11th International Workshop on Semantic Evaluation (SemEval 2017)

Vancouver, Canada
3 – 4 August 2017

Volume 1 of 2

ISBN: 978-1-5108-4563-3

11th International Workshop on Semantic Evaluation (SemEval 2017)

Vancouver, Canada
3 – 4 August 2017

Volume 1 of 2

ACL 2017

11th International Workshop on Semantic Evaluations (SemEval-2017)

Proceedings of the Workshop

August 3 - 4, 2017
Vancouver, Canada

Welcome to SemEval-2017

The Semantic Evaluation (SemEval) series of workshops focuses on the evaluation and comparison of systems that can analyse diverse semantic phenomena in text with the aim of extending the current state of the art in semantic analysis and creating high quality annotated datasets in a range of increasingly challenging problems in natural language semantics. SemEval provides an exciting forum for researchers to propose challenging research problems in semantics and to build systems/techniques to address such research problems.

SemEval-2017 is the eleventh workshop in the series of International Workshops on Semantic Evaluation. The first three workshops, SensEval-1 (1998), SensEval-2 (2001), and SensEval-3 (2004), focused on word sense disambiguation, each time growing in the number of languages offered, in the number of tasks, and also in the number of participating teams. In 2007, the workshop was renamed to SemEval, and the subsequent SemEval workshops evolved to include semantic analysis tasks beyond word sense disambiguation. In 2012, SemEval turned into a yearly event. It currently runs every year, but on a two-year cycle, i.e., the tasks for SemEval-2017 were proposed in 2016.

SemEval-2017 was co-located with the 55th annual meeting of the Association for Computational Linguistics (ACL'2017) in Vancouver, Canada. It included the following 12 shared tasks organized in three tracks:

Semantic comparison for words and texts

- Task 1: Semantic Textual Similarity

- Task 2: Multi-lingual and Cross-lingual Semantic Word Similarity

- Task 3: Community Question Answering

Detecting sentiment, humor, and truth

- Task 4: Sentiment Analysis in Twitter

- Task 5: Fine-Grained Sentiment Analysis on Financial Microblogs and News

- Task 6: #HashtagWars: Learning a Sense of Humor

- Task 7: Detection and Interpretation of English Puns

- Task 8: RumourEval: Determining rumour veracity and support for rumours

Parsing semantic structures

- Task 9: Abstract Meaning Representation Parsing and Generation

- Task 10: Extracting Keyphrases and Relations from Scientific Publications

- Task 11: End-User Development using Natural Language

- Task 12: Clinical TempEval

This volume contains both Task Description papers that describe each of the above tasks and System Description papers that describe the systems that participated in the above tasks. A total of 12 task description papers and 169 system description papers are included in this volume.

We are grateful to all task organizers as well as the large number of participants whose enthusiastic participation has made SemEval once again a successful event. We are thankful to the task organizers who also served as area chairs, and to task organizers and participants who reviewed paper submissions. These proceedings have greatly benefited from their detailed and thoughtful feedback. We also thank the ACL 2017 conference organizers for their support. Finally, we most gratefully acknowledge the support of our sponsor, the ACL Special Interest Group on the Lexicon (SIGLEX).

The SemEval-2017 organizers,

Steven Bethard, Marine Carpuat, Marianna Apidianaki, Saif M. Mohammad, Daniel Cer, David Jurgens

Organizers:

Steven Bethard, University of Arizona
Marine Carpuat, University of Maryland
Marianna Apidianaki, LIMSI, CNRS, University Paris-Saclay
Saif M. Mohammad, National Research Council Canada
Daniel Cer, Google Research
David Jurgens, Stanford University

Task Selection Committee:

Yejin Choi, University of Washington
Paul Cook, University of New Brunswick
Lea Frermann, University of Edinburgh
Spence Green, Lilt
Kazi Saidul Hasan, IBM
Anna Korhonen, University of Cambridge
Omer Levy, Technion – Israel Institute of Technology
Mike Lewis, Facebook AI Research
Rada Mihalcea, University of Michigan
Preslav Nakov, Qatar Computing Research Institute
Vivi Nastase, Universität Heidelberg
Vincent Ng, University of Texas at Dallas
Brendan O'Connor, University of Massachussets
Ted Pedersen, University of Minnesota Duluth
Sasa Petrovic, Google
Mohammad Taher Pilehvar, University of Cambridge
Maria Pontiki, Institute for Language and Speech Processing, Athena R.C.
Simone Paolo Ponzetto, Universität Mannheim
Verónica Pérez-Rosas, University of Michigan
Anna Rumshisky, University of Massachusetts Lowell
Derek Ruths, McGill University
Carlo Strapparava, Fondazione Bruno Kessler
Svitlana Volkova, Pacific Northwest National Laboratory
Sida I. Wang, Stanford University
Wei Xu, Ohio State University
Wen-tau Yih, Microsoft Research
Luke Zettlemoyer, University of Washington
Renxian Zhang, Tongji University

Task Organizers:

Eneko Agirre, University of Basque Country
Isabelle Augenstein, University College London
Timothy Baldwin, The University of Melbourne
Steven Bethard, University of Arizona
Kalina Bontcheva, University of Sheffield
José Camacho-Collados, Sapienza University of Rome
Daniel Cer, Google Research

Nigel Collier, University of Cambridge
Keith Cortis, University of Passau
Mrinal Das, University of Massachusetts Amherst
Tobias Daudert, INSIGHT Centre for Data Analytics
Leon Derczynski, University of Sheffield
Mona Diab, George Washington University
Noura Farra, Columbia University
Andre Freitas, University of Passau
Iryna Gurevych, Technische Universität Darmstadt
Siegfried Handschuh, University of Passau
Christian F. Hempelmann, Texas A&M University-Commerce
Doris Hoogeveen, The University of Melbourne
Manuela Huerlimann, INSIGHT Centre for Data Analytics
Maria Liakata, University of Warwick
Iñigo Lopez-Gazpio, University of Basque Country
Lluís Màrquez, Qatar Computing Research Institute, HBKU
Jonathan May, University of Southern California Information Sciences Institute
Andrew McCallum, University of Massachusetts Amherst
Tristan Miller, Technische Universität Darmstadt
Alessandro Moschitti, Qatar Computing Research Institute, HBKU
Hamdy Mubarak, Qatar Computing Research Institute, HBKU
Preslav Nakov, Qatar Computing Research Institute, HBKU
Preslav Nakov, Qatar Computing Research Institute, HBKU
Roberto Navigli, Sapienza University of Rome
Martha Palmer, University of Colorado
Mohammad Taher Pilehvar, University of Cambridge
Peter Potash, University of Massachusetts Lowell
Rob Procter, University of Warwick
James Pustejovsky, Brandeis University
Sebastian Riedel, University College London
Alexey Romanov, University of Massachusetts Lowell
Sara Rosenthal, IBM Research
Anna Rumshisky, University of Massachusetts Lowell
Juliano Sales, University of Passau
Guergana Savova, Harvard University
Lucia Specia, University of Sheffield
Karin Verspoor, The University of Melbourne
Lakshmi Vikraman, University of Massachusetts Amherst
Geraldine Wong Sak Hoi, swissinfo.ch
Manel Zarrouk, INSIGHT Centre for Data Analytics
Arkaitz Zubiaga, University of Warwick

Table of Contents

Conference Program

3 August 2017

09:00–09:15   *Welcome / Opening Remarks*

09:15–10:30   *Invited Talk: From Naive Physics to Connotation: Modeling Commonsense in Frame Semantics*
Yejin Choi

10:30–11:00   *Coffee*

11:00–12:30   **Task Descriptions**

11:00–11:15   *SemEval-2017 Task 1: Semantic Textual Similarity Multilingual and Crosslingual Focused Evaluation*
Daniel Cer, Mona Diab, Eneko Agirre, Inigo Lopez-Gazpio and Lucia Specia

11:15–11:30   *SemEval-2017 Task 2: Multilingual and Cross-lingual Semantic Word Similarity*
Jose Camacho-Collados, Mohammad Taher Pilehvar, Nigel Collier and Roberto Navigli

11:30–11:45   *SemEval-2017 Task 3: Community Question Answering*
Preslav Nakov, Doris Hoogeveen, Lluís Màrquez, Alessandro Moschitti, Hamdy Mubarak, Timothy Baldwin and Karin Verspoor

11:45–12:00   *SemEval-2017 Task 6: #HashtagWars: Learning a Sense of Humor*
Peter Potash, Alexey Romanov and Anna Rumshisky

12:00–12:15   *SemEval-2017 Task 7: Detection and Interpretation of English Puns*
Tristan Miller, Christian Hempelmann and Iryna Gurevych

12:15–12:30   *SemEval-2017 Task 8: RumourEval: Determining rumour veracity and support for rumours*
Leon Derczynski, Kalina Bontcheva, Maria Liakata, Rob Procter, Geraldine Wong Sak Hoi and Arkaitz Zubiaga

12:30–14:00   *Lunch*

3 August 2017 (continued)

14:00–15:30   Best Of SemEval

14:00–14:15   *BIT at SemEval-2017 Task 1: Using Semantic Information Space to Evaluate Semantic Textual Similarity*
Hao Wu, Heyan Huang, Ping Jian, Yuhang Guo and Chao Su

14:15–14:30   *ConceptNet at SemEval-2017 Task 2: Extending Word Embeddings with Multilingual Relational Knowledge*
Robert Speer and Joanna Lowry-Duda

14:30–14:45   *IIT-UHH at SemEval-2017 Task 3: Exploring Multiple Features for Community Question Answering and Implicit Dialogue Identification*
Titas Nandi, Chris Biemann, Seid Muhie Yimam, Deepak Gupta, Sarah Kohail, Asif Ekbal and Pushpak Bhattacharyya

14:45–15:00   *HumorHawk at SemEval-2017 Task 6: Mixing Meaning and Sound for Humor Recognition*
David Donahue, Alexey Romanov and Anna Rumshisky

15:00–15:15   *Idiom Savant at Semeval-2017 Task 7: Detection and Interpretation of English Puns*
Samuel Doogan, Aniruddha Ghosh, Hanyang Chen and Tony Veale

15:15–15:30   *Turing at SemEval-2017 Task 8: Sequential Approach to Rumour Stance Classification with Branch-LSTM*
Elena Kochkina, Maria Liakata and Isabelle Augenstein

15:30–16:00   *Coffee*

16:00–16:30   *Discussion*

16:30–17:30 **Poster Session**

16:30–17:30 *CompiLIG at SemEval-2017 Task 1: Cross-Language Plagiarism Detection Methods for Semantic Textual Similarity*
Jérémy Ferrero, Laurent Besacier, Didier Schwab and Frédéric Agnès

16:30–17:30 *UdL at SemEval-2017 Task 1: Semantic Textual Similarity Estimation of English Sentence Pairs Using Regression Model over Pairwise Features*
Hussein T. Al-Natsheh, Lucie Martinet, Fabrice Muhlenbach and Djamel Abdelkader ZIGHED

16:30–17:30 *DT_Team at SemEval-2017 Task 1: Semantic Similarity Using Alignments, Sentence-Level Embeddings and Gaussian Mixture Model Output*
Nabin Maharjan, Rajendra Banjade, Dipesh Gautam, Lasang J. Tamang and Vasile Rus

16:30–17:30 *FCICU at SemEval-2017 Task 1: Sense-Based Language Independent Semantic Textual Similarity Approach*
Basma Hassan, Samir AbdelRahman, Reem Bahgat and Ibrahim Farag

16:30–17:30 *HCTI at SemEval-2017 Task 1: Use convolutional neural network to evaluate Semantic Textual Similarity*
Yang Shao

16:30–17:30 *LIM-LIG at SemEval-2017 Task1: Enhancing the Semantic Similarity for Arabic Sentences with Vectors Weighting*
El Moatez Billah NAGOUDI, Jérémy Ferrero and Didier Schwab

16:30–17:30 *OPI-JSA at SemEval-2017 Task 1: Application of Ensemble learning for computing semantic textual similarity*
Martyna Śpiewak, Piotr Sobecki and Daniel Karaś

16:30–17:30 *Lump at SemEval-2017 Task 1: Towards an Interlingua Semantic Similarity*
Cristina España-Bonet and Alberto Barrón-Cedeño

16:30–17:30 *QLUT at SemEval-2017 Task 1: Semantic Textual Similarity Based on Word Embeddings*
Fanqing Meng, Wenpeng Lu, Yuteng Zhang, Jinyong Cheng, Yuehan Du and Shuwang Han

16:30–17:30 *ResSim at SemEval-2017 Task 1: Multilingual Word Representations for Semantic Textual Similarity*
Johannes Bjerva and Robert Östling

16:30–17:30 *ITNLP-AiKF at SemEval-2017 Task 1: Rich Features Based SVR for Semantic Textual Similarity Computing*
Wenjie Liu, Chengjie Sun, Lei Lin and Bingquan Liu

3 August 2017 (continued)

16.30–17:30   *Turing at SemEval-2017 Task 8: Sequential Approach to Rumour Stance Classification with Branch-LSTM*
Elena Kochkina, Maria Liakata and Isabelle Augenstein

16:30–17:30   *Mama Edha at SemEval-2017 Task 8: Stance Classification with CNN and Rules*
Marianela García Lozano, Hanna Lilja, Edward Tjörnhammar and Maja Karasalo

16:30–17:30   *DFKI-DKT at SemEval-2017 Task 8: Rumour Detection and Classification using Cascading Heuristics*
Ankit Srivastava, Georg Rehm and Julian Moreno Schneider

16:30–17:30   *ECNU at SemEval-2017 Task 8: Rumour Evaluation Using Effective Features and Supervised Ensemble Models*
Feixiang Wang, Man Lan and Yuanbin Wu

16:30–17:30   *IITP at SemEval-2017 Task 8 : A Supervised Approach for Rumour Evaluation*
Vikram Singh, Sunny Narayan, Md Shad Akhtar, Asif Ekbal and Pushpak Bhattacharyya

4 Aug 2017

09:00–09:30   SemEval 2018 Tasks

09:30–10:30   State of SemEval Discussion

10:30–11:00   Coffee

4 Aug 2017 (continued)

11:00–12:30   **Task Descriptions**

11:00–11:15   *SemEval-2017 Task 4: Sentiment Analysis in Twitter*
Sara Rosenthal, Noura Farra and Preslav Nakov

11:15–11:30   *SemEval-2017 Task 5: Fine-Grained Sentiment Analysis on Financial Microblogs and News*
Keith Cortis, André Freitas, Tobias Daudert, Manuela Huerlimann, Manel Zarrouk, Siegfried Handschuh and Brian Davis

11:30–11:45   *SemEval-2017 Task 9: Abstract Meaning Representation Parsing and Generation*
Jonathan May and Jay Priyadarshi

11:45–12:00   *SemEval 2017 Task 10: ScienceIE - Extracting Keyphrases and Relations from Scientific Publications*
Isabelle Augenstein, Mrinal Das, Sebastian Riedel, Lakshmi Vikraman and Andrew McCallum

12:00–12:15   *SemEval-2017 Task 11: End-User Development using Natural Language*
Juliano Sales, Siegfried Handschuh and André Freitas

12:15–12:30   *SemEval-2017 Task 12: Clinical TempEval*
Steven Bethard, Guergana Savova, Martha Palmer and James Pustejovsky

12:30–14:00   ***Lunch***

14:00–15:30	**Best Of SemEval**

14:00–14:15   *BB_twtr at SemEval-2017 Task 4: Twitter Sentiment Analysis with CNNs and LSTMs*
Mathieu Cliche

14:15–14:30   *Lancaster A at SemEval-2017 Task 5: Evaluation metrics matter: predicting sentiment from financial news headlines*
Andrew Moore and Paul Rayson

14:30–14:45   *Sheffield at SemEval-2017 Task 9: Transition-based language generation from AMR.*
Gerasimos Lampouras and Andreas Vlachos

14:45–15:00   *The AI2 system at SemEval-2017 Task 10 (ScienceIE): semi-supervised end-to-end entity and relation extraction*
Waleed Ammar, Matthew Peters, Chandra Bhagavatula and Russell Power

15:00–15:15   *LIMSI-COT at SemEval-2017 Task 12: Neural Architecture for Temporal Information Extraction from Clinical Narratives*
Julien Tourille, Olivier Ferret, Xavier Tannier and Aurélie Névéol

15:30–16:00   *Coffee*

16:00–16:30   *Discussion*

16:30–17:30   **Poster Session**

16:30–17:30   *OMAM at SemEval-2017 Task 4: Evaluation of English State-of-the-Art Sentiment Analysis Models for Arabic and a New Topic-based Model*
Ramy Baly, Gilbert Badaro, Ali Hamdi, Rawan Moukalled, Rita Aoun, Georges El-Khoury, Ahmad Al Sallab, Hazem Hajj, Nizar Habash, Khaled Shaban and Wassim El-Hajj

16:30–17:30   *NILC-USP at SemEval-2017 Task 4: A Multi-view Ensemble for Twitter Sentiment Analysis*
Edilson Anselmo Corrêa Júnior, Vanessa Queiroz Marinho and Leandro Borges dos Santos

16:30–17:30   *deepSA at SemEval-2017 Task 4: Interpolated Deep Neural Networks for Sentiment Analysis in Twitter*
Tzu-Hsuan Yang, Tzu-Hsuan Tseng and Chia-Ping Chen

16:30–17:30   *MI&T Lab at SemEval-2017 task 4: An Integrated Training Method of Word Vector for Sentiment Classification*
Jingjing Zhao, Yan Yang and Bing Xu

16:30–17:30   *SiTAKA at SemEval-2017 Task 4: Sentiment Analysis in Twitter Based on a Rich Set of Features*
Mohammed Jabreel and Antonio Moreno

16:30–17:30   *Senti17 at SemEval-2017 Task 4: Ten Convolutional Neural Network Voters for Tweet Polarity Classification*
Hussam Hamdan

16:30–17:30   *DUTH at SemEval-2017 Task 4: A Voting Classification Approach for Twitter Sentiment Analysis*
Symeon Symeonidis, Dimitrios Effrosynidis, John Kordonis and Avi Arampatzis

16:30–17:30   *SSN_MLRG1 at SemEval-2017 Task 4: Sentiment Analysis in Twitter Using Multi-Kernel Gaussian Process Classifier*
Angel Deborah S, S Milton Rajendram and T T Mirnalinee

16:30–17:30   *YNUDLG at SemEval-2017 Task 4: A GRU-SVM Model for Sentiment Classification and Quantification in Twitter*
Ming Wang, Biao Chu, Qingxun Liu and Xiaobing Zhou

16:30–17:30   *LSIS at SemEval-2017 Task 4: Using Adapted Sentiment Similarity Seed Words For English and Arabic Tweet Polarity Classification*
Amal Htait, Sébastien Fournier and Patrice Bellot

16:30–17:30   *ELiRF-UPV at SemEval-2017 Task 4: Sentiment Analysis using Deep Learning*
José-Ángel González, Ferran Pla and Lluís-F. Hurtado

16:30–17:30   *XJSA at SemEval-2017 Task 4: A Deep System for Sentiment Classification in Twitter*
Yazhou Hao, YangYang Lan, Yufei Li and Chen Li

16:30–17:30   *Adullam at SemEval-2017 Task 4: Sentiment Analyzer Using Lexicon Integrated Convolutional Neural Networks with Attention*
Joosung Yoon, Kigon Lyu and Hyeoncheol Kim

16:30–17:30   *EICA at SemEval-2017 Task 4: A Simple Convolutional Neural Network for Topic-based Sentiment Classification*
wang maoquan, Chen Shiyun, Xie yufei and Zhao lu

16:30–17:30   *funSentiment at SemEval-2017 Task 4: Topic-Based Message Sentiment Classification by Exploiting Word Embeddings, Text Features and Target Contexts*
Quanzhi Li, Armineh Nourbakhsh, Xiaomo Liu, Rui Fang and Sameena Shah

16:30–17:30   *Fortia-FBK at SemEval-2017 Task 5: Bullish or Bearish? Inferring Sentiment towards Brands from Financial News Headlines*
Youness Mansar, Lorenzo Gatti, Sira Ferradans, Marco Guerini and Jacopo Staiano

16:30–17:30   *SSN_MLRG1 at SemEval-2017 Task 5: Fine-Grained Sentiment Analysis Using Multiple Kernel Gaussian Process Regression Model*
Angel Deborah S, S Milton Rajendram and T T Mirnalinee

16:30–17:30   *IBA-Sys at SemEval-2017 Task 5: Fine-Grained Sentiment Analysis on Financial Microblogs and News*
Zarmeen Nasim

16:30–17:30   *HHU at SemEval-2017 Task 5: Fine-Grained Sentiment Analysis on Financial Data using Machine Learning Methods*
Tobias Cabanski, Julia Romberg and Stefan Conrad

16:30–17:30   *INF-UFRGS at SemEval-2017 Task 5: A Supervised Identification of Sentiment Score in Tweets and Headlines*
Tiago Zini, Karin Becker and Marcelo Dias

16:30–17:30   *HCS at SemEval-2017 Task 5: Polarity detection in business news using convolutional neural networks*
Lidia Pivovarova, Llorenç Escoter, Arto Klami and Roman Yangarber

16:30–17:30   *NLG301 at SemEval-2017 Task 5: Fine-Grained Sentiment Analysis on Financial Microblogs and News*
Chung-Chi Chen, Hen-Hsen Huang and Hsin-Hsi Chen

16:30–17:30   *funSentiment at SemEval-2017 Task 5: Fine-Grained Sentiment Analysis on Financial Microblogs Using Word Vectors Built from StockTwits and Twitter*
Quanzhi Li, Sameena Shah, Armineh Nourbakhsh, Rui Fang and Xiaomo Liu

16:30–17:30   *SentiHeros at SemEval-2017 Task 5: An application of Sentiment Analysis on Financial Tweets*
Narges Tabari, Armin Seyeditabari and Wlodek Zadrozny

16:30–17:30   *DUTH at SemEval-2017 Task 5: Sentiment Predictability in Financial Microblogging and News Articles*
Symeon Symeonidis, John Kordonis, Dimitrios Effrosynidis and Avi Arampatzis

16:30–17:30   *TakeLab at SemEval-2017 Task 5: Linear aggregation of word embeddings for fine-grained sentiment analysis of financial news*
Leon Rotim, Martin Tutek and Jan Šnajder

16:30–17:30   *UW-FinSent at SemEval-2017 Task 5: Sentiment Analysis on Financial News Headlines using Training Dataset Augmentation*
Vineet John and Olga Vechtomova

16:30–17:30   *LIPN at SemEval-2017 Task 10: Filtering Candidate Keyphrases from Scientific Publications with Part-of-Speech Tag Sequences to Train a Sequence Labeling Model*
Simon David Hernandez, Davide Buscaldi and Thierry Charnois

16:30–17:30   *EUDAMU at SemEval-2017 Task 11: Action Ranking and Type Matching for End-User Development*
Marek Kubis, Paweł Skórzewski and Tomasz Ziętkiewicz

16:30–17:30   *Hitachi at SemEval-2017 Task 12: System for temporal information extraction from clinical notes*
Sarath P R, Manikandan R and Yoshiki Niwa

16:30–17:30   *NTU-1 at SemEval-2017 Task 12: Detection and classification of temporal events in clinical data with domain adaptation*
Po-Yu Huang, Hen-Hsen Huang, Yu-Wun Wang, Ching Huang and Hsin-Hsi Chen

16:30–17:30   *XJNLP at SemEval-2017 Task 12: Clinical temporal information ex-traction with a Hybrid Model*
Yu Long, Zhijing Li, Xuan Wang and Chen Li

16:30–17:30   *ULISBOA at SemEval-2017 Task 12: Extraction and classification of temporal expressions and events*
Andre Lamurias, Diana Sousa, Sofia Pereira, Luka Clarke and Francisco M Couto

16:30–17:30   *GUIR at SemEval-2017 Task 12: A Framework for Cross-Domain Clinical Temporal Information Extraction*
Sean MacAvaney, Arman Cohan and Nazli Goharian

16:30–17:30   *KULeuven-LIIR at SemEval-2017 Task 12: Cross-Domain Temporal Information Extraction from Clinical Records*
Artuur Leeuwenberg and Marie-Francine Moens

SemEval-2017 Task 1: Semantic Textual Similarity Multilingual and Cross-lingual Focused Evaluation

Daniel Cer[a], Mona Diab[b], Eneko Agirre[c], Iñigo Lopez-Gazpio[c], and Lucia Specia[d]

[a]Google Research
Mountain View, CA

[b]George Washington University
Washington, DC

[c]University of the Basque Country
Donostia, Basque Country

[d]University of Sheffield
Sheffield, UK

Abstract

Semantic Textual Similarity (STS) measures the meaning similarity of sentences. Applications include machine translation (MT), summarization, generation, question answering (QA), short answer grading, semantic search, dialog and conversational systems. The STS shared task is a venue for assessing the current state-of-the-art. The 2017 task focuses on multilingual and cross-lingual pairs with one sub-track exploring MT quality estimation (MTQE) data. The task obtained strong participation from 31 teams, with 17 participating in *all language tracks*. We summarize performance and review a selection of well performing methods. Analysis highlights common errors, providing insight into the limitations of existing models. To support ongoing work on semantic representations, the *STS Benchmark* is introduced as a new shared training and evaluation set carefully selected from the corpus of English STS shared task data (2012-2017).

1 Introduction

Semantic Textual Similarity (STS) assesses the degree to which two sentences are semantically equivalent to each other. The STS task is motivated by the observation that accurately modeling the meaning similarity of sentences is a foundational language understanding problem relevant to numerous applications including: machine translation (MT), summarization, generation, question answering (QA), short answer grading, semantic search, dialog and conversational systems. STS enables the evaluation of techniques from a diverse set of domains against a shared interpretable performance criteria. Semantic inference tasks related to STS include textual entailment (Bentivogli et al., 2016; Bowman et al., 2015; Dagan et al., 2010), semantic relatedness (Bentivogli et al., 2016) and paraphrase detection (Xu et al., 2015; Ganitkevitch et al., 2013; Dolan et al., 2004). STS differs from both textual entailment and paraphrase detection in that it captures *gradations of meaning overlap* rather than making binary classifications of particular relationships. While semantic relatedness expresses a graded semantic relationship as well, it is non-specific about the nature of the relationship with contradictory material still being a candidate for a high score (e.g., "night" and "day" are highly related but not particularly similar).

To encourage and support research in this area, the STS shared task has been held annually since 2012, providing a venue for evaluation of state-of-the-art algorithms and models (Agirre et al., 2012, 2013, 2014, 2015, 2016). During this time, diverse similarity methods and data sets[1] have been explored. Early methods focused on lexical semantics, surface form matching and basic syntactic similarity (Bär et al., 2012; Šarić et al., 2012a; Jimenez et al., 2012a). During subsequent evaluations, strong new similarity signals emerged, such as Sultan et al. (2015)'s alignment based method. More recently, deep learning became competitive with top performing feature engineered systems (He et al., 2016). The best performance tends to be obtained by ensembling feature engineered and deep learning models (Rychalska et al., 2016).

Significant research effort has focused on STS over English sentence pairs.[2] English STS is a

---

[1]i.a., news headlines, video and image descriptions, glosses from lexical resources including WordNet (Miller, 1995; Fellbaum, 1998), FrameNet (Baker et al., 1998), OntoNotes (Hovy et al., 2006), web discussion fora, plagiarism, MT post-editing and Q&A data sets. Data sets are summarized on: `http://ixa2.si.ehu.es/stswiki`.

[2]The 2012 and 2013 STS tasks were English only. The 2014 and 2015 task included a Spanish track and 2016 had a

Proceedings of the 11th International Workshop on Semantic Evaluations (SemEval-2017), pages 1–14,
Vancouver, Canada, August 3 - 4, 2017. ©2017 Association for Computational Linguistics

well-studied problem, with state-of-the-art systems often achieving 70 to 80% correlation with human judgment. To promote progress in other languages, the 2017 task emphasizes performance on Arabic and Spanish as well as cross-lingual pairings of English with material in Arabic, Spanish and Turkish. The *primary* evaluation criteria combines performance on all of the different language conditions except English-Turkish, which was run as a surprise language track. Even with this departure from prior years, the task attracted 31 teams producing 84 submissions.

STS shared task data sets have been used extensively for research on sentence level similarity and semantic representations (i.a., Arora et al. (2017); Conneau et al. (2017); Mu et al. (2017); Pagliardini et al. (2017); Wieting and Gimpel (2017); He and Lin (2016); Hill et al. (2016); Kenter et al. (2016); Lau and Baldwin (2016); Wieting et al. (2016b,a); He et al. (2015); Pham et al. (2015)). To encourage the use of a common evaluation set for assessing new methods, we present the STS Benchmark, a publicly available selection of data from English STS shared tasks (2012-2017).

2   Task Overview

STS is the assessment of pairs of sentences according to their degree of semantic similarity. The task involves producing real-valued similarity scores for sentence pairs. Performance is measured by the Pearson correlation of machine scores with human judgments. The ordinal scale in Table 1 guides human annotation, ranging from 0 for no meaning overlap to 5 for meaning equivalence. Intermediate values reflect interpretable levels of partial overlap in meaning. The annotation scale is designed to be accessible by reasonable human judges without any formal expertise in linguistics. Using reasonable human interpretations of natural language semantics was popularized by the related textual entailment task (Dagan et al., 2010). The resulting annotations reflect both pragmatic and world knowledge and are more interpretable and useful within downstream systems.

3   Evaluation Data

The Stanford Natural Language Inference (SNLI) corpus (Bowman et al., 2015) is the primary evaluation data source with the exception that one of the

---

5	*The two sentences are completely equivalent, as they mean the same thing.*
	The bird is bathing in the sink. Birdie is washing itself in the water basin.
4	*The two sentences are mostly equivalent, but some unimportant details differ.*
	Two boys on a couch are playing video games. Two boys are playing a video game.
3	*The two sentences are roughly equivalent, but some important information differs/missing.*
	John said he is considered a witness but not a suspect. "He is not a suspect anymore." John said.
2	*The two sentences are not equivalent, but share some details.*
	They flew out of the nest in groups. They flew into the nest together.
1	*The two sentences are not equivalent, but are on the same topic.*
	The woman is playing the violin. The young lady enjoys listening to the guitar.
0	*The two sentences are completely dissimilar.*
	The black dog is running through the snow. A race car driver is driving his car through the mud.

Table 1: Similarity scores with explanations and English examples from Agirre et al. (2013).

cross-lingual tracks explores data from the WMT 2014 quality estimation task (Bojar et al., 2014).[3]

Sentences pairs in SNLI derive from Flickr30k image captions (Young et al., 2014) and are labeled with the entailment relations: entailment, neutral, and contradiction. Drawing from SNLI allows STS models to be evaluated on the type of data used to assess textual entailment methods. However, since entailment strongly cues for semantic relatedness (Marelli et al., 2014), we construct our own sentence pairings to deter gold entailment labels from informing evaluation set STS scores.

Track 4b investigates the relationship between STS and MT quality estimation by providing STS labels for WMT quality estimation data. The data includes Spanish translations of English sentences from a variety of methods including RBMT, SMT, hybrid-MT and human translation. Translations are annotated with the time required for human correction by post-editing and Human-targeted Translation Error Rate (HTER) (Snover et al., 2006).[4] Participants are not allowed to use the gold quality estimation annotations to inform STS scores.

---

pilot track on cross-lingual Spanish-English STS. The English tracks attracted the most participation and have the largest use of the evaluation data in ongoing research.

[3]Previous years of the STS shared task include more data sources. This year the task draws from two data sources and includes a diverse set of languages and language-pairs.

[4]HTER is the minimal number of edits required for correction of a translation divided by its length after correction.

Track	Language(s)	Pairs	Source
1	Arabic (ar-ar)	250	SNLI
2	Arabic-English (ar-en)	250	SNLI
3	Spanish (es-es)	250	SNLI
4a	Spanish-English (es-en)	250	SNLI
4b	Spanish-English (es-en)	250	WMT QE
5	English (en-en)	250	SNLI
6	Turkish-English (tr-en)	250	SNLI
	Total	1750	

Table 2: STS 2017 evaluation data.

3.1 Tracks

Table 2 summarizes the evaluation data by track. The six tracks span four languages: Arabic, English, Spanish and Turkish. Track 4 has subtracks with 4a drawing from SNLI and 4b pulling from WMT's quality estimation task. Track 6 is a surprise language track with no annotated training data and the identity of the language pair first announced when the evaluation data was released.

3.2 Data Preparation

This section describes the preparation of the evaluation data. For SNLI data, this includes the selection of sentence pairs, annotation of pairs with STS labels and the translation of the original English sentences. WMT quality estimation data is directly annotated with STS labels.

3.3 Arabic, Spanish and Turkish Translation

Sentences from SNLI are human translated into Arabic, Spanish and Turkish. Sentences are translated independently from their pairs. Arabic translation is provided by CMU-Qatar by native Arabic speakers with strong English skills. Translators are given an English sentence and its Arabic machine translation[5] where they perform post-editing to correct errors. Spanish translation is completed by a University of Sheffield graduate student who is a native Spanish speaker and fluent in English. Turkish translations are obtained from SDL.[6]

3.4 Embedding Space Pair Selection

We construct our own pairings of the SNLI sentences to deter gold entailment labels being used to inform STS scores. The *word embedding similarity* selection heuristic from STS 2016 (Agirre et al., 2016) is used to find interesting pairs. Sentence embeddings are computed as the sum of in-

dividual word embeddings, $\mathbf{v}(s) = \sum_{w \in s} \mathbf{v}(w)$.[7] Sentences with likely meaning overlap are identified using cosine similarity, Eq. (1).

$$\text{sim}_{\mathbf{v}}(s_1, s_2) = \frac{\mathbf{v}(s_1)\mathbf{v}(s_2)}{\|\mathbf{v}(s_1)\|_2 \|\mathbf{v}(s_2)\|_2} \quad (1)$$

4 Annotation

Annotation of pairs with STS labels is performed using Crowdsourcing, with the exception of Track 4b that uses a single expert annotator.

4.1 Crowdsourced Annotations

Crowdsourced annotation is performed on Amazon Mechanical Turk.[8] Annotators examine the STS pairings of English SNLI sentences. STS labels are then transferred to the translated pairs for cross-lingual and non-English tracks. The annotation instructions and template are identical to Agirre et al. (2016). Labels are collected in batches of 20 pairs with annotators paid $1 USD per batch. Five annotations are collected per pair. The MTurk *master*[9] qualification is required to perform the task. Gold scores average the five individual annotations.

4.2 Expert Annotation

English-Spanish WMT quality estimation pairs for Track 4b are annotated for STS by a University of Sheffield graduate student who is a native speaker of Spanish and fluent in English. This track differs significantly in label distribution and the complexity of the annotation task. Sentences in a pair are translations of each other and tend to be more semantically similar. Interpreting the potentially subtle meaning differences introduced by MT errors is challenging. To accurately assess STS performance on MT quality estimation data, no attempt is made to balance the data by similarity scores.

5 Training Data

The following summarizes the training data: Table 3 English; Table 4 Spanish;[10] Table 5 Spanish-English; Table 6 Arabic; and Table 7 Arabic-English. Arabic-English parallel data is supplied by translating English training data, Table 8.

---

[7]We use 50-dimensional GloVe word embeddings (Pennington et al., 2014) trained on a combination of Gigaword 5 (Parker et al., 2011) and English Wikipedia available at `http://nlp.stanford.edu/projects/glove/`.

[8]`https://www.mturk.com/`

[9]A designation that statistically identifies workers who perform high quality work across a diverse set of tasks.

[10]Spanish data from 2015 and 2014 uses a 5 point scale that collapses STS labels 4 and 3, removing the distinction between unimportant and important details.

[5]Produced by the Google Translate API.

[6]`http://www.sdl.com/languagecloud/managed-translation/`

Year	Data set	Pairs	Source
2012	MSRpar	1500	newswire
2012	MSRvid	1500	videos
2012	OnWN	750	glosses
2012	SMTnews	750	WMT eval.
2012	SMTeuroparl	750	WMT eval.
2013	HDL	750	newswire
2013	FNWN	189	glosses
2013	OnWN	561	glosses
2013	SMT	750	MT eval.
2014	HDL	750	newswire headlines
2014	OnWN	750	glosses
2014	Deft-forum	450	forum posts
2014	Deft-news	300	news summary
2014	Images	750	image descriptions
2014	Tweet-news	750	tweet-news pairs
2015	HDL	750	newswire headlines
2015	Images	750	image descriptions
2015	Ans.-student	750	student answers
2015	Ans.-forum	375	Q&A forum answers
2015	Belief	375	committed belief
2016	HDL	249	newswire headlines
2016	Plagiarism	230	short-answer plag.
2016	post-editing	244	MT postedits
2016	Ans.-Ans.	254	Q&A forum answers
2016	Quest.-Quest.	209	Q&A forum questions
2017	Trial	23	Mixed STS 2016

Table 3: English training data.

Year	Data set	Pairs	Source
2014	Trial	56	
2014	Wiki	324	Spanish Wikipedia
2014	News	480	Newswire
2015	Wiki	251	Spanish Wikipedia
2015	News	500	Sewswire
2017	Trial	23	Mixed STS 2016

Table 4: Spanish training data.

Year	Data set	Pairs	Source
2016	Trial	103	Sampled $\leq$ 2015 STS
2016	News	301	en-es news articles
2016	Multi-source	294	en news headlines, short-answer plag., MT postedits, Q&A forum answers, Q&A forum questions
2017	Trial	23	Mixed STS 2016
2017	MT	1000	WMT13 Translation Task

Table 5: Spanish-English training data.

Year	Data set	Pairs	Source
2017	Trial	23	Mixed STS 2016
2017	MSRpar	510	newswire
2017	MSRvid	368	videos
2017	SMTeuroparl	203	WMT eval.

Table 6: Arabic training data.

English, Spanish and English-Spanish training data pulls from prior STS evaluations. Arabic and Arabic-English training data is produced by translating a subset of the English training data and transferring the similarity scores. For the MT quality estimation data in track 4b, Spanish sentences are translations of their English counterparts, differing substantially from existing Spanish-English STS data. We release one thousand new Spanish-English STS pairs sourced from the 2013 WMT translation task and produced by a phrase-based Moses SMT system (Bojar et al., 2013). The data is expert annotated and has a similar label distribution to the track 4b test data with 17% of the pairs scoring an STS score of less than 3, 23% scoring 3, 7% achieving a score of 4 and 53% scoring 5.

5.1 Training vs. Evaluation Data Analysis

Evaluation data from SNLI tend to have sentences that are slightly shorter than those from prior years of the STS shared task, while the track 4b MT quality estimation data has sentences that are much longer. The track 5 English data has an average sentence length of 8.7 words, while the English sentences from track 4b have an average length of 19.4. The English training data has the following average lengths: 2012 10.8 words; 2013 8.8 words (excludes restricted SMT data); 2014 9.1 words; 2015 11.5 words; 2016 13.8 words.

Similarity scores for our pairings of the SNLI sentences are slightly lower than recent shared task years and much lower than early years. The change is attributed to differences in data selection and filtering. The average 2017 similarity score is 2.2 overall and 2.3 on the track 7 English data. Prior English data has the following average similarity scores: 2016 2.4; 2015 2.4; 2014 2.8; 2013 3.0; 2012 3.5. Translation quality estimation data from track 4b has an average similarity score of 4.0.

6 System Evaluation

This section reports participant evaluation results for the SemEval-2017 STS shared task.

6.1 Participation

The task saw strong participation with 31 teams producing 84 submissions. 17 teams provided 44 systems that participated in all tracks. Table 9 summarizes participation by track. Traces of the focus on English are seen in 12 teams participating just in track 5, English. Two teams participated exclusively in tracks 4a and 4b, English-Spanish. One team took part solely in track 1, Arabic.

Year	Data set	Pairs	Source
2017	Trial	23	Mixed STS 2016
2017	MSRpar	1020	newswire
2017	MSRvid	736	videos
2017	SMTeuroparl	406	WMT eval.

Table 7: Arabic-English training data.

Year	Data set	Pairs	Source
2017	MSRpar	1039	newswire
2017	MSRvid	749	videos
2017	SMTeuroparl	422	WMT eval.

Table 8: Arabic-English parallel data.

6.2 Evaluation Metric

Systems are evaluated on each track by their Pearson correlation with gold labels. The overall ranking averages the correlations across tracks 1-5 with tracks 4a and 4b individually contributing.

Track	Language(s)	Participants
1	Arabic	49
2	Arabic-English	45
3	Spanish	48
4a	Spanish-English	53
4b	Spanish-English MT	53
5	English	77
6	Turkish-English	48
Primary	All except Turkish	44

Table 9: Participation by shared task track.

6.3 CodaLab

As directed by the SemEval workshop organizers, the CodaLab research platform hosts the task.[11]

6.4 Baseline

The baseline is the cosine of binary sentence vectors with each dimension representing whether an individual word appears in a sentence.[12] For cross-lingual pairs, non-English sentences are translated into English using state-of-the-art machine translation.[13] The baseline achieves an average correlation of 53.7 with human judgment on tracks 1-5 and would rank 23rd overall out the 44 system submissions that participated in all tracks.

---

[11]https://competitions.codalab.org/competitions/16051

[12]Words obtained using Arabic (ar), Spanish (es) and English (en) Treebank tokenizers.

[13]http://translate.google.com

6.5 Rankings

Participant performance is provided in Table 10. ECNU is best overall (avg r: 0.7316) and achieves the highest participant evaluation score on: track 2, Arabic-English (r: 0.7493); track 3, Spanish (r: 0.8559); and track 6, Turkish-English (r: 0.7706). BIT attains the best performance on track 1, Arabic (r: 0.7543). CompiLIG places first on track 4a, SNLI Spanish-English (r: 0.8302). SEF@UHH exhibits the best correlation on the difficult track 4b WMT quality estimation pairs (r: 0.3407). RTV has the best system for the track 5 English data (r: 0.8547), followed closely by DT_Team (r: 0.8536).

Especially challenging tracks with SNLI data are: track 1, Arabic; track 2, Arabic-English; and track 6, English-Turkish. Spanish-English performance is much higher on track 4a's SNLI data than track 4b's MT quality estimation data. This highlights the difficulty and importance of making fine grained distinctions for certain downstream applications. Assessing STS methods for quality estimation may benefit from using alternatives to Pearson correlation for evaluation.[14]

Results tend to decrease on cross-lingual tracks. The baseline drops > 10% relative on Arabic-English and Spanish-English (SNLI) vs. monolingual Arabic and Spanish. Many participant systems show smaller decreases. ECNU's top ranking entry performs slightly better on Arabic-English than Arabic, with a slight drop from Spanish to Spanish-English (SNLI).

6.6 Methods

Participating teams explore techniques ranging from state-of-the-art deep learning models to elaborate feature engineered systems. Prediction signals include surface similarity scores such as edit distance and matching n-grams, scores derived from word alignments across pairs, assessment by MT evaluation metrics, estimates of conceptual similarity as well as the similarity between word and sentence level embeddings. For cross-lingual and non-English tracks, MT was widely used to convert the two sentences being compared into the same language.[15] Select methods are highlighted below.

---

[14]e.g., Reimers et al. (2016) report success using STS labels with alternative metrics such as normalized Cumulative Gain (nCG), normalized Discounted Cumulative Gain (nDCG) and F1 to more accurately predict performance on the downstream tasks: text reuse detection, binary classification of document relatedness and document relatedness within a corpus.

[15]Within the highlighted submissions, the following use a monolingual English system fed by MT: ECNU, BIT, HCTI

Team	Primary	Track 1 AR-AR	Track 2 AR-EN	Track 3 SP-SP	Track 4a SP-EN	Track 4b SP-EN-WMT	Track 5 EN-EN	Track 6 EN-TR
ECNU (Tian et al., 2017)	73.16	**74.40**	**74.93**•	**85.59**•	**81.31**	**33.63**	**85.18**	**77.06**•
ECNU (Tian et al., 2017)	70.44	**73.80**	71.26	**84.56**	74.95	**33.11**	**81.81**	73.62
ECNU (Tian et al., 2017)	69.40	**72.71**	69.75	82.47	76.49	**26.33**	**83.87**	74.20
BIT (Wu et al., 2017)*	67.89	**74.17**	69.65	**84.99**	78.28	11.07	**84.00**	**73.05**
BIT (Wu et al., 2017)*	67.03	75.35	70.07	83.23	78.13	7.58	81.61	73.27
BIT (Wu et al., 2017)	66.62	**75.43**•	69.53	**82.89**	77.61	5.84	**82.22**	**72.80**
HCTI (Shao, 2017)	65.98	**71.30**	68.36	**82.63**	76.21	14.83	81.13	67.41
MITRE (Henderson et al., 2017)	65.90	**72.94**	67.53	82.02	78.02	15.98	80.53	64.30
MITRE (Henderson et al., 2017)	65.87	**73.04**	67.40	82.01	77.99	15.74	80.48	64.41
FCICU (Hassan et al., 2017)	61.90	**71.58**	67.82	**84.84**	69.26	2.54	**82.72**	54.52
neobility (Zhuang and Chang, 2017)	61.71	68.21	64.59	79.28	71.69	2.00	79.27	66.96
FCICU (Hassan et al., 2017)	61.66	**71.58**	67.81	**84.89**	68.54	2.14	**82.80**	53.90
STS-UHH (Kohail et al., 2017)	60.58	67.81	63.07	77.13	72.01	4.81	79.89	59.37
RTV	60.50	67.13	55.95	74.85	70.50	7.61	**85.41**	62.04
HCTI (Shao, 2017)	59.88	43.73	68.36	67.09	76.21	14.83	**81.56**	67.41
RTV	59.80	66.89	54.82	74.24	69.99	7.34	**85.41**	59.89
MatrusriIndia	59.60	68.60	54.64	76.14	71.18	5.72	77.44	63.49
STS-UHH (Kohail et al., 2017)	57.25	61.04	59.10	72.04	63.38	12.05	73.39	59.72
SEF@UHH (Duma and Menzel, 2017)	56.76	57.90	53.84	74.23	58.66	18.02	72.56	62.11
SEF@UHH (Duma and Menzel, 2017)	56.44	55.88	47.89	74.56	57.39	**30.69**	78.80	49.90
RTV	56.33	61.43	48.32	68.63	61.40	8.29	**85.47**•	60.79
SEF@UHH (Duma and Menzel, 2017)	55.28	57.74	48.13	69.79	56.60	**34.07**•	71.86	48.78
neobility (Zhuang and Chang, 2017)	51.95	13.69	62.59	77.92	69.30	0.44	75.56	64.18
neobility (Zhuang and Chang, 2017)	50.25	3.69	62.07	76.90	69.47	1.47	75.35	62.79
MatrusriIndia	49.75	57.03	43.40	67.86	55.63	8.57	65.79	49.94
NLPProxem	49.02	51.93	53.13	66.42	51.44	9.96	62.56	47.67
UMDeep (Barrow and Peskov, 2017)	47.92	47.53	49.39	51.65	56.15	16.09	61.74	52.93
NLPProxem	47.90	55.06	43.69	63.81	50.79	14.14	64.63	43.20
UMDeep (Barrow and Peskov, 2017)	47.73	45.87	51.99	51.48	52.32	13.00	62.22	57.25
Lump (España Bonet and Barrón-Cedeño, 2017)*	47.25	60.52	18.29	75.74	43.27	1.16	73.76	58.00
Lump (España Bonet and Barrón-Cedeño, 2017)*	47.04	55.08	13.57	76.76	48.25	11.12	72.69	51.79
Lump (España Bonet and Barrón-Cedeño, 2017)*	44.38	62.87	18.05	73.80	44.47	1.51	73.47	36.52
NLPProxem	40.70	53.27	47.73	0.16	55.06	14.40	66.81	47.46
RTM (Biçici, 2017)*	36.69	33.65	17.11	69.90	60.04	14.55	54.68	6.87
UMDeep (Barrow and Peskov, 2017)	35.21	39.05	37.13	45.88	34.82	5.86	47.27	36.44
RTM (Biçici, 2017)*	32.91	33.65	0.25	56.82	50.54	13.68	64.05	11.36
RTM (Biçici, 2017)*	32.78	41.56	13.32	48.41	45.83	23.47	56.32	0.55
ResSim (Bjerva and Östling, 2017)	31.48	28.92	10.45	66.13	23.89	3.05	69.06	18.84
ResSim (Bjerva and Östling, 2017)	29.38	31.20	12.88	69.20	10.02	1.62	68.77	11.95
ResSim (Bjerva and Östling, 2017)	21.45	0.33	10.98	54.65	22.62	1.99	50.57	9.02
LIPN-IIMAS (Arroyo-Fernández and Meza Ruiz, 2017)	10.67	4.71	7.69	15.27	17.19	14.46	7.38	8.00
LIPN-IIMAS (Arroyo-Fernández and Meza Ruiz, 2017)	9.26	2.14	12.92	4.58	1.20	1.91	20.38	21.68
hjpwhu	4.80	4.12	6.39	6.17	2.04	6.24	1.14	7.53
hjpwhu	2.94	4.77	2.04	7.63	0.46	2.57	0.69	2.46
compiLIG (Ferrero et al., 2017)					**83.02**•	15.50		
compiLIG (Ferrero et al., 2017)					76.84	14.64		
compiLIG (Ferrero et al., 2017)					79.10	14.94		
DT_TEAM (Maharjan et al., 2017)							**85.36**	
DT_TEAM (Maharjan et al., 2017)							**83.60**	
DT_TEAM (Maharjan et al., 2017)							83.29	
FCICU (Hassan et al., 2017)							**82.17**	
ITNLPAiKF (Liu et al., 2017)							82.31	
ITNLPAiKF (Liu et al., 2017)							82.31	
ITNLPAiKF (Liu et al., 2017)							81.59	
L2F/INESC-ID (Fialho et al., 2017)*				76.16	1.91	5.44	78.11	2.93
L2F/INESC-ID (Fialho et al., 2017)							69.52	
L2F/INESC-ID (Fialho et al., 2017)*				63.85	15.61	5.24	66.61	3.56
LIM-LIG (Nagoudi et al., 2017)		**74.63**						
LIM-LIG (Nagoudi et al., 2017)		**73.09**						
LIM-LIG (Nagoudi et al., 2017)		59.57						
MatrusriIndia		68.60		76.14	71.18	5.72	77.44	63.49
NRC*					42.25	0.23		
NRC					28.08	11.33		
OkadaNaoya							77.04	
OPI-JSA (Śpiewak et al., 2017)							78.50	
OPI-JSA (Śpiewak et al., 2017)							73.42	
OPI-JSA (Śpiewak et al., 2017)							67.96	
PurdueNLP (Lee et al., 2017)							79.28	
PurdueNLP (Lee et al., 2017)							55.35	
PurdueNLP (Lee et al., 2017)							53.11	
QLUT (Meng et al., 2017)*							64.33	
QLUT (Meng et al., 2017)							61.55	
QLUT (Meng et al., 2017)*							49.24	
SIGMA							80.47	
SIGMA							80.08	
SIGMA							79.12	
SIGMA_PKU_2							81.34	
SIGMA_PKU_2							81.27	
SIGMA_PKU_2							80.61	
STS-UHH (Kohail et al., 2017)							80.93	
UCSC-NLP							77.29	
UdL (Al-Natsheh et al., 2017)							80.04	
UdL (Al-Natsheh et al., 2017)*							79.01	
UdL (Al-Natsheh et al., 2017)							78.05	
cosine baseline	53.70	60.45	51.55	71.17	62.20	3.20•	72.78	54.56

* Corrected or late submission

Table 10: STS 2017 rankings ordered by average correlation across tracks 1-5. Performance is reported by convention as Pearson's $r \times 100$. For tracks 1-6, the top ranking result is marked with a • symbol and results in bold have no statistically significant difference with the best result on a track, $p > 0.05$ Williams' t-test (Diedenhofen and Musch, 2015).

ECNU (Tian et al., 2017) The best overall system is from ENCU and ensembles well performing a feature engineered models with deep learning methods. Three feature engineered models use Random Forest (RF), Gradient Boosting (GB) and XGBoost (XGB) regression methods with features based on: n-gram overlap; edit distance; longest common prefix/suffix/substring; tree kernels (Moschitti, 2006); word alignments (Sultan et al., 2015); summarization and MT evaluation metrics (BLEU, GTM-3, NIST, WER, METEOR, ROUGE); and kernel similarity of bags-of-words, bags-of-dependencies and pooled word-embeddings. ECNU's deep learning models are differentiated by their approach to sentence embeddings using either: averaged word embeddings, projected word embeddings, a deep averaging network (DAN) (Iyyer et al., 2015) or LSTM (Hochreiter and Schmidhuber, 1997). Each network feeds the element-wise multiplication, subtraction and concatenation of paired sentence embeddings to additional layers to predict similarity scores. The ensemble averages scores from the four deep learning and three feature engineered models.[16]

BIT (Wu et al., 2017) Second place overall is achieved by BIT primarily using sentence information content (IC) informed by WordNet and BNC word frequencies. One submission uses sentence IC exclusively. Another ensembles IC with Sultan et al. (2015)'s alignment method, while a third ensembles IC with cosine similarity of summed word embeddings with an IDF weighting scheme. Sentence IC in isolation outperforms all systems except those from ECNU. Combining sentence IC with word embedding similarity performs best.

HCTI (Shao, 2017) Third place overall is obtained by HCTI with a model similar to a convolutional Deep Structured Semantic Model (CDSSM) (Chen et al., 2015; Huang et al., 2013). Sentence embeddings are generated with twin convolutional neural networks (CNNs). The embeddings are then compared using cosine similarity and element wise difference with the resulting values fed to additional layers to predict similarity labels. The architecture is abstractly similar to ECNU's deep learning models. UMDeep (Barrow and Peskov, 2017) took a similar approach using LSTMs rather than CNNs for the sentence embeddings.

MITRE (Henderson et al., 2017) Fourth place overall is MITRE that, like ECNU, takes an ambitious feature engineering approach complemented by deep learning. Ensembled components include: alignment similarity; TakeLab STS (Šarić et al., 2012b); string similarity measures such as matching n-grams, summarization and MT metrics (BLEU, WER, PER, ROUGE); a RNN and recurrent convolutional neural networks (RCNN) over word alignments; and a BiLSTM that is state-of-the-art for textual entailment (Chen et al., 2016).

FCICU (Hassan et al., 2017) Fifth place overall is FCICU that computes a sense-base alignment using BabelNet (Navigli and Ponzetto, 2010). Babel-Net synsets are multilingual allowing non-English and cross-lingual pairs to be processed similarly to English pairs. Alignment similarity scores are used with two runs: one that combines the scores within a string kernel and another that uses them with a weighted variant of Sultan et al. (2015)'s method. Both runs average the Babelnet based scores with soft-cardinality (Jimenez et al., 2012b).

CompiLIG (Ferrero et al., 2017) The best Spanish-English performance on SNLI sentences was achieved by CompiLIG using features including: cross-lingual conceptual similarity using DBNary (Serasset, 2015), cross-language Multi-Vec word embeddings (Berard et al., 2016), and Brychcin and Svoboda (2016)'s improvements to Sultan et al. (2015)'s method.

LIM-LIG (Nagoudi et al., 2017) Using only weighted word embeddings, LIM-LIG took second place on Arabic.[17] Arabic word embeddings are summed into sentence embeddings using uniform, POS and IDF weighting schemes. Sentence similarity is computed by cosine similarity. POS and IDF outperform uniform weighting. Combining the IDF and POS weights by multiplication is reported by LIM-LIG to achieve r 0.7667, higher than all submitted Arabic (track 1) systems.

DT_Team (Maharjan et al., 2017) Second place on English (track 5)[18] is DT_Team using feature en-

---

and MITRE. HCTI submitted a separate run using ar, es and en trained models that underperformed using their en model with MT for ar and es. CompiLIG's model is cross-lingual but includes a word alignment feature that depends on MT. SEF@UHH built ar, es, and en models and use bi-directional MT for cross-lingual pairs. LIM-LIG and DT_Team only participate in monolingual tracks.

[16]The two remaining ECNU runs only use either RF or GB and exclude the deep learning models.

[17]The approach is similar to SIF (Arora et al., 2017) but without removal of the common principle component

[18]RTV took first place on track 5, English, but submitted no system description paper.

Genre	Train	Dev	Test	Total
news	3299	500	500	4299
caption	2000	625	525	3250
forum	450	375	254	1079
total	5749	1500	1379	8628

Table 11: STS Benchmark annotated examples by genres (rows) and by train, dev. test splits (columns).

gineering combined with the following deep learning models: DSSM (Huang et al., 2013), CDSSM (Shen et al., 2014) and skip-thoughts (Kiros et al., 2015). Engineered features include: unigram overlap, summed word alignments scores, fraction of unaligned words, difference in word counts by type (all, adj, adverbs, nouns, verbs), and min to max ratios of words by type. Select features have a multiplicative penalty for unaligned words.

SEF@UHH (Duma and Menzel, 2017) First place on the challenging Spanish-English MT pairs (Track 4b) is SEF@UHH. Unsupervised similarity scores are computed from paragraph vectors (Le and Mikolov, 2014) using cosine, negation of Bray-Curtis dissimilarity and vector correlation. MT converts cross-lingual pairs, L_1-L_2, into two monolingual pairs, L_1-L_1 and L_2-L_2, with averaging used to combine the monolingual similarity scores. Bray-Curtis performs well overall, while cosine does best on the Spanish-English MT pairs.

7 Analysis

Figure 1 plots model similarity scores against human STS labels for the top 5 systems from tracks 5 (English), 1 (Arabic) and 4b (English-Spanish MT). While many systems return scores on the same scale as the gold labels, 0-5, others return scores from approximately 0 and 1. Lines on the graphs illustrate perfect performance for both a 0-5 and a 0-1 scale. Mapping the 0 to 1 scores to range from 0-5,[20] approximately 80% of the scores from top performing English systems are within 1.0 pt of the gold label. Errors for Arabic are more broadly distributed, particularly for model scores between 1 and 4. The English-Spanish MT plots the weak relationship between the predicted and gold scores.

Table 12 provides examples of difficult sentence pairs for participant systems and illustrates common sources of error for even well-ranking systems including: (i) *word sense disambiguation* "making"

and "preparing" are very similar in the context of "food", while "picture" and "movie" are not similar when picture is followed by "day"; (ii) *attribute importance* "outside" vs. "deserted" are smaller details when contrasting "The man is in a deserted field" with "The man is outside in the field"; (iii) *compositional meaning* "A man is carrying a canoe with a dog" has the same content words as "A dog is carrying a man in a canoe" but carries a different meaning; (iv) *negation* systems score "...with goggles and a swimming cap" as nearly equivalent to "...without goggles or a swimming cap". Inflated similarity scores for examples like "There is a young girl" vs. "There is a young boy with the woman" demonstrate (v) *semantic blending*, whereby appending "with a woman" to "boy" brings its representation closer to that of "girl".

For multilingual and cross-lingual pairs, these issues are magnified by translation errors for systems that use MT followed by the application of a monolingual similarity model. For track 4b Spanish-English MT pairs, some of the poor performance can in part be attributed to many systems using MT to re-translate the output of another MT system, obscuring errors in the original translation.

7.1 Contrasting Cross-lingual STS with MT Quality Estimation

Since MT quality estimation pairs are translations of the same sentence, they are expected to be minimally on the same topic and have an STS score ≥ 1.[21] The actual distribution of STS scores is such that only 13% of the test instances score below 3, 22% of the instances score 3, 12% score 4 and 53% score 5. The high STS scores indicate that MT systems are surprisingly good at preserving meaning. However, even for a human, interpreting changes caused by translations errors can be difficult due both to disfluencies and subtle errors with important changes in meaning.

The Pearson correlation between the gold MT quality scores and the gold STS scores is 0.41, which shows that translation quality measures and STS are only moderately correlated. Differences are in part explained by translation quality scores penalizing all mismatches between the source segment and its translation, whereas STS focuses on differences in meaning. However, the difficult interpretation work required for STS annotation may

---

[19]ECNU, BIT and LIM-LIG are scaled to the range 0-5.

[20]$s_{new} = 5 \times \frac{s - min(s)}{max(s) - min(s)}$ is used to rescale scores.

[21]The evaluation data for track 4b does in fact have STS scores that are ≥ 1 for all pairs. In the 1,000 sentence training set for this track, one sentence that received a score of zero.

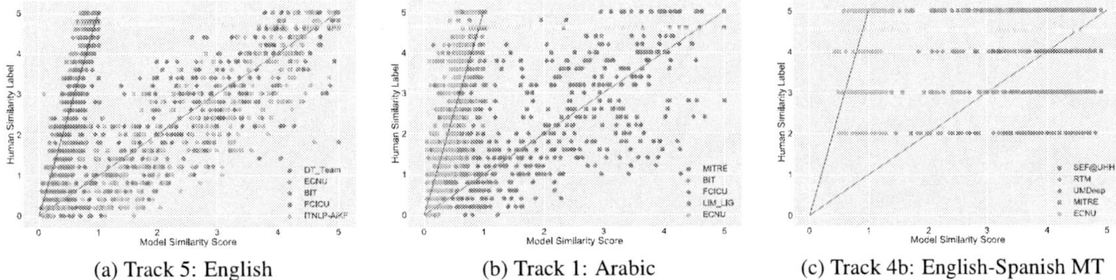

(a) Track 5: English	(b) Track 1: Arabic	(c) Track 4b: English-Spanish MT

Figure 1: Model vs. human similarity scores for top systems.

Pairs	Human	DT_Team	ECNU	BIT	FCICU	ITNLP-AiKF
There is a cook preparing food. A cook is making food.	5.0	4.1	4.1	3.7	3.9	4.5
The man is in a deserted field. The man is outside in the field.	4.0	3.0	3.1	3.6	3.1	2.8
A girl in water without goggles or a swimming cap. A girl in water, with goggles and swimming cap.	3.0	4.8	4.6	4.0	4.7	0.1
A man is carrying a canoe with a dog. A dog is carrying a man in a canoe.	1.8	3.2	4.7	4.9	5.0	4.6
There is a young girl. There is a young boy with the woman.	1.0	2.6	3.3	3.9	1.9	3.1
The kids are at the theater watching a movie. it is picture day for the boys	0.2	1.0	2.3	2.0	0.8	1.7

Table 12: Difficult English sentence pairs (Track 5) and scores assigned by top performing systems.[19]

Genre	File	Yr.	Train	Dev	Test
news	MSRpar	12	1000	250	250
news	headlines	13/6	1999	250	250
news	deft-news	14	300	0	0
captions	MSRvid	12	1000	250	250
captions	images	14/5	1000	250	250
captions	track5.en-en	17	0	125	125
forum	deft-forum	14	450	0	0
forum	ans-forums	15	0	375	0
forum	ans-ans	16	0	0	254

Table 13: STS Benchmark detailed break-down by files and years.

increase the risk of inconsistent and subjective labels. The annotations for MT quality estimation are produced as by-product of post-editing. Humans fix MT output and the edit distance between the output and its post-edited correction provides the quality score. This post-editing based procedure is known to produce relatively consistent estimates across annotators.

8 STS Benchmark

The STS Benchmark is a careful selection of the English data sets used in SemEval and *SEM STS shared tasks between 2012 and 2017. Tables 11 and 13 provide details on the composition of the benchmark. The data is partitioned into training, development and test sets.[22] The development set can be used to design new models and tune hyperparameters. The test set should be used sparingly and only after a model design and hyperparameters have been locked against further changes. Using the STS Benchmark enables comparable assessments across different research efforts and improved tracking of the state-of-the-art.

Table 14 shows the STS Benchmark results for some of the best systems from Track 5 (EN-EN)[23] and compares their performance to competitive baselines from the literature. All baselines were run by the organizers using canonical pre-trained models made available by the originator of each method,[24] with the exception of PV-DBOW that

[22]Similar to the STS shared task, while the training set is provided as a convenience, researchers are encourage to incorporate other supervised and unsupervised data as long as no supervised annotations of the test partitions are used.

[23]Each participant submitted the run which did best in the development set of the STS Benchmark, which happened to be the same as their best run in Track 5 in all cases.

[24]**sent2vec:** https://github.com/epfml/ sent2vec, trained model sent2vec_twitter_unigrams; **SIF:** https://github.com/epfml/sent2vec Wikipedia trained word frequencies enwiki_vocab_min200.txt, https://github.com/alexandres/lexvec embeddings from lexvec.commoncrawl.300d.W+C.pos.vectors, first 15 principle components removed, $\alpha = 0.001$, dev

STS 2017 Participants on STS Benchmark				
Name	Description		Dev	Test
ECNU	Ensemble (Tian et al., 2017)		84.7	81.0
BIT	WordNet+Embeddings (Wu et al., 2017)		82.9	80.9
DT_TEAM	Ensemble (Maharjan et al., 2017)		83.0	79.2
HCTI	CNN (Shao, 2017)		83.4	78.4
SEF@UHH	Doc2Vec (Duma and Menzel, 2017)		61.6	59.2
Sentence Level Baselines				
sent2vec	Sentence spanning CBOW with words & bigrams (Pagliardini et al., 2017)		78.7	75.5
SIF	Word embedding weighting & principle component removal (Arora et al., 2017)		80.1	72.0
InferSent	Sentence embedding from bi-directional LSTM trained on SNLI (Conneau et al., 2017)		80.1	75.8
C-PHRASE	Prediction of syntactic constituent context words (Pham et al., 2015)		74.3	63.9
PV-DBOW	Paragraph vectors, Doc2Vec DBOW (Le and Mikolov, 2014; Lau and Baldwin, 2016)		72.2	64.9
Averaged Word Embedding Baselines				
LexVec	Weighted matrix factorization of PPMI (Salle et al., 2016a,b)		68.9	55.8
FastText	Skip-gram with sub-word character n-grams (Joulin et al., 2016)		65.3	53.6
Paragram	Paraphrase Database (PPDB) fit word embeddings (Wieting et al., 2015)		63.0	50.1
GloVe	Word co-occurrence count fit embeddings (Pennington et al., 2014)		52.4	40.6
Word2vec	Skip-gram prediction of words in a context window (Mikolov et al., 2013a,b)		70.0	56.5

Table 14: STS Benchmark. Pearson's $r \times 100$ results for select participants and baseline models.

uses the model from Lau and Baldwin (2016) and InferSent which was reported independently. When multiple pre-trained models are available for a method, we report results for the one with the best dev set performance. For each method, input sentences are preprocessed to closely match the tokenization of the pre-trained models.[25] Default

experiments varied α, principle components removed and whether GloVe, LexVec, or Word2Vec word embeddings were used; **C-PHRASE**: http://clic.cimec.unitn.it/composes/cphrase-vectors.html; **PV-DBOW**: https://github.com/jhlau/doc2vec, AP-NEWS trained apnews_dbow.tgz; **LexVec**: https://github.com/alexandres/lexvec, embedddings lexvec.commoncrawl.300d.W.pos.vectors.gz; **FastText**: https://github.com/facebookresearch/fastText/blob/master/pretrained-vectors.md, Wikipedia trained embeddings from wiki.en.vec; **Paragram**: http://ttic.uchicago.edu/~wieting/, embeddings trained on PPDB and tuned to WS353 from Paragram-WS353; **GloVe**: https://nlp.stanford.edu/projects/glove/, Wikipedia and Gigaword trained 300 dim. embeddings from glove.6B.zip; **Word2vec**: https://code.google.com/archive/p/word2vec/, Google News trained embeddings from GoogleNews-vectors-negative300.bin.gz.

[25]**sent2vec**: results shown here tokenized by tweetTokenize.py constrasting dev experiments used wikiTokenize.py, both distributed with sent2vec. **LexVec**: numbers were converted into words, all punctuation was removed, and text is lowercased; **FastText**: Since, to our knowledge, the tokenizer and preprocessing used for the pre-trained FastText embeddings is not publicly described. We use the following heuristics to preprocess and tokenize sentences for Fast-Text: numbers are converted into words, text is lowercased, and finally prefixed, suffixed and infixed punctuation is recursively removed from each token that does not match an entry in the model's lexicon; **Paragram**: Joshua (Matt Post, 2015) pipeline to pre-process and tokenized English text; **C-PHRASE, GloVe, PV-DBOW & SIF**: PTB tokenization provided by Stanford CoreNLP (Manning et al., 2014) with post-processing based on dev OOVs; **Word2vec**: Similar to Fast-

inference hyperparameters are used unless noted otherwise. The *averaged word embedding baselines* compute a sentence embedding by averaging word embeddings and then using cosine to compute pairwise sentence similarity scores.

While state-of-the-art baselines for obtaining sentence embeddings perform reasonably well on the benchmark data, improved performance is obtained by top 2017 STS shared task systems. There is still substantial room for further improvement. To follow the current state-of-the-art, visit the leaderboard on the STS wiki.[26]

9 Conclusion

We have presented the results of the 2017 STS shared task. This year's shared task differed substantially from previous iterations of STS in that the primary emphasis of the task shifted from English to multilingual and cross-lingual STS involving four different languages: Arabic, Spanish, English and Turkish. Even with this substantial change relative to prior evaluations, the shared task obtained strong participation. 31 teams produced 84 system submissions with 17 teams producing a total of 44 system submissions that processed pairs in all of the STS 2017 languages. For languages that were part of prior STS evaluations

Text, to our knowledge, the preprocessing for the pre-trained Word2vec embeddings is not publicly described. We use the following heuristics for the Word2vec experiment: All numbers longer than a single digit are converted into a '#' (e.g., 24 → ##) then prefixed, suffixed and infixed punctuation is recursively removed from each token that does not match an entry in the model's lexicon.

[26]http://ixa2.si.ehu.es/stswiki/index.php/STSbenchmark

(e.g., English and Spanish), state-of-the-art systems are able to achieve strong correlations with human judgment. However, we obtain weaker correlations from participating systems for Arabic, Arabic-English and Turkish-English. This suggests further research is necessary in order to develop robust models that can both be readily applied to new languages and perform well even when less supervised training data is available. To provide a standard benchmark for English STS, we present the STS Benchmark, a careful selection of the English data sets from previous STS tasks (2012-2017). To assist in interpreting the results from new models, a number of competitive baselines and select participant systems are evaluated on the benchmark data. Ongoing improvements to the current state-of-the-art is available from an online leaderboard.

Acknowledgments

We thank Alexis Conneau for the evaluation of InferSent on the STS Benchmark. This material is based in part upon work supported by QNRF-NPRP 6 - 1020-1-199 OPTDIAC that funded Arabic translation, and by a grant from the Spanish MINECO (projects TUNER TIN2015-65308-C5-1-R and MUSTER PCIN-2015-226 cofunded by EU FEDER) that funded STS label annotation and by the QT21 EU project (H2020 No. 645452) that funded STS labels and data preparation for machine translation pairs. Iñigo Lopez-Gazpio is supported by the Spanish MECD. Any opinions, findings, and conclusions or recommendations expressed in this material are those of the authors and do not necessarily reflect the views of QNRF-NPRP, Spanish MINECO, QT21 EU, or the Spanish MECD.

References

Eneko Agirre, Carmen Banea, Claire Cardie, Daniel Cer, Mona Diab, Aitor Gonzalez-Agirre, Weiwei Guo, Iñigo Lopez-Gazpio, Montse Maritxalar, Rada Mihalcea, German Rigau, Larraitz Uria, and Janyce Wiebe. 2015. SemEval-2015 Task 2: Semantic Textual Similarity, English, Spanish and Pilot on Interpretability. In *Proceedings of SemEval 2015*. http://www.aclweb.org/anthology/S15-2045.

Eneko Agirre, Carmen Banea, Claire Cardie, Daniel Cer, Mona Diab, Aitor Gonzalez-Agirre, Weiwei Guo, Rada Mihalcea, German Rigau, and Janyce Wiebe. 2014. SemEval-2014 Task 10: Multilingual semantic textual similarity. In *Proceedings of SemEval 2014*. http://www.aclweb.org/anthology/S14-2010.

Eneko Agirre, Carmen Banea, Daniel Cer, Mona Diab, Aitor Gonzalez-Agirre, Rada Mihalcea, German Rigau, and Janyce Wiebe. 2016. Semeval-2016 task 1: Semantic textual similarity, monolingual and cross-lingual evaluation. In *Proceedings of the SemEval-2016*. http://www.aclweb.org/anthology/S16-1081.

Eneko Agirre, Daniel Cer, Mona Diab, and Aitor Gonzalez-Agirre. 2012. SemEval-2012 Task 6: A pilot on semantic textual similarity. In *Proceedings of *SEM 2012/SemEval 2012*. http://www.aclweb.org/anthology/S12-1051.

Eneko Agirre, Daniel Cer, Mona Diab, Aitor Gonzalez-Agirre, and Weiwei Guo. 2013. *SEM 2013 shared task: Semantic Textual Similarity. In *Proceedings of *SEM 2013*. http://www.aclweb.org/anthology/S13-1004.

Hussein T. Al-Natsheh, Lucie Martinet, Fabrice Muhlenbach, and Djamel Abdelkader ZIGHED. 2017. UdL at SemEval-2017 Task 1: Semantic textual similarity estimation of english sentence pairs using regression model over pairwise features. In *Proceedings of SemEval-2017*. http://www.aclweb.org/anthology/S17-2013.

Sanjeev Arora, Yingyu Liang, and Tengyu Ma. 2017. A simple but tough-to-beat baseline for sentence embeddings. In *Proceedings of ICLR 2017*. https://openreview.net/pdf?id=SyK00v5xx.

Ignacio Arroyo-Fernández and Ivan Vladimir Meza Ruiz. 2017. LIPN-IIMAS at SemEval-2017 Task 1: Subword embeddings, attention recurrent neural networks and cross word alignment for semantic textual similarity. In *Proceedings of SemEval-2017*. http://www.aclweb.org/anthology/S17-2031.

Collin F. Baker, Charles J. Fillmore, and John B. Lowe. 1998. The Berkeley FrameNet Project. In *Proceedings of COLING '98*. http://aclweb.org/anthology/P/P98/P98-1013.pdf.

Daniel Bär, Chris Biemann, Iryna Gurevych, and Torsten Zesch. 2012. Ukp: Computing semantic textual similarity by combining multiple content similarity measures. In *Proceedings of *SEM 2012/SemEval 2012*. http://www.aclweb.org/anthology/S12-1059.

Joe Barrow and Denis Peskov. 2017. UMDeep at SemEval-2017 Task 1: End-to-end shared weight LSTM model for semantic textual similarity. In *Proceedings of SemEval-2017*. http://www.aclweb.org/anthology/S17-2026.

Luisa Bentivogli, Raffaella Bernardi, Marco Marelli, Stefano Menini, Marco Baroni, and Roberto Zamparelli. 2016. SICK through the SemEval glasses. lesson learned from the evaluation of compositional distributional semantic models on full sentences through semantic relatedness and textual entailment. *Lang Resour Eval* 50(1):95–124. https://doi.org/10.1007/s10579-015-9332-5.

Alexandre Berard, Christophe Servan, Olivier Pietquin, and Laurent Besacier. 2016. MultiVec: a multilingual and multilevel representation learning toolkit for NLP. In *Proceedings of LREC 2016*. http://www.lrec-conf.org/proceedings/lrec2016/pdf/666_Paper.pdf.

Ergun Biçici. 2017. RTM at SemEval-2017 Task 1: Referential translation machines for predicting semantic similarity. In *Proceedings of SemEval-2017*. http://www.aclweb.org/anthology/S17-2030.

Johannes Bjerva and Robert Östling. 2017. ResSim at SemEval-2017 Task 1: Multilingual word representations for semantic textual similarity. In *Proceedings of SemEval-2017*. http://www.aclweb.org/anthology/S17-2021.

Ondrej Bojar, Christian Buck, Christian Federmann, Barry Haddow, Philipp Koehn, Johannes Leveling, Christof Monz, Pavel Pecina, Matt Post, Herve Saint-Amand, Radu Soricut, Lucia Specia, and Aleš Tamchyna. 2014. Findings of the 2014 workshop on statistical machine translation. In *Proceedings of WMT 2014*. http://www.aclweb.org/anthology/W/W14/W14-3302.pdf.

Ondřej Bojar, Christian Buck, Chris Callison-Burch, Christian Federmann, Barry Haddow, Philipp Koehn, Christof Monz, Matt Post, Radu Soricut, and Lucia Specia. 2013. Findings of the 2013 Workshop on Statistical Machine Translation. In *Proceedings of WMT 2013*. http://www.aclweb.org/anthology/W13-2201.

Samuel R. Bowman, Gabor Angeli, Christopher Potts, and Christopher D. Manning. 2015. A large annotated corpus for learning natural language inference. In *Proceedings of EMNLP 2015*. http://aclweb.org/anthology/D/D15/D15-1075.pdf.

Tomas Brychcin and Lukas Svoboda. 2016. UWB at SemEval-2016 Task 1: Semantic textual similarity using lexical, syntactic, and semantic information. In *Proceedings of SemEval 2016*. https://www.aclweb.org/anthology/S/S16/S16-1089.pdf.

Qian Chen, Xiaodan Zhu, Zhen-Hua Ling, Si Wei, and Hui Jiang. 2016. Enhancing and combining sequential and tree LSTM for natural language inference. *CoRR* abs/1609.06038. http://arxiv.org/abs/1609.06038.

Yun-Nung Chen, Dilek Hakkani-Tür, and Xiaodong He. 2015. Learning bidirectional intent embeddings by convolutional deep structured semantic models for spoken language understanding. In *Proceedings of NIPS-SLU, 2015*. https://www.microsoft.com/en-us/research/publication/learning-bidirectional-intent-embeddings-by-convolutional-deep-structured-semantic-models-for-spoken-language-understanding/.

Alexis Conneau, Douwe Kiela, Holger Schwenk, Loïc Barrault, and Antoine Bordes. 2017. Supervised learning of universal sentence representations from natural language inference data. *CoRR* abs/1705.02364. http://arxiv.org/abs/1705.02364.

Ido Dagan, Bill Dolan, Bernardo Magnini, and Dan Roth. 2010. Recognizing textual entailment: Rational, evaluation and approaches. *J. Nat. Language Eng.* 16:105–105. https://doi.org/10.1017/S1351324909990234.

Birk Diedenhofen and Jochen Musch. 2015. cocor: A comprehensive solution for the statistical comparison of correlations. *PLoS ONE* 10(4). http://dx.doi.org/10.1371/journal.pone.0121945.

Bill Dolan, Chris Quirk, and Chris Brockett. 2004. Unsupervised construction of large paraphrase corpora: Exploiting massively parallel news sources. In *Proceedings of COLING 04*. http://aclweb.org/anthology/C/C04/C04-1051.pdf.

Mirela-Stefania Duma and Wolfgang Menzel. 2017. SEF@UHH at SemEval-2017 Task 1: Unsupervised knowledge-free semantic textual similarity via paragraph vector. In *Proceedings of SemEval-2017*. http://www.aclweb.org/anthology/S17-2024.

Cristina España Bonet and Alberto Barrón-Cedeño. 2017. Lump at SemEval-2017 Task 1: Towards an interlingua semantic similarity. In *Proceedings of SemEval-2017*. http://www.aclweb.org/anthology/S17-2019.

Christiane Fellbaum. 1998. *WordNet: An Electronic Lexical Database*. MIT Press. https://books.google.com/books?id=Rehu8OOzMIMC.

Jérémy Ferrero, Laurent Besacier, Didier Schwab, and Frédéric Agnès. 2017. CompiLIG at SemEval-2017 Task 1: Cross-language plagiarism detection methods for semantic textual similarity. In *Proceedings of SemEval-2017*. http://www.aclweb.org/anthology/S17-2012.

Pedro Fialho, Hugo Patinho Rodrigues, Luísa Coheur, and Paulo Quaresma. 2017. L2f/inesc-id at semeval-2017 tasks 1 and 2: Lexical and semantic features in word and textual similarity. In *Proceedings of SemEval-2017*. http://www.aclweb.org/anthology/S17-2032.

Juri Ganitkevitch, Benjamin Van Durme, and Chris Callison-Burch. 2013. PPDB: The paraphrase database. In *Proceedings of NAACL/HLT 2013*. http://cs.jhu.edu/ ccb/publications/ppdb.pdf.

Basma Hassan, Samir AbdelRahman, Reem Bahgat, and Ibrahim Farag. 2017. FCICU at SemEval-2017 Task 1: Sense-based language independent semantic textual similarity approach. In *Proceedings of SemEval-2017*. http://www.aclweb.org/anthology/S17-2015.

Hua He, Kevin Gimpel, and Jimmy Lin. 2015. Multi-perspective sentence similarity modeling with convolutional neural networks. In *Proceedings of EMNLP*. pages 1576–1586. http://aclweb.org/anthology/D15-1181.

Hua He and Jimmy Lin. 2016. Pairwise word interaction modeling with deep neural networks for semantic similarity measurement. In *Proceedings of NAACL/HLT*. http://www.aclweb.org/anthology/N16-1108.

Hua He, John Wieting, Kevin Gimpel, Jinfeng Rao, and Jimmy Lin. 2016. UMD-TTIC-UW at SemEval-2016 Task 1: Attention-based multi-perspective convolutional neural networks for textual similarity measurement. In *Proceedings of SemEval 2016*. http://www.anthology.aclweb.org/S/S16/S16-1170.pdf.

John Henderson, Elizabeth Merkhofer, Laura Strickhart, and Guido Zarrella. 2017. MITRE at SemEval-2017 Task 1: Simple semantic similarity. In *Proceedings of SemEval-2017*. http://www.aclweb.org/anthology/S17-2027.

Felix Hill, Kyunghyun Cho, and Anna Korhonen. 2016. Learning distributed representations of sentences from unlabelled data. In *Proceedings of NAACL/HLT*. http://www.aclweb.org/anthology/N16-1162.

Sepp Hochreiter and Jürgen Schmidhuber. 1997. Long short-term memory. *Neural Comput.* 9(8):1735–1780. http://dx.doi.org/10.1162/neco.1997.9.8.1735.

Eduard Hovy, Mitchell Marcus, Martha Palmer, Lance Ramshaw, and Ralph Weischedel. 2006. OntoNotes: The 90% solution. In *Proceedings of NAACL/HLT 2006*. http://aclweb.org/anthology/N/N06/N06-2015.pdf.

Po-Sen Huang, Xiaodong He, Jianfeng Gao, Li Deng, Alex Acero, and Larry Heck. 2013. Learning deep structured semantic models for web search using clickthrough data. In *Proceedings of CIKM*. https://www.microsoft.com/en-us/research/publication/learning-deep-structured-semantic-models-for-web-search-using-clickthrough-data/.

Mohit Iyyer, Varun Manjunatha, Jordan Boyd-Graber, and Hal Daumé III. 2015. Deep unordered composition rivals syntactic methods for text classification. In *Proceedings of ACL/IJCNLP*. http://www.aclweb.org/anthology/P15-1162.

Sergio Jimenez, Claudia Becerra, and Alexander Gelbukh. 2012a. Soft cardinality: A parameterized similarity function for text comparison. In *Proceedings of *SEM 2012/SemEval 2012*. http://www.aclweb.org/anthology/S12-1061.

Sergio Jimenez, Claudia Becerra, and Alexander Gelbukh. 2012b. Soft Cardinality: A parameterized similarity function for text comparison. In *Proceedings of *SEM 2012/SemEval 2012*. http://aclweb.org/anthology/S/S12/S12-1061.pdf.

Armand Joulin, Edouard Grave, Piotr Bojanowski, and Tomas Mikolov. 2016. Bag of tricks for efficient text classification. *CoRR* abs/1607.01759. http://arxiv.org/abs/1607.01759.

Tom Kenter, Alexey Borisov, and Maarten de Rijke. 2016. Siamese cbow: Optimizing word embeddings for sentence representations. In *Proceedings of ACL*. http://www.aclweb.org/anthology/P16-1089.

Ryan Kiros, Yukun Zhu, Ruslan Salakhutdinov, Richard S. Zemel, Antonio Torralba, Raquel Urtasun, and Sanja Fidler. 2015. Skip-thought vectors. *CoRR* abs/1506.06726. http://arxiv.org/abs/1506.06726.

Sarah Kohail, Amr Rekaby Salama, and Chris Biemann. 2017. STS-UHH at SemEval-2017 Task 1: Scoring semantic textual similarity using supervised and unsupervised ensemble. In *Proceedings of SemEval-2017*. http://www.aclweb.org/anthology/S17-2025.

Jey Han Lau and Timothy Baldwin. 2016. An empirical evaluation of doc2vec with practical insights into document embedding generation. In *Proceedings of ACL Workshop on Representation Learning for NLP*. http://www.aclweb.org/anthology/W/W16/W16-1609.pdf.

Quoc V. Le and Tomas Mikolov. 2014. Distributed representations of sentences and documents. *CoRR* abs/1405.4053. http://arxiv.org/abs/1405.4053.

I-Ta Lee, Mahak Goindani, Chang Li, Di Jin, Kristen Marie Johnson, Xiao Zhang, Maria Leonor Pacheco, and Dan Goldwasser. 2017. PurdueNLP at SemEval-2017 Task 1: Predicting semantic textual similarity with paraphrase and event embeddings. In *Proceedings of SemEval-2017*. http://www.aclweb.org/anthology/S17-2029.

Wenjie Liu, Chengjie Sun, Lei Lin, and Bingquan Liu. 2017. ITNLP-AiKF at SemEval-2017 Task 1: Rich features based svr for semantic textual similarity computing. In *Proceedings of SemEval-2017*. http://www.aclweb.org/anthology/S17-2022.

Nabin Maharjan, Rajendra Banjade, Dipesh Gautam, Lasang J. Tamang, and Vasile Rus. 2017. Dt_team at semeval-2017 task 1: Semantic similarity using alignments, sentence-level embeddings and gaussian mixture model output. In *Proceedings of SemEval-2017*. http://www.aclweb.org/anthology/S17-2014.

Christopher D. Manning, Mihai Surdeanu, John Bauer, Jenny Finkel, Steven J. Bethard, and David McClosky. 2014. The Stanford CoreNLP natural language processing toolkit. In *Proceedings of ACL 2014 Demonstrations*. http://www.aclweb.org/anthology/P/P14/P14-5010.

Marco Marelli, Stefano Menini, Marco Baroni, Luisa Bentivogli, Raffaella Bernardi, and Roberto Zamparelli. 2014. A SICK cure for the evaluation of compositional distributional semantic models. In *Proceedings of LREC 14*. http://www.lrec-conf.org/proceedings/lrec2014/pdf/363_Paper.pdf.

Yuan Cao Gaurav Kumar Matt Post. 2015. Joshua 6: A phrase-based and hierarchical statistical machine translation. *The Prague Bulletin of Mathematical Linguistics* 104:516. https://ufal.mff.cuni.cz/pbml/104/art-post-cao-kumar.pdf.

Fanqing Meng, Wenpeng Lu, Yuteng Zhang, Jinyong Cheng, Yuehan Du, and Shuwang Han. 2017. QLUT at SemEval-2017 Task 1: Semantic textual similarity based on word embeddings. In *Proceedings of SemEval-2017*. http://www.aclweb.org/anthology/S17-2020.

Tomas Mikolov, Kai Chen, Greg Corrado, and Jeffrey Dean. 2013a. Efficient estimation of word representations in vector space. *CoRR* abs/1301.3781. http://arxiv.org/abs/1301.3781.

Tomas Mikolov, Ilya Sutskever, Kai Chen, Greg S Corrado, and Jeff Dean. 2013b. Distributed representations of words and phrases and their compositionality. In *Proceedings of NIPS 2013*. http://papers.nips.cc/paper/5021-distributed-representations-of-words-and-phrases-and-their-compositionality.pdf.

George A. Miller. 1995. WordNet: A lexical database for english. *Commun. ACM* 38(11):39–41. https://doi.org/10.1145/219717.219748.

Alessandro Moschitti. 2006. Efficient convolution kernels for dependency and constituent syntactic trees. In *Proceedings of ECML'06*. http://dx.doi.org/10.1007/11871842_32.

Jiaqi Mu, Suma Bhat, and Pramod Viswanath. 2017. Representing sentences as low-rank subspaces. *CoRR* abs/1704.05358. http://arxiv.org/abs/1704.05358.

El Moatez Billah Nagoudi, Jérémy Ferrero, and Didier Schwab. 2017. LIM-LIG at SemEval-2017 Task1: Enhancing the semantic similarity for arabic sentences with vectors weighting. In *Proceedings of SemEval-2017*. http://www.aclweb.org/anthology/S17-2017.

Roberto Navigli and Simone Paolo Ponzetto. 2010. BabelNet: Building a very large multilingual semantic network. In *Proceedings of ACL 2010*. http://aclweb.org/anthology/P/P10/P10-1023.pdf.

Matteo Pagliardini, Prakhar Gupta, and Martin Jaggi. 2017. Unsupervised Learning of Sentence Embeddings using Compositional n-Gram Features. *arXiv* https://arxiv.org/pdf/1703.02507.pdf.

Robert Parker, David Graff, Junbo Kong, Ke Chen, and Kazuaki Maeda. 2011. *Gigaword Fifth Edition LDC2011T07*. Linguistic Data Consortium. https://catalog.ldc.upenn.edu/ldc2011t07.

Jeffrey Pennington, Richard Socher, and Christopher D. Manning. 2014. GloVe: Global Vectors for Word Representation. In *Proceedings of EMNLP 2014*. http://www.aclweb.org/anthology/D14-1162.

Nghia The Pham, Germán Kruszewski, Angeliki Lazaridou, and Marco Baroni. 2015. Jointly optimizing word representations for lexical and sentential tasks with the c-phrase model. In *Proceedings of ACL/IJCNLP*. http://www.aclweb.org/anthology/P15-1094.

Nils Reimers, Philip Beyer, and Iryna Gurevych. 2016. Task-oriented intrinsic evaluation of semantic textual similarity. In *Proceedings of COLING 2016*. http://aclweb.org/anthology/C16-1009.

Barbara Rychalska, Katarzyna Pakulska, Krystyna Chodorowska, Wojciech Walczak, and Piotr Andruszkiewicz. 2016. Samsung Poland NLP Team at SemEval-2016 Task 1: Necessity for diversity; combining recursive autoencoders, wordnet and ensemble methods to measure semantic similarity. In *Proceedings of SemEval-2016*. http://www.aclweb.org/anthology/S16-1091.

Alexandre Salle, Marco Idiart, and Aline Villavicencio. 2016a. Enhancing the lexvec distributed word representation model using positional contexts and external memory. *CoRR* abs/1606.01283. http://arxiv.org/abs/1606.01283.

Alexandre Salle, Marco Idiart, and Aline Villavicencio. 2016b. Matrix factorization using window sampling and negative sampling for improved word representations. In *Proceedings of ACL*. http://aclweb.org/anthology/P16-2068.

Gilles Serasset. 2015. DBnary: Wiktionary as a lemon-based multilingual lexical resource in RDF. *Semantic Web Journal (special issue on Multilingual Linked Open Data)* 6:355–361. https://doi.org/10.3233/SW-140147.

Yang Shao. 2017. HCTI at SemEval-2017 Task 1: Use convolutional neural network to evaluate semantic textual similarity. In *Proceedings of SemEval-2017*. http://www.aclweb.org/anthology/S17-2016.

Yelong Shen, Xiaodong He, Jianfeng Gao, Li Deng, and Gregoire Mesnil. 2014. A latent semantic model with convolutional-pooling structure for information retrieval. In *Proceedings of CIKM '14*. https://www.microsoft.com/en-us/research/publication/a-latent-semantic-model-with-convolutional-pooling-structure-for-information-retrieval/.

Matthew Snover, Bonnie Dorr, Richard Schwartz, Linnea Micciulla, and John Makhoul. 2006. A study of translation edit rate with targeted human annotation. In *Proceedings of AMTA 2006*. http://mt-archive.info/AMTA-2006-Snover.pdf.

Martyna Śpiewak, Piotr Sobecki, and Daniel Karaś. 2017. OPI-JSA at SemEval-2017 Task 1: Application of ensemble learning for computing semantic textual similarity. In *Proceedings of SemEval-2017*. http://www.aclweb.org/anthology/S17-2018.

Md Arafat Sultan, Steven Bethard, and Tamara Sumner. 2015. DLS@CU: Sentence similarity from word alignment and semantic vector composition. In *Proceedings of SemEval 2015*. http://aclweb.org/anthology/S/S15/S15-2027.pdf.

Junfeng Tian, Zhiheng Zhou, Man Lan, and Yuanbin Wu. 2017. ECNU at SemEval-2017 Task 1: Leverage kernel-based traditional nlp features and neural networks to build a universal model for multilingual and cross-lingual semantic textual similarity. In *Proceedings of SemEval-2017*. http://www.aclweb.org/anthology/S17-2028.

Frane Šarić, Goran Glavaš, Mladen Karan, Jan Šnajder, and Bojana Dalbelo Bašić. 2012a. Takelab: Systems for measuring semantic text similarity. In *Proceedings of *SEM 2012/SemEval 2012*. http://www.aclweb.org/anthology/S12-1060.

Frane Šarić, Goran Glavaš, Mladen Karan, Jan Šnajder, and Bojana Dalbelo Bašić. 2012b. TakeLab: Systems for measuring semantic text similarity. In *Proceedings of SemEval 2012*. http://www.aclweb.org/anthology/S12-1060.

John Wieting, Mohit Bansal, Kevin Gimpel, and Karen Livescu. 2015. From paraphrase database to compositional paraphrase model and back. *Transactions of the ACL (TACL)* 3:345–358. http://aclweb.org/anthology/Q/Q15/Q15-1025.pdf.

John Wieting, Mohit Bansal, Kevin Gimpel, and Karen Livescu. 2016a. Charagram: Embedding words and sentences via character n-grams. In *Proceedings of EMNLP*. https://aclweb.org/anthology/D16-1157.

John Wieting, Mohit Bansal, Kevin Gimpel, and Karen Livescu. 2016b. Towards universal paraphrastic sentence embeddings. In *Proceedings of ICLR 2016*. http://arxiv.org/abs/1511.08198.

John Wieting and Kevin Gimpel. 2017. Revisiting recurrent networks for paraphrastic sentence embeddings. *CoRR* abs/1705.00364. http://arxiv.org/abs/1705.00364.

Hao Wu, Heyan Huang, Ping Jian, Yuhang Guo, and Chao Su. 2017. BIT at SemEval-2017 Task 1: Using semantic information space to evaluate semantic textual similarity. In *Proceedings of SemEval-2017*. http://www.aclweb.org/anthology/S17-2007.

Wei Xu, Chris Callison-Burch, and William B. Dolan. 2015. SemEval-2015 Task 1: Paraphrase and semantic similarity in Twitter (PIT). In *Proceedings of SemEval 2015*. http://www.aclweb.org/anthology/S15-2001.

Peter Young, Alice Lai, Micah Hodosh, and Julia Hockenmaier. 2014. From image descriptions to visual denotations: New similarity metrics for semantic inference over event descriptions. *TACL* 2:67–78. http://aclweb.org/anthology/Q14-1006.

WenLi Zhuang and Ernie Chang. 2017. Neobility at SemEval-2017 Task 1: An attention-based sentence similarity model. In *Proceedings SemEval-2017*. http://www.aclweb.org/anthology/S17-2023.

SemEval-2017 Task 2:
Multilingual and Cross-lingual Semantic Word Similarity

Jose Camacho-Collados[*][1]**, Mohammad Taher Pilehvar**[*][2]**,**
Nigel Collier[2] **and Roberto Navigli**[1]

[1]Department of Computer Science, Sapienza University of Rome
[2]Department of Theoretical and Applied Linguistics, University of Cambridge
[1]{collados,navigli}@di.uniroma1.it
[2]{mp792,nhc30}@cam.ac.uk

Abstract

This paper introduces a new task on Multilingual and Cross-lingual Semantic Word Similarity which measures the semantic similarity of word pairs within and across five languages: English, Farsi, German, Italian and Spanish. High quality datasets were manually curated for the five languages with high inter-annotator agreements (consistently in the 0.9 ballpark). These were used for semi-automatic construction of ten cross-lingual datasets. 17 teams participated in the task, submitting 24 systems in subtask 1 and 14 systems in subtask 2. Results show that systems that combine statistical knowledge from text corpora, in the form of word embeddings, and external knowledge from lexical resources are best performers in both subtasks. More information can be found on the task website: http://alt.qcri.org/semeval2017/task2/.

1 Introduction

Measuring the extent to which two words are semantically similar is one of the most popular research fields in lexical semantics, with a wide range of Natural Language Processing (NLP) applications. Examples include Word Sense Disambiguation (Miller et al., 2012), Information Retrieval (Hliaoutakis et al., 2006), Machine Translation (Lavie and Denkowski, 2009), Lexical Substitution (McCarthy and Navigli, 2009), Question Answering (Mohler et al., 2011), Text Summarization (Mohammad and Hirst, 2012), and Ontology Alignment (Pilehvar and Navigli, 2014). Moreover, word similarity is generally accepted as the most direct in-vitro evaluation framework for

word representation, a research field that has recently received massive research attention mainly as a result of the advancements in the use of neural networks for learning dense low-dimensional semantic representations, often referred to as word embeddings (Mikolov et al., 2013; Pennington et al., 2014). Almost any application in NLP that deals with semantics can benefit from efficient semantic representation of words (Turney and Pantel, 2010).

However, research in semantic representation has in the main focused on the English language only. This is partly due to the limited availability of word similarity benchmarks in languages other than English. Given the central role of similarity datasets in lexical semantics, and given the importance of moving beyond the barriers of the English language and developing language-independent and multilingual techniques, we felt that this was an appropriate time to conduct a task that provides a reliable framework for evaluating multilingual and cross-lingual semantic representation and similarity techniques. The task has two related subtasks: multilingual semantic similarity (Section 1.1), which focuses on representation learning for individual languages, and cross-lingual semantic similarity (Section 1.2), which provides a benchmark for multilingual research that learns unified representations for multiple languages.

1.1 Subtask 1: Multilingual Semantic Similarity

While the English community has been using standard word similarity datasets as a common evaluation benchmark, semantic representation for other languages has generally proved difficult to evaluate. A reliable multilingual word similarity benchmark can be hugely beneficial in evaluating the robustness and reliability of semantic

---

Authors marked with * contributed equally.

Proceedings of the 11th International Workshop on Semantic Evaluations (SemEval-2017), pages 15–26,
Vancouver, Canada, August 3 - 4, 2017. ©2017 Association for Computational Linguistics

representation techniques across languages. Despite this, very few word similarity datasets exist for languages other than English: The original English RG-65 (Rubenstein and Goodenough, 1965) and WordSim-353 (Finkelstein et al., 2002) datasets have been translated into other languages, either by experts (Gurevych, 2005; Joubarne and Inkpen, 2011; Granada et al., 2014; Camacho-Collados et al., 2015), or by means of crowdsourcing (Leviant and Reichart, 2015), thereby creating equivalent datasets in languages other than English. However, the existing English word similarity datasets suffer from various issues:

1. The similarity scale used for the annotation of WordSim-353 and MEN (Bruni et al., 2014) does not distinguish between similarity and relatedness, and hence conflates these two. As a result, the datasets contain pairs that are judged to be highly similar even if they are not of similar type or nature. For instance, the WordSim-353 dataset contains the pairs *weather-forecast* or *clothes-closet* with assigned similarity scores of 8.34 and 8.00 (on the [0,10] scale), respectively. Clearly, the words in the two pairs are (highly) related, but they are not similar.

2. The performance of state-of-the-art systems have already surpassed the levels of human inter-annotator agreement (IAA) for many of the old datasets, e.g., for RG-65 and WordSim-353. This makes these datasets unreliable benchmarks for the evaluation of newly-developed systems.

3. Conventional datasets such as RG-65, MC-30 (Miller and Charles, 1991), and WS-Sim (Agirre et al., 2009) (the similarity portion of WordSim-353) are relatively small, containing 65, 30, and 200 word pairs, respectively. Hence, these benchmarks do not allow reliable conclusions to be drawn, since performance improvements have to be large to be statistically significant (Batchkarov et al., 2016).

4. The recent SimLex-999 dataset (Hill et al., 2015) improves both the size and consistency issues of the conventional datasets by providing word similarity scores for 999 word pairs on a consistent scale that focuses on similarity only (and not relatedness). However,

the dataset suffers from other issues. First, given that SimLex-999 has been annotated by turkers, and not by human experts, the similarity scores assigned to individual word pairs have a high variance, resulting in relatively low IAA (Camacho-Collados and Navigli, 2016). In fact, the reported IAA for this dataset is 0.67 in terms of average pairwise correlation, which is considerably lower than conventional expert-based datasets whose IAA are generally above 0.80 (Rubenstein and Goodenough, 1965; Camacho-Collados et al., 2015). Second, similarly to many of the above-mentioned datasets, SimLex-999 does not contain named entities (e.g., *Microsoft*), or multiword expressions (e.g., *black hole*). In fact, the dataset includes only words that are defined in WordNet's vocabulary (Miller et al., 1990), and therefore lacks the ability to test the reliability of systems for WordNet out-of-vocabulary words. Third, the dataset contains a large number of antonymy pairs. Indeed, several recent works have shown how significant performance improvements can be obtained on this dataset by simply tweaking usual word embedding approaches to handle antonymy (Schwartz et al., 2015; Pham et al., 2015; Nguyen et al., 2016).

Since most existing multilingual word similarity datasets are constructed on the basis of conventional English datasets, any issues associated with the latter tend simply to be transferred to the former. This is the reason why we proposed this task and constructed new challenging datasets for five different languages (i.e., English, Farsi, German, Italian, and Spanish) addressing all the above-mentioned issues. Given that multiple large and high-quality verb similarity datasets have been created in recent years (Yang and Powers, 2006; Baker et al., 2014; Gerz et al., 2016), we decided to focus on nominal words.

1.2 Subtask 2: Cross-lingual Semantic Similarity

Over the past few years multilingual embeddings that represent lexical items from multiple languages in a unified semantic space have garnered considerable research attention (Zou et al., 2013; de Melo, 2015; Vulić and Moens, 2016; Ammar et al., 2016; Upadhyay et al., 2016), while at the same time cross-lingual applications have also been increasingly studied (Xiao and Guo, 2014; Franco-Salvador et al., 2016). However, there have been very few reliable datasets for evaluating cross-lingual systems. Similarly to the case of multilingual datasets, these cross-lingual datasets have been constructed on the basis of conventional English word similarity datasets: MC-30 and WordSim-353 (Hassan and Mihalcea, 2009), and RG-65 (Camacho-Collados et al., 2015). As a result, they inherit the issues affecting their parent datasets mentioned in the previous subsection: while MC-30 and RG-65 are composed of only 30 and 65 pairs, WordSim-353 conflates similarity and relatedness in different languages. Moreover, the datasets of Hassan and Mihalcea (2009) were not re-scored after having been translated to the other languages, thus ignoring possible semantic shifts across languages and producing unreliable scores for many translated word pairs.

For this subtask we provided ten high quality cross-lingual datasets, constructed according to the procedure of Camacho-Collados et al. (2015), in a semi-automatic manner exploiting the monolingual datasets of subtask 1. These datasets constitute a reliable evaluation framework across five languages.

2 Task Data

Subtask 1, i.e., multilingual semantic similarity, has five datasets for the five languages of the task, i.e., English, Farsi, German, Italian, and Spanish. These datasets were manually created with the help of trained annotators (as opposed to Mechanical Turk) that were native or fluent speakers of the target language. Based on these five datasets, 10 cross-lingual datasets were automatically generated (described in Section 2.2) for subtask 2, i.e., cross-lingual semantic similarity.

In this section we focus on the creation of the evaluation test sets. We additionally created a set of small trial datasets by following a similar process. These datasets were used by some participants during system development.

2.1 Monolingual datasets

As for monolingual datasets, we opted for a size of 500 word pairs in order to provide a large enough set to allow reliable evaluation and comparison of the systems. The following procedure was used for the construction of multilingual datasets: (1) we first collected 500 English word pairs from a

Animals	Language and linguistics
Art, architecture and archaeology	Law and crime
Biology	Literature and theatre
Business, economics, and finance	Mathematics
Chemistry and mineralogy	Media
Computing	Meteorology
Culture and society	Music
Education	Numismatics and currencies
Engineering and technology	Philosophy and psychology
Farming	Physics and astronomy
Food and drink	Politics and government
Games and video games	Religion, mysticism and mythology
Geography and places	Royalty and nobility
Geology and geophysics	Sport and recreation
Health and medicine	Textile and clothing
Heraldry, honors, and vexillology	Transport and travel
History	Warfare and defense

Table 1: The set of thirty-four domains.

wide range of domains (Section 2.1.1), (2) through translation of these pairs, we obtained word pairs for the other four languages (Section 2.1.2) and, (3) all word pairs of each dataset were manually scored by multiple annotators (Section 2.1.3).

2.1.1 English dataset creation

Seed set selection. The dataset creation started with the selection of 500 English words. One of the main objectives of the task was to provide an evaluation framework that contains named entities and multiword expressions and covers a wide range of domains. To achieve this, we considered the 34 different domains available in BabelDomains[1] (Camacho-Collados and Navigli, 2017), which in the main correspond to the domains of the *Wikipedia featured articles page*[2]. Table 1 shows the list of all the 34 domains used for the creation of the datasets. From each domain, 12 words were sampled in such a way as to have at least one multiword expression and two named entities. In order to include words that may not belong to any of the pre-defined domains, we added 92 extra words whose domain was not decided beforehand. We also tried to sample these seed words in such a way as to have a balanced set across occurrence frequency.[3] Of the 500 English seed words, 84 (17%) and 83 were, respectively, named entities and multiwords.

Similarity scale. For the annotation of the datasets, we adopted the five-point Likert scale of the SemEval-2014 task on Cross-Level Semantic

---

[1]http://lcl.uniroma1.it/babeldomains/
[2]https://en.wikipedia.org/wiki/
Wikipedia:Featured_articles
[3]We used the Wikipedia corpus for word frequency calculation during the dataset construction.

4	Very similar	The two words are synonyms (e.g., *midday-noon* or *motherboard-mainboard*).
3	Similar	The two words share many of the important ideas of their meaning but include slightly different details. They refer to similar but not identical concepts (e.g., *lion-zebra* or *firefighter-policeman*).
2	Slightly similar	The two words do not have a very similar meaning, but share a common topic/domain/function and ideas or concepts that are related (e.g., *house-window* or *airplane-pilot*).
1	Dissimilar	The two words describe clearly dissimilar concepts, but may share some small details, a far relationship or a domain in common and might be likely to be found together in a longer document on the same topic (e.g., *software-keyboard* or *driver-suspension*).
0	Totally dissimilar and unrelated	The two words do not mean the same thing and are not on the same topic (e.g., *pencil-frog* or *PlayStation-monarchy*).

Table 2: The five-point Likert scale used to rate the similarity of item pairs. See Table 4 for examples.

Similarity (Jurgens et al., 2014) which was designed to systematically order a broad range of semantic relations: synonymy, similarity, relatedness, topical association, and unrelatedness. Table 2 describes the five points in the similarity scale along with example word pairs.

Pairing word selection. Having the initial 500-word seed set at hand, we selected a pair for each word. The selection was carried out in such a way as to ensure a uniform distribution of pairs across the similarity scale. In order to do this, we first assigned a random intended similarity to each pair. The annotator then had to pick the second word so as to match the intended score. In order to allow the annotator to have a broader range of candidate words, the intended score was considered as a similarity interval, one of [0-1], [1-2], [2-3] and [3,4]. For instance, if the first word was *helicopter* and the presumed similarity was [3-4], the annotator had to pick a pairing word which was "semantically similar" (see Table 2) to *helicopter*, e.g., *plane*. Of the 500 pairing words, 45 (9%) and 71 (14%) were named entities and multiwords, respectively. This resulted in an English dataset comprising 500 word pairs, 105 (21%) and 112 (22%) of which have at least one named entity and multiword, respectively.

2.1.2 Dataset translation

The remaining four multilingual datasets (i.e., Farsi, German, Italian, and Spanish) were constructed by translating words in the English dataset to the target language. We had two goals in mind while selecting translation as the construction strategy of these datasets (as opposed to independent word samplings per language): (1) to have comparable datasets across languages in terms of domain coverage, multiword and named entity distribution[4] and (2) to enable an automatic construction of cross-lingual datasets (see Section 2.2).

Each English word pair was translated by two independent annotators. In the case of disagreement, a third annotator was asked to pick the preferred translation. While translating, the annotators were shown the word pair along with their initial similarity score, which was provided to help them in selecting the correct translation for the intended meanings of the words.

2.1.3 Scoring

The annotators were instructed to follow the guidelines, with special emphasis on distinguishing between similarity and relatedness. Furthermore, although the similarity scale was originally designed as a Likert scale, annotators were given flexibility to assign values between the defined points in the scale (with a step size of 0.25), indicating a blend of two relations. As a result of this procedure, we obtained 500 word pairs for each of the five languages. The pairs in each language were shuffled and their initial scores were discarded. Three annotators were then asked to assign a similarity score to each pair according to our similarity scale (see Section 2.1.1).

Table 3 (first row) reports the average pairwise Pearson correlation among the three annotators for each of the five languages. Given the fact that our word pairs spanned a wide range of domains, and that there was a possibility for annotators to misunderstand some words, we devised a procedure to check the quality of the annotations and to improve the reliability of the similarity scores. To this end, for each dataset and for each annotator

---

[4] Apart from the German dataset in which the proportion of multiwords significantly reduces (from 22% of English to around 11%) due to the compounding nature of the German language, other datasets maintain similar proportions of multiwords to those of the English dataset.

	English	Farsi	German	Italian	Spanish
Initial scores	0.836	0.839	0.864	0.798	0.829
Revised scores	0.893	0.906	0.916	0.900	0.890

Table 3: Average pairwise Pearson correlation among annotators for the five monolingual datasets.

MONOLINGUAL			
DE	Tuberkulose	LED	0.25
ES	zumo	batido	3.00
EN	Multiple Sclerosis	MS	4.00
IT	Nazioni Unite	Ban Ki-moon	2.25
FA	شام آخر	لئوناردو دا وینچی	2.08

CROSS-LINGUAL			
DE-ES	Sessel	taburete	3.08
DE-FA	Lawine	برف	2.25
DE-IT	Taifun	ciclone	3.46
EN-DE	pancreatic cancer	Chemotherapie	1.75
EN-ES	Jupiter	Mercurio	3.25
EN-FA	film	پوچ‌گرایی	0.25
EN-IT	island	penisola	3.08
ES-FA	duna	بیابان	2.25
ES-IT	estrella	pianeta	2.83
IT-FA	avvocato	نمایشگر	0.08

Table 4: Example pairs and their ratings (EN: English, DE: German, ES: Spanish, IT: Italian, FA: Farsi).

	EN	DE	ES	IT	FA
EN	500	914	978	970	952
DE	-	500	956	912	888
ES	-	-	500	967	967
IT	-	-	-	500	916
FA	-	-	-	-	500

Table 5: Number of word pairs in each dataset. The cells in the main diagonal of the table (e.g., EN-EN) correspond the monolingual datasets of subtask 1.

we picked the subset of pairs for which the difference between the assigned similarity score and the average of the other two annotations was more than 1.0, according to our similarity scale. The annotator was then asked to revise this subset performing a more careful investigation of the possible meanings of the word pairs contained therein, and change the score if necessary. This procedure resulted in considerable improvements in the consistency of the scores. The second row in Table 3 ("Revised scores") shows the average pairwise Pearson correlation among the three revised sets of scores for each of the five languages. The inter-annotator agreement for all the datasets is consistently in the 0.9 ballpark, which demonstrates the high quality of our multilingual datasets thanks to careful annotation of word pairs by experts.

2.2 Cross-lingual datasets

The cross-lingual datasets were automatically created on the basis of the translations obtained with the method described in Section 2.1.2 and using the approach of Camacho-Collados et al. (2015).[5] By intersecting two aligned translated pairs across

[5] http://lcl.uniroma1.it/
similarity-datasets/

two languages (e.g., *mind-brain* in English and *mente-cerebro* in Spanish), the approach creates two cross-lingual pairs between the two languages (*mind-cerebro* and *brain-mente* in the example). The similarity scores for the constructed cross-lingual pairs are computed as the average of the corresponding language-specific scores in the monolingual datasets. In order to avoid semantic shifts between languages interfering in the process, these pairs are only created if the difference between the corresponding language-specific scores is lower than 1.0. The full details of the algorithm can be found in Camacho-Collados et al. (2015). The approach has been validated by human judges and shown to achieve agreements of around 0.90 with human judges, which is similar to inter-annotator agreements reported in Section 2.1.3. See Table 4 for some sample pairs in all monolingual and cross-lingual datasets. Table 5 shows the final number of pairs for each language pair.

3 Evaluation

We carried out the evaluation on the datasets described in the previous section. The experimental setting is described in Section 3.1 and the results are presented in Section 3.2.

3.1 Experimental setting

3.1.1 Evaluation measures and official scores

Participating systems were evaluated according to standard Pearson and Spearman correlation measures on all word similarity datasets, with the final official score being calculated as the harmonic mean of Pearson and Spearman correlations (Jurgens et al., 2014). Systems were allowed to participate in either multilingual word similarity, cross-lingual word similarity, or both. Each participating system was allowed to submit a maximum of two runs.

For the multilingual word similarity subtask, some systems were multilingual (applicable to different languages), whereas others were monolingual (only applicable to a single language). While monolingual approaches were evaluated in their respective languages, multilingual and language-independent approaches were additionally given a global ranking provided that they tested their systems on at least four languages. The final score of a system was calculated as the average harmonic mean of Pearson and Spearman correlations of the four languages on which it performed best.

Likewise, the participating systems of the cross-lingual semantic similarity subtask were allowed to provide a score for a single cross-lingual dataset, but must have provided results for at least six cross-lingual word similarity datasets in order to be considered for the final ranking. For each system, the global score was computed as the average harmonic mean of Pearson and Spearman correlation on the six cross-lingual datasets on which it provided the best performance.

3.1.2 Shared training corpus

We encouraged the participants to use a shared text corpus for the training of their systems. The use of the shared corpus was intended to mitigate the influence that the underlying training corpus might have upon the quality of obtained representations, laying a common ground for a fair comparison of the systems.

- **Subtask 1.** The common corpus for subtask 1 was the Wikipedia corpus of the target language. Specifically, systems made use of the Wikipedia dumps released by Al-Rfou et al. (2013).[6]

- **Subtask 2.** The common corpus for subtask 2 was the Europarl parallel corpus[7]. This corpus is available for all languages except

Farsi. For pairs involving Farsi, participants were allowed to use the OpenSubtitles2016 parallel corpora[8]. Additionally, we proposed a second type of multilingual corpus to allow the use of different techniques exploiting comparable corpora. To this end, some participants made use of Wikipedia.

3.1.3 Participating systems

This task was targeted at evaluating multilingual and cross-lingual word similarity measurement techniques. However, it was not only limited to this area of research, as other fields such as semantic representation consider word similarity as one of their most direct benchmarks for evaluation. All kinds of semantic representation techniques and semantic similarity systems were encouraged to participate.

In the end we received a wide variety of participants: proposing distributional semantic models learnt directly from raw corpora, using syntactic features, exploiting knowledge from lexical resources, and hybrid approaches combining corpus-based and knowledge-based clues. Due to lack of space we cannot describe all the systems in detail, but we recommend the reader to refer to the system description papers for more information about the individual systems: HCCL (He et al., 2017), Citius (Gamallo, 2017), jmp8 (Melka and Bernard, 2017), l2f (Fialho et al., 2017), QLUT (Meng et al., 2017), RUFINO (Jimenez et al., 2017), MERALI (Mensa et al., 2017), Luminoso (Speer and Lowry-Duda, 2017), hhu (Qasem-iZadeh and Kallmeyer, 2017), Mahtab (Ranjbar et al., 2017), SEW (Delli Bovi and Raganato, 2017) and Wild_Devs (Rotari et al., 2017), and OoO.

3.1.4 Baseline

As the baseline system we included the results of the concept and entity embeddings of NASARI (Camacho-Collados et al., 2016). These embeddings were obtained by exploiting knowledge from Wikipedia and WordNet coupled with general domain corpus-based Word2Vec embeddings (Mikolov et al., 2013). We performed the evaluation with the 300-dimensional English embedded vectors (version 3.0)[9] and used them for all languages. For the comparison within and

---

System	English			Farsi			German			Italian			Spanish		
	r	ρ	Final	r	ρ	Final	r	ρ	Final	r	ρ	Final	r	ρ	Final
Luminoso_run2	**0.78**	**0.80**	**0.79**	0.51	0.50	0.50	**0.70**	**0.70**	**0.70**	**0.73**	**0.75**	**0.74**	**0.73**	**0.75**	**0.74**
Luminoso_run1	**0.78**	0.79	**0.79**	0.51	0.50	0.50	0.69	0.69	0.69	**0.73**	**0.75**	**0.74**	**0.73**	**0.75**	**0.74**
QLUT_run1*	**0.78**	0.78	0.78	-	-	-	-	-	-	-	-	-	-	-	-
hhu_run1*	0.71	0.70	0.70	0.54	0.59	0.56	-	-	-	-	-	-	-	-	-
HCCL_run1*	0.68	0.70	0.69	0.42	0.45	0.44	0.58	0.61	0.59	0.63	0.67	0.65	0.69	0.72	0.70
NASARI (baseline)	0.68	0.68	0.68	0.41	0.40	0.41	0.51	0.51	0.51	0.60	0.59	0.60	0.60	0.60	0.60
hhu_run2*	0.66	0.70	0.68	0.61	0.60	0.60	-	-	-	-	-	-	-	-	-
QLUT_run2*	0.67	0.67	0.67	-	-	-	-	-	-	-	-	-	-	-	-
RUFINO_run1*	0.65	0.66	0.66	0.38	0.34	0.36	0.54	0.54	0.54	0.48	0.47	0.48	0.53	0.57	0.55
Citius_run2	0.60	0.71	0.65	-	-	-	-	-	-	-	-	-	0.44	0.64	0.52
l2f_run2 (a.d.)	0.64	0.65	0.65	-	-	-	-	-	-	-	-	-	-	-	-
l2f_run1 (a.d.)	0.64	0.65	0.64	-	-	-	-	-	-	-	-	-	-	-	-
Citius_run1*	0.57	0.65	0.61	-	-	-	-	-	-	-	-	-	0.44	0.63	0.51
MERALI_run1*	0.59	0.60	0.59	-	-	-	-	-	-	-	-	-	-	-	-
Amateur_run1*	0.58	0.59	0.59	-	-	-	-	-	-	-	-	-	-	-	-
Amateur_run2*	0.58	0.59	0.59	-	-	-	-	-	-	-	-	-	-	-	-
MERALI_run2*	0.57	0.58	0.58	-	-	-	-	-	-	-	-	-	-	-	-
SEW_run2 (a.d.)	0.56	0.58	0.57	0.38	0.40	0.39	0.45	0.45	0.45	0.57	0.57	0.57	0.61	0.62	0.62
jmp8_run1*	0.47	0.69	0.56	-	-	-	0.26	0.51	0.35	0.41	0.64	0.50	-	-	-
Wild_Devs_run1	0.46	0.48	0.47	-	-	-	-	-	-	-	-	-	-	-	-
RUFINO_run2*	0.39	0.40	0.39	0.25	0.26	0.26	0.38	0.36	0.37	0.30	0.31	0.31	0.40	0.41	0.41
SEW_run1	0.37	0.41	0.39	0.38	0.40	0.39	0.45	0.45	0.45	0.57	0.57	0.57	0.61	0.62	0.62
hjpwhuer_run1	-0.04	-0.03	0.00	0.00	0.00	0.00	0.02	0.02	0.02	0.05	0.05	0.05	-0.06	-0.06	0.00
Mahtab_run2*	-	-	-	**0.72**	**0.71**	**0.71**	-	-	-	-	-	-	-	-	-
Mahtab_run1*	-	-	-	**0.72**	**0.71**	**0.71**	-	-	-	-	-	-	-	-	-

Table 6: Pearson (r), Spearman (ρ) and official (Final) results of participating systems on the five monolingual word similarity datasets (subtask 1).

across languages NASARI relies on the lexicalizations provided by BabelNet (Navigli and Ponzetto, 2012) for the concepts and entities in each language. Then, the final score was computed through the conventional closest senses strategy (Resnik, 1995; Budanitsky and Hirst, 2006), using cosine similarity as the comparison measure.

3.2 Results

We present the results of subtask 1 in Section 3.2.1 and subtask 2 in Section 3.2.2.

3.2.1 Subtask 1

Table 6 lists the results on all monolingual datasets.[10] The systems which made use of the shared Wikipedia corpus are marked with * in Table 6. Luminoso achieved the best results in all languages except Farsi. Luminoso couples word embeddings with knowledge from ConceptNet (Speer et al., 2017) using an extension of Retrofitting (Faruqui et al., 2015), which proved highly effective. This system additionally proposed two fallback strategies to handle

System	Score	Official Rank
Luminoso_run2	0.743	1
Luminoso_run1	0.740	2
HCCL_run1*	0.658	3
NASARI (baseline)	0.598	-
RUFINO_run1*	0.555	4
SEW_run2 (a.d.)	0.552	-
SEW_run1	0.506	5
RUFINO_run2*	0.369	6
hjpwhuer_run1	0.018	7

Table 7: Global results of participating systems on subtask 1 (multilingual word similarity).

out-of-vocabulary (OOV) instances based on loanwords and cognates. These two fallback strategies proved essential given the amount of rare words or domain-specific words which were present in the datasets. In fact, most systems fail to provide scores for all pairs in the datasets, with OOV rates close to 10% in some cases.

The combination of corpus-based and knowledge-based features was not unique to

---

[10] Systems followed by (a.d.) submitted their results after the official deadline.

System	German-Spanish			German-Farsi			German-Italian			English-German			English-Spanish		
	r	ρ	Final	r	ρ	Final	r	ρ	Final	r	ρ	Final	r	ρ	Final
Luminoso_run2	**0.72**	**0.74**	**0.73**	**0.59**	**0.59**	**0.59**	**0.74**	**0.75**	**0.74**	**0.76**	**0.77**	**0.76**	**0.75**	**0.77**	**0.76**
Luminoso_run1	**0.72**	0.73	0.72	**0.59**	**0.59**	**0.59**	0.73	0.74	0.73	0.75	**0.77**	**0.76**	**0.75**	**0.77**	**0.76**
NASARI (baseline)	0.55	0.55	0.55	0.46	0.45	0.46	0.56	0.56	0.56	0.60	0.59	0.60	0.64	0.63	0.63
OoO_run1	0.54	0.56	0.55	-	-	-	0.54	0.55	0.55	0.56	0.58	0.57	0.58	0.59	0.58
SEW_run2 (a.d.)	0.52	0.54	0.53	0.42	0.44	0.43	0.52	0.52	0.52	0.50	0.53	0.51	0.59	0.60	0.59
SEW_run1	0.52	0.54	0.53	0.42	0.44	0.43	0.52	0.52	0.52	0.46	0.47	0.46	0.50	0.51	0.50
HCCL_run2* (a.d.)	0.42	0.39	0.41	0.33	0.28	0.30	0.38	0.34	0.36	0.49	0.48	0.48	0.55	0.56	0.55
RUFINO_run1[†]	0.31	0.32	0.32	0.23	0.25	0.24	0.32	0.33	0.33	0.33	0.34	0.33	0.34	0.34	0.34
RUFINO_run2[†]	0.30	0.30	0.30	0.26	0.27	0.27	0.22	0.24	0.23	0.30	0.30	0.30	0.34	0.33	0.34
hjpwhu_run2	0.05	0.05	0.05	0.01	0.01	0.01	0.06	0.05	0.05	0.04	0.04	0.04	0.04	0.04	0.04
hjpwhu_run1	0.05	0.05	0.05	0.01	0.01	0.01	0.06	0.05	0.05	-0.01	-0.01	0.00	0.04	0.04	0.04
HCCL_run1*	0.03	0.02	0.02	0.03	0.02	0.02	0.03	-0.01	0.00	0.34	0.28	0.31	0.10	0.08	0.09
UniBuc-Sem_run1*	–	–	–	-	-	-	-	-	-	0.05	0.06	0.06	0.08	0.10	0.09
Citius_run1[†]	–	–	–	-	-	-	-	-	-	-	-	-	0.57	0.59	0.58
Citius_run2[†]	–	–	–	-	-	-	-	-	-	-	-	-	0.56	0.58	0.57

System	English-Farsi			English-Italian			Spanish-Farsi			Spanish-Italian			Italian-Farsi		
	r	ρ	Final	r	ρ	Final	r	ρ	Final	r	ρ	Final	r	ρ	Final
Luminoso_run2	**0.60**	**0.59**	**0.60**	**0.77**	**0.79**	**0.78**	**0.62**	**0.63**	**0.63**	**0.74**	**0.77**	**0.75**	**0.60**	**0.61**	**0.60**
Luminoso_run1	**0.60**	**0.59**	**0.60**	0.76	0.78	0.77	**0.62**	**0.63**	**0.63**	**0.74**	0.76	**0.75**	**0.60**	0.60	**0.60**
hhu_run1	0.49	0.54	0.51	-	-	-	-	-	-	-	-	-	-	-	-
NASARI (baseline)	0.52	0.49	0.51	0.65	0.65	0.65	0.49	0.47	0.48	0.60	0.59	0.60	0.50	0.48	0.49
hhu_run2	0.43	0.58	0.49	-	-	-	-	-	-	-	-	-	-	-	-
SEW_run2 (a.d.)	0.46	0.49	0.48	0.58	0.60	0.59	0.50	0.53	0.52	0.59	0.60	0.60	0.48	0.50	0.49
HCCL_run2* (a.d.)	0.44	0.42	0.43	0.50	0.49	0.49	0.37	0.33	0.35	0.43	0.41	0.42	0.33	0.28	0.30
SEW_run1	0.41	0.43	0.42	0.52	0.53	0.53	0.50	0.53	0.52	0.59	0.60	0.60	0.48	0.50	0.49
RUFINO_run2[†]	0.37	0.37	0.37	0.24	0.23	0.24	0.30	0.30	0.30	0.28	0.29	0.29	0.21	0.21	0.21
RUFINO_run1[†]	0.26	0.25	0.25	0.34	0.34	0.34	0.25	0.26	0.26	0.35	0.36	0.36	0.25	0.25	0.25
HCCL_run1*	0.02	0.01	0.01	0.12	0.07	0.09	0.05	0.05	0.05	0.08	0.06	0.06	0.02	0.00	0.00
hjpwhu_run1	0.00	-0.01	0.00	-0.05	-0.05	0.00	0.01	0.00	0.01	0.03	0.03	0.03	0.02	0.02	0.02
hjpwhu_run2	0.00	-0.01	0.00	-0.05	-0.05	0.00	0.01	0.00	0.01	0.03	0.03	0.03	0.02	0.02	0.02
OoO_run1	-	-	-	0.58	0.59	0.58	-	-	-	0.57	0.57	0.57	-	-	-
UniBuc-Sem_run1*	-	-	-	0.08	0.10	0.09	-	-	-	-	-	-	-	-	-

Table 8: Pearson (r), Spearman (ρ) and the official (Final) results of participating systems on the ten cross-lingual word similarity datasets (subtask 2).

Luminoso. In fact, most top performing systems combined these two sources of information. For Farsi, the best performing system was Mahtab, which couples information from Word2Vec word embeddings (Mikolov et al., 2013) and knowledge resources, in this case FarsNet (Shamsfard et al., 2010) and BabelNet. For English, the only system that came close to Luminoso was QLUT, which was the best-performing system that made use of the shared Wikipedia corpus for training. The best configuration of this system exploits the Skip-Gram model of Word2Vec with an additive compositional function for computing the similarity of multiwords. However, Mahtab and QLUT only performed their experiments in a single language (Farsi and English, respectively).

For the systems that performed experiments in at least four of the five languages we computed a global score (see Section 3.1.1). Global rankings and results are displayed in Table 7. Luminoso clearly achieves the best overall results. The second-best performing system was HCCL, which also managed to outperform the baseline. HCCL exploited the Skip-Gram model of Word2Vec and performed hyperparameter tuning on existing word similarity datasets. This system did not make use of external resources apart from the shared Wikipedia corpus for training. RUFINO, which also made use of the Wikipedia corpus only, attained the third overall position. The system exploits PMI and an association measure to capture second-order relations between words based on the Jaccard distance (Jimenez et al., 2016).

3.2.2 Subtask 2

The results for all ten cross-lingual datasets are shown in Table 8. Systems that made use of the shared Europarl parallel corpus are marked with * in the table, while systems making use of

System	Score	Official Rank
Luminoso_run2	0.754	1
Luminoso_run1	0.750	2
NASARI (baseline)	0.598	-
OoO_run1*	0.567	3
SEW_run2 (a.d.)	0.558	-
SEW_run1	0.532	4
HCCL_run2* (a.d.)	0.464	-
RUFINO_run1†	0.336	5
RUFINO_run2†	0.317	6
HCCL_run1*	0.103	7
hjpwhu_run2	0.039	8
hjpwhu_run1	0.034	9

Table 9: Global results of participating systems in subtask 2 (cross-lingual word similarity).

Wikipedia are marked with †. Luminoso, the best-performing system in Subtask 1, also achieved the best overall results on the ten cross-lingual datasets. This shows that the combination of knowledge from word embeddings and the ConceptNet graph is equally effective in the cross-lingual setting.

The global ranking for this subtask was computed by averaging the results of the six datasets on which each system performed best. The global rankings are displayed in Table 9. Luminoso was the only system outperforming the baseline, achieving the best overall results. OoO achieved the second best overall performance using an extension of the Bilingual Bag-of-Words without Alignments (BilBOWA) approach of Gouws et al. (2015) on the shared Europarl corpus. The third overall system was SEW, which leveraged Wikipedia-based concept vectors (Raganato et al., 2016) and pre-trained word embeddings for learning language-independent concept embeddings.

4 Conclusion

In this paper we have presented the SemEval 2017 task on *Multilingual and Cross-lingual Semantic Word Similarity*. We provided a reliable framework to measure the similarity between nominal instances within and across five different languages (English, Farsi, German, Italian, and Spanish). We hope this framework will contribute to the development of distributional semantics in general and for languages other than English in particular, with a special emphasis on multilin-

gual and cross-lingual approaches. All evaluation datasets are available for download at `http://alt.qcri.org/semeval2017/task2/`.

The best overall system in both tasks was Luminoso, which is a hybrid system that effectively integrates word embeddings and information from knowledge resources. In general, this combination proved effective in this task, as most other top systems somehow combined knowledge from text corpora and lexical resources.

Acknowledgments

The authors gratefully acknowledge the support of the MRC grant No. MR/M025160/1 for PheneBank and ERC Starting Grant MultiJEDI No. 259234. Jose Camacho-Collados is supported by a Google Doctoral Fellowship in Natural Language Processing.

We would also like to thank Ángela Collados Ais, Claudio Delli Bovi, Afsaneh Hojjat, Ignacio Iacobacci, Tommaso Pasini, Valentina Pyatkin, Alessandro Raganato, Zahra Pilehvar, Milan Gritta and Sabine Ullrich for their help in the construction of the datasets. Finally, we also thank Jim McManus for his suggestions on the manuscript and the anonymous reviewers for their helpful comments.

References

Eneko Agirre, Enrique Alfonseca, Keith Hall, Jana Kravalova, Marius Paşca, and Aitor Soroa. 2009. A study on similarity and relatedness using distributional and WordNet-based approaches. In *Proceedings of NAACL*. pages 19–27.

Rami Al-Rfou, Bryan Perozzi, and Steven Skiena. 2013. Polyglot: Distributed word representations for multilingual nlp. In *Proceedings of the Seventeenth Conference on Computational Natural Language Learning*. Sofia, Bulgaria, pages 183–192.

Waleed Ammar, George Mulcaire, Yulia Tsvetkov, Guillaume Lample, Chris Dyer, and Noah A Smith. 2016. Massively multilingual word embeddings. *arXiv preprint arXiv:1602.01925* .

Simon Baker, Roi Reichart, and Anna Korhonen. 2014. An unsupervised model for instance level subcategorization acquisition. In *Proceedings of EMNLP*. pages 278–289.

Miroslav Batchkarov, Thomas Kober, Jeremy Reffin, Julie Weeds, and David Weir. 2016. A critique of word similarity as a method for evaluating distributional semantic models. In *Proceedings of the ACL Workshop on Evaluating Vector Space Representations for NLP*. Berlin, Germany, pages 7–12.

Elia Bruni, Nam-Khanh Tran, and Marco Baroni. 2014. Multimodal distributional semantics. *J. Artif. Intell. Res.(JAIR)* 49(1-47).

Alexander Budanitsky and Graeme Hirst. 2006. Evaluating WordNet-based measures of Lexical Semantic Relatedness. *Computational Linguistics* 32(1):13–47.

José Camacho-Collados and Roberto Navigli. 2016. Find the word that does not belong: A framework for an intrinsic evaluation of word vector representations. In *Proceedings of the ACL Workshop on Evaluating Vector Space Representations for NLP*. Berlin, Germany, pages 43–50.

Jose Camacho-Collados and Roberto Navigli. 2017. BabelDomains: Large-Scale Domain Labeling of Lexical Resources. In *Proceedings of EACL (2)*. Valencia, Spain, pages 223–228.

José Camacho-Collados, Mohammad Taher Pilehvar, and Roberto Navigli. 2015. A Framework for the Construction of Monolingual and Cross-lingual Word Similarity Datasets. In *Proceedings of ACL (2)*. Beijing, China, pages 1–7.

José Camacho-Collados, Mohammad Taher Pilehvar, and Roberto Navigli. 2016. Nasari: Integrating explicit knowledge and corpus statistics for a multilingual representation of concepts and entities. *Artificial Intelligence* 240:36–64.

Gerard de Melo. 2015. Wiktionary-based word embeddings. *Proceedings of MT Summit XV* pages 346–359.

Claudio Delli Bovi and Alessandro Raganato. 2017. Sew-embed at semeval-2017 task 2: Language-independent concept representations from a semantically enriched wikipedia. In *Proceedings of the 11th International Workshop on Semantic Evaluation (SemEval-2017)*. Association for Computational Linguistics, Vancouver, Canada, pages 261–266. http://www.aclweb.org/anthology/S17-2041.

Manaal Faruqui, Jesse Dodge, Sujay K. Jauhar, Chris Dyer, Eduard Hovy, and Noah A. Smith. 2015. Retrofitting word vectors to semantic lexicons. In *Proceedings of NAACL*. pages 1606–1615.

Pedro Fialho, Hugo Patinho Rodrigues, Luísa Coheur, and Paulo Quaresma. 2017. L2f/inesc-id at semeval-2017 tasks 1 and 2: Lexical and semantic features in word and textual similarity. In *Proceedings of the 11th International Workshop on Semantic Evaluation (SemEval-2017)*. Association for Computational Linguistics, Vancouver, Canada, pages 213–219. http://www.aclweb.org/anthology/S17-2032.

Lev Finkelstein, Gabrilovich Evgenly, Matias Yossi, Rivlin Ehud, Solan Zach, Wolfman Gadi, and Ruppin Eytan. 2002. Placing search in context: The concept revisited. *ACM Transactions on Information Systems* 20(1):116–131.

Marc Franco-Salvador, Paolo Rosso, and Manuel Montes-y Gómez. 2016. A systematic study of knowledge graph analysis for cross-language plagiarism detection. *Information Processing & Management* 52(4):550–570.

Pablo Gamallo. 2017. Citius at semeval-2017 task 2: Cross-lingual similarity from comparable corpora and dependency-based contexts. In *Proceedings of the 11th International Workshop on Semantic Evaluation (SemEval-2017)*. Association for Computational Linguistics, Vancouver, Canada, pages 226–229. http://www.aclweb.org/anthology/S17-2034.

Daniela Gerz, Ivan Vulić, Felix Hill, Roi Reichart, and Anna Korhonen. 2016. Simverb-3500: A large-scale evaluation set of verb similarity. In *Proceedings of EMNLP*. Austin, USA.

Stephan Gouws, Yoshua Bengio, and Greg Corrado. 2015. Bilbowa: Fast bilingual distributed representations without word alignments. In *Proceedings of the 32nd International Conference on Machine Learning (ICML-15)*. pages 748–756.

Roger Granada, Cassia Trojahn, and Renata Vieira. 2014. Comparing semantic relatedness between word pairs in Portuguese using Wikipedia. In *Computational Processing of the Portuguese Language*, Springer, pages 170–175.

Iryna Gurevych. 2005. Using the structure of a conceptual network in computing semantic relatedness. In *Natural Language Processing–IJCNLP 2005*, Springer, pages 767–778.

Samer Hassan and Rada Mihalcea. 2009. Cross-lingual semantic relatedness using encyclopedic knowledge. In *Proceedings of EMNLP*. pages 1192–1201.

Junqing He, Long Wu, Xuemin Zhao, and Yonghong Yan. 2017. Hccl at semeval-2017 task 2: Combining multilingual word embeddings and transliteration model for semantic similarity. In *Proceedings of the 11th International Workshop on Semantic Evaluation (SemEval-2017)*. Association for Computational Linguistics, Vancouver, Canada, pages 220–225. http://www.aclweb.org/anthology/S17-2033.

Felix Hill, Roi Reichart, and Anna Korhonen. 2015. Simlex-999: Evaluating semantic models with (genuine) similarity estimation. *Computational Linguistics* .

Angelos Hliaoutakis, Giannis Varelas, Epimenidis Voutsakis, Euripides GM Petrakis, and Evangelos Milios. 2006. Information retrieval by semantic similarity. *International Journal on Semantic Web and Information Systems* 2(3):55–73.

Sergio Jimenez, George Dueñas, Lorena Gaitan, and Jorge Segura. 2017. Rufino at semeval-2017 task 2: Cross-lingual lexical similarity by extending pmi and word embeddings systems with a swadesh's-like list. In *Proceedings of the*

11th International Workshop on Semantic Evaluation (SemEval-2017). Association for Computational Linguistics, Vancouver, Canada, pages 239–244. http://www.aclweb.org/anthology/S17-2037.

Sergio Jimenez, Fabio A. Gonzalez, and Alexander Gelbukh. 2016. Mathematical properties of soft cardinality: Enhancing jaccard, dice and cosine similarity measures with element-wise distance. *Information Sciences* 367:373–389.

Colette Joubarne and Diana Inkpen. 2011. Comparison of semantic similarity for different languages using the Google n-gram corpus and second-order co-occurrence measures. In *Advances in Artificial Intelligence*, Springer, pages 216–221.

David Jurgens, Mohammad Taher Pilehvar, and Roberto Navigli. 2014. Semeval-2014 task 3: Cross-level semantic similarity. *SemEval 2014* pages 17–26.

Alon Lavie and Michael J. Denkowski. 2009. The Meteor metric for automatic evaluation of Machine Translation. *Machine Translation* 23(2-3):105–115.

Ira Leviant and Roi Reichart. 2015. Judgment language matters: Multilingual vector space models for judgment language aware lexical semantics. *CoRR, abs/1508.00106* .

Diana McCarthy and Roberto Navigli. 2009. The English lexical substitution task. *Language Resources and Evaluation* 43(2):139–159.

Josué Melka and Gilles Bernard. 2017. Jmp8 at semeval-2017 task 2: A simple and general distributional approach to estimate word similarity. In *Proceedings of the 11th International Workshop on Semantic Evaluation (SemEval-2017)*. Association for Computational Linguistics, Vancouver, Canada, pages 230–234. http://www.aclweb.org/anthology/S17-2035.

Fanqing Meng, Wenpeng Lu, Yuteng Zhang, Ping Jian, Shumin Shi, and Heyan Huang. 2017. Qlut at semeval-2017 task 2: Word similarity based on word embedding and knowledge base. In *Proceedings of the 11th International Workshop on Semantic Evaluation (SemEval-2017)*. Association for Computational Linguistics, Vancouver, Canada, pages 235–238. http://www.aclweb.org/anthology/S17-2036.

Enrico Mensa, Daniele P. Radicioni, and Antonio Lieto. 2017. Merali at semeval-2017 task 2 subtask 1: a cognitively inspired approach. In *Proceedings of the 11th International Workshop on Semantic Evaluation (SemEval-2017)*. Association for Computational Linguistics, Vancouver, Canada, pages 245–249. http://www.aclweb.org/anthology/S17-2038.

Tomas Mikolov, Kai Chen, Greg Corrado, and Jeffrey Dean. 2013. Efficient estimation of word representations in vector space. *CoRR* abs/1301.3781. http://arxiv.org/abs/1301.3781.

George A. Miller, R.T. Beckwith, Christiane D. Fellbaum, D. Gross, and K. Miller. 1990. WordNet: an online lexical database. *International Journal of Lexicography* 3(4):235–244.

George A. Miller and Walter G. Charles. 1991. Contextual correlates of semantic similarity. *Language and Cognitive Processes* 6(1):1–28.

Tristan Miller, Chris Biemann, Torsten Zesch, and Iryna Gurevych. 2012. Using distributional similarity for lexical expansion in knowledge-based word sense disambiguation. In *Proceedings of COLING.* pages 1781–1796.

Saif Mohammad and Graeme Hirst. 2012. Distributional measures of semantic distance: A survey. *CoRR* abs/1203.1858. http://arxiv.org/abs/1203.1858.

Michael Mohler, Razvan Bunescu, and Rada Mihalcea. 2011. Learning to grade short answer questions using semantic similarity measures and dependency graph alignments. In *Proceedings of the 49th Annual Meeting of the Association for Computational Linguistics: Human Language Technologies - Volume 1*. Portland, Oregon, HLT'11, pages 752–762.

Roberto Navigli and Simone Paolo Ponzetto. 2012. BabelNet: The automatic construction, evaluation and application of a wide-coverage multilingual semantic network. *Artificial Intelligence* 193:217–250.

Kim Anh Nguyen, Sabine Schulte im Walde, and Ngoc Thang Vu. 2016. Integrating distributional lexical contrast into word embeddings for antonym-synonym distinction. In *Proc. of ACL.* pages 454–459.

Jeffrey Pennington, Richard Socher, and Christopher D Manning. 2014. GloVe: Global vectors for word representation. In *Proceedings of EMNLP.* pages 1532–1543.

Nghia The Pham, Angeliki Lazaridou, and Marco Baroni. 2015. A multitask objective to inject lexical contrast into distributional semantics. In *Proceedings of ACL.* pages 21–26.

Mohammad Taher Pilehvar and Roberto Navigli. 2014. A robust approach to aligning heterogeneous lexical resources. In *Proceedings of ACL.* pages 468–478.

Behrang QasemiZadeh and Laura Kallmeyer. 2017. Hhu at semeval-2017 task 2: Fast hash-based embeddings for semantic word similarity assessment. In *Proceedings of the 11th International Workshop on Semantic Evaluation (SemEval-2017)*. Association for Computational Linguistics, Vancouver, Canada, pages 250–255. http://www.aclweb.org/anthology/S17-2039.

Alessandro Raganato, Claudio Delli Bovi, and Roberto Navigli. 2016. Automatic Construction and Evaluation of a Large Semantically Enriched Wikipedia. In

Proceedings of IJCAI. New York City, USA, pages 2894–2900.

Niloofar Ranjbar, Fatemeh Mashhadirajab, Mehrnoush Shamsfard, Rayeheh Hosseini pour, and Aryan Vahid pour. 2017. Mahtab at semeval-2017 task 2: Combination of corpus-based and knowledge-based methods to measure semantic word similarity. In *Proceedings of the 11th International Workshop on Semantic Evaluation (SemEval-2017)*. Association for Computational Linguistics, Vancouver, Canada, pages 256–260. http://www.aclweb.org/anthology/S17-2040.

Philip Resnik. 1995. Using information content to evaluate semantic similarity in a taxonomy. In *Proceedings of IJCAI*. pages 448–453.

Răzvan-Gabriel Rotari, Ionut Hulub, Stefan Oprea, Mihaela Plamada-Onofrei, Alina Beatrice Lorent, Raluca Preisler, Adrian Iftene, and Diana Trandabat. 2017. Wild devs' at semeval-2017 task 2: Using neural networks to discover word similarity. In *Proceedings of the 11th International Workshop on Semantic Evaluation (SemEval-2017)*. Association for Computational Linguistics, Vancouver, Canada, pages 267–270. http://www.aclweb.org/anthology/S17-2042.

Herbert Rubenstein and John B. Goodenough. 1965. Contextual correlates of synonymy. *Communications of the ACM* 8(10):627–633.

Roy Schwartz, Roi Reichart, and Ari Rappoport. 2015. Symmetric pattern based word embeddings for improved word similarity prediction. *CoNLL 2015* pages 258–267.

Mehrnoush Shamsfard, Akbar Hesabi, Hakimeh Fadaei, Niloofar Mansoory, Ali Famian, Somayeh Bagherbeigi, Elham Fekri, Maliheh Monshizadeh, and S Mostafa Assi. 2010. Semi automatic development of farsnet; the persian wordnet. In *Proceedings of 5th Global WordNet Conference, Mumbai, India*. volume 29.

Robert Speer, Joshua Chin, and Catherine Havasi. 2017. Conceptnet 5.5: An open multilingual graph of general knowledge. In *Proceedings of AAAI*. San Francisco, USA.

Robert Speer and Joanna Lowry-Duda. 2017. Conceptnet at semeval-2017 task 2: Extending word embeddings with multilingual relational knowledge. In *Proceedings of the 11th International Workshop on Semantic Evaluation (SemEval-2017)*. Association for Computational Linguistics, Vancouver, Canada, pages 85–89. http://www.aclweb.org/anthology/S17-2008.

Peter D. Turney and Patrick Pantel. 2010. From frequency to meaning: Vector space models of semantics. *Journal of Artificial Intelligence Research* 37:141–188.

Shyam Upadhyay, Manaal Faruqui, Chris Dyer, and Dan Roth. 2016. Cross-lingual models of word embeddings: An empirical comparison. In *Proceedings of ACL*. Berlin, Germany, pages 1661–1670. http://www.aclweb.org/anthology/P16-1157.

Ivan Vulić and Marie-Francine Moens. 2016. Bilingual distributed word representations from document-aligned comparable data. *Journal of Artificial Intelligence Research* 55:953–994.

Min Xiao and Yuhong Guo. 2014. Semi-supervised matrix completion for cross-lingual text classification. In *Proceedings of AAAI*. pages 1607–1614.

Dongqiang Yang and David MW Powers. 2006. Verb similarity on the taxonomy of wordnet. In *Proceedings of the Third International WordNet Conference*. Jeju Island, Korea, pages 121–128.

Will Y. Zou, Richard Socher, Daniel M. Cer, and Christopher D Manning. 2013. Bilingual word embeddings for phrase-based machine translation. In *Proceedings of EMNLP*. pages 1393–1398.

SemEval-2017 Task 3: Community Question Answering

Preslav Nakov[1]   Doris Hoogeveen[2]   Lluís Màrquez[1]   Alessandro Moschitti[1]
Hamdy Mubarak[1]   Timothy Baldwin[2]   Karin Verspoor[2]
[1]ALT Research Group, Qatar Computing Research Institute, HBKU
[2]The University of Melbourne

Abstract

We describe SemEval2017 Task 3 on Community Question Answering. This year, we reran the four subtasks from SemEval-2016: (A) *Question–Comment Similarity*, (B) *Question–Question Similarity*, (C) *Question–External Comment Similarity*, and (D) *Rerank the correct answers for a new question in Arabic*, providing all the data from 2015 and 2016 for training, and fresh data for testing. Additionally, we added a new subtask E in order to enable experimentation with *Multi-domain Question Duplicate Detection* in a larger-scale scenario, using StackExchange subforums. A total of 23 teams participated in the task, and submitted a total of 85 runs (36 primary and 49 contrastive) for subtasks A–D. Unfortunately, no teams participated in subtask E. A variety of approaches and features were used by the participating systems to address the different subtasks. The best systems achieved an official score (MAP) of 88.43, 47.22, 15.46, and 61.16 in subtasks A, B, C, and D, respectively. These scores are better than the baselines, especially for subtasks A–C.

1 Introduction

Community Question Answering (CQA) on web forums such as Stack Overflow[1] and Qatar Living,[2] is gaining popularity, thanks to the flexibility of forums to provide information to a user (Moschitti et al., 2016). Forums are moderated only indirectly via the community, rather open, and subject to few restrictions, if any, on who can post and answer a question, or what questions can be asked. On the positive side, a user can freely ask any question and can expect a variety of answers. On the negative side, it takes efforts to go through the provided answers of varying quality and to make sense of them. It is not unusual for a popular question to have hundreds of answers, and it is very time-consuming for a user to inspect them all.

Hence, users can benefit from automated tools to help them navigate these forums, including support for finding similar existing questions to a new question, and for identifying good answers, e.g., by retrieving similar questions that already provide an answer to the new question.

Given the important role that natural language processing (NLP) plays for CQA, we have organized a challenge series to promote related research for the past three years. We have provided datasets, annotated data and we have developed robust evaluation procedures in order to establish a common ground for comparing and evaluating different approaches to CQA.

In greater detail, in SemEval-2015 Task 3 "Answer Selection in Community Question Answering" (Nakov et al., 2015),[3] we mainly targeted conventional Question Answering (QA) tasks, i.e., answer selection. In contrast, in SemEval-2016 Task 3 (Nakov et al., 2016b), we targeted a fuller spectrum of CQA-specific tasks, moving closer to the real application needs,[4] particularly in Subtask C, which was defined as follows: "given (*i*) a new question and (*ii*) a large collection of question-comment threads created by a user community, rank the comments that are most useful for answering the new question". A test question is new with respect to the forum, but can be related to one or more questions that have been previously asked in the forum. The best answers can come from different question–comment threads. The threads are independent of each other, the lists of comments are chronologically sorted, and there is meta information, e.g., date of posting, who is the user who asked/answered the question, category the question was asked in, etc.

---

[1]http://stackoverflow.com/
[2]http://www.qatarliving.com/forum

[3]http://alt.qcri.org/semeval2015/task3
[4]A system based on SemEval-2016 Task 3 was integrated in Qatar Living's betasearch (Hoque et al., 2016):
http://www.qatarliving.com/betasearch

27

Proceedings of the 11th International Workshop on Semantic Evaluations (SemEval-2017), pages 27–48,
Vancouver, Canada, August 3 - 4, 2017. ©2017 Association for Computational Linguistics

The comments in a thread are intended to answer the question initiating that thread, but since this is a resource created by a community of casual users, there is a lot of noise and irrelevant material, in addition to the complications of informal language use, typos, and grammatical mistakes. Questions in the collection can also be related in different ways, although there is in general no explicit representation of this structure.

In addition to Subtask C, we designed subtasks A and B to give participants the tools to create a CQA system to solve subtask C. Specifically, Subtask A (*Question-Comment Similarity*) is defined as follows: "given a question from a question–comment thread, rank the comments according to their relevance (similarity) with respect to the question." Subtask B (*Question-Question Similarity*) is defined as follows: "given a new question, rerank all similar questions retrieved by a search engine, assuming that the answers to the similar questions should also answer the new question."

The relationship between subtasks A, B, and C is illustrated in Figure 1. In the figure, q stands for the new question, q' is an existing related question, and c is a comment within the thread of question q'. The edge $\overline{qc}$ relates to the main CQA task (subtask C), i.e., deciding whether a comment for a potentially related question is a good answer to the original question. This relation captures the *relevance* of c for q. The edge $\overline{qq'}$ represents the similarity between the original and the related questions (subtask B). This relation captures the *relatedness* of q and q'. Finally, the edge $\overline{q'c}$ represents the decision of whether c is a good answer for the question from its thread, q' (subtask A). This relation captures the *appropriateness* of c for q'. In this particular example, q and q' are indeed related, and c is a good answer for both q' and q.

The participants were free to approach Subtask C with or without solving Subtasks A and B, and participation in the main subtask and/or the two subtasks was optional.

We had three objectives for the first two editions of our task: (*i*) to focus on semantic-based solutions beyond simple "bag-of-words" representations and "word matching" techniques; (*ii*) to study new NLP challenges arising in the CQA scenario, e.g., relations between the comments in a thread, relations between different threads, and question-to-question similarity; and (*iii*) to facilitate the participation of non-IR/QA experts.

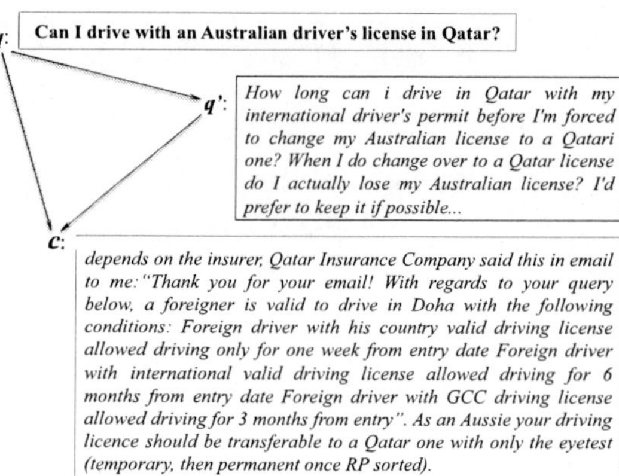

Figure 1: The similarity triangle for CQA, showing the three pairwise interactions between the original question q, the related question q', and a comment c in the related question's thread.

The third objective was achieved by providing the set of potential answers and asking the participants to (re)rank the answers, and also by defining two optional subtasks (A and B), in addition to the main subtask (i.e., C).

Last year, we were successful in attracting a large number of participants to all subtasks. However, as the task design was new (we added subtasks B and C in the 2016 edition of the task), we felt that participants would benefit from a rerun, with new test sets for subtasks A–C.

We preserved the multilinguality aspect (as in 2015 and 2016), providing data for two languages: English and Arabic. In particular, we had an Arabic subtask D, which used data collected from three medical forums. This year, we used a slightly different procedure for the preparation of test set compared to the way the training, development, and test data for subtask D was collected last year.

Additionally, we included a new subtask, subtask E, which enables experimentation on *Question–Question Similarity* on a large-scale CQA dataset, i.e., StackExchange, based on the CQADupStack data set (Hoogeveen et al., 2015). Subtask E is a *duplicate question detection* task, and like Subtask B, it is focused on question–question similarity. Participants were asked to rerank 50 candidate questions according to their relevance with respect to each query question. The subtask included several elements that differentiate it from Subtask B (see Section 3.2).

28

We provided manually annotated training data for both languages and for all subtasks. All examples were manually labeled by a community of annotators using a crowdsourcing platform. The datasets and the annotation procedure for the old data for subtasks A, B and C are described in (Nakov et al., 2016b). In order to produce the new data for Subtask D, we used a slightly different procedure compared to 2016, which we describe in Section 3.1.1.

The remainder of this paper is organized as follows: Section 2 introduces related work. Section 3 gives a more detailed definition of the subtasks; it also describes the datasets and the process of their creation, and it explains the evaluation measures we used. Section 4 presents the results for all subtasks and for all participating systems. Section 5 summarizes the main approaches used by these systems and provides further discussion. Finally, Section 6 presents the main conclusions.

2 Related Work

The first step to automatically answer questions on CQA sites is to retrieve a set of questions similar to the question that the user has asked. This set of similar questions is then used to extract possible answers for the original input question. Despite its importance, question similarity for CQA is a hard task due to problems such as the "lexical gap" between the two questions.

Question-question similarity has been featured as a subtask (subtask B) of SemEval-2016 Task 3 on Community Question Answering (Nakov et al., 2016b); there was also a similar subtask as part of SemEval-2016 Task 1 on Semantic Textual Similarity (Agirre et al., 2016). Question-question similarity is an important problem with application to question recommendation, question duplicate detection, community question answering, and question answering in general. Typically, it has been addressed using a variety of textual similarity measures. Some work has paid attention to modeling the question topic, which can be done explicitly, e.g., using question topic and focus (Duan et al., 2008) or using a graph of topic terms (Cao et al., 2008), or implicitly, e.g., using a language model with a smoothing method based on the category structure of Yahoo! Answers (Cao et al., 2009) or using LDA topic language model that matches the questions not only at the term level but also at the topic level (Zhang et al., 2014).

Another important aspect is syntactic structure, e.g., Wang et al. (2009) proposed a retrieval model for finding similar questions based on the similarity of syntactic trees, and Da San Martino et al. (2016) used syntactic kernels. Yet another emerging approach is to use neural networks, e.g., dos Santos et al. (2015) used convolutional neural networks (CNNs), Romeo et al. (2016) used long short-term memory (LSTMs) networks with neural attention to select the important part of text when comparing two questions, and Lei et al. (2016) used a combined recurrent–convolutional model to map questions to continuous semantic representations. Finally, translation (Jeon et al., 2005; Zhou et al., 2011) and cross-language models (Da San Martino et al., 2017) have also been popular for question-question similarity.

Question-answer similarity has been a subtask (subtask A) of our task in its two previous editions (Nakov et al., 2015, 2016b). This is a well-researched problem in the context of general question answering. One research direction has been to try to match the syntactic structure of the question to that of the candidate answer. For example, Wang et al. (2007) proposed a probabilistic quasi-synchronous grammar to learn syntactic transformations from the question to the candidate answers. Heilman and Smith (2010) used an algorithm based on Tree Edit Distance (TED) to learn tree transformations in pairs. Wang and Manning (2010) developed a probabilistic model to learn tree-edit operations on dependency parse trees. Yao et al. (2013) applied linear chain conditional random fields (CRFs) with features derived from TED to learn associations between questions and candidate answers. Moreover, syntactic structure was central for some of the top systems that participated in SemEval-2016 Task 3 (Filice et al., 2016; Barrón-Cedeño et al., 2016).

Another important research direction has been on using neural network models for question-answer similarity (Feng et al., 2015; Severyn and Moschitti, 2015; Wang and Nyberg, 2015; Tan et al., 2015; Barrón-Cedeño et al., 2016; Filice et al., 2016; Mohtarami et al., 2016). For instance, Tan et al. (2015) used neural attention over a bidirectional long short-term memory (LSTM) neural network in order to generate better answer representations given the questions. Another example is the work of Tymoshenko et al. (2016), who combined neural networks with syntactic kernels.

Yet another research direction has been on using machine translation models as features for question-answer similarity (Berger et al., 2000; Echihabi and Marcu, 2003; Jeon et al., 2005; Soricut and Brill, 2006; Riezler et al., 2007; Li and Manandhar, 2011; Surdeanu et al., 2011; Tran et al., 2015; Hoogeveen et al., 2016a; Wu and Zhang, 2016), e.g., a variation of IBM model 1 (Brown et al., 1993), to compute the probability that the question is a "translation" of the candidate answer. Similarly, (Guzmán et al., 2016a,b) ported an entire machine translation evaluation framework (Guzmán et al., 2015) to the CQA problem.

Using information about the answer thread is another important direction, which has been explored mainly to address Subtask A. In the 2015 edition of the task, the top participating systems used thread-level features, in addition to local features that only look at the question–answer pair. For example, the second-best team, HITSZ-ICRC, used as a feature the position of the comment in the thread, such as whether the answer is first or last (Hou et al., 2015). Similarly, the third-best team, QCRI, used features to model a comment in the context of the entire comment thread, focusing on user interaction (Nicosia et al., 2015). Finally, the fifth-best team, ICRC-HIT, treated the answer selection task as a sequence labeling problem and proposed recurrent convolutional neural networks to recognize good comments (Zhou et al., 2015b).

In follow-up work, Zhou et al. (2015a) included long-short term memory (LSTM) units in their convolutional neural network to model the classification sequence for the thread, and Barrón-Cedeño et al. (2015) exploited the dependencies between the thread comments to tackle the same task. This was done by designing features that look globally at the thread and by applying structured prediction models, such as CRFs.

This research direction was further extended by Joty et al. (2015), who used the output structure at the thread level in order to make more consistent global decisions about the goodness of the answers in the thread. They modeled the relations between pairs of comments at any distance in the thread, and combined the predictions of local classifiers using graph-cut and Integer Linear Programming. In follow up work, Joty et al. (2016) proposed joint learning models that integrate inference within the learning process using global normalization and an Ising-like edge potential.

Question–External comment similarity is our main task (subtask C), and it is inter-related to subtasks A and B, as described in the triangle of Figure 1. This task has been much less studied in the literature, mainly because its definition is specific to our SemEval Task 3, and it first appeared in the 2016 edition (Nakov et al., 2016b). Most of the systems that took part in the competition, including the winning system of the SUper team (Mihaylova et al., 2016), approached the task indirectly by solving subtask A at the thread level and then using these predictions together with the reciprocal rank of the related questions in order to produce a final ranking for subtask C. One exception is the *KeLP* system (Filice et al., 2016), which was ranked second in the competition. This system combined information from different subtasks and from all input components. It used a modular kernel function, including stacking from independent subtask A and B classifiers, and applying SVMs to train a Good vs. Bad classifier (Filice et al., 2016). In a related study, Nakov et al. (2016a) discussed the input information to solve Subtask C, and concluded that one has to model mainly question-to-question similarity (Subtask B) and answer goodness (subtask A), while modeling the direct relation between the new question and the candidate answer (from a related question) was found to be far less important.

Finally, in another recent approach, Bonadiman et al. (2017) studied how to combine the different CQA subtasks. They presented a multitask neural architecture where the three tasks are trained together with the same representation. The authors showed that the multitask system yields good improvement for Subtask C, which is more complex and clearly dependent on the other two tasks.

Some notable features across all subtasks. Finally, we should mention some interesting features used by the participating systems across all three subtasks. This includes fine-tuned word embeddings[5] (Mihaylov and Nakov, 2016b); features modeling text complexity, veracity, and user trollness[6] (Mihaylova et al., 2016); sentiment polarity features (Nicosia et al., 2015); and PMI-based goodness polarity lexicons (Balchev et al., 2016; Mihaylov et al., 2017a).

---

[5] https://github.com/tbmihailov/semeval2016-task3-cqa

[6] Using a heuristic that if several users call somebody a troll, then s/he should be one (Mihaylov et al., 2015a,b; Mihaylov and Nakov, 2016a; Mihaylov et al., 2017b).

Category	Train+Dev+Test from SemEval-2015	Train(1,2)+Dev+Test from SemEval-2016	Test
Original Questions	–	(200+67)+50+70	**88**
Related Questions	**2,480+291+319**	**(1,999+670)+500+700**	**880**
– Perfect Match	–	(181+54)+59+81	24
– Relevant	–	(606+242)+155+152	139
– Irrelevant	–	(1,212+374)+286+467	717
Related Comments (with respect to Original Question)	–	**(19,990+6,700)+5,000+7,000**	**8,800**
– Good	–	(1,988+849)+345+654	246
– Bad	–	(16,319+5,154)+4,061+5,943	8,291
– Potentially Useful	–	(1,683+697)+594+403	263
Related Comments (with respect to Related Question)	**14,893+1,529+1,876**	**(14,110+3,790)+2,440+3,270**	**2,930**
– Good	7,418+813+946	(5,287+1,364)+818+1,329	1,523
– Bad	5,971+544+774	(6,362+1,777)+1,209+1,485	1,407
– Potentially Useful	1,504+172+156	(2,461+649)+413+456	0

Table 1: Statistics about the English CQA-QL dataset. Note that the *Potentially Useful* class was merged with *Bad* at test time for SemEval-2016 Task 3, and was eliminated altogether at SemEval-2017 task 3.

3 Subtasks and Data Description

The 2017 challenge was structured as a set of five subtasks, four of which (A, B, C and E) were offered for English, while the fifth (D) one was for Arabic. We leveraged the data we developed in 2016 for the first four subtasks, creating only new test sets for them, whereas we built a completely new dataset for the new Subtask E.

3.1 Old Subtasks

The first four tasks and the datasets for them are described in (Nakov et al., 2016b). Here we review them briefly.

English subtask A *Question-Comment Similarity*. Given a question Q and the first ten comments[7] in its question thread $(c_1, \ldots, c_{10})$, the goal is to rank these ten comments according to their relevance with respect to that question.

Note that this is a ranking task, not a classification task; we use mean average precision (MAP) as an official evaluation measure. This setting was adopted as it is closer to the application scenario than pure comment classification. For a perfect ranking, a system has to place all "Good" comments above the "PotentiallyUseful" and the "Bad" comments; the latter two are not actually distinguished and are considered "Bad" at evaluation time. This year, we elliminated the "PotentiallyUseful" class for test at annotation time.

English subtask B *Question-Question Similarity*. Given a new question Q (aka *original question*) and the set of the first ten related questions from the forum $(Q_1, \ldots, Q_{10})$ retrieved by a search engine, the goal is to rank the related questions according to their similarity with respect to the original question.

In this case, we consider the "PerfectMatch" and the "Relevant" questions both as good (i.e., we do not distinguish between them and we will consider them both "Relevant"), and they should be ranked above the "Irrelevant" questions. As in subtask A, we use MAP as the official evaluation measure. To produce the ranking of related questions, participants have access to the corresponding related question-thread.[8] Thus, being more precise, this subtask could have been named *Question — Question+Thread Similarity*.

English subtask C *Question-External Comment Similarity*. Given a new question Q (also known as the *original question*), and the set of the first ten related questions $(Q_1, \ldots, Q_{10})$ from the forum retrieved by a search engine for Q, each associated with its first ten comments appearing in Q's thread $(c_1^1, \ldots, c_1^{10}, \ldots, c_{10}^1, \ldots, c_{10}^{10})$, the goal is to rank these $10 \times 10 = 100$ comments $\{c_i^j\}_{i,j=1}^{10}$ according to their relevance with respect to the original question Q.

---

[7] We limit the number of comments we consider to the first ten only in order to spare some annotation efforts.

[8] Note that the search engine indexes entire Web pages, and thus, the search engine has compared the original question to the related questions together with their comment threads.

This is the main English subtask. As for subtask A, we want the "Good" comments to be ranked above the "PotentiallyUseful" and the "Bad" comments, which will be considered just bad in terms of evaluation. Although, the systems are supposed to work on 100 comments, we take an application-oriented view in the evaluation, assuming that users would like to have good comments concentrated in the first ten positions. We believe users care much less about what happens in lower positions (e.g., after the 10th) in the rank, as they typically do not ask for the next page of results in a search engine such as Google or Bing. This is reflected in our primary evaluation score, MAP, which we restrict to consider only the top ten results for subtask C.

Arabic subtask D *Rank the correct answers for a new question.* Given a new question Q (aka the original question), the set of the first 30 related questions retrieved by a search engine, each associated with one correct answer $((Q_1, c_1) \ldots, (Q_{30}, c_{30}))$, the goal is to rank the 30 question-answer pairs according to their relevance with respect to the original question. We want the "Direct" and the "Relevant" answers to be ranked above the "Irrelevant" answers; the former two are considered "Relevant" in terms of evaluation. We evaluate the position of "Relevant" answers in the rank, and this is again a ranking task. Unlike the English subtasks, here we use 30 answers since the retrieval task is much more difficult, leading to low recall, and the number of correct answers is much lower. Again, the systems were evaluated using MAP, restricted to the top-10 results.

3.1.1 Data Description for A–D

The English data for subtasks A, B, and C comes from the Qatar Living forum, which is organized as a set of seemingly independent question–comment threads. In short, for subtask A, we annotated the comments in a question-thread as "Good", "PotentiallyUseful" or "Bad" with respect to the question that started the thread. Additionally, given original questions, we retrieved related question–comment threads and annotated the related questions as "PerfectMatch", "Relevant", or "Irrelevant" with respect to the original question (Subtask B). We then annotated the comments in the threads of related questions as "Good", "PotentiallyUseful" or "Bad" with respect to the original question (Subtask C).

For Arabic, the data was extracted from medical forums and has a different format. Given an original question, we retrieved pairs of the form (related_question, answer_to_the_related_question). These pairs were annotated as "Direct" answer, "Relevant" and "Irrelevant" with respect to the original question.

For subtasks A, B, and C we annotated new English test data following the same setup as for SemEval-2016 Task 3 (Nakov et al., 2016b), except that we elliminated the "Potentially Useful" class for subtask A. We first selected a set of questions to serve as original questions. In a real-world scenario those would be questions that had never been asked previously, but here we used existing questions from Qatar Living.

From each original question, we generated a query, using the question's subject (after some word removal if the subject was too long). Then, we executed the query against Google, limiting the search to the Qatar Living forum, and we collected up to 200 resulting question-comment threads as related questions. Afterwards, we filtered out threads with less than ten comments as well as those for which the question was more than 2,000 characters long. Finally, we kept the top-10 surviving threads, keeping just the first 10 comments in each thread.

We formatted the results in XML with UTF-8 encoding, adding metadata for the related questions and for their comments; however, we did not provide any meta information about the original question, in order to emulate a scenario where it is a new question, never asked before in the forum. In order to have a valid XML, we had to do some cleansing and normalization of the data. We added an XML format definition at the beginning of the XML file and we made sure it validated.

We organized the XML data as a sequence of original questions (OrgQuestion), where each question has a subject, a body, and a unique question identifier (ORGQ_ID). Each such original question is followed by ten threads, where each thread consists of a related question (from the search engine results) and its first ten comments.

We made available to the participants for training and development the data from 2016 (and for subtask A, also from 2015), and we created a new test set of 88 new questions associated with 880 question candidates and 8,800 comments; details are shown in Table 1.

Category	SemEval-2016 data			Test-2017
	Train	**Dev**	**Test**	
Questions	**1,031**	**250**	**250**	**1,400**
QA Pairs	**30,411**	**7,384**	**7,369**	**12,600**
– Direct	917	70	65	891
– Related	17,412	1,446	1,353	4,054
– Irrelevant	12,082	5,868	5,951	7,655

Table 2: Statistics about the CQA-MD corpus.

For subtasks D we had to annotate new test data. In 2016, we used data from three Arabic medical websites, which we downloaded and indexed locally using Solr.[9] Then, we performed 21 different query/document formulations, and we merged the retrieved results, ranking them according to the reciprocal rank fusion algorithm (Cormack et al., 2009). Finally, we truncated the result list to the 30 top-ranked question–answer pairs.

This year we only used one of these websites, namely `Altibbi.com`[10] First, we selected some questions from that website to be used as original questions, and then we used Google to retrieve potentially related questions using the `site:*` filter.

We turned the question into a query as follows: We first queried Google using the first thirty words from the original question. If this did not return ten results, we reduced the query to the first ten non-stopwords[11] from the question, and if needed we further tried using the first five non-stopwords only. If we did not manage to obtain ten results, we discarded that original question.

If we managed to obtain ten results, we followed the resulting links and we parsed the target page to extract the question and the answer, which is given by a physician, as well as some metadata such as date, question classification, doctor's name and country, etc.

In many cases, Google returned our original question as one of the search results, in which case we had to exclude it, thus reducing the results to nine. In the remaining cases, we excluded the 10th result in order to have the same number of candidate question–answer pairs for each original question, namely nine. Overall, we collected 1,400 original questions, with exactly nine potentially related question–answer pairs for each of them, i.e., a total of 12,600 pairs.

We created an annotation job on CrowdFlower to obtain judgments about the relevance of the question–answer pairs with respect to the original question. We controlled the quality of annotation using a hidden set of 50 test questions. We had three judgments per example, which we combined using the CrowdFlower mechanism. The average agreement was 81%. Table 2 shows statistics about the resulting dataset, together with statistics about the datasets from 2016, which could be used for training and development.

3.1.2 Evaluation Measures for A–D

The official evaluation measure we used to rank the participating systems is Mean Average Precision ("MAP"), calculated over the top-10 comments as ranked by a participating system. We further report the results for two unofficial ranking measures, which we also calculated over the top-10 results only: Mean Reciprocal Rank ("MRR") and Average Recall ("AvgRec"). Additionally, we report the results for four standard classification measures, which we calculate over the full list of results: Precision, Recall and F_1 (with respect to the Good/Relevant class), and Accuracy.

We released a specialized scorer that calculates and returns all the above-mentioned scores.

3.2 The New Subtask E

Subtask E is a duplicate question detection task, similar to Subtask B. Participants were asked to rerank 50 candidate questions according to their relevance with respect to each query question. The subtask included several elements that distinguish it from Subtask B:

- Several meta-data fields were added, including the tags that are associated with each question, the number of times a question has been viewed, and the score of each question, answer and comment (the number of upvotes it has received from the community, minus the number of downvotes), as well as user statistics, containing information such as user reputation and user badges.[12]

- At test time, two extra test sets containing data from two surprise subforums were provided, to test the participants' system's cross-domain performance.

---

[9]`https://lucene.apache.org/solr/`

[10]`http://www.altibbi.com/`أسئلة-طبية

[11]We used the following Arabic stopword list: `https://sites.google.com/site/kevinbouge/stopwords-lists`

[12]The complete list of available meta-data fields can be found on the Task website.

Subforums	Train	Development	Test
Android	10,360	3,197	3,531
English	20,701	6,596	6,383
Gaming	14,951	4,964	4,675
Wordpress	13,733	5,007	3,816
Surprise 1	—	—	5,123
Surprise 2	—	—	4,039

Table 3: Statistics on the data for Subtask E. Shown is the number of query questions; for each of them, 50 candidate questions were provided.

- The participants were asked to truncate their result list in such a way that only "Perfect-Match" questions appeared in it. The evaluation metrics were adjusted to be able to handle empty result lists (see Section 3.2.2).

- The data was taken from StackExchange instead of the Qatar Living forums, and reflected the real-world distribution of duplicate questions in having many query questions with zero relevant results.

The cross-domain aspect was of particular interest, as it has not received much attention in earlier duplicate question detection research.

3.2.1 Data Description for E

The data consisted of questions from the following four StackExchange subforums: *Android, English, Gaming*, and *Wordpress*, derived from a data set known as CQADupStack (Hoogeveen et al., 2015). Data size statistics can be found in Table 3. These subforums were chosen due to their size, and to reflect a variety of domains.

The data was provided in the same format as for the other subtasks. Each original question had 50 candidate questions, and these related questions each had a number of comments. On top of that, they had a number of answers, and each answer potentially had individual comments. The difference between answers and comments is that answers should contain a well-formed answer to the question, while comments contain things such as requests for clarification, remarks, and small additions to someone else's answer. Since the content of StackExchange is provided by the community, the precise delineation between comments and the main body of a post can vary across forums.

The relevance labels in the development and in the training data were sourced directly from the users of the StackExchange sites, who can vote for questions to be closed as duplicates: these are the questions we labeled as *PerfectMatch*.

The questions labeled as *Related* are questions that are not duplicates, but that are somehow similar to the original question, also as judged by the StackExchange community. It is possible that some duplicate labels are missing, due to the voluntary nature of the duplicate labeling on StackExchange. The development and training data should therefore be considered a silver standard (Hoogeveen et al., 2016b).

For the test data, we started an annotation project together with StackExchange.[13] The goal was to obtain multiple annotations per question pair in the test set, from the same community that provided the labels in the development and in the training data. We expected the community to react enthusiastically, because the data would be used to build systems that can improve duplicate question detection on the site, ultimately saving the users manual effort. Unfortunately, only a handful of people were willing to annotate a sizeable set of question pairs, thus making their annotations unusable for the purpose of this shared task.

An example that includes a query question from the English subforum, a duplicate of that question, and a non-duplicate question (with respect to the query) is shown below:

- Query: *Why do bread companies add sugar to bread?*

- Duplicate: *What is the purpose of sugar in baking plain bread?*

- Non-duplicate: *Is it safe to eat potatoes that have sprouted?*

3.2.2 Evaluation Measure for E

In CQA archives, the majority of new questions do not have a duplicate in the archive. We maintained this characteristic in the training, in the development, and in the test data, to stay as close to a real world setting as possible. This means that for most query questions, the correct result is an empty list.

---

[13] A post made by StackExchange about the project can be found here: `http://meta.stackexchange.com/questions/286329/project-reduplication-of-deduplication-has-begun`

This has two consequences: (1) a system that always returns an empty list is a challenging baseline to beat, and (2) standard IR evaluation metrics like MAP, which is used in the other subtasks, cannot be used, because they break down when the result list is empty or there are no relevant documents for a given query.

To solve this problem we used a modified version of MAP, as proposed by Liu et al. (2016). To make sure standard IR evaluation metrics do not break down on empty result list queries, Liu et al. (2016) add a nominal terminal document to the end of the ranking returned by a system, to indicate where the number of relevant documents ended. This terminal document has a corresponding gain value of:

$$r_t = \begin{cases} 1 & \text{if } R = 0 \\ \sum_{i=1}^{d} r_i / R & \text{if } R > 0 \end{cases}$$

The result of this adjustment is that queries without relevant documents in the index, receive a MAP score of 1.0 for an empty result ranking. This is desired, because in such cases, the empty ranking is the correct result.

4 Participants and Results

The list of all participating teams can be found in Table 4. The results for subtasks A, B, C, and D are shown in tables 5, 6, 7, and 8, respectively. Unfortunately, there were no official participants in Subtask E, and thus we present baseline results in Table 9. In all tables, the systems are ranked by the official MAP scores for their primary runs[14] (shown in the third column). The following columns show the scores based on the other six unofficial measures; the ranking with respect to these additional measures are marked with a subindex (for the primary runs).

Twenty two teams participated in the challenge presenting a variety of approaches and features to address the different subtasks. They submitted a total of 85 runs (36 primary and 49 contrastive), which breaks down by subtask as follows: The English subtasks A, B and C attracted 14, 13, and 6 systems and 31, 34 and 14 runs, respectively. The Arabic subtask D got 3 systems and 6 runs. And there were no participants for subtask E.

<hr>

The best MAP scores had large variability depending on the subtask, going from 15.46 (best result for subtask C) to 88.43 (best result for subtask A). The best systems for subtasks A, B, and C were able to beat the baselines we provided by sizeable margins. In subtask D, only the best system was above the IR baseline.

4.1 Subtask A, English (Question-Comment Similarity)

Table 5 shows the results for subtask A, English, which attracted 14 teams (two more than in the 2016 edition). In total 31 runs were submitted: 14 primary and 17 contrastive. The last four rows of the table show the performance of four baselines. The first one is the chronological ranking, where the comments are ordered by their time of posting; we can see that all submissions but one outperform this baseline on all three ranking measures. The second baseline is a random baseline, which is 10 MAP points below the chronological ranking. Baseline 3 classifies all comments as Good, and it outperforms all but three of the primary systems in terms of F_1 and one system in terms of Accuracy. However, it should be noted that the systems were not optimized for such measures. Finally, baseline 4 classifies all comments as Bad; it is outperformed by all primary systems in terms of Accuracy.

The winner of Subtask A is *KeLP* with a MAP of 88.43, closely followed by *Beihang-MSRA*, scoring 88.24. Relatively far from the first two, we find five systems, *IIT-UHH*, *ECNU*, *bunji*, *EICA* and *SwissAlps*, which all obtained an MAP of around 86.5.

4.2 Subtask B, English (Question-Question Similarity)

Table 6 shows the results for subtask B, English, which attracted 13 teams (3 more than in last year's edition) and 34 runs: 13 primary and 21 contrastive. This is known to be a hard task. In contrast to the 2016 results, in which only 6 out of 11 teams beat the strong IR baseline (i.e., ordering the related questions in the order provided by the search engine), this year 10 of the 13 systems outperformed this baseline in terms of MAP, AvgRec and MRR. Moreover, the improvements for the best systems over the IR baseline are larger (reaching > 7 MAP points absolute). This is a remarkable improvement over last year's results.

The random baseline outperforms two systems in terms of Accuracy. The "all-good" baseline is below almost all systems on F_1, but the "all-false" baseline yields the best Accuracy results. This is partly because the label distribution in the dataset is biased (81.5% of negative cases), but also because the systems were optimized for MAP rather than for classification accuracy (or precision/recall).

The winner of the task is *SimBow* with a MAP of 47.22, followed by *LearningToQuestion* with 46.93, *KeLP* with 46.66, and *Talla* with 45.70. The other nine systems scored sensibly lower than them, ranging from about 41 to 45. Note that the contrastive1 run of *KeLP*, which corresponds to the *KeLP* system from last year (Filice et al., 2016), achieved an even higher MAP of 49.00.

4.3 Subtask C, English (Question-External Comment Similarity)

The results for subtask C, English are shown in Table 7. This subtask attracted 6 teams (sizable decrease compared to last year's 10 teams), and 14 runs: 6 primary and 8 contrastive. The test set from 2017 had much more skewed label distribution, with only 2.8% positive instances, compared to the ~10% of the 2016 test set. This makes the overall MAP scores look much lower, as the number of examples without a single positive comment increased significantly, and they contribute 0 to the average, due to the definition of the measure. Consequently, the results cannot be compared directly to last year's.

All primary systems managed to outperform all baselines with respect to the ranking measures. Moreover, all but one system outperformed the "all true" system on F_1, and all of them were below the accuracy of the "all false" baseline, due to the extreme class imbalance.

The best-performing team for subtask C is *IIT-UHH*, with a MAP of 15.46, followed by *bunji* with 14.71, and *KeLP* with 14.35. The contrastive1 run of *bunji*, which used a neural network, obtained the highest MAP, 16.57, two points higher than their primary run, which also uses the comment plausibility features. Thus, the difference seems to be due to the use of comment plausibility features, which hurt the accuracy. In their SemEval system paper, Koreeda et al. (2017) explain that the similarity features are more important for Subtask C than plausibility features.

Indeed, Subtask C contains many comments that are not related to the original question, while candidate comments for subtask A are almost always on the same topic. Another explanation may be the overfitting to the development set since the authors manually designed plausibility features using that set. As a result, such features perform much worse on the 2017 test set.

4.4 Subtask D, Arabic (Reranking the Correct Answers for a New Question)

Finally, the results for subtask D, Arabic are shown in Table 8. This year, subtask D attracted only 3 teams, which submitted 6 runs: 3 primary and 3 contrastive. Compared to last year, the 2017 test set contains a significantly larger number of positive question–answer pairs (~40% in 2017, compared to ~20% in 2016), and thus the MAP scores are higher this year. Moreover, this year, the IR baseline is coming from Google and is thus very strong and difficult to beat. Indeed, only the best system was able to improve on it (marginally) in terms of MAP, MRR and AvgRec.

As in some of the other tasks, the participants in Subtask D did not concentrate on optimizing for precision/recall/F_1/accuracy and they did not produce sensible class predictions in most cases.

The best-performing system is *GW_QA* with a MAP score of 61.16, which barely improves over the IR baseline of 60.55. The other two systems *UPC-USMBA* and *QU_BIGIR* are about 3-4 points behind.

4.5 Subtask E, English (Multi-Domain Question Duplicate Detection)

The baselines for Subtask E can be found in Table 9. The IR baseline is BM25 with perfect truncation after the final relevant document for a given document (equating to an empty result list if there are no relevant documents). The zero results baseline is the score for a system that returns an empty result list for every single query. This is a high number for each subforum because for many queries there are no duplicate questions in the archive.

As previously stated, there are no results submitted by participants to be discussed for this subtask. Eight teams signed up to participate, but unfortunately none of them submitted test results.

5 Discussion and Conclusions

In this section, we first describe features that are common across the different subtasks. Then, we discuss the characteristics of the best systems for each subtask with focus on the machine learning algorithms and the instance representations used.

5.1 Feature Types

The features the participants used across the subtasks can be organized into the following groups:

(*i*) *similarity features* between questions and comments from their threads or between original questions and related questions, e.g., cosine similarity applied to lexical, syntactic and semantic representations, including distributed representations, often derived using neural networks;

(*ii*) *content features*, which are special signals that can clearly indicate a bad comment, e.g., when a comment contains "thanks";

(*iii*) *thread level/meta features*, e.g., user ID, comment rank in the thread;

(*iv*) *automatically generated features* from syntactic structures using tree kernels.

Generally, similarity features were developed for the subtasks as follows:

Subtask A. Similarities between question subject vs. comment, question body vs. comment, and question subject+body vs. comment.

Subtask B. Similarities between the original and the related question at different levels: subject vs. subject, body vs. body, and subject+body vs. subject+body.

Subtask C. The same as above, plus the similarities of the original question, subject and body at all levels with the comments from the thread of the related question.

Subtask D. The same as above, without information about the thread, as there is no thread.

The similarity scores to be used as features were computed in various ways, e.g., most teams used dot product calculated over word n-grams (n=1,2,3), character n-grams, or with TF-IDF weighting. Simple word overlap, i.e., the number of common words between two texts, was also considered, often normalized, e.g., by question/comment length. Overlap in terms of nouns or named entities was also explored.

5.2 Learning Methods

This year, we saw variety of machine learning approaches, ranging from SVMs to deep learning.

The *KeLP* system, which performed best on Subtask A, was SVM-based and used syntactic tree kernels with relational links between questions and comments, together with some standard text similarity measures linearly combined with the tree kernel. Variants of this approach were successfully used in related research (Tymoshenko et al., 2016; Da San Martino et al., 2016), as well as in last year's *KeLP* system (Filice et al., 2016).

The best performing system on Subtask C, *IIT-UHH*, was also SVM-based, and it used textual, domain-specific, word-embedding and topic-modeling features. The most interesting aspect of this system is their method for dialogue chain identification in the comment threads, which yielded substantial improvements.

The best-performing system on Subtask B was *SimBow*. They used logistic regression on a rich combination of different unsupervised textual similarities, built using a relation matrix based on standard cosine similarity between bag-of-words and other semantic or lexical relations.

This year, we also saw a jump in the popularity of deep learning and neural networks. For example, the *Beihang-MSRA* system was ranked second with a result very close to that of *KeLP* for Subtask A. They used gradient boosted regression trees, i.e., XgBoost, as a ranking model to combine (*i*) TF×IDF, word sequence overlap, translation probability, (*ii*) three different types of tree kernels, (*iii*) subtask-specific features, e.g., whether a comment is written by the author of the question, the length of a comment or whether a comment contains URLs or email addresses, and (*iv*) neural word embeddings, and the similarity score from Bi-LSTM and 2D matching neural networks.

LearningToQuestion achieved the second best result for Subtask B using SVM and Logistic Regression as integrators of rich feature representations, mainly embeddings generated by the following neural networks: (*i*) siamese networks to learn similarity measures using GloVe vectors (Pennington et al., 2014), (*ii*) bidirectional LSTMs, (*iii*) gated recurrent unit (GRU) used as another network to generate the neural embeddings trained by a siamese network similar to Bi-LSTM, (*iv*) and convolutional neural networks to generate embeddings inside the siamese network.

The *bunji* system, second on Subtask C, produced features using neural networks that capture the semantic similarities between two sentences as well as comment plausibility. The neural similarity features were extracted using a decomposable attention model (Parikh et al., 2016), which can model alignment between two sequences of text, allowing the system to identify possibly related regions of a question and of a comment, which then helps it predict whether the comment is relevant with respect to the question. The model compares each token pair from the question tokens and comment tokens associating them with an attention weight. Each question-comment pair is mapped to a real-value score using a neural network with shared weights and the prediction loss is calculated listwise. The plausibility features are task-specific, e.g., is the person giving the answer actually trying to answer the question or is s/he making remarks or asking for more information. Other features are the presence keywords such as *what, which, who, where* within the question. There are also features about the question and the comment length. All these features were merged in a CRF.

Another interesting system is that of *Talla*, which consists of an ensemble of syntactic, semantic, and IR-based features, i.e., semantic word alignment, term frequency Kullback-Leibler divergence, and tree kernels. These were integrated in a pairwise-preference learning handled with a random forest classifier with 2,000 weak estimators. This system achieved very good performance on Subtask B.

Regarding Arabic, *GW_QA*, the best-performing system for Subtask D, used features based on latent semantic models, namely, weighted textual matrix factorization models (WTMF), as well as a set of lexical features based on string lengths and surface-level matching. WTMF builds a latent model, which is appropriate for semantic profiling of a short text. Its main goal is to address the sparseness of short texts using both observed and missing words to explicitly capture what the text is and is not about. The missing words are defined as those of the entire training data vocabulary minus those of the target document. The model was trained on text data from the Arabic Gigaword as well as on Arabic data that we provided in the task website, as part of the task. For Arabic text processing, the MADAMIRA toolkit was used.

The second-best team for Arabic, *QU-BIGIR*, used SVM-rank with two similarity feature sets. The first set captured similarity between pairs of text, i.e., synonym overlap, language model score, cosine similarity, Jaccard similarity, etc. The second set used word2vec to build average word embedding and covariance word embedding similarity to build the text representation.

The third-best team for Arabic, *UPC-USMBA*, combined several classifiers, including (*i*) lexical string similarities in vector representations, and (*ii*) rule-based features. A core component of their approach was the use of medical terminology covering both Arabic and English terms, which was organized into the following three categories: body parts, drugs, and diseases. In particular, they translated the Arabic dataset into English using the Google Translate service. The linguistic processing was carried out with Stanford CoreNLP for English and MADAMIRA for Arabic. Finally, WordNet synsets both for Arabic and English were added to the representation without performing word sense disambiguation.

6 Conclusions

We have described SemEval-2017 Task 3 on Community Question Answering, which extended the four subtasks at SemEval-2016 Task 3 (Nakov et al., 2016b) with a new subtask on multi-domain question duplicate detection. Overall, the task attracted 23 teams, which submitted 85 runs; this is comparable to 2016, when 18 teams submitted 95 runs. The participants built on the lessons learned from the 2016 edition of the task, and further experimented with new features and learning frameworks. The top systems used neural networks with distributed representations or SVMs with syntactic kernels for linguistic analysis. A number of new features have been tried as well.

Apart from the new lessons learned from this year's edition, we believe that the task has another important contribution: the datasets we have created as part of the task, and which we have released for use to the research community, should be useful for follow-up research beyond SemEval.

Finally, while the new subtask E did not get any submissions, mainly because of the need to work with a large amount of data, we believe that it is about an important problem and that it will attract the interest of many researchers of the field.

Acknowledgements

This research was performed in part by the Arabic Language Technologies (ALT) group at the Qatar Computing Research Institute (QCRI), HBKU, part of Qatar Foundation. It is part of the Interactive sYstems for Answer Search (IYAS) project, which is developed in collaboration with MIT-CSAIL. This research received funding in part from the Australian Research Council.

References

Eneko Agirre, Carmen Banea, Daniel Cer, Mona Diab, Aitor Gonzalez-Agirre, Rada Mihalcea, German Rigau, and Janyce Wiebe. 2016. SemEval-2016 Task 1: Semantic textual similarity, monolingual and cross-lingual evaluation. In *Proceedings of the Workshop on Semantic Evaluation*. San Diego, California, USA, SemEval '2016, pages 497–511.

Surya Agustian and Hiroya Takamura. 2017. UINSUSKA-TiTech at SemEval-2017 task 3: Exploiting word importance levels as similarity features for CQA. In *Proceedings of the 11th International Workshop on Semantic Evaluation*. Vancouver, Canada, SemEval '17, pages 370–374.

Nada Almarwani and Mona Diab. 2017. GW_QA at SemEval-2017 task 3: Question answer re-ranking on Arabic fora. In *Proceedings of the 11th International Workshop on Semantic Evaluation*. Vancouver, Canada, SemEval '17, pages 344–348.

Giuseppe Attardi, Antonio Carta, Federico Errica, Andrea Madotto, and Ludovica Pannitto. 2017. FA3L at SemEval-2017 task 3: A three embeddings recurrent neural network for question answering. In *Proceedings of the 11th International Workshop on Semantic Evaluation*. Vancouver, Canada, SemEval '17, pages 300–304.

Daniel Balchev, Yasen Kiprov, Ivan Koychev, and Preslav Nakov. 2016. PMI-cool at SemEval-2016 Task 3: Experiments with PMI and goodness polarity lexicons for community question answering. In *Proceedings of the 10th International Workshop on Semantic Evaluation*. San Diego, California, USA, SemEval '16, pages 844–850.

Alberto Barrón-Cedeño, Simone Filice, Giovanni Da San Martino, Shafiq Joty, Lluís Màrquez, Preslav Nakov, and Alessandro Moschitti. 2015. Thread-level information for comment classification in community question answering. In *Proceedings of the 53rd Annual Meeting of the Association for Computational Linguistics and the 7th International Joint Conference on Natural Language Processing*. Beijing, China, ACL-IJCNLP '15, pages 687–693.

Alberto Barrón-Cedeño, Giovanni Da San Martino, Shafiq Joty, Alessandro Moschitti, Fahad A. Al Obaidli, Salvatore Romeo, Kateryna Tymoshenko, and Antonio Uva. 2016. ConvKN at SemEval-2016 Task 3: Answer and question selection for question answering on Arabic and English fora. In *Proceedings of the 10th International Workshop on Semantic Evaluation*. San Diego, California, USA, SemEval '16, pages 896–903.

Asma Ben Abacha and Dina Demner-Fushman. 2017. NLM_NIH at SemEval-2017 task 3: from question entailment to question similarity for community question answering. In *Proceedings of the 11th International Workshop on Semantic Evaluation*. Vancouver, Canada, SemEval '17, pages 349–352.

Adam Berger, Rich Caruana, David Cohn, Dayne Freitag, and Vibhu Mittal. 2000. Bridging the lexical chasm: Statistical approaches to answer-finding. In *Proceedings of the 23rd Annual International ACM SIGIR Conference on Research and Development in Information Retrieval*. Athens, Greece, SIGIR '00, pages 192–199.

Daniele Bonadiman, Antonio Uva, and Alessandro Moschitti. 2017. Effective shared representations with multitask learning for community question answering. In *Proceedings of the Conference of the European Chapter of the Association for Computational Linguistics*. Valencia, Spain, pages 726–732.

Peter Brown, Vincent Della Pietra, Stephen Della Pietra, and Robert Mercer. 1993. The mathematics of statistical machine translation: Parameter estimation. *Comput. Linguist.* 19(2):263–311.

Xin Cao, Gao Cong, Bin Cui, Christian Søndergaard Jensen, and Ce Zhang. 2009. The use of categorization information in language models for question retrieval. In *Proceedings of the 18th ACM Conference on Information and Knowledge Management*. Hong Kong, China, CIKM '09, pages 265–274.

Yunbo Cao, Huizhong Duan, Chin-Yew Lin, Yong Yu, and Hsiao-Wuen Hon. 2008. Recommending questions using the MDL-based tree cut model. In *Proceedings of the International Conference on World Wide Web*. Beijing, China, WWW '08, pages 81–90.

Delphine Charlet and Geraldine Damnati. 2017. SimBow at SemEval-2017 task 3: Soft-cosine semantic similarity between questions for community question answering. In *Proceedings of the 11th International Workshop on Semantic Evaluation*. Vancouver, Canada, SemEval '17, pages 315–319.

Gordon V Cormack, Charles LA Clarke, and Stefan Buettcher. 2009. Reciprocal rank fusion outperforms condorcet and individual rank learning methods. In *Proceedings of the 32nd international ACM SIGIR conference on Research and development in information retrieval*. Boston, Massachusetts, USA, SIGIR '09, pages 758–759.

Giovanni Da San Martino, Alberto Barrón Cedeño, Salvatore Romeo, Antonio Uva, and Alessandro

Moschitti. 2016. Learning to re-rank questions in community question answering using advanced features. In *Proceedings of the 25th ACM International on Conference on Information and Knowledge Management*. Indianapolis, Indiana, USA, CIKM '16, pages 1997–2000.

Giovanni Da San Martino, Salvatore Romeo, Alberto Barrón-Cedeño, Shafiq Joty, Lluís Màrquez, Alessandro Moschitti, and Preslav Nakov. 2017. Cross-language question re-ranking. In *Proceedings of the 40th International ACM SIGIR Conference on Research and Development in Information Retrieval*. Tokyo, Japan, SIGIR '17.

Jan Milan Deriu and Mark Cieliebak. 2017. SwissAlps at SemEval-2017 task 3: Attention-based convolutional neural network for community question answering. In *Proceedings of the 11th International Workshop on Semantic Evaluation*. Vancouver, Canada, SemEval '17, pages 334–338.

Cicero dos Santos, Luciano Barbosa, Dasha Bogdanova, and Bianca Zadrozny. 2015. Learning hybrid representations to retrieve semantically equivalent questions. In *Proceedings of the 53rd Annual Meeting of the Association for Computational Linguistics and the 7th International Joint Conference on Natural Language Processing*. Beijing, China, ACL-IJCNLP '15, pages 694–699.

Huizhong Duan, Yunbo Cao, Chin-Yew Lin, and Yong Yu. 2008. Searching questions by identifying question topic and question focus. In *Proceedings of the 46th Annual Meeting of the Association for Computational Linguistics*. Columbus, Ohio, USA, pages 156–164.

Abdessamad Echihabi and Daniel Marcu. 2003. A noisy-channel approach to question answering. In *Proceedings of the 41st Annual Meeting of the Association for Computational Linguistics*. Sapporo, Japan, ACL '03, pages 16–23.

Yassine El Adlouni, Imane LAHBARI, Horacio Rodriguez, Mohammed Meknassi, Said Ouatik El Alaoui, and Noureddine Ennahnahi. 2017. UPC-USMBA at SemEval-2017 task 3: Combining multiple approaches for CQA for Arabic. In *Proceedings of the 11th International Workshop on Semantic Evaluation*. Vancouver, Canada, SemEval '17, pages 276–280.

Minwei Feng, Bing Xiang, Michael R. Glass, Lidan Wang, and Bowen Zhou. 2015. Applying deep learning to answer selection: a study and an open task. In *Proceedings of the Workshop on Automatic Speech Recognition and Understanding*. Scottsdale, Arizona, USA, ASRU '15, pages 813–820.

Simone Filice, Danilo Croce, Alessandro Moschitti, and Roberto Basili. 2016. KeLP at SemEval-2016 Task 3: Learning semantic relations between questions and answers. In *Proceedings of the Workshop on Semantic Evaluation*. San Diego, California, USA, SemEval '16, pages 1116–1123.

Simone Filice, Giovanni Da San Martino, and Alessandro Moschitti. 2017. KeLP at SemEval-2017 task 3: Learning pairwise patterns in community question answering. In *Proceedings of the 11th International Workshop on Semantic Evaluation*. Vancouver, Canada, SemEval '17, pages 327–334.

Byron Galbraith, Bhanu Pratap, and Daniel Shank. 2017. Talla at SemEval-2017 task 3: Identifying similar questions through paraphrase detection. In *Proceedings of the 11th International Workshop on Semantic Evaluation*. Vancouver, Canada, SemEval '17, pages 375–379.

Naman Goyal. 2017. LearningToQuestion at SemEval 2017 task 3: Ranking similar questions by learning to rank using rich features. In *Proceedings of the International Workshop on Semantic Evaluation*. Vancouver, Canada, SemEval '17, pages 310–314.

Francisco Guzmán, Shafiq Joty, Lluís Màrquez, and Preslav Nakov. 2015. Pairwise neural machine translation evaluation. In *Proceedings of the 53rd Annual Meeting of the Association for Computational Linguistics and the 7th International Joint Conference on Natural Language Processing*. Beijing, China, ACL-IJCNLP '15, pages 805–814.

Francisco Guzmán, Lluís Màrquez, and Preslav Nakov. 2016a. Machine translation evaluation meets community question answering. In *Proceedings of the 54th Annual Meeting of the Association for Computational Linguistics*. Berlin, Germany, ACL '16, pages 460–466.

Francisco Guzmán, Preslav Nakov, and Lluís Màrquez. 2016b. MTE-NN at SemEval-2016 Task 3: Can machine translation evaluation help community question answering? In *Proceedings of the International Workshop on Semantic Evaluation*. San Diego, California, USA, SemEval '16, pages 887–895.

Michael Heilman and Noah A. Smith. 2010. Tree edit models for recognizing textual entailments, paraphrases, and answers to questions. In *Human Language Technologies: The 2010 Annual Conference of the North American Chapter of the Association for Computational Linguistics*. Los Angeles, California, USA, ACL '10, pages 1011–1019.

Doris Hoogeveen, Yitong Li, Huizhi Liang, Bahar Salehi, Timothy Baldwin, and Long Duong. 2016a. UniMelb at SemEval-2016 Task 3: Identifying similar questions by combining a CNN with string similarity measures. In *Proceedings of the International Workshop on Semantic Evaluation*. San Diego, California, USA, SemEval '16, pages 851–856.

Doris Hoogeveen, Karin Verspoor, and Timothy Baldwin. 2016b. CQADupStack: Gold or silver? In *Proceedings of the SIGIR 2016 Workshop on Web Question Answering Beyond Factoids*. Pisa, Italy, WebQA '16.

Doris Hoogeveen, Karin M. Verspoor, and Timothy Baldwin. 2015. CQADupStack: A benchmark data set for community question-answering research. In *Proceedings of the 20th Australasian Document Computing Symposium*. Parramatta, NSW, Australia, ADCS '15, pages 3:1–3:8.

Enamul Hoque, Shafiq Joty, Lluís Màrquez, Alberto Barrón-Cedeño, Giovanni Da San Martino, Alessandro Moschitti, Preslav Nakov, Salvatore Romeo, and Giuseppe Carenini. 2016. An interactive system for exploring community question answering forums. In *Proceedings of the 26th International Conference on Computational Linguistics: System Demonstrations*. Osaka, Japan, COLING '16, pages 1–5.

Yongshuai Hou, Cong Tan, Xiaolong Wang, Yaoyun Zhang, Jun Xu, and Qingcai Chen. 2015. HITSZ-ICRC: Exploiting classification approach for answer selection in community question answering. In *Proceedings of the 9th International Workshop on Semantic Evaluation*. Denver, Colorado, USA, SemEval '15, pages 196–202.

Jiwoon Jeon, W. Bruce Croft, and Joon Ho Lee. 2005. Finding similar questions in large question and answer archives. In *Proceedings of the 14th ACM International Conference on Information and Knowledge Management*. Bremen, Germany, CIKM '05, pages 84–90.

Shafiq Joty, Alberto Barrón-Cedeño, Giovanni Da San Martino, Simone Filice, Lluís Màrquez, Alessandro Moschitti, and Preslav Nakov. 2015. Global thread-level inference for comment classification in community question answering. In *Proceedings of the 2015 Conference on Empirical Methods in Natural Language Processing*. Lisbon, Portugal, EMNLP '15, pages 573–578.

Shafiq Joty, Lluís Màrquez, and Preslav Nakov. 2016. Joint learning with global inference for comment classification in community question answering. In *Proceedings of the 2016 Conference of the North American Chapter of the Association for Computational Linguistics: Human Language Technologies*. San Diego, California, USA, NAACL-HLT '16.

Yuta Koreeda, Takuya Hashito, Yoshiki Niwa, Misa Sato, Toshihiko Yanase, Kenzo Kurotsuchi, and Kohsuke Yanai. 2017. bunji at SemEval-2017 task 3: Combination of neural similarity features and comment plausibility features. In *Proceedings of the International Workshop on Semantic Evaluation*. Vancouver, Canada, SemEval '17, pages 353–359.

Tao Lei, Hrishikesh Joshi, Regina Barzilay, Tommi S. Jaakkola, Kateryna Tymoshenko, Alessandro Moschitti, and Lluís Màrquez. 2016. Semi-supervised question retrieval with gated convolutions. In *Proceedings of the 15th Annual Conference of the North American Chapter of the Association for Computational Linguistics: Human Language Technologies*. San Diego, California, USA, NAACL-HLT '16, pages 1279–1289.

Shuguang Li and Suresh Manandhar. 2011. Improving question recommendation by exploiting information need. In *Proceedings of the 49th Annual Meeting of the Association for Computational Linguistics*. Portland, Oregon, USA, ACL '11, pages 1425–1434.

Fei Liu, Alistair Moffat, Timothy Baldwin, and Xiuzhen Zhang. 2016. Quit while ahead: Evaluating truncated rankings. In *Proceedings of the 39th International ACM SIGIR Conference on Research and Development in Information Retrieval*. Pisa, Italy, SIGIR '16, pages 953–956.

Todor Mihaylov, Daniel Balchev, Yasen Kiprov, Ivan Koychev, and Preslav Nakov. 2017a. Large-scale goodness polarity lexicons for community question answering. In *Proceedings of the 40th International Conference on Research and Development in Information Retrieval*. Tokyo, Japan, SIGIR '17.

Todor Mihaylov, Georgi Georgiev, and Preslav Nakov. 2015a. Finding opinion manipulation trolls in news community forums. In *Proceedings of the Nineteenth Conference on Computational Natural Language Learning*. Beijing, China, CoNLL '15, pages 310–314.

Todor Mihaylov, Ivan Koychev, Georgi Georgiev, and Preslav Nakov. 2015b. Exposing paid opinion manipulation trolls. In *Proceedings of the International Conference Recent Advances in Natural Language Processing*. Hissar, Bulgaria, RANLP'15, pages 443–450.

Todor Mihaylov, Tsvetomila Mihaylova, Preslav Nakov, Lluís Màrquez, Georgi Georgiev, and Ivan Koychev. 2017b. The dark side of news community forums: Opinion manipulation trolls. *Internet Research* .

Todor Mihaylov and Preslav Nakov. 2016a. Hunting for troll comments in news community forums. In *Proceedings of the 54th Annual Meeting of the Association for Computational Linguistics*. Berlin, Germany, ACL '16, pages 399–405.

Todor Mihaylov and Preslav Nakov. 2016b. SemanticZ at SemEval-2016 Task 3: Ranking relevant answers in community question answering using semantic similarity based on fine-tuned word embeddings. In *Proceedings of the 10th International Workshop on Semantic Evaluation*. San Diego, California, USA, SemEval '16, pages 879–886.

Tsvetomila Mihaylova, Pepa Gencheva, Martin Boyanov, Ivana Yovcheva, Todor Mihaylov, Momchil Hardalov, Yasen Kiprov, Daniel Balchev, Ivan Koychev, Preslav Nakov, Ivelina Nikolova, and Galia Angelova. 2016. SUper Team at SemEval-2016 Task 3: Building a feature-rich system for community question answering. In *Proceedings of the Workshop on Semantic Evaluation*. San Diego, California, USA, SemEval '16, pages 836–843.

Mitra Mohtarami, Yonatan Belinkov, Wei-Ning Hsu, Yu Zhang, Tao Lei, Kfir Bar, Scott Cyphers, and Jim Glass. 2016. SLS at SemEval-2016 Task 3: Neural-based approaches for ranking in community question answering. In *Proceedings of the International Workshop on Semantic Evaluation*. San Diego, California, USA, SemEval '16, pages 828–835.

Alessandro Moschitti, Lluís Márquez, Preslav Nakov, Eugene Agichtein, Charles Clarke, and Idan Szpektor. 2016. SIGIR 2016 workshop WebQA II: Web question answering beyond factoids. In *Proceedings of the 39th International Conference on Research and Development in Information Retrieval*. ACM, Pisa, Italy, SIGIR '16, pages 1251–1252.

Preslav Nakov, Lluís Màrquez, and Francisco Guzmán. 2016a. It takes three to tango: Triangulation approach to answer ranking in community question answering. In *Proceedings of the 2016 Conference on Empirical Methods in Natural Language Processing*. Austin, Texas, USA, pages 1586–1597.

Preslav Nakov, Lluís Màrquez, Walid Magdy, Alessandro Moschitti, Jim Glass, and Bilal Randeree. 2015. SemEval-2015 task 3: Answer selection in community question answering. In *Proceedings of the International Workshop on Semantic Evaluation*. Denver, Colorado, USA, SemEval '15, pages 269–281.

Preslav Nakov, Lluís Màrquez, Alessandro Moschitti, Walid Magdy, Hamdy Mubarak, abed Alhakim Freihat, Jim Glass, and Bilal Randeree. 2016b. SemEval-2016 task 3: Community question answering. In *Proceedings of the 10th International Workshop on Semantic Evaluation*. San Diego, California, USA, SemEval '16, pages 525–545.

Titas Nandi, Chris Biemann, Seid Muhie Yimam, Deepak Gupta, Sarah Kohail, Asif Ekbal, and Pushpak Bhattacharyya. 2017. IIT-UHH at SemEval-2017 task 3: Exploring multiple features for community question answering and implicit dialogue identification. In *Proceedings of the 11th International Workshop on Semantic Evaluation*. Vancouver, Canada, SemEval '17, pages 91–98.

Massimo Nicosia, Simone Filice, Alberto Barrón-Cedeño, Iman Saleh, Hamdy Mubarak, Wei Gao, Preslav Nakov, Giovanni Da San Martino, Alessandro Moschitti, Kareem Darwish, Lluís Màrquez, Shafiq Joty, and Walid Magdy. 2015. QCRI: Answer selection for community question answering - experiments for Arabic and English. In *Proceedings of the Workshop on Semantic Evaluation*. Denver, Colorado, USA, SemEval '15, pages 203–209.

Ankur Parikh, Oscar Täckström, Dipanjan Das, and Jakob Uszkoreit. 2016. A decomposable attention model for natural language inference. In *Proceedings of the 2016 Conference on Empirical Methods in Natural Language Processing*. Austin, Texas, USA, EMNLP '16, pages 2249–2255.

Jeffrey Pennington, Richard Socher, and Christopher Manning. 2014. Glove: Global vectors for word representation. In *Proceedings of the Conference on Empirical Methods in Natural Language Processing*. Doha, Qatar, EMNLP '14, pages 1532–1543.

Le Qi, Yu Zhang, and Ting Liu. 2017. SCIR-QA at SemEval-2017 task 3: CNN model based on similar and dissimilar information between keywords for question similarity. In *Proceedings of the 11th International Workshop on Semantic Evaluation*. Vancouver, Canada, SemEval '17, pages 305–309.

Mohammed R. H. Qwaider, Abed Alhakim Freihat, and Fausto Giunchiglia. 2017. TrentoTeam at SemEval-2017 task 3: An application of Grice Maxims principles in ranking community question answers. In *Proceedings of the 11th International Workshop on Semantic Evaluation*. Vancouver, Canada, SemEval '17, pages 272–275.

Stefan Riezler, Alexander Vasserman, Ioannis Tsochantaridis, Vibhu Mittal, and Yi Liu. 2007. Statistical machine translation for query expansion in answer retrieval. In *Proceedings of the 45th Annual Meeting of the Association of Computational Linguistics*. Prague, Czech Republic, ACL '07, pages 464–471.

Miguel J. Rodrigues and Francisco M Couto. 2017. MoRS at SemEval-2017 task 3: Easy to use SVM in ranking tasks. In *Proceedings of the 11th International Workshop on Semantic Evaluation*. Vancouver, Canada, SemEval '17, pages 288–292.

Salvatore Romeo, Giovanni Da San Martino, Alberto Barrón-Cedeño, Alessandro Moschitti, Yonatan Belinkov, Wei-Ning Hsu, Yu Zhang, Mitra Mohtarami, and James Glass. 2016. Neural attention for learning to rank questions in community question answering. In *Proceedings of the 26th International Conference on Computational Linguistics: Technical Papers*. Osaka, Japan, COLING '2016, pages 1734–1745.

Aliaksei Severyn and Alessandro Moschitti. 2015. Learning to rank short text pairs with convolutional deep neural networks. In *Proceedings of the 38th International ACM SIGIR Conference on Research and Development in Information Retrieval*. Santiago, Chile, SIGIR '15, pages 373–382.

Radu Soricut and Eric Brill. 2006. Automatic question answering using the web: Beyond the factoid. *Inf. Retr.* 9(2):191–206.

Mihai Surdeanu, Massimiliano Ciaramita, and Hugo Zaragoza. 2011. Learning to rank answers to non-factoid questions from web collections. *Comput. Linguist.* 37(2):351–383.

Ming Tan, Bing Xiang, and Bowen Zhou. 2015. Lstm-based deep learning models for non-factoid answer selection. *arXiv preprint arXiv:1511.04108* .

Marwan Torki, Maram Hasanain, and Tamer Elsayed. 2017. QU-BIGIR at SemEval-2017 task 3: Using similarity features for Arabic community question answering forums. In *Proceedings of the 11th International Workshop on Semantic Evaluation*. Vancouver, Canada, SemEval '17, pages 360–364.

Quan Hung Tran, Vu Tran, Tu Vu, Minh Nguyen, and Son Bao Pham. 2015. JAIST: Combining multiple features for answer selection in community question answering. In *Proceedings of the 9th International Workshop on Semantic Evaluation*. Denver, Colorado, USA, SemEval '15, pages 215–219.

Kateryna Tymoshenko, Daniele Bonadiman, and Alessandro Moschitti. 2016. Learning to rank nonfactoid answers: Comment selection in web forums. In *Proceedings of the 25th ACM International on Conference on Information and Knowledge Management*. Indianapolis, Indiana, USA, CIKM '16, pages 2049–2052.

Filip Šaina, Toni Kukurin, Lukrecija Puljić, Mladen Karan, and Jan Šnajder. 2017. TakeLab-QA at SemEval-2017 task 3: Classification experiments for answer retrieval in community QA. In *Proceedings of the Workshop on Semantic Evaluation*. Vancouver, Canada, SemEval '17, pages 339–343.

Di Wang and Eric Nyberg. 2015. A long short-term memory model for answer sentence selection in question answering. In *Proceedings of the 53rd Annual Meeting of the Association for Computational Linguistics and the 7th International Joint Conference on Natural Language Processing*. Beijing, China, ACL-IJCNLP '15, pages 707–712.

Kai Wang, Zhaoyan Ming, and Tat-Seng Chua. 2009. A syntactic tree matching approach to finding similar questions in community-based QA services. In *Proceedings of the 32nd International ACM SIGIR Conference on Research and Development in Information Retrieval*. Boston, Massachusetts, USA, SIGIR '09, pages 187–194.

Mengqiu Wang and Christopher D. Manning. 2010. Probabilistic tree-edit models with structured latent variables for textual entailment and question answering. In *Proceedings of the 23rd International Conference on Computational Linguistics*. Beijing, China, COLING '10, pages 1164–1172.

Mengqiu Wang, Noah A. Smith, and Teruko Mitamura. 2007. What is the Jeopardy model? A quasi-synchronous grammar for QA. In *Proceedings of the 2007 Joint Conference on Empirical Methods in Natural Language Processing and Computational Natural Language Learning*. Prague, Czech Republic, EMNLP-CoNLL '07, pages 22–32.

Guoshun Wu, Yixuan Sheng adn Man Lan, and Yuanbin Wu. 2017a. ECNU at SemEval-2017 task 3: Using traditional and deep learning methods to address community question answering task. In *Proceedings of the Workshop on Semantic Evaluation*. Vancouver, Canada, SemEval '17, pages 365–369.

Yu Wu, WenZheng Feng, Wei Wu, Ming Zhou, and Zhoujun Li. 2017b. Beihang-MSRA at SemEval-2017 task 3: A ranking system with neural matching features for Community Question Answering. In *Proceedings of the 11th International Workshop on Semantic Evaluation*. Vancouver, Canada, SemEval '17, pages 281–287.

Yunfang Wu and Minghua Zhang. 2016. ICL00 at SemEval-2016 Task 3: Translation-based method for CQA system. In *Proceedings of the Workshop on Semantic Evaluation*. San Diego, California, USA, SemEval '16, pages 857–860.

Yufei Xie, Maoquan Wang, Jing Ma, Jian Jiang, and Zhao Lu. 2017. EICA team at SemEval-2017 task 3: Semantic and metadata-based features for Community Question Answering. In *Proceedings of the International Workshop on Semantic Evaluation*. Vancouver, Canada, SemEval '17, pages 293–299.

Xuchen Yao, Benjamin Van Durme, Chris Callison-Burch, and Peter Clark. 2013. Answer extraction as sequence tagging with tree edit distance. In *Proceedings of the Conference of the North American Chapter of the Association for Computational Linguistics*. NAACL-HLT '13, pages 858–867.

Kai Zhang, Wei Wu, Haocheng Wu, Zhoujun Li, and Ming Zhou. 2014. Question retrieval with high quality answers in community question answering. In *Proceedings of the 23rd ACM International Conference on Information and Knowledge Management*. Shanghai, China, CIKM '14, pages 371–380.

Sheng Zhang, Jiajun Cheng, Hui Wang, Xin Zhang, Pei Li, and Zhaoyun Ding. 2017. FuRongWang at SemEval-2017 task 3: Deep neural networks for selecting relevant answers in community question answering. In *Proceedings of the 11th International Workshop on Semantic Evaluation*. Vancouver, Canada, SemEval '17, pages 320–325.

Guangyou Zhou, Li Cai, Jun Zhao, and Kang Liu. 2011. Phrase-based translation model for question retrieval in community question answer archives. In *Proceedings of the 49th Annual Meeting of the Association for Computational Linguistics*. Portland, Oregon, USA, ACL '11, pages 653–662.

Xiaoqiang Zhou, Baotian Hu, Qingcai Chen, Buzhou Tang, and Xiaolong Wang. 2015a. Answer sequence learning with neural networks for answer selection in community question answering. In *Proceedings of the 53rd Annual Meeting of the Association for Computational Linguistics and the 7th International Joint Conference on Natural Language Processing*. Beijing, China, ACL-IJCNLP '15, pages 713–718.

Xiaoqiang Zhou, Baotian Hu, Jiaxin Lin, Yang Xiang, and Xiaolong Wang. 2015b. ICRC-HIT: A deep learning based comment sequence labeling system for answer selection challenge. In *Proceedings of the 11th International Workshop on Semantic Evaluation*. Denver, Colorado, USA, SemEval '15, pages 210–214.

Team ID	Team Affiliation
Beihang-MSRA	Beihang University, Beijing, China; Microsoft Research, Beijing, China (Wu et al., 2017b)
bunji	Hitachi Ltd., Japan (Koreeda et al., 2017)
ECNU	East China Normal University, P.R. China; Shanghai Key Laboratory of Multidimensional Information Processing, P.R. China (Wu et al., 2017a)
EICA	East China Normal University, Shanghai, P.R.China (Xie et al., 2017)
FuRongWang	National University of Defense Technology, P.R. China (Zhang et al., 2017)
FA3L	University of Pisa, Italy (Attardi et al., 2017)
GW_QA	The George Washington University, D.C. USA (Almarwani and Diab, 2017)
IIT-UHH	Indian Institute of Technology Patna, India; University of Hamburg, Germany (Nandi et al., 2017)
KeLP	University of Roma, Tor Vergata, Italy; Qatar Computing Research Institute, HBKU, Qatar (Filice et al., 2017)
MoRS	Universidade de Lisboa, Portugal (Rodrigues and Couto, 2017)
LearningToQuestion	Georgia Institute of Technology, Atlanta, GA, USA (Goyal, 2017)
LS2N	LS2N [no paper submitted]
NLM_NIH	U.S. National Library of Medicine, Bethesda, MD, USA (Ben Abacha and Demner-Fushman, 2017)
QU-BIGIR	Qatar University, Qatar (Torki et al., 2017)
SCIR-QA	Harbin Institute of Technology, P.R. China (Qi et al., 2017)
SimBow	Orange Labs, France (Charlet and Damnati, 2017)
SnowMan	Harbin Institute of Technology, P.R. China [no paper submitted]
SwissAlps	Zurich University of Applied Sciences, Switzerland (Deriu and Cieliebak, 2017)
TakeLab-QA	University of Zagreb, Croatia (Šaina et al., 2017)
Talla	Talla, Boston, MA, USA (Galbraith et al., 2017)
TrentoTeam	University of Trento, Italy (Qwaider et al., 2017)
UINSUSKA-TiTech	UIN Sultan Syarif Kasim Riau, Indonesia; Tokyo Institute of Technology, Japan (Agustian and Takamura, 2017)
UPC-USMBA	Universitat Politècnica de Catalunya, Spain; Sidi Mohamed Ben Abdellah University, Morocco (El Adlouni et al., 2017)

Table 4: The participating teams and their affiliations.

	Submission	MAP	AvgRec	MRR	P	R	F1	Acc
1	**KeLP-primary**	**88.43**$_1$	**93.79**$_2$	**92.82**$_1$	**87.30**$_3$	**58.24**$_9$	**69.87**$_5$	**73.89**$_3$
2	**Beihang-MSRA-primary**	**88.24**$_2$	**93.87**$_1$	**92.34**$_2$	**51.98**$_{14}$	**100.00**$_1$	**68.40**$_6$	**51.98**$_{13}$
	Beihang-MSRA-contrastive2	88.18	93.91	92.45	51.98	100.00	68.40	51.98
	Beihang-MSRA-contrastive1	88.17	93.82	92.17	51.98	100.00	68.40	51.98
3	**IIT-UHH-primary**	**86.88**$_3$	**92.04**$_7$	**91.20**$_5$	**73.37**$_{11}$	**74.52**$_3$	**73.94**$_2$	**72.70**$_4$
	ECNU-contrastive1	86.78	92.41	92.65	83.05	66.91	74.11	75.70
4	**ECNU-primary**	**86.72**$_4$	**92.62**$_4$	**91.45**$_3$	**84.09**$_6$	**72.16**$_4$	**77.67**$_1$	**78.43**$_1$
	EICA-contrastive2	86.60	92.25	90.67	88.50	31.32	46.27	62.18
5	**bunji-primary**	**86.58**$_5$	**92.71**$_3$	**91.37**$_4$	**84.59**$_4$	**63.43**$_5$	**72.50**$_3$	**74.98**$_2$
6	**EICA-primary**	**86.53**$_6$	**92.50**$_5$	**89.57**$_8$	**88.29**$_2$	**30.20**$_{12}$	**45.01**$_{12}$	**61.64**$_{11}$
	EICA-contrastive1	86.48	92.18	90.69	88.43	29.61	44.37	61.40
	IIT-UHH-contrastive1	86.35	91.74	91.40	79.42	51.94	62.80	68.02
7	**SwissAlps-primary**	**86.24**$_7$	**92.28**$_6$	**90.89**$_6$	**90.78**$_1$	**28.43**$_{13}$	**43.30**$_{13}$	**61.30**$_{12}$
	SwissAlps-contrastive1	85.53	91.98	90.52	90.37	24.03	37.97	59.18
	bunji-contrastive1	85.29	91.77	91.48	83.14	56.34	67.16	71.37
	IIT-UHH-contrastive2	85.24	91.37	90.38	81.22	57.65	67.43	71.06
8	***FuRongWang-primary**	**84.26**$_8$	**90.79**$_8$	**89.40**$_9$	**84.58**$_5$	**48.98**$_{10}$	**62.04**$_{10}$	**68.84**$_7$
	bunji-contrastive2	84.01	90.45	89.17	81.88	59.03	68.60	71.91
9	**FA3L-primary**	**83.42**$_9$	**89.90**$_9$	**90.32**$_7$	**73.82**$_{10}$	**59.62**$_6$	**65.96**$_9$	**68.02**$_8$
	ECNU-contrastive2	83.15	90.01	89.46	75.06	78.86	76.91	75.39
	LS2N-contrastive2	82.91	89.70	89.58	72.19	71.77	71.98	70.96
	FA3L-contrastive1	82.87	89.64	89.98	77.28	56.27	65.12	68.67
	SnowMan-contrastive1	82.01	89.36	88.56	75.92	73.47	74.67	74.10
10	**SnowMan-primary**	**81.84**$_{10}$	**88.67**$_{10}$	**87.21**$_{12}$	**79.54**$_8$	**58.44**$_7$	**67.37**$_7$	**70.58**$_5$
11	**TakeLab-QA-primary**	**81.14**$_{11}$	**88.48**$_{12}$	**87.51**$_{11}$	**78.72**$_9$	**58.31**$_8$	**66.99**$_8$	**70.14**$_6$
12	**LS2N-primary**	**80.99**$_{12}$	**88.55**$_{11}$	**87.92**$_{10}$	**80.07**$_7$	**43.27**$_{11}$	**56.18**$_{11}$	**64.91**$_{10}$
	TakeLab-QA-contrastive1	79.71	87.31	87.03	73.88	62.77	67.87	69.11
	TakeLab-QA-contrastive2	78.98	86.33	87.13	80.06	56.66	66.36	70.14
13	**TrentoTeam-primary**	**78.56**$_{13}$	**86.66**$_{13}$	**85.76**$_{13}$	**65.59**$_{12}$	**75.71**$_2$	**70.28**$_4$	**66.72**$_9$
	LS2N-contrastive1	74.08	81.88	81.66	70.66	28.30	40.41	56.62
14	**MoRS-primary**	**63.32**$_{14}$	**71.67**$_{14}$	**71.99**$_{14}$	**59.23**$_{13}$	**5.06**$_{14}$	**9.32**$_{14}$	**48.84**$_{14}$
	Baseline 1 (chronological)	**72.61**	**79.32**	**82.37**	—	—	—	—
	Baseline 2 (random)	62.30	70.56	68.74	53.15	75.97	62.54	**52.70**
	Baseline 3 (all 'true')	—	—	—	51.98	100.00	**68.40**	51.98
	Baseline 4 (all 'false')	—	—	—	—	—	—	48.02

Table 5: **Subtask A, English (Question-Comment Similarity)**: results for all submissions. The first column shows the rank of the primary runs with respect to the official MAP score. The second column contains the team's name and its submission type (primary vs. contrastive). The following columns show the results for the primary, and then for other, unofficial evaluation measures. The subindices show the rank of the primary runs with respect to the evaluation measure in the respective column. All results are presented as percentages. The system marked with a * was a late submission.

	Submission	MAP	AvgRec	MRR	P	R	F1	Acc
	KeLP-contrastive1	49.00	83.92	52.41	36.18	88.34	51.34	68.98
	SimBow-contrastive2	47.87	82.77	50.97	27.03	93.87	41.98	51.93
1	**SimBow-primary**	**47.22**$_1$	**82.60**$_1$	**50.07**$_3$	**27.30**$_{10}$	**94.48**$_3$	**42.37**$_9$	**52.39**$_{11}$
	LearningToQuestion-contrastive2	47.20	81.73	53.22	18.52	100.00	31.26	18.52
	LearningToQuestion-contrastive1	47.03	81.45	52.47	18.52	100.00	31.26	18.52
2	**LearningToQuestion-primary**	**46.93**$_2$	**81.29**$_4$	**53.01**$_1$	**18.52**$_{12}$	**100.00**$_1$	**31.26**$_{12}$	**18.52**$_{12}$
	SimBow-contrastive1	46.84	82.73	50.43	27.80	94.48	42.96	53.52
3	**KeLP-primary**	**46.66**$_3$	**81.36**$_3$	**50.85**$_2$	**36.01**$_3$	**85.28**$_5$	**50.64**$_1$	**69.20**$_5$
	Talla-contrastive1	46.54	82.15	49.61	30.39	76.07	43.43	63.30
	Talla-contrastive2	46.31	81.81	49.14	29.88	74.23	42.61	62.95
4	**Talla-primary**	**45.70**$_4$	**81.48**$_2$	**49.55**$_5$	**29.59**$_9$	**76.07**$_8$	**42.61**$_8$	**62.05**$_8$
	Beihang-MSRA-contrastive2	44.79	79.13	49.89	18.52	100.00	31.26	18.52
5	**Beihang-MSRA-primary**	**44.78**$_5$	**79.13**$_7$	**49.88**$_4$	**18.52**$_{13}$	**100.00**$_2$	**31.26**$_{13}$	**18.52**$_{13}$
	NLM_NIH-contrastive1	44.66	79.66	48.08	33.68	79.14	47.25	67.27
6	**NLM_NIH-primary**	**44.62**$_6$	**79.59**$_5$	**47.74**$_6$	**33.68**$_5$	**79.14**$_6$	**47.25**$_3$	**67.27**$_6$
	UINSUSKA-TiTech-contrastive1	44.29	78.59	48.97	34.47	68.10	45.77	70.11
	NLM_NIH-contrastive2	44.29	79.05	47.45	33.68	79.14	47.25	67.27
	Beihang-MSRA-contrastive1	43.89	79.48	48.18	18.52	100.00	31.26	18.52
7	**UINSUSKA-TiTech-primary**	**43.44**$_7$	**77.50**$_{11}$	**47.03**$_9$	**35.71**$_4$	**67.48**$_{11}$	**46.71**$_4$	**71.48**$_4$
8	**IIT-UHH-primary**	**43.12**$_8$	**79.23**$_6$	**47.25**$_7$	**26.85**$_{11}$	**71.17**$_{10}$	**38.99**$_{10}$	**58.75**$_{10}$
	UINSUSKA-TiTech-contrastive2	43.06	76.45	46.22	35.71	67.48	46.71	71.48
9	**SCIR-QA-primary**	**42.72**$_9$	**78.24**$_9$	**46.65**$_{10}$	**31.26**$_8$	**89.57**$_4$	**46.35**$_5$	**61.59**$_9$
	SCIR-QA-contrastive1	42.72	78.24	46.65	32.69	83.44	46.98	65.11
	ECNU-contrastive2	42.48	79.44	45.09	36.47	78.53	49.81	70.68
	IIT-UHH-contrastive2	42.38	78.59	46.82	32.99	59.51	42.45	70.11
	ECNU-contrastive1	42.37	78.41	45.04	34.34	83.44	48.66	67.39
	IIT-UHH-contrastive1	42.29	78.41	46.40	32.66	59.51	42.17	69.77
10	**FA3L-primary**	**42.24**$_{10}$	**77.71**$_{10}$	**47.05**$_8$	**33.17**$_6$	**40.49**$_{13}$	**36.46**$_{11}$	**73.86**$_2$
	LS2N-contrastive1	42.06	77.36	47.13	32.01	59.51	41.63	69.09
11	**ECNU-primary**	**41.37**$_{11}$	**78.71**$_8$	**44.52**$_{13}$	**37.43**$_1$	**76.69**$_7$	**50.30**$_2$	**71.93**$_3$
12	**EICA-primary**	**41.11**$_{12}$	**77.45**$_{12}$	**45.57**$_{12}$	**32.60**$_7$	**72.39**$_9$	**44.95**$_6$	**67.16**$_7$
	EICA-contrastive1	41.07	77.70	46.38	32.30	70.55	44.32	67.16
13	**LS2N-primary**	**40.56**$_{13}$	**76.67**$_{13}$	**46.33**$_{11}$	**36.55**$_2$	**53.37**$_{12}$	**43.39**$_7$	**74.20**$_1$
	EICA-contrastive2	40.04	76.98	44.00	31.69	71.17	43.86	66.25
	Baseline 1 (IR)	**41.85**	77.59	46.42	—	—	—	—
	Baseline 2 (random)	29.81	62.65	33.02	18.72	75.46	30.00	34.77
	Baseline 3 (all 'true')	—	—	—	18.52	100.00	**31.26**	18.52
	Baseline 4 (all 'false')	—	—	—	—	—	—	81.48

Table 6: **Subtask B, English (Question-Question Similarity):** results for all submissions. The first column shows the rank of the primary runs with respect to the official MAP score. The second column contains the team's name and its submission type (primary vs. contrastive). The following columns show the results for the primary, and then for other, unofficial evaluation measures. The subindices show the rank of the primary runs with respect to the evaluation measure in the respective column. All results are presented as percentages.

	Submission	MAP	AvgRec	MRR	P	R	F1	Acc
	bunji-contrastive2	16.57	30.98	17.04	19.83	19.11	19.46	95.58
1	**IIT-UHH-primary**	**15.46**$_1$	**33.42**$_1$	**18.14**$_1$	8.41$_3$	51.22$_3$	14.44$_2$	83.03$_4$
	IIT-UHH-contrastive1	15.43	33.78	17.52	9.45	54.07	16.08	84.23
2	**bunji-primary**	**14.71**$_2$	29.47$_4$	16.48$_2$	20.26$_1$	19.11$_4$	19.67$_1$	95.64$_2$
	EICA-contrastive1	14.60	32.71	16.14	10.80	9.35	10.02	95.31
3	**KeLP-primary**	**14.35**$_3$	30.74$_2$	16.07$_3$	6.48$_5$	89.02$_2$	12.07$_4$	63.75$_5$
	IIT-UHH-contrastive2	14.00	30.53	14.65	5.98	85.37	11.17	62.06
4	**EICA-primary**	**13.48**$_4$	24.44$_6$	16.04$_4$	7.69$_4$	0.41$_6$	0.77$_6$	97.08$_1$
	ECNU-contrastive2	13.29	30.15	14.95	13.86	26.42	18.18	93.35
5	***FuRongWang-primary**	**13.23**$_5$	29.51$_3$	14.27$_5$	2.80$_6$	100.00$_1$	5.44$_5$	2.80$_6$
	EICA-contrastive2	13.18	25.16	15.05	10.00	0.81	1.50	97.02
6	**ECNU-primary**	**10.54**$_6$	25.56$_5$	11.09$_6$	13.44$_2$	13.82$_5$	13.63$_3$	95.10$_3$
	ECNU-contrastive1	10.54	25.56	11.09	13.83	14.23	14.03	95.13
	bunji-contrastive1	8.19	15.12	9.25	0.00	0.00	0.00	97.20
	Baseline 1 (IR)	**9.18**	21.72	10.11	—	—	—	—
	Baseline 2 (random)	5.77	7.69	5.70	2.76	73.98	5.32	26.37
	Baseline 3 (all 'true')	—	—	—	2.80	100.00	**5.44**	2.80
	Baseline 4 (all 'false')	—	—	—	—	—	—	97.20

Table 7: **Subtask C, English (Question-External Comment Similarity):** results for all submissions. The first column shows the rank of the primary runs with respect to the official MAP score. The second column contains the team's name and its submission type (primary vs. contrastive). The following columns show the results for the primary, and then for other, unofficial evaluation measures. The subindices show the rank of the primary runs with respect to the evaluation measure in the respective column. All results are presented as percentages. The system marked with a * was a late submission.

	Submission	MAP	AvgRec	MRR	P	R	F1	Acc
1	**GW_QA-primary**	**61.16**$_1$	85.43$_1$	66.85$_1$	0.00$_3$	0.00$_3$	0.00$_3$	60.77$_2$
	QU_BIGIR-contrastive2	59.48	83.83	64.56	55.35	70.95	62.19	66.15
	QU_BIGIR-contrastive1	59.13	83.56	64.68	49.37	85.41	62.57	59.91
2	**UPC-USMBA-primary**	**57.73**$_2$	81.76$_3$	62.88$_2$	63.41$_1$	33.00$_2$	43.41$_2$	66.24$_1$
3	**QU_BIGIR-primary**	**56.69**$_3$	81.89$_2$	61.83$_3$	41.59$_2$	70.16$_1$	52.22$_1$	49.64$_3$
	UPC-USMBA-contrastive1	56.66	81.16	62.87	45.00	64.04	52.86	55.18
	Baseline 1 (IR)	**60.55**	85.06	66.80	—	—	—	—
	Baseline 2 (random)	48.48	73.89	53.27	39.04	66.43	49.18	46.13
	Baseline 3 (all 'true')	—	—	—	39.23	100.00	**56.36**	39.23
	Baseline 4 (all 'false')	—	—	—	—	—	—	60.77

Table 8: **Subtask D, Arabic (Reranking the correct answers for a new question):** results for all submissions. The first column shows the rank of the primary runs with respect to the official MAP score. The second column contains the team's name and its submission type (primary vs. contrastive). The following columns show the results for the primary, and then for other, unofficial evaluation measures. The subindices show the rank of the primary runs with respect to the evaluation measure in the respective column. All results are presented as percentages.

Baseline	TMAP
Android Baseline 1 (IR oracle)	99.00
Android Baseline 2 (all empty results)	98.56
English Baseline 1 (IR oracle)	98.05
English Baseline 2 (all empty results)	97.65
Gaming Baseline 1 (IR oracle)	99.18
Gaming Baseline 2 (all empty results)	98.73
Wordpress Baseline 1 (IR oracle)	99.21
Wordpress Baseline 2 (all empty results)	98.98

Table 9: **Subtask E, English (Multi-Domain Duplicate Detection):** Baseline results on the test dataset. The empty result baseline has an empty result list for all queries. The IR baselines are the results of applying BM25 with perfect truncation. All results are presented as percentages.

SemEval-2017 Task 6: #HashtagWars: Learning a Sense of Humor

Peter Potash, Alexey Romanov, Anna Rumshisky
University of Massachusetts Lowell
Department of Computer Science
{ppotash, aromanov, arum}@cs.uml.edu

Abstract

This paper describes a new shared task for humor understanding that attempts to eschew the ubiquitous binary approach to humor detection and focus on comparative humor ranking instead. The task is based on a new dataset of funny tweets posted in response to shared hashtags, collected from the 'Hashtag Wars' segment of the TV show @midnight. The results are evaluated in two subtasks that require the participants to generate either the correct pairwise comparisons of tweets (subtask A), or the correct ranking of the tweets (subtask B) in terms of how funny they are. 7 teams participated in subtask A, and 5 teams participated in subtask B. The best accuracy in subtask A was 0.675. The best (lowest) rank edit distance for subtask B was 0.872.

1 Introduction

Most work on humor detection approaches the problem as binary classification: humor or not humor. While this is a reasonable initial step, in practice humor is continuous, so we believe it is interesting to evaluate different degrees of humor, particularly as it relates to a given person's sense of humor. To further such research, we propose a dataset based on humorous responses submitted to a Comedy Central TV show, allowing for computational approaches to comparative humor ranking.

Debuting in Fall 2013, the Comedy Central show @midnight[1] is a late-night "game-show" that presents a modern outlook on current events by focusing on content from social media. The show's contestants (generally professional comedians or actors) are awarded points based on how funny their answers are. The segment of the show that best illustrates this attitude is the Hashtag Wars (HW). Every episode the show's host proposes a topic in the form of a hashtag, and the show's contestants must provide tweets that would have this hashtag. Viewers are encouraged to tweet their own responses. From the viewers' tweets, we are able to apply labels that determine how relatively humorous the show finds a given tweet.

Because of the contest's format, it provides an adequate method for addressing the selection bias (Heckman, 1979) often present in machine learning techniques (Zadrozny, 2004). Since each tweet is intended for the same hashtag, each tweet is effectively drawn from the same sample distribution. Consequently, tweets are seen not as humor/non-humor, but rather varying degrees of wit and cleverness. Moreover, given the subjective nature of humor, labels in the dataset are only "gold" with respect to the show's sense of humor. This concept becomes more grounded when considering the use of supervised systems for the dataset.

The idea of the dataset is to learn to characterize the sense of humor represented in this show. Given a set of hashtags, the goal is to predict which tweets the show will find funnier within each hashtag. The degree of humor in a given tweet is determined by the labels provided by the show. We propose two subtasks to evaluate systems on the dataset. The first subtask is pairwise comparison: given two tweets, select the funnier tweet, and the pairs will be derived from the labels assigned by the show to individual tweets. The second subtask is to rank the the tweets based on the comparative labels provided by the show. This is a semi-ranking task because most labels are applied to more than one tweet. Seen as a classification task, the labels are comparative, because there is a notion of distance. We introduce a new edit distance-

---

[1]http://www.cc.com/shows/-midnight

Proceedings of the 11th International Workshop on Semantic Evaluations (SemEval-2017), pages 49–57,
Vancouver, Canada, August 3 - 4, 2017. ©2017 Association for Computational Linguistics

inspired metric for this subtask.

A number of different computational approaches to humor have been proposed within the last decade (Yang et al., 2015; Mihalcea and Strapparava, 2005; Zhang and Liu, 2014; Radev et al., 2015; Raz, 2012; Reyes et al., 2013; Barbieri and Saggion, 2014; Shahaf et al., 2015; Purandare and Litman, 2006; Kiddon and Brun, 2011). In particular, Zhang and Liu (2014); Raz (2012); Reyes et al. (2013); Barbieri and Saggion (2014) focus on recognizing humor in Twitter. However, the majority of this work focuses on distinguishing humor from non-humor.

This representation has two shortcomings: (1) it ignores the continuous nature of humor, and (2) it does not take into account the subjectivity in humor perception. Regarding the first issue, we believe that shifting away from the binary approach to humor detection as done in the present task is a good pathway towards advancing this work. Regarding the second issue, consider a humour annotation task done by Shahaf et al. (2015), in which the annotators looked at pairs of captions from the New Yorker Caption Content[2], Shahaf et al. (2015) report that "Only 35% of the unique pairs that were ranked by at least five people achieved 80% agreement..." In contrast, the goal of the present task is to not to identify humour that is universal, but rather, to capture the specific sense of humour represented in the show.

2   Related Work

Mihalcea and Strapparava (2005) developed a humor dataset of puns and humorous one-liners intended for supervised learning. In order to generate negative examples for their experimental design, the authors used news titles from Reuters and the British National Corpus, as well as proverbs. Recently, Yang et al. (2015) used the same dataset for experimental purposes, taking text from AP News, New York Times, Yahoo! Answers, and proverbs as their negative examples. To further reduce the bias of their negative examples, the authors selected negative examples with a vocabulary that is in the dictionary created from the positive examples. Also, the authors forced the negative examples to have a similar text length compared to the positive examples.

Zhang and Liu (2014) constructed a dataset for recognizing humor in Twitter in two parts. First,

the authors use the Twitter API with targeted user mentions and hashtags to produce a set of 1,500 humorous tweets. After manual inspections, 1,267 of the original 1,500 tweets were found to be humorous, of which 1,000 were randomly sampled as positive examples in the final dataset. Second, the authors collect negative examples by extracting 1,500 tweets from the Twitter Streaming API, manually checking for the presence of humor. Next, the authors combine these tweets with tweets from part one that were found to actually not contain humor. The authors argue this last step will partly assuage the selection bias of the negative examples.

In Reyes et al. (2013) the authors create a model to detect ironic tweets. To construct their dataset they collect tweets with the following hashtags: irony, humor, politics, and education. Therefore, a tweet is considered ironic solely because of the presence of the appropriate hashtag. Barbieri and Saggion (2014) also use this dataset for their work.

Finally, recently researchers have developed a dataset similar to our HW dataset based on the New Yorker Caption Contest (NYCC) (Radev et al., 2015; Shahaf et al., 2015). Whereas for the HW segment, viewers submit a tweet in response to a hashtag, for the NYCC readers submit humorous captions in response to a cartoon. It is important to note this key distinction between the two datasets, because we believe that the presence of the hashtag allows for further innovative NLP methodologies aside from solely analyzing the tweets themselves. In Radev et al. (2015), the authors developed more than 15 unsupervised methods for ranking submissions for the NYCC. The methods can be categorized into broader categories such as originality and content-based.

Alternatively, Shahaf et al.(2015) approach the NYCC dataset with supervised models, evaluating on a pairwise comparison task, upon which we base our evaluation methodology. The features to represent a given caption fall in the general areas of Unusual Language, Sentiment, and Taking Expert Advice. For a single data point (which represents two captions), the authors concatenate the features of each individual caption, as well as encoding the difference between each caption's vector. The authors' best-performing system records a 69% accuracy on the pairwise evaluation task. Note that for this evaluation task, random baseline is 50%.

---

[2]http://contest.newyorker.com/

3 #HashtagWars Dataset

3.1 Data collection

The following section describes our data collection process. First, when a new episode airs (which generally happens four nights a week), a new hashtag will be given. We wait until the following morning to use the public Twitter search API[3] to collect tweets that have been posted with the new hashtag. Generally, this returns 100-200 tweets. We wait until the following day to allow for as many tweets as possible to be submitted. The day of the ensuing episode (i.e. on a Monday for a hashtag that came out for a Thursday episode), @midnight creates a Tumblr post[4] that announces the top-10 tweets from the previous episode's hashtag (the tweets are listed as embedded images, as is often done for sharing public tweets on websites). If they're not already present, we add the tweets from the top-10 to our existing list of tweets for the hashtag. We also perform automated filtering to remove redundant tweets. Specifically, we see that the text of tweets (aside from hashtags and user mentions) are not the same. The need for this results from the fact that some viewers submit identical tweets.

Using both the @midnight official Tumblr account, as well as the show's official website where the winning tweet is posted, we annotate each tweet with labels 0, 1 and 2. Label 2 designates the winning tweet. Thus, the label 2 only occurs once for each hashtag. Label 1 indicates that the tweet was selected as a top-10 tweet (but *not* the winning tweet) and label 0 is assigned for all other tweets. It is important to note that every time we collect a tweet, we must also collect its tweet ID. While this was initially done to comply with Twitter's terms of use[5], which disallows the public distribution of users' tweets, The presence of tweet IDs allows us to easily handle the evaluation process when referencing tweets (see Section 4). The need to determine the tweet IDs for tweets that weren't found in the initial query (i.e. tweets added from the top 10) makes the data collection process slightly laborious, since the top-10 list doesn't contain the tweet ID. In fact, it doesn't even contain the text itself since it's actually an

image.

3.1.1 A Semi-Automated System for Data Collection

Because the data collection process is continuously repeated and requires a non-trivial amount of human labor, we have built a helper system that can partially automate the process of data collection. This system is organized as a website with a convenient user interface.

On the start page the user enters the id of the Tumblr post with the tweets in the top 10. Next, we invoke Tesseract[6], an OCR command-line utility, to recognize the textual content of the tweet images. Using the recognized content, the system forms a webpage on which the user can simultaneously see the text of the tweets as well as the original images. On this page, the user can query the Twitter API to search by text, or click the button "Open twitter search" to open the Twitter Search page if the API returns zero results. We note that the process is not fully automated because a given text query can we return redundant results, and we primarily check to make sure we add the tweet that came from the appropriate user. With the help of this system, the process of collecting the top-10 tweets (along with their tweet IDs) takes roughly 2 minutes. Lastly, we note that the process for annotating the winning tweet (which is already included in the top-10 posted in the Tumblr list) is currently manual, because it requires going to the @midnight website. This is another aspect of the data collection system that could potentially be automated.

3.2 Dataset

Data collection occurred for roughly eight months, producing a total of 12,734 tweets for 112 hashtags. The resulting dataset is what we used for the task.

The distribution of the number of tweets per hashtag is represented in Figure 1. For 71% of hashtags, we have at least 90 tweets. The files of the individual hashtags are formatted so that the individual hashtag tokens are easily recoverable. Specifically, tokens are separated by the '_' character. For example, the hashtag *FastFoodBooks* has the file name "fast_food_books.tsv".

Figure 2 represents an example of the tweets collected for the hashtag *FastFoodBooks*. Ob-

---

[3]https://dev.twitter.com/rest/public/search
[4]http://atmidnightcc.tumblr.com/
[5]https://dev.twitter.com/overview/terms

[6]https://github.com/tesseract-ocr/tesseract

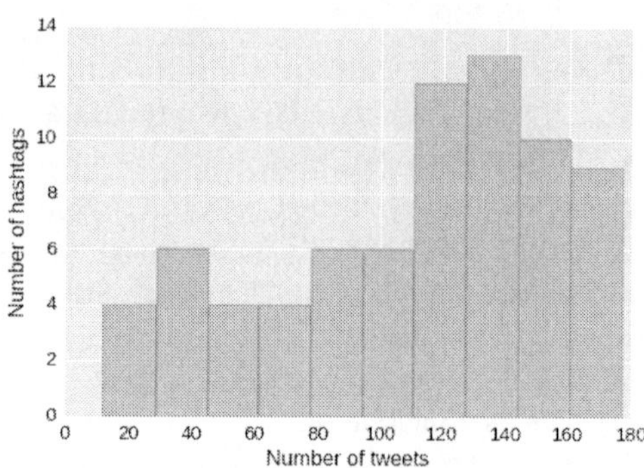

Figure 1: Distribution of the numbers of tweets per hashtag

serve that this hashtag requires external knowledge about fast food and books in order to understand the humor. Furthermore, this hashtag illustrates how prevalent puns are in the dataset, especially related to certain target hashtags. In contrast, the hashtag *IfIWerePresident* (see Figure 3) does not require external knowledge and the tweets are understandable without awareness of any specific concepts.

For the purpose of our task, we released 5 files/660 tweets as the trial data, 101 files/11,325 tweets (separate from the trial data) as the training data, and 6 files/749 tweets as the evaluation data. The 6 evaluation files were chosen based on the following logic: first, we examined the results of our own systems on individual hashtags using leave-one-out evaluation (Potash et al., 2016). We looked for a mixture of hashtags that had high, average, and low performance. Secondly, we wanted a mixture of hashtags that promote different types of humor, such as puns that use external knowledge (for example the hashtag *FastFoodBooks* in Figure 3.2), or hashtags that seek to express more general humor (for example the hashtag *IfIWerePresident* in Figure 3.2).

4 Subtasks

In this task, the results are evaluated in two subtasks. Subtask A requires the participants to generate the correct pairwise comparisons of tweets to determine which tweet is funnier according to the TV show @midnight. Subtask B asks for the correct ranking of tweets in terms of how funny they are (again, according to @midnight).

As I Lay Dying of congestive heart failure @midnight #FastFoodBooks
Harry Potter and the Order of the Big Mac #FastFoodBooks @midnight
The Girl With The Jared Tattoo #FastFoodBooks @midnight
A Room With a Drive-thru @midnight #FastFoodBooks

Figure 2: An example of the items in the dataset for the hashtag *FastFoodBooks* that requires external knowledge in order to understand the humor. Furthermore, the tweets for this hashtag are puns connecting book titles and fast food-related language

#IfIWerePresident my Cabinet would just be cats. @midnight
Historically, I'd oversleep and eventually get fired. @midnight #IfIWerePresident
#IfIWerePresident I'd pardon Dad so we could be together again... @midnight
#IfIWerePresident my estranged children would finally know where I was @midnight

Figure 3: An example of the items in the dataset for the hashtag *IfIWerePresident* that does not require external knowledge in order to understand the humor

4.1 Subtask A: Pairwise Comparison

For the first subtask, we follow the approach taken by Shahaf et al. (2015) and make predictions on pairs of tweets with the goal of determining which tweet is funnier. Using the tweets for each hashtag, we construct pairs of tweets in which one tweet is judged by the show to be funnier than the other. The pairs used for evaluation are constructed as follows:

(1) The tweets that are the top-10 funniest tweets are paired with the tweets not in the top-10.

(2) The winning tweet is paired with the other tweets in the top-10.

If we have n tweets for a given hashtag, (1) will produce $10(n - 10)$ pairs, and (2) will produce 9 pairs, giving us $10n - 91$ data points for a single hashtag. Constructing the pairs for evaluation in this way ensures that one of the tweets in each pair has been judged to be funnier than the other. We follow Shahaf et al. and use the label 1 to denote that the first tweet is funnier, and 0 to denote that the second tweet is funnier. However, this labeling is counter-intuitive to zero-indexing, and could be changed to avoid confusion in labeling (see Section 5).

Since we only provide teams with files containing tweet ID, tweet text, and tweet label (gold label: 0, 1, or 2), it is up to the teams to form the appropriate pairs with the correct labels. In order to produce balanced training data, we recommend that the ordering of tweets in a pair be determined by a coin-flip. At evaluation time, we provide the teams with hashtag files with tweet id and tweet text. We then ask the teams to provide predictions for every possible tweet combination. Our evaluation script then chooses only the tweet pairs where two different labels are present. The pairs can be listed in either ordering of the tweets because the scorer accounts for the two possible orderings for each pair. We decided against the idea of providing the appropriate pairs themselves for evaluation because it is very easy to use frequencies of tweet IDs in the pairs to determine overall tweet label.

The evaluation measure for subtask A is the micro average of accuracy across the individual evaluation hashtags. For a given hashtag, the accuracy is the number of correctly predicted pairs divided by the total number of pairs. Therefore, random guessing will produce 50% accuracy on this task.

4.2 Subtask B: Ranking

The second subtask asks teams to use the same input data for training and evaluation as subtask A. However, whereas subtask A creates pairs of tweets based on the labeling, subtask B asks teams to predict the labels directly. For this dataset, the number of tweets per class is known. Moreover, since the labels describe a partial ordering, predicting the labels is akin to providing a ranking of tweets in order of how funny they are. Therefore, for subtask B, we ask the teams to provide prediction files where the tweets are ranking by how funny they are. From the provided ranking we infer the labeling: the first tweet is labeled 2, the next nine labeled 1, and the rest labeled 0.

The metric for evaluating subtask B is inspired by a notion of edit distance, because standard clas-

sification metrics do not take into account class' comparative rankings. Treating labels as buckets, the metric determines, for a predicted label, how many 'moves' are needed to place it in the correct bucket. For example, if the correct label is 1 and the predicted label is 0, the edit distance is 1. Similarly, if the correct label is 0 and the predicted label is 2, the edit distance is 2. For a given hashtag file, the maximum edit distance for all tweets is 22. As a result, the edit distance for a given hashtag file is the total number of moves for all tweets divided by 22. This gives a normalized metric between 0 and 1 where a lower value is better. For the final distance metric, we micro-average across all evaluation files.

5 Results

Three teams participated only in subtask A, one team participated only in subtask B, and four teams participated in both subtasks. The official results for participating teams are shown in Tables 1 and 2 for subtasks A and B, respectively. Note that due to space constraints we use short versions of hashtag names in the tables. Namely, "Christmas" corresponds to the hashtag *RuinAChristmasMovie*, "Shakespeare" corresponds to *ModernShakespeare*, "Bad Job" to *BadJobIn5Words*, "Break Up" to *BreakUpIn5Words*, "Broadway" to *BroadwayACeleb*, and "Cereal" to *CerealSongs*.

We report the results broken down by hashtag, as well as the overall micro-average. This table records results that were submitted to the CodaLab competition pages[7]. TakeLab (Kukovačec et al., 2017) submitted predictions with the labels flipped, which causes each run to appear in the table twice. The corrected files are not given an official ranking. After the release of the labeled evaluation data, many teams reported improved results. We have accrued these new results and combined them with the official submission rankings to produce Tables 3 and 4. The goal of these tables is to report the most up-to-date results on the evaluation set. Moreover, all results that do not have an official ranking in these tables are results that are reported individually by the teams in their system papers (except for TakeLab's results) after the gold evaluation labels were released.

53

Rank	Team	Run	Hashatag						Average
			Christmas	Shakespeare	Bad Job	Break Up	Broadway	Cereal	
1	HumorHawk	2	0.673	**0.789**	0.704	0.723	0.643	0.492	**0.675** (±0.101)
	TakeLab	2	**0.683**	0.543	0.641	0.576	**0.716**	**0.704**	0.641 (±0.071)
2	HumorHawk	1	0.650	0.726	0.603	0.620	0.627	0.588	0.637 (±0.049)
3	DataStories	1	0.641	0.714	**0.828**	0.686	0.496	0.479	0.632 (±0.134)
4	Duluth	2	0.485	0.585	0.557	**0.913**	0.527	0.589	0.627 (±0.154)
	TakeLab	1	0.575	0.550	0.620	0.563	0.603	0.689	0.597 (±0.051)
5	SRHR	1	0.520	0.451	0.606	0.505	0.550	0.524	0.523 (±0.051)
6	SVNIT	1	0.455	0.353	0.395	0.654	0.542	0.563	0.506 (±0.113)
7	TakeLab	1	0.425	0.450	0.380	0.437	0.397	0.311	0.403 (±0.051)
8	Duluth	1	0.441	0.445	0.417	0.240	0.470	0.402	0.397 (±0.083)
9	TakeLab	2	0.317	0.457	0.359	0.424	0.284	0.296	0.359 (±0.071)
10	QUB	1	0.165	0.343	0.229	0.165	0.091	0.154	0.187 (±0.086)
Average			0.529 (±0.157)	0.550 (±0.156)	0.560 (±0.171)	0.565 (±0.221)	0.527 (±0.170)	0.518 (±0.158)	0.542 (±0.150)

Table 1: The official results for the subtask A broken down by hashtag. Bold indicates the best run for the given hashtag. "Christmas" corresponds to the hashtag *RuinAChristmasMovie*, "Shakespeare" corresponds to *ModernShakespeare*, "Bad Job" to *BadJobIn5Words*, "Break Up" to *BreakUpIn5Words*, "Broadway" to *BroadwayACeleb*, and "Cereal" to *CerealSongs*.

Rank	Team	Run	Hashatag						Average
			Christmas	Shakespeare	Bad Job	Break Up	Broadway	Cereal	
1	Duluth	2	**0.818**	0.909	1.000	**0.636**	1.000	0.909	**0.872** (±0.137)
2	TakeLab	1	0.909	0.909	1.000	0.818	1.000	**0.818**	0.908 (±0.081)
3	QUB	1	**0.818**	0.909	**0.818**	1.000	1.000	0.909	0.924 (±0.081)
3	QUB	2	**0.818**	0.909	**0.818**	1.000	1.000	0.909	0.924 (±0.081)
5	SVNIT	2	**0.818**	1.000	0.909	1.000	1.000	**0.818**	0.938 (±0.089)
6	TakeLab	2	**0.818**	1.000	1.000	0.909	1.000	0.909	0.944 (±0.074)
7	SVNIT	1	1.000	**0.818**	1.000	0.909	1.000	1.000	0.949 (±0.076)
8	Duluth	1	1.000	1.000	1.000	1.000	**0.909**	0.909	0.967 (±0.047)
9	#WarTeam	1	1.000	1.000	1.000	1.000	1.000	1.000	1.000 (±0.000)
Average			0.889 (±0.088)	0.939 (±0.064)	0.949 (±0.08)	0.919 (±0.124)	0.990 (±0.030)	0.909 (±0.064)	0.936 (±0.036)

Table 2: The official results for the subtask B broken down by hashtag. Bold indicates the best run for the given hashtag. "Christmas" corresponds to the hashtag *RuinAChristmasMovie*, "Shakespeare" corresponds to *ModernShakespeare*, "Bad Job" to *BadJobIn5Words*, "Break Up" to *BreakUpIn5Words*, "Broadway" to *BroadwayACeleb*, and "Cereal" to *CerealSongs*.

6 Discussion

6.1 Task Analysis

The last row of Table 1 shows the average accuracy of each hashtag across all systems (the official results of the TakeLab systems are not included in this average since we also include in the average the unofficial, corrected results). The two easiest hashtags are ones that require less external knowledge compared to the other four. These four hashtags specifically riff on a particular Christmas movie, Shakespeare quote, celebrity/Broadway play, or cereal/song. Consequently, one single system did best in three out of four of these hashtags (TakeLab). It is not coincidence, since this system made extensive use of external knowledge bases. Furthermore, the three hashtags where it did best required knowledge of specific entities, whereas the knowledge required in the hashtag *ModernShakespeare* is the actual lines from Shakespeare plays.

As we mentioned in Section 3.2, the evaluation hashtags were chosen partly because of our own system performance on the hashtags (Potash et al., 2016). One of the most difficult hashtags from our initial experiments was the hashtag *CerealSongs*, which was the hashtag systems performed the worse on in this task. We believe this is because the humor in this hashtag is based on *two* sources of external knowledge: cereals and songs. Correspondingly, the hashtag with the second worse performance also requires two sources of external knowledge: Broadway plays and celebrities (this hashtag was originally chosen as a representative of the hashtags our systems recorded average performance). The hashtag *BadJobIn5Words* was one that had high performance by our own systems, and that continued in this task. This hashtag had the second highest accuracy, and would have had the highest if the Duluth team (Yan and Pedersen, 2017) did not have such remarkable success on the highest accuracy hashtag, *BreakUpIn5Words*.

The poor performance for the hashtags *CerealSongs* and *BroadwayACeleb* is also interesting

Official Ranking	Team	Accuracy	Notes
	SVNIT	0.751	An SVM classifier with incongruity, ambiguity, and stylistic features
	DataStories	0.711	Siamese biderectional LSTM with attention
	HumorHawk	0.683	Embedding/Character Joint Humor Model
1	HumorHawk	0.675	XGBoost ensemble of feature-based and emedding models
	TakeLab	0.641	Gradient boosting classifier with a rich set of features, including cultural references
2	HumorHawk	0.637	Embedding/Character Joint Humor Model
3	DataStories	0.632	Siamese biderectional LSTM with attention
4	Duluth	0.627	Trigram language model (news dataset)
	SRHR	0.564	Random Forest classifier with word association and sematic relatedness features
5	SRHR	0.523	Random Forest classifier with word association and sematic relatedness features
6	SVNIT	0.506	Multilayer perceptron with incongruity, ambiguity, and stylistic features
7	TakeLab	0.403	Gradient boosting classifier with a rich set of features, including cultural references (reversed labels)
8	Duluth	0.397	Trigram language model (tweets dataset)
9	TakeLab	0.359	Gradient boosting classifier with a rich set of features, including cultural references (reversed labels)
10	QUB	0.187	A set of imblanaced classifiers with n-gram features

Table 3: Unofficial results for the subtask A on the released evaluation set reported by the participating teams

Official Ranking	Team	Score	Notes
	Duluth	0.853	Bigram language model (news dataset)
1	Duluth	0.872	Trigram language model (news dataset)
2	TakeLab	0.908	Gradient boosting classifier with a rich set of features, including cultural references
3	QUB	0.924	A set of imblanaced classifiers with n-gram features
3	QUB	0.924	A set of imblanaced classifiers with n-gram features
5	SVNIT	0.938	Multilayer perceptron with incongruity, ambiguity, and stylistic features
6	TakeLab	0.944	Gradient boosting classifier with a rich set of features, including cultural references
7	SVNIT	0.949	A Naive Bayes classifier with incongruity, ambiguity, and stylistic features
8	Duluth	0.967	Trigram language model (tweets dataset)
9	#WarTeam	1.000	A word-based voting algorithm of a Naive Bayes and neural network word scorers

Table 4: Unofficial results for the subtask B on the released evaluation set reported by the participating teams

to note since they were chosen because the hashtag names had strong similarity to hashtags in the training data. For example, 12 hashtags in the training data had the word 'Song'. Likewise, five hashtags had the word 'Celeb', and there was one more hashtag with the word 'Broadway'. Alternatively, The two hashtags with the best performance followed the 'X in X words' format, for which there were 16 such hashtags in the training data. Regarding the hashtag *BadJobIn5Words*, there are six hashtags in the training data beginning with the word 'Bad'.

Our current task analysis has focused on subtask A. The primary reason for this is that the performance on subtask B was relatively poor. To put the results in perspective, we created random guesses for subtask B, and these random guesses recorded an average distance of 0.880. From the results, only one team was able to beat this score. We can see that two of the three highest performing teams in subtask A did not participate in subtask B, and the other team that did participate approached subtask B as a secondary task (see Section 6.2).

6.2 System Analysis

For the teams that participated in both subtasks, they used the output of a single system to predict for both subtasks. Two teams, SVNIT (Mahajan and Zaveri, 2017) and QUB (Han and Toner, 2017) , initially predicted the labels of each tweet based on the output of a supervised classifier, and then used these labels to both rank the tweets and make pairwise predictions for the subtasks. Duluth took a similar approach, but used the output of a language model to rank the tweets, as opposed to labels provided by a classifier. Conversely, TakeLab sought to solve subtask A first, then used the frequencies of a tweet being chosen as funnier in a pair to provide a single, ordered metric to make predictions for subtask B. The team that only participated in subtask B, #WarTeam, also used the output of a supervised classifier to label the tweets, which in turn provided the ranking. One of interesting results from having the two subtasks (which are effectively two different ways of evaluating the same overall task) is to see how it distinguishes the unified approaches to solving both subtasks. We can see that, in fact, the top team is not consistent between the two subtasks. It is not a surprise to see that the best performing team (out of the four that participated in both subtasks) in subtask A was TakeLab, who focused primarily on this task. Conversely, TakeLab finished second in subtask B to Duluth, who focused on creating an ordered metric for ranking via language models.

In terms of overall system approach, we can analyze how heavily systems rely on feature-engineering, verse using learned representations from neural networks. Three of the top four systems for subtask A leveraged neural network architectures. Two of these systems used only pretrained word representations as external knowledge for the neural network systems. This is in opposition to other systems that relied on the output of separate tools, or looking up terms in corpora. Some teams, such as HumorHawk[8] (Donahue et al., 2017) and #WarTeam, used a combination of these two types of systems, and notably, the system that was ranked first in Subtask A (HumorHawk) was an ensemble system that utilized prediction from both feature-based and neural networks-based models.

As for the feature-based systems, one trend we observed is that many teams tried to capture the incongruity aspect of humor (Cattle and Ma, 2017) , often present in the dataset. The approaches used by teams varied from n-gram language models, word association, to semantic relatedness features. In addition, the TakeLab team used cultural reference features, such as movie and song references, and Google Trends features for named entities. During the performed analysis, the team found these features most useful for the model.

Considering neural network-based systems, LSTMs were used the most, which is expected given the sequential nature of text data. Plain LSTM models alone, using pretrained word embeddings, achieved competitive results, and DataStories (Baziotis et al., 2017) ranked third using a siamese bidirectional LSTM model with attention.

One key difference between the dataset used in this task and the datasets based on the NYCC (Radev et al., 2015; Shahaf et al., 2015) is the presence of the hashtag. Some teams used additional hashtag-based features in their systems.

For example, humor patterns, defined by the hashtag, were one of the most important features for the TakeLab team. Other teams used semantic distances between the hashtag and tweets as features.

Table 1 also includes the standard deviation of system scores across the hashtags. Looking at the numbers there appears to be little in the way of a pattern regarding the standard deviation numbers. When correlated with system accuracy, the results is 0.11, which supports the idea that consistency across the hashtags has no relation to overall system performance. Even between the two purest neural network-based systems, DataStories and HumorHawk run 1, the standard deviations vary greatly: 0.134 (DataStories) and 0.049 (HumorHawk run 1). In fact, 0.049 was the lowest standard deviation across all systems. Duluth recorded the highest standard deviation across the datasets, primarily due to the fact that it had the single highest accuracy on any hashtag (0.913 for the hashtag *BreakUpIn5Words*), as well as the lowest single hashtag score for any system with an overall accuracy greater than 0.600 (0.485 for the hashtag *RuinAChristmasMovie*). One possibility for this high standard deviation is that this is the only unsupervised system. However, the other run submitted by Duluth (whose primary difference is that its language model was trained on a dataset of tweets as opposed to news articles) has a both a significantly lower accuracy and standard deviation.

7 Conclusion

We have presented the results of the SemEval 2017 shared task: #HashtagWars: Learning a Sense of Humor. It was the first year this task was presented, attracting 8 teams and 19 systems across two substasks. The top performing systems achieved 0.675 accuracy in subtask A and 0.872 score on subtask B, advancing the difficult task of humor understanding. Interestingly, the top-ranked system used an ensemble of both feature-based and neural network-based systems, suggesting that despite the overwhelming success of neural networks in the past few years, human intuition is still important for systems that seek to automatically understand humor.

References

Francesco Barbieri and Horacio Saggion. 2014. Automatic detection of irony and humour in twitter.

---

[8]Two of the organizers were members of this team. They were not involved in the data selection process. They had no knowledge of which files were selected for evaluation, nor how these files were chosen.

In *Proceedings of the International Conference on Computational Creativity*.

Christos Baziotis, Nikos Pelekis, and Christos Doulkeridis. 2017. Datastories at semeval-2017 task 6: Siamese lstm with attention for humorous text comparison. In *Proceedings of the 11th International Workshop on Semantic Evaluation (SemEval-2017)*. Association for Computational Linguistics, Vancouver, Canada, pages 389–394. http://www.aclweb.org/anthology/S17-2065.

Andrew Cattle and Xiaojuan Ma. 2017. Srhr at semeval-2017 task 6: Word associations for humour recognition. In *Proceedings of the 11th International Workshop on Semantic Evaluation (SemEval-2017)*. Association for Computational Linguistics, Vancouver, Canada, pages 400–405. http://www.aclweb.org/anthology/S17-2067.

David Donahue, Alexey Romanov, and Anna Rumshisky. 2017. Humorhawk at semeval-2017 task 6: Mixing meaning and sound for humor recognition. In *Proceedings of the 11th International Workshop on Semantic Evaluation (SemEval-2017)*. Association for Computational Linguistics, Vancouver, Canada, pages 98–102. http://www.aclweb.org/anthology/S17-2010.

Xiwu Han and Gregory Toner. 2017. Qub at semeval-2017 task 6: Cascaded imbalanced classification for humor analysis in twitter. In *Proceedings of the 11th International Workshop on Semantic Evaluation (SemEval-2017)*. Association for Computational Linguistics, Vancouver, Canada, pages 379–383. http://www.aclweb.org/anthology/S17-2063.

James J Heckman. 1979. Sample selection bias as a specification error. *Econometrica: Journal of the econometric society* pages 153–161.

Chloe Kiddon and Yuriy Brun. 2011. That's what she said: double entendre identification. In *Proceedings of the 49th Annual Meeting of the Association for Computational Linguistics: Human Language Technologies: short papers-Volume 2*. Association for Computational Linguistics, pages 89–94.

Marin Kukovačec, Juraj Malenica, Ivan Mršić, Antonio Šajatović, Domagoj Alagić, and Jan Šnajder. 2017. Takelab at semeval-2017 task 6: #rankinghumorin4pages. In *Proceedings of the 11th International Workshop on Semantic Evaluation (SemEval-2017)*. Association for Computational Linguistics, Vancouver, Canada, pages 395–399. http://www.aclweb.org/anthology/S17-2066.

Rutal Mahajan and Mukesh Zaveri. 2017. Svnit @ semeval 2017 task-6: Learning a sense of humor using supervised approach. In *Proceedings of the 11th International Workshop on Semantic Evaluation (SemEval-2017)*. Association for Computational Linguistics, Vancouver, Canada, pages 410–414. http://www.aclweb.org/anthology/S17-2069.

Rada Mihalcea and Carlo Strapparava. 2005. Making computers laugh: Investigations in automatic humor recognition. In *Proceedings of the Conference on Human Language Technology and Empirical Methods in Natural Language Processing*. Association for Computational Linguistics, pages 531–538.

Peter Potash, Alexey Romanov, and Anna Rumshisky. 2016. #hashtagwars: Learning a sense of humor. *arXiv preprint arXiv:1612.03216* .

Amruta Purandare and Diane Litman. 2006. Humor: Prosody analysis and automatic recognition for f* r* i* e* n* d* s*. In *Proceedings of the 2006 Conference on Empirical Methods in Natural Language Processing*. Association for Computational Linguistics, pages 208–215.

Dragomir Radev, Amanda Stent, Joel Tetreault, Aasish Pappu, Aikaterini Iliakopoulou, Agustin Chanfreau, Paloma de Juan, Jordi Vallmitjana, Alejandro Jaimes, Rahul Jha, et al. 2015. Humor in collective discourse: Unsupervised funniness detection in the new yorker cartoon caption contest. *arXiv preprint arXiv:1506.08126* .

Yishay Raz. 2012. Automatic humor classification on twitter. In *Proceedings of the 2012 Conference of the North American Chapter of the Association for Computational Linguistics: Human Language Technologies: Student Research Workshop*. Association for Computational Linguistics, pages 66–70.

Antonio Reyes, Paolo Rosso, and Tony Veale. 2013. A multidimensional approach for detecting irony in twitter. *Language resources and evaluation* 47(1):239–268.

Dafna Shahaf, Eric Horvitz, and Robert Mankoff. 2015. Inside jokes: Identifying humorous cartoon captions. In *Proceedings of the 21th ACM SIGKDD International Conference on Knowledge Discovery and Data Mining*. ACM, pages 1065–1074.

Xinru Yan and Ted Pedersen. 2017. Duluth at semeval-2017 task 6: Language models in humor detection. In *Proceedings of the 11th International Workshop on Semantic Evaluation (SemEval-2017)*. Association for Computational Linguistics, Vancouver, Canada, pages 384–388. http://www.aclweb.org/anthology/S17-2064.

Diyi Yang, Alon Lavie, Chris Dyer, and Eduard Hovy. 2015. Humor recognition and humor anchor extraction pages 2367–2376.

Bianca Zadrozny. 2004. Learning and evaluating classifiers under sample selection bias. In *Proceedings of the twenty-first international conference on Machine learning*. ACM, page 114.

Renxian Zhang and Naishi Liu. 2014. Recognizing humor on twitter. In *Proceedings of the 23rd ACM International Conference on Conference on Information and Knowledge Management*. ACM, pages 889–898.

SemEval-2017 Task 7: Detection and Interpretation of English Puns

Tristan Miller[*†] and **Christian F. Hempelmann**[†] and **Iryna Gurevych**[*]

[*]Ubiquitous Knowledge Processing Lab (UKP-TUDA/UKP-DIPF)
Department of Computer Science
Technische Universität Darmstadt
`https://www.ukp.tu-darmstadt.de`

[†]Ontological Semantic Technology Lab
Texas A&M University-Commerce
`http://www.tamuc.edu/ontology`

Abstract

A pun is a form of wordplay in which a word suggests two or more meanings by exploiting polysemy, homonymy, or phonological similarity to another word, for an intended humorous or rhetorical effect. Though a recurrent and expected feature in many discourse types, puns stymie traditional approaches to computational lexical semantics because they violate their one-sense-per-context assumption. This paper describes the first competitive evaluation for the automatic detection, location, and interpretation of puns. We describe the motivation for these tasks, the evaluation methods, and the manually annotated data set. Finally, we present an overview and discussion of the participating systems' methodologies, resources, and results.

1 Introduction

Word sense disambiguation (WSD), the task of identifying a word's meaning in context, has long been recognized as an important task in computational linguistics, and has been the focus of a considerable number of Senseval/SemEval evaluation tasks. Traditional approaches to WSD rest on the assumption that there is a single, unambiguous communicative intention underlying each word in the document. However, there exists a class of language constructs known as *puns*, in which lexical-semantic ambiguity is a *deliberate* effect of the communication act. That is, the speaker or writer intends for a certain word or other lexical item to be interpreted as simultaneously carrying two or more separate meanings. Though puns are a recurrent and expected feature in many discourse types, they have attracted relatively little attention in the fields of computational linguistics and natural language processing in general, or WSD in particular. In this document, we describe a shared task for evaluating computational approaches to the detection and semantic interpretation of puns.

A pun is a form of wordplay in which one sign (*e.g.,* a word or phrase) suggests two or more meanings by exploiting polysemy, homonymy, or phonological similarity to another sign, for an intended humorous or rhetorical effect (Aarons, 2017; Hempelmann and Miller, 2017). For example, the first of the following two punning jokes exploits the sound similarity between the surface sign "propane" and the latent target "profane", while the second exploits contrasting meanings of the word "interest":

(1) When the church bought gas for their annual barbecue, proceeds went from the sacred to the propane.

(2) I used to be a banker but I lost interest.

Puns where the two meanings share the same pronunciation are known as *homophonic* or *perfect*, while those relying on similar- but not identical-sounding signs are known as *heterophonic* or *imperfect*. Where the signs are considered as written rather than spoken sequences, a similar distinction can be made between *homographic* and *heterographic* puns.

Conscious or tacit linguistic knowledge—particularly of lexical semantics and phonology—is an essential prerequisite for the production and interpretation of puns. This has long made them an attractive subject of study in theoretical linguistics, and has led to a small but growing body of research into puns in computational linguistics. Most computational treatments of puns to date have focused on generative algorithms (Binsted and Ritchie, 1994,

Proceedings of the 11th International Workshop on Semantic Evaluations (SemEval-2017), pages 58–68,
Vancouver, Canada, August 3 - 4, 2017. ©2017 Association for Computational Linguistics

1997; Ritchie, 2005; Hong and Ong, 2009; Waller et al., 2009; Kawahara, 2010) or modelling their phonological properties (Hempelmann, 2003a,b). However, several studies have explored the detection and interpretation of puns (Yokogawa, 2002; Taylor and Mazlack, 2004; Miller and Gurevych, 2015; Kao et al., 2015; Miller and Turković, 2016; Miller, 2016); the most recent of these focus squarely on computational semantics. In this paper, we present the first organized public evaluation for the computational processing of puns.

We believe computational interpretation of puns to be an important research question with a number of real-world applications. For example:

- It has often been argued that humour can enhance human–computer interaction (HCI) (Hempelmann, 2008), and at least one study (Morkes et al., 1999) has already shown that incorporating canned humour into a user interface can increase user satisfaction without adversely affecting user efficiency. An interactive system that is able to recognize and produce contextually appropriate responses to users' puns could further enhance the HCI experience.

- Recognizing humorous ambiguity is also important in machine translation, particularly for sitcoms and other comedic works, which feature puns and other forms of wordplay as a recurrent and expected feature (Schröter, 2005). Puns can be extremely difficult for non-native speakers to detect, let alone translate. Future automatic translation aids could scan source texts, flagging potential puns for special attention, and perhaps even proposing ambiguity-preserving translations that best match the original pun's double meaning.

- Wordplay is a perennial topic of scholarship in literary criticism and analysis, with entire books (*e.g.,* Wurth, 1895; Rubinstein, 1984; Keller, 2009) having been dedicated to cataloguing the puns of certain authors. Computer-assisted detection and classification of puns could help digital humanists in producing similar surveys of other œuvres.

2 Data sets

The pun processing tasks at SemEval-2017 used two manually annotated data sets, both of which we are freely releasing to the research community.[1]

Our first data set, containing English homographic puns, is based on the one described by Miller and Turković (2016) and Miller (2016).[2] It contains punning and non-punning jokes, aphorisms, and other short, self-contained contexts sourced from professional humorists and online collections. For the purposes of deciding which contexts contain a pun, we used a somewhat weaker definition of homography: the lexical units corresponding to a pun's two distinct meanings must be spelled exactly the same way, with the exception that inflections and particles (*e.g.,* the prepositions or dummy object pronouns in phrasal verbs such as "duke it out") may be disregarded. The contexts have the following characteristics:

- Each context contains a maximum of one pun.

- Each pun (and its latent target) contains exactly one *content word* (*i.e.,* a noun, verb, adjective, or adverb) and zero or more *non-content words* (*e.g.,* prepositions or articles). Here "word" is defined as a sequence of letters delimited by space or punctuation. This means that puns and targets do not include hyphenated words, and they do not consist of multi-word expressions containing more than one content word, such as "get off the ground" or "state of the art". Puns and targets may be multi-word expressions containing only one content word—this includes phrasal verbs such as "take off" or "put up with".

- Each pun (and its target) has a lexical entry in WordNet 3.1. However, the *sense* of the pun or the target may or may not exist in WordNet 3.1.

The homographic data set contains 2250 contexts, of which 1607 (71%) contain a pun. Sense annotation was carried out by three trained human judges, two of whom independently applied sense keys from WordNet 3.1. Each pun word was annotated with two sets of sense keys, one for each meaning of the pun. As in previous Senseval/SemEval word sense annotation tasks, annotators were permitted to select more than one sense key per meaning, or to indicate that the meaning was not listed in

---

[1] https://www.ukp.tu-darmstadt.de/data/sense-labelling-resources/sense-annotated-english-puns/

[2] The only significant difference is that we removed several hundred of the contexts not containing puns and added them to our new heterographic data set.

pun type	subtask	contexts	words	words / context		
				min	mean	max
homographic	detection	2 250	24 499	2	10.9	44
homographic	location	1 607	18 998	3	11.8	44
homographic	interpretation	1 298	15 510	3	11.9	44
heterographic	detection	1 780	19 461	2	10.9	69
heterographic	location	1 271	15 145	3	11.9	69
heterographic	interpretation	1 098	13 258	3	12.1	69

Table 1: Data set statistics

WordNet. Interannotator agreement, as measured by Krippendorff's (1980) α and a variation of the MASI set comparison metric (Passonneau, 2006; Miller, 2016), was 0.777. Disagreements were resolved automatically by taking the intersection of the corresponding sense sets; for contexts where this was not possible, the third judge manually adjudicated the disagreements. Of the 1607 puns, 1298 (81%) have both meanings in WordNet.

The second data set is similar to the first, except that the puns are heterographic rather than homographic. It was constructed in a similar manner, including the use of two annotators and an adjudicator. However, as heterographic puns have an extra level of complexity (it being sometimes necessary to discuss or explain an obscure joke before one "gets it"), the annotators were given an opportunity to resolve their disagreements themselves before passing the remainder on to the adjudicator. Pre-adjudication agreement for the sense annotations was $\alpha = 0.838$. The final data set contains 1780 contexts, of which 1271 (71%) contain a pun. Of the puns, 1098 (86%) have both meanings in WordNet.

As described in the following section, the two data sets are used in three subtasks—pun detection, pun location, and pun interpretation. The pun detection subtask uses the full data sets, while the other two subtasks use subsets of the full data sets. Table 1 presents some statistics on the size of each subtask's data set in terms of the number of contexts and word tokens.

3 Task definition

Participating systems competed in any or all of the following three subtasks, evaluated consecutively. Within each subtask, participants had the choice of running their system on either or both data sets.

Subtask 1: Pun detection. For this subtask, participants were given an entire raw data set. For each context in the data set, the system had to decide whether or not it contains a pun. For example, take the following two contexts:

(2) I used to be a banker but I lost interest.

(3) What if there were no hypothetical questions?

For (2), the system should have returned "pun", whereas for (3) the system should have returned "non-pun".

Systems had to classify *all* contexts in the data set. Scores were calculated using the standard precision, recall, accuracy, and F-score measures as used in classification (Manning et al., 2008, §8.3):

$$P = \frac{TP}{TP + FP}$$

$$R = \frac{TP}{TP + FN}$$

$$A = \frac{TP + TN}{TP + TN + FP + FN}$$

$$F_1 = \frac{2PR}{P + R}$$

where *TP*, *TN*, *FP*, and *FN* are the numbers of true positives, true negatives, false positives, and false negatives, respectively.

Subtask 2: Pun location. For this subtask, the contexts not containing puns were removed from the data sets. For any or all of the contexts, systems had to make a single guess as to which word is the pun. For example, given context (2) above, the system should have indicated that the tenth word, "interest", is the pun.

Scores were calculated using the standard coverage, precision, recall, and F-score measures as used in word sense disambiguation (Palmer et al., 2007):

$$C = \frac{\text{\# of guesses}}{\text{\# of contexts}}$$

$$P = \frac{\text{\# of correct guesses}}{\text{\# of guesses}}$$

$$R = \frac{\text{\# of correct guesses}}{\text{\# of contexts}}$$

$$F_1 = \frac{2PR}{P + R}.$$

Note that, according to the above definitions, it is always the case that $P \geq R$, and $F_1 = P = R$ whenever $P = R$.

Subtask 3: Pun interpretation. For this subtask, the pun word in each context is marked, and contexts where the pun's two meanings are not found in WordNet are removed from the data sets. For any or all of the contexts, systems had to annotate the two meanings of the given pun by reference to WordNet sense keys. For example, given context (2), the system should have returned the WordNet sense keys `interest%1:09:00::` (glossed as "a sense of concern with and curiosity about someone or something") and `interest%1:21:00::` ("a fixed charge for borrowing money; usually a percentage of the amount borrowed").

As with the pun location subtask, scores were calculated using the coverage, precision, recall, and F-score measures from word sense disambiguation. A guess is considered to be "correct" if one of its sense lists is a non-empty subset of one of the sense lists from the gold standard, and the other of its sense lists is a non-empty subset of the other sense list from the gold standard. That is, the order of the two sense lists is not significant, nor is the order of the sense keys within each list. If the gold standard sense lists contain multiple senses, then it is sufficient for the system to correctly guess only one sense from each list.

4 Baselines

For each subtask, we provide results for various baselines:

Pun detection. The only baseline we use for this subtask is a random classifier. It makes no assumption about the underlying class distribution, labelling each context as "pun" or "non-pun" with equal probability. On average, its recall and accuracy will therefore be 0.5, and its precision equal to the proportion of contexts containing puns.

Pun location. For this subtask we present the results of three naïve baselines. The first simply selects one of the context words at random. The second baseline always selects the last word of the context as a pun. It is informed by empirical studies of large joke corpora, which have found that punchlines tend to occur in a terminal position (Attardo, 1994). The third baseline is a slightly more sophisticated pun location baseline inspired by Mihalcea et al. (2010). In that study, genuine joke punchlines were selected among several non-humorous alternatives by finding the candidate whose words have the highest mean polysemy. We adapt this technique by selecting as the pun the word with the highest polysemy (counting together senses from all parts of speech). In the case of a tie, we choose the most polysemous word nearest to the end of the context.

Pun interpretation. Following the practice in traditional word sense disambiguation, we present the results of the random and most frequent sense baselines, as adapted to pun annotation.

The random baseline attempts to lemmatize the pun word, looks it up in WordNet, and selects two of its senses at random, one for each meaning of the pun. It scores

$$P = R = \frac{1}{n} \sum_{i=1}^{n} \frac{G_1^i \cdot G_2^i}{\binom{S^i}{2}},$$

where n is the number of contexts, G_j^i is the number of gold-standard sense keys in the jth meaning of the pun word in context i, and S^i is the number of sense keys WordNet contains for the pun word in context i. We compute the random baseline only for the homographic data set. (It would in principle be adaptable to the heterographic data set, though the large number of potential target words means the scores would be negligible.)

The most frequent sense (MFS) baseline is a supervised baseline in that it depends on a manually sense-annotated background corpus. As its name suggests, it involves always selecting from the candidates that sense that has the highest frequency in the corpus. For the homographic data set, our MFS implementation attempts to lemmatize the pun word (if necessary, building a list of candidate lemmas) and then selects the two most frequent senses of these lemmas according to WordNet's built-in sense frequency counts.[3] For the heterographic data set, only the first sense is selected from the list of candidate lemmas. A second list is constructed by finding all other lemmas in WordNet

---

[3] These counts come from the SemCor (Miller et al., 1993) corpus.

with the minimum Levenshtein (1966) distance to the lemmas in the first list. The most frequent sense of the lemmas in the second list is selected as the second meaning of the pun.

In addition to the two naïve baselines, we also provide scores for the homographic pun interpretation system described by Miller and Gurevych (2015). This system works by running each pun through a variation of the Lesk (1986) algorithm that scores each candidate sense according to the lexical overlap with the pun's context. The two top-scoring senses are then selected; in case of ties, the system attempts to select senses which are not closely related to each other, and at least one of whose parts of speech matches the one applied to the pun by a POS tagger.

The baseline pun interpretation scores presented in this paper differ slightly from those given in Miller and Gurevych (2015) and Miller (2016). This is because the scoring program used in those studies compared sense keys on the basis of their underlying WordNet synsets, whereas in this shared task the sense keys are compared directly.

5 Participating systems

Our shared task saw participation from ten systems:

BuzzSaw (Oele and Evang, 2017). BuzzSaw assumes that each meaning of the pun will exhibit high semantic similarity with one and only one part of the context. The system's approach to homographic pun interpretation is to compute the semantic similarity between the two halves of every possible contiguous, binary partitioning of the context, retaining the partitioning with the lowest similarity between the two parts. A Lesk-like WSD algorithm based on word and sense embeddings is then used to disambiguate the pun word separately with respect to each part of the context.

The pun interpretation system is also used for homographic pun location. First, the interpretation system is run once for each polysemous word in the context. The word whose two disambiguated senses have maximum cosine distance between their sense embeddings is selected as the pun word.

Duluth (Pedersen, 2017). For pun detection, the Duluth system assumes that all-words WSD systems will have difficulties in consistently assigning sense labels to contexts containing puns. The system therefore disambiguates each context with four slightly different configurations of the same WSD algorithm. If more than two sense labels differ across runs, the context is assumed to contain a pun. For pun location, the system selects the word whose sense label changed across runs; if multiple words changed senses, then the system selects the one closest to the end of the context.

Homographic pun interpretation is carried out by running various configurations of a WSD algorithm on the pun word and selecting the two most frequently returned senses. For heterographic puns, the system attempts to recover the target form either by generating a list of WordNet lemmas with minimal edit distance to the pun word, or by querying the Datamuse API for words with similar spellings, pronunciations, and meanings. WSD algorithms are then run separately on the pun and the set of target candidates, with the best matching pun and target senses retained.

ECNU (Xiu et al., 2017). ECNU uses a supervised approach to pun detection. The authors collected a training set of 60 homographic and 60 heterographic puns, plus 60 proverbs and famous sayings, from various Web sources. The data is then used to train a classifier, using features derived from Word-Net and word2vec embeddings. The ECNU pun locator is knowledge-based, determining each context word's likelihood of being the pun on the basis of the distance between its sense vectors, or between its senses and the context.

ELiRF-UPV (Hurtado et al., 2017). This system's approach to homographic pun location rests on two hypotheses: that the pun will be semantically very similar to one of the non-adjacent words in the sentence, and that the pun will be located near the end of the sentence. The system therefore calculates the similarity between every pair of non-adjacent words in the context using word2vec, retaining the pair with the highest similarity. The word in the pair that is closer to the end of the context is selected as the pun.

To interpret homographic puns, ELiRF-UPV first finds the two context words whose word embeddings are closest to that of the pun.

Then, for each context word, the system builds a bag-of-words representation for each of its candidate senses, and for each of the pun word's candidate senses, using information from WordNet. The lexical overlap between every pair of pun and context senses is calculated, and the pun sense with the highest overlap is selected as one of the meanings of the pun.

Fermi (Indurthi and Oota, 2017). Fermi takes a supervised approach to the detection of homographic puns. Unlike ECNU, the authors did not construct their own data set of puns, but rather split the shared task data set into separate training and test sets, the first of which they manually annotated. A bi-directional RNN then learns a classification model, using distributed word embeddings as input features.

Fermi's approach to pun location is a knowledge-based approach similar to that of ELiRF-UPV. For every pair of words in the context, a similarity score is calculated on the basis of the maximum pairwise similarity of their WordNet synsets. In the highest-scoring pair, the word closest to the end of the context is selected as the pun.

Idiom Savant (Doogan et al., 2017). Idiom Savant uses a variety of different methods depending on the subtask and pun type, but which are generally based on Google *n*-grams and word2vec. Target recovery in heterographic puns involves computing phonetic distance with the aid of the CMU Pronouncing Dictionary. Uniquely among participating systems, Idiom Savant attempts to flag and specially process Tom Swifties, a genre of punning jokes commonly seen in the test data.

JU_CSE_NLP (Pramanick and Das, 2017). As a supervised approach, JU_CSE_NLP relies on a manually annotated data set of 413 puns sourced by the authors from Project Gutenberg. The data is used to train a hidden Markov model and cyclic dependency network, using features from a part-of-speech tagger and a syntactic parser. The classifiers are applied to the pun detection and location subtasks.

PunFields (Mikhalkova and Karyakin, 2017). PunFields uses separate methods for pun

detection, location, and interpretation; central to all of them is the notion of semantic fields. The system's approach to pun detection is a supervised one, with features being vectors tabulating the number of words in the context that appear in each of the 34 sections of *Roget's Thesaurus*. For pun location, PunFields uses a weakly supervised approach that scores candidates on the basis of their presence in *Roget's* sections, their position within the context, and their part of speech.

For pun interpretation, the system partitions the context on the basis of semantic fields, and then selects as the first sense of the pun the one whose WordNet gloss has the greatest number of words in common with the first partition. For homographic puns, the second sense selected is the one with the highest frequency count in WordNet (or the next-highest frequency count, in case the first selected sense already has the highest frequency). For heterographic puns, a list of candidate target words is produced using Damerau-Levenshtein (1964) distance. Among their corresponding WordNet senses, the system selects the one whose definition has the highest lexical overlap with the second partition.

UWaterloo (Vechtomova, 2017). UWaterloo is a rule-based pun locator that scores candidate words according to eleven simple heuristics. These heuristics involve the position of the word within the context or relative to certain punctuation or function words, the word's inverse document frequency in a large reference corpus, normalized pointwise mutual information (PMI) with other words in the context, and whether the word exists in a reference set of homophones and similar-sounding words. Only words in the second half of the context are scored; in the event of a tie, the system chooses the word closer to the end of the context.

UWAV (Vadehra, 2017). UWAV participated in the pun detection and location subtasks. The detection component is another supervised system, taking the votes of three classifiers (support vector machine, naïve Bayes, and logistic regression) trained on lexical-semantic and word embedding features of a manually annotated data set.

For pun location, UWAV splits the context in half and checks whether any word in the second half is in some predefined lists of homonyms, homophones, and antonyms. If so, one of those words is selected as the pun. Otherwise, word2vec similarity is calculated between every pair of words in the context. In the highest-scoring word pair, the word closest to the end of the context is selected.

One further team submitted answers after the official evaluation period was over:

N-Hance (Sevgili et al., 2017). The N-Hance system assumes every pun has a particularly strong association with exactly one other word in the context. To detect and locate puns, then, it calculates the PMI between every pair of words in the context. If the PMI of the highest-scoring pair exceeds a certain threshold relative to the other pairs' PMI scores, then the context is assumed to contain a pun, with the pun being the word in the pair closest to the end of the context. Otherwise, the context is assumed to have no pun.

For homographic pun interpretation, the first sense is selected by finding the maximum overlap between the candidate sense definitions and the pun's context. N-Hance then finds the word in the context that has the highest PMI score with the pun. The system selects as the second sense of the pun that sense whose synonyms have the greatest word2vec cosine similarity with the paired word.

6 Results and analysis

Tables 2 through 4 show the results for each of the three subtasks and two data sets. Results for the participating systems are shown in the upper section of each table; the lower section shows the baselines and the N-Hance system entered out of competition. Pun detection results for ECNU and Fermi are also in the non-competition section, since their training data, by accident or design, included some contexts from the test data. To calculate the pun detection scores for these two systems, we first removed the overlapping contexts from the test set.[4] The PunFields pun locator is also marked

as it makes use of POS frequency counts of the homographic data set that were published in Miller and Gurevych (2015).

For each metric, the result of the best-performing participating system is shown in boldface. Where a baseline or non-competition entry matched or outperformed the best participating system, its result is also shown in boldface. Generally only the best-scoring run submitted by each system is shown;[5] we have made an exception for Duluth's Datamuse- and edit distance–based pun interpretation variations ("DM" and "ED", respectively), neither of which outperformed the other on all metrics.

Subtask 1: Pun detection. No one system emerged as the clear winner for this subtask, making it hard to draw conclusions on what approaches work best. Among the participating systems for the homographic data set, Punfields achieved the highest precision (0.7993), JU_CSE_NLP the highest recall (0.9079), and Duluth the highest accuracy and F-score (0.7364 and 0.8254, respectively). N-Hance equalled or outperformed the participating systems on recall, accuracy, and F-score. For the heterographic data set, Idiom Savant had the highest precision, accuracy, and F-score (0.8704, 0.7837, and 0.8439, respectively), while JU_CSE_NLP achieved the best recall (0.9402). N-Hance performed about as well as Idiom Savant in terms of F-Score (0.8440). For both data sets, all systems outperformed the random baseline.

Subtask 2: Pun location. The last word baseline (F_1 = 0.4704 and 0.5704 for homographic and heterographic puns, respectively) turned out to be surprisingly hard to beat for this subtask. For the homographic data set, this baseline was exceeded only by Idiom Savant (F_1 = 0.6631) and UWaterloo (F_1 = 0.6523). For the heterographic puns, it was bested only by Idiom Savant (F_1 = 0.6845), UWaterloo (F_1 = 0.7964), and N-Hance (F_1 = 0.6553).

Idiom Savant was not the only system to measure semantic relatedness via word2vec, though it was the only one to do so with n-grams from a large background corpus. It was also the only system to directly (albeit simplistically) measure phonetic

---

[4]Two further supervised pun detection systems, UWAV and Punfields, were found to have inadvertently used training contexts that also appear in the test data. In these two cases, however, the authors removed the overlapping contexts from

their training data, retrained their systems, and submitted new results, which we report here.

[5]Participants were permitted to submit the results of up to two runs for each subtask and data set. The intention was to allow participants the opportunity to fix problems in the formatting of their output files, or to try minor variations of the same system.

	homographic				heterographic			
system	P	R	A	F_1	P	R	A	F_1
Duluth	0.7832	0.8724	**0.7364**	**0.8254**	0.7399	0.8662	0.6871	0.7981
Idiom Savant	—	—	—	—	**0.8704**	0.8190	**0.7837**	**0.8439**
JU_CSE_NLP	0.7251	**0.9079**	0.6884	0.8063	0.7367	**0.9402**	0.7174	0.8261
PunFields	**0.7993**	0.7337	0.6782	0.7651	0.7580	0.5940	0.5747	0.6661
UWAV	0.6838	0.4723	0.4671	0.5587	0.6523	0.4178	0.4253	0.5094
random	0.7142	0.5000	0.5000	0.5882	0.7140	0.5000	0.5000	0.5882
ECNU*	0.7127	0.6474	0.5628	0.6785	0.7807	0.6761	0.6333	0.7247
Fermi†	**0.9024**	0.8970	**0.8533**	**0.8997**	—	—	—	—
N-Hance	0.7553	**0.9334**	**0.7364**	**0.8350**	0.7725	0.9300	0.7545	**0.8440**

Table 2: Pun detection results

	homographic				heterographic			
system	C	P	R	F_1	C	P	R	F_1
BuzzSaw	**1.0000**	0.2775	0.2775	0.2775	—	—	—	—
Duluth	**1.0000**	0.4400	0.4400	0.4400	**1.0000**	0.5311	0.5311	0.5311
ECNU	**1.0000**	0.3373	0.3373	0.3373	**1.0000**	0.5681	0.5681	0.5681
ELiRF-UPV	**1.0000**	0.4462	0.4462	0.4462	—	—	—	—
Fermi	**1.0000**	0.5215	0.5215	0.5215	—	—	—	—
Idiom Savant	0.9988	**0.6636**	**0.6627**	**0.6631**	**1.0000**	0.6845	0.6845	0.6845
JU_CSE_NLP	**1.0000**	0.3348	0.3348	0.3348	**1.0000**	0.3792	0.3792	0.3792
PunFields‡	**1.0000**	0.3279	0.3279	0.3279	**1.0000**	0.3501	0.3501	0.3501
UWaterloo	0.9994	0.6526	0.6521	0.6523	0.9976	**0.7973**	**0.7954**	**0.7964**
UWAV	**1.0000**	0.3410	0.3410	0.3410	**1.0000**	0.4280	0.4280	0.4280
random	**1.0000**	0.0846	0.0846	0.0846	**1.0000**	0.0839	0.0839	0.0839
last word	**1.0000**	0.4704	0.4704	0.4704	**1.0000**	0.5704	0.5704	0.5704
max. polysemy	**1.0000**	0.1798	0.1798	0.1798	**1.0000**	0.0110	0.0110	0.0110
N-Hance	0.9956	0.4269	0.4250	0.4259	0.9882	0.6592	0.6515	0.6553

Table 3: Pun location results

	homographic				heterographic			
system	C	P	R	F_1	C	P	R	F_1
BuzzSaw	0.9761	0.1563	**0.1525**	0.1544	—	—	—	—
Duluth (DM)	0.8606	**0.1683**	0.1448	**0.1557**	**0.9791**	0.0009	0.0009	0.0009
Duluth (ED)	0.9992	0.1480	0.1479	0.1480	0.9262	0.0315	0.0291	0.0303
ELiRF-UPV	0.9646	0.1014	0.0978	0.0996	—	—	—	—
Idiom Savant	**0.9900**	0.0778	0.0770	0.0774	0.8434	**0.0842**	**0.0710**	**0.0771**
PunFields	0.8760	0.0484	0.0424	0.0452	0.9709	0.0169	0.0164	0.0166
random	**1.0000**	0.0931	0.0931	0.0931	—	—	—	—
MFS	**1.0000**	0.1348	0.1348	0.1348	**0.9800**	0.0716	0.0701	0.0708
Miller & Gurevych	0.6826	**0.1975**	0.1348	**0.1603**	—	—	—	—
N-Hance	0.9831	0.0204	0.0200	0.0202	—	—	—	—

Table 4: Pun interpretation results

*Evaluated on 2237 of the 2250 homographic contexts, and 1778 of the 1780 heterographic contexts.

†Evaluated on 675 of the 2250 homographic contexts.

‡Uses POS frequency counts from the homographic test set.

distance using a pronunciation dictionary, and the only system that flagged puns of a certain genre for special processing. These features, alone or in combination, may have contributed to the system's success.

UWaterloo and N-Hance were the only systems making use of pointwise mutual information, to which their success might be credited. Evidently the notion of a unique "trigger" word in the context that activates the pun is an important one to model. UWaterloo also shares with Idiom Savant the use of hand-crafted rules based on real-world knowledge of punning jokes.

Subtask 3: Pun interpretation. As in the pun detection subtask, no one approach worked best here, at least for the homographic data set. Only two systems (BuzzSaw and Duluth) were able to beat the most frequent sense baseline. The Miller and Gurevych (2015) system remains the best-performing pun interpreter in terms of precision (0.1975) and F-score (0.1603), though BuzzSaw was able to exceed it in terms of recall (0.1525). Both BuzzSaw and Miller and Gurevych (2015) apply Lesk-like algorithms to "disambiguate" the pun word. However, lexical overlap approaches are also used by most of the lower-performing systems. For heterographic pun interpretation, Idiom Savant achieved the highest scores ($P = 0.0842$, $R = 0.0710$, $F_1 = 0.0771$), though its recall is not much higher than the most frequent sense baseline (0.0701).

It seems that for probabilistic approaches like those submitted, classifying texts as puns and, to a lesser degree, pinpointing the punning lexical material are easier than actual semantic tasks like our Subtask 3. This may be because probabilistic approaches cannot, in principle, see past the arbitrariness of the linguistic sign, instead relying on context to reflect meaning. We assume that producing a full semantic analysis in terms of a knowledge-based system, akin to those proposed in Bar-Hillel's (1960) famous evaluation of fully automatic high-quality translation, might be necessary, because only these approaches can get beyond observed shared features to natural language meaning. Such knowledge-based approaches to meaning in humour, based on relevant semantic humour theories (Raskin, 1985; Attardo and Raskin, 1991), have been in development since Raskin et al. (2009) and one recent (albeit non-scalable) approach, Kao et al. (2015), has already shown very interesting results.

7 Concluding remarks

In this paper we have introduced SemEval-2017 Task 7, the first shared task for the computational processing of puns. We have described the rules for three subtasks—pun detection, pun location, and pun interpretation—and described the manually annotated data sets used for their evaluation. Both data sets are now freely available for use by the research community. We have also described the approaches and presented the results of ten participating teams, as well as several baseline algorithms and a further system entered out of competition.

We observe most systems performed well on the pun detection task, with F-scores in the range of 0.5587 to 0.8440. However, only a few systems beat a simple baseline on pun location. Pun interpretation remains an extremely challenging problem, with most systems failing to exceed the baselines, and with sense assignment accuracy much lower than what is seen with traditional word sense disambiguation. Interestingly, though there exists a considerable body of research in linguistics on phonological models of punning (Hempelmann and Miller, 2017) and on semantic theories of humour (Raskin, 2008), little to none of this work appeared to inform the participating systems.

Acknowledgments

This work has been supported by the German Institute for Educational Research (DIPF). The authors thank Edwin Simpson for helping build the heterographic data set.

References

Debra Aarons. 2017. Puns and tacit linguistic knowledge. In Salvatore Attardo, editor, *The Routledge Handbook of Language and Humor*, Routledge, New York, NY, Routledge Handbooks in Linguistics, pages 80–94.

Salvatore Attardo. 1994. *Linguistic Theories of Humor*, Mouton de Gruyter, Berlin, chapter 2: The Linear Organization of the Joke. https://doi.org/10.1515/9783110219029.

Salvatore Attardo and Victor Raskin. 1991. Script theory revis(it)ed: Joke similarity and joke representation model. *Humor: International Journal of Humor Research* 4(3–4):293–348. https://doi.org/10.1515/humr.1991.4.3-4.293.

Yehoshua Bar-Hillel. 1960. The present status of automatic translation of languages. In Franz L. Alt, editor, *Advances in Computers*, Academic Press, volume 1, pages 91–163.

Kim Binsted and Graeme Ritchie. 1994. An implemented model of punning riddles. In *Proceedings of the Twelfth National Conference on Artificial Intelligence: AAAI-94*. pages 633–638.

Kim Binsted and Graeme Ritchie. 1997. Computational rules for generating punning riddles. *Humor: International Journal of Humor Research* 10(1):25–76. https://doi.org/10.1515/humr.1997.10.1.25.

Fred J. Damerau. 1964. A technique for computer detection and correction of spelling errors. *Communications of the ACM* 7(3):171–176. https://doi.org/10.1145/363958.363994.

Samuel Doogan, Aniruddha Ghosh, Hanyang Chen, and Tony Veale. 2017. Idiom Savant at SemEval-2017 Task 7: Detection and interpretation of English puns. In *Proceedings of the 11th International Workshop on Semantic Evaluation (SemEval-2017)*. pages 103–108.

Christian F. Hempelmann. 2003a. *Paronomasic Puns: Target Recoverability Towards Automatic Generation*. Ph.D. thesis, Purdue University, West Lafayette, IN.

Christian F. Hempelmann. 2003b. YPS – The Ynperfect Pun Selector for computational humor. In *Proceedings of the CHI 2003 Workshop on Humor Modeling in the Interface*.

Christian F. Hempelmann. 2008. Computational humor: Beyond the pun? In Victor Raskin, editor, *The Primer of Humor Research*, Mouton de Gruyter, Berlin, number 8 in Humor Research, pages 333–360. https://doi.org/10.1515/9783110198492.333.

Christian F. Hempelmann and Tristan Miller. 2017. Puns: Taxonomy and phonology. In Salvatore Attardo, editor, *The Routledge Handbook of Language and Humor*, Routledge, New York, NY, Routledge Handbooks in Linguistics, pages 95–108.

Bryan Anthony Hong and Ethel Ong. 2009. Automatically extracting word relationships as templates for pun generation. In *Computational Approaches to Linguistic Creativity: Proceedings of the Workshop*. pages 24–31.

Lluís-F. Hurtado, Encarna Segarra, Ferran Pla, Pascual Andrés Carrasco Gómez, and José Ángel González. 2017. ELiRF-UPV at SemEval-2017 Task 7: Pun detection and interpretation. In *Proceedings of the 11th International Workshop on Semantic Evaluation (SemEval-2017)*. pages 439–442.

Vijayasaradhi Indurthi and Subba Reddy Oota. 2017. Fermi at SemEval-2017 Task 7: Detection and interpretation of homographic puns in English language. In *Proceedings of the 11th International Workshop on Semantic Evaluation (SemEval-2017)*. pages 456–459.

Justine T. Kao, Roger Levy, and Noah D. Goodman. 2015. A computational model of linguistic humor in puns. *Cognitive Science* 40(5):1270–1285. https://doi.org/10.1111/cogs.12269.

Shigeto Kawahara. 2010. Papers on Japanese imperfect puns. Online collection of previously published journal and conference articles. http://user.keio.ac.jp/~kawahara/pdf/punbook.pdf.

Stefan Daniel Keller. 2009. *The Development of Shakespeare's Rhetoric: A Study of Nine Plays*. Number 136 in Swiss Studies in English. Narr, Tübingen.

Klaus Krippendorff. 1980. *Content Analysis: An Introduction to Its Methodology*. Number 5 in The Sage CommText Series. Sage Publications, Beverly Hills, CA.

Michael Lesk. 1986. Automatic sense disambiguation using machine readable dictionaries: How to tell a pine cone from a ice cream cone. In Virginia DeBuys, editor, *SIGDOC '86: Proceedings of the 5th Annual International Conference on Systems Documentation*. pages 24–26. https://doi.org/10.1145/318723.318728.

Vladimir I. Levenshtein. 1966. Binary codes capable of correcting deletions, insertions, and reversals. *Soviet Physics Doklady* 10(8):707–710.

Christopher D. Manning, Prabhakar Raghavan, and Hinrich Schütze. 2008. *Introduction to Information Retrieval*. Cambridge University Press, Cambridge.

Rada Mihalcea, Carlo Strapparava, and Stephen Pulman. 2010. Computational models for incongruity detection in humour. In Alexander Gelbukh, editor, *Computational Linguistics and Intelligent Text Processing: 11th International Conference, CICLing 2010*. Springer, Berlin/Heidelberg, number 6008 in Theoretical Computer Science and General Issues, pages 364–374. https://doi.org/10.1007/978-3-642-12116-6_30.

Elena Mikhalkova and Yuri Karyakin. 2017. PunFields at SemEval-2017 Task 7: Employing *Roget's Thesaurus* in automatic pun recognition and interpretation. In *Proceedings of the 11th International Workshop on Semantic Evaluation (SemEval-2017)*. pages 425–430.

George A. Miller, Claudia Leacock, Randee Tengi, and Ross T. Bunker. 1993. A semantic concordance. In *Human Language Technology: Proceedings of a Workshop Held at Plainsboro, New Jersey*. San Francisco, CA, pages 303–308. https://doi.org/10.3115/1075671.1075742.

Tristan Miller. 2016. *Adjusting Sense Representations for Word Sense Disambiguation and Automatic Pun Interpretation*. Dr.-Ing. thesis, Department of Computer Science, Technische Universität Darmstadt.

Tristan Miller and Iryna Gurevych. 2015. Automatic disambiguation of English puns. In *The 53rd Annual Meeting of the Association for Computational Linguistics and the 7th International Joint Conference on Natural Language Processing of the Asian Federation of Natural Language Processing: Proceedings of the Conference.* volume 1, pages 719–729.

Tristan Miller and Mladen Turković. 2016. Towards the automatic detection and identification of English puns. *European Journal of Humour Research* 4(1):59–75.

John Morkes, Hadyn K. Kernal, and Clifford Nass. 1999. Effects of humor in task-oriented human–computer interaction and computer-mediated communication: A direct test of SRCT theory. *Human–Computer Interaction* 14(4):395–435. https://doi.org/10.1207/S15327051HCI1404_2.

Dieke Oele and Kilian Evang. 2017. BuzzSaw at SemEval-2017 Task 7: Global vs. local context for interpreting and locating homographic English puns with sense embeddings. In *Proceedings of the 11th International Workshop on Semantic Evaluation (SemEval-2017).* pages 443–447.

Martha Palmer, Hwee Tou Ng, and Hoa Trang Dang. 2007. Evaluation of wsd systems. In Eneko Agirre and Philip Edmonds, editors, *Word Sense Disambiguation: Algorithms and Applications*, Springer, number 33 in Text, Speech, and Language Technology, chapter 4, pages 75–106.

Rebecca J. Passonneau. 2006. Measuring agreement on set-valued items (MASI) for semantic and pragmatic annotation. In *5th Edition of the International Conference on Language Resources and Evaluation.* pages 831–836.

Ted Pedersen. 2017. Duluth at SemEval-2017 Task 7: Puns upon a midnight dreary, lexical semantics for the weak and weary. In *Proceedings of the 11th International Workshop on Semantic Evaluation (SemEval-2017).* pages 384–388.

Aniket Pramanick and Dipankar Das. 2017. JU_CSE_NLP at SemEval-2017 Task 7: Employing rules to detect and interpret English puns. In *Proceedings of the 11th International Workshop on Semantic Evaluation (SemEval-2017).* pages 431–434.

Victor Raskin. 1985. *Semantic Mechanisms of Humor.* Number 24 in Studies in Linguistics and Philosophy. Springer Netherlands. https://doi.org/10.1007/978-94-009-6472-3.

Victor Raskin, editor. 2008. *The Primer of Humor Research.* Number 8 in Humor Research. Mouton de Gruyter, Berlin. https://doi.org/10.1515/9783110198492.

Victor Raskin, Christian F. Hempelmann, and Julia M. Taylor. 2009. How to understand and assess a theory: The evolution of SSTH into the GTVH and now into the OSTH. *Journal of Literary Theory* 3(2):285–312. https://doi.org/10.1515/JLT.2009.016.

Graeme D. Ritchie. 2005. Computational mechanisms for pun generation. In Graham Wilcock, Kristiina Jokinen, Chris Mellish, and Ehud Reiter, editors, *Proceedings of the 10th European Workshop on Natural Language Generation (ENLG-05).* pages 125–132.

Frankie Rubinstein. 1984. *A Dictionary of Shakespeare's Sexual Puns and Their Significance.* Macmillan, London.

Thorsten Schröter. 2005. *Shun the Pun, Rescue the Rhyme? The Dubbing and Subtitling of Languageplay in Film.* Ph.D. thesis, Karlstad University.

Özge Sevgili, Nima Ghotbi, and Selma Tekir. 2017. N-Hance at SemEval-2017 Task 7: A computational approach using word association for puns. In *Proceedings of the 11th International Workshop on Semantic Evaluation (SemEval-2017).* pages 435–438.

Julia M. Taylor and Lawrence J. Mazlack. 2004. Computationally recognizing wordplay in jokes. In Kenneth Forbus, Dedre Gentner, and Terry Regier, editors, *Proceedings of the Twenty-sixth Annual Conference of the Cognitive Science Society.* pages 1315–1320.

Ankit Vadehra. 2017. UWAV at SemEval-2017 Task 7: Automated feature-based system for locating puns. In *Proceedings of the 11th International Workshop on Semantic Evaluation (SemEval-2017).* pages 448–451.

Olga Vechtomova. 2017. UWaterloo at SemEval-2017 Task 7: Locating the pun using syntactic characteristics and corpus-based metrics. In *Proceedings of the 11th International Workshop on Semantic Evaluation (SemEval-2017).* pages 420–424.

Annalu Waller, Rolf Black, David A. O'Mara, Helen Pain, Graeme Ritchie, and Ruli Manurung. 2009. Evaluating the STANDUP pun generating software with children with cerebral palsy. *ACM Transactions on Accessible Computing* 1(3):1–27. https://doi.org/10.1145/1497302.1497306.

Leopold Wurth. 1895. *Das Wortspiel bei Shakspere.* Wilhelm Braumüller, Vienna.

Yuhuan Xiu, Man Lan, and Yuanbin Wu. 2017. ECNU at SemEval-2017 Task 7: Using supervised and unsupervised methods to detect and locate English puns. In *Proceedings of the 11th International Workshop on Semantic Evaluation (SemEval-2017).* pages 452–455.

Toshihiko Yokogawa. 2002. Japanese pun analyzer using articulation similarities. In *Proceedings of the 2002 IEEE International Conference on Fuzzy Systems: FUZZ 2002.* volume 2, pages 1114–1119. https://doi.org/10.1109/FUZZ.2002.1006660.

SemEval-2017 Task 8: RumourEval: Determining rumour veracity and support for rumours

Leon Derczynski♡* and **Kalina Bontcheva**♡ and **Maria Liakata**♣
and **Rob Procter**♣ and **Geraldine Wong Sak Hoi**◇ and **Arkaitz Zubiaga**♣

♡: Department of Computer Science, University of Sheffield, S1 4DP, UK
♣: Department of Computer Science, University of Warwick, CV4 7AL, UK
◇: swissinfo.ch, Bern, Switzerland
*: leon.d@shef.ac.uk

Abstract

Media is full of false claims. Even Oxford Dictionaries named "post-truth" as the word of 2016. This makes it more important than ever to build systems that can identify the veracity of a story, and the nature of the discourse around it. RumourEval is a SemEval shared task that aims to identify and handle rumours and reactions to them, in text. We present an annotation scheme, a large dataset covering multiple topics – each having their own families of claims and replies – and use these to pose two concrete challenges as well as the results achieved by participants on these challenges.

1 Introduction and Motivation

Rumours are rife on the web. False claims affect people's perceptions of events and their behaviour, sometimes in harmful ways. With the increasing reliance on the Web – social media, in particular – as a source of information and news updates by individuals, news professionals, and automated systems, the potential disruptive impact of rumours is further accentuated.

The task of analysing and determining veracity of social media content has been of recent interest to the field of natural language processing. After initial work (Qazvinian et al., 2011), increasingly advanced systems and annotation schemas have been developed to support the analysis of rumour and misinformation in text (Kumar and Geethakumari, 2014; Zhang et al., 2015; Shao et al., 2016; Zubiaga et al., 2016b). Veracity judgment can be decomposed intuitively in terms of a comparison between assertions made in – and entailments from – a candidate text, and external world knowledge. Intermediate linguistic cues have also been

shown to play a role. Critically, based on recent work the task appears deeply nuanced and very challenging, while having important applications in, for example, journalism and disaster mitigation (Hermida, 2012; Procter et al., 2013a; Veil et al., 2011).

We propose a shared task where participants analyse rumours in the form of claims made in user-generated content, and where users respond to one another within conversations attempting to resolve the veracity of the rumour. We define a rumour as a "circulating story of questionable veracity, which is apparently credible but hard to verify, and produces sufficient scepticism and/or anxiety so as to motivate finding out the actual truth" (Zubiaga et al., 2015b). While breaking news unfold, gathering opinions and evidence from as many sources as possible as communities react becomes crucial to determine the veracity of rumours and consequently reduce the impact of the spread of misinformation.

Within this scenario where one needs to listen to, and assess the testimony of, different sources to make a final decision with respect to a rumour's veracity, we ran a task in SemEval consisting of two subtasks: (a) stance classification towards rumours, and (b) veracity classification. Subtask A corresponds to the core problem in crowd response analysis when using discourse around claims to verify or disprove them. Subtask B corresponds to the AI-hard task of assessing directly whether or not a claim is false.

1.1 Subtask A - SDQC Support/ Rumour stance classification

Related to the objective of predicting a rumour's veracity, Subtask A deals with the complementary objective of tracking how other sources orient to the accuracy of the rumourous story. A key step in the analysis of the surrounding discourse is to

Proceedings of the 11th International Workshop on Semantic Evaluations (SemEval-2017), pages 69–76,
Vancouver, Canada, August 3 - 4, 2017. ©2017 Association for Computational Linguistics

---

SDQC support classification. Example 1:

u1: We understand there are two gunmen and up to a dozen hostages inside the cafe under siege at Sydney.. ISIS flags
. remain on display #7News **[support]**
    u2: @u1 not ISIS flags **[deny]**
    u3: @u1 sorry - how do you know it's an ISIS flag? Can you actually confirm that? **[query]**
        u4: @u3 no she can't cos it's actually not **[deny]**
    u5: @u1 More on situation at Martin Place in Sydney, AU –LINK– **[comment]**
    u6: @u1 Have you actually confirmed its an ISIS flag or are you talking shit **[query]**

SDQC support classification. Example 2:

u1: These are not timid colours; soldiers back guarding Tomb of Unknown Soldier after today's shooting #StandforCanada
–PICTURE– **[support]**
    u2: @u1 Apparently a hoax. Best to take Tweet down. **[deny]**
    u3: @u1 This photo was taken this morning, before the shooting. **[deny]**
    u4: @u1 I don't believe there are soldiers guarding this area right now. **[deny]**
        u5: @u4 wondered as well. I've reached out to someone who would know just to confirm that. Hopefully get
response soon. **[comment]**
            u4: @u5 ok, thanks. **[comment]**

Figure 1: Examples of tree-structured threads discussing the veracity of a rumour, where the label associated with each tweet is the target of the SDQC support classification task.

determine how other users in social media regard the rumour (Procter et al., 2013b). We propose to tackle this analysis by looking at the conversation stemming from direct and nested replies to the tweet originating the rumour (source tweet).

To this effect RumourEval provided participants with a tree-structured conversation formed of tweets replying to the originating rumourous tweet, directly or indirectly. Each tweet presents its own type of support with respect to the rumour (see Figure 1). We frame this in terms of supporting, denying, querying or commenting on (SDQC) the original rumour (Zubiaga et al., 2016b). Therefore, we introduce a subtask where the goal is to label the type of interaction between a given statement (rumourous tweet) and a reply tweet (the latter can be either direct or nested replies).

We note that superficially this subtask may bear similarity to SemEval-2016 Task 6 on stance detection from tweets (Mohammad et al., 2016), where participants are asked to determine whether a tweet is in favour, against or neither, of a given target entity (e.g. Hillary Clinton) or topic (e.g. climate change). Our SQDC subtask differs in two aspects. Firstly, participants needed to determine the objective support towards a rumour, an entire statement, rather than individual target concepts. Moreover, they are asked to determine additional response types to the rumourous tweet that are relevant to the discourse, such as a request for more information (questioning, Q) and making a com-

ment (C), where the latter doesn't directly address support or denial towards the rumour, but provides an indication of the conversational context surrounding rumours. For example, certain patterns of comments and questions can be indicative of false rumours and others indicative of rumours that turn out to be true.

Secondly, participants need to determine the type of response towards a rumourous tweet from a tree-structured conversation, where each tweet is not necessarily sufficiently descriptive on its own, but needs to be viewed in the context of an aggregate discussion consisting of tweets preceding it in the thread. This is more closely aligned with stance classification as defined in other domains, such as public debates (Anand et al., 2011). The latter also relates somewhat to the SemEval-2015 Task 3 on Answer Selection in Community Question Answering (Moschitti et al., 2015), where the task was to determine the quality of responses in tree-structured threads in CQA platforms. Responses to questions are classified as 'good', 'potential' or 'bad'. Both tasks are related to textual entailment and textual similarity. However, Semeval-2015 Task3 is clearly a question answering task, the platform itself supporting a QA format in contrast with the more free-form format of conversations in Twitter. Moreover, as a question answering task Semeval-2015 Task 3 is more concerned with relevance and retrieval whereas the task we propose here is about whether support or denial can be inferred towards the original statement (source tweet) from the reply tweets.

Each tweet in the tree-structured thread is categorised into one of the following four categories, following Procter et al. (2013b):

- **Support:** the author of the response supports the veracity of the rumour.
- **Deny:** the author of the response denies the veracity of the rumour.
- **Query:** the author of the response asks for additional evidence in relation to the veracity of the rumour.
- **Comment:** the author of the response makes their own comment without a clear contribution to assessing the veracity of the rumour.

Prior work in the area has found the task difficult, compounded by the variety present in language use between different stories (Lukasik et al., 2015; Zubiaga et al., 2017). This indicates it is challenging enough to make for an interesting SemEval shared task.

1.2 Subtask B - Veracity prediction

The goal of this subtask is to predict the veracity of a given rumour. The rumour is presented as a tweet, reporting an update associated with a newsworthy event, but deemed unsubstantiated at the time of release. Given such a tweet/claim, and a set of other resources provided, systems should return a label describing the anticipated veracity of the rumour as true or false – see Figure 2.

The ground truth of this task has been manually established by journalist members of the team who identified official statements or other trustworthy sources of evidence that resolved the veracity of the given rumour. Examples of tweets annotated for veracity are shown in Figure 2.

The participants in this subtask chose between two variants. In the first case – the *closed* variant – the veracity of a rumour had to be predicted solely from the tweet itself (for example (Liu et al., 2015) rely only on the content of tweets to assess the veracity of tweets in real time, while systems such as Tweet-Cred (Gupta et al., 2014) follow a tweet level analysis for a similar task where the credibility of a tweet is predicted). In the second case – the *open* variant – additional context was provided as input to veracity prediction systems; this context consists of a Wikipedia dump. Critically, no external resources could be used that contained information from after the rumour's resolu-

tion. To control this, we specified precise versions of external information that participants could use. This was important to make sure we introduced time sensitivity into the task of veracity prediction. In a practical system, the classified conversation threads from Subtask A could be used as context.

We take a simple approach to this task, using only true/false labels for rumours. In practice, however, many claims are hard to verify; for example, there were many rumours concerning Vladimir Putin's activities in early 2015, many wholly unsubstantiable. Therefore, we also expect systems to return a confidence value in the range of 0-1 for each rumour; if the rumour is unverifiable, a confidence of 0 should be returned.

1.3 Impact

Identifying the veracity of claims made on the web is an increasingly important task (Zubiaga et al., 2015b). Decision support, digital journalism and disaster response already rely on picking out such claims (Procter et al., 2013b). Additionally, web and social media are a more challenging environment than e.g. newswire, which has traditionally provided the mainstay of similar tasks (such as RTE (Bentivogli et al., 2011)). Last year we ran a workshop at WWW 2015, Rumors and Deception in Social Media: Detection, Tracking, and Visualization (RDSM 2015)[1] which garnered interest from researchers coming from a variety of backgrounds, including natural language processing, web science and computational journalism.

2 Data & Resources

To capture web claims and the community reaction around them, we take data from the "model organism" of social media, Twitter (Tufekci, 2014). Data for the task is available in the form of online discussion threads, each pertaining to a particular event and the rumours around it. These threads form a tree, where each tweet has a parent tweet it responds to. Together these form a conversation, initiated by a source tweet (see Figure 1). The data has already been annotated for veracity and SDQC following a published annotation scheme (Zubiaga et al., 2016b), as part of the PHEME project (Derczynski and Bontcheva, 2014), in which the task organisers are partners.

---

[1]http://www.pheme.eu/events/rdsm2015/

Veracity prediction examples:

u1: Hostage-taker in supermarket siege killed, reports say. #ParisAttacks –LINK– **[true]**

u1: OMG. #Prince rumoured to be performing in Toronto today. Exciting! **[false]**

Figure 2: Examples of source tweets with a veracity value, which has to be predicted in the veracity prediction task.

	S	D	Q	C
Subtask A				
Train	910	344	358	2,907
Test	94	71	106	778

	T	F	U
Subtask B			
Train	137	62	98
Test	8	12	8

Table 1: Label distribution of training and test datasets.

2.1 Training Data

Our training dataset comprises 297 rumourous threads collected for 8 events in total, which include 297 source and 4,222 reply tweets, amounting to 4,519 tweets in total. These events include well-known breaking news such as the Charlie Hebdo shooting in Paris, the Ferguson unrest in the US, and the Germanwings plane crash in the French Alps. The size of the dataset means it can be distributed without modifications, according to Twitter's current data usage policy, as JSON files.

This dataset is already publicly available (Zubiaga et al., 2016a) and constitutes the training and development data.

2.2 Test Data

For the test data, we annotated 28 additional threads. These include 20 threads extracted from the same events as the training set, and 8 threads from two newly collected events: (1) a rumour that Hillary Clinton was diagnosed with pneumonia during the 2016 US election campaign, and (2) a rumour that Youtuber Marina Joyce had been kidnapped.

The test dataset includes, in total, 1,080 tweets, 28 of which are source tweets and 1,052 replies. The distribution of labels in the training and test datasets is summarised in Table 1.

2.3 Context Data

Along with the tweet threads, we also provided additional context that participants could make use of. The context we provided was two-fold: (1) **Wikipedia articles** associated with the event in question. We provided the last revision of the article prior to the source tweet being posted, and (2) **content of linked URLs**, using the Internet Archive to retrieve the latest revision prior to the link being tweeted, where available.

2.4 Data Annotation

The annotation of rumours and their subsequent interactions was performed in two steps. In the first step, we sampled a subset of likely rumourous tweets from all the tweets associated with the event in question, where we used the high number of retweets as an indication of a tweet being potentially rumourous. These sampled tweets were fed to an annotation tool, by means of which our expert journalist annotators members manually identified the ones that did indeed report unverified updates and were considered to be rumours. Whenever possible, they also annotated rumours that had ultimately been proven true or the ones that had been debunked as false stories; the rest were annotated as "unverified". In the second step, we collected conversations associated with those rumourous tweets, which included all replies succeeding a rumourous source tweet. The type of support (SDQC) expressed by each participant in the conversation was then annotated through crowdsourcing. The methodology for performing this crowdsourced annotation process has been previously assessed and validated (Zubiaga et al., 2015a), and is further detailed in (Zubiaga et al., 2016b). The overall inter-annotator agreement rate of 63.7% showed the task to be challenging, and easier for source tweets (81.1%) than for replying tweets (62.2%).

The evaluation data was not available to those participating in any way in the task, and selection decisions were taken only by organisers not connected with any submission, to retain fairness across submissions.

Figure 1 shows an example of what a data instance looks like, where the source tweet in the tree presents a rumourous statement that is supported, denied, queried and commented on by others. Note that replies are nested, where some tweets reply directly to the source, while other tweets reply to earlier replies, e.g., u4 and u5 engage in a short conversation replying to each other in the second example. The input to the veracity prediction task is simpler than this; here participants had to determine if a rumour was true or false by only looking at the source tweet (see Figure 2), and optionally making use of the additional context provided by the organisers.

To prepare the evaluation resources, we collected and sampled the tweets around which there is most interaction, placed these in an existing annotation tool to be annotated as rumour vs. non-rumour, categorised them into rumour sub-stories, and labelled them for veracity.

For Subtask A, the extra annotation for support / deny / question / comment at the tweet level within the conversations were performed through crowdsourcing – as performed to satisfactory quality already with the existing training data (Zubiaga et al., 2015a).

3 Evaluation

The two subtasks were evaluated as follows.

SDQC stance classification: The evaluation of the SDQC needed careful consideration, as the distribution of the categories is clearly skewed towards comments. Evaluation is through classification accuracy.

Veracity prediction: The evaluation of the predicted veracity, which is either true or false for each instance, was done using macroaveraged accuracy, hence measuring the ratio of instances for which a correct prediction was made. Additionally, we calculated RMSE ρ for the difference between system and reference confidence in correct examples and provided the mean of these scores. Incorrect examples have an RMSE of 1. This is normalised and combined with the macroaveraged accuracy to give a final score; e.g. $acc = (1 - \rho)acc$.

The baseline is the most common class. For

Team	Score
DFKI DKT	0.635
ECNU	0.778
IITP	0.641
IKM	0.701
Mama Edha	0.749
NileTMRG	0.709
Turing	0.784
UWaterloo	0.780
Baseline (4-way)	0.741
Baseline (SDQ)	0.391

Table 2: Results for Task A: support/deny/query/comment classification.

Task A, we also introduce a baseline excluding the common, low-impact "comment" class, considering accuracy over only support, deny and query. This is included as the SDQ baseline.

4 Participant Systems and Results

We have had 13 system submissions at RumourEval, eight submissions for Subtask A (Kochkina et al., 2017; Bahuleyan and Vechtomova, 2017; Srivastava et al., 2017; Wang et al., 2017; Singh et al., 2017; Chen et al., 2017; García Lozano et al., 2017; Enayet and El-Beltagy, 2017), the identification of stance towards rumours, and five submissions for Subtask B (Srivastava et al., 2017; Wang et al., 2017; Singh et al., 2017; Chen et al., 2017; Enayet and El-Beltagy, 2017), the rumour veracity classification task, with participant teams coming from four continents (Europe: Germany, Sweden, UK; North America: Canada; Asia: China, India, Taiwan; Africa: Egypt), showing the global reach of the issue of rumour veracity on social media.

Most participants tackled Subtask A, which involves classifying a tweet in a conversation thread as either supporting (S), denying (D), querying (Q) or commenting on (C) a rumour. Results are given in Table 2 The distribution of SDQC labels in the training, development and test sets favours comments (see Table 1. Including and recognising the items that fit in this class is important for reducing noise in the other, information-bearing classifications (support, deny and query). In actual fact, comments are often express implicit support; the absence of dispute is a soft signal of agreement.

Systems generally viewed this task as a four-way single tweet classification task, with the exception of the best performing system (Turing), which addressed it as a sequential classification problem, where the SDQC label of each tweet depends on the features and labels of the previous tweets, and the ECNU and IITP systems. The IITP system takes as input pairs of source and reply tweets whereas the ECNU system addressed class imbalance by decomposing the problem into a two step classification task (comment vs. non-comment), and all non-comment tweets classified as SDQ. Half of the systems employed ensemble classifiers, where classification was obtained through majority voting (ECNU, MamaEdha, UWaterloo, DFKI-DKT). In some cases the ensembles were hybrid, consisting both of machine learning classifiers and manually created rules, with differential weighting of classifiers for different class labels (ECNU, MamaEdha, DFKI-DKT). Three systems used deep learning, with team Turing employing LSTMs for sequential classification, team IKM using convolutional neural networks (CNN) for obtaining the representation of each tweet, assigned a probability for a class by a softmax classifier and team Mama Edha using CNN as one of the classifiers in their hybrid conglomeration. The remaining two systems NileTMRG and IITP used support vector machines with linear and polynomial kernel respectively. Half of the systems invested in elaborate feature engineering including cue words and expressions denoting Belief, Knowledge, Doubt and Denial (UWaterloo) as well as Tweet domain features including meta-data about users, hashtags and event specific keywords (ECNU, UWaterloo, IITP, NileTMRG). The systems with the least elaborate features were IKM and Mama Edha for CNNs (word embeddings), DFKI-DKT (sparse word vectors as input to logistic regression) and Turing (average word vectors, punctuation, similarity between word vectors in current tweet, source tweet and previous tweet, presence of negation, picture, URL). Five out of the eight systems used pre-trained word embeddings, mostly Google News word2vec embeddings, while ECNU used four different types of embeddings. Overall, elaborate feature engineering and a strategy for addressing class imbalance seemed to pay off, as can be seen by the success of the high performance of the UWaterloo and ECNU systems. The success of the best performing system (Turing) can be attributed both to the use of LSTM to address

Team	Score	Confidence RMSE	
IITP	0.393		0.746

Table 3: Results for Task B: Rumour veracity - open variant.

Team	Score	Confidence RMSE	
DFKI DKT	0.393		0.845
ECNU	0.464		0.736
IITP	0.286		0.807
IKM	0.536		0.763
NileTMRG	0.536		0.672
Baseline	0.571		–

Table 4: Results for Task B: Rumour veracity - closed variant.

the problem as a sequential task and the choice of word embeddings.

Subtask B, veracity classification of a source tweet, was viewed as either a three-way (NileTMRG, ECNU, IITP) or two-way (IKM, DFKI-DKT) single tweet classification task. Results are given in Table 3 for the open variant, where external resources may be used,[2] and Table 4 for the closed variant – with no external resource use permitted. The systems used mostly similar features and classifiers to those in Subtask A, though some added features more specific to the distribution of SDQC labels in replies to the source tweet (e.g. the best performing system in this task, NileTMRG, considered the percentage of reply tweets classified as either S, D or Q).

5 Conclusion

Detecting and verifying rumours is a critical task and in the current media landscape, vital to populations so they can make decisions based on the truth. This shared task brought together many approaches to fixing veracity in real media, working through community interactions and claims made on the web. Many systems were able to achieve good results on unravelling the argument around various claims, finding out whether a discussion supports, denies, questions or comments on rumours.

The commentary around a story often helps determine how true that story is, so this advance is a great positive. However, finding out accurately

---

[2]Namely, the 20160901 English Wikipedia dump.

whether a story is false or true remains really tough. Systems did not reach the most-common-class baseline, despite the data not being exceptionally skewed. even the best systems could have the wrong level of confidence in a true/false judgment, weakly verifying stories that are true and so on. This tells us that we are making progress, but that the problem is so far very hard.

RumourEval leaves behind competitive results, a large number of approaches to be dissected by future researchers, and a benchmark dataset of thousands of documents and novel news stories. This sets a good baseline for the next steps in the area of fake news detection, as well as the material anyone needs to get started on the problem and evaluate and improve their systems.

Acknowledgments

This work is supported by the European Commission's 7th Framework Programme for research, under grant No. 611223 PHEME. This work is also supported by the European Unions Horizon 2020 research and innovation programme under grant agreement No. 687847 COMRADES. We are grateful to Swissinfo.ch for their extended support in the form of journalistic advice, keeping the task well-grounded, and annotation and task design efforts. We also extend our thanks to the SemEval organisers for their sustained hard work, and to our participants for bearing with us during the first shared task of this nature and all the joy and trouble that comes with it.

References

Pranav Anand, Marilyn Walker, Rob Abbott, Jean E. Fox Tree, Robeson Bowmani, and Michael Minor. 2011. Cats rule and dogs drool!: Classifying stance in online debate. In *Proceedings of the 2Nd Workshop on Computational Approaches to Subjectivity and Sentiment Analysis*. Association for Computational Linguistics, Stroudsburg, PA, USA, WASSA '11, pages 1–9. http://dl.acm.org/citation.cfm?id=2107653.2107654.

Hareesh Bahuleyan and Olga Vechtomova. 2017. UWaterloo at SemEval-2017 Task 8: Detecting Stance towards Rumours with Topic Independent Features. In *Proceedings of SemEval*. ACL.

Luisa Bentivogli, Peter Clark, Ido Dagan, Hoa Dang, and Danilo Giampiccolo. 2011. The seventh Pascal Recognizing Textual Entailment challenge. In *Proceedings of the Text Analysis Conference*. NIST.

Yi-Chin Chen, Zhao-Yand Liu, and Hung-Yu Kao. 2017. IKM at SemEval-2017 Task 8: Convolutional Neural Networks for Stance Detection and Rumor Verification. In *Proceedings of SemEval*. ACL.

Leon Derczynski and Kalina Bontcheva. 2014. Pheme: Veracity in digital social networks. In *UMAP Workshops*.

Omar Enayet and Samhaa R. El-Beltagy. 2017. NileTMRG at SemEval-2017 Task 8: Determining Rumour and Veracity Support for Rumours on Twitter. In *Proceedings of SemEval*. ACL.

Marianela García Lozano, Hanna Lilja, Edward Tjörnhammar, and Maja Maja Karasalo. 2017. Mama Edha at SemEval-2017 Task 8: Stance Classification with CNN and Rules. In *Proceedings of SemEval*. ACL.

Aditi Gupta, Ponnurangam Kumaraguru, Carlos Castillo, and Patrick Meier. 2014. Tweetcred: Real-time credibility assessment of content on twitter. In *SocInfo*. pages 228–243. https://doi.org/10.1007/978-3-319-13734-6_16.

Alfred Hermida. 2012. Tweets and truth: Journalism as a discipline of collaborative verification. *Journalism Practice* 6(5-6):659–668.

Elena Kochkina, Maria Liakata, and Isabelle Augenstein. 2017. Turing at SemEval-2017 Task 8: Sequential Approach to Rumour Stance Classification with Branch-LSTM. In *Proceedings of SemEval*. ACL.

KP Krishna Kumar and G Geethakumari. 2014. Detecting misinformation in online social networks using cognitive psychology. *Human-centric Computing and Information Sciences* 4(1):1–22.

Xiaomo Liu, Armineh Nourbakhsh, Quanzhi Li, Rui Fang, and Sameena Shah. 2015. Real-time rumor debunking on twitter. In *Proceedings of the 24th ACM International on Conference on Information and Knowledge Management*. ACM, pages 1867–1870.

Michal Lukasik, Trevor Cohn, and Kalina Bontcheva. 2015. Classifying tweet level judgements of rumours in social media. In *Proceedings of the Conference on Empirical Methods in Natural Language Processing*. volume 2, pages 2590–2595.

Saif M Mohammad, Svetlana Kiritchenko, Parinaz Sobhani, Xiaodan Zhu, and Colin Cherry. 2016. SemEval-2016 Task 6: Detecting Stance in Tweets. In *Proceedings of the Workshop on Semantic Evaluation*.

Alessandro Moschitti, Preslav Nakov, Lluis Marquez, Walid Magdy, James Glass, and Bilal Randeree. 2015. Semeval-2015 task 3: Answer selection in community question answering. *SemEval-2015* page 269.

Rob Procter, Jeremy Crump, Susanne Karstedt, Alex Voss, and Marta Cantijoch. 2013a. Reading the riots: What were the Police doing on Twitter? *Policing and Society* 23(4):413–436.

Rob Procter, Farida Vis, and Alex Voss. 2013b. Reading the riots on twitter: methodological innovation for the analysis of big data. *International journal of social research methodology* 16(3):197–214.

Vahed Qazvinian, Emily Rosengren, Dragomir R Radev, and Qiaozhu Mei. 2011. Rumor has it: Identifying misinformation in microblogs. In *Proceedings of the Conference on Empirical Methods in Natural Language Processing*. Association for Computational Linguistics, pages 1589–1599.

Chengcheng Shao, Giovanni Luca Ciampaglia, Alessandro Flammini, and Filippo Menczer. 2016. Hoaxy: A platform for tracking online misinformation. *arXiv preprint arXiv:1603.01511* .

Vikram Singh, Sunny Narayan, Md Shad Akhtar, Asif Ekbal, and Pushpak Bhattacharya. 2017. IITP at SemEval-2017 Task 8: A Supervised Approach for Rumour Evaluation. In *Proceedings of SemEval*. ACL.

Ankit Srivastava, Rehm Rehm, and Julian Moreno Schneider. 2017. DFKI-DKT at SemEval-2017 Task 8: Rumour Detection and Classification using Cascading Heuristics. In *Proceedings of SemEval*. ACL.

Zeynep Tufekci. 2014. Big questions for social media big data: Representativeness, validity and other methodological pitfalls. In *Proceedings of the AAAI International Conference on Weblogs and Social Media*.

Shari R Veil, Tara Buehner, and Michael J Palenchar. 2011. A work-in-process literature review: Incorporating social media in risk and crisis communication. *Journal of contingencies and crisis management* 19(2):110–122.

Feixiang Wang, Man Lan, and Yuanbin Wu. 2017. ECNU at SemEval-2017 Task 8: Rumour Evaluation Using Effective Features and Supervised Ensemble Models. In *Proceedings of SemEval*. ACL.

Qiao Zhang, Shuiyuan Zhang, Jian Dong, Jinhua Xiong, and Xueqi Cheng. 2015. Automatic detection of rumor on social network. In *Natural Language Processing and Chinese Computing*, Springer, pages 113–122.

Arkaitz Zubiaga, Ahmet Aker, Kalina Bontcheva, Maria Liakata, and Rob Procter. 2017. Detection and resolution of rumours in social media: A survey. *arXiv preprint arXiv:1704.00656* .

Arkaitz Zubiaga, Maria Liakata, Rob Procter, Kalina Bontcheva, and Peter Tolmie. 2015a. Crowdsourcing the annotation of rumourous conversations in social media. In *Proceedings of the 24th International Conference on World Wide Web: Companion volume*. International World Wide Web Conferences Steering Committee, pages 347–353.

Arkaitz Zubiaga, Maria Liakata, Rob Procter, Kalina Bontcheva, and Peter Tolmie. 2015b. Towards detecting rumours in social media. In *Proceedings of the AAAI Workshop on AI for Cities*.

Arkaitz Zubiaga, Maria Liakata, Rob Procter, Geraldine Wong Sak Hoi, and Peter Tolmie. 2016a. PHEME rumour scheme dataset: Journalism use case. doi:10.6084/m9.figshare.2068650.v1.

Arkaitz Zubiaga, Maria Liakata, Rob Procter, Geraldine Wong Sak Hoi, and Peter Tolmie. 2016b. Analysing how people orient to and spread rumours in social media by looking at conversational threads. *PLoS ONE* 11(3):1–29. https://doi.org/10.1371/journal.pone.0150989.

BIT at SemEval-2017 Task 1: Using Semantic Information Space to Evaluate Semantic Textual Similarity

Hao Wu, Heyan Huang,* **Ping Jian, Yuhang Guo, Chao Su**
Beijing Engineering Research Center of High Volume Language Information Processing
and Cloud Computing Applications, School of Computer Science,
Beijing Institute of Technology, Beijing, China
{wuhao123, hhy63, pjian, guoyuhang, suchao}@bit.edu.cn

Abstract

This paper presents three systems for semantic textual similarity (STS) evaluation at SemEval-2017 STS task. One is an unsupervised system and the other two are supervised systems which simply employ the unsupervised one. All our systems mainly depend on the *semantic information space* (SIS), which is constructed based on the semantic hierarchical taxonomy in WordNet, to compute non-overlapping information content (IC) of sentences. Our team ranked 2nd among 31 participating teams by the primary score of Pearson correlation coefficient (PCC) mean of 7 tracks and achieved the best performance on Track 1 (AR-AR) dataset.

1 Introduction

Given two snippets of text, semantic textual similarity (STS) measures the degree of equivalence in the underlying semantics. STS is a basic but important issue with multitude of application areas in natural language processing (NLP) such as example based machine translation (EBMT), machine translation evaluation, information retrieval (IR), question answering (QA), text summarization and so on.

The SemEval STS task has become the most famous activity for STS evaluation in recent years and the STS shared task has been held annually since 2012 (Agirre et al., 2012, 2013, 2014, 2015, 2016; Cer et al., 2017), as part of the SemEval/*SEM family of workshops. The organizers have set up publicly available datasets of sentence pairs with similarity scores from human annotators, which are up to more than 16,000

sentence pairs for training and evaluation, and attracted a large number of teams with a variety of systems to participate the competitions.

Generally, STS systems could be divided into two categories: One kind is unsupervised systems (Li et al., 2006; Mihalcea et al., 2006; Islam and Inkpen, 2008; Han et al., 2013; Sultan et al., 2014b; Wu and Huang, 2016), some of which are appeared for a long time when there wasn't enough training data; The other kind is supervised systems (Bär et al., 2012; Šarić et al., 2012; Sultan et al., 2015; Rychalska et al., 2016; Brychcín and Svoboda, 2016) applying machine learning algorithms, including deep learning, after adequate training data has been constructed. Each kind of methods has its advantages and application areas. In this paper, we present three systems, one unsupervised system and two supervised systems which simply make use of the unsupervised one.

2 Preliminaries

Following the standard argumentation of information theory, Resnik (1995) proposed the definition of the information content (IC) of a concept as follows:

$$IC(c) = -\log P(c), \tag{1}$$

where $P(c)$ refers to statistical frequency of concept c.

Since information content (IC) for multiple words, which sums the non-overlapping concepts IC, is a computational difficulties for knowledge based methods. For a long time, IC related methods were usually used as word similarity (Resnik, 1995; Jiang and Conrath, 1997; Lin, 1997) or word weight (Li et al., 2006; Han et al., 2013) rather than the core evaluation modules of sentence similarity methods (Wu and Huang, 2016).

---

*Corresponding author

Proceedings of the 11th International Workshop on Semantic Evaluations (SemEval-2017), pages 77–84,
Vancouver, Canada, August 3 - 4, 2017. ©2017 Association for Computational Linguistics

2.1 STS evaluation using SIS

To apply non-overlapping IC of sentences in STS evaluation, we construct the semantic information space (SIS), which employs the super-subordinate (is-a) relation from the hierarchical taxonomy of WordNet (Wu and Huang, 2016). The space size of a concept is the information content of the concept. SIS is not a traditional orthogonality multidimensional space, while it is the space with inclusion relation among concepts. Sentences in SIS are represented as a real physical space instead of a point in vector space.

We have the intuitions about similarity: The similarity between A and B is related to their commonality and differences, the more commonality and the less differences they have, the more similar they are; The maximum similarity is reached when A and B are identical, no matter how much commonality they share(Lin, 1998). The principle of Jaccard coefficient (Jaccard, 1908) is accordance with the intuitions about similarity and we define the similarity of two sentences S_a and S_b based on it:

$$sim\,(s_a, s_b) = \frac{IC\,(s_a \cap s_b)}{IC\,(s_a \cup s_b)}. \tag{2}$$

The quantity of the intersection of the information provided by the two sentences can be obtained through that of the union of them:

$$IC\,(s_a \cap s_b) = IC\,(s_a) + IC\,(s_b) - IC\,(s_a \cup s_b)\,. \tag{3}$$

So the remaining problem is how to compute the quantity of the union of non-overlapping information of sentences. We calculate it by employing the inclusion-exclusion principle from combinatorics for the total IC of sentence s_a and the same way is used for sentence s_b and both sentences:

$$
\begin{aligned}
IC\,(s_a) &= IC\left(\bigcup_{i=1}^{n} c_i^a\right) \\
&= \sum_{k=1}^{n} (-1)^{k-1} \sum_{1 \le i_1 < \cdots < i_k \le n} IC\left(c_{i_1}^a \cap \cdots \cap c_{i_k}^a\right).
\end{aligned} \tag{4}
$$

For the IC of n-concepts intersection in Equation (4), we use the following equation[1]:

[1] For the sake of high computational complexity introduced by Equation (4), we simplify the calculation of common IC of n-concepts and use the approximate formula in Equation (6). The accurate formula of common IC is:

$$commonIC\,(c_1, \cdots, c_n) = IC\left(\bigcap_{i=1}^{n} c_i\right) = IC\left(\bigcup_{j=1}^{m} c_j\right), \tag{5}$$

Algorithm 1: $getInExTotalIC(S)$

Input: $S : \{c_i | i = 1, 2, \ldots, n; n = |S|\}$

Output: tIC: Total IC of input S

1 **if** $S = \varnothing$ **then**
2   **return** 0

3 Initialize: $tIC \leftarrow 0$
4 **for** $i = 1; i \le n; i + + $ **do**
5   **foreach** $comb$ in $C(n, i)$-combinations **do**
6         $cIC \leftarrow commonIC\,(comb)$
7         $tIC + = (-1)^{i-1} \cdot cIC$

8 **return** tIC

$$
\begin{aligned}
commonIC\,(c_1, \cdots, c_n) &= IC\left(\bigcap_{i=1}^{n} c_i\right) \\
&\approx \max_{c \in subsum(c_1, \cdots, c_n)} [-\log P(c)],
\end{aligned} \tag{6}
$$

where, $subsum\,(c_1, \cdots, c_n)$ is the set of concepts that subsume all the concepts of $c_1, \cdots, c_n$ in SIS.

Algorithm 1 is according to Equation (4) and (6), here $C(n, i)$ is the number of combinations of i-concepts from n-concepts, $commonIC(comb)$ is calculated through Equation (6).

For more details about this section, please see the paper (Wu and Huang, 2016) for reference.

2.2 The Efficient Algorithm for Sentence IC

According to the Binomial Theorem, the amount of combinations for $commonIC(comb)$ calculation from Equation (4) is:

$$C\,(n, 1) + \cdots + C\,(n, n) = 2^n - 1. \tag{7}$$

Searching subsumers in the hierarchical taxonomy of WordNet is the most time-consuming operation. Define one time searching between concepts be the minimum computational unit. Considering searching subsumers among multiple concepts, the real computational complexity is more than $0 * C(n, 1) + 1 * C(n, 2) + \cdots + (n - 1) * C(n, n)$.

Note that the computational complexity through the inclusion-exclusion principle is more than $O(2^n)$. To decrease the computational complexity, we exploit the efficient algorithm for precise non-overlapping IC computing of sentences by making use of the thinking of the different set in hierarchical network (Wu and Huang,

---

where $c_j \in subsum\,(c_1, \cdots, c_n)$, m is the total number of c_j. We could see Equation.(4) and (5) are indirect recursion.

Algorithm 2: *getTotalIC(S)*

Input: S : $\{c_i | i = 1, 2, \ldots, n; n = |S|\}$

Output: tIC: Total IC of input S

1 **if** $S = \varnothing$ **then**
2 $\quad$ **return** 0

3 Initialize: $tIC \leftarrow 0, Root(0) \leftarrow \varnothing$
4 **for** $i = 1; i \le n; i + + $ **do**
5 $\quad$ $Intersect(i|i-1), Root(i) \leftarrow$
  $\quad$ $getIntersect(c_i, Root(i-1))$
6 $\quad$ $ICG \leftarrow$
  $\quad$ $IC(c_i) - getTotalIC(Intersect(i|i-1))$
7 $\quad$ $tIC+ = ICG$

8 **return** tIC

Algorithm 3: *getIntersect(c_i, Root(i − 1))*

Input: c_i, $Root(i-1)$

Output: $Intersect(i|i-1), Root(i)$

1 Initialize: get $Root(c_i)$ from WordNet
  $Intersect(i|i-1) \leftarrow \varnothing; Root(i) \leftarrow Root(i-1)$
2 **if** $Root(i) = \varnothing$ **then** $\qquad$ /* $i = 1$ */
3 $\quad$ $Root(i) \leftarrow Root(c_i)$
4 $\quad$ **return** $Intersect(i|i-1), Root(i)$

5 **foreach** $r_i \in Root(c_i)$ **do**
6 $\quad$ $pos \leftarrow depth(r_i) - 1$ /* $pos \Leftrightarrow$ root */
7 $\quad$ **foreach** $r_{i-1} \in Root(i-1)$ **do**
8 $\quad\quad$ $(p, q) \leftarrow$ deepest common node
  $\quad\quad$ position: p in r_i, q in r_{i-1}
9 $\quad\quad$ **if** $p = 0$ **then** $\qquad$ /* r_i in r_{i-1} */
10 $\quad\quad\quad$ add c_i to $Intersect(i|i-1)$
11 $\quad\quad\quad$ break the outer foreach loop

12 $\quad\quad$ **if** $q = 0$ **then** $\qquad$ /* r_{i-1} in r_i */
13 $\quad\quad\quad$ remove r_{i-1} from $Root(i)$

14 $\quad\quad$ **if** $p < pos$ **then** /* r_{i-1} intersect
  $\quad\quad$ at deeper node in r_i */
15 $\quad\quad\quad$ $pos \leftarrow p$

16 $\quad$ add r_i to $Root(i)$
17 $\quad$ add $c_{pos} \in r_i$ to $Intersect(i|i-1)$

18 **return** $Intersect(i|i-1), Root(i)$

2017): We add the words into the SIS one by one each time and sum the gain IC of $ICG(c_i)$ from the newly added concept c_i. For sentence $S = \{c_i | i = 1, 2, \ldots, n; n = |S|\}$, where c_i is the concept of the i-th concept in S, $|S|$ is concept count of S, the formula of $ICG(c_i)$ is as follows:

$$IC(S) = \sum_{i=1}^{n} ICG(c_i) \qquad (8)$$

For convenience in the expression of $ICG(c_i)$, we define some functions: $Root(c_i)$ indicates the set of paths, each path is the node list **from c_i to the root** in the nominal hierarchical taxonomy of WordNet. $Root(n)$ is the short form of $Root(c_1, \cdots, c_n)$. Formally, let $Set(p)$ be the set of nodes in path p, $Root(n) = \{p_k | \forall p_k \in Root(c_i), \nexists p_t \in Root(c_j), Set(p_k) \subseteq Set(p_t).i = 1, 2, \ldots, n; j = 1, 2, \ldots, n\}$. $|Root(c_i)|$ means the number of paths in $Root(c_i)$. $HSN(c_i)$ expresses the set of nodes in any of path in $Root(c_i)$. $HSN(n)$ is the short form of $HSN(c_1, \cdots, c_n)$, formally, $HSN(n) = \{c_k | c_k \in HSN(c_i).i = 1, 2, \ldots, n\}$.

Let $depth(c)$ be the max depth from concept c to the root. We define $Intersect(n + 1|n) = \{c_i | \forall c_i \in \{Set(p_t) \wedge HSN(n)\}, \nexists c_j \in \{Set(p_t) \wedge HSN(n)\}, depth(c_i) \le depth(c_j).p_t \in Root(c_{n+1}); t = 1, \cdots, |Root(c_{n+1})|\}$ and $totalIC(c_1, \cdots, c_n)$ is the quantity of total information of n-concepts. We have

$$ICG(C_i) = IC(c_i) - totalIC(Intersect(i|i-1)). \qquad (9)$$

Algorithm 2 and 3 are according to Equation (8) and (9). Algorithm 3 is approximately equal to one time subsumer searching between concepts, thus the computational complexity of Algorithm 2 is $O(n)$. This indicates SIS methods could be applied to any length of sentences even short paragraphs. The open source implementations of Algorithm 2 and 3 with related library are also available at GitHub[2].

Theoretical system with lemmas and theorems has been established for supporting the correctness of Equation (8) and (9). For more details about this section, please see the paper (Wu and Huang, 2017) for reference.

2.3 Increasing Word Recall Rate for SIS

We made three aspects improvements in our another previous work:

First, we utilize WordNet to directly obtain the nominal forms of a content word which is not a noun mainly through derivational pointers in WordNet. The word formation helps enhance the recall rate of known content words in sentence-to-SIS mappings. Second, name entity (NE) recognition tool (Manning et al., 2014) and the alignment

---

[2] https://github.com/hao123wu/STS

tool (Sultan et al., 2014a) are employed to obtain non-overlapping unknown NEs, which are used for simulating non-overlapping IC in SIS. The alignment tool is mainly used for finding actually same NEs with different string forms and inconsistent NE annotations by the NE recognition tool. Through the statistic values of known NEs of the same kinds from previous datasets, we simulate the IC of out-of-vocabulary NEs in SIS. Finally, sentence IC is augmented by word weights which could deem as the importance of words.

The above contents of this subsection is mainly based on the work which is currently under review.

3 System Overview

We submitted three systems: One is the unsupervised system of exploiting non-overlapping IC in SIS, the other two are supervised systems of making use of the methods of sentence alignment and word embedding respectively.

3.1 Preprocessing

First of all, we translated all the other languages into English by employing Google machine translation system[3] and preprocessed the test datasets with *tokenizer.perl* and *truecase.perl*, which are the tools from Moses machine translation toolkit (Koehn et al., 2007), then utilized the preprocessed datasets to do POS obtaining and lemmatization by utilizing NLTK (Bird, 2006), and finally made use of lemma to do sentence alignment (Sultan et al., 2014a) and name entity recognition (Manning et al., 2014). We use the lemma instead of the original word in all the situations where need words to participate for the consideration of simplicity.

We also developed a word spelling correction module based on Levenshtein distance which is special for the spelling mistakes in STS datasets. It proved important for the eventual performances in previous years, however, it was not so critical this year.

3.2 Run 1: Unsupervised SIS

Run 1 is from the unsupervised system constructed using the framework described in Section 2 and the implementation is as follows:

Word IC calculation employs Equation (1) and

---

the probability of a concept c is:

$$P(c) = \frac{\sum_{n \in words(c)} count(n)}{N} \tag{10}$$

where *words*(c) is the set of all the words contained in concept c **and its sub-concepts** in WordNet, N is the sum of frequencies of words contained in all the concepts in the hierarchy of semantic net. The word statistics are from British National Corpus (BNC) obtained by NLTK (Bird, 2006). Sentence IC computation applies Equation (9).

For the simplification, we choose the concept of a word with the minimal IC, which denotes the most common sense of a word, in all the circumstances of conversion of word-to-concept and the selection between two aligned words, instead of word sense disambiguation (WSD).

3.3 Run 2: Supervised IC and Alignment

As the aligner of Sultan et al. (2014a) is successfully applied in STS evaluation, we should leverage its advantage of finding potential word aligned pairs from both sentences, especially for different surface forms. However, we did not obtain the global inverse document frequency (IDF) data on time, thus we did not employ the aligner of Brychcín and Svoboda (2016), which is the improved version of Sultan et al. (2014a), that introduces IDF information of words in the similarity formula.

In this run, we use support vector machines (Chang and Lin, 2011) (SVM) for regression, more specifically sequential minimal optimization (Shevade et al., 2000) (SMO). There two features: One is the output of SIS, the other is that of unsupervised method of Sultan et al. (2015).

Actually, we tested some other regression methods. We found that LR and SVM always outperform the others. The tool for regression methods are implemented in WEKA (Hall et al., 2009).

3.4 Run 3: Supervised IC and Embeddings

Deep learning has become a hot topic in recent years and many supervised methods of STS incorporate deep learning models. At SemEval 2016 STS task, at least top 5 teams included deep learning modules according to incomplete statistics (Agirre et al., 2016).

In this run, we take advantage of the embeddings that obtained information from large scale

---

[3]http://translate.google.com

Track	Dataset	Total	GS Pairs
Track 1	Arabic-Arabic	250	250
Track 2	Arabic-English	250	250
Track 3	Spanish-Spanish	250	250
Track 4a	Spanish-English	250	250
Track 4b	Spanish-English-WMT	250	250
Track 5	English-English	250	250
Track 6	English-Turkish	500	250
Sum		2000	1750

Table 1: Test sets at SemEval 2017 STS task.

corpora and train the linear regression (LR) model. There two features: One is the outputs of SIS, the other is from a modified version of basic sentence embedding which is the simply combination of word embeddings.

The word embedding vectors are generated from word2vec (Mikolov et al., 2013) over the 5th edition of the Gigaword (LDC2011T07) (Parker et al., 2011). We also preprocess the Gigaword data with *tokenizer.perl* and *truecase.perl*. We modify this basic sentence embedding by importing domain IDF information. The domain IDFs of words could be obtained from the current test dataset by deeming each sentence as a document. We did not directly use the domain IDFs d as the weight of a word embedding. On previous datasets, we found $d^{0.8}$ as its weight performed nearly the best.

4 Data

SemEval 2017 STS task assesses the ability of systems to determine the degree of semantic similarity between monolingual and cross-lingual sentences in Arabic, English, Spanish and a surprise language of Turkish. The shared task is organized into a set of secondary sub-tracks and a single combined primary track. Each secondary sub-track involves providing STS scores for monolingual sentence pairs in a particular language or for cross-lingual sentence pairs from the combination of two particular languages. Participation in the primary track is achieved by submitting results for all of the secondary sub-tracks (Cer et al., 2017).

As shown in Table 1, the SemEval 2017 STS shared task contains 1750 pairs with gold standard (GS) out of total 2000 pairs from 7 different tracks. Systems were required to annotate all the pairs and performance was evaluated on all pairs or a subset with GS in the datasets. The GS for each pair ranges from 0 to 5, with the values indicating the corresponding interpretations:

5 indicates completely equivalence; 4 expresses mostly equivalent with differences only in some unimportant details; 3 means roughly equivalent but with differences in some important details; 2 means non-equivalence but sharing some details; 1 means the pairs only share the same topic; and 0 represents no overlap in similarity.

5 Evaluation

The evaluation metric is the Pearson product-moment correlation coefficient (PCC) between semantic similarity scores of machine assigned and human judgements. PCC is used for each individual test set, and the primary evaluation is measured by weighted mean of PCC on all datasets (Cer et al., 2017).

Performances of our three runs on each of SemEval 2017 STS test set are shown in Table 2. Bold numbers represents the best scores from any our system on each test set, including the primary scores. *Cosine Baseline* utilizes basic sentence embedding method for monolingual similarity (Track 1, 3 and 5) provided officially by STS organizers; *Best system* denotes all the scores are from the state-of-the-art system; *All Systems Best* means the best scores from all the systems participated in each track, regardless of whether they come from the same system; *Differences* indicates the differences between the best scores from our three systems and *All Single Best* in each track, primary difference is between our best system and state-of-the-art system. *Team Rankings* show the rankings of our best scores from that of other teams. *Team Rankings* of Primary could be the most important ranking for participants who submitted scores for all tracks.

Our team ranked 2nd for the primary score and achieved the best performance in Track 1 (Arabic-Arabic). Track 1 is the only track that totally employed new languages which has no references from the past (cross-lingual evaluation contains English sentences).

The very failing performance is in Track 4b. We guess the reasons could be the followings and further research is needed on this issue:

1) Our methods, especially for unsupervised SIS, ignore some important information as the embedding methods and are currently not suit for complicated post-editing sentences. We tested basic sentence embedding method in isolation which could achieve the score of more than 0.16,

	Primary	Track 1	Track 2	Track 3	Track 4a	Track 4b	Track 5	Track 6
Run 1	0.6703	0.7535	**0.7007**	0.8323	0.7813	0.0758	0.8161	**0.7327**
Run 2	0.6662	**0.7543**	0.6953	0.8289	0.7761	0.0584	0.8222	0.7280
Run 3	**0.6789**	0.7417	0.6965	**0.8499**	**0.7828**	**0.1107**	**0.8400**	0.7305
Cosine Baseline	0.5370	0.6045	0.5155	0.7117	0.6220	0.0320	0.7278	0.5456
Best System	0.7316	0.7440	0.7493	0.8559	0.8131	0.3363	0.8518	0.7706
All Single Best	-	0.7543	0.7493	0.8559	0.8302	0.3407	0.8547	0.7706
Differences	5.3%	-0.8%	4.9%	0.6%	4.7%	23.0%	1.5%	3.8%
Team Rankings	2	1	2	2	3	14	4	2

Table 2: Performances on SemEval 2017 STS evaluation datasets.

much better than our IC based systems of Run 1 (0.0758) and Run 2 (0.0584),which are without embedding modules.

2) The translation quantity for long sentences by machine translation may be not good enough as that for short sentences. The translation results may lose some information in the original sentences for SIS and introduce more noise.

6 STS benchmark

In order to provide a standard benchmark to compare among the state-of-the-art in Semantic Textual Similarity for English, the organizers of SemEval STS tasks are already setting a leaderboard this year which includes results of some selected systems. The benchmark comprises a selection of the English datasets used in the STS tasks in the context of SemEval from 2012 to 2017 and it is organized into train, development and test (Cer et al., 2017).

Our systems are selected by the organizers to submit the results for STS benchmark. We employ the models that described above, but a small difference is in Run 3: $d^{0.9}$ was used as the weights of word embeddings, which could achieve the best performance of cosine similarity from the summed word embeddings in isolation. As our models need not tune hyperparameters, the train part is used for tuning parameters and training models while the development part and the test part are used for the testing of the final systems. Table 3 shows the performances of our systems.

From the table we could see Run 3 provides the best performance in benchmark, which is in accordance with the results in SemEval 2017 STS task. Our best system ranks 2nd at present. More details about STS benchmark and the real-time leaderboard could be find in the official website[4].

---

[4]http://ixa2.si.ehu.es/stswiki/index.php/STSbenchmark

Set	Size	Run 1	Run 2	Run 3
Development	1500	0.8194	0.8240	**0.8291**
Test	1379	0.7942	0.7962	**0.8085**

Table 3: Performances of runs on STS benchmark.

7 Conclusions

At SemEval 2017 STS task, we introduced a unsupervised knowledge based method, SIS, which could be new at SemEval. SIS is the extension of information content for STS evaluation. The performance of SIS is pretty good on STS test sets for it's just a new unsupervised method with room to improve. Currently, our main concern is how to gain the information contained in word embeddings, which may be lost in knowledge based SIS, and combine it with SIS to improve STS performance.

Acknowledgments

The work described in this paper is mainly supported by National Programs for Fundamental Research and Development of China (973 Program) under Grant 2013CB329303.

The authors would like to thank Daniel Cer and Eneko Agirre for their insightful comments to the improvement in technical contents and paper presentation.

References

Eneko Agirre, Carmen Banea, Claire Cardie, Daniel Cer, Mona Diab, Aitor Gonzalez-Agirre, Weiwei Guo, Inigo Lopez-Gazpio, Montse Maritxalar, Rada Mihalcea, German Rigau, Larraitz Uria, and Janyce Wiebe. 2015. SemEval-2015 Task 2: Semantic Textual Similarity, English, Spanish and Pilot on Interpretability. In *Proceedings of the 9th International Workshop on Semantic Evaluation (SemEval 2015)*. Association for Computational Linguistics, pages 252–263. https://doi.org/10.18653/v1/S15-2045.

Eneko Agirre, Carmen Banea, Claire Cardie, Daniel

Cer, Mona Diab, Aitor Gonzalez-Agirre, Weiwei Guo, Rada Mihalcea, German Rigau, and Janyce Wiebe. 2014. SemEval-2014 Task 10: Multilingual Semantic Textual Similarity. In *Proceedings of the 8th International Workshop on Semantic Evaluation (SemEval 2014)*. Association for Computational Linguistics, pages 81–91. https://doi.org/10.3115/v1/S14-2010.

Eneko Agirre, Carmen Banea, Daniel Cer, Mona Diab, Aitor Gonzalez-Agirre, Rada Mihalcea, German Rigau, and Janyce Wiebe. 2016. SemEval-2016 Task 1: Semantic Textual Similarity, Monolingual and Cross-Lingual Evaluation. In *Proceedings of the 10th International Workshop on Semantic Evaluation (SemEval-2016)*. Association for Computational Linguistics, pages 497–511. https://doi.org/10.18653/v1/S16-1081.

Eneko Agirre, Daniel Cer, Mona Diab, and Aitor Gonzalez-Agirre. 2012. SemEval-2012 Task 6: A Pilot on Semantic Textual Similarity. In **SEM 2012: The First Joint Conference on Lexical and Computational Semantics – Volume 1: Proceedings of the main conference and the shared task, and Volume 2: Proceedings of the Sixth International Workshop on Semantic Evaluation (SemEval 2012)*. Association for Computational Linguistics, pages 385–393. http://aclweb.org/anthology/S12-1051.

Eneko Agirre, Daniel Cer, Mona Diab, Aitor Gonzalez-Agirre, and Weiwei Guo. 2013. *SEM 2013 shared task: Semantic Textual Similarity. In *Second Joint Conference on Lexical and Computational Semantics (*SEM), Volume 1: Proceedings of the Main Conference and the Shared Task: Semantic Textual Similarity*. Association for Computational Linguistics, pages 32–43. http://aclweb.org/anthology/S13-1004.

Daniel Bär, Chris Biemann, Iryna Gurevych, and Torsten Zesch. 2012. Ukp: Computing semantic textual similarity by combining multiple content similarity measures. In **SEM 2012: The First Joint Conference on Lexical and Computational Semantics – Volume 1: Proceedings of the main conference and the shared task, and Volume 2: Proceedings of the Sixth International Workshop on Semantic Evaluation (SemEval 2012)*. Association for Computational Linguistics, pages 435–440. http://aclweb.org/anthology/S12-1059.

Steven Bird. 2006. NLTK: The Natural Language Toolkit. In *Proceedings of the COLING/ACL 2006 Interactive Presentation Sessions*. Association for Computational Linguistics, pages 69–72. http://aclweb.org/anthology/P06-4018.

Tomáš Brychcín and Lukáš Svoboda. 2016. UWB at SemEval-2016 Task 1: Semantic Textual Similarity using Lexical, Syntactic, and Semantic Information. In *Proceedings of the 10th International Workshop on Semantic Evaluation (SemEval-2016)*. Association for Computational Linguistics, pages 588–594. https://doi.org/10.18653/v1/S16-1089.

Daniel Cer, Mona Diab, Eneko Agirre, Inigo Lopez-Gazpio, and Lucia Specia. 2017. Semeval-2017 task 1: Semantic textual similarity multilingual and crosslingual focused evaluation. In *Proceedings of the 11th International Workshop on Semantic Evaluation (SemEval-2017)*. Association for Computational Linguistics, Vancouver, Canada, pages 1–14. http://www.aclweb.org/anthology/S17-2001.

Chih-Chung Chang and Chih-Jen Lin. 2011. LIBSVM: a library for support vector machines. *ACM Transactions on Intelligent Systems and Technology (TIST)* 2(3):27.

Mark Hall, Eibe Frank, Geoffrey Holmes, Bernhard Pfahringer, Peter Reutemann, and Ian H Witten. 2009. The weka data mining software: an update. *ACM SIGKDD explorations newsletter* 11(1):10–18.

Lushan Han, Abhay L. Kashyap, Tim Finin, James Mayfield, and Jonathan Weese. 2013. UMBC_EBIQUITY-CORE: Semantic Textual Similarity Systems. In *Second Joint Conference on Lexical and Computational Semantics (*SEM), Volume 1: Proceedings of the Main Conference and the Shared Task: Semantic Textual Similarity*. Association for Computational Linguistics, pages 44–52. http://aclweb.org/anthology/S13-1005.

Aminul Islam and Diana Inkpen. 2008. Semantic text similarity using corpus-based word similarity and string similarity. *ACM Transactions on Knowledge Discovery from Data (TKDD)* 2(2):10.

Paul Jaccard. 1908. *Nouvelles recherches sur la distribution florale*.

Jay J Jiang and David W Conrath. 1997. Semantic similarity based on corpus statistics and lexical taxonomy. In *Proceedings of International Conference Research on Computational Linguistics (ROCLING X)*.

Philipp Koehn, Hieu Hoang, Alexandra Birch, Chris Callison-Burch, Marcello Federico, Nicola Bertoldi, Brooke Cowan, Wade Shen, Christine Moran, Richard Zens, Chris Dyer, Ondrej Bojar, Alexandra Constantin, and Evan Herbst. 2007. Moses: Open Source Toolkit for Statistical Machine Translation. In *Proceedings of the 45th Annual Meeting of the Association for Computational Linguistics Companion Volume Proceedings of the Demo and Poster Sessions*. Association for Computational Linguistics, pages 177–180. http://aclweb.org/anthology/P07-2045.

Yuhua Li, David McLean, Zuhair A Bandar, James D O'shea, and Keeley Crockett. 2006. Sentence similarity based on semantic nets and corpus statistics. *IEEE Transactions on Knowledge and Data Engineering* 18(8):1138–1150.

Dekang Lin. 1997. Using Syntactic Dependency as Local Context to Resolve Word Sense Ambiguity. In *35th Annual Meeting of the*

Association for Computational Linguistics. http://aclweb.org/anthology/P97-1009.

Dekang Lin. 1998. An information-theoretic definition of similarity. In *ICML*. Citeseer, volume 98, pages 296–304.

Christopher Manning, Mihai Surdeanu, John Bauer, Jenny Finkel, Steven Bethard, and David McClosky. 2014. The Stanford CoreNLP Natural Language Processing Toolkit. In *Proceedings of 52nd Annual Meeting of the Association for Computational Linguistics: System Demonstrations*. Association for Computational Linguistics, pages 55–60. https://doi.org/10.3115/v1/P14-5010.

Rada Mihalcea, Courtney Corley, and Carlo Strapparava. 2006. Corpus-based and knowledge-based measures of text semantic similarity. In *AAAI*. volume 6, pages 775–780.

Tomas Mikolov, Kai Chen, Greg Corrado, and Jeffrey Dean. 2013. Efficient estimation of word representations in vector space. *arXiv preprint arXiv:1301.3781* .

Robert Parker, David Graff, Junbo Kong, Ke Chen, and Kazuaki Maeda. 2011. English gigaword fifth edition ldc2011t07, 2011. *URL https://catalog. ldc. upenn. edu/LDC2011T07.[Online]* .

Philip Resnik. 1995. Using information content to evaluate semantic similarity in a taxonomy. *International Joint Conference on Artificial Intelligence (IJCAI)* .

Barbara Rychalska, Katarzyna Pakulska, Krystyna Chodorowska, Wojciech Walczak, and Piotr Andruszkiewicz. 2016. Samsung poland nlp team at semeval-2016 task 1: Necessity for diversity; combining recursive autoencoders, wordnet and ensemble methods to measure semantic similarity. In *Proceedings of the 10th International Workshop on Semantic Evaluation (SemEval-2016)*. Association for Computational Linguistics, pages 602–608. https://doi.org/10.18653/v1/S16-1091.

Frane Šarić, Goran Glavaš, Mladen Karan, Jan Šnajder, and Bojana Dalbelo Bašić. 2012. Takelab: Systems for measuring semantic text similarity. In **SEM 2012: The First Joint Conference on Lexical and Computational Semantics – Volume 1: Proceedings of the main conference and the shared task, and Volume 2: Proceedings of the Sixth International Workshop on Semantic Evaluation (SemEval 2012)*. Association for Computational Linguistics, pages 441–448. http://aclweb.org/anthology/S12-1060.

Shirish Krishnaj Shevade, S Sathiya Keerthi, Chiranjib Bhattacharyya, and Karaturi Radha Krishna Murthy. 2000. Improvements to the smo algorithm for svm regression. *IEEE transactions on neural networks* 11(5):1188–1193.

Arafat Md Sultan, Steven Bethard, and Tamara Sumner. 2014a. Back to Basics for Monolingual Alignment: Exploiting Word Similarity and Contextual Evidence. *Transactions of the Association of Computational Linguistics* 2:219–230. http://aclweb.org/anthology/Q14-1018.

Arafat Md Sultan, Steven Bethard, and Tamara Sumner. 2014b. DLS@CU: Sentence Similarity from Word Alignment. In *Proceedings of the 8th International Workshop on Semantic Evaluation (SemEval 2014)*. Association for Computational Linguistics, pages 241–246. https://doi.org/10.3115/v1/S14-2039.

Arafat Md Sultan, Steven Bethard, and Tamara Sumner. 2015. DLS@CU: Sentence Similarity from Word Alignment and Semantic Vector Composition. In *Proceedings of the 9th International Workshop on Semantic Evaluation (SemEval 2015)*. Association for Computational Linguistics, pages 148–153. https://doi.org/10.18653/v1/S15-2027.

Hao Wu and Heyan Huang. 2016. Sentence similarity computational model based on information content. *IEICE TRANSACTIONS on Information and Systems* 99(6):1645–1652.

Hao Wu and Heyan Huang. 2017. Efficient algorithm for sentence information content computing in semantic hierarchical network. *IEICE TRANSACTIONS on Information and Systems* 100(1):238–241.

ConceptNet at SemEval-2017 Task 2: Extending Word Embeddings with Multilingual Relational Knowledge

Robert Speer
Luminoso Technologies, Inc.
675 Massachusetts Avenue
Cambridge, MA 02139
`rspeer@luminoso.com`

Joanna Lowry-Duda
Luminoso Technologies, Inc.
675 Massachusetts Avenue
Cambridge, MA 02139
`jlowry-duda@luminoso.com`

Abstract

This paper describes Luminoso's participation in SemEval 2017 Task 2, "Multilingual and Cross-lingual Semantic Word Similarity", with a system based on ConceptNet. ConceptNet is an open, multilingual knowledge graph that focuses on general knowledge that relates the meanings of words and phrases. Our submission to SemEval was an update of previous work that builds high-quality, multilingual word embeddings from a combination of ConceptNet and distributional semantics. Our system took first place in both subtasks. It ranked first in 4 out of 5 of the separate languages, and also ranked first in all 10 of the cross-lingual language pairs.

1 Introduction

ConceptNet 5 (Speer and Havasi, 2013) is a multilingual, domain-general knowledge graph that connects words and phrases of natural language (*terms*) with labeled, weighted edges. Compared to other knowledge graphs, it avoids trying to be a large gazetteer of named entities. It aims most of all to cover the frequently-used words and phrases of every language, and to represent generally-known relationships between the meanings of these terms.

The paper describing ConceptNet 5.5 (Speer et al., 2017) showed that it could be used in combination with sources of distributional semantics, particularly the word2vec Google News skip-gram embeddings (Mikolov et al., 2013) and GloVe 1.2 (Pennington et al., 2014), to produce new embeddings with state-of-the-art performance across many word-relatedness evaluations. The three data sources are combined using an extension of the technique known as retrofitting (Faruqui et al.,

2015). The result is a system of pre-computed word embeddings we call "ConceptNet Numberbatch".

The system we submitted to SemEval-2017 Task 2, "Multilingual and Cross-lingual Semantic Word Similarity", is an update of that system, coinciding with the release of version 5.5.3 of ConceptNet[1]. We added multiple fallback methods for assigning vectors to out-of-vocabulary words. We also experimented with, but did not submit, systems that used additional sources of word embeddings in the five languages of this SemEval task.

This task (Camacho-Collados et al., 2017) evaluated systems at their ability to rank pairs of words by their semantic similarity or relatedness. The words are in five languages: English, German, Italian, Spanish, and Farsi. Subtask 1 compares pairs of words within each of the five languages; subtask 2 compares pairs of words that are in different languages, for each of the ten pairs of distinct languages.

Our system took first place in both subtasks. Detailed results for our system appear in Section 3.4.

2 Implementation

The way we built our embeddings is based on retrofitting (Faruqui et al., 2015), and in particular, the elaboration of it we call "expanded retrofitting" (Speer et al., 2017). Retrofitting, as originally described, adjusts the values of existing word embeddings based on a new objective function that also takes a knowledge graph into account. Its output has the same vocabulary as its input. In expanded retrofitting, on the other hand, terms that are only present in the knowledge graph are added to the vocabulary and are also assigned

---

[1]Data and code are available at `http://conceptnet.io`.

Proceedings of the 11th International Workshop on Semantic Evaluations (SemEval-2017), pages 85–89,
Vancouver, Canada, August 3 - 4, 2017. ©2017 Association for Computational Linguistics

vectors.

2.1 Combining Multiple Sources of Vectors

As described in the ConceptNet 5.5 paper (Speer et al., 2017), we apply expanded retrofitting separately to multiple sources of embeddings (such as pre-trained word2vec and GloVe), then align the results on a unified vocabulary and reduce its dimensionality.

First, we make a unified matrix of embeddings, M_1, as follows:

- Take the subgraph of ConceptNet consisting of nodes whose degree is at least 3. Remove edges corresponding to negative relations (such as *NotUsedFor* and *Antonym*). Remove phrases with 4 or more words.

- Standardize the sources of embeddings by case-folding their terms and L_1-normalizing their columns.

- For each source of embeddings, apply expanded retrofitting over that source with the subgraph of ConceptNet. In each case, this provides vectors for a vocabulary of terms that includes the ConceptNet vocabulary.

- Choose a unified vocabulary (described below), and look up the vectors for each term in this vocabulary in the expanded retrofitting outputs. If a vector is missing from the vocabulary of a retrofitted output, fill in zeroes for those components.

- Concatenate the outputs of expanded retrofitting over this unified vocabulary to give M_1.

2.2 Vocabulary Selection

Expanded retrofitting produces vectors for all the terms in its knowledge graph and all the terms in the input embeddings. Some terms from outside the ConceptNet graph have useful embeddings, representing knowledge we would like to keep, but using all such terms would be noisy and wasteful.

To select the vocabulary of our term vectors, we used a heuristic that takes advantage of the fact that the pre-computed word2vec and GloVe embeddings we used have their rows (representing terms) sorted by term frequency.

To find appropriate terms, we take all the terms that appear in the first 500,000 rows of both the word2vec and GloVe inputs, and appear in the first 200,000 rows of at least one of them. We take the union of these with the terms in the ConceptNet subgraph described above. The resulting vocabulary, of 1,884,688 ConceptNet terms plus 99,869 additional terms, is the vocabulary we use in the system we submitted and its variants.

2.3 Dimensionality Reduction

The concatenated matrix M_1 has k columns representing features that may be redundant with each other. Our next step is to reduce its dimensionality to a smaller number k', which we set to 300, the dimensionality of the largest input matrix. Our goal is to learn a projection from k dimensions to k' dimensions that removes the redundancy that comes from concatenating multiple sources of embeddings.

We sample 5% of the rows of M_1 to get M_2, which we will use to find the projection more efficiently, assuming that its vectors represent approximately the same distribution as M_1.

M_2 can be approximated with a truncated SVD: $M_2 \approx U\Sigma^{1/2}V^T$, where Σ is truncated to a $k' \times k'$ diagonal matrix of the k' largest singular values, and U and V are correspondingly truncated to have only these k' columns.

U is a matrix mapping the same vocabulary to a smaller set of features. Because V is orthonormal, $U\Sigma$ is a rotation and truncation of the original data, where each feature contributes the same amount of variance as it did in the original data. $U\Sigma^{1/2}$ is a version that removes some of the variance that came from redundant features, and also is analogous to the decomposition used by Levy et al. (2015) in their SVD process.

We can solve for the operator that projects M_2 into $U\Sigma^{1/2}$:

$$U\Sigma^{1/2} \approx M_2 V \Sigma^{-1/2}$$

$V\Sigma^{-1/2}$ is therefore a $k \times k'$ operator that, when applied on the right, projects vectors from our larger space of features to our smaller space of features. It can be applied to any vector in the space of M_1, not just the ones we sampled. $M_3 = M_1 V \Sigma^{-1/2}$ is the projection of the selected vocabulary into k' dimensions, which is the matrix of term vectors that we output and evaluate.

2.4 Don't Take "OOV" for an Answer

Published evaluations of word embeddings can be inconsistent about what to do with out-of-vocabulary (OOV) words, those words that the system has learned no representation for. Some evaluators, such as Bojanowski et al. (2016), discard all pairs containing an OOV word. This makes different systems with different vocabularies difficult to compare. It enables gaming the evaluation by limiting the system's vocabulary, and gives no incentive to expand the vocabulary.

This SemEval task took a more objective position: no word pairs may be discarded. Every system must submit a similarity value for every word pair, and "OOV" is no excuse. The organizers recommended using the midpoint of the similarity scale as a default.

In our previous work with ConceptNet, we eliminated one possible cause of OOV terms. A term that is outside of the selected vocabulary, perhaps because its degree in ConceptNet is too low, can still be assigned a vector. When we encounter a word with no computed vector, we look it up in ConceptNet, find its neighbors, and take the average of whatever vectors those neighboring terms have. This approximates the vector the term would have been assigned if it had participated in retrofitting. If the term has no neighbors with vectors, it remains OOV.

For this SemEval task, we recognized the importance of minimizing OOV terms, and implemented two additional fallback strategies for the terms that are still OOV.

It is unavoidable that training data in non-English languages will be harder to come by and sparser than data in English. It is also true that some words in non-English languages are borrowed directly from English, and are therefore exact cognates for English words.

As such, we used a simple strategy to further increase the coverage of our non-English vocabularies: if a term is not associated with a vector in matrix M_3, we first look up the vector for the term that is spelled identically in English. If that vector is present, we use it.

This method is in theory vulnerable to false cognates, such as the German word *Gift* (meaning "poison"). However, false cognates tend to appear among common words, not rare ones, so they are unlikely to use this fallback strategy. Our German embeddings do contain a vector for "Gift", and it is similar to English "poison", not English "gift".

As a second fallback strategy, when a term cannot be found in its given language or in English,

we look for terms in the vocabulary that have the given term as a prefix. If we find none of those, we drop a letter from the end of the unknown term, and look for that as a prefix. We continue dropping letters from the end until a result is found. When a prefix yields results, we use the mean of all the resulting vectors as the word's vector.

3 Results

In this task, systems were scored by the harmonic mean of their Pearson and Spearman correlation with the test set for each language (or language pair in Subtask 2). Systems were assigned aggregate scores, averaging their top 4 languages on Subtask 1 and their top 6 pairs on Subtask 2.

3.1 The Submitted System: ConceptNet + word2vec + GloVe

The system we submitted applied the retrofitting-and-merging process described above, with ConceptNet 5.5.3 as the knowledge graph and two well-regarded sources of English word embeddings. The first source is the word2vec Google News embeddings[2], and the second is the GloVe 1.2 embeddings that were trained on 840 billion tokens of the Common Crawl[3].

Because the input embeddings are only in English, the vectors in other languages depended entirely on propagating these English embeddings via the multilingual links in ConceptNet.

This system appears in the results as "Luminoso-run2". Run 1 was similar, but it was looking up neighbors in an unreleased version of the ConceptNet graph with fewer edges from DBPedia in it.

This system's aggregate score on subtask 1 was 0.743. Its combined score on subtask 2 (averaged over its six best language pairs) was 0.754.

3.2 Variant A: Adding Polyglot Embeddings

Instead of relying entirely on English knowledge propagated through ConceptNet, it seemed reasonable to also include pre-calculated word embeddings in other languages as inputs. In Variant A, we added inputs from the Polyglot embeddings (Al-Rfou et al., 2013) in German, Spanish, Italian, and Farsi as four additional inputs to the retrofitting-and-merging process.

---

[2]https://code.google.com/archive/p/
word2vec/
[3]http://nlp.stanford.edu/projects/
glove/

The results of this variant on the trial data were noticeably lower, and when we evaluate it on the test data in retrospect, its test results are lower as well. Its aggregate scores are .720 on subtask 1 and .736 on subtask 2.

3.3 Variant B: Adding Parallel Text from OpenSubtitles

In Variant B, we calculated our own multilingual distributional embeddings from word co-occurrences in the OpenSubtitles2016 parallel corpus (Lison and Tiedemann, 2016), and used this as a third input alongside word2vec and GloVe.

For each pair of aligned subtitles among the five languages, we combined the language-tagged words into a single set of n words, then added $1/n$ to the co-occurrence frequency of each pair of words, yielding a sparse matrix of word co-occurrences within and across languages. We then used the SVD-of-PPMI process described by Levy et al. (2015) to convert these sparse co-occurrences into 300-dimensional vectors.

On the trial data, this variant compared inconclusively to Run 2. We submitted Run 2 instead of Variant B because Run 2 was simpler and seemed to perform slightly better on average.

However, when we run variant B on the released test data, we note that it would have scored better than the system we submitted. Its aggregate scores are .759 on subtask 1 and .767 on subtask 2.

3.4 Comparison of Results

The released results[4] show that our system, listed as Luminoso-Run2, got the highest aggregate score on both subtasks, and the highest score on each test set except the monolingual Farsi set.

Table 1 compares the results per language of the system we submitted, the same system without our OOV-handling strategies, variants A and B, and the baseline Nasari (Camacho-Collados et al., 2016) system.

Variant B performed the best in the end, so we will incorporate parallel text from OpenSubtitles in the next release of the ConceptNet Numberbatch system.

4 Discussion

The idea of producing word embeddings from a combination of distributional and relational

[4] http://alt.qcri.org/semeval2017/
task2/index.php?id=results

Eval.	Base	Ours	−OOV	Var. A	Var. B
en	.683	.789	.747	.778	**.796**
de	.513	.700	.599	.673	**.722**
es	.602	.743	.611	.716	**.761**
it	.597	.741	.606	.711	**.756**
fa	.412	.503	.363	.506	**.541**
Score 1	.598	.743	.641	.720	**.759**
en-de	.603	.763	.696	.749	**.767**
en-es	.636	.761	.675	.752	**.778**
en-it	.650	.776	.677	.759	**.786**
en-fa	.519	.598	.502	.590	**.634**
de-es	.550	.728	.620	.704	**.747**
de-it	.565	.741	.612	.722	**.757**
de-fa	.464	.587	.501	.586	**.610**
es-it	.598	.753	.613	.732	**.765**
es-fa	.493	.627	.482	.623	**.646**
it-fa	.497	.604	.474	.599	**.635**
Score 2	.598	.754	.649	.736	**.767**

Table 1: Evaluation scores by language. "Score 1" and "Score 2" are the combined subtask scores. "Base" is the Nasari baseline, "Ours" is Luminoso-Run2 as submitted, "−OOV" removes our OOV strategy, and "Var. A" and "Var. B" are the variants we describe in this paper.

knowldedge has been implemented by many others, including Iacobacci et al. (2015) and various implementations of retrofitting (Faruqui et al., 2015). ConceptNet is distinguished by the large improvement in evaluation scores that occurs when it is used as the source of relational knowledge. This indicates that ConceptNet's particular blend of crowd-sourced, gamified, and expert knowledge is providing valuable information that is not learned from distributional semantics alone.

The results transfer well to other languages, showing ConceptNet's usefulness as "multilingual glue" that can combine knowledge in multiple languages into a single representation.

Our submitted system relies heavily on interlanguage links in ConceptNet that represent direct translations, as well as exact cognates. We suspect that this makes it perform particularly well at directly-translated English. It would have more difficulty determining the similarity of words that lack direct translations into English that are known or accurate. This is a weak point of many current word-similarity evaluations: The words that are vague when translated, or that have language-specific connotations, tend not to appear.

On a task with harder-to-translate words, we may have to rely more on observing the distributional semantics of corpus text in each language, as we did in the unsubmitted variants.

References

Rami Al-Rfou, Bryan Perozzi, and Steven Skiena. 2013. Polyglot: Distributed word representations for multilingual NLP. In *Proceedings of the Seventeenth Conference on Computational Natural Language Learning*. Association for Computational Linguistics, Sofia, Bulgaria, pages 183–192. http://www.aclweb.org/anthology/W13-3520.

Piotr Bojanowski, Edouard Grave, Armand Joulin, and Tomas Mikolov. 2016. Enriching word vectors with subword information. *arXiv preprint arXiv:1607.04606* https://arxiv.org/pdf/1607.04606.

Jose Camacho-Collados, Mohammad Taher Pilehvar, Nigel Collier, and Roberto Navigli. 2017. SemEval-2017 Task 2: Multilingual and cross-lingual semantic word similarity. In *Proceedings of SemEval*. Vancouver, Canada.

José Camacho-Collados, Mohammad Taher Pilehvar, and Roberto Navigli. 2016. Nasari: Integrating explicit knowledge and corpus statistics for a multilingual representation of concepts and entities. *Artificial Intelligence* 240:36–64.

Manaal Faruqui, Jesse Dodge, Sujay K. Jauhar, Chris Dyer, Eduard Hovy, and Noah A. Smith. 2015. Retrofitting word vectors to semantic lexicons. In *Proceedings of NAACL*. http://arxiv.org/abs/1411.4166.

Ignacio Iacobacci, Mohammad Taher Pilehvar, and Roberto Navigli. 2015. SensEmbed: Learning sense embeddings for word and relational similarity. In *ACL (1)*. pages 95–105.

Omer Levy, Yoav Goldberg, and Ido Dagan. 2015. Improving distributional similarity with lessons learned from word embeddings. *Transactions of the Association for Computational Linguistics* 3:211–225. http://www.aclweb.org/anthology/Q15-1016.

Pierre Lison and Jörg Tiedemann. 2016. OpenSubtitles2016: Extracting large parallel corpora from movie and TV subtitles. In *Proceedings of the 10th International Conference on Language Resources and Evaluation*.

Tomas Mikolov, Kai Chen, Greg Corrado, and Jeffrey Dean. 2013. Efficient estimation of word representations in vector space. *CoRR* abs/1301.3781. http://arxiv.org/abs/1301.3781.

Jeffrey Pennington, Richard Socher, and Christopher D Manning. 2014. GloVe: Global vectors for word representation. *Proceedings of the Empiricial Methods in Natural Language Processing (EMNLP 2014)* 12:1532–1543. http://www-nlp.stanford.edu/pubs/glove.pdf.

Robert Speer, Joshua Chin, and Catherine Havasi. 2017. ConceptNet 5.5: An open multilingual graph of general knowledge. San Francisco. http://arxiv.org/abs/1612.03975.

Robert Speer and Catherine Havasi. 2013. ConceptNet 5: A large semantic network for relational knowledge. In *The People's Web Meets NLP*, Springer, pages 161–176.

IIT-UHH at SemEval-2017 Task 3: Exploring Multiple Features for Community Question Answering and Implicit Dialogue Identification

Titas Nandi[1], **Chris Biemann**[2], **Seid Muhie Yimam**[2],
Deepak Gupta[1], **Sarah Kohail**[2], **Asif Ekbal**[1] and **Pushpak Bhattacharyya**[1]

[1]Indian Institute of Technology Patna
[2]Universität Hamburg Germany
{titas.ee13,deepak.pcs16,asif,pb}@iitp.ac.in
{biemann,yimam,kohail}@informatik.uni-hamburg.de

Abstract

In this paper we present the system for Answer Selection and Ranking in Community Question Answering, which we build as part of our participation in SemEval-2017 Task 3. We develop a Support Vector Machine (SVM) based system that makes use of textual, domain-specific, word-embedding and topic-modeling features. In addition, we propose a novel method for dialogue chain identification in comment threads. Our primary submission *won* subtask C, outperforming other systems in all the primary evaluation metrics. We performed well in other English subtasks, ranking *third* in subtask A and *eighth* in subtask B. We also developed open source toolkits for all the three English subtasks by the name cQARank[1].

1 Introduction

This paper presents the system built for participation in the SemEval-2017 Shared Task 3 on Community Question Answering (CQA). The task aims to classify and rank a candidate text c in relevance to a target text t. Based on the nature of the candidate and target texts, the main task is subdivided into three subtasks in which the teams are expected to solve the problem of Question-Comment similarity, Question-Question similarity and Question-External Comment similarity (Nakov et al., 2017).

In this work, we propose a rich feature-based system for solving these problems. We create an architecture which integrates textual, semantic and domain-specific features to achieve good results in the proposed task. Due to the extremely noisy nature of the social forum data, we also develop a

customized preprocessing pipeline, rather than using the standard tools. We use Support Vector Machine (SVM) (Cortes and Vapnik, 1995) for classification, and its confidence score for ranking.

We initially define a generic set of features to develop a robust system for all three subtasks, then include additional features based on the nature of the subtasks. To adapt the system to subtasks B and C, we include features extracted from the scores of the other subtasks, propagating meaningful information essential in an incremental setting. We propose a novel method for identification of dialogue groups in the comment thread by constructing a user interaction graph and also incorporate features from this graph in our system. Our algorithm outputs mutually disjoint groups of users who are involved in conversation with each other in the comment thread.

The rest of the paper is organized as follows: Section 2 describes the related work. Sections 3, 4, and 5 elucidate the system architecture, features used and algorithms developed. Section 6 provides experimentation details and reports the official results.

2 Related Work

In Question Answering, answer selection and ranking has been a major research concern in Natural Language Processing (NLP) during the past few years. The problem becomes more interesting for Community Question Answering due to the highly unstructured and noisy nature of the data. Also, domain knowledge plays a major role in such an environment, where meta data of users and context based learning can capture trends well. The task on Community Question Answering in SemEval began in 2015, where the objective was to classify comments in a thread as *Good*, *Bad* or *PotentiallyUseful*. In subsequent years, the task

---

[1]https://github.com/TitasNandi/cQARank

Proceedings of the 11th International Workshop on Semantic Evaluations (SemEval-2017), pages 90–97,
Vancouver, Canada, August 3 - 4, 2017. ©2017 Association for Computational Linguistics

was extended and modified to focus on ranking and duplicate question detection in a cross domain setting.

In their 2015 system, Belinkov (2015) used word vectors of the question and of the comment, various text-based similarities and meta data features. Nicosia (2015) derived features from a comment in the context of the entire thread. They also modelled potential dialogues by identifying interlacing comments between users. Establishing similarity between Questions and External comments (subtask C) is quite challenging, which can be tackled by propagating useful context and information from other subtasks. Filice (2016) introduced an interesting approach of stacking classifiers across subtasks and Wu & Lan (2016) proposed a method of reducing the errors that propagated as a result of this stacking.

3 System Description

3.1 System Pipeline

The system architecture of our submission to subtask A is depicted in Figure 1. We explain the pre-processing pipeline in the next subsection. The cleaned data is fed into our supervised machine learning framework. We train our word-embedding model on the unannotated and training data[2] provided by the organizers, and train a probabilistic topic model on the training data. The detailed description of features is provided in the following section. After obtaining the feature vectors, we perform feature selection using wrapper methods to maximize the accuracy on the development set. We Z-score normalize the feature vectors and feed them to a SVM. We tune the hyperparameters of SVM and and generate classification labels and probabilities, the latter being used for computing the MAP score.

3.2 Preprocessing Pipeline

Due to the highly unstructured, spelling and grammatical error-prone nature of the data, adaptation of any standard tokenization pipeline was not well motivated. We customized the preprocessing according to the nature of the data. We unescaped HTML special characters and removed URLs, e-mails, HTML tags, image description tags, punctuations and slang words (from a defined dictionary). Finally, we expanded apostrophe words and

---

[2]http://alt.qcri.org/semeval2017/
task3/index.php?id=data-and-tools

removed stopwords.

The cleaned data is then used in all further experiments.

4 Features

We use a rich set of features to capture the textual and semantic relevance between two snippets of text. These features are categorized into several broad classes:

4.1 String Similarity Features

This set of features makes use of a number of string matching algorithms to compute the string similarity between the question and comment. This generates a continuous set of values for every comment, and is apt for a baseline system. The bag of algorithms used is a careful combination of various string similarity, metric distances and normalized string distance methods, capturing the overall profiling of texts. The string similarity functions used include Longest Common Subsequence (LCS), Q-Gram ($q = 1,2,3$), Weighted Levenshtein and Optimal String Alignment. The normalized similarity algorithms used are Jaro-Winkler, Normalized Levenshtein, n-gram ($n = 1,2,3$), cosine-similarity ($n = 1,2,3$), Jaccard Index ($n = 1,2,3$), and Sorensen-Dice coefficient ($n = 1,2,3$). The metric distance methods implemented are Levenshtein, Damerau, and Metric LCS.

4.2 Word Embedding Features

Semantic features constitute the core of our feature engineering pipeline. These try to capture the proximity between the meanings encoded in the word sequences of question and comments. We train word embeddings using Word2Vec (Mikolov et al., 2013) on the unannotated and given training data. The unannotated data is in the same format as the training data, except that the comments are not annotated. We performed experiments with different vector sizes ($N = 100, 200, 300$), and finally settled on using 100 dimensional word vectors. We also used a pre-trained model on *Google News* dataset in order to compare the performance of the two models. Interestingly, the domain-specific model trained on the unannotated and training data proved to be better than the one trained on Google News dataset, hence we used the former in building our final system.

Since we wanted a feature vector corresponding to each comment in the thread, we had to transform

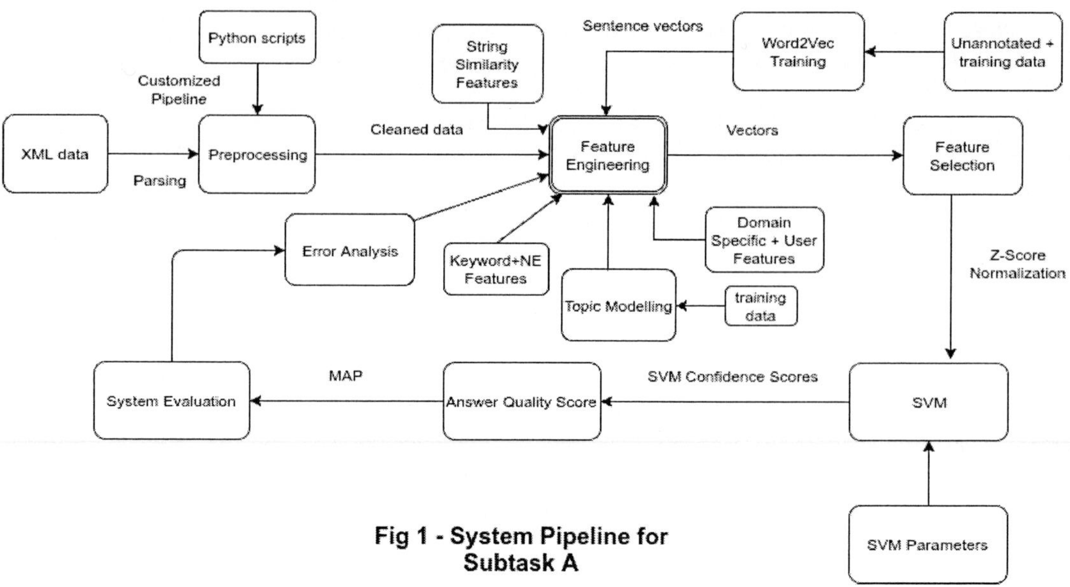

Fig 1 - System Pipeline for Subtask A

these trained word vectors into sentence vectors. Two approaches were considered for this:

- Construct the sentence vector by taking an average of the vectors of all words that constitute the sentence.
- Construct the sentence vector as a weighted average of all the word vectors constituting that sentence. Here the weight corresponds to the *Inverse Document Frequency* (IDF) value of the word in the thread.

Although the first approach has an evident disadvantage of not assigning importance to the keywords in the sentence (which is why we resorted to the IDF-based weighted averaging), it yielded better results, which is why we included it in our final system.

We extract two sets of features from these sentence vectors:

- The vector subtraction of the comment vector from the vector of the question at the head of the thread is used as the scoring vector for that comment.
- We calculate the cosine similarity, Euclidean and Manhattan distances between question and comment vectors.

4.3 Topic Modeling Features

To capture the thematic similarity between the question and comment texts, we train a LDA topic model on the training data using Mallet (McCallum, 2002). We perform different experiments by varying the number of topics ($n = 10, 20, 50, 100$) and obtain the best performance with 20 topics. We generate a topic vocabulary of 50 words for each topic class. The following features were entailed from these topic distributions and words:

- The vector subtraction of question and comment topic vectors, measuring the topical distance between the two snippets of text.
- Cosine, Euclidean and Manhattan distance between the topic vectors.
- We generate a vocabulary for each text by taking the union of topic words of its first 10 most probable topic classes.

$$\text{Vocabulary}(T) = \bigcup_{i=1}^{10} topic\_words(t_i)$$

where each t_i represents one of the top 10 topic classes for comment or question T.

We then determine the word overlap of the topic vocabulary of the question with *(i)* the entire comment string and *(ii)* the topic vocabulary of the comment.

4.4 Domain Specific Features

In CQA sites, comments in a thread typically reflect an underlying discussion about a question, and there is usually a strong correlation among the nearby comments in the thread. Users reply to each other, ask for further details, can acknowledge others' answers or can tease other users. Therefore, as discussed in (Barrón-Cedeño et al., 2015), comments in a common thread are strongly interconnected.

We extract various features from the meta data of the thread and from our surface observation of the thread's structure and properties. We extract if the comment is written by the asker of the question. In the case of repeated comments by the asker, we monitor if the comment is an acknowledgement (*thanks*, *thank you*, *appreciate*) or a further question. With the likely assumption that the comments at the beginning of a thread will be more relevant to the question, we have a feature capturing the position of comment in the thread. We also compute the coverage (the ratio of the number of tokens) of question by the comment and comment by the question.

We further try to model explicit conversations among users in the thread. We do it in two ways:

- Repeated and interlacing comments by a user in the same thread
- Explicitly mentioning the name of some previous user in the comment

The case of implicit dialogues (where the intent of the conversation has to be inferred solely from the context of the comment by a user) is discussed in a separate section later. These domain-specific features proved to be quite effective in classification, and thus form an integral part of our system.

4.5 Keyword and Named Entity Features

Finding the focus of the question and comment is important in measuring if the comment specifically covers the aspects of the question. We extract keywords from the texts using the RAKE keyword extraction algorithm (Rose et al., 2010), and derive features from the keyword match between question and comment. We also use the relative importance of common keywords as feature values.

In case of factoid questions, or especially in subtask B, *Named Entity Recognition* becomes an important tool for computing the relevance of a text. We extract named entities using the Stanford Named Entity Recognizer (Finkel et al., 2005) and classify words into seven entity categories including PERSON, LOCATION, ORGANIZATION, DATE, MONEY, PERCENT, and TIME. We compute if both question and comment have named entities, and if these belong to the same classes, if the named entity is an answer to a *Wh-type* question or not.

4.6 Implicit Dialogue Identification

Data driven error analysis on the *Qatar Living Data* indicated the presence of implicit dialogue chains. Users were almost always engaging in conversations with each other but this could only be captured by the content of their comment. Here we propose a novel algorithm based on construction of a user interaction graph to model these potential dialogues. The components of our construction are as follows:

- **Vertices** - Users in the comment thread and the Question
- **Edges** - Directed edges showing interaction
- **Edge Weights** - Numerical estimate of the interaction

Algorithm 1 Dialogue Group Detection

1: **Initialize:**
    $U \to$ User Graph   ▷ Initially Empty
    $D \to$ Dialogue Graph   ▷ Initially Empty
    $Q \to$ Question node   ▷ Node indexed 0
2: **procedure** DIALOGUE IDENTIFICATION
3:    $V(U) \leftarrow V(U) \cup \{Q\}$ ▷ Add Q to vertex set of U
4:    **for** each comment c_x in thread **do**
5:       u_i commented c_x
6:       **if** u_i is a new user **then**
7:          $V(U) \leftarrow V(U) \cup \{u_i\}$
8:          $V(D) \leftarrow V(D) \cup \{u_i\}$
9:       **end if**
10:      **for** Q and each previous comment c_y **do**
11:         u_j commented c_y
12:         **if** $i \neq j$ and e_{ij} doesn't exist in $E(U)$ **then**
13:            Add e_{ij} in $E(U)$ ▷ Add e_{ij} in edge set of U
14:         **end if**
15:         $w(e_{ij}) \leftarrow$ Compute_Weight(c_x, c_y, i, j)
16:      **end for**
17:      $e \leftarrow max_j \; w(e_{ij})$ ▷ Pick max outgoing edge
18:      **if** $j \neq 0$ and e does not exist in $E(D)$ **then**
19:         Add e in $E(D)$
20:      **end if**
21:    **end for**
22:    Find weakly connected components in D
23: **end procedure**

The algorithm to construct this dynamic graph is given in Algorithm 1. We simultaneously construct two graphs, a user graph and a dialogue graph. Initially, the user graph has the question node and the dialogue graph is empty. We add new users to the graphs according to the timestamp of their occurrence in the thread. For each new comment, we add edges to each previous user and the question, in the user graph for the user who commented. Then we pick the maximum outgoing edge to some previous user from the user who commented, and add that edge in the dialogue graph. Finally, we find the *weakly connected components* (WCCs) in the dialogue graph and the users in each such WCC are in mutual dialogue. Note that the user graph at the end of each iteration depicts the current conversational interaction of the user who commented, with respect to all other users in the thread.

Algorithm 2 Compute Weight Function

1: **procedure** COMPUTE_WEIGHT(c_x, c_y, i, j)
2:      u_i commented c_x
3:      u_j commented c_y
4:      $e_{ij} \leftarrow 0.0$
5:      **if** user u_i explicitly mentions user u_j in comment **then**
6:          $e_{ij} \leftarrow e_{ij} + 1.0$ ▷ Explicit dialogue
7:      **end if**
8:      $c_x \rightarrow \{w_1, w_2, ..., w_k\}$ ▷ w_i is the ith word in c_x
9:      $c_y \rightarrow \{w'_1, w'_2, ..., w'_l\}$
10:     $tr\_score \leftarrow (\sum_{1 \leq m \leq k} \max_{1 \leq n \leq l} cos(\vec{v_{w_m}}, \vec{v_{w'_n}}))/k$
11:     $\vec{t_x} \leftarrow$ topic vector for c_x
12:     $\vec{t_y} \leftarrow$ topic vector for c_y
13:     $to\_score \leftarrow cos(\vec{t_x}, \vec{t_y})$ ▷ Topic similarity score
14:     $e_{ij} \leftarrow e_{ij} + tr\_score + to\_score$ ▷ Edge weight
15:     **return** e_{ij}
16: **end procedure**

The main part of the algorithm is where we compute the edge weights between a pair of users after some comment, see Algorithm 2 for details. We have three components that constitute the weight:

- if the user mentions the other user explicitly
- we calculate the score of reformulating one comment from the other by closest word match based on cosine scores of word vectors (*tr_score*)
- cosine of the topic vectors of a pair of comments (*to_score*)

In addition to identifying latent dialogue groups, we also extract features from this graph and these features prove to be very helpful in classification.

4.7 Classifier

We use an SVM classifier as implemented in Lib-SVM (Chang and Lin, 2011) for classification. We experiment with different kernels (Hsu et al., 2003), and achieve the best results with the RBF kernel, which we use to train the model for our primary submission. We also achieve comparable re-sults with the linear kernel and L2-regularized logistic regression. The ranking score for a question-comment pair in subtask A is the calculated probability of the pair to be classified as *Good*.

The ranking score for subtask B is the SVM probability score for the original question-related question pair multiplied by the reciprocal search engine rank provided in the data.

For subtask C, the scoring value is the sum of the log probabilities of the SVM scores of all subtasks

$$final\_score = \log(svm\_A) + \log(svm\_B) + \log(svm\_C)$$

5 Stacking features for other subtasks

We implemented a generic system for tackling semantic similarity for any two snippets of text. We further fine tuned it with domain specific features for subtask A. For subtasks B and C, we again adopted this generic system with slight modifications. But, the strong interconnectivity and incremental nature of the subtasks motivated the development of a stacking strategy where we propagate useful information from other subtasks as features for the present subtask and re-run the classifier. Filice (2016) developed a stacking strategy that we adopt with modifications.

For subtask B, we consider the scores for subtasks A and C as probability distributions and calculate various features and correlation coefficients (*Spearmann, Kendall, Pearson*) over these distributions.

For subtask C, we calculate feature values from the SVM scores of all three subtasks, and re-run our system with these stacking features. These features include average, minimum and maximum of subtask A and B scores, and binary features capturing if these probability scores are above 0.5.

6 Experimentation and Results

We extensively experimented with a lot of feature engineering. Notable features that were discarded in the feature ablation process are:

- **Statistical Paraphrasing**: We found the top 10 semantically related words corresponding to every word in the comment, based on word vectors and did an n-gram matching ($n = 1,2,3$) on the extended wordlist.

- **Doc2Vec**: We also used Doc2Vec (Le and Mikolov, 2014) to generate sentence vectors directly, but these degraded the results.

Features	Development Set 2017						
Subtask A	**MAP**	**AvgRec**	**MRR**	**P**	**R**	**F1**	**Accuracy**
All Features	*65.50*	*84.86*	*71.96*	*58.43*	*62.71*	*60.50*	*72.54*
All — string features	65.53	84.90	72.19	57.84	62.71	60.18	72.17
All — embedding features	62.11	81.23	69.00	53.03	53.42	53.23	68.52
All — domain features	61.85	81.06	69.80	54.46	54.52	54.49	69.47
All — topic features	65.15	84.79	72.37	59.02	61.98	60.47	72.83
All — keyword features	65.73	84.65	71.94	57.98	62.59	60.20	72.25
IR Baseline	*53.84*	*72.78*	*63.13*	-	-	-	-
Subtask B							
All Features	*73.03*	*88.77*	*78.33*	*72.39*	*45.33*	*55.75*	*69.20*
All — string features	73.46	88.83	78.95	72.87	43.93	54.81	69.00
All — embedding features	73.91	89.11	79.33	71.53	45.79	55.84	69.00
All — domain features	73.07	88.77	78.33	71.77	41.59	52.66	68.00
All — topic features	72.95	88.07	78.17	67.86	44.39	53.67	67.20
All — keyword features	73.55	88.99	79.33	72.93	45.33	55.91	69.40
All — stacking features	72.95	88.64	78.67	71.90	40.65	51.94	67.80
IR Baseline	*71.35*	*86.11*	*76.67*	-	-	-	-
Subtask C							
All Features	*36.09*	*41.13*	*39.89*	*18.42*	*37.10*	*24.62*	*84.32*
All — string features	36.85	40.27	39.72	16.81	35.07	22.72	83.54
All — embedding features	39.39	45.09	45.01	17.48	47.83	25.60	80.82
All — domain features	36.83	40.68	39.69	17.21	35.07	23.09	83.88
All — topic features	35.89	41.18	40.50	16.98	38.84	23.63	82.68
All — keyword features	35.39	41.17	38.57	18.58	37.97	24.95	84.24
All — stacking features	36.57	41.85	40.80	16.80	36.81	23.07	83.06
IR Baseline	*30.65*	*34.55*	*35.97*	-	-	-	-
Runs	Test Set 2017						
Subtask A	**MAP**	**AvgRec**	**MRR**	**P**	**R**	**F1**	**Accuracy**
Primary	*86.88*	*92.04*	*91.20*	*73.37*	*74.52*	*73.94*	*72.70*
Contrastive 1	86.35	91.74	91.40	79.42	51.94	62.80	68.02
Contrastive 2	85.24	91.37	90.38	81.22	57.65	67.43	71.06
IR Baseline	*72.61*	*79.32*	*82.37*	-	-	-	-
Subtask B							
Primary	*43.12*	*79.23*	*47.25*	*26.85*	*71.17*	*38.99*	*58.75*
Contrastive 1	42.29	78.41	46.40	32.66	59.51	42.17	69.77
Contrastive 2	42.38	78.59	46.82	32.99	59.51	42.45	70.11
IR Baseline	*41.85*	*77.59*	*46.42*	-	-	-	-
Subtask C							
Primary	*15.46*	*33.42*	*18.14*	*08.41*	*51.22*	*14.44*	*83.03*
Contrastive 1	15.43	33.78	17.52	09.45	54.07	16.08	84.23
Contrastive 2	14.00	30.53	14.65	05.98	85.37	11.17	62.06
IR Baseline	*09.18*	*21.72*	*10.11*	-	-	-	-

Table 1: Feature Ablation Results on Development Set and Runs on Test Set

Our primary submission for subtasks A and B uses SVM with an RBF kernel for classification as this yielded the best results on the dev set. We also achieved similar results with the linear and L2-regularized logistic regression classifiers and we use these for our contrastive submissions. All the submissions comprised of same number of features. For subtask C, we oversample the training data using the SMOTE (Chawla et al., 2002) technique in the ImbalancedLearn[3] toolkit, due to the highly skewed distribution of labels. We use regular SMOTE for our primary and SMOTE SVM for our first contrastive submission. For the sec-

ond contrastive submission, we integrate the feature sets of subtasks A and B directly in the feature set of subtask C.

The feature ablation results on the development set and the results of different runs on the test set are presented in Table 1. It reports the system performance on all evaluation metrics including Mean Average Precision (*MAP*), Average Recall (*AvgRec*), Mean Reciprocal Rank (*MRR*), Precision (*P*), Recall (*R*), F1-score (*F1*) and Accuracy.

7 Conclusion

We establish the importance of domain specific and dialogue identification features in tackling the given task. In future work, we would like to fo-

[3]https://github.com/
scikit-learn-contrib/imbalanced-learn

cus on extracting more information from inter-comment dependencies. This should improve our algorithm for dialogue group detection and model conversational activity better. We also wish to work on a Deep Learning architecture for handling this, as in (Wu and Lan, 2016) and (Guzmán et al., 2016). The problem can be modeled as a semi-supervised classification task, where the unanno-tated data can help supervised classification. Sub-task C still presents a challenging research prob-lem and we will investigate novel methods to in-tegrate results from other subtasks to tackle this subtask better.

References

Alberto Barrón-Cedeño, Simone Filice, Giovanni Da San Martino, Shafiq Joty, Lluís Màrquez, Preslav Nakov, and Alessandro Moschitti. 2015. Thread-Level Information for Comment Classification in Community Question Answering. In *Proceedings of the 53rd Annual Meeting of the Association for Computational Linguistics and the 7th International Joint Conference on Natural Language Processing (Volume 2: Short Papers)*. Association for Compu-tational Linguistics, Beijing, China, pages 687–693. http://www.aclweb.org/anthology/P15-2113.

Yonatan Belinkov, Mitra Mohtarami, Scott Cyphers, and James Glass. 2015. VectorSLU: A Continu-ous Word Vector Approach to Answer Selection in Community Question Answering Systems. In *Pro-ceedings of the 9th International Workshop on Se-mantic Evaluation (SemEval 2015)*. Association for Computational Linguistics, Denver, Colorado, pages 282–287. http://www.aclweb.org/anthology/S15-2048.

Chih-Chung Chang and Chih-Jen Lin. 2011. LIBSVM: A library for support vector machines. *ACM TIST* 2(3):27:1–27:27. https://doi.org/10.1145/1961189.1961199.

Nitesh V. Chawla, Kevin W. Bowyer, Lawrence O. Hall, and W. Philip Kegelmeyer. 2002. SMOTE: synthetic minority over-sampling technique. *Jour-nal of artificial intelligence research* 16:321–357.

Corinna Cortes and Vladimir Vapnik. 1995. Support-vector networks. *Machine learning* 20(3):273–297.

Simone Filice, Danilo Croce, Alessandro Moschitti, and Roberto Basili. 2016. KeLP at SemEval-2016 Task 3: Learning Semantic Relations be-tween Questions and Answers. In *Proceedings of the 10th International Workshop on Semantic Evaluation (SemEval-2016)*. Association for Com-putational Linguistics, San Diego, California, pages 1116–1123. http://www.aclweb.org/anthology/S16-1172.

Jenny Rose Finkel, Trond Grenager, and Christopher Manning. 2005. Incorporating Non-local Informa-tion into Information Extraction Systems by Gibbs Sampling. In *Proceedings of the 43rd Annual Meet-ing of the Association for Computational Linguis-tics (ACL'05)*. Association for Computational Lin-guistics, Ann Arbor, Michigan, pages 363–370. https://doi.org/10.3115/1219840.1219885.

Francisco Guzmán, Preslav Nakov, and Lluís Màrquez. 2016. MTE-NN at SemEval-2016 Task 3: Can Machine Translation Evaluation Help Community Question Answering? In *Proceedings of the 10th International Workshop on Semantic Evalu-ation (SemEval-2016)*. Association for Computa-tional Linguistics, San Diego, California, pages 887–895. http://www.aclweb.org/anthology/S16-1137.

Chih-Wei Hsu, Chih-Chung Chang, and Chih-Jen Lin. 2003. A practical guide to support vec-tor classification. Technical report, Department of Computer Science, National Taiwan University. http://www.csie.ntu.edu.tw/ cjlin/papers.html.

Quoc V. Le and Tomas Mikolov. 2014. Dis-tributed Representations of Sentences and Docu-ments. In *Proceedings of the 31th International Conference on Machine Learning, ICML 2014, Bei-jing, China, 21-26 June 2014*. pages 1188–1196. http://jmlr.org/proceedings/papers/v32/le14.html.

Andrew Kachites McCallum. 2002. MAL-LET: A Machine Learning for Lan-guage Toolkit. Http://mallet.cs.umass.edu. http://mallet.cs.umass.edu.

Tomas Mikolov, Ilya Sutskever, Kai Chen, Gregory S. Corrado, and Jeffrey Dean. 2013. Distributed Representations of Words and Phrases and their Compositionality. In *Advances in Neural In-formation Processing Systems 26: 27th Annual Conference on Neural Information Processing Sys-tems 2013. Proceedings of a meeting held December 5-8, 2013, Lake Tahoe, Nevada, United States.*. pages 3111–3119. http://papers.nips.cc/paper/5021-distributed-representations-of-words-and-phrases-and-their-compositionality.

Preslav Nakov, Doris Hoogeveen, Lluís Màrquez, Alessandro Moschitti, Hamdy Mubarak, Timothy Baldwin, and Karin Verspoor. 2017. SemEval-2017 Task 3: Community Question Answering. In *Pro-ceedings of the 11th International Workshop on Se-mantic Evaluation*. Association for Computational Linguistics, Vancouver, Canada, SemEval '17.

Massimo Nicosia, Simone Filice, Alberto Barrón-Cedeno, Iman Saleh, Hamdy Mubarak, Wei Gao, Preslav Nakov, Giovanni Da San Martino, Alessan-dro Moschitti, Kareem Darwish, et al. 2015. QCRI: Answer selection for community question answering-experiments for Arabic and English. In *Proceedings of the 9th International Workshop on Semantic Evaluation, SemEval*. volume 15, pages 203–209.

Stuart Rose, Dave Engel, Nick Cramer, and Wendy Cowley. 2010. Automatic keyword extraction from individual documents. In Michael W. Berry and Jacob Kogan, editors, *Text Mining. Applications and Theory*, John Wiley and Sons, Ltd, pages 1–20. https://doi.org/10.1002/9780470689646.ch1.

Guoshun Wu and Man Lan. 2016. ECNU at SemEval-2016 Task 3: Exploring Traditional Method and Deep Learning Method for Question Retrieval and Answer Ranking in Community Question Answering. In *Proceedings of the 10th International Workshop on Semantic Evaluation (SemEval-2016)*. Association for Computational Linguistics, San Diego, California, pages 872–878. http://www.aclweb.org/anthology/S16-1135.

HumorHawk at SemEval-2017 Task 6: Mixing Meaning and Sound for Humor Recognition

David Donahue, Alexey Romanov, Anna Rumshisky
Dept. of Computer Science
University of Massachusetts Lowell
198 Riverside St, Lowell, MA 01854
`david_donahue@student.uml.edu`
`{aromanov, arum}@cs.uml.edu`

Abstract

This paper describes the winning system for SemEval-2017 Task 6: #HashtagWars: Learning a Sense of Humor. Humor detection has up until now been predominantly addressed using feature-based approaches. Our system utilizes recurrent deep learning methods with dense embeddings to predict humorous tweets from the @midnight show #HashtagWars. In order to include both meaning and sound in the analysis, GloVe embeddings are combined with a novel phonetic representation to serve as input to an LSTM component. The output is combined with a character-based CNN model, and an XGBoost component in an ensemble model which achieved 0.675 accuracy in the official task evaluation.

1 Introduction

Computational approaches to how humour is expressed in language have received relatively limited attention up until very recently. With few exceptions, they have used feature-based machine learning techniques (Zhang and Liu, 2014; Radev et al., 2015) drawing on hand-engineered features such as sentence length, the number of nouns, number of adjectives, and tf-idf-based LexRank (Erkan and Radev, 2004). Among the recent proposals, puns have been emphasized as a crucial component of humor expression (Jaech et al., 2016). Others have proposed that text is perceived as humorous when it deviates in some way from what is expected (Radev et al., 2015). One of the reasons for such dominant position of the feature-based approaches is the fact that the datasets have been relatively small, rendering deep learning methods ineffective. Furthermore, existing humour detection datasets tended to treat humor as a classification task in which text has to be labeled as funny or not funny, with nothing in between, which makes the task considerably simpler. In contrast, the #HashtagWars dataset (Potash et al., 2016b) provided for SemEval-2016 Task 6 assumes that humor can be evaluated on a scale, reflecting the reality that humor is non-binary and some things may be seen as funnier than others. It is also large in size, making it better suited to the application of deep learning techniques.

SemEval 2017 Task 6 used the tweets posted by the viewers of the Comedy Central's @midnight show, the #HashtagWars segment. Our team participated in subtask A, which was as follows: given a pair of tweets supplied for a given hashtag by the viewers, the goal was to identify the tweet that the show judged to be funnier (Potash et al., 2017). This paper describes the winning submission, and specifically, our systems that took first and second place in the official rankings for the task.

Our goal was to create a model that could represent both meaning and sound, thus covering different aspects of the tweet that might make it funny. Word embeddings have been used in a variety of applications, but phonetic information can provide new insights into the punchline of humor not present in traditional embeddings. The pronunciation of a sentence is important to the delivery of a punchline, and can connect sound-alike words.

In our first submission for Subtask A, semantic information for each word is provided to the model in the form of a GloVe embedding. We then provide the model with a novel phonetic representation of each word, in the form of a learned phonetic embedding taken as an intermediate state from an encoder-decoder character-to-phoneme model. With access to both meaning and

Proceedings of the 11th International Workshop on Semantic Evaluations (SemEval-2017), pages 98–102,
Vancouver, Canada, August 3 - 4, 2017. ©2017 Association for Computational Linguistics

sound embeddings, the model learns to read each tweet using a Long Short-Term Memory (LSTM) Recurrent Neural Network (RNN) encoder. The encoded state of each tweet passes into dense layers, where a prediction is made as to which tweet is funnier.

In addition to the embedding model described above, we construct a Convolutional Neural Network (CNN) to process each tweet character by character. This character-level model was used by Potash et al. (2016b), and serves as a baseline. The output of the CNN feeds into the same final dense layers as the embedding LSTM tweet encoders. This model achieved 63.7% accuracy in the official task evaluation, placing it second in the official task rankings.

To boost prediction performance further, we built an ensemble model over different model configurations. In addition to the model above, we provided an embedding-LSTM-only model and a character-CNN-only model as input to the ensemble. Inspired by previous work in NLP, we added an XGBoost feature-based model as input to the ensemble. This system was our second submission. The predictions of the ensemble model achieved 67.5% accuracy, placing it first in the official rankings for the task.

We also report experiments we conducted after the release of the test data, in which a few of the bugs present in the original submissions were addressed, and in which the best model achieves the accuracy of 68.3%.

2   Previous Work

Considerable research has gone into understanding the properties of humor in text. Radev et al. (2015) used a feature-bucket approach to analyze captions from the New Yorker Caption Contest. They noted that negative sentiment, human-centeredness and lexical centrality were their most important model features. Zhang and Liu (2014) trained a classifier using tweets that use the hashtag #Humor for positive examples. They concluded that tweet part-of-speech ratios are a major factor in humor detection. They also showed that sexuality and politics are popular topics in Twitter jokes that can boost humor perception. Jaech et al. (2016) and Miller and Turković (2016) explored the complicated nature of puns and their role in humor. Barbieri and Saggion (2014) explored the concept of irony in humor and used a large va-

riety of syntactic and semantic features to detect irony in tweets. To summarize, negative sentiment, human-centeredness, lexical centrality, syntax, puns, and irony represent just a few of many aspects that characterize humor in text.

The majority of attempts at humor detection, including those listed above, rely on hand-engineered features to distinguish humor from non-humor. However, recently deep learning strategies have also been employed. Chen and Lee (2017) used convolutional networks to make predictions on humorous/non-humorous sentences in a TED talk corpus. Bertero and Fung (2016) predicted punchlines using textual and audio features from the popular sitcom The Big Bang Theory. While feature-based solutions use linguistic properties of text to detect humour, our hope in experimenting with deep learning models for this task was that they could capture such properties in a more unstructured form, without pre-determined hand-engineered indicators.

3   System Description

In order to identify the funnier tweet in each pair, as required by the task setup, we build the following models:

- Character-to-Phoneme Model (C2P)
- Embedding Humor Model (EHM)
- Character Humor Model (CHM)
- Embedding/Character Joint Model (ECJM)
- XGBoost Feature-Based Model (XGBM)
- Ensemble Model (ENSEMBLE)

3.1   Character-to-Phoneme Model

In addition to understanding the meaning of each word in the sentence and how those meanings fit together, some words sound funnier to the ear than others. The sound of a sentence might also reveal the power of its punchline.

To give the model a representation of sound (i.e., pronunciation) for each word, we train an encoder-decoder LSTM model to convert a sequence of characters (via learned character embeddings) into a sequence of phonemes. Much like other sequence-to-sequence models, our model learns how to convert an English word into a sequence of phonemes that determine how that word is pronounced (see Figure 1).

We train and evaluate this model on the CMU Pronouncing Dictionary corpus (Lenzo, 2017), which contains mappings from each word to its

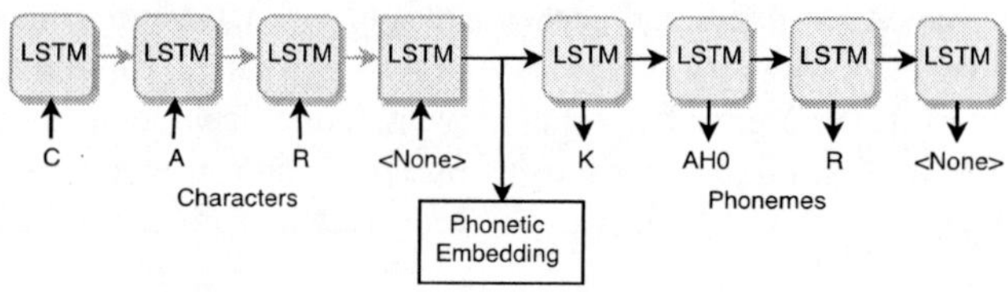

Figure 1: Character-to-Phoneme Model

corresponding phonemes. We use a 0.6/0.4 train-test split. Once the model is trained, we extract the intermediate embedding state (200 dim) between the encoder and decoder; this acts as a phonetic embedding, containing all information needed to pronounce the word. The resulting phonetic embedding for each word is concatenated with a semantic embedding to serve as the input for the embedding humor model (see below). Table 3.1 shows sample output of the model.

3.2   Embedding Humor Model

For both tweets in a tweet pair, a concatenation of a GloVe word embedding (Pennington et al., 2014) and phonetic embedding is processed by an LSTM encoder at each time-step (per word). We use word embeddings pre-trained on a Twitter corpus, available on the GloVe website[1]. Zero padding is added to the end of each tweet for a maximum length of 20 words/tweet. The output of each LSTM encoder (800 dim) is inserted into dense layers, and a binary classification decision is generated.

3.3   Character Humor Model

The character-based humor model processes each tweet as a sequence of characters with a CNN (Koushik, 2016). 30-dimensional embeddings are learned per character as input. The output of the CNN for both tweets in the pair are inserted into dense layers.

3.4   XGBoost Feature-Based Model

In order to approach the problem from a different prospective, in addition to the neural network-based systems described above, we constructed a feature-based model using XGBoost (Chen and Guestrin, 2016). In line with previous work (Radev et al., 2015; Zhang and Liu, 2014), we used the following features as input to the model:

1. Sentiment of each tweet in a pair, obtained with TwitterHawk, a state-of-the-art sentiment analysis system for Twitter (Boag et al., 2015).
2. Sentiment of the tokenized hashtag.
3. Length of each tweet in both tokens and characters (a very long tweet might not be funny)
4. Distance of the average GloVe embeddings of the tokens of the tweets to the global centroid of the embeddings of all tweets for the given hashtag.
5. Minimum, maximum and average distance from each token in a tweet to the hashtag.
6. Number of tokens belonging to the top-10 most frequent POS tags on the training data.

3.5   Embedding/Character Joint Model

The output of the embedding model LSTM encoders and the character model CNN encoders are fed into dense layers. For encoder input N, the three dense layers are of size $(3/4)N$, $(1/2)N$, and 1. Each layer gradually reduces dimensionality to final binary decision.

3.6   Ensemble Model

Inspired by the success of ensemble models in other tasks (Potash et al., 2016a; Rychalska et al., 2016) we built an ensemble model that combines the predictions of the character-based model, embedding-based model, the character/embedding joint humor model, and the feature-based XGBoost model to make the final prediction which incorporates different views of the input data. For the ensemble model itself, we use an XGBoost model again. Input predictions are obtained by using 5-fold cross-validation on the training data.

4   Results

Accuracies are calculated over three run average. Embedding/character models trained for five epochs with a learning rate of 1e-5 using the Adam optimizer (Kingma and Ba, 2014). Parameters are

---

[1]`https://nlp.stanford.edu/projects/glove/`

Word	Model Output	CMU Dictionary
rupard	R UW0 P ER0 D D	R UW1 P ER0 D
disabling	D AY1 S EY1 B L IH0 NG	D IH0 S EY1 B AH0 L IH0 NG
clipping	K L IH1 P IH0 NG	K L IH1 P IH0 NG
enfranchised	IH0 N F R AE1 N SH AY2 D D	EH0 N F R AE1 N CH AY2 Z D
eimer	AY1 M ER0	AY1 M ER0
dowel	D AW1 AH0 L	D AW1 AH0 L
vasilly	V AE1 S IH0 L IY0	V AH0 S IH1 L IY0

Table 1: Sample character-to-phoneme model output.

Model Configuration/Features	Trial Acc	Evaluation Acc	Official Evaluation Acc
ENSEMBLE	64.02%	65.99 %	**67.5%** (Run #2)
ECJM	59.31%	**68.30%**	63.7% (Run #1)
ECJM (GloVe-only)	64.42%	65.95%	
EHM	58.09%	67.56%	
EHM (GloVe-only)	**64.76%**	67.44%	
EHM (Phonetic-only)	54.55%	65.93%	
CHM	59.59%	63.52%	
XGBM	57.02%	60.35%	

Table 2: Model performance (accuracy). Official results reported for joint and ensemble models.

tuned to the trial set, which contained five hashtags. Train, trial and evaluation datasets were provided by task organizers, with the evaluation data containing six hashtags. Table 2 shows the results obtained by different models on the evaluation data. Note that the reported figures were obtained in additional experiments after a few of the bugs present in the original submission were addressed. For completeness, we also report the official results obtained by our system submissions (runs #1 and #2).

5 Discussion

The ensemble model performed the best during the official evaluation, placing it 1st among 10 runs, submitted by the 7 participating teams. Note that accuracies on evaluation hashtags are on average 5.36% higher than on trial hashtags (see Table 2). This suggests each dataset contains different hashtag types, and that the evaluation set more closely matches the training set. For example, phonetic embeddings reduce performance in the trial set and improve performance in the evaluation set. We hypothesize that phonetic embeddings are not important for some hashtags, and that the evaluation set contains more such hashtags .

While adding phonetic embeddings and/or the character model yields inconsistent results across the trial and evaluation sets, adding the GloVe representation produced the best scores for both datasets. From these results, token-based semantic knowledge appears to be the most important factor in humor recognition for this dataset. These results differ from that of Potash et al. (2016b), who report that a CNN-based character model achieves the highest accuracy on leave-one-out evaluation.

The character-to-phoneme model yields very interesting results upon testing. The model correctly classifies 75% of phonemes in the test set. As shown in Table 3.1, the model often guesses a similar-sounding phoneme in cases when the correct phoneme is not guessed. For example, in 'vasilly', AE1 is guessed instead of AH0.

6 Conclusion

The learned character embeddings achieved reasonable results on both trial and evaluation data. The incorporation of phonetic embeddings in humor prediction, on the other hand, appears to yield inconsistent performance across different hashtags. The ensemble model improved performance on the official data. Overall, GloVe embeddings consistently improved performance, highlighting the importance of lexical semantic information for this humour classification task.

References

Francesco Barbieri and Horacio Saggion. 2014. Automatic detection of irony and humour in twitter. In *Proceedings of the International Conference on Computational Creativity*.

Dario Bertero and Pascale Fung. 2016. Deep learning of audio and language features for humor prediction. In *International Conference on Language Resources and Evaluation (LREC)*.

William Boag, Peter Potash, and Anna Rumshisky. 2015. Twitterhawk: A feature bucket approach to sentiment analysis. *SemEval-2015* page 640.

Lei Chen and Chong MIn Lee. 2017. Convolutional neural network for humor recognition. *arXiv preprint arXiv:1702.02584* .

Tianqi Chen and Carlos Guestrin. 2016. Xgboost: A scalable tree boosting system. In *Proceedings of the 22Nd ACM SIGKDD International Conference on Knowledge Discovery and Data Mining*. ACM, pages 785–794.

Günes Erkan and Dragomir R Radev. 2004. Lexrank: Graph-based lexical centrality as salience in text summarization. *Journal of Artificial Intelligence Research* 22:457–479.

Aaron Jaech, Rik Koncel-Kedziorski, and Mari Ostendorf. 2016. Phonological pun-derstanding. In *Proceedings of NAACL-HLT*. pages 654–663.

Diederik Kingma and Jimmy Ba. 2014. Adam: A method for stochastic optimization. *arXiv preprint arXiv:1412.6980* .

Jayanth Koushik. 2016. Understanding convolutional neural networks. *arXiv preprint arXiv:1605.09081* .

Kevin Lenzo. 2017. The cmu pronouncing dictionary. https://doi.org/http://www.speech.cs.cmu.edu/cgi-bin/cmudict.

Tristan Miller and Mladen Turković. 2016. Towards the automatic detection and identification of english puns. *The European Journal of Humour Research* 4(1):59–75.

Jeffrey Pennington, Richard Socher, and Christopher D Manning. 2014. Glove: Global vectors for word representation. In *EMNLP*. volume 14, pages 1532–1543.

Peter Potash, William Boag, Alexey Romanov, Vasili Ramanishka, and Anna Rumshisky. 2016a. Simihawk at semeval-2016 task 1: A deep ensemble system for semantic textual similarity. *Proceedings of SemEval* pages 741–748.

Peter Potash, Alexey Romanov, and Anna Rumshisky. 2016b. # hashtagwars: Learning a sense of humor. *arXiv preprint arXiv:1612.03216* .

Peter Potash, Alexey Romanov, and Anna Rumshisky. 2017. SemEval-2017 Task 6: #HashtagWars: Learning a Sense of Humor. In *Proceedings of the 11th International Workshop on Semantic Evaluation (SemEval 2017)*. Association for Computational Linguistics.

Dragomir Radev, Amanda Stent, Joel Tetreault, Aasish Pappu, Aikaterini Iliakopoulou, Agustin Chanfreau, Paloma de Juan, Jordi Vallmitjana, Alejandro Jaimes, Rahul Jha, et al. 2015. Humor in collective discourse: Unsupervised funniness detection in the new yorker cartoon caption contest. *arXiv preprint arXiv:1506.08126* .

Barbara Rychalska, Katarzyna Pakulska, Krystyna Chodorowska, Wojciech Walczak, and Piotr Andruszkiewicz. 2016. Samsung poland nlp team at semeval-2016 task 1: Necessity for diversity; combining recursive autoencoders, wordnet and ensemble methods to measure semantic similarity. In *Proceedings of the 10th International Workshop on Semantic Evaluation (SemEval-2016)*. Association for Computational Linguistics, San Diego, California, pages 602–608. http://www.aclweb.org/anthology/S16-1091.

Renxian Zhang and Naishi Liu. 2014. Recognizing humor on twitter. In *Proceedings of the 23rd ACM International Conference on Conference on Information and Knowledge Management*. ACM, pages 889–898.

Idiom Savant at Semeval-2017 Task 7: Detection and Interpretation of English Puns

Samuel Doogan Aniruddha Ghosh Hanyang Chen Tony Veale
Department of Computer Science and Informatics
University College Dublin
Dublin, Ireland
{samuel.doogan, aniruddha.ghosh, hanyang.chen}@ucdconnect.ie
tony.veale@ucd.ie

Abstract

This paper describes our system, entitled *Idiom Savant*, for the 7th Task of the Semeval 2017 workshop, "Detection and interpretation of English Puns". Our system consists of two probabilistic models for each type of puns using Google n-grams and Word2Vec. Our system achieved f-score of 0.84, 0.663, and 0.07 in homographic puns and 0.8439, 0.6631, and 0.0806 in heterographic puns in task 1, task 2, and task 3 respectively.

1 Introduction

A pun is a form of wordplay, which is often profiled by exploiting polysemy of a word or by replacing a phonetically similar sounding word for an intended humorous effect. From Shakespeare's works to modern advertisement catchphrases (Tanaka, 1992), puns have been widely used as a humorous and rhetorical device. For a polysemous word, the non-literal meaning is addressed when contextual information has low accordance with it's primary or most prominent meaning (Giora, 1997). A pun can be seen as a democratic form of literal and non-literal meaning. In using puns, the author alternates an idiomatic expression to a certain extent or provides enough context for a polysemous word to evoke non-literal meaning without attenuating literal meaning completely (Giora, 2002).

Task 7 of the 2017 SemEval workshop (Miller et al., 2017) involves three subtasks. The first subtask requires the system to classify a given context into two binary categories: puns and non-puns. The second subtask concerns itself with finding the word producing the punning effect in a given context. The third and final subtask involves annotating puns with the dual senses with which the

punning effect is being driven.

In a written context, puns are classified into 2 categories. Homographic puns shown in example 1, exploits polysemy of the language by using a word or phrase which has multiple coherent meanings given its context; And heterographic puns shown in example 2, humorous effect is often induced by adding incongruity by replacing a phonetically similar word which is semantically distant from the context.

(1) Tires are fixed for a *flat* rate.

(2) A dentist hates having a bad day at the *orifice*.

The rest of the paper is organized as follows. Section 2 give a general description of our approach. Section 3 and 4 illustrate the detailed methodologies used for detecting and locating Heterographic and Homographic puns respectively. In section 5, we provided an analysis of the system along with experimental results and finally section 6 contains some closing remarks and conclusion.

2 General Approach

We argue that the detection of heterographic puns rests on two assumptions. Firstly, the word being used to introduce the punning effect is phonetically similar to the intended word, so that the reader can infer the desired meaning behind the pun. Secondly, the context in which the pun takes place is a subversion of frequent or idiomatic language, once again so that the inference appropriately facilitated. This introduces two computational tasks - designing a model which ranks pairs of words based on their phonetic similarity, and introducing a means by which we can determine the normativeness of the context in question. The sys-

103

Proceedings of the 11th International Workshop on Semantic Evaluations (SemEval-2017), pages 103–108,
Vancouver, Canada, August 3 - 4, 2017. ©2017 Association for Computational Linguistics

tem is attempting to recreate how a human mind might recognize a pun. Take this example:

(3) "Acupuncture is a *jab* well done"

It is immediately noticeable that this sentence is not a normative use of language. However, we can easily recognize the familiar idiom "a job well done", and it is easy to make this substitution due to the phonetic overlap between the words "job" and "jab". Our system is therefore trying to mimic two things: the detection of an infrequent (or even semantically incoherent) use of language, and the detection of the intended idiom by means of phonetic substitution. To model the detection of subverted uses of idioms, we use the Google n-gram corpus (Brants and Franz, 2006). We assume that the normativeness of a context is represented by the n-gram frequency provided by this corpus. The system then replaces phonetically similar words in the non-normative context in an attempt to produce an idiomatic use of language. We determine an idiomatic use of language to be one that has an adequately high frequency in the Google n-gram corpus. We argue that if, by replacing a word in an infrequent use of language with a phonetically similar word, we arrive at a very frequent use of language, we have derived an indicator for the usage of puns. For example, the quadgram "a jab well done" occurs 890 times in the corpus. By replacing the word "jab" with "job", the new quadgram occurs 203575 times. This increase in frequency suggests that a pun is taking place. The system uses several methods to examine such changes in frequency, and outputs a "score", or the estimated likelihood that a pun is being used. The way in which these scores are computed is detailed below.

Homographic puns are generally figurative in nature. Due to identical spelling, interpretation of literal and non-literal meaning is solely dependent on the context information. Literal and non-literal meaning of a polysemous word are referred by different slices of context, which is termed as "double grounding" by Feyaerts and Brône (2002). Considering example 1, it is easily noticeable that two coherent meanings of 'flat', 'a deflated pneumatic tire' and 'commercially inactive', have been referred by 'Tires' and 'rate' respectively. Thus detection of homographic puns involves establishing links between concepts present in context with meanings of polysemous word.

From the general description of different types of puns, it is evident that detection of pun is complex and challenging. To keep the complexity at its minimum, *Idiom Savant* contains two distinct models to handle homographic and heterographic pun tasks.

3 Heterographic Puns

Idiom Savant calculates scores for all possible ngram pairs for a given context. To generate pairs, the system first separates the context into n-grams. For each of these original n-grams, the corpus is searched for n-grams that are at most one word different. The pairs are then scored using the metric described below. The scores for these pairs are then used to tackle each subtask, which is covered below. Since heterographic puns are fabricated by replacing phonetically similar words, classification and identification requires a phonetic knowledge of the language. To obtain phonetic representation of a word, CMU pronouncing dictionary[1] was used. We have ignored the lexical stresses in the pronunciation, as experimentation showed that coarser definitions led to better results. To measure the phonetic distance between a phoneme representation of a pair of words, we have employed three different strategies which use Levenshtein distances. The first distance formula, d_{ph}, calculates Levenshtein distance between two words by considering each CMU phoneme of a word as a single unit. Take the pun word and intended word from example 2:

$$d_{ph}(\{\text{AO, F, AH, S}\}, \{\text{AO, R, AH, F, AH, S}\}) = 2$$

Our second strategy treats the phonetic representation as a concatenated string and calculates Levenshtein distance d_{phs}.

$$d_{phs}(\text{"AOFAHS", "AORAHFAHS"}) = 3$$

With this metric, the distance reflects the similarity between phonemes such as "AH" and "AA", which begin with the same vowel sounds. The fallback method for out-of-vocabulary words uses the original Levenshtein string distance.

$$d_{ch}(\text{"office", "orifice"}) = 2$$

---

[1] http://www.speech.cs.cmu.edu/cgi-bin/cmudict

The system normalizes these distances with respect to the length of the phonetic representation of the target words to reduce the penalty caused by word length. By converting distance measures into similarity ratios, longer words remain candidates for possible puns, even though Levenshtein distances will be greater than the shorter counterparts. The system chooses the maximum positive ratio from all possible phonetic representations. If no positive ratio exists, the target word is discarded as a possible candidate.

$$ratio_f(w_1, w_2) = \frac{\min_{w \in w_1, w_2} ||w||_f - d_f(w_1, w_2)}{\min_{w \in w_1, w_2} ||w||_f}$$

where $f \in \{ph, phs, ch\}$

$$ratio = max(ratio_{ph}, ratio_{phs}, ratio_{ch})$$

We choose the maximum ratio in order to minimize the drawbacks inherent in each metric. The assumption is that the maximum ratio between all three methods is the most reflective of the real phonetic similarity between a pair of words. The final score is calculated as the inverted ratio subtracted from the difference between the ngram pair's frequency.

$$score = (freq_{ngram'} - freq_{ngram}) - \frac{1}{ratio^n}$$

Deducting the original n-gram's frequency from the new frequency effectively ignores normal uses of language which do not relate to pun language. The value of the exponent introduces a trade off between phonetic similarity and frequency. The frequencies of certain n-grams are so high that if n is too low, even words with very little phonetic similarity will score high using this method. In our experiments, an optimal value of 10 was found for this trade off.

3.1 Binary Classification

Tto classify a context as a pun or non pun, *Idiom Savant* finds the maximum score from all possible n-gram pairs. If the maximum score found exceeds a threshold value, the context is classified as a pun.

Finding the correct threshold value to accurately classify contexts is discussed below in the Experiments and Results section.

3.2 Locating Pun Word

By maximizing the score when replacing all potential lexical units, the system also produces a candidate word. Whichever replacement word used to produce the top n-gram pair is returned as the candidate word. The system only examines the last two ngrams. Those grams, the system annotates the POS tag and only the content words — nouns, verbs, adverbs and adjectives— are considered as candidate words. The system uses a fall back by choosing the last word in the context when no adequate substitution is found.

3.3 Annotating senses for pun meanings

Subtask 3 introduces an added difficulty with regards to heterographic puns. The system needs to correctly identify the two senses involved of pun, which is based on the accuracy of selecting target words. The system produce a ranked list of n-gram pairs using single word substitution. The highest ranked pair then contains the new or replaced word with which we search for a sense in WordNet (Fellbaum, 1998). For this particular task, the pun word are already given, so the system chooses only the n-grams which contain this word, and only needs to replace this word in order to produce pairs.

Once both words are found, we apply the semantic similarity measure akin to the one used in our systems approach to homographic puns described in Section 4. Both the original and target word is compared to a list of wordnet glosses corresponding to the senses available for each word. *Idiom Savant* uses Word2Vec cosine similarity between the words and their sense glosses to choose the best sense key.

3.4 Tom Swifties

"Tom Swifty" (Lessard and Levison, 1992) is one type of pun often found in the test data set. An example found is " It's March 14th, Tom said piously". Such puns frequently use adverbs to introduce the contextual ties inherent in heterographic puns. Despite that, most of these adverbs occurred in the test data set show little connection with their contexts, rather they are specifically used for ironic purpose. As such, our system did not adequately recognize these instances, so we designed a separate procedure for these cases. To flag whether a pun might be of a Tom Swifty type, the system uses a Part of Speech tagger from

NLTK (Bird, 2006) and also analyses the suffixes of the last word in the context (for example, words ending in "ly").

With relation to tasks 1, an amalgamation of this approach and the original is performed. If the highest score does not exceed the threshold, we check to see if the pun is of type Tom Swifty. If this is the case, then we mark the context as a pun. Task 2 operates similarly - if the pun is flagged as a Tom Swifty, then the last adverb is returned as a candidate. For task 3 however, we need to transform the adverb into the intended word in order to get the appropriate sense entry in WordNet.

To do so we build two prefix trees: one is a phonetic prefix tree based on CMU pronunciation dictionary; the other is a string prefix tree, to cover the exception cases where the adverb is not present in the CMU. If the word is in the phonetic prefix tree, the program returns all words which share at least two common prefix phonemes. For example, given the adverb "punctually", the words "puncture", "punk", "pun" and so on will be returned as candidates. If the string prefix tree is used, the program returns words which share at least the first three characters found in th input word. For the word "dogmatically", "dogmatic", "dogma", and "dog" will be returned as candidates. The list of such candidates is then used to replace the ngrams in which they occur, and the new ngram pairs are ranked according to the metric described at the beginning of 3. The highest scoring prefix is then used to search the appropriate WordNet sense tags.

4 Homographic Puns

Since polysemous words have identical spelling but different meanings, detecting homographic puns is solely dependent on context information. Following double grounding theory, if the ith word of input sentence $W = w_{1:n}$ has a higher possibility to be the punning word, two senses of w_i should infer a higher similarity score with two different components in its context $c_i = w_{1:i-1,i+1:n}$. In the baseline model we design, the pun potential score of a word w_i is computed as the sum of cosine similarities between the word w_i and every word in context $w_j \in c_i$, using distributed representation *Word2Vec* (Mikolov et al., 2013). The word with highest score is returned as the punning word.

Furthermore, as additional context information, w_i were replaced with set of gloss information ex-

tracted from its different senses, noted as g_i, obtained from WordNet. While calculating similarity between g_i and c_i, two different strategies were employed. In the first strategy, the system computes similarities between every combination of g_i and c_i, and sum of similarity scores is the score for w_i. In the second strategy, similarity score were calculated between g_i and g_j, the gloss of $w_j \in c_i$. In most of the cases, pun words and their grounding words in the context do not share the same part-of-speech (POS) tags. In the latter strategy, we added a POS damping factor, noted as p_{ij} of 0.2 if the POS tags of w_i and w_j are equal. Following Optimal Innovation hypothesis, the similarity of a punning word and its grounding word should neither be too high or too low in order to evoke the non-literal meaning. We applied following correction on computed similarities.

$$ f_{ws}(x) = \begin{cases} 0 & x < 0.01 \\ 1 - x & x >= 0.01 \end{cases} $$

In puns, punning words and grounding words in context are often not adjacent. Thus the system does not consider the adjacent words of the candidate word. The system also ignored stopwords offered by *NLTK*. We noticed that words with high frequency other than stopwords overshadow low frequency words since every word with high frequency poses certain similarity score with every other phrases. Thus we added a frequency damping factor(f_{ij}) of 0.1 to the score for whose words have frequencies more than 100 in *Brown Corpus* (Francis and Kucera, 1979). The final scoring function is shown as follows.

$$ score(W, i) = \sum_{j=1}^{n} p_{ij} f_{ij} \sum_{k=1}^{l} \sum_{m=1}^{q} f_{ws}\left(\frac{g_k g_m}{|g_k||g_m|}\right) $$

n is the number of words in c_i and l and q is number of senses of w_i and w_j. g_k and g_m are gloss of the kth sense and m^{th} sense of w_i and w_j respectively.

For task 3, in order to obtain the sense keys of intended meaning from *Wordnet*, we chose the top two glosses of the pun word based on similarity score between gloss and word in context. For adding more context, instead of comparing only with words in context, we performed similarity measurement among the glosses.

For subtask 1, for each word we calculated similarity with other words and we averaged the top two similarity score. We have considered a word as a pun if the average score is more than threshold of 0.6, which we chose empirically after observing a number of examples. For subtask 3, we chose the top two senses of the word ranked by the gloss similarity as candidate senses of punned word.

5 Experiment results and analysis

5.1 Heterographic Puns Processing

ID	Method	P	R	F
1	Infrequent Quadgram	**0.90**	0.71	0.79
	Trigram Score	0.82	**0.87**	**0.84**
2	Last Word	0.55	0.55	0.55
	BestQuadGramPairs	**0.68**	**0.68**	**0.68**
3	TopSenses	**0.14**	**0.11**	**0.12**
	GlossSim	0.08	0.07	0.07

Table 1: The precision, recall, and F-score value of heterographic pun subtasks

The experiment results for the heterographic pun subtasks are shown in Table 5.1. For subtask 1, the baseline *infrequent quadgram* is created: if a pun contains no infrequent quadgrams, which have a frequency less than 150 in Ngram corpus, then it is labeled as a non pun. The system uses trigram in subtask 1 because it is computationally feasible to search the ngram space, whilst still being representative of typical uses of language. We set a balanced threshold value of -14 by observing the first 200 samples in the test set.

The high precision score indicates the underlying mechanism behind such puns: a mutation of a typical use of language needs to take place. However the recall for this baseline is poor. A large portion of puns de facto use frequent language usages as targets for linguistic perversion, which this baseline method fails.

Our system outperforms the baseline about five percentage of F-score. The largest factor regarding improper classifications of our model is false positives. Not all infrequent uses of language are heterographic puns. *Idiom Savant*'s technique would sometimes misread a context, modify an infrequent trigram that was not the source of a pun to produce a much more frequent trigram. These false positives are the result of the enormous amount of possible uses in the English language. Infrequent yet "normal" trigrams are an important caveat when using frequency based techniques such as *Idiom Savant*. Hence we see the differ-

ence between our model and the simple baseline: although the puns that were detected were very precise, the baseline failed to detect more subtle puns, where normal uses of language are still using phonetic translations to introduce ambiguity.

For subtask 2, *Idiom Savant* uses quadgrams to produce the scores. This is possible because the system employs a number of methods to reduce the search space created when attempting to replace quadgrams. Firstly, the system won't search the Tom Swifty puns in ngrams corpus. Analysing the first 200 samples in the test data, which is not Tom Swifty puns, we found that roughly half all pun words are the last words in the context. Using this method on the whole corpus produced the *LastWord* baseline seen above. When expanding that to quadgrams and thus enlarging the window, an even greater ratio presents itself. Of the same 200 samples, three fourth of punning words are present in the last quadgram. In the gold standard, ninety percent of pun words appear in the last quadgram. We apply the same scoring technique as described above and achieved the performance presented in the table. We find an increase of 13% as compared to the last word baseline across the board.

To create a baseline for subtask 3, we followed the approach described in (Miller and Gurevych, 2015). and choose the top WordNet senses for each word selected as pun word. As WordNet ranks each sense with their associated frequency of usage, the baseline simply selects the most frequent sense for the pun word and replaced word respectively. As the replaced word are produced by the system, the possibility of error even with the baseline approach is affected by the accuracy of previous steps. When an incorrect word is produced, the sense key attached is by default incorrect and thus the precision, recall, and F scores suffer. The baseline outperforms our system to choose the best sense keys by approximately 6 percentage points. Our method involves Word2Vec is insufficient for solving this subtask, which is evidently much more difficult than the previous subtasks.

5.2 Homographic Pun Processing

For homographic pun processing, we participated in subtask 2 and 3. We calculated scores of subtask 1 on test data after task. For subtask 1, our system achieves 0.84 F-score, which outperforms the all positive baseline. For subtask 2, our system achieves 0.66 F-score. We observed that our system performed well on long sentences. However, for short sentences, most frequent word in the sentence were selected as pun word. This may be caused by lack of context.

Our system does not perform well on subtask 3 as it could not pick the apt sense intended in the pun. We noticed that the system can not pinpoint the apt senses whose glosses are not long enough.

Task	Method	P	R	F-score
Task 1	AllPositive	0.71	**1.00**	0.83
	WordPairSim	**0.73**	0.98	**0.84**
Task 2	WordSim	0.57	0.54	0.55
	WordGlossSim	**0.66**	**0.66**	**0.66**
Task 3	GlossSim	0.08	0.08	0.08

Table 2: The precision, recall, and F-score value of homographic pun processing subtasks

6 Concluding Remarks

We introduced *Idiom Savant*, a computational system that capable of classifying and analyzing heterographic and homographic puns. We show that using n-grams in combination with the CMU dictionary can accurately model heterographic pun.

There are however a number of drawbacks to this approach. We hypothesize that using a larger corpus would increase the performance of heterograhic pun processing. And we may combine different length grams to search for these idiomatic uses of language, which would more accurately model how human recognizes heterographic puns. Furthermore, the system has no means of checking whether the candidate words offered up by *Idiom Savant* are correlated to the rest of the context. Our system suffers intensely for short sentences and short gloss information, since *Word2Vec* doesn't offer context information.

References

Steven Bird. 2006. NLTK: The Natural Language Toolkit. In *Proceedings of the COLING/ACL 2006 Interactive Presentation Sessions*. Association for Computational Linguistics, Sydney, Australia, pages 69–72.

Thorsten Brants and Alex Franz. 2006. Web 1t 5-gram version 1. *Linguistic Data Consortium* .

Christiane Fellbaum, editor. 1998. *WordNet: An Electronic Lexical Database*. Massachusetts Institute of Technology.

Kurt Feyaerts and Geert Brône. 2002. Humor through double grounding: Structural interaction of optimality principles. *Odense Working Papers in Language and Communication* (23):312–336.

W. Nelson Francis and Henry Kucera. 1979. Brown corpus manual. *Brown University* .

Rachel Giora. 1997. Understanding figurative and literal language: The graded salience hypothesis. *Cognitive Linguistics (includes Cognitive Linguistic Bibliography)* 8(3):183–206.

Rachel Giora. 2002. Optimal innovation and pleasure. In *Stock, O., Strapparva, C. and A. Nijholt (eds.) Processing of The April Fools Day Workshop on Computational Humour*. Citeseer, pages 11–28.

Greg Lessard and Michael Levison. 1992. Computational modelling of linguistic humour: Tom swifties. In *ALLC/ACH Joint Annual Conference, Oxford*. pages 175–178.

Tomas Mikolov, Ilya Sutskever, Kai Chen, Greg S Corrado, and Jeff Dean. 2013. Distributed representations of words and phrases and their compositionality. In *Advances in neural information processing systems*. pages 3111–3119.

Tristan Miller and Iryna Gurevych. 2015. Automatic disambiguation of english puns. In *Proceedings of the 53rd Annual Meeting of the Association for Computational Linguistics and the 7th International Joint Conference on Natural Language Processing (Volume 1: Long Papers)*. Association for Computational Linguistics, Beijing, China, pages 719–729.

Tristan Miller, Christian F. Hempelmann, and Iryna Gurevych. 2017. SemEval-2017 Task 7: Detection and interpretation of English puns. In *Proceedings of the 11th International Workshop on Semantic Evaluation (SemEval-2017)*.

Keiko Tanaka. 1992. The pun in advertising: A pragmatic approach. *Lingua* 87(1):91 – 102.

CompiLIG at SemEval-2017 Task 1: Cross-Language Plagiarism Detection Methods for Semantic Textual Similarity

Jérémy Ferrero
Compilatio
276 rue du Mont Blanc
74540 Saint-Félix, France
LIG-GETALP
Univ. Grenoble Alpes, France
jeremy.ferrero@imag.fr

Laurent Besacier
LIG-GETALP
Univ. Grenoble Alpes, France
laurent.besacier@imag.fr

Didier Schwab
LIG-GETALP
Univ. Grenoble Alpes, France
didier.schwab@imag.fr

Frédéric Agnès
Compilatio
276 rue du Mont Blanc
74540 Saint-Félix, France
frederic@compilatio.net

Abstract

We present our submitted systems for Semantic Textual Similarity (STS) Track 4 at SemEval-2017. Given a pair of Spanish-English sentences, each system must estimate their semantic similarity by a score between 0 and 5. In our submission, we use syntax-based, dictionary-based, context-based, and MT-based methods. We also combine these methods in unsupervised and supervised way. Our best run ranked 1st on track 4a with a correlation of 83.02% with human annotations.

1 Introduction

CompiLIG is a collaboration between Compilatio[1] - a company particularly interested in cross-language plagiarism detection - and LIG research group on natural language processing (GETALP). Cross-language semantic textual similarity detection is an important step for cross-language plagiarism detection, and evaluation campaigns in this new domain are rare. For the first time, SemEval STS task (Agirre et al., 2016) was extended with a Spanish-English cross-lingual sub-task in 2016. This year, sub-task was renewed under track 4 (divided in two sub-corpora: track 4a and track 4b).

Given a sentence in Spanish and a sentence in English, the objective is to compute their semantic textual similarity according to a score from 0 to 5, where 0 means *no similarity* and 5 means *full semantic similarity*. The evaluation metric is a Pearson correlation coefficient between the submitted scores and the gold standard scores from human annotators. Last year, among 26 submissions from 10 teams, the method that achieved the best performance (Brychcin and Svoboda, 2016) was a supervised system (SVM regression with RBF kernel) based on word alignment algorithm presented in Sultan et al. (2015).

Our submission in 2017 is based on cross-language plagiarism detection methods combined with the best performing STS detection method published in 2016. CompiLIG team participated to SemEval STS for the first time in 2017. The methods proposed are syntax-based, dictionary-based, context-based, and MT-based. They show additive value when combined. The submitted runs consist in (1) our best single unsupervised approach (2) an unsupervised combination of best approaches (3) a fine-tuned combination of best approaches. The best of our three runs ranked 1st with a correlation of 83.02% with human annotations on track 4a among all submitted systems (51 submissions from 20 teams for this track). Correlation results of all participants (including ours) on track 4b were much lower and we try to explain why (and question the validity of track 4b) in the last part of this paper.

---

[1]www.compilatio.net

Proceedings of the 11th International Workshop on Semantic Evaluations (SemEval-2017), pages 109–114,
Vancouver, Canada, August 3 - 4, 2017. ©2017 Association for Computational Linguistics

2 Cross-Language Textual Similarity Detection Methods

2.1 Cross-Language Character N-Gram (CL-C*n*G)

CL-CnG aims to measure the syntactical similarity between two texts. It is based on Mcnamee and Mayfield (2004) work used in information retrieval. It compares two texts under their n-grams vectors representation. The main advantage of this kind of method is that it does not require any translation between source and target text.

After some tests on previous year's dataset to find the best n, we decide to use the Potthast et al. (2011)'s *CL-C3G* implementation. Let S_x and S_y two sentences in two different languages. First, the alphabet of these sentences is normalized to the ensemble $\sum = \{a - z, 0 - 9, \quad \}$, so only spaces and alphanumeric characters are kept. Any other diacritic or symbol is deleted and the whole text is lower-cased. The texts are then segmented into 3-grams (sequences of 3 contiguous characters) and transformed into *tf.idf* vectors of character 3-grams. We directly build our *idf* model on the evaluation data. We use a double normalization K (with $K = 0.5$) as *tf* (Manning et al., 2008) and a inverse document frequency smooth as *idf*. Finally, a cosine similarity is computed between the vectors of source and target sentences.

2.2 Cross-Language Conceptual Thesaurus-based Similarity (CL-CTS)

CL-CTS (Gupta et al., 2012; Pataki, 2012) aims to measure the semantic similarity between two vectors of concepts. The model consists in representing texts as bag-of-words (or concepts) to compare them. The method also does not require explicit translation since the matching is performed using internal connections in the used "ontology".

Let S a sentence of length n, the n words of the sentence are represented by w_i as:

$$S = \{w_1, w_2, w_3, ..., w_n\} \qquad (1)$$

S_x and S_y are two sentences in two different languages. A bag-of-words S' from each sentence S is built, by filtering stop words and by using a function that returns for a given word all its possible translations. These translations are jointly given by a linked lexical resource, *DBNary* (Sérasset, 2015), and by cross-lingual word embeddings. More precisely, we use the top 10 closest words in the embeddings model and all the available translations from *DBNary* to build the bag-of-words of a word. We use the *MultiVec* (Berard et al., 2016) toolkit for computing and managing word embeddings. The corpora used to build the embeddings are Europarl and Wikipedia sub-corpus, part of the dataset of Ferrero et al. (2016)[2]. For training our embeddings, we use CBOW model with a vector size of 100, a window size of 5, a negative sampling parameter of 5, and an alpha of 0.02.

So, the sets of words S'_x and S'_y are the conceptual representations in the same language of S_x and S_y respectively. To calculate the similarity between S_x and S_y, we use a syntactically and frequentially weighted augmentation of the Jaccard distance, defined as:

$$J(S_x, S_y) = \frac{\Omega(S'_x) + \Omega(S'_y)}{\Omega(S_x) + \Omega(S_y)} \qquad (2)$$

where S_x and S_y are the input sentences (also represented as sets of words), and Ω is the sum of the weights of the words of a set, defined as:

$$\Omega(S) = \sum_{i=1 \, , \, w_i \in S}^{n} \varphi(w_i) \qquad (3)$$

where w_i is the ith word of the bag S, and φ is the weight of word in the Jaccard distance:

$$\varphi(w) = pos\_weight(w)^{1-\alpha} \cdot idf(w)^{\alpha} \qquad (4)$$

where *pos_weight* is the function which gives the weight for each universal part-of-speech tag of a word, *idf* is the function which gives the inverse document frequency of a word, and . is the scalar product. Equation (4) is a way to syntactically (*pos_weight*) and frequentially (*idf*) weight the contribution of a word to the Jaccard distance (both contributions being controlled with the α parameter). We assume that for one word, we have its part-of-speech within its original sentence, and its inverse document frequency. We use *TreeTagger* (Schmid, 1994) for POS tagging, and we normalize the tags with *Universal Tagset* of Petrov et al. (2012). Then, we assign a weight for each of the 12 universal POS tags. The 12 POS weights and the value α are optimized with *Condor* (Berghen and Bersini, 2005) in the same way as in Ferrero et al. (2017). *Condor* applies a Newton's method with a trust region algorithm

---

[2]https://github.com/FerreroJeremy/Cross-Language-Dataset

to determinate the weights that optimize a desired output score. No re-tuning of these hyper-parameters for SemEval task was performed.

2.3 Cross-Language Word Embedding-based Similarity

CL-WES (Ferrero et al., 2017) consists in a cosine similarity on distributed representations of sentences, which are obtained by the weighted sum of each word vector in a sentence. As in previous section, each word vector is syntactically and frequentially weighted.

If S_x and S_y are two sentences in two different languages, then *CL-WES* builds their (bilingual) common representation vectors V_x and V_y and applies a cosine similarity between them. A distributed representation V of a sentence S is calculated as follows:

$$V = \sum_{i=1\,,\,w_i \in S}^{n} (vector(w_i) . \varphi(w_i)) \qquad (5)$$

where w_i is the ith word of the sentence S, *vector* is the function which gives the word embedding vector of a word, φ is the same that in formula (4), and . is the scalar product. We make this method publicly available through *MultiVec*[3] (Berard et al., 2016) toolkit.

2.4 Translation + Monolingual Word Alignment (T+WA)

The last method used is a two-step process. First, we translate the Spanish sentence into English with *Google Translate* (*i.e.* we are bringing the two sentences in the same language). Then, we align both utterances. We reuse the monolingual aligner[4] of Sultan et al. (2015) with the improvement of Brychcin and Svoboda (2016), who won the cross-lingual sub-task in 2016 (Agirre et al., 2016). Because this improvement has not been released by the initial authors, we propose to share our re-implementation on *GitHub*[5].

If S_x and S_y are two sentences in the same language, then we try to measure their similarity with the following formula:

$$J(S_x, S_y) = \frac{\omega(A_x) + \omega(A_y)}{\omega(S_x) + \omega(S_y)} \qquad (6)$$

---

[3]https://github.com/eske/multivec
[4]https://github.com/ma-sultan/
monolingual-word-aligner
[5]https://github.com/FerreroJeremy/
monolingual-word-aligner

where S_x and S_y are the input sentences (represented as sets of words), A_x and A_y are the sets of aligned words for S_x and S_y respectively, and ω is a frequency weight of a set of words, defined as:

$$\omega(A) = \sum_{i=1\,,\,w_i \in A}^{n} idf(w_i) \qquad (7)$$

where *idf* is the function which gives the inverse document frequency of a word.

2.5 System Combination

These methods are syntax-, dictionary-, context- and MT- based, and are thus potentially complementary. That is why we also combine them in unsupervised and supervised fashion. Our unsupervised fusion is an average of the outputs of each method. For supervised fusion, we recast fusion as a regression problem and we experiment all available methods in *Weka* 3.8.0 (Hall et al., 2009).

3 Results on SemEval-2016 Dataset

Table 1 reports the results of the proposed systems on SemEval-2016 STS cross-lingual evaluation dataset. The dataset, the annotation and the evaluation systems were presented in the SemEval-2016 STS task description paper (Agirre et al., 2016), so we do not re-detail them here. The lines in bold represent the methods that obtain the best mean score in each category of system (best method alone, unsupervised and supervised fusion). The scores for the supervised systems are obtained with 10-folds cross-validation.

4 Runs Submitted to SemEval-2017

First, it is important to mention that our outputs are linearly re-scaled to a real-valued space $[0\,;5]$.

Run 1: Best Method Alone. Our first run is only based on the best method alone during our tests (see Table 1), *i.e.* Cross-Language Conceptual Thesaurus-based Similarity (*CL-CTS*) model, as described in section 2.2.

Run 2: Fusion by Average. Our second run is a fusion by average on three methods: *CL-C3G*, *CL-CTS* and *T+WA*, all described in section 2.

Run 3: M5′ Model Tree. Unlike the two precedent runs, the third run is a supervised system. We have selected the system that obtained the best score during our tests on SemEval-2016 evaluation dataset (see Table 1), which is the M5′ model tree (Wang and Witten, 1997) (called M5P in

Methods	News	Multi	Mean
Unsupervised systems			
CL-C3G (1)	0.7522	0.6550	0.7042
CL-CTS (2)	**0.9072**	**0.8283**	**0.8682**
CL-WES (3)	0.7028	0.6312	0.6674
T+WA (4)	0.9060	0.8144	0.8607
Average (1-2-3-4)	0.8589	0.7824	0.8211
Average (1-2-4)	**0.9051**	**0.8347**	**0.8703**
Average (2-3-4)	0.8923	0.8239	0.8585
Average (2-4)	0.9082	0.8299	0.8695
Supervised systems (fine-tuned fusion)			
GaussianProcesses	0.8712	0.7884	0.8303
LinearRegression	0.9099	0.8414	0.8761
MultilayerPerceptron	0.8966	0.7999	0.8488
SimpleLinearRegression	0.9048	0.8144	0.8601
SMOreg	0.9071	0.8375	0.8727
Ibk	0.8396	0.7330	0.7869
Kstar	0.8545	0.8173	0.8361
LWL	0.8572	0.7589	0.8086
DecisionTable	0.9139	0.8047	0.8599
M5Rules	0.9146	0.8406	0.8780
DecisionStump	0.8329	0.7380	0.7860
M5P	**0.9154**	**0.8442**	**0.8802**
RandomForest	0.9109	0.8418	0.8768
RandomTree	0.8364	0.7262	0.7819
REPTree	0.8972	0.7992	0.8488

Table 1: Results of the methods on SemEval-2016 STS cross-lingual evaluation dataset.

Weka 3.8.0 (Hall et al., 2009)). Model trees have a conventional decision tree structure but use linear regression functions at the leaves instead of discrete class labels. The first implementation of model trees, M5, was proposed by Quinlan (1992) and the approach was refined and improved in a system called M5′ by Wang and Witten (1997). To learn the model, we use all the methods described in section 2 as features.

5 Results of the 2017 evaluation and Discussion

Dataset, annotation and evaluation systems are presented in SemEval-2017 STS task description paper (Cer et al., 2017). We can see in Table 2 that our systems work well on SNLI[6] (Bowman et al., 2015) (track 4a), on which we ranked 1st with more than 83% of correlation with human annotations. Conversely, correlations on the WMT corpus (track 4b) are strangely low. This difference is notable on the scores of all participating teams (Cer et al., 2017)[7]. This might be explained by the fact that WMT was annotated by only one

---

[6]http://nlp.stanford.edu/projects/snli/

[7]The best score for this track is 34%, while for the other tracks it is around 85%.

annotator, while the SNLI corpus was annotated by many.

Methods	SNLI (4a)	WMT (4b)	Mean
CL-CTS	0.7684	0.1464	0.4574
Average	0.7910	0.1494	0.4702
M5P	0.8302	0.1550	0.4926

Table 2: Official results of our submitted systems on SemEval-2017 STS track 4 evaluation dataset.

Methods	SNLI (4a)	WMT (4b)	Mean
Our Annotations			
CL-CTS	0.7981	0.5248	0.6614
Average	0.8105	0.4031	0.6068
M5P	0.8622	0.5374	0.6998
SemEval Gold Standard			
CL-CTS	0.8123	0.1739	0.4931
Average	0.8277	0.2209	0.5243
M5P	0.8536	0.1706	0.5121

Table 3: Results of our submitted systems scored on our 120 annotated pairs and on the same 120 SemEval annotated pairs.

To investigate deeper on this issue, we manually annotated 60 random pairs of each sub-corpus (120 annotated pairs among 500). These annotations provide a second annotator reference. We can see in Table 3 that, on SNLI corpus (4a), our methods behave the same way for both annotations (a difference of about 1.3%). However, the difference in correlation is huge between our annotations and SemEval gold standard on the WMT corpus (4b): 30% on average. The Pearson correlation between our annotated pairs and the related gold standard is 85.76% for the SNLI corpus and 29.16% for the WMT corpus. These results question the validity of the WMT corpus (4b) for semantic textual similarity detection.

6 Conclusion

We described our submission to SemEval-2017 Semantic Textual Similarity task on track 4 (Sp-En cross-lingual sub-task). Our best results were achieved by a M5′ model tree combination of various textual similarity detection techniques. This approach worked well on the SNLI corpus (4a - finishes 1st with more than 83% of correlation with human annotations), which corresponds to a real cross-language plagiarism detection scenario. We also questioned WMT corpus (4b) validity providing our own manual annotations and showing low correlations with those of SemEval.

References

Eneko Agirre, Carmen Banea, Daniel Cer, Mona Diab, Aitor Gonzalez-Agirre, Rada Mihalcea, and Janyce Wiebe. 2016. SemEval-2016 Task 1: Semantic Textual Similarity, Monolingual and Cross-Lingual Evaluation. In *Proceedings of the 10th International Workshop on Semantic Evaluation (SemEval 2016)*. Association for Computational Linguistics, San Diego, CA, USA, pages 497–511. http://www.aclweb.org/anthology/S16-1081.

Alexandre Berard, Christophe Servan, Olivier Pietquin, and Laurent Besacier. 2016. MultiVec: a Multilingual and Multilevel Representation Learning Toolkit for NLP. In *Proceedings of the Tenth International Conference on Language Resources and Evaluation (LREC'16)*. European Language Resources Association (ELRA), Portoroz, Slovenia, pages 4188–4192.

Frank Vanden Berghen and Hugues Bersini. 2005. CONDOR, a new parallel, constrained extension of Powell's UOBYQA algorithm: Experimental results and comparison with the DFO algorithm. *Journal of Computational and Applied Mathematics* 181:157–175. https://doi.org/10.1016/j.cam.2004.11.029.

Samuel R. Bowman, Gabor Angeli, Christopher Potts, and Christopher D. Manning. 2015. A Large Annotated Corpus for Learning Natural Language Inference. In *Proceedings of the 2015 Conference on Empirical Methods in Natural Language Processing (EMNLP)*. Association for Computational Linguistics, Lisbon, Portugal, pages 632–642. http://aclweb.org/anthology/D/D15/D15-1075.pdf.

Tomas Brychcin and Lukas Svoboda. 2016. UWB at SemEval-2016 Task 1: Semantic textual similarity using lexical, syntactic, and semantic information. In *Proceedings of the 10th International Workshop on Semantic Evaluation (SemEval 2016)*. San Diego, CA, USA, pages 588–594. https://www.aclweb.org/anthology/S/S16/S16-1089.pdf.

Daniel Cer, Mona Diab, Eneko Agirre, Inigo Lopez-Gazpio, and Lucia Specia. 2017. Semeval-2017 task 1: Semantic textual similarity multilingual and crosslingual focused evaluation. In *Proceedings of the 11th International Workshop on Semantic Evaluation (SemEval-2017)*. Association for Computational Linguistics, Vancouver, Canada, pages 1–14. http://www.aclweb.org/anthology/S17-2001.

Jérémy Ferrero, Frédéric Agnès, Laurent Besacier, and Didier Schwab. 2016. A Multilingual, Multi-style and Multi-granularity Dataset for Cross-language Textual Similarity Detection. In *Proceedings of the Tenth International Conference on Language Resources and Evaluation (LREC'16)*. European Language Resources Association (ELRA), Portoroz, Slovenia, pages 4162–4169. ISLRN: 723-785-513-738-2. http://islrn.org/resources/723-785-513-738-2.

Jérémy Ferrero, Laurent Besacier, Didier Schwab, and Frédéric Agnès. 2017. Using Word Embedding for Cross-Language Plagiarism Detection. In *Proceedings of the 15th Conference of the European Chapter of the Association for Computational Linguistics, (EACL 2017)*. Association for Computational Linguistics, Valencia, Spain, volume 2, pages 415–421. http://aclweb.org/anthology/E/E17/E17-2066.pdf.

Parth Gupta, Alberto Barrón-Cedeño, and Paolo Rosso. 2012. Cross-language High Similarity Search using a Conceptual Thesaurus. In *Information Access Evaluation. Multilinguality, Multimodality, and Visual Analytics*. Springer Berlin Heidelberg, Rome, Italy, pages 67–75. https://doi.org/10.1007/978-3-642-33247-0_8.

Mark Hall, Eibe Frank, Geoffrey Holmes, Bernhard Pfahringer, Peter Reutemann, and Ian H. Witten. 2009. The WEKA Data Mining Software: An Update. In *SIGKDD Explorations*. volume 11, pages 10–18. https://doi.org/10.1145/1656274.1656278.

Christopher D. Manning, Prabhakar Raghavan, and Hinrich Schütze. 2008. *Introduction to Information Retrieval*, Cambridge University Press, New York, chapter 6 - "Scoring, term weighting, and the vector space model", pages 109–133. ISBN: 9780511809071. https://doi.org/10.1017/CBO9780511809071.007.

Paul Mcnamee and James Mayfield. 2004. Character N-Gram Tokenization for European Language Text Retrieval. In *Information Retrieval Proceedings*. Kluwer Academic Publishers, volume 7, pages 73–97.

Màté Pataki. 2012. A New Approach for Searching Translated Plagiarism. In *Proceedings of the 5th International Plagiarism Conference*. Newcastle, UK, pages 49–64.

Slav Petrov, Dipanjan Das, and Ryan McDonald. 2012. A universal part-of-speech tagset. In *Proceedings of the Eight International Conference on Language Resources and Evaluation (LREC'12)*. European Language Resources Association (ELRA), Istanbul, Turkey, pages 2089–2096.

Martin Potthast, Alberto Barrón-Cedeño, Benno Stein, and Paolo Rosso. 2011. Cross-Language Plagiarism Detection. In *Language Ressources and Evaluation*. volume 45, pages 45–62. https://doi.org/10.1007/s10579-009-9114-z.

J. R. Quinlan. 1992. Learning with continuous classes. In Eds. Adams & Sterling, editor, *Proceedings of the Fifth Australian Joint Conference on Artificial Intelligence*. World Scientific, Singapore, pages 343–348.

Helmut Schmid. 1994. Probabilistic Part-of-Speech Tagging Using Decision Trees. In *Proceedings of the International Conference on New Methods in Language Processing*. Manchester, UK, pages 44–49.

Gilles Sérasset. 2015. DBnary: Wiktionary as a Lemon-Based Multilingual Lexical Resource in RDF. In *Semantic Web Journal (special issue on Multilingual Linked Open Data)*. volume 6, pages 355–361. https://doi.org/10.3233/SW-140147.

Md Arafat Sultan, Steven Bethard, and Tamara Sumner. 2015. DLS@CU: Sentence similarity from word alignment and semantic vector composition. In *Proceedings of the 9th International Workshop on Semantic Evaluation (SemEval 2015)*. Denver, CO, USA, pages 148–153. http://www.aclweb.org/anthology/S15-2027.

Yong Wang and Ian H. Witten. 1997. Induction of model trees for predicting continuous classes. In *Proceedings of the poster papers of the European Conference on Machine Learning*. Prague, Czech Republic, pages 128–137.

UdL at SemEval-2017 Task 1: Semantic Textual Similarity Estimation of English Sentence Pairs Using Regression Model over Pairwise Features

Hussein T. Al-Natsheh [123], Lucie Martinet [124], Fabrice Muhlenbach [15], Djamel A. Zighed [12]

[1]Université de Lyon,

[2]Lyon 2, ERIC EA 3083, 5 Avenue Pierre Mendès France, F69676 Bron Cedex - France

[3]CNRS, ISH FRE 3768, 14 Avenue Berthelot, F-69007 Lyon, France

[4]CESI EXIA/LINEACT, 19 Avenue Guy de Collongue, F-69130 Écully, France

[5]UJM-Saint-Etienne, CNRS, Laboratoire Hubert Curien UMR 5516, F-42023 Saint Etienne, France

`hussein.al-natsheh@cnrs.fr, lucie.martinet@eric.univ-lyon2.fr`
`fabrice.muhlenbach@univ-st-etienne.fr, djamel@zighed.com`

Abstract

This paper describes the model UdL we proposed to solve the semantic textual similarity task of SemEval 2017 workshop. The track we participated in was estimating the semantics relatedness of a given set of sentence pairs in English. The best run out of three submitted runs of our model achieved a Pearson correlation score of 0.8004 compared to a hidden human annotation of 250 pairs. We used random forest ensemble learning to map an expandable set of extracted pairwise features into a semantic similarity estimated value bounded between 0 and 5. Most of these features were calculated using word embedding vectors similarity to align Part of Speech (PoS) and Name Entities (NE) tagged tokens of each sentence pair. Among other pairwise features, we experimented a classical tf–idf weighted Bag of Words (BoW) vector model but with character-based range of n-grams instead of words. This sentence vector BoW-based feature gave a relatively high importance value percentage in the feature importances analysis of the ensemble learning.

1 Introduction

Semantic Textual Similarity (STS) is a shared task that have been running every year by SemEval workshop since 2012. Each year, the participating teams are encouraged to utilize the previous years data sets as a training set for their models. The teams are then ranked by their test score on a hidden human annotated pairs of sentences. After the end of the competition, the organizers publish the gold standards and ask the teams of the coming year task to use it as a training set and so on. The description of STS2017 task is reported in (Cer et al., 2017). In STS2017 , the primary task consisted in 6 tracks covering both monolingual and cross-lingual sentence pairs for the languages Spanish, English, Arabic, and Turkish. Our team, UdL, only participated in the English monolingual track (Track 5).

The data consist in thousands of pairs of sentences from various resources like (Twitter news, image captions, news headline, questions, answers, paraphrasing, post-editing...). For each pair, a human annotated score (from 0 to 5) is assigned and indicates the semantic similarity values of the two sentences. The challenge is then to estimate the semantic similarity of 250 sentence pairs with hidden similarity values. The quality of the proposed models would then be evaluated by the Pearson correlation between the estimated and the human annotated hidden values.

In section 2, we link to some related work to this problem. The data preparation method followed by a full description of the model pipeline and its implementation are then presented in sections 3, 4, and 5. Results of the model selection experiments and the final task results are shown in section 6.

2 Related Work

The general description of the methodologies proposed by the task previous year winners are discussed in Agirre et al. (2016). However, there were many other related work to solve the issue of encoding semantics of short text, i.e., sentences or paragraphs. Many of them tend to reuse word embeddings (Pennington et al., 2014) as an input for sentence embedding, while others (Shen et al., 2014; Le and Mikolov, 2014) propose to directly learn the sentence semantics features. Most of these embedding techniques are based on large

115

Proceedings of the 11th International Workshop on Semantic Evaluations (SemEval-2017), pages 115–119,
Vancouver, Canada, August 3 - 4, 2017. ©2017 Association for Computational Linguistics

text corpus where each word or short text dense vector representations (i.e., word embedding) are learned from the co-occurrence frequencies with other words in the context. Other methodologies are based on matrix decomposition of the Bag of Word (BoW) matrix using Latent Semantic Analysis (LSA) techniques like Singular Value Decomposition (SVD) or Non-Negative Matrix Factorization (NMF). According to a comparable transfer learning strategy (Bottou, 2014), if we are able to build a model consisting in (1) a pairwise transformer (i.e., feature extractor), and (2) a comparator that can well-predict if the two elements of the input are of the same class or not, then the learned transformer could be reused to easily train a classifier to label a single element. A good example to understand such system is face recognition, e.g., it is considered impossible to have all human faces images to train the best features set of a face, however, a learned model that can tell if two given face-images are of the same person or not, could guide us to define a set of good representative features to recognize a person given one face image. We can generate $\frac{2^n}{2}$ comparative pairs from n examples. Similarly, we cannot have all possible sentences to identify the sentence semantics, but we can generate a lot of comparative sentence pairs to learn the best semantics features set, i.e., sentence dense vector representation. Thus we consider our pairwise feature-based model as an initial step to build a sentence dense vector semantics representation that can perform very well in many applications like semantics highlighter, question answering system and semantics-based information retrieval system.

3   Data Set Preparation

The data set provided for the STS task consists in a set of tab-separated values data files from different text types accommodated year-after-year since 2012. Each year, the task organizers provide additional data files from different text sources. The text sources vary between classical narrative sentences, news headlines, image captions or forum questions or even chat Twitter news. The source types used in the task are listed in Table 1.

Each files pair consists of a first file containing, at each line, the two sentences to be compared and some information about the sources of these sentences if any. The second file contains, at each line, the similarity score of the corresponding pair

of sentences that is presented in the first file. In addition, for the data extracted from the previous years, we have one directory for the training set and another one for tests. We noticed that the separator format for the data file is not optimized since using a tabulator can make things confused because it is also a character used in some cases inside the text. This could be solved only by hand, after a first automatic preprocessing. After that, we can read the file by line, looking for the good characters and line format. We are also grateful that our predecessors, e.g., Tan et al. (2015), who shared some of their aggregated data that we could also add to our training set. In the end, we used the set of data of all the previous years since 2012. An additional step we considered was the spell-checker correction using *Enchant* software. We assume that such preprocessing step could enhance the results. However, this step was not used in our submitted system. Finally, we also consider a version of the data set where we filtered out the hash-tag symbol from the Twitter news sentence pairs.

4   Model Description

Our approach is based on the comparable transfer learning systems discussed in section 2. Accordingly, our model pipeline mainly consists in 2 phases: (1) pairwise feature extraction, i.e., feature transformer, and (2) regression estimator. While many related work either use words embedding as an input for learning the sentence semantics representation or learning such semantics features directly, our model is able to reuse both types as input for the pairwise feature transformer. For example, as listed in Table 2, we used features that is based on word vectors similarity of aligned words while we also have a feature that consider the whole sentence vector, i.e., sparse BoW. The model can also use, but not yet used in this paper, unsupervised learned sentence representation out of methods like BoW *matrix decomposition*, *paragraph vector*, or *sent2vec* methods as input to our pairwise features transformer.

4.1   Pairwise Feature Extraction

We used different feature types as in Table 2. The first two types are based on aligning PoS and NE tagged words and then compute the average word vectors cosine similarity (CS) of the paired tags. The process of extracting these type of pairwise

Source Types (as named in the source file)	Manually Assigned Domain Class
FNWN, OnWN, surprise.OnWN	Definition
MSRpar, belief, plagiarism, postediting	Paraphrasing
MSRvid, images	Image-captions
SMT, SMTeuroparl, deft-news, headlines, surprise.SMTnews, tweet-news	News
answer-answer, answers-forums, answers-students, deft-forum, question-question	Question-answer

Table 1: Sentence pairs data source types and its manually annotated domain class.

Algorithm 1: The pairwise features extraction process of aligned PoS and NE tagged tokens.

Input: Sentence pair

1. Extract a PoS type or a NE type word tokens from both sentences
2. Pair each tagged word-token in one sentence to all same tagged tokens in the other sentence
3. Get the word vector representations of both tokens of each paired tokens
4. Compute the vector representations of both tokens of each paired tokens
5. Align words if the cosine similarity (CS) is above a threshold value
6. Solve alignment conflicts, if any, based on the higher CS value
7. Compute the average CS of the aligned tokens and use it as the pairwised feature value

---

features are resumed in the algorithm 1.

The third feature is extracted by transforming each sentence to its BoW vector representation. This sparse vector representation is weighted by tf–idf. The vocabulary of the BoW is the character grams range between 2 and 3. This BoW vocabulary source is only the data set of the task itself and not a general large text corpus like the ones usually used for word embedding. We are planning to try out a similar feature, but unsupervised, where we consider a corpus like Wikipedia dump as a source for the BoW. Another feature we plan to consider as a future work is the dense decomposed BoW using SVD or NMF. Finally, we can also consider unsupervised sentence vectors using *paragraph vectors* or *sent2vec* methods.

Features number 4 is extracted by computing the absolute difference of the summation of all numbers in each sentence. To achieve that, we transferred any spelled number, e.g., "sixty-five", to its numerical value, e.g., 65. The fifth pairwise

feature we used was simply based on the sentence length. The last feature is extracted by mapping each sentence pair source to a manually annotated domain class as in Table 1. However, in order to use this feature, we would need to specify the domain class of the sentence pairs of the test data set. Manually checking the test data and also based on some replies found from the task organizers about the source of the test data, we classified them all as "Image-captions".

4.2 Regression

We have mainly evaluated two regression estimators for this task. The first estimator was random forests (RF) and the other was Lasso (least absolute shrinkage and selection operator). Based on a 10-fold cross-validation (CV), we set the number of estimators of 1024 for RF and a maximum depth of 8. For Lasso CV, we finally set the number of iterations to 512.

5 Implementation

Our Python model implementation is available for reproducing the results on GitHub[1]. For PoS and RE tagging, we utilized both polyglot (Al-Rfou et al., 2013) and spaCy. We used a pre-trained GloVe (Pennington et al., 2014) word vectors of a size 300. The pipeline of the transformer and the regression estimator was built on scikit-learn API. Finally, we used pair-wise feature combiners similar to the ones used in Louppe et al. (2016).

6 Results

6.1 Regression Estimator Selection

First, we run few experiments to decide on using RF or Lasso CV. The experimental results of these runs are listed in Table 3. The feature-importances analysis are shown in the right column of Table 2.

---

[1]https://github.com/natsheh/sensim

	Feature	Pair Combiner	Importance
1	Aligned PoS tags (17 tags)	Average of w2v CS of all PoS tag pairs	0.113
2	Aligned NE tags (10 tags)	Average of w2v CS of all NE tag pairs	0.003
3	TFIDF char ngrams BoW	Cosine similarity of the sentence BoW vector pair	0.847
4	Numbers	Absolute difference of the number summation	0.006
5	Sentence length	Absolute difference of the number of characters	0.032
6	Domain class of the pair	N/A	N/A

Table 2: Pairwise features set.

Regressor	PoS	word_vectors	images	answers_students	headlines_2016	Mean
Lasso CV	polyglot	GloVe	0.82	0.74	0.80	0.79
Lasso CV	spaCy	spaCy	0.82	0.74	0.79	0.79
RF	spaCy	spaCy	0.85	0.78	0.80	0.81
RF	polyglot	spaCy	0.85	0.77	0.80	0.81

Table 3: Regression estimator selection based on experimental evaluation score over a few data sets.

6.2 System Configuration Selection

We experimented different settings varying the feature transformation design parameters and trying out three different training set versions for RF. We show the 3 selected settings for submission and the test score of a few evaluation data-sets from previous years in Table 4.

6.3 Final Results

We finally submitted three runs of our model UdL for the task official evaluation. The settings of these three runs are shown in Table 4. The summary of the evaluation score with the baseline (0.7278), the best score run model (0.8547), the least (0.0069), the median (0.7775) and the mean (0.7082) are shown in Figure 1. Run1 was our best run with Pearson correlation score of (0.8004), At this run, we used RF for regression estimator on our all extracted pairwise features except the domain class feature. Run2 (0.7805) was same as Run1 except that we used the domain class feature. Finally, Run3, submission correction phase (0.7901), used a different data set were we filtered-out hash-tag symbol from Twitter-news sentence pairs.

7 Conclusion and Future Work

We proposed UdL, a model for estimating sentence pair semantic similarity. The model mainly utilizes two types of pairwise features which are (1) the aligned part-of-speech and named-entities tags and (2) the tf–idf weighted BoW vector model of character-based n-gram range instead of words. The evaluation results shows that Random Forest regression estimator on our extracted pairwise fea-

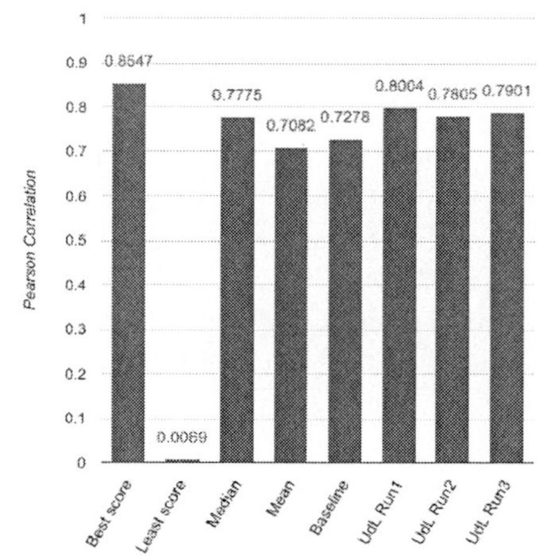

Figure 1: Track 5 results summary in comparison to UdL three runs;*: submission correction.

tures provided 80% of Pearson correlation with hidden human annotation values. The model was implemented in a scalable pipeline architecture and is now made available to the public where the user can add and experiment any additional features or even any other regression models. Since the sentence vector BoW-based pairwise feature showed high percentage in the feature importances analysis of the Random Forest estimator, we are going to try other, but dense, sentence vector representation, e.g., in Shen et al. (2014); Le and Mikolov (2014). We are also planning to use and evaluate the model in some related applications in-

Submission	data set	DF	PoS	vectors	images	AS	H16	AA	QQ	plagiarism	mean
-	small	no	polyglot	spaCy	0.85	0.77	0.80	0.47	0.54	0.82	0.71
-	small	yes	polyglot	spaCy	0.82	0.75	0.79	0.53	0.56	0.84	0.72
Run2 settings	big	yes	spaCy	spaCy	0.82	0.74	0.79	0.54	0.61	0.84	0.72
-	big	yes	polyglot	spaCy	0.82	0.75	0.79	0.52	0.55	0.84	0.71
-	big	no	spaCy	spaCy	0.82	0.78	0.80	0.46	0.60	0.82	0.71
-	big	no	polyglot	spaCy	0.85	0.77	0.80	0.51	0.56	0.82	0.72
Run1 settings	big	no	polyglot	spaCy	0.85	0.77	0.80	0.46	0.54	0.82	0.71
Run3 settings	BH	no	polyglot	spaCy	0.85	0.77	0.80	0.51	0.58	0.82	0.72
-	BH	no	polyglot	GloVe	0.85	0.77	0.80	0.46	0.57	0.81	0.71

Table 4: Evaluation 2-decimal-rounded score on some testsets. DF: domain feature, AA:answer-answer, AS:answers_students, H16:headlines_2016, QQ:question-question, BH:bigger data set size where hashtags are filtered

cluding a semantic sentences highlighter, a topic-diversified document recommender system as well as a question-answering system.

Acknowledgments

We would like to thank ARC6 Auvergne-Rhône-Alpes that funds the current PhD studies of the first author and the program "Investissements d'Avenir" ISTEX for funding the post-doctoral position of the second author.

References

Eneko Agirre, Carmen Banea, Daniel Cer, Mona Diab, Aitor Gonzalez-Agirre, Rada Mihalcea, German Rigau, and Janyce Wiebe. 2016. Semeval-2016 task 1: Semantic textual similarity, monolingual and cross-lingual evaluation. In Steven Bethard, Daniel Cer, Marine Carpuat, David Jurgens, Preslav Nakov, and Torsten Zesch, editors, *Proceedings of the 10th International Workshop on Semantic Evaluation (SemEval-2016)*. Association for Computational Linguistics, San Diego, California, pages 497–511.

Rami Al-Rfou, Bryan Perozzi, and Steven Skiena. 2013. Polyglot: Distributed word representations for multilingual NLP. In Julia Hockenmaier and Sebastian Riedel, editors, *Proceedings of the Seventeenth Conference on Computational Natural Language Learning, CoNLL 2013, Sofia, Bulgaria, August 8-9, 2013*. ACL, pages 183–192.

Léon Bottou. 2014. From machine learning to machine reasoning - an essay. *Machine Learning* 94(2):133–149.

Daniel Cer, Mona Diab, Eneko Agirre, Inigo Lopez-Gazpio, and Lucia Specia. 2017. Semeval-2017 task 1: Semantic textual similarity multilingual and crosslingual focused evaluation. In *Proceedings of the 11th International Workshop on Semantic Evaluation (SemEval-2017)*. Association for Computational Linguistics, Vancouver, Canada, pages 1–14. http://www.aclweb.org/anthology/S17-2001.

Quoc V. Le and Tomas Mikolov. 2014. Distributed representations of sentences and documents. In *Proceedings of the 31th International Conference on Machine Learning, ICML 2014, Beijing, China, 21-26 June 2014*. JMLR.org, volume 32 of *JMLR Workshop and Conference Proceedings*, pages 1188–1196.

Gilles Louppe, Hussein T. Al-Natsheh, Mateusz Susik, and Eamonn James Maguire. 2016. Ethnicity sensitive author disambiguation using semi-supervised learning. In Axel-Cyrille Ngonga Ngomo and Petr Kremen, editors, *Knowledge Engineering and Semantic Web - 7th International Conference, KESW 2016, Prague, Czech Republic, September 21-23, 2016, Proceedings*. Springer, volume 649 of *Communications in Computer and Information Science*, pages 272–287.

Jeffrey Pennington, Richard Socher, and Christopher D. Manning. 2014. Glove: Global vectors for word representation. In Alessandro Moschitti, Bo Pang, and Walter Daelemans, editors, *Proceedings of the 2014 Conference on Empirical Methods in Natural Language Processing, EMNLP 2014, October 25-29, 2014, Doha, Qatar, A meeting of SIGDAT, a Special Interest Group of the ACL*. ACL, pages 1532–1543.

Yelong Shen, Xiaodong He, Jianfeng Gao, Li Deng, and Grégoire Mesnil. 2014. A latent semantic model with convolutional-pooling structure for information retrieval. In Jianzhong Li, Xiaoyang Sean Wang, Minos N. Garofalakis, Ian Soboroff, Torsten Suel, and Min Wang, editors, *Proceedings of the 23rd ACM International Conference on Conference on Information and Knowledge Management, CIKM 2014, Shanghai, China, November 3-7, 2014*. ACM, pages 101–110.

Liling Tan, Carolina Scarton, Lucia Specia, and Josef van Genabith. 2015. USAAR-SHEFFIELD: semantic textual similarity with deep regression and machine translation evaluation metrics. In *Proceedings of the 9th International Workshop on Semantic Evaluation, SemEval@NAACL-HLT 2015, Denver, Colorado, USA, June 4-5, 2015*. The Association for Computer Linguistics, pages 85–89.

DT_Team at SemEval-2017 Task 1: Semantic Similarity Using Alignments, Sentence-Level Embeddings and Gaussian Mixture Model Output

Nabin Maharjan, Rajendra Banjade, Dipesh Gautam, Lasang J. Tamang and Vasile Rus
Department of Computer Science / Institute for Intelligent Systems
The University of Memphis
Memphis, TN, USA
`{nmharjan,rbanjade,dgautam,ljtamang,vrus}@memphis.edu`

Abstract

We describe our system (*DT_Team*) submitted at SemEval-2017 Task 1, Semantic Textual Similarity (STS) challenge for English (Track 5). We developed three different models with various features including similarity scores calculated using word and chunk alignments, word/sentence embeddings, and Gaussian Mixture Model (GMM). The correlation between our system's output and the human judgments were up to 0.8536, which is more than 10% above baseline, and almost as good as the best performing system which was at 0.8547 correlation (the difference is just about 0.1%). Also, our system produced leading results when evaluated with a separate STS benchmark dataset. The word alignment and sentence embeddings based features were found to be very effective.

1 Introduction

Measuring the Semantic Textual Similarity (STS) is to quantify the semantic equivalence between given pair of texts (Banjade et al., 2015; Agirre et al., 2015). For example, a similarity score of 0 means that the texts are not similar at all while a score of 5 means that they have same meaning. In this paper, we describe our system *DT_Team* and the three different runs that we submitted to this year's SemEval shared task on STS English track (Track 5; Agirre et al. (2017)). We applied Support Vector Regression (SVR), Linear Regression (LR) and Gradient Boosting Regressor (GBR) with various features (see § 3.4) in order to predict the semantic similarity of texts in a given pair. We also report the results of our models when evaluated with a separate STS benchmark dataset created recently by the STS task organizers.

2 Preprocessing

The preprocessing step involved tokenization, lemmatization, POS-tagging, name-entity recognition and normalization (e.g. pc, pct, % are normalized to pc). The preprocessing steps were same as our DTSim system (Banjade et al., 2016).

3 Feature Generation

We generated various features including similarity scores generated using different methods. We describe next the word-to-word and sentence-to-sentence similarity methods used in our system.

3.1 Word-to-Word Similarity

We used the word2vec (Mikolov et al., 2013)[1] vectorial word representation, PPDB database (Pavlick et al., 2015)[2], and WordNet (Miller, 1995) to compute similarity between words. Please see DTSim system description (Banjade et al., 2016) for additional details.

3.2 Sentence-to-Sentence Similarity

3.2.1 Word Alignment Method

We lemmatized all content words and aligned them optimally using the Hungarian algorithm (Kuhn, 1955) implemented in the SEMILAR Toolkit (Rus et al., 2013). The process is the same as finding the maximum weight matching in a weighted bi-partite graph. The nodes are words and the weights are the similarity scores between the word pairs computed as described in § 3.1. In order to avoid noisy alignments, we reset the similarity score below 0.5 (empirically set threshold) to 0. The similarity score was computed as the sum of the scores for all aligned word-pairs divided by the total length of the given sentence pair.

---

[1] http://code.google.com/p/word2vec/
[2] http://www.cis.upenn.edu/ ccb/ppdb/

Proceedings of the 11th International Workshop on Semantic Evaluations (SemEval-2017), pages 120–124,
Vancouver, Canada, August 3 - 4, 2017. ©2017 Association for Computational Linguistics

In some cases, we also applied a penalty for un-aligned words which we describe in § 3.3

3.2.2 Interpretable Similarity Method

We aligned chunks across sentence-pairs and labeled the alignments, such as Equivalent or Specific as described in Maharjan et al. (2016). Then, we computed the interpretable semantic score as in the DTSim system (Banjade et al., 2016).

3.2.3 Gaussian Mixture Model Method

Similar to the GMM model we have proposed for assessing open-ended student answers (Maharjan et al., 2017), we represented the sentence pair as a feature vector consisting of feature sets $\{7, 8, 9, 10, 14\}$ from § 3.4 and modeled the semantic equivalence levels [0 5] as multivariate Gaussian densities of feature vectors. We then used GMM to compute membership weights to each of these semantic levels for a given sentence pair. Finally, the GMM score is computed as:

$$mem\_wt_i = w_i N(x|\mu_i, \sum_i), \ i \in [0, 5]$$

$$gmm\_score = \sum_{i=0}^{5} mem\_wt_i * i$$

3.2.4 Compositional Sentence Vector Method

We used both Deep Structured Semantic Model (DSSM; Huang et al. (2013)) and DSSM with convolutional-pooling (CDSSM; Shen et al. (2014); Gao et al. (2014)) in the Sent2vec tool[3] to generate the continuous vector representations for given texts. We then computed the similarity score as the cosine similarity of their representations.

3.2.5 Tuned Sentence Representation Based Method

We first obtained the continuous vector representations V_A and V_B for sentence pair A and B using the Sent2Vec DSSM or CDSSM models or skip-thought model[4] (Zhu et al., 2015; Kiros et al., 2015). Inspired by Tai et al. (2015), we then represented the sentence pairs by the features formed by concatenating element-wise dot product $V_A.V_B$ and absolute difference $|V_A - V_B|$. We used these features in our logistic regression model which produces the output $\hat{p}_\theta$. Then, we predicted the similarity between the texts in the target pair as

[3]https://www.microsoft.com/en-us/download/details.aspx?id=52365
[4]https://github.com/ryankiros/skip-thoughts

$\hat{y} = r^T \hat{p}_\theta$, where $r^T = \{1, 2, 3, 4, 5\}$ is the ordinal scale of similarity. To enforce that $\hat{y}$ is close to the gold rating y, we encoded y as a sparse target distribution p such that $y = r^T p$ as:

$$p_i = \begin{cases} y - \lfloor y \rfloor, i = \lfloor y \rfloor + 1 \\ \lfloor y \rfloor - y + 1, i = \lfloor y \rfloor \\ 0, \ otherwise \end{cases}$$

where $1 \le i \le 5$ and, $\lfloor y \rfloor$ is $floor$ operation. For instance, given $y = 3.2$, it would give sparse p = [0 0 0.8 0.2 0]. For building logistic model, we used training data set from our previous DTSim system (Banjade et al., 2016) and used image test data from STS-2014 and STS-2015 as validation data set.

3.2.6 Similarity Vector Method

We generated a vocabulary V of unique words from the given sentence pair (A, B). Then, we generated sentence vectors as in the followings: $V_A = (w_{1a}, w_{2a}, ..w_{na})$ and $V_B = (w_{1b}, w_{2b}, ...w_{nb})$, where $n = |V|$ and $w_{ia} = 1$, if $word_i$ at position i in V has a synonym in sentence A. Otherwise, w_{ia} is the maximum similarity between $word_i$ and any of the words in A, computed as: $w_{ia} = max_{j=1}^{j=|A|} sim(w_j, word_i)$. The $sim(w_j, word_i)$ is cosine similarity score computed using the word2vec model. Similarly, we compute V_B from sentence B.

3.2.7 Weighted Resultant Vector Method

We combined word2vec word representations to obtain sentence level representations through vector algebra. We weighted the word vectors corresponding to content words. We generated resultant vector for A as $R_A = \sum_{i=1}^{i=|A|} \theta_i * word_i$, where the weight θ_i for $word_i$ was chosen as $word_i \in$ {noun = 1.0, verb = 1.0, adj = 0.2, adv = 0.4, others (e.g. number) = 1.0}. Similarly, we computed resultant vector R_B for text B. The weights were set empirically from training data. We then computed a similarity score as the cosine of R_A and R_B. Finally, we penalized the similarity score by the unalignment score (see § 3.3).

3.3 Penalty

We applied the following two penalization strategies to adjust the sentence-to-sentence similarity score. It should be noted that only certain similarity scores used as features of our regression models were penalized but we did not penalize the scores obtained from our final models. Unless specified, similarity scores were not penalized.

3.3.1 Crossing Score

Crossing measures the spread of the distance between the aligned words in a given sentence pair. In most cases, sentence pairs with higher degree of similarity have aligned words in same position or its neighborhood. We define crossing crs as:

$$crs = \frac{\sum_{w_i \in A,\ w_j \in B,\ aligned(w_i, w_j)} |i - j|}{max(|A|, |B|) * (\#alignments)}$$

where $aligned(w_i, w_j)$ refers to word w_i at index i in A and w_j at index j in B are aligned. Then, the similarity score was reset to 0.3 if $crs > 0.7$. The threshold 0.7 was empirically set based on evaluations using the training data.

3.3.2 Unalignment Score

We define unalignment score similar to alignment score (see § 3.2.1) but this time the score is calculated using unaligned words in both A and B as:
$unalign\_score = \frac{|A|+|B|-2*(\#alignments)}{|A|+|B|}$. Then, the similarity score was penalized as in the followings:

$$score^* = (1 - 0.4 * unalign\_score) * score$$

where the weight 0.4 was empirically chosen.

3.4 Feature Selection

We generated and experimented with many features. We describe here only those features used directly or indirectly by our three submitted runs which we describe in § 4. We used word2vec representation and WordNet antonym and synonym for word similarity unless anything else is mentioned specifically.

1. $\{w2v\_wa,\ ppdb\_wa,\ ppdb\_wa\_pen\_ua\}$: similarity scores generated using word alignment based methods (pen_ua for scores penalized by unalignment score).

2. $\{gmm\}$: output of Gaussian Mixture Model.

3. $\{dssm,\ cdssm\}$: similarity scores using DSSM and CDSSM models (see § 3.2.4).

4. $\{dssm\_lr,\ skipthought\_lr\}$: similarity scores using logistic model with sentence representations from DSSM and skip-thought models (see § 3.2.5).

5. $\{sim\_vec\}$: score using similarity vector method (see § 3.2.6).

6. $\{res\_vec\}$: score using the weighted resultant vector method (see § 3.2.7).

7. $\{interpretable\}$: score calculated using interpretable similarity method (§ 3.2.2).

8. $\{noun\_wa,\ verb\_wa,\ adj\_wa,\ adv\_wa\}$: Noun-Noun, Adjective-Adjective, Adverb-Adverb, and Verb-Verb alignment scores using word2vec for word similarity.

9. $\{noun\_verb\_mult\}$: multiplication of Noun-Noun similarity scores and Verb-Verb similarity scores.

10. $\{abs\_diff\_t\}$: absolute difference as $\frac{|C_{ta}-C_{tb}|}{C_{ta}+C_{tb}}$ where C_{ta} and C_{ta} are the counts of tokens of type $t \in \{$all tokens, adjectives, adverbs, nouns, and verbs$\}$ in sentence A and B respectively.

11. $\{overlap\_pen\}$: unigram overlap between text A and B with synonym check given by: $score = \frac{2*overlap\_count}{|A|+|B|}$. Then penalized by crossing followed by unalignment score.

12. $\{noali\}$: number of NOALI relations in aligning chunks between texts relative to the total number of alignments (see § 3.2.2).

13. $\{align,\ unalign\}$: fraction of aligned/non-aligned words in the sentence pair.

14. $\{mmr\_t\}$: min to max ratio as $\frac{C_{t1}}{C_{t2}}$ where C_{t1} and C_{t2} are the counts of type $t \in \{$all, adjectives, adverbs, nouns, and verbs$\}$ for shorter text 1 and longer text 2 respectively.

4 Model Development

Training Data. We used data released in previous shared tasks (see Table 1) for the model development (see § 5 for STS benchmarking).

Models and Runs. Using the combination of features described in § 3.4, we built three different models corresponding to the three runs (R1-3) submitted.

R1. Linear SVM Regression model (SVR; $\epsilon = 0.1$, $C = 1.0$) with a set of 7 features: $overlap\_pen$, $ppdb\_wa\_pen\_ua$, $dssm$, $dssm\_lr$, $noali$, $abs\_diff\_all\_tkns$, mmr_all_tkns.

R2. Linear regression model (LR; default weka settings) with a set of 8 features: $dssm$, $cdssm$, gmm, res_vec, $skipthought\_lr$, sim_vec, $aligned$, $noun\_wa$.

Data set	Count	Release time
Deft-news	299	STS2014-Test
Images	749	STS2014-Test
Images	750	STS2015-Test
Headlines	742	STS2015-Test
Answer-forums	375	STS2015-Test
Answer-students	750	STS2015-Test
Belief	375	STS2015-Test
Headlines	244	STS2016-Test
Plagiarism	230	STS2016-Test
Total	**4514**	

Table 1: Summary of training data.

R1	R2	R3	Baseline	1st
0.8536	0.8360	0.8329	0.7278	**0.8547**

Table 2: Results of our submitted runs on test data (1st is the best result among the participants).

R3. Gradient boosted regression model (GBR; $estimators = 1000$, $max\_depth = 3$) which includes 3 additional features: $w2v\_wa$, $ppdb\_wa$, $overlap$ to feature set used in Run 2.

We used SVR and and LR models in Weka 3.6.8. We used GBR model using sklearn python library. We evaluated our models on training data using 10-fold cross validation. The correlation scores in the training data were 0.797, 0.816 and 0.845 for R1, R2, and R3, respectively.

5 Results

Table 2 presents the correlation (r) of our system outputs with human ratings in the evaluation data (250 sentence pairs from Stanford Natural Language Inference data (Bowman et al., 2015)). The correlation scores of all three runs are 0.83 or above, on par with top performing systems. All of our systems outperform the baseline by a large margin of above 10%. Interestingly, R1 system is at par with the 1st ranked system differing by a very small margin of 0.009 (<0.2%). Figure 1 presents the graph showing R1 system output against human judgments (gold scores). It shows that our system predicts relatively better for similarity scores between 3 to 5 while the system slightly overshoots the prediction for the gold ratings in the range of 0 to 2. In general, it can be seen that our system works well across all similarity levels.

Our 11 features had a correlation of 0.75 or

$dssm$ (0.8254), $ppdb\_wa\_pen\_ua$ (0.8273), $ppdb\_wa$ (0.8139), $cdssm$ (0.8013), $dssm\_lr$ (0.8135), $overlap$ (0.8048)

Table 3: A set of highly correlated features with gold scores in test data.

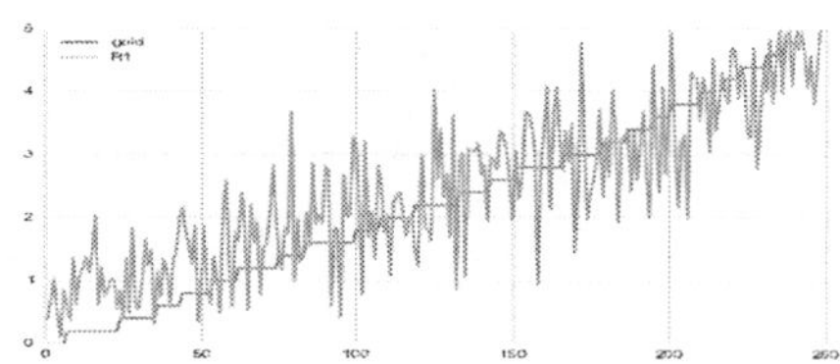

Figure 1: R1 system output in evaluation data plotted against human judgments (in ascending order).

above when compared with gold scores in test data. In Table 3, we list only those features having correlations of 0.8 or above. Similarity scores computed using word alignment and compositional sentence vector methods were the best predictive features.

STS Benchmark (Agirre et al., 2017). We also evaluated our models on a benchmark dataset which consists of 1379 pairs and was created by the task organizers. We trained our three runs with the benchmark training data under identical settings. We used benchmark development data only for generating features from § 3.2.5 (as validation dataset). The correlation scores for $R1$, $R2$ and $R3$ systems were:

In **Dev**: 0.800, 0.822, **0.830** and
In **Test**: 0.755, 0.787, **0.792**

All of our systems outperformed best baseline benchmark system (**Dev** = 0.77, **Test** = 0.72). Interestingly, $R3$ was the best performing while $R1$ was the least performing among the three. As such, generalization was found to improve with increasing number of features (#features: 7, 8 and 11 for $R1$, $R2$ and $R3$ respectively).

6 Conclusion

We presented our *DT_Team* system submitted in SemEval-2017 Task 1. We developed three different models using SVM regression, Linear regression and Gradient Boosted regression for predicting textual semantic similarity. Overall, the outputs of our models highly correlate (correlation up to 0.85 in STS 2017 test data and up to 0.792 on benchmark data) with human ratings. Indeed, our methods yielded highly competitive results.

References

Eneko Agirre, , Daniel Cer, Mona Diabe, , Inigo Lopez-Gazpioa, and Specia Lucia. 2017. Semeval-2017 task 1: Semantic textual similarity multilingual and crosslingual focused evaluation.

Eneko Agirre, Carmen Baneab, Claire Cardiec, Daniel Cer, Mona Diabe, Aitor Gonzalez-Agirrea, Weiwei Guof, Inigo Lopez-Gazpioa, Montse Maritxalara, Rada Mihalceab, et al. 2015. Semeval-2015 task 2: Semantic textual similarity, english, spanish and pilot on interpretability. In *Proceedings of the 9th international workshop on semantic evaluation (SemEval 2015)*. pages 252–263.

Rajendra Banjade, Nabin Maharjan, Dipesh Gautam, and Vasile Rus. 2016. Dtsim at semeval-2016 task 1: Semantic similarity model including multi-level alignment and vector-based compositional seman- tics. *Proceedings of SemEval* pages 640–644.

Rajendra Banjade, Nobal B Niraula, Nabin Mahar- jan, Vasile Rus, Dan Stefanescu, Mihai Lintean, and Dipesh Gautam. 2015. Nerosim: A system for mea- suring and interpreting semantic textual similarity. In *Proceedings of the 9th International Workshop on Semantic Evaluation (SemEval 2015)*. pages 164– 171.

Samuel R Bowman, Gabor Angeli, Christopher Potts, and Christopher D Manning. 2015. A large anno- tated corpus for learning natural language inference. *arXiv preprint arXiv:1508.05326* .

Jianfeng Gao, Li Deng, Michael Gamon, Xiaodong He, and Patrick Pantel. 2014. Modeling interest- ingness with deep neural networks. US Patent App. 14/304,863.

Po-Sen Huang, Xiaodong He, Jianfeng Gao, Li Deng, Alex Acero, and Larry Heck. 2013. Learning deep structured semantic models for web search using clickthrough data. In *Proceedings of the 22nd ACM international conference on Conference on informa- tion & knowledge management*. ACM, pages 2333– 2338.

Ryan Kiros, Yukun Zhu, Ruslan Salakhutdinov, Richard S Zemel, Antonio Torralba, Raquel Urta- sun, and Sanja Fidler. 2015. Skip-thought vectors. *arXiv preprint arXiv:1506.06726* .

Harold W Kuhn. 1955. The hungarian method for the assignment problem. *Naval research logistics quar- terly* 2(1-2):83–97.

Nabin Maharjan, Rajendra Banjade, Nobal B Niraula, and Vasile Rus. 2016. Semaligner: A method and tool for aligning chunks with semantic relation types and semantic similarity scores. *CRF* 82:62–56.

Nabin Maharjan, Rajendra Banjade, and Vasile Rus. 2017. Automated assessment of open-ended student answers in tutorial dialogues using gaussian mixture models (in press). In *FLAIRS Conference*.

Tomas Mikolov, Ilya Sutskever, Kai Chen, Greg S Cor- rado, and Jeff Dean. 2013. Distributed representa- tions of words and phrases and their compositional- ity. In *Advances in neural information processing systems*. pages 3111–3119.

George A Miller. 1995. Wordnet: a lexical database for english. *Communications of the ACM* 38(11):39– 41.

Ellie Pavlick, Pushpendre Rastogi, Juri Ganitkevitch, Benjamin Van Durme, and Chris Callison-Burch. 2015. Ppdb 2.0: Better paraphrase ranking, fine- grained entailment relations, word embeddings, and style classification .

Vasile Rus, Mihai C Lintean, Rajendra Banjade, Nobal B Niraula, and Dan Stefanescu. 2013. Semi- lar: The semantic similarity toolkit. In *ACL (Confer- ence System Demonstrations)*. Citeseer, pages 163– 168.

Yelong Shen, Xiaodong He, Jianfeng Gao, Li Deng, and Grégoire Mesnil. 2014. A latent semantic model with convolutional-pooling structure for information retrieval. In *Proceedings of the 23rd ACM Inter- national Conference on Conference on Information and Knowledge Management*. ACM, pages 101– 110.

Kai Sheng Tai, Richard Socher, and Christopher D Manning. 2015. Improved semantic representations from tree-structured long short-term memory net- works. *arXiv preprint arXiv:1503.00075* .

Yukun Zhu, Ryan Kiros, Richard Zemel, Ruslan Salakhutdinov, Raquel Urtasun, Antonio Torralba, and Sanja Fidler. 2015. Aligning books and movies: Towards story-like visual explanations by watch- ing movies and reading books. *arXiv preprint arXiv:1506.06724* .

FCICU at SemEval-2017 Task 1: Sense-Based Language Independent Semantic Textual Similarity Approach

Basma Hassan[1]   **Samir AbdelRahman[2]**   **Reem Bahgat[2]**   **Ibrahim Farag[2]**

[1]Faculty of Computers and Information
Fayoum University, Fayoum, Egypt
`bhassan@fayoum.edu.eg`

[2] Faculty of Computers and Information
Cairo University, Giza, Egypt
`{s.abdelrahman, r.bahgat, i.farag}@fci-cu.edu.eg`

Abstract

This paper describes FCICU team systems that participated in SemEval-2017 Semantic Textual Similarity task (Task1) for monolingual and cross-lingual sentence pairs. A sense-based language independent textual similarity approach is presented, in which a proposed alignment similarity method coupled with new usage of a semantic network (BabelNet) is used. Additionally, a previously proposed integration between sense-based and surface-based semantic textual similarity approach is applied together with our proposed approach. For all the tracks in Task1, Run1 is a string kernel with alignments metric and Run2 is a sense-based alignment similarity method. The first run is ranked 10th, and the second is ranked 12th in the primary track, with correlation 0.619 and 0.617 respectively.

1 Introduction

Semantic Textual Similarity (STS) is the task of measuring the similarity between two short texts semantically. STS is very important because a wide range of Natural Language Processing (NLP) applications rely heavily on such task.

This paper describes our participation in the STS task (Task1) at SemEval 2017 in all the six monolingual and cross-lingual tracks (Cer et al., 2017). The STS task seeks to calculate a graded similarity score from 0 to 5 between two sentences according to their meaning, i.e. semantically. The monolingual tracks are Arabic, English, and Spanish sentence-pairs (track1, track3, and track5 respectively), while the cross-lingual tracks are Arabic, Spanish, and Turkish sentences paired with English sentences (track2, track4a-4b, and track6 respectively). An additional Primary track is provided that presents the mean score of the results of all the other tracks.

The similarity between two natural language sentences can be inferred from the quantity/quality of aligned constituents in both sentences. Such alignments provide valuable information regarding how and to what extent the two sentences are related or semantically similar, where semantically equivalent text pairs are likely to have a successful alignment between their words. Our proposed sense-based approach employs this aspect to calculate the similarity between sentence-pairs regardless of their language. This is achieved through a proposed word-sense aligner that relies mainly on a new usage of the semantic network BabelNet. BabelNet utilization compensates the need of a machine translation module that is most commonly used to transfer cross-lingual STS to monolingual. Besides, the proposed sense-based similarity score is combined with a surface-based similarity score.

The paper is organized as follows. Section 2 explains our main multilingual sense-based aligner. Section 3 describes our system that participated in all tracks. Section 4 shows the experiments conducted and analyzes the results achieved. Section 5 concludes the paper and mentions some future directions.

2 Multilingual Sense-Based Aligner

Highly semantically similar sentences should also have a high degree of conceptual alignment between their semantic units: words, tokens,

Proceedings of the 11th International Workshop on Semantic Evaluations (SemEval-2017), pages 125–129,
Vancouver, Canada, August 3 - 4, 2017. ©2017 Association for Computational Linguistics

phrases, etc. Several STS methods that use alignments in their calculations have been proposed in literature. Many of those methods were very successful and were among the top performing methods during the last years of SemEval 2013-2016 (Han et al., 2013; Han et al., 2015; Hänig et al., 2015; Sultan et al., 2014a; Sultan et al., 2014b; Sultan et al., 2015).

From this point, we present a sense-based STS approach that produces a similarity score between texts by means of a multilingual word-sense aligner. The following subsections describe in detail the main resource utilized in our STS approach, namely BabelNet (details in subsection 2.1), and our proposed word-sense aligner that our sense-based similarity method relies on (subsection 2.2).

2.1 BabelNet

BabelNet[1] is a rich semantic knowledge resource that covers a wide range of concepts and named entities connected with large numbers of semantic relations (Navigli and Ponzetto, 2010). Concepts and relations are gathered from different lexical resources such as: WordNet, Wikipedia, Wikidata, Wiktionary, FrameNet, ImageNet, and others.

BabelNet is made up of about 14 million entries called *Babel synsets*. Each Babel synset is a set of multilingual lexicalizations (each being a Babel Sense) that represents a given meaning, either concept or named entity, and contains all the synonyms which express that meaning in a range of different languages. For example, the concept '*A motor vehicle with four wheels*' is represented by the synset {car_{en}, $auto_{en}$, $automobile_{en}$, $automobile_{fr}$, $voiture_{fr}$, $auto_{fr}$, $automóvil_{es}$, $auto_{es}$, $coche_{es}$, $otomobil_{tr}$, $araba_{tr}$, سيارة$_{ar}$, مركبة$_{ar}$, عربة$_{ar}$}[2], this synset contains synonyms in English (EN), French (FR), Spanish (ES), Turkish (TR), and Arabic (AR) languages.

BabelNet semantic knowledge is encoded as a labeled directed graph, where vertices are Babel synset (concepts or named entities), and edges connect pairs of synsets with a label indicating the type of the semantic relation between them.

2.2 Word-Sense Aligner

Alignment is the task of discovering and aligning similar semantic units in a pair of sentences expressed in a natural language.

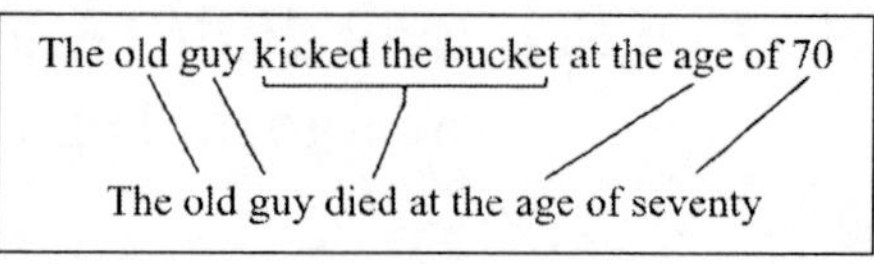

Figure 1: Token alignments using our aligner between monolingual English - English sentence pair example.

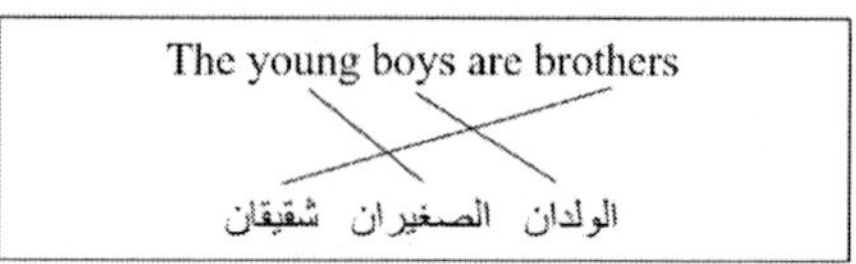

Figure 2: Token alignments using our aligner between cross-lingual English - Arabic sentence pair from SemEval 2017-Track2 dataset.

Our proposed multilingual aligner aligns tokens across two sentences based on the similarity of their corresponding Babel synsets. A token can be in the form of a single word or a multi-words token. When alignment of a single word token fails, its multi-words synonyms are retrieved from BabelNet. The proposed aligner aligns only a token that is neither a stop word nor a punctuation mark.

Figure 1 shows an example of alignments between English monolingual sentence-pairs using our aligner. In this figure the idiom "kicked the bucket" is considered as a single token of multiple words, and it was successfully aligned with the token "died" in the other sentence because both tokens are synonyms to each other in BabelNet. Figure 2 illustrates an example of direct token alignments between English-Arabic cross-lingual sentence pairs without using any machine translation module for translating one sentence language to the other.

Token-pairs are aligned one-to-one in decreasing order of their Babel synsets similarity score (s) using Equation (1). The most commonly used Babel synset of each token is selected.
$$Al_{S1,S2} = \{(t, t', s) : t \in T_1, t' \in T_2, \text{ and } s > \delta \};$$
where T_i is a set of tokens of sentence i, and δ is a threshold parameter for alignment score ($\delta = 0.5$)[3]

2.3 Synset Similarity Measure

Finding similarity between synsets is a fundamental part of our aligner. Hence, we proposed a synset similarity measure based on the hypothesis

---

[1] http://babelnet.org/
[2] Each word is a Babel sense in the subscripted language.
[3] According to experimental results conducted, we found that the best value for this threshold is 0.5.

that highly semantically similar concepts have high degree of common neighbor synsets. From this standpoint, this measure calculates the similarity between Babel synset pairs (bs_i, bs_j) based on the overlap between their directly connected synsets. The overlap-coefficient is used, which is defined as the size of the intersection divided by the smaller of the size of the two sets. That is:

$$sim_{synset}(bs_i, bs_j) = \frac{\left| NS_i \cap NS_j \right|}{\min(| NS_i |, | NS_j |)} \quad (1)$$

where NS_i and NS_j are the sets of all neighbor Babel synsets having a connected edge with bs_i and bs_j in the BabelNet network respectively. Since synonyms are belong to the same synset, their similarity score is equal to 1.

3   System Description

Our systems are based on the past successful integrated architecture of sense-based and surface-based similarity functions presented in SemEval-2015 system (Hassan et al., 2015). We use the integration in the latter system unchanged (Equation 2), where the current results are provided by taking the arithmetic mean of: 1) $sim_{proposed}$: a proposed sentence-pair semantic similarity score (differs in each Run, details in subsection 3.2), and 2) sim_{SC} : the surface-based similarity function proposed by Jimenez et al. (2012). Hence,

$$sim(S_1, S_2) = \frac{sim_{proposed}(S_1, S_2) + sim_{SC}(S_1, S_2)}{2} \quad (2)$$

The approach presented in (Jimenez et al., 2012) represents sentence words as sets of q-grams and measures semantic similarity based on soft cardinality computed from sentence q-grams similarity. Our system employs this approach, with the following parameters setup: $p=2$, bias=0, and $\alpha=0.5$.

In this section, the text preprocessing details is firstly explained in subsection 3.1, and then each submitted Run is described in subsection 3.2.

3.1   Text Preprocessing

The given multilingual input sentences are preprocessed beforehand to map the raw natural language text into structured representation that can be processed. This process is including only four different tasks: (1) tokenization, (2) stopwords removal, (3) lemmatization, and (4) sense tagging.

Tokenization: is carried out using Stanford CoreNLP[4] (Manning et al., 2014), in which the input raw sentence text, in any language, is broken down into a set of tokens.

Stopwords removal: is the task of removing all tokens that are either a stop word or a punctuation mark.

Lemmatization: is a language-dependent task, in which each token is annotated with its lemma. English tokens are lemmatized using Stanford CoreNLP (Manning et al., 2014). Spanish tokens are lemmatized using a freely available lemma-token pairs dataset[5]. Arabic tokens are lemmatized using Madamira[6] (Pasha et al., 2014). For Turkish tokens, lemmatization is not carried out.

Sense tagging: is the task of attaching the Babel synsets (bs) to each sentence token (t). It is achieved by retrieving all the Babel synsets of token's lemma.

On completion of the text preprocessing phase, each sentence is represented by a set of tokens (T), in which each token (t) is annotated by its original word (t_{word}), lemma (t_{lemma}), and a set of Babel synsets (bs_t). This structured representation is then used as an input to our proposed aligner (subsection 2.3), and from which a set of aligned tokens across two sentences S_1 and S_2 is formed ($Al_{S1,S2}$).

3.2   Submitted Runs

We made two system submissions to participate in all the provided monolingual and cross-lingual tracks, named Run1 and Run2. Each run proposes a new different sense-based similarity method between sentence-pairs. The proposed similarity score is then applied in Equation (2), $sim_{proposed}$, resulting in the final similarity score between two sentences in each run. In the following, each of the two runs is described.

Run1: String Kernel with Alignments

A kernel can be interpreted as a similarity measure between two sentences, it is a simple way of computing the inner product of two data points in a feature space directly as a function of their original space variables (Liang et al., 2011). At SemEval 2015, a string kernel was presented, which relied on the hypothesis that the greater the

---

[4]http://nlp.stanford.edu/software/corenl p.shtml
[5]http://www.lexiconista.com/datasets/lem matization/
[6]http://camel.abudhabi.nyu.edu/madamira/

similarity of word senses between two texts, the higher their semantic equivalence will be (Hassan et al., 2015). Accordingly, this run employs the string kernel presented in (Hassan et al., 2015) in which the alignments obtained from our proposed aligner is used in mapping a sentence to feature space. The changed kernel mapping function is given by:

$$\phi_t(S) = \max_{1 \le i \le n} \left\{ sim(t, t_i) \right\} \qquad (3)$$

where $sim(t, t_i)$ is the alignment score s of the two tokens if $(t, t_i, s) \in Al_{S1,S2}$, and is equal to 0 otherwise, and n is the number of tokens contained in sentence S, i.e. $| T |$.

The normalized string kernel between two sentences S_1 and S_2 is calculated as follows (Shawe-Taylor and Cristianini, 2004):

$$\kappa_{NS}(S_1, S_2) = \frac{\kappa_S(S_1, S_2)}{\sqrt{\kappa_S(S_1, S_1)\kappa_S(S_2, S_2)}} \qquad (4)$$

$$\kappa_S(S_1, S_2) = \langle \phi(S_1), \phi(S_2) \rangle = \sum_{t \in T} \phi_t(S_1) \cdot \phi_t(S_2)$$

where T is the set of all tokens in both S_1 and S_2.

Given two sentences, S_1 and S_2, our similarity score between S_1 and S_2 proposed by this run is the value of the normalized string kernel function between the two sentences (Equation 4). That is:

$$sim_{proposed}(S_1, S_2) = \kappa_{NS}(S_1, S_2) \qquad (5)$$

Run2: Alignment-Based Similarity Metric

Alignment-based semantic similarity approaches presented in (Sultan et al., 2014a; Sultan et al., 2014b; Sultan et al., 2015) relied only on the proportions of the aligned content words on the two sentences. We hypothesized that alignments are not of the same importance, an alignment of synonym tokens with alignment score 1 is not the same as an alignment of two semantically related tokens with score 0.5. Hence, the proposed similarity score between S_1 and S_2 proposed for this run is based on the alignment scores as well as their proportion to the number of tokens in both sentences. It is given by:

$$sim_{proposed}(S_1, S_2) = \frac{2 * \sum_{al \in Al_{S1,S2}} al.s}{| T_1 | + | T_2 |} \qquad (6)$$

where T_i is a set of tokens in sentence i, and $al.s$ is the score calculated for the alignment al.

Track	Run1	Run2	Baseline	Best Score
1 : AR-AR	.7158	**.7158**	.6045	.7543
2 : AR-EN	**.6782**	.6781		.7493
3 : SP-SP	.8484	**.8489**	.7117	.8559
4a: SP-EN	**.6926**	.6854		.8302
4b: SP-EN	**.0254**	.0214		.3407
5 : EN-EN	.8272	**.8280**	.7278	.8547
6 : TR-EN	**.5452**	.5390		.7706
Primary	**.6190**	**.6166**		**.7316**

Table 1: System performance on SemEval-2107 datasets.

4   Experimental Results

The main evaluation measure selected by the task organizers was the Pearson correlation between the system scores and the gold standard scores. Table 1 presents the official results of our submissions in SemEval2017-Task1 for both Run1 and Run2 in the six tracks as well as the primary track. The best performing score obtained in each track is included as well alongside with the baseline system results announced by the task organizers. Our best system (Run1) achieved 0.619 correlation and ranked the 10th run and the 5th team out of 84 runs and 31 teams respectively.

Although the performance of the two Runs differs slightly, it is noticeable from the table that Run1 (Kernel) performs better with cross-lingual sentence-pairs, while Run2 (Alignments) performs better with monolingual sentence-pairs. Hence, relying on aligned tokens only in cross-lingual sentences is insufficient.

5   Conclusions and Future work

Experimental results proved that, in spite of the fact that our proposed simple unsupervised approach relies only on BabelNet and token alignments, it is capable of assessing the semantic similarity between two sentences in different languages with good performance, 10th run rank and 5th team rank. Also, the proposed approach demonstrates the effectiveness and usefulness of using the BabelNet semantic network in solving the STS task. Some potential future work includes enhancing our proposed synset similarity method, and exploiting the extraction of promising content words in the given sentences.

References

Daniel Cer, Mona Diab, Eneko Agirre, Iñigo Lopez-Gazpio, and Lucia Specia. 2017. SemEval-2017 Task 1: Semantic Textual Similarity Multilingual and Crosslingual Focused Evaluation. In *Proceedings of the 11th International Workshop on Semantic Evaluation (SemEval 2017)*, pages 1–14, Vancouver, Canada.

Lushan Han, Abhay Kashyap, Tim Finin, James Mayfield, and Jonathan Weese. 2013. UMBC EBIQUITY-CORE: Semantic textual similarity systems. In *Proceedings of the Second Joint Conference on Lexical and Computational Semantics*, pages. 44-52, Atlanta, Georgia, USA

Lushan Han, Justin Martineau, Doreen Cheng, and Christopher Thomas. 2015. Samsung: Align-and-differentiate approach to semantic textual similarity. In *Proceedings of the 9th International Workshop on Semantic Evaluation (SemEval 2015)*, pages 172–177, Denver, Colorado, USA

Christian Hänig, Robert Remus, and Xose De La Puente. 2015. ExB Themis: Extensive feature extraction from word alignments for semantic textual similarity. In *Proceedings of the 9th International Workshop on Semantic Evaluation (SemEval 2015)*, pages 264–268, Denver, Colorado, USA

Basma Hassan, Samir AbdelRahman, and Reem Bahgat. (2015). FCICU: The Integration between Sense-Based Kernel and Surface-Based Methods to Measure Semantic Textual Similarity. In *Proceedings of the 9th International Workshop on Semantic Evaluation (SemEval 2015)*, pages 154–158, Denver, Colorado, USA.

Sergio Jimenez, Claudia Becerra, and Alexander Gelbukh. 2012. Soft Cardinality: A Parameterized Similarity Function for Text Comparison. In *Proceedings of the First Joint Conference on Lexical and Computational Semantics (*SEM)*, pages 449–453, Montreal, Canada.

Yizeng Liang, Qing-Song Xu, Hong-Dong Li, and Dong-Sheng Cao. 2011. *Support Vector Machines and Their Application in Chemistry and Biotechnology*. CRC Press.

Christopher D. Manning, Mihai Surdeanu, John Bauer, Jenny Finkel, Steven J. Bethard, and David McClosky. 2014. The Stanford CoreNLP Natural Language Processing Toolkit. In *Proceedings of the 52nd Annual Meeting of the Association for Computational Linguistics: System Demonstrations*, pages 55–60, Baltimore, Maryland.

Roberto Navigli and Simone Paolo Ponzetto. 2010. BabelNet: Building a Very Large Multilingual Semantic Network. In *Proceedings of the 48th Annual Meeting of the Association for Computational Linguistics*, pages 216–225, Uppsala, Sweden.

Arfath Pasha, Mohamed Al-Badrashiny, Mona Diab, Ahmed El Kholy, Ramy Eskander, Nizar Habash, Manoj Pooleery, Owen Rambow, and Ryan Roth. 2014. MADAMIRA: A Fast, Comprehensive Tool for Morphological Analysis and Disambiguation of Arabic. In Proceedings of the 9th International Conference on Language Resources and Evaluation (LREC'14), pages 1094–1101, Reykjavik, Iceland.

Md Arafat Sultan, Steven Bethard, and Tamara Sumner. 2014a. Back to Basics for Monolingual Alignment: Exploiting Word Similarity and Contextual Evidence. *Transactions of the Association for Computational Linguistics*, 2:219–230.

Md Arafat Sultan, Steven Bethard, and Tamara Sumner. 2014b. DLS@CU: Sentence Similarity from Word Alignment. In *Proceedings of the 8th International Workshop on Semantic Evaluation (SemEval 2014)*, pages 241–246, Dublin, Ireland.

Md Arafat Sultan, Steven Bethard, and Tamara Sumner. 2015. DLS@CU: Sentence Similarity from Word Alignment and Semantic Vector Composition. In *Proceedings of the 9th International Workshop on Semantic Evaluation (SemEval 2015)*, pages 148–153, Denver, Colorado, USA.

John Shawe-Taylor and Nello Cristianini. 2004. *Kernel Methods for Pattern Analysis*. Cambridge University Press.

HCTI at SemEval-2017 Task 1: Use convolutional neural network to evaluate Semantic Textual Similarity

Yang SHAO

Hitachi, Ltd. / Higashi koigakubo 1-280, Kokubunji-shi, Tokyo, Japan

`yang.shao.kn@hitachi.com`

Abstract

This paper describes our convolutional neural network (CNN) system for the Semantic Textual Similarity (STS) task. We calculated semantic similarity score between two sentences by comparing their semantic vectors. We generated a semantic vector by max pooling over every dimension of all word vectors in a sentence. There are two key design tricks used by our system. One is that we trained a CNN to transfer GloVe word vectors to a more proper form for the STS task before pooling. Another is that we trained a fully-connected neural network (FCNN) to transfer the difference of two semantic vectors to the probability distribution over similarity scores. All hyperparameters were empirically tuned. In spite of the simplicity of our neural network system, we achieved a good accuracy and ranked 3rd on primary track of SemEval 2017.

1 Introduction

Semantic Textual Similarity (STS) is the task of determining the degree of semantic similarity between two sentences. STS task is a building block of many natural language processing (NLP) applications. Therefore, it has received a significant amount of attention in recent years. STS tasks in SemEval have been held from 2012 to 2017 (Cer et al., 2017). Successfully estimating the degree of semantic similarity between two sentences requires a very deep understanding of both sentences. Well performing STS methods can be applied to many other natural language understanding tasks including paraphrasing, entailment detection, answer selection, hypothesis evidencing, machine translation (MT) evaluation and

quality estimation, summarization, question answering (QA) and short answer grading.

Measuring sentence similarity is challenging for two reasons. One is the variability of linguistic expression and the other is the limited amount of annotated training data. Therefore, conventional NLP approaches, such as sparse, hand-crafted features are difficult to use. However, neural network systems (He et al., 2015a; He and Lin, 2016) can alleviate data sparseness with pre-training and distributed representations. We propose a convolutional neural network system with 5 components:

1) Enhance GloVe word vectors by adding hand-crafted features.

2) Transfer the enhanced word vectors to a more proper form by a convolutional neural network.

3) Max pooling over every dimension of all word vectors to generate semantic vector.

4) Generate semantic difference vector by concatenating the element-wise absolute difference and the element-wise multiplication of two semantic vectors.

5) Transfer the semantic difference vector to the probability distribution over similarity scores by fully-connected neural network.

2 System Description

Figure 1 provides an overview of our system. The two sentences to be semantically compared are first pre-processed as described in subsection 2.1. Then the CNN described in subsection 2.2 combines the word vectors from each sentence into an appropriate sentence level embedding. After that, the methods described in subsection 2.3 are used to compute representations that compare paired sentence level embeddings. Then, a fully-connected neural network (FCNN) described in subsection 2.4 transfers the semantic difference vector to a probability distribution over similarity

Proceedings of the 11th International Workshop on Semantic Evaluations (SemEval-2017), pages 130–133,
Vancouver, Canada, August 3 - 4, 2017. ©2017 Association for Computational Linguistics

scores. All hyperparameters in our system were empirically tuned for the STS task and shown in Table 1. We implemented our neural network system by using Keras[1] (Chollet, 2015) and Tensor-Flow[2] (Abadi et al., 2016).

2.1 Pre-process

Several text preprocessing operations were performed before feature engineering:

1) All punctuations are removed.

2) All words are lower-cased.

3) All sentences are tokenized by Natural Language Toolkit (NLTK) (Bird et al., 2009).

4) All words are replaced by pre-trained GloVe word vectors (Common Crawl, 840B tokens) (Pennington et al., 2014). Words that do not exist in the pre-trained embeddings are set to the zero vector.

5) All sentences are padded to a static length $l = 30$ with zero vectors (He et al., 2015a).

Several hand-crafted features are added to enhance the GloVe word vectors:

1) If a word appears in both sentences, add a TRUE flag to the word vector, otherwise, add a FALSE flag.

2) If a word is a number, and the same number appears in the other sentence, add a TRUE flag to the word vector of the matching number in each sentence, otherwise, add a FALSE flag.

3) The part-of-speech (POS) tag of every word according to NLTK is added as a one-hot vector.

2.2 Convolutional neural network (CNN)

Our CNN consists of $n = 300$ one dimensional filters. The length of the filters is set to be the same as the dimension of the enhanced word vectors. The activation function of the CNN is set to be $relu$ (Nair and Hinton, 2010). We did not use any regularization or drop out. Early stopping triggered by model performance on validation data was used to avoid overfitting. The number of layers is set to be 1. We used the same model weights to transfer each of the words in a sentence. Sentence level embeddings are calculated by max pooling (Scherer et al., 2010) over every dimension of the transformed word level embedding.

---

[1]http://github.com/fchollet/keras
[2]http://github.com/tensorflow/tensorflow

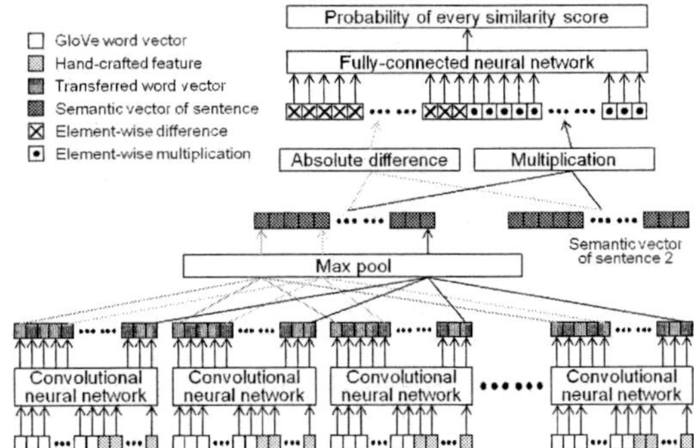

Figure 1: Overview of system

2.3 Comparison of semantic vectors

To calculate the semantic similarity score of two sentences, we generate a semantic difference vector by concatenating the element-wise absolute difference and the element-wise multiplication of the corresponding paired sentence level embeddings. The calculation equation is

$$S\vec{D}V = (|S\vec{V}1 - S\vec{V}2|, S\vec{V}1 \circ S\vec{V}2) \qquad (1)$$

Here, $S\vec{D}V$ is the semantic difference vector, $S\vec{V}1$ and $S\vec{V}2$ are the semantic vectors of the two sentences, and $\circ$ is Hadamard product which generate the element-wise multiplication of two semantic vectors.

2.4 Fully-connected neural network (FCNN)

An FCNN is used to transfer the semantic difference vector (600 dimension) to a probability distribution over the six similarity labels used by STS. The number of layers is set to be 2. The first layer uses 300 units with a $tanh$ activation function. The second layer produces the similarity label probability distribution with 6 units combined with a $softmax$ activation function. We train without using regularization or drop out.

3 Experiments and Results

We randomly split all dataset files of SemEval-2012–2015 (Agirre et al., 2012, 2013, 2014, 2015) into ten. We used the preparation of the data from (Baudis et al., 2016). We used 90% of the pairs in each individual dataset file for training and the other 10% for validation. We tested our model in the English dataset of SemEval-2016 (Agirre et al., 2016). Our objective function is the Pearson correlation coefficient computed over each batch. ADAM was used as the gradient descent optimization method. All parameters are set to the values

Table 1: Hyperparameters

Sentence pad length	30
Dimension of GloVe vectors	300
Number of CNN layers	1
Dimension of CNN filters	1
Number of CNN filters	300
Activation function of CNN	$relu$
Initial function of CNN	$he\_uniform$
Number of FCNN layers	2
Dimension of input layer	600
Dimension of first layer	300
Dimension of second layer	6
Activation of first layer	$tanh$
Activation of second layer	$softmax$
Initial function of layers	$he\_uniform$
Optimizer	$ADAM$
Batch size	339
Max epoch	6
Run times	8

suggested by (P.Kingma and Ba, 2015): learning rate is 0.001, $\beta1$ is 0.9, $\beta2$ is 0.999, ϵ is 1e-08. $he\_uniform$ (He et al., 2015b) was used as the initial function of layers. We did the experiment 8 times and choose the model that achieved the best performance on the validation dataset. Our system got a Pearson correlation coefficient result of 0.7192±0.0062.

We also used the same model design to take part in all tracks of SemEval-2017. We submitted two runs. One with machine translation (MT) and another without (non-MT). In MT run, we translated all the other languages in the test dataset into English by Google Translate[3] and used the English model to evaluate all similarity scores. For the monolingual tracks, we also tried non-MT run, which means we trained the models directly from the English, Spanish and Arabic data. Here, we independently trained another English model for each run. The difference between English-English performance from MT and non-MT is caused by the random shuffling of data during training.

We also trained another English model with same design to evaluate the STS benchmark dataset (Cer et al., 2017)[4]. We used only the Train part for training and the Dev. part to fine tune. We also run our system without any hand-crafted features. The purely sentence representation system

[3]http://translate.google.com
[4]http://ixa2.si.ehu.es/stswiki/index.php/STSbenchmark

Table 2: Pearson correlation coefficient with the golden standard of 2017 test dataset

Tracks	CNN	Best	Diff.(Rank)
STS 2016	0.7192	0.7781	$0.0589(14^{th})$
	±0.0062		
STS 2017 (MT)			
Primary	0.6598	0.7316	$0.0718(3^{rd})$
1 AR-AR	0.7130	0.7543	$0.0413(6^{th})$
2 AR-EN	0.6836	0.7493	$0.0657(3^{rd})$
3 SP-SP	0.8263	0.8559	$0.0296(4^{th})$
4a SP-EN	0.7621	0.8302	$0.0681(5^{th})$
4b SP-EN	0.1483	0.3407	$0.1924(7^{th})$
5 EN-EN	0.8113	0.8547	$0.0434(8^{th})$
6 EN-TR	0.6741	0.7706	$0.0965(3^{rd})$
STS 2017 (non-MT)			
1 AR-AR	0.4373	0.7543	$0.3170(15^{th})$
3 SP-SP	0.6709	0.8559	$0.1850(15^{th})$
5 EN-EN	0.8156	0.8547	$0.0391(7^{th})$
STS benchmark (hand-craft)			
Dev.	0.8343	0.8470	$0.0127(4^{th})$
Test	0.7842	0.8100	$0.0258(4^{th})$
STS benchmark (no hand-craft)			
Dev.	0.8236	0.8470	$0.0234(4^{th})$
Test	0.7833	0.8100	$0.0267(4^{th})$

also got a good accuracy. The results are shown in Table 2. Our model achieves 4th place on the STS benchmark[5].

4 Discussion

The difference between our model's performance and that of the best participating system are relative small for all tracks except track 4b and 6. We note that the sentences in track 4b are significantly longer than the sentences in other tracks. We speculate that the results of our system in track 4b were pulled down by the decision to use static padding of length 30 within our model.

Another trend that could be observed is that the results of non-MT were likely harmed by the smaller amounts of available training data. We had over 10,000 training pairs for English, but only 1634 pairs in Spanish and 1104 in Arabic. Correspondingly, for our non-MT models, we achieved our best Pearson correlation scores on English with diminished results on Spanish and our worst results on Arabic. Notably, the results obtained by combining our English model with MT to handle Spanish and Arabic were not affected by the

[5]As of April 17, 2017

limited amount of training data for these two languages and provided better performance.

5 Conclusion

We proposed a simple convolutional neural network system for the STS task. First, it uses a convolutional neural network to transfer hand-crafted feature enhanced GloVe word vectors. Then, it calculates a semantic vector representation of each sentence by max pooling every dimension of their transformed word vectors. After that, it generates a semantic difference vector between two paired sentences by concatenating their element-wise absolute difference and the element-wise multiplication of their semantic vectors. Next, it uses a fully-connected neural network to transfer the semantic difference vector to a probability distribution over similarity scores.

In spite of the simplicity of our neural network system, the difference in performance between our proposed model and the best performing systems that participated in the STS shared task are less than 0.1 absolute in almost all STS tracks and result in our model being ranked 3rd on primary track of SemEval STS 2017.

References

Martín Abadi, Paul Barham, Jianmin Chen, Zhifeng Chen, Andy Davis, Jeffrey Dean, Matthieu Devin, Sanjay Ghemawat, Geoffrey Irving, Michael Isard, Manjunath Kudlur, Josh Levenberg, Rajat Monga, Sherry Moore, Derek G. Murray, Benoit Steiner, Paul Tucker, Vijay Vasudevan, Pete Warden, Martin Wicke, Yuan Yu, and Xiaoqiang Zheng. 2016. Tensorflow: A system for large-scale machine learning. In *Proceedings of the 12th USENIX Conference on Operating Systems Design and Implementation*. USENIX Association, Berkeley, CA, USA, OSDI'16, pages 265–283.

Eneko Agirre, Carmen Banea, Claire Cardie, Daniel Cer, Mona Diab, Aitor Gonzalez-Agirre, Weiwei Guo, Inigo Lopez-Gazpio, Montse Maritxalar, Rada Mihalcea, German Rigau, Larraitz Uria, and Janyce Wiebe. 2015. Semeval-2015 task 2: Semantic textual similarity, english, spanish and pilot on interpretability. In *Proceedings of the 9th International Workshop on Semantic Evaluation*. pages 252–263.

Eneko Agirre, Carmen Banea, Claire Cardie, Daniel Cer, Mona Diab, Aitor Gonzalez-Agirre, Weiwei Guo, Rada Mihalcea, German Rigau, and Janyce Wiebe. 2014. Semeval-2014 task 10: Multilingual semantic textual similarity. In *Proceedings of the 8th International Workshop on Semantic Evaluation*. pages 81–91.

Eneko Agirre, Carmen Banea, Daniel Cer, Mona Diab, Aitor Gonzalez-Agirre, Rada Mihalcea, German Rigau, and Janyce Wiebe. 2016. Semeval-2016 task 1: Semantic textual similarity, monolingual and cross-lingual evaluation. In *Proceedings of the 10th International Workshop on Semantic Evaluation*. Association for Computational Linguistics, San Diego, California, pages 497–511.

Eneko Agirre, Daniel Cer, Mona Diab, Aitor Gonzalez-Agirre, and Weiwei Guo. 2013. Sem 2013 shared task: Semantic textual similarity. In *Proceedings of the Main Conference and the Shared Task: Semantic Textual Similarity*. pages 32–43.

Eneko Agirre, Mona Diab, Daniel Cer, and Aitor Gonzalez-Agirre. 2012. Semeval-2012 task 6: A pilot on semantic textual similarity. In *Proceedings of the First Joint Conference on Lexical and Computational Semantics*. pages 385–393.

Petr Baudis, Jan Pichl, Tomas Vyskocil, and Jan Sedivy. 2016. Sentence pair scoring: Towards unified framework for text comprehension. *arXiv preprint arXiv:1603.06127* .

Steven Bird, Ewan Klein, and Edward Loper. 2009. *Natural Language Processing with Python*. O'Reilly Media.

Daniel Cer, Mona Diab, Eneko Agirre, Inigo Lopez-Gazpio, and Lucia Specia. 2017. Semeval-2017 task 1: Semantic textual similarity multilingual and crosslingual focused evaluation. In *Proceedings of the 11th International Workshop on Semantic Evaluation (SemEval-2017)*. Association for Computational Linguistics, Vancouver, Canada, pages 1–14. http://www.aclweb.org/anthology/S17-2001.

François Chollet. 2015. Keras. `https://github.com/fchollet/keras`.

Hua He, Kevin Gimpel, and Jimmy Lin. 2015a. Multiperspective sentence similarity modelling with convolutional neural networks. In *Proceedings of the 2015 Conference on Empirical Methods in Natural Language Processing*. pages 1576–1586.

Hua He and Jimmy Lin. 2016. Pairwise word interaction modelling with deep neural networks for semantic similarity measurement. In *Proceedings of the 2016 Conference of the North American Chapter of the Association for Computational Linguistics: Human Language Technologies*.

Kaiming He, Xiangyu Zhang, Shaoqing Ren, and Jian Sun. 2015b. Delving deep into rectifiers: Surpassing human-level performance on imagenet classification. In *Proceedings of the International Conference on Computer Vision (ICCV)*.

Vinod Nair and Geoffrey Hinton. 2010. Rectified linear units improve restricted boltzmann machines. In *Proceedings of the 27th International Conference on Machine Learning (ICML)*.

Jeffrey Pennington, Richard Socher, and Christopher D. Manning. 2014. Glove: Global vectors for word representation. In *Empirical Methods in Natural Language Processing*. pages 1532–1543.

Diederik P.Kingma and Jimmy Lei Ba. 2015. Adam: A method for stochastic optimization. In *Proceedings of the 3rd International Conference on Learning Representations (ICLR)*.

Dominik Scherer, Andreas C. Muller, and Sven Behnke. 2010. Evaluation of pooling operations in convolutional architectures for object recognition. In *Proceedings of 20th International Conference on Artificial Neural Networks (ICANN)*. pages 92–101.

LIM-LIG at SemEval-2017 Task1: Enhancing the Semantic Similarity for Arabic Sentences with Vectors Weighting

El Moatez Billah Nagoudi
Laboratoire d'Informatique
et de Mathématiques
LIM
Université Amar Telidji
de Laghouat, Algérie
e.nagoudi@lagh-univ.dz

Jérémy Ferrero
Compilatio
276 rue du Mont Blanc
74540 Saint-Félix, France
LIG-GETALP
Univ. Grenoble Alpes, France
jeremy.ferrero@imag.fr

Didier Schwab
LIG-GETALP
Univ. Grenoble Alpes
France
didier.schwab@imag.fr

Abstract

This article describes our proposed system named *LIM-LIG*. This system is designed for SemEval 2017 Task1: Semantic Textual Similarity (Track1). *LIM-LIG* proposes an innovative enhancement to word embedding-based model devoted to measure the semantic similarity in Arabic sentences. The main idea is to exploit the word representations as vectors in a multidimensional space to capture the semantic and syntactic properties of words. IDF weighting and Part-of-Speech tagging are applied on the examined sentences to support the identification of words that are highly descriptive in each sentence. *LIM-LIG* system achieves a Pearsons correlation of 0.74633, ranking 2nd among all participants in the Arabic monolingual pairs STS task organized within the SemEval 2017 evaluation campaign.

1 Introduction

Semantic Textual Similarity (STS) is an important task in several application fields, such as information retrieval, machine translation, plagiarism detection and others. STS measures the degree of similarity between the meanings of two text sequences (Agirre et al., 2015). Since SemEval 2013, STS has been one of the official shared tasks.

This is the first year in which SemEval has organized an Arabic monolingual pairs STS. The challenge in this task lies in the interpretation of the semantic similarity of two given Arabic sentences, with a continuous valued score ranging from 0 to 5. The Arabic STS measurement could be very useful for several areas, including: disguised plagiarism detection, word-sense disambiguation, la-

tent semantic analysis (LSA) or paraphrase identification. A very important advantage of SemEval evaluation campaign, is enabling the evaluation of several different systems on a common datasets. Which makes it possible to produce a novel annotated datasets that can be used in future NLP research.

In this article we present our LIM-LIG system devoted to enhancing the semantic similarity between Arabic sentences. In STS task (Arabic monolingual pairs) SemEval 2017, the LIM-LIG system propose three methods to measure this similarity: No weighting, IDF weighting and Part-of-speech weighting Method. The best submitted method (Part-of-speech weighting) achieves a Pearsons correlation of 0.7463, ranking 2nd in the Arabic monolingual STS task. In addition, we have proposed another method (after the competition) named Mixed method, with this method, the correlation rate reached 0.7667, which represent the best score among the different submitted methods involved in the Arabic monolingual STS task.

2 Word Embedding Models

In the literature, several techniques are proposed to build word-embedding model.

For instance, Collobert and Weston (2008) have proposed a unified system based on a deep neural network architecture. Their word embedding model is stored in a matrix $M \in R^{d*|D|}$, where D is a dictionary of all unique words in the training data, and each word is embedded into a $d\text{-}dimensional$ vector. Mnih and Hinton (2009) have proposed the Hierarchical Log-Bilinear Model (HLBL). The HLBL Model concatenates the $n - 1$ first embedding words $(w_1..w_{n-1})$ and learns a neural linear model to predicate the last word w_n.

Mikolov et al. (2013a, 2013b) have proposed

Proceedings of the 11th International Workshop on Semantic Evaluations (SemEval-2017), pages 134–138,
Vancouver, Canada, August 3 - 4, 2017. ©2017 Association for Computational Linguistics

two other approaches to build a words representations in vector space. The first one named the
continuous bag of word model CBOW (Mikolov
et al., 2013a), predicts a pivot word according
to the context by using a window of contextual
words around it. Given a sequence of words
$S = w_1, w_2, ..., w_i$, the CBOW model learns
to predict all words w_k from their surrounding
words $(w_{k-l}, ..., w_{k-1}, w_{k+1}, ..., w_{k+l})$. The second model SKIP-G, predicts surrounding words of
the current pivot word w_k (Mikolov et al., 2013b).

Pennington et al.(2014) proposed a Global Vectors (GloVe) to build a words representations
model, GloVe uses the global statistics of word-
word co-occurrence to calculate the probability of
word w_i to appear in the context of another word
w_j, this probability $P(i/j)$ represents the relationship between words.

3   System Description

3.1   Model Used

In Mikolov et al. (2013a), all the methods
(Collobert and Weston, 2008), (Turian et al.,
2010), (Mnih and Hinton, 2009), (Mikolov et al.,
2013c) have been evaluated and compared, and
they show that CBOW and SKIP-G are significantly faster to train with better accuracy compared to these techniques. For this reason, we have
used the CBOW word representations for Arabic
model[1] proposed by Zahran et al. (2015). To
train this model, they have used a large collection
from different sources counting more than 5.8 billion words including: Arabic Wikipedia (WikiAr,
2006), BBC and CNN Arabic corpus (Saad and
Ashour, 2010), Open parallel corpus (Tiedemann,
2012), Arabase Corpus (Raafat et al., 2013), Osac
corpus (Saad and Ashour, 2010), MultiUN corpus (Chen and Eisele, 2012), KSU corpus (ksucorpus, 2012), Meedan Arabic corpus (Meedan,
2012) and other (see Zahran et al. 2015).

3.2   Words Similarity

We used CBOW model in order to identify the
near matches between two words w_i and w_j. The
similarity between w_i and w_j is obtained by comparing their vector representations v_i and v_j respectively. The similarity between v_i and v_j can
be evaluated using the cosine similarity, euclidean
distance, manhattan distance or any other similarity measure functions. For example, let "الجامعة"

---

[1] https://sites.google.com/site/mohazahran/data

(*university*), "المساء" (*evening*) and "الكلية" (*faculty*)
be three words. The similarity between them is
measured by computing the cosine similarity between their vectors as follows:

$$sim(الجامعة, المساء) = cos(V(الجامعة), V(المساء)) = 0.13$$
$$sim(الجامعة, الكلية) = cos(V(الجامعة), V(الكلية)) = 0.72$$

That means that, the words "الكلية" (*faculty*) and
"الجامعة" (*university*) are semantically closer than
"المساء" (*evening*) and "الجامعة" (*university*).

3.3   Sentences similarity

Let $S_1 = w_1, w_2, ..., w_i$ and $S_2 = w'_1, w'_2, ..., w'_j$
be two sentences, their words vectors representa-
tions are $(v_1, v_2, ..., v_i)$ and $(v'_1, v'_2, ..., v'_j)$ respectively. There exist several ways to compare two
sentences. For this purpose, we have used four
methods to measure the similarity between sentences. Figure 1 illustrates an overview of the procedure for computing the similarity between two
candidate sentences in our system.

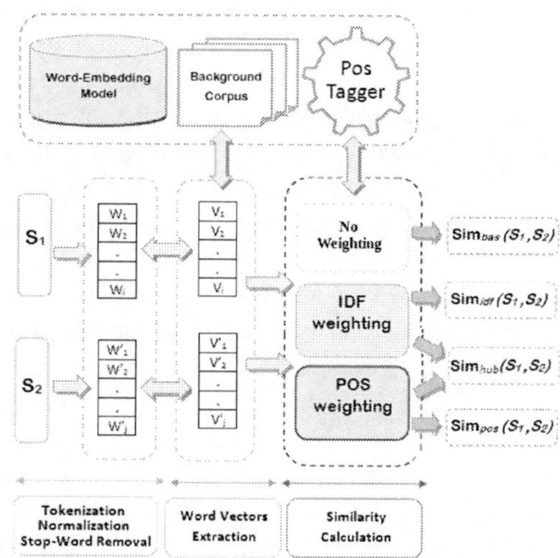

Figure 1: Architecture of the proposed system.

In the following, we explain our proposed methods to compute the semantic similarity among sentences.

3.3.1   No Weighting Method

A simple way to compare two sentences, is to sum
their words vectors. In addition, this method can
be applied to any size of sentences. The similarity
between S_1 and S_2 is obtained by calculating the
cosine similarity between V_1 and V_2, where:

$$\begin{cases} V_1 = \sum_{k=1}^{i} v_k \\ V_2 = \sum_{k=1}^{j} v'_k \end{cases}$$

For example, let S_1 and S_2 be two sentences:
$S_1 = $ "ذهب يوسف إلى الكلية" (*Joseph went to college*).

$S_2 = $ "يوسف يمضى مسرعا للجامعة" (*Joseph goes quickly to university*).

The similarity between S_1 and S_2 is obtained as follows:

Step 1: Sum of the word vectors
$$V_1 = V(الكلية) + V(يوسف) + V(ذهب)$$
$$V_2 = V(للجامعة) + V(مسرعا) + V(يمضى) + V(يوسف)$$

Step 2: Calculate the similarity

The similarity between S_1 and S_2 is obtained by calculating the cosine similarity between V_1 and V_2: $sim(S_1, S_2) = cos(V_1, V_2) = 0.71$

In order to improve the similarity results, we have used two weighting functions based on the Inverse Document Frequency IDF (Salton and Buckley, 1988) and the Part-Of-Speech tagging (POS tagging) (Schwab, 2005) (Lioma and Blanco, 2009).

3.3.2 IDF Weighting Method

In this variant, the Inverse Document Frequency IDF concept is used to produce a composite weight for each word in each sentence. The *idf weight* serves as a measure of how much information the word provides, that is, whether the term that occurs infrequently is good for discriminating between documents (in our case sentences). This technique uses a large collection of document (background corpus), generally the same genre as the input corpus that is to be semantically verified. In order to compute the *idf weight* for each word, we have used the BBC and CNN Arabic corpus[2] (Saad and Ashour, 2010) as a background corpus. In fact, the *idf* of each word is determined by using the formula: $idf(w) = log(\frac{S}{WS})$, where S is the total number of sentences in the corpus and WS is the number of sentences containing the word w. The similarity between S_1 and S_2 is obtained by calculating the cosine similarity between V_1 and V_2, $cos(V_1, V_2)$ where:

$$\begin{cases} V_1 & = & \sum_{k=1}^{i} idf(w_k) * v_k \\ V_2 & = & \sum_{k=1}^{j} idf(w'_k) * v'_k \end{cases}$$

and $idf(w_k)$ is the weight of the word w_k in the background corpus.

Example: let us continue with the sentences of the previous example, and suppose that IDF weights of their words are:

ذهب	يوسف	الكلية	يمضى	مسرعا	الجامعة
0.27	0.37	0.31	0.29	0.22	0.34

Step 1: Sum of vectors with IDF weights
$$V_1 = V(الكلية) * 0.31 + V(يوسف) * 0.37 + V(ذهب) * 0.27$$
$$V_2 = V(الجامعة) * 0.34 + V(مسرعا) * 0.22 + V(يمضى) * 0.29$$
$$+ V(يوسف) * 0.37$$

Step 2: Calculate the similarity

The cosine similarity is applied to computed a similarity score between V_1 and V_2.
$$sim(S_1, S_2) = cos(V_1, V_2) = 0.78$$
We note that the similarity result between the two sentences is better than the previous method.

3.3.3 Part-of-speech weighting Method

An alternative technique is the application of the Part-of-Speech tagging (POS tag) for identification of words that are highly descriptive in each input sentence (Lioma and Blanco, 2009). For this purpose, we have used the POS tagger for Arabic language proposed by G. Braham et al. (2012) to estimate the part-of-speech of each word in sentence. Then, a weight is assigned for each type of tag in the sentence. For example, $verb = 0.4$, $noun = 0.5$, $adjective = 0.3$, $preposition = 0.1$, etc.

The similarity between S_1 and S_2 is obtained in three steps (Ferrero et al., 2017) as follows:

Step 1: POS tagging

In this step the POS tagger of G. Braham et al. (2012) is used to estimate the POS of each word in sentence.

$$\begin{cases} Pos\_tag(S_1) = Pos_{w_1}, Pos_{w_2}, ..., Pos_{w_i} \\ Pos\_tag(S_2) = Pos_{w'_1}, Pos_{w'_2}, ..., Pos_{w'_j} \end{cases}$$

The function $Pos\_tag(S_i)$ returns for each word w_k in S_i its estimated part of speech Pos_{w_k}.

Step 2: POS weighting

At this point we should mention that, the weight of each part of speech can be fixed empirically. Indeed, we based on the training data of SemEval-2017 (Task 1)[3] to fix the POS weights.

$$\begin{cases} V_1 & = & \sum_{k=1}^{i} Pos\_weight(Pos_{w_k}) * v_k \\ V_2 & = & \sum_{k=1}^{j} Pos\_weight(Pos_{w'_k}) * v'_k \end{cases}$$

where $Pos\_weight(Pos_{w_k})$ is the function which return the weight of POS tagging of w_k.

Step 3: Calculate the similarity

Finally, the similarity between S_1 and S_2 is obtained by calculating the cosine similarity between V_1 and V_2 as follows: $sim(S_1, S_2) = cos(V_1, V_2)$.

---

[2]https://sourceforge.net/projects/ar-text-mining/files/Arabic-Corpora/

[3]http://alt.qcri.org/semeval2017/task1/data/uploads/

Example:
Let us continue with the same example, and suppose that POS weights are:

verb	noun	noun_prop	adj	prep
0.4	0.5	0.7	0.3	0.1

Step 1: Pos tagging
The function $Pos\_tag(S_i)$ is applied to each sentence.

$$\begin{cases} Pos\_tag(S_1) = verb\ noun\_prop\ noun \\ Pos\_tag(S_2) = noun\_prop\ verb\ adj\ noun \end{cases}$$

Step 2: Sum of vectors with POS weighting

$$V_1 = V(\text{الكلية}) * 0.5 + V(\text{يوسف}) * 0.7 + V(\text{ذهب}) * 0.4$$

$$V_2 = V(\text{الجامعة}) * 0.5 + V(\text{مسرعا}) * 0.3 + V(\text{يمضى}) * 0.4 + V(\text{يوسف}) * 0.7$$

Step 3: Calculate the similarity

$$sim(S_1, S_2) = cos(V_1, V_2) = 0.82$$

3.3.4 Mixed weighting

We have proposed another method (after the competition), this method propose to use both IDF and the POS weightings simultaneously. The similarity between S_1 and S_2 is obtained as follows:

$$\begin{cases} V_1 = \sum_{k=1}^{i} idf(w_k) * Pos\_weight(Pos_{w_k}) * v_k \\ V_2 = \sum_{k=1}^{j} idf(w'_k) * Pos\_weight(Pos_{w'_k}) * v'_k \end{cases}$$

If we apply this method to the previous example, using the same weights in Section 3.2 and 3.3, we will have: $Sim(S_1, S_2) = Cos(V_1, V_2) = 0,87$.

4 Experiments And Results

4.1 Preprocessing

In order to normalize the sentences for the semantic similarity step, a set of preprocessing are performed on the data set. All sentences went through by the following steps:

1. Remove Stop-word, punctuation marks, diacritics and non letters.

2. We normalized أ ، إ ، آ to ا and ة to ه.

3. Replace final ى followed by ء with ئ.

4. Normalizing numerical digits to Num.

4.2 Tests and Results

To evaluate the performance of our system, our four approaches were assessed based on their accuracy on the 250 sentences in the STS 2017 Monolingual Arabic Evaluation Sets v1.1[4]. We calculate the Pearson correlation between our assigned semantic similarity scores and human judgements. The results are presented in Table 1.

[4] http://alt.qcri.org/semeval2017/task1/data/uploads/sts2017.eval.v1.1.zip

Approach	Correlation
Basic method (run 1)	0.5957
IDF-weighting method (run 2)	0.7309
POS tagging method (run 3)	0.7463
Mixed method	0.7667

Table 1: Correlation results

These results indicate that when the no weighting method is used the correlation rate reached 59.57%. Both IDF-weighting and POS tagging approaches significantly outperformed the correlation to more than 73% (respectively 73.09% and 74.63%). We noted that, the Mixed method achieve the best correlation (76.67%) of the different techniques involved in the Arabic monolingual pairs STS task.

5 Conclusion and Future Work

In this article, we presented an innovative word embedding-based system to measure semantic relations between Arabic sentences. This system is based on the semantic properties of words included in the word-embedding model. In order to make further progress in the analysis of the semantic sentence similarity, this article showed how the IDF weighting and Part-of-Speech tagging are used to support the identification of words that are highly descriptive in each sentence. In the experiments we have shown how these techniques improve the correlation results. The performance of our proposed system was confirmed through the Pearson correlation between our assigned semantic similarity scores and human judgements. As future work, we are going to combine these methods with those of other classical techniques in NLP field such as: n-gram, fingerprint and linguistic resources.

Acknowledgments

This work was carried out as part of a PNE scholarship funded by Ministry of Higher Education and Scientific Research of Algeria, with an international collaboration between two research laboratories: LIM Laboratoire d'Informatique et de Mathmatiques Laghouat, Algeria and LIG Laboratoire d'Informatique de Grenoble (GETALP Team), France.

References

Eneko Agirre, Carmen Baneab, Claire Cardiec, Daniel Cerd, Mona Diabe, Aitor Gonzalez-Agirrea, Weiwei Guof, Inigo Lopez-Gazpioa, Montse Maritxalara, Rada Mihalceab, et al. 2015. Semeval-2015 task 2: Semantic textual similarity, english, spanish and pilot on interpretability. In *Proceedings of the 9th international workshop on semantic evaluation (SemEval 2015)*, pages 252–263.

Yu Chen and Andreas Eisele. 2012. Multiun v2: Un documents with multilingual alignments. In *LREC*, pages 2500–2504.

Ronan Collobert and Jason Weston. 2008. A unified architecture for natural language processing: Deep neural networks with multitask learning. In *Proceedings of the 25th international conference on Machine learning*, pages 160–167. ACM.

Jérémy Ferrero, Frédéric Agnès, Laurent Besacier, and Didier Schwab. 2017. Using Word Embedding for Cross-Language Plagiarism Detection. In *European Association for Computational Linguistics (EACL)*, Volume "short papers" EACL 2017, Valence, Spain, April.

ksucorpus. 2012. King saud university corpus, http://ksucorpus.ksu.edu.sa/ar/ (accessed january 20,2017).

Christina Lioma and Roi Blanco. 2009. Part of speech based term weighting for information retrieval. In *European Conference on Information Retrieval*, pages 412–423. Springer.

Meedan. 2012. Meedan's open source arabic english, https://github.com/anastaw/meedan-memory, (accessed january 20,2017).

Tomas Mikolov, Kai Chen, Greg Corrado, and Jeffrey Dean. 2013a. Efficient estimation of word representations in vector space. In *In: ICLR: Proceeding of the International Conference on Learning Representations Workshop Track*, pages 1301–3781.

Tomas Mikolov, Ilya Sutskever, Kai Chen, Greg S Corrado, and Jeff Dean. 2013b. Distributed representations of words and phrases and their compositionality. In *Advances in neural information processing systems*, pages 3111–3119.

Tomas Mikolov, Wen-tau Yih, and Geoffrey Zweig. 2013c. Linguistic regularities in continuous space word representations. In *Hlt-naacl*, volume 13, pages 746–751.

Andriy Mnih and Geoffrey E Hinton. 2009. A scalable hierarchical distributed language model. In D. Koller, D. Schuurmans, Y. Bengio, and L. Bottou, editors, *Advances in Neural Information Processing Systems 21*, pages 1081–1088. Curran Associates, Inc.

Hazem M Raafat, Mohamed A Zahran, and Mohsen Rashwan. 2013. Arabase-a database combining different arabic resources with lexical and semantic information. In *KDIR/KMIS*, pages 233–240.

Motaz K Saad and Wesam Ashour. 2010. Osac: Open source arabic corpora. In *6th ArchEng Int. Symposiums, EEECS*, volume 10.

Gerard Salton and Christopher Buckley. 1988. Term-weighting approaches in automatic text retrieval. *Information processing & management*, 24(5):513–523.

Didier Schwab. 2005. *Approche hybride-lexicale et thématique-pour la modélisation, la détection et lexploitation des fonctions lexicales en vue de lanalyse sémantique de texte*. Ph.D. thesis, Université Montpellier II.

Jörg Tiedemann. 2012. Parallel data, tools and interfaces in opus. In *LREC*, volume 2012, pages 2214–2218.

Joseph Turian, Lev Ratinov, and Yoshua Bengio. 2010. Word representations: a simple and general method for semi-supervised learning. In *Proceedings of the 48th annual meeting of the association for computational linguistics*, pages 384–394. Association for Computational Linguistics.

WikiAr. 2006. Arabic wikipedia corpus, http://linguatools.org/tools/corpora/wikipedia-monolingual-corpora/, (accessed january 21,2017).

OPI-JSA at SemEval-2017 Task 1:
Application of Ensemble learning for computing semantic textual similarity

Martyna Śpiewak, Piotr Sobecki and Daniel Karaś
National Information Processing Institute
al. Niepodległości 188b, 00-608 Warsaw, Poland
{mspiewak, psobecki, dkaras}@opi.org.pl

Abstract

Semantic Textual Similarity (STS) evaluation assesses the degree to which two parts of texts are similar, based on their semantic evaluation. In this paper, we describe three models submitted to STS SemEval 2017. Given two English parts of a text, each of proposed methods outputs the assessment of their semantic similarity.

We propose an approach for computing monolingual semantic textual similarity based on an ensemble of three distinct methods. Our model consists of recursive neural network (RNN) text auto-encoders ensemble with supervised a model of vectorized sentences using reduced part of speech (PoS) weighted word embeddings as well as unsupervised a method based on word coverage (TakeLab). Additionally, we enrich our model with additional features that allow disambiguation of ensemble methods based on their efficiency. We have used Multi-Layer Perceptron as an ensemble classifier basing on estimations of trained Gradient Boosting Regressors.

Results of our research proves that using such ensemble leads to a higher accuracy due to a fact that each member-algorithm tends to specialize in particular type of sentences. Simple model based on PoS weighted Word2Vec word embeddings seem to improve performance of more complex RNN based auto-encoders in the ensemble. In the monolingual English-English STS subtask our Ensemble based model achieved mean Pearson correlation of .785 compared with human annotators.

1 Introduction

The objective of a system for evaluating semantic textual similarity, is to produce a value which serves as a rating of semantic similarity between pair of text samples. Such task certainly could not be regarded as toy problem, the results could be used to solve multiple real-world problems, e.g. plagiarism detection. We used described methods in STS task in the SemEval 2017 competition (Bethard et al., 2017).

2 Methods

2.1 Data

For the purpose of this research we have used datasets provided by the SemEval challenge organizers containing English sentence pairs coming from several sources. STS Task objective is to produce a value in the range between 0.0 and 5.0, which assessing semantic similarity of a given pair of sentences. Intermediate levels are corresponding to partial similarity such as rough or topical equivalence but with differing details. In this study, we have used all English datasets provided by the challenge organizers until this year to train our supervised models.

2.2 Models

The core of the system is based on widely used Gradient Boosting algorithm. The main novelty of described system lies in the formulation of its feature vectors.

Each feature vector can be divided into two main parts: similarity scores and sentences' descriptors. The process of feature extraction compiles similarity scores of three distinct methods (described later in detail) — effectively forming an ensemble. Additionally, for every pair of sentences, following descriptors are also attached to feature vector:

Proceedings of the 11th International Workshop on Semantic Evaluations (SemEval-2017), pages 139–143,
Vancouver, Canada, August 3 - 4, 2017. ©2017 Association for Computational Linguistics

lengths of the evaluated sentences, Word2Vec coverage as well as two boolean predicates — one of them indicates if a sentence is a question and another one indicating if sentence contains numbers. Word2Vec coverage is defined as follows:

$$G_{lv}(S_i) = \frac{|S_i \cap G|}{|S_i|}$$

where S_i denotes set of all words present in ith sentence and G is a set of all words available in Word2Vec.

The logic behind introduction of these descriptors is based on observations made during evaluation of each separate method. Overall they all achieved a similar Pearson score, but accuracy of every method in context of particular instances of sentence pairs was different. For example, model based on cosine similarity of Word2Vec vectors performed worse in case of long sentences and when the sentences contained words not present in Word2Vec. Ideally introduction of sentences' descriptors to feature vectors would let the regressor "pick" the right method for each case by learning the correlations between features exhibited by sentences and performance of particular method. This hypothesis has been proven true, which is further backed by achieved results.

We used the implementation of Gradient Boosting and Multi-layer Perceptron (MLP) from scikit-learn library (Pedregosa et al., 2011). Facilities present in mentioned library were also used for evaluation using 3-fold crossvalidation and hyperparameters optimization using grid search method. We have used low number of folds in Cross Validation to prevent over-fitting.

2.2.1 TakeLab

This method contributes three components for feature vector used by the meta-regressor. These components correspond to three word similarity measures defined by (Šarić et al., 2012) — ngram overlap, weighted word overlap and WordNet-augmented word overlap. Authors of (Šarić et al., 2012) use Google Books Ngrams for computing information content used in the weighted word overlap measure — we, in comparison, use the frequency list from British National Corpus (Leech, 2016).

Mentioned overlaps were implemented in Java programming language. The WS4J library was used for computing the WordNet path lengths between words with Wu-Palmer method. The OpenNLP library was used for both lemmatization and PoS-tagging. For complete overview of TakeLab measures see (Šarić et al., 2012).

2.2.2 Run 1: Part of Speech weighted Word2Vec Similarity (PoS-Word2Vec)

Described model is based on a well-documented Word2Vec (Mikolov et al., 2013) method of textual information encoding that allows vectorized representation of words, enforces vector space proximity for semantically similar words.

Given sentence pairs (x, y) of words length (n_i, n_j), part of speech (PoS) weights of words w_{x_n} and w_{y_n} and vector representation of words v_{x_n} and v_{y_n} coming from given sentences x and y, respectively. To evaluate vector similarity we have used cosine similarity between vectors x and y:

$$cos(x, y) = \frac{x \cdot y}{||x|| \cdot ||y||}$$

We have extracted following features for each sentence pair, to produce resulting vector r:

- cosine similarity of the mean of word vectors in each sentence

$$r(0) = cos\left(\frac{\sum_{k=1}^{n_i} v_{x_k}}{n_i}, \frac{\sum_{k=1}^{n_j} v_{y_k}}{n_j}\right)$$

- cosine similarity of the mean of word vectors in each sentence weighted by the PoS of the word

$$r(1) = cos\left(\frac{\sum_{k=1}^{n_i} w_{x_k} \cdot v_{x_k}}{\sum_{k=1}^{n_i} w_{x_k}}, \frac{\sum_{k=1}^{n_j} w_{y_k} \cdot v_{y_k}}{\sum_{k=1}^{n_j} w_{y_k}}\right)$$

Furthermore, we have analyzed cross sentence word-wise cosine similarity:

$$M(i, j) = cos(v_{x_i}, v_{y_j}),$$

and obtained maximum, PoS weighted, cross sentence word similarity vector v:

$$v(k) = \max_{j=1,\ldots,n_j} M(k, j) \cdot w_x,$$

for $k = 1, \ldots, n_i$, and

$$v(k) = \max_{i=1,\ldots,n_i} M(i, k - n_i) \cdot w_y,$$

for $k = n_i, \ldots, n_i + n_j$.

We have extracted following statistical features from the resulting vector v and added to the resulting vector r:, Mean , Kurtosis, Skewness, Standard deviation, Maximum value, Minimum value, Percentiles (5th, 25th, 75th and 95th).

$$r(3) = \text{mean}(v)$$
$$r(4) = \text{kurtosis}(v)$$
$$r(5) = \text{skewness}(v)$$
$$r(6) = \text{sd}(v)$$
$$r(7) = \text{max}(v)$$
$$r(8) = \text{min}(v)$$
$$r(9) = \text{percentile}(v, 5)$$
$$r(10) = \text{percentile}(v, 25)$$
$$r(11) = \text{percentile}(v, 75)$$
$$r(12) = \text{percentile}(v, 95)$$

We have used precomputed Word2Vec vectors from GloVe dataset (300 dimensions) (Pennington et al., 2014) for words in sentence pairs and British National Corpus dataset (Leech, 2016) to obtain information about PoS of given word. PoS weights have been experimentally assigned using results from random walk evaluated using Spearman correlation. Statistical moments and percentiles have been experimentally selected during manual trial and error optimization. We trained Gradient Boosting Regressor on the extracted features and evaluated it using 3 fold cross validation to prevent over-fitting.

2.2.3 Run 2: Skip Thoughts Vectors

Skip-thought vectors is an encoder-decoder model (Kiros et al., 2015), which is based on an RNN encoder with GRU acivations and an RNN decoder with a conditional GRU. Instead, in our approach, we only used skip-thought vectors' encoder pretrained on the BookCorpus dataset (Zhu et al., 2015), which maps words to a sentence vector. We determined skip-thought vectors as generic features for all sentences.

Next, we computed component-wise features for given pair of sentences. Denoting a and b as two skip-thought vectors, we computed their component-wise features: product $a \cdot b$, absolute difference $|a - b|$, and the other statistics between sentence pairs used by (Socher et al., 2011). For two compared sentenced the used statistics are as follows:

- 1 if sentences contain exactly the same numbers or no numbers and 0 otherwise,

- 1 if both sentences contain the same numbers,
- 1 if the set of numbers in one sentence is a strict subset of the numbers in the second sentence,
- the percentage of words in one sentence which are in the second sentence and vice-versa,
- the mean of the ratios the number of words in one sentence by the numbers of words in the other sentence.

Finally, we concatenated all aforementioned features together as a final features vector. Again Gradient Boosting Regressor was trained on the obtained features.

2.2.4 Run 3: Ensemble

Using all English pair of sentences from previous years of this task with the available gold scores we computed TakeLab score and trained Gradient Boosting algorithm on PoS weighted Word2Vec features (Run 1) and skip thoughts vectors (Run 2). We used GridSearchCV function with 3 fold cross validation from scikit-learn library to determine the best parameters of Gradient Boosting algorithm according to Pearson measure, separately for each run. Next, we obtained three values as features of Multi-layer Perceptron to determined the final predicted gold scores for each pair of sentences.

3 Results

The purpose of the STS task is to assess the semantic similarity of two sentences. Sentences are scored using the continuous interval $[0, 5]$, where 0 denotes a complete dissimilarity and 5 implies a complete semantic equivalence between the sentences. The final result is the Pearson score between the fixed gold scores and the predicted values from the user system (Agirre et al., 2016).

Table 1: The official results on the test dataset for Subtask 5 (english-english).

Method	Pearson score
Run 3: Ensemble	0.7850
Run 2: Skip Thoughts Vectors	0.7342
STS Baseline	0.7278
Run 1: PoS-Word2Vec	0.6796

As mentioned above, our intention was to create a system to measure the level of paraphrasing, which may be applied to Polish pair of sentences in a relatively easy way in the future. It is worth noticing that the Run 1 and the Run 2 strongly depend on particular language tools, e.g. Word2Vec or a corpus using to train Skip Thoughts Vectors. Furthermore, we did not have appropriate datasets to train these tools for other languages, so we decided to only take part in the Subtask 5 for English pair of sentences. In Table 1 we present the official results only for this subtask.

As was expected the best score was obtained for the ensemble approach. Due to the fact that used pair of sentences had a different format, the final regressor chose which method is better for a particular type of sentence (see Table 2).

Analysis of PoS-Word2Vec method clearly shows that overestimation occurs when subject in compared sentences differs. However cases of underestimation display lack of representation of idioms and use of informal speech. Overall the method seems to be too focused on the meaning of particular words. On the other hand, TakeLab exhibits poor performance in case of nearly-duplicate pairs of sentences. This doesn't come as much of surprise due to the way all TakeLab measures estimate similarity between sentences. This in turn translates to overestimation in cases when two sentences have high word coverage, but effectively differ in semantic meaning (see first example in Table 2). Skip thoughts vectors approach has the biggest problem with significant differences between the length of compared sentences, then there are also over and underestimation error. Also, this method does not handle near-duplicated sentences that sentences differ in only one or two words, and the different words are not synonyms.

4 Conclusion

In this paper, we have presented the OPI-JSA system submitted by our team for SemEval 2017, Task 1, Subtask 5. The proposed system uses a lot of different tools to encode a sentence to a features vector. We used machine learning algorithms to predict the gold score for given pairs of sentences which measure their similarity. Additionally, we showed that an ensemble method improved the performance of our system. The best results we have obtained is equal to 0.785 according to a Pearson's correlation while placing OPI - JSA as 36 of all reported solutions (77) and 16 of 32 teams in the Subtask 5.

Table 2: Examples of maximum over and underestimation of STS evaluation for proposed methods and sentence pairs. Error corresponds to difference between assessed STS and gold scores.

TakeLab	Overestimation	Error
What kind of socket is this?	What kind of bug is this?	4,54
The act of annoying someone or something	The act of liberating someone or something.	4,36
What is the difference between shawarma and gyros?	What is the difference between portamento and glissando?	4,26

TakeLab	Underestimation	Error
The lady peeled the potatoe.	A woman is peeling a potato.	-4,05
Utter fucking nonsense.	That doesn't make any sense.	-3,96
Eurozone backs Greek bailout	Eurozone agrees Greece bail-out	-3,87

PoS-Word2Vec	Overestimation	Error
The activity of examining or assessing something	The activity of protecting someone or something.	3,88
What is the significance of the cat?	What is the significance of the artwork?	3,72
Live Blog: Ukraine In Crisis	Live Blog: Iraq In Turmoil	3,71

PoS-Word2Vec	Underestimation	Error
Murray ends 77-year wait for British win	Murray wins Wimbledon title ends Britains 77year agony	-3,94
The process must happen in the blink of an eye.	The process must be held in a heartbeat.	-3,87
What the what?! ?: Voice of Charlie Brown arrested, charged. ?	Good grief! Charlie Brown actor charged	-3,45

Skip Thoughts Vectors	Overestimation	Error
Vietnamese citizens need a visa to visit the USA.	Nepalese citizens require a visa to visit the UK.	2,52
The PCA (format used by the company and its Apple iPods taken from them), meanwhile, is less course.	AAC (the format used by Apple and its iPods), meanwhile, is less current.	2,18
The act of purchasing back something previously sold.	The act of explaining	2,08

Skip Thoughts Vectors	Underestimation	Error
This frame covers words that name locations as defined politically, or administratively.	The territory occupied by a nation	-2,57
Someone or something that is the agent of fulfilling desired expectations	Someone (or something) on which expectations are centered.	-1,88
The quality of being important, worthy of attention	The quality of being important and worthy of note.	-1,76

References

Eneko Agirre, Carmen Banea, Daniel M. Cer, Mona T. Diab, Aitor Gonzalez-Agirre, Rada Mihalcea, German Rigau, and Janyce Wiebe. 2016. Semeval-2016 task 1: Semantic textual similarity, monolingual and cross-lingual evaluation. In Steven Bethard, Daniel M. Cer, Marine Carpuat, David Jurgens, Preslav Nakov, and Torsten Zesch, editors, *SemEval@NAACL-HLT*. The Association for Computer Linguistics, pages 497–511.

Steven Bethard, Marine Carpuat, Marianna Apidianaki, Saif M. Mohammad, Daniel Cer, and David Jurgens, editors. 2017. *Proceedings of the 11th International Workshop on Semantic Evaluation (SemEval-2017)*. Association for Computational Linguistics, Vancouver, Canada. http://www.aclweb.org/anthology/S17-2.

Ryan Kiros, Yukun Zhu, Ruslan Salakhutdinov, Richard S. Zemel, Antonio Torralba, Raquel Urtasun, and Sanja Fidler. 2015. Skip-thought vectors. *CoRR* abs/1506.06726. http://arxiv.org/abs/1506.06726.

Geoffrey Leech. 2016. *Word frequencies in written and spoken english: based on the british national corpus*. Routlege.

Tomas Mikolov, Ilya Sutskever, Kai Chen, Greg S Corrado, and Jeff Dean. 2013. Distributed representations of words and phrases and their compositionality. In C. J. C. Burges, L. Bottou, M. Welling, Z. Ghahramani, and K. Q. Weinberger, editors, *Advances in Neural Information Processing Systems 26*, Curran Associates, Inc., pages 3111–3119. http://papers.nips.cc/paper/5021-distributed-representations-of-words-and-phrases-and-their-compositionality.pdf.

F. Pedregosa, G. Varoquaux, A. Gramfort, V. Michel, B. Thirion, O. Grisel, M. Blondel, P. Prettenhofer, R. Weiss, V. Dubourg, J. Vanderplas, A. Passos, D. Cournapeau, M. Brucher, M. Perrot, and E. Duchesnay. 2011. Scikit-learn: Machine learning in Python. *Journal of Machine Learning Research* 12:2825–2830.

Jeffrey Pennington, Richard Socher, and Christopher Manning. 2014. Glove: Global vectors for word representation. *Proceedings of the 2014 Conference on Empirical Methods in Natural Language Processing (EMNLP)* https://doi.org/10.3115/v1/d14-1162.

Richard Socher, Eric H. Huang, Jeffrey Pennington, Andrew Y. Ng, and Christopher D. Manning. 2011. Dynamic pooling and unfolding recursive autoencoders for paraphrase detection. In *Proceedings of the 24th International Conference on Neural Information Processing Systems*. Curran Associates Inc., USA, NIPS'11, pages 801–809. http://dl.acm.org/citation.cfm?id=2986459.2986549.

Frane Šarić, Goran Glavaš, Mladen Karan, Jan Šnajder, and Bojana Dalbelo Bašić. 2012. Takelab: Systems for measuring semantic text similarity. In *Proceedings of the First Joint Conference on Lexical and Computational Semantics - Volume 1: Proceedings of the Main Conference and the Shared Task, and Volume 2: Proceedings of the Sixth International Workshop on Semantic Evaluation*. Association for Computational Linguistics, Stroudsburg, PA, USA, SemEval '12, pages 441–448. http://dl.acm.org/citation.cfm?id=2387636.2387708.

Yukun Zhu, Ryan Kiros, Richard Zemel, Ruslan Salakhutdinov, Raquel Urtasun, Antonio Torralba, and Sanja Fidler. 2015. Aligning books and movies: Towards story-like visual explanations by watching movies and reading books. *arXiv preprint arXiv:1506.06724* .

Lump at SemEval-2017 Task 1:
Towards an Interlingua Semantic Similarity

Cristina España-Bonet
[1]University of Saarland
[2]DFKI, German Research Center
for Artificial Intelligence
Saarbrücken, Germany
cristinae@dfki.de

Alberto Barrón-Cedeño
Qatar Computing Research Institute
HBKU, Qatar
albarron@hbku.edu.qa
albarron@gmail.com

Abstract

This is the Lump team participation at SemEval 2017 Task 1 on Semantic Textual Similarity. Our supervised model relies on features which are multilingual or interlingual in nature. We include lexical similarities, cross-language explicit semantic analysis, internal representations of multilingual neural networks and interlingual word embeddings. Our representations allow to use large datasets in language pairs with many instances to better classify instances in smaller language pairs avoiding the necessity of translating into a single language. Hence we can deal with all the languages in the task: Arabic, English, Spanish, and Turkish.

1 Introduction

The Semantic Textual Similarity (STS) task poses the following challenge. Let s and t be two text snippets. Determine the degree of equivalence $\alpha(s, t) \mid \alpha \in [0, 5]$. Whereas 0 represents complete independence, 5 reflects semantic equivalence. The current edition (Cer et al., 2017) includes the monolingual ar–ar, en–en, and es–es, as well as the cross-language ar–en, es–en, and tr–en language pairs. We use the two-letter ISO 639-1 codes: ar=Arabic, en=English, es=Spanish, and tr=Turkish.

Multilinguality is the premise of the Lump approach: we use representations which lie towards language-independence as we aim to be able to approach similar tasks on other languages, paying the least possible effort. Our regression model relies on different kinds of features, from simple length-based and lexical similarities to more sophisticated embeddings and deep neural net internal representations.

2 Features Description

The main algorithm used in this work is the support vector regressor from LibSVM (Chang and Lin, 2011). We use an RBF kernel and greedily select the best parameters by 5-fold cross-validation. In addition, we experiment with a different machine learning component built with gradient boosting algorithms as implemented by the XGBoost package.[1]

We describe the features in growing level of complexity: from language flags up to embeddings derived from neural machine translation.

2.1 Language-Identification Flags (6 feats.)

The novelty of the cross-language tasks causes a noticeable language imbalance in the amount of data (cf. Table 1). To deal with this issue, one of our systems learns on the instances in all the language pairs jointly. In order to reduce the clutter of the different data distributions, we devised six binary features that mark the languages of each pair. $lang1$, $lang2$ and $lang3$ are set to 1 if s is written in either ar, en, or es, respectively. The other three features, $lang4$, $lang5$, and $lang6$, provide the same information for t. For instance, the value for the six features for a pair en–ar would be 0 1 0 1 0 0.

2.2 Lengths (3 feats.)

Intuitively, if s and t have a similar length, being semantically similar is more plausible. Hence, we consider two integer features tok_s and tok_t: the number of tokens in s and t. We also use a length model (Pouliquen et al., 2003) len, defined as

$$\varrho(s, t) = e^{-0.5 \left(\frac{\frac{|t|}{|s|} - \mu}{\sigma} \right)^2}, \quad (1)$$

---

[1]http://xgboost.readthedocs.io

Proceedings of the 11th International Workshop on Semantic Evaluations (SemEval-2017), pages 144–149,
Vancouver, Canada, August 3 - 4, 2017. ©2017 Association for Computational Linguistics

where μ and σ are the mean and standard deviation of the character lengths ratios between translations of documents from L into L'; $|\cdot|$ represents the length of $\cdot$ in characters. If the ratio of lengths of s and t is far from the mean for related snippets, $\varrho(s,t)$ is rather low. This has shown useful in similar cross-language tasks (Barrón-Cedeño et al., 2010; Potthast et al., 2011). The parameters for the different language pairs are $\mu_{en-ar} = 1.23 \pm 0.60$, $\mu_{en-es} = 1.13 \pm 0.41$, $\mu_{en-tr} = 1.04 \pm 0.56$, and $\mu_{x-x} = 1.00 \pm 0.32$ for monolingual pairs.

2.3 Lexical Similarities (5 feats.)

We compute cosine similarities between character n-gram representations of s and t, with $n = [2,5]$ ($2grm,\ldots,5grm$). The pre-processing in this case is casefolding and diacritics removal. The fifth feature cog is the cosine similarity computed over "pseudo-cognate" representations. From an NLP point of view, cognates are "words that are similar across languages" (Manning and Schütze, 1999). We relax this concept and consider as pseudo-cognates any words in two languages that share prefixes. To do so, we discard tokens shorter than four characters, unless they contain non-alphabetical characters, and cut off the resulting tokens to four characters (Simard et al., 1992).

This kind of representations is used on European languages with similar alphabets (McNamee and Mayfield, 2004; Simard et al., 1992). We apply Buckwalter transliteration to texts in `ar` and remove vowels from the snippets written in latin alphabets. For the pseudo-cognates computations, we use three characters instead of four.

2.4 Explicit Semantic Analysis (1 feat.)

We compute the similarity between s and t by means of explicit semantic analysis (ESA) (Gabrilovich and Markovitch, 2007). ESA is a distributional-semantics model in which texts are represented by means of their similarity against a large reference collection. CL-ESA —its cross-language extension (Potthast et al., 2008)— relies on a comparable collection. We compute a standard cosine similarity of the resulting vectorial representations of s and t. Our reference collection consists of $12k$ comparable Wikipedia articles from the `ar`, `en`, and `es` 2015 editions. We did not compile a reference collection for `tr`.

2.5 Context Vectors in a Neural Machine Translation Engine (2 feats.)

Hidden units in neural networks learn to interpret the input and generate a new representation of it. We take advantage of this characteristic and train a multilingual neural machine translation (NMT) system to obtain a representation in a common space for sentences in all the languages. We build the NMT system in the same philosophy of Johnson et al. (2016) using and adapting the Nematus engine (Sennrich et al., 2016). The multilingual system is able to translate between any combination of languages `ar`, `en`, and `es`. It was trained on $60\,k$ parallel sentences ($20\,k$ per language pair) using 512-dimensional word embeddings, 1024 hidden units, a minibatch of 200 samples, and applying Adadelta optimisation. The parallel corpus includes data from United Nations (Rafalovitch and Dale, 2009), Common Crawl[2], News Commentary[3] and IWSLT.[4]

We are not interested in the translations but in the context vectors output of the hidden layers of the encoder, as these are supposed to have learnt an interlingua representation of the input. We compute the cosine similarity between 2048-dimensional context vectors from the internal representation when the encoder is fed with s and t. Two independent systems, one trained with words and another one trained with lemmas[5] provide our two features $lNMT$ and $wNMT$.

2.6 Embeddings for Babel Synsets (2 feats.)

BabelNet is a multilingual semantic network connecting concepts via *Babel synsets* (Navigli and Ponzetto, 2012). Each concept, or word, is identified by its ID irrespective of its language, making these IDs interlingua. For this feature, we gather corpora in the three languages, convert them into sequences of BabelNet IDs, and estimate 300-dimensional word embeddings using the CBOW algorithm, as implemented in the `Word2Vec`

---

[2]`http://commoncrawl.org/`
[3]`http://www.casmacat.eu/corpus/news-commentary.html`
[4]`https://sites.google.com/site/iwsltevaluation2016/mt-track/`
[5]We built a version of the lemma translator with an extra language: Babel synsets (cf. Section 2.6), representing sentences with BabelNet IDs instead of words. The purpose was to extract also this feature for the `tr` surprise language, since it could be used for every language once the input sentences are converted into BabelNet IDs. However, the training was not advanced enough before the deadline and we could not include the results.

2017 Track	L–L'	Instances	Pctge.
1	ar–ar	1,081	5.11
2	ar–en	2,162	10.21
3	es–es	1,555	7.34
4	es–en	1,595	7.53
5	en–en	14,778	69.80
6	tr–en	0*	0.00
total		21,171	100

Table 1: Instances provided in the history of STS. (*No training data exists for this pair.)

package (Mikolov et al., 2013), with a 5-token window. We use the same corpora described before for training the NMT system with the addition of parts of Wikipedia and Gigaword to estimate the embeddings. For these experiments we annotated $1.7\,G$ tokens for ar, $1.1\,G$ for en, and $0.9\,G$ for es. As we are not interested in all the words of a sentence to represent its semantics, we restrict the extraction of Babel synsets to adjectives, adverbs, nouns, and verbs. Negations are considered tagging them with a special label. The global embeddings are then estimated from $1.9\,G$ synsets ($0.9\,G$ ar, $0.5\,G$ en, and $0.4\,G$ es).

Our two features consist of the cosine similarity between the embeddings of the two snippets. The full embedding of a snippet is obtained as the sum of the embeddings if its tokens. The difference between the two features lies in the corpus from which we estimate the embeddings. For $BNall$ we used the full collection of corpora in the three languages. For $BNsub$ we only used the subcollection of data coming from the languages involved in the pair. Significant differences in the performance of these two features will allow us to discern weather the interlinguality of these embeddings is a fair assumption or not (even if synsets are interlingua, its embeddings do not need to be).

2.7 Additional Features

We produced variations of the described features. We used other similarity measures than cosine: modified versions of the weighted Jaccard similarity, and the Kullback–Leibler and Jensen–Shannon divergences). We replicated the features described in Sections 2.3 to 2.6 with their monolingual counterpart. We obtained the counterpart translating ar and es snippets into en for Tracks 1-4 and 6, and en snippets into es for Track 5 with the multilingual NMT system (cf. Section 2.5). We used Google Translate for tr.

3 Experiments

For training, we used all the annotated datasets released both in the current and in previous editions.[6] Table 1 shows the size of the different language collections. Note the important imbalance: there are more than ten times more instances available in en only than in the rest of languages. We used the test set from the 2016 edition (only in English) (Agirre et al., 2016) as our internal test set.

Using the features in Sections 2.1 to 2.6, we train two regressors by:

Sys1 learning one SVM per each language pair

Sys2 learning one single SVM for all the language pairs together.

We experiment with a third system using all the extensions of Section 2.7 on XGBoost. The purpose of this system is to analyse and compare different assumptions made for Sys1 and Sys2:

Sys3 learning one single XGB for all the language pairs with an extended set of features.

Table 2 shows the results of the three settings; including the average Pearson correlation for mono- and cross-language tracks. Comparing Sys1 and Sys2, we see that in the case of en–en the best performance is obtained when training on en only. Adding instances in other languages slightly confuses our regressor, but differences are small; the number of examples added is only a 30%. Nevertheless, considering together different language pairs does help when dealing with less-represented pairs. This is the case of ar–ar, es–es, and es–en where the inclusion of more than ten times more instances in other languages boosts the performance. We did not observe this behaviour in the rest of language pairs. The worst case is that of the surprise pair tr–en. The reason could be that we could not compute all the features for these instances and instead, we used equivalents for en. Regarding the performance of our models on mono- and cross-language pairs, considering one single classifier versus one per language pair makes no difference when dealing with monolingual instances. This reflects the nature of the data: 82% of the training set is monolingual. The story is different when dealing with cross-language instances. Further experiments are necessary using one classifier with cross-language instances only.

---

[6] In order to combine all the datasets we had to do some cleaning and adaptation. For instance, the similarity values in some of the subsets ranged $[0, 4]$ rather than $[0, 5]$.

Track	L–L'	Sys1	Sys2	Sys3
Primary	all	0.4725	0.4438	0.4704
1	ar–ar	0.6052	0.6287	0.5508
2	ar–en	0.1829	0.1805	0.1357
3	es–es	0.7574	0.7380	0.7676
4a	es–en	0.4327	0.4447	0.4825
4b	es–en	0.0116	0.0151	0.1112
5	en–en	0.7376	0.7347	0.7269
6	tr–en	0.5800	0.3652	0.5179
avg$_{mono}$		0.7001	0.7005	0.6818
avg$_{cross}$		0.3359	0.2899	0.3435

Table 2: Official Pearson correlation performance for our three submissions. Average correlations for *mono-* and *cross*-language tracks at the bottom.

Regarding Sys3, we observe a lost in performance with respect to Sys1 and Sys2, except for the tracks involving es. The system introduces three variations with respect to Sys2: the learning model, the addition of several similarity measures for each representation, and the addition of new representations obtained after translating the input into en (es). A deeper analysis shows that the performance drop is due to the learning algorithm. XGBoost is performing better than SVM in our cross-validation. However, the loss function we use is a mean squared error and the evaluation is done via Pearson correlation. We attribute the discrepancy to this fact. Still, except for en–en, the inclusion of the two families of features improves the results of the basic features set.

Gradient boosting methods allow to estimate the importance of each feature in a very natural way: the more a feature is used to take the decisions in the construction of the boosted trees, the more important it is (Hastie, 2013). The complete analysis is out of the scope of this paper, but some comments and remarks can be made in the light of their relative importance. Figure 1 shows the relative importance of the features given by three XGBoost regressors: one trained only with en monolingual data, one for en–es cross-language data, and one for all the languages trained together. The concrete distribution of features depends on the specific language pair, but the set $\{len, 2grm, (CL)ESA, lNMT, wNMT, BNsub, BNall\}$ stands out among the full set. Notice that language identifiers are not relevant at all for the joint model and the regressor practically neglects them.

In general, the internal representation of the neural network is more important for cross-language pairs and Babel embeddings are more relevant for monolingual pairs. In the latter, we observe almost no difference between the relative importance of $BNsub$ and $BNall$, confirming the assumption of the interlinguality of the embeddings. (CL-)ESA is always among the most informative features. Finally, the high contribution of two simple scores is worth noting: len and $2grm$. This comes at no surprise for len (Barrón-Cedeño et al., 2014). Regarding the n-grams similarity, in general $\{3,4\}$-grams perform better in similar tasks (e.g., comparable corpora parallelisation (Barrón-Cedeño et al., 2015)), but no important difference exist with respect to using 2-grams.

4 Conclusions and Future Work

Our approach to the SemEval 2017 task on semantic textual similarity focused on designing text representations which could be equivalent across languages. For example, instead of using standard monolingual or bilingual word embeddings, we build embeddings for the interlingua Babel synsets or let an autoencoder learn representations in the multilingual space. In internal experiments, monolingual word embeddings performed better than BabelNet embeddings for the monolingual tracks, but the advantage of the latter is that the same embeddings can be used for the seven tracks. This is useful for less-resourced languages and for easy porting of the system to new languages. That was true for the tr–en track but, at the moment, the huge difference between the performance of our systems across tracks does not allow us to go further with this conclusion.

In the future we want to take advantage of the amount of information that BabelNet has and we aim at including synsets for multiword expressions and exploiting translations to be able to extract the same sense in all the languages. We are also studying the behaviour of the internal representation of NMT systems in order to determine the appropriate configuration of the translation system to be used for this purpose. To the best of our knowledge, the internal representation and the importance of its dimensionality has not been studied as an interlingual space.

Acknowledgements

Part of this work has been funded by the Leibniz Gemeinschaft via the SAW-2016-ZPID-2 project. The research work of the second author is carried out in the framework of the Interactive sYstems for Answer Search project (IYAS), at the Qatar Computing Research Institute, HBKU.

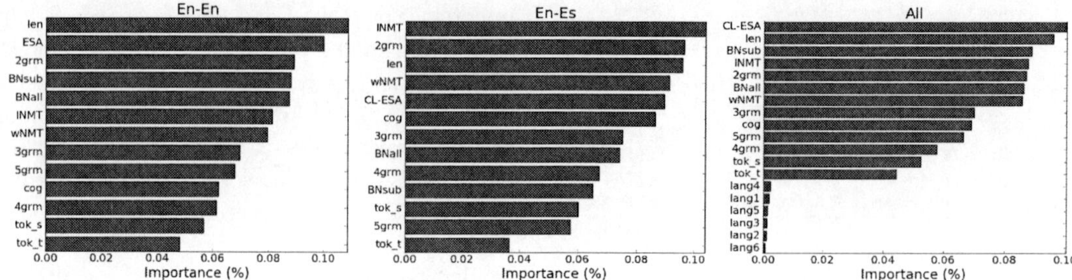

Figure 1: Relative importance of the features in the XGBoost regressors for the monolingual en–en Track 5, the cross-language en–es Track 4, and the all joint training.

References

Eneko Agirre, Carmen Banea, Daniel Cer, Mona Diab, Aitor Gonzalez-Agirre, Rada Mihalcea, German Rigau, and Janyce Wiebe. 2016. Semeval-2016 task 1: Semantic textual similarity, monolingual and cross-lingual evaluation. In *Proceedings of the 10th International Workshop on Semantic Evaluation (SemEval-2016)*. Association for Computational Linguistics, San Diego, CA, pages 497–511.

Alberto Barrón-Cedeño, Cristina Españ-Bonet, Josu Boldoba, and Lluís Màrquez. 2015. A Factory of Comparable Corpora from Wikipedia. In *Proceedings of the Eighth Workshop on Building and Using Comparable Corpora*. Beijing, China.

Alberto Barrón-Cedeño, Monica Paramita Lestari, Paul Clough, and Paolo Rosso. 2014. A Comparison of Approaches for Measuring Cross-Lingual Similarity of Wikipedia Articles. In Maarten de Rijke, Tom Kenter, Arjen P. de Vries, ChengXiang Zhai, Franciska de Jong, Kira Radinsky, and Katja Hofmann, editors, *Advances in Information Retrieval*, Springer International Publishing, volume 8416 of *Lecture Notes in Computer Science*, pages 424–429.

Alberto Barrón-Cedeño, Paolo Rosso, Eneko Agirre, and Gorka Labaka. 2010. Plagiarism Detection across Distant Language Pairs. In Chu-Ren Huang and Dan Jurafsky, editors, *Proceedings of the 23rd International Conference on Computational Linguistics (COLING 2010)*. COLING 2010 Organizing Committee, Beijing, China, pages 37–45.

Daniel Cer, Mona Diab, Eneko Agirre, Inigo Lopez-Gazpio, and Lucia Specia. 2017. Semeval-2017 task 1: Semantic textual similarity multilingual and crosslingual focused evaluation. In *Proceedings of the 11th International Workshop on Semantic Evaluation (SemEval-2017)*. Association for Computational Linguistics, Vancouver, Canada, pages 1–14.

Chih-Chung Chang and Chih-Jen Lin. 2011. LIB-SVM: A library for support vector machines. *ACM Transactions on Intelligent Systems and Technology* 2:27:1–27:27.

Evgeniy Gabrilovich and Shaul Markovitch. 2007. Computing Semantic Relatedness Using Wikipedia-based Explicit Semantic Analysis. In *Proceedings of the 20th International Joint Conference on Artificial Intelligence*. Morgan Kaufmann Publishers Inc., San Francisco, CA, USA, pages 1606–1611.

Trevor Hastie. 2013. *The elements of statistical learning: data mining, inference, and prediction.* Springer series in statistics. Springer, New York, NY, 2nd ed. corr. 7th printing 2013 edition.

Melvin Johnson, Mike Schuster, Quoc V. Le, Maxim Krikun, Yonghui Wu, Zhifeng Chen, Nikhil Thorat, Fernanda B. Viégas, Martin Wattenberg, Greg Corrado, Macduff Hughes, and Jeffrey Dean. 2016. Google's multilingual neural machine translation system: Enabling zero-shot translation. *CoRR* abs/1611.04558.

Christopher D. Manning and Hinrich Schütze. 1999. *Foundations of Statistical Natural Language Processing*. The MIT Press.

Paul McNamee and James Mayfield. 2004. Character N-Gram Tokenization for European Language Text Retrieval. *Information Retrieval* 7(1-2):73–97.

Tomas Mikolov, Kai Chen, Greg Corrado, and Jeffrey Dean. 2013. Efficient Estimation of Word Representations in Vector Space. In *Proceedings of Workshop at ICLR*. http://code.google.com/p/word2vec.

Roberto Navigli and Simone Paolo Ponzetto. 2012. BabelNet: The automatic construction, evaluation and application of a wide-coverage multilingual semantic network. *Artificial Intelligence* 193:217–250.

Martin Potthast, Alberto Barrón-Cedeño, Benno Stein, and Paolo Rosso. 2011. Cross-language plagiarism detection. *Language Resources and Evaluation (LRE), Special Issue on Plagiarism and Authorship Analysis* 45(1):1–18.

Martin Potthast, Benno Stein, and Maik Anderka. 2008. A Wikipedia-Based Multilingual Retrieval Model. *Advances in Information Retrieval, 30th European Conference on IR Research* LNCS (4956):522–530. Springer-Verlag.

Bruno Pouliquen, Ralf Steinberger, and Camelia Ignat. 2003. Automatic Identification of Document Translations in Large Multilingual Document Collections. In *Proceedings of the International Conference on Recent Advances in Natural Language Processing (RANLP-2003)*. Borovets, Bulgaria, pages 401–408.

Alexandre Rafalovitch and Robert Dale. 2009. United Nations General Assembly Resolutions: A Six-Language Parallel Corpus. In *Proceedings of the Machine Translation Summit XII*. International Association of Machine Translation, pages 292–299.

Rico Sennrich, Barry Haddow, and Alexandra Birch. 2016. Edinburgh Neural Machine Translation Systems for WMT 16. In *Proceedings of the First Conference on Machine Translation (WMT16)*.

Michel Simard, George F. Foster, and Pierre Isabelle. 1992. Using Cognates to Align Sentences in Bilingual Corpora. In *Proceedings of the Fourth International Conference on Theoretical and Methodological Issues in Machine Translation*.

QLUT at SemEval-2017 Task 1: Semantic Textual Similarity Based on Word Embeddings

Fanqing Meng, Wenpeng Lu[*], Yuteng Zhang, Jinyong Cheng, Yuehan Du, Shuwang Han
Institute of Intelligent Information Processing, School of Information
QiLu University of Technology, Jinan, Shandong, China
mengfanqing678@163.com, lwp@qlu.edu.cn, zhangyuteng1029@163.com,
cjy@qlu.edu.cn, amaris_du@163.com, hanshuwang0909@163.com

Abstract

This paper reports the details of our submissions in the task 1 of SemEval 2017. This task aims at assessing the semantic textual similarity of two sentences or texts. We submit three unsupervised systems based on word embeddings. The differences between these runs are the various preprocessing on evaluation data. The best performance of these systems on the evaluation of Pearson correlation is 0.6887. Unsurprisingly, results of our runs demonstrate that data preprocessing, such as tokenization, lemmatization, extraction of content words and removing stop words, is helpful and plays a significant role in improving the performance of models.

1 Introduction

Semantic Textual Similarity (STS) has been held in SemEval since 2012 (Agirre et al., 2012; Agirre et al., 2013; Agirre et al., 2014; Agirre et al., 2015; Agirre et al., 2016), which is a basic task in natural language processing (NLP) field. It aims at computing the semantic similarity of two short texts or sentences, and the result will be evaluated on a gold standard set, which is made by several official annotators (Cer et al., 2017). In recent years, as an unsupervised method, word embedding (Mikolov et al., 2013a) becomes more and more popular in SemEval (Jimenez, 2016; Wu et al., 2016).

The paper describes the submission of our systems to STS 2017, which utilize word embedding method. Different from some teams who have

____
[*]Corresponding author

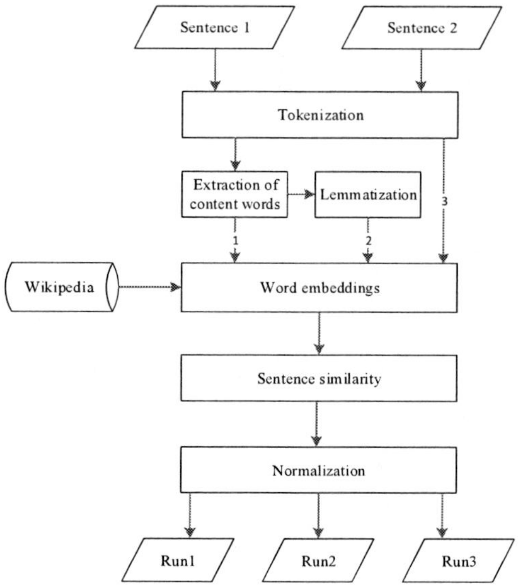

Figure 1: Framework of system.

used word embedding described above, what we pay attention to is the point of preprocessing evaluation data. With this consideration, we process the evaluation data with different method in order to verify whether it works or not.

The framework of our systems is showed in Figure 1. Its simple description is as follows:

Tokenization: This is to tokenize the two sentences of the system's input. Though the English sentence is tokenized naturally, the punctuations are not. For instance, the sentence "A person is on a baseball team." will be tokenized to "A person is on a baseball team .".

Extraction of content words: In this process, content words of the tokenized sentence will be extracted. For example, the tokenized sentence

Proceedings of the 11th International Workshop on Semantic Evaluations (SemEval-2017), pages 150–153,
Vancouver, Canada, August 3 - 4, 2017. ©2017 Association for Computational Linguistics

"A person is on a baseball team ." turns into "person is baseball team". In this paper, content words include nouns, verbs, adverbs or adjectives.

Lemmatization: It is known that words in English sentences have a variety of forms. This operation will lemmatize these words to their basic forms, for example, word "made" and "making" will be changed to "make". In addition, this process also convert the uppercase to lowercase, for instance, "Make" will be changed to "make".

Word embeddings: This process utilizes the word2vec toolkit[1] to train on the Wikipedia corpus, then the word embeddings can be obtained.

Sentence similarity: The similarity of two sentences is computed as the cosine of their sentence embeddings, which can be gotten easily (see 2.3).

Normalization: Due to the different range of the results of runs, similarity scores are normalized to meet the official standard.

2 System Overview

In STS 2017, we submit three system runs, all of which are unsupervised and utilize word embedding method after preprocessing.

2.1 Data Set

Test Set: The test set of the Track 5 (English monolingual pairs) consists of 250 sentence pairs. Each of these sentence pairs is in a line, split by tab.

Gold Standard Set: This set is the gold standard similarity score of 250 sentence pairs in the test set. The range of the score is from 0 to 5. More specially, 0 denotes that the two sentences are completely dissimilar; 1 means that the two sentences only have the same topic; 2 represents that the two sentences only have some details in common; 3 shows that the two sentences are approximately equivalent but they have some differences in the important details; 4 implies that the two sentences are roughly equivalent and some differences they have are not important; 5 indicates that the two sentences are completely equivalent.

2.2 Wikipedia Corpus

We use the unlabeled corpus, i.e., the English Wikipedia corpus, which have been processed by Rami Al-Rfou'[2]. The processed Wikipedia dumps have been tokenized in text format for all the languages which are considered in the evaluation. What we use in the system run is the English Wikipedia dump, after unzipped, a text file can be gotten and its size is 15.8 GB.

2.3 Method

In this competition, we use the word2vec toolkit on the Wikipedia corpus described above to train word embeddings. Before training word embeddings, we preprocess the text file in the corpus to transform its charset from Unicode to UTF-8, because UTF-8 is the default charset for us to run the word2vec toolkit. We set the training window size to 5 and default dimensions to 200, and choose the Skip-gram model. After trained on the corpus, the word2vec can generate a word embeddings file, in which each word in the corpus can be mapped to a word embedding of 200 dimensions. Each dimension of the word embedding is of floating point type double.

Mikolov has explained that the word embedding has semantic meaning (Mikolov et al., 2013a). Therefore, given two words, the semantic similarity of words can be easily obtained by the cosine of their word embeddings. Moreover, we can extend this to the semantic sentence similarity. Inspired by (Mikolov et al., 2013b; Wu et al., 2016), the sentence embedding of a sentence can be gained by accumulating the word embedding of all the words in it. Then by computing the cosine of two sentence embeddings, the semantic sentence similarity can be gotten as follows:

$$sim_{vec}(s_1, s_2) = \frac{\sum_{i=1}^{|s_1|} vec(w_i) \sum_{j=1}^{|s_2|} vec(w_j)}{\left|\sum_{i=1}^{|s_1|} vec(w_i)\right| \left|\sum_{j=1}^{|s_2|} vec(w_j)\right|}, \quad (1)$$

where $|s_1|$ and $|s_2|$ are the number of tokens, which sentence s_1 and s_2 include, respectively. Word w_i represents the word, which belongs to s_1.

2.4 Runs

All of our runs utilize the same method described above, i.e., word emdeddings method. The only difference among them lies that each of these runs have different details in preprocessing the evaluation data. Here we clearly show their preprocessing operations in details.

Run1: We firstly use the Stanford CoreNLP toolkit[3] (Manning et al., 2014) to split each token for the sentence pairs in the evaluation data. Then

---

[1] https://code.google.com/p/word2vec/
[2] https://sites.google.com/site/rmyeid/projects/polyglot
[3] http://stanfordnlp.github.io/CoreNLP/

Data set	Run1	Run2	Run3	Run3'
Track 5	0.6155	**0.6433**	0.4924	0.5299

Table 1: Official evaluation results of our submitted runs on Track 5.

Data set	Run1-	Run2-	Run3-	Run3'-
Track 5	0.6473	**0.6887**	0.6341	0.6683

Table 2: Official evaluation results of our submitted runs after removing stop words on Track 5.

we tokenize all words with the help of the Stanford CoreNLP toolkit, then extract content words of the sentence pairs in the evaluation data.

Run2: As the operations of Run1, we tokenize the sentence pairs and extract content words for the sentence pairs in the evaluation data. Beyond that, we get the lemmas of these content words with the Stanford CoreNLP toolkit.

Run3: The only operation we do is to tokenize the sentence pairs of the evaluation data. Compared with Run1, all words are reserved in this run.

At last, in order to carry on the following evaluation, we normalize the output of these systems from [0, 1] to [0, 5].

The three runs are submitted to official evaluation, which are compared in Table 1.

In order to further consider the influence of stop words, we perform another group of experiences. Based on the runs in Table 1, we remove stop words which is from NLTK package. The corresponding results are shown in Table 2.

3 Evaluation

In the task, the official evaluation tool is based on Pearson correlation. A system run in each test set is evaluated by its Pearson correlation with the official provided gold standard set.

The results in Table 1 above shows that the system Run2 get the best performance of 0.6433. Compared with Run1, Run2 achieves a 2.78% improvement, which implies that to lemmatize content words can be helpful. The difference of 12.31% between Run1 and Run3 indicates that the extraction of content words can make a larger improvement for the similarity computation of the sentence pairs.

In order to further know the effect of lemmatization with Run3, we make the system Run3'. The only difference between them is that in the operation of preprocessing the data, Run3' makes the lemmatization of the sentence pairs in the data, on the contrary, Run3 do not do it. The contrast of Run3 and Run3' again confirms that lemmatization for computing the similarity of the sentence pairs can be effective.

As is shown in Table 2, the relative performance of each run is similar with Table 1. Run2- get the best performance of 0.6887, which demonstrate the effectiveness of content words extraction and lemmatization. Each run in Table 2 achieves a better performance than that in Table 1, which demonstrates that it is necessary to remove stop words.

4 Conclusions and Future Work

The best Pearson correlation of our runs is 0.6887. Although our runs do not get the state-of-the-art performance, the result of these runs is acceptable. And it shows that word embeddings method is effective. Besides, in the competition, we can conclude that the appropriate preprocessing operation (such as tokenization, lemmatization, extraction of content words and removing stop words) for the data is helpful and necessary. In the future, with the help of word embeddings, we will explore some improved method to get a better performance.

Acknowledgments

The work described in this paper is mainly supported by Natural Science Foundation of China under Grant 61502259 and 61202244, Natural Science Foundation of Shandong Province under Grant ZR2011FQ038. Thanks for the reviewers for their helpful suggestions.

References

Eneko Agirre, Daniel Cer, Mona Diab and Aitor Gonzalez-Agirre. 2012. Semeval-2012 task 6: A pilot on semantic textual similarity. In *SEM 2012: The First Joint Conference on Lexical and Computational Semantics -- Volume 1: Proceedings of the main conference and the shared task, and Volume 2: Proceedings of the Sixth International Workshop on Semantic Evaluation (SemEval 2012)*. Association for Computational Linguistics, Montreal, Canada, pages 385--393. http://www.aclweb.org/anthology/S12-1051.

Eneko Agirre, Daniel Cer, Mona Diab, Aitor Gonzalez-Agirre and Weiwei Guo. 2013. *sem 2013 shared task: Semantic textual similarity. In *the Second Joint Conference on Lexical and Computational Semantics (*SEM), Volume 1: Proceedings of the Main Conference and the Shared Task: Semantic Textual Similarity*. Association for Computational Linguistics, Atlanta, Georgia, pages 32--43. http://www.aclweb.org/anthology/S13-1004.

Eneko Agirre, Carmen Banea, Claire Cardie, Daniel Cer, Mona Diab, Aitor Gonzalez-Agirre, Weiwei Guo, Rada Mihalcea, German Rigau and Janyce Wiebe. 2014. Semeval-2014 task 10: Multilingual semantic textual similarity. In *Proceedings of the 8th International Workshop on Semantic Evaluation (SemEval 2014)*. Association for Computational Linguistics and Dublin City University, Dublin, Ireland, pages 81--91. http://www.aclweb.org/anthology/S14-2010.

Eneko Agirre, Carmen Banea, Claire Cardie, Daniel Cer, Mona Diab, Aitor Gonzalez-Agirre, Weiwei Guo, Inigo Lopez-Gazpio, Montse Maritxalar, Rada Mihalcea, German Rigau, Larraitz Uria and Janyce Wiebe. 2015. Semeval-2015 task 2: Semantic textual similarity, english, spanish and pilot on interpretability. In *Proceedings of the 9th International Workshop on Semantic Evaluation (SemEval 2015)*. Association for Computational Linguistics, Denver, Colorado, pages 252--263. http://www.aclweb.org/anthology/S15-2045.

Eneko Agirre, Carmen Banea, Daniel Cer, Mona Diab, Aitor Gonzalez-Agirre, Rada Mihalcea, German Rigau and Janyce Wiebe. 2016. Semeval-2016 task 1: Semantic textual similarity, monolingual and cross-lingual evaluation. In *Proceedings of the 10th International Workshop on Semantic Evaluation (SemEval-2016)*. Association for Computational Linguistics, San Diego, California, pages 497--511. http://www.aclweb.org/anthology/S16-1081.

Daniel Cer, Mona Diab, Eneko Agirre, Inigo Lopez-Gazpio and Lucia Specia. 2017. Semeval-2017 task 1: Semantic textual similarity multilingual and crosslingual focused evaluation. In *Proceedings of the 11th International Workshop on Semantic Evaluation (SemEval-2017)*. Association for Computational Linguistics, Vancouver, Canada, pages 1--14. http://www.aclweb.org/anthology/S17-2001.

Sergio Jimenez. 2016. Sergiojimenez at semeval-2016 task 1: Effectively combining paraphrase database, string matching, wordnet, and word embedding for semantic textual similarity. In *Proceedings of the 10th International Workshop on Semantic Evaluation (SemEval-2016)*. Association for Computational Linguistics, San Diego, California,

pages 749--757. http://www.aclweb.org/anthology/S16-1116.

Christopher D. Manning, Mihai Surdeanu, John Bauer, Jenny Finkel, Steven J. Bethard and David McClosky. 2014. The stanford corenlp natural language processing toolkit. In *Association for Computational Linguistics (ACL) System Demonstrations*. pages 55--60. http://www.aclweb.org/anthology/P/P14/P14-5010.

Tomas Mikolov, Kai Chen, Greg Corrado and Jeffrey Dean. 2013a. Efficient estimation of word representations in vector space. *arXiv preprint arXiv:1301.3781*. https://arxiv.org/abs/1301.3781.

Tomas Mikolov, Ilya Sutskever, Kai Chen, Greg S Corrado and Jeff Dean. 2013b. Distributed representations of words and phrases and their compositionality. *arXiv preprint arXiv:1310.4546*. https://arxiv.org/abs/1310.4546.

Hao Wu, Heyan Huang and Wenpeng Lu. 2016. Bit at semeval-2016 task 1: Sentence similarity based on alignments and vector with the weight of information content. In Proceedings of the 10th International Workshop on Semantic Evaluation (SemEval-2016). Association for Computational Linguistics, San Diego, California, pages 686-690. http://www.aclweb.org/anthology/S16-1105.

ResSim at SemEval-2017 Task 1: Multilingual Word Representations for Semantic Textual Similarity

Johannes Bjerva
Center for Language and Cognition Groningen
University of Groningen
The Netherlands
j.bjerva@rug.nl

Robert Östling
Department of Linguistics
Stockholm University
Sweden
robert@ling.su.se

Abstract

Shared Task 1 at SemEval-2017 deals with assessing the semantic similarity between sentences, either in the same or in different languages. In our system submission, we employ multilingual word representations, in which similar words in different languages are close to one another. Using such representations is advantageous, since the increasing amount of available parallel data allows for the application of such methods to many of the languages in the world. Hence, semantic similarity can be inferred even for languages for which no annotated data exists. Our system is trained and evaluated on all language pairs included in the shared task (English, Spanish, Arabic, and Turkish). Although development results are promising, our system does not yield high performance on the shared task test sets.

1 Introduction

Semantic Textual Similarity (STS) is the task of assessing the degree to which two sentences are semantically similar. Within the SemEval STS shared tasks, this is measured on a scale ranging from 0 (no semantic similarity) to 5 (complete semantic similarity) (Cer et al., 2017). Monolingual STS is an important task, for instance for evaluation of machine translation (MT) systems, where estimating the semantic similarity between a system's translation and the gold translation can aid both system evaluation and development. The task is already a challenging one in a monolingual setting, e.g., when estimating the similarity between two English sentences. In this paper, we tackle the more difficult case of cross-lingual STS, e.g., estimating the similarity between an English and an Arabic sentence.

Previous approaches to this problem have focussed on two main approaches. On the one hand, MT approaches have been attempted (e.g. Lo et al. (2016)), which allow for monolingual similarity assessment, but suffer from the fact that involving a fully-fledged MT system severely increases system complexity. Applying bilingual word representations, on the other hand, bypasses this issue without inducing such complexity (e.g. Aldarmaki and Diab (2016)). However, bilingual approaches do not allow for taking advantage of the increasing amount of STS data available for more than one language pair.

Currently, there are several methods available for obtaining high quality multilingual word representations. It is therefore interesting to investigate whether language can be ignored entirely in an STS system after mapping words to their respective representations. We investigate the utility of multilingual word representations in a cross-lingual STS setting. We approach this by combining multilingual word representations with a deep neural network, in which all parameters are shared, regardless of language combinations.

The contributions of this paper can be summed as follows: i) we show that multilingual input representations in some cases can be used to train an STS system without access to training data for a given language; ii) we show that access to data from other languages in some cases improves system performance for a given language.

2 Multilingual Word Representations

2.1 Multilingual Skip-gram

The skip-gram model has become one of the most popular manners of learning word representations in NLP (Mikolov et al., 2013). This is in part owed to its speed and simplicity, as well as the per-

Proceedings of the 11th International Workshop on Semantic Evaluations (SemEval-2017), pages 154–158,
Vancouver, Canada, August 3 - 4, 2017. ©2017 Association for Computational Linguistics

formance gains observed when incorporating the resulting word embeddings into almost any NLP system. The model takes a word w as its input, and predicts the surrounding context c. Formally, the probability distribution of c given w is defined as

$$p(c|w; \theta) = \frac{\exp(\vec{c}^T \vec{w})}{\Sigma_{c \in V} \exp(\vec{c}^T \vec{w})}, \qquad (1)$$

where V is the vocabulary, and θ the parameters of word emeddings ($\vec{w}$) and context embeddings ($\vec{c}$). The parameters of this model can then be learned by maximising the log-likelihood over (w, c) pairs in the dataset D,

$$J(\theta) = \sum_{(w,c) \in D} \log p(c|w; \theta). \qquad (2)$$

Guo et al. (2016) provide a multilingual extension for the skip-gram model, by requiring the model to not only learn to predict English contexts, but also multilingual ones. This can be seen as a simple adaptation of Firth (1957, p.11), i.e., you shall judge a word by the *multilingual* company it keeps. Hence, the vectors for, e.g., *dog* and *perro* ought to be close to each other in such a model. This assumes access to multilingual parallel data, as word alignments are used in order to determine which words comprise the multilingual context of a word. Whereas Guo et al. (2016) only evaluate their approach on the relatively similar languages English, French and Spanish, we explore a more typological diverse case, as we apply this method to English, Spanish and Arabic. We use the same parameter settings as Guo et al. (2016).

2.2 Learning embeddings

We train 100-dimensional multilingual embeddings on the Europarl (Koehn, 2005) and UN corpora (Ziemski et al., 2016). Word alignment, which is required for the training of multilingual embeddings, is performed using the Efmaral word-alignment tool (Östling and Tiedemann, 2016). This allows us to extract a large amount of multilingual (w, c) pairs. We then use these pairs in order to learn multilingual embeddings, by applying the *word2vecf* tool (Levy and Goldberg, 2014).

3 Method

3.1 System architecture

We use a relatively simple neural network architecture, consisting of an input layer with pre-

trained word embeddings and a network of fully connected layers. Given word representations for each word in our sentence, we take the simplistic approach of averaging the vectors across each sentence. The resulting sentence-level representations are then concatenated and passed through a single fully connected layer, prior to the output layer. In order to prevent any shift from occurring in the embeddings, we do not update these during training. The intuition here, is that we do not want the representation for, e.g., *dog* to be updated, which might push it further away from that of *perro*. We expect this to be especially important in cases where we train on a single language, and evaluate on another.

We apply dropout ($p = 0.5$) between each layer (Srivastava et al., 2014). All weights are initialised using the approach in Glorot and Bengio (2010). We use the Adam optimisation algorithm (Kingma and Ba, 2014), monitoring the categorical cross entropy of a one-hot representation of the (rounded) sentence similarity score, while sanity-checking against the scores obtained as measured with Pearson correlation. All systems are trained using a batch size of 40 sentence pairs, over a maximum of 50 epochs, using early stopping. Hyperparameters are kept constant in all conditions.

3.2 Data

We use all available data from previous editions of the SemEval shared tasks on (cross-lingual) STS. An overview of the available data is shown in Table 1.

Language pair	N sentences
English / English	3750
English / Spanish	1000
English / Arabic	2162
Spanish / Spanish	1620
Arabic / Arabic	1081

Table 1: Available data for (cross-lingual) STS from the SemEval shared task series.

4 Experiments and Results

We aim to investigate whether using a multilingual input representation and shared weights allow us to ignore languages in STS. We first train and evaluate single-source trained systems (i.e. on a single language pair), and evaluate this both using the same language pair as target, and on all other target language pairs.[1] Secondly, we investigate the effect of bundling training data together, investigating which language pairings are helpful for each other. We measure performance between gold similarities and system output using the Pearson correlation measure, as this is standard in the SemEval STS shared tasks. We first present results on the development sets, and finally the official shared task evaluation results.

4.1 Single-source training

Results when training on a single source corpus are shown in Table 2. Training on the target language pair generally yields the highest results, except for one case. When evaluating on Arabic/Arabic sentence pairs, training on English/Arabic texts yields comparable, or slightly better, performance than when training on Arabic/Arabic.

Test \ Train	en/en	en/es	en/ar	es/es	ar/ar
en/en	**0.69**	0.07	-0.04	0.64	0.54
en/es	0.19	**0.27**	0.00	0.18	-0.04
en/ar	-0.44	0.37	**0.73**	-0.10	0.62
es/es	0.61	0.07	0.12	**0.65**	0.50
ar/ar	0.59	0.52	**0.73**	0.59	0.71

Table 2: Single-source training results (Pearson correlations). Columns indicate training language pairs, and rows indicate testing language pairs. Bold numbers indicate best results per row.

4.2 Multi-source training

We combine training corpora in order to investigate how this affects evaluation performance on the language pairs in question. In the first condition, we copy the single-source setup, except for that we also add in the data belonging to the source-pair at hand, e.g., training on both English/Arabic and Arabic/Arabic when evaluating on Arabic/Arabic (see Table 3).

We observe that the monolingual language pairings (en/en, es/es, ar/ar) appear to be beneficial for one another. We therefore run an ablation experiment, in which we train on two out of three of these language pairs, and evaluate on all three. Not

Test \ Train	en/en	en/es	en/ar	es/es	ar/ar
en/en	0.69	0.68	0.67	0.69	**0.71**
en/es	0.22	0.27	**0.30**	0.22	0.24
en/ar	0.72	0.72	**0.73**	0.71	0.72
es/es	0.63	0.60	0.63	0.65	**0.66**
ar/ar	0.71	0.72	**0.75**	0.70	0.71

Table 3: Training results with one source in addition to in-language data (Pearson correlations). Columns indicate added training language pairs, and rows indicate testing language pairs. Bold numbers indicate best results per row.

including any Spanish training data yields comparable performance to including it (Table 4).

Test \ Ablated	en/en	es/es	ar/ar	none
en/en	**0.60**	0.69	0.69	0.65
es/es	0.64	**0.64**	0.67	0.60
ar/ar	0.68	0.66	**0.58**	0.72

Table 4: Ablation results (Pearson correlations). Columns indicate ablated language pairs, and rows indicate testing language pairs. The *none* column indicates no ablation, i.e., training on all three monolingual pairs. Bold indicates results when not training on the language pair evaluated on.

4.3 Shared Task Test Results

The results from the official SemEval-2017 evaluation are shown in Table 5. Although our results for Spanish/Spanish and English/English are in line with our development results, the results for all other language pairs are far lower than expected. This might be explained by overfitting to the training/dev sets we use. After the official evaluation period ended, we also attempted to perform a sanity check. We allowed our model to tune on the gold data, which surprisingly did not increase performance particularly much. We therefore suspect that the poor system performance we observe, may be partially owed to two factors: i) overfitting on the tracks involving Arabic, as we did not apply any type of pre-processing, and our vector set was tuned on relatively little Arabic data; ii) discrepancies between the mix of training-data (and possibly annotators) from previous editions of the

---

[1] This setting can be seen as a sort of model transfer.

	Primary	ar/ar	ar/en	es/es	es/en	es/en (wmt)	en/en	en/tr
Single-source	0.3148	0.2892	0.1045	0.6613	0.2389	0.0305	0.6906	0.1884
Multi-source	0.2938	0.3120	0.1288	0.6920	0.1002	0.0162	0.6877	0.1195
Ablation	0.2145	0.0033	0.1098	0.5465	0.2262	0.0199	0.5057	0.0902

Table 5: Results on SemEval-2017 Shared Task Test sets.

shared task, and test data in this year's edition.

An interesting option to attempt to solve part of this problem, would be to frame this as a multi-task learning problem. This could be done by assigning each year's data set a separate output layer. Should annotator conventions differ, e.g., if a score of 2.5 in 2015 is equivalent to a score of 3.5 in 2016, the network should be able to learn this and compensate for such effects.

5 Discussion

In all cases, training on the target language pair is beneficial. We also observe that using multilingual embeddings is crucial for multilingual approaches, as monolingual embeddings naturally only yield on-par results in monolingual settings. This is due to the fact that using the shared language-agnostic input representation allows us to take advantage of linguistic regularities across languages, which we obtain solely from observing distributions between languages in parallel text. Using monolingual word representations, however, there is no similarity between, e.g., *dog* and *perro* to rely on to guide learning.

For the single-source training, we in one case observe somewhat better performance using other training sets than the in-language one: training on English/Arabic outperforms training on Arabic/Arabic, when evaluating on Arabic/Arabic. We expected this to be due to differing data set sizes (English/Arabic is about twice as big). Controlling for this does, indeed, bring the performance of training on English/Arabic close to training on Arabic/Arabic. However, combining these datasets increases performance further (Table 3).

In single-source training, we also observe that certain source languages do not offer any generalisation over certain target languages. Interestingly, certain combinations of training/testing language pairs yield very poor results. For instance, training on English/English yields very poor results when evaluating on English/Arabic, and vice versa. The same is observed for the combination Spanish/Spanish and English/Arabic. This may be explained by domain differences in training and evaluation data. A general trend appears to be that either monolingual training pairs and evaluation pairs, or cross-lingual pairs with some overlap (e.g. English/Arabic, Arabic/Arabic) is beneficial.

The positive results on pairings without any language overlap are particularly promising. Training on English/English yields results not too far from training on the source language pairs, for Spanish/Spanish and Arabic/Arabic. Similar results are observed when training on Spanish/Spanish and evaluating on English/English and Arabic/Arabic, as well as when training on Arabic/Arabic and evaluating on English/English and Spanish/Spanish. This indicates that we can estimate STS relatively reliably, even without assuming any existing STS data for a given language.

6 Conclusions and Future Work

Multilingual word representations allow us to leverage more available data for multilingual learning of semantic textual similarity. We have shown that relatively high STS performance can be achieved for languages without assuming existing STS annotation, and relying solely on parallel texts. An interesting direction for future work is to investigate how multilingual character-level representations can be included, perhaps learning morpheme-level representations and mappings between these across languages. Leveraging approaches to learning multilingual word representations from smaller data sets would also be interesting. For instance, learning such representations from only the New Testament, would allow for STS estimation for more than 1,000 languages.

Acknowledgments

We would like to thank the Center for Information Technology of the University of Groningen for providing access to the Peregrine high performance computing cluster.

References

Hanan Aldarmaki and Mona Diab. 2016. GWU NLP at SemEval-2016 Shared Task 1: Matrix factorization for crosslingual STS. In *Proceedings of SemEval 2016*. pages 663–667.

Daniel Cer, Mona Diab, Eneko Agirre, Inigo Lopez-Gazpio, and Lucia Specia. 2017. Semeval-2017 task 1: Semantic textual similarity multilingual and crosslingual focused evaluation. In *Proceedings of the 11th International Workshop on Semantic Evaluation (SemEval-2017)*. Association for Computational Linguistics, Vancouver, Canada, pages 1–5. http://www.aclweb.org/anthology/S17-2001.

John R Firth. 1957. *A synopsis of linguistic theory, 1930-1955*. Blackwell.

Xavier Glorot and Yoshua Bengio. 2010. Understanding the difficulty of training deep feedforward neural networks. In *Aistats*. volume 9, pages 249–256.

Jiang Guo, Wanxiang Che, David Yarowsky, Haifeng Wang, and Ting Liu. 2016. A representation learning framework for multi-source transfer parsing. In *Proc. of AAAI*.

Diederik Kingma and Jimmy Ba. 2014. Adam: A method for stochastic optimization. *arXiv preprint arXiv:1412.6980*.

Philipp Koehn. 2005. Europarl: A parallel corpus for statistical machine translation. In *The Tenth Machine Translation Summit.*. Phuket, Thailand.

Omer Levy and Yoav Goldberg. 2014. Dependency-based word embeddings. In *ACL*. pages 302–308.

Chi-kiu Lo, Cyril Goutte, and Michel Simard. 2016. Cnrc at semeval-2016 task 1: Experiments in crosslingual semantic textual similarity. *Proceedings of SemEval 2016* pages 668–673.

Tomas Mikolov, Kai Chen, Greg Corrado, and Jeffrey Dean. 2013. Efficient estimation of word representations in vector space. *arXiv preprint arXiv:1301.3781*.

Robert Östling and Jörg Tiedemann. 2016. Efficient word alignment with markov chain monte carlo. *The Prague Bulletin of Mathematical Linguistics* 106(1):125–146.

Nitish Srivastava, Geoffrey E Hinton, Alex Krizhevsky, Ilya Sutskever, and Ruslan Salakhutdinov. 2014. Dropout: a simple way to prevent neural networks from overfitting. *Journal of Machine Learning Research* 15(1):1929–1958.

Micha Ziemski, Marcin Junczys-Dowmunt, and Bruno Pouliquen. 2016. The united nations parallel corpus v1.0. In Nicoletta Calzolari, Khalid Choukri, Thierry Declerck, Sara Goggi, Marko Grobelnik, Bente Maegaard, Joseph Mariani, Helene Mazo, Asuncion Moreno, Jan Odijk, and Stelios Piperidis, editors, *Proceedings of the Tenth International Conference on Language Resources and Evaluation (LREC 2016)*. European Language Resources Association (ELRA), Paris, France.

ITNLP-AiKF at SemEval-2017 Task 1: Rich Features Based SVR for Semantic Textual Similarity Computing

Wenjie Liu, Chengjie Sun, Lei Lin and Bingquan Liu
School of Computer Science and Technology
Harbin Institute of Technology
Harbin, China
`{wjliu, cjsun, linl, liubq}@insun.hit.edu.cn`

Abstract

Semantic Textual Similarity (STS) devotes to measuring the degree of equivalence in the underlying semantic of the sentence pair. We proposed a new system, ITNLP-AiKF, which applies in the SemEval 2017 Task1 Semantic Textual Similarity track 5 English monolingual pairs. In our system, rich features are involved, including Ontology based, word embedding based, Corpus based, Alignment based and Literal based feature. We leveraged the features to predict sentence pair similarity by a Support Vector Regression (SVR) model. In the result, a Pearson Correlation of 0.8231 is achieved by our system, which is a competitive result in the contest of this track.

1 Introduction

Semantic Evaluation (SemEval) contest devotes to pushing the research of semantic analysis, which attracts many participants and promote a lot of groundbreaking achievements in natural language processing (NLP) field. Semantic textual similarity (STS) task works for computing word and text semantics, which has made extensive attraction to the researchers and NLP community since SemEval 2012 (Agirre et al., 2012).

In STS 2017, The organizers added monolingual Arabic and Cross-lingual Arabic-English semantic calculation in order to increase the difficulty in the contest. The task definition is given two sentences participating systems are asked to predict a continuous similarity score on a scale from 0 to 5 of the sentence pair, with 0 indicating that the semantics of the sentences completely independent and 5 semantic equivalence. The evaluation criterion uses Pearson Correlation Coefficient, which computing the correlation between golden standard scores and semantic system predicted scores.

In our system, in order to predict similarity score of two sentences, we trained a Support Vector Regression (SVR) model with abundant features including Ontology based features, Word Embedding based features, Corpus based features, Alignment based features and Literal based features. All the English training, trial and evaluation data set released by previous STS tasks in SemEval were used to construct our system. Our best system achieved 0.8231 Pearson Correlation coefficient in the SemEval 2017 evaluation data set, and the winner achieved 0.8547.

2 Feature Engineering

In our system, many features are tried to promote the performance of our system. Five kinds of features are used: Ontology based features, Word Embedding based features, Corpus based features, Alignment based features and Literal based features.The following is a detailed description of the five kinds features.

2.1 Ontology Based Features

WordNet (Miller, 1995) is used to exploit Ontology based features. WordNet is a large lexical database of English. In WordNet, nouns, verbs, adjectives and adverbs are divided into sets of cognitive synonyms called synsets. Each synonym expresses a distinct concept. WordNet measures two words similarity based on Path_similarity, Res_similarity, Lin_similarity, Wup_similarity, Lch_similarity and so on. In our system, we directly use WordNet APIs provided by NLTK toolkit (Bird, 2006) to calculate the similarity of two words.

Path_similarity measure is based on the shortest path similarity measure. The Path_similarity for-

Proceedings of the 11th International Workshop on Semantic Evaluations (SemEval-2017), pages 159–163,
Vancouver, Canada, August 3 - 4, 2017. ©2017 Association for Computational Linguistics

mula is defined as Eq 1:

$$Sim_{path}(c_1, c_2) = 2 * deep\_max - len(c_1, c_2) \tag{1}$$

where c_1 and c_2 are concepts, $deep\_max$ is a fixed value of the WordNet and $len(c_1, c_2)$ is the shortest path of concepts c_1 an c_2 in WordNet.

Lch_similarity (Leacock et al., 1998) measure two words similarity by using the depth of concepts in the WordNet hierarchy tree. The Lch_similarity formula is as Eq 2:

$$Sim_{lch}(c_1, c_2) = -log(\frac{len(c_1, c_2)}{2 * deep\_max}) \tag{2}$$

Res_similarity (Resniks Measure) calculates similarity based on two concepts common information content in the taxonomy. The Res_similarity formula is defined as Eq 3:

$$Sim_{res}(c_1, c_2) = -\log P(lso(c_1, c_2)) \\ = IC(lso(c_1, c_2)) \tag{3}$$

where $lso(c_1, c_2)$ is the lowest subsumer of concepts c_1 and c_2 in the taxonomy. The value of Lch_similarity and Res_similarity is not in $[0, 1]$, so we need to scale features into $[0, 1]$.

Lin_similarity (Lin, 1998) considers the similarity depending on the commonality and differences of the information contained in the different meaning concepts. The Lin_similarity formula is defined as Eq 4:

$$Sim_{lin}(c_1, c_2) = \frac{2 * IC(lso(c_1, c_2))}{IC(c_1) + IC(c_2)} \tag{4}$$

Wup_similarity (Wu and Palmer, 1994) measures similarity based on the path of conception node, shared parent node and root node. The Wup_similarity formula is defined as Eq 5:

$$sim_{wup}(c_1, c_2) = \\ \frac{2 * depth(lso(c_1, c_2))}{len(c_1, c_2) + 2 * depth(lso(c_1, c_2))} \tag{5}$$

We can use two vectors S_1 and S_2 to represent two sentences. For each word in S_1 or S_2, search for the most similar word in another sentence by above methods. For S_1, add all elements together, which are divided by the length of S_1, and then get

the value of V_1. Do the same calculation for S_2, and then get the value of V_2. Computing the harmonic mean (denoted by harmonic_mean) of V_1 and V_2, and the result is the similarity of the two sentences. The harmonic mean is defined as Eq 6:

$$harmonic\_mean = \frac{2}{\frac{1}{V_1} + \frac{1}{V_2}} \tag{6}$$

2.2 Word Embedding Based Features

Word Embedding maps words or phrases from defined vocabulary with dense vectors of real values, which have been applied as features in document classification (Sebastiani, 2002), question answering (Tellex et al., 2003), and named entity recognition (Turian et al., 2010) tasks. In our system, we obtained word vectors using two kinds of unsupervised models: Word2Vec (Mikolov et al., 2013) and Global Vectors (GloVe) (Pennington et al., 2014), which can produce high-quality word vectors from millions of corpus data. With the obtained word vectors, the following sentences similarities are calculated: W2V_similarity, IDFV_similarity, S2V_similarity, Text_similarity, WFSV_similarity.

In order to get a better word vector, we used full Wikipedia English corpus to train Word2Vec vectors (400 dimensions) and the Global vector of twitter (200 dimensions) provided by GloVe.

W2V_similarity measures two sentences similarity by using word vectors. The W2V_similarity formula is defined as Eq 7:

$$W2V\_Sim(S_1, S_2) = Cos\_Dis(\frac{\sum_{w \in S_1} W2V(w)}{len(S_1)} \\ , \frac{\sum_{w \in S_2} W2V(w)}{(len(S_2)}) \tag{7}$$

where $W2V(w)$ is the word embedding vector, and $len(S_1)$, $len(S_2)$ is the length of sentence.

The cosine similarity is defined as Eq 8:

$$Cos\_Dis(V_1, V_2) = \frac{V_1 \cdot V_2}{\|V_1\| \cdot \|V_2\|} \tag{8}$$

S2V_similarity is another method that measures two sentences similarity directly, by using the following formula as Eq 9:

$$S2VSim(S_1, S_2) =$$

$$\frac{1}{\frac{len(S_1)}{\sum_{w \in S_1} maxSim(w, S_2)} + \frac{len(S_2)}{\sum_{w \in S_2} maxSim(w, S_1)}} \quad (9)$$

maxSim(w,S) is to find the maximum similarity value between one word in one sentence and all words in another sentence, which is defined as Eq 10.

$$maxSim(w, S) =$$
$$Max\{Cos\_Dis(W2V(w), W2V(w_s)), w_s \in S\} \quad (10)$$

Text_similarity uses maxSim method and the weight of tf-idf to calculate the pair of sentence. Text_similarity measures (Mihalcea et al., 2006) two sentences similarity uses the following formula as Eq 11:

$$Text\_sim(S_1, S_2)$$
$$= \frac{1}{2}\left(\frac{\sum_{w \in S_1}(maxSim(w, S_2) * idf(w))}{\sum_{w \in S_1} idf(w)} \right. \quad (11)$$
$$\left. + \frac{\sum_{w \in S_2}(maxSim(w, S_1) * idf(w))}{\sum_{w \in S_2} idf(w)}\right)$$

IDF_W2V similarity and Freq_W2V similarity represent sentence vector with word embedding, word frequency and word tf-idf. IDF_W2V similarity and Freq_W2V similarity formula are as Eq 12 and Eq 13:

$$IDFV(S) = \sum_{w \in S} IDF(w) * \frac{W2V(w)}{norm(W2V(w))} \quad (12)$$

$$WFSV(S) = \sum_{w \in S} WF(w) * \frac{W2V(w)}{norm(W2V(w))} \quad (13)$$

where IDF(w) and WF(w) are the word tf-idf and frequency based on all Wikipedia english corpus.

After getting the sentence vectors, comput cosine distance between two vectors and the value is a feature of two sentences.

2.3 Corpus Based Features

Latent semantic analysis (LSA) is a technique of global matrix factorization methods, to analyse the relationships between a set of documents and the words. Based on optimal vector space structure, LSA method can leverage statistical information efficiently, and be always used to measure word-to-word similarity.

There are several publicly available tools to construct LSA models, such as SemanticVectors Package (Widdows and Ferraro, 2008) and S-Space Package (Jurgens and Stevens, 2010) can be used to generate LSA space vectors. For this part, we directly use the word vectors provided by SEMILAR[1] (Stefanescu et al., 2014) to calculate the features: W2V_LSI_similarity, S2V_LSI_similarity, Text_LSI_similarity, IDF_LSI_similarity, WFSV_LSI_similarity.

2.4 Alignment Based Features

Alignment similarity based on monolingual alignment measures sentences similarity. Alignment try to discover similar meaning word pairs by exploiting the semantic and contextual similarities. In our work, we directly use the monolingual word aligner provided by (Sultan et al., 2014a,b). Alignment similarity uses the following formula Eq 14:

$$sts(S_1, S_2) = \frac{n_c^a(S_1) + n_c^a(S_2)}{n_c(S_1) + n_c(S_2)} \quad (14)$$

where $n_c^a(S_1)$ and $n_c^a(S_2)$ is the amount of word alignment in two sentences, and $n_c(S_1)$ and $n_c(S_2)$ is the length of sentence.

2.5 Literal Based Features

For literal similarity, we use the edit distance and jaccard distance to calculate sentences similarity. Edit distance also known as Levenshtein Distance, is the minimum step of editing operations from one sentence to another.

Firstly, for jaccard distance, we extracted part-of-speech tagging of each word from a sentence. Then calculate jaccard distance by using the formula defined by Eq 15:

$$J(S_1, S_2) = \frac{|S_1 \cap S_2|}{|S_1 \cup S_2|} \quad (15)$$

where S_1 and S_2 are the tag of each word in a sentence, which ignores the order. We use the NLTK toolkit part-of-speech tagging.

---

[1] http://www.semanticsimilarity.org/

	Ans-Ans	**Qus-Qus**	**HDL**	**Postediting**	**Plagiarism**
Ontology Based	**0.5926**	**0.6041**	0.7192	0.8136	0.7349
Word2vec Based	0.5838	0.6012	**0.7395**	**0.8233**	**0.8053**
GloVe Based	0.5360	0.5827	0.7172	0.7508	0.7478
Corpus Based	0.3737	0.4378	0.6157	0.7334	0.7356
Alignment Based	0.4842	0.5827	0.7172	0.7508	0.7478
Literal Based	0.4860	0.5232	0.6715	0.8108	0.7339
All	0.6248	0.6315	0.8106	0.8307	0.8132

Table 1: The Pearson Correlation on SemEval 2016 evaluation data sets.

3 Experiments and Results

In our system, We build our data set by collecting all off-the-shelf English data sets which released by prior STS evaluations (except the evaluation data set of STS 2016). After that, 80% data set are used as train data set and 20% as valid data set. In our system, we trained SVR model, and the SVR parameters are set as Table 2.

parameter	kernel	C	gamma	epsilon
value	rbf	0.1	auto	0.0

Table 2: parameter setting in SVR.

Ontology based, Word embedding based, Corpus based, Alignment based and Literal based features are used in SVR model respectively, in order to explore the effect of each kind of features. We used SemEval 2016 evaluation data set to test the performance of different feature set, and the results of Pearson Correlation coefficients are shown in Table 1.

The Table 1 indicates Word2Vec performed better in HDL, Postediting, Plagiarism data set, and WordNet performed better in Ans-Ans, Qus-Qus data set. The reason maybe that training Word2vec uses all the English corpus of Wikipedia, and it can learn better word vectors. WordNet can make full uses of lexical information to match the synonyms between two sentences.

We also used SemEval 2017 evaluation data to test our system, and adding each kind of feature one by one. The result of Pearson Correlation coefficients are shown in Table 3.

From Table 3, we can see Ontology based features, Corpus based features and Literal based features outperformed others in SemEval 2017 evaluation data set.

Feature	**Pearson correlation**
Alignment Based	0.7527
Ontology Based	0.7816
Word2vec Based	0.7823
GloVe Based	0.7836
Corpus Based	0.8104
Literal Based	0.8231
All	0.8231

Table 3: The Pearson Correlation on SemEval 2017 evaluation data sets.

4 Conclusion and Future Works

In this paper, we describe our system in the Semantic Textual Similarity task1 subtask 5 English monolingual similarity in SenEval 2017. We used 5 kinds of features and SVR model to build the ultimate system. We find that Ontology based feature, Word Embedding based feature and Alignment based feature performed better in some aspects of semantic similarity calculation. With the limitation of time, we do not try other methods. In our future work, we are going to attempt LSTM tree method to calculate sentences similarity.

Acknowledgment

This work is sponsored by the National High Technology Research and Development Program of China (2015AA015405) and National Natural Science Foundation of China (61572151 and 61602131).

References

Eneko Agirre, Daniel M. Cer, Mona T. Diab, and Aitor Gonzalez-Agirre. 2012. Semeval-2012 task 6: A pilot on semantic textual similarity. In *Proceedings of the 6th International Workshop on Semantic Evaluation, SemEval@NAACL-HLT 2012,*

Montréal, Canada, June 7-8, 2012. pages 385–393. http://aclweb.org/anthology/S/S12/S12-1051.pdf.

Steven Bird. 2006. NLTK: the natural language toolkit. In *ACL 2006, 21st International Conference on Computational Linguistics and 44th Annual Meeting of the Association for Computational Linguistics, Proceedings of the Conference, Sydney, Australia, 17-21 July 2006.* http://aclweb.org/anthology/P06-4018.

David Jurgens and Keith Stevens. 2010. The s-space package: An open source package for word space models. In *ACL 2010, Proceedings of the 48th Annual Meeting of the Association for Computational Linguistics, July 11-16, 2010, Uppsala, Sweden, System Demonstrations.* pages 30–35. http://www.aclweb.org/anthology/P10-4006.

Claudia Leacock, Martin Chodorow, and George A. Miller. 1998. Using corpus statistics and wordnet relations for sense identification. *Computational Linguistics* 24(1):147–165.

Dekang Lin. 1998. An information-theoretic definition of similarity. In *Proceedings of the Fifteenth International Conference on Machine Learning (ICML 1998), Madison, Wisconsin, USA, July 24-27, 1998.* pages 296–304.

Rada Mihalcea, Courtney Corley, and Carlo Strapparava. 2006. Corpus-based and knowledge-based measures of text semantic similarity. In *Proceedings, The Twenty-First National Conference on Artificial Intelligence and the Eighteenth Innovative Applications of Artificial Intelligence Conference, July 16-20, 2006, Boston, Massachusetts, USA.* pages 775–780. http://www.aaai.org/Library/AAAI/2006/aaai06-123.php.

Tomas Mikolov, Kai Chen, Greg Corrado, and Jeffrey Dean. 2013. Efficient estimation of word representations in vector space. *CoRR* abs/1301.3781. http://arxiv.org/abs/1301.3781.

George A. Miller. 1995. Wordnet: A lexical database for english. *Commun. ACM* 38(11):39–41. https://doi.org/10.1145/219717.219748.

Jeffrey Pennington, Richard Socher, and Christopher D. Manning. 2014. Glove: Global vectors for word representation. In *Proceedings of the 2014 Conference on Empirical Methods in Natural Language Processing, EMNLP 2014, October 25-29, 2014, Doha, Qatar, A meeting of SIGDAT, a Special Interest Group of the ACL.* pages 1532–1543. http://aclweb.org/anthology/D/D14/D14-1162.pdf.

Fabrizio Sebastiani. 2002. Machine learning in automated text categorization. *ACM Comput. Surv.* 34(1):1–47. https://doi.org/10.1145/505282.505283.

Dan Stefanescu, Rajendra Banjade, and Vasile Rus. 2014. Latent semantic analysis models on wikipedia and TASA. In *Proceedings of the Ninth International Conference on Language Resources and Evaluation, LREC 2014, Reykjavik, Iceland, May 26-31, 2014..* pages 1417–1422. http://www.lrec-conf.org/proceedings/lrec2014/summaries/403.html.

Md. Arafat Sultan, Steven Bethard, and Tamara Sumner. 2014a. Back to basics for monolingual alignment: Exploiting word similarity and contextual evidence. *TACL* 2:219–230. https://tacl2013.cs.columbia.edu/ojs/index.php/tacl/article/view/292.

Md. Arafat Sultan, Steven Bethard, and Tamara Sumner. 2014b. Dls$@$cu: Sentence similarity from word alignment. In *Proceedings of the 8th International Workshop on Semantic Evaluation, SemEval@COLING 2014, Dublin, Ireland, August 23-24, 2014..* pages 241–246. http://aclweb.org/anthology/S/S14/S14-2039.pdf.

Stefanie Tellex, Boris Katz, Jimmy J. Lin, Aaron Fernandes, and Gregory Marton. 2003. Quantitative evaluation of passage retrieval algorithms for question answering. In *SIGIR 2003: Proceedings of the 26th Annual International ACM SIGIR Conference on Research and Development in Information Retrieval, July 28 - August 1, 2003, Toronto, Canada.* pages 41–47. https://doi.org/10.1145/860435.860445.

Joseph P. Turian, Lev-Arie Ratinov, and Yoshua Bengio. 2010. Word representations: A simple and general method for semi-supervised learning. In *ACL 2010, Proceedings of the 48th Annual Meeting of the Association for Computational Linguistics, July 11-16, 2010, Uppsala, Sweden.* pages 384–394. http://www.aclweb.org/anthology/P10-1040.

Dominic Widdows and Kathleen Ferraro. 2008. Semantic vectors: a scalable open source package and online technology management application. In *Proceedings of the International Conference on Language Resources and Evaluation, LREC 2008, 26 May - 1 June 2008, Marrakech, Morocco.* http://www.lrec-conf.org/proceedings/lrec2008/summaries/300.html.

Zhibiao Wu and Martha Stone Palmer. 1994. Verb semantics and lexical selection. In *32nd Annual Meeting of the Association for Computational Linguistics, 27-30 June 1994, New Mexico State University, Las Cruces, New Mexico, USA, Proceedings..* pages 133–138. http://aclweb.org/anthology/P/P94/P94-1019.pdf.

Neobility at SemEval-2017 Task 1: An Attention-based Sentence Similarity Model

WenLi Zhuang [*]
Shan-Si Elementary School
ChangHua County, Taiwan
bibo9901@gmail.com

Ernie Chang
Department of Linguistics
University of Washington
Seattle, WA 98195, USA
cyc025@uw.edu

Abstract

This paper describes a neural-network model which performed competitively (top 6) at the SemEval 2017 cross-lingual Semantic Textual Similarity (STS) task. Our system employs an attention-based recurrent neural network model that optimizes the sentence similarity. In this paper, we describe our participation in the multilingual STS task which measures similarity across English, Spanish, and Arabic.

1 Introduction

Semantic textual similarity (STS) measures the degree of equivalence between the meanings of two text sequences (Agirre et al., 2016). The similarity of the text pair can be represented as discrete or continuous values ranging from irrelevance (1) to exact semantic equivalence (5). It is widely applicable to many NLP tasks including summarization (Wong et al., 2008; Nenkova et al., 2011), generation and question answering (Vo et al., 2015), paraphrase detection (Fernando and Stevenson, 2008), and machine translation (Corley and Mihalcea, 2005).

In this paper, we describe a system that is able to learn context-sensitive features within the sentences. Further, we encode the sequential information with Recurrent Neural Network (RNN) and perform attention mechanism (Bahdanau et al., 2015) on RNN outputs for both sentences. Attention mechanism was performed to increase sensitivity of the system to words of similarity significance. We also optimize directly on the Pearson correlation score as part of our neural-based approach. Moreover, we include a pair feature

adapter module that could be used to include more features to further improve performance. However, for this competition we include merely the TakeLab features (Šarić et al., 2012). [1]

2 Related Works

Most proposed approaches in the past adopted a hybrid of varying text unit sizes ranging from character-based, token-based, to knowledge-based similarity measure (Gomaa and Fahmy, 2013). The linguistic depths of these measures often vary between lexical, syntactic, and semantic levels.

Most solutions include an ensemble of modules that employs features coming from different unit sizes and depths. More recent approaches generally include the word embedding-based similarity (Liebeck et al., 2016; Brychcín and Svoboda, 2016) as a component of the final ensemble. The top performing team in 2016 (Rychalska et al., 2016) uses an ensemble of multiple modules including recursive autoencoders with WordNet and monolingual aligner (Sultan et al., 2016). UMD-TTIC-UW (He et al., 2016) proposes the MPCNN model that requires no feature engineering and managed to perform competitively at the 6th place. MPCNN is able to extract the hidden information using the Convolutional Neural Network (CNN) and adds an attention layer to extract the vital similarity information.

3 Methods

3.1 Model

Given two sentences $I_1 = \{w_1^1, w_2^1, ..., w_{n^1}^1\}$ and $I_2 = \{w_1^2, w_2^2, ..., w_{n^2}^2\}$, where w_{ij} denote the jth token of the ith sentence, embedded using a function ϕ that maps each token to a D-dimension trainable vector. Two sentences are encoded with

---

[*] The author is currently serving in his Alternative Military Service of Education.

[1] Our system and data is available at github.com/iamalbert/semval2017task1

Proceedings of the 11th International Workshop on Semantic Evaluations (SemEval-2017), pages 164–169,
Vancouver, Canada, August 3 - 4, 2017. ©2017 Association for Computational Linguistics

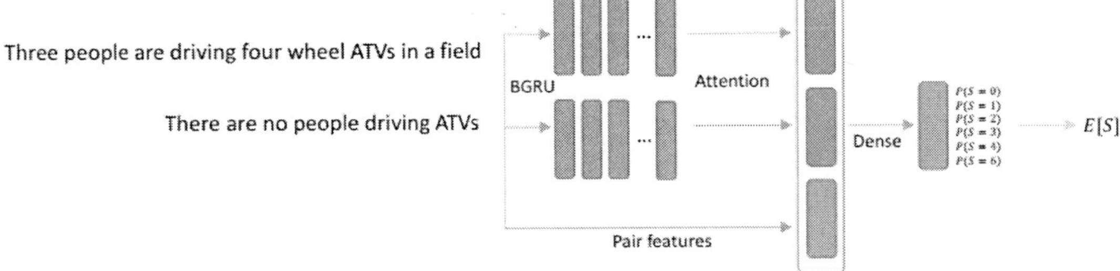

Figure 1: Illustration of model architecture

an attentitve RNN to obtain sentence embeddings u^1, u^2, respectively.

Sentence Encoder   For each sentence, the RNN firstly converts w_j^i into $x_j^i \in R^{2H}$, using an bidirectional Gated Recurrent Unit (GRU) (Cho et al., 2014) [2] by sequentially feeding w_j^i into the unit, in both forward and backward directions. The superscripts of w, x, a, u, n are omitted for clear notation.

$$x_i = [x_i^F; x_i^B]$$
$$x_i^F = \text{GRU}(x_{i-1}^F, w_i) \qquad (1)$$
$$x_i^B = \text{GRU}(x_{i+1}^B, w_i)$$

Then, we attend each word x_j for different salience a_j and blend the memories $x_{1:n}$ into sentence embedding u:

$$a_j \propto \exp(r^T \tanh(W x_i))$$
$$u = \sum_{j=1}^{n} a_j x_j \qquad (2)$$

where $W \in R^{2H \times 2H}$ and $r \in R^{2H}$ are trainable parameters.

Surface Features   Inspired by the *simple* system described in (Šarić et al., 2012), We also extract surface features from the sentence pair as following:

•**Ngram Overlap Similarity:** These are features drawn from external knowledge like Word-Net (Miller, 1995) and Wikipedia. We use both PathLen similarity (Leacock and Chodorow, 1998) and Lin similarity (Lin et al., 1998) to compute similarity between pairs of words w_i^1 and w_j^2 in I_1 and I_2, respectively. We employ the suggested preprocessing step (Šarić et al., 2012), and add

both WordNet and corpus-based information to ngram overlap scores, which is obtained with the harmonic mean of the degree of overlap between the sentences.

•**Semantic Sentence Similarity:** We also compute token-based alignment overlap and vector space sentence similarity (Šarić et al., 2012). Semantic alignment similarity is computed greedily between all pairs of tokens using both the knowledge-based and corpus-based similarity. Scores are further enhanced with the aligned pair information. We obtain the weighted form of latent semantic analysis vectors (Turney and Pantel, 2010) for each word w, before computing the cosine similarity. As such, sentence similarity scores are enhanced with corpus-based information for tokens. The features are concatenated into a vector, denoted as m.

Scoring   Let S be a descrete random variable over $\{0, 1, ..., 4, 5\}$ describing the similarity of the given sentence pair $\{I_1, I_2\}$. The representation of the given pair is the concatenation of u^1, u^2, and m, which is fed into an MLP with one hidden layer to calculate the estimated distribution of S.

$$p = \begin{bmatrix} P(S = 0) \\ P(S = 1) \\ \vdots \\ P(S = 5) \end{bmatrix}$$
$$= \text{softmax}(V \tanh(U \begin{bmatrix} u^1 \\ u^2 \\ m \end{bmatrix})) \qquad (3)$$

Therefore, the score y is the expected value of

---

[2] We also explored Longer Short-Term Memory (LSTM), but find it more overfitting than GRU.

S:

$$y = E[S] = \sum_{i=0}^{5} iP(S = i) = v^T p \qquad (4)$$

, where $v = [0, 1, 2, 3, 4, 5]^T$. The entire system is shown in Figure 1.

3.2 Word Embedding

We explore initializing word embeddings randomly or with pre-trained word2vec (Mikolov et al., 2013) of dimension 50, 100, 300, respectively. We found that the system works the best with 300-dimension word2vec embeddings.

3.3 Optimization

Let p^n, y^n be the predicted probability density and expected score and $\hat{y}^n$ be the annotated gold score of the n-th sample. Most of the previous learning-based models are trained to minimize the following objectives on a batch of N samples:

- Negative Log-likelihood (NLL) of p and $\hat{p}$ (Aker et al., 2016). The task is viewed as a classification problem for 6 classes.

$$L_{\text{NLL}} = \sum_{n=1}^{N} -\log p_{t^n}^n$$

, where t^n is $\hat{y}^n$ rounded to the nearest integer.

- Mean square error (MSE) between y^n and $\hat{y}^n$ (Brychcín and Svoboda, 2016).

$$L_{\text{MSE}} = \frac{1}{N} \sum_{n=1}^{N} (y^n - \hat{y}^n)^2$$

- Kullback-Leibler divergence (KLD) of p^n and gold distribution $\hat{p}^n$ estimated by $\hat{y}^n$:

$$L_{\text{KLD}} = \sum_{n=1}^{N} \left(\sum_{i=1}^{6} \hat{p}_i^n \log \frac{\hat{p}_i^n}{p_i^n} \right)$$

where

$$\hat{p}_i^n = \begin{cases} \hat{y}^n - \lfloor \hat{y}^n \rfloor, & \text{if } i = \lfloor \hat{y}^n \rfloor + 1 \\ \lfloor \hat{y}^n \rfloor + 1 - \hat{y}^n, & \text{if } i = \lfloor \hat{y}^n \rfloor \\ 0, & \text{otherwise} \end{cases}$$

(Li and Huang, 2016; Tai et al., 2015). For each n, there exists some k such that $\hat{p}_k^n = 1$ and $\forall h \neq k, \hat{p}_h^n = 0$, KLD is identical to NLL.

However, the evaluation metric of this task is Pearson Correlation Coefficient (PCC), which is invariant to changes in location and scale of y^n but none of the above objectives can reflect it. Here we use an example to illustrate that MSE and KLD can even report an inverse tendency. In Table 1, group A has lower MSE and KLD loss than group B, but its PCC is also lower.

To solve this problem, we train the model to maximize PCC directly. Hence, the loss function is given by:

$$L_{\text{PCC}} = -\frac{\sum_{n=1}^{N} (y^n - \bar{y})(\hat{y}^n - \bar{\hat{y}})}{\sqrt{\sum_{n=1}^{N} (y^n - \bar{y})^2} \sqrt{\sum_{n=1}^{N} (\hat{y}^n - \bar{\hat{y}})^2}} \tag{5}$$

where $\bar{y} = \frac{1}{N} \sum_{n=1}^{N} y^n$ and $\bar{\hat{y}} = \frac{1}{N} \sum_{n=1}^{N} \hat{y}^n$. Since N is fixed for every batch, L_{PCC} is differentiable with respect to y^n, which means we can apply back propagation to train the network. To the best of our knowledge, we are the first team to adopt this training objective.

Group	A			B		
Gold Score	3	4	5	3	4	5
$P(S=0)$	0.05	0.05	0.05	0.15	0.05	0.1
$P(S=1)$	0.05	0.05	0.05	0.3	0.2	0.1
$P(S=2)$	0.15	0.1	0.05	0.25	0.3	0.2
$P(S=3)$	0.5	0.35	0.0	0.1	0.25	0.3
$P(S=4)$	0.15	0.4	0.1	0.1	0.1	0.2
$P(S=5)$	0.1	0.05	0.7	0.1	0.1	0.1
$E[S]$	2.95	3.15	4.2	2.0	2.45	2.7
	MSE	KLD	PCC	MSE	KLD	PCC
	0.455	**1.966**	0.931	2.90	6.91	**0.987**

Table 1: Example of lower MSE and KLD not indicating higher PCC.

4 Evaluation

4.1 Data

Dataset	Pairs
Training	22,401
Validation	5,601

Table 2: Training and validation Data sets (STS 2012-2016 and SICK).

We gather dataset from SICK (Marelli et al., 2014) and past STS across years 2012, 2013, 2014, 2015, and 2016 (Agirre et al., 2012, 2013, 2014, 2015, 2016) for both cross-lingual and monolingual subtasks. We shuffle and split them according to the ratio 80:20 into training set and validation set, respectively. Table 2 indicates the size of training set and validation set. All non-English sentence appearing in training, validation, and test set are translated into English with Google Cloud Translation API.

4.2 Experiments

In the experiment, the size of output of GRU is set to be $H = 200$. We use ADAM algorithm to optimize the parameters with mini-batches of 125. The learning rate is set to 10^{-4} at the beginning and reduced by half for every 5 epochs. We trained the network for 15 epochs.

Word embeddings In Table 3, we demonstrate that the system performs better with pretrained word vectors (WI) than randomly initialized (RI).

	D	PCC on validation set
RI	50	0.7904
	300	0.8091
WI	50	0.7974
	300	**0.8174**

Table 3: System performance with different dimensions of word embeddings, using either randomly initialized or pre-trained word embedding.

Loss function We display performances with systems optimized with KLD, MSE, and PCC. It shows that when using L_{PCC} as the training objective, our system not only performs the best but also converges the fastest. As shown in Table 4 and Figure 2.

Loss function	PCC
L_{KLD}	0.6839
L_{MSE}	0.7863
L_{PCC}	**0.8174**

Table 4: Influence of different loss objectives on the system performance measured using PCC on our validation set.

4.3 Final System Results

We tune the model on validation set, and select the set of hyper-parameters that yields the best performance to obtain the scores of test data. We report the official provisional results in Table 5. There is an obvious performance drop in track4b, which happens to all teams. We hypothesize that the sentences in track4b (en_es) are collected from a special domain, due to the fact that the number of

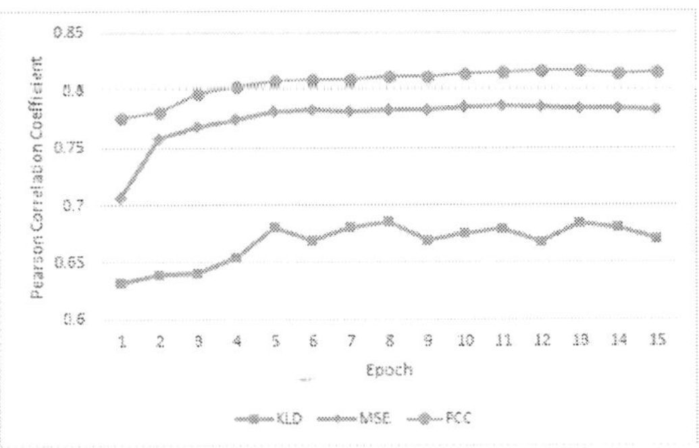

Figure 2: Performance of different loss functions

out-of-vocabulary words in track 4b is many times more than that in other tracks.

Track	PCC	mean	median	max
Primary	0.6171	0.66	0	28
1	0.6821	0.53	0	3
2	0.6459	0.50	0	3
3	0.7928	0.35	0	4
4a	0.7169	0.35	0	4
4b	0.0200	2.54	2	28
5	0.7927	0.36	0	4
6	0.6696	0.33	0	5

Table 5: Final system results and statistics of the number of OOV words within a pair

5 Conclusion

We propose a simple neural-based system with a novel means of optimization. We adopt a simple neural network with surface features which leads to a promising performance. We also revise several popular training objectives and empirically show that optimizing directly on Pearson's correlation coefficient achieved the best scores and perform competitively on STS-2017.

References

Eneko Agirre, Carmen Banea, Claire Cardie, Daniel Cer, Mona Diab, Aitor Gonzalez-Agirre, Weiwei Guo, Inigo Lopez-Gazpio, Montse Maritxalar, Rada Mihalcea, German Rigau, Larraitz Uria, and Janyce Wiebe. 2015. Semeval-2015 task 2: Semantic textual similarity, english, spanish and pilot on interpretability. In *Proceedings of the 9th International Workshop on Semantic Evaluation (SemEval 2015)*. Association for Computational Linguistics, Denver, Colorado, pages 252–263. http://www.aclweb.org/anthology/S15-2045.

Eneko Agirre, Carmen Banea, Claire Cardie, Daniel Cer, Mona Diab, Aitor Gonzalez-Agirre, Weiwei Guo, Rada Mihalcea, German Rigau, and Janyce Wiebe. 2014. Semeval-2014 task 10: Multilingual semantic textual similarity. In *Proceedings of the 8th International Workshop on Semantic Evaluation (SemEval 2014)*. Association for Computational Linguistics and Dublin City University, Dublin, Ireland, pages 81–91. http://www.aclweb.org/anthology/S14-2010.

Eneko Agirre, Carmen Banea, Daniel Cer, Mona Diab, Aitor Gonzalez-Agirre, Rada Mihalcea, German Rigau, and Janyce Wiebe. 2016. Semeval-2016 task 1: Semantic textual similarity, monolingual and cross-lingual evaluation. In *Proceedings of the 10th International Workshop on Semantic Evaluation*. Association for Computational Linguistics, San Diego, California, pages 497–511. http://www.aclweb.org/anthology/S16-1081.

Eneko Agirre, Daniel Cer, Mona Diab, and Aitor Gonzalez-Agirre. 2012. Semeval-2012 task 6: A pilot on semantic textual similarity. In **SEM 2012: The First Joint Conference on Lexical and Computational Semantics – Volume 1: Proceedings of the main conference and the shared task, and Volume 2: Proceedings of the Sixth International Workshop on Semantic Evaluation (SemEval 2012)*. Association for Computational Linguistics, Montréal, Canada, pages 385–393. http://www.aclweb.org/anthology/S12-1051.

Eneko Agirre, Daniel Cer, Mona Diab, Aitor Gonzalez-Agirre, and Weiwei Guo. 2013. *sem 2013 shared task: Semantic textual similarity. In *Second Joint Conference on Lexical and Computational Semantics (*SEM), Volume 1: Proceedings of the Main Conference and the Shared Task: Semantic Textual Similarity*. Association for Computational Linguistics, Atlanta, Georgia, USA, pages 32–43. http://www.aclweb.org/anthology/S13-1004.

Ahmet Aker, Frederic Blain, Andres Duque, Marina Fomicheva, Jurica Seva, Kashif Shah, and Daniel Beck. 2016. Usfd at semeval-2016 task 1: Putting different state-of-the-arts into a box. In *Proceedings of the 10th International Workshop on Semantic Evaluation (SemEval-2016)*. Association for Computational Linguistics, San Diego, California, pages 609–613. http://www.aclweb.org/anthology/S16-1092.

Dzmitry Bahdanau, Kyunghyun Cho, and Yoshua Bengio. 2015. Neural machine translation by jointly learning to align and translate. In *Proc. ICLR*.

Tomáš Brychcín and Lukáš Svoboda. 2016. Uwb at semeval-2016 task 1: Semantic textual similarity using lexical, syntactic, and semantic information. In *Proceedings of the 10th International Workshop on Semantic Evaluation (SemEval-2016)*. Association for Computational Linguistics, San Diego, California, pages 588–594. http://www.aclweb.org/anthology/S16-1089.

Kyunghyun Cho, Bart van Merrienboer, Caglar Gulcehre, Dzmitry Bahdanau, Fethi Bougares, Holger Schwenk, and Yoshua Bengio. 2014. Learning phrase representations using rnn encoder–decoder for statistical machine translation. In *Proceedings of the 2014 Conference on Empirical Methods in Natural Language Processing (EMNLP)*. Association for Computational Linguistics, Doha, Qatar, pages 1724–1734. http://www.aclweb.org/anthology/D14-1179.

Courtney Corley and Rada Mihalcea. 2005. Measuring the semantic similarity of texts. In *Proceedings of the ACL workshop on empirical modeling of semantic equivalence and entailment*. Association for Computational Linguistics, pages 13–18.

Samuel Fernando and Mark Stevenson. 2008. A semantic similarity approach to paraphrase detection. In *Proceedings of the 11th Annual Research Colloquium of the UK Special Interest Group for Computational Linguistics*. Citeseer, pages 45–52.

Wael H Gomaa and Aly A Fahmy. 2013. A survey of text similarity approaches. *International Journal of Computer Applications* 68(13).

Hua He, John Wieting, Kevin Gimpel, Jinfeng Rao, and Jimmy Lin. 2016. Umd-ttic-uw at semeval-2016 task 1: Attention-based multi-perspective convolutional neural networks for textual similarity measurement. In *Proceedings of the 10th International Workshop on Semantic Evaluation (SemEval-2016)*. Association for Computational Linguistics, San Diego, California, pages 1103–1108. http://www.aclweb.org/anthology/S16-1170.

Claudia Leacock and Martin Chodorow. 1998. Combining local context and wordnet similarity for word sense identification. *WordNet: An electronic lexical database* 49(2):265–283.

Peng Li and Heng Huang. 2016. Uta dlnlp at semeval-2016 task 1: Semantic textual similarity: A unified framework for semantic processing and evaluation. In *Proceedings of the 10th International Workshop on Semantic Evaluation (SemEval-2016)*. Association for Computational Linguistics, pages 584–587. https://doi.org/10.18653/v1/S16-1088.

Matthias Liebeck, Philipp Pollack, Pashutan Modaresi, and Stefan Conrad. 2016. Hhu at semeval-2016 task 1: Multiple approaches to measuring semantic textual similarity. In *Proceedings of the 10th International Workshop on Semantic Evaluation (SemEval-2016)*. Association for Computational Linguistics, San Diego, California, pages 595–601. http://www.aclweb.org/anthology/S16-1090.

Dekang Lin et al. 1998. An information-theoretic definition of similarity. In *ICML*. Citeseer, volume 98, pages 296–304.

Marco Marelli, Stefano Menini, Marco Baroni, Luisa Bentivogli, Raffaella Bernardi, and Roberto Zamparelli. 2014. A sick cure for the evaluation of compositional distributional semantic models. In Nicoletta Calzolari (Conference Chair), Khalid Choukri, Thierry Declerck, Hrafn Loftsson, Bente Maegaard, Joseph Mariani, Asuncion Moreno, Jan Odijk, and Stelios Piperidis, editors, *Proceedings of the Ninth International Conference on Language Resources and Evaluation (LREC'14)*. European Language Resources Association (ELRA), Reykjavik, Iceland.

Tomas Mikolov, Ilya Sutskever, Kai Chen, Greg S Corrado, and Jeff Dean. 2013. Distributed representations of words and phrases and their compositionality. In *Advances in neural information processing systems*. pages 3111–3119.

George A Miller. 1995. Wordnet: a lexical database for english. *Communications of the ACM* 38(11):39–41.

Ani Nenkova, Kathleen McKeown, et al. 2011. Automatic summarization. *Foundations and Trends® in Information Retrieval* 5(2–3):103–233.

Barbara Rychalska, Katarzyna Pakulska, Krystyna Chodorowska, Wojciech Walczak, and Piotr Andruszkiewicz. 2016. Samsung poland nlp team at semeval-2016 task 1: Necessity for diversity; combining recursive autoencoders, wordnet and ensemble methods to measure semantic similarity. In *Proceedings of the 10th International Workshop on Semantic Evaluation (SemEval-2016)*. Association for Computational Linguistics, pages 602–608. https://doi.org/10.18653/v1/S16-1091.

Frane Šarić, Goran Glavaš, Mladen Karan, Jan Šnajder, and Bojana Dalbelo Bašić. 2012. Takelab: Systems for measuring semantic text similarity. In **SEM 2012: The First Joint Conference on Lexical and Computational Semantics – Volume 1: Proceedings of the main conference and the shared task, and Volume 2: Proceedings of the Sixth International Workshop on Semantic Evaluation (SemEval 2012)*. Association for Computational Linguistics, pages 441–448. http://aclweb.org/anthology/S12-1060.

Arafat Md Sultan, Steven Bethard, and Tamara Sumner. 2016. Dls\$@\$cu at semeval-2016 task 1: Supervised models of sentence similarity. In *Proceedings of the 10th International Workshop on Semantic Evaluation (SemEval-2016)*. Association for Computational Linguistics, pages 650–655. https://doi.org/10.18653/v1/S16-1099.

Kai Sheng Tai, Richard Socher, and Christopher D. Manning. 2015. Improved semantic representations from tree-structured long short-term memory networks. In *Proceedings of the 53rd Annual Meeting of the Association for Computational Linguistics and the 7th International Joint Conference on Natural Language Processing (Volume 1: Long Papers)*. Association for Computational Linguistics, Beijing, China, pages 1556–1566. http://www.aclweb.org/anthology/P15-1150.

Peter D Turney and Patrick Pantel. 2010. From frequency to meaning: Vector space models of semantics. *Journal of artificial intelligence research* 37:141–188.

Ngoc Phuoc An Vo, Simone Magnolini, and Octavian Popescu. 2015. Fbk-hlt: An application of semantic textual similarity for answer selection in community question answering. In *Proceedings of the 9th International Workshop on Semantic Evaluation, SemEval*. volume 15, pages 231–235.

Frane Šarić, Goran Glavaš, Mladen Karan, Jan Šnajder, and Bojana Dalbelo Bašić. 2012. Takelab: Systems for measuring semantic text similarity. In **SEM 2012: The First Joint Conference on Lexical and Computational Semantics – Volume 1: Proceedings of the main conference and the shared task, and Volume 2: Proceedings of the Sixth International Workshop on Semantic Evaluation (SemEval 2012)*. Association for Computational Linguistics, Montréal, Canada, pages 441–448. http://www.aclweb.org/anthology/S12-1060.

Kam-Fai Wong, Mingli Wu, and Wenjie Li. 2008. Extractive summarization using supervised and semi-supervised learning. In *Proceedings of the 22nd International Conference on Computational Linguistics-Volume 1*. Association for Computational Linguistics, pages 985–992.

SEF@UHH at SemEval-2017 Task 1: Unsupervised Knowledge-Free Semantic Textual Similarity via Paragraph Vector

Mirela-Stefania Duma and Wolfgang Menzel

University of Hamburg

Natural Language Systems Division

{mduma, menzel}@informatik.uni-hamburg.de

Abstract

This paper describes our unsupervised knowledge-free approach to the SemEval-2017 Task 1 Competition. The proposed method makes use of Paragraph Vector for assessing the semantic similarity between pairs of sentences. We experimented with various dimensions of the vector and three state-of-the-art similarity metrics. Given a cross-lingual task, we trained models corresponding to its two languages and combined the models by averaging the similarity scores. The results of our submitted runs are above the median scores for five out of seven test sets by means of Pearson Correlation. Moreover, one of our system runs performed best on the Spanish-English-WMT test set ranking first out of 53 runs submitted in total by all participants.

1 Introduction

Semantic Textual Similarity (STS) aims to assess the degree to which two snippets of text are related in meaning to each other. The SemEval annual competition offers a track on STS (Cer et al., 2017) where submitted STS systems are evaluated in terms of the Pearson correlation between machine assigned semantic similarity scores and human judgments.

We participated in both monolingual sub-tracks and cross-lingual sub-tracks. Given a sentence pair in the same language, the SemEval STS task is to assign a similarity score to it ranging from 0 to 5, with 0 implying that the semantics of the sentences are completely independent and 5 denoting semantic equivalence (Cer et al., 2017). The cross-lingual side of STS is similar to the initial task, but differs in the input sentences which come from two languages.

This year's shared task features six sub-tasks: Arabic-Arabic, Arabic-English, Spanish-Spanish, Spanish-English (two test sets), English-English and a surprise task (Turkish-English) for which no annotated data is offered.

For example, for the English monolingual STS track, the pair of sentences below had a score of 3 assigned by human annotators, meaning that the two sentences are roughly equivalent, but some essential information differs or is missing (Cer et al., 2017).

Bayes' theorem was named after Rev Thomas Bayes and is a method used in probability theory.

As an official theorem, Bayes' theorem is valid in all universal interpretations of probability.

We present an unsupervised, knowledge-free approach that utilizes Paragraph Vector (Le and Mikolov, 2014) to represent sentences by means of continuous distributed vectors. In addition to experimenting with feature spaces of different dimensionality, we also compare three state-of-the-art similarity metrics (Cosine, Bray-Curtis and Correlation) for calculating the STS scores. We do not make use of any lexical or semantic resources, nor hand-annotated labeled corpora in addition to the distributed representations trained on non-annotated text. The approach gives promising results on all sub-tasks, with our submitted systems ranking first out of 53 for one Spanish-English sub-track and above the median scores for five out of seven test sets.

We first shortly summarize related work in STS and describe Paragraph Vector in Section 2. Then we present our method in Section 3 along with the corpora we used in training the Paragraph Vector models. Section 4 contains an overview of the evaluation and the results.

Proceedings of the 11th International Workshop on Semantic Evaluations (SemEval-2017), pages 170–174,
Vancouver, Canada, August 3 - 4, 2017. ©2017 Association for Computational Linguistics

2   Related Work

2.1   Semantic Textual Similarity

We present in this subsection the state-of-the-art in STS-Task 1 using Paragraph Vector since it is the most relevant to our work. King et al. (2016), for instance make use of Paragraph Vectors as one approach in the English monolingual sub-task. Results are reported for a single vector size and the Cosine metric which is employed in obtaining the similarity score between sentences. Brychcín and Svoboda (2016) follow a similar approach but apply it also to the cross-lingual task.

We raise three research questions regarding the usage of Paragraph Vector in STS:

- To which degree does the vector size matter?

- What could be a better alternative to the traditional Cosine metric for measuring the similarity between two vectors (obtained with Doc2Vec[1])?

- Given a cross-lingual task, does averaging the similarity scores obtained using the Doc2Vec models trained on both language corpora result in an improvement over using only the scores from one model?

2.2   Paragraph Vector

In order to assess the semantic textual similarity of two sentences, methods of representing them are crucial. Le and Mikolov (2014) propose a continuous, distributed vector representation of phrases, sentences and documents, Paragraph Vectors. It is a continuation of the work in Mikolov et al. (2013a) where word vectors (embeddings) are introduced in order to semantically represent words.

The strength of capturing the semantics of words via word embeddings is visible not only when considering words with similar meaning like "strong" and "powerful" (Le and Mikolov, 2014), but also in learning relationships such as *male/female* where the vector representation for *King - Man + Woman* results in a vector very close to *Queen* (Mikolov et al., 2013b).

In the Paragraph Vector framework, the paragraph vectors are concatenated with the word vectors to form one vector. The paragraph vector acts as a memory of what is missing in the current context. The word vectors are shared across all paragraphs, while the paragraph vector is shared across all contexts generated from the same paragraph. The vectors are trained using stochastic gradient descent with backpropagation (Le and Mikolov, 2014).

Since the STS task requires assigning a similarity score between two sentences, we apply Paragraph Vector at the sentence level. The models are trained using the Gensim library (Řehůřek and Sojka, 2010).

3   Semantic Textual Similarity via Paragraph Vector

3.1   Corpora

For training the Doc2Vec models we used various corpora available for the different language pairs. Following the rationale from Lau and Baldwin (2016), we concatenated to the corpora the test set too as the Doc2Vec training is purely unsupervised. The corpora we used are made available by Opus (Tiedemann, 2012) (except Commoncrawl[2] and SNLI (Bowman et al., 2015)): Wikipedia (Wolk and Marasek, 2014), TED[3], MultiUN (Eisele and Chen, 2010), EUBookshop (Skadiņš et al., 2014), SETIMES[4], Tatoeba[5], WMT[6] and News Commentary[7]. The following table presents which corpora were used and how many sentences they consist of. The corpora marked with * were used only for the third run.

Track / Corpora	AR-AR	AR-EN	ES-ES	ES-EN	EN-EN	TR-EN
Commoncrawl	-	-	1.84M	-	2.39M	-
Wikipedia	151K	151K	-	1.81M	-	160K
TED	152K	152K	-	157K	-	137K
MultiUN	1M	1M	-	-	-	-
EUBookshop	-	-	-	-	-	23K
SETIMES	-	-	-	-	-	207K
Tatoeba	-	-	-	-	-	156K
SNLI*	-	150K	-	150K	150K	150K
WMT*	-	16K	-	16K	16K	16K
News Commentary*	-	238K	-	238K	238K	238K

Table 1: Corpora used in training Doc2Vec models

The SNLI, WMT and News Commentary corpora were used for run 3 in some sub-tasks where we aimed to assess whether using more data makes

---

[1]The terms Paragraph Vector and Doc2Vec are used interchangeably as follows.

[2]http://commoncrawl.org/
[3]http://www.casmacat.eu/corpus/ted2013.html
[4]http://nlp.ffzg.hr/resources/corpora/setimes/
[5]http://tatoeba.org/
[6]http://www.statmt.org/wmt14/
[7]http://www.casmacat.eu/corpus/news-commentary

a difference. For training the English models only the EN side of the ES-EN language pair was used.

3.2 Preprocessing

For the sub-tasks that included the Arabic language we utilized the Stanford Arabic Segmenter (Monroe et al., 2014) in order to reduce lexical sparsity. For all the other sub-tasks, we performed text normalization, tokenization and lowercasing using the scripts available in the Moses Machine Translation Toolkit (Koehn et al., 2007).

3.3 Methods

We assess the semantic similarity between two sentences based on their continuous vector representations obtained by means of various Paragraph Vector models. A similarity metric is applied afterwards in order to determine the proximity between the two vectors. This measure is directly used as the similarity score of the two sentences.

For all sub-tasks we experiment with the PV-DBOW training algorithm, various vector sizes (200, 300 and 400) and with various state-of-the-art similarity metrics (Cosine, Bray-Curtis, Correlation) defined as:

$$\text{Cosine: } 1 - \frac{u \cdot v}{||u||_2 ||v||_2}$$

$$\text{Bray-Curtis: } \frac{\sum |u_i - v_i|}{\sum |u_i + v_i|}$$

$$\text{Correlation: } 1 - \frac{(u - \bar{u}) \cdot (v - \bar{v})}{||(u - \bar{u})||_2 ||(v - \bar{v})||_2}$$

where u and v are the vector representations of the two sentences, $\bar{u}$ and $\bar{v}$ denote the mean value of the elements of u and and v, and $x \cdot y$ is the dot product of x and y.

The Cosine metric is directly available from the *Gensim* library, while the Bray-Curtis and Correlation metrics are part of the *spatial* library from *scipy*[8]. We need to invert the score produced by the *spatial* library as it provides dissimilarity scores instead of the required similarity measures.

Given a monolingual sub-task $L_1 - L_1$ and multiple bilingual corpora, the L_1 side of the corpora is used to train Doc2Vec models. For all cross-lingual sub-tasks $L_1 - L_2$ we used Google Translate to obtain the test set translation from L_1 to L_2 and vice versa. Then we trained the Doc2Vec models for the two languages separately and combined the similarity scores obtained by the two models by averaging. Since the scores are in the

range $(0, 1]$ we multiply them by 5 in order to return a continuous valued similarity score on a scale from 0 to 5, as the competition requires.

We submitted three runs to the competition:

run	
run1	Model(size=200), Cosine similarity EN-ES: Model_ES AR-EN: Model_AR TR-EN: Model_TR
run2	Model(size=400), Cosine similarity EN-ES: Model_ES AR-EN: Model_AR TR-EN: Model_TR
run3	Model(size=200), Bray-Curtis similarity, more training data EN-ES: Model_EN AR-EN: Model_EN TR-EN: Model_EN

Table 2: Submitted runs settings

4 Evaluation and Results

The similarity scores are evaluated by computing the Pearson Correlation between them and human judgments for the same sentence pairs. This section presents our results for all sub-tasks of the 2017 test sets and also for the STS Benchmark[9] (Cer et al., 2017).

4.1 STS 2017 Test Sets

When considering all 85 submitted runs (including the monolingual runs and the baseline), our best runs ranked 26 out of 49 for AR-AR, 21 out of 45 for AR-EN, 22 out of 48 for ES-ES, 28 out of 53 for ES-EN-a, 1 out of 53 for ES-EN-b, 35 out of 77 for EN-EN and 16 out of 48 for TR-EN (Cer et al., 2017).

Several experiments were conducted with size 200, 300 and 400 for the Doc2Vec vectors, training on both sides of the corpora for the cross-lingual tasks and applying Cosine, Bray-Curtis and Correlation similarity metrics. We detail in Table 3 the Pearson Correlation scores obtained.

The results indicate that the Bray-Curtis metric performs better than the other two in five out of seven test sets, with a tie on the EN-EN test set. Regarding the dimension of the Doc2Vec vectors, a conclusion cannot be simply drawn from these results, since size 200 leads to best results for ES-ES, ES-EN-a and EN-EN, size 300 gives best results for AR-AR, size 400 for AR-EN and ES-EN-b and a tie for TR-EN when using sizes 300 and 400. It is also important to note that the

---

[8]https://docs.scipy.org/doc/scipy-0.18.1/reference/spatial.html

[9]http://ixa2.si.ehu.es/stswiki/index.php/STSbenchmark

Task	Cosine			Bray-Curtis			Correlation		
AR-AR									
200		0.5587			0.5790			0.5579	
300		0.5825			**0.5984**			0.58	
400		0.5773			0.5943			0.5767	
AR-EN	AR	EN	Mean	AR	EN	Mean	AR	EN	Mean
200	0.4789	0.4971	0.5221	0.755	0.503	0.5268	0.4779	0.4997	0.5227
300	0.4963	0.5141	0.5429	0.502	0.5085	0.5432	0.4963	0.5154	0.5437
400	0.4813	0.5266	0.5381	0.4949	0.5288	**0.5469**	0.4796	0.5275	0.5372
ES-ES									
200		**0.7455**			0.7423			0.7434	
300		0.7002			0.7054			0.6991	
400		0.6979			0.7072			0.6982	
ES-EN-a	ES	EN	Mean	ES	EN	Mean	ES	EN	Mean
200	0.5738	0.6021	0.6212	0.5852	0.6208	**0.6353**	0.5748	0.6041	0.6227
300	0.5676	0.6162	0.6219	0.5793	0.6253	0.6299	0.566	0.6171	0.6213
400	0.566	0.6092	0.6187	0.5767	0.6162	0.6253	0.5643	0.606	0.6163
ES-EN-b	ES	EN	Mean	ES	EN	Mean	ES	EN	Mean
200	0.3069	0.1933	0.3111	0.306	0.1686	0.2953	0.307	0.1919	0.31
300	0.3234	0.1784	0.3193	0.3187	0.1685	0.3099	0.323	0.1826	0.3222
400	0.3407	0.1873	0.3303	**0.3436**	0.1575	0.3113	0.342	0.1854	0.3284
EN-EN									
200		**0.7880**			**0.7880**			0.7871	
300		0.7237			0.7396			0.7249	
400		0.7185			0.7264			0.7178	
TR-EN	TR	EN	Mean	TR	EN	Mean	TR	EN	Mean
200	0.4990	0.5554	0.5804	0.5080	0.5577	0.5846	0.5052	0.5540	0.5837
300	0.4919	0.5718	0.5792	0.4869	**0.6001**	0.5879	0.4909	0.5705	0.5770
400	0.4878	0.5832	0.5775	0.5024	**0.6000**	0.5930	0.4857	0.5836	0.5772

Table 3: Pearson Correlation results for various parameters

Pearson correlation scores range from 0.1575 to 0.3436 for the ES-EN-b test set and from 0.7178 to 0.788 for the EN-EN test set which suggests that experimenting with various sizes of Doc2Vec vectors is worth investigating, contrary to the common practice of experimenting with just a single vector size.

Averaging the similarity scores for the source and the target language also seems to be a promising approach. This combination led to best Pearson correlation scores for two of the four cross-lingual test sets (AR-EN and ES-EN-a).

We report in Table 4 the Pearson correlation results of the runs we submitted to the competition. For the first two runs we used Cosine for computing the similarity between the sentence pairs and for the third run we used Bray-Curtis.

	average	AR-AR	AR-EN	ES-ES	ES-EN-a	ES-EN-b	EN-EN	TR-EN
run 1	0.5644	0.5588	0.4789	0.7456	0.5739	0.3069	0.7880	0.4990
run 2	0.5528	0.5774	0.4813	0.6979	0.5660	0.3407	0.7186	0.4878
run 3	**0.5676**	0.5790	0.5384	0.7423	0.5866	0.1802	0.7256	0.6211

Table 4: Results for the submitted runs

The non-English language side of the corpora was used for training the Doc2Vec models for the cross-lingual tasks in the first two runs, while for the third run we trained the Doc2Vec models on the English side of the corpora. In the third run we also included additional data (except for AR-AR and ES-ES) in order to assess how the size of the training corpus for the Doc2Vec models influences the results. For the AR-EN, ES-EN-b and TR-EN sub-tasks the scores improved when using more training data, but the differences were small.

4.2 STS Benchmark

The Semeval STS organizers made available the STS Benchmark for the EN-EN task with the purpose of creating state-of-the-art approaches and collecting their results on standard data sets. The benchmark data consist of a selection of previous data sets used in the competition between 2012 and 2017.

Since the methods we presented are unsupervised and knowledge-free, we did not make use of the annotated training data when computing the similarity scores for the development and test sets. We tested two approaches for obtaining similarity scores on the EN-EN sub-task: the first infers the vectors for the development and test set sentences from the already trained Doc2Vec models (**Post-training inference**) and the other one retrains from scratch new models by adding the development and test sets to the initial Doc2Vec training data (**New-Model**).

As it can be noted in Table 4, the best Pearson correlation result for EN-EN was obtained using the settings from our submitted run 1. These settings also gave the best results for the STS Benchmark test data (Table 5).

Approach	Development set	Test set
Post-training inference	0.6670	0.5915
New-Model	0.6158	0.5922

Table 5: Results for the STS Benchmark

5 Conclusions

We presented in this paper our unsupervised knowledge-free approach to the STS task. A wide range of experiments were carried out in order to assess the impact of the similarity metric if Paragraph Vector is used to represent sentences. Our results indicate that Bray-Curtis might be a good choice, because it outperformed the commonly used Cosine metric on five out of seven test sets. Moreover, training the Doc2Vec models on both sides of the language corpora and averaging their similarity scores seems to be a promising approach for the cross-lingual STS task.

The proposed method achieved encouraging results as we ranked first on the EN-ES-b sub-task and obtained Pearson correlation scores above the median score for five out of seven test sets.

References

Samuel R. Bowman, Gabor Angeli, Christopher Potts, and Christopher D. Manning. 2015. A large annotated corpus for learning natural language inference. In *Proceedings of the 2015 Conference on Empirical Methods in Natural Language Processing*. Association for Computational Linguistics.

Tomáš Brychcín and Lukáš Svoboda. 2016. Uwb at semeval-2016 task 1: Semantic textual similarity using lexical, syntactic, and semantic information. In *Proceedings of the 10th International Workshop on Semantic Evaluation (SemEval-2016)*. Association for Computational Linguistics, pages 588–594.

Daniel Cer, Mona Diab, Eneko Agirre, Inigo Lopez-Gazpio, and Lucia Specia. 2017. Semeval-2017 task 1: Semantic textual similarity multilingual and crosslingual focused evaluation. In *Proceedings of the 11th International Workshop on Semantic Evaluation (SemEval-2017)*. Association for Computational Linguistics, Vancouver, Canada, pages 1–14. http://www.aclweb.org/anthology/S17-2001.

Andreas Eisele and Yu Chen. 2010. Multiun: A multilingual corpus from united nation documents. In *LREC*.

Milton King, Waseem Gharbieh, SoHyun Park, and Paul Cook. 2016. Unbnlp at semeval-2016 task 1: Semantic textual similarity: A unified framework for semantic processing and evaluation. In *Proceedings of the 10th International Workshop on Semantic Evaluation (SemEval-2016)*. ACL, San Diego, California, pages 732–735.

Philipp Koehn, Hieu Hoang, Alexandra Birch, Chris Callison-Burch, Marcello Federico, Nicola Bertoldi, Brooke Cowan, Wade Shen, Christine Moran, Richard Zens, Chris Dyer, Ondřej Bojar, Alexandra Constantin, and Evan Herbst. 2007. Moses: Open source toolkit for statistical machine translation. In *Proceedings of the 45th Annual Meeting of the ACL on Interactive Poster and Demonstration Sessions*. ACL, Stroudsburg, PA, USA.

Jey Han Lau and Timothy Baldwin. 2016. An empirical evaluation of doc2vec with practical insights into document embedding generation. In *Proceedings of the 1st Workshop on Representation Learning for NLP*. Association for Computational Linguistics.

Quoc V. Le and Tomas Mikolov. 2014. Distributed representations of sentences and documents. In *Proceedings of the 31th International Conference on Machine Learning, ICML 2014, Beijing, China, 21-26 June 2014*. pages 1188–1196.

Tomas Mikolov, Ilya Sutskever, Kai Chen, Gregory S. Corrado, and Jeffrey Dean. 2013a. Distributed representations of words and phrases and their compositionality. In *Advances in Neural Information Processing Systems 26: 27th Annual Conference on Neural Information Processing Systems 2013*. pages 3111–3119.

Tomas Mikolov, Wen-tau Yih, and Geoffrey Zweig. 2013b. Linguistic regularities in continuous space word representations. In *Human Language Technologies: Conference of the North American Chapter of the Association of Computational Linguistics, Proceedings, June 9-14, 2013, Westin Peachtree Plaza Hotel, Atlanta, Georgia, USA*. pages 746–751.

Will Monroe, Spence Green, and Christopher D. Manning. 2014. Word segmentation of informal arabic with domain adaptation. In *Association for Computational Linguistics (ACL)*.

Radim Řehůřek and Petr Sojka. 2010. Software framework for topic modelling with large corpora. In *Proceedings of the LREC 2010 Workshop on New Challenges for NLP Frameworks*. ELRA, pages 45–50.

Raivis Skadiņš, Jörg Tiedemann, Roberts Rozis, and Daiga Deksne. 2014. Billions of parallel words for free: Building and using the eu bookshop corpus. In *Proceedings of the 9th International Conference on Language Resources and Evaluation (LREC-2014)*. European Language Resources Association (ELRA), Reykjavik, Iceland.

Jörg Tiedemann. 2012. Parallel data, tools and interfaces in opus. In Nicoletta Calzolari (Conference Chair), Khalid Choukri, Thierry Declerck, Mehmet Ugur Dogan, Bente Maegaard, Joseph Mariani, Asuncion Moreno, Jan Odijk, and Stelios Piperidis, editors, *Proceedings of the Eight International Conference on Language Resources and Evaluation (LREC'12)*. European Language Resources Association (ELRA), Istanbul, Turkey.

Krzysztof Wolk and Krzysztof Marasek. 2014. Building subject-aligned comparable corpora and mining it for truly parallel sentence pairs. In *Procedia Technology, 18*. Elsevier, pages 126 – 132.

STS-UHH at SemEval-2017 Task 1: Scoring Semantic Textual Similarity Using Supervised and Unsupervised Ensemble

Sarah Kohail[*]
LT Group
CS Department
Universität Hamburg

Amr Rekaby Salama[*]
NATS Group
CS Department
Universität Hamburg

Chris Biemann
LT Group
CS Department
Universität Hamburg

`{kohail,salama,biemann}@informatik.uni-hamburg.de`

Abstract

This paper reports the STS-UHH participation in the SemEval 2017 shared Task 1 of Semantic Textual Similarity (STS). Overall, we submitted 3 runs covering monolingual and cross-lingual STS tracks. Our participation involves two approaches: unsupervised approach, which estimates a word alignment-based similarity score, and supervised approach, which combines dependency graph similarity and coverage features with lexical similarity measures using regression methods. We also present a way on ensembling both models. Out of 84 submitted runs, our team best multi-lingual run has been ranked 12th in overall performance with correlation of 0.61, 7th among 31 participating teams.

1 Introduction

Semantic Textual Similarity (STS) measures the degree of semantic equivalence between a pair of sentences. Accurate estimation of semantic similarity would benefit many Natural Language Processing (NLP) applications such as textual entailment, information retrieval, paraphrase identification and plagiarism detection (Agirre et al., 2016). In an attempt to support the research efforts in STS, the SemEval STS shared Task (Agirre et al., 2017) offers an opportunity for developing creative new sentence-level semantic similarity approaches and to evaluate them on benchmark datasets. Given a pair of sentences, the task is to provide a similarity score on a scale of 0..5 according to the extent to which the two sentences are considered semantically similar, with 0 indicating that the semantics of the sentences are

completely unrelated and 5 signifying semantic equivalence. Final performance is measured by computing the Pearson's correlation (ρ) between machine-assigned semantic similarity scores and gold standard scores provided by human annotators. Since last year, the STS task have been extended to involve additional subtasks for cross-lingual STS. Similar to the monolingual STS task, the cross-lingual task requires the semantic similarity measurement for two snippets of text that are written in different languages. In contrast to last year's edition (Agirre et al., 2016), the task is organized into 6 sub-tracks and a primary track, which is the average of all of the secondary sub-tracks results. Secondary sub-tracks involve scoring similarity for monolingual sentence pairs in one language (Arabic, English, Spanish), and cross-lingual sentence pairs from the combination of two different languages (Arabic-English, Spanish-English, Turkish-English).

Our paper proposes both supervised and unsupervised systems to automatically scoring semantic similarity between monolingual and cross-lingual short sentences. The two systems are then combined with an average ensemble to strengthen the similarity scoring performance. Out of 84 submissions, our system is placed 12th with an overall primary score of 0.61.

2 Related Work

Since 2012 (Agirre et al., 2012), the STS shared task has been one of the official shared tasks in SemEval and has attracted many researchers from the computational linguistics community (Agirre et al., 2017). Most of the state-of-the-art approaches often focus on training regression models on traditional lexical surface overlap features. Recently, deep learning models have achieved very promising results in semantic textual sim-

---

*These authors contributed equally to this work

Proceedings of the 11th International Workshop on Semantic Evaluations (SemEval-2017), pages 175–179,
Vancouver, Canada, August 3 - 4, 2017. ©2017 Association for Computational Linguistics

ilarity. The top three best performing systems from STS 2016 used sophisticated deep learning based models (Rychalska et al., 2016; Brychcín and Svoboda, 2016; Afzal et al., 2016). The highest correlation score was obtained by Rychalska et al. (2016). They proposed a textual similarity model that combines recursive auto-encoders (RAE) from deep learning with WordNet award penalty, which helps to adjusts the Euclidean distance between word vectors.

3 System Description

Our contribution in the STS shared task includes three different systems: supervised, unsupervised and supervised-unsupervised ensemble. Our models are mainly developed to measure semantic similarity between monolingual sentences in English. For the cross-lingual tracks, we leverage the Google translate API to automatically translate other languages into English. In the following subsections, we describe our data preprocessing and present our three systems.

3.1 Data Preprocessing

We use all the previously released datasets since 2012 to train and evaluate our models. The final total number of training examples is 14 619. We use StanfordCoreNLP[1] pipeline to tokenize, lemmatize, dependency parse, and annotate the dataset for lemmas, part-of-speech (POS) tags, and named entities (NE). Stopwords are removed for the purpose of topic modeling and TfIdf computation.

3.2 Unsupervised Model

Inspired by (Sultan et al., 2015; Brychcín and Svoboda, 2016), our unsupervised solution calculates a similarity score based on the alignment of the input pair of sentences. As presented in Figure 1, given a pair of sentences $S1, S2$, the alignment task builds a set of matched pair of words $match(w_i, w_j)$ where w_i is a word in sentence $S1$, and w_j is a word in sentence $S2$. Each matched pair has a score on the scale [0-1]. This matching score indicates the strength of the semantic similarity between the aligned pair of words, with 1 representing the highest similarity match.

As shown in Figure 2, after preprocessing, the system starts with matching exact similar words

[1]http://stanfordnlp.github.io/CoreNLP/

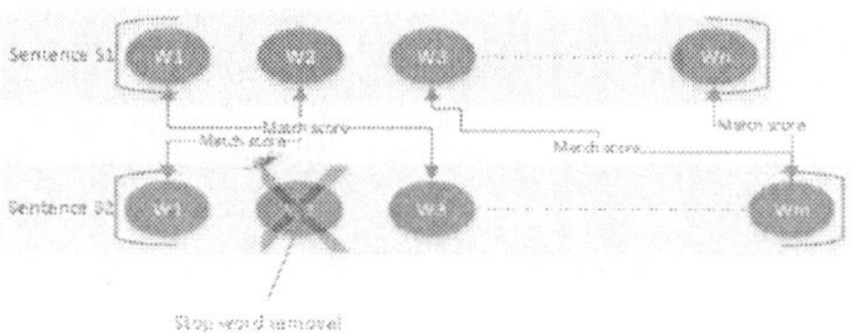

Figure 1: Unsupervised sentence alignment

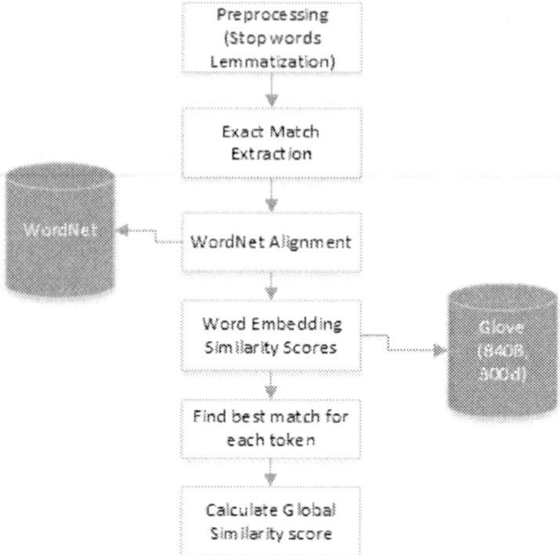

Figure 2: Unsupervised solution overview

(lemmas), and words that share similar WordNet hierarchy (synonyms, hyponyms, and hypernyms). We consider these two types of aligning as exact match with score 1.

As a last step of the alignment process, we handle the words that have not been matched in the preceding steps. The solution uses Glove word embeddings (Pennington et al., 2014) to calculate the matching score. Glove (840B tokens, 2.2M vocab) represent the word embeddings in 300d vector. We calculate the cosine distance between the unmatched words and all the words in the other sentence. Using a greedy strategy, we pick up the best match of each word.

The global similarity is calculated using a weighted matches scores as shown in equation (1).

$$Score = \frac{\sum TfIdf(w_i) * match(w_i, w_j)}{\sum TfIdf(S1, S2)} \quad (1)$$

For all w_i in $S1$ or $S2$, and $match(w_i, w_j)$ is the best match score for W_i with word W_j from the other sentence. $TfIdf(S1, S2)$ is the sum of the term frequency inverse document frequency of the words in $S1, S2$. The final alignment score is [0-

1], so we scale it into the [0-5] range.

3.3 Supervised Model

To generate our supervised model, we extract the following features:

I **Bag-of-Words:** for each sentence a $|V|$-dimension vector is generated, where V includes the unique vocabulary from both sentences. Entries in single vectors correspond to the frequency of the word in the respective sentence. Cosine similarity between these vectors serves as a feature.

II **Distributional Thesaurus (DTs) Expansion Feature:** Each non-stopword is expanded to its most similar top 10 words using the API for the Distributional Thesaurus (DTs) by Biemann and Riedl (2013).

III **POS Tags Longest Common Subsequence:** We measure the length of the longest common subsequence of POS tags between sentence pairs. Additionally, we also average this length by dividing it by the total number of tokens in each sentence separately.

IV **Topic Similarity Feature:** To model the topical similarity between two documents, we use Latent Dirichlet Allocation (LDA, (Blei et al., 2003))[2] model trained on a recent Wikipedia dump. To guarantee topic distribution stability, we run LDA for 100 repeated inferences. Then for each token, we assign the most frequent topic ID (Riedl and Biemann, 2012).

V **Dependency-Graph Features:** Following Kohail (2015), each sentence S is converted into a graph using dependency relations obtained from the parser. We define the dependency graph $G_S = \{V_S, E_S\}$, where the graph vertices $V_S = \{w_1, w_2, \ldots, w_n\}$ represent the tokens in a sentence, and E_S is a set of edges. Each edge e_{iy} represents a directed dependency relation between w_i and w_y. We calculate TfIdf on three levels and weight our dependency graph using the following conditions:
Word TfIdf: Considering only those words that satisfy the condition: TfIdf $(w_i) > \alpha_1$
Pair TfIdf: Word pair are filtered based on the condition: TfIdf $(w_i, w_y) > \alpha_2$
Triplet TfIdf: Considering only those triples (word, pair and relation), which satisfies the condition: TfIdf $(w_i, w_y, e_{iy}) > \alpha_3$
Similarities are then measured on three levels by representing each sentence as a vector of words, pairs and triples, where each entry in one vector is weighted using TfIdf. We used New York Times articles within the years 2004-2006, as a background corpus for TfIdf calculation.

VI **Coverage Features:** As a text gets longer, term frequency factors increase, and thus having a high similarity score is likelier for longer than for shorter texts. Coverage features measures the number of one-to-one tokens, edges and relations correspondence between the dependency graphs of a pair sentences as described in (Kohail and Biemann, 2017).

VII **NE Similarity:** We measure similarity based on the shared named entities between the pair of text.

VIII **Unsupervised Dependency Alignment score:** Using a Glove word embedding, we include the score of the cosine similarity between the syntactic heads of the matched words aligned in the unsupervised model (Sec. 3.2), as presented in equation (2).

$$score = \frac{\sum TfIdf(\widehat{w_i}) * Cos\_sim(\widehat{w_i}, \widehat{w_j})}{\sum TfIdf(S1, S2)} \tag{2}$$

For all w_i in $S1$ or $S2$, we calculate the weighted cosine similarity between its syntactic dependency head: $\widehat{w_i}$ and the syntactic head of the matched word: $\widehat{w_j}$.

These features are fed into three different regression methods[3]: Multilayer Perceptron (MLP)[4] neural network, Linear Regression (LR) and Regression Support Vector Machine (RegSVM). To evaluate our preliminary pre-testing models, we perform 10-fold cross-validation.

---

[2]The implementation was used in this work is available at: http://gibbslda.sourceforge.net/

[3]We used the WEKA (Witten et al., 2016) implementation with default parameters, if not mentioned otherwise
[4]Hidden layers = 2, Learning rate = 0.4, momentum = 0.2

System	Primary	Track 1 AR-AR	Track 2 AR-EN	Track 3 SP-SP	Track 4a SP-EN	Track 4b SP-EN	Track 5 EN-EN	Track 6 EN-TR
Run1	0.57	0.61	0.59	0.72	0.63	0.12	0.73	0.60
Run2	**0.61**	0.68	0.63	0.77	0.72	0.05	0.80	0.59
Run3	-	-	-	-	-	-	**0.81**	-
Ens.*	0.63	0.68	0.66	0.80	0.73	0.11	0.82	0.63
Basel.	-	0.60	-	0.71	-	-	0.73	-
Top	0.73	0.75	0.75	0.85	0.83	0.34	0.85	0.77

Table 1: Results obtained in terms of Pearson correlation over three runs for all the six sub-tracks in comparison with the baseline and the top obtained correlation in each track. The primary score represents the weighted mean correlation. Ens.* represents the results after adding the expansion and topic modeling features.

3.4 Ensembling Supervised and Unsupervised models

We create an ensemble model by by averaging the supervised and unsupervised models predictions.

4 Experimental Results

We report our results in Table 1. Overall we submitted 3 runs: **Run1** uses the unsupervised approach discussed earlier in Sec. 3.2, **Run2** uses a supervised MLP neural network trained as described in Sec. 3.3, and **Run3** uses the ensemble average system described in Sec. 3.4. Due to time constraints and technical issues, only evaluation for English monolingual track was given. Additionally, we were not able to compute the topic modeling and expansion features. We included the missing features later after the task deadline. Final ensemble results are given under Ens.*. According to the results, we can make following observations:

- Our results significantly outperform the baseline provided by the task organizers for monolingual tracks by a large margin.

- The ensemble outperforms the individual ensemble members.

- Results obtained in monolingual, especially English, are markedly higher than in crosslingual tracks. This might be due to noise introduced by the automatic translation.

- Results of track 4b appears to be significantly worse compared to other tracks results. In addition to the machine translation accuracy challenge, the difficulty of this track lies in providing longer sentences with less informative surface overlap between the sentences compared to other tracks.

5 Conclusion

We have presented and discussed our results on the task of Semantic Textual Similarity (STS). We have shown that combining supervised and unsupervised models in an ensemble provides better results than when each is used in isolation. 31 teams participated in the task with 84 runs. Our best system achieves an overall mean Pearson's correlation of 0.61, ranking 7th among all teams, 12th among all submissions. Future work includes building a real multi-lingual model by projecting phrases from different languages into the same embedding space. In the current solution, we consider hyponyms/hypernyms as synonyms. The system gives an exact match score for these word pairs. In the future, we tackle finding a way to give calculated dynamic scores for such kind of alignment to do not equalize them with exact matches.

Acknowledgment

This research was supported by the Deutscher Akademischer Austauschdienst (DAAD).

References

Naveed Afzal, Yanshan Wang, and Hongfang Liu. 2016. MayoNLP at SemEval-2016 Task 1: Semantic Textual Similarity based on Lexical Semantic Net and Deep Learning Semantic Model. In *Proceedings of the 10th International Workshop on Semantic Evaluation (SemEval-2016)*. San Diego, California, pages 674–679.

Eneko Agirre, Carmen Banea, Daniel Cer, Mona Diab, Aitor Gonzalez-Agirre, Rada Mihalcea, German Rigau, and Janyce Wiebe. 2016. Semeval-2016 task 1: Semantic textual similarity, monolingual and cross-lingual evaluation. In *Proceedings of SemEval*. San Diego, California, pages 497–511.

Eneko Agirre, Daniel Cer, Mona Diab, Iigo Lopez-Gazpio, and Lucia Specia. 2017. SemEval-2017 Task 1: Semantic Textual Similarity Multilingual and Crosslingual Focused Evaluation. In *Proceedings of SemEval*. Vancouver, Canada.

Eneko Agirre, Mona Diab, Daniel Cer, and Aitor Gonzalez-Agirre. 2012. SemEval-2012 Task 6: A Pilot on Semantic Textual Similarity. In *Proceedings of the First Joint Conference on Lexical and Computational Semantics - Volume 1: Proceedings of the Main Conference and the Shared Task, and Volume 2: Proceedings of the Sixth International Workshop on Semantic Evaluation*. Montreal, Canada, SemEval '12, pages 385–393.

Chris Biemann and Martin Riedl. 2013. Text: Now in 2D! a framework for lexical expansion with contextual similarity. *Journal of Language Modelling* 1(1):55–95.

David M. Blei, Andrew Y. Ng, and Michael I. Jordan. 2003. Latent Dirichlet Allocation. *J. Mach. Learn. Res.* 3:993–1022.

Tomáš Brychcín and Lukáš Svoboda. 2016. UWB at SemEval-2016 Task 1: Semantic Textual Similarity using Lexical, Syntactic, and Semantic Information. In *Proceedings of the 10th International Workshop on Semantic Evaluation (SemEval-2016)*. San Diego, California, pages 588–594.

Sarah Kohail. 2015. Unsupervised Topic-Specific Domain Dependency Graphs for Aspect Identification in Sentiment Analysis. In *Proceedings of the Student Research Workshop associated with RANLP*. Hissar, Bulgaria, pages 16–23.

Sarah Kohail and Chris Biemann. 2017. Matching, Re-ranking and Scoring: Learning Textual Similarity by Incorporating Dependency Graph Alignment and Coverage Features. In *18th International Conference on Computational Linguistics and Intelligent Text Processing*. Budapest, Hungary.

Jeffrey Pennington, Richard Socher, and Christopher D. Manning. 2014. GloVe: Global Vectors for Word Representation. In *Empirical Methods in Natural Language Processing (EMNLP)*. pages 1532–1543.

Martin Riedl and Chris Biemann. 2012. Sweeping through the topic space: Bad luck? roll again! In *Proceedings of the Joint Workshop on Unsupervised and Semi-Supervised Learning in NLP*. Association for Computational Linguistics, Avignon, France, ROBUS-UNSUP '12, pages 19–27.

Barbara Rychalska, Katarzyna Pakulska, Krystyna Chodorowska, Wojciech Walczak, and Piotr Andruszkiewicz. 2016. Samsung Poland NLP Team at SemEval-2016 Task 1: Necessity for diversity; combining recursive autoencoders, WordNet and ensemble methods to measure semantic similarity. In *Proceedings of the 10th International Workshop on Semantic Evaluation (SemEval-2016)*. San Diego, California, pages 602–608.

Md Arafat Sultan, Steven Bethard, and Tamara Sumner. 2015. Dls@cu: Sentence similarity from word alignment and semantic vector composition. In *Proceedings of the 9th International Workshop on Semantic Evaluation (SemEval 2015)*. Association for Computational Linguistics, Denver, Colorado, pages 148–153.

Ian H. Witten, Eibe Frank, Mark A. Hall, and Christopher J. Pal. 2016. *Data Mining: Practical machine learning tools and techniques*. Morgan Kaufmann.

UMDeep at SemEval-2017 Task 1: End-to-End Shared Weight LSTM Model for Semantic Textual Similarity

Joe Barrow
University of Maryland
Computer Science
`jdbarrow@cs.umd.edu`

Denis Peskov
University of Maryland
Computer Science
`dpeskov@cs.umd.edu`

Abstract

We describe a modified shared-LSTM network for the Semantic Textual Similarity (STS) task at SemEval-2017. The network builds on previously explored Siamese network architectures. We treat max sentence length as an additional hyperparameter to be tuned (beyond learning rate, regularization, and dropout). Our results demonstrate that hand-tuning max sentence training length significantly improves final accuracy. After optimizing hyperparameters, we train the network on the multilingual semantic similarity task using pre-translated sentences. We achieved a correlation of 0.4792 for all the subtasks. We achieved the fourth highest team correlation for Task 4b, which was our best relative placement.

1 Introduction

Semantic Textual Similarity (STS) has been a staple of the SemEval competition and requires systems that automatically identify the semantic relatedness of two sentences. The resulting system could be used down-stream in many important NLP tasks, such as scoring the output of a machine translation system or finding related document/query pairs in web search.

The data available for this competition has been updated annually and contains gold-label, human-evaluated scores based on sentence pairs across multiple languages ((Agirre et al., 2012), (Agirre et al., 2013), (Agirre et al., 2014), (Agirre et al., 2015)). The gold label for each sentence pair is in the range $[0, 5]$, with 0 being *the sentences are completely dissimilar* to 5 being *the sentences are completely equivalent*. (Agirre et al., 2016)

The task is not restricted to English or monolingual similarity scoring. The 2017 SemEval task consists of seven different tracks, each with a different language pair: Arabic-Arabic, Arabic-English, Spanish-Spanish, Spanish-English, an additional Spanish-English track, English-English, and English-Turkish. We avoid language-specific feature engineering and take a representation learning approach to STS. This requires constructing directly-comprable sentence representations that can be induced from the limited amounts of annotated STS training data.

We present a modified version of the Siamese Long Short-Term Memory (LSTM) network to solve this problem. (Mueller and Thyagarajan, 2016) A Siamese network is one in which parameters between layers are shared, and are updated in parallel during the learning phase. For the semantic relatedness task, this allows two sentences to be encoded into the same space using a single shared recurrent neural network. The dual-encoding enables the use of end-to-end supervised deep learning, using only the surface forms of the sentences and the gold labels.

We extend the Siamese LSTM in two ways. First, we consider the semantic relatedness as a classification, rather than a regression problem. Initially, semantic relatedness appears to be a continuous one-dimensional measure suitable for regression. However, there are many subtleties within the bands of scores, as sentences can differ along more than a single dimension. Thus, rather than regressing over the label, our model generates a distribution over possible labels. Second, we use a different concatenative dense layer on top of the dual LSTMs to better model the classification problem (Tai et al., 2015), and train using KL-Divergence as the loss function for training.

Our results did not achieve the state-of-the-art performance possible with a Siamese LSTM ar-

180

Proceedings of the 11th International Workshop on Semantic Evaluations (SemEval-2017), pages 180–184,
Vancouver, Canada, August 3 - 4, 2017. ©2017 Association for Computational Linguistics

chitecture. Despite this set-back, we are able to demonstrate the effect of sentence training length on a LSTM. Additionally, all foreign languages were translated through Google Translate and the same model was used for the seven tracks. This standardization provides insight into the quality of Google Translate and the negative effect of machine translation on correlation.

The following section provides detail on our system and the training process. As our submission is focused on the use of end-to-end deep learning in semantic relatedness, we do not use hand-crafted features from external data, except for pre-trained word embeddings to speed up training. A visual overview of the shared LSTM model can be seen in Figure 1.

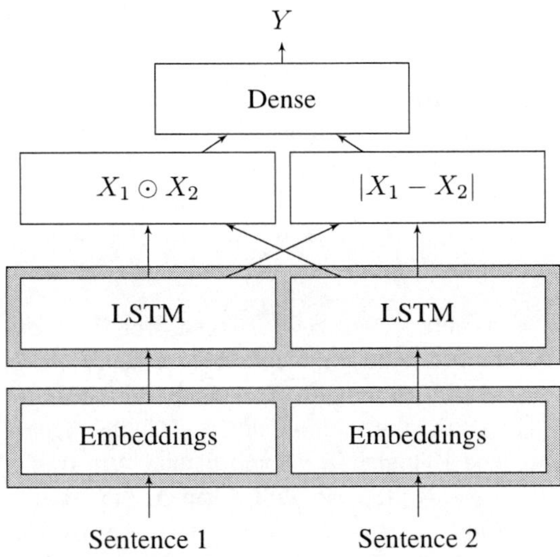

Figure 1: The end-to-end shared-LSTM model. Note that the shaded boxes represent shared parameters that are updated in parallel when the error is backpropagated. In this model, both the embeddings and the LSTM weights are shared, meaning the sentences are encoded into the same space. The model was implemented in Lasagne. (Dieleman et al., 2015)

2   End-to-End Shared LSTM

We use a shared-parameter LSTM model, also known as a Siamese LSTM model, as a completely end-to-end deep learning model. (Mueller and Thyagarajan, 2016; Tai et al., 2015)

Shared Parameters. In the siamese LSTM, the embedding layers share weights with each other,

as do the LSTM layers. These weights are shared throughout the entire training process, so updates applied to one are applied to both. Each sentence was transformed into a sequence of embeddings and then encoded into a sentence vector by the LSTM, and since the embedding and LSTM layers were the same for both sentences, both sentences were encoded into the same space. The sentence embeddings were the final vector in the LSTM.

Word Embeddings.   The model was initialized with GloVe word embeddings. (Pennington et al., 2014) Our experiments with both GloVe and the Paragram (Wieting et al., 2015) embeddings showed only a negligible difference in the final performance of the model. This difference disappeared when embeddings were made trainable.

Should one include all the embeddings or simply the subset seen in the training data? If all the embeddings are included, then the model should theoretically generalize better, as there are fewer UNKNOWN's in the validation and testing data. However, if all the embeddings are included and the embeddings are trainable, then only the seen portion of the embedding space is updated, which could hurt model generalization.

Our model uses the whole embedding space, but also updates the embeddings after each batch. Although updating only part of the space could risk damaging model generalizability, our experiments found that we actually saw an improvement in generalizability with both the whole embedding space and trainable embeddings.

Dense Concatenative Layer. The original equation for the dense layer is: $exp(-||X_1 - X_2||_1)$. (Mueller and Thyagarajan, 2016) However, as shown in Figure 1, our dense layer takes the concatenation of two different transformations: $|X_1 - X_2|$ and $X_1 \odot X_2$. This is used to capture both the difference in the angle and the absolute difference of the two sentences. (Tai et al., 2015)

Training Objective.   In order to use Kullback-Leiber divergence (KL divergence) as the objective function, we had to convert the gold labels into probability distributions: (Tai et al., 2015)

$$p_i = \begin{cases} y - \lfloor y \rfloor, & i = \lfloor y \rfloor + 1 \\ \lfloor y \rfloor - y + 1, & i = \lfloor y \rfloor \\ 0 & otherwise \end{cases}$$

Thus, a label of 4.7 would distribute 70% of its probability mass to the category 5, and 30% of its probability mass to the category 4. To convert from a probability distribution to a prediction, simply take the dot product of the ordered vector $< 0, 1, 2, 3, 4, 5 >$ and the distribution.

Then, the loss for each example was computed using the standard KL divergence formula, with some minor smoothing to disallow zeros: $D_{KL}(P||Q) = \sum_i P(i) log\frac{P(i)}{Q(i)}$.

3 Experiments and Results

We opted for minimal preprocessing in our final model: merely tokenizing and lower-casing the input. Lemmatizing the words did not lead to a notable improvement, and hence was omitted. Additionally, experimenting with targeted Part of Speech exclusion (removing all articles, increasing weight of proper nouns, etc.) did not produce dramatically higher results. Therefore, we decided to let the LSTM learn for itself.

Our final results on the 2017 data are shown in Table 1. Retrospectively, we saw that the 2016 postediting data (65.13% accuracy when 2016 data was held out from training) would have served as a close proxy for 2017 En-En performance. Our three submissions to the 2017 Semeval task were trained treating maximum training sentence length as a hyperparameter. Our results show that this parameter can have a large impact on the final outcome of the model.

The cosine baseline provided by SemEval organizers achieved a 0.72 correlation for the English-English sentences, which was roughly 0.07 higher than our best performance on the same dataset. Although disheartening, a Siamese LSTM model is capable of performing dramatically better with curated training data, whereas the baseline approach cannot be significantly modified.

Network Architecture and Parameters. Our final model used length 300 GloVe embeddings, 100 LSTM cells, 50 neurons in the final dense layer, and 6 output neurons, one for each class. We used the Kullback-Leibler Divergence of the output distribution and the gold label distribution as the objective function.

Data. We used all available past STS Task 1 datasets and no external data. In order to participate in the non-English tracks, we used Google Translate to translate all the sentence pairs into English. We then used the model trained on the English-English pairs on the translated-English data.

4 Discussion

Length. As shown in Table 1, the best identified length was 20. Meanwhile, the median length for the labeled sentences was below 11. Training on the max length saw an improvement on the English-English dataset, but an overall decrease in performance on the other datasets, in particular the SP-EN-WMT dataset, which contained very long English-Spanish sentence pairs. This is likely due to the network capturing long-term dependencies present in the native English sentence pairs that weren't present in the translated sentence pairs.

Translations. Our results demonstrate that the introduction of machine translation into the pipeline damages performance. The drop for non-English monolingual tasks exceeds that for English cross-lingual tasks, as translation is only applied to one side in the latter.

- **Spanish** - On the translated Spanish-Spanish sentence pairs, our correlation went down from 0.62 to 0.52. However, the drop was only to 0.56 on the English-Spanish sentence pairs, likely because half of the data was the native English used in training.

- **Arabic** - We saw a larger drop in accuracy on the Arabic-Arabic sentence pairs, from 0.62 to 0.48. This likely demonstrates that the translation quality of Google Translate is higher for Spanish than for Arabic. As was the case with Spanish, the Arabic-English pairs did better than the Arabic-Arabic pairs, achieving a correlation of 0.49 with the length 20 model, and 0.52 with the max length model.

- **Turkish** - Although there was no Turkish-Turkish track this year, our system performed roughly as expected on the Turkish-English track, given its performance on the Spanish-English and Arabic-English tracks. Uniquely in Turkish, accuracy spikes between the length 20 and max length models: from .53 to over .57 respectively.

Overall, we found the superior translation of Spanish unsurprising given the similarity of the languages and the large corpora available for Spanish-English translations.

Investigating the Results. Table 2 shows a selection of sentence pairs, their gold labels, and our

2017 Language Pairs	Number of Pairs	Length 11 (ρ)	Length 20 (ρ)	Max Length (ρ)
AR-AR	250	0.3905	0.4753	0.4587
AR-EN	250	0.3713	0.4939	0.5199
SP-SP	250	0.4588	0.5165	0.5148
SP-EN	250	0.3482	0.5615	0.5232
SP-EN-WMT	250	0.0586	0.1609	0.1300
EN-EN	250	0.4727	0.6174	0.6222
EN-TR	250	0.3644	0.5293	0.5725
Weighted Mean	-	**0.3521**	**0.4792**	**0.4773**

Table 1: Results in the different tracks of SemEval-2017. The lengths refer to the maximum lengths of the sentences used for training the model.

Sentence 1	Sentence 2	Gold	Pred.
A man is performing labor.	A man is performing today.	2.8	1.5
A kid sits on a soccer ball outside.	A kid sitting on a soccer ball at the park.	4.2	4.2
The player shoots the winning points.	The basketball player is about to score points for his team.	2.8	2.7
The yard has a dog.	The dog is running after another dog.	1.6	4.1
the people are running a marathon	People are running a marathon	5.0	0.9

Table 2: A selection of results showing the successes and failures of our shared-LSTM architecture. These sentences were selected to show areas in which our system excels or under-performs.

system's predicted score. There were many cases in which our system achieved very precise scoring, as included in the table. The examples on which the end-to-end model failed prove more interesting.

There were many simple examples that fooled our system. The most notable one is the pair ("the people are running a marathon", "People are running a marathon"). In this case, the only difference is the inclusion of the determiner "the" at the start of the sentence, as the capitalization of people would have been removed during preprocessing. Yet our system predicts the relatedness to be 0.9, rather than 5.0. This example shows that, although the sentences are theoretically encoded into the same space, the series of transformations that the sentence undergoes is complex and imperfect. Another such example is the pair ("The yard has a dog.", "The dog is running after another dog.") The fact that a dog exists in both sentences should not merit such a high score alone. This trend of attributing similarity to sentences with similar subjects percolates throughout our results.

The sentence pair ("A man is performing labor.", "A man is performing today.) demonstrates the learning potential of our model's predictions. These sentences are identical in length and the surface forms are 80% similar as only the final word differs. However, the different sense of perform make these sentences mostly unrelated. The difference is subtle, and unlikely to be picked up by a more naive system. Some basic ability to disambiguate different word senses is suggested by the shared weight LSTM's 1.5 assignment.

5 Conclusion and Future Work

A Siamese LSTM architecture has the potential for generating sophisticated predictions, but relies heavily on selecting appropriate training data. Our results show that hand-tweaking the maximum length of training sentences can significantly affect model output. Additionally, we show that the LSTM model performs worse on machine-translated data than on native English sentences.

There are several possible extensions of the proposed shared LSTM framework, such as a tree-structured, rather than linear LSTM. This uses the sentence parse as a "feature" for structuring the model, and can provide significant improvements over a purely linear LSTM for semantic relatedness. (Tai et al., 2015)

References

Eneko Agirre, Carmen Banea, Claire Cardie, Daniel Cer, Mona Diab, Aitor Gonzalez-Agirre, Weiwei Guo, Rada Mihalcea, German Rigau, and Janyce Wiebe. 2014. Semeval-2014 task 10: Multilingual semantic textual similarity. In *Proceedings of the 8th international workshop on semantic evaluation (SemEval 2014)*. Association for Computational Linguistics Dublin, Ireland, pages 81–91.

Eneko Agirre, Carmen Baneab, Claire Cardiec, Daniel Cerd, Mona Diabe, Aitor Gonzalez-Agirrea, Weiwei Guof, Inigo Lopez-Gazpioa, Montse Maritxalara, Rada Mihalceab, et al. 2015. Semeval-2015 task 2: Semantic textual similarity, english, spanish and pilot on interpretability. In *Proceedings of the 9th international workshop on semantic evaluation (SemEval 2015)*. pages 252–263.

Eneko Agirre, Carmen Baneab, Daniel Cerd, Mona Diabe, Aitor Gonzalez-Agirrea, Rada Mihalceab, German Rigaua, Janyce Wiebef, and Basque Country Donostia. 2016. Semeval-2016 task 1: Semantic textual similarity, monolingual and cross-lingual evaluation. *Proceedings of SemEval* pages 497–511.

Eneko Agirre, Daniel Cer, Mona Diab, Aitor Gonzalez-Agirre, and Weiwei Guo. 2013. sem 2013 shared task: Semantic textual similarity, including a pilot on typed-similarity. In *In* SEM 2013: The Second Joint Conference on Lexical and Computational Semantics. Association for Computational Linguistics.* Citeseer.

Eneko Agirre, Mona Diab, Daniel Cer, and Aitor Gonzalez-Agirre. 2012. Semeval-2012 task 6: A pilot on semantic textual similarity. In *Proceedings of the First Joint Conference on Lexical and Computational Semantics-Volume 1: Proceedings of the main conference and the shared task, and Volume 2: Proceedings of the Sixth International Workshop on Semantic Evaluation.* Association for Computational Linguistics, pages 385–393.

Sander Dieleman, Jan Schlter, Colin Raffel, Eben Olson, Sren Kaae Snderby, Daniel Nouri, et al. 2015. Lasagne: First release. https://doi.org/10.5281/zenodo.27878.

Jonas Mueller and Aditya Thyagarajan. 2016. Siamese recurrent architectures for learning sentence similarity. In *AAAI*. pages 2786–2792.

Jeffrey Pennington, Richard Socher, and Christopher D Manning. 2014. Glove: Global vectors for word representation. In *EMNLP*. volume 14, pages 1532–1543.

Kai Sheng Tai, Richard Socher, and Christopher D Manning. 2015. Improved semantic representations from tree-structured long short-term memory networks. *arXiv preprint arXiv:1503.00075* .

John Wieting, Mohit Bansal, Kevin Gimpel, and Karen Livescu. 2015. Towards universal paraphrastic sentence embeddings. *arXiv preprint arXiv:1511.08198* .

MITRE at SemEval-2017 Task 1: Simple Semantic Similarity

John Henderson, Elizabeth M. Merkhofer, Laura Strickhart and **Guido Zarrella**
The MITRE Corporation
202 Burlington Road
Bedford, MA 01730-1420, USA
`{jhndrsn,emerkhofer,lstrickhart,jzarrella}@mitre.org`

Abstract

This paper describes MITRE's participation in the Semantic Textual Similarity task (SemEval-2017 Task 1), which evaluated machine learning approaches to the identification of similar meaning among text snippets in English, Arabic, Spanish, and Turkish. We detail the techniques we explored, ranging from simple bag-of-ngrams classifiers to neural architectures with varied attention and alignment mechanisms. Linear regression is used to tie the systems together into an ensemble submitted for evaluation. The resulting system is capable of matching human similarity ratings of image captions with correlations of 0.73 to 0.83 in monolingual settings and 0.68 to 0.78 in cross-lingual conditions.

1 Introduction

Semantic Textual Similarity (STS) measures the degree to which two snippets of text convey the same meaning. Cross-lingual STS measures the same for sentence pairs written in two different languages. Automatic identification of semantically similar text has practical applications in domains such as evaluation of machine translation outputs, discovery of parallel sentences in comparable corpora, essay grading, and news summarization. It serves as an easily explained assay for systems modeling semantics.

SemEval-2017 marked the sixth consecutive year of a shared task measuring progress in STS. Current machine learning approaches to measuring semantic similarity vary widely. One design decision for STS systems is whether to explicitly align words between paired sentences. Wieting et al. (2016) demonstrate that sentence embeddings without explicit alignment or atten-tion can often provide reasonable performance on STS tasks. Related work in textual entailment offers evidence that neural models with soft alignment outperform embeddings-only approaches Chen et al. (2016); Parikh et al. (2016). However these results were obtained on a dataset multiple orders of magnitude larger than existing STS datasets. In absence of large datasets, word alignments similar to those used in statistical machine translation have proven to be useful (Zarrella et al., 2015; Itoh, 2016).

In this effort we explored diverse methods for aligning words in pairs of candidate sentences: translation-inspired hard word alignments as well as soft alignments learned by deep neural networks with attention. We also examined a variety of approaches for comparing aligned words, ranging from bag-of-ngrams features leveraging hand-engineered lexical databases, to recurrent and convolutional neural networks operating over distributed representations. Although an ideal cross-lingual STS system might operate directly on input sentences in their original language, we used machine translation to convert all the inputs into English. The paucity of in-domain training data and the simplicity of the image caption genre made the translation approach reasonable. Our contribution builds on approaches developed for English STS but points a way forward for progress on knowledge-lean, fully-supervised methods for semantic comparison across different languages.

2 Task, Data and Evaluation

Semantic Textual Similarity was a shared task organized within SemEval-2017 (Agirre et al., 2017). The task organizers released 1,750 sentence pairs of evaluation data organized into six tracks: Arabic, Spanish, and English monolingual, as well as Arabic-English, Spanish-English, and

Proceedings of the 11th International Workshop on Semantic Evaluations (SemEval-2017), pages 185–190,
Vancouver, Canada, August 3 - 4, 2017. ©2017 Association for Computational Linguistics

Turkish-English cross-lingual.

Most of this evaluation data was sourced from the Stanford Natural Language Inference corpus (Bowman et al., 2015). The sentences are English-language image captions, grouped into pairs and human-annotated on a scale of 0 to 5 for semantic similarity. In the monolingual English task, the average sentence length was 8.7 words, and the average rating was 2.3 (e.g. *The woman had brown hair.* and *The woman has gray hair.*) There was a roughly balanced distribution of highly rated pairs (e.g. *A woman is bungee jumping.* and *A girl is bungee jumping.*) and poorly rated pairs (e.g. *The yard has a dog.* and *The dog is running after another dog.*) Annotated sentence pairs were manually translated from English into other languages to create additional tracks.

For each pair, task participants predicted a similarity score. Systems were evaluated by Pearson correlation with the human ratings.

3 System Overview

We created an ensemble of five systems which each independently predicted a similarity score. Some features were reused among many components, including word embeddings, machine translations, alignments, and dependency parses.

3.1 English Word Embeddings

We used word2vec (Mikolov et al., 2013) to learn distributed representations of words from the text of the English Wikipedia. We applied word2phrase twice to identify phrases of up to four words, and trained a skip-gram model of size 256 for the 630,902 vocabulary items which appeared at least 100 times, using a context window of 10 words and 15 negative samples per example.

3.2 Machine Translation

Sentences in the image caption genre tend to be short and use a simple vocabulary. To test the extent to which this is true of SNLI data, we trained a small unregularized neural language model which achieved a perplexity of 18.9 on a held-out test set. The same parameterization achieved a perplexity of 114.5 in experiments on the Penn Treebank (Zaremba et al., 2014). We proceeded to translate all non-English sentences to English, recognizing that modern MT systems are sufficient to provide high quality translations for simple sentences. We used the Google Translate API in mid-

January 2017.

3.3 Dependency Parses

The dependency parse arcs were used as features to assist in aligning and comparing pairs of words. The Stanford Parser library produced these typed dependency representations (Chen and Manning, 2014). The English PCFG model with basic dependencies was used rather than the default collapsed dependencies to ensure that the parser gave us exactly one parse arc for each token.

3.4 Alignment

Comparing sentences can be a tallying process. One can find all associated atomic pairs in the left hand and right hand sides, cross them off, and judge the dissimilarity based on the remaining residuals. This process is reminiscent of finding translation equivalences for training machine translation systems (Al-Onaizan et al., 1999).

To this end, we built an alignment system on top of word embeddings. First, the *min alignment* is produced to maximize the sum of cosine similarities ($sim(w_i, w_j) = 1 + \cos(w_i, w_j)$) of word vectors corresponding to aligned word pairs under the constraint that no word is aligned more than once. The *max alignment* is constrained such that each word must be paired with at least one other, and the total number of edges in the alignment can be no more than word count of the longer string. In both cases, LPSOLVE was employed to find the assignment maximizing these criteria (Berkelaar et al., 2004).

Dependency parses constructed in Section 3.3 were aligned in a similar way. Consider dependency arcs a_i : $head \rightarrow dep$ Instead of the sum of cosine similarities as atoms in the linear program, however, we used $sim(a_1, a_2) = sim(head(a_1), head(a_2)) + 10sim(dep(a_1), dep(a_2))$ to give preference to matching dependency arcs a_1 and a_2 with similar heads.

3.5 Ensemble Components

TakeLab The open source TakeLab Semantic Text Similarity System was incorporated as a baseline (Šarić et al., 2012). Specifically we use LIBSVM to train a support vector regression model with an RBF kernel, cost parameter of 20, gamma of 0.2, and epsilon of 0.5. Input features were comprised of TakeLab-computed n-gram overlap and word similarity metrics.

Recurrent Convolutional Neural Network We recreate the recurrent neural network (RNN) model described in Zarrella et al. (2015) and train it using the embeddings and parse-aware alignments described above. Briefly, this 16-dimensional RNN operates over a sequence of aligned word pairs, comparing each pair according to features that encode embedding similarity, word position, and unsupervised string similarity.

We extended this model with four new feature categories. The first was a binary variable that indicates whether both words in the pair were determined to have the same dependency type in their respective parses. We also added three convolutional recurrent neural networks (CRNNs), each of which receive as input a sequence of word embeddings, and which learn STS features via 256 1D convolutional filters connected (with 50% dropout) to a 128-dimensional LSTM. For each aligned word pair, the first CRNN operates on the embeddings of the aligned words, the second CRNN operates on the squared difference of the embeddings of the aligned words, and the final CRNN operates on the embeddings of the parent words selected by the dependency parse. All above RNN outputs were concatenated to form a sequence of 400-dimensional (16+128*3) timesteps, which fed a 128-dimensional LSTM connected to a single sigmoidal output unit.

We unrolled this network to a zero-padded sequence length of 60 and trained it to convergence using Adam with a mean average error loss function (Kingma and Ba, 2014). The embeddings were not updated during training. We ensembled eight instances of this network trained from different random initializations.

Paris: String Similarity More than a decade ago, MITRE entered a system based on string similarity metrics in the 2004 Pascal RTE competition (Bayer et al., 2005). The `libparis` code base implements eight different string similarity and machine translation evaluation algorithms; measures include an implementation of the MT evaluation BLEU (Papineni et al., 2002); WER, a common speech recognition word error rate based on Levenshtein distance (Levenshtein, 1966); WER-g (Foster et al., 2003); ROUGE (Lin and Och, 2004); a simple position-independent error rate similar to PER (Leusch et al., 2003); both global and local similarity metrics often used for biological string comparison (Gusfield, 1997).

Finally, there are precision and recall measures based on bags of *all* substrings (or n-grams in word tokenization).

In total, the package computes 22 metrics for a pair of strings. The metrics were run on both case-folded and original versions as well as on word tokens and characters, yielding 88 string similarity features. Some of the metrics are not symmetric, so they were run both forward and reversed based on presentation in the dataset yielding 176 features. Finally, for each feature value x, $\log(x)$ was added as a feature, producing a final count of 352 string similarity features. `LIBLINEAR` used these features to build a L1-regularized logistic regression model. This system was unchanged, except for retraining, from the system described in Zarrella et al. (2015)

Simple Alignment Measures Section 3.4 describes methods we used for aligning two strings. L2-regularized logistic regression was used to combine 16 simple features calculated as side-effects of alignment. Details are described in Zarrella et al. (2015).

Enhanced BiLSTM Inference Model (EBIM) We recreated the neural model described in Chen et al. (2016) which reports state-of-the-art performance on the task of finding entailment in the SNLI corpus. The model encodes each sentence with a bidirectional LSTM over word embeddings, uses a parameter-less attention mechanism to produce a soft alignment matrix for the two sentences, and then does inference over each timestep and its alignment using another LSTM. Two fully-connected layers complete the prediction. Chen et al. (2016) improves performance by concatenating the final LSTM representation from EBIM with that of a similar model where a modified LSTM operates over a syntax tree; we did not include this extension in our submission.

Our implementation kept most hyperparameters described in the paper. However, we used the word2vec embeddings described above and found that freezing the embeddings produced better performance for this small dataset. We also found our models worked better without dropout on the embedding layer. Where the original model chooses a class via softmax, we output a semantic similarity score trained to minimize mean squared error.

	Primary	Track 1 AR-AR	Track 2 AR-EN	Track 3 ES-ES	Track 4a ES-EN	Track 4b ES-EN news	Track 5 EN-EN	Track 6 TR-EN
Official Score	0.6590	0.7294	0.6753	0.8202	0.7802	0.1598	0.8053	0.6430
Corrected Score	**0.6687**	0.7294	0.6753	0.8202	0.7802	0.1598	**0.8329**	**0.6831**

Table 1: Pearson correlations on official test set. Corrected ensemble effects in bold.

	Factored		Ablated	
Component	dev	test	dev	test
TakeLab	.8724	.6503	.8739	.6454
CRNNs-8	.8621	.6379	.8846	.6551
Paris	.8074	.5524	.8891	.6666
EBIM	.7742	.4760	.8886	.6687
Align	.7607	.5037	**.8910**	**.6722**
All In			.8900	.6687

Table 2: Factored and ablated system components evaluated on our dev set and the official test set.

3.6 Ensemble

The semantic similarity estimates of the predictors described above contributed to the final prediction with a weighting determined by L2-regularized logistic regression.

4 Experiment Details

We used as training data a selection of English monolingual sentence pairs released during prior SemEval STS evaluations. Specifically, we trained on 6,898 pairs of news and caption genre data from the 2012-2014 and 2016 evaluations. We used an additional 400 and 350 captions from the 2015 evaluation as development and tuning sets, respectively. We did not use out-of-genre data (e.g. dictionary definitions, Europarl, web forums, student essays) or the newly-released multilingual 2017 training data. The dev set was used to select hyperparameters for individual components, while the tuning set was used to select the hyperparameters for the final ensemble.

5 Results

The evaluation of our components on the competition test set is shown in Table 1. The official similarity score produced by this approach achieved 0.6590 correlation with expert judgment averaged across all tracks. A misfiling during construction of the ensemble submission for tracks 5 and 6 reduced the official score from 0.6687.

The dev columns of Table 2 show the ability of each individual system in isolation on the dev data ("Factored") as well as the performance of the ensemble when the individual system was removed ("Ablated"). Note that the *Align* system should have been ablated from the final system to achieve a higher score. Presumably its capability was strictly dominated by the CRNNs that used many of the same features.

The test scores for individual CRNN models ranged from 0.605 to 0.636, highlighting the volatility inherent in the process. The CRNN-ensemble improved slightly over the best single model, with a score of 0.638.

6 Conclusion

Five models of semantic similarity constructed from 2004 to 2016 were combined for paraphrase detection in image captions. The TakeLab bag-of-features SVM developed and open-sourced in 2012, when trained on our selection of in-genre data and evaluated on a machine translated version of the test set, performed well enough in isolation to place fourth out of seventeen in the Primary Track of the Semantic Textual Similarity competition organized within SemEval-2017 Task 1, which had submissions from 31 teams in total.

Inclusion of explicit word alignments, a neural attention model, and recurrent networks accounting for sequences of syntactic dependencies yielded an improvement in Pearson correlation from 0.650 to 0.672, a modest improvement which increased the corrected system's ranking to third. This surprising result is perhaps an indication that image captions have few of the complex linguistic dependencies that typically make estimating semantic similarity a difficult task. Future work could focus on testing whether this result holds when performing crosslingual STS without explicit machine translation.

Acknowledgments

This work was funded under the MITRE Innovation Program. Approved for Public Release; Distribution Unlimited: 17-0970.

References

Eneko Agirre, Daniel Cer, Mona Diab, Iigo Lopez-Gazpio, and Lucia Specia. 2017. SemEval-2017 task 1: Semantic textual similarity multilingual and crosslingual focused evaluation. In *Proceedings of the 11th International Workshop on Semantic Evaluation (SemEval 2017)*.

Y. Al-Onaizan, J. Curin, M. Jahr, K. Knight, J. Lafferty, I. D. Melamed, F-J. Och, D. Purdy, N. A. Smith, and D. Yarowsky. 1999. Statistical machine translation: Final report. Technical report, JHU Center for Language and Speech Processing.

Samuel Bayer, John Burger, Lisa Ferro, John Henderson, and Alexander Yeh. 2005. MITRE's submissions to the EU Pascal RTE challenge. In *Proceedings of the Pattern Analysis, Statistical Modelling, and Computational Learning (PASCAL) Challenges Workshop on Recognising Textual Entailment*.

Michel Berkelaar, Kjell Eikland, and Peter Notebaert. 2004. lp_solve 5.5, open source (mixed-integer) linear programming system. Software. http://lpsolve.sourceforge.net/5.5/.

Samuel R. Bowman, Gabor Angeli, Christopher Potts, and Christopher D. Manning. 2015. A large annotated corpus for learning natural language inference. In *Proceedings of the 2015 Conference on Empirical Methods in Natural Language Processing (EMNLP)*. Association for Computational Linguistics. http://www.anthology.aclweb.org/D/D15/D15-1075.pdf.

Danqi Chen and Christopher D Manning. 2014. A fast and accurate dependency parser using neural networks. In *Proceedings of EMNLP*. http://www.aclweb.org/anthology/D14-1082.

Qian Chen, Xiaodan Zhu, Zhenhua Ling, Si Wei, and Hui Jiang. 2016. Enhancing and combining sequential and tree LSTM for natural language inference. *arXiv preprint arXiv:1609.06038* .

George Foster, Simona Gandrabur, Cyril Goutte, Erin Fitzgerald, Alberto Sanchis, Nicola Ueffing, John Blatz, and Alex Kulesza. 2003. Confidence estimation for machine translation. Technical report, JHU Center for Language and Speech Processing.

Dan Gusfield. 1997. *Algorithms on Strings, Trees, and Sequences: Computer Science and Computational Biology*. Cambridge University Press.

Hideo Itoh. 2016. RICOH at SemEval-2016 task 1: IR-based semantic textual similarity estimation. *Proceedings of SemEval* https://www.aclweb.org/anthology/S/S16/S16-1106.pdf.

Diederik Kingma and Jimmy Ba. 2014. Adam: A method for stochastic optimization. *arXiv preprint arXiv:1412.6980* .

G. Leusch, N. Ueffing, and H. Ney. 2003. A novel string-to-string distance measure with applications to machine translation evaluation. In *Proc. of the Ninth MT Summit*.

V. I. Levenshtein. 1966. Binary codes capable of correcting deletions, insertions and reversals. *Soviet Physics Doklady* 10(8):707–710.

Chin-Yew Lin and Franz Josef Och. 2004. ORANGE: a method for evaluating automatic evaluation metrics for machine translation. In *Proceedings of the 20th International Conference on Computational Linguistics (COLING 2004)*. Geneva, Switzerland. http://www.aclweb.org/anthology/C04-1072.

Tomas Mikolov, Ilya Sutskever, Kai Chen, Greg S Corrado, and Jeff Dean. 2013. Distributed representations of words and phrases and their compositionality. In *Advances in Neural Information Processing Systems*.

Kishore Papineni, Salim Roukos, Todd Ward, and Wei-Jing Zhu. 2002. Bleu: A method for automatic evaluation of machine translation. In *Proceedings of the 40th Annual Meeting on Association for Computational Linguistics*. ACL '02.

Ankur P Parikh, Oscar Täckström, Dipanjan Das, and Jakob Uszkoreit. 2016. A decomposable attention model for natural language inference. *arXiv preprint arXiv:1606.01933* .

Frane Šarić, Goran Glavaš, Mladen Karan, Jan Šnajder, and Bojana Dalbelo Bašić. 2012. Takelab: Systems for measuring semantic text similarity. In *Proceedings of the Sixth International Workshop on Semantic Evaluation (SemEval 2012)*. http://www.aclweb.org/anthology/S12-1060.

John Wieting, Mohit Bansal, Kevin Gimpel, and Karen Livescu. 2016. Towards universal paraphrastic sentence embeddings. In *Proceedings of ICLR*.

Wojciech Zaremba, Ilya Sutskever, and Oriol Vinyals. 2014. Recurrent neural network regularization. *arXiv preprint arXiv:1409.2329* .

Guido Zarrella, John Henderson, Elizabeth M Merkhofer, and Laura Strickhart. 2015. MITRE: Seven systems for semantic similarity in tweets. *Proceedings of SemEval* http://www.aclweb.org/anthology/S15-2002.

A   Supplemental Material

These *min alignment* examples all come from Track 5.

Example 1: Similarity 5.0.

	the	boy	is	taking	a	test	at	school
a	1.69	1.32	1.56	1.36	[2.00]	1.26	1.47	1.31
boy	1.30	[2.00]	1.22	1.30	1.32	1.21	1.23	1.41
is	1.58	1.22	[2.00]	1.28	1.56	1.24	1.48	1.30
at	1.56	1.23	1.48	1.35	1.47	1.25	[2.00]	1.34
school	1.28	1.41	1.30	1.21	1.31	1.24	1.34	[2.00]
taking	1.39	1.30	1.28	[2.00]	1.36	1.34	1.35	1.21
a	[1.69]	1.32	1.56	1.36	2.00	1.26	1.47	1.31
test	1.23	1.21	1.24	1.34	1.26	[2.00]	1.25	1.24

Example 2: Similarity 2.6.

	two	men	standing	in	the	surf	on	a	beach
a	1.41	1.29	1.36	1.64	1.69	1.20	1.52	[2.00]	1.28
pair	[1.54]	1.33	1.38	1.35	1.40	1.21	1.34	1.37	1.28
of	1.42	1.34	1.35	[1.66]	1.79	1.18	1.53	1.60	1.30
men	1.29	[2.00]	1.40	1.35	1.36	1.25	1.27	1.29	1.33
walk_along	1.26	1.25	1.43	1.25	1.30	[1.44]	1.39	1.29	1.60
the	1.47	1.36	1.42	1.73	[2.00]	1.25	1.57	1.69	1.30
beach	1.31	1.33	1.36	1.30	1.30	1.66	1.33	1.28	[2.00]

Example 3: Similarity 0.0.

	men	are	trying	to	remove	oil	from	a_body	of	water
adding	1.12	1.21	1.29	1.21	[1.40]	1.07	1.18	1.15	1.16	1.18
aspirin	1.16	[1.15]	1.17	1.17	1.23	1.32	1.15	1.11	1.17	1.27
to	1.33	1.44	1.31	[2.00]	1.34	1.25	1.62	1.06	1.59	1.35
the	1.36	1.49	1.26	1.64	1.23	1.31	[1.58]	1.10	1.79	1.37
water	1.21	1.32	1.10	1.35	1.21	1.50	1.34	1.10	1.36	[2.00]
could	1.31	1.34	[1.51]	1.48	1.36	1.20	1.30	1.13	1.31	1.18
kill	[1.30]	1.26	1.41	1.35	1.44	1.18	1.27	1.19	1.32	1.19
the	1.36	1.49	1.26	1.64	1.23	1.31	1.58	1.10	[1.79]	1.37
plant	1.19	1.30	1.18	1.33	1.26	[1.47]	1.29	1.07	1.32	1.41

ECNU at SemEval-2017 Task 1: Leverage Kernel-based Traditional NLP features and Neural Networks to Build a Universal Model for Multilingual and Cross-lingual Semantic Textual Similarity

Junfeng Tian[1], Zhiheng Zhou[1], Man Lan[1,2*], Yuanbin Wu[1,2]
[1]Department of Computer Science and Technology,
East China Normal University, Shanghai, P.R.China
[2]Shanghai Key Laboratory of Multidimensional Information Processing
{jftian, zhzhou}@stu.ecnu.edu.cn
{mlan, ybwu}@cs.ecnu.edu.cn

Abstract

To model semantic similarity for multilingual and cross-lingual sentence pairs, we first translate foreign languages into English, and then build an efficient monolingual English system with multiple NLP features. Our system is further supported by deep learning models and our best run achieves the mean Pearson correlation 73.16% in primary track.

1 Introduction

Sentence semantic similarity is the building block of natural language understanding. Previous Semantic Textual Similarity (STS) tasks in SemEval focused on judging sentence pairs in English and achieved great success. In SemEval-2017 STS shared task concentrates on the evaluation of sentence semantic similarity in multilingual and cross-lingual (Agirre et al., 2017). There are two challenges in modeling multilingual and cross-lingual sentence similarity. On the one hand, this task requires human linguistic expertise to design specific features due to the different characteristics of languages. On the other hand, lack of enough training data for a particular language would lead to a poor performance.

The SemEval-2017 STS shared task assesses the ability of participant systems to estimate the degree of semantic similarity between monolingual and cross-lingual sentences in Arabic, English and Spanish, which is organized into a set of six secondary sub-tracks (Track 1 to Track 6) and a single combined primary track (Primary Track) achieved by submitting results for all of the secondary sub-tracks. Specifically, track 1, 3 and 5 are to determine STS scores for monolingual sentence pairs in Arabic, Spain and English, respectively. Track 2, 4, and 6 involve estimat-

ing STS scores for cross-lingual sentence pairs from the combination of two particular languages, i.e., Arabic-English, Spanish-English and surprise language (here is Turkish)-English cross-lingual pairs. Given two sentences, a continuous valued similarity score on a scale from 0 to 5 is returned, with 0 indicating that the semantics of the sentences are completely independent and 5 signifying semantic equivalence. The system is assessed by computing the Pearson correlation between system returned semantic similarity scores and human judgements.

To address this task, we first translate all sentences into English through the state-of-the-art machine translation (MT) system, i.e., Google Translator[1]. Then we adopt a combination method to build a universal model to estimate semantic similarity, which consists of traditional natural language processing (NLP) methods and deep learning methods. For traditional NLP methods, we design multiple effective NLP features to depict the semantic matching degree and then supervised machine learning-based regressors are trained to make prediction. For neural networks methods, we first obtain distributed representations for each sentence in sentence pairs and then feed these representations into end-to-end neural networks to output similarity scores. Finally, the scores returned by the regressors with traditional NLP methods and by the neural network models are equally averaged to get a final score to estimate semantic similarity.

2 System Description

Figure 1 shows the overall architecture of our system, which consists of the following three modules:

---

[1]https://cloud.google.com/translate/

Proceedings of the 11th International Workshop on Semantic Evaluations (SemEval-2017), pages 191–197,
Vancouver, Canada, August 3 - 4, 2017. ©2017 Association for Computational Linguistics

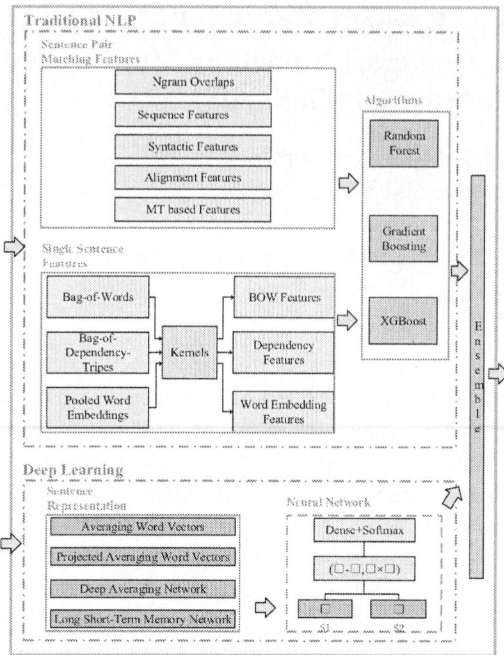

Figure 1: The system architecture

Traditional NLP Module is to extracts two kinds of NLP features. The sentence pair matching features are to directly calculate the similarity of two sentences from several aspects and the single sentence features are to first represent each sentence in NLP method and then to adopt kernel-based method to calculate the similarity of two sentences. All these NLP-based similarity scores act as features to build regressors to make prediction.

Deep Learning Module is to encode input sentence pairs into distributed vector representations and then to train end-to-end neural networks to obtain similarity scores.

Ensemble Module is to equally average the above two modules to get a final score.

Next, we will describe the system in detail.

2.1 Traditional NLP Module

In this section, we give the details of feature engineering and learning algorithms.

2.1.1 Sentence Pair Matching Features

Five types of sentence pair matching features are designed to directly calculate the similarity of two sentences based on the overlaps of character/word/sequence, syntactic structure, alignment and even MT metrics.

***N*-gram Overlaps:** Let S_i be the sets of consecutive n-grams, and the n-gram overlap (denoted as ngo) is defined as (Šarić et al., 2012):

$$\text{ngo}(S_1, S_2) = 2 \cdot \left(\frac{|S_1|}{|S_1 \cap S_2|} + \frac{|S_2|}{|S_1 \cap S_2|} \right)^{-1}$$

We obtain n-grams at three different levels (i.e., the original and lemmatized word, the character level), where $n = \{1, 2, 3\}$ are used for word level and $n = \{2, 3, 4, 5\}$ are used for character level. Finally, we collect 10 features.

Sequence Features: Sequence features are designed to capture more enhanced sequence information besides the n-gram overlaps. We compute the *longest common prefix / suffix / substring / sequence* and *levenshtein distance* for each sentence pair. Note that the stopwords are removed and each word is lemmatized so as to estimate sequence similarity more accurately. As a result, we get 5 features.

Syntactic Parse Features: In order to model tree structured similarity between two sentences rather than sequence-based similarity, inspired by Moschitti (2006), we adopt tree kernels to calculate the similarity between two syntactic parse trees. In particular, we calculate the number of common substructures in three different kernel spaces, i.e., *subtree* (ST), *subset tree* (SST), *partial tree* (PT). Thus we get 3 features.

Alignment Features: Sultan et al. (2015) used word aligner to align matching words across a pair of sentences, and then computes the proportion of aligned words as follows:

$$sim(S_1, S_2) = \frac{n_a(S_1) + n_a(S_2)}{n(S_1) + n(S_2)}$$

where $n_a(S)$ and $n(S)$ is the number of aligned and non-repeated words in sentence S.

To assign appropriate weights to different words, we adopt two weighting methods: i) weighted by five POS tags (i.e., noun, verb, adjective, adverb and others; we first group words in two sentences into 5 POS categories, then for each POS category we compute the proportion of aligned words, and we get 5 features as a result. ii) weighted by IDF values (calculated in each dataset separately). Totally, we collect 7 alignment features.

MT based Features: Following previous work in (Zhao et al., 2014) and (Zhao et al., 2015), we use MT evaluation metrics to measure the semantic equivalence of the given sentence pairs. Nine

MT metrics (i.e., *BLEU, GTM-3, NIST, -WER, -PER, Ol, -TERbase, METEOR-ex, ROUGE-L*) are used to assess the similarity. These 9 MT based features are calculated using the Asiya Open Toolkit[2].

Finally, we collect a total of 34 sentence pair matching features.

2.1.2 Single Sentence Features

Unlike above sentence pair matching features to directly estimate matching score between two sentences, the single sentence features are to represent each sentence in the same vector space to calculate the sentence similarity. We design the following three types of features.

BOW Features: Each sentence is represented as a Bag-of-Words (BOW) and each word (i.e., dimension) is weighted by its IDF value.

Dependency Features: For each sentence, its dependency tree is interpreted as a set of triples, i.e., (dependency-label, governor, subordinate). Similar to BOW, we treat triples as words and represent each sentence as Bag-of-Triples.

Word Embedding Features: Each sentence is represented by concatenating *min/max/average* pooling of vector representations of words. Note that for each word, its vector is weighted by its IDF value. Table 1 lists four the state-of-the-art pretrained word embeddings used in this work.

Embedding	Dimension	Source
word2vec Mikolov et al. (2013)	300d	GoogleNews-vectors-negative300.bin
GloVe Pennington et al. (2014)	100d	glove.6B.100d.txt
	300d	glove.6B.300d.txt
paragram Wieting et al. (2015)	300d	paragram_300_sl999.txt

Table 1: Four pretrained word embeddings

However, in comparison with the number of sentence pair matching features (33 features), the dimensionality of single sentence features is huge (approximately more than $71K$ features) and thus it would suppress the discriminating power of sentence pair matching features. Therefore, In order to reduce the high dimensionality of single sentence features, for each single sentence feature, we use 11 kernel functions to calculate sentence pair similarities. Table 2 lists the 11 kernel functions we used in this work. In total we collect 33 single sentence features, which is of the same order of magnitude as sentence pair matching features.

Type	Measures
linear kernel	Cosine distance, Manhanttan distance, Euclidean distance, Chebyshev distance
stat kernel	Pearson coefficient, Spearman coefficient, Kendall tau coefficient
non-linear kernel	polynomial, rbf, laplacian, sigmoid

Table 2: List of 11 kernel functions

Finally, these 67 NLP features are standardized into $[0, 1]$ using max-min normalization before building regressor models.

2.1.3 Regression Algorithms

Five learning algorithms for regression are explored, i.e., Random Forests (RF), Gradient Boosting (GB) Support Vector Machines (SVM), Stochastic Gradient Descent (SGD) and XGBoost (XGB). Specially, the first four algorithms are implemented in scikit-learn toolkit[3], and XGB is implemented in xgboost[4]. In preliminary experiments, SVM and SGD underperformed the other three algorithms and thus we adopt RF, GB and XGB in following experiments.

2.2 Deep Learning Module

Unlike above method adopting manually designed NLP features, deep learning based models are to calculate semantic similarity score with the pretrained word vectors as inputs. Four pretrained word embeddings listed in Table 1 are explored and the paragram embeddings achieved better results in preliminary experiments. We analyze and find the possible reason may be that the paragram embeddings are trained on Paraphrase Database[5], which is an extensive semantic resource that consists of many phrase pairs. Therefore, we use paragram embeddings to initialize word vectors.

Based on pretrained word vectors, we adopt the following four methods to obtain single sentence vector as (Wieting et al., 2015):

(1) by simply averaging the word vectors in single sentence;

(2) after (1), the resulting averaged vector is multiplied by a projection matrix;

(3) by using deep averaging network (DAN, Iyyer et al. (2015)) consisting of multiple layers as well as nonlinear activation functions;

---

[2]http://asiya.cs.upc.edu/demo/asiya_online.php

[3]http://scikit-learn.org/stable/
[4]https://github.com/dmlc/xgboost
[5]http://www.cis.upenn.edu/~ccb/ppdb/

(4) by using long short-term memory network (LSTM, Hochreiter and Schmidhuber (1997)) to capture long-distance dependencies information.

In order to obtain the vector of sentence pair, given two single sentence vectors, we first use a element-wise subtraction and a multiplication and then concatenate the two values as the final vector of sentence pair representation. At last, we use a fully-connected neural network and output the probability of similarity based on a softmax function. Thus we obtain 4 deep learning based scores.

To learn model parameters, we minimize the KL-divergence between the outputs and gold labels, as in Tai et al. (2015). We adopt Adam (Kingma and Ba, 2014) as optimization method and set learning rate of 0.01.

2.3 Ensemble Module

The NLP-based scores and the deep learning based scores are averaged in the ensemble module to obtain the final score.

3 Experimental Settings

Datasets: SemEval-2017 provided 7 tracks in monolingual and cross-lingual language pairs. We first translate all sentences into English via Google Translator and then we build a universal model on only English pairs. The training set we used is all the monolingual English dataset from SemEval STS task (2012-2015) consisting of $13,592$ sentence pairs.

For each track, we grant the training datasets provided by SemEval-2017 as development set. Table 3 lists the statistics of the development and the test data for each track in SemEval-2017.

Track	Language Pair	Development		Test
		Pairs	Dataset	Pairs
Track 1	Arabic-Arabic (AR-AR)	1088	MSRpar, MSRvid, SMTeuroparl (2017)	250
Track 2	Arabic-English (AR-EN)	2176	MSRpar, MSRvid, SMTeuroparl (2017)	250
Track 3	Spanish-Spanish (SP-SP)	1555	News, Wiki (2014, 2015)	250
Track 4a	Spanish-English (SP-EN)	595	News, Multi-source (2016)	250
Track 4b	Spanish-English WMT news data (SP-EN-WMT)	1000	WMT (2017)	250
Track 5	English-English (EN-EN)	1186	Plagiarsism, Postediting, Ans.-Ans., Quest.-Quest., HDL (2016)	250
Track 6	English-Turkish (EN-TR)	-	-	500

Table 3: The statistics of development and test set.

Almost all test data is from *SNLI*, except for Track 4b from *WMT*. This can explain why on *Track 4b SP-EN-WMT*, the performance is very poor. So we perform $10 - fold$ cross validation (CV) on *Track 4b SP-EN-WMT*.

Preprocessing: All sentences are translated into English via Google Translator. The Stanford CoreNLP (Manning et al., 2014) is used for tokenization, lemmatization, POS tagging and dependency parsing.

Evaluation: For Track 1 to Track 6, Pearson correlation coefficient is used to evaluate each individual test set. For Primary Track, since it is achieved by submitting results of all the secondary sub-tracks, a macro-averaged weighted sum of all correlations on sub-tracks is used for evaluation.

4 Results on Training Data

A series of comparison experiments on *English STS 2016* training set have been performed to explore different features and algorithms.

4.1 Comparison of NLP Features

Table 4 lists the results of different NLP features with GB learning algorithm. We find that: (1) the simple *BOW Features* with kernel functions are effective for sentence semantic similarity. (2) The combination of all these NLP features achieved the best results, which indicates that all features make contributions. Therefore we do not perform feature selection and use all these NLP features in following experiments.

4.2 Comparison of Learning Algorithms

Table 5 lists the results of different algorithms using all NLP features as well as deep learning scores. We find:

(1) Regarding machine learning algorithms, RF and GB achieve better results than XGB. GB performs the best on 3 and RF performs the best on 2 of 5 datasets.

(2) Regarding deep learning models, DL-word and DL-proj outperform the other 2 non-linear models on all the 5 datasets. This result is consistent with the findings in (Wieting et al., 2015):"In out-of-domain scenarios, simple architectures such as word averaging vastly outperform LSTMs."

(3) All ensemble methods significantly improved the performance. The ensemble of 3 machine learning algorithms (RF+GB+XGB) outperforms any single learning algorithm. Similarly, the ensemble of the 4 deep learning models (DL-all) promotes the performance to 75.28%, which is sig-

English STS 2016						
NLP Features	**Postediting**	**Ques.-Ques.**	**HDL**	**Plagiarism**	**Ans.-Ans.**	**Weighted mean**
BOW features	0.8388	0.6577	0.7338	0.7817	0.6302	0.7322
Alignment Features	0.8125	0.6243	0.7642	0.7883	**0.6432**	0.7312
Ngram Overlaps	0.8424	0.5864	0.7581	0.8070	0.5756	0.7203
Sequence Features	**0.8428**	0.6115	0.7337	0.7983	0.4838	0.7000
Word Embedding Features	0.8128	0.6378	0.7625	0.7955	0.4598	0.6992
MT based Features	0.8412	0.5558	0.7259	0.7617	0.5084	0.6851
Dependency Features	0.7264	0.5381	0.4634	0.5820	0.3431	0.5328
Syntactic Parse Features	0.5773	0.0846	0.4940	0.3976	0.0775	0.3376
All Features	0.8357	**0.6967**	**0.7964**	**0.8293**	0.6306	**0.7618**
Rychalska et al. (2016)	0.8352	0.6871	**0.8275**	**0.8414**	**0.6924**	**0.7781**
Brychcín and Svoboda (2016)	0.8209	0.7020	0.8189	0.8236	0.6215	0.7573
Afzal et al. (2016)	**0.8484**	**0.7471**	0.7726	0.8050	0.6143	0.7561

Table 4: Feature comparison on English STS 2016, the last three are top three systems in STS 2016

	English STS 2016						
	Algorithm	**Postediting**	**Ques.-Ques.**	**HDL**	**Plagiarism**	**Ans.-Ans.**	**Weighted mean**
Single Model	RF	0.8394	0.6858	0.7966	0.8259	0.5882	0.7518
	GB	0.8357	0.6967	0.7964	0.8293	0.6306	0.7618
	XGB	0.7917	0.6237	0.7879	0.8175	0.6190	0.7333
	DL-word	0.8097	0.6635	0.7839	0.8003	0.5614	0.7283
	DL-proj	0.7983	0.6584	0.7910	0.7892	0.5573	0.7234
	DL-dan	0.7695	0.4200	0.7411	0.6876	0.4756	0.6274
	DL-lstm	0.7864	0.5895	0.7584	0.7783	0.5182	0.6921
Ensemble	RF+GB+XGB	0.8298	0.6969	0.8086	0.8313	0.6234	0.7622
	DL-all	0.8308	0.6817	0.8160	0.8261	0.5854	0.7528
	EN-seven	**0.8513**	**0.7077**	**0.8288**	**0.8515**	**0.6647**	**0.7851**

Table 5: Algorithms comparison on English STS 2016 datasets

nificantly better than single model and is comparable to the result using expert knowledge. Furthermore, the ensemble of 3 machine learning algorithms and 4 deep learning models by averaging these 7 scores (EN-seven), achieves the best results on all of the development set in *English STS 2016*. It suggests that the traditional NLP methods and the deep learning models are complementary to each other and their combination achieves the best performance.

4.3 Results on Cross-lingual Data

To address cross-lingual, we first translate cross-lingual pairs into monolingual pairs and then adopt the universal model to estimate semantic similarity. Thus, language translation is critical to the performance. The first straightforward way for translation (Strategy 1) is to translate foreign language into English. We observe that it is more likely to produce synonyms when using Strategy 1. For example: one English-Spanish pair

```
The respite was short.
La tregua fue breve.
```

is translated into English-English pair,

```
The respite was short.
```

```
The respite was brief.
```

where *short* and *brief* are synonyms produced by MT rather than their actual literal meaning expressed in original languages. Reminding that one MT system may be in favour of certain words and it also can translate English into foreign language. Thus we propose Strategy 2 for translation, i.e., we first translate the English sentence into foreign target language and then roll back to English via MT again. Under Strategy 2, the above example English-Spanish pair is translated into the same English sentence:

```
The respite was brief.
```

Table 6 compares the results of the two strategies on cross-lingual data. It is clear that Strategy 2 achieves better performance, which indicates that the semantic difference between synonyms in cross-lingual pairs resulting from MT are different from that in monolingual pairs.

4.4 Results on Spanish-English WMT

On Spanish-English WMT dataset, the system performance dropped dramatically. The possible reason may lie in that they are from different domains. Therefore, we use 10-fold cross validation on

Cross-lingual STS 2016			
Algorithm		news	multisource	Weighted mean
Stategy 1	RF[1]	0.9101	0.8259	0.8686
	GB[1]	0.8911	0.8220	0.8570
	XGB[1]	0.8795	0.7984	0.8394
Stategy 2	RF[2]	0.9009	0.8405	0.8711
	GB[2]	0.9122	0.8441	0.8786
	XGB[2]	0.8854	0.8265	0.8563
	RF+GB+XGB[2]	**0.9138**	**0.8474**	**0.8810**
	DL-all[2]	0.8016	0.7442	0.7732
	EN-seven[2]	0.8832	0.8291	0.8565
Brychcín and Svoboda (2016)		0.9062	0.8190	0.8631

Table 6: Pearson correlations on Cross-lingual STS 2016, the last row is the top system in 2016.

this dataset for evaluation. Table 7 list the results on Spanish-English WMT, where the last column (wmt(CV)) of show that using the in-domain dataset achieves better performance.

Take a closer look at this dataset, we find that several original Spanish sentences are meaningless. For example, the English-Spanish pair

```
His rheumy eyes began to cloud.
A sus ojos rheumy comenzóa nube.
```

has a score of 1 as the second is not a proper Spanish sentence. Since there are many meaningless Spanish sentences in this dataset sourced from MT evaluation, we speculate that these meaningless sentences are made to be used as negative training samples for MT model. Thus, only on this dataset, we grant Spanish as target language and translate English sentences into Spanish sentences. After that, we use 9 MT evaluation metrics (mentioned in Section 2.1) to generate **MT based Features**. Then these 9 MT metrics are averaged as the similarity score ($MT(es)^3$).

Spanish-English WMT		
Algorithm	wmt	wmt(CV)
RF[2]	0.1761	0.2635
GB[2]	0.1661	0.2053
XGB[2]	0.1627	0.2620
RF+GB+XGB[2]	0.1739	0.2677
DL-all[2]	0.0780	-
EN-seven[2]	0.1393	-
$MT(es)^3$	0.2858	0.2858
RF+GB+XGB[2]+$MT(es)^3$	**0.2889**	**0.3789**
EN-seven[2]+$MT(es)^3$	0.2847	-

Table 7: Pearson correlations on Spanish-English WMT. $MT(es)^3$ is calculated using their translated Spanish-Spanish form. We did not perform cross validation in deep learning models and did not ensemble them due to time constraint.

From Table 7, we see that the $MT(es)^3$ score

alone achieves 0.2858 on *wmt* in terms of Pearson correlation, which even surpasses the best performance (0.2677) of ensemble model. Based on this, we also combine the ensemble model with $MT(es)^3$ and their averaged score achieves 0.3789 in terms of Pearson correlation.

4.5 System Configuration

Based on the above results, we configure three following systems:

Run 1: all features using RF algorithms. (RF)

Run 2: all features using GB algorithms. (GB)

Run 3: ensemble of three algorithms and four deep learning scores. (EN-seven)

Particularly, we train *Track 4b SP-EN-WMT* using the *wmt* dataset provided in SemEval-2017 and Run 2 and Run 3 on this track are combined with $MT(es)^3$ features.

5 Results on Test Data

Table 8 lists the results of our submitted runs on test datasets. We find that: (1) GB achieves slightly better performance than RF, which is consistent to that in training data; (2) the ensemble model significantly improves the performance on all datasets and enhance the performance of *Primary Track* by about 3% in terms of Pearson coefficient; (3) on *Track 4b SP-EN-WMT*, combining with $MT(es)^3$ significantly improves the performance.

The last three rows list the results of two top systems and one baseline system provided by organizer. The baseline is to use the *cosine* similarity of one-hot vector representations of sentence pairs. On all language pairs, our ensemble system achieves the best performance. This indicates that both the traditional NLP methods and the deep learning methods make contribution to performance improvement.

6 Conclusion

To address mono-lingual and cross-lingual sentence semantic similarity evaluation, we build a universal model in combination of traditional NLP methods and deep learning methods together and the extensive experimental results show that this combination not only improves the performance but also increases the robustness for modeling similarity of multilingual sentences. Our future work will concentrate on learning reliable sentence pair representations in deep learning.

Run	Primary	Track 1 AR-AR	Track 2 AR-EN	Track 3 SP-SP	Track 4a SP-EN	Track 4b SP-EN-WMT	Track 5 EN-EN	Track 6 EN-TR
Run 1: RF	0.6940	0.7271	0.6975	0.8247	0.7649	0.2633	0.8387	0.7420
Run 2: GB	0.7044	0.7380	0.7126	0.8456	0.7495	0.3311*	0.8181	0.7362
Run 3: EN-seven	**0.7316**	**0.7440**	**0.7493**	**0.8559**	**0.8131**	**0.3363***	**0.8518**	**0.7706**
Rank 2: BIT	0.6789	0.7417	0.6965	0.8499	0.7828	0.1107	0.8400	0.7305
Rank 3: HCTI	0.6598	0.7130	0.6836	0.8263	0.7621	0.1483	0.8113	0.6741
Baseline	0.5370	0.6045	0.5155	0.7117	0.6220	0.0320	0.7278	0.5456

Table 8: The results of our three runs on STS 2017 test datasets.

Acknowledgments

This research is supported by grants from Science and Technology Commission of Shanghai Municipality (14DZ2260800 and 15ZR1410700), Shanghai Collaborative Innovation Center of Trustworthy Software for Internet of Things (ZF1213) and NSFC (61402175).

References

Naveed Afzal, Yanshan Wang, and Hongfang Liu. 2016. Mayonlp at semeval-2016 task 1: Semantic textual similarity based on lexical semantic net and deep learning semantic model. In *Proceedings of SemEval 2016*. San Diego, California.

Eneko Agirre, Daniel Cer, Mona Diab, Lopez-Gazpio Inigo, and Specia Lucia. 2017. Semeval-2017 task 1: Semantic textual similarity multilingual and crosslingual focused evaluation. In *Proceedings of SemEval 2017*.

Tomáš Brychcín and Lukáš Svoboda. 2016. Uwb at semeval-2016 task 1: Semantic textual similarity using lexical, syntactic, and semantic information. In *Proceedings of SemEval 2016*. San Diego, California, pages 588–594.

Sepp Hochreiter and Jürgen Schmidhuber. 1997. Long short-term memory. *Neural computation* 9(8):1735–1780.

Mohit Iyyer, Varun Manjunatha, Jordan Boyd-Graber, and Hal Daumé III. 2015. Deep unordered composition rivals syntactic methods for text classification. In *Proceedings of ACL 2015*.

Diederik P. Kingma and Jimmy Ba. 2014. Adam: A method for stochastic optimization. *CoRR* abs/1412.6980.

Christopher D. Manning, Mihai Surdeanu, John Bauer, Jenny Finkel, Steven J. Bethard, and David McClosky. 2014. The Stanford CoreNLP natural language processing toolkit. In *Proceedings of ACL 2014*. pages 55–60.

Tomas Mikolov, Ilya Sutskever, Kai Chen, Greg S Corrado, and Jeff Dean. 2013. Distributed representations of words and phrases and their compositionality. In *NIPS 2013*. pages 3111–3119.

Alessandro Moschitti. 2006. Efficient convolution kernels for dependency and constituent syntactic trees. In *ECML 2006*. Springer, pages 318–329.

Jeffrey Pennington, Richard Socher, and Christopher D. Manning. 2014. Glove: Global vectors for word representation. In *Proceedings of EMNLP 2014*. pages 1532–1543.

Barbara Rychalska, Katarzyna Pakulska, Krystyna Chodorowska, Wojciech Walczak, and Piotr Andruszkiewicz. 2016. Samsung poland nlp team at semeval-2016 task 1: Necessity for diversity; combining recursive autoencoders, wordnet and ensemble methods to measure semantic similarity. In *Proceedings of SemEval 2016*. San Diego, California, pages 602–608.

Md Arafat Sultan, Steven Bethard, and Tamara Sumner. 2015. Dls@cu: Sentence similarity from word alignment and semantic vector composition. In *Proceedings of SemEval 2015*. Denver, Colorado.

Kai Sheng Tai, Richard Socher, and Christopher D Manning. 2015. Improved semantic representations from tree-structured long short-term memory networks. *arXiv preprint arXiv:1503.00075* .

Frane Šarić, Goran Glavaš, Mladen Karan, Jan Šnajder, and Bojana Dalbelo Bašić. 2012. Takelab: Systems for measuring semantic text similarity. In *Proceedings of SemEval 2012*. Montréal, Canada, pages 441–448.

John Wieting, Mohit Bansal, Kevin Gimpel, and Karen Livescu. 2015. Towards universal paraphrastic sentence embeddings. *arXiv preprint arXiv:1511.08198* .

Jiang Zhao, Man Lan, and Jun Feng Tian. 2015. Ecnu: Using traditional similarity measurements and word embedding for semantic textual similarity estimation. In *Proceedings of SemEval 2015*. Denver, Colorado.

Jiang Zhao, Tiantian Zhu, and Man Lan. 2014. Ecnu: One stone two birds: Ensemble of heterogeneous measures for semantic relatedness and textual entailment. In *Proceedings of SemEval 2014*. Dublin, Ireland.

PurdueNLP at SemEval-2017 Task 1: Predicting Semantic Textual Similarity with Paraphrase and Event Embeddings

I-Ta Lee, Mahak Goindani, Chang Li, Di Jin, Kristen Marie Johnson
Xiao Zhang, Maria Leonor Pacheco, Dan Goldwasser
Department of Computer Science, Purdue University
West Lafayette, IN 47907
`{lee2226,mgoindan,li1873,jind,john1187,`
`zhang923,pachecog,dgoldwas}@purdue.edu`

Abstract

This paper describes our proposed solution for SemEval 2017 Task 1: Semantic Textual Similarity (Daniel Cer and Specia, 2017). The task aims at measuring the degree of equivalence between sentences given in English. Performance is evaluated by computing Pearson Correlation scores between the predicted scores and human judgements. Our proposed system consists of two subsystems and one regression model for predicting STS scores. The two subsystems are designed to learn Paraphrase and Event Embeddings that can take the consideration of paraphrasing characteristics and sentence structures into our system. The regression model associates these embeddings to make the final predictions. The experimental result shows that our system acquires 0.8 of Pearson Correlation Scores in this task.

1 Introduction

The SemEval Semantic Textual Similarity (STS) task (Daniel Cer and Specia, 2017) is to assess the degree of similarity between two given sentences and assign a score on a scale from 0 to 5. A score of 0 indicates that the two sentences are completely dissimilar, while a score of 5 indicates that the sentences have the same meaning. Predicting the similarity between pieces of texts finds utility in many NLP tasks such as question-answering, and plagiarism detection.

In this paper, we proposed a system to facilitate STS task. Our system includes training two types of embeddings–Paraphrase Embeddings (PE) and Event Embeddings (EE)–as features to assess STS. For the first type of embeddings, PE, we exploit two crucial properties for measuring

sentence similarity: paraphrasing characteristics and sentence structures. The paraphrasing characteristics help identifying if two sentences share the same meaning. Our system incorporates it using an unsupervised learning step over the Paraphrase Database (PPDB; Ganitkevitch et al. 2013), which is inspired by Wieting et al. 2015a. The sentence structure, on the other hand, can detect structural differences, which reflect different aspects of the similarity between the input sentences. Our system employs a Convolutional Neural Network (CNN) to strengthen the embedding by including the sentence structure into our representation. The second type of embeddings, EE, conveys the distributional semantics of events in a narrative setting, associating a vector with each event.

In the last part of our system, we build a regression model that associates the two distributed representations and predicts the similarity scores.

2 System Description

Our system builds two types of embedding models, Paraphrase Embeddings (PE) and Event Embeddings (EE), and trains a regression model for predicting the similarity score between two sentences, which is described in this Section 2.3.

2.1 Paraphrase Embeddings

The Paraphrase Database (PPDB) is a large scale database containing millions of automatically extracted paraphrases. Wieting et al. 2015a show that by training word embeddings on PPDB (Ganitkevitch et al., 2013), paraphrase information can be captured by the embeddings, which is very useful for the STS task. Their system works well when word overlaps reflect sentence similarities, which is the most common case in the STS dataset. We extend their work by introducing a Convolutional Neural Network (CNN) model, because it better accounts for sentence structure.

Proceedings of the 11th International Workshop on Semantic Evaluations (SemEval-2017), pages 198–202,
Vancouver, Canada, August 3 - 4, 2017. ©2017 Association for Computational Linguistics

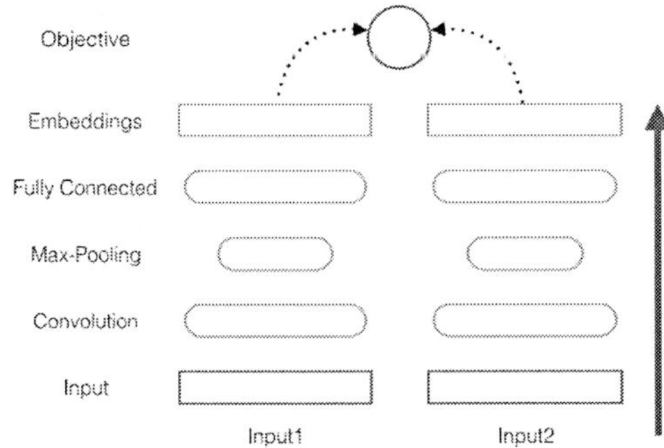

Figure 1: The convolutional neural network architecture consists of two networks that share the network parameters. The networks are constructed by a convolutional layer, a max-pooling layer, and two fully connected layers.

Figure 1 describes our network architecture. Each input example consists of a pair of sentences/phrases. The initial input representation for each sentence is created by averaging the word vectors of the words in the sentence. The initial word vectors can rely on pre-trained word embeddings, such as Word2Vec (Mikolov et al., 2013) or Glove (Pennington et al., 2014).

This input layer is followed by a convolutional layer, a max-pooling layer, and two fully connected layers. The projected outputs (the embeddings layer in Figure 1) comprise the PE that will later be used for regression. Note that the two networks in Figure 1 share the network parameters. During training, the errors back-propagate not only to the network, but also to the embeddings. To train PE, we adopt a 2-step framework inspired by Wieting et al. 2015a and initialize our word embedding look-up table with the best performing embeddings they released–*PARAGRAM-PHRASE XXL*. In the first step, we train the CNN on PPDB 2.0 (Pavlick et al., 2015) and aim at making PE a quality representation for paraphrase-related tasks. The objective function here is a margin-based ranking loss (Wieting et al., 2015a):

$$\min_{W_c, W_w} \Bigg(\sum_{<x_1, x_2> \in X} max(0, \delta - cos(g(x_1), g(x_2))$$
$$+ cos(g(x_1), g(t_1)))$$
$$+ max(0, \delta - cos(g(x_1), g(x_2)))$$
$$+ cos(g(x_2), g(t_2)) \Bigg)$$
$$+ \lambda_c ||W_c||^2 + \lambda_w ||W_{init} - W_w||^2,$$

where X is all the positive paraphrasing pairs; δ is the margin [1]; $g(\cdot)$ is the functional representation of CNN; λ_c and λ_w are two hyperparameters for L2-regularization; W_c is the parameters to be trained; W_w is the most recent word embeddings; W_{init} is the initial word embeddings; and t_1 and t_2 are negative examples. The negative examples are randomly and uniformly selected from other examples. That is, for x_1, we randomly select a phrase t_1 from the corpus, which is nearly unlikely to be a paraphrase to x_1. The same strategy is also applied to select t_2 for x_2.

In the second step, we fine-tune the PE by fitting it to SemEval STS data. This is a supervised regression task, with an objective function that considers both the distances and angles of the two projected embeddings. This regression objective is the same as the one that we will describe in Section 2.3. Although the objective function used here and in Section 2.3 are the same, they are used differently. The intention of using it in this step is to adjust the PE representations, while the regression model in Section 2.3 is used for combining different embeddings for regression. More details will be discussed in Section 2.3.

2.2 Event Embeddings

Word embeddings capture distributional semantics. It is a function that maps a word to a dense, low-dimension vector. With the same concept in mind, we can infer event semantics by exploring its contextual events to build EE. Similar ideas have be explored in several recent works (Granroth-Wilding and Clark, 2016; Pichotta and Mooney, 2016; Pacheco et al., 2016).

Our EE model is constructed as follows: first, we extract event tokens, similar to narrative scripts construction (Chambers and Jurafsky, 2008). We resolve co-referent entities and run a dependency parser on all documents [2]. For each entity in a co-reference chain, we represent an event token e by its predicate $p(e)$, a dependency relation to the entity $d(e)$, and animacy of the entity $a(e)$; resulting in a triplet $((p(e), d(e), a(e)))$. An event chain thus can be constructed by corresponding all the entities in a co-reference chain to event tokens.

We extend the definition of the event predicate $p(e)$ to include lemmatized verbs and predicative adjectives. These extensions are useful as they

---

[1] δ is tuned over $\{0.4, 1\}$ in our evaluation.
[2] we use Stanford CoreNLP library (Manning et al., 2014)

capture important information about the state of the entity. For example, "Jim was hungry. He ate a sub". The word "hungry" captures meaningful narrative information that should be included in the event chain of the entity "Jim", so the resulting chain here should be: *(hungry, subj, animate), (eat, subj, animate)*. Moreover, relying on verb predicates alone is sometimes insufficient, when the verbs are too ambiguous on their own, e.g., verbs like *go*, *get*, and *have*. For such weak verbs, we include their particles and clausal complement (xcomp) in the predicates, e.g., "have to sleep" will be represented as one predicate– *have_to_sleep*. Lastly, negations to the predicate matter a lot to event semantics, so we also include it as a part of predicates. For instance, "did not sleep" will be represented as *not_sleep*.

For dependencies $d(e)$, we only consider subjects, objects, and indirect objects in the dependency tree. Argument animacy information $a(e)$ is also included, because the entity's animacy often changes the event semantics. For instance, the difference in meaning of the phrases "killed a joke" and "killed a person" is hard to identify without including the object's animacy information. There are three possible animacy types that are represented in our triplet: *animate, inanimate,* or *unknown*.

The Skip-Gram model (Mikolov et al., 2013), which predicts contextual tokens given a current token, is then used for training EE. The model treats each event token as a word and each event chain as a sentence, and learns EE by optimizing the following objective:

$$p(C(e)|e) = \prod_{e' \in C(e)} P(e'|e)$$

$$= \prod_{e' \in C(e)} \frac{exp(v_{e'}, v_e)}{\sum_{e^* \in E} exp(v_{e^*}, v_e)},$$

where e is the current event, $C(e)$ is the contextual events of e, and v_e is the embedding representation of e.

To make the computation feasible, the negative sampling strategy is again used here. For each pair of event tokens in a sliding window, we sample k negative tokens. Other optimizing strategies for improve embedding quality used by Mikolov et al. 2013 are also applied here, such as subsampling for high-frequency tokens and filtering low-frequency tokens. The followings are the hyperparameters related to PE that are used in our

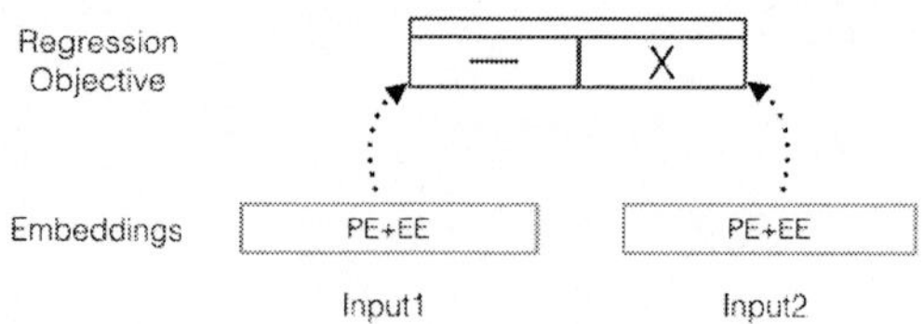

Figure 2: The regression model that considers the distance and angle between the two inputs.

system: the sub-sampling rate is empirically set to 0.001; the minimum count of tokens is set to 5; the sliding window size and k are set to 5; and the vector dimension is set to 300.

2.3 Regression

In this section, we discuss how to fuse the different embedding representations in the final regression model that predicts a similarity score between the two input sentences. The objective function is shown below:

$$h_* = v_{e1} \otimes v_{e2} \tag{1}$$
$$h_\triangle = |v_{e1} - v_{e2}| \tag{2}$$
$$h = \tanh(W_* \cdot h_* + W_\triangle \cdot h_\triangle) \tag{3}$$
$$p = \text{softmax}(W \cdot h), \tag{4}$$

where v_{e1} and v_{e2} are vector representations of input 1 and input 2 respectively; $W_* \in R^{d \times k}$, $W_\triangle \in R^{d \times k}$, and $W \in R^{6 \times k}$ are the parameters to be trained; d is the total dimension of PE and EE; k is a hyperparameter of hidden layer size (the 6 in the first dimension of W is from the softmax layer outputs which account for the probabilities of integer scores between 0-5). The final score is calculated by taking the mean of the 6 softmax outputs. This regression model is visualized in Figure 2. The PE and EE are concatenated to represent each input. They are fixed representations that will not be updated during the regression. The "X" and "-" shown in Figure 2 are element-wise products and element-wise differences between two input representations (Equation (1) and (2)). They represent the angles and distances between the input sentences. This regression objective has been shown to be very useful in text similarity tasks (Tai et al., 2015).

3 Evaluation

We train PE using two datasets, PPDB 2.0 (Pavlick et al., 2015) and SemEval STS data. These are

	Train	Dev.	Test
W2V	0.3060	0.2442	0.2641
EE	0.2491	0.2458	0.3545
paragram-small	0.6723	0.5446	0.6989
paragram-XXL	0.6639	0.6610	0.7322
PE	0.8138	0.6896	0.7979
PE+W2V	0.8214	0.6879	0.7961
PE+EE (official)	-	-	0.7928
PE+EE	0.8243	**0.6932**	**0.8015**
Winner STS2017	-	-	0.8547

Table 1: Pearson Correlation Scores for the models we tested, where the Train data is STS2012-2015, Dev. data is STS2016, Test data is STS2017. The best scores of our model are in bold fonts.

used in the first (Section 2.1) and second steps (Section 2.2) respectively. We used the New York Times (NYT) section of the Gigaword corpus (Parker et al., 2011) for training EE and our baselines. The SemEval STS data is also used in training the final regression model. The data splits are as follows: SemEval STS2012-2015 was used as the training set, STS2016 data was used as the development set, and STS2017 was used as the test set. After the development stage was finished, the training and development sets were both used to train a final model with the best hyperparameters.

To update the parameters, Mini-batch Stochastic Gradient Descent is used for optimizing the parameters and Adagrad (Duchi et al., 2011) is used to update the learning rate while training. The batch size is set to 100 and the number of epochs is set to 10. $L2$-regularization is included in all the objective functions and the λ is tuned over $\{1e-5, 1e-6, 1e-7, 1e-8\}$. Both PE and EE's dimensions are set to 300.

The first baseline we compare with is the Word2Vec Skip-Gram (W2V; Mikolov et al. 2013) model, one of the most popular universal word embeddings. It was trained over the same corpus as EE (NYT section of Gigaword). The second baseline (paragram-small) and third baseline (paragram-XXL) are the best performing word embeddings for STS tasks shown in Wieting et al. 2015b,a. In order to represent the input sentences with the word embeddings, we average the word embeddings based on the words in the input sentences. This approach has been shown to be effective in Wieting et al. 2015a,

Table 1 lists the Pearson Correlation Score of

SemEval 2017 STS tasks. We can see that the general embedding models, (W2V and EE), do not perform well as their general purpose representation does not fit the textual similarity task. On the other hand, paragram-small and paragram-XXL which were trained with the textual-similarity-related data (PPDB and STS data) perform reasonably well. The PE model, which takes paragram-XXL as the initial embeddings and tunes all the parameters on a CNN, gets higher score in both development and test sets. The performance further increases as we introduce EE to be parts of input representations (PE+EE), while the W2V does not provide such improvement (PE+W2V).

PE is specifically designed for identifying paraphrasing characteristics and sentence structures, which we believe are the keys to STS task, resulting in the strongest feature set in our system. We do not expect that using EE alone will give high performance, since considerable amounts of information are filtered out during event chain extraction. In addition, EE does not use any STS-related data during training. However, it is still helpful for capturing high-level event semantics, which can be a complement to our PE.

The official result of PE+EE is also included in Table 1. Our best results improve on it, by fine tuning the model's hyperparameters. In addition, the best performing system of SemEval STS2017 acquires the score of 0.8547, outperforming our model. However, it is not clear that what external resources or hand-crafted features were used in their work. Our system, nevertheless, can accommodate additional resources and features. We believe that our results can be further improved by including such information and we will look into it in the future.

4 Conclusion

In this paper, we describe our system for SemEval 2017 STS task which consists three key components relevant to this task: paraphrasing characteristics, sentence structures, and event-level semantics. To incorporate the first two ideas into the system, PE–a CNN model trained with a paraphrase database–is used. It measures sentence similarity in terms of paraphrasing and structure similarities. We capture event semantics using EE, and include it in our system. It complements the PE and further boosts performance. Our full system was able to achieve a 0.8 of Pearson Correlation Score.

References

Nathanael Chambers and Daniel Jurafsky. 2008. Unsupervised learning of narrative event chains. In *ACL*. Citeseer, volume 94305, pages 789–797.

Mona Diab Eneko Agirre Inigo Lopez-Gazpio Daniel Cer and Lucia Specia. 2017. Semeval-2017 task 1: Semantic textual similarity multilingual and crosslingual focused evaluation. *Proceedings of SemEval* .

John Duchi, Elad Hazan, and Yoram Singer. 2011. Adaptive subgradient methods for online learning and stochastic optimization. *Journal of Machine Learning Research* 12(Jul):2121–2159.

Juri Ganitkevitch, Benjamin Van Durme, and Chris Callison-Burch. 2013. PPDB: The paraphrase database. In *Proceedings of NAACL-HLT*. Association for Computational Linguistics, Atlanta, Georgia, pages 758–764. http://cs.jhu.edu/ ccb/publications/ppdb.pdf.

Mark Granroth-Wilding and Stephen Clark. 2016. What happens next? event prediction using a compositional neural network model. In *AAAI*. pages 2727–2733.

Christopher D. Manning, Mihai Surdeanu, John Bauer, Jenny Finkel, Steven J. Bethard, and David McClosky. 2014. The Stanford CoreNLP natural language processing toolkit. In *Association for Computational Linguistics (ACL) System Demonstrations*. pages 55–60. http://www.aclweb.org/anthology/P/P14/P14-5010.

Tomas Mikolov, Kai Chen, Greg Corrado, and Jeffrey Dean. 2013. Efficient estimation of word representations in vector space. *arXiv preprint arXiv:1301.3781* .

Maria Leonor Pacheco, I-Ta Lee, Xiao Zhang, Abdullah Khan Zehady, Pranjal Daga, Di Jin, Ayush Parolia, and Dan Goldwasser. 2016. Adapting event embedding for implicit discourse relation recognition. *ACL 2016* page 136.

Robert Parker, David Graff, Junbo Kong, Ke Chen, and Kazuaki Maeda. 2011. English gigaword. *Linguistic Data Consortium* .

Ellie Pavlick, Pushpendre Rastogi, Juri Ganitkevitch, Benjamin Van Durme, and Chris Callison-Burch. 2015. Ppdb 2.0: Better paraphrase ranking, fine-grained entailment relations, word embeddings, and style classification .

Jeffrey Pennington, Richard Socher, and Christopher D Manning. 2014. Glove: Global vectors for word representation. In *EMNLP*. volume 14, pages 1532–1543.

Karl Pichotta and Raymond J Mooney. 2016. Learning statistical scripts with lstm recurrent neural networks. In *AAAI*. pages 2800–2806.

Kai Sheng Tai, Richard Socher, and Christopher D Manning. 2015. Improved semantic representations from tree-structured long short-term memory networks. *arXiv preprint arXiv:1503.00075* .

John Wieting, Mohit Bansal, Kevin Gimpel, and Karen Livescu. 2015a. Towards universal paraphrastic sentence embeddings. *arXiv preprint arXiv:1511.08198* .

John Wieting, Mohit Bansal, Kevin Gimpel, Karen Livescu, and Dan Roth. 2015b. From paraphrase database to compositional paraphrase model and back. *arXiv preprint arXiv:1506.03487* .

RTM at SemEval-2017 Task 1: Referential Translation Machines for Predicting Semantic Similarity

Ergun Biçici

orcid.org/0000-0002-2293-2031

bicici.github.com

Abstract

We use referential translation machines for predicting the semantic similarity of text in all STS tasks which contain Arabic, English, Spanish, and Turkish this year. RTMs pioneer a language independent approach to semantic similarity and remove the need to access any task or domain specific information or resource. RTMs become 6th out of 52 submissions in Spanish to English STS. We average prediction scores using weights based on the training performance to improve the overall performance.

1 Referential Translation Machines (RTMs)

Semantic textual similarity (STS) task (Cer et al., 2017) at SemEval-2017 (Bethard et al., 2017) is about quantifying the degree of similarity between two given sentences S_1 and S_2 in the same language or in different languages. RTMs use interpretants, data close to the task instances, to derive features measuring the closeness of the test sentences to the training data, the difficulty of translating them, and to identify translation acts between any two data sets for building prediction models. RTMs are applicable in different domains and tasks and in both monolingual and bilingual settings. Figure 1 depicts RTMs and explains the model building process.

RTMs use ParFDA (Biçici, 2016a) for instance selection and machine translation performance prediction system (MTPPS) (Biçici and Way, 2015) for generating features for the training and the test set mapping both to the same space where the total number of features in each task becomes 368. The new features we include are about punctuation: number of tokens about punc-

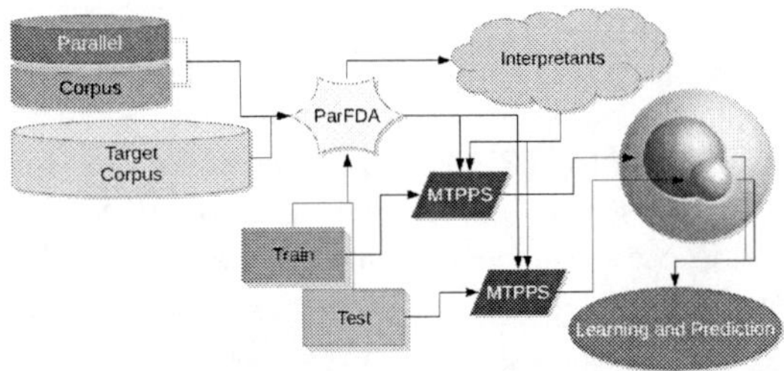

Figure 1: RTM depiction: ParFDA selects interpretants close to the training and test data using parallel corpus in bilingual settings and monolingual corpus in the target language or just the monolingual target corpus in monolingual settings; an MTPPS use interpretants and training data to generate training features and another use interpretants and test data to generate test features in the same feature space; learning and prediction takes place taking these features as input.

tuation (Kozlova et al., 2016) and the cosine between the punctuation vectors.

RTMs are providing a language independent text processing and machine learning model able to use predictions from different predictors. We use ridge regression (RR), k-nearest neighors (KNN), support vector regression (SVR), AdaBoost (Freund and Schapire, 1997), and extremely randomized trees (TREE) (Geurts et al., 2006) as learning models in combination with feature selection (FS) (Guyon et al., 2002) and partial least squares (PLS) (Wold et al., 1984). For most of the models, we use `scikit-learn`. [1] We optimize the models using a subset of the training data for the following parameters: λ for RR, k for KNN, γ, C, and ϵ for SVR, minimum number of samples for leaf nodes and for splitting an in-

---

[1] `http://scikit-learn.org/`. For RR, contains different solvers, support for sparse matrices, and checks for size and errors.

Proceedings of the 11th International Workshop on Semantic Evaluations (SemEval-2017), pages 203–207,
Vancouver, Canada, August 3 - 4, 2017. ©2017 Association for Computational Linguistics

	all	Tr.1	Tr.2	Tr.3	Tr.4a	Tr.4b	Tr.5	Tr.6
		ar-ar	ar-en	es-es	es-en	en-es	en-en	en-tr
test		250	250	250	250	250	250	500
ranks	34	'34'	34	'27'	26	6	61	'39'
out of	44	48	44	47	52	52	78	47
r	0.37	0.34	0.17	0.7	0.6	0.15	0.55	0.07

Table 1: RTM ranks and the number of instances in the STS test sets with abbreviations: Arabic (ar), English (en), Spanish (es), Turkish (tr). Only 250 instances are evaluated in en-tr. Results within single quotes used mismatching corpora and therefore we reran our experiments (Section 3).

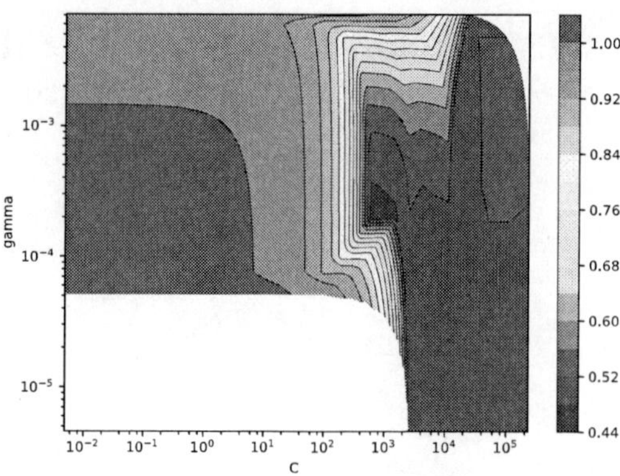

Figure 2: Sample SVR optimization plot (en-en).

ternal node for TREE, the number of features for FS, and the number of dimensions for PLS. For AdaBoost, we do not optimize but use exponential loss and 500 estimators like we use also with the TREE model. We use grid search for SVR. Figure 2 plots sample search contours.

Evaluation metrics we use are Pearson's correlation (r), mean absolute error (MAE), relative absolute error (RAE), MAER (mean absolute error relative), and MRAER (mean relative absolute error relative) (Biçici and Way, 2015). Official evaluation metric is r.

This year, we experiment with averaging scores from different models. The predictions, $\hat{y}$, are sorted according to their performance on the training set and the mean of the top k predictions (equally weighted averaging) or their weighted average according to their performance are used:

$$\hat{y}_{\mu_k} = \frac{1}{k} \sum_{i=1}^{k} \hat{y}_i \qquad (1)$$

$$\hat{y}_{w_k} = \frac{1}{\sum_{i=1}^{k} \frac{1}{w_i}} \sum_{i=1}^{k} \frac{1}{w_i} \hat{y}_i \qquad (2)$$

The weights are inverted since we are trying to decrease MAER and normalize by the sum. We use MAER for sorting and selecting predictions.

2 SemEval-17 STS Results

SemEval-2017 STS contains STS sentence pairs from the languages listed in Table 1 where the top r from among our officially submitted results are listed, which contain a mean averaged, a weight averaged, and a top prediction corresponding to weight 3, mean 3, and SVR model predictions. These results do not contain AdaBoost results and

they are optimized less. We build individual RTM models for each subtask with RTM team name. Interpretants are selected from the corpora distributed by the translation task of WMT17 (Bojar et al., 2017) and they consist of monolingual sentences used to build the LM and parallel sentence pair instances used by MTPPS to derive the features. For monolingual STS, we use the corresponding monolingual corpora. We built RTM models using:

- 275 thousand sentences for en-en, 200 thousand sentences for en-tr, and 250 thousand sentences for others for training data

- 7 million sentences for the language model

which are close to the fixed training set size setting in (Biçici and Way, 2015).

We identified numeric expressions using regular expressions as a pre-processing step, which replaces them with a label. Identification of numerics improve the performance on the test set (Biçici, 2016b). For en-es or es-en, we did not use any language identification tool and separated sentences based on left/right difference rather than using the mixed format that was made available to the participants even though identification of the language increase r on the test set from 0.5375 to 0.6066 while decreasing error (Biçici, 2016b). For en-tr, we were not provided any training data; therefore, we used the training data from other subtasks.

3 Experiments After the Challenge

Table 2 compares the top averaging result with the top result without averaging on the test set. The

Task	r	MAE	RAE	MAER	MRAER	model
ar-ar	0.5302	1.4072	1.122	1.3068	1.331	weight 7
ar-ar	0.5286	1.3909	1.109	1.2941	1.304	TREE
ar-en	0.2144	1.5793	1.276	1.4937	1.456	mean 2
ar-en	0.2235	1.565	1.264	1.4556	1.432	FS-SVR
es-es	0.7398	0.9689	0.708	0.7756	0.746	weight 4
es-es	0.7409	0.9673	0.7072	0.7739	0.7467	FS-TREE
es-en	0.5481	1.4072	1.137	1.3229	1.362	mean 3
es-en	0.5197	1.4176	1.146	1.3483	1.328	FS-TREE
en-es	0.1101	1.3122	1.305	0.3306	1.377	weight 2
en-es	0.0847	1.3263	1.319	0.3351	1.388	TREE
en-en	0.7103	1.0261	0.852	0.8678	1.042	weight 11
en-en	0.6528	1.0644	0.883	0.9126	1.052	FS+PLS-SVR
en-tr	-0.0204	1.6094	1.2849	1.4614	1.3533	weight 8
en-tr	-0.0527	1.7121	1.3669	1.4955	1.4569	FS+PLS SVR
all	0.4105	averaging				
all	0.4011	others				

Table 2: RTM top averaged result compared with the top non averaged result on the test set. Averaging improve the performance on the test set.

	all	Tr.1	Tr.2	Tr.3	Tr.4a	Tr.4b	Tr.5	Tr.6
		ar-ar	ar-en	es-es	es-en	en-es	en-en	en-tr
ranks	33	33	34	25	33	6	53	45
out of	44	48	44	47	52	52	78	47

Table 3: RTM ranks in the STS test sets with results from Table 2.

results warn us that ar-ar, ar-en, en-es, and es-en obtain MRAER larger than 1 suggesting more work towards these tasks. en-en has slightly more than 1 in MRAER and this is worse than the 0.719 MRAER obtained by RTMs in STS in 2016. For es-es, we obtain slightly lower results compared with 0.729 MRAER of RTMs in STS in 2016 where we used language identification. The test set domain is different this year; Stanford Natural Language Inference corpus (Bowman et al., 2015) is focusing on inference and entailment tasks and entailment assumes direction and in contrast the goal in STS is the bidirectional grading of equivalence (Agirre et al., 2015). Table 3 list the ranks we can obtain with RTMs these new results. Figure 3 plots the performance on the test set where instances are sorted according to the magnitude of the target scores.

Also in this section, we present results about transfer of learning. Transfer learning attempt to re-use and transfer knowledge from models developed in different domains or for different tasks such as using models developed for handwritten digit recognition for handwritten character recognition (Guyon et al., 2012). We cross use RTM SVR models developed for different tasks as a cross-task TL [2] and present the results in Table 4 with #train listing the size of the training set used for each task. Cross use of RTM es-es model increase r for en-en from 0.71 to 0.75 and for en-ar from 0.19 to 0.50 while making all tasks except 4b en-es below the 1 MRAER threshold we seek for showing improvements in prediction performance relatively better than a predictor knowing and using the mean of the target scores on the test set.

4 Conclusion

Referential translation machines pioneer a clean and intuitive computational model for automatic prediction of semantic similarity by measuring the acts of translation involved. Averaging predictions improve the correlation on the test set.

References

Eneko Agirre, Carmen Banea, Claire Cardie, Daniel Cer, Mona Diab, Aitor Gonzalez-Agirre, Weiwei Guo, Inigo Lopez-Gazpio, Montse Maritxalar, Rada

---

[2] `www.youtube.com/watch?v=9ChVn3xVNDI`; we have the same domain of STS but we use the models for different tasks.

| | | | | test | | | |
r	#train	ar-ar	en-ar	es-es	es-en	en-es	en-en	en-tr
ar-ar	1105	0.4391	0.1053	0.0885	-0.0153	-0.0554	0.5535	-0.1235
en-ar	2186	-0.0773	0.1938	0.0596	-0.1587	-0.0138	-0.0861	0.0036
es-es	1644	0.5235	0.4953	**0.7342**	0.4051	0.0238	**0.7503**	0.3888
es-en	1722	**0.5947**	0.3572	0.6886	0.4017	0.1591	0.6798	0.4781
en-es	1722	0.5643	**0.5616**	0.666	**0.6052**	**0.2141**	0.6794	**0.4998**
en-en	15672	0.57	0.2963	0.6841	0.2213	-0.0933	0.7109	0.0817
en-tr	22329	0.4242	0.2222	0.3914	-0.0671	-0.0638	0.4075	-0.0074
MAER	# train	ar-ar	en-ar	es-es	es-en	en-es	en-en	en-tr
ar-ar	1105	1.2202	1.5205	1.4414	1.5653	0.3624	1.0899	1.676
en-ar	2186	1.6913	1.5928	1.6145	1.819	0.4261	1.6371	1.8628
es-es	1644	**0.8667**	**0.9702**	**0.7136**	**0.9997**	0.3966	**0.6175**	**1.0874**
es-en	1722	1.332	1.4329	1.3814	1.444	**0.3051**	1.2728	1.4783
en-es	1722	1.012	1.1449	0.978	1.099	0.3246	0.8882	1.2638
en-en	15672	0.9224	1.3786	0.9324	1.3048	0.4329	0.8031	1.4932
en-tr	22329	1.044	1.2837	1.1252	1.3961	0.4787	1.0383	1.4959
MRAER	# train	ar-ar	en-ar	es-es	es-en	en-es	en-en	en-tr
ar-ar	1105	1.24	1.357	1.251	1.459	1.549	1.16	1.415
en-ar	2186	1.775	1.6	1.546	1.731	1.663	1.648	1.644
es-es	1644	**0.943**	**0.935**	**0.759**	**0.962**	1.896	**0.735**	**0.934**
es-en	1722	1.168	1.203	1.126	1.21	1.408	1.08	1.173
en-es	1722	1.2	1.249	1.038	1.25	**1.385**	1.104	1.193
en-en	15672	1.127	1.434	0.982	1.297	1.785	1.081	1.446
en-tr	22329	1.271	1.415	1.146	1.416	1.97	1.169	1.492

Table 4: RTM SVR model (rows) r, MAER, and MRAER results on the test sets (columns).

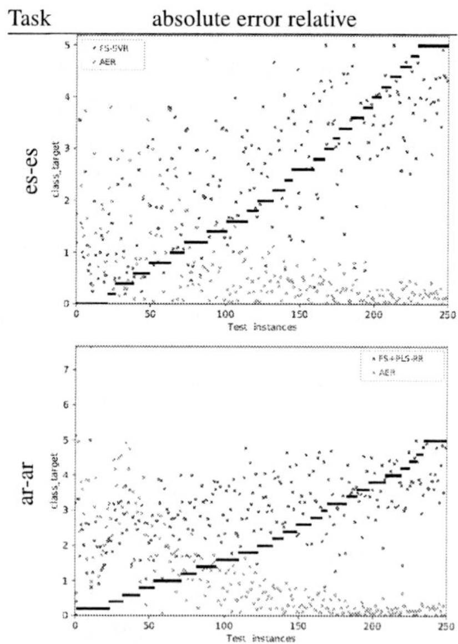

Figure 3: RTM's top predictor's absolute errors relative to the magnitude of the target.

Mihalcea, German Rigau, Larraitz Uria, and Janyce Wiebe. 2015. Semeval-2015 task 2: Semantic textual similarity, english, spanish and pilot on interpretability. In *Proc. of the 9th International Workshop on Semantic Evaluation (SemEval 2015)*. Association for Computational Linguistics, Denver, Colorado, pages 252–263. www.aclweb.org/anthology/S15-2045.

Steven Bethard, Marine Carpuat, Marianna Apidianaki, Saif M. Mohammad, Daniel Cer, and David Jurgens. 2017. Proc. of the 11th international workshop on semantic evaluation (semeval-2017). In *Proc. of the 11th International Workshop on Semantic Evaluation (SemEval-2017)*. Association for Computational Linguistics.

Ergun Biçici. 2016a. ParFDA for instance selection for statistical machine translation. In *Proc. of the First Conference on Statistical Machine Translation (WMT16)*. Association for Computational Linguistics, Berlin, Germany. http://aclanthology.info/papers/parfda-for-instance-selection-for-statistical-machine-translation.

Ergun Biçici. 2016b. RTM at SemEval-2016 task 1: Predicting semantic similarity with referential translation machines and related statistics. In *SemEval-2016: Semantic Evaluation Exercises - International Workshop on Semantic Evaluation*. San Diego, CA, USA. http://aclanthology.info/papers/rtm-at-semeval-2016-task-1-predicting-semantic-similarity-with-referential-translation-machines-and-related-statistics.

Ergun Biçici and Andy Way. 2015. Referential translation machines for predicting semantic similarity. *Language Resources and Evaluation* pages 1–27. https://doi.org/10.1007/s10579-015-9322-7.

Ondrej Bojar, Christian Buck, Rajen Chatterjee, Christian Federmann, Barry Haddow, Matthias Huck, Jimeno Antonio Yepes, Julia Kreutzer, Varvara Logacheva, Aurelie Neveol, Mariana Neves, Philipp Koehn, Christof Monz, Matteo

Negri, Matt Post, Stefan Riezler, Artem Sokolov, Lucia Specia, Karin Verspoor, and Marco Turchi. 2017. Proc. of the second conference on Machine Translation. In *Proc. of the Second Conference on Machine Translation*. Association for Computational Linguistics, Copenhagen, Denmark.

Samuel R. Bowman, Gabor Angeli, Christopher Potts, and Christopher D. Manning. 2015. A large annotated corpus for learning natural language inference. In *Proceedings of the 2015 Conference on Empirical Methods in Natural Language Processing (EMNLP)*. Association for Computational Linguistics.

Daniel Cer, Mona Diab, Eneko Agirre, Inigo Lopez-Gazpio, and Lucia Specia. 2017. SemEval-2017 Task 1: Semantic textual similarity multilingual and crosslingual focused evaluation. In *Proceedings of the 11th International Workshop on Semantic Evaluation (SemEval-2017)*. Association for Computational Linguistics, Vancouver, Canada, pages 1–14. http://www.aclweb.org/anthology/S17-2001.

Yoav Freund and Robert E Schapire. 1997. A decision-theoretic generalization of on-line learning and an application to boosting. *Journal of Computer and System Sciences* 55(1):119–139. https://doi.org/10.1006/jcss.1997.1504.

Pierre Geurts, Damien Ernst, and Louis Wehenkel. 2006. Extremely randomized trees. *Machine Learning* 63(1):3–42.

Isabelle Guyon, Gideon Dror, Vincent Lemaire, Graham W. Taylor, and Daniel L. Silver, editors. 2012. *Unsupervised and Transfer Learning - Workshop held at ICML 2011, Bellevue, Washington, USA, July 2, 2011*, volume 27 of *JMLR Proceedings*. JMLR.org. http://clopinet.com/ul.

Isabelle Guyon, Jason Weston, Stephen Barnhill, and Vladimir Vapnik. 2002. Gene selection for cancer classification using support vector machines. *Machine Learning* 46(1-3):389–422. https://doi.org/10.1023/A:1012487302797.

Anna Kozlova, Mariya Shmatova, and Anton Frolov. 2016. Ysda participation in the wmt'16 quality estimation shared task. In *Proceedings of the First Conference on Machine Translation*. Association for Computational Linguistics, Berlin, Germany, pages 793–799. http://www.aclweb.org/anthology/W/W16/W16-2385.

S. Wold, A. Ruhe, H. Wold, and W. J. III Dunn. 1984. The collinearity problem in linear regression. the partial least squares (pls) approach to generalized inverses. *SIAM Journal on Scientific and Statistical Computing* 5:735–743.

LIPN-IIMAS at SemEval-2017 Task 1: Subword Embeddings, Attention Recurrent Neural Networks and Cross Word Alignment for Semantic Textual Similarity

Ignacio Arroyo-Fernández
Universidad Nacional
Autonoma de Mexico, Mexico
`iaf@ciencias.unam.mx`

Ivan Meza
Instituto de Investigaciones
en Matematicas Aplicadas y en Sistemas
Universidad Nacional
Autonoma de Mexico, Mexico
`ivanvladimir@turing.iimas.unam.mx`

Abstract

In this paper we report our attempt to use, on the one hand, state-of-the-art neural approaches that are proposed to measure Semantic Textual Similarity (STS). On the other hand, we propose an unsupervised cross-word alignment approach, which is linguistically motivated. The neural approaches proposed herein are divided into two main stages. The first stage deals with constructing neural word embeddings, the components of sentence embeddings. The second stage deals with constructing a semantic similarity function relating pairs of sentence embeddings. Unfortunately our competition results were poor in all tracks, therefore we concentrated our research to improve them for Track 5 (EN-EN).

1 Introduction

Semantic Textual Similarity (STS) refers to the Natural Language Processing (NLP) task which is aimed at measuring the degree of similarity/dissimilarity between two text units (Agirre et al., 2012, 2016). In other words given a pair of text snippets (generally a pair of sentences) the task is to determine a real value (the semantic similarity score) in the interval between 0.0 and 5.0, which represents how much similar are the two sentences of a given pair.

There are two main types of proposed systems in prior editions of the competition: supervised and unsupervised systems. While supervised systems are expected to be highly reliable because of that they use human-annotated gold standards, unsupervised systems also are highly reliable by using modest levels of linguistic knowledge. In this work we report results from both, unsupervised and supervised systems.

Currently the STS task involves tracks of different nature, i.e. the monolingual and cross-lingual ones. In this paper we investigate the underlying properties in text which are relevant to measure semantic similarity, thus we focus our major efforts into the English-English Track 5.

2 Data

We tested a couple of supervised systems. We prepared the STS monolingual English datasets from years 2012, 2013, 2015 and 2016. After discarding sentence pairs whose similarity score was absent from the corresponding gold standard files, we obtained a dataset consisted of $10,592$ sentence pairs ($6,858$ are already marked as training pairs and $3,734$ are already marked as test pairs).

In order to obtain subword embeddings we trained the *"fastText"* method for 20, 50, 100, 200 and 300 dimensions by using the English Wikipedia (Bojanowski et al., 2016). We decided to take advantage of the capability of this method for inferring out-of-vocabulary words. This advantage is mainly due to the fastText's character level n-gram approach, which represents a meaningful performance difference both in training and in testing.

3 Systems Description

Multiple Neural Network architectures were used to model similarity measuring in supervised settings. Also an unsupervised system[1] was directly tested on this year's evaluation dataset.

3.1 Word embeddings + RNN

We see the Recurrent Neural Networks (RNN) as intuitive models for observing relevance of sentence elements; in particular the Long-Short Term Memories (LSTMs). These kind of networks are

---

[1] `https://github.com/iarroyof/sts_align`

Proceedings of the 11th International Workshop on Semantic Evaluations (SemEval-2017), pages 208–212,
Vancouver, Canada, August 3 - 4, 2017. ©2017 Association for Computational Linguistics

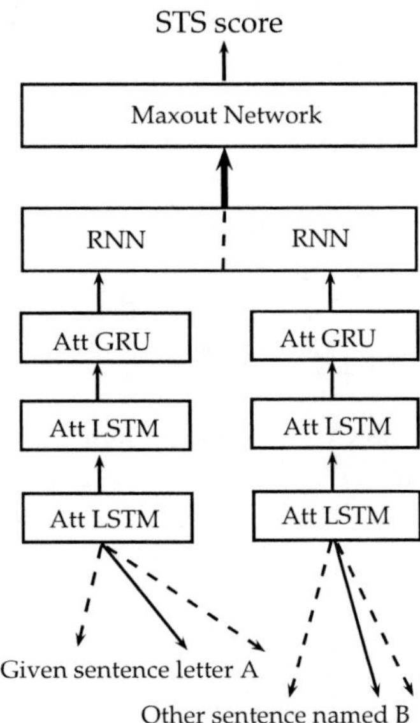

Figure 1: Attentional architecture for detecting relevant parts of each sentence within a pair of sentences.

well documented as suitable for modeling sequentiality of lexical units within sentences whereas avoiding the gradient vanishing of long term patterns (Hochreiter and Schmidhuber, 1997).

In the case of Attention LSTMs, they capture additional features of the sequential process they model. The additional features are encoded into an attention vector. This attention vector indicates to the network which segments of the sequence (sentence) are statistically more relevant than the other ones according to the training set.

In this paper we used the architecture proposed by (Vinyals et al., 2015), where the authors used a stacked Attention LSTM for PoS tagging. In Figure 1 we show a modified version of the mentioned architecture, which consists of two attention LSTM layers on the bottom, one Gated Recurrent Unit (GRU) at the middle and a simple RNN on top (Cho et al., 2014). Notice that this description corresponds to each of the twin networks showed in the figure, which is our adaptation to the STS task. This recurrent architecture is followed by a Maxout Network (Goodfellow et al., 2013), which has a monolithic output layer (i.e. the similarity score $y_i \in [1, 5] \subset \mathbb{R}$).

3.2 Sentence embeddings + MLP

The word/sentence embedding stage was modeled via the *doc2vec* method (Le and Mikolov, 2014),

which is based on the *word2vec* word embedding method (Mikolov et al., 2013). For each pair of sentences, we obtained a pair of sentence embeddings $(s_a, s_b) \in \mathbb{R}^d \times \mathbb{R}^d$. Thus each pair was concatenated to form a pair vector $p_i = s_a \| s_b \in \mathbb{R}^{2d}$. In this way, we obtained a training set $(p_1, y_1), ..., (p_m, y_m)$ which was feed to a simple MLP. The output layer of the MLP is a 6-node softmax, so we have six possible output similarity values, i.e. $y_i \in \{0, ..., 5\}$.

3.3 Cross word aligner

We proposed an unsupervised system which is motivated by linguistic elements we identified as highly relevant accordingly to linguistic theories. General linguistics states that we can know what is being said about something by seeing at the predicative structure. The theories by Harris (1968) inspire NLP algorithms where it is said that word use leads to meaning (which is commonly interpreted as word co-occurrence). Harris also said that combinatorics of words is more informative in the predicates, where redundancy is needed by speakers to provide integrity to a message.

In an attempt to follow these statements and also inspired by success obtained by authors like Han et al. (2013) and Rychalska et al. (2016), we implemented a word alignment system. Unlike previous works, our system considers that verbs operate on nouns. We used Open Information Extraction algorithms (openIE) for detecting predicates $(\mathcal{P}_a, \mathcal{P}_b)$ of the form (NP, VP, NP) within each sentence of the pair (S_a, S_b) (Fader et al., 2011).

Similarly to the word analogies commonly used for word embedding evaluations (Mikolov et al., 2013), our system considers that verbs frequently operate on nouns. Thus, it is measured how similar each verb $v_a \in \mathcal{P}_a$ of a sentence S_a is, with respect to its combination with each noun $n_b \in \mathcal{P}_b$ of a sentence S_b, i.e. $d_c(S_a, S_b)$. Given that the relationship $d_c(\cdot, \cdot)$ is not commutative this similarity also is computed from S_b to S_a, i.e.

$$d_c(S_a, S_b) = \frac{1}{N_{v,a}} \sum_{v_a \in S_a} \frac{1}{N_{n,b}} \sum_{n_b \in S_b} \theta(v_a, n_b)$$

(1a)

$$d_c(S_b, S_a) = \frac{1}{N_{v,b}} \sum_{v_b \in S_b} \frac{1}{N_{n,a}} \sum_{n_a \in S_a} \theta(v_b, n_a),$$

(1b)

where $\theta(\cdot, \cdot)$ is the cosine similarity and $v_a, n_a \in \mathbb{R}^d$ are word embeddings categorized as verbs

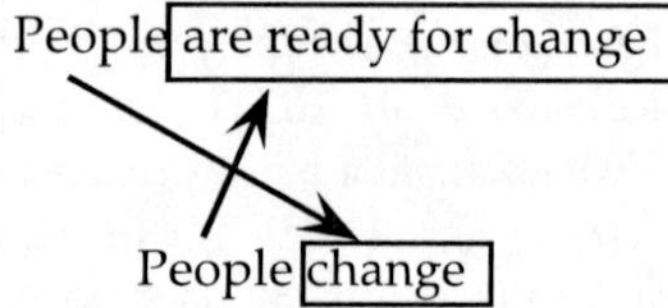

Figure 2: General scheme for the vector similarities of cross word alignments with respect to structural categories.

	LSTM	Attention
Track 1	0.0471	0.0214
Track 2	0.0769	0.1292
Track 3	0.1527	0.0458
Track 4	0.1719	0.0120
Track 5	0.1446	0.0191
Track 6	0.0738	0.2038
Track 7	0.0800	0.2168
Overall	0.1067	0.0926

Table 1: LSTM network without/with attention mechanism. Official results of the competition in this year's evaluation.

and nouns within the sentence S_a, respectively. $N_{v,a}, N_{n,a}$ are the number of verbs and nouns considered in S_a (same for S_b). Overall, equations (1a) and (1b) are the average vector similarities of *cross word alignments* with respect to structural categories between S_a and S_b. For example, in Figure 2 the sentence "People are ready for change" $[S_a]$ is compared against the phrase "people change" $[S_b]$. The main idea, in one direction $[S_b] \rightarrow [S_a]$, is to quantify how the word "people" is used along the conjugated form "are" (which forms a predicate together with the noun phrase "ready for change"). This operation is also performed in the inverted direction $[S_a] \rightarrow [S_b]$.

The kind of predicates showed in Figure 2 are often part of more complex sentences, e.g. "It is clear that future is near and people is ready for change". We extracted these predicates by using the openIE algorithm implemented in the coreNLP[2] library.

There are cases in the STS corpora where no extractions are made. This is due to the low recall openIE systems offer until now (Xu et al., 2013). That is, many openIE algorithms can extract neither implicit relations (e.g. "Mexico City, where Aztecs live") nor short phrases (e.g. "The white house"). We assume that these snippets are expressed in their minimum form, so things like "people changes" are embedded word by word. The embeddings are then compared either to embeddings of other equally short phrases or to embeddings of openIE extractions. The global score is simply the average of all distances:

$$s_f = \frac{d_c(S_a, S_b) + d_c(S_b, S_a)}{2}$$

4   Results

Our systems passed through several refinement stages. Unfortunately, the submitted runs were

to early stages and did not reach competitive performance as can be seen in Table 1. We transformed the multi-lingual data onto English using the Google Translate API and trained a unique model on resulting data. We submitted two LSTM models, with and without attention mechanism. The models were selected by monitoring the best test score after 25 training epochs. Additional systems were tested after-competition. Our best results are considered as such given its absolute value (inverse correlations can be reinterpreted in-system in the case we reach higher values).

4.1   Word embeddings + RNN

A sentence can be seen as a sequence of word embeddings which are appended in order to form a sentence matrix. For this system we used FastText word embeddings. Given a sentence pair, each sentence matrix is fed to each of the multi-layered RNNs described in Section 3.1. We used the last-top hidden states (or time steps) of the two networks as sentence embeddings. We concatenated these sentence embeddings. In this way, we obtained pair vectors $p_1, ..., p_m \subset \mathbb{R}^{2t}$ that were feed to the top Maxout network (herein t is the number of hidden states each of the top RNN layers has in Figure 1).

The networks showed in Table 2 were trained over 1500 pairs from data described in Section 2 (1050 for training and 450 for test). As shown in the table, we fed the networks with word embeddings of 200, 100 and 50 dimensions. Results are much better for the architecture formed by word embeddings of 200 dimensions, 50 hidden states and 100 hidden Maxout nodes.

---

[2]`http://stanfordnlp.github.io/CoreNLP/`

Time steps	Hidden Maxout	Embe-dding di-mension	Correlation/ MSE
50	100	200	-0.2951/1.2
100	40	100	-0.2848/1.8567
25	10	50	-0.0103/2.0738
10	40	50	-0.0123/2.0252

Table 2: Twin Attention LSTM-GRU-RNN-Maxout architecture and performance (**after-official evaluation**) on the 2017 track 5.

4.2 Sentence embeddings + MLP

We trained Doc2vec sentence embeddings $s_a, s_b \in \mathbb{R}^d$ of different dimensions (i.e. d=100, 200, 300, 500, 600) by using the whole data described in Section 2. All values of d other than 300 showed very poor learning in the MLP stage. Thus, we reported only results produced by 300-dimensional sentence embeddings.

Hidden layers	MSE (%)	Correlation
[210, 45]	64.56	0.0777
[260, 66]	64.67	0.0349
[250, 75]	64.94	0.0140
[80]	62.95	-0.0058
[270, 60]	65.32	0.0139

Table 3: Multilayer Perceptron architecture and performance in this year's evaluation (track 5).

In Table 3 we depict the Mean Squared Error (MSE) for the test set and the Pearson's weighted correlation coefficient for the track 5 evaluation. Many combinations in the architecture during the training showed that even the minimum test MSE is very high. Therefore our setting Doc2vec+MLP did not allow for good generalization.

4.3 Cross word aligner

The cross word alignment system is unsupervised and we tested it directly on some of the most popular past year's datasets. We used fastText word embeddings of different dimensions. A good choice for semantic assessment is 100 dimensions (Bojanowski et al., 2016). Additionally we reported results for 300, 200, 50 and 20 dimensions.

On top of Table 4 we show our best result (after official evaluation), which is that for 200 dimensions. Furthermore we noticed our engineered features are sensitive to text properties, e.g. domains

Corpus	Dim.	Correlation
Eval. 2017	200	-0.4599
Eval. 2017	100	-0.4557
Eval. 2017	50	-0.4291
Eval. 2017	20	-0.3716
Eval. 2017	300	-0.3597
OnWN	200	-0.4389
Plagiarism	100	-0.1851
Headlines	20	-0.1481

Table 4: Cross word aligner results. This year's evaluation and best results for popular STS data.

and, therefore, writing styles are very different between Headlines and Eval. 2017. It is needed to say that we tested direct word alignments (i.e. verb-verb, noun-noun) without success.

5 Conclusions

Despite of the success that RNNs have recently showed, we observed that even when they do not require feature engineering, instead they require training time, large data amounts, high computational power and architecture engineering. The results we showed in Section 4.1 are not good. The reason is very probably one the aforementioned and it needs to be improved. We think the amount of sequential patterns with which we trained our networks was not enough. Such patterns are based on punctual lexical items (each particular word embedding), but not in generalized sequential and semantic patterns.

Our cross word alignment system is based on feature engineering, in such a way that we showed that when a simple cosine similarity focuses on relevant segments of sentences, the performance can be progressively improved (probably by improving feature engineering and adding external resources not considered at this moment). This reasoning is consistent with much other unsupervised approaches. It is needed to say that even when we performed simple feature engineering, a critical part of our method was the use of word embeddings, which are barely based on linguistic feature engineering.

Acknowledgments

We thank to *Laboratorio Universitario de Cómputo de Alto Rendimiento* (IIMAS-UNAM); to The CONACyT (grant No. 386128) and to the CS graduate program (UNAM).

References

Eneko Agirre, Carmen Banea, Daniel Cer, Mona Diab, Aitor Gonzalez-Agirre, Rada Mihalcea, German Rigau, and Janyce Wiebe. 2016. Semeval-2016 task 1: Semantic textual similarity, monolingual and cross-lingual evaluation. *Proceedings of SemEval* pages 497–511.

Eneko Agirre, Mona Diab, Daniel Cer, and Aitor Gonzalez-Agirre. 2012. Semeval-2012 task 6: A pilot on semantic textual similarity. In *Proceedings of the First Joint Conference on Lexical and Computational Semantics-Volume 1: Proceedings of the main conference and the shared task, and Volume 2: Proceedings of the Sixth International Workshop on Semantic Evaluation*. Association for Computational Linguistics, pages 385–393.

Piotr Bojanowski, Edouard Grave, Armand Joulin, and Tomas Mikolov. 2016. Enriching word vectors with subword information. *arXiv preprint arXiv:1607.04606* .

Kyunghyun Cho, Bart Van Merriënboer, Caglar Gulcehre, Dzmitry Bahdanau, Fethi Bougares, Holger Schwenk, and Yoshua Bengio. 2014. Learning phrase representations using rnn encoder-decoder for statistical machine translation. *arXiv preprint arXiv:1406.1078* .

Anthony Fader, Stephen Soderland, and Oren Etzioni. 2011. Identifying relations for open information extraction. In *Proceedings of the Conference on Empirical Methods in Natural Language Processing*. Association for Computational Linguistics, pages 1535–1545.

Ian J Goodfellow, David Warde-Farley, Mehdi Mirza, Aaron C Courville, and Yoshua Bengio. 2013. Maxout networks. *ICML (3)* 28:1319–1327.

Lushan Han, Abhay Kashyap, Tim Finin, James Mayfield, and Jonathan Weese. 2013. Umbc ebiquitycore: Semantic textual similarity systems. *Atlanta, Georgia, USA* 44.

Zellig S. Harris. 1968. *Mathematical Structures of Language*. Wiley, New York, NY, USA.

Sepp Hochreiter and Jürgen Schmidhuber. 1997. Long short-term memory. *Neural computation* 9(8):1735–1780.

Quoc Le and Tomas Mikolov. 2014. Distributed representations of sentences and documents. In *31th International Conference on Machine Learning, ICML 2014, Beijing, China, 21-26 June 2014*. pages 1188–1196. http://jmlr.org/proceedings/papers/v32/le14.html.

Tomas Mikolov, Kai Chen, Greg Corrado, and Jeffrey Dean. 2013. Efficient estimation of word representations in vector space. *arXiv preprint arXiv:1301.3781* .

Barbara Rychalska, Katarzyna Pakulska, Krystyna Chodorowska, Wojciech Walczak, and Piotr Andruszkiewicz. 2016. Samsung poland nlp team at semeval-2016 task 1: Necessity for diversity; combining recursive autoencoders, wordnet and ensemble methods to measure semantic similarity. In *Proceedings of the 10th International Workshop on Semantic Evaluation (SemEval 2016), San Diego, CA, USA*.

Oriol Vinyals, Łukasz Kaiser, Terry Koo, Slav Petrov, Ilya Sutskever, and Geoffrey Hinton. 2015. Grammar as a foreign language. In *Advances in Neural Information Processing Systems*. pages 2773–2781.

Ying Xu, Mi-Young Kim, Kevin Quinn, Randy Goebel, and Denilson Barbosa. 2013. Open information extraction with tree kernels. In *HLT-NAACL*. pages 868–877.

L2F/INESC-ID at SemEval-2017 Tasks 1 and 2: Lexical and semantic features in word and textual similarity

Pedro Fialho, Hugo Rodrigues, Luísa Coheur and Paulo Quaresma

Spoken Language Systems Lab (L2F), INESC-ID
Rua Alves Redol 9
1000-029 Lisbon, Portugal
`name.surname@l2f.inesc-id.pt`

Abstract

This paper describes our approach to the SemEval-2017 "Semantic Textual Similarity" and "Multilingual Word Similarity" tasks. In the former, we test our approach in both English and Spanish, and use a linguistically-rich set of features. These move from lexical to semantic features. In particular, we try to take advantage of the recent Abstract Meaning Representation and SMATCH measure. Although without state of the art results, we introduce semantic structures in textual similarity and analyze their impact. Regarding word similarity, we target the English language and combine WordNet information with Word Embeddings. Without matching the best systems, our approach proved to be simple and effective.

1 Introduction

In this paper we present two systems that competed in SemEval-2017 tasks "Semantic Textual Similarity" and "Multilingual Word Similarity", using supervised and unsupervised techniques, respectively.

For the first task we used lexical features, as well as a semantic feature, based in the Abstract Meaning Representation (AMR) and in the SMATCH measure. AMR is a semantic formalism, structured as a graph (Banarescu et al., 2013). SMATCH is a metric for comparison of AMRs (Cai and Knight, 2013). To the best of our knowledge, these were not yet applied to Semantic Textual Similarity. In this paper we focus on the contribution of the SMATCH score as a semantic feature for Semantic Textual Similarity, relative to a model based on lexical clues only.

For word similarity, we test semantic equivalence functions based on WordNet (Miller, 1995) and Word Embeddings (Mikolov et al., 2013). Experiments are performed on test data provided in the SemEval-2017 tasks, and yielded competitive results, although outperformed by other approaches in the official ranking.

The document is organized as follows: in Section 2 we briefly discuss some related work; in Sections 3 and 4, we describe our systems regarding the "Semantic Textual Similarity" and "Multilingual Word Similarity" tasks, respectively. In Section 5 we present the main conclusions and point to future work.

2 Related work

The general architecture of our STS system is similar to that of Brychcín and Svoboda (2016), Potash et al. (2016) or Tian and Lan (2016), but we employ more lexical features and AMR semantics.

Brychcín and Svoboda (2016) model feature dependence in Support Vector Machines by using the product between pairs of features as new features, while we rely on neural networks. In Potash et al. (2016) it is concluded that feature based systems have better performance than structural learning with syntax trees. A fully-connected neural network is employed on hand engineered features and on an ensemble of predictions from feature based and structural based systems. We also employ a similar neural network on hand engineered features, but use semantic graphs to obtain one of such features.

For word similarity, our approach isolates the micro view approach seen in (Tian and Lan, 2016), where word embeddings are applied to measure the similarity of word pairs in an unsupervised manner. This work also describes supervised experiments on a macro/sentence view, which em-

Proceedings of the 11th International Workshop on Semantic Evaluations (SemEval-2017), pages 213–219,
Vancouver, Canada, August 3 - 4, 2017. ©2017 Association for Computational Linguistics

ploy hand engineered features and the Gradient Boosting algorithm, as in our STS system.

Henry and Sands (2016) employ WordNet for their sentence and chunk similarity metric, as also occurs in our system for word similarity.

3 Task 1 - Semantic textual similarity

In this section we describe our participation in Task 1 of SemEval-2017 (Cer et al., 2017), aimed at assessing the ability of a system to quantify the semantic similarity between two sentences, using a continuous value from 0 to 5 where 5 means semantic equivalence. This task is defined for monolingual and cross-lingual pairs. We participated in the monolingual evaluation for English, and we also report results for Spanish, both with test sets composed by 250 pairs. Most of our lexical features are language independent, thus we use the same model.

For a pair of sentences, our system collects the numeric output of metrics that assess their similarity relative to lexical or semantic aspects. Such features are supplied to a machine learning algorithm to: a) build a model, using pairs labeled with an equivalence value (compliant with the task), or b) predict such value, using the model.

3.1 Features

In our system, the similarity between two sentences is represented by multiple continuous values, obtained from metrics designed to leverage lexical or semantic analysis on the comparison of sequences or structures. Lexical features are also applied to alternative views of the input text, such as character or metaphone[1] sequences. A total of 159 features was gathered, from which one relies on semantic representations.

Lexical features are obtained from INESC-ID@ASSIN (Fialho et al., 2016), such as TER, edit distance and 17 others. These are applied to 6 representations of an input pair, totaling 96 features since not all representations are valid on all metrics (for instance, TER is not applicable on character trigrams). Its metrics and input representations rely on linguistic phenomena, such as the BLEU score on metaphones of input sentences.

We also gather lexical features from HARRY[2], where 21 similarity metrics are calculated for bits,

bytes and tokens of a pair of sentences, except for the Spectrum kernel on bits (as it is not a valid combination), resulting in 62 of our 159 features.

The only semantic feature is the SMATCH score (Cai and Knight, 2013) which represents the similarity among two AMR graphs (Banarescu et al., 2013). The AMR for each sentence in a pair is generated with JAMR[3], and then supplied to SMATCH, which returns a numeric value between 0 and 1 denoting their similarity.

In SMATCH, an AMR is translated into triples that represent variable instances, their relations, and global attributes such as the start node and literals. The final SMATCH score is the maximum F score of matching triples, according to various variable mappings, obtained by comparing their instance tokens. These are converted into lower case and then matched for exact equality.

3.2 Experimental setup

We applied all metrics to the train, test and trial examples of the SICK corpus (Marelli et al., 2014) and train and test examples from previous Semantic Textual Similarity in SemEval, as compiled by Tan et al. (2015).

Thus, our training dataset is comprised of 24623 vectors (with 9841 from SICK) assigned to a continuous value ranging from 0 to 5. Each vector contains our 159 feature values for the similarity among the sentences in an example pair.

We standardized the features by removing the mean and scaling to unit variance and norm. Then, machine learning algorithms were applied to the feature sets to train a model of our Semantic Textual Similarity representations. Namely, we employed ensemble learning by gradient boosting with decision trees, and feedforward neural networks (NN) with 1 and 2 fully connected hidden layers.

SMATCH is not available for Spanish, therefore this feature was left out when evaluating Spanish pairs (es-es). For English pairs (en-en), the scenarios include: a) only lexical features, or b) an ensemble with lexical features and the SMATCH score (without differentiation).

Gradient boosting was applied with the default configuration provided in scikit-learn (Pedregosa et al., 2011). NN were configured with single and multiple hidden layers, both with a rectifier as activation function. The first layer combines the 159

---

[1] Symbols representing how a word sounds, according to the Double Metaphone algorithm.

[2] http://www.mlsec.org/harry/

[3] https://github.com/jflanigan/jamr

input features (or 158 when not using SMATCH) into 270 neurons, which are either combined into a second layer with 100 neurons, or to the output layer (with 1 neuron). Finally, we employed the mean square error cost function and the ADAM optimizer (Kingma and Ba, 2014), and fit a model in 100 epochs and batches of 5.

Our experiments were run with Tensorflow 0.11 (Abadi et al., 2015), with NN implementations from the Keras framework[4]. Gradient boosting implementation is from scikit-learn.

3.3 Results

System performance in the Semantic Textual Similarity task was measured with the Pearson coefficient. A selection of results is shown in Table 1, featuring our different scenarios/configurations, our official scores (in bold), and systems that achieved results similar to ours or are the best of each language/track. Variations of our system are identified by the "*l2f*" prefix.

System	es-es	en-en
RTV (best of *en-en*)	0.6863	0.8547
ECNU (best of *es-es*)	0.8559	0.8518
neobility	0.7928	0.7927
l2f G. boost	0.7620	0.7919
l2f G. boost (+smatch)	-	**0.7811**
UdL	-	0.7805
MatrusriIndia	0.7614	0.7744
cosine baseline	0.71169	0.7278
l2f NN-1 (+smatch)	-	0.6998
l2f NN-1	0.6808	**0.6952**
l2f NN-2	0.6065	0.6832
l2f NN-2 (+smatch)	-	**0.6661**

Table 1: Pearson scores on monolingual evaluation, in descending order of performance on the English track.

We should mention that, afterwards, we ran our experiments with Theano 0.8.2, which yielded different results. As an example, on the English track, using the same settings (network topology, training data and normalization) of run "*l2f* NN-2 (+smatch)" resulted in a Pearson score of 0.72374. More recently, Tensorflow released version 1.0, which resulted in a score of 0.70437 for the same setup[5].

---

[4]https://keras.io/
[5]https://www.tensorflow.org/install/ migration#numeric_differences

In order to evaluate the contribution of SMATCH, we analyzed some examples where SMATCH led to a lower deviation from the gold standard, and, at the same time, higher deviation from runs without SMATCH.

On 15 pairs, SMATCH based predictions were consistently closer to the gold standard, across all learning algorithms, with an average difference of 0.27 from non SMATCH predictions. However, after analyzing the resulting AMR of some of these cases, we noticed that information was lost during AMR conversion. For instance, consider the following examples, which led to the results presented in Table 2.

(A) *The player shoots the winning points. / The basketball player is about to score points for his team.*, with a gold score of 2.8.

(B) *A woman jumps and poses for the camera. / A woman poses for the camera.*, with a gold score of 4.0.

(C) *Small child playing with letter P / 2 young girls are sitting in front of a bookcase and 1 is reading a book.*, with a gold score of 0.8.

Considering example A, we can see the information lost during the AMR conversion in the following.

```
(w / win-01
 :ARG1 (p / point))
vs.
(b / basketball                        (1)
 :ARG1-of (s / score-01
 :ARG2 (t / team
 :location-of (p / point))))
```

The top structure (until "vs.") is the AMR for the first sentence, where "winning" is incorrectly identified as a verb, and the actual verb ("shoot") and its subject ("player") are missing. The same subject is also missing in the bottom AMR. For a comprehensive understanding of the AMR notation and the parser we employed please see Banarescu et al. (2013) and Flanigan et al. (2014), respectively.

The same happened with example B (and C, al-

	Algorithm	SMATCH	no SMATCH	Gold
	G. boost	2.77	2.93	
A	NN-1	3.31	1.82	2.8
	NN-2	2.00	1.74	
	G. boost	4.13	4.15	
B	NN-1	4.00	4.31	4.0
	NN-2	4.05	4.34	
	G. boost	1.76	1.89	
C	NN-1	1.01	1.66	0.8
	NN-2	1.32	1.89	

Table 2: Predictions for pairs A, B and C where SMATCH excels, grouped by pair.

though not presented here):

```
(a / and
 :op1 (p / pose-02
  :ARG0 (w / woman)
  :ARG1 (c / camera)))
vs.
(p / pose-02
 :ARG0 (w / woman)
 :location (c / camera))
```
(2)

Thus, we could not identify specific situations to which AMR explicitly contributed, since examples where using SMATCH yielded better results reveal that SMATCH was applied to AMR with less information than in the source sentence.

To conclude, we should say that 20 pairs were consistently better predicted without SMATCH, with an average difference to SMATCH based predictions of 0.38.

4 Task 2.1 - Multilingual word similarity: English

In this section we report the experiments conducted for the second task of 2017 SemEval (Camacho-Collados et al., 2017). The task consists of, given a pair of words, automatically measuring their semantic similarity, in a continuous range of $[0 - 4]$, from unrelated to totally similar. The test set was composed of 500 pairs of tokens (which can be words or multiple-word expressions); a small trial of 18 pairs set was also provided by the organizers.

For this task we used a family of equivalence functions, from now on $equiv(t_1, t_2)$, where t_1 and t_2 are the tokens to be compared. $equiv$ functions return a value in the range $[0 - 1]$. This value was later scaled into the goal's range. Then, we

analyzed how to combine them. In the following subsections we detail our approach.

4.1 Equivalence functions

Two functions were considered:

- $equiv_{WN}$, which uses WordNet (Miller, 1995).

- $equiv_{W2V}$, which employs Word2Vec vectors (Mikolov et al., 2013) to compare the two tokens – we use the pre-trained vectors model available, trained on the Google News dataset[6].

$equiv_{WN}(t_1, t_2)$ is defined as:

$$equiv_{WN} = \begin{cases} 1 & \text{if } syn(t_1) = syn(t_2) \\ x & \text{if } syn\big(hyp(t_1)\big) \supset hyp(t_2) \\ x & \text{if } hyp(t_1) \subset syn\big(hyp(t_2)\big) \\ 0 & \text{otherwise,} \end{cases}$$

where:

- $syn(t)$ gives the synset of the token t;

- $hyp(t)$ gives the hypernyms of t;

- $x = 1 - max(n \times 0.1, m \times 0.1)$, with n and m being the number of nodes traversed in the synsets of t_1 and t_2, respectively.

$equiv_{WN}$ matches, thus, two tokens if they have a common hypernym (Resnik, 1995) in their synset path. We compute the path distance by traversing the synsets upwards until finding the least common hypernym. For each node up, a decrement of 0.1 is awarded, starting at 1.0. If no concrete common hypernym is found, then 0 is the result returned.

Token 1	Token 2	$equiv_{WN}(\times 4)$	$equiv_{W2V}(\times 4)$	Gold
eagle	falcon	0.8 (3.20)	0.44 (1.76)	3.72
keyboard	light	0.7 (2.80)	0.02 (0.09)	0.24
science fiction	comedy	0.0 (0.00)	0.34 (1.37)	2.78
sunset	string	0.0 (0.00)	0.09 (0.36)	0.05

Table 3: Results of our functions in some instances of the trial set.

TeamName	Pearson	Spearman	Final
Luminoso_run2	0.783	0.795	0.789
Luminoso_run1	0.781	0.794	0.788
QLUT_run1	0.775	0.781	0.778
hhu_run1	0.71	0.699	0.704
HCCL*_run1	0.675	0.7	0.687
...			
l2f(a.d.)_run2	0.644	0.654	0.649
l2f(a.d.)_run1	0.637	0.648	0.643
...			
SEW_run1	0.373	0.414	0.392
hjpwhuer_run1	-0.037	-0.032	0.0

Table 4: Results for the runs submitted for Task 2.1 - English.

For example, *laptop* and *notebook* have the common synset `Portable Computer`, one node above both words, which results in a score of $1 - 0.1 = 0.9$. *Crocodile* and *lizard* return 0.8, as one needs to go up two nodes in both tokens to find the common synset `Diapsid`. We do not consider generic synsets such as `artifact` or `item`.

Regarding $equiv_{W2V}$, it computes the cosine similarity between the vectors representing the two tokens:

$$equiv_{W2V}(t_1, t_2) = \cos\big(W2V(t_1), W2V(t_2)\big),$$

where $W2V(t)$ is the vector representing the word embedding for the token t. If the token is composed by more than one word, their vectors are added before computing the cosine similarity. For example, *self-driving car* and *autonomous car* obtain a cosine similarity of 0.53 (showing a degree of similarity, resulting from multiple-word tokens), while *brainstorming* and *telescope* result in a score of 0.04, which means the tokens are not related. Note that the scores are rounded to 0 if they are negative.

[6]`https://code.google.com/archive/p/word2vec/`

4.2 Combining the equivalence functions

We started by applying the $equiv(t_1, t_2)$ to the trial set. Table 3 shows some results for this experience. As one can see, in certain cases it would be better to use $equiv_{WN}$, and in others the $equiv_{W2V}$ function.

Just these few examples show how hard it is to combine these functions. Although we did not expect to accomplish relevant results with such approach, we decided to train a linear regression model in Weka (Hall et al., 2009) with the (very small) provided example set.

The final result obtained was $C_1 = 5.0381 \times equiv_{w2v} + 0.6355$, which only uses one of the functions. We used this equation in one of our runs, `RunW2V`, with a modified version: $C' = min(C_1, 4)$.

Believing $equiv_{WN}$ had potential to be important in certain cases, we manually designed a weighed function to combine both functions. The threshold was decided by analyzing the trial set only. We ended up with the following decision function:

$$C_2 = \begin{cases} equiv_{WN} \times 4 & \text{if } equiv_{W2V} < 0.12 \\ C' & \text{otherwise.} \end{cases}$$

The idea behind it is the following: when $equiv_{W2V}$ is below a threshold (set to 0.12), we use $equiv_{WN}$. Then either $equiv_{WN}$ does not find a relation as well (and probably has a value of 0.0), or it finds one and it is probably correct (see *sunset/string* in Table 3). This led to our second run, `RunMix`.

4.3 Results

Results for the task are presented in Table 4, with our runs in bold as submitted (`run1` is `RunW2V` and `run2` is `RunMix`). Both our runs attain a similar score, which is somehow surprising given how differently the scores were calculated. We placed at the middle of the table, although only a few points short from the 5th best ranked run - a difference of less than 0.04 on both Pearson and final score. This ends up being an interesting result, based on how simple our approach was, and the lack of data to properly learn a function to combine our *equiv* functions.

5 Conclusions and Future Work

In this paper we present our results on two tasks of 2017 SemEval competition, "Semantic Textual Similarity" and "Multilingual Word Similarity". The results obtained yielded competitive results, although being outperformed by other approaches in the official ranking.

For the "Semantic Textual Similarity" task, our models performed similarly for multilingual data, since most features are language independent, and essentially rely on matching tokens among input sentences. Therefore, our method is feasible for all monolingual pairs.

We could not identify situations where the SMATCH metric improved the results, although in 15 cases SMATCH based predictions were closer to the gold standard, across all learning algorithms.

Future work includes replacing the exact instance matching in SMATCH with our word similarity module, and using the SMATCH representation in a structural learning method such as Tree-LSTM (Tai et al., 2015), or in a more balanced/weighed ensemble with the lexical features.

In what respects the "Multilingual Word Similarity" task, we believe that our participation was simple, but still effective. We used two semantic resources (WordNet and Word2Vec), a weighting function learned on a small trial set, and a hand-crafted formula to combine the similarity scores of our two functions, which makes it an approach lacking ground. The results were still promising, given the simplicity of our approach.

As future work, the word similarity module itself could be largely improved by automatically learning a set of weights to combine the two functions. For instance, the gold standard, now available, can be a useful tool for this task, as other large datasets like Simlex-999 (Hill et al., 2014).

References

Martín Abadi, Ashish Agarwal, Paul Barham, Eugene Brevdo, Zhifeng Chen, Craig Citro, Greg S. Corrado, Andy Davis, Jeffrey Dean, Matthieu Devin, Sanjay Ghemawat, Ian Goodfellow, Andrew Harp, Geoffrey Irving, Michael Isard, Yangqing Jia, Rafal Jozefowicz, Lukasz Kaiser, Manjunath Kudlur, Josh Levenberg, Dan Mané, Rajat Monga, Sherry Moore, Derek Murray, Chris Olah, Mike Schuster, Jonathon Shlens, Benoit Steiner, Ilya Sutskever, Kunal Talwar, Paul Tucker, Vincent Vanhoucke, Vijay Vasudevan, Fernanda Viégas, Oriol Vinyals, Pete Warden, Martin Wattenberg, Martin Wicke, Yuan Yu, and Xiaoqiang Zheng. 2015. TensorFlow: Large-scale machine learning on heterogeneous systems. Software available from tensorflow.org. http://tensorflow.org/.

Laura Banarescu, Claire Bonial, Shu Cai, Madalina Georgescu, Kira Griffitt, Ulf Hermjakob, Kevin Knight, Philipp Koehn, Martha Palmer, and Nathan Schneider. 2013. Abstract meaning representation for sembanking. In *Proceedings of the 7th Linguistic Annotation Workshop and Interoperability with Discourse*. Association for Computational Linguistics, Sofia, Bulgaria, pages 178–186. http://www.aclweb.org/anthology/W13-2322.

Steven Bethard, Daniel M. Cer, Marine Carpuat, David Jurgens, Preslav Nakov, and Torsten Zesch, editors. 2016. *Proceedings of the 10th International Workshop on Semantic Evaluation, SemEval@NAACL-HLT 2016, San Diego, CA, USA, June 16-17, 2016*. The Association for Computer Linguistics. http://aclweb.org/anthology/S/S16/.

Tomás Brychcín and Lukás Svoboda. 2016. UWB at semeval-2016 task 1: Semantic textual similarity using lexical, syntactic, and semantic information. In (Bethard et al., 2016), pages 588–594. http://aclweb.org/anthology/S/S16/S16-1089.pdf.

Shu Cai and Kevin Knight. 2013. Smatch: an evaluation metric for semantic feature structures. In *Proceedings of the 51st Annual Meeting of the Association for Computational Linguistics, ACL 2013, 4-9 August 2013, Sofia, Bulgaria, Volume 2: Short Papers*. The Association for Computer Linguistics, pages 748–752.

Jose Camacho-Collados, Mohammad Taher Pilehvar, Nigel Collier, and Roberto Navigli. 2017. Semeval-2017 task 2: Multilingual and cross-lingual semantic word similarity. In *Proceedings of the 11th International Workshop on Semantic Evaluation (SemEval-2017)*. Association for Computational Linguistics, Vancouver, Canada, pages 15–26. http://www.aclweb.org/anthology/S17-2002.

Daniel Cer, Mona Diab, Eneko Agirre, Inigo Lopez-Gazpio, and Lucia Specia. 2017. Semeval-2017 task 1: Semantic textual similarity multilingual and crosslingual focused evaluation. In *Proceedings of the 11th International Workshop on Semantic Evaluation (SemEval-2017)*. Association for Computational Linguistics, Vancouver, Canada, pages 1–14. http://www.aclweb.org/anthology/S17-2001.

Pedro Fialho, Ricardo Marques, Bruno Martins, Luísa Coheur, and Paulo Quaresma. 2016. Inesc-id@assin: Medição de similaridade semântica e reconhecimento de inferência textual. *Linguamática* 8(2):33–42.

Jeffrey Flanigan, Sam Thomson, Jaime Carbonell, Chris Dyer, and Noah A. Smith. 2014. A discriminative graph-based parser for the abstract meaning representation. In *Proceedings of the 52nd Annual Meeting of the Association for Computational Linguistics*. Association for Computational Linguistics, volume 1, pages 1426–1436.

Mark Hall, Eibe Frank, Geoffrey Holmes, Bernhard Pfahringer, Peter Reutemann, and Ian H. Witten. 2009. The weka data mining software: An update. *SIGKDD Explor. Newsl.* 11(1):10–18. https://doi.org/10.1145/1656274.1656278.

Sam Henry and Allison Sands. 2016. Vrep at semeval-2016 task 1 and task 2: A system for interpretable semantic similarity. In (Bethard et al., 2016), pages 577–583. http://aclweb.org/anthology/S/S16/S16-1087.pdf.

Felix Hill, Roi Reichart, and Anna Korhonen. 2014. Simlex-999: Evaluating semantic models with (genuine) similarity estimation. *CoRR* abs/1408.3456. http://arxiv.org/abs/1408.3456.

Diederik P. Kingma and Jimmy Ba. 2014. Adam: A method for stochastic optimization. *CoRR* abs/1412.6980. http://arxiv.org/abs/1412.6980.

Marco Marelli, Stefano Menini, Marco Baroni, Luisa Bentivogli, Raffaella Bernardi, and Roberto Zamparelli. 2014. A SICK cure for the evaluation of compositional distributional semantic models. In Nicoletta Calzolari, Khalid Choukri, Thierry Declerck, Hrafn Loftsson, Bente Maegaard, Joseph Mariani, Asunción Moreno, Jan Odijk, and Stelios Piperidis, editors, *Proceedings of the Ninth International Conference on Language Resources and Evaluation, LREC 2014, Reykjavik, Iceland, May 26-31, 2014.*. European Language Resources Association (ELRA), pages 216–223. http://www.lrec-conf.org/proceedings/lrec2014/summaries/363.html.

Tomas Mikolov, Kai Chen, Greg Corrado, and Jeffrey Dean. 2013. Efficient estimation of word representations in vector space. *CoRR* abs/1301.3781.

George A. Miller. 1995. Wordnet: a lexical database for english. *Commun. ACM* 38:39–41.

F. Pedregosa, G. Varoquaux, A. Gramfort, V. Michel, B. Thirion, O. Grisel, M. Blondel, P. Prettenhofer, R. Weiss, V. Dubourg, J. Vanderplas, A. Passos, D. Cournapeau, M. Brucher, M. Perrot, and E. Duchesnay. 2011. Scikit-learn: Machine learning in Python. *Journal of Machine Learning Research* 12:2825–2830.

Peter Potash, William Boag, Alexey Romanov, Vasili Ramanishka, and Anna Rumshisky. 2016. Simihawk at semeval-2016 task 1: A deep ensemble system for semantic textual similarity. In (Bethard et al., 2016), pages 741–748. http://aclweb.org/anthology/S/S16/S16-1115.pdf.

Philip Resnik. 1995. Using information content to evaluate semantic similarity in a taxonomy. In *Proceedings of the 14th International Joint Conference on Artificial Intelligence - Volume 1*. Morgan Kaufmann Publishers Inc., San Francisco, CA, USA, IJCAI'95, pages 448–453.

Kai Sheng Tai, Richard Socher, and Christopher D. Manning. 2015. Improved semantic representations from tree-structured long short-term memory networks. In *Proceedings of the 53rd Annual Meeting of the Association for Computational Linguistics and the 7th International Joint Conference on Natural Language Processing of the Asian Federation of Natural Language Processing, ACL 2015, July 26-31, 2015, Beijing, China, Volume 1: Long Papers*. The Association for Computer Linguistics, pages 1556–1566. http://aclweb.org/anthology/P/P15/P15-1150.pdf.

Li Ling Tan, Carolina Scarton, Lucia Specia, and Josef van Genabith. 2015. Usaar-sheffield: Semantic textual similarity with deep regression and machine translation evaluation metrics. In *Proceedings of the 9th International Workshop on Semantic Evaluation*. o.A., pages 85–89.

Junfeng Tian and Man Lan. 2016. ECNU at semeval-2016 task 1: Leveraging word embedding from macro and micro views to boost performance for semantic textual similarity. In (Bethard et al., 2016), pages 621–627.

HCCL at SemEval-2017 Task 2: Combining Multilingual Word Embeddings and Transliteration Model for Semantic Similarity

Junqing He[1,3], Long Wu[1,3], Xuemin Zhao[1], Yonghong Yan[1,2,3]
[1]The Key Laboratory of Speech Acoustics and Content Understanding
Institute of Acoustics, Chinese Academy of Sciences
[2]Xinjiang Laboratory of Minority Speech and Language Information Processing
Xinjiang Technical Institute of Physics and Chemistry, Chinese Academy of Sciences
[3]University of Chinese Academy of Sciences
{hejunqing,wulong,zhaoxuemin,yonghongyan}@hccl.ioa.ac.cn

Abstract

In this paper, we introduce an approach to combining word embeddings and machine translation for multilingual semantic word similarity, the task2 of SemEval-2017. Thanks to the unsupervised transliteration model, our cross-lingual word embeddings encounter decreased sums of OOVs. Our results are produced using only monolingual Wikipedia corpora and a limited amount of sentence-aligned data. Although relatively little resources are utilized, our system ranked 3rd in the monolingual subtask and can be the 6th in the cross-lingual subtask.

1 Introduction

With convenient word representation methods being proposed, word embeddings are successfully utilized in state-of-the-art systems ranging from text classification (Kim, 2014), opinion categorization (Enríquez et al., 2016), machine translation (Zou et al., 2013), to stock price prediction (Peng and Jiang, 2016) and so on.

In earlier studies, the latent semantic analysis (LSA) was introduced by Deerwester (1990). It is called topic model because terms are represented as the vectors of topics and was popularized by Landauer (1997). In 2003, researchers developed the topic model based on latent Dirichlet allocation(LDA) (Blei et al., 2003). LDA did not widely spread until the Gibbs sampling was applied to the on-line training of LDA (Hoffman et al., 2010). Another traditional distributional method, pointwise mutual information metric was proposed by Turney and Pental (2010). Recently, fast distributed embeddings like (Mikolov et al., 2013c) and GloVe (Pennington et al., 2014) are based on the assumption that the meaning of a word depends on its context. As Levy et al. (2015) pointed out, there is no significant performance difference between them.

For cross-lingual word representation, there are generally four categories: Monolingual mapping (Mikolov et al., 2013b), pseudo-cross-lingual training (Gouws and Søgaard, 2015), cross-lingual training (Hermann and Blunsom, 2014) and joint optimization (Coulmance et al., 2015). As presented in (Mogadala and Rettinger, 2016) , the joint optimization method represents the state-of-the-art level in cross-lingual text classification and translation. These methods train embeddings both on monolingual and parallel corpora by jointly optimizing the losses. However, they are rarely used in word similarity due to the unsatisfying performance.

In this task, we adopt different strategies for the two subtasks. We use word2vec for subtask1, monolingual word similarity. For the subtask2, cross-lingual word similarity, we use jointly optimized cross-lingual word representation in addition to transliteration model. We build a cross-lingual word embedding system and a special machine translation system. Our approach has the following characteristics:

- Fast and efficient. Both word2vec and the cross-lingual word embeddgings tool have impressive speed (Coulmance et al., 2015) and not need expensive annotated word-aligned data.

- Decreasing OOVs. Our translation system is featured by its transliteration model that deal with OOVs outside the parallel corpus.

We constructed a naive system and did not try out the parameters for embeddings and translation models in limited time.

Proceedings of the 11th International Workshop on Semantic Evaluations (SemEval-2017), pages 220–225,
Vancouver, Canada, August 3 - 4, 2017. ©2017 Association for Computational Linguistics

2 Our Approach

We use skip-gram word embeddings directly for monolingual subtask. For cross-lingual subtask, we use English as pivot language and train multilingual word embeddings using monolingual corpora and sentence-aligned parallel data. A translation model is also trained by our statistical machine translation system. Subsequently, we translate the words in the test set into English and look up their word embeddings. For those out of English word embeddings, we check them from original language word embeddings.

2.1 Word Embeddings

For monolingual task, we choose word2vec to generate our word representations for robustness reason. Mikolov (2013c) modeled input word embeddings $\vec{w}$ as the weights from the input layer to the projection layer and its output vector $\vec{w}_o$ as weights from the projection layer to the one-hot output layer.

Skip-gram Model. The skip-gram model assumes that $P(w|c) = \sigma(\vec{w} \cdot \vec{c})$, with c as the embedding of context. Then minimize the loss function which is simplified as:

$$J = \sum_{s \in C} \sum_{w \in s} \sum_{c \in s[w-l:w+l]} -\log \sigma(\vec{w} \cdot \vec{c}) \quad (1)$$

where C is the sentence set of training corpus, s means a sentence and l is the window length. σ is the sigmoid function. Negative sampling is ignored in the equation for simplification.

Trans-gram Model. With skip-gram model introduced, we now extend it to the trans-gram model (Coulmance et al., 2015) for cross-lingual task. For sentence aligned data $A_{s,t}$, where s is the source language and t is the target language, we consider the whole sentence s_t as the context of each word w_s in sentence s_s. The loss for the source language is written as:

$$J_{s,t} = \sum_{s_s \in C_s} \sum_{w_s \in s_s} \sum_{c_t \in s_t} -\log \sigma(\vec{w_s} \cdot \vec{c_t}) \quad (2)$$

The skip-gram model also adopts the negative sampling.

The skip-gram model is famous for its efficiency (Mikolov et al., 2013a). The trans-gram model is of the same computational complexity, thus has the same speed. Although the cross-lingual embeddings can be trained fast, their performance on word similarity task is unsatisfying

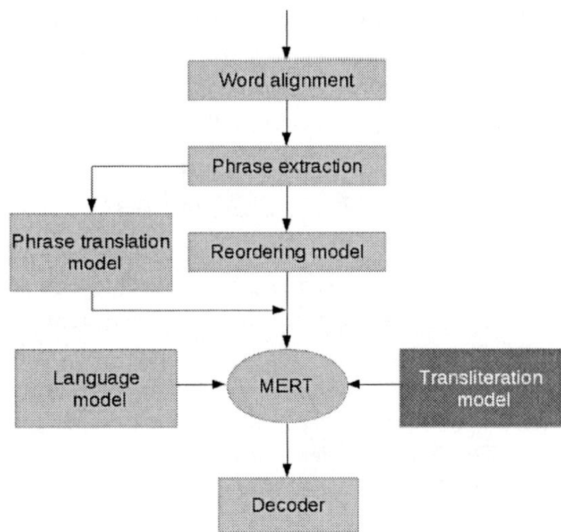

Figure 1: Framework of our translation system.

(0.493 of correlation) with word aligned data (Luong et al., 2015). So we turn to machine translation for steady performance with assistance of these word embeddings.

2.2 Machine Translation System

We constructed a phrase-based statistical machine translation (SMT) system with the transliteration model (TM) (Durrani et al., 2014). Our SMT system is illustrated in Figure 1. Like most of the phrased-based machine translation model, our system follow the steps which are shallow gray in the diagram. First we use GIZA++ (Och and Ney, 2003) as our aligner to align words and get lexical translation table. Then phrases are extracted and we estimate their translation scores directly and inversely by refining the word alignments heuristically. Subsequently, a distance-based bidirectional reordering model conditioned on both source and target language is built to arrange the word orders. For more details, please see (Koehn et al., 2003). Since our SMT system is a discriminative model, after all the features are captured, their weights are tuned using minimum error rate training (MERT) (Och, 2003). We choose KenLM (Heafield et al., 2013) as our language model and a stack decoder (Zens and Ney, 2008) with beam search for our system.

Transliteration model. Since the parallel corpus is of small size and the coverage of words is very limited, we apply a transliteration model to translate the OOVs. It models the character relationships between words and generate words at the character level. For the word alignments with character relationship, consider a word pair (e, f), the transliteration model is defined as:

$$p_{tr}(e, f) = \sum_{a \in Align(e,f)} \prod_{j=1}^{|a|} p(q_j) \qquad (3)$$

where $Align(e, f)$ is the set of possible character alignment sequence, a is one of the alignment sequences, q_j is one alignment. For word pairs without character relation, it is modeled by multiplying source and target character unigram models. The whole model is defined as the combination of transliteration and non-transliteration submodel, where λ is the prior probability of non-transliteration:

$$p_{ntr}(e, f) = \prod_{i=1}^{|e|} p_E(e_i) \prod_{j=1}^{|f|} p_F(f_i) \qquad (4)$$

$$p(e, f) = (1 - \lambda)p_{tr}(e, f) + \lambda p_{ntr}(e, f) \qquad (5)$$

The transliteration model learns the character alignment using expectation maximization (EM) over the character pairs. λ is computed in the tuning stage of the whole system.

3 Experiments

3.1 Implementation

Word representations based on different corpus may have a significant gap on the performance. Larger corpus typically generate better word embeddings. But we only use the shared corpus for comparison.

Data. We use the benchmark monolingual Wikipedia and Europarl copora in the task description (Camacho-Collados et al., 2017) as our data. Especially, we only utilize the EN-DE, EN-ES, EN-it, EN-FA parallel data for translation and cross-lingual embedding training, where EN: English, DE: German, FA: Farsi, ES: Spanish, IT: Italian.

Preprocessing. For Wikipedia data, we first filter out the stop words using the list from RANKS NL[1]. Then we clean up digits and normalize the marks. Empty lines and web tags are deleted further. For parallel data, we just filter out the stop words and normalize the marks. Parallel data are split with 99% as training set and 1% as develop set for tuning in translation system.

---

[1] http://www.ranks.nl/stopwords

similarity score. We use the cosine distance of two embeddings as the similarity score of a word pair. Its range is [-1,1].

3.2 Monolingual Experiments

We conduct an experiment on English word embeddings to see the performance of our vectors. We use phrasing and positional context when training. The phrasing is to extract phrased based on co-occurence and the threshold is 400. Positional context treats the same word in different position as different words. Our monolingual embeddings are trained with 500 dimension, 5 iterations, 15 negative samples, `win=5` and `mincount=10`. We use similary part of WordSim353 (Agirre et al., 2009), MEN (Bruni et al., 2012) , M.Turk (Radinsky et al., 2011), Rare Words (Luong et al., 2013) and SimLex (Hill et al.) as test sets, which contain 203, 3000, 287, 2034 and 999 word pairs respectively. The results of our embeddings and in (Levy et al., 2015) of the same window size without phrasing and positional context are listed in Table 1.

The performance of the submitted systems (extra resources are used) including ours (in bold) and RUFINO (the other system uses the same corpus) on all languages are listed in Table 2.

3.3 Cross-lingual Experiments

In the cross-lingual word similarity subtask each word pair is composed by words in different languages. This subtask consists of ten cross-lingual word similarity datasets: EN-DE, EN-ES, EN-FA, EN-IT, DE-ES, DE-FA, DE-IT, ES-FA, ES-IT, and FA-IT. We define the OOVs as the words that can either be found in parallel data or word embeddings. In this subtask, due to the limited amount of parallel data, OOVs occupy a large proportion in the test sets. We show the statistics of OOVs in test sets before, after transliteration model and their final counts after looking up cross-lingual word embeddings in Table 3.

In subtask 2, for the sake of limited time, we did not use phrasing and positional context like in subtask1. For phrases in test sets, we sum up the vectors of all word in the phrase as its embedding. The results of random embeddings that equal to random guess without any semantics, correct results of our system and the top system (Luminoso2) are listed in Table 4.

	WordSim353s		MEN		M.Turk		RareWords		SimLex	
correlation	sp	pr	sp	pr	sp	pr	sp	pr	sp	pr
our embeddings	.814	.800	.769	.756	.650	.684	.444	.416	.436	.435
(Levy et al., 2015)	.772	-	.772	-	.663	-	.454	-	.403	-

Table 1: Performance of English word embeddings on different test sets. sp is short for Spearman correlation, pr is short for Pearson correlation.

	EN	DE	IT	FA	ES
Luminoso2	.789	.700	.741	.503	.743
Luminoso1	.788	.693	.738	.501	.740
HCCL	**.687**	**.594**	**.651**	**.436**	**.701**
NASARI	.682	.514	.596	.405	.600
RUFINO1	.656	.539	.476	.360	.549
...			...		
hjpwhuer	.0	.024	.048	.0	.0

Table 2: Results on subtask1.

	before TM	after TM		final
EN-DE	117	85	-27.4%	31
EN-ES	71	46	-35.2%	11
EN-IT	72	51	-29.2%	11
EN-FA	120	68	-43.3%	27
DE-ES	166	11	-33.1%	31
DE-IT	156	110	-29.5%	27
DE-FA	190	124	-34.7%	27
ES-IT	119	80	-32.8%	8
ES-FA	153	88	-42.5%	23
IT-FA	155	96	-38.1%	25

Table 3: Counts of OOVs after each steps.

	random	HCCL	Luminoso2
EN-DE	.083	.484	.763
EN-ES	.022	.554	.761
EN-IT	.040	.427	.776
EN-FA	.074	.493	.598
DE-ES	.031	.408	.728
DE-IT	.035	.303	.741
DE-FA	.056	.361	.567
ES-IT	.039	.350	.753
ES-FA	.034	.420	.627
IT-FA	.014	.303	.604
GLOBAL	.053	.464	.754

Table 4: Results on subtask2.

4 Results

Compared with the results in (Levy et al., 2015), our embeddings have an improvement of 4.2% on WordSim353s and 3.3% on SimLex while have a slight decline of 0.3% on MEN, 1.3% on M.Turk and 1.0% on RareWords. Thus phrasing and positional context fail to benefit word embeddings on some test sets. It is also concluded that the embeddings we trained are comparable.

Table 2 shows that our system is ranked 3rd and behave steadily better than RUFINO for subtask1. With phrasing and positional context, Word2vec can achieve satisfying performance.

As we can see in Table 3, up to 43.3% of OOVs are significantly reduced , which are generated at the character level with transliteration model and proved to be real words. It is revealed that our transliteration model can saliently reduce OOVs.

Our cross-lingual system was ranked 8th in official results because of using mismatched data. We rerun our model using the correct data and our true results (will be mentioned in task description paper) listed in Table 4 can rank the 6th. It can be seen that our results for subtask2 are much better than that of the random embeddings, which is equal to guess blindly. However, the gap between the best system and ours is significant. Not enough parallel data and training epochs for non-English embeddings may account for this.

5 Conclusion

For mono-lingual subtask, we train word2vec based word embeddings with positional context and phrasing. For cross-lingual subtask, we built a cross-lingual word representation model and statistical machine translation system with an unsupervised transliteration model, which can greatly translate OOVs. We are the only team that uses the benchmark corpus and achieve good performance on both subtasks. But in global ranking for open resources, there is much space for improvement, i.e. using more iterations, resources and advanced models.

Acknowledgments

We genuinely appreciate Omer Levy for his advice on the monolingual subtask.

This work is partially supported by the National Natural Science Foundation of China (Nos. 11461141004, 61271426, 11504406, 11590770, 11590771, 11590772, 11590773, 11590774), the Strategic Priority Research Program of the Chinese Academy of Sciences (Nos. XDA06030100, XDA06030500, XDA06040603), National 863 Program (No. 2015AA016306), National 973 Program (No. 2013CB329302) and the Key Science and Technology Project of the Xinjiang Uygur Autonomous Region (No. 201230118-3).

References

Eneko Agirre, Enrique Alfonseca, Keith Hall, Jana Kravalova, Marius Paşca, and Aitor Soroa. 2009. A study on similarity and relatedness using distributional and wordnet-based approaches. In *Proceedings of Human Language Technologies: The 2009 Annual Conference of the North American Chapter of the Association for Computational Linguistics*. Association for Computational Linguistics, pages 19–27.

David M Blei, Andrew Y Ng, and Michael I Jordan. 2003. Latent dirichlet allocation. *Journal of machine Learning research* 3(Jan):993–1022.

Elia Bruni, Gemma Boleda, Marco Baroni, and Nam-Khanh Tran. 2012. Distributional semantics in technicolor. In *Proceedings of the 50th Annual Meeting of the Association for Computational Linguistics: Long Papers-Volume 1*. Association for Computational Linguistics, pages 136–145.

Jose Camacho-Collados, Mohammad Taher Pilehvar, Nigel Collier, and Roberto Navigli. 2017. SemEval-2017 Task 2: Multilingual and Cross-lingual Semantic Word Similarity. In *Proceedings of SemEval*. Vancouver, Canada.

Jocelyn Coulmance, Jean-Marc Marty, Guillaume Wenzek, and Amine Benhalloum. 2015. Transgram, fast cross-lingual word-embeddings. In *Proceedings of the 2015 Conference on Empirical Methods in Natural Language Processing*. Association for Computational Linguistics, Lisbon, Portugal, pages 1109–1113. http://aclweb.org/anthology/D15-1131.

Scott Deerwester, Susan T Dumais, George W Furnas, Thomas K Landauer, and Richard Harshman. 1990. Indexing by latent semantic analysis. *Journal of the American society for information science* 41(6):391.

Nadir Durrani, Hassan Sajjad, Hieu Hoang, and Philipp Koehn. 2014. Integrating an unsupervised transliteration model into statistical machine translation. In *Proceedings of the 14th Conference of the European Chapter of the Association for Computational Linguistics, volume 2: Short Papers*. Association for Computational Linguistics, Gothenburg, Sweden, pages 148–153. http://www.aclweb.org/anthology/E14-4029.

Fernando Enríquez, José A Troyano, and Tomás López-Solaz. 2016. An approach to the use of word embeddings in an opinion classification task. *Expert Systems with Applications* 66:1–6.

Stephan Gouws and Anders Søgaard. 2015. Simple task-specific bilingual word embeddings. In *Proceedings of the 2015 Conference of the North American Chapter of the Association for Computational Linguistics: Human Language Technologies*. Association for Computational Linguistics, Denver, Colorado, pages 1386–1390. http://www.aclweb.org/anthology/N15-1157.

Kenneth Heafield, Ivan Pouzyrevsky, Jonathan H. Clark, and Philipp Koehn. 2013. Scalable modified Kneser-Ney language model estimation. In *Proceedings of the 51st Annual Meeting of the Association for Computational Linguistics*. Sofia, Bulgaria, pages 690–696.

Karl Moritz Hermann and Phil Blunsom. 2014. Multilingual models for compositional distributed semantics. In *Proceedings of the 52nd Annual Meeting of the Association for Computational Linguistics (Volume 1: Long Papers)*. Association for Computational Linguistics, Baltimore, Maryland, pages 58–68. http://www.aclweb.org/anthology/P14-1006.

Felix Hill, Roi Reichart, and Anna Korhonen. ????. Simlex-999: Evaluating semantic models with (genuine) similarity estimation. *Computational Linguistics* 41(4):665–695.

Matthew Hoffman, Francis R. Bach, and David M. Blei. 2010. Online learning for latent dirichlet allocation. In J. D. Lafferty, C. K. I. Williams, J. Shawe-Taylor, R. S. Zemel, and A. Culotta, editors, *Advances in Neural Information Processing Systems 23*, Curran Associates, Inc., pages 856–864. http://papers.nips.cc/paper/3902-online-learning-for-latent-dirichlet-allocation.pdf.

Yoon Kim. 2014. Convolutional neural networks for sentence classification. In *Proceedings of the 2014 Conference on Empirical Methods in Natural Language Processing (EMNLP)*. Association for Computational Linguistics, Doha, Qatar, pages 1746–1751. http://www.aclweb.org/anthology/D14-1181.

Philipp Koehn, Franz Josef Och, and Daniel Marcu. 2003. Statistical phrase-based translation. In *Proceedings of the 2003 Conference of the North American Chapter of the Association for Computational Linguistics on Human Language Technology-Volume 1*. Association for Computational Linguistics, pages 48–54.

Thomas K Landauer and Susan T Dumais. 1997. A solution to plato's problem: The latent semantic analysis theory of acquisition, induction, and representation of knowledge. *Psychological review* 104(2):211.

Omer Levy, Yoav Goldberg, and Ido Dagan. 2015. Improving distributional similarity with lessons learned from word embeddings. *Transactions of the Association for Computational Linguistics* 3:211–225.

Thang Luong, Hieu Pham, and Christopher D Manning. 2015. Bilingual word representations with monolingual quality in mind. In *Proceedings of the 1st Workshop on Vector Space Modeling for Natural Language Processing*. pages 151–159.

Thang Luong, Richard Socher, and Christopher D Manning. 2013. Better word representations with recursive neural networks for morphology. In *CoNLL*. pages 104–113.

Tomas Mikolov, Kai Chen, Greg Corrado, and Jeffrey Dean. 2013a. Efficient estimation of word representations in vector space. *CoRR* abs/1301.3781. http://arxiv.org/abs/1301.3781.

Tomas Mikolov, Quoc V. Le, and Ilya Sutskever. 2013b. Exploiting similarities among languages for machine translation. *CoRR* abs/1309.4168. http://arxiv.org/abs/1309.4168.

Tomas Mikolov, Ilya Sutskever, Kai Chen, Greg S Corrado, and Jeff Dean. 2013c. Distributed representations of words and phrases and their compositionality. In *Advances in neural information processing systems*. pages 3111–3119.

Aditya Mogadala and Achim Rettinger. 2016. Bilingual word embeddings from parallel and non-parallel corpora for cross-language text classification. In *Proceedings of the 2016 Conference of the North American Chapter of the Association for Computational Linguistics: Human Language Technologies*. Association for Computational Linguistics, San Diego, California, pages 692–702. http://www.aclweb.org/anthology/N16-1083.

Franz Josef Och. 2003. Minimum error rate training in statistical machine translation. In *Proceedings of the 41st Annual Meeting on Association for Computational Linguistics - Volume 1*. Association for Computational Linguistics, Stroudsburg, PA, USA, ACL '03, pages 160–167. https://doi.org/10.3115/1075096.1075117.

Franz Josef Och and Hermann Ney. 2003. A systematic comparison of various statistical alignment models. *Computational linguistics* 29(1):19–51.

Yangtuo Peng and Hui Jiang. 2016. Leverage financial news to predict stock price movements using word embeddings and deep neural networks. In *Proceedings of NAACL-HLT*. pages 374–379.

Jeffrey Pennington, Richard Socher, and Christopher D Manning. 2014. Glove: Global vectors for word representation. In *EMNLP*. volume 14, pages 1532–1543.

Kira Radinsky, Eugene Agichtein, Evgeniy Gabrilovich, and Shaul Markovitch. 2011. A word at a time: Computing word relatedness using temporal semantic analysis. In *Proceedings of the 20th International Conference on World Wide Web*. ACM, New York, NY, USA, WWW '11, pages 337–346. https://doi.org/10.1145/1963405.1963455.

Peter D Turney and Patrick Pantel. 2010. From frequency to meaning: Vector space models of semantics. *Journal of artificial intelligence research* 37:141–188.

Richard Zens and Hermann Ney. 2008. Improvements in dynamic programming beam search for phrase-based statistical machine translation. In *Proceedings of the International Workshop on Spoken Language Translation (IWSLT)*. pages 195–205.

Y. Will Zou, Richard Socher, Daniel Cer, and D. Christopher Manning. 2013. Bilingual word embeddings for phrase-based machine translation. In *Proceedings of the 2013 Conference on Empirical Methods in Natural Language Processing*. Association for Computational Linguistics, pages 1393–1398. http://aclweb.org/anthology/D13-1141.

Citius at SemEval-2017 Task 2: Cross-Lingual Similarity from Comparable Corpora and Dependency-Based Contexts

Pablo Gamallo
Centro Singular de Investigación en
Tecnoloxías da Información (CiTIUS)
Universidade de Santiago de Compostela, Galiza
`pablo.gamallo@usc.es`

Abstract

This article describes the distributional strategy submitted by the Citius team to the SemEval 2017 Task 2. Even though the team participated in two sub-tasks, namely monolingual and cross-lingual word similarity, the article is mainly focused on the cross-lingual sub-task. Our method uses comparable corpora and syntactic dependencies to extract count-based and transparent bilingual distributional contexts. The evaluation of the results show that our method is competitive with other cross-lingual strategies, even those using aligned and parallel texts.

1 Introduction

A comparable corpus consists of documents in two or more languages or varieties which are not translation of each other and deal with similar topics. Comparable corpora are by definition multilingual and cross-lingual text collections. The use of comparable corpora for word similarity is a well-known task (Fung and McKeown, 1997; Rapp, 1999; Saralegi et al., 2008; Gamallo, 2007; Gamallo and Pichel, 2008; Ansari et al., 2014; Hazem and Morin, 2014). The main advantage of comparable corpora is that the Web can be used as a huge resource of multilingual texts. In contrast, their main drawback is the low performance of the extraction systems based on them. According to (Nakagawa, 2001), word similarity extraction from comparable corpora is a too difficult and ambitious objective, and much more complex than extraction from parallel and aligned corpora. However, the reasonable results our comparable-corpus method achieved in the cross-lingual sub-task of SemEval 2017 Task 2 (Camacho-Collados et al., 2017) show that the gap between paral-lel and comparable corpora for word similarity is shortening. In this article, we describe our comparable-corpus method for cross-lingual similarity in the next section (2).Then Section 3 describes the experiments and the evaluation and, finally, a discusion is addressed in Section 4.

2 The Cross-Lingual Strategy

The best known strategy to extract bilingual correspondences from comparable corpora works as follows: a word w_2 in the target language is semantically related to w_1 in the source language if the context expressions with which w_2 co-occurs tend to be translations of the context expressions with which w_1 co-occurs. The basis of the method is to find the target words that have the most similar distributions with a given source word. The starting point of this strategy is a seed list of bilingual expressions that are used to build the context vectors defining all words in both languages. This seed list is usually provided by an external bilingual dictionary. In our approach, the seed expressions used as cross-language pivot contexts are not bilingual pairs of words as in related work, but bilingual pairs of lexico-syntactic contexts.

The process of building a list of seed bilingual lexico-syntactic contexts consists of two steps: first, we generate a large list of bilingual correlations between lexico-syntactic patterns using an external bilingual dictionary, syntactic parsing and syntactic-based transfer rules. Second, this list is reduced by filtering out those pairs of patterns that do not occur in the comparable corpus. We also remove those that are sparse or unbalanced in the corpus. It results in a list of *seed bilingual contexts*.

To take an example, let us suppose that an English-Spanish dictionary translates the noun *import* into the Spanish counterpart *importación*. To

Proceedings of the 11th International Workshop on Semantic Evaluations (SemEval-2017), pages 226–229,
Vancouver, Canada, August 3 - 4, 2017. ©2017 Association for Computational Linguistics

English	Spanish
(*import*, of|to|in|for|by|with, N)	(*importación*, de|a|en|para|por|con, N)
(N, of|to|in|for|by|with, *import*)	(N, de|a|en|para|por|con, *importación*)
(V, obj, *import*)	(V, obj, *importación*)
(V, subj, *import*)	(V, subj, *importación*)
(V, of|to|in|for|by|with, *import*)	(V, de|a|en|para|por|con, *importación*)
(*import*, mod, A)	(*importación*, mod, A)

Table 1: Bilingual correlations between lexico-syntactic patterns generated from the translation pair: import-importación. A patterns is a dependency triple (head, relation, dependent). The head and dependent can be lexical units (e.g. *import*) or Part-of-Speech tags (e.g. N, V, A)

generate bilingual pairs of lexico-syntactic patterns from these two nouns, we follow basic transfer rules such as: (1) if *import* is the subject of a verb, then its Spanish equivalent, *importación*, is also the subject; (2) if *import* is modified by an adjective at the left position, then its Spanish equivalent is modified by an adjective at the right position; (3) if *import* is restricted by a prepositional complement headed by the preposition *in*, then its Spanish counterpart is restricted by a prepositional complement headed by the preposition *en*. The third rule needs a closed list of English prepositions and their more usual Spanish translations. For each entry (noun, verb, or adjective), we only generated a subset of all possible patterns. Notice that prepositions are encoded not as lexical units, but as syntactic dependencies. Table 1 depicts the bilingual pairs of patterns generated from the bilingual word pair *import-importación* and a restricted set of rules.

Finally, the comparable corpus allows us to filter out missing and sparse patterns, for instance: $(import, with, N/importación, con, N)$. The resulting bilingual lexico-syntactic patterns are used as distributional contexts to build the vector space.

The distributional vector space we have adopted is a transparent count-based model with explicit and sparse dimensions. Sparseness reduction is performed by selecting the most relevant contexts per word using a filtering strategy (Bordag, 2008; Gamallo and Bordag, 2011; Gamallo, 2016). The filtering strategy to select the most relevant contexts consists in selecting, for each word, the R (relevant) contexts with highest lexical association scores and computed with loglikelihood measure (Dunning, 1993). The top R contexts are considered to be the most *relevant* and informative for each word. R is a global, arbitrarily defined constant whose usual values range from 10 to 1000 (Biemann et al., 2013; Padró et al., 2014). In short,

we keep at most the R most relevant contexts for each target word. This is an explicit and transparent representation giving rise to a non-zero matrix. Methods based on dimensionality reduction and embeddings, by contrast, make the vector space more compact with dimensions that are not transparent in linguistic terms (Gamallo, 2016).

3 Experiments

3.1 Data and Tools

We have participated at the cross-lingual word similarity subtask of SemEval 2017 Task 2 (Camacho-Collados et al., 2017), where each word pair is composed by ten cross-lingual word similarity datasets (Camacho-Collados et al., 2015). More precisely, we sent two different runs to be evaluated against the English-Spanish dataset. In this subtask, we used as comparable corpora the English and Spanish tokenized Wikipedia dumps in text format, which are available at `https://sites.google.com/site/rmyeid/projects/polyglot`. The difference between the two runs (Citius_run1 and Citius_run2) we have submitted is in the training corpus. While Citius_run1 is only trained with the two above mentioned Wikipedias, Citius_run2 uses additional text created with BootCat (Baroni et al., 2006) and seed words that do not occur in the two Wikipedias.

To process the corpus, we used the multilingual PoS tagger of LinguaKit[1] (Garcia and Gamallo, 2015) and DepPattern, a rule-based and multilingual dependency parser (Gamallo and González, 2011; Gamallo, 2015). Named entities were identified with the NER module provided by LinguaKit while multi-words were extracted by means of an ad-hoc procedure that just selects those appearing in the test dataset.

---

[1] `https://github.com/citiususc/Linguakit`

TeamName	Pear.	Spear.	Final
Luminoso_run2	0.75	0.772	0.761
Luminoso_run1	0.748	0.772	0.76
NASARI(baseline)	0.636	0.63	0.633
OoO_run1	0.579	0.59	0.584
Citius_run1&	0.565	0.589	0.577
Citius_run2	0.556	0.576	0.566
SEW_run1	0.495	0.514	0.505
RUFINO_run1&	0.339	0.341	0.34
RUFINO_run2&	0.342	0.333	0.337
UniBuc-Sem_run1*	0.084	0.096	0.09
HCCL_run1*	0.101	0.077	0.087
hjpwhu_run2	0.043	0.041	0.042
hjpwhu_run1	0.043	0.041	0.042
HCCL_run1*	0.04	0.04	0.04

Table 2: Results for the cross-lingual English-Spanish task.

To build the distributional models, target words appearing less than 100 times were filtered out. Similarly, bilingual contexts with frequency less than 50 were removed. The English-Spanish dictionary used to select the seed contexts required by the acquisition algorithm contains 10,828 entries, which is the lexical resource integrated in Apertium, an open source machine translation system[2]. Then, for each word, we selected the 500 most relevant contexts. The final model resulted in a bilingual non-zero matrix of about 440k target words and over 208k different dependency-based contexts. In total we built a non-zero matrix with about 100 billion word-context pairs, which is a relatively easy-to-handle matrix, and even smaller in size than an equivalent dense matrix with 440k words and 500 dimensions. This is the the co-occurrence matrix used by Citius_run1. A version of the system is publicly available at http://gramatica.usc.es/~gamallo/prototypes.htm. A second matrix (used by Citius_run2) was built by searching for new occurrences with BootCat for those test words that were filtered out from the previous co-occurrence matrix.

3.2 Results

Table 2 shows the results for the English-Spanish dataset. Citius_run1 is the 5th best system (out of 14). However, if we only consider the runs using

[2]https://sourceforge.net/projects/apertium/

a comparable-based strategy with the Wikipedia dumps (marked with "&" in the table), Citius_run1 is the first out of three, leading by 23 points the second one. It is also noticeable that our comparable-corpus strategy is in a competitive position with other methods based on aligned and parallel corpora, which are most of systems participating at the subtask.

We also participated at the monolingual word similarity task for English and Spanish by making use of the same distributional vector space we have adopted for the cross-lingual task and reported in Gamallo (2016). The results we obtained are reasonable for the two languages, in particular if we only consider the Spearman correlation. According to this measure, Citius_run2 is the 4th best run in English (out of 23), and is also the 4th best system in Spanish (out of 11).

4 Discussion

We have reached interesting results by making use of a traditional and transparent distributional model instead of dense and embedding representations. Besides, in the cross-lingual task, we have built the models with non-parallel corpora instead of using aligned and parallel texts. However, our method is language dependent since it requires syntactic information and specific language processing. Finally, we must also point out that the test dataset is not well suited to the characteristics of our syntax-based strategy. The test dataset includes semantically related word pairs that are not functionally equivalents, such as for instance *globalism / visa* or *nepotism / king* in the English pairs. Even if *globalism* is semantically related to *visa*, they occur in different syntactic positions with different syntactic functions. Models without syntactic contexts (i.e. *bag-of-words* models) tend to perform well in tasks oriented to identify semantic relatedness and analogies (Levy and Goldberg, 2014; Gamallo, 2016). By contrast, syntax-based methods, as the one we have proposed, tend to outperform bag-of-words techniques when the objective is to compute semantic similarity between functional (or paradigmatic) equivalent words, such as detection of synonym, co-hyponym or hypernym word relations (Padó and Lapata, 2007; Peirsman et al., 2007; Gamallo, 2009).

Acknowledgments

This work has received financial support from a 2016 BBVA Foundation Grant for Researchers and Cultural Creators, TelePares (MINECO, ref:FFI2014-51978-C2-1-R), the Consellería de Cultura, Educación e Ordenación Universitaria (accreditation 2016-2019, ED431G/08) and the European Regional Development Fund (ERDF).

References

Ebrahim Ansari, M. H. Sadreddini, Alireza Tabebordbar, and Mehdi Sheikhalishahi. 2014. Combining different seed dictionaries to extract lexicon from comparable corpus. *Indian Journal of Science and Technology* 7(9):1279–1288.

Marco Baroni, Adam Kilgarriff, Jan Pomikálek, and Pavel Rychlý. 2006. Webbootcat: a web tool for instant corpora. In Cristina Onesti Elisa Corino, Carla Marello, editor, *EURALEX International Congress*. Edizioni dell'Orso, Torino, Italy, pages 123–131.

Biemann, C., and Riedl M. 2013. Text: Now in 2d! a framework for lexical expansion with contextual similarity. *Journal of Language Modelling* 1(1):55–95.

Stefan Bordag. 2008. A Comparison of Co-occurrence and Similarity Measures as Simulations of Context. In *9th CICLing*. pages 52–63.

José Camacho-Collados, Mohammad Pilehvar, Nigel Collier, and Roberto Navigli. 2017. Semeval-2017 task 2: Multilingual and cross-lingual semantic word similarity. In *SemEval*. Vancouver, Canada.

José Camacho-Collados, Mohammad Taher Pilehvar, and Roberto Navigli. 2015. A framework for the construction of monolingual and cross-lingual word similarity datasets. In *ACL, Beijing, China*. pages 1–7.

Ted Dunning. 1993. Accurate methods for the statistics of surprise and coincidence. *Computational Linguistics* 19(1):61–74.

Pascale Fung and Kathleen McKeown. 1997. Finding terminology translation from non-parallel corpora. In *5th Annual Workshop on Very Large Corpora*. Hong Kong, pages 192–202.

Pablo Gamallo. 2007. Learning Bilingual Lexicons from Comparable English and Spanish Corpora. In *Machine Translation SUMMIT XI*. Copenhagen, Denmark.

Pablo Gamallo. 2009. Comparing different properties involved in word similarity extraction. In *14th Portuguese Conference on Artificial Intelligence (EPIA'09), LNCS, Vol. 5816*. Springer-Verlag, Aveiro, Portugal, pages 634–645.

Pablo Gamallo. 2015. Dependency parsing with compression rules. In *International Workshop on Parsing Technology (IWPT 2015)*. Bilbao, Spain.

Pablo Gamallo. 2016. Comparing explicit and predictive distributional semantic models endowed with syntactic contexts. *Language Resources and Evaluation* First online: 13 May 2016.

Pablo Gamallo and Stefan Bordag. 2011. Is singular value decomposition useful for word simalirity extraction. *Language Resources and Evaluation* 45(2):95–119.

Pablo Gamallo and Isaac González. 2011. A grammatical formalism based on patterns of part-of-speech tags. *International Journal of Corpus Linguistics* 16(1):45–71.

Pablo Gamallo and José Ramom Pichel. 2008. Learning Spanish-Galician Translation Equivalents Using a Comparable Corpus and a Bilingual Dictionary. *LNCS* 4919:413–423.

Marcos Garcia and Pablo Gamallo. 2015. Yet another suite of multilingual nlp tools. In *Symposium on Languages, Applications and Technologies (SLATE 2015)*. Madrid, Spain, pages 81–90.

Amir Hazem and Emmanuel Morin. 2014. Improving bilingual lexicon extraction from comparable corpora using window-based and syntax-based models. *Lecture Notes in Computer Science* 8404:310–323.

Omer Levy and Yoav Goldberg. 2014. Dependency-based word embeddings. In *Proceedings of the 52nd Annual Meeting of the Association for Computational Linguistics, ACL 2014, June 22-27, 2014, Baltimore, MD, USA*. pages 302–308.

Hiroshi Nakagawa. 2001. Disambiguation of single noun translations extracted from bilingual comparable corpora. *Terminology* 7(1):63–83.

Sebastian Padó and Mirella Lapata. 2007. Dependency-Based Construction of Semantic Space Models. *Computational Linguistics* 33(2):161–199.

Muntsa Padró, Marco Idiart, Aline Villavicencio, and Carlos Ramisch. 2014. Nothing like good old frequency: Studying context filters for distributional thesauri. In *EMNLP*. pages 419–424.

Yves Peirsman, Kris Heylen, and Dirk Speelman. 2007. Finding semantically related words in Dutch. Co-occurrences versus syntactic contexts. In *CoSMO Workshop*. Roskilde, Denmark, pages 9–16.

Reinhard Rapp. 1999. Automatic Identification of Word Translations from Unrelated English and German Corpora. In *ACL'99*. pages 519–526.

X. Saralegi, I. San Vicente, and A. Gurrutxaga. 2008. Automatic generation of bilingual lexicons from comparable corpora in a popular science domain. In *LREC 2008 Workshop on Building and Using Comparable Corpora*.

Jmp8 at SemEval-2017 Task 2: A simple and general distributional approach to estimate word similarity

Josué Melka
LIASD - Université Paris 8
jmelka@ai.univ-paris8.fr

Gilles Bernard
LIASD - Université Paris 8
gb@ai.univ-paris8.fr

Abstract

We have built a simple corpus-based system to estimate words similarity in multiple languages with a count-based approach. After training on Wikipedia corpora, our system was evaluated on the multilingual subtask of SemEval-2017 Task 2 and achieved a good level of performance, despite its great simplicity. Our results tend to demonstrate the power of the distributional approach in semantic similarity tasks, even without knowledge of the underlying language. We also show that dimensionality reduction has a considerable impact on the results.

1 Introduction

Despite the crucial importance of semantic similarity in NLP, the vast majority of experiments have been conducted on the English language, which raises the question whether the developed approaches can be generalized.

SemEval-2017 Task 2 provides us with a framework for evaluating semantic representations in multiple languages and compare them. We focus here on the **multilingual** subtask, which consists of five monolingual word similarity datasets.

Our submission is based on the well known statistical approach which uses *bag-of-contexts* representation of words in a vector space model. We run two versions of our system, the first one using a direct sparse representation and the second one with compressed dense representation (detailed below). This second version was evaluated after the official evaluation deadline, and produced superior results as will appear below.

We briefly describe the multilingual subtask in section 2. Next, in section 3, we detail our system and its parameters. The results are presented and analyzed in section 4, and then we conclude in section 5.

2 Task description

Camacho-Collados et al. (2017) describes the task as follows:

> Given a pair of words, the task is to automatically measure their semantic similarity. All pairs in our datasets are scored according to a [0-4] similarity scale, where 4 denotes that the two words are synonymous and 0 indicates that they are completely dissimilar.

Multilingual word similarity This subtask provides five monolingual word similarity datasets in English, German, Italian, Spanish and Farsi. The subtask is intended to test not only monolingual approaches but also multilingual and language-independent techniques.

The individual score of the systems is defined by the authors as the harmonic mean of Pearson and Spearman correlations on the corresponding dataset. However, as our analysis lead us to take into account the separate behavior of both measures, we did not focus here on the final score.

3 Our system

Our system is *corpus-based* only, and uses a few well known ideas from the distributional approach in word semantic similarity.

3.1 The training corpus

We have used the *Wikipedia corpus* taken from `https://sites.google.com/site/rmyeid/projects/polyglot` as recommended by the authors of the task in order to compare fairly with other corpus-based systems.

Proceedings of the 11th International Workshop on Semantic Evaluations (SemEval-2017), pages 230–234,
Vancouver, Canada, August 3 - 4, 2017. ©2017 Association for Computational Linguistics

Some properties of these corpora are given in Table 1. It should be noted that no preprocessing was made on the corpora documents.

Table 1: Statistics of the Wikipedia corpora

	size	lines	words	uniques
en	8.7G	70.9M	1 392M	5.3M
de	3.5G	32.2M	482M	5.7M
it	1.8G	11.9M	265M	1.9M
es	2.1G	14.8M	338M	2.3M

3.2 Language model

Our model is *count-based*, and we have used the same parameters for all languages.

First, we counted occurrences of alphabetic words in each corpus (barring words with non alphabetic characters), and kept the 100,000 most frequent for context words and the 300,000 most frequent as vocabulary. These arbitrary limits are justified by physical constraints of memory and time.

Contexts

The context we use for a given word w_i is defined as $w_{i-L}, \ldots, w_{i-1}, w_{i+1}, \ldots, w_{i+L}$. In this work we use a context length $L = 4$.

For each context word w_{i-k} we apply a weight of $\frac{1}{k}$ to give a stronger influence to nearest words in the context.

Then we built a *word-context* matrix by summing the weighted context occurrences for each word in the vocabulary.

PPMI

Pointwise Mutual Information (PMI) introduced by Ward Church and Hanks (1989) is one of the popular ways to measure the semantic association between words and their textual context as defined above, and can be easily estimated from the word-context matrix M, as:

$$\text{PMI}(w_i, c_j) = \log \frac{M_{ij} \sum_k \sum_n M_{kn}}{\sum_k M_{ik} \sum_n M_{nj}}$$

Bullinaria and Levy (2007) argue that the Positive PMI (PPMI) outperforms the other variants of PMI for semantic similarity tasks.

$$\text{PPMI}(w, c) = \max\left(0, \text{PMI}(w, c)\right)$$

Vector compression

A common approach inspired by Latent Semantic Analysis (Deerwester et al., 1990) is to use truncated singular value decomposition (SVD) to reduce the vector dimensionality. The SVD factorization of the PPMI matrix is $M^{\text{PPMI}} = U \cdot \Sigma \cdot V^\top$, and can be truncated to the first d components.

In our experiments, we have used the symmetric variant proposed by Levy et al. (2015) using only the U_d matrix for representing word vectors, and we chose $d = 500$. Randomized SVD (Halko et al., 2009) from Scikit-learn was used to produce the matrix decomposition.

3.3 Evaluating word pairs similarity

Basically, we have used the cosine similarity to compare the word vectors.

Multi-word expressions

While some special features of the present task (such as *domain-specific* terms and *named entities*) do not necessarily require a special adaptation, *multi-word* expressions cannot be compared directly with single-word vectors. For this reason, we simply sum the vectors of every word in a multi-word expression to give the corresponding vector estimation.

See in section 4.3 a discussion about the results of this method.

Out of vocabulary words

Some words of the test dataset do not appear in our vocabulary, and we choose to give the median value .5 to the similarity of pairs including one or more out of vocabulary (OOV) words. Table 2 shows the numbers of such pairs for each language.

Table 2: pairs with OOV words

	pairs	*%*
en	21	4.2
de	68	13.6
it	24	4.8
es	17	3.4

A closer look shows that some words (such as "Brexit" or "DeepMind") were missed because they appeared too recently to be in our corpus, others because they contain non-alphabetic characters (like apostrophes or dashes), and the main part because they were not frequent enough to have been retained in our vocabulary.

The fact that the German language presents a higher OOV rate is not surprising, due to the morphological richness of this language. This can be improved by using a larger vocabulary and/or

using morphological approaches such as Bojanowski et al. (2016).

4   Results

We report the results obtained with our system
(**Jmp8**) on four different languages in Table 3 and
Table 4. Note that, due to a bug correction, the data
is not exactly the same as in the official evaluation,
though the magnitudes are similar. Moreover, the
results of our second version have not been submitted for the challenge due to lack of time.

Luminoso is the best performer on this subtask,
and **HCCL** is, to our knowledge, the best system
which is corpus based and uses the shared training corpora. **NASARI** (Camacho-Collados et al.,
2016) is the baseline proposed by the authors of
the task.

Table 3: Pearson correlation

	en	de	it	es
Luminoso	0.783	0.7	0.728	0.732
HCCL	0.675	0.576	0.635	0.688
Jmp8-1	0.516	0.286	0.436	0.455
Jmp8-2	0.687	0.578	0.652	0.685
NASARI	0.683	0.513	0.597	0.602

Table 4: Spearman correlation

	en	de	it	es
Luminoso	0.795	0.7	0.754	0.754
HCCL	0.7	0.614	0.668	0.715
Jmp8-1	0.652	0.502	0.635	0.643
Jmp8-2	0.731	0.604	0.695	0.727
NASARI	0.681	0.514	0.594	0.597

4.1   Comparison of both Jmp8 versions

Jmp8-1 simply uses the PPMI matrix to compute
similarities with sparse vectors of 100,000 components, while the second version, Jmp8-2, is based on a truncated SVD matrix which represents
words as dense vectors of 500 components.

It turns out that Jmp8-1 produces a very important difference between Pearson and Spearman
correlations, while Jmp8-2 provides more consistent results, and also better ones. In fact, Jmp8-2
outperforms **NASARI** in all cases, and achieves
similar performance to **HCCL**.

Interpretation

The important difference between both Jmp8 versions is explained by the fact that Jmp8-1 presents
a non-linear relationship with the gold standard, as
depicted in Figure 1.

Figure 1: Comparison of both versions (en)

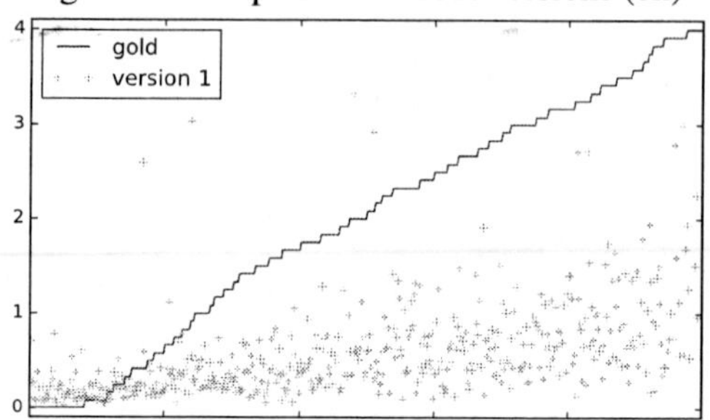

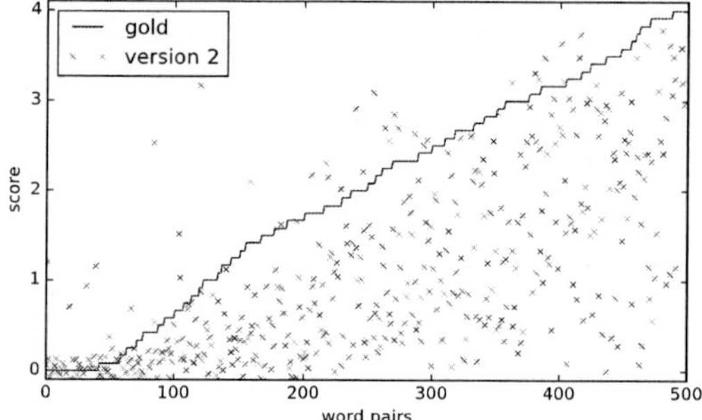

4.2   Language independence

These results suggest that our method (especially
the second version) generalizes well for different
languages, even if there are differences.

Our interpretation is that the English language
is favored because its corpus is the biggest; Italian and Spanish results indicate that our approach remains interesting even with a much smaller corpus. The results are significantly lower for
the German language despite the size of its corpus
(this is true for all methods mentioned here), presumably because there are many out of vocabulary
words.

This is supported by the fact that we found the
correlations to be much higher (comparable to Italian and Spanish values), if, instead of using .5 median value for OOV pairs, we simply deleted these
pairs from the dataset.

With SVD approach, these deletions improved
correlations by about 20% ($p = 0.65$ and $s = 0.67$) for German and by less than 3% for other
languages. Note that these numbers should be ta-

ken with caution because missing data can introduce bias.

4.3 Multi-word influence

To show the effect of the number of words in expressions on global performances, we calculated and plotted for each language the correlation with the gold standard separately for each number of words by expression (Figure 2). The size of the circles indicates the amount of pairs in each group.

For multiple reasons, it is somewhat difficult to analyze the influence of multi-word expressions on the overall performance. However, as one can expect, our simplistic method appears to degrade performance when the number of words in expressions increases. It is rather surprising that our results are still quite good despite this negative influence, but this should be mitigated by the number of pairs involved.

Figure 2: Multi-word influence in a pair (Jmp8-2)

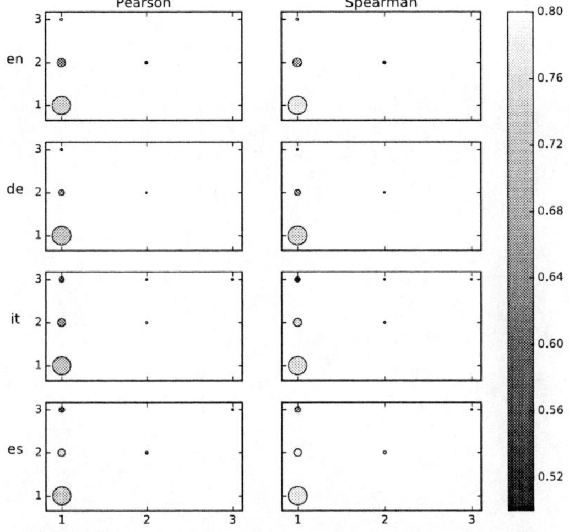

Another approach such as phrasing (Mikolov et al., 2013) can be applied as well to address this issue.

4.4 Comparison with WordSim-353 dataset

Leviant and Reichart (2015) has translated the WordSim-353 dataset into several languages [1], and we have tested our system with the similarity subset (Agirre et al., 2009), which contains 201 pairs of words. It should be noted that WS353 uses single words only, and we have very few OOV

---

[1] http://technion.ac.il/~ira.leviant/Multilingual_SimLex_Wordsim.html

words (0 in English, 4 in German and 1 in Italian). Table 5 shows our results.

Table 5: Correlations on WS353-sim dataset

		en	de	it
Jmp8-1	P	0.608	0.461	0.447
	S	0.667	0.547	0.592
Jmp8-2	P	0.722	0.654	0.600
	S	0.737	0.676	0.602

The gap between Pearson and Spearman correlations is still present for Jmp8-1, confirming that sparse vectors do not perform well in semantic similarity tasks.

Another interesting point is that the correlations for the German language are significantly higher than for the present task, which can be explained by the lower OOV rate in this dataset, as discussed above (section 4.2).

Surprisingly, contrary to the results of the present task, Italian results are significantly lower than for the other languages, though less so than were German results in the present task. We have not yet found a good explanation for this, as it is clear that OOV words are out of the picture.

5 Conclusion

We have shown that it is possible to achieve a good level of performance in multilingual word semantic similarity task with a rather simple but generalist approach.

While one should take these results with caution, some important conclusions can be drawn from our work. First, it is confirmed that the raw sparse PPMI representation is less adapted to similarity measure than the compressed dense SVD representation. Second, a specific approach needs to be developed to address multi-word expressions, although the vector addition seems to work moderately well for 2-words. And last, we have seen that OOV pairs can be problematic for a systematic comparison between systems and/or languages.

The ability of our method to handle multiple languages seems good, but needs further investigation in those directions with more extensive test sets in order to yield a refined analysis.

Finally, we are considering the combination of this method with other approaches, both from *word embeddings* methods and from supervised techniques.

References

Eneko Agirre, Enrique Alfonseca, Keith Hall, Jana Kravalova, Marius Pasca, and Aitor Soroa. 2009. A study on similarity and relatedness using distributional and wordnet-based approaches. In *Proceedings of Human Language Technologies: The 2009 Annual Conference of the North American Chapter of the Association for Computational Linguistics*. Association for Computational Linguistics, pages 19–27. http://aclweb.org/anthology/N09-1003.

Piotr Bojanowski, Edouard Grave, Armand Joulin, and Tomas Mikolov. 2016. Enriching word vectors with subword information. *CoRR* abs/1607.04606. http://arxiv.org/abs/1607.04606.

John A Bullinaria and Joseph P Levy. 2007. Extracting semantic representations from word co-occurrence statistics: A computational study. *Behavior research methods* 39(3):510–526.

Jose Camacho-Collados, Mohammad Taher Pilehvar, Nigel Collier, and Roberto Navigli. 2017. Semeval-2017 task 2: Multilingual and cross-lingual semantic word similarity. In *Proceedings of the 11th International Workshop on Semantic Evaluation (SemEval-2017)*. Association for Computational Linguistics, Vancouver, Canada, pages 15–26. http://www.aclweb.org/anthology/S17-2002.

José Camacho-Collados, Mohammad Taher Pilehvar, and Roberto Navigli. 2016. Nasari: Integrating explicit knowledge and corpus statistics for a multilingual representation of concepts and entities. *Artificial Intelligence* 240:36–64.

Scott Deerwester, Susan T Dumais, George W Furnas, Thomas K Landauer, and Richard Harshman. 1990. Indexing by latent semantic analysis. *Journal of the American society for information science* 41(6):391.

Nathan Halko, Per-Gunnar Martinsson, and Joel A. Tropp. 2009. Finding structure with randomness: Probabilistic algorithms for constructing approximate matrix decompositions. *CoRR* abs/0909.4061. http://arxiv.org/abs/0909.4061.

Ira Leviant and Roi Reichart. 2015. Separated by an Un-common Language: Towards Judgment Language Informed Vector Space Modeling. *CoRR* abs/1508.00106. http://arxiv.org/abs/1508.00106.

Omer Levy, Yoav Goldberg, and Ido Dagan. 2015. Improving distributional similarity with lessons learned from word embeddings. *Transactions of the Association of Computational Linguistics* 3:211–225. http://aclweb.org/anthology/Q15-1016.

Tomas Mikolov, Ilya Sutskever, Kai Chen, Greg S Corrado, and Jeff Dean. 2013. Distributed representations of words and phrases and their compositionality. In *Advances in neural information processing systems*. pages 3111–3119.

F. Pedregosa, G. Varoquaux, A. Gramfort, V. Michel, B. Thirion, O. Grisel, M. Blondel, P. Prettenhofer, R. Weiss, V. Dubourg, J. Vanderplas, A. Passos, D. Cournapeau, M. Brucher, M. Perrot, and E. Duchesnay. 2011. Scikit-learn: Machine learning in Python. *Journal of Machine Learning Research* 12:2825–2830.

Peter D Turney and Patrick Pantel. 2010. From frequency to meaning: Vector space models of semantics. *Journal of artificial intelligence research* 37:141–188.

Kenneth Ward Church and Patrick Hanks. 1989. Word association norms, mutual information, and lexicography. In *27th Annual Meeting of the Association for Computational Linguistics*. http://aclweb.org/anthology/P89-1010.

A Supplemental Material

We made our source code and outputs available at
`https://github.com/yoch/jmp8`

QLUT at SemEval-2017 Task 2: Word Similarity Based on Word Embedding and Knowledge Base

Fanqing Meng[1], Wenpeng Lu[*1], Yuteng Zhang[1], Ping Jian[2], Shumin Shi[2], Heyan Huang[2]
[1]School of Information, QiLu University of Technology, Jinan, Shandong, China
[2]School of Computer, Beijing Institute of Technology, Beijing, China
mengfanqing678@163.com, lwp@qlu.edu.cn, zhangyuteng1029@163.com,
pjian@bit.edu.cn, bjssm@bit.edu.cn, hhy63@bit.edu.cn

Abstract

This paper shows the details of our system submissions in the task 2 of SemEval 2017. We take part in the subtask 1 of this task, which is an English monolingual subtask. This task is designed to evaluate the semantic word similarity of two linguistic items. The results of runs are assessed by standard Pearson and Spearman correlation, contrast with official gold standard set. The best performance of our runs is 0.781 (Final). The techniques of our runs mainly make use of the word embeddings and the knowledge-based method. The results demonstrate that the combined method is effective for the computation of word similarity, while the word embeddings and the knowledge-based technique, respectively, needs more deeply improvement in details.

1 Introduction

Semantic word similarity aims at measuring the extent to which two words are similar (Camacho-Collados et al., 2017). Given two words, the runs in this competition should give a score which indicates the similarity between them, and it will be evaluated by the official gold standard set. This task doesn't offer any annotated corpus and the organizers encourage systems to utilize unlabeled corpus. With the development of word embeddings technique, more and more attentions are paid to it (Mikolov et al., 2013a; Mikolov et al., 2013b). We also adopt the word embeddings

method in our runs.

Besides the word embeddings method, another knowledge-based method is proposed by us, which is based on BabelNet (Navigli and Ponzetto, 2012). Integrating Wikipedia and WordNet, BabelNet is a multilingual encyclopedic and lexicographic knowledge base, which builds an enormous semantic network linking concepts and named entities with the aid of a large semantic relations.

Based on the word embedding method and the knowledge-based method, a combined method is implemented, which achieves the best performance.

2 System Overview

In the subtask 1 (English monolingual word similarity) of this task, we have submitted two system runs, both of which are unsupervised. We mainly utilize the word embeddings method and the combined method.

The Figure 1 shows the framework of our system runs. In the top part of the figure, *word1* and *word2* are the input of our systems. Run1 utilizes the word embeddings method. Run2 utilizes the combined method, which is based on the word embeddings and knowledge-based method.

2.1 DataSet

Test Set: In this task, we submit our runs on the English monolingual word similarity dataset, which includes 500 word pairs. These word pairs

---

*Corresponding author

Proceedings of the 11th International Workshop on Semantic Evaluations (SemEval-2017), pages 235–238,
Vancouver, Canada, August 3 - 4, 2017. ©2017 Association for Computational Linguistics

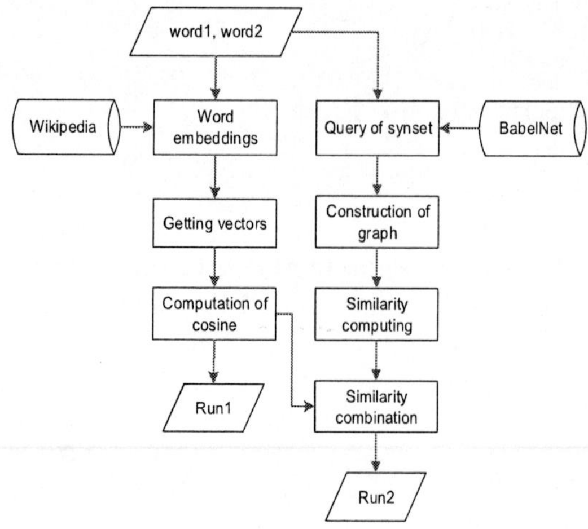

Figure 1: The framework of our system runs.

may be concepts or named entities, which are tab-separated.

Gold Standard Set: This set is gold standard set, which is annotated by official annotators. Each line in this set is a similarity value according to the test set describe above in [0-4] rating scale. 4 shows that the two words are very similar, i.e., synonyms; 3 means that the two words are similar, but have slightly different details; 2 represents that the two words are slightly similar, having a topic/domain/function and ideas or related concepts in common; 1 shows that the two words are dissimilar, which only having some small details in common. 0 means that the two words are totally dissimilar.

2.2 Word Embeddings Method

In this competition, we use the word2vec toolkit[1] to train word embeddings on the English Wikipedia corpus[2]. Before training word embedding, we preprocess the text file of the corpus to change its character encoding form from Unicode to UTF-8, because it is the default set to run the word2vec toolkit. We set the training window size to 5 and default dimensions to 200, and choose the Skipgram model. After training on the corpus, word2vec toolkit generates a word embeddings file, in which each word in the Wikipedia corpus can be mapped to a word embedding of 200 dimensions. Each dimension of the word embedding is a double value.

---

[1] https://code.google.com/p/word2vec/
[2] https://sites.google.com/site/rmyeid/projects/polyglot

Word Similarity: Mikolov has explained that the word embedding has semantic meaning (Mikolov et al., 2013a). Therefore, given two words, the semantic word similarity can be easily attained by the cosine of their word embeddings:

$$sim_{vec}(w_1, w_2) = \frac{Vec(w_1)\,Vec(w_2)}{|Vec(w_1)||Vec(w_2)|}, \qquad (1)$$

where $vec(w_1)$ is the word embedding of word w_1 and, $|vec(w_1)|$ and $|vec(w_2)|$ are the length of $vec(w_1)$ and $vec(w_2)$, respectively.

Phrase Similarity: As Mikolov has presented that phrase vector can be easily gotten by simple vector addition (Mikolov et al., 2013b), we can gain the phrase similarity between two phrases as follows:

$$sim_{vec}(p_1, p_2) = \frac{\sum_{i=1}^{|p_1|} vec(w_i) \sum_{j=1}^{|p_2|} vec(w_j)}{\left|\sum_{i=1}^{|p_1|} vec(w_i)\right|\left|\sum_{j=1}^{|p_2|} vec(w_j)\right|}, \qquad (2)$$

where $|p_1|$ and $|p_2|$ are the number of the words, which phrase p_1 and p_2 contain respectively. Word w_i represents the word, which belongs to p_1.

2.3 Knowledge-based Method

Thanks to the BabelNet, which provides a large coverage of concepts and named entities connected in a large semantic relations, such as synonymy, hypernymy and hyponymy, we can get the semantic relations between the two given words (each being a concept or named entity) by the BabelNet API[3]. In order to easily compute the similarity of two words, we implement the following algorithm.

Algorithm 1:

```
Input: word1, word2
Output: the semantic similarity be-
tween word1 and word2
Procedure:
1:  if word1(or word2) isn't found
2:    then sim = 0.5, return sim;
3:  if word1 and word2 are synset
4:    then sim = 1.0;
5:  else{
6:    search their related words;
7:    if the search steps step > γ
8:      then sim = 0.0;
9:    else{
10:     construct a graph;
11:     get the shortest path path;
12:     get the similarity sim;
13:    }
14: }
15: return sim;
```

---

[3] http://babelnet.org/download

Lines 1-2, we make the similarity of 0.5 according to the official suggestion if the systems can't cover the words in the evaluation data. Lines 3-4, if the two items of input are synset, then we assign 1.0 as its similarity. Lines 5-6, if the two words do not have this relationship, the program will iteratively search the related synsets of *word1* and *word2*, respectively, until they have common related synset(s) or the search steps *step* beyond a set threshold γ beforehand. Due to the large cost of the subsequent graph computation, we simply set 10 steps as the maximum iterative steps (i.e., γ). Lines 7-8, If the steps *step* is beyond γ, we consider that it may cost more than 10 steps to get the common synset which connect them in the graph, or even not get anything. In other words, the two words may be weakly similar, then we just simply set 0.0 as their similarity. Lines 9-14, if the steps *step* do not reach the threshold γ, we begin to construct the graph with *word1*, *word2* and their related synset by means of JUNG toolkit[4] and then traverse the graph to get the Dijkstra shortest path *path* between the input *word1* and *word2*. And we make the reciprocal of the *path* power of μ as their similarity *sim*:

$$sim = 1/(\mu^{path}), \qquad (3)$$

where *path* is the Dijkstra shortest path described above, and μ is set to 1.4 manually, which is used to adjust the similarity *sim* to be in a proper range (see 2.1). At last (line 15), it return the similarity *sim*.

2.4 Combined Method

This method is directly generated by combining the two methods described above, i.e., the word embeddings method and the knowledge-based method. We make this method, in order to leverage the performance of the two methods. More specially, we use the following equation to get the final similarity.

$$sim_{final} = \alpha * sim_{vec} + (1 - \alpha) * sim_{kb}, \qquad (4)$$

where sim_{kb} represents the semantic similarity of the knowledge-based method and sim_{vec} stands for the semantic similarity of the word embedding method. The parameter α is the manually factor for balancing the results of the two methods. And it is set to 0.6 manually. sim_{final} is the final result.

---

[4] http://jrtom.github.io/jung/

Runs	Pearson	Spearman	Final
Run1	0.669	0.673	0.671
Run2	**0.774**	**0.780**	**0.777**
NASARI	0.683	0.681	0.682

Table 1: Results of our runs and baseline.

μ	Pearson	Spearman	Final
1.0	-0.025	-0.020	-0.022
1.2	**0.653**	0.652	0.652
1.4	**0.653**	**0.656**	**0.654**
1.6	0.644	**0.656**	0.650
1.8	0.633	**0.656**	0.644
2.0	0.621	0655	0.637

Table 2: Results of Run$_{kb}$ with various parameters.

α	Pearson	Spearman	Final
0.0	0.653	0.656	0.654
0.2	0.731	0.747	0.739
0.4	**0.777**	**0.786**	**0.781**
0.6	0.774	0.780	0.777
0.8	0.731	0.735	0.733
1.0	0.669	0.673	0.671

Table 3: Results of Run2 with various parameters.

3 Evaluation

Run1: This run uses the word embeddings method described in Section 2.2. Given two words or phrases, it can get the semantic similarity by computing the cosine between their word vectors.

Run2: This run use the combined method described in Section 2.4. It can leverage the word embeddings method and knowledge-based method.

Run$_{kb}$: This run use the knowledge-based method which is described in Section 2.3.

The runs are evaluated according to the measures of standard Pearson and Spearman correlation. The final score (see the last column in Table 1) is the harmonic mean of Pearson and Spearman correlations. NASARI in Table 1 (the last row) is the baseline system which is created by the official of this task.

As we can see in Table 1 that the system Run2 make a 9.5% (Final) improvement in contrast with the baseline system (NASARI), and achieves the best performance. The performance of the system Run1 does not exceed the baseline system. Table 2 shows that the system Run_{kb} get its best performance when μ is set to 1.4 (see 2.3). Table 3 shows that Run2 get its best performance when α is set to 0.4 instead of 0.6 (see 2.4). These results show that the word embeddings method and the knowledge-based method, respectively, are not enough effective while the combined method of them makes the best performance of 0.781 in all our runs.

4   Conclusions and Future Work

Our best run achieves the performance of 0.781 (Final). It shows that the combined method is more effective for the computation of word similarity than the word embeddings method and the knowledge-based method, respectively. There are a large room to improve the performance of the word embeddings method and the knowledge-based method. In the future, we will refine the various relations among words to improve knowledge-based method.

Acknowledgments

The work described in this paper is mainly supported by National Programs for Fundamental Research and Development of China (973 Program) under Grant 2013CB329303, and National Natural Science Foundation of China under Grant 61502259, 61671064 and 61202244.

References

Jose Camacho-Collados, Mohammad Taher Pilehvar, Nigel Collier and Roberto Navigli. 2017. Semeval-2017 task 2: Multilingual and cross-lingual semantic word similarity. In *Proceedings of the 11th International Workshop on Semantic Evaluation (SemEval-2017)*. Vancouver, Canada, pages 15--26. http://www.aclweb.org/anthology/S17-2002.

Tomas Mikolov, Kai Chen, Greg Corrado and Jeffrey Dean. 2013a. Efficient estimation of word representations in vector space. *arXiv preprint arXiv:1301.3781*. https://arxiv.org/abs/1301.3781.

Tomas Mikolov, Ilya Sutskever, Kai Chen, Greg S Corrado and Jeff Dean. 2013b. Distributed representations of words and phrases and their compositionality. *arXiv preprint arXiv:1310.4546*. https://arxiv.org/abs/1310.4546.

Roberto Navigli and Simone Paolo Ponzetto. 2012. Babelnet: The automatic construction, evaluation and application of a wide-coverage multilingual semantic network. *Artificial Intelligence*, 193:217-250. http://dx.doi.org/10.1016/j.artint.2012.07.001.

RUFINO at SemEval-2017 Task 2: Cross-lingual lexical similarity by extending PMI and word embeddings systems with a Swadesh's-like list

Sergio Jimenez
Instituto Caro y Cuervo
Bogotá, Colombia
`sergio.jimenez`
`@caroycuervo`
`.gov.co`

George Dueñas
Instituto Caro y Cuervo
Bogotá, Colombia
`george.duenas`
`@caroycuervo`
`.gov.co`

Lorena Gaitan
Universidad Cooperativa
de Colombia
Bogotá, Colombia
`lorena.gaitanb`
`@campusucc.edu.co`

Jorge Segura
Universidad Nacional
de Colombia
Bogotá, Colombia
`jaseguran`
`@unal.edu.co`

Abstract

The RUFINO team proposed a non-supervised, conceptually-simple and low-cost approach for addressing the Multi-lingual and Cross-lingual Semantic Word Similarity challenge at SemEval 2017. The proposed systems were cross-lingual extensions of popular monolingual lexical similarity approaches such as PMI and word2vec. The extensions were possible by means of a small parallel list of concepts similar to the Swadesh's list, which we obtained in a semi-automatic way. In spite of its simplicity, our approach showed to be effective obtaining statistically-significant and consistent results in all datasets proposed for the task. Besides, we provide some research directions for improving this novel and affordable approach.

1 Introduction

Pairwise semantic lexical similarity is a core component in NLP systems that tackle fundamental NLP tasks such as word sense disambiguation (Camacho-Collados et al., 2015), semantic textual similarity (Agirre et al., 2017) and many others. Since more than two decades, the problem has been addressed mainly for the English language, but only recently, other languages have been considered. The task 2 in SemEval 2017 (Camacho-Collados et al., 2017) proposes a public challenge for this task in 5 languages (English, Spanish, Italian, German and Farsi) and an additional cross-lingual challenge in their 10 possible combinations. This paper describes the participating systems of the RUFINO team in these challenges.

Lexical-similarity systems receive two words as input and return a numerical score that reflects the

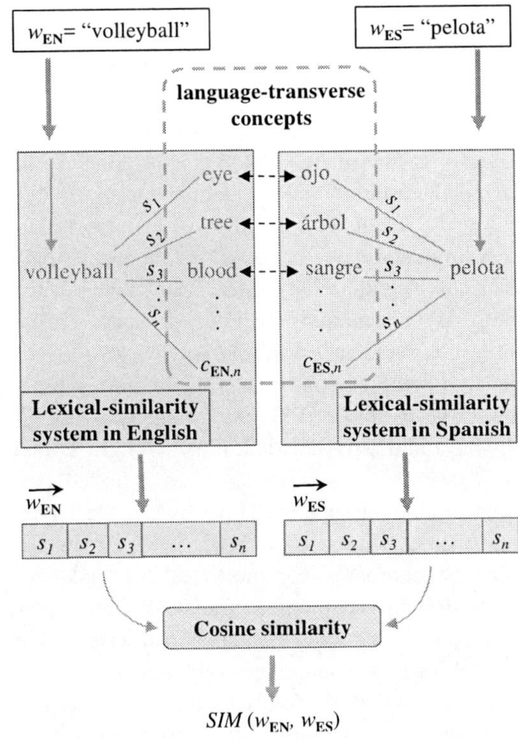

Figure 1: Architecture of the cross-lingual system

similarity or relatedness between them. Cross-lingual systems extends the idea to words in different languages. The evaluation of such systems consist in measuring the correlation of the scores obtained by several word pairs against the consensus of human judgments (gold standard).

The main fundamental resources used by lexical similarity systems are monolingual corpora, parallel corpora and knowledge-based resources such as WordNet (Miller, 1995) and Babelnet (Navigli and Ponzetto, 2012). Among them, monolingual corpora are the cheapest and most available resource in the majority of the languages. Aiming to propose a lexical similarity system with easy

Proceedings of the 11th International Workshop on Semantic Evaluations (SemEval-2017), pages 239–244,
Vancouver, Canada, August 3 - 4, 2017. ©2017 Association for Computational Linguistics

replicability, beyond the 5 languages of the challenge, the RUFINO team proposed a system based mainly on monolingual corpora.

Like monoligual lexical similarity, the cross-lingual variant of this task aims to establish quantitatively the degree of similarity between two words, but with the added complexity of being in different languages. This task contributes to solve other higher level task such as cross-lingual text similarity and entailment (Jimenez et al., 2012, 2013). However, to the best of our knowledge, it is not possible to build a cross-lingual system between two non-similar languages based solely on monolingual corpora. For that, we proposed a resource inspired by the well-known Swadesh's list. The Swadesh's list (Swadesh, 1950, 1952) is comprised of approximately 200 concepts aimed to be universal, culturally independent and transverse to almost any language for the purposes of comparative linguistics. We used Wikipedia and Google Translate to build a list for the 5 languages of the competition containing 66 concepts with similar properties to the ones proposed by Swadesh. Since the alignment of concepts grouped into synsets among WordNets in different languages is not always available, we decided to use Google Translate. In case of considering a not included language among the supported ones by Google Translate (they are more than 100), we estimated it could be comparatively more feasible and economic to build an automatic translator from a parallel corpus than the manual construction of a WordNet for that language. Nevertheless, a resource like BabelNet, for instance, could also provide accurate translations of transverse concepts. Our goal, is to build cross-lingual systems starting from monolingual systems connected across languages by the proposed list of concepts. Figure 1 provides a general overview of the general architecture of the proposed system.

The organizers of the challenge proposed a benchmark corpus for the sake of comparison of the participating systems. The systems proposed by our team used for training the Wikipedias in the 5 languages, which is the benchmark corpora for the monolingual sub-task. The benchmark corpus for the cross-lingual systems is the Europarl parallel corpus[1].Alternatively, our cross-lingual systems used the proposed list of language-traverse concepts, which is considerably smaller, simpler

------

[1]http://www.statmt.org/europarl/

and cheaper than the Europarl corpus. Although, the results obtained by our systems were in the middle range of the general ranking of official results, all of them were statistically significant and consistent across all datasets. Moreover, in some cases our results were comparable to other systems relying in considerably larger, more complex and more expensive resources.

The rest of the paper contains the following sections. In section 2, we present the motivation for our approach. Section 3 contains the detailed description of our participating systems. In section 4 the obtained results are presented and discussed. Finally, in section 5 we provide some concluding remarks.

2 Motivation

A concept list of basic vocabulary items showing the universality of certain parts of the lexicon of human languages was initially proposed by Morris Swadesh (Swadesh, 1950, 1952). Swadesh claimed that certain morphemes and everyday words such as *mother, son, hand, head, sun, warm, water, tree*, etc. connected with concepts and experiences common to all human groups are relatively stable over time. Since then, many concepts lists following the same characteristics have been compiled for several purposes in descriptive linguistics.

Considering that concepts are not only transverse to languages, but they also share some proximity when they are semantically close. For instance, *mother* and *son* are more semantically close than *mother* and *sun* independently of the language. Our approach is based on the idea that a set of transverse concepts to languages serve as a support to index a vectorial representation of the words of a given language. In order to obtain such representation for just one language, it is required the lexicalization of that set of transverse concepts and a lexical-similarity (or distance) system of that language. This semantic representation is cross-lingual since it only depends on the relative similarities (or distances) of each one of the words to be represented to the set of transverse concepts. Therefore, the representation of a particular word w is a vector where each dimension corresponds to the similarity score between w and each word from the set of transversal concepts.

Intuitively, three conditions that a set of transverse concepts for a set of languages should follow were considered. First, these concepts should be relatively frequent in all the given languages due to the fact that infrequent words tend to produce low-quality measurements in the required lexical similarity systems based either on knowledge or corpus. Second, it is preferable that the transverse concepts are lexicalized in each one of the languages with just one word. This condition could anticipate problems with the rules of the usage of multi-words in each language. Third, the monolingual lexical similarity systems should be similar in their construction and used resources. The latter improves the conditions so that the distances and similarities among concepts could be proportional through the different languages.

As a result, the list of transverse concepts, a relatively simple resource to obtain, can be useful to turn a set of monolingual systems into a cross-lingual system.

3   Methods

We build two groups of monolingual lexical similarity systems and other two groups of cross-lingual systems. For both, monolingual and cross-lingual sub-tasks, the systems labeled as *run1* rely mainly on Pointwise Mutual Information (PMI) (Church and Hanks, 1990), and those labeled as *run2* were based on Polyglot's word embeddings (Al-Rfou et al., 2013). The following subsections describe such systems.

3.1   Monolingual systems

3.1.1   *run1*: PMI and common contexts

PMI is a simple corpus-based information-theoretical method for finding associations between pairs of words using the distributional hypothesis, which states that associations between words depend on the coocurrences of the words in a large corpus. The PMI score between two words a and b can be computed with this formula:

$$PMI(a, b) = -\log\left(\frac{P(a \wedge b)}{P(a)P(b)}\right).$$

Probabilities can be estimated by the following expressions:

$$P(a) = \frac{o_a}{N}; \; P(b) = \frac{o_b}{N}; \; P(a \wedge b) = \frac{o_{a \wedge b}}{N - 1}$$

Where o_a and o_b are the number or occurrences of words a and b in the corpus, $o_{a \wedge b}$ is the number of coocurrences, and N the total number of words in the corpus (all occurrences). We used the benchmark corpora proposed for the task, that is, Wikipedia's dumps for the 5 languages downloaded in October 2016. The preprocessing comprised lower-casing and stopwords[2] removal. For obtaining $o_{a \wedge b}$, each coocurrence of a followed by b or vice-versa was counted. N was the total number of non-stopwords on each corpus.

The PMI scores computed using coocurrences is a low-cost and effective tool for finding word associations. However, associations between synonyms or words in the same category cannot be detected with such method because they do not tend occur consecutively in text. For capturing these second-order relationships, we proposed an association measure based in the proportion of common contexts between pairs of words. For that, we defined the context of a word as a duple of its left and right neighbor words (after removing stopwords). During the process of context definiction, we also tried other context settings such as two neighbor words before and after, two before/one after, one before/ two after, just one before, just one after, just two before and just two after (we even attempted not to remove the stopwords). However, we observed that when using the trial data, the setting with the best performance was a neighbor word before and after. Thus, we collected for each word a the set of its contexts C_a. The Jaccard coefficient (Jaccard, 1901; Jimenez et al., 2016) was used for comparing pairs of words represented as their sets of contexts:

$$JCC(a, b) = \frac{|C_a \cap C_b|}{|C_a \cup C_b|}$$

The final similarity score for a pair of words was the average of previously scaled PMI and JCC scores.

$$SIM(a, b) = 0.5\left(\frac{PMI(a, b)}{\max PMI} + \frac{JCC(a, b)}{\max JCC}\right)$$

Here, $\max PMI$ and $\max JCC$ are the maximum scores of the corresponding measures within the entire dataset of word pairs being compared. In our implementation, if PMI produced a mathematical error such as division by zero or logarithm of a negative number, then the PMI score was replaced by the average of the scores obtained by the same measure for the other non-erroneous word pairs in the dataset.

---

[2]urls of stopwords

English	Spanish	Italian	German	Farsi	English	Spanish	Italian	German	Farsi
angel	ángel	angelo	Engel	فرشته	background	fondo	sfondo	Hintergrund	زمینه
animal	animal	animale	Tier	حیوان	ministry	ministerio	ministero	Ministerium	وزارت
artist	artista	artista	Künstler	هنرمند	birth	nacimiento	nascita	Geburt	تولد
metal	metal	metallo	Metall	فلز	musician	músico	musicista	Musiker	نوازنده
poet	poeta	poeta	Dichter	شاعر	newspaper	periódico	giornale	Zeitung	روزنامه
minute	minuto	minuto	Minute	دقیقه	novel	novela	romanzo	Roman	رمان
blood	sangre	sangue	Blut	خون	christians	cristianos	cristiani	Christen	مسیحیان
ring	anillo	anello	Ring	حلقه	piano	piano	pianoforte	Klavier	پیانو
painter	pintor	pittore	Maler	نقاش	beautiful	hermoso	bello	schön	زیبا
comedy	comedia	commedia	Komödie	کمدی	composer	compositor	compositore	Komponist	آهنگساز
price	precio	prezzo	Preis	قیمت	quality	calidad	qualitf	Qualität	کیفیت
concert	concierto	concerto	Konzert	کنسرت	contract	contrato	contratto	Vertrag	قرارداد
sale	venta	vendita	Verkauf	فروش	religion	religión	religione	Religion	دین
read	leer	leggere	lesen	خواندن	candidate	candidato	candidato	Kandidat	نامزد
crisis	crisis	crisi	Krise	بحران	congress	congreso	congresso	Kongress	کنگره
train	tren	treno	Zug	قطار	scene	escena	scena	Szene	صحنه
tree	árbol	albero	Baum	درخت	shipyard	astillero	cantiere navale	Werft	کشتیسازی کارخانه
texts	textos	testi	Texte	متون	sister	hermana	sorella	Schwester	خواهر
domain	dominio	dominio	Domain	دامنه	soldier	soldado	soldato	Soldat	سرباز
doubt	duda	dubbio	Zweifel	شک	speed	velocidad	velocità	Geschwindigkeit	سرعت
drama	drama	dramma	Drama	درام	engines	motores	motori	Motoren	موتورهای
statue	estatua	statua	Statue	مجسمه	structure	estructura	struttura	Struktur	ساختار
error	error	errore	Fehler	خطا	discovery	descubrimiento	scoperta	Entdeckung	کشف
eye	ojo	occhio	Auge	چشم	depth	profundidad	profonditf	Tiefe	عمق
factory	fábrica	fabbrica	Fabrik	کارخانه	translation	traducción	traduzione	Übersetzung	ترجمه
weapon	arma	arma	Waffe	سلاح	device	dispositivo	dispositivo	Gerät	دستگاه
friend	amigo	amico	Freund	دوست	identity	identidad	identitf	Identität	هویت
guitar	guitarra	chitarra	Gitarre	گیتار	violence	violencia	violenza	Gewalt	خشونت
hand	mano	mano	Hand	دست	founder	fundador	fondatore	Gründer	موسس
value	valor	valore	Wert	ارزش	weight	peso	peso	Gewicht	وزن
wind	viento	vento	Wind	باد	important	importante	importante	wichtig	مهم
window	ventana	finestra	Fenster	پنجره	marriage	matrimonio	matrimonio	Ehe	ازدواج
word	palabra	parola	Wort	کلمه	message	mensaje	messaggio	Nachricht	پیام

Table 1: List of 66 language-transverse concepts in the 5 target languages

3.1.2 *run2*: Polyglot's embeddings

Our second monolingual system used the pre-trained Polyglot's word embeddings (Al-Rfou et al., 2013), which were obtained using the *word2vec* algorithm (Mikolov et al., 2013) applied to Wikipedia as corpus for a large number of languages. For each pair of target words a and b, their 64-dimensional vector representations (64 is the number of dimmensions in Polyglot's vectors) were obtained from Polyglot's files and then compared using cosine similarity. If a target word started with a capital letter and it was not found in the database of embeddings, then the word is lowercased and searched again. Similarity, if multi-words targets are not found we used the vectorial summation of the representations of the composing words. After that, if some target is still not found, as before, we used the average score of non-erroneous word pairs in the dataset.

3.2 Obtaining a Swadesh-like list

For obtaining a list of concepts with similar properties to the Swadesh's list, first we collected the lists of the top-5000 more frequent terms from the Wikipedia for each one of the 5 target languages. Next, each word on each list was translated to the other 4 languages and the translations were translated back to the original language. All translations were obtained using the GOOGLE-TRANSLATE() function in the spreadsheet editor of Google Drive. On each list, we preserved only the rows whose all 4 back translations coincided with the original word. Finally, the 5 list were merged and aligned for identify terms that occurred in the 5 languages. Only the terms occurring exactly in the 5 languages were preserved.

From the previous selection, we obtained a list containing 172 concepts with their lexicalizations in the 5 target languages. This initial list was purged manually by removing proper names, cardinals, stopwords and other unwanted forms. The final result is an aligned list of 66 concepts of fre-

Method→	PMI-JCC	Polyglot	NASARI
language	*run1*	*run2*	baseline
English	0.656	0.394	0.682
Spanish	0.549	0.406	0.600
Italian	0.476	0.306	0.596
German	0.539	0.369	0.514
Farsi	0.360	0.256	0.405
Average	0.481	0.334	0.529

Table 2: Results for the monolingual sub-task (values are the harmonic mean between Pearson's and Spearman's correlation coefficients).

Method→	PMI-JCC	Polyglot	NASARI
languages	*run1*	*run2*	baseline
it-fa	0.249	0.210	0.486
es-it	0.356	0.288	0.595
es-fa	0.257	0.300	0.479
en-it	0.342	0.238	0.648
en-fa	0.253	0.373	0.505
en-es	0.340	0.337	0.633
en-de	0.330	0.303	0.598
de-it	0.327	0.232	0.561
de-fa	0.240	0.267	0.458
de-es	0.318	0.302	0.549
Average	0.301	0.285	0.551

Table 3: Results for the cross-lingual sub-task (values are the harmonic mean between Pearson's and Spearman's correlation coefficients).

quent words in 5 languages. Besides, all possible combination pair from the 5 words on each concept are common translations of the others. The obtained list is shown in Table 1. That is the proposed list of language-traverse concepts used for enhancing the previously described monolingual lexical-similarity systems to support cross-linguality.

3.3 Cross-lingual systems

The proposed lexical cross-lingual systems were built by combining the monolingual systems described in subsections 3.1.1 and 3.1.2, with the list of 66 language-traverse concepts proposed in the previous subsection. The method for that is straightforward and depicted in Figure 1. Basically, for obtaining a vectorial representation of a word in a particular language, such word is compared using a monolingual lexical-similarity system for that language, against the 66 lexicalizations of the transverse concepts in that language. The result is a 66-dimensional vector, which is a language-independent representation the word. For comparing a pair of words in two different languages, their language-independent vectorial representations are obtained using their respective monolingual systems and the aligned list of concepts. Then the final similarity score is obtained computing the cosine similarity between the two vectors. We built two cross-lingual systems labeled as *run1*, using the monolingual systems described in subsection 3.1.1, and *run2*, with the systems described in subsection 3.1.2.

4 Results and discussion

Results obtained by our monolingual systems (*run1* and run2) are shown in Table 2. *Run1* averaged relatively close to the baseline, which in

fact, is a very strong baseline based in knowledge from Babelnet (Camacho-Collados et al., 2016). The system that outperformed the baseline was the $PMI\text{-}JCC$ monolingual system (*run1*) for German. *Run2*, based on Polyglot's embeddings, was consistently worse than *run1*. Although, both systems use the same corpora, the difference in performance is significant. As regards our runs, we suggest that $PMI\text{-}JCC$ is a method that takes better advantage of small corpora in comparison with the *word2vec* algorithm used in the construction of Polyglot's embeddings.

Unlike the results of monolingual systems, the results for *run1* and *run2* in the cross-lingual task had a similar performance and were considerably less than the baseline (see Table 3). An interesting question we asked was to what extent the results of monolingual systems predict the performance of bilingual systems. In order to answer this question, we measured Pearson's correlation (r) between the result of the bilingual system and the minimum between the results of the two monolingual systems for the 10 language combinations. The result was $r_{run1} = 0.883$, $r_{run2} = 0.263$, and $r_{baseline} = 0.950$. Clearly, the results of monolingual systems based on $PMI\text{-}JCC$ and NASARI are good predictors of the results of bilingual systems.

5 Conclusions and future directions

From our participation in the task 2 in SemEval 2017 we can gather several conclusions. First, the proposed lexical-monolingual systems based respectively on PMI-JCC and Polyglot's embeddings (i.e. *word2vec*) obtained considerably different results, in spite of being constructed using the same corpus (i.e. Wikipedia). This result suggest that, for inferring lexical relationships, relatively small corpora can be better exploited by simpler methods such as PMI, which is convenient for under-resourced languages. Second, the proposed approach of using a parallel list of language-transverse concepts for building lexical cross-lingual systems from monolingual resources showed to be effective with a good cost-benefit ratio. Third, there is an important performance gap between the proposed approach and the knowledge-based baseline approach.

However, the monolingual versions of both our approach (*run1*) and that baseline share the property of being good predictors of the performance of the cross-lingual versions. Therefore, we conclude that a straightforward way to improve the proposed system is to use better monolingual systems. Additionally, the method for selecting the set of language-traverse concepts can be improved by considering the transversality of the relationships and by the use of size-balanced multilingual corpora.

Acknowledgments

We are grateful to Nestor Ruiz of the Instituto Caro y Cuervo for supporting and promoting the participation in this competition by the students of the graduate course in computational analysis of the language. We would also like to thank María Catalina Suárez, Karen González and María Camila Escobar for their helpful discussions, valuable comments and suggestions.

References

Eneko Agirre, Daniel Cer, Mona Diab, Iñigo Lopez-Gazpio, and Lucia Specia. 2017. Semeval-2017 task 1: Semantic textual similarity multilingual and crosslingual focused evaluation. In *Proceedings of SemEval*.

Rami Al-Rfou, Bryan Perozzi, and Steven Skiena. 2013. Polyglot: Distributed word representations for multilingual nlp. In *Proceedings of the Seventeenth Conference on Computational Natural Language Learning*. ACL, pages 183–192.

Jose Camacho-Collados, Mohammad Taher Pilehvar, Nigel Collier, and Roberto Navigli. 2017. Semeval-2017 task 2: Multilingual and cross-lingual semantic word similarity. In *Proceedings of the 11th International Workshop on Semantic Evaluation (SemEval-2017)*. Association for Computational Linguistics, Vancouver, Canada, pages 15–26.

José Camacho-Collados, Mohammad Taher Pilehvar, and Roberto Navigli. 2015. A framework for the construction of monolingual and cross-lingual word similarity datasets. In *Proceedings of the Association for Computational Linguistics*. pages 1–7.

José Camacho-Collados, Mohammad Taher Pilehvar, and Roberto Navigli. 2016. Nasari: Integrating explicit knowledge and corpus statistics for a multilingual representation of concepts and entities. *Artificial Intelligence* 240:36–64.

Kenneth Ward Church and Patrick Hanks. 1990. Word association norms, mutual information, and lexicography. *Computational linguistics* 16(1):22–29.

Paul Jaccard. 1901. *Etude comparative de la distribution florale dans une portion des Alpes et du Jura*. Impr. Corbaz.

Sergio Jimenez, Claudia Becerra, and Alexander Gelbukh. 2012. Soft cardinality+ ml: learning adaptive similarity functions for cross-lingual textual entailment. In *Proceedings of the Sixth International Workshop on Semantic Evaluation, SemEval*. ACL, pages 684–688.

Sergio Jimenez, Claudia Becerra, and Alexander Gelbukh. 2013. Softcardinality: Learning to identify directional cross-lingual entailment from cardinalities and smt. In *Second Joint Conference on Lexical and Computational Semantics (* SEM)*. volume 2, pages 34–38.

Sergio Jimenez, Fabio A. Gonzalez, and Alexander Gelbukh. 2016. Mathematical properties of soft cardinality: Enhancing jaccard, dice and cosine similarity measures with element-wise distance. *Information Sciences* 367:373–389.

Tomas Mikolov, Kai Chen, Greg Corrado, and Jeffrey Dean. 2013. Efficient estimation of word representations in vector space. In *Proceedings of ICLR*.

George Miller. 1995. Wordnet: a lexical database for english. *Communications of the ACM* 38(11):39–41.

Roberto Navigli and Simone Paolo Ponzetto. 2012. Babelnet: The automatic construction, evaluation and application of a wide-coverage multilingual semantic network. *Artificial Intelligence* 193:217–250.

Morris Swadesh. 1950. Salish internal relationships. *International Journal of American Linguistics* 16(4):157–167.

Morris Swadesh. 1952. Lexico-statistic dating of prehistoric ethnic contacts: with special reference to north american indians and eskimos. *Proceedings of the American philosophical society* 96(4):452–463.

MERALI at SemEval-2017 Task 2 Subtask 1: a Cognitively Inspired approach

Enrico Mensa
University of Turin, Italy
Dipartimento di Informatica
mensa@di.unito.it

Daniele P. Radicioni
University of Turin, Italy
Dipartimento di Informatica
radicion@di.unito.it

Antonio Lieto
University of Turin, Italy
ICAR-CNR, Palermo, Italy
lieto@di.unito.it

Abstract

In this paper we report on the participation of the MERALI system to the SemEval Task 2 Subtask 1. The MERALI system approaches conceptual similarity through a simple, cognitively inspired, heuristics; it builds on a linguistic resource, the $\text{TTCS}^{\mathcal{E}}$, that relies on Babel-Net, NASARI and ConceptNet. The linguistic resource in fact contains a novel mixture of common-sense and encyclopedic knowledge. The obtained results point out that there is ample room for improvement, so that they are used to elaborate on present limitations and on future steps.

1 Introduction

Defining conceptual representations along with their associated reasoning procedures required and still requires truly interdisciplinary efforts, involving psychologists (Miller and Charles, 1991; Barsalou, 1999; Malt et al., 2015), philosophers (Machery, 2009; Gärdenfors, 2014), neuroscientists (Vigliocco et al., 2014), and computer scientists (Resnik, 1998; Agirre et al., 2009; Pilehvar and Navigli, 2015). Today, the ever-growing number of applications of semantic technologies demand for further investigation on concepts' meaning: this fact explains the popularity of issues rooted in and related to conceptual similarity, and the success of the present Semantic Word Similarity task (Camacho-Collados et al., 2017).

In this paper we present an approach to the computation of conceptual similarity based on a novel lexical resource, the $\text{TTCS}^{\mathcal{E}}$—so dubbed after Terms to Conceptual Spaces-Extended— that has been acquired by integrating two different sorts of linguistic resources, such as the encyclopedic knowledge available in BabelNet (Nav-

igli and Ponzetto, 2012) and NASARI (Camacho-Collados et al., 2015), and the common-sense grasped by ConceptNet (Speer and Havasi, 2012). The resulting representation enjoys the interesting property of being anchored to both resources, thereby providing a uniform conceptual access grounded on the sense identifiers provided by BabelNet.

The $\text{TTCS}^{\mathcal{E}}$ provides a conceptual representation inspired to Conceptual Spaces (CSs), a geometric representation framework where knowledge is represented as a set of limited though cognitively relevant quality dimensions (Gärdenfors, 2014). The CSs framework has been recently used to extend and complement the representational and inferential power allowed by formal ontologies with special emphasis on dealing with the corresponding typicality-based conceptual reasoning (Lieto et al., 2015, 2017); in this setting, the $\text{TTCS}^{\mathcal{E}}$ aims at providing a wide-coverage, cognitively based linguistic resource for this sort of knowledge, by extending previous work (Lieto et al., 2016; Mensa et al., 2017).

2 Concept Representation in the $\text{TTCS}^{\mathcal{E}}$

Concepts representation in the $\text{TTCS}^{\mathcal{E}}$ is consistent with CSs: each concept c is provided with a vector representation $\vec{c}$ providing information on the given concept along some semantic dimensions d. All concepts included in such description are referred to through BabelNet synset IDs, and dimensions themselves are a subset of the relationships available in ConceptNet. Such relations report common-sense information like, e.g., IsA, AtLocation, UsedFor, PartOf, MadeOf, HasA, CapableOf, etc.. For a full description of the employed properties we refer the reader to (Mensa et al., 2017).

Let D be the set of N dimensions. Each con-

Proceedings of the 11th International Workshop on Semantic Evaluations (SemEval-2017), pages 245–249,
Vancouver, Canada, August 3 - 4, 2017. ©2017 Association for Computational Linguistics

RelatedTo	*tool, food, table, cutlery, eating, knife, spoon, utensil*
IsA	*tool, cutlery, utensil*
AtLocation	*table, desk, plate*
UsedFor	*eating*
Antonym	*knife, spoon*
MadeOf	*metal*

Figure 1: Example of representation for the concept FORK (BN:00035902N). The representation has been made human-readable by displaying concept lexicalizations in place of their actual Babel synset IDs.

cept c_i in the linguistic resource is defined as a vector $\vec{c}_i = [s^i_1, .., s^i_N]$, where each s^i_h constitutes the set of concepts filling the dimension $d_h \in D$. Each s can contain an arbitrary number of values, or be empty. For example, the representation for the concept FORK includes information about 6 dimensions that are filled with overall 18 concepts, like illustrated in Figure 1.

The TTCS$^\mathcal{E}$ resource contains $14,677$ concepts, and it was built by starting from the $10K$ most frequent nouns present in the Corpus of Contemporary American English (COCA),[1] browsing over $11M$ associations available in ConceptNet and the $2.8M$ NASARI vectors. Concepts in the TTCS$^\mathcal{E}$ are filled, on average, with 14.90 (concept) values.[2]

3 Conceptual similarity with the TTCS$^\mathcal{E}$

Our similarity metrics does not employ WordNet taxonomy and distances between pairs of nodes, such as in (Wu and Palmer, 1994; Leacock et al., 1998), nor it depends on information content accounts either, such as in (Resnik, 1998).

Conversely, given the aforementioned representation for concepts, one principal assumption underlying our approach is that two concepts are

---

[1] http://corpus.byu.edu/full-text/.

[2] The final resource is available for download at the URL http://ttcs.di.unito.it.

similar insofar as they share values on the same dimension, such as when they are both used for the same ends, they share the same components, *etc..* Given two concepts $\vec{c}_i$ and $\vec{c}_j$, the conceptual similarity along each dimension —filled in both vectors— should be ideally computed as a function of the cardinality of the intersection between overlapping dimensions

$$\text{sim}(\vec{c}_i, \vec{c}_j) = \sum_{k=1}^{N} |s^i_k \cap s^j_k|$$

where s^i_k is the set of concepts filling the k-th dimension in the vector $\vec{c}_i$ representing the concept c_i. The rationale underlying this formula is to grasp shared features, thereby allowing us to provide an explanation based on common-sense accounts. For example, rather than computing a distance on WordNet or observing how frequently they co-occur, to justify the similarity score for the pair ⟨*bird, cock*⟩ we consider that each concept IsA 'animal'; and that both of them are RELATEDTO 'feather', 'chicken', 'roosting' and 'vertebrate'.

However, our approach is presently limited by the actual average filling factor, and by the noise that can be possibly collected by an automatic procedure built on top of the BabelNet and ConceptNet resources. To handle the possibly unbalanced number of concepts that characterize the different dimensions and to prevent the computation from being biased by more richly defined concepts, we adopt the Symmetrical Tversky's Ratio Model (Jimenez et al., 2013).

$$\text{sim}(\vec{c}_i, \vec{c}_j) = \frac{1}{N^*} \cdot \sum_{k=1}^{N^*} \frac{|s^i_k \cap s^j_k|}{\beta\,(\alpha a + (1-\alpha)\,b) + |s^i_k \cap s^j_k|}$$

where $|s^i_k \cap s^j_k|$ counts the number of shared concepts that are used as fillers for the dimension d_k in the concept $\vec{c}_i$ and $\vec{c}_j$, respectively; and a and b are computed as $a = \min(|s^i_k - s^j_k|, |s^j_k - s^i_k|)$, $b = \max(|s^i_k - s^j_k|, |s^j_k - s^i_k|)$; and N^* counts the dimensions actually filled with at least one concept in both vectors. The Symmetrical Tversky's Ratio Model allows us to tune the balance between cardinality differences (through the parameter α), and between $|s^i_k \cap s^j_k|$ and $|s^i_k - s^j_k|, |s^j_k - s^i_k|$ (through the parameter β). The parameters α and β were set to .8 and .2 for the experimentation, based on a parameter tuning performed on the RG, MC and WS-sim datasets (Rubenstein and Goodenough, 1965;

Dimension (h)	Dim. score	$\|s_h^{bird}\|$	$\|s_h^{cock}\|$	shared values
RELATEDTO	0.68	44	06	*feather, chicken roosting, vertebrate*
ISA	0.58	07	04	*animal*

Table 1: Example of computation of the conceptual similarity for the pair 'bird' and 'cock', by inspecting the actual content of the $\text{TTCS}^{\mathcal{E}}$ resource.

Miller and Charles, 1991; Agirre et al., 2009).

For example, in order to compute the semantic similarity between the concepts $bird$ and $cock$ the $\text{TTCS}^{\mathcal{E}}$ finds that the ISA and RELATEDTO dimensions are filled in both $\vec{c}_{bird}$ and $\vec{c}_{cock}$, thus $N^* = 2$ in the present setting. Figures in column $\|s_h^{bird}\|$ and $\|s_h^{cock}\|$ report about how many concepts were retrieved that fill each dimension; elements in the 'shared values' column detail how many concepts were found in common to be part of both concept descriptions along the given dimension. The final similarity score obtained by the $\text{TTCS}^{\mathcal{E}}$ is 0.63, against the 0.65 assigned in the gold standard.

4 Evaluation

The dataset proposed for the experimentation included 500 word pairs; thanks to the mixture of abstract/concrete concepts and named entities it can be considered as a very complete and challenging test bed. Results have been computed through Pearson and Spearman correlations (respectively, r and ρ) and their harmonic mean; the latter measure ranges between 0.789 (obtained by the LUMINOSO team) and 0, as displayed in Figure 2. In particular, MERALI obtained 0.589 (r), 0.600 (ρ) and 0.594, respectively. We presently focus on this run of the system and disregard the other one that attained substantially similar results, stemming from a slightly different parameters setting.

We dissected the dataset, to identify our system's weaknesses, to the ends of improving both the conceptual similarity computation procedures and the lexical resource. We noticed that out of the 500 overall word pairs, 405 involve concept comparisons, while in the reminder pairs we have at least one entity at stake (namely, 45 entity-entity pairs and 50 entity-concept pairs).

Comparisons involving entities are somehow different from those involving only concepts: for example, the cases where the semantic similarity is computed between a concept and an entity (e.g., in 'Darwin-evolution', 'Gauss-scientist',

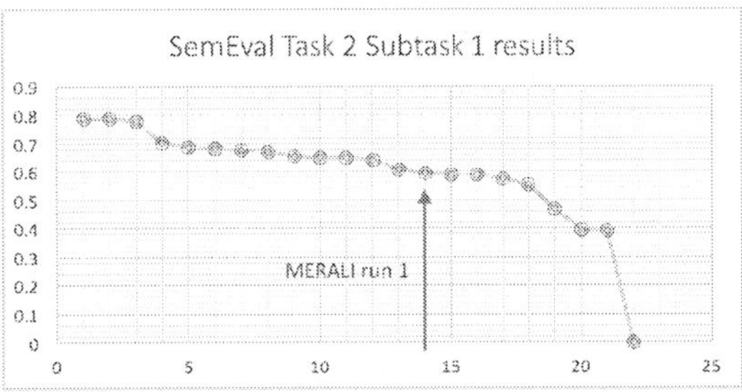

Figure 2: Results of the SemEval Task 2 Subtask 1 (English): harmonic mean between Spearman and Pearson correlations for each team.

'Siemens-electric train') pose additional problems with respect to cases in which two entities are considered (such as for 'Juventus-Bayern Munich', 'Plato-Aristotle', and 'Alexander Fleming-Penicillin'). Under an ontological perspective, individual entities act like instances, whilst concepts can be considered as classes: one thus wonders what does comparing individuals and classes mean. Moreover, according to the Conceptual Spaces framework, individuals can be thought of as points, while concepts are represented as regions over the multidimensional conceptual space. Comparisons between a class and an individual are intuitively harder in that they require i) to find the relations relating the individual and the class being examined; and ii) in a CSs perspective, to compare a point with a region. Furthermore, under a cognitive perspective, it is difficult to follow the strategy adopted by humans in providing a score for pairs such as 'Zara-leggings' (gold standard similarity judgement: 1.67): directly comparing a manufacturer and a product is nearly unfeasible, since their features can be hardly compared. Justifying the answer is perhaps helpful to give some information on the argumentative paths that can be followed to assess semantic similarity. One major risk, in these respects, is that instead of *similarity*, the scores provided by human annotators rather refer to generic *relatedness*. For example, let us consider the pair 'tail-Boeing 747' (gold standard similarity judgement: 1.92): although each Boeing 747 has a tail, the whole plane (holonym) cannot be conceptually similar to its tail (meronym), in the same way a door is not similar to its knob.

So we have re-run the statistical tests to compute Spearman and Pearson correlations over the three subsets (entity-entity, entity-concept, concept-concept); the partial results are reported

	# pairs	r	ρ	harm.mean
entire data	500	0.59	0.60	0.59
entity-entity	45	0.69	0.70	0.69
entity-concept	50	0.72	0.66	0.69
concept-concept	405	0.56	0.57	0.56

Table 2: Spearman (ρ) and Pearson (r) correlations (and their harmonic mean) obtained by the MERALI system over the three subsets.

in Table 2.

It turned out that, against our intuition, the MERALI system has better accuracy on word pairs including an entity; so we further examined the latter subset (concept-concept), where we obtained poorer results. Here we notice that in many cases (22, that is over 5% of this subset) overly high scores were determined by the maximization implemented in the word-similarity: in such cases, in fact, semantic similarity is usually computed as the similarity of the closest senses underlying the given terms (Budanitsky and Hirst, 2006). An example of this sort of errors is the pair 'apocalypse-fire' (gold standard similarity judgement: 1.25), where the MERALI system returned a value by far higher than the expected value (namely, 3.85): fires can legitimately be interpreted as apocalyptic events, but only in a figurative way. Similar, though distinct, differences in score are observed when comparing two identical concepts: not always human beings provide the maximum (equality) score, sometimes in unexpected way like for, e.g., 'movie-film' (gold standard similarity judgement: 3.92), 'multiple sclerosis-MS' (gold standard similarity judgement: 3.92). Out of 24 such cases, for 13 pairs (3% of this subset) we over-estimated the semantic similarity. As regards as fully different concept pairs (46, over 11%), in half cases we have over-estimated the similarity, perhaps due to a too permissive enriching routine that sometimes accepts noisy concepts as dimension fillers.

However, the main issue of the first version of the MERALI system is that the overall amount of information available to the system is often not enough to fully assess the semantic similarity between concepts. Sometimes concepts themselves have been missing, and missing concepts may be lacking in (at least one of) the resources upon which the TTCS$^\mathcal{E}$ is built. Also, difficulties stemmed from insufficient information for the concepts at stake: this phenomenon was observed, e.g., when both concepts have been found, but no common dimension has been filled. This sort of difficulty shows that the coverage of the resource still needs to be enhanced, especially by improving the extraction phase, so to add further concepts *per* dimension, and to fill more dimensions.

5 Conclusions

We have illustrated the system MERALI, that relies on a novel resource, the TTCS$^\mathcal{E}$. The underlying representation is compatible with the Conceptual Spaces framework and aims at putting together encyclopedic and common-sense knowledge. The results of the MERALI system have been illustrated and discussed. The experimentation clearly showed that there is room for improving the system along two main axes: dimensions must be filled with further information, and the quality of the extracted information should be improved. Also the computation of the similarity can be refined by testing further heuristics, so to reduce the cases of over-estimation of semantic similarity. All mentioned aspects will be addressed in our future work.

References

Eneko Agirre, Enrique Alfonseca, Keith Hall, Jana Kravalova, Marius Paşca, and Aitor Soroa. 2009. A study on similarity and relatedness using distributional and wordnet-based approaches. In *Proceedings of NAACL*. Association for Computational Linguistics, NAACL '09, pages 19–27.

Lawrence W Barsalou. 1999. Perceptions of perceptual symbols. *Behavioral and brain sciences* 22(04):637–660.

Alexander Budanitsky and Graeme Hirst. 2006. Evaluating wordnet-based measures of lexical semantic relatedness. *Computational Linguists* 32(1):13–47.

Jose Camacho-Collados, Mohammad Taher Pilehvar, Nigel Collier, and Roberto Navigli. 2017. Semeval-2017 task 2: Multilingual and cross-lingual semantic word similarity. In *Proceedings of the 11th International Workshop on Semantic Evaluation (SemEval 2017)*. Vancouver, Canada.

José Camacho-Collados, Mohammad Taher Pilehvar, and Roberto Navigli. 2015. NASARI: a novel approach to a semantically-aware representation of items. In *Proceedings of NAACL*. pages 567–577.

Peter Gärdenfors. 2014. *The geometry of meaning: Semantics based on conceptual spaces*. MIT Press.

Sergio Jimenez, Claudia Becerra, Alexander Gelbukh, Av Juan Dios Bátiz, and Av Mendizábal. 2013. Softcardinality-core: Improving text overlap with distributional measures for semantic textual similarity. In *Proceedings of *SEM 2013*. volume 1, pages 194–201.

Claudia Leacock, George A Miller, and Martin Chodorow. 1998. Using corpus statistics and wordnet relations for sense identification. *Computational Linguistics* 24(1):147–165.

Antonio Lieto, Enrico Mensa, and Daniele P. Radicioni. 2016. A Resource-Driven Approach for Anchoring Linguistic Resources to Conceptual Spaces. In *Procs of the XV International Conference of the Italian Association for Artificial Intelligence*. Springer, volume 10037 of *LNAI*, pages 435–449. https://doi.org/10.1007/978-3-319-49130-1.

Antonio Lieto, Andrea Minieri, Alberto Piana, and Daniele P. Radicioni. 2015. A knowledge-based system for prototypical reasoning. *Connection Science* 27(2):137–152.

Antonio Lieto, Daniele P. Radicioni, and Valentina Rho. 2017. Dual PECCS: A Cognitive System for Conceptual Representation and Categorization. *Journal of Experimental & Theoretical Artificial Intelligence* 29(2):433–452. https://doi.org/10.1080/0952813X.2016.1198934.

Edouard Machery. 2009. *Doing without concepts*. Oxford University Press.

Barbara C Malt, Silvia P Gennari, Mutsumi Imai, Eef Ameel, Noburo Saji, and Asifa Majid. 2015. 11 where are the concepts? what words can and cant reveal. *The conceptual mind: New directions in the study of concepts* page 291.

Enrico Mensa, Daniele P. Radicioni, and Antonio Lieto. 2017. TTCS$^\mathcal{E}$: a Vectorial Resource for Computing Conceptual Similarity. In *Proceedings of the 1st Workshop on Sense, Concept and Entity Representations and their Applications*. Association for Computational Linguistics, Valencia, Spain, pages 96–101. http://www.aclweb.org/anthology/W17-1912.

George A Miller and Walter G Charles. 1991. Contextual correlates of semantic similarity. *Language and cognitive processes* 6(1):1–28.

Roberto Navigli and Simone Paolo Ponzetto. 2012. BabelNet: The automatic construction, evaluation and application of a wide-coverage multilingual semantic network. *Artif. Intell.* 193:217–250.

Mohammad Taher Pilehvar and Roberto Navigli. 2015. From senses to texts: An all-in-one graph-based approach for measuring semantic similarity. *Artif. Intell.* 228:95–128.

Philip Resnik. 1998. Semantic similarity in a taxonomy: An information-based measure and its application to problems of ambiguity in natural language. *Journal of Artificial Intelligence Research* 11(1).

Herbert Rubenstein and John B Goodenough. 1965. Contextual correlates of synonymy. *Communications of the ACM* 8(10):627–633.

Robert Speer and Catherine Havasi. 2012. Representing General Relational Knowledge in ConceptNet 5. In *LREC*. pages 3679–3686.

Gabriella Vigliocco, Stavroula-Thaleia Kousta, Pasquale Anthony Della Rosa, David P Vinson, Marco Tettamanti, Joseph T Devlin, and Stefano F Cappa. 2014. The neural representation of abstract words: the role of emotion. *Cerebral Cortex* 24(7):1767–1777.

Zhibiao Wu and Martha Palmer. 1994. Verbs semantics and lexical selection. In *Proceedings of the 32nd annual meeting on Association for Computational Linguistics*. ACL, pages 133–138.

HHU at SemEval-2017 Task 2:
Fast Hash-Based Embeddings for Semantic Word Similarity Assessment

Behrang Qasemizadeh
DFG SFB 991
Universität Düsseldorf
Düsseldorf, Germany
zadeh@phil.hhu.de

Laura Kallmeyer
DFG SFB 991
Universität Düsseldorf
Düsseldorf, Germany
kallmeyer@phil.hhu.de

Abstract

This paper describes the HHU system that participated in Task 2 of SemEval 2017, Multilingual and Cross-lingual Semantic Word Similarity. We introduce our unsupervised embedding learning technique and describe how it was employed and configured to address the problems of monolingual and multilingual word similarity measurement. This paper reports from empirical evaluations on the benchmark provided by the task's organizers.

1 Introduction

The goal of Task 2 of SemEval-2017 is to provide a reliable benchmark for the evaluation of monolingual and multilingual semantic representations (Camacho-Collados et al., 2017). The proposed evaluation benchmark goes beyond classic semantic relatedness tests by providing both monolingual and cross-lingual data sets that include multiword expressions, domain-specific terms, and named entities for five languages. To measure 'semantic similarity' between pairs of lexical items, the HHU system uses the algorithm proposed in (QasemiZadeh et al., 2017), which is based on a derandomization of the 'random positive-only projections' method proposed by QasemiZadeh and Kallmeyer (2016).

Word embedding techniques (i.e., using distributional frequencies to produce word vectors of reduced dimensionality) are one of the most popular approaches to semantic word similarity problems. These methods are often rationalized using Harris' Distributional Hypothesis that words of similar linguistic properties appear with/within a similar set of 'contexts' (Harris, 1954). For example, words of related meanings co-occur with similar context words $\{c_1, \ldots c_n\}$.

This hypothesis implies that if these context words are grouped randomly into m buckets, e.g. $\{\{c_1 \ldots c_x\}_1, \ldots, \{c_y, \ldots c_n\}_m\}$, then co-related words still co-occur with similar sets of buckets. QasemiZadeh and Kallmeyer (2016) exploit this assumption and propose random positive-only projections for building word vectors directly at a reduced dimensionality m. In this paper, we propose a derandomization of this method and a hash-based technique for learning word embeddings. In Section 2, we describe our method. In Section 3, we report results obtained by applying this method to the shared-task benchmark. Finally, we conclude in Section 4.

2 Method

Our method consists of two logical routines: (a) a *text skimmer* to collect co-occurrence information; and (b) a *hash-based encoder* to build low-dimensional vectors from collected co-occurrences in (a). Evidently, these procedures can be merged and ordered differently to meet requirements of an application.

To build an m-dimensional embedding for an entity w (such as a word or phrase) that co-occurs with (or within) some context elements c (resulting from the skimming routine), we take the following steps:

Algorithm 1 : Encoding Co-Occurrences

1:   $\vec{w} = \vec{0}$
2: **for each** c co-occurring with w **do**
3:     d $\leftarrow$ abs(hash(c) % m)
4:     $\vec{w}_\mathrm{d} = \vec{w}_\mathrm{d} + 1$
   return $\vec{w}$

Here, w_d is the dth component of $\vec{w}$. The hash function assigns a hash code (e.g., an integer) to each context element c. The abs function returns the absolute value of its input number and % is the

Proceedings of the 11th International Workshop on Semantic Evaluations (SemEval-2017), pages 250–255,
Vancouver, Canada, August 3 - 4, 2017. ©2017 Association for Computational Linguistics

modulus operator and it gives the remainder of the division of the generated hash code by the chosen value m. We use the following `hash` function:[1]

```
int hash(byte[] key) {
  int i = 0;
  int hash = 0;
  while (i != key.length) {
    hash += key[i++];
    hash += hash << 10;
    hash ^= hash >> 6;
  }
  hash += hash << 3;
  hash ^= hash >> 11;
  hash += hash << 15;
  return hash;
}
```

Our choice for `hash` is motivated by its low collision rate for short words (byte sequences) and the closer resemblance of computed ds to an independent and identical distribution (i.i.d). It can be verified that the procedure proposed above implements a derandomization of QasemiZadeh and Kallmeyer's PoP method: The generated modulus of hash codes from context elements constitutes a random positive-only projection matrix, and the component-wise additions compute the multiplication of this randomly generated matrix with the original high-dimensional vectors (QasemiZadeh et al., 2017).

2.1 Computing Similarities

Once $\vec{w}$s are constructed, they are weighted by the expected and marginal frequencies, e.g., using positive pointwise mutual information (PPMI) (Church and Hanks, 1990; Turney, 2001). Let $\mathbf{W}_{p \times m}$ (consisting of p row vectors $\vec{w}$ of dimensionality m) be the set of embeddings in our model (i.e., the output of Algorithm 1). The PPMI weight for a component w_{xy} in $\mathbf{W}$ is given by:

$$ppmi(w_{xy}) = \max(0, \log \frac{w_{xy} \times \sum_{i=1}^{p} \sum_{j=1}^{m} w_{ij}}{\sum_{i=1}^{p} w_{iy} \times \sum_{j=1}^{m} w_{xj}}).$$

For this task, however, we adopt *cascaded PPMI weightings*: PPMI-weighted vectors are weighted once more using the above-mentioned formula, i.e., we compute $ppmi(ppmi(\mathbf{W}_{p \times m}))$. We believe this cascaded weighting yields better results by providing a well-balanced scaling of the original PPMI weights. Note that the weighting process is fast since it is carried out on vectors of small dimensionality m.

---

[1]Designed by Bob Jenkins (2006); see http://www.burtleburtle.net/bob/hash/doobs.html.

Finally, we compute similarities between these weighted vectors using a correlation measure. QasemiZadeh and Kallmeyer (2016) suggest Pearson's r for PPMI weighted vectors. Later, in QasemiZadeh et al. (2017), they suggest Goodman and Kruskal's γ coefficient (Goodman and Kruskal, 1954). To compute γ, *concordant* and *discordant* pairs must be counted. Given any pairs such as (x_i, y_i) and (x_j, y_j) from two m-dimensional vectors $\vec{x}$ and $\vec{y}$ and the value $v = (x_i - x_j)(y_i - y_j)$, these two pairs are concordant if $v > 0$ and discordant if $v < 0$. If $v = 0$, the pair is neither concordant nor discordant. Let p and q be the number of concordant and discordant pairs, then γ is given by (Chen and Popovich, 2002, p. 86):

$$\gamma = \frac{p - q}{p + q}.$$

In this paper, we suggest a new estimator based on Lin's information theoretic definition of similarity (Lin, 1998):

$$sim_{lin} = \log\left(\frac{2 \times \sum_{i=1}^{m}(x_i y_i)(1 + \log(2 + x_i y_i))}{\sum_{i=1}^{m} x_i^2 + \sum_{i=1}^{m} y_i^2}\right).$$

2.2 Extending the Method to Cross-Lingual Tasks

The proposed method can also be employed in a cross-lingual setting. However, this requires a small dictionary (translation-memory) and an additional pre-processing step.

In the pre-processing step, all pairs of lexical items in the input dictionary must be first mapped onto a common symbol space. Let's assume that the input dictionary consists of entries of the form $l \mapsto \{t_1, \ldots, t_n\}$ (i.e., l is a lexical item in the source language which has a number of t_i translations in the target language). To build the common symbol space, we generate all possible (l, t_i) tuples and we assign them *unique* identifiers—i.e., $(l, t_i) \mapsto s$. Finally, these tuples and their assigned identifiers are flattened in a symbol table t: for instance, if (l, t_i) are assigned to the unique identifier s, then the entries of (l, s) and (t_i, s) are stored in this table t. Note that the mappings in t are not necessarily one-to-one.

To build cross-lingual vectors for lexical items w in any of the input languages, similar to the monolingual setting, input corpora are scanned to collect context elements c. However, only those context elements that can be found in t are encoded into models. If t contains an identifier symbol s for a given context element c, then s is passed to Algorithm 1 to update vector $\vec{w}$.

3 Reports from Empirical Evaluation

3.1 General Settings

As input, we use the Wikipedia text corpora provided by the task organizers.[2] In our reports, we include results from the sense-based NASARI vectors (i.e., the baseline introduced by the organizers): 300-dimensional embeddings obtained using a hybrid approach (Camacho-Collados et al., 2016). The evaluation metric is the harmonic mean (H) of Pearson's r and Spearman ρ correlations between the test datasets (i.e., gold data constructed from scores assigned by humans to word pairs) and the corresponding system generated ones.

We treat multi-word expressions similar to single-token words. Given a list of tokens, instead of collecting co-occurrence information only for single tokens, we extend our scan of input corpora to contiguous n-gram sequences of tokens for which n is decided by the maximum length of items in the evaluation test sets. In effect, we limit the active vocabulary of our system and collect co-occurrence information only for those lexical items in the task's test sets.

3.2 Monolingual Subtask

To collect co-occurrence information from input corpora, given the small size of input corpora, we adapt a greedy approach. Input corpora are read line by line; if a lexical item w_t in our target vocabulary appears in a line at span i to j, we update $\vec{w}_t$ by passing the following items as context element to Algorithm 1:

Feature Sets:

- The whole line (as one unit): this is done to capture information about possible co-occurrences of test lexical items within a large context (such as done in word-by-document models).

- All the tokens from position $i - 20$ to $j + 20$ (i.e., including w_t), i.e., the classic sliding context window. We include w_t to enforce similarity between a pair of multiword lexical items of similar constituent tokens.

[2]https://sites.google.com/site/rmyeid/projects/polyglot

Lang	r	ρ	H	m	Weighting	Similarity	RUN
FA	.541	.585	.562	2000	Cascaded-PPMI	r	1
FA	.606	.601	.604	2500	Cascaded-PPMI	sim_{lin}	2
EN	.71	.699	.704	2500	Cascaded-PPMI	sim_{lin}	1
EN	.656	.697	.676	2500	Cascaded-PPMI	r	2

Table 1: Results for our official submissions.

- All n-grams ($n \in \{3, 4\}$) generated from each of the tokens appearing in the above sliding context window: this is done to capture information about the morphological structure of the context words.

Table 1 summarizes the results and configurations that we have used in our official submissions. For Farsi, for the first run, we built vectors of dimension $m = 2000$, weighted them using cascaded-PPMI (see Section 2.1) and used Pearson's r as a similarity measure. Evaluated by the organisers, this resulted in $r = 0.541$, $\rho = 0.585$, and the official score of $H = 0.562$. In the second run, however, we built vectors of dimensionality $m = 2500$ and after cascaded-PPMI weighting, similarities were computed using sim_{lin}. This resulted in scores of $r = 0.606$, $\rho = 0.601$, and $H = 0.604$. To choose these configurations, we relied on the trial data as well as resources introduce in Camacho-Collados et al. (2015). For English, we observed that adding n-gram features deteriorates results; hence, we removed this set of features from our model of dimensionality $m = 2500$. In both runs, we used cascaded-PPMI. As a similarity measure, we used sim_{lin} and Pearson's r in the first and second run, respectively. This produced a score of $r = 0.71$, $\rho = 0.699$, and $H = 0.704$ for the first run, and $r = 0.656$, $\rho = 0.697$, and $H = 0.676$ over the second run. Note that for both languages, we could build any vectors for a number lexical items since they did not occur in the input corpora (see the last column of Table 2 for details).

3.2.1 Extended Evaluations

While our official submissions are limited to English and Farsi, to provide a better understanding of the method's performance, we provide results for all the five languages in the monolingual subtask. To build models, we use the feature sets described in the previous section. The remaining hyper-parameter of our method is m (the dimensionality of models); we report results for $m \in \{300, 700, 2000\}$. Results obtained using various

| Lang | Baseline | | | Hash Method - WPPMI - SimPearson | | | | | | | | | #M |
| | | | | Dim =300 | | | Dim = 700 | | | Dim = 2000 | | | |
	r	ρ	H	r	ρ	H	r	ρ	H	r	ρ	H	
DE	0.513	0.514	**0.514**	0.439	0.436	**0.438**	0.537	0.574	**0.555** [↑]	0.603	0.655	**0.628** [↑]	16
EN	0.683	0.681	**0.682**	0.428	0.474	**0.450**	0.535	0.598	**0.564**	0.614	0.652	**0.632**	3
ES	0.602	0.597	**0.600**	0.512	0.568	**0.539**	0.576	0.644	**0.608** [↑]	0.665	0.719	**0.691** [↑]	7
FA	0.412	0.398	**0.405**	0.475	0.496	**0.486** [↑]	0.512	0.535	**0.523** [↑]	0.538	0.569	**0.553** [↑]	25
IT	0.597	0.594	**0.596**	0.469	0.503	**0.485**	0.537	0.589	**0.562**	0.616	0.674	**0.643** [↑]	12

Table 2: Results for vectors of various dimensionality (denoted by dim), and when using PPMI for weighting and Pearson's r for measuring similarity between them. H denotes the harmonic mean of r and ρ (i.e., the task's official score). #M is the number of lexical items which have not occurred in our input corpora; for pairs containing these items, we use 0 as a default value for similarity. Those settings that yield better results than the baseline are marked using ↑.

| Lang | Dim =300 | | | Dim = 700 | | | Dim = 2000 | | |
	r	ρ	H	r	ρ	H	r	ρ	H
DE	.576	.577	**.576** [↑]	.609	.609	**.609** [↑]	.619	.617	**.618** [↑]
EN	.633	.627	**.630**	.659	.653	**.656**	.644	.633	**.638**
ES	.660	.659	**.659** [↑]	.675	.670	**.673** [↑]	.669	.669	**.669** [↑]
FA	.449	.439	**.444** [↑]	.468	.458	**.463** [↑]	.517	.506	**.512** [↑]
IT	.609	.601	**.605** [↑]	.617	.611	**.614** [↑]	.618	.612	**.615** [↑]

Table 3: Method's performance when using PPMI for weighting and Goodman and Kruskal's γ for a similarity measurement. This combination gives the best performance for models of small dimensionality such as $m = 300$.

| Lang | Dim =300 | | | Dim = 700 | | | Dim = 2000 | | |
	r	ρ	H	r	ρ	H	r	ρ	H
DE	.392	.377	**.384**	.511	.515	**.513**	.616	.624	**.620** [↑]
EN	.435	.436	**.436**	.548	.553	**.551**	.632	.630	**.631**
ES	.506	.505	**.506**	.583	.578	**.580**	.673	.683	**.678** [↑]
FA	.477	.501	**.488** [↑]	.518	.540	**.529** [↑]	.551	.573	**.562** [↑]
IT	.445	.443	**.444**	.532	.534	**.533**	.643	.650	**.646** [↑]

Table 4: Method's performance when using the combination of PPMI and sim_{lin}.

| Lang | Dim =300 | | | Dim = 700 | | | Dim = 2000 | | |
	r	ρ	H	r	ρ	H	r	ρ	H
DE	.486	.486	**.486**	.587	.626	**.606** [↑]	.630	.675	**.651** [↑]
EN	.519	.538	**.528**	.608	.647	**.627**	.639	.668	**.653**
ES	.572	.626	**.598**	.646	.695	**.670** [↑]	.683	.721	**.701** [↑]
FA	.507	.521	**.514** [↑]	.535	.565	**.550** [↑]	.552	.595	**.573** [↑]
IT	.516	.538	**.527**	.597	.638	**.617** [↑]	.626	.670	**.647** [↑]

Table 5: Method's performance when using the combination of cascaded-PPMI and Pearson's r.

| Lang | Dim =300 | | | Dim = 700 | | | Dim = 2000 | | |
	r	ρ	H	r	ρ	H	r	ρ	H
DE	.551	.556	**.553** [↑]	.630	.633	**.631** [↑]	.648	.652	**.650** [↑]
EN	.608	.603	**.606**	.659	.653	**.656**	.661	.648	**.655**
ES	.647	.650	**.649** [↑]	.692	.688	**.690** [↑]	.688	.684	**.686** [↑]
FA	.500	.487	**.493** [↑]	.528	.517	**.523** [↑]	.559	.551	**.555** [↑]
IT	.593	.598	**.595**	.640	.633	**.636** [↑]	.637	.631	**.634** [↑]

Table 6: Method's performance when using the combination of cascaded-PPMI and γ.

combinations of weighting techniques and similarity measure are summarized in Table 2 to 7.[3]

Disregarding the choice of weighting technique and similarity measure, an increase in m often produces better results, but at the expense of higher computational cost. In addition, as suggested in Section 2.1, by comparing results between Table 2 to 4 and Table 5 to 7, we observe that using cascaded-PPMI weighting instead of simple PPMI weighting often yields better scores. The

| Lang | Dim =300 | | | Dim = 700 | | | Dim = 2000 | | |
	r	ρ	H	r	ρ	H	r	ρ	H
DE	.434	.454	**.444**	.597	.614	**.605** [↑]	.665	.686	**.675** [↑]
EN	.497	.508	**.502**	.641	.644	**.643**	.684	.677	**.680**
ES	.575	.589	**.582**	.677	.683	**.680** [↑]	.727	.733	**.730** [↑]
FA	.537	.557	**.547** [↑]	.582	.592	**.587** [↑]	.589	.605	**.597** [↑]
IT	.513	.513	**.513**	.634	.641	**.637** [↑]	.690	.693	**.692** [↑]

Table 7: Method's performance for the combination of cascaded-PPMI and sim_{lin}: This combination proves to provide the best results for high-dimensional models.

---

[3]Slight improvements in results for Farsi are due to homogenizing character encoding: Zero-width non-joiner characters (U+200c) are replaced by the space character (U+0020); the Arabic letter Kaf (U+0643) is replaced by the Farsi letter Kaf U+06A9, and the Arabic letter Yeh (U+064A) is replaced by the Farsi letter Yeh (U+FBFC).

Lang	r	ρ	H	RUN
EN-FA	0.519	0.492	0.505	Baseline
EN-FA	0.485	0.544	0.513	1
EN-FA	0.429	0.582	0.494	2

Table 8: Results for EN-FA detest.

only exception is when m is small (e.g., $m = 300$) and γ is used to measure similarities. For small $m = 300$, this combination of PPMI weighting and γ gives the best performance (Table 3); we witness that for $m = 300$, this combination also gives the best results for Camacho-Collados et al.'s data sets.

3.3 Cross-Lingual Subtask

We applied the methodology described in Section 2.2 to build cross-lingual embeddings for the pair emphEnglish and Farsi. To build the common symbol space, we extracted an English-to-Farsi translation dictionary from the English Wiktionary dump of January 2017, containing translations for 7500 lexical items in English. These 7500 entries were converted to a symbol table t of size 17760. We then augmented this table with Wikipedia's title translations. As a result, the number of entries in t increased to 1,299,770.

For each w in the test data set, we collected co-occurrences from a context window (extended 20 tokens at each side of w) for both words and multiword expressions that appear in t. Note that the sole input to our method was unaligned text from the English and Farsi Wikipedia corpus (similar to the monolingual setting). In both runs, we used vectors of dimensionality $m = 3000$ and the proposed sim_{lin} measure to compute similarities between vectors. To weight vectors, in the first run, we used cascaded-PPMI while we used simple PPMI for the second run. Table 8 provides a summary of the method's performance. Surprisingly, our simple methodology performs at least as well as the baseline technique.

Results reported in Table 8 can be easily improved by feeding in additional input, particularly parallel corpora. For instance, we observe that using the Open Subtitles corpus in addition to the Wikipedia corpus can enhance the results for the combination of cascaded-PPMI and sim_{lin} (Run 1) from $H = 0.505$ to 0.575.

4 Conclusion

This paper described the methodology behind the HHU system that participated in the SemEval 2017 shared task on semantic word similarity. The proposed technique uses a hash-based algorithm for building embeddings. The method is fast and simple, and it demands only a small amount of computational resources to build a model. As shown by empirical evaluations, our method shows acceptable performance in semantic similarity tasks. Our code is available for download (https://user.phil.hhu.de/~zadeh/ material/hash-vectors/) in order to replicate the results reported in this paper.

Acknowledgments

This work was supported by the CRC 991 "The Structure of Representations in Language, Cognition, and Science" funded by the German Research Foundation (DFG). We would like to thank Matthias Liebeck and Pashutan Modaresi for their comments and suggestions.

References

Jose Camacho-Collados, Mohammad Taher Pilehvar, Nigel Collier, and Roberto Navigli. 2017. Semeval-2017 task 2: Multilingual and cross-lingual semantic word similarity. In *Proceedings of the 11th International Workshop on Semantic Evaluation (SemEval-2017)*. Association for Computational Linguistics, Vancouver, Canada, pages 15–26. http://www.aclweb.org/anthology/S17-2002.

José Camacho-Collados, Mohammad Taher Pilehvar, and Roberto Navigli. 2015. A unified multilingual semantic representation of concepts. In *Proceedings of the 53rd Annual Meeting of the Association for Computational Linguistics and the 7th International Joint Conference on Natural Language Processing (Volume 1: Long Papers)*. Association for Computational Linguistics, Beijing, China, pages 741–751. http://www.aclweb.org/anthology/P15-1072.

José Camacho-Collados, Mohammad Taher Pilehvar, and Roberto Navigli. 2016. Nasari: Integrating explicit knowledge and corpus statistics for a multilingual representation of concepts and entities. *Artif. Intell.* 240:36–64. https://doi.org/10.1016/j.artint.2016.07.005.

Peter Y. Chen and Paula M. Popovich. 2002. *Correlation: Parametric and Nonparametric Measures*. Quantitative Applications in the Social Sciences. Sage Publications.

Kenneth Ward Church and Patrick Hanks. 1990. Word association norms, mutual information, and lexicography. *Comput. Linguist.* 16(1):22–29. http://dl.acm.org/citation.cfm?id=89086.89095.

Leo A. Goodman and William H. Kruskal. 1954. Measures of association for cross classifications. *Journal of the American Statistical Association* 49(268):732–764. http://www.jstor.org/stable/2281536.

Zellig S Harris. 1954. Distributional structure. *Word* 10(2-3):146–162.

Dekang Lin. 1998. An information-theoretic definition of similarity. In *Proceedings of the Fifteenth International Conference on Machine Learning*. Morgan Kaufmann Publishers Inc., San Francisco, CA, USA, ICML '98, pages 296–304. http://dl.acm.org/citation.cfm?id=645527.657297.

B. QasemiZadeh, L. Kallmeyer, and P. Passban. 2017. Sketching Word Vectors Through Hashing. *ArXiv e-prints* abs/1002.0035. https://arxiv.org/abs/1705.04253v1.

Behrang QasemiZadeh and Laura Kallmeyer. 2016. Random positive-only projections: PPMI-Enabled incremental semantic space construction. In *Proceedings of the Fifth Joint Conference on Lexical and Computational Semantics*. Association for Computational Linguistics, Berlin, Germany, pages 189–198. http://anthology.aclweb.org/S16-2024.

Behrang QasemiZadeh, Laura Kallmeyer, and Aurelie Herbelot. 2017. Projection aleatoire non-negative pour le calcul de word embedding. In *Proceedings of TALN 2017*.

Peter D. Turney. 2001. Mining the web for synonyms: PMI-IR versus LSA on TOEFL. In *Proceedings of the 12th European Conference on Machine Learning*. Springer-Verlag, London, UK, UK, EMCL '01, pages 491–502. http://dl.acm.org/citation.cfm?id=645328.650004.

Mahtab at SemEval-2017 Task 2: Combination of Corpus-based and Knowledge-based Methods to Measure Semantic Word Similarity

Niloofar Ranjbar
ni.ranjbar@Mail.sbu.ac.ir
Fatemeh Mashhadirajab
fa.mashhadi@gmail.com
Mehrnoush Shamsfard
m-shams@sbu.ac.ir
Rayehe Hosseini pour
Hosseinipour.r1@gmail.com
Aryan Vahid pour
aryanvahidpour@gmail.com
Faculty of Computer Science and Engineering / Shahid Beheshti University

Abstract

In this paper, we describe our proposed method for measuring semantic similarity for a given pair of words at SemEval-2017 monolingual semantic word similarity task. We use a combination of knowledge-based and corpus-based techniques. We use FarsNet, the Persian Word-Net, besides deep learning techniques to extract the similarity of words. We evaluated our proposed approach on Persian (Farsi) test data at SemEval-2017. It outperformed the other participants and ranked the first in the challenge.

1 Introduction

Semantic similarity represents a special case of semantic relatedness: for example, cars and gasoline would seem to be more closely related than, say, cars and bicycles, but the latter pair are certainly more similar(Resnik et al., 1999). Semantic similarity has been used in many application in natural language processing. At SemEval-2017 monolingual semantic word similarity task, given a pair of words, we have to automatically measure their semantic similarity and score them according to a [0-4] similarity scale where 4 denotes that the two words are synonymous and 0 indicates that they are completely dissimilar(Camacho-Collados et al., 2017). In subtask 1 in which we participated, the two words in the pair belong to the same language. This subtask provides five monolingual word similarity datasets in English, German, Italian, Spanish and Farsi. The language whose dataset we used is Farsi.

The rest of the paper is organized as follows. Section 2 reviews published work related to the semantic word similarity task. Section 3 explains the proposed algorithm. The experimental results are discussed in Section 4 and the conclusion and future work are reported in Section 5.

2 Related Works

There are different methods for finding semantic similarity and relation between two words. Christoph(Christoph, 2015)generally divides similarity measurement techniques into two categories: knowledge-based and corpus-based techniques. Some of the available techniques use a combination of these two methods. In knowledge-based techniques, a taxonomy or ontology like WordNet(Miller, 1995) usually is used to extract taxonomic information like path length and depth in the hierarchy(Pilehvar and Navigli, 2015). For example, the proposed methods by Resnik(Resnik, 1995), Lin(Lin et al., 1998)and FaITH(Pirró and Euzenat, 2010) fall in this category. In corpus-based techniques, usually a large corpus is used to extract statistical information. Christoph(Christoph, 2015) also divides corpus-based methods into two categories. One category contains simple distributional approaches, which check co-occurrences of words like SemSim(Bollegala et al., 2007) and PMI(Church and Hanks, 1990) . Another category contains dense vector representations-based methods, which usually use dimensionally reduction techniques in vector representations. LSA(tefănescu et al., 2014) , SGNS(Mikolov et al., 2013), SVD(Levy and Goldberg, 2014)and GLOVE(Pennington et al., 2014) are some methods which fall in this category.

In the proposed method, we use a combination of both knowledge-based and corpus-based

Proceedings of the 11th International Workshop on Semantic Evaluations (SemEval-2017), pages 256–260,
Vancouver, Canada, August 3 - 4, 2017. ©2017 Association for Computational Linguistics

techniques. On the one side, we have used FarsNet(Shamsfard et al., 2010a) ontology to enable knowledge-based techniques and on the other side we have used corpus-based techniques like Word2Vec(Mikolov et al., 2013) in order to improve results.

3 The Proposed Method

One of the corpus-based methods is continuous vector representation, also known as word embedding. For using this method, first we preprocess the Wikipedia corpus downloaded from Polyglot (Al-Rfou et al., 2013) and then we use Word2Vec toolkit, which is represented by deeplearnig4j library(Team, 2016) in java. Furthermore, we use some Lexical Resources such as FarsNet(Shamsfard et al., 2010a) (the Persian WordNet) and BabelNet(Navigli and Ponzetto, 2012) in order to measure similarity between pair of words. We explain this method in detail in sections 3.1 and 3.2.

3.1 Corpus-based Method

Preprocessing:Preprocessing includes four steps: stop-words removal, removing punctuations and numbers, stemming and normalizing multi word expressions by replacing all space characters with "zero-width non-joining" character.

First, we remove all Persian stop-words according to "ranks" website[1] , and then we remove punctuation marks and all English and Persian numbers in the text. After that, we replace plural words with their singular form and remove inflectional suffixes using STeP-1(Shamsfard et al., 2010b). Finally, we detect multi-word expressions, which appeared in corpus and contain only two words, by checking all bi-grams of corpus in FarsVaje Lexicon[2] and normalize them by replacing all space characters with "zero-width non-joining" character. We also replace multi-word expressions, which appeared in test dataset, with their normalized form.

Word2Vec: "Word2Vec is a two-layer neural network that processes text. Its input is a text corpus and its output is a set of vectors: feature vectors for words in that corpus. Deeplearning4j(Team, 2016) implements a distributed form of Word2vec for Java"[3].

---

[1]http://www.ranks.nl/stopwords/persian
[2]A lexicon developed at NLP lab of Shahid beheshti University and is used in Negar (Shamsfard et al., 2016)
[3]https://deeplearning4j.org/word2vec

To measure the similarity of two words first we measure the similarity of their corresponding synonyms. If there are n synonyms for the first word and m synonyms for the second, we will calculate the similarity for n*m pairs which are made of the Cartesian product of two synonym sets extracted from FarsNet (Word2Vec gives us cosine similarity and we consider it as similarity between a pair of words). At last, we choose maximum value of similarities as score of a pair of words. We use default tokenizer factory for tokenizing the corpus, which tokenizes the text by spaces and is useful for our purpose. We set Word2Vec parameters as below: minWord-Frequency= 1, iterations=1, layer Size=100, seed=42 and windowSize=5.

3.2 Knowledge-based Methods

FarsNet: FarsNet is a Lexical ontology for Persian language. This ontology is designed to contain a Persian WordNet with about 42000 synset in the last version, which we use to measure similarities. In this section, we will explain the approach we use to measure semantic distance between two words using some rules and then introduce a function, which map the measured distance to similarity score. First, we explain some strict rules introduced by(Rychalska et al., 2016) and then we explain some less strict rules:

1. If two words are exactly the same or are two different writing forms of one word or belong to the same synset, the distance will be zero ($D(x,y)=0$).

2. If two words have more than four common senses in their corresponding synsets, the distance will be one ($D(x, y) =1$).

3. If there is a direct or two-level hypernym relation between the corresponding synsets of words, the distance will be two ($D(x, y) =2$).

4. If two words share any common sense, the distance will be three ($D(x, y) =3$).

5. If two words are derivationally related, the distance will be four ($D(x, y) =4$).

If none of these rules met, we use the following rules, which are less strict:

1. If there is any relation except hypernym between synsets of two words, the distance will be three ($D(x, y) =3$).

257

2. If there is any two-links relation except hypernym between synsets of two words, the distance will be four (D(x, y) =4).

3. If there is any three-links relation between synsets of two words, the distance will be five (D(x, y) =5).

After all, if no relation is found between a pair of word to measure the distance between them, the distance will set to -1 and then we calculate similarity score using equation 1 introduced by(Rychalska et al., 2016):

$$A(x.y) = \begin{cases} \beta e^{-\alpha D(x,y)} & if\, D(x,y) \geq 0 \\ 0 & otherwise \end{cases} \quad (1)$$

We set α to 0.25 and β to 1 as these values seemed to yield the best results.

BabelNet: BabelNet is a very large, wide coverage multilingual semantic network. We use the version of Babel Net which was available on September 2016.

Semantic distance D is measured using the following rules for these pairs of words:

1. If words are exactly the same or one of them is main sense for another, the distance will be zero (D(x, y) =0).

2. If there is a direct named-relation between pairs, the distance will be one (Un-named relations are filtered e.g. semantically related) (D(x, y) =1).

3. If words share more than four common sense the distance will be two (D(x, y) =2).

4. If words share any common sense, the distance will be three (D(x, y) =3).

5. If their synsets share any important domain, the distance will be four (domains like media which are too general to be considered as a similarity measure are filtered) (D(x, y) =4).

6. If the main gloss of one of the words contains the other one the distance will be five (D(x, y) =5).

7. If there is a 2-link (indirect) n amed-relation between them, the distance will be six (D(x, y) =6).

If none of these rules met, D will set to -1 then we calculate similarity score using equation 1.

Gloss: We also use gloss of words extracted from FarsNet and BabelNet to measure similarity of a pair of words. A combination of the following methods is used (note that in all methods finally we calculate sum of intersections)

1. Gloss-Gloss: In this method, the intersection between glosses of both words is calculated.

2. Hyper-Hyper: In this method, the intersection between glosses of Hypernyms of both words is calculated.

3. Hypo-Hypo: In this method, the intersection between glosses of Hyponyms of both words is calculated.

4. Gloss-Hyper: In this method, we calculate the intersection between glosses of Hypernyms of the first word and glosses of the second word and vice versa (the intersection between glosses of Hypernyms of the second word and glosses of the first word) and finally we calculate sum of both intersections.

In order to calculate intersections, we use following method:

First, we remove stop-words from sentences and extract words, after that we choose longest common subsequence in each iteration and calculate square of its length as its score in that iteration. For example, suppose that we have two following sequences:

1,2,3,4,5 and 1,2,7,4.

In the first iteration 1, 2 is LCS and its length is 2 so the score in this iteration will be 4.

In the second iteration, we have two following sequences: 3,4,5 and 7,4 and 4 is LCS of these sequences with length of 1 so the final score will be 1+4=5.

After measuring all scores, we normalize all of them between 0 and 1 using following equations:

$$mean = \frac{1}{n} \sum_{i=1}^{n} x_i \quad (2)$$

$$variance = \frac{1}{n-1} \sum_{i=1}^{n} (x_i - mean)^2 \quad (3)$$

$$y = \frac{x_i - mean}{2 * \sqrt{variance}} \quad (4)$$

$$x = \frac{1}{1 + e^{-y}} \quad (5)$$

3.3 Combination of methods

To obtain the final similarity score for a pair of words, we calculate their normalized weighted sum using equations 6 and 7 :

$$score_{knowledge-based} =$$

$$score_{Farsnet} + 0.3 * score_{Babelnet} + 0.15 * score_{Gloss} \tag{6}$$

$$FinalScore =$$

$$\frac{score_{knowledge-based} + 0.75 * score_{W2V}}{2.2} \tag{7}$$

4 Experimental Results

We evaluated our proposed approach at SemEval 2017 and ranked first among the participants in task2, subtask1 for Farsi.Table 1 shows the results of the submitted runs on test data from SemEval 2017 task2-subtask1 for Farsi. Test data at SemEval 2017 task2 is available at :

```
alt.qcri.org/semeval2017/task2/
data/uploads/semeval17_task2_
test.zip
```

The test data for Farsi language contains 500 pairs of Farsi words that we have to measure their semantic similarity.

Farsi Test Data	Pearson	Spearman	Final
Mahtab	0.719	0.711	0.715
hhu_run2	0.606	0.601	0.604
hhu_run1	0.541	0.585	0.562
Luminoso_run2	0.507	0.498	0.503
Luminoso_run1	0.506	0.496	0.501
HCCL_run1	0.424	0.45	0.436
NASARI(baseline)	0.412	0.398	0.405
SEW_run1	0.383	0.404	0.393
RUFINO_run1	0.378	0.344	0.36
RUFINO_run2	0.25	0.262	0.256
hjpwhuer_run1	0.002	-0.003	0.0

Table 1: The results of the submitted runs on Farsi test data at SemEval 2017 task2_subtask1.

5 Conclusions and Future Work

This paper described our proposed method, a combination of corpus-based techniques like Word2Vec and knowledge-based techniques using FarsNet to measure semantic similarity between given pairs of words. The results show that our method achieved good results, better than other participants in the challenge. Future work will focus on enhancing the similarity measures besides using other corpus-based techniques like GloVe and LSA.

References

Rami Al-Rfou, Bryan Perozzi, and Steven Skiena. 2013. Polyglot: Distributed word representations for multilingual nlp. *arXiv preprint arXiv:1307.1662* .

Danushka Bollegala, Yutaka Matsuo, and Mitsuru Ishizuka. 2007. Measuring semantic similarity between words using web search engines. *www* 7:757–766.

Jose Camacho-Collados, Mohammad Taher Pilehvar, Nigel Collier, and Roberto Navigli. 2017. SemEval-2017 Task 2: Multilingual and Cross-lingual Semantic Word Similarity. In *Proceedings of SemEval*. Vancouver, Canada.

LOFI Christoph. 2015. Measuring semantic similarity and relatedness with distributional and knowledge-based approaches. *Information and Media Technologies* 10(3):493–501.

Kenneth Ward Church and Patrick Hanks. 1990. Word association norms, mutual information, and lexicography. *Computational linguistics* 16(1):22–29.

Omer Levy and Yoav Goldberg. 2014. Neural word embedding as implicit matrix factorization. In *Advances in neural information processing systems*. pages 2177–2185.

Dekang Lin et al. 1998. An information-theoretic definition of similarity. In *ICML*. Citeseer, volume 98, pages 296–304.

Tomas Mikolov, Kai Chen, Greg Corrado, and Jeffrey Dean. 2013. Efficient estimation of word representations in vector space. *arXiv preprint arXiv:1301.3781* .

George A Miller. 1995. Wordnet: a lexical database for english. *Communications of the ACM* 38(11):39–41.

Roberto Navigli and Simone Paolo Ponzetto. 2012. Babelnet: The automatic construction, evaluation and application of a wide-coverage multilingual semantic network. *Artificial Intelligence* 193:217–250.

Jeffrey Pennington, Richard Socher, and Christopher D Manning. 2014. Glove: Global vectors for word representation. In *EMNLP*. volume 14, pages 1532–1543.

Mohammad Taher Pilehvar and Roberto Navigli. 2015. From senses to texts: An all-in-one graph-based approach for measuring semantic similarity. *Artificial Intelligence* 228:95–128.

Giuseppe Pirró and Jérôme Euzenat. 2010. A feature and information theoretic framework for semantic similarity and relatedness. In *International semantic web conference*. Springer, pages 615–630.

Philip Resnik. 1995. Using information content to evaluate semantic similarity in a taxonomy. *arXiv preprint cmp-lg/9511007* .

Philip Resnik et al. 1999. Semantic similarity in a taxonomy: An information-based measure and its application to problems of ambiguity in natural language. *J. Artif. Intell. Res.(JAIR)* 11:95–130.

Barbara Rychalska, Katarzyna Pakulska, Krystyna Chodorowska, Wojciech Walczak, and Piotr Andruszkiewicz. 2016. Samsung poland nlp team at semeval-2016 task 1: Necessity for diversity; combining recursive autoencoders, wordnet and ensemble methods to measure semantic similarity. In *Proceedings of the 10th International Workshop on Semantic Evaluation (SemEval 2016)*.

M Shamsfard, H Fadaiei, and H.S Jafari. 2016. Negar: Persian Standardization System. Technical report, Shahid Beheshti University ,NLP Research Lab.

Mehrnoush Shamsfard, Akbar Hesabi, Hakimeh Fadaei, Niloofar Mansoory, Ali Famian, Somayeh Bagherbeigi, Elham Fekri, Maliheh Monshizadeh, and S Mostafa Assi. 2010a. Semi automatic development of farsnet; the persian wordnet. In *Proceedings of 5th Global WordNet Conference*. volume 29.

Mehrnoush Shamsfard, Hoda Sadat Jafari, and Mahdi Ilbeygi. 2010b. Step-1: A set of fundamental tools for persian text processing. In *LREC*.

Deeplearning4j Development Team. 2016. Deeplearning4j: Open-source distributed deep learning for the jvm. *Apache Software Foundation License* 2.0. http://deeplearning4j.org.

Dan tefănescu, Rajendra Banjade, and Vasile Rus. 2014. Latent semantic analysis models on wikipedia and tasa. In *Language Resources Evaluation Conference (LREC)*.

SEW-EMBED at SemEval-2017 Task 2: Language-Independent Concept Representations from a Semantically Enriched Wikipedia

Claudio Delli Bovi and **Alessandro Raganato**
Department of Computer Science
Sapienza University of Rome
`{dellibovi,raganato}@di.uniroma1.it`

Abstract

This paper describes SEW-EMBED, our language-independent approach to multilingual and cross-lingual semantic word similarity as part of the SemEval-2017 Task 2. We leverage the Wikipedia-based concept representations developed by Raganato et al. (2016), and propose an embedded augmentation of their explicit high-dimensional vectors, which we obtain by plugging in an arbitrary word (or sense) embedding representation, and computing a weighted average in the continuous vector space. We evaluate SEW-EMBED with two different off-the-shelf embedding representations, and report their performances across all monolingual and cross-lingual benchmarks available for the task. Despite its simplicity, especially compared with supervised or overly tuned approaches, SEW-EMBED achieves competitive results in the cross-lingual setting (3rd best result in the global ranking of subtask 2, score 0.56).

1 Introduction

Semantic similarity is a well established research area of Natural Language Processing, concerned with measuring the extent to which two linguistic items are similar (Budanitsky and Hirst, 2006). In particular, word similarity is nowadays a widely used evaluation benchmark for word and sense representations (Turney and Pantel, 2010).

While many classical approaches to word similarity have been limited to the English language (Gabrilovich and Markovitch, 2007; Mihalcea, 2007; Pilehvar et al., 2013; Baroni et al., 2014), a growing interest for multilingual and

cross-lingual models is emerging (Hassan and Mihalcea, 2011; Camacho Collados et al., 2016) and it is accompanied by the development of multilingual benchmarks (Gurevych, 2005; Granada et al., 2014; Camacho Collados et al., 2015).

In this respect Wikipedia, as one of the most popular semi-structured resources in the field (Hovy et al., 2013), provides a convenient bridge to multilinguality, with several million inter-language links among articles refferring to the same concept or entity. In fact, a number of successful approaches to semantic similarity make explicit use of Wikipedia, from ESA (Gabrilovich and Markovitch, 2007) to NASARI (Camacho Collados et al., 2016). Others, like SENSEMBED (Iacobacci et al., 2015), report state-of-the-art results when trained on an automatically disambiguated version of a Wikipedia dump. Regardless of whether Wikipedia is seen as a multilingual semantic network of concepts and entities or as a sense-annotated corpus, *hyperlinks* (inter-page links) constitute its key structural property: in light of this, Raganato et al. (2016) addressed the sparsity problem of original hyperlinks and developed SEW[1], a semantically enriched Wikipedia where the overall number of linked mentions has been more than tripled by solely exploiting the structure of Wikipedia itself and the wide-coverage sense inventory of Babel-Net (Navigli and Ponzetto, 2012)[2].

In addition to building the corpus, the authors used SEW's sense annotations to construct vector representations of concepts and entities from the BabelNet sense inventory, and tested them on multiple semantic similarity tasks. Being defined at the concept level, SEW's representations are inherently multilingual: however, they consist of high-

---

[1] `http://lcl.uniroma1.it/sew`
[2] `http://babelnet.org`

Proceedings of the 11th International Workshop on Semantic Evaluations (SemEval-2017), pages 261–266,
Vancouver, Canada, August 3 - 4, 2017. ©2017 Association for Computational Linguistics

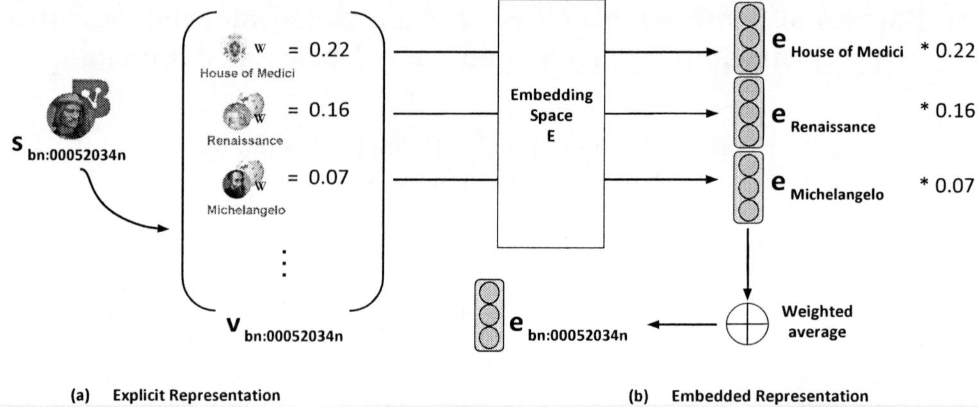

Figure 1: Illustrative example of SEW-EMBED's embedded representation (*b*) for the BabelNet entity *Lorenzo de Medici* (`bn:00052034n`) obtained from the corresponding explicit representation (*a*).

dimensional sparse vectors, not immediately comparable with existing approaches, especially those based on word embeddings, and less flexible to use within downstream applications.

In this paper we propose SEW-EMBED, an embedded augmentation of SEW's original representations in which sparse vectors, defined in the high-dimensional space of Wikipedia pages, are mapped to continuous vector representations via a weighted average of embedded vectors from an arbitrary, pre-specified word (or sense) representation. Regardless of the particular representation used, the resulting vectors are still defined at the concept level, and hence immediately expendable in a multilingual and cross-lingual setting.

We describe and evaluate SEW-EMBED with two off-the-shelf embedded representations: the popular word embeddings of Word2Vec (Mikolov et al., 2013a) and the embedded concept representations of NASARI (Camacho Collados et al., 2016)[3]. We report and discuss the results obtained by both versions on all monolingual and cross-lingual benchmarks available for the task (Camacho Collados et al., 2017), and include a comparison with the original explicit representations of Raganato et al. (2016).

2 Background: Developing a Semantically Enriched Wikipedia

The approach used by Raganato et al. (2016) to develop SEW relies on a cascade of *hyperlink propagation heuristics*, applied to an English Wikipedia

dump after some standard pre-processing. In general terms, each propagation heuristic identifies a list of BabelNet synsets to be propagated across a given Wikipedia page p; then, for each synset, occurrences of any of its potential lexicalizations are detected and added as new sense annotations for p. Raganato et al. (2016) distinguishes between intra-page and inter-page heuristics (depending on whether the synsets propagated across p are collected from the same page), but all of them share a common assumption: every occurrence of an ambiguous mention within p refers to the same underlying sense (*one sense per page*) and hence it is annotated with the same synset.[4] After all heuristics have been applied, overlapping mentions and duplicates are removed by enforcing a conservative policy which favors intra-page annotations over inter-page ones, and selects the longest match in case of overlapping annotations of the same type.

The result of this process is SEW, a Wikipedia-based corpus with over 200 million sense annotations of BabelNet synsets for all open-class parts of speech (nouns, verbs, adjectives, and adverbs).

3 SEW-EMBED: Building Vectors from Sense Annotations

In this section we provide the details of SEW-EMBED. We start by briefly describing the original explicit representations based on SEW (Section 3.1) and then our embedded augmentation (Section 3.2). The workflow of our procedure is depicted in Figure 1 with an illustrative example.

---

[3] `http://lcl.uniroma1.it/nasari`

[4] Although restrictive, this assumption is surprisingly accurate, as shown also in previous work (Wu and Giles, 2015).

3.1 Explicit Representation

As a starting point, we consider the Wikipedia-based representation (WB-SEW) by Raganato et al. (2016), in which each concept or entity s in the BabelNet sense inventory is represented as a vector v_s where dimensions are Wikipedia pages. For each Wikipedia page p in SEW, the corresponding component of v_s is computed as the estimated frequency of s appearing as sense annotation in p. Frequency is estimated using *lexical specificity* (Lafon, 1980), a statistical measure based on the hypergeometric distribution, particularly suitable for extracting an accurate set of representative terms for a given subcorpus SC of a reference corpus RC. We applied the procedure described by Camacho Collados et al. (2016), with the single page p as SC and the whole SEW as RC. As a result we obtain v_s, a rather sparse vector in which non-zero components correspond to the Wikipedia pages where s appears as a hyperlink; the weight ω_p associated with each component reflects the representativeness of s in the context described by p (Figure 1a).

3.2 Embedded Representation

In order to compute the embedded augmentation of an explicit vector v_s, obtained as in Section 3.1 for a given concept or entity s, we follow Camacho Collados et al. (2016) and exploit the compositionality of word embeddings (Mikolov et al., 2013b). According to this property, the representation of an arbitrary compositional phrase can be expressed as the combination (typically the average) of its constituents' representations. We build on this property and plug a pre-trained embedding representation into the explicit representation of Raganato et al. (2016). In particular, we consider each dimension p (i.e. Wikipedia page, cf. Section 3.1) of v_s and map it to the embedding space E provided by the pre-trained representation to obtain an embedded vector e_p. Such mapping depends on the specific embedding representation:

- In case of a *word* embedding representation we consider the Wikipedia page title as lexicalization of p and then retrieve the associated pre-trained embedding. If the title is a multi-word expression and no embedding is available for the whole expression, we exploit compositionality again and average the embedding vectors of its individual tokens;

- In case of a *sense* or *concept* embedding representation we instead exploit BabelNet's inter-resource links, and map p to the target sense inventory for which the corresponding embedding vector can be retrieved.

The embedded representation e_s of s (Figure 1b) is then computed as the weighted average over all the embedded vectors e_p associated with the dimensions of v_s:

$$e_s = \frac{\sum_{p \in v_s} \omega_p \, e_p}{\sum_{p \in v_s} \omega_p} \tag{1}$$

where ω_p is the lexical specificity weight of dimension p. In contrast to a simple average, here we exploit the ranking of each dimension p (represented by ω_p) and hence give more importance to the higher weighted dimensions of v_s.

3.3 Word Similarity

In order to calculate similarity at the word level, we follow other sense-based approaches (Pilehvar et al., 2013; Camacho Collados et al., 2016) and adopt a strategy that selects, for a given word pair w_1 and w_2, the *closest* pair of candidate senses:

$$Sim(w_1, w_2) = \max_{s_1 \in S_{w_1}, s_2 \in S_{w_2}} \sigma(\vec{s_1}, \vec{s_2}) \tag{2}$$

where S_w is the set of candidate senses of w in the BabelNet sense inventory, and $\vec{s}$ is the vector representation associated with $s \in S_w$. As similarity measure σ we use standard *cosine similarity* for SEW-EMBED (Section 3.2), and *weighted overlap* (Pilehvar et al., 2013) for the explicit representations based on SEW (Section 3.1).

Finally, we rely on a back-off strategy that set $Sim(w_1, w_2) = 0.5$ (i.e. the middle point in our similarity scale) when no candidate sense is found for either w_1 or w_2.

4 Experiments

In this section we report and discuss the performance of SEW-EMBED on the monolingual and cross-lingual benchmark of the Semeval 2017 Task 2 (Camacho Collados et al., 2017). We consider two versions of SEW-EMBED: one based on the pre-trained word embeddings of Word2Vec (Mikolov et al., 2013a, **SEW-EMBED**$_{w2v}$)[5], and another one based on the

---

[5] We utilized the pre-trained models available at `https://code.google.com/archive/p/word2vec`. These models were trained on a Google News corpus of about 100 billion words.

	EN			FA			DE			IT			ES		
	r	ρ	Mean	r	ρ	Mean	r	ρ	Mean	r	ρ	Mean	r	ρ	Mean
SEW-EMBED$_{w2v}$	0.56	0.58	0.57	0.38	0.40	0.39	0.45	0.45	0.45	0.57	0.57	0.57	0.61	0.62	0.62
SEW-EMBED$_{Nasari}$	0.57	0.61	0.59	0.30	0.40	0.34	0.38	0.45	0.42	0.56	0.62	0.59	0.59	0.64	0.62
SEW	0.61	0.67	0.64	**0.51**	**0.56**	**0.53**	**0.51**	0.53	0.52	**0.63**	**0.70**	**0.66**	**0.60**	**0.66**	**0.63**
NASARI	**0.68**	**0.68**	**0.68**	0.41	0.40	0.41	**0.51**	0.51	0.51	0.60	0.59	0.60	**0.60**	0.60	0.60

Table 1: Results on the multilingual word similarity benchmarks (subtask 1) of Semeval 2017 task 2, in terms of Pearson correlation (r), Spearman correlation (ρ), and the harmonic mean of r and ρ.

	DE-ES			DE-FA			DE-IT			EN-DE			EN-ES		
	r	ρ	Mean	r	ρ	Mean	r	ρ	Mean	r	ρ	Mean	r	ρ	Mean
SEW-EMBED$_{w2v}$	0.52	0.54	0.53	0.42	0.44	0.43	0.52	0.52	0.52	0.50	0.53	0.51	0.59	0.60	0.59
SEW-EMBED$_{Nasari}$	0.47	0.55	0.51	0.35	0.45	0.39	0.47	0.55	0.51	0.46	0.55	0.50	0.59	0.63	0.61
SEW	**0.57**	**0.61**	**0.59**	**0.53**	**0.58**	**0.56**	**0.59**	**0.64**	**0.61**	0.58	**0.62**	**0.60**	0.61	**0.63**	0.61
NASARI	0.55	0.55	0.55	0.46	0.45	0.46	0.56	0.56	0.56	**0.60**	0.59	**0.60**	**0.64**	**0.63**	**0.63**

	EN-FA			EN-IT			ES-FA			ES-IT			IT-FA		
	r	ρ	Mean	r	ρ	Mean	r	ρ	Mean	r	ρ	Mean	r	ρ	Mean
SEW-EMBED$_{w2v}$	0.46	0.49	0.48	0.58	0.60	0.59	0.50	0.53	0.52	0.59	0.60	0.60	0.48	0.50	0.49
SEW-EMBED$_{Nasari}$	0.41	0.52	0.46	0.59	0.65	0.62	0.44	0.54	0.48	0.58	0.64	0.61	0.42	0.52	0.47
SEW	**0.58**	**0.63**	**0.61**	0.64	**0.71**	**0.68**	**0.59**	**0.65**	**0.62**	**0.63**	**0.70**	**0.66**	**0.59**	**0.65**	**0.62**
NASARI	0.52	0.49	0.51	**0.65**	0.65	0.65	0.49	0.47	0.48	0.60	0.59	0.60	0.50	0.48	0.49

Table 2: Results on the cross-lingual word similarity benchmarks (subtask 2) of Semeval 2017 task 2, in terms of Pearson correlation (r), Spearman correlation (ρ), and the harmonic mean of r and ρ.

embedded concept vectors of NASARI (Camacho Collados et al., 2016, **SEW-EMBED**$_{Nasari}$). In all test sets, the figures of **SEW-EMBED**$_{w2v}$ correspond to the results of SEW-EMBED reported in the task description paper (Camacho Collados et al., 2017). We additionally include the results obtained by the original explicit representations based on SEW (cf. Section 3.1) and by the NASARI baseline, and use them as comparison systems across Sections 4.1 and 4.2.[6]

4.1 Subtask 1: Multilingual Word Similarity

Table 1 shows the overall performance on multilingual word similarity for each monolingual dataset. Both **SEW-EMBED**$_{w2v}$ and **SEW-EMBED**$_{Nasari}$ achieve comparable results: their correlation figures are in the same ballpark as the NASARI baseline for Italian, Farsi, and Spanish; instead, they lag behind in English and German. Most surprisingly, however, the explicit representations based on SEW show an impressive performance, and reach the best result overall in 4 out of 5 benchmarks: this might suggest that many word pairs across the test sets are actually being associated with concepts or entities that are well

connected in the semantically enriched Wikipedia, and hence the corresponding sparse vectors are representative enough to provide meaningful comparisons. In general, the performance decrease on German and Farsi for all comparison systems is connected to the lack of coverage: both SEW and SEW-EMBED use the back-off strategy (cf. Section 3.3) 70 times for Farsi (14%) and 54 times (10.8%) for German.

4.2 Subtask 2: Cross-lingual Word Similarity

Table 2 reports the overall performance on cross-lingual word similarity for each language pair. Consistently with the multilingual evaluation (Section 4.1), both **SEW-EMBED**$_{w2v}$ and **SEW-EMBED**$_{Nasari}$ achieve comparable results in the majority of benchmarks. All approaches based on SEW seem to perform globally better in a cross-lingual setting: on average, the harmonic mean of r and ρ is 2.2 points below the NASARI baseline (compared to 3.2 points in the evaluation of Section 4.1). This suggests the potential of Wikipedia as a bridge to multilinguality: in fact, even though SEW was constructed automatically on the English Wikipedia, knowledge transfers rather well via inter-language links and has a considerable impact on the cross-lingual performance.

---

[6]For an extensive comparison including all participating systems in the task, the reader is referred to the task description paper (Camacho Collados et al., 2017).

Again, the best figures are consistently achieved by the explicit representations based on SEW: the improvement in terms of harmonic mean of r and ρ is especially notable in benchmarks that include a less-resourced language such as Farsi (+11.75% on average compared to the NASARI baseline). This improvement does not occur with SEW-EMBED, since in that case sparse vectors are eventually mapped to an embedding space trained specifically on an English corpus.

4.3 General Discussion

Overall, SEW-EMBED reached the 4th and 3rd positions in the global rankings of subtask 1 and 2 respectively (with scores 0.552 and 0.558, not including the NASARI baseline). Thus, perhaps surprisingly, the embedded augmentation yielded a considerable decrease in terms of global performance in both subtasks, where the original explicit representations of SEW achieved a global score of 0.615 in subtask 1, and a global score of 0.63 in subtask 2 (cf. Sections 4.1-4.2).[7]

Intuitively, multiple factors might have influenced this negative result:

- **Dimensionality Reduction.** Converting an explicit vector (with around 4 million dimensions) into a latent vector of a few hundred dimensions leads inevitably to losing some valuable information, and hence to a decrease in the representational power of the model. Such a phenomenon was also shown by Camacho Collados et al. (2016), where the lexical and unified representations of NASARI tend to outperform the embedded representation on several word similarity and sense clustering benchmarks;

- **Lexical Ambiguity.** While the original concept vectors of SEW are defined in the unambiguous semantic space of Wikipedia pages, we constructed their embedded counterparts via the word-level representations of their lexicalized dimensions (Section 3.2); hence, when moving to the word level, we ended up conflating the different meanings of an ambiguous word or expression;[8]

- **Non-Compositionality.** The compositional properties of word embeddings that we assumed in Section 3.2 falls short in many cases, such as idiomatic expressions or named entity mentions (e.g. *Wall Street*, or *New York*). The explicit vectors of SEW, instead, do not require the compositional assumption and always consider a multi-word expression as a whole.

Even though the embedded representations of SEW do not match up to the accuracy of explicit ones on experimental benchmarks, they are on the other hand more convenient in terms of compactness and flexibility (due to the reduced dimensionality), and also in terms of comparability, as they are defined in the same vector space of Word2Vec-based representations such as the embedded vectors of NASARI (Camacho Collados et al., 2016) or DECONF (Pilehvar and Collier, 2016).

5 Conclusion

In this paper we presented SEW-EMBED, a language-independent concept representation approach which we put forward as a competitor system in the Semeval-2017 Task 2 (Camacho Collados et al., 2017). SEW-EMBED is tied to a Wikipedia-based sense-annotated corpus, SEW (Raganato et al., 2016), obtained automatically by exploiting the hyperlink structure of Wikipedia and the wide-coverage sense inventory of BabelNet. SEW is used to construct sparse vector representations in the space of Wikipedia pages, which are then mapped to an embedded representation by plugging in an arbitrary word (or sense) embedding model and computing a weighted average. We described and evaluated SEW-EMBED on all benchmarks available for the task, together with the explicit sparse vectors originally proposed by Raganato et al. (2016). In spite of the methodological simplicity of the approach (which was designed as an extrinsic test bed for the quality of SEW's annotations), global figures put SEW-EMBED close to, or on par with, state-of-the-art approaches such as NASARI. In particular, we showed that a cross-lingual setting yields the best overall improvement for concept representations based entirely on SEW, suggesting its potential for multilingual and cross-lingual applications.

---

[7] The global score is computed as the average harmonic mean of Pearson and Spearman correlation on the best four (subtask 1) and six (subtask 2) individual benchmarks (Camacho Collados et al., 2017).

[8] E.g., in SEW-EMBED$_{w2v}$, the distinct explicit dimensions represented in SEW by the Wikipedia pages BANK and BANK (GEOGRAPHY) were both mapped to the Word2Vec embedding of *bank*.

References

Marco Baroni, Georgiana Dinu, and Germán Kruszewski. 2014. Don't count, predict! A systematic comparison of context-counting vs. context-predicting semantic vectors. In *Proc. of ACL*. pages 238–247.

Alexander Budanitsky and Graeme Hirst. 2006. Evaluating WordNet-based Measures of Lexical Semantic Relatedness. *Computational Linguistics* 32(1):13–47.

José Camacho Collados, Mohammad Taher Pilehvar, Nigel Collier, and Roberto Navigli. 2017. SemEval-2017 Task 2: Multilingual and Cross-lingual Semantic Word Similarity. In *Proc. of SemEval*. pages 15–26.

José Camacho Collados, Mohammad Taher Pilehvar, and Roberto Navigli. 2015. A Framework for the Construction of Monolingual and Cross-lingual Word Similarity Datasets. In *Proc. of ACL*. pages 1–7.

José Camacho Collados, Mohammad Taher Pilehvar, and Roberto Navigli. 2016. Nasari: Integrating explicit knowledge and corpus statistics for a multilingual representation of concepts and entities. *Artificial Intelligence* 240:36–64.

Evgeniy Gabrilovich and Shaul Markovitch. 2007. Computing Semantic Relatedness Using Wikipedia-based Explicit Semantic Analysis. In *Proc. of IJCAI*. pages 1606–1611.

Roger Granada, Cassia Trojahn, and Renata Vieira. 2014. Comparing Semantic Relatedness between Word Pairs in Portuguese using Wikipedia. In *Computational Processing of the Portuguese Language*. pages 170–175.

Iryna Gurevych. 2005. Using the Structure of a Conceptual Network in Computing Semantic Relatedness. In *Proceedings of the Second International Joint Conference on Natural Language Processing*. pages 767–778.

Samer Hassan and Rada Mihalcea. 2011. Semantic Relatedness Using Salient Semantic Analysis. In *Proc. of AAAI*. pages 884–889.

Eduard Hovy, Roberto Navigli, and Simone Paolo Ponzetto. 2013. Collaboratively built semi-structured content and Artificial Intelligence: The story so far. *Artificial Intelligence* 194:2–27.

Ignacio Iacobacci, Mohammad Taher Pilehvar, and Roberto Navigli. 2015. SensEmbed: Learning Sense Embeddings for Word and Relational Similarity. In *Proc. of ACL*. pages 95–105.

Pierre Lafon. 1980. Sur la variabilité de la fréquence des formes dans un corpus. *Mots* 1(1):127–165.

Rada Mihalcea. 2007. Using Wikipedia for Automatic Word Sense Disambiguation. In *Proc. of NAACL-HLT*. pages 196–203.

Tomas Mikolov, Kai Chen, Greg Corrado, and Jeffrey Dean. 2013a. Efficient estimation of word representations in vector space. In *ICLR Workshop*.

Tomas Mikolov, Ilya Sutskever, Kai Chen, Greg Corrado, and Jeffrey Dean. 2013b. Distributed Representations of Words and Phrases and Their Compositionality. In *Proc. of NIPS*. pages 3111–3119.

Roberto Navigli and Simone Paolo Ponzetto. 2012. BabelNet: The Automatic Construction, Evaluation and Application of a Wide-Coverage Multilingual Semantic Network. *Artificial Intelligence* 193:217–250.

Mohammad Taher Pilehvar and Nigel Collier. 2016. De-conflated semantic representations. In *Proc. of EMNLP*. pages 1680–1690.

Mohammad Taher Pilehvar, David Jurgens, and Roberto Navigli. 2013. Align, Disambiguate and Walk: a Unified Approach for Measuring Semantic Similarity. In *Proc. of ACL*. pages 1341–1351.

Alessandro Raganato, Claudio Delli Bovi, and Roberto Navigli. 2016. Automatic Construction and Evaluation of a Large Semantically Enriched Wikipedia. In *Proc. of IJCAI*. pages 2894–2900.

Peter D. Turney and Patrick Pantel. 2010. From Frequency to Meaning: Vector Space Models of Semantics. *Journal of Artificial Intelligence Research* 37(1):141–188.

Zhaohui Wu and C. Lee Giles. 2015. Sense-aware Semantic Analysis: A Multi-prototype Word Representation Model using Wikipedia. In *Proc. of AAAI*. pages 2188–2194.

Wild Devs' at SemEval-2017 Task 2: Using Neural Networks to Discover Word Similarity

Răzvan-Gabriel Rotari, Ionuț Hulub, Ștefan Oprea, Mihaela Plămadă-Onofrei, Alina
Beatrice Lorenț, Raluca Preisler, Adrian Iftene, Diana Trandabăț

University Alexandru Ioan Cuza of Iași, Romania
{razvan.rotari, ionut.hulub, stefan.oprea, mihaela.onofrei,
alina.lorent, raluca.preisler, adiftene, dtrandabat}@info.uaic.ro

Abstract

This paper presents Wild Devs' participation in the SemEval-2017 Task 2 "Multilingual and Cross-lingual Semantic Word Similarity", which tries to automatically measure the semantic similarity between two words. The system was build using neural networks, having as input a collection of word pairs, whereas the output consists of a list of scores, from 0 to 4, corresponding to the degree of similarity between the word pairs.

1 Introduction

The Wild Dev's team participated this year in SemEval 2017 Task 2, subtask 1, in the evaluation for the English language. The system is based on a neural network, trained on an enriched corpus of word pairs.

The paper is structured in 4 sections: this section discusses existing approaches to similarity using word embedding, before presenting the architecture of our system in Section 2. The next section briefly analyses the results, while Section 4 drafts some conclusions and further work.

In natural language processing, one of the most important challenges is to understand the meaning of words.

The organizers of Task 2 (Task2, 2017) state that this task "provides a reliable benchmark for the development, evaluation and analysis" of:

- Word embeddings, monolingual word embeddings, as well as bilingual and multilingual word embeddings which have a unified semantic space for the languages;

- Similarity measures that use lexical resources;

- Supervised systems that combine multiple measures.

Our initial option was word embedding. The most prominent word embedding software tools are:

1. Word2Vec (Mikolov et al., 20013) is an algorithm with the explicit goal of producing word embeddings that encode general semantic relations (Collobert et al., 2011).

2. GloVe (Pennington et al., 2014) has a similar aim as Word2Vec. Its authors present GloVe mainly as an unsupervised learning algorithm, also offering an implementation.

3. Deeplearning4j is an open source deep learning library for Java which implements both Word2Vec and GloVe, among other algorithms (Deeplearning4j, 2017).

4. Principal Component Analysis (Jolliffe, 2002) and T-Distributed Stochastic Neighbor Embedding (van der Maaten 2008) are two algorithms that reduce the dimensionality of already generated word embedding vectors.

After initial tests using the data provided by the task organizers, we realized that it would yield better results to aggregate multiple techniques, and thus resolved to use a supervised system which combines multiple techniques. Recent studies show that neural-network-inspired word embedding models exceed the traditional count-based distributional models on word similarity.

267

Proceedings of the 11th International Workshop on Semantic Evaluations (SemEval-2017), pages 267–270,
Vancouver, Canada, August 3 - 4, 2017. ©2017 Association for Computational Linguistics

The supervised system we propose is a neural network trained on a list of gold standard word pairs. Three individual models (word embedding, definition comparison, synonyms, detailed in the next section) are run on the collection of word pairs and different lists of scores are obtained. The neural network is trained by comparing the lists of scores to the gold standard.

In order to develop a gold standard, we collected a set of word pairs and designed a web site that allowed human annotators to rate each word pair on the scale of 0 to 4. The users were students from the Faculty of Letters, who thus had a proficient and professional knowledge of the English language.

2 Methodology

Nowadays, there is a huge mass of textual data in electronic format, and this fact increased the need for fast and accurate techniques for textual data processing. Despite the evolution of the field, evaluation still rely (most of the time) on a comparison between the output of a statistical system on the one hand, and a hand-crafted gold standard, on the other hand. Generally, a gold standard provides an interesting basis for the comparison of systems against the same set of data, or for the comparison of the evolution of the performance of the different versions of a system performing a certain task.

2.1 Increased Gold Standard

In order to train the neural network, we needed a set of word pairs and a gold standard. The task's website affirmed that a human-generated gold standard is used, therefore we decided to increase its size by building a collection of word pairs manually rated according to their similarity.

For building the list of word pairs, we used Daniel Defoe's novel "Robinson Crusoe"[1]. We picked nouns at random from the novel and built pairs (for testing that a word is a noun, we used WordNet). A web interface (figure 1) was developed to allow user to validate the similarity between word pairs. Most word pairs obtained scores between 0 and 2. In order to obtain higher scores (3 and 4), meaning higher similarity, we built some pairs using a noun from the novel and one of the synonyms in its synset from WordNet.

---

[1] The novel is in the public domain and is available on Project Gutenberg

The group of annotators was composed of students from the Faculty of Letters who had proficient and professional knowledge of the English language. To assist their voting, we built a web site (Figure 1) that offers word pairs and saves the votes in a database. We used a session cookie to avoid giving the same word pair to a session twice.

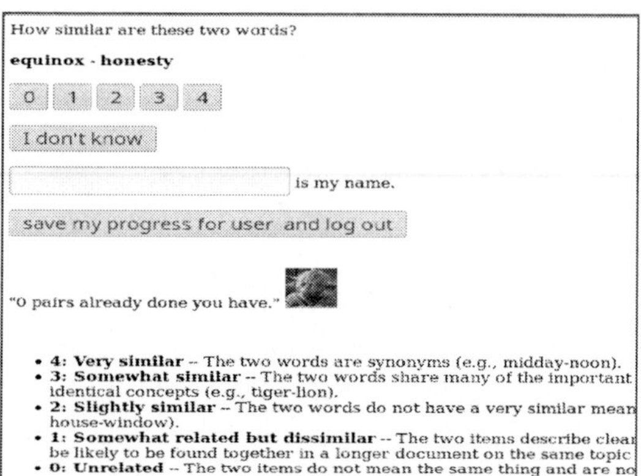

Figure 1. The website for rating word pairs

After the website was up, we added a username field to sessions, as well as a statistics page which collected the total number of votes for a student for all his sessions.

One of our priorities has been the maintenance of the website and quick fixing of bugs, in order to avoid losing data about sessions and the number of votes each student has done. As always when using volunteers, the danger exists that some users could cheat by scoring the word pairs at random. We took the precaution that we kept a record of all votes for a word pair, and thus could single out a suspect-looking vote. In order to insure inter-annotator agreement, each pair of words was evaluated by 5 different users.

The site also contained the original description of the rating scale, from the SemEval website, such that our gold standard would be similar to that used by the organizers.

In this way, we obtained a gold standard of 5747 word pairs, and the distribution of scores is satisfactory. The collection will be made publically available.

After having the corpus, we built our system using neural networks. The architecture of our systems is presented in figure 2.

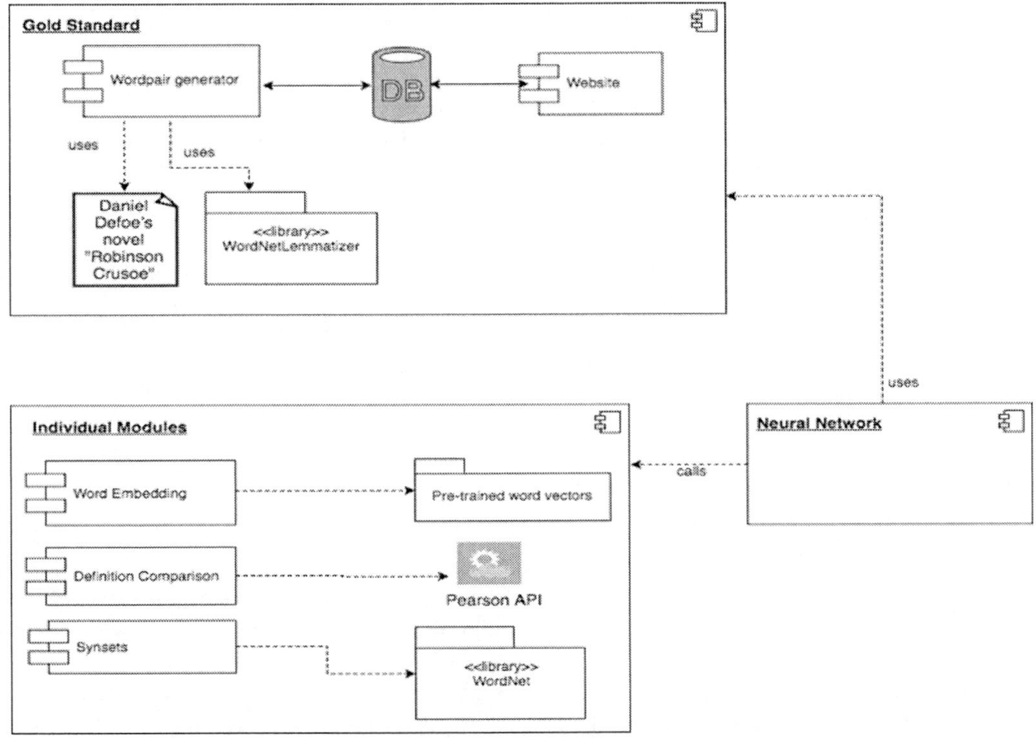

Figure 2. Architecture

2.2 Word Embeddings

From word vectors, we can find out the similarity of two words using the dot product of their vectors. One drawback is that most existing implementations load all vectors into RAM, which requires gigabytes of RAM. Given word vector files which can be obtained from various word embedding algorithms, our supervised system can use each of those vectors to obtain a score file, and train the neural network.

2.3 Definition Comparison

This module calculates the similarity of two words by comparing their definitions using the Levenshtein distance as a String metric.

An initial check is performed to verify if the words are identical, in which case the score will be 4, or if they are pairs of antonyms formed by derivation from the same root (e.g. hopeful <-> hopeless, legal <-> illegal), in which case the score will be 0. If it is not the case, the program goes on.

For each of the two words, a call is made to the API offered by the Pearson Publishing House.

The result is a JSON which can contain one or more entries, depending on how many meanings the word has. Our program parses the JSON and extracts only the definitions, which are then stored in an array.

Thus we have two arrays of definitions, one for each word, we iterate through the first array and we compare every definition to all the definitions of the other word. For this purpose, we use the Levenshtein distance (the minimum number of single-character edits, i.e. insertions, deletions or substitutions, required to change one word into the other). To calculate the Levenshtein distance we use Java's StringUtils library.

This score is increased by our program if one word includes the other (e.g. flower-sunflower) or if at least one of the words can be found in the definition of the other. From all the scores we get from comparing the definitions, only the biggest will be kept. Because the scores obtained by applying the Levenshtein distance to dictionary entries have very small values (between 0 și 1.5 out of 100), we process them to get one of the values: 0, 1, 2, 3, 4.

If one or both words cannot be found in the dictionary or if an error occurs during the execution, the returned score is 0.

The program can support a limited number of multi-word expressions and personal names, if they can be found in the Pearson dictionary.

2.4 Synonymy

This module calculates the similarity of two words using Wordnet, by comparing their synsets. For each word pair, the list of synsets is retrieved, and the sets of synonyms are compared two by two in order to count the common words. A score is thus obtained, to be compared to the score given by users (mainly to check the user's credibility). Additionally, the list of word pairs having higher scores has been increased by using synonyms of these words, extracted from Wordnet.

3 Evaluation

We performed an internal evaluation of our system on the training data and obtained a score of 0.372 (Pearson: 0.385, Spearman: 0.357). The results show that we have managed to accomplish the main objective of this project, to outperform the random strategy. The lower scores have been obtained for named entities and multiword expressions, instances which do not exist in our gold standard, for which we plan to add dedicated modules.

Our team participated in task 1 for English, and was officially evaluated with a Pearson score of 0.459 and a Spearman score of 0.477, giving a total of 0.468.

4 Conclusions

This paper explores word similarities by using a supervised system that aggregated corpus based techniques, as well as word embedding techniques. It also exposes the need for more experiments that should be done in this field, and we take into account the possibility to create such a solution for the Romanian language.

In the future, we will refine the components of the supervised system. Given more time, we could get an even larger gold standard using our site, which will allow us to even better train our neural network.

We could also implement word embedding software that efficiently uses hard disk space, ra-ther than loading all vectors into RAM at once, or use a distributed computing approach.

There are some other aspects that we are interested to tackle in the future, such as named entity recognition and multiword expressions recognition.

References

Collobert, R., Weston, J., Bottou, L., Karlen, M., Kavukcuoglu, K., & Kuksa, P. (2011). Natural Language Processing (almost) from Scratch. Journal of Machine Learning Research, 12 (Aug), 2493–2537. Retrieved from http://arxiv.org/abs/1103.0398

Deeplearning4j Development Team. (2017) *Deeplearning4j: Open-source distributed deep learning for the JVM*, Apache Software Foundation License 2.0. http://deeplearning4j.org

Jolliffe I.T. (2002) *Principal Component Analysis*, Series: Springer Series in Statistics, 2nd ed., Springer, NY, 2002, XXIX, 487 p. 28 illus. ISBN 978-0-387-95442-4

Mikolov Tomas, Kai Chen, Greg Corrado, Jeffrey Dean (2013) Efficient Estimation of Word Representations in Vector Space, arXiv:1301.3781.

Pennington, Jeffrey, (2014) Richard Socher, and Christopher D. Manning. "Glove: Global Vectors for Word Representation." EMNLP. Vol. 14. 2014.

Jose Camacho-Collados, Mohammad Taher Pilehvar, Nigel Collier and Roberto Navigli (2017) *SemEval-2017 Task 2: Multilingual and Cross-lingual Semantic Word Similarity*. In Proceedings of the 11th International Workshop on Semantic Evaluation (SemEval 2017). Vancouver, Canada.

van der Maaten, L.J.P.; Hinton, G.E. (2008). *Visualizing High-Dimensional Data Using t-SNE*. Journal of Machine Learning Research. 9: 2579–2605.

TrentoTeam at SemEval-2017 Task 3: An application of Grice Maxims in Ranking Community Question Answers

Mohammed R. H. Qwaider
Fondazione Bruno Kessler
Via Sommarive, 18
Trento, Italy.
qwaider@fbk.eu

Abed Alhakim Freihat
University of Trento
Via Sommarive, 19
Trento, Italy.
abed.freihat@unitn.it

Fausto Giunchiglia
University of Trento
Via Sommarive, 19
Trento, Italy.
fausto@unitn.it

Abstract

In this paper, we present a community answers ranking system which is based on Grice Maxims. In particular, we describe a ranking system which is based on answer relevancy scores, assigned by three main components: Named entity recognition, similarity score, and sentiment analysis.

1 Introduction

This paper describes the Grice Ranking system which participated to SemEval 2017 Task 3 (Nakov et al., 2017) subtask A competition[1]. The SemEval 2017 Task 3 (Nakov et al., 2017) sub-task A focuses on raking a list of answers (10 in our case) as follows. Given a question Q and a list of answers $\langle a_1, ..., a_n \rangle$. Rank these answers according to their relevancy with respect to the question Q. Our participation to the task was mainly motivated by our interest in applying Grice maxims (Grice, 1975) principles to a ranking task to define standards of Grice maxims for ranking tasks. The system follows 3 steps: similarity, entity recognition, and sentiment analysis.

2 Grice maxims principles

Grice main idea is that communication between human beings is logic and rational. Following this idea, any conversation assumes cooperation between the conversation parties. This cooperation supposes in essence four maxims that usually hold in dialogues or conversations. These maxims are:

1. **Quality**: Say only true things.

2. **Quantity**: Be informative.

3. **Relation**: Be relevant in your conversation.

---

[1] http://alt.qcri.org/semeval2016/task3/

4. **Manner**: Be direct and straightforward.

These maxims have been intensively researched in the domain of linguistics and pragmatics in the last decades, where the researchers focused on how to use Grice theory to explain speaker intention when he says some thing. For example, these maxims explain that the speaker B understands the intention of the speaker A. The same holds for A who understands the indirect Answer of B.

A *What is the time?*

B *The bus left five minutes ago.*

In this work, we use these maxims partially to measure the appropriateness or relevancy of answer(s) of a given question. In this approach, we do not try to understand what the speaker (intentional) means. Instead, we try to understand if the speaker contribution contains (extensional) elements that comply with Grice maxims.

In the following, we explain how we interpret the quantity, relation and manner maxims in our approach. We do not use the quality maxim and it is beyond the scope of our research.

2.1 Quantity

We interpret this maxim as how much an answer is informative by examining whether an answer contains the following informative elements?

1. **Named entities**: A named entity here refers to person, organization, location, or product.

2. **References**: References include web urls, emails, and phone numbers.

3. **Currency**: We consider the presence of currency in an answer as informative element.

4. **Numbers**: In some cases, phone numbers, or currency are not recognized because they are

Proceedings of the 11th International Workshop on Semantic Evaluations (SemEval-2017), pages 271–274,
Vancouver, Canada, August 3 - 4, 2017. ©2017 Association for Computational Linguistics

implicit such as *20000 is a good salary*. For this reason, we consider the presence of numbers (2 digits or more) in answers as an informative element.

Of course, this list is not exhaustive. However, these are the informative elements that we utilize in our approach.

2.2 Relation

We think that defining what is a relevant contribution in the relation maxim is still an open issue (Frederking, 1996). At the same time, we try to discover relevancy indicators and use them in our algorithm. Accordingly, we consider the following as relevancy indicators.

1. **Similarity**: Similarity between the question and the answer.

2. **Imperatives**: Answers that contain imperative verbs such as *try*, *go to*, or *check* indicate that the answerer is explaining a way to solve the problem being discussed.

3. **Expression of politeness**: Expressions of politeness *I would*, *I suggest*, or *I recommend* are usually polite alternatives for imperatives.

4. **Factoid answer particles**: For factoid questions *is/are* or *does/do*, the answer particles *yes/no* indicate the relevancy of the answer.

5. **Domain specific terms**: Domain specific terms indicate relevancy. For example, terms such as *CV*, *NOC*, *torrent*,... are domain specific terms . Using such terms indicates also that the answerer is trying to explain how to solve the problem being discussed.

Again, this list is not exhaustive and it would be much better for our approach if we could use more concrete criteria that indicate the relation maxim.

2.3 Manner

Grice summarizes this maxim as (a speaker contribution is expected to be clear) and he gives four criteria that indicate not violating this maxim: *Avoid obscurity of expressions, avoid ambiguity, be brief*, and *be orderly*. We did not use these criteria for the difficulty of applying them. Instead, we give the following criteria that can be used to judge that a speaker contribution complies with or violates the manner maxim.

1. **Be positive**: By this criterion, we mean that the speaker contribution is expected to be tolerant and permissive.

2. **Avoid frustrating utterances**: Answers that contain such expressions are usually not useful in the conversation.

3. **Avoid ironic and humbling expressions**: We mean here that the answer tends to be formal and professional and that the answerer is aiming to give a direct useful contribution.

4. **Avoid insulting and degrading expressions**: Answers that contain such expressions are not expected to be be useful.

We may also consider the grammatical and orthographic correctness as a criterion. We did not consider it because many of the members of Qatar Living are not native speakers of English.

3 Implementation

In the following, we present the ranking algorithm , where we start with explaining the used resources. Then, we illustrate some experiments that we have conducted in the framework of our approach, and finally we describe the Grice Ranking system.

3.1 Resources

We used the following resources in our algorithm.
Quality: No resources and this maxim was not used in the implementation.
Quantity: We adopted pre-trained openNLP[2] name finder model for named entity recognition (NER) to our domain data. we needed this model because of the low performance of the state of the art NER systems on the training data. We have trained the openNLP NER system on an self annotated subset of the training data set. The generated model reached 87% F1-measure. Both the annotated corpus and the model are downloadable online[3].
Relation: We have used the following resources:

a) *Similarity*: We used Word2Vec[4](Turian et al., 2010) and Brown and clark (Agerri and Rigau, 2016) embeddings.

---

[2]https://opennlp.apache.org/
[3]https://www.researchgate.net/project/Named-Entity-Recognizer-For-Qatar
[4]https://github.com/ragerri/cluster-preprocessing/

b) *Imperatives and Expression of politeness*: We used an OpenNLP POS-tagger to detect these expressions. We reward answers that contains such expressions.

c) *Domain specific terms*: Using the training data, we have compiled a small dictionary that contains domain specif terms such as *router, CV, NOC, torrent,....* The terms in the dictionary are not classified and of course they are not exhaustive. Answers that contain such expressions are also rewarded.

Manner: We used two sentiment polarity lists[5], one positive sentiment list and other negative sentiment list.

a) *Be positive*: We used the positive sentiment list to reward answers that contain positive expressions.

b) *Avoid frustrating expressions*: We used the negative sentiment list to penalize answers that contain such expressions.

c) *Avoid ironic and humbling expressions*: The negative sentiment list includes some of the ironic and humbling expressions. We used the training data to extend the list with new expressions that we found in the training data. Answers that contain such expressions are penalized.

d) *Avoid insulting and degrading expressions*: The negative sentiment list includes some of these expressions. We have extended the list with new expressions that we found in the training data. We penalize answers that contain such expressions.

3.2 Experiments

In the following, we describe some of the experiments that we conducted to evaluate the proposed algorithm which is described in next section. We evaluate the systems using the test set taken from SemEval 2016 (Nakov et al., 2016), where we used MAP (mean average precision) as performance measure.

Experiment 1 (similarity run): Rank the answers of a question using TF-IDF as a similarity function from the most similar answer to less relevant one.

Experiment 2 (clusters/word representation 1): We experimented mixing different combinations of word embeddings and similarity measure to rank the answers. We used Brown embedding with N-grams level, with a weight of 0.5 to embedding similarity and 0.5 to string similarity.

Experiment 3 (clusters/word representation 2): Using Brown and Clark with weight of 0.3 to string similarity and 0.7 to cluster similarity.

Experiment 4 (clusters/word representation 3): Including word2vec to Brown and clark, with a low-level features, like word shape with the same weight of 0.3 to string similarity and 0.7 to cluster similarity.

Experiment 5 (similarity rule based): In this experiment, we run the system in two phases:

1. Rank the comments depending on their token-based similarity score.

2. Re-rank them based on background rules such as downgrading the answers of the same person which we considered as duplicates.

3.3 Grice Maxims Based Ranking Algorithm

In the following, we present the ranking algorithm.[6].

Input: Q: $\langle p, qText \rangle$, L: $\langle a_1, ..., a_n \rangle$
   p: The person who is asking
   $qText$: The question text.
   $a_i = \langle p_i, aText_i, score_i \rangle$.
   p_i: The person who answered a_i
   $qText_i$: The answer text of a_i
   $score_i$: The relevancy of a_i.
Output: L: The input list after sorting.
algorithm `GriceMaximsRanking(`Q`, `L`)`
begin
   foreach answer a_i **in** L
     if $p_i = p$ **then** $score_i = i * -100$
     else
       $score_i = |SM_{qi}| + |NE_i| + |RE_i| + |CN_i| + |IM_i| + |DT_i| + |PS_i|$;
       $score_i - = |NS_i| + |IR_i| + |ID_i|$;
   sort L ;
   return L;
end

---

[6] SM: Similarity between question and answer. NE: Named entities. RE: Reference expressions. CN: Currency and numbers. IM: Imperative and polite expressions. DT: Domain specific terms. PS: Positive sentiment words. NS: Negative sentiment words. IR: Ironic and humbling words. ID: Insulting and degrading words. p: Refers to the person who is asking. $qText$: Refers to the question text

---

[5]https://github.com/jeffreybreen/twitter-sentiment-analysis-tutorial-201107

The algorithm works in four steps as follows.

1. The algorithm checks whether the answerer is the same person who asked the question. The answers made by person who asked the question are downgraded such that they become the last answers in the list.

2. For the rest of the answers, we compute the similarity between the question Q and the answer a_i, where $0 \leq SM_{qi} \leq n$ $(n = |L|)$.

3. Then, based on Grice maxims, the answers are rewarded or penalized as follows.

    a The answer a_i is rewarded according to the number of entities, reference expressions, currency and numbers, imperatives, domain specific terms, and positive sentiment words.

    b On the other hand, a_i is penalized according to the number of negative sentiment, ironic, and insulting words.

4. After rewarding and penalizing all answers, we then sort the list of answers according to their achieved scores in a descending order. Best answer is the first answer in the list and so on.

Evaluating the algorithm on the same test set in the previous experiments, we get MAP=0.7151. The best system in SemEval 2016 (Filice et al., 2016) achieved MAP=79.19 as shown in Table 1.

System	MAP
Baseline	0.5280
Experiment 3	0.5596
Experiment 1	0.5839
Experiment 2	0.6089
SemEval-2016 Worst System	0.6224
Experiment 5	0.6403
Experiment 4	0.6422
Our System	0.7151
SemEval-2016 Best System	0.7919

Table 1: Results of some community Question Answer Ranking approaches in SemEval 2016.

4 Results

Our system obtained a rank[7] of 12 out of 13 participated systems and a MAP of 78.56. It beat the IR baseline by 6 points, and the last system LaSIGE-primary by 15 points, with a difference of 10 points from the best system.

References

Rodrigo Agerri and German Rigau. 2016. Robust multilingual named entity recognition with shallow semi-supervised features. *Artificial Intelligence* 238:63 – 82.

Simone Filice, Danilo Croce, Alessandro Moschitti, and Roberto Basili. 2016. Kelp at semeval-2016 task 3: Learning semantic relations between questions and answers. In *Proceedings of the 10th International Workshop on Semantic Evaluation (SemEval-2016)*. Association for Computational Linguistics, San Diego, California, pages 1116–1123. http://www.aclweb.org/anthology/S16-1172.

R. Frederking. 1996. Grice's maxims: do the right thing. *Proc. of AAAI SpringSymp. on Compl. Implicature: Computational Approaches to Interpreting and Generating Conversational Implicature* .

H. P. Grice. 1975. Logic and conversation. In P. Cole and J. L. Morgan, editors, *Syntax and Semantics: Vol. 3: Speech Acts*, Academic Press, San Diego, CA, pages 41–58.

Preslav Nakov, Doris Hoogeveen, Lluís Màrquez, Alessandro Moschitti, Hamdy Mubarak, Timothy Baldwin, and Karin Verspoor. 2017. SemEval-2017 task 3: Community question answering. In *Proceedings of the 11th International Workshop on Semantic Evaluation*. Association for Computational Linguistics, Vancouver, Canada, SemEval '17.

Preslav Nakov, Lluís Màrquez, Alessandro Moschitti, Walid Magdy, Hamdy Mubarak, abed Alhakim Freihat, Jim Glass, and Bilal Randeree. 2016. Semeval-2016 task 3: Community question answering. In *Proceedings of the 10th International Workshop on Semantic Evaluation (SemEval-2016)*. Association for Computational Linguistics, San Diego, California, SemEval '16, pages 525–545. http://www.aclweb.org/anthology/S16-1083.

Joseph Turian, Lev-Arie Ratinov, and Yoshua Bengio. 2010. Word representations: A simple and general method for semi-supervised learning. In *Proceedings of the 48th Annual Meeting of the Association for Computational Linguistics*. Association for Computational Linguistics, Uppsala, Sweden, pages 384–394. http://www.aclweb.org/anthology/P10-1040.

[7]http://alt.qcri.org/semeval2017/task3/

UPC-USMBA at SemEval-2017 Task 3: Combining Multiple Approaches for CQA for Arabic

Yassine El Adlouni
USMBA
Fes, Morocco
yeladlouni@gmail.com

Imane Lahbari
USMBA
Fes, Morocco
imane.lahbari@usmba.ac.ma

Horacio Rodríguez
UPC
Barcelona, Spain
horacio@cs.upc.edu

Mohammed Meknassi
USMBA
Fes, Morocco
m.meknassi@gmail.com

Said Ouatik El Alaoui
USMBA
Fes, Morocco
s_ouatik@yahoo.com

Noureddine Ennahnahi
USMBA
Fes, Morocco
nahnnourd@yahoo.fr

Abstract

This paper presents a description of the participation of the UPC-USMBA team in the SemEval 2017 Task 3, subtask D, Arabic. Our approach for facing the task is based on a performance of a set of atomic classifiers (lexical string-based, vectorial, and rule-based) whose results are later combined. Our primary submission has obtained good results: 2nd (from 3 participants) in *MAP*, and 1st in in *accuracy*.

1 Introduction

The SemEval Task 3 subtask D, (Nakov et al., 2017), asks, given a query, consisting of a question, and a set of 30 question-answer pairs, to re-rank the question-answer pairs according to their relevance with respect to the original question.

Question Answering, QA, i.e. querying a computer using Natural Language, is a traditional objective of Natural Language Processing. *CQA* differs from conventional QA systems basically on three aspects: The source of the possible answers, that are the threads of queries and answers activated from the original query, the structure of the threads and the available metadata can be exploited for the task, types of questions include the frequent use of complex questions, as definitional, why, consequences, how_to_proceed, etc. One factor that makes very attractive the task is that many approaches, rule-based, pattern-based, Statistical, ML, have been applied to face it. See (Nakov et al., 2017) for an overview of frequently used techniques. See also the overviews of past contests, (Nakov et al., 2016a) and (Nakov et al., 2016b).

2 Our Approach

Due to the negative results in last year participation, for this year we present a system that combines different classifiers, going beyond the two classifiers, Arabic and English shallow features-based ones, used last year. The new classifiers follow approaches that have produced good results in systems as (Barrón-Cedeño et al., 2016), (Mihaylov and Nakov, 2016), and (Joty et al., 2016). We will refer in what follows to these classifiers as atomic ones and they are further combined for obtaining the final results.

Proceedings of the 11th International Workshop on Semantic Evaluations (SemEval-2017), pages 275–279,
Vancouver, Canada, August 3 - 4, 2017. ©2017 Association for Computational Linguistics

The overall architecture of our system is presented in Figure 1. As can be seen, the system performs in four steps, a preliminary step, aiming at collecting needed resources, basically Arabic and English classified medical terminologies, a learning step, for getting the models, a classification step, for applying them to the test dataset, and a last step combining the results of the atomic classifiers that are described next.

2.1 Overall description

A core component of our approach is the use of a medical terminology, covering both Arabic and English terms and organized into three categories: *body parts*, *drugs*, and *diseases*. See (Adlouni et al., 2016).

After downloading the training (resp. test) Arabic dataset we translate into English all the Arabic query texts and all the Arabic texts corresponding to each of the query/answers pairs. For doing so we have used the Google Translate API[1]. The texts are then processed using for English the Stanford CoreNLP toolbox[2] (Manning et al., 2014) and for Arabic *Madamira*[3] (Pasha et al., 2015). The results are then enriched with WordNet synsets and with Named Entities included in the medical dictionaries for both Arabic and English. Then a process of feature extraction is carried out. This process is different for each atomic classifier and will be described next. Finally, a process of learning (resp. classification) is performed. Also these processes differ depending on the involved classifiers.

2.2 Atomic Classifiers

The atomic classifiers[4] used by our system are the following:

- *Basic lexical string-based classifiers*, i.e. *Basic_ar* and *Basic_en*, identical to the ones used last year. The basic classifiers use three sets of features[5]: shallow linguistic features, vectorial features, and domain-based features. Details can be seen in (Adlouni et al., 2016). We have used for learning the

Logistic Regression classifier included in the Weka toolkit[6], (Hall et al., 2009).

- A simple IR system, using *LUCENE* engine, with different combinations served as index, Question, Answer and Question concatenated with the Answer.

- Latent Semantic Indexing (LSI), learned from different datasets, was used to get dense representations of our sentences by using SVD (Singular Value Decomposition). These vectorial representations are then used to measure the similarity between each pair Q_o/Q_i where Q_o denote the original question and Q_i denote the i^{st} Question within the set of questions to rank. Various corpora was used for that matter including Wikipedia, Webteb.com, altibbi.com and dailymedical-info.com which are specialized Arabic websites for medical domain articles. The preprocessing step consisted of denoising collected articles, extracting paragraphs, removing stopwords, diacritics, tokenizing, normalizing and lemmatizing. The same pipeline is used later for the query and for each pair of Question/Answer. The implementation used for LSI is from gensim (Řehůřek and Sojka, 2010). After the SVD decomposition, cosine similarity measure is calculated for each pair which are ordered for each query and a quartile approach is taken to decide if the pair is relevant or not.

- A topic-based LDA using the same training datasets that for LSI. We used the implementation of Rehurek's gensim[7].

- *Embedding* systems. We have tried several embeddings with no remarkable results. Specifically we tried *Word2Vec*[8], *Glove*[9], and *doc2vec*[10]. The last one produced the best results but was outperformed by the combination of LDA and LSI.

- A *Rulebased* system, with rulesets for Arabic and English. The motivation of rule-based classifiers is that for some queries both the original questions and some of the questions

---

[1]translate.google.com

[2]http://stanfordnlp.github.io/CoreNLP/

[3]http://nlp.ldeo.columbia.edu/madamira/

[4]In fact the classifiers, besides classifying each pair as relevant or not, use their confidence scores for obtaining the score of each pair and, thus, their relative order. We can, so, define them as regressors or rankers.

[5]Extracted independently for each language.

[6]http://www.cs.waikato.ac.nz/ml/weka/

[7]http://radimrehurek.com/gensim/models/ldamodel.html

[8]http://deeplearning4j.org/word2vec.html

[9]http://nlp.stanford.edu/projects/glove/

[10]http://radimrehurek.com/gensim/models/doc2vec.html

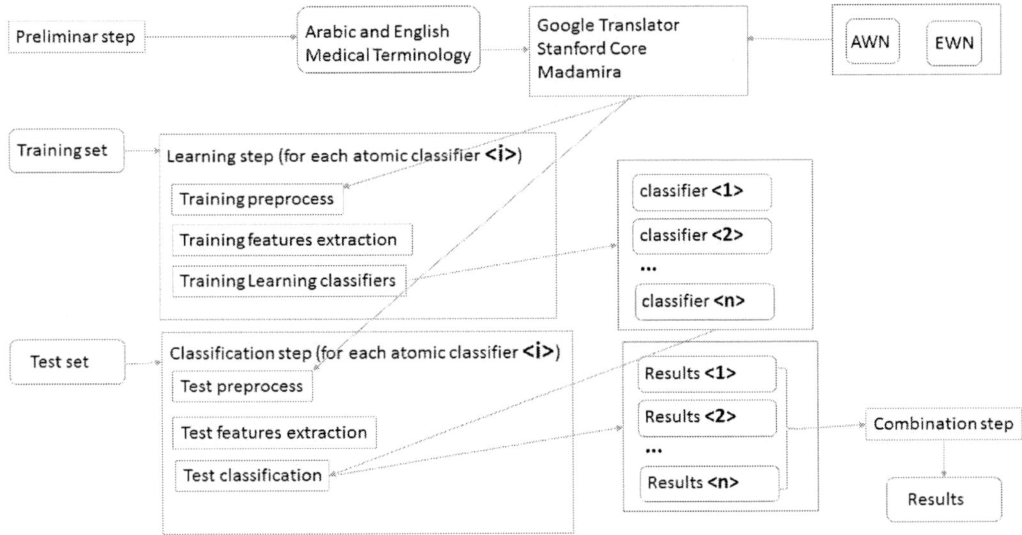

Figure 1: Train and testing pipelines

included into the thread are short questions involving a clear objective. We can manually build *condition rules* for recognizing these questions and extracting their objectives. Consider, for instance, a question beginning with "What is the cause of", and containing close to it a disease name. This question can be easily classified with the Question type (*QT*) *CauseDisease* and parameterized with the tag *Disease* with the extracted name as value. Similarly we can build *answer rules* for detecting whether the answer part of a pair satisfy the objective (in this example) an occurrence of the disease name. If the original question fires a *condition rule* and is classified with a *QT* with some associated tag and some of its questions within the thread are also classified with the same *QT* being their tags compatible, it is highly likely that the corresponding pairs are relevant for the original query. Moreover, if the answer part of the pair satisfy the associated *answer rule* the confidence (and, thus, the score) of the pair increases. Unfortunately although the precision of *condition rules* is high, recall is very low. Our hope is that with careful engineering of the rules and this kind of atomic classifier if not alone could contribute to improve the performance of other classifiers. 13 QTs were used for Arabic and 16 QTs for En-

glish, with a total of 75 rules.

2.3 Combinations

Output of the atomic classifiers are further combined. We have evaluated the powerset of the atomic classifiers for looking for the best combination using the training set. However, no more than 3 atomic classifiers produced good results and the best one resulted from the combination of one of the LSI and one of the LDA classifiers. The parameters used for learning the combiner are the following:

- *scoring form*, i.e. 'max' or 'ave', defining how for each pair i of each query q the scores of the different atomic components s are combined.

- *thresholding form*, i.e. None, 'global' or 'local', defining whether a threshold has to be used for getting the result of each pair i.

- *thresholding level*, i-e. 0.2, 0.4, 0.6, 0.8.

- *result form*, i.e. 'max', 'voting', 'coincidence'.

3 Experimental framework

We carried out all the processes depicted in Figure 1, for preprocessing and training using the training dataset. Besides, we tried all the possible

Team	Rank	MAP	Accuracy
GW_QA-primary	1	0.6116	0.6077
UPC-USMBA-primary	2	0.5773	0.6624
QU_BIGIR-primary	3	0.56695	0.4964

Table 1: Official results of the task

combinations of atomic classifiers. The best results were obtained for the combination LDA and LSI learned from Webteb, lemmatized. This combination was our primary run. As we were interested on the performance of our manual rules we submitted, too, a contrastive run including a combination of *basic_ar* and *basic_en* with *rule_based*. We were interested on analyzing two measures *MAP* as official measure and *accuracy* as the measure based on the individual results and not in the order. As our classifiers are not true rankers, analyzing the two measures seemed more appropriate for evaluating our system and proposing ways of improvement.

4 Results

In Table 1 a summary of the Official results of Semeval 2017 Task 3 Subtask D, corresponding to primary runs is presented.

Regarding *MAP*, and so, looking at the official rank, we are placed in the middle (2nd from 3 participants). Regarding *accuracy*, that is important for us as argued in previous section, we are placed on the top of the rank. We analyzed the results in the test dataset of our atomic classifiers (with different parameterization) and combinations. Due to space constraints we cannot include the whole results. The *MAP* for the atomic classifiers (using the best parameters got in training) range from 55 to 58.32. All the atomic results were outperformed by our primary run but *Lucene* obtaining our best result, 58.32.

5 Conclusions and future work

This year our results have been rather good, second (but from only 3 teams) in *MAP* and first in *accuracy*.

From our contrastive run we need more time for analyzing the results. The accuracy of each rule of each language should be measured and some rules should be refined, some others removed and probably more rules are needed.

Our next steps will be:

- Performing an in depth analysis of the performance of our two rulesets, analyzing the accuracy of each rule and cross comparing the rules fired in each language. It is likely that if a rule has been correctly applied to a pair for a language a corresponding rule in the other languages should be applied as well, so modifying an existing rule or including a new one could be possible. Learning a rule classifier is another possibility to examine.

- Using a final ranker over the results of our atomic classifiers for trying to improve our *MAP*.

- Trying others NN models as CNN and LSTM.

- Extending the coverage of our medical terminologies to other medical entities (procedures, clinical signs, etc).

Acknowledgments

We are grateful for the comments and suggestions from four anonimous reviewers. Dr. Rodríguez has been partially funded by Spanish project "GraphMed" (TIN2016-77820-C3-3R).

References

Yassine El Adlouni, Imane Lahbari, Horacio Rodríguez, Mohammed Meknassi, Said Ouatik El Alaoui, and Noureddine Ennahnahi. 2016. Upcusmba participation in semeval 2016 task 3, subtask d: Cqa for arabic. In *NAACL HLT 2016, At San Diego, CA, Volume: In Proceedings of the 10th International Workshop on Semantic Evaluation, SemEval 16*.

Alberto Barrón-Cedeño, Giovanni Da San Martino, Shafiq R. Joty, Alessandro Moschitti, Fahad Al-Obaidli, Salvatore Romeo, Kateryna Tymoshenko, and Antonio Uva. 2016. Convkn at semeval-2016 task 3: Answer and question selection for question answering on arabic and english fora. In *Proceedings of the 10th International Workshop on Semantic Evaluation, SemEval@NAACL-HLT 2016, San Diego, CA, USA, June 16-17, 2016*, pages 896–903.

Mark Hall, Eibe Frank, Geoffrey Holmes, Bernhard Pfahringer, Peter Reutemann, and Ian Witten. 2009. The WEKA Data Mining Software: An Update. In *SIGKDD Explorations*.

Shafiq R. Joty, Lluís Màrquez, and Preslav Nakov. 2016. Joint learning with global inference for comment classification in community question answering. In *NAACL HLT 2016, The 2016 Conference of the North American Chapter of the Association for Computational Linguistics: Human Language Technologies, San Diego California, USA, June 12-17, 2016*, pages 703–713.

Christopher Manning, Mihai Surdeanu, John Bauer, Jenny Finkel, Steven Bethard, and David McClosky. 2014. The Stanford CoreNLP natural language processing toolkit. In *Association for Computational Linguistics (ACL) System Demonstrations*, pages 55–60.

Todor Mihaylov and Preslav Nakov. 2016. Semanticz at semeval-2016 task 3: Ranking relevant answers in community question answering using semantic similarity based on fine-tuned word embeddings. In *Proceedings of the 10th International Workshop on Semantic Evaluation, SemEval@NAACL-HLT 2016, San Diego, CA, USA, June 16-17, 2016*, pages 879–886.

Preslav Nakov, Lluís Màrquez, Alessandro Moschitti, Walid Magdy, Hamdy Mubarak, Abed Alhakim Freihat, Jim Glass, and Bilal Randeree. 2016a. SemEval-2016 Task 3: Community Question Answering. In *Proceedings of the 10th International Workshop on Semantic Evaluation*, SemEval '16, San Diego, California, June. Association for Computational Linguistics.

Preslav Nakov, Lluís Màrquez, Alessandro Moschitti, Walid Magdy, Hamdy Mubarak, Abed Alhakim Freihat, Jim Glass, and Bilal Randeree. 2016b. Semeval-2016 task 3: Community question answering. In *Proceedings of the 10th International Workshop on Semantic Evaluation, SemEval@NAACL-HLT 2016, San Diego, CA, USA, June 16-17, 2016*, pages 525–545.

Preslav Nakov, Doris Hoogeveen, Lluís Màrquez, Alessandro Moschitti, Hamdy Mubarak, Timothy Baldwin, and Karin Verspoor. 2017. SemEval-2017 task 3: Community question answering. In *Proceedings of the 11th International Workshop on Semantic Evaluation*, SemEval '17, Vancouver, Canada, August. Association for Computational Linguistics.

Arfath Pasha, Mohammad Al-Badrashiny, Mona Diab, Nizar Habash, Manoj Pooleery, Owen Rambow, and Ryan Roth. 2015. Madamira 2.1. In *Center for Computational Learning Systems Columbia University, April 2015*, pages 55–60.

Radim Řehůřek and Petr Sojka. 2010. Software framework for topic modelling with large corpora. In *Proceedings of the LREC 2010 Workshop on New Challenges for NLP Frameworks*, pages 45–50, Valletta, Malta, May. ELRA.

Beihang-MSRA at SemEval-2017 Task 3: A Ranking System with Neural Matching Features for Community Question Answering

Wenzheng Feng[†], Yu Wu[†], Wei Wu[‡], Zhoujun Li[†*], Ming Zhou[‡]
[†]State Key Lab of Software Development Environment, Beihang University, Beijing, China
[‡] Microsoft Research, Beijing, China
{wuyu,lizj,wenzhengfeng}@buaa.edu.cn {wuwei,mingzhou}@microsoft.com

Abstract

This paper presents the system in SemEval-2017 Task 3, Community Question Answering (CQA). We develop a ranking system that is capable of capturing semantic relations between text pairs with little word overlap. In addition to traditional NLP features, we introduce several neural network based matching features which enable our system to measure text similarity beyond lexicons. Our system significantly outperforms baseline methods and holds the second place in Subtask A and the fifth place in Subtask B, which demonstrates its efficacy on answer selection and question retrieval.

1 Introduction

In task 3 of SemEval 2017, participants are required to address typical problems in modern CQA forums. We participate two subtasks: question-comment similarity (Subtask A) and question-question similarity (Subtask B). In Subtask A, given a question and 10 comments in its comment thread, one is required to re-rank the 10 comments according to their relevance with the question. Subtask B gives a question and asks participants to re-rank 10 related questions according to their similarity to the input question.

The challenge of both subtasks is that two natural language sentences often express similar meanings with different but semantically related words, which results in semantic gaps between them. To bridge the semantic gaps, we build a ranking system with a variety of features. In addition to traditional NLP features such as tf-idf (Salton and Buckley, 1988), the longest common subsequence (Allison and Dix, 1986), translation models (Jeon

---

* Corresponding Author

et al., 2005), and tree kernels (Schlkopf et al., 2003; Collins and Duffy, 2002; Moschitti, 2006), which match sentences based on word overlap, syntax (tree kenerls), and word-word translations (translation models), we also introduce neural network based matching models into the system as features. The neural matching features, including a long short term memory network (LSTM) (Schuster and Paliwal, 1997) and a 2D matching network which is a variant of our model in (Wu et al., 2016), can extract high level matching signals from distributed representations of the sentences and capture their similarity beyond lexicons. We also design some specific features for each subtask. All the features are combined as a ranking model by a gradient boosted regression tree which is implemented by Xgboost (Chen and Guestrin, 2016). Our system significantly outperforms baseline methods on the two subtasks. On Subtask A, it holds the second place and is comparable with the best system. On Subtask B, it holds the fifth place. The results demonstrate that our system can alleviate the semantic gaps in the tasks of CQA and effectively rank relevant comments and similar questions to high positions.

2 System Description

Our system is built under a learning to rank framework (Liu et al., 2009). It takes a question and a group of candidates (comments or related questions) as input, and outputs a ranking list of the candidates based on scores of question-candidate pairs. The ranking scores are calculated in three steps: text preprocessing, feature extraction, and feature combination. In preprocessing, we replace special characters and punctuations with spaces, normalize all letters to their lowercase, remove stop-words, and conduct stemming and syntax analysis. Subsequently, we extract a variety of fea-

Proceedings of the 11th International Workshop on Semantic Evaluations (SemEval-2017), pages 280–286,
Vancouver, Canada, August 3 - 4, 2017. ©2017 Association for Computational Linguistics

tures from text pairs including traditional NLP features and neural matching features for both subtasks and some task-specific features. Finally, we feed the features to a ranking model which is trained under a pairwise loss using the training data provided in the subtasks to calculate the ranking scores.

In the following, we will describe details of preprocessing, features, and feature combination.

2.1 Preprocessing

We exploit NLTK toolkit (Loper and Bird, 2002) to conduct stemming, tokenization, and POS tagging. We use Stanford PCFG parser (Klein and Manning, 2003) to get the parse tree of each sentence.

2.2 Traditional NLP Features

The following features are designed based on words and syntactic analysis.

Tf-idf cosine: each piece of text is converted to a one hot representation weighted by tf-idf values, where tf is the term frequency in the text, and idf is calculated using the unannotated Qatar corpora (Nakov et al., 2017). The cosine of representations of the two pieces of text is used as a feature.

Longest common subsequence: we measure the lexical similarity of each text pair with the term-level longest common subsequence (LCS) (Allison and Dix, 1986). The length of LCS is normalized by dividing the maximum length of the two pieces of text.

Word overlap: we calculate the normalized count of common ngrams (n=1,2,3) and nouns.

Tree kernels: tree kernels are similarity functions used to measure the syntactic similarity of a text pair. We compute the subtree kernel (ST) (Schlkopf et al., 2003), the subset tree kernel (SST) (Collins and Duffy, 2002), and the partial tree kernel (PTK) (Moschitti, 2006) on the parse trees of a text pair.

Translation probability: we learn word-to-word translation probabilities using GIZA++ [1] with the unannotated Qatar Living data. In training, we regard questions as source language and their answers as target language. Following (Jeon et al., 2005), we use translation probability $p(\text{qusetion A}|\text{question B})$ and $p(\text{comment}|\text{question})$ as features for a question-

[1] http://www.statmt.org/moses/giza/GIZA++.html

question pair and a question-comment pair respectively.

In Subtask A, we compute the features on both (question body, comment) and (question subject, comment), and in Subtask B, we compute the features on (question body, question body) and (question subject, question subject).

2.3 Neural Matching Features

In addition to the traditional NLP features, we also use neural matching features to measure text similarity based on their distributed representations. These neural network based models have proven their effectiveness in previous works (Zhang et al., 2016; Fang et al., 2016; Wu et al., 2016; Zhao et al., 2016).

Word embedding cosine: we employ a pre-trained word embedding from `https://github.com/tbmihailov/semeval2016-task3-cqa`, where the dimensionality of word vectors is 200. We average the embedding of words in a piece of text as its representation, and compute the cosine of the representations of two pieces of text as a feature.

Bi-LSTM: long short term memory (LSTM) is an advanced type of recurrent neural network which leverages memory cells and gates to learn long-term dependencies within a sequence (Hochreiter and Schmidhuber, 1997). We use a bidirectional LSTM (bi-LSTM) with a multi-layer perceptron (MLP) to calculate a matching score for a text pair as a feature.

Specifically, given a text pair (S_x, S_y), the model looks up an embedding table to convert S_x and S_y to $\mathbf{S}_x = [e_{x,1}, ..., e_{x,i}, ..., e_{x,I}]$ and $\mathbf{S}_y = [e_{y,1}, ..., e_{y,i}, ..., e_{y,J}]$ respectively, where $e_{x,i}, e_{y,i}$ are the embeddings of the i-th words of S_x and S_y respectively. Then $\mathbf{S}_x$ and $\mathbf{S}_y$ are encoded in hidden sequences by a bi-LSTM which consists of a forward LSTM and a backward LSTM. The forward LSTM reads $\mathbf{S}_x$ in its order (i.e., from $w_{x,1}$ to $w_{x,I}$) and transforms it to a forward hidden sequence $\{\overrightarrow{h}_{x,i}\}_{i=1}^{I}$. $\forall i \in \{1, ..., I\}$, $\overrightarrow{h}_{x,i}$ is defined by:

$$i_i = \sigma(W^{(i)}e_{x,i} + U^{(i)}h_{x,i-1} + b^{(i)})$$
$$f_i = \sigma(W^{(f)}e_{x,i} + U^{(f)}h_{x,i-1} + b^{(f)})$$
$$o_i = \sigma(W^{(o)}e_{x,i} + U^{(o)}h_{x,i-1} + b^{(o)})$$
$$u_i = \tanh(W^{(u)}e_{x,i} + U^{(u)}h_{x,i-1} + b^{(u)})$$
$$c_i = i_i \otimes u_i + f_i \otimes c_{(i-1)}$$
$$h_i = o_i \otimes \tanh(c_i),$$

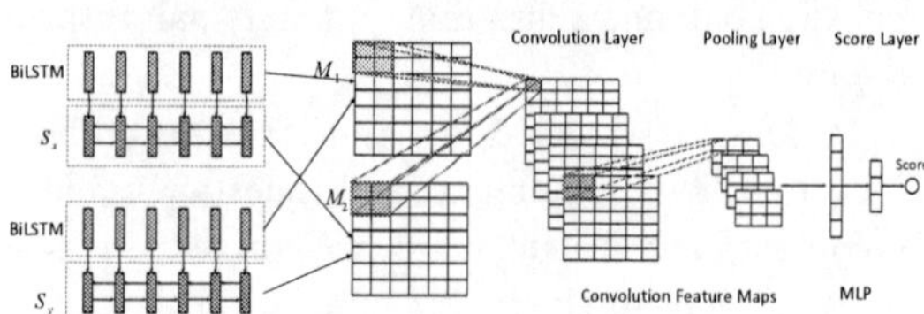

Figure 1: Architecture of 2D matching network

where $\sigma(\cdot)$ is a sigmoid function and $\tanh(\cdot)$ is a hyperbolic tangent function. $W^{(i)}$, $W^{(f)}$, $W^{(o)}$, $W^{(u)}$ $U^{(i)}$, $U^{(f)}$, $U^{(o)}$, $U^{(u)}$, $b^{(i)}$, $b^{(f)}$, $b^{(o)}$, and $b^{(u)}$ are parameters. Similarly, the backward LSTM reads $\mathbf{S}_x$ in its reverse order (i.e., from $w_{x,I}$ to $w_{x,1}$) and transforms it to a backward hidden sequence $\{\overleftarrow{h}_{x,i}\}_{i=1}^{I}$. Then $\forall i \in \{1, \ldots, I\}$, we concatenate $\overleftarrow{h}_{x,i}$ and $\overrightarrow{h}_{x,i}$ as $h_{x,i}$, and then represent S_x as $v_x = average(h_{x,1}, ..., h_{x,I})$. Following the same procedure, we have v_y as the representation of S_y. Finally, we concatenate (v_x, v_y) as an input of a multi-layer perceptron (MLP) to calculate a score.

2D matching network: the model is a variant of the one proposed in (Wu et al., 2016) which has proven effective on the data of SemEval-2015. The model in (Wu et al., 2016) leverages prior knowledge and performs text matching with multiple channels. In our system, we only use two channels, which means we do not take prior knowledge such as knowledge base (Zheng et al., 2016) and topic information into consideration. The architecture is shown in Figure 1. Given a text pair (S_x, S_y), their word embedding representations $\mathbf{S}_x$, $\mathbf{S}_y$ and their bi-LSTM representations $\{h_{x,i}\}_{i=1}^{I}$ and $\{h_{y,i}\}_{i=1}^{J}$, we compute a word similarity matrix $\mathbf{M}_1 = [m_{1,i,j}]_{I \times J}$ and a sequence similarity matrix $\mathbf{M}_2 = [m_{2,i,j}]_{I \times J}$. $\forall i, j$, the (i, j)-th element of $\mathbf{M}_1$ is defined by

$$m_{1,i,j} = e_{u,i}^{\top} \cdot e_{r,j}. \tag{1}$$

where $e_{u,i}$ is the i-th word embedding of the utterance, and $e_{r,j}$ is the j-th word embedding of the response. The (i, j)-th element of $\mathbf{M}_2$ is defined by

$$m_{2,i,j} = h_{u,i}^{\top} \mathbf{A} h_{r,j}, \tag{2}$$

where $\mathbf{A}$ is a parameter. After that, a convolutional neural network (CNN) takes $\mathbf{M}_1$ and $\mathbf{M}_2$ as input channels, and alternates convolution and max-pooling operations (The system only has one convolution and one pooling layer). Suppose that

$z^{(l,f)} = \left[z_{i,j}^{(l,f)}\right]_{I^{(l,f)} \times J^{(l,f)}}$ denotes the output of feature maps of type-f on layer-l, where $z^{(0,f)} = \mathbf{M}_f$, $\forall f = 1, 2$. On convolution layers, we employ a 2D convolution operation with a window size $r_w^{(l,f)} \times r_h^{(l,f)}$, and define $z_{i,j}^{(l,f)}$ as

$$z_{i,j}^{(l,f)} = \sigma(\sum_{f'=0}^{F_{l-1}} \sum_{s=0}^{r_w^{(l,f)}} \sum_{t=0}^{r_h^{(l,f)}} \mathbf{w}_{s,t}^{(l,f)} \cdot z_{i+s,j+t}^{(l-1,f')} + b^{l,k}), \tag{3}$$

where $\sigma(\cdot)$ is a ReLU (Nair and Hinton, 2010), and $\mathbf{w}^{(l,f)} \in \mathbb{R}^{r_w^{(l,f)} \times r_h^{(l,f)}}$ and $b^{l,k}$ are parameters of the f-th feature map on the l-th layer, and F_{l-1} is the number of feature maps on the $(l-1)$-th layer. A max pooling operation can be formulated as

$$z_{i,j}^{(l,f)} = \max_{p_w^{(l,f)} > s \geq 0} \max_{p_h^{(l,f)} > t \geq 0} z_{i+s,j+t}. \tag{4}$$

Feature vectors at the last pooling layer are concatenated to form a similarity vector v, which is fed to an MLP to predict the final similarity score.

We learn the bi-LSTM and the 2D matching network by minimizing cross entropy on training data. Let Θ denote the parameters, then the objective function can be formulated as

$$-\sum_{i=1}^{N} [l_i log(f(s_{x,i}, s_{y,i})) + (1 - l_i) log(1 - f(s_{x,i}, s_{y,i}))], \tag{5}$$

where $l_i \in \{0, 1\}$ is a label, $f(s_{x,i}, s_{y,i})$ is the neural network we want to learn, and N is the number of instances in the training data.

We use two data sets to learn the neural networks, which means we obtain two features from each model. The first one is the training data provided by SemEval-2017 task 3, and the other one is 2 million Yahoo! Answer data we crawled, which is released in (Zhang et al., 2016). In both data, question subjects and question bodies are concatenated together. In SemEval-2017 data, comments in Subtask A are annotated as Good, PotentiallyUseful, and Bad, and we treat "Good" as 1 and the others as 0. In Subtask B, each related question is annotated as PerfectMatch, Relevant, and Irrelevant, and we treat "PerfectMatch" and "Relevant" as 1 and "Irrelevant" as "0". The Yahoo Answer data is only used to learn the neural networks for Subtask A, in which we take a question and its best answer as a positive instance, and randomly sample an answer from other questions as a negative instance. The motivation of leveraging external data is that the training data of SemEval-2017 is small, which may cause overfitting in learning of neural networks.

	Subtask A				Subtask B			
	Train			Test	Train			Test
	2016-train	2016-dev	2016-test	2017-test	2016-train	2016-dev	2016-test	2017-test
Original questions	-	-	-	-	267	50	70	88
Related questions	6154	244	327	293	2670	500	700	880
Comments	37848	2440	3270	2930	-	-	-	

Table 1: Statistics of the datasets

2.4 Task Specific Features

The features described above are used in both Subtask A and Subtask B. In addition to them, we also design some specific features for each subtask.

In Subtask A, we design some features based on heuristic rules which might indicate whether a comment is good or not: (i) whether a comment is written by the author of the question. (ii) the length of a comment. (iii) whether a comment contains URLs or email addresses. (iv) whether a comment contains positive or negative smileys, e.g., ;), :), ;(, :(.

In Subtask B, a related question has a metadata field that shows its relative rank in an external search engine by considering its similarity with the original question. We use the relative rank as a feature for subtask B.

2.5 Feature Combination

Since both Subtask A and Subtask B are ranking problems, we learn gradient boosted regression trees using XgBoost (Chen and Guestrin, 2016) as ranking models to combine all features. The ranking models are learned by minimizing pairwise loss on training instances provided by the subtasks.

3 Experiments

3.1 Data Sets and Evaluation Metrics

We used the data sets provided by SemEval-2017 (Nakov et al., 2017). Table 1 gives the statistics. We employed Mean Average Precision (MAP), Average Recall (AveRec), and Mean Reciprocal Rank (MRR) as evaluation metrics.

3.2 Parameter Tuning and Feature Selection

We tuned parameters according to average MAP on 5-fold cross validation (CV) with grid search algorithm. There are three sensitive parameters of XGBoost that should be tuned in training, namely *gamma*, *subsample*, *colsample_bytree*. The best parameters of two subtasks is shown in Table 2.

	Subtask A	Subtask B
gamma	19	10
subsample	0.5	1
colsample_bytree	0.5	0.2
bst:max_depth	10	10
bst:eta	0.01	0.01
scale_pos_weight	0.7	0.7

Table 2: Parameters of XgBoost

	Bi-LSTM	2D MN
Two LSTMs	not shared	shared
Dim. of embedding	200	200
Dim. of hidden states	200	200
# CNN filters	-	8
CNN filter size	-	(3,3)
nodes of MLP	(200,50,2)	(400,50,2)

Table 3: Parameters of neural networks

We adopted Adagrad (Duchi et al., 2011) which is a stochastic gradient descent method to optimize the neural network models. In order to prevent overfitting, we used early-stopping (Lawrence and Giles, 2000) and dropout (Srivastava et al., 2014) with rate of 0.5. In bi-LSTM and 2D matching network (2D MN), the dimensionality of word embedding is 200. Word embedding was initialized by the result of word2vec (Mikolov et al., 2013) trained on unannotated Qatar data (Nakov et al., 2017) and updated in training. We set the initial learning rate and batch size as 0.001 and 30 respectively. The other parameters of the two models are listed in Table 3.

We conducted feature selection by 5-fold CV to filter out useless features for the two subtasks. Our approach is that we first used all features and obtained an MAP on 5-fold CV, then we removed the features one by one and checked how MAP changes. If MAP increased significantly by removing that feature, we removed the feature. The final result is that we preserved all features for Subtask A, and removed neural matching features for Subtask B. Details of feature contributions will be described in Section 3.5.

Apart from the primary submission, we also

Features	5-fold cross validation			Test-2017		
	MAP	AvgRec	MRR	MAP	AvgRec	MRR
All	70.65	88.54	76.17	88.24	93.87	92.34
- traditional NLP features	69.06	87.94	75.16	87.83	93.60	92.73
- tf-idf cosine	70.28	88.21	76.23	87.88	93.75	92.21
- LCS	69.95	88.01	76.15	88.04	93.90	92.21
- word overlap	69.69	88.10	75.41	88.62	94.14	92.97
- tree kernels	69.50	87.98	95.38	87.97	93.84	92.38
- translation probability	69.77	88.25	75.50	87.81	93.77	92.59
- neural matching features	64.81	82.85	71.91	85.06	91.40	91.52
- word embedding cosine	69.90	88.28	76.24	88.31	93.81	92.40
- bi-LSTM	67.57	86.67	74.54	88.02	93.90	92.54
- 2D MN	69.72	88.01	75.86	88.17	94.04	92.50
- meta-data features	68.09	86.75	74.90	86.54	92.58	91.66

Table 4: Subtask A: results of ablation experiments

Features	5-fold cross validation			Test-2017		
	MAP	AvgRec	MRR	MAP	AvgRec	MRR
All	77.13	91.86	83.89	44.78	79.13	49.89
- tf-idf cosine	72.81	87.85	79.91	44.80	78.60	49.89
- LCS	74.25	88.95	80.90	42.93	78.59	46.94
- word overlap	74.04	88.79	80.67	45.19	80.63	49.65
- tree kernels	76.10	90.98	82.88	45.48	80.63	49.65
- translation probability	75.99	90.35	82.20	44.89	79.57	49.18
- meta-data feature	76.14	91.16	82.98	47.00	80.31	50.83
+ neural matching features*	71.32	86.74	78.21	42.77	77.23	45.98
+ word embedding cosine*	74.76	89.31	81.21	43.59	78.76	46.83
+ bi-LSTM*	71.43	86.88	78.39	42.89	77.89	46.65
+ 2D MN*	70.39	85.49	77.53	43.46	78.60	46.71

Table 5: Subtask B: results of ablation experiments. * means we did not use it in our submitted system for its bad performance on CV.

submitted two contrastive results. The only difference is the parameter setting of XgBoost. In the primary submission, we selected the parameters with which our system achieved the best performance on 5-fold CV, while in the two contrastive submissions, we selected two parameter combinations that correspond to the smallest and the second smallest variance of MAP on 5 runs.

Submission	MAP	AvgRec	MRR
primary	88.24	93.87	92.34
contrastive1	88.17	93.82	92.17
contrastive2	88.18	93.91	92.45
KeLP (first)	88.43	93.79	92.82
Baseline (IR)	72.61	79.32	82.37

Table 6: Subtask A: results of our system on test set

3.3 Baseline

We selected the relative rank provided by the search engine, Google, as a baseline method, and denote it as IR baseline.

3.4 Overall results

We show the primary and contrastive results of Subtask A and Subtask B in Table 6 and Table 7 respectively. There is no significant difference between our primary and contrastive results, indicating that the final result is not sensitive to our parameter selection of Xgboost. On subtask A, the primary and contrastive results significantly outperform the baseline method with a big margin. The primary result, achieving 88.24 on MAP, is ranked second in all submitted systems, demonstrating that neural matching features are effective

Submission	MAP	AvgRec	MRR
primary	44.78	79.13	49.88
contrastive1	43.89	79.48	48.18
contrastive2	44.79	79.13	49.89
simbow (first)	47.22	82.60	50.07
Baseline (IR)	41.85	77.59	46.42

Table 7: Subtask B: results of our system on test set

on the task of answer selection. Our improvement is not big on Subtask B, which is only 3 points on MAP score. This is because we only use shallow features on this task and neural matching features are useless according to our experiments. There are two reasons why neural matching fails on this task: (1) training data provided by SemEval-2017 is too small to train a neural network, and our external data only consists of question-answer pairs which does not support learning neural networks for question-question similarity; (2) a question and its question often share most of words and are only different on a small proportion of function words. Neural matching models, however, are not good at capturing such difference.

3.5 Feature Contribution

We conducted ablation experiments on training data with 5-fold CV and on test data to examine the usefulness of features. The conclusion is that traditional NLP features are effective on both subtasks, while neural matching features can only improve the system performance on Subtask A.

In Table 4, we present the results on Subtask A, including our system with all features and the system with one of the features excluded. We can observe that all features are useful on training data, but the system can achieve a better result on test data if we exclude the word overlap feature. Neural matching features are important on Subtask A, with which we obtain 5 point gain on training data and 3 point gain on test data. Meta-data features are also useful, indicating that they are good complementary to the similarity based features.

In Table 5, we show the results of ablation experiments on Subtask B. Neural matching features caused performance drop on this task, therefore we did not include them in our submitted system. Although all the traditional NLP features are useful on training data, *word overlap*, *tree kernels*, and *meta-data feature* hurt the performance on the test data. It is also worth noting that our system

can be further improved on the test data if the meta-data feature, i.e., relative rank of Google, is excluded from our system.

4   Conclusion

We developed a ranking system with neural matching features for Subtask A and Subtask B in SemEval-2017. The system holds the second place in Subtask A and the fifth place in Subtask B, which demonstrates its efficacy on answer selection and similar question retrieval.

5   Acknowledgment

Thanks for the valuable comments given by anonymous reviewers and the discussion with Zhao Yan. This work was supported by the National Natural Science Foundation of China (Grand Nos. 61672081,U1636211, 61370126), Beijing Advanced Innovation Center for Imaging Technology (No.BAICIT-2016001), National High Technology Research and Development Program of China (No.2015AA016004),the Fund of the State Key Laboratory of Software Development Environment (No.SKLSDE-2015ZX-16).

References

L Allison and T I Dix. 1986. A bit-string longest-common-subsequence algorithm. *Information Processing Letters* 23(5):305–310.

Tianqi Chen and Carlos Guestrin. 2016. Xgboost: A scalable tree boosting system. In *ACM SIGKDD International Conference on Knowledge Discovery and Data Mining*. pages 785–794.

Michael Collins and Nigel Duffy. 2002. New ranking algorithms for parsing and tagging: kernels over discrete structures, and the voted perceptron. In *Meeting on Association for Computational Linguistics*. pages 263–270.

John Duchi, Elad Hazan, and Yoram Singer. 2011. Adaptive subgradient methods for online learning and stochastic optimization. *Journal of Machine Learning Research* 12(7):2121–2159.

Hanyin Fang, Fei Wu, Zhou Zhao, Xinyu Duan, Yueting Zhuang, and Martin Ester. 2016. Community-based question answering via heterogeneous social network learning. In *Proceedings of the Thirtieth AAAI Conference on Artificial Intelligence*. AAAI Press, pages 122–128.

S Hochreiter and J Schmidhuber. 1997. Long short-term memory. *Neural Computation* 9(8):1735–1780.

Jiwoon Jeon, W. Bruce Croft, and Joon Ho Lee. 2005. Finding similar questions in large question and answer archives. In *ACM International Conference on Information and Knowledge Management*. pages 84–90.

Dan Klein and Christopher D Manning. 2003. Accurate unlexicalized parsing. In *Meeting on Association for Computational Linguistics*. pages 423–430.

Steve Lawrence and C. Lee Giles. 2000. Overfitting and neural networks: Conjugate gradient and back-propagation 1:114–119 vol.1.

Tie-Yan Liu et al. 2009. Learning to rank for information retrieval. *Foundations and Trends® in Information Retrieval* 3(3):225–331.

Edward Loper and Steven Bird. 2002. Nltk: the natural language toolkit. In *ACL 2006, International Conference on Computational Linguistics and Meeting of the Association for Computational Linguistics, Proceedings of the Conference, Sydney, Australia, 17-21 July*. pages 63–70.

Tomas Mikolov, Ilya Sutskever, Kai Chen, Greg Corrado, and Jeffrey Dean. 2013. Distributed representations of words and phrases and their compositionality. *Advances in Neural Information Processing Systems* 26:3111–3119.

Alessandro Moschitti. 2006. Efficient convolution kernels for dependency and constituent syntactic trees. In *European Conference on Machine Learning*. pages 318–329.

Vinod Nair and Geoffrey E Hinton. 2010. Rectified linear units improve restricted boltzmann machines. In *Proceedings of the 27th international conference on machine learning (ICML-10)*. pages 807–814.

Preslav Nakov, Doris Hoogeveen, Lluís Màrquez, Alessandro Moschitti, Hamdy Mubarak, Timothy Baldwin, and Karin Verspoor. 2017. SemEval-2017 task 3: Community question answering. In *Proceedings of the 11th International Workshop on Semantic Evaluation*. Association for Computational Linguistics, Vancouver, Canada, SemEval '17.

Gerard Salton and Christopher Buckley. 1988. Term-weighting approaches in automatic text retrieval. *Information processing & management* 24(5):513–523.

B Schlkopf, K Tsuda, and J Vert. 2003. Fast kernels for string and tree matching. *Advances in Neural Information Processing Systems* 15(1):296.

Mike Schuster and Kuldip K Paliwal. 1997. Bidirectional recurrent neural networks. *IEEE Transactions on Signal Processing* 45(11):2673–2681.

Nitish Srivastava, Geoffrey Hinton, Alex Krizhevsky, Ilya Sutskever, and Ruslan Salakhutdinov. 2014. Dropout: a simple way to prevent neural networks from overfitting. *Journal of Machine Learning Research* 15(1):1929–1958.

Yu Wu, Wei Wu, Zhoujun Li, and Ming Zhou. 2016. Knowledge enhanced hybrid neural network for text matching. *arXiv preprint arXiv:1611.04684* .

Kai Zhang, Wei Wu, Fang Wang, Ming Zhou, and Zhoujun Li. 2016. Learning distributed representations of data in community question answering for question retrieval. In *Proceedings of the Ninth ACM International Conference on Web Search and Data Mining*. ACM, pages 533–542.

Zhou Zhao, Qifan Yang, Deng Cai, Xiaofei He, and Yueting Zhuang. 2016. Expert finding for community-based question answering via ranking metric network learning. In *Proceedings of the Twenty-Fifth International Joint Conference on Artificial Intelligence*. AAAI Press, pages 3000–3006.

Hao Zheng, Zhoujun Li, Senzhang Wang, Zhao Yan, and Jianshe Zhou. 2016. Aggregating inter-sentence information to enhance relation extraction. In *Proceedings of the Thirtieth AAAI Conference on Artificial Intelligence*. AAAI Press, pages 3108–3114.

MoRS At SemEval-2017 Task 3: Easy To Use SVM In Ranking Tasks

Miguel J. Rodrigues[‡] and Francisco Couto[1]

[1]LaSIGE, Faculdade de Ciências, Universidade de Lisboa, Portugal
mrodrigues@lasige.di.fc.ul.pt, fcouto@di.fc.ul.pt

Abstract

This paper describes our system, dubbed MoRS (Modular Ranking System), pronounced 'Morse', which participated in Task 3 of SemEval-2017. We used MoRS to perform the Community Question Answering Task 3, which consisted on reordering a set of comments according to their usefulness in answering the question in the thread. This was made for a large collection of questions created by a user community. As for this challenge we wanted to go back to simple, easy-to-use, and somewhat forgotten technologies that we think, in the hands of non-expert people, could be reused in their own data sets. Some of our techniques included the annotation of text, the retrieval of meta-data for each comment, POS tagging and Named Entity Recognition, among others. These gave place to syntactical analysis and semantic measurements. Finally we show and discuss our results and the context of our approach, which is part of a more comprehensive system in development, named MoQA.

1 Credits

This work was supported by FCT through funding of LaSIGE Research Unit, ref. UID/CEC/00408/2013.

2 Introduction

The main difference between Question Answering (QA) and Community Question Answering (cQA) is, while QA systems rely on a user query in order to search and prepare an answer based on the searching capabilities it already has and its documents, in cQA the query and respective related answers are already provided, being only necessary a reordering by relevance of such answers, or perhaps even a rephrasing of such an answer in order to suit better the query.

In recent times, QA systems have attracted great interest in the information retrieval community, and also in the cQA (Höffner et al., 2016).

A characteristic of cQA, is that a user resorts to the web for answers without a given structured knowledge base. The arbitrariness of cQA forums, the dependence and waiting time on their results, may slow the gathering of answers in real time. Also, public forums are dependent of the users input (i.e. answers), which might be rather unstructured, not straight to the point, not related to the question at hand, not well written (i.e. grammatically), lengthy or even incorrect. Our team shares this exact same interest and continuous development in this area.

Our participation focused on the Community Question Answering (CQA) Task 3 SubTask A of 2017 SemEval edition [1] (Nakov et al., 2017), which consisted on reordering a set of comments according to their usefulness in answering the question in the thread. This was made for a large collection of questions created by a user community, provided by the task organizers. Succinctly, Subtask A: Question-Comment Similarity, involved ranking "Good" comments above the "PotentiallyUseful" or "Bad" comments, where there was no distinction between them, since their difference was not important for the task's evaluation method. Finally, the result file was to be a ranked list of the probability of the comments according to their relevance.

We developed MoRS (pronounced "morse"),

Corresponding author: mrodrigues@lasige.di.fc.ul.pt

[1]`http://alt.qcri.org/semeval2017/task3/`

Proceedings of the 11th International Workshop on Semantic Evaluations (SemEval-2017), pages 287–291,
Vancouver, Canada, August 3 - 4, 2017. ©2017 Association for Computational Linguistics

which went back to simple and rather effective technologies, making it available at a later stage to the public, with minimal pre-requisites and ease of (re)use. MoRS addressed Subtask A of Task 3 by first recognizing relevant terms in each query and also in the respective comments in the thread related to the question being analyzed. Next, the system builds its features by passing through a submodule which analyzes each question and respective comments. Then, MoRS compares named entities from the questions and comments and cross-references them. It also identifies the comments that shared most concepts with the ones associated to the thread question. MoRS employed a semantic similarity to measure how close in meaning both comments and questions are even if they do no share the same exact concepts.(Couto and Pinto, 2013) Additionally, MoRS used Machine Learning (Pedregosa et al., 2011) techniques to classify if a comment as "Good", as explained in the description of the Subtask, and "Not Good" according to the comment's relevance.

The paper also describes the main system where MoRS is part of, which is a larger and modular pipeline, MoQA (Modular Question Answering, pronounced "mocha") and also presents the result measure values obtained in Subtask A. Despite successful implementation we did not get the desired results due to data set corruption found only after result submission.

The following section, Section 3, approaches some works that have inspired our system overall, Section 4 explains its composing sub-modules, in Section 5, we present and discuss our results, and finally in sections 6 and 7 we talk about our conclusions and how we plan to approach the future work and applicability of MoRS.

3   Related Work

When coming upon methodology and features to use, the most important ones features came from (Mihaylova et al., 2016), from where we could see such features like: (1) the number of question marks in the documents, (2) whether it contains smileys, e-mails, "thank you" phrases, (3) number of offensive words from a predefined list, (4) length of the answer (in characters), (5) if it includes a first person singular, or (6) plural pronoun, or even (7) if the author of the comment is the same as he author of the question at hand. Moreover, we could use, if available, character-

istics such as the position of the comment in the thread, and the ID of the author of the comment. After tokenization, another metric used is the ratio of the comment length and of the question length (in of number of tokens), the number of comments from the same user the thread and the order in which they are written by him. Other aspect of meta-data worthy of exploration is the presence and the number of links in the question and in the comment (inbound or outbound), taking into consideration that the presence of a reference to another resource is indicative of a relevant comment(Mohtarami et al., 2016). These features were the ones we explored in the development of MoRS.

The modularity promoted by OAQA (Yang et al., 2015) and YodaQA (Baudiš, 2015) along with an also modular and reusable and reshapable implementation developed in WS4A (Rodrigues et al., 2016), shaped the idea of a system for lay users, using resources easily available.

4   MoRS Pipeline

As we can see in Figure 1, the system is separated and defined in several modules that work as a pipeline, where each module was designed to be as much independent from the others as possible. The most complex module is the Scorer, which will be detailed in this section. The first step, takes the xml files provided by the organization that go through our xml parser (a). This parser is specific to the format of the xml file, and in principle is the only module that has to be user defined for future use in other projects. The information that comes out of this parsing is the question itself, its author, and from each comment, the author, the text that compose the comment and, if in training phase, the golden score of the comment. The comment then goes through the Scorer module (b), and each comment goes through various scoring methods already described in section 2 which involve, (1) cross-matching of Named Entities (exact and partial tokens), using Stanford Named Entities Recognition (Finkel et al., 2005), determining the number of named entities that the comment has in common with the question; (2) if the author of the comment is the same as the author of the question, giving it away that such a comment would not be fit, since the questioner only on rare occasions answers his own question; (3) if the comment has any question marks, proving that

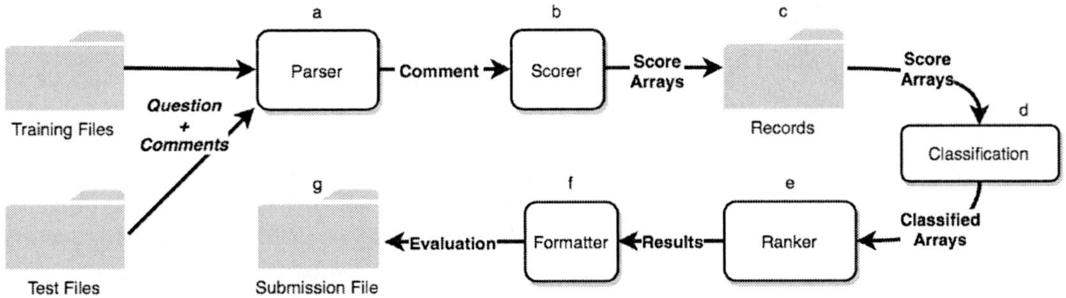

Figure 1: The pipeline of MoRS with its main modules

that comment does not answer the question by not being assertive; (4) if there is any swear words or even (5) misspelled words (from a given list), that may demonstrate a lack of zeal in the answer, plain ignorance or at least lack of effort from the author when answering; (6) sentence semantic similarity score for sentences between the question and the comment, based on the Wu-Palmer metric [2]; (7) if there are any personal pronouns, making the notion of opinion making, which may indicate an answer to the question; (8) the presence of other question URLs or even (9) image URLs which might indicate that a question might be already answered in another thread; (10) the existence of nouns in common may point to similar concepts in discussion in the comment; (11) the presence of smileys, from related work showed that they are not a good sign or assurance in this way, because they did not show seriousness from the comment's author; (12) the number of comments from that author, in which a relative large number indicates that the author has many comments in that thread that at least do not answer correctly the question, therefore the need of other comments. Finally,(13) the length of the comment and it's ratio (14) with the length of the question.

After each set of question plus ten comments, the resulting arrays are written to the Records file (c) for the next step: the classification phase (d): after all questions and correspondent answers are dealt with, we use Machine Learning, more specifically Support Vector Machines (SVM), to classify between "Good" comments and other comments, based on the information provided in the training files.

The "training" phase from the classification

ends here, in step (d).

In the second phase, the test files go through the same modules as the training files did, with the difference that in the classification module, the resulting arrays are classified as "Good" or not, and then they go through an implementation of SVM^{light}, SVMrank (e).

SVMrank is an instance of SVMstruct (Joachims, 2002) which mainly features: a fast optimization algorithm, a working set selection based on steepest feasible descent, the ability to handle thousands of support vectors and training examples.

The classified arrays are then transformed in the following format, where the first digit is the importance/relevance of that comment. The larger this first number, more important is the comment, qid denotes the question number, for classification within that question, and the 1:, 2:, 3:, etc. are the scores for each feature. Here follows an example:

```
1 qid:2 1:0 2:0 3:1 4:0.2
2 qid:2 1:1 2:0 3:1 4:0.4
1 qid:2 1:0 2:0 3:1 4:0.1
1 qid:2 1:0 2:0 3:1 4:0.2
```

SVMrank has also a learning phase, where the scored arrays from the training files were provided. After the ranking scores for each question is given, these are run through the Formatter module (f), where the submission file is prepared according to the Subtask's requirements specified in the instructions (g).

5   Results

Our results placed us on the bottom of the table, with the best MAP result belonging to the KeLP team of 88.43, our result of 63.32, and the baseline just slightly lower of 62.30.

Comparing to last year's standards and to our

---

[2] http://sujitpal.blogspot.pt/2014/12/semantic-similarity-for-short-sentences.html

Submission	MAP	AvgRec	MRR	P	R	F1	Acc
KeLP	79.19	88.82	86.42	76.96	55.30	64.36	75.11
MoRS	*81.15*	*81.42*	*88.44*	*74.37*	*99.94*	*85.28*	*74.34*
Baseline	45.56	65.42	53.50	34.44	76.41	47.47	43.32

Table 1: MoRS' comparison to last year's task 3 results.

Submission	MAP	AvgRec	MRR	P	R	F1	Acc
Beihang	0.714	89.2	77.265	-	-	-	-
MoRS	*79.91*	*80.02*	*86.51*	*74.39*	*100*	*85.31*	*74.39*
Baseline	45.56	65.4	53.50	-	-	-	-

Table 2: MoRS' results for the development set of 2017.

team's surprise, MoRS was far from achieving a comparable performance. After verifying our classification module of "Good" and not "Good" answers, we noticed that our module was defect, lacking about 95% of the arrays necessary to build it, due to a small pipeline error which did not warn us about this mistake, and continued regardless.

After re-running MoRS, and also verifying every step of our system, we compared the results of MoRS with the data-sets from last years' task (Table 1) and with the development set of 2017 (Table 2), and confirmed that in fact, this year's results would have been much better if the models were correctly built.

To our surprise, our scores were significantly lower than what we were experiencing during our scores during the development phase, which achieved very similar results, consisting in a MAP score of 79.91. Highlight to a maximum score of 100 in the Recall.

Another thing we noticed is that the SVMrank had quite the same behavior in both cases, so the issue of the results was exactly the classification of good answers, which brought the results to a surprising first place if it had participated in SemEval 2016 Task3. This was mainly because of our research in the features used by the teams in that year's task and choosing what we thought best fit the purpose of this task. The scores for both 2016 test set and 2017 dev set are available in `https://github.com/migueljrodrigues/MoRS-Scores`.

6 Conclusion

As for this challenge we wanted to go back to simple, easy-to-use, and somewhat forgotten technologies (some going back to 2002) that we think, in the hands of non-experts, could be reused in their own data sets. To simplify the task of fu-

ture users, we implemented a pipeline, where only the data set provided has some restrictions of format (xml), and we took to a minimum the prerequisites necessary to run the same pipeline (xml files of training and testing), which does not need any computational requisites unavailable to those that do not have large processing resources. The result in this challenge is negative due to a pipeline error. Despite this, after solving the problem, MoRS achieved top results comparing to last year's scores and this year's development set, and so we believe in bringing an easy and simple system to the hands of non-experts in this area, while taking advantage of its capabilities.

7 Future Work

For the algorithm in itself, and since the system is already in place, we pretend to take part in next years Task, maybe with a larger participation in the other subtasks of Task 3. Also, some immediate improvements are to be regarded, such as the handling of empty questions, that represented in the subject, and even use the subject to better grab a context of the question in itself.

In the future, we intend to assimilate this module into MoQA, a Modular Question Answering system, already in development. This system intends to make use of the capabilities developed here in order to rank answers from biomedical articles (from PubMed) taking into account a user query. The system, besides the biomedical example, is to be modular to any domain knowledge, if the correct data-set is to be provided. This system also has the ability to adapt to general questions without a specific domain knowledge, thanks to implementation of DBpedia [3] RDF queries through a Web Service. Finally, MoQA will be easy to understand and reshape according to the users' likeness, if they want to, due to its' modular nature and clear and simple division of the same modules.

References

Petr Baudiš. 2015. Yodaqa: a modular question answering system pipeline. In *POSTER 2015-19th International Student Conference on Electrical Engineering*. pages 1156–1165.

Francisco M Couto and H Sofia Pinto. 2013. The next generation of similarity measures that fully ex-

---

[3] http://dbpedia.org

plore the semantics in biomedical ontologies. *Journal of bioinformatics and computational biology* 11(05):1371001.

Jenny Rose Finkel, Trond Grenager, and Christopher Manning. 2005. Incorporating non-local information into information extraction systems by gibbs sampling. In *Proceedings of the 43rd annual meeting on association for computational linguistics*. Association for Computational Linguistics, pages 363–370.

Konrad Höffner, Sebastian Walter, Edgard Marx, Ricardo Usbeck, Jens Lehmann, and Axel-Cyrille Ngonga Ngomo. 2016. Survey on challenges of question answering in the semantic web. *Submitted to the Semantic Web Journal* .

Thorsten Joachims. 2002. Optimizing search engines using clickthrough data. In *Proceedings of the eighth ACM SIGKDD international conference on Knowledge discovery and data mining*. ACM, pages 133–142.

Tsvetomila Mihaylova, Pepa Gencheva, Martin Boyanov, Ivana Yovcheva, Todor Mihaylov, Momchil Hardalov, Yasen Kiprov, Daniel Balchev, Ivan Koychev, Preslav Nakov, et al. 2016. Super team at semeval-2016 task 3: Building a feature-rich system for community question answering. *Proceedings of SemEval* pages 836–843.

Mitra Mohtarami, Yonatan Belinkov, Wei-Ning Hsu, Yu Zhang, Tao Lei, Kfir Bar, D. Scott Cyphers, and Jim Glass. 2016. Sls at semeval-2016 task 3: Neural-based approaches for ranking in community question answering. In *SemEval@NAACL-HLT*.

Preslav Nakov, Doris Hoogeveen, Lluís Márquez, Alessandro Moschitti, Hamdy Mubarak, Timothy Baldwin, and Karin Verspoor. 2017. SemEval-2017 task 3: Community question answering. In *Proceedings of the 11th International Workshop on Semantic Evaluation*. Association for Computational Linguistics, Vancouver, Canada, SemEval '17.

Fabian Pedregosa, Gaël Varoquaux, Alexandre Gramfort, Vincent Michel, Bertrand Thirion, Olivier Grisel, Mathieu Blondel, Peter Prettenhofer, Ron Weiss, Vincent Dubourg, et al. 2011. Scikit-learn: Machine learning in python. *Journal of Machine Learning Research* 12(Oct):2825–2830.

Miguel J. Rodrigues, Miguel Falé, Andre Lamurias, and Francisco M. Couto. 2016. WS4A: a biomedical question and answering system based on public web services and ontologies. *CoRR* abs/1609.08492. http://arxiv.org/abs/1609.08492.

Zi Yang, Niloy Gupta, Xiangyu Sun, Di Xu, Chi Zhang, and Eric Nyberg. 2015. Learning to answer biomedical factoid & list questions: Oaqa at bioasq 3b. In *CLEF (Working Notes)*.

EICA Team at SemEval-2017 Task 3: Semantic and Metadata-based Features for Community Question Answering

Yufei Xie, Maoquan Wang, Jing Ma, Jian Jiang, Zhao Lu
Department of Computer Science and Technology,
East China Normal University, Shanghai, P.R.China
yufeixie@ica.stc.sh.cn, zlu@cs.ecnu.edu.cn

Abstract

We describe our system for participating in SemEval-2017 Task 3 on Community Question Answering. Our approach relies on combining a rich set of various types of features: semantic and metadata. The most important types turned out to be the metadata feature and the semantic vectors trained on QatarLiving data. In the main Subtask C, our primary submission was ranked fourth, with a MAP of 13.48 and accuracy of 97.08. In Subtask A, our primary submission get into the top 50%.

1 Introduction

SemEval-2017 Task 3 on Community Question Answering (Nakov et al., 2017) aims to solve a real-life application problem. The main subtask C (Question-External Comment Similarity) asks to find an answer in the forum that is appropriate as a response to a newly posted question. This is achieved by retrieving similar questions and ranking their answers with respect to the new question. Three additional supporting subtasks are defined:

Subtask A (Question-Comment Similarity): Given a question from a question-comment thread, rank the comments within the thread based on their relevance with respect to the question. The comments in a question-comment thread are annotated as *Good, PotentiallyUseful* and *Bad*. A good ranking is the one that ranks all *Good* comments above *PotentiallyUseful* and *Bad* ones.

Subtask B (Question-Question Similarity): Given a new question, re-rank the similar questions retrieved by a search engine with respect to that question. The potentially relevant questions are annotated as *PerfectMatch, Relevant* and *Irrelevant* with respect to the original question. A good ranking is the one that the *PerfectMatch* and the *Relevant* questions are both ranked above the *Irrelevant* ones.

Subtask C (Question-External Comment Similarity): Given a new question and the set of the first 10 related questions (retrieved by a search engine), each associated with its first 10 comments appearing in its thread. Re-rank the 100 comments (10 questions × 10 comments) according to their relevance with respect to the original question.

2 Related Work

This year's SemEval-2017 Task3 is a follow up of SemEval-2016 Task3 (Nakov et al., 2016) on Answer Reranking in Community Question Answering. There are three reranking subtasks associated with the English dataset. Subtask A is the same as subtask A at SemEval-2015 Task 3 (Joty et al., 2015), but with slightly different annotation and a different evaluation measure.

The research of rerank can be classified into two categories, traditional feature engineering and newest deep neural network employing. The first type of method pays more attention on textural features exploiting. Textual features have been exploited well, including lexical features (e.g., n-grams), syntactic features (such as parse trees) and semantic features (for instance wordnet-based). Some work exploit various feature extraction approaches and indicates the importance of feature selection in the rerank task. (Filice et al., 2016; Franco-Salvador et al., 2016; Mihaylova et al., 2016). However those methods all face the problem of feature merging, due to many features may affect each other.

Most recently, convolution neural networks (C-NN) and recurrent neural networks (RNN) are employed in the task of text rerank (Wu and Lan, 2016; Qiu and Huang, 2015). Wu's team use both convolutional neural network and long-short ter-

Proceedings of the 11th International Workshop on Semantic Evaluations (SemEval-2017), pages 292–298,
Vancouver, Canada, August 3 - 4, 2017. ©2017 Association for Computational Linguistics

m memory network (Wu and Lan, 2016) to train the model. Qiu's model (Qiu and Huang, 2015) integrates sentence modeling and semantic matching into a single model, which can not only capture the useful information with convolutional and pooling layers, but also learn the matching metrics between the question and its answer. However, these methods all face the problem of too many parameters in the model and it is hard to choose the best parameters.

We build our system on top of the framework developed by (Mihaylov and Nakov, 2016). In addition, we extract more different kinds of features. In order to solve the problem of feature merging, we just try different combinations of features and choose the best one in the development set.

3 Data

There are 6,398 questons and 40,288 comments for subtask A, 317 original + 3,169 related questions for subtask B, and 317 original questions + 3,169 related questions + 31,690 comments for subtask C (Nakov et al., 2016).

We also used semantic vectors pretrained on Qatar Living Forum: 200 dimensional vectors, available for 472,100 words and phrases.

4 Method

In particular, we formulate all the three tasks as classification problems.

We use various of features like question and comment metadata; distance measures between the question and the comment; lexical semantics vectors for the question and for the comment.

4.1 Features

We use several semantic vector similarity and metadata feature groups. For the similarity measures mentioned below, we use cosine similarity (Nguyen and Bai, 2010):

$$1 - \frac{a.b}{\|a\|.\|b\|} \qquad (1)$$

Semantic Word Embeddings. We use semantic word embeddings obtained from Word2Vec models trained on different unannotated data sources including the QatarLiving and DohaNews (Abbar et al., 2016). For each piece of text such as comment text, question body and question subject, we construct the centroid vector from the vectors of all words in that text.

$$centroid(w_{1..n}) = \frac{\sum_{i=1}^{n} w_i}{n} \qquad (2)$$

4.1.1 Semantic Features

We use various similarity features calculated using the centroid word vectors on the question body, on the question subject and on the comment text, as well as on parts thereof:

Question to Answer similarity. We assume that a relevant answer should have a centroid vector that is close to that for the question (Min et al., 2017). We use the question body to comment text similarity, and question subject to comment text similarity.

Maximized similarity. We rank each word in the answer text to the question body centroid vector according to their similarity and we take the max similarity of the top N words (Fu and Murata, 2016). We take the top 1,2 and 3 similarities as features. The assumption here is that if the average similarity for the top N most similar words is high, then the answer might be relevant.

Aligned similarity. For each word in the question body, we choose the most similar word from the comment text and we take the average of all best word pair similarities as suggested in (Tran et al., 2015)

Dependency syntax tree based word vector similarities. We obtain the dependency syntax tree with the Stanford parser (De Marneffe and Manning, 2008), and we take similarities between centroid vectors of noun phrases from the comment text and the centroid vector of the noun phrases from the question body text. The assumption is that same parts of dependency syntax tree between the question and the comment might be closer than other parts of dependency tree.

Word clusters (WC) similarity. We cluster the word vectors from the Word2Vec vocabulary into 500 clusters (with 400 words per cluster on average) using K-Means clustering (Basu et al., 2002). We then calculate the cluster similarity between the question body word clusters and the answer text word clusters. For all experiments, we use clusters obtained from the Word2Vec model trained on QatarLiving forums with vector size of 100, window size 10, minimum words frequency of 5, and skip-gram 1.

LDA topic similarity. We perform topic clustering using Latent Dirichlet Allocation (LDA) as implemented in the gensim toolkit (Rehurek and

Sojka, 2010)on Train1+Train2 questions and comments. We build topic models with 150 topics. For each question body and comment text, we get the corresponding distribution, and calculated similarity. The assumption here is that if the question and the comment share similar topics, they are more likely to be relevant to each other.

Semantic features above can fully represent the similarity between the question and the comment, which is very important in the next classification part.

4.1.2 Metadata-based Features

Metadata-based features provide clues about the social aspects of the community (Kıcıman, 2010). Thus, except for the semantic features described above, we also used some common sense metadata features:

Answer containing a question mark. We think if the comment has a question mark, it may be another question, which might indicate a bad answer (Katzman et al., 2017).

The presence and the number of links in the question and in the comment. We count both inbound and outbound links. Our hypothesis is that the presence of a reference to another resource is indicative of a relevant comment (Newton et al., 2017).

Answer length. The assumption here is that longer answers could bring more useful detail (Yang et al., 2017).

Question length. If the question is longer, it may be more clear, which may help users give a more relevant answer (Figueroa, 2017).

Question to comment length. If the question is long and the answer is short, it may be less relevant.

The comment is written by the author of the question If the answer is posted by the same user who posted the question and it is relevant, why has he/she asked the question in the first place?

Answer rank in the thread. Earlier answers could be posted by users who visit the forum more often, and they may have read more similar questions and answers. Moreover, discussion in the forum tends to diverge from the question over time.

4.1.3 Other-extra Features

Some features neither belong to the semantic nor metadata-based features, we call them extra features. They are also useful in the task of rerank.

Special symbols. We think whether the comment text contains smiley, e-mails, phone numbers, only laughter, "thank you" phrases, personal opinions, or disagreement is an important feature (Toba et al., 2014).

Numbers of special part of speech We extract statistics about the number of verbs, nouns, pronouns, and adjectives in the question and in the comment, as well as the number of numbers.

Numbers of misspelled words We obtain the features relate to spelling and include number of misspelled words that are within edit distance 2 from a word in our vocabulary and number of offensive words from a predefined list (Agichtein et al., 2008).

4.2 Classifier

For each Question and Comment pair, we firstly extract the features described above from the Question body and the comment text. Then we concatenate the extracted features in a bag of features vector and have them normalized. After the normalization, the value are mapped to interval [-1,1]. At last, we input them into the classifier. In our experiments, we use L2-regularized logistic regression classifier (Buitinck et al., 2013) and SVM classifier (Zweigenbaum and Lavergne, 2016) respectively. For the logistic regression classifier, we tune the classifier with different values of the C (cost) parameter (Aono et al., 2016), and we take the one that yield the best accuracy on 10-fold cross-validation on the training set. For the SVM classifier, we choose different kernels (Moreno et al., 2003) and achieve the best results with RBF kernel. We only show the better results of above two classifiers in the next section. We use binary classification Good vs. Bad (including both Bad and Potentially Useful original labels). The output of the evaluation for each test example is a label, either Good or Bad, and the probability of being Good in the 0 to 1 range. We then use this output probability as a relevance rank for each Comment in the Question thread.

5 Experiments and Evalution

This section presents the evaluation of the SemEval-2017 Task 3 on CQA (Nakov et al., 2017). Note that for our system EICA we did not use data from SemEval-2015 CQA. The best result of each partition and subtask is highlighted. Our percentage comparisons all use absolute values.

Table 1

Results of Subtask A: English Question-Comment Similarity(test set for 2016).

Model	MAP	AvgRec	MRR	P	R	F_1	Acc
Random baseline	52.80	66.52	58.71	40.56	74.57	52.55	45.26
Search engine	59.53	72.60	67.83	–	–	–	–
Kelp (Top 1)	**79.19**	88.82	86.42	76.96	55.30	64.36	75.11
ConvKN (Top 2)	77.66	88.05	84.93	75.56	58.84	66.16	75.54
SemanticZ (Top 3)	77.58	88.14	85.21	74.13	53.05	61.84	73.39
EICA	77.68	87.94	84.89	**81.90**	34.39	48.44	70.24

Table 2

Results of Subtask A: English Question-Comment Similarity(test set for 2017).

Model	MAP	AvgRec	MRR	P	R	F_1	Acc
Random baseline	62.30	70.56	68.74	53.15	75.97	62.54	52.70
Search engine	72.61	79.32	82.37	–	–	–	–
KeLP (Top 1)	**88.43**	93.79	92.82	87.30	58.24	69.87	73.89
Beihang-MSRA (Top 2)	88.24	93.87	92.34	51.98	100.00	68.40	51.98
IIT-UHH (Top 3)	86.88	92.04	91.20	73.37	74.52	73.94	72.70
EICA	86.53	92.50	89.57	**88.29**	30.20	45.01	61.64

Table 3

Results of Subtask B: English Question-Question Similarity(test set for 2016).

Model	MAP	AvgRec	MRR	P	R	F_1	Acc
Random baseline	46.98	67.92	50.96	32.58	73.82	45.20	40.43
Search engine	74.75	88.30	83.79	–	–	–	–
UH-PRHLT (Top 1)	**76.70**	90.31	83.02	63.53	69.53	66.39	76.57
ConvKN (Top 2)	76.02	90.70	84.64	68.58	66.52	67.54	78.71
Kelp (Top 3)	75.83	91.02	82.71	66.79	75.97	71.08	79.43
EICA	76.34	90.67	83.68	**70.59**	61.80	65.90	78.71

Table 4

Results of Subtask B: English Question-Question Similarity(test set for 2017).

Model	MAP	AvgRec	MRR	P	R	F_1	Acc
Random baseline	29.81	62.65	33.02	18.72	75.46	30.00	34.77
Search engine	41.85	77.59	46.42	–	–	–	–
simbow (Top 1)	**47.22**	82.60	50.07	27.30	94.48	42.37	52.39
LearningToQuestion (Top 2)	46.93	81.29	53.01	18.52	100.00	31.26	18.52
KeLP (Top 3)	46.66	81.36	50.85	36.01	85.28	50.64	69.20
EICA	41.11	77.45	45.57	32.60	72.39	44.95	67.16

Table 5

Results of Subtask C: English Question-External Comment Similarity(test set for 2016).

Model	MAP	AvgRec	MRR	P	R	F_1	Acc
Random baseline	15.01	11.44	15.19	9.40	75.69	16.73	29.59
Search engine	40.36	45.97	45.83	–	–	–	–
SUper_team (Top 1)	**55.41**	60.66	61.48	18.03	63.15	28.05	69.73
Kelp (Top 2)	52.95	59.27	59.23	33.63	64.53	44.21	84.79
SemanticZ (Top 3)	51.68	53.43	55.96	17.11	57.65	26.38	69.94
EICA	48.57	46.90	54.80	**56.48**	9.33	16.01	**90.86**

Table 6

Results of Subtask C: English Question-External Comment Similarity(test set for 2017).

Model	MAP	AvgRec	MRR	P	R	F_1	Acc
Random baseline	5.77	7.69	5.70	2.76	73.98	5.32	26.37
Search engine	9.18	21.72	10.11	–	–	–	–
IIT-UHH (Top 1)	**15.46**	33.42	18.14	8.41	51.22	14.44	83.03
BUNJI (Top 2)	14.71	29.47	16.48	20.26	19.11	19.67	95.64
KeLP (Top 3)	14.35	30.74	16.07	6.48	89.02	12.07	63.75
EICA	13.48	24.44	16.04	7.69	0.41	0.77	**97.08**

5.1 SemEval-2016 Task 3 Results

We can see the results of Subtask A (question-comment similarity ranking) in Table 1. In terms of ranking measures, our system outperform both the random and the search engine baseline. We observe a MAP improvement of 18.15% compare with the results obtained by the search engine. We obtain the second rank in SemEval-2016 (Nakov et al., 2016).

Similar to Subtask A ,the performance of our approach is also superior in Subtask B (question-question similarity ranking). As we can see in Table 3, using the test set for 2016, the improvement of MAP and AvgRec has been of 1.59%, 2.37% respectively compare to the search engine baseline. In this case, the improvements in performance are slightly reduced. We obtain the second rank in SemEval-2016 (Nakov et al., 2016).

For Subtask C, the results are shown in Table 5. Using the test set for 2016, the improvement of MAP and AvgRec has been of 8.21%, 0.93% respectively compare to the search engine baseline (Nakov et al., 2016).

5.2 SemEval-2017 Task 3 Results

We can see the results of Subtask A (question-comment similarity ranking) in Table 2. In terms of ranking measures, our system also outperform both the random and the search engine baseline. Using the test set for 2017 (Nakov et al., 2017), we observe a MAP improvement of 13.92% compare with the results obtained by the search engine.

Similar to Subtask A ,the performance of our approach is also superior in Subtask B (question-related question similarity ranking). As shown in Table 4, using the test set for 2017 (Nakov et al., 2017), we obtain the MAP of 41.11% and AvgRec of 77.45.

For Subtask C, we can see the results in Table 6. Using the test set for 2017 (Nakov et al., 2017), the improvement of MAP and AvgRec is 4.3%, 2.72% respectively compare to the search engine baseline.

The results in both SemEval-2016 (Nakov et al., 2016) and SemEval-2017 (Nakov et al., 2017) prove that features we use are quite useful for ranking comments with respect to a given question (Subtask A and C), but they do not achieve as similar results when ranking questions with respect to other questions(Subtask B).

6 Conclusion

We have described our system for SemEval-2017, Task 3 on Community Question Answering. Our approach rely on semantic and metadata-based features. In the main Subtask C, our primary submission is ranked fourth, with a MAP of 13.48 and accuracy of 97.08, which is the highest. In Subtask A, our primary submission is sixth, with MAP of 86.53 and accuracy of 61.64.

In future work, we plan to use our best feature combinations in a deep learning architecture, as in the Qiu's system (Qiu and Huang, 2015), which outperforms the other methods on two matching tasks. We also want to use information from entire threads (Joty et al., 2015) to make better predictions. How to combine them efficiently in the system is an interesting research question.

Acknowledgments

This research was supported in part by Science and Technology Commission of Shanghai Municipality (No.16511102702).

References

Sofiane Abbar, Tahar Zanouda, Laure Berti-Equille, and Javier Borge-Holthoefer. 2016. Using twitter to understand public interest in climate change: The case of qatar. *arXiv preprint arXiv:1603.04010* .

Eugene Agichtein, Carlos Castillo, Debora Donato, Aristides Gionis, and Gilad Mishne. 2008. Finding high-quality content in social media. In *Proceedings of the 2008 international conference on web search and data mining*. ACM, pages 183–194.

Yoshinori Aono, Takuya Hayashi, Le Trieu Phong, and Lihua Wang. 2016. Scalable and secure logistic regression via homomorphic encryption. In *Proceedings of the Sixth ACM Conference on Data and Application Security and Privacy*. ACM, pages 142–144.

Sugato Basu, Arindam Banerjee, and Raymond Mooney. 2002. Semi-supervised clustering by seeding. In *In Proceedings of 19th International Conference on Machine Learning (ICML-2002*. Citeseer.

Lars Buitinck, Gilles Louppe, Mathieu Blondel, Fabian Pedregosa, Andreas Mueller, Olivier Grisel, Vlad Niculae, Peter Prettenhofer, Alexandre Gramfort, Jaques Grobler, et al. 2013. Api design for machine learning software: experiences from the scikit-learn project. *arXiv preprint arXiv:1309.0238* .

Marie-Catherine De Marneffe and Christopher D Manning. 2008. The stanford typed dependencies representation. In *Coling 2008: Proceedings of the workshop on Cross-Framework and Cross-Domain Parser Evaluation*. Association for Computational Linguistics, pages 1–8.

Alejandro Figueroa. 2017. Automatically generating effective search queries directly from community question-answering questions for finding related questions. *Expert Systems with Applications* 77:11–19.

Simone Filice, Danilo Croce, Alessandro Moschitti, and Roberto Basili. 2016. Kelp at semeval-2016 task 3: Learning semantic relations between questions and answers. *Proceedings of SemEval* 16:1116–1123.

Marc Franco-Salvador, Sudipta Kar, Thamar Solorio, and Paolo Rosso. 2016. Uh-prhlt at semeval-2016 task 3: Combining lexical and semantic-based features for community question answering. *Proceedings of SemEval* 16:814–821.

Liya Fu and Tomohiro Murata. 2016. Configuration design of virtual cellular manufacturing system with batch splitting operations. In *Advanced Applied Informatics (IIAI-AAI), 2016 5th IIAI International Congress on*. IEEE, pages 1010–1015.

Shafiq Joty, Alberto Barrón-Cedeno, Giovanni Da San Martino, Simone Filice, Lluıs Marquez, Alessandro Moschitti, and Preslav Nakov. 2015. Global thread-level inference for comment classification in community question answering. In *Proceedings of the Conference on Empirical Methods in Natural Language Processing, EMNLP*. volume 15.

Debra K Katzman, Sloane Madden, Dasha Nicholls, Karizma Mawjee, and Mark L Norris. 2017. From questions to answers: Examining the role of pediatric surveillance units in eating disorder research. *International Journal of Eating Disorders* .

Emre Kıcıman. 2010. Language differences and metadata features on twitter. In *Web N-gram Workshop*. page 47.

Todor Mihaylov and Preslav Nakov. 2016. Semanticz at semeval-2016 task 3: Ranking relevant answers in community question answering using semantic similarity based on fine-tuned word embeddings. *Proceedings of SemEval* pages 879–886.

Tsvetomila Mihaylova, Pepa Gencheva, Martin Boyanov, Ivana Yovcheva, Todor Mihaylov, Momchil Hardalov, Yasen Kiprov, Daniel Balchev, Ivan Koychev, Preslav Nakov, et al. 2016. Super team at semeval-2016 task 3: Building a feature-rich system for community question answering. *Proceedings of SemEval* pages 836–843.

Sewon Min, Minjoon Seo, and Hannaneh Hajishirzi. 2017. Question answering through transfer learning from large fine-grained supervision data. *arXiv preprint arXiv:1702.02171* .

Pedro J Moreno, Purdy P Ho, and Nuno Vasconcelos. 2003. A kullback-leibler divergence based kernel for svm classification in multimedia applications. In *Advances in neural information processing systems*. page None.

Preslav Nakov, Doris Hoogeveen, Lluís Màrquez, Alessandro Moschitti, Hamdy Mubarak, Timothy Baldwin, and Karin Verspoor. 2017. SemEval-2017 task 3: Community question answering. In *Proceedings of the 11th International Workshop on Semantic Evaluation*. Association for Computational Linguistics, Vancouver, Canada, SemEval '17.

Preslav Nakov, Lluís Màrquez, Alessandro Moschitti, Walid Magdy, Hamdy Mubarak, Abed Alhakim Freihat, Jim Glass, and Bilal Randeree. 2016. SemEval-2016 task 3: Community question answering. In *Proceedings of the 10th International Workshop on Semantic Evaluation*. Association for Computational Linguistics, San Diego, California, SemEval '16.

John N Newton, Julia Verne, Mark Dancox, and Nicholas Young. 2017. are fluoride levels in drinking water associated with hypothyroidism prevalence in england? a large observational study of g-p practice data and fluoride levels in drinking water: comments on the authors' response to earlier criticism. *Journal of Epidemiology and Community Health* pages jech–2016.

Hieu V Nguyen and Li Bai. 2010. Cosine similarity metric learning for face verification. In *Asian Conference on Computer Vision*. Springer, pages 709–720.

Xipeng Qiu and Xuanjing Huang. 2015. Convolutional neural tensor network architecture for community-based question answering. In *IJCAI*. pages 1305–1311.

Radim Rehurek and Petr Sojka. 2010. Software framework for topic modelling with large corpora. In *In Proceedings of the LREC 2010 Workshop on New Challenges for NLP Frameworks*. Citeseer.

Hapnes Toba, Zhao-Yan Ming, Mirna Adriani, and Tat-Seng Chua. 2014. Discovering high quality answers in community question answering archives using a hierarchy of classifiers. *Information Sciences* 261:101–115.

Quan Hung Tran, Vu Tran, Tu Vu, Minh Le Nguyen, and Son Bao Pham. 2015. Jaist: Combining multiple features for answer selection in community question answering. In *Proceedings of the 9th International Workshop on Semantic Evaluation, SemEval*. volume 15, pages 215–219.

Guoshun Wu and Man Lan. 2016. Ecnu at semeval-2016 task 3: Exploring traditional method and deep learning method for question retrieval and answer ranking in community question answering. *Proceedings of SemEval* pages 872–878.

Shuo Yang, Lei Zou, Zhongyuan Wang, Jun Yan, and Ji-Rong Wen. 2017. Efficiently answering technical questionsła knowledge graph approach .

Pierre Zweigenbaum and Thomas Lavergne. 2016. Hybrid methods for icd-10 coding of death certificates. *EMNLP 2016* page 96.

FA3L at SemEval-2017 Task 3: A ThRee Embeddings Recurrent Neural Network for Question Answering

Giuseppe Attardi, Antonio Carta, Federico Errica, Andrea Madotto, Ludovica Pannitto

Department of Computer Science, University of Pisa

Largo B. Pontecorvo, 3

`attardi@di.unipi.it, a.carta@outlook.it, f.errica@protonmail.com`
`andreamad8@gmail.com, ellepannitto@gmail.com`

Abstract

In this paper we present ThReeNN, a model for Community Question Answering, Task 3, of SemEval-2017. The proposed model exploits both syntactic and semantic information to build a single and meaningful embedding space. Using a dependency parser in combination with word embeddings, the model creates sequences of inputs for a Recurrent Neural Network, which are then used for the ranking purposes of the Task. The score obtained on the official test data shows promising results.

1 Introduction

Community Question Answering (cQA) systems have proven to be useful for a long time and they still are an invaluable source of information. However, due to their rapid growth and to the large amount of data provided it is not easy to find a relevant answer or a good related question amongst all the others. For these reasons we present a model which tries to tackle these problems. The subtasks we have worked on can be described as follows:

A) Question-Comment Similarity - Given a question q and 10 comments $c_1, \ldots, c_{10}$, rank such comments from the most relevant to the least one with respect to q, and assign to each one a label which can be "Good" or "Bad".

B) Question-Question Similarity - Given a question q and a set of 10 related questions $q_1, \ldots, q_{10}$, rank the 10 questions from "Relevant" to "Irrelevant", according to q.

A more detailed description of the task can be found in (Nakov et al., 2017).

Our work has been inspired by studies regarding embedding spaces. Indeed, in (Hsu et al., 2016) GloVe embeddings (Pennington et al., 2014) are used to solve the same subtasks as ours, achieving good results using just word embeddings which encode semantic information into a vector. Moreover, the model proposed in (Yu et al., 2013), where autoencoders are used to build an embedding space, has been exploited to propose an approach that mixes semantic and syntactic information through the use of word embeddings and dependency parsing. These are then put together and become an input for the neural network. In this way we try to enhance the capability of the learning system.

In principle, our approach aims at enriching semantic information with syntactic relations holding between elements of the couples (question-comment or question-question). This should serve well for both subtasks A and B, since the model will learn relations between a question and a comment or between a question and another one. However, further research would be useful to understand to what extent there exist differences in the kind of relations learnt, and therefore in the subtasks.

The paper is organised as follows: Section 2 outlines the preprocessing and additional features used by the model, while Section 3 describes the key models used. Section 4 shows the model selection strategy and the alternatives we explored with respect to word embeddings and their combination. Finally, Section 5 reports performances on different models and Section 6 wraps up everything and discusses about future works. From now on, we will refer to "comment" for indicating both a comment (Subtask A) or a related question (Subtask B), since our model does not make distinctions between them. We participated to Semeval 2017, ranking 8th in Subtask A and 10th in Subtask B.

Proceedings of the 11th International Workshop on Semantic Evaluations (SemEval-2017), pages 299–304,
Vancouver, Canada, August 3 - 4, 2017. ©2017 Association for Computational Linguistics

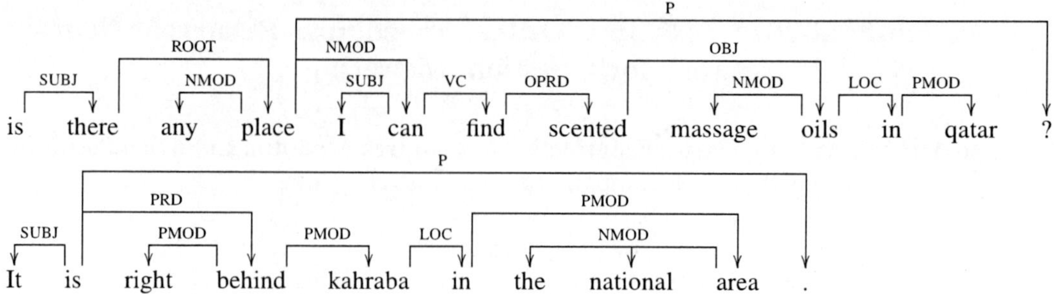

Figure 1: Dependency parsing of two sentences taken from a question and a comment in the training set. In this example the first input $x(t)$ of the RNN is going to be: <"is",SUBJ,"there","is",SUBJ,"It">.

2 Data Preprocessing

We applied standard preprocessing to question and comment body, so as to achieve better performance during syntactic parsing and a better alignment of our vocabulary to the GloVe one. Each question also includes the subject of the topic. Preprocessing included the following steps:

- Portions of text that include HTML tags and special sequences were removed or substituted with simpler strings.

- Using a set of regular expressions, we replaced URLs, nicknames, email addresses with a placeholder for each category.

- Too long repetitions of characters inside tokens were replaced by a single character (e.g. *loooot* became *lot*). Indeed, in the language spoken on community forums, letters are often repeated to emphasize words; with our approach we were able to reconstruct their standard form. Moreover, multiple punctuation was also collapsed.

- Standard use of spacing after punctuation was restored, in order to avoid problems during tokenization.

- Using a hand-written dictionary, the most common abbreviations were replaced with the corresponding extended form.

We then performed sentence splitting and tokenization using *nltk* (Bird et al., 2009). During the tokenization step, we performed spelling corrections.

Finally, texts were analyzed using Tanl pipeline (Attardi et al., 2007), adding morpho-syntactic

and syntactic information (i.e., part of speech tagging and dependency parsing). Figure 1 shows an example of a question and a comment which are parsed accordingly.

2.1 Additional Features

After that, we generated several features, representing both metadata and some properties of the couple Question-Comment. These features have been commonly used in literature, both with Neural Networks (as in (Mohtarami et al., 2016)), linear or SVM models as in (Mihaylova et al., 2016), in order to include additional and potentially relevant information not easily conveyed through semantic representations. In our case, they are used as additional input beside the RNN output. Features can be grouped as follows:

- Features encoding information about standard similarity between question and comment (all measures are expressed in terms of number of tokens):

  - size of intersection between question and comment
  - Jaccard Coeffcient (ratio between intersection size and union size of question and comment)
  - comment length
  - ratio between comment length and question length
  - length of the longest common subsequence between question and comment

- Features encoding metadata information, in particular:

  - number of the comment in default ordering

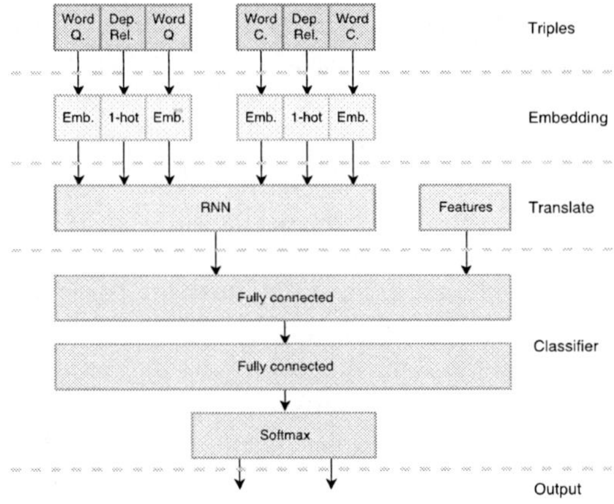

Figure 2: Conceptual schema of the model used for the classification.

- whether the comment was posted by the same user asking the question
- whether the user posting the comment had already posted a comment for the same question

- Features encoding presence of certain elements in comment body, in particular we looked for:

  - presence of question marks
  - presence of URLs (through regex)
  - presence of username (through regex)
  - presence of a username among those that are authors of comments preceeding the considered one

3 Model

The proposed model[1] makes use of the previous steps (i.e. a dependency parser) whose output is a tree, to generate a sequence of triples. The ith triple is made of $< W_i, rel, W_r >$, where W_i is the ith word of the text and W_r is the word associated through rel (i.e. the dependency relation extracted by the parser). Then triples $< e_i, rel, e_r >$ are generated, where e_i and e_r are word-embeddings vectors for the two words, and rel is a 1-hot-encoding of the dependency relations. The kth input to be fed to the RNN is simply made by concatenating the kth embedding triple of

---

[1]An implementation is available at https://github.com/AntonioCarta/ThreeRNN

the comment with the kth one of the question. Figure 1 shows an example of how to obtain a valid input for our model. Our goal is to let the system learn the correct composition rule through syntactic dependencies.

Hence, the input of our model is dual: a sequence of triples which represents the question and another sequence for the comments. These are then passed to a sentence encoder, which is a Recurrent Neural Network (RNN), that is used to return a single output aiming to represent the entire sequences. In particular we describe a Long Short Term Memory (Hochreiter and Schmidhuber, 1997) which are capable of learning long-term dependencies; Then, given x as input in the form:

$$x^{(t)} = < e_{Qi}^{(t)}, Rel_Q^{(t)}, e_{Qr}^{(t)}, e_{Ci}^{(t)}, Rel_C^{(t)}, e_{Cr}^{(t)} >$$

we have:

$$f^{(t)} = \sigma\left(U^f x^{(t)} + W^f h^{(t-1)} + b^f\right)$$
$$g^{(t)} = \sigma\left(U^g x^{(t)} + W^g h^{(t-1)} + b^g\right)$$
$$y^{(t)} = \sigma\left(U^i x^{(t)} + W^i h^{(t-1)} + b^i\right)$$
$$s^{(t)} = f^{(t)} \odot s^{(t-1)} + g^{(t)} \odot y^{(t)}$$
$$o^{(t)} = \sigma\left(U^o x^{(t)} + W^o h^{(t-1)}\right)$$
$$h^{(t)} = tanh(s^{(t)}) \odot o^{(t)}$$

where $f^{(t)}$ is the forget gate, $g^{(t)}$ the input gate, $s^{(t)}$ the state, $o^{(t)}$ the output gate and $h^{(t)}$ the hidden state. U and W are the weight matrices for each gate (e.g., U^o refers to the matrix for the output gate) and $\odot$ is the Hadamard product. Then the RNN output, along with a vector made up of additional features, become the inputs passed to the final feed-forward layers which performs the scoring.

Each layer of the final network uses a sigmoid activation function. Hence, given x, the layer input, W and b the layer matrix and bias, the output y is defined as

$$y = \sigma(Wx + b)$$

The final output o of the network uses a softmax activation, thus we have:

$$o_i = \frac{exp(y_i)}{\sum_{j=0}^{n} exp(y_j)}$$

Where n is the length of the vector y. The latter provides a distribution over two classes: 'Good' and 'Bad/Partially Useful' for subtask A, 'PerfectMatch/Relevant' and 'Irrelevant' for subtask B. To obtain the final ranking we took the probability of a given input to be labeled as the positive class. The entire network is trained with back-propagation using a cross-entropy loss function. Figure 2 shows the conceptual schema of the model.

4 Experiments

To perform model selection we merged *training* and *development* files provided by Semeval organisers, then we shuffled and extracted a training and a validation set. We selected various hyperparameters, shown with their values in Table 4, such as learning rate, number of hidden units and hidden layers for the recurrent and feedforward layers, dropout (Srivastava et al., 2014), L2 regularization, activation functions (i.e. ReLu (Nair and Hinton, 2010), sigmoid and hyperbolic tangent), optimization algorithms (i.e. adam (Kingma and Ba, 2014) and rmsprop (Tieleman and Hinton, 2012)). The length threshold for the number of triples in input to the RNN as been also added as hyper-parameter (i.e., Max length); if the comment/question is shorter, it is filled up with zeros ("null triples"). Since each training required quite a large amount of time, we opted for a random search technique (Bergstra and Bengio, 2012).

Parameter	Values
RNN	<u>LSTM</u>, **GRU**, SUM
RNN layer	1,**2**
Hidden layer	1,2,**3**
Embeddings size	**100**, <u>200</u>, 300
Hidden size	**50**, 100, <u>200</u>
Max length	5,**10**,25,<u>50</u>,75,100,150
Dropout	0, **0.1**, 0.2, <u>0.3</u>, 0.4
L2	<u>0.01</u>, **0.001**, 0.0001, 0.00001
Activation	ReLu, tanh, **sigmoid**
Optimizer	<u>**adam**</u>, rmsprop

Table 1: Hyper-parameters used during model selection. The selected parameters for Subtask A are in bold, and underlined for Subtask B.

The embeddings layer uses pretrained embeddings which are fixed during the training phase. We tried to update them together with the entire network during training but the resulting network always

ended up to over-fit. Two different types of embeddings have been evaluated: GloVe (Pennington et al., 2014), which are trained using Wikipedia, and embeddings trained directly with questions and answers extracted from the Qatar Living forum (Mihaylov and Nakov, 2016). However, in our model both embeddings worked well, thus with the latter we did not obtained any particular improvements.

To encode the RNN input into a single embedding we compare three different approaches: SUM (which sums all the triples given as input), LSTM (Hochreiter and Schmidhuber, 1997) and GRU (Cho et al., 2014).

Finally, the neural network model was implemented using Keras (Chollet, 2015), which provides an efficient and easy-to-use deep learning utilities.

5 Results

The results obtained in the test set, in both sub-task A and B, are summarized in Table 2. The primary submission uses LSTM for subtask A and GRU for subtask B. Instead, the contrastive model uses SUM as aggregation and it has been submitted just for the subtask A. Using the SUM model, which is computationally less expensive than RNN, we obtained just a slightly worst MAP (i.e. around 0.5%), which suggests we could further improve the performance by making the RNN exploit better the sequence in input. Moreover, there is a trade-off between representation length and computational costs, achieved with the use of the length threshold; this may be regarded as a crucial choice for our model.

	Subtask A		Subtask B	
	MAP	Acc	MAP	Acc
Baseline (IR)	72.61	-	41.85	-
Primary	83.42	68.02	42.24	73.86
Contrastive	82.87	68.67	-	-

Table 2: Summary of the results of the submitted model on subtask A and B

6 Conclusions

To sum up, we have developed a model which tries to combine semantic and syntactic information into a single vector space. We will further investigate this combination, through the use of syntactic relations holding between content words, rather than exploiting the whole set of dependency relations (e.g. different tag-sets, partial or shallow parsing of sentences etc.). Our experiments have explored different possibilities regarding the choice of the word embedding system; all of them proved in the end to achieve similar results. However, it may be worth trying to build an ad-hoc embedding space which mixes parsing and lexical information, aiming to improve the performances of our model. Future works may include improvements to the RNN in order to better represent longer sentences, or the use of recursive neural network that directly use the tree structure given by the dependency parsing, with different weights matrices for each dependency relation.

References

Giuseppe Attardi, Felice Dell'Orletta, Maria Simi, Atanas Chanev, and Massimiliano Ciaramita. 2007. Multilingual dependency parsing and domain adaptation using desr. In *EMNLP-CoNLL*. pages 1112–1118.

James Bergstra and Yoshua Bengio. 2012. Random search for hyper-parameter optimization. *Journal of Machine Learning Research* 13(Feb):281–305.

Steven Bird, Ewan Klein, and Edward Loper. 2009. *Natural language processing with Python: analyzing text with the natural language toolkit.* " O'Reilly Media, Inc.".

Kyunghyun Cho, Bart Van Merriënboer, Dzmitry Bahdanau, and Yoshua Bengio. 2014. On the properties of neural machine translation: Encoder-decoder approaches. *arXiv preprint arXiv:1409.1259* .

François Chollet. 2015. Keras. https://github.com/fchollet/keras.

Sepp Hochreiter and Jürgen Schmidhuber. 1997. Long short-term memory. *Neural computation* 9(8):1735–1780.

Wei-Ning Hsu, Yu Zhang, and James Glass. 2016. Recurrent neural network encoder with attention for community question answering. *arXiv preprint arXiv:1603.07044* .

Diederik Kingma and Jimmy Ba. 2014. Adam: A method for stochastic optimization. *arXiv preprint arXiv:1412.6980* .

Todor Mihaylov and Preslav Nakov. 2016. Semanticz at semeval-2016 task 3: Ranking relevant answers in community question answering using semantic similarity based on fine-tuned word

embeddings. In *Proceedings of the 10th International Workshop on Semantic Evaluation (SemEval 2016)*. Association for Computational Linguistics, San Diego, California, pages 804 – 811. http://www.aclweb.org/anthology/S16.

Tsvetomila Mihaylova, Pepa Gencheva, Martin Boyanov, Ivana Yovcheva, Todor Mihaylov, Momchil Hardalov, Yasen Kiprov, Daniel Balchev, Ivan Koychev, Preslav Nakov, Ivelina Nikolova, and Galia Angelova. 2016. Super team at semeval-2016 task 3: Building a feature-rich system for community question answering. In *Proceedings of the 10th International Workshop on Semantic Evaluation (SemEval-2016)*. Association for Computational Linguistics, San Diego, California, pages 836–843. http://www.aclweb.org/anthology/S16-1129.

Mitra Mohtarami, Yonatan Belinkov, Wei-Ning Hsu, Yu Zhang, Tao Lei, Kfir Bar, Scott Cyphers, and Jim Glass. 2016. Sls at semeval-2016 task 3: Neural-based approaches for ranking in community question answering. In *Proceedings of the 10th International Workshop on Semantic Evaluation (SemEval-2016)*. Association for Computational Linguistics, San Diego, California, pages 828–835. http://www.aclweb.org/anthology/S16-1128.

Vinod Nair and Geoffrey E Hinton. 2010. Rectified linear units improve restricted boltzmann machines. In *Proceedings of the 27th international conference on machine learning (ICML-10)*. pages 807–814.

Preslav Nakov, Doris Hoogeveen, Lluís Màrquez, Alessandro Moschitti, Hamdy Mubarak, Timothy Baldwin, and Karin Verspoor. 2017. Semeval-2017 task 3: Community question answering. In *Proceedings of the 11th International Workshop on Semantic Evaluation (SemEval-2017)*. Association for Computational Linguistics, Vancouver, Canada, pages 27–48. http://www.aclweb.org/anthology/S17-2003.

Jeffrey Pennington, Richard Socher, and Christopher D. Manning. 2014. Glove: Global vectors for word representation. In *Empirical Methods in Natural Language Processing (EMNLP)*. pages 1532–1543. http://www.aclweb.org/anthology/D14-1162.

Nitish Srivastava, Geoffrey E Hinton, Alex Krizhevsky, Ilya Sutskever, and Ruslan Salakhutdinov. 2014. Dropout: a simple way to prevent neural networks from overfitting. *Journal of Machine Learning Research* 15(1):1929–1958.

T Tieleman and G Hinton. 2012. Rmsprop: Divide the gradient by a running average of its recent magnitude. coursera: Neural networks for machine learning. Technical report, Technical report.

Wenchao Yu, Guangxiang Zeng, Ping Luo, Fuzhen Zhuang, Qing He, and Zhongzhi Shi. 2013. Embedding with autoencoder regularization. In *Joint Euro-*

pean Conference on Machine Learning and Knowledge Discovery in Databases. Springer, pages 208–223.

SCIR-QA at SemEval-2017 Task 3: CNN Model Based on Similar and Dissimilar Information between Keywords for Question Similarity

Le Qi, Yu Zhang, Ting Liu
Research Center for Social Computing
and Information Retrieval
Harbin Institute of Technology
`lqi,zhangyu,tliu@ir.hit.edu.cn`

Abstract

We describe a method of calculating the similarity between questions in community QA. Questions in cQA are usually very long and there are a lot of useless information about calculating the similarity between questions. Therefore, we implement a CNN model based on similar and dissimilar information on questions keywords. We extract the keywords of questions, and then model the similar and dissimilar information between the keywords, and use the CNN model to calculate the similarity.

1   Introduction

We participate in SemEval-2017 Task 3 Subtask B (Nakov et al., 2017) on Community Question Answering. In this task, we are given a question from community forum (named original question) and 10 related questions. We need to re-rank the related questions according to their similarity between the origin question.

Both the original question and the related question have question subject and question body. The subject is short. The body is long and contains a lot of useless information. In our system, we try to use keywords to replace questions to locate more important information on the question, so we use a keyword extraction algorithm that combines syntactic information to get more accurate keywords. Then we use a CNN model based on similar and dissimilar information between questions to calculate the similarity of questions. The model can make good use of similar information and dissimilar information between questions to get better results.

The paper is organized as follows: Section 2 introduces our system. Section 3 introduces the experiment. And in section 4, there are the conclusions.

2   Model

In this section we describe our system in detail. In Section 2.1 we show how we extract keywords from the subject and body, and then in Section 2.2 we describe how to construct the CNN model based on similar and dissimilar information on question keywords.

2.1   Keyword extraction

First, we cut the question subject and question body. Then, we extract keywords from each sub-sentence. We combine all the extracted keywords together as a result.

We use an unsupervised keyword extraction method based on dependency analysis. The method uses syntactic dependency relations between words as clues. For the given question, we not only use the statistical information and word vector information, but also construct the dependency graph to calculate the correlation intensity between words, and then construct the weighted graph according to the dependency degree, and use the TextRank algorithm (Mihalcea and Tarau, 2004) to iterate to calculate the word importance score. The main steps include preprocessing, the construction of the non-directional weighted graph, graph ranking, and the selection of the t words with the highest score as keywords of the question, as shown in Figure 1.

Preprocess: The preprocessing process includes word segmentation and removing the stop words. We use the remaining words as the candidate words of the keywords.

Construct the undirected weighted graph: After preprocessing, all candidate words are represented as vertices of the graph. If two words co-occur in a sentence, there is an edge to the two

305

Proceedings of the 11th International Workshop on Semantic Evaluations (SemEval-2017), pages 305–309,
Vancouver, Canada, August 3 - 4, 2017. ©2017 Association for Computational Linguistics

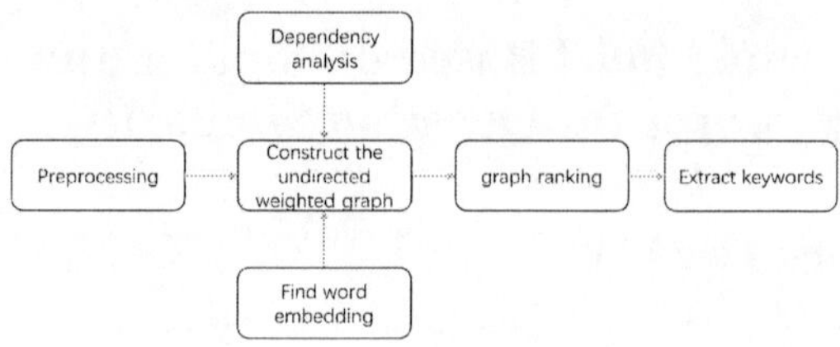

Figure 1: Keywords extraction

vertices. The weight of the edge is calculated by the statistical information on words, the word vector information and the dependent syntax analysis information.

The methods that can be used to calculate the correlation between two words are: Pointwise Mutual Information (PMI), Average Mutual Information(AMI) (Terra and Clarke, 2004), etc. However, these methods only consider the statistical information between words, and do not consider the syntactic dependencies. The syntactic dependency between words has a positive effect on measuring the importance of words.

The result of the dependency syntax analysis is analogous to the tree structure. If we remove its root node, and ignore the arc of the point, we can get an undirected dependency diagram $G' = (V', E'), V' = w_1, w_2, ..., w_n, E' = e_1, e_2, ..., e_m$, where w_i denotes a word and e_j denotes an undirected relationship between two words. The undirected dependency graph guarantees that there is a dependency path between any two words in the question, and the length of the dependency path reflects the intensity of the dependency relationship. Therefore, we introduce the concept of dependency degree according to the length of the dependent path (Zhang et al., 2012), as shown in Equation(1), where $dr\_path\_len(w_i, w_j)$ represents the dependency path length between words w_i and w_j, b is the superparameter.

$$Dep(w_i, w_j) = \frac{1}{b^{dr\_path\_len(w_i, w_j)}} \quad (1)$$

The degree of correlation between two words, that is, the weight of the edge is multiplied by the gravitational value of the two words by the length of the dependent path, as shown in Equation(2).

$$weight(w_i, w_j) = Dep(w_i, w_j) * f(w_i, w_j) \quad (2)$$

Among them, the concept of gravitational values proposed by (Wang et al., 2015), inspired by gravitation. The word frequency is regarded as the object mass, and the distance between the words is taken as the distance of the object. The gravitational value $f(w_i, w_j)$ of the two words is given by the Equation(3).

$$f(w_i, w_j) = \frac{freq(w_i) * freq(w_j)}{d^2} \quad (3)$$

Graph ranking: We use the weighted TextRank algorithm to sort the graph. In the undirected graph $G = (V, E)$, V is the set of vertices, E is the set of edges, and $C(v_i)$ is the set of vertices connected to the vertex v_i. The score of the vertex v_i is calculated from the Equation(4), where $weight(w_i, w_j)$ is calculated from the Equation(3), d is the damping coefficient.

$$ws(v_i) = (1-d)+d* \sum_{v_j \in C(v_i)} \frac{weight(v_i, v_j)}{\sum_{v_k \in C(v_j)} weight(v_j, v_k)} \quad (4)$$

Then we select the t words with the highest score as the keywords.

2.2 CNN model based on similar and dissimilar information

We use a CNN model based on similar parts and dissimilar parts between two sentences to get sentence similarity. This model is proposed by (Wang et al., 2016), now we will introduce the model briefly. Figure 2 shows the structure of the model.

Given a sentence pair, the model represents each keyword as a vector, and calculates a semantic matching vector for each keyword based on part of keywords in the other sentence. Then each word vector is decomposed into two components based on the semantic matching vector: a similar component and a dissimilar component. After this, we use a two-channel CNN to compose the similar and dissimilar components into a feature vector. Finally, a fully connected neural network is used to predict the sentence similarity through the composed feature vector.

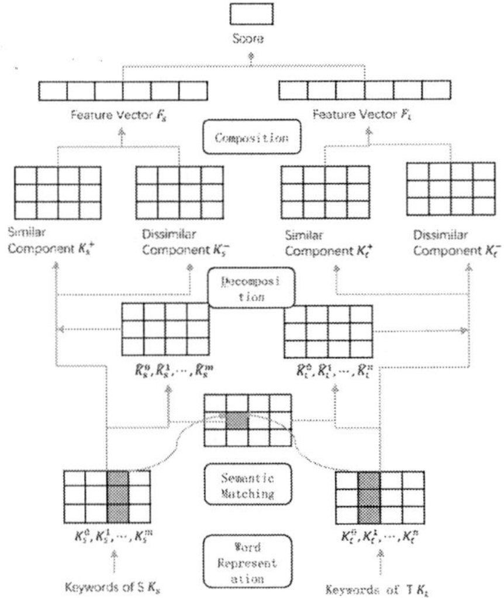

First, with word embedding pre-trained by Stanford using GloVe's model (Pennington et al., 2014), we transform keywords of question S and T into matrix $S = [s_1, s_2, ..., s_m]$ and $T = [t_1, t_2, ..., t_n]$, where s_i and t_j are 300-dimention vectors of corresponding keywords, and m and n are the length of keywords of S and T. Second, for judging the similarity between two sentences, we check whether each keyword in one sentence can be covered by the other sentence. For a sentence pair S and T, we first calculate a similarity matrix $A_{(m \times n)}$, where each element $a_{(i,j)} \in A_{(m \times n)}$ computes cosine similarity between words s_i and t_j as

$$a_{(i,j)} = \frac{s_i^T t_j}{||s_i|| \cdot ||t_j||} \quad \forall s_i \in S, \forall t_j \in T \quad (5)$$

We calculate a semantic matching vector $\hat{s_i}$ for each word s_i by composing part of word vectors in the other sentence T. In this way, we can match a keyword s_i to some keywords in T. Similarly, we also calculate all semantic matching vectors $\hat{t_i}$ in T. We define a semantic matching functions over $A_{(m \times n)}$

$$f_{match}(s_i, T) = \frac{\sum_{j=k-w}^{k+w} a_{i,j} t_j}{\sum_{j=k-w}^{k+w} a_{i,j}} \quad (6)$$

where

$$k = argmax_j a_{i,j}$$

w indicates the size of the window to consider centered at k (the most similar word position). So the semantic matchisng vector is a weighted average vector from t_{k-w} to t_{k+w}.

Third, after semantic matching, we have the semantic matching vectors of $\hat{s_i}$ and $\hat{t_j}$. Take s as an example. We interpret $\hat{s_i}$ as a semantic coverage of word s_i by the sentence T. However, there must be some difference between s_i and $\hat{s_i}$. So based on its semantic matching vector $\hat{s_i}$, our model further decomposes word s_i into two components: similar component $\hat{s_i}^+$ and dissimilar component $\hat{s_i}^-$. Then we choose a linear decomposition method. The motivation for the linear decomposition is that the more similar between s_i and $\hat{s_i}$, the higher proportion of s_i should be assigned to the similar component. First, we calculate the cosine similarity between s_i and $\hat{s_i}$. Then, we decompose s_i linearly based on α. Eq.(7) gives the corresponding definition:

$$a_{(i,j)} = \frac{s_i^T \hat{s_i}}{||s_i|| \cdot ||\hat{s_i}||}$$

$$\hat{t_j}^+ = \alpha s_i$$

$$\hat{s_i}^- = (1 - \alpha)s_i \quad (7)$$

Finally, due to the dissimilar and similar components have strong connections, we use a two-channel CNN model (Kim, 2014) to compose them together. In the CNN model, we have three layers. The first is a convolution layer. We define a list of filters w_o. The shape of each filter is d h, where d is the dimension of word vectors and h is the window size. Each filter is applied to two patches (a window size h of vectors) from both similar and dissimilar channels, and generates a feature. Eq.(8) expresses this process:

$$c_{o,i} = f(w_o * S_{[i:i+h]}^+ + w_o * S_{[i:i+h]}^- + b_o) \quad (8)$$

The second layer is a pooling layer. We choose max-pooling method to deal with variable feature size. And the last layer is a full-connected layer. We use a sigmoid function to constrain the result within the range [0,1].

3 Experiment

We experimented with the corpus provided by SemEval-2017 task3. Training set has 267 questions, each question has 10 related questions, a total of 2670 question pairs. Development set has 50 questions, 500 question pairs. The test set has 88 questions, 880 question pairs. We do the experiment without preprocessing. We use Stanfod Parser (De Marneffe and Manning, 2008) to parse sentences. And we use the keyword extraction algorithm described in 2.1, for each sub-sentence we extract 1/3 of the words as keywords and set b = 1.4, d = 0.8. In the CNN model, we set up the filter shape is 3*300. The number of filters is 500. We set the similarity threshold of 0.5, that is, a score greater than 0.5 is considered a positive case. And we set the learning rate as 0.001. After 20 rounds of training, we got the result in devlopment set and test set.

Team	MAP	AvgRec	MRR
Baseline(IR)	41.85	77.59	46.42
Baseline(Random)	29.81	62.65	33.02
simbow	47.22	82.60	50.07
LearningToQuestion	46.93	81.29	53.01
SCIR-QA	42.72	78.24	46.65

Table 1: Test Result

User or Team Name	MAP	AvgRec	MRR
Sagustian	79.6	94.3	86.0
BeiHang	76.9	91.2	83.5
naman	75.1	90.8	81.33
LS2NSEMEVAL	74.4	88.3	79.5
NLMNIH	73.7	88.2	79.33
IIT-UHH	73.6	89.0	79.33
Organizers	71.4	86.1	76.67
MIT-QCRI	71.4	86.1	76.67
SCIR-QA	70.8	87.5	77.25
preslav	55.9	73.2	62.23

Table 2: Develop Result

The results in test set are shown in Table 1, the first two lines are the baseline, the next two lines are the best results, the last line is our result. And results in development set are shown in Table 2. In test set, our results are better than the baseline, but there is still some distance from the best results. In development set, our result is all not so good.

We think that because we do the experiment without preprocessing, there exists too many unknown words in word embeddings, which results in poor system performance. On the other hand, because the training corpus is too small, the neural network can not be well trained and can not find meaningful features. Therefore, in the future work, we will add features of artificial extraction into neural network to improve performance. And we will add features of artificial extraction into neural network to improve performance.

4 Result and Future Work

We implement a CNN model based on similar and dissimilar information between questions keywords, and experiment on SemEval-2017 corpus. The experimental results show that our method is better than baseline, we can extract the key information from the long sentence to model the question better, which helps us to calculate the similarity of the question. We think that keyword extraction is important in this task, and in the future we will try other keyword extraction methods to achieve better results.

Acknowledgments

This work was supported by the National High Technology Development 863 Program of China (No.2015AA015407), National Natural Science Foundation of China (No.61472105 and No.61472107). And I am grateful to Professor Zhang Yu for his guidance to my work. And I also appreciate the support of SCIR laboratory.

References

Marie-Catherine De Marneffe and Christopher D Manning. 2008. Stanford typed dependencies manual. Technical report, Technical report, Stanford University.

Yoon Kim. 2014. Convolutional neural networks for sentence classification. In *EMNLP*.

Rada Mihalcea and Paul Tarau. 2004. Textrank: Bringing order into texts. *Unt Scholarly Works* pages 404–411.

Preslav Nakov, Doris Hoogeveen, Lluís Màrquez, Alessandro Moschitti, Hamdy Mubarak, Timothy Baldwin, and Karin Verspoor. 2017. SemEval-2017 task 3: Community question answering. In *Proceedings of the 11th International Workshop on Semantic Evaluation*. Association for Computational Linguistics, Vancouver, Canada, SemEval '17.

Jeffrey Pennington, Richard Socher, and Christopher D. Manning. 2014. Glove: Global vectors for word representation. In *Empirical Methods in Natural Language Processing (EMNLP)*. pages 1532–1543. http://www.aclweb.org/anthology/D14-1162.

Egidio Terra and C. L. A Clarke. 2004. Frequency estimates for statistical word similarity measures. In *Naacl 03 Conference of the North American Chapter of the Association for Co*. pages 244–251.

Rui Wang, Wei Liu, and Chris McDonald. 2015. Corpus-independent generic keyphrase extraction using word embedding vectors.

Zhiguo Wang, Haitao Mi, and Abraham Ittycheriah. 2016. Sentence similarity learning by lexical decomposition and composition. In *COLING*.

Weinan Zhang, Zhaoyan Ming, Yu Zhang, Liqiang Nie, Ting Liu, and Tat-Seng Chua. 2012. The use of dependency relation graph to enhance the term weighting in question retrieval. In *COLING*. pages 3105–3120.

LearningToQuestion at SemEval 2017 Task 3: Ranking Similar Questions by Learning to Rank Using Rich Features

Naman Goyal
Georgia Institute of Technology
`naman.goyal21@gmail.com`

Abstract

This paper describes our official entry LearningToQuestion for SemEval 2017 task 3 community question answer, subtask B. The objective is to rerank questions obtained in web forum as per their similarity to original question. Our system uses pairwise learning to rank methods on rich set of hand designed and representation learning features. We use various semantic features that help our system to achieve promising results on the task. The system achieved second highest results on official metrics MAP and good results on other search metrics.

1   Introduction

In online forums question answering is one of the most popular way for users to share information between each other. Due to the unstructured nature of these forums, it's a problem to find relevant information from the already existing information for users. One way to solve this problem is to design systems to automatically find similar content (question, answer, comment) to the user's posted question. SemEval-2017 task 3 (Nakov et al., 2017) focuses on solving this problem in community question answer by various subtasks of ranking relevant information in Qatar living forums data. The system presented in this paper focuses on **subtask B**, to re-rank given set of questions retrieved by search engine, in their similarity to original question.

The system is mainly designed by employing learning to rank methods on the rich feature set obtained by text processing of the question text.

2   Data

We primarily use the annotated training, development and testing dataset provided by the SemEval-2017 task 3 organizers. The dataset is collected by organizers from Qatar living forum. It's in the form of an original question and set of related questions. Each related question in training and development dataset is annotated with one of the 3 possible tags, *PerfectMatch*, *Relevant* or *Irrelevant*. A ranking task is required to rank both *PerfectMatch* and *Relevant* above *Irrelevant* questions without any distinction between the first two. The train dataset for subtask B consists of 317 original questions and 3169 retrieved questions by search engine roughly 10 related questions per original question. The organizers have also provided annotated test dataset from SemEval-2016 challenge.

Along with these we also used Glove embeddings (Pennington et al., 2014) which were pretrained using 6 billion tokens from Wikipedia-2014 and Gigaword dataset.

3   System

Since the task is a ranking task, our system uses learning to rank (Trotman, 2005) to model the ranking of questions. Learning to rank refers to various machine learning techniques used in ranking tasks. These have been studied in information retrieval literature and they power many of the industrial search engines. These systems mainly fall into 3 categories: pointwise, pairwise and listwise as described in (Liu et al., 2009). We use pairwise methods for our system with rich feature set. Our feature set is combination of various hand generated features and semantic features learned by neural network. In the following section we first describe these features and then the learning to rank method used.

Proceedings of the 11th International Workshop on Semantic Evaluations (SemEval-2017), pages 310–314,
Vancouver, Canada, August 3 - 4, 2017. ©2017 Association for Computational Linguistics

3.1 Features

3.1.1 Neural Embedding Similarity Feature

We use various neural network learned embeddings as similarity feature in our system. The system uses Siamese network to learn these similarity measures. Siamese nets were first introduced in the early 1990s by (Bromley et al., 1993) to solve signature verification as an image matching problem. A siamese neural network consists of twin networks which accept distinct inputs but are joined by an energy function at the top. This function computes some metric between the highest level feature representation on each side. The weights between both the networks are shared generally, so that they project the similar texts not far in the embedding dimension. We use contrastive loss described in (Chopra et al., 2005) as the loss function to the Siamese network. Glove pretrained vectors (300 dimension) are fed as input to the neural network. The final neural embeddings are generated by various architectures.

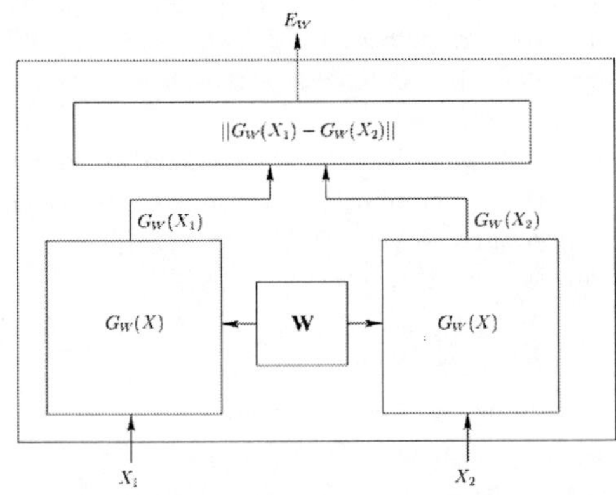

Figure 1: Simaese network

Figure 1 shows a siamese network, where X_1 represents the original question text and X_2 represents the candidate question text. G_W represents a complex nonlinear function which is represented by neural network having weights W. The euclidean distance of the vectors is used to compute the contrastive loss. The goal is to minimize the distance in the embedding space of the similar question text and maximize for non similar pairs. The contrastive loss can be given by following equation:

$$L = Y||G_W(X_1), G_W(X_2)||^2 + (1 - Y)$$
$$max(0, m - ||G_W(X_1), G_W(X_2)||^2)$$

where Y is annotated tag, 1 if X_1 and X_2 are similar, 0 otherwise. m is margin parameter for hinge loss, which is kept 1 for all our networks. We use following networks to generate text embedding:

Long Short Term Memory LSTM (Hochreiter and Schmidhuber, 1997) are popular variant of the the recurrent neural network architecture that captures the long term dependency in text and deals with vanishing gradient problem. Recently LSTMs have been very successful in various NLP tasks.

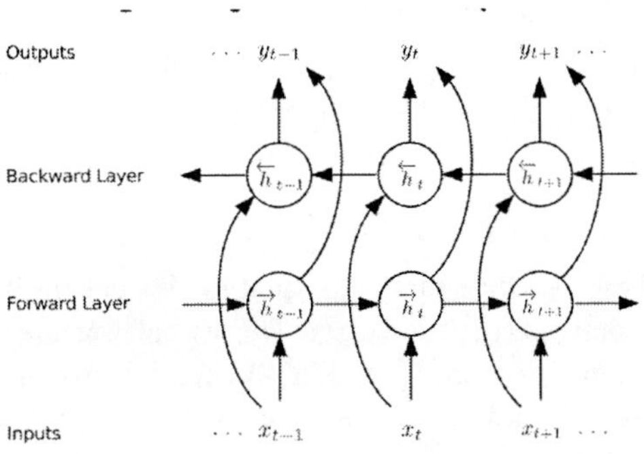

Figure 2: Bidirectional recurrent neural network

Figure 2 shows a bidirectional recurrent neural network architecture. Bi-directional RNN processes the text in both directions with separate hidden units and these hidden representations are concatenated together to create final hidden embedding. For bi-directional LSTM, the hidden unit is a LSTM cell combining of various gates. We use a bidirectional LSTM to generate a 256 dimensional vector for pair of text and train the model by back propagation using contrastive loss.

Gated Recurrent Unit Gated recurrent unit (GRU) (Chung et al., 2014) is another variant of RNN which were introduced recently as compared to LSTM. They also have seen similar success as LSTM in various NLP tasks. We use Bi-GRU as another network to generate the neural embeddings trained by siamese network similar to Bi-LSTM. The final hidden embedding size is 256 dimension for our Bi-GRU network also.

Convolution Net We also use convolution networks as another neural network architecture to generate embeddings inside the siamese network. We use 1D-convolution with 128 kernels, stride of 5 followed by 1D-max pool with pool-size of 5 and finally a dense layer to create a 128 dimension vector.

Implementation Details We use Keras [1] library with Theano (Theano Development Team, 2016) backend to train above 3 models. The batch size is set to 64 and dropout rate is 0.25. We run 25 epochs for each of these 3 networks training. It takes couple of hours to train on CPU. Instead of using the entire vectors into our final classifier, we compute cosine similarity of learned vectors of both the question text (for each of the 3 networks) and use that as a feature in our system.

3.1.2 Rank Features

We use rank given by the search engine as a feature in our system. This gives the system the baseline accuracy of the search engine.

3.1.3 Lexical Features

These set of features represent the lexical similarity between question texts. The lexical used are the common n-gram ($n = 1, 2, 3$) counts between the original question and a candidate question. Apart from these features, we compute a count vector and a tfidf vector for n-grams ($n = 1, 2, 3$) for both the question and candidate question and compute the cosine similarity between them.

3.1.4 Syntactical Features

These features represent the syntactical similarity between the texts of questions. This is represented by cosine similarity of POS count vector for n-gram ($n = 1, 2, 3$).

3.1.5 Semantic Features

Apart from the neural network learned semantic features, we also employ semantic similarity between question text generated by semantic net. We use the sentence similarity described in (Li et al., 2006) using WordNet as semantic net. The paper describes various heuristics used to generate this sentence similarity. First, word pair similarity is generated as a function of the shortest path between the words and height of their lowest common subsumer (LCS). This combines the word

---

[1] https://github.com/fchollet/keras

similarity with their specificity (abstract vs specific concept).

Then the sentence similarity is obtained as a linear combination of semantic similarity and the word order similarity. To generate semantic similarity, cosine between semantic vectors is obtained. The semantic vectors are generated by creating sentence vector of word presence and their similarity. Word order similarity is computed in the similar way as semantic similarity but the position of word in the sentence is used to generate the word order vector. Finally a linear combination of these two similarity features is used as the similarity measure between question texts. We use the same hyper-parameters as original paper that give the best results i.e. $\alpha = 0.2, \beta = 0.45, \eta = 0.4, \phi = 0.2, \delta = 0.85$.

The feature encodes semantic similarity and gives boost to system, shown in the results table.

3.1.6 Summarization Metrics Feature

There has been a lot of research in machine translation and summarization community to find metrics that correlate with human judgement on these tasks. We compute BLEU (Papineni et al., 2002) metrics for $1, 2, 3$ and 4 grams and compute a weighted addition (weights $= 0.1, 0.1, 0.3, 0.5$). We also compute ROUGE-L (Lin, 2004), which is recall oriented similarity measure based on longest common subsequence (LCS), as a feature in our system.

3.1.7 Length feature

We compute the heuristic based on length in tokens of both the texts as $f(l_1, l_2) = \frac{abs(l_1 - l_2)}{l_1 + l_2}$.

3.1.8 Topic Similarity Feature

Topic modeling is used to generate the salient topics in the text. We use Latent Dirichlet allocation (LDA) (Blei et al., 2003) to compute topic similarity between texts. We train LDA topic model using the whole text (body and subject) as corpus. Then a topic distribution over the 50 topics is computed for both the text and cosine similarity is used as a feature in the system.

3.1.9 Other Features

We use count of 10 selected common question words also as a feature in the system.

All of the above features are calculated for both the question subject and body separately.

Features	Dev 2017 as test set		Test 2017 as test set	
	MAP	MRR	MAP	MRR
Baseline	71.35	76.67	41.85	46.42
Above + length features	70.92	76.73	41.60	46.35
Above + common ngram counts	71.36	77.79	43.06	46.08
Above + cosine count ngram	71.23	78.33	43.45	45.41
Above + cosine tfidf ngram	73.10	80.73	43.34	49.29
Above + cosine pos ngram	72.98	80.73	44.96	49.10
Above + semantic similarity	73.29	81.17	45.52	50.05
Above + GRU embeddings	74.21	81.17	45.61	50.05
Above + LSTM embeddings	74.43	81.17	45.91	51.15
Above + Convnet embeddings	74.60	81.17	45.91	51.15
Above + BLEU, ROUGE L	74.88	81.17	46.17	52.02
Above + common question word	74.88	81.17	46.45	52.88
Above + topic similarity	75.10	81.33	46.93	53.01
primary	75.10	81.33	46.93	**53.01**
contrastive-1	74.88	81.17	47.03	52.47
contrastive-2	74.60	81.17	47.23	53.22
All features (Pointwise)	74.43	81.17	45.89	51.07
Best Primary	-	-	**47.22**	50.07
Best Overall	-	-	49.00	52.41

Table 1: Results on dev and test set with various features

3.2 Learning to rank

We use pairwise learning to rank for ranking task which poses the ranking problem as classification problem to minimize the average number of inversions in ranking. This formulation is more closer to ranking task than predicting relevance as regression and also has theoretical guarantees of maximizing the MAP in ranking (Chen et al., 2009).

First, we create these pairs by taking original question Q_o and two candidate questions of which one was relevant and other one not, Q_{c1} and Q_{c2}. Then we generate above mentioned feature vectors $f(Q_o, Q_{c1})$, $f(Q_o, Q_{c2})$ and use feature difference $f(Q_o, Q_{c1}) - f(Q_o, Q_{c2})$ to the classifier. In total, 5949 such pairs are used for training. Logistic regression is used for our *primary* submission and linear kernel *SVM* with regularization parameter as 1 for our both contrastive submissions. The submitted systems *primary* and *contrastive-1* use train, development as training and *contrastive-2* uses test-2016 in concatenation for training.

4 Results

The results generated by the system on test data were submitted as an entry to SemEval-2017 task 3 subtask B. Our primary entry achieved second place on the MAP which was official metric for ranking. Also it achieved highest MRR amongst all the primary submissions.

Table 1 shows the dev and test set accuracy for our system with each feature applied incrementally. Our both *contrastive* submissions trained on SVM achieved better test accuracy than training on Logistic Regression. Thus the Ranking-SVM is able to generalize better.

We also experimented with pointwise learning to rank method and got inferior results thus corroborating the fact that pairwise methods are helping our system in achieving better accuracy.

5 Conclusion and Future Work

This paper presented a system which uses sophisticated learning to rank method with semantic features to obtain promising results on ranking similar questions. The paper shows that semantic features and pairwise learning are essential components to the system by ablation tests.

In future, we would like to extend our neural architecture to attention based models which have shown success in recent times. We also plan to use Triplet loss (Hoffer and Ailon, 2015) which captures ranking task in better way. Another direction is to use state-of-art listwise learning to rank methods that can directly optimize MAP.

References

David M Blei, Andrew Y Ng, and Michael I Jordan. 2003. Latent dirichlet allocation. *Journal of machine Learning research* 3(Jan):993–1022.

Jane Bromley, James W. Bentz, Léon Bottou, Isabelle Guyon, Yann LeCun, Cliff Moore, Eduard Säckinger, and Roopak Shah. 1993. Signature verification using a "siamese" time delay neural network. *IJPRAI* 7(4):669–688.

Wei Chen, Tie-Yan Liu, Yanyan Lan, Zhi-Ming Ma, and Hang Li. 2009. Ranking measures and loss functions in learning to rank. In *Advances in Neural Information Processing Systems*. pages 315–323.

Sumit Chopra, Raia Hadsell, and Yann LeCun. 2005. Learning a similarity metric discriminatively, with application to face verification. In *Computer Vision and Pattern Recognition, 2005. CVPR 2005. IEEE Computer Society Conference on*. IEEE, volume 1, pages 539–546.

Junyoung Chung, Caglar Gulcehre, KyungHyun Cho, and Yoshua Bengio. 2014. Empirical evaluation of gated recurrent neural networks on sequence modeling. *arXiv preprint arXiv:1412.3555* .

Sepp Hochreiter and Jürgen Schmidhuber. 1997. Long short-term memory. *Neural computation* 9(8):1735–1780.

Elad Hoffer and Nir Ailon. 2015. Deep metric learning using triplet network. In *International Workshop on Similarity-Based Pattern Recognition*. Springer, pages 84–92.

Yuhua Li, David McLean, Zuhair A Bandar, James D O'shea, and Keeley Crockett. 2006. Sentence similarity based on semantic nets and corpus statistics. *IEEE transactions on knowledge and data engineering* 18(8):1138–1150.

Chin-Yew Lin. 2004. Rouge: A package for automatic evaluation of summaries. In *Text summarization branches out: Proceedings of the ACL-04 workshop*. Barcelona, Spain, volume 8.

Tie-Yan Liu et al. 2009. Learning to rank for information retrieval. *Foundations and Trends® in Information Retrieval* 3(3):225–331.

Preslav Nakov, Doris Hoogeveen, Lluís Màrquez, Alessandro Moschitti, Hamdy Mubarak, Timothy Baldwin, and Karin Verspoor. 2017. SemEval-2017 task 3: Community question answering. In *Proceedings of the 11th International Workshop on Semantic Evaluation*. Association for Computational Linguistics, Vancouver, Canada, SemEval '17.

Kishore Papineni, Salim Roukos, Todd Ward, and Wei-Jing Zhu. 2002. Bleu: a method for automatic evaluation of machine translation. In *Proceedings of the 40th annual meeting on association for computational linguistics*. Association for Computational Linguistics, pages 311–318.

Jeffrey Pennington, Richard Socher, and Christopher D Manning. 2014. Glove: Global vectors for word representation. In *EMNLP*. volume 14, pages 1532–1543.

Theano Development Team. 2016. Theano: A Python framework for fast computation of mathematical expressions. *arXiv e-prints* abs/1605.02688. http://arxiv.org/abs/1605.02688.

Andrew Trotman. 2005. Learning to rank. *Information Retrieval* 8(3):359–381.

SimBow at SemEval-2017 Task 3: Soft-Cosine Semantic Similarity between Questions for Community Question Answering

Delphine Charlet and Géraldine Damnati
Orange Labs
Lannion, France
`delphine.charlet,geraldine.damnati@orange.com`

Abstract

This paper describes the SimBow system submitted at SemEval2017-Task3, for the question-question similarity subtask B. The proposed approach is a supervised combination of different unsupervised textual similarities. These textual similarities rely on the introduction of a relation matrix in the classical cosine similarity between bag-of-words, so as to get a soft-cosine that takes into account relations between words. According to the type of relation matrix embedded in the soft-cosine, semantic or lexical relations can be considered. Our system ranked first among the official submissions of subtask B.

1 Introduction

Social networks enable people to post questions, and to interact with other people to obtain relevant answers. The popularity of forums show that they are able to propose reliable answers. Due to this tremendous popularity, forums are growing fast, and the first reflex for an internet user is to check with his favorite search engine if a similar question has already been posted.Community Question Answering at SemEval focuses on this task, with 3 different subtasks. SubtaskA (resp. subtaskC) aims at re-ranking the comments of one original question (resp. the comments of a set of 10 related questions), regarding the relevancy to the original questions. SubtaskB aims at re-ranking 10 related questions proposed by a search engine, regarding the relevancy to the original question. Subtasks A and C are question-answering tasks. SubtaskB can be viewed as a pure semantic textual similarity task applied on community questions, with noisy user-generated texts, making it different from SemEval-Task1 (Agirre et al.,

2016), which focuses on semantic similarity between short well-formed sentences.

In this paper, we only focus on subtaskB, with the purpose of developing semantic textual similarity measures for such noisy texts. Question-question similarity appeared in SemEval2016 (Nakov et al., 2016), and is pursued in SemEval2017 (Nakov et al., 2017). The approaches explored last year were mostly supervised fusion of different similarity measures, some being unsupervised, others supervised. Among the unsupervised measures, many were based on overlap count between components (from n-grams of words or characters to knowledge-based components such as named entities, frame representations, knowledge graphs, e.g. (Franco-Salvador et al., 2016)...). Much attention was also paid for the use of word embeddings (e.g. (Mihaylov and Nakov, 2016)), with question-level averaged vectors used directly with a cosine similarity or as input of a neural classifier. Finally, fusion was often performed with SVMs (Filice et al., 2016)

Our motivation in this work was slightly different: we considered that forum data were too noisy to get reliable outputs from linguistic analysis and we wanted to focus on core textual semantic similarity. Hence, we avoided using any metadata analysis (such as user profile...) to get results that could easily generalize to other similarity tasks.Thus, we explore unsupervised similarity measures, with no external resources, hardly any linguistic processing (except a list of stopwords), relying only on the availability of sufficient unannotated corpora representative of the data. And we fuse them in a robust and simple supervised framework (logistic regression).

The rest of the paper is organized as follows: in section 2, the core unsupervised similarity measure is presented, the submitted systems are described in section 3, and section 4 presents results.

Proceedings of the 11th International Workshop on Semantic Evaluations (SemEval-2017), pages 315–319,
Vancouver, Canada, August 3 - 4, 2017. ©2017 Association for Computational Linguistics

2 Soft-Cosine Similarity Measure

In a classical bag-of-words approach, texts are represented by a vector of TF-IDF coefficients of size N, N being the number of different words occurring in the texts. Computing a cosine similarity between 2 vectors is directly related to the amount of words which are in common in both texts.

$$cos(X, Y) = \frac{X^t.Y}{\sqrt{X^t.X}\sqrt{Y^t.Y}} \text{ whith } X^t.Y = \sum_{i=1}^{n} x_i y_i \quad (1)$$

When there are no words in common between texts X and Y (*i.e.* no index i for which both x_i and y_i are not equal to zero), cosine similarity is null. However, even with no words in common, texts can be semantically related when the words are themselves semantically related. Hence we propose to take into account word-level relations by introducing in the cosine similarity formula a relation matrix M, as suggested in equation 2.

$$cos_M(X, Y) = \frac{X^t.M.Y}{\sqrt{X^t.M.X}\sqrt{Y^t.M.Y}} \quad (2)$$

$$X^t.M.Y = \sum_{i=1}^{n}\sum_{j=1}^{n} x_i m_{i,j} y_j \quad (3)$$

where M is a matrix whose element $m_{i,j}$ expresses some relation between word i and word j. With such a metric, the similarity between two texts is non null as soon as the texts share related words, even if they have no words in common. Introducing the relation matrix in the denominator normalization factors ensures that the reflexive similarity is 1. If the words are only related with themselves ($m_{i,i} = 1$ and $m_{i,j} = 0 \; \forall i, j$ with $i \neq j$), M is the identity matrix and the *soft*-cosine turns out to be the cosine.

We first investigated this modified cosine similarity in the context of topic segmentation of TV Broadcast News (Bouchekif et al., 2016), using semantic relations between words to improve the computation of semantic cohesion between consecutive snippets. Other researchers have also proposed this measure (e.g (Sidorov et al., 2014)) along with the *soft-cosine* denomination, where the matrix was based for instance on Levenshtein distance between n-grams. In this work, we investigate different kinds of word relations that can be used for computing M.

2.1 Semantic relations

Distributed representations of words, such as the word2vec approach proposed by (Mikolov et al.,

2013) have known a tremendous success recently. They enable to obtain relevant semantic relations between words, based on a simple similarity measure (e.g. cosine) between the vector representations of these words.

In this work, 2 distributed representations of words are computed, using the word2vec toolkit, in the cbow configuration: one is estimated on English Wikipedia, and the other is estimated using the unannotated corpus of questions and comments on Qatar-Living forum, distributed in the campaign, which contains 100 millions of words. The vectors dimension is 300 (experiments with various vector dimensions didn't provide any significant difference), and only the words with a minimal frequency of 50 are taken into account.

Once the word2vec representations of words are available, M can be computed in different ways. We have explored different variants, and the best results were obtained with the following framework, where v_i stands for the word2vec reprsentation of word w_i:

$$m_{i,j} = max(0, cosine(v_i, v_j))^2 \quad (4)$$

Grounding to 0 is motivated by the observation that negative *cosine* between words are hard to interpret, and often irrelevant. Squaring is applied to emphasize the dynamics of the semantic relations: insisting more on strong semantic relations, and flattening weak semantic relations. Actually we have observed in several applicative domains that high semantic similarities derived from word embedding are more significant than low similarities.

2.2 Edit-distance based relations

Using a Levenshtein distance between words, an edit relation between words can be computed: it enables to cope, for instance, with little typographic errors which are frequent in social user-generated corpora such as Qatar Living forum. It is defined as $m_{i,i} = 1$ and for $i \neq j$:

$$m_{i,j} = \alpha * \left(1 - \frac{Levenshtein(w_i, w_j)}{max(||w_i||, ||w_j||)}\right)^{\beta} \quad (5)$$

$||w||$ is the number of characters of the word, α is a weighting factor relatively to diagonal elements, and β is a factor that enables to emphasize the score dynamics. Experiments on train and dev led to set $\alpha = 1.8$ and $\beta = 5$.

3 System Description

3.1 Data pre-processing

Some basic preprocessing steps are applied on the text: lowercase, suppression of punctuation marks and stopwords, replacing urls and images with the generic terms "_url_" and "_img_". As for the bag of word representation, TF-IDF coefficients are computed in a specific way: TF coefficients are computed in the text under consideration as usual but IDF coefficients are computed from the large unannotated Qatar Living forum corpus.

3.2 Supervised combination of unsupervised similarities

For a given pair of texts to compare, 3 textual similarity measures are considered: cos_{Mrel} (soft-cosine with semantic relations), cos_{Mlev} (soft-cosine with Levenshtein distance), $wavg\_word2vec$ (cosine between weighted averaged `word2vec`). Soft-cosine measures are computed as explained in section 2. For the latter, weights are given by the TF-IDF coefficients computed as described in section3.1.

Each original question contains a *subject* and a *body*. Each related question additionally contains a thread of *comments*. We have considered several variants for text selection: (*subject*, *body*, *subject+body*, or *comments*). The 3 textual similarities are then computed between every possible 12 text pairings (3 possible texts for original questions $\times$ 4 possible texts for relative questions), constituting the set of 36 potential features. We also include in this set the IR system reciprocal rank rrk. Logistic regressions, combining these features, is then trained on the "train-part1" set of 1999 paired texts of SemEval2016. Thus, we evaluate all possible subsets of features among the set of 37 potential features, and we keep for our primary submission the one that gave the best result on average on dev and test2016. *contrastive1* was chosen as the best candidate including only soft-cosine metrics and rrk and *contrastive2* was chosen as the best candidate system with the lowest amount of features.

4 Evaluation

In this section, we present detailed evaluations of Task3/subtaskB. Given a new question (aka original question), the task consists in reranking the 10 questions (aka related questions) proposed by a search engine. A precise description of the corpus and metrics can be found in Task3 description paper (Nakov et al., 2017). Results are presented with the MAP evaluation measure, on 3 corpora: dev (50 original questions $\times$ 10 related questions), test2016 (70 original questions $\times$ 10 related questions) and test2017 (88 original questions $\times$ 10 related questions).

It is worth noticing that the MAP scorer used in this campaign is sensitive to the amount of original questions which don't have any relevant related questions in the gold labels. In fact, these questions always account for a precision of 0 in the MAP scoring. Hence, an Oracle evaluation, giving a score of 1 to all related questions labeled as "true", and a score of 0 to all related questions labeled as "false" in the gold labels, doesn't provide a 100% MAP but an Oracle MAP which corresponds to the proportion of original questions that have at least 1 relevant related question. Hence the upper bound of MAP performances is 86.00% for dev, 88.57% for test2016, and only 67.05% for test2017 (29 original questions without any relevant related question out of 88). Another difference between test2016 and test2017 is the average number of "true" labels for questions that have at least one relevant associated question (3.7 for test2016 and 2.7 for test2017). On the overall test2017 is more difficult for the Task.

4.1 Unsupervised textual similarity measures

Table 1 presents the MAP results obtained for different unsupervised textual similarities. Here, the focus is made on unsupervised textual similarity measure, and we only present results for the *subject+body* configuration for both the original and related questions. Performances of the Information Retrieval system (IR), and of the best system submitted at SemEval2016 (Franco-Salvador et al., 2016) are reported for comparison purpose.

similarity	dev	test 2016	test 2017
IR	71.35	74.75	41.85
best SemEval2016	-	77.33	-
baseline_token_cos	62.22	68.54	40.88
baseline_pp_cos	67.49	71.05	42.80
baseline_pp_cos_tfidf	69.41	75.53	44.37
cos_{Mrel} relations WP	72.25	77.11	45.38
cos_{Mrel} relations QL	**75.24**	**77.96**	45.27
cos_{Mlev} Levenshtein	70.02	76.34	46.10
wavg-word2vec on QL	73.31	75.77	**46.99**

Table 1: MAP results for unsupervised textual similarity measures

As a baseline, we use the *baseline_token_cos* defined in SemEval2015-Task2 (Agirre et al., 2015), for semantic textual similarity between sentences. It is a simple cosine similarity between bag-of-tokens binary vectors (a token is a non-white-space sequence between 2 white spaces, and weights are 1 or 0). Performances of *baseline_pp_cos*, which is also a cosine of binary vectors but obtained after the pre-processing step show the importance of suitable pre-processing. *baseline_pp_cos_tfidf* show the influence of appropriate term weighting over simple binary coefficients. Next results reveal significant improvements when introducing a relation matrix M in the soft-cosine metric (cos_M). When M contains semantic relations, a significant difference is observed on dev, between relations estimated on a general corpus WP (Wikipedia, 2.7 Bwords) and on a specialized corpus QL (Qatar Living, 100 Mwords). The difference is much lower for test2016, and even negative for test2017. On the contrary, the Levenshtein-based M matrix performs best on test2017, whereas its gain is only marginal for dev and test2016. In all cases, introducing a carefully chosen relation matrix M in the cosine-based similarity measure improves performances. Finally, the cosine between TF-IDF weighted average `word2vec` is less effective on dev and test2016, but performs well on test2017.

It is worth noticing that the mere cos_{Mrel} soft-cosine on QL would have won the 2016 challenge.

4.2 Evaluation of supervised combination

Table 2 presents the MAP obtained for different supervised combinations of similarity measures.

First, for a given unsupervised textual similarity measure, all the possible combinations of paired texts are evaluated, and we give the result of the subset which gives the best performance on average on dev, test2016, and test2017. Interestingly, it is the same combination of paired texts which performs best for the 3 textual similarity measure: similarity between *subject+body* for both questions and *subject+body* for the original question and *comments* for the related question. This last pairing performs poorly alone but is interesting in combination with the first one.

Then we report the results of the submitted systems to the official evaluation. As can be seen in Table 2, *contrastive2* was more robust to the more difficult conditions of test2017. Additionally, as the IR performs really worse in test2017,

similarity	dev	test 2016	test 2017
IR	71.35	74.75	41.85
best SemEval2016	-	77.33	-
text combination			
cos_{Mrel} relations QL	75.76	78.76	46.67
cos_{Mlev} Levenshtein	72.26	78.19	47.48
wavg-word2vec on QL	75.91	76.70	47.40
submissions			
primary	**77.30**	**79.77**	**47.22**
contrastive1	77.04	79.12	46.84
contrastive2	77.30	79.43	**47.87**
removing rrk			
primary$-rrk$	76.71	78.61	47.68
contrastive1$-rrk$	76.09	78.90	46.96
contrastive2$-rrk$	76.73	78.97	**48.38**

Table 2: MAP results for supervised combination of textual similarity measures

we re-trained the systems excluding rrk from features. Actually, if rrk was helpful for both dev and test2016 corpora, we can see that removing rrk provides better results on test2017, yielding a maximum MAP score of 48.38. This performance is obtained with the following set of similarities: cos_{Mrel} between $subject+body$, cos_{Mlev} between $subject + body$ and $subject$ of the original question and $body$ of the relative question, and $wavg - w2v$ between $subject + body$ and between $subject + body$ of the original question and $comments$ of the relative question.

5 Conclusion

In this work, we have explored a modified version of the cosine similarity between bag-of-words representation of texts. In this so-called *soft-cosine* similarity, a relation matrix M is embedded, allowing relations between words to be taken into account. The computation of M is unsupervised, and can be derived from distributed representations of words. *soft-cosine* performed well at SemEval-Taks3 question-question similarity subtaskB. A simple supervised logistic regression combination of different unsupervised similarity measures over different text selection strategies ranked first at the official evaluation. In the future, we plan to pursue the work on *soft-cosine* in two directions: including other relations between words, for instance using semantic role labeling, and studying how this matrix M, efficiently initialized in an unsupervised way, could be further trained for specific tasks.

References

Eneko Agirre, Carmen Banea, Claire Cardie, Daniel Cer, Mona Diab, Aitor Gonzalez-Agirre, Weiwei Guo, Inigo Lopez-Gazpio, Montse Maritxalar, Rada Mihalcea, German Rigau, Larraitz Uria, and Janyce Wiebe. 2015. Semeval-2015 task 2: Semantic textual similarity, english, spanish and pilot on interpretability. In *Proceedings of the 9th International Workshop on Semantic Evaluation (SemEval 2015)*. Association for Computational Linguistics, Denver, Colorado, pages 252–263. http://www.aclweb.org/anthology/S15-2045.

Eneko Agirre, Carmen Banea, Daniel M. Cer, Mona T. Diab, Aitor Gonzalez-Agirre, Rada Mihalcea, German Rigau, and Janyce Wiebe. 2016. Semeval-2016 task 1: Semantic textual similarity, monolingual and cross-lingual evaluation. In *Proceedings of the 10th International Workshop on Semantic Evaluation, SemEval@NAACL-HLT 2016, San Diego, CA, USA, June 16-17, 2016*. pages 497–511.

Abdessalam Bouchekif, Géraldine Damnati, Delphine Charlet, Nathalie Camelin, and Yannick Estève. 2016. Title assignment for automatic topic segments in TV broadcast news. In *2016 IEEE International Conference on Acoustics, Speech and Signal Processing, ICASSP 2016, Shanghai, China, March 20-25, 2016*. pages 6100–6104.

Simone Filice, Danilo Croce, Alessandro Moschitti, and Roberto Basili. 2016. Kelp at semeval-2016 task 3: Learning semantic relations between questions and answers. In *SemEval@NAACL-HLT*.

Marc Franco-Salvador, Sudipta Kar, Thamar Solorio, and Paolo Rosso. 2016. UH-PRHLT at semeval-2016 task 3: Combining lexical and semantic-based features for community question answering. In *Proceedings of the 10th International Workshop on Semantic Evaluation, SemEval@NAACL-HLT 2016, San Diego, CA, USA, June 16-17, 2016*. pages 814–821.

Todor Mihaylov and Preslav Nakov. 2016. Semanticz at semeval-2016 task 3: Ranking relevant answers in community question answering using semantic similarity based on fine-tuned word embeddings. *Proceedings of SemEval* pages 879–886.

Tomas Mikolov, Kai Chen, Greg Corrado, and Jeffrey Dean. 2013. Efficient estimation of word representations in vector space. *arXiv preprint arXiv:1301.3781*.

Preslav Nakov, Doris Hoogeveen, Lluís Màrquez, Alessandro Moschitti, Hamdy Mubarak, Timothy Baldwin, and Karin Verspoor. 2017. SemEval-2017 task 3: Community question answering. In *Proceedings of the 11th International Workshop on Semantic Evaluation*. Association for Computational Linguistics, Vancouver, Canada, SemEval '17.

Preslav Nakov, Lluís Màrquez, Alessandro Moschitti, Walid Magdy, Hamdy Mubarak, abed Alhakim Freihat, Jim Glass, and Bilal Randeree. 2016. Semeval-2016 task 3: Community question answering. In *Proceedings of the 10th International Workshop on Semantic Evaluation (SemEval-2016)*. Association for Computational Linguistics, San Diego, California, pages 525–545. http://www.aclweb.org/anthology/S16-1083.

Grigori Sidorov, Alexander F. Gelbukh, Helena Gómez-Adorno, and David Pinto. 2014. Soft similarity and soft cosine measure: Similarity of features in vector space model. *Computación y Sistemas* 18(3). http://cys.cic.ipn.mx/ojs/index.php/CyS/article/view/2043.

FuRongWang at SemEval-2017 Task 3: Deep Neural Networks for Selecting Relevant Answers in Community Question Answering

Sheng Zhang, Jiajun Cheng, Hui Wang,
Xin Zhang, Pei Li and Zhaoyun Ding
College of Information Systems and Management,
National University of Defense Technology,
Changsha, P. R. China
{zhangsheng,jiajun.cheng,huiwang,
zhangxin,peili,zyding}@nudt.edu.cn

Abstract

We describe deep neural networks frameworks in this paper to address the community question answering (cQA) ranking task (SemEval-2017 task 3). Convolutional neural networks and bi-directional long-short term memory networks are applied in our methods to extract semantic information from questions and answers (comments). In addition, in order to take the full advantage of question-comment semantic relevance, we deploy interaction layer and augmented features before calculating the similarity. The results show that our methods have the excellent effectiveness for both subtask A and subtask C.

1 Introduction

Answer selection is regarded as a key step in question answering tasks, especially for community question answering (cQA), which is greatly valuable for user to retrieve information. Some cQA forums, such as Quora, Qatar Living and Stack Overflow, are quite open to users, providing a convenient platform for asking and answering questions. Hence, the development of cQA forums makes it urgent to answer questions automatically.

SemEval-2017 (Bethard et al., 2017) task 3 (Nakov et al., 2017) is the task for selecting relevant answers (or comments) for questions in community question answering (cQA). The data is collected from an online cQA forum, Qatar Living, which is close to some real application needs. The task consists of several subtasks, which are described briefly as follows:

- **Question-Comment Similarity**: Given one question and ten candidates comments $\{c_1, c_2, \cdots, c_n\}$, the goal is to rank these

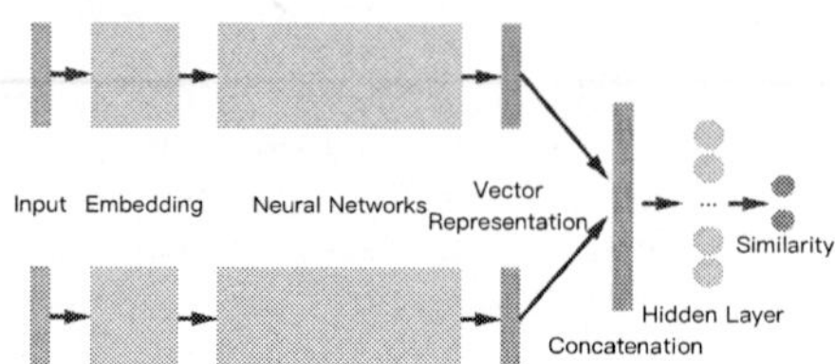

Figure 1: One Basic Deep Learning cQA Framework. The question and the comment are mapped into fixed-length word vectors. After that, they are fed into the neural network framework to extract features. Through a fully connected neural network, the framework outputs the similarity of the question and the comment.

comments according to their relevance to the question.

- **Question-External Comment Similarity**: Given one question and ten candidate questions, which also have ten candidate comments. The questions can be relevant or completely irrelevant. As for the original question, the target is to rank the top ten relevant comments from these 100 candidate comments.

The relevance between the question and the comment can be divided as "Good", "PotentiallyUseful" and "Bad". "PotentiallyUseful" and "Bad" do not make a clear distinction. "Good" comments are considered useful and should be ranked before "PotentiallyUseful" and "Bad" comments. From the above description, these tasks can be regarded as a binary classification tasks: the relation between the question and the comment is divided into "Relevant" or "Irrelevant".

Deep neural networks techniques accelerate the development of automatic question answering,

Proceedings of the 11th International Workshop on Semantic Evaluations (SemEval-2017), pages 320–325,
Vancouver, Canada, August 3 - 4, 2017. ©2017 Association for Computational Linguistics

which due to the great capability of capturing the semantic meaning of texts. Our work is mainly motivated by the previous work (Tan et al., 2016; Feng et al., 2015; Cui et al., 2016; Hu et al., 2014), which utilizes neural networks to extract features from texts. We deploy a deep neural networks framework to measure the relevance of questions and comments in the cQA task, and then rank the candidates according to their similarity to the original question. In this study, methods based on deep neural networks extract semantic features from the question and the comment respectively, which involve little manual operation and show an advantage on the huge amount of data.

In addition, to increase the connection between the question and the comment, we apply an interaction layer before calculating the similarity. Then, we add augmented features to improve the performance of deep neural networks. Finally, the system we proposed are used to address subtask A and subtask C, and the results significantly surpass the baselines provided by the organizers.

2 Methodology

Neural networks are increasingly applied in various of natural language processing tasks, due to the capability of capturing semantic meaning of texts. Our models are fundamentally motivated by previous work in Question Answering.

One basic deep learning architecture for cQA is shown as Figure 1, which is used in a great many papers (Tan et al., 2015; dos Santos et al., 2016; Feng et al., 2015; Cui et al., 2016; Hu et al., 2014). The question and the comment are mapped into fixed-length word vectors. After that, they are fed into the neural network framework to extract features. The frameworks output semantic vectors of the question and the comment, which are then concatenated into a vector. Through a fully connected neural network, the architecture outputs the similarity of the question and the comment. Finally, the similarity value can be the criteria to rank the candidate comments according to the original question.

Currently, convolutional neural networks (CNNs) have proved superiority in a variety of tasks due to the ability of learning the representation of short texts or sentences. Meanwhile, recurrent neural networks (RNNs), especially the variant: long short term memory networks (LSTMs), successfully model the long and short term information of the sequence.

2.1 CNN-based Architecture

The question and the comment are represented by word embedding sequences with a fixed length: $\{w_1, \cdots, w_l\}$, each element is real-valued and $w \in \mathbb{R}^d$. Each sentence is normalized to a fixed length sequence by adding paddings if the sentence is short or truncating the excess otherwise. After embeddings, each sentence can be presented by a matrix $S \in \mathbb{R}^{l \times d}$.

In order to capture higher semantic information of sentences, convolutional layer is applied after embeddings, which consists of several convolutional feature maps. Suppose we have k feature maps $z_i \in \mathbb{R}^{s \times d}$, after convolutional operation, the outputs of CNN is $C \in \mathbb{R}^{(l-s+1) \times k}$.

A pooling layer is added after the convolutional layer. Max pooling and average pooling are commonly used in the model, which choose the max or average value of the features extracted from the former layer to reduce the presentation. In this study, we use 1-max pooling as our methods to select the max value of each filter, and the question and the comment vectors generated by neural networks are $q, c \in \mathbb{R}^k$ respectively.

In order to extract features from different scales, we use different types of feature maps altogether. These feature maps have different width to capture information from different contexts, which contribute to the feature extraction of CNNs.

2.2 LSTM-based Architecture

The long short term memory (LSTM) network is a variant of recurrent neural network (RNN) which has recently received great results on various of sequence modeling tasks. LSTM overcomes the shortcoming of RNN in handling "long-term dependencies". Memory cells and forget gates are the key points of the LSTM: they make it capable of handling both long and short sequences through controlling the information flow of a sequence. A LSTM network is made up of several cells with the following formula:

$$f_t = \sigma(W_f \cdot [h_{t-1}, x_t] + b_f), \tag{1}$$

$$i_t = \sigma(W_i \cdot [h_{t-1}, x_t] + b_i), \tag{2}$$

$$\tilde{C}_t = tanh(W_C \cdot [h_{t-1}, x_t] + b_C) \tag{3}$$

$$C_t = f_t \odot C_{t-1} + i_t \odot \tilde{C}_t, \tag{4}$$

$$o_t = \sigma(W_o \cdot [h_{t-1}, x_t] + b_o), \tag{5}$$

$$h_t = o_t \odot tanh(C_t), \tag{6}$$

where W and b are parameters which are trained and shared by all cells, and $\odot$ indicates element-wise production. C_t is the memory cell, which stores previous values. The forget gate f_t and the input gate i_t control the percentage of information from the previous memory and new inputs respectively, while the output gate o_t controls the output of hidden states. $\sigma(\cdot)$ indicates the sigmoid function.

Single directional LSTM only utilizes the former information of a sequence, while bi-directional LSTMs utilize the information both forward and afterward. Usually, in order to capture more information of the sequence, bi-directional LSTMs are adopted, with the one processes information from the front to the end of a sequence while the other processes information in the reverse direction. The output of bi-directional LSTMs can be the concatenation of two output vectors from both direction, i.e. $h_t = \overrightarrow{h_t} || \overleftarrow{h_t}$.

2.3 Augmented Features

In general, neural networks are able to extract features automatically. However, (Fu et al., 2016) and (Yu et al., 2014) have shown that augmented features contribute to the behavior of neural networks. Some commonly used augmented features such as word overlap indices, part-of-speech tags, position indices, etc.

In this work, we use word overlap indices as augmented features. Given a question $q_i = (x_1^q, x_2^q, \cdots, x_m^q)$ and a comment $c_i = (x_1^c, x_2^c, \cdots, x_m^c)$, the overlap features q_{feat} and c_{feat} are calculated as follows:

$$q_{feat}^{(i)} = \begin{cases} 1 & x_i^q \in c_i, \\ 0 & \text{otherwise}, \end{cases} \tag{7}$$

$$c_{feat}^{(i)} = \begin{cases} 1 & x_i^c \in q_i, \\ 0 & \text{otherwise}, \end{cases} \tag{8}$$

where $q_{feat}^{(i)}$ is the ith element of q_{feat}, so is $c_{feat}^{(i)}$.

As shown in Figure 2, q_{feat} and c_{feat} are added at the tail of sequence embeddings. Also, their concatenation x_{feat} is regarded as augmented features before feeding into the fully connected networks.

2.4 Interaction Layer

In order to make full use of the connection of the question and the comment, we design an interaction layer to capture the relevance of them, which is shown in Figure 2.

Given a question vector $q \in \mathbb{R}^k$ and a comment vector $c \in \mathbb{R}^k$ produced by neural networks, the interaction layer calculates the matrix multiplication as follows:

$$z_{int} = f(q^T W c), \tag{9}$$

where $z_{int} \in \mathbb{R}$ is the output of interaction layer, and $M \in \mathbb{R}^{k \times k}$ is the parameter of the layer and updated when training, while $f(\cdot)$ is the activation function.

2.5 Objective Function and Optimizer

Features extracted by deep neural networks are concatenated with extra features, which are then fed into a fully connected neural network altogether.

$$o_i^h = f(W_o[q, c, x_{feat}, z_{int}] + b_o), \tag{10}$$

where o_i^h is the output of hidden layer node i, and x_{feat} is the augmented features. W_o and b_o are the weight and the bias of the hidden layer respectively.

After that, the softmax function is applied to obtain the similarity of the question and the comment:

$$o_i = Softmax(W_s \cdot o_i^h + b_s), \tag{11}$$

where $o_i \in [0, 1]$ is the output of the network, which satisfies $\sum_i o_i = 1$. W_s and b_s are the weight and the bias of the output layer respectively.

The objective function in this study is cross entropy, which is illustrated as follows:

$$\mathcal{L} = -\frac{1}{N} \sum_{i \in N} \{ y_i \log o_i + (1 - y_i) \log (1 - o_i) \}, \tag{12}$$

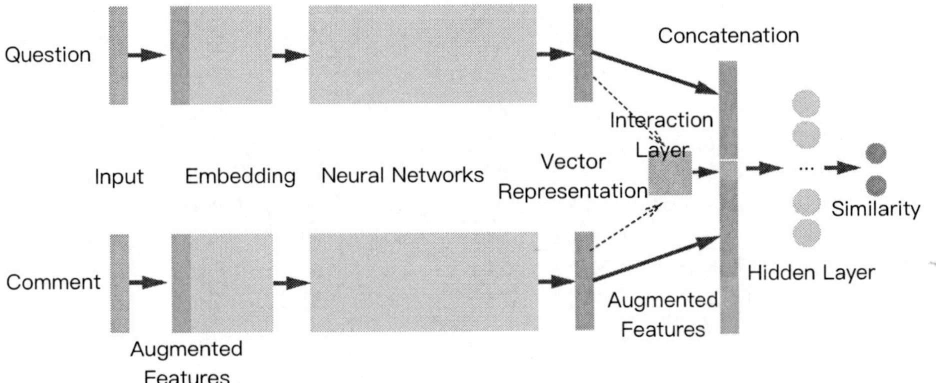

Figure 2: The deep neural network frameworks for cQA. The question and the answer are represented by word vectors, with augmented features added at the end. Then the vectors are fed into neural networks, such as CNN or LSTM, to extract vectors. Interaction layer compute the similarity of vectors, which are then concatenated with extracted vectors together. Through a fully connected neural network, the framework outputs the similarity of the question and the comment.

where $y_i \in \{0, 1\}$ is the ground truth label of the question-comment relation. N is the number of samples.

The relation of the question and the comment is divided to two classes, "Good" and "Bad" ("PotentiallyUseful" is regraded as "Bad"). To train the parameters in networks, Adagrad optimizer (Duchi et al., 2011) is applied. Adagrad is an algorithm designed for gradient-based optimization, which adapt the learning rate for better convergence when training the parameters. (Dean et al., 2012) point out that Adagrad increase the robustness of stochastic gradient descent when training large-scale neural networks.

3 Experimental Results

In this section, we describe the detail of training deep neural networks, including the datasets, metrics, baseline, parameters settings and so on. Then, we present the results and give a brief analysis of these results.

3.1 Data Description

Datasets provided by the organizers are collected from Qatar Living forum, which is an online cQA website. The components of the datasets are shown as Table 3.1:

In our experiment, datasets "train_1", "train_2" and "dev" are used to train neural networks. In addition, dataset "test_2016" is used for development

Dataset	train_1	train_2	dev
Questions	1999	670	500
Dataset	test_2016	test_2017	
Questions	700	880	

Table 1: The components of the datasets.

and parameters searching, and dataset "test_2017" is submitted for evaluation.

3.2 Metrics and Baselines

The official evaluation metrics in this task is Mean Average Precision (MAP), which is used for ranking submissions from different teams. MAP is often used to measure the quality of ranking in information retrieval. In addition, Average Recall (AvgRec), Mean Reciprocal Rank (MRR), Accuracy (Acc), etc. are also reported by the official scorer.

Baselines are given by the organizer, which consists of Information Retrieval (IR) baseline and random baseline. IR baseline is the rank of candidates given by a search engine, such as Google or Bing. Random baseline is the results of given a random number (from 0 to 1) to rank each candidate.

3.3 Experimental Setup

Our models in this work are mainly implemented with tensorflow v1.0 (Abadi et al., 2016) from a scratch. The code runs on a GTX 1080 GPU and

Datasets	test_2016			test_2017		
Methods	MAP	AvgRec	MRR	MAP	AvgRec	MRR
Random (baseline)	52.80	66.52	58.71	62.30	70.56	68.74
IR (baseline)	59.53	72.60	67.83	72.61	79.32	82.37
CNN	73.13	84.25	79.74	82.93	89.94	88.28
multi-CNN	74.38	85.24	**81.58**	83.42	90.13	88.96
+Augmented Features	73.86	84.99	80.81	83.52	90.48	89.60
+Interaction Layer (Pri)	**74.94**	**85.85**	81.10	**84.26**	**90.79**	89.40
biLSTM	74.02	84.97	80.79	83.57	90.28	89.42
+Augmented Features	73.57	84.66	79.94	84.06	90.56	**89.74**
+Interaction Layer	74.72	85.59	81.22	83.96	90.70	89.49

Table 2: Results on Subtask A

Datasets	test_2016			test_2017		
Methods	MAP	AvgRec	MRR	MAP	AvgRec	MRR
Random (baseline)	15.01	11.44	15.19	5.77	7.69	5.70
IR (baseline)	40.36	45.97	45.83	9.18	21.72	10.11
CNN	47.62	50.25	52.64	12.57	29.00	14.06
multi-CNN	48.85	51.56	55.11	12.55	**29.65**	**14.64**
+Augmented Features	49.81	52.04	55.68	**13.55**	29.45	**14.63**
+Interaction Layer (Pri)	**50.15**	**53.58**	54.56	13.23	29.51	14.27
biLSTM	46.31	51.64	55.39	12.78	26.48	14.25
+Augmented Features	47.29	51.72	**55.91**	12.73	26.48	14.24
+Interaction Layer	48.06	52.72	53.70	13.23	26.13	14.52

Table 3: Results on Subtask C

it is about 100 epochs that the model become to converge.

All texts from questions and comments are used at first to train Word2Vec vectors (Mikolov et al., 2013a,b) by a Python package gensim [1], whose length is fixed to 100. The max sequence length of the question and the comment are fixed to 200. We add paddings if the sequence is short or truncate the excess otherwise.

The single-type CNN networks have the filter size of 3, and 800 feature maps, while the multi-type CNN networks have the filter sizes of 1,2,3 and 5 with 800 feature maps each. The bi-LSTMs have the output length of 400 of each direction, and the hidden states are outputted directly for the higher layer. The number of nodes in hidden layer is 256 and the activation function used in fully connected neural networks is ReLu. The optimizer is set to AdagradOptimizer and the learning rate is set to 0.01 initially.

3.4 Results on subtask A

Table 3.1 summarizes the results on subtask A: Question-Comment Similarity. The first two rows illustrate the random baseline and the IR baseline, follow by 4 rows of CNN results. The last three rows are the results of LSTMs. As shown in the table, our results significantly outperform the baselines. Neural network based methods perform quite stable, the differences between their results are less than 1%.

The multiCNN along with augmented features and interaction layer achieves the best MAP scores among these methods, although it does not rank the first as for MRR scores. It is also clear that interaction layer and augmented features contribute to the behavior of neural networks.

3.5 Results on subtask C

Table 3.1 illustrates the results on subtask C: Question-External Comment Similarity. It should be noted that we use the reciprocal rank of questions to improve the rank of the comments.

From the table, our methods surpass the baselines and the best method obtains the MAP of

[1] https://radimrehurek.com/gensim/

13.55. The circumstance is quite similar to subtask
A, which has proved that our deep neural based architectures are of great stability. However, LSTM-
based architectures is far behind CNN-based architectures in terms of MAP and AvgRec scores,
but have the advantage in terms of MRR scores.

4 Conclusion

In this paper, we present deep neural networks
frameworks to address community question answering tasks. CNNs and biLSTMs are used to extract the semantic features of questions and comments. We add an interaction layer and augmented
features to improve the performance of the framework. The results illustrate that our methods are
greatly superior to the baselines provided by organizers both in subtask A and subtask C.

Acknowledgments

The research is supported by National Natural
Science Foundation of China (No.71331008) and
(No.61105124).

References

Martín Abadi, Ashish Agarwal, Paul Barham, Eugene
Brevdo, Zhifeng Chen, Craig Citro, Greg S Corrado,
Andy Davis, Jeffrey Dean, Matthieu Devin, et al.
2016. Tensorflow: Large-scale machine learning on
heterogeneous distributed systems. *arXiv preprint
arXiv:1603.04467* .

Steven Bethard, Marine Carpuat, Marianna Apidianaki, Saif M. Mohammad, Daniel Cer, and
David Jurgens, editors. 2017. *Proceedings
of the 11th International Workshop on Semantic Evaluation (SemEval-2017)*. Association for
Computational Linguistics, Vancouver, Canada.
http://www.aclweb.org/anthology/S17-2.

Yiming Cui, Zhipeng Chen, Si Wei, Shijin Wang,
Ting Liu, and Guoping Hu. 2016. Attention-over-
attention neural networks for reading comprehension. *arXiv preprint arXiv:1607.04423* .

Jeffrey Dean, Greg Corrado, Rajat Monga, Kai Chen,
Matthieu Devin, Mark Mao, Andrew Senior, Paul
Tucker, Ke Yang, Quoc V Le, et al. 2012. Large
scale distributed deep networks. In *Advances in
neural information processing systems*. pages 1223–
1231.

Cicero Nogueira dos Santos, Ming Tan, Bing Xiang,
and Bowen Zhou. 2016. Attentive pooling networks. *CoRR, abs/1602.03609* .

John Duchi, Elad Hazan, and Yoram Singer. 2011.
Adaptive subgradient methods for online learning
and stochastic optimization. *Journal of Machine
Learning Research* 12(Jul):2121–2159.

Minwei Feng, Bing Xiang, Michael R Glass, Lidan
Wang, and Bowen Zhou. 2015. Applying deep
learning to answer selection: A study and an open
task. In *Automatic Speech Recognition and Understanding (ASRU), 2015 IEEE Workshop on*. IEEE,
pages 813–820.

Jian Fu, Xipeng Qiu, and Xuanjing Huang. 2016. Convolutional deep neural networks for document-based
question answering. In *International Conference
on Computer Processing of Oriental Languages*.
Springer, pages 790–797.

Baotian Hu, Zhengdong Lu, Hang Li, and Qingcai
Chen. 2014. Convolutional neural network architectures for matching natural language sentences. In
Advances in neural information processing systems.
pages 2042–2050.

Tomas Mikolov, Kai Chen, Greg Corrado, and Jeffrey Dean. 2013a. Efficient estimation of word
representations in vector space. *arXiv preprint
arXiv:1301.3781* .

Tomas Mikolov, Ilya Sutskever, Kai Chen, Greg S Corrado, and Jeff Dean. 2013b. Distributed representations of words and phrases and their compositionality. In *Advances in neural information processing
systems*. pages 3111–3119.

Preslav Nakov, Doris Hoogeveen, Lluís Màrquez,
Alessandro Moschitti, Hamdy Mubarak, Timothy
Baldwin, and Karin Verspoor. 2017. Semeval-2017
task 3: Community question answering. In *Proceedings of the 11th International Workshop on Semantic
Evaluation (SemEval-2017)*. Association for Computational Linguistics, Vancouver, Canada, pages
27–48. http://www.aclweb.org/anthology/S17-
2003.

Ming Tan, Cicero dos Santos, Bing Xiang, and Bowen
Zhou. 2015. Lstm-based deep learning models
for non-factoid answer selection. *arXiv preprint
arXiv:1511.04108* .

Ming Tan, Cicero Dos Santos, Bing Xiang, and Bowen
Zhou. 2016. Improved representation learning for
question answer matching. In *Meeting of the Association for Computational Linguistics*. pages 464–
473.

Lei Yu, Karl Moritz Hermann, Phil Blunsom, and
Stephen Pulman. 2014. Deep learning for answer
sentence selection. *arXiv preprint arXiv:1412.1632*
.

KeLP at SemEval-2017 Task 3:
Learning Pairwise Patterns in Community Question Answering

Simone Filice[1], Giovanni Da San Martino[2] and **Alessandro Moschitti[2]**

[1] DICII, University of Roma, Tor Vergata
[2] ALT, Qatar Computing Research Institute, HBKU

`filice.simone@gmail.com`
`{gmartino,amoschitti}@hbku.edu.qa`

Abstract

This paper describes the KeLP system participating in the SemEval-2017 community Question Answering (cQA) task. The system is a refinement of the kernel-based sentence pair modeling we proposed for the previous year challenge. It is implemented within the Kernel-based Learning Platform called KeLP, from which we inherit the team's name. Our primary submission ranked first in subtask A, and third in subtasks B and C, being the only systems appearing in the top-3 ranking for all the English subtasks. This shows that the proposed framework, which has minor variations among the three subtasks, is extremely flexible and effective in tackling learning tasks defined on sentence pairs.

1 Introduction

This paper describes the KeLP system participating in the SemEval-2017 cQA challenge (Nakov et al., 2017). The task setting for the English part is the same as the previous edition (Nakov et al., 2016): the corpus is extracted from *Qatar Living*[1], a web forum where people pose questions about multiple aspects of their daily life in Qatar, and three subtasks are defined:

Subtask A: Given a question q and its first 10 comments $c_1, \ldots, c_{10}$ in its question thread, re-rank these 10 comments according to their relevance with respect to the question, i.e., the *good* comments have to be ranked above *potential* or *bad* comments.

Subtask B: Given a new question o and the set of the first 10 related questions $q_1, \ldots, q_{10}$ (retrieved by a search engine), re-rank the related questions according to their similarity with respect

to o, i.e., the *perfect match* and *relevant* questions should be ranked above the *irrelevant* ones.

Subtask C: Given a new question o, and the set of the first 10 related questions, $q_1, \ldots, q_{10}$, (retrieved by a search engine), each one associated with its first 10 comments, $c_1^q, \ldots, c_{10}^q$, appearing in its thread, re-rank the 100 comments according to their relevance with respect to o, i.e., the *good* comments are to be ranked above *potential* or *bad* comments.

We participated to the previous year edition, where our system (Filice et al., 2016) achieved very good results, i.e., first in subtask A, third in B and second in C. For the new year challenge, we therefore decided to reuse the same system applied to a new method for selecting tree structures, (Barrón-Cedeño et al., 2016; Romeo et al., 2016) summarized in Sec. 3.

We modeled the three subtasks as binary classification problems: kernel-based classifiers are trained and the classification score is used to sort the instances and produce the final ranking. We implemented models within the Kernel-based Learning Platform[2] (KeLP) (Filice et al., 2015a), which determined the team's name. Our tests provide two main contributions: (*i*) we asses the results obtained in (Filice et al., 2016), demonstrating that our kernel-based models for relational learning tasks between two texts (Filice et al., 2015b) are effective for community Question Answering. (*ii*) We studied the impact of text selection described in (Barrón-Cedeño et al., 2016).

Our primary submission ranked first in subtask A, and third in subtasks B and C, demonstrating that the proposed method is very accurate and adaptable to different learning problems. At the moment, we could not find out if text selection is always useful as our contrastive submission not

---

[1] `http://www.qatarliving.com/forum`

[2] `http://www.kelp-ml.org/`

Proceedings of the 11th International Workshop on Semantic Evaluations (SemEval-2017), pages 326–333,
Vancouver, Canada, August 3 - 4, 2017. ©2017 Association for Computational Linguistics

using it turned out to be much more accurate for Task B.

In the reminder, Section 2 introduces the proposed kernel-based system, Section 3 describes the pruning technique to select the relevant parts from the input sentences, while Section 4 reports official results.

2 The KeLP system: kernel-based learning from text pairs

In the three subtasks, the underlying problem is to understand if two texts are related. Thus, in subtasks A and C, each pair, (question, comment), generates a training instance for a binary Support Vector Machine (SVM) (Chang and Lin, 2011), where the positive label is associated with a *good* comment and the negative label includes the *potential* and *bad* comments. In subtask B, we evaluated the similarity between two questions. Each pair generates a training instance for SVM, where the positive label is associated with the *perfect match* or *relevant* classes and the negative label is associated with the *irrelevant*; the resulting classification score is used to rank the question pairs.

In KeLP, the SVM learning algorithm operates on a kernel combination of tree kernels and a linear kernel. In particular the linear kernel is applied on feature vectors containing (*i*) linguistic similarities between the texts in a pair (Section 2.1); (*ii*) task-specific features (Section 2.3).

Tree kernels are applied to evaluate inter-pair similarities between sentence pairs, in order to automatically discover pairwise relational patterns.

2.1 Intra-pair similarities

In subtasks A and C, a *good* comment is likely to share similar terms with the question. In subtask B a question that is relevant to another probably shows common words. Following this intuition, given a text pair (either question/comment or question/question), we define a feature vector whose dimensions reflect the following similarity metrics:

- **Lexical Similarities:** *Cosine similarity, Jaccard coefficient* (Jaccard, 1901) and *containment measure* (Broder, 1997) of *n*-grams of word lemmas ($n = 1, 2, 3, 4$ was used in all experiments); *Longest common substring measure* (Gusfield, 1997), *Longest common subsequence measure* (Allison and

Dix, 1986), and *Greedy String Tiling* (Wise, 1996).

- **Syntactic Similarities:** *Cosine similarity* of *n*-grams of part-of-speech tags. It considers a shallow syntactic similarity ($n = 1, 2, 3, 4$ was used in all experiments); *Partial tree kernel* (Moschitti, 2006) between the parse tree of the sentences.

- **Semantic Similarities:** *Cosine similarity* between additive representations of word embeddings generated by applying word2vec (Mikolov et al., 2013) to the entire Qatar Living corpus from SemEval 2015[3]. Five features are derived considering (*i*) only nouns, (*ii*) only adjectives, (*iii*) only verbs, (*iv*) only adverbs and (*v*) all the above words.

These metrics are computed in all the subtasks between the two elements within a pair, i.e., q and c_i for subtask A, q and o for subtask B, o and c_i for subtask C. In addition, in subtasks B and C, the similarity metrics (except the Partial Tree Kernel similarity) are computed between o and the entire thread of q, concatenating q with its answers. Similarities between q and o are also employed in subtask C.

2.2 Inter-pair kernel methods

In tasks A and C, some question types may have an expected answering form. Similarly, in Task B, related questions may be characterized by the application of some latent paraphrasing rules. Such pairwise patterns cannot be captured by any intra-pair similarity feature, and require an alternative approach. Specific features may be manually defined, but this would require a complex feature engineering.

To automatize relational learning between pairs of texts, one of the early works is (Moschitti et al., 2007; Moschitti, 2008). This approach was improved in several subsequent researches (Severyn and Moschitti, 2012; Severyn et al., 2013a,b; Severyn and Moschitti, 2013; Tymoshenko et al., 2014; Tymoshenko and Moschitti, 2015), exploiting relational tags and linked open data. In particular, in (Filice et al., 2015b), we defined new inter-pair methods to directly employ text pairs into a kernel-based learning framework.

The kernels we proposed can be directly applied to subtask B and to subtasks A and C for learn-

---

[3]http://alt.qcri.org/semeval2015/task3

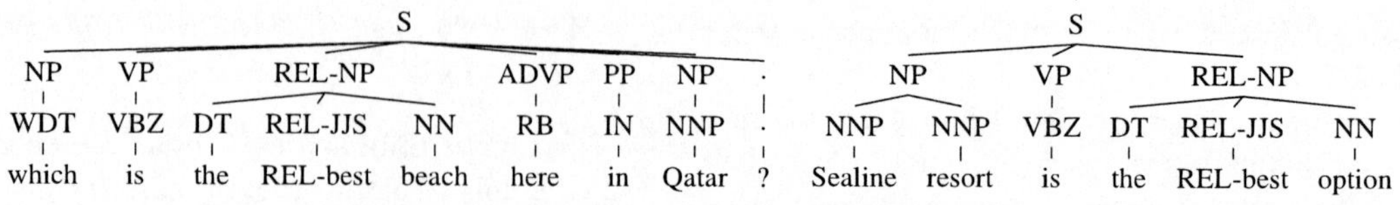

$$
\text{S} \qquad\qquad\qquad\qquad \text{S}
$$

NP	VP	REL-NP		ADVP	PP	NP	.	NP	VP	REL-NP	
WDT	VBZ	DT	REL-JJS	NN	RB	IN	NNP	.	NNP	NNP	VBZ	DT	REL-JJS	NN
which	is	the	REL-best	beach	here	in	Qatar	?	Sealine	resort	is	the	REL-best	option

Figure 1: Structural Representation of a question-answer pair.

ing question-question and question-answer pairwise patterns (see also (Tymoshenko et al., 2016; Da San Martino et al., 2016). As shown in Figure 1, a pair of sentences is represented as pair of their corresponding shallow parse trees, where common or semantically similar lexical nodes are linked using a tagging strategy (which is propagated to their upper constituents). This method discriminates aligned sub-fragments from non-aligned ones, allowing the learning algorithm to capture relational patterns, e.g., *the* REL-*best beach* and *the* REL-*best option*. Thus, given two pairs of sentences $p_a = \langle a_1, a_2 \rangle$ and $p_b = \langle b_1, b_2 \rangle$, some tree kernel combinations can be defined:

$$
\text{PTK}^+(p_a, p_b) = \text{PTK}(a_1, b_1) + \text{PTK}(a_2, b_2)
$$
$$
\text{PTK}^\times(p_a, p_b) = \text{PTK}(a_1, b_1) \times \text{PTK}(a_2, b_2)
$$

where PTK is the Partial Tree Kernel (PTK) (Moschitti, 2006). Tree kernels, computing the shared substructures between parse trees, are effective in evaluating the syntactic similarity between two texts. The proposed tree kernel combinations extend such reasoning to text pairs.

2.3 Task Specific Features

While the features described so far can be effectively applied to any sentence pair modeling task, in this section, we describe features specifically developed for the cQA domain.

- **Ranking Features:** The ten questions related to an original question are retrieved using a search engine. We use their absolute and relative ranks[4] as features for subtasks B and C (for the latter the question rank is given to all the comments within the related question thread).

- **Heuristics:** We adopt the heuristic features described in (Barrón-Cedeño et al., 2015), which can be applied to subtasks A and C.

---

[4]Some of the results retrieved by the search engine were filtered out, because they were threads with less than 10 comments, or documents out of Qatar Living. Therefore, the threads in the dataset may have an associated rank higher than 10. The relative rank maps such absolute values into [1;10].

In particular, forty-five features capture some comment characteristics such as its length, its category (*Socializing*, *Life in Qatar*, etc.), whether it includes URLs, emails, or other particular words, etc.

- **Thread-based features:** As discussed in (Barrón-Cedeño et al., 2015), comments in a common thread are strongly interconnected: users replicate to each others and start a concrete discussion. We used some specific features for subtasks A and C that aim at capturing some thread-level dependencies, such as whether a comment is part of a dialogue or whether a comment is followed by an acknowledgment from the user who asked the question

- **Stacking features:** A *good* comment for a question q should be also *good* for an original question o if q and o are strongly related, i.e., q is *relevant* or a *perfect match* to o. We thus developed a stacking strategy for Subtask C that uses the following scores in the classification step, w.r.t. an original question o and the comment c_i from the thread of q:
    - p_{q,c_i}, which is the score of the pair $\langle q, c_i \rangle$ provided by the model trained on Subtask A;
    - p_{o,c_i}, which is the score of the pair $\langle o, c_i \rangle$ provided by the model trained on Subtask A;
    - $p_{o,q}$, which is the score of the pair $\langle o, q \rangle$ provided by the model trained on Subtask B.

Starting from these scores, we built the following features: (*i*) values and signs of p_{q,c_i}, p_{o,c_i} and $p_{o,q}$ (6 feats); (*ii*) a boolean feature indicating whether both p_{q,c_i} and $p_{o,q}$ are positive; (*iii*) *min value* $= min(p_{q,c_i}, p_{o,q})$; (*iv*) *max value* $= max(p_{q,c_i}, p_{o,q})$; (*v*) *average value* $= \frac{1}{2}(p_{q,c_i} + p_{o,q})$.

3 Tree Pruning Techniques

We propose to reduce the size of the input trees by removing all nodes and branches that are less discriminative for the task. To determine such fragments, we use the supervised approach described in (Barrón-Cedeño et al., 2016). After training a tree kernel, $K()$, on pairs of trees, the solution of the dual optimization problem is expressed as a linear combination of a subset of the training examples, i.e., the support vectors: $M = \{(\alpha_j, (a_j, b_j))\}$, where the $(a_j, b_j) \in A \times B$ is a pair of parse trees (a_j could be the one of an original or related question and b_j the one of a related question or a comment, depending on the subtask) and α_j are the coefficients of the combination. The classification of a new example is obtained as the sign of the score function $f()$:

$$f(a, b) = \sum_{1 \leq j \leq |M|} \alpha_j K\left((a, b), (a_j, b_j)\right), \quad (1)$$

where $|M|$ is the number of support vectors, i.e., the number of elements of the set M. The higher the absolute value of the score of an example, the more confident the learning algorithm is in classifying it. We exploit such property to devise a strategy for determineing the importance $w(n)$ of a node. Let n be a node of a tree t, $\overset{n}{\triangle}$ is the proper sub-tree rooted at n, i.e., the tree composed of n and all its descendants in t. We use the score of $\overset{n}{\triangle}$ with respect to M to assess the importance of n:

$$w(n) = \begin{cases} \displaystyle\sum_{1 \leq j \leq |M|} \alpha_j PTK(\overset{n}{\triangle}, a_j) & \text{if } n \in a, a \in A \\ \displaystyle\sum_{1 \leq j \leq |M|} \alpha_j PTK(\overset{n}{\triangle}, b_j) & \text{if } n \in b, b \in B. \end{cases} \quad (2)$$

In order to be consistent, only the parse trees of $a_j \in A$ will be used to compute $w(n)$, if n belongs to the first tree of the pair $(a_j, b_j) \in M$. Conversely if n belongs to the second tree of the pair (a_j, b_j) only the parse trees of $b_i \in B$ will be used.

Now we can proceed to prune a tree on the basis of the $w(n)$ importance estimated by model M for each of its nodes and a user-defined threshold. We prune a leaf node n if $-h < w(n) < h$. If n is not a leaf, then it is removed if all its children are going to be removed. Note that the threshold h determines the number of pruned nodes. Our algorithm has a constraint: REL-tagged nodes are never pruned, regardless of their estimated importance. This is because a REL tag indicates that a and b share a common leaf in $\overset{n}{\triangle}$, which conveys useful information, e.g., for paraphrasing (Filice et al., 2015b).

		MAP	AvgR	MRR	P	R	F_1	Acc
2016	IR	59.53	72.60	67.83	-	-	-	-
	KeLP	**79.19**	88.82	86.42	76.96	55.30	64.36	75.11
2017	IR	72.61	79.32	82.37	-	-	-	-
	KeLP	**88.43**	93.79	92.82	87.30	58.24	69.87	73.89

Table 1: Results on subtask A on the 2016 and 2017 official testsets. IR is the baseline system based on the search engine results.

4 Submission and Results

We chose parameters using the 2016 official test set as validation set, and we trained on the official train and development sets[5]. In Subtask C, the stacking features (Section 2.3) need the scores provided by the models on subtasks A and B. Such scores are generated with a 10-fold cross validation. For the final submissions we used all the 2016 data (including the testset) as training. We used the OpenNLP pipeline for lemmatization, POS tagging and chunking to generate the tree representations described in Section 2.2. All the kernel-based learning models are implemented in KeLP (Filice et al., 2015a). For all the tasks, we used the C-SVM learning algorithm (Chang and Lin, 2011). The MAP@10 was the official metric. In addition, results are also reported in Average Recall (AvgR), Mean Reciprocal Rank (MRR), Precision (P), Recall (R), F_1, and Accuracy (Acc).

4.1 Subtask A

Model: The learning model operates on question-comment pairs $p = \langle q, c \rangle$. The kernel is $PTK^+(p_a, p_b) + LK_A(p_a, p_b)$. Such kernel linearly combines $PTK^+(p_a, p_b) = PTK(q_1, q_2) + PTK(c_1, c_2)$ (see Section 2.2) with a linear kernel LK_A that operates on feature vectors including: (*i*) the similarity metrics between q and c described in Section 2.1; (*ii*) the heuristic features and (*iii*) the thread-based features discussed in Section 2.3. PTK uses the default parameters (Moschitti, 2006), while the best SVM regularization parameter we estimated was $C = 1$. This system is identical to the one we proposed in the previous year.

Results: Table 1 reports the results on subtask A. We confirmed the excellent results of 2016: the model is very accurate and achieved the first position among 13 systems in terms of MAP.

---

[5]We merged the official Train1, Train2 and Dev sets.

		MAP	AvgR	MRR	P	R	F_1	Acc
	IR	74.75	88.30	83.79	-	-	-	-
2016	KeLP	**78.50**	91.95	84.52	71.30	70.39	70.84	80.71
	KC1	75.47	90.68	82.48	70.42	72.53	71.46	80.71
	IR	41.85	77.59	46.42	-	-	-	-
2017	KeLP	46.66	81.36	50.85	36.01	85.28	50.64	69.20
	KC1	**49.00**	83.92	52.41	36.18	88.34	51.34	68.98

Table 2: Results on subtask B on the 2016 and 2017 official test sets. KeLP is our primary submission, while KC1 is the contrastive one. IR is the baseline system based on the search engine results.

4.2 Subtask B

Model: The proposed system operates on question-question pairs $p = \langle o, q \rangle$. The kernel is $\text{PTK}^\times(p_a, p_b) + \text{LK}_B(p_a, p_b)$, by adopting the kernels defined in Section 2.2. The product in the $\text{PTK}^\times$ combination acts like a *logic and*, as, when comparing two pairs, we want a strict match in which both the elements of the first pair must be similar to the counterpart elements in the second pair. Conversely, in subtasks A and C, the adopted $\text{PTK}^+(p_a, p_b)$ applies a sort of *logic or* as we noticed that some form of comments may be considered *good* (or *bad*) regardless the question they are answering. We pruned the question trees according to the criterion described in Section 3. The best pruning threshold we estimated on the 2016 test set was $h = 0.91$. The previous year model adopted the Smoothed Partial Tree Kernel (SPTK) (Croce et al., 2011) in place of the PTK. This year we decided to use the PTK kernel as our preliminary experiments did not justified the usage of the slower SPTK.

LK_B is a linear kernel that operates on feature vectors including: (*i*) the similarity metrics between o and q, and between o and the entire answer thread of q, as described in Section 2.1; (*ii*) ranking features, described in Section 2.3. With respect to the previous year challenge we did not include some features derived from subtask A, because in subsequent experiments they did not demonstrate a significant impact.

The best SVM regularization parameter estimated during the tuning stage is $C = 1$.

We made an additional submission in which the pruning in not applied.

Results: Table 2 shows the results on subtask B. On the official test set, our primary submission achieved the third position w.r.t. MAP among 13 systems. Differently from what observed in the

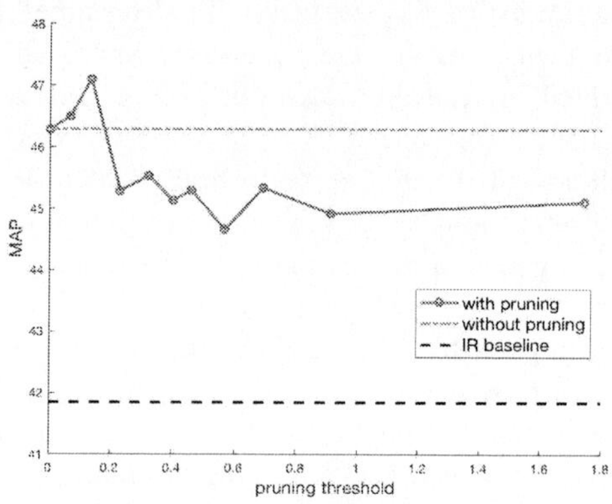

Figure 2: 10 fold cross validation results on the official 2017 test set with different pruning thresholds on subtask B.

tuning stage, on the official test set the contrastive system achieves the highest MAP and would have ranked first in the challenge.

In general, the difference between the system accuracy obtained in 2016 and 2017 suggests that the two test sets are rather different. To verify this hypothesis, we performed a 10-fold cross validation using only the data from 2017 test set. We kept the same pruning strategy and weights computed on the 2016 training set that we applied to the entire test set of 2017 for our official submission. We evaluated different pruning thresholds. Figure 2 reports the MAP averaged over the results of a 10 fold cross validation on the official 2017 test set (the 2016 dataset is not used at all).

The results show that (*i*) our best system with or without pruning is less accurate than the submitted results, i.e., producing an MAP of 46.29: this is reasonable since the model uses less training data. (*ii*) our pruning can improve our best system from 46.29 to 47.10 MAP.

Thus, it would seem that the difference between 2016 and 2017 dataset plays an important role for the pruning approach as removing some subtrees makes the TK approach more effective but probably also more specific to the data used for training the model. Another possible explanation is that it is easier to improve a weaker model, using less data. Finding out the properties of tree pruning is surely an interesting research line we would like to pursue in the future.

		MAP	AvgR	MRR	P	R	F_1	Acc
2016	IR	40.36	45.97	45.83	-	-	-	-
	KeLP	**55.91**	59.57	60.99	52.16	22.17	31.12	90.83
2017	IR	9.18	21.72	10.11	-	-	-	-
	KeLP	**14.35**	30.74	16.07	6.48	89.02	12.07	63.75

Table 3: Results on subtask C on the 2016 and 2017 official test sets. KeLP is our primary submission, while IR is the baseline system based on the search engine results.

4.3 Subtask C

Model: The learning model operates on the triplet, $\langle o, q, c \rangle$, using the kernel, $\mathrm{PTK}^+(p_a, p_b) + \mathrm{LK}_C(t_a, t_b)$, where $\mathrm{PTK}^+(p_a, p_b) = \mathrm{PTK}(o_1, o_2) + \mathrm{PTK}(c_1, c_2)$ (see Section 2.2) and LK_C is a linear kernel operating on feature vectors, which include: (*i*) the similarity metrics between o and c, between o and q, and between o and the entire thread of q, as described in Section 2.1; (*ii*) the heuristic features, (*iii*) the thread-based features, (*iv*) the ranking features, and (*v*) the features derived from the scores of subtasks A and B, described in Section 2.3. PTK uses the default parameters. The subtask training data is rather imbalanced, as the number of negative examples is about 10 times the positive ones. We took this into account by setting the regularization parameter for the positive class, $C_p = \frac{\#negatives}{\#positives} C$, as in (Morik et al., 1999). The best SVM regularization parameter estimated during the tuning stage is $C = 5$. The system is identical to the one proposed the previous year.

Results: Table 3 shows the results for subtask C. Our primary submission achieved the third highest MAP among 5 systems. The large difference among the 2016 and 2017 MAP is mainly due to the much lower presence of relevant examples in the 2017 test set, indeed, more than 97% of instances are *irrelevant*.

Acknowledgements

This work has been partially supported by the EC project CogNet, 671625 (H2020-ICT-2014-2, Research and Innovation action).

References

Lloyd Allison and Trevor I. Dix. 1986. A bit-string longest-common-subsequence algorithm. *Inf. Process. Lett.* 23(6):305–310. http://dl.acm.org/citation.cfm?id=8871.8877.

Alberto Barrón-Cedeño, Simone Filice, Giovanni Da San Martino, Shafiq Joty, Lluís Màrquez, Preslav Nakov, and Alessandro Moschitti. 2015. Thread-level information for comment classification in community question answering. In *Proceedings of the 53rd Annual Meeting of the Association for Computational Linguistics and the 7th International Joint Conference on Natural Language Processing (Volume 2: Short Papers)*. Beijing, China, pages 687–693. http://www.aclweb.org/anthology/P15-2113.

Alberto Barrón-Cedeño, Giovanni Da San Martino, Salvatore Romeo, and Alessandro Moschitti. 2016. Selecting sentences versus selecting tree constituents for automatic question ranking. In *COLING 2016, 26th International Conference on Computational Linguistics, Proceedings of the Conference: Technical Papers, December 11-16, 2016, Osaka, Japan*. pages 2515–2525.

A. Broder. 1997. On the resemblance and containment of documents. In *Proceedings of the Compression and Complexity of Sequences 1997*. IEEE Computer Society, Washington, DC, USA, SEQUENCES '97, pages 21–. http://dl.acm.org/citation.cfm?id=829502.830043.

Chih-Chung Chang and Chih-Jen Lin. 2011. LIB-SVM: A library for support vector machines. *ACM Transactions on Intelligent Systems and Technology* 2:27:1–27:27.

Danilo Croce, Alessandro Moschitti, and Roberto Basili. 2011. Structured lexical similarity via convolution kernels on dependency trees. In *Proceedings of the Conference on Empirical Methods in Natural Language Processing*. Association for Computational Linguistics, Stroudsburg, PA, USA, EMNLP '11, pages 1034–1046. http://dl.acm.org/citation.cfm?id=2145432.2145544.

Giovanni Da San Martino, Alberto Barrón-Cedeño, Salvatore Romeo, Antonio Uva, and Alessandro Moschitti. 2016. Learning to re-rank questions in community question answering using advanced features. In *Proceedings of the 25th ACM International on Conference on Information and Knowledge Management, CIKM 2016, Indianapolis, IN, USA, October 24-28, 2016*. pages 1997–2000. https://doi.org/10.1145/2983323.2983893.

Simone Filice, Giuseppe Castellucci, Danilo Croce, Giovanni Da San Martino, Alessandro Moschitti, and Roberto Basili. 2015a. KeLP: a Kernel-based Learning Platform in java. In *The workshop on Machine Learning Open Source Software (MLOSS): Open Ecosystems*. International Conference of Machine Learning, Lille, France.

Simone Filice, Danilo Croce, Alessandro Moschitti, and Roberto Basili. 2016. KeLP at SemEval-2016 task 3: Learning semantic relations between questions and comments. In *Proceedings of the 10th International Workshop on Semantic Evaluation*. San Diego, California, SemEval '16.

Simone Filice, Giovanni Da San Martino, and Alessandro Moschitti. 2015b. Structural representations for learning relations between pairs of texts. In *Proceedings of the 53rd Annual Meeting of the Association for Computational Linguistics and the 7th International Joint Conference on Natural Language Processing (Volume 1: Long Papers)*. Beijing, China, pages 1003–1013. http://www.aclweb.org/anthology/P15-1097.

Dan Gusfield. 1997. *Algorithms on Strings, Trees, and Sequences: Computer Science and Computational Biology*. Cambridge University Press, New York, NY, USA.

Paul Jaccard. 1901. Étude comparative de la distribution florale dans une portion des Alpes et des Jura. *Bulletin del la Société Vaudoise des Sciences Naturelles* 37:547–579.

Tomas Mikolov, Kai Chen, Greg Corrado, and Jeffrey Dean. 2013. Efficient estimation of word representations in vector space. *CoRR* abs/1301.3781. http://arxiv.org/abs/1301.3781.

Katharina Morik, Peter Brockhausen, and Thorsten Joachims. 1999. Combining statistical learning with a knowledge-based approach - a case study in intensive care monitoring. In *ICML*. Morgan Kaufmann Publishers Inc., San Francisco, CA, USA, pages 268–277.

Alessandro Moschitti. 2006. Efficient convolution kernels for dependency and constituent syntactic trees. In *ECML*. Machine Learning: ECML 2006, 17th European Conference on Machine Learning, Proceedings, Berlin, Germany, pages 318–329.

Alessandro Moschitti. 2008. Kernel Methods, Syntax and Semantics for Relational Text Categorization. In *Proceeding of ACM 17th Conf. on Information and Knowledge Management (CIKM'08)*. Napa Valley, CA, USA.

Alessandro Moschitti, Silvia Quarteroni, Roberto Basili, and Suresh Manandhar. 2007. Exploiting syntactic and shallow semantic kernels for question answer classification. In *Proceedings of the 45th Annual Meeting of the Association of Computational Linguistics*. Association for Computational Linguistics, Prague, Czech Republic, pages 776–783. http://www.aclweb.org/anthology/P07-1098.

Preslav Nakov, Doris Hoogeveen, Lluís Màrquez, Alessandro Moschitti, Hamdy Mubarak, Timothy Baldwin, and Karin Verspoor. 2017. SemEval-2017 task 3: Community question answering. In *Proceedings of the 11th International Workshop on Semantic Evaluation*. Association for Computational Linguistics, Vancouver, Canada, SemEval '17.

Preslav Nakov, Lluís Màrquez, Alessandro Moschitti, Walid Magdy, Hamdy Mubarak, Abed Alhakim Freihat, Jim Glass, and Bilal Randeree. 2016. SemEval-2016 task 3: Community question answering. In *Proceedings of the 10th International Workshop on Semantic Evaluation*. Association for Computational Linguistics, San Diego, California, SemEval '16.

Salvatore Romeo, Giovanni Da San Martino, Alberto Barrón-Cedeño, Alessandro Moschitti, Yonatan Belinkov, Wei-Ning Hsu, Yu Zhang, Mitra Mohtarami, and James R. Glass. 2016. Neural attention for learning to rank questions in community question answering. In *COLING 2016, 26th International Conference on Computational Linguistics, Proceedings of the Conference: Technical Papers, December 11-16, 2016, Osaka, Japan*. pages 1734–1745.

Aliaksei Severyn and Alessandro Moschitti. 2012. Structural relationships for large-scale learning of answer re-ranking. In *Proceedings of the 35th International ACM SIGIR Conference on Research and Development in Information Retrieval*. ACM, New York, NY, USA, SIGIR '12, pages 741–750. https://doi.org/10.1145/2348283.2348383.

Aliaksei Severyn and Alessandro Moschitti. 2013. Automatic feature engineering for answer selection and extraction. In *EMNLP*. ACL, pages 458–467.

Aliaksei Severyn, Massimo Nicosia, and Alessandro Moschitti. 2013a. Building structures from classifiers for passage reranking. In *Proceedings of the 22nd ACM international Conference on Information and Knowledge Management*. ACM, New York, NY, USA, CIKM '13, pages 969–978. https://doi.org/10.1145/2505515.2505688.

Aliaksei Severyn, Massimo Nicosia, and Alessandro Moschitti. 2013b. Learning adaptable patterns for passage reranking. In *Proceedings of the Seventeenth Conference on Computational Natural Language Learning*. Association for Computational Linguistics, Sofia, Bulgaria, pages 75–83. http://www.aclweb.org/anthology/W13-3509.

Kateryna Tymoshenko, Daniele Bonadiman, and Alessandro Moschitti. 2016. Learning to rank nonfactoid answers: Comment selection in web forums. In *Proceedings of the 25th ACM International on Conference on Information and Knowledge Management, CIKM 2016, Indianapolis, IN, USA, October 24-28, 2016*. pages 2049–2052. https://doi.org/10.1145/2983323.2983906.

Kateryna Tymoshenko and Alessandro Moschitti. 2015. Assessing the impact of syntactic and semantic structures for answer passages reranking. In *Proceedings of the 24th ACM International on Conference on Information and Knowledge Management*. ACM, New York, NY, USA, CIKM '15, pages 1451–1460. https://doi.org/10.1145/2806416.2806490.

Kateryna Tymoshenko, Alessandro Moschitti, and Aliaksei Severyn. 2014. *Encoding semantic resources in syntactic structures for passage reranking*, Association for Computational Linguistics (ACL), pages 664–672.

Michael J. Wise. 1996. Yap3: Improved detection of similarities in computer program and other texts. In *Proceedings of the Twenty-seventh SIGCSE Technical Symposium on Computer Science Education.* ACM, New York, NY, USA, SIGCSE '96, pages 130–134. https://doi.org/10.1145/236452.236525.

SwissAlps at SemEval-2017 Task 3: Attention-based Convolutional Neural Network for Community Question Answering

Jan Deriu
Zurich University of Applied Sciences
`deri@zhaw.ch`

Mark Cieliebak
Zurich University of Applied Sciences
`ciel@zhaw.ch`

Abstract

In this paper we propose a system for re-ranking answers for a given question. Our method builds on a siamese CNN architecture which is extended by two attention mechanisms. The approach was evaluated on the datasets of the SemEval-2017 competition for Community Question Answering (cQA), where it achieved 7th place obtaining a MAP score of 86.24 points on the *Question-Comment Similarity* subtask.

1 Introduction

Community Question Answering (cQA) describes the task of finding a relevant answer to a never-before seen question (Nakov et al., 2017). The cQA task in SemEval-2017 is subdivided into three subtasks: (a) *Question-Comment Similarity*, (b) *Question-Question Similarity*, and (c) *Question-External Comment Similarity*. We participated at the *Question-Comment Similarity* subtask, which consists of re-ranking a set of 10 answers to a given question, such that all the relevant answers are ranked higher than the irrelevant answers. We evaluated this system on the dataset provided by SemEval-2017 for the *Question-Comment Similarity* subtask, wich consits of approximately 2000 questions with 10 answers each. Our system ranked 7th place, achieving a MAP score of 86.2 which was outperformed by 2 points by the 1st ranked system. In this paper we describe the implementation details of our system, which follows a siamese CNN architecture based on (Severyn and Moschitti, 2015) extended by the attention mechanisms introduced by (Yin et al., 2015).

Siamese Architecture Siamese architectures usually consist of two parallel CNNs, each processing one sentence and then using the representations for the classification. Siamese architectures have been proposed for various tasks, e.g. (Bromley et al., 1993) used the structure for signature verification, and they have been shown to be very useful for modelling sentence pairs: (He et al., 2015), (Severyn and Moschitti, 2015), and (Tan et al., 2015) used the siamese architecture to generate representations for both sentences which then are used for classification.

Attention Mechanisms Recently the notion of attention has been introduced in neural network architectures to mimic human behaviour, as we tend to focus on key parts of the sentences to extract relevant parts. Most of the work on attention mechanisms is focused on LSTMs: for instance in (Bahdanau et al., 2014) the authors use an attention mechanism for language translation, and in (Vinyals et al., 2015) the authors use it for generating parse trees. Regarding attention mechanisms for CNNs, we are only aware of (Yin et al., 2015), on which our system is based on.

The rest of the paper is structured as follows: in Section 2 we present our model showing the siamese architecture augmented with two different attention mechanisms. In Section 3 we describe our experimental setup and show the results obtained with our system. We conclude our discussion in Section 4.

2 Model

The input to the system are pairs of questions and answer candidates where the model should classify if the answer candidate is relevant to the question, thus, being a binary classification problem. Given such an input a question and an answer candidate, the parallel CNNs produce a representation

Proceedings of the 11th International Workshop on Semantic Evaluations (SemEval-2017), pages 334–338,
Vancouver, Canada, August 3 - 4, 2017. ©2017 Association for Computational Linguistics

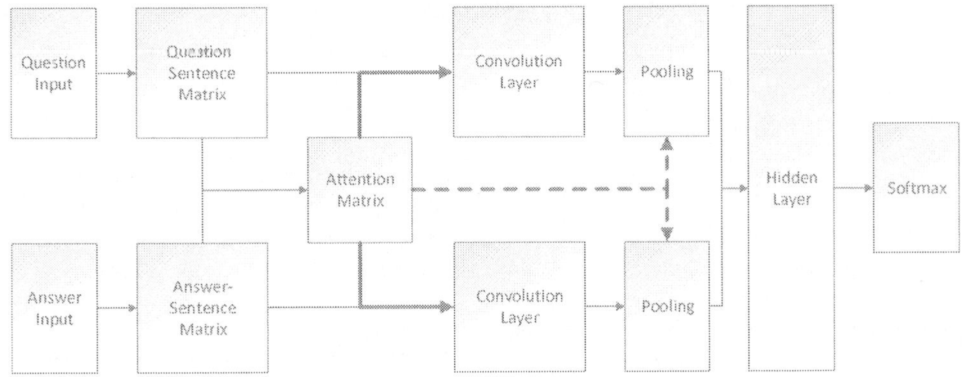

Figure 1: The architecture of the attention-based CNN used in our approach. The bold part highlights the first attention mechanism the dotted line highlight the second attention mechanism.

for both sentences, which are then concatenated and fed into a fully connected hidden layer before being fed into a softmax layer for classification (see Figure 1). The model is extended with two attention mechanisms: one modifies the input to the convolution and the second modifies the output of the convolution. Both methods aim at giving more weight to relevant parts of the sentences.

2.1 Language Model

We use word embeddings based on word2vec (Mikolov et al., 2013) as input to the convolutions. As described in (Mikolov et al., 2013) we first learn representations for phrases by learning which bigrams and trigrams appear frequently together. These n-grams are replaced by a unique token, e.g. 'New York' is replaced by the token 'New_York'. The word embeddings are generated using the skip-gram model setting the context window to 5 and the dimensionality to $d = 200$. The data used to create the word embeddings is a large corpus of 200M English Twitter messages. The word embeddings are stored as a matrix $E \in \mathbb{R}^{n \times d}$ where n is the number of tokens in the vocabulary. We generate a mapping V from each token t to the index of the corresponding word vector in the matrix E where $V(t)$ denotes the index of token t.

2.2 Siamese CNN Architecture

Input Layer A minimal preprocessing is applied to both sentences. First, each sentence is lower-cased and tokenized. Each token t is replaced with the corresponding vocabulary index $V(t)$. Thus, each sentence is represented as a vec-

tor s of indices. We denote the length of the vector as s_q for the length of the question and s_a for the length of the answer.

Embedding Layer The embedding layer uses the indices provided by the input layer to select and concatenate the vectors from the embedding matrix E, thus, creating a matrix representation S for the sentence. For the question we have $S^q \in \mathbb{R}^{s_q \times d}$ and for the answer candidate $S^a \in \mathbb{R}^{s_a \times d}$.

Convolution Layer This layer applies a set of m convolutional filters of length h over the sentence matrix $S \in \{S^q, S^a\}$. Let $S_{[i:i+h]}$ denote the concatenation of word vectors S_i to S_{i+h}. A feature c_i is generated for a given filter $\mathbb{F}$ by:

$$c_i := \sum_{k,j} (S_{[i:i+h]})_{k,j} \cdot \mathbb{F}_{k,j} \qquad (1)$$

The concatenation of all vectors in a sentence defines a feature vector $c \in \mathbb{R}^{s-h+1}$, where s denotes the sentence length. The vectors are then aggregated from all m filters into a feature map matrix $C \in \mathbb{R}^{m \times (s-h+1)}$. The output of the convolutional layer is passed through the *relu*-activation function (Nair and Hinton, 2010), before entering a pooling layer.

Zero Padding When computing the convolution at the boundary of the sentence, the convolutional filter is off the edge. Zero Padding is applied by adding $h - 1$ zero vectors at the beginning and the end of the sentence matrix. The padded sentence matrix is of the form: $S^{zq} \in \mathbb{R}^{s_q + 2*(h-1) \times d}$ and $S^{za} \in \mathbb{R}^{s_a + 2*(h-1) \times d}$ for the question and answer candidate respectively. Note that the feature map matrix has the form: $C \in \mathbb{R}^{m \times (s+h-1)}$ if the input is padded.

Pooling Layer The pooling layer aggregates the vectors in the feature map matrix C by taking the maximum value for each feature vector. This reduces the representation of both the question and the answer candidate to $c_{q,pooled}, c_{a,pooled} \in \mathbb{R}^m$.

Hidden Layer The two vectors $c_{q,pooled}$ and $c_{a,pooled}$ are concatenated to a vector $x \in \mathbb{R}^{2m}$ and passed into a fully connected hidden layer which computes the following transformation: $x_h = relu(W * x + b)$, where $W \in \mathbb{R}^{2m \times 2m}$ is the weight matrix and $b \in \mathbb{R}^{2m}$ the bias vector.

Softmax Finally, the outputs of the previous layer $x \in \mathbb{R}^{2m}$ are fully connected to a softmax regression layer, which returns the class $\hat{y} \in [1, K]$ with largest probability, i.e.,

$$\hat{y} = \arg\max_{j} P(y = j \mid \mathbf{x}, \mathbf{w}, \mathbf{a})$$
$$= \arg\max_{j} \frac{e^{\mathbf{x}^\mathsf{T}\mathbf{w}_j + a_j}}{\sum_{k=1}^{K} e^{\mathbf{x}^\mathsf{T}\mathbf{w}_k + a_k}}, \tag{2}$$

where $\mathbf{w}_j$ and a_j denotes the weights and bias of class j.

2.3 Attention Mechanism

We implemented the two different ways of introducing an attention mechanism into the siamese structure. The first manipulates the input to the convolution directly, the second modifies output to the convolution. Both approaches are based on an attention matrix.

Attention Matrix The attention matrix $A \in \mathbb{R}^{s_q \times s_a}$ is derived from the sentence matrices S_q and S_a by computing the pairwise Euclidean similarity between the word embeddings of S_q and the word embeddings of S_a. Thus, $A_{i,j} = (1 + |S_{q_i} - S_{a_j}|)^{-1}$ denotes the similarity of the i-th word in the question with the j-th word in the answer candidate.

Convolution Modification The first mechanism modifies the input to the convolution by applying a linear transformation to the attention matrix A to create the attention features. For this, two weight matrices are used: one for the question $W_q \in \mathbb{R}^{s_c \times d}$ and one for the answer candidate $W_a \in \mathbb{R}^{s_q \times d}$. To attention matrix is multiplied with the weight matrices to generate the attention features: $A_q = A * W_q$ and $A_a = A^T * W_a$

with $A_q \in \mathbb{R}^{s_q \times d}$ and $A_a \in \mathbb{R}^{s_a \times d}$, where the weight matrices are learned during the training phase. The attention features are stacked on top of the sentence matrix, creating an order-3-tensor: $S_q^2 \in \mathbb{R}^{s_q \times d \times 2}$ for the question and $S_a^2 \in \mathbb{R}^{s_a \times d \times 2}$ for the answer candidate. These tensors are used as the input into the convolution layer, giving more weight to the relevant regions in the sentence. As in (Yin et al., 2015) we refer to this architecture as *ABCNN 1*.

Attention Based Pooling The second mechanism modifies the output of the convolution. First a sliding window is applied on h consecutive columns of the feature map matrix $C_{:,i}^w = \sum_{k=i:i+h} C_{:,k}$ where $i \in [1..s_q]$ and the window size h is the same as the filter length h used for the convolution. The values of the resulting feature map matrix $C^w \in \mathbb{R}^{m \times s_q}$ are weighted to include the attention values. The attention values are generated by summing the attention matrix column-wise for the question and row-wise for the answer candidate. Thus, $a^q = \sum A_{j,:} \in \mathbb{R}^{s_q}$ and $a^a = \sum A_{:,j} \in \mathbb{R}^{s_a}$ represent the attention values for each token in the question and the answer candidate, respectively. These vectors are used to weight the feature map matrix, thus, we get $C_{:,i}^q = a_i^q * C_{:,i}^{wq}$ for the question and $C_{:,i}^a = a_i^a * C_{:,i}^{wa}$ where C^{wq} and C^{wa} denote the window averaged feature map matrices for the question and answer candidate, respectively. Finally, standard max pooling is applied to the attention weighted feature map matrices. As in (Yin et al., 2015) we refer to this architecture as *ABCNN 2*.

3 Experiments

For the experiments we compared the three different architectures: (i) the siamese architecture without the attention mechanism; we refer to this as *siamese CNN* (sCNN) (ii) the *ABCNN 1* architecture, and (iii) the *ABCNN 2* architecture.

3.1 Setup

For all experiments we used the same pre-trained 200-dimensional word embeddings introduced in Section 2.1. We employ *AdaDelta* (Zeiler, 2012) as optimizer and L_2 regularization to avoid overfitting. Table 1 gives an overview of the hyperparameters chosen via grid search. Furthermore we employ early stopping on the *SemEval-2016 test-set*, using a patience of 50 epochs. The final

	lr	ϵ	ρ	m	h	L_2
sCNN	0.1	$1e^{-6}$	0.95	500	3	0.001
ABCNN1	0.05	$1e^{-8}$	0.95	200	3	0.0005
ABCNN2	0.01	$1e^{-8}$	0.95	200	3	0.0001

Table 1: Hyperparameters of the system. lr: learning rate, ρ and ϵ: AdaDelta hyperparameters , h: filter width, m: number of filters

ranking of the answer candidates for a question is derived from the softmax probability, i.e. the answer candidates are sorted by their probability of being relevant.

3.2 Data

The training data provided by SemEval consist of approx. 2000 questions with 10 answer candidates each. Each answer candidate is manually labelled as either *Relevant*, *Irrelevant*, or *Potentially Useful*. Table 2 gives an overview of the data. For the training phase we combined the *Training Part 1*, *Training Part 2*, and *Dev 2016*, and we used *Test 2016* as validation set for early stopping. Furthermore, we aggregated the *Irrelevant* and the *Potentially Useful* pairs to reduce the problem to a binary classification task.

	Relevant	Irrelevant	Pot. Useful	Total
Training Part 1	5287	6362	2461	14110
Training Part 2	1364	1777	649	3790
Dev 2016	2440	1209	413	818
Test 2016	1329	1485	456	3270

Table 2: Overview of the datasets used for training and validation.

3.3 Results

Table 3 shows the results obtained by the systems on the *Test 2016*. The results show that the attention based mechanism boosts the MAP score by 3-4 points, the AvgRec by 3 points, and the MRR score by 3-4 points compared to the *sCNN* architecture. We also observe that *ABCNN2* outperforms *ABCNN1* by 1 point in every metric.

	MAP	AvgRec	MRR	Prec	Rec	F1	Acc
sCNN	0.741	0.854	0.806	0.589	0.815	0.684	0.693
ABCNN1	0.776	0.878	0.833	0.807	0.313	0.451	0.690
ABCNN2	0.788	0.883	0.845	0.798	0.352	0.489	0.700

Table 3: Resutls on the *Test 2016* set.

Based on these results we decided to use *ABCNN2* as our primary submission and *ABCNN1* as the contrastive submission. Table 4 shows

the results obtained on the *SemEval-2017 test-set*. We observe the same pattern as with *Test 2016*, i.e. *ABCNN2* outperforms *ABCNN1* by 1 point. We included the scores of the 1st, 2nd, and 3rd placed submissions for comparison. Our system is outperformed by 2 points by the *KeLP* and the *Beihang-MSRA* submission and by only 0.6 points by the *IIT-UHH* submission.

	MAP	AvgRec	MRR	Prec	Rec	F1	Acc
ABCNN1	0.855	0.919	0.905	0.903	0.240	0.379	0.591
ABCNN2	0.862	0.922	0.908	0.907	0.284	0.433	0.613
KeLP(1st)	0.884	0.937	0.928	0.873	0.582	0.698	0.738
Beihang-MSRA(2nd)	0.882	0.938	0.923	0.519	1.0	0.684	0.519
IIT-UHH (3rd)	0.868	0.920	0.912	0.733	0.745	0.739	0.727

Table 4: Resutls on the *Test 2017* set.

4 Conclusion

We described a deep learning approach to question-answering. The proposed architecture is based on parallel CNNs that compute a sentence representation for the question and the answer. These representations are then concatenated and used to predict whether the answer is relevant to the question. The architecture is augmented by two different attention mechanisms which improve the performance. Our system was evaluated on the SemEval-2017 competition for Community Question Answering, where it ranked 7th on the *Question-Comment* subtask. Our system performed poorly on the other two subtasks, thus, for future work we will improve our system to tackle these tasks with high performance.

References

Dzmitry Bahdanau, Kyunghyun Cho, and Yoshua Bengio. 2014. Neural machine translation by jointly learning to align and translate. *arXiv preprint arXiv:1409.0473* .

Jane Bromley, Isabelle Guyon, Yann LeCun, Eduard Sackinger, and Roopak Shah. 1993. Signature verification using a "siamese" time delay neural network. In *International Journal of Pattern Recognition and Artificial Intelligence*.

Hua He, Kevin Gimpel, and Jimmy J Lin. 2015. Multi-perspective sentence similarity modeling with convolutional neural networks. In *EMNLP*. pages 1576–1586.

Tomas Mikolov, Ilya Sutskever, Kai Chen, Greg S Corrado, and Jeff Dean. 2013. Distributed representations of words and phrases and their compositionality. In *Advances in neural information processing systems*. pages 3111–3119.

Vinod Nair and Geoffrey E Hinton. 2010. Rectified linear units improve restricted boltzmann machines. In *Proceedings of the 27th International Conference on Machine Learning (ICML-10)*. pages 807–814.

Preslav Nakov, Doris Hoogeveen, Lluís Màrquez, Alessandro Moschitti, Hamdy Mubarak, Timothy Baldwin, and Karin Verspoor. 2017. SemEval-2017 task 3: Community question answering. In *Proceedings of the 11th International Workshop on Semantic Evaluation*. Association for Computational Linguistics, Vancouver, Canada, SemEval '17.

Aliaksei Severyn and Alessandro Moschitti. 2015. Learning to rank short text pairs with convolutional deep neural networks. In *Proceedings of the 38th International ACM SIGIR Conference on Research and Development in Information Retrieval*. ACM, pages 373–382.

Ming Tan, Cicero dos Santos, Bing Xiang, and Bowen Zhou. 2015. Lstm-based deep learning models for non-factoid answer selection. *arXiv preprint arXiv:1511.04108* .

Oriol Vinyals, Łukasz Kaiser, Terry Koo, Slav Petrov, Ilya Sutskever, and Geoffrey Hinton. 2015. Grammar as a foreign language. In *Advances in Neural Information Processing Systems*. pages 2773–2781.

Wenpeng Yin, Hinrich Schütze, Bing Xiang, and Bowen Zhou. 2015. Abcnn: Attention-based convolutional neural network for modeling sentence pairs. *arXiv preprint arXiv:1512.05193* .

Matthew D Zeiler. 2012. Adadelta: an adaptive learning rate method. *arXiv preprint arXiv:1212.5701* .

TakeLab-QA at SemEval-2017 Task 3: Classification Experiments for Answer Retrieval in Community QA

Filip Šaina, Toni Kukurin, Lukrecija Puljić,
Mladen Karan, Jan Šnajder
Text Analysis and Knowledge Engineering Lab
Faculty of Electrical Engineering and Computing, University of Zagreb
Unska 3, 10000 Zagreb, Croatia
{name.surname}@fer.hr

Abstract

In this paper we present the TakeLab-QA entry to SemEval 2017 task 3, which is a question-comment re-ranking problem. We present a classification based approach, including two supervised learning models – Support Vector Machines (SVM) and Convolutional Neural Networks (CNN). We use features based on different semantic similarity models (e.g., Latent Dirichlet Allocation), as well as features based on several types of pre-trained word embeddings. Moreover, we also use some hand-crafted task-specific features. For training, our system uses no external labeled data apart from that provided by the organizers. Our primary submission achieves a MAP-score of 81.14 and F1-score of 66.99 – ranking us 10th on the SemEval 2017 task 3, subtask A.

1 Introduction

The ever-growing *Community Question Answering* (CQA) on-line services are gaining popularity at an increasing rate. However, there are some problems inherent to question-answer collections created by on-line communities. A major issue is the sheer volume of CQA collections, which makes finding an answer to a user question infeasible without some kind of an automated retrieval system. Consequently, information retrieval on CQA collections has gained increased focus in the research community, giving rise to several shared tasks on SemEval (Nakov et al., 2017).

From a natural language processing perspective, this is a difficult task due to high variance in the quality of questions and answers in CQA collections (Màrquez et al., 2015). The cause of this is the self-moderated nature of CQA sites, which implies that there are few restrictions on who is allowed to answer a question.

In this paper we describe our entries for the SemEval 2017 Question-Comment Similarity subtask (Nakov et al., 2017). Given a question q and a comment list C, the task is to rank the comments in C according to their relevance with respect to q. Datasets for this task were extracted from Qatar Living, a web forum where people pose questions about various aspects of their daily life in Qatar.

Following Filice et al. (2016), we framed the task as a binary classification problem. We experimented with two classification approaches – Support Vector Machines (SVM) (Cortes and Vapnik, 1995) and Convolutional Neural Networks (CNN) (Kim, 2014). Most of the features we use follow the work of Barrón-Cedeno et al. (2015) and Nicosia et al. (2015). Moreover, we use embedding-based (Mihaylov and Nakov, 2016) features for both models.

The CNN model with the full feature set has proven to be the most successful, ranking 10th in the competition with a MAP-score of 81.14 and an F1-score of 66.99.

The rest of this paper is structured as follows. Section 2 gives a brief overview of the data set. A detailed description of the our models is given in Section 3. Section 4 outlines our experiments and results. Finally, we present our conclusions in Section 5.

2 Dataset

The dataset we used was provided by the shared-task organizers. Incoming user queries are denoted as *original questions*. For each original question, we are provided with 10 annotated threads. Each thread consists of a *related question*[1] and a set of

---

[1]Related questions are questions that have been asked in the past, and have a set of posted comments.

Proceedings of the 11th International Workshop on Semantic Evaluations (SemEval-2017), pages 339–343,
Vancouver, Canada, August 3 - 4, 2017. ©2017 Association for Computational Linguistics

	relevant	non-relevant	% relevant
training	14,418	18,872	43.3
dev	2,198	3,152	41.1
overall	16,616	22,024	43.0

Table 1: Class distribution statistics.

10 comments posted as answers to the related question. Subtask A, the main focus of this work, is concerned with correctly ranking the 10 comments with respect to a related question (henceforth: question). Every *question-comment pair* contains a classification label *Good*, *Bad*, or *PotentiallyUseful*. In our experiments, labels *Bad* and *PotentiallyUseful* are both considered *non-relevant* and the label *Good* is considered *relevant*. Table 1 shows the class distribution of *question-comment* pairs in the shared task dataset. There is a slight bias towards the *non-relevant* class, but no mechanisms were implemented to address this. The official split allocates 86% of the data to the train set and 14% to the development set. For further information on the collection we refer to (Nakov et al., 2017).

3 System Description

Considering we have class labels available for each question-comment pair, it is natural to frame this ranking task as a supervised classification problem. The input of the classifier is a vector of features that represents the question-comment pair (q, c). The output is a class – *relevant* or *non-relevant* – indicating whether c is relevant with respect to q. We have experimented with two supervised approaches for classifying the data, SVM and CNN, which were shown to be very successful in question-comment re-ranking tasks in previous work (Nakov et al., 2016). Note that both of these variants of our system fall into the *pointwise* category of the *learning-to-rank* paradigm (Cao et al., 2007). We next describe all our systems' components in detail.

3.1 Preprocessing

We have preprocessed all entries by tokenizing them, stemming the tokens, and removing stopwords using the NLTK toolkit.[2] These tokens were used as input to the feature extraction pipeline.

3.2 Embedding-Based Features

As observed by Socher et al. (2011), in the case where a large training set is not available, using word embeddings obtained from an unsupervised language model can be an efficient method for improving performance. More specifically, in our scenario embeddings alleviate lexical gap that often arises when comparing a question to a relevant comment.

We use two types of embeddings. First, *word2vec* embeddings trained on Quatar Living questions and comments that was used by last year's participants (Mihaylov and Nakov, 2016). We used 800-dimensional word vectors.[3] Secondly, we use the *PARAGRAM*[4] model introduced by Wieting et al. (2016), which produces 300-dimensional word embeddings specifically tuned to work well when aggregated by a simple operation such as the average.

After some experimentation, we found the following embedding features offered the best performance boosts on the development set:

- **Question and Answer Embeddings** – using the *PARAGRAM* embeddings, we compute the vector representation of both the question and comment by averaging their corresponding content-word vectors. This yields two 300-dimensional vectors, which are fed into our models as 600 numerical features;

- **Word2vec average cosine similarity** – we compute vector representations of the question and comment in the same manner as for the previous feature, but using *word2vec* word vectors. We then introduce into our models a single numerical feature computed as the cosine similarity of the question and comment vector representations.

3.3 SEMILAR Features

Features listed under this group were all obtained from SEMILAR[5] (Rus et al., 2013). This is a library that implements a multitude of popular semantic similarity measures for text. We use it to calculate the similarity of the question to the candidate comment, and include each measure as a

---

[3] These vectors alone can produce a MAP-score of 78.45 on subtask A, and can be obtained from `https://github.com/tbmihailov/semeval2016-task3-cqa`

[4] We use the SL999 variant available at – `http://ttic.uchicago.edu/~wieting/`

[5] `http://deeptutor2.memphis.edu/Semilar-Web/`

[2] `http://www.nltk.org`

numerical feature. In our experiments we include similarity measures based on:

- Lexical overlap – two variants, overlap before preprocessing and overlap after preprocessing;

- WordNet (Fellbaum, 1998);

- Latent Semantic Analysis (Landauer et al., 1998);

- Latent Dirichlet Allocation (Blei et al., 2003);

- BLEU (Papineni et al., 2002);

- Meteor (Denkowski and Lavie, 2011);

- Pointwise Mutual Information (Church and Hanks, 1990).

3.4 Other Features

In this group we list hand-crafted features, as well as features that do not fit into the previous two groups:

- **Words contained in comment** – we have tested each comment for some words that often seem to be useful in distinguishing good from bad comments in the previous editions of the task (Barrón-Cedeno et al., 2015). More specifically, we checked whether the comment contains words *yes, ok, sorry, no, sure*, or *can*, and encoded them as binary numerical features;

- **Answer contains question mark** – another binary numerical feature that has previously been proven useful is whether the comment body contains a question mark (Barrón-Cedeno et al., 2015);

- **Answer length** – longer comments tend to be better thought-out and, consequently, more useful with respect to the question at hand. This numerical feature represents the number of words in the comment after preprocessing;

- **Tf-Idf cosine similarity** – we determine *Tf-Idf* vectors for each question and comment, respectively. We then compute the cosine similarity of these vectors and include it as a numerical feature for our models.

3.5 SVM

We use the SVM classifier (Cortes and Vapnik, 1995) from ScikitLearn.[6] The relevance score of comment c with respect to question q is the confidence of the SVM classifier that the class is *relevant*, when presented (q, c) as input.

3.6 CNN

We follow the work of Severyn and Moschitti (2015). The overall architecture of the network includes two convolutional layers and the corresponding information flow:[7]

- The question q and comment c at the input are represented as matrices containing the *word2vec* embeddings of their words. They are the input of two separate convolutional layers that perform feature extraction;

- The max-pooling operation is applied to the resulting feature-maps;

- This results in task-specific representation vectors of the question and the comment. These vectors are concatenated and fed into a fully connected hidden layer, along with other features that we wish to include. Note that the extra features could be especially helpful in cases where many words in q and c that are not covered by the *word2vec* model, which may lead to meaningless features extracted by the convolutional layers;

- Finally, a fully connected softmax layer calculates the probability distribution over the output label.

The network is trained by mini-batch stochastic gradient descent, minimizing the cross-entropy loss. To combat overfitting we use both early stopping and dropout (Srivastava et al., 2014).

The score of comment c with respect to question q is the probability that the network assigns to the *relevant* class when presented with (q, c) as input.

4 Evaluation

4.1 Hyperparameters

We optimizeed the hyperparameters of the SVM classifier using cross-validation on the train set. We

---

[6] http://scikit-learn.org/

[7] The most notable difference is that we ommit the the similarity matrix present in their network.

varied the C and γ parameters [8], and experimented with both linear and non-linear kernels. We found that the RBF kernel with C set to 5 and γ set to 0.01 was the best performing combination.

For CNN hyperparameters we used as a starting point the values proposed by Kim (2014), and then tuned them empirically, to find the setting that optimizes the performance on the development set. More specifically, we used filter windows of size 3, 4, 5, with 64 feature maps for each window, a dropout rate of 0.7, and mini-batch size of 64.

4.2 Evaluation

Participants were allowed to make three submissions and mark them as *primary*, *contrastive1*, or *contrastive2*. All submissions were evaluated but only the *primary* was considered for the competition system ranking.

For our *contrastive1* run we submitted an SVM classifier trained on features from the *embedding-based* and *other* groups. We denote this model as *SVM-EO*.

In our *contrastive2* run we submitted a completely different combination: the CNN classifier with the *SEMILAR* features as additional input to the hidden layer. We refer to this variant of the model as *CNN-S*.

The last combination we considered was the CNN classifier with all the other features provided as additional input to the hidden layer. We refer to this submission as *CNN-EOS*. This model has access to both the feature representations generated by the convolutional layers, as well as to all other features. Thus, expectedly, it performed best on the development set,[9] and we decided to submit it as our *primary* run.

4.3 Results

Final evaluation results released by the shared-task organizers are shown in Table 2. [10] Our primary submission was ranked at 10th place, achieving a MAP-score of 81.14.

Our contrastive submissions, both SVM and CNN based, achieve comparable performances. The CNN seems to outperform SVM only when new features are added, suggesting that the features work best when used jointly.

	MAP	F1	Acc
Best system (KeLP)	88.43	69.87	73.89
CNN-EOS (primary)	**81.14**	66.99	**70.14**
SVM-EO	79.71	**67.87**	69.11
CNN-S	78.98	62.54	**70.14**
Baseline 1 (IR)	72.61	–	–
Baseline 2 (random)	62.30	66.36	52.70

Table 2: Submission results summary.

Furthermore, while the CNN model did prove to be better on the MAP metric, SVM outperforms it on the F1-score. This indicates that maximizing F1-score may not always maximize MAP-score.

5 Conclusion

In this paper we presented a re-ranking system developed to participate in SemEval 2017 Task 3 – Community Question Answering. The system consists of two supervised learning approaches – Support Vector Machines (SVM) and Convoluational Neural Networks (CNN), which outperformed the baseline model. While our models were trained only on the official dataset, better results may have been attained with additional training data.

For future work we would like to include additional features, such as tree kernels (Filice et al., 2016) and sentiment-specific word embeddings proposed by Tang et al. (2014). We would also like to experiment with different classification models. An intriguing venue would be obtaining more training data from other popular CQA sites, and explore if some cross-domain information transfer that could benefit ranking models is possible. Finally, as indicated by our experiments, we would like to consider approaches that optimize the ranking model explicitly for the MAP-score.

---

[8]γ only for the RBF kernel.

[9]Prediction accuracy – number of correct predictions over all pairs, is used as a overall training and development performance metric.

[10]http://alt.qcri.org/semeval2017/task3/data/uploads/semeval2017_task3_results.pdf

References

Alberto Barrón-Cedeno, Simone Filice, Giovanni Da San Martino, Shafiq R Joty, Lluís Màrquez, Preslav Nakov, and Alessandro Moschitti. 2015. Thread-level information for comment classification in community question answering. In *Proceedings of the meeting of the Association for Computational Linguistics.* pages 687–693.

David M Blei, Andrew Y Ng, and Michael I Jordan. 2003. Latent dirichlet allocation. *Journal of machine Learning research* 3(Jan):993–1022.

Zhe Cao, Tao Qin, Tie-Yan Liu, Ming-Feng Tsai, and Hang Li. 2007. Learning to rank: from pairwise approach to listwise approach. In *Proceedings of the 24th international conference on Machine learning*. ACM, pages 129–136.

Kenneth Ward Church and Patrick Hanks. 1990. Word association norms, mutual information, and lexicography. *Computational linguistics* 16(1):22–29.

Corinna Cortes and Vladimir Vapnik. 1995. Support-vector networks. *Machine learning* 20(3):273–297.

Michael Denkowski and Alon Lavie. 2011. Meteor 1.3: Automatic metric for reliable optimization and evaluation of machine translation systems. In *Proceedings of the Sixth Workshop on Statistical Machine Translation*. Association for Computational Linguistics, pages 85–91.

Christiane Fellbaum. 1998. *WordNet: An Electronic Lexical Database.*. Bradford Books.

Simone Filice, Danilo Croce, Alessandro Moschitti, and Roberto Basili. 2016. Kelp at SemEval-2016 task 3: Learning semantic relations between questions and answers. *Proceedings of SemEval* 16:1116–1123.

Yoon Kim. 2014. Convolutional neural networks for sentence classification. In *Proceedings of the Conference on Empirical Methods in Natural Language Processing*.

Thomas K Landauer, Peter W Foltz, and Darrell Laham. 1998. An introduction to latent semantic analysis. *Discourse processes* 25(2-3):259–284.

Lluís Màrquez, James Glass, Walid Magdy, Alessandro Moschitti, Preslav Nakov, and Bilal Randeree. 2015. SemEval-2015 task 3: Answer selection in community question answering. In *Proceedings of the 9th International Workshop on Semantic Evaluation (SemEval 2015)*.

Todor Mihaylov and Preslav Nakov. 2016. Semanticz at SemEval-2016 task 3: Ranking relevant answers in community question answering using semantic similarity based on fine-tuned word embeddings. In *Proceedings of the 10th International Workshop on Semantic Evaluation (SemEval 2016)*. Association for Computational Linguistics, San Diego, California, pages 804 – 811. http://www.aclweb.org/anthology/S16.

Preslav Nakov, Doris Hoogeveen, Lluís Màrquez, Alessandro Moschitti, Hamdy Mubarak, Timothy Baldwin, and Karin Verspoor. 2017. SemEval-2017 task 3: Community question answering. In *Proceedings of the 11th International Workshop on Semantic Evaluation*. Association for Computational Linguistics, Vancouver, Canada, SemEval '17.

Preslav Nakov, Lluís Màrquez, Alessandro Moschitti, Walid Magdy, Hamdy Mubarak, Abed Alhakim Freihat, Jim Glass, and Bilal Randeree. 2016. SemEval-2016 task 3: Community question answering. In *Proceedings of the 10th International Workshop on Semantic Evaluation*. Association for Computational Linguistics, San Diego, California, SemEval '16.

Massimo Nicosia, Simone Filice, Alberto Barrón-Cedeno, Iman Saleh, Hamdy Mubarak, Wei Gao, Preslav Nakov, Giovanni Da San Martino, Alessandro Moschitti, Kareem Darwish, et al. 2015. Qcri: Answer selection for community question answering-experiments for arabic and english. In *Proceedings of the 9th International Workshop on Semantic Evaluation, SemEval*. volume 15, pages 203–209.

Kishore Papineni, Salim Roukos, Todd Ward, and Wei-Jing Zhu. 2002. Bleu: a method for automatic evaluation of machine translation. In *Proceedings of the 40th annual meeting on association for computational linguistics*. Association for Computational Linguistics, pages 311–318.

Vasile Rus, Mihai C Lintean, Rajendra Banjade, Nobal B Niraula, and Dan Stefanescu. 2013. Semilar: The semantic similarity toolkit. In *Association for Computational Linguistics (Conference System Demonstrations)*. pages 163–168.

Aliaksei Severyn and Alessandro Moschitti. 2015. Learning to rank short text pairs with convolutional deep neural networks. In *Proceedings of the 38th International ACM SIGIR Conference on Research and Development in Information Retrieval*. ACM, pages 373–382.

Richard Socher, Jeffrey Pennington, Eric H. Huang, Andrew Y. Ng, and Christopher D. Manning. 2011. Semi-supervised recursive autoencoders for predicting sentiment distributions. In *Proceedings of the Conference on Empirical Methods in Natural Language Processing*. Association for Computational Linguistics, Stroudsburg, PA, USA, EMNLP '11, pages 151–161. http://dl.acm.org/citation.cfm?id=2145432.2145450.

Nitish Srivastava, Geoffrey E Hinton, Alex Krizhevsky, Ilya Sutskever, and Ruslan Salakhutdinov. 2014. Dropout: a simple way to prevent neural networks from overfitting. *Journal of Machine Learning Research* 15(1):1929–1958.

Duyu Tang, Furu Wei, Nan Yang, Ming Zhou, Ting Liu, and Bing Qin. 2014. Learning sentiment-specific word embedding for twitter sentiment classification. In *Proceedings of the meeting of the Association for Computational Linguistics*. pages 1555–1565.

John Wieting, Mohit Bansal, Kevin Gimpel, and Karen Livescu. 2016. Towards universal paraphrastic sentence embeddings. In *Proceedings of the International Conference on Learning Representations*.

GW_QA at SemEval-2017 Task 3: Question Answer Re-ranking on Arabic Fora

Nada Almarwani and **Mona Diab**
Department of Computer Science
The George Washington University
{nadaoh;mtdiab}@gwu.edu

Abstract

This paper describes our submission to SemEval-2017 Task 3 Subtask D, "Question Answer Ranking in Arabic Community Question Answering". In this work, we applied a supervised machine learning approach to automatically re-rank a set of QA pairs according to their relevance to a given question. We employ features based on latent semantic models, namely WTMF, as well as a set of lexical features based on string length and surface level matching. The proposed system ranked first out of 3 submissions, with a MAP score of 61.16%.

1 Introduction

Nowadays Community Question Answering (CQA) websites provide a virtual place for users to share and exchange knowledge about different topics. In most cases, users freely express their concerns and hope for some reliable answers from specialists or other users. In addition, they can search for an answer from previously posted question-answers (QA) that are similar to their question. Although posting a question and looking for a direct or related answer in CQA sounds appealing, the number of unanswered questions are relatively high. According to Baltadzhieva and Chrupała (2015) the number of unanswered questions in Stack Overflow[1] and Yahoo! Answers[2] are approximately 10.9% and 15%, respectively. Interestingly, as noted in (Asaduzzaman et al., 2013), the high percentage of unanswered questions is due to the duplicate question problem, i.e. the existence of a similar question that had been addressed before, which

makes users not re-address the question again. Hence, it is the asker's role to review the site looking for an answer before posting a new question. This is a task that requires searching related questions from a hundred others posted on a daily basis. Thus, in a good forum there should be an automatic search functionality to retrieve the set of QA that are more likely to be related to the new question being asked. As a result, the number of duplications and unanswered questions will be limited.

In order to find a solution to this and other problems in CQA, the SemEval 2015, 2016, and 2017 Task 3 have been dedicated to dealing with "Answer Selection in Community Question Answering" (Nakov et al., 2017, 2016; AlessandroMoschitti et al., 2015). There are 5 different subtasks, one of which has been proposed for Arabic. The specific task for Arabic in the SemEval 2016-2017 Task 3, subtask D, was to re-rank the possible related question-answer pairs to a given question.

The Arabic task is especially difficult due to its challenging characteristics. Arabic is one of the most complex languages to process due to its morphological richness, with relative free word order, and its diglossic nature (where the standard and the dialects mix in most genres of data).

The rest of this paper is organized as follows: Section 2 gives an overview of the task and data, Section 3 describes the proposed system, Section 4 presents a discussion of the experiments and results, Section 5 outlines the error analysis, and Section 6 concludes.

2 Task and Data Description

Arabic by nature has different characteristics that make it one of the most challenging languages to process from an NLP perspective. It is a morphologically rich language, flexible word order, and

---

[1] A programming CQA forum
[2] A community-driven question-and-answer site

Proceedings of the 11th International Workshop on Semantic Evaluations (SemEval-2017), pages 344–348,
Vancouver, Canada, August 3 - 4, 2017. ©2017 Association for Computational Linguistics

in most typical genres and domains available online, we note a significant mix of the standard form of Arabic (MSA) and dialectical variants (DA). In fact, the use of dialectical Arabic in fora such as the CQA presents a special challenge for processing Arabic. The SemEval 2017 subtask D targets the Arabic language. In particular, the task is to re-rank a given set of QA pairs with respect to their relatedness to a given query. Therefore, the top of the ranked list is either a directly related pair, "Direct"; a "Relevant" pair, which is not directly related but includes relevant information; or an "Irrelevant" pair, at the end of the list. These are the three labels used for the task. The organizers cast the task as both a ranking problem with the three possible ranks as well as a binary classification problem where they grouped the labels Direct and Relevant as true, while Irrelevant is deemed False.

The Arabic dataset was extracted from medical fora, where users ask question(s) about medical concerns and the answers are generally from doctors. The dataset contains: a training of 1,031 questions and 30,411 potentially related QA pairs, a development set of 250 questions and 7,385 potentially related QA pairs, and a test set of 1400 questions associated with 8 to 9 potentially related QA pairs for each.[3]

3 Approach

In this work, we are interested in studying the effect of using semantic textual similarity (STS) based on latent semantic representations and surface level similarity features derived from the given triple: User new Question Q_u, and the retrieved Question Answer (QA) pairs which we will refer to as R_Q and R_A, respectively. Therefore, we casted the problem as a ranking problem that orders the QA pairs according to their relatedness to a given query Q_u. We used a supervised framework SVM_{rank} (Manning et al., 2008).

In order to extract the features set between the Q_u and QA pair, we extracted a set of features shared between the (Q_u, R_Q) and shared between the (Q_u, R_A) and then we used the concatenation of both as a feature vector for each triple.

In the following subsection, we describe in detail the preprocessing steps we applied to the raw data and the set of features we used in the submit-

ted model.

3.1 Preprocessing and Features

3.1.1 Text Preprocessing

Text preprocessing is especially important for this CQA dataset. Therefore, in this section we briefly outline the preprocessing we applied before the feature extraction. First of all, we used SPLIT (Al-Badrashiny et al., 2016) to check if a token is a number, date, URL, or punctuation. All URLs and punctuation are removed and numbers and dates are normalized to Num and Date, respectively. Alef and Yaa characters are normalized each to a single form which is typical in large scale Arabic NLP applications to overcome and avoid writing variations. For tokenization, lemmatization and stemming we used MADAMIRA (Pasha et al., 2014) (a D3 tokenization scheme which segments determiners as well as proclitics and enclitics). Finally, we removed stop words based on a list.[4]

3.1.2 Features

1 . Latent Semantics Features: a latent semantic representation transforms the high dimensional representation of text into a low dimensional latent space and thus overcomes the problem of standard bag-of-words representation by assigning a semantic profile to the text, which captures implicit syntactic and semantic information. There are various models such as Latent Dirichlet Allocation (LDA) (Blei et al., 2003), which rely on observed words to find text distribution over "K" topics. These models in general are applied to relatively lengthy pieces of text or documents. However, texts such as question and answer pairs found in CQA are relatively short pieces of text with two to three sentences on average. Therefore, we used the Weighted Textual Matrix Factorization (WTMF) (Guo and Diab, 2012) latent model, which is more appropriate for semantic profiling of a short text.

The main goal of the WTMF model is to address the sparseness of such short text by relying on both observed and missing words to explicitly model what the text is and is **not** about. The missing words as defined by the model are the whole vocabulary of the training data minus the ones observed in the given

---

[3]For more details refer to the task description paper at (Nakov et al., 2017)

[4]https://pypi.python.org/pypi/many-stop-words

	Gigword Sample	Unlabeled data
Tokens	45,302,744	16,101
Stem Types	153,452	2234

Table 1: Statistic of the raw Arabic corpora used for building the WTMF model

document.

We used the implementation of WTMF,[5] with a modification in the preprocessing pipeline to accommodate Arabic, i.e. we used the same preprocessing steps in 3.1.1. We used the stems of the word as the level of representation. To train the model we used a sample data from Arabic Gigaword (Parker et al., 2011) with the UNANNOTATED Arabic data provided in the task website.[6] We used the default parameters except for the number of dimensions, which we set to 500. Table 1 shows Training data statistics.

For feature generation, we first generated vector representation for Q_u, R_Q, and R_A using the above model. Then, we used Euclidean distance, Manhattan distance, and Cosine distance to calculate the overall semantic relatedness scores between (Q_u, R_Q) and between (Q_u, R_A).

2 . Lexical Features: similar pairs are more likely to share more words and hence they are more likely to be related. Following this assumption, the following set of features are used to record the length information of a given pair using the following measures: $|B - A|$, $|A \cap B|$, $\frac{(|B|-|A|)}{|A|}$, $\frac{(|A|-|B|)}{|B|}$, $\frac{|A \cap B|}{|B|}$ where $|A|$ represents the number of unique instances in A, $|B - A|$ refers to the number of unique instances that are in B but not in A, and $|A \cap B|$ represents the number of instances that are in both A and B. To account for word forms variations, we applied them at the token, lemma and stem levels.

4   Experiments and Results

Our ranking system is a supervised model using SVM_{rank}, a variation of SVM (Hearst et al., 1998) for ranking. We tested different types of

kernels, and the best result was obtained using a linear kernel, which we used to train our model. Furthermore, we tuned the cost factor parameter C of the linear kernel on the development set and we obtained the best result with C=3, which we set during the testing of our model. The outputs of the SVM_{rank} are mainly used for ordering and they do not have any meaning of relatedness.[7] For binary classification, "Direct" and "Relevant" are mapped to "True" and "Irrelevant" is mapped to "False" for the classification task. We employed a logistic regression (LR) classifier, LIBLINEAR classifier with the default parameters, implemented using WEKA package (Witten and Frank, 2005).

We report results on the development tuning set, **DEV**, and **TEST** set. Furthermore, we report the results of different experimental setups to show the performance over different feature sets. We report results using lexical features (**LEX**), using WTMF features (**WTMF**), and with combined features (**WTMF+LEX**). The latter is our primary submission to the SemEval-2017 subtask D. It is worth noting that we only officially participated in the ranking task. In addition, we report the binary classification results, which we did not officially submit. Furthermore, we compare our results to subtask D baselines and we report the results using the official metrics.

As can be seen in Table 2, the combined WTMF+LEX setting outperformed the other settings, WTMF and LEX, individually. This indicates that the combination of LEX features with WTMF provide complementary information about the relatedness at the explicit matching level for the model. Specifically, the **WTMF+LEX** based system improved the MAP by about 1% increase from the **WTMF** and the **LEX** based system. Furthermore, we obtain a significant improvement over the baselines for the DEV set and relatively modest improvements in the TEST set, with MAP 45.73 and 61.16, respectively.

Table 3 on the other hand, presents the results of the binary classification on the TEST set using the WTMF+LEX setting along with the baseline and the results submitted by the two other participants. As can be seen in the the table, we achieved the best result on all metrics except for precision.

---

[5]http://www.cs.columbia.edu/ weiwei/code.html

[6]http://alt.qcri.org/semeval2016/task3/data/uploads/Arabic. DataDump.txt.gz

[7]https://www.cs.cornell.edu/people/tj/svm_light /svm_rank.html

	DEV			TEST		
	MAP	AvgRec	MRR	MAP	AvgRec	MRR
LEX	42.40	47.84	49.78	59.19	83.55	64.6678
WTMF	44.97	49.99	50.63	59.31	83.85	64.8225
WTMF+LEX	**45.73**	**51.48**	**53.08**	**61.16**	**85.43**	**66.85**
Baseline 1 (IR)	28.55	27.96	31.39	60.55	85.06	66.80
Baseline 2 (random)	-	-	-	48.48	73.89	53.27

Table 2: Ranking Results on the development and test sets using official metrics

	TEST			
	P	R	F1	Acc
WTMF+LEX	55.63	77.45	64.75	66.92
UPC-USMBA-primary	**63.41**	33.00	43.41	66.24
QU BIGIR-primary	41.59	70.16	52.22	49.64
Baseline 2 (random)	39.04	66.43	49.18	46.13
Baseline 3 (all 'true')	39.23	100	56.36	39.23
Baseline 4 (all 'false')	-	-	-	60.77

Table 3: Binary Classification Results using our LR classifier with combined features WTMF+LEN on the Test set

5 Error Analysis

There were different challenges faced during the ranking and classification of a given question. We observed that False positive (FP) and False negative (FN) examples fall in one of the following categories:

1. Mixed Arabic variants and Mixed Languages: this is one of the challenges proposed by the task. Table4 shows an example of this from the SemEval-2017 test data. The mix in either dialect with standard Arabic, or Arabic with a foreign language (English), or both. This affected FP and FN cases produced by our system as follows:

   (a) WTMF Model: we had a mismatch between the data genre used to train the WTMF model and our test data resulting in a high out of vocabulary (OOV) rate in the pair of text snippets compared;

   (b) . Lexical feature: mixes in either dialect/standard, or Arabic with foreign language, or both resulted in a low overlap between the pair.

2. Noise: even though we removed a list of stop words, there are other words that are considered noise words in this task that affect the overlap similarities in both the FP and

1	اجرى زوجى فحص وكانت النتيجة to-tal sperm 300 millions sperm [—] S- second h فهل هذا الفحص 60% سليم ؟	My husband was checked and the result was total sperm 300 milions sperm [—]S-second h 60% does this check up sound correct?
2	انا (بقالى) فتره (بعانى) من حكه فى اليدين والارجل وينتج (مع—]عنها احمرار العلم بانى كل ما (احط ايدى) على مكان الحكه (الاقيها ورمت واحمرت	For a while I have been suffering from itching in my hands and legs resulting in redness[—]Knowing that when I put my hand on the itch place I find it burning and swelling

Table 4: 1 is an example of Mixed Languages and 2 is an example of Mixed between Dialectal,words between parentheses, and Modern Standard Arabic. Both types of mix resulted in wrong prediction of the relatedness relation

FN categories. For example, words describing personal information such as weight, age, or gender are not directly related to the medical concern being asked and are considered noise. Therefore, this data needed a hand crafted list to be used for cleaning.

6 Conclusion

We have presented in this paper the submission of the GW_QA team in SemEval-2017 Task 3 subtask D on Arabic CQA ranking. We used a supervised machine learning ranker based on a combination of latent Semantics based similarity and lexical features. We submitted a primary result using the SVM_{rank} and we used Logistic regression for the binary classification setting, not an official submission. Our primary submission MAP official score ranked first for the Arabic subtask D. Furthermore, we analyzed the performance of our model and outlined the limitations that caused false positive and false negative predictions.

References

Mohamed Al-Badrashiny, Arfath Pasha, Mona Diab, Nizar Habash, Owen Rambow, Wael Salloum, and Ramy Eskander. 2016. Split: Smart preprocessing (quasi) language independent tool. In *10th International Conference on Language Resources and Evaluation (LREC'16)*. European Language Resources Association (ELRA), Portorož, Slovenia.

PreslavNakov LluısMarquez WalidMagdy AlessandroMoschitti, James Glass, and Bilal Randeree. 2015. Semeval-2015 task 3: Answer selection in community question answering. *SemEval-2015* 269.

Muhammad Asaduzzaman, Ahmed Shah Mashiyat, Chanchal K Roy, and Kevin A Schneider. 2013. Answering questions about unanswered questions of stack overflow. In *Mining Software Repositories (MSR), 2013 10th IEEE Working Conference on*. IEEE, pages 97–100.

Antoaneta Baltadzhieva and Grzegorz Chrupała. 2015. Question quality in community question answering forums: a survey. *Acm Sigkdd Explorations Newsletter* 17(1):8–13.

David M Blei, Andrew Y Ng, and Michael I Jordan. 2003. Latent dirichlet allocation. *Journal of machine Learning research* 3(Jan):993–1022.

Weiwei Guo and Mona Diab. 2012. Modeling sentences in the latent space. In *Proceedings of the 50th Annual Meeting of the Association for Computational Linguistics: Long Papers-volume 1*. Association for Computational Linguistics, pages 864–872.

Marti A. Hearst, Susan T Dumais, Edgar Osuna, John Platt, and Bernhard Scholkopf. 1998. Support vector machines. *IEEE Intelligent Systems and their Applications* 13(4):18–28.

Christopher D Manning, Prabhakar Raghavan, Hinrich Schütze, et al. 2008. *Introduction to information retrieval*, volume 1. Cambridge university press Cambridge.

Preslav Nakov, Doris Hoogeveen, Lluís Màrquez, Alessandro Moschitti, Hamdy Mubarak, Timothy Baldwin, and Karin Verspoor. 2017. SemEval-2017 task 3: Community question answering. In *Proceedings of the 11th International Workshop on Semantic Evaluation*. Association for Computational Linguistics, Vancouver, Canada, SemEval '17.

Preslav Nakov, Lluís Màrquez, Alessandro Moschitti, Walid Magdy, Hamdy Mubarak, Abed Alhakim Freihat, Jim Glass, and Bilal Randeree. 2016. SemEval-2016 task 3: Community question answering. In *Proceedings of the 10th International Workshop on Semantic Evaluation*. Association for Computational Linguistics, San Diego, California, SemEval '16.

Robert Parker, David Graff, Ke Chen, Junbo Kong, and Kazuaki Maeda. 2011. Arabic gigaword fifth edition ldc2011t11. *Philadelphia: Linguistic Data Consortium* .

Arfath Pasha, Mohamed Al-Badrashiny, Mona T Diab, Ahmed El Kholy, Ramy Eskander, Nizar Habash, Manoj Pooleery, Owen Rambow, and Ryan Roth. 2014. Madamira: A fast, comprehensive tool for morphological analysis and disambiguation of arabic. In *LREC*. volume 14, pages 1094–1101.

Ian H Witten and Eibe Frank. 2005. *Data Mining: Practical machine learning tools and techniques*. Morgan Kaufmann.

NLM_NIH at SemEval-2017 Task 3: from Question Entailment to Question Similarity for Community Question Answering

Asma Ben Abacha
U.S. National Library of Medicine,
Bethesda, MD
asma.benabacha@nih.gov

Dina Demner-Fushman
U.S. National Library of Medicine,
Bethesda, MD
ddemner@mail.nih.gov

Abstract

This paper describes our participation in SemEval-2017 Task 3 on Community Question Answering (cQA). The Question Similarity subtask (B) aims to rank a set of related questions retrieved by a search engine according to their similarity to the original question. We adapted our feature-based system for Recognizing Question Entailment (RQE) to the question similarity task. Tested on cQA-B-2016 test data, our RQE system outperformed the best system of the 2016 challenge in all measures with 77.47 MAP and 80.57 Accuracy. On cQA-B-2017 test data, performances of all systems dropped by around 30 points. Our primary system obtained 44.62 MAP, 67.27 Accuracy and 47.25 F1 score. The cQA-B-2017 best system achieved 47.22 MAP and 42.37 F1 score. Our system is ranked sixth in terms of MAP and third in terms of F1 out of 13 participating teams.

1 Introduction

SemEval-2017 Task 3[1] on Community Question Answering (cQA) focuses on answering new questions by retrieving related answered questions in community forums (Nakov et al., 2017). This task extends the previous SemEval-2015 and SemEval-2016 cQA tasks.

This year, five subtasks were proposed: English Question-Comment Similarity (subtask A), English Question-Question Similarity (subtask B), English Question-External Comment Similarity (subtask C), Arabic Answer Re-rank (subtask D) and English Multi-Domain Duplicate Question Detection (subtask E).

Subtask B (Question Similarity) aims to re-rank a set of similar questions retrieved by a search engine with respect to the original question, with the idea that the answers to the similar questions should also be answers to the new question. For a given question, a set of ten similar questions is provided for re-ranking.

2 Data

The cQA task covers two languages: English and Arabic. The English dataset (CQA-QL corpus) is based on data from the Qatar Living forum. The CQA-QL corpus consists of a list of original questions, having each ten related questions from Qatar Living, and the first ten comments from their threads. For subtask B, questions are annotated as *PerfectMatch*, *Relevant* and *Irrelevant* with respect to the original question. Both *PerfectMatch* and *Relevant* questions are considered as good without distinction.

For the cQA-B-2017 task, training and development datasets are the cQA-B-2016 datasets. A total of 3,869 question pairs is available for training including cQA-2016 test questions. cQA-B-2017 test data is composed of 880 question pairs.

3 Question Similarity vs. Question Entailment

In addition to the efforts within the semEval cQA tasks since 2015, earlier definitions and methods were proposed for Question Similarity based on different elements such as the question topic and question type (Burke et al., 1997; Jeon et al., 2005; Duan et al., 2008). But other definitions using specific kinds of question similarity such as entailment and paraphrases are not yet very developed for Question Answering (QA).

In a previous effort (Ben Abacha and Demner-Fushman, 2016), we introduced a new task called

---

[1]http://alt.qcri.org/semeval2017/task3

349

Proceedings of the 11th International Workshop on Semantic Evaluations (SemEval-2017), pages 349–352,
Vancouver, Canada, August 3 - 4, 2017. ©2017 Association for Computational Linguistics

Recognizing Question Entailment (RQE), which tackles a specific kind of question similarity. As question entailment has not previously been proposed for automatic QA, we proposed a new RQE definition: *A question PQ entails a question HQ if every answer to HQ is also an exact or partial answer to PQ.*

The RQE task is proposed to automatically provide an existing answer if an entailment relation exists between a new question and an existing answered question. Considering the example of a question PQ asking about medications for a pregnant woman, the entailed question should include this specificity too, otherwise the question is not entailed from a semantic standpoint since its answer is not relevant to the original question PQ. This answer-related definition makes question entailment a relevant extension of textual entailment for QA.

Also, our definition includes partial answers (e.g. an answer of only one sub-question of a question PQ asking about causes, diagnoses and treatments of a specific disease). Partial answers are crucial in dealing with complex questions including more than one sub-question.

Our RQE system obtained 75% F1 score on medical questions when using training data constructed automatically (Ben Abacha and Demner-Fushman, 2016). Our RQE method is applied to answer consumer health questions received by the U.S. National Library of Medicine[2] (NLM).

4   System

Our RQE System uses a supervised machine learning approach to determine whether or not a question HQ can be inferred from a question PQ. We use Logistic Regression with a set of lexical and morpho-syntactic features. The used features were selected empirically after numerous tests on Recognizing Question Entailment (RTE) datasets.

4.1   Preprocessing

For each question, we remove stop words and perform word stemming using the Porter algorithm (Porter, 1980).

4.2   Similarity Features

We compute different similarity measures between the pre-processed questions and use their values as features:

- Selected similarity measures are Word Overlap, the Dice coefficient based on the number of common bigrams, cosine distance, Levenshtein distance, and Jaccard distance.

- The feature list also includes the maximum and average values among the five similarity measures and the questions length ratio.

4.3   Morpho-syntactic Feature

We use TreeTagger (Schmid, 1994) for POS tagging. We generate an additional feature for the number of common nouns and verbs between the two questions.

4.4   Question Similarity System

For cQA-B-2017, we used our RQE classifier trained on semEval-2016 datasets (3,869 question pairs). In cQA-B-2016, the IR baseline system provided interesting results. We used a weight-based method to combine the scores provided by the Logistic Regression model and the IR baseline ranks. We used a reciprocal rank to convert the IR baseline rank and a weight w fixed after several empirical tests on cQA-2016 data. The formula that we used for combination is: $score = LogisticRegression\_score + w \times \frac{1}{IR\_rank}$

5   Results

Systems are scored according to Mean Average Precision (MAP), Mean Reciprocal Rank (MRR), Average Recall (AvgRec), Precision (P), Recall (R), F1 and Accuracy (Acc). The official evaluation measure used to rank the participating systems is MAP.

For the final evaluation we submitted 3 runs. We only changed the weighting coefficient. For **NLM_NIH-primary**, the combination weight was the one that gave the best results on the 2016 test data ($w = 7.9$). For **NLM_NIH-contrastive1**, we used the combination weight that performed the best on the 2016 development data ($w = 8.9$), which had a slightly better impact on MAP on the new 2017 test data (44.66 vs. 44.62 MAP). For **NLM_NIH-contrastive2**, we used a third combination weight ($w = 6.8$).

Table 1 presents the results on cQA-B-2017 test data. Our primary system obtained 44.62 MAP and was ranked sixth over 13 participating teams. The best system obtained 47.22 MAP. The IR baseline based on the order provided by the search engine obtained 41.85 MAP.

[2]http://www.nlm.nih.gov

System	MAP	AvgRec	MRR	P	R	F1	Acc
NLM_NIH-primary	44.62	79.59	47.74	**33.68**	79.14	**47.25**	**67.27**
NLM_NIH-contrastive1	44.66	79.66	48.08	**33.68**	79.14	**47.25**	**67.27**
NLM_NIH-contrastive2	44.29	79.05	47.45	**33.68**	79.14	**47.25**	**67.27**
cQA-B-2017 Best System	**47.22**	**82.60**	**50.07**	27.30	**94.48**	42.37	52.39
cQA-B-2017 IR Baseline	41.85	77.59	46.42	–	–	–	–

Table 1: cQA-B-2017 Official Results (Nakov et al., 2017)

System	MAP	AvgRec	MRR	P	R	F1	Acc
Our RQE System (Ben Abacha and Demner-Fushman, 2016)	**77.47**	**91.39**	**83.79**	**70.29**	**72.10**	**71.19**	**80.57**
cQA-B-2016 Best System (Franco-Salvador et al., 2016)	76.70	90.31	83.02	63.53	69.53	66.39	76.57
cQA-B-2016 IR Baseline (Nakov et al., 2016)	74.75	88.30	83.79	–	–	–	–

Table 2: Results on cQA-B-2016-Test data. RQE system trained on cQA-B-2016 training and development datasets (3,169 pairs)

Table 2 presents the results using the test data from cQA-B-2016. We used the same system with the best combination weight according to the development data ($w = 8.9$). Our results outperformed the best system on the 2016 test data. A general drop of 30 points on performance for all systems can be observed with the cQA-B-2017 test data.

6 Conclusion

In this paper, we described our participation in the task 3-B of SemEval 2017. We explored the adequacy of our question entailment system for the question similarity task. Despite the general drop of performance with regards the 2016 test data for all participating systems, we obtained good results on the 2017 test data with 44.62 MAP, 67.27 Accuracy and 47.25 F1 score. Our system is ranked sixth in terms of MAP and third in terms of F1 out of 13 participating teams.

Acknowledgments

This research was supported by the Intramural Research Program at the U.S. National Library of Medicine, National Institutes of Health.

References

Asma Ben Abacha and Dina Demner-Fushman. 2016. Recognizing question entailment for medical question answering. In *AMIA 2016, American Medical Informatics Association Annual Symposium, Chicago, IL, USA, November 12-16, 2016*. https://lhncbc.nlm.nih.gov/system/files/pub9456.pdf.

Robin D Burke, Kristian J Hammond, Vladimir Kulyukin, Steven L Lytinen, Noriko Tomuro, and Scott Schoenberg. 1997. Question answering from frequently asked question files: Experiences with the faq finder system. *AI magazine* 18(2):57.

Huizhong Duan, Yunbo Cao, Chin-Yew Lin, and Yong Yu. 2008. Searching questions by identifying question topic and question focus.

Marc Franco-Salvador, Sudipta Kar, Thamar Solorio, and Paolo Rosso. 2016. UH-PRHLT at semeval-2016 task 3: Combining lexical and semantic-based features for community question answering. In *Proceedings of the 10th International Workshop on Semantic Evaluation, SemEval@NAACL-HLT 2016, San Diego, CA, USA, June 16-17, 2016*. pages 814–821. http://aclweb.org/anthology/S/S16/S16-1126.pdf.

Jiwoon Jeon, W. Bruce Croft, and Joon Ho Lee. 2005. Finding similar questions in large question and answer archives. In *Proceedings of the 14th ACM International Conference on Information and Knowledge Management*. ACM, New York, NY, USA, CIKM '05, pages 84–90. https://doi.org/10.1145/1099554.1099572.

Preslav Nakov, Doris Hoogeveen, Lluís Màrquez, Alessandro Moschitti, Hamdy Mubarak, Timothy Baldwin, and Karin Verspoor. 2017. SemEval-2017 task 3: Community question answering. In *Proceedings of the 11th International Workshop on Semantic Evaluation*. Association for Computational Linguistics, Vancouver, Canada, SemEval '17.

Preslav Nakov, Lluís Màrquez, Alessandro Moschitti, Walid Magdy, Hamdy Mubarak, Abed Alhakim Freihat, Jim Glass, and Bilal Randeree. 2016. Semeval-2016 task 3: Community question answering. In *Proceedings of the 10th International Workshop on Semantic Evaluation, SemEval@NAACL-HLT 2016, San Diego, CA, USA, June 16-17, 2016.* pages 525–545. http://aclweb.org/anthology/S/S16/S16-1083.pdf.

M. Porter. 1980. An Algorithm for Suffix Stripping. *Program* 14(3):130–137.

Helmut Schmid. 1994. Probabilistic part-of-speech tagging using decision trees. In *Proceedings of the International Conference on New Methods in Language Processing.* Manchester, UK.

bunji at SemEval-2017 Task 3: Combination of Neural Similarity Features and Comment Plausibility Features

Yuta Koreeda[1], Takuya Hashito[2], Yoshiki Niwa[1], Misa Sato[1],
Toshihiko Yanase[1], Kenzo Kurotsuchi[1], and Kohsuke Yanai[1]

[1]Research & Development Group, Hitachi, Ltd.
[2]Industry & Distribution Business Unit, Hitachi, Ltd.
{yuta.koreeda.pb, takuya.hashito.qk, yoshiki.niwa.tx,
misa.sato.mw toshihiko.yanase.gm,
kenzo.kurotsuchi.qs, kohsuke.yanai.cs}@hitachi.com

Abstract

This paper describes a text-ranking system developed by bunji team in SemEval-2017 Task 3: Community Question Answering, Subtask A and C. The goal of the task is to re-rank the comments in a question-and-answer forum such that useful comments for answering the question are ranked high. We proposed a method that combines neural similarity features and hand-crafted comment plausibility features, and we modeled inter-comments relationship using conditional random field. Our approach obtained the fifth place in the Subtask A and the second place in the Subtask C.

1 Introduction

This paper explains the participation of the bunji team in SemEval-2017 Task 3 on Community Question Answering (CQA) (Nakov et al., 2017), Subtask A and Subtask C. The goal of the task is to re-rank the comments in a question-and-answer forum such that useful comments for answering the question are ranked high. Subtask A is extraction of relevant answers from comments in a question thread. Given a question and its comments, the system must re-rank the comments according to their relevance with respect to the question. Subtask C is extraction of relevant answers from comments in different question threads. Given a question (the original question), questions that are possibly related to the original question (the relevant questions) and comments to the relevant questions, the system must re-rank the comments according to their relevance with respect to the original question. Since the task is ranking, the primary metric is mean average precision (MAP).

Our model consists of three elements; use of similarity features, use of comment plausibility features and a supervised scoring method that models inter-comments relationship. The similarity features are designed to capture the similarities between a question and a comment because a valid answer should be on the same topic as the question. Similarity features were utilized by many teams in SemEval-2016 (Nakov et al., 2016). In this work, we take a deep learning approach to extract similarity features.

The comment plausibility features are designed to capture characteristics that relevant answers tend to have. Similar concept was proposed by Mihaylova et al. (2016), who tried to model readability, credibility, sentiment and trollness. The comment plausibility features were hand-crafted to incorporate human knowledge about CQA.

In past CQA tasks, some teams incorporated inter-comments relationship. An example of such relationship is acknowledgement, where a good answer is likely to be followed by acknowledgement of the questioner. Barrn-Cedeo et al. (2015) modeled inter-comments relationship by taking distance to nearest acknowledgement as a feature and using Conditional Random Field (CRF) to model transition probability between relevant and irrelevant comments. In our work, we try to model inter-comments relationship in much simpler way; by concatenating features of adjacent comments and by utilizing CRF for final ranking function.

2 Method

Our proposed method is constructed in following steps:

(i) Neural network is trained to extract similarity features independently to the rest of the system,

(ii) comment plausibility features are extracted with hand-crafted rules,

Proceedings of the 11th International Workshop on Semantic Evaluations (SemEval-2017), pages 353–359,
Vancouver, Canada, August 3 - 4, 2017. ©2017 Association for Computational Linguistics

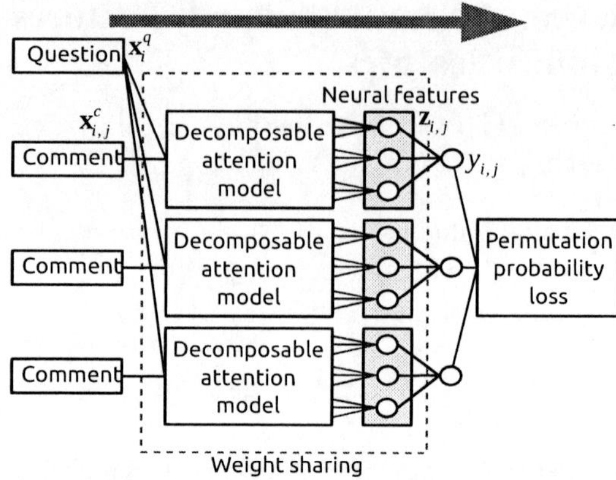

Figure 1: Neural feature extraction

(iii) neural similarity features and comment plausibility features are concatenated to form the combined features, and

(iv) CRF is optimized on the combined features while keeping the neural network fixed.

We used almost identical method for Subtask C. The differences in the system for Subtask A and for C are discussed in Section 2.4.

2.1 Neural Similarity Features

One of the challenges in the CQA task is that question and comment texts tend to be long. This makes use of recurrent neural network difficult, because recurrent neural network is known to be less effective against a long sequence (Lai et al., 2015). In this work, we make assumption that only a very small region of a question and a comment is needed to decide whether the comment is relevant. For example, given a 62-words question,

> *... and would like to know the typical business dress code in Doha for Non Nationals. Is it OK for men to wear short sleeve shirts? For women; I am assuming the more conservative; ...*[1]

and a 50-words comment,

> *I agree with MR M;its not much to worry of your dress.. its not an issue over here ;just be modest...*[1]

We only need underlined parts of the question and the answer to identify that the comment is relevant.

[1]From SemEval-2017 data (Nakov et al., 2017) (http://alt.qcri.org/semeval2017/task3/index.php?id=data-and-tools)

We propose a feature extraction method based on a decomposable attention model (Parikh et al., 2016). This method is designed to model alignment between two sequences of text, allowing the system to jointly identify informative region and predict whether the comment is relevant.

The overview of our neural network is shown in Figure 1. Each question-comments thread (one question and multiple comments) is mapped to a real value score using a decomposable attention model. The loss for stochastic gradient decent is calculated for each thread using list-wise ranking loss.

As preprocessing, we remove HTML tags, apply tokenization and lowercase all characters. Named entities, image tags, URLs and numerics are each converted to special symbols. A question subject text is prepended to the corresponding question text. We truncate question and comment text to first 50 tokens.

The c-th token of j-th comment text ($1 \leq j \leq N$) in i-th thread is then mapped to word vector representation $\mathbf{x}_{i,j,c}^C \in \mathbb{R}^M$ and the q-th token of the question text in i-th thread to $\mathbf{x}_{i,q}^Q \in \mathbb{R}^M$. The word vector was pretrained with the raw forum text provided by the organizers which contained approximately 100 million words. We only use 50,000 most frequent words and the rest of the words are mapped to an averaged vector of 50 least frequent words.

Each combination of a comment $\mathbf{x}_{i,j}^C = \{\mathbf{x}_{i,j,c}^C\}_{1 \leq c \leq L^C}$ and a question $\mathbf{x}_i^Q = \{\mathbf{x}_{i,q}^Q\}_{1 \leq q \leq L^Q}$ is mapped to a question-comment vector $\mathbf{z}_{i,j}$ using the decomposable attention model. First, the model compares and calculates attention $e_{i,j,c,q}$ for each token combination,

$$e_{i,j,c,q} = F\left(\mathbf{x}_{i,j,c}^C\right)^T F\left(\mathbf{x}_{i,q}^Q\right), \qquad (1)$$

where F is a feed forward neural network. Then, the model extracts subphrase of $\mathbf{x}_{i,j}^C$ that is soft-aligned against $\mathbf{x}_i^Q$ using attention mechanism:

$$\bar{e}_{i,j,c,q}^C = \frac{\exp(e_{i,j,c,q})}{\sum_{s=1}^{L^C} \exp(e_{i,j,s,q})} \qquad (2)$$

$$\chi_{i,j,q}^C = \sum_{c=1}^{L^C} \bar{e}_{i,j,c,q}^C \mathbf{x}_{i,j,c}^C, \qquad (3)$$

Then we compare the word vector to the soft-aligned subphrase and aggregate all the combinations:

$$\mathbf{v}_{i,j}^{Q} = \sum_{q=1}^{L^{Q}} G([\chi_{i,j,q}^{C}, \mathbf{x}_{i,q}^{Q}]), \qquad (4)$$

where G is a feed forward neural network and $[\bullet, \bullet]$ denotes the concatenation of vectors. This is calculated vice-versa for $\mathbf{v}_{i,j}^{C}$. Finally, we map $\mathbf{v}_{i,j}^{Q}$ and $\mathbf{v}_{i,j}^{C}$ to a score $y_{i,j} \in \mathbb{R}$:

$$\mathbf{z}_{i,j} = H([\mathbf{v}_{i,j}^{Q}, \mathbf{v}_{i,j}^{C}]) \qquad (5)$$

$$y_{i,j} = \sigma(\mathbf{z}_{i,j}) \cdot \mathbf{W} + \mathbf{b}, \qquad (6)$$

where H is a feed forward neural network, σ is an activation function, and $\mathbf{W}$ and $\mathbf{b}$ are model parameters. The representation $\mathbf{z}_{i,j}$ is used as the neural features, which is combined with comments plausibility features to form our final model.

The scores $\mathbf{y}_i = \{y_{i,j}\}$ are optimized to predict ground truth label sequence $\mathbf{t}_i = \{t_{i,j}\}$ with permutation probability loss (Cao et al., 2007). A ground truth label is set 1 if it is labeled "Good" and 0 if it is labeled "PotentiallyUseful" or "Bad" in accordance to the task rules (Nakov et al., 2017). We use $k = 1$ permutation probability distribution function $P : \mathbb{R}^N \mapsto \mathbb{R}^N$, such that

$$P(\mathbf{y}_i) = \left[\frac{\exp(y_{i,j})}{\sum_n^N \exp(y_{i,n})} \right]_{j \in \{1,2,\dots,N\}}. \qquad (7)$$

The permutation probability loss is defined as $D_{KL}(P(\mathbf{t}_i) \| P(\mathbf{y}_i))$ where D_{KL} is Kullback-Leibler divergence between two distributions.

Since decomposable attention model and permutation probability loss are fully differentiable, we can optimize the whole network with minibatch stochastic gradient descent with backpropagation. We use rmsprop with momentum (Graves, 2013) and learning rate reduction of 1% for every 100 batches. Dropout (Srivastava et al., 2014) and L2-norm regularization are applied to each layer of feed forward neural network to avoid overfitting. Batch normalization (Ioffe and Szegedy, 2015) is applied and gradient norm is clipped to 5.0 to improve the training stability. We use leaky rectified linear unit for activation function σ as shown in Equation (8) to stabilize the training.

$$\sigma(x) = \max(x, 0.2x) \qquad (8)$$

Other hyperparameters are shown in Table 1. Above model selection and hyperparameters were manually tuned by validation against SemEval-2016 test data.

Parameter	Subtask A	Subtask C
Number of layers in F and H	3	3
Number of layers in G	3	3
Dimension of $z_{i,j}$	200	50
Dimensions of other layers	200	200
Word vector dimension M	200	200
Dropout rate	0.1	0.1
L2 regularization coefficient	0.1×10^{-4}	0.2×10^{-4}
L2 regularization coefficient for W	0.2×10^{-4}	0.3×10^{-5}
Initial learning rate	0.5×10^{-5}	0.5×10^{-5}
Mini-batch size	2	1
Max tokens	50	30
Training epochs	50	30

Table 1: Hyperparameters of the neural network

?, !, what, which, who, where, when, why, whom, how, hi, $\langle$what, which, who, where, when, why, whom, how, hi$\rangle$, $\langle$yes, yep, year$\rangle$, $\langle$no, nope, nah$\rangle$, $\langle$thank, thanks, tnx, thx$\rangle$, $\langle$you, u$\rangle$, $\langle$good, greate, nice$\rangle$, $\langle$bad, not, non$\rangle$

Table 2: Lexicons used in function-of-a-comment features. $\langle\bullet\rangle$ denotes a feature that is positive when any of the words are present in the comment.

2.2 Comment Plausibility Features

Comment plausibility features are designed to extract information that is not captured by neural similarity features. These features are divided into five groups: (1) function of a comment, (2) answer adequacy, (3) dialog structure, (4) answerer's meta-information, and (5) miscellaneous.

Part of speech tagging and named entity recognition for comment plausibility features are carried out using Stanford CoreNLP (Manning et al., 2014).

2.2.1 Function of a Comment

This group of 39 features is designed to capture the function of a comment; e.g. trying to answer the question, making remarks, or asking the questioner for more information. This group of features is extracted from each comment.

The occurrence of each word in Table 2 within each comment is extracted as a binary feature. We use the part of speech tag for the first and the final word of the comment. This is expressed as one-hot representation of whether the first/final word is noun, adjective, adverb, verb, auxiliary verb, conjunction (for the final word only) or interjection. We also added a feature whether the first word is "is."

We also use ratio of each part of speech tag to the number of tokens.

#	Comparing			IDF source					
				Per thread			All dataset		
	S	Q	C	S	Q	C	S	Q	C
1		o	o		o	o			
2		o	o	o	o	o			
3	o		o	o		o			
4	o		o	o	o	o			
5		o	o					o	o
6		o	o				o	o	o
7	o		o				o		o
8	o		o				o	o	o

S = question subject, Q = question text, C = comment text

Table 3: Types of TF-IDFs for calculating cosine distance. Column *Comparing* shows text blocks to extract and compare TF-IDF. Column *IDF source* shows the documents used to calculate IDF, where each text block is regarded as a single document.

2.2.2 Answer Adequacy

This group of 27 features is designed to capture whether the comment has adequate information to answer the question. For this purpose, this group of features is extracted from each question-answer pair.

The presence of each word (what, which, who, where, when, why, whom, how, hi, and any of do, does, or did) within a question is extracted as a binary feature. The presence of each type of named entities (location, person, organization, money, percent, date and time) and the presence of any type of the named entities, numerics, image tags and URLs in each comment are also extracted.

The relative length of a comment to a question is also extracted. This is based on the idea that the answer tends to be long when a question is long. This relative length is calculated for 6 variants; i.e. the number of words/characters in a comment divided by,

 (i) the total number of words/characters in the question and the comment,
 (ii) the total number of words/characters in the question subject, text and the comment text, and
(iii) the total number of words/characters in the question subject and the comment text.

2.2.3 Dialog Structure

This group of four features is designed to capture the dialog structure of comments. For this purpose, this group of features is extracted for each comment using the whole thread.

Dialog structure features include the binary fea-

tures for each of the following statements:
 (i) If the comment is posted by the question author.
 (ii) If the comment contains the name of the question author.
(iii) If the comment contains a name of the user other than the question author (comment contains a string with "@" prefix).

We use reciprocal chronological order (e.g. $1/3$ for the third comment) to capture the global position of a comment.

2.2.4 Answerer's Meta-information

This group of two features is designed to capture the answerer's meta-information. For this purpose, this group of features is extracted for each comment using the whole dataset.

For example, whether a comment is written by the author of the question is important information because he or she hardly ever knows the answer.

Answerer's meta-information features are binary features for each of the following statements:
 (i) If the comment author is anonymous.
 (ii) If the comment author has posted a comment elsewhere in the dataset.

2.2.5 Miscellaneous

To further improve the performance, we adopted a lexicon of 23 words with the lowest semantic orientation in CQA (Balchev et al., 2016) and extracted the occurrence of these words from the comments.

We also use the cosine distance between the term frequency-inverse document frequency (TF-IDF) vectors of a question and a comment. We use eight types of TF-IDF as listed in Table 3, each characterized by document blocks (question subject, question text or comment text) to compare and to calculate IDF. We also used presence of word overwrap in the question-comment and the subject-comment pair as binary features. While redundant to neural similarity features, redundant features increase the overall performance by acting like an ensemble.

We use the cosine distance between the TF-IDF vector of a comment and an averaged TF-IDF vector of all comments in thread. This is extracted for an averaged TF-IDF vector of all comments in dataset, as well. These features are intended to capture amount of distinctive information that each comment contains.

Submission	Subtask A				Subtask C			
	Position	MAP	AvgRec	MRR	Position	MAP	AvgRec	MRR
Primary*	5	86.58	92.71	91.37	2	14.71	29.47	16.48
Contrastive 1[†]	7	85.29	91.77	91.48	5	8.19	15.12	9.25
Contrastive 2[‡]	7	84.01	90.45	89.17	1	16.57	30.98	17.04
Top team	1	88.43	93.79	92.82	1	15.46	33.42	18.14
baseline(IR)	-	72.61	79.32	82.37	-	9.18	21.72	10.11

* Combined   [†] Comment plausibility features   [‡] Neural features

Table 4: 2017 official result

Submission	Subtask A		Subtask C	
	2017	2016	2017	2016
Primary	86.58	75.6	14.71	39.9
Contrastive 1	85.29	74.4	8.19	38.0
Contrastive 2	84.01	71.4	16.57	28.0
Top team	88.43	79.2	15.46	55.4
IR baseline	72.61	59.5	9.18	40.3

Table 5: Comparison of MAP scores in 2016 and 2017 test dataset

2.3 Combined features

The neural features and the comment plausibility features are concatenated to form Primary run for Subtask A and C. The features are further extended by concatenating features from two comments before and after the target comment, resulting in concatenated features over five comments. This allows extending the dialog structure features (Section 2.2.3) without adding too many features, as described in Section 1.

We use first order linear CRF by regarding each comment as an observation and a thread as a sequence. Along with concatenated features, CRF allows non-local optimization of inter-comments relationship. For example, presence of "yes" after a good answer is likely to be acknowledgement by the questioner. In this case, effect of "yes" is conditioned on the label of the previous comment.

CRF is trained using L-BFGS with L1 regularization coefficient of 1.0 and L2 regularization coefficient of 0.001. We use CRFsuite (Okazaki, 2007) as an implementation of CRF.

2.4 Modification for Subtask C

For neural similarity features, hyperparameters were manually tuned for Subtask C as shown in Table 1. On training neural models for Subtask C, we added all the question-comment pairs from Subtask A to augment the data.

For comment plausibility feature, we ap-plied greedy stepwise backward elimination using SemEval-2016 test data as validation data. We tested the deletion of each feature and removed the feature whose deletion gives the best MAP improvement. We repeated the process until MAP no longer improves. The process removed following features:

(i) Presence of any of words ⟨what, which, who, where, when, why, whom, how, hi⟩.

(ii) The relative length of a comment (Section 2.2.2, (ii)).

(iii) Reference to the question author (Section 2.2.3, (i) and (ii)).

(iv) Answerer's meta-information.

(v) TF-IDF (Table 3, #1 and #4).

3 Experiments

Our Primary submission was CRF with combined features. Contrastive 1 was CRF with only the comment plausibility features. Contrastive 2 was CRF with only the neural similarity features.

The official results for the 2017 test data are shown in Table 4. The Primary obtained the fifth and the second in Subtask A and C, respectively.

The combined features (Primary) was much better than Contrastive 1 and 2 in Subtask A, as expected. The large increase of 1.29 MAP score from Contrastive 1 to the Primary implies that the neural features and comment plausibility features were capturing different aspects of the problem.

On the other hand, Contrastive 1 performed poorly in Subtask C. This was partially because the similarity was more important in Subtask C, which contained many unrelated comments. Thus neural similarity features performed much better than in Subtask A and comment plausibility feature did much worse. Another reason for Contrastive 1's poor performance may have been due to the over-fitting to development dataset, as implied by large performance drop from 2016 dataset (Table 5).

Feature	MAP
All features	76.23
− Author's comment or not	74.80
− Reciprocal of answer's number	75.00
− Word "?"	75.64
− First word is an auxiliary verb	75.65
− Word "avatar"	75.66
− Word "whom"	75.70
− First word is adjective	75.72
− TF-IDF (Table 3, #1)	75.73

Table 6: The top 8 contributing comment plausibility features in Subtask A

Feature	MAP
All features	38.70
− Word "do," "does" or "did"	37.24
− Word "who"	37.63
− Word "fs"	37.93
− Final word is an adverb	38.13
− Word "what" in the comment	38.23
− First word is a noun	38.33
− Word "?"	38.35
− Cosine distance between a comment TF-IDF and an averaged TF-IDF over all comments in thread	38.39

Table 7: The top 8 contributing comment plausibility features in Subtask C

To identify the contributing features within the comment plausibility features, we carried out additional experiments on 2016 test dataset where we eliminated each feature one by one from the Primary system. The top 8 contributing features are shown in Table 6 (Subtask A) and 7 (Subtask C). From the result, the comment plausibility features seem to work as a blacklist for comments that are unlikely to be an answer. For example, occurrence of words "?," "do," "does," "did," and "what" all contribute to identifying a question which are less likely to be a comment.

Our neural similarity feature performed worse than the previous application of recurrent neural network to Subtask A (MAP scores of 75.7 against our 71.4) and to Subtask C (MAP scores of 47.2 against our 28.0) (Wu and Lan, 2016). The reason for the inferior performance may be due to very large vocabulary of CQA, which caused the neural network to fall back to only using commonly appearing words in many cases. As a supporting observation, attention weight seem to localize on very few commonly appearing words instead of on

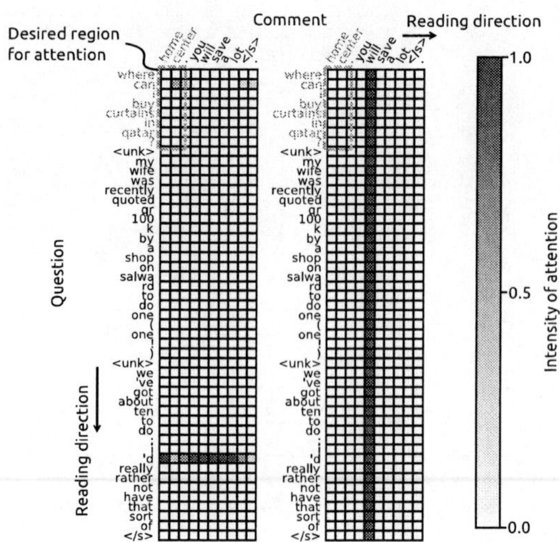

Figure 2: Visualization of attention ($\bar{e}^{Q}_{i,j,c,q}$ on left and $\bar{e}^{C}_{i,j,c,q}$ on right) in failing case. Attention had concentrated on commonly appearing words rather than more informative regions.

more meaningful region of text (Figure 2). Use of sub-word vocabulary can help overcome this problem (Yoon Kim et al., 2016; Wu et al., 2016). Also, we manually tuned the hyperparamters for neural network. Random searching for better hyperparameters can improve the overall performance.

4 Conclusions

This paper explains the participation in SemEval-2017 Task 3, Subtask A and Subtask C, which is a problem of ranking the comments in community question answering forum according to their relevance to the question. We proposed a method that combines neural similarity features and comment plausibility features, and modeled inter-comments relationship. Our approach obtained the fifth place in the Subtask A and the second place in the Subtask C.

For future work, we will improve the neural method so that it can better handle large vocabulary of CQA. We will also incorporate systematic end-to-end tuning on both feature selection and neural method to deal with over-fitting problem.

References

Daniel Balchev, Yasen Kiprov, Ivan Koychev, and Preslav Nakov. 2016. PMI-cool at SemEval-2016 Task 3: Experiments with PMI and Goodness Polarity Lexicons for Community Question Answering. In *Proceedings of the 10th International Workshop on Semantic Evaluation (SemEval-2016)*. pages 844–850.

Alberto Barrn-Cedeo, Simone Filice, Giovanni Da San Martino, Shafiq Joty, Llus Mrquez, Preslav Nakov, and Alessandro Moschitti. 2015. Thread-Level Information for Comment Classification in Community Question Answering. In *Proceedings of the 53rd Annual Meeting of the Association for Computational Linguistics and the 7th International Joint Conference on Natural Language Processing*. pages 687–693.

Zhe Cao, Tao Qin, Tie-Yan Liu, Ming-Feng Tsai, and Hang Li. 2007. Learning to Rank: From Pairwise Approach to Listwise Approach. In *Proceedings of the 24th International Conference on Machine Learning*. pages 129–136.

Alex Graves. 2013. Generating Sequences With Recurrent Neural Networks. *arXiv* .

Sergey Ioffe and Christian Szegedy. 2015. Batch Normalization: Accelerating Deep Network Training by Reducing Internal Covariate Shift. In *Proceedings of the 32nd International Conference on Machine Learning*. volume 37, pages 448–456.

Siwei Lai, Liheng Xu, Kang Liu, and Jun Zhao. 2015. Recurrent Convolutional Neural Networks for Text Classification. In *Proceedings of the Twenty-Ninth AAAI Conference on Artificial Intelligence*. pages 2267–2273.

Christopher D. Manning, Mihai Surdeanu, John Bauer, Jenny Finkel, Steven J. Bethard, and David Mc-Closky. 2014. The Stanford CoreNLP Natural Language Processing Toolkit. In *Association for Computational Linguistics (ACL) System Demonstrations*. pages 55–60.

Tsvetomila Mihaylova, Pepa Gencheva, Martin Boyanov, Ivana Yovcheva, Todor Mihaylov, Momchil Hardalov, Yasen Kiprov, Daniel Balchev, Ivan Koychev, Preslav Nakov, Ivelina Nikolova, and Galia Angelova. 2016. SUper Team at SemEval-2016 Task 3: Building a Feature-Rich System for Community Question Answering. In *Proceedings of the 10th International Workshop on Semantic Evaluation (SemEval-2016)*. pages 836–843.

Preslav Nakov, Doris Hoogeveen, Lluís Màrquez, Alessandro Moschitti, Hamdy Mubarak, Timothy Baldwin, and Karin Verspoor. 2017. SemEval-2017 Task 3: Community Question Answering. In *Proceedings of the 11th International Workshop on Semantic Evaluation (SemEval-2017)*. pages 27–48.

Preslav Nakov, Llus Mrquez, Alessandro Moschitti, Walid Magdy, Hamdy Mubarak, abed Alhakim Freihat, Jim Glass, and Bilal Randeree. 2016. SemEval-2016 Task 3: Community Question Answering. In *Proceedings of the 10th International Workshop on Semantic Evaluation (SemEval-2016)*. pages 525–545.

Naoaki Okazaki. 2007. Crfsuite: a fast implementation of conditional random fields (CRFs). http://www.chokkan.org/software/crfsuite/.

Ankur Parikh, Oscar Täckström, Dipanjan Das, and Jakob Uszkoreit. 2016. A Decomposable Attention Model for Natural Language Inference. In *Proceedings of the 2016 Conference on Empirical Methods in Natural Language Processing*. pages 2249–2255.

Nitish Srivastava, Geoffrey Hinton, Alex Krizhevsky, Ilya Sutskever, and Ruslan Salakhutdinov. 2014. Dropout: A Simple Way to Prevent Neural Networks from Overfitting. *Journal of Machine Learning Research* 15:1929–1958.

Guoshun Wu and Man Lan. 2016. ECNU at SemEval-2016 Task 3: Exploring Traditional Method and Deep Learning Method for Question Retrieval and Answer Ranking in Community Question Answering. In *Proceedings of the 10th International Workshop on Semantic Evaluation (SemEval-2016)*. pages 872–878.

Yonghui Wu, Mike Schuster, Zhifeng Chen, Quoc V. Le, Mohammad Norouzi, Wolfgang Macherey, Maxim Krikun, Yuan Cao, Qin Gao, Klaus Macherey, Jeff Klingner, Apurva Shah, Melvin Johnson, Xiaobing Liu, ukasz Kaiser, Stephan Gouws, Yoshikiyo Kato, Taku Kudo, Hideto Kazawa, Keith Stevens, George Kurian, Nishant Patil, Wei Wang, Cliff Young, Jason Smith, Jason Riesa, Alex Rudnick, Oriol Vinyals, Greg Corrado, Macduff Hughes, and Jeffrey Dean. 2016. Google's Neural Machine Translation System: Bridging the Gap between Human and Machine Translation. Technical report.

Yoon Kim, Yacine Jernite, David Sontag, and Alexander Rush. 2016. Character-Aware Neural Language Models. In *Proceedings of the Thirtieth AAAI Conference on Artificial Intelligence*. pages 2741–2749.

QU-BIGIR at SemEval 2017 Task 3: Using Similarity Features for Arabic Community Question Answering Forums

Marwan Torki and **Maram Hasanain** and **Tamer Elsayed**

Qatar University

Department of Computer Science & Engineering

Doha, Qatar

{mtorki,maram.hasanain,telsayed}@qu.edu.qa

Abstract

In this paper, we describe our QU-BIGIR system for the Arabic subtask D of the SemEval 2017 Task 3. Our approach builds on our participation in the past version of the same subtask. This year, our system uses different similarity features that encodes lexical and semantic pairwise similarity of text pairs. In addition to well-known similarity measures such as cosine similarity, we use other measures based on the summary statistics of word embedding representation for a given text. To rank a list of candidate question-answer pairs for a given question, we train a linear SVM classifier over our similarity features. Our best resulting run came second in subtask D with a very competitive performance to the first-ranking system.

1 Introduction

The ubiquitous presence of community question answering (CQA) websites has motivated research on building automatic question answering (QA) systems that can benefit from previously-answered questions to answer newly-posed ones (Shtok et al., 2012). A core functionality of such systems is their ability to effectively rank previously-suggested answers with respect to their degree/probability of relevance to a posted question. Ranking is vital to push away irrelevant and low quality answers, which are commonplace in CQA as they are generally open with no restrictions on who can post or answer questions.

To this effect, SemEval 2017 Task 3 "Community Question Answering" has emphasized the ranking component in the main task of the challenge. We have participated in Task 3-Subtask D (Arabic Subtask) which is confined to the main

Question: ما هي الدوالي وما هي اسبابها

Candidate question-answer pairs (QApairs):

Q : هل لدوالي القدم اعراض يوجد معي دوالي في القدم ولكن اطلب منكم تزويدي باعراض الدوالي والمشاكل التي يسببها

A : العرض الأكثر شيوعا هو ظهور الأوردة منتفخة على واجهة الساق واالتشخيص يكون من خلال الفحص الطبي المباشر والعلاج سيكون وفق السبب

Q : ماهى دوالى الدرجه الثالثه وما اسبابها وكيف يتم الوقايه منها

A : الدوالي هي عباره عن توسع في الاورده العلويه للمنطقه المصابه ولها الكثير من الاسباب كالحمل والسمنه والجلوس لمده طويله جدا ويتم الوقايه منها عن طريق عدم الوقوف لمده طويله وممارسة الرايضه بشكل اكبر ولبس جوارب مخصصه لهذه الحالات لمنع التفاقم

Q: هل العروق الملتويه بشكل واضح في القدم تعتبر من الدوالي وهل الدوالي لها اخطار اذا لم يتم علاجها

A: يمكن أن تنفجر الدوالي تحت الجلد وتؤدى إلى كدمات وترسبات دموية وتصبغات تحت الجلد ويمكن أن تؤدي إلى تقرحات. قد يشمل علاج دوالي الساقين عدد من التدابير التي تهدف الى التخفيف من حدة الأعراض أو الحد من تطورها

Q: انا شاب عمري ٣٧سنة وأعاني من من دوالي الأوردة في الساقين فكيف أزيلها

A: الغالب أنه بحاجة لاستئصال إذا كانت كبيرة ومزعجة راجع اختصاصي جراحة عامة أو جراحة الأوعية الدموية لتقييم الحالة

Figure 1: A question and 4 of its given 30 candidate QA-pairs

task of ranking answers; given a new question and a set of 30 question-answer pairs (QApairs) retrieved by a search engine, re-rank those QApairs by their degree/probability of relevance to the new question. Figure 1 shows an example of a question and four of its 30 given candidate question-answer pairs. Further details about SemEval 2017 Task 3 can be found in (Nakov et al., 2017).

In this paper, we describe the system we developed to participate in that task. The system leverages a supervised learning approach over similarity features. We utilize two types of similarity features. First, we employ similarity features based on term representation for a given pairs of text. Second, we utilize word2vec to build text representation following the same approach as in our last year's submission for the same subtask (Malhas et al., 2016). We used similarity features based on that text representation to encode the semantic similarity for pairs of texts.

The rest of the paper is organized as follows; the approach and description of features are in-

360

Proceedings of the 11th International Workshop on Semantic Evaluations (SemEval-2017), pages 360–364,
Vancouver, Canada, August 3 - 4, 2017. ©2017 Association for Computational Linguistics

troduced in section 2; the experimental setup followed in our submitted runs and the results are presented in section 3. Finally we conclude our study with final remarks in section 4.

2 Approach

We tackled the answer ranking task with a supervised learning approach that uses linear SVM models. The features used in classification are designed to capture both lexical and semantic information of pairs of texts.

2.1 Data Setup

We are given a set of questions Q; each is associated with P question-answer pairs. To compute our features, we define a text pair $< T_1, T_2 >$ according to three setups:

- **QQA:** We consider T_1 to be the original question q and the concatenation of one **pair** p of its associated question-answer pairs as T_2.

- **QA:** We consider T_1 to be the original question q and one **answer** of its associated question-answer pairs as T_2.

- **QQ:** We consider T_1 to be the original question q and one **question** of its associated question-answer pairs as T_2.

2.2 Term-based Similarity Features

A recent study has showed that simple features like MK features (Metzler and Kanungo, 2008) can be very effective for re-ranking candidate question answer pairs (Yang et al., 2016). We specifically use the following features described by Yang et al. (Yang et al., 2016). For all features, we assume the input to be two pieces of text: T_1 and T_2 as defined by any of the setups illustrated in section 2.1.

- **SynonymsOverlap:** Before computing this feature, we first apply light text normalization to T_1 and T_2 including special character (e.g., ',', '.', etc.) and diacritics removal. The feature is then computed as the portion of T_1 terms that have a synonym or the original term in T_2. Synonyms are extracted from the Arabic WordNet.[1]

---

[1]Described here: `http://bit.ly/2mzfc7X`

To compute the remaining features, we normalize T_1 and T_2 following the same approach when computing SynonymsOverlap feature. We also apply preprocessing steps including stemming and stopwords removal.

- **LMScore:** The language model score is computed as the Dirichlet-smoothed log-likelihood score of generating T_1 given T_2. The score is computed using the following equation:

$$LMScore(T_1, T_2) = \sum_{w \in T_1} tf_{w,T_1} \log \frac{tf_{w,T_2} + \mu P(w|C)}{|T_2| + \mu} \quad (1)$$

where tf_{w,T_1} and tf_{w,T_2} is the frequency of term w in T_1 and T_2 respectively. $P(w|C)$ is the background language model computed using the maximum likelihood estimate with term statistics extracted from a recent large-scale crawl of the Arabic Web called ArabicWeb16 (Suwaileh et al., 2016). We set μ to 2000 as this is the default value used in Lucene's language modeling retrieval model.[2]

- **CosineSimilarty**. This feature computes the cosine similarity between T_1 and T_2 as follows.

$$CS(T_1, T_2) = \frac{\vec{T_1} \cdot \vec{T_2}}{||\vec{T_1}|| \, ||\vec{T_2}||} \quad (2)$$

where $\vec{T_1}$ and $\vec{T_2}$ is the vector representation of T_1 and T_2 respectively and $||\vec{T_1}||$ and $||\vec{T_2}||$ is the Euclidean lengths of vectors $\vec{T_1}$ and $\vec{T_2}$. We represent texts as vectors using TF-IDF representation where term statistics are extracted from ArabicWeb16 (Suwaileh et al., 2016).

- **JaccardSimilarty**. This feature computes the Jaccard similarity between T_1 and T_2 as follows.

$$JS(T_1, T_2) = \frac{|\vec{T_1} \cap \vec{T_2}|}{|\vec{T_1} \cup \vec{T_2}|} \quad (3)$$

- **JaccardSimilartyV1**. This is a variant of Jaccard similarity computed as follows.

$$JS_1(T_1, T_2) = \frac{|\vec{T_1} \cap \vec{T_2}|}{|\vec{T_1}|} \quad (4)$$

---

[2]`http://bit.ly/2lOOdqw`

- **JaccardSimialirtyV2**. This is a second variant of Jaccard similarity computed as follows.

$$JS_2(T_1, T_2) = \frac{|\vec{T_1} \cap \vec{T_2}|}{|\vec{T_2}|} \qquad (5)$$

2.3 Semantic word2vec Similarity Features

Every text snippet T has a set of words. Each word has a fixed-length word embedding representation, $w \in \mathbb{R}^d$, where d is the dimensionality of the word embedding. Thus for a text snippet T we define $T = \{w_1, \cdots, w_k\}$, where k is the number of words in T. The word embedding representation is computed offline following Mikolov et al. approach (Mikolov et al., 2013).

To compute similarity scores, we represent each text snippet by a feature vector; different alternatives for feature representations are adopted as described next.

2.3.1 Average Word Embedding Similarity

For a text snippet T that has k words, we compute the average vector as follows:

$$T^\mu = \frac{\sum_{i=1}^{k}(w_i)}{k} \qquad (6)$$

Notice that $T^\mu = \in \mathbb{R}^d$. This leads to the following cosine similarity feature.

$$CS_\mu(T_1, T_2) = \frac{\vec{T_1^\mu} \cdot \vec{T_2^\mu}}{||\vec{T_1^\mu}|| \, ||\vec{T_2^\mu}||} \qquad (7)$$

2.3.2 Covariance Word Embedding Similarity

Instead of computing the average vector, we can compute a covariance matrix $C \in \mathbb{R}^{d \times d}$. The covariance matrix C is computed by treating each dimension as a random variable and every entry in $C_{u,v}$ is the covariance between the pair of variables (u, v). The covariance between two random variables u and v is computed as in eq. 8, where k is the number of observations (words).

$$C_{u,v} = \frac{\sum_{i=1}^{k}(u_i - \bar{u})(v_i - \bar{v})}{k - 1} \qquad (8)$$

The matrix $C \in \mathbb{R}^{d \times d}$ is a symmetric matrix. We compute a vectorized representation of the matrix C as the stacking of the lower triangular part of matrix C as in eq. 9. This process produces a vector $T^{Cov} \in \mathbb{R}^{d \times (d+1)/2}$

$$T^{Cov} = \mathbf{vect}(C) = \{C_{u,v} : u \in \{1, \cdots, d\}, v \in \{u, \cdots, d\}\} \qquad (9)$$

This leads to the following cosine similarity feature.

$$CS_{Cov}(T_1, T_2) = \frac{T_1^{\vec{Cov}} \cdot T_2^{\vec{Cov}}}{||T_1^{\vec{Cov}}|| \, ||T_2^{\vec{Cov}}||} \qquad (10)$$

2.4 Ranking Using SVM

Although Subtask D is a re-ranking task, it has also a classification task where answers need to be ranked and labeled with either *true* or *false*; the former designates a *Direct* or *Relevant* answer to the new question, and the latter designates an *Irrelevant* answer. In our last year's submission (Malhas et al., 2016) we used learning-to-rank module for re-ranking pairs, but we used a simple heuristic to give labels to the candidate question-answer pairs. This year we use SVM to give a label for every candidate pair using the SVM model. In addition to labeling pairs, we use the decision scores from the SVM model for re-ranking the candidate question-answer pairs.

3 Experimental Evaluation

In this section we present the experimental setup and results of our primary, contrastive-1 and contrastive-2 submissions.

3.1 Experimental Setup

We used the Arabic collection of questions and their potentially related question-answer pairs provided by Task 3 organizers to train our word embedding model. The Gensim[3] tool was used to generate the word2vec model from training data[4], setting $d = 100$. We used the learned model to compute our features as described in section 2. Features were generated for the three data setups described in section 2.1.

3.2 Submissions and Results

The differences among our submitted runs is based on the selection of the features. In all cases we use linear SVM for classifying and ranking question-answer pairs. Details on our official submissions

---

[3] http://radimrehurek.com/gensim/
[4] Testing data are held out during the computation of the word2vec model.

	MAP	AvgRec	MRR	P	R	F1	Acc
QU-BigIR Contrastive 2	59.48	83.83	64.56	55.35	70.95	62.19	66.15
QU-BigIR Contrastive 1	59.13	83.56	64.68	49.37	85.41	62.57	59.91
QU-BigIR Primary	56.69	81.89	61.83	41.59	70.16	52.22	49.64
Baseline 1 (IR)	60.55	85.06	66.08	-	-	-	-
Baseline 2 (Random)	48.48	73.89	53.27	39.04	66.43	49.18	46.13
Baseline 3 (all true)	-	-	-	39.23	100	56.36	39.23
Baseline 4 (all false)	-	-	-	-	-	-	60.77

Table 1: The official scores attained by our primary and contrastive submissions to SemEval 2017 Task 3-SubTask D

are summarized next. Table 1 presents the official results of our submissions.

Contrastive-1. We use the set of term-based similarity features defined in section 2.2. We compute these features for all data setups defined in section 2.1. This results in 18 features in total. Six features for every data setup **(QQ, QA and QQA)**. We tuned the parameter C for the linear SVM on the development set.

Contrastive-2. In addition to the features used in Contrastive-1 submission, we use the set of semantic word2vec based similarity features defined in section 2.3. This results in 24 features in total; eight features for every data setup **(QQ, QA and QQA)**. This submission produced our best MAP results.

Primary. We use the full set of similarity features defined in section 2.2 and section 2.3. In addition, we performed a weighted score fusion with an SVM model based on fixed length representation using Covariance word embedding. The feature vectors we used are computed using equation 9. We tuned the model weights using the development set. Table 2 shows that this setup gets the best MAP results on the development set.

	MAP
QU-BigIR Contrastive 1	42.54
QU-BigIR Contrastive 2	42.87
QU-BigIR Primary	43.41
Baseline (Random)	29.79

Table 2: The development set MAP scores obtained by our primary and contrastive submissions.

3.3 Discussion

- Our best official submission is Contrastive-2 using both term-based similarity features and semantic word2vec similarity features. This indicates that the two similarity features types are complementing each other.

- Our results justify the usage of SVM model for labeling and re-ranking question-answer pairs. This is clear in the **P, R, F1** and **Acc** scores reported across all other baselines. We report very competitive MAP scores to the best performing ranking systems which are not using any form of labeling such as IR-baseline.

- Score fusion in our primary run did not achieve best results on the official test set while it was the best run in our experiments on the development set. We believe that this happened due to the difference in the source of question-answer pairs in the development set compared to the the official test set where the test set contains only medical questions.

4 Conclusion

This paper describes the system we developed to participate in SemEval-2017 Task 3 on Community Question Answering. Our system has focused on the Arabic Subtask D which is confined to Answer Selection in Community Question Answering, i.e., finding good answers for a given new question.

We have adopted a supervised learning approach where linear SVM models were trained over similarity features. In our best submission, term-based similarity features and word2vec similarity features were both used; our system ranked second among the other participating teams.

Acknowledgments

This work was made possible by NPRP grant# NPRP 6-1377-1-257 from the Qatar National Research Fund (a member of Qatar Foundation). The statements made herein are solely the responsibility of the authors.

References

Rana Malhas, Marwan Torki, and Tamer Elsayed. 2016. QU-IR at SemEval 2016 Task 3: Learning to Rank on Arabic Community Question Answering Forums with Word Embedding. In *Proceedings of the 10th International Workshop on Semantic Evaluation (SemEval-2016)*. Association for Computational Linguistics, San Diego, California, pages 866–871.

Donald Metzler and Tapas Kanungo. 2008. Machine learned sentence selection strategies for query-biased summarization. In *SIGIR Learning to Rank Workshop*. pages 40–47.

Tomas Mikolov, Kai Chen, Greg Corrado, and Jeffrey Dean. 2013. Efficient estimation of word representations in vector space. *arXiv preprint arXiv:1301.3781* .

Preslav Nakov, Doris Hoogeveen, Lluís Màrquez, Alessandro Moschitti, Hamdy Mubarak, Timothy Baldwin, and Karin Verspoor. 2017. SemEval-2017 task 3: Community question answering. In *Proceedings of the 11th International Workshop on Semantic Evaluation*. Association for Computational Linguistics, Vancouver, Canada, SemEval '17.

Anna Shtok, Gideon Dror, Yoelle Maarek, and Idan Szpektor. 2012. Learning from the past: answering new questions with past answers. In *Proceedings of the 21st international conference on World Wide Web*. ACM, pages 759–768.

Reem Suwaileh, Mucahid Kutlu, Nihal Fathima, Tamer Elsayed, and Matthew Lease. 2016. Arabicweb16: A new crawl for today's arabic web. In *Proceedings of the 39th International ACM SIGIR Conference on Research and Development in Information Retrieval*. SIGIR '16, pages 673–676.

Liu Yang, Qingyao Ai, Damiano Spina, Ruey-Cheng Chen, Liang Pang, W. Bruce Croft, Jiafeng Guo, and Falk Scholer. 2016. Beyond factoid qa: Effective methods for non-factoid answer sentence retrieval. In *Advances in Information Retrieval: 38th European Conference on IR Research, ECIR 2016, Padua, Italy, March 20–23, 2016. Proceedings*, Springer International Publishing, pages 115–128.

ECNU at SemEval-2017 Task 3: Using Traditional and Deep Learning Methods to Address Community Question Answering Task

Guoshun Wu[1], Yixuan Sheng[1], Man Lan[1,2*], Yuanbin Wu[1,2]
[1]Department of Computer Science and Technology,
East China Normal University, Shanghai, P.R.China
[2]Shanghai Key Laboratory of Multidimensional Information Processing
51141201064,51164500026@stu.ecnu.edu.cn
mlan,ybwu@cs.ecnu.edu.cn

Abstract

This paper describes the systems we submitted to the task 3 (Community Question Answering) in SemEval 2017 which contains three subtasks on english corpora, i.e., subtask A: Question-Comment Similarity, subtask B: Question-Question Similarity, and subtask C: Question-External Comment Similarity. For subtask A, we combined two different methods to represent question-comment pair, i.e., supervised model using traditional features and Convolutional Neural Network. For subtask B, we utilized the information of snippets returned from Search Engine with question subject as query. For subtask C, we ranked the comments by multiplying the probability of the pair "related question - comment" being Good by the reciprocal rank of the related question.

1 Introduction

The purpose of Community Question Answering task in SemEval 2017 (Nakov et al., 2017) is to provide a platform for finding good answers to new questions in a community-created discussion forum, where the main task (subtask C) is defined as follows: given a new question and a large collection of question-comment threads created by a user community, participants are required to rank the comments that are most useful for answering the new question. Obviously, this main task consists of two optional subtasks, i.e., Question-Comment Similarity (subtask A, also known as *answer ranking*), which is to re-rank comments/answers according to their relevance with respect to the question, and Question-Question Similarity (i.e., subtask B, also known as *question retrieval*), which is to retrieve the simi-

lar questions according to their semantic similarity with respect to the original question. More, a new subtask: Multi-Domain Duplicate Detection Subtask (i.e., subtask E) which is to identify duplicate questions in StackExchange has been added to SemEval 2017 task 3.

To address subtask A, we explored a traditional machine learning method which uses multiple types of features, e.g., Word Match Features, Topic Model-based Features, and Lexical Semantic Similarity Features. Additionally, for subtask A, we also built a Convolutional Neural Network (CNN) model to learn joint representation for question-comment (Q-C) pair. For subtask B, we utilized the information of snippets returned from Search Engine with question subject as query, e.g., we counted the frequency of each word in each snippets list and added the words which appear in the subject of original question and the frequency is more than 1 to the subject of related question. Since subtask C can be regarded as a joint work of the two above-mentioned subtasks, we ranked the comments by multiplying the probability of the pair "related question - comment" being Good by the reciprocal rank of the related question. As for subtask E, we did not submit the results because of the large amount of dataset.

The rest of this paper is organized as follows. Section 2 describes our system. Section 3 describes experimental setting. Section 4 and 5 report results on training and test sets. Finally, Section 6 concludes this work.

2 Systems Description

For subtask A, we presented two different methods i.e., using traditional linguistic features and learning a CNN model to represent question and comment sentences. For subtask B, besides Word

Proceedings of the 11th International Workshop on Semantic Evaluations (SemEval-2017), pages 365–369,
Vancouver, Canada, August 3 - 4, 2017. ©2017 Association for Computational Linguistics

Match, Topic Model based, and Lexical Semantic Similarity features, we also extracted Search Engine Extensional feature. For subtask C, we ranked the comments by multiplying the probability of the pair "relevant question – comment" being Good by the reciprocal rank of the related question.

2.1 Features Engineering

All three subtasks can be regarded as an estimation task of sentence semantic measures which can be modeled by various types of features. Besides Word Match, Topic Model Based, Lexical Semantic Similarity, and Comment Information Features used in our previous work (Wu and Lan, 2016), we also extract three types of novel features, i.e., Meta Data Features, Google Ranking Feature, and Search Engine Extensional Features. The details of features are described as follows. Here we took the Q-Q pair for example.

Word Matching Feature (WM): Inspired by the work of (Zhao et al., 2015), we adopt word matching feature in our system. This feature represents the the proportions of co-occurred words that between a given sentence pair. Given a Q-Q pair, this feature is expressed in the following nine measures: $|Q_0 \cap Q_1|, |Q_0 \cap Q_1|/|Q_0|, |Q_0 \cap Q_1|/|Q_1|, |Q_1 - Q_0|/|Q_1|, |Q_0 - Q_1|/|Q_0|, |Q_0 \cap Q_1|/|Q_0 - Q_1|, |Q_0 \cap Q_1|/|Q_1 - Q_0|, |Q_0 \cap Q_1|/|Q_0 \cup Q_1|, 2*|Q_0 \cap Q_1|/(|Q_0|+|Q_1|)$, where $|Q_0|$ and $|Q_1|$ are the number of the words of Q_0 and Q_1.

Topic Model based Feature (TMB): Topic model based feature has been proved beneficial for question retrieval and answer ranking tasks by the work of (Duan et al., 2008; Qin et al., 2009). We use the *GibbsLDA++* (Phan and Nguyen, 2007) Toolkit with 100,000 random sampling question and answer pairs from Qatar Living data to train the topic model. In training and test phase, Q_0 and Q_1 are transformed into an 100-dimensional topic-based vectors using pre-trained topic model. After that we calculate the cosine similarity, Manhattan distance and Euclidean distance between these two vectors and regard the scores as TMB feature. Inspired by the work of (Filice et al., 2016), we also adopt four kinds of nonlinear kernel functions to calculate the distance between two vectors, i.e., "polynomial", "rbf", "laplacian" and "sigmoid".

Lexical Semantic Similarity Feature (LSS): Inspired by (Yih et al., 2013a), we included the lexical semantic similarity feature in our model. Two types of 300-dimensional vectors are pre-trained on Qatar Living data with word2vec (Yih et al., 2013b) and Glove (Pennington et al., 2014) toolkits. We select the maximum, minimum and average values for each dimension of words vectors to make up a vector to represent the sentence. After obtained the vector representation of Q_0 and Q_1, we also calculated the nine distance measures mentioned in **TMB**.

Note that all above three types of features are adopted in both answer ranking and question retrieval tasks.

Search Engine Extensional Feature (SEE):
We first got two lists of 10 snippets returned by search engine (i.e., Google, Bing) with the subjects of original question Q_0 and related question Q_1 as query. Then we counted the frequency of each word in each snippets list and added the words which appear in the Q_1/Q_0 and the frequency is more than 1 to the subject of Q_0/Q_1. Finally, the *WM* features are calculated based the changed subjects of Q_0 and Q_1.

Google Ranking Feature (GR): The reciprocal rank of the related question as given by Google is regarded as one dimensional feature.

Meta Data Feature (MD): Meta data is often helpful for finding good answers and question category distribution of user posted answers is an important meta data information. There are 28 question categories in the training data, we calculate the following values as features, i.e., the numbers of answers answered by all users in a certain category and the numbers of answers answered by a single user in all categories are normalized using max-min scaling, forming two 28-dimensional vectors. We also take the quality (i.e., Good, PotentiallyUseful, and Bad) of answers into consideration. The numbers of different quality answers answered by all users under a category and the numbers of different quality answers answered by a users in all categories are normalized using max-min scaling, forming two 3*28-dimensional vectors.

Comment Information Feature (CI):
We also extracted following comment information features to measure the informativeness of a comment text: (1) comment unigram feature, we constructed a vocabulary with the words appeared more than twice in the training data, generating a 9000-dimensional vector of one-hot for-

m for each comment. (2) comment ner feature, we extracted nine types of name entity information in the comment, i.e., "Duration", "Location", "Person", "Organization", "Percent", "Ordinal", "Time", "Date", and "Money" with the *CoreNLP* tool, generating a nine-dimensional one-hot forming vector. (3) comment special characters feature, We extracted the following five special characters features from the comment, i.e., email, url, "@", "...", and "?", generating a 5-dimensional vector of one-hot form for every comment.

Note that **MD** and **CI** features are used in answer ranking task only. **GR** and **SEE** features are used in question retrieval task only.

2.2 CNN to address subtask A

We proposed a convolutional neural network to model question-comment sentence. As illustrated in Figure 1, it first takes the embeddings (here we used 300-dimensional Glove vectors) (Pennington et al., 2014) of question and comment words as inputs and then summarizes the meaning of question and comment through convolution and pooling. Finally the softmax output of *Good* classes is regarded as ranking score between question and comment by a simple hidden layer building on the concatenation of two feature vectors and softmax operation. For CNN model, we set the filter numbers as 1,2,3 and 4 with same feature map of 100 and the stochastic gradient descent algorithm is used to update the parameters with learning rate of 0.001 and cross entropy as loss function.

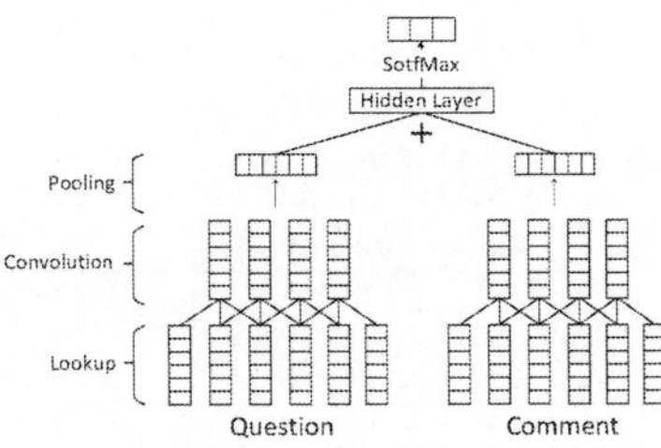

Figure 1: An illustration of CNN for question-comment similarity estimation.

3 Experimental Setting

3.1 Datasets

Table 1 shows the statistics of training, development, test data sets of SemEval 2016 and test data sets of SemEval 2017, where the #_ original, #_ related, and #_ answers represent the number of original questions, related questions and answers, respectively. The types of comments with respect to original question and related question fall into three classes: *Good*, *PotentiallyUseful* and *Bad*. The types of related question with respect to original question fall into three classes: *PerfectMatch*, *Relevant* and *Irrelevant*.

Subtask	Data	#_original	#_related	#_answers
A	train	–	5,898	37,848
	dev	–	500	5,000
	2016 test	–	327	3,270
	2017 test	–	293	2,930
B	train	267	2,669	26,690
	dev	50	500	5,000
	2016 test	70	700	7,000
	2017 test	88	880	8,800
C	train	267	2,669	26,690
	dev	50	500	5,000
	2016 test	70	700	7,000
	2017 test	88	880	8,800

Table 1: Statistics of datasets.

3.2 Preprocessing

Firstly, we removed stop words and punctuation, and changed words to their lowercase. After that, we performed tokenization and stemming using NLTK[1] Toolkit.

3.3 Learning Algorithm

We compared various machine learning algorithms such as Logistic Regression, Random Forest and AdaBoost implemented by SKLearn[2] with default parameters setting for their good performance in preliminary experiments. The probabilistic scores of *PerfectMatch* and *Good* classes returned by classifiers are regarded as ranking scores of question-question pair and question-comment pair. According to their performances with diverse features in three subtasks, they are used in different subtasks in our final submitted results.

4 Experiments on Training Data

4.1 Results on Subtask A

Table 2 shows the results of subtask A with two different methods on SemEval 2016 Test data sets.

---

[1] http://www.nltk.org/
[2] http://scikit-learn.org/stable/

Methods	Features	Test MAP(%)
Traditional NLP Features	All	77.82
	All - WM	76.60
	All - TMB	77.46
	All - MD	73.53
	All - CI	76.56
	All - LSS	76.43
CNN	–	77.76
Tra + CNN	–	**79.30**

Table 2: Results of subtask A with two different methods. "All" means to all features and "-" means to exclude some feature groups.

4.2 Results on Subtask B

Table 3 summarizes the results of subtask B on SemEval 2016 Test data sets with different features and algorithms.

Features	Algorithms		
	LR	AdaBoost	RandomForest
All	**75.43**	75.14	74.85
All - WM	74.31	74.78	74.14
All - GR	71.33	73.43	71.33
All - TMB	74.34	74.65	74.25
All - SEE	72.34	73.65	74.10
All - LSS	73.65	74.51	74.21

Table 3: Results of subtask B.

4.3 Results on Subtask C

Table 2 shows the results of subtask C with different algorithms and features on SemEval 2016 Test data sets.

Features	Algorithms		
	AdaBoost	Random Forest	LR
All	52.04	50.89	48.39
All - WM	51.70	50.63	47.59
All - TMB	51.82	49.05	47.59
All - MD	**52.35**	50.90	49.12
All - CI	49.19	48.93	46.75
All - LSS	50.54	49.48	47.73

Table 4: Results of subtask C.

4.4 Conclusion on Experimental results

Based on above experimental results, we find that

(1) For subtask A, all the features (e.g., WM, TMB, MD, CI and LSS) make contribution to the improvement of performance. The CNN based model achieves comparable performance with traditional method and with the average value of scores returned by two methods as ranking score achieves the best performance.

(2) For subtask B, three algorithms such as Logistic Regression, AdaBoost and Random Forest achieve comparable results with traditional NLP features. Specially, LR with all features achieve the best performance.

(3) For subtask C, AdaBoost with all features (excluding MD feature) makes the best result compared with Random Forest and Logistic Regression.

4.5 Systems Configuration

Based on above experimental analysis, the three system configurations on SemEval 2017 Test data sets are listed as followings:

(1) subtask A: We used the combination of traditional method and CNN as primary run. Traditional method and CNN serve as contrastive1 run and contrastive2 run.

(2) subtask B: Logistic Regression with all NLP features is used as primary run. AdaBoost and Random Forest with all NLP features are used as contrastive1 run and contrastive2 run.

(3) subtask C: AdaBoost with all NLP features is used as primary run in the test set. Random Forest and Logistic Regression with all NLP features are used as contrastive1 run and contrastive2 run.

5 Results on 2017 Test Data

Table 5 shows the results on SemEval 2017 test set which are released by the organizers.

subtask	run(rank)	MAP(%)
A	ECNU-primary(4)	86.72
	ECNU-contrastive1	86.78
	ECNU-contrastive2	83.15
	Kelp-primary(1)	88.43
B	ECNU-primary(11)	41.37
	ECNU-contrastive1	42.37
	ECNU-contrastive2	42.48
	simbow-primary(1)	47.22
C	ECNU-primary(5)	10.54
	ECNU-contrastive1	10.54
	ECNU-contrastive2	13.29
	IIT-UHH-primary(1)	15.46

Table 5: Our results and the best results on three subtasks test sets. The numbers in the brackets are the official ranking.

From the results, we find: (1) In subtask A, the combination of two methods does not make obvious contribution and the CNN based method has a certain gap with traditional method, which is inconsistent with the results on training data as our expectation. (2) In subtask B, the result using LR does not make expected result compared with AdaBoost and Random Forest algorithms. (3) In subtask C, beyond our expectation, the method using LR algorithm achieved the best result.

6 Conclusion

In this paper, we proposed multiple strategies (i.e., traditional method of extracting features and deep learning models) to address Community Question Answering task in SemEval 2017. For subtask A, we train a classifier and learn the question-comment representation based CNN. For subtask B, we we utilized the information of snippets searching from Search Engine with question as query. For subtask C, We ranked the comments by multiplying the probability of the pair "relevant question – comment" being Good by the reciprocal rank of the related question.

Acknowledgments

This research is supported by grants from Science and Technology Commission of Shanghai Municipality (14DZ2260800 and 15ZR1410700), Shanghai Collaborative Innovation Center of Trustworthy Software for Internet of Things (ZF1213) and NSFC (61402175)

References

Huizhong Duan, Yunbo Cao, Chin-Yew Lin, and Yong Yu. 2008. Searching questions by identifying question topic and question focus. In *ACL*, pages 156–164.

Simone Filice, Danilo Croce, Alessandro Moschitti, and Roberto Basili. 2016. Kelp at semeval-2016 task 3: Learning semantic relations between questions and answers. In *Proceedings of the 10th International Workshop on Semantic Evaluation (SemEval-2016)*, pages 1116–1123, San Diego, California, June. Association for Computational Linguistics.

Preslav Nakov, Doris Hoogeveen, Lluís Màrquez, Alessandro Moschitti, Hamdy Mubarak, Timothy Baldwin, and Karin Verspoor. 2017. SemEval-2017 task 3: Community question answering. In *Proceedings of the 11th International Workshop on Semantic Evaluation*, SemEval '17, Vancouver, Canada, August. Association for Computational Linguistics.

Jeffrey Pennington, Richard Socher, and Christopher D. Manning. 2014. Glove: Global vectors for word representation. In *Proceedings of the 2014 Conference on Empirical Methods in Natural Language Processing (EMNLP 2014)*, pages 1532–1543.

Xuan-Hieu Phan and Cam-Tu Nguyen. 2007. Gibbslda++: Ac/c++ implementation of latent dirichlet allocation (lda).

Zengchang Qin, Marcus Thint, and Zhiheng Huang. 2009. Ranking answers by hierarchical topic models. In *Next-Generation Applied Intelligence*, pages 103–112. Springer.

Guoshun Wu and Man Lan. 2016. Ecnu at semeval-2016 task 3: Exploring traditional method and deep learning method for question retrieval and answer ranking in community question answering. In *Proceedings of the 10th International Workshop on Semantic Evaluation (SemEval-2016)*, pages 872–878, San Diego, California, June. Association for Computational Linguistics.

Wen-tau Yih, Ming-Wei Chang, Christopher Meek, and Andrzej Pastusiak. 2013a. Question answering using enhanced lexical semantic models.

Wen-tau Yih, Ming-Wei Chang, Christopher Meek, and Andrzej Pastusiak. 2013b. Question answering using enhanced lexical semantic models. In *Proceedings of the 51st Annual Meeting of the Association for Computational Linguistics (Volume 1: Long Papers)*, pages 1744–1753, Sofia, Bulgaria, August. Association for Computational Linguistics.

Jiang Zhao, Man Lan, and Jun Feng Tian. 2015. Ecnu: Using traditional similarity measurements and word embedding for semantic textual similarity estimation. In *Proceedings of the 9th International Workshop on Semantic Evaluation (SemEval 2015)*, pages 117–122, Denver, Colorado, June. Association for Computational Linguistics.

UINSUSKA-TiTech at SemEval-2017 Task 3: Exploiting Word Importance Levels for Similarity Features for CQA

Surya Agustian[1,2] and **Hiroya Takamura**[2]

[1]Teknik Informatika, UIN Sultan Syarif Kasim Riau, Indonesia

[1]Computational Intelligence & System Science, Tokyo Institute of Technology, Japan

[2]Institute of Innovative Research, Tokyo Institute of Technology, Japan

sagustian{@uin-suska.ac.id, @lr.pi.titech.ac.jp}, takamura@pi.titech.ac.jp

Abstract

The majority of core techniques to solve many problems in Community Question Answering (CQA) task rely on similarity computation. This work focuses on similarity between two sentences (or questions in subtask B) based on word embeddings. We exploit words importance levels in sentences or questions for similarity features, for classification and ranking with machine learning. Using only 2 types of similarity metric, our proposed method has shown comparable results with other complex systems. This method on subtask B 2017 dataset is ranked on position 7 out of 13 participants. Evaluation on 2016 dataset is on position 8 of 12, outperforms some complex systems. Further, this finding is explorable and potential to be used as baseline and extensible for many tasks in CQA and other textual similarity based system.

1 Introduction

Community Question Answering (CQA) is getting popular for requesting valid information from experienced people. However, waiting for such favorable answers for a new submitted question, is a boring task for users once querying to online community forums. IR system can utilize thread in online community forum for question queries. Even so, the appropriate answers are often mixed among snippets of many irrelevant documents, and opening full articles is still required. A post-processing system is needed in order to obtain the most relevant answers. CQA tasks want to address this need, to help user get the most favorable answers by improving IR system results.

SemEval CQA Task 3 is designed to gather some possible solutions, in five coherent subtasks (Nakov et al., 2017). Since some subtasks are related, we focus only on subtask B, with goal to provide a good basis framework for solving problem in other subtasks.

In Task 3 of the previous year, word embeddings obtained with a tool such as word2vec (Mikolov et al., 2013, 2013b) contributed to the best systems for all subtasks. In addition, machine learning based methods were mostly ranked in the top positions for all subtasks. The most popular machine learning approach was SVM for classification, regression and ranking, while neural networks, even though widely used, did not win any subtasks (Nakov et al., 2016).

Most machine learning approaches rely on several similarity features as the basis. Various techniques to compute semantic similarity based on word embeddings, were used by Franco-Salvador et al. (2016), Filice et al. (2016), Mohtarami et al. (2016), Wu and Lan (2016), and Mihaylov and Nakov (2016). Besides, they also used various lexical and semantic similarities including simple match counts on words or n-grams. Specifically, Franco-Salvador et al. (2016), also used nouns and n-grams overlaps, distributed word alignments, knowledge graphs, and common frame.

Interestingly, Mihaylova et al. (2016) used cosine distance between topic pairs, and text distance for SVM learning features, rather than using similarity features. They also implemented other Boolean and Qatar Living Forum users as task specific features.

Filice et al. (2016) constructed many types of similarity based on text pairs, e.g. n-grams of word lemmas, n-grams of POS tags, parse tree, and LCS for SVM learning features. Then they stack the classifiers across subtasks to solve substasks B and C in such a way that utilizes other subtasks' results. This task-specific features seem to be the key success for the team to get the relatively best performance on all English subtasks.

Proceedings of the 11th International Workshop on Semantic Evaluations (SemEval-2017), pages 370–374,
Vancouver, Canada, August 3 - 4, 2017. ©2017 Association for Computational Linguistics

In this CQA task, we focus on machine learning approaches with a small number of features. We attempt to find an effective way to use word embeddings as the basis of our similarity features. We also make use of the words (lemmas) that are frequent in a thread or small document collection (i.e. the original and the 10 related questions), in the calculation of similarity between sentences. We create several sets of words with different 'word importance levels', from which we derive similarity features for machine learning methods.

The experiment on this 2017 shared task (subtask B) shows good results with respect to MAP scores. Our method also surpasses IR baseline and achieved the 7th position out of 13 teams for the primary submission.

2 System Description

The framework of our system contains three main phases, i.e. (1) pre-processing, (2) feature generation, and (3) training and classification.

2.1 Pre-processing

From each dataset, i.e. development, train and test sets, we extract the questions to form threads for subtask B. Each thread contains one original question (orgQ) and the 10 related questions (relQ). We use the term 'collection of documents' for the thread, which contains questions (each with subject and body[1]) as the documents.

From each collection of documents, we extract all lemmas and select only content words: nouns, verbs, adjectives, named entities, question words, and foreign words. For this need we use lemmatizer, POS tagger and Named Entity Recognizer from Stanford CoreNLP (Manning et al., 2014). We also count each lemma's frequency in each collection of documents for each certain thread, not from the whole dataset.

Intuitively, in a QA forum, if the frequency of a word is high in a certain thread, the word is likely to be an important matter in the conversation discussed by majority users. For this reason, we rank the words by their frequencies. We list top-N rank of words[2] for next process. In our experiments, we set N to 4.

2.2 Word Importance Level

We first derive several sets of content words from orgQ$_{subj}$ (the set of words in the subject of orgQ), orgQ$_{body}$ (the set of words in the body of orgQ), and TopN consisting the top N words in the ranking obtained in Section 2.1. Specifically, the following sets are supposed to have different levels of importance:

L1=$orgQ_{sub} \cap TopN$,
L2=$TopN \cap (orgQ_{sub} \cup orgQ_{body})$,
L3=$TopN$,
L4=$orgQ_{sub} \cup TopN$,
L5=$orgQ_{sub} \cup orgQ_{body}$,
L6=$\neg(TopN \cap (orgQ_{sub} \cup orgQ_{body}))$.

For example, the words in L1 belong to both set of orgQ-subject and TopN, and thus supposed to be very important.

2.3 Similarity Feature

We next calculate a number of similarities between two sets of content words: C_{orgQ} representing orgQ such as L1 and L2, and C_{relQ} representing relQ such as relQ$_{sub}$, relQ$_{body}$, and their union. We later use these similarities as features for the classifier as in Table 1.

Semantic Similarity

The first semantic similarity type in this work is the cosine similarity (Equation (2)) between the sums (resultant R as in Equation (1)) of word embeddings of the words w in the sets.

$$R = \sum_{i=1}^{n} w_i \tag{1}$$

$$Sim(C_{orgQ}, C_{relQ}) = cos\theta = \frac{R_{orgQ} \cdot R_{relQ}}{|R_{orgQ}||R_{relQ}|} \tag{2}$$

As word embeddings, we use the pre-trained Google 1B words dataset, with 300-dimensional word vectors (Mikolov et al., 2013b).

Lexical Semantic Similarity

For the second type of similarity, we use lexical semantic similarity, which is similar to Konopík et al. (2016). We denote the union of C_{orgQ} and C_{relQ} by C (i.e., $C = C_{orgQ} \cup C_{relQ}$, which consists of m unique words $\{b_1, ..., b_m\}$.

Given two sets C_{orgQ} and C_{relQ}, we derive their m-dimensional lexical vector representations LV_{orgQ} and LV_{relQ} respectively. For each word b_i in C, we calculate the maximum cosine similar-

---

[1] If body is empty, we copy the subject for the body.
[2] Only words with frequency count $\geq$ 2 are taken into consideration.

ity score between the embeddings of b_i and a word in C_{orgQ}, which we regard as an element of LV_{orgQ}:

$$LV_{orgQ} = \left\{ \max_{w \in C_{orgQ}} \left(Sim(b_1, w)\right), \dots, \max_{w \in C_{orgQ}} \left(Sim(b_m, w)\right)\right\}. \tag{3}$$

Similarly, we calculate each element of LV_{relQ} from C_{relQ}. Lastly, we calculate the cosine similarity between LV_{orgQ} and LV_{relQ} to form a new feature.

2.4 Feature Generation

For our supervised learning, we compose feature sets as Table 1 below. Semantic cosine similarity is indexed with i in $\{1, \dots, 10\}$ and lexical semantic similarity with j in $\{11, \dots, 20\}$.

F_i	F_j	C_{orgQ}	C_{relQ}
F_1	F_{11}	L1	$relQ_{sub}$
F_2	F_{12}	L1	$relQ_{sub} \cup relQ_{body}$
F_3	F_{13}	L3	$relQ_{sub}$
F_4	F_{14}	L3	$relQ_{sub} \cup relQ_{body}$
F_5	F_{15}	L4	$relQ_{sub}$
F_6	F_{16}	L4	$relQ_{sub} \cup relQ_{body}$
F_7	F_{17}	L5	$relQ_{sub} \cup relQ_{body}$
F_8	F_{18}	L6	$relQ_{sub} \cup relQ_{body}$
F_9	F_{19}	L2	$relQ_{sub} \cup relQ_{body}$
F_{10}	F_{20}	NE	$relQ_{sub} \cup relQ_{body}$

Table 1: Similarity Feature Composition

As additional features, we investigated influence of named entities (NE) in F_{10} and F_{20}. We extract only sentences or questions containing NE-words in orgQ subject and body as C_{orgQ}.

2.5 Learning, Classification and Ranking

We use machine learning for relevance classification and ranking tasks on the same feature combinations. We extract gold annotations (i.e., relevance and score) from the training set and compose separate SVM input files for both tasks. We run the training to produce models for both tasks.

For classification task, SVM binary classifier with a linear kernel (Joachims, 1999) is used to assign label on each relQ, relevant (true) or not relevant (false) on the test set. For ranking task, SVM rank (Joachims, 2002) is used to produce scores. The score assigned to each relQ is regarded as rank, where a higher score means more related to the orgQ. Then, we take both results (relevance and score) into a system prediction file.

3 Experiments and Results

3.1 Dataset

We use 2016 Task 3 datasets provided by the organizer[3], i.e. TRAIN-part1, DEV and TEST. We do not use TRAIN-part2 for it is less reliable and contains more noise as informed in the readme-file. We also conduct experiments on TEST-2016 dataset to test our system performance and compare it with the published official scores in Nakov et al. (2016) as seen in Table 4.

3.2 Feature Selection

We create a simple baseline, which uses only a single similarity feature. This baseline only computes semantic cosine similarity of F_7, i.e. using all content words in orgQ and relQ (word importance level L5). For tuning the parameters and seeking the best combination of features, we train SVM with a linear kernel on TRAIN dataset, and applied the model on DEV dataset. We choose two best cost-parameters C with specific feature combinations in Table 2.

Features	Feature Description	$C=1$	$C=100$
7	Base (L5)	69.56	69.56
7,8	Base (L5) + L6	69.76	68.23
7,6	Base (L5) + L4	69.73	69.72
7,4	Base (L5) + L3	69.31	70.06
7,9	Base (L5) + L2	71.09	70.37
7,2	Base (L5) + L1	72.06	72.30
7,1,2	L5+ L1* + L1	70.86	72.09
7,1,2,9	L5+ L1* + L1 + L2	72.33	72.50
7,1,2,9, 17,11,12,19	L5+ L1* + L1 + L2 (both similarity types)	72.26	73.10
1-20	All features, both sim types	**74.04**	**73.19**

L1* means the similarity is computed between L1 and relQ subject only.

Table 2: MAP Scores on DEV

The official score for CQA Task is MAP (Mean Average Precision), besides other complementary scores, i.e. Average Recall, MRR (Mean Reciprocal Rank) Precision, Recall, F_1 and Accuracy (Nakov et al., 2016, 2017).

To analyze the influence of each feature, we conducted experiments on many possible combinations as in Table 2. We combine each word important level from the lowest level (i.e. L6, L4, L3, L2, L1), with baseline (L5) and see how it influences the MAP score. Generally, by combining with other single word importance level features,

---

[3] http://alt.qcri.org/semeval2017/task3/index.php?id=data-and-tools

the MAP score is increased. Combined feature set $F_{7,9}$, i.e. word important level L2 (top-N words appear in orgQ subject and body) improves the MAP score by about 1 point when compared with single baseline feature L5. Moreover, we get more improvement when baseline is combined with word important level L1, i.e. top-N words in orgQ subject only (experiment with feature set $F_{7,2}$).

We are also curious to join more word importance level features, to compute using both similarity types, and to use different content words of relQ, e.g. content words that appear in subject only or in both subject and body. Some interesting results are also reported in Table 2.

When adding the similarity between L1 and relQ subject only ($F_{7,1,2}$), the MAP score slightly decreases for C=100, but decreases by more than 1 point for C=1. Interestingly, adding one more feature from L2 ($F_{7,1,2,9}$), gives the better score than the aforementioned features.

L1 and L2 tend to have higher influence on the MAP score, compared with L3, L4, and L6. When combining with their lexical semantic similarity features ($F_{7,1,2,9,17,11,12,19}$), L1 and L2 increase MAP score for C=100, but a little bit decrease the score for C=1. Considering that each of L3 to L6 has its own contribution to the improvement of the baseline, we incorporate all features and use both similarity types. The results give the two best MAP scores among all our experiments in this parameter tuning and feature selection phase.

3.3 Final Results

For our participation in Subtask B, we use combination of F_1 - F_{20}, and TRAIN-part1 for training. We choose C=1 and C=100, as the primary and contrastive Con-1 respectively. For contrastive Con-2, we use C=1 and join TRAIN-part1+TEST-2016 for training.

Method	MAP	AvgR	MRR	P	R	F_1	Acc
IR	41.85	77.59	46.42	-	-	-	-
Best	**47.22**	82.60	50.07	27.30	94.48	42.37	52.39
Lowest	40.56	76.67	46.33	36.55	53.37	43.39	74.20
Random	29.81	62.65	33.02	18.72	75.46	30.00	34.77
Primary	43.44	77.50	47.03	35.71	67.48	46.71	71.48
Con-1	44.29	78.59	48.97	34.47	68.10	45.77	70.11
Con-2	43.06	76.45	46.22	35.71	67.48	46.71	71.48

Table 3: Final Result on Task B

Our system achieved the 7th position out of 13 teams for the primary submission with MAP score is 43.44. Our contrastive-1 has the best score

among our three submissions, i.e. 44.29, which is nearly about 1 point higher than the primary submission.

Method	MAP	AvgR	MRR	P	R	F_1	Acc
IR	74.75	88.30	83.79	-	-	-	-
Best	**76.70**	90.31	83.02	63.53	69.53	66.39	76.57
Lowest	69.04	84.53	79.55	39.53	64.81	49.11	55.29
Random	46.98	67.92	50.96	40.43	32.58	73.82	45.20
Con-1	72.49	87.77	81.95	64.32	58.88	61.43	75.43

Table 4: Experiment on SemEval 2016 subtask B

We also conduct experiment to test our system performance on TEST-2016 dataset. We use model from TRAIN-part1 dataset training with C=100 (our best result as in Table 3, i.e. Constrastive-1). In respect of previous year results, this result achieved the 8th position out of 12 teams, if it is put into the leaderboard. In respect of the scores, our results in the 2017 and 2016 dataset are consistently in the middle range between the top and the lowest MAP score as seen in Table 4.

4 Conclusion and Future Work

As many CQA tasks rely on similarity measure as the basis, utilizing word importance classes in such a way for semantic similarity metrics can increase the MAP score significantly. Taking into consideration the top-n words in a thread, can contribute to find alternative words, which are unseen in the original question.

Our future work is to implement this method as baseline for other subtasks, and later combine with rich features, which involve various task-specific operations to solve the main problem in CQA.

Acknowledgements

First author would like to acknowledge the Indonesia Endowment Fund for Education (LPDP), Ministry of Finance of the Republic of Indonesia who support his study and research in Japan.

We also would like to thank Prof. Manabu Okumura for the generous support on writing this paper.

References

Guoshun Wu and Man Lan. 2016. *ECNU at SemEval-2016 Task 3: Exploring traditional method and deep learning method for question retrieval and answer ranking in community question answering.*

In Proceedings of the 10th International Workshop on Semantic Evaluation, SemEval '16, San Diego, CA. https://aclweb.org/anthology/S/S16/S16-1135.pdf

Manning, Christopher D., Mihai Surdeanu, John Bauer, Jenny Finkel, Steven J. Bethard, and David McClosky. 2014. *The Stanford CoreNLP Natural Language Processing Toolkit*. In Proceedings of the 52nd Annual Meeting of the Association for Computational Linguistics: System Demonstrations, pp. 55-60.

Marc Franco-Salvador, Sudipta Kar, Thamar Solorio, and Paolo Rosso. 2016. *UH-PRHLT at SemEval-2016 Task 3: Combining lexical and semantic-based features for community question answering*. In Proceedings of the 10th International Workshop on Semantic Evaluation, SemEval '16, San Diego, CA. https://aclweb.org/anthology/S/S16/S16-1126.pdf

Mitra Mohtarami, Yonatan Belinkov, Wei-Ning Hsu, Yu Zhang, Tao Lei, Kfir Bar, Scott Cyphers, and Jim Glass. 2016. *SLS at SemEval-2016 Task 3: Neuralbased approaches for ranking in community question answering*. In Proceedings of the 10th International Workshop on Semantic Evaluation, SemEval '16, San Diego, CA.
https://aclweb.org/anthology/S/S16/S16-1128.pdf

Miloslav Konopík, Ondrej Prazak, David Steinberger, and Tomáš Brychcín. 2016. *UWB at semeval-2016 task 2: Interpretable semantic textual similarity with distributional semantics for chunks*. In Proceedings of the 10th International Workshop on Semantic Evaluation (SemEval 2016), San Diego, California, June. Association for Computational Linguistics.
https://aclweb.org/anthology/S/S16/S16-1124.pdf

Preslav Nakov, Lluís Màrquez, Walid Magdy, Alessandro Moschitti, Jim Glass, and Bilal Randeree. 2016. *SemEval-2016 Task 3: Community Question Answering*. In Proceedings of the 10th International Workshop on Semantic Evaluation, SemEval '16, San Diego, California, June. Association for Computational Linguistics.
https://aclweb.org/anthology/S/S16/S16-1083.pdf

Preslav Nakov, Doris Hoogeveen, Lluís Màrquez, Alessandro Moschitti, Hamdy Mubarak, Timothy Baldwin, and Karin Verspoor. 2017. *SemEval-2017 Task 3: Community Question Answering*. In Pro ceedings of the 11th International Workshop on Semantic Evaluation, SemEval '17, Vancouver, Canada, August. Association for Computational Linguistics.

Simone Filice, Danilo Croce, Alessandro Moschitti, and Roberto Basili. 2016. *KeLP at SemEval-2016 Task 3: Learning semantic relations between questions and answers*. In Proceedings of the 10th In-

ternational Workshop on Semantic Evaluation, SemEval '16, San Diego, CA.
https://aclweb.org/anthology/S/S16/S16-1172.pdf

T. Joachims. 2002. *Optimizing Search Engines Using Clickthrough Data*, Proceedings of the ACM Conference on Knowledge Discovery and Data Mining (KDD), ACM, 2002.

T. Joachims, 1999 in: *Making large-Scale SVM Learning Practical*. Advances in Kernel Methods - Support Vector Learning, B. Schölkopf and C. Burges and A. Smola (ed.), MIT Press, 1999.

Todor Mihaylov and Preslav Nakov. 2016. *SemanticZ at SemEval-2016 Task 3: Ranking relevant answers in community question answering using semantic similarity based on fine-tuned word embeddings*. In Proceedings of the 10th International Workshop on Semantic Evaluation, SemEval '16, San Diego, CA. https://aclweb.org/anthology/S/S16/S16-1136.pdf

Tomas Mikolov, Kai Chen, Greg Corrado, and Jeffrey Dean. 2013. *Efficient Estimation of Word Representations in Vector Space*. In Proceedings of Workshop at ICLR, 2013.

Tomas Mikolov, Ilya Sutskever, Kai Chen, Greg Corrado, and Jeffrey Dean. 2013b. *Distributed Representations of Words and Phrases and their Compositionality*. In Proceedings of NIPS, 2013.

Tsvetomila Mihaylova, Pepa Gencheva, Martin Boyanov, Ivana Yovcheva, Todor Mihaylov, Momchil Hardalov, Yasen Kiprov, Daniel Balchev, Ivan Koychev, Preslav Nakov, Ivelina Nikolova, and Galia Angelova. 2016. SUper Team at SemEval-2016 Task 3: Building a feature-rich system for community question answering. In Proceedings of the 10th International Workshop on Semantic Evaluation, SemEval '16, San Diego, CA. https://aclweb.org/anthology/S/S16/S16-1129.pdf

Talla at SemEval-2017 Task 3: Identifying Similar Questions Through Paraphrase Detection

Byron V. Galbraith, Bhanu Pratap, Daniel Shank

Talla

Boston, MA, USA

`{byron, bhanu, daniel}@talla.com`

Abstract

This paper describes our approach to the SemEval-2017 shared task of determining question-question similarity in a community question-answering setting (Task 3B). We extracted both syntactic and semantic similarity features between candidate questions, performed pairwise-preference learning to optimize for ranking order, and then trained a random forest classifier to predict whether the candidate questions were paraphrases of each other. This approach achieved a MAP of 45.7% out of max achievable 67.0% on the test set.

1 Introduction

A large amount of information of interest to users of community forums is stored in semi-structured text, but surfacing that information can be challenging given the variety of ways users can phrase their search queries. Question-answering is a significant task for both natural language processing (NLP) and information retrieval (IR), as both the actual terms used in the query plus the semantic intent of the query itself need to be accounted for in surfacing relevant potential answers. The Community Question Answering (cQA) task of SemEval-2017 (Nakov et al., 2017) seeks to address this problem through several related subtasks around effectively determining and ranking the relevance of related stored questions and associated answers.

We chose to focus on subtask B: question-question similarity. This problem can be seen as one of paraphrase detection – determine if two questions have the same meaning. We reviewed existing performant paraphrase detection methods and selected several to implement and ensemble (Ji and Eisenstein, 2013; Wan et al., 2006; Wang and Ittycheriah, 2015; Filice et al., 2015) along with the related question IR system rank provided in the dataset. As paraphrase detection is a classification problem while subtask B is a ranking problem, we also incorporated pairwise-preference learning (Joachims, 2002; Fürnkranz and Hüllermeier, 2003) to aid in improving the key metric of mean average precision (MAP).

The rest of the paper is organized as follows. Section 2 provides a detailed description of our system, including the key identified features that were extracted, while Section 3 provides the results from experiments used to evaluate the system. Section 4 concludes the paper with a summary of the work and directions for future exploration.

2 System Description

Our approach consisted of four parts: data preparation, feature extraction, pairwise-preference learning, and paraphrase classification. All code was implemented in Python 3.5. For data extraction, we converted the XML documents provided by (Nakov et al., 2017) into pandas DataFrames, retaining the subject text, body text, and metadata related to the original and related questions. The feature extraction and the pairwise-preference learning phase are described below. Classification was handled with a random forest classifier containing 2000 weak estimators.

2.1 Feature Extraction

We computed features as described in several leading paraphrase detection method papers. One of which, fine-grained textual features (Wan et al., 2006), failed to produce any significant value during further evaluation for this task and so were discarded. In addition to the paraphrase detection features, we also incorporated the reciprocal of the

Proceedings of the 11th International Workshop on Semantic Evaluations (SemEval-2017), pages 375–379,
Vancouver, Canada, August 3 - 4, 2017. ©2017 Association for Computational Linguistics

reported IR system rank of the related question as an additional feature.

Unless otherwise noted, question texts for feature extraction were created by concatenating the subject and body fields of the question, all terms were made lowercase, and stop words were removed.

2.1.1 Tree Kernels

Tree kernel (TK) features (Filice et al., 2015) were derived by generating parse trees of the two sentences, then defining a kernel that allows for a numerical distance to be computed. The kernel takes all possible valid (not necessarily terminal) partial tree structures within the sentence parse trees and counts the amount of overlap between the two. The result is a score for every pair of sentences.

The kernel function $K(S_1, S_2)$ for two trees S_1 and S_2 is defined as follows:

$$K(S_1, S_2) = \sum_{n_1 \in N_{S_1}} \sum_{n_2 \in N_{S_2}} \Delta(n_1, n_2)$$

where $\Delta(n_1, n_2)$ is the Partial Tree Kernel (PTK) function as defined in (Filice et al., 2015). A standard kernel norm is then applied, given by:

$$\frac{K(S_1, S_2)}{\sqrt{K(S_1, S_1)K(S_2, S_2)}}.$$

We computed distances for both constituency trees and dependency trees. For constituency parse trees, words that occur in both sentences were marked along with their part of speech in order to increase the effect of shared terms belonging to similar subtrees. Dependency parse trees, on the other hand, were constructed so that non-leaf nodes are made up entirely of dependency types (rather than parts of speech). For example a single ROOT node may have nodes *nsubj* and *dobj* as children. Leaves were all tokens representing words themselves, and every interior node had a child that was a leaf. The final features produced were the result of the kernel applied to the constituency parse tree and that result multiplied by the result from the kernel applied to the dependency parse tree.

2.1.2 TF-KLD

TF-KLD (Term Frequency Kullback-Leibler Divergence) (Ji and Eisenstein, 2013) is a supervised TF weighting scheme based on modeling probability distributions of phrases being aligned with or without the presence of a particular term. More formally:

We assume labeled sentence pairs $\langle \vec{w}_i^{(2)}, \vec{w}_i^{(2)}, r_i \rangle$, where $\vec{w}_i^{(1)}$ is the binarized vector of bigram and unigram occurrence for the first sentence, $\vec{w}_i^{(2)}$ is the bigram and unigram occurrence vector for the second, and $r_i \in \{0, 1\}$ is an indicator of whether the two sentences match. We assume the order of the sentences are irrelevant, and for each feature with index k we define two Bernoulli distributions:

$$p_k = P(w_{ik}^{(1)} | w_{ik}^{(2)}, r_i = 1)$$

which is the probability that feature k appears in the first sentence given that k appears in the second and both are matched, and

$$q_k = P(w_{ik}^{(1)} | w_{ik}^{(2)}, r_i = 0)$$

which is the probability that feature k appears in the first sentence given that k appears in the second and both are not matched.

The Kullback-Leibler divergence is a premetric over probability distributions, defined as $KL(p_k || q_k) = \sum_x p_k(x) \log \frac{p_k(x)}{q_k(x)}$. We calculate a KLD score for each feature k, then use this to weight the vector of non-binarized occurrences. The sparse TF-KLD vector then undergoes dimensionality reduction by means of rank-100 nonnegative matrix factorization. Finally, the cosine similarity of individual vectors is taken to give a single feature for each pair of sentences.

2.1.3 Semantic Word Alignment

Semantic word alignment (WA) (Wang and Ittycheriah, 2015) used word embeddings to infer semantic similarity between documents at the individual word level. For embeddings we used the pre-trained 300-dimensional GloVe vectors (Pennington et al., 2014).

Given a source question Q and reference question R, let $Q = \{q_0, q_1, ..., q_m\}$ and $R = \{r_0, r_1, ..., r_n\}$ denote the words in each question text. First, the cosine-similarity between all pairs of the words (q_i, r_j) was computed to form a similarity matrix (Figure 1). Next we denote the word alignment position for each query word q_i as $align_i$, similarity score as sim_i, and the inverse document frequency as idf_i. Word alignment position $align_i$ for a query word q_i in Q w.r.t words in R is equal to the position of a word r_j in R at

	Submission	MAP	AvgRec	MRR	P	R	F1	Acc
	Talla-constrastive1	46.50	82.15	49.61	30.39	76.07	43.43	63.30
	Talla-contrastive2	46.31	81.81	49.14	29.88	74.23	42.61	62.95
4	**Talla-primary**	**45.70**$_4$	**81.48**$_2$	**49.55**$_5$	**29.59**$_9$	**76.07**$_8$	**42.61**$_8$	**62.05**$_8$
	Baseline 1 (IR)	41.85	77.59	46.42	-	-	-	-
	Baseline 2 (random)	29.81	62.65	33.02	18.72	75.46	30.00	34.77
	Baseline 3 (all 'true')	-	-	-	18.52	100.00	31.26	18.52
	Baseline 3 (all 'false')	-	-	-	-	-	-	81.48

Table 1: System performance on the SemEval-2017 test dataset

which q_i has maximum similarity score sim_i. Finally, we compute a set of distinct word alignment features as:

- **similarity:** $f_0 = \sum_i sim_i * idf_i / \sum_i idf_i$. This feature represents question similarity based on the aligned words.

- **dispersion:** $f_1 = \sum_i (|align_i - align_{i-1} - 1|)$. This feature is a measure of contiguously aligned words.

- **penalty:** If we denote the position of unaligned words (where $sim_i = 0$) as $unalign_i$, then this feature penalizes pairs with unaligned question words and was calculated as $f_2 = \sum_{unalign_i} idf_i / \sum_i idf_i$.

- **five important words:** $f_{i_{th}} = sim_{i_{th}} * idf_{i_{th}}$. This feature set included the similarity score of the top five important words in the question text, where importance of a word was based on its IDF score.

The first three features were computed in both directions i.e. for (Q_i, R_j) and (R_j, Q_i). The cosine similarity of the aggregate of all embeddings in the questions was also computed. This process was repeated separately for both question subjects and bodies (instead of on the combined concatenated text) for a total of 24 distinct features.

2.2 Pairwise-Preference Learning

Since the official evaluation metric for Subtask B was MAP, we adopted a ranking approach to indirectly optimize for MAP. Given an original question Q_i and its list of corresponding related questions $\{R_1, R_2, ..R_{10}\}$, we are interested in learning a ranking of this list, where relevant questions are ranked higher than irrelevant ones. An alternative way to learn this ranking is to classify if a pair from a set of pairs formed within one group,

	r_1	r_2	r_3	r_4	r_5	r_6
q_1	0.2	0.7	0	0	0	0.4
q_2	0	0.1	0.4	0.2	0	0
q_3	0.3	0.2	0	0	0.5	0

	r_1	r_2	r_3	r_4	r_5	r_6
q_1		X				
q_2			X			
q_3					X	

Figure 1: Word alignment matrix example. The upper table contains the cosine similarity scores between words in questions Q and R, while the lower table contains the corresponding word-alignment.

where a group is formed for each original question Q_i is correctly ordered or not. This principle is called "pairwise-preference learning" (Joachims, 2002; Fürnkranz and Hüllermeier, 2003).

To make use of this approach we transformed the datasets from question-question(or question-comment) pairs into a set of instance pairs. That is, we presented a pair of answers with one correct and one incorrect answer to the same question. Number of features were kept constant, while feature values were equal to the difference between the values of two answers in the instance pair.

In training phase, for each question group $(Q_i, \{R_1, R_2, ..R_{10}\})$ we generated labeled pairs as "correct-pair(Q_i, R_j) minus incorrect-pair(Q_i, R_k)" with label *true* and "incorrect-pair(Q_i, R_k) minus correct-pair(Q_i, R_j)" with label *false*. In this way, we generated $2 * (n_c + n_i)$ instance pairs for each question group, where n_c and n_i is the number of correct pairs and number of incorrect pairs within a group respectively.

In testing phase, number of instance pairs generated for a question group$(Q_i, \{R_1, R_2, ..R_{10}\})$ were equal to the number of all possible pairs within that question group. Then, our model assigned a probability to each of these instance pairs that it is correctly ordered. To create a final score for each related-question R_j, we took the sum of probabilities over all pairs in which R_j was ranked first. This final score was then used to create a ranked list of related-questions R_j for each original question Q_i.

3 Experiments and Evaluation

We combined the provided training and dev datasets as our system training set and used the provided SemEval-2016 test data with gold labels as our test set. No additional external data, other than pre-trained word embeddings, were used. We evaluated different classifier hyperparameters using 10-fold cross-validation and ultimately chose a random forest classifier with 2000 trees as our final model.

This system achieved fourth place overall (Table 1) on the SemEval-2017 test dataset, and while both contrastive submissions placed higher than the primary, nether was able to achieve a greater MAP than the third place entry. Contrastive1 was identical in feature set to the primary submission, but included the SemEval-2016 test dataset as part of the training data, suggesting that MAP can be improved by increasing the amount of examples used to train the system. Contrastive2 did not include the extra data and also omitted the TF-KLD features. Comparing the effects of ablating the other individual features (Table 2) across both SemEval-2016 and SemEval-2017 test datasets demonstrated that both the TF-KLD and TK features were minimally effective. The IR system features had a dramatic difference between the two years – in 2016 it accounted for a 0.022 gain in MAP, while in 2017 it produced a 0.010 reduction. In both cases the WA features contributed the most, with gains of 0.041 and 0.034, respectively.

Subtask B of Task 3 combines the PerfectMatch and Relevant classes into a single positive class for purposes of evaluation. Given that this approach treated question-question similarity as a paraphrase detection problem, the expectation was that this model would do better on the PerfectMatch and Irrelevant samples, but have a harder time with Relevant questions. This is seen in the SemEval-2016 data (Figure 2), where there is good separation between the computed pairwise-preference scores of Irrelevant and PerfectMatch

| | MAP | |
Features	2016	2017
Max	0.886	0.670
All features	0.781	0.457
All - TK	0.775	0.452
All - TF-KLD	0.773	0.464
All - IR	0.759	0.467
All - WA	**0.740**	**0.423**
Baseline 1 (IR)	0.748	0.419
Baseline 2 (random)	0.470	0.298

Table 2: Ablation studies of the four ensembled feature sources against SemEval-2016 and SemEval-2017 test data. Bolded values indicate the largest loss due to ablation.

samples while the Relevant class is spread evenly between the other two. Surprisingly, this dynamic changed when applied to the SemEval-2017 data, resulting in improved separation for the Relevant class, but worse for both Irrelevant and PerfectMatch classes.

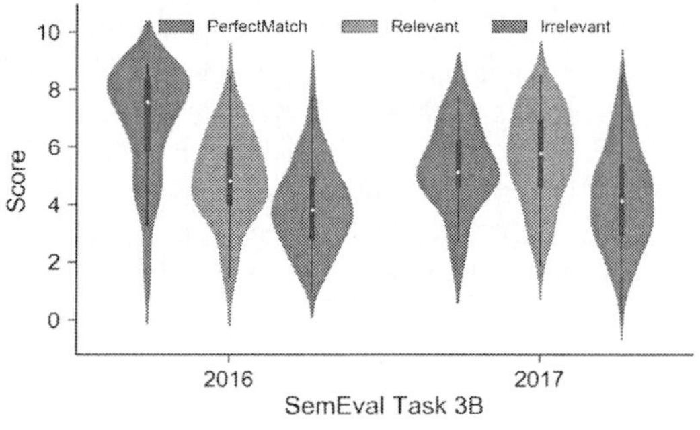

Figure 2: Our model was unable to consistently score PerfectMatch class questions over Irrelevant ones across SemEval datasets, suggesting that it overfit to the distribution of the training data.

Both the significant swing in IR feature contribution and drop in ability to detect PerfectMatch samples as positive examples of question-question similarity are reflected in the change in makeup of the dataset (Table 3). The train + dev dataset we used for general training was more closely aligned with the distribution of class labels in 2016 than in 2017, suggesting a potential i.i.d. data dependence on this approach to produce good results on test data.

Dataset	n	PM	R	I
train	2669	0.09	0.32	0.59
dev	500	0.12	0.31	0.57
test-2016	700	0.11	0.22	0.67
test-2017	880	0.03	0.16	0.81

Table 3: Distribution of the PerfectMatch (PM), Relevant (R), and Irrelevant (I) classes within the datasets.

4 Summary

We described a system that relies on an ensemble of syntactic, semantic, and IR features to detect question-question similarity and demonstrated it on the SemEval-2017 community question answering shared task. Of the four feature sources we evaluated, the semantic word alignment features provided the largest contributed and consistent boost in MAP. Features derived from TF-KLD and tree kernel methods had modest effects. The efficacy of the IR-derived features varied from providing a noticeable gain on historical data vs a significant drop on the current test set, likely attributable to the significant increase in the number of Irrelevant class samples. Future work will explore how to compensate for highly unbalanced class scenarios.

References

Simone Filice, Giovanni Da San Martino, and Alessandro Moschitti. 2015. Structural representations for learning relations between pairs of texts. In *Proceedings of the 53rd Annual Meeting of the Association for Computational Linguistics and the 7th International Joint Conference on Natural Language Processing of the Asian Federation of Natural Language Processing, ACL 2015, July 26-31, 2015, Beijing, China, Volume 1: Long Papers*. pages 1003–1013. http://aclweb.org/anthology/P/P15/P15-1097.pdf.

Johannes Fürnkranz and Eyke Hüllermeier. 2003. Pairwise preference learning and ranking. In Nada Lavrač, Dragan Gamberger, Hendrik Blockeel, and L. Todorovski, editors, *Proceedings of the 14th European Conference on Machine Learning (ECML-03)*. Springer-Verlag, Cavtat, Croatia, volume 2837 of *Lecture Notes in Artificial Intelligence*, pages 145–156. http://www.ke.tu-darmstadt.de/ juffi/publications/ecml-03.pdf.

Yangfeng Ji and Jacob Eisenstein. 2013. Discriminative improvements to distributional sentence similarity. In *Proceedings of the 2013 Conference on Empirical Methods in Natural Language Processing, EMNLP 2013, 18-21 October 2013, Grand Hyatt Seattle, Seattle, Washington, USA, A meeting of SIGDAT, a Special Interest Group of the ACL*. pages 891–896. http://aclweb.org/anthology/D/D13/D13-1090.pdf.

Thorsten Joachims. 2002. Optimizing search engines using clickthrough data. In *Proceedings of the Eighth ACM SIGKDD International Conference on Knowledge Discovery and Data Mining*. ACM, New York, NY, USA, KDD '02, pages 133–142. https://doi.org/10.1145/775047.775067.

Preslav Nakov, Doris Hoogeveen, Lluís Màrquez, Alessandro Moschitti, Hamdy Mubarak, Timothy Baldwin, and Karin Verspoor. 2017. SemEval-2017 task 3: Community question answering. In *Proceedings of the 11th International Workshop on Semantic Evaluation*. Association for Computational Linguistics, Vancouver, Canada, SemEval '17.

Jeffrey Pennington, Richard Socher, and Christopher D. Manning. 2014. Glove: Global vectors for word representation. In *Empirical Methods in Natural Language Processing (EMNLP)*. pages 1532–1543. http://www.aclweb.org/anthology/D14-1162.

Stephen Wan, Mark Dras, Robert Dale, and Cécile Paris. 2006. Using dependency-based features to take the "para-farce" out of paraphrase. In *Proceedings of the Australasian Language Technology Workshop*. volume 2006.

Zhiguo Wang and Abraham Ittycheriah. 2015. Faq-based question answering via word alignment. *CoRR* abs/1507.02628. http://arxiv.org/abs/1507.02628.

QUB at SemEval-2017 Task 6: Cascaded Imbalanced Classification for Humor Analysis in Twitter

Xiwu Han and Gregory Toner
Queen's University Belfast
Belfast, BT7 1NN, UK
x.han@qub.ac.uk; g.toner@qub.ac.uk

Abstract

This paper presents our submission to SemEval-2017 Task 6: #HashtagWars: Learning a Sense of Humor. There are two subtasks: A. Pairwise Comparison, and B. Semi-Ranking. Our assumption is that the distribution of humorous and non-humorous texts in real life language is naturally imbalanced. Using Naïve Bayes Multinomial with standard text-representation features, we approached Subtask B as a sequence of imbalanced classification problems, and optimized our system per the macro-average recall. Subtask A was then solved via the Semi-Ranking results. On the final test, our system was ranked 10th for Subtask A, and 3rd for Subtask B.

1 Introduction

Humor is an essential trait of human intelligence that has not yet been addressed extensively in current AI research[1]. It's certainly one of the most interesting and puzzling research areas in the field of natural language understanding, and developing techniques that enable computers to understand humor in human languages deserves research attention (Yang et al., 2015).

Humor recognition or analysis by computers aims to determine whether a sentence in context expresses a certain degree of humor. This can be extremely challenging (Attardo, 1994) because no universal definition of humor has been achieved, humor is highly contextual, and there are many different types of humor with different characteristics (Raz, 2012). Previous studies (Mihalcea and

Strapparava, 2005; Yang et al., 2015; Zhang and Liu, 2014; Purandare and Litman, 2006; Bertero and Fung, 2016) dealt with the humor recognition task as a binary classification task, which was to categorize a given text as humorous or non-humorous (Li et al., 2016). Textual data consisting of comparable amounts of humorous texts and non-humorous texts were collected, and a classification model was then built using textual features. Barbieri and Saggion (2014) examined cross-domain application of humor detection using Twitter data. Purandare and Litman (2006) used data from a famous TV series, *Friends*. Speakers' turns which occurred right before simulated laughter were defined as humorous ones and the other turns as non-humorous ones. They also used speakers' acoustic characteristics as features. Bertero and Fung (2016) pursued a similar hypothesis. Their target was to categorize an utterance in a sitcom, *The Big Bang Theory*, into those followed by laughter or not. They were the first to use a deep learning algorithm for humor classification. Besides, because genre bias can be problematic, Yang et al. (2015) tried to minimize genre differences between humorous and non-humorous texts.

SemEval-2017 Task 6 aims to encourage the development of methods that should take into account the continuous nature of humor, on the one hand, and to characterize the sense of humor of a particular source, on the other. The dataset was based on humorous responses submitted to a Comedy Central TV show *@midnight*[2]. There are two subtasks: A. Pairwise Comparison, where a successful system should be able to predict among a pair of tweets which is funnier; and B. Semi-Ranking, where, given a file of tweets for a hashtag, systems

---

[1] http://alt.qcri.org/semeval2017/task6/

[2] http://www.cc.com/shows/-midnight

Proceedings of the 11th International Workshop on Semantic Evaluations (SemEval-2017), pages 380–384,
Vancouver, Canada, August 3 - 4, 2017. ©2017 Association for Computational Linguistics

should produce a ranking of tweets from funniest to least funny.

Since automatic humor analysis is difficult, our goal is only to provide computer assistance to human experts. We approached Subtask B as a sequence of imbalanced classification problems, and optimized our system per the macro-average recall. Subtask A was then solved simply via the Semi-Ranking results of Subtask B.

2　Data and Our Features

The training and trial data consists of 106 files, and the test data consists of 6 files. Each file corresponds to a single hashtag, and is named accordingly. For example, for the hashtag #DogSongs, the file is called Dog_Songs. The tweets are labeled 0, 1, or 2. 0 corresponds to a tweet not in the top 10 (i.e. not considered funny). 1 corresponds to a tweet in the top 10, but not the funniest tweet. 2 corresponds to the funniest tweet. Figure 1 shows the distribution of these three classes on the training and trial data sets. This is unlike existing relevant research, which involved comparable amounts of humorous and non-humorous texts.

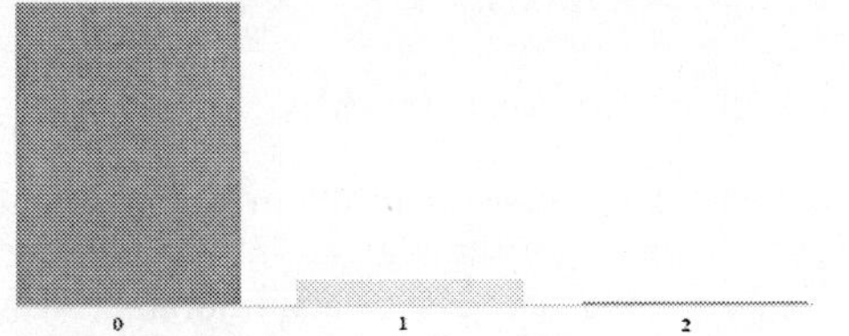

Figure 1: Imbalanced distribution of humor degrees on the training and trial data sets.

However, this distribution might be more pragmatic for analyzing humor in real life languages. Though humor is as important to our life as is spice to our food[3], it's just a small part of the whole matter. The distribution of humor vs. non-humor might be naturally imbalanced. The nature of Subtask A is also imbalanced. Although only tweet pairs with differing humor degrees are evaluated in the final test, those pairs with the same degree of humor will occupy by far the larger proportion of all tweet pairs for a given hashtag. We chose to solve Subtask A simply from ranking results of Subtask B.

A better semantic understanding of the hashtag will contribute to a better performance in the task. For example, named entities obviously form an important part of contextual knowledge. The task organizers allow participants to manually annotate

the trial and training data, such as annotating the proper nouns referenced in a tweet. However, the automatic annotating performance could be unreliable and be detrimental to the hashtag understanding. Besides, the manual annotation of around ten thousand tweets is not a trivial task. Therefore, we only included the tweets and the relevant hashtags for classification features. They were regarded as two textual features, with the hashtag parsed into a sequence of words.

3　Our Approach

We first focused on Subtask B, solving it by cascaded imbalanced classification. In our daily life, there exists similar imbalanced distribution to that shown in Figure 1, such as the World Cup and beauty contests. In such cases, there can be n predefined levels or ranks, the number of participants or survivors allowed for each higher rank is usually exponentially smaller than its lower ranks. In a cascaded way, a such n-rank machine learning task could be solved by $n-1$ imbalanced classifiers.

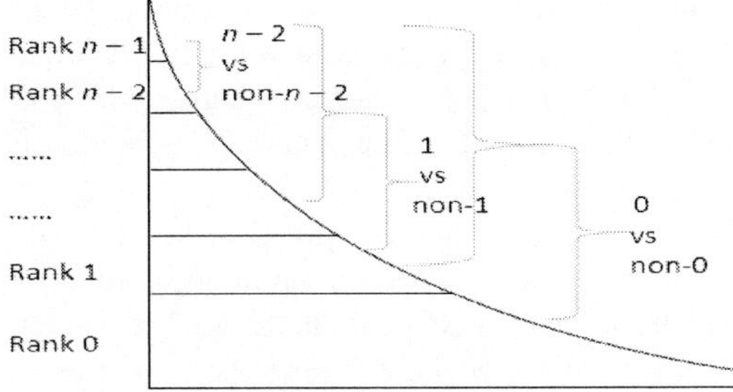

Figure 2: Cascaded imbalanced classification.

The cascaded method is illustrated in Figure 2, and a pseudo algorithm for training the classifiers, classifying a query, and semi-ranking, is detailed in Table 1. Each binary imbalanced classifier in the cascade is trained to distinguish the data points of one rank and those of its higher ranks, while data points in any lower ranks are not counted in. All the $n-1$ classifiers work one by one in the ranking order to complete the election or filtering process.

For imbalanced classification, there are many existing solutions (Kotsiantis et al., 2006; Sun et al., 2009; Galar et al., 2012). The solutions can be based on data resampling, algorithm adjustment, cost-sensitive tuning, boosting approaches, or hybrid methods. Since humor distribution might be naturally imbalanced, we chose to tune the classifying cost matrix and prediction confidence.

---

[3] http://www.aath.org/humor-the-spice-of-life.

Input: Training set X of data point x labeled with n ranks $\{0, 1, …, n-1\}$, and a test set T of data point t with no labels.
Output: Set F of $n-1$ imbalanced classifiers, and semi-ranked T of data point t labeled with ranks $\{0, 1, …, n-1\}$.
1. **for** rank r ($0 <= r < n-1$), remove from X any x labeled with r' ($r' < r$). 2.   Re-label any x within rank r'' ($r''>r$) as *non-r*. 3.   Train an imbalanced binary classifier $f_r(x)$ on the re-labeled X, and set F as $F \bigcup \{f_r(x)\}$. 4. **end for** 5. Given t in T, for $0 <= r < n-1$, apply $f_r(t)$, **end for**. 6. Label t with r^*, the highest rank predicted. 7. Set the ranking score of t as $r^* + C_{fr^*(t)}$, where $C_{fr^*(t)}$ is prediction confidence of $f_{r^*}(t)$. 8. Sort T per the ranking scores, and return T.

Table 1: Algorithm for solving Subtask B.

A cost matrix is used to represent the differing cost of each type of misclassification (Elkan, 2001). Typically, each row in the matrix is used to represent the predicted label and each column corresponds to the actual label of gold standard. The matrix entry C_{ij} is the cost of predicting the ith label when the jth label is actually correct. In general, $C_{ij} > C_{jj}$ when $i \neq j$, i.e. a correct prediction is less costly than an incorrect prediction. Usually the entries C_{jj} along the main diagonal will all be zero.

For a classifier that can output the full probability distribution over all class labels, prediction confidence is defined as the difference between the estimated probability of the true class and that of the most likely predicted class other than the true class. By tuning prediction confidence for one class, we can easily balance the weight distribution between this class and other classes. Tuning the cost matrix and prediction confidence could be done via optimizing a given performance measurement on a held-out development set or by cross-validation. Since our goal is to provide computer assistance to human experts in humor analysis, we chose macro-average recall as the performance measurement to be optimized. The parameters for imbalanced classification could be tuned in a pipeline way, i.e. for each classifier $f_r(x)$ we first tuned the cost sensitive matrix and then tuned the prediction confidence.

Though Subtask A aims to predict among a pair of tweets which is funnier, its evaluation requires a system to return all tweet pairs with different humor degrees for a given hashtag. More generally, a pairwise comparison problem with n predefined ranks of data points could be solved simply by the algorithm in Table 2, once the semi-ranking results have been obtained for Subtask B.

Input: Semi-ranked set T of data point t labeled with ranks $\{0, 1, …, n-1\}$.
Output: Set of tweet pairs $P = \{(t_i, t_j)\mid i > j, 0 < i < n, 0 <= j < n-1\}$.
1. **for** $i = n-1; i > 0$: 2.   **for** $j = n-2; j >= 0$: 3. $P = P \bigcup \{(t_i, t_j)\}$. 4.   **end for** 5. **end for** 6. Return P.

Table 2: Algorithm for solving Subtask A.

The algorithm in Table 2 depends on the predicted ranks, thus it will result in better recall of data pairs with different ranking degrees, and human experts will have more choices. However, better precision or F-measure could be achieved by exploiting the semi-ranking order and limiting the number of data points in each rank as required by the concrete task. For example, the number in rank 2 is 1, and in rank 1 it is 9 for a given hashtag in SemEval-2017 Task 6.

4 Experiment and Results

This task is a 3-partite problem that could be solved via the algorithms given in Table 1 and 2. Using Java and Naïve Bayes Multinomial (NBM) classification of Weka 3.7[4] (Witten et al, 2011), we did the experiment with the training and trial data as training set. As for classification features, our present research simply chose word n-grams with n = 1, 2, and 3. By optimizing the macro-average recall of an NBM classifier on the training set with all original class labels, 3200 word types were kept before vectorization. Figure 3 gives some results of a part of the optimizing process. The star denotes the optimized point. For tuning the cost matrix and prediction confidence, we used 10-fold cross validation. The parameter values of the largest macro-average recall and the least standard deviation were returned for training final NBM classifiers on the whole training set and predicting for the final test set.

Table 3 lists the results of tuning cost matrix and prediction confidence. We first tuned the cost matrices, and the best macro-average recalls are marked with [1] in Table 3.

---

[4] http://www.cs.waikato.ac.nz/ml/weka/downloading.html

Figure 3: Selecting word n-gram types before vectorization.

NBM Classifiers	0 vs non-0	1 vs non-1
Positive Class	0	1
Negative Class	1	2
Cost of False Positive	1	1
Cost of False Negative	46	5
Macro-average Recall[1]	$0.698_{\pm0.11}$	$0.617_{\pm0.14}$
Negative Confidence	0.01	0.96
Macro-average Recall[2]	$0.713_{\pm0.09}$	$0.623_{\pm0.12}$

Table 3: Tuning results for cost matrix and prediction confidence

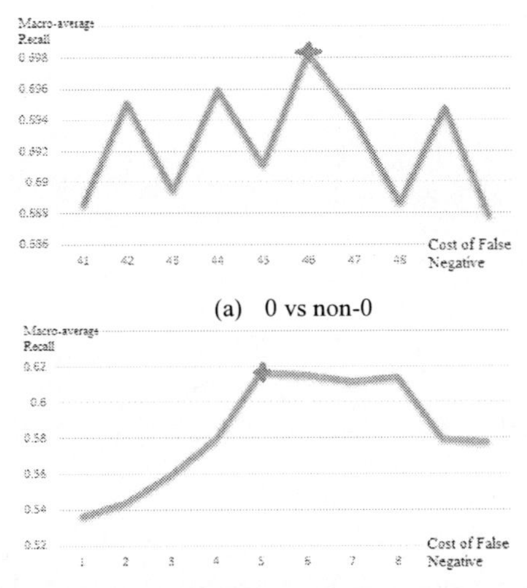

(a) 0 vs non-0

(b) 1 vs non-1

Figure 4: Tuning the cost of false negative.

Figure 4 gives parts of the cost matrix tuning process nearby the optimization points (denoted with stars). To make the tuning less expensive, we fixed the cost for false positive as 1, and only tuned the cost for false positive. Then, with the optimized cost matrices for NBM classifiers, we tuned the confidence for predicting negative items, and the best macro-average recalls are marked with [2] in Table 3. Figure 5 gives parts of the prediction confidence tuning process near the optimization points (denoted with stars). We finally trained our system on the whole training set with the tuned parameters, and applied this system on the evaluation set. For Subtask A, our submission is ranked 10th, with a micro-averaged accuracy of 0.187. For Subtask B, our submission is ranked 3rd, with an edit distance of 0.924.

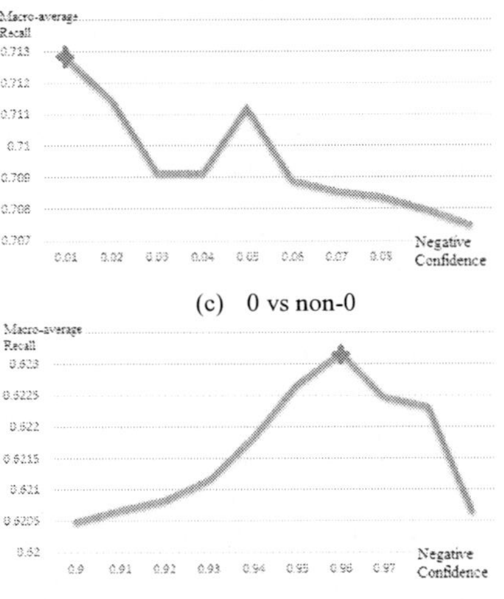

(c) 0 vs non-0

(d) 1 vs non-1

Figure 5: Tuning prediction confidence

5   Conclusion

For detecting humor, we assume that the distribution of humorous and non-humorous texts in a language is naturally imbalanced. Instead of aiming at an automatic humor analysis system, our goal for solving SemEval-2017 Task 6 is to provide computer assistance to human experts. Therefore, macro-average recall was employed as the major measurement for training. We approached Subtask B as a sequence of imbalanced classification problems, and optimized our system per the macro-average recall. Subtask A was then solved via the Semi-Ranking results. In future research, we plan to employ more classification features and other imbalanced machine learning techniques.

Acknowledgments

This research is sponsored by the Leverhulme Trust project with grant number of RPG-2015-089.

References

Salvatore Attardo. 1994. *Linguistic theories of humor*, volume 1. Walter de Gruyter.

Francesco Barbieri and Horacio Saggion. 2014. Automatic detection of irony and humour in Twitter. *Proceedings of the Fifth International Conference on Computational Creativity*, Ljubljana, Slovenia, jun. Josef Stefan Institute.

Dario Bertero and Pascale Fung. 2016. A long short-term memory framework for predicting humor in dialogues. *Proceedings of the 2016 Conference of the North American Chapter of the Association for Computational Linguistics: Human Language Technologies*, 130-135, SanDiego, California, June.

C. Elkan. 2001. The Foundations of Cost-sensitive Learning. *International Joint Conference on Artificial Intelligence*, LAWRENCE ERLBAUM ASSOCIATES LTD, 17.1: 973-978.

M. Galar, A. Fernandez, E. Barrenechea, H. Bustince, and F. Herrera. 2012. A review on ensembles for the class imbalance problem: bagging-, boosting-, and hybrid-based approaches. *IEEE Transactions on Systems, Man, and Cybernetics, Part C (Applications and Reviews)*, 42(4), 463-484.

Sotiris Kotsiantis, Dimitris Kanellopoulos, and Panayiotis Pintelas. 2006. Handling imbalanced datasets: A review. *GESTS International Transactions on Computer Science Engineering*, 30.1: 25-36.

Jiwei Li, Xinlei Chen, Eduard H. Hovy, and Dan Jurafsky. 2016. Visualizing and understanding neural models in NLP. *The 2016 Conference of the North American Chapter of the Association for Computational Linguistics: Human Language Technologies*, San Diego California, USA, 681-691.

Rada Mihalcea and Carlo Strapparava. 2005. Making computerslaugh: Investigationsinautomatichumor recognition. *Proceedings of the Conference on Human Language Technology and Empirical Methods in Natural Language Processing*, 531- 538. Association for Computational Linguistics.

Amruta Purandare and Diane Litman. 2006. Humor: Prosody analysis and automatic recognition for f*r*i*e*n*d*s*. *Proceedings of the 2006 Conference on Empirical Methods in Natural Language Processing, EMNLP '06*, 208-215, Stroudsburg, PA. Association for Computational Linguistics.

Yishay Raz. 2012. Automatic humor classification on twitter. *Proceedings of the 2012 Conference of the North American Chapter of the Association for Computational Linguistics: Human Language Technologies: Student Research Workshop*, 66-70. Association for Computational Linguistics.

Yanmin Sun, Andrew KC Wong, and Mohamed S. Kamel. 2009. Classification of imbalanced data: A review. *International Journal of Pattern Recognition and Artificial Intelligence*, 23.04: 687-719.

Ian H Witten, Eibe Frank, and Mark A Hall. 2011. *Data Mining: Practical machine learning tools and techniques*. Morgan Kaufmann, Third edition, ISBN: 978-0-12-374856-0.

Diyi Yang, Alon Lavie, Chris Dyer and Eduard Hovy. 2015. Humor Recognition and Humor Anchor Extraction. *Proceedings of the 2015 Conference on Empirical Methods in Natural Language Processing*, 2367-2376, Lisbon, Portugal.

Renxian Zhang and Naishi Liu. 2014. Recognizing humor on twitter. *Proceedings of the 23rd ACM International Conference on Information and Knowledge Management*, 889-898. ACM.

Duluth at SemEval-2017 Task 6: Language Models in Humor Detection

Xinru Yan & Ted Pedersen
Department of Computer Science
University of Minnesota Duluth
Duluth, MN, 55812 USA
{yanxx418,tpederse}@d.umn.edu

Abstract

This paper describes the Duluth system that participated in SemEval-2017 Task 6 #HashtagWars: Learning a Sense of Humor. The system participated in Subtasks A and B using N-gram language models, ranking highly in the task evaluation. This paper discusses the results of our system in the development and evaluation stages and from two post-evaluation runs.

1 Introduction

Humor is an expression of human uniqueness and intelligence and has drawn attention in diverse areas such as linguistics, psychology, philosophy and computer science. *Computational humor* draws from all of these fields and is a relatively new area of study. There is some history of systems that are able to generate humor (e.g., (Stock and Strapparava, 2003), (Özbal and Strapparava, 2012)). However, *humor detection* remains a less explored and challenging problem (e.g., (Mihalcea and Strapparava, 2006), (Zhang and Liu, 2014), (Shahaf et al., 2015), (Miller and Gurevych, 2015)).

SemEval-2017 Task 6 (Potash et al., 2017) also focuses on *humor detection* by asking participants to develop systems that learn a sense of humor from the Comedy Central TV show, *@midnight with Chris Hardwick*. Our system ranks tweets according to how funny they are by training N-gram language models on two different corpora. One consisting of funny tweets provided by the task organizers, and the other on a freely available research corpus of news data. The funny tweet data is made up of tweets that are intended to be humorous responses to a hashtag given by host Chris Hardwick during the program.

2 Background

Training **Language Models** (LMs) is a straightforward way to collect a set of rules by utilizing the fact that words do not appear in an arbitrary order; we in fact can gain useful information about a word by knowing the company it keeps (Firth, 1968). A statistical language model estimates the probability of a sequence of words or an upcoming word. An N-gram is a contiguous sequence of N words: a unigram is a single word, a bigram is a two-word sequence, and a trigram is a three-word sequence. For example, in the tweet

tears in Ramen #SingleLifeIn3Words

"tears", "in", "Ramen" and "#SingleLifeIn3Words" are unigrams; "tears in", "in Ramen" and "Ramen #SingleLifeIn3Words" are bigrams and "tears in Ramen" and "in Ramen #SingleLifeIn3Words" are trigrams.

An N-gram model can predict the next word from a sequence of N-1 previous words. A trigram Language Model (LM) predicts the conditional probability of the next word using the following approximation:

$$P(w_n|w_1^{n-1}) \approx P(w_n|w_{n-2}, w_{n-1}) \quad (1)$$

The assumption that the probability of a word depends only on a small number of previous words is called a **Markov** assumption (Markov, 2006). Given this assumption the probability of a sentence can be estimated as follows:

$$P(w_1^n) \approx \prod_{k=1}^{n} P(w_k|w_{k-2}, w_{k-1}) \quad (2)$$

In a study on how phrasing affects memorability, (Danescu-Niculescu-Mizil et al., 2012) take a language model approach to measure the distinctiveness of memorable movie quotes. They do this

Proceedings of the 11th International Workshop on Semantic Evaluations (SemEval-2017), pages 385–389,
Vancouver, Canada, August 3 - 4, 2017. ©2017 Association for Computational Linguistics

by evaluating a quote with respect to a "common language" model built from the newswire sections of the Brown corpus (Kucera and Francis, 1967). They find that movie quotes which are less like "common language" are more distinctive and therefore more memorable. The intuition behind our approach is that humor should in some way be memorable or distinct, and so tweets that diverge from a "common language" model would be expected to be funnier.

In order to evaluate how funny a tweet is, we train language models on two datasets: the tweet data and the news data. Tweets that are more probable according to the tweet data language model are ranked as being funnier. However, tweets that have a lower probability according to the news language model are considered the funnier since they are the least like the (unfunny) news corpus. We relied on both bigrams and trigrams when training our models.

We use KenLM (Heafield et al., 2013) as our language modeling tool. Language models are estimated using modified Kneser-Ney smoothing without pruning. KenLM also implements a back-off technique so if an N-gram is not found, KenLM applies the lower order N-gram's probability along with its back-off weights.

3 Method

Our system[1] estimated tweet probability using N-gram LMs. Specifically, it solved the comparison (Subtask A) and semi-ranking (Subtask B) subtasks in four steps:

1. Corpus preparation and pre-processing: Collected all training data into a single file. Pre-processing included filtering and tokenization.

2. Language model training: Built N-gram language models using KenLM.

3. Tweet scoring: Computed log probability for each tweet based on trained N-gram language model.

4. Tweet prediction: Based on the log probability scores.

   - Subtask A – Given two tweets, compare and predict which one is funnier.

   - Subtask B – Given a set of tweets associated with one hashtag, rank tweets from the funniest to the least funny.

3.1 Corpus Preparation and Pre-processing

The tweet data was provided by the task organizers. It consists of 106 hashtag files made up of about 21,000 tokens. The hashtag files were further divided into a development set *trial_dir* of 6 hashtags and a training set of 100 hashtags *train_dir*. We also obtained 6.2 GB of English news data with about two million tokens from the News Commentary Corpus and the News Crawl Corpus from 2008, 2010 and 2011[2]. Each tweet and each sentence from the news data is found on a single line in their respective files.

3.1.1 Preparation

During the development of our system we trained our language models solely on the 100 hashtag files from *train_dir* and then evaluated our performance on the 6 hashtag files found in *trial_dir*. That data was formatted such that each tweet was found on a single line.

3.1.2 Pre-processing

Pre-processing consists of two steps: filtering and tokenization. The filtering step was only for the tweet training corpus. We experimented with various filtering and tokenziation combinations during the development stage to determine the best setting.

   - Filtering removes the following elements from the tweets: URLs, tokens starting with the "@" symbol (Twitter user names), and tokens starting with the "#" symbol (Hashtags).

   - Tokenization: Text in all training data was split on white space and punctuation

3.2 Language Model Training

Once we had the corpora ready, we used the KenLM Toolkit to train the N-gram language models on each corpus. We trained using both bigrams and trigrams on the tweet and news data. Our language models accounted for unknown words and were built both with and without considering sentence or tweet boundaries.

---

[1]https://xinru1414.github.io/HumorDetection-SemEval2017-Task6/

[2]http://www.statmt.org/wmt11/featured-translation-task.html

3.3 Tweet Scoring

After training the N-gram language models, the next step was scoring. For each hashtag file that needed to be evaluated, the logarithm of the probability was assigned to each tweet in the hashtag file based on the trained language model. The larger the probability, the more likely that tweet was according to the language model. Table 1 shows an example of two scored tweets from hashtag file *Bad_Job_In_5_Words.tsv* based on the tweet data trigram language model. Note that KenLM reports the log of the probability of the N-grams rather than the actual probabilities so the value closer to 0 (-19) has the higher probability and is associated with the tweet judged to be funnier.

3.4 Tweet Prediction

The system sorts all the tweets for each hashtag and orders them based on their log probability score, where the funniest tweet should be listed first. If the scores are based on the tweet language model then they are sorted in ascending order since the log probability value closest to 0 indicates the tweet that is most like the (funny) tweets model. However, if the log probability scores are based on the news data then they are sorted in descending order since the largest value will have the smallest probability associated with it and is therefore least like the (unfunny) news model.

For Subtask A, the system goes through the sorted list of tweets in a hashtag file and compares each pair of tweets. For each pair, if the first tweet was funnier than the second, the system would output the tweet_ids for the pair followed by a "1". If the second tweet is funnier it outputs the tweet_ids followed by a "0". For Subtask B, the system outputs all the tweet_ids for a hashtag file starting from the funniest.

4 Experiments and Results

In this section we present the results from our development stage (*Table 2*), the evaluation stage (*Table 3*), and two post-evaluation results (*Table 3*). Since we implemented both bigram and trigram language models during the development stage but only results from trigram language models were submitted to the task, we evaluated bigram language models in the post-evaluation stage. Note that the accuracy and distance measurements listed in Table 2 and Table 3 are defined by the task organizers (Potash et al., 2017).

Table 2 shows results from the development stage. These results show that for the tweet data the best setting is to keep the # and @, omit sentence boundaries, be case sensitive, and ignore tokenization. While using these settings the trigram language model performed better on Subtask B (.887) and the bigram language model performed better on Subtask A (.548). We decided to rely on trigram language models for the task evaluation since the advantage of bigrams on Subtask A was very slight (.548 versus .543). For the news data, we found that the best setting was to perform tokenization, omit sentence boundaries, and to be case sensitive. Given that trigrams performed most effectively in the development stage, we decided to use those during the evaluation.

Table 3 shows the results of our system during the task evaluation. We submitted two runs, one with a trigram language model trained on the tweet data, and another with a trigram language model trained on the news data. In addition, after the evaluation was concluded we also decided to run the bigram language models as well. Contrary to what we observed in the development data, the bigram language model actually performed somewhat better than the trigram language model. In addition, and also contrary to what we observed with the development data, the news data proved generally more effective in the post–evaluation runs than the tweet data.

5 Discussion and Future Work

We relied on bigram and trigram language models because tweets are short and concise, and often only consist of just a few words.

The performance of our system was not consistent when comparing the development to the evaluation results. During development language models trained on the tweet data performed better. However during the evaluation and post-evaluation stage, language models trained on the news data were significantly more effective. We also observed that bigram language models performed slightly better than trigram models on the evaluation data. This suggests that going forward we should also consider both the use of unigram and character–level language models.

These results suggest that there are only slight differences between bigram and trigram models, and that the type and quantity of corpora used to train the models is what really determines the re-

The hashtag: #BadJobIn5Words		
tweet_id	tweet	score
705511149970726912	The host of Singled Out #BadJobIn5Words @midnight	-19.923433303833008
705538894415003648	Donut receipt maker and sorter #BadJobIn5Words @midnight	-27.67446517944336

Table 1: Scored tweets according to the trigram LM. The log probability scores computed based on the trigram LM are shown in the third column.

DataSet	N-gram	# and @ removed	Sentence Boundaries	Lowercase	Tokenization	Subtask A Accuracy	Subtask B Distance
tweets	**trigram**	**False**	**False**	**False**	**False**	**0.543**	**0.887**
tweets	bigram	False	False	False	False	0.548	0.900
tweets	trigram	False	True	True	False	0.522	0.900
tweets	bigram	False	True	True	False	0.534	0.887
news	**trigram**	**NA**	**False**	**False**	**True**	**0.539**	**0.923**
news	bigram	NA	False	False	True	0.524	0.924
news	trigram	NA	False	False	False	0.460	0.923
news	bigram	NA	False	False	False	0.470	0.900

Table 2: Development results based on *trial_dir* data. The settings we chose to train LMs are in bold.

DataSet	N-gram	# and @ removed	Sentence Boundaries	Lowercase	Tokenization	Subtask A Accuracy	Subtask B Distance
tweets	**trigram**	**False**	**False**	**False**	**False**	**0.397**	**0.967**
tweets	bigram	False	False	False	False	0.406	0.944
news	**trigram**	**NA**	**False**	**False**	**True**	**0.627**	**0.872**
news	bigram	NA	False	False	True	0.624	0.853

Table 3: Evaluation results (bold) and post-evaluation results based on *evaluation_dir* data. The trigram LM trained on the news data ranked 4th place on Subtask A and 1st place on Subtask B.

sults.

The task description paper (Potash et al., 2017) reported system by system results for each hashtag. We were surprised to find that our performance on the hashtag file *#BreakUpIn5Words* in the evaluation stage was significantly better than any other system on both Subtask A (with accuracy of 0.913) and Subtask B (with distance score of 0.636). While we still do not fully understand the cause of these results, there is clearly something about the language used in this hashtag that is distinct from the other hashtags, and is somehow better represented or captured by a language model. Reaching a better understanding of this result is a high priority for future work.

The tweet data was significantly smaller than the news data, and so certainly we believe that this was a factor in the performance during the evaluation stage, where the models built from the news data were significantly more effective. Going forward we plan to collect more tweet data, particularly those that participate in #HashtagWars. We also intend to do some experiments where we cut the amount of news data and then build models to see how those compare.

While our language models performed well, there is some evidence that neural network models can outperform standard back-off N-gram models (Mikolov et al., 2011). We would like to experiment with deep learning methods such as recurrent neural networks, since these networks are capable of forming short term memory and may be better suited for dealing with sequence data.

References

Cristian Danescu-Niculescu-Mizil, Justin Cheng, Jon Kleinberg, and Lillian Lee. 2012. You had me at hello: How phrasing affects memorability. In *Proceedings of the 50th Annual Meeting of the Association for Computational Linguistics: Long Papers - Volume 1*. Association for Computational Linguistics, Stroudsburg, PA, USA, ACL '12, pages 892–901.

J. Firth. 1968. A synopsis of linguistic theory 1930-1955. In F. Palmer, editor, *Selected Papers of J. R. Firth*, Longman.

Kenneth Heafield, Ivan Pouzyrevsky, Jonathan H. Clark, and Philipp Koehn. 2013. Scalable modified Kneser-Ney language model estimation. In *Proceedings of the 51st Annual Meeting of the Association for Computational Linguistics*. Sofia, Bulgaria, pages 690–696.

Henry Kucera and W. Nelson Francis. 1967. *Computational Analysis of Present-day American English*. Brown University Press, Providence, RI, USA.

A. A. Markov. 2006. An example of statistical investigation of the text *Eugene Onegin* concerning the connection of samples in chains. *Science in Context* 19(4):591–600.

Rada Mihalcea and Carlo Strapparava. 2006. Learning to laugh (automatically): Computational models for humor recognition. *Computational Intelligence* 22(2):126–142.

Tomáš Mikolov, Stefan Kombrink, Lukáš Burget, Jan Černocký, and Sanjeev Khudanpur. 2011. Extensions of recurrent neural network language model. In *Acoustics, Speech and Signal Processing (ICASSP), 2011 IEEE International Conference on*. IEEE, pages 5528–5531.

Tristan Miller and Iryna Gurevych. 2015. Automatic disambiguation of English puns. In *Proceedings of the 53rd Annual Meeting of the Association for Computational Linguistics and the 7th International Joint Conference on Natural Language Processing (Volume 1: Long Papers)*. Association for Computational Linguistics, Beijing, China, pages 719–729.

Gözde Özbal and Carlo Strapparava. 2012. A computational approach to the automation of creative naming. In *Proceedings of the 50th Annual Meeting of the Association for Computational Linguistics: Long Papers-Volume 1*. Association for Computational Linguistics, pages 703–711.

Peter Potash, Alexey Romanov, and Anna Rumshisky. 2017. SemEval-2017 Task 6: #HashtagWars: learning a sense of humor. In *Proceedings of the 11th International Workshop on Semantic Evaluation (SemEval-2017)*. Vancouver, BC.

Dafna Shahaf, Eric Horvitz, and Robert Mankoff. 2015. Inside jokes: Identifying humorous cartoon captions. In *Proceedings of the 21th ACM SIGKDD International Conference on Knowledge Discovery and Data Mining*. ACM, New York, NY, USA, KDD '15, pages 1065–1074.

Oliviero Stock and Carlo Strapparava. 2003. Getting serious about the development of computational humor. In *Proceedings of the Eighteenth International Joint Conference on Artificial Intelligence*. Acapulco, pages 59–64.

Renxian Zhang and Naishi Liu. 2014. Recognizing humor on Twitter. In *Proceedings of the 23rd ACM International Conference on Conference on Information and Knowledge Management*. ACM, New York, NY, USA, CIKM '14, pages 889–898.

DataStories at SemEval-2017 Task 6: Siamese LSTM with Attention for Humorous Text Comparison

Christos Baziotis, Nikos Pelekis, Christos Doulkeridis

University of Piraeus - Data Science Lab

Piraeus, Greece

`mpsp14057@unipi.gr, npelekis@unipi.gr, cdoulk@unipi.gr`

Abstract

In this paper we present a deep-learning system that competed at SemEval-2017 Task 6 "#HashtagWars: Learning a Sense of Humor". We participated in Subtask A, in which the goal was, given two Twitter messages, to identify which one is funnier. We propose a Siamese architecture with bidirectional Long Short-Term Memory (LSTM) networks, augmented with an attention mechanism. Our system works on the token-level, leveraging word embeddings trained on a big collection of unlabeled Twitter messages. We ranked 2nd in 7 teams. A post-completion improvement of our model, achieves state-of-the-art results on #HashtagWars dataset.

1 Introduction

Computational humor (Stock and Strapparava, 2003) is an area in computational linguistics and natural language understanding. Most computational humor tasks focus on the problem of humor detection. However SemEval-2017 Task 6 (Potash et al., 2017) explores the subjective nature of humor, using a dataset of Twitter messages posted in the context of the TV show "@midnight". At each episode during the segment "Hashtag Wars", a topic in the form of a hashtag is given and viewers of the show post funny tweets including that hashtag. In the next episode, the show selects the ten funniest tweets and a final winning tweet.

In the past, computational humor tasks have been approached using hand-crafted features (Hempelmann, 2008; Mihalcea and Strapparava, 2006; Kiddon and Brun, 2011; Yang et al., 2015). However, these approaches require a laborious feature-engineering process, which usually leads to missing or redundant features, especially in the case of humor, which is hard to define and con-

sequently hard to model. Recently, approaches using neural networks, that perform feature-learning, have shown great results (Chen and Lee, 2017; Potash et al., 2016; Bertero and Fung, 2016a,b) outperforming the traditional methods.

In this paper, we present a deep-learning system that we developed for subtask A - "Pairwise Comparison". The goal of the task is, given two tweets about the same topic, to identify which one is funnier. The labels are applied using the show's relative ranking. This is a very challenging task, because humor is subjective and the machine learning system must develop a sense of humor similar to that of the show, in order to perform well.

We employ a Siamese neural network, which generates a dense vector representation for each tweet and then uses those representations as features for classification. For modeling the Twitter messages we use Long Short-Term Memory (LSTM) networks augmented with a context-aware attention mechanism (Yang et al., 2016). Furthermore, we perform thorough text preprocessing that enables our neural network to learn better features. Finally, our approach does not rely on any hand-crafted features.

2 System Overview

2.1 External Data and Word Embeddings

We collected a big dataset of 330M English Twitter messages, which is used (1) for calculating word statistics needed for word segmentation and spell correction and (2) for training word embeddings. Word embeddings are dense vector representations of words (Collobert and Weston, 2008; Mikolov et al., 2013), capturing their semantic and syntactic information. We leverage our big Twitter dataset to train our own word embeddings, using GloVe (Pennington et al., 2014). The word embeddings are used for initializing the weights of the first layer (embedding layer) of our network.

Proceedings of the 11th International Workshop on Semantic Evaluations (SemEval-2017), pages 390–395,
Vancouver, Canada, August 3 - 4, 2017. ©2017 Association for Computational Linguistics

2.2 Text Preprocessing [1]

For preprocessing the text we perform the following steps: tokenization, spell correction, word normalization, word segmentation (for splitting hashtags) and word annotation (with special tags).

Tokenizer. Our tokenizer is able to identify most emoticons, emojis, expressions like dates (e.g. 07/11/2011, April 23rd), times (e.g. 4:30pm, 11:00 am), currencies (e.g. $10, 25mil, 50€), acronyms, censored words (e.g. s**t), words with emphasis (e.g. *very*) and more. This way we keep all these expressions as one token, so later we can normalize them, or annotate them (with special tags) reducing the vocabulary size and enabling our model to learn more abstract features.

Postprocessing. After the tokenization we add an extra postprocessing step, where we perform spell correction, word normalization, word segmentation (for splitting a hashtag to its constituent words) and word annotation. We use the Viterbi algorithm in order to perform spell correction (Jurafsky and Martin, 2000) and word segmentation (Segaran and Hammerbacher, 2009), utilizing word statistics (unigrams and bigrams) from our big Twitter dataset. Finally, we lowercase all words, and replace URLs, emails and user handles (@user), with special tags.

2.3 Recurrent Neural Networks

In computational humor tasks, the most popular approaches that utilize neural networks involve, Convolutional Neural Networks (CNN) (Chen and Lee, 2017; Potash et al., 2016; Bertero and Fung, 2016a) and Recurrent Neural Networks (RNN) (Bertero and Fung, 2016b). We model the text of the Twitter messages using RNNs, because CNNs have no notion of order, therefore losing the information of the word order. However, RNNs are designed for processing sequences, where the order of the elements matters. An RNN performs the same computation, $h_t = f_W(h_{t-1}, x_t)$, on every element of a sequence, where h_t is the hidden state at time-step t, and W the weights of the network. The hidden state at each time-step depends on the previous hidden states. As a result, RNNs utilize the information of word order and are able to handle inputs of variable length.

RNNs are difficult to train (Pascanu et al., 2013), because of the vanishing and exploding gradients problem, where gradients may grow or

decay exponentially over long sequences (Bengio et al., 1994; Hochreiter et al., 2001). We overcome this limitation by using one of the more sophisticated variants of the regular RNN, the Long Short-Term Memory (LSTM) network (Hochreiter and Schmidhuber, 1997), which introduces a gating mechanism, that ensures proper gradient propagation through the network.

2.3.1 Attention Mechanism

An RNN can generate a fixed representation for inputs of variable length. It reads each element sequentially and updates its hidden state, which holds a summary of the processed information. The hidden state at the last time-step, is used as the representation of the input. In some cases, especially in long sequences, the RNN might not be able to hold all the important information in its final hidden state. In order to amplify the contribution of important elements (i.e. words) in the final representation, we use an attention mechanism (Rocktäschel et al., 2015), that aggregates all the intermediate hidden states using their relative importance (Fig. 1).

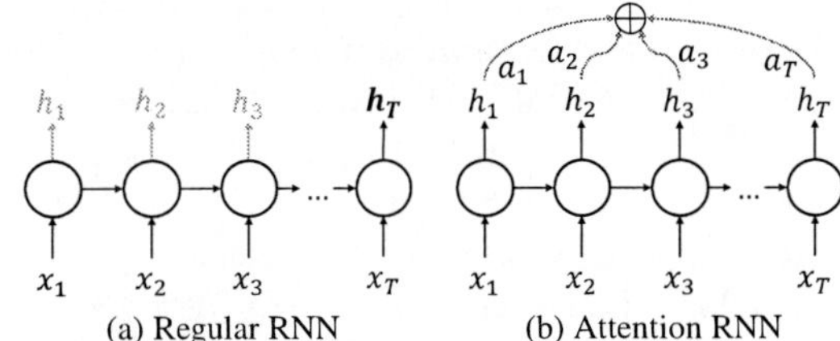

Figure 1: Regular RNN and RNN with attention.

3 Model Description

In our approach, we adopt a Siamese architecture (Bromley et al., 1993), in which we create two identical sub-networks. Each sub-network reads a tweet and generates a fixed representation. Both subnetworks share the *same* weights, in order to project both tweets to the *same* vector space and thus be able to make a meaningful comparison between them. The Siamese sub-networks involve the Embedding layer, BiLSTM layer and Attention layer.

The network has two inputs, the sequence of words in the first tweet $X_1 = (x_1^1, x_2^1, ..., x_{T_1}^1)$, where T_1 the number of words in the first tweet, and the sequence words of the second tweet $X_2 = (x_1^2, x_2^2, ..., x_{T_2}^2)$, where T_2 the number of words of the second tweet.

---

[1] github.com/cbaziotis/ekphrasis

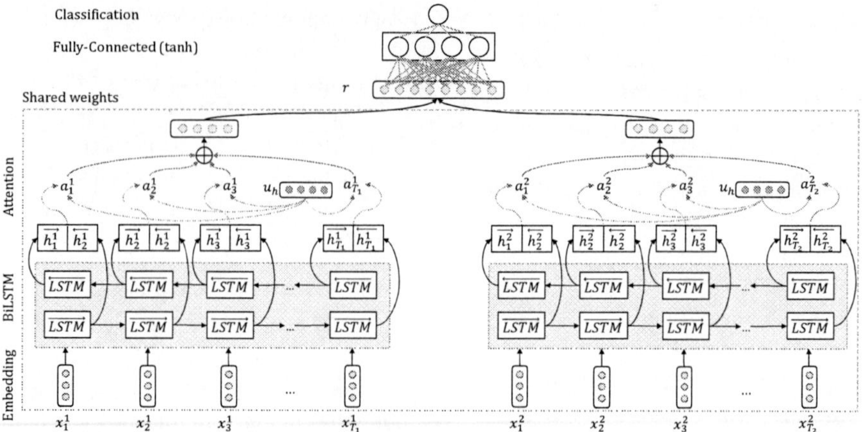

Figure 2: Siamese Bidirectional LSTM with context-aware attention mechanism.

Embedding Layer. We use an Embedding layer to project the words to a low-dimensional vector space R^E, where E is the size of the Embedding layer. We initialize the weights of the Embedding layer using our pre-trained word embeddings.

BiLSTM Layer. An LSTM takes as input the words of a tweet and produces the word annotations $H = (h_1, h_2, ..., h_T)$, where h_i is the hidden state of the LSTM at time-step i, summarizing all the information of the sentence up to x_i. We use bidirectional LSTM (BiLSTM) in order to get annotations for each word that summarize the information from both directions of the message. A bidirectional LSTM consists of a forward LSTM $\overrightarrow{f}$ that reads the sentence from x_1 to x_T and a backward LSTM $\overleftarrow{f}$ that reads the sentence from x_T to x_1. We obtain the final annotation for each word x_i, by concatenating the annotations from both directions,

$$h_i = \overrightarrow{h_i} \parallel \overleftarrow{h_i}, \quad h_i \in R^{2L} \tag{1}$$

where $\parallel$ denotes the concatenation operation and L the size of each LSTM.

Context-Attention Layer. An attention mechanism assigns a weight a_i to each word annotation, which reflects its importance. We compute the fixed representation r of the whole message as the weighted sum of all the word annotations using the attention weights. We use a context-aware attention mechanism as in (Yang et al., 2016). This attention mechanism introduces a context vector u_h, which can be interpreted as a fixed query, that helps to identify the informative words and it is randomly initialized and jointly learned with the rest of the attention layer weights. Formally,

$$e_i = tanh(W_h h_i + b_h), \quad e_i \in [-1, 1] \tag{2}$$

$$a_i = \frac{exp(e_i^\top u_h)}{\sum_{t=1}^{T} exp(e_t^\top u_h)}, \quad \sum_{i=1}^{T} a_i = 1 \tag{3}$$

$$r = \sum_{i=1}^{T} a_i h_i, \quad r \in R^{2L} \tag{4}$$

where W_h, b_h and u_h are the layer's weights.

Fully-Connected Layer. Each Siamese subnetwork produces a fixed representation for each tweet, r_1 and r_2 respectively, that we concatenate to produce the final representation r.

$$r = r_1 \parallel r_2, \quad r \in R^{4L} \tag{5}$$

We pass the vector r, to a fully-connected feedforward layer with a $tanh$ (hyperbolic tangent) activation function. This layer learns a non-linear function of the input vector, enabling it to perform the complex task of humor comparison.

$$c = tanh(W_c r + b_c) \tag{6}$$

Output Layer. The output c of the comparison layer is fed to a final single neuron layer, that performs binary classification (logistic regression) and identifies which tweet is funnier.

3.1 Regularization

At first we adopt the simple but effective technique of dropout (Srivastava et al., 2014), in which we randomly turn-off a percentage of the neurons of a layer in our network. Dropout prevents co-adaptation of neurons and can also be thought as a form of ensemble learning, because for each training example a subpart of the whole network is trained. Additionally, we apply dropout to the recurrent connections of the LSTM as suggested in (Gal and Ghahramani, 2016). Moreover, we add L_2 regularization penalty (weight decay) to the loss function to discourage large weights. Also, we stop the training of the network, after the validation loss stops decreasing (early-stopping). Lastly, we apply Gaussian noise and dropout at the embedding layer. As a result, the network never sees the exact same sentence during training, thus making it more robust to overfitting.

3.2 Training

We train our network to minimize the cross-entropy loss, using back-propagation with stochastic gradient descent and mini-batches of size 256, with the Adam optimizer (Kingma and Ba, 2014) and we clip the gradients at unit norm.

In order to find good hyper-parameter values in a relative short time, compared to grid or random search, we adopt the Bayesian optimization (Bergstra et al., 2013) approach. The size of the embedding layer is 300, the size of LSTM layers is 50 (100 for BiLSTM) and the size of the $tanh$ layer is 25. We insert Gaussian noise with $\sigma = 0.2$ and dropout of 0.3 at all layers. Moreover we apply dropout 0.2 at the recurrent connections of the LSTMs. Finally, we add L_2 regularization of 0.0001 at the loss function.

4 Results

Subtask A Results. The official evaluation metric of Subtask A is micro-averaged accuracy. Our team ranked 2nd in 7 teams, with score 0.632. A post-completion bug-fix improved significantly the performance of our model (Table 2).

	training	testing
hashtags	106	6
tweet pairs	109309	48285

Table 1: Dataset Statistics for Subtask A.

System	Acc Micro Avg
HumorHawk	0.675
DataStories (official)	0.632
Duluth	0.627
DataStories (fixed)	0.711

Table 2: The Results of our submitted and fixed models, evaluated on the official Semeval test set. The updated model would have ranked 1st.

#HastagWars Dataset Results. Furthermore, we compare the performance of our system on the #HastagWars dataset (Potash et al., 2016). Table 3 shows that our improved model outperforms the other approaches. The reported results are the average of 3 Leave-One-Out runs, in order to be comparable with (Potash et al., 2016). Figure 3 shows the detailed results of our model on the #HastagWars dataset, with the accuracy distribution over the hashtags.

System	Acc Micro Avg
LSTM (token) (Potash et al., 2016)	0.554 ($\pm$ 0.0085)
CNN (char) (Potash et al., 2016)	0.637 ($\pm$ 0.0074)
DataStories (fixed)	**0.696 ($\pm$ 0.0075)**

Table 3: Comparison on #HastagWars dataset.

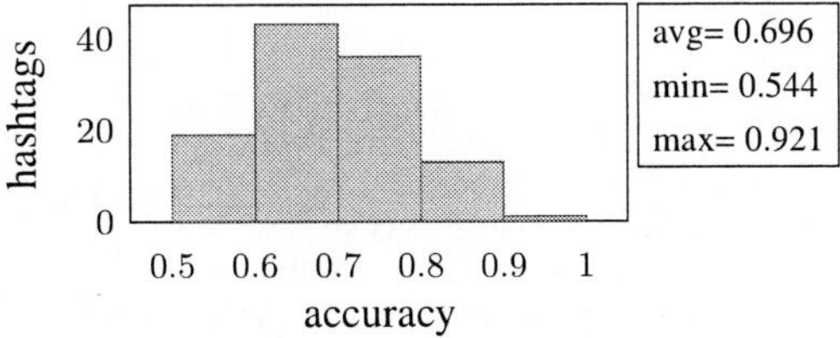

Figure 3: Detailed results on #HastagWars dataset.

Experimental Setup. For developing our models we used Keras (Chollet, 2015), Theano (Theano Dev Team, 2016) and Scikit-learn (Pedregosa et al., 2011). We trained our neural networks on a GTX750Ti(4GB), with each model taking approximately 30 minutes to train. Our source code is available to the research community[2].

5 Conclusion

In this paper we present our submission at SemEval-2017 Task 6 "#HashtagWars: Learning a Sense of Humor". We participated in Subtask A and ranked 2nd out of 7 teams. Our neural network uses a BiLSTM equipped with an attention mechanism in order to identify the most informative words. The network operates on the word level, leveraging word embeddings trained on a big collection of tweets. Despite the good results of our system, we believe that a character-level network will perform even better in computational humor tasks, as it will be able to capture the morphological characteristics of the words and possibly to identify word puns. We would like to explore this approach in the future.

---

[2]https://github.com/cbaziotis/
datastories-semeval2017-task6

References

Yoshua Bengio, Patrice Y. Simard, and Paolo Frasconi. 1994. Learning long-term dependencies with gradient descent is difficult. *IEEE Trans. Neural Networks* 5(2):157–166.

James Bergstra, Daniel Yamins, and David D. Cox. 2013. Making a Science of Model Search: Hyperparameter Optimization in Hundreds of Dimensions for Vision Architectures. *Proceedings of ICML* 28:115–123.

Dario Bertero and Pascale Fung. 2016a. Deep learning of audio and language features for humor prediction. In *Proceedings of LREC*.

Dario Bertero and Pascale Fung. 2016b. A long short-term memory framework for predicting humor in dialogues. In *Proceedings of NAACL-HLT*. pages 130–135.

Jane Bromley, James W. Bentz, Léon Bottou, Isabelle Guyon, Yann LeCun, Cliff Moore, Eduard Säckinger, and Roopak Shah. 1993. Signature Verification Using A "Siamese" Time Delay Neural Network. *IJPRAI* 7(4):669–688.

Lei Chen and Chong Min Lee. 2017. Convolutional Neural Network for Humor Recognition. *arXiv preprint arXiv:1702.02584* .

François Chollet. 2015. Keras. `https://github.com/fchollet/keras`.

Ronan Collobert and Jason Weston. 2008. A unified architecture for natural language processing: Deep neural networks with multitask learning. In *Proceedings ICML*. pages 160–167.

Yarin Gal and Zoubin Ghahramani. 2016. A theoretically grounded application of dropout in recurrent neural networks. In *Proceedings of NIPS*. pages 1019–1027.

Christian F. Hempelmann. 2008. Computational humor: Beyond the pun? *The Primer of Humor Research. Humor Research* 8:333–360.

Sepp Hochreiter, Yoshua Bengio, Paolo Frasconi, and Jürgen Schmidhuber. 2001. *Gradient Flow in Recurrent Nets: The Difficulty of Learning Long-Term Dependencies*. A field guide to dynamical recurrent neural networks. IEEE Press.

Sepp Hochreiter and Jürgen Schmidhuber. 1997. Long short-term memory. *Neural Computation* 9(8):1735–1780.

Daniel Jurafsky and James H. Martin. 2000. *Speech and Language Processing: An Introduction to Natural Language Processing, Computational Linguistics, and Speech Recognition*. Prentice Hall PTR, 1st edition.

Chloe Kiddon and Yuriy Brun. 2011. That's what she said: Double entendre identification. In *Proceedings of ACL*. pages 89–94.

Diederik Kingma and Jimmy Ba. 2014. Adam: A method for stochastic optimization. *arXiv preprint arXiv:1412.6980* .

Rada Mihalcea and Carlo Strapparava. 2006. Learning to laugh (automatically): Computational models for humor recognition. *Computational Intelligence* 22(2):126–142.

Tomas Mikolov, Ilya Sutskever, Kai Chen, Greg S. Corrado, and Jeff Dean. 2013. Distributed representations of words and phrases and their compositionality. In *Proceedings of NIPS*. pages 3111–3119.

Razvan Pascanu, Tomas Mikolov, and Yoshua Bengio. 2013. On the difficulty of training recurrent neural networks. In *Proceedings of ICML*. pages 1310–1318.

Fabian Pedregosa, Gaël Varoquaux, Alexandre Gramfort, Vincent Michel, Bertrand Thirion, Olivier Grisel, Mathieu Blondel, Peter Prettenhofer, Ron Weiss, Vincent Dubourg, and others. 2011. Scikit-learn: Machine learning in Python. *Journal of Machine Learning Research* 12:2825–2830.

Jeffrey Pennington, Richard Socher, and Christopher D. Manning. 2014. Glove: Global Vectors for Word Representation. In *Proceedings of EMNLP*. volume 14, pages 1532–1543.

Peter Potash, Alexey Romanov, and Anna Rumshisky. 2016. # HashtagWars: Learning a Sense of Humor. *arXiv preprint arXiv:1612.03216* .

Peter Potash, Alexey Romanov, and Anna Rumshisky. 2017. SemEval-2017 Task 6: #HashtagWars: Learning a Sense of Humor. In *Proceedings of SemEval*.

Tim Rocktäschel, Edward Grefenstette, Karl Moritz Hermann, Tomáš Kočiskáž, and Phil Blunsom. 2015. Reasoning about entailment with neural attention. *arXiv preprint arXiv:1509.06664* .

Toby Segaran and Jeff Hammerbacher. 2009. *Beautiful Data: The Stories Behind Elegant Data Solutions*. "O'Reilly Media, Inc.".

Nitish Srivastava, Geoffrey E. Hinton, Alex Krizhevsky, Ilya Sutskever, and Ruslan Salakhutdinov. 2014. Dropout: A simple way to prevent neural networks from overfitting. *Journal of Machine Learning Research* 15(1):1929–1958.

Oliviero Stock and Carlo Strapparava. 2003. Getting serious about the development of computational humor. In *Proceedings of IJCAI*. pages 59–64.

Theano Dev Team. 2016. Theano: A Python framework for fast computation of mathematical expressions. *arXiv e-prints* abs/1605.02688.

Diyi Yang, Alon Lavie, Chris Dyer, and Eduard H. Hovy. 2015. Humor Recognition and Humor Anchor Extraction. In *Proceedings of EMNLP*. pages 2367–2376.

Zichao Yang, Diyi Yang, Chris Dyer, Xiaodong He, Alex Smola, and Eduard Hovy. 2016. Hierarchical attention networks for document classification. In *Proceedings of NAACL-HLT*. pages 1480–1489.

TakeLab at SemEval-2017 Task 6: #RankingHumorIn4Pages

Marin Kukovačec, Juraj Malenica, Ivan Mršić, Antonio Šajatović,
Domagoj Alagić, Jan Šnajder
Text Analysis and Knowledge Engineering Lab
Faculty of Electrical Engineering and Computing, University of Zagreb
Unska 3, 10000 Zagreb, Croatia
`{name.surname}@fer.hr`

Abstract

This paper describes our system for humor ranking in tweets within the SemEval 2017 Task 6: #HashtagWars (6A and 6B). For both subtasks, we use an off-the-shelf gradient boosting model built on a rich set of features, handcrafted to provide the model with the external knowledge needed to better predict the humor in the text. The features capture various cultural references and specific humor patterns. Our system ranked 2nd (officially 7th) among 10 submissions on the Subtask A and 2nd among 9 submissions on the Subtask B.

1 Introduction

While extremely interesting, understanding humor expressed in text is a challenging natural language problem. Besides standard ambiguity of natural language, humor is also highly subjective and lacks an universal definition (Mihalcea and Strapparava, 2005). Moreover, humor should almost never be taken at face value, as its understanding often requires a broader context – external knowledge and common sense. On top of that, what is funny today might not be funny tomorrow, as humor goes hand in hand with ever-changing trends of popular culture.

Even though there has been some work on humor generation (Petrović and Matthews, 2013; Valitutti et al., 2013), most work has been concerned with humor detection, a task of classifying whether a given text snippet is humorous (Mihalcea and Strapparava, 2005; Kiddon and Brun, 2011; Yang et al., 2015; Chen and Lee, 2017). However, this research was mostly focused on a simple binary detection of humor.

In this paper, we describe a system for ranking humor in tweets, which we participated with in the SemEval-2017 Task 6 (Potash et al., 2017). It comprised two subtasks, one dealing with predicting which tweet out of two is more humorous, and other with ranking a set of tweets by their humorousness. Even though these tasks can be both posed and tackled differently, we straightforwardly used the obtained pairwise classifications from the first task in coming up with ranked lists for the second. Our system uses a standard gradient boosting classifier (GB) based on a rich set of features and collections of external knowledge. We ranked 2nd among 10 submissions (7th officially) at the Subtask 6A, and 2nd among 9 submissions at the Subtask 6B.

2 Task Description

The dataset provided by the task organizers comprises the tweets collected from many episodes of the Comedy Central show @midnight.[1] This game show is based around contestants and viewers providing humorous and witty tweets in response to a given topic (hashtag), which are then ranked by their humorousness. The compiled dataset consists of 11,685 tweets grouped into 106 hashtags. Each group is further split into three bins: the most humorous tweet (denoted 1), nine less humorous tweets (denoted 2), and a varying number of the least humorous tweets (denoted 0). The test set consists of 749 tweets grouped into 6 hashtags not present in the train set.

The task is divided into subtasks 6A and 6B. In the first subtask, participants must recognize the more humorous tweet of the two, whereas the second subtask asks for a complete tripartite ranking of all tweets under a given hashtag. This basically means that the order of the tweets is not important as long they are placed in the correct bin. For more details consult (Potash et al., 2017).

---

[1] `http://www.cc.com/shows/-midnight`

Proceedings of the 11th International Workshop on Semantic Evaluations (SemEval-2017), pages 396–400,
Vancouver, Canada, August 3 - 4, 2017. ©2017 Association for Computational Linguistics

3 Model

We tackle both subtasks with a single base model. For the subtask A, we trained a model that predicts which tweet of the given two is more humorous, and then used this information to rank the tweets for the subtask B. More specifically, we counted how many times a tweet was more humorous than other tweets, and ranked the tweets by that number. Note that this resulted in a complete ranking, which we reorganized into bins (which is possible as the cardinality of the two out of three bins is known). In the following sections, we describe our rich set of features and model optimization.

3.1 Features

We used Twitter-specialized preprocessing tools. More precisely, we first tokenize the dataset and then obtain the part-of-speech (POS) tags with Twokenizer.[2] This tool also accounts for the normalization of the elongated vowels (e.g., "heeeeello"→"hello"). For dependency parsing, we use TweeboParser.[3] We lemmatize the obtained words using the NLTK toolkit (Bird et al., 2009). In the end, we obtain a 140-dimensional feature vector of a tweet.[4] Below we describe the features grouped into categories (number of features per group given in parentheses).

Cultural reference features (96). By inspecting the dataset, we noticed that, at least within the @midnight game show, most jokes are based solely on taking the names of famous people, movies, TV series, and other culture references, and modifying them in an unexpected, yet humorous way. To this end, we acquired a number of collections covering such references, so that our model could recognize them within the tweets. The collections comprise, among others, movie titles, song names, book titles, TV series titles, cartoon titles, people names and their professions, nationality, and birth year (Yu et al., 2016) (Table 1). To obtain the features, we first calculate the tf-idf-weighted bag-of-words (BoW) vectors of all tweets and all items in the acquired collections. Then, for each collection, we construct a single feature that denotes the maximum cosine similar-

Collection	Number of items
Movie titles	6,609
Song names	3,820
Book titles	191
TV series titles	228
Cartoon titles	183
People information	10,951
One-line jokes	2,868
Curse words	165

Table 1: External knowledge collections we used in the model.

ity between a given tweet's vector and those of the items from the collection. We also construct a one-hot-encoded vector of professions of a person mentioned in the text (the resource covers 88 different occupations). In the case no person is mentioned in a tweet, this vector is set to a zero vector. Additionally, we specifically check whether there is a USA citizen mentioned in a tweet and fetch an average Google Trends[5] rank of all the named entities found within a tweet.

Binary and count-based features (15). Besides simple tweet length in characters, we also measure the common noun, proper noun, pronoun, adjective, and verb to token ratios. Analogously, we measure the punctuation count and punctuation to character ratio. Besides this, we detect whether time and place deixes occur in a tweet (Zhang and Liu, 2014) using a precompiled list of deixes. Furthermore, we used binary features that denote whether the tweet contains a exclamation mark, negation, hashtag, or a URL. On top of these features, we calculated how much times single words are repeated in a tweet.

Readability-based features (3). Our intuition tells us that good jokes "flow": they are catchy and easily pronounceable. To capture this, we used the features that gauge tweet readability. First, we employ the Flesch reading-ease test (Flesch, 1948). Secondly, we follow the work of Zhang and Liu (2014) and extract all the alliteration chains (sequences of at least two words that start with the same phone). We construct the alliteration feature as a total length of alliteration chains divided by the number of tweet tokens. Lastly, we measure the vowels to characters ratio.

---

[2] https://github.com/brendano/ark-tweet-nlp/

[3] https://github.com/ikekonglp/TweeboParser

[4] Note that this has nothing to do with the character limit on Twitter, which is coincidentally also 140.

[5] https://trends.google.com/trends/

Humor-specific features (25). As the simplest feature in this category, we measure the number of tokens between the root of a dependency-parsed sentence and furthest node pointing to it. With this feature we hope to capture punchlines, whose common characteristic is that they are usually found at the end of a sentence.

Additionally, by examining the dataset, we noticed that humor often arises from the use of a modifier that does not seem to fit with the word it modifies. For instance, in the case of "Conan the Apologizer" (orig. "Conan the Barbarian"), the tweet is humorous because Conan is never attributed with such a trait, as he never apologizes. To detect this disparity, we measure the cosine similarity of skip-gram (SG) embeddings (Mikolov et al., 2013) between certain parts of a tweet: the root and the subject, the root and the object, and the root and all of its modifiers. In the last case, we sum all the similarities. We use the freely-available pre-trained vectors.[6]

To detect puns, we use a simple heuristic – a tweet contains a pun if it matches in all but one word with any of the items from our collections. We also acquired a collection of one-line jokes and curse words (Table 1). For one-line jokes, we realized that it would be unreasonable to expect having a complete joke within a tweet. To account for this, we simply counted how many words from the collection of one-line jokes are present in a tweet. This way we hope to capture the characteristic words found in one-line jokes. Lastly, we map the tweet's hashtag to a predefined set of humor patterns, which we manually compiled out of all the hashtags from the dataset: *Movie, Song, Book, Cartoon, Show, Sci*Fi, Celeb, Food, *Words, Add*, Make*, If*, Before*, *Because, One*letter, Ruin*, Sexy*, y** (where * denotes a wildcard). We construct a one-hot-encoded vector of these patterns, which is set to zero if a new hashtag could not match to any of these patterns.

Sentiment-based features (1). We used the output of model for sentiment classification of tweets (Lozić et al., 2017) as one of our features.

3.2 Model Optimization

Considering that we tackle both subtasks using a binary classification model, we construct the instances by concatenating feature vectors of both

tweets in a pair. The pairs are constructed as a Cartesian product between all the tweets in all different bin pairings. Note that this results in an extremely large number of instances, as there are $1 \cdot 9 + 1 \cdot (n - 10) + 9 \cdot (n - 10)$ different pairs, where n denotes the number of tweets under a given hashtag. Additionally, to help the model learn the symmetric predictions, we include these pairs' symmetric counterparts as well, which doubles the total number.

Due to resource constraints, we decided to start off with a variety of readily-available models and rule out those that perform badly in our rough preliminary evaluation. Specifically, we trained a selection of models with their default hyperparameters on the train set and evaluated them on the trial set. Surprisingly, a single model, gradient boosting (GB) with variance loss, performed the best, so we decided to use it in as our base model. We used a GB implementation of the scikit-learn package (Pedregosa et al., 2011). We ran a fine-grained 5-fold cross-validation over two GB hyperparameters: number of estimators and maximum tree depth. As we are working with tweets grouped into hashtags, the folds actually contained whole hashtags. Additionally, note that we used a random sample of 80% of pairs for training in order to reduce the computation costs.

4 Evaluation

The subtask 6A was evaluated in terms of accuracy (higher is better), whereas the subtask 6B was evaluated in terms of a metric inspired by edit distance. The metric captures how many moves the tweet must make to fall into a correct bin (lower is better). This metric was normalized by the maximum possible edit distance. Both metrics were micro-averaged across hashtags.

4.1 Feature Analysis

A gradient boosting model allowed us to effortlessly acquire the list of feature importances. We report the top ten most relevant features, according to the model, in Figure 1. Most notably, five cultural reference features found their spot within this list. This confirmed our earlier intuition that, at least within the @midnight game show, most jokes are based on culture references, which are slightly transformed to induce a comical feel.

---

[6]https://code.google.com/archive/p/word2vec/

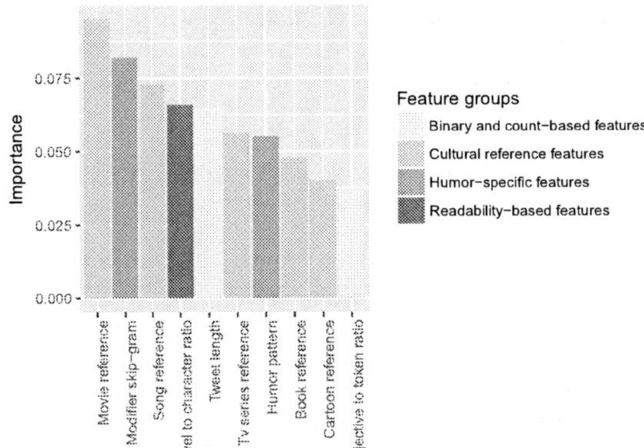

Figure 1: Top ten most important features, according to the trained GB model.

4.2 Model Variants

The two models we submitted for the subtask 6A are effectively identical. The only thing that makes them different is the size of the hyperparameter search space used model optimization: the second model used a more fine-grained grid of values and thus expectedly performed better. Our best (unofficial) model, denoted *TakeLab-2*, ranked 2nd (officially 7th) among 10 submissions with the accuracy of 0.641. Other participants' scores can be found in Table 2. We also included our official submissions (*TakeLab-official-1* and *TakeLab-official-2* along their non-official counterparts.[7]

As mentioned earlier, to obtain the tripartite ranking for the subtask 6B, we used the pairwise classifications obtained by the model used in the subtask 6A. This brought us to the distance metric value of 0.908, placing us at the 2nd place out of 9 submissions. Additionally, we experimented with LambdaMART algorithm to see how a full-fledged learning-to-rank algorithm would perform at this subtask. To that end, we explored two different variants of the model: one using all the described features (denoted *LambdaMART-all*) and one only the top ten features according to the model we used in subtask 6A (denoted *LambdaMART-10*). In comparison to the models we submitted, it is intriguing to see that both of these models perform only slightly worse. What is more, model variant trained using only the top ten features would rank third among all submissions.

---

[7]Unfortunately, we accidentally swapped the labels in the submission file so we had to unofficially submit a fixed file.

Team name	Accuracy
HumorHawk-2	0.675
TakeLab-2	**0.641**
HumorHawk-1	0.637
DataStories-1	0.632
Duluth-2	0.627
TakeLab-official-1	**0.597**
SRHR	0.523
SVNIT@SemEval	0.506
TakeLab-1	**0.403**
Duluth-1	0.397
TakeLab-official-2	**0.359**
QUB	0.187

Table 2: Final rankings on the subtask 6A. Our submissions are bolded.

Team name	Distance
Duluth-2	0.872
TakeLab-1	**0.908**
LambdaMART-10	**0.912**
QUB-1	0.924
QUB-2	0.924
SVNIT@SemEval-2	0.938
TakeLab-2	**0.944**
LambdaMART-all	**0.946**
SVNIT@SemEval-1	0.949
Duluth-1	0.967
# WarTeam-1	1.000

Table 3: Final rankings on the subtask 6B. Our submissions are bolded.

5 Conclusion

We described the system for humor detection which we participated with in the SemEval-2017 Task 6 (subtasks A and B). The gist of our system lies in an off-the-shelf gradient boosting model built on a rich set of handcrafted features. Knowing that humor understanding requires a broader context that also asks for external knowledge, we manually compiled a series of features that can capture the cultural references in a tweet – celebrities, movies, TV series, books, and so on. Besides that, we also included pronounciation-based, as well as humor-specific features that can recognize one-line jokes and puns, hoping to capture the humor patterns used throughout the @midnight game show. Future work includes experiments with full-fledged learning-to-rank models and a more detailed investigation of linguistically-motivated humor features, both backed up by exhaustive cross-dataset analyses.

References

Steven Bird, Ewan Klein, and Edward Loper. 2009. *Natural language processing with Python: analyzing text with the natural language toolkit.* O'Reilly Media, Inc.

Lei Chen and Chong Min Lee. 2017. Convolutional neural network for humor recognition. *arXiv preprint arXiv:1702.02584* .

Rudolph Flesch. 1948. A new readability yardstick. *Journal of applied psychology* 32(3):221.

Chloe Kiddon and Yuriy Brun. 2011. That's what she said: double entendre identification. In *Proceedings of the 49th Annual Meeting of the Association for Computational Linguistics: Human Language Technologies (ACL HLT 2011)*. Portland, Oregon, USA, pages 89–94.

David Lozić, Doria Šarić, Ivan Tokić, Zoran Medić, and Jan Šnajder. 2017. TakeLab at SemEval-2017 Task 4: Recent deaths and the power of nostalgia in sentiment analysis in Twitter. In *Proceedings of the 11th International Workshop on Semantic Evaluation (SemEval-2017)*. Vancouver, Canada, pages 782–787.

Rada Mihalcea and Carlo Strapparava. 2005. Making computers laugh: Investigations in automatic humor recognition. In *Proceedings of the 2005 Conference on Human Language Technology and Empirical Methods in Natural Language Processing (HIT EMNLP 2005)*. Vancouver, B.C., Canada, pages 531–538.

Tomas Mikolov, Ilya Sutskever, Kai Chen, Greg S Corrado, and Jeff Dean. 2013. Distributed representations of words and phrases and their compositionality. In *Proceedings of the Neural Information Processing Systems Conference (NIPS 2013)*. Lake Tahoe, USA, pages 3111–3119.

Fabian Pedregosa, Gaël Varoquaux, Alexandre Gramfort, Vincent Michel, Bertrand Thirion, Olivier Grisel, Mathieu Blondel, Peter Prettenhofer, Ron Weiss, Vincent Dubourg, Jake Vanderplas, Alexandre Passos, David Cournapeau, Matthieu Brucher, Matthieu Perrot, and Édouard Duchesnay. 2011. Scikit-learn: Machine learning in Python. *Journal of Machine Learning Research* 12:2825–2830.

Sasa Petrović and David Matthews. 2013. Unsupervised joke generation from big data. In *Proceedings of the 51st Annual Meeting of the Association for Computational Linguistics (ACL 2013)*. Sofia, Bulgaria, pages 228–232.

Peter Potash, Alexey Romanov, and Anna Rumshisky. 2017. SemEval-2017 Task 6: #HashtagWars: Learning a sense of humor. In *Proceedings of the 11th International Workshop on Semantic Evaluation (SemEval-2017)*. Vancouver, Canada, pages 49–57.

Alessandro Valitutti, Hannu Toivonen, Antoine Doucet, and Jukka M. Toivanen. 2013. "Let everything turn well in your wife": Generation of adult humor using lexical constraints. In *Proceedings of the 51st Annual Meeting of the Association for Computational Linguistics (ACL 2013)*. Sofia, Bulgaria, pages 243–248.

Diyi Yang, Alon Lavie, Chris Dyer, and Eduard H. Hovy. 2015. Humor recognition and humor anchor extraction. In *Proceedings of the 2015 Conference on Empirical Methods in Natural Language Processing (EMNLP 2015)*. Lisbon, Portugal, pages 2367–2376.

Amy Zhao Yu, Shahar Ronen, Kevin Hu, Tiffany Lu, and César A Hidalgo. 2016. Pantheon 1.0, a manually verified dataset of globally famous biographies. *Scientific data* 3.

Renxian Zhang and Naishi Liu. 2014. Recognizing humor on Twitter. In *Proceedings of the 23rd ACM International Conference on Information and Knowledge Management (CIKM 2014)*. ACM, Shanghai, China, pages 889–898.

SRHR at SemEval-2017 Task 6: Word Associations for Humour Recognition

Andrew Cattle   **Xiaojuan Ma**
Hong Kong University of Science and Technology
Department of Computer Science and Engineering
Clear Water Bay, Hong Kong
{acattle,mxj}@cse.ust.hk

Abstract

This paper explores the role of semantic relatedness features, such as word associations, in humour recognition. Specifically, we examine the task of inferring pairwise humour judgments in Twitter hashtag wars. We examine a variety of word association features derived from the University of Southern Florida Free Association Norms (USF) (Nelson et al., 2004) and the Edinburgh Associative Thesaurus (EAT) (Kiss et al., 1973) and find that word association-based features outperform Word2Vec similarity, a popular semantic relatedness measure. Our system achieves an accuracy of 56.42% using a combination of unigram perplexity, bigram perplexity, $\text{EAT}^{\text{tweet-avg}}_{\text{difference}}$, $\text{USF}^{\text{max}}_{\text{forward}}$, $\text{EAT}^{\text{word-avg}}_{\text{difference}}$, $\text{USF}^{\text{word-avg}}_{\text{difference}}$, $\text{EAT}^{\text{min}}_{\text{forward}}$, $\text{USF}^{\text{tweet-max}}_{\text{difference}}$, and $\text{EAT}^{\text{min}}_{\text{backward}}$.

1 Introduction

What makes something funny? Humour is very personal; what is funny to one person may not be funny to another. Yet, there are still certain works which seem to have widespread appeal, from comedian Louis C.K. to sitcom The Big Bang Theory. What makes these works more humorous to the average person than similar ones? A good place to start might be with the show *@midnight* and their nightly *Hashtag Wars* segment. Each night viewers are given a prompt in the form of a Twitter hashtag and asked to tweet their funniest responses. Given two such tweets, how can we decide which is funnier?

This paper largely focuses on semantic relatedness-based features and their application in humour recognition. It is reasonable to assume

that a punchline should be related to a setup; that is to say, a tweet's relevance to its hashtag prompt should be apparent. Similarly, it is reasonable to assume that punchlines should have a certain amount of unexpectedness; in other words, funnier tweets should be harder to guess. As such, it follows that semantic relation strength in general should serve as a barometer for humour where weaker relations are less understandable and stronger relations are more obvious (Cattle and Ma, 2016). Moreover, we hypothesize that the interplay between this understandability and unexpectedness should provide an even more powerful indication of humour.

2 Previous Work

Early work on computational humour focused more on humour generation in specific contexts, such as punning riddles (Binsted and Ritchie, 1994; Ritchie et al., 2007), humorous acronyms (Stock and Strapparava, 2003), or jokes in the form of "I like my X like I like my Y" (Petrovic and Matthews, 2013). Labutov and Lipson (2012) offered a slightly more generalized approach using Semantic Script Theory of Humour.

Recently, humour recognition has gained increasing attention. Taylor and Mazlack (2004) presented a method for recognizing wordplay in "Knock Knock" jokes. Mihalcea and Strapparava (2005) used stylistic features, such as alliteration and antonymy, to identify humorous one-liners. Mihalcea and Pulman (2007) expanded on this approach, finding that human-centeredness and negative sentiment are both useful in not only identifying humorous one-liners, but also distinguishing satirical news articles from genuine ones. Related to humor recognition, irony identification (Davidov et al., 2010; Tsur et al., 2010; Reyes et al., 2012) typically uses n-gram and sentiment fea-

Proceedings of the 11th International Workshop on Semantic Evaluations (SemEval-2017), pages 401–406,
Vancouver, Canada, August 3 - 4, 2017. ©2017 Association for Computational Linguistics

tures to distinguish ironic from non-ironic tweets.

Shahaf et al. (2015) and Radev et al. (2016) examine humour recognition as a ranking task. Both works aim to identify the funnier of a pair of cartoon captions taken from submissions to The New Yorker's Cartoon Caption Contest[1]. Each week, New Yorker readers are presented "a cartoon in need of a caption" and encouraged to submit their own humorous suggestions. Shahaf et al. (2015) found that simpler grammatical structures, less reliance on proper nouns, and shorter joke phrases all lead to funnier captions. Radev et al. (2016) showed that in addition to human-centeredness and sentiment, high LexRank score was a strong indication of humour, where LexRank is a graph-based text summarization technique introduced in Erkan and Radev (2004).

Cattle and Ma (2016) noted that cartoon caption contests and hashtag wars are very similar in that they both involve short, humorous texts written as a response to an external stimulus. Furthermore, Cattle and Ma (2016) explored the role of semantic relatedness between setups and punchlines in perceived humour and found USF Free Association Norm- (Nelson et al., 2004) and Normalized Google Distance-based features (Cilibrasi and Vitanyi, 2007) to be useful in identifying funnier tweets. However, the results of Cattle and Ma (2016) were based on a small dataset of only four hashtag prompts, inferred humour judgments from Twitter likes and retweets, and relied on human annotations to identify both setups and punchlines.

3 System Definition

3.1 Dataset

We performed all training and testing on the dataset introduced in Potash et al. (2017) specifically for this task. The dataset consists of response tweets to 112 hashtags created by @midnight. The tweets are separated into files according to their respective hashtags, each hashtag file containing an average of 114 tweets. Each tweet includes a label specifying whether it was deemed to be funniest, in the top ten, or neither for that particular hashtag according to the @midnight staff. Potash et al. (2017) further divides the hashtags into three sets: Trial, Training, and Evaluation containing five, 101, and six hashtags, respectively.

3.2 Preprocessing and Baseline Features

Before feature extraction, tweets went through a preprocessing procedure. Each tweet was lowercased and then tokenized and POS tagged using Tweet NLP (Gimpel et al., 2011; Owoputi et al., 2013). English stop words were removed along with any punctuation, discourse markers (e.g. "RT"), interjections, emoticons, and URLs according to Tweet NLP's POS tags. Furthermore, prepositions, postpositions, subordinating conjunctions, coordinating conjunctions, verb particles, and predeterminers were also removed as these tended to be closed-class words (Gimpel et al., 2011) which do not affect the word-level semantic relationships this paper focuses on. Any references to the @*midnight* Twitter account or the relevant hashtag prompt were also removed. Each hashtag prompt was tokenized according to the hashtag segmentations included with the dataset. English stop words were removed along with any single digit numbers and the words "in" and "words". This was to omit the collocation "in # words", a common type of hashtag prompt, which does not affect semantic meaning.

Following the model of Shahaf et al. (2015), unigram and bigram bag-of-words features were extracted for each tweet. Furthermore, both unigram and bigram perplexities were calculated based on a simple language model created using n-gram counts from the Rovereto Twitter N-Gram Corpus (Herdağdelen, 2013). For simplicity, our language model uses add-one smoothing, although we intend to explore more complex smoothing techniques in future works. These features were intended to serve as a baseline for semantic relatedness-based features.

3.3 Semantic Relatedness Features

The results of Cattle and Ma (2016) suggest that University of Southern Florida Free Association Norm-based features are useful in humour recognition. Given two words, *A* and *B*, the USF Free Association Norms (USF) report the *forward strength*, i.e. proportion of participants who, when given word *A*, produce word *B* as their first reaction (Nelson et al., 2004). The USF dataset was represented as a graph where each node *U* referred to a word in the vocabulary and each edge from *U* to *V* had a weight proportional to the negative log of the forward strength form word *U* to word *V*. By representing the forward strengths as their negative logs, finding the shortest path between two nodes using Dijkstra's Algorithm is equivalent to finding the path with the maximal product of forward strengths. Using this information we can easily estimate the forward strength between any two words in the USF vocabulary.

Word association is unidirectional; given the word "beer" a participant might say "glass" but given "glass" they might not say "beer" (Ma, 2013). Thus, we collect both $USF_{forward}$, representing how strongly the words in the hashtag prompt are associated with the words in the tweet's content, and $USF_{backward}$, representing how strongly the tweet's content is associated with the hashtag. These can be roughly interpreted as how easy a punchline is to guess given only the setup and how easy a punchline is to understand in context, respectively. Unlike Cattle and Ma (2016), which used human annotations to limit their scope to only punch words, we consider all hashtag-word/tweet-word pairs. We record the maximum, minimum, and average values for each feature across all such pairs.

Since we expect tweets which are relatively unexpected, i.e. low $USF_{forward}$, but also relatively easy to understand, i.e. high $USF_{backward}$, to be deemed funnier, we also collect $USF_{difference}$, the difference between the two values. $USF_{difference}$ is calculated both at word-level, e.g. $USF_{difference}^{word-max}$ refers to the maximal difference for a single word, and tweet-level, e.g. $USF_{difference}^{tweet-max}$ refers to the difference between $USF_{forward}^{max}$ and $USF_{backward}^{max}$.

In addition to USF association-based features, we also extract an identical set of features in the same manner but using the association strengths reported in the Edinburgh Associative Thesaurus (EAT) (Kiss et al., 1973).

To test the effectiveness of association-based features, we also collected the maximum, minimum, and average Word2Vec (Mikolov et al., 2013) cosine similarities across all hashtag-word/tweet-word pairs to serve as a semantic-feature baseline. We used Google's pre-trained Word2Vec embeddings[2].

3.4 Classifier

Features were extracted for each tweet following the methodology presented in the previous sections. Next, for each hashtag, tweet pairs were generated such that the two tweets had different humour judgment labels, i.e. one of the tweets is judged funnier according to the gold standard ratings. Each tweet pair then became two ordered training examples; one where the funnier of the two tweets was on the left and one where the funnier tweet was on the right, with appropriate training labels. For each training example, the left tweet's feature vector was concatenated with that of the right tweet's as well as the difference between the two. These training vectors were then used to train a Random Forest Classifier using scikit-learn[3], a popular Python machine learning library, using default settings and 100 estimators.

4 Results and Discussion

Feature selection experiments were performed using Training data for training and Trial data as a validation set to identify the best performing features. Using these features, we trained a new classifier on a combination of Training and Trial data and evaluated its performance on Evaluation data. The results in Table 1 show that the highest performing features in the validation test were $EAT_{difference}^{tweet-avg}$, $USF_{forward}^{max}$, $EAT_{difference}^{word-avg}$, $USF_{difference}^{word-avg}$, $EAT_{forward}^{min}$, $USF_{difference}^{tweet-max}$, and $EAT_{backward}^{min}$. The results using only these features are reported as **Best Features**. We also evaluated the performance of two more feature combinations: best features plus perplexity and n-gram features, as **Best Features+**, and best feature plus perplexity features only, as **Best Features+ (no n-gram)**.

Interestingly, although n-gram features on their own performed no better than chance in both validation and evaluation tests, their addition to the Best Features resulted in a large 8% point gain in validation tests compared to the same features minus n-grams (p=0.02 for paired t-test on file-level accuracies). However, their addition resulted in a drop in performance in evaluation tests, although this result was not statistically significant. Considering the dataset contains under 13,000 unique tweets, this extreme variation in performance might be due to n-gram features overfitting on the small dataset. By comparison, Shahaf et al. (2015) found n-grams alone offered a 55% accuracy on the similar task of selecting the funnier of two cartoon captions but their dataset contained over four times as many unique documents.

Another problem facing n-gram features is that

---

[2]https://code.google.com/archive/p/word2vec/

[3]http://scikit-learn.org/

Features		Accuracy %	
		Trial	Evaluation
baseline	n-grams	50.42	50.20
	unigram perplexity	53.05	50.27
	bigram perplexity	54.29	53.78
	Word2Vec Sim	50.72	50.76
Best Features	$EAT_{difference}^{tweet\text{-}avg}$	57.40	46.54
	$USF_{forward}^{max}$	55.15	48.33
	$EAT_{difference}^{word\text{-}avg}$	54.80	46.18
	$USF_{difference}^{word\text{-}avg}$	54.80	51.63
	$EAT_{forward}^{min}$	53.84	47.29
	$USF_{difference}^{tweet\text{-}max}$	52.44	50.58
	$EAT_{backward}^{min}$	51.94	44.33
Best Features		**53.42**	**52.40**
Best Features+		**61.51**	**53.72**
Best Features+ (no n-gram)		**53.39**	**56.42**

Table 1: Accuracy by feature on Trial and Evaluation data

compared to cartoon captions, hashtag wars have a higher incidence of novel word-forms, typically in service of a pun, which occur only a few times for a particular hashtag prompt and never again. E.g. "HELLMFAO. #SpookyBands @midnight", or "Purrassic Park #CatBooks @Midnight". Simple n-gram models, such as the one used in this paper, are ill-equipped to deal with these types of out-of-vocabulary words.

Compared to Word2Vec, association-based features proved more discerning. One possible explanation for this is that word association is a more flexible relatedness measure than similarity. It is hard to find examples of similar concepts which are not also associated, but easy to find examples of associated concepts which are not similar. E.g. "red" and "green" would be similar in that they are both colours and associated in that they appear together at Christmas. However, "green" and "grass" are associated in that grass is green but the two words are very different.

Another possible explanation is that word associations are unidirectional while most similarity or distance metrics are not. The fact that four of the top seven best features are some variation of association difference seems to support our hypothesis that the interplay between a joke's unexpectedness and its understandability serves as a useful indication of humour.

Cattle and Ma (2016) noted that their USF performance was hurt by a lack of coverage. This seems to be the case for us as well. Less than 65%

of tweets contained a valid $USF_{forward}$ strength, with valid $USF_{backward}$ and $USF_{difference}$ strengths appearing in only 70% and less than 60%, respectively. By comparison, almost 95% of tweets contained a valid Word2Vec similarity. EAT showed slightly better coverage with valid $EAT_{forward}$ and $EAT_{backward}$ strengths each appearing in almost 75% of tweets and $EAT_{difference}$ appearing in just under 70%. This may explain why EAT features outperformed USF in the validation tests. This was expected given that EAT contains twice as many words as USF and four times as many edges.

In order to avoid using human annotations, such as those in Cattle and Ma (2016), USF, EAT, and Word2Vec features were calculated across all hashtag-word/tweet-word pairs. Even though the bag-of-words was heavily filtered by POS to leave only words which carry more word-level semantic meaning, this is a shotgun-like approach which likely added noise to the data. This may explain why only two of the top seven word association features use min values. The punchline makes up only a small part of the tweet and it is expected that the remainder would not show any strong associations. Some kind of automatic punchline identification would help in this respect but may exacerbate the aforementioned coverage issue faced by USF and EAT.

5 Conclusion and Future Work

Humour recognition in general is a very difficult task and humour recognition in hashtag wars is no exception. The majority of features tested performed only slightly better than chance if better than chance at all. Our optimal result was only a 56.42% accuracy on Evaluation data and was obtained using only the features unigram perplexity, bigram perplexity, $EAT_{difference}^{tweet\text{-}avg}$, $USF_{forward}^{max}$, $EAT_{difference}^{word\text{-}avg}$, $USF_{difference}^{word\text{-}avg}$, $EAT_{forward}^{min}$, $USF_{difference}^{tweet\text{-}max}$, and $EAT_{backward}^{min}$. Although our accuracy is fairly low we believe semantic relatedness features, and word association-based features in particular, are worthy of further study.

Our system could be improved by using automatic punchline detection to cut down on the noise in our word association features. Furthermore, a larger vocabulary or even the ability to automatically infer association strength would increase the usefulness of word association features. Finally, a larger dataset may be needed to rule out the efficacy of n-gram features.

References

Kim Binsted and Graeme Ritchie. 1994. An implemented model of punning riddles. In *Proceedings of the Twelfth AAAI National Conference on Artificial Intelligence*. AAAI Press, pages 633–638.

Andrew Cattle and Xiaojuan Ma. 2016. Effects of semantic relatedness between setups and punchlines in twitter hashtag games. *PEOPLES 2016* page 70.

Rudi L Cilibrasi and Paul MB Vitanyi. 2007. The google similarity distance. *IEEE Transactions on knowledge and data engineering* 19(3).

Dmitry Davidov, Oren Tsur, and Ari Rappoport. 2010. Semi-supervised recognition of sarcastic sentences in twitter and amazon. In *Proceedings of the fourteenth conference on computational natural language learning*. Association for Computational Linguistics, pages 107–116.

Günes Erkan and Dragomir R Radev. 2004. Lexrank: Graph-based lexical centrality as salience in text summarization. *Journal of Artificial Intelligence Research* 22:457–479.

Kevin Gimpel, Nathan Schneider, Brendan O'Connor, Dipanjan Das, Daniel Mills, Jacob Eisenstein, Michael Heilman, Dani Yogatama, Jeffrey Flanigan, and Noah A Smith. 2011. Part-of-speech tagging for twitter: Annotation, features, and experiments. In *Proceedings of the 49th Annual Meeting of the Association for Computational Linguistics: Human Language Technologies: short papers-Volume 2*. Association for Computational Linguistics, pages 42–47.

Amaç Herdağdelen. 2013. Twitter n-gram corpus with demographic metadata. *Language resources and evaluation* 47(4):1127–1147.

George R Kiss, Christine Armstrong, Robert Milroy, and James Piper. 1973. An associative thesaurus of english and its computer analysis. *The computer and literary studies* pages 153–165.

Igor Labutov and Hod Lipson. 2012. Humor as circuits in semantic networks. In *Proceedings of the 50th Annual Meeting of the Association for Computational Linguistics: Short Papers-Volume 2*. Association for Computational Linguistics, pages 150–155.

Xiaojuan Ma. 2013. Evocation: analyzing and propagating a semantic link based on free word association. *Language resources and evaluation* 47(3):819–837.

Rada Mihalcea and Stephen Pulman. 2007. Characterizing humour: An exploration of features in humorous texts. In *International Conference on Intelligent Text Processing and Computational Linguistics*. Springer, pages 337–347.

Rada Mihalcea and Carlo Strapparava. 2005. Making computers laugh: Investigations in automatic humor recognition. In *Proceedings of the Conference on Human Language Technology and Empirical Methods in Natural Language Processing*. Association for Computational Linguistics, pages 531–538.

Tomas Mikolov, Ilya Sutskever, Kai Chen, Greg S Corrado, and Jeff Dean. 2013. Distributed representations of words and phrases and their compositionality. In *Advances in neural information processing systems*. pages 3111–3119.

Douglas L Nelson, Cathy L McEvoy, and Thomas A Schreiber. 2004. The university of south florida free association, rhyme, and word fragment norms. *Behavior Research Methods, Instruments, & Computers* 36(3):402–407.

Olutobi Owoputi, Brendan O'Connor, Chris Dyer, Kevin Gimpel, Nathan Schneider, and Noah A Smith. 2013. Improved part-of-speech tagging for online conversational text with word clusters. Association for Computational Linguistics.

Sasa Petrovic and David Matthews. 2013. Unsupervised joke generation from big data. In *ACL (2)*. Citeseer, pages 228–232.

Peter Potash, Alexey Romanov, and Anna Rumshisky. 2017. Semeval-2017 task 6: #hashtagwars: Learning a sense of humor. In *Proceedings of the 11th International Workshop on Semantic Evaluation (SemEval-2017)*. Association for Computational Linguistics, Vancouver, Canada, pages 49–57. http://www.aclweb.org/anthology/S17-2004.

Dragomir Radev, Amanda Stent, Joel Tetreault, Aasish Pappu, Aikaterini Iliakopoulou, Agustin Chanfreau, Paloma de Juan, Jordi Vallmitjana, Alejandro Jaimes, Rahul Jha, and Robert Mankoff. 2016. Humor in collective discourse: Unsupervised funniness detection in the new yorker cartoon caption contest. In Nicoletta Calzolari (Conference Chair), Khalid Choukri, Thierry Declerck, Sara Goggi, Marko Grobelnik, Bente Maegaard, Joseph Mariani, Helene Mazo, Asuncion Moreno, Jan Odijk, and Stelios Piperidis, editors, *Proceedings of the Tenth International Conference on Language Resources and Evaluation (LREC 2016)*. European Language Resources Association (ELRA), Paris, France.

Antonio Reyes, Paolo Rosso, and Davide Buscaldi. 2012. From humor recognition to irony detection: The figurative language of social media. *Data & Knowledge Engineering* 74:1–12.

Graeme Ritchie, Ruli Manurung, Helen Pain, Annalu Waller, Rolf Black, and Dave OMara. 2007. A practical application of computational humour. In *Proceedings of the 4th International Joint Conference on Computational Creativity*. pages 91–98.

Dafna Shahaf, Eric Horvitz, and Robert Mankoff. 2015. Inside jokes: Identifying humorous cartoon captions. In *Proceedings of the 21th*

ACM SIGKDD International Conference on Knowledge Discovery and Data Mining. ACM, New York, NY, USA, KDD '15, pages 1065–1074. https://doi.org/10.1145/2783258.2783388.

Oliviero Stock and Carlo Strapparava. 2003. Hahacronym: Humorous agents for humorous acronyms. *Humor* 16(3):297–314.

Julia M Taylor and Lawrence J Mazlack. 2004. Computationally recognizing wordplay in jokes. In *Proceedings of the Cognitive Science Society*. volume 26.

Oren Tsur, Dmitry Davidov, and Ari Rappoport. 2010. Icwsm-a great catchy name: Semi-supervised recognition of sarcastic sentences in online product reviews. In *ICWSM*. pages 162–169.

#WarTeam at SemEval-2017 Task 6: Using Neural Networks for Discovering Humorous Tweets

Iuliana Alexandra Fleşcan-Lovin-Arseni, Ramona Andreea Turcu, Cristina Sîrbu,
Larisa Alexa, Sandra Maria Amarandei, Nichita Herciu, Constantin Scutaru,
Diana Trandabăţ, Adrian Iftene

University Alexandru Ioan Cuza of Iaşi, Romania
{alexandra.flescan, ramona.turcu, cristina.sirbu, larisa.alexa,
sandra.amarandei, nichita.herciu, dtrandabat, adiftene}@info.uaic.ro

Abstract

This paper presents the participation of #WarTeam in Task 6 of SemEval2017 with a system classifying humor by comparing and ranking tweets. The training data consists of annotated tweets from the *@midnight* TV show. #WarTeam's system uses a neural network (TensorFlow) having inputs from a Naïve Bayes humor classifier and a sentiment analyzer.

1 Introduction

One of the most recent direction in Artificial Intelligence is related to humor and, in recent years, comedy based computing such as Manatee (Gustin, 2014), the joke writing computer, STANDUP - System to Augment Non-Speakers' Dialogue Using Puns (Waller et al., 2009); SASI the sarcasm-detector (Davidov et al., 2010), or DeviaNT (Kiddon and Brun, 2011) were developed, with more or less success (Leybovich 2017). If the well-hidden structure of humor, from which are derived all uncertainties, would be uncovered, it would have great applicability in social networks and human computer interactive systems. In time, research has been made and progress is undeniable. However, most recent studies are concerned with a binary perspective over humor where two main features are ignored: its continuous nature and subjectivity.

Our objectives in Task 6 of SemEval 2017 (Potash et al., 2017) were: (1) to build an application able to score the degree of humor in tweets from the Midnight TV show, the Hashtag War section and (2) to discover ways to automatically determine amusement and how to quantify it.

The paper is structured in 5 sections: Section 2 discusses existing approaches to humor detection and Section 3 presents the methodology of our system. Section 4 briefly analyses the obtained results, before Section 5 drafting some conclusions and further work.

2 State of the Art

In the area of identifying, describing and evaluating humor, the majority of studies succeeded only to describe if something is funny or not. The actual tendency is to move forward to something more specific, namely to the value or the degree of humor. Currently, studies are mainly concerned with the binary evaluation of humor, whether it is funny or not. Their object of study is different as some of them focused on evaluating humor in videos and images, while others in texts expressed in natural language.

As for the studies related to identifying humor in pictures (Chandrasekaran et al., 2016), theories in this area suggest that humor's key components are qualities such as unexpectedness, incongruity, pain, as observed by analyzing a database of 6,400 funny and not funny images.

The linguistic side of this computational approach identifies the mechanisms for humor detection with a formal model of the semantic and syntactic regularities underlying some of the simpler types of punning riddles (Mulder and Nijholt, 2002).

Barbieri and Saggion (Barbieri and Saggion, 2014) represents the task as a classification problem, applying supervised machine learning methods taking into account a group of features: frequency, written-spoken style uses; intensity of ad-

Proceedings of the 11th International Workshop on Semantic Evaluations (SemEval-2017), pages 407–410,
Vancouver, Canada, August 3 - 4, 2017. ©2017 Association for Computational Linguistics

verbs and adjectives; structure (length, punctuation, emoticons, links), sentiments (gap between positive and negative terms); common vs. rare synonyms use; ambiguity (measure of possible ambiguities). In a part of their research, they treat irony and humor as a single class called figurative language and, by using specially designed humor characteristics, obtain accuracy around 76%.

A similar direction is investigated in (Yang et al., 2015), where they first formulate the task as a traditional text classification problem, to further apply Random Forest. At the same time, semantic structures behind humor are analyzed in terms of meaning incongruity, ambiguity, phonetic style and personal affect. A simple and effective method of Maximal Decrement is proposed. The phonetic style (alliteration, rhyme, word repetition etc.) of a joke is regarded as being at least as important as its content.

Several studies agree that humor has at its basis incongruity. In (Mihalcea et al., 2010), models are analyzed based on their features:

(1) semantic relatedness, where the intuition is that the correct punch line will have a minimum relatedness with respect to the set-up: knowledge-based metrics and corpus-based metrics (vector space model and pointwise mutual information), based on word co-occurrence over very large corpora, and domain fitness obtained from WordNet domains; and

(2) joke-specific features: polysemy and latent semantic analysis trained on joke data that contains one-linears (short sentences with comic effects, simple syntax, rhetoric devices and creative language constructions). As the authors confess, the difficulty in detecting incongruity is that it has to satisfy to opposite requirements, namely to be coherent but to produce a surprising effect. Using a combined model consisting of an SVM learning system trained on a combination of knowledge-based, corpus-based, and joke-specific features, they obtained a precision of 84%.

The most common and efficiently used text classifiers are Naive Bayes and Support Vector Machines (Mihalcera and Pulman, 2007).

The first one is used to estimate the probability of a category using joint probabilities. The second ones are binary classifiers that seek to find the hyperplane that best separates a set of positive examples from a set of negative examples, with maximum margin.

Our approach proposes the use of neural networks as an interface between a Naïve Bayes classifier and a sentiment analyzer, trained on the data provided by SemEval 2017 task 6 organizers.

3 Methodology

#WildDev's team developed a system for classifying humor by comparing and ranking a set of tweets on the basis of a collection of hashtags from @midnight show. Our approach considered using two machine learning techniques: neural networks and Naïve Bayes.

The format of the trial and training data was established by the task organizers (Potash et al., 2017), having the following structure:

"720293211374104578 Honey, I lost the house. #VegasMovies @midnight   0"

with a tweet ID, the text of the tweet, the hashtag it related to in the #HashtagWar at @midnight show, and a score.

Each tweet in a set of tweets is evaluated with a score of 0, 1, or 2, where 2 corresponds to the funniest tweet in the set, 1 corresponds to a tweet in the top 10 funniest tweets, and 0 corresponds to a tweet not in the top 10 funniest tweets (most of the tweets in a file). This way, the continuous nature of humor can be investigated.

The architecture of the #WarTeam is presented in figure 1 and includes four modules: a pre-processing task; a Naïve Bayes classification algorithm for identifying humorous vs. non-humorous instances; a simple, dictionary-based sentiment analyzer and a neural network supervised algorithm. Each specific module is further detailed below.

3.1 Pre-processing

The first module consists in a pre-processing phase, a component responsible with cleaning each tweet before passing it to the machine learning algorithms. The goal of this module is to remove unneeded data which might have a bad impact on the learning algorithm.

The pre-processor module is a JAVA standalone application that receives as input a file with multiple tweets, one per line, and returns a list with processed tweets. Several rules are applied in the process of cleaning tweets. The most important one is removing frequent hashtags.

We consider a hashtag to be frequent when it appears in at least two of the tweets given as input. This rule was established due to our belief

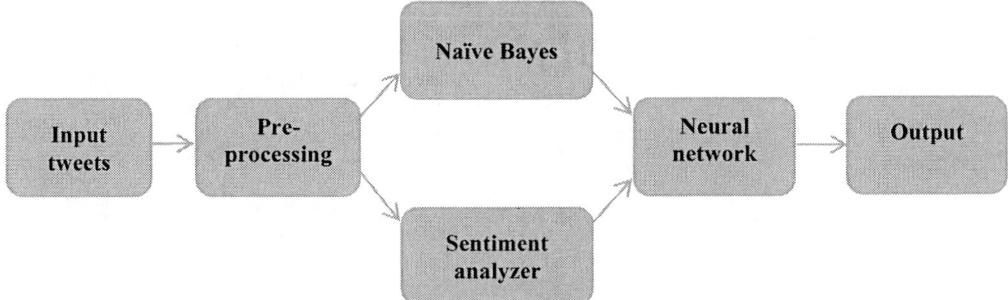

Figure 1. System Architecture

that humor, in the sense of the TV show *@midnight* from Comedy Central, from which the training data was collected, arises mostly from new, creative content.

If the hashtag is unique, the pre-processor will try to split it into separate words (this rule applies only for hashtags written with camel case).

After all hashtags have been processed and any other irrelevant data removed (e.g links, punctuation), the tweets are lemmatized and each word is replaced with the corresponding lemma. This will help the learning algorithm find more matches in the list of tweets, than it would if word forms were used.

This module uses two language processing libraries: Stanford parser (Klein and Manning, 2003) for tokenization and WordNet[1] for finding a word's lemma.

3.2 Naïve Bayes

Two machine learning algorithms were used to extract humor from tweets: a Naïve Bayes and a neural network, trained on the data provided by SemEval 2017 Task 6 organizers.

The first solution we adopted was to train binary Naïve Bayes algorithms on the training data, for each category of scores. As features for the Naïve Bayes classifiers, we used data from the pre-processing module (lemmas)
However, the classifiers turned out to be rather biased, since only one most funny tweet (score 2) and top ten funniest tweets (score 1) are annotated for each set of tweets, and the majority of tweets have the score 0.

3.3 Sentiment analyzer

Trying to improve the results of the classifier, we developed a further module responsible for attaching a polarity score to each word in the tweet:
"<word>" : <polarity_score>,

This simple sentiment analyzer used a manually acquired dictionary of about 2500 lemmas annotated with a sentiment score ranging from -5 (corresponding to the extreme negative sentiment) to +5 (the extreme positive one). The words not included in this list were considered neutral and received the polarity_score 0.

Using a python program, the input tweets and the dictionary of polarity scores, a list of word pairs with corresponding scores was generated.
"<word1> <word2>" : <score>,
The main idea behind this approach is that there are contrastive bigrams more frequently indicating humor, such as "black milk".

3.4 Neural network

The output of the Naïve Bayes classifier, along with the scores generated by the sentiment analyzer, are inputs for a neural network algorithm. Additionally, a manually generated corpus of celebrity names was also used as input.
"<name>" : <score>,
This was motivated b the observation that tweets containing celebrity names were considered more attractive.

A neural network with 101 neurons was trained to rate the tweets in their final form. This algorithm can be used for a file or only for one tweet. Thus, each tweet will have a score from the different machine learning algorithms that represents a value on the 'funny' scale (greater value = funnier), in the [0,1] interval. Based on these scores, the tweets are ordered and the first tweet is awarded the final score 2, the next 9 tweets receive 1, and the rest a score of 0.

---

[1] Java WordNet Library from https://sourceforge.net/projects/jwordnet/

4 Evaluation

The running time for the pre-processing phase is less than 2.5 seconds and for the neural network and rating algorithms is less than 7.0 seconds per file for 101 neurons. The size of the created corpuses are: polarity scores dictionary with about 2500 words, bigram lists with about 2000 word pairs, and the celebrities corpus with 50 names.

The implemented neural network algorithm returns a label for every tweet provided as input. Testing the algorithm using training data provided (10 fold cross validation), the accuracy of the algorithm proved to be 10286 of 11325 tweets correctly identified (mostly the ones with a 0 score).

5 Conclusions

Classifying and ranking humor is certainly a challenging task. The major challenge comes from the subjective nature of humor and the influence of the cultural background on identifying humorous situations.

#Warteam participated in SemEval 2017 Task 6 with a system combining Naïve Bayes and neural networks. This participation was an excellent way to consolidate natural language skills, while being involved in an international competition.

For a first try, the results are satisfying, given the fact that our algorithm succeeded to identify humor rules similar to the ones identified by human while looking through training data.

Although our system needs improvements, the research interest for this field was open and progress was done. Taking this into consideration, the improvements we consider for our system implies: better scoring algorithm to provide higher credibility to either of the two learning algorithms we used for each individual file, not at a whole as we currently do; improve running time for the neural network, enrich the corpora using assisted automatic web crawling techniques, but also use an API to identify positive and negative sentiments.

But the most challenging research direction yet to be investigated is how to incorporate cultural background when classifying tweets for their humor.

References

Barbieri, Francesco, and Horacio Saggion (2014) *Automatic detection of irony and humour in twitter,* in Proceedings of the Int. Conf. on Computational Creativity.

Chandrasekaran Arjun, Ashwin K. Vijayakumar, Stanislaw Antol, Mohit Bansal, Dhruv Batra, C. Lawrence Zitnick, Devi Parikh (2016) *We Are Humor Beings: Understanding and Predicting Visual Humor,* arXiv:1512.04407

Dan Klein and Christopher D. Manning. (2003). *Accurate Unlexicalized Parsing.* Proceedings of the 41st Meeting of the Association for Computational Linguistics, pp. 423-430.

Davidov, Dmitry, Oren Tsur, and Ari Rappoport. (2010) *Semi-supervised recognition of sarcastic sentences in twitter and amazon,* in Proceedings of the fourteenth conference on computational natural language learning. ACL, 2010.

Ilya Leybovich (2017) *Is Humor the Final Barrier for Artificial Intelligence?* from https://iq.intel.com/is-humor-the-final-barrier-for-artificial-intelligence/.

Kiddon, C., & Brun, Y. (2011). *That's what she said: double entendre identification.* In Proceedings of the 49th Annual Meeting of the Association for Computational Linguistics: Human Language Technologies: short papers-Volume 2 (pp. 89-94). Association for Computational Linguistics.

M.P. Mulder, A. Nijholt. (2002) *Humour Research: State of the Art,* Technical Report CTIT-02-34.

Mihalcea, Rada, and Stephen Pulman. (2007) *Characterizing humour: An exploration of features in humorous texts* in Int. Conf. on Intelligent Text Processing and Computational Linguistics.

Mihalcea, Rada, Carlo Strapparava, and Stephen Pulman. (2010) *Computational models for incongruity detection in humour.* in Int. Conf. on Intelligent Text Processing and Computational Linguistics.

Potash Peter, Romanov Alexey and Rumshisky Anna (2017) *SemEval-2017 Task 6: #HashtagWars: Learning a Sense of Humor*, in Proceedings of the 11th International Workshop on Semantic Evaluation (SemEval 2017).

Sam Gustin (2014) *It's Comedian vs. Computer in a Battle for Humor Supremacy*, from https://www.wired.com/2014/04/underwire_0401_funnycomputer/

Waller, A., Black, R., O'Mara, D.A., Pain, H., Ritchie, G., Manurung, R. (2009) *Evaluating the STANDUP Pun Generating Software with Children with Cerebral Palsy.* ACM Transactions on Accessible Computing (TACCESS) Volume 1, Issue 3 (February 2009) Article No. 16.

Yang, D., Lavie, A., Dyer, C., & Hovy, E. H. (2015). Humor Recognition and Humor Anchor Extraction. In EMNLP (pp. 2367-2376).

SVNIT @ SemEval 2017 Task-6: Learning a Sense of Humor Using Supervised Approach

Rutal Mahajan,   Mukesh Zaveri
Computer Engineering Department
S.V. National Institute of Technology, Surat
{rutal.mahajan, mazaveri}@gmail.com

Abstract

This paper describes the system developed for SemEval 2017 task 6: #HashTagWars - Learning a Sense of Humor. Learning to recognize sense of humor is the important task for language understanding applications. Different set of features based on frequency of words, structure of tweets and semantics are used in this system to identify the presence of humor in tweets. Supervised machine learning approaches, Multilayer perceptron and Naïve Bayes are used to classify the tweets in to three levels of sense of humor. For given Hashtag, the system finds the funniest tweet and predicts the amount of funniness of all the other tweets. In official submitted runs, we have achieved 0.506 accuracy using multilayer perceptron in subtask-A and 0.938 distance in subtask-B. Using Naïve bayes in subtask-B, the system achieved 0.949 distance. Apart from official runs, this system have scored 0.751 accuracy in subtask-A using SVM.

1   Introduction

Humor is an integral aspect of human beings that requires self-awareness, spontaneity, linguistic sophistication and empathy. Generating and recognizing humor is not an easy task to be carried out by machines. Generating and understanding humor can be useful in many NLP tasks. (Azizinezhad & Hashemi, 2011) have described the use of humor as the pedagogical tool for language learners, as it helps to keep students interested and motivated. Moreover, recognizing humor is also important in sentiment analysis and opinion mining because it can be useful to get the actual meaning out of figurative sentence.

Research on modeling humor such as (Barbieri & Saggion, 2014)(Raz, 2012)is focused on classifying humor into binary classes as humor and non-humor. In (Reyes, Rosso, & Buscaldi, 2012), humor is modeled by a binary classifier as well as by a multi-class classifier. It classifies different figurative sentences into humor, irony, politics, technology and general sentences. But all these approaches ignore the continuous nature of humor. Hence in task 6 of SemEval 2017 HashTag Wars: Learning a sense of humor (Potash, Romanov, & Rumshisky,2016), humor in tweet should be modeled in its continuous form instead of binary. The participating groups are asked to predict the amount of funniness of the tweet for particular hashtag according to gold labels of tweet. Tweets are labeled with 0, 1, or 2. 0 corresponds to tweet not in top 10. 1 corresponds to tweet in top 10 but not winning tweet and 2 corresponds to winning tweet. There are two subtasks: A) pairwise comparison- a task of predicting which tweet is funnier from given two tweets according to gold labels of tweets. In given pair of tweets, the tweet with higher label is said to be funnier. B) Semi-ranking- a task to predict ranking of tweets from funniest to least funny for given file of tweets for a hashtag.

The remainder of this paper is structured as follows: In section 2, description about overall system architecture is given. It covers pre-processing stage, feature extraction, simple machine learnings approaches for classification and comparator for ranking of tweets. Section 3 describes the results of experiments carried out for subtask A and subtask B by our system followed by conclusion in section 4.

2   System Architecture

This section describes the system architecture submitted for subtask A and B of HashTagWars by the team SVNIT @ SemEval.

Proceedings of the 11th International Workshop on Semantic Evaluations (SemEval-2017), pages 411–415,
Vancouver, Canada, August 3 - 4, 2017. ©2017 Association for Computational Linguistics

As shown in Figure 1, our system uses simple set of features adapted from (Barbieri & Saggion, 2014) and classifier from weka[1] toolkit.

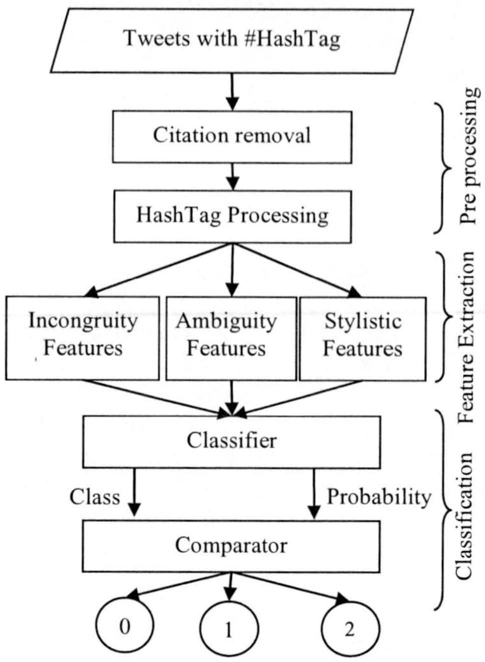

Figure 1: System Architecture of SVNIT@SemEval for HashTag Wars

In the next subsections, different stages of our system for obtaining results of subtask A and B are described.

2.1 Pre-processing

In this stage, the systems takes individual tweets and perform cleaning steps. It removes the references to tweeter username such as @midnight and also processes hash tags. It removes the hash tag from the given tweet and replaces it with corresponding word. E.g. consider tweet in dataset, "See Cats Run. @midnight #CatBooks". Here #CatBooks is replaced with "Cat Books".

2.2 Feature Extraction

After pre-processing of the given tweet, three main set of features are extracted to detect the humor level: 1) Incongruity features; 2) ambiguity features; and 3) stylistic features. Incongruity features checks incongruous or incompatible words in text. E.g. clean *desk* is a sign of cluttered *desk drawer.* Here we use 3 frequency related features of incongruity, and 3 written spoken features. These

features are implemented with the help of ANC[2] (American National Corpus). Ambiguity features are important to capture humor in the text as humor is found in two cases: 1) when text has different interpretation and 2) those interpretations are opposed to each other. Here 3 ambiguity related features are used to capture humor in text, which is based on WordNet. Other set of features are Stylistic features, which include 16 features related to structure of the tweet and 8 features related to intensity of adjectives and adverbs. These features are used to detect signatures, unexpectedness and style which is useful for identifying humor in given text (Reyes et al., 2013). Table 1 shows categorization of different features used in this

Feature name	No. of features	Type
Frequency related features	3	Incongruity features
Written Spoken Style features	3	
Structure related features	16	Stylistic features
Intensity related features	8	
Synonym related features	4	
Ambiguity related features	3	Ambiguity features

Table 1: Categorization of features based on incongruity, ambiguity and stylistic properties captured by them

system according to incongruity, ambiguity and stylistic properties captured by them. These groups of features are described below:

Frequency Related Features: Presence of commonly used words and rarest words in tweets are useful to detect unexpectedness and incongruity (Lucariello, 2007; Venour, 2013). We have used ANC frequency corpus for calculating these features. There are three features in this group: 1) Frequency mean is the arithmetic average of frequencies of all words. 2) Rarest word is the frequency value of the rarest word. 3) Frequency gap is the difference between maximum and minimum frequency. For the tweet "A flashlight that doubles as a flesh light. @midnight #BadInventions ", frequency features can be calculated as in Table 2: . For each POS tagged word in tweet written-spoken frequency, written frequency and spoken frequency is calculated respectively as below from

---

[1] http://www.cs.waikato.ac.nz/ml/weka/

[2] The American National Corpus (http://www.anc.org/) is a massive electronic collection of American English Words (15 million)

ANC corpus. These frequencies are used for the calculation of different frequency features given in Table 2.

A, a: 490433, 406057, 84376

flashlight: 38, 34, 4

that: 98949, 51493, 47456

doubles: 9, 9, 0

as: 107588, 98598, 8990

flesh: 265, 246,19

light: 952,898, 54

Written-Spoken style related features: Informal spoken English is used in many tweets. These features are designed to detect the Incongruity caused by using spoken English in written text or vice versa (Barbieri and Horacio, 2014) (Barbieri and Horacio, 2016). There are three features in this group: 1) Written mean is a mean of frequency values in written ANC corpora. 2) Spoken mean is a mean of frequency values in spoken ANC corpora. 3) Written Spoken gap is the difference between written mean and spoken mean. The example of these feature is given in Table 2.

Feature name	Value
Frequency mean	118896.9
Rarest word	0.0
Frequency gap	Max. frequency- Min. frequency = 490433.0
Written Frequency mean	96369.0
Spoken frequency mean	22527.9
Written-Spoken frequency gap	73841.1

Table 3: Example of incongruity features calculation

Structure related features: This group of feature analyzes the structure of given tweet as in (Bertero and Fung, 2016). It uses different structure related features: 1) length is the number of characters in the tweet. 2) Number of words. 3) Word length mean is the mean of word length. 4-7) Number of verbs, nouns, adjectives and adverbs. 8-11) Ratio of above four to total number of words. 6) Number of commas, full stops, ellipsis, exclamation marks and quotation marks.

Intensity related features: We have used Potts (2011) intensity scores to calculate the intensity of adjectives and adverbs. This group of features includes 1) adjective total is the sum of all the adjectives scores. 2) Adjective mean is adjective total divided by number of adjectives. 3) Adjective max is the maximum adjective score. 4) Adjective gap is the difference between adjective max and adjective mean. Similarly, 5) Adverb to-

tal 6) adverb mean 7) adverb max and 8) adverb gap is calculated.

Synonyms related features: Some of the humorous tweets convey two messages at the same time (Veale 2004). To identify such a tweet we used this group of features. There are four features in this group. To calculate these features system finds synonyms of all the words using Word-Net (Miller 1995) and sorts them according to their ANC frequencies.

This group of features includes 1) synonyms lower mean is the mean of all the synonyms lower. Synonym lower is number of synonyms of word whose frequency is lower than the word's frequency. 2) Synonym lower gap is the difference between word lowest synonym and synonyms lower mean. Word lowest synonym is maximum of synonyms lower. 3) Synonyms greater mean is the mean of all the synonyms greater. Synonym greater is number of synonyms of word whose frequency is greater than the word's frequency. 4) Synonym greater gap is the difference between word greatest synonym and synonyms greater mean. Word greatest synonym is minimum of synonyms greater. For the tweet " Dwarf Cannon. Oh shit, that's actually an AWESOME invention!! #BadInventions @midnight", stylistic feature calculation is given in Table 3.

Feature name	Value
Length of tweet	77.0
Number of Words in tweet	13.0
Words Length Mean	4.92307
Number of Verbs	2.0
Number of Nouns	6.0
Number of Adjectives	2.0
Number of Adverbs	1.0
Verb Ratio= Number of Verbs / Total number of words	0.15384
Noun Ratio= Number of Nouns / Total number of words	0.46153
Adjective Ratio= Number of Adjectives / Total number of words	0.15384
Adverb Ratio= Number of Adverbs / Total number of words	0.07692
Number of Commas	1.0
Number of Fullstops	1.0
Number of Ellipsis	0.0
Number of Exclamation	2.0
Number of Quotation	1.0
synoLower Mean	3.18181
synoLower Gap	33.18181
synoGreater Mean	0.0
Syno Greater Gap:0.0	0.0

Table 2: Example of Stylistic features calculation

413

Ambiguity related features: Three features are used to capture the aspect of Ambiguity as in (Bertero and Fung, 2016). Ambiguity (Bucaria, 2004), the disambiguation of words with multiple meanings (Bekinschtein et al., 2011), is a crucial component of many humor jokes (Miller and Gurevych, 2015; Yang et al., 2015). Features included are 1) synset mean: it is a mean of the number of synsets of each word of the tweet; 2) Max synset: it is a greatest number of synsets that a single word has. 3) Synset gap is a difference between max synset and synset mean.

2.3 Classifiers and Comparator

For classification, we have used simple learning algorithms from Weka, such as implementation of Naïve Bayes classifier and Multilayer perceptron in official submission of subtask A and subtask B. We have also used support vector machine for subtask A and taken results other than official submissions.

In subtask A, we have used Multilayer perceptron (MLP) for pairwise comparison, which initially classifies both the tweets into different classes (0, 1, or 2) then comparator compares the class label of two tweets. Tweet containing higher class label in the pair is considered as funnier tweet.

Participating System	Subtask A (Accuracy)	Subtask B (Distance)
SVNIT@SemEval (unofficial) -SVM	**0.751**	-
HumorHawk -run2	**0.675**	-
TakeLab-run2 (unofficial)	0.641	-
HumorHawk -run1	0.637	-
DataStories-run1	0.632	-
Duluth -run2	0.627	**0.872**
TakeLab-run1 (unofficial)	0.597	-
SRHR -run1	0.523	-
SVNIT@SemEval run1- MLP	0.506	0.949
SVNIT@SemEval run2 - NB	-	0.938
TakeLab-run1	0.403	0.908
Duluth-run1	0.397	0.967
TakeLab-run2	0.359	0.944
QUB-run1	0.187	0.924
QUB-run2	-	0.924
#WarTeam	-	1.0

Table 4: result of HashtagWars subtask A and subtask B for all participating systems including unofficial results

Comparator uses all features and compares given two tweets for the level of humor.

In subtask B, using Naïve Bayes classifier and multilayer perceptron tweets are classified into classes among 0, 1 and 2 same as done in subtask A. Tweets with class 1 label are ranked according to their probabilities of class for ranking in funnier to least funny tweet.

3 Experimental Results

In this section, we describe the experiment carried out for the different subtasks and the datasets provided by the organizers. The dataset is composed of 9658 tweets for 86 hashtags roughly collected over seven months of period. Table 4 represents the comparison of result of our system with other systems in subtask A and subtask B as per the results declared on SemEval portal. Scores with bold are best scores of respective system in that subtask.

Our system has scored average in subtask A using Multilayer perceptron classifier with 0.506 accuracy in official submitted runs. In the same subtask our system scored 0.751 accuracy, when evaluated with given evaluation script, which is higher than the highest scoring system. In subtask B, our system have ranked the tweets with 0.938 distance using multilayer perceptron and with 0.949 distance using Naïve Bayes classifier. This edit distance should be as low as possible because it evaluate the system according to how many moves for each tweet need to be occur for placing it at right place.

4 Conclusion

This paper describes the participation of SVNIT at SemEval 2017 task 6 Hashtag wars: learning a sense of humor. We have participated with the system implemented using simplest machine learning algorithms and set of features for humor recognition. Overall our approach using described set of features looks promising but still there is wide room for improvement. We want to improve our machine learning part and set of features by doing error analysis on the achieved results.

References

Azizinezhad Masoud and Hashemi Masoud 2011. Humour: A pedagogical tool for language learners. Procedia - Social and Behavioral Sciences, 30: pages 2093-2098.

http://dx.doi.org/10.1016/j.sbspro.2011.10.407

Barbieri Francesco and Saggion Horacio, 2014. Automatic Detection of Irony and Humor in Twitter. In *Proceedings of the 5th International Conference on Computing Creativity*. Ljubljana, Slovenia, June.

Barbieri Francesco and Saggion Horacio, 2016. Irony Detection in Twitter: The Role of Affective Content. *ACM Transactions on Internet Technology (TOIT)*, 16(3), July, pages 19:1—19:24. http://doi.acm.org/10.1145/2930663

Dario Bertero and Pascale Fung, 2016. Predicting humor response in dialogues from TV sitcoms. In *Proceedings of IEEE International Conference on Acoustics, Speech and Signal Processing (ICASSP)*, Shanghai March 20-25, pages 5780-5784.
http://ieeexplore.ieee.org/stamp/stamp.jsp?tp=&arnumber=7472785&isnumber=7471614

Diyi Yang, Alon Lavie, Chris Dyer and Eduard Hovy, 2015. Humor Recognition and Humor Anchor Extraction, In *Proceedings of 2015 Conference on Empirical Methods in Natural Language Processing*, Lisbon, Portugal, September 17-20, Association for Computational Linguistics, pages 2367-2376.http://aclweb.org/anthology/D/D15/D15-1284.pdf

Peter Potash, Alexey Romanov and Anna Rumshisky, 2017. SemEval-2017 Task 6: #HashTagWars: Learning Sense of Humor. In *Proceedings of the 11th International Workshop on Semantic Evaluation (SemEval 2017)*. August. Association for Computational Linguistics.

Raz Yishay. 2012. Automatic Humor Classification on Twitter. *Proceedings of the NAACL HLT 2012 Student Research Workshop*, Montreal, Canada. Association for Computational Linguistics, pages 66–70.http://www.aclweb.org/anthology/N12-2012

Reyes Antonio, Rosso Paolo and Buscaldi Davide. 2012. From humor recognition to irony detection: The figurative language of social media." *Data and Knowledge Engineering*, 74, April, pages 1–12. https://doi.org/10.1016/j.datak.2012.02.005

Reyes Antonio, Rosso Paolo and Veale Tony, 2013. A multidimensional approach for detecting irony in twitter. *Language Resources and Evaluation*, Springer-Verlag New York, 47(1): pages 239-268. http://dx.doi.org/10.1007/s10579-012-9196-x

Veale Tony, 2004. The challenge of creative information retrieval. In *Proceedings of Computational Linguistics and Intelligent Text Processing:5th International Conference, CICLing*. February 15-21, Springer Berlin Heidelberg, pages 457–467. http://dx.doi.org/10.1007/978-3-540-24630-5_56

Venour Chris. 2013. A computational model of lexical incongruity in humorous text. Ph.D. Dissertation, University of Aberdeen.

Duluth at SemEval-2017 Task 7:
Puns Upon a Midnight Dreary, Lexical Semantics for the Weak and Weary

Ted Pedersen
Department of Computer Science
University of Minnesota
Duluth, MN 55812 USA
`tpederse@d.umn.edu`

Abstract

This paper describes the Duluth systems that participated in SemEval-2017 Task 7 : Detection and Interpretation of English Puns. The Duluth systems participated in all three subtasks, and relied on methods that included word sense disambiguation and measures of semantic relatedness.

1 Introduction

Puns represent a broad class of humorous word play. This paper focuses on two types of puns, *homographic* and *heterographic*.

A *homographic* pun is characterized by an oscillation between two senses of a single word, each of which leads to a different but valid interpretation:

> I'd like to tell you a chemistry joke but
> I'm afraid of your reaction.

Here the oscillation is between two senses of *reaction*. The first that comes to mind is perhaps that of a person revealing their true feelings about something (how they react), but then the relationship to *chemistry* emerges and the reader realizes that *reaction* can also mean the chemical sense, where substances change into others.

Homographic puns can also be created via compounding:

> He had a collection of candy that was in
> mint condition.

The pun relies on the oscillation between the flavor *mint* and the compound *mint condition*, where *candy* interacts with *mint* and *mint condition* interacts with *collection*.

A *heterographic* pun relies on a different kind of oscillation, that is between two words that nearly sound alike, rhyme, or are nearly spelled the same.

> The best angle from which to solve a
> problem is the try angle.

Here the oscillation is between *try angle* and *triangle*, where *try* suggests that the best way to solve a problem is to try harder, and *triangle* is (perhaps) the best kind of angle.

This example illustrates one of the main challenges of heterographic puns, and that is identifying multi word expressions that are used as a kind of compound, but without being a standard or typical compound (like the very non-standard *try angle*). One reading treats *try angle* as a kind of misspelled version of *triangle* while the other treats them as two distinct words (*try* and *angle*). There is also a kind of oscillation between senses here, since *try angle* can waver back and forth between the geometric sense and the one of making effort.

During our informal study of both heterographic and homographic puns, we observed a fairly clear pattern where a punned word will occur towards the end of a sentence and has a sense that is semantically related to an earlier word, and another sense that fits the immediate context in which it occurs. It often seemed that the sense that fits the immediate context is a more conventional usage (as in *afraid of your reaction*) and the more amusing sense is that which connects to an earlier word via some type of semantic relation (*chemical reaction*). This is more complicated in the case of heterographic puns since the punned word can rely on pronunciation or spelling to create the effect (i.e., *try angle* versus *triangle*). In this work we focused on exploiting these long distance semantic relations, although in future work we plan to consider the use of language models to identify more conventional usages.

We used two versions of the WordNet SenseRelate word sense disambiguation algorithm[1] : Tar-

---

[1] `http://senserelate.sourceforge.net`

Proceedings of the 11th International Workshop on Semantic Evaluations (SemEval-2017), pages 416–420,
Vancouver, Canada, August 3 - 4, 2017. ©2017 Association for Computational Linguistics

getWord (Patwardhan et al., 2005) and AllWords (Pedersen and Kolhatkar, 2009). Both have the goal of finding the assignment of senses in a context that maximizes their overall semantic relatedness (Patwardhan et al., 2003) according to measures in WordNet::Similarity[2] (Pedersen et al., 2004). We relied on the Extended Gloss Overlaps measure (lesk) (Banerjee and Pedersen, 2003) and the Gloss vector measure (vector) (Patwardhan and Pedersen, 2006).

The intuition behind a Lesk measure is that related words will be defined using some of the same words, and that recognizing these overlaps can serve as a means of identifying relationships between words (Lesk, 1986). The Extended Gloss overlap measure (hereafter simply lesk) extends this idea by considering not only the definitions of the words themselves, but also concatenates the definitions of words that are directly related via hypernym, hyponym, and other relations according to WordNet.

The Gloss Vector measure (hereafter simply vector) extends this idea by representing each word in a concatenated definition with a vector of co-occurring words, and then creating a representation of this definition by averaging together all of these vectors. The relatedness between two word senses can then be measured by finding the cosine between their respective vectors.

2   Systems

The evaluation data for each subtask was individual sentences that are independent of each other. All sentences were tokenized so that each alphanumeric string was separated from any adjacent punctuation, and all text was converted to lowercase. Multi-word expressions (compounds) found in WordNet were identified.

SemEval–2017 Task 7 (Miller et al., 2017) focused on pun identification, and was divided into three subtasks.

2.1   Subtask 1

The problem in Subtask 1 was to identify if a sentence contains a pun (or not). We relied on the premise that a sentence will have one unambiguous assignment of senses, and that this should be true even as the parameters of a word sense disambiguation algorithm are varied. Thus, if a sentence has multiple possible assignments of senses based

on the results of different runs of a word sense disambiguation algorithm, then there is a possibility that a pun exists. To investigate this hypothesis we ran the WordNet::SenseRelate::AllWords algorithm using four different configurations, and then compared the four sense tagged sentences with each other. If there were more than two differences in the sense assignments that resulted from these different runs, then the sentence is presumed to contain a pun.

WordNet::SenseRelate::AllWords takes measures of semantic relatedness between all the pairwise combinations of words in a sentence that occur within a certain number of positions of each other (the window size), and assigns the sense to each content word that results in the maximum relatedness among the words in that window. The assumption that underlies this method is that words in a window will be semantically related, at least to an extent, so when choices among word senses are made, those that are most related to other words in the window will be selected.

The four configurations include two where the window of context is the entire sentence (a wide window) and another two where the window of context is only one word to the left and one word to the right (a narrow window). In addition these two configurations were carried out with and without compounding of words being performed prior to disambiguation. In all four configurations the Gloss Vector measure WordNet::Similarity::vector was used as the measure of semantic relatedness. If more than two sense changes result from these different configurations, then we say that a pun has occurred in the sentence.

2.2   Subtask 2

In Subtask 2 the evaluation data consists of the instances from Subtask 1 that contain puns. The task is to identify the punning word.

We took two approaches to this subtask, however both were informed by our observation that punned words often occur later in sentences. The first (run 1) was to rely on our word sense disambiguation results from Subtask 1 and identify the last word which changed senses between different runs of the WordNet::SenseRelate::AllWords disambiguation algorithm. We relied on two of the four configurations used in Subtask 1. We used the narrow and wide contexts from Subtask 1 without

[2] http://wn-similarity.sourceforge.net

finding compounds. We realized that this might cause us to miss some cases where a pun was created with a compound, but our intuition was that the more common cases (especially for homographic puns) would be those without compounds. Our second approach (run 2) was a simple baseline where the last content word in the sentence was simply assumed to be the punned word.

2.3 Subtask 3

The evaluation data for Subtask 3 includes heterographic and homographic instances from Subtask 2 where the word being punned has been identified. The task is to determine which two senses of the punned word are creating the pun.

We used the word sense disambiguation algorithm WordNet::SenseRelate::TargetWord, which assigns a sense to a single word in context (whereas AllWords assigns a sense to every word in a context). However, both TargetWord and All-Words have the same underlying premise, and that is that words in a sentence should be assigned the senses that are most related to the senses of other words in that sentence.

We tried various combinations of TargetWord configurations, where each would produce their own verdict on the sense of the punned word. We took the two most frequent senses assigned by these variations and used them as the sense of the punned word. Note that for the heterographic puns there was an additional step, where alternative spellings of the target word were included in the disambiguation algorithm. For example :

The dentist had a bad day at the orifice.

Orifice is already identified as the punned word, and one of the intended senses would be that of an opening, but the other is the somewhat less obvious spelling variation *office*, as in *a bad day at the office*.

For the first variation (run 1) we used both the local and global options from TargetWord. The local option measures the semantic relatedness of the target word with all of the other members of the window of context, whereas the global option measures the relatedness among all of the words in the window of context (not just the target word). We also varied whether the lesk or vector measure was used, if a narrow or wide window was used, and if compounds were identified. We took all possible combinations of these variations, which resulted in 16 possible configurations.

To this we added a WordNet sense one baseline with and without finding compounds, and a randomly assigned sense baseline. Thus, there were 19 variations in our run 1 ensemble. We took this approach with both the homographic and heterographic puns, although for the heterographic puns we also replaced the target word with all of the words known to WordNet that differed by one edit distance. The premise of this was to detect minor misspellings that might enable a heterographic pun.

For run 2 we only used the local window of context with WordNet::SenseRelate::TargetWord, but added to lesk and vector the Resnik measure (res) and the shortest path (path) measure. We carried out each of these with and without identifying compounds, which gives us a total of eight different combinations. We also tried a much more ambitious substitution method for the heterographic puns, where we queried the Datamuse API in order to find words that were rhymes, near rhymes, homonyms, spelled like, sound like, related, and means like words for the target word. This created a large set of candidate target words, and all of these were disambiguated to find out which sense of which target word was most related to the surrounding context.

3   Results

We review our results in the three subtasks in this section. Table 1 refers to homographic results as *hom* and heterographic as *het*. Thus the first run of the Duluth systems on homographic data is denoted as Duluth-hom1, and the first run on heterographic data is Duluth-het1. The highest ranking system is indicated via High-hom and High-het. P and R as column headers stand for precision and recall, A stands for accuracy, and C is for coverage. Rank x/y indicates that this system was ranked x of y participating systems.

3.1   Subtask 1

Puns were found in 71% (1,271) of the heterographic and 71% of the homographic instances (1,607). This suggests this subtask would have a relatively high baseline performance, for example if a system simply predicted that every sentence contained a pun. Given this we do not want to make too strong a claim about our approach, but it does seem that focusing on sentences that have multiple possible (and valid) sense assignments

Table 1: Subtask 1, 2, 3 results

Subtask 1	P	R	A	F1	rank
High-hom	.97	.80	.84	.87	1 / 9
Duluth-hom1	.87	.78	.74	.83	2 / 9
High-het	.87	.82	.78	.84	1 / 7
Duluth-het1	.87	.74	.69	.80	3 / 7
Subtask 2	P	R	C	F1	rank
High-hom	.66	.66	1.0	.66	1 / 15
Duluth-hom1	.37	.36	.99	.37	7 / 15
Duluth-hom2	.44	.44	1.0	.44	6 / 15
High-het	.80	.80	1.0	.80	1 / 11
Duluth-het1	.18	.18	.99	.18	11 / 11
Duluth-het2	.53	.53	1.0	.53	4 / 11
Subtask 3	P	R	C	F1	rank
High-hom	.17	.14	.86	.16	1 / 8
Duluth-hom2	.17	.14	.86	.16	1 / 8
Duluth-hom1	.15	.15	1.0	.15	3 / 8
High-het	.08	.07	.83	.08	1 / 6
Duluth-het1	.03	.03	1.0	.03	3 / 6
Duluth-het2	.001	.001	.98	.001	6 / 6

is promising for pun identification. Our method tended to over-predict puns, reporting that a pun occurred in 84% (1,489 of 1,780 instances) of the heterographic data, and 80% (1,791 of 2,250 instances) of the homographic.

3.2 Subtask 2

Subtask 2 consists of all the instances from Subtask 1 that included a pun. This leads to 1,489 heterographic puns and 1,791 homographic.

We see that our simple baseline method of choosing the last content word as the punned word (run 2) significantly outperformed our more elaborate method (run 1) of identifying which word experienced more changes of senses across multiple variations of the disambiguation algorithm. We can also see that run 1 did not fare very well with heterographic puns. In general we believe the difficulty that run 1 experienced was due to the overall noisiness that is characteristic of word sense disambiguation algorithms.

3.3 Subtask 3

Subtask 3 consists of 1,298 homograph instances and 1,098 heterographic instances. We see that for homographs our method fared very well, and was the top ranked of participating systems. On the other hand our heterographic approach was

not terribly successful. We believe that the idea of generating alternative target words for heterographic puns is necessary, since without this it would be impossible to identify one of the senses of the punned word. However, our run 1 approach of simply using target word variations with an edit distance of one did not capture the variations present in heterographic puns (e.g., *orifice* and *office* have an edit distance of 2). Our run 2 approach of finding many different target words via the Datamuse API resulted in an overwhelming number of possibilities where the intended target word was very difficult to identify.

4   Discussion and Future Work

One limitation of our approach is the uncertain level of accuracy of word sense disambiguation algorithms, which vary from word to word and domain to domain. Finding multiple possible senses for a single word may signal a pun or expose the limits of a particular WSD algorithm.

In addition, the contexts used in this evaluation were all single sentences, and were relatively short. Whether or not having more context available would help or hinder these approaches is an interesting question.

Heterographic puns posed a host of challenges, in particular mapping clever near spellings and near pronunciations into the intended form (e.g., *try angle* as *triangle*). Simply trying to assign senses to *try angle* will obviously miss the pun, and so the ability to map similar sounding phrases to the intended word is a capability that our systems were not terribly successful with. However, we were better able to identify compounds in homographic puns (e.g., *mint condition*) since those were written literally and could be found (if in WordNet) via a simple subsequence search.

While our reliance on word sense disambiguation and semantic relatedness served us well for homographic puns, it was clearly not sufficient for heterographic. Moving forward it seems important to have a reliable mechanism to map the spelling and pronunciation variations that characterize heterographic puns to their intended forms. While dictionaries of rhyming and sound-alike words are certainly helpful, they typically introduce too many possibilities from which to make a reliable selection. Language modeling seems like a promising way to winnow that space, so that we can get from a *try angle* to a *triangle*.

References

Satanjeev Banerjee and Ted Pedersen. 2003. Extended gloss overlaps as a measure of semantic relatedness. In *Proceedings of the Eighteenth International Joint Conference on Artificial Intelligence.* Acapulco, pages 805–810.

M.E. Lesk. 1986. Automatic sense disambiguation using machine readable dictionaries : How to tell a pine cone from an ice cream cone. In *Proceedings of the 5th Annual International Conference on Systems Documentation.* ACM Press, pages 24–26.

Tristan Miller, Christian F. Hempelmann, and Iryna Gurevych. 2017. SemEval-2017 Task 7: Detection and interpretation of English puns. In *Proceedings of the 11th International Workshop on Semantic Evaluation (SemEval-2017).* Vancouver, BC.

S. Patwardhan, S. Banerjee, and T. Pedersen. 2003. Using measures of semantic relatedness for word sense disambiguation. In *Proceedings of the Fourth International Conference on Intelligent Text Processing and Computational Linguistics.* Mexico City, pages 241–257.

S. Patwardhan, S. Banerjee, and T Pedersen. 2005. SenseRelate::TargetWord - a generalized framework for word sense disambiguation. In *Proceedings of the Demonstration and Interactive Poster Session of the 43rd Annual Meeting of the Association for Computational Linguistics.* Ann Arbor, MI, pages 73–76.

S. Patwardhan and T. Pedersen. 2006. Using WordNet-based Context Vectors to Estimate the Semantic Relatedness of Concepts. In *Proceedings of the EACL 2006 Workshop on Making Sense of Sense: Bringing Computational Linguistics and Psycholinguistics Together.* Trento, Italy, pages 1–8.

T. Pedersen and V. Kolhatkar. 2009. WordNet::SenseRelate::AllWords - a broad coverage word sense tagger that maximizes semantic relatedness. In *Proceedings of the North American Chapter of the Association for Computational Linguistics - Human Language Technologies 2009 Conference.* Boulder, CO, pages 17–20.

T. Pedersen, S. Patwardhan, and J. Michelizzi. 2004. Wordnet::Similarity - Measuring the relatedness of concepts. In *Proceedings of Fifth Annual Meeting of the North American Chapter of the Association for Computational Linguistics.* Boston, MA, pages 38–41.

UWaterloo at SemEval-2017 Task 7: Locating the Pun Using Syntactic Characteristics and Corpus-based Metrics

Olga Vechtomova
University of Waterloo
Waterloo, ON, Canada
ovechtom@uwaterloo.ca

Abstract

The paper presents a system for locating a pun word. The developed method calculates a score for each word in a pun, using a number of components, including its Inverse Document Frequency (IDF), Normalized Pointwise Mutual Information (NPMI) with other words in the pun text, its position in the text, part-of-speech and some syntactic features. The method achieved the best performance in the Heterographic category and the second best in the Homographic. Further analysis showed that IDF is the most useful characteristic, whereas the count of words with which the given word has high NPMI has a negative effect on performance.

1 Introduction

The pun is defined as "A joke exploiting the different possible meanings of a word or the fact that there are words which sound alike but have different meanings" (Oxford University Press, 2017). When a pun is a spoken utterance, two types of puns are commonly distinguished: homophonic puns, which exploit different meanings of the same word, and heterophonic puns, in which one or more words have similar but not identical pronunciations to some other word or phrase that is alluded to in the pun. The SemEval Task 7 (Miller et al., 2017) focused on the identification of puns as written texts, rather than spoken utterances, and hence distinguished between homographic and heterographic puns.

We participated in Subtask 2: Pun location, which required participating systems to identify which word is the pun. Only the cases which contain exactly one pun word were given to the participants in each of the two categories: homographic

and heterographic puns.

Our approach to identifying the pun word is to rank words in the pun text by a score calculated as the sum of values of eleven features. The feature values are calculated using a combination of corpus statistics and rule-based methods. The word with the highest score is considered to be the pun word. The method is described in detail in Section 2. In developing the word ranking method, we were guided by a number of intuitions, outlined below.

The punchline in a pun or a joke is almost always close to the end, since it is at the end that the reader is expected to uncover the second hidden (non-obvious) meaning of the pun. This intuition is consistent with Ruskin's Script-based Semantic Theory of humour (Ruskin, 1985). The system therefore only assigns scores to words located in the second half of the pun text.

What makes a homographic pun humorous is the simultaneous perception by a reader of two conflicting meanings of the same pun word. The pun author can achieve this by using words that are associated with (or evoke) different senses of the pun word. For example in "Why don't programmers like nature? It has too many bugs" The word "programmers" is associated with one sense of "bugs", but the word "nature" is associated with another sense. We operationalize this intuition by calculating Normalized Pointwise Mutual Information (NPMI) between pairs of words to find words that are semantically associated with each other.

Heterographic puns often contain one or more words that are associated with either the pun word itself or its similarly sounding word. In the case of "What did the grape say when it got stepped on? Nothing - but it let out a little whine." The pun word "whine" has a similarly sounding word "wine", which is associated with the preceding

421

Proceedings of the 11th International Workshop on Semantic Evaluations (SemEval-2017), pages 421–425,
Vancouver, Canada, August 3 - 4, 2017. ©2017 Association for Computational Linguistics

word "grape". To operationalize this intuition, we used a dictionary of similarly sounding words. If for a given word in the pun text there exists a similarly sounding word (or words), we calculate NPMI between it and each other word in the text. We also calculate NPMI between the original word as it appears in the pun and each other word. We hypothesize that if a similarly sounding word is more strongly associated (i.e. has higher NPMI) with other words in the text, compared to the original word, it is likely to be the pun word, and receives an additional weight.

The pun word has to stand out from the rest of the text and attract the reader's attention, as it is the realization of the joke's punchline. One possible reason why it stands out is because it is a more rare word compared to the surrounding words. Inverse Document Frequency (IDF) is a measure of how rare the word is in a corpus. The less frequent the word is in a corpus, the higher is its IDF. We hypothesize that a word, which has the highest IDF in the second half of the text is more likely to be the pun word than words with lower IDFs. We thus assign an additional weight to such a word. Furthermore, only nouns, adjectives, adverbs and verbs are assigned scores by our system.

Sometimes, a pun word is a made up word, e.g. "velcrows" in "There is a special species of bird that is really good at holding stuff together. They are called velcrows." We assign an additional weight to words that have zero frequency in a large corpus.

A number of intuitions were guided by the syntactic structure of the text. Thus, we hypothesize that if the pun text consists of two sentences, the pun word is located in the second sentence, as it is most likely to contain the punchline. Therefore, all words in the second sentence receive an additional weight. In a similar vein, if the text contains a comma or the words "then" or "but", all words following them receive additional weights. These clues can signal a pause, a shift in the narrative or a juxtaposition, which all precede the punchline.

2 Methodology

Each test case is tokenized and POS-tagged using Stanford CoreNLP toolkit (Manning et al., 2014). For each word w that is either a noun, an adjective, an adverb or a verb (henceforth referred to as *content words*), the IDF is calculated as $IDF_w = log(N/n_w)$, where n_w is the number of documents in the corpus containing w, and N is the total number of documents in the corpus. For calculating IDF we used ClueWeb09 TREC Category B corpus (Language Technologies Institute, 2009), consisting of 50 million English webpages. To obtain term frequencies, the corpus was indexed and queried using the Wumpus Search Engine (Buettcher, 2007).

For each content word w, the system also calculates pairwise Normalized Pointwise Mutual Information (NPMI) (Bouma, 2009) with each other content word present in the text.

$$NPMI(x,y) = \left(\ln \frac{p(x,y)}{p(x)p(y)} \right) \Big/ - \ln p(x,y)$$

$$(1)$$

where $p(x, y)$ is calculated as $f(x, y)/N$, in which $f(x, y)$ is the number of times y occurs within the span of s words before or after x in the corpus, and N is the number of word occurrences (tokens) in the corpus; $p(x) = f(x)/N$; $p(y) = f(y)/N$. The co-occurrence span size s was set in our system to 20.

In some puns, the pun word may be hyphenated, where the string after the hyphen can be associated with other content words in the sentence, for example, in "The one who invented the door knocker got a *No-bell* prize." "bell" is associated with "knocker". To account for these cases, we check if a word has a hyphen, extract its second half, lemmatize it, and calculate its NPMI with all other content words present in the text. Given a word pair (x, y), where x is hyphenated and z is the string after the hyphen, calculate $NPMI(x, y)$ and $NPMI(z, y)$. If $NPMI(z, y) > NPMI(x, y)$, then assign the $NPMI(z, y)$ value to $NPMI(x, y)$. We did not experiment with calculating NPMI for the string before the hyphen.

In heterographic puns, a word that is spelled differently, but has similar pronunciation to a word present in the pun, may be associated with other words in the text. A list of 2167 similarly sounding words was compiled from two publicly available resources [1,2]. For each content word, the system checks if it has at least one similarly sounding word in the list, and if so, creates a set of

---

[1] http://www.zyvra.org/lafarr/hom.htm
[2] http://www.singularis.ltd.uk/bifroest/misc/homophones-list.html

f1	Number of content words in the text of the pun that have a lower NPMI with the word x than with any of its similarly sounding words.
f2	Number of content words in the text of the pun that have a lower NPMI with the word x than with its substring following the hyphen (for hyphenated words).
f3	1 - word x has zero frequency in the ClueWeb09 corpus.
f4	1 - word x has a similarly sounding word.
f5	Number of content words y for which $NPMI(x, y) > m$.
f6	1 - word x is located in the third quarter of the text; 2 - in the fourth quarter.
f7	2 - word x is located in the second sentence.
f8	1- word x is located after the earliest occurrence of a comma.
f9	1- word x is located after the earliest occurrence of "then".
f10	1- word x is located after the earliest occurrence of "but".
f11	1 - word x has the highest IDF in the second half of the text.

Table 1: Components of the score calculated for every content word x in the text of the pun.

Method	Precision (rank)	Recall (rank)	F1 score (rank)	Coverage (rank)
Heterographic	0.7973 (1)	0.7954 (1)	0.7964 (1)	0.9976(2)
Homographic (submission 1)	0.6526 (2)	0.6521 (2)	0.6523 (2)	0.9994 (2)
Homographic (submission 2)	0.6519	0.6503	0.6511	0.9975

Table 2: Submission results

similarly sounding words H, including the original word. For each $h \in H$ it calculates its NPMI with each other content word in the text. Given a word pair (x, y), where $x \in H$, $NPMI(x, y) = \max_{h \in H} NPMI(h, y)$. For each content word x in the pun text the system counts the number of content words y for which $NPMI(x, y) > m$ (feature f5 in Table 1), where m is set to 0.3. The system also counts the number of content words y, which have lower NPMI with the original word x, than with any of its similarly sounding words (feature f1).

For every word in the second half of the text, the score is calculated as the sum of values of the features presented in Table 1. The word that has the highest score is selected to be the pun word. If there are ties, the word closer to the end is selected.

3   Results

We made one submission in the Heterographic category and two in the Homographic category (Table 2). Our submission in the Heterographic category achieved the best result among all submissions, exceeding the second-best one in F1 score by 16%. Our best submission in the Homographic category achieved the second best result, with F1 being only 0.02% lower than that of the best submission. Our submission in the Heterographic category and Submission 1 in the Homographic category use all features listed in Table 1. The system used to generate submission 2 in the Homographic category does not use the list of similarly sounding words, hence does not use features f1 and f4.

4   Extensions

After the submission, we noticed that puns may consist of more than two sentences, therefore, we modified feature f7 to assign one point to the last sentence, instead of the second. This resulted in slight improvement ("Submitted (corrected)" in Table 3).

Following the submission we developed another component (f12) to the system presented in Section 2. We were guided by the intuition that in heterographic puns, word x may have the strongest association with word y, however its similarly sounding word h may have the strongest association with a different word z, but the two words z and y are not associated. For example, in "A chicken farmer's favorite car is a coupe." the word "coupe" (x) is strongly associated with "car" (z), however its similarly sounding word "coop" is strongly associated with "chicken" (y). The words "chicken" and "car" however do not have a strong association. We operationalize it as follows. When a word x has a similarly sounding word h, the system finds a word z among all content words W in text with $\max_{z \in W} NPMI(h, z)$. Similarly, for the word x the system finds a word y among all content words W in text with $\max_{y \in W} NPMI(x, y)$. If $NPMI(z, y) < t$ the system adds one point to the score of the word x. Different t values (0.1, 0.2, 0.3, 0.4, 0.5) were evaluated, with $t = 0.2$ showing the best results. The addition of this new feature (row "f12 added" in Table 3 showed some improvement.

Method	Effect on performance	Precision	Recall	F1 score	Coverage
Submitted (corrected)		0.7981	0.7962	0.7971	0.9976
f12 added	+	0.8052	0.8033	0.8043	0.9976
f13 added	+	0.8368	0.8348	0.8358	0.9976
f1 removed	+	0.7744	0.7726	0.7735	0.9976
f2 removed	0	0.7981	0.7962	0.7971	0.9976
f3 removed	0	0.7981	0.7962	0.7971	0.9976
f4 removed	+	0.7926	0.7907	0.7916	0.9976
f5 removed	−	0.8407	0.8387	0.8397	0.9976
f6 removed	+	0.7926	0.7907	0.7916	0.9976
f7 removed	+	0.795	0.7931	0.794	0.9976
f8 removed	+	0.7926	0.7907	0.7916	0.9976
f9 removed	−	0.7989	0.797	0.7979	0.9976
f10 removed	+	0.7965	0.7946	0.7955	0.9976
f11 removed	+	0.6025	0.6011	0.6018	0.9976
f1+f4+f6+f7+f8+f10+f11+f12+f13		**0.8502**	**0.8482**	**0.8492**	**0.9976**

Table 3: Post-submission results with added/removed features (Heterographic puns)

Next, we evaluated component f13, which adds one point to the word's score if its IDF is above threshold i. The i values evaluated were 2, 3, 4 and 5, with $i = 3$ showing the best results. Addition of this feature ("f13 added" in Table 3) led to an improvement of 4.9% over the submitted result.

In order to determine which features contributed positively or negatively to performance, we removed each component one by one (Table 3). The second column in Table 3 shows the effect that the given feature has on the overall performance, e.g. if the removal of the feature causes drop in performance, the feature has a positive effect, indicated by a "+" sign. The component that has the strongest positive contribution to the system's performance is f11, which assigns one point to the word with the highest IDF in the second half of the text. The component that has the strongest negative impact is f5 (number of content words with which the given word has high NPMI). The number of words in the sentence that are more strongly related to the word's similarly sounding word (f1) is also a useful component. Based on this analysis, we modified the system to use only the positively contributing features (last row in Table 3, which outperformed our submitted method in all measures, achieving F1 score of 0.8492 (6.6% improvement).

5 Conclusions and future work

The paper described a method for identifying the location of a pun word using corpus-based characteristics of a word, such as its IDF and NPMI with other words in the pun text, as well its position in the text, part-of-speech and some syntactic features, such as presence of comma and words "but" and "then" prior to the given word's occurrence. The method achieved the best performance in the Heterographic category and the second best in the Homographic. Further analysis showed that IDF is the most useful characteristic, whereas the count of words with which the given word has high NPMI has a negative effect on performance.

Possible future improvements to the presented system are proposed below. In the Homographic pun category, some puns make use of idiomatic expressions. The joke exploits the dual interpretation of an idiomatic expression as, on the one hand, a combination of the literal meanings of its words, and on the other hand, its idiomatic meaning. For example, in "Luggage salespeople have to make a good case for you to buy." it would be useful if the system recognized the phrase "make a good case" as an idiomatic expression.

We used a rather limited list of similarly sounding words. A better way to find similarly sounding words and phrases would be useful, especially in those cases where a combination of words is pronounced similarly to one word, e.g. "There was a big paddle sale at the boat store. It was quite an *oar deal.*"

Currently, the feature weights are selected empirically. A possible avenue for future work is to develop an automatic method for selecting the best feature weights.

References

Gerlof Bouma. 2009. Normalized (pointwise) mutual information in collocation extraction. In *Proceedings of the Biennial GSCL Conference*.

Stephan Buettcher. 2007. The Wumpus Infor-

mation Retrieval system. `http://www.
wumpus-search.org/docs/wumpus_
tutorial.pdf`. Last accessed: 2017-02-15.

CMU Language Technologies Institute. 2009. The ClueWeb09 dataset. `http://lemurproject.
org/clueweb09/`. Last accessed: 2017-02-15.

Christopher D Manning, Mihai Surdeanu, John Bauer, Jenny Rose Finkel, Steven Bethard, and David McClosky. 2014. The Stanford CoreNLP Natural Language Processing Toolkit. In *ACL (System Demonstrations)*. pages 55–60.

Tristan Miller, Christian F. Hempelmann, and Iryna Gurevych. 2017. SemEval-2017 Task 7: Detection and interpretation of English puns. In *Proceedings of the 11th International Workshop on Semantic Evaluation (SemEval-2017)*.

Oxford University Press. 2017. Oxford dictionary. `https://en.oxforddictionaries.
com/definition/pun`. Last accessed: 2017-02-17.

Victor Ruskin. 1985. *Semantic Mechanisms of Humor*. D. Reidel Publishing Company.

PunFields at SemEval-2017 Task 7: Employing Roget's Thesaurus in Automatic Pun Recognition and Interpretation

Elena Mikhalkova
Institute of Philology
and Journalism
Tyumen State University
Tyumen, Russia, 625003
`e.v.mikhalkova@utmn.ru`

Yuri Karyakin
Institute of Mathematics
and Computer Science
Tyumen State University
Tyumen, Russia, 625003
`y.e.karyakin@utmn.ru`

Abstract

The article describes a model of automatic interpretation of English puns, based on Roget's Thesaurus, and its implementation, PunFields. In a pun, the algorithm discovers two groups of words that belong to two main semantic fields. The fields become a semantic vector based on which an SVM classifier learns to recognize puns. A rule-based model is then applied for recognition of intentionally ambiguous (target) words and their definitions. In SemEval Task 7 PunFields shows a considerably good result in pun classification, but requires improvement in searching for the target word and its definition.

1 Introduction

The following terminology is basic in our research of puns. **A pun** is a) a short humorous genre where a word or phrase is intentionally used in two meanings, b) a means of expression the essence of which is to use a word or phrase so that in the given context the word or phrase can be understood in two meanings simultaneously. **A target word** is a word that appears in two meanings. **A homographic pun** is a pun that "exploits distinct meanings of the same written word" (Miller and Gurevych, 2015) (these can be meanings of a polysemantic word or homonyms, including homonymic word forms). **A heterographic pun** is a pun in which the target word resembles another word or phrase in spelling; we will call the latter **the second target word**. Consider the following example (the Banker joke):

> "I used to be a banker, but I lost interest."

The Banker joke is a homographic pun; *interest* is the target word. Unlike it, the Church joke be-

low is a heterographic pun; *propane* is the target word, *profane* is the second target word:

> "When the church bought gas for their annual barbecue, proceeds went from the sacred to the propane."

Our model of automatic pun analysis is based on the following premise: in a pun, there are two groups of words and their meanings that indicate the two meanings of the target word. These groups can overlap, i.e. contain the same polysemantic words used in different meanings.

In the Banker joke, words and collocations *banker*, *lost interest* point at the professional status of the narrator and his/her career failure. At the same time, *used to*, *lost interest* tell a story of losing emotional attachment to the profession: the narrator became disinterested. The algorithm of pun recognition that we suggest discovers these two groups of words based on common semes[1] (Subtask 1), finds the words that belong to the both groups, and chooses the target word (Subtask 2), and, based on the common semes, picks up the best suitable meaning which the target word exploits (Subtask 3). In case of heterographic puns, in Subtask 2, the algorithm looks for the word or phrase that appears in one group and *not* in the other.

2 Subtask 1: Mining Semantic Fields

We will call a semantic field a group of words and collocations that share a common seme. In taxonomies like WordNet (Kilgarriff and Fellbaum, 2000) and Roget's Thesaurus (Roget, 2004) (further referred to as Thesaurus) semes appear as hierarchies of word meanings. Top-levels attract

---

[1] Bits of meaning. Semes are some parts of meaning present both in the word and in its hypernym. Moving up the taxonomy like Thesaurus or WordNet, hypernyms become more general, and the seme connecting them to the word becomes more general, too.

Proceedings of the 11th International Workshop on Semantic Evaluations (SemEval-2017), pages 426–431,
Vancouver, Canada, August 3 - 4, 2017. ©2017 Association for Computational Linguistics

words with more general meanings (hypernyms). For example, Thesaurus has six top-level Classes that divide into Divisions that divide into Sections and so on, down to the fifth lowest level[2]. Applying such dictionaries to get semantic fields (the mentioned common groups of words) in a pun is, therefore, the task of finding two most general hypernyms in WordNet or two relevant Classes among the six Classes in Thesaurus. We chose Thesaurus, as its structure is only five levels deep, Classes labels are not lemmas themselves, but arbitrary names (we used numbers instead). Also, it allows parsing on a certain level and insert corrections (adding lemmas, merging subsections, etc.[3]). After some experimentation, instead of Classes, we chose to search for relevant Sections that are 34 subdivisions of the six Classes[4].

After normalization (including change to lowercase; part-of-speech tagging, tokenization, and lemmatization with NLTK tools (Bird et al., 2009); collocation extraction[5]; stop-words removal[6]), the algorithm collects Section numbers for every word and collocation and removes duplicates (in Thesaurus, homonyms proper can belong to different subdivisions in the same or different Sections). Table 1 shows what Sections words of the Banker joke belong to.

Then, the semantic vector of a pun is calculated. Every pun p is a vector in a 34-dimensional space:

$$p_i = p_i(s_{1i}, s_{2i}, ..., s_{34i})$$

The value of every element s_{ki} equals the number of words and collocations in a pun that belong to a Section S_k. The algorithm passes from a Section to a Section each time checking every word and collocation w_{ji} in the bunch of extracted items l_i. If a word or collocation belongs to a Section, the value of s_{ki} increases by 1:

$$s_{ki} = \sum_{j=1}^{l_i} \{1 | w_{ji} \in S_k\},$$

$$k = 1, 2, ..., 34, i = 1, 2, 3...$$

For example, the semantic vector of the Banker joke looks as follows: see Table 2.

To test the algorithm, we, first, collected 2,484 puns from different Internet resources and, second, built a corpus of 2,484 random sentences of length 5 to 25 words from different NLTK corpora (Bird et al., 2009) plus several hundred aphorisms and proverbs from different Internet sites. We shuffled and split the sentences into two equal groups, the first two forming a training set and the other two a test set. The classification was conducted, using different Scikit-learn algorithms (Pedregosa et al., 2011). We also singled out 191 homographic puns and 198 heterographic puns and tested them against the same number of random sentences.

In all the preliminary tests, the Scikit-learn algorithm of SVM with the Radial Basis Function (RBF) kernel produced the highest average F-measure results ($\bar{f} = \frac{f_{puns} + f_{random}}{2}$) for the class of puns. Table 3 illustrates results of different algorithms. The results were higher for the split selection, reaching 0.79 (homographic) and 0.78 (heterographic) scores of F-measure. The common selection got the maximum of 0.7 for average F-measure in several tests. We are inclined to think that higher results of split selection may be due to a larger training set.

3 Subtask 2: Hitting the Target Word

We suggest that, in a homographic pun, the target word is a word that immediately belongs to two semantic fields; in a heterographic pun, the target word belongs to at least one discovered semantic field and does not belong to the other. However, in reality, words in a sentence tend to belong to too many fields, and they create noise in the search. To reduce influence of noisy fields, we included such non-semantic features in the model as the

---

[2]The hierarchical structure of WordNet is not so transparent. According to WordNet documentation, it is rather a union of four nets: nouns, verbs, adjectives, and adverbs. Their grouping depends on the semantic mark-up. Thus, it resembles a folksonomy and its structure changes implicitly. At the same time, the documentation mentions "forty-five lexicographer files based on syntactic category and logical groupings" (wordnet.princeton.edu/wordnet/man/lexnames.5WN.html) which can count as "owner-prescribed" structural subdivisions. Hypernymic relations are more specific among verbs and nouns, whereas adjectives often relate antonymically. Also, all WordNet nouns finally relate to the synset "entity".

[3]We edited Thesaurus by adding words that were absent in it. If a word in a pun was missing in Thesaurus, the system checked up for its hypernyms in Wordnet and added the word to those Sections in Thesaurus that contained the hypernyms. We merged some small closely-related Sections, as well. Originally, there used to be 39 Sections. Editing was done after experimenting with training data.

[4]Sections are not always *immediate* subdivisions of a Class. Some Sections are grouped in Divisions.

[5]To extract collocations and search for them in Thesaurus, we applied our own procedure based on the part-of-speech analysis.

[6]After lemmatization, all words are analyzed in collocations, but only nouns, adjectives, and verbs compose a list of separate words.

Word	Section No., Section name in Thesaurus
I	-
use	24, Volition In General
	30, Possessive Relations
to	-
be	0, Existence
	19, Results Of Reasoning
a	-
banker	31, Affections In General
	30, Possessive Relations
but	-
lose	21, Nature Of Ideas Communicated
	26, Results Of Voluntary Action
	30, Possessive Relations
	19, Results Of Reasoning
interest	30, Possessive Relations
	25, Antagonism
	24, Volition In General
	7, Causation
	31, Affections In General
	16, Precursory Conditions And Operations
	1, Relation

Table 1: Semantic fields in the Banker joke

$$p_{Banker} \quad \{1, 1, 0, 0, 0, 0, 0, 1, 0, 0, 0, 0, 0, 0, 0, 0, 0, 1, 0, 0, 2, 0, 1, 0, 0, 2, 1, 1, 0, 0, 0, 4, 2, 0, 0\}$$

Table 2: Semantic vector of the Banker joke

Method	Precision	Recall	F-measure
Common selection			
SVM with linear kernel	0.67	0.68	0.67
SVM with polynomial kernel	0.65	0.79	0.72
SVM with Radial Basis Function (RBF) kernel	0.70	0.70	0.70
SVM with linear kernel, normalized data	0.62	0.74	0.67
Homographic puns			
SVM with RBF kernel	0.79	0.80	0.79
Multinomial Naive Bayes	0.71	0.80	0.76
Logistic Regression, standardized data	0.77	0.71	0.74
Heterographic puns			
SVM with RBF kernel	0.77	0.79	0.78
Logistic Regression	0.74	0.75	0.74

Table 3: Tests for pun recognition.

tendency of the target word to occur at the end of a sentence and part-of-speech distribution, given in (Miller and Gurevych, 2015). A-group (W_A) and B-group (W_B) are groups of words in a pun that belong to the two semantic fields sharing the target word. Thus, for some s_{ki}, k becomes A or B [7]. A-group attracts the maximum number of words in a pun:

$$s_{Ai} = \max_k s_{ki}, k = 1, 2, ..., 34$$

In the Banker joke, $s_{Ai} = 4, A = 30$ (Possessive Relations); words that belong to this group are *use, lose, banker, interest*. B-group is the second largest group in a pun:

$$s_{Bi} = \max_k(s_{ki}/s_{Ai}), k = 1, 2, ..., 34$$

In the Banker joke, $s_{Bi} = 2$. There are three groups of words that have two words in them: $B_1 = 19$, Results Of Reasoning: *be, lose*; $B_2 = 24$, Volition In General: *use, interest*; $B_3 = 31$, Affections In General: *banker, interest*. Ideally, there should be a group of about three words, and collocations, describing a person's inner state (*used to be, lose, interest*), and two words (*lose, interest*) in W_A are a target phrase. However, due to the shortage of data about collocations in dictionaries and weak points of collocation extraction, W_B splits into several smaller groups. Consequently, to find the target word, we have to appeal to other word features. Testing the system on homographic puns, we relied on the polysemantic character of words. If in a joke, there is more than one value of B, W_B candidates merge into one, with duplicates removed, and every word in W_B becomes the target word candidate: $c \in W_B$. In the Banker joke, W_B is a list of *be, lose, use, interest, banker*; $B = \{19, 24, 31\}$. Based on the definition of the target word in a homographic pun, words from W_B that are also found in W_A should have a privilege. Therefore, the first value v_α assigned to each word is the output of the Boolean function:

$$v_\alpha(c) = \begin{cases} 2 & \text{if}(c \in W_A) \wedge (c \in W_B) \\ 1 & \text{if}(c \notin W_A) \wedge (c \in W_B) \end{cases}$$

The second value v_β is the absolute frequency of a word in the union of B_1, B_2 etc., including duplicates: $v_\beta(c) = f_c(W_{B_1} \cup W_{B_2} \cup W_{B_3})$.

Word form	v_α	v_β	v_γ	v_δ	$v_{W_{Bk}}$
be	1	1	4	0.338	1.352
lose	2	1	9	0.338	6.084
use	2	1	2	0.338	1.352
interest	2	2	10	0.502	**20.08**
banker	2	1	6	0.502	6.024

Table 4: Values of the Banker joke.

The third value v_γ is a word's position in the sentence: the closer the word is to the end, the bigger this value is. If the word occurs several times, the algorithm counts the average of the sums of position numbers.

The fourth value is part-of-speech probability v_δ. Depending on the part of speech, the word belongs to, it gets the following rate:

$$v_\delta(c) = \begin{cases} 0.502 & if \quad c \quad - \quad Noun \\ 0.338 & if \quad c \quad - \quad Verb \\ 0.131 & if \quad c \quad - \quad Adjective \\ 0.016 & if \quad c \quad - \quad Adverb \\ 0.013 & otherwise \end{cases}$$

The final step is to count rates using multiplicative convolution and choose the word with the maximum rate:

$$z_1(W_B) = \left\{ c \middle| \max_c(v_\alpha \times v_\beta \times v_\gamma \times v_\delta) \right\}$$

Values of the Banker joke are illustrated in Table 4.

In the solution for heterographic puns, we built a different model of B-group. Unlike homographic puns, here the target word is missing in W_B (the reader has to guess the word or phrase homonymous to the target word). Accordingly, we rely on the completeness of the union of W_A and W_B: among the candidates for W_B (the second largest groups), such groups are relevant that form the longest list with W_A (duplicates removed). In Ex. 2 (the Church joke), $W_A = go, gas, annual, barbecue, propane$, and two groups form the largest union with it: $W_B = buy, proceeds + sacred, church$. Every word in W_A and W_B can be the target word. The privilege passes to words used only in one of the groups. Ergo, the first value is:

$$v_\alpha(c) = \begin{cases} 2 & \text{if}(c \in W_A) \oplus (c \in W_B) \\ 1 & \text{otherwise} \end{cases}$$

Frequencies are not calculated; values of position in the sentence and part-of-speech distribution remain the same. The output of the function is:

$$z_1(W_B) = \left\{ c \middle| \max_c(v_\alpha \times v_\gamma \times v_\delta) \right\}$$

Word form	v_α	v_γ	v_δ	$v_{W_{Ak}}, v_{W_{Bk}}$
propane	2	18	0.502	**18.072**
annual	2	8	0.131	2.096
gas	2	5	0.502	5.02
sacred	2	15	0.338	10.14
church	2	3	0.502	3.012
barbecue	2	9	0.502	9.036
go	2	12	0.338	8.112
proceeds	2	11	0.502	11.044
buy	2	4	0.338	2.704

Table 5: Values of the Church joke.

Values of the Church joke are illustrated in Table 5.

4 Subtask 3: Mapping Roget's Thesaurus to Wordnet

In the last phase, we implemented an algorithm that maps Roget's Sections to synsets in Wordnet. In homographic puns, definitions of a word in Wordnet are analyzed similarly to words in a pun when searching for semantic fields the words belong to. For example, words from the definitions of the synset *interest* belong to the following Roget's Sections: Synset(interest.n.01)=a sense of concern with and curiosity about someone or something: (21, 19, 31, 24, 1, 30, 6, 16, 3, 31, 19, 12, 2, 0); Synset(sake.n.01)=a reason for wanting something done: 15, 24, 18, 7, 19, 11, 2, 31, 24, 30, 12, 2, 0, 26, 24, etc. When A-Section is discovered (for example, in the Banker joke, A=30 (Possessive Relations)), the synset with the maximum number of words in its definition that belong to A-Section becomes the A-synset. The B-synset is found likewise for the B-group, with the exception that it should not coincide with A-synset. In heterographic puns, the B-group is also a marker of the second target word. Every word in the index of Roget's Thesaurus is compared to the known target word using Damerau-Levenshtein distance. The list is sorted in the increasing order, and the algorithm begins to check what Roget's Sections every word belongs to, until it finds the word that belongs to a Section (or the Section if there is only one) in the B-group. This word becomes the second target word.

Nevertheless, as we did not have many trial data, but for the four examples released before the competition, the first trials of the program on a large collection returned many errors, so we changed the algorithm for the B-group as follows.

Homographic puns, first run. B-synset is calculated on the basis of sense frequencies (the output is the most frequent sense). If it coincides with A-synset, the program returns the second frequent synset.

Homographic puns, second run. B-synset is calculated on the basis of Lesk distance using built-in NLTK Lesk function (Bird et al., 2009). If it coincides with A-synset, the program returns another synset based on sense frequencies, as in the first run.

Heterographic puns, first run. The second target word is calculated based on Thesaurus and Damerau-Levenshtein distance; words missing in Thesaurus are analyzed as their WordNet hypernyms. In both runs for heterographic puns, synsets are calculated using the Lesk distance.

Heterographic puns, second run. The second target word is calculated on the basis of Brown corpus (NLTK (Bird et al., 2009)): if the word stands in the same context in Brown as it is in the pun, it becomes the target word. The size of the context window is (0; +3) for verbs, (0;+2) for adjectives; (-2;+2) for nouns, adverbs, and other parts of speech within the sentence where a word is used.

5 Results

Table 6 illustrates SemEval results (Miller et al., 2017) of our system PunFields[8] (Ho. - homographic, He. - heterographic).

In one of the reviews, we were prompted to check if the training and test set overlap. The overlap was 742 puns (30% of the pun training set). When we removed them and an equal number of random sentences from the training set and recalcualted the result using Gold set, the result fell within the scope of 4.5% which puts PunFields at the same place in the scoring table. We tend to think that the results went down not only because of the overlap removal, but also due to the reduction of the training set by 30%. This encourages us to state that the sematic fields hypothesis on which we build the classification model was tested successfully.

Type of pun	Precision	Recall	F1
Ho.	0.7993	0.7337	0.7651
Change	-0.0026	-0,0448	-0,0249
He.	0.7580	0.5940	0.6661
Change	-0.0005	-0,0386	-0,0237

Table 7: Task 1, overlap removed.

---

[8]https://github.com/evrog/PunFields

Task	Precision	Recall	Accuracy	F1
1, Ho.	0.7993	0.7337	0.6782	0.7651
1, He.	0.7580	0.5940	0.5747	0.6661

Task	Coverage	Precision	Recall	F1
2, Ho., run 1	1.0000	0.3279	0.3279	0.3279
2, Ho., run 2	1.0000	0.3167	0.3167	0.3167
2, He., run 1	1.0000	0.3029	0.3029	0.3029
2, He., run 2	1.0000	0.3501	0.3501	0.3501
3, Ho., run 1	0.8760	0.0484	0.0424	0.0452
3, Ho., run 2	1.0000	0.0331	0.0331	0.0331
3, He., run 1	0.9709	0.0169	0.0164	0.0166
3, He., run 2	1.0000	0.0118	0.0118	0.0118

Table 6: Competition results.

In comparison with the results of other systems, PunFields showed its best performance in classification which is probably due to the following factors. First, supervised learning algorithms like SVM have been historically very efficient in classification tasks. Although they fail on short texts more often than on long ones. Second, the training set was rather large (twice larger than during experimentation). However, the results for heterographic puns are lower than even in the preliminary tests. Probably, our training set contains too few heterographic puns, or their vectors are more alike with random sentences (or, rather, more scattered across the vector space).

The rule-based system of finding the target word and its WordNet meaning turned out to be less successful. Although later after fixing some programming errors, we managed to improve the result for Subtask 2[9]. Furthermore, multiplying values turned out to be a wrong decision, and the reasons for it will be reflected in a further publication. As for Subtask 3, we tried to combine two very different dictionaries: Roget's Thesaurus and Wordnet. When used in Subtask 1, Thesaurus provided reliable information on meanings of puns and was more or less successful in Subtask 2 (considering the mentioned improvements). But in Subtask 3 it was very much below the baseline results suggested by the Task Organizers. At the same time, we did not have any experimental data to test different variations of the algorithm before the competition. Especially, it concerns combinations of the own system with existing methods of WordNet (Lesk and sense frequencies). Initially, employing Thesaurus instead of WordNet was a solution made for convenience of parsing and experimenting with data. Further research will show whether these dictionaries can combine and solve issues together, or one of them should become a more preferrable source of data.

References

Steven Bird, Ewan Klein, and Edward Loper. 2009. *Natural language processing with Python: analyzing text with the natural language toolkit*. O'Reilly Media, Inc.

Adam Kilgarriff and Christiane Fellbaum. 2000. Wordnet: An electronic lexical database.

Tristan Miller and Iryna Gurevych. 2015. Automatic disambiguation of English puns. In *ACL (1)*. pages 719–729.

Tristan Miller, Christian Hempelmann, and Iryna Gurevych. 2017. Semeval-2017 task 7: Detection and interpretation of english puns. In *Proceedings of the 11th International Workshop on Semantic Evaluation (SemEval-2017)*. Association for Computational Linguistics, Vancouver, Canada, pages 60–70. http://www.aclweb.org/anthology/S17-2005.

Fabian Pedregosa, Gaël Varoquaux, Alexandre Gramfort, Vincent Michel, Bertrand Thirion, Olivier Grisel, Mathieu Blondel, Peter Prettenhofer, Ron Weiss, Vincent Dubourg, et al. 2011. Scikit-learn: Machine learning in Python. *Journal of Machine Learning Research* 12(Oct):2825–2830.

Peter Mark Roget. 2004. Roget's thesaurus of English words and phrases. Project Gutenberg.

---

[9]The current result is 0.5145 for homographic puns, 0.3879 for heterographic puns.

JU_CSE_NLP at SemEval 2017 Task 7: Employing Rules to Detect and Interpret English Puns

Dipankar Das and **Aniket Pramanick**
Department of Computer Science and Engineering
Jadavpur University, Kolkata, India
dipankar.dipnil2005@gmail.com
abcdefgh.ABCD65@gmail.com

Abstract

The problem of detection and interpretation of English puns falls under the area of word sense disambiguation in natural language processing, which deals with the sense of a word used in a sentence from the readers' perspective. We have tried to design a system to identify puns from a sentence by developing a cyclic dependency–based system which is implemented based on some rules which are actually statistical inferences taken from a set of random data collected from the Web.

1 Introduction

Extensive research has been done in the field of modelling and detecting puns (Hempelmann, 2003; Miller and Gurevych, 2015). The context or the sense depends largely on the perspective and knowledge of the reader about a particular language. For example, in the sentence, 'I was a banker but I lost *interest*,' the word in italics conveys two different meanings or 'senses' in the sentence. So, the word 'interest' could be called a pun. A *pun* is the exploitation of the various meanings of a word or words with phonetic similarity but different meanings.

Our system is a rule-based implementation of a dependency network and a hidden Markov model.

2 Dataset and Preprocessing

In the present shared task (Miller et al., 2017), participants are provided with a trial dataset and a test dataset. No training data was supplied due to the large cardinality of such words or contexts in general. In case of the subtask on pun detection (Subtask 1), the test data was subdivided into two sets: a *homographic* set containing 2250 contexts, and a *heterographic* set containing 1780 contexts.

On the other hand, in case of Subtask 2, another set of data was provided and that set was also subdivided into homographic and heterographic sets.

For training purposes, or rather to analyze the contexts statistically, a dataset was collected from random sources, mostly form *Project Gutenberg* and used in our present experiments. This dataset contains 413 sentences and is not subdivided into homographic and heterographic subsets.

The given data containing English contexts is preprocessed and each word of a sentence is tagged with its part of speech using NLTK, an open-source package for NLP written in Python. For example, the sentence, 'I was a banker but I lost interest.' is tagged using the Stanford NLP parser as follows:

> [('I', 'PRP'), ('was', 'VBD'), ('a', 'DT'),
> ('banker', 'NN'), ('but', 'CC'), ('I',
> 'PRP'), ('lost', 'VBD'), ('interest', 'NN'),
> ('.', '.')]

We also generate the parse tree for the sentence, which looks as in Figure 1. Using such parse trees, the clauses are identified and used for our further tasks.

3 System Framework

We have used a hidden Markov model (Ghahramani, 2001) and incorporated cyclic dependency (Toutanova et al., 2003) in order to detect points of pun occurrences in English sentences. The probability has been calculated with respect to each word being pun in a sentence. To calculate the probability, the parts of speech of the words immediately surrounding the target word are considered and the probability is increased accordingly.

3.1 Features

To train the system, 413 sentences, each containing a pun, has been analyzed. The probability of stop

Proceedings of the 11th International Workshop on Semantic Evaluations (SemEval-2017), pages 432–435,
Vancouver, Canada, August 3 - 4, 2017. ©2017 Association for Computational Linguistics

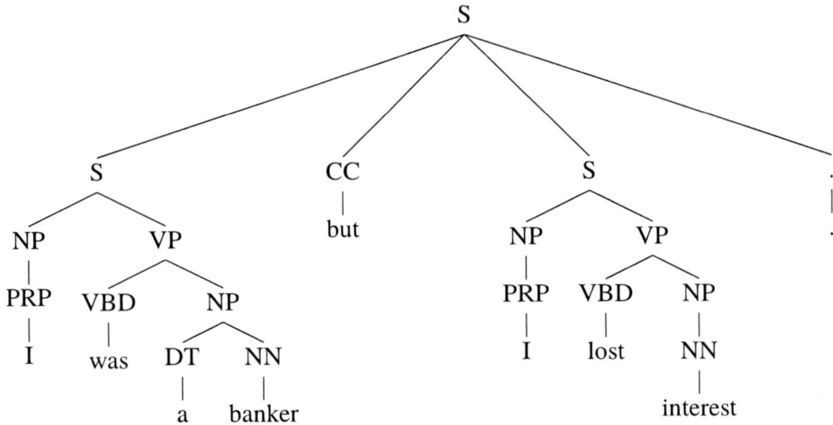

Figure 1: Parse tree for 'I was a banker but I lost interest.'

words such as articles, prepositions, 'be'-verbs, conjunctions, and infinitives are assumed to be 0 as they cannot be a pun. The probability of each part of speech being a pun is calculated from the training data and is given in Table 1.

Part of Speech	Probability
Noun	0.1538
Adjective	0.1111
Verb	0.0806
Others	1/(Sentence Length)

Table 1: Pun probability by part of speech.

Since in the task it is explicitly mentioned that each sentence will contain at most one pun, *sentence length* in this context has been defined as the number of words in the sentence. Each word of a smaller sentence will have higher probability of being pun.

The concept of clauses has been used in order to modify the probability. The clauses are extracted from the parse tree generated by the Stanford Parser. And clauses are classified as follows:

Type 1: Any clause that doesn't contain any other clauses falls under this category. A word which belongs to this type of clause has a pretty low probability of being pun.

Type 2: Any clause that contains only Type 1 clauses falls under this category. A word which belongs to this type of clause has a medium probability of being pun.

Type 3: Any clause that contains Type 1, Type 2, or other Type 3 clauses falls under this category.

A word which belongs to this type of clause has a very high probability of being pun.

Thus, the probability is increased according to the occurrence of the words within the aforementioned category of puns. Data collected from the trial set tells that a word that belongs to the Type 3 clause has 0.1 higher probability approximately than the words that belong to the clauses of other types.

Furthermore, it has been observed that if a word ends with '-ing' or '-ed', the probability of the word being a pun increases by 0.01.

It has also been observed that this probability depends on the parts of speech of the words adjacent to the target words. This is given in Tables 2 and 3.

POS of previous word	Increase Factor
Infinitive	0.02
Noun	0.01
Punctuations	0.014

Table 2: Pun probability by POS of previous word.

POS of next word	Increase Factor
Infinitive	0.02
Noun	0.01
Preposition	0.01
Punctuations	0.014

Table 3: Pun probability by POS of next word.

If the word is situated at the end of the sentence then its probability is increased by 0.02. The probability assigned to stop words and punctuation is 0.

3.2 Rule Definitions

Since this system is a rule-based implementation, a few rules are defined in order to identify the puns. These are as follows:

Rule 1: The probability of stop words (i.e., articles, prepositions, infinitives, and pronouns) being puns is trivially 0. 'Be'-verbs can also never be a pun in any English sentence. For example, in the sentence, 'I am a good boy,' the stop words words 'a' and 'am' cannot be puns in any case.

Rule 2: The probability of a word being a pun increases if it is a noun. It has been seen from the set of sentences collected from the Web that out of 195 words which are nouns, 30 are puns. This is highest among all parts of speech. For instance, in the sentence 'She thought it was a real horse, but it was a phony,' the pun 'phony' is a noun.

Rule 3: If a word belongs to a higher-level clause, then its probability of being pun increases. That is, if a word belongs to a Type 3 clause, its probability of being pun will be higher than a word that belongs to a Type 2 or Type 1 clause.

Rule 4: The probability of a word being a pun depends on the parts of speech of the words before and after it in a wrap-around fashion. For example, in the sentence 'She thought it was a real horse , but it was a phony,' the word just before the word 'phony' is 'a', an article, and thus 'phony' will have a greater probability of being pun than the other words in the sentence.

Rule 5: A probability of being a pun is associated to every part of speech, which is furnished in Table 1.

Rule 6: It has been observed that if a word ends with '-ed' or '-ing', it will have greater chance of being a pun.

3.3 Inference from Rules

In our system, we have used rules to determine the probability of each word in a sentence being a pun. We have used the basic statistical formula of determining the probability for dependent events in this respect: $P(A|B) = P(A \cap B)/P(B)$ and $P(A \cup B) = P(A) + P(B) - P(A \cap B)$.

Using standard formulas related to probability we have calculated the cumulative probability obtained by the cumulative effect of all the rules. Since in the task it is given that a given sentence in the test data could contain at most one word that could be determined a pun, we have only considered simple cases. For a random sentence that could potentially contain unknown number of puns, complex rules must be developed and the dependency among the rules to be determined.

3.4 Result

Assigning probability to each of the word of the sentence by the rules defined in the previous sections gives a vector whose length equals the length of the sentence. For example the sentence 'I was a banker but I lost interest.' gives the vector [0.000, 0.201, 0.000, 0.274, 0.000, 0.000, 0.261, 0.314, 0.000]. We denote this vector the *pun vector*.

It has been observed that if the maximum value among the components of this pun vector is less than or equal to 0.25, then the sentence does not contain any pun. On the other hand, if the maximum value among the components of the vector exceeds the value 0.25, then the sentence must contain a pun and the word corresponding to the maximum-valued component can be declared as a pun.

Applying this concept to the test data provided by the organizers, we obtained the coverage (C), precision (P), accuracy (A), recall (R), and F-score (F_1) shown in Tables 4 and 5.

Type	P	A	R	F_1
Homo	0.7251	0.6884	0.9079	0.8063
Hetero	0.7369	0.7174	0.9402	0.8261

Table 4: Results on Subtask 1.

Type	P	C	R	F_1
Homo	0.3348	1.0000	0.3348	0.3348
Hetero	0.3792	1.0000	0.3792	0.3792

Table 5: Results on Subtask 2.

4 Conclusion

In this paper we have presented a system based on a dependency probabilistic model to detect and identify puns from a given English sentence. Undoubtedly, the problem will become far more complex if the sentence contains more than one pun and the task is to identify each of those words individually.

In the test dataset, various non-pun words have been identified as puns because not only the context between pun and a non-pun is very narrow but the structural discrimination between the pun and the non-pun word in a sentence sometimes becomes very difficult even considering all aspects of the sentence including meanings and parts of speech of individual words.

Thus identifying a pun is pretty complex task and we believe that this model could be extended to identify complex cases. Apart from this, solutions to this problem will have tremendous effect in emotions recognition and analysis.

References

Zoubin Ghahramani. 2001. An introduction to hidden Markov models and Bayesian networks. *International Journal of Pattern Recognition and Artificial Intelligence* 15(1):9–42. https://doi.org/10.1142/S0218001401000836.

Christian F. Hempelmann. 2003. *Paronomasic Puns: Target Recoverability Towards Automatic Generation*. Ph.D. thesis, Purdue University, West Lafayette, IN.

Tristan Miller and Iryna Gurevych. 2015. Automatic disambiguation of English puns. In *The 53rd Annual Meeting of the Association for Computational Linguistics and the 7th International Joint Conference on Natural Language Processing of the Asian Federation of Natural Language Processing: Proceedings of the Conference*. volume 1, pages 719–729.

Tristan Miller, Christian F. Hempelmann, and Iryna Gurevych. 2017. SemEval-2017 Task 7:Detection and interpretation of English puns. In *Proceedings of the 11th International Workshop on Semantic Evaluation (SemEval-2017)*.

Kristina Toutanova, Dan Klein, Christopher D. Manning, and Yoram Singer. 2003. Feature-rich part-of-speech tagging with a cyclic dependency network. In *Proceedings of the 2003 Conference of the North American Chapter of the Association for Computational Linguistics on Human Language Technology*. volume 1, pages 173–180. https://doi.org/10.3115/1073445.1073478.

N-Hance at SemEval-2017 Task 7: A Computational Approach using Word Association for Puns

Özge Sevgili
İzmir Institute of Technology,
Computer Engineering, Urla,
İzmir, Turkey
ozgesevgili@iyte.edu.tr

Nima Ghotbi
İzmir Institute of Technology,
Computer Engineering, Urla,
İzmir, Turkey
nimaghotbi
@iyte.edu.tr

Selma Tekir
İzmir Institute of Technology,
Computer Engineering, Urla,
İzmir, Turkey
selmatekir@iyte.edu.tr

Abstract

This paper presents a system developed for SemEval-2017 Task 7, Detection and Interpretation of English Puns consisting of three subtasks; pun detection, pun location, and pun interpretation, respectively. The system stands on recognizing a distinctive word which has a high association with the pun in the given sentence. The intended humorous meaning of pun is identified through the use of this word. Our official results confirm the potential of this approach.

1 Introduction

Word Sense Disambiguation (WSD) (Navigli, 2009) is the task of determining the sense of a word in a specific context computationally. In the general case, a polysemous word's a single, specific sense is meant in a given context. However, a type of wordplay called pun suggests two or more meanings, by exploiting multiple meanings of words, or of similar-sounding words. Understanding the linguistic realization of puns and automatically detecting and disambiguating them are important for computational linguistics. Machine learning-based approaches are too expensive and impractical for this area as these humour constructs employ lexical-semantic anomalies and they are hard to be found in regular training sets. Thus, knowledge-based and unsupervised methods are prevalent. There are three tasks in the detection and interpretation of English puns: pun detection-the given context contains a pun or not, pun identification-location of the pun word, and pun disambiguation-identifying the two meanings referred by the pun in the given context.

Current approaches to pun interpretation rely on Lesk (1986), which considers the highest overlap between the context and gloss in order to return the target sense (two senses) for the pun. Miller and Gurevych (2015) performs automatic pun disambiguation in a comprehensive experimental setup for the first time using three Lesk variants along with Random and MFS (Most Frequent Sense) baselines. The general conclusion is that pun disambiguation results are poorer when compared with traditional WSD and traditional WSD must be extended with pun-specific features to increase accuracy in this area.

Our consideration for the task of detection and interpretation of English puns is mainly based on the assumption that pun containing contexts include a distinctive word that can be paired with the pun. This word has a central role in the wordplay such that the intended humorous meaning of pun is in connection with this word. This claim implies that this word's association with a pun is considerably greater than the other words' association scores with the pun. As the threshold to be used here is determined using all the sentences (either pun or not), the unsupervised nature of our method is preserved. In the computation of word association scores; we used the information-theoretic measure, Pointwise Mutual Information (PMI) (Church and Hanks, 1990). Our experiments support this claim computationally. The results both in homographic and heterographic puns are promising in detecting whether the given context is a pun or not.

In the remainder of this paper, we describe our system including the components for pun detection, pun location, and pun interpretation. In Section 3 we present our performance results. Finally, we summarize our findings and give comment on possible future extensions.

Proceedings of the 11th International Workshop on Semantic Evaluations (SemEval-2017), pages 436–439,
Vancouver, Canada, August 3 - 4, 2017. ©2017 Association for Computational Linguistics

2 System Description

First of all, we performed exploratory analysis on both homographic and heterographic trial datasets. We observed that sentences containing a pun have a distinctive word that has a high semantic/phonetic association with the pun. In accordance with this observation, for a sentence, all the pairwise word associations should be calculated to determine the most correlated word pair. If an element of this most correlated word pair has a second sense/spelling, it's an evidence of being a pun. To illustrate; in the following sentence, "banker-interest" word pair has the highest correlation and the word "interest" of this pair has a second sense, making it a good candidate for the pun.

I used to be a banker but I lost interest.

We used PMI to measure the association between words. PMI distinguishes the relevant word pairs (e.g. banker-interest) from the irrelevant ones (e.g. used-interest) because word co-occurrence frequencies are normalized by the individual word frequencies, as seen in 1.

$$pmi(w1, w2) = log_2 \frac{p(w1, w2)}{p(w1)p(w2)} \quad (1)$$

To calculate the PMI scores, we used a subset of Wikipedia data[1]. Because pun words seldom appear in Wikipedia, we added test datasets to guarantee words co-occur at least once and thus the system is able to compute PMI scores for each word pair. We calculated PMI scores using nltk library (Bird et al., 2009)[2] using bigram collocation with a window size of 20.

2.1 Pun Detection

This subtask requires deciding whether a given sentence contains a pun or not. In order to accomplish this, we followed a process that consists of the following steps:

- Converting each sentence into tokens.

- Stopword removal.

- Generating word pairs preserving word order in the sentence (leaving out the reverse of each ordered pair).

- Calculating PMI scores for each pair and sorting the list of scores for each sentence.

For instance, if the input of the system is the sentence below:

They threw a party for the inventor of the toaster. And he was toasted.

The following sorted PMI scores of word pairs are given as output (Table 1).

Pair of words	PMI score
toaster, toasted	11.6896
threw, toasted	7.9549
threw, toaster	7.8618
inventor, toasted	7.4851
inventor, toaster	7.3920
threw, inventor	3.6572
party, toasted	3.1461
party, toaster	3.0530
threw, party	1.6402
party, inventor	-1.1516

Table 1: Sorted PMI scores for each pair in the sentence.

In the realization of this subtask, we ask whether the highest PMI score is distinctively higher than the others. In order to answer this, we need a global threshold value to be used for the whole set of sentences (either pun or not). To determine this threshold value, we used the interquartile range (IQR) of the set of sorted PMI scores of every sentence. IQR is preferred because it is able to eliminate outliers.

To sum up, we had an IQR value for each sentence and we took their median as the threshold value because median and IQR are consistent with each other. Our threshold value for homographic sentences was 2.458 and for heterographic sentences was 2.940. Thus, if the difference between the highest PMI score and the succeeding one in a sentence was higher than the threshold value, the sentence was marked as containing a pun.

2.2 Pun Location

The main aim of the subtask is to find the location of pun in pun containing sentences. Here we assumed that the second element of the pair with the highest PMI score in a sentence is the pun using the observation that pun word usually is located at the end of the sentence.

---

[1]https://dumps.wikimedia.org/enwiki/latest/enwiki-latest-pages-articles.xml.bz2

[2]http://www.nltk.org/howto/collocations.html

2.3 Pun Interpretation

In this subtask, we are given the location of the pun word and we are required to find the two relevant senses of it. We provided a solution only for the homographic dataset for this subtask.

In order to identify the first relevant sense in the context, we used lesk method which predicts the answer on the basis of the overlap between the given sentence and the dictionary entries. It is appropriate because we need a context-based prediction. As an implementation detail, we used pywsd (Tan, 2014)[3] library that includes simple lesk algorithm implementation.

As for the second sense of the pun word, we again rely on our assumption that the given sentence has a target word that can be paired with the pun by its highest correlation. In order to determine this target word, we get help from pairwise associations using PMI scores. Then, the second sense of the pun word can be predicted by finding the highest similar sense to this target word. This final step requires to find all senses of the pun word and choose the highest similar sense among them, respectively. Here, we represented each individual sense of pun by its synonym. We used wordnet (Miller, 1995)[4] dictionary to extract all senses and synonyms for a given word.

To measure similarity, we used word2vec (Mikolov et al., 2013)[5] method in which words are represented by local vectors to be used in a computational manner. The similarity of two words are calculated by taking cosine of vectors of those words. We used the gensim library (Řehůřek and Sojka, 2010)[6] to calculate word2vec for each word. To feed word2vec, we used, again, Wikipedia data. Our vector size was set as 128-dimensional and our window size was 10.

To sum up, we selected pun's best word pair with respect to the PMI score. Then, we took every sense of the pun and retrieved the synonymous words for every sense. After that, we calculated cosine similarity between each sense and pun's word pair. As a result, the sense with the highest similarity is recognized as the second suggested meaning of pun. To illustrate, in the following sentence, the word pair "room - admitted" is the most correlated with the PMI score of 0.6130:

"There's room for one more," Tom admitted.

All senses of the pun word, namely "admitted", and their synonymous words were taken. Then, using their word vectors, cosine similarities between the synonyms and the word, "room" were calculated, as seen in Table 2.

word and synonym	cosine similarity
room, admit	-0.0113
room, accommodate	0.2292
room, accept	-0.0972

Table 2: Cosine similarity values between synonymous words of the senses of pun and its highest correlated word in the sentence.

According to the cosine similarity values, as the second sense of pun "accommodate" ("accommodate.v.04") which means "have room for; hold without crowding" was chosen. As we said before, the first sense was identified using the simple lesk algorithm. For the above example sentence, the algorithm returned the result "admit.v.08" which means "serve as a means of entrance".

3 Evaluation Results

Table 3 presents the official scores[7] of our system. As results show, our main success comes from the task of pun detection. We have 0.7553 precision for homographic and 0.7725 for heterographic datasets and around 0.93 recall value for both of them. The relatively lower precision scores we get can be attributed to the general feature of unsupervised methods when compared with that of their supervised counterparts. In our implementation, there are minor errors while extracting pairs or calculating PMI scores. In those inconvenience cases, our system predicts randomly, for exactly 22 sentences in homographic dataset and 28 sentences in heterographic one which may cause a wrong decision.

For pun detection and pun location, our results for heterographic sentences are better than the homographic ones. Actually, it is because our pairwise association is more appropriate for heterographic sentences in which two words are distinctively correlated in one spelling than the others.

For pun interpretation, our results are lower than the other subtasks. To begin with; in identifying

---

[3]https://github.com/alvations/pywsd
[4]http://www.nltk.org/howto/wordnet.html
[5]https://code.google.com/p/word2vec/
[6]https://radimrehurek.com/gensim/models/word2vec.html
[7]system submitted after the official end of the evaluation

dataset	subtask	precision	recall	F1
homographic	pun detection	0.7553	0.9334	0.8350
	pun location	0.4269	0.4250	0.4259
	pun interpretation	0.0204	0.0200	0.0202
heterographic	pun detection	0.7725	0.9300	0.8440
	pun location	0.6592	0.6515	0.6553

Table 3: The performances of our system for three subtasks in each dataset.

the first sense of pun, we are limited by the performance of simple Lesk algorithm, $50 - 70\%$, as Lesk (1986) explained. Therefore, another algorithm for WSD may enable us to reach better results. As for disambiguating the second sense of the pun word, we utilize synonymous words for each sense of pun, however, there is sometimes none or limited synonymous words for an input sense. This may result in reaching a wrong decision.

4 Conclusion

We have described the system submitted to the SemEval-2017 Task 7, Detection and Interpretation of English Puns. For participated system descriptions and their highlighted ideas, please refer to the task description paper by Miller et al. (2017). Our system uses word association scores based on PMI to determine a target word that can be paired with the pun. The substantially high association score of this target word with pun is used as an indicator that the given sentence is a pun. Moreover, this word can be exploited to disambiguate the second meaning of a pun. The evaluation results show that the idea of this word pair association could reasonably accomplish the goal of the subtasks especially the task of pun detection.

This work suggests an interesting further direction to use PMI scores in conjunction with local vector similarities to identify pun-specific features in WSD.

References

Steven Bird, Ewan Klein, and Edward Loper. 2009. *Natural Language Processing with Python*. O'Reilly Media.

Kenneth Ward Church and Patrick Hanks. 1990. Word association norms, mutual information, and lexicography. *Comput. Linguist.* 16(1):22–29. http://dl.acm.org/citation.cfm?id=89086.89095.

Michael Lesk. 1986. Automatic sense disambiguation using machine readable dictionaries: How to tell a pine cone from an ice cream cone. In *Proceedings of the 5th Annual International Conference on Systems Documentation*. ACM, New York, NY, USA, SIGDOC '86, pages 24–26. https://doi.org/10.1145/318723.318728.

Tomas Mikolov, Kai Chen, Greg Corrado, and Jeffrey Dean. 2013. Efficient estimation of word representations in vector space. *CoRR* abs/1301.3781. http://arxiv.org/abs/1301.3781.

George A. Miller. 1995. Wordnet: A lexical database for english. *Commun. ACM* 38(11):39–41. https://doi.org/10.1145/219717.219748.

Tristan Miller and Iryna Gurevych. 2015. Automatic disambiguation of english puns. In *Proceedings of the 53rd Annual Meeting of the Association for Computational Linguistics and the 7th International Joint Conference on Natural Language Processing (ACL-IJCNLP 2015)*.

Tristan Miller, Christian Hempelmann, and Iryna Gurevych. 2017. Semeval-2017 task 7: Detection and interpretation of english puns. In *Proceedings of the 11th International Workshop on Semantic Evaluation (SemEval-2017)*. Association for Computational Linguistics, Vancouver, Canada, pages 58–68. http://www.aclweb.org/anthology/S17-2005.

Roberto Navigli. 2009. Word sense disambiguation: A survey. *ACM Comput. Surv.* 41(2):10:1–10:69. https://doi.org/10.1145/1459352.1459355.

Radim Řehůřek and Petr Sojka. 2010. Software Framework for Topic Modelling with Large Corpora. In *Proceedings of the LREC 2010 Workshop on New Challenges for NLP Frameworks*. ELRA, Valletta, Malta, pages 45–50. http://is.muni.cz/publication/884893/en.

Liling Tan. 2014. Pywsd: Python implementations of word sense disambiguation (wsd) technologies [software]. https://github.com/alvations/pywsd.

ELiRF-UPV at SemEval-2017 Task 7: Pun Detection and Interpretation

Lluís-F. Hurtado, Encarna Segarra, Ferran Pla, Pascual Carrasco, José-Ángel González
Universitat Politècnica de València
Camí de Vera sn, 46022, València
{lhurtado|esegarra|fpla|pascargo|jogonba2}@dsic.upv.es

Abstract

This paper describes the participation of ELiRF-UPV team at task 7 (subtask 2: homographic pun detection and subtask 3: homographic pun interpretation) of SemEval2017. Our approach is based on the use of word embeddings to find related words in a sentence and a version of the Lesk algorithm to establish relationships between synsets. The results obtained are in line with those obtained by the other participants and they encourage us to continue working on this problem.

1 Introduction

Pun is a figure of speech that consists of a deliberate confusion of similar words or phrases for rhetorical effect, whether humorous or serious. In (Giorgadze, 2014), the author analyzed, from a linguistic point of view, the pun as one of the categories of wordplay and its manifestation in one-liner jokes in English. Pun is a way of using the characteristics of the language to cause a word, a sentence or a discourse to involve two or more different meanings. Therefore, humorous or any other effects created by puns depend upon the ambiguities of these words.

Pun detection is closely related to the Word Sense Disambiguation (WSD) problem, but in this case we need to select two senses of the pun (Miller and Gurevych, 2015; Miller and Turkovi, 2016).

The interpretation of puns has been subject of study in theoretical linguistics, and has led to a small but growing body of research in computational linguistics. In the task 7 of the SemEval 2017 competition, organizers proposed three challenges (subtasks): pun detection, pun location and pun interpretation (Miller et al., 2017).

In this work, we present a proposal for two subtasks: homographic pun location (subtask2), and homographic pun interpretation (subtask3).

Our proposal for both subtasks lies in the hypothesis that the two senses of the pun in the sentence are possible thanks to the coexistence of the pun with other words in that sentence that are semantically close to the pun. According to this hypothesis, our method for pun detection consists of finding pairs of words more semantically related in the sentence. In addition, our method for pun interpretation is based on the detection of words in the sentence, different from the pun, that help to find the two senses of the pun. The selection of these words is also based on the criterion of the semantic proximity to the pun.

2 Subtask 2: Pun location process

Pun localization consists of identifying which word is the pun given a sentence that contains a pun. Our proposal is based on two hypotheses: i) to find the most semantically related pair of words (one of these words should be the pun); ii) the pun should be at the end of the sentence.

Our approach to the pun location process is made following the Algorithm 1. As a previous step, the sentence is processed in order to eliminate punctuation marks and stop words, and to convert uppercase to lowercase. As a result of this process a set of semantically relevant tokens is obtained. This process removes from the sentences those tokens without semantics. Each token is represented by its embedding obtained from a pretrained word embedding model (Mikolov et al., 2013) trained on part of Google News dataset (3 million words). The embedding dimension was fixed to 300.

For all the pairs of tokens, the cosine distance of their corresponding embedding representation

Proceedings of the 11th International Workshop on Semantic Evaluations (SemEval-2017), pages 440–443,
Vancouver, Canada, August 3 - 4, 2017. ©2017 Association for Computational Linguistics

is calculated. The pairs are ranked according to this distance and the pair of less distance is selected. Finally, the pun selection is performed applying two heuristics:

- First, we assume that consecutive words in a sentence are semantically close, but the words that help the pun to be interpretable are not placed next to the pun. Therefore, we do not consider those pairs that correspond to consecutive words in the sentence.

- Second, we assume that the words that help the pun to be interpretable are placed before the pun in the sentence. Therefore, we selected as pun the word in the pair that is situated closer to the end of the sentence.

Algorithm 1: Selection of the pun of a sentence, task2

Input: s, the sentence that contains a pun

Result: w_k, the word in s that we guess is the pun

begin
  $k, b \leftarrow$ -1, ∞
  $t \leftarrow$ remove_stopwords(tokenize(s))
  foreach $w_i \in t$ **do**
    $e_i \leftarrow$ embedding(w_i)
    foreach $w_j \in t$: $i < j - 1$ **do**
      $e_j \leftarrow$ embedding(w_j)
      $d \leftarrow$ cosine_distance(e_i, e_j)
      if $d < b$ **then**
        $b, k \leftarrow d, j$

  if $k > -1$ **then**
    return w_k
  else
    return $w_{|t|-1}$

Table 1 shows the results for the subtask 2 (Homographic pun location). Although our results present a wide room for improvement (0.4462 for $F1$), they are in line with those obtained by other participants. We achieved the fourth place in the competition being the best result 0.6631 for $F1$.

In order to test the two heuristics applied in the pun selection, we additionally computed some statistics comparing our results with those of the gold standard.

We assumed that the words that help the pun to be interpretable are placed before the pun in the

$F1$	0.4462
recall	0.4462
precision	0.4462
coverage	1.0000

Table 1: Results of subtask 2: Homographic pun location.

sentence in most of the cases. The number of pairs of tokens selected by our approach that contain the pun is 767. In 702 of these pairs (91,5%), the pun was the second component of the pair, and, only in 65 (8,5%) the pun was the first component. These percentages confirm the goodness of this heuristic for subtask 2.

We also assumed that the words that help the pun to be interpretable are not placed next to the pun; therefore, we did not consider as candidates the consecutive words. If this heuristic is not applied, the number of pairs of tokens selected by our approach that contains the pun is 672, fewer than 767 pairs in case the heuristics was applied. In these 672 pairs, there are 580 where the pun is the word selected by our approach, and in 92 pairs, the selected word was the first component of the pair, that is more than the 65 pairs in case the heuristics was applied.

3 Subtask 3: Pun interpretation process

The process of pun interpretation is described by Algorithm 2. The interpretation process of our proposal is made following several steps:

- Selection of the two words semantically closest to the pun.

  In a similar way that stated for subtask 2 (Section 2), the sentence is processed in order to eliminate punctuation marks and stop words, and uppercase are converted to lowercase.

  Given the set of tokens, a sorted list of pairs of different tokens is generated, where, the first component of the pair is the pun w_p and the second component is any of the other tokens in the sentence whenever is not consecutive to the pun. For each pair of tokens, the cosine distance of their corresponding embedding representation is calculated.

  We selected the two first pairs in the above sorted list, $(w_p, w_1), (w_p, w_2)$, that is, we selected the two words in the sentence most

---

Algorithm 2: Selection of the two synsets of the pun on a sentence, task3

Input: s, the sentence that contains a pun

w_p, the word in the sentence, at position p, that is the pun

Result: (sy_1, sy_2), the two synsets of the pun w_p in the sentence s

---

Function *get_closest_words (s, w_p)*

    $t \leftarrow$ remove_stopwords(tokenize(s))

    $w_1, w_2, b_1, b_2 \leftarrow$ null, null, ∞, ∞

    $e_p \leftarrow$ embedding_representation(w_p)

    foreach $w_i \in t \mid (i < p - 1) \vee (i > p + 1)$ **do**

        $e_i \leftarrow$ embedding_representation(w_i)

        $d \leftarrow$ cosine_distance(e_p, e_i)

        if $(d < b_1) \wedge (d < b_2)$ **then**

            $b_1, b_2, w_1, w_2 \leftarrow d, b_1, w_i, w_1$

        else if $d < b_2$ **then**

            $b_2, w_2 \leftarrow d, w_i$

    return (w_1, w_2)

Function *get_context (synset)*

    $d \leftarrow$ get_definition($synset$)

    $w \leftarrow \{w_i \in$ tokenize(lemmatize(d)) $\mid w_i \notin$ stopword_list$\}$

    foreach $e_i \in$ *get_examples(synsets)* **do**

        $w \leftarrow w \cup \{w_i : w_i \in$ tokenize(lemmatize(e) $\mid w_i \notin$ stopword_list)$\}$

    return w

Function *synset_similarity(sy_1, sy_2)*

    $c_1 \leftarrow$ get_context(sy_1)

    $c_2 \leftarrow$ get_context(sy_2)

    return $\|c_1 \cap c_2\|$

begin

    $w_i, w_j =$ get_closest_words(s, w_p)

    $sy_1, b \leftarrow null, -\infty$

    foreach $sy_p \in synsets(w_p)$ **do**

        foreach $sy_i \in synsets(w_i)$ **do**

            $s \leftarrow$ synset_similarity(sy_p, sy_i)

            if $s > b$ **then**

                $sy_1, b \leftarrow sy_p, s$

    $sy_2, b \leftarrow null, -\infty$

    foreach $sy_p \in synsets(w_p)$ **do**

        foreach $sy_j \in synsets(w_j) \mid sy_j \neq sy_1$ **do**

            $s \leftarrow$ synset_similarity(sy_p, sy_i)

            if $s > b$ **then**

                $sy_2, b \leftarrow sy_p, s$

    return (sy_1, sy_2)

---

closely related to the pun from a semantic point of view. The cosine distance of (w_p, w_1) is the smallest and the cosine distance of (w_p, w_2) is the next smaller one.

In Algorithm 2, this step corresponds to the *get_closest_words* function.

- Generation of a bag-of-words per synset.

For each synset of the pun (w_p) and for each synset of both closest words (w_1, w_2), we obtain a bag-of-words that includes: i) all the lemmas in the gloss of the synset; ii) the own name of the synset; and iii) the lemmas in all the example sentences. Before getting the lemmas, the sentences are processed in order to convert to lowercase and to eliminate punctuation marks and stop-words.

This step corresponds to the *get_context* function in Algorithm 2.

- Synsets selection.

The final goal of the subtask is to select one pair of synsets (sy_1, sy_2) of the pun that represent its two different meanings in the sentence. Our hypothesis is that one synset of the pair (sy_1) is related to one synset of w_1 and the other synset of the pair (sy_2) is related to one synset of w_2. In a similar way that *Lesk algorithm* (Lesk, 1986), we used as measure of similarity between two synsets, the overlapping between the bags-of-words of both synsets.

In this way, we select the first synset (sy_1) of the pun that maximizes the overlapping with one synsets of w_1. After that, we select other synset of the pun (sy_2, $sy_2 \neq sy_1$) that maximizes the overlapping with one synset of w_2.

Table 2 shows the results of subtask 3 (Homographic pun interpretation). Our results are low, but are in line with the results of the rest of the participants. We achieved 0.0996 for $F1$ (the third place), being the best result 0.1557.

$F1$	0.0996
recall	0.0978
precision	0.1014
coverage	0.9646

Table 2: Results of subtask 3: Homographic pun interpretation.

As in the subtask 2, we calculated some statistics comparing our results with those of the gold-standard. The number of correct pairs of synsets was 127 of the 1252 analyzed sentences, however, there were 255 additional sentences for which one synset was correct.

4 Conclusions

In this work, we have presented our participation at task 7 (subtask 2: homographic pun detection and subtask 3: homographic pun interpretation) of SemEval2017. Our approach is based on the use of word embeddings to find related words in a sentence and a version of the Lesk algorithm to establish relationships between synsets. We achieved the fourth place in subtask 2 (Homographic pun location) and the third place in subtask 3 (Homographic pun interpretation).

The results obtained are in line with those obtained by the other participants and they encourage us to continue working on this problem.

As future work we plan to adapt state-of-the-art WSD techniques to tackle with the pun interpretation problem.

Acknowledgements

This work has been partially funded by the Spanish MINECO and FEDER founds under project ASLP-MULAN: Audio, Speech and Language Processing for Multimedia Analytics, TIN2014-54288-C4-3-R.

References

Meri Giorgadze. 2014. Linguistic features of pun, its typology and classification. *European Scientific Journal* .

Michael Lesk. 1986. Automatic sense disambiguation using machine readable dictionaries: How to tell a pine cone from an ice cream cone. In *Proceedings of the 5th Annual International Conference on Systems Documentation*. ACM, New York, NY, USA, SIGDOC '86, pages 24–26. https://doi.org/10.1145/318723.318728.

Tomas Mikolov, Kai Chen, Greg Corrado, and Jeffrey Dean. 2013. Efficient estimation of word representations in vector space. *CoRR* abs/1301.3781. http://arxiv.org/abs/1301.3781.

Tristan Miller and Iryna Gurevych. 2015. Automatic disambiguation of english puns. In *Proceedings of the 53rd Annual Meeting of the Association for Computational Linguistics and the 7th International Joint Conference on Natural Language Processing (ACL-IJCNLP 2015)*. page 719729.

Tristan Miller, Christian F. Hempelmann, and Iryna Gurevych. 2017. SemEval-2017 Task 7: Detection and interpretation of English puns. In *Proceedings of the 11th International Workshop on Semantic Evaluation (SemEval-2017)*.

Tristan Miller and Mladen Turkovi. 2016. Towards the automatic detection and identification of english puns. *European Journal of Humour Research* 4(1):59–75.

BuzzSaw at SemEval-2017 Task 7: Global vs. Local Context for Interpreting and Locating Homographic English Puns with Sense Embeddings

Dieke Oele
CLCG
University of Groningen
The Netherlands
d.oele@rug.nl

Kilian Evang
CLCG
University of Groningen
The Netherlands
k.evang@rug.nl

Abstract

This paper describes our system participating in the SemEval-2017 Task 7, for the subtasks of homographic pun location and homographic pun interpretation. For pun interpretation, we use a knowledge-based Word Sense Disambiguation (WSD) method based on sense embeddings. Pun-based jokes can be divided into two parts, each containing information about the two distinct senses of the pun. To exploit this structure we split the context that is input to the WSD system into two local contexts and find the best sense for each of them. We use the output of pun interpretation for pun location. As we expect the two meanings of a pun to be very dissimilar, we compute sense embedding cosine distances for each sense-pair and select the word that has the highest distance. We describe experiments on different methods of splitting the context and compare our method to several baselines. We find evidence supporting our hypotheses and obtain competitive results for pun interpretation.

1 Introduction

A pun is a word used in a context to evoke two or more distinct senses for humorous effect. For example, in the 1987 movie "The Running Man", Arnold Schwarzenegger's character cuts his enemy Buzzsaw in half with a chainsaw, then announces: "He had to split." The verb *split* is the pun here, evoking two senses in the context: that of leaving, and that of disintegrating into two parts.

Recognizing and appreciating puns requires sophisticated feats of intelligence currently unique to humans. A recently proposed set of artificial intelligence tasks (Miller et al., 2017) challenges computers to try their hand at it: *pun detection* (tell whether or not a text contains a pun), *pun location* (given a text with a pun, tell which word is the pun) and *pun interpretation* (given a pun in context, tell which senses it evokes).

Pun interpretation is closely related to the task of Word Sense Disambiguation. A typical WSD system chooses that sense of a word which fits best in the context the word appears in. A pun interpretation system, however, should return not one but two different senses of a word. Miller and Turković (2016) suggest a straightforward extension of the WSD approach to pun interpretation: choose the best scoring sense and second-best scoring sense for the word in its context. However, this approach does not take into account the specific structure of pun-based jokes. In most cases, such jokes can be divided into two parts, where in the first part cues for one sense are concentrated, and in the second part, cues for another sense. Figure 1 shows examples of such cases.

A pun interpretation system could exploit this two-part structure by splitting the global context of the entire joke into two local contexts and performing WSD separately for each local context, choosing the best sense for each of the two. As this process makes each context more informative for the respective sense, we hypothesize that it leads to more accurate pun interpretation than the simple approach which uses the top-scoring two senses according to the global context.

Additionally, we believe that we can use the output of our pun interpretation system for pun location. We hypothesize that the two senses of a pun are typically very dissimilar, as this is important for the joke to be recognizable. We therefore attempt to locate puns by selecting the polysemous word with the most dissimilar two senses.

Proceedings of the 11th International Workshop on Semantic Evaluations (SemEval-2017), pages 444–448,
Vancouver, Canada, August 3 - 4, 2017. ©2017 Association for Computational Linguistics

The first time he put the horses on the carriage, it went without a **hitch**.
If a priest is called a white collar worker, a nun would be a creature of **habit**.
Television sets in Britain have to cross the English **Channel**.
Old math teachers never die, they just become **irrational**.
In the winter my dog wears his coat, but in the summer he wears his coat and **pants**.

Figure 1: Examples of pun-based jokes. The pun is typeset in boldface. Words that we judge to be cues for one sense are marked with a dashed underline, words and n-grams that we judge to be cues for the other sense are marked with a dotted underline. Note that the cues for the two senses tend to divide the jokes into two non-overlapping parts.

2 Method

Similar to Miller and Gurevych (2015) we use a knowledge-based WSD system and apply it to pun annotation. Our method is loosely based on the Lesk algorithm exploiting both the context of the words and the definitions (hereafter referred to as glosses) of the senses (Oele and van Noord, 2017). Given a word, Lesk selects the sense whose definition has the highest number of words in common with the context. In our method, which we call Lesk++, instead of counting the number of words that overlap between the gloss of a sense and its context, word and sense embeddings are used to compute the similarity between the gloss of a sense and the context.

2.1 Word Sense Disambiguation

Our WSD method takes sentences as input and outputs a preferred sense for each polysemous word. Given a sentence $w_1 \ldots w_i$ of i words, we retrieve a set of word senses from the sense inventory for each word w and sort them in ascending order. Then, for each sense s of each word w, we consider the similarity of its lexeme (the combination of a word and one of its senses (Rothe and Schütze, 2015)) with the context and the similarity of the gloss with the context.

For each potential sense s of word w, the cosine similarity is computed between its gloss vector G_s and its context vector C_w and between the context vector C_w and the lexeme vector $L_{s,w}$. The score of a given word w and sense s is thus defined as follows:

$$\text{Score}(s,w) = cos(G_s, C_w) + cos(L_{s,w}, C_w) \quad (1)$$

The sense with the highest score is chosen. When no gloss is found for a given sense, only the second part of the equation is used.

Prior to disambiguation itself, we sort the words by the number of senses, so that the word with the fewest senses will be considered first. The idea behind this is that words that have fewer senses are easier to disambiguate (Chen et al., 2014). As the algorithm relies on the words in the context which may themselves be ambiguous, if words in the context have been disambiguated already, this information can be used for the ambiguous words that follow. We therefore use the resulting sense of each word for the disambiguation of the following words, starting with the "easiest" words.

Our method requires lexeme embeddings $L_{s,w}$ for each sense s. For this we use AutoExtend (Rothe and Schütze, 2015) to create additional embeddings for senses from WordNet on the basis of word embeddings. AutoExtend is an auto-encoder that relies on the relations present in WordNet to learn embeddings for senses and lexemes. To create these embeddings, a neural network containing lexemes and sense layers is built, while the WordNet relations are used to create links between each layer. The advantage of their method is that it is flexible: it can take any set of word embeddings and any lexical database as input and produces embeddings of senses and lexemes, without requiring any extra training data.

Ultimately, for each word W we need a vector for the context C_w, and for each sense s of word w we need a gloss vector G_s. The context vector C_w is defined as the mean of all the content word representations in the sentence: if a word in the context has already been disambiguated, we use the corresponding sense embedding; otherwise we use the word embedding. For each sense s, we take its gloss as provided in WordNet. In line with Banerjee and Pedersen (2002), we expand this gloss with the glosses of related meanings, excluding antonyms. Similar to the creation of the context vectors, the gloss vector G_s is created by averaging the word embeddings of all the content words in the gloss.

2.2 Pun Interpretation: the Context Had to Split

The WSD method that we described above returns the sense with the highest score taking into account the whole context. For pun interpretation, we could simply adapt it to return the best and second-best sense. However, to exploit the two-part structure of pun-based jokes, we instead split the context into two local contexts, run WSD for each local context and then return the best sense according to each of the two.

Ideally, we want to split the context so that all cues for one sense are in one local context, and all cues for the other sense are in the other. We therefore split the context so as to maximize the semantic dissimilarity between both parts. For each possible split of the text into two contiguous parts, we create a vector for each part by taking the means of all content words, as described earlier, and compute the cosine distance between both vectors. The pair of parts with the highest distance are used as local contexts for the WSD system.

For each polysemous word in the sentence, the WSD system is applied twice, using a different part of the context. The highest scoring sense for each run is chosen. As both runs could assign the same sense to the word, the second best sense of the first run is chosen in this case.

2.3 Pun Location: Attracting Opposites

We attempt to locate the pun in a sentence by selecting the polysemous word with the two most dissimilar senses. In order to do this, we use the two senses as determined by the pun interpretation system for each ambiguous word in the sentence. We therefore retrieve the two best senses for each polysemous word in the sentence and compute the cosine distance between their embeddings. The word that has the maximum distance between its senses is chosen as the answer.

3 Experiments

We use the sense and lexeme embeddings from Rothe and Schütze (2015)[1]. They lie within the same vector space as the pre-trained word embeddings by Mikolov et al. (2013)[2]. This model contains 300-dimensional vectors for 3 million words and phrases from the Google News dataset. Our

sense inventory is Princeton WordNet 3.1 (Fellbaum, 1998).

Although a pun can have two or more different part-of-speech tags, our method does not account for this. Instead, we use the POS that was assigned by the Stanford POS tagger (Toutanova et al., 2003).

3.1 Development Data

For the development of our system, we gathered and annotated a small dataset of 91 puns from the website "Pun of the Day"[3]. We used instances that have the same characteristics as in the data for the subtasks we consider (one pun per text, one content word per pun, target exists in WordNet 3.1, pun is homographic). From a small set of downloaded texts, both authors first independently selected the texts that meet all of these criteria. This was followed by a round of adjudication by discussion to determine the texts to use. We then used a similar process to annotate each pun for its two senses.

3.2 Pun Interpretation

We compare our pun interpretation method to three baselines: a random baseline, a most frequent sense baseline and a WSD system that does not use context splitting. The latter was modified to return the two senses with the highest score instead of one.

In addition, we compared different ways of splitting the context of the pun. Next to splitting on the basis of the maximal cosine distance between two possible parts of the context we also ran the WSD system with contexts that were split in half and with contexts that were split at the first punctuation symbol.

3.3 Pun Location

For pun location, we compared our system's performance to two baselines. One baseline randomly selects one content word from the text as the pun, and the other baseline always selects the *last* content word in the text as the pun. In addition, we used the output of all experimental setups of pun interpretation to assess the influence of the quality of assigned senses on pun location.

---

[1] http://www.cis.lmu.de/ sascha/AutoExtend/
[2] see https://code.google.com/p/word2vec/

[3] http://www.punoftheday.com/

4 Results

Results of the experiments for pun interpretation can be found in Table 1[4].

Table 1: Results for pun interpretation on the shared task test data.

System	Coverage	Precision
Random baseline	98.92	7.24
MFS baseline	98.92	11.21
Lesk++, no splitting	98.23	15.45
Lesk++, split in half	98.23	16.39
Lesk++, split by punctuation	98.23	15.53
Lesk++, optimal split	98.23	15.53

Our system easily outperforms both the random baseline and the most frequent sense baseline. Also, if we split the context before disambiguating the target word, we gain higher scores as compared to a system that selects the two best scoring senses. We do not, however, gain higher scores when we split the contexts on the basis of maximum semantic dissimilarity. Instead we observe that a system that splits the context in half performs better.

Table 2 shows results for pun location using the output of our system for pun interpretation. Our system scores well above our random baseline. However, the baseline selecting the last content word is much stronger, as the pun often appears at the end of the joke in the data.

Table 2: Results for pun location on the shared task test data.

	Coverage	Precision
Random content word	100.00	13.20
Last content word	100.00	52.96
Lesk++, optimal split	100.00	27.69

Results of the experiments for pun location using the output of our system compared to all baselines for pun interpretation and different splitting setups are shown in Table 3. Using the output of our system, with or without context splitting, performs better compared to systems that use random or most frequent output. The output of systems that use splitting modules and the ones that do not seem to not make a big difference for pun location.

---

[4]Lesk++, optimal split, was the submitted system. Numbers differ slightly due to a fixed inconsistency in how words are handled for which only one sense could be found.

Table 3: Results for pun location on the shared task test data.

Pun interpretation system	Coverage	Precision
Random baseline	100.00	17.24
MFS baseline	100.00	18.48
Lesk++, no splitting	100.00	27.75
Lesk++, split in half	100.00	27.75
Lesk++, split by punctuation	100.00	28.44
Lesk++, optimal split	100.00	27.69

5 Discussion

Our method for pun interpretation does not yet deal with puns where each sense has a different part of speech. A solution to this would be the use of the senses of the word's second best option of a part-of-speech tagger as well. Also, our method does not deal with phrasal verbs and multi-word expressions.

Our method for pun location works much better than chance, but much worse than a simple heuristic exploiting the fact puns typically appear at the end in the data. It would be interesting to see if both methods can be combined, e.g. using confidence scores and the heuristic as a fallback. It would also be interesting to see if the heuristic can be applied to other types of data, such as movie scripts.

6 Conclusions

We hypothesized that the idea that pun-based jokes can be divided into two parts, each containing information about the two distinct senses of the pun, can be exploited for pun interpretation. Experiments were done splitting the context that is input to a WSD system into two parts, run WSD for each context and return the best sense for pun interpretation. Results of our experiments show that, on the pun interpretation task, systems that use such a module outperform a WSD system that returns the two best senses. Also, our system performs better compared to both the random and the most frequent baseline.

As we expected the two meanings of a pun to be very dissimilar, we used the output of pun interpretation for pun location. Computing cosine distances between each sense-pair and select the one that has the highest distance gains higher scores as compared to a system that randomly selects a content word to be the pun.

References

Satanjeev Banerjee and Ted Pedersen. 2002. An adapted Lesk algorithm for word sense disambiguation using WordNet. In *Proceedings of the Third International Conference on Computational Linguistics and Intelligent Text Processing*. Springer-Verlag, London, UK, UK, CICLing '02, pages 136–145. http://dl.acm.org/citation.cfm?id=647344.724142.

Xinxiong Chen, Zhiyuan Liu, and Maosong Sun. 2014. A Unified Model for Word Sense Representation and Disambiguation. In *Proceedings of the 2014 Conference on Empirical Methods in Natural Language Processing, EMNLP 2014, October 25-29, 2014, Doha, Qatar, A meeting of SIGDAT, a Special Interest Group of the ACL.* pages 1025–1035. http://aclweb.org/anthology/D/D14/D14-1110.pdf.

Christiane Fellbaum, editor. 1998. *WordNet An Electronic Lexical Database.* The MIT Press, Cambridge, MA ; London.

Tomas Mikolov, Kai Chen, Greg Corrado, and Jeffrey Dean. 2013. Efficient estimation of word representations in vector space. *CoRR* abs/1301.3781. http://dblp.uni-trier.de/db/journals/corr/corr1301.html.

Tristan Miller and Iryna Gurevych. 2015. Automatic disambiguation of English puns. In *Proceedings of the 53rd Annual Meeting of the Association for Computational Linguistics and the 7th International Joint Conference on Natural Language Processing (Volume 1: Long Papers)*. Association for Computational Linguistics, Beijing, China, pages 719–729. http://www.aclweb.org/anthology/P15-1070.

Tristan Miller, Christian F. Hempelmann, and Irina Gurevych. 2017. Semeval-2017 task 7: Detection and interpretation of English puns. In *Proceedings of the 11th International Workshop on Semantic Evaluation (SemEval-2017)*.

Tristan Miller and Mladen Turković. 2016. Towards the automatic detection and identification of English puns. *European Journal of Humour Research* 4.

Dieke Oele and Gertjan van Noord. 2017. Distributional Lesk: Effective multilingual knowledge-based word sense disambiguation. Submitted for publication.

Sascha Rothe and Hinrich Schütze. 2015. Autoextend: Extending word embeddings to embeddings for synsets and lexemes. In *Proceedings of the 53rd Annual Meeting of the Association for Computational Linguistics and the 7th International Joint Conference on Natural Language Processing (Volume 1: Long Papers)*. Association for Computational Linguistics, pages 1793–1803. https://doi.org/10.3115/v1/P15-1173.

Kristina Toutanova, Dan Klein, Christopher D. Manning, and Yoram Singer. 2003. Feature-rich part-of-speech tagging with a cyclic dependency network. In *Proceedings of the 2003 Human Language Technology Conference of the North American Chapter of the Association for Computational Linguistics.* http://aclweb.org/anthology/N03-1033.

UWAV at SemEval-2017 Task 7: Automated feature-based system for locating puns

Ankit Vadehra

University of Waterloo

`avadehra@uwaterloo.ca`

Abstract

In this paper we describe our system created for SemEval-2017 Task 7: Detection and Interpretation of English Puns(Miller et al., 2017). We tackle subtask 1, pun detection, by leveraging features selected from sentences to design a classifier that can disambiguate between the presence or absence of a pun. We address subtask 2, pun location, by utilizing a decision flow structure that uses presence or absence of certain features to decide the next action. The results obtained by our system are encouraging, considering the simplicity of the system. We consider this system as a precursor for deeper exploration on efficient feature selection for pun detection.

1 Introduction

Puns are ambiguous word pairs in language that play on the different meaning of the word (polysemy), or utilize similarly pronounced sounds (phonology) often for a humorous effect(Miller and Turković, 2016). They are widely used in written and spoken literature, intended as jokes. The task tries to detect whether a sentence is a pun or not (Subtask 1). If a pun is detected, we try to detect which word in the sentence was meant as a pun (Subtask2). For example, the sentence, *"I'd tell you a chemistry joke, but, I know I wouldn't get a reaction."* is a play on the word *reaction*, which is a common phrase. But, including it after *chemistry*, which deals with chemical reactions; gives it a humorous intent. Another example, the sentence, *"I used to meditate a lot, but now I only do it every now and zen."* plays on the similar pronunciation of the words zen and then. Puns often require knowledge about syntactic similarity between words and phrases like meditation and zen,

chemistry and reaction, etc.

Recently, a definite trend is noticeable in developing a system that can automatically detect puns efficiently so that the humorous nature of the pun can be captured. Pun detection is of high importance for language modeling, machine translation and sentiment analysis task so that the actual meaning of terms can be understood. This allows effectively utilizing the intended meaning rather than just the words themselves.

The absence of any unified global word knowledge base makes detections of puns difficult since automatic selection of intended meaning is hard. There exist many Word Sense Disambiguation (WSD) approaches, but they are inefficient in capturing the word play(Miller and Gurevych, 2015). This makes pun detection a very interesting area to work on.

Due to the ambiguous nature of the words used, sentences containing puns are often wrongly classified. Due to an absence of a globally used pun dataset, all work in this area utilize self-accumulated and tagged datasets. This makes it difficult to compare the performance of different approaches.

We use the SemEval2017 Task7 dataset and design a classifier system that can detect the presence and location of puns. We explain the features selected and extracted that can efficiently detect puns in Section 2.1.1. In Section 2.2.1, we propose our decision flow based algorithm that utilizes features to locate the word in the sentence that was intended as the pun. We show and explain our results in Section 3 .

2 System Overview

We use this section to explain details of the system we designed for the task. The task was distributed in different subtasks and each subtask had two

Proceedings of the 11th International Workshop on Semantic Evaluations (SemEval-2017), pages 449–452,
Vancouver, Canada, August 3 - 4, 2017. ©2017 Association for Computational Linguistics

tasks for Homographic puns and Heterographic puns. Homographic puns play on the two distinct meanings of a word, whereas, Heterographic puns deal with the similar phonological pronunciation between words. For each subtask we design a single system, to tackle both Heterographic and Homographic puns, since in real life, we don't find a distinction between the two types. We try to present a system that could identify puns, irrespective of their type.

2.1 Subtask 1: Pun Detection

In this section we present the description of the classifier system used for detecting whether a sentence contains a pun or not.

2.1.1 Feature Set

For an efficient classifier we extract the following binary features from the sentence. The value for each feature is either 1 or 0, denoting the presence or absence of that feature in that sentence. We select the features that were generally found in puns.

- **Homophone:** Homophones are a set of words that have the same pronunciation but different meaning like "knew" and "new". We utilize two sources[1,2] from the Internet to create a list of homophones. This list is in no way exhaustive but covers the most frequent homophones.

- **Antonym:** Antonyms are pair of words that are opposite in meaning, like "good" and "bad". We utilize the WordNet (Miller, 1995) library to check whether the sentence contains any antonym pairs.

- **Idioms:** Idioms are group of words that are used together as an expression having a specific meaning. For example the phrase "blue moon" means something rare. We create a list of the most common idioms from the Englishclub website[3].

- **Homonym:** Homonyms are words that have more than one definitions. For example the word 'fine'. We create a list of the most common homonyms from Wikipedia[4] and Alphalink[5].

- **word2vec similarity:** We utilize the word2vec word representations(Mikolov et al., 2013) pre-

---

[1]http://www.zyvra.org/lafarr/hom.htm
[2]http://www.singularis.ltd.uk/
bifroest/misc/homophones-list.html
[3]https://www.englishclub.com/ref/
Idioms/
[4]https://en.wikipedia.org/wiki/List_
of_true_homonyms
[5]http://home.alphalink.com.au/
~umbidas/homonym_main.htm

trained on the 100 billion Google News words[6]. We construct a set of unique pair of words from the sentence and check the similarity score between them. If a score higher than the threshold (set to 0.30) is obtained for any pair, we assume that a word2vec similar word pair exists.

- **WordNet similarity:** We can utilize the WordNet (Miller, 1995) tree to calculate the distance between two words. Similar words are relatively closer and have high similarity score. If any pair of words has score higher than threshold (set to 0.30) we assume that a WordNet similar pair exists.

The threshold similarity value was set by manually calculating the similarity score for some similar words like *ketchup* and *mustard*.

2.1.2 Classification

Extracting the six binary features, described in the previous section, from our training dataset (explained in Section 3.1.1) we train three classifiers.

- **Support Vector Machine(SVM):** We use an SVM with a linear kernel, C=1, a squared-hinge loss function, and L2 loss penalty (Pedregosa et al., 2011).

- **Naive Bayes(NB):** We use Binomial variant with Laplace smoothing parameter = 1 (Pedregosa et al., 2011).

- **Logistic Regression(LR):** We use Logistic Regression with L2 loss penalty, and C=1 (Pedregosa et al., 2011).

The classifier gives an output of 1 or 0, denoting the presence or absence of a pun. We use the best-of-three approach, pooling the results of all three classifiers and selecting the highest occurring value (1 or 0).

2.2 Subtask 2: Pun Location

In this section we describe the decision flow based algorithm to expose the word in the sentence that represents the pun.

2.2.1 Algorithm Design

We present the decision flow algorithm used to detect the pun word in the sentence in Algorithm 1.

We start by utilizing the list of homophones and homonyms as described in Section 2.1.1. We utilize the word2vec pre-trained vectors (Mikolov et al., 2013) and the WordNet library (Miller,

---

[6]https://code.google.com/archive/p/
word2vec/

1995) to calculate similarity score using *calcScore* function.

Algorithm 1 Algorithm to detect location of pun word in sentence.

Require: hph = list of homophones; hom = list of homonym; wn = WordNet Library; w2v = word2vec pre-trained vectors; S = Sentence to test;

1: $sHalf \leftarrow$ Second Half of words in S
2: $sHalf \leftarrow$ Reverse words in $sHalf$
3: $flag = 0$
4: **for** $word \in sHalf$ **do**
5:    **if** $length(word) > 3$ **then**
6:       **if** $word \in (hph \cup hom)$ **then**
7:          $pun \leftarrow word$
8:          flag = 1; break;
9:       **end if**
10:       **if** $antonym(word) \in S$ **then**
11:          $pun \leftarrow word$
12:          flag = 1; break;
13:       **end if**
14:    **end if**
15: **end for**
16: **if** $flag = 0$ **then**
17:    $prevScore = 0$
18:    $revS \leftarrow$ Reverse of words in S
19:    $wP \leftarrow$ Pairs of words $\in$ revS
20:    **for** $p \in wP$ **do** $\triangleright p = (word1, word2)$
21:       $score \leftarrow calcScore(word1, word2)$
22:       **if** $score > prevScore$ **then**
23:          $prevScore \leftarrow score$
24:          $pun \leftarrow word1$
25:       **end if**
26:    **end for**
27: **end if**
28: **if** $prevScore = 0$ **then**
29:    $pun \leftarrow$ Last word of S
30: **end if**

We break the sentence into its constituent words, and check whether any word in the second half of the sentence is a homophone/homonym. If any such word is found, it is considered as the pun word. If no such match is found, we check whether any word in the second half has an antonym (Section 2.1.1) in the sentence. If an antonym pair is found, that word is considered as the pun.

If no match is found then we consider the unique pair combinations of words in the sentence and calculate the word similarity. The word from the back of the sentence that has the highest similarity score with any other word in the sentence is considered as the pun word. If all decisions fail, the last word in the sentence is considered as the pun word.

3 Experiment and Results

3.1 Subtask 1: Pun Detection

We extract features and design a classifier for Subtask 1.

3.1.1 Dataset

We created the dataset for the classifier by gathering puns from the punoftheday[7] website. The website consists of user aggregated puns of all types. A collection of 5316 puns were accumulated.

For non-pun sentences multiple sources were used. Sentences containing homophones and homonyms were extracted from WordNet (Miller, 1995). We also utilized the SemEval2012 - Task 6[8] training dataset by taking a single sentence from each dataset item. The BBC dataset (Greene and Cunningham, 2006) of news articles was also used[9]. We extracted the first sentence for each news article. Compiling all these sources gave us a set of 4848 non-pun sentences.

3.1.2 Result

We tabulate the results achieved in the SemEval 2017 Task 7 in Table 1.

Table 1: Official SemEval Results for Subtask1.

PunTask	Precision	Recall	Accuracy	F1
Homographic	0.78	0.61	0.60	0.68
Heterographic	0.79	0.62	0.61	0.69

3.1.3 Limitations

On deeper analysis of the training dataset we found that the final testing dataset contained items from the punoftheday[7] website too. This made multiple items from the test dataset present in our training dataset. In total, 1145 items from the Homographic task and 715 items from the Heterographic task were present in our training set.

Due to this unfortunate coincidence, we recreated our training set, eliminating all the items that

---

[7] http://www.punoftheday.com/
[8] https://www.cs.york.ac.uk/semeval-2012/task6.html
[9] http://mlg.ucd.ie/datasets/bbc.html

were present in the SemEval Test set. This reduced our dataset to 3456 puns and 4848 nonpuns. Retesting on this dataset provided us with the following results as mentioned in Table 2:

Table 2: Recalculated Results for Subtask1.

PunTask	Precision	Recall	Accuracy	F1
Homographic	0.68	0.47	0.47	0.56
Heterographic	0.65	0.42	0.43	0.51

3.2 Subtask2: Pun Location

For this task we run the testing dataset through our algorithm proposed in Section 2.2.1. We submitted two runs for this subtask, using WordNet Path Similarity for one run and word2vec word similarity for the other.

3.2.1 Result

The results achieved using WordNet as a similarity metric are tabulated in Table 3, whereas Table 4 tabulates the results obtained using word2vec as a similarity measure.

Table 3: SemEval Subtask2 results using WordNet as similarity measure.

PunTask	Precision	Recall	F1
Homographic	0.315	0.315	0.315
Heterographic	0.357	0.357	0.357

Table 4: SemEval Subtask2 results using word2vec as similarity measure.

PunTask	Precision	Recall	F1
Homographic	0.341	0.341	0.341
Heterographic	0.428	0.428	0.428

4 Conclusion

Based on our submissions and the results for SemEval2017 Task7, we believe that efficient feature selection may be a feasible approach for automatic detection of sentences containing puns. We propose to integrate language models and word substitution in future work to perform deeper analysis on the dataset.

Even though our system was not the best one, we do believe that the simplicity of its design is a highly attractive feature. We selected features for our system that are generally found in puns. We found that some of the features like homophones resulted in poor performance for Subtask 2. Future work on efficient feature selection might allow us to get much higher results.

References

Derek Greene and Pádraig Cunningham. 2006. Practical solutions to the problem of diagonal dominance in kernel document clustering. In *Proc. 23rd International Conference on Machine learning (ICML'06)*. ACM Press, pages 377–384.

Tomas Mikolov, Ilya Sutskever, Kai Chen, Greg S Corrado, and Jeff Dean. 2013. Distributed representations of words and phrases and their compositionality. In *Advances in neural information processing systems*. pages 3111–3119.

George A Miller. 1995. Wordnet: a lexical database for english. *Communications of the ACM* 38(11):39–41.

Tristan Miller and Iryna Gurevych. 2015. Automatic disambiguation of english puns. In *ACL (1)*. pages 719–729.

Tristan Miller, Christian F. Hempelmann, and Iryna Gurevych. 2017. SemEval-2017 Task 7: Detection and interpretation of English puns. In *Proceedings of the 11th International Workshop on Semantic Evaluation (SemEval-2017)*.

Tristan Miller and Mladen Turković. 2016. Towards the automatic detection and identification of english puns. *The European Journal of Humour Research* 4(1):59–75.

Fabian Pedregosa, Gaël Varoquaux, Alexandre Gramfort, Vincent Michel, Bertrand Thirion, Olivier Grisel, Mathieu Blondel, Peter Prettenhofer, Ron Weiss, Vincent Dubourg, et al. 2011. Scikit-learn: Machine learning in python. *Journal of Machine Learning Research* 12(Oct):2825–2830.

ECNU at SemEval-2017 Task 7: Using Supervised and Unsupervised Methods to Detect and Locate English Puns

Yuhuan Xiu[1], Man Lan[1,2*], Yuanbin Wu[1,2]
[1]Department of Computer Science and Technology,
East China Normal University, Shanghai, P.R.China
[2]Shanghai Key Laboratory of Multidimensional Information Processing
51164500032@stu.ecnu.edu.cn
mlan,ybwu@cs.ecnu.edu.cn

Abstract

This paper describes our submissions to task 7 in SemEval 2017, i.e., Detection and Interpretation of English Puns. We participated in the first two subtasks, which are to detect and locate English puns respectively. For subtask 1, we presented a supervised system to determine whether or not a sentence contains a pun using similarity features calculated on sense vectors or cluster center vectors. For subtask 2, we established an unsupervised system to locate the pun by scoring each word in the sentence and we assumed that the word with the smallest score is the pun.

1 Introduction

A pun is a form of wordplay in which one signifier (e.g., a word or phrase) suggests two or more meanings by exploiting polysemy, or phonological similarity to another signifier, for an intended humorous or rhetorical effect. The study of puns can be seen as a respectable research topic in traditional linguistics and the cognitive sciences.

Semeval 2017 task 7(Miller et al., 2017) contains three subtasks, i.e., pun detection, pun location, and pun interpretation. And we participated in the first two subtasks. The detection and location of English puns are to determine whether or not a sentence contains a pun and which word is a pun respectively, which differ from traditional word sense disambiguation (WSD). WSD is to determine an exact meaning of the target word in the given context. However, WSD algorithms could provide the lexical-semantic understanding for pun detection and location. And we adopted a knowledge-based WSD algorithm to obtain possible *senses*[1] for each word in the sentence.

There are two types of puns: some are homographic puns and the others are heterographic puns. A homographic pun exploits distinct meanings of the same written word, and a heterographic pun exploits distinct meanings of the similar but not exactly the same spoken word. The organizers provided two test datasets about homographic puns and heterographic puns respectively for each subtask. Since they did not provide official training datasets, we collected our own positive samples(each sentence contains a pun) from the *Pun of the Day website*[2], which conclude 60 homographic puns and 60 heterographic puns. Besides, we also assembled a raw dataset of 120 negative samples(sentences that do not contain puns) from the Internet. Then, we combined 120 negative samples with 60 homographic puns or 60 heterographic puns into homographic or heterographic training dataset. Then, we did the same data preprocessing for both training and test datasets. Firstly, we performed part-of-speech(POS) tagging using *Stanford CoreNLP tools*(Manning et al., 2014). Secondly, we removed the stop words in sentences. The words produced after this series of processing are denoted as *target words* for each sentence.

Since there are two different puns, we adopted different methods for them to detect and locate English puns. For homographic puns, we calculated the semantic similarity between sense vectors of each target word in the sentence to obtain a vector representation of a sentence and score each target word in the sentence, and for heterographic puns, we computed the semantic similarity between cluster center vectors of each sentence for the same purpose.

---

[1]The sense is the gloss provided by WordNet

[2]http://www.punoftheday.com/

Proceedings of the 11th International Workshop on Semantic Evaluations (SemEval-2017), pages 453–456,
Vancouver, Canada, August 3 - 4, 2017. ©2017 Association for Computational Linguistics

2   Homographic Puns Detection and Location

To detect and locate homographic puns, we performed exploratory analysis on training dataset. We found that the degree of semantic similarity between two meanings of a pun is supposed not to be high, where the semantic similarity between meanings is measured by calculating the distance between sense vectors.

(Miller and Turković, 2016) makes a case for research into computational methods for detection of puns in running context. Inspired by their work, for subtask 1, we presented a supervised system using similarity features which are calculated on sense vectors of each target word to create each target word vector, and to obtain the vector representation of the sentence. For subtask 2, we located the pun by scoring each target word in the sentence.

2.1   Pun Detection

This subtask is to determine whether or not a given sentence contains a pun. To address this subtask, we performed the process that consists of the following steps:

- For each *target word* in the sentence, we adopted Simplified Lesk algorithm(Kilgarriff and Rosenzweig, 2000) with respect to its POS to select the possible *senses*. Simplified Lesk disambiguates a word by examining the *definitions*[3] and selecting the single sense with the highest *overlap score*[4]. In our case, we selected the possible senses which *overlap scores* are higher than or equal to the second highest *overlap score*.

- In order to obtain the sense vector for each sense, we used 300-dimensional word vectors which are pre-trained Google word vectors downloaded from Internet[5] to represent each word in the *sense* and the simple *min, max, average* pooling strategies were adopted to concatenate sense vector representations with dimensionality of 900.

- For each *target word* in the sentence, we calculated the similarity between its sense vectors using six kernel functions, i.e., cosine similarity, manhattan distance, euclidean distance, pearsonr distance, Spearman's rho distance and sigmoid function. Note that, the instruction of sigmoid function is : Firstly, compute the dot product of two vectors to obtain the value of K. Secondly, update K by K=tanh(K/D+1), where D is the dimension of the vector. Finally, we denote K as the similarity score calculated by sigmoid function.

- For each *target word* in the sentence, we combined each minimum score calculated by each kernel function into target word vector(6-dimensional).

- In order to obtain the sentence vector(18-dimensional), we simply adopted the *min, max, mean* pooling strategies on all target words in the sentence.

we explored two supervised machine learning algorithms to build the classifiers: AdaBoost(AB) and RandomForest(RF) both implemented in *scikit-learn tools*[6].

2.2   Pun Loaction

This subtask is to decide which word in the sentence is the pun. We scored each target word by averaging the elements of its target word vector described in section 2.1. Finally, we assumed that the word with the smallest score is a homographic pun.

3   Heterographic Puns Detection and Location

A heterographic pun corresponds to another word with similar spoken but distinct meaning. That is different from a homographic pun, which exploits distinct meanings of exactly one word. Therefore, we adopted different methods for heterographic puns. Through an artificial analysis on heterographic puns, we found that the original meaning of the heterographic pun differs greatly from the meanings of other words in the sentence. Therefore, we clustered all words in training and test datasets in order to cluster words with high degree of semantic similarity into the same cluster. Firstly, we used pre-trained Google word vectors

---

[3]In our implementation, the definitions are formed by concatenating the synonyms, gloss, and example sentences provided by WordNet

[4]Overlap score is the number of words in common with the context

[5]https://code.google.com/archive/p/word2vec

[6]http://scikit-learn.org/stable

to represent each word. Secondly, we clustered those word vectors into 100 clusters using k-means(k=100) clustering algorithm. Finally, we obtained a cluster center vector(300-dimensional) for each cluster by averaging the word vectors belonging to this cluster. Moreover, the semantic similarity between words in the sentence is measured by calculating the distance between cluster center vectors.

For subtask 1, we presented a supervised system using similarity features which are calculated on cluster center vectors to represent a sentence. For subtask 2, we selectively scored target word in the sentence.

3.1 Pun Detection

To address this subtask, we used the following two steps to implement our approach.

- We clustered the target words in a sentence into several clusters. If the number of clusters of all taget words in a sentence is exactly one, we assumed that this sentence does not contain a pun. If not, we calculated the similarity between those cluster center vectors using the six kernel functions adopted in section 2.1.

- We took the min, max, and mean scores calculated by each kernel function as a vector representation(18-dimensional) of the sentence.

we also explored two same classification algorithms as for homographic puns detection.

3.2 Pun Loaction

To locate the pun in the sentence, we split the location process into three steps.

- We calculated the similarity scores between a cluster center and other cluster centers using the six kernel functions to find the outlier cluster, then we computed the average value of those similarity scores as a score for each cluster center. We chose the cluster center with the smallest score as the outlier cluster.

- If there is only one word in the outlier cluster, we selected this word as a pun. If not, for each candidate word, we calculated the similarity scores between the *top-sense vector*[7] of

---

[7]Top-sense is the definition of top-scoring synset returned by Simplified Lesk algorithm and we used the method described in Section 2.1 to obtain top-sense vector

it and every cluster center except the outlier one using the six kernel functions. Finally, We calculated the average value of these similarity scores as a score for each candidate word.

- We supposed that the word with the smallest score is a heterographic pun.

Particularly, if the number of clusters of all target words in a sentence is less than three, we could not find the outlier cluster. Therefore we calculated the similarity scores between *top-sense vectors* of target words in the sentence. We scored each target word by averaging all the similarity scores that are relevant to that target word.

4 Experiments

4.1 Datasets

Although organizers did not provide the training datasets, we collected our own training datasets. Table 1 shows the statistics of the datasets we used in our experiments.

Pun	Dataset	Positive	Negative	Total
homographic	training	60(33%)	120(67%)	180
	test	1,607(71%)	643(29%)	2,250
heterographic	training	60(33%)	120(67%)	180
	test	1,271(71%)	509(29%)	1,780

Table 1: Statistics of datasets in training and test data. The number in brackets are the percentages of different classes in each dataset.

4.2 Evaluation Metrics

For both subtask 1 and 2, the three widely-used evaluation measures *precision(P)*, *recall(R)* and F_1 are adopted. Moreover, for subtask 1, *accuracy(Acc)* is also included and for subtask 2, *coverage(C)* is used. *Coverage* is defined as the ratio of sentence for which a location assignment was attempted.

4.3 Experiment on Training Data For Subtask 1

Table 2 and 3 show the results of different algorithms of subtask 1 on homographic and heterographic training datasets respectively. The 5-fold cross validation is performed for system development. From Table 2 and Table 3, we find that AdaBoost outperforms RandomForest algorithm and the ensemble method performed best on homographic pun. Therefore we chose the ensemble classifier for homographic pun and the AdaBoost algorithm for heterographic pun.

Method	Algorithm	P	R	Acc	F_1
Single	AB	0.7945	0.6836	0.6667	0.7349
	RF	0.7814	0.6733	0.6346	0.7233
Ensemble	AB+RF	0.8013	0.6955	0.6835	0.7747

Table 2: Results of subtask 1 on homographic training dataset.

Method	Algorithm	P	R	Acc	F_1
Single	AB	0.8401	0.8233	0.8833	0.8316
	RF	0.7107	0.4833	0.77.22	0.57.59
Ensemble	AB+RF	0.8880	0.4500	0.8056	0.5973

Table 3: Results of subtask 1 on heterographic training dataset.

4.4 Results and Discussion on Test Data

Table 4 and Table 5 show the results of our systems and the top-ranked systems provided by organizers for subtask 1 and subtask 2 respectively. Compared with the top ranked systems, there is much room for improvement in our work. The reason for the poor performance may be that the constructing method of sense vectors is simple and straightforward, which neglects the word sequence and the sentence structure of the sense. We find that detecting puns at the sentence level is more effective than locating puns at the word level, and our systems performed better on heterographic puns.

Pun	System(rank)	P	R	Acc	F_1
Homographic	ECNU(6)	0.7127	0.6474	0.5628	0.6785
	PunFields(1)	0.8091	0.7785	0.7044	0.7900
	Duluth(2)	0.7832	0.8724	0.7364	0.8254
	UWAV(3)	0.7806	0.6067	0.5973	0.6828
Heterographic	ECNU(2)	0.7807	0.6761	0.6333	0.7247
	Idiom Savant(1)	0.8704	0.8190	0.7837	0.8439
	N-Hance(3)	0.7725	0.9300	0.7545	0.8440

Table 4: Performance of our systems and the top-ranked(ranked by P) systems. The numbers in the brackets are the official ranking

5 Conclusion

In this paper, we presented systems to detect and locate a pun in the sentence on both homographic and heterographic puns datasets. For homographic puns, we calculated the semantic similarity between sense vectors of each target word in the sentence to obtain its sentence vector and score each target word. And for heterographic puns, we

Pun	System(rank)	C	P	R	F_1
Homographic	ECNU(8)	1.0000	0.3373	0.3373	0.3373
	Idiom Savant(1)	0.9988	0.6636	0.6627	0.6631
	UWaterloo(2)	0.9994	0.6526	0.6521	0.6523
	Fermi(3)	1.0000	0.5215	0.5215	0.5215
Heterographic	ECNU(4)	1.0000	0.5681	0.5681	0.5681
	UWaterloo(1)	0.9976	0.7973	0.7954	0.7964
	Idiom Savant(2)	1.0000	0.6845	0.6845	0.6845
	N-Hance(3)	0.9882	0.6592	0.6515	0.6553

Table 5: Performance of our systems and the top-ranked(ranked by P) systems. The numbers in the brackets are the official ranking

computed the semantic similarity between cluster center vectors of each sentence for the same purpose. In the future, we will explore the requisite problem of pun interpretation, where the objection is to determine two senses of the pun.

Acknowledgements

This research is supported by grants from Science and Technology Commission of Shanghai Municipality(14DZ2260800 and 15ZR1410700), Shanghai Collaborative Innovation Center of Trustworthy Software for Internet of Things (ZF1213) and NSFC (61402175).

References

Adam Kilgarriff and Joseph Rosenzweig. 2000. Framework and results for english senseval. *Computers and the Humanities* 34(1):15–48.

Christopher D Manning, Mihai Surdeanu, John Bauer, Jenny Rose Finkel, Steven Bethard, and David McClosky. 2014. The stanford corenlp natural language processing toolkit. In *ACL (System Demonstrations)*. pages 55–60.

Tristan Miller, Christian F. Hempelmann, and Iryna Gurevych. 2017. SemEval-2017 Task 7: Detection and interpretation of English puns. In *Proceedings of the 11th International Workshop on Semantic Evaluation (SemEval-2017)*.

Tristan Miller and Mladen Turković. 2016. Towards the automatic detection and identification of english puns. *The European Journal of Humour Research* 4(1):59–75.

Fermi at SemEval-2017 Task 7: Detection and Interpretation of Homographic puns in English Language

Vijayasaradhi Indurthi
SIEL, IIIT Hyderabad
vijaya.saradhi@research.iiit.ac.in

Oota Subba Reddy
SIEL, IIIT Hyderabad
oota.subba@students.iiit.ac.in

Abstract

This paper describes our system for detection and interpretation of English puns. We participated in 2 subtasks related to homographic puns achieve comparable results for these tasks. Through the paper we provide detailed description of the approach, as well as the results obtained in the task.

Our models achieved an F1-score of 77.65% for Subtask 1 and 52.15% for Subtask 2.

1 Introduction

The pun, also called paronomasia, is a form of word play that suggests two or more meanings, by exploiting multiple meanings of words, or of similar-sounding words, for an intended humorous or rhetorical effect. A pun is also a special form of ambiguity (mostly lexical) that is consciously used to create statements with ambiguous-distinct-meanings. These ambiguities can arise from the intentional use of homophonic, homographic, metonymic, or figurative language. A homographic pun exploits distinct meanings of the same written word, and a homophonic pun exploits distinct meanings of the same spoken word.

Examples of homographic puns.

- *"I used to be a banker but I lost interest"*,

- *"Tires are fixed for a flat rate"*

- *"Getting rid of your boat for another could cause a whole raft of problems"*

In the first example, the word interest is the pun denoting interest as willingness and also as a fixed charge for borrowing money. In the second example, the word flat is the pun denoting flat as in a flat

tyre and flat as in flat rate. The third example, the word raft is the pun denoting raft as a batch and raft as a type of boat.

In the present work, we focus on homographic puns. We present methods to a) identify a pun sentence, b) identify the pun word given a pun sentence and c) interpret the different word senses of the pun word. The details of the shared task are available at (Tristan Miller and Hempelmann, 2017)

2 Subtask 1 - Pun detection

In this task, for each sentence, the system must decide whether it contains a pun or not. While this task is mostly unsupervised, we cast this problem as a supervised learning classification problem. We have randomly selected part of the dataset and manually annotated them as a pun sentence or a non-pun. We decided to leverage on models that try to model sequences of word vectors. We can view the each sentence as a sequence where we only have one label at the end. This many-to-one mapping lends itself nicely to Recurrent Neural Network. Due to this reason, we used a recurrent neural network to train the classifier and generate the model. Using this model we classify the remaining dataset.

We used two settings for the train and test split. In setting 1, we used 70% of the dataset for training and 30% of the data for testing. In Setting 2, we used 30% of the dataset for training and the remaining 70% of the data for testing.

Recent research has shown that deep learning methods can minimize the reliance on feature engineering by automatically extracting meaningful features from raw text (Collobert, 2012). Thus, we propose to use distributed word embeddings which capture lexical and semantic features as input features to our neural network model.

Proceedings of the 11th International Workshop on Semantic Evaluations (SemEval-2017), pages 457–460,
Vancouver, Canada, August 3 - 4, 2017. ©2017 Association for Computational Linguistics

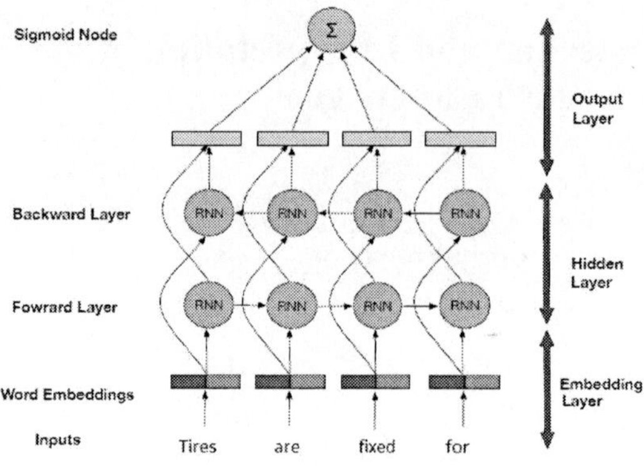

Figure 1: BiDirectional RNN architecture for detecting puns

Distributed word embeddings map words in a language to high dimensional real-valued vectors in order to capture hidden semantic and syntactic properties of words. These embeddings are typically learned from large unlabeled text corpora. In our work, we use the pre-trained 50 dimensional GloVe embeddings (Pennington et al., 2014) which were trained on about 6B words from the twitter using the Continuous Bag of Words architecture.

2.1 Model

The network architecture of our model as illustrated in Figure 1 has the following structure

- Embedding Layer: This layer transforms each word into embedded features. The embedded features are a concatenation of the words Distributed word embeddings. The embedding layer acts as input to the hidden layer.

- Hidden Layer: The hidden layer consists of a Bi-Directional RNN. The output of the RNN is a fixed sized representation of its input.

- Output Layer: In the output layer, the representation learned from the RNN is passed through a fully connected neural network with a sigmoid output node that classifies the sentence as a pun or a non-pun.

2.2 Performance

We train the network for 25 epochs. The following table describes the results on the pun dataset.

Table 1 shows the performance of our classifier on the two settings.

2.3 Discussion

While the pun classification was supposed to be an unsupervised classification problem, we cast the problem into a supervised classification problem by annotating the data partially. This might be a reason for very high precision for the Setting 1 as the classifier might have overfit the model to a wider range of training data than in the second setting. We used a dropout of 0.5 in Bi-Direction RNN to avoid the overfitting problem.

3 Subtask 2 - Pun location

In this task, for each sentence containing a pun, the system must identify the pun word. We introduce the algorithm which takes a sentence containing a pun as an input and returns the pun word.

3.1 Observations

Empirical observations of the puns show the following characteristics of the pun word

- The pun word usually appears towards the end of the pun (Miller, 2014)

- There exists a non-pun word whose similarity is more than a threshold, than any other word to word similarity in the sentence.

- Stopwords and non content words can not be puns

- The pun word will have atleast two word senses in the wordnet corpus (Miller, 1995)

3.2 Methodology

From the examples given in section 1, we see that the pun word interest is semantically close to the word banker and its root bank. In the next example, we observe that the word flat is semantically close to the word tires because tires can go flat. In the last example the word raft is semantically close to the word boat as both are used as transport objects in water.

Based on the above observations, we propose the following algorithm to identify the pun word in a sentence having a pun. The function FIND_PUN takes a sentence containing a pun as an input and returns the pun word discussed in Algorithm 1. First, a list of probable pun words is generated by removing the stopwords and punctuation in the

Setting	Train	Test	Precision	Recall	Accuracy.	F1
Setting 1	70%	30%	0.9697	0.7953	0.8360	0.8738
Setting 2	30%	70%	0.8918	0.6876	0.7173	0.7765

Table 1: Performance of the pun classifier using Bidirectional RNN in 2 settings for Subtask 1

sentence. Next, all words which have less than 2 entries in the wordnet are removed. If there is only 1 word left, we return this word as a pun word. In case multiple words are present in the probable puns list, then a list of pairs with all combination of words in the sentence with all the possible words in the probable puns is made. For every pair in the list of pairs, the similarity of the two words is calculated. The similarity of two words is also calculated by expanding the synsets of both the words and finding the most similar pair between the pairs of every synset in word 1 with every synset in word2.

Algorithm 1 PUN Detection Algorithm

1: **INPUT** Sentence
2: **OUTPUT** PUN word.
3: **Step 1:** Tokenize the input sentence.
4: **Step 2:** Remove punctuations and stop words
5: from the tokens.
6: **Step 3:** Remove tokens which have less than
7: 2 entries from the wordnet.
8: **if** Only one Word in list **then**
9:    return Word(PUN word)
10: **else**
11:    **for** All pair of words in sentence **do**
12:       Bestpair=MAXSIM(Pair of words)
13:    **end for**
14:    return Word $\in$ Bestpair which occurs
15:    towards end of the sentence.
16: **end if**

The MAXSIM function takes two words as input and returns the maximum similarity between all pairs of words in their synsets. The algorithm is described in 2.

For every possible pair between synsets1 and synsets2, calculate the word to word similarity using the word embeddings. Return the pair which has the maximum similarity.

For the pun example 3, the following table shows the similarity between all pairs of the words in the descending order of the similarity.

Algorithm 2 MAXSIM Model

1: **INPUT** Words={Word1, Word2}
2: **Initialization** MaxSimilarity=0
3: **OUTPUT** Maximum similarity between all pairs of words in their synsets
4: **Step 1:** synsets1 = get the synsets of word1
5: **Step 2:** synsets2 = get the synsets of word2
6: **for** pairword1 in synsets1 **do**
7:    **for** pairword2 in synsets2 **do**
8:       **Step 3:**WordSimilarity=
9: similarity(pairword1,pairword2)
10:       **if** MaxSimilarity $\leq$ WordSimilarity **then**
11:          **a:**MaxSimilarity= WordSimilarity
12:       **end if**
13: **end for**
14: **end for**
15: **Step 4:**return MaxSimilarity

Word 1	Word 2	Max similarity
boat	**raft**	**0.68**
boat	whole	0.61
getting	whole	0.5
rid	whole	0.5
getting	problems	0.46
getting	raft	0.4
rid	raft	0.4
getting	boat	0.28
boat	problems	0.26
boat	whole	0.24
rid	raft	0.23
rid	whole	0.21
rid	problems	0.20

Table 2: All word similarity pairs for the example pun 3

Precision	Recall	Coverage.	F1
0.5215	0.5215	1	0.5215

Table 3: Performance of the pun word identification using MAXSIM for Subtask 2

In the first step, the following non content words

are removed - of, your, for, could, cause. The remaining words are - rid, boat, getting, whole, problems. Table 2 shows the similarities between all pairs of the words. The highest pair boat-raft is returned by the maxsim function. Since the word raft appears later in the sentence, the word raft is identified as the pun word.

3.3 Performance

Table 2 describes the result of our teams run for Subtask 2.

3.4 Discussion

We have observed that our algorithm maxsim has performed decently for pun sentences which are short in length having up to 10 words in the sentence. We observed that as the length of the sentence increases, there are more number of words which are similar together and the accuracy of pun word identification decreased.

4 Subtask 3 - Pun interpretation

In this subtask, the pun word is given and the system has to annotate the word with the right Word-Net sense keys. While we did not participate in this subtask, it is trivial to extend the work done for Subtask 2 to achieve the objective of Subtask 3.

5 Conclusion

Classifying an English sentence as a pun or not is a non trivial task. It is much more difficult and challenging to solve this problem as an unsupervised classification task. Experimentation can be done to use LSTMs, and BiDirectional LSTMs to improve the performance of the classifier. Character Level Embeddings can be used as features to capture orthographic and morphological features of a word. word2vec embeddings from the Google News dataset can be evaluated as alternative features for GloVe vectors. For pun identification task, cluster based approaches can be explored specifically for the long sentences. As the interpretation of most of the puns relies on specific domain knowledge, additional corpora can be used to augment our models for better performance.

References

R. Weston J. Bottou L. Karlen M. Kavukcuoglu K. Kuksa P Collobert. 2012. Natural language processing (almost) from scratch. journal of machine learning research.

George A Miller. 1995. Wordnet: A lexical database for english. communications of the acm vol. 38, no. 11: 39-41.

Tristan Miller. 2014. Towards the automatic detection and identification of english puns.

Jeffrey Pennington, Richard Socher, and Christopher D. Manning. 2014. Glove: Global vectors for word representation. In *Empirical Methods in Natural Language Processing (EMNLP)*. pages 1532–1543. http://www.aclweb.org/anthology/D14-1162.

Iryna Gurevych Tristan Miller and Christian F. Hempelmann. 2017. Systemdescription paper for semeval 2017 task 7. In *Proceedings of the 11th Annual Meeting of the SemEval)*. Association for Computational Linguistics.

UWaterloo at SemEval-2017 Task 8: Detecting Stance towards Rumours with Topic Independent Features

Hareesh Bahuleyan and **Olga Vechtomova**
University of Waterloo, ON, Canada
`{hpallika, ovechtomova}@uwaterloo.ca`

Abstract

This paper describes our system for subtask-A: SDQC for RumourEval, task-8 of SemEval 2017. Identifying rumours, especially for breaking news events as they unfold, is a challenging task due to the absence of sufficient information about the exact rumour stories circulating on social media. Determining the stance of Twitter users towards rumourous messages could provide an indirect way of identifying potential rumours. The proposed approach makes use of topic independent features from two categories, namely cue features and message specific features to fit a gradient boosting classifier. With an accuracy of 0.78, our system achieved the second best performance on subtask-A of RumourEval.

1 Introduction

In the recent years, with the increasing popularity of smartphones, social media has become one of the top sources of news. However, because all the content is user-generated, the truth behind such news stories may become difficult to verify. Spread of misinformation during the event of an emergency can potentially have negative impacts. Although a few studies in the literature have developed rumour classification algorithms for Twitter (Qazvinian et al., 2011), these studies assume that the circulating stories about a topic or an event are known *a priori* (Eg: *Is Barack Obama muslim ?*). On the other hand, identifying rumour stories for breaking news events, as they unfold, is even more challenging (Zubiaga et al., 2016b). This is because during these early stages, the exact rumour stories propagating about the event are still unknown.

In such a scenario, studying the conversation between users discussing the event on Twitter can possibly give insights about the veracity of a circulating rumour story (Zubiaga et al., 2016c). By making use of the so-called 'wisdom of the crowd', the idea here is to understand how other users respond to rumourous tweets. It would be useful to identify if users may reply with an intent to support the story, deny the rumour by providing counter evidence or pose questions about the information stated (Zubiaga et al., 2016a). Collating the stance of other users could indirectly help in resolving the veracity of a rumour.

The rest of this paper is organized as follows. Section 2 is a brief overview of the task. The features used and the modeling technique are described in section 3. The results are analyzed in section 4 and the conclusions from the study are provided in section 5.

2 Task Description

The objective of subtask-A of RumourEval was to identify the stance of Twitter users towards rumour tweets. Given a rumourous tweet (source) and its conversation thread, the participants were required to classify the stance of each tweet (including the source tweet) with respect to the underlying rumour (Derczynski et al., 2017). The type of interaction could be one of the following:

1. Support(S): responding user supports the veracity of the rumour
2. Deny(D): responding user denies the veracity of the rumour
3. Query(Q): responding user demands additional evidence
4. Comment(C): responding user's tweet is not useful in determining the veracity of the rumour

The training dataset consisted of 4519 tweets from

Proceedings of the 11th International Workshop on Semantic Evaluations (SemEval-2017), pages 461–464,
Vancouver, Canada, August 3 - 4, 2017. ©2017 Association for Computational Linguistics

eight breaking news stories. The test set had 1049 tweets corresponding to a mix of topics from different events.

3 System Description

Breaking news events, as they unfold on social media, may not have sufficient topic-specific information that could assist in rumour identification. For this reason, we chose to design topic independent features for the task of rumour stance classification. Our hypothesis was that the presence of specific words in the reply tweets could potentially be indicative of reply type.

Prior to feature extraction, the following data pre-processing steps were carried out: (1) removal of quoted text (reply tweets at times quote the source tweet), (2) discarding URLs, unicode characters, HTML tags, and (3) stripping out the extra whitespaces and carriage returns in the text.

We began by manually inspecting tweet messages in the training dataset to come up with an initial hand-curated list of word features. On further analyzing these features, it was found that these words could be categorized into meaningful groups. Such 'cue words' have previously been reported to be useful in identifying an author's certainty in journalism (Soni et al., 2014), determining veracity of rumours (Reichel and Lendvai, 2016) and detecting disagreement in online dialogue (Misra and Walker, 2013). As listed in Table 1, the first five categories of the cue features are **Belief**, **Report**, **Doubt**, **Knowledge**, **Denial**. The presence of belief or knowledge words could be indicative of a reply where the author expresses his support. As for doubt or denial word cues, they are more likely to be used when the replying author wishes to convey his disagreement. On the other hand, report cue words could be present in either a supporting tweet or a denying tweet. Table 2 provides example tweet messages containing different cue words and their corresponding true class-labels from the original dataset .

Internet slang and curse words are more likely to be present in reply tweets which are of type 'comment'. While negation words were useful in identifying denying replies, the occurrence of question words in the text were very informative in capturing query type replies. We have a list of certain other cue words, which could not be fit into any particular category, but were useful in this 4-class classification problem. The cue word feature

categories along with examples are shown in Table 1. In total, there were 153 such features.[1]

Feature	Example Words
Belief	*assume, believe, apparent, perhaps, suspect, think, thought, consider*
Report	*evidence, source, official, footage, capture, assert, told, claim, according*
Doubt	*wonder, allege, unsure, guess, speculate, doubt*
Knowledge	*confirm, definitely, admit*
Denial	*refuse, reject, rebuff, dismiss, contradict, oppose*
Curse Words & Internet Slang	*lol, rofl, lmfao, yeah, stfu, aha, wtf, shit*
Negation Words	*no, not, no one, nothing, never, don't, can't, hardly*
Question Words	*when, which, what, who, how, whom, why whose*
Others	*irresponsible, careless, liar, false, witness, untrue, neglect, integrity, murder, fake*

Table 1: Set of cue features and examples

Example Tweet	Cue Word Type	Reply Type
@TroyBramston Source from Ray Hadley shows **confirmed** *same report of gunman claiming there are four packages around Sydney*	Knowledge/ Report	Support
@PhilSerrin Me thinks you like to emote in suppositions. Truth is, you don't know what happened, but want to **speculate.**	Doubt	Deny
@DaveBeninger @SheilaGunnReid Canadian news **contradicts** *this*	Denial	Deny
@Manning_Eli_1 @TheAnonMessage2 I **thought** *the same thing*	Belief	Support

Table 2: Example tweets with cue words

Apart from the cue word features discussed earlier, certain other tweet specific features were also used as part of our model. These message level features provide information about the writing style, such as the presence of punctuation marks, Twitter-specific characters (such as #, @) and number of words/characters in the message. The entire list of features under this category have been summarized in Table 3. For calculating the sentiment polarity score, the lexicon based social media sentiment calculator, VADER, developed by Hutto and Gilbert (2014), was used.

---

[1]The cue word feature list used in this study is available at `https://github.com/HareeshBahuleyan/rumour-eval/blob/master/cue_word_list.txt`

It is to be noted that all of the features discussed in this section (except for *similarity*) were extracted from the reply tweets in the dataset. The task also required the source tweet to be classified as one of the four reply types. Since there wasn't enough data to train a separate model for predicting the label of source tweets, we made an assumption that all source tweets were 'supporting' the rumour, which was the majority class in the training set.

Feature	Description
Word Count	Number of words in the tweet
Capital Words	Count of words in ALL CAPS
Punctuation	Number of '?', '!' and '.'
Character Count	Number of characters
Sentiment	VADER sentiment score
Similarity	Cosine similarity between source and reply tweets
Hashtag	Count of hashtags
@user	Count of @*user* mentions
Part-of-Speech	A vector of POS tag counts

Table 3: Set of tweet features and description

The numeric features, most of which were counts of specific characters or words, were used for training a supervised classification algorithm, specifically Gradient Boosting. Boosting is an additive and iterative tree-based supervised machine learning approach where a strong classifier is sequentially constructed from multiple weak learners. The XGBoost implementation of the gradient boosting algorithm was utilized in this study (Chen and Guestrin, 2016). The hyperparameters were tuned and set to be as follows:

1. **n_estimators** = 100: Refers to the number of trees to be grown to fit the model.
2. **max_depth** = 9: Number of splits for each of the weak learner trees.
3. **sub_sample** = 0.8; Each tree uses a random subset of size 80% of the original training set size.

Baseline: We also construct a unigram model as a baseline, which is compared against the proposed model that uses topic independent features. Because the unigram terms are unfiltered, the baseline model uses topic specific features as well.

4   Results

In this section, we discuss the performance of the model with topic independent features. We also compare it against the unigram baseline. Classification accuracy was the evaluation metric for this RumourEval subtask. However, since a majority of the tweets (about 70%) in the dataset belonged to the class label 'comment', we also report the macro-averaged F-score here.

The development set provided by the organizers was the set of tweets corresponding to the topic *germanwings-crash*. This was used for validating the model and determining the best combination of features from among the ones listed in the previous section. The results of the proposed model, in terms of accuracy and F-score, on the development set are shown in Table 4. The model with the proposed set of features is observed to have a reasonable accuracy and F-score for all class labels, except for the 'deny' label, which it found difficult to identify.

The results on the actual test set, which was a mix of all topics, are summarized in Table 5. All models performed similarly in terms of accuracy because a large proportion of the predicted labels belong to 'comment' class. However, the models with the topic independent features outperformed the baseline unigram model in terms of F-score. While the baseline model had an F-score of 0.31, the best combination of the proposed features resulted in an F-score of 0.45. The features were chosen by running validations with different feature combinations on the development dataset. The highest accuracy and F-score was obtained when the following features were discarded from the model: @user, hashtag, similarity, sentiment, characters. The submission with this model made our system the one with the second best performance for subtask A of RumourEval.

We also tried out models with features only from one category. When the cue features alone were used, the F-score was 0.34. On the other hand, the model with only the message specific features provided a higher F-score of 0.42. When all the proposed features were used for the classification task, it resulted in an accuracy of 0.77 with an F-score of 0.44, suggesting that, when used in tandem, the features yield a better result than using only a single category of features.

5   Conclusions

This paper provides a description of our submission for subtask A of RumourEval in which the participants were required to classify the stance of tweets towards rumours. The proposed model used topic independent features from two categories: cue features and message specific features.

Features	Accuracy	F-score	Comment	Deny	Query	Support
Unigrams (Baseline)	0.690	0.32	0.799	0.000	0.000	0.489
Only Cue Features	0.697	0.38	0.804	**0.153**	0.067	0.489
Only Message Specific Features	0.718	0.46	0.802	0.000	0.428	**0.621**
All Proposed Features	**0.729**	**0.51**	**0.813**	**0.153**	**0.450**	0.617
All Features -{@user, hashtag, similarity, sentiment, characters}	0.718	**0.51**	0.803	**0.153**	0.465	0.608

Table 4: Results for different feature combinations on the Development Set - Accuracy and F-score (macro-averaged and per class)

Features	Accuracy	F-score	Comment	Deny	Query	Support
Unigrams (Baseline)	0.750	0.31	0.856	0.000	0.000	0.386
Only Cue Features	0.757	0.34	0.860	0.000	0.085	**0.406**
Only Message Specific Features	0.763	0.42	0.858	0.000	0.432	0.400
All Proposed Features	0.770	0.44	0.867	0.027	0.473	0.388
All Features -{@user, hashtag, similarity, sentiment, characters}	**0.780**	**0.45**	**0.869**	**0.052**	**0.494**	0.397

Table 5: Results for different feature combinations on the Test Set - Accuracy and F-score (macro-averaged and per class)

A gradient boosting classifier was implemented for this 4-class classification problem. Our system ranked second in terms of accuracy. For future work, we plan to investigate if the tree structure of the conversation could provide insights about the reply type.

References

Tianqi Chen and Carlos Guestrin. 2016. Xgboost: A scalable tree boosting system. *arXiv preprint arXiv:1603.02754* .

Leon Derczynski, Kalina Bontcheva, Maria Liakata, Rob Procter, Geraldine Wong Sak Hoi, and Arkaitz Zubiaga. 2017. SemEval-2017 Task 8: RumourEval: Determining rumour veracity and support for rumours. In *Proceedings of SemEval*. ACL.

Clayton J Hutto and Eric Gilbert. 2014. Vader: A parsimonious rule-based model for sentiment analysis of social media text. In *Eighth International AAAI Conference on Weblogs and Social Media.*

Amita Misra and Marilyn A Walker. 2013. Topic independent identification of agreement and disagreement in social media dialogue. In *Conference of the Special Interest Group on Discourse and Dialogue.* page 920.

Vahed Qazvinian, Emily Rosengren, Dragomir R Radev, and Qiaozhu Mei. 2011. Rumor has it: Identifying misinformation in microblogs. In *Proceedings of the Conference on Empirical Methods in Natural Language Processing*. Association for Computational Linguistics, pages 1589–1599.

Uwe D Reichel and Piroska Lendvai. 2016. Veracity computing from lexical cues and perceived certainty trends. *arXiv preprint arXiv:1611.02590* .

Sandeep Soni, Tanushree Mitra, Eric Gilbert, and Jacob Eisenstein. 2014. Modeling factuality judgments in social media text. In *ACL (2)*. pages 415–420.

Arkaitz Zubiaga, Elena Kochkina, Maria Liakata, Rob Procter, and Michal Lukasik. 2016a. Stance classification in rumours as a sequential task exploiting the tree structure of social media conversations. *arXiv preprint arXiv:1609.09028* .

Arkaitz Zubiaga, Maria Liakata, and Rob Procter. 2016b. Learning reporting dynamics during breaking news for rumour detection in social media. *arXiv preprint arXiv:1610.07363* .

Arkaitz Zubiaga, Maria Liakata, Rob Procter, Geraldine Wong Sak Hoi, and Peter Tolmie. 2016c. Analysing how people orient to and spread rumours in social media by looking at conversational threads. *PloS one* 11(3):e0150989.

IKM at SemEval-2017 Task 8: Convolutional Neural Networks for Stance Detection and Rumor Verification

Yi-Chin Chen, Zhao-Yang Liu, Hung-Yu Kao

Department of Computer Science and Information Engineering
National Cheng Kung University
Tainan, Taiwan, ROC
{kimberycc,kjes89011}@gmail.com
hykao@mail.ncku.edu.tw

Abstract

This paper describes our approach for SemEval-2017 Task 8. We aim at detecting the stance of tweets and determining the veracity of the given rumor. We utilize a convolutional neural network for short text categorization using multiple filter sizes. Our approach beats the baseline classifiers on different event data with good F_1 scores. The best of our submitted runs achieves rank 1st among all scores on subtask B.

1 Introduction

Rumors in social networks are widely noticed due to the broad success of online social media. Unconfirmed rumors usually spark discussion before being verified. These have created cost for society and panic among people. Rather than relying on human observers to identify trending rumors, it would be helpful to detect them automatically and limit the damage immediately. However, identifying false rumors early is a hard task without sufficient evidence such as responses, retweet and fact checking sites. Instead of propagation structure, context-level patterns are more obvious and useful for the identification of rumors at this stage – in particular, observing the different patterns of stances amongst participants (Qazvinian et al., 2011).

Recent research has proposed a 4-way classification task to encompass all the different kinds of reactions to rumors (Arkaitz et al., 2016). A schema of classifications including supporting, deny-ing, querying and commenting (SDQC) is applied in SemEval2017 Task 8.

In this paper, we describe a system for stance classification and rumor verification in tweets. For the first task, we are given tree-structured conversations, where replies are triggered by a source tweet. We need to categorize the replies into one of the SDQC categories by reply-source pairs. The second task is about rumor verification. Our system is for the closed variant – which means the veracity of a rumor will have to be predicted solely without external data.

It is a challenging NLP task. Statements containing sarcasm, irony and metaphor often need personal experience to be able to infer their broader context (Kreuz and Caucci, 2007). Furthermore, lots of background knowledge is required to do the fact checking (Reichel and Lendvai, 2016).

In this paper, we develop convolutional neural network models for both tasks. Our system relies on a supervised classifier, using text features of different word representation methods such as learning word embedding through training and pre-trained word embedding model like GloVe (Pennington et al., 2014). The experiment section presents our results and discusses the performance of our work.

2 Related Work

Rumor verification from online social media has developed into a popular subject in recent years. The most common features were proposed by Castillo (2011) who classified useful features into

Proceedings of the 11th International Workshop on Semantic Evaluations (SemEval-2017), pages 465–469,
Vancouver, Canada, August 3 - 4, 2017. ©2017 Association for Computational Linguistics

four categories: message-based features, user-based features, topic-based features, and propagation-based features. However, this approach is limited because of the data skew problem when false rumors are less common. Thus, most existing approaches attempt to classify truthfulness by utilizing information beyond the content of the posts – propagation structure, for example. Ke Wu (2015) et al., proposed a novel message propagation pattern based on the users who transmit this message. But most of these features are available only when the rumors have been responded to by many users. Our task, on the other hand, is to do the initial classification on content features which are available much earlier.

3 System Overview

Our system employs a convolutional neural network mainly inspired by Kim (2014). We chose models by testing on LOO (Leave One Out) validation performance. LOO can be simply explained as that we test on each conversation thread by retraining models on the other threads. In the following section, our CNN Tweet Model is briefly explained.

3.1 Data Preprocessing

Before applying the models, we need to do some transforms of the irregular input text. At first, we remove URLs and username with '@' tags that do not contribute to sentiment analysis. In this case, URLs and usernames are considered as noise without external data. Furthermore, we convert all letters to lower case. Besides removal, it is worth mentioning that we leave important clues such as hashtags and some special characters. Question marks and exclamation marks, for example, have proven to be helpful (Zhao, 2015).

3.2 Convolutional Model

There are two steps for the process of encoding tweets into matrices that are then passed to the input layer. This model is illustrated in Figure 1. First, we use word embedding to convert each word in the tweet into a vector. We randomly initialize the word embedding matrix. Each row of this matrix is a vector that represents a word in the vocabulary. Then we learn the embedding weights during the training process. Second, we concatenate these word vectors to produce a matrix representing the sentence. In the matrix, each row

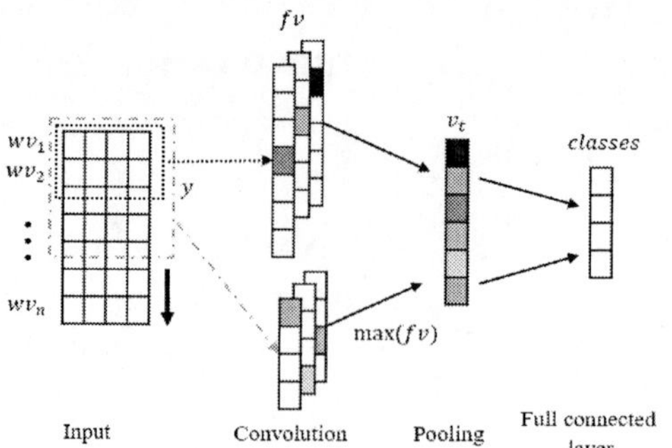

Figure 1: Architecture of Word-Embedding Convolutional Model

represents one word in the tweet as follows:

$$tm = \begin{bmatrix} wv_1 \\ wv_2 \\ \vdots \\ wv_n \end{bmatrix}_{n \times d} \qquad (1)$$

Where tm is a word matrix formed by the concatenation of each word vector.

In the convolutional layer, we use tm as input and select a window size y to slide over the matrix. To extract local features in the region of the window, a filter matrix $fm \in R^{y \times d}$ is used to produce element-wise multiplication and non-linear operations on the matrix values in the window at every position. The following is an example of this operation:

$$el_i = g \left(fm \cdot \begin{bmatrix} wv_i \\ \vdots \\ wv_{i+y-1} \end{bmatrix} + b \right) \qquad (2)$$

Where fm is the filter matrix. The values of the filter matrix will be learned by the CNN from the training process. b is the bias term, g is the non-linear function, and el_i is an element of a local feature vector. After we slide the window through the whole matrix, we get a local feature vector of the input tweet as:

$$fv = \begin{bmatrix} el_1, el_2, \cdots, el_{n-y+1} \end{bmatrix} \qquad (3)$$

Where $fv \in R^{n-y+1}$ is a local feature vector with $n-y+1$ elements.

For the purpose of dealing with continuous n words which may represent special meaning in NLP (e.g. "Boston Globe"), we use multiple window sizes to produce different feature vectors. Thus, the idea of a different window size applied to capturing features is similar to n-grams. Meanwhile, we use different filter matrices to extract different local features of the tweet in each window.

A pooling layer is used for simplifying the information of the output from the convolutional layer. We extract the maximum value from each local feature vector to form a condensed representation vector. For every local feature vector, only the most important feature is extracted and noise is ignored. After the max-pooling operation, we can concatenate all maximum values of each column as follows:

$$v_t = \begin{bmatrix} max(fv_1) \\ \vdots \\ max(fv_m) \end{bmatrix} \quad (4)$$

Where v_t is the global feature vector representing the tweet.

Through the pooling layer, if we use the same window size and filter matrix on different tweets, we can make sure the global feature size is fixed.

For classification, we feed the global feature vectors of the tweet into a fully connected layer to calculate the probability distribution. A softmax activation function is applied as follows:

$$P(y = i|v_t, b) = \frac{e^{w^T_i v_t + b_i}}{\sum_{i'=1} e^{w^T_{i'} v_t + b_{i'}}} \quad (5)$$

Where v_t is the input vector, $w^T_{i'}$ is the i'-th column of weight matrix W. With the probabilities over the four classes, we take the class with the maximum value as the label for the given input tweet.

4   Tasks and Model Training

During the training phase, our CNN model automatically learns the values of its filters based on the task.

In task A, the tweets are classified into four categories: supporting, denying, querying and commenting. We defined the ground truth vector p as a one-hot vector. The parameter d used in the word embedding is 128. The number of filters in the convolutional layers is 128. The probability of dropout is set to 0.5. Adam Optimization algorithm is used to optimize our network's loss function. Moreover, there are three filter region sizes in our system: 2, 3 and 4, each of which has 2 filters.

In order to deal with the imbalance of classes in the data, balanced mini-batching was applied. In the statistics, more than 64% of the instances belong to the commenting class. We chose 16 instances with each class from training set randomly, which means that there are 64 instances in a batch.

A voting scheme is applied to decrease the uncertainty of training on randomly selected samples. We trained 5 models to predict the same testing data and took a vote for the final prediction. By performing training multiple times independently we achieved more robust results.

In subtask B, most of the parameter settings were the same as in Task A. Because the output classes are rumor and non-rumor, we discard the label "unverified". In addition, we use the probability in section 3.2 to define the credibility of our answer c. The credibility in the interval [0, 1] is normalized as:

$$c = \frac{max(P(y=0,1|v_t,b))}{\sum_{i=0,1} P(y=i|v_t,b)} \quad (6)$$

5   Evaluation

We conduct experiments using the rumor datasets annotated for stance (Zubiaga et al., 2016). The statistics of the datasets are shown in Table 1. For subtask B, conversation threads are not available for the participants and the use of external data is forbidden on the closed variant.

Subtask A			
Stance	Support	Deny	Query	Comment
Training	841(20%)	333(8%)	330(8%)	2734(65%)
Testing	94(9%)	71(7%)	106(10%)	778(74%)
Subtask B			
Veracity	True	False	unverified
Training	127(47%)	50(18%)	95(35%)
Testing	8(40%)	12(60%)	0

Table 1: Statistics of datasets for subtask A and B.

5.1   Baselines

We compare our result with Lukasik's (2016) in Table 2. We follow their LOO settings and test on the same dataset. The report includes accuracy (Acc) and macro average of F_1 scores across all labels (F_1) from Lukasik's baseline.

The results show our deep learning model is the best method in terms of F1 score. Especially, the CNN model beats all the other methods. While the RNN method is not performing well on this task. Another issue is the GloVe embedding – the pre-training model sometimes lacks some of the vocabulary from new events. Nevertheless, GloVe is still competitive with the CNN method for the Ferguson event.

Event	Ottawa		Ferguson	
	Acc	F_1	Acc	F_1
GP	62.28	42.41	64.31	32.9
Lang. model	53.2	42.66	49.56	34.35
NB	61.76	40.64	62.05	31.29
HP Approx.	67.77	32.29	68.44	25.99
HP Grad.	63.43	42.4	63.23	33.14
CNN	61.74	**44.9**	62.31	36.49
CNN(GloVe)	59.61	38.87	63.03	**39.48**
RNN(GloVe)	52.49	38.66	51.49	32.52

Table 2: Accuracy and F_1 scores for different methods across datasets. The upper lines of the results are our baseline.

Window Sizes	Precision	Recall	F_1
3	0.39	0.42	0.40
3,4	0.43	0.42	0.43
2,3,4	0.43	0.40	0.42
3,4,5	**0.45**	**0.45**	**0.45**
2,3,4,5	0.44	0.45	0.44

Table 3: results of using different window sizes.

5.2 Window Sizes for Filters

Table 3 lists the results of using different window sizes for the filters in the tweet encoding process. We set different window sizes to observe the impact. The experiment was performed with the same settings as in section 5.1 for the Ottawa event. We obtain the best performance when the window size combination is (3, 4, 5). Different window sizes 2, 3 and 4 correspond to the encoding for the bigrams, trigrams and four-grams of the tweets respectively. We can see that the performance decrease slightly with the window size increases. That is, insufficient grams can lose some features while too many grams can bring noise.

5.3 Official Results[1]

Our submission results to the subtask A achieve an accuracy of 0.701. The statistical details of each class are given in Table 4. We notice that the comment stance is the easiest to detect, since they take a large part of the data. The number of query stances are similar to support and deny, while it has much better precision and recall because the features of queries are more obvious. Likewise, there are some negative words in the deny stance

Stance	Precision	Recall	Accuracy
Support	0.19	0.20	0.20
Deny	0.31	0.07	0.07
Query	0.58	0.45	0.45
Comment	0.78	0.85	0.85

Table 4: Result on test data for subtask A.

Team	Score	RMSE
DFKI DKT	0.393	0.845
ECNU	0.464	0.736
IITP	0.286	0.807
IKM	**0.536**	**0.763**
NileTMRG	0.536	0.672

Table 5: Rank on test data for subtask B.

as features. However, it is challenging to extract features of supporting which results in a poorer performance.

The rank of subtask B is summarized in Table 5. As we can see our model performs best among the official scores. Our code is available on github for anyone who has interest in further exploration[2].

6 Conclusion

We develop a convolutional neural network system for detecting twitter stance and rumor veracity determination in this paper. Compared with the baseline approach, our system obtains good results on stance detection. In addition, on the test set of SemEval2017 Task8B, we ranked 2nd in the official evaluation run.

Reference

Castillo, Carlos, Marcelo Mendoza, and Barbara Poblete. "Information credibility on twitter. " *Proceedings of the 20th international conference on World wide web.* ACM, 2011.

Wu Ke, Song Yang, and Kenny Q. Zhu. "False rumors detection on sina weibo by propagation structures." *Data Engineering (ICDE), 2015 IEEE 31st International Conference on.* IEEE, 2015.

Yoon Kim. "Convolutional neural networks for sentence classification." *arXiv preprint arXiv:1408.5882* (2014).

Lukasik, Michal, Srijith, P.K, Vu, Duy, Bontcheva, Kalina, Zubiaga, Arkaitz and Cohn. "Hawkes processes for continuous time sequence classification: an application to rumor stance classification in

---

[1] Results and task detail can be found on http://alt.qcri.org/semeval2017/task8/

[2] https://github.com/kimber-chen/Twitter-stance-classification-by-TensorFlow

twitter." Proceedings of 54th Annual Meeting of the Association for Computational Linguistics. Association for Computational Linguistics, 2016.

Jeffrey Pennington, Richard Socher, and Christopher D Manning. 2014. Glove: Global vectors for word representation. In *EMNLP*, volume 14, pages 1532–1543.

Vahed Qazvinian, Emily Rosengren, Dragomir R. Radev, and Qiaozhu Mei. 2011. Rumor has it: Identifying misinformation in microblogs. In *Proceedings of the Conference on Empirical Methods in Natural Language Processing, EMNLP '11*, pages 1589–1599.

Kreuz, Roger J., and Gina M. Caucci. "Lexical influences on the perception of sarcasm." *Proceedings of the Workshop on computational approaches to Figurative Language*. Association for Computational Linguistics, 2007.

Reichel, Uwe D., and Piroska Lendvai. "Veracity computing from lexical cues and perceived certainty trends." *arXiv preprint arXiv:1611.02590* (2016).

Zhao, Zhe, Paul Resnick, and Qiaozhu Mei. "Enquiring minds: Early detection of rumors in social media from enquiry posts." *Proceedings of the 24th International Conference on World Wide Web*. ACM, 2015.

Arkaitz Zubiaga ,Maria Liakata,Rob Procter, Geraldine Wong Sak Hoi, and Peter Tolmie. "Analysing how people orient to and spread rumors in social media by looking at conversational threads." *PloS one* 11.3 (2016): e0150989.

Arkaitz Zubiaga, Elena Kochkina, Maria Liakata, Rob Procter, and Michal Lukasik. "Stance classification in rumors as a sequential task exploiting the tree structure of social media conversations." *arXiv preprint arXiv:1609.09028* (2016)

NileTMRG at SemEval-2017 Task 8: Determining Rumour and Veracity Support for Rumours on Twitter

Omar Enayet and Samhaa R. El-Beltagy

Center for informatics sciences

Nile University

Giza, Egypt

omar.enayet@gmail.com, samhaa@computer.org

Abstract

This paper presents the results and conclusions of our participation in SemEval-2017 task 8: Determining rumour veracity and support for rumours. We have participated in 2 subtasks: SDQC (Subtask A) which deals with tracking how tweets orient to the accuracy of a rumourous story, and Veracity Prediction (Subtask B) which deals with the goal of predicting the veracity of a given rumour. Our participation was in the closed task variant, in which the prediction is made solely from the tweet itself. For subtask A, linear support vector classification was applied to a model of bag of words, and the help of a naïve Bayes classifier was used for semantic feature extraction. For subtask B, a similar approach was used. Many features were used during the experimentation process but only a few proved to be useful with the data set provided. Our system achieved 71% accuracy and ranked 5th among 8 systems for subtask A and achieved 53% accuracy with the lowest RMSE value of 0.672 ranking at the first place among 5 systems for subtask B.

1 Introduction

Over the past 15 years, and in a gradual manner, social media has started to become a main source of news. However, social media has also become a ripe ground for rumours, spreading them in a matter of a few minutes. A rumour is defined as a claim that could be true or false. False rumours may greatly affect the social, economic and political stability of any society around the world, hence the need for tools to help people, especially journalists, analyze the spread of rumours and their effect on the society as well as determine their veracity.

Twitter is a famous social media platform capable of spreading breaking news, thus most of rumour related research uses Twitter feed as a basis for research.

SemEval (Semantic Evaluation) is an ongoing series of evaluations of computational semantic analysis systems. Task 8 (RumourEval) (Derczynski, et al. (2017)) is one of 12 tasks presented in SemEval 2017. This paper describes the system that we have used to participate in this task. The task consists of 2 subtasks: SDQC (Subtask A) which has the objective of tracking how other tweets orient to the accuracy of a rumourous story, and Veracity Prediction (Subtask B) for which has the goal to predict the veracity of a given rumour. Task B has two variants: an open variant and a closed one. We have only participated in the closed variant, in which the prediction should be made solely from the tweet itself.

Scientific literature related to rumours on social media has started to emerge over the past 7 years. It can be categorized into 4 main categories: 1) the detection of the spreading of a rumour, 2) the determination of the veracity of a rumour, 3) the analysis of the rumour propagation through a social network and 4) speech act analysis of different online replies to the rumour. Subtask A belongs to the 4th category, while subtask B belongs to the 2nd category.

The rest of the paper is organized as follows: section 2 briefly overviews related work, section 3 provides task description details, section 4 provides a detailed system description covering pre-processing, feature extraction and selection, learning model and evaluation done for both subtasks A and B. In the end a conclusion is given with the future work needed.

Proceedings of the 11th International Workshop on Semantic Evaluations (SemEval-2017), pages 470–474,
Vancouver, Canada, August 3 - 4, 2017. ©2017 Association for Computational Linguistics

2 Related Work

Zubiaga et al. (2016), presented a methodology that enabled them to collect, identify and annotate a big data set of rumours associated with multiple newsworthy events, and analyzed how people orient to and spread rumours in social media. This data set was used for task 8 of SemEval 2017: RumourEval. Qazvinian et al. (2011), addressed the problem of automatic rumour detection in microblogs as well as identifying users that support or deny or question the rumour. They achieved this by exploring the effectiveness of 3 categories of features: content-based, network-based and micro-blog specific memes. Vosoughi et al. (2015), addressed the problem of rumour detection via a speech act classifier that detects assertions using different semantic and syntactic features in addition to a clustering algorithm to cluster groups of rumourous tweets talking about the same topic together. Hamidiain et al. (2015), Castillo et al. (2011), Vosoughi et al. (2015) and Giasemidis et al. (2016) addressed the issue of detecting the veracity of rumours using manually selected and annotated rumours on Twitter using linguistic, user, rumour, pragmatic, content, twitter-specific and propagation features and the latter developed a software demonstration that provides a visual user interface to allow the user to examine the analysis. Chua et al. (2016), concentrated on linguistic features such as comprehensibility, sentiment and writing style to predict rumour veracity, ignoring all non-linguistic features. Galitsky et al. (2015), also concentrated on linguistic features to detect disinformation by comparing the text to search results using the significant sentences in that text. Liu et al. (2015), proposed the first real time rumour debunking algorithm for Twitter while Zhao et al. (2015), concentrated on identifying a trending rumour as early as possible without trying to assess its veracity.

3 Task Description

Below is a brief overview of each subtask. For more details, please refer to RumourEval (Derczynski, et al. (2017))

Subtask A: The input to this task is a set of tweets each replying to a rumourous tweet, which we name the rumour source tweet. The training data is composed of the tweet content and its speech act class. A tweet can be classified to be a support, deny, query or a comment.

Subtask B: The input to this task is a set of tweets each representing a source of a rumour. The training data is composed of the tweet content and its veracity. A tweet's veracity can be either true, false or unknown. Also, a confidence value which is a float from 0 to 1 is required for each tweet.

4 System Overview

The systems used for both subtasks A and B were very similar, except that each focused on a different set of features. Python libraries scikit-learn (Buitinck et al. (2013)) and NLTK (Bird et al., 2009) were mainly used to implement this work. Below are the general system specifications. All classifiers were adjusted to use their default parameters.

4.1 Preprocessing and feature extraction

The system depends on performing some preprocessing on the tweets' texts, extracting simple bag of words features from them, and then extracting additional higher level features from them as well as from the entire twitter feed provided. These steps were carried out with the aid of the NLTK Tweet Tokenizer (2015).

Preprocessing also included the removal of stop words, punctuation characters and twitter specific words such as 'rt' and 'via'.

No further pre-processing was performed. Below are some notes in this context:

- The case of the words could be useful in showing the sentiment and the context of the word, thus all words were kept in their original case.
- Performing stemming or lemmatization caused worse performance as keeping the word in its original form proved to be useful.
- Removing URLs from text yielded worse performance, as tweets using the same URL usually shared the same speech act, so the URL word token acted as an important feature.
- Using bi-grams resulted in noise being added to the training data, causing the classifier's performance to degrade.

4.2 Features Selection

The following feature selection and dimensionality reduction methods were used on the basic bag of words features, before adding higher level features:

- Chi-Squared Feature selection. (2010)
- Variance Threshold Feature selection. (2010)
- Truncated SVD dimensionality reduction. (2010)

None of the above algorithms were used, as they all yielded worse results when the model was cross-validated. We attribute this to the fact that the number of features were not big enough.

Additional features were manually selected by measuring the performance of the classifier on training data when adding/removing each additional feature. Features with big numerical values were scaled down to the range between 0 and 1.

4.3 Additional features extraction

Several features were extracted though not all of them proved useful in the classification process.

Below is the complete list of features which apply for **both subtask A and B**.

- **Question Existence:** The relationship between a question and a query is tight. A question is often a query and a query is often a question. Also, if a tweet is a question, then it is highly unlikely that it is a normal comment; it is more likely it is a support or a denial, if not a query. Thus, being a question is an important feature to consider. A question detection module was built for this purpose. Below are details for this module:

- An assumption was made that any sentence containing a question mark is considered a question.
- In case the question mark was absent, any sentence classified as a question should contain at least one of the following keywords used in WH-questions: "what, why, how, when, where" or in Yes/No questions: "did, do, does, have, has, am, is, are, can, could, may, would, will" as well as their negations. It is highly unlikely that a question does not have one of these words.
- A utility classifier was used for further detection of questions; we performed speech act recognition using a Naive Bayes classifier on NLTK corpus 'nps_chat' (2015). On cross validating that classifier, we got an accuracy of 67%. If this utility classifier marks the tweet as a Yes-No question or a wh-question, the tweet is considered to be a question.

- **Denial term detection:** We found that explicitly specifying the existence of a denial word within a tweet, to be a useful feature for generalizing over the data. The list of words used are: 'not true', 'don't agree', 'impossible', 'false', 'shut'.

- **Support words detection:** Like denial words, we included another feature for signaling the existence of a support term. These were detected based on the following list of common support words: 'true', 'exactly', 'yes', 'indeed', 'omg', 'know'

- **Hashtag Existence**

- **URL Existence**

- **Tweet is reply:** This feature specifies whether the tweet was a reply to another tweet or whether it is a source tweet. Source tweets are rarely queries, and not often a denial or support. Most of them are normal comments.

- **Tweet's words' sentiments:** Simple sentiment prediction was performed on each tweet's text though counting the number of positive and negative sentiment in the tweet using the NLTK opinion lexicon (2015). If the positive words exceeded negative words, the feature got a value of 1, otherwise, it got a value of 0. If there were no sentiment words o or if the positive and negative words were equal, this feature value was set to a 0.5.

- **Tweet sentiment:** A utility classifier was used for further detection of sentiment. For setting this feature, a naïve Bayes classifier was trained using the NLTK movie reviews corpus (2015) for sentiment analysis. It would be better of course to train this classifier using tagged tweets, which is what we intend to do in future work.

- **Is User verified**

- **Number of followers**

- **Number of user's past tweets**

- **Number of user's friends**

- **Retweet Ratio:** This feature represents the ratio between the numbers of retweets of the target tweet over the number of retweets of the rumour source tweet.

- **Photo Existence**
- **Days since user creation:** This feature represents the number of days since user account was created on Twitter. Older accounts may have more credibility than new ones.
- **Source tweet user is verified:** This feature represents whether the tweeter of the rumour source has a verified account or not.

The following list of features applies to **subtask A only**:

- **User 'replied to' is verified**
- **Cosine similarity with root rumourous tweet and the 'replied to' tweet:** Using the same words may imply more that the tweet is a support.

Finally, the following features applies to **subtask B only**:

- **Percentage of replying tweets classified as queries, denies or support:** These 3 features represent the percentage of tweets classified as different classes via the system implemented for Task A, for this rumour's source tweet.

5   Evaluation

Several scikit-learn classifiers were used during experimentation before deciding on the final model.

For subtask A, the linear support vector machine classifier (Linear SVC) proved to be the most accurate during cross validation, however, logistic regression generalized the best on test data. During cross-validation the macro-averaged F1 measure was used to evaluate the classifiers and choose the best amongst them, as the distribution of categories was clearly skewed towards comments.

For subtask B, Linear SVC proved to be the best in terms of accuracy and the confidence root mean square error (RMSE).

Table 1 shows the features used for each subtask along with its type. Type 'Content' refers to the features determined from the tweet's text, 'user' refers to the features determined from the user who tweeted and his behavior, 'twitter' refers to twitter specific features used. Table 2 compares the accuracy of different classifiers for each subtask.

Feature	Type	A	B
Question Existence	content	Y	N
Denial term detection	content	Y	N
Support words detection	content	Y	N
Hashtag existence	twitter	N	Y
URL existence	content	Y	Y
Tweet is reply	twitter	Y	-
Tweets' words' sentiments	content	Y	N
Tweet sentiment	content	N	N
Is User Verified	user	N	N
Number of followers	user	Y	N
Number of user's past tweets	user	N	N
Number of user's friends	user	N	N
Retweet Ratio	twitter	N	N
Photo Existence	content	N	N
Days since user creation	user	N	N
Source tweet user is verified	user	Y	N
User 'replied to' is verified	user	Y	-
Cosine similarity with root rumourous tweet	content	Y	-
Cosine similarity with the 'replied to' tweet	content	N	-
Percentage of replying tweets classified as queries, denies or support	content	-	Y

Table 1 – Features found useful for each subtask and used in final evaluation.

Classifier	A	B	B(RMSE)
Linear SVC	0.71	**0.53**	**0.67**
Random Forest	0.75	0.39	0.77
Linear SVM with SGD learning	0.72	0.5	0.73
Logistic Regression	**0.76**	0.53	0.71
Decision Tree	0.71	0.46	0.73

Table 2 – The resultant accuracy and confidence RMSE for subtasks A and B

6   Conclusion

In this paper, we have performed a quick analysis of using different pre-processing, features extraction and selection, learning classifiers which achieved good results in the RumourEval task. For subtask A, a combination of different types of content, twitter and user specific features were used. For subtask B, it was clear that only content and twitter features were useful. User based features didn't enhance the performance for the latter subtask, thus we conclude that the identity and behavior of the user didn't affect much the credibility of the rumour he/she is spreading, at least for the data set provided.

7   Future Work

Additional features could be extracted that can play a better role in classifying each tweet or rumour. On the tweet text level, better linguistic features could be extracted. A better sentiment analysis model could be employed. On the rumour level, network-based features maybe extracted such as the work done by Vosoughi, et. al. (2015). Time-based analysis could be performed to detect certain patterns in the change of reactions to the rumour.

8 References

Derczynski, Leon and Bontcheva, Kalina and Liakata, Maria and Procter, Rob and Wong Sak Hoi, Geraldine and Zubiaga, Arkaitz, 2017. SemEval-2017 Task 8: RumourEval: Determining rumour veracity and support for rumours. Proceedings of SemEval 2017.

Zubiaga, A., Liakata, M., Procter, R., Hoi, G.W.S. and Tolmie, P., 2016. Analysing how people orient to and spread rumours in social media by looking at conversational threads. PloS one, 11(3), p.e0150989.

Vosoughi, S., 2015. Automatic detection and verification of rumors on Twitter (Doctoral dissertation, Massachusetts Institute of Technology).

Qazvinian, V., Rosengren, E., Radev, D.R. and Mei, Q., 2011, July. Rumor has it: Identifying misinformation in microblogs. In Proceedings of the Conference on Empirical Methods in Natural Language Processing (pp. 1589-1599). Association for Computational Linguistics.

Giasemidis, G., Singleton, C., Agrafiotis, I., Nurse, J.R., Pilgrim, A., Willis, C. and Greetham, D.V., 2016, November. Determining the veracity of rumours on Twitter. In International Conference on Social Informatics (pp. 185-205). Springer International Publishing.

Castillo, C., Mendoza, M. and Poblete, B., 2011, March. Information credibility on twitter. In Proceedings of the 20th international conference on World wide web (pp. 675-684). ACM.

Hamidiain, S. and Diab, M., 2015. Rumor detection and classification for twitter data. In The Fifth International Conference on Social Media Technologies, Communication, and Informatics, SOTICS, IARIA (pp. 71-77).

Liu, X., Nourbakhsh, A., Li, Q., Fang, R. and Shah, S., 2015, October. Real-time rumor debunking on twitter. In Proceedings of the 24th ACM International on Conference on Information and Knowledge Management (pp. 1867-1870). ACM.

Zhao, Z., Resnick, P. and Mei, Q., 2015, May. Enquiring minds: Early detection of rumors in social media from enquiry posts. In Proceedings of the 24th International Conference on World Wide Web (pp. 1395-1405). ACM.

Galitsky, B., 2015, March. Detecting Rumor and Disinformation by Web Mining. In 2015 AAAI Spring Symposium Series.

Bird, Steven, Edward Loper and Ewan Klein (2009), Natural Language Processing with Python. O'Reilly Media Inc.

NLTK Tweet Tokenizer (2015). Retrieved April 1, 2017, from http://www.nltk.org/api/nltk.tokenize.html

Scikit-learn Chi-Squared Feature Selection, 2010. Retrieved April 1, 2017, from http://scikit-learn.org/stable/modules/generated/sklearn.feature_selection.chi2.html

Scikit-learn Variance Threshold Feature Selection, 2010. Retrieved April 1, 2017, from http://scikit-learn.org/stable/modules/generated/sklearn.feature_selection.VarianceThreshold.html

Scikit-learn Truncated SVD, 2010. Retrieved April 1, 2017, from http://scikit-learn.org/stable/modules/generated/sklearn.decomposition.TruncatedSVD.html

NLTK NPS Chat Corpus Reader, 2015. Retrieved April 1, 2017, from http://www.nltk.org/_modules/nltk/corpus/reader/nps_chat.html

NLTK Opinion Lexicon Corpus Reader, 2015. Retrieved April 1, 2017, from http://www.nltk.org/_modules/nltk/corpus/reader/opinion_lexicon.html

NLTK Categorized Sentences Corpus Reader. Retrieved April 1, 2017, from http://www.nltk.org/_modules/nltk/corpus/reader/categorized_sents.html

Buitinck, L., Louppe, G., Blondel, M., Pedregosa, F., Mueller, A., Grisel, O., Niculae, V., Prettenhofer, P., Gramfort, A., Grobler, J. and Layton, R., 2013. API design for machine learning software: experiences from the scikit-learn project. arXiv preprint arXiv:1309.0238.

Chua, A.Y. and Banerjee, S., 2016. Linguistic Predictors of Rumor Veracity on the Internet. In Proceedings of the International MultiConference of Engineers and Computer Scientists (Vol. 1).

Turing at SemEval-2017 Task 8: Sequential Approach to Rumour Stance Classification with Branch-LSTM

Elena Kochkina[12]**, Maria Liakata**[12]**, Isabelle Augenstein**[3]
[1] University of Warwick, Coventry, United Kingdom
[2] Alan Turing Institute, London, United Kingdom
[3] University College London, London, United Kingdom
{E.Kochkina, M.Liakata}@warwick.ac.uk, I.Augenstein@ucl.ac.uk

Abstract

This paper describes team Turing's submission to SemEval 2017 RumourEval: Determining rumour veracity and support for rumours (SemEval 2017 Task 8, Subtask A). Subtask A addresses the challenge of rumour stance classification, which involves identifying the attitude of Twitter users towards the truthfulness of the rumour they are discussing. Stance classification is considered to be an important step towards rumour verification, therefore performing well in this task is expected to be useful in debunking false rumours. In this work we classify a set of Twitter posts discussing rumours into either supporting, denying, questioning or commenting on the underlying rumours. We propose a LSTM-based sequential model that, through modelling the conversational structure of tweets, which achieves an accuracy of 0.784 on the RumourEval test set outperforming all other systems in Subtask A.

1 Introduction

In stance classification one is concerned with determining the attitude of the author of a text towards a target (Mohammad et al., 2016). Targets can range from abstract ideas, to concrete entities and events. Stance classification is an active research area that has been studied in different domains (Ranade et al., 2013; Chuang and Hsieh, 2015). Here we focus on stance classification of tweets towards the truthfulness of rumours circulating in Twitter conversations in the context of breaking news. Each conversation is defined by a tweet that initiates the conversation and a set of nested replies to it that form a conversation thread. The goal is to classify each of the tweets in the conversation thread as either *supporting*, *denying*, *querying* or *commenting* (*SDQC*) on the rumour initiated by the source tweet. Being able to detect stance automatically is very useful in the context of events provoking public resonance and associated rumours, as a first step towards verification of early reports (Zhao et al., 2015). For instance, it has been shown that rumours that are later proven to be false tend to spark significantly larger numbers of denying tweets than rumours that are later confirmed to be true (Mendoza et al., 2010; Procter et al., 2013; Derczynski et al., 2014; Zubiaga et al., 2016b).

Here we focus on exploiting the conversational structure of social media threads for stance classification and introduce a novel LSTM-based approach to harness conversations.

2 Related Work

Single Tweet Stance Classification Stance classification for rumours was pioneered by Qazvinian et al. (2011) as a binary classification task (support/denial). Zeng et al. (2016) perform stance classification for rumours emerging during crises. Both works use tweets related to the same rumour during training and testing.

A model based on bidirectional LSTM encoding of tweets conditioned on targets has been shown to achieve state-of-the-art on the SemEval-2016 task 6 dataset (Augenstein et al., 2016). However the RumourEval task is different as it addresses conversation threads.

Sequential Stance Classification Lukasik et al. (2016) and Zubiaga et al. (2016a) consider the sequential nature of tweet threads in their works. Lukasik et al. (2016) employ Hawkes processes to classify temporal sequences of tweets. They show the importance of using both the textual content and temporal information about the tweets, disregarding the discourse structure. Zubiaga et

Proceedings of the 11th International Workshop on Semantic Evaluations (SemEval-2017), pages 475–480,
Vancouver, Canada, August 3 - 4, 2017. ©2017 Association for Computational Linguistics

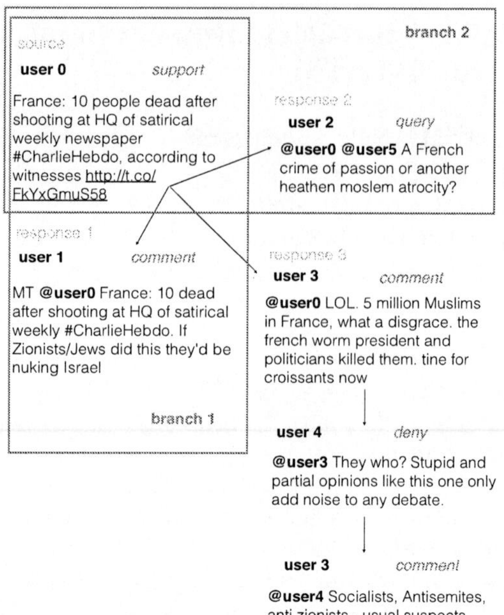

Figure 1: Example of a conversation thread from the dataset with three branches, two of which are highlighted. The conversation has a tree structure, which can be split into individual branches by taking each leaf node with all its direct parents.

al. (2016a) model the conversational structure of source tweets and subsequent replies: as a linear chain and as a tree. They use linear- and tree- versions of a CRF classifier, outperforming the approach by Lukasik et al. (2016).

3 Dataset

The dataset provided for this task contains Twitter conversation threads associated with rumours around ten different events in breaking news, including the Paris shootings in Charlie Hebdo, the Ferguson unrest, the crash of a Germanwings plane. These events include 325 conversation threads consisting of 5568 underlying tweets annotated for stance at the tweet level (breakdown between training, testing and development sets is shown in Table 1) (Derczynski et al., 2017).

	# threads	# branches	# tweets
Development	25	215	281
Testing	28	772	1049
Training	272	3030	4238
Total	**325**	**4017**	**5568**

Table 1: Number of threads, branches and tweets in the training, development and testing sets.

	S	D	Q	C
Development	69	11	28	173
Testing	94	71	106	778
Training	841	333	330	2734
Total	**1004**	**415**	**464**	**3685**

Table 2: Per-class distribution of tweets in the training, development and testing sets.

Each thread includes a source tweet that initiates a conversation and nested tweets responding to either the source tweet or earlier replies. The thread can be split into linear branches of tweets, where a branch is defined as a chain of tweets that starts with a leaf tweet including its direct parent tweets, all the way up to the source tweet. Figure 1 shows an example of a conversation along with its annotations represented as a tree structure with highlighted branches. The depth of a tweet is the number of its parents starting from the root node. Branches 1 and 2 in Figure 1 have depth one whereas branch 3 has depth three. There is a clear class imbalance in favour of *commenting* tweets (66%) and *supporting* tweets (18%), whereas the *denying* (8%) and *querying* classes (8%) are under-represented (see Table 2). While this imbalance poses a challenge, it is also indicative of the realistic scenario where only a few users question the veracity of a statement.

4 System Description

4.1 Features

Prior to generating features for the tweets, we perform a pre-processing step where we remove non-alphabetic characters, convert all words to lower case and tokenise texts.[1] Once tweet texts are pre-processed, we extract the following features:

- **Word vectors:** we use a word2vec (Mikolov et al., 2013) model pre-trained on the Google News dataset (300d) [2] using the gensim package (Řehůřek and Sojka, 2010).
- **Tweet lexicon:** (1) count of negation words[3] and (2) count of swear words.[4]

---

[1] For implementation of all pre-processing routines we use Python 2.7 with the NLTK package.

[2] We have also tried using Glove word embeddings trained on Twitter dataset, but it lead to a decrease in performance on both development and testing sets comparing to the Google News word vectors

[3] A presence of any of the following words would be considered as a presence of negation: not, no, nobody, nothing, none, never, neither, nor, nowhere, hardly, scarcely, barely, don't, isn't, wasn't, shouldn't, wouldn't, couldn't, doesn't

[4] A list of 458 bad words was taken from http://urbanoalvarez.es/blog/2008/04/04/bad-words-list/

> [As querying] @username Weren't you the one who abused her?
>
> [As supporting] "Go online & amp; put down 'Hillary Clinton illness,'" Rudy says. Yes – but look up the truth – not health smears https://t.co/EprqiZhAxM
>
> [As supporting] @username I demand you retract the lie that people in #Ferguson were shouting "kill the police", local reporting has refuted your ugly racism
>
> [As commenting] @FoxNews six years ago... real good evidence. Not!

Figure 2: Examples of misclassified denying tweets.

- **Punctuation:** (1) presence of a period, (2) presence of an exclamation mark, (3) presence of a question mark, (4) ratio of capital letters.
- **Attachments:** (1) presence of a URL and (2) presence of images.
- **Relation to other tweets** (1) Word2Vec cosine similarity wrt source tweet, (2) Word2Vec cosine similarity wrt preceding tweet, and (3) Word2Vec cosine similarity wrt thread
- **Content length:** (1) word count and (2) character count.
- **Tweet role:** whether the tweet is a source tweet of a conversation.

Tweet representations are obtained by averaging word vectors in a tweet and then concatenating with the additional features into a single vector, at the preprocessing step. This set of features have shown to be the best comparing to using word2vec features on their own or any of the reduced combinations of these features.

4.2 Branch - LSTM Model

To tackle the task of rumour stance classificaiton, we propose *branch-LSTM*, a neural network architecture that uses layers of LSTM units (Hochreiter and Schmidhuber, 1997) to process the whole branch of tweets, thus incorporating structural information of the conversation (see the illustration of the *branch-LSTM* on the Figure 3). The input at each time step i of the LSTM layer is the representation of the tweet as a vector. We record the

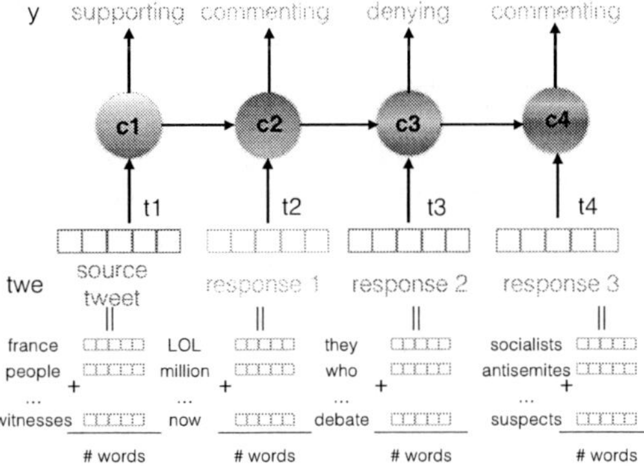

Figure 3: Illustration of the input/output structure of the branch-nestedLSTM model.

output of each time step so as to attach a label to each tweet in a branch[5]. This output is fed through several dense ReLU layers, a 50% dropout layer, and then through a softmax layer to obtain class probabilities. We use zero-padding and masks to account for the varying lengths of tweet branches. The model is trained using the categorical cross entropy loss function. Since there is overlap between branches originating from the same source tweet, we exclude the repeating tweets from the loss function using a mask at the training stage. The model uses tweet representation as the mean average of word vectors concatenated with extra features described above. Due to the short length of tweets, using more complex models for learning tweet representations, such as an LSTM that takes each word as input at each time step and returns the representation at the final time step, does not lead to a noticeable difference in the performance based on cross-validation experiments on the training and development sets, while taking significantly longer to train. We experimented with replacing the unidirectional LSTMs with bidirectional LSTMs but could observe no improvements in accuracy (using cross-validation results on the training and development set).

5   Experimental Setup

The dataset is split into training, development and test sets by the task organisers. We determined the optimal set of hyperparameters via testing the performance of our model on the development set for different parameter combinations. We used the

---

[5]For implementation of all models we used Python libraries Theano (Bastien et al., 2012) and Lasagne (Dieleman et al., 2015).

	Accuracy	Macro F	S	D	Q	C
Development	0.782	0.561	0.621	0.000	0.762	0.860
Testing	**0.784**	0.434	0.403	0.000	0.462	0.873

Table 3: Results on the development and testing sets. Accuracy and F1 scores: macro-averaged and per class (S: *supporting*, D: *denying*, Q: *querying*, C: *commenting*).

Depth	# tweets	# S	# D	# Q	# C	Accuracy	MacroF	S	D	Q	C
0	28	26	2	0	0	0.929	0.481	**0.963**	0.000	0.000	0.000
1	704	61	60	81	502	0.739	0.348	0.000	0.000	**0.550**	**0.842**
2	128	3	6	7	112	0.875	0.233	0.000	0.000	0.000	**0.933**
3	60	2	1	5	52	0.867	0.232	0.000	0.000	0.000	**0.929**
4	41	0	0	3	38	0.927	0.481	0.000	0.000	0.000	**0.962**
5	27	1	0	1	25	0.926	0.321	0.000	0.000	0.000	**0.961**
6+	61	1	2	9	49	0.803	0.223	0.000	0.000	0.000	**0.891**

Table 4: Number of tweets per depth and performance at each of the depths.

Tree of Parzen Estimators (TPE) algorithm [6] to search the parameter space, which is defined as follows: the number of dense ReLU layers varies from one to four; the number of LSTM layers is one or two; the mini-batch size is either 32 or 64; the number of units in the ReLU layer is one of $\{100, 200, 300, 400, 500\}$, and in the LSTM layer one of $\{100, 200, 300\}$; the strength of the L2 regularisation is one of $\{0.0, 1e\text{-}4, 3e\text{-}4, 1e\text{-}3\}$ and the number of epochs is selected from $\{30, 50, 70, 100\}$. We performed 100 trials of different parameter combinations optimising for accuracy on the development set in order to choose the best combination. We fixed hyperparameters to train the model on combined training and development sets and evaluated on the held out test set.

6   Results

The performance of our model on the testing and development set is shown in Table 3. Together with the accuracy we show macro-averaged F-score and per-class macro-averaged F-scores as these metrics account for the class imbalance. The difference in accuracy between testing and development set is minimal, however we see significant difference in Macro-F score due to different class balance in these sets. Macro-F score could be improved if we used it as a metric for optimising hyper-parameters. The *branch-LSTM* model predicts *commenting*, the majority class well, however it is unable to pick out any *denying*, the most-challenging under-represented class. Most *deny-*

Label \ Prediction	C	D	Q	S
Commenting	760	0	12	6
Denying	68	0	1	2
Querying	69	0	36	1
Supporting	67	0	1	26

Table 5: Confusion matrix for testing set predictions

ing instances get misclassified as *commenting* (see Table 5), with only one tweet misclassified as *querying* and two as *supporting* (Figure 2). An increased amount of labelled data would be helpful to improve performance of this model. As we were considering conversation branches, it is interesting to analyse the performance distribution across different tweet depths (see Table 4). Maximum depth/branch length in the testing set is 13 with most tweets concentrated at depths from 0 to 3. Source tweets (depth zero) are usually *supporting* and the model predicts these very well, but performance of *supporting* tweets at other depths decreases. The model does not show a noticeable difference in performance on tweets of varying lengths.

7   Conclusions

This paper describes the Turing system entered in the SemEval-2017 Task 8 Subtask A. Our method decomposes the tree structure of conversations into linear sequences and achieves accuracy 0.784 on the testing set and sets the state-of-the-art for rumour stance classification. In future work we plan to explore different methods for modelling tree-structured conversations.

---

[6]We used the implementation of the TPE algorithm in the hyperopt package (Bergstra et al., 2013)

Acknowledgments

This work was supported by The Alan Turing Institute under the EPSRC grant EP/N510129/1. Cloud computing resource were kindly provided through a Microsoft Azure for Research Award. Work by Elena Kochkina was partially supported by the Leverhulme Trust through the Bridges Programme.

References

Isabelle Augenstein, Tim Rocktäschel, Andreas Vlachos, and Kalina Bontcheva. 2016. Stance Detection with Bidirectional Conditional Encoding. In *Proceedings of EMNLP*.

Frédéric Bastien, Pascal Lamblin, Razvan Pascanu, James Bergstra, Ian Goodfellow, Arnaud Bergeron, Nicolas Bouchard, David Warde-Farley, and Yoshua Bengio. 2012. Theano: new features and speed improvements. *arXiv preprint arXiv:1211.5590* .

James Bergstra, Daniel Yamins, and David D Cox. 2013. Making a science of model search: Hyperparameter optimization in hundreds of dimensions for vision architectures. *ICML (1)* 28:115–123.

Ju-han Chuang and Shukai Hsieh. 2015. Stance classification on ptt comments. In *Proceedings of the 29th Pacific Asia Conference on Language, Information and Computation*.

Leon Derczynski, Kalina Bontcheva, Maria Liakata, Rob Procter, Geraldine Wong Sak Hoi, and Arkaitz Zubiaga. 2017. Semeval-2017 task 8: Rumoureval: Determining rumour veracity and support for rumours. In *Proceedings of the 11th International Workshop on Semantic Evaluation (SemEval-2017)*. Association for Computational Linguistics, Vancouver, Canada, pages 69–76. http://www.aclweb.org/anthology/S17-2006.

Leon Derczynski, Kalina Bontcheva, Michal Lukasik, Thierry Declerck, Arno Scharl, Georgi Georgiev, Petya Osenova, Toms Pariente Lobo, Anna Kolliakou, Robert Stewart, et al. 2014. Pheme: computing veracity: the fourth challenge of big social data. In *Proceedings of ESWC EU Project Networking*.

Sander Dieleman, Jan Schlüter, Colin Raffel, Eben Olson, Sren Kaae Sønderby, Daniel Nouri, Daniel Maturana, Martin Thoma, Eric Battenberg, Jack Kelly, Jeffrey De Fauw, Michael Heilman, Diogo Moitinho de Almeida, Brian McFee, Hendrik Weideman, Gbor Takács, Peter de Rivaz, Jon Crall, Gregory Sanders, Kashif Rasul, Cong Liu, Geoffrey French, and Jonas Degrave. 2015. Lasagne: First release. https://doi.org/10.5281/zenodo.27878.

Sepp Hochreiter and Jürgen Schmidhuber. 1997. Long short-term memory. *Neural computation* 9(8):1735–1780.

Michal Lukasik, P. K. Srijith, Duy Vu, Kalina Bontcheva, Arkaitz Zubiaga, and Trevor Cohn. 2016. Hawkes processes for continuous time sequence classification: an application to rumour stance classification in twitter. In *Proceedings of the 54th Meeting of the Association for Computational Linguistics*. Association for Computer Linguistics, pages 393–398.

Marcelo Mendoza, Barbara Poblete, and Carlos Castillo. 2010. Twitter under crisis: Can we trust what we RT? In *1st Workshop on Social Media Analytics*. SOMA'10, pages 71–79.

Tomas Mikolov, Kai Chen, Greg Corrado, and Jeffrey Dean. 2013. Efficient estimation of word representations in vector space. *arXiv preprint arXiv:1301.3781* .

Saif M Mohammad, Svetlana Kiritchenko, Parinaz Sobhani, Xiaodan Zhu, and Colin Cherry. 2016. Semeval-2016 task 6: Detecting stance in tweets. In *Proceedings of the International Workshop on Semantic Evaluation, SemEval*. volume 16.

Rob Procter, Farida Vis, and Alex Voss. 2013. Reading the riots on twitter: methodological innovation for the analysis of big data. *International journal of social research methodology* 16(3):197–214.

Vahed Qazvinian, Emily Rosengren, Dragomir R Radev, and Qiaozhu Mei. 2011. Rumor has it: Identifying misinformation in microblogs. In *Proceedings of the Conference on Empirical Methods in Natural Language Processing*. Association for Computational Linguistics, pages 1589–1599.

Sarvesh Ranade, Rajeev Sangal, and Radhika Mamidi. 2013. Stance classification in online debates by recognizing users' intentions. In *Proceedings of the SIGDIAL 2013 Conference*. pages 61–69.

Radim Řehůřek and Petr Sojka. 2010. Software Framework for Topic Modelling with Large Corpora. In *Proceedings of the LREC 2010 Workshop on New Challenges for NLP Frameworks*. ELRA, Valletta, Malta, pages 45–50. http://is.muni.cz/publication/884893/en.

Li Zeng, Kate Starbird, and Emma S Spiro. 2016. #unconfirmed: Classifying rumor stance in crisis-related social media messages. In *Tenth International AAAI Conference on Web and Social Media*.

Zhe Zhao, Paul Resnick, and Qiaozhu Mei. 2015. Enquiring minds: Early detection of rumors in social media from enquiry posts. In *Proceedings of the 24th International Conference on World Wide Web*. ACM, pages 1395–1405.

Arkaitz Zubiaga, Elena Kochkina, Maria Liakata, Rob Procter, and Michal Lukasik. 2016a. Stance classification in rumours as a sequential task exploiting the tree structure of social media conversations. In *Proceedings of COLING, the International Conference on Computational Linguistics*.

Arkaitz Zubiaga, Maria Liakata, Rob Procter, Geraldine Wong Sak Hoi, and Peter Tolmie. 2016b. Analysing how people orient to and spread rumours in social media by looking at conversational threads. *PloS one* 11(3):e0150989.

Mama Edha at SemEval-2017 Task 8: Stance Classification with CNN and Rules

Marianela García Lozano[*,†], Hanna Lilja[*], Edward Tjörnhammar[†], and Maja Karasalo[*]

[*]FOI Swedish Defence Research Agency
[*]{garcia, hanna.lilja, maja.karasalo}@foi.se
[†]KTH Royal Institute of Technology
[†]{mgl, edwardt}@kth.se

Abstract

For the competition SemEval-2017 we investigated the possibility of performing stance classification (support, deny, query or comment) for messages in Twitter conversation threads related to rumours. Stance classification is interesting since it can provide a basis for rumour veracity assessment. Our ensemble classification approach of combining convolutional neural networks with both automatic rule mining and manually written rules achieved a final accuracy of 74.9% on the competition's test data set for Task 8A. To improve classification we also experimented with data relabeling and using the grammatical structure of the tweet contents for classification.

1   Introduction

The task of determining the veracity of a rumour is sometimes a difficult one, even with the reasoning power of a human being. This paper presents an approach to an automatic analysis of discussion elements with respect to rumours. Discussion structure and analysis can well play a part in a broader effort to assess rumour veracity, and the expectation is that the results presented here is one step of the way towards that end goal.

The research presented in this paper is a submission to SemEval-2017, Task 8 (RumourEval: Determining rumour veracity and support for rumours), Subtask A (SDQC) (Derczynski et al., 2017). The objective of this subtask is to classify the relation between a tweet and the rumour it is related to in terms of support, deny, query or comment.

Our approach to this classification task is building three different classifiers and combining the predictions in an ensemble method. The general idea is that different types of classifiers may learn different concepts and hence complement each other, resulting in a better prediction capability for the joint classifier. Furthermore we tested the accuracy in applying our ensemble approach to both originally labeled and relabeled data.

The remainder of this paper is organized as follows: Section 2 describes the data given in the task and our observations on irregularities in the data labeling. Section 3 contains a description of the process and used methods employed for the experiments. Sections 4 and 5 describe the results and discusses the findings. Finally, we conclude the work in Section 6.

2   Data Inconsistencies

The data used in the SemEval-2017 Task 8A is a subset of the PHEME data set of social media rumours (Zubiaga et al., 2016).

When studying the dataset, it was discovered that for some tweets, the annotation is somewhat inconsistent, e.g., tweets with very similar contents have sometimes received different annotations. For example, despite being nearly identical replies to the same source tweet, the first is annotated with (C) and the second with (S):

> I just feel sick RT @[user]: At least 12 dead in Paris shooting. Updated story:[link]
>
> Awful. RT @[user]: At least 12 dead in the Paris shooting. [link]

Other found issues were that tweets were sometimes labeled (Q) although they contained no query. Some tweets were labelled with respect to its direct predecessor in the conversation thread, as opposed to with respect to the source tweet. Also, some tweets were annotated (S) for simply

Proceedings of the 11th International Workshop on Semantic Evaluations (SemEval-2017), pages 481–485,
Vancouver, Canada, August 3 - 4, 2017. ©2017 Association for Computational Linguistics

expressing empathy or concern, without any input on the veracity of the rumour.

3 Method

For solving the task we had an approach of multiple parallel data pipelines, for our workflow schema, see Figure 1. The following sections and subsections describe the parts of the figure.

3.1 Data Processing

Chosen parts of the raw data were extracted into new subsets of attributes, tailored for each type of classifier. Among the extracted data attributes were the text content of the tweets, metadata related to the tweets (such as time of posting) and metadata related to the users (such as number of followers). In terms of training, development and test data we used the data split provided by the SemEval Task organizers.

To investigate whether the inconsistencies in the annotation would affect the results of the experiments, we constructed a separate data set in which we tried to remedy the found inconsistencies.iIn uncertain cases, the original annotation was used.

3.2 Feature Engineering

Most of the metadata attributes from the raw data could be used as features for classification without further processing. However, some attributes (the text data in particular) required preprocessing and feature engineering in order to be a useful representation of the data.

3.2.1 Preprocessing

Tweets have limited space (only 140 characters) and hence, symbols, abbreviations, slang and contractions are used in an effort to increase the information ratio. The downside of this is that the tweets tend to appear noisy to NLP software and some preprocessing is usually needed. The measures we applied were, e.g., splitting contractions and stemming the words. For the stemming we employed the Python package "Snowballstemmer". Also, in an effort to avoid training the classifiers on data that could be too context specific, e.g., a link or a user name. We elected to remove mentions and links, replacing them with a simple "@" and "http://".

3.2.2 Grammatical Representation Generation

We investigated whether the grammatical structure could be useful as a replacement of the tweets themselves. We chose to use a pretrained model on the English language for the initial tweet to Part Of Speech (POS) Tagging, i.e., Parsey Mc-Parseface[1] (Andor et al., 2016). Further; We relied on CoNLL-U (Nivre, 2015), a unicode version of CoNNL-X (Buchholz and Marsi, 2006) as our data format for the POS tagging. Input tweets were not stemmed but otherwise preprocessed.

We utilized the same rule encoding as (Feng et al., 2012) and chose the one level neighbourhood semantic rules, i.e. the $\hat{r}*$ notational case, i.e., unlexicalized production rules combined with the grandparent node.

3.2.3 Word2vec Embeddings

We used word2vec vectors learned using the skip-gram model which predicts the linear context of the words surrounding the target words (Mikolov et al., 2013)[2].

3.3 Classification

In our method we used an ensemble approach consisting of combining several classifiers and using their individual strengths in the final voting.

3.3.1 CNN

In our experiments we followed (Kim, 2014)'s architecture[3]. We experimented with different CNN model versions, see all paths that lead to CNN in Figure 1. We used a non static setting for the word embeddings which, as previously mentioned, came from the pretrained word2vec corpus. Due to the skewed nature of the training data with two classes being significantly more common than the other two we adjusted the weights to reflect this relationship, i.e., $w[S, D, Q, C] = [0.157, 0.396, 0.399, 0.048]$. We used no regularization.

---

[1] The environment containing the trained Parsey McParseface model is available at docker hub as `edwtjo/syntaxnet:conll`

[2] The pretrained corpus `GoogleNews-vectors-negative300.bin.gz` can be downloaded from `https://code.google.com/archive/p/word2vec/`.

[3] As a starting point for the CNN-implementation we used Denny Brick's version of (Kim, 2014)'s Theano implementation. The code can be found at `https://github.com/dennybritz/cnn-text-classification-tf`

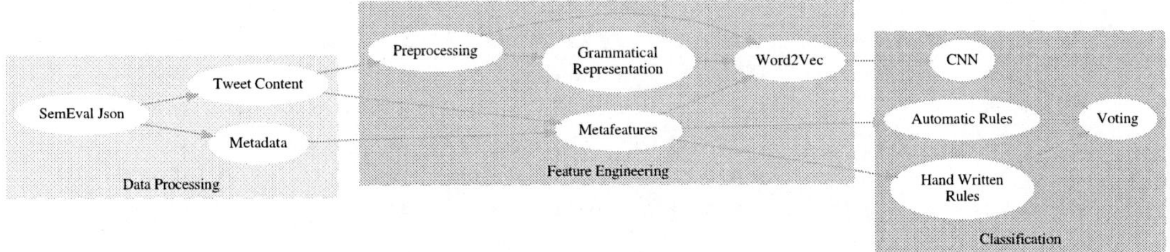

Figure 1: Workflow schematic for our data pipeline

3.3.2 Automatic Rule Mining

Classification through automatic rule mining was done with the WEKA (Witten et al., 2016) implementation of PART (Frank and Witten, 1998). PART was used with the confidence factor set to 0.25 and the minimum number of instances per rule set to 2. For this classifier the data was represented in terms of a number of metadata features: i) Number of ".", "?", "!", and negations in the tweet. ii) Number of statuses, followers and friends, and favourites of the user. iii) Whether the user is verified or not. iv) Whether the tweet was a reply or not and its conversation depth. The conversation depth of a tweet is here defined as 0 for a source tweet, 1 for a reply to a source tweet, and so forth.

3.3.3 Hand Written Rules

The classifier based on hand written rules (HWR) relies on a small set of rules to classify tweets. The rules are designed to favour precision over recall, and were constructed through manual inspection of the training data. The default class is *comment*. One type of rule checks if any predefined key phrases are present in the tweet and if so classifies the tweet accordingly. An example of such a rule is: *If sentence contains phrase 'not believable': → assign class **deny*** The second type of rule checks for certain combinations of occurrences of "@"-mentions, "#", and urls in the whole text, as well as "?" in the first 5 tokens of the tweet. An example of this type of rule is: *If sentence contains an **url** and does **not start** with an **@-mention**: → assign class **support***

3.3.4 Voting

The final prediction of the class of a data instance is achieved through a voting procedure. As different classifiers have different strenghts and weaknesses, which vary over classes as well as between precision and recall, not all votes are counted as equal. A vote on a certain class from a classifier with high precision on said class is deemed more important.

4 Results

In addition to the results on the test data, results on the development data are also provided.

		Label	
	original (%)	our (%)	diff (pp)
S	910 (20.1)	955 (21.1)	+44 (+1)
D	344 (7.6)	230 (5.1)	-114 (-2.5)
Q	358 (7.9)	326 (7.2)	-32 (-0.7)
C	2907 (64.3)	3009 (66.6)	+102 (+2.3)

Table 1: Distribution of tweets between classes using original labels and our new labels.

4.1 Relabeling

Out of 4519 tweets we relabeled 846, or about 19%. The distribution of tweets between classes before and after relabeling is shown in Table 1.

4.2 Development Data Performance

The CNN trained using preprocessed tweet contents, together with each tweets absolute time (counting from its source tweet as point zero), and dynamic word2vec settings reached an accuracy of 0.715 on the development set. The PART rules reached an accuracy of 0.701 on the development set. The hand written rules reached an accuracy of 0.733 on the development set.

After tweaking of the voting schema to make use of the strengths of the different methods an accuracy of 0.758 on the development set was reached. The best accuracy on the development data was achieved with the following priority order of votes from the classifiers: 1) CNN vote on support, 2) HWR vote on deny or query, 3) PART vote on query, 4) CNN vote on deny or query, 5) HWR vote on support, 6) Default class comment.

Model	Accuracy	Precision				Recall			
		S	D	Q	C	S	D	Q	C
HWR	0.751	0.55	0.053	**0.605**	0.783	0.319	0.014	0.217	0.943
PART	0.745	0.423	0.105	0.553	0.802	0.319	0.028	0.396	0.910
PART$_R$	0.732	0.343	0.167	0.558	**0.811**	0.383	0.042	**0.453**	0.875
CNN	**0.752**	**0.622**	0.0	0.333	0.761	0.298	0.0	0.009	**0.977**
CNN$_G$	0.633	0.563	**0.2**	0.286	0.681	**0.391**	**0.182**	0.071	0.850
CNN$_R$	0.745	0.538	0.0	0.333	0.758	0.298	0.0	0.009	0.968
Voting	*0.749*	*0.5*	*0.05*	*0.525*	*0.812*	*0.372*	*0.014*	*0.5*	*0.896*

Table 2: Results on test data set, comparison between classifiers. Subscript R after the classifier name stands for "Relabeled" and subscript G stands for "Grammatical Representation". The best result in each column is marked with bold face.

4.3 Test Data Performance

Table 2 shows performance measures for our classifiers, evaluated on the test data. In the Table we have also included the results of training both with the new labels, marked with subscript R, and training a CNN model with only the grammatical representation of the tweet contents and absolute time, marked with subscript G.

5 Discussion

The data set class distribution is rather skewed, with the vast majority of the tweets classified as comments. In fact, using a simple majority classifier would result in an accuracy of 64.3%, i.e., the ratio of tweets classified as comments. This might be considered an evaluation baseline. In our experiments with relabeling the data to try and remedy the found inconsistencies we changed almost one fifth of the labels. Which could indicate that the labels are highly subjective. A reason for this could be that the overall rumour was not given in the data. A downside of the relabeling was that the two largest classes, i.e., S and C, became even more prevalent.

There was a great difference in the performance of the models on the development and test data, e.g., the CNN model went from an accuracy of 71.5% to 75.2%. This indicates that the development data might not be representative for the test data and that methods developed for this task should take care to avoid being too domain specific.

The CNN based models show consistently best accuracy for a few epochs, on average around 8 epochs, and after that the models become overfitted. We tested with regularization to avoid overfitting, but to no avail. This only prolongs the number of epochs necessary for training. Note that we did not do experiments with more than 200 epochs. A theory is that the data set is simply so small that it is easy to overfit a CNN-model and the number of epochs thus must be carefully monitored.

For this competition it became apparent, during the development phase and tuning of hyper parameters, that the grammar structure of tweets had little impact on the overall accuracy of the model, see CNN$_G$ results in Table 2. There are many possible reasons for this but the most likely is that tweets follow a very reduced grammatical structure due to their inherent shortness and as such exhibit similar distributions over the possible output classes. But, there was one class in which the CNN$_G$ model had much better precision than all other models, i.e., the elusive deny class.

The hand written rules performed remarkably well considering their simplicity. A possible explanation for this is of course that the person constructing the rules will make use of general language and world knowledge that a machine may not have access to. A potential problem with this approach is that it might be difficult to significantly improve the performance, at least without a substantial manual effort. Some metadata and text meta features are less intuitive for a human to manually write rules based upon. The PART classifier could more easily handle these features and so discover rules that would have been difficult for a human to come up with.

The main goal of the voting procedure is to exploit the strengths of different types of classifiers. We decided to rank votes per classifier and class, rather than a more complex weighting scheme or a simple majority vote. A motivation for this was the tendency of the classifiers to favour precision over recall (in the case of HWR) or to be heavily biased towards the comment class due to the class imbalance of the data set.

6 Conclusions

The key contributions of this paper are, among other, approaching the task of stance classification with an ensemble method combining CNNs with both automatic rule mining and manually written rules. Interesting feature engineering was done by, among other things, relabeling the data and using the grammatical structure of the tweet contents.

Utilizing each method's strengths the results were weighted with a voting system developed for the task. The submitted system achieved a final accuracy of 74.9% on the competition's test data set, placing the team at a fourth place on the SemEval-2017 RumourEval task 8A.

Acknowledgments

PhD. M. Rosell suggested relabeling the data.

References

Daniel Andor, Chris Alberti, David Weiss, Aliaksei Severyn, Alessandro Presta, Kuzman Ganchev, Slav Petrov, and Michael Collins. 2016. Globally normalized transition-based neural networks. *arXiv preprint arXiv:1603.06042* .

Sabine Buchholz and Erwin Marsi. 2006. CoNLL-X Shared Task on Multilingual Dependency Parsing. In *Proceedings of the Tenth Conference on Computational Natural Language Learning*. Association for Computational Linguistics, pages 149–164.

Leon Derczynski, Kalina Bontcheva, Maria Liakata, Rob Procter, Geraldine Wong Sak Hoi, and Arkaitz Zubiaga. 2017. Semeval-2017 task 8: Rumoureval: Determining rumour veracity and support for rumours. In *Proceedings of the 11th International Workshop on Semantic Evaluation (SemEval-2017)*. Association for Computational Linguistics, Vancouver, Canada, pages 69–76. http://www.aclweb.org/anthology/S17-2006.

Song Feng, Ritwik Banerjee, and Yejin Choi. 2012. Syntactic Stylometry for Deception Detection. In *Proceedings of the 50th Annual Meeting of the Association for Computational Linguistics: Short Papers-Volume 2*. Association for Computational Linguistics, pages 171–175.

Eibe Frank and Ian H. Witten. 1998. Generating Accurate Rule Sets Without Global Optimization. Morgan Kaufmann, pages 144–151.

Yoon Kim. 2014. Convolutional Neural Networks for Sentence Classification. *CoRR abs/1408.5882*.

Tomas Mikolov, Ilya Sutskever, Kai Chen, Greg S Corrado, and Jeff Dean. 2013. Distributed Representations of Words and Phrases and Their Compositionality. In *Advances in Neural Information Processing Systems*. pages 3111–3119.

Joakim Nivre. 2015. Towards a Universal Grammar for Natural Language Processing. In *International Conference on Intelligent Text Processing and Computational Linguistics*. Springer, pages 3–16.

Ian H. Witten, Eibe Frank, Mark A. Hall, and Christopher J. Pal. 2016. *The WEKA Workbench. Online Appendix for "Data Mining: Practical Machine Learning Tools and Techniques"*. Morgan Kaufmann, 4 edition.

Arkaitz Zubiaga, Maria Liakata, Rob Procter, Geraldine Wong Sak Hoi, and Peter Tolmie. 2016. Analysing How People Orient to and Spread Rumours in Social Media by Looking at Conversational Threads. *PloS one* 11(3):e0150989.

DFKI-DKT at SemEval-2017 Task 8:
Rumour Detection and Classification using Cascading Heuristics

Ankit Kumar Srivastava

DFKI GmbH
Alt-Moabit 91c, 10559 Berlin, DE
ankit.srivastava@dfki.de

Georg Rehm

DFKI GmbH
Alt-Moabit 91c, 10559 Berlin, DE
georg.rehm@dfki.de

Julian Moreno Schneider

DFKI GmbH
Alt-Moabit 91c, 10559 Berlin, DE
julian.moreno_schneider@dfki.de

Abstract

We describe our submissions for
SemEval-2017 Task 8, Determining
Rumour Veracity and Support for Rumours. The Digital Curation Technologies
(DKT) (Rehm and Sasaki, 2016, 2015)
team at the German Research Center for
Artificial Intelligence (DFKI) participated
in two subtasks: Subtask A (determining
the stance of a message) and Subtask B
(determining veracity of a message, closed
variant). In both cases, our implementation consisted of a Multivariate Logistic
Regression (Maximum Entropy) classifier
coupled with hand-written patterns and
rules (heuristics) applied in a post-process
cascading fashion. We provide a detailed
analysis of the system performance and
report on variants of our systems that were
not part of the official submission.

1 Introduction

In today's digital age, the social, political and economic relevance of online media and online content is becoming more and more relevant. Accordingly, the task of analysing and determining the
veracity of online content is receiving a growing
amount of attention by the NLP community. The
ability to detect whether a piece of news is fake or
not, and to do so automatically, is a very timely
language technology application (Zubiaga and Ji,
2014). Through these shared tasks, we intend to
address which linguistic and contextual features
characterise a rumour.

SemEval2017 Task 8 (Derczynski et al., 2017)
provided all participants with a dataset consisting
of tweets in response to breaking news stories. It
contains conversations responding to rumourous
tweets. These tweets have been annotated for sup-

port, deny, query or comment (SDQC). The competition consisted of two subtasks:

- **Subtask A:** Determining whether response
  tweets support, deny, query or comment
  (SDQC) on rumours (source tweet)

- **Subtask B:** Given a tweet, determine
  whether the statement is true or false (i. e.,
  a rumour). This subtask featured two variants: closed (determining veracity from the
  tweet alone) and open (determining veracity
  from additional context). We participated in
  the closed task.

Our approach to both subtasks involved extracting relevant features from the provided data and
training a classifier followed by a set of heuristics implemented in a cascading decision tree style
(Minguillon, 2002). These rules, applied as a post-
process, help induce a better mapping from classification results to rumour categorisation and veracity detection because they take into account specific features characterising a particular class.

In this paper we seek to answer two questions
using Rumour Detection and Classification as a
case-study:

- Which features comprise the set of post-
  process rules?

- What is the optimal technique to implement
  these heuristics (cascading order)?

This paper is structured as follows. Section 2
gives a bird's eye overview of our systems submitted for evaluation. Section 3 describes the various
rumour detection and classification models as well
as experimental setups (not part of the official submission). Section 4 displays the results and analyses them. Section 5 contains a discussion of the
task in general followed by an explanation of some
design decisions.

Proceedings of the 11th International Workshop on Semantic Evaluations (SemEval-2017), pages 486–490,
Vancouver, Canada, August 3 - 4, 2017. ©2017 Association for Computational Linguistics

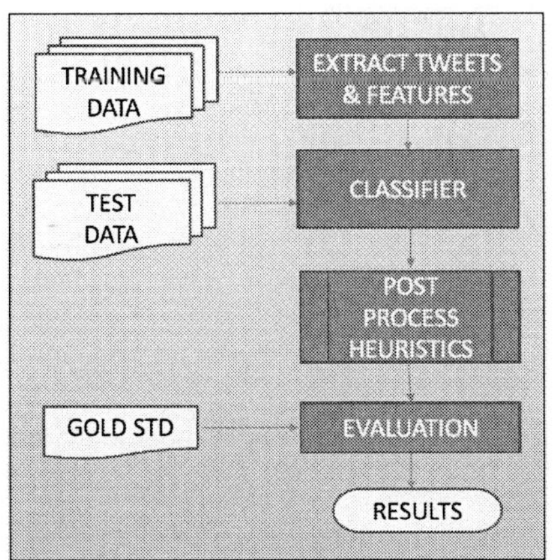

Figure 1: Workflow of the DFKI-DKT System for both tasks

Category	Subtask A	Subtask B
Training	4238 tweets	272 tweets
Development	281 tweets	25 tweets
Test	1049 tweets	28 tweets

Table 1: Overview of Training and Testing data

2 DFKI-DKT's Submission Overview

Our submissions can be categorised as hybrid systems since they consist of both machine learning and rule-based (heuristics) modules.

The first step was to extract contextual features (tweet text) and metadata features (Twitter user account properties and message properties) from the provided test data. We then trained a Maximum Entropy classifier (Malouf, 2002) followed by a set of heuristics (if-then clauses) implemented in a cascading decision tree style (Minguillon, 2002), see Figure 1.

2.1 Data and Tools

In terms of tools and resources we did not use any external data. All models were trained on the provided twitter dataset. Table 1 gives an overview of the size of the data for subtasks A and B. We implemented feature vector-based text classification models using the Mallet Machine Learning Toolkit (McCallum, 2002) in Java. The heuristics were implemented in the form of an experimentally determined sequence of if-then decision rules written in Python. Evaluation was performed using the scoring scripts provided by the task organisers.

2.2 Preprocessing

We employed the standard tokenisation scripts while extracting the feature vectors for training a classifier. We did not implement any other preprocessing step. In fact, it was discovered that cleaning the tweets actually impacted the classification algorithm in a negative way. We believe that certain as-is characteristics of the text (uppercase, spelling errors, emoticons, etc.) help in better distinguishing the used categories (SDQC).

2.3 Subtask A Heuristics

The classifier was trained on four classes (SDQC). This was followed by a post-processing module of decision rules based on linguistic patterns and Twitter metadata. The heuristics were as follows:

- **If** a tweet begins with a wh-word (where, when, how, what, why, which) and/or ends with a question mark, **then** classify it as *query*

- **If** a tweet contains a negation, **then** classify it as *denial*

- **If** a tweet is a retweet, **then** classify it as *support*

- **If** more than 70% of the text is all uppercase, **then** classify it as *comment*

2.4 Subtask B (closed) Heuristics

The classifier was trained on two classes (true, false). This was followed by a post-processing module of decision rules based on linguistic patterns and Twitter metadata. The heuristics were as follows:

- **If** a tweet begins with a wh-word (where, when, how, what, why, which) and/or ends with a question mark, **then** classify it as *false*

- **If** the tweet has been retweeted x number of times, **then** classify it as *true*

- **If** more than 70% of the text is all uppercase, **then** classify it as *false*

- **If** the tweet contains more than three @usernames and hashtags, **then** classify it as *false*

- **If** the author of the tweet as more than 10000 followers, **then** classify it as *true*

Pattern	Support	Query	Deny	Comment
RT (retweet)	**7.5%**	2.6%	6.2%	5.7%
@username (replies)	64.7%	**95.9%**	88.9%	92.1%
! (exclamation mark)	7.5%	6.7%	11.1%	**12.2%**
Negative emoticons	0.2%	0.3%	0.3%	**1.0%**
Positive emoticons	0%	**0.9%**	0.5%	0.2%
? (question mark)	6.7%	**65.8%**	14.9%	10.3%
Wh-word	6.5%	**21.3%**	13.4%	10.3%
"" (quotation marks)	5.2%	2.3%	**6.5%**	4.8%
Abusive language	2.5%	2.0%	**12.9%**	9.4%

Table 2: Percentage of tweets in the four categories of training data containing a specific feature.

3 Models and Experiments

In this section, we describe the details of the features used in our models as well as the different experimental settings.

3.1 Models

We trained three different classifiers, followed by applying the heuristics model described in Sections 2.3 and 2.4:

- Maximum Entropy classification (MaxEnt) (Malouf, 2002), also known as Multivariate Logistic Regression.

- Naive Bayes classification (Frank and Bouckaert, 2006) assumes independence of the features while counting.

- Winnow classification (Winnow2) (Littlestone, 1988) is similar to the perceptron model but uses a multiplicative weight update scheme rather than an additive method.

While we submitted only the MaxEnt model due to time constraints, we also include the results and analysis of the performance of the Naive Bayes and Winnow classifiers. We also computed an ensemble classifier, i. e., a voting-based combination of the three models' results using the following algorithm:

- Count the number of votes (MaxEnt, Naive Bayes, Winnow) for each of the categories (four for Subtask A, two for Subtask B)

- Select the category with the maximum number of votes

- If there is a tie, select the result of MaxEnt classifier

3.2 Useful Features

For subtask A (determining the category of a message), we compiled a list of distinctive features[1] characteristic of each of the stances: support, query, deny, comment. We conducted an investigation into linguistic and context-specific patterns that may distinguish one stance from the other. For example, query messages almost always have a wh-word and a question mark.

1. Message is a retweet, i. e., begins with *RT*

2. Message is a reply (*@usernames*)

3. Message contains exclamation marks

4. Message is a question (question mark or wh-word: who/what/when/why/where/how)

5. Message contains emoticons (smileys)

6. At least 70% of the message is in uppercase

7. Message contains negations (not, doesn't)

8. Message contains expletives or abuse

Table2 gives a snapshot of the frequency of the patterns on the training data in each of the SQDC categories.

3.3 Experimental Setup

The features used in the classification algorithms consisted of a vector of the words (twitter text). When we attempted to incorporate some of the features described above in the classification algorithm, the performance deteriorated. This led us to implement a post-process heuristic module and subject the results of the classification to a second

---

[1] After conducting a statistical analysis of the training data, we also used some of these features in determining the rumour veracity in subtask B, see Section 2.4.

System	Subtask	
	A	**B**
MaxEnt+Heuristics	0.635	0.393
NaiveBayes+Heuristics	0.621	0.387
Winnow+Heuristics	0.630	0.400
Ensemble+Heuristics	0.705	0.422

Table 3: Evaluation scores of submitted system (first row) as well as other runs of our system.

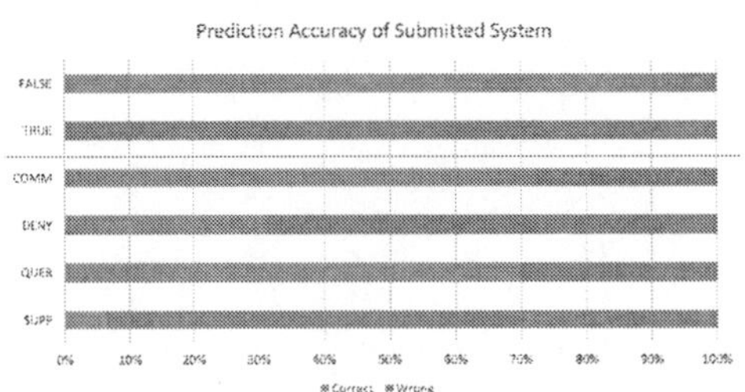

Figure 2: Prediction Accuracy of Submitted Systems in Subtask B and Subtask A

stage of assigning labels. For example, over 60% of the messages containing a question mark were queries. Hence any message containing a question mark was tagged as a query.

4 Results

Table 3 shows the results of our experiments. We submitted the MaxEnt results. However, the ensemble method (combination of all three models) shows a much better performance.

Figure 2 demonstrates the number of correct categories we classified accurately (blue bar). Our systems performed best at predicting the "comment" and "query" in subtask A and "false" in subtask B. The poor performance on "support" in subtask A and "true" in subtask B can be attributed to our post-process framework, i.e. our rules are not sufficiently discriminative. A work-around is to label all tweets as "support" and then implement the if-then rules.

5 Discussion

In this section, we briefly touch upon a few observations from our experiments. First, the actual twitter text should not be cleaned in any way, i. e., errors, misspellings, acronyms etc. contained in the text help in the task. Using rule-based heuristics derived from a statistical analysis of the characteristics of the training data, helps in a post-

processing step to improve the classification performance of test data.

6 Conclusion

We implemented hybrid systems, i. e., combinations of statistical (classifier) and rule-based (heuristics) modules. It can be observed that textual features and metadata benefit both tasks. In terms of future work, we plan to implement a better cascading model, i. e., to assign probabilities to the heuristics.

Acknowledgments

We would like to thank the anonymous reviewers for their insight and helpful comments on our first draft. The project Digitale Kuratierungstechnologien (DKT) is supported by the German Federal Ministry of Education and Research (BMBF), Unternehmen Region, instrument Wachstumskern-Potenzial (No. 03WKP45). More information on the project can be found online at http://www.digitale-kuratierung.de.

References

Leon Derczynski, Kalina Bontcheva, Maria Liakata, Rob Procter, Geraldine Wong Sak Hoi, and Arkaitz Zubiaga. 2017. Semeval-2017 task 8: Rumoureval: Determining rumour veracity and support for rumours. In *Proceedings of the 11th International Workshop on Semantic Evaluation (SemEval-2017)*. Association for Computational Linguistics, Vancouver, Canada, pages 60–67. http://www.aclweb.org/anthology/S17-2006.

Eibe Frank and Remco R. Bouckaert. 2006. Naive Bayes for text classification with unbalanced classes. In *Proc 10th European Conference on Principles and Practice of Knowledge Discovery in Databases*. Springer, Berlin, Germany, pages 503–510.

Nick Littlestone. 1988. Learning quickly when irrelevant attributes abound: A new linear-threshold algorithm. *Machine Learning* 2(4):285–318. https://doi.org/10.1023/A:1022869011914.

Robert Malouf. 2002. A comparison of algorithms for maximum entropy parameter estimation. In *Proceedings of the 6th Conference on Natural Language Learning - Volume 20*. Association for Computational Linguistics, Stroudsburg, PA, USA, COLING-02, pages 1–7. https://doi.org/10.3115/1118853.1118871.

Andrew Kachites McCallum. 2002. Mallet: A machine learning for language toolkit. http://mallet.cs.umass.edu.

Julia Minguillon. 2002. *On Cascading Small Decision Trees*. Ph.D. thesis, Universitat Autonoma de Barcelon.

Georg Rehm and Felix Sasaki. 2015. Digitale Kuratierungstechnologien – Verfahren für die effiziente
Verarbeitung, Erstellung und Verteilung qualitativ
hochwertiger Medieninhalte. In *Proceedings der
Frühjahrstagung der Gesellschaft für Sprachtech-
nologie und Computerlinguistik (GSCL 2015)*. Duis-
burg, pages 138–139. 30. September–2. Oktober.

Georg Rehm and Felix Sasaki. 2016. Digital Curation Technologies. In *Proceedings of the 19th Annual Conference of the European Association for
Machine Translation (EAMT 2016)*. Riga, Latvia.

Arkaitz Zubiaga and Heng Ji. 2014. Tweet, but verify:
epistemic study of information verification on twitter. *Social Network Analysis and Mining* 4(1):163.
https://doi.org/10.1007/s13278-014-0163-y.

ECNU at SemEval-2017 Task 8: Rumour Evaluation Using Effective Features and Supervised Ensemble Models

Feixiang Wang[1], Man Lan[1,2]*, Yuanbin Wu[1,2]
[1]Department of Computer Science and Technology,
East China Normal University, Shanghai, P.R.China
[2]Shanghai Key Laboratory of Multidimensional Information Processing
51151201049@stu.ecnu.edu.cn, {mlan, ybwu}@cs.ecnu.edu.cn

Abstract

This paper describes our submissions to task 8 in SemEval 2017, i.e., *Determining rumour veracity and support for rumours*. Given a rumoured tweet and a plethora of replied tweets, subtask A is to label whether these tweets are *support*, *deny*, *query* or *comment*, and subtask B aims to predict the veracity (i.e., *true*, *false*, and *unverified*) with a confidence (in range of 0-1) of the given rumoured tweet. For both subtasks, we adopted supervised machine learning methods incorporating rich features. Since the training data is imbalanced, we specifically designed a two-step classifier to address subtask A .

1 Introduction

With the rapid development of social media in recent years, people cannot only stay abreast of ongoing events and breaking news, but also express their own views freely. News can spread quickly in social media platforms through a large amount of users, whilst those pieces of unverified information often spawn rumours. The RumourEval (Derczynski et al., 2017) task aims to identify how users in social media networks regard the originating rumours and reply to them, as well as analysis and determining veracity of rumoured tweets. The organizer provides tree-structured conversations that are associated with breaking news and consisting of originating rumoured tweets and tweets replying to them.

There are two subtasks in RumourEval. The propose of subtask A is, given the related breaking news, to predict the class (i.e., *support*, *deny*, *query*, and *comment*) of the originating rumoured tweet (i.e., source tweet) and reactions (i.e., replied tweets). The goal of subtask B is to determine the veracity and confidence of the given rumoured tweet, participants are required to return a label of rumour as *true*, *false* or *unverified*, with a confidence value in the range of 0-1.

We treated the two subtasks as multi-classification problems, and designed multiple effective natural language processing (NLP) features to build classifiers to make predictions. Besides, rumour detection is relevant to sentiment analysis, for example, *support* and *deny* can be viewed as positive and negative sentiment respectively. Therefore, we solved the problem with the aid of a number of sentiment-related features. Due to the imbalanced characteristic of the training data, we specifically adopted a two-step classifier to deal with subtask A. Firstly, tweets would be separated into two categories: *comment* and *non-comment*, then the tweets labeled as *non-comment* would be classified as *support*, *deny* or *query*. On the other hand, we directly adopted a three-classification system for subtask B to label rumoured tweets as *true*, *false* or *unverified* along with confidence.

2 System Description

For both subtask, we extracted rich features from the training data and then built classifiers to make predictions. For subtask A, we designed a two-step classification system. The first step (1-step) classifier is to discriminate *comment* tweets from *non-comment* tweets. And the second step (2-step) classifier is to identify whether a tweet is *support*, *deny* or *query* towards the rumour if the tweet was labeled as *non-comment* in the 1-step classification. The 1-step can be viewed as determining whether a tweet is *objective* (*comment*) or *subjective* (*non-comment*). The 2-step is actually to classify a *non-comment* tweet that expresses positive (*support*), negative (*deny*) or doubtful (*query*)

Proceedings of the 11th International Workshop on Semantic Evaluations (SemEval-2017), pages 491–496,
Vancouver, Canada, August 3 - 4, 2017. ©2017 Association for Computational Linguistics

sentiment. While for subtask B, we simply implemented a three-classification system to determine whether the given rumoured tweet is *true, false* or *unverified* and returned a confidence of label.

2.1 Feature Engineering

In this section, we give the detail of feature engineering. Five types of NLP features are designed to capture effective information from the given tweets.

Linguistic-informed Features

- **Word N-grams:** We extracted word n-grams features ($n = 1, 2$) from tweets. However, a word has various forms, therefore we also constructed lemmatization and stem word n-grams features ($n = 1, 2$). To accomplish that, we acquired the lemmatization and stem of words from the pending sentences, using the *Stanford CoreNLP tools*[1].

- **NER:** There are different types of words in tweets, such as a tweet "*Gunman Takes Hostages In Sydney Cafe*" that has useful information like person and location to help to detect rumours. NER feature can effectively express aforesaid information. The 12 types (i.e., *DURATION, SET, NUMBER, LOCATION, PERSON, ORGANIZATION, PERCENT, MISC, ORDINAL, TIME, DATE, MONEY*) named entities are labeled by *Stanford CoreNLP tools*. We used a 12-dimensions binary feature to indicate the entities in tweet.

There are some particular elements in tweets, that can help to predict labels of tweets. For instance, hashtag and mentioned entity (e.g., "#semeval", "@YouTube") express the topic information of the tweets, and several special punctuation and emotions (e.g., "!", "?", and ":)") reveal the sentiment information of users.

Tweet domain Features

We collected all the hashtags and mentioned entities appeared in training tweets, using unigram feature to imply whether a tweet contained such information.

- **Punctuation:** Considering that users often use exclamation marks and question marks to express strongly surprised and questioned

feelings, we extracted 7-dimensions punctuation features by recording rules of punctuation marks in the tweets (i.e., whether there is one or more question marks or exclamation marks, whether there is a question mark or an exclamation mark in the end of sentence).

- **Emoticon:** We collected 67 emoticons labeled with positive and negative scores from the Internet[2], and used a 67-dimensions feature to record the sentiment score of the emoticon in tweets.

- **Event:** Training data consists of plenty of tree-structured conversations that cover eight breaking news. We gathered several keywords[3] about these events from the Internet to extract corresponding unigram feature.

Metadata contains important information and can indicate the popularity of a tweet and the credibility of the author of a tweet. For example, features like "*favorite_count: 1340*", "*retweet_count: 500*" may indicate whether the tweet is being watched; "*verified: false*", "*protected: true*" perhaps imply whether the author is trustworthy.

Tweet metadata Features

We extracted two types of metadata information:

- **Tweet metadata:** We designed a 5-dimensions feature that consists of *tweet favorite count, retweet count, pre-retweet count* (i.e., the retweet count of the last replied tweet), *create time gap* (i.e., the time interval between the tweet and previous replied tweet) and *tweet level* (i.e., the layer of the tweet in a tweet conversation flow). These numerical characteristics are normalized by *0-1* normalization.

- **User metadata:** In addition to the metadata of a tweet, users also have some instrumentally valuable metadata as follows: *list count, followers count, user favourites count, friends count, verified, protected, default profile, profile use background image,* and *geo*

---

[2] https://github.com/haierlord/resource/blob/master/Emoticon.txt

[3] We enter the hashtag of source tweet on the Internet, to collect keywords from the headlines of relevant news. For example, we manually extracted "charlie", "hebdo", "attack" and "terror" from the title "Charlie Hebdo attack: Three days of terror - BBC News".

---

[1] http://stanfordnlp.github.io/CoreNLP/

enabled. The first four are numerical features that need normalization, and others are binary features. The aforementioned features form a 9-dimensions feature.

Word Vector Features

A lot of recent studies on NLP applications are reported to have good performance using word vectors, such as ducument classification (Sebastiani, 2002), parsing (Socher et al., 2013), and question answering (Lan et al., 2016a), We adopted two widely-used word vectors, i.e., GoogleW2V (Mikolov et al., 2013) and GloVe (Pennington et al., 2014). However, semantic word vectors find similar words with similar context rather than similar sentiment information. Several recent works focused on sentiment word vectors using neural network based models (Lan et al., 2016b). In this work, we also adopted two sentiment word vectors, one is SSWE (Tang et al., 2014) and the other is a home-made sentiment word vector from our previous work. To obtain the representation of a tweet, for each word in a tweet, we concatenated the maximum, minimum and mean of each dimension as a tweet vector [*min-max-mean*].

- **GoogleW2V:** We adopted the pre-trained available 300-dimensions word vectors that were trained on 100 billion words from Google News by word2vec tool[4]

- **GloVe:** The 100-dimensions word vectors we used were trained on 2 billion tweets and supplied in *GloVe*[5].

- **SSWE:** The sentiment-specific word embeddings were trained by using multi-hidden-layers nerual network with a vector size of 50.

- **ZSWE:** The 200-dimensions home-made sentiment word vectors were trained with NRC140 tweet corpus by the *Combined-Sentiment Word Embedding* Model.

Word-cluster Feature

To further group similar words into a small set and to make better use of word semantic information, we clustered all the words of tweets by k-means algorithm. The pending words were firstly represented as 300-dimensions word vectors by

looking up pre-trained GoogleW2V, then grouped into 80 clusters. Thus we adopted 80-dimensions binary feature to mark whether the words of a certain cluster appeared in the tweet.

2.2 Learning algorithms and Evaluation metrics

Based on above multiple features, we explored several learning algorithms to build classification models, e.g., Logistic Regression (LR), supplied in *liblinear tools*[6], Support Vector Machines (SVM), Decision Trees (DT), Random Forests (R-F), AdaBoost (ADB), and Gradient Tree Boosting (GDB), implemented in *scikit-learn*[7]. We also ensembled the effective learning algorithms using majority vote strategy.

The official evaluation measure for both subtasks is *accuracy*.

3 Experiments and Results

3.1 Datasets

The statistics of the datasets provided by SemEval 2017 task 8 are shown in Table 1.

Subtask A	support(%)	query(%)	deny(%)	comment(%)
train	841(19.8)	330(7.8)	333(7.9)	2, 734(64.5)
dev	69(24.6)	28(10.0)	11(3.9)	173(61.6)
test	94(9.0)	106(10.1)	71(6.8)	778(74.2)

Subtask B	true(%)	false(%)	unverified(%)	-
train	127(46.7)	50(18.4)	95(34.9)	-
dev	10(40.0)	12(48.0)	3(12.0)	-
test	8(28.6)	12(42.9)	8(28.6)	-

Table 1: Statistics of training (train), development (dev) and testing (test) data sets in SemEval 2017 Task 8.

The train and dev sets are associated with eight different breaking news in English, i.e., *charliehebdo*, *ebola-essien*, *ferguson*, *germanwings-crash*, *ottawashooting*, *prince-toronto*, *putinmissing*, and *sydneysiege*. They are made up of 297 Twitter conversations including $4,519$ tweets in total. Apart from the eight original breaking news, the test set adds two new, i.e., *hillaryshealth* and *save-marinajoyce*, and it contains 28 conversations and $1,049$ tweets. This corpus is collected using the method described in (Zubiaga et al., 2016).

3.2 Data Preprocessing

To deal with the informal characteristic of tweets, we performed tweet normalization to convert elon-

---

[4]https://code.google.com/archive/p/word2vec
[5]http://nlp.stanford.edu/projects/glove/
[6]https://www.csie.ntu.edu.tw/ cjlin/liblinear/
[7]http://scikit-learn.org/

Subtask	Algorithm	Subtask A									Subtask B			
		1-step				2-step					-			
		LR	SVM	DT	ADB	LR	SVM	RF	ADB	GDB	LR	SVM	RF	GDB
Tweet domain	Hashtag					✓				✓	✓	✓	✓	✓
	Mentioned_entity	✓	✓	✓		✓	✓			✓			✓	
	Punctuation	✓	✓	✓	✓	✓	✓	✓		✓		✓	✓	✓
	Emoticon		✓	✓		✓	✓					✓		✓
	Event										✓		✓	✓
Metadata	Tweet metadata	✓	✓	✓	✓	✓						✓	✓	
	User metadata	✓	✓			✓	✓		✓					
Word-cluster	Word-cluster		✓		✓	✓		✓			✓	✓	✓	
Linguistic	unigram			✓				✓	✓					
	unigram_lemma						✓			✓	✓	✓	✓	
	unigram_stem					✓								✓
	bigram													
	bigram_lemma							✓				✓		
	bigram_stem					✓								
	ner							✓			✓		✓	✓
Word Vector	GoogleW2V					✓								
	GloVe	✓	✓				✓							
	SSWE									✓				
	ZSWE							✓						
Accuracy (%)		80.07	81.14	79.36	81.14	**81.49**	81.14	80.07	80.43	81.39	70.03	70.70	64.98	67.34
Ensemble (%)		**83.99**				**80.07**					**71.04**			

Table 2: Results of feature and algorithm selection experiments for both Subtask A and Subtask B. 1-step, 2-step represent the first and second classification of subtask A respectively,

gated words and slang words into original word. For elongated word (e.g., *"sooo"*), we implemented a home-made application to transform it into *"so"*, and for slang words, we collected a big dictionary[8] from the Internet to convert *"LOL"* into *"laugh out loud"*. Then we conducted tokenization, lemmatization and stemming with the aid of *Stanford CoreNLP tools*[9].

3.3 Experiments on training data

The Table 2 lists the results of the best feature set with respect to top learning algorithms on two subtasks. Note that for subtask A, we adopted a two-step classification. The accuracy of 1-step is calculated on two classes (i.e., *comment* and *non-comment*), and that of 2-step is calculated on four classes (i.e., *support*, *deny*, *query* and *comment*). Since the dev set of subtask B is not enough (only 25 samples), we combined train and dev sets and performed a 2-fold cross-validation. Furthermore, we also performed ensemble to combine the results of top learning algorithms with their optimum feature sets, which are shown as the last row in Table 2.

From Table 2, we observe the findings as follows:
(1) Among 7 algorithms, LR and SVM consistently perform well in the three classifications. Besides, ADB does a good job in two classifications in subtask A, RF and GBD have a good perfor-

mance in 2-step of subtask A and subtask B.
(2) Generally, Tweet domain, metadata and Word-cluster features make a considerable contribution for both subtasks, and they can achieve promising performance with different algorithms. The possible reasons are: (a) Tweet domain features not only contain sentiment information (e.g., Punctuation and Emoticon), but also include topic information (e.g., Hashtag, Mentioned_entity, and Event). (b) The numerical characteristic (e.g, tweet favorite count, retweet count, etc) of metadata can indicate that whether a tweet is being closely watched and worthy of commenting. Binary features (e.g., friends count, is-verified, is-protected, etc) reveal that whether the author of a tweet is trustworthy. (c) The Word-cluster feature provides semantic information.
(3) The performance of Linguistic-informed and Word vector features in three classifications is mixed. The Linguistic-informed features do not work in the 1-step, however they contribute to the 2-step classification and subtask B. By observation, the lemmatization and stem n-gram outperform the original n-gram probably because that lemmatization and stem unify the form of words, thus reducing the dimension of feature and unnecessary noise. For Word vector, GloVe slightly outperforms other word vectors.
(4) From the algorithm comparison experiments, the ensemble models for 1-step of subtask A and subtask B are superior to the models using single algorithms, different learning algorithms

---

[8] https://github.com/haierlord/resource/blob/master/slangs
[9] http://stanfordnlp.github.io/CoreNLP/

contribute differently to the classification performance, that is why we conduct majority vote to ensemble those effective learning algorithms. However, we directly use the LR algorithm in 2-step on account of its best performance.

3.4 System Configuration

Based on the above experimental results, we constructed our submissions as follows: For subtask A, we employed an ensemble model incorporating LR, SVM, DT, and ADB for 1-step classification, while used LR directly for 2-step classification. For subtask B, we also adopted an ensemble model with LR, SVM, RF, GDB to predict labels of rumoured tweets, and probabilities of labels returned as confidence values. The parameters of every algorithms are listed as follows: LR with $c=1$, SVM with $kernel=linear$, $c=0.1$, RF with $n\_estimators=10$, ADB with $n\_estimators=100$, GDB with $n\_estimators=100$, and DT with default parameters.

3.5 Results on test data

Tabel 3 shows the officially-released results of our models and top-ranked teams. We ranked the third for both subtasks in terms of *accuracy*, the second for subtask B on the *RMSE* evaluation (a higher *accuracy* is better, while a lower *RMSE* is better). The predict results of test data are inferior to the results of dev set, especially for subtask B. we partly blame it for two reasons: (1) The addition of two breaking news (i.e., *hillaryshealth* and *save-marinajoyce*). The feature set used in subtask B can not capture unseen words in new topics, so the model may have a limited generalizability. (2) The test set is too small (only 28 samples).

Subtask	System	Accuracy(%)	RMSE
	ECNU	**77.8(3)**	-
Subtask A	Turing	78.4(1)	-
	Uwaterloo	78.0(2)	-
	ECNU	**46.4(3)**	**0.736(2)**
Subtask B	NileTMRG	53.6(1)	0.672(1)
	IKM	53.6(2)	0.763(3)

Table 3: Performance of our models and top-ranked teams on both two subtasks. The numbers in the brackets are the official rankings.

4 Conclusion

For both subtasks, we adopted supervised machine learning methods incorporating rich features. We adopted a two-step classifier to address subtask A to solve the imbalance of training data, and a simplified three-classification for subtask B. We originally thought that features with good generalization performance, such as Linguistic-informed and Word vector features would perform well in both subtasks, but in fact that was not the case. On the contrary, good performance can be achieved with several features like Tweet domain and Metadata features closely related with the tweets. From the final results in test data, in the future work, we need to build a topic independent model to achieve better generalizability.

Acknowledgments

This research is supported by grants from Science and Technology Commission of Shanghai Municipality (14DZ2260800 and 15ZR1410700), Shanghai Collaborative Innovation Center of Trustworthy Software for Internet of Things (ZF1213) and NSFC (61402175).

References

Leon Derczynski, Kalina Bontcheva, Maria Liakata, Rob Procter, Geraldine Wong Sak Hoi, and Arkaitz Zubiaga. 2017. SemEval-2017 Task 8: RumourEval: Determining rumour veracity and support for rumours. In *Proceedings of SemEval*. ACL.

Man Lan, Guoshun Wu, Chunyun Xiao, Yuanbin Wu, and Ju Wu. 2016a. Building mutually beneficial relationships between question retrieval and answer ranking to improve performance of community question answering. In *Neural Networks (IJCNN), 2016 International Joint Conference on*. IEEE, pages 832–839.

Man Lan, Zhihua Zhang, Yue Lu, and Ju Wu. 2016b. Three convolutional neural network-based models for learning sentiment word vectors towards sentiment analysis. In *Neural Networks (IJCNN), 2016 International Joint Conference on*. IEEE, pages 3172–3179.

Tomas Mikolov, Ilya Sutskever, Kai Chen, Greg S Corrado, and Jeff Dean. 2013. Distributed representations of words and phrases and their compositionality. In *Advances in neural information processing systems*. pages 3111–3119.

Jeffrey Pennington, Richard Socher, and Christopher D Manning. 2014. Glove: Global vectors for word representation. In *EMNLP*. volume 14, pages 1532–1543.

Fabrizio Sebastiani. 2002. Machine learning in automated text categorization. *ACM computing surveys (CSUR)* 34(1):1–47.

Richard Socher, John Bauer, Christopher D Manning, and Andrew Y Ng. 2013. Parsing with composition-al vector grammars. In *ACL (1)*. pages 455–465.

Duyu Tang, Furu Wei, Nan Yang, Ming Zhou, Ting Li-u, and Bing Qin. 2014. Learning sentiment-specific word embedding for twitter sentiment classification. In *ACL (1)*. pages 1555–1565.

Arkaitz Zubiaga, Maria Liakata, Rob Procter, Geral-dine Wong Sak Hoi, and Peter Tolmie. 2016. Analysing how people orient to and spread rumours in social media by looking at conversational threads. *PloS one* 11(3):e0150989.

IITP at SemEval-2017 Task 8 : A Supervised Approach for Rumour Evaluation

Vikram Singh, Sunny Narayan, Md Shad Akhtar, Asif Ekbal, Pushpak Bhattacharyya
Indian Institute of Technology Patna, India
{vikram.mtcs15,sunny.cs13,shad.pcs15,asif,pb}@iitp.ac.in

Abstract

This paper describes our system participation in the SemEval-2017 Task 8 'RumourEval: Determining rumour veracity and support for rumours'. The objective of this task was to predict the stance and veracity of the underlying rumour. We propose a supervised classification approach employing several lexical, content and twitter specific features for learning. Evaluation shows promising results for both the problems.

1 Introduction

Twitter along with Facebook is widely used social networking site which generates tons of authentic and unauthentic information. The purpose of twitter varies from people to people. Twitter has been greatly used as a communication channel and also as an information source (Zhao and Rosson, 2009). However, Twitter like any other social media platform does not always poses authentic information. It also brings a negative by-product called rumour (Castillo et al., 2011; Derczynski and Bontcheva, 2014; Qazvinian et al., 2011). Rumours are the statement which cannot be verified for its correctness. These rumours may confuse people with the unverified information and drive them in poor decision making. In many organizations(political, administration etc.), detection and support for rumour invites great interest from the concerned authorities.

Recently, researchers across the globe have started addressing the challenges related to rumours. A time sequence classification technique has been proposed for detecting the stance against a rumor (Lukasik et al., 2016). Zubiaga et al. (2016) used sequence of label transitions in tree-structured conversations for classifying stance. A

study on speech act classifier for veracity prediction is proposed in (Vosoughi, 2015). One of the earlier work reported on rumour detection and classification had used twitter specific and content based features for the prediction (Qazvinian et al., 2011).

In this paper we present our proposed system submitted as part of the SemEval-2017 shared task on "RumourEval: Determining rumour veracity and support for rumours". Our system is supervised in nature and uses a diverse set of features (c.f. Section 2.3) for training. The task involves Twitter conversation thread where for every source tweet a number of direct and nested reply tweets are present. An example thread is depicted in Table 1. The task defines two separate sub-problems: A) **S**upport, **D**eny, **Q**uery & **C**omment (SDQC) classification and B) veracity prediction. The first subtask checks the stance of any tweet(source or reply) w.r.t. the underlying rumour. Reply tweet can be direct or nested. Second subtask predicts the veracity of a rumour i.e. *true (rumour)*, *false (not rumour)* or *unverified (its veracity cannot be verified)*. Further, there were two variants of the veracity task: closed and open variants. In closed variant, the veracity prediction has to be made solely from the tweet text only. In addition usage of extra data (Wikipedia article, news article etc.) was allowed for the open variant.

The rest of the paper is organized as follows: Section 2 presents a brief description of the proposed approach. Experimental results and discussion is furnished in Section 3. Finally, we conclude in Section 4.

2 System Overview

We adopted a supervised classification approach for both the tasks. We use Decision Tree (DT), Naive Bayes (NB) and Support Vector Machine

Proceedings of the 11th International Workshop on Semantic Evaluations (SemEval-2017), pages 497–501,
Vancouver, Canada, August 3 - 4, 2017. ©2017 Association for Computational Linguistics

Tweet conversation thread	Stance
Src: Very good on #Putin coup by @CoalsonR: Three Scenarios For A Succession In Russia http://t.co/fotdqxDfEV	Support
Rep1: @andersostlund @CoalsonR @RFERL And how Europe will behave in such a case?	Deny
Rep2: @andersostlund @RFERL Putin'll be made a tsar (and the newborn an heir). Back 2 serfdom as Zorkin suggested.	Comment
Rep3: @andersostlund @CoalsonR @RFERL uhmmm botox sesions far more likely anyway	Comment
Rep4: @andersostlund What are your thoughts on #WhereIsPutin?	Query
Rep5: @tulipgrrl Either a simple flue, more serious illness or serious domestic political problems.	Comment
Rep6: @andersostlund @tulipgrrl :mask:	Deny

Table 1: Twitter conversational thread. Src: Source tweet; Rep#: Replies.

(SVM) as base classifier for prediction of veracity. For stance detection, every instance consists of a pair of source-reply tweet. We extracted features for both the tweets and fed it to the system for the classification. In subsequent subsections we describe dataset, preprocessing and list of features that we use in this work.

2.1 Dataset

The training dataset consists of 272 source tweets for which 3966 replies tweet are present. For tuning the system, validation set contains 256 replies across 25 source tweets. Each source and reply tweet has one of the four label for stance detection namely, *support*, *deny*, *query* and *comment*. For veracity prediction, each of the source tweets belongs to one of the three classes i.e. *true*, *false* and *unverified*. The gold standard test dataset has 28 source and 1021 reply tweets. A detailed statistics is depicted in Table 2.

2.2 Preprocessing

The distribution of different classes in the dataset is very skewed so the first step that we perform is to extract and over sample the under represented class. Classes *support*, *deny* and *comment* were sampled by a factor of 4, 7 and 7 respectively. Afterwards, we perform normalization of urls and usernames in which all urls and username were replaced by keyword someurl and @someuser respectively.

2.3 Features

In this section we describe features that we employed for building the system. We use following set of features for both Subtask A and B.

- **Word Embedding**: Word vectors has been proved to be an efficient technique in capturing semantic property of a word. We use 200-dimension pretrained GloVe model[1] for computing the word embeddings. Sentence embedding is computed by concatenating embeddings of all the words in a tweet. We fix the length of each tweet by padding it to the maximum number of tokens.

- **Vulgar words**: Conversations on Twitter are usually very informal and usage of vulgar words are often in practice. The presence of vulgar words in a sentence declines the orientation of it being a fact, hence, less chances of it being a rumour. We use a list of vulgars words[2][3] and define a binary feature that takes a value '1' if a token is present in the list, otherwise '0'.

- **Twitter specific features**: We use presence and absence of following twitter specific features in this work.

  - **URL and Media**: The presence of metadata indicates that the user is providing with more authentic information. Hence less chances of it being a rumour. For subtask A, a user reply with metadata suggests it to be a *support* or *deny*.

  - Punctuation, Emoticons and Abbreviation.

- **Word count** : Rumour sentences tend to be more elaborative and hence longer while factual data is generally short and precise. Also, user tends to deny a claim in shorter sentence. We, therefore, define number of words in a sentence (excluding stop words and punctuations), as a feature.

- **POS tag**: We use unigram and bigram POS tags extracted from CMU's ARK[4] tool.

In addition, we also implement few of the task specific features listed below. **Subtask A: SDQC**

---

[1]http://nlp.stanford.edu/data/glove.6B.zip

[2]http://fffff.at/googles-official-list-of-bad-words/
[3]http://www.noswearing.com/dictionary
[4]http://www.cs.cmu.edu/ ark/TweetNLP/

Dataset	Overall		Subtask A: SDQC				Subtask B: Veracity		
	Source	Reply	Support	Deny	Query	Comment	True	False	Unverified
Train	272	3966	841	333	330	2734	127	50	95
Dev	25	256	69	11	28	173	10	12	3
Test	28	1021	94	71	106	778	8	12	8

Table 2: Distribution of source and reply tweets with their labels in the dataset

- **Negation words**: Presence of negation word in a tweet signals it to be a denial case. Therefore, we use a binary feature indicating the presence of negation words in the tweet. There were 27 negation words taken into account. The following are the list - no, not, nobody, nothing, none, never, neither, nor, nowhere, hardly, scarcely, barely, don't, isn't, wasn't, shouldn't, wouldn't, couldn't, doesn't, hasn't, haven't, didn't, ain't, can't, doesn't and won't.

- *Wh-* **words:** Query usually contains *Wh-* words (What, Where, Which, When, Who, Why, Whom, Whose). We define a binary feature that fires when a tweet contains one of these words.

Subtask B: Veracity prediction

- **Presence of Opinion words**: An opinion carrying sentence cannot be a fact, hence, makes it a probable candidate for rumour. We define two features based on MPQA subjectivity lexicon (Wilson et al., 2005). The first feature takes opinion word count, whereas, the second feature checks the presence of at least one strongly subjective token in a tweet.

- **Number of adjectives**: An interesting relation between presence of adjectives in a sentence and its subjectivity has been explored in (Hatzivassiloglou and Wiebe, 2000). As per (Wiebe, 2000) the probability of a sentence being subjective, given that there is at least one adjective in the sentence, is 0.545. If a sentence is objective then its chances of being a rumour is very low. Therefore, we use a binary feature that denotes presence/absence of adjectives in a tweet.

Since, prediction in close variants has the limitation of using the tweet only, we also extracted 'presence of media' as a binary feature value for the open variant only.

3   Experiments and Results

We use scikit learn machine learning package[5] for the implementation. As defined by shared task, we use classification accuracy and micro-average accuracy as evaluation metrics for SDQC and veracity prediction respectively. For subtask A, we try various feature combinations to train a SVM classifier. Table 3 reports the validation accuracy for SDQC subtasks. As a result we select the feature combination that performs best during the validation phase and submit it for the final prediction on the test dataset. In veracity prediction task, we em-

	Features	Accuracy
A.	Unigram	54.2969%
B.	Unigram + POS	62.1093%
C.	W.E.	61.3281%
D.	(C + POS)	63.2813%
E.	(D + URL and Media)	62.8906%
F.	(E + Twitter Specific)	63.2813%
G.	(F + Negation words)	63.2813%
H.	(G + Wh-Word)	63.6719%
I.	**(H + Vulgar words)**	**64.0625%**
J.	(I + Punctuation)	63.6719%
K.	**(J + Word count)**	**64.0625%**

Table 3: SDQC: Accuracy on Development Set

ploy three classifiers i.e. Decision Tree, SVM and Naive Bayes to the evaluate our system. We observe that the among three classifiers performance of Naive Bayes is comparatively better than others as shown in Table 4. For evaluation of test dataset we use our best classifier i.e. Naive Bayes. Our system reports an accuracy of 64.1% for the SDQC classification. For subtask B, we also compute a confidence score for each prediction. We obtain micro-average accuracies of 39.28% and 28.57% respectively for the open and close variants. Reported root mean squared error (RMSE) for the two variants are 0.746 and 0.807. It should be noted that we were the only team which submit-

---

[5] http://scikit-learn.org

ted their system in open variant category. Table 5 depicts the evaluation result on test dataset.

Classifiers	Micro-average Accuracy	
	Open	Closed
Decision Tree	58.23%	54.54%
SVM	58.75%	59.09%
Naive Bayes	59.09%	**63.0%**

Table 4: Veracity: Accuracy on Development Set

Task	Accuracy	RMSE
Subtask A	64.1%	-
Subtask B(Open)	39.28%	0.746
Subtask B(Closed)	28.57%	0.807

Table 5: Evaluation results on test set.

Further, we perform error analysis on the results. Confusion matrix for SDQC classification is depicted in Table 6. We observe that most of the classes were confused with the *comment* class. The possible reason could be the presence of relatively high number instances for the comment 'class'. Similarly, Table 7 & 8 shows confusion matrix for both open and closed variants of subtask B. Recall for 'true' is encouraging i.e. 75% but the problem lies with the precision which is merely 28% & 25% for open and close variants respectively.

	Support	Deny	Query	Comment
Support	**42**	2	2	48
Deny	11	**9**	2	49
Query	9	7	**35**	55
Comment	125	35	32	**586**

Table 6: SDQC: Confusion Matrix on test set (S: support, D: deny, Q: query, C: comment)

	True	False	Unverified
True	**6**	2	0
False	7	**5**	0
Unverified	8	0	**0**

Table 7: Veracity (Open): Confusion Matrix on test set

4 Conclusion

In this paper we proposed a supervised approach for determining the support and veracity of a rumour as part of the SemEval-2017 shared task on

	True	False	Unverified
True	**6**	2	0
False	10	**2**	0
Unverified	8	0	**0**

Table 8: Veracity (Closed): Confusion Matrix on test set

rumour evaluation. As base classification algorithm we use Naive Bayes, Support Vector Machine and Decision Tree for building the model. In future, we would like to explore deep learning technique and other relevant features to further improve the performance of the system.

References

Carlos Castillo, Marcelo Mendoza, and Barbara Poblete. 2011. Information credibility on twitter. In *Proceedings of the 20th international conference on World wide web*. ACM, pages 675–684.

Leon Derczynski and Kalina Bontcheva. 2014. Pheme: Veracity in digital social networks. In *UMAP Workshops*.

Vasileios Hatzivassiloglou and Janyce M Wiebe. 2000. Effects of adjective orientation and gradability on sentence subjectivity. In *Proceedings of the 18th conference on Computational linguistics-Volume 1*. Association for Computational Linguistics, pages 299–305.

Michal Lukasik, PK Srijith, Duy Vu, Kalina Bontcheva, Arkaitz Zubiaga, and Trevor Cohn. 2016. Hawkes processes for continuous time sequence classification: an application to rumour stance classification in twitter. In *Proceedings of 54th Annual Meeting of the Association for Computational Linguistics*. Association for Computational Linguistics, pages 393–398.

Vahed Qazvinian, Emily Rosengren, Dragomir R Radev, and Qiaozhu Mei. 2011. Rumor has it: Identifying misinformation in microblogs. In *Proceedings of the Conference on Empirical Methods in Natural Language Processing*. Association for Computational Linguistics, pages 1589–1599.

Soroush Vosoughi. 2015. *Automatic detection and verification of rumors on Twitter*. Ph.D. thesis, Massachusetts Institute of Technology.

Janyce Wiebe. 2000. Learning subjective adjectives from corpora. In *AAAI/IAAI*. pages 735–740.

Theresa Wilson, Janyce Wiebe, and Paul Hoffmann. 2005. Recognizing contextual polarity in phrase-level sentiment analysis. In *Proceedings of the conference on human language technology and empirical methods in natural language processing*. Association for Computational Linguistics, pages 347–354.

Dejin Zhao and Mary Beth Rosson. 2009. How and why people twitter: the role that micro-blogging plays in informal communication at work. In *Proceedings of the ACM 2009 international conference on Supporting group work*. ACM, pages 243–252.

Arkaitz Zubiaga, Elena Kochkina, Maria Liakata, Rob Procter, and Michal Lukasik. 2016. Stance classification in rumours as a sequential task exploiting the tree structure of social media conversations. *arXiv preprint arXiv:1609.09028* .

SemEval-2017 Task 4: Sentiment Analysis in Twitter

Sara Rosenthal♣, Noura Farra◇, Preslav Nakov♡
♡Qatar Computing Research Institute, Hamad bin Khalifa University, Qatar
◇Department of Computer Science, Columbia University
♣IBM Research, USA

Abstract

This paper describes the fifth year of the *Sentiment Analysis in Twitter task*. SemEval-2017 Task 4 continues with a rerun of the subtasks of SemEval-2016 Task 4, which include identifying the *overall sentiment* of the tweet, *sentiment towards a topic* with classification on a two-point and on a five-point ordinal scale, and *quantification* of the distribution of sentiment towards a topic across a number of tweets: again on a two-point and on a five-point ordinal scale. Compared to 2016, we made two changes: (*i*) we introduced a new language, Arabic, for all subtasks, and (*ii*) we made available information from the profiles of the Twitter users who posted the target tweets. The task continues to be very popular, with a total of 48 teams participating this year.

1 Introduction

The identification of sentiment in text is an important field of study, with social media platforms such as Twitter garnering the interest of researchers in language processing as well as in political and social sciences. The task usually involves detecting whether a piece of text expresses a POSITIVE, a NEGATIVE, or a NEUTRAL sentiment; the sentiment can be general or about a specific topic, e.g., a person, a product, or an event.

The *Sentiment Analysis in Twitter* task has been run yearly at SemEval since 2013 (Nakov et al., 2013; Rosenthal et al., 2014; Nakov et al., 2016b), with the 2015 task introducing sentiment towards a topic (Rosenthal et al., 2015) and the 2016 task introducing tweet quantification and five-point ordinal classification (Nakov et al., 2016a).

SemEval is the International Workshop on Semantic Evaluation, formerly SensEval. It is an ongoing series of evaluations of computational semantic analysis systems, organized under the umbrella of SIGLEX, the Special Interest Group on the Lexicon of the Association for Computational Linguistics. Other related tasks at SemEval have explored sentiment analysis of product review and their aspects (Pontiki et al., 2014, 2015, 2016), sentiment analysis of figurative language on Twitter (Ghosh et al., 2015), implicit event polarity (Russo et al., 2015), detecting stance in tweets (Mohammad et al., 2016a), out-of-context sentiment intensity of words and phrases (Kiritchenko et al., 2016), and emotion detection (Strapparava and Mihalcea, 2007). Some of these tasks featured languages other than English, such as Arabic (Pontiki et al., 2016; Mohammad et al., 2016a); however, they did not target tweets, nor did they focus on sentiment towards a topic.

This year, we performed a re-run of the subtasks in SemEval-2016 Task 4, which, in addition to the overall sentiment of a tweet, featured classification, ordinal regression, and quantification with respect to a topic. Furthermore, we introduced a new language, Arabic. Finally, we made available to the participants demographic information about the users who posted the tweets, which we extracted from the respective public profiles.

Ordinal Classification As last year, SemEval-2017 Task 4 includes sentiment analysis on a five-point scale {HIGHLYPOSITIVE, POSITIVE, NEUTRAL, NEGATIVE, HIGHLYNEGATIVE}, which is in line with product ratings occurring in the corporate world, e.g., Amazon, TripAdvisor, and Yelp. In machine learning terms, moving from a categorical two-point scale to an ordered five-point scale means moving from binary to *ordinal classification* (aka *ordinal regression*).

Proceedings of the 11th International Workshop on Semantic Evaluations (SemEval-2017), pages 502–518,
Vancouver, Canada, August 3 - 4, 2017. ©2017 Association for Computational Linguistics

Tweet Quantification SemEval-2017 Task 4 includes *tweet quantification* tasks along with tweet classification tasks, also on 2-point and 5-point scales. While the tweet classification task is concerned with whether a specific tweet expresses a given sentiment towards a topic, the tweet quantification task looks at estimating the *distribution* of tweets about a given topic across the different sentiment classes. Most (if not all) tweet sentiment classification studies within political science (Borge-Holthoefer et al., 2015; Kaya et al., 2013; Marchetti-Bowick and Chambers, 2012), economics (Bollen et al., 2011; O'Connor et al., 2010), social science (Dodds et al., 2011), and market research (Burton and Soboleva, 2011; Qureshi et al., 2013), study Twitter with an interest in aggregate statistics about sentiment and are *not* interested in the sentiment expressed in individual tweets. We should also note that quantification is not a mere byproduct of classification, as it can be addressed using different approaches and it also needs different evaluation measures (Forman, 2008; Esuli and Sebastiani, 2015).

Analysis in Arabic This year, we added a new language, Arabic, in order to encourage participants to experiment with multilingual and cross-lingual approaches for sentiment analysis. Our objective was to expand the Twitter sentiment analysis resources available to the research community, not only for general multilingual sentiment analysis, but also for multilingual sentiment analysis *towards a topic*, which is still a largely unexplored research direction for many languages and in particular for morphologically complex languages such as Arabic.

Arabic has become an emergent language for sentiment analysis, especially as more resources and tools for it have recently become available. It is also both interesting and challenging due to its rich morphology and abundance of dialectal use in Twitter. Early Arabic studies focused on sentiment analysis in newswire (Abdul-Mageed and Diab, 2011; Elarnaoty et al., 2012), but recently there has been a lot more work on social media, especially Twitter (Mourad and Darwish, 2013; Abdul-Mageed et al., 2014; Refaee and Rieser, 2014; Salameh et al., 2015), where the challenges of sentiment analysis are compounded by the presence of multiple dialects and orthographical variants, which are frequently used in conjunction with the formal written language.

Some work studied the utility of machine translation for sentiment analysis of Arabic texts (Salameh et al., 2015; Mohammad et al., 2016b; Refaee and Rieser, 2015), identification of sentiment holders (Elarnaoty et al., 2012), and sentiment targets (Al-Smadi et al., 2015; Farra et al., 2015; Farra and McKeown, 2017). We believe that the development of a standard Arabic Twitter dataset for sentiment, and particularly with respect to topics, will encourage further research in this regard.

User Information Demographic information in Twitter has been studied and analyzed using network analysis and natural language processing (NLP) techniques (Mislove et al., 2011; Nguyen et al., 2013; Rosenthal and McKeown, 2016). Recent work has shown that user information and information from the network can help sentiment analysis in other corpora (Hovy, 2015) and in Twitter (Volkova et al., 2013; Yang and Eisenstein, 2015). Thus, this year we encouraged participants to use information from the public profiles of Twitter users such as demographics (e.g., age, location) as well as information from the rest of the social network (e.g., sentiment of the tweets of friends), with the goal of analyzing the impact of this information on improving sentiment analysis.

The rest of this paper is organized as follows. Section 2 presents in more detail the five subtasks of SemEval-2017 Task 4. Section 3 describes the English and the Arabic datasets and how we created them. Section 4 introduces and motivates the evaluation measures for each subtask. Section 5 presents the results of the evaluation and discusses the techniques and the tools that the participants used. Finally, Section 6 concludes and points to some possible directions for future work.

2 Task Definition

SemEval-2017 Task 4 consists of five subtasks, each offered for both Arabic and English:

1. **Subtask A:** Given a tweet, decide whether it expresses POSITIVE, NEGATIVE or NEUTRAL sentiment.

2. **Subtask B:** Given a tweet and a topic, classify the sentiment conveyed towards that topic on a two-point scale: POSITIVE vs. NEGATIVE.

3. **Subtask C:** Given a tweet and a topic, classify the sentiment conveyed in the tweet towards that topic on a five-point scale: STRONGLYPOSITIVE, WEAKLYPOSITIVE, NEUTRAL, WEAKLYNEGATIVE, and STRONGLYNEGATIVE.

4. **Subtask D:** Given a set of tweets about a topic, estimate the *distribution* of tweets across the POSITIVE and NEGATIVE classes.

5. **Subtask E:** Given a set of tweets about a topic, estimate the *distribution* of tweets across the five classes: STRONGLYPOSITIVE, WEAKLYPOSITIVE, NEUTRAL, WEAKLYNEGATIVE, and STRONGLYNEGATIVE.

Languages: English and Arabic			
	Goal	**Granularity**	**Topic**
A	Classification	3-point	No
B	Classification	2-point	Yes
C	Classification	5-point	Yes
D	Quantification	2-point	Yes
E	Quantification	5-point	Yes

Table 1: Summary of the subtasks.

Each subtask is run for both English and Arabic. Subtask A has been run in all previous editions of the task and continues to be the most popular one (see section 5.) Subtasks B-E have all been run at SemEval-2016 Task 4 (Nakov et al., 2016a), with variants running in 2015 (Rosenthal et al., 2015). Table 1 shows a summary of the subtasks.

3 Datasets

Our datasets consist of tweets annotated for sentiment on a 2-point, 3-point, and 5-point scales. We made available to participants all the data from previous years (Nakov et al., 2016a) for the English training sets, and we collected new training data for Arabic, as well as new test sets for both English and Arabic. The annotation scheme remained the same as last year (Nakov et al., 2016a), with the key new contribution being to apply the task and instructions to Arabic as well as providing a script to download basic user information. All annotations were performed on CrowdFlower. Note that we release all our datasets to the research community to be used freely beyond SemEval.

3.1 Tweet Collection

We chose English and Arabic topics based on popular current events that were trending on Twitter, both internationally and in specific Arabic-speaking countries, using local and global Twitter trends.[1] The topics included a range of named entities (e.g., *Donald Trump, iPhone*), geopolitical entities (e.g., *Aleppo, Palestine*), and other entities (e.g., *Syrian refugees, Dakota Access Pipeline, Western media, gun control,* and *vegetarianism*). We then used the Twitter API to download tweets, along with corresponding user information, containing mentions of these topics in the specified language. We intentionally chose to use some overlapping topics between the two languages in order to encourage cross-language approaches.

We automatically filtered the tweets for duplicates and we removed those for which the bag-of-words cosine similarity exceeded 0.6. We then retained only the topics for which at least 100 tweets remained. The training tweets for Arabic were collected over the period of September-November 2016 and all test tweets were collected over the period of December 2016-January 2017.

For both English and Arabic, the topics for the test dataset were different from those in the training and in the development datasets.

3.2 Annotation using CrowdFlower

We used CrowdFlower to annotate the new training and testing tweets. The annotators were asked to indicate the overall polarity of the tweet (on a five-point scale) as well as the polarity of the tweet towards the given target topic (again, on a five-point scale), as described in (Nakov et al., 2016a). We also provided additional examples, some of which are shown in Tables 2 and 3. In particular, we stressed that topic-level positive or negative sentiment needed to express an opinion about the topic itself rather than about a positive or a negative event occurring in the context of the topic (see for example, the third row of Table 3).

Each tweet was annotated by at least five people, and we created many hidden tests for quality control, which we used to reject annotations by contributors who missed a large number of the hidden tests. We also created pilot runs, which helped us adjust the annotation instructions until we found, based on manual inspection, the quality of the annotated tweets to be satisfactory.

---

[1] https://trends24.in/

504

Tweet	Overall Sentiment	Topic-level Sentiment
Who are you tomorrow? Will you make me smile or just bring me sorrow? #HottieOfTheWeek Demi Lovato	NEUTRAL	Demi Lovato: POSITIVE
Saturday without Leeds United is like Sunday dinner it doesn't feel normal at all (Ryan)	WEAKLYNEGATIVE	Leeds United: HIGHLYPOSITIVE
Apple releases a new update of its OS	NEUTRAL	Apple: NEUTRAL

Table 2: Some English example annotations that we provided to the annotators.

Tweet	Overall Sentiment	Topic-level Sentiment
أبل تطلق النسخة التجريبية الرابعة لنظام التشغيل *Apple releases a fourth beta of its OS*	NEUTRAL	أبل *Apple*: NEUTRAL
المايسترو ... الاسطورة روجر فدرر ملك اللّعب الخلفي من اجمل لقطاته *The maestro ... the legend Roger Federer king of the back-hand game one of his best shots*	HIGHLYPOSITIVE	فدرر *Federer*: HIGHLYPOSITIVE
اللّاجئون يواجهون الصعوبات *Refugees are facing difficulties*	WEAKLYNEGATIVE	اللّاجئون *Refugees* : NEUTRAL

Table 3: Some Arabic example annotations that we provided to the annotators.

For Arabic, the contributors tended to annotate somewhat conservatively, and thus a very small number of HIGHLYPOSITIVE and HIGHLYNEG-ATIVE annotations were consolidated, despite us having provided examples of such annotations.

3.3 Consolidating the Annotations

As the annotations are on a five-point scale, where the expected agreement is lower, we used a two-step procedure. If three out of the five annotators agreed on a label, we accepted the label. Otherwise, we first mapped the categorical labels to the integer values -2, -1, 0, 1, 2. Then we calculated the average, and finally we mapped that average to the closest integer value. In order to counter-balance the tendency of the average to stay away from the extreme values -2 and 2, and also to prefer 0, we did not use rounding at ±0.5 and ±1.5, but at ±0.4 and ±1.4 instead. Finally, note that the values -2, -1, 0, 1, 2 are to be interpreted as STRONGLYNEGATIVE, WEAKLYNEGATIVE, NEUTRAL, WEAKLYPOSI-TIVE, and STRONGLYPOSITIVE, respectively.

3.4 Data Statistics

The English training and development data this year consisted of the data from all previous editions of this task (Nakov et al., 2013; Rosenthal et al., 2014, 2015; Nakov et al., 2016b). Unlike in previous years, we did not set aside data to assess progress compared to prior years. Therefore, we allowed all data to be used for training and development.

For evaluation, we used the newly-created data described in the previous subsection. Tables 4 and 5 show the statistics for the English and Arabic data. For English, we only show the aggregate statistics for the training data; the breakdown from prior years can be found in (Nakov et al., 2016a). Note that the same tweets were annotated for multiple subtasks, so there is overlap between the tweets across the tasks. Duplicates may have occurred where the same tweet was extracted for multiple topics.

As Arabic is a new language this year, we created for it a default train-development split of the Arabic data for the participants to use if they wished to do so.

3.5 Data Distribution

As in previous years, we provided the participants with a script[2] to download the training tweets given IDs. In addition, this year we also included in the script the option to download basic user information for the author of each tweet: user id, follower count, status count, description, friend count, location, language, name, and time zone. To ensure a fair evaluation, the test set was provided via download and included the tweets as well as the basic user information provided by the download script. The training and the test data is available for downloaded on our task page.[3]

---

[2]https://github.com/seirasto/twitter_download

[3]http://alt.qcri.org/semeval2017/task4/index.php?id=data-and-tools

Dataset	Subtask	Topics	Positive		Neutral	Negative		Total
			2	**1**	**0**	**−1**	**−2**	
Train	A	N/A	19,902		22,591	7,840		50,333
	B, D	373	14,951		1,544	4,013		20,508
	C, E	200	1,020	12,922	12,993	3,398	299	30,632
Test	A	N/A	2375		5,937	3,972		12,284
	B, D	125	2,463		—	3,722		6,185
	C, E	125	131	2,332	6,194	3,545	177	12,379

Table 4: Statistics about the English training and testing datasets. The training data is the aggregate of all data from prior years, while the testing data is new.

Dataset	Subtask	Topics	Positive		Neutral	Negative		Total
			2	**1**	**0**	**−1**	**−2**	
Train	A	N/A	743		1,470	1,142		3,355
	B, D	34	885		—	771		1,656
	C, E	34	1	884	1699	770	1	3,355
Test	A	N/A	1,514		2,364	2,222		6,100
	B, D	61	1,561		—	1,196		2,757
	C, E	61	13	1,548	3,343	1,175	21	6,100

Table 5: Statistics about the newly collected Arabic training and testing datasets.

4 Evaluation Measures

This section describes the evaluation measures for our five subtasks. Note that for Subtasks B to E, the datasets are each subdivided into a number of topics, and the subtask needs to be carried out independently for each topic. As a result, each of the evaluation measures will be "macroaveraged" across the topics, i.e., we compute the measure individually for each topic, and we then average the results across the topics.

4.1 Subtask A: Overall Sentiment of a Tweet

Our primary measure is AvgRec, or *average recall*, which is recall averaged across the POSITIVE (P), NEGATIVE (N), and NEUTRAL (U) classes. This measure has desirable theoretical properties (Sebastiani, 2015), and is also the one we use as primarily for Subtask B. It is computed as follows:

$$AvgRec = \frac{1}{3}(R^P + R^N + R^U) \qquad (1)$$

where R^P, R^N and R^U refer to recall with respect to the POSITIVE, the NEGATIVE, and the NEUTRAL class, respectively. See (Nakov et al., 2016a) for more detail.

AvgRec ranges in $[0, 1]$, where a value of 1 is achieved only by the perfect classifier (i.e., the classifier that correctly classifies all items), a value of 0 is achieved only by the perverse classifier (the classifier that misclassifies all items), while 0.3333 is both (*i*) the value for a trivial classifier (i.e., one that assigns all tweets to the same class – be it POSITIVE, NEGATIVE, or NEUTRAL), and (*ii*) the expected value of a random classifier.

The advantage of *AvgRec* over "standard" accuracy is that it is more robust to class imbalance. The accuracy of the majority-class classifier is the relative frequency (aka "prevalence") of the majority class, that may be much higher than 0.5 if the test set is imbalanced. Standard F_1 is also sensitive to class imbalance for the same reason. Another advantage of *AvgRec* over F_1 is that *AvgRec* is invariant with respect to switching POSITIVE with NEGATIVE, while F_1 is not. See (Sebastiani, 2015) for more detail on *AvgRec*.

We further use two secondary measures: accuracy and F_1^{PN}. The latter was the primary evaluation measure for Subtask A in previous editions of the task. It is macro-average F_1, calculated over the POSITIVE and the NEGATIVE classes (note the exclusion of NEUTRAL). This year, we demoted F_1^{PN} to a secondary evaluation measure. It is calculated as follows:

$$F_1^{PN} = \frac{1}{2}(F_1^P + F_1^N) \qquad (2)$$

where F_1^P and F_1^N refer to F_1 with respect to the POSITIVE and the NEGATIVE class, respectively.

4.2 Subtask B: Topic-Based Classification on a 2-point Scale

As in 2016, our primary evaluation measure for subtask B is average recall, or AvgRec (note that there are only two classes for this subtask):

$$AvgRec = \frac{1}{2}(R^P + R^N) \qquad (3)$$

We further use accuracy and F_1 as secondary measures for subtask B. Finally, as subtask B is topic-based, we computed each metric individually for each topic, and we then averaged the result across the topics to yield the final score.

4.3 Subtask C: Topic-based Classification on a 5-point Scale

Subtask C is an *ordinal classification* (also known as *ordinal regression*) task, in which each tweet must be classified into exactly one of the classes in $\mathcal{C}$={HIGHLYPOSITIVE, POSITIVE, NEUTRAL, NEGATIVE, HIGHLYNEGATIVE}, represented in our dataset by numbers in $\{+2,+1,0,-1,-2\}$, with a total order defined on $\mathcal{C}$.

We adopt an evaluation measure that takes the order of the five classes into account. For instance, misclassifying a HIGHLYNEGATIVE example as HIGHLYPOSITIVE is a bigger mistake than misclassifying it as NEGATIVE or as NEUTRAL.

As in SemEval-2016 Task 4, we use *macro-average mean absolute error* (MAE^M) as the main ordinal classification measure:

$$MAE^M(h, Te) = \frac{1}{|\mathcal{C}|} \sum_{j=1}^{|\mathcal{C}|} \frac{1}{|Te_j|} \sum_{\mathbf{x}_i \in Te_j} |h(\mathbf{x}_i) - y_i|$$

where y_i denotes the true label of item $\mathbf{x}_i$, $h(\mathbf{x}_i)$ is its predicted label, Te_j denotes the set of test documents whose true class is c_j, $|h(\mathbf{x}_i) - y_i|$ denotes the "distance" between classes $h(\mathbf{x}_i)$ and y_i (e.g., the distance between HIGHLYPOSITIVE and NEGATIVE is 3), and the "M" superscript indicates "macroaveraging".

The advantage of MAE^M over "standard" mean absolute error, which is defined as

$$MAE^\mu(h, Te) = \frac{1}{|Te|} \sum_{\mathbf{x}_i \in Te} |h(\mathbf{x}_i) - y_i| \qquad (4)$$

is that it is robust to class imbalance (which is useful, given the imbalanced nature of our dataset). On perfectly balanced datasets MAE^M and MAE^μ are equivalent.

MAE^M is an extension of macro-average recall for ordinal regression; yet, it is a measure of error, and thus lower values are better. We also use MAE^μ as a secondary measure, in order to provide better consistency with Subtasks A and B. These measures are computed for each topic, and the results are then averaged across all topics to yield the final score. See (Baccianella et al., 2009) for more detail about MAE^M and MAE^μ.

4.4 Subtask D: Tweet Quantification on a 2-point Scale

Subtask D assumes a binary quantification setup, in which each tweet is classified as POSITIVE or NEGATIVE, and the distribution across classes must be estimated. The difference with binary classification is that errors of different polarity (e.g., a false positive and a false negative for the same class) can compensate for each other in quantification. Quantification is thus a more lenient task than classification, since a perfect classifier is also a perfect quantifier, but a perfect quantifier is not necessarily a perfect classifier.

For evaluating binary quantification, we keep the *Kullback-Leibler Divergence (KLD)* measure used in 2016 along with additive smoothing (Nakov et al., 2016a; Forman, 2005). KLD was proposed as a quantification measure in (Forman, 2005), and is defined as follows:

$$KLD(\hat{p}, p, \mathcal{C}) = \sum_{c_j \in \mathcal{C}} p(c_j) \log_e \frac{p(c_j)}{\hat{p}(c_j)} \qquad (5)$$

KLD is a measure of the error made in estimating a true distribution p over a set $\mathcal{C}$ of classes by means of a predicted distribution $\hat{p}$. Like MAE^M, KLD is a measure of error, which means that lower values are better. KLD ranges between 0 (best) and $+\infty$ (worst).

Note that the upper bound of KLD is not finite since Equation 5 has predicted prevalences, and not true prevalences, at the denominator: that is, by making a predicted prevalence $\hat{p}(c_j)$ infinitely small we can make KLD infinitely large. To solve this problem, in computing KLD we smooth both $p(c_j)$ and $\hat{p}(c_j)$ via additive smoothing, i.e.,

$$p^s(c_j) = \frac{p(c_j) + \epsilon}{(\sum_{c_j \in \mathcal{C}} p(c_j)) + \epsilon \cdot |\mathcal{C}|}$$
$$= \frac{p(c_j) + \epsilon}{1 + \epsilon \cdot |\mathcal{C}|} \qquad (6)$$

where $p^s(c_j)$ denotes the smoothed version of $p(c_j)$ and the denominator is just a normalizer (same for the $\hat{p}^s(c_j)$'s); the quantity $\epsilon = \frac{1}{2 \cdot |Te|}$ is used as a smoothing factor, where Te denotes the test dataset.

The smoothed versions of $p(c_j)$ and $\hat{p}(c_j)$ are used in place of their original versions in Equation 5; as a result, KLD is always defined and still returns a value of 0 when p and $\hat{p}$ coincide.

Like MAE^M, KLD is a measure of error, which means that lower values are better. We further use two secondary error-based evaluation measures: *absolute error* (AE), and *relative absolute error* (RAE).

Again, the measures are computed individually for each topic, and the results are averaged across the topics to yield the final score.

4.5 Subtask E: Tweet Quantification on a 5-point Scale

Subtask E is an ordinal quantification task. As in binary quantification, the goal is to compute the distribution across classes, this time assuming a quantification setup.

Here each tweet belongs exactly to one of the classes in $C=\{$HIGHLYPOSITIVE, POSITIVE, NEUTRAL, NEGATIVE, HIGHLYNEGATIVE$\}$, where there is a total order on C. As in binary quantification, the task is to compute an estimate $\hat{p}(c_j)$ of the relative frequency $p(c_j)$ in the test tweets of all the classes $c_j \in C$.

The measure we adopt for ordinal quantification is the *Earth Mover's Distance* (Rubner et al., 2000), also known as the *Vaseršteĭn metric* (Rüschendorf, 2001), a measure well-known in the field of computer vision. EMD is currently the only known measure for ordinal quantification. It is defined for the general case in which a distance $d(c', c'')$ is defined for each $c', c'' \in C$. When there is a total order on the classes in C and $d(c_i, c_{i+1}) = 1$ for all $i \in \{1, ..., (C-1)\}$, the Earth Mover's Distance is defined as

$$EMD(\hat{p}, p) = \sum_{j=1}^{|C|-1} |\sum_{i=1}^{j} \hat{p}(c_i) - \sum_{i=1}^{j} p(c_i)| \quad (7)$$

and can be computed in $|C|$ steps from the estimated and true class prevalences.

Like KLD, EMD is a measure of error, so lower values are better; EMD ranges between 0 (best) and $|C| - 1$ (worst). See (Esuli and Sebastiani, 2010) for more detail on EMD.

As before, EMD is computed individually for each topic, and the results are then averaged across all topics to yield the final score. For more detail on EMD, the reader is referred to (Esuli and Sebastiani, 2010) and to last year's task description paper (Nakov et al., 2016a).

5 Participants and Results

A total of 48 teams participated in SemEval-2017 Task 4 this year. As in previous years, the most popular subtask this year was Subtask A, with 38 teams participating in the English subtask A, and 8 teams participating in the Arabic subtask A. Overall, there were 46 teams who participated in some English subtask and 9 teams that participated in some Arabic subtask. There were 28 teams that participated in a subtask other than subtask A. Moreover, two teams (OMAM and ELiRF-UPV) participated in all English and in all Arabic subtasks. There were 9 teams that participated in the topic versions of the subtasks but not in subtask A, reflecting a growing interest among researchers in developing systems for topic-specific analysis.

5.1 Common Resources and Methods

In terms of methods, the use of deep learning stands out in particular, and we also see an increase over the last year. There were at least 20 teams who used deep learning and neural network methods such as CNN and LSTM networks. Supervised SVM and Liblinear were also very popular, with several participants combining SVM with neural network methods or SVM with dense word embedding features. Other teams used classifiers such as Maximum Entropy, Logistic Regression, Random Forest, Naïve Bayes classifier, and Conditional Random Fields.

Common software used included Python (with the sklearn and numpy libraries), Java, Tensorflow, Weka, NLTK, Keras, Theano, and Stanford CoreNLP. The most common external datasets used were sentiment140 as a lexicon, pre-trained word2vec embeddings. Many teams further gathered additional tweets using the Twitter API that were not annotated for sentiment. These were used for distant supervision, lexicon building, and word vector training.

In the following subsections, we present the results and the ranking for each subtask, and we highlight the best-performing systems for each subtask.

#	System	$AvgRec$	F_1^{PN}	Acc
1	DataStories	**0.681**$_1$	0.677$_2$	0.651$_5$
	BB_twtr	**0.681**$_1$	0.685$_1$	0.658$_3$
3	LIA	**0.676**$_3$	0.674$_3$	0.661$_2$
4	Senti17	**0.674**$_4$	0.665$_4$	0.652$_4$
5	NNEMBs	**0.669**$_5$	0.658$_5$	0.664$_1$
6	Tweester	**0.659**$_6$	0.648$_6$	0.648$_6$
7	INGEOTEC	**0.649**$_7$	0.645$_7$	0.633$_{11}$
8	SiTAKA	**0.645**$_8$	0.628$_9$	0.643$_9$
9	TSA-INF	**0.643**$_9$	0.620$_{11}$	0.616$_{17}$
10	UCSC-NLP	**0.642**$_{10}$	0.624$_{10}$	0.565$_{30}$
11	HLP@UPENN	**0.637**$_{11}$	0.632$_8$	0.646$_8$
12	YNU-HPCC	**0.633**$_{12}$	0.612$_{15}$	0.647$_7$
	SentiME++	**0.633**$_{12}$	0.613$_{13}$	0.601$_{23}$
14	ELiRF-UPV	**0.632**$_{14}$	0.619$_{12}$	0.599$_{24}$
15	ECNU	**0.628**$_{15}$	0.613$_{13}$	0.630$_{12}$
16	TakeLab	**0.627**$_{16}$	0.607$_{16}$	0.628$_{14}$
17	DUTH	**0.621**$_{17}$	0.605$_{17}$	0.640$_{10}$
18	CrystalNest	**0.619**$_{18}$	0.593$_{19}$	0.629$_{13}$
19	deepSA	**0.618**$_{19}$	0.587$_{20}$	0.616$_{17}$
20	NILC-USP	**0.612**$_{20}$	0.595$_{18}$	0.617$_{16}$
21	Ti-Senti	**0.607**$_{21}$	0.577$_{22}$	0.627$_{15}$
22	BUSEM	**0.605**$_{22}$	0.587$_{20}$	0.603$_{22}$
23	EICA	**0.595**$_{23}$	0.555$_{24}$	0.599$_{24}$
24	OMAM	**0.590**$_{24}$	0.542$_{26}$	0.615$_{19}$
25	Adullam	**0.589**$_{25}$	0.552$_{25}$	0.614$_{20}$
26	NileTMRG	**0.578**$_{26}$	0.515$_{32}$	0.606$_{21}$
27	Amobee-C-137	**0.575**$_{27}$	0.520$_{30}$	0.587$_{27}$
28	ej-za-2017	**0.571**$_{28}$	0.539$_{27}$	0.582$_{28}$
	LSIS	**0.571**$_{28}$	0.561$_{23}$	0.521$_{34}$
30	XJSA	**0.556**$_{30}$	0.519$_{31}$	0.575$_{29}$
31	Neverland-THU	**0.555**$_{31}$	0.507$_{33}$	0.597$_{26}$
32	MI&T-Lab	**0.551**$_{32}$	0.522$_{29}$	0.561$_{31}$
33	diegoref	**0.546**$_{33}$	0.527$_{28}$	0.540$_{33}$
34	xiwu	**0.479**$_{34}$	0.365$_{34}$	0.547$_{32}$
35	SSN_MLRG1	**0.431**$_{35}$	0.344$_{35}$	0.439$_{35}$
36	YNUDLG	**0.340**$_{36}$	0.201$_{37}$	0.387$_{36}$
37	WarwickDCS	**0.335**$_{37}$	0.221$_{36}$	0.382$_{37}$
	Avid	**0.335**$_{37}$	0.163$_{38}$	0.206$_{38}$
B1	All POSITIVE	**0.333**	0.162	0.193
B2	All NEGATIVE	**0.333**	**0.244**	0.323
B3	All NEUTRAL	**0.333**	0.000	**0.483**

Table 6: **Results for Subtask A "Message Polarity Classification", English.** The systems are ordered by average recall *AvgRec* (higher is better). In each column, the rankings according to the corresponding measure are indicated with a subscript. Bx indicates a baseline.

#	System	$AvgRec$	F_1^{PN}	Acc
1	NileTMRG	**0.583**$_1$	0.610$_1$	0.581$_1$
2	SiTAKA	**0.550**$_2$	0.571$_2$	0.563$_2$
3	ELiRF-UPV	**0.478**$_3$	0.467$_4$	0.508$_3$
4	INGEOTEC	**0.477**$_4$	0.455$_5$	0.499$_4$
5	OMAM	**0.438**$_5$	0.422$_6$	0.430$_8$
	LSIS	**0.438**$_5$	0.469$_3$	0.445$_6$
7	Tw-StAR	**0.431**$_7$	0.416$_7$	0.454$_5$
8	HLP@UPENN	**0.415**$_8$	0.320$_8$	0.443$_7$
B1	All POSITIVE	**0.333**	0.199	0.248
B2	All NEGATIVE	**0.333**	**0.267**	0.364
B3	All NEUTRAL	**0.333**	0.000	**0.388**

Table 7: **Results for Subtask A "Message Polarity Classification", Arabic.** The systems are ordered by average recall *AvgRec* (higher is better). In each column, the rankings according to the corresponding measure are indicated with a subscript. Bx indicates a baseline.

Both teams participated in all English subtasks and were also ranked in first (*BB_twtr*) and second (*DataStories*) place for subtasks B-D; *BB_twtr* was also ranked first for subtask E.

The top 5 teams for English were very closely scored. The following four best-ranked teams all used deep learning or deep learning ensembles. Three of the top-10 scoring teams (*INGEOTEC*, *SiTAKA*, and *UCSC-NLP*) used SVM classifiers instead, with various surface, lexical, semantic, and dense word embedding features. The use of ensembles clearly stood out, with five of the top-10 scoring systems (*BB_twtr*, *LIA*, *NNEMBs*, *Tweester*, and *INGEOTEC*) using ensembles, hybrid, stacking or some kind of mix of learning methods. All teams beat the baseline on macro-average recall; however, a few teams did not beat the harsher average F-measure and accuracy baselines.

For Arabic the best-ranked team was *NileTMRG*, and it achieved a score of 0.583. They used a Naïve Bayes classifier with a combination of lexical and sentiment features; they further augmented the training dataset to about 13K examples using external tweets. The *SiTAKA* team was ranked second with a score of 0.55. Their system used a feature-rich SVM with lexical features and embedding representations. Except for *EliRF-UPV*, who used multi-layer neural networks (CRNNs), the remaining teams used SVM and Naïve Bayes classifiers, genetic algorithms, or conditional random fields (CRFs). All teams managed to beat all baselines for all metrics.

5.2 Results for Subtask A: Overall Sentiment in a Tweet

Tables 6 and 7 show the results for Subtask A in English and Arabic, respectively, where the teams are ranked by macro-average recall.

For English the best ranking teams were *BB_twtr* and *DataStories*, both achieving a macro-average recall of 0.681. Both top teams used deep learning; *BB_twtr* used an ensemble of LSTMs and CNNs with multiple convolution operations, while *DataStories* used deep LSTM networks with an attention mechanism.

The difference in the absolute scores for the two languages is probably partially due to the difference in the amount of training data available for Arabic, which was much smaller compared English, even when external datasets were taken into account. The results also reflect the linguistic complexity of Arabic as it is used in social media, which is characterized by the abundant use of dialectal forms and spelling variants. Overall, participants preferred to focus on developing Arabic-specific systems (varying in the extent to which they applied Arabic-specific preprocessing) rather than trying to leverage cross-language models that would enable them to use English data to augment their Arabic models.

#	System	$AvgRec$	F_1	Acc
1	BB_twtr	$\mathbf{0.882}_1$	0.890_1	0.897_1
2	DataStories	$\mathbf{0.856}_2$	0.861_2	0.869_2
3	Tweester	$\mathbf{0.854}_3$	0.856_3	0.863_3
4	TopicThunder	$\mathbf{0.846}_4$	0.847_4	0.854_4
5	TakeLab	$\mathbf{0.845}_5$	0.836_5	0.840_6
6	funSentiment	$\mathbf{0.834}_6$	0.824_8	0.827_8
	YNU-HPCC	$\mathbf{0.834}_6$	0.816_{10}	0.818_{10}
8	WarwickDCS	$\mathbf{0.829}_8$	0.834_6	0.843_5
9	CrystalNest	$\mathbf{0.827}_9$	0.822_9	0.827_8
10	Ti-Senti	$\mathbf{0.826}_{10}$	0.830_7	0.838_7
11	Amobee-C-137	$\mathbf{0.822}_{11}$	0.801_{12}	0.802_{12}
12	SINAI	$\mathbf{0.818}_{12}$	0.806_{11}	0.809_{11}
13	NRU-HSE	$\mathbf{0.798}_{13}$	0.787_{13}	0.790_{13}
14	EICA	$\mathbf{0.790}_{14}$	0.775_{14}	0.777_{16}
15	OMAM	$\mathbf{0.779}_{15}$	0.762_{17}	0.764_{17}
16	NileTMRG	$\mathbf{0.769}_{16}$	0.774_{15}	0.789_{15}
17	ELiRF-UPV	$\mathbf{0.766}_{17}$	0.773_{16}	0.790_{13}
18	DUTH	$\mathbf{0.663}_{18}$	0.600_{18}	0.607_{18}
19	ej-za-2017	$\mathbf{0.594}_{19}$	0.486_{21}	0.518_{19}
20	SSN_MLRG1	$\mathbf{0.586}_{20}$	0.494_{20}	0.518_{19}
21	YNUDLG	$\mathbf{0.516}_{21}$	0.499_{19}	0.499_{21}
22	TM-Gist	$\mathbf{0.499}_{22}$	0.428_{22}	0.444_{22}
23	SSK_JNTUH	$\mathbf{0.483}_{23}$	0.372_{23}	0.412_{23}
B1	All POSITIVE	**0.500**	0.285	0.398
B2	All NEGATIVE	**0.500**	**0.376**	**0.602**

Table 8: **Results for Subtask B "Tweet classification according to a two-point scale", English.** The systems are ordered by average recall $AvgRec$ (higher is better). Bx indicates a baseline.

#	System	$AvgRec$	F_1	Acc
1	NileTMRG	$\mathbf{0.768}_1$	0.767_1	0.770_1
2	ELiRF-UPV	$\mathbf{0.721}_2$	0.724_2	0.734_2
3	ASA	$\mathbf{0.693}_3$	0.670_4	0.672_4
4	OMAM	$\mathbf{0.687}_4$	0.678_3	0.679_3
B1	All POSITIVE	**0.500**	**0.362**	**0.566**
B2	All NEGATIVE	0.500	0.303	0.434

Table 9: **Results for Subtask B "Tweet classification according to a two-point scale", Arabic.** The systems are ordered by average recall $AvgRec$ (higher is better). Bx indicates a baseline.

5.3 Results for Subtasks B and C: Topic-Based Classification

The results of Subtasks B and C are shown in Tables 8–11. We can see that the system scores for subtask B are higher than those for subtask A, with the best team achieving 0.882 accuracy for English (compared to 0.681 for subtask A) and 0.768 for Arabic (compared to 0.583 for subtask A). However, this is primarily due to the fact there are two classes for subtask B, while there are three classes for subtask A.

#	System	MAE^M	MAE^μ
1	BB_twtr	$\mathbf{0.481}_1$	0.554_6
2	DataStories	$\mathbf{0.555}_2$	0.543_4
3	Amobee-C-137	$\mathbf{0.599}_3$	0.582_{10}
4	Tweester	$\mathbf{0.623}_4$	0.734_{13}
5	TwiSe	$\mathbf{0.640}_5$	0.616_{12}
6	CrystalNest	$\mathbf{0.698}_6$	0.571_9
7	ELiRF-UPV	$\mathbf{0.806}_7$	0.586_{11}
8	EICA	$\mathbf{0.823}_8$	0.509_2
9	funSentiment	$\mathbf{0.842}_9$	0.530_3
10	DUTH	$\mathbf{0.895}_{10}$	0.544_5
	OMAM	$\mathbf{0.895}_{10}$	0.475_1
12	YNU-HPCC	$\mathbf{0.925}_{12}$	0.567_8
13	NRU-HSE	$\mathbf{0.928}_{13}$	0.557_7
14	YNU-1510	$\mathbf{1.262}_{14}$	0.764_{14}
15	SSN_MLRG1	$\mathbf{1.325}_{15}$	0.985_{15}
B1	HIGHLYNEGATIVE	2.000	1.895
B2	NEGATIVE	1.400	0.923
B3	NEUTRAL	**1.200**	**0.525**
B4	POSITIVE	1.400	1.127
B5	HIGHLYPOSITIVE	2.000	2.105

Table 10: **Results for Subtask C "Tweet classification according to a five-point scale", English.** The systems are ordered by their MAE^M score (lower is better). Bx indicates a baseline.

#	System	MAE^M	MAE^μ
1	OMAM	$\mathbf{0.943}_1$	0.646_1
2	ELiRF-UPV	$\mathbf{1.264}_2$	0.787_2
B1	HIGHLYNEGATIVE	2.000	2.059
B2	NEGATIVE	1.400	1.065
B3	NEUTRAL	**1.200**	**0.458**
B4	POSITIVE	1.400	0.946
B5	HIGHLYPOSITIVE	2.000	1.941

Table 11: **Results for Subtask C "Tweet classification according to a five-point scale", Arabic.** The systems are ordered by their MAE^M score (lower is better). Bx indicates a baseline.

For English the *BB_twtr* system, ranked first, modeled topics by concatenating the topical information at the word level. The second-best system, *DataStories*, also accounted for topics by producing topic annotations and a context-aware attention mechanism.

#	System	KLD	AE	RAE
1	BB_twtr	$\mathbf{0.036}_1$	0.080_1	0.598_1
2	DataStories	$\mathbf{0.048}_2$	0.095_2	0.848_2
3	TakeLab	$\mathbf{0.050}_3$	0.096_3	1.057_5
4	CrystalNest	$\mathbf{0.056}_4$	0.104_5	1.202_6
5	Tweester	$\mathbf{0.057}_5$	0.103_4	1.051_4
6	funSentiment	$\mathbf{0.060}_6$	0.109_6	0.939_3
7	NileTMRG	$\mathbf{0.077}_7$	0.120_7	1.228_7
8	NRU-HSE	$\mathbf{0.078}_8$	0.132_8	1.528_8
9	EICA	$\mathbf{0.092}_9$	0.143_9	1.922_9
10	THU_HCSI_IDU	$\mathbf{0.129}_{10}$	0.179_{10}	2.428_{11}
11	Amobee-C-137	$\mathbf{0.149}_{11}$	0.179_{10}	2.168_{10}
12	OMAM	$\mathbf{0.164}_{12}$	0.204_{12}	2.790_{12}
13	SSK_JNTUH	$\mathbf{0.421}_{13}$	0.314_{13}	2.983_{13}
14	ELiRF-UPV	$\mathbf{1.060}_{14}$	0.593_{15}	7.991_{15}
15	YNU-HPCC	$\mathbf{1.142}_{15}$	0.592_{14}	7.859_{14}
B1	(0 1)	1.518	0.422	**2.645**
B2	macro-avg on 2016 data	0.554	0.423	6.061
B3	micro-avg on 2016 data	0.591	0.432	6.169
B4	macro-avg on 2015-6 data	**0.534**	**0.418**	6.000
B5	micro-avg on 2015-6 data	0.587	0.431	6.157

Table 12: **Results for Subtask D "Tweet quantification according to a two-point scale", English.** The systems are ordered by their KLD score (lower is better). Bx indicates a baseline.

#	System	KLD	AE	RAE
1	NileTMRG	$\mathbf{0.127}_1$	0.170_1	2.462_1
2	OMAM	$\mathbf{0.202}_2$	0.238_2	4.835_2
3	ELiRF-UPV	$\mathbf{1.183}_3$	0.537_3	11.434_3
B1	(0 1)	1.518	0.422	**2.645**
B2	macro-avg on train-2017	0.296	0.322	6.600
B3	micro-avg on train-2017	**0.295**	**0.321**	6.692

Table 13: **Results for Subtask D "Tweet quantification according to a two-point scale", Arabic.** The systems are ordered by their KLD score (lower is better). Bx indicates a baseline.

funSentiment, ranked 6th and 9th for subtasks B and C, respectively, modeled the sentiment towards the topic using the left and the right context around a topic mention in the tweet. *WarwickDCS*, ranked 8th, used simple tweet-level classification, while ignoring the topic. Overall, almost all teams managed to outperform the majority class baseline for subtask B, but only two teams outperformed the NEUTRAL class baseline for subtask C.

For Arabic four teams participated in Subtask B and two teams in Subtask C. *NileTMRG* was once again ranked first for Subtask B, with a system based on ensembles of topic-specific and topic-agnostic models. For subtask C, *OMAM* also used combinations of such models applied in succession. All teams easily outperformed the baselines for Subtask B, but only the *OMAM* team managed to do so for Subtask C.

#	System	EMD
1	BB_twtr	0.245
2	TwiSe	0.269
3	funSentiment	0.273
4	ELiRF-UPV	0.306
5	NRU-HSE	0.317
6	Amobee-C-137	0.345
7	OMAM	0.350
8	Tweester	0.365
9	THU_HCSI_IDU	0.385
10	YNU-HPCC	0.447
11	DataStories	0.595
12	EICA	1.461
B1	(0 0 0 1 0)	1.123
B2	macro-avg on 2016 data	0.583
B3	micro-avg on 2016 data	**0.552**

Table 14: **Results for Subtask E "Tweet quantification according to a five-point scale", English.** The systems are ordered by their EMD score (lower is better). Bx indicates a baseline.

#	System	EMD
1	OMAM	0.548
2	ELiRF-UPV	0.564
B1	(0 0 1 0 0)	0.458
B2	macro-avg on train-2017	**0.440**
B3	micro-avg on train-2017	**0.440**

Table 15: **Results for Subtask E "Tweet quantification according to a five-point scale", Arabic.** The systems are ordered by their EMD score (lower is better). Bx indicates a baseline.

5.4 Results for Subtasks D and E: Tweet Quantification

Tables 12–15 show the results for the tweet quantification subtasks. The bottom of the tables report the result of a baseline system, B1, that assigns a prevalence of 1 to the majority class (which is the POSITIVE class for subtask D, and the WEAKLYPOSITIVE/NEUTRAL class for subtask E, English/Arabic) and 0 to the other class(es).

We further show the results for a smarter "maximum likelihood" baseline, which assigns to each test topic the distribution of the training tweets (the union of TRAIN, DEV, DEVTEST) across the classes. This is the "smartest" among the trivial policies that attempt to maximize KLD. For this baseline, for English we use for training either (*i*) the 2016 data only, or (*ii*) data from both 2015 and 2016; we also experiment with (*i*) micro-averaging and (*ii*) macro-averaging over the topics. It turns out that macro-averaging over 2015+2016 data is the strongest baseline in terms of KLD. For Arabic, we use the train-2017 data, and micro-averaging works better there.

There were 15 participating teams competing in Subtask D: 15 for English and 3 for Arabic (these 3 teams all participated in English). As in the other subtasks, *BB_twtr* was ranked first in English. They achieved an improvement of .50 points absolute in KLD over the best baseline, and a .01 improvement over the next best team, *DataStories*. For Arabic, the best team was *NileTMRG* With improvement of .17 over the best baseline and of .08 over the next best team, *OMAM*. All but the last two teams in English and the last team for Arabic outperformed all baselines.

In Subtask E, there were 12 participating teams, with *OMAM* and *EliRF-UPV* competing for both English and Arabic. Once again, *BB_twtr* was the best for English, improving over the best baseline by .31 EMD points absolute. Interestingly, this is the first subtask where *DataStories* was not the second-ranked team. *BB_twtr* outperformed the second-best team, *TwiSe*, by .02 points. For English, all but the last two teams outperformed the baselines. However, for Arabic, none of the two participating teams could do so.

5.5 User Information

This year, we encouraged teams to explore using in their models information about the user who wrote the tweet, which can be extracted from the public user profiles of the respective Twitter users. Participants could also try features about following relations and the structure of the social network in general, as well as could make use of other tweets by the target user when analyzing one particular tweet. Four teams tried that: *SINAI*, *ECNU*, *TakeLab*, and *OMAM*. *OMAM* and *TakeLab* did not find any improvements, and ultimately decided not to use any user information. *ECNU* used profile information such as favorited, favorite count, retweeted, and retweet count. They ended up 15th in Subtask A. *SINAI* used the last 200 tweets from the person's timeline. They ranked 12th in Subtask B. They generated a user model from the timeline of a given target user. They built a general SVM model on word2vec embeddings. Then, for each user in the test set, they downloaded the last 200 tweets published by the user and classified their sentiment using that SVM classifier. If the classified user tweets achieved an accuracy above a threshold (0.7), the user model was applied on the authored tweets from the test set. If not, the general SVM model was used.

It is difficult to judge whether and by how much user information could help the best approaches as they did not try to use such information. However, we believe that building and using a Twitter user profile is a promising research direction, and that participants should learn how to make this work in the future. Thus, we would like to encourage more teams to try to explore using this information. We would also like to provide more user information such as age and gender, which we can predict automatically (Rosenthal and McKeown, 2016), when it is not directly available from the user profile. Another promising direction is to make use of "conversations" in Twitter, i.e., take into account the replies to tweets in Twitter. For example, previous work (Vanzo et al., 2014) has shown that it is beneficial to model the polarity detection problem as a sequential classification task over streams of tweets, where the stream is a "conversation" on Twitter containing tweets, replies to these tweets, replies to these replies, etc.

6 Conclusion and Future Work

Sentiment Analysis in Twitter continues to be a very popular task, attracting 48 teams this year. The task provides immense value to the sentiment community by providing a large accessible benchmark dataset containing over 70,000 tweets across two languages for researchers to evaluate and compare their method to the state of the art. This year, we introduced a new language for the first time and also encouraged the use of user information. These additions drew new participants and ideas to the task. The Arabic tasks drew nine participants and four teams took advantage of user information. Although a respectable amount of participants for its inaugural year, further exploration into both of these areas would be useful in the future, such as collecting more training data for Arabic and encouraging the use of cross-lingual training data. In the future, we would like to include exploring additional languages, providing further user information, and other related tasks such as irony and emotion detection. Finally, deep learning continues to be popular and employed by the state of the art approaches. We expect this trend to continue in sentiment analysis research, but also look forward to new innovative ideas that are discovered.

Team ID	Affiliation	Country	Subtasks (English)					Subtasks (Arabic)					Paper
			A	B	C	D	E	A	B	C	D	E	
Adullam	Korea University	South Korea	A										(Yoon et al., 2017)
Amobee C-137	Amobee	USA	A	B	C	D	E						(Rozental and Fleischer, 2017)
ASA	Al-Imam Muhammad Ibn Saud Islamic University.	Saudi Arabia							B				N/A
Avid	N/A	N/A	A										N/A
BB_twtr	Bloomberg	USA	A	B	C	D	E						(Cliche, 2017)
BUSEM	Bogazici University	Turkey	A										(Ayata et al., 2017)
CrystalNest	Institute of High Performance Computing (IHPC)	Singapore	A	B	C	D							(Gupta and Yang, 2017)
DataStories	Data Science Lab at University of Piraeus	Greece	A	B	C	D	E						(Baziotis et al., 2017)
deepSA	National Sun Yat-sen University	Taiwan	A										(Yang et al., 2017)
diegoref	N/A	N/A	A										N/A
DUTH	Democritus University of Thrace	Greece	A	B	C								(Symeonidis et al., 2017)
ECNU	East China Normal University	China	A										(Zhou et al., 2017)
EICA	East China Normal University	China	A	B	C	D	E						(Maoquan et al., 2017)
ej-sa-2017	University of Evora	Portugal	A	B									(Dovdon and Saias, 2017)
ELiRF-UPV	Universitat Politécnica de Valéncia	Spain	A	B	C	D	E	A	B	C	D	E	(González et al., 2017)
funSentiment	Thomson Reuters	USA		B	C	D	E						(Li et al., 2017)
HLP@UPENN	University of Pennsylvania	USA	A					A					(Sarker and Gonzalez, 2017)
INGEOTEC	CONACYT-INFOTEC/CENTROGEO	Mexico	A					A					(Miranda-Jiménez et al., 2017)
LIA	LIA	France	A										(Rouvier, 2017)
LSIS	Aix-Marseille University	France	A					A					(Htait et al., 2017)
MI&T Lab	Harbin Institute of Technology	China	A										(Zhao et al., 2017)
Neverland-THU	N/A	N/A	A										N/A
NILC-USP	Institute of Mathematics and Computer Science, University of So Paulo	Brazil	A										(Anselmo Corrêa Júnior et al., 2017)
NileTMRG	Nile University	Egypt	A	B		D		A	B		D		(El-Beltagy et al., 2017)
NNEMBs	Peking University	China	A										(Yin et al., 2017)
NRU-HSE	National Research University Higher School of Economics	Russia		B	C	D	E						(Karpov, 2017)
OMAM	American University of Beirut, Universiti Teknologi Malaysia, Cairo University, New York University Abu Dhabi, Qatar University	Egypt, Lebanon, Malaysia, Qatar, United Arab Emirates	A	B	C	D	E	A	B	C	D	E	(Baly et al., 2017; Onyibe and Habash, 2017)
QUB	Queen's University Belfast	Ireland	A										
senti17	Lip6, UPMC	France	A										(Hamdan, 2017)
SentiME++	EURECOM	France	A										(Troncy et al., 2017)
SINAI	Universidad de Jaén	Spain		B									(Jiménez-Zafra et al., 2017)
SiTAKA	iTAKA, Universitat Rovira i Virgili; Hodeidah University	Spain, Yemen	A					A					(Jabreel and Moreno, 2017)
SSK_JNTUH	J.N.T.U.H College of Engg Jagtial and BVRIT Hyderabad College of Engineering for Women	India		B		D							N/A
SSN_MLRG1	Department of CSE, SSN College of Engineering	India	A	B	C								(Deborah et al., 2017)
TakeLab	TakeLab, University of Zagreb	Croatia	A	B		D							(Lozić et al., 2017)
THU_HCSI_IDU	Human Computer Speech Interaction Research Group, Tsinghua University	China				D	E						
Ti-Senti	N/A	N/A	A	B									N/A
TM-Gist	N/A	N/A		B									N/A
TopicThunder	N/A	N/A		B									N/A
TSA-INF	Infosys Limited	India	A										(Deshmane and Friedrichs, 2017)
Tw-StAR	Selcuk University, Universit Libre de Bruxelles (ULB)	Belgium, Turkey						A					(Mulki et al., 2017)
Tweester	National Technical University of Athens, University of Athens, "Athena" Research and Innovation Center, Signal Analysis and Interpretation Laboratory (SAIL), USC	Greece, USA	A	B	C	D	E						(Kolovou et al., 2017)
TwiSe	University of Grenoble-Alps	France			C		E						(Balikas, 2017)
UCSC-NLP	Catholic University of the Most Holy Conception	Chile	A										(Castro et al., 2017)
WarwickDCS	Department of Computer Science, University of Warwick	UK	A	B									N/A
XJSA	Xi'an JiaoTong University	China	A										(Hao et al., 2017)
YNU-HPCC	Yunnan University	China	A	B	C	D	E						(Zhang et al., 2017)
YNUDLG	Yunnan University	China	A	B	C								(Wang et al., 2017)
TOTAL			38	23	15	15	12	8	4	2	3	2	

Table 16: Alphabetical list of the participating teams, their affiliation, country, the subtasks they participated in, and the system description paper that they contributed to SemEval-2017. Teams whose *Affiliation* column is typeset on more than one row include researchers from different institutions, which have collaborated to build a joint system submission. An *N/A* entry for the *Paper* column indicates that the team did not contribute a system description paper. Finally, the last row gives statistics about the total number of system submissions for each subtask.

513

References

Muhammad Abdul-Mageed, Mona Diab, and Sandra Kübler. 2014. Samar: Subjectivity and sentiment analysis for Arabic social media. *Computer Speech & Language* 28(1):20–37.

Muhammad Abdul-Mageed and Mona T. Diab. 2011. Subjectivity and sentiment annotation of modern standard Arabic newswire. In *Proceedings of the 5th Linguistic Annotation Workshop*. Portland, Oregon, USA, LAW '11, pages 110–118.

Mohammad Al-Smadi, Omar Qawasmeh, Bashar Talafha, and Muhannad Quwaider. 2015. Human annotated Arabic dataset of book reviews for aspect based sentiment analysis. In *Proceedings of the 3rd International Conference on Future Internet of Things and Cloud*. Rome, Italy, FiCloud '15, pages 726–730.

Edilson Anselmo Corrêa Júnior, Vanessa Marinho, and Leandro Santos. 2017. NILC-USP at SemEval-2017 Task 4: A Multi-view Ensemble for Twitter Sentiment Analysis. In *Proceedings of the 11th International Workshop on Semantic Evaluation*. Vancouver, Canada, SemEval '17, pages 610–614.

Deger Ayata, Murat Saraclar, and Arzucan Ozgur. 2017. BUSEM at SemEval-2017 Task 4A: Sentiment Analysis with Word Embedding and Long Short Term Memory RNN Approaches. In *Proceedings of the 11th International Workshop on Semantic Evaluation*. Vancouver, Canada, SemEval '17, pages 776–782.

Stefano Baccianella, Andrea Esuli, and Fabrizio Sebastiani. 2009. Evaluation measures for ordinal regression. In *Proceedings of the 9th IEEE International Conference on Intelligent Systems Design and Applications*. Pisa, Italy, ISDA '09, pages 283–287.

Georgios Balikas. 2017. TwiSe at SemEval-2017 Task 4: Five-point Twitter Sentiment Classification and Quantification. In *Proceedings of the 11th International Workshop on Semantic Evaluation*. Vancouver, Canada, SemEval '17, pages 754–758.

Ramy Baly, Gilbert Badaro, Ali Hamdi, Rawan Moukalled, Rita Aoun, Georges El-Khoury, Ahmad Al Sallab, Hazem Hajj, Nizar Habash, Khaled Shaban, and Wassim El-Hajj. 2017. OMAM at SemEval-2017 Task 4: Evaluation of English State-of-the-Art Sentiment Analysis Models for Arabic and a New Topic-based Model. In *Proceedings of the 11th International Workshop on Semantic Evaluation*. Vancouver, Canada, SemEval 17, pages 602–609.

Christos Baziotis, Nikos Pelekis, and Christos Doulkeridis. 2017. DataStories at SemEval-2017 Task 4: Deep LSTM with Attention for Message-level and Topic-based Sentiment Analysis. In *Proceedings of the 11th International Workshop on Semantic Evaluation*. Vancouver, Canada, SemEval '17, pages 746–753.

Johan Bollen, Huina Mao, and Xiao-Jun Zeng. 2011. Twitter mood predicts the stock market. *Journal of Computational Science* 2(1):1–8.

Javier Borge-Holthoefer, Walid Magdy, Kareem Darwish, and Ingmar Weber. 2015. Content and network dynamics behind Egyptian political polarization on Twitter. In *Proceedings of the 18th ACM Conference on Computer Supported Cooperative Work and Social Computing*. Vancouver, Canada, CSCW '15, pages 700–711.

Suzan Burton and Alena Soboleva. 2011. Interactive or reactive? Marketing with Twitter. *Journal of Consumer Marketing* 28(7):491–499.

Iván Castro, Sebastián Oliva, José Abreu, Claudia Martínez, and Yoan Gutiérrez. 2017. UCSC-NLP at SemEval-2017 Task 4: Sense n-grams for sentiment analysis in Twitter. In *Proceedings of the 11th International Workshop on Semantic Evaluation*. Vancouver, Canada, SemEval '17, pages 806–810.

Mathieu Cliche. 2017. BB_twtr at SemEval-2017 Task 4: Twitter Sentiment Analysis with CNNs and LSTMs. In *Proceedings of the 11th International Workshop on Semantic Evaluation*. Vancouver, Canada, SemEval '17, pages 572–579.

Angel Deborah, Milton Rajendram, and T. Mirnalinee. 2017. SSN_MLRG1 at SemEval-2017 Task 4: Sentiment Analysis in Twitter Using Multi-Kernel Gaussian Process Classifier . In *Proceedings of the 11th International Workshop on Semantic Evaluation*. Vancouver, Canada, SemEval '17.

Amit Ajit Deshmane and Jasper Friedrichs. 2017. TSA-INF at SemEval-2017 Task 4: An ensemble of deep learning architectures including lexicon features for Twitter sentiment analysis. In *Proceedings of the 11th International Workshop on Semantic Evaluation*. Vancouver, Canada, SemEval '17, pages 801–805.

Peter S. Dodds, Kameron D. Harris, Isabel M. Kloumann, Catherine A. Bliss, and Christopher M. Danforth. 2011. Temporal patterns of happiness and information in a global social network: Hedonometrics and Twitter. *PLoS ONE* 6(12).

Enkhzol Dovdon and José Saias. 2017. ej-sa-2017 at SemEval-2017 Task 4: Experiments for target oriented sentiment analysis in Twitter. In *Proceedings of the 11th International Workshop on Semantic Evaluation*. Vancouver, Canada, SemEval '17, pages 643–646.

Samhaa R. El-Beltagy, Mona El Kalamawy, and Abu Bakr Soliman. 2017. NileTMRG at SemEval-2017 Task 4: Arabic sentiment analysis. In *Proceedings of the 11th International Workshop on Semantic Evaluation*. Vancouver, Canada, SemEval '17, pages 789–794.

Mohamed Elarnaoty, Samir AbdelRahman, and Aly Fahmy. 2012. A machine learning approach for opinion holder extraction in Arabic language. *arXiv preprint arXiv:1206.1011* .

Andrea Esuli and Fabrizio Sebastiani. 2010. Sentiment quantification. *IEEE Intelligent Systems* 25(4):72–75.

Andrea Esuli and Fabrizio Sebastiani. 2015. Optimizing text quantifiers for multivariate loss functions. *ACM Transactions on Knowledge Discovery and Data* 9(4):Article 27.

Noura Farra and Kathleen McKeown. 2017. SMARTies: Sentiment models for Arabic target entities. In *Proceedings of the 15th Conference of the European Chapter of the Association for Computational Linguistics*. Valencia, Spain, EACL '17.

Noura Farra, Kathy McKeown, and Nizar Habash. 2015. Annotating targets of opinions in Arabic using crowdsourcing. In *Proceedings of the Second Workshop on Arabic Natural Language Processing*. Beijing, China, ANLP '17, pages 89–98.

George Forman. 2005. Counting positives accurately despite inaccurate classification. In *Proceedings of the 16th European Conference on Machine Learning*. Porto, Portugal, ECML '05, pages 564–575.

George Forman. 2008. Quantifying counts and costs via classification. *Data Mining and Knowledge Discovery* 17(2):164–206.

Aniruddha Ghosh, Guofu Li, Tony Veale, Paolo Rosso, Ekaterina Shutova, John Barnden, and Antonio Reyes. 2015. SemEval-2015 Task 11: Sentiment analysis of figurative language in Twitter. In *Proceedings of the 9th International Workshop on Semantic Evaluation*. Denver, Colorado, USA, SemEval '15, pages 470–478.

José Ángel González, Ferran Pla, and Lluís-F Hurtado. 2017. ELiRF-UPV at SemEval-2017 Task 4: Sentiment Analysis using Deep Learning. In *Proceedings of the 11th International Workshop on Semantic Evaluation*. Vancouver, Canada, SemEval '17, pages 722–726.

Raj Kumar Gupta and Yinping Yang. 2017. CrystalNest at SemEval-2017 Task 4: Using sarcasm detection for enhancing sentiment classification and quantification. In *Proceedings of the 11th International Workshop on Semantic Evaluation*. Vancouver, Canada, SemEval '17, pages 625–632.

Hussam Hamdan. 2017. Senti17 at SemEval-2017 Task 4: Ten convolutional neural network voters for tweet polarity classification. In *Proceedings of the 11th International Workshop on Semantic Evaluation*. Vancouver, Canada, SemEval '17, pages 699–702.

Yazhou Hao, YangYang Lan, Yufei Li, and Chen Li. 2017. XJSA at SemEval-2017 Task 4: A deep system for sentiment classification in Twitter. In *Proceedings of the 11th International Workshop on Semantic Evaluation*. Vancouver, Canada, SemEval '17, pages 727–730.

Dirk Hovy. 2015. Demographic factors improve classification performance. In *Proceedings of the 53rd Annual Meeting of the Association for Computational Linguistics and the 7th International Joint Conference on Natural Language Processing (Volume 1: Long Papers)*. Beijing, China, ACL-IJCNLP '17, pages 752–762.

Amal Htait, Sébastien Fournier, and Patrice Bellot. 2017. LSIS at SemEval-2017 Task 4: Using adapted sentiment similarity seed words for English and Arabic tweet polarity classification. In *Proceedings of the 11th International Workshop on Semantic Evaluation*. Vancouver, Canada, SemEval '17, pages 717–721.

Mohammed Jabreel and Antonio Moreno. 2017. SiTAKA at SemEval-2017 Task 4: Sentiment analysis in Twitter based on a rich set of features. In *Proceedings of the 11th International Workshop on Semantic Evaluation*. Vancouver, Canada, SemEval '17, pages 693–698.

Salud María Jiménez-Zafra, Arturo Montejo-Ráez, M. Teresa Martín-Valdivia, and L. Alfonso Ureña López. 2017. SINAI at SemEval-2017 Task 4: User based classification. In *Proceedings of the 11th International Workshop on Semantic Evaluation*. Vancouver, Canada, SemEval '17, pages 633–638.

Nikolay Karpov. 2017. NRU-HSE at SemEval-2017 Task 4: Tweet quantification using deep learning architecture. In *Proceedings of the 11th International Workshop on Semantic Evaluation*. Vancouver, Canada, SemEval '17, pages 682–687.

Mesut Kaya, Guven Fidan, and Ismail Hakki Toroslu. 2013. Transfer learning using Twitter data for improving sentiment classification of Turkish political news. In *Proceedings of the 28th International Symposium on Computer and Information Sciences*. Paris, France, ISCIS '13, pages 139–148.

Svetlana Kiritchenko, Saif Mohammad, and Mohammad Salameh. 2016. SemEval-2016 Task 7: Determining sentiment intensity of English and Arabic phrases. In *Proceedings of the 10th International Workshop on Semantic Evaluation*. San Diego, California, USA, SemEval '16, pages 42–51.

Athanasia Kolovou, Filippos Kokkinos, Aris Fergadis, Pinelopi Papalampidi, Elias Iosif, Nikolaos Malandrakis, Elisavet Palogiannidi, Haris Papageorgiou, Shrikanth Narayanan, and Alexandro Potamianos. 2017. Tweester at SemEval-2017 Task 4: Fusion of semantic-affective and pairwise classification models for sentiment analysis in Twitter. In *Proceedings of the 11th International Workshop on Seman-*

tic Evaluation. Vancouver, Canada, SemEval '17, pages 674–681.

Quanzhi Li, Armineh Nourbakhsh, Xiaomo Liu, Rui Fang, and Sameena Shah. 2017. funSentiment at SemEval-2017 Task 4: Topic-based message sentiment classification by exploiting word embeddings, text features and target contexts. In *Proceedings of the 11th International Workshop on Semantic Evaluation*. Vancouver, Canada, SemEval '17, pages 740–745.

David Lozić, Doria Šarić, Ivan Tokić, Zoran Medić, and Jan Šnajder. 2017. TakeLab at SemEval-2017 Task 4: Recent deaths and the power of nostalgia in sentiment analysis in Twitter. In *Proceedings of the 11th International Workshop on Semantic Evaluation*. Vancouver, Canada, SemEval '17, pages 783–788.

Wang Maoquan, Chen Shiyun, Xie Yufei, and Zhao Lu. 2017. EICA at SemEval-2017 Task 4: A simple convolutional neural network for topic-based sentiment classification. In *Proceedings of the 11th International Workshop on Semantic Evaluation*. Vancouver, Canada, SemEval '17, pages 293–299.

Micol Marchetti-Bowick and Nathanael Chambers. 2012. Learning for microblogs with distant supervision: Political forecasting with Twitter. In *Proceedings of the 13th Conference of the European Chapter of the Association for Computational Linguistics*. Avignon, France, EACL '12, pages 603–612.

Sabino Miranda-Jiménez, Mario Graff, Eric Sadit Tellez, and Daniela Moctezuma. 2017. INGEOTEC at SemEval 2017 Task 4: A B4MSA ensemble based on genetic programming for Twitter sentiment analysis. In *Proceedings of the 11th International Workshop on Semantic Evaluation*. Vancouver, Canada, SemEval '17, pages 770–775.

Alan Mislove, Sune Lehmann, Yong-Yeol Ahn, Jukka-Pekka Onnela, and J Niels Rosenquist. 2011. Understanding the demographics of Twitter users. In *Proceedings of the 9th AAAI International Conference on Web and Social Media*. Barcelona, Spain, ICWSM '11, pages 554–557.

Saif Mohammad, Svetlana Kiritchenko, Parinaz Sobhani, Xiao-Dan Zhu, and Colin Cherry. 2016a. SemEval-2016 Task 6: Detecting stance in tweets. In *Proceedings of the 10th International Workshop on Semantic Evaluation*. San Diego, California, USA, SemEval '16, pages 31–41.

Saif M Mohammad, Mohammad Salameh, and Svetlana Kiritchenko. 2016b. How translation alters sentiment. *J. Artif. Intell. Res.(JAIR)* 55:95–130.

Ahmed Mourad and Kareem Darwish. 2013. Subjectivity and sentiment analysis of modern standard Arabic and Arabic microblogs. In *Proceedings of the 4th workshop on computational approaches to subjectivity, sentiment and social media analysis*. Atlanta, Georgia, USA, WASSA '13, pages 55–64.

Hala Mulki, Hatem Haddad, Mourad Gridach, and Ismail Babaolu. 2017. Tw-StAR at SemEval-2017 Task 4: Sentiment classification of Arabic tweets. In *Proceedings of the 11th International Workshop on Semantic Evaluation*. Vancouver, Canada, SemEval '17, pages 663–668.

Preslav Nakov, Alan Ritter, Sara Rosenthal, Fabrizio Sebastiani, and Veselin Stoyanov. 2016a. SemEval-2016 task 4: Sentiment analysis in Twitter. In *Proceedings of the 10th International Workshop on Semantic Evaluation*. San Diego, California, USA, SemEval '16, pages 1–18.

Preslav Nakov, Sara Rosenthal, Svetlana Kiritchenko, Saif M. Mohammad, Zornitsa Kozareva, Alan Ritter, Veselin Stoyanov, and Xiaodan Zhu. 2016b. Developing a successful SemEval task in sentiment analysis of Twitter and other social media texts. *Language Resources and Evaluation* 50(1):35–65.

Preslav Nakov, Sara Rosenthal, Zornitsa Kozareva, Veselin Stoyanov, Alan Ritter, and Theresa Wilson. 2013. SemEval-2013 Task 2: Sentiment analysis in Twitter. In *Proceedings of the 7th International Workshop on Semantic Evaluation*. Atlanta, Georgia, USA, SemEval '13, pages 312–320.

Dong Nguyen, Rilana Gravel, Dolf Trieschnigg, and Theo Meder. 2013. "How old do you think I am?" A study of language and age in Twitter. In *Proceedings of the Seventh International Conference on Weblogs and Social Media*. Cambridge, Massachusetts, USA, ICWSM '13, pages 439–448.

Brendan O'Connor, Ramnath Balasubramanyan, Bryan R. Routledge, and Noah A. Smith. 2010. From tweets to polls: Linking text sentiment to public opinion time series. In *Proceedings of the Fourth International Conference on Weblogs and Social Media*. Washington, DC, USA, ICWSM '10, pages 122–129.

Chukwuyem Onyibe and Nizar Habash. 2017. OMAM at SemEval-2017 Task 4: English sentiment analysis with conditional random fields. In *Proceedings of the 11th International Workshop on Semantic Evaluation*. Vancouver, Canada, SemEval '17, pages 669–673.

Maria Pontiki, Dimitris Galanis, Haris Papageorgiou, Ion Androutsopoulos, Suresh Manandhar, Mohammad AL-Smadi, Mahmoud Al-Ayyoub, Yanyan Zhao, Bing Qin, Orphee De Clercq, Veronique Hoste, Marianna Apidianaki, Xavier Tannier, Natalia Loukachevitch, Evgeniy Kotelnikov, Núria Bel, Salud María Jiménez-Zafra, and Gülşen Eryiğit. 2016. SemEval-2016 Task 5: Aspect based sentiment analysis. In *Proceedings of the 10th International Workshop on Semantic Evaluation*. San Diego, California, USA, SemEval '16, pages 19–30.

Maria Pontiki, Dimitris Galanis, Haris Papageorgiou, Suresh Manandhar, and Ion Androutsopoulos. 2015. SemEval-2015 Task 12: Aspect based sentiment analysis. In *Proceedings of the 9th International Workshop on Semantic Evaluation*. Denver, Colorado, USA, SemEval '15, pages 486–495.

Maria Pontiki, Dimitris Galanis, John Pavlopoulos, Harris Papageorgiou, Ion Androutsopoulos, and Suresh Manandhar. 2014. SemEval-2014 Task 4: Aspect based sentiment analysis. In *Proceedings of the 8th International Workshop on Semantic Evaluation*. Dublin, Ireland, SemEval '14, pages 27–35.

Muhammad A. Qureshi, Colm O'Riordan, and Gabriella Pasi. 2013. Clustering with error estimation for monitoring reputation of companies on Twitter. In *Proceedings of the 9th Asia Information Retrieval Societies Conference*. Singapore, AIRS '13, pages 170–180.

Eshrag Refaee and Verena Rieser. 2014. Subjectivity and sentiment analysis of Arabic Twitter feeds with limited resources. In *Workshop on Free/Open-Source Arabic Corpora and Corpora Processing Tools*. Reykjavik, Iceland, pages 16–21.

Eshrag Refaee and Verena Rieser. 2015. Benchmarking machine translated sentiment analysis for Arabic tweets. In *Proceedings of the 2015 Conference of the North American Chapter of the Association for Computational Linguistics: Human Language Technologies*. Denver, Colorado, USA, NAACL-HLT '15, pages 71–78.

Sara Rosenthal and Kathy McKeown. 2016. Social proof: The impact of author traits on influence detection. In *Proceedings of the First Workshop on NLP and Computational Social Science*. Austin, Texas, USA, pages 27–36.

Sara Rosenthal, Preslav Nakov, Svetlana Kiritchenko, Saif Mohammad, Alan Ritter, and Veselin Stoyanov. 2015. SemEval-2015 Task 10: Sentiment analysis in Twitter. In *Proceedings of the 9th International Workshop on Semantic Evaluation*. Denver, Colorado, USA, SemEval '15, pages 451–463.

Sara Rosenthal, Alan Ritter, Preslav Nakov, and Veselin Stoyanov. 2014. SemEval-2014 task 9: Sentiment analysis in Twitter. In *Proceedings of the 8th International Workshop on Semantic Evaluation*. Dublin, Ireland, SemEval '14, pages 73–80.

Mickael Rouvier. 2017. LIA at SemEval-2017 Task 4: An ensemble of neural networks for sentiment classification. In *Proceedings of the 11th International Workshop on Semantic Evaluation*. Vancouver, Canada, SemEval '17, pages 759–764.

Alon Rozental and Daniel Fleischer. 2017. Amobee at SemEval-2017 Task 4: Deep learning system for sentiment detection on Twitter. In *Proceedings of the 11th International Workshop on Semantic Evaluation*. Vancouver, Canada, SemEval '17, pages 652–657.

Yossi Rubner, Carlo Tomasi, and Leonidas J. Guibas. 2000. The Earth Mover's Distance as a metric for image retrieval. *International Journal of Computer Vision* 40(2):99–121.

Ludger Rüschendorf. 2001. Wasserstein metric. In Michiel Hazewinkel, editor, *Encyclopaedia of Mathematics*, Kluwer Academic Publishers, Dordrecht, Netherlands.

Irene Russo, Tommaso Caselli, and Carlo Strapparava. 2015. SemEval-2015 Task 9: CLIPEval implicit polarity of events. In *Proceedings of the 9th International Workshop on Semantic Evaluation*. Denver, Colorado, USA, SemEval '15, pages 443–450.

Mohammad Salameh, Saif Mohammad, and Svetlana Kiritchenko. 2015. Sentiment after translation: A case-study on Arabic social media posts. In *Proceedings of the 2015 Conference of the North American Chapter of the Association for Computational Linguistics: Human Language Technologies*. Denver, Colorado, USA, NAACL-HLT '15, pages 767–777.

Abeed Sarker and Graciela Gonzalez. 2017. HLP@UPenn at SemEval-2017 Task 4A: A simple, self-optimizing text classification system combining dense and sparse vectors. In *Proceedings of the 11th International Workshop on Semantic Evaluation*. Vancouver, Canada, SemEval '17, pages 639–642.

Fabrizio Sebastiani. 2015. An axiomatically derived measure for the evaluation of classification algorithms. In *Proceedings of the 2015 International Conference on The Theory of Information Retrieval*. Northampton, Massachusetts, USA, ICTIR '15, pages 11–20.

Carlo Strapparava and Rada Mihalcea. 2007. SemEval-2007 Task 14: Affective text. In *Proceedings of the Fourth International Workshop on Semantic Evaluations*. Prague, Czech Republic, SemEval '07, pages 70–74.

Symeon Symeonidis, Dimitrios Effrosynidis, John Kordonis, and Avi Arampatzis. 2017. DUTH at SemEval-2017 Task 4: A voting classification approach for Twitter sentiment analysis. In *Proceedings of the 11th International Workshop on Semantic Evaluation*. Vancouver, Canada, SemEval '17, pages 703–707.

Raphael Troncy, Enrico Palumbo, Efstratios Sygkounas, and Giuseppe Rizzo. 2017. SentiME++ at SemEval-2017 Task 4: Stacking state-of-the-art classifiers to enhance sentiment classification. In *Proceedings of the 11th International Workshop on Semantic Evaluation*. Vancouver, Canada, SemEval '17, pages 647–651.

Andrea Vanzo, Danilo Croce, and Roberto Basili. 2014. A context-based model for sentiment analysis in Twitter. In *Proceedings of the 25th International*

Conference on Computational Linguistics: Technical Papers. Dublin, Ireland, COLING '14, pages 2345–2354.

Svitlana Volkova, Theresa Wilson, and David Yarowsky. 2013. Exploring demographic language variations to improve multilingual sentiment analysis in social media. In *Proceedings of the Conference on Empirical Methods in Natural Language Processing*. Seattle, Washington, USA, EMNLP '13, pages 1815–1827.

Ming Wang, Biao Chu, Qingxun Liu, and Xiaobing Zhou. 2017. YNUDLG at SemEval-2017 Task 4: A GRU-SVM model for sentiment classification and quantification in Twitter. In *Proceedings of the 11th International Workshop on Semantic Evaluation*. Vancouver, Canada, SemEval '17, pages 712–716.

Tzu-Hsuan Yang, Tzu-Hsuan Tseng, and Chia-Ping Chen. 2017. deepSA at SemEval-2017 Task 4: Interpolated deep neural networks for sentiment analysis in Twitter. In *Proceedings of the 11th International Workshop on Semantic Evaluation*. Vancouver, Canada, SemEval '17, pages 615–619.

Yi Yang and Jacob Eisenstein. 2015. Putting things in context: Community-specific embedding projections for sentiment analysis. *CoRR* abs/1511.06052.

Yichun Yin, Yangqiu Song, and Ming Zhang. 2017. NNEMBs at SemEval-2017 Task 4: Neural Twitter sentiment classification: a simple ensemble method with different embeddings. In *Proceedings of the 11th International Workshop on Semantic Evaluation*. Vancouver, Canada, SemEval '17, pages 620–624.

Joosung Yoon, Hyeoncheol Kim, and Kigon Lyu. 2017. Adullam at SemEval-2017 Task 4: Sentiment analyzer using lexicon integrated convolutional neural networks with attention. In *Proceedings of the 11th International Workshop on Semantic Evaluation*. Vancouver, Canada, SemEval '17, pages 731–735.

Haowei Zhang, Jin Wang, Jixian Zhang, and Xuejie Zhang. 2017. YNU-HPCC at SemEval 2017 Task 4: Using a multi-channel CNN-LSTM model for sentiment classification. In *Proceedings of the 11th International Workshop on Semantic Evaluation*. Vancouver, Canada, SemEval '17, pages 795–800.

Jingjing Zhao, Yan Yang, and Bing Xu. 2017. MI&T Lab at SemEval-2017 Task 4: An integrated training method of word vector for sentiment classification. In *Proceedings of the 11th International Workshop on Semantic Evaluation*. Vancouver, Canada, SemEval '17, pages 688–692.

Yunxiao Zhou, Man Lan, and Yuanbin Wu. 2017. ECNU at SemEval-2017 Task 4: Evaluating effective features on machine learning methods for Twitter message polarity classification. In *Proceedings of the 11th International Workshop on Semantic Evaluation*. Vancouver, Canada, Semeval 2017, pages 811–815.

Association for Computational Linguistics
209 N. Eighth Street
Stroudsburg, Pennsylvania 18360

ISBN 978-1-5108-4563-3

11th International Workshop on Semantic Evaluation (SemEval 2017)

Vancouver, Canada
3 – 4 August 2017

Volume 2 of 2

11th International Workshop on Semantic Evaluation (SemEval 2017)

Vancouver, Canada
3 – 4 August 2017

Volume 2 of 2

ISBN: 978-1-5108-4563-3

ACL 2017

11th International Workshop on Semantic Evaluations (SemEval-2017)

Proceedings of the Workshop

August 3 - 4, 2017
Vancouver, Canada

Welcome to SemEval-2017

The Semantic Evaluation (SemEval) series of workshops focuses on the evaluation and comparison of systems that can analyse diverse semantic phenomena in text with the aim of extending the current state of the art in semantic analysis and creating high quality annotated datasets in a range of increasingly challenging problems in natural language semantics. SemEval provides an exciting forum for researchers to propose challenging research problems in semantics and to build systems/techniques to address such research problems.

SemEval-2017 is the eleventh workshop in the series of International Workshops on Semantic Evaluation. The first three workshops, SensEval-1 (1998), SensEval-2 (2001), and SensEval-3 (2004), focused on word sense disambiguation, each time growing in the number of languages offered, in the number of tasks, and also in the number of participating teams. In 2007, the workshop was renamed to SemEval, and the subsequent SemEval workshops evolved to include semantic analysis tasks beyond word sense disambiguation. In 2012, SemEval turned into a yearly event. It currently runs every year, but on a two-year cycle, i.e., the tasks for SemEval-2017 were proposed in 2016.

SemEval-2017 was co-located with the 55th annual meeting of the Association for Computational Linguistics (ACL'2017) in Vancouver, Canada. It included the following 12 shared tasks organized in three tracks:

Semantic comparison for words and texts

- Task 1: Semantic Textual Similarity

- Task 2: Multi-lingual and Cross-lingual Semantic Word Similarity

- Task 3: Community Question Answering

Detecting sentiment, humor, and truth

- Task 4: Sentiment Analysis in Twitter

- Task 5: Fine-Grained Sentiment Analysis on Financial Microblogs and News

- Task 6: #HashtagWars: Learning a Sense of Humor

- Task 7: Detection and Interpretation of English Puns

- Task 8: RumourEval: Determining rumour veracity and support for rumours

Parsing semantic structures

- Task 9: Abstract Meaning Representation Parsing and Generation

- Task 10: Extracting Keyphrases and Relations from Scientific Publications

- Task 11: End-User Development using Natural Language

- Task 12: Clinical TempEval

This volume contains both Task Description papers that describe each of the above tasks and System Description papers that describe the systems that participated in the above tasks. A total of 12 task description papers and 169 system description papers are included in this volume.

We are grateful to all task organizers as well as the large number of participants whose enthusiastic participation has made SemEval once again a successful event. We are thankful to the task organizers who also served as area chairs, and to task organizers and participants who reviewed paper submissions. These proceedings have greatly benefited from their detailed and thoughtful feedback. We also thank the ACL 2017 conference organizers for their support. Finally, we most gratefully acknowledge the support of our sponsor, the ACL Special Interest Group on the Lexicon (SIGLEX).

The SemEval-2017 organizers,

Steven Bethard, Marine Carpuat, Marianna Apidianaki, Saif M. Mohammad, Daniel Cer, David Jurgens

Nigel Collier, University of Cambridge
Keith Cortis, University of Passau
Mrinal Das, University of Massachusetts Amherst
Tobias Daudert, INSIGHT Centre for Data Analytics
Leon Derczynski, University of Sheffield
Mona Diab, George Washington University
Noura Farra, Columbia University
Andre Freitas, University of Passau
Iryna Gurevych, Technische Universität Darmstadt
Siegfried Handschuh, University of Passau
Christian F. Hempelmann, Texas A&M University-Commerce
Doris Hoogeveen, The University of Melbourne
Manuela Huerlimann, INSIGHT Centre for Data Analytics
Maria Liakata, University of Warwick
Iñigo Lopez-Gazpio, University of Basque Country
Lluís Màrquez, Qatar Computing Research Institute, HBKU
Jonathan May, University of Southern California Information Sciences Institute
Andrew McCallum, University of Massachusetts Amherst
Tristan Miller, Technische Universität Darmstadt
Alessandro Moschitti, Qatar Computing Research Institute, HBKU
Hamdy Mubarak, Qatar Computing Research Institute, HBKU
Preslav Nakov, Qatar Computing Research Institute, HBKU
Preslav Nakov, Qatar Computing Research Institute, HBKU
Roberto Navigli, Sapienza University of Rome
Martha Palmer, University of Colorado
Mohammad Taher Pilehvar, University of Cambridge
Peter Potash, University of Massachusetts Lowell
Rob Procter, University of Warwick
James Pustejovsky, Brandeis University
Sebastian Riedel, University College London
Alexey Romanov, University of Massachusetts Lowell
Sara Rosenthal, IBM Research
Anna Rumshisky, University of Massachusetts Lowell
Juliano Sales, University of Passau
Guergana Savova, Harvard University
Lucia Specia, University of Sheffield
Karin Verspoor, The University of Melbourne
Lakshmi Vikraman, University of Massachusetts Amherst
Geraldine Wong Sak Hoi, swissinfo.ch
Manel Zarrouk, INSIGHT Centre for Data Analytics
Arkaitz Zubiaga, University of Warwick

Table of Contents

Conference Program

3 August 2017

09:00–09:15 *Welcome / Opening Remarks*

09:15–10:30 *Invited Talk: From Naive Physics to Connotation: Modeling Commonsense in Frame Semantics*
Yejin Choi

10:30–11:00 *Coffee*

11:00–12:30 **Task Descriptions**

11:00–11:15 *SemEval-2017 Task 1: Semantic Textual Similarity Multilingual and Crosslingual Focused Evaluation*
Daniel Cer, Mona Diab, Eneko Agirre, Inigo Lopez-Gazpio and Lucia Specia

11:15–11:30 *SemEval-2017 Task 2: Multilingual and Cross-lingual Semantic Word Similarity*
Jose Camacho-Collados, Mohammad Taher Pilehvar, Nigel Collier and Roberto Navigli

11:30–11:45 *SemEval-2017 Task 3: Community Question Answering*
Preslav Nakov, Doris Hoogeveen, Lluís Màrquez, Alessandro Moschitti, Hamdy Mubarak, Timothy Baldwin and Karin Verspoor

11:45–12:00 *SemEval-2017 Task 6: #HashtagWars: Learning a Sense of Humor*
Peter Potash, Alexey Romanov and Anna Rumshisky

12:00–12:15 *SemEval-2017 Task 7: Detection and Interpretation of English Puns*
Tristan Miller, Christian Hempelmann and Iryna Gurevych

12:15–12:30 *SemEval-2017 Task 8: RumourEval: Determining rumour veracity and support for rumours*
Leon Derczynski, Kalina Bontcheva, Maria Liakata, Rob Procter, Geraldine Wong Sak Hoi and Arkaitz Zubiaga

12:30–14:00 *Lunch*

16:30–17:30   Poster Session

16:30–17:30   *CompiLIG at SemEval-2017 Task 1: Cross-Language Plagiarism Detection Methods for Semantic Textual Similarity*
Jérémy Ferrero, Laurent Besacier, Didier Schwab and Frédéric Agnès

16:30–17:30   *UdL at SemEval-2017 Task 1: Semantic Textual Similarity Estimation of English Sentence Pairs Using Regression Model over Pairwise Features*
Hussein T. Al-Natsheh, Lucie Martinet, Fabrice Muhlenbach and Djamel Abdelkader ZIGHED

16:30–17:30   *DT_Team at SemEval-2017 Task 1: Semantic Similarity Using Alignments, Sentence-Level Embeddings and Gaussian Mixture Model Output*
Nabin Maharjan, Rajendra Banjade, Dipesh Gautam, Lasang J. Tamang and Vasile Rus

16:30–17:30   *FCICU at SemEval-2017 Task 1: Sense-Based Language Independent Semantic Textual Similarity Approach*
Basma Hassan, Samir AbdelRahman, Reem Bahgat and Ibrahim Farag

16:30–17:30   *HCTI at SemEval-2017 Task 1: Use convolutional neural network to evaluate Semantic Textual Similarity*
Yang Shao

16:30–17:30   *LIM-LIG at SemEval-2017 Task1: Enhancing the Semantic Similarity for Arabic Sentences with Vectors Weighting*
El Moatez Billah NAGOUDI, Jérémy Ferrero and Didier Schwab

16:30–17:30   *OPI-JSA at SemEval-2017 Task 1: Application of Ensemble learning for computing semantic textual similarity*
Martyna Śpiewak, Piotr Sobecki and Daniel Karaś

16:30–17:30   *Lump at SemEval-2017 Task 1: Towards an Interlingua Semantic Similarity*
Cristina España-Bonet and Alberto Barrón-Cedeño

16:30–17:30   *QLUT at SemEval-2017 Task 1: Semantic Textual Similarity Based on Word Embeddings*
Fanqing Meng, Wenpeng Lu, Yuteng Zhang, Jinyong Cheng, Yuehan Du and Shuwang Han

16:30–17:30   *ResSim at SemEval-2017 Task 1: Multilingual Word Representations for Semantic Textual Similarity*
Johannes Bjerva and Robert Östling

16:30–17:30   *ITNLP-AiKF at SemEval-2017 Task 1: Rich Features Based SVR for Semantic Textual Similarity Computing*
Wenjie Liu, Chengjie Sun, Lei Lin and Bingquan Liu

16:30–17:30   *Jmp8 at SemEval-2017 Task 2: A simple and general distributional approach to estimate word similarity*
Josué Melka and Gilles Bernard

16:30–17:30   *QLUT at SemEval-2017 Task 2: Word Similarity Based on Word Embedding and Knowledge Base*
Fanqing Meng, Wenpeng Lu, Yuteng Zhang, Ping Jian, Shumin Shi and Heyan Huang

16:30–17:30   *RUFINO at SemEval-2017 Task 2: Cross-lingual lexical similarity by extending PMI and word embeddings systems with a Swadesh's-like list*
Sergio Jimenez, George Dueñas, Lorena Gaitan and Jorge Segura

16:30–17:30   *MERALI at SemEval-2017 Task 2 Subtask 1: a Cognitively Inspired approach*
Enrico Mensa, Daniele P. Radicioni and Antonio Lieto

16:30–17:30   *HHU at SemEval-2017 Task 2: Fast Hash-Based Embeddings for Semantic Word Similarity Assessment*
Behrang QasemiZadeh and Laura Kallmeyer

16:30–17:30   *Mahtab at SemEval-2017 Task 2: Combination of Corpus-based and Knowledge-based Methods to Measure Semantic Word Similarity*
Niloofar Ranjbar, Fatemeh Mashhadirajab, Mehrnoush Shamsfard, Rayeheh Hosseini pour and Aryan Vahid pour

16:30–17:30   *Sew-Embed at SemEval-2017 Task 2: Language-Independent Concept Representations from a Semantically Enriched Wikipedia*
Claudio Delli Bovi and Alessandro Raganato

16:30–17:30   *Wild Devs' at SemEval-2017 Task 2: Using Neural Networks to Discover Word Similarity*
Răzvan-Gabriel Rotari, Ionut Hulub, Stefan Oprea, Mihaela Plamada-Onofrei, Alina Beatrice Lorent, Raluca Preisler, Adrian Iftene and Diana Trandabat

16:30–17:30   *TrentoTeam at SemEval-2017 Task 3: An application of Grice Maxims in Ranking Community Question Answers*
Mohammed R. H. Qwaider, Abed Alhakim Freihat and Fausto Giunchiglia

16:30–17:30   *UPC-USMBA at SemEval-2017 Task 3: Combining multiple approaches for CQA for Arabic*
Yassine El Adlouni, Imane Lahbari, Horacio Rodriguez, Mohammed Meknassi, Said Ouatik El Alaoui and Noureddine Ennahnahi

16:30–17:30   *Beihang-MSRA at SemEval-2017 Task 3: A Ranking System with Neural Matching Features for Community Question Answering*
Wenzheng Feng, Yu Wu, Wei Wu, Zhoujun Li and Ming Zhou

16:30–17:30   *MoRS at SemEval-2017 Task 3: Easy to use SVM in Ranking Tasks*
Miguel J. Rodrigues and Francisco M Couto

16:30–17:30   *EICA Team at SemEval-2017 Task 3: Semantic and Metadata-based Features for Community Question Answering*
Yufei Xie, Maoquan Wang, Jing Ma, Jian Jiang and Zhao Lu

16:30–17:30   *FA3L at SemEval-2017 Task 3: A ThRee Embeddings Recurrent Neural Network for Question Answering*
Giuseppe Attardi, Antonio Carta, Federico Errica, Andrea Madotto and Ludovica Pannitto

16:30–17:30   *SCIR-QA at SemEval-2017 Task 3: CNN Model Based on Similar and Dissimilar Information between Keywords for Question Similarity*
Le Qi, Yu Zhang and Ting Liu

16:30–17:30   *LearningToQuestion at SemEval 2017 Task 3: Ranking Similar Questions by Learning to Rank Using Rich Features*
Naman Goyal

16:30–17:30   *SimBow at SemEval-2017 Task 3: Soft-Cosine Semantic Similarity between Questions for Community Question Answering*
Delphine Charlet and Geraldine Damnati

16:30–17:30   *FuRongWang at SemEval-2017 Task 3: Deep Neural Networks for Selecting Relevant Answers in Community Question Answering*
Sheng Zhang, Jiajun Cheng, Hui Wang, Xin Zhang, Pei Li and Zhaoyun Ding

16:30–17:30   *KeLP at SemEval-2017 Task 3: Learning Pairwise Patterns in Community Question Answering*
Simone Filice, Giovanni Da San Martino and Alessandro Moschitti

16:30–17:30   *SwissAlps at SemEval-2017 Task 3: Attention-based Convolutional Neural Network for Community Question Answering*
Jan Milan Deriu and Mark Cieliebak

16:30–17:30   *TakeLab-QA at SemEval-2017 Task 3: Classification Experiments for Answer Retrieval in Community QA*
Filip Šaina, Toni Kukurin, Lukrecija Puljić, Mladen Karan and Jan Šnajder

16:30–17:30   *GW_QA at SemEval-2017 Task 3: Question Answer Re-ranking on Arabic Fora*
Nada Almarwani and Mona Diab

16:30–17:30   *NLM_NIH at SemEval-2017 Task 3: from Question Entailment to Question Similarity for Community Question Answering*
Asma Ben Abacha and Dina Demner-Fushman

16:30–17:30   *bunji at SemEval-2017 Task 3: Combination of Neural Similarity Features and Comment Plausibility Features*
Yuta Koreeda, Takuya Hashito, Yoshiki Niwa, Misa Sato, Toshihiko Yanase, Kenzo Kurotsuchi and Kohsuke Yanai

4 Aug 2017 (continued)

11:00–12:30   Task Descriptions

11:00–11:15   *SemEval-2017 Task 4: Sentiment Analysis in Twitter*
Sara Rosenthal, Noura Farra and Preslav Nakov

11:15–11:30   *SemEval-2017 Task 5: Fine-Grained Sentiment Analysis on Financial Microblogs and News*
Keith Cortis, André Freitas, Tobias Daudert, Manuela Huerlimann, Manel Zarrouk, Siegfried Handschuh and Brian Davis

11:30–11:45   *SemEval-2017 Task 9: Abstract Meaning Representation Parsing and Generation*
Jonathan May and Jay Priyadarshi

11:45–12:00   *SemEval 2017 Task 10: ScienceIE - Extracting Keyphrases and Relations from Scientific Publications*
Isabelle Augenstein, Mrinal Das, Sebastian Riedel, Lakshmi Vikraman and Andrew McCallum

12:00–12:15   *SemEval-2017 Task 11: End-User Development using Natural Language*
Juliano Sales, Siegfried Handschuh and André Freitas

12:15–12:30   *SemEval-2017 Task 12: Clinical TempEval*
Steven Bethard, Guergana Savova, Martha Palmer and James Pustejovsky

12:30–14:00   *Lunch*

14:00–15:30   **Best Of SemEval**

14:00–14:15   *BB_twtr at SemEval-2017 Task 4: Twitter Sentiment Analysis with CNNs and LSTMs*
Mathieu Cliche

14:15–14:30   *Lancaster A at SemEval-2017 Task 5: Evaluation metrics matter: predicting sentiment from financial news headlines*
Andrew Moore and Paul Rayson

14:30–14:45   *Sheffield at SemEval-2017 Task 9: Transition-based language generation from AMR.*
Gerasimos Lampouras and Andreas Vlachos

14:45–15:00   *The AI2 system at SemEval-2017 Task 10 (ScienceIE): semi-supervised end-to-end entity and relation extraction*
Waleed Ammar, Matthew Peters, Chandra Bhagavatula and Russell Power

15:00–15:15   *LIMSI-COT at SemEval-2017 Task 12: Neural Architecture for Temporal Information Extraction from Clinical Narratives*
Julien Tourille, Olivier Ferret, Xavier Tannier and Aurélie Névéol

15:30–16:00   *Coffee*

16:00–16:30   *Discussion*

16:30–17:30   **Poster Session**

16:30–17:30   *OMAM at SemEval-2017 Task 4: Evaluation of English State-of-the-Art Sentiment Analysis Models for Arabic and a New Topic-based Model*
Ramy Baly, Gilbert Badaro, Ali Hamdi, Rawan Moukalled, Rita Aoun, Georges El-Khoury, Ahmad Al Sallab, Hazem Hajj, Nizar Habash, Khaled Shaban and Wassim El-Hajj

16:30–17:30   *NILC-USP at SemEval-2017 Task 4: A Multi-view Ensemble for Twitter Sentiment Analysis*
Edilson Anselmo Corrêa Júnior, Vanessa Queiroz Marinho and Leandro Borges dos Santos

16:30–17:30   *deepSA at SemEval-2017 Task 4: Interpolated Deep Neural Networks for Sentiment Analysis in Twitter*
Tzu-Hsuan Yang, Tzu-Hsuan Tseng and Chia-Ping Chen

16:30–17:30   *LIPN at SemEval-2017 Task 10: Filtering Candidate Keyphrases from Scientific Publications with Part-of-Speech Tag Sequences to Train a Sequence Labeling Model*
Simon David Hernandez, Davide Buscaldi and Thierry Charnois

16:30–17:30   *EUDAMU at SemEval-2017 Task 11: Action Ranking and Type Matching for End-User Development*
Marek Kubis, Paweł Skórzewski and Tomasz Ziętkiewicz

16:30–17:30   *Hitachi at SemEval-2017 Task 12: System for temporal information extraction from clinical notes*
Sarath P R, Manikandan R and Yoshiki Niwa

16:30–17:30   *NTU-1 at SemEval-2017 Task 12: Detection and classification of temporal events in clinical data with domain adaptation*
Po-Yu Huang, Hen-Hsen Huang, Yu-Wun Wang, Ching Huang and Hsin-Hsi Chen

16:30–17:30   *XJNLP at SemEval-2017 Task 12: Clinical temporal information ex-traction with a Hybrid Model*
Yu Long, Zhijing Li, Xuan Wang and Chen Li

16:30–17:30   *ULISBOA at SemEval-2017 Task 12: Extraction and classification of temporal expressions and events*
Andre Lamurias, Diana Sousa, Sofia Pereira, Luka Clarke and Francisco M Couto

16:30–17:30   *GUIR at SemEval-2017 Task 12: A Framework for Cross-Domain Clinical Temporal Information Extraction*
Sean MacAvaney, Arman Cohan and Nazli Goharian

16:30–17:30   *KULeuven-LIIR at SemEval-2017 Task 12: Cross-Domain Temporal Information Extraction from Clinical Records*
Artuur Leeuwenberg and Marie-Francine Moens

SemEval-2017 Task 5: Fine-Grained Sentiment Analysis on Financial Microblogs and News

Keith Cortis[*], André Freitas[*], Tobias Daudert[**], Manuela Hürlimann[**],
Manel Zarrouk[**], Siegfried Handschuh[*], and Brian Davis[**]

[*]Department of Computer Science and Mathematics, University of Passau, Germany
[**]Insight Centre for Data Analytics, National University of Ireland, Galway

Abstract

This paper discusses the "Fine-Grained Sentiment Analysis on Financial Microblogs and News" task as part of SemEval-2017, specifically under the "Detecting sentiment, humour, and truth" theme. This task contains two tracks, where the first one concerns Microblog messages and the second one covers News Statements and Headlines. The main goal behind both tracks was to predict the sentiment score for each of the mentioned companies/stocks. The sentiment scores for each text instance adopted floating point values in the range of -1 (very negative/bearish) to 1 (very positive/bullish), with 0 designating neutral sentiment. This task attracted a total of 32 participants, with 25 participating in Track 1 and 29 in Track 2.

1 Overview

Our task is focused on Sentiment Analysis in the domain of financial microblogs and news. Domain-specific Sentiment Analysis has received much attention within the NLP community, motivated by the highly domain-dependent language used to express sentiment (Liu, 2012). Domain-specificity impacts all levels of analysis. On the lexical level, which is crucial in sentiment analysis, Liu (2012) notes that positive words in one domain can be negative in another, and vice versa. For instance, Loughran and McDonald (2011a) show that many words which are considered negative in general-purpose polarity lexicon have a neutral meaning in the financial domain (e.g. "liability"). This makes it difficult to transport sentiment classifiers across domains and underlines the need for domain-specific tools.

The financial domain is a high-impact use case for Sentiment Analysis because it has been shown that sentiments and opinions can affect market dynamics (Goonatilake and Herath, 2007; de Kauter et al., 2015). Sentiments are in some cases derived from news which discuss macroeconomic factors, company-specific, or political information as all of these can be market-relevant (Sinha, 2014). Good news tends to lift markets and increase optimism (de Kauter et al., 2015; Schuster, 2003). Evidence has been found that both quantitative measures (e.g. the quantity of news, market fluctuation) and qualitative indicators, (e.g. linguistic style and tone) affect investors' behaviour (Tetlock et al., 2008; Loughran and McDonald, 2011a; Takala et al., 2014). (Bollen et al., 2011) showed that changes in public mood reflect value shifts in the Dow Jones Industrial Index three to four days later.

Given the link between sentiment and market dynamics, the analysis of public sentiment becomes a powerful method to predict the market reaction. However, the accuracy of machine learning-based sentiment analysis approaches rarely exceeds seventy percent (Takala et al., 2014; Eagle Alpha, 2016). Research effort is required to overcome and address complex linguistic issues, such as sarcasm, irony and poorly-structured and/or colloquial language (Eagle Alpha, 2016). In addition, text that is short in length (such as microblog messages) can be quite opinionated, dense in information, dependent on the modelling of economic context and challenging to parse, due to the different vocabularies used (Sinha, 2014). Our task is motivated by the interest of this field and the great potential for improvement. It aims at assessing the overall market sentiment as well as sentiment about specific stocks and thus to make use of their predictive power.

More specifically, the aim of organising this task and creating this test collection was to achieve the following goals:

1. Developing state-of-the-art on classification

Proceedings of the 11th International Workshop on Semantic Evaluations (SemEval-2017), pages 519–535,
Vancouver, Canada, August 3 - 4, 2017. ©2017 Association for Computational Linguistics"

methods for sentiment analysis in the domain of financial short texts.

2. Incentivising the creation of new lexical resources for the financial domain.

3. Understanding how state-of-the-art sentiment analysis performs on a domain-specific / highly technical corpus.

4. Improving the understanding of linguistic phenomena and the creation of semantic models for the financial domain.

The domain of finance has unique linguistic and semantic features, whose interpretation depends on the formulation of semantic models which reflect the economic and mathematical tools used by the experts to assess financial information. Moreover, the accurate interpretation of financial text requires the orchestration of large volumes of common sense and domain-specific financial/economic knowledge. Additionally, as much of the financial discourse is mediated by terms which demand precise definitions, many times associated with the quantification of economic phenomena, the semantic interpretation processes in the financial domain require fine-grained semantic interpretation approaches.

From a linguistic standpoint, topics of interest in this task include (but are not limited to):

- Low-level linguistic analysis tools for the financial domain (e.g. tokenization, part-of-speech tagging, parsing)

- Sentiment classification on financial texts;

- Understanding of linguistic phenomena associated with financial tweets;

- New semantic models for finance;

- Construction and application of distributional semantic models on finance;

- Sentiment compositionality;

- Machine learning approaches for sentiment classification;

- Lexical resources for the financial domain;

2 Data

2.1 Tracks

The test collection consists of two tracks:

1. **Microblog Messages** derived from two sources:

   (a) *StockTwits Messages*: Consists of microblog messages focusing on stock market events and assessments from investors and traders, exchanged via the StockTwits microblogging platform[1]. Typical stocktwits consist of references to company stock symbols (so-called cashtags - a stock symbol preceded by "$", e.g. "$AAPL" for the company Apple Inc.), a short supporting text or references to a link or pictures (typically containing charts showing stock values analysis).

   (b) *Twitter Messages*: Some stock market discussion also takes place on the Twitter platform[2]. In order to extend and diversify our data sources, we extract Twitter posts containing company stock symbols (cashtags).

2. **News Statements & Headlines** Sentences have been taken from news headlines as well as news text. The textual content was crawled from different sources on the Internet, such as Yahoo Finance[3]. The Enterprise identification for this track was based on company names and abbreviations, as cashtags are not typically used in news statements and headlines.

2.2 Corpus Creation

The corpus of statements was created by conducting random sampling and an initial filtering process over a pool of StockTwits messages, tweets and RSS News feeds.

While the random sampling ensured an unbiased set of statements, the filtering mechanism aimed at removing messages from the set microblog messages which are spam. The filtering mechanism was based on a manual curation of the set of microblog users which are classified as spammers. The goal of data sampling is to come up with a most representative and manageable amount of data for manual annotation. The first step in our case is to ap-

---

ply a stratified random sampling by objects δ per the smallest time unit level θ we determine (in our case it is stock's messages per day) to ensure that all different objects are adequately represented in the sample with respect to their distribution in the population. Then, the random samples of a time-unit level θ_i are pooled into a time-unit level θ_{i+1} and randomly sampled.

The purpose of re-sampling at different time-unit levels is to make the resulted random sample more random, more balanced and more representative of the entire time-span of our data. A general negative sentiment in a certain sub-sample will be counter-balanced by the other sub-samples.

StockTwits data have been provided by Stock-Twits in a batch export and refer to the period from October 2011 to June 2015. The original pool before sampling contains 27 million StockTwits, from which 1847 messages were sampled. Twitter data was collected between March 11th and 18th 2016 using the official Streaming APIs. Sampling was also applied to this data and resulted in a sample of 1591 messages.

The News Statements and Headlines have been collected from a pool of 20.000 RSS feeds in the period between August and November 2015 (e.g. AP News, Reuters, Handelsblatt, Bloomberg and Forbes). A final set of about 1780 News Statements and Headlines has been produced.

2.3 Annotation

To create the Gold Standard, the final sample has been annotated by 3 independent financial expert annotators using a Web platform developed for that purpose and according to the annotations guidelines we defined. A fourth domain expert consolidated the ratings to create the final data set. The total time the experts spend on annotating and consolidating the data set is 120 hours (30 hours per expert). The costs of annotation and consolidation have been covered by ICT-15-2014 Grant: 645425 (SSIX project).

Each statement (instance) is annotated with the following information:

- **Cashtag (subtask1) / Company (subtask2)**: A stock company symbol (for microblogs) or reference to a company (for news/headlines) to which a sentiment score is assigned.

- **Sentiment Score**: A sentiment between -1 (very negative/bearish) and 1 (very positive/bullish), with 0 representing neutral/no sentiment is assigned to each cashtag or company. The sentiment is assigned from the point of view of an investor and the sentiment annotation is carried out by domain experts. Textual data containing information implying a positive prospective trend for a company or stock, the markets, or the economy, in general, constitutes a positive sentiment, whereas information revealing negative trends constitutes a negative sentiment since it may impact companies, markets or the economy negatively.

- **Span (subtask 1)**: extract of a text string in which sentiment is expressed.

- **Message (subtask 1) / Title (subtask2)**: Text string in which sentiment is expressed.

- **Source (subtask 1)**: Either "twitter" or "stock-twits" dependent on the origin of the text message.

Examples of annotated microblog messages and news headlines are provided in Section 2.6 below.

The quality of the annotations was assessed following a similar methodology as proposed in Takala et al. (2014), where inter-annotator agreements measures for continuous data is calculated for the sentiment classifications. Spearman's Rank Correlation on sentiment scores was calculated for each pair of annotators, then averaged across annotator pairs. This yielded the following results: 0.54 for news headlines (three annotators, three pairs) and 0.69 for microblogs (four annotators, six pairs).

2.4 Gold Standard

After annotating and consolidating the data, the gold standard for subtask 1 consists of 2510 Twitter and StockTwit messages. The gold standard for subtask 2 contains 1647 Headlines and News Statements.

2.5 Task Formulation

Participating systems needed to fulfil the following task: given a text instance (microblog message in Track 1, news statement or headline in Track 2; cp. Section 2.1), predicting the sentiment score for each of the companies/stocks mentioned. Sentiment values needed to be floating point values within the range of -1 (very negative/bearish) to 1 (very positive/bullish), with 0 designating neutral sentiment.

2.6 Examples

Below we present annotated example statements, two for microblogs and one for news. Please note that sentiment score agreement as per Section 2.3 is not given as annotations for these examples were provided by a single expert. Also, the string covered by the 'span' is given for ease of reading.

Microblogs

> Este Lauder beats on Revenues and EPS and boosts dividend 25% - global growth in the Middle Class trend continues. $EL $NKE $SBUX $AAPL

- **Sentiment Score**:
    - $EL: 0.95
    - $NKE: 0.5
    - $SBUX: 0.5
    - $AAPL : 0.5

- **Cashtag**
    - $EL
    - $NKE
    - $SBUX
    - $AAPL

- **Span**
    - $EL:
        * (13, 38) - "beats on Revenues and EPS"
        * (43, 62) - "boosts dividend 25%"
        * (65, 144) - "global growth in the Middle Class trend continues"
    - $NKE, $SBUX, $AAPL:
        * (65, 144) - "global growth in the Middle Class trend continues"

> Awaiting These Sell Signals on the $SPY & $QQQ - https://t.co/GF9PRk5OUF $TQQQ $SQQQ https://t.co/W97yN4Zb4N

- **Sentiment Score**:
    - $SPY: -0.25
    - $QQQ: -0.15
    - $TQQQ: -0.15
    - $SQQQ : 0.10

- **Cashtag**
    - $SPY
    - $QQQ
    - $TQQQ
    - $SQQQ

- **Span**
    - $SPY:
        * (0, 41) - "Awaiting These Sell Signals on the $SPY"
        * (From the blog post) - "this bearish rising wedge for the next sell signal in the SPY"
        * (From the blog post) - Chart shows a bearish rising wedge
    - $QQQ, $TQQQ:
        * The message and blog make reference to shorting the SPY, but as but indexes are strongly correlated so some of the sentiment for SPY could be transferred to these ETFs.
    - $SQQQ:
        * The message and blog make reference to shorting the SPY, but as indexes are strongly correlated so some of the sentiment for SPY could be transferred to this ETF but inverted.

News Statements & Headlines

> First Solar, Vivint Solar Lead Short Interest Trend

- **Sentiment Score**:
    - First Solar: -0.7
    - Vivint Solar: -0.7

- **Company**

  - First Solar
  - Vivint Solar

2.7 Assessment Infrastructure & Baselines

Two classification baselines were provided:

- **Random selection:** Consists of a random number generated within the sentiment range.

- **SentiWordNet-based average and maximum functions:** Consist of the maximum and averaging of all the sentiment words using a simple SentiWordNet-based lookup.

For the Microblogs test set, SentiWordNet lexicon-based look-up (average) achieved an average score of 0.3021, while the same look-up method using the max/min score achieved 0.2428. The random baseline achieved 0.0148.

For the Financial Headlines test set, a SentiWordNet lexicon-based look-up classifier, which averages all the sentiment scores of individual lemmatised words, achieved a score of 0.290, while the same look-up method using a max/min score achieved 0.2184. The random baseline achieved 0.1064.

3 Pilot Task

A pilot dataset consisting of financial social data was collected from two on-line social networking services, specifically Twitter and StockTwits, as part of a pilot study carried out within the **SSIX: Social Sentiment analysis financial IndeXes**[4] project as part of the European Horizon 2020 Research and Innovation programme (Davis et al., 2016). A domain expert experienced in trading annotated 100 tweets and 100 StockTwits messages selected randomly. He annotated the messages for sentiment following the guideline of assuming the point of view of an investor in the given stock(s) (see Section 2.3 above).

The results from the pilot study provided valuable insights with regards to the distribution of sentiment and the need for improved filtering (Figures 3 and 2). These insights proved to be valuable when building the data set for this task, enabling us to provide a higher-quality data collection.

The results (Figure 1) showed a relatively even distribution of positive and negative sentiment, with slight differences between the StockTwits and Twitter sources as regards the intensity of the sentiment

[4]http://ssix-project.eu/

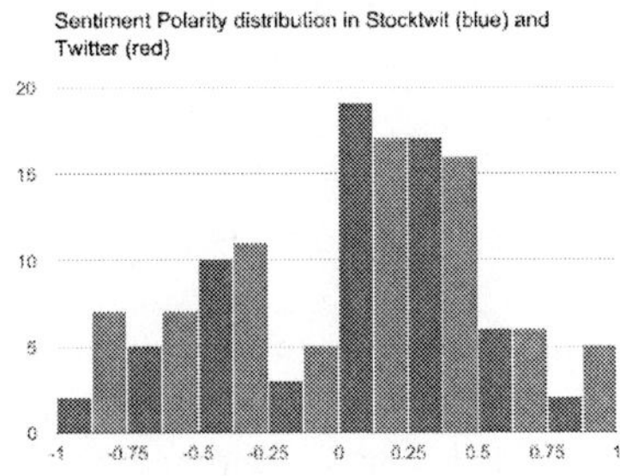

Figure 1: Pilot results on sentiment distribution for StockTwits and Twitter

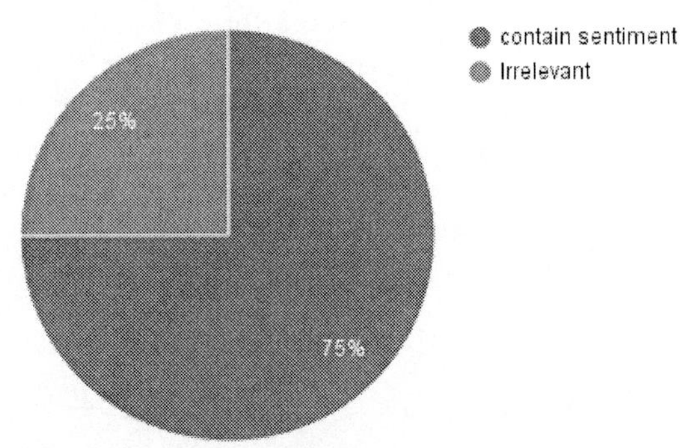

Figure 2

Pilot results on percentage of sentiment-containing and irrelevant messages on Twitter.

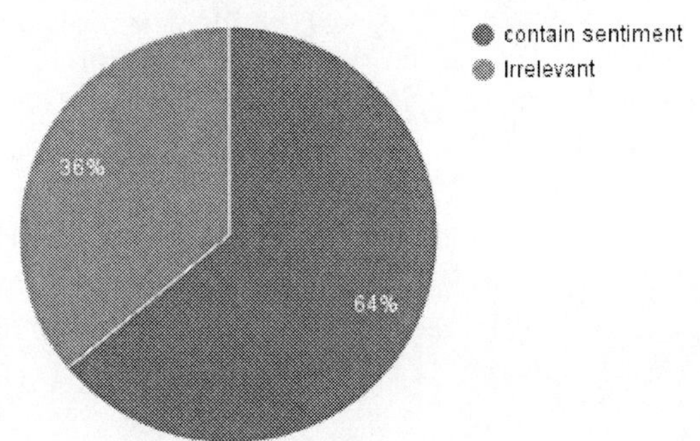

Figure 3

Pilot results on percentage of sentiment-containing and irrelevant messages on StockTwits.

The pilot study also pointed to the need to improve the filtering phase as 25% - 36% of Twitter and StockTwits messages, respectively, have been deemed irrelevant (i.e. spam and/or not providing any relevant financial sentiment) by the annotator (figure 3 and 2). As a consequence, filtering rules have been added to the filtering phase and the data for the gold standard proposed in this task underwent additionally manual post-filtering by a domain expert prior to sentiment annotation. This is ensuring that only relevant messages are included in the data set.

4 Evaluation

The Evaluation of the participating systems was based on cosine similarity, in a spirit similar to Ghosh et al. (2015). As the sentiment scores to be predicted by systems lie on a continuous scale between -1 and 1 (cp. Section 2.5), cosine enables us to compare the proximity between gold standard and predicted results (conceptualized as vectors), while not requiring exact correspondence between the gold and predicted score for a given instance. An instance is a message or headline which can include several entities (companies or cashtags). Cosine similarity is calculated according to equation (1), where G is the vector of gold standard scores and P is the vector of corresponding scores predicted by the system:

$$cosine(G, P) = \frac{\sum\limits_{i=1}^{n} G_i \times P_i}{\sqrt{\sum\limits_{i=1}^{n} G_i^2} \times \sqrt{\sum\limits_{i=1}^{n} P_i^2}} \quad (1)$$

In order to reward systems which attempt to answer all problems in the gold standard, the final score is obtained by weighting the cosine similarity from (1) with the ratio of answered problems (scored instances), given in (2) in line with Ghosh et al. (2015).

$$cos\_weight = \frac{|P|}{|G|} \quad (2)$$

The equation for the final score is the product of the cosine similarity (1) and the weight (2), given in (3).

$$final\_score = cos\_weight \times cosine(G, P) \quad (3)$$

5 Results and Participants

Task 5 attracted a total of 32 participants: 25 teams participated in Track 1 and 29 in Track 2, of which 22 teams addressed both tracks. The analysis and results for each track are discussed in more detail in the sub-sections below. Given that 19 out of the 32 participants submitted a paper with their approach and findings, we opted to include the system analysis and ranking of results of only the submitted participants.

Analysis of the systems consisted of the following criteria: pre-processing methods, techniques used, external sources, data sets and/or lexica used, tools utilised, why the adopted approach was chosen and if it is (i) multilingual/cross-lingual and/or (ii) domain dependent/independent, any issues encountered and how they were tackled and potentially solved.

5.1 Track 1 - Microblog Messages

Figure 4 shows the results of the 25 participants in Track 1. Results of all participants were ranked (first column) according to the evaluation metric (last column) described in the Section 4 - Evaluation. The second column specifies the team's/participant's name. Please note that the analysis of systems discussed in this sub-section includes only the participants highlighted in yellow since only these submitted a paper with their approach and findings.

Track 1 - Microblog Messages			
Rank	Team Name		Score
1	ECNU	Jiang et al. (2017)	0.778
	CodersGoneCrazy		0.760
	zhiqiang		0.759
2	IITP	Ghosal et al. (2017)	0.751
3	SSN_MLRG1	Deborah et al. (2017)	0.735
4	HHU	Cabanski et al. (2017)	0.730
5	IITPB	Kumar et al. (2017)	0.726
6	RiTUAL-UH	Kar et al. (2017)	0.723
7	IBA-Sys	Nasim (2017)	0.720
	cbaziotis		0.714
8	SentiHeros	Seyeditabari et al. (2017)	0.707
	mattia-atzeni		0.703
9	FEUP	Saleiro et al. (2017)	0.693
10	funSentiment	Li et al. (2017)	0.677
	hittle2008		0.655
	xiwu		0.636
11	INF-UFRGS	Zini et al. (2017)	0.614
	lhurtado		0.614
12	HCS	Pivovarova et al. (2017)	0.607
	amouma		0.507
13	NLG301	Chen et al. (2017)	0.383
	vpekar		0.337
	four_u		0.314
	gloncakv		0.186
14	DUTH	Symeonidis et al. (2017)	0.003

Figure 4: Track 1 Results

5.1.1 Pre-processing

In terms of pre-processing, all 14 participants adopted some methods in order to clean the microblog messages before further processing. The most common methods used were: removal of special characters and/or punctuations, removal of URLs and user mentions ('@username') and/or substitution of certain expressions by specific words (e.g., replace 'full urls' with 'url' and 'company names' with 'company'), stop word removal, tokenisation, lemmatisation and lowercase conversion. Some participants also performed Named Entity Recognition (NER), emoticon removal, Part-of-Speech (POS) tagging, stemming and URL resolution, besides other specific tasks, such as concatenation of spans to form a unified string (Nasim, 2017). NLTK[5] was the tool mostly used (Seyeditabari et al., 2017; Deborah et al., 2017; Kumar et al., 2017; Symeonidis et al., 2017; Jiang et al., 2017) for pre-processing tasks, such as lemmatisation, stemming and lowercase conversion.

5.1.2 Techniques

All the techniques used by each system of the 14 participants are shown in Figure 5. Each system was analysed and in-turn categorised under one of the following techniques: Hybrid, Machine Learning (ML), Deep Learning (DL) and Lexicon-based (Lex).

It is clear that most techniques were of a Hybrid nature with the Machine Learning and Lexicon-based approach being the most popular choice, followed by Machine Learning-based approaches. Authors of some systems experimented with multiple approaches to find the one that fared best in the competition. In fact, Cabanski et al. (2017) implemented two-hybrid techniques (as noted above), where the Hybrid (DL, Lex) approach produced their best result for this track. On the other hand, Kumar et al. (2017) implemented two Hybrid (ML, Lex) systems, one adopting Support Vector Machine and Logistic Regression and the other adopting SVR.

The Hybrid (ML, Lex) technique by Jiang et al. (2017) ranked first for this track, whereas the Hybrid (DL, Lex) technique by Ghosal et al. (2017) ranked second. The system placing third (Deborah et al., 2017) adopted a ML technique.

The Machine Learning-based techniques made use of the following algorithms:

- Artificial Neural Network (ANN) - adopted by Li (2017); Symeonidis et al. (2017); Saleiro et al. (2017)

- Random Forests - adopted by Seyeditabari et al. (2017); Symeonidis et al. (2017); Jiang et al. (2017); Saleiro et al. (2017)

- Support Vector Machine (SVM) - adopted by Seyeditabari et al. (2017); Cabanski et al. (2017); Kumar et al. (2017); Saleiro et al. (2017)

- Support Vector Regression (SVR) - adopted by Zini et al. (2017); Kumar et al. (2017); Chen et al. (2017); Jiang et al. (2017)

- Linear Regression (LiR) - adopted by Symeonidis et al. (2017)

- Logistic Regression (LoR) - adopted by Seyeditabari et al. (2017); Kumar et al. (2017)

- Naive Bayes (NB) - adopted by Seyeditabari et al. (2017)

- Multi-Kernel Gaussian Process (MKGP) - adopted by Deborah et al. (2017)

- XGBoost Regressor (XGB) - adopted by Nasim (2017); Jiang et al. (2017)

- Boosted Decision Tree Regression (BDTR) - adopted by Symeonidis et al. (2017)

- AdaBoost Regressor (ABR) - adopted by Jiang et al. (2017)

- Bagging Regressor (BR) - adopted by Jiang et al. (2017)

- Gradient Boosting Regressor (GBR) - adopted by Jiang et al. (2017)

- Least Absolute Shrinkage and Selection Operator (LASSO) - adopted by Jiang et al. (2017)

The most common ML techniques used overall –by 4 participants– were RF, SVM and SVR. The SVR was part of the ensemble regression model used by the system that ranked first for this track (Jiang et al., 2017). The RF classifier was ultimately used by Seyeditabari et al. (2017), since it is the best performer in terms of tweets classification. Regarding the ANN computational approach, both Li (2017) and Symeonidis et al. (2017) use a regression method, whereas Saleiro et al. (2017) use a Multilayer Perceptron (MLP).

The Deep Learning-based techniques made use of the following algorithms:

---

[5]http://www.nltk.org/

Technique	System
Hybrid (ML, Lex)	Nasim (2017), Seyeditabari et al. (2017), Cabanski et al. (2017), Kumar et al. (2017), Chen et al. (2017), Jiang et al. (2017), Saleiro et al. (2017)
Hybrid (DL, Lex)	Ghosal et al. (2017), Cabanski et al. (2017), Kar et al. (2017)
ML	Li (2017), Zini et al. (2017), Symeonidis et al. (2017), Deborah et al. (2017)
DL	Pivovarova et al. (2017)

Figure 5: Techniques used by systems in Track 1

- Convolution Neural Network (CNN) - adopted by Pivovarova et al. (2017); Kar et al. (2017); Ghosal et al. (2017)

- Recurrent Neural Network (RNN) : Long Short-Term Memory (LSTM) - adopted by Cabanski et al. (2017); Ghosal et al. (2017)

- Bidirectional Gated Recurrent Unit (Bi-GRU) - adopted by Kar et al. (2017)

The MLP based ensemble model in Ghosal et al. (2017) that combines the CNN and LSTM Deep Learning algorithms ranked second in this track. In Cabanski et al. (2017), their best submission for this track was provided by the RNN (as opposed to SVR).

Lexicon-based methods made use of the following known sentiment lexica:

- Loughran and McDonald Sentiment Word Lists (Loughran and McDonald, 2011b) - adopted by Nasim (2017); Seyeditabari et al. (2017); Saleiro et al. (2017); Ghosal et al. (2017)

- Stock Market Lexicon[6] - adopted by Nasim (2017)

- SentiWordNet[7] - adopted by Cabanski et al. (2017); Chen et al. (2017); Jiang et al. (2017)

- SenticNet 4[8] - adopted by Chen et al. (2017); Kar et al. (2017)

- VADER (Hutto and Gilbert, 2014) - adopted by Cabanski et al. (2017)

- Opinion Lexicon(Hu and Liu, 2004) - adopted by Cabanski et al. (2017); Kumar et al. (2017); Jiang et al. (2017); Ghosal et al. (2017)

- MPQA Subjectivity Lexicon (Wilson et al., 2009) - adopted by Kumar et al. (2017); Jiang et al. (2017); Saleiro et al. (2017); Ghosal et al. (2017)

- NRC Hashtag Sentiment Lexicon (Kiritchenko et al., 2014) - adopted by Cabanski et al. (2017); Kumar et al. (2017); Jiang et al. (2017); Ghosal et al. (2017)

- NRC Hashtag Emotion Lexicon (Kiritchenko et al., 2014) - adopted by Chen et al. (2017)

- NRC Hashtag Affirmative Context Sentiment Lexicon (Kiritchenko et al., 2014) - adopted by Chen et al. (2017); Ghosal et al. (2017)

- NRC Hashtag Negated Context Sentiment Lexicon (Kiritchenko et al., 2014) - adopted by Chen et al. (2017)

- NRC Word-Emotion Association Lexicon / NRC Emotion Lexicon (Kiritchenko et al., 2014) - adopted by (Chen et al., 2017)

- Emoticon Lexicon / Sentiment140 Lexicon[9] - adopted by Chen et al. (2017); Jiang et al. (2017); Ghosal et al. (2017)

- Sentiment140 Affirmative Context Lexicon (Kiritchenko et al., 2014) - adopted by Ghosal et al. (2017); Chen et al. (2017)

- Yelp Restaurant Sentiment Lexicon[10] - adopted by Chen et al. (2017)

- Amazon Laptop Sentiment Lexicon[11] - adopted by Chen et al. (2017)

- Macquarie Semantic Orientation Lexicon[12] - adopted by Chen et al. (2017)

---

[6]https://github.com/nunomroliveira/stock_market_lexicon

[7]http://sentiwordnet.isti.cnr.it/

[8]http://sentic.net/senticnet-4.pdf

[9]http://saifmohammad.com/Lexicons/Sentiment140-Lexicon-v0.1.zip

[10]http://saifmohammad.com/Lexicons/Yelp-restaurant-reviews.zip

[11]http://saifmohammad.com/Lexicons/Amazon-laptop-electronics-reviews.zip

[12]http://saifmohammad.com/Lexicons/MSOL-June15-09.txt.zip

- Harvard's General Inquirer Lexicon[13] - adopted by Jiang et al. (2017); Ghosal et al. (2017)

- IMDB (Zhu et al., 2013) - adopted by Jiang et al. (2017)

- AFINN[14] - adopted by Jiang et al. (2017)

- Corpus of Business News (Pivovarova et al., 2013) - adopted by Pivovarova et al. (2017)

The following three lexica listed are the ones mostly used overall: (i) the Loughran and McDonald Sentiment Word (rank 2), (ii) Opinion Lexicon (rank 1, 2) and (iii) MPQA Subjectivity Lexicon (rank 1, 2). An interesting observation is that the systems that ranked first (Jiang et al., 2017) and second (Ghosal et al., 2017) in this track utilised all three lexicons (ranked system using the particular lexicon represented next to each name), whereby lexica (ii) and (iii) were used by both.

Seyeditabari et al. (2017) extended Loughran and McDonald's word list of positive and negative words with 10,000 financial reports containing a summary of the company's performances in order to add features to the training dataset In Cabanski et al. (2017), the authors, besides using the sentiment lexica identified above, also built and used a custom Financial Sentiment Lexicon.

5.2 Track 2 - News Statements and Headlines

Figure 6 shows the results of the 29 participants in Track 2. Results of all participants were ranked (first column) according to the evaluation metric (last column) described in Section 4 - Evaluation. The second column specifies the team/participant name. Please note that the analysis of systems discussed in this sub-section includes only the participants highlighted in yellow, which are the participants who submitted a paper with their approach and findings.

5.2.1 Pre-processing

In terms of pre-processing – same as for Track 1 – all 17 participants adopted some methods in order to clean the news statements and headlines before further processing. The most common methods used were: removal of numbers, special characters and/or punctuations, removal of URLs and user mentions and/or substitution of certain expressions with tags (e.g. replace 'company name' with

Track 2 - News Statements & Headlines			
Rank	Team Name	Reference	Score
1	Fortia-FBK	Mansar et al. (2017)	0.745
2	RiTUAL-UH	Kar et al. (2017)	0.744
3	TakeLab	Rotim et al. (2017)	0.733
4	Lancaster A	Moore and Rayson (2017)	0.732
	CodersGoneCrazy		0.726
5	ECNU	Jiang et al. (2017)	0.710
6	HHU	Cabanski et al. (2017)	0.702
7	IITP	Ghosal et al. (2017)	0.697
8	IITPB	Kumar et al. (2017)	0.696
	cbaziotis		0.686
	zhiqiang		0.681
9	COMMIT	Schouten et al. (2017)	0.681
10	HCS	Pivovarova et al. (2017)	0.680
11	FEUP	Saleiro et al. (2017)	0.670
12	SSN_MLRG1	Deborah et al. (2017)	0.666
13	IBA-Sys	Nasim (2017)	0.656
14	UW-FinSent	John and Vechtomova (2017)	0.645
	MarinaChern		0.627
	bonson		0.615
	mattia-atzeni		0.613
15	INF-UFRGS	Zini et al. (2017)	0.608
	lhurtado		0.607
	xiwu		0.603
16	DUTH	Symeonidis et al. (2017)	0.588
	amouma		0.431
17	NLG301	Chen et al. (2017)	0.415
	vpekar		0.352
	hittle2008		0.251
	four_u		0.016

Figure 6: Track 2 Results

'⟨company⟩' and 'numbers' with '⟨number⟩'), stop word removal, tokenisation, lemmatisation, lowercase conversion and NER on certain entities (e.g., Organisation and Person). Some participants also performed dependency parsing, POS tagging, stemming and URL resolution, besides other specific tasks, such as filtering out all named entities and keeping only "general" tokens given that they are generally the ones carrying the sentiment (Rotim et al., 2017). Same as track 1, NLTK was the tool mostly used (Ghosal et al., 2017; Deborah et al., 2017; Kumar et al., 2017; Symeonidis et al., 2017; Jiang et al., 2017) for pre-processing, whereas Stanford CoreNLP[15] was used for performing NER, sentence breaking and parsing. (Nasim, 2017; Rotim et al., 2017; Schouten et al., 2017; Chen et al., 2017; Jiang et al., 2017)

5.2.2 Techniques

Figure 7 shows all the techniques used by each system of the 17 participants. Each system has been analysed and categorised under one of the following techniques: Hybrid, Machine Learning (ML), Deep Learning (DL), Lexicon (Lex) and Ontology (Ont).

Similar to track 1, the Machine Learning and a Machine Learning/Lexicon-based Hybrid approach were the ones mostly used (six participants). However, the techniques were more balanced in this track, with six participants adopting a Machine Learning-based approach. It is worth noting that one of the systems used a Machine Learning and Ontology-based Hybrid approach, which technique is unique in both tracks. In this system,Schouten et al. (2017) used the SVR algorithm with ontology features (including features derived from ontology reasoning), which ontology was self-designed by the authors. Multiple techniques were used by some authors in order to find the best one to use in this competition within their system. Moore and Rayson (2017) experimented with an ML and DL algorithm respectively, with the latter performing better. On the other hand, Cabanski et al. (2017) implemented two-hybrid techniques, where the Hybrid (DL, Lex) approach produced their best result for this track , same as for track 1.

The systems that ranked first (Mansar et al., 2017) and second (Kar et al., 2017) both adopted a Hybrid (DL, Lex) technique, whereas an ML technique was used by the system in rank three.

The Machine Learning-based techniques made use of the following algorithms:

- Artificial Neural Network (ANN) - adopted by Symeonidis et al. (2017)

- Random Forests - adopted by Symeonidis et al. (2017); Jiang et al. (2017); Saleiro et al. (2017)

- Support Vector Machine (SVM) - adopted by Kumar et al. (2017); Saleiro et al. (2017)

- Support Vector Regression (SVR) - adopted by Rotim et al. (2017); Schouten et al. (2017); Moore and Rayson (2017); John and Vechtomova (2017); Zini et al. (2017); Cabanski et al. (2017); Kumar et al. (2017); Chen et al. (2017); Jiang et al. (2017)

- Linear Regression (LiR) - adopted by John and Vechtomova (2017); Symeonidis et al. (2017)

- Logistic Regression (LoR) - adopted by Kumar et al. (2017)

- Multi-Kernel Gaussian Process (MKGP) - adopted by Deborah et al. (2017)

- XGBoost Regressor (XGB) - adopted by Nasim (2017); John and Vechtomova (2017); Jiang et al. (2017)

- Boosted Decision Tree Regression (BDTR) - adopted by Symeonidis et al. (2017)

- AdaBoost Regressor (ABR) - adopted by Jiang et al. (2017)

- Bagging Regressor (BR) - adopted by Jiang et al. (2017)

- Gradient Boosting Regressor (GBR) - adopted by Jiang et al. (2017)

- Least Absolute Shrinkage and Selection Operator (LASSO) - adopted by Jiang et al. (2017)

As can be seen above, the most common ML technique used within the systems was SVR by 9 participants. This was used by the system that ranked third for this track (Rotim et al., 2017).

The Deep Learning-based techniques made use of the following algorithms:

- Convolution Neural Network (CNN) - adopted by Mansar et al. (2017); Pivovarova et al. (2017); Ghosal et al. (2017); Kar et al. (2017)

- Recurrent Neural Network (RNN) : Long Short-Term Memory (LSTM) - adopted by Ghosal et al. (2017); Cabanski et al. (2017)

- RNN : Bidirectional Long Short-Term Memory (BLSTM) - adopted by Moore and Rayson (2017)

- Bidirectional Gated Recurrent Unit (Bi-GRU) - adopted by Kar et al. (2017)

The CNN algorithm was the most popular amongst all Deep Learning-based techniques, with both systems ranking first (Mansar et al., 2017) and second (Kar et al., 2017) using it.

Lexicon-based methods made use of the following known sentiment lexica:

- Loughran and McDonald Sentiment Word Lists - adopted by Nasim (2017); Ghosal et al. (2017); Kumar et al. (2017); Saleiro et al. (2017)

Technique	System
Hybrid (ML, Lex)	Nasim (2017), Cabanski et al. (2017), Kumar et al. (2017), Chen et al. (2017), Jiang et al. (2017), Saleiro et al. (2017)
Hybrid (DL, Lex)	Mansar et al. (2017), Ghosal et al. (2017), Cabanski et al. (2017), Kar et al. (2017)
Hybrid (DL, Ont)	Schouten et al. (2017)
ML	Rotim et al. (2017), Moore and Rayson (2017), John and Vechtomova (2017), Deborah et al. (2017), Zini et al. (2017), Symeonidis et al. (2017)
DL	Moore and Rayson (2017), Pivovarova et al. (2017)

Figure 7: Techniques used by systems in Track 2

- SentiWordNet - adopted by Cabanski et al. (2017); Kumar et al. (2017); Chen et al. (2017); Jiang et al. (2017)

- SenticNet 4 - adopted by Chen et al. (2017); Kar et al. (2017)

- VADER - adopted by Mansar et al. (2017); Cabanski et al. (2017)

- Opinion Lexicon - adopted by Ghosal et al. (2017); Cabanski et al. (2017); Kumar et al. (2017); Jiang et al. (2017)

- MPQA Subjectivity Lexicon - adopted by Ghosal et al. (2017)

- NRC Hashtag Sentiment Lexicon - adopted by Cabanski et al. (2017); Nasim (2017); Ghosal et al. (2017); Jiang et al. (2017)

- NRC Hashtag Emotion Lexicon - adopted by Chen et al. (2017)

- NRC Hashtag Affirmative Context Sentiment Lexicon - adopted by Ghosal et al. (2017); Chen et al. (2017)

- NRC Hashtag Negated Context Sentiment Lexicon - adopted by Chen et al. (2017)

- NRC Word-Emotion Association Lexicon / NRC Emotion Lexicon - adopted by Chen et al. (2017)

- Emoticon Lexicon / Sentiment140 Lexicon - adopted by Ghosal et al. (2017); Jiang et al. (2017); Chen et al. (2017)

- Sentiment140 Affirmative Context Lexicon - adopted by Ghosal et al. (2017); Chen et al. (2017)

- Yelp Restaurant Sentiment Lexicon - adopted by Chen et al. (2017)

- Amazon Laptop Sentiment Lexicon - adopted by Chen et al. (2017)

- Macquarie Semantic Orientation Lexicon - adopted by Chen et al. (2017)

- Harvard's General Inquirer Lexicon - adopted by Nasim (2017); Ghosal et al. (2017); Kumar et al. (2017); Jiang et al. (2017)

- IMDB - adopted by Jiang et al. (2017)

- AFINN - adopted by Jiang et al. (2017)

- DepecheMood Affective Lexicon (Staiano and Guerini, 2014) - adopted by Mansar et al. (2017)

- Amazon Product Reviews[16] - adopted by John and Vechtomova (2017)

- Financial Phrasebank (Malo et al., 2014a) - adopted by John and Vechtomova (2017)

- Corpus of Business News - adopted by Pivovarova et al. (2017)

In total, four lexica listed above are the ones mostly used (all by 4 participants each): (i) the Loughran and McDonald Sentiment Word, (ii) SentiWordNet, (iii) Opinion Lexicon and (iv) Harvard's General Inquirer Lexicon. Unlike the case in track 1, none of the participants ranked first till third used one of these four lexica.

Some authors constructed their own lexica from external sources, such as Moore and Rayson (2017) (rank four) who manually downloaded 189,206 financial articles which contain 161,877,425 tokens from Factiva[17] (articles come from sources such as Financial Times that relate to United States companies only).

---

[16] http://jmcauley.ucsd.edu/data/amazon/
[17] https://global.factiva.com

5.2.3 Tools used in both tracks

Several tools were used within the participants' systems, with the following (Figure 8) being the most popular:

Scikit-learn is a Machine Learning kit (in Python) that offers simple efficient tools (e.g., classification and regression algorithms) for data mining and data analysis. This is the tool mostly used by the participants of our task (42% in total) to compute their results. Similarly, Weka –a collection of machine learning algorithms for data mining tasks– was used by 2 participants. The Keras Deep Learning library was used by 2 participants, whereas TensorFlow – an open source software library for numerical computation using data flow graph– was also used by 3 participants (work in Pivovarova et al. (2017) built their implementation on top of it).

GloVe, an unsupervised learning algorithm for obtaining vector representations of words, was used by 6 participants for word embeddings. Word2vec –an efficient implementation of the continuous bag-of-words and skip-gram architectures for computing vector representations of words– was also used for the same purpose by 4 participants.

5.3 General assessment of the task

The approaches proposed by the participating systems explored a combination of machine learning methods using lexical features, sentiment lexical resources (both generic and specific to finance) and pre-trained word embedding models. Novel features specific to the task included the creation of a domain-specific ontology (Schouten et al., 2017), a stocktwits-based embedding model and distance supervision model (Li, 2017) and domain-specific lexica (Moore and Rayson, 2017). Moreover, due to the emphasis of the task on the sentiment classification on a continuous scale, many approaches targeted regression-based models.

With the exception of Cabanski et al. (2017), few approaches explicitly tackled the problem of compositionality (Sales et al., 2016), valency shifting (Malo et al., 2014a), and clausal disembedding (Niklaus et al., 2016), a fact that is reflected by the lack of submissions which explored syntactic features.

With regard to language transportability, most approaches have a medium level of transportability, being dependent on the translation of the sentiment lexica, but not depending on syntactic parser.

Important specific aspects proposed by the task remained unexplored or poorly explored, including:

(i) the use of quantitative background knowledge (e.g. stock price, financial report data), (ii) the use of the annotated text spans.

6 Alternative Evaluation Metric

Based on the evaluation metric as stated in Section 4, another evaluation metric has been developed during the competition. The intention to propose a modified way of evaluation was based on the fact that the cosine similarity (1) is treating all predicted scores with the same weight. This approach is not exploiting all information given in the data set, in specific it is not taking the link between entities and instances into consideration.

6.1 First Modification

Therefore, we proposed an approach which is using multiple vectors (one per instance) instead of only two. These instance vectors are containing one score per corresponding entity. Cosine similarity scores are calculated for each instance and added up to then divide the sum of all similarity scores by the number of submitted instance predictions in order to retrieve an average cosine similarity score.

While considering this modified evaluation metric a drawback, dividing the predictions on one hand into a regression problem but on the other hand into a classification problem, was noticed. The cosine similarity (1) for vectors with a length of 1 is resulting in either +1 or -1. However, the cosine similarity for vectors with a length greater than 1 is resulting in a floating point value. Thus, another modification of the initial evaluation formula has been conducted.

6.2 Second Modification

The second modification of the initial evaluation metric is also using one vector per instance containing one score per corresponding entity. Those instance vectors are populated into either a gold standard (GS) or predicted system (PS) vector. As both vectors are populated according to matching instances and entities, both vectors should be the same length. In contrast to the first modification (6.1), the second modification is using two different methods of evaluating the given scores dependent on the length of a vector. For each instance vector in GS/PS which has a length of 1, the absolute distance between both scores (4) is added to the total similarity score (6).

$$s\_similarity(G, P) = 1 - |G_0 - P_0| \quad (4)$$

Tool	System
scikit-learn[18]	Nasim (2017), Moore and Rayson (2017), John and Vechtomova (2017), Cabanski et al. (2017), Kumar et al. (2017), Symeonidis et al. (2017), Kar et al. (2017), Jiang et al. (2017)
word2vec[19]	Li (2017), Ghosal et al. (2017), Kumar et al. (2017), Saleiro et al. (2017)
Weka[20]	Seyeditabari et al. (2017), Zini et al. (2017)
GloVe[21]	Seyeditabari et al. (2017), Mansar et al. (2017), Rotim et al. (2017), Pivovarova et al. (2017), Ghosal et al. (2017), Kumar et al. (2017)
LIBSVM[22]	Rotim et al. (2017)
LIBLINEAR[23]	Rotim et al. (2017), Jiang et al. (2017)
Keras[24]	Moore and Rayson (2017), Ghosal et al. (2017)
XGBoost[25]	John and Vechtomova (2017), Jiang et al. (2017)
gensim[26]	John and Vechtomova (2017), Cabanski et al. (2017)
TensorFlow[27]	John and Vechtomova (2017), Pivovarova et al. (2017), Cabanski et al. (2017)

Figure 8: Tools used by systems in both tracks

For each instance vector with a length greater than 1, the cosine similarity is "length times" added to the total similarity score (5).

$$m\_similarity(G, P) = |P| \times cosine(G, P) \quad (5)$$

$$total\_similarity(GS, PS) =$$

$$\sum_{i=1}^{|PS|} \begin{cases} |PS_i| = 1 & s\_similarity(GS_i, PS_i) \\ |PS_i| > 1 & m\_similarity(GS_i, PS_i) \end{cases} \quad (6)$$

Once the similarity scores are calculated for each instance vector and added to the total_similarity, the final score is calculated by dividing the total similarity score by the number of predicted entities to then multiply the quotient with a weight which consists of the quotient of all predicted entities divided by all possible entity predictions (7). In contrast to the cosine weight as stated in (2), this weight is calculated on an entity level.

$$final\_score(GS, PS) =$$

$$\frac{\sum_{i=1}^{|PS|} |PS_i|}{\sum_{i=1}^{|GS|} |GS_i|} \times \frac{total\_similarity(GS, PS)}{\sum_{i=1}^{|PS|} |PS_i|} \quad (7)$$

Similarity scores produced using this alternative evaluation metric can be found in the appendix A.

6.3 Pros and Cons

On one hand, the evaluation metric as stated in 6.2 differentiating between vectors according to their lengths avoids the regression/classification problem as described in 6.1. In addition, it is considering the link between instances and entities in the final score.

On the other hand, one disadvantage of this is approach is the linearity / non-linearity of the two sub-methods used ((4), (5)). One could argue that both sub-methods are not equally impacting the total score. Balancing would be one approach to reducing discrepancy but also be subjectively influenced.

7 Related Initiatives

A number of projects have addressed questions pertaining to Sentiment Analysis and Finance. The FIRST (2010-2013) FP7 European project [28] provides sentiment extraction and analysis of market participants from social media networks in near real-time, for detecting and predicting financial market events, such as insights about financial market movements and financial market abuse. The developed tool consists of a decision support model based on Web sentiment as found within textual data extracted from Twitter or blogs, for the financial domain.

The TrendMiner (2011-2014) FP7 European project [29], presents an innovative and portable open-source real-time method for cross-lingual mining and summarisation of large-scale social media streams, such as weblogs, Twitter, Facebook, etc. One high profile case study was a financial decision support (with analysts, traders, regulators and economists).

---

[28] http://project-first.eu/
[29] http://www.trendminer-project.eu/

StockWatcher (Micu et al., 2008) provides a customised, aggregated view of news categorised by different topics, where it performs sentiment analysis - positive, negative or neutral effect - on particular news messages about a particular company. This tool enables the extraction of relevant news items from RSS feeds concerning the NASDAQ-100 listed companies. The sentiment of the news messages directly affects a company's respective stock price.

Mirowski et al. (Mirowski et al., 2010) present an algorithm for topic modelling, text classification and retrieval from time-stamped documents. This algorithm has been applied to predict the stock market volatility using financial news from Bloomberg. The volatility considered is estimated from daily stock prices of a particular company.

Several data sets have been created which are relevant in the context of our current endeavour. (Sanders, 2011) provide the Sanders Twitter Sentiment corpus, consisting of 5513 tweets about four topics/companies (Apple, Google, Microsoft, Twitter). One annotator manually assigned a positive, negative, neutral or irrelevant annotation to each tweet, depending on the sentiment expressed towards the given topic (company). This can refer to any aspect of the company, e.g. the service at the Apple store or the features of the iPhone in the case of Apple Inc. The current proposal will instead focus on a much larger range of companies and evaluate them specifically with respect to their stock market value. Furthermore, sentiment scoring will be more fine-grained as it will consist of floating-point numbers in the range of -1 (very negative/bearish) and 1 (very positive/bullish), with 0 representing neutral sentiment.

(Malo et al., 2014b) present the Financial Phrase Bank, a resource containing around 5000 sentences from English-language news about companies listed on the Helsinki stock exchange. Annotations at the level of syntactic phrases assigned one of three sentiment classes (positive, negative, neutral), based on the expected influence on the stock price. Each phrase was scored by between five and eight annotators. In our proposed task, the sentiment was also assigned with a view to the stock price or market development. However, our annotation is more fine-grained, ranging on a scale from -1 to 1. Furthermore, we annotate at the target (stock or company entity) rather than the phrase-level.

Over the years, many shared tasks in SemEval have focused on Sentiment Analysis, exploring various angles within the field. A series of tasks have concentrated on Sentiment Analysis in Twitter (Nakov et al., 2013; Rosenthal et al., 2014; Rosenthal and Stoyanov, 2015). They have covered tasks such as Polarity Disambiguation, document- and topic-level Polarity Classification, and topic-based Sentiment Aggregation. These tasks targeted open domains, with topics being determined using Named Entity Recognition (e.g. celebrities, places, sports clubs). The sentiment was assigned on two-point (positive, negative), three-point (positive, negative, neutral) or five-point (strongly positive, weakly positive, neutral, weakly negative, strongly negative) scales. In contrast, our proposed task aims to detect fine-grained sentiment, a scoring company- and stock-level sentiment on a floating point scale between -1 and 1. Furthermore, the data in our proposed task focuses only on the financial domain and its particular semantic challenges.

Aspect-based Sentiment Analysis has also emerged in recent editions of SemEval (Pontiki et al., 2014, 2015). Depending on the subtask, entities and their aspects are provided to the participants or need to be identified. Sentiment for entity-aspect pairs is scored according to four categories: positive, negative, neutral and conflict. In terms of data, while the 2014 task focused on isolated sentences from customer reviews, the 2015 edition dealt with full reviews. Again, our proposed task differs in the assignment of fine-grained sentiment, in the short nature of the text instances and in terms of the domain.

8 Conclusions and Future Work

We presented a new task on fine-grained sentiment analysis for the financial domain, where a sentiment in range (-1, 1) is assigned to entities. In our two subtasks, we focussed on two distinct data sources: financial microblogs (Twitter and StockTwits), where the target entities are company stock symbols ("cashtags"), and financial news headlines, where sentiment needs to be assigned to companies.

Deep Learning (word embeddings) and more traditional Machine Learning techniques account for the majority of contributions. Many participants made use of sentiment lexica, both finance-specific (e.g. the word lists from (Loughran and McDonald, 2011b)) and general domain (e.g. (Hu and Liu, 2004; Wilson et al., 2009)), as well as custom lexica created in the context of this task. A review of the results obtained by participants shows that three of the systems that performed best (top three in each track) adopted a Hybrid (Deep Learning, Lexicon) technique, while the other three used a Machine Learning-based approach.

For a future edition of this task, we will focus on enhancing the evaluation metric in the light of the discussion in Section 6. It would be interesting to add subtasks with different sources, perhaps broadening the scope to include longer texts, such as full news articles from financial newspapers, or Facebook posts.

Acknowledgements

Horizon 2020 ICT Program Project SSIX: Social Sentiment analysis financial IndeXes, has received funding from the European Union's Horizon 2020 Research and Innovation Program ICT 2014 - Information and Communications Technologies under grant agreement No. 645425.

References

Johan Bollen, et al. 2011. Twitter mood predicts the stock market. *Journal of Computational Science* 2(1):1–8.

Tobias Cabanski, et al. 2017. Hhu at semeval-2017 task 5: Fine-grained sentiment analysis on financial data using machine learning methods. In *Proceedings of the 11th International Workshop on Semantic Evaluation (SemEval-2017)*. Association for Computational Linguistics, Vancouver, Canada. http://alt.qcri.org/semeval2017/.

Chung-Chi Chen, et al. 2017. Nlg301 at semeval-2017 task 5: Fine-grained sentiment analysis on financial microblogs and news. In *Proceedings of the 11th International Workshop on Semantic Evaluation (SemEval-2017)*. Association for Computational Linguistics, Vancouver, Canada. http://alt.qcri.org/semeval2017/.

Brian Davis, et al. 2016. Social sentiment indices powered by x-scores. In *2nd International Conference on Big Data, Small Data, Linked Data and Open Data, ALLDATA 2016.*

Marjan Van de Kauter, et al. 2015. Fine-grained analysis of explicit and implicit sentiment in financial news articles. *Expert Systems with Applications* 42:4999–5010.

Angel Deborah, et al. 2017. Ssn_mlrg1 at semeval-2017 task 5: Fine-grained sentiment analysis using multiple kernel gaussian process regression model. In *Proceedings of the 11th International Workshop on Semantic Evaluation (SemEval-2017)*. Association for Computational Linguistics, Vancouver, Canada. http://alt.qcri.org/semeval2017/.

Eagle Alpha. 2016. Sentiment analysis in the financial domain. does it work? https://medium.com/eagle-alpha/sentiment-analysis-in-the-financial-domain-does-it-work-36fa974ea3cb#.o793xdr9h. Accessed 23-March-2016.

Deepanway Ghosal, et al. 2017. Iitp at semeval-2017 task 5: An ensemble of deep learning and feature based models for financial sentiment analysis. In *Proceedings of the 11th International Workshop on Semantic Evaluation (SemEval-2017)*. Association for Computational Linguistics, Vancouver, Canada. http://alt.qcri.org/semeval2017/.

Aniruddha Ghosh, et al. 2015. Semeval-2015 task 11: Sentiment analysis of figurative language in twitter. In *Proceedings of the 9th International Workshop on Semantic Evaluation (SemEval 2015)*. pages 470–478.

Rohitha Goonatilake and Susantha Herath. 2007. The volatility of the stock market and news. *International Research Journal of Finance and Economics* 3(11):53–65.

Minqing Hu and Bing Liu. 2004. Mining and summarizing customer reviews. In *Proceedings of the tenth ACM SIGKDD international conference on Knowledge discovery and data mining*. ACM, pages 168–177.

Clayton J Hutto and Eric Gilbert. 2014. Vader: A parsimonious rule-based model for sentiment analysis of social media text. In *Eighth International AAAI Conference on Weblogs and Social Media*.

Mengxiao Jiang, et al. 2017. Ecnu at semeval-2017 task 5: An ensemble of regression algorithms with effective features for fine-grained sentiment analysis in financial domain. In *Proceedings of the 11th International Workshop on Semantic Evaluation (SemEval-2017)*. Association for Computational Linguistics, Vancouver, Canada. http://alt.qcri.org/semeval2017/.

Vineet John and Olga Vechtomova. 2017. Uw-finsent at semeval-2017 task 5: Fine-grained sentiment analysis on financial microblogs and news. In *Proceedings of the 11th International Workshop on Semantic Evaluation (SemEval-2017)*. Association for Computational Linguistics, Vancouver, Canada. http://alt.qcri.org/semeval2017/.

Sudipta Kar, et al. 2017. Ritual-uh at semeval-2017 task 5: Sentiment analysis on financial data using neural networks. In *Proceedings of the 11th International Workshop on Semantic Evaluation (SemEval-2017)*. Association for Computational Linguistics, Vancouver, Canada. http://alt.qcri.org/semeval2017/.

Svetlana Kiritchenko, et al. 2014. Sentiment analysis of short informal texts. *Journal of Artificial Intelligence Research* 50:723–762.

Abhishek Kumar, et al. 2017. Iitpb at semeval-2017 task 5: Sentiment prediction in financial text. In *Proceedings of the 11th International Workshop on Semantic Evaluation (SemEval-2017)*. Association for Computational Linguistics, Vancouver, Canada. http://alt.qcri.org/semeval2017/.

Quanzhi Li. 2017. funsentiment at semeval-2017 task 5: Fine-grained sentiment analysis on financial microblogs using different word embeddings and target contexts. In *Proceedings of the 11th International Workshop on Semantic Evaluation (SemEval-2017)*. Association for Computational Linguistics, Vancouver, Canada. http://alt.qcri.org/semeval2017/.

Bing Liu. 2012. Sentiment analysis and opinion mining. *Synthesis lectures on human language technologies* 5(1):1–167.

Tim Loughran and Bill McDonald. 2011a. "when is a liability not a liability? textual analysis, dictionaries, and 10-ks". *The Journal of Finance* 66(1):35–65.

Tim Loughran and Bill McDonald. 2011b. When is a liability not a liability? textual analysis, dictionaries, and 10-ks. *The Journal of Finance* 66(1):35–65.

Pekka Malo, et al. 2014a. Good debt or bad debt: Detecting semantic orientations in economic texts. *Journal of the Association for Information Science and Technology* 65(4):782–796.

Pekka Malo, et al. 2014b. Good debt or bad debt: Detecting semantic orientations in economic texts. *Journal of the Association for Information Science and Technology* 65(4):782–796.

Youness Mansar, et al. 2017. Fortia-fbk at semeval-2017 task 5:bullish or bearish? inferring sentiment towards brands from financial news headlines. In *Proceedings of the 11th International Workshop on Semantic Evaluation (SemEval-2017)*. Association for Computational Linguistics, Vancouver, Canada. http://alt.qcri.org/semeval2017/.

Alex Micu, et al. 2008. Financial news analysis using a semantic web approach.

Piotr Mirowski, et al. 2010. Dynamic auto-encoders for semantic indexing. In *NIPS 2010 Workshop on Deep Learning*.

Andrew Moore and Paul Rayson. 2017. Lancaster a at semeval-2017 task 5: Evaluation metrics matter: predicting sentiment from financial news headlines. In *Proceedings of the 11th International Workshop on Semantic Evaluation (SemEval-2017)*. Association for Computational Linguistics, Vancouver, Canada. http://alt.qcri.org/semeval2017/.

Preslav Nakov, et al. 2013. Semeval-2013 task 2: Sentiment analysis in twitter .

Zarmeen Nasim. 2017. Iba-sys at semeval-2017 task 5: Fine-grained sentiment analysis on financial microblogs and news. In *Proceedings of the 11th International Workshop on Semantic Evaluation (SemEval-2017)*. Association for Computational Linguistics, Vancouver, Canada. http://alt.qcri.org/semeval2017/.

Christina Niklaus, et al. 2016. A sentence simplification system for improving relation extraction. In *26th International Conference on Computational Linguistics*.

Lidia Pivovarova, et al. 2017. Hcs at semeval-2017 task 5: Polarity detection in business news using convolutional neural networks. In *Proceedings of the 11th International Workshop on Semantic Evaluation (SemEval-2017)*. Association for Computational Linguistics, Vancouver, Canada. http://alt.qcri.org/semeval2017/.

Lidia Pivovarova, et al. 2013. Event representation across genres. In *NAACL HLT*. volume 2013, page 29.

Maria Pontiki, et al. 2015. Semeval-2015 task 12: Aspect based sentiment analysis. In *Proceedings of the 9th International Workshop on Semantic Evaluation (SemEval 2015), Association for Computational Linguistics, Denver, Colorado*. pages 486–495.

Maria Pontiki, et al. 2014. Semeval-2014 task 4: Aspect based sentiment analysis. In *Proceedings of the 8th international workshop on semantic evaluation (SemEval 2014)*. pages 27–35.

Sara Rosenthal, et al. 2014. Semeval-2014 task 9: Sentiment analysis in twitter. In *Proceedings of the 8th International Workshop on Semantic Evaluation (SemEval 2014)*. pages 73–80.

Sara Rosenthal and Veselin Stoyanov. 2015. Semeval-2015 task 10: Sentiment analysis in twitter. *Proceedings of SemEval-2015* .

Leon Rotim, et al. 2017. Takelab at semeval-2017 task 5: Linear aggregation of word embeddings for fine-grained sentiment analysis of financial news. In *Proceedings of the 11th International Workshop on Semantic Evaluation (SemEval-2017)*. Association for Computational Linguistics, Vancouver, Canada. http://alt.qcri.org/semeval2017/.

Pedro Saleiro, et al. 2017. Feup at semeval-2017 task 5: Predicting sentiment polarity and intensity with financial word embeddings. In *Proceedings of the 11th International Workshop on Semantic Evaluation (SemEval-2017)*. Association for Computational Linguistics, Vancouver, Canada. http://alt.qcri.org/semeval2017/.

Juan Efson Sales, et al. 2016. A compositional-distributional semantic model for searching complex entity categories. In *5th Joint Conference on Lexical and Computational Semantics (*SEM)*.

Niek J. Sanders. 2011. Sanders-twitter sentiment corpus. http://www.sananalytics.com/lab/twitter-sentiment. Accessed 30-March-2016.

Kim Schouten, et al. 2017. Commit at semeval-2017 task 5: Ontology-based method for sentiment analysis of financial headlines. In *Proceedings of the 11th International Workshop on Semantic Evaluation (SemEval-2017)*. Association for Computational Linguistics, Vancouver, Canada. http://alt.qcri.org/semeval2017/.

Thomas Schuster. 2003. Meta-communication and market dynamics. reflexive interactions of financial markets and the mass media .

Armin Seyeditabari, et al. 2017. Sentiheros at semeval-2017 task 5: An application of sentiment analysis on financial tweets. In *Proceedings of the 11th International Workshop on Semantic Evaluation (SemEval-2017)*. Association for Computational Linguistics, Vancouver, Canada. http://alt.qcri.org/semeval2017/.

Nitish Sinha. 2014. Using big data in finance: Example of sentiment-extraction from news articles. `http://www.federalreserve.gov/econresdata/notes/feds-notes/2014/using-big-data-in-finance-example-of-sentiment-extraction-from-news-articles-20140326.html`. Accessed 29-March-2016.

Jacopo Staiano and Marco Guerini. 2014. Depechemood: A lexicon for emotion analysis from crowd-annotated news. *arXiv preprint arXiv:1405.1605* .

Symeon Symeonidis, et al. 2017. Duth at semeval-2017 task 5: Sentiment predictability in financial microblogging and news articles. In *Proceedings of the 11th International Workshop on Semantic Evaluation (SemEval-2017)*. Association for Computational Linguistics, Vancouver, Canada. http://alt.qcri.org/semeval2017/.

Pyry Takala, et al. 2014. Gold-standard for topic-specific sentiment analysis of economic texts. In *LREC*. Citeseer, volume 2014, pages 2152–2157.

Paul C Tetlock, et al. 2008. More than words: Quantifying language to measure firms' fundamentals. *The Journal of Finance* 63(3):1437–1467.

Theresa Wilson, et al. 2009. Recognizing contextual polarity: An exploration of features for phrase-level sentiment analysis. *Computational linguistics* 35(3):399–433.

Tian Tian Zhu, et al. 2013. Ecnucs: A surface information based system description of sentiment analysis in twitter in the semeval-2013 (task 2). *Atlanta, Georgia, USA* page 408.

Tiago Zini, et al. 2017. Inf-ufrgs at semeval-2017 task 5: A supervised identification of sentiment score in tweets and headlines. In *Proceedings of the 11th International Workshop on Semantic Evaluation (SemEval-2017)*. Association for Computational Linguistics, Vancouver, Canada. http://alt.qcri.org/semeval2017/.

A Supplemental Material

Similarity scores calculated using the evaluation metric as proposed in Section 6.2:

`http://alt.qcri.org/semeval2017/task5/data/uploads/results/subtask1-microblogs-siscosim.pdf`

`http://alt.qcri.org/semeval2017/task5/data/uploads/results/subtask2-headlines-siscosim.pdf`

SemEval-2017 Task 9: Abstract Meaning Representation Parsing and Generation

Jonathan May and Jay Priyadarshi
Information Sciences Institute
Computer Science Department
University of Southern California
`jonmay@isi.edu, jpriyada@usc.edu`

Abstract

In this report we summarize the results of the 2017 AMR SemEval shared task. The task consisted of two separate yet related subtasks. In the parsing subtask, participants were asked to produce Abstract Meaning Representation (AMR) (Banarescu et al., 2013) graphs for a set of English sentences in the biomedical domain. In the generation subtask, participants were asked to generate English sentences given AMR graphs in the news/forum domain. A total of five sites participated in the parsing subtask, and four participated in the generation subtask. Along with a description of the task and the participants' systems, we show various score ablations and some sample outputs.

1 Introduction

Abstract Meaning Representation (AMR) is a compact, readable, whole-sentence semantic annotation (Banarescu et al., 2013). It includes entity identification and typing, PropBank semantic roles (Kingsbury and Palmer, 2002), individual entities playing multiple roles, as well as treatments of modality, negation, etc. AMR abstracts in numerous ways, e.g., by assigning the same conceptual structure to *fear* (v), *fear* (n), and *afraid* (adj). Figure 1 gives an example.

In 2016 an AMR parsing shared task was held at SemEval (May, 2016). Task participants demonstrated several new directions in AMR parsing technology and also validated the strong performance of existing parsers. We sought, in 2017, to focus AMR parsing performance on the biomedical domain, for which a not insignificant but still relatively small training corpus had been produced. While sentences from this domain are quite

```
(f / fear-01
  :polarity "-"
  :ARG0 ( s / soldier )
  :ARG1 ( d / die-01
          :ARG1 s ))
```

The soldier was not afraid of dying.
The soldier was not afraid to die.
The soldier did not fear death.

Figure 1: An Abstract Meaning Representation (AMR) with several English renderings. Example borrowed from Pust et al. (2015).

formal compared to some of those evaluated in last year's task, they are also very complex, and have many terms unique to the domain. An example is shown in Figure 2. We continue to use Smatch (Cai and Knight, 2013) as a metric for AMR parsing, but we perform additional ablative analysis using the approach proposed by Damonte et al. (2016).

Along with parsing into AMR, it is important to encourage improvements in automatic *generation* of natural language (NL) text from AMR. Humans favor communication in NL. An AI that is able to parse text into AMR at a quality level indistinguishable from humans may be said to understand NL, but without the ability to render its own semantic representations into NL no human will ever be able to appreciate this.

The advent of several systems that generate English text from AMR input (Flanigan et al., 2016b; Pourdamghani et al., 2016) inspired us to conduct a generation-based shared task from AMRs in the news/discussion forum domain. For the generation subtask, we solicited human judgments of sentence quality. We followed the precedent established by the Workshop in Machine Translation (Bojar et al., 2016) and used the Appraise solicitation system (Federmann, 2012), lightly mod-

536

```
Interestingly, serpinE2 mRNA and protein
were also markedly enhanced in human CRC
cells exhibiting mutation in
<i>KRAS </i>and <i>BRAF</i>.

(e / enhance-01 :li 2
 :ARG1 (a3 / and
  :op1 (n6 / nucleic-acid
     :name (n / name :op1 "mRNA")
   :ARG0-of (e2 / encode-01
     :ARG1 p))
  :op2 (p / protein
     :name (n2 / name :op1 "serpinE2")))
 :manner (m / marked)
 :mod (a2 / also)
 :location (c / cell
  :ARG0-of (e3 / exhibit-01
   :ARG1 (m2 / mutate-01
    :ARG1 (a4 / and
     :op1 (g / gene
        :name (n4 / name :op1 "KRAS"))
     :op2 (g2 / gene
        :name (n5 / name :op1 "BRAF")))))
  :mod (h / human)
  :mod (d / disease
     :name (n3 / name :op1 "CRC")))
 :manner (i / interesting))
```

Figure 2: One of the simpler biomedical domain sentences and its AMR. Note the italics markers in the original sentence are preserved, as they are semantically important to the sentence's understanding.

ified, to gather human rankings, then TrueSkill (Sakaguchi et al., 2014) to elicit an overall system ranking.

Since the same training data and tools are available to both subtasks (though, in the case of the generation subtask, the utility of the Bio-AMR corpus is unclear), we will describe all the resources for both subtasks in Sections 2 and 3 but then will handle descriptions and ablations for the parsing and generation subtasks separately, in, respectively, Sections 4 and 5. Readers interested in only one of these subtasks should not feel compelled to read the other section. We will reconvene in Section 6 to conclude and discuss hardware, as we continue the tradition established last year in the awarding of trophies to the declared winners of each subtask.

2 Data

LDC released a new corpus of AMRs (LDC2016E25), created as part of the DARPA DEFT program, in March of 2016. The new corpus, which was annotated by teams at SDL, LDC, and the University of Colorado, and su-

pervised by Ulf Hermjakob at USC/ISI, is an extension of previous releases (LDC2015E86, LDC2014E41 and LDC2014T12). It contains 39,260 sentences (subsuming, in turn, the 19,572 AMRs from LDC2015E86, the 18,779 AMRs from LDC2014E41, and the 13,051 AMRs from LDC2014T12), partitioned into training, development, and test splits, from a variety of news and discussion forum sources. Participants in the generation task *only* were provided with AMRs for an additional 1,293 sentences for evaluation; the original sentences were also provided, as needed, to human evaluators during the human evaluation phase of the generation subtask (see Section 5.2). These sentences and their corresponding AMRs were sequestered and never released as data before the evaluation phase.

We also made available the Bio-AMR corpus version 0.8, which consists of 6,452 AMR annotations of sentences from cancer-related PubMed articles, covering 3 full papers[1] as well as the result sections of 46 additional PubMed papers. The corpus also includes about 1000 sentences each from the BEL BioCreative training corpus and the Chicago Corpus. The Bio-AMR corpus was partitioned into training, development, and test splits. An additional 500 sentences and their AMRs were sequestered until the evaluation phase, at which point the sentences were provided to parsing task participants *only*. Table 1 summarizes the available data, including the split sizes.

3 Other Resources

We made the following resources available to participants:

- The tokenizer (from Ulf Hermjakob) used to produce the tokenized sentences in the training corpus.[2]

- The AMR specification, used by annotators in producing the AMRs.[3]

- The JAMR (Flanigan et al., 2014)[4] and CAMR (Wang et al., 2015a)[5] parsers, as strong parser baselines.

---

[1]PMIDs 24651010, 11777939, and 15630473
[2] http://alt.qcri.org/semeval2016/task8/data/uploads/tokenizer.tar.gz
[3] https://github.com/kevincrawfordknight/amr-guidelines/blob/master/amr.md
[4] https://github.com/jflanigan/jamr
[5] https://github.com/c-amr/camr

Corpus	Domain	Train	Dev	Test	Eval
LDC2016E25	News/Forum	36,521	1,368	1,371	N/A
Bio-AMR v0.8	Biomedical	5,452	500	500	N/A
Parsing evaluation set	Biomedical	N/A	N/A	N/A	500
Generation evaluation set (LDC2016R33)	News/Form	N/A	N/A	N/A	1,293

Table 1: A summary of data used in this task; split sizes indicate the number of AMRs per sub-corpus.

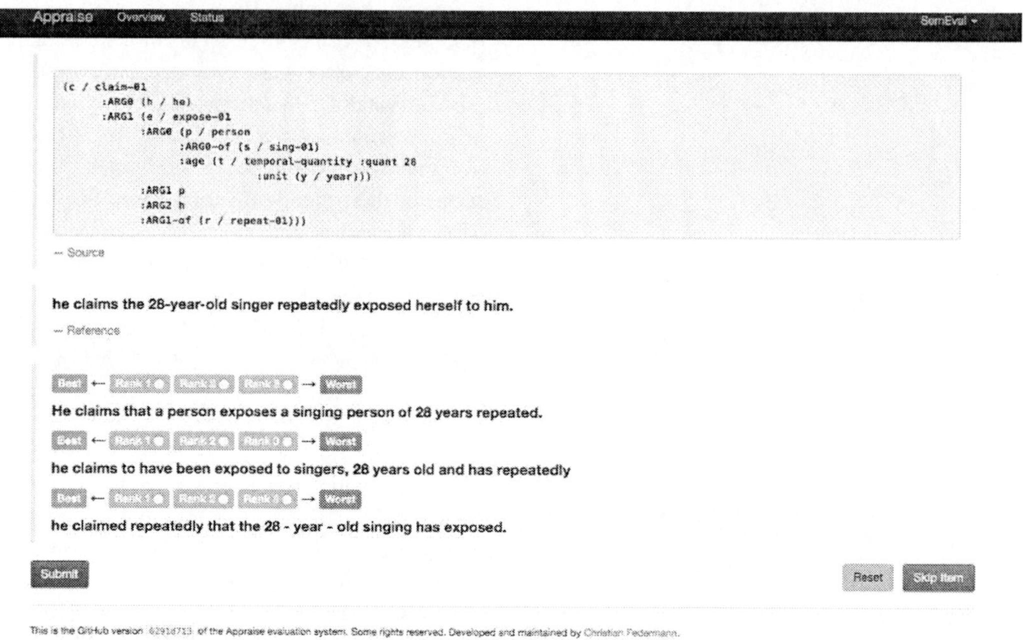

Figure 3: The Appraise interface, adapted for AMR generation evaluation.

- The JAMR (Flanigan et al., 2016b) generation system, as a strong generation baseline.

- An unsupervised AMR-to-English aligner (Pourdamghani et al., 2014).[6]

- The same Smatch (Cai and Knight, 2013) scoring script used in the evaluation.[7]

- A Python AMR manipulation library, from Nathan Schneider.[8]

4 Parsing Sub-Task

In the parsing sub-task, participants were given 500 previously sequestered Bio-AMRs and were asked to produce AMR graphs. Main results and ablative results are shown in Table 2.

4.1 Systems

Five teams participated in the task, a noticeable decline from last year's task, which saw eleven full participants. One team submitted two systems for a total of six distinct systems. Two teams were repeats from last year: CMU and RIGOTRIO (previously RIGA). Below are brief descriptions of each of the various systems, based on summaries provided by the system authors. Readers are encouraged to consult individual system description papers or relevant conference paper descriptions for more details.

4.1.1 The Meaning Factory (van Noord and Bos, 2017)

This team submitted two parsers. TMF-1 is a character-level sequence-to-sequence deep learn-

---

[6] http://isi.edu/~damghani/papers/Aligner.zip

[7] https://github.com/snowblink14/smatch

[8] https://github.com/nschneid/amr-hackathon

	Smatch	Unlab.	No WSD	NER	Wiki
TMF-1	0.46	0.5	0.46	0.51	0.46
TMF-2	0.58	0.63	0.58	0.58	0.4
UIT-DANGNT-CLNLP	**0.61**	**0.65**	**0.61**	**0.66**	0.35
Oxford	0.59	0.63	0.59	**0.66**	0.18
CMU	0.44	0.47	0.44	0.48	**0.59**
RIGOTRIO	0.54	0.59	0.54	0.46	0

(a) Main parsing results and four ablations

	Smatch	Neg.	Concepts	Reent.	SRL
TMF-1	0.46	0	0.63	0.29	0.43
TMF-2	0.58	0.24	0.76	0.35	0.54
UIT-DANGNT-CLNLP	**0.61**	0.24	**0.78**	0.37	0.56
Oxford	0.59	0.27	0.74	**0.43**	**0.57**
CMU	0.44	**0.33**	0.65	0.27	0.41
RIGOTRIO	0.54	0.31	0.71	0.34	0.51

(b) Main parsing results and four other ablations

Table 2: Main parsing results: For Smatch, a mean of ten runs with ten restarts per run is shown; standard deviation was about 0.0003 per system. For the remaining ablations, a single run was used.

ing model[9] similar to that of Barzdins and Gosko (2016), but with a number of pre- and post-processing changes to improve results. TMF-2 is an ensemble of CAMR (Wang et al., 2015b) models trained on different data sets and the seq-to-seq model to find the best CAMR parse.

4.1.2 UIT-DANGNT-CLNLP
(Nguyen and Nguyen, 2017)

This team implemented two wrapper layers for CAMR (Wang et al., 2015a). The first layer standardizes and adds additional information to input sentences to eliminate the weakness of the dependency parser observed when parsing scientific quotations, figures, formulas, etc. The second layer wraps the output data of CAMR. It is based on a prebuilt list of (biology term–AMR structure) pairs to fix the output data of CAMR. This makes CAMR deal with unknown scientific concepts better.

4.1.3 Oxford
(Buys and Blunsom, 2017)

This is a neural encoder-decoder AMR parser modeling the alignment between graph nodes and sentence tokens explicitly with a pointer mechanism. Candidate lemmas are predicted as a pre-processing step so that the lemmas of lexical node labels are factored out of the graph linearization.

4.1.4 CMU

This was the same JAMR parsing system used in last year's evaluation (Flanigan et al., 2016a). The participants declined to submit a new system description paper.

4.1.5 RIGOTRIO
(Gruzitis et al., 2017)

This team extended their CAMR-based AMR parser from last year's shared task (Barzdins and Gosko, 2016) with a gazetteer for recognizing as named entities the biomedical compounds frequently mentioned in the biomedical texts. The gazetteer was populated from the provided biomedical AMR training data.

4.2 Quantitative Ablation

We made use of the analysis scripts produced by Damonte et al. (2016) to conduct a more fine-grained ablation of scores. As noted in that work, Smatch provides full-sentence analysis but some aspects of an AMR are more difficult to parse correctly than others. The ablation study considers only (or excludes) an aspect of the AMR and then calculates Smatch (or F1, when no heuristic matching is needed) with that limitation in place. Ablation scores are shown in Table 2. The ablations are:[10]

---

[9] https://www.tensorflow.org/tutorials/seq2seq/

[10] see Damonte et al. (2016) for more details

- Unlabeled: All argument labels (e.g. `ARG0`, `location`) are replaced with a single common label

- No WSD: Propbank frames indicating different senses (such as `die-01` vs `die-02`) are conflated

- NER: Only named entities are scored; that is, in both reference and hypothesis AMR, only nodes with an incoming arc labeled `name` are considered.

- Wiki: Only wikifications are scored; this is achieved in a manner similar to NER but with the incoming arc labeled `wiki`.

- Negation: Only concepts with an outgoing `polarity` arc are considered. In practice this arc is only used to indicate negation.

- Concepts: Only concepts, not relations, are scored.

- Reentrancies: Only concepts with two or more incoming relations are scored. Reentrancies occur when a concept has several mentions in a sentence, or where an 'inverted' relation (one that ends in `-of`) occurs, implying inverse dependency. In practice the latter is much more often the cause of a re-entrancy.

- Semantic Role Labeling (SRL): only relations corresponding to roles in PropBank, i.e. those named `ARG0` and the like, are scored.

The ablation results show that superior performance in Smatch correlates with superior performance in the Unlabeled, No-WSD, NER, and Concepts performance. Additionally, Figure 4, which plots each ablation score against Smatch and induces a linear regression, shows that six of the eight ablation sub-metrics are well correlated with Smatch; only wikification and negation are not. Wikification is generally handled as a separate process on top of overall AMR parsing; this may explain that discrepancy. We have no great explanation for negation's weak correlation but note that it is generally considered a difficult task in semantics.

4.3 Discussion

It is interesting to note that the top-scoring system was, as in last year's shared task, based on

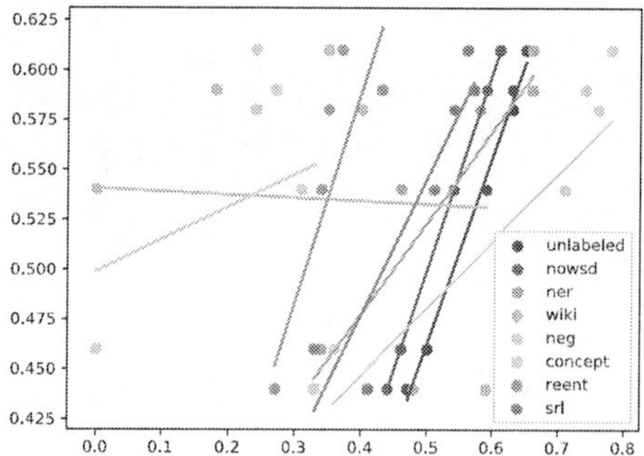

Figure 4: Relationship between each of the eight quantitative ablation studies from Damonte et al. (2016) and Smatch; six of the eight metrics are well-correlated with Smatch.

CAMR (Wang et al., 2015b). It is also interesting to note that, in the Oxford team's submission, once again, a pure neural system is nearly as good as the CAMR system, despite having rather little data to train on. The Oxford system appears to be quite different from last year's neural submission (Foland and Martin, 2016) but nevertheless is a strong competitor. Finally, the top-scoring system, that of UIT-DANGNT-CLNLP, got a 0.61 Smatch, while last year's top scoring systems (Barzdins and Gosko, 2016; Wang et al., 2016) scored a 0.62, practically the same score. This, despite the fact that the evaluation corpora were quite different. One might expect the biomedical corpus to be easier to parse than the news/forum corpus, since its sentences are rather formal, and do not use slang or incorrect syntax. On the other hand, the sentences in the biomedical corpus are on average longer than those in the news/forum corpus (on average 25 words in bio vs. 14.5 in news/forum) and the biomedical corpus contains many unknown words, corresponding to domain terminology not in general use (1-count words are 9% of tokens in bio training, vs. 7.2% in news/forum). The news/forum corpus has, in its forum content, colloquialisms and writing variants that are very difficult to automatically analyze. Perhaps the relatively 'easy' and 'hard' parts of each corpus canceled each other out, yielding corpora that were about the same level of difficulty to parse. Nevertheless, it is somewhat concerning that AMR parsing quality appears to have stalled, as parsing performance remains in the low 0.60 range.

5 Generation Sub-Task

As AMR provides full-sentence semantics, it may be a suitable formalism for semantics-to-text generation. This subtask explored the suitability of that hypothesis. Given that AMRs do not capture non-semantic surface phenomena nor some essential properties of realized text such as tense, we incorporated human judgments into our evaluation, since automatic metrics against a single reference were practically guaranteed to be inadequate.

5.1 Systems

Four teams participated in the task. We also included a submission from Pourdamghani et al. (2016) run by the organizer, though *a priori* declared that submission to be non-competitive due to a conflict of interest. Below we provide short summaries of each team's approach.

5.1.1 CMU

This was the JAMR generation system described in (Flanigan et al., 2016b). The participants declined to submit a system description paper.

5.1.2 Sheffield
(Lampouras and Vlachos, 2017)

This team's method is based on inverting previous work on transition-based parsers, and casts NLG from AMR as a sequence of actions (e.g., insert/remove/rename edges and nodes) that progressively transform the AMR graph into a syntactic parse tree. It achieves this by employing a sequence of four classifiers, each focusing on a subset of the transition actions, and finally realizing the syntactic parse tree into the final sentence.

5.1.3 RIGOTRIO
(Gruzitis et al., 2017)

For generation, this team's approach was to write transformation rules for converting AMR into Grammatical Framework (Ranta, 2004) abstract syntax from which semantically correct English text can be rendered automatically. In reality the approach worked for 10% of AMRs. For the submission the remaining 90% AMRs were converted to text using the JAMR (Flanigan et al., 2014) tool.

5.1.4 FORGe
(Simon Mille and Wanner, 2017)

UPF-TALN's generation pipeline comprises a series of rule-based graph-transducers, for the syntacticization of the input graphs (converted to CoNLL format) and the resolution of morphological agreements, and an off-the-shelf statistical linearization component.

5.1.5 ISI

This was an internal, non-trophy-eligible submission based on the work of Pourdamghani et al. (2016). It views generation as phrase based machine translation and learns a linearization of AMR such that the result can be used in an off-the-shelf Moses (Koehn et al., 2007) PBMT implementation.

5.2 Manual Evaluation

We used Appraise (Federmann, 2012), an open-source system for manual evaluation of machine translation, to conduct a human evaluation of generation quality. The system asks human judges to rank randomly selected systems' translations of sentences from the test corpus. This in turn yields pairwise preference information that can be used to effect an overall system ranking.

For the purposes of this task we needed to adapt the Appraise system to admit nested representations of AMRs, and to be compatible with our IT infrastructure. A screen shot is shown in Figure 3.

5.3 Scoring

We provided BLEU as a potentially helpful automatic metric but consider several metrics induced over pairwise comparisons induced by manual evaluation to be the "true" evaluation metric for the purposes of trophy-awarding:

- Win+tie percentage: This is simply the percentage "wins" (better pairwise comparisons) plus "ties" (equal comparisons) of the total number of its pairwise comparisons. This metric was largely used to induce rankings from human judgments through WMT 2011.

- Win percentage: This is a "harsher" version of Win+tie; the percentage is $\frac{\text{wins}}{\text{wins+ties+losses}}$. Essentially, ties are judged as losses. This was used in WMT 2011 and 2012.

- TrueSkill (Sakaguchi et al., 2014). This is an adaptation of a metric developed for player rankings in ongoing competitions such as on Microsoft Xbox Live. The metric maintains estimates of player (i.e., generation system)

	Win	Win+Tie	Trueskill	BLEU
RIGOTRIO	**54.91**	**81.49**	**1.07**	18.82
CMU	50.36	72.48	0.85	**19.01**
FORGe	43.64	57.43	0.45	4.74
ISI	26.05	38.39	-1.19	10.92
Sheffield	8.38	21.16	-2.20	3.32

Table 3: Main generation results: The three manually-derived metrics agree on the systems' relative rankings.

	Win	Win+Tie	Trueskill
RIGOTRIO	**53.00**	**79.98**	**1.03**
CMU	50.02	71.91	0.819
FORGe	44.49	58.57	0.458
ISI	26.40	38.60	-1.172
Sheffield	9.46	22.84	-2.132

Table 4: Human judgments of generation results after self-judgments are removed: The results are fundamentally the same

ability as Gaussian distributions and rewards events (i.e., pairwise rankings of outputs) that are unexpected, such as a poorly ranked player outperforming a highly-ranked player, more than expected events.

We note that the three metrics derived from human pairwise rankings agree with the relative ordering of the submitted systems' abilities on the evaluation data, while the BLEU metric does not. It is not terribly surprising the BLEU does not correlate with human judgment; it was designed for a very different task.

Since the participants in this task were also judges in the human evaluation, we were somewhat concerned that implicit bias might lead to a skewing of the results, even though system identification was not available during evaluation. We thus removed all judgments that involved self-scoring and recalculated results. The results, shown in Table 4, show little difference from the main results.

5.4 Qualitative Analysis

The generation task was quite challenging, as generation from AMR is still a nascent field. Table 5 shows an example of a single AMR and the content generated by each system for it, along with the number of wins, ties, and losses per system by the human evaluations (note: not all segments were scored for all systems, and not all systems received the same number of comparisons). Some systematic errors, such as incorporating label text into the generation, could lead to improvements, as could a stronger language model; generated output is often disfluent.

6 Conclusion

Both biomedical AMR parsing and generation from AMRs appear to be challenging tasks; perhaps too challenging, as the number of participants in either subtask was significantly lower than the participation rate from a year ago. However, we observed that AMR parsing quality on the seemingly more difficult biomedical domain was no worse than that observed on the news/forum domain. In fact, the same fundamental technology that dominated in last year's evaluation once again reigned supreme. A concern that Smatch was too coarse a metric to evaluate AMRs was not borne out, as scores in an ablation study tracked well with the overall Smatch score. We are pleased to award the parsing trophy to the UIT-DANGNT-CLNLP team, which added domain-specific modification to the strong CAMR (Wang et al., 2015b) parsing platform.

On the generation side, it seems that there is still a long way to go to reach fluency. We note that BLEU, which is often used as a generation metric, is woefully inadequate compared to human evaluation. We hope the analysis presented here will lead to better generation systems in the future. It was clear from the human evaluations, however, that the RIGOTRIO team prevailed and will receive the generation trophy.

Acknowledgments

We were overjoyed to be offered volunteer human judgments by Nathan Schneider and his class at Georgetown: Austin Blodgett, Emma Manning, Harry Eldridge, Joe Garman, Lucia Donatelli, Sean MacAvaney, Max Kim, Nicholas Chapman, Mohammad Ali Yekataie, and Yushi Zhao. Thanks to Marco Damonte and Shay Cohen for reaching out regarding Smatch ablations and providing scoring code. The human evaluations would not have been possible without the use of the Appraise system, which was shared by Christian Federmann and Matt Post. Many thanks to the AMR creation team: Kira Griffitt, Ulf Hermjakob, Kevin Knight, and Martha Palmer. Thanks also to

```
(a / and
  :op1 (r / remain-01
     :ARG1 (c / country :wiki "Bosnia_and_Herzegovina"
        :name (n / name :op1 "Bosnia"))
     :ARG3 (d / divide-02
        :ARG1 c
        :topic (e / ethnic)))
  :op2 (v / violence
     :time (m / match-03
        :mod (f2 / football)
        :ARG1-of (m2 / major-02))
     :location (h / here)
     :frequency (o / occasional))
  :time (f / follow-01
     :ARG2 (w / war-01
        :time (d2 / date-interval
           :op1 (d3 / date-entity :year 1992)
           :op2 (d4 / date-entity :year 1995)))))
```

Source	Text	W	T	L
Reference	following the 1992-1995 war bosnia remains ethnically divided and violence during major football matches occasionally occurs here.			
RIGOTRIO	following the 1992 1995 war, bosnia has remained an ethnic divide, and the major football matches occasionally violence in here.	1	2	1
CMU	following the 1992 1995 war , bosnia remains divided in ethnic and the occasional football match in major violence in here	2	0	0
FORGe	Bosnia and Herzegovina remains under about ethnic the Bosnia and Herzegovina divide and here at a majored match a violence.	0	0	4
ISI	following war between 1992 and 1995 , the country :wiki bosnia_and_herzegovina bosnia remain divided on ethnic and violence in football match by major here from time to time	3	0	1
Sheffield	Remain Bosnia ethnic divid following war 920000 950000 major match footbal occasional here violency	0	2	0

Table 5: Examples of an AMR from the Generation subtask and each system's generation for it (W = # wins, T = # ties, L = # losses in human evaluation).

the SemEval organizers: Steven Bethard, Marine Carpuat, Marianna Apidianaki, Saif Mohammad, Daniel Cer, and David Jurgens. We also gratefully acknowledge the participating teams' efforts. This work was sponsored by DARPA DEFT (FA8750-13-2-0045).

References

Laura Banarescu, Claire Bonial, Shu Cai, Madalina Georgescu, Kira Griffitt, Ulf Hermjakob, Kevin Knight, Philipp Koehn, Martha Palmer, and Nathan Schneider. 2013. Abstract Meaning Representation for sembanking. In *Proceedings of the 7th Linguistic Annotation Workshop and Interoperability with Discourse*. Association for Computational Linguistics, Sofia, Bulgaria, pages 178–186. http://www.aclweb.org/anthology/W13-2322.

Guntis Barzdins and Didzis Gosko. 2016. RIGA at

SemEval-2016 task 8: Impact of Smatch extensions and character-level neural translation on AMR parsing accuracy. In *Proceedings of the 10th International Workshop on Semantic Evaluation (SemEval 2016)*. Association for Computational Linguistics, San Diego, California.

Ondřej Bojar, Rajen Chatterjee, Christian Federmann, Yvette Graham, Barry Haddow, Matthias Huck, Antonio Jimeno Yepes, Philipp Koehn, Varvara Logacheva, Christof Monz, Matteo Negri, Aurelie Neveol, Mariana Neves, Martin Popel, Matt Post, Raphael Rubino, Carolina Scarton, Lucia Specia, Marco Turchi, Karin Verspoor, and Marcos Zampieri. 2016. Findings of the 2016 conference on machine translation. In *Proceedings of the First Conference on Machine Translation*. Association for Computational Linguistics, Berlin, Germany, pages 131–198. http://www.aclweb.org/anthology/W/W16/W16-2301.

Jan Buys and Phil Blunsom. 2017. Oxford at SemEval-

2017 task 9: Neural AMR parsing with pointer-augmented attention. In *Proceedings of the 11th International Workshop on Semantic Evaluation (SemEval 2017)*. Association for Computational Linguistics, Vancouver, Canada.

Shu Cai and Kevin Knight. 2013. Smatch: an evaluation metric for semantic feature structures. In *Proceedings of the 51st Annual Meeting of the Association for Computational Linguistics (Volume 2: Short Papers)*. Association for Computational Linguistics, Sofia, Bulgaria, pages 748–752. http://www.aclweb.org/anthology/P13-2131.

Marco Damonte, Shay B. Cohen, and Giorgio Satta. 2016. An incremental parser for abstract meaning representation. *CoRR* abs/1608.06111. http://arxiv.org/abs/1608.06111.

Christian Federmann. 2012. Appraise: An open-source toolkit for manual evaluation of machine translation output. *The Prague Bulletin of Mathematical Linguistics* 98:25–35.

Jeffrey Flanigan, Chris Dyer, Noah A. Smith, and Jaime Carbonell. 2016a. CMU at SemEval-2016 task 8: Graph-based AMR parsing with infinite ramp loss. In *Proceedings of the 10th International Workshop on Semantic Evaluation (SemEval 2016)*. Association for Computational Linguistics, San Diego, California.

Jeffrey Flanigan, Chris Dyer, Noah A. Smith, and Jaime Carbonell. 2016b. Generation from abstract meaning representation using tree transducers. In *Proceedings of the 2016 Conference of the North American Chapter of the Association for Computational Linguistics: Human Language Technologies*. Association for Computational Linguistics, San Diego, California, pages 731–739. http://www.aclweb.org/anthology/N16-1087.

Jeffrey Flanigan, Sam Thomson, Jaime Carbonell, Chris Dyer, and Noah A. Smith. 2014. A discriminative graph-based parser for the Abstract Meaning Representation. In *Proceedings of the 52nd Annual Meeting of the Association for Computational Linguistics (Volume 1: Long Papers)*. Association for Computational Linguistics, Baltimore, Maryland, pages 1426–1436. http://www.aclweb.org/anthology/P14-1134.

William Foland and James H. Martin. 2016. CU-NLP at SemEval-2016 task 8: AMR parsing using LSTM-based recurrent neural networks. In *Proceedings of the 10th International Workshop on Semantic Evaluation (SemEval 2016)*. Association for Computational Linguistics, San Diego, California.

Normunds Gruzitis, Didzis Gosko, and Guntis Barzdins. 2017. RIGOTRIO at SemEval-2017 task 9: Combining machine learning and grammar engineering for AMR parsing and generation. In *Proceedings of the 11th International Workshop on Semantic Evaluation (SemEval 2017)*. Association for Computational Linguistics, Vancouver, Canada.

Paul Kingsbury and Martha Palmer. 2002. From Treebank to Propbank. In *Language Resources and Evaluation*.

Philipp Koehn, Hieu Hoang, Alexandra Birch, Chris Callison-Burch, Marcello Federico, Nicola Bertoldi, Brooke Cowan, Wade Shen, Christine Moran, Richard Zens, Chris Dyer, Ondrej Bojar, Alexandra Constantin, and Evan Herbst. 2007. Moses: Open source toolkit for statistical machine translation. In *Proceedings of the 45th Annual Meeting of the Association for Computational Linguistics Companion Volume Proceedings of the Demo and Poster Sessions*. Association for Computational Linguistics, Prague, Czech Republic, pages 177–180. http://www.aclweb.org/anthology/P07-2045.

Gerasimos Lampouras and Andreas Vlachos. 2017. Sheffield at SemEval-2017 task 9: Transition-based language generation from AMR. In *Proceedings of the 11th International Workshop on Semantic Evaluation (SemEval 2017)*. Association for Computational Linguistics, Vancouver, Canada.

Jonathan May. 2016. Semeval-2016 task 8: Meaning representation parsing. In *Proceedings of the 10th International Workshop on Semantic Evaluation (SemEval-2016)*. Association for Computational Linguistics, San Diego, California, pages 1063–1073. http://www.aclweb.org/anthology/S16-1166.

Khoa Nguyen and Dang Nguyen. 2017. UIT-DANGNT-CLNLP at SemEval-2017 task 9: Building scientific concept fixing patterns for improving CAMR. In *Proceedings of the 11th International Workshop on Semantic Evaluation (SemEval 2017)*. Association for Computational Linguistics, Vancouver, Canada.

Nima Pourdamghani, Yang Gao, Ulf Hermjakob, and Kevin Knight. 2014. Aligning English strings with Abstract Meaning Representation graphs. In *Proceedings of the 2014 Conference on Empirical Methods in Natural Language Processing (EMNLP)*. Association for Computational Linguistics, Doha, Qatar, pages 425–429. http://www.aclweb.org/anthology/D14-1048.

Nima Pourdamghani, Kevin Knight, and Ulf Hermjakob. 2016. Generating English from Abstract Meaning Representations. In *Proceedings of the 9th International Natural Language Generation conference*. Association for Computational Linguistics, Edinburgh, UK, pages 21–25.

Michael Pust, Ulf Hermjakob, Kevin Knight, Daniel Marcu, and Jonathan May. 2015. Parsing English into Abstract Meaning Representation using syntax-based machine translation. In *Proceedings of the 2015 Conference on Empirical Methods in Natural Language Processing*. Association for Computational Linguistics, Lisbon, Portugal, pages 1143–1154. http://aclweb.org/anthology/D15-1136.

Aarne Ranta. 2004. Grammatical framework. *Journal of Functional Programming* 14(2):145189. https://doi.org/10.1017/S0956796803004738.

Keisuke Sakaguchi, Matt Post, and Benjamin Van Durme. 2014. Efficient elicitation of annotations for human evaluation of machine translation. In *Proceedings of the Ninth Workshop on Statistical Machine Translation*. Association for Computational Linguistics, Baltimore, Maryland, USA, pages 1–11. http://www.aclweb.org/anthology/W14-3301.

Roberto Carlini Alicia Burga Simon Mille and Leo Wanner. 2017. FORGe at SemEval-2017 task 9: Deep sentence generation based on a sequence of graph transducers. In *Proceedings of the 11th International Workshop on Semantic Evaluation (SemEval 2017)*. Association for Computational Linguistics, Vancouver, Canada.

Rik van Noord and Johan Bos. 2017. The meaning factory at SemEval-2017 task 9: Producing AMRs with neural semantic parsing. In *Proceedings of the 11th International Workshop on Semantic Evaluation (SemEval 2017)*. Association for Computational Linguistics, Vancouver, Canada.

Chuan Wang, Nianwen Xue, and Sameer Pradhan. 2015a. Boosting transition-based AMR parsing with refined actions and auxiliary analyzers. In *Proceedings of the 53rd Annual Meeting of the Association for Computational Linguistics and the 7th International Joint Conference on Natural Language Processing (Volume 2: Short Papers)*. Association for Computational Linguistics, Beijing, China, pages 857–862. http://www.aclweb.org/anthology/P15-2141.

Chuan Wang, Nianwen Xue, and Sameer Pradhan. 2015b. A transition-based algorithm for AMR parsing. In *Proceedings of the 2015 Conference of the North American Chapter of the Association for Computational Linguistics: Human Language Technologies*. Association for Computational Linguistics, Denver, Colorado, pages 366–375. http://www.aclweb.org/anthology/N15-1040.

Chuan Wang, Nianwen Xue, Sameer Pradhan, Xiaoman Pan, and Heng Ji. 2016. CAMR at SemEval-2016 task 8: An extended transition-based AMR parser. In *Proceedings of the 10th International Workshop on Semantic Evaluation (SemEval 2016)*. Association for Computational Linguistics, San Diego, California.

SemEval 2017 Task 10: ScienceIE - Extracting Keyphrases and Relations from Scientific Publications

Isabelle Augenstein[1], Mrinal Das[2], Sebastian Riedel[1], Lakshmi Vikraman[2], and Andrew McCallum[2]

[1]Department of Computer Science, University College London (UCL), UK

[2]College of Information and Computer Sciences, University of Massachusetts Amherst, USA

Abstract

We describe the SemEval task of extracting keyphrases and relations between them from scientific documents, which is crucial for understanding which publications describe which processes, tasks and materials. Although this was a new task, we had a total of 26 submissions across 3 evaluation scenarios. We expect the task and the findings reported in this paper to be relevant for researchers working on understanding scientific content, as well as the broader knowledge base population and information extraction communities.

1 Introduction

Empirical research requires gaining and maintaining an understanding of the body of work in specific area. For example, typical questions researchers face are which papers describe which tasks and processes, use which materials and how those relate to one another. While there are review papers for some areas, such information is generally difficult to obtain without reading a large number of publications.

Current efforts to address this gap are search engines such as Google Scholar,[1] Scopus[2] or Semantic Scholar,[3] which mainly focus on navigating author and citations graphs.

The task tackled here is mention-level identification and classification of keyphrases, e.g. Keyphrase_Extraction (TASK), as well as extracting semantic relations between keywords, e.g. Keyphrase_Extraction HYPONYM-OF Information_Extraction. These tasks are related to the tasks of named entity recognition, named entity

classification and relation extraction. However, keyphrases are much more challenging to identify than e.g. person names, since they vary significantly between domains, lack clear signifiers and contexts and can consist of many tokens. For this purpose, a double-annotated corpus of 500 publications with mention-level annotations was produced, consisting of scientific articles of the Computer Science, Material Sciences and Physics domains.

Extracting keyphrases and relations between them is of great interest to scientific publishers as it helps to recommend articles to readers, highlight missing citations to authors, identify potential reviewers for submissions, and analyse research trends over time. Note that organising keyphrases in terms of synonym and hypernym relations is particularly useful for search scenarios, e.g. a reader may search for articles on information extraction, and through hypernym prediction would also receive articles on named entity recognition or relation extraction.

We expect the outcomes of the task to be relevant to the wider information extraction, knowledge base population and knowledge base construction communities, as it offers a novel application domain for methods researched in that area, while still offering domain-related challenges.

Since the dataset is annotated for three tasks dependent on one another, it could also be used as a testbed for joint learning or structured prediction approaches to information extraction (Kate and Mooney, 2010; Singh et al., 2013; Augenstein et al., 2015; Goyal and Dyer, 2016).

Furthermore, we expect the task to be interesting for researchers studying tasks aiming at understanding scientific content, such as keyphrase extraction (Kim et al., 2010b; Hasan and Ng, 2014; Sterckx et al., 2016; Augenstein and Søgaard, 2017), semantic relation extraction (Tateisi et al.,

---

[1]https://scholar.google.co.uk/

[2]http://www.scopus.com/

[3]https://www.semanticscholar.org/

Proceedings of the 11th International Workshop on Semantic Evaluations (SemEval-2017), pages 546–555,
Vancouver, Canada, August 3 - 4, 2017. ©2017 Association for Computational Linguistics

2014; Gupta and Manning, 2011; Marsi and
Öztürk, 2015), topic classification of scientific articles (Ó Séaghdha and Teufel, 2014), citation context extraction (Teufel, 2006; Kaplan et al., 2009), extracting author and citation graphs (Peng and McCallum, 2006; Chaimongkol et al., 2014; Sim et al., 2015) or a combination of those (Radev and Abu-Jbara, 2012; Gollapalli and Li, 2015; Guo et al., 2015).

The expected impact of the task is an interest of the above mentioned research communities beyond the task due to the release of a new corpus, leading to novel research methods for information extraction from scientific documents. What will be particularly useful about the proposed corpus are annotations of hypernym and synonym relations on mention-level, as existing hypernym and synonym relation resources are on type-level, e.g. WordNet.[4] Further, we expect that these methods will directly impact industrial solutions to making sense of publications, partly due to the task organisers' collaboration with Elsevier.[5]

2   Task Description

The task is divided into three subtasks:

A) Mention-level keyphrase identification

B) Mention-level keyphrase classification. Keyphrase types are PROCESS (including methods, equipment), TASK and MATERIAL (including corpora, physical materials)

C) Mention-level semantic relation extraction between keyphrases with the same keyphrase types. Relation types used are HYPONYM-OF and SYNONYM-OF.

We will refer to the above subtasks as Subtask A, Subtask B, and Subtask C respectively.

A shortened (artificial) example of a data instance for the Computer Science area is displayed in Example 1, examples for Material Science and Physics are included in the appendix. The first part is the plain text paragraph (with keyphrases in italics for better readability), followed by stand-off keyphrase annotations based on character offsets, followed relation annotations.

Example 1.

Text: *Information extraction* is the process of extracting structured data from unstructured text, which is relevant for several end-to-end tasks, including *question answering*. This paper addresses the tasks of *named entity recognition (NER)*, a subtask of *information extraction*, using *conditional random fields (CRF)*. Our method is evaluated on the *ConLL-2003 NER corpus*.

ID	Type	Start	End
0	TASK	0	22
1	TASK	150	168
2	TASK	204	228
3	TASK	230	233
4	TASK	249	271
5	PROCESS	279	304
6	PROCESS	306	309
7	MATERIAL	343	364

ID1	ID2	Type
2	0	HYPONYM-OF
2	3	SYNONYM-OF
5	6	SYNONYM-OF

3   Resources for SemEval-2017 Task

3.1   Corpus

A corpus for the task was built from ScienceDirect[6] open access publications and was available freely for participants, without the need to sign a copyright agreement. Each data instance consists of one paragraph of text, drawn from a scientific paper.

Publications were provided in plain text, in addition to xml format, which included the full text of the publication as well as additional metadata. 500 paragraphs from journal articles evenly distributed among the domains Computer Science, Material Sciences and Physics were selected.

---

[4]https://wordnet.princeton.edu/
[5]https://www.elsevier.com/

[6]http://www.sciencedirect.com/

The training data part of the corpus consists of 350 documents, 50 for development and 100 for testing. This is similar to the pilot task described in Section 5, for which 144 articles were used for training, 40 for development and for 100 testing.

We present statistics about the dataset in Table 1. Notably, the dataset contains many long keyphrases. 22% of all keyphrases in the training set consist of words of 5 or more tokens. This contributes to making the task of keyphrase identification very challenging. However, 93% of those keyphrases are noun phrases[7], which is valuable information for simple heuristics to identify keyphrase candidates. Lastly, 31% of keyphrases contained in the training dataset only appear in it once, systems will have do generalise to unseen keyphrases well.

3.2 Annotation Process

Mention-level annotation is very time-consuming, and only a handful of semantic relations such as hypernymy and synonymy can be found in each publication. We therefore only annotate paragraphs of publications likely to contain relations.

We originally intended to identify suitable documents by automatically extracting a knowledge graph of relations from a large scientific dataset using Hearst-style patterns (Hearst, 1991; Snow et al., 2005), then using those to find potential relations in a distinct set of documents, similar to the distant supervision (Mintz et al., 2009; Snow et al., 2005) heuristic. Documents containing a high number of such potential relations would then be selected. However, this requires automatically learning to identify keyphrases between which those potential relations hold, and requires relations to appear several times in a dataset for such a knowledge graph to be useful.

In the end, this strategy was not feasible due to the difficulty of learning to detect keyphrases automatically and only a small overlap between relations in different documents. Instead, keyphrase-dense paragraphs were detected automatically using a coarse unsupervised approach (Mikolov et al., 2013) and those likely to contain relations were selected manually for annotation.

For annotation, undergraduate student volunteers studying Computer Science, Material Science or Physics were recruited using UCL's student newsletter, which reaches all of its students. Students were shown example annotations and the annotation guidelines, and if they were still interested in participating in the annotation exercise, afterwards asked to select beforehand how many documents they wanted to annotate. Approximately 50% of students were still interested, having seen annotated documents and read annotation guidelines. They were then given two weeks to annotate documents with the BRAT tool (Stenetorp et al., 2012), which was hosted on an Amazon EC2 instance as a web service. Students were compensated for annotations per document. Annotation time was estimated as approximately 12 minutes per document and annotator, on which basis they were paid roughly 10 GBP per hour. They were only compensated upon completion of all annotations, i.e. compensation was conditioned on annotating all documents. The annotation cost was covered by Elsevier. To develop annotation guidelines, a small pilot annotation exercise on 20 documents was performed with one annotator after which annotation guidelines were refined.[8]

We originally intended for student annotators to triple annotate documents and apply majority voting on the annotations, but due to difficulties with recruiting high-quality annotators we instead opted to double-annotate documents, where the second annotator was an expert annotator. Where annotations disagreed, we opted for the expert's annotation. Pairwise inter-annotator agreement between the student annotator and the expert annotator measured with Cohen's kappa is shown in Table 2. The * indicates annotation quality decreased over time, ending with the annotator not completing annotating all documents. To account for this, documents for which no annotations are given are excluded from computing inter-annotator agreement. Out of the annotators completing the annotation exercise, Cohen's kappa ranges between 0.45 and 0.85, with half of them having a substantial agreement of 0.6 or higher. For future iterations of this task, we recommend to invest significant efforts into recruiting high-quality annotators, perhaps with more pre-annotation quality screening.

---

[7] Parts of speech are determined automatically, using the nltk POS tagger

[8] Annotation guidelines were available to task participants, they can be found here: https://scienceie.github.io/resources.html

Characteristic	
Labels	Material, Process, Task
Topics	Computer Science, Physics, Material Science
Number all keyphrases	5730
Number unique keyphrases	1697
% singleton keyphrases	31%
% single-word mentions	18%
% mentions, word length $>= 3$	51%
% mentions, word length $>= 5$	22%
% mentions, noun phrases	93%
Most common keyphrases	'Isogeometric analysis', 'samples', 'calibration process','Zirconium alloys'

Table 1: Characteristics of SemEval 2017 Task 10 dataset, statistics of training sets

Student Annotator	IAA
1	0.85
2	0.66
3	0.63
4	0.60
5	0.50
6	0.48
7	0.47
8	0.45
9*	0.25
10*	0.22
11*	0.20
12*	0.15
13*	0.06

Table 2: Inter-annotator agreement between the student annotator and the expert annotator, measured with Cohen's Kappa

4 Evaluation

SemEval 2017 Task 10 offers three different evaluation scenarios:

1) Only plain text is given (Subtasks A, B, C).

2) Plain text with manually annotated keyphrase boundaries are given (Subtasks B, C).

3) Plain text with manually annotated keyphrases and their types are given (Subtask C).

We refer to the above scenarios as Scenario 1, Scenario 2, and Scenario 3 respectively.

4.1 Metrics

Keyphrase identification (Subtask A) has traditionally been evaluated by calculating the exact matches with the gold standard. There is existing work for capturing semantically similar keyphrases (Zesch and Gurevych, 2009; Kim et al., 2010a), however since these are captured using relations, similar to the pilot task on keyphrase extraction (Section 5) we evaluate keyphrases, keyphrase types and relations with exact match criteria. The output of systems is matched exactly against the gold standard. The traditionally used metrics of precision, recall and F1-score are computed and the micro-average of those metrics across publications of the three genres are calculated. These metrics are also calculated for Subtasks B and C. In addition, for Subtasks B and C, participants are given the option of using text manually annotated with keyphrase mentions and types.

5 Pilot Task

A pilot task on keyphrase extraction from scientific documents was run by other organisers at SemEval 2010 (Kim et al., 2010b). The task was to extract a list of keyphrases representing key topics from scientific documents, i.e. similar to the first part of our proposed Subtask A, only on type-level. Participants were allowed to submit up to 3 runs and were required to submit a list of 15 keyphrases for each document, ranked by the probability of being reader-assigned phrases. Data was collected from the ACM Digital Library for the research areas Distributed Systems, Information Search and Retrieval, Distributed Artificial Intelligence Multiagent Systems and Social and Behavioral Sciences Economics. Participants were provided with 144 training, 40 development and 100 test articles, each set containing a mix of articles of the different research areas. The data was provided in plain text, converted from pdf with pdftotext. Publications were annotated with keyphrases by 50 Computer Science students and added to author-provided keyphrases required by the journals they were published in. Guidelines were for the keyphrases to exactly appear anywhere in the text of the paper, in reality 15% of annotator-provided keyphrases did not, as well as 19% of author-provided keyphrases. The number of author-specified keywords was 4 on average, whereas annotators identified 12 on average. Returned phrases are considered correct if they are exact matches of either the annotator- or author-assigned keyphrases, allowing for minor syntactic variations (A of B $\rightarrow$ B A ; A's B $\rightarrow$ A B). Precision, recall and F1 is calculated for the top 5, top 10 and all keywords. 19 systems were submitted to the task, the best one achieving an F1 of 27.5% on the combined author-assigned and annotator-assigned keywords.

Lessons learned from the task were that performance varies depending on how many keywords are to be extracted, the task organisers recommend against fixing a threshold for a number of keyphrases to extract lead. They further recommend a more semantically-motivated task, taking into account synonyms of keyphrases instead of requiring exact matches. Both of those recommendations will be taken into account for future task design. To fulfill the latter, we will ask annotator to assign types to the identified keywords (process, task, material) and identify semantic relations between them (hypernym, synonym).

6 Existing Resources

As part of the FUSE project with IARPA, we created a small annotated corpus of 100 noun phrases generated from the titles and abstracts derived from the Web Of Science corpora[9] of the domains Physics, Computer Science, Chemistry and Computer Science. These corpora cannot be distributed publicly and were made available by the IARPA funding agency. Annotation was performed by 3 annotators using 14 fine-grained types, including PROCESS.

We measured inter-annotator agreement among the three annotators for the 14 categories using Fleiss' Kappa. The k value was found to be 0.28 which implies that there was fair agreement between them, however distinguishing between the fine-grained types added significantly to the annotation time. Therefore we only use three main types for the SemEval 2017 Task 10.

There are some existing keyphrase extraction corpora, however, they are not similar enough to the proposed task to justify reuse. Below is a description of existing corpora.

The SemEval 2010 Keyphrase Extraction corpus (Kim et al., 2010b)[10] consists of a handful of document-level keyphrases per article. In contrast to the task proposed, the keyphrases are annotated on type-level and not further classified as process, task or material and semantic relations are not annotated. Further, the domains considered are different and mostly sub-domains of Computer Science.

The corpus released by Tateisi et al. (2014)[11] contains sentence-level fine-grained semantic annotations for 230 publication abstracts in Japanese and 400 in English. In contrast to what we propose, the annotations are more fine-grained and annotations are only available for abstracts.

Gupta and Manning (2011) studied keyphrase extraction from ACL Anthology articles, applying a pattern-based bootstrapping approach based on 15 016 documents and assigning the types FOCUS, TECHNIQUE and DOMAIN. Performance was evaluated on 30 manually annotated documents. Although the latter corpus is related to what we propose, manual annotation is only available for a small number of documents and only for the Natural Language Processing domain.

The ACL RD-TEC 2.0 dataset (QasemiZadeh and Schumann, 2016) consists of 300 ACL Anthology abstracts annotated on mention-level with seven different types of keyphrases. Unlike our dataset, it does not contain relation annotations. Note that this corpus was created at the same time as the one SemEval 2017 Task 10 dataset and thus we did not have the chance to build on it. A more in-depth comparison between the two datasets as well as keyphrase identification and classification methods evaluated on them can be found in Augenstein and Søgaard (2017).

6.1 Baselines

We frame the task as a sequence-to-sequence prediction task. We preprocess the files by splitting documents into sentences and tokenising them with nltk, then aligning span annotations from .ann files to tokens. Each sentence is regarded as one sequence. We then split the task into the

---

[9] http://thomsonreuters. com/en/products-services/ scholarly-scientific-research/ scholarly-search-and-discovery/ web-of-science.html

[10] https://github.com/snkim/ AutomaticKeyphraseExtraction

[11] https://github.com/mynlp/ranis

three subtasks, keyphrase boundary identification, keyphrase classification and relation classification and add three output layers. We predict the following types, for the three subtasks respectively:

Subtask A: $t_A = O, B, I$ for tokens being outside, at the beginning, or inside a keyphrase

Subtask B: $t_B = O, M, P, T$ for tokens being outside a keyphrase, or being part of a material, process or task

Subtask C: $t_C = O, S, H$ for Synonym-of and Hyponym-of relations. For Subtask A and B, we predict one output label per input token. For Subtask C we predict a vector for each token, that encodes what the relationship between that token and every other token in the sequence is for the first token in each keyphrase. After predictions for tokens are obtained, these are converted back to spans and relations between them in a post-processing step.

We report results for two simple models: one to estimate the *upper bound*, that converts .ann files into instances, as described above, then converts them back into .ann files. Next, to estimate a lower bound, a *random baseline*, that for each token assigns a random label for each of the subtasks.

The *upper bound* span-token-span round-trip conversion performance, an F1 of 0.84, shows that we already lose a significant amount of performance due to sentence splitting and tokenisation alone. The *random* baseline further shows hard especially the keyphrase boundary identification task is and as a result the overall task, since the subtasks depend on one another. For Subtask A, a random baseline achieves an F1 of 0.03. The overall tasks gets easier if keyphrase boundaries are given, resulting in F1 of 0.23 for keyphrase classification, and if keyphrase types are given, an F1 of 0.04 are achieved with the random baseline for Subtask C.

7 Summary of Participating Systems

In this section, we summarise the outcome of the competition. For more details please refer to the respective system description papers and the task website `https://scienceie.github.io/`.

We had three subtasks, described in Sec 2, which were grouped together in three evaluation scenarios, described in Sec 4. The competition was hosted in CodaLab[12] in two phases: (i) development phase and (ii) testing phase. Fifty four teams participated in the development phase, and out of them twenty six teams participated in the final competition. One of the major success of the competition is due to such wide participation and application of various different techniques starting from neural networks, supervised classification with careful feature engineering to simple rule based methods. We present a summary of approaches used by task participants below.

7.1 Evaluation Scenario 1

In this scenario teams need to solve all three subtasks A, B, and C; where no annotation information was given. Some teams participated only in Subtask A, or B; but the overall micro F1 performance across subtasks is considered for the ranking of the teams. Seventeen teams participated in this scenario. The F1 scores range from 0.04 to 0.43. Complete results are given in Table 3.

Various different types of methods have been applied by different teams with various levels of supervision. The best three teams TTI_COIN, TIAL_UW, and s2_end2end have used recurrent neural network (RNN) based approaches to obtain F1 scores of 0.38, 0.42 and 0.43 respectively. However, TIAL_UW, and s2_end2end, by using a conditional random fields (CRF) layer on top of RNNs achieve a higher F1 in Subtask A compared to TTI_COIN.

The fourth team PKU_ICL with an F1 of 0.37 found classification models based on random forest and support vector machines (SVM) useful with carefully engineered feature such as TF-IDF over a very large external corpus, IDF weighted word-embeddings etc, along with an existing taxonomy. SciX on the other hand used noun phrase chunking and trained an SVM classifier on provided training data to classify phrases, and used a CRF to predict labels of the phrases. CRF based methods with parts-of-speech (POS) tagging and orthographic features such as presence of symbols and capitalisation have been tried by several teams (NTNU, SZTE-NLP, WING-NUS) and they leading to a reasonable performance (F1: 0.23, 0.26, and 0.27, respectively).

Noun phrase extraction with length constraint by HCC-NLP, and using a global list of keyphrases by NITK_IT_PG are found not to perform satisfactorily (F1: 0.16 and 0.14 respectively). The

---

Teams	Overall	A	B	C
s2_end2end (Ammar et al., 2017)	**0.43**	0.55	**0.44**	**0.28**
TIAL_UW	0.42	**0.56**	**0.44**	
TTI_COIN (Tsujimura et al., 2017)	0.38	0.5	0.39	0.21
PKU_ICL (Wang and Li, 2017)	0.37	0.51	0.38	0.19
NTNU-1 (Marsi et al., 2017)	0.33	0.47	0.34	0.2
WING-NUS (Prasad and Kan, 2017)	0.27	0.46	0.33	0.04
Know-Center (Kern et al., 2017)	0.27	0.39	0.28	
SZTE-NLP (Berend, 2017)	0.26	0.35	0.28	
NTNU (Lee et al., 2017b)	0.23	0.3	0.24	0.08
LABDA (Segura-Bedmar et al., 2017)	0.23	0.33	0.23	
LIPN (Hernandez et al., 2017)	0.21	0.38	0.21	0.05
SciX	0.2	0.42	0.21	
IHS-RD-BELARUS	0.19	0.41	0.19	
HCC-NLP	0.16	0.24	0.16	
NITK_IT_PG	0.14	0.3	0.15	
Surukam	0.1	0.24	0.1	0.13
GMBUAP (Flores et al., 2017)	0.04	0.08	0.04	
upper bound	0.84	0.85	0.85	0.77
random	0.00	0.03	0.01	0.00

Table 3: F1 scores of teams participating in Scenario 1 and baseline models for Overall, Subtask A, Subtask B, and Subtask C. Ranking of the teams is based on overall performance measured in Micro F1.

former is surprising, as keyphrases are with an overwhelming majority noun phrases, the latter not as much, many keyphrases only appear once in the dataset (see Table 1). GMBUAP further tried using empirical rules obtained by observing the training data for Subtask A, and a Naive Bayes classifier trained on provided training data for Subtask B. Such simple methods on their own prove not to be accurate enough. Attempts of such give us additional insight about the hardness of the problem and applicability of simple methods to the task.

7.2 Evaluation Scenario 2

In this scenario teams needed to solve sub-tasks B, and C. Partial annotation was provided to the teams, that is, solution to the Subtask A. Four teams participated in this scenario with F1 cores ranging from 0.43 to 0.64. Please refer to Table 4 for complete result.

Except MayoNLP, other three teams participated only in Subtask B. Although ranking is done based on overall performance, but in this scenario

rankings are consistent in each category. BUAP with the worst F1 score for Subtask B (0.45), is still better than the best team in Scenario 1 s2_end2end for Subtask B (0.44). Partial annotation or accuracy for Subtask A proves to be critical, reinforcing again that identifying keyphrase boundaries is the most difficult part of the shared task.

Unlike the Scenario 1, in this case the top two teams used classifiers with lexical features (F1: 0.64) as well as neural networks (F1: 0.63). The first team MayoNLP used SVM with rich feature sets like n-grams, lexical features, orthographic features, whereas the second team UKP/EELECTION used used three different neural network approaches and subsequently combined them via majority voting. Both these methods perform quite similarly. However, a CRF based approach and an SVM with simpler feature sets attempted by the two teams LABDA and BUAP are found to be less effective in this scenario.

MayoNLP applied a simple rule based method for synonym-of relation extraction, and Hearst patterns for hyponym-of relation detection. The rules for synonym-of detection is based on presence of phrases such as *in terms of, equivalently,*

---

[13]After the end of the evaluation period, team UKP/EELECTION discovered those results were based on training on the development set. For training on the training set, their results are: 0.69 F1 overall and 0.72 F1 for Subtask B only

Teams	Overall	B	C
MayoNLP (Liu et al., 2017)	**0.64**	**0.67**	**0.23**
UKP/EELECTION (Eger et al., 2017)[13]	0.63	0.66	
LABDA (Segura-Bedmar et al., 2017)	0.48	0.51	
BUAP (Alemán et al., 2017)	0.43	0.45	
upper bound	0.84	0.85	0.77
random	0.15	0.23	0.01

Table 4: F1 scores of teams participating in Scenario 2 and baseline models for Overall, Subtask B, and Subtask C. Ranking of the teams is based on overall performance measured in Micro F1. Teams participating in Scenario 2 received partial annotation with respect to Subtask A.

Teams	Overall
MIT (Lee et al., 2017a)	**0.64**
s2_rel (Ammar et al., 2017)	0.54
NTNU-2 (Barik and Marsi, 2017)	0.5
LaBDA (Suárez-Paniagua et al., 2017)	0.38
TTI_COIN_rel (Tsujimura et al., 2017)[15]	0.1
upper bound	0.84
random	0.04

Table 5: F1 scores of teams participating in Scenario 3 and baseline models. Teams participating in Scenario 3 received partial annotation with respect to Subtask A, and Subtask B. Ranking of the teams is based on overall performance measured in Micro F1.

which are called etc in the text between two keyphrases. Interestingly, the RNN based approach of s2_end2end in Scenario 1 performs better than MayoNLP without using partial annotation of Subtask A.

7.3 Evaluation Scenario 3

In this scenario, teams need to solve only Subtask C. Partial annotations were provided to the teams for Subtask B and C. Five teams participated in this scenario, and F1 scores ranged from 0.1 to 0.64. Please refer to Table 5 for complete result.

Neural network (NN) based models are found to perform better than other methods in this scenario. The best method by MIT uses a convolutional NN (CNN). The other method uses two phases of NN and found to be reasonably effective (F1: 0.54).

On the other hand, application of supervised classification with five different classifiers (SVM, decision tree, random forest, multinomial naive Bayes and k-nearest neighbour) using three different feature selection techniques (chi square, decision tree, and recursive feature elimination) found close accuracy (F1: 0.5) with the top performing ones.

LaBDA also use a CNN based method. However, the rule based post-processing and argument ordering strategy applied by MIT seemed to give additional advantage as also observed by them.

However most of the teams in this scenario outperform, all teams from other scenarios (who did not have access to partial information for Subtask B, and C) in relation prediction. This also asserts the significance of accuracy on Subtask A, and B in order to perform accurately on Subtask C.

8 Conclusion

In this paper, we present the setup and discuss participating systems of SemEval 2017 Task 10 on identifying and classifying keyphrases and relations between them from scientific articles, to which 26 systems were submitted. Successful systems vary in their approaches. Most of them use RNNs, often in combination with CRFs as well as CNNs, however the system performing best for evaluation scenario 1 uses an SVM with a well-engineered lexical feature set. Identifying keyphrases is the most challenging subtask, since the dataset contains many long and infrequent keyphrases, and systems relying on remembering them do not perform well.

Acknowledgments

We would like to thank Elsevier for supporting this shared task. Special thanks go to Ronald Daniel Jr. for his feedback on the task setup and Pontus Stenetorp for his advice on brat and shared task organisation.

---

[15]After the end of the evaluation period, team TTI_COIN_rel discovered a bug in preprocessing, leading to low results. Their overall result after having corrected for that error is a Macro F1 of 0.48.

References

Yuridiana Alemán, Darnes Vilariño, and Josefa So-
modevilla. 2017. BUAP at SemEval-2017 Task 10.
In *Proceedings of SemEval*.

Waleed Ammar, Matthew Peters, Chandra Bhagavatula, and Russell Power. 2017. The AI2 system at SemEval-2017 Task 10 (ScienceIE): semi-
supervised end-to-end entity and relation extraction.
In *Proceedings of SemEval*.

Isabelle Augenstein and Anders Søgaard. 2017. Multi-
Task Learning of Keyphrase Boundary Classification. In *Proceedings of ACL*.

Isabelle Augenstein, Andreas Vlachos, and Diana
Maynard. 2015. Extracting Relations between Non-
Standard Entities using Distant Supervision and Im-
itation Learning. In *Proceedings of EMNLP*.

Biswanath Barik and Erwin Marsi. 2017. NTNU-
2@ScienceIE: Identifying Synonym and Hyponym
Relations among Keyphrases in Scientific Documents. In *Proceedings of SemEval*.

Gábor Berend. 2017. SZTE-NLP at SemEval-2017
Task 10: A High Precision Sequence Model for
Keyphrase Extraction Utilizing Sparse Coding for
Feature Generation. In *Proceedings of SemEval*.

Panot Chaimongkol, Akiko Aizawa, and Yuka Tateisi.
2014. Corpus for Coreference Resolution on Scientific Papers. In *Proceedings of LREC*.

Steffen Eger, Erik-Lân Do Dinh, Ilia Kuznetsov, Masoud Kiaeeha, and Iryna Gurevych. 2017. EELEC-
TION at SemEval-2017 Task 10: Ensemble of nEural Learners for kEyphrase ClassificaTION. In *Proceedings of SemEval*.

Gerardo Flores, Mireya Tovar, and José A. Reyes-
Ortiz. 2017. GMBUAP at SemEval-2017 Task
10: A First Approach Based Empirical Rules and
n-grams for the Extraction and Classification of
Keyphrases. In *Proceedings of SemEval*.

Sujatha Das Gollapalli and Xiaoli Li. 2015. EMNLP
versus ACL: Analyzing NLP research over time. In
Proceedings of EMNLP.

Kartik Goyal and Chris Dyer. 2016. Posterior regularization for Joint Modelling of Multiple Structured
Prediction Tasks with Soft Constraints. In *Proceedings of EMNLP*.

Yufan Guo, Roi Reichart, and Anna Korhonen. 2015.
Unsupervised Declarative Knowledge Induction for
Constraint-Based Learning of Information Structure
in Scientific Documents. *Transactions of the Association for Computational Linguistics* 3:131–143.

Sonal Gupta and Christopher Manning. 2011. Ana-
lyzing the Dynamics of Research by Extracting Key
Aspects of Scientific Papers. In *Proceedings of IJC-
NLP*.

Kazi Saidul Hasan and Vincent Ng. 2014. Automatic
Keyphrase Extraction: A Survey of the State of the
Art. In *Proceedings of ACL*.

Marti Hearst. 1991. Noun Homograph Disambiguation
Using Local Context in Large Text Corpora. *Using
Corpora* pages 185–188.

Simon David Hernandez, Davide Buscaldi, and Thierry
Charnois. 2017. LIPN at SemEval-2017 Task 10:
Selecting Candidate Phrases with Part-of-Speech
Tag Sequences from the training data. In *Proceed-
ings of SemEval*.

Dain Kaplan, Ryu Iida, and Takenobu Tokunaga. 2009.
Automatic Extraction of Citation Contexts for Research Paper Summarization: A Coreference-chain
based Approach. In *Proceedings of NLPIR4DL
workshop at ACL-IJCNLP*.

Rohit J Kate and Raymond J Mooney. 2010. Joint
Entity and Relation Extraction using Card-Pyramid
Parsing. In *Proceedings of CoNLL*.

Roman Kern, Stefan Falk, and Andi Rexha. 2017.
Know-Center at SemEval-2017 Task 10: CODE annotator. In *Proceedings of SemEval*.

Su Nam Kim, Timothy Baldwin, and Min-Yen Kan.
2010a. Evaluating n-gram based evaluation metrics
for automatic keyphrase extraction. In *Proceedings
of Coling*.

Su Nam Kim, Olena Medelyan, Min-Yen Kan, and
Timothy Baldwin. 2010b. SemEval-2010 Task 5 :
Automatic Keyphrase Extraction from Scientific Articles. In *Proceedings of the 5th International Workshop on Semantic Evaluation*. Association for Computational Linguistics, Uppsala, Sweden, pages 21–
26.

Ji Young Lee, Franck Dernoncourt, and Peter
Szolovits. 2017a. MIT at SemEval-2017 Task 10:
Relation Extraction with Convolutional Neural Net-
works. In *Proceedings of SemEval*.

Lung-Hao Lee, Kuei-Ching Lee, and Yuen-Hsien
Tseng. 2017b. The NTNU System at SemEval-2017
Task 10: Extracting Keyphrases and Relations from
Scientific Publications Using Multiple Conditional
Random Fields. In *Proceedings of SemEval*.

Sijia Liu, Shen Feichen, Vipin Chaudhary, and Hong-
fang Liu. 2017. MayoNLP at SemEval 2017
Task 10: Word Embedding Distance Pattern for
Keyphrase Classification in Scientific Publications.
In *Proceedings of SemEval*.

Erwin Marsi and Pinar Öztürk. 2015. Extraction and
generalisation of variables from scientific publications. In *Proceedings of EMNLP*.

Erwin Marsi, Utpal Kumar Sikdar, Cristina Marco,
Biswanath Barik, and Rune Sætre. 2017. NTNU-
1@ScienceIE at SemEval-2017 Task 10: Identifying
and Labelling Keyphrases with Conditional Random
Fields. In *Proceedings of SemEval*.

Tomas Mikolov, Ilya Sutskever, Kai Chen, Greg S Corrado, and Jeff Dean. 2013. Distributed Representations of Words and Phrases and their Compositionality. In *Proceedings of NIPS*.

M. Mintz, S. Bills, R. Snow, and D. Jurafsky. 2009. Distant supervision for relation extraction without labeled data. In *Proceedings of ACL-IJCNLP*.

Diarmuid Ó Séaghdha and Simone Teufel. 2014. Unsupervised learning of rhetorical structure with untopic models. In *Proceedings of Coling*.

Fuchun Peng and Andrew McCallum. 2006. Information extraction from research papers using conditional random fields. *Information Processing and Management* 42(4):963–979.

Animesh Prasad and Min-Yen Kan. 2017. WING-NUS at SemEval-2017 Task 10: Keyphrase Extraction and Classification as Joint Sequence Labeling. In *Proceedings of SemEval*.

Behrang QasemiZadeh and Anne-Kathrin Schumann. 2016. The ACL RD-TEC 2.0: A Language Resource for Evaluating Term Extraction and Entity Recognition Methods. In *Proceedings of LREC*.

Dragomir Radev and Amjad Abu-Jbara. 2012. Rediscovering ACL Discoveries Through the Lens of ACL Anthology Network Citing Sentences. In *Proceedings of the ACL-2012 Special Workshop on Rediscovering 50 Years of Discoveries*.

Isabel Segura-Bedmar, Cristóbal Colón-Ruiz, and Paloma Martínez. 2017. LABDA at SemEval-2017 Task 10: Extracting Keyphrases from Scientific Publications by combining the BANNER tool and the UMLS Semantic Network. In *Proceedings of SemEval*.

Yanchuan Sim, Bryan Routledge, and Noah A. Smith. 2015. A Utility Model of Authors in the Scientific Community. In *Proceedings of EMNLP*.

Sameer Singh, Sebastian Riedel, Brian Martin, Jiaping Zheng, and Andrew McCallum. 2013. Joint Inference of Entities, Relations, and Coreference. In *Proceedings of the 2013 Workshop on Automated Knowledge Base Construction (AKBC)*.

R. Snow, D. Jurafsky, and A.Y. Ng. 2005. Learning syntactic patterns for automatic hypernym discovery. *Advances in Neural Information Processing Systems* 17:1297–1304.

Pontus Stenetorp, Sampo Pyysalo, Goran Topić, Tomoko Ohta, Sophia Ananiadou, and Jun'ichi Tsujii. 2012. BRAT: a Web-based Tool for NLP-Assisted Text Annotation. In *Proceedings of EACL System Demonstrations*.

Lucas Sterckx, Cornelia Caragea, Thomas Demeester, and Chris Develder. 2016. Supervised Keyphrase Extraction as Positive Unlabeled Learning. In *Proceedings of EMNLP*.

Víctor Suárez-Paniagua, Isabel Segura-Bedmar, and Paloma Martínez. 2017. LaBDA Team at SemEval-2017 Task C: Relation Classification between keyphrases via Convolutional Neural Network. In *Proceedings of SemEval*.

Yuka Tateisi, Yo Shidahara, Yusuke Miyao, and Akiko Aizawa. 2014. Annotation of Computer Science Papers for Semantic Relation Extraction. In Nicoletta Calzolari, Khalid Choukri, Thierry Declerck, Hrafn Loftsson, Bente Maegaard, Joseph Mariani, Asuncin Moreno, Jan Odijk, and Stelios Piperidis, editors, *Proceedings of LREC*.

Simone Teufel. 2006. Argumentative Zoning for Improved Citation Indexing. In James G. Shanahan, Yan Qu, and Janyce Wiebe, editors, *Computing Attitude and Affect in Text*, Springer, volume 20 of *The Information Retrieval Series*, pages 159–169.

Tomoki Tsujimura, Makoto Miwa, and Yutaka Sasaki. 2017. TTI-COIN at SemEval-2017 Task 10: Investigating Embeddings for End-to-End Relation Extraction from Scientific Papers. In *Proceedings of SemEval*.

Liang Wang and Sujian Li. 2017. PKU_ICL at SemEval-2017 Task 10: Keyphrase Extraction with Model Ensemble and External Knowledge. In *Proceedings of SemEval*.

Torsten Zesch and Iryna Gurevych. 2009. Approximate Matching for Evaluating Keyphrase Extraction. In *Proceedings of RANLP*.

SemEval-2017 Task 11: End-User Development using Natural Language

Juliano Efson Sales, Siegfried Handschuh, André Freitas
Department of Computer Science and Mathematics
University of Passau, Germany
{juliano-sales, siegfried.handschuh, andre.freitas}@uni-passau.de

Abstract

This task proposes a challenge to support the interaction between users and applications, micro-services and software APIs using natural language. It aims to support the evaluation and evolution of the discussions surrounding the application natural language processing techniques within the context of end-user natural language programming, under scenarios of high lexical and semantic heterogeneity.

1 Introduction

The specific syntax of traditional programming languages and the user effort associated with finding, understanding and integrating multiple interfaces within a software development task, defines the intrinsic complexity of programming. Despite the widespread demand for automating actions within a digital environment, even the basic software development tasks require previous (usually extensive) software development expertise. Domain experts processing data, analysts automating recurrent tasks, or a businessman testing an idea on the web depend on the mediation of programmers to materialise their demands, independently of the simplicity of the task to be addressed and on the availability of existing services and libraries.

Recent advances in natural language processing bring the opportunity of improving the interaction between users and software artefacts, supporting users to program tasks using natural language-based communication. This ability to match users' actions intents and information needs to formal actions within an *application programming interface* (API), using the semantics of natural language as the mediation layer between both, can drastically impact the accessibility of software development. Despite the fact that some software development tasks with stricter requirements will always depend on the precise semantic definition of programming languages, there is a vast spectrum of applications with softer formalisation requirements. This subset of applications can be defined and built with the help of natural language descriptions.

This SemEval task aims to develop the state-of-the-art discussions and techniques concerning the semantic interpretation of natural language commands and user action intents, bridging the semantic gap between users and software artefacts. The practical relevance of the challenge lies in the fact that addressing this task supports improving the accessibility of programming (meaning a systematic specification of computational operations) to a large spectrum of users which have the demand for increasing automation within some specific tasks. Moreover, with the growing availability of software artefacts, such as APIs and services, there is a higher demand to support the discoverability of these resources, i.e. devising principled semantic interpretation approaches to semantically match interface descriptions with the intent from users.

The proposed task also intersects with demands from the field of robotics, as part of the human-robot interaction area, which depends on a systematic ability to address user commands that lie beyond navigational tasks.

From the point-of-view of computational linguistics, this challenge aims to catalyse the discussions in the following dimensions:

- Semantic parsing of natural language commands;

- Semantic representation of software interfaces;

Proceedings of the 11th International Workshop on Semantic Evaluations (SemEval-2017), pages 556–564,
Vancouver, Canada, August 3 - 4, 2017. ©2017 Association for Computational Linguistics

- Statistical and ontology-based semantic matching techniques;

- Compositional models for natural language command interpretation (NLCI);

- Machine learning models for NLCI;

- API/Service composition and associated planning techniques;

- Linguistic aspects of user action intents.

2 Commands & Programming in Natural Language

The use of natural language to instruct robots and computational systems, in general, is an active research area since the 70's and 80's (Maas and Suppes, 1985; Guida and Tasso, 1982) (and within references). Initiatives vary over a large spectrum of application domains including operating system's functions (Manaris and Dominick, 1993), web services choreography (Englmeier et al., 2006), mobile programming by voice (Amos Azaria, 2016), domain-specific natural programming languages (Pane and Myers, 2006), industrial robots (Stenmark and Nugues, 2013) and home care assistants.

The variability of domains translates into a wide number of research communities comprising different foci and being expressed by distinct terms such as *natural language interfaces*, *end-user development*, *natural programming*, *programming by example* and *trigger-action development*. Some of these terms embrace wide domains, also including non-verbal (visual) approaches.

2.1 Semantic Parsing & Matching

The interpretation of natural language commands is typically associated with the task of parsing the natural language input to an internal representation of the target system. This internal representation is usually associated with a *n*-ary predicate-argument structure which represents the interface for an action within the system. The identification of which action the command refers to and its potential parameters are at the centre of this task.

Taking as an example the natural language command:

Please convert US$ 475 to the Japanese currency and send this value to John Smith by SMS.

We can conceptualise the challenges involved in the command interpretation process in three dimensions: *command chunking*, *term type identification* and *semantic matching*. The chunking dimension comprises the identification of terms and segments in the original sentence that can potentially map to the system actions and parameters. The example command embodies two actions: *converting currency* and *sending SMS*. For the first action, the command interpreter needs to identify the currencies involved in the transaction and the financial amount (term type identification).

Other semantic interpretation processes might be involved. In the case of the second action, besides identifying *John Smith* as the message's receiver, the interpreter also needs to resolve the co-reference of *this value* to the currency conversion result and instantiate it as a parameter in the content of the message. This first level of interpretation of the command would generate an output such as:

SEQUENCY {
ACTION: [convert currency]
PARAMS: [US$ 475] - [(to) Japanese currency]

ACTION: [send sms]
PARAMS: [this value] - [(to) John Smith]
}

The *matching process* corresponds to the mapping between terms from the user vocabulary to the terms used in the internal representation of the system (the API). In the given example, the system should find an action that can convert currencies and another that can send SMS messages.

In the example, depending on the parametrisation of the command interface, the value *[US$ 475]* needs to be split into two parameters, and these parts, mapped to the internal vocabulary of the system (*US$* need to be interpreted as *USD* while *Japanese currency* needs to be translated to *JPY*. For the second action, similarly, *John Smith* will be used to retrieve a phone number from a user personal data source.

The final execution command is the result of the matching processing, as shown below:

ACTION ENDPOINT: *[action id]*
PARAMS:

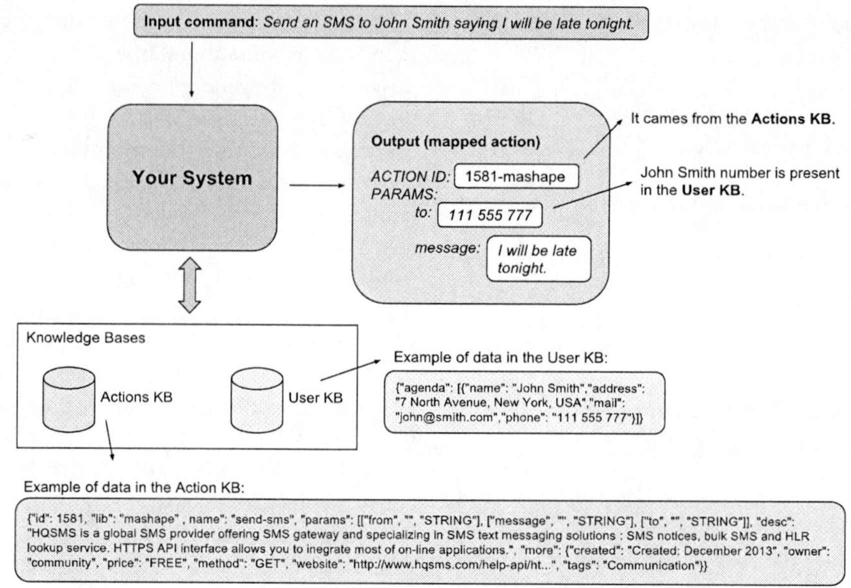

Figure 1: An overview of the task.

from: "USD"

to: "JPY"

from_amount: 475

The task can be addressed using different semantic interpretation abstractions: shallow parsing, lambda-calculus-based semantic parsing (Artzi et al., 2014), compositional-distributional models (Freitas and Curry, 2014; Freitas, 2015), information retrieval approaches (Sales et al., 2016). Additionally, pre-processing techniques such as clausal disembedding (Niklaus et al., 2016) and co-reference resolution are central components within the task.

While approaches and test collections emphasising the shallow parsing aspect of the problem are more present in the literature (Section 3), others focusing on a semantic matching process involving a broader vocabulary gap (Furnas et al., 1987) are less prevalent. Part of this can be explained by the domain-specific nature of previous works (e.g. focus on spatial commands (Dukes, 2014)).

In contrast, this task emphasises the creation of a test collection targeting an open domain scenario, with a large-scale set of target actions, assessing the ability of command interpretation approaches to address a larger vocabulary gap. This scenario aims to instantiate a real use case for end-user natural language programming, since the action knowledge base used in the test collection maps to real-world APIs and so a semantic interpreter developed over this test collection can become a concrete end-user programming environment.

3 Similar Initiatives

Most of the applications related to the parsing of natural language commands are within the context of human-robot interaction. The *Human Robot Interaction Corpus* (HuRIC) describes a list of spoken commands between humans and robots. It is composed of three datasets which were developed under the context of three different events. They are annotated using Frame Semantics together with Holistic Spatial Semantics (Bastianelli et al., 2014).

Artzi et al. (2014) and Tellex et al. (2014) give a more focused contribution in the interpretation of spatial elements. In both cases, the vocabulary variability is more constrained. Similar vocabulary variability assumptions are present in Thomason et al. (2015) and Azaria et al. (2016).

In 2014, SemEval hosted a task related to the parsing of natural language spatial commands (Dukes, 2014), also targeting a robotics scenario. More specifically, the task proposed the parsing of commands to move a robot arm that moved objects within a spatial region.

The proposed task can be contrasted with these previous initiatives in the following dimensions: (*i*) more comprehensive knowledge base of actions, (*ii*) generic (open domain) user programming scenarios and (*iii*) exploration of the interaction between actions and user personal information (Section 4).

The work that has more similarity with this test collection is the problem defined by Quirk et al. (2015) under the *ifttt.com* platform, which targets the creation of an if-then receipt from a natural language description provided by the user. The first difference between the two tasks is the fact that, while the program structure is limited to if-then recipes in Quirk et al., other more complex structures are supported in this task. Secondly, in the case of Quirk et al., the task requires only the mapping of the actions that comprise the recipe, keeping aside the instantiation of the parameter values, while our proposed task emphasises both. Finally, the presence of these two characteristics introduces the challenge of mapping co-references and metonymy within the task.

4 Task Definition

The task comprises 210 scenarios which consist of a total of 438 natural language commands. Figures 1 and 2 depicts an overview of the task. A *scenario* is a set of sentences that defines a program in natural language. The excerpt below shows an example of a scenario:

> *"When a message from Enrico Hernandez arrives, get the necklace price; Convert it from Chilean Pesos to Euro; If it costs less than 100 EUR, send to him a message asking him to buy it; If not, write saying I am not interested."*

Associated with each scenario, there is a program which is composed of actions from the Action Knowledge Base (Action KB). In addition to the actions, the program also uses `If` and `Foreach` constructors, having the same semantics commonly expressed in programming languages to define the execution flow.

Like a programming language function, an action can have input parameters and return values. Table 1 shows examples of natural language commands describing scenarios.

Natural language scenario commands
If a receive a deposit from John Sanders in my bank account, send this message to him: "Hello John, thanks for your gift, I receive your deposit of some money to me, thanks a lot, buddy."
Send an email to Mark asking him for the picture we took in Munich. When I receive the answer, get the attached image and publish it on my Flickr account with the tags #munich, #germany, #my-love
Find "Bachianas N.5 of Villa-Lobos" on Youtube. Get the link and send to my mum.
List tweets containing #ChampionsLeague.
Find a picture of Darth Vader on Flickr. Post this text to my friends on Facebook with the picture of Darth Vader: May The Force Be With Us Next Friday!!!
Search on eBay for the iPhone 7 with the maximum price of 700 Euro and send the result list by e-mail to my wife.
Message Dr Brown by email, asking a suitable day for a meeting; When I receive the information, sent to my wife by email;
Search for a picture of Yoda. Attach that image in a Facebook post and write this: Friends, let's go to the cinema to the see Star Wars on Friday.
When I receive an email from Helena, get the attachment. Print it and write to Mr Sanders by Skype: Hi Mr Sanders, the document is in the printer.
If someone reports a problem in GitHub, send the problem title by Skype to John, if the project name is FinanceSystem. For all other systems, send a message to the Tech Manager.
If Manchester United wins, put Thriller of Michael Jackson in Spotify "celebrations" playlist and call me to say "we are the champions, my friends".
Open the door always when reached Central Park.
Get a quote about science. Get a photo of Paris. Attach the photo in an email, write the quote and send to maria@hotmail.com.
Get the translation of the hashtag #sqn. Convert it to a QR code and send to my Skype account.

Table 1: Examples of natural language commands describing scenarios.

The values of the parameters map to constants (e.g. integer numbers, string values) or to *tags*, which represent returning data from previously executed actions. There are two types of tags.

- <**returnX**> The return tag represents the content returned by the action X, where X is a sequential identifier.

- <**item**> The item tag is used only in the context of Foreach constructors. It represents an iterated item.

Both types of tags have some additional naming assumptions in order to simplify the syntax of the generated program. Examples of valid tags are:

- <**return1**> - meaning the data returned by the first action in the scenario.

- **<item>.url** - represent the attribute *url* of the item.

In addition to the scenarios, the test collection consists of:

- **Action KB**: The set of available API functions along with their respective documentation. The information describing the API functions does not follow a strict pattern. While some documentation has rich natural language descriptions or show usage examples, others are succinct and just contain the frame and parameter names. The same occurs concerning data format, data type and returning data. This test collection reflects the variability and heterogeneity that we find in real-world APIs.

- **User KB**: A personal user information dataset, which is necessary to make commands more natural by supporting co-reference resolution. It allows commands like "Call John", once the system can identify the proper phone number from the User KB.

An example excerpt of the User KB is described below:

```
[
  {
    "name": "Maria Alice",
    "address": "Rua Central, 35,
                Rio de Janeiro,
                Brasil",
    "facebook": "malice",
    "group": "classmates",
    "mail": "maria@alice.com.br",
    "phone": "555 111 222",
    "skype": "maria.alice",
    "tags": "my wife",
    "twitter": "malice"
  },
  {
    "name": "John Sanders",
    "address": "7 North Avenue,
                New York, USA",
    "facebook": "jsanders",
    "group": null,
    "mail": "john@fam.com",
    "phone": "111 555 777",
    "skype": "johnjohn",
    "tags": null,
```

id	action_name(params*)
700000	make_a_payment(invoice)
600603	send_an_email(attachment_url)
700002	read_file_content(file)
700003	extract_content(info)
503679	convert(to)
700005	get_contacts(group)
600490	upload_public_photo_from_url(tags)
700006	search_image_on_Flickr(query)
700007	search_video_on_YouTube(query)
600431	create_a_link_post(link_url)
601733	post_a_tweet_with_image(image_url)
700008	tweets_from_search(search_for)
502328	directions(starting)
600352	new_item_from_search(search_terms)
600979	share_a_link(image_url)
700009	create_calendar_item(which_day?)
600761	print_document(document_url)
601535	post_message(user_name)
500797	convert-file(file)
700011	any_new_post_by_someone(user)
600591	any_new_issue(user)
601206	new_article_in_section(section)
600187	add_a_bitlink(url)
601732	post_a_tweet(tweet_text)
601888	picture_of_the_day(section)
600840	add_photo_to_album(album_name)
600408	new_final_score(team)
601684	new_story_from_section(which_section?)
600596	create_an_issue(body)
601791	air_quality_changed(device)
503062	search(depart-date)
502335	check(text)
600326	take_snapshots(which_camera?)
503155	get-top-definition(hashtag)

Table 2: Examples of action frames used in the scenarios.

```
    "twitter": "jsanders"
  },
  ...
]
```

The natural language scenarios, Action KB and User KB are all described using JSON as a serialisation format. The Action KB is composed of about 3800 micro-services from Mashape (mashape.com) and 1900 actions and triggers from the ifttt.com platform. APIs from Mashape and ifttt.com are public, and their instantiation for the challenge was approved by the platform owners.

Table 2 shows examples of action frames used in the dataset and Table 3 shows metrics about the scenarios, actions and the associated natural language commands, showing the natural language signature of the test collection.

metric	training	test	total
# of scenarios	179	31	210
avg # of sentences per scenario	2.72	2.35	2.66
# of actions	374	64	438
avg # of actions per scenario	2.08	2.06	2.08
avg # of params per action	1.59	1.22	1.52
# of conditionals in actions	53	14	67
# of co-references in actions	124	17	141
# of metonymy in actions	94	11	105

Table 3: Metrics about the scenarios, actions and the associated natural language command.

4.1 Annotation

The scenarios containing the natural language commands were created using high-level task descriptions. These high-level task descriptions were sent to a crowdsourcing platform (CrowdFlower), in which workers were requested to express in natural language the commands which entail the scenario descriptions. Motivated by those scenario descriptions, the users proposed a set of commands which addresses the specification.

The excerpt below shows an example of a scenario description:

> *You are arranging a meeting with some people in Andre's office. Adamantios is coming for that meeting, but he does not know how to drive in Passau. Additionally, you do not know where the office is.*

One possible output for that description is:

- Ask Andre for the address of his office;

- Make a map from the university to it;

- Send the map to Adamantios including driving directions.

For each scenario description, in average ten workers were invited to suggest the natural language commands. The crowdsourcing process was followed by a data curation process which discarded 70% of the commands due to low quality issues. The other part of the sample was reviewed to correct misspelling and adjusted to comply with the task requirements while preserving the original syntactic structure and vocabulary.

5 Analysis of The Task Complexity

The task aims to explore vocabulary and syntactic structure variation within the natural language commands. It also targets the orchestration of different natural language processing techniques, including syntactic parsing, semantic role labelling, fine-grained semantic approximation and co-reference resolution.

5.1 Semantic approximation

Different actions and parameters can be expressed using distinct lexicalizations (synonymy) and abstraction levels. For example:

> *"If someone reports a problem in GitHub, send the problem's headline by Skype to John."*

In the examples, the action in the knowledge base is expressed as *"any new issue"*, while intended *"headline"* in the returned value is expressed as *"Issue Title"*. Given the context, it is expected the system to be able to identify the equivalence between the pairs of terms (*problem, issue*) and (*title, headline*).

5.2 Syntactic variation

Additionally, interpreters are expected to cope with syntactic variation.

> *"If Manchester United wins, call me."*

> *"Get ready to call me in the case of victory of Manchester United."*

5.3 Co-reference and metonymy resolution

The first type of resolution needed is the pronominal co-reference, where a pronoun refers to a constant which was previously mentioned within the context of the same scenario. The metonymy resolution consists of using the reference to an attribute or type to refer to a constant or to a different attribute of a constant. For example:

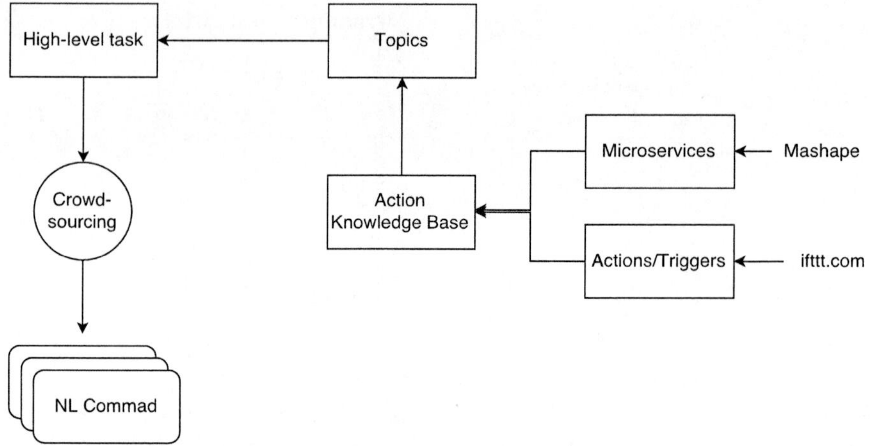

Figure 2: The scenario creation workflow.

*"If an issue is created, send **its** content to the **Tech Manager**."*

This excerpt shows both cases. The bold **its** makes reference to **an issue**, while **Tech Manager** is a metonymy for the Tech Manager's email (sandra@andrade.com.br according to the user KB).

6 Evaluation

The final dataset contains commands and their associated mappings to the Action KB. Given a command in natural language, it is expected that the participating systems provide:

- The correct action;

- The correct mapping of text chunks in the natural commands to parameters;

The participating systems were evaluated considering four criteria:

1. Resolved individual actions ignoring parameter values;

2. Resolved individual actions considering parameter values;

3. Resolved scenarios ignoring parameter values;

4. Resolved scenarios considering parameter values.

Criteria 1 and 2 are quantified by using precision and recall, while 3 and 4 are quantified by the percentage of the total number of scenarios which were addressed.

Participating teams were allowed to use external linguistic resources and external tools such as taggers and parsers.

7 Participants and Results

Initially, nine teams demonstrated interest in the tasks, but only one participated in the challenge.

Kubis et al. (2017) proposed the EUDAMU system, which implements an action ranking model based on TF/IDF and a type matching system.

The EUDAMU system is composed of a pipeline divided into six steps. It starts by preprocessing the dataset using three tools (NLTK, Core-NLP and SyntaxNet). In the pre-processing step, natural language commands are tokenized and each token is enriched with its lemma, part-of-speech and named entity labels. Additionally, it also adds the constituent and dependency structures associated with the commands. The final pre-processing step annotates the commands with types which supports the system to resolve co-references between the actions and references from the User KB. The same procedure (with the exception of the last step) is applied for the Action KB.

The preprocessing phase is followed by the *Discourse Tagger*, which is responsible for individualising the command from the paragraph description of the scenario. The team implemented this component using a rule-based approach. The next step is *Action Ranker*, which applies a TF-IDF

Criterion	Metric	Value
Individual actions solved ignoring parameter values	precision	0.5490
	recall	0.7066
Individual actions solved considering parameter values	precision	0.0533
	recall	0.0533
Scenarios solved ignoring parameter values	accuracy	41.93%
Scenarios solved considering parameter values	accuracy	0%

Table 4: Results from Kubis et al.

model to rank the actions. The model was indexed using all textual content present in the Action KB, plus the actions which were mapped with in the training mappings file. The next step is the *Reference Matcher* that is designed to identify which output of a given action act as the parameters of a subsequent action. The next step is the *Parameter Matcher*. It infers parameter and value types which can serve as a support to the action matching process. Finally, based on the knowledge generated and stored in the previous steps, the rule-based *Statement Mapper* provides a list of up to 10 elements of possible matching action instances. Additional details of the proposed method can be found in the original paper (Kubis et al., 2017). Table 4 shows its results.

While the proposed solution has a high recall for the number of resolved actions, it fails mainly in providing the correct value for all the required parameters. Two types of linguistic settings showed to be more challenging:

- Description of commands split into two sentences. For example:

  "Get the price of the book The Intelligent Investor. If it costs less than 25 Euros, buy it."

  where "*25 Euros*" is the parameter value of the action defined in the first sentence.

- Capturing actions with more specific/fine-grained semantics. For example:

  "Once I have bet my running distance target of the week, set my current weight as 100 Kg in Fitbit."

  where the system ignored the temporal expression "*of the week*" and suggested the "*Daily step goal achieved*" instead of "*Weekly distance goal reached*" action. A second example of the same case is expressed in the command:

  "Suspend the execution of my Samsung washer."

where the term "*Samsung*" was ignored when selecting actions.

8 Summary

In the Semeval 2017 Task 11 we developed a test collection to support the creation of semantic interpretation methods for end-user programming environments. The test collection focuses on the following features in comparison with existing approaches: (*i*) open domain, (*ii*) large syntactic and vocabulary variability, (*iii*) dependent of co-reference and metonymy resolution. Moreover, as the test collection uses APIs available on the open web, it can be used to build real end-user programming environments. While there is space for the improvement of the precision and recall on the identification of the command actions, the main challenge remains in the matching of the parameters between natural language commands and the API.

References

Jayant Krishnamurthy Tom M. Mitchel Amos Azaria. 2016. Instructable intelligent personal. In *Proceedings of the Thirtieth AAAI Conference on Artificial Intelligence*. AAAI'16.

Yoav Artzi, Dipanjan Das, and Slav Petrov. 2014. Learning compact lexicons for ccg semantic parsing. In *Proceedings of the 2014 Conference on Empirical Methods in Natural Language Processing (EMNLP)*. Association for Computational Linguistics, Doha, Qatar, pages 1273–1283. http://www.aclweb.org/anthology/D14-1134.

Emanuele Bastianelli, Giuseppe Castellucci, Danilo Croce, Luca Iocchi, Roberto Basili, and Daniele Nardi. 2014. Huric: a human robot interaction corpus. In Nicoletta Calzolari (Conference Chair), Khalid Choukri, Thierry Declerck, Hrafn

Loftsson, Bente Maegaard, Joseph Mariani, Asuncion Moreno, Jan Odijk, and Stelios Piperidis, editors, *Proceedings of the Ninth International Conference on Language Resources and Evaluation (LREC'14)*. European Language Resources Association (ELRA), Reykjavik, Iceland.

Kais Dukes. 2014. Semeval-2014 task 6: Supervised semantic parsing of robotic spatial commands. In *Proceedings of the 8th International Workshop on Semantic Evaluation (SemEval 2014)*. Association for Computational Linguistics and Dublin City University, Dublin, Ireland, pages 45–53. http://www.aclweb.org/anthology/S14-2006.

Kurt Englmeier, Javier Pereira, and Josiane Mothe. 2006. Choreography of web services based on natural language storybooks. In *Proceedings of the 8th International Conference on Electronic Commerce: The New e-Commerce: Innovations for Conquering Current Barriers, Obstacles and Limitations to Conducting Successful Business on the Internet*. ACM, New York, NY, USA, ICEC '06, pages 132–138. https://doi.org/10.1145/1151454.1151485.

André Freitas. 2015. Schema-agnostic queries over large-schema databases: a distributional semantics approach. PhD Thesis.

Andre Freitas and Edward Curry. 2014. Natural language queries over heterogeneous linked data graphs: A distributional-compositional semantics approach. In *Proceedings of the 19th International Conference on Intelligent User Interfaces*. ACM, New York, NY, USA, IUI '14, pages 279–288. https://doi.org/10.1145/2557500.2557534.

George W. Furnas, Thomas K. Landauer, Louis M. Gomez, and Susan T. Dumais. 1987. The vocabulary problem in human-system communication. *Commun. ACM* 30(11):964–971. https://doi.org/10.1145/32206.32212.

Giovanni Guida and Carlo Tasso. 1982. Nli: a robust interface for natural language person-machine communication. *International Journal of Man-Machine Studies* 17(4):417 – 433. https://doi.org/http://dx.doi.org/10.1016/S0020-7373(82)80042-4.

Marek Kubis, Pawel Skorzewski, and Tomasz Zietkiewicz. 2017. EUDAMU at SemEval-2017 Task 11: Action ranking and type matching for end-user development. In *"Proceedings of the 11th International Workshop on Semantic Evaluation (SemEval-2017)"*. Association for Computational Linguistics.

Robert Elton Maas and Patrick Suppes. 1985. Natural-language interface for an instructable robot. *International Journal of Man-Machine Studies* 22(2):215 – 240. https://doi.org/http://dx.doi.org/10.1016/S0020-7373(85)80071-7.

Bill Z. Manaris and Wayne D. Dominick. 1993. Nalige: a user interface management system for the development of natural language interfaces. *International Journal of Man-Machine Studies* 38(6):891 – 921. https://doi.org/http://dx.doi.org/10.1006/imms.1993.1042.

Christina Niklaus, Bernhard Bermeitinger, Siegfried Handschuh, and André Freitas. 2016. A sentence simplification system for improving relation extraction. In *Proceedings of COLING 2016, the 26th International Conference on Computational Linguistics: System Demonstrations*. The COLING 2016 Organizing Committee, Osaka, Japan, pages 170–174. http://aclweb.org/anthology/C16-2036.

John F. Pane and Brad A. Myers. 2006. *"End User Development"*, "Springer Netherlands", "Dordrecht", chapter "More Natural Programming Languages and Environments", pages "31–50". https://doi.org/"10.1007/1-4020-5386-X_3".

Chris Quirk, Raymond Mooney, and Michel Galley. 2015. Language to code: Learning semantic parsers for if-this-then-that recipes. In *Proceedings of the 53rd Annual Meeting of the Association for Computational Linguistics (ACL-15)*. Beijing, China, pages 878–888. http://www.cs.utexas.edu/users/ai-lab/pub-view.php?PubID=127514.

Juliano Efson Sales, Andre Freitas, Brian Davis, and Siegfried Handschuh. 2016. A compositional-distributional semantic model for searching complex entity categories. In *Proceedings of the Fifth Joint Conference on Lexical and Computational Semantics*. Association for Computational Linguistics, Berlin, Germany, pages 199–208. http://anthology.aclweb.org/S16-2025.

M. Stenmark and P. Nugues. 2013. Natural language programming of industrial robots. In *Robotics (ISR), 2013 44th International Symposium on.* pages 1–5. https://doi.org/10.1109/ISR.2013.6695630.

Jesse Thomason, Shiqi Zhang, Raymond Mooney, and Peter Stone. 2015. Learning to interpret natural language commands through human-robot dialog. In *Proceedings of the 24th International Conference on Artificial Intelligence*. AAAI Press, IJCAI'15, pages 1923–1929. http://dl.acm.org/citation.cfm?id=2832415.2832516.

Matthew R. Walter, Sachithra Hemachandra, Bianca Homberg, Stefanie Tellex, and Seth Teller. 2014. A framework for learning semantic maps from grounded natural language descriptions. *International Journal of Robotics Research* 31(9):1167–1190.

SemEval-2017 Task 12: Clinical TempEval

Steven Bethard
University of Arizona
Tucson, AZ 85721, USA
bethard@email.arizona.edu

Guergana Savova
Harvard Medical School
Boston, MA 02115, USA
Guergana.Savova@childrens.harvard.edu

Martha Palmer
University of Colorado Boulder
Boulder, CO 80309
martha.palmer@colorado.edu

James Pustejovsky
Brandeis University
Waltham, MA 02453, USA
jamesp@cs.brandeis.edu

Abstract

Clinical TempEval 2017 aimed to answer the question: how well do systems trained on annotated timelines for one medical condition (colon cancer) perform in predicting timelines on another medical condition (brain cancer)? Nine sub-tasks were included, covering problems in time expression identification, event expression identification and temporal relation identification. Participant systems were evaluated on clinical and pathology notes from Mayo Clinic cancer patients, annotated with an extension of TimeML for the clinical domain. 11 teams participated in the tasks, with the best systems achieving F1 scores above 0.55 for time expressions, above 0.70 for event expressions, and above 0.30 for temporal relations. Most tasks observed about a 20 point drop over Clinical TempEval 2016, where systems were trained and evaluated on the same domain (colon cancer).

1 Introduction

The TempEval shared tasks have, since 2007, provided a focus for research on temporal information extraction (Verhagen et al., 2007, 2010; UzZaman et al., 2013). In recent years the community has moved toward testing such information extraction systems on clinical data, to address a common need of doctors and clinical researchers to search over timelines of clinical events like symptoms, diseases, and procedures. In the Clinical TempEval shared tasks (Bethard et al., 2015, 2016), participant systems have competed to identify critical components of the timeline of a clinical text: time expressions, event expressions, and temporal relations. For example, Figure 1 shows the annotations that a system is expected to produce when given the text:

> April 23, 2014: The patient did not have any postoperative bleeding so we'll resume chemotherapy with a larger bolus on Friday even if there is slight nausea.

Clinical TempEval 2017 introduced a new aspect to this problem: domain adaptation. Whereas in Clinical TempEval 2015 and 2016, systems were both trained and tested on notes from colon cancer patients, in 2017, systems were trained on colon cancer patients, but tested on brain cancer patients. The diseases, symptoms, procedures, etc. vary widely across these two patient populations, and the doctors treating these different kinds of cancer make a variety of different linguistic choices when discussing such patients. As a result, systems that participated in Clinical TempEval 2017 were faced with a much more challenging task than systems from 2015 or 2016.

2 Data

The Clinical TempEval corpus was based on a set of clinical notes and pathology reports from 200 colon cancer patients and 200 brain cancer patients at the Mayo Clinic. These notes were manually de-identified by the Mayo Clinic to replace names, locations, etc. with generic placeholders, but time expressions were not altered. The notes were then manually annotated by the THYME project (thyme.healthnlp.org) using an extension of ISO-TimeML for the annotation of times, events and temporal relations in clinical notes (Styler, IV et al., 2014b). This extension includes additions such as new time expression types (e.g., PRE-POSTEXP for expressions like *postoperative*), new EVENT attributes (e.g., DEGREE=LITTLE for expressions like *slight nausea*), and an increased focus on temporal relations of type CONTAINS (a.k.a. INCLUDES).

The annotation procedure was as follows:

Proceedings of the 11th International Workshop on Semantic Evaluations (SemEval-2017), pages 565–572,
Vancouver, Canada, August 3 - 4, 2017. ©2017 Association for Computational Linguistics

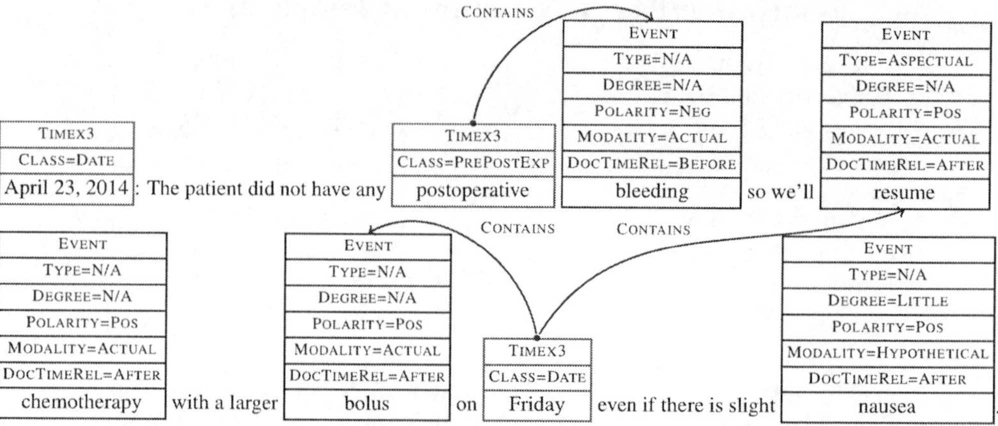

Figure 1: Example Clinical TempEval annotations

1. Annotators identified time and event expressions, along with their attributes

2. Adjudicators revised and finalized the time and event expressions and their attributes

3. Annotators identified temporal relations between pairs of events and events and times

4. Adjudicators revised and finalized the temporal relations

More details on the corpus annotation process are documented in Styler, IV et al. (2014a).

Because the data contained incompletely de-identified clinical data (the time expressions were retained), participants were required to sign a data use agreement with the Mayo Clinic to obtain the raw text of the clinical notes and pathology reports.[1] The event, time and temporal relation annotations were distributed separately from the text, in an open source repository[2] using the Anafora standoff format (Chen and Styler, 2013).

Each corpus (colon cancer and brain cancer) was split into three portions: Train (50%), Dev (25%) and Test (25%). Patients were sorted by patient number (an integer arbitrarily assigned by the de-identification process) and stratified across these splits. Table 1 shows the number of documents, event expressions (EVENT annotations), time expressions (TIMEX3 annotations) and narrative container relations (TLINK annotations with TYPE=CONTAINS attributes) in the Train, Dev, and Test portions of each corpus.

The raw text of both the colon cancer and brain cancer corpora were already released as part of Clinical TempEval 2015 and 2016, as were the time, event, and temporal relation annotations for the colon cancer corpus. However, none of the annotations for the brain cancer corpus were previously released.

Clinical TempEval 2017 ran several phases of evaluation, where different data were released for training and testing sets[3].

Trial This phase replicated the Clinical TempEval 2016 setup: systems were expected to train on the colon cancer Train and Dev sets, and were tested on the colon cancer Test set. This phase was organized primarily to allow participants to validate the format of their system output.

Unsupervised Domain Adaptation In this phase, systems were expected to train on all the colon cancer annotations (released in previous Clinical TempEvals) and were tested on the annotations of the brain cancer Test set. No brain cancer annotations were provided for training, though systems were free to use the raw brain cancer text if they had a way to do so.

Supervised Domain Adaptation This phase released annotations for the first 10 patients in the brain cancer Train data (Train-10 in Table 1). Systems were expected to train on these brain cancer annotations, in addition to the colon cancer annotations provided previously, and were

---

[1]Details on the data use agreement process can be found at: http://thyme.healthnlp.org/

[2]https://github.com/stylerw/thymedata

[3]All releases were made at the CodaLab site: https://competitions.codalab.org/competitions/15621

	Colon Cancer			Brain Cancer			
	Train	Dev	Test	Train-10	Train	Dev	Test
Documents	293	147	151	30	298	149	148
Timex3s	3833	2078	1952	350	3527	1498	1552
Events	38890	20974	18990	2557	26210	11162	11510
TLinks with Type=Contains	11150	6163	5894	624	3938	1641	1759

Table 1: Number of documents, event expressions, time expressions and narrative container relations in Train, Dev, and Test portions of the THYME data. All colon cancer data was released as part of Clinical TempEval 2015 and 2016. The Train-10 column is the data from the first 10 patients of the brain cancer Train data, which was the only additional training data released in Clinical TempEval 2017.

tested on the annotations of the brain cancer Test set. Systems were again free to use all the raw brain cancer text if they had a way to do so.

Note that across all phases, the only brain cancer data released was the Train-10 set. The remainder of the brain cancer data was reserved for future evaluations.

3   Tasks

Nine tasks were included (the same as those of Clinical TempEval 2015 and 2016), grouped into three categories:

- Identifying time expressions (TIMEX3 annotations in the THYME corpus) consisting of the following components:

    - The span (character offsets) of the expression in the text
    - Class: Date, Time, Duration, Quantifier, PrePostExp, or Set

- Identifying event expressions (EVENT annotations in the THYME corpus) consisting of the following components:

    - The span (character offsets) of the expression in the text
    - Contextual Modality: Actual, Hypothetical, Hedged, or Generic
    - Degree: Most, Little, or N/A
    - Polarity: Pos or Neg
    - Type: Aspectual, Evidential, or N/A

- Identifying temporal relations between events and times, focusing on the following types:

    - Relations between events and the document creation time (Before, Overlap, Before-Overlap, or After), represented by Doc-TimeRel annotations.

- Narrative container relations (Pustejovsky and Stubbs, 2011), which indicate that an event or time is temporally contained in (i.e., occurred during) another event or time, represented by TLink annotations with Type=Contains.

4   Evaluation Metrics

All of the tasks were evaluated using the standard metrics of precision (P), recall (R) and F_1:

$$P = \frac{|S \cap H|}{|S|} \quad R = \frac{|S \cap H|}{|H|} \quad F_1 = \frac{2 \cdot P \cdot R}{P + R}$$

where S is the set of items predicted by the system and H is the set of items annotated by the humans. Applying these metrics only requires a definition of what is considered an "item" for each task.

- For evaluating the spans of event expressions or time expressions, items were tuples of (begin, end) character offsets. Thus, systems only received credit for identifying events and times with exactly the same character offsets as the manually annotated ones.

- For evaluating the attributes of event expressions or time expressions – Class, Contextual Modality, Degree, Polarity and Type – items were tuples of (begin, end, value) where begin and end are character offsets and value is the value that was given to the relevant attribute. Thus, systems only received credit for an event (or time) attribute if they both found an event (or time) with the correct character offsets and then assigned the correct value for that attribute.

- For relations between events and the document creation time, items were tuples of (begin, end, value), just as if it were an event attribute. Thus, systems only received credit if they found a correct event and assigned the correct relation

(BEFORE, OVERLAP, BEFORE-OVERLAP, or AFTER) between that event and the document creation time.

- For narrative container relations, items were tuples of ((begin$_1$, end$_1$), (begin$_2$, end$_2$)), where the begins and ends corresponded to the character offsets of the events or times participating in the relation. Thus, systems only received credit for a narrative container relation if they found both events/times and correctly assigned a CONTAINS relation between them.

For narrative container relations, the P and R definitions were modified to take into account *temporal closure*, where additional relations are deterministically inferred from other relations (e.g., A CONTAINS B and B CONTAINS C, so A CONTAINS C):

$$P = \frac{|S \cap \text{closure}(H)|}{|S|} \qquad R = \frac{|\text{closure}(S) \cap H|}{|H|}$$

Similar measures were used in prior work (UzZaman and Allen, 2011) and TempEval 2013 (UzZaman et al., 2013), following the intuition that precision should measure the fraction of system-predicted relations that can be verified from the human annotations (either the original human annotations or annotations inferred from those through closure), and that recall should measure the fraction of human-annotated relations that can be verified from the system output (either the original system predictions or predictions inferred from those through closure).

5 Human Agreement

We also provide two types of human agreement on the tasks, measured with the same evaluation metrics as the systems:

ann-ann Inter-annotator agreement between the two independent human annotators who annotated each document. This is the most commonly reported type of agreement, and often considered to be an upper bound on system performance.

adj-ann Inter-annotator agreement between the adjudicator and the two independent annotators. This is usually a better bound on system performance in adjudicated corpora, since the models are trained on the adjudicated data, not on the individual annotator data.

Only F_1 is reported in these scenarios since precision and recall depend on the arbitrary choice of one annotator as human (H) and the other as system (S).

6 Baseline Systems

Two rule-based systems were used as baselines to compare the participating systems against.

memorize For all tasks but the narrative container task, a memorization baseline was used.

To train the model, all phrases annotated as either events or times in the training data were collected. All exact character matches for these phrases in the training data were then examined, and only phrases that were annotated as events or times greater than 50% of the time were retained. For each phrase, the most frequently annotated type (event or time) and attribute values for instances of that phrase were determined.

To predict with the model, the raw text of the test data was searched for all exact character matches of any of the memorized phrases, preferring longer phrases when multiple matches overlapped. Wherever a phrase match was found, an event or time with the memorized (most frequent) attribute values was predicted.

closest For the narrative container task, a proximity baseline was used. Each time expression was predicted to be a narrative container, containing only the closest event expression to it in the text.

7 Participating Systems

11 teams submitted a total of 28 runs, 10 for the unsupervised domain adaptation phase, and 18 for the supervised domain adaptation phase. All participating systems trained some form of supervised classifiers, with common features including character n-grams, words, part-of-speech tags, and Unified Medical Language System (UMLS) concept types. Below is a brief description of each participating team, and a note if they performed any more elaborate domain adaptation than simply adding the extra 30 brain cancer notes to their training data.

GUIR (MacAvaney et al., 2017) combined conditional random fields, rules, and decision tree ensembles, with features including character n-grams, words, word shapes, word clusters, word embeddings, part-of-speech tags, syntactic and dependency tree paths, semantic roles, and UMLS concept types.

Hitachi (P R et al., 2017) combined conditional random fields, rules, neural networks, and decision tree ensembles, with features including character n-grams, word n-grams, word shapes, word embeddings, verb tense, section headers, and sentence embeddings.

KULeuven-LIIR (Leeuwenberg and Moens, 2017) combined support vector machines and structured perceptrons with features including words and part-of-speech tags. For domain adaptation, KULeuven-LIIR tried assigning higher weight to the brain cancer training data, and representing unknown words in the input vocabulary.

LIMSI-COT (Tourille et al., 2017) combined recurrent neural networks with character and word embeddings, and support vector machines with features including words and part-of-speech tags. For domain adaptation, LIMSI-COT tried disallowing modification of pre-trained word embeddings, and representing unknown words in the input vocabulary.

NTU-1 (Huang et al., 2017) combined support vector machines and conditional random fields with features including word n-grams, part-of-speech tags, word shapes, named entities, dependency trees, and UMLS concept types.

ULISBOA (Lamurias et al., 2017) combined conditional random fields and rules with features including character n-grams, words, part-of-speech tags, and UMLS concept types.

XJNLP (Long et al., 2017) combined rules, support vector machines, and recurrent and convolutional neural networks, with features including words, word embeddings, and verb tense.

Several other teams (WuHanNLP, UNICA, UTD, and IIIT) also competed, but did not submit a system description.

8   Evaluation Results

Tables 2 to 4 show the results of the evaluation. In all tables, the best system score from each column is in bold. Systems marked with † were submitted after the competition deadline, and are thus not considered part of the official evaluation.

Team	time span			time span + class		
	F1	P	R	F1	P	R
Unsupervised domain adaptation						
GUIR	**0.57**	0.61	0.53	0.51	0.55	0.47
KULeuven-LIIR	0.56	**0.72**	0.46	**0.53**	**0.68**	0.43
LIMSI-COT	0.51	0.42	**0.66**	0.49	0.40	**0.63**
ULISBOA	0.48	0.44	0.54	0.43	0.39	0.48
Hitachi	0.43	0.63	0.33	-	-	-
baseline	0.36	**0.72**	0.24	0.32	0.63	0.21
WuHanNLP	0.31	0.65	0.20	0.27	0.57	0.18
Supervised domain adaptation						
GUIR	**0.59**	0.57	0.62	**0.56**	0.54	0.59
LIMSI-COT	0.58	0.51	**0.67**	0.55	0.49	**0.64**
NTU-1	0.58	**0.58**	0.58	0.54	0.54	0.54
KULeuven-LIIR	0.56	0.57	0.55	0.54	**0.55**	0.53
ULISBOA	0.55	0.52	0.60	0.52	0.48	0.56
UTD	0.54	0.56	0.52	0.44	0.46	0.43
Hitachi	0.51	0.53	0.48	-	-	-
WuHanNLP	0.43	0.45	0.41	0.40	0.42	0.38
XJNLP†	0.41	0.33	0.52	0.35	0.29	0.45
UNICA	0.37	0.31	0.45	0.31	0.26	0.38
baseline	0.35	0.53	0.26	0.32	0.49	0.24
IIIT	0.31	0.39	0.25	0.19	0.24	0.16
Annotator agreement						
ann-ann	0.81	-	-	0.79	-	-
adj-ann	0.86	-	-	0.85	-	-

Table 2: System performance and annotator agreement on TIMEX3 tasks: identifying the time expression's span (character offsets) and class (DATE, TIME, DURATION, QUANTIFIER, PREPOSTEXP or SET).

8.1   Time Expressions

Table 2 shows results on the time expression tasks. The GUIR system had the top F1 in almost all time expression tasks across both unsupervised and supervised domain adaptation phases, achieving F1s between 0.51 and 0.59. Compared to human agreement, the best systems were more than 0.20 lower than the inter-annotator agreement (and further, of course, from the annotator-adjudicator agreement).

In Clinical TempEval 2016, for comparison, when models were both trained and tested on colon cancer notes, the top system achieved 0.80 F1 for time spans, and 0.77 F1 for time types. This suggests that a time expression system trained on one clinical condition (e.g., colon cancer) can expect a 20+ point drop when tested on another clinical condition (e.g., brain cancer). Providing 30 annotated notes in the target domain narrowed that gap by only a few points.

The drop in performance can probably be partly attributed to differences in time expressions across the two corpora. For example, *post-op* is 26.5 times more common in brain cancer (212 occurrences in brain cancer data vs. 27 occurrences in colon cancer data), *overnight* is 13 times more common (148

Team	event span			event span + modality			event span + degree			event span + polarity			event span + type		
	F1	P	R	F1	P	R	F1	P	R	F1	P	R	F1	P	R
Unsupervised domain adaptation															
LIMSI-COT	**0.72**	0.62	**0.84**	**0.64**	0.55	**0.75**	**0.71**	0.62	**0.83**	**0.69**	0.60	**0.82**	**0.70**	0.61	**0.82**
GUIR	0.71	0.64	0.80	0.56	0.50	0.64	0.68	0.61	0.77	0.65	0.59	0.74	0.68	0.61	0.76
KULeuven-LIIR	0.68	**0.70**	0.67	0.62	**0.63**	0.61	0.67	**0.69**	0.66	0.67	**0.68**	0.65	0.66	**0.67**	0.65
ULISBOA	0.68	0.62	0.77	0.61	0.55	0.68	0.68	0.61	0.76	0.66	0.60	0.74	0.66	0.60	0.74
Hitachi	0.68	0.67	0.69	-	-	-	-	-	-	-	-	-	-	-	-
baseline	0.63	0.65	0.61	0.55	0.57	0.54	0.62	0.64	0.60	0.58	0.60	0.56	0.60	0.62	0.59
WuHanNLP	0.62	0.59	0.66	0.55	0.52	0.58	0.61	0.58	0.65	0.6	0.57	0.63	0.60	0.57	0.63
Supervised domain adaptation															
LIMSI-COT	**0.76**	**0.69**	0.85	**0.69**	**0.63**	**0.78**	**0.75**	**0.68**	0.84	**0.75**	**0.68**	0.83	**0.75**	**0.68**	0.83
GUIR	0.74	0.68	0.82	0.66	0.60	0.72	0.73	0.67	0.80	0.58	0.54	0.64	0.72	0.66	0.79
NTU-1	0.73	0.62	**0.87**	0.63	0.54	0.75	0.72	0.62	**0.86**	0.70	0.60	**0.84**	0.70	0.60	**0.85**
ULISBOA	0.73	0.65	0.83	0.64	0.57	0.73	0.72	0.64	0.82	0.71	0.63	0.81	0.71	0.63	0.80
KULeuven-LIIR	0.72	0.67	0.78	0.66	0.61	0.71	0.71	0.66	0.77	0.71	0.66	0.76	0.70	0.65	0.76
Hitachi	0.71	0.67	0.76	-	-	-	-	-	-	-	-	-	-	-	-
baseline	0.70	0.67	0.74	0.62	0.59	0.65	0.69	0.66	0.73	0.66	0.62	0.69	0.68	0.65	0.72
UTD	0.66	0.62	0.71	0.57	0.53	0.61	-	-	-	-	-	-	-	-	-
WuHanNLP	0.65	0.59	0.72	0.58	0.53	0.64	0.64	0.58	0.71	0.63	0.57	0.70	0.63	0.57	0.70
IIIT	0.62	**0.69**	0.56	0.51	0.57	0.47	0.61	0.67	0.55	0.58	0.64	0.52	0.59	0.66	0.54
XJNLP†	0.61	0.55	0.68	0.51	0.46	0.57	0.59	0.54	0.67	0.54	0.49	0.61	0.58	0.52	0.66
UNICA	0.50	0.39	0.71	0.43	0.34	0.61	0.49	0.38	0.70	0.47	0.37	0.66	0.47	0.37	0.67
Annotator agreement															
ann-ann	0.79	-	-	0.72	-	-	0.78	-	-	0.78	-	-	0.76	-	-
adj-ann	0.87	-	-	0.84	-	-	0.86	-	-	0.86	-	-	0.85	-	-

Table 3: System performance and annotator agreement on EVENT tasks: identifying the event expression's span (character offsets), contextual modality (ACTUAL, HYPOTHETICAL, HEDGED or GENERIC), degree (MOST, LITTLE or N/A), polarity (POS or NEG) and type (ASPECTUAL, EVIDENTIAL or N/A).

in brain vs. 11 in colon), and *intraoperative* is 2.3 times more common (156 in brain vs. 68 in colon). Formatting is also different across the corpora. For example, *POST-OP* (all capitals) occurs 161 times in all the brain cancer data, but never occurs with this capitalization in any of the colon cancer data.

8.2 Event Expressions

Table 3 shows results on the event expression tasks. The LIMSI-COT system achieved the best F1 on all event expression tasks for both the unsupervised and supervised domain adaptation phases, achieving around 0.70 F1 for most subtasks in the unsupervised setting, and around 0.75 F1 in the supervised setting. Compared to human agreement, the LIMSI-COT system ranged between 0.06 and 0.09 below the inter-annotator agreement.

In Clinical TempEval 2016, for comparison, the top system achieved F1s of 0.92, 0.87, 0.91, 0.90, and 0.89 for event spans, modality, degree, polarity, and type, respectively. This suggests that, much like for time expressions, an event expression system trained on one clinical condition (e.g., colon cancer) can expect a 20+ point drop when tested on another clinical condition (e.g., brain cancer). Providing 30 annotated notes in the target domain again narrows the gap by only a few points.

The drop in performance can again probably be attributed to differences across the two corpora. Even more so than time expressions, event expressions for brain cancer are very different from event expressions for colon cancer. For example, *craniotomy*, *glioma*, *glioblastoma*, *oligoastrocytoma*, *aphasia*, and *temozolomide* all occur as events more than 150 times in the brain cancer data, but do not occur as events even once in the colon cancer data.

8.3 Temporal Relations

Table 4 shows performance on the temporal relation tasks. The LIMSI-COT system had the top F1 in almost all of the temporal relation tasks in both the unsupervised and supervised domain adaptation settings, achieving above 0.50 F1 in linking events to the document creation time, and above 0.30 F1 for linking events to their narrative containers. Compared to humans, the LIMSI-COT system was more than 0.30 below inter-annotator agreement for narrative container relations, but above inter-annotator agreement (though still below annotator-adjudicator agreement) on document time relations when using the additional target domain (brain cancer) training data.

In Clinical TempEval 2016, for comparison, the top system achieved F1s of 0.76 for document time

	To document time			Narrative containers		
	F1	P	R	F1	P	R
	Unsupervised domain adaptation					
LIMSI-COT	**0.51**	0.44	**0.60**	0.33	0.28	**0.40**
KULeuven-LIIR	0.49	**0.50**	0.48	0.32	0.33	0.30
GUIR	0.40	0.36	0.45	**0.34**	**0.52**	0.25
Hitachi	0.45	0.44	0.45	0.23	0.23	0.22
baseline	0.38	0.39	0.37	0.14	0.39	0.08
ULISBOA	0.41	0.37	0.45	-	-	-
WuHanNLP	0.41	0.39	0.43	-	-	-
	Supervised domain adaptation					
LIMSI-COT	**0.59**	**0.53**	**0.66**	**0.32**	0.25	**0.43**
KULeuven-LIIR	0.56	0.52	0.61	0.28	0.23	0.35
GUIR	0.50	0.45	0.55	0.25	**0.59**	0.16
NTU-1	0.49	0.42	0.59	0.26	0.20	0.37
Hitachi	0.52	0.49	0.55	0.16	0.11	0.27
baseline	0.46	0.43	0.48	0.14	0.27	0.09
WuHanNLP	0.46	0.42	0.51	0.12	0.16	0.09
UTD	0.45	0.42	0.48	0.11	0.08	0.16
ULISBOA	0.44	0.39	0.51	-	-	-
IIIT	0.36	0.40	0.33	0.05	0.03	0.08
UNICA	0.20	0.15	0.28	-	-	-
	Annotator agreement					
ann-ann	0.52	-	-	0.66	-	-
adj-ann	0.71	-	-	0.80	-	-

Table 4: System performance and annotator agreement on temporal relation tasks: identifying relations between events and the document creation time (DOCTIMEREL), and identifying narrative container relations (CONTAINS).

relations, and 0.48 for narrative containers. Again we see a major drop when training on one condition (e.g., colon cancer) and testing on another (e.g., brain cancer): a 20+ point drop for document time relations, and around a 15 point drop for narrative containers.

9 Discussion

Clinical TempEval 2017 showed that developing clinical timeline extraction tools that generalize across domains is still a challenging problem. Almost across the board, we saw 20+ point drops in performance when systems were trained on one domain (colon cancer) and tested on another (brain cancer), as compared to systems that were trained and tested on a single domain (colon cancer, as in Clinical TempEval 2016). And across the board, providing a small amount of target domain (brain cancer) training data narrowed that gap only by a couple of points. This is an important finding because it stresses how much work remains to build robust clinical information extraction tools that are useful across a wide range of medical applications.

Though the focus in Clinical TempEval 2017 was on domain adaptation, only a small number of fairly simple domain adaptation techniques were applied by participants, probably because producing even an initial system for all the Clinical TempEval sub-tasks is already a significant effort. Two participants (LIMSI-COT and KULeuven-LIIR, two of the top ranking systems) included special handling of unknown words to try to increase generalization power. Other approaches attempted by participants included giving a heavier weight to the target domain (brain cancer) training data, and using pre-trained domain independent word embeddings. A wide variety of more sophisticated domain adaptation techniques exist that were not applied by participants, and we expect that some of these will make future progress in reducing the cross-domain performance degradation that was observed in Clinical TempEval 2017.

Acknowledgements

The project described was supported in part by R01LM010090 (THYME) from the National Library Of Medicine. The content is solely the responsibility of the authors and does not necessarily represent the official views of the National Institutes of Health.

References

Steven Bethard, Leon Derczynski, Guergana Savova, James Pustejovsky, and Marc Verhagen. 2015. SemEval-2015 Task 6: Clinical TempEval. In *Proceedings of the 9th International Workshop on Semantic Evaluation (SemEval 2015)*. Association for Computational Linguistics, Denver, Colorado, pages 806–814. http://www.aclweb.org/anthology/S15-2136.

Steven Bethard, Guergana Savova, Wei-Te Chen, Leon Derczynski, James Pustejovsky, and Marc Verhagen. 2016. SemEval-2016 Task 12: Clinical TempEval. In *Proceedings of the 10th International Workshop on Semantic Evaluation (SemEval-2016)*. Association for Computational Linguistics, San Diego, California, pages 1052–1062. http://www.aclweb.org/anthology/S16-1165.

Wei-Te Chen and Will Styler. 2013. Anafora: A web-based general purpose annotation tool. In *Proceedings of the 2013 NAACL HLT Demonstration Session*. Association for Computational Linguistics, Atlanta, Georgia, pages 14–19. http://www.aclweb.org/anthology/N13-3004.

Po-Yu Huang, Hen-Hsen Huang, Yu-Wun Wang, Ching Huang, and Hsin-Hsi Chen. 2017. NTU-1 at SemEval-2017 Task 12: Detection and classification of temporal events in clinical data with domain adaptation. In *Proceedings of the 11th International*

Workshop on Semantic Evaluation (SemEval-2017). Association for Computational Linguistics, Vancouver, Canada, pages 1007–1010. `http://www.aclweb.org/anthology/S17-2177`.

Andre Lamurias, Diana Sousa, Sofia Pereira, Luka Clarke, and Francisco M Couto. 2017. ULISBOA at SemEval-2017 Task 12: Extraction and classification of temporal expressions and events. In *Proceedings of the 11th International Workshop on Semantic Evaluation (SemEval-2017)*. Association for Computational Linguistics, Vancouver, Canada, pages 1016–1020. `http://www.aclweb.org/anthology/S17-2179`.

Artuur Leeuwenberg and Marie-Francine Moens. 2017. KULeuven-LIIR at SemEval-2017 Task 12: Cross-domain temporal information extraction from clinical records. In *Proceedings of the 11th International Workshop on Semantic Evaluation (SemEval-2017)*. Association for Computational Linguistics, Vancouver, Canada, pages 1027–1031. `http://www.aclweb.org/anthology/S17-2181`.

Yu Long, Zhijing Li, Xuan Wang, and Chen Li. 2017. XJNLP at SemEval-2017 Task 12: Clinical temporal information extraction with a hybrid model. In *Proceedings of the 11th International Workshop on Semantic Evaluation (SemEval-2017)*. Association for Computational Linguistics, Vancouver, Canada, pages 1011–1015. `http://www.aclweb.org/anthology/S17-2178`.

Sean MacAvaney, Arman Cohan, and Nazli Goharian. 2017. GUIR at SemEval-2017 Task 12: A framework for cross-domain clinical temporal information extraction. In *Proceedings of the 11th International Workshop on Semantic Evaluation (SemEval-2017)*. Association for Computational Linguistics, Vancouver, Canada, pages 1021–1026. `http://www.aclweb.org/anthology/S17-2180`.

Sarath P R, Manikandan R, and Yoshiki Niwa. 2017. Hitachi at SemEval-2017 Task 12: System for temporal information extraction from clinical notes. In *Proceedings of the 11th International Workshop on Semantic Evaluation (SemEval-2017)*. Association for Computational Linguistics, Vancouver, Canada, pages 1002–1006. `http://www.aclweb.org/anthology/S17-2176`.

James Pustejovsky and Amber Stubbs. 2011. Increasing informativeness in temporal annotation. In *Proceedings of the 5th Linguistic Annotation Workshop*. Association for Computational Linguistics, Portland, Oregon, USA, pages 152–160. `http://www.aclweb.org/anthology/W11-0419`.

William F. Styler, IV, Steven Bethard, Sean Finan, Martha Palmer, Sameer Pradhan, Piet de Groen, Brad Erickson, Timothy Miller, Chen Lin, Guergana Savova, and James Pustejovsky. 2014a. Temporal annotation in the clinical domain. *Transactions of the Association for Computational Linguistics* 2:143–154. `https://tacl2013.cs.columbia.edu/ojs/index.php/tacl/article/view/305`.

William F. Styler, IV, Guergana Savova, Martha Palmer, James Pustejovsky, Tim O'Gorman, and Piet C. de Groen. 2014b. THYME annotation guidelines. `http://clear.colorado.edu/compsem/documents/THYMEGuidelines.pdf`.

Julien Tourille, Olivier Ferret, Xavier Tannier, and Aurélie Névéol. 2017. LIMSI-COT at SemEval-2017 Task 12: Neural architecture for temporal information extraction from clinical narratives. In *Proceedings of the 11th International Workshop on Semantic Evaluation (SemEval-2017)*. Association for Computational Linguistics, Vancouver, Canada, pages 595–600. `http://www.aclweb.org/anthology/S17-2098`.

Naushad UzZaman and James Allen. 2011. Temporal evaluation. In *Proceedings of the 49th Annual Meeting of the Association for Computational Linguistics: Human Language Technologies*. Association for Computational Linguistics, Portland, Oregon, USA, pages 351–356. `http://www.aclweb.org/anthology/P11-2061`.

Naushad UzZaman, Hector Llorens, Leon Derczynski, James Allen, Marc Verhagen, and James Pustejovsky. 2013. SemEval-2013 Task 1: TempEval-3: Evaluating time expressions, events, and temporal relations. In *Second Joint Conference on Lexical and Computational Semantics (*SEM), Volume 2: Proceedings of the Seventh International Workshop on Semantic Evaluation (SemEval 2013)*. Association for Computational Linguistics, Atlanta, Georgia, USA, pages 1–9. `http://www.aclweb.org/anthology/S13-2001`.

Marc Verhagen, Robert Gaizauskas, Frank Schilder, Mark Hepple, Graham Katz, and James Pustejovsky. 2007. SemEval-2007 Task 15: TempEval temporal relation identification. In *Proceedings of the Fourth International Workshop on Semantic Evaluations (SemEval-2007)*. Association for Computational Linguistics, Prague, Czech Republic, pages 75–80. `http://www.aclweb.org/anthology/S/S07/S07-1014`.

Marc Verhagen, Roser Sauri, Tommaso Caselli, and James Pustejovsky. 2010. SemEval-2010 Task 13: TempEval-2. In *Proceedings of the 5th International Workshop on Semantic Evaluation*. Association for Computational Linguistics, Uppsala, Sweden, pages 57–62. `http://www.aclweb.org/anthology/S10-1010`.

BB_twtr at SemEval-2017 Task 4: Twitter Sentiment Analysis with CNNs and LSTMs

Mathieu Cliche

Bloomberg

`mcliche@bloomberg.net`

Abstract

In this paper we describe our attempt at producing a state-of-the-art Twitter sentiment classifier using Convolutional Neural Networks (CNNs) and Long Short Term Memory (LSTMs) networks. Our system leverages a large amount of unlabeled data to pre-train word embeddings. We then use a subset of the unlabeled data to fine tune the embeddings using distant supervision. The final CNNs and LSTMs are trained on the SemEval-2017 Twitter dataset where the embeddings are fined tuned again. To boost performances we ensemble several CNNs and LSTMs together. Our approach achieved first rank on all of the five English subtasks amongst 40 teams.

1 Introduction

Determining the sentiment polarity of tweets has become a landmark homework exercise in natural language processing (NLP) and data science classes. This is perhaps because the task is easy to understand and it is also easy to get good results with very simple methods (e.g. positive - negative words counting). The practical applications of this task are wide, from monitoring popular events (e.g. Presidential debates, Oscars, etc.) to extracting trading signals by monitoring tweets about public companies. These applications often benefit greatly from the best possible accuracy, which is why the SemEval-2017 Twitter competition promotes research in this area. The competition is divided into five subtasks which involve standard classification, ordinal classification and distributional estimation. For a more detailed description see (Rosenthal et al., 2017).

In the last few years, deep learning techniques have significantly out-performed traditional methods in several NLP tasks (Chen and Manning, 2014; Bahdanau et al., 2014), and sentiment analysis is no exception to this trend (Rojas-Barahona, 2016). In fact, previous iterations of the SemEval Twitter sentiment analysis competition have already established their power over other approaches (Nakov et al., 2016; Severyn and Moschitti, 2015; Deriu et al., 2016). Two of the most popular deep learning techniques for sentiment analysis are CNNs and LSTMs. Consequently, in an effort to build a state-of-the-art Twitter sentiment classifier, we explore both models and build a system which combines both.

This paper is organized as follows. In sec. 2 we describe the architecture of the CNN and the LSTM used in our system. In sec. 3 we expand on the three training phases used in our system. In sec. 4 we discuss the various tricks that were used to fine tune the system for each individual subtasks. Finally in sec. 5 we present the performance of the system and in sec. 6 we outline our main conclusions.

2 System description

2.1 CNN

Let us now describe the architecture of the CNN we worked with. Its architecture is almost identical to the CNN of Kim (2014). A smaller version of our model is illustrated on Fig. 1. The input of the network are the tweets, which are tokenized into words. Each word is mapped to a word vector representation, i.e. a word embedding, such that an entire tweet can be mapped to a matrix of size $s \times d$, where s is the number of words in the tweet and d is the dimension of the embedding space (we chose $d = 200$). We follow Kim (2014) zero-

Proceedings of the 11th International Workshop on Semantic Evaluations (SemEval-2017), pages 573–580,
Vancouver, Canada, August 3 - 4, 2017. ©2017 Association for Computational Linguistics

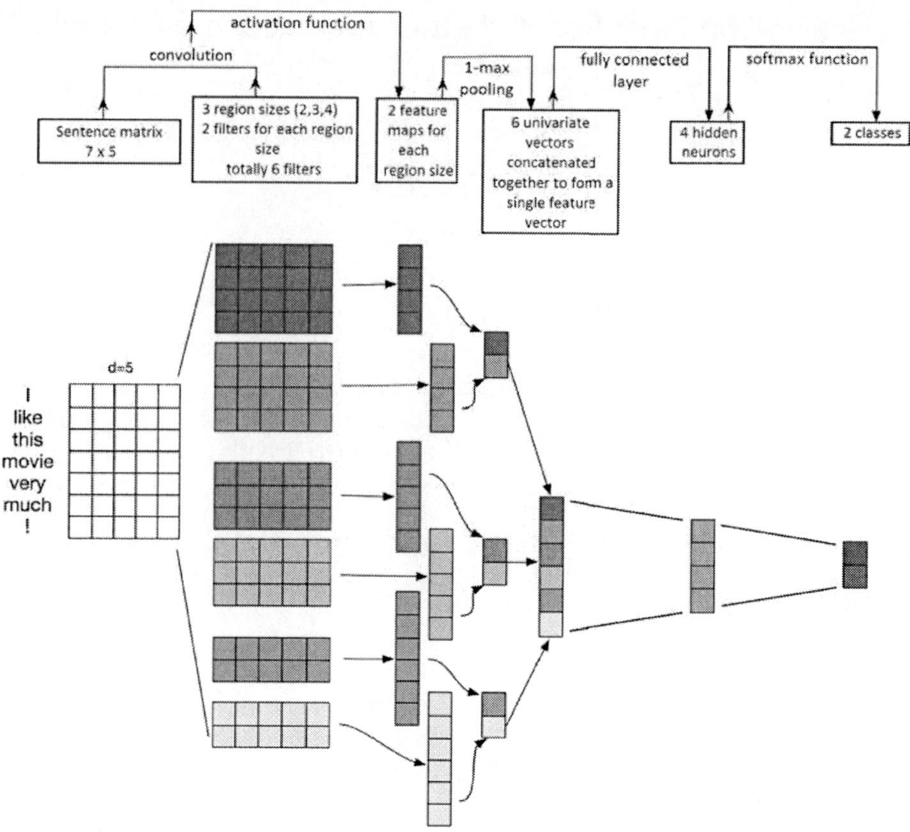

Figure 1: Architecture of a smaller version of the CNN used. Picture is taken from (Zhang and Wallace, 2015) with minor modifications.

padding strategy such that all tweets have the same matrix dimension $X \in \mathbb{R}^{s' \times d}$, where we chose $s' = 80$. We then apply several convolution operations of various sizes to this matrix. A single convolution involves a filtering matrix $w \in \mathbb{R}^{h \times d}$ where h is the size of the convolution, meaning the number of words it spans. The convolution operation is defined as

$$c_i \;=\; f\left(\sum_{j,k} w_{j,k} \left(X_{[i:i+h-1]}\right)_{j,k} + b\right) \quad (1)$$

where $b \in \mathbb{R}$ is a bias term and f(x) is a non-linear function, which we chose to be the relu function. The output $c \in \mathbb{R}^{s'-h+1}$ is therefore a concatenation of the convolution operator over all possible window of words in the tweet. Note that because of the zero-padding strategy we use, we are effectively applying wide convolutions (Kalchbrenner et al., 2014). We can use multiple filtering matrices to learn different features, and

additionally we can use multiple convolution sizes to focus on smaller or larger regions of the tweets. In practice, we used three filter sizes (either $[1, 2, 3]$, $[3, 4, 5]$ or $[5, 6, 7]$ depending on the model) and we used a total of 200 filtering matrices for each filter size.

We then apply a max-pooling operation to each convolution $c_{\max} = \max(c)$. The max-pooling operation extracts the most important feature for each convolution, independently of where in the tweet this feature is located. In other words, the CNN's structure effectively extracts the most important n-grams in the embedding space, which is why we believe these systems are good at sentence classification. The max-pooling operation also allows us to combine all the $c_{\max}$ of each filter into one vector $\mathbf{c}_{\max} \in \mathbb{R}^{m}$ where m is the total number of filters (in our case $m = 3 \times 200 = 600$). This vector then goes through a small fully connected hidden layer of size 30, which is then in

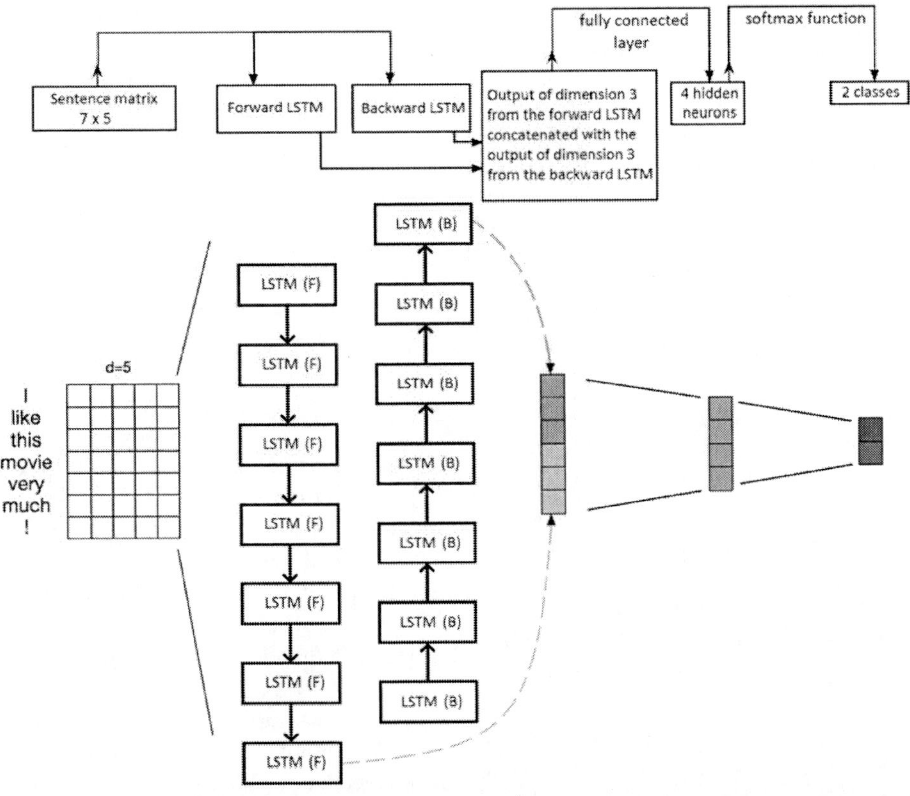

Figure 2: Architecture of a smaller version of the bi-directional LSTM used. Picture is inspired by Figure 1 of (Zhang and Wallace, 2015).

turn passed through a softmax layer to give the final classification probabilities. To reduce overfitting, we add a dropout layer (Srivastava et al., 2014) after the max-pooling layer and after the fully connected hidden layer, with a dropout probability of 50% during training.

2.2 LSTM

Let us now describe the architecture of the LSTM system we worked with. A smaller version of our model is illustrated on Fig. 2. Its main building blocks are two LSTM units. LSTMs are part of the recurrent neural networks (RNN) family, which are neural networks that are constructed to deal with sequential data by sharing their internal weights across the sequence. For each element in the sequence, that is for each word in the tweet, the RNN uses the current word embedding and its previous hidden state to compute the next hidden state. In its simplest version, the hidden state $h_t \in \mathbb{R}^m$ (where m is the dimension of the RNN, which we pick to be $m = 200$) at time t is computed by

$$h_t = f(W_h \cdot x_t + U_h \cdot h_{t-1} + b_h) \quad (2)$$

where x_t is the current word embedding, $W_h \in \mathbb{R}^{m \times d}$ and $U_h \in \mathbb{R}^{m \times m}$ are weight matrices, $b_h \in \mathbb{R}^m$ is a bias term and $f(x)$ is a non-linear function, usually chosen to be tanh. The initial hidden state is chosen to be a vector of zeros. Unfortunately this simple RNN suffers from the exploding and vanishing gradient problem during the backpropagation training stage (Hochreiter, 1998). LSTMs solve this problem by having a more complex internal structure which allows LSTMs to remember information for either long or short terms (Hochreiter and Schmidhuber, 1997). The hidden state of an LSTM unit is computed by (Zaremba et al., 2014)

$$
\begin{aligned}
f_t &= \sigma(W_f \cdot x_t + U_f \cdot h_{t-1} + b_f) \\
i_t &= \sigma(W_i \cdot x_t + U_i \cdot h_{t-1} + b_i) \\
o_t &= \sigma(W_o \cdot x_t + U_o \cdot h_{t-1} + b_o)
\end{aligned}
$$

$$
\begin{aligned}
c_t &= f_t \circ c_{t-1} \\
&\quad + i_t \circ \tanh\left(W_c \cdot x_t + U_c \cdot h_{t-1} + b_c\right) \\
h_t &= o_t \circ \tanh\left(c_t\right)
\end{aligned}
\tag{3}
$$

where i_t is called the input gate, f_t is the forget gate, c_t is the cell state, h_t is the regular hidden state, σ is the sigmoid function, and $\circ$ is the Hadamard product.

One drawback from the LSTM is that it does not sufficiently take into account post word information because the sentence is read only in one direction; forward. To solve this problem, we use what is known as a bidirectional LSTM, which is two LSTMs whose outputs are stacked together. One LSTM reads the sentence forward, and the other LSTM reads it backward. We concatenate the hidden states of each LSTM after they processed their respective final word. This gives a vector of dimension $2m = 400$, which is fed to a fully connected hidden layer of size 30, and then passed through a softmax layer to give the final classification probabilities. Here again we use dropout to reduce over-fitting; we add a dropout layer before and after the LSTMs, and after the fully connected hidden layer, with a dropout probability of 50% during training.

3 Training

To train those models we had access to 49,693 human labeled tweets for subtask A, 30,849 tweets for subtasks (C, E) and 18,948 tweets for subtasks (B, D). In addition to this human labeled data, we collected 100 million unique unlabeled English tweets using the Twitter streaming API. From this unlabeled dataset, we extracted a distant dataset of 5 million positive tweets and 5 million negative tweets. To extract this distant dataset we used the strategy of Go et al. (2009), that is we simply associate positive tweets with the presence of positive emoticons (e.g. ":)") and vice versa for negative tweets. Those three datasets (unlabeled, distant and labeled) were used separately in the three training stages which we now present. Note that our training strategy is very similar to the one used in (Severyn and Moschitti, 2015; Deriu et al., 2016).

3.1 Pre-processing

Before feeding the tweets to any training stage, they are pre-processed using the following procedure:

- URLs are replaced by the <url> token.

- Several emoticons are replaced by the tokens <smile>, <sadface>, <lolface> or <neutralface>.

- Any letter repeated more than 2 times in a row is replaced by 2 repetitions of that letter (for example, "sooooo" is replaced by "soo").

- All tweets are lowercased.

3.2 Unsupervised training

We start by using the 100 million unlabeled tweets to pre-train the word embeddings which will later be used in the CNN and LSTM. To do so, we experimented with 3 unsupervised learning algorithms, Google's Word2vec (Mikolov et al., 2013a,b), Facebook's FastText (Bojanowski et al., 2016) and Stanford's GloVe (Pennington et al., 2014). Word2vec learns word vector representations by attempting to predict context words around an input word. FastText is very similar to Word2vec but it also uses subword information in the prediction model. GloVe on the other hand is a model based on global word-word co-occurrence statistics. For all three algorithms we used the code provided by the authors with their default settings.

3.3 Distant training

The embeddings learned in the unsupervised phase contain very little information about the sentiment polarity of the words since the context for a positive word (ex. "good") tends to be very similar to the context of a negative word (ex. "bad"). To add polarity information to the embeddings, we follow the unsupervised training by a fine tuning of the embeddings via a distant training phase. To do so, we use the CNN described in sec. 2 and initialize the embeddings with the ones learned in the unsupervised phase. We then use the distant dataset to train the CNN to classify noisy positive tweets vs. noisy negative tweets. The first epoch of the training is done with the embeddings frozen in order to minimize large changes in the embeddings. We then unfreeze the embeddings and train for 6 more epochs. After this training stage, words with very different sentiment polarity (ex. "good" vs. "bad") are far apart in the embedding space.

3.4 Supervised training

The final training stage uses the human labeled data provided by SemEval-2017. We initialize the embeddings in the CNN and LSTM models with the fine tuned embeddings of the distant training phase, and freeze them for the first ~ 5 epochs. We then train for another ~ 5 epochs with unfrozen embeddings and a learning rate reduced by a factor of 10. We pick the cross-entropy as the loss function, and we weight it by the inverse frequency of the true classes to counteract the imbalanced dataset. The loss is minimized using the Adam optimizer (Kingma and Ba, 2014) with initial learning rate of 0.001. The models were implemented in TensorFlow and experiments were run on a GeForce GTX Titan X GPU.

To reduce variance and boost accuracy, we ensemble 10 CNNs and 10 LSTMs together through soft voting. The models ensembled have different random weight initializations, different number of epochs (from 4 to 20 in total), different set of filter sizes (either $[1, 2, 3]$, $[3, 4, 5]$ or $[5, 6, 7]$) and different embedding pre-training algorithms (either Word2vec or FastText).

4 Subtask specific tricks

The models described in sec. 2 and the training method described in sec. 3 are used in the same way for all five subtasks, with a few special exceptions which we now address. Clearly, the output dimension differs depending on the subtask, for subtask A the output dimension is 3, while for B and D it is 2 and for subtask C and E it is 5. Furthermore, for quantification subtasks (D and E), we use the probability average approach of Bella et al. (2010) to convert the output probabilities into sentiment distributions.

Finally for subtasks that have a topic associated with the tweet (B, C, D and E), we add two special steps which we noticed improves the accuracy during the cross-validation phase. First, if any of the words in the topic is not explicitly mentioned in the tweet, we add those missing words at the end of the tweet in the pre-processing phase. Second, we concatenate to the regular word embeddings another embedding space of dimension 5 which has only 2 possible vectors. One of these 2 vectors indicates that the current word is part of the topic, while the other vector indicates that the current word is not part of the topic.

5 Results

Let us now discuss the results obtained from this system. In order to assess the performance of each model and their variations, we first show their scores on the historical Twitter test set of 2013, 2014, 2015 and 2016 without using any of those sets in the training dataset, just like it was required for the 2016 edition of this competition. For brevity, we only focus on task A since it tends to be the most popular one. Moreover, in order to be consistent with historical editions of this competition, we use the average F_1 score of the positive and negative class as the metric of interest. This is different from the macro-average recall which is used in the 2017 edition, but this should not affect the conclusions of this analysis significantly since we found that the two metrics were highly correlated. The results are summarized in Table 1. This table is not meant to be an exhaustive list of all the experiments performed, but it does illustrate the relative performances of the most important variations on the models explored here.

We can see from Table 1 that the GloVe unsupervised algorithm gives a lower score than both FastText and Word2vec. It is for this reason that we did not include the GloVe variation in the ensemble model. We also note that the absence of class weights or the absence of a distant training stage lowers the scores significantly, which demonstrates that these are sound additions. Except for these three variations, the other models have similar scores. However, the ensemble model effectively outperforms all the other individual models. Indeed, while these individual models give similar scores, their outputs are sufficiently uncorrelated such that ensembling them gives the score a small boost. To get a sense of how correlated with each other these models are, we can compute the Pearson correlation coefficient between the output probabilities of any pairs of models, see Table 2. From this table we can see that the most uncorrelated models come from different supervised learning models (CNN vs. LSTM) and from different unsupervised learning

System	2013	2014	2015	2016
Logistic regression on 1-3 grams baseline	0.627	0.629	0.586	0.558
CNN (word2vec, convolution size=[3,4,5])	0.715	0.723	**0.688**	0.643
CNN (fasttext, convolution size=[3,4,5])	0.720	0.733	0.665	0.640
CNN (glove, convolution size=[3,4,5])	0.709	0.714	0.660	0.637
CNN (word2vec, convolution size=[1,2,3])	0.712	0.735	0.673	0.642
CNN (word2vec, convolution size=[5,6,7])	0.710	0.732	0.676	0.646
CNN (word2vec, convolution size=[3,4,5], no class weights)	0.682	0.679	0.659	0.640
CNN (word2vec, convolution size=[3,4,5], no distant training)	0.698	0.716	0.660	0.636
CNN (word2vec, convolution size=[3,4,5], no fully connected layer)	0.715	0.724	0.683	0.641
LSTM (word2vec)	0.720	0.733	0.677	0.636
LSTM (fasttext)	0.712	0.730	0.666	0.633
LSTM (glove)	0.710	0.730	0.658	0.630
LSTM (word2vec, no class weights)	0.689	0.661	0.652	0.643
LSTM (word2vec, no distant training)	0.698	0.719	0.647	0.629
LSTM (word2vec, no fully connected layer)	0.719	0.725	0.675	0.634
Ensemble model	0.725	**0.748**	0.679	**0.648**
Previous best historical scores	**0.728**	0.744	0.671	0.633

Table 1: Validation results on the historical test sets of subtask A. Bold values represent the best score for a given test set. The 2013 test set contains 3,813 tweets, the 2014 test set contains 1,853 tweets, the 2015 test set contains 2,392 tweets and the 2016 test set contains 20,632 tweets. Word2vec, fasttext and glove refer to the choice of algorithm in the unsupervised phase. No class weights means no weights were used in the cost function to counteract the imbalanced classes. No distant training means that we used the embeddings from the unsupervised phase without distant training. No fully connected layer means we removed the fully connected hidden layer from the network. Ensemble model refers to the ensemble model described in Sec. 3.4. The previous best historical scores were collected from (Nakov et al., 2016). They do not come from a single system or from a single team; they are the best previous scores obtained for each test set over the years.

algorithms (Word2vec vs. FastText).

For the predictions on the 2017 test set, the system is retrained on all available training data, which includes previous years testing data. The results of our system on the 2017 test set are shown on Table 3. Our system achieved the best scores on all of the five English subtasks. For subtask A, there is actually a tie between our submission and another team (DataStories), but note that with respect to the other metrics (accuracy and F_1^{PN} score) our submission ranks higher.

6 Conclusion

In this paper we presented the system we used to compete in the SemEval-2017 Twitter sentiment analysis competition. Our goal was to experiment with deep learning models along with modern training strategies in an effort to build the best possible sentiment classifier for tweets. The final model we used was an ensemble of 10 CNNs and 10 LSTMs with different hyper-parameters and different pre-training strategies. We participated in all of the English subtasks, and obtained first rank in all of them.

For future work, it would be interesting to explore systems that combine a CNN and an LSTM more organically than through an ensemble model, perhaps a model similar to the one of Stojanovski et al. (2016). It would also be interesting to analyze the dependence of the amount of unlabeled and distant data on the performance of the models.

Acknowledgments

We thank Karl Stratos, Anju Kambadur, Liang Zhou, Alexander M. Rush, David Rosenberg and Biye Li for their help on this project.

System/System	System 1	System 2	System 3	System 4	System 5	System 6
System 1	1.0	0.95	0.97	0.97	0.93	0.91
System 2	0.95	1.0	0.95	0.95	0.91	0.92
System 3	0.97	0.95	1.0	0.96	0.92	0.91
System 4	0.97	0.95	0.96	1.0	0.92	0.91
System 5	0.93	0.91	0.92	0.92	1.0	0.95
System 6	0.91	0.92	0.91	0.91	0.95	1.0

Table 2: Correlation matrix for the most important models. System 1: CNN (word2vec, convolution size=[3,4,5]), System 2: CNN (fasttext, convolution size=[3,4,5]), System 3: CNN (word2vec, convolution size=[1,2,3]), System 4: CNN (word2vec, convolution size=[5,6,7]), System 5: LSTM (word2vec), System 6: LSTM (fasttext).

Subtask	Metric	Rank	BB_twtr submission	Next best submission
A	Macroaveraged recall	1/38	0.681	0.681
B	Macroaveraged recall	1/23	0.882	0.856
C	Macroaveraged mean absolute error	1/15	0.481	0.555
D	Kullback-Leibler divergence	1/15	0.036	0.048
E	Earth movers distance	1/12	0.245	0.269

Table 3: Results on the 2017 test set. The 2017 test set contains 12,379 tweets. For a description of the subtasks and metrics used, see (Rosenthal et al., 2017). For subtask A and B, higher is better, while for subtask C, D and E, lower is better.

References

Dzmitry Bahdanau, Kyunghyun Cho, and Yoshua Bengio. 2014. Neural machine translation by jointly learning to align and translate. *arXiv preprint arXiv:1409.0473* .

Antonio Bella, Cesar Ferri, José Hernández-Orallo, and Maria Jose Ramirez-Quintana. 2010. Quantification via probability estimators. In *Data Mining (ICDM), 2010 IEEE 10th International Conference on*. IEEE, pages 737–742.

Piotr Bojanowski, Edouard Grave, Armand Joulin, and Tomas Mikolov. 2016. Enriching word vectors with subword information. *arXiv preprint arXiv:1607.04606* .

Danqi Chen and Christopher D Manning. 2014. A fast and accurate dependency parser using neural networks. In *EMNLP*. pages 740–750.

Jan Deriu, Maurice Gonzenbach, Fatih Uzdilli, Aurelien Lucchi, Valeria De Luca, and Martin Jaggi. 2016. Swisscheese at semeval-2016 task 4: Sentiment classification using an ensemble of convolutional neural networks with distant supervision. In *Proceedings of the 10th International Workshop on Semantic Evaluation (SemEval-2016)*. Association for Computational Linguistics, San Diego, California, pages 1124–1128. http://www.aclweb.org/anthology/S16-1173.

Alec Go, Richa Bhayani, and Lei Huang. 2009. Twitter sentiment classification using distant supervision. *CS224N Project Report, Stanford* 1(12).

Sepp Hochreiter. 1998. The vanishing gradient problem during learning recurrent neural nets and problem solutions. *International Journal of Uncertainty, Fuzziness and Knowledge-Based Systems* 6(02):107–116.

Sepp Hochreiter and Jürgen Schmidhuber. 1997. Long short-term memory. *Neural computation* 9(8):1735–1780.

Nal Kalchbrenner, Edward Grefenstette, and Phil Blunsom. 2014. A convolutional neural network for modelling sentences. *arXiv preprint arXiv:1404.2188* .

Yoon Kim. 2014. Convolutional neural networks for sentence classification. *arXiv preprint arXiv:1408.5882* .

Diederik Kingma and Jimmy Ba. 2014. Adam: A method for stochastic optimization. *arXiv preprint arXiv:1412.6980* .

Tomas Mikolov, Kai Chen, Greg Corrado, and Jeffrey Dean. 2013a. Efficient estimation of word representations in vector space. *arXiv preprint arXiv:1301.3781* .

Tomas Mikolov, Ilya Sutskever, Kai Chen, Greg S Corrado, and Jeff Dean. 2013b. Distributed representations of words and phrases and their compositionality. In *Advances in neural information processing systems*. pages 3111–3119.

Preslav Nakov, Alan Ritter, Sara Rosenthal, Veselin Stoyanov, and Fabrizio Sebastiani. 2016. SemEval-2016 task 4: Sentiment analysis in Twitter. In *Proceedings of the 10th International Workshop on Semantic Evaluation*. Association for Computational Linguistics, San Diego, California, SemEval '16.

Jeffrey Pennington, Richard Socher, and Christopher D. Manning. 2014. Glove: Global vectors for word representation. In *Empirical Methods in Natural Language Processing (EMNLP)*. pages 1532–1543. http://www.aclweb.org/anthology/D14-1162.

Lina Maria Rojas-Barahona. 2016. Deep learning for sentiment analysis. *Language and Linguistics Compass* 10(12):701–719.

Sara Rosenthal, Noura Farra, and Preslav Nakov. 2017. SemEval-2017 task 4: Sentiment analysis in Twitter. In *Proceedings of the 11th International Workshop on Semantic Evaluation*. Association for Computational Linguistics, Vancouver, Canada, SemEval '17.

Aliaksei Severyn and Alessandro Moschitti. 2015. Unitn: Training deep convolutional neural network for twitter sentiment classification. In *Proceedings of the 9th International Workshop on Semantic Evaluation (SemEval 2015)*. Association for Computational Linguistics, Denver, Colorado, pages 464–469. http://www.aclweb.org/anthology/S15-2079.

Nitish Srivastava, Geoffrey E Hinton, Alex Krizhevsky, Ilya Sutskever, and Ruslan Salakhutdinov. 2014. Dropout: a simple way to prevent neural networks from overfitting. *Journal of Machine Learning Research* 15(1):1929–1958.

Dario Stojanovski, Gjorgji Strezoski, Gjorgji Madjarov, and Ivica Dimitrovski. 2016. Finki at semeval-2016 task 4: Deep learning architecture for twitter sentiment analysis. In *Proceedings of the 10th International Workshop on Semantic Evaluation (SemEval-2016)*. Association for Computational Linguistics, San Diego, California, pages 149–154. http://www.aclweb.org/anthology/S16-1022.

Wojciech Zaremba, Ilya Sutskever, and Oriol Vinyals. 2014. Recurrent neural network regularization. *arXiv preprint arXiv:1409.2329* .

Ye Zhang and Byron Wallace. 2015. A sensitivity analysis of (and practitioners' guide to) convolutional neural networks for sentence classification. *arXiv preprint arXiv:1510.03820* .

Lancaster A at SemEval-2017 Task 5: Evaluation metrics matter: predicting sentiment from financial news headlines

Andrew Moore and Paul Rayson

School of Computing and Communications, Lancaster University, Lancaster, UK

`initial.surname@lancaster.ac.uk`

Abstract

This paper describes our participation in Task 5 track 2 of SemEval 2017 to predict the sentiment of financial news headlines for a specific company on a continuous scale between -1 and 1. We tackled the problem using a number of approaches, utilising a Support Vector Regression (SVR) and a Bidirectional Long Short-Term Memory (BLSTM). We found an improvement of 4-6% using the LSTM model over the SVR and came fourth in the track. We report a number of different evaluations using a finance specific word embedding model and reflect on the effects of using different evaluation metrics.

1 Introduction

The objective of Task 5 Track 2 of SemEval (2017) was to predict the sentiment of news headlines with respect to companies mentioned within the headlines. This task can be seen as a finance-specific aspect-based sentiment task (Nasukawa and Yi, 2003). The main motivations of this task is to find specific features and learning algorithms that will perform better for this domain as aspect based sentiment analysis tasks have been conducted before at SemEval (Pontiki et al., 2014).

Domain specific terminology is expected to play a key part in this task, as reporters, investors and analysts in the financial domain will use a specific set of terminology when discussing financial performance. Potentially, this may also vary across different financial domains and industry sectors. Therefore, we took an exploratory approach and investigated how various features and learning algorithms perform differently, specifically SVR and BLSTMs. We found that BLSTMs outperform an SVR without having any knowledge of the company that the sentiment is with respect to. For replicability purposes, with this paper

we are releasing our source code[1] and the finance specific BLSTM word embedding model[2].

2 Related Work

There is a growing amount of research being carried out related to sentiment analysis within the financial domain. This work ranges from domain-specific lexicons (Loughran and McDonald, 2011) and lexicon creation (Moore et al., 2016) to stock market prediction models (Peng and Jiang, 2016; Kazemian et al., 2016). Peng and Jiang (2016) used a multi layer neural network to predict the stock market and found that incorporating textual features from financial news can improve the accuracy of prediction. Kazemian et al. (2016) showed the importance of tuning sentiment analysis to the task of stock market prediction. However, much of the previous work was based on numerical financial stock market data rather than on aspect level financial textual data.

In aspect based sentiment analysis, there have been many different techniques used to predict the polarity of an aspect as shown in SemEval-2016 task 5 (Pontiki et al., 2014). The winning system (Brun et al., 2016) used many different linguistic features and an ensemble model, and the runner up (Kumar et al., 2016) used uni-grams, bi-grams and sentiment lexicons as features for a Support Vector Machine (SVM). Deep learning methods have also been applied to aspect polarity prediction. Ruder et al. (2016) created a hierarchical BLSTM with a sentence level BLSTM inputting into a review level BLSTM thus allowing them to take into account inter- and intra-sentence context. They used only word embeddings making their system less dependent on extensive feature engineering or manual feature creation. This system outperformed all others on certain languages

---

[1] `https://github.com/apmoore1/semeval`
[2] `https://github.com/apmoore1/semeval/tree/master/models/word2vec_models`

Proceedings of the 11th International Workshop on Semantic Evaluations (SemEval-2017), pages 581–585,
Vancouver, Canada, August 3 - 4, 2017. ©2017 Association for Computational Linguistics

on the SemEval-2016 task 5 dataset (Pontiki et al., 2014) and on other languages performed close to the best systems. Wang et al. (2016) also created an LSTM based model using word embeddings but instead of a hierarchical model it was a one layered LSTM with attention which puts more emphasis on learning the sentiment of words specific to a given aspect.

3 Data

The training data published by the organisers for this track was a set of headline sentences from financial news articles where each sentence was tagged with the company name (which we treat as the aspect) and the polarity of the sentence with respect to the company. There is the possibility that the same sentence occurs more than once if there is more than one company mentioned. The polarity was a real value between -1 (negative sentiment) and 1 (positive sentiment).

We additionally trained a word2vec (Mikolov et al., 2013) word embedding model[3] on a set of 189,206 financial articles containing 161,877,425 tokens, that were manually downloaded from Factiva[4]. The articles stem from a range of sources including the Financial Times and relate to companies from the United States only. We trained the model on domain specific data as it has been shown many times that the financial domain can contain very different language.

4 System description

Even though we have outlined this task as an aspect based sentiment task, this is instantiated in only one of the features in the SVR. The following two subsections describe the two approaches, first SVR and then BLSTM. Key implementation details are exposed here in the paper, but we have released the source code and word embedding models to aid replicability and further experimentation.

4.1 SVR

The system was created using ScitKit learn (Pedregosa et al., 2011) linear Support Vector Regression model (Drucker et al., 1997). We exper-

imented with the following different features and parameter settings:

4.1.1 Tokenisation

For comparison purposes, we tested whether or not a simple whitespace tokeniser can perform just as well as a full tokeniser, and in this case we used Unitok[5].

4.1.2 N-grams

We compared word-level uni-grams and bi-grams separately and in combination.

4.1.3 SVR parameters

We tested different penalty parameters C and different epsilon parameters of the SVR.

4.1.4 Word Replacements

We tested replacements to see if generalising words by inserting special tokens would help to reduce the sparsity problem. We placed the word replacements into three separate groups:

1. Company - When a company was mentioned in the input headline from the list of companies in the training data marked up as aspects, it was replaced by a company special token.

2. Positive - When a positive word was mentioned in the input headline from a list of positive words (which was created using the N most similar words based on cosine distance) to 'excellent' using the pre-trained word2vec model.

3. Negative - The same as the positive group however the word used was 'poor' instead of 'excellent'.

In the positive and negative groups, we chose the words 'excellent' and 'poor' following Turney (2002) to group the terms together under non-domain specific sentiment words.

4.1.5 Target aspect

In order to incorporated the company as an aspect, we employed a boolean vector to represent the sentiment of the sentence. This was done in order to see if the system could better differentiate the sentiment when the sentence was the same but the company was different.

---

[3]For reproducibility, the model can be downloaded, however the articles cannot be due to copyright and licence restrictions.

[4]`https://global.factiva.com/factivalogin/login.asp?productname=global`

[5]`http://corpus.tools/wiki/Unitok`

4.2 BLSTM

We created two different Bidirectional (Graves and Schmidhuber, 2005) Long Short-Term Memory (Hochreiter and Schmidhuber, 1997) using the Python Keras library (Chollet, 2015) with tensor flow backend (Abadi et al., 2016). We choose an LSTM model as it solves the vanishing gradients problem of Recurrent Neural Networks. We used a bidirectional model as it allows us to capture information that came before and after instead of just before, thereby allowing us to capture more relevant context within the model. Practically, a BLSTM is two LSTMs one going forward through the tokens the other in reverse order and in our models concatenating the resulting output vectors together at each time step.

The BLSTM models take as input a headline sentence of size L tokens[6] where L is the length of the longest sentence in the training texts. Each word is converted into a 300 dimension vector using the word2vec model trained over the financial text[7]. Any text that is not recognised by the word2vec model is represented as a vector of zeros; this is also used to pad out the sentence if it is shorter than L.

Both BLSTM models have the following similar properties:

1. Gradient clipping value of 5 - This was to help with the exploding gradients problem.

2. Minimised the Mean Square Error (MSE) loss using RMSprop with a mini batch size of 32.

3. The output activation function is linear.

The main difference between the two models is the use of drop out and when they stop training over the data (epoch). Both models architectures can be seen in figure 1.

4.2.1 Standard LSTM (SLSTM)

The BLSTMs do contain drop out in both the input and between the connections of 0.2 each. Finally the epoch is fixed at 25.

4.2.2 Early LSTM (ELSTM)

As can be seen from figure 1, the drop out of 0.5 only happens between the layers and not the

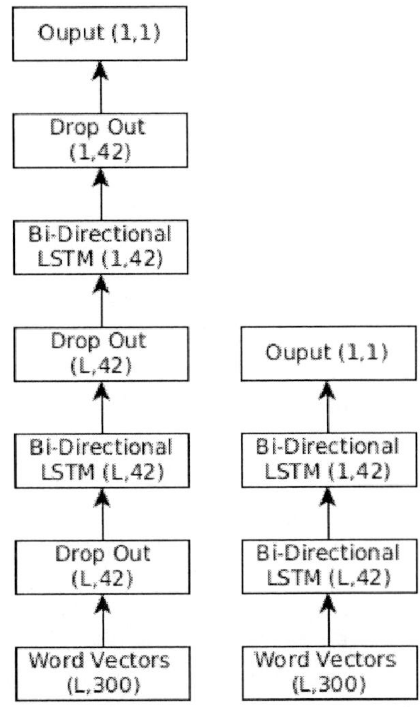

Figure 1: Left hand side is the ELSTM model architecture and the right hand side shows the SLSTM. The numbers in the parenthesis represent the size of the output dimension where L is the length of the longest sentence.

connections as in the SLSTM. Also the epoch is not fixed, it uses early stopping with a patience of 10. We expect that this model can generalise better than the standard one due to the higher drop out and that the epoch is based on early stopping which relies on a validation set to know when to stop training.

5 Results

We first present our findings on the best performing parameters and features for the SVRs. These were determined by cross validation (CV) scores on the provided training data set using cosine similarity as the evaluation metric.[8] We found that using uni-grams and bi-grams performs best and using only bi-grams to be the worst. Using the Unitok tokeniser always performed better than simple whitespace tokenisation. The binary presence of tokens over frequency did not alter performance.

---

[6]Tokenised by Unitok

[7]See the following link for detailed implementation details `https://github.com/apmoore1/semeval#finance-word2vec-model`

[8]All the cross validation results can be found here `https://github.com/apmoore1/semeval/tree/master/results`

The C parameter was tested for three values; 0.01, 0.1 and 1. We found very little difference between 0.1 and 1, but 0.01 produced much poorer results. The eplison parameter was tested for 0.001, 0.01 and 0.1 the performance did not differ much but the lower the higher the performance but the more likely to overfit. Using word replacements was effective for all three types (company, positive and negative) but using a value N=10 performed best for both positive and negative words. Using target aspects also improved results. Therefore, the best SVR model comprised of: Unitok tokenisation, uni- and bi- grams, word representation, C=0.1, eplison=0.01, company, positive, and negative word replacements and target aspects.

$$\frac{\sum_{n=1}^{N} \text{Cosine similarity}(\hat{y}_n, y_n)}{N} \quad (1)$$

The main evaluation over the test data is based on the best performing SVR and the two BLSTM models once trained on all of the training data. The result table 1 shows three columns based on the three evaluation metrics that the organisers have used. Metric 1 is the original metric, weighted cosine similarity (the metric used to evaluate the final version of the results, where we were ranked 5th; metric provided on the task website[9]). This was then changed after the evaluation deadline to equation 1[10] (which we term metric 2; this is what the first version of the results were actually based on, where we were ranked 4th), which then changed by the organisers to their equation as presented in Cortis et al. (2017) (which we term metric 3 and what the second version of the results were based on, where we were ranked 5th).

Model	Metric 1	Metric 2	Metric 3
SVR	62.14	54.59	62.34
SLSTM	72.89	61.55	68.64
ELSTM	73.20	61.98	69.24

Table 1: Results

As you can see from the results table 1, the difference between the metrics is quite substantial. This is due to the system's optimisation being based on metric 1 rather than 2. Metric 2 is a classification metric for sentences with one aspect as it penalises values that are of opposite sign (giving -1 score) and rewards values with the same sign (giving +1 score). Our systems are not optimised for this because it would predict scores of -0.01 and true value of 0.01 as very close (within vector of other results) with low error whereas metric 2 would give this the highest error rating of -1 as they are not the same sign. Metric 3 is more similar to metric 1 as shown by the results, however the crucial difference is that again if you get opposite signs it will penalise more.

We analysed the top 50 errors based on Mean Absolute Error (MAE) in the test dataset specifically to examine the number of sentences containing more than one aspect. Our investigation shows that no one system is better at predicting the sentiment of sentences that have more than one aspect (i.e. company) within them. Within those top 50 errors we found that the BLSTM systems do not know which parts of the sentence are associated to the company the sentiment is with respect to. Also they do not know the strength/existence of certain sentiment words.

6 Conclusion and Future Work

In this short paper, we have described our implemented solutions to SemEval Task 5 track 2, utilising both SVR and BLSTM approaches. Our results show an improvement of around 5% when using LSTM models relative to SVR. We have shown that this task can be partially represented as an aspect based sentiment task on a domain specific problem. In general, our approaches acted as sentence level classifiers as they take no target company into consideration. As our results show, the choice of evaluation metric makes a great deal of difference to system training and testing. Future work will be to implement aspect specific information into an LSTM model as it has been shown to be useful in other work (Wang et al., 2016).

Acknowledgements

We are grateful to Nikolaos Tsileponis (University of Manchester) and Mahmoud El-Haj (Lancaster University) for access to headlines in the corpus of financial news articles collected from Factiva. This research was supported at Lancaster University by an EPSRC PhD studentship.

---

[9] http://alt.qcri.org/semeval2017/task5/index.php?id=evaluation

[10] Where N is the number of unique sentences, $\hat{y}_n$ is the predicted and y_n are the true sentiment value(s) of all sentiments in sentence n.

References

Martín Abadi, Ashish Agarwal, Paul Barham, Eugene Brevdo, Zhifeng Chen, Craig Citro, Greg S Corrado, Andy Davis, Jeffrey Dean, Matthieu Devin, et al. 2016. Tensorflow: Large-scale machine learning on heterogeneous distributed systems. *arXiv preprint arXiv:1603.04467* .

Caroline Brun, Julien Perez, and Claude Roux. 2016. Xrce at semeval-2016 task 5: Feedbacked ensemble modelling on syntactico-semantic knowledge for aspect based sentiment analysis. *Proceedings of SemEval* pages 277–281.

François Chollet. 2015. Keras. `https://github.com/fchollet/keras`.

Keith Cortis, André Freitas, Tobias Dauert, Manuela Huerlimann, Manel Zarrouk, Siegfried Handschuh, and Brian Davis. 2017. Semeval-2017 task 5: Fine-grained sentiment analysis on financial microblogs and news. In *Proceedings of the 11th International Workshop on Semantic Evaluation (SemEval-2017)*. Association for Computational Linguistics, Vancouver, Canada, pages 517–533. http://www.aclweb.org/anthology/S17-2089.

Harris Drucker, Christopher JC Burges, Linda Kaufman, Alex Smola, Vladimir Vapnik, et al. 1997. Support vector regression machines. *Advances in neural information processing systems* 9:155–161.

Alex Graves and Jürgen Schmidhuber. 2005. Framewise phoneme classification with bidirectional lstm and other neural network architectures. *Neural Networks* 18(5):602–610.

Sepp Hochreiter and Jürgen Schmidhuber. 1997. Long short-term memory. *Neural computation* 9(8):1735–1780.

Siavash Kazemian, Shunan Zhao, and Gerald Penn. 2016. Evaluating sentiment analysis in the context of securities trading. In *Proceedings of the 54th Annual Meeting of the Association for Computational Linguistics*. Association for Computational Linguistics, pages 2094–2103. https://doi.org/10.18653/v1/P16-1197.

Ayush Kumar, Sarah Kohail, Amit Kumar, Asif Ekbal, and Chris Biemann. 2016. Iit-tuda at semeval-2016 task 5: Beyond sentiment lexicon: Combining domain dependency and distributional semantics features for aspect based sentiment analysis. *Proceedings of SemEval* pages 1129–1135.

Tim Loughran and Bill McDonald. 2011. When is a liability not a liability? textual analysis, dictionaries, and 10-ks. *The Journal of Finance* 66(1):35–65.

Tomas Mikolov, Kai Chen, Greg Corrado, and Jeffrey Dean. 2013. Efficient estimation of word representations in vector space. *arXiv preprint arXiv:1301.3781* .

Andrew Moore, Paul Rayson, and Steven Young. 2016. Domain adaptation using stock market prices to refine sentiment dictionaries. In *Proceedings of the 10th edition of Language Resources and Evaluation Conference (LREC2016)*. European Language Resources Association (ELRA).

Tetsuya Nasukawa and Jeonghee Yi. 2003. Sentiment analysis: Capturing favorability using natural language processing. In *Proceedings of the 2nd international conference on Knowledge capture*. ACM, pages 70–77.

Fabian Pedregosa, Gaël Varoquaux, Alexandre Gramfort, Vincent Michel, Bertrand Thirion, Olivier Grisel, Mathieu Blondel, Peter Prettenhofer, Ron Weiss, Vincent Dubourg, et al. 2011. Scikit-learn: Machine learning in python. *Journal of Machine Learning Research* 12(Oct):2825–2830.

Yangtuo Peng and Hui Jiang. 2016. Leverage financial news to predict stock price movements using word embeddings and deep neural networks. In *Proceedings of the 2016 Conference of the North American Chapter of the Association for Computational Linguistics: Human Language Technologies*. Association for Computational Linguistics, pages 374–379. https://doi.org/10.18653/v1/N16-1041.

Maria Pontiki, Dimitris Galanis, John Pavlopoulos, Harris Papageorgiou, Ion Androutsopoulos, and Suresh Manandhar. 2014. Semeval-2014 task 4: Aspect based sentiment analysis. *Proceedings of SemEval* pages 27–35.

Sebastian Ruder, Parsa Ghaffari, and G. John Breslin. 2016. A hierarchical model of reviews for aspect-based sentiment analysis. In *Proceedings of the 2016 Conference on Empirical Methods in Natural Language Processing*. Association for Computational Linguistics, pages 999–1005. http://aclweb.org/anthology/D16-1103.

Peter D Turney. 2002. Thumbs up or thumbs down?: semantic orientation applied to unsupervised classification of reviews. In *Proceedings of the 40th annual meeting on association for computational linguistics*. Association for Computational Linguistics, pages 417–424.

Yequan Wang, Minlie Huang, xiaoyan zhu, and Li Zhao. 2016. Attention-based lstm for aspect-level sentiment classification. In *Proceedings of the 2016 Conference on Empirical Methods in Natural Language Processing*. Association for Computational Linguistics, pages 606–615. http://aclweb.org/anthology/D16-1058.

Sheffield at SemEval-2017 Task 9: Transition-based language generation from AMR.

Gerasimos Lampouras
Department of Computer Science
University of Sheffield, UK
`g.lampouras@sheffield.ac.uk`

Andreas Vlachos
Department of Computer Science
University of Sheffield, UK
`a.vlachos@sheffield.ac.uk`

Abstract

This paper describes the submission by the University of Sheffield to the SemEval 2017 Abstract Meaning Representation Parsing and Generation task (SemEval 2017 Task 9, Subtask 2). We cast language generation from AMR as a sequence of actions (e.g., insert/remove/rename edges and nodes) that progressively transform the AMR graph into a dependency parse tree. This transition-based approach relies on the fact that an AMR graph can be considered structurally similar to a dependency tree, with a focus on content rather than function words. An added benefit to this approach is the greater amount of data we can take advantage of to train the parse-to-text linearizer. Our submitted run on the test data achieved a BLEU score of 3.32 and a Trueskill score of -2.204 on automatic and human evaluation respectively.

1 Introduction

Abstract meaning representation (AMR) is a formalism representing the meaning of a sentence (or multiple sentences) as a directed, acyclic graph, where each node represents a concept, and each edge represents a relation between concepts (Banarescu et al., 2013). Natural language generation (NLG) from AMRs introduces challenges, as AMR abstracts away from syntactic structure, function words, or inflections. Flanigan et al. (2016) were the first work to perform NLG from AMR; they used a weighted combination of a tree-to-string transducer and a language model to transform the AMR graph into English. Later work by Song et al. (2016) proposed segmenting the AMR graph into fragments and generating subphrases from them, using a set of subgraph-to-string rules. They then cast the problem of ordering these subphrases as a travelling salesman problem. Pourdamghani et al. (2016) suggested linearizing the AMR graph using a maximum entropy classifier. The linearization is then used as input to a phrase-based machine translation system, to produce the final sentence.

Our submission to SemEval task 9 on AMR-to-English Generation is based on inverting previous work on transition-based parsers (Goodman et al., 2016a,b), which was in turn based on the previous work of Wang et al. (2015). Beyond inverting the transition from AMR graph to dependency tree, our system also separates the transition in three passes. Briefly, during the first pass we convert the AMR concepts into content words, during the second pass the structure of the tree is modified (e.g. by inserting, deleting, and moving nodes and edges), while in the third pass missing function words are inserted, and existing words realized in their final form. To form a natural language sentence, the dependency tree needs only to be linearized; we note that this is not part of the transition, but should be considered a separate post-processing step. We train a separate classifier for each pass, to learn which action should be taken at each time-step.

2 System description

2.1 Pre-processing

During pre-processing the graph structure of the AMR is converted to a tree by identifying each node n with multiple incoming edges in the graph. Each additional incoming edge is redirected to a duplicate node n' (as shown in the transition between stage a and b in Figure 1). These duplicate nodes are inserted as leaves in the structure, and maintain no edges to the n's children. The system randomly determines which of the incoming edges will remain connected with n, and lets the transition system remove duplicate nodes, or move any

Proceedings of the 11th International Workshop on Semantic Evaluations (SemEval-2017), pages 586–591,
Vancouver, Canada, August 3 - 4, 2017. ©2017 Association for Computational Linguistics

of n's descendants as required.

During training, we employ the SpaCy dependency parser (Honnibal and Johnson, 2015) to construct the dependency tree of the training sentence and obtain part-of-speech tags; the dataset's sentences are already split into tokens. Heuristics are used to normalize all date occurrences and numeric expressions in both the sentence and dependency tree, to help our system handle temporal and numerical AMR concepts and structures. Additionally, we construct a simplified version of the dependency tree where articles, auxiliary words, and punctuation, are removed. This simplified tree is useful for the first and second phases of the transition where the focus is on content words.

2.2 Phase 1

Phase 1 is initialized with a stack σ containing all nodes in the AMR tree, with the leaf nodes first; in subsequent phases, σ is initialized with the nodes of the modified tree of the previous phase. A second stack β is initialized with the children of the top node in σ. At each time-step the transition system considers the current state, which consists of the aforementioned stacks, and the tree (which may be in any intermediate stage between an AMR tree and a dependency tree). Each phase concludes once σ is exhausted, with both σ and β stacks being reinitiated for the next phase as needed.

All transition actions are detailed in Table 1, separated according to which phase they may be applied. Some actions may appear in multiple phases (e.g. the NextNode and NextEdge actions, which are primarily used to traverse the σ and β stacks) but note that their outcome may slightly differ from phase to phase. Particularly, during phase 1 the action NextNode is also used to modify the labels of the graph, in effect transforming AMR concepts to content words. If a content word is determined to be a verb, noun, adjective or adverb, a parameter l_n is used which consists of the word's stem and the appropriate part-of-speech tag. The stem is obtained by applying Porter's stemmer to the AMR concept identifier.[1] The intuition here is that, while the stem and part-of-speech tag may be useful in structuring the dependency tree in phase 2, the inflected form of each word can more accurately be determined after the dependency tree is finalized (i.e. after phase 2).

The NextEdge action is used to traverse the β

---

stack, alternating with MergeNode actions. The latter are applied when two AMR concepts should be combined to form a single content word, e.g. the negation concept "-" and concept "security" combining to form the word "insecurity". Additionally, during phase 1, certain AMR fragments with typified structure (e.g., `name`, `date-entity`, `time`) are collapsed into single nodes, and occurrences of `wiki` relations are removed. Consult stage c of Figure 1 for an example.

2.3 Phase 2

In phase 2, the transition actions aim to transform the structure of the tree. They are based on the actions used by Goodman et al. (2016a,b), with some alterations due to σ being initialized by traversing the tree from leaves to root, namely the Insert action is allowed to add a parent node above the current one, but limited to adding only leaf nodes as children. Similarly to Wang et al. (2015), but unlike Goodman et al. (2016a,b), the Reattach, SwapEdge, InsertParent, and InsertLeaf actions are parameterized with an edge label l_e. The NextNode action in phase 2 simply traverses σ.

To improve runtime, the Reattach, InsertParent, and InsertLeaf actions are allowed only to σ_0 nodes they were applied to in the training data, and will not be considered otherwise. Similarly, labels l_n, l_e are limited to those observed during training.

Finally, all actions preserve full connectivity of the tree, and any Reattach actions that would introduce a cycle are not considered. To avoid conflicts between actions, the following restrictions are enforced: a DeleteLeaf or ReplaceHead action cannot delete a previously inserted node, and vice-versa; a SwapEdge action cannot swap a previously swapped edge; a Reattach action cannot move a previously reattached or inserted node.

Stages d, e, f, and g of Figure 1 show the intermediate trees produced in phase 2. The double-bordered nodes denote nodes already visited via NextNode actions and thus no longer in σ.

2.4 Phase 3

During phase 3, InsertParent and InsertLeaf actions are used to add any closed-set function words (e.g. auxiliary verbs and articles) and punctuation that are missing from the dependency tree. The ModifyNode action is a variant of the NextNode action, which modifies (rather than replaces) any temporary labels with a suffix operation (i.e. "-s", "-ing") that, when combined with the stem of

Action name	β status	Parameters	Action outcome
Phase 1: Convert AMR concepts to content words.			
NextNode	empty	l_n	Set label of node σ_0 to l_n. Pop σ_0, and initialize β.
MergeNode	non-empty	l_n	Set label of node σ_0 to l_n. Pop β_0, and remove it from the tree. The children of β_0 are attached as children to σ_0.
NextEdge	non-empty	-	Pop β_0.
Phase 2: Modify the structure of the tree.			
InsertParent	-	l_n, l_e	Insert new node δ with label l_n as the parent of σ_0, via dependency label l_e. Insert δ into σ.
InsertLeaf	empty	l_n, l_e	Insert new node δ with label l_n as a child of **leaf node** σ_0, via dependency label l_e. Insert δ into σ.
NextEdge	non-empty	l_e	Set label of edge (σ_0, β_0) to l_e. Pop β_0.
SwapEdge	non-empty	l_e	Reverse edge (σ_0, β_0) to (β_0, σ_0), and set its label to l_e. β_0 becomes the parent of σ_0 and its subgraph, while the previous parent of σ_0 becomes the parent of β_0. Pop β_0.
ReplaceHead	non-empty	-	Pop σ_0, delete it from the graph. Attach β_0 as a child to the previous parent of σ_0. All other children of σ_0 become children of β_0. Insert β_0 at the head of σ, initialize β.
DeleteLeaf	empty	-	Pop **leaf node** σ_0, delete it from the graph. Initialize β.
Reattach	non-empty	p, l_e	Change edge (σ_0, β_0) to (p, β_0), where p is an existing node in the graph. p becomes the parent of β_0 and its subgraph. Pop β_0, and insert p to σ.
NextNode	empty	-	Pop σ_0, and initialize β.
Phase 3: Insert function words, punctuation, and determine the proper inflection of content words.			
InsertParent	-	l_n, l_e	Insert new node δ with label l_n as the parent of σ_0, via dependency label l_e. Insert δ into σ.
InsertLeaf	-	l_n, l_e	Insert new node δ with label l_n as a child of **leaf node** σ_0, via dependency label l_e. Insert δ into σ.
ModifyNode	-	m_n	Modify label of node σ_0 by m_n. Pop σ_0, and initialize β.

Table 1: Available actions per phase, for transition-based transformation of AMR graphs to parse trees.

the label, can properly inflect the word (e.g. modify "make_VB" with "-s" to construct "makes"). Stage h of Figure 1 shows the outcome of phase 3.

2.5 Expert policy

During training, an expert policy (also known as oracle) is constructed to determine which action should be performed given a particular state. By consulting the alignments between the concepts of each AMR graph and the words of the corresponding sentence in the training data, the expert policy detects any unaligned AMR concepts to be deleted by appropriate actions, as well as any unaligned words in the dependency tree to be inserted; other actions can be similarly inferred. During phases 1 and 2 we consider the simplified dependency tree, where function words have been removed, and in phase 3 we consider the full tree. The alignments were provided in the dataset using the system of Pourdamghani et al. (2014).

2.6 Post-processing

In post-processing, the dependency tree constructed by the transition needs to be linearized into a sentence. Tree linearization has most commonly been addressed by overgenerating word sequences and ranking (e.g. according to a trigram language model); however there has been a lot of recent research studying this topic (Filippova and Strube, 2009; He et al., 2009; Belz et al., 2011; Bohnet et al., 2011; Zhang, 2013; Futrell and Gibson, 2015). Our approach in this paper is to simply order the nodes in each subtree using a classifier, in effect creating ordered subphrases of the tree. The subtrees are thus incrementally ordered, in a bottom-up approach, and subsequently formed into a natural language sentence. Any date occurrences or numerical expressions that were normalized during pre-processing, are restored to their original form. It is also important to note again, that the structure of this approach allows it to take

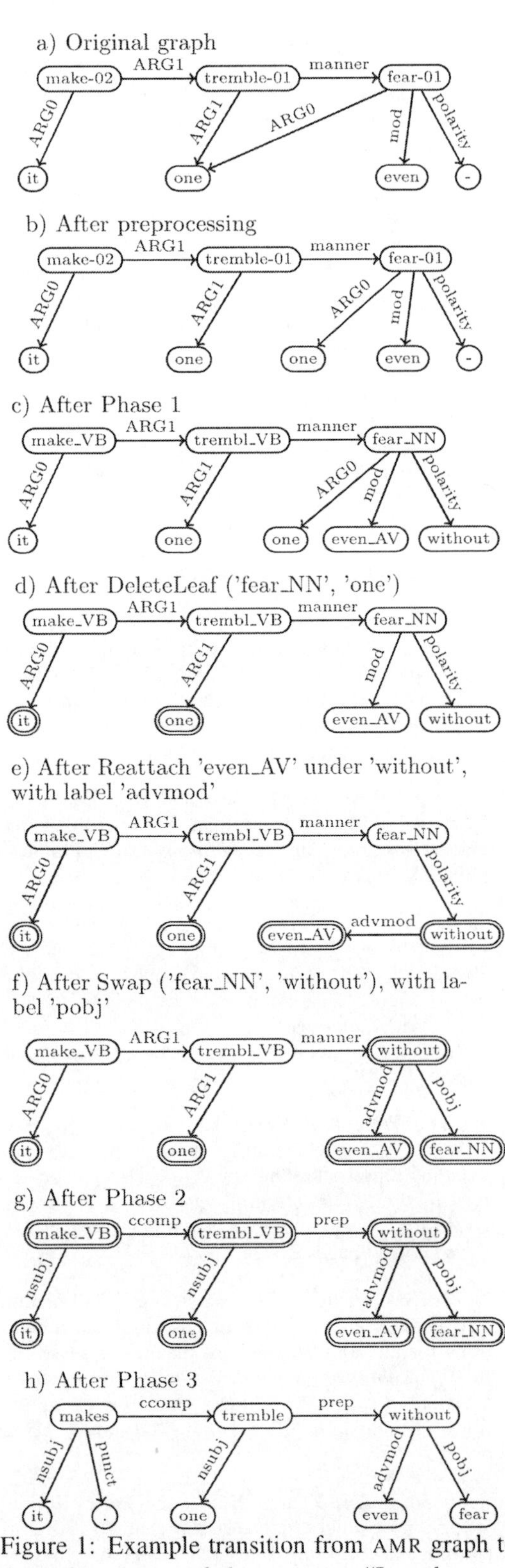

Figure 1: Example transition from AMR graph to dependency tree of the sentence "It makes one tremble even without fear."

advantage of additional parse-tree datasets to augment the training of the post-precessing step.

3 Results

We use the adaptive regularization of weight vectors (AROW) algorithm (Crammer et al., 2013) for all aforementioned classifiers. All the features we use are boolean indicators and similar to those proposed by Goodman et al. (2016a,b) and Wang et al. (2015). All classifiers were trained on the same corpus of AMRs released by LDC, and created as part of tehe DARPA DEFT program (LDC2016E25); we hope to augment the linearization's training with other dependency parse datasets in future work. To provide further speed improvement in testing time, we filter actions (conditioned on specific parameters) that appear infrequently in the training set.

Table 2 shows the ablation results of our system on the test set of the task. For Phase 1 we calculate the precision of the labels in the output tree compared to the labels of the dependency parse, while on phases 2 and 3 we calculate the unlabeled and labeled attachment scores. We also include the BLEU (Papineni et al., 2002) and Trueskill (Sakaguchi et al., 2014) scores achieved by our submitted run on the task's test data. In future work, we would like to examine the effect of error propagation from phase to phase.

	Precision	
Phase 1	0.45	
	UAS	LAS
Phase 2	0.16	0.11
Phase 3	0.08	0.06
	BLEU	Trueskill
Realization	3.32	−2.204

Table 2: Ablation results on the testing set.

4 Conclusion

We proposed a three-phase transition-based system for transforming an AMR graph into a dependency tree; the final sentence can then be acquired via a tree linearizer. Our results suggest there is much room for improvement; we hope to continuously refine the proposed action space and expert policy, and develop and apply a more complex linearizer to the constructed parse trees. Finally, we believe that by using imitation learning algorithms, the transition sequences could be improved to generalize better to unseen data.

Acknowledgements

This research is supported by the EPSRC grant Diligent (EP/M005429/1).

References

Laura Banarescu, Claire Bonial, Shu Cai, Madalina Georgescu, Kira Griffitt, Ulf Hermjakob, Kevin Knight, Philipp Koehn, Martha Palmer, and Nathan Schneider. 2013. Abstract meaning representation for sembanking. In *Proceedings of the 7th Linguistic Annotation Workshop and Interoperability with Discourse*. Association for Computational Linguistics, Sofia, Bulgaria, pages 178–186.

Anja Belz, Michael White, Dominic Espinosa, Eric Kow, Deirdre Hogan, and Amanda Stent. 2011. The first surface realisation shared task: Overview and evaluation results. In *Proceedings of the 13th European Workshop on Natural Language Generation*. Association for Computational Linguistics, Stroudsburg, PA, USA, ENLG '11, pages 217–226.

Bernd Bohnet, Simon Mille, Benoît Favre, and Leo Wanner. 2011. StuMaBa : From deep representation to surface. In *ENLG 2011 - Proceedings of the 13th European Workshop on Natural Language Generation, 28-30 September 2011, Nancy, France.* pages 232–235.

Koby Crammer, Alex Kulesza, and Mark Dredze. 2013. Adaptive regularization of weight vectors. *Machine Learning* 91:155–187.

Katja Filippova and Michael Strube. 2009. Tree linearization in english: Improving language model based approaches. In *Proceedings of Human Language Technologies: The 2009 Annual Conference of the North American Chapter of the Association for Computational Linguistics, Companion Volume: Short Papers*. Association for Computational Linguistics, Stroudsburg, PA, USA, NAACL-Short '09, pages 225–228.

Jeffrey Flanigan, Chris Dyer, Noah A. Smith, and Jaime G. Carbonell. 2016. Generation from abstract meaning representation using tree transducers. In *NAACL HLT 2016, The 2016 Conference of the North American Chapter of the Association for Computational Linguistics: Human Language Technologies, San Diego California, USA, June 12-17, 2016*. pages 731–739.

Richard Futrell and Edward Gibson. 2015. Experiments with generative models for dependency tree linearization. In *Proceedings of the 2015 Conference on Empirical Methods in Natural Language Processing, EMNLP 2015, Lisbon, Portugal, September 17-21, 2015*. pages 1978–1983.

James Goodman, Andreas Vlachos, and Jason Naradowsky. 2016a. Noise reduction and targeted exploration in imitation learning for abstract meaning representation parsing. In *Proceedings of the 54th Annual Meeting of the Association for Computational Linguistics (Volume 1: Long Papers)*. Association for Computational Linguistics, Berlin, Germany, pages 1–11.

James Goodman, Andreas Vlachos, and Jason Naradowsky. 2016b. Ucl+sheffield at semeval-2016 task 8: Imitation learning for amr parsing with an alpha-bound. In *Proceedings of the 10th International Workshop on Semantic Evaluation (SemEval-2016)*. Association for Computational Linguistics, San Diego, California, pages 1167–1172.

Wei He, Haifeng Wang, Yuqing Guo, and Ting Liu. 2009. Dependency based chinese sentence realization. In *Proceedings of the Joint Conference of the 47th Annual Meeting of the ACL and the 4th International Joint Conference on Natural Language Processing of the AFNLP: Volume 2 - Volume 2*. Association for Computational Linguistics, Stroudsburg, PA, USA, ACL '09, pages 809–816.

Matthew Honnibal and Mark Johnson. 2015. An improved non-monotonic transition system for dependency parsing. In *Proceedings of the 2015 Conference on Empirical Methods in Natural Language Processing*. Association for Computational Linguistics, Lisbon, Portugal, pages 1373–1378.

K. Papineni, S. Roukos, T. Ward, and W. J. Zhu. 2002. BLEU: a method for automatic evaluation of machine translation. In *Proceedings of ACL*. Philadelphia, PA, pages 311–318.

Nima Pourdamghani, Yang Gao, Ulf Hermjakob, and Kevin Knight. 2014. Aligning english strings with abstract meaning representation graphs. In *Proceedings of the 2014 Conference on Empirical Methods in Natural Language Processing (EMNLP)*. Association for Computational Linguistics, Doha, Qatar, pages 425–429.

Nima Pourdamghani, Kevin Knight, and Ulf Hermjakob. 2016. Generating english from abstract meaning representations. In *INLG 2016 - Proceedings of the Ninth International Natural Language Generation Conference, September 5-8, 2016, Edinburgh, UK*. pages 21–25.

Keisuke Sakaguchi, Matt Post, and Benjamin Van Durme. 2014. Efficient elicitation of annotations for human evaluation of machine translation. In *Proceedings of the Ninth Workshop on Statistical Machine Translation*. Association for Computational Linguistics, Baltimore, Maryland, USA, pages 1–11.

Linfeng Song, Yue Zhang, Xiaochang Peng, Zhiguo Wang, and Daniel Gildea. 2016. Amr-to-text generation as a traveling salesman problem. In *Proceedings of the 2016 Conference on Empirical Methods in Natural Language Processing, EMNLP 2016, Austin, Texas, USA, November 1-4, 2016*. pages 2084–2089.

Chuan Wang, Nianwen Xue, and Sameer Pradhan. 2015. A transition-based algorithm for AMR parsing. In *NAACL HLT 2015, The 2015 Conference of the North American Chapter of the Association for Computational Linguistics: Human Language Technologies, Denver, Colorado, USA, May 31 - June 5, 2015*. pages 366–375.

Yue Zhang. 2013. Partial-tree linearization: Generalized word ordering for text synthesis. In *IJCAI 2013, Proceedings of the 23rd International Joint Conference on Artificial Intelligence, Beijing, China, August 3-9, 2013*. pages 2232–2238.

The AI2 system at SemEval-2017 Task 10 (ScienceIE): semi-supervised end-to-end entity and relation extraction

Waleed Ammar   Matthew E. Peters   Chandra Bhagavatula   Russell Power
Allen Institute for Artificial Intelligence, Seattle, WA, USA
{waleeda,matthewp,chandrab,russellp}@allenai.org

Abstract

This paper describes our submission for the ScienceIE shared task (SemEval-2017 Task 10) on entity and relation extraction from scientific papers. Our model is based on the end-to-end relation extraction model of Miwa and Bansal (2016) with several enhancements such as semi-supervised learning via neural language models, character-level encoding, gazetteers extracted from existing knowledge bases, and model ensembles. Our official submission ranked first in end-to-end entity and relation extraction (scenario 1), and second in the relation-only extraction (scenario 3).

1   Task overview

The ScienceIE shared task (Augenstein et al., 2017) focuses on information extraction from scientific papers. In the end-to-end evaluation scenario, participants were provided with a paragraph and asked to extract typed entities (Task, Material or Process) and relations (Hyponym-of or Synonym-of) in different scientific domains.

Running example.   Consider the following input sentence: *"Here, we consider a radical pair in which the first electron spin is devoid of hyperfine interactions, while the second electron spin interacts isotropically with one spin-1 nucleus, e.g. nitrogen."*   The provided human labeled entity annotations for this sentence include: *"electron spin"* of type Process, *"spin-1 nucleus"* of type Material, and *"nitrogen"* of type Material. The only positive relation annotation labeled for this sentence is: Hyponym-of(*"nitrogen"*, *"spin-1 nucleus"*). We will use this example

throughout the paper to illustrate various parts of our system (see Fig. 1).

2   System description

In this section, we describe the components in our system.

Text preprocessing.   We process the input text using spaCy[1] which provides sentence segmentation, tokenization, part-of-speech (POS) tagging and labeled dependency parsing.

Label encoding.   We use the BILOU tagging scheme to encode the annotations for each of the three entity types. For a given entity type, each token in a sentence is labeled with: O if it does not belong to any entity, U if it belongs to a single-token entity, B if it is the beginning of a multi-word entity, L if it is the end of a multi-word entity, and I if it is inside a multi-word entity. In order to allow the same token to participate in multiple entities of different types, each token is assigned three labels (one for each entity type).[2]

The labeled data specify two kinds of relations: a directional relation (Hyponym-of) and an undirectional relation (Synonym-of). In our system, we automatically convert Hyponym-of(e2,e1) into a new label Hypernym-of(e1,e2) when e2 follows e1 in the sentence. We generate the label No-relation(e1,e2) as needed in order to have a label for each pair (e1, e2) where e1 precedes e2 in a sentence. This encoding allows us to only consider entity pairs in the order in which they appear in the sentence. In other

---

[1] https://spacy.io/

[2] In a small number of cases, the human labels specified at the character level did not coincide with our tokenization. In these cases we used the human annotations to override the tokenization. When two entity annotations of the same entity type overlap, we only keep the longer one.

Proceedings of the 11th International Workshop on Semantic Evaluations (SemEval-2017), pages 592–596,
Vancouver, Canada, August 3 - 4, 2017. ©2017 Association for Computational Linguistics

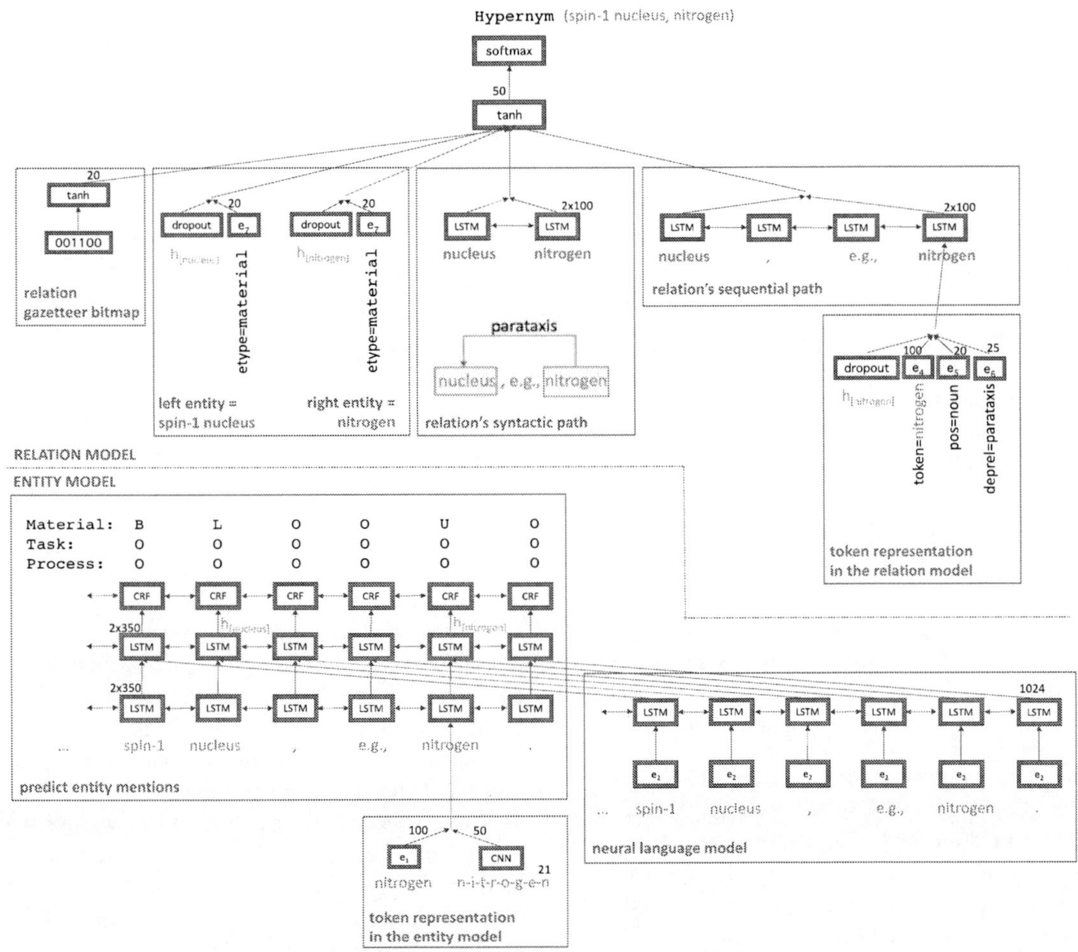

Figure 1: Schematic diagram of the end-to-end model for entity and relation extraction. **Bottom part:** the main components of the entity model (see §2.1 for details). **Top part:** the main components of the relation model (see §2.2 for details).

words, all relations (including `No-relation` are modeled as directional relations. In a post-processing step, `Hypernym-of(e1,e2)` relations are deterministically converted to `Hyponym-of(e2,e1)` relations.

2.1 Entity model

In this section, we describe the entity model, which is illustrated in the bottom part of Fig. 1. Given the token sequence $(t_1, t_2, \ldots, t_N)$, this model predicts a sequence of `BILOU` labels for each entity type.

Token representation. We first form a token representation, $\mathbf{x}_k = [\mathbf{c}_k; \mathbf{w}_k]$, by concatenating a character based representation $\mathbf{c}_k$ with a token embedding $\mathbf{w}_k$. The character representation, $\mathbf{c}_k$, is parameterized as a convolutional neutral network (CNN) with a filter width of 3 characters.[3] The token embeddings, $\mathbf{w}_k$, are initialized using pre-trained GloVe word embeddings (Pennington et al., 2014) and fine tuned during training. This component is illustrated at the bottom of Fig. 1.

Neural language model. In addition to using unlabeled data to learn feature representations of individual word types, we also learn feature representations of words in a particular context using neural language models. Following Józefowicz

---

[3]The filter width was decided based on preliminary experiments on the development set.

et al. (2016), we feed the output of the embedding layer through one or two layers of LSTMs (Hochreiter and Schmidhuber, 1997) to embed the history $(t_1, t_2, \ldots, t_k)$ into a fixed dimensional vector $\overrightarrow{\mathbf{h}}_k^{LM}$, the *forward LM embedding* of the token at position k. While training the parameters of the language model, a softmax layer over words in the vocabulary is used to predict the probability of token t_{k+1}.

In order to capture future context in the LM embeddings, we also use a *backward LM embedding* $\overleftarrow{\mathbf{h}}_k^{LM}$ which predicts the previous token t_{k-1} given the following tokens $(t_k, t_{k+1}, \ldots, t_N)$. In our formulation, the forward and backward LMs are independent, without any shared parameters.

In our final system, after pre-training the forward and backward LMs separately, we remove the top layer softmax and concatenate the forward and backward LM embeddings to form bidirectional LM embeddings, i.e., $\mathbf{h}_k^{LM} = [\overrightarrow{\mathbf{h}}_k^{LM}; \overleftarrow{\mathbf{h}}_k^{LM}]$, and use it in the sequence tagging model, which is explained next. This component is illustrated at the bottom right corner of Fig. 1.

Sequence tagging model. We employ two layers of bidirectional LSTMs, followed by a conditional random field (CRF) layer to predict entity mentions of each type (see Fig. 1). For each token position, k, the hidden state of the first bidirectional LSTM layer is formed by concatenating the hidden states from the forward and backward LSTMs. We also concatenate the LM embeddings $\mathbf{h}^{LM}$ with the output from the first LSTM layer before feeding it into the second LSTM layer.

The output of the second LSTM layer $\mathbf{h}_k$ is used to predict a score for each possible tag. To predict token tags from $\mathbf{h}_k$ we use a dense layer for each entity type and compute the conditional random field (CRF) loss (Lafferty et al., 2001) using the forward-backward algorithm at training time, and using the Viterbi algorithm to find the most likely tag sequence at test time, similar to Collobert et al. (2011). In this layer, we use different parameters for each entity type in order to allow for overlapping entities of different types.

Entity gazetteer features. We use lists of scientific terms collected from the web[4] and several topics from freebase,[5] and add them as features in the sequence tagging model. Given an input token sequence, we found all phrases which match one or more of the gazetteers. We encode this information at the token level using a binary feature for each gazetteer (i.e., the number of binary features $= N \times$ the number of gazetteers). The binary features for each token feeds into a dense `tanh` layer which is concatenated to the output of the top LSTM layer. This component was omitted from Fig. 1 to simplify the exposition.

2.2 Relation model

In this subsection, we describe the relation model, which is illustrated in the top part of Fig. 1. Given a pair of entity mention spans and their entity types, this model predicts the relation between the two mentions by feeding a context-sensitive representation of the relation into a dense tanh layer, followed by a softmax layer to predict the label.

Left and right entities. We represent each of the left and right entities by concatenating an embedding of its entity type with a hidden representation based on the sequence tagging model.

Since many entity mentions consist of multiple tokens, we need to compress their representations to obtain a fixed size encoding. First, we use the dependency tree to identify the syntactic head of the each entity mention. If none of the words in the entity mention qualifies as a direct or indirect head of all other words in the entity mention, we use the last word in the mention, which is often the head in English. For example, 'nucleus' is the head of the entity mention "spin-1 nucleus" in our running example, because there is a direct dependency where 'nucleus' is the head of 'spin-1' with relation type 'compound'. After identifying the head word in an entity mention, we then use the input to the CRF layer from the sequence tagging model at this position, feed it into a dropout layer, and concatenate it with the entity type embedding. This component is second to the left in the top part of Fig. 1.

Syntactic and sequential path. We use a bidirectional LSTM layer to encode the shortest path in a dependency tree between the heads of the left and right entities. The input to the LSTM layer at each node in the dependency path concatenates four components: a context-sensitive embedding

---

[4]We thank Peter Turney for providing this list.

[5]The freebase topics we used are 'dissertation', 'material', 'scholarly work', 'task', 'chemical element', 'competitive space', 'invention', 'drug', 'project_focus', 'literature_subject', 'patent', 'project', 'field_of_study' and 'industry'.

of the word (the input to the CRF layer followed by a dropout layer), a context-insensitive embedding of the word, an embedding of the POS tag, and an embedding of the dependency relation between this node and its direct head.

In addition to encoding the dependency path between the two entities, we also found it useful to encode the sequential path (i.e., the tokens between the two heads in the sentence). We again use a bidirectional LSTM layer and use the same four components to represent the LSTM input at each position in the sequential path. The hidden states at both ends of the syntactic and sequential path are then concatenated (simple concatenation) with the left and right entity representations. This component is illustrated in the right most three boxes in the top part of Fig. 1.

Relation gazetteer features. We use two publicly available knowledge bases (Wikipedia and freebase) to derive gazetteer-like features in the relation model. We also encode three features as implicit gazetteers to indicate whether one of the two entities is an acronym, a suffix, or an exact copy of the other. For a given entity pair, we compute input binary features which indicate whether the entity pair matches each gazetteer. The input binary features feed into a dense layer as illustrated in the left-most box in the top part of Fig. 1.

2.3 Training

Although we combine the entity model and the relation model at test time, each model is trained separately.[6] Joint training adds some practical complexities, but may result in better results.

Hyperparameters. We use performance on development set to guide our selection of hyperparameters. The numbers on the arrows in Fig. 1 correspond to the size of the hidden layers (or the number of filters in the CNN module) in the best performing single model.

We initialize the word embeddings using GloVe (Pennington et al., 2014). For the pre-trained language models, we use the single best forward model from Józefowicz et al. (2016) with two LSTM layers, and a backward LM with one LSTM layer with 2048 hidden units and a 512 dimension projection. These models have test set perplex-

ity of 30.0 and 47.7 on the 1B Word Benchmark (Chelba et al., 2014), respectively.

We use the Adam optimizer (Kingma and Ba, 2014) with learning rate of 0.001 and 0.0003 and gradient norms clipped at 5.0 and 1.0 for the entity and relation models, respectively. We use early stopping by monitoring development set performance.

Model	F_1
Our best model without language model	49.9
Our best model with language model	54.1
Our 15-model ensemble	55.2

Table 1: Development set entity only F_1 comparison.

Team	End-to-end	Entities	Relations
Ours	**0.43**	0.55	**0.28**
Team_24	0.42	**0.56**	-
Team_21	0.38	0.50	0.21
Team_19	0.37	0.51	0.19
Team_14	0.33	0.47	0.20

Table 2: Final test set F_1 for top five teams in Scenario 1, end-to-end extraction.

Ensembles. While tuning the hyperparameters of the models, we save the models with the best results on a development set and use them to create an ensemble. The entity model ensemble averages the label predictions at each position, while the relation model ensemble only predicts a positive relation if 50% of the individual models predict the same relation. Our final submission uses an ensemble of 15 entity models and 8 relation models.

Differences between Scenario 1 and Scenario 3. While training the relation model in Scenario 1, we use both the gold entities and the entities predicted by the entity model to generate candidate relations. In Scenario 3, only gold entities are used to generate candidate relations for training.

To make predictions on the test set, only entities predicted by the entity model were used to generate candidate relations in Scenario 1. In Scenario 3, only gold entities were used to generate candidate relations for the test set.

---

[6]All parameters (including word and character embeddings) in each model are trained. None of the parameters are fixed.

3 Results

We compare three variants of our entity extraction model on the development set in Table 1. Adding a bidirectional LM to our sequence tagging model amounts to an improvement of 4.2 F_1, while using an ensemble of 15 models amounts to a further improvement of 1.1 F_1.

In Scenario 1, our submission ranked first with F_1 of 0.43%, second in the entity only subtask (0.55% F_1) and first in the relation only subtask for end-to-end extraction (0.28% F_1), as shown in Table 2. In Scenario 3, our submission ranked second with 0.54% F_1.

Acknowledgements

We thank the shared task organizers for their efforts and the anonymous reviewers for their helpful comments.

References

Isabelle Augenstein, Mrinal Kanti Das, Sebastian Riedel, Lakshmi Nair Vikraman, and Andrew McCallum. 2017. SemEval 2017 Task 10: ScienceIE - Extracting Keyphrases and Relations from Scientific Publications. In *Proceedings of the International Workshop on Semantic Evaluation*. Association for Computational Linguistics, Vancouver, Canada.

Ciprian Chelba, Tomas Mikolov, Mike Schuster, Qi Ge, Thorsten Brants, and Phillipp Koehn. 2014. One billion word benchmark for measuring progress in statistical language modeling. *CoRR* abs/1312.3005.

Ronan Collobert, Jason Weston, Léon Bottou, Michael Karlen, Koray Kavukcuoglu, and Pavel P. Kuksa. 2011. Natural language processing (almost) from scratch. In *JMLR*.

Sepp Hochreiter and Jürgen Schmidhuber. 1997. Long short-term memory. *Neural Computation* 9:1735–1780.

Rafal Józefowicz, Oriol Vinyals, Mike Schuster, Noam Shazeer, and Yonghui Wu. 2016. Exploring the limits of language modeling. *CoRR* abs/1602.02410.

Diederik P. Kingma and Jimmy Ba. 2014. Adam: A method for stochastic optimization. *CoRR* abs/1412.6980.

John D. Lafferty, Andrew McCallum, and Fernando Pereira. 2001. Conditional random fields: Probabilistic models for segmenting and labeling sequence data. In *ICML*.

Makoto Miwa and Mohit Bansal. 2016. End-to-end relation extraction using lstms on sequences and tree structures. In *ACL*.

Jeffrey Pennington, Richard Socher, and Christopher D. Manning. 2014. Glove: Global vectors for word representation. In *EMNLP*.

LIMSI-COT at SemEval-2017 Task 12: Neural Architecture for Temporal Information Extraction from Clinical Narratives

Julien Tourille[1,2,3], Olivier Ferret[4], Xavier Tannier[1,2,3], Aurélie Névéol[1,3]

[1] LIMSI, CNRS
[2] Univ. Paris-Sud
[3] Université Paris-Saclay
[4] CEA, LIST, Gif-sur-Yvette, F-91191 France.
`firstname.lastname@limsi.fr, olivier.ferret@cea.fr`

Abstract

In this paper we present our participation to SemEval 2017 Task 12. We used a neural network based approach for entity and temporal relation extraction, and experimented with two domain adaptation strategies. We achieved competitive performance for both tasks.

1 Introduction

SemEval 2017 Task 12 offers 6 subtasks addressing medical event recognition and temporal reasoning in the clinical domain using the THYME corpus (Styler IV et al., 2014). Similarly to the two previous editions of the challenge (Bethard et al., 2015, 2016), the first group of subtasks concerns medical event (EVENT) and temporal expression (TIMEX3) extraction from raw text. In a second group of subtasks, participants are challenged to extract containment (CONTAINS) relations between EVENT and/or TIMEX3 as well as Document Creation Time (DCT) relations between EVENT entities and documents in which they are embedded. The novelty of the 2017 edition lies in the difference of domains between train and test corpora. More details about the task and the definition of each subtask can be found in Bethard et al. (2017).

The task has been offered by SemEval over the past two years. Concerning the first group of subtasks, different approaches have been implemented by the participants including Conditional Random Fields (CRF) (AAl Abdulsalam et al., 2016; Caselli and Morante, 2016; Chikka, 2016; Cohan et al., 2016; Grouin and Moriceau, 2016; Hansart et al., 2016) and deep learning models (Fries, 2016; Chikka, 2016; Li and Huang, 2016). Similarly, CRF and neural networks models have been used for the second group of subtasks (AAl Abdulsalam et al., 2016; Cohan et al.,

2016; Lee et al., 2016). Other approaches include Support Vector Machines (SVM) (AAl Abdulsalam et al., 2016; Tourille et al., 2016).

2 Methodology

The EVENT and TIMEX3 entity extraction subtasks can be seen as two sequence labeling problems where each token of a given sentence is assigned a label. Entities can spread over several tokens and therefore, we used the IOB format (Inside, Outside, Beginning) for label representation. Each token can be at the beginning of an entity (B), inside an entity (I) or outside (O). EVENT entities are characterized by a *type* attribute that we used in our IOB scheme resulting in 7 possible labels. Similarly, TIMEX3 entities are characterized by a *class* attribute that we used in our IOB scheme resulting in 13 possible labels.

The container relation extraction task can be cast as a 3-class classification problem. For each combination E1 – E2 of EVENT and/or TIMEX3 from left to right, three cases are possible:

- E1 temporally *contains* E2,
- E1 *is* temporally *contained* by E2,
- there is no relation between E1 and E2.

Intra- and inter-sentence relation detection can be seen as two different tasks with specific features. Intra-sentence relations can benefit from intra-sentential clues such as adverbs (e.g. *during*) or pronouns (e.g. *which*) which are not available at the inter-sentence level. Furthermore, past work on the topic seems to indicate that this differentiation improves overall performance (Tourille et al., 2016). We have adopted this approach by building two separate classifiers, one for intra-sentence relations and one for inter-sentence relations.

If we were to consider all combinations of entities within documents for inter-sentence relations, it would result in a very large training corpus with very few positive examples. In order to cope with this issue, we limit our experiments to inter-

597

Proceedings of the 11th International Workshop on Semantic Evaluations (SemEval-2017), pages 597–602,
Vancouver, Canada, August 3 - 4, 2017. ©2017 Association for Computational Linguistics

sentence relations that do not span over more than three sentences. By doing so, we obtain a manageable training corpus size with less unbalanced classes while keeping a good coverage.

3 Corpus Preprocessing

We preprocessed the corpus using cTAKES 3.2.2 (Savova et al., 2010), an open-source natural language processing system for the extraction of information from electronic health records. We extracted sentence and token boundaries, as well as token types and semantic types of the entities that have a span overlap with a least one gold standard EVENT entity of the THYME corpus. This information was added to the set of gold standard attributes available for EVENT entities in the corpus.

We also preprocessed the corpus using HeidelTime 2.2.1 (Strötgen and Gertz, 2015), a multilingual domain-sensitive temporal tagger, and used the results to further extend our feature set.

4 Models

4.1 Entity Extraction

Our approach relies on Long Short-Term Memory Networks (LSTMs) (Hochreiter and Schmidhuber, 1997). The architecture of our model is presented in Figure 1. For a given sequence of tokens, represented as vectors, we compute representations of left and right contexts of the sequence at every token. These representations are computed using two LSTMs (forward and backward LSTM in figure 1). Then these representations are concatenated and linearly projected to a n-dimensional vector representing the number of categories. Finally, as Huang et al. (2015), we add a CRF layer to take into account the previous label during prediction. Following preliminary experiments, we built one specific classifier for each entity type (EVENT or TIMEX3).

4.2 Event Attribute and Document Creation Time Relation Extraction

We treated each EVENT attribute (*ContextualModality*, *Degree*, *Polarity*) extraction subtask as a supervised classification problem. We built a common architecture for all attributes based on a linear SVM. Concerning DCT relation extraction subtask, we used the same architecture. We trained a separate classifier for each of the four subtasks based on lexical, contextual and structural features extracted from the documents:

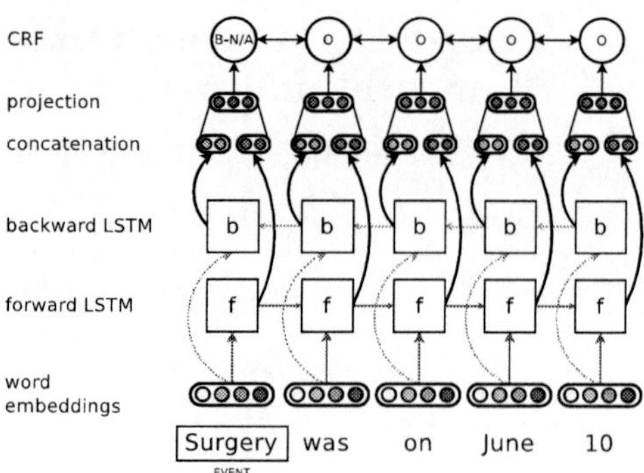

Figure 1: Neural model for EVENT extraction.

- EVENT type attribute,
- EVENT plain lexical form,
- EVENT position within the document,
- POS tags of the verbs within the right and left contexts of the considered entity,
- EVENT POS tag,
- type or class of the other entities that are present within the left and right contexts,
- token unigrams and bigrams within a window around the entity.

4.3 Temporal Relation Extraction

Similarly to our entity extraction approach, we built a system based on LSTMs for CONTAINS relation extraction. The architecture of our model is presented in Figure 2. For a given sequence of tokens between two entities (EVENT and/or TIMEX3), we compute a representation by scanning the sequence from left to right (forward LSTM in Figure 2). As LSTMs tend to be biased toward the most recent inputs, this model is biased toward the second entity of each pair processed by the network. To counteract this effect, we compute the reverse representation with an LSTM reading the sequence from right to left (backward LSTM in Figure 2). The two final states are then concatenated and linearly transformed into a 3-dimensional vector representing the number of categories (concatenation and projection in figure 2). Finally, a softmax function is applied.

4.4 Input Word Embeddings

Input vectors are built differently depending on the subtask. For the entity extraction subtask, vectors representing tokens are built by concatenating a character-based embedding and a word embedding. Whether we are dealing with EVENT or TIMEX3 entities, we add one embedding per

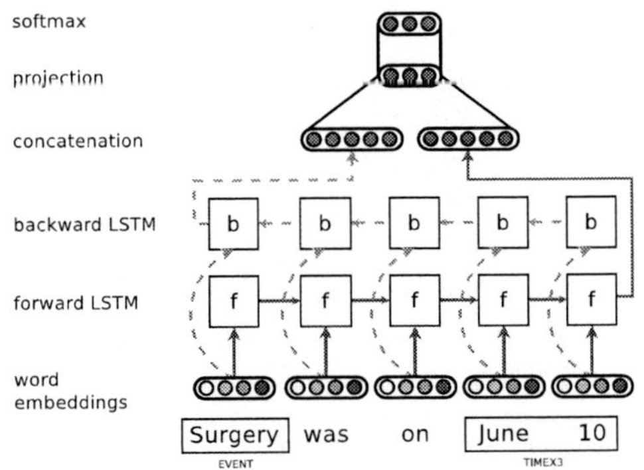

Figure 2: Neural architecture for `CONTAINS` relation extraction.

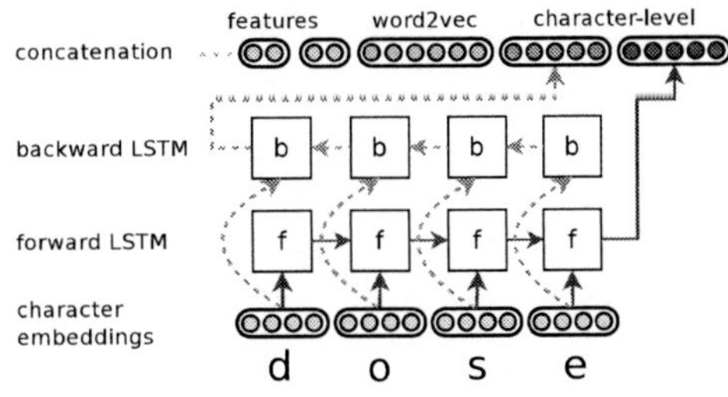

Figure 3: Model for character-based embeddings.

cTAKES attribute or one embedding representing the `TIMEX3` *class* as detected by HeidelTime. Concerning the containment relation subtask, input vectors are built by concatenating a character-based embedding, a word embedding, one embedding per Gold Standard attribute and one embedding for the type of DCT relations (*before ...*).

An overview of the embedding computation is presented in Figure 3. Following Lample et al. (2016), the character-based representation is constructed with a Bi-LSTM[1]. First, a random embedding is generated for every character in the training corpus. Token characters are then processed with a forward and backward LSTM architecture similar to the one of our entity extraction model. The final character-based representation results from the concatenation of the forward and backward representations. Since medical terms often include prefixes and suffixes derived from ancient Greek and classical Latin (Namer and Zweigenbaum, 2004), we believe that both entity and containment relation extractions can particularly benefit from this character-based representation of tokens for terms that have not been seen during training or that don't have a pretrained word embedding.

We use pretrained word embeddings computed with *word2vec* (Mikolov et al., 2013)[2] on the Mimic 3 corpus (Johnson et al., 2016) and the colon cancer part of the THYME corpus. In order to account for unknown tokens during the test phase, we train a special embedding UNK by replacing randomly some singletons with the UNK embedding (probability of replacement = 0.5). In

the inter-sentence relation classifier, we introduce a specific token for identifying sentence breaks. This token is composed of one distinctive character and it is associated to a specific word embedding. Similarly to the character embeddings, we randomly initialize one embedding per token attribute value, with an embedding size of 4. All these embeddings are then concatenated.

4.5 Network Training

We implemented the two neural networks models described in the previous section using Tensor-Flow 0.12 (Abadi et al., 2015). We trained our networks with mini-batch Stochastic Gradient Descent using Adam (Kingma and Ba, 2014)[3]. We use dropout training to avoid overfitting. We apply dropout on input embeddings with a rate of 0.5.

The optimization of hyperparameters for the attribute and DCT relation extraction subtasks was addressed by using a Tree-structured Parzen Estimator approach (Bergstra et al., 2011) and applied to the hyperparameter C of the linear SVM, the lookup window around entities and the percentile of features to keep. For the latter we used the ANOVA F-value as selection criterion.

5 Domain Adaptation Strategies

We implemented two strategies for domain adaptation during the first phase. In the first strategy, we blocked further training of the pretrained word embeddings during network training. Since a large number of medical events mentioned in the test set are not seen during training, we believe that our system should rely on untuned word embeddings to make its prediction.

In the second strategy we randomly replaced tokens that composed EVENT entities by the *unknown* token[4]. Given the fact that our word em-

---

[1] Embedding size = 8; hidden layer size = 25.

[2] Parameters used during computation: algorithm = CBOW; min-count = 4; vector size = 100; window = 8.

[3] Learning rate = 0.001; hidden layer sizes = 256.

[4] Replacement probability = 0.2.

| | Phase 1 | | | | | | Phase 2 | | | | | |
| | STATIC | | | REPLACE | | | ALL | | | 30-30 | | |
	P	R	F1	P	R	F1	P	R	F1	P	R	F1
EVENT Span	.622	.843	**.716**	.606	.841	.705	.691	.854	**.764**	.660	.865	.749
EVENT Modality	.553	.749	**.636**	.537	.745	.624	.628	.775	**.694**	.598	.784	.679
EVENT Degree	.616	.834	**.708**	.600	.831	.697	.682	.843	**.754**	.652	.854	.739
EVENT Polarity	.603	.816	**.693**	.588	.815	.683	.676	.835	**.747**	.644	.844	.731
EVENT Type	.608	.823	**.699**	.592	.821	.688	.675	.834	**.746**	.641	.841	.728
EVENT All attributes	.374	.507	**.431**	.365	.507	.425	.468	.578	**.517**	.440	.577	.500
TIMEX3 Span	.421	.660	.514	.421	.660	.514	.510	.671	**.579**	.452	.621	.523
TIMEX3 Class	.401	.630	.490	.401	.630	.490	.487	.641	**.553**	.430	.591	.498
DCT Relation	.443	.599	**.509**	.436	.604	.506	.535	.661	**.591**	.511	.670	.580
CONTAINS	.280	.396	**.328**	.264	.408	.320	.244	.438	**.316**	.211	.422	.282

Table 1: Results obtained by our system across our four runs. We report Precision (P), Recall (R) and F1-measure (F1). The best F1 performance in each phase is bolded.

beddings are pretrained on the Mimic 3 corpus and on the colon cancer part of the THYME corpus, a number of tokens (and therefore EVENTs) of the test part of the corpus may not have a specific word embedding. By replacing randomly EVENT token, we force our networks to look at other contextual clues within the sentence. Both strategies were applied on EVENT entity and CONTAINS relation extraction subtasks.

Phase 2 was addressed by implementing two strategies. In the first one, we mixed the 30 texts about brain cancer to the 591 texts about colon cancer. In the second one, we randomly chose 30 texts related to colon cancer and combined them to the 30 texts about brain cancer, resulting in a balanced training corpus. Both strategies were applied on EVENT, TIMEX3 and CONTAINS extraction subtasks.

6   Results and Discussion

Results for our four runs are presented in Table 1. The two strategies implemented for Phase 1 yield similar results (0.01 difference in F1-measure at most), with only a very slight advantage for the strategy blocking further training of the word embeddings (STATIC strategy in the table). In Phase 2, the two strategies also yield close results (0.04 difference in F1-measure) for the EVENT entity extraction and temporal relation subtasks. However, the strategy consisting in taking all available annotations (ALL strategy in the table) outperforms slightly the training on a balanced corpus, especially for the extraction of CON-TAINS relations. The same strategy seems to perform much better for the TIMEX3 entity ex-traction subtask where the gap in F1-measure reaches 0.06. This superiority agrees the general observation that the size of the training corpus has often a greater impact on results than its strict matching with the target domain. Overall, in both phases and for all strategies, results are competi-tive for entity and temporal relation extraction.

The performance obtained by our system re-lies in part on corpus tayloring. Some sections of the test corpus related to *medication* and *diet* are not to be annotated according to the annotation guidelines. However, these sections are not for-mally delimited within the documents. To avoid annotating them during test time, we developed a semi-automatic approach for detecting these sec-tions and put them aside.

Other aspects linked to the corpus limit the per-formance. Some sections should not be annotated as they are duplicate of other sections found in the corpus as a whole. However, we have no infor-mation on how to formally identify these sections. Furthermore, a number of temporal expressions are annotated as SECTIONTIME or DOCTIME entities. Detecting TIMEX3 entities instead de-creases the precision of our model.

In future work, we plan to explore additional strategies. For instance, adding a feature predict-ing whether a given EVENT entity is a container or not has proved useful in previous work (Tourille et al., 2016), but was not implemented in our sys-tem due to time constraints.

Acknowledgements   This work was supported by Labex Digicosme, operated by the Foundation for Scientific Cooperation (FSC) Paris-Saclay, un-der grant CÔT.

References

Abdulrahman AAl Abdulsalam, Sumithra Velupillai, and Stephane Meystre. 2016. UtahBMI at SemEval-2016 Task 12: Extracting Temporal Information from Clinical Text. In *Proceedings of the 10th International Workshop on Semantic Evaluation (SemEval-2016)*. Association for Computational Linguistics, San Diego, California, pages 1256–1262.

Martín Abadi, Ashish Agarwal, Paul Barham, Eugene Brevdo, Zhifeng Chen, Craig Citro, Greg S. Corrado, Andy Davis, Jeffrey Dean, Matthieu Devin, Sanjay Ghemawat, Ian Goodfellow, Andrew Harp, Geoffrey Irving, Michael Isard, Yangqing Jia, Rafal Jozefowicz, Lukasz Kaiser, Manjunath Kudlur, Josh Levenberg, Dan Mané, Rajat Monga, Sherry Moore, Derek Murray, Chris Olah, Mike Schuster, Jonathon Shlens, Benoit Steiner, Ilya Sutskever, Kunal Talwar, Paul Tucker, Vincent Vanhoucke, Vijay Vasudevan, Fernanda Viégas, Oriol Vinyals, Pete Warden, Martin Wattenberg, Martin Wicke, Yuan Yu, and Xiaoqiang Zheng. 2015. TensorFlow: Large-Scale Machine Learning on Heterogeneous Systems. Software available from tensorflow.org.

James S. Bergstra, Rémi Bardenet, Yoshua Bengio, and Balázs Kégl. 2011. Algorithms for Hyper-Parameter Optimization. In J. Shawe-Taylor, R. S. Zemel, P. L. Bartlett, F. Pereira, and K. Q. Weinberger, editors, *Advances in Neural Information Processing Systems 24*, Curran Associates, Inc., pages 2546–2554.

Steven Bethard, Leon Derczynski, Guergana Savova, James Pustejovsky, and Marc Verhagen. 2015. SemEval-2015 Task 6: Clinical TempEval. In *Proceedings of the 9th International Workshop on Semantic Evaluation (SemEval 2015)*. Association for Computational Linguistics, Denver, USA, pages 806–814.

Steven Bethard, Guergana Savova, Wei-Te Chen, Leon Derczynski, James Pustejovsky, and Marc Verhagen. 2016. SemEval-2016 Task 12: Clinical TempEval. In *Proceedings of the 10th International Workshop on Semantic Evaluation (SemEval-2016)*. Association for Computational Linguistics, San Diego, California, pages 1052–1062.

Steven Bethard, Guergana Savova, Martha Palmer, and James Pustejovsky. 2017. Semeval-2017 task 12: Clinical tempeval. In *Proceedings of the 11th International Workshop on Semantic Evaluation (SemEval-2017)*. Association for Computational Linguistics, Vancouver, Canada.

Tommaso Caselli and Roser Morante. 2016. VUA-CLTL at SemEval 2016 Task 12: A CRF Pipeline to Clinical TempEval. In *Proceedings of the 10th International Workshop on Semantic Evaluation (SemEval-2016)*. Association for Computational Linguistics, San Diego, California, pages 1241–1247.

Veera Raghavendra Chikka. 2016. CDE-IIITH at SemEval-2016 Task 12: Extraction of Temporal Information from Clinical documents using Machine Learning techniques. In *Proceedings of the 10th International Workshop on Semantic Evaluation (SemEval-2016)*. Association for Computational Linguistics, San Diego, California, pages 1237–1240.

Arman Cohan, Kevin Meurer, and Nazli Goharian. 2016. Guir at semeval-2016 task 12: Temporal information processing for clinical narratives. In *Proceedings of the 10th International Workshop on Semantic Evaluation (SemEval-2016)*. Association for Computational Linguistics, San Diego, California, pages 1248–1255.

Jason Fries. 2016. Brundlefly at semeval-2016 task 12: Recurrent neural networks vs. joint inference for clinical temporal information extraction. In *Proceedings of the 10th International Workshop on Semantic Evaluation (SemEval-2016)*. Association for Computational Linguistics, San Diego, California, pages 1274–1279.

Cyril Grouin and Véronique Moriceau. 2016. LIMSI at SemEval-2016 Task 12: machine-learning and temporal information to identify clinical events and time expressions. In *Proceedings of the 10th International Workshop on Semantic Evaluation (SemEval-2016)*. Association for Computational Linguistics, San Diego, California, pages 1225–1230.

Charlotte Hansart, Damien De Meyere, Patrick Watrin, André Bittar, and Cédrick Fairon. 2016. CENTAL at SemEval-2016 Task 12: a linguistically fed CRF model for medical and temporal information extraction. In *Proceedings of the 10th International Workshop on Semantic Evaluation (SemEval-2016)*. Association for Computational Linguistics, San Diego, California, pages 1286–1291.

Sepp Hochreiter and Jürgen Schmidhuber. 1997. Long short-term memory. *Neural computation* 9(8):1735–1780.

Zhiheng Huang, Wei Xu, and Kai Yu. 2015. Bidirectional LSTM-CRF models for sequence tagging. *arXiv preprint* arXiv:1508.01991.

Alistair E. W. Johnson, Tom J. Pollard, Lu Shen, Liwei H. Lehman, Mengling Feng, Mohammad Ghassemi, Benjamin Moody, Peter Szolovits, Leo A. Celi, and Roger G. Mark. 2016. MIMIC-III, a freely accessible critical care database. *Scientific Data* 3.

Diederik P. Kingma and Jimmy Ba. 2014. Adam: A Method for Stochastic Optimization. *CoRR* abs/1412.6980.

Guillaume Lample, Miguel Ballesteros, Sandeep Subramanian, Kazuya Kawakami, and Chris Dyer. 2016. Neural Architectures for Named Entity Recognition. In *Proceedings of the 2016 Conference of the North American Chapter of the Association for*

Computational Linguistics: Human Language Technologies. Association for Computational Linguistics, San Diego, California, pages 260–270.

Hee-Jin Lee, Hua Xu, Jingqi Wang, Yaoyun Zhang, Sungrim Moon, Jun Xu, and Yonghui Wu. 2016. UTHealth at SemEval-2016 Task 12: an End-to-End System for Temporal Information Extraction from Clinical Notes. In *Proceedings of the 10th International Workshop on Semantic Evaluation (SemEval-2016)*. Association for Computational Linguistics, San Diego, California, pages 1292–1297.

Peng Li and Heng Huang. 2016. Uta dlnlp at semeval-2016 task 12: Deep learning based natural language processing system for clinical information identification from clinical notes and pathology reports. In *Proceedings of the 10th International Workshop on Semantic Evaluation (SemEval-2016)*. Association for Computational Linguistics, San Diego, California, pages 1268–1273.

Tomas Mikolov, Kai Chen, Greg Corrado, and Jeffrey Dean. 2013. Efficient Estimation of Word Representations in Vector Space. *CoRR* abs/1301.3781. http://arxiv.org/abs/1301.3781.

Fiammetta Namer and Pierre Zweigenbaum. 2004. Acquiring meaning for French medical terminology: contribution of morphosemantics. In *Proceedings of the 10th World Congress on Medical Informatics (MEDINFO)*. pages 535–539.

Guergana K Savova, James J Masanz, Philip V Ogren, Jiaping Zheng, Sunghwan Sohn, Karin C Kipper-Schuler, and Christopher G Chute. 2010. Mayo clinical Text Analysis and Knowledge Extraction System (cTAKES): architecture, component evaluation and applications. *Journal of the American Medical Informatics Association* 17(5):507–513.

Jannik Strötgen and Michael Gertz. 2015. A Baseline Temporal Tagger for all Languages. In *Proceedings of the 2015 Conference on Empirical Methods in Natural Language Processing*. Association for Computational Linguistics, Lisbon, Portugal, pages 541–547.

William Styler IV, Steven Bethard, Sean Finan, Martha Palmer, Sameer Pradhan, Piet de Groen, Brad Erickson, Timothy Miller, Chen Lin, Guergana Savova, and James Pustejovsky. 2014. Temporal Annotation in the Clinical Domain. *Transactions of the Association for Computational Linguistics* 2:143–154.

Julien Tourille, Olivier Ferret, Aurélie Névéol, and Xavier Tannier. 2016. LIMSI-COT at SemEval-2016 Task 12: Temporal relation identification using a pipeline of classifiers. In *Proceedings of the 10th International Workshop on Semantic Evaluation (SemEval-2016)*. Association for Computational Linguistics, San Diego, California, pages 1136–1142.

OMAM at SemEval-2017 Task 4: Evaluation of English State-of-the-Art Sentiment Analysis Models for Arabic and a New Topic-based Model

Ramy Baly[1], **Gilbert Badaro**[1], **Ali Hamdi**[2]
Rawan Moukalled[1], **Rita Aoun**[1], **Georges El-Khoury**[1], **Ahmad El-Sallab**[3]
Hazem Hajj[1], **Nizar Habash**[4], **Khaled Bashir Shaban**[5], **Wassim El-Hajj**[6]

[1] Department of Electrical and Computer Engineering, American University of Beirut
[2] Faculty of Computing, Universiti Teknologi Malaysia
[3] Computer Engineering Department, Cairo University
[4] Computational Approaches to Modeling Language Lab, New York University Abu Dhabi
[5] Computer Science and Engineering Department, Qatar University
[6] Department of Computer Science, American University of Beirut

`{rgb15,ggb05,rrm32,rra47,gbe03,hh63,we07}@mail.aub.edu,`
`nizar.habash@nyu.edu, ali@alihamdi.com`
`ahmad.elsallab@gmail.com, khaled.shaban@qu.edu.qa`

Abstract

While sentiment analysis in English has achieved significant progress, it remains a challenging task in Arabic given the rich morphology of the language. It becomes more challenging when applied to Twitter data that comes with additional sources of noise including dialects, misspellings, grammatical mistakes, code switching and the use of non-textual objects to express sentiments. This paper describes the "OMAM" systems that we developed as part of SemEval-2017 task 4. We evaluate English state-of-the-art methods on Arabic tweets for subtask A. As for the remaining subtasks, we introduce a topic-based approach that accounts for topic specificities by predicting topics or domains of upcoming tweets, and then using this information to predict their sentiment. Results indicate that applying the English state-of-the-art method to Arabic has achieved solid results without significant enhancements. Furthermore, the topic-based method ranked 1st in subtasks C and E, and 2nd in subtask D.

1 Introduction

Sentiment Analysis (SA) is a fundamental problem aiming to allow machines to automatically extract subjectivity information from text (Turney, 2002), whether at the sentence or the document level (Farra et al., 2010). This field has been attracting attention in the research and business communities due to the complexity of human language, and given the range of applications that are interested in harvesting public opinion in different domains such as politics, stocks and marketing.

The interest in SA from Arabic tweets has increased since Arabic has become a key source of the Internet content (Miniwatts, 2016), with Twitter being one of the most expressive social media platforms. While models for SA from English tweets have achieved significant success, Arabic methods continue to lag. Opinion mining in Arabic (OMA) is a challenging task given: (1) the morphological complexity of Arabic (Habash, 2010), (2) the excessive use of dialects that vary significantly across the Arab world, (3) the significant amounts of misspellings and grammatical errors due to length restriction in Twitter, (4) the variations in writing styles, topics and expressions used across the Arab world due to cultural diversity (Baly et al., 2017), and (5) the existence of Twitter-specific tokens (hashtags, mentions, multimedia objects) that may have subjective information embedded in them. Further details on challenging issues in Arabic SA are discussed in (Hamdi et al., 2016).

In this paper, we present the different systems we developed as part of our participation in SemEval-2017 Task 4 on Sentiment Analysis in Twitter (Rosenthal et al., 2017). This task covers both English and Arabic languages. Our systems work on Arabic, but is submitted as part of the OMAM (Opinion Mining for Arabic and More) team that also submitted a system that analyzes sentiment in English (Onyibe and Habash, 2017).

Proceedings of the 11th International Workshop on Semantic Evaluations (SemEval-2017), pages 603–610,
Vancouver, Canada, August 3 - 4, 2017. ©2017 Association for Computational Linguistics

The first system extends English state-of-the-art feature engineering methods, and is based on training sentiment classifiers with different choices of surface, syntactic and semantic features. The second is based on clustering the data into groups of semantically-related tweets and developing a sentiment classifier for each cluster. The third extends recent advances in deep learning methods. The fourth is a topic-based approach for twitter SA that introduces a mechanism to predict the topics of tweets, and then use this information to predict their sentiment polarity. It further allows operating at the domain-level as a form of generalization from topics. We evaluate these models for message polarity classification (subtask A), topic-based polarity classification (subtasks B-C) and tweet quantification (subtasks D-E). Experimental results show that English state-of-the-art methods achieved reasonable results in Arabic without any customization, with results being in the middle of the group in subtask A. For the remaining subtasks, the topic-based approach ranked 2nd in subtask D and 1st in subtasks C and E.

The rest of this paper is organized as follows. Section 2 describes previous efforts on the given task. Section 3 presents the details of the Arabic OMAM systems. Section 4 illustrates the performances achieved for each subtask. We conclude in Section 5 with remarks on future work.

2 Related Work

SA models for Arabic are generally developed by training machine learning classifiers using different choices of features. The most common features are the word n-grams features that were used to train Support Vector Machines (SVM) (Rushdi-Saleh et al., 2011; Aly and Atiya, 2013; Shoukry and Rafea, 2012), Naïve Bayes (Mountassir et al., 2012; Elawady et al., 2014) and ensemble classifiers (Omar et al., 2013). Word n-grams were also used with syntactic features (root and part-of-speech n-grams) and stylistic features (digit and letter n-grams, word length, etc.) and achieved good performances after applying the Entropy-Weighted Genetic Algorithm for feature reduction (Abbasi et al., 2008). Sentiment lexicons also provided an additional source of features that proved useful for the task (Abdul-Mageed et al., 2011; Badaro et al., 2014, 2015)

A framework was developed for tweets written in Modern Standard Arabic (MSA) and containing Jordanian dialects, Arabizi (Arabic words written using Latin characters) and emoticons. This framework was realized by training different classifiers using features that capture the different linguistic phenomena (Duwairi et al., 2014). A distant-based approach showed improvement over existing fully-supervised models for subjectivity classification (Refaee and Rieser, 2014a). A subjectivity and sentiment analysis system for Arabic tweets used a feature set that includes different forms of the word (lexemes and lemmas), POS tags, presence of polar adjectives, writing style (MSA or DA), and genre-specific features including the user's gender and ID (Abdul-Mageed et al., 2014). Machine translation was used to apply existing state-of-the-art models for English to translations of Arabic tweets. Despite slight accuracy drop caused by translation errors, these models are still considered efficient and effective, especially for low-resource languages (Refaee and Rieser, 2014b; Mohammad et al., 2016).

We briefly mention the state-of-the-art performances achieved in English SA. A new class of machine learning models based on deep learning have recently emerged. These models achieved high performances in both Arabic and English, such as the Recursive Auto Encoders (RAE) (Socher et al., 2011; Al Sallab et al., 2015), the Recursive Neural Tensor Networks (Socher et al., 2013), the Gated Recurrent Neural Networks (Tang et al., 2015) and the Dynamic Memory Networks (Kumar et al., 2015). These models were only evaluated on reviews documents, and were never tested against the irregularities and noise that exist in Twitter data. A framework to automate the human reading process improved the performance of several state-of-the-art models (Baly et al., 2016; Hobeica et al., 2011).

3 OMAM Systems

In this section, we present the four OMAM systems that we investigated to perform the different subtasks of SemEval-2017 Task 4. These systems were explored during the development phase, and those that achieved best performances for each subtask were then used to submit the test results.

3.1 System 1: English State-of-the-Art SA

The state-of-the-art system selected from English was the winner of SemEval-2016 Subtask C "Five-point scale Tweet classification" in English (Balikas and Amini, 2016). To apply it for Arabic, we derived an equivalent set of features to train a similar model for sentiment classification in Arabic tweets. The derived features are listed here:

- Word n-grams, where $n \in [1, 4]$. To account for the morphological complexity and sparsity of Arabic language, lemma n-grams are extracted since they have better generalization capabilities than words (Habash, 2010)

- Character n-grams, where $n \in [3, 5]$

- Counts of exclamation marks, question marks, and both marks

- Count of elongated words

- Count of negated contexts; a negated context is any phrase that occurs between a negation particle and the next punctuation

- Counts of positive emoticons and negative emoticons, in addition to a binary feature indicating if emoticons exist in a given tweet

- Counts of each part-of-speech tag in the tweet

- Counts of positive and negative words based on ArSenL (Badaro et al., 2014), AraSenti (Al-Twairesh et al., 2016) and ADHL (Mohammad et al., 2016) lexicons

We also added two additional binary features that indicate the presence of (1) user mentions and (2) URL or any other media content.

3.2 System 2: Cluster-based SA

This system is based on grouping semantically-related tweets, then training different sentiment classifiers for each group independently. At test time, each upcoming tweet is assigned to one of the pre-defined clusters, and the corresponding sentiment classifier is used to predict its polarity. Clusters are identified by applying the k-means algorithm to cluster the word embedding space that is generated using the skip-gram embedding model (Mikolov et al., 2013). Consequently, each cluster corresponds to a collection of semantically-related word vectors, and each tweet is assigned to the cluster whose word vectors are most similar (closest) to the tweet's words' vectors. Tweets that are assigned to the same cluster are used together to train a sentiment classifier using n-gram features. We trained several classifiers including the logistic regression, linear and non-linear SVM, Bernoulli Naive Bayes, Multinomial

Bayes Naive. During model development, we only tuned the number of clusters k, whereas we used the default parameters of the different classifiers as implemented in scikit-learn (Pedregosa et al., 2011).

3.3 System 3: Recursive Auto Encoders

We trained the RAE deep learning model that achieved high performances in both English (Socher et al., 2011) and Arabic (Al Sallab et al., 2015). Briefly, the RAE model derive a sentence representation by combining word embeddings, two at a time, following the structure of a syntactic parse tree. The sentence representation is then used to train a softmax sentiment classifier. We followed the setup proposed by (Al Sallab et al., in press 2017) by applying RAE to morphologically tokenized text which proved to improve the performance by reducing the lexical sparsity of the language. We also use a broader semantic representation of words by concatenating word embeddings trained using the skip-gram model (Mikolov et al., 2013) with sentiment embeddings trained using the ArSenL sentiment lexicon (Badaro et al., 2014).

3.4 System 4: Topic-based SA

This system is based on the assumption that tweets discussing a particular topic are likely to share some unique semantic features. Figure 1 shows the architecture of this system. It is composed of several modules; (A) unsupervised topic classifier, (B) supervised topic classifier, (C) supervised domain classifier, in addition to a (D) generic sentiment classifier. The idea behind this system is that, since the test tweets may belong to topics that are not present in the training set, the different modules attempt to predict the topic and then classify the tweet's sentiment given the predicted topic. Before running the system in Figure 1, topic-specific and domain-specific sentiment classifiers are trained offline. Tweets belonging to each topic or domain in the train set are used, along with their sentiment labels, to train sentiment classifiers that are specific to the corresponding topic or domain. These classifiers are used with the above-mentioned modules as follows.

(M_1) Unsupervised Topic Classification Since the topic of each new tweet is unknown and can be different from those in the training set, we aim to discover which of the training topics is closest

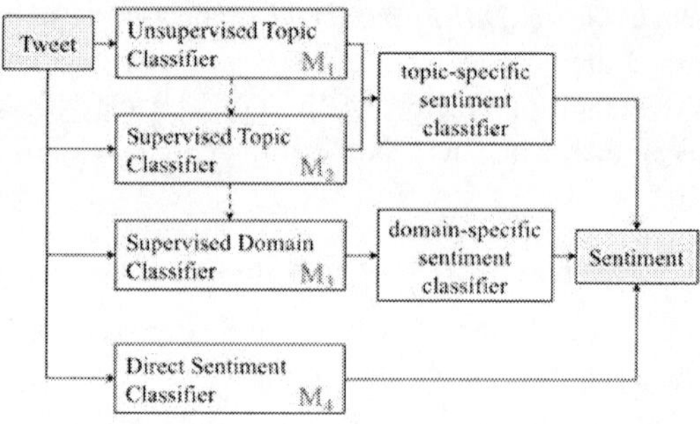

Figure 1: Architecture of the topic-based sentiment analysis system.

(or mostly related) to that of the tweet. This is achieved by training an embedding model, similar to that in System 2. Then, for each new tweet the system checks the similarity between the vector of each of the training topics and those of the tweet's words. The tweet is then assigned to the topic with the highest similarity, and its sentiment polarity is predicted using the sentiment classifier that is trained using instances of that particular topic.

(M_2) Supervised Topic Classification In many cases, all similarity values turn out to be small and close to 0. This is possible if the test tweet's topic is totally different from those in the train set, or if the tweet's words are implicitly related to the discussed topic. In such cases, we refer to a supervised topic classifier; a multi-class classifier, where the number of classes is equal to the number of topics in the training set. The topic classifier is trained using n-gram features extracted from all training tweets. Once the topic of the test tweet is predicted, its sentiment polarity is predicted using the sentiment classifier that is trained using instances of that particular topic.

(M_3) Supervised Domain Classification Some topics may not have sufficient instances to train an accurate sentiment classifier, therefore we introduce the concept of "domain"; a generalized form of the topic. A supervised domain classifier is a multi-class classifier, where the number of classes is equal to the number of domains in the training set. The domain classifier is trained using n-gram features extracted from all training tweets. Once the domain of the test tweet is predicted, its sentiment polarity is predicted using the sentiment classifier that is trained using instances of that particular domain.

(M_4) Direct Sentiment Classification In addition to the topic-specific and domain-specific classifiers, we also experiment with the direct sentiment classifier that ignores the topic information and is trained using all tweets in the training set.

We evaluated the following sequences of these modules: [M_1 →M_2 →M_3], [M_2 →M_3], [M_3] or [M_4]. For instance, in the first sequence, the tweet's topic is predicted using the unsupervised module (M_1), and then its polarity is predicted using the sentiment classifier for that topic. If no similarity was detected, we proceed to module (M_2) to predict the tweet's topic using the topic classifier, and then predict its sentiment using the sentiment classifier for that topic. If the topic is rare and no sentiment classifier exists for that topic, we proceed to module (M_3) to predict the tweet's domain using the domain classifier, and then predict its sentiment using the sentiment classifier for that domain.

4 Experiments and Results

In this section, we describe the experiments and results we achieved as part of our participation in SemEval-2017 Task 4. We describe the datasets we used, the preprocessing steps we applied and the performance of the different systems for each subtask. Table 1 illustrates the design of the evaluation experiments, highlighting the systems that were evaluated for each subtask. The system that achieved the best evaluation results, for each subtask, was then used to submit the test results.

Subtask	Systems
Message Polarity Classification (A)	Systems 1, 2, 3
Topic-based Polarity Classification (B-C)	Systems 1, 4
Tweet Quantification (D-E)	Systems 1, 4

Table 1: Design of evaluation experiments.

4.1 Datasets and Preprocessing

To run our experiments, we used datasets provided by the task organizers (Rosenthal et al., 2017) as follows. During evaluation, we trained our models on the TRAIN set, and evaluated our different systems on the DEV set. During testing, the system that achieved the best development results is trained using the combination of TRAIN and DEV sets, and tested the model on the TEST set.

For the English state-of-the-art approach (System 1), tweets are preprocessed by (1) replacing mentions and URLs with special tokens, (2) extracting emoticons and emojis and replacing them with special tokens using the emojis sentiment lexicon (Novak et al., 2015) and a in-home emoticons lexicon, (3) normalizing hashtags by removing the # symbol and the underscores that connect words in composite hashtags, and (4) normalizing letter repetitions (elongations). Then features are extracted by performing lemmatization and POS tagging using MADAMIRA v2.1, the state-of-the-art morphological analyzer and disambiguator in Arabic (Pasha et al., 2014), that uses the Standard Arabic Morphological Analyzer (SAMA) (Maamouri et al., 2010). We only included n-grams that occurred more than a pre-defined threshold t, where $t \in [3, 5]$ is tuned on the "DEV" set.

For the cluster-based SA approach (System 2), we trained the skip-gram word embedding model using a collection of datasets including the TRAIN and the DEV tweets provided by the organizers, the Qatar Arabic Language Bank (QALB) (Zaghouani et al., 2014) and several Arabic Twitter corpora from (Nabil et al., 2015; Refaee and Rieser, 2014b). We also used the k-means algorithm to cluster the embedding space into k clusters, with k ranging between 1 (no clustering) and 12. Best results during development were obtained using $k = 4$ and 5.

For the RAE approach (System 3), tweets are processed similar to System 1. We used MADAMIRA v2.1 to perform morphological tokenization following the ATB scheme (Habash and Sadat, 2006). We also used the Stanford parser (Green and Manning, 2010) to generate the syntactic parse trees. Since the resulting trees are not necessarily binary, and hence cannot be used to train recursive models, we used left-factoring to transform the trees to the Chomsky Normal Form (CNF) grammar that only contains unary and binary production rules.

For the topic-based approach (System 4), tweets are preprocessed by applying normalization and stemming using the NLTK ISRI stemmer (Taghva et al., 2005) and stopword removal. Then, n-grams are extracted using SKlearn TFiDFvectorizer (Pedregosa et al., 2011), with a variance threshold for feature reduction. The tweets in the training set that is provided by the task organizers pertain to 34 topics. We came up with a list of 8 generic do-

mains that correspond to these topics, as shown in Table 2.

Domains	Topics
technology	ويندوز ١٠، جوجل، بوكيمونأندرويد، غوغل، ايفون، آبل
shopping	غوتشي، أمازون
sports	برشلونة، ريال مدريد، ميسي، فيدرير
media	هاري بوتر، جستن بيبر، بيونسيه
religion	رمضان، الاسلام
politics_isis	داعش، الارهاب
politics_me	بشار، اردوغان، إيران، سوريا، سورية، حلب، الأسد العراق، السعودية، سيسي
politics_us	هيلاري كلنتون، دونالد ترامب، باراك أوباما، اوباما

Table 2: The list of 8 generalized domains corresponding to the 34 topics in the training dataset.

4.2 Message Polarity Classification (A)

For this subtask, we evaluated the English state-of-the-art approach (System 1), the cluster-based SA approach (System 2) and RAE (System 3). The development and test results are illustrated in Table 3. It can be observed that System 1 achieved the best development results, and hence was used at the test phase. System 2 achieved slightly lower recall and higher accuracy, which indicates the potential benefits of training different sentiment classifiers for different clusters. Also, the inferior performance produced by System 3 can be due to its reliance on Arabic NLP tools, such as the syntactic parser, that are trained on MSA data, whereas the evaluation data are tweets that are likely to be noisy in terms of containing significant amounts of misspellings and grammatical errors.

	Model	Avg-R	Avg-F1	Acc.
	Sys 1	**0.458**	**0.434**	**0.453**
DEV	*Sys 2*	0.455	0.401	0.477
	Sys 3	0.424	0.394	0.410
TEST	*Sys 1*	0.438	0.422	0.430

Table 3: Results for subtask A (rank: #5/8).

4.3 Topic-based Polarity Classification (B-C)

For these subtasks, we evaluated the English state-of-the-art approach (System 1) and the different configurations of the topic-based SA approach (System 4) as discussed in subsection 3.2. The development and testing results for the 2-point and the 5-point scale predictions are illustrated in Table 4 and 5, respectively.

	System	Avg-F1	Avg-R	Acc.
DEV	Sys 1	0.551	0.611	0.654
	Sys 4 [$M_1 \rightarrow M_2 \rightarrow M_3$]	0.473	0.536	0.554
	Sys 4 [$M_2 \rightarrow M_3$]	0.487	0.553	0.569
	Sys 4 [CM_3]	0.495	0.576	0.569
	Sys 4 [M_4]	**0.581**	**0.640**	**0.690**
TEST	Sys 4 [M_4]	0.678	0.687	0.679

Table 4: Results for subtask B (rank: #4/4).

	System	$\mathbf{MAE}_M$	$\mathbf{MAE}_\mu$
DEV	Sys 1	0.410	0.568
	Sys 4 [$M_1 \rightarrow M_2 \rightarrow M_3$]	**0.387**	**0.551**
	Sys 4 [$M_2 \rightarrow M_3$]	0.414	0.648
	Sys 4 [M_3]	0.436	0.665
	Sys 4 [M_4]	0.422	0.647
TEST	Sys 4 [$M_1 \rightarrow M_2 \rightarrow M_3$]	0.943	0.646

Table 5: Results for subtask C (rank: #1/2).

For Subtask B, it can be observed that ignoring the topic and domain information achieves highest performances. It can also be observed that generalizing from topics to domains in System 4 achieves better results than working at the topic-level only. As for Subtask C, results indicate that using topic-specific sentiment classifiers, and backing them with domain-specific sentiment classifiers, achieves the best performance in the competition on that subtask.

4.4 Tweet Quantification (D-E)

For these subtasks, we evaluated the English state-of-the-art approach (System 1) and the different configurations of the topic-based SA approach (System 4). The development and testing results for the 2-point and the 5-point scale quantifications are illustrated in Table 6 and 7, respectively.

	System	KLD	AE	RAE
DEV	Sys 1	**0.277**	**0.316**	**2.442**
	Sys 4 [$M_1 \rightarrow M_2 \rightarrow M_3$]	0.240	0.257	2.125
	Sys 4 [$M_2 \rightarrow M_3$]	0.319	0.668	2.783
	Sys 4 [M_3]	0.258	0.298	2.322
	Sys 4 [M_4]	0.581	0.640	0.690
TEST	Sys 1	0.202	0.238	4.835

Table 6: Results for subtask D (rank: #2/3).

For both subtasks, it can be observed that ignoring the topic and domain information achieves the best performances. For subtask D, using the features from System 1 achieved best development

	System	EMD
DEV	Sys 1	0.436
	Sys 4 [$M_1 \rightarrow M_2 \rightarrow M_3$]	0.473
	Sys 4 [$M_2 \rightarrow M_3$]	0.474
	Sys 4 [M_3]	0.458
	Sys 4 [M_4]	**0.426**
TEST	Sys 4 [M_4]	0.548

Table 7: Results for subtask E (rank: #1/2).

results, and ranked 2nd in the competition. On the other hand, for subtask E, it turns out that using the simple n-gram features for direct sentiment classification ranked 1st in the competition.

5 Conclusion

In this paper, we evaluated the application of recent state-of-the-art English models for sentiment analysis in Arabic tweets. These systems were used to perform all Arabic-related subtasks in SemEval-2017 Task 4.

In some cases, such as for message polarity classification (subtask A), the feature-based approach outperformed a RAE deep learning approach and another system that is based on creating semantic clusters for the tweets and training a sentiment classifier for each cluster.

For topic-based polarity classification (subtasks B and C) and topic-based tweet quantification (subtasks D and E), we evaluated a system that predicts the topic of upcoming tweets, and then predicts their sentiment using topic-specific sentiment classifiers. We allow this system to generalize from topics to domains. Results indicate that ignoring the topic and the domain information achieves better performances, with an exception for subtask C, where using topic-specific classifiers and backing them with domain-specific classifiers performs better.

As part of our future work, we will focus on developing SA models for different Arabic dialects, and also to perform cross-regional evaluations to confirm whether different models are needed for different regions and dialects, or a general model can work for any tweet regardless of its origins.

Acknowledgments

This work was made possible by NPRP 6-716-1-138 grant from the Qatar National Research Fund (a member of Qatar Foundation). The statements made herein are solely the responsibility of the authors.

References

Ahmed Abbasi, Hsinchun Chen, and Arab Salem. 2008. Sentiment analysis in multiple languages: Feature selection for opinion classification in web forums. *ACM Transactions on Information Systems (TOIS)* 26(3):12.

Muhammad Abdul-Mageed, Mona Diab, and Sandra Kübler. 2014. Samar: Subjectivity and sentiment analysis for arabic social media. *Computer Speech & Language* 28(1):20–37.

Muhammad Abdul-Mageed, Mona T Diab, and Mohammed Korayem. 2011. Subjectivity and sentiment analysis of modern standard arabic. In *Proceedings of the 49th Annual Meeting of the Association for Computational Linguistics: Human Language Technologies: short papers-Volume 2*. Association for Computational Linguistics, pages 587–591.

Ahmad A Al Sallab, Ramy Baly, Gilbert Badaro, Hazem Hajj, Wassim El Hajj, and Khaled B Shaban. 2015. Deep learning models for sentiment analysis in arabic. In *ANLP Workshop 2015*. page 9.

Ahmad A Al Sallab, Ramy Baly, Gilbert Badaro, Hazem Hajj, Wassim El Hajj, and Khaled B Shaban. in press 2017. Aroma: A recursive deep learning model for opinion mining in arabic as a low resource language. *ACM Transactions on Asian and Low-Resource Language Information Processing* .

Nora Al-Twairesh, Hend Al-Khalifa, and AbdulMalik Al-Salman. 2016. Arasenti: Large-scale twitter-specific arabic sentiment lexicons. *Proceedings of the 54th Annual Meeting of the Association for Computational Linguistics* pages 697–705.

Mohamed A Aly and Amir F Atiya. 2013. Labr: A large scale arabic book reviews dataset. In *ACL (2)*. pages 494–498.

Gilbert Badaro, Ramy Baly, Rana Akel, Linda Fayad, Jeffrey Khairallah, Hazem Hajj, Wassim El-Hajj, and Khaled Bashir Shaban. 2015. A light lexicon-based mobile application for sentiment mining of arabic tweets. In *ANLP Workshop 2015*. page 18.

Gilbert Badaro, Ramy Baly, Hazem Hajj, Nizar Habash, and Wassim El-Hajj. 2014. A large scale arabic sentiment lexicon for arabic opinion mining. *ANLP 2014* 165.

Georgios Balikas and Massih-Reza Amini. 2016. Twise at semeval-2016 task 4: Twitter sentiment classification. *arXiv preprint arXiv:1606.04351* .

Ramy Baly, Gilbert Badaro, Georges El-Khoury, Rawan Moukalled, Rita Aoun, Hazem Hajj, Wassim El-Hajj, Nizar Habash, and Khaled Bashir Shaban. 2017. A characterization study of arabic twitter data with a benchmarking for state-of-the-art opinion mining models. *ANLP 2017* .

Ramy Baly, Roula Hobeica, Hazem Hajj, Wassim El-Hajj, Khaled Bashir Shaban, and Ahmad Al-Sallab. 2016. A meta-framework for modeling the human reading process in sentiment analysis. *ACM Transactions on Information Systems (TOIS)* 35(1):7.

RM Duwairi, Raed Marji, Narmeen Sha'ban, and Sally Rushaidat. 2014. Sentiment analysis in arabic tweets. In *Information and communication systems (icics), 2014 5th international conference on*. IEEE, pages 1–6.

Rasheed M Elawady, Sherif Barakat, and Nora M Elrashidy. 2014. Different feature selection for sentiment classification. *International Journal of Information Science and Intelligent System* 3(1):137–150.

Noura Farra, Elie Challita, Rawad Abou Assi, and Hazem Hajj. 2010. Sentence-level and document-level sentiment mining for arabic texts. In *Data Mining Workshops (ICDMW), 2010 IEEE International Conference on*. IEEE, pages 1114–1119.

Spence Green and Christopher D Manning. 2010. Better arabic parsing: Baselines, evaluations, and analysis. In *Proceedings of the 23rd International Conference on Computational Linguistics*. Association for Computational Linguistics, pages 394–402.

Nizar Habash and Fatiha Sadat. 2006. Arabic preprocessing schemes for statistical machine translation. In *Proceedings of the Human Language Technology Conference of the NAACL, Companion Volume: Short Papers*. Association for Computational Linguistics, pages 49–52.

Nizar Y Habash. 2010. Introduction to arabic natural language processing. *Synthesis Lectures on Human Language Technologies* 3(1):1–187.

Ali Hamdi, Khaled Shaban, and Zainal Anazida. 2016. A review on challenging issues in arabic sentiment analysis. *Journal of Computer Science* 12(9):471–481.

Roula Hobeica, Hazem Hajj, and Wassim El Hajj. 2011. Machine reading for notion-based sentiment mining. In *Data Mining Workshops (ICDMW), 2011 IEEE 11th International Conference on*. IEEE, pages 75–80.

Ankit Kumar, Ozan Irsoy, Jonathan Su, James Bradbury, Robert English, Brian Pierce, Peter Ondruska, Ishaan Gulrajani, and Richard Socher. 2015. Ask me anything: Dynamic memory networks for natural language processing. *CoRR, abs/1506.07285* .

Mohamed Maamouri, Dave Graff, Basma Bouziri, Sondos Krouna, Ann Bies, and Seth Kulick. 2010. Standard arabic morphological analyzer (sama) version 3.1. *Linguistic Data Consortium, Catalog No.: LDC2010L01* .

Tomas Mikolov, Ilya Sutskever, Kai Chen, Greg S Corrado, and Jeff Dean. 2013. Distributed representations of words and phrases and their compositionality. In *Advances in neural information processing systems*. pages 3111–3119.

Miniwatts. 2016. Internet world users by language. http://www.internetworldstats.com/stats7.htm.

Saif M Mohammad, Mohammad Salameh, and Svetlana Kiritchenko. 2016. How translation alters sentiment. *J. Artif. Intell. Res.(JAIR)* 55:95–130.

Asmaa Mountassir, Houda Benbrahim, and Ilham Berrada. 2012. An empirical study to address the problem of unbalanced data sets in sentiment classification. In *Systems, Man, and Cybernetics (SMC), 2012 IEEE International Conference on*. IEEE, pages 3298–3303.

Mahmoud Nabil, Mohamed A Aly, and Amir F Atiya. 2015. Astd: Arabic sentiment tweets dataset. In *EMNLP*. pages 2515–2519.

Petra Kralj Novak, Jasmina Smailović, Borut Sluban, and Igor Mozetič. 2015. Sentiment of emojis. *PloS one* 10(12):e0144296.

Nazlia Omar, Mohammed Albared, Adel Qasem Al-Shabi, and Tareq Al-Moslmi. 2013. Ensemble of classification algorithms for subjectivity and sentiment analysis of arabic customers' reviews. *International Journal of Advancements in Computing Technology* 5(14):77.

Chukwuyem J. Onyibe and Nizar Habash. 2017. OMAM at SemEval-2017 task 4: English sentiment analysis with conditional random fields. In *Proceedings of the 11th International Workshop on Semantic Evaluation*. Association for Computational Linguistics, Vancouver, Canada, SemEval '17.

Arfath Pasha, Mohamed Al-Badrashiny, Mona T Diab, Ahmed El Kholy, Ramy Eskander, Nizar Habash, Manoj Pooleery, Owen Rambow, and Ryan Roth. 2014. Madamira: A fast, comprehensive tool for morphological analysis and disambiguation of arabic. In *LREC*. volume 14, pages 1094–1101.

Fabian Pedregosa, Gaël Varoquaux, Alexandre Gramfort, Vincent Michel, Bertrand Thirion, Olivier Grisel, Mathieu Blondel, Peter Prettenhofer, Ron Weiss, Vincent Dubourg, et al. 2011. Scikit-learn: Machine learning in python. *Journal of Machine Learning Research* 12(Oct):2825–2830.

Eshrag Refaee and Verena Rieser. 2014a. Can we read emotions from a smiley face? emoticon-based distant supervision for subjectivity and sentiment analysis of arabic twitter feeds. In *5th International Workshop on Emotion, Social Signals, Sentiment and Linked Open Data, LREC*.

Eshrag Refaee and Verena Rieser. 2014b. Subjectivity and sentiment analysis of arabic twitter feeds with limited resources. In *Workshop on Free/Open-Source Arabic Corpora and Corpora Processing Tools Workshop Programme*. page 16.

Sara Rosenthal, Noura Farra, and Preslav Nakov. 2017. SemEval-2017 task 4: Sentiment analysis in Twitter. In *Proceedings of the 11th International Workshop on Semantic Evaluation*. Association for Computational Linguistics, Vancouver, Canada, SemEval '17.

Mohammed Rushdi-Saleh, M Teresa Martín-Valdivia, L Alfonso Ureña-López, and José M Perea-Ortega. 2011. Oca: Opinion corpus for arabic. *Journal of the American Society for Information Science and Technology* 62(10):2045–2054.

Amira Shoukry and Ahmed Rafea. 2012. Sentence-level arabic sentiment analysis. In *Collaboration Technologies and Systems (CTS), 2012 International Conference on*. IEEE, pages 546–550.

Richard Socher, Jeffrey Pennington, Eric H Huang, Andrew Y Ng, and Christopher D Manning. 2011. Semi-supervised recursive autoencoders for predicting sentiment distributions. In *Proceedings of the conference on empirical methods in natural language processing*. Association for Computational Linguistics, pages 151–161.

Richard Socher, Alex Perelygin, Jean Y Wu, Jason Chuang, Christopher D Manning, Andrew Y Ng, Christopher Potts, et al. 2013. Recursive deep models for semantic compositionality over a sentiment treebank. In *Proceedings of the conference on empirical methods in natural language processing (EMNLP)*. Citeseer, volume 1631, page 1642.

Kazem Taghva, Rania Elkhoury, and Jeffrey Coombs. 2005. Arabic stemming without a root dictionary. In *Information Technology: Coding and Computing, 2005. ITCC 2005. International Conference on*. IEEE, volume 1, pages 152–157.

Duyu Tang, Bing Qin, and Ting Liu. 2015. Document modeling with gated recurrent neural network for sentiment classification. In *EMNLP*. pages 1422–1432.

Peter D Turney. 2002. Thumbs up or thumbs down?: semantic orientation applied to unsupervised classification of reviews. In *Proceedings of the 40th annual meeting on association for computational linguistics*. Association for Computational Linguistics, pages 417–424.

Wajdi Zaghouani, Behrang Mohit, Nizar Habash, Ossama Obeid, Nadi Tomeh, Alla Rozovskaya, Noura Farra, Sarah Alkuhlani, and Kemal Oflazer. 2014. Large scale arabic error annotation: Guidelines and framework. In *LREC*. pages 2362–2369.

NILC-USP at SemEval-2017 Task 4: A Multi-view Ensemble for Twitter Sentiment Analysis

Edilson A. Corrêa Jr., Vanessa Queiroz Marinho, Leandro Borges dos Santos
Institute of Mathematics and Computer Science
University of São Paulo (USP)
São Carlos, São Paulo, Brazil
{edilsonacjr,vanessaqm,leandrobs}@usp.br

Abstract

This paper describes our multi-view ensemble approach to SemEval-2017 Task 4 on Sentiment Analysis in Twitter, specifically, the Message Polarity Classification subtask for English (subtask A). Our system is a voting ensemble, where each base classifier is trained in a different feature space. The first space is a bag-of-words model and has a Linear SVM as base classifier. The second and third spaces are two different strategies of combining word embeddings to represent sentences and use a Linear SVM and a Logistic Regressor as base classifiers. The proposed system was ranked 18th out of 38 systems considering F1 score and 20th considering recall.

1 Introduction

Twitter is a microblogging service that has 313 million monthly active users [1]. In this social media platform, users interact through short messages, so-called *tweets*. The company estimates that over 500 million tweets are sent each day [2]. Despite of their size, at most 140 characters, these messages provide rich data because users generally write about their thoughts, opinions and sentiments. Therefore, applications in several domains, such as commercial (Jansen et al., 2009) and political (Tumasjan et al., 2010; Wang et al., 2012), may benefit from the automatic classification of sentiment in tweets.

In this paper we show that a multi-view ensemble approach that leverages simple representations of texts may achieve good results in the task of message polarity classification. The proposed system consists of three base classifiers, each of them

with a specific text representation technique (bag-of-words or word embeddings combination). As base classifiers, we use Support Vector Machines (SVM) and Logistic Regression. The proposed approach was evaluated on the SemEval-2017 Task 4 Subtask A for English and was ranked 18th out of 38 participating systems considering F1 score and 20th considering recall.

This paper is organized as follows: Section 2 describes our system, the feature spaces and the classifiers we employed. The training and evaluation datasets are presented in Section 3. In addition, Section 3 also describes the preprocessing steps and some details about the word embeddings. We present our results in Section 4. Finally, Section 5 outlines our conclusions and remarks on future work.

2 System Description

The proposed system consists of a multi-view ensemble with three base classifiers with different text representation techniques (feature spaces), that is, all base classifiers are trained on the same dataset but with a different representation or feature space. The first is a Linear SVM and the tweets are represented using bag-of-words (Section 2.1.1). The second is another Linear SVM and the tweets are represented by averaging the word embeddings (Section 2.1.2). The third is a Logistic Regressor and the tweets are represented by averaging the weighted word embeddings (Section 2.1.2). In these systems, a class of a given instance is decided as the class which maximizes the sums of the predicted probabilities (soft-voting).

The idea of using a multi-view ensemble is to explore different feature spaces without the need of combining all features in the same space, since this combination may lead to the insertion of noise. Moreover, there is no straightforward way

---

[1] https://about.twitter.com/company
[2] https://business.twitter.com/en/basics.html

611

Proceedings of the 11th International Workshop on Semantic Evaluations (SemEval-2017), pages 611–615,
Vancouver, Canada, August 3 - 4, 2017. ©2017 Association for Computational Linguistics

of combining them. Other important aspect of this technique is the possibility of assigning different weights to each pair of classifier/features (view) or even learn the weights by a regression method (Xu et al., 2013).

The process of choosing the best classifier for each feature space was done by executing a Grid Search with state-of-art classifiers (k-NN, Decision Trees, Naive Bayes, Random Forest, AdaBoost, SVM and Logistic Regression), which led to the selection of SVM and Logistic Regression. In the following subsections, the text representations and the classifiers are described. The complete system will be made available [3].

2.1 Text representations

In this work, tweets were modeled using three types of text representation. The first one is a bag-of-words model weighted by *tf-idf* (term frequency - inverse document frequency) (Section 2.1.1). The second represents a sentence by averaging the word embeddings of all words (in the sentence) and the third represents a sentence by averaging the weighted word embeddings of all words, the weight of a word is given by *tf-idf* (Section 2.1.2).

2.1.1 Bag-of-words

The bag-of-words model is a popular approach to represent text (documents, sentences, queries and others) in Natural Language Processing and Information Retrieval. In this model, a text is represented by its set of words, this representation can be binary, in which a word receives 1 if it is in the text or 0 otherwise, considering a predefined vocabulary. An alternative is a representation weighted by some specific information, such as frequency. The representation adopted by this work is the bag-of-words weighted by *tf-idf* (Salton, 1989), where each tweet is represented as $tweet_i = (a_{i1}, a_{i2}, ..., a_{im})$, where a_{ij} is given by the frequency of term t_j in the tweet i weighted by the total number of tweets divided by the amount of tweets containing the term t_j.

2.1.2 Word embeddings

Word embeddings, a concept introduced by Bengio et al. (2003), is a distributional representation of words, where each word is represented by a dense, real-valued vector. These vectors are learned by neural networks trained

in language modeling (Bengio et al., 2003) or similar tasks (Collobert et al., 2011; Mikolov et al., 2013a,b). In this work, the Word2Vec model (Mikolov et al., 2013a,b) is used, in which the vectors are learned by training the neural network to perform context (skip-gram) or word (CBOW) prediction.

In addition to capture syntactic and semantic information, the vectors produced by Word2Vec have geometric properties such as *compositionality* (Mikolov et al., 2013b), which allow larger blocks of information (such as sentences and paragraphs) to be represented by the combination of the embeddings of the words contained in the block. This approach has been adopted by a considerable number of works in several areas, such as question answering (Belinkov et al., 2015), semantic textual similarity (Sultan et al., 2015), word sense disambiguation (Iacobacci et al., 2016) and even sentiment analysis (Socher et al., 2013).

In our work we adopted two combination approaches. The first is a simple combination, where each tweet is represented by the average of the word embedding vectors of the words that compose the tweet. The second approach also averages the word embedding vectors, but each embedding vector is now weighted (multiplied) by the *tf-idf* of the word it represents. A similar approach has been used in Zhao et al. (2015).

2.2 Classifiers

For both classifiers we used the well-known *Scikit-learn* (Pedregosa et al., 2011) implementation (with default parameters).

2.2.1 Logistic Regression

Logistic Regression is a linear classifier that predicts the class probabilities of a binary classification problem. It is also known as logit regression because a sigmoid function outputs the class probabilities. To tackle multiclass problems, the training algorithm uses the one-vs-rest approach (Murphy, 2012).

2.2.2 Support Vector Machines

Support Vector Machines (SVMs) classifiers find the decision boundary that maximizes the margin between two classes. However, when data is intrinsically nonlinear, SVM classifiers cannot properly separate between classes. A possible solution is to map the data points into a higher-dimensional feature space. By doing so, the data becomes lin-

---

early separable (Murphy, 2012). To apply the algorithm to our multiclass problem, we used the one-vs-one approach.

3 Data

To evaluate our system we used the training and development datasets provided by the SemEval-2017 competition (specifically Twitter2016-train and Twitter2016-dev). For testing, in addition to the previous year's testing datasets (Twitter2016-test, SMS2013, Tw2014-sarcasm, LiveJournal2014), a new dataset (Twitter2017-test) was made available. A summary of the datasets is given in Table 1.

Dataset	Total	Pos.	Neg.	Neut.
Twitter2016-train	6000	3094	863	2043
Twitter2016-dev	2000	844	765	391
Twitter2016-test	20632	7059	10342	3231
Twitter2017-test	12284	2375	3972	5937
SMS2013	2093	492	394	1207
Tw2014-sarcasm	86	33	40	13
LiveJournal2014	1142	427	304	411

Table 1: Datasets used in the training and evaluation of the system.

Data preprocessing. Before extracting features, the tweets were preprocessed. First, we tokenized the text considering HTML tags, mentions/usernames, URLs, numbers, words (including hyphenated words) and emoticons. Then, the text was set to lowercase and stopwords (words with low semantic value such as prepositions and articles), punctuation marks, hashtags and mentions/usernames were removed.

Word embeddings. We used the pre-trained word embeddings [4], generated with the Word2Vec model (Mikolov et al., 2013a,b) and trained on part of Google News dataset, which is composed of approximately 100 billion words. The model comprises 3 million words and phrases and the embedding vectors have 300 dimensions. Words out of the vocabulary were disregarded and when all words in a tweet had no pre-trained vectors, a randomly initialized vector of 300 dimensions was assigned.

[4]code.google.com/archive/p/word2vec/

4 Results

To evaluate, compare and rank the participating systems, F1 score (average), recall (average) and accuracy were chosen by the organizers. Our system was ranked 18th out of 38 systems, with a F1 score of 0.595 on the Twitter2017-test, ranked 20th considering recall (0.612) and ranked 16th with 0.617 of accuracy. The full ranking and other details of the competition may be found in Rosenthal et al. (2017).

Dataset	F1 score	recall	accuracy
Twitter2016-test	0.523	0.527	0.542
Twitter2017-test	0.595	0.612	0.617
SMS2013	0.381	0.494	0.609
Tw2014-sarcasm	0.339	0.536	0.442
LiveJournal2014	0.573	0.569	0.588

Table 2: Results obtained by our systems in different evaluation datasets.

In the Twitter2016-test evaluation, only Twitter2016-train and Twitter2016-dev were used in training. In the rest of the evaluations, Twitter2016-train, Twitter2016-dev, Twitter2016-test were used. Despite of the availability of other datasets for training, we chose to use only the three. The results obtained by our system are summarized in Table 2.

From the results it is possible to notice that the system is impaired in datasets of different origin, such as SMS2013, this may occur due to the use of a distinct and specific vocabulary. In the case of Tw2014-sarcasm, the major problem is that our representations do not consider the order of words in the sentence which can make it difficult to identify sarcasm or modifiers. In the LiveJournal2014 dataset the system remained stable even though it is a dataset of another domain, probably because it is similar to the Twitter datasets.

5 Conclusion and Future Work

In this paper, we presented a multi-view ensemble approach to message polarity classification that participated in the SemEval-2017 Task 4 on Sentiment Analysis in Twitter (subtask A English). Our system was ranked 18th out of 38 participants.

The results indicated that a multi-view ensemble approach that leverages simple representations of texts may achieve good results in the task of message polarity classification with almost no intervention or special preprocessing.

In our approach, tweets with opposite polarities might end up with the same vector representation in the cases they present the same words, such as *"It isn't horrible, it's perfect"* and *"It isn't perfect, it's horrible"*. To solve this problem, we plan to combine our model with other techniques that consider the ordering of words, such as word n-grams. In the future, we also plan to use approaches for the normalization of informal texts in order to capture particularities of the social media language. In informal texts, a word or a sequence of words can be intentionally replaced, for example *you*, *are* and *see you* can be written as *u*, *r* and *cu*. Because these forms are not mapped into the original words, they are seen as different tokens. In addition, commonly used abbreviations, such as *omg* and *wth*, may express sentiment and their expansion could lead to model improvements. Other improvements that may lead to a better system is the use of word embeddings trained to capture sentiment information and the use of autoencoders to generate sentence/document embeddings.

Acknowledgments

E.A.C.J. acknowledge financial support from Google (Google Research Awards in Latin America grant) and CAPES (Coordination for the Improvement of Higher Education Personnel). V.Q.M. acknowledge financial support from FAPESP (grant no. 15/05676-8). L.B.S. acknowledge financial support from Google (Google Research Awards in Latin America grant) and CNPq (National Council for Scientific and Technological Development, Brazil).

References

Yonatan Belinkov, Mitra Mohtarami, Scott Cyphers, and James Glass. 2015. Vectorslu: A continuous word vector approach to answer selection in community question answering systems. In *Proceedings of the 9th International Workshop on Semantic Evaluation (SemEval 2015)*. pages 282–287.

Yoshua Bengio, Réjean Ducharme, Pascal Vincent, and Christian Jauvin. 2003. A neural probabilistic language model. *Journal of Machine Learning Research* 3(Feb):1137–1155.

Ronan Collobert, Jason Weston, Léon Bottou, Michael Karlen, Koray Kavukcuoglu, and Pavel Kuksa. 2011. Natural language processing (almost) from scratch. *Journal of Machine Learning Research* 12(Aug):2493–2537.

Ignacio Iacobacci, Mohammad Taher Pilehvar, and Roberto Navigli. 2016. Embeddings for word sense disambiguation: An evaluation study. In *Proceedings of the 54th Annual Meeting of the Association for Computational Linguistics*. volume 1, pages 897–907.

Bernard J. Jansen, Mimi Zhang, Kate Sobel, and Abdur Chowdury. 2009. Twitter power: Tweets as electronic word of mouth. *Journal of the American Society for Information Science and Technology* 60(11):2169–2188.

Tomas Mikolov, Kai Chen, Greg Corrado, and Jeffrey Dean. 2013a. Efficient estimation of word representations in vector space. *arXiv preprint arXiv:1301.3781* .

Tomas Mikolov, Ilya Sutskever, Kai Chen, Greg S Corrado, and Jeff Dean. 2013b. Distributed representations of words and phrases and their compositionality. In *Advances in neural information processing systems*. pages 3111–3119.

Kevin P. Murphy. 2012. *Machine Learning: A Probabilistic Perspective*. The MIT Press.

Fabian Pedregosa, Gaël Varoquaux, Alexandre Gramfort, Vincent Michel, Bertrand Thirion, Olivier Grisel, Mathieu Blondel, Peter Prettenhofer, Ron Weiss, Vincent Dubourg, et al. 2011. Scikit-learn: Machine learning in python. *Journal of Machine Learning Research* 12(Oct):2825–2830.

Sara Rosenthal, Noura Farra, and Preslav Nakov. 2017. SemEval-2017 task 4: Sentiment analysis in Twitter. In *Proceedings of the 11th International Workshop on Semantic Evaluation*. Association for Computational Linguistics, Vancouver, Canada, SemEval '17.

Gerard Salton. 1989. Automatic text processing: The transformation, analysis, and retrieval of. *Reading: Addison-Wesley* .

Richard Socher, Alex Perelygin, Jean Y Wu, Jason Chuang, Christopher D Manning, Andrew Y Ng, Christopher Potts, et al. 2013. Recursive deep models for semantic compositionality over a sentiment treebank. In *Proceedings of the conference on empirical methods in natural language processing (EMNLP)*. volume 1631, page 1642.

Md Arafat Sultan, Steven Bethard, and Tamara Sumner. 2015. Dls@ cu: Sentence similarity from word alignment and semantic vector composition. In *Proceedings of the 9th International Workshop on Semantic Evaluation*. pages 148–153.

Andranik Tumasjan, Timm O. Sprenger, Philipp G. Sandner, and Isabell M. Welpe. 2010. Predicting elections with twitter: What 140 characters reveal about political sentiment. In *Proceedings of the Fourth International AAAI Conference on Weblogs and Social Media*. pages 178–185.

Hao Wang, Dogan Can, Abe Kazemzadeh, François
Bar, and Shrikanth Narayanan. 2012. A system
for real-time twitter sentiment analysis of 2012 u.s.
presidential election cycle. In *Proceedings of the
ACL 2012 System Demonstrations*. Association for
Computational Linguistics, Stroudsburg, PA, USA,
ACL '12, pages 115–120.

Chang Xu, Dacheng Tao, and Chao Xu. 2013. A
survey on multi-view learning. *arXiv preprint
arXiv:1304.5634* .

Jiang Zhao, Man Lan, and Jun Feng Tian. 2015. Ecnu:
Using traditional similarity measurements and word
embedding for semantic textual similarity estimation. In *Proceedings of the 9th International Workshop on Semantic Evaluation (SemEval 2015)*. page
117.

System Implementation for SemEval-2017 Task 4 Subtask A
Based on Interpolated Deep Neural Networks

[1]**Tzu-Hsuan Yang**, [2]**Tzu-Hsuan Tseng**, and [3]**Chia-Ping Chen**
Department of Computer Science and Engineering
National Sun Yat-sen University
Kaohsiung, Taiwan
[1]m043040003@student.nsysu.edu.tw
[2]m043040013@student.nsysu.edu.tw
[3]cpchen@cse.nsysu.edu.tw

Abstract

In this paper, we describe our system implementation for sentiment analysis in Twitter. This system combines two models based on deep neural networks, namely a convolutional neural network (CNN) and a long short-term memory (LSTM) recurrent neural network, through interpolation. Distributed representation of words as vectors are input to the system, and the output is a sentiment class. The neural network models are trained exclusively with the data sets provided by the organizers of SemEval-2017 Task 4 Subtask A. Overall, this system has achieved 0.618 for the average recall rate, 0.587 for the average F1 score, and 0.618 for accuracy.

1 Introduction

Analysis of digital content created and spread in social networks are becoming instrumental in public affairs. Twitter is one of the popular social networks, so there are more and more researches on Twitter recently, including sentiment analysis, which predicts the polarity of a message.

A message submitted to Twitter is called a tweet. Millions of tweets are created every hour, expressing users' views or emotions towards all sorts of topics. Different from a document or an article, a tweet is limited in length to 140 characters. In addition, tweets are often colloquial and may contain emotional symbols called emoticons.

For sentiment analysis, deep learning-based approaches have performed well in recent years. For example, convolution neural networks (CNN) with word embeddings have been implemented for text classification (Kim, 2014), and have achieved state-of-the-art results in SemEval 2015 (Severyn and Moschitti, 2015).

In this paper, we describe our system for SemEval-2017 Task 4 Subtask A for message polarity classification (Rosenthal et al., 2017). It classifies the sentiment of a tweet as positive, neutral, or negative. Our system combines a CNN and a recurrent neural network (RNN) based on long short-term memory (LSTM) cells. We use word embeddings in both models and interpolate them. Our submission achieved 0.618 for average recall, which ranked 19th out of 39 participating teams for subtask A.

This paper is organized as follows. In Section 2, we review previous studies on sentiment analysis in Twitter. In Section 3, we describe data, preprocessing steps, model architectures, and tools used in developing our system. In Section 4, we present the evaluation results along with our comments. In Section 5, we draw conclusion and discuss future works.

2 Related Works

In this section, we briefly review the research works of sentiment analysis in Twitter based on deep neural networks. A one-layer convolution neural network with embeddings can achieve high performance on sentiment analysis (Kim, 2014). In SemEval 2016, quite a few submissions were based on neural networks. A CNN model with word embedding is implemented for all subtasks (Ruder et al., 2016). The model performs well on three-point scale sentiment classification, while performing poorly on five-point scale sentiment classification. A GRU-based model with two kinds of embedding used for general and task-specific purpose can be more efficient than CNN models (Nabil et al., 2016).

Proceedings of the 11th International Workshop on Semantic Evaluations (SemEval-2017), pages 616–620,
Vancouver, Canada, August 3 - 4, 2017. ©2017 Association for Computational Linguistics

	Vocab.	Pos.	Neu.	Neg.	Total
train	29039	2607	1712	713	5032
test		5939	8672	2596	17207

Table 1: Statistics of SemEval-2016.

	Vocab.	Pos.	Neu.	Neg.	Total
train	38532	12844	12249	4609	29702
dev		7059	10341	3231	20632

Table 2: Statistics of SemEval-2017.

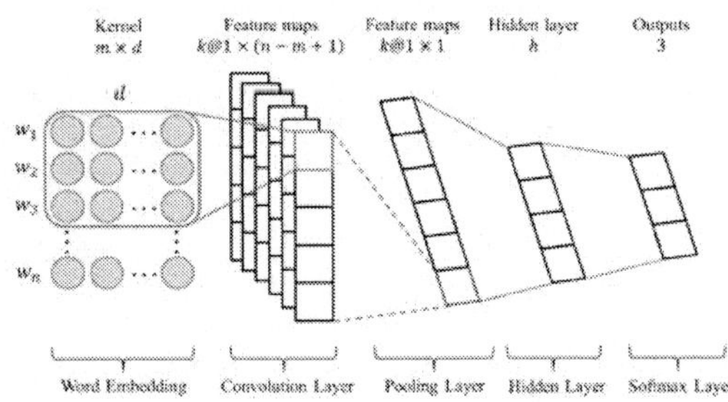

Figure 1: CNN architecture.

3 Experiment

3.1 Data

We use two datasets called SemEval-2016 and SemEval-2017. Tables 1 and 2 summarize the statistics of these datasets.

For the set of SemEval-2016, we obtain 5032 tweets for train data and 17207 tweets for test data from twitter API, respectively. Although some of the original tweets were not available in the beginning, we still use this SemEval-2016 data set for evaluating different models and tuning hyperparameters.

The SemEval-2017 is provided by task organizers. It contains SemEval data used in the years from 2013 to 2016. We use 2013-train, 2013-dev, 2013-test, 2014-sarcasm, 2014-test, 2015-train, 2015-test, 2016-train, 2016-dev, and 2016-devtest as train data. The 2017-dev data is used for test data, which is almost the same as the 2016-test. The models trained with SemEval-2017 data is used for final submission.

A tweet is pre-processed before it is used in the neural networks. First, we use a tokenizer to split a tweet into words, emoticons and punctuation marks. Then, we replace URLs and USERs with normalization patterns <URL> and <USER>, respectively. All uppercase letters are converted to lowercase letters. Word list contains different words in the training data, and vocabulary size is the size of word list. During test, words not in the word list are removed. After pre-processing, words are converted to vectors by GloVe (Pennington et al., 2014). Then the sequence of embedding word vectors are input to neural networks.

3.2 System

3.2.1 CNN

The CNN model we use is the architecture used by Kim (Kim, 2014), which consists of a non-linear convolution layer, max-pooling layer, one hidden layer, and softmax layer. Figure 1 depicts our CNN model.

The input of this model is a pre-processed tweet, which is treated as a sequence of words. We pad input texts with zeros to the length n.

A pre-processed tweet $w_{1:n}$ is represented by the corresponding word embedding $x_{1:n}$, where x_i is the d-dimensional word vector of i-th word. The word embedding is a parameterized function mapping words to vectors as a lookup table parameterized by a matrix. Through word-embedding, input words are embedded into dense representation, and then feed to the convolution layer. Words out-of-embeddings will be represented by zero vector. And each input texts will be mapped to a $n \times d$ input matrix.

At the convolution layer, filters of size $m \times d$ slide over the input matrix and creates $(n - m + 1)$ features each filter. We use k filters to create k feature maps. Thus, the size of the convolutional layer is $k \times 1 \times (n - m + 1)$.

We apply the max pooling operation over each feature map (Kim, 2014). After max pooling, we use dropout by randomly drop out some activation values while training for regularization in order to prevent the model from overfitting (Srivastava et al., 2014). Then we add a hidden layer to get the appropriate representation and a dense layer with softmax function to get probabilities for classification.

3.2.2 RNN

Figure 2 shows our architecture of RNN-based model, which contains input layer, embedding layer, hidden layer and softmax layer.

At the input layer, each tweet is treated as a sequence of words $w_1, w_2, ..., w_n$, where n is the maximum tweet length. In order to fix the length

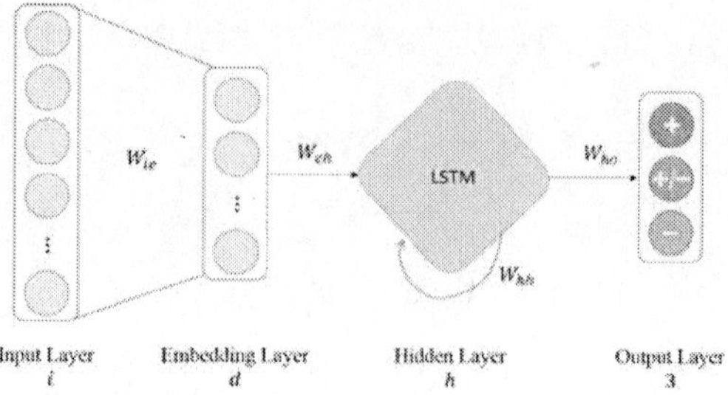

Figure 2: LSTM-based RNN architecture.

of tweet, we pad zero at beginning of tweets whose length is less than n. The size of input layer is equal to the size of word list, and each word is represented by a one-hot vector.

At the embedding layer, each word is converted to a word vector. We use pre-trained word vectors, GloVe, where word vectors are stored in a matrix. Specifically, a word in the word list is represented by the corresponding row vector (or a leading subvector), while a word not in the word list is represented by a zero vector.

At the hidden layer, we choose LSTM memory cell (Hochreiter and Schmidhuber, 1997) for its long-range dependency. It is argued that LSTM can get better results than simple RNN. The model contains one hidden layer, which size is h. The hidden states of first word to $(n-1)$-th word in a tweet connect to the hidden state of the next word. Only the hidden state of n-th word connect to the next (output) layer. Also, we add dropout to the hidden layer for regularization.

At the softmax layer, output values through a softmax function model the probabilities of three classes. During test phase, the sentiment class with the greatest probability is the output sentiment.

3.2.3 Interpolation

On SemEval-2016 data, performances of SA systems with respect to different sentiment classes have shown significant difference. Thus, we interpolate them to achieve better generalisation. After models are trained respectively, we interpolate them with weight λ

$$p_{\text{interp}} = \lambda \times p_{\text{lstm}} + (1 - \lambda) \times p_{\text{cnn}} \quad (1)$$

where p_{lstm} and p_{cnn} are the probability of the LSTM and CNN model, respectively, and p_{interp} is the interpolated probability.

3.2.4 Settings

The maximum length for the tweets in SemEval-2017 data set is $n = 99$. The dimension of word vector is set to $d = 100$ at first, and then varied to a few values.

For CNN model, we choose $k = 50$ filters with size 3×100 with stride $s = 1$ over the input matrix. Max pooling is applied over each feature map. Then, we drop activations randomly with the probability $p = 0.2$ and feed to the hidden layer with size $h = 20$.

For RNN-based model, input size i is the size of word list and hidden size h is 50. We drop input units for input gates and recurrent connections with same probability $p = 0.2$.

We have tried rectified linear units (ReLU) and hyperbolic tangent (tanh) function for the activation function, and it seems that tanh performs better than ReLU in our experiments. We use cross entropy for the objective function and Adam algorithm for optimization. Finally, the CNN and LSTM models are interpolated with weight $\lambda = 0.6$ through a grid search.

3.3 Tool

The tokenizer for text pre-processing is the Happytokenizer[1]. All models we use in our experiments are implemented using Keras[2] with Tensorflow[3] backend.

4 Result

4.1 Comparison of Representations

First, we compare one-hot representation (sparse) and word vector representation (distributed). We train simple RNN and LSTM-based model and evaluate them on SemEval-2016 data. Each model contains one hidden layer with 50 hidden units. For models using word embeddings, the dimension of a word vector is $d = 100$.

The results are shown in Table 3. We can see that word vectors work better than one-hot vectors, except for the F1 score of RNN. We also observe that RNN model with embedding is prone to predict negative class as positive, and LSTM model predicts more accurately over all classes.

---

[1] http://sentiment.christopherpotts.net/tokenizing.html
[2] https://keras.io/
[3] https://www.tensorflow.org/

	RNN		LSTM	
	sparse	dist.	sparse	dist.
R_{pos}	0.634	0.867	0.726	0.807
R_{neu}	0.339	0.401	0.377	0.444
R_{neg}	0.227	0.014	0.271	0.344
Avg R	0.400	0.427	0.458	0.532
Avg F1	0.365	0.310	0.427	0.515
Acc.	0.424	0.503	0.482	0.554

Table 3: One-hot (sparse) vs. word vector (dist.).

system ID	Avg R	Avg F1	Acc.
RNN-50-20	0.417	0.319	0.485
RNN-100-50	0.427	0.310	0.503
RNN-200-50	0.436	0.410	0.453
LSTM-50-20	0.504	0.496	0.516
LSTM-100-50	0.532	0.515	0.554
LSTM-200-50	0.537	0.522	0.549
LSTM-200-100	0.512	0.500	0.523

Table 4: RNN vs. LSTM. The numbers in a system ID indicate the dimension of word vector and the number of neurons in the hidden layer.

4.2 Comparison of RNN and LSTM

Table 4 list the results of the comparison of RNN and LSTM using SemEval-2016 data. The results of LSTM model are better than RNN model, showing that long-range dependency within text message is useful in sentiment analysis.

4.3 Comparison of Data Amounts

Table 5 shows the results of LSTM and CNN on SemEval-2016 and SemEval-2017 data. As expected, various measures of performance are improved with an increase in the amount of train data.

4.4 Model Interpolation

From Table 5, we can see that CNN performs better than LSTM on negative class, and LSTM performs better than CNN on positive and neutral classes. Thus, by combining their strengths, better generalization can often be achieved than an individual system.

We tune hyper-parameter λ of interpolation via a grid search. We choose word vector size $d = 100$ for both models, one hidden layer with 50 hidden neurons for LSTM model, and number of filters $k = 50$ and fully connected size $h = 20$ for CNN model.

Model	LSTM-100-50		CNN-100-50-20	
	2016	2017	2016	2017
R_{pos}	0.807	0.729	0.824	0.697
R_{neu}	0.444	0.633	0.335	0.502
R_{neg}	0.344	0.451	0.344	0.606
Avg R	0.532	0.604	0.501	0.602
Avg F1	0.515	0.581	0.487	0.564
Acc.	0.554	0.637	0.505	0.585

Table 5: Comparison of LSTM and CNN using different amounts of data. Here the numbers in a CNN system ID indicate the dimension of word vector, the number of filters, and the size of the hidden layer.

		Avg R	Avg F1	Acc.
	baseline	0.333	0.255	0.342
2017	LSTM	0.604	0.581	0.637
dev	CNN	0.602	0.564	0.585
	interpolation	0.631	0.604	0.640
2017	baseline	0.333	0.162	0.193
test	interpolation	0.618	0.587	0.616

Table 6: Results on SemEval-2017 data with interpolation weight $\lambda = 0.6$.

Eventually, the interpolated system gets 0.618 for average recall rate on subtask A on SemEval 2017 test data, as shown in Table 6.

5 Conclusion

We implemented CNN and LSTM models with word embedding for sentiment analysis in Twitter data organized in SemEval 2017. Our experiments reveled an interesting point that LSTM model performs well on positive and neutral classes, while CNN model performs average on all classes. The final submission is based on model interpolation, with the weight decided by development set. It achieved 0.618 for 3-class average recall rate, 0.587 for 2-class average F1-score, and 0.618 for accuracy.

For near-future works, we hope to get closer in performance to the leaders on the board, respectively 0.681, 0.685, and 0.657. We will start by looking at methods that deal with data imbalance, as well as adversarial training approaches.

Acknowledgments

We thank the Ministry of Science and Technology of Taiwan, ROC for funding this research.

References

Sepp Hochreiter and Jürgen Schmidhuber. 1997. Long short-term memory. *Neural computation* 9(8):1735–1780.

Yoon Kim. 2014. Convolutional neural networks for sentence classification. *arXiv preprint arXiv:1408.5882* .

Mahmoud Nabil, Amir Atyia, and Mohamed Aly. 2016. Cufe at semeval-2016 task 4: A gated recurrent model for sentiment classification. In *Proceedings of the 10th International Workshop on Semantic Evaluation (SemEval-2016)*.

Jeffrey Pennington, Richard Socher, and Christopher D. Manning. 2014. Glove: Global vectors for word representation. In *Empirical Methods in Natural Language Processing (EMNLP)*. pages 1532–1543. http://www.aclweb.org/anthology/D14-1162.

Sara Rosenthal, Noura Farra, and Preslav Nakov. 2017. SemEval-2017 task 4: Sentiment analysis in Twitter. In *Proceedings of the 11th International Workshop on Semantic Evaluation*. Association for Computational Linguistics, Vancouver, Canada, SemEval '17.

Sebastian Ruder, Parsa Ghaffari, and John G Breslin. 2016. Insight-1 at semeval-2016 task 4: Convolutional neural networks for sentiment classification and quantification. *arXiv preprint arXiv:1609.02746* .

Aliaksei Severyn and Alessandro Moschitti. 2015. Unitn: Training deep convolutional neural network for twitter sentiment classification. In *Proceedings of the 9th International Workshop on Semantic Evaluation (SemEval 2015), Association for Computational Linguistics, Denver, Colorado*. pages 464–469.

Nitish Srivastava, Geoffrey E Hinton, Alex Krizhevsky, Ilya Sutskever, and Ruslan Salakhutdinov. 2014. Dropout: a simple way to prevent neural networks from overfitting. *Journal of Machine Learning Research* 15(1):1929–1958.

NNEMBs at SemEval-2017 Task 4: Neural Twitter Sentiment Classification: a Simple Ensemble Method with Different Embeddings

Yichun Yin
Peking University
`yichunyin@pku.edu.cn`

Yangqiu Song
HKUST
`yqsong@cse.ust.hk`

Ming Zhang
Peking University
`mzhang_cs@pku.edu.cn`

Abstract

Recently, neural twitter sentiment classification has become one of state-of-the-arts, which requires less feature engineering work compared with traditional methods. In this paper, we propose a simple and effective ensemble method to further boost the performances of neural models. We collect several word embedding sets which are publicly released (often are learned on different corpus) or constructed by running Skip-gram on released large-scale corpus. We make an assumption that different word embeddings cover different words and encode different semantic knowledge, thus using them together can improve the generalizations and performances of neural models. In the SemEval 2017, our method ranks 1st in Accuracy, 5th in AverageR. Meanwhile, the additional comparisons demonstrate the superiority of our model over these ones based on only one word embedding set. We release our code [1] for the method replicability.

1 Introduction

Twitter sentiment classification has attracted a lot of attention (Dong et al., 2015; Nakov et al., 2016; Rosenthal et al., 2017), which aims to classify a tweet into three sentiment categories: negative, neutral, and positive. Tweet text has several features: written by the informal language, hash-tags and emoticons indicate sentiments, and sometimes is sarcasm, which make decisions of tweet sentiment hard for machines. With releases of annotated datasets, more researchers prefer to use the

twitter sentiment classification as one testbed to evaluate their proposed models.

Traditional methods (Mohammad et al., 2013) for twitter sentiment classification use a variety of hand-crafted features including surface-form, semantic and sentiment lexicons. The performances of these methods often depend on the quality of feature engineering work, and building a state-of-the-art system is difficult for novices. Moreover, these designed features are presented by the one-hot representation which cannot capture the semantic relativeness of different features and proposes a problem of feature sparsity. To address this, Tang et al. (2014) induced sentiment-specific low-dimensional, real-valued embedding features for twitter classification, which encode both semantics and sentiments of words. In the experiments, the embedding features and hand-crafted features obtain similar results, and also they are complementary for each other in the system. With the developments of neural networks in natural language processing, neural sentiment classification (Severyn and Moschitti, 2015; Deriu et al., 2016) has attracted a lot of attention recently and become the state-of-the-arts. These methods first learn word embeddings from large-scale twitter corpus, then tune neural networks by the tweets which have distant labels, and finally fine-tune the proposed models by the annotated datasets.

Learning word embeddings using in-domain data is an effective way to boost model performances (Mikolov et al., 2013; Yin et al., 2016). However, collecting large-scale twitter corpus is often time-consuming. In this paper, we use the different word embedding sets to boost the performances of our neural networks, which only include released different word embeddings sets and the word embedding set derived from the released Yelp large-scale datasets by Skip-gram (Mikolov et al., 2013). A simple and effective ensemble

---

[1] https://github.com/zwjyyc/NNEMBs

Proceedings of the 11th International Workshop on Semantic Evaluations (SemEval-2017), pages 621–625,
Vancouver, Canada, August 3 - 4, 2017. ©2017 Association for Computational Linguistics

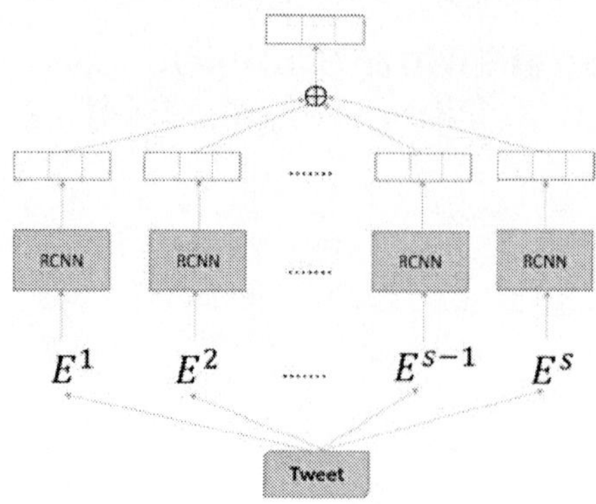

Figure 1: Overview of our method.

method is proposed, which takes different word embedding sets as input to train neural networks and predicts labels of testing tweets by merging all output of neural models. Our ensemble method show its effectiveness in SemEval 2017, though most of used word embedding sets are not learned from twitter corpus, which can be explained that different embedding sets has different vocabularies and encode different parts of sentiment knowledge. Moreover, we conduct additional experiments to analyze our model.

2 Method

In this section, we describe the details of our method, which is illustrated in Figure 1. We feed different word embedding sets into neural networks and train these neural networks separately. When predicting the labels of tweets in testing set, we sum label probabilities of all neural network to make final decisions.

2.1 Neural Network

We have many choices of neural networks (e.g., LSTM, RNN and GRU) for our method, here we consider RCNN (Lei et al., 2016) in our method. RCNN has non-consecutive convolution and adaptive gated decay, which aims to capture longer-range, non-consecutive patterns in a weighted manner.

Given a sequence of words which are denoted as $\{x_i\}_{i=1}^{l}$, the corresponding word embeddings $\{\mathbf{x}_i\}_{i=1}^{l}$ are derived using the embedding matrix E. Then, RCNN obtains their corresponding hidden vectors $\{\mathbf{h}_i\}_{i=1}^{l}$ using the convolution operation and gating mechanism. After obtaining hidden vectors, RCNN uses a pooling operation to get fixed-sized vector presentation, which is fed

into softmax layer to finish the prediction. The n-gram convolution operation and gating decay are described as follows:

$$\lambda_t = \sigma(\mathbf{W}^\lambda \mathbf{x}_t + \mathbf{U}^\lambda \mathbf{h}_{t-1} + \mathbf{b}^\lambda),$$
$$\mathbf{c}_t^{(1)} = \lambda_t \odot \mathbf{c}_{t-1}^{(1)} + (1 - \lambda_t) \odot (\mathbf{W}_1 \mathbf{x}_t),$$
$$\mathbf{c}_t^{(2)} = \lambda_t \odot \mathbf{c}_{t-1}^{(2)} + (1 - \lambda_t) \odot (\mathbf{c}_{t-1}^{(1)} + \mathbf{W}_2 \mathbf{x}_t),$$
$$\cdots,$$
$$\mathbf{c}_t^{(n)} = \lambda_t \odot \mathbf{c}_{t-1}^{(n)} + (1 - \lambda_t) \odot (\mathbf{c}_{t-1}^{(n-1)} + \mathbf{W}_n \mathbf{x}_t),$$
$$\mathbf{h}_t = \tanh(\mathbf{c}_t^{(n)} + \mathbf{b}),$$

where $\mathbf{W}^\lambda$, $\mathbf{U}^\lambda$, $\mathbf{b}^\lambda$, $\mathbf{b}$ and $\mathbf{W}_*$ are learnable parameters, σ is sigmoid function which rescales the value into $(0, 1)$, $\odot$ is dot product, λ_t is gating value determining how much information of $\mathbf{x}_t$ and previous patterns is added into the hidden vector, $\mathbf{c}_t^{(i)}$ refer to the vector for accumulated previous patterns which are ended with x_t include i consecutive tokens. When $\lambda_t = 0$, the convolution becomes a standard n-gram convolution.

We also can build a deep RCNN by adding several convolution layer on top of hidden vectors derived from the bottom convolution layer. Here we consider the RCNN with d convolution layers, which outputs $\{\mathbf{h}_i^d\}_{i=1}^{l}$. Then, a last pooling operation is conducted on hidden vectors to obtain text representation $\mathbf{r}$. Finally, text representation is fed into a softmax layer. The softmax layer outputs the probability distribution over $|\mathcal{Y}|$ categories for the distributed representation, which is defined as:

$$\mathbf{p}(\mathbf{r}) = \text{softmax}(\mathbf{W}_k^{class} \mathbf{r}).$$

The cross-entropy objective function is used to optimize the RCNN model.

2.2 Prediction

We learn different RCNN models with different embedding sets as input. Formally, we have s embedding sets which are denoted as $\{\mathbf{E}^1, \mathbf{E}^2, \cdots, \mathbf{E}^s\}$, and feed them into s RCNN models, then learn RCNN models separately. We predict sentiment label of testing tweet based on these learned RCNN models, which are described by following functions:

Sets	Corpus	Scale	Algorithm	Dimension	Source	Vocab
gloveG	General	840B	GloVec	300	**R**	2.2M
gloveT	Twitter	27B	GloVec	200	**R**	1.2M
word2vecGN	Google News	100B	Word2Vec	300	**R**	3.0M
word2vecY	Yelp Reviews	0.3B	Word2Vec	300	**S**	0.2M
Ensemble	-	-	-	-	-	5.4M

Table 1: Statistics of the embedding sets. **R** means the embedding set is publicly released and **S** means the embedding set is self-contained. GloVec (Mikolov et al., 2013) and Word2Vec (Pennington et al., 2014) are most popular embedding algorithms. Scale means the size of tokens in corpus, M and B refer to million and billion respectively. The embedding set word2vecY are trained by Word2Vec with default settings and Yelp reviews are available at https://www.yelp.com/dataset_challenge.

Dataset	#num	#category_ratio
Previous SemEvals	50032	1.5/4.7/3.8
SemEval 2017 Test	12284	3.2/4.8/2.0

Table 2: Statistics of datasets.

$$\mathbf{p}_1 = \text{RCNN}_1(\{x_i\}_{i=1}^l, \mathbf{E}^1),$$

$$\mathbf{p}_2 = \text{RCNN}_2(\{x_i\}_{i=1}^l, \mathbf{E}^2),$$

$$\cdots,$$

$$\mathbf{p}_s = \text{RCNN}_s(\{x_i\}_{i=1}^l, \mathbf{E}^s),$$

$$\mathbf{p}' = \sum_{1 \le i \le s} \mathbf{p}_i.$$

$$y = \text{argmax}_{1 \le i \le |\mathcal{Y}|} \mathbf{P}_i',$$

where y is the predicted label.

3 Experiment

3.1 Datasets and Settings

We use 4 embedding sets which are described in Table 1. Meanwhile, we crawl and merge all annotated datasets of previous SemEvals, and split them into training, development, and testing sets with ratio 8:1:1, which are shown in Table 2 together with testing set of SemEval 2017. From the table, we can see that testing set of SemEval 2017 has big differences on the category ratio (negative:neutral:positive), compared with the previous SemEval datasets.

For the model settings, all RCNN models have same configurations but different word embedding sets. We set dimensions of hidden vectors to 250 and depths d to 2. To avoid model over-fitting, we use dropout and regularization as follows: (1) the regularization parameter is set to *1e-5*; (2) the

dropout rate is set to 0.3, which is applied in the final text representation. All parameters are learned by Adam optimizer (Kingma and Ba, 2014) with the learning rate 0.001. Note that, all word embedding sets are fixed when training. All models are tuned by the development set in Training.

3.2 Results and Analysis

In this section, we first report the results on datasets of previous SemEvals, which are described in Table 3. Then, we report the performances of our method on SemEval 2017 in Table 4.

From the Table 3, we observe that gloveT performs worst though it is trained on in-domain twitter dataset and the word2vecY performs best though it is derived from yelp reviews. As far as we known, Yelp data is constructed by carefully filtering and is high-quality. Thus, we can include that the quality of corpus is also important as the size of corpus and domain in twitter sentiment classification. Additionally, we can infer that word2vecGN outperforms others in recall of negative category, word2vecY performs best in recall of neutral category, and gloveT is best in recall of positive category. Different embedding sets propose different characteristics. Additionally, the ensemble method obtains a significant improvement of 4%.

In the Table 4, we compare our method with best and median systems in SemEval 2017, and report the results of individual embedding sets. Our method outperforms other systems in accuracy, but performs worse in R_Average, especially in R_Negative. Compared with the median system, our method has improvements of about 5% in both accuracy and R_Average. Different from the results in Table 3, the word2vecY performs

Embeddings	Accuracy	R_Negative	R_Neutral	R_Positive	R_Average
gloveG	70.6	66.3	66.4	77.7	70.1
gloveT	68.3	66.8	61.2	77.9	68.7
word2vecGN	70.5	70.2	68.3	73.5	70.7
word2vecY	72.2	65.0	71.3	76.2	70.8
Ensemble	**74.6**	**72.1**	**71.2**	**80.0**	**74.5**

Table 3: Results on datasets of previous SemEval. R_* means recall value.

Embeddings	Accuracy	R_Negative	R_Neutral	R_Positive	R_Average
Best_system	65.1	**82.9**	51.2	**70.2**	**68.1**
Median_system	61.6	53.1	**65.0**	67.4	61.8
gloveG	62.9	63.0	61.3	66.7	63.7
gloveT	63.7	70.5	57.4	68.2	65.4
word2vecGN	62.9	68.4	60.0	60.8	63.1
word2vecY	61.6	59.1	63.8	60.5	61.1
Our	**66.4**	69.8	64.0	66.8	66.9

Table 4: Results on SemEval 2017. The median system is the system of rank 19th among 38 teams.

worse among these embedding sets, while the gloveT obtains best performances. Additionally, we can observe that gloveT performs best both in R_Negative and R_Positive, and word2vecY performs best in R_Neutral. Compared with the embedding baselines, our ensemble method obtains improvements of 2.7% and 1.5% in accuracy and R_Average respectively, which demonstrates the effectiveness of the proposed method.

3.3 Error Analysis

In this section, we analyze the incorrect predictions of our system in SemEval 2017.

We summarize four kinds of errors in our system. The first one is that some decisions need domain knowledge, which our method only can learn from the labeled datasets. The instances are as follows:

Messi's 100 international goals for Barcelona #fcblive https://t.co/fMkglvusL1 [via @thereisagenius]. Predicted label: **neutral**, golden label: **positive**

#Trudeau gives your cash to #Terrorist #Hamas-influenced group - #UNRWA - @CandiceMalcolm https://t.co/5i5o2qwRWl Predicted label: **neutral**, golden label: **negative**

Messis 9 goals in CL are more than 20 of the 32 teams in the competition have scored in total, and hes tied with five other sides #fcblive Predicted label: **neutral**, golden label: **positive**

The second one is emoticons in tweet, as most of word embedding sets do not include emoticon embeddings and emoticons are always with senti-

Figure 2: Emoticon instances.

ments. The instances are described in Figure 2

The third one is that sentiments are not consistent in sentences. For example, the first half part is positive, while the second half part is negative, in this case, our system would predict 'positive' or 'negative', the golden label is neutral.

@jimmyfallon 1. Emily 2. Michel 3. Kirk 4. TJ. Love the quirky ones and Emily coz she's such a BIATCH! #gilmoregirlstop4. predicted label **positive**, golden label: **neutral**

The fourth one is the sarcasm, such as: *#Hamas leader: #Trump may be a #Jew https://t.co/jGFZTvj2pF.* predicted label **positive**, golden label: **negative**

4 Conclusion

We propose a simple and effective ensemble method to boost the neural twitter sentiment classification. By using different embedding sets, the system can cover more words and encode more sentiment information. The results on datasets of previous SemEval and SemEval 2017 show the effectiveness of our method. Moreover, error analysis is conducted to propose the main challenges for our method. We release our code for system duplicability.

References

Jan Deriu, Maurice Gonzenbach, Fatih Uzdilli, Aurélien Lucchi, Valeria De Luca, and Martin Jaggi. 2016. Swisscheese at semeval-2016 task 4: Sentiment classification using an ensemble of convolutional neural networks with distant supervision. In *Proceedings of the 10th International Workshop on Semantic Evaluation, SemEval@NAACL-HLT 2016, San Diego, CA, USA, June 16-17, 2016.* pages 1124–1128. http://aclweb.org/anthology/S/S16/S16-1173.pdf.

Li Dong, Furu Wei, Yichun Yin, Ming Zhou, and Ke Xu. 2015. Splusplus: A feature-rich two-stage classifier for sentiment analysis of tweets. *SemEval-2015* page 515.

Diederik P. Kingma and Jimmy Ba. 2014. Adam: A method for stochastic optimization. *CoRR* abs/1412.6980. http://arxiv.org/abs/1412.6980.

Tao Lei, Hrishikesh Joshi, Regina Barzilay, Tommi S. Jaakkola, Kateryna Tymoshenko, Alessandro Moschitti, and Lluís Màrquez. 2016. Semi-supervised question retrieval with gated convolutions. In *NAACL HLT 2016, The 2016 Conference of the North American Chapter of the Association for Computational Linguistics: Human Language Technologies, San Diego California, USA, June 12-17, 2016.* pages 1279–1289. http://aclweb.org/anthology/N/N16/N16-1153.pdf.

Tomas Mikolov, Ilya Sutskever, Kai Chen, Gregory S. Corrado, and Jeffrey Dean. 2013. Distributed representations of words and phrases and their compositionality. In *Advances in Neural Information Processing Systems 26: 27th Annual Conference on Neural Information Processing Systems 2013. Proceedings of a meeting held December 5-8, 2013, Lake Tahoe, Nevada, United States..* pages 3111–3119. http://papers.nips.cc/paper/5021-distributed-representations-of-words-and-phrases-and-their-compositionality.

Saif Mohammad, Svetlana Kiritchenko, and Xiaodan Zhu. 2013. Nrc-canada: Building the state-of-the-art in sentiment analysis of tweets. In *Proceedings of the 7th International Workshop on Semantic Evaluation, SemEval@NAACL-HLT 2013, Atlanta, Georgia, USA, June 14-15, 2013.* pages 321–327. http://aclweb.org/anthology/S/S13/S13-2053.pdf.

Preslav Nakov, Alan Ritter, Sara Rosenthal, Fabrizio Sebastiani, and Veselin Stoyanov. 2016. Semeval-2016 task 4: Sentiment analysis in twitter. In *Proceedings of the 10th International Workshop on Semantic Evaluation, SemEval@NAACL-HLT 2016, San Diego, CA, USA, June 16-17, 2016.* pages 1–18. http://aclweb.org/anthology/S/S16/S16-1001.pdf.

Jeffrey Pennington, Richard Socher, and Christopher D. Manning. 2014. Glove: Global vectors for word representation. In *Proceedings of the 2014 Conference on Empirical Methods in Natural Language Processing, EMNLP 2014, October 25-29, 2014, Doha, Qatar, A meeting of SIGDAT, a Special Interest Group of the ACL.* pages 1532–1543. http://aclweb.org/anthology/D/D14/D14-1162.pdf.

Sara Rosenthal, Noura Farra, and Preslav Nakov. 2017. SemEval-2017 task 4: Sentiment analysis in Twitter. In *Proceedings of the 11th International Workshop on Semantic Evaluation.* Association for Computational Linguistics, Vancouver, Canada, SemEval '17.

Aliaksei Severyn and Alessandro Moschitti. 2015. UNITN: training deep convolutional neural network for twitter sentiment classification. In *Proceedings of the 9th International Workshop on Semantic Evaluation, SemEval@NAACL-HLT 2015, Denver, Colorado, USA, June 4-5, 2015.* pages 464–469. http://aclweb.org/anthology/S/S15/S15-2079.pdf.

Duyu Tang, Furu Wei, Nan Yang, Ming Zhou, Ting Liu, and Bing Qin. 2014. Learning sentiment-specific word embedding for twitter sentiment classification. In *Proceedings of the 52nd Annual Meeting of the Association for Computational Linguistics (Volume 1: Long Papers).* Association for Computational Linguistics, Baltimore, Maryland, pages 1555–1565. http://www.aclweb.org/anthology/P14-1146.

Yichun Yin, Furu Wei, Li Dong, Kaimeng Xu, Ming Zhang, and Ming Zhou. 2016. Unsupervised word and dependency path embeddings for aspect term extraction. In *Proceedings of the Twenty-Fifth International Joint Conference on Artificial Intelligence, IJCAI 2016, New York, NY, USA, 9-15 July 2016.* pages 2979–2985. http://www.ijcai.org/Abstract/16/423.

CrystalNest at SemEval-2017 Task 4: Using Sarcasm Detection for Enhancing Sentiment Classification and Quantification

Raj Kumar Gupta and **Yinping Yang**[*]
Institute of High Performance Computing (IHPC)
Agency for Science, Technology and Research (A*STAR), Singapore
{*gupta-rk, yangyp*}@ihpc.a-star.edu.sg

Abstract

This paper describes a system developed for a shared sentiment analysis task and its subtasks organized by SemEval-2017. A key feature of our system is the embedded ability to detect sarcasm in order to enhance the performance of sentiment classification. We first constructed an affect-cognition-sociolinguistics sarcasm features model and trained a SVM-based classifier for detecting sarcastic expressions from general tweets. For sentiment prediction, we developed *CrystalNest*—a two-level cascade classification system using features combining sarcasm score derived from our sarcasm classifier, sentiment scores from Alchemy, NRC lexicon, n-grams, word embedding vectors, and part-of-speech features. We found that the sarcasm detection derived features consistently benefited key sentiment analysis evaluation metrics, in different degrees, across four subtasks A-D.

1 Introduction

Sentiment analysis, also known as opinion mining, is the study of the feelings and opinions from user-generated content. Sarcasm detection, though very related, is a different topic of interest. As a classification task, the primary objective of sentiment analysis is to determine if a message is positive, negative, or neutral. In contrast, the objective of sarcasm detection is to determine if a message is sarcastic or not sarcastic.

To illustrate, let us look at two short text examples. Example 1 expresses a positive sentiment which has a slight mixed feeling, but it is not sarcastic. A very similar-looking Example 2 is sarcastic, and its underlying sentiment is negative.

Ex 1. Love my new phone! Only that the battery runs out very fast.

Ex 2. Love my new phone that runs out battery so fast!

In computational linguistics and NLP, detecting sarcasm is receiving increasing research interest (e.g., González-Ibáñez et al., 2011; Reyes et al., 2012; Liebrecht et al., 2013; Riloff et al., 2013; Rajadesingan et al., 2015; Bamman and Smith, 2015). While these studies recognized the linkage between sarcasm and sentiment and have proposed various techniques for detecting sarcasm, none directly studied the impact of sarcasm detection on sentiment analysis. Maynard and Greenwood (2014) is among the first to explore how to use sarcasm-related information to improve sentiment analysis. They proposed a rule-based method involving five rules such as using "#sarcasm" to flip a sentiment from positive to negative. However, their evaluation was performed on a relatively small test dataset of 400 tweets.

We believe that sentiment analysis systems will benefit from a systematically embedded ability to detect sarcasm. In the following, we describe our approach and present supportive findings evaluated on a large set of test data provided by SemEval-2017 Task 4 (Rosenthal et al., 2017).

2 Sarcasm Detection: An Affect-Cognition-Sociolinguistics (ACS) Feature Model

In order to capture discriminative and explainable sarcasm features, we sought to design a feature model based on review and synthesis across related studies such as natural language processing, linguistics, psychology, speech and communication, as well as neuroscience. Our

---

[*]Both authors contributed to this research equally. For correspondence, please contact yangyp@ihpc.a-star.edu.sg.

Proceedings of the 11th International Workshop on Semantic Evaluations (SemEval-2017), pages 626–633,
Vancouver, Canada, August 3 - 4, 2017. ©2017 Association for Computational Linguistics

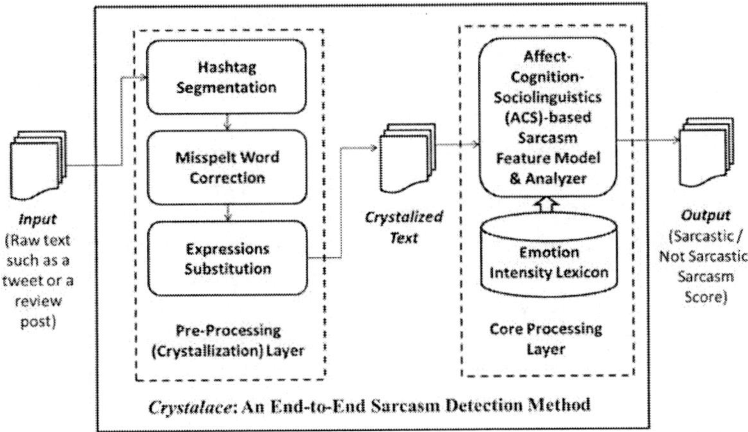

Figure 1: The Key Components of the *Crystalace* Sarcasm Detection Method

model characterizes sarcasm with three key feature groups: affect-related, cognition-related, and sociolinguistics-related features.

Figure 1 presents an overview of the proposed sarcasm detection method that we name it as "Crystalace". *Crystalace* will subsequently produce a key feature, i.e. sarcasm score, for the final *CrystalNest* sentiment analysis system. *Crystalace*'s core processing layer is the affect-cognition-sociolinguistics sarcasm feature model (sections 2.1-2.4). *Crystalace* also includes a supporting layer that pre-processes raw text into crystallized text (section 2.5) for effective feature extraction.

2.1 Affect-related features

A fundamental understanding of sarcasm is that it involves a negative emotional connotation through a seemingly positive expression (Brant, 2012). Riloff et al. (2013) suggested that *count* of positive and negative words, *location* and *order* of positive words and negative words are useful features in sarcasm detection. Rajadesingan et al. (2015) further used *strength* of positive words and negative words and found that strength-related features (e.g., count of very positive words in a tweet) are among top ten sarcasm features in their study.

In our model, beyond the valence and strength-related features, we propose to incorporate the intensity aspect of affective expressions. Conceptually, psychologists characterized emotion with two fundamental dimensions: the strength dimension (Osgood et al., 1957 called it "evaluation") in that an expression would have a positive or negative meaning that is strong, moderate or weak, and the intensity dimension (Shaver et al., 1987) which

further concerns what Osgood et al. called motivational "potency" and physical "activity"[1]. With the intensity dimension, anger-based expressions (high in potency), for example, can be differentiated from sadness-based expressions (low in potency). Because sarcasm is featured with an underlying emotional connation (Brant, 2012), it is conceivable that expressers would tend to leverage seemingly positive emotions such as joy or gratitude words to implicate underlying negative mental experiences such as contempt or disapproval. Thus, in addition to the strength dimension, we explore capturing the emotional intensity variances to further differentiate sarcastic from non-sarcastic expressions.

Other than using words, Twitter users often use special punctuations to highlight their affective experiences, which can be useful cues to sarcasm. For example, users tend to capitalize certain letters to express strong feelings. Others may also use repetitive exclamations marks "!!!". Therefore, we consider these special punctuations as affect-related features. Lastly, we consider percentage of first-persons singular pronouns (I, me, mine etc.) as a feature as research in linguistic psychology has indicated that such words give an expresser power to make an emotional connection with the audience (Cohen, 2014).

2.2 Cognition-related features

Besides affect, sarcasm is also significantly associated with cognitive processes. As Haiman (1998) puts it, what is essential to sarcasm is that it is

---

[1] It is worth noting that other psychologists (e.g., Russell, 1980; Plutchik, 1980; Mehrabian, 1980) have also proposed other emotion dimensions.

"overt irony intentionally used by the speaker as a form of verbal aggression". Neuropsychology studies also indicated that damage of certain cognitive functions in the brain harms people's ability in recognizing sarcasm (Shamay-Tsoory et al., 2005; Davis et al., 2016). Because sarcasm is intentional, there is a degree of deliberation in order to construct sarcasm. Thus, if a sarcastic tweet is produced, the tweet is probably manifested with a high degree of lexical complexity which is also likely constructed by a high cognitive complexity individual. Conversely, a low cognitive complexity individual would tend to be more straightforward to communicate their feelings.

In linguistics, certain words have been found to reveal "depth of thinking" (Tausczik and Pennebaker, 2009). These include cognitive processes words (e.g., *because*), conjunctions (e.g., *although*), prepositions (e.g., *to*) and words greater than six letters. In addition, psycholinguistic analysis of tweets has suggested that a well-prepared and constructed tweet is correlated with higher lexical density, which is marked by information-carrying words (Hu et al., 2013). Therefore, we include nouns, negation, verbs, adjectives, numbers, and quantifiers which are information-carrying words in this feature category.

2.3 Sociolinguistics-related features

In verbal communication, average pitch, pitch slop, and laughter or responses to questions have been found to be prosodic cues to sarcasm utterances (Tepperman et al., 2006). In online digital platforms such as Twitter, users do not have facial and vocal cues at their disposal to communicate sarcastic expressions (Burgers, 2010). In consequence, they would find some alternative and "creative" ways to effectively express sarcasm cues as a hint to their intended audiences. Users would use hashtags to highlight a specific key phrase for easy search by others, use at-mentions to bring attention to a specific user, or use emoticons to provide cues to the underlying feelings. Therefore, we incorporate user-created hashtags, at-mentions, URLs and emoticons in our feature model.

2.4 Features Extraction

In total, our proposed sarcasm feature model includes a total of 82 features. The *affect-related* features include 50 valence-based features, strength-based features, intensity-based fea-

tures and other indirect affective features. The *cognition-related* features include a total of 26 depth-of-thinking features (e.g., prep, conj). The *sociolinguistics-related* features refer to 6 Twitter-specific contextual cues features (e.g., #, @).

In order to capture the complementary benefits from different lexical sources, we used three lexicons, i.e., Opinion Lexicon[2] (Hu and Liu, 2004), SentiStrength Lookup Dictionary[3] (Thelwall et al., 2012), and our Emotion Intensity Lexicon[4], in conjunction with two linguistic sources, i.e., LIWC 2015[5] (Pennebaker et al., 2015) and TweetPOS[6] (Owoputi et al., 2013) to extract the relevant features.

Appendix A shows the full list of the 82 features, the feature codes and the respective linguistic resources/tools used for the features extraction.

2.5 Tweets Preprocessing

For supporting effective feature extraction, we designed a procedure to pre-process raw tweets. The first step is *hashtag segmentation* (Davidov et al., 2010), which involves tokenizing each hashtag such that the words can be more readily captured by existing lexical sources (e.g., *#shitnooneeversay* will be *shit no one ever say*). The second step is *misspelt word correction*, which converts words with more than two consecutive letters into those with two consecutive letters (e.g., *greaaat* will be *greaat*, *awwww* will be *aww*), such that intentionally misspelt words are standardized for the subsequent step. The third step is *expressions substi-*

---

[2] https://www.cs.uic.edu/~liub/FBS/sentiment-analysis.html#lexicon

[3] http://sentistrength.wlv.ac.uk/

[4] No major sentiment or emotion lexicons developed to date cover the intensity dimension of emotions. Hence, we developed "Emotion Intensity (EI) Lexicon" for the purpose of more effectively distinguishing emotion-related words and phrases in different degrees of valence, strength and intensity. The EI Lexicon consists of 3,204 lexicon items including classic emotion-carrying English words, common social media slangs and emoticons, where each item is coded with a strength score as well as an intensity score in the range of [-3, -2, -1, 0, 1, 2, 3]. For example, items such as *excited*, *astonished* and *thrill* are coded as "3" (high-intensity, positive). Items such as *thank*, *cooperative*, *concern*, *:)* and *:d* are coded as "1" (low-intensity, positive). Items such as *sorry*, *agh* and *:/* are coded "-2" (medium-intensity, negative). Items such as *hate*, *resented* and *D:* are coded "-3" (high-intensity, negative). Words such as *great*, *haze*, *fulfill*, *sick* and *sleepy* are coded as "0" as they are related to emotions, but are not "genuine emotions" (Clore et al., 1987; Ortony et al., 1987). We will make this lexicon and its upgraded versions available for the research community.

[5] http://liwc.wpengine.com/

[6] http://www.cs.cmu.edu/ ark/TweetNLP/#pos

Method	Precision	Recall	F_1
Random Classifier	.22	.48	.30
N-grams Classifier	.54	.44	.48
Riloff et al. (2013)'s bootstrapped lexicon-based method	.62	.44	.51
Our proposed ACS model-based method (*Crystalace*)	**.52**	**.70**	**.60**

Table 1: Performance of Sarcasm Classification

tution. Even after the first two steps, many tweets could still contain a great variety of unusual expressions. Therefore, we constructed a mapped list of such expressions with more common words or phrases that carry a similar meaning, referencing Internet resources such as Urban Dictionary and Wikipedia. For example, *gonna* will be *going to*, *:/* will be *annoyed*, *aww* will be *sweet*, *classier* will be *excellent*, *rainy* will be *bad weather*, and *sneezing* will be *poor health*.

Note that we do not remove stop words, as removing stop words that helps in classic NLP tasks has been found to harm sentiment analysis performance (Saif et al., 2014).

2.6 Sarcasm Classifier

To train and evaluate our sarcasm classifier, we downloaded the annotated tweets dataset from Riloff et al. (2013), pre-processed the tweets, and trained a linear SVM classifier using our ACS-based features model. Similar to the final condition reported in Riloff et al. (2013), we also added unigrams and bigrams features to complement the theoretical features model. We then ran 10-fold cross validations to evaluate our method's performance. The results in Table 1 show that our ACS-based method obtained F_1-score of .60, which gained an additional .09 as compared to the best condition reported in Riloff et al.'s original study. Based on the results, we trained the final *Crystalace* sarcasm classifier using the full dataset.

3 System Description

Our sarcasm detection-enhanced sentiment analysis system, *CrystalNest*, is designed with five features groups and a cascade classifier with two levels of training. The following provides the development details.

3.1 Sarcasm and Sentiment Features

We used our *Crystalace* sarcasm classifier and Alchemy Language API[7] to form a two-dimensional feature vector. Alchemy Language is a component of the cognitive APIs offered on IBM Watson Developer Cloud. The first dimension of this feature vector contains the confidence score obtained using the sarcasm classifier and the second dimension contains the confidence score that has been obtained by calling Alchemy.

3.2 NRC SemEval-2015 English Twitter Lexicons Features

We also leveraged NRC SemEval-2015 English Twitter Sentiment Lexicons[8] which aims to capture the degree of the positiveness of a given word or phrase (Rosenthal et al., 2015) and a list of negator[9] words to extract a six-dimensional feature vector for each tweet. This feature vector contains the counts of positive, negative, neutral, negators words respectively, as well as maximum and minimum strengths of sentiment for a given tweet.

3.3 N-grams Features

N-grams are a common feature used for sentiment analysis. We extracted unigrams and bigrams from each tweet without removing stop words. To build the n-gram dictionary, we downloaded 25,000 general tweets using Twitter's Streaming API and extracted all possible unigrams and bigrams from those tweets. After extraction, we filtered these unigrams and bigrams based on their occurrences and removed all that appeared less than three times in our tweets dataset. We then used this n-gram dictionary to represent a tweet into the feature space where each of the feature dimensions represents the number of occurrences of that n-gram in the tweet.

3.4 Word Embedding Features

Word embedding has been used in recent Twitter sentiment analysis methods (Zhang et al., 2015; Rouvier and Favre, 2016) due to its ability to represent the semantic and syntactic meaning of

---

[7] https://www.ibm.com/watson/developercloud/alchemy-language.html

[8] http://saifmohammad.com/WebPages/lexicons.html

[9] http://dictionary.cambridge.org/grammar/british-grammar/questions-and-negative-sentences/negation and https://www.grammarly.com/handbook/sentences/negatives/1/negatives/

the word into a low-dimensional feature vector. Here, we used Gensim[10] based Sentence2Vec[11] to convert the tweets into 500-dimensional feature vectors. To train the word-embedding model, we downloaded approximately 8 million general tweets from Twitter using Twitter Streaming API.

3.5 Tweet Part-of-Speech (POS) Features

Lastly, we extracted 25-dimensional part-of-speech (Owoputi et al., 2013) features for each tweet *without* any preprocessing, as the TweetPOS tool has been specially designed to capture tweets-specific linguistic elements. These features help to capture cues such as tweets-specific linguistic counts, punctuation, as well as conversational markers including hashtags, at-mentions, emoticons and URLs.

3.6 Cascade Sentiment Classifier

For our final system, we used a cascade classification approach to predict the sentiment outcome. Before extracting the features, tweets are preprocessed as described in Section 2.5. For each of the five feature groups described in sections 3.1-3.5, we used linear SVM to train three different classifiers using one-against-all approach for positive, negative and neutral classes. For each of these classifiers (first-level classification), we used SemEval-2013 training data for training and SemEval-2016 and SemEval-2017 test tweets for final evaluation.

After obtaining the outputs from all three classifiers of each feature group, we formed a 15-dimensional feature vector and used Naive Bayes classifier to train the final classifier. In this final classifier (second-level classification), we used SemEval-2016 test data for training[12] and SemEval-2017 test data for final evaluation.

For topic-based tweet quantification subtask D, we calibrated *CrystalNest* using a dynamic base-sentiment selection approach as there was no clear prior knowledge to determine if topic-specific information would be benefiting or harming the quantification performance. We first obtained two sets of sentiment scores (*sentiment_general*

and *sentiment_topic*) by using Alchemy to process each individual tweet's sentiment score *with* and *without* using the specific topic information. Then when *sentiment_general* and *sentiment_topic* converged on the same polarity, we used the converged consensus. When *sentiment_general* and *sentiment_topic* produced conflicting polarity for a given tweet, we used the "majority voted" polarity from the other tweets under the same topic to assign the polarity to the particular tweet that received conflicting polarity values. Using this dynamic approach, we found the error terms were reduced as compared to those resulted from simply relying on any of the individual *sentiment_general* and *sentiment_topic* base sentiment features.

4   Results

We evaluated the proposed approach using the official test datasets provided by SemEval-2017 Task 4's subtasks A-D. Tables 2-4 summarize the results. For subtasks A & B, recall and F_1 scores are assessed as averaged scores according to the task organizers (see Rosenthal et al. 2017 for detailed discussion on the evaluation metrics).

System	$Recall(\rho)$	F_1^{PN}	Acc
Subtask A Message Polarity Classification			
Alchemy	.589	.577	.586
Alchemy+Sarcasm	.591	.575	.581
CyrstalNest	**.619**	**.593**	**.629**
Subtask B Topic-based Two-point Scale Classification			
Alchemy	.657	.651	.719
Alchemy+Sarcasm	.820	.816	.821
CyrstalNest	**.827**	**.822**	**.827**

Table 2: *CrystalNest* Results for Subtasks A & B

System	MAE^M	MAE^μ
Subtask C Topic-based Five-point Scale Classification		
Alchemy	.758	.591
Alchemy+Sarcasm	.760	.564
CyrstalNest	**.698**	**.571**

Table 3: *CrystalNest* Results for Subtask C (MAE is an error term; the lower MAE is, the better the system is)

System	KLD	AE	RAE
Subtask D Topic-based Two-point Scale Quantification			
Alchemy	.357	.270	1.718
Alchemy+Sarcasm	.061	.111	1.346
CyrstalNest	**.056**	**.104**	**1.202**

Table 4: *CrystalNest* Results for Subtask D (KLD, AE and RAE are error terms; the lower they are, the better the system is)

---

[10] https://github.com/RaRe-Technologies/gensim

[11] https://github.com/klb3713/sentence2vec

[12] Note that for all the above-mentioned system training, we used only the classic general message-level sentiment (subtask A) data. This could limit the effectiveness of the training, and we plan to expand with more training data for future system enhancement.

The test data provided by SemEval-2017 Task 4 is so far one of the largest annotated sentiment analysis test datasets. Subtask A consists of 12,284 annotated tweets, Subtasks B and D consist of 6,185 annotated tweets, and Subtask C consists of 12,379 annotated tweets. The results indicated that *CrystalNest* consistently benefited the performance more than the full-fledged, off-the-shelf sentiment analysis service offered by Alchemy. Furthermore, when we experimented with the subsystem combining only Alchemy and sarcasm features, the enhancements from sarcasm classifier over Alchemy's base sentiment features were also found in subtasks A, B and D, in particular in the two two-point subtasks B and D.

In comparison with other participating systems, *CrystalNest* obtained relatively good rankings in subtask A (#18 out of 37 systems), subtask B (#9 out of 23), subtask C (#6 out of 15) and subtask D (#4 out of 15).

5 Conclusion

This paper described a new sentiment analysis system featuring a sarcasm detection classifier in conjunction with other complementary features derived from Alchemy, NRC sentiment lexicon, n-grams, word embedding vectors, and part-of-speech features. The evaluation results using sentiment analysis subtasks A-D test data provided initial evidence on the value of embedding sarcasm detection in sentiment analysis systems. For future work, we plan to explore deep learning methods and conduct more experiments to further augment the system performance.

Acknowledgment

This research is supported by the Social Technologies+ Programme funded by A*STAR Joint Council Office. We thank Tong Joo Chuan for the encouragement to pursue this research. The authors are grateful to Faith Tng Hui En and Tng Tai Hou for proofreading assistance and to anonymous reviewers for providing constructive comments that helped to improve this paper.

References

David Bamman and Noah Smith. 2015. Contextualized sarcasm detection on twitter. *International Conference on Weblogs and Social Media* pages 574–577.

William Brant. 2012. Critique of sarcastic reason: The epistemology of the cognitive neurological ability called 'theory-of-mind' and deceptive reasoning. *Südwestdeutscher Verlag für Hochschulschriften* .

Christian Frederik Burgers. 2010. Verbal irony: Use and effects in written discourse. *Ipskamp, UB Nijmegen, The Netherlands* .

Gerald L. Clore, Andrew Ortony, and Mark A. Foss. 1987. The psychological foundations of the affective lexicon. *Journal of Personality and Social Psychology* 53(4):751–766.

Georgy Cohen. 2014. The power of the first-person perspective. *http://meetcontent.com/blog/power-first-person-perspective/* .

Dmitry Davidov, Oren Tsur, and Ari Rappoport. 2010. Enhanced sentiment learning using twitter hashtags and smileys. *COLING* pages 241–249.

Cameron L. Davis, Kenichi Oishi, Andreia V. Faria, John Hsu, Yessenia Gomez, Susumu Mori, and Argye E. Hillis. 2016. White matter tracts critical for recognition of sarcasm. *Neurocase* 22(1):22–29.

Roberto González-Ibáñez, Smaranda Muresan, and Nina Wacholder. 2011. Identifying sarcasm in twitter: A closer look. *ACL: HLT* pages 581–586.

John Haiman. 1998. Talk is cheap: Sarcasm, alienation and the evolution of language. *Oxford University Press* page 20.

Minqing Hu and Bing Liu. 2004. Mining and summarizing customer reviews. *ACM SIGKDD* pages 168–177.

Yuheng Hu, Kartik Talamadupula, and Subbarao Kambhampati. 2013. Dude, srsly?: The surprisingly formal nature of twitter's language. *ICWSM* pages 244–253.

Christine Liebrecht, Florian Kunneman, and Antal Van Den Bosch. 2013. The perfect solution for detecting sarcasm in tweets #not. *Workshop on Computational Approaches to Subjectivity, Sentiment and Social Media Analysis* pages 29–37.

Diana Maynard and Mark A. Greenwood. 2014. Who cares about sarcastic tweets? investigating the impact of sarcasm on sentiment analysis. *LREC* pages 4238–4243.

Albert Mehrabian. 1980. Basic dimensions for a general psychological theory: Implications for personality, social, environmental, and developmental studies. *Oelgeschlager, Gunn & Hain* pages 39–53.

Andrew Ortony, Gerald L. Clore, and Mark A. Foss. 1987. The referential structure of the affective lexiconn. *Cognitive Science* 11(3):341–364.

Charles Egerton Osgood, George J. Suci, and Percy H. Tannenbaum. 1957. The measurement of meaning. *University of Illinois Press* .

Olutobi Owoputi, Brendan O'Connor, Chris Dyer, Kevin Gimpel, Nathan Schneider, and Noah A. Smith. 2013. Improved part-of-speech tagging for online conversational text with word clusters. *NAACL: HLT* pages 380–390.

James W. Pennebaker, Roger J. Booth, Ryan L. Boyd, and Martha E. Francis. 2015. Linguistic inquiry and word count: LIWC2015. *Austin, TX: Pennebaker Conglomerates* .

Robert Plutchik. 1980. Emotion: A psychoevolutionary synthesis. *New York: Harper and Row* .

Ashwin Rajadesingan, Reza Zafarani, and Huan Liu. 2015. Sarcasm detection on twitter: A behavioral modeling approach. *ACM WSDM* pages 97–106.

Antonio Reyes, Paolo Rosso, and Davide Buscaldi. 2012. From humor recognition to irony detection: The figurative language of social media. *Data & Knowledge Engineering* pages 1–12.

Ellen Riloff, Ashequl Qadir, Prafulla Surve, Lalindra De Silva, Nathan Gilbert, and Ruihong Huang. 2013. Sarcasm as contrast between a positive sentiment and negative situation. *Empirical Methods on Natural Language Processing* pages 704–714.

Sara Rosenthal, Noura Farra, and Preslav Nakov. 2017. SemEval-2017 task 4: Sentiment analysis in Twitter. *SemEval* .

Sara Rosenthal, Preslav Nakov, Svetlana Kiritchenko, Saif M Mohammad, Alan Ritter, and Veselin Stoyanov. 2015. SemEval-2015 task 10: Sentiment analysis in twitter. *SemEval* pages 451–463.

Mickael Rouvier and Benoit Favre. 2016. SENSEI-LIF at SemEval-2016 task 4: Polarity embedding fusion for robust sentiment analysis. *SemEval* pages 202–208.

James A Russell. 1980. A circumplex model of affect. *Journal of Personality and Social Psychology* 39(6):1161–1178.

Hassan Saif, Miriam Fernndez, Yulan He, and Harith Alani. 2014. On stopwords, filtering and data sparsity for sentiment analysis of twitter. *LREC* pages 810–817.

Simone G. Shamay-Tsoory, Rachel Tomer, and Judith Aharon-Peretz. 2005. The neuroanatomical basis of understanding sarcasm and its relationship to social cognition. *Neuropsychology* pages 288–300.

Phillip Shaver, Judith Schwartz, Donald Kirson, and Cary O'Connor. 1987. Emotion knowledge: Further exploration of a prototype approach. *Journal of Personality and Social Psychology* 52(6):1061–1086.

Yla R. Tausczik and James W. Pennebaker. 2009. The psychological meaning of words: LIWC and computerized text analysis methods. *Journal of Language and Social Psychology* 29(1):24–54.

Joseph Tepperman, David R. Traum, and Shrikanth Narayanan. 2006. yeah right: sarcasm recognition for spoken dialogue systems. *INTERSPEECH* pages 1838–1841.

Mike Thelwall, Kevan Buckley, and Georgios Paltoglou. 2012. Sentiment strength detection for the social web. *Journal of the American Society for Information Science and Technology* 63(1):163–173.

Zhihua Zhang, Guoshun Wu, and Man Lan. 2015. Ecnu: Multi-level sentiment analysis on twitter usning traditional linguistic features and word embedding features. *SemEval* pages 561–567.

Appendix A Full List of Features in the Affect-Cognition-Sociolinguistics Sarcasm Feature Model

Features (example words)	Feature codes	Extraction source/tool
Affect-related Features (50)		
Count of +ive words (advanced, foolproof)	$pcountOL$	Opinion Lexicon
Count of −ive words (crashed, drunken)	$ncountOL$	Opinion Lexicon
Count of both +ive and −ive words	$pncountOL$	Opinion Lexicon
Starting position of first positive word (-1 if no positive word)	$pstartOL$	Opinion Lexicon
Starting position of first negative word (-1 if no positive word)	$nstartOL$	Opinion Lexicon
Order of the +ive and −ive words (1 if +ive words appear before−ive; -1 otherwise. 0 if no +ive/−ive words)	$pnorderOL$	Opinion Lexicon
Count of positive words (2,3,4 scored) (care, bff)	$pcountSS$	SentiStrength Lookup Dictionary
Count of negative words (-2,-3,-4 scored) (dizzy, provoke)	$ncountSS$	SentiStrength Lookup Dictionary
Count of both positive and negative words	$pncountSS$	SentiStrength Lookup Dictionary
Starting position of first positive word	$pstartSS$	SentiStrength Lookup Dictionary
Starting position of first negative word	$nstartSS$	SentiStrength Lookup Dictionary
Order of the position of the positive and negative words	$pnorderSS$	SentiStrength Lookup Dictionary
Count of 4-scored words (loving, magnific* [*: all words starting with magnific])	$pos4SS$	SentiStrength Lookup Dictionary
Count of 3-scored words (awesome, fantastic, great, wow*, joy*)	$strengthp3SS$	SentiStrength Lookup Dictionary
Count of 2-scored words (fun, glad, thank, nice*, brillian*)	$strengthp2SS$	SentiStrength Lookup Dictionary
Count of 1-scored words (ok, peace*)	$strengthp1SS$	SentiStrength Lookup Dictionary
Count of -1-scored words (dark, lost)	$strengthn1SS$	SentiStrength Lookup Dictionary
Count of -2-scored words (against, aloof)	$strengthn2SS$	SentiStrength Lookup Dictionary
Count of -3-scored words (envy*, foe*)	$strengthn3SS$	SentiStrength Lookup Dictionary
Count of -4-scored words (cry, fear)	$strengthn4SS$	SentiStrength Lookup Dictionary
Absolute value of highest positive strength score of words (e.g., 3 is returned if a tweet contains "excitement" and "amused", which have SentiStrength scores of 3 and 2 respectively)	$maxpstrengthSS$	SentiStrength Lookup Dictionary
Absolute value of lowest negative strength score of words (e.g., 4 is returned if a tweet contains "anguish" and "alone", which have SentiStrength scores of -4 and -2 respectively)	$minnstrengthSS$	SentiStrength Lookup Dictionary

Appendix A Full List of Features in the Affect-Cognition-Sociolinguistics Sarcasm Feature Model (continued...)

Features (example words)	Feature codes	Extraction source/tool
Affect-related Features (50) (continued...)		
Count of positive words (feeling-high, heartening, aww, =))	$pcountEI$	Emotion Intensity Lexicon
Count of negative words (uncared-for, weird, agh, :/)	$ncountEI$	
Count of both positive and negative words	$pncountEI$	
Starting position of first positive word	$pstartEI$	
Starting position of first negative word	$nstartEI$	
Order of the position of the positive and negative words	$pnorderEI$	
Count of 3-scored strength words (love, awesome)	$strengthp3EI$	
Count of 2-scored strength words (lucky, surprising)	$strengthp2EI$	
Count of 1-scored strength words (compassion, curious)	$strengthp1EI$	
Count of 0-scored strength words (refreshed, sleepy)	$strength0EI$	
Count of -1-scored strength words (nervous, sorrow)	$strengthn1EI$	
Count of -2-scored strength words (tense, bitter)	$strengthn2EI$	
Count of -3-scored strength words (woesome, hating)	$strengthn3EI$	
Absolute value of highest positive score of strength words	$maxpstrengthEI$	
Absolute value of highest negative score of strength words	$maxnstrengthEI$	
Count of 3-scored intensity words (excited, astonished, thrill)	$intensityp3EI$	
Count of 2-scored intensity words (love, awesome, glad, fun,:P,=D)	$intensityp2EI$	
Count of 1-scored intensity words (thank, cooperative, concern, :), :d)	$intensityp1EI$	
Count of 0-scored intensity words (great, haze, fulfill, sick, sleepy)	$intensity0EI$	
Count of -1-scored intensity words (anger, annoyed)	$intensityn1EI$	
Count of -2-scored intensity words (sorry, agh, :/)	$intensityn2EI$	
Count of -3-scored intensity words (hate, resented, D:)	$intensityn3EI$	
Absolute value of highest positive score of intensity words	$maxpintensityEI$	
Absolute value of lowest negative score of intensity words	$minnintensityEI$	
Percentage of uppercase characters	$uppcase$	LIWC2015
Percentage of question marks (?)	$qmark$	
Percentage of exclamation marks (!)	$exclamark$	
Percentage of first persons singular (I, me, mine)	i	
Cognition-related Features (26)		
Count of total words	WC	
Count of total characters	$charcount$	
Frequency of words greater than 6 letters	$sixltr$	
Percentage of negation words (no, never)	$negate$	
Percentage of certainty words	$certain$	
Percentage of preposition words	$prep$	
Percentage of conjunction words	$conj$	
Count of common nouns (books, someone)	N	TweetPOS
Count of pronoun (personal/WH; not possessive)	O	
Count of nominal + possessive words (books', someone's)	S	
Count of proper nouns (lebron, usa, iPad)	$\hat{}$	
Count of proper nouns + possessive (America's)	Z	
Count of nominal _ verbal (I'm), verbal + nominal (let's)	L	
Count of proper noun + verbal (Mark'll)	M	
Count of verbs incl. copula and auxiliaries (might, ought, couldn't, is, eats)	V	
Count of adjectives (good, fav, lil)	A	
Count of adverbs (2, i.e., too)	R	
Count of interjections (lol, haha, FTW, yea, right)	$!$	
Count of determiner words (the, the, its, it's)	D	
Count of pre- or postpositions or subordinating conjunction (while, to, for, 2[to], 4[for])	P	
Count of coordinating conjunctions (and, n, &, +, BUT)	$\&$	
Count of verb particles (out, off, Up, UP)	T	
Count of existential there, predeterminers (both)	X	
Count of existential there, predeterminers, verbal (there's, all's)	Y	
Count of numerals (2010, four, 9:30)	$\$$	
Count of punctuations (#,$,(,))	$,$	
Sociolinguistics-related Features (6)		
Count of hashtags (#acl)	$\#$	
Count of at-mentions (@BarackObama)	$@$	
Count of discourse markers (RT @user : hello)	$\sim$	
Count of URLs or email address (http://t.co/rsxZxhnU)	U	
Count of emoticons (:) :b (: <3 o_O)	E	
Count of other abbreviations, foreign words etc. (ily (I love you) wby (what about you) 's –>awesome...I'm)	G	

SINAI at SemEval-2017 Task 4: User based classification

Salud María Jiménez-Zafra, Arturo Montejo-Ráez,
M. Teresa Martín-Valdivia, L. Alfonso Ureña-López
Computer Science Department, Escuela Politécnica Superior de Jaén
Universidad de Jaén, 23071 - Jaén (Spain)
`{sjzafra, amontejo, maite, laurena}@ujaen.es`

Abstract

This document describes our participation in SemEval-2017 Task 4: Sentiment Analysis in Twitter. We have only reported results for subtask B - English, determining the polarity towards a topic on a two point scale (positive or negative sentiment). Our main contribution is the integration of user information in the classification process. A SVM model is trained with Word2Vec vectors from user's tweets extracted from his timeline. The obtained results show that user-specific classifiers trained on tweets from user timeline can introduce noise as they are error prone because they are classified by an imperfect system. This encourages us to explore further integration of user information for author-based Sentiment Analysis.

1 Introduction

Task 4 of SemEval 2017, Sentiment Analysis in Twitter (Rosenthal et al., 2017), has included some new subtasks this year. One of these subtasks considers user information to be also integrated in proposed systems. We have participated in subtask B consisting of, given a message and a topic, classify the message on a two-point scale (positive or negative sentiment towards that topic). Actually, organizers provide scripts to download user profile information such as age, location, followers... We have taken advantage of this information to expand a SVM model trained with Word2Vec vectors from user publications on this social media.

In this paper, we present our approach to classify tweets in a two point scale (positive and negative) by combining Support Vector Machine (SVM), Word2Vec (Mikolov et al., 2013) and user information. We have decided to combine these technologies for several reasons. Firstly, we have applied SVM many different tasks including tweet polarity classification with good results (Saleh et al., 2011). Secondly, after a revision of the systems presented in the last year for the same task (Nakov et al., 2016), it seems that better results are achieved by using word embeddings representations, so we have decided to test how it works on user modeling. Finally, this year for the first time, organizers include user information. We consider that it is very interesting to integrate this contextual information to improve tweets sentiment classification. Actually, polarity classification on a per-user basis has been found to be useful in tasks like collaborative filtering (García-Cumbreras et al., 2013). Besides, the generation of user profiles in Twitter has attracted the attention of many researches in recent years, enabling the prediction of user behavior as in election processes (Pennacchiotti and Popescu, 2011).

In Section 2 we explain the data used in our approach. Section 3 presents the system description. Experiments and results are expounded in Section 4 and they are analyzed in Section 5. Finally, in Section 6, conclusions and future work are commented.

2 Data

The organizers provided English data from previous years (2015 and 2016). The test set corresponding to 2016 was also supplied for development purposes but, since then, it can be used for training too. In the experimentation phase, the training set is composed by the development, training and test datasets of 2015 and the development and training datasets of 2016. For our participation in task 4 we used all this data for training. In Table 1, it can be seen the distribution of tweets used in the experimentation and testing phases.

Proceedings of the 11th International Workshop on Semantic Evaluations (SemEval-2017), pages 634–639,
Vancouver, Canada, August 3 - 4, 2017. ©2017 Association for Computational Linguistics

Set	Positive	Negative	Total
training_dev	6,739	1,674	8,413
dev	8,212	2,339	10,551
training_test	14,951	4,013	18,964
test	2,463	3,722	6,185

Table 1: Number of tweets provided for experimentation and testing.

3 System description

The system presented is based on user modeling. It determines the user opinion on a tweet according to a user model generated from his timeline. In our experiments, all tweets are vectorized using Word2Vec. First, a general SVM model on training vectors is generated. Then, for each user in the test set, the system downloads the last 200 tweets published by the user and classifies them using a general SVM classifier, the one resulting from the training set. If the classified tweets from the timeline contains positive and negative tweets and an specific SVM model of the timeline reports an accuracy over 0.7 on leave-one-out cross-validation, the user model is applied on authored tweets from the test set; if not, the general SVM model is applied. Thus, we try to train a per-user classifier, whenever feasible.

For the Word2Vec representation of the tweets, it has been used the software[1] developed by the authors of the method (Mikolov et al., 2013). In order to get representative vectors for each word, it is needed to generate a model from a large text volume. To this end, a Wikipedia[2] dump in English of the articles in XML was downloaded, and the text from them was extracted. The parameters used have been those that provided better results in previous experiments with Spanish tweets (Montejo-Ráez and Díaz-Galiano, 2016; Montejo-Ráez et al., 2014): a window of 5 terms, the CBOW model and a number of dimensions expected of 300. In this way, each tweet of the training and test set has been represented with the resultant vector of calculating the average and standard deviation of the Word2Vec vectors from words in the tweet text, resulting in a final vector of 600 features. Previously, a simple normalization has been performed on each tweet: repeated letters have been eliminated, stop words have been

removed and all words have been transformed to lowercase.

The SVM implementation selected is that based on LibSVM (Chang and Lin, 2011) provided by the Scikit-learn library (Pedregosa et al., 2011).

4 Experiments and results

Three different experiments were conducted over the development set as follows (Fig. 1 and Fig. 2):

- Experiment 1: a general SVM model on Word2Vec representations of training tweets was generated. Each tweet of the development set was vectorized using Word2Vec and classified with the model obtained previously.

- Experiment 2: each tweet vector was expanded with a user vector. A general SVM model was also generated, but on both the Word2Vec representation of the training tweets and user timeline. For every user in the training tweets, the last 200 tweets from his timeline were downloaded. These tweets were used to enrich the vector of each individual tweet. Each tweet of the development set along with user timeline who posted it were vectorized using Word2Vec and the tweet was classified with the model.

- Experiment 3: the general SVM model of experiment 1 was used but one model per user was also defined. In order to define the user model, the last 200 tweets published by the user were retrieved and each of them was vectorized and classified using the general SVM model. Each tweet of the development set was vectorized using Word2Vec and classified according to the following approach: if the model corresponding to the user contains positive and negative tweets and the leave-one-out cross-validation reports an accuracy over 0.7%, the tweet is classified with the user model; if not, it is classified with the general SVM model.

The results obtained in the development phase are shown in Table 2. Although experiment 1 was the one that provided the best results, for our participation in the task, we selected the approach developed in experiment 3 because it takes into account user information, one of the challenges of this year. Experiment 2 also considers user information and got better results than experiment

---

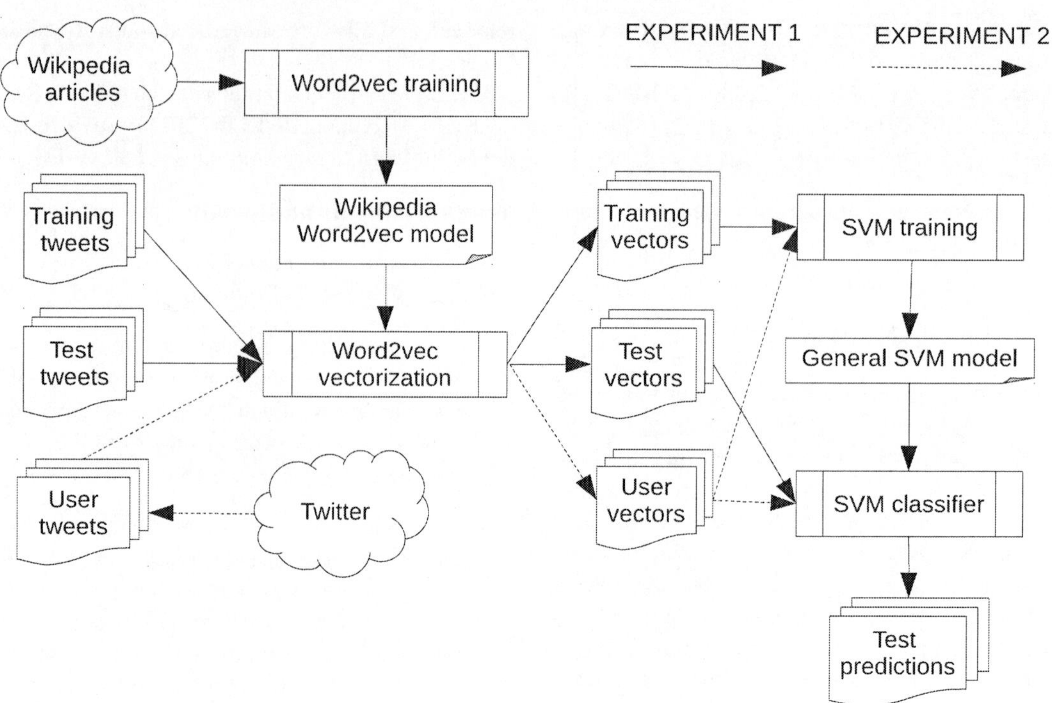

Figure 1: Data flow for experiment 1 and 2.

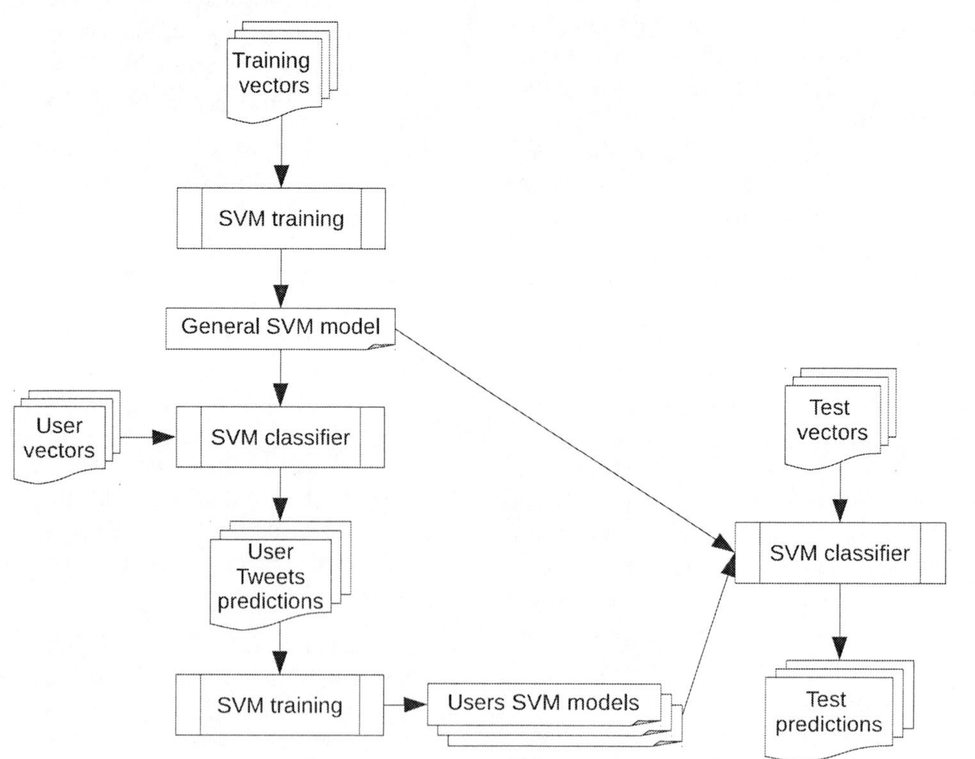

Figure 2: Data flow for experiment 3.

	Exp_1	Exp_2	Exp_3
P positive	0.856	0.854	0.842
P negative	0.764	0.757	0.772
R positive	0.962	0.962	0.970
R negative	0.432	0.422	0.363
Avg. F1	0.729	0.723	0.698
Avg. R	0.697	0.692	0.666
Acc.	0.845	0.842	0.835

Table 2: Results for the development phase.

#	System	AvgR	AvgF1	Acc
1	BB_twtr	0.882_1	0.890_1	0.897_1
2	DataStories	0.856_2	0.861_2	0.869_2
3	Tweester	0.854_3	0.856_3	0.863_3
4	TopicThunder	0.846_4	0.847_4	0.854_4
5	TakeLab	0.845_5	0.836_5	0.840_6
6	funSentiment	0.834_6	0.824_8	0.827_8
7	YNU-HPCC	0.834_6	0.816_{10}	0.818_{10}
8	WarwickDCS	0.829_8	0.834_6	0.843_5
9	CrystalNest	0.827_9	0.822_9	0.827_8
10	zhangweida2080	0.826_{10}	0.830_7	0.838_7
11	Amobee-C-137	0.822_{11}	0.801_{12}	0.802_{12}
12	**SINAI**	$\mathbf{0.818_{12}}$	$\mathbf{0.806_{11}}$	$\mathbf{0.809_{11}}$
13	NRU-HSE	0.798_{13}	0.787_{13}	0.790_{13}
14	EICA	0.790_{14}	0.775_{14}	0.777_{16}
15	OMAM	0.779_{15}	0.762_{17}	0.764_{17}
16	NileTMRG	0.769_{16}	0.774_{15}	0.789_{15}
17	ELiRF-UPV	0.766_{17}	0.773_{16}	0.790_{13}
18	DUTH	0.663_{18}	0.600_{18}	0.607_{18}
19	ej-za-2017	0.594_{19}	0.486_{21}	0.518_{19}
20	SSN_MLRG1	0.586_{20}	0.494_{20}	0.518_{19}
21	YNU-1510	0.516_{21}	0.499_{19}	0.499_{21}
22	TM-Gist	0.499_{22}	0.428_{22}	0.444_{22}
23	SSK_JNTUH	0.483_{23}	0.372_{23}	0.412_{23}
	baseline 1: all POSITIVE	0.500	0.285	0.398
	baseline 2: all NEGATIVE	0.500	0.376	0.602

Table 3: Results for SemEval-2017 Task 4, subtask B - English.

3 in the development phase, but we did not select it because we considered that the fact of adding tweets without more sense was not a good idea. Experiment 3 makes more sense, since it defines a personal model for each user based on the way he thinks.

The results for all participants in the test phase can be seen in Table 3 and the detailed report of the results for all participants can be found at (Rosenthal et al., 2017).

Once the gold standard corresponding to the test phase was released, we also conducted other experiments that we defined in the development phase. The results related to the test set in all the experiments are shown in Table 4. Following, in the next section, an in-depth analysis of the results obtained is performed.

	Exp_1	Exp_2	Exp_3
P positive	0.735	0.730	0.718
P negative	0.897	0.890	0.893
R positive	0.862	0.851	0.859
R negative	0.794	0.791	0.777
Avg. F1	0.818	0.812	0.806
Avg. R	0.828	0.821	0.818
Acc.	0.821	0.815	0.809

Table 4: Results for the test phase.

5 Analysis of results

The results obtained do not seem to support the integration of content from users' timelines. In Table 4 we can see that using word embeddings in tweet words straightforward yielded the best results. Adding further user information did not improve the first setup. A model of the user under the form of an aggregated vector computed from his timeline, or a specific polarity classifier for each user involves, first, to download hundreds of tweets for every single user in the data set and, second, use these tweets to compute a final user model.

It is important to note that the SemEval data set is very unbalanced, and that can affect the generation of user classifiers. Besides, not additional data has been used to determine the polarity of tweets in the timeline, so the effects of a bad performance might be, therefore, amplified. Anyhow, experiment 3 shows similar results as the other two approaches, despite the potential bias that recent tweets from the timeline may have on the classification process.

6 Conclusion

Working on timelines has been found interesting as a source of information to generate user profiles (Bollen et al., 2011). Actually, as more text is obtained, further analysis on user behavior or personality can be performed (Diakopoulos and Shamma, 2010).

We will continue exploring how the timeline could be better integrated or analyzed for an effective user modeling process. As the timeline is provided on recent tweets, it could be worth downloading those closer to the moment when the tweet to analyze was published, so the context would be more coherent.

Acknowledgments

This work has been partially supported by a Grant from the Ministerio de Educación, Cultura y Deporte (MECD - scholarship FPU014/00983), Fondo Europeo de Desarrollo Regional (FEDER) and REDES project (TIN2015-65136-C2-1-R) from the Ministerio de Economía y Competitividad.

References

Johan Bollen, Huina Mao, and Alberto Pepe. 2011. Modeling public mood and emotion: Twitter sentiment and socio-economic phenomena. *ICWSM* 11:450–453.

Chih-Chung Chang and Chih-Jen Lin. 2011. Libsvm: a library for support vector machines. *ACM Transactions on Intelligent Systems and Technology (TIST)* 2(3):27.

Nicholas A. Diakopoulos and David A. Shamma. 2010. Characterizing debate performance via aggregated twitter sentiment. In *Proceedings of the SIGCHI Conference on Human Factors in Computing Systems*. ACM, New York, NY, USA, CHI '10, pages 1195–1198. https://doi.org/10.1145/1753326.1753504.

Miguel Á. García-Cumbreras, Arturo Montejo-Ráez, and Manuel C. Díaz-Galiano. 2013. Pessimists and optimists: Improving collaborative filtering through sentiment analysis. *Expert Systems with Applications* 40(17):6758 – 6765.

Tomas Mikolov, Kai Chen, Greg Corrado, and Jeffrey Dean. 2013. Efficient estimation of word representations in vector space. *arXiv preprint arXiv:1301.3781* .

A Montejo-Ráez and MC Diaz-Galiano. 2016. Participación de sinai en tass 2016. *Comité organizador* page 41.

Arturo Montejo-Ráez, MA García-Cumbreras, and M Carlos Díaz-Galiano. 2014. Participación de sinai word2vec en tass 2014. In *Proceedings of the TASS workshop at SEPLN*.

Preslav Nakov, Alan Ritter, Sara Rosenthal, Fabrizio Sebastiani, and Veselin Stoyanov. 2016. Semeval-2016 task 4: Sentiment analysis in twitter. *Proceedings of SemEval* pages 1–18.

Fabian Pedregosa, Gaël Varoquaux, Alexandre Gramfort, Vincent Michel, Bertrand Thirion, Olivier Grisel, Mathieu Blondel, Peter Prettenhofer, Ron Weiss, Vincent Dubourg, et al. 2011. Scikit-learn: Machine learning in python. *Journal of Machine Learning Research* 12(Oct):2825–2830.

Marco Pennacchiotti and Ana-Maria Popescu. 2011. A machine learning approach to twitter user classification. *Icwsm* 11(1):281–288.

Sara Rosenthal, Noura Farra, and Preslav Nakov. 2017. SemEval-2017 task 4: Sentiment analysis in Twitter. In *Proceedings of the 11th International Workshop on Semantic Evaluation*. Association for Computational Linguistics, Vancouver, Canada, SemEval '17.

M Rushdi Saleh, Maria Teresa Martín-Valdivia, Arturo Montejo-Ráez, and LA Ureña-López. 2011.

Experiments with svm to classify opinions in different domains. *Expert Systems with Applications*
38(12):14799–14804.

HLP@UPenn at SemEval-2017 Task 4A: A simple, self-optimizing text classification system combining dense and sparse vectors

Abeed Sarker   **Graciela Gonzalez**

Institute of Biomedical Informatics

Department of Biostatistics, Epidemiology and Informatics

The Perelman School of Medicine

University of Pennsylvania

`{abeed, gragon}@upenn.edu`

Abstract

We present a simple supervised text classification system that combines sparse and dense vector representations of words, and the generalized representations of words via clusters. The sparse vectors are generated from word n-gram sequences (1-3). The dense vector representations of words (embeddings) are learned by training a neural network to predict neighboring words in a large unlabeled dataset. To classify a text segment, the different vector representations of it are concatenated, and the classification is performed using Support Vector Machines (SVMs). Our system is particularly intended for use by non-experts of natural language processing and machine learning, and, therefore, the system does not require any manual tuning of parameters or weights. Given a training set, the system automatically generates the training vectors, optimizes the relevant hyper-parameters for the SVM classifier, and trains the classification model. We evaluated this system on the SemEval-2017 English sentiment analysis task. In terms of average F1-Score, our system obtained 8th position out of 39 submissions (F1-Score: 0.632, average recall: 0.637, accuracy: 0.646).

1 Introduction

Text classification is one of the most fundamental natural language processing tasks, and involves the categorization of texts based on their lexical contents. In its simplest form, text classification is binary in nature, such as the categorization of spam *vs.* non-spam email (Youn and McLeod, 2007). Researchers from distinct fields are exposed to a wide range of text classification problems. Even within a specific domain, such as the medical domain, there is a multitude of text classification tasks and problems, such as assessing the qualities of published papers (Kilicoglu et al., 2009; Sarker et al., 2015), outcome polarity classification (Sarker et al., 2011), biomarker classification (Davis et al., 2015), and adverse drug reaction mention detection (Sarker and Gonzalez, 2015) to name a few. Early automated text classification systems were rule-based in nature (*e.g.*, Sarker and Mollá-Aliod (2010)) mostly because of the absence of sufficient annotated data. However, such rule-based systems are generally limited in terms of performance and/or overfit to the target problem. They particularly suffer in terms of performance when exposed to unseen datasets. With the rapid increase in text-based data in all domains (*e.g.*, the largest medical database, Medline,[1] now indexes over 23 million articles), most efficient text classification systems now use machine learning. Such systems utilize annotated data, and automatically extract features from large volumes of annotated text to perform classification. The rules that are used in classification are not hard-coded or predetermined, but are learned from the annotated data automatically. Text classification strategies for various tasks have been thoroughly explored in the literature, and relatively recent progress has seen the use of techniques such as distant supervision (Mintz et al., 2009).

While the automated classification of text is useful for numerous tasks involving natural language, and in a variety of domains, setting up and running text classification systems is very challenging for non-experts. The task generally requires in-depth knowledge of natural language processing (NLP), particularly for preprocessing,

---

[1] `https://www.nlm.nih.gov/bsd/pmresources.html`. Accessed: 2/17/2017.

Proceedings of the 11th International Workshop on Semantic Evaluations (SemEval-2017), pages 640–643,
Vancouver, Canada, August 3 - 4, 2017. ©2017 Association for Computational Linguistics

feature extraction/generation and analysis, and at least basic knowledge of machine learning so that the classification system can be optimized. For researchers working on interdisciplinary projects (*e.g.*, clinicians working on biomedical informatics projects), the time or opportunity to learn the relevant topics are often unavailable. While state-of-the-art classification techniques now apply sophisticated techniques such as deep neural networks (*e.g.*, Lai et al. (2015)), such techniques are rarely used by non-experts of machine learning in practice. Therefore, there is motivation to design simple text classification systems that are easy to setup and run, and also perform well on real-world text classification problems.

In this paper, we describe a simple text classification system that was initially designed to teach text classification to biomedical informatics students from non-computing backgrounds. The system was modified for application to a 3-class problem (from its initial implementation for binary classification).[2] The system employs a Support Vector Machines (SVMs) (Vapnik, 1995) classifier and some simple features. SVMs are particularly useful for text classification as they are capable of handling large feature vectors. However, to optimize the performance of the SVM classifiers, several hyperparameters have to be tuned (Chang and Lin, 2011). In our system, the *cost* parameter of the classifier and weights for classes (useful for imbalanced datasets) are learned automatically via 5-fold cross validation over the training set. To evaluate the performance of our simple system, we used it for the SemEval-2017 sentiment analysis task in English language (task 4). Our system obtained an average F1-Score of 0.632 (8th out of 39 teams), average recall of 0.637, and accuracy of 0.646. The balance in simplicity and performance of the system suggests that it can be very useful for researchers who are non-experts in the natural language processing and machine learning domains. The system is publicly available, and is open source.[3]

2 Methods

The sentiment analysis task for SemEval Task-4A requires the classification of English tweets into one of three sentiment classes: *positive*, *negative* and *neutral*. For the 2017 task, all Twitter sentiment annotations from past years were made available. We downloaded all these annotations and used them for training our system. Specific details about the task can be found in Rosenthal et al. (2017).[4] We used a total of 49,484 tweets from the past annotations of which 19,597 (39.6%) were tagged as positive, 7692 (15.5%) as negative, and 22,195 (44.9%) as neutral. We used an SVM classifier with an RBF kernel for the classification task. In our system, the training set was used to compute suitable weights for each of the classes and an optimal value for the *cost* parameter via 5-fold cross validation. We now briefly discuss our features and parameter/weight optimization approach.

2.1 Feature sets

We used three simple feature sets, which are as follows:

2.1.1 N-grams

To generate sparse vectors, we used traditional word n-grams (n = 1–3). Standard preprocessing steps such as stemming and lowercasing was performed prior to generating the sparse vectors. Stemming was performed using the Porter stemmer (Porter, 1980). We limited the total number of features to 5000.

2.1.2 Word clusters

In an attempt to include more generalized representations of terms, we used word clusters, which have proven to be useful for Twitter-based classification tasks in our past work. The clusters represent groups of terms that are semantically similar. We used a set of publicly available word clusters[5] that were generated by first learning distributed representations of Twitter terms and then clustering the word vectors (Owoputi et al., 2012). The clusters are used in a bag-of-words manner, and feature vectors are generated for these in the same way as the n-gram features.

---

[2]Notes for the workshop for training students about the system are available at: `http://diego.asu.edu/Publications/Textclassif_workshop_v2-3.pdf`.

[3]Available at: `https://bitbucket.org/pennhlp/hlp-upenn_semeval_2017_task4`.

[4]The task website is: `http://alt.qcri.org/semeval2017/task4/`. Accessed: 2/20/2017.

[5]Available at: `http://www.cs.cmu.edu/~ark/TweetNLP/`. Accessed: 2/20/2016

2.1.3 Dense vectors

We obtained dense vector representations of each tweet simply by adding dense representations of individual terms. To obtain dense vector representations of the terms, we used publicly available pretrained vectors[6] (Godin et al., 2015). The vectors were learned from 400 million tweets, and each word is represented using a dense vector of size 400.

2.2 Optimization and classification

A good value for the cost parameter of the SVM classifier was determined via grid search. The grid search included all powers of 2 between 1 and 5. Ideally, identifying the optimal value requires a more thorough search, with an extended search space. We used this small search space to speed up the searching process. To determine the appropriate weight for each class, first each of the three classes were assigned a weight which is equal to the total number of instances in the training set divided by the number of instances for that class in the training set. Thus, for example, the initial weight assigned to the neutral class was $\frac{49484}{22195} = 2.23$. Iterating through possible weights in imbalanced classification tasks can be a tricky problem, and require some expertise in applied machine learning. Without optimization of weights, classification problems involving imbalanced datasets may perform poorly. As mentioned, our system was originally designed to provide simple text classification solutions to non-experts. Therefore, we devised a simple weight optimization strategy. First, the search *interval* is computed as the *variance* of the vector of the initial weight values. For a given class, the possible weight then lies in the range given by Equation 1:

$$range = [max(0.1, class\_weight \\ - (2 \times interval)), \quad (1) \\ class\_weight + (2 \times interval)]$$

Possible values for weight for the class can then be iterated through within the given range using suitable step sizes. In our work, the initial weight of the positive class (middle class), was kept constant while a range of values were iterated through for the neutral (larger class) and negative (smaller class). Within a given range, we used step sizes of $\frac{interval}{2}$, and chose the weight combination that

---

[6]Available at: `http://www.fredericgodin.com/software/`. Accessed: 2/20/2016

produced the best results for the cross validation task. A larger search space is likely to result in a better classifier, but also requires longer time for searching.

As described in the previous subsections, during feature generation, a single vector (dense or sparse) is generated for each feature set for each instance. All the three feature vectors for an instance are simply concatenated to form a single vector prior to training. For the system used for this task, each combined vector consisted of a total of 6400 features.

3 Results, Comments and Conclusion

Despite the simplicity of our approach, and limited tuning, it obtained 8th position in terms of average F1-Score out of 39 systems. In addition, the system obtained average recall of 0.637 (11th), and accuracy of 0.646 (8th). Due to time-constraints associated with the submission deadline for the shared task, we only performed 5-fold cross validation, and estimated optimal class weights and values for the cost parameter from a small set of possibilities, as described in the previous section. Therefore, we suspect that the performance of the system could be further improved by searching through a larger set of values. Furthermore, our system was optimized for average F1-Score, resulting in better overall ranking for F1-Score, rather than for average recall.

The key advantage of our system is its simplicity. The parameter optimization is handled automatically, and does not require any manual interpretation. At the same time, the optimization approach is easily interpretable and customizable by non-experts. For example, if better accuracy is required for a specific task, a more thorough search for optimal weights can be performed simply by increasing the number of steps. Such modification does not require deep understanding of SVMs.

Our system is simple and is applicable to any social media text classification task. In the future, we will assess the true performance of the optimized system over the SemEval-2017 test set, via more thorough automated optimization. We will also compare the performance of our simple system with other similar automated systems (*e.g.*, the TPOT system Olson et al. (2016)) in terms of speed and performance.

Acknowledgments

This work was supported by National Institutes of Health (NIH) National Library of Medicine (NLM) grant number NIH NLM 5R01LM011176. The content is solely the responsibility of the authors and does not necessarily represent the official views of the NLM or NIH.

References

Chih-Chung Chang and Chih-Jen Lin. 2011. LIBSVM: A library for support vector machines. *ACM Transactions on Intelligent Systems and Technology* 2(27).

J. Davis, M. Maes, A. Andreazza, J. J. McGrath, S. J. Tye, and M. Berk. 2015. Towards a classification of biomarkers of neuropsychiatric disease: from encompass to compass. *Molecular Psychiatry* 20:152–153.

Fréderic Godin, Baptist Vandersmissen, Wesley De Neve, and Rik Van de Walle. 2015. Multimedia Lab @ ACL W-NUT NER Shared Task: Named Entity Recognition for Twitter Microposts using Distributed Word Representations. In *Proceedings of the ACL 2015 Workshop on Noisy User-generated Text*. pages 146–153.

Halil Kilicoglu, Dina Demner-Fushman, Thomas C. Rindflesch, Nancy L. Wilczynski, and Brian Hynes. 2009. Towards Automatic Recognition of Scientifically Rigorous Clinical Reserc Evidence. *Journal of the American Medical Informatics Association* 16(1):25–31.

Siwei Lai, Liheng Xu, Kang Liu, and Jun Zhao. 2015. Recurrent convolutional neural networks for text classification. In *Proceedings of the Conference of the Association for the Advancement of Artificial Intelligence (AAAI)*. pages 2267–2273.

Mike Mintz, Steven Bills, Rion snow, and Dan Jurafsky. 2009. Distant supervision for relation extraction without labeled data. In *Proceedings of the Joint Conference of the 47th Annual Meeting of the ACL and the 4th International Joint Conference on Natural Language Processing of the AFNLP*. pages 1003–1011.

Randal S. Olson, Ryan J. Urbanowicz, Peter C. Andrews, Nicole A. Lavender, La Creis Kidd, and Jason H. Moore. 2016. *Applications of Evolutionary Computation: 19th European Conference, EvoApplications 2016, Porto, Portugal, March 30 – April 1, 2016, Proceedings, Part I*, Springer International Publishing, chapter Automating Biomedical Data Science Through Tree-Based Pipeline Optimization, pages 123–137.

Olutobi Owoputi, Brendan O'Connor, Chris Dyer, Kevin Gimpel, and Nathan Schneider. 2012. Part-of-speech tagging for twitter: Word clusters and other advances. Technical report, Carnegie Mellon University. http://www.cs.cmu.edu/ ark/TweetNLP/owoputi+etal.tr12.pdf.

Martin F. Porter. 1980. An algorithm for suffix stripping. *Program* 14(3):130–137.

Sara Rosenthal, Noura Farra, and Preslav Nakov. 2017. SemEval-2017 task 4: Sentiment analysis in Twitter. In *Proceedings of the 11th International Workshop on Semantic Evaluation*. Association for Computational Linguistics, Vancouver, Canada, SemEval '17.

Abeed Sarker and Graciela Gonzalez. 2015. Portable automatic text classification for adverse drug reaction detection via multi-corpus training. *Journal of Biomedical Informatics* 53:196 – 207.

Abeed Sarker, Diego Mollá, and Cécile Paris. 2011. Outcome Polarity Identification of Medical Papers. In *Proceedings of the ALTW 2011*. pages 105–114.

Abeed Sarker, Diego Mollá, and Cécile Paris. 2015. Automatic evidence quality prediction to support evidence-based decision making. *Artificial Intelligence in Medicine* 64(2):89–103.

Abeed Sarker and Diego Mollá-Aliod. 2010. A Rule-based Approach for Automatic Identification of Publication Types of Medical Papers. In *Proceedings of the ADCS Annual Symposium*. Melbourne, Australia, pages 84–88.

Vladimir N. Vapnik. 1995. *The nature of statistical learning theory*. Springer-Verlag New York, Inc., New York, NY, USA. http://portal.acm.org/citation.cfm?id=211359.

Seongwook Youn and Dennis McLeod. 2007. Spam Email Classification using an Adaptive Ontology. *Journal of Software* 2(3):43–55.

ej-sa-2017 at SemEval-2017 Task 4: Experiments for Target oriented Sentiment Analysis in Twitter

Enkhzol Dovdon and José Saias

DI - ECT - Universidade de Évora
Rua Romão Ramalho, 59
7000-671 Évora, Portugal
`d36506@alunos.uevora.pt, jsaias@uevora.pt`

Abstract

This paper describes the system we have used for participating in Subtasks A (Message Polarity Classification) and B (Topic-Based Message Polarity Classification according to a two-point scale) of SemEval-2017 Task 4 Sentiment Analysis in Twitter. We used several features with a sentiment lexicon and NLP techniques, Maximum Entropy as a classifier for our system.

1 Introduction

Text data has been growing dramatically. We have demands to process and mine from Social networks and online platforms. Opinions in user-generated content, are valuable for market and trend analysis. Processing of sentiment analysis helps us to automatically distinguish from these written opinions.

This paper describes a participation in SemEval-2017 Task 4 with the *ej-sa-2017* system. We have participated in SemEval-2017 Task 4 on Sentiment Analysis in Twitter, subtasks A (Message Polarity Classification), B (Topic-Based Message Polarity Classification)(Rosenthal et al., 2017). Subtask A is to classify message polarity from given a message that is of positive, negative, or neutral sentiment. Subtask B is to classify positive or negative sentiment of a tweet towards that topic on a two-point scale.

We utilized a supervised machine learning classifier, having bag-of-word (BoW), lemmas, bigrams of adjective, punctuation based features, and lexicon-based features. The rest of the paper is structured as follows: In Section 2, we present some related work in features and approaches with a lexicon. In Section 3, this section describes the algorithm and feature representation used to detect sentiment of text. In Section 4, the experimental results are introduced. Finally, the conclusions as well as further work are described in Section 5.

2 Related Work

There are many works associated with the target-oriented sentiment analysis. Some of these works have focused on probability distribution model of particular features and approach. The system of *Sentiue* (Saias, 2015) used a separate MaxEnt classifier of MALLET (MAchine Learning for LanguagE Toolkit) (McCallum, 2002) with bag-of-word like features (lemmas, bigram, presences, etc.) for Aspect based Sentiment Analysis in SemEval-2015 Task 12 and accuracy was approximately 79%. Kamps (Kamps et al., 2004) developed a simple distance measure, that focuses almost exclusively on taxonomic relations and WordNet and determined usage of the semantic orientation of adjectives. Pak (Pak and Paroubek, 2010) utilized the presence of n-grams, for $n \in \{1, 2, 3\}$, as a binary feature of a BoW representation using TreeTagger. They collected a corpus of 300000 text posts from Twitter. Fong (Fong et al., 2013) focused on news articles, which tend to use a more neutral vocabulary using MALLET to implement and train six classifiers for sentiment analysis and compared them. Their experimental results show that the Naive Bayes classifier performs the best of six algorithms. Singh (Singh et al., 2013) have been implemented double Machine Learning based classifiers (Naive Bayes as a 2-class text classification problem and SVM with tf.idf vectors), the Unsupervised Semantic Orientation approach with POS tagging and the SentiWordNet approaches for sentiment classification of a huge amount of movie reviews. Their used priority scoring Adjective + Adverb combine scheme of SentiWordNet approach was performed

Proceedings of the 11th International Workshop on Semantic Evaluations (SemEval-2017), pages 644–647,
Vancouver, Canada, August 3 - 4, 2017. ©2017 Association for Computational Linguistics

0.811 F1-score in their experiments.

3   Method

This section describes feature extraction and a classifier of the sentiment analysis for our system. We used the tool MALLET that supports a variety of supervised classifiers, which makes it ideal for the comparative study of our experiences. We developed the current system using several valuable ideas from previous work (Saias, 2015) for Target and Aspect based Sentiment Analysis.

3.1   Feature extraction

We have performed standard data preprocessing steps on the system of tweets prior to classification. Text preprocessing consists of tokenization, removing all capitalization, stop word removal, POS tagging, and lemmatization with Stanford CoreNLP (Manning et al., 2014) and MALLET. An instance was created for each tweet text which includes extracted features. Some features are used additional lexicon resources such as Senti-WordNet lexicon (Baccianella et al., 2010).

Subtask A (Message Polarity Classification). The below features to represent each instance in Subtask A were:

- BoW with a feature for each token text;

- lemmas for nouns, verbs, adjectives and adverbs;

- a polarized term for each word;

- average polarized term for each instance;

- presence of negation terms.

The polarized terms based on SentiWordNet and used count of positive or negative polarity words using polarity scores. Some words appear more than once in this lexicon. For an example: "easy", this word is used in 28 different sentences on SentiWordNet. In other words, there are 28 use cases of the word and diverse polarity scores (positive or negative score). Thus, we have chosen an approximate use case of the word from the lexicon using BoW.

Subtask B (Topic-Based Message Polarity Classification). The below features to extract from each instance in Subtask B were:

- BoW with a feature for each token text after target position;

- lemmas for nouns, verbs, adjectives and adverbs with next to target position;

- polarized term for unigram and bigram words after given-target (topic) position in a text;

- presence of negation terms;

- presence of exclamation/question mark.

In this case, a polarized term was based on average polarity score which was created using all used cases of a word in SentiWordNet records. If any of an adjective appears next to target in a text, it will be chosen as the polarized term feature and set a tag as a positive, negative or neutral. Some features of an example tweet presented are:
Target: *"denzel"*; Tweet:*"Gotta go see Flight tomorrow Denzel is the greatest actor ever!"*; Extracted features: *(1) #AFTER.VBZ.positive for "is", (2) #AFTER.JJS.positive for "greatest", (3) #AFTER.NN.neutral for "actor" (4) #AFTER.RB.neutral for "ever" (5) #polExclMark.positive for "!".*

After this step, each text document in the system will be represented by a feature vector using MALLET.

3.2   Classifier training

The classifier algorithm was Maximum Entropy and the classifier model features were previously mentioned features. MaxEnt seeks the probability distribution model that best fits the features observed in the text. We have trained a classifier with instance list where each tweet text had been created as an instance with feature vectors using MALLET pipeline. A single label multiclass classification is used for the training in subtask A. Each tweet must be classified into exactly one of the following three classes (positive, neutral and negative). We also used a binary classification (positive or negative) for the training in subtask B. A single sentence in a tweet may have several sentiment polarities about different aspects. Thus, we tried to consider it in feature selection phase that has to choose correct sensitive words as a feature depends on a target.

4   Results

In this section, the results obtained with the proposed system and datasets are written. The preliminary experiments, we performed for the system were carried out by training and testing our models on datasets generated in editions of previous years of the tasks (see Table 1 and 2). All tweets are annotated for polarity by the organizers. Unbalanced training corpus is used where there are more positive tweets than others.

Dataset	All	Pos.	Neg.	Neut.
twitter-2013 -train-A	9684	3640	1458	4586
twitter-2013 -dev-A	1654	575	340	739
twitter-2014 -sarcasm-A	86	33	40	13
twitter-2015 -train-A	489	170	66	253
twitter-2016 -train-A	6000	3094	863	2043
twitter-2016 -dev-A	1999	843	391	765
twitter-2016 -devtest-A	2000	994	325	681
Total (no duplication)	21403	9171	3412	8820

Table 1: Trainset for our system in Task 4-A.

Dataset	All	Pos.	Neg.
twitter-2015 -train-BD	198	142	56
twitter-2015 -testBD	1127	867	260
twitter-2016 -train-BD.txt	4346	3591	755
twitter-2016 -dev-BD	1325	986	339
twitter-2016 -devtest-BD	1417	1153	264
twitter-2016 -test-BD	10551	8212	2339
Total	18964	14951	4013

Table 2: Trainset for our system in Task 4-B.

The classification results are presented in Table 3. In Subtask A, 37 submissions evaluated, the best F1-score value was 0.685, while our result F1-score was 0.539. There are 24 submissions in Subtask B, the best F1-score was 0.89 and our F1-score was 0.486.

5   Conclusions

We have presented an approach that incorporates the MaxEnt with various features to solve the over-

Subtask	F1	Recall	Acc
A	0.539	0.571	0.582
B	0.486	0.594	0.518

Table 3: Results achieved by our system

all polarity and topic-based message polarity. Our system is part of first author's work on text classification, included in PhD ongoing work. From the results, we noticed that our system was unsatisfactory compared to other teams. However, this evaluation became a good experience for us. Many people usually use an entirely different language on social media sites such as Twitter and Facebook. Thus, we will focus on social media and informal language learning. As further work we propose the following:

- compare the classical approaches with common features

- investigate the usage of a combination of classical approaches

- explore different techniques that can be used in target-oriented sentiment analysis

- investigate efficient features and new feature

- use more lexicons such as AFINN (Nielsen, 2011) and NRC Emoticon (Mohammad and Turney, 2010)

- develop the possibility of the system on multilingual

6   Acknowledgments

We would like to thank the gLINK project of *"Erasmus Mundus Programme, Action 2 - STRAND 1, Lot 5, Asia (East)"*. We would also like to thank the LabInterop project, for providing the infrastructure. LabInterop is funded by *Programa Operacional Regional do Alentejo* (INA-LENTEJO).

References

Stefano Baccianella, Andrea Esuli, and Fabrizio Sebastiani. 2010. Sentiwordnet 3.0: An enhanced lexical resource for sentiment analysis and opinion mining. In *LREC*. volume 10, pages 2200–2204.

Simon Fong, Yan Zhuang, Jinyan Li, and Richard Khoury. 2013. Sentiment analysis of online news using mallet. In *Computational and Business Intelligence (ISCBI), 2013 International Symposium on*. IEEE, pages 301–304.

Jaap Kamps, Maarten Marx, Robert J Mokken, Maarten De Rijke, et al. 2004. Using wordnet to measure semantic orientations of adjectives. In *LREC*. Citeseer, volume 4, pages 1115–1118.

Christopher D Manning, Mihai Surdeanu, John Bauer, Jenny Rose Finkel, Steven Bethard, and David McClosky. 2014. The stanford corenlp natural language processing toolkit. In *ACL (System Demonstrations)*. pages 55–60.

Andrew Kachites McCallum. 2002. Mallet: A machine learning for language toolkit .

Saif M Mohammad and Peter D Turney. 2010. Emotions evoked by common words and phrases: Using mechanical turk to create an emotion lexicon. In *Proceedings of the NAACL HLT 2010 workshop on computational approaches to analysis and generation of emotion in text*. Association for Computational Linguistics, pages 26–34.

Finn Årup Nielsen. 2011. A new anew: Evaluation of a word list for sentiment analysis in microblogs. *arXiv preprint arXiv:1103.2903* .

Alexander Pak and Patrick Paroubek. 2010. Twitter as a corpus for sentiment analysis and opinion mining. In *LREc*. volume 10.

Sara Rosenthal, Noura Farra, and Preslav Nakov. 2017. SemEval-2017 task 4: Sentiment analysis in Twitter. In *Proceedings of the 11th International Workshop on Semantic Evaluation*. Association for Computational Linguistics, Vancouver, Canada, SemEval '17.

José Saias. 2015. Sentiue: Target and aspect based sentiment analysis in semeval-2015 task 12. Association for Computational Linguistics.

VK Singh, R Piryani, A Uddin, P Waila, et al. 2013. Sentiment analysis of textual reviews; evaluating machine learning, unsupervised and sentiwordnet approaches. In *Knowledge and Smart Technology (KST), 2013 5th International Conference on*. IEEE, pages 122–127.

SentiME++ at SemEval-2017 Task 4: Stacking State-of-the-Art Classifiers to Enhance Sentiment Classification

Enrico Palumbo[**,*], Efstratios Sygkounas[*], Raphaël Troncy[*] and Giuseppe Rizzo[**]

[*]EURECOM, Sophia Antipolis, France
[**]ISMB, Turin, Italy

Abstract

In this paper, we describe the participation of the SentiME++ system to the SemEval 2017 Task 4A "Sentiment Analysis in Twitter" that aims to classify whether English tweets are of positive, neutral or negative sentiment. SentiME++ is an ensemble approach to sentiment analysis that leverages stacked generalization to automatically combine the predictions of five state-of-the-art sentiment classifiers. SentiME++ achieved officially 61.30% F1-score, ranking 12th out of 38 participants.

1 Introduction

The SemEval-2017 Task 4 (Rosenthal et al., 2017) focuses on the classification of tweets into positive, neutral and negative sentiment classes. In 2015, the Webis system (Hagen et al., 2015) showed the effectiveness of ensemble methods for sentiment classification by winning the SemEval-2015 Task 10 "polarity detection" challenge through the combination of four classifiers that had participated to previous editions of SemEval. In 2016, we have combined the original public release of the Webis system with the Stanford Sentiment System (Socher et al., 2013) using bagging, creating the SentiME system (Sygkounas et al., 2016b,a) which won the ESWC2016 Semantic Sentiment Analysis challenge. In bagging, the predictions of the classifiers trained on different bootstrap samples (bags) are simply averaged to obtained a final prediction. In this paper, we propose SentiME++, an enhanced version of the SentiME system that combines the predictions of the base classifiers through stacked generalization. In Section 2, we detail our approach to stack a meta-learner on top of five state-of-the-art sentiment classifiers to combine their predictions. In

Section 3, we describe the experimental setup of our participation to SemEval and we report the results we obtained in Section 4. Finally, we conclude the paper in Section 5.

2 Approach

2.1 Preliminaries

SentiME++ is based on the predictions of five state-of-the-art sentiment classifiers:

NRC-Canada: winner of SemEval 2013, trains a linear kernel SVM classifier on a set of linguistic and semantic features to extract sentiment from tweets (Mohammad et al., 2013);

GU-MLT-LT: 2nd ranked at SemEval 2013, uses a linear classifier trained by stochastic gradient descent with hinge loss and elastic net regularization for their predictions on a set of linguistic and semantic features (Günther and Furrer, 2013);

KLUE: 5th ranked at SemEval 2013, feeds a simple bag-of-words model into popular machine learning classifiers such as Naive Bayes, Linear SVM and Maximum Entropy (Proisl et al., 2013);

TeamX: winner of SemEval 2014, uses a variety of pre-processors and features, fed into a supervised machine learning algorithm which utilizes Logistic Regression (Miura et al., 2014);

Stanford Sentiment System: one of the subsystems of the Stanford NLP Core toolkit[1], contains the Stanford Tree Parser, a machine-learning model that can parse the input text into Stanford Tree format and the Stanford Sentiment Classifier, which takes as input Stanford Trees and outputs the classification results. The output of the Stanford Sentiment System belongs to one of five classes (very positive, positive, neutral, negative, very negative) which differs from the three classes defined in SemEval. In a previous work (Sygkounas et al., 2016b), we have tested different con-

---

[1]http://stanfordnlp.github.io/CoreNLP/

Proceedings of the 11th International Workshop on Semantic Evaluations (SemEval-2017), pages 648–652,
Vancouver, Canada, August 3 - 4, 2017. ©2017 Association for Computational Linguistics

figurations for mapping the Stanford Sentiment System classification to the three classes of the SemEval competition and finally decided to use the following strategy: very positive and positive are mapped to positive, neutral is mapped to neutral and negative and very negative are mapped to negative. The Stanford Sentiment System is used as an off-the-self classifier and is not trained with SemEval data.

2.2 Bootstrap samples

The first step in the SentiME++ approach consists in training separately the first four classifiers, using a uniform random sampling with replacement (bootstrap sampling) to generate four different training sets T_i for each of the four sub-classifiers from the initial training set T. In Section 3, we report the results of the experiments that we have conducted to determine the optimal size of the samples T_i. Note that these samples are also called 'bags'. At this point, the SentiME system combines the predictions on the models trained on these bags using a simple average, while SentiME++ uses stacked generalization, as described in the next section.

2.3 Stacking

Stacked Generalization (or simply stacking) (Wolpert, 1992) is based on the idea of creating an ensemble of base classifiers and then combining them by means of a supervised classifier, also called 'meta-learner'. Stacking typically leverages the complementarity among the base classifiers to obtain a better global performance than any of the individual models. The base classifiers are trained separately and, for each input, output their prediction. The meta-learner, which is 'stacked' on top of the base classifiers, is trained on the base classifiers' predictions and aims to correct the prediction errors of the base classifiers. SentiME++ trains separately four models, uses the Stanford Sentiment System without training and uses these five outputs as a feature vector for a stacked supervised learner (Fig. 1). In detail, the SentiME++ approach works can be divided in a training and a testing phase:

Training phase: (1) generate four bootstrap samples T_i by sampling n tweets from the original training set T, where $n = s * |T|$ and s is a parameter that has to be fixed experimentally (2) train separately NRC-CANADA, GU-MLT-LT, KLUE, TeamX classifiers on the samples T_i and store the

trained models; (3) use the four trained models and the Stanford Sentiment System to predict the sentiment of each tweet $t \in T$, producing a training set for the stacking layer T_{stack}; (4) Train the meta-learner on T_{stack}.

Testing phase: (1) use the four trained models and the Stanford Sentiment System to predict the sentiment of each tweet $t \in T_{test}$ producing a test set for the stacking layer T_{test}; (2) test the trained meta-learner on T_{test}.

Note that the described approach is slightly different from the standard procedure of Stacked Generalization described in (Wolpert, 1992), which is normally not based on bootstrap samples, but rather on disjoint splits of the training set. This variation is mainly due to the will of building SentiME++ as an incremental enhancement of the existing SentiMe system, without disrupting its base training mechanism. The meta-learner that is used as default in SentiME++ is a Support Vector Machine (SVM) with a Radial Basis Function (RBF) kernel (Scholkopf et al., 1997). Different choices are possible, but Support Vector Machines are well-studied methods in machine learning, able to be trained efficiently and to limit over-fitting. This method depends on two hyper-parameters, i.e. parameters that are not automatically learnt and that constitutes parameters of the algorithm itself: the regularization constant C and the parameter of the radial basis function γ. In order to optimize the performance of the stacking layer, we have chosen these parameters using a grid-search cross validation approach (Hsu et al., 2003). The process works as follows: (1) define a range for hyper-parameters $C \in [C_1...C_m]$ and $\gamma \in [\gamma_1...\gamma_n]$; (2) train the model with all possible pairs (C_i, γ_j); (3) compute scores with k-fold cross validation for (C_i, γ_j) pair; (4) find the best pair (C_i, γ_j) according to k-fold cross validation score.

SentiME is implemented in Java and the stacking process that characterizes SentiME++ is performed by a python script working on top of the results obtained by the SentiME system. The source code is available on github[2]. It uses a variety of lexicons (Table 1).

---

[2] https://github.com/
MultimediaSemantics/sentime

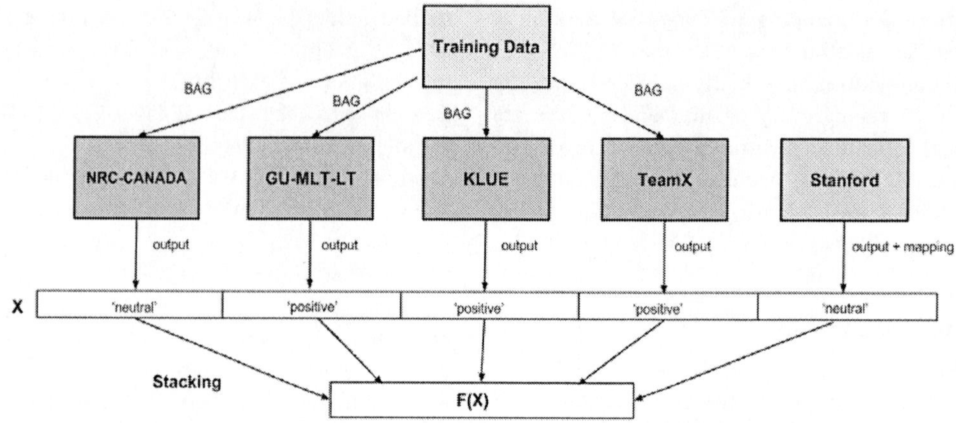

Figure 1: Illustration of the SentiME++ approach: bootstrap samples (bags) are generated to train four state-of-the-art sentiment classifiers, the Stanford System is used without training and their predictions are used as a feature vector for a meta-learner.

Lexicon	# of Words and phrases	Classifiers
AFINN-111	2477	TeamX
Bingliu	6800	NRC-Canada,TeamX
Hashtag	16,862 unigrams	NRC-Canada
NRC-emotion-lexicon-v0.92	14,182 unigrams	NRC-Canada,TeamX
Sentiment140	62,468 unigrams	NRC-Canada,TeamX
SentiWordNet_3.0.0	155.287	NRC-Canada,GU-MLT-LT,TeamX
SentiStrength	16,000 social web texts	KLUE

Table 1: Lexicons used by each sub-classifier included into SentiME++

3 Experimental Setup

In this section, we describe the experimental setup of the SentiME++ system for the participation to the SemEval2017 Task4A challenge.

3.1 Bootstrap samples size

One of the parameters of the SentiME++ model is the size of the bootstrap samples T_i. Different sampling sizes have been experimented, ranging from 33% to 175% of the size of the initial training set T. In order to determine an optimal size, we have tested the SentiME bagging approach, which simply averages the predictions of the base classifiers, on the SemEval2013-test-B dataset training the models with different random extractions of the SemEval2013-train+dev-B dataset. The experiment was repeated three times to mitigate the randomness due to the random extractions and we observed that a 150% size[3] led to the best per-

formance on SemEval2013-test-B dataset (Sygkounas et al., 2016a).

3.2 Encoding categorical features

In order to use the predicted sentiment classes as features for a meta-learner in the stacking layer, it is necessary to specify an encoding scheme, which allows the system to interpret the class values 'Positive', 'Neutral' and 'Negative'. These values could be simply mapped to integers $0, 1, 2$, but the meta-learner, expecting continuous or binary inputs, would interpret it as an ordered sequence of real values. To avoid this, we use a one-hot encoding scheme, i.e. m categorical values are turned into a m dimensional binary vector where only one element at the time is active. In this specific case, the encoding that we have used is: 'positive'=$[0, 0, 1]$, 'neutral'=$[0, 1, 0]$, 'negative'=$[1, 0, 0]$.

3.3 Hyper-parameters optimization

In order to optimize the performance of the SVM meta-learner, we have performed the grid-search

---

[3]Note that this implies that there are duplicates among the training examples

cross validation described in Section 2 on the SemEval2013-train+dev-B dataset using 10-folds. The experiment has been performed using as a range an array of 30 logarithmically spaced values for γ from 10^{-9} to 10^3 and for C from 10^{-2} to 10^{10}. The best obtained (C, γ) pair, i.e. the pair producing the best prediction score, which has been used for the participation to the challenge is: $(C, \gamma) = (0.174, 0.028)$. The implementation of the SVM classifier and of the grid-search cross validation procedure has been carried out using the python library scikit-learn[4].

4 Results

We started our experiments by training the system on different combinations of SemEval datasets, thus producing different trained models: **model 1**: SemEval2013-train+dev; **model 2**: model 1 + SemEval2013-test + SemEval2014-test + Twitter2014-sarcasm + SemEval2015-train + SemEval2015-test; **model 3**: model 2 + SemEval2016-dev + SemEval2016-test.

In order to compare the performance of these different trained models, we have chosen as a test set the SemEval2016-test dataset, as it is the largest in size (33k tweets) and the most recent of SemEval test sets. The results obtained from this experiment are illustrated in Table 2. We observe

	Model 1	Model 2	Model 3
SentiME++	65.69	71.24	94.80
SentiME	64.35	70.23	86.87

Table 2: Comparison among trained models on SemEval2016-test dataset for SentiME and SentiME++ according to F1 scores

that for all models, SentiME++ performs better than SentiME, proving the efficiency of stacked generalization with respect to bagging for combining the predictions of classifiers. For Model 1 and Model 2 the difference is around 1% and for Model 3 around 8%. Model 2 performs about 6% better than Model 1: this can be explained by the size of the training set which is bigger. Model 3 achieves the highest performance but the test dataset is part of the training dataset. While being aware that this introduces a bias in this evaluation, we also see that using more training data enhances the performance of the system and thus

---

[4]http://scikit-learn.org/stable/

we opt for using SentiME++ with Model 3 for the final submission. Being the process of bootstrap sampling stochastic, we ran the system four times and computed the F1-score on the SemEval2017 development dataset and, after the release of the gold standard for the test set, on the SemEval2017 test dataset (Tab. 3). Run 4 has been submitted as

SentiME++	Run 1	Run 2	Run 3	Run 4
Dev	84.63	86.15	85.13	**86.16**
Test	60.70	60.90	**63.40**	61.30

Table 3: Comparison among runs on SemEval2017-dev and SemEval2017-test dataset for SentiME++ according to F1 scores.

it was the best performing on the development set, but, a posteriori, we can observe that Run 3 performs better on the test set. We also observe a significant performance drop from the development to the test set. We believe that this might be due to the marked difference in the category distributions of the tweets in the two datasets (see Tab.4 in (Rosenthal et al., 2017)). The best SentiME++ run at SemEval2017 Task 4 Sub-Task A would rank 8th out of 38 participants.

5 Conclusion

In this paper, we have presented SentiME++, a sentiment classifier that combines the predictions of five state-of-the-art systems through stacking. SentiME++ achieved officially 61.30% F1-score, ranking 12th out of 38 participants. We have shown how stacking can improve the combination of the classifiers with respect to bagging, implemented in the previous version of SentiME, evaluating it on SemEval2017 Challenge datasets. We have described an experimental procedure to determine an appropriate size of the bootstrap samples and optimize hyper-parameters of the meta-learner. In general, we provide a further evidence of the power of the ensemble approach applied to sentiment analysis. As a future work, we plan to improve the bootstrap sampling process by taking into account the class distributions of the tweets, to determine the bag sizes directly using SentiME++, to include more base classifiers and experiment different meta-learners.

Acknowledgments

This work was partially supported by the innovation activity PasTime (17164) of EIT Digital.

References

Tobias Günther and Lenz Furrer. 2013. GU-MLT-LT: Sentiment Analysis of Short Messages using Linguistic Features and Stochastic Gradient Descent. In 7th *International Workshop on Semantic Evaluation (SemEval)*.

Matthias Hagen, Martin Potthast, Michel Büchner, and Benno Stein. 2015. Webis: An Ensemble for Twitter Sentiment Detection. In 9th *International Workshop on Semantic Evaluation (SemEval)*.

Chih-Wei Hsu, Chih-Chung Chang, Chih-Jen Lin, et al. 2003. A practical guide to support vector classification. `http://www.csie.ntu.edu.tw/~cjlin/papers/guide/guide.pdf`.

Yasuhide Miura, Shigeyuki Sakaki, Keigo Hattori, and Tomoko Ohkuma. 2014. TeamX: A Sentiment Analyzer with Enhanced Lexicon Mapping and Weighting Scheme for Unbalanced Data. In 8th *International Workshop on Semantic Evaluation (SemEval)*.

Saif Mohammad, Svetlana Kiritchenko, and Xiaodan Zhu. 2013. NRC-Canada: Building the State-of-the-Art in Sentiment Analysis of Tweets. In 7th *International Workshop on Semantic Evaluation (SemEval)*.

Thomas Proisl, Paul Greiner, Stefan Evert, and Besim Kabashi. 2013. KLUE: Simple and robust methods for polarity classification. In 7th *International Workshop on Semantic Evaluation (SemEval)*.

Sara Rosenthal, Noura Farra, and Preslav Nakov. 2017. SemEval-2017 Task 4: Sentiment Analysis in Twitter. In 11th *International Workshop on Semantic Evaluation (SemEval)*. Vancouver, Canada.

Bernhard Scholkopf, Kah-Kay Sung, Christopher JC Burges, Federico Girosi, Partha Niyogi, Tomaso Poggio, and Vladimir Vapnik. 1997. Comparing support vector machines with gaussian kernels to radial basis function classifiers. *IEEE transactions on Signal Processing* 45(11):2758–2765.

Richard Socher, Alex Perelygin, Jean Y. Wu, Jason Chuang, Christopher D. Manning, Andrew Y. Ng, and Christopher Potts. 2013. Recursive Deep Models for Semantic Compositionality Over a Sentiment Treebank. In *Conference on Empirical Methods in Natural Language Processing (EMNLP)*.

Efstratios Sygkounas, Giuseppe Rizzo, and Raphaël Troncy. 2016a. A Replication Study of the Top Performing Systems in SemEval Twitter Sentiment Analysis. In 15th *International Semantic Web Conference (ISWC)*.

Efstratios Sygkounas, Giuseppe Rizzo, and Raphaël Troncy. 2016b. Sentiment Polarity Detection From Amazon Reviews: An Experimental Study. In 13th *European Semantic Web Conference (ESWC), Semantic Sentiment Analysis Challenge*. pages 108–120.

David H. Wolpert. 1992. Stacked generalization. *Neural networks* 5(2):241–259.

Amobee at SemEval-2017 Task 4: Deep Learning System for Sentiment Detection on Twitter

Alon Rozental[*] **, Daniel Fleischer**[*]

Amobee, Tel Aviv, Israel

{arozental,danielf}@amobee.com

Abstract

This paper describes the Amobee sentiment analysis system, adapted to compete in SemEval 2017 task 4. The system consists of two parts: a supervised training of RNN models based on a Twitter sentiment treebank, and the use of feedforward NN, Naive Bayes and logistic regression classifiers to produce predictions for the different sub-tasks. The algorithm reached the 3rd place on the 5-label classification task (sub-task C).

1 Introduction

Sentiment detection is the process of determining whether a text has a positive or negative attitude toward a given entity (topic) or in general. Detecting sentiment on Twitter—a social network where users interact via short 140-character messages, exchanging information and opinions—is becoming ubiquitous. Sentiment in Twitter messages (tweets) can capture the popularity level of political figures, ideas, brands, products and people. Tweets and other social media texts are challenging to analyze as they are inherently different; use of slang, mis-spelling, sarcasm, emojis and co-mentioning of other messages pose unique difficulties. Combined with the vast amount of Twitter data (mostly public), these make sentiment detection on Twitter a focal point for data science research.

SemEval is a yearly event in which teams compete in natural language processing tasks. Task 4 is concerned with sentiment analysis in Twitter; it contains five sub-tasks which include classification of tweets according to 2, 3 or 5 labels and quantification of sentiment distribution regarding topics mentioned in tweets; for a complete description of task 4 see Rosenthal et al. (2017).

This paper describes our system and participation in all sub-tasks of SemEval 2017 task 4. Our system consists of two parts: a recurrent neural network trained on a private Twitter dataset, followed by a task-specific combination of model stacking and logistic regression classifiers.

The paper is organized as follows: section 2 describes the training of RNN models, data being used and model selection; section 3 describes the extraction of semantic features; section 4 describes the task-specific workflows and scores. We review and summarize in section 5. Finally, section 6 describes our future plans, mainly the development of an LSTM algorithm.

2 RNN Models

The first part of our system consisted of training recursive-neural-tensor-network (RNTN) models (Socher et al., 2013).

2.1 Data

Our training data for this part was created by taking a random sample[1] from Twitter and having it manually annotated on a 5-label basis to produce fully sentiment-labeled parse-trees, much like the Stanford sentiment treebank. The sample contains twenty thousand tweets with sentiment distribution as following:

	v-neg.	neg.	neu.	pos.	v-pos.
Train	8.4%	23.2%	31.7%	25.3%	11.4%
Test	8.6%	23.0%	33.2%	24.8%	10.4%

2.2 Preprocessing

First we build a custom dictionary by means of crawling Wikipedia and extracting lists of brands,

---

[*]These authors contributed equally to this work.

[1]Amobee is an official Twitter partner and as such has access to its global stream of data.

Proceedings of the 11th International Workshop on Semantic Evaluations (SemEval-2017), pages 653–658,
Vancouver, Canada, August 3 - 4, 2017. ©2017 Association for Computational Linguistics

celebrities, places and names. The lists were then pruned manually. Then we define the following steps when preprocessing tweets:

1. Standard tokenization of the sentences, using the Stanford coreNLP tools (Manning et al., 2014).

2. Word-replacement step using the Wiki dictionary with representative keywords.

3. Lemmatization, using coreNLP.

4. Emojis: removing duplicate emojis, clustering them according to sentiment and replacing them with representative keywords, e.g. "happy-emoji".

5. Regex: removing duplicate punctuation marks, replacing URLs with a keyword, removing Camel casing.

6. Parsing: parts-of-speech and constituency parsing using a shift-reduce parser[2], which was selected for its speed over accuracy.

7. NER: using entity recognition annotator[3], replacing numbers, dates and locations with representative keywords.

8. Wiki: second step of word-replacement using our custom wiki dictionary.

2.3 Training

We used the Stanford coreNLP sentiment annotator, introduced by Socher et al. (2013). Words are initialized either randomly as d dimensional vectors, or given externally as word vectors. We used four versions of the training data; with and without lemmatization and with and without pre-trained word representations[4] (Pennington et al., 2014).

2.4 Tweet Aggregation

Twitter messages can be comprised of several sentences, with different and sometimes contrary sentiments. However, the trained models predict sentiment on individual sentences. We aggregated the sentiment for each tweet by taking a linear combination of the individual sentences comprising the

tweet with weights having the following power dependency:

$$h(f, l, \mathrm{pol}) = (1 + f)^{\alpha}\, l^{\beta}\, (1 + \mathrm{pol})^{\gamma} + 1, \quad (1)$$

where α, β, γ are numerical factors to be found, f, l, pol are the fraction of known words, length of the sentence and polarity, respectively, with polarity defined by:

$$\mathrm{pol} = |10 \cdot \mathrm{vn} + \mathrm{n} - \mathrm{p} - 10 \cdot \mathrm{vp}|, \quad (2)$$

where vn, n, p, vp are the probabilities as assigned by the RNTN for very-negative, negative, positive and very-positive label for each sentence. We then optimized the parameters α, β, γ with respect to the true labels.

2.5 Model Selection

After training dozens of models, we chose to combine only the best ones using stacking, namely combining the models output using a supervised learning algorithm. For this purpose, we used the Scikit-learn (Pedregosa et al., 2011) recursive feature elimination (RFE) algorithm to find both the optimal number and the actual models, thus choosing the best five models. The models chosen include a representative from each type of the data we used and they were:

- Training data without lemmatization step, with randomly initialized word-vectors of size 27.

- Training data with lemmatization step, with pre-trained word-vectors of size 25.

- 3 sets of training data with lemmatization step, with randomly initialized word-vectors of sizes 24, 26.

The five models output is concatenated and used as input for the various tasks, as described in 4.1.

3 Features Extraction

In addition to the RNN trained models, our system includes feature extraction step; we defined a set of lexical and semantical features to be extracted from the original tweets:

- In-subject, In-object: whether the entity of interest is in the subject or object.

- Containing positive/negative adjectives that describe the entity of interest.

---

[2]http://nlp.stanford.edu/software/srparser.shtml.

[3]http://nlp.stanford.edu/software/CRF-NER.shtml.

[4]Twitter pre-trained word vectors were used, http://nlp.stanford.edu/projects/glove/

- Containing negation, quotations or perfect progressive forms.

For this purpose, we used the Stanford deterministic coreference resolution system (Lee et al., 2011; Recasens et al., 2013).

4 Experiments

The experiments were developed by using Scikit-learn machine learning library and Keras deep learning library with TensorFlow backend (Abadi et al., 2016). Results for all sub-tasks are summarized in table 1.

4.1 General Workflow

For each tweet, we first ran the RNN models and got a 5-category probability distribution from each of the trained models, thus a 25-dimensional vector. Then we extracted sentence features and concatenated them with the RNN vector. We then trained a Feedforward NN which outputs a 5-label probability distribution for each tweet. That was the starting point for each of the tasks; we refer to this process as the pipeline.

4.2 Task A

The goal of this task is to classify tweets sentiment into three classes (negative, neutral, positive) where the measured metric is a macro-averaged recall.

We used the SemEval 2017 task A data in the following way: using SemEval 2016 TEST as our TEST, partitioning the rest into TRAIN and DEV datasets. The test dataset went through the previously mentioned pipeline, getting a 5-label probability distribution.

We anticipated the sentiment distribution of the test data would be similar to the training data—as they may be drawn from the same distribution. Therefore we used re-sampling of the training dataset to obtain a skewed dataset such that a logistic regression would predict similar sentiment distributions for both the train and test datasets. Finally we trained a logistic regression on the new dataset and used it on the task A test set. We obtained a macro-averaged recall score of $\rho = 0.575$ and accuracy of $Acc = 0.587$.

Apparently, our assumption about distribution similarity was misguided as one can observe in the next table.

	Negative	Neutral	Positive
Train	15.5%	41.1%	43.4%
Test	32.3%	48.3%	19.3%

4.3 Tasks B, D

The goals of these tasks are to classify tweets sentiment regarding a given entity as either positive or negative (task B) and estimate sentiment distribution for each entity (task D). The measured metrics are macro-averaged recall and KLD, respectively.

We started with the training data passing our pipeline. We calculated the mean distribution for each entity on the training and testing datasets. We trained a logistic regression from a 5-label to a binary distribution and predicted a positive probability for each entity in the test set. This was used as a prior distribution for each entity, modeled as a Beta distribution. We then trained a logistic regression where the input is a concatenation of the 5-labels with the positive component of the probability distribution of the entity's sentiment and the output is a binary prediction for each tweet. Then we chose the label—using the mean positive probability as a threshold. These predictions are submitted as task B. We obtained a macro-averaged recall score of $\rho = 0.822$ and accuracy of $Acc = 0.802$.

Next, we took the predictions mean for each entity as the likelihood, modeled as a Binomial distribution, thus getting a Beta posterior distribution for each entity. These were submitted as task D. We obtained a score of $KLD = 0.149$.

4.4 Tasks C, E

The goals of these tasks are to classify tweets sentiment regarding a given entity into five classes—very negative, negative, neutral, positive, very positive—(task C) and estimate sentiment distribution over five classes for each entity (task E). The measured metrics are macro-averaged MAE and earth-movers-distance (EMD), respectively.

We first calculated the mean sentiment for each entity. We then used bootstrapping to generate a sample for each entity. Then we trained a logistic regression model which predicts a 5-label distribution for each entity. We modified the initial 5-label probability distribution for each tweet using

Task	A	B	C	D	E
	3-class.	2-class.	5-class.	2-quant.	5-quant.
Metric	ρ	ρ	MAE^M	KLD	EMD
Score	0.575	0.822	0.599	0.149	0.345
Rank	27/37	11/23	3/15	11/15	6/12

Table 1: Summary of evaluation results, metrics used and rank achieved, for all sub tasks. ρ is macro-averaged recall, MAE^M is macro-averaged mean absolute error, KLD is Kullback-Leibler divergence and EMD is earth-movers distance.

the following formula:

$$p^{\text{new}}(t_0, c_0) = \sum_{c \in C} \frac{p(t_0, c) \cdot p^{\text{entity-LR}}(t_0, c_0)}{\sum_{t \in T} p(t, c)},$$

$$(3)$$

where t_0, c_0 are the current tweet and label, $p^{\text{entity-LR}}$ is the sentiment prediction of the logistic regression model for an entity, T is the set of all tweets and $C = \{\text{vn, n, neu, p, vp}\}$ is the set of labels. We trained a logistic regression on the new distribution and the predictions were submitted as task C. We obtained a macro-averaged MAE score of $MAE^M = 0.599$.

Next, we defined a loss function as follows:

$$\text{loss}(t_0, c_0) = \sum_{c \in C} |c - c_0| \cdot \frac{p(t_0, c)}{\sum_{t \in T} p(t, c)}, \quad (4)$$

where the probabilities are the predicted probabilities after the previous logistic regression step. Finally we predicted a label for each tweet according to the lowest loss, and calculated the mean sentiment for each entity. These were submitted as task E. We obtained a score of $EMD = 0.345$.

5 Review and Conclusions

In this paper we described our system of sentiment analysis adapted to participate in SemEval task 4. The highest ranking we reached was third place on the 5-label classification task. Compared with classification with 2 and 3 labels, in which we scored lower, and the fact we used similar workflow for tasks A, B, C, we speculate that the relative success is due to our sentiment treebank ranking on a 5-label basis. This can also explain the relatively superior results in quantification of 5 categories as opposed to quantification of 2 categories.

Overall, we have had some unique advantages and disadvantages in this competition. On the one hand, we enjoyed an additional twenty thousand tweets, where every node of the parse tree was labeled for its sentiment, and also had the manpower

to manually prune our dictionaries, as well as the opportunity to get feedback from our clients. On the other hand, we did not use any user information and/or metadata from Twitter, nor did we use the SemEval data for training the RNTN models. In addition, we did not ensemble our models with any commercially or freely available pre-trained sentiment analysis packages.

6 Future Work

We have several plans to improve our algorithm and to use new data. First, we plan to extract more semantic features such as verb and adverb classes and use them in neural network models as additional input. Verb classification was used to improve sentiment detection (Chesley et al., 2006); we plan to label verbs according to whether their sentiment changes as we change the tense, form and active/passive voice. Adverbs were also used to determine sentiment (Benamara et al., 2007); we plan to classify adverbs into sentiment families such as intensifiers ("very"), diminishers ("slightly"), positive ("delightfully") and negative ("shamefully").

Secondly, we can use additional data from Twitter regarding either the users or the entities-of-interest.

Finally, we plan to implement a long short-term memory (LSTM) network (Hochreiter and Schmidhuber, 1997) which trains on a sentence together with all the syntax and semantic features extracted from it. There is some work in the field of semantic modeling using LSTM, e.g. Palangi et al. (2014, 2016). Our plan is to use an LSTM module to extend the RNTN model of Socher et al. (2013) by adding the additional semantic data of each phrase and a reference to the entity-of-interest. An illustration of the computational graph for the proposed model is presented in figure 1. The inputs/outputs are: V is a word vector representation of dimension d, D encodes the parts-of-speech (POS) tagging, syntactic cate-

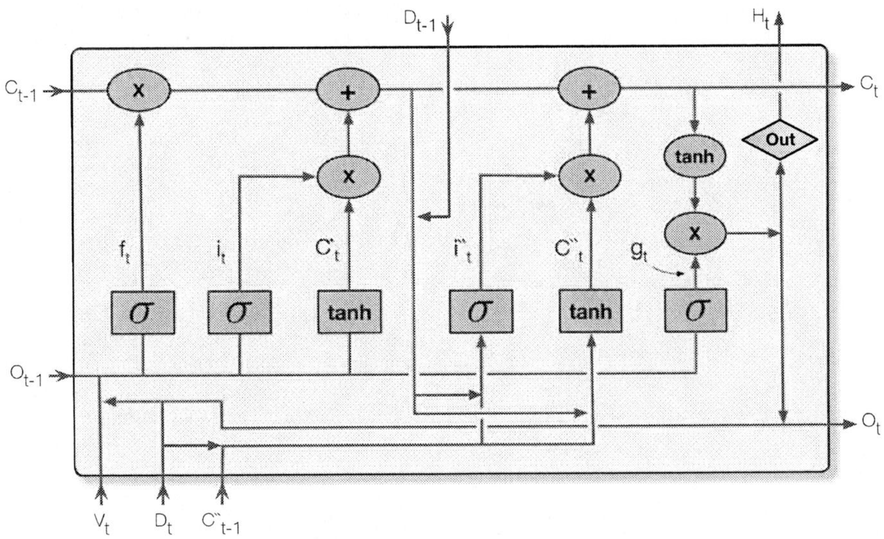

Figure 1: LSTM module; round purple nodes are element-wise operations, turquoise rectangles are neural network layers, orange rhombus is a dim-reducing matrix, splitting line is duplication, merging lines is concatenation.

gory and an additional bit indicating whether the entity-of-interest is present in the expression—all encoded in a 7 dimensional vector, C is a control channel of dimension d, O is an output layer of dimension $d + 7$ and H is a sentiment vector of dimension s.

The module functions are defined as following:

$$
\begin{aligned}
f_t &= \sigma \left[L_f \left([V_t, D_t], O_{t-1} \right) \right] \\
i_t &= \sigma \left[L_i \left([V_t, D_t], O_{t-1} \right) \right] \\
C_t' &= \tanh \left[L_{C'} \left([V_t, D_t], O_{t-1} \right) \right] \\
i_t'' &= \sigma \left[L_{i''} \left([C_{t-1}'', D_t], [C_{t-1}, D_{t-1}] \right) \right] \\
C_t'' &= \tanh \left[L_{C''} \left([C_{t-1}'', D_t], [C_{t-1}, D_{t-1}] \right) \right] \\
g_t &= \sigma \left[L_g \left([V_t, D_t], O_{t-1} \right) \right] \\
C_t &= C_{t-1} \odot f_t + C_t' \odot i_t + i_t'' \odot C_t'' \\
H_t &= W_{\text{out}} \cdot \left(g_t \odot \tanh \left(C_t \right) \right) \\
O_t &= \left[D_t, \left(g_t \odot \tanh \left(C_t \right) \right) \right],
\end{aligned}
\tag{5}
$$

where $W_{\text{out}} \in \mathbb{R}^{s \times d}$ is a matrix to be learnt, $\odot$ denotes Hadamard (element-wise) product and $[.,.]$ denotes concatenation. The functions L_i are the six NN computations, given by:

$$
\begin{aligned}
L^k \left(S_{ij} \right) &= S_{ij} T^{k,[1:d]} S_{ij}^\top + I_{0,0} W_{0,0}^k S_{ij}^\top \\
&\quad + I_{0,1} W_{0,1}^k S_{ij}^\top + I_{1,0} W_{1,0}^k S_{ij}^\top \\
&\quad + I_{1,1} W_{1,1}^k S_{ij}^\top \\
S_{ij} &= \left((v_i, s_i, e_i), (v_j, s_j, e_j) \right),
\end{aligned}
\tag{6}
$$

where (v_i, s_i, e_i) are the d dimensional word embedding, 6-bit encoding of the syntactic category and an indication bit of the entity-of-interest for the ith phrase, respectively, S_{ij} encodes the inputs of a left descendant i and a right descendant j in a parse tree and $k \in \{1, \ldots, 6\}$. Define $D = 2d + 14$, then $T^{[1:d]} \in \mathbb{R}^{D \times D \times d}$ is a tensor defining bilinear forms, $I_{I,J}$ with $I, J \in \{0, 1\}$ are indication functions for having the entity-of-interest on the left and/or right child and $W_{I,J} \in \mathbb{R}^{d \times D}$ are matrices to be learnt.

The algorithm processes each tweet according to its parse tree, starting at the leaves and going up combining words into expressions; this is different than other LSTM algorithms since the parsing data is used explicitly. As an example, figure 2 presents the simple sentence "Amobee is awesome" with its parsing tree. The leaves are given by d-dimensional word vectors together with their POS tagging, syntactic categories (if defined for the leaf) and an entity indicator bit. The computation takes place in the inner nodes; "is" and "awesome" are combined in a node marked by "VP" which is the phrase category. In terms of our terminology, "is" and "awesome" are the i, j nodes, respectively for "VP" node calculation. We define C_{t-1}'' as the cell's state for the *left* child, in this case the "is" node. Left and right are concatenated as input V_t and the metadata D_t is from the *right* child while D_{t-1} is the metadata from the *left* child. The second calculation takes place at the

657

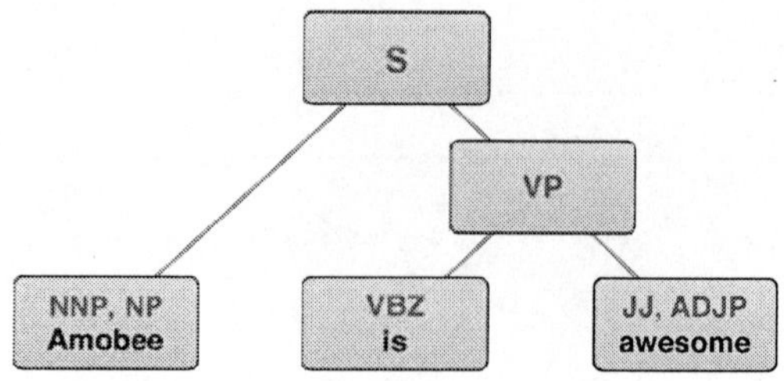

Figure 2: Constituency-based parse tree; the LSTM module runs on the internal nodes by concatenating the left and right nodes as its input.

root "S"; the input V_t is now a concatenation of "Amobee" word vector, the input O_{t-1} holds the O_t output of the previous step in node "VP"; the cell state C''_{t-1} comes from the "Amobee" node.

References

Martín Abadi, Ashish Agarwal, Paul Barham, Eugene Brevdo, Zhifeng Chen, Craig Citro, Greg S Corrado, Andy Davis, Jeffrey Dean, Matthieu Devin, et al. 2016. Tensorflow: Large-scale machine learning on heterogeneous distributed systems. *arXiv preprint arXiv:1603.04467* .

Farah Benamara, Carmine Cesarano, Antonio Picariello, Diego Reforgiato Recupero, and Venkatramana S Subrahmanian. 2007. Sentiment analysis: Adjectives and adverbs are better than adjectives alone. In *ICWSM*. Citeseer.

Paula Chesley, Bruce Vincent, Li Xu, and Rohini K Srihari. 2006. Using verbs and adjectives to automatically classify blog sentiment. *Training* 580(263):233.

Sepp Hochreiter and Jürgen Schmidhuber. 1997. Long short-term memory. *Neural computation* 9(8):1735–1780.

Heeyoung Lee, Yves Peirsman, Angel Chang, Nathanael Chambers, Mihai Surdeanu, and Dan Jurafsky. 2011. Stanford's multi-pass sieve coreference resolution system at the conll-2011 shared task. In *Proceedings of the Fifteenth Conference on Computational Natural Language Learning: Shared Task*. Association for Computational Linguistics, pages 28–34.

Christopher D. Manning, Mihai Surdeanu, John Bauer, Jenny Finkel, Steven J. Bethard, and David McClosky. 2014. The Stanford CoreNLP natural language processing toolkit. In *Association for Computational Linguistics (ACL) System Demonstrations*. pages 55–60. http://www.aclweb.org/anthology/P/P14/P14-5010.

Hamid Palangi, Li Deng, Yelong Shen, Jianfeng Gao, Xiaodong He, Jianshu Chen, Xinying Song, and Rabab Ward. 2016. Deep sentence embedding using long short-term memory networks: Analysis and application to information retrieval. *IEEE/ACM Trans. Audio, Speech and Lang. Proc.* 24(4):694–707. http://dl.acm.org/citation.cfm?id=2992449.2992457.

Hamid Palangi, Li Deng, Yelong Shen, Jianfeng Gao, Xiaodong He, Jianshu Chen, Xinying Song, and Rabab K. Ward. 2014. Semantic modelling with long-short-term memory for information retrieval. *CoRR* abs/1412.6629. http://arxiv.org/abs/1412.6629.

F. Pedregosa, G. Varoquaux, A. Gramfort, V. Michel, B. Thirion, O. Grisel, M. Blondel, P. Prettenhofer, R. Weiss, V. Dubourg, J. Vanderplas, A. Passos, D. Cournapeau, M. Brucher, M. Perrot, and E. Duchesnay. 2011. Scikit-learn: Machine learning in Python. *Journal of Machine Learning Research* 12:2825–2830.

Jeffrey Pennington, Richard Socher, and Christopher D. Manning. 2014. Glove: Global vectors for word representation. In *Empirical Methods in Natural Language Processing (EMNLP)*. pages 1532–1543. http://www.aclweb.org/anthology/D14-1162.

Marta Recasens, Marie-Catherine de Marneffe, and Christopher Potts. 2013. The life and death of discourse entities: Identifying singleton mentions. In *North American Association for Computational Linguistics (NAACL)*.

Sara Rosenthal, Noura Farra, and Preslav Nakov. 2017. SemEval-2017 task 4: Sentiment analysis in Twitter. In *Proceedings of the 11th International Workshop on Semantic Evaluation*. Association for Computational Linguistics, Vancouver, Canada, SemEval '17.

Richard Socher, Alex Perelygin, Jean Y Wu, Jason Chuang, Christopher D Manning, Andrew Y Ng, Christopher Potts, et al. 2013. Recursive deep models for semantic compositionality over a sentiment treebank. In *Proceedings of the conference on empirical methods in natural language processing (EMNLP)*. Citeseer, volume 1631, page 1642.

TWINA at SemEval-2017 Task 4: Twitter Sentiment Analysis with Ensemble Gradient Boost Tree Classifier

Naveen Kumar Laskari

Assistant Professor of IT
BVRIT Hyderabad
naveen.laskari@gmail.com

Suresh Kumar Sanampudi

Head of the Department, IT
JNTUH College of Engineering Jagitial
sureshsanampudi@gmail.com

Abstract

This paper describes the TWINA system, with which we participated in SemEval-2017 Task 4B (Topic Based Message Polarity Classification – Two point scale) and 4D (Two-point scale Tweet Quantification). We implemented ensemble based Gradient Boost Trees Classification method for both the tasks. Our system could perform well for the task 4D and ranked 13th among 15 teams, for the task 4B our model ranked 23rd position.

1 Introduction

Twitter, as a social networking service and microblogging service has gained great success in the recent years. It attracted millions of users to disseminate most up-to-date information, which resulted in generating massive amounts of information every day. Users share their opinions and experience on Twitter with the limit of 140 characters length text called as Tweet. Many applications in the field of Natural Language processing (NLP) and Information Retrieval (IR) are suffering severely from noisy in such a short 140 character length text.

This paper describes the system, with which we participated in Task 4 (Sentiment Analysis in Twitter) of SemEval – 2017 (Rosenthal et al., 2017). Organizers have given five different subtasks in task 4, they are:

* Task-4A: Message Polarity Classification
* Task-4B: Two-point scale Topic Based Message Polarity Classification
* Task-4C: Five-point scale Topic-Based Message Polarity Classification
* Task-4D: Two-point scale-Tweet quantification
* Task-4E: Five-point scale - Tweet quantification

We participated in only two subtasks B and D. With our submissions, we could stand in 13th position among 15 participants of task 4D and ranked 23rd position in task 4B. For both the tasks B and D, we implemented basic model of ensemble based Gradient Boost Tree Classifier and applied parameter optimization technique to improve the results.

The rest of the paper is organized as follows: In section 2 we describe the datasets, section 3 pre-processing of data for analysis, section 4 describes the model implementation using ensemble based Gradient Boost Trees Classification technique, section 5 gives results and section 6 gives conclusion and future work.

2 Datasets

In implementing the solution for SemEval Task 4, for every subtask the organizers provide training, development testing and testing datasets for training and testing. In addition to, the organizers made 2015 datasets available for training and tuning. We have used 4896 tweets for training the model and 20632 to test the model during the development. Final test of the model has been done on 12284 tweets.

Proceedings of the 11th International Workshop on Semantic Evaluations (SemEval-2017), pages 659–663,
Vancouver, Canada, August 3 - 4, 2017. ©2017 Association for Computational Linguistics

3 Pre-processing

Twitter has a constraint that, Tweet should not exceed 140 characters to convey the information or message. This makes the users to use unpredictable ways of expressing themselves. To find out sentiment from these kinds of tweets is very challenging task. In addition to, short text users are using different emoticons to express their opinions and feelings. Dealing with emoticons is a challenging task. To get the better results, we have to apply some pre-processing steps in order to clean Tweets for not to have unnecessary information. Initially each tweet converted into lower case and all URLS and HTML parts, Hash tags are removed from these tweets. Basically, emoticons has considered as

Original Tweet	Look @Qualcomm I found the 1st #Snapdragon Phone in my stuff from #Toshiba and @Microsoft. Still Working :) http://t.co/dLbuag6QDU
After Preprocessing	look found 1st snapdragon phone stuff toshiba still working HAPPY
Original Tweet	@darebeark @alyaeldeeb12345 my memory doesnt have more space. So i cant download it :(but i'll try to download it tomorrow from iPad
After Preprocessing	memory does not space cant download SAD try download tomorrow ipad
Original Tweet	Don't forget to collect the bills and win free ipod nano 7th generation & 17% CK vouchers of total bills , we...http://t.co/CNn4Ln9swy
After Preprocessing	do not forget collect bills win free ipod nano 7th generation 17% ck vouchers total bills

Table 1: Tweet Pre-processing

two categories SAD and HAPPY, to deal with emoticons, each of the emoticons has been replaced with its category label either SAD or HAPPY. The Table 1 shows how the pre-processing step is applied, for the original Tweet and pre-processed Tweet can be seen.

4 Implementation

To train and test our model implementations, we have downloaded the training, development testing and testing datasets provided by the SemEval-2017 Task 4 organizers. After pre-processing the Tweet, we extracted word2vec features using genism models. These word2vec features are used to train the Gradient Boost Tree Classifier (GBC). After training the GBC model, development test dataset has been used to validate the model and final test dataset has been used to evaluate the model.

4.1 Word2Vec

Word2vec[1] model is used for learning the vector representations of words called word embeddings (Mikolov et al., 2013; Pennington et al.,2014). Word2vec is computationally efficient predictive model for learning word embeddings. It comes in two flavors, the Continuous Bag-of-Words model (CBOW) and the Skip-Gram model. Algorithmically, these models are similar, except that CBOW predicts target words from source context words, while the skip-gram does the inverse and predicts source context-words from the target words. The amazing property of these word embeddings is that, it effectively captures the semantic meanings of the words.

4.2 Gradient Boost Tree Classifier

Gradient Boosting is a machine learning technique for regression and classification problems, it builds an ensemble of trees one-by-one, and then the predictions of individual trees are summed.
Gradient Boosting involves three elements:
- A loss function to be optimized
- A weak learner to make predictions
- An additive model to add weak learner to minimize the loss function.

Decision trees are used as weak learners in gradient boosting. Trees are constructed in greedy manner by choosing the best split points. Trees are added one at a time, and existing trees in the model are not changed.

As we have used Scikit-learn[2] for our model implementation. It is a free software library for machine learning in python. Scikit-learn come with various classification, regression and clustering techniques. It is designed to interoperate with Python numerical and scientific libraries NumPy and SciPy.

Gradient Boosting is typically used with decision trees. In constructing the decision trees in Gradient Boosting method various parameters are used for defining a tree are - 'n_estimators', 'max_depth', 'subsample', 'min_samples_leaf', 'learning_rate', 'random_state '.

min_samples_leaf is the minimum observations or samples required in leaf or terminal node. Lower values can be picked to control the over fitting problem and solve class imbalance problem, so we fixed with 1.

n_estimators is the number of sequential trees to be modeled. In GBC is fairly robust for the higher values of trees, but it can still over fit from point on. Hence, we checked various combinations of values and fixed with 2500.

max_depth is the maximum depth of the tree. Appropriate value has to be picked to control overfitting, because as the higher depth tree will allow the model to learn very specific relations, which leads to overfitting. So we fixed with 7.

subsample is the fraction of observations to be used for each construction. Selection of the subsample is done by purely random sampling approach. The value slightly less than 1 makes the model robust. We fixed at 0.75.

random_state is the random number seed used to generate the same random numbers every time. This is very important parameter. If we don't fix the random number, then we will have different outcomes for subsequent runs on the same parameters. We fixed with 3.

learning_rate is the parameter which determines the impact of each tree on the final outcome. Learning rate controls the magnitude of change in the estimates. Lower values are suitable to make the model more robust, but need to construct more number of trees to model all the relations, which actually computationally expensive. We fixed with 0.005.

We have tested Gradient Boost Tree Classifier model with various combinations of values for the above parameters, and for every combination the accuracy of the model has been evaluated. We could arrive at comparatively best results for the above combinations.

5 Results

We participated in only two sub tasks (Task 4B & 4D) of SemEval-2017 Task 4. We have used ensemble based Gradient Boost Trees Classification technique for both the subtasks. For Task 4B we classified the polarity of the Tweet with respect to a particular entity either positive or negative.

For Task 4D, we assigned the probability score for each Tweet and computed mean value of the positive and negative probabilities for entity level. The computed mean probability of the entity is considered as the final score for the Tweet quantification towards the entity.

	Precision	Recall	F1-Score
Positive	0.389	0.834	0.530
Negative	0.546	0.133	0.214
Average		0.483	0.372
Overall Score : 0.483			
Accuracy : 0.412			

Table 2: Results for subtask- 4B

---

[1]https://radimrehurek.com/gensim/models/word2vec.html

[2]http://scikitlearn.org/stable/modules/generated/sklearn.ensemble.GradientBoostingClassifier.html

[3]https://www.analyticsvidhya.com/blog/2016/02/complete-guide-parameter-tuning-gradient-boosting-gbm-python/

The organizers have defined various baselines for measuring the performance of submissions. For task 4B average recall and accuracy for each class is considered as baseline. For task 4D five baselines have been defined. Baseline 2 is macro-averaged KLD, AE and RAE on train, dev, devtest and test from 2016. Baseline 3 is micro-averaged KLD, AE and RAE on train, dev, devtest, and test from 2016. Baseline 4 is micro-averaged KLD, AE and RAE on train, dev, devtest and test from 2016. Baseline 5 is micro-averaged KLD, AE and RAE on train, dev, devtest and test from 2015 and 2016.

S.No	System	ρ	F_1^{PN}	Acc
1	BB_twtr	0.882	0.890	0.897
2	DataStories	0.856	0.861	0.869
3	Tweester	0.854	0.856	0.863
4	TopicThunder	0.846	0.847	0.854
5	TakeLab	0.845	0.836	0.840
6	funSentiment	0.834	0.824	0.827
7	YNU-HPCC	0.834	0.816	0.818
8	WarwickDCS	0.829	0.834	0.843
9	CrystalNest	0.827	0.822	0.827
10	Zhangweuda2080	0.826	0.830	0.838
11	Amobee-C-137	0.822	0.801	0.802
12	SINAI	0.818	0.806	0.809
13	NRU-HSC	0.798	0.787	0.790
14	EICA	0.790	0.775	0.777
15	OMAM	0.779	0.762	0.764
16	NileTMRG	0.769	0.774	0.789
17	EliRF-UPV	0.766	0.773	0.790
18	DUTH	0.663	0.600	0.607
19	Ej-za-2017	0.594	0.486	0.518
20	SSN_MLRGI	0.586	0.494	0.518
21	YNU_1510	0.516	0.499	0.499
22	TM_Gist	0.499	0.428	0.444
23	**SSK_JNTUH**	**0.483**	**0.372**	**0.412**
	Baseline 1 : All POSITIVE	**0.500**	**0.285**	**0.398**
	Baseline 2: All NEGATIVE	**0.500**	**0.376**	**0.602**

Table 3: Comparative Results for subtask- 4B

6 Conclusions and Future work

In this paper we presented TWINA system, with which we participated in two sub tasks of SemEval-2017. This is the first time we participated in SemEval Task; there is much scope for the improvement. We have used very simple feature extraction technique like word2vec, and ensemble based Gradient Boost Tree Classification method. We can get better results with the implementation of good feature engineering techniques and use of deep neural networks for classification task.

S. No	System	KLD	AE	RAE
1	BB_twtr	0.036	0.080	0.598
2	DataStories	0.048	0.095	0.848
3	TakeLab	0.050	0.096	1.057
4	CrystalNest	0.056	0.104	1.202
5	Tweester	0.057	0.103	1.051
6	funSentiment	0.060	0.109	0.939
7	NileTMRG	0.077	0.120	1.228
8	NRU-HSC	0.078	0.132	1.528
9	Ecnucsy	0.092	0.143	1.922
10	THU_HCSI_IDU	0.129	0.179	2.428
11	Amobee-C-137	0.149	0.179	2.168
12	OMAM	0.164	0.204	2.790
13	**SSK_JNTUH**	**0.421**	**0.314**	**2.983**
14	EliRF-UPV	1.060	0.593	7.991
15	YNU-HPCC	1.142	0.592	7.859
	Baseline 1	**1.518**	**0.422**	**2.645**
	Baseline 2	**0.554**	**0.423**	**6.061**
	Baseline 3	**0.591**	**0.432**	**6.169**
	Baseline 4	**0.534**	**0.418**	**6.000**
	Baseline 5	**0.587**	**0.431**	**6.157**

Table 4: Comparative Results for subtask- 4D

7 References

Chikersal, Prerna, Soujanya Poria, and Erik Cambria. "SeNTU: sentiment analysis of tweets by combining a rule-based classifier with supervised learning." Proceedings of the International Workshop on Semantic Evaluation, SemEval. 2015.

Kharde, Vishal, and Prof Sonawane. "Sentiment analysis of twitter data: A survey of techniques." arXiv preprint arXiv: 1601. 06971(2016).

Liu, Bing. "Sentiment analysis and opinion mining." Synthesis lectures on human language technologies 5.1 (2012): 1-167.

Meyer, David. "How exactly does word2vec work?." (2016).

Nakov, Preslav, Alan Ritter, Sara Rosenthal, Fabrizio Sebastiani, and Veselin Stoyanov. "SemEval-2016 task 4: Sentiment analysis in Twitter." Proceedings of SemEval (2016): 1-18.

Roe, Byron P., et al. "Boosted decision trees as an alternative to artificial neural networks for particle identification." Nuclear Instruments and Method in Physics Research Section A: Accelerators, Spectrometers, Detectors and Associated Equipment 543.2 (2005): 577-584.

Sara Rosenthal, Noura Farra, and Preslav Nakov. 2017. SemEval-2017 task 4: Sentiment analysis in Twitter. In Proceedings of the 11th International Workshop on Semantic Evaluation. Vancouver, Canada, SemEval '17

Sara Rosenthal, Preslav Nakov, Svetlana Kiritchenko, Saif Mohammad, Alan Ritter, and Veselin Stoyanov. 2015. SemEval-2015 task 10: Sentiment analysis in Twitter. In Proceedings of the 9th International Workshop on Semantic Evaluation. Denver, Colorado, SemEval '15, pages 451–463.

Tw-StAR at SemEval-2017 Task 4: Sentiment Classification of Arabic Tweets

Hala Mulki [1], Hatem Haddad [2], Mourad Gridach [3] and Ismail Babaoglu [1]

[1] Department of Computer Engineering, Selcuk University, Konya, Turkey
[2] Department of Computer and Decision Engineering, Université Libre de Bruxelles, Belgium
[3] High Institute of Technology, Ibn Zohr University, Agadir, Morocco
`halamulki@selcuk.edu.tr,Hatem.Haddad@ulb.ac.be`
`m.gridach@uiz.ac.ma,ibabaoglu@selcuk.edu.tr`

Abstract

In this paper, we present our contribution in SemEval 2017 international workshop. We have tackled task 4 entitled "Sentiment analysis in Twitter", specifically subtask 4A-Arabic. We propose two Arabic sentiment classification models implemented using supervised and unsupervised learning strategies. In both models, Arabic tweets were preprocessed first then various schemes of bag-of-N-grams were extracted to be used as features. The final submission was selected upon the best performance achieved by the supervised learning-based model. Nevertheless, the results obtained by the unsupervised learning-based model are considered promising and evolvable if more rich lexica are adopted in further work.

1 Introduction

Social media is literally shaping decision making processes in many aspects of our daily lives. Exploring online opinions is therefore becoming the focus of many analytical studies. Twitter is one of the most popular microblogging systems that enables a real-time tracking of opinions towards ongoing events (Saif et al., 2016). Hence, it provides the needed feedback information for analytical studies in several domains such as politics and targeted advertising (El-Makky et al., 2014). Sentiment analysis plays an essential role in performing such studies as it can extract the sentiments out of the opinions and classify them into polarities (Tang et al., 2015). Arabic language has recently been considered as one of the most growing languages on Twitter with more than 10.8 million tweets per day (Alhumoud et al., 2015). Yet, Arabic is remarkably less tackled in the research

of Sentiment Analysis (Nabil et al., 2015; ElSahar and El-Beltagy, 2015). With more resources and tools for Arabic Natural Language Processing (NLP) becoming available, and with the recent developed sentiment lexica for Modern Standard Arabic (MSA) and dialectal Arabic, this year, SemEval contest offers the opportunity to apply sentiment classification on Arabic tweets through subtask 4A-Arabic (Rosenthal et al., 2017). Analyzing Arabic tweets is significantly challenging due to the complex nature and morphology of the Arabic language. Furthermore, Arabic tweets are mostly informal and written in different dialects in which same words or expressions may have drastically different sentiments. For example, العافية يعطيك is a compliment of a positive sentiment that means "May GOD grant you health" in the Levantine dialect while it has an aggressive meaning of "burn in fire" in the Moroccan and Tunisian dialects (El-Makky et al., 2014). Additionally, tweeters tend to use abbreviations, neologisms, emoji and sarcasm frequently (Maas et al., 2011; Rajadesingan et al., 2015), and sometimes in the same 140-characters tweet (Maas et al., 2011).

Here, we describe our participation in Task 4, subtask 4A-Arabic of SemEval 2017 under the team name "Tw-StAR" (Twitter-Sentiment analysis team for ARabic). The task requires classifying the sentiment of single Arabic tweets into one of the classes: positive, negative or neutral (Rosenthal et al., 2017). To accomplish this mission, we have used two classification models:

- Supervised learning-based model: bag-of-N-grams features of different schemes have been adopted to train the model. Support Vector Machines (SVM) and naïve Bayes (NB) algorithms have been used as classification algorithms.

Proceedings of the 11th International Workshop on Semantic Evaluations (SemEval-2017), pages 664–669,
Vancouver, Canada, August 3 - 4, 2017. ©2017 Association for Computational Linguistics

- Unsupervised learning-based (lexicon-based) model: in which a merged MSA/multi-dialectal sentiment lexica along with the constant weighting strategy have been employed to classify the tweets' sentiment.

The remainder of the paper is organized as follows: in Section 2, we describe the preprocessing step. In Section 3, we identify the extracted feature sets. Section 4 introduces the learning strategies used in the presented models. Results are reviewed and discussed in Section 5 while Section 6 concludes the study and future work.

2 Data Preprocessing

In this step, we have first cleaned the tweets from the unsentimental content such as URLs, Username, dates, hashtags, retweet symbols, punctuation, emotions and non-Arabic characters to get the Arabic text only as in (Shoukry and Rafea, 2012; Al-Osaimi and Badruddin, 2014). Secondly, the input data has been filtered from the words that do not affect the text meaning, the so called stopwords (El-Makky et al., 2014). Since our data contains several dialects we had to use an already built stopwords list of 244 words for MSA and Egyptian dialect used in (Shoukry and Rafea, 2012) merged with a manually-built list of 12 words from the Levantine and Gulf dialects such as شو, فين which mean"where" and "what" in the Gulf and Levantine dialects respectively. Furthermore, MSA/dialectal negation words such as ما, مش that mean "not" in Levantine and Egyptian dialects respectively, have been excluded from the used stopwords lists, as they may reverse the polarity of a tweet (Duwairi et al., 2014). Thus, a tweet such as "https://t.co/wPg3KEz4bW-ما يدور في رأس دونالد ترامب" which means "what is going on in Trump's mind" becomes "ما يدور رأس دونالد ترامب" after preprocessing. Lastly, for the ulexicon-based model, we have subjected each tweet to tokenization then to stemming to facilitate the words lookup process in the lexica. Stemming has been carried out using the Information Science Research Institute's (ISRI) Arabic stemmer provided by NLTK library (Bird, 2006). ISRI is a root-extraction stemmer that can provide a normalized form of unstemmed words rather than leaving them unchanged. Moreover, being a context-sensitive stemmer prevents ISRI from producing insensible and invalid roots (Dahab et al., 2015).

3 Feature Extraction

Bag-of-N-grams features have been adopted to be used in both of the presented models (Shoukry and Rafea, 2012; Abdulla et al., 2013; Ahmed et al., 2013). N-grams represent a sequence of adjoining N items collected from a given corpus. Extracting N-grams can be thought of as exploring a large piece of text through a window of a fixed size (Pagolu et al., 2016). Features selection has been performed using NLTK module FreqDist which gives a list of the distinct words ordered by their frequency of appearance in the corpus (Bird, 2006). A specific number of features was defined (equals to 40100 for the combination of unigrams+bigrams+trigrams) in order to be selected from the FreqDist's list . The feature extraction pipeline is illustrated in Figure 1. For a certain

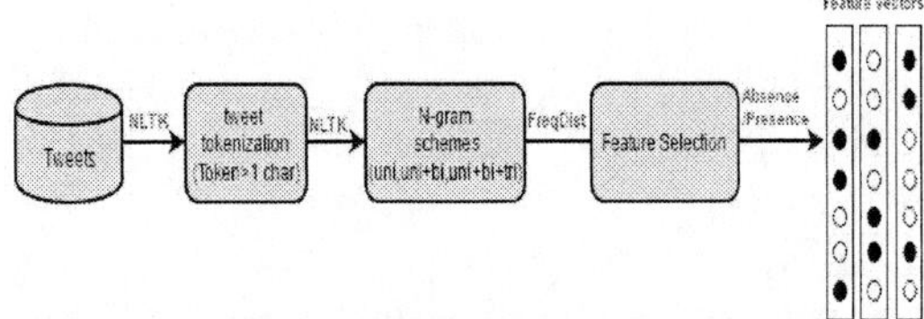

Figure 1: Feature extraction pipeline

N-grams scheme, a tweet's feature vector is constructed via examining the presence/absence of the N-grams features among the tweet's tokens. Consequently, the feature vector's values are identified as True (presence) or False (absence).

4 Learning Strategies

In this section, we describe the learning strategies adopted by the presented models. The mechanism of each strategy is briefly reviewed, in addition to an introduction of the python[1] supported tools used by these strategies to build the classification models.

4.1 Supervised learning

Supervised learning requires a labeled corpus to train the classifier on the text polarity prediction (Biltawi et al., 2016). In our case, a polarity labeled dataset of (3355) Arabic tweets provided by SemEval 2017 has been used such that 2684 tweets were dedicated to train the model while 671 tweets were used to tune it. The learning process

---

[1] https://www.python.org

has been carried out by inferring that a combination of specific features of a tweet yields a specific class (Shoukry and Rafea, 2012). We have used Naïve Bayes (NB) from Scikit-Learn (Pedregosa et al., 2011) since it is as powerful as Logistic Regression (Räbigera et al., 2016) and has proved its efficiency in classifying sentiment of multi-dialectal datasets (Itani et al., 2012). Additionally, linear SVM from LIBSVM was employed for its robustness and ease of implementation (Chang and Lin, 2011). Regarding used features, and as higher-order N-grams performed better compared to unigrams (Rushdi-Saleh et al., 2011). We have adopted N-grams schemes ranging from unigrams up to trigrams.

4.2 Unsupervised learning (lexicon-based)

In this strategy, neither labeled data nor training step are required to train the classifier. The polarity of a word or a sentence is determined using a sentiment lexicon or lexica that can be either pre-built or manually-built (Abdulla et al., 2013). Sentiment lexica usually contain subjective words along with their polarities (positive, negative). For each polarity, a sentiment weight is assigned using one of these weighting algorithms:

- Sum method: adopts the constant weight strategy to assign weights to the lexicon's entries, where negative words have the weight of -1 while positive ones have the weight of 1. The polarity of a given text is thus calculated by accumulating the weights of negative and positive terms. Then, the total polarity is determined by the sign of the resulted value (Abdulla et al., 2016).

- Double Polarity (DP) method: assigns both a positive and a negative weight for each term in the lexicon. For example, if a positive term in the lexicon has a weight of 0.8, then its negative weight will be: -1+0.8 = -0.2. Similarly, a negative term of -0.6 weight has a 0.4 positive weight. Polarity is calculated by summing all the positive weights and all the negative weights in the input text. Consequently, the final polarity is determined according to the greater absolute value of the resulted sum (El-Makky et al., 2014).

Having the MSA/dialectal combination of our training dataset defined by manual annotation (see Table 1), we have adopted a merged of pre-built and manually-built sentiment lexica with 6587 total entries of single and compound terms.

Arabic Type	Number of Tweets
MSA	2643
Egyptian	247
Levantine	69
Gulf	393
Moroccan	3
Total	3355

Table 1: Dataset MSA/Dialectal combination.

The pre-built lexica included NileULex (El-Beltagy, 2016) for MSA and Egyptian, Arabic Emotion Lexicon (Salameh et al., 2015) for emojis and Arabic Hashtag Lexicon (Salameh et al., 2015; Mohammad et al., 2016) for MSA/multiple dialects. Levantine and Gulf dialects were targeted through two manually-built lexica. Table 2 lists the used lexica and their sizes.

Sentiment Lexicon Used	Size
NileULex	5953
Arabic Emotion Lexicon (seeds)	23
Arabic Hashtag Lexicon (seeds)	230
Levantine Lexicon (manually-built)	281
Gulf Lexicon (manually-built)	100

Table 2: Used lexica.

As in (Abdulla et al., 2013; El-Beltagy and Ali, 2013), we have used the Sum method to determine the tweets' polarity. The polarity calculation procedure involved looking for entries that match the tweet's unigrams or bigrams in the lexica. Besides, we have provided the ability to look for the stemmed word if the unstemmed one could not be found (Al-Horaibi and Khan, 2016). Stop-words and negation words were kept to increase the possibility of matching a tweet's token with the compound terms of the merged lexica. Thus, for a tweet such غوغل مبدعة شي خرافي means "Google is incredibly creative" the polarity is calculated by summing the polarity values of its tokens "google+incredibly+creative= 0+1+1=+2 >0 " hence, it is positive.

5 Results and Discussion

The provided dataset consists of three parts: TRAIN (2684 tweets) for training models, DEV (671 tweets) for tuning models, and TEST (6100 tweets) for the official evaluation. Data pre-processing involved using regular expressions recognition and substitution provided by the re Python module[2]. N-grams feature schemes (unigrams+bigrams+trigrams) have been generated via NLTK [3]. Having the data preprocessed and the features extracted, we have trained the supervised learning-based model then classified the sentiment of the DEV set. The used classification algorithms were SVM from LIBSVM [4] and NB from Scikit-Learn [5]. Table 4 lists the results of these two classification algorithms. Considering the baseline results reviewed in Table 3, it can be observed that a slight improvement was achieved by NB compared to the baseline. While SVM outperformed both the baseline and NB by achieving an average F-score (AVG F1) of 0.384 and an average Recall (AVG R) of 0.459.

	AVG F1	AVG R
Baseline	0.249	0.333

Table 3: The baseline results for DEV set.

Algorithm	AVG F1	AVG R
SVM	**0.384**	**0.459**
NB	0.284	0.418

Table 4: The performance of the supervised learning-based model on DEV dataset.

For the lexicon-based model, the tweet's tokens (unigrams+bigrams) have been looked up in the lexica to calculate the tweet's polarity using the Sum method. The lookup process involved looking for the stemmed token if the unstemmed one is not found in the lexica. In Table 5, we notice that when stemming assists the lookup process, the performance degraded from 0.342 to 0.309 in terms of F-score value. This is because dialectal words may not be stemmed correctly by ISRI stemmer[6] (Dahab et al., 2015). For example, the term أبغى means "I want" in the Gulf dialect and has a neutral sentiment, while its stem using ISRI

is بغى means "injustice" that has a negative polarity. However, the experiment in which stemmer was not used achieved quite a close performance to that of the supervised model as it yielded 0.448 and 0.342 for average recall and average F-score respectively. This is due to the fact that MSA/Egyptian and Gulf/Levantine dialects were efficiently supported by the used lexica.

Stemming	AVG F1	AVG R
Available	0.309	0.367
Not available	**0.342**	**0.448**

Table 5: Lexicon-based model performance on DEV dataset.

Considering the results in Table 4 and Table 5, the supervised learning-based model with SVM algorithm achieved the best average F-score and Recall values compared to the lexicon-based model. So, we selected it to provide the TEST set classification results for the final submission. Table 6 reviews the scores and the ranking of our system in the official evaluation.

Metric	Value	Ranking
Average F1	0.416	7/8
Average R	0.431	7/8
Average Accuracy	0.454	5/8

Table 6: Final submission evaluation of supervised learning-based model for the TEST dataset.

6 Conclusion and Future work

We have investigated sentiment classification of Arabic tweets via two classification models of various features and two learning strategies. Relatively, satisfying results were obtained by the supervised and lexicon-based models. For the final submission, we selected the supervised learning-based model, as it achieved the best average F-score and Recall values. However, the lexicon-based model has also yielded good results when the lookup process was not assisted by stemming. We noticed that MSA/multi-dialectal content has been efficiently handled by the merged lexica. Further improvement can be obtained in the future if Levantine/Gulf dialects are more efficiently supported by using their current lexica entries as seeds to produce a richer lexicon.

---

[2]https://docs.python.org/3/library/re.html

[3]http://www.nltk.org/

[4]https://www.csie.ntu.edu.tw/~cjlin/libsvm/

[5]http://scikit-learn.org/stable/modules/naive_bayes.html

[6]http://www.nltk.org/_modules/nltk/stem/isri.html

References

Nawaf A Abdulla, Nizar A Ahmed, Mohammed A Shehab, and Mahmoud Al-Ayyoub. 2013. Arabic sentiment analysis: Lexicon-based and corpus-based. In *2013 IEEE Jordan Conference on Applied Electrical Engineering and Computing Technologies (AEECT)*. pages 1–6.

Nawaf A Abdulla, Nizar A Ahmed, Mohammed A Shehab, Mahmoud Al-Ayyoub, Mohammed N Al-Kabi, and Saleh Al-rifai. 2016. Towards improving the lexicon-based approach for arabic sentiment analysis. In *Big Data: Concepts, Methodologies, Tools, and Applications*. IGI Global, pages 1970–1986.

Soha Ahmed, Michel Pasquier, and Ghassan Qadah. 2013. Key issues in conducting sentiment analysis on Arabic social media text. In *2013 9th International Conference on Innovations in Information Technology (IIT)*. IEEE, pages 72–77.

Lamia Al-Horaibi and Muhammad Badruddin Khan. 2016. Sentiment Analysis of Arabic Tweets Using Semantic Resources. *International Journal of Computing & Information Sciences* 12(2):149.

Salha Al-Osaimi and Khan Muhammad Badruddin. 2014. Role of Emotion icons in Sentiment classification of Arabic Tweets. In *Proceedings of the 6th international conference on management of emergent digital ecosystems*. Association for Computing Machinery (ACM), pages 167–171.

Sarah O Alhumoud, Mawaheb I Altuwaijri, Tarfa M Albuhairi, and Wejdan M Alohaideb. 2015. Survey on Arabic Sentiment Analysis in Twitter. *International Science Index* 9(1):364–368.

Mariam Biltawi, Wael Etaiwi, Sara Tedmori, Amjad Hudaib, and Arafat Awajan. 2016. Sentiment classification techniques for Arabic language: A survey. In *2016 7th International Conference on Information and Communication Systems (ICICS)*. IEEE, pages 339–346.

Steven Bird. 2006. NLTK: the natural language toolkit. In *Proceedings of the COLING/ACL on Interactive presentation sessions*. Association for Computational Linguistics, pages 69–72.

Chih-Chung Chang and Chih-Jen Lin. 2011. LIBSVM: A Library for Support Vector Machines. *ACM Trans. Intell. Syst. Technol.* 2(3):1–27.

Mohamed Y Dahab, Al Ibrahim, and Rihab Al-Mutawa. 2015. A comparative study on arabic stemmers. *International Journal of Computer Applications* 125(8):38–47.

R M Duwairi, Raed Marji, Narmeen Sha'ban, and Sally Rushaidat. 2014. Sentiment analysis in arabic tweets. In *2014 5th International Conference on Information and Communication Systems (ICICS)*. IEEE, pages 1–6.

Samhaa R. El-Beltagy. 2016. Nileulex: A phrase and word level sentiment lexicon for egyptian and modern standard arabic. In *Proceedings of the Tenth International Conference on Language Resources and Evaluation (LREC 2016)*. European Language Resources Association (ELRA).

Samhaa R El-Beltagy and Ahmed Ali. 2013. Open issues in the sentiment analysis of Arabic social media: A case study. In *9th the International Conference on Innovations and Information Technology (IIT2013)*. IEEE, pages 215–220.

Nagwa El-Makky, Khaled Nagi, Alaa El-Ebshihy, Esraa Apady, Omneya Hafez, Samar Mostafa, and Shimaa Ibrahim. 2014. Sentiment analysis of colloquial Arabic tweets. In *ASE Big-Data/SocialInformatics/PASSAT/BioMedCom 2014 Conference, Harvard University*.

Hady ElSahar and Samhaa R El-Beltagy. 2015. Building large arabic multi-domain resources for sentiment analysis. In *International Conference on Intelligent Text Processing and Computational Linguistics*. Springer, pages 23–34.

M M Itani, R N Zantout, L Hamandi, and I Elkabani. 2012. Classifying sentiment in arabic social networks: Naïve search versus Naïve Bayes. In *2012 2nd International Conference on Advances in Computational Tools for Engineering Applications (ACTEA)*. IEEE, pages 192–197.

Andrew L Maas, Raymond E Daly, Peter T Pham, Dan Huang, Andrew Y Ng, and Christopher Potts. 2011. Learning word vectors for sentiment analysis. In *Proceedings of the 49th Annual Meeting of the Association for Computational Linguistics: Human Language Technologies-Volume 1*. Association for Computational Linguistics, pages 142–150.

Saif M Mohammad, Mohammad Salameh, and Svetlana Kiritchenko. 2016. How Translation Alters Sentiment. *J. Artif. Intell. Res.(JAIR)* 55:95–130.

Mahmoud Nabil, Mohamed A Aly, and Amir F Atiya. 2015. ASTD: Arabic Sentiment Tweets Dataset. In *Empirical Methods on Natural Language Processing (EMNLP)*. pages 2515–2519.

Venkata Sasank Pagolu, Kamal Nayan Reddy Challa, Ganapati Panda, and Babita Majhi. 2016. Sentiment Analysis of Twitter Data for Predicting Stock Market Movements. In *2016 International Conference on Signal Processing, Communication, Power and Embedded System*.

Fabian Pedregosa, Gaël Varoquaux, Alexandre Gramfort, Vincent Michel, Bertrand Thirion, Olivier Grisel, Mathieu Blondel, Peter Prettenhofer, Ron Weiss, Vincent Dubourg, and Others. 2011. Scikit-learn: Machine learning in Python. *Journal of Machine Learning Research* 12:2825–2830.

Stefan Räbigera, Mishal Kazmia, Yücel Saygına, Peter Schüllerb, and Myra Spiliopoulouc. 2016. SteM at SemEval-2016 Task 4: Applying active learning to improve sentiment classification. *Proceedings of SemEval* pages 64–70.

Ashwin Rajadesingan, Reza Zafarani, and Huan Liu. 2015. Sarcasm detection on twitter: A behavioral modeling approach. In *Proceedings of the Eighth ACM International Conference on Web Search and Data Mining*. ACM, pages 97–106.

Sara Rosenthal, Noura Farra, and Preslav Nakov. 2017. SemEval-2017 task 4: Sentiment analysis in Twitter. In *Proceedings of the 11th International Workshop on Semantic Evaluation*. Association for Computational Linguistics, Vancouver, Canada, SemEval '17.

Mohammed Rushdi-Saleh, M Teresa Martín-Valdivia, L Alfonso Ureña-López, and José M Perea-Ortega. 2011. OCA: Opinion corpus for Arabic. *Journal of the American Society for Information Science and Technology* 62(10):2045–2054.

Hassan Saif, Yulan He, Miriam Fernandez, and Harith Alani. 2016. Contextual semantics for sentiment analysis of Twitter. *Information Processing & Management* 52(1):5–19.

Mohammad Salameh, Saif Mohammad, and Svetlana Kiritchenko. 2015. Sentiment after Translation: A Case-Study on Arabic Social Media Posts. In *2015 Conference of the North American Chapter of the Association for Computational Linguistics: Human Language Technologies*. The Association for Computational Linguistics, pages 767–777.

Amira Shoukry and Ahmed Rafea. 2012. Sentence-level Arabic sentiment analysis. In *2012 International Conference on Collaboration Technologies and Systems (CTS)*. IEEE, pages 546–550.

Duyu Tang, Bing Qin, and Ting Liu. 2015. Deep learning for sentiment analysis: Successful approaches and future challenges. *Wiley Int. Rev. Data Min. and Knowl. Disc.* 5(6):292–303.

OMAM at SemEval-2017 Task 4:
English Sentiment Analysis with Conditional Random Fields

Chukwuyem J. Onyibe and Nizar Habash

Computational Approaches to Modeling Language (CAMeL) Lab

Computer Science Program

New York University Abu Dhabi, Abu Dhabi, UAE

`{chukwuyem.onyibe, nizar.habash}@nyu.edu`

Abstract

We describe a supervised system that uses optimized Conditional Random Fields and lexical features to predict the sentiment of a tweet. The system was submitted to the English version of all subtasks in SemEval-2017 Task 4.

1 Introduction

Sentiment analysis, sometimes known as opinion mining, is the process of detecting the contextual polarity of text. That is, given a text (of any length), subjective information pertaining to the sentiment attached to the text is derived using natural language processing tools (Pang et al., 2008; Cambria et al., 2013). Sentiment analysis could be approached in two ways. General sentiment analysis, often termed sentence-level sentiment analysis, extracts the general sentiment of the text based solely on its contents. The sentiment is not related or based on any external entity. On the other hand, topic-level sentiment analysis infers the sentiment of the given text based on a specific topic. This branch of sentiment analysis has been further explored under the term Stance Detection (Faulkner, 2014; Anand et al., 2011). With the rapid increase in different forms of online expression like reviews, political criticism, ratings and punditry, social media has become an invaluable source of data for research in sentiment analysis. With data from social media, sentiment analysis can show the public sentiment towards current topics of public discourse. Twitter is one of the largest of such social media platforms and a prominent source of data for sentiment research (Pak and Paroubek, 2010; Wang et al., 2011; Rajadesingan and Liu, 2014). In this paper, we describe the components and results of a system for English sentiment analysis with which participated in an international shared task on sentiment analysis for Twitter data.

2 Shared Task Description

The SemEval-2017 Task 4 (Rosenthal et al., 2017) (henceforth SemEval) is aimed at categorizing tweets from Twitter. This task is composed of five subtasks. Subtask A is a message polarity classification task where tweets are classified on general sentiment (not directed at any topic) on a three-way scale: *Negative, Neutral and Positive* (henceforth, -1, 0, $+1$). Subtask B is a topic-based message polarity classification where tweets are classified on sentiment towards a given topic on a two-way scale: *Negative and Positive* (henceforth, -1, $+1$). Subtask C is the same topic-based task as B, except that it uses a five-point sentiment scale (-2, -1, 0, $+1$, $+2$), where -2 is *very negative* and $+2$ is *very positive*. Both subtasks D and E are tweet quantification tasks based on subtasks B and C, respectively. In both D and E, given the same datasets from B and C, the distribution of the tweets for each topic across each label of the given scales is estimated.

This task is a rerun of SemEval-2016 Task 4 (Nakov et al., 2016), with some changes. For this task, user profile information of the author of each tweet were made available. Also, this task included an Arabic language version. Our system works on English but is submitted as part of the OMAM (Opinion Mining for Arabic and More) team that also submitted a system that analyzes sentiment in Arabic (Baly et al., 2017).

3 Approach

For all subtasks, we used the same setup (process and system). We used CRF++ (Kudo, 2005), which is an implementation of Conditional Random Fields (CRF), as the underlying machine learning component. We were inspired by the work of Yang et al. (2007) who used CRFs to determine sentiment of web blogs, training at the sentence level and classifying at the document

Proceedings of the 11th International Workshop on Semantic Evaluations (SemEval-2017), pages 670–674,
Vancouver, Canada, August 3 - 4, 2017. ©2017 Association for Computational Linguistics

level where the sentences sequence was taken in consideration. For this shared task, however, the tweets are not ordered, so there is no sequence information to be exploited. Nevertheless, we were interested in benchmarking how CRFs will fare in this scenario. We optimized the lexical features as well as the CRF++ parameters for each subtask independently against the specific subtask metrics. Although some subtasks involved topic-level sentiment analysis (i.e. sentiment towards a target), we ignored the topics for all subtasks. This idea is taken from the top scoring submission to SemEval-2016 Task 4C, TwiSE (Balikas and Amini, 2016), who used a single-label multiclass classifier and ignored topics altogether. For the tweet quantification tasks, we used a simple aggregation script (supplied by SemEval for a previous iteration of this task).

3.1 Data Preprocessing

We make use of all the data provided by SemEval for training and testing for all five subtasks. Additionally, we use a data set of 4,000 tweets available from SentiStrength.[1] In the SemEval data, each tweet is paired with a $TweetID$, $Topic$ and $Label$, except for subtask A data which has no $Topic$. For the SentiStrength data, each tweet is assigned two values representing positive and negative sentiment.

In order to use the training data from other subtasks and from SentiStrength in a subtask, we convert across the different label sets. For **subtask A** (three-point scale), we mapped subtask C's data's five-point scale labels -2 and $+2$ to -1 and $+1$, respectively; but used subtask B's data as is. We also added the SentiStrength data's two values and mapped them to $(-1, 0, +1)$. For **subtask B (and D)** (two-point scale), we folded the five-point labels as above and had two options regarding neutral values: remove the *neutral* tweets or duplicate them and relabel them as *positive* once and *negative* once. We also explored classifying with higher point scales and mapping down. Details are discussed in Section 4.2. For **subtask C (and E)** (five-point scale), we converted data labels from other subtasks using duplication and relabeling: tweets with positive labels were duplicated and labeled with $+1$ and $+2$; tweets with negative labels were duplicated and labeled with -1 and -2; and the neutral labels (0) were simply duplicated to maintain balance. When converting subtask A

---

[1] http://sentistrength.wlv.ac.uk/

data for use in other subtasks, a placeholder topic column was added. This did not influence the system as topics are not considered in any of the subtasks. The SentiStrength data was first mapped to subtask A format, then duplicated and relabeled.

3.2 Lexical Features

We considered the following lexical features with the CRF++ system. The unigram feature was always used, but feature combinations were explored for the other lexical features.

- **Unigrams** The unique words in each tweet consisting of alphanumeric characters and punctuation.
- **Tweet length (twtlen)** The number of words in the tweet.
- **Tweet length binned (twtlenbin)** The number of words in the tweet arbitrarily binned as LOW ($twtlen \leq 11$), MID ($12 \leq twtlen \leq 22$) and HIGH ($23 \leq twtlen$).
- **Bigrams** The unique bigrams in the tweet.
- **SentiStrength (senti)** The SentiStrength tool estimates the strength of positive and negative sentiment in short texts (Thelwall et al., 2010). The tool returns two values representing negative sentiment (range -1 to -5) and positive sentiment (range $+1$ to $+5$). Both values are used, as well as their sum, and a mapped value (onto the range of -2 to $+2$).
- **Removed URL (rurl)** All URLs are replaced with the string 'EXTERNALURL'. If the removed URL feature is *true*, that string is removed.
- **Stopwords (stpwrd)** This feature removes all stopwords in the tweet.

3.3 Model Optimization

We optimize the CRF++ model on the training data in two phases. First, the seven lexical features discussed above are exhaustively combined to identify the best feature combination for each subtask separately. Additionally, we explored combinations of different data sets, e.g., using SentiStrength data and/or subtask A data for subtask C. Using all of the available data for each subtask produced the best results. During this phase, the CRF++ is run with default parameter values. Next, the model is further optimized by tuning the CRF++ parameters c and f. The c value controls the hyper-parameter for the CRF to balance between overfitting and underfitting. The f parameter

Features	$AvgR$	$AvgF1$	Acc
unigram; senti	**0.623**	**0.596**	**0.686**
unigram; twtlenbin; rurl; senti	0.621	0.593	0.667
unigram; stpwrd; twtlen; bigram; senti	0.613	0.584	0.667
unigram; twtlen; rurl; senti	0.613	0.583	0.686
unigram; twtlen; senti	0.613	0.580	0.688

Table 1: Scores of lexical feature combinations for subtask A

$-f$	$-c$	$AvgR$	$AvgF1$	Acc
1	8.5	**0.634**	**0.612**	**0.695**
1	4.0	0.626	0.599	0.694
1	1.0	0.623	0.596	0.686
4	7.5	0.615	0.587	0.680
2	6.0	0.613	0.585	0.682

Table 2: Scores of CRF++ parameters combinations for subtask A

sets the cut-off threshold for the features. We explored all combinations of c and f ranging between 0.5 and 10.0 (in increments of 0.5) and 1 to 4 (in increments of 1), respectively.

3.4 Evaluation Metrics

Each subtask had its own target metric (Rosenthal et al., 2017). Subtasks A and B use $AvgR$, macro-averaged recall (recall averaged across the targeted labels). Subtask C uses MAE^M, macro-averaged mean absolute error. Subtask D uses KL, Kullback-Leibler Divergence. Subtask E uses EMD, Earth Mover's Distance.

4 Results

4.1 Subtask A

For subtask A, we used the following data sets for training: SemEval 2016 task 4A data (train, dev and devtest), SemEval 2016 task 4C data (train, test, dev and devtest) and SentiStrength twitter data. Table 1 shows the five top performing combinations from the lexical feature optimization phase. The *senti* feature with *unigrams* were the best features. Table 2 shows the five top performing combinations for the CRF parameter optimization phase. The best setup, with c value 8.5, f value 1 and features *unigram and senti*, was used to produce the predicted file submitted for subtask A for SemEval 2017. Our submission received the following scores and ranks (in subscript) out of 38 systems: average recall $AvgR = 0.590_{24}$, $AvgF1 = 0.542_{26}$, $Acc = 0.615_{19}$.

4.2 Subtasks B and D

For subtasks B and D, we explored the possibility of training and predicting in five-point scale space and then mapping to two-point scale space. In the mapping, -2 and $+2$ map to -1 and $+1$, respectively. When the system predicts the *neutral* label (0), we select the next most probable label determined using CRF++'s *verbose* mode. For subtask B and D, we used the following training data: SemEval task 4B data, SemEval task 4A data, SemEval task 4C data and SentiStrength twitter data.

Table 3(a) shows the five top performing lexical feature combinations for subtask B. All features combinations in Table 3(a) were from the setup where classification is done in two-point format and the neutral tweets from subtask A and C data were removed.

Table 3(b) shows the five top performing c and f value combinations for subtask B. The highest performing setup, with c value 0.5 and f value 1 and features *twtlenbin, rurl, bigram and senti*, was used to produce the predicted file submitted for subtask B for SemEval 2017. Our submission received the following scores and ranks (in subscript) out of 23 systems: average recall $AvgR = 0.779_{15}$, $AvgF1 = 0.762_{17}$, $Acc = 0.764_{17}$.

For subtask D, the five top performing feature combinations are shown in Table 5. All combinations in Table 5, except the second, are from the setup that predicts on five-point labeled data where the neutral tweets are preserved and duplicated. The second combination, *unigram; stpwrd; twtlen; senti*, is from the setup the predicts on five-point labeled data where the neutral tweets are removed.

The combination with the best score, used the following features: *unigram; twtlenbin, rurl, senti*. This was used for prediction for the test file which was later aggregated and submitted for subtask D. Our submission received the following scores and ranks (in subscript) out of 15 systems: $KL = 0.164_{12}$, $AE = 0.204_{12}$, $RAE = 2.790_{12}$.

Features	$AvgR$
unigram; twtlenbin; rurl; bigram; senti	**0.785**
unigram; stpwrd; twtlenbin; rurl; bigram; senti	0.783
unigram; twtlen; rurl; bigram; senti	0.783
unigram; stpwrd; rurl; bigram; senti	0.782
unigram; twtlenbin; bigram; senti	0.782

(a) lexical feature combinations

$-f$	$-c$	$AvgR$
1	**0.5**	**0.786**
2	0.5	0.786
1	2.0	0.786
1	2.0	0.785
3	1.0	0.782

(b) CRF++ parameters

Table 3: Optimization scores for subtask B

Features	MAE^M
unigram; twtlen; twtlenbin; rurl; senti	**0.74**
unigram; stpwrd; twtlen; rurl; senti	0.77
unigram; stpwrd; rurl; bigram; senti	0.77
unigram; stpwrd; twtlenbin; senti	0.77
unigram; senti	0.77

(a) lexical feature combinations

$-f$	$-c$	MAE^M
2	**10.0**	**0.71**
1	0.5	0.74
1	1.0	0.74
2	5.5	0.75
2	7.5	0.75

(b) CRF++ parameters

Table 4: Optimization scores for subtask C

Features	KL
unigram; twtlenbin; rurl; senti	**0.035**
unigram; stpwrd; twtlen; senti	0.036
unigram; rurl; bigram; senti	0.037
unigram; stpwrd; twtlenbin; rurl; senti	0.038
unigram; twtlenbin; rurl; senti	0.038

Table 5: Scores of lexical feature combinations for Subtask D

Features	EMD
unigram; twtlenbin; rurl; senti	**0.070**
unigram; twtlen; twtlenbin; senti	0.087
unigram; twtlenbin; rurl	0.087
unigram; senti	0.088
unigram; twtlen; twtlenbin; rurl; senti	0.088

Table 6: Scores of lexical feature combinations for Subtask E

4.3 Subtasks C and E

For subtask C and E, we used the following data for training: SemEval 2016 task4A data, SemEval 2016 task 4C data and SentiStrength twitter data. Table 4(a) shows the five top performing lexical feature combinations for subtask C. Table 4 shows the five top performing c and f value combinations for subtask C.

The highest performing setup, with c value 10.0 and f value 2 and features *unigram; twtlen, twtlenbin, rurl and senti*, was used to produce the prediction file submitted for subtask C for SemEval 2017. Our submission received the following scores and ranks (in subscript) out of 15 systems: $MAE^M = 0.895_{10}$, $MAE^\mu = 0.475_1$.

For subtask E, Table 6 shows the five top performing lexical combinations.

The combination with the best score, used the following features: *unigram twtlenbin, rurl, senti*. This was used for creating the prediction file which was later aggregated and submitted for subtask E. Our submission received the following scores and ranks (in subscript) out of 12 systems: $EMD = 0.350_7$.

5 Conclusion and Future Work

In this paper, we presented a system for English sentence-level sentiment analysis of twitter using CRF++ and optimized lexical features. We explore feature combinations and tune CRF++ parameters values to find the best setup for each subtask. Overall, the unigram and SentiStrength (*senti*) features were always present in the best performing setups for all subtasks. In all subtasks other than A, binned tweet length (*twtlenbin*) and removing URLs (*rurl*) consistently helped.

We used this system to participate in the SemEval-2017 Task 4. The system's performance was middle of the pack, which was accomplished while ignoring topics in the topic-level tasks.

In the future, we will explore more lexical features and other CRF and SVM implementations. We also look forward to applying the same setup to other languages.

References

Pranav Anand, Marilyn Walker, Rob Abbott, Jean E Fox Tree, Robeson Bowmani, and Michael Minor. 2011. Cats rule and dogs drool!: Classifying stance in online debate. In *Proceedings of the 2nd workshop on computational approaches to subjectivity and sentiment analysis*. Association for Computational Linguistics, pages 1–9.

Georgios Balikas and Massih-Reza Amini. 2016. Twise at semeval-2016 task 4: Twitter sentiment classification. *arXiv preprint arXiv:1606.04351* .

Ramy Baly, Gilbert Badaro, Ali Hamdi, Rawan Moukalled, Rita Aoun, Georges El-Khoury, Ahmad Al Sallab, Hazem Hajj, Nizar Habash, Khaled Shaban, and Wassim El-Hajj. 2017. Omam at semeval-2017 task 4: Evaluation of english state-of-the-art sentiment analysis models for arabic and a new topic-based model. In *Proceedings of the 11th International Workshop on Semantic Evaluation (SemEval-2017)*. Association for Computational Linguistics, Vancouver, Canada, pages 601–608. http://www.aclweb.org/anthology/S17-2099.

Erik Cambria, Björn Schuller, Yunqing Xia, and Catherine Havasi. 2013. New avenues in opinion mining and sentiment analysis. *IEEE Intelligent Systems* 28(2):15–21.

Adam Faulkner. 2014. Automated classification of stance in student essays: An approach using stance target information and the wikipedia link-based measure. *Science* 376(12):86.

Taku Kudo. 2005. Crf++: Yet another crf toolkit. *Software available at http://taku910.github.io/crfpp/* .

Preslav Nakov, Alan Ritter, Sara Rosenthal, Veselin Stoyanov, and Fabrizio Sebastiani. 2016. SemEval-2016 task 4: Sentiment analysis in Twitter. In *Proceedings of the 10th International Workshop on Semantic Evaluation*. Association for Computational Linguistics, San Diego, California, SemEval '16.

Alexander Pak and Patrick Paroubek. 2010. Twitter as a corpus for sentiment analysis and opinion mining. In *LREC*.

Bo Pang, Lillian Lee, et al. 2008. Opinion mining and sentiment analysis. *Foundations and Trends® in Information Retrieval* 2(1–2):1–135.

Ashwin Rajadesingan and Huan Liu. 2014. Identifying users with opposing opinions in twitter debates. In *International Conference on Social Computing, Behavioral-Cultural Modeling, and Prediction*. Springer, pages 153–160.

Sara Rosenthal, Noura Farra, and Preslav Nakov. 2017. Semeval-2017 task 4: Sentiment analysis in twitter. In *Proceedings of the 11th International Workshop on Semantic Evaluation (SemEval-2017)*. Association for Computational Linguistics, Vancouver, Canada, pages 501–516. http://www.aclweb.org/anthology/S17-2088.

Mike Thelwall, Kevan Buckley, Georgios Paltoglou, Di Cai, and Arvid Kappas. 2010. Sentiment strength detection in short informal text. *Journal of the American Society for Information Science and Technology* 61(12):2544–2558.

Xiaolong Wang, Furu Wei, Xiaohua Liu, Ming Zhou, and Ming Zhang. 2011. Topic sentiment analysis in twitter: a graph-based hashtag sentiment classification approach. In *Proceedings of the 20th ACM international conference on Information and knowledge management*. ACM, pages 1031–1040.

Changhua Yang, Kevin Hsin-Yih Lin, and Hsin-Hsi Chen. 2007. Emotion classification using web blog corpora. In *Web Intelligence, IEEE/WIC/ACM International Conference on*. IEEE, pages 275–278.

Tweester at SemEval-2017 Task 4: Fusion of Semantic-Affective and pairwise classification models for sentiment analysis in Twitter

Athanasia Kolovou [2,3]**, Filippos Kokkinos** [1]**, Aris Fergadis** [1,3]**, Pinelopi Papalampidi** [1]
Elias Iosif [1,3]**, Nikolaos Malandrakis** [4]**, Elisavet Palogiannidi** [1]**, Harris Papageorgiou** [3]
Shrikanth Narayanan [4]**, Alexandros Potamianos** [1,3]

[1]School of ECE, National Technical University of Athens, Zografou 15780, Athens, Greece
[2] Department of Informatics, University of Athens, Athens, Greece
[3] "Athena" Research and Innovation Center, Maroussi 15125, Athens, Greece
[4] Signal Analysis and Interpretation Laboratory (SAIL), USC, Los Angeles, CA 90089, USA
`akolovou@di.uoa.gr, el11142@mail.ntua.gr`
`fergadis@central.ntua.gr, el12003@central.ntua.gr`
`iosife@central.ntua.gr, malandra@usc.edu`
`epalogiannidi@gmail.com, xaris@ilsp.athena-innovation.gr`
`shri@sipi.usc.edu, potam@central.ntua.gr`

Abstract

In this paper, we describe our submission to SemEval2017 Task 4: Sentiment Analysis in Twitter. Specifically the proposed system participated both to tweet polarity classification (two-, three- and five class) and tweet quantification (two and five-class) tasks. The submitted system is based on "Tweester" (Palogiannidi et al., 2016) that participated in last year's Sentiment analysis in Twitter Tasks A and B. Specifically it comprises of multiple independent models such as neural networks, semantic-affective models and affective models inspired by topic modeling that are combined in a late fusion scheme.

1 Introduction

Tweets are short length pieces of text, usually written in informal style that contain abbreviations, misspellings and creative syntax (like emoticons, hashtags etc). The challenging nature of sentiment analysis in Twitter motivated the organization of numerous tasks within the Semantics Evaluation (SemEval) workshop. In this paper, we show how our sentiment analysis framework called "Tweester" (winner of Subtask B in SemEval-2016 (Palogiannidi et al., 2016)), can be applied to all subtasks, namely Subtask A (message polarity classification), Subtask B (tweet classification according to a two-point scale), Subtask C (sentiment conveyed by a tweet towards the topic on a five-point scale), Subtask D (estimate the distribution of the tweets across a two-point scale), Subtask E (estimate the distribution

of the tweets across a five-point scale). The system achieved high performance ranking 5th, 3rd, 4th, 5th and 8th for Subtasks A, B, C, D, and E, respectively (S.Rosenthal et al., 2017). In Section 2 we provide more details on the individual systems as well as the fusion scheme. Experimental procedure is described in Section 3 and some concluding remarks as well as an outlook on future work are presented in Section 4.

2 System Description

The submitted system is based on the fusion of several systems. Specifically the system consists of: 1) the semantic-affective system (submitted to the SemEval 2016 Task 4 (Palogiannidi et al., 2016)) that incorporates affective, semantic-similarity, sarcasm/irony and topic modeling features, 2) a single and a two-step convolutional neural network, 3) a system based on word embeddings, 4) a "stacking" based system that transforms the 3-class polarity problem of Subtask A, into 2-class binary problems and finally 5) the open-source system submitted to the SemEval 2015 Task 10 (Rosenthal et al., 2015a).

2.1 Preprocessing

We hypothesize that **hashtags** are able to express user's sentiment with regard to some topic or events (e.g., "Jazz all day #lovemusic"). Following this assumption, hashtag expansion into word strings (Palogiannidi et al., 2016) was performed using the Viterbi algorithm (Forney, 1973). The absolute and relative frequencies of hashtags to be expanded are used as features, as well as the binary indicators that a tweet contains hashtags that

675

Proceedings of the 11th International Workshop on Semantic Evaluations (SemEval-2017), pages 675–682,
Vancouver, Canada, August 3 - 4, 2017. ©2017 Association for Computational Linguistics

require expansion. **POS-tagging / Tokenization** is performed using the ARK NLP tweeter tagger (Owoputi et al., 2013). The Gensim model (Řehůřek and Sojka, 2010) is used which can automatically detect common **multi-word expressions (MWE)** from a stream of sentences. After we detect MWE, we select only the ones that consist up to two words, which we treat as a single token. **Negations** are usually expressions that are used to alter the sentiment orientations. We claim that not all parts of the tweet convey equally important information and some parts, like negated parts or the last words of a tweet may express an opposite meaning of what is literally said. The underlying intuition here is the cognitive dissonance phenomenon that is associated with the existence of ironic content, sarcasm and humour (Reyes and Rosso, 2014). Based on this claim, we detect the negation part of a tweet using the list proposed by (Potts, 2011). Specifically, when a negation token is detected, the tokens that follow are marked as negated until a punctuation mark is reached. Then, we extract features in the negated part. We also apply **context windows** on each tweet, in order to keep selected words. "Prefix" context windows are the first two and three tokens of the tweet, however , "suffix" windows change analogously to the length of the tweet, selecting the 20%, 50% and 70% of the last tokens.

2.2 Semantic-Affective system

The Semantic-Affective based system is the core model of "Tweester" which is based on previous work by (Malandrakis et al., 2014). The majority of the features used are affective ratings that have been estimated by semantic affective models, however, numerous non-affective or semantic features are also used.

2.2.1 Affective lexica

Using the semantic affective model described in (1) we created affective lexica by estimating continuous (in [-1,1]) ratings for unknown words. This model that was first proposed by (Malandrakis et al., 2013) and enhanced by (Palogiannidi et al., 2015) relies on the assumption that "semantic similarity implies affective similarity". First, a semantic model is built and then affective ratings are estimated for unknown tokens. This approach uses a set of words with known affective ratings, usually referred as seed words, as a starting point. The English manual annotated affective

lexicon ANEW (Bradley and Lang, 1999) is used for selecting the seed words. The model is applicable both to single words or multi-word expression tokens:

$$\hat{v}(w) = \alpha_0 + \sum_{i=1}^{M} \alpha_i v(t_i) S(t_i, w), \qquad (1)$$

where $t_1...t_M$ are the seed words, $v(t_i)$ is the affective rating for seed word t_i, α_i is a trainable weight corresponding to seed t_i and $S(\cdot)$ is the semantic similarity metric between two tokens. The semantic model is built as shown in (Palogiannidi et al., 2015) using word-level contextual feature vectors and adopting a scheme based on mutual information for feature weighting. From the affective ratings we retain only the polarity features (instead of using additional affective dimensions, namely arousal and dominance). Affective lexica were created using a Twitter corpus, which we call *task-dependent corpus* and a generic corpus, which we call *out-of-domain* (see Section 3.1). In an attempt to create task-dependent affective lexica we use the out-of-domain corpus and follow a domain adaptation technique. Specifically, we build a language model using domain relevant sentences, i.e., tweets. Then, we estimate the perplexity of each out-of-domain sentence in order to evaluate its relevance to the language model. In this context, instances that are lexically more similar to the instances in the task-dependent corpus will be assigned lower perplexity scores. We create four adapted lexica selecting from the out-of-domain corpus the top 10%, 30%, 50% and 70% of the most relevant sentences to the language model.

Third party affective lexica are also used. Those include AFFIN ((Nielsen, 2011), NRC and nrctag (Mohammad et al., 2013)). Given the affective ratings, the next step is combining them through statistics. We use simple statistics grouped by part of speech tags. Specifically we compute: length (cardinality), min, max, max amplitude, sum, average, range (max minus min), standard deviation and variance. The results are statistics like "maximum valence among adjectives", "mean valence among proper nouns", "number of verbs and nouns", etc. All features mentioned above are not only extracted on the token-level, but also on the prefix and suffix parts of each tweet and the MWEs.

2.2.2 Additional features

In addition to the affective features, we also incorporate morphology, character and word embedding based features.

Character features include the frequencies of selected characters like capitalized letters, punctuation marks, emoticons and character repetition.

Word embeddings are utilized for the semantic similarity estimation. They were derived using word2vec (Mikolov et al., 2013b), representing each word as a d-dimensional vector. For each tweet the corresponding vectors of its constituent words are averaged to get a sentence-level feature vector.

As **subjectivity features** we use the absolute and the relative frequencies of the strong positive/negative and weak positive/negative words taken from a subjectivity lexicon (Wilson et al., 2005).

The detection of **irony** in tweets is mainly constituted from the detection of disagreement between what someone says and what he actually believes. According to this assumption, features that measure the level of opposition between literal and intended meanings in a tweet are extracted. Similar to (Barbieri and Saggion, 2014), we extracted the following features: i) *frequency based* which are features that are derived from the mean frequency of common and rare words in a tweet, as well as the difference between them. Word frequencies are indicated in the ANC Frequency Data corpus (Ide and Macleod, 2001), ii) *written-spoken gap* where we calculate the difference between the number of words that are considered "formal" vs. the "informal" ones in each tweet. Those words are also identified in the ANC corpus, iii) *sentiment distances* for which we first apply a threshold that separates words into positive and negative, based on polarity ratings from the lexica we describe in Section 2.2.1. For each tweet we compute: total sentiment range (average positive minus average negative), positive range (max positive minus tweet average), negative range (max negative minus tweet average) and iv) following the approach proposed by (Barbieri and Saggion, 2014), we use the same feature selection process related to synonyms, since they may be high indicators of irony.

A **topic modeling** method (described in Section 2.6), provides additional features to this system.

2.3 Convolutional Neural Network

In our framework we propose the combination of two neural networks. Specifically, we develop a deep Convolutional Neural Network (CNN) and a two-step Convolutional Neural Network. The neural network architecture is inspired by sentence classification tasks (Severyn and Moschitti, 2015; Kalchbrenner et al., 2014; Kim, 2014). Each tweet is represented by a sentence matrix $\mathbf{D}$ that is created as follows. First, each word is represented as a d-dimensional vector using word2vec (Mikolov et al., 2013b), and then, the word vectors are concatenated as follows:

$$\mathbf{D} = W_1 \oplus W_2 \oplus W_3 \oplus \cdots \oplus W_n., D \in \mathbb{R}^{d \times n} \quad (2)$$

where $\oplus$ indicates the concatenation operation. Each column i of $\mathbf{D}$ is a vector $W \in \mathbb{R}^d$ that corresponds to the ith word of the tweet. This way the sequence of the words in the tweet is kept. In order to preserve the same length for all tweets, zero padding is applied by concatenating zero word vectors until the length n of the longest tweet is reached. The size of $\mathbf{D}$ is $d \times n$, where d is the dimension of the word embedding and n is the maximum number of words.

The matrix $\mathbf{D}$ is the input to the network, where a convolution operation is performed between $\mathbf{D}$ and a filter $F \in \mathbb{R}^{d \times m}$ which is applied to a window of m words to produce a new feature. The result of the convolutional layer is a vector $c \in \mathbb{R}^{n-h+1}$ (Kim, 2014). The network uses multiple m filters, with varying sliding windows and generates multiple features that are aggregated into a feature matrix $C \in IR^{mx(n-h+1)}$. The filters are learned during the training phase of the neural network (the exact parameter values are presented in Table 3). These features are the inputs to the next layer which selects the maximum value of each feature by applying a max-over-time pooling operation (max-pooling layer) (Collobert et al., 2011). Max pooling reduces the dimensionality of the input feature matrix and allows the "strongest" information to be considered in the resulting feature representation. The output pooled feature map matrix of this step has the form: $C_{pooled} \in \mathbb{R}^{m \times \frac{n-h+1}{s}}$ (Kalchbrenner et al., 2014) where s is the length of each region. The next layer is a fully connected hidden layer that computes the following transformation: $\alpha(W_{hidden} * x + b_{hidden})$ as explained in (Nair and Hinton, 2010) where α is the rectified

linear activation function $relu(x) = max(0, x)$
, $W_{hidden} \in \mathbb{R}^{m \times m}$ is the weight matrix and
$b_{hidden} \in R^m$ is the bias. The output vector of this
layer, $x \in R^m$ are the sentence embeddings for
each tweet. Finally we add a soft-max layer that
classifies the outputs of the hidden layer $x \in R^m$
to one of the possible classes.

Two-step CNN: In the case of 3-class problem
of Subtask A we propose an additional two-step
system. This process requires the re-annotation
of the train datasets as follows. We separate the
neutral tweets, while positive and negative tweets
are annotated as "emotional". Then, we apply the
aforementioned CNN model architecture which is
trained on the re-annotated data. The output is predictions on neutral and "emotional" tweets. The
next step involves the classification of the tweets
that were found to belong to "emotional" category, into positive and negative. This step requires
only the "emotional" tweets for training the CNN
model.

2.4 Word2vec

This system uses word embeddings to predict the
sentiment of each tweet in a supervised approach,
using a classifier which is trained with the available labeled data. The vector for each word is
a semantic description of how that word is used
in context, so words that are used similarly in
text will get similar vector representations. Motivated by this, we build this separate system that
relies exclusively on tweets' semantic representation. Specifically the word embeddings of each
tweet word are first extracted. Then, the vectors of
each tweets' constituent words are averaged and
form utterance-level vectors used for training the
classifier.

2.5 Stacking

The main idea of this technique is to reduce a
multi-class problem into binary 2-class problems
and train one separate classifier for each pair of
classes (Savicky and Fürnkranz, 2003). In the second step, the predictions of the binary classifiers
are combined using a separate classifier. This process is referred to as stacking (Fürnkranz, 2001).

2.6 Topic modeling

Here, we perform sentence-level adaptation from
the semantic space to the affective space. For the
adaptation of the semantic space of each tweet we
split a large Twitter corpus (see Section 3.1) in

topics using LDA (Blei et al., 2003). We create
a number of topics and an equal number of clusters with the following procedure. For each tweet
we get the LDA posteriors which give the probabilities by which the tweet belongs to certain topics. The tweet is assigned to those clusters if the
probability is above a threshold. Each cluster constitutes a sub-corpus for which a semantic model
is built using word embeddings as features. The
purpose of those steps is to calculate a new similarity score between a lexical token t_j and a seed
word w_i using a semantic mixture of the above
mentioned models as follows:

$$S(t_j, w_i) = \frac{\sum_{n=1}^{T} p(n|s) \cdot S_n(t_j, w_i)}{\sum_{n=1}^{T} p(n|s)}, \quad (3)$$

where $s = \{t_0, t_1, \ldots, t_j, \ldots, t_k\}$ are the tweet's
tokens, w_i is the i_{th} seed word, T is the number
of topics-clusters, $p(n|s)$ is the posterior probabil-
ity for s to contain topic n and $S_n(\cdot)$ is the cosine
similarity between t_j and w_i, obtained from cluster n. The similarities computed in (3) are used
in (1). This enables the computation of affective
scores for tweet tokens based on which the following statistics are computed: *max, min, mean,
variance, standard deviation, range* (max - min),
extremum (larger absolute value) and *sum*. We also
compute the same statistics for the following POS
tags of each tweet, *N, O, S, ^, Z, L, V, A, R, !*, using the ARK NLP tweeter tagger (Owoputi et al.,
2013) getting max score over all nouns, min score
over all nouns etc. Those values are normalized by
dividing with the corresponding score computed
over all tokens, e.g. the min score over all nouns
is divided by the min score over all tokens.

2.7 Webis

We also incorporated the Webis system (Büchner
and Stein, 2015), which is the ensemble of different subsystems (namely NRC, GUMLT, KlUE,
TeamX) that ranked at the top of SemEval 2013
and 2014 Sentiment Analysis tasks (Nakov et al.,
2013; Rosenthal et al., 2015b)

2.8 Fusion of systems

The last step of the "Tweester" framework is the
combination of all the aforementioned systems
that have been trained on different feature spaces.
Specifically, this step applies late fusion by averaging the output posterior probabilities from each
classifier.

3 Experimental procedure and results

3.1 Data

We train our systems using both general purpose and Twitter data. The training set is composed by the training, development and development-time testing data of SemEval-2013 and SemEval-2016, as described in Table 1. We also add to the train set, the test data from SemEval-2015 and SemEval-2014. We omit the SemEval-2016 test data, which are kept for testing and experimenting with our models. For the procedure of adaptive lexica creation we used a general purpose corpus that contains 116M sentences that was created by posing queries on a web search engine and aggregating the resulting snippets of web documents(Iosif et al., 2016). In addition, a Twitter-specific dataset is created and consists of 300M tweets (T-300M). Finally the ANEW lexicon (Bradley and Lang, 1999) is used for selecting the initial set of seed words of (1).

	Training Set
Subtask A	28,061
Subtask B & D	6,680
Subtask C & E	9,070

Table 1: Number of tweets used for training.

3.2 Systems

The **Semantic-Affective system** (see Section 2.2) is trained using the SemEval datasets of Table 1 for each subtask. We perform feature selection on the massive set of candidate features. Specifically, we perform a forward stepwise feature selection using a correlation criterion (Hall, 1999) that extracts the most informative features. For classification, a Naive Bayes tree classifier is trained. Naive Bayes trees proved superior to other types of trees during our testing, presumably due to the smoothing of observation distributions. This model is used for Subtasks A,B and D combined with the other systems, however in Subtask C and E it is used as a standalone system.

For the **word2vec-based system** (see Section 2.4) we trained a Random Forest classifier with 100 trees using the tweet-level vectors described in Section 2.4. The word embeddings are initialized using word2vec (Mikolov et al., 2013a,b) and are trained using the T-300M corpus (see Section 3.1). We apply a skip-gram model of window size 5 while the words with frequency less than 50 were not taken into consideration. The dimensionality of the word vectors used is $d = 50$. Words that appear in the tweet but do not have a vector representation, are initialized randomly from a uniform distribution.

The **stacking based system** (see Section 2.5) is used in Subtask A and requires that the training data is split into subsets using only examples from each of the two classes (i.e, positive-negative, positive-neutral and negative-neutral). We form tweet-level vectors (set to d=50), as in the word2vec based system, for each of the aforementioned subsets. Then, we train separate Random Forest classifiers with 100 trees, using the tweet-level vectors. After the training phase, each classifier is tested not only on the provided test data but also on the training data. The posterior probabilities from this step constitute the features for the classifier in the final step, which is a nearest neighbor classifier (Savicky and Fürnkranz, 2003).

We run a series of experiments with the **topic modeling system** (see Section 2.6) in which we fine-tune the following parameters. *Word2vec parameters* of topic clusters which are, size of word vectors, max skip length between words and the model's architecture, i.e. Continuous Bag-of-Words (CBOW) or skip-gram, the *number of topics* to extract from the T-300M, the *probability threshold* for grouping tweets into clusters (as described in Section 2.6) and the *number of seed words* to use from the ANEW lexicon in order to estimate the affective scores, as described in (1) and (3). Each experiment produces a different feature set. In order to select the best set for the semantic-affective based system, we evaluate them against the SemEval labeled data using a Naive Bayes tree classifier. The feature set that gives the best performance is selected for each subtask.

	Parameters
Number of convolutional filters	m = 200
Filter window size h	[3,4,5]
Size of max-pooling interval	width = 6, s = 2
Activation function	relu
Adadelta parameters	$\epsilon = 10^{-6}$ and $\rho = 0.95$

Table 3: Summary of CNN parameters used.

For the **CNN model** we first run a distant-

| | | | | | | | Tweester Systems | | | | |
Subtask	Perf.	Rank	NRC	GUMLT	KlUE	TeamX	Sem-Affect	CNN	2step CNN	Word2vec	Stack
A	0.659	5	0.617	0.613	0.593	0.615	0.606	0.621	0.613	0.593	0.575
B	0.854	3	×	0.752	×	×	0.843	0.851	×	0.791	×
C	0.623	4	×	×	×	×	0.623	×	×	×	×
D	0.057	5	×	0.093	×	×	0.062	0.052	×	0.079	×
E	0.365	8	×	×	×	×	0.365	×	×	×	×

Table 2: Individual system combinations and their performance.

supervised phase where we use emoticons to infer the polarity of a balanced set of 15M tweets. The word-embeddings, $D \in \mathbb{R}^{d \times n}$ are updated during both the distant and the supervised training phases, as back-propagation is applied through the entire network. The neural network is trained on the 15M tweets for one epoch, followed by a supervised training phase using SemEval labeled data. The dimensionality of the vector representation in the sentence matrix is set to $d = 50$. The same parameters are used in both single and 2-step CNN models. The CNN model is not used in Task C and D due to the lack of a large distant training dataset annotated in 5 classes. The network parameters are summarized in Table 3.

3.3 Results

In Table 2 the integrated systems' performances are depicted along with the submitted combination for each subtask (the omitted systems are denoted with ×). For Subtasks A and B the evaluation metric is macro-averaged recall (AvgR), for Subtask C it is the macro-averaged mean absolute error (MAE^M), for Subtask D the normalized cross-entropy (KLD) is used and for Subtask E the metric is called the Earth Mover's Distance (EMD). All the aforementioned metrics are defined in (Rosenthal et al., 2014).

For Subtask A we combined all individual systems and achieved an AvgR of 0.659. CNN proved to be the most robust individual system, achieving the highest performance (0.621) among the others. The two-step CNN achieved a slightly lower score compared to the single-step model. Since the CNN model is quite robust in distinguishing positive vs negative tweets it seems that the 2-step model makes more errors on the first step, which is the distinction between neutral and emotional class. For Subtasks B and D the stepwise based systems are omitted (since they involve binary classification). The selected combi-

nations are based on our empirical results using SemEval-2016 test dataset. Particularly, in Subtask B, where we decided to omit three subsystems from Webis, the model was ranked at the 3rd place with 0.854 AvgR. Similarly, in Subtask D we omitted the same systems as in B and ranked in 5th place. The results for B and D show that the highest performance is achieved by the CNN followed by the semantic-affective system. However, in Subtask D the selected combination degraded the best performing system. Finally, for Subtasks C and E we submitted only the semenatic-affective based system, based on experiments conducted on SemEval-2016 test dataset.

4 Conclusions

We presented a system for the sentiment classification of tweets for the SemEval 2017 Task 4: Sentiment analysis in twitter. The system participated in Subtasks A, B, C, D and E and proved very successful, ranking on the top 5 places for the first four subtasks. Our framework is improved using a two-step CNN, a stacking-based approach for the 3-class problem and we incorporate new features using the adaptation of the semantic space to each tweet. Future work should focus on domain adaptation technique as we believe there is still room for improvement. Also, we aim to investigate in more depth the fusion of different systems.

Acknowledgments

This work has been partially funded by the Baby-Robot project supported by the EU Horizon 2020 Programme, grant number 687831. We would like to thank Fenia Christopoulou for providing the implementation of the topic modeling system. Also, the authors would like to thank NVIDIA for supporting this work by donating a TitanX GPU and the members of the Computing Systems Laboratory (CSLab) of The National Technical University of Athens (NTUA) for their technical support.

References

F. Barbieri and H. Saggion. 2014. Automatic detection of irony and humour in twitter. In *Proceedings of International Conference on Computational Creativity*.

DM. Blei, A. Ng, and M. Jordan. 2003. Latent dirichlet allocation. *Journal of machine Learning research* 3(Jan):993–1022.

M. Bradley and P. Lang. 1999. Affective norms for English words (ANEW): Instruction Manual and Affective Ratings. Technical report.

M. Büchner and B. Stein. 2015. Webis: An Ensemble for Twitter Sentiment Detection. *Proceedings of the 9th International Workshop on Semantic Evaluation (SemEval 2015)* page 582.

R. Collobert, J. Weston, L. Bottou, M. Karlen, K. Kavukcuoglu, and P. Kuksa. 2011. Natural language processing (almost) from scratch. *Journal of Machine Learning Research* 12(Aug):2493–2537.

G.D Forney. 1973. The viterbi algorithm. *Proceedings of the IEEE* 61(3):268–278.

J. Fürnkranz. 2001. Round robin rule learning. In *Proceedings of the 18th International Conference on Machine Learning (ICML-01): 146–153*.

M.A Hall. 1999. *Correlation-based feature selection for machine learning*. Ph.D. thesis, The University of Waikato.

N. Ide and C. Macleod. 2001. The American National Corpus: A standardized resource for American English. In *Proceedings of Corpus Linguistics*. page 831836.

E. Iosif, S. Georgiladakis, and A. Potamianos. 2016. Cognitively Motivated Distributional Representations of Meaning. In *Proc. of the Language Resources and Evaluation Conference (LREC)*.

N. Kalchbrenner, E. Grefenstette, and P. Blunsom. 2014. A convolutional neural network for modelling sentences. *CoRR* abs/1404.2188.

Y. Kim. 2014. Convolutional neural networks for sentence classification. *CoRR* abs/1408.5882.

N. Malandrakis, M. Falcone, C. Vaz, J. Bisogni, A. Potamianos, and S. Narayanan. 2014. SAIL: Sentiment Analysis using Semantic Similarity and Contrast Features. In *Proc. of the 8th International Workshop on Semantic Evaluation (SemEval)*. pages 512–516.

N. Malandrakis, A. Potamianos, E. Iosif, and S. Narayanan. 2013. Distributional semantic models for affective text analysis. *IEEE Transactions on Audio, Speech and Language Processing* 21(11):2379–2392.

T. Mikolov, K. Chen, G. Corrado, and J. Dean. 2013a. Efficient estimation of word representations in vector space. *CoRR* abs/1301.3781.

T. Mikolov, I. Sutskever, K. Chen, G. S. Corrado, and J. Dean. 2013b. Distributed representations of words and phrases and their compositionality. In *Proc of. Advances in Neural Information Processing systems (NIPS)*. pages 3111–3119.

S. M. Mohammad, S. Kiritchenko, and X. Zhu. 2013. NRC-Canada: Building the State-of-the-Art in Sentiment Analysis of Tweets. In *Proc. of the 7th International Workshop on Semantic Evaluation (SemEval)*. pages 321–327.

V. Nair and GE. Hinton. 2010. Rectified linear units improve restricted boltzmann machines. In *Proceedings of the 27th International Conference on Machine Learning (ICML-10)*. pages 807–814.

P. Nakov, Z. Kozareva, A. Ritter, S. Rosenthal, V. Stoyanov, and T. Wilson. 2013. Semeval-2013 task 2: Sentiment analysis in twitter. In *Proc. of the 10th International Workshop on Semantic Evaluation (SemEval)*.

F. Å. Nielsen. 2011. A new ANEW: Evaluation of a word list for sentiment analysis in microblogs. In *Proc. of the ESWC Workshop on Making Sense of Microposts*. pages 93–98.

O. Owoputi, B. O'Connor, C. Dyer, K. Gimpel, N. Schneider, and N. A Smith. 2013. Improved part-of-speech tagging for online conversational text with word clusters. In *In Proceedings of the North American Chapter of the Association for Computational Linguistics*.

E. Palogiannidi, E. Iosif, P. Koutsakis, and A. Potamianos. 2015. Valence, Arousal and Dominance Estimation for English, German, Greek, Portuguese and Spanish Lexica using Semantic Models. In *Proc. of Interspeech*. pages 1527–1531.

E. Palogiannidi, A. Kolovou, F. Christopoulou, E. Iosif, N. Malandrakis, H. Papageorgiou, S. Narayanan, and A. Potamianos. 2016. Tweester at SemEval 2016: Sentiment Analysis in Twitter using Semantic-Affective Model Adaptation. In *Proc. of the 10th International Workshop on Semantic Evaluation (SemEval)*. pages 155–163.

C. Potts. 2011. Sentiment symposium tutorial. In *Proc. of Sentiment Symposium Tutorial*.

R. Řehůřek and P. Sojka. 2010. Software Framework for Topic Modelling with Large Corpora. In *Proc. of the Language Resources and Evaluation Conference (LREC) Workshop on New Challenges for NLP Frameworks*. pages 45–50.

A. Reyes and P. Rosso. 2014. On the difficulty of automatically detecting irony: beyond a simple case of negation. *Knowledge and Information Systems* 40(3):595–614.

S. Rosenthal, P. Nakov, S. Kiritchenko, S. M. Moham-
mad, A. Ritter, and V. Stoyanov. 2015a. Semeval-
2015 Task 10: Sentiment Analysis in Twitter. In
*Proceedings of the 9th International Workshop on
Semantic Evaluation (SemEval)*. Association for
Computational Linguistics (ACL), pages 451–463.

S. Rosenthal, P. Nakov, S. Kiritchenko, S. M Mohammad, A. Ritter, and V. Stoyanov. 2015b. Semeval-
2015 task 10: Sentiment analysis in twitter. *Proceedings of the 9th International Workshop on Semantic Evaluation (SemEval 2015)* .

S. Rosenthal, A. Ritter, P. Nakov, and V. Stoyanov.
2014. SemEval-2014 task 9: Sentiment Analysis
in Twitter. In *Proceedings of the 8th International
Workshop on Semantic Evaluation (SemEval)*. Association for Computational Linguistics (ACL), pages
73–80.

P. Savicky and J. Fürnkranz. 2003. Combining pairwise classifiers with stacking. In *International Symposium on Intelligent Data Analysis*. Springer, pages
219–229.

A. Severyn and A. Moschitti. 2015. Unitn: Training
deep convolutional neural network for twitter sentiment classification. In *Proceedings of the 9th International Workshop on Semantic Evaluation (SemEval 2015), Association for Computational Linguistics*. pages 464–469.

S.Rosenthal, N.Farra, and P.Nakov. 2017. SemEval-
2017 task 4: Sentiment analysis in Twitter. In *Proceedings of the 11th International Workshop on Semantic Evaluation*. Association for Computational
Linguistics, SemEval '17.

T. Wilson, J. Wiebe, and P. Hoffmann. 2005. Recognizing contextual polarity in phrase-level sentiment
analysis. In *Proc. of the Conference on Human
Language Technology and Empirical Methods in
Natural Language Processing (HLT/EMNLP)*. pages
347–354.

NRU-HSE at SemEval-2017 Task 4: Tweet Quantification Using Deep Learning Architecture

Nikolay Karpov

National Research University Higher School of Economics
25/12 Bolshaja Pecherskaja str. 603155
Nizhny Novgorod, Russia
`nkarpov@hse.ru`

Abstract

In many areas, such as social science, politics or market research, people need to deal with dataset shifting over time. Distribution drift phenomenon usually appears in the field of sentiment analysis, when proportions of instances are changing over time. In this case, the task is to correctly estimate proportions of each sentiment expressed in the set of documents (quantification task). Basically, our study was aimed to analyze the effectiveness of a mixture of quantification technique with one of deep learning architecture. All the techniques are evaluated using the SemEval-2017 Task4 dataset and source code, mentioned in this paper and available online in the Python programming language. The results of an application of the quantification techniques are discussed.

1 Introduction

A traditional classification task is often based on the assumption that data for training a classifier represent test data. But in many areas, such as customer-relationship management or opinion mining, people need to deal with dataset shift or population drift phenomenon. The simplest type of dataset shift is when training set and test set vary only in the distribution of the classes of the instances aka distribution drift. If we would like to measure this variation, the task of accurate classification of each item is replaced by the task of providing accurate proportions of instances from each class (quantification). George Forman suggested defining the 'quantification task' as finding the best estimate for the amount of cases in each class in a test set, using a training set with a substantially different class distribution (Forman, 2008).

Application of the quantification approach in opinion mining (Esuli et al., 2010), network-behavior analysis (Tang et al., 2010), word-sense disambiguation (Chan and Ng, 2006), remote sensing (Guerrero-Curieses et al., 2009), quality control (Sánchez et al., 2008), monitoring support-call logs (Forman et al., 2006) and credit scoring (Hand and others, 2006) showed high performance even with a relatively small training set.

Although quantification techniques are able to provide accurate sentiment analysis of proportions in situations of distribution drift, the question of an optimal technique for analysis of tweets still raises a lot of questions. It is worth mentioning that sentiment analysis of tweets presents additional challenges to natural language processing, because of the small amount of text (less than 140 characters in each document), usage of creative spelling (e.g. "happpyyy", "some1 yg bner2 tulus"), abbreviations (such as "wth" or "lol"), informal constructions ("hahahaha yava quiet so !ma I m bored av even home nw") and hashtags (BREAKING: US GDP growth is back! #kidding), which are a type of tagging for Twitter messages.

We participated in D and E subtasks of the tweet sentiment quantification competition SemEval-2017 Task 4. To solve them we used a quantification method, which showed good accuracy last year (Karpov et al., 2016) and deep learning architecture mentioned in literature for text classification task.

The paper is organized as follows. In Section 2, we first look at the notation, then we briefly overview a method to solve the quantification problem. Section 3 describes a deep learning architec-

Proceedings of the 11th International Workshop on Semantic Evaluations (SemEval-2017), pages 683–688,
Vancouver, Canada, August 3 - 4, 2017. ©2017 Association for Computational Linguistics

ture and approach to train our network. In Section 4 we show an experiment methodology. Section 5 describes the results of our experiments, while Section 6 concludes the work defining open research issues for further investigation.

2 Quantification Method

In this section, we describe methods used to handle changes in class distribution.

First, let us give some definition of notation.
X: vector representation of observation x;
$C = \{c_1, ..., c_n\}$: classes of observations, where n is the number of classes;
$p_S(c)$: a true a priori probability (aka "prevalence" of class c in the set S;
$p_S(c_j)$: estimated prevalence of c_j using the set S;
$p_S^M(c_j)$: estimated $p_S(c_j)$ obtained via method M;
$p(c_j/x)$: a posteriori probability to classify an observation x to the class c_j;
$TRAIN$, $TEST$: training and test sets of observations, respectively;
$TEST_c$: a subset of $TEST$ set where each observation falls within class c;
$TEST\_CD = \{p_{TEST}(c_i)\}$; $i=\overline{1,n}$: class probability distribution of the test set;
$TRAIN\_CD = \{p_{TRAIN}(c_i)\}$; $i=\overline{1,n}$: class probability distribution of the training set;

The problem we study has some training set, which provides us with a set of labeled examples – TRAIN, with class distribution TRAIN_CD. At some point, the distribution of data changes to a new, but unknown class distribution – TEST_CD, and this distribution provides a set of unlabeled examples – TEST. Given this terminology, we can state our quantification problem more precisely.

2.1 Expectation Maximization

A simple procedure to adjust the outputs of a classifier to a new a priori probability is described in the study by (Saerens et al., 2002).

$$p(c_j/x_k) = \frac{\frac{p_{TEST}(c_j)}{p_{TRAIN}(c_j)}\hat{p}(c_j/x_k)}{\sum_{i=1}^{n}\frac{p_{TEST}(c_i)}{p_{TRAIN}(c_i)}\hat{p}(c_i/x_k)} \quad (1)$$

It is important that authors suggest using not only a well-known formula (1) to compute the corrected a posteriori probabilities, but also an iterative procedure to adjust the outputs of the trained classifier with respect to these new a priori probabilities, without having to refit the mod-

el, even when these probabilities are not known in advance.

To make the Expectation Maximization (EM) method clear, we specify its algorithm in Figure1 using a pseudo-code. The algorithm begins with counting start values for class probability distribution, using labels on the training set TRAIN (line 1), then builds an initial classifier C_i from the TRAIN set (line 2) and classifies each item in the unlabeled TEST set (line3), where the `classify` functions return the a posteriori probabilities (TEST_prob) for the specified datasets. The algorithm then iterates in lines 4-9 until the maximum number of iterations (`maxIterations`) is reached. In this loop, the algorithm first uses the previous a posteriori probabilities TEST_prob to estimate a new a priori probability (line 6). Then, in line 7, a posteriori probabilities are computed using Equation (1). Finally, once the loop terminates, the last a posteriori probabilities return (line 9).

```
EM (TRAIN, TEST)
1.TEST_CD = prevalence(TRAIN)
2.C_i = build_clf(TRAIN)
3.TEST_prob = classify(C_i, TEST)
4.for (i=1; i<maxIterations; i++)
5.{
6.TEST_CD = prevalence(TEST_prob)
7.TEST_prob=bayes(TEST_CD,
TEST_prob)
8.}
9.return TEST_CD
```

Figure 1: Pseudo-code for the EM algorithm.

To build a classifier in the function `build_clf`, we use support vector machines (SVM) with a linear kernel.

2.2 Iterative Class Distribution Estimation

Another interesting method is iterative cost-sensitive class distribution estimation (CDE-Iterate) described in the study by (Xue and Weiss, 2009).

The main idea of this method is to retrain a classifier at each iteration, where the iterations progressively improve the quantification accuracy of performing the «classify and count» method via generated cost-sensitive classifiers.

For the CDE-based method, the final prevalence is induced from the TRAIN labeled set with the cost of classes COST. The COST value is computed with Equation (2), utilizing the class distribution calculated during the previous step TEST_CD. For each iteration, we recalculate:

$$COST = \frac{TEST\_CD}{TRAIN\_CD} \qquad (2)$$

The CDE-Iterate algorithm is specified in Figure 2, using the pseudo-code. The algorithm begins with counting the class distribution TRAIN_CD for training labels TRAIN (line 1). Then it builds an initial classifier `C_i` from the TRAIN set (line 2). In a loop, this algorithm uses the previous classifier `C_i` to classify the unlabeled TEST set by estimating a posterior probability `TEST_prob` for each item in a test set (line 5). Then in line 6, the a priory probability distribution is computed and the cost ratio information is updated (line 7). In line 8, a new cost-sensitive classifier `C_i` is generated using the TRAIN set with the updated cost ratio COST. The algorithm then iterates in lines 4-9 until the maximum number of iterations (`maxIterations`) is reached. Finally, once the loop terminates, the last a priory probability distribution of classes is returned TEST_CD (line 10).

```
CDE-Iterate(TRAIN, TEST, COST_start)
1. TRAIN_CD = prevalence(TRAIN)
2. C_i = build_clf(TRAIN,
COST_start)
3. for (i=1; i<maxIterations; i++)
4. {
5.   TEST_prob= classify(C_i, TEST)
6.   TEST_CD = prevalence(TEST_prob)
7.   COST = TEST_CD/TRAIN_CD
8.   C_i = build_clf(TRAIN, COST)
9. }
10.return TEST_CD
```

Figure 2: Pseudo-code for the CDE-Iterate algorithm.

Last year we did not find any open library where baseline quantification methods were implemented. We, therefore, shared all the algorithms, which we had programmed using the Python language, on the Github repository[1]. We believe that this library can help to pool information on quantification.

3 Deep Learning Architecture

As the classifier for quantification algorithm, we used a neural network with traditional architecture for text classification task. In this section, we briefly describe our choice of architecture, a regularization method and a training algorithm.

3.1 Pre-trained Embedding Layer

The organizers provided a dataset of messages of SemEval Task4 since 2013 till 2016. But it still contained not so many samples to effectively train deep architecture. Therefore, we additionally used weekly labeled Sentiment140 corpus of tweets, (Go et al., 2009), to pre-train our network so as to learn semantic and sentiment specific representation of words and phrases.

A sequence of words of the input tweet maps to the corresponding real-valued vectors by the embedding layer. The length of its vector is called the dimension of the embeddings. To find out good embeddings we utilize GenSim[2] to pre-trained CBOW model for vectors with a dimensionality of 300. We choose these over the CBOW embeddings trained on Twitter data because of the higher dimensionality, considerably larger training corpus and vocabulary of unique words.

Word vectors from GenSim used as a starting point and they have updated during network training by back-propagating the classification errors.

3.2 Recurrent layers

Recurrent layers are proved to be useful in handling variable length sequences (Tang et al., 2015). We use two series-connected long short-term memory (LSTM) cells to compute continuous representations of tweets with semantic composition.

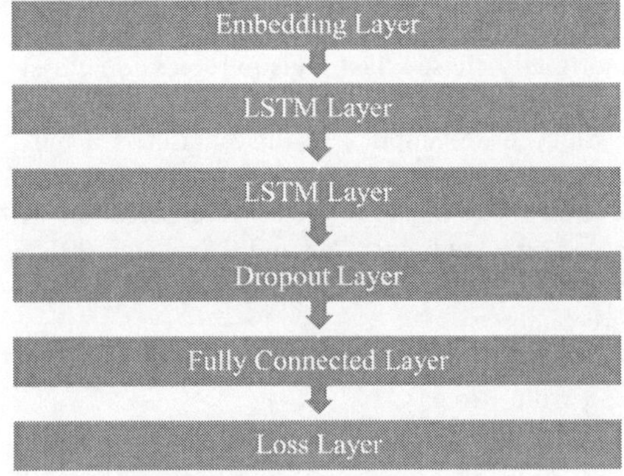

Figure 3: Neural network structure.

3.3 Regularization

We use dropout as the regularizer to prevent our network from overfitting (Srivastava, 2013). Our

---

[1]https://github.com/Arctickirillas/Rubrication

[2]http://radimrehurek.com/gensim/

dropout layer selects a half of the hidden units at random and sets their output to zero and thus prevents co-adaptation of the features.

3.4 Training algorithm

The Sentiment140 dataset and all messages from SemEval Task4 competition since 2013 till 2016 were used (except sarcasm dataset) to pre-train neural network layers. Then we fine tuned them on the train subsets for extract subtask. We used Adam method for stochastic optimization of an objective function.

4 Experiment Methodology

This section describes our experimental setup for participation in the SemEval-2017 Task 4 called "Sentiment Analysis in Twitter". Task 4 consists of five subtasks, but we only participated in topic-based message polarity quantification – subtasks D, E according to a two-point scale and five-point scale, respectively. Its dataset consists of Twitter messages (aka observations) divided into several topics. These subtasks are evaluated independently for different topics, and the final result is counted as an average of evaluation measure out of all the topics (Rosenthal et al., 2017).

For the quantification algorithm described in Section 2, we need to build a cost-sensitive classifier in the function `build_clf`.

4.1 Approach 2016

Last year we tried few cost-sensitive classifiers and finally chose a fast logistic regression classifier.

Since observation x in this dataset is a message written in a natural language, we first need to transform it to a vector representation X. Based on a study by (Gao and Sebastiani, 2015), we choose the following components of the feature vector:

- TF-IDF for word n-grams with n varies from 1 to 4
- TF-IDF character n-grams where n varies from 3 to 5.

A feature vector is extracted with a Scikit_Learn tool[3]. We also perform data preprocessing. Several text patterns (e.g. links, emoti-

cons, and numbers) were replaced with their substitutes. For word n-grams we apply lemmatization using WordNetLemmatizer.

It is interesting to characterize messages using the SentiWordNet library. For each token x_i in document X we obtain its polarity value from the SentiWordNet. First, we recognize the part of speech using a speech tagger from the NLTK library (Bird et al., 2009). Second, we get the SentiWordNet first polarity value for this token using the part of speech information.

The organizers provide a default split of the SemEval2016 data into training, development, development-time testing and testing datasets. The algorithms evaluation is performed using these subsets. The training, development and development-time testing subsets are used as a TRAIN set. The testing subset is used as a TEST set.

4.2 Approach 2017

This year we try to apply neural network as a cost-sensitive classifier.

We remove punctuations from input text message. Then we split tweets into words and transform them into a sequence of word index with fixed length. All preprocessing is performed using Keras[4] library with Tensor Flow backend. We do not apply character sequences and lemmatization or stemming of words. As a TRAIN set, we use all datasets provided by organizers of topic-based message polarity challenge.

The chosen parameters of our network are as follows: the maximum input sequence length is set to 30, vocabulary size is 300000, the dimensionality of word embedding is 300, LSTM units hidden state vector size is 64, two LSTM layers and dropout of 50% while training. We use the dense layer with output dimension equals to one for subtask D and five for subtask E with sigmoid activation.

The metrics that we use to evaluate the classifier performance are described in (Rosenthal et al., 2017) and are not described here.

5 Experiment Results

The results of five point scale subtask are shown in Table 1. During the development period, we compare our system with last year one on the last year dataset. New system produced an EMD

[3]http://scikit-learn.org/stable/modules/generated/sklearn.feature_extractio
n.text.TfidfVectorizer.html

[4]https://keras.io

measure of 0.347 while last year system was slightly better - 0.334. We explain this by the fact that dataset for network fine-tuning was relatively small last year. This year training dataset is three times bigger, that is why we decide to submit results from the new version of the algorithm.

EMD of our new system on the new dataset is 0.317 while the best system scored 0.245.

Settings	EMD
Approach and dataset 2017	0.317 (5)
Approach 2017, dataset 2016	0.347
Approach and dataset 2016	0.334 (4)

Table 1: Results of Task 4E.

The results of two-point scale subtask are shown in Table 2. Our algorithm shows KLD equals to 0.078 while the best system is 0.036.

Settings	KLD	RAE
Approach and dataset 2017	0.078 (8)	1.528 (8)
Approach and dataset 2016	0.084 (7)	0.767 (4)

Table 2: Results of Task 4D.

6 Conclusion and future work

The aim of this research was to try to solve sentiment quantification task with deep learning architecture. We compared our deep learning approach used this year with an approach without deep learning used last year.

For tweet quantification on a five-point scale (Subtask E) and a two-point scale (Subtask D), we used the same iterative method proposed by (Xue and Weiss, 2009). As a classifier we used deep learning network which was retrained on the big corpus and fine tune on the small. These approaches showed the 5-th and the 8-th best places in the competition subtasks E and D respectively.

In our future work, we are planning to move in two directions. First, we plan to apply new deep architecture and pre-train it using more data. Second, we want to explore the bias property of the CDE-Iterate quantification method.

Acknowledgments

The reported study was funded by RFBR under research Project No. 16-06-00184 A, the Academic Fund Program at the National Research University Higher School of Economics (HSE) in 2017 (grant N17-05-0007) and by the Russian Academic Excellence Project "5-100".

References

Steven Bird, Ewan Klein, and Edward Loper. 2009. *Natural language processing with Python.* O'Reilly Media, Inc.

Yee Seng Chan and Hwee Tou Ng. 2006. Estimating class priors in domain adaptation for word sense disambiguation. In *Proceedings of the 21st International Conference on Computational Linguistics and the 44th annual meeting of the Association for Computational Linguistics*, pages 89–96. Association for Computational Linguistics.

Andrea Esuli, Fabrizio Sebastiani, and Ahmed ABBASI. 2010. Sentiment quantification. *IEEE intelligent systems*, 25(4):72–79.

George Forman. 2008. Quantifying counts and costs via classification. *Data Mining and Knowledge Discovery*, 17(2):164–206, June.

George Forman, Evan Kirshenbaum, and Jaap Suermondt. 2006. Pragmatic text mining: minimizing human effort to quantify many issues in call logs. In *Proceedings of the 12th ACM SIGKDD international conference on Knowledge discovery and data mining*, pages 852–861. ACM.

Wei Gao and Fabrizio Sebastiani. 2015. Tweet Sentiment: From Classification to Quantification. In *Proceedings of the 2015 IEEE/ACM International Conference on Advances in Social Networks Analysis and Mining 2015*, pages 97–104. ACM.

Alec Go, Richa Bhayani, and Lei Huang. 2009. Twitter sentiment classification using distant supervision. *CS224N Project Report, Stanford*, 1(12).

A. Guerrero-Curieses, R. Alaiz-Rodriguez, and J. Cid-Sueiro. 2009. Cost-sensitive and modular landcover classification based on posterior probability estimates. *International Journal of Remote Sensing*, 30(22):5877–5899.

David J. Hand and others. 2006. Classifier technology and the illusion of progress. *Statistical science*, 21(1):1–14.

Nikolay Karpov, Alexander Porshnev, and Kirill Rudakov. 2016. NRU-HSE at SemEval-2016 Task 4: Comparative Analysis of Two Iterative Methods Using Quantification Library. In *Proceedings of the 10th International Workshop on Semantic Evaluation (SemEval-2016)*, pages 171–177, San Diego, California, June. Association for Computational Linguistics.

Sara Rosenthal, Noura Farra, and Preslav Nakov. 2017. SemEval-2017 Task 4: Sentiment Analysis in Twitter. In *Proceedings of the 11th International Workshop on Semantic Evaluation*, Vancouver, Canada, August. Association for Computational Linguistics.

Marco Saerens, Patrice Latinne, and Christine Decaestecker. 2002. Adjusting the outputs of a classifier to new a priori probabilities: a simple procedure. *Neural computation*, 14(1):21–41.

Lidia Sánchez, Víctor González, Enrique Alegre, and Rocío Alaiz. 2008. Classification and quantification based on image analysis for sperm samples with uncertain damaged/intact cell proportions. In *Image Analysis and Recognition*, pages 827–836. Springer.

Nitish Srivastava. 2013. *Improving neural networks with dropout*. phdthesis, University of Toronto.

Duyu Tang, Bing Qin, and Ting Liu. 2015. Document Modeling with Gated Recurrent Neural Network for Sentiment Classification. In *EMNLP*, pages 1422–1432.

Lei Tang, Huiji Gao, and Huan Liu. 2010. Network quantification despite biased labels. In *Proceedings of the Eighth Workshop on Mining and Learning with Graphs*, pages 147–154. ACM.

Jack Chongjie Xue and Gary M Weiss. 2009. Quantification and semi-supervised classification methods for handling changes in class distribution. In *Proceedings of the 15th ACM SIGKDD international conference on Knowledge discovery and data mining*, pages 897–906. ACM.

MI&T Lab at SemEval-2017 task 4: An Integrated Training Method of Word Vector for Sentiment Classification

Jingjing Zhao, Yan Yang, Bing Xu

Laboratory of Machine Intelligence and Translation, Harbin Institute of Technology

School of Computer Science and Technology, Harbin Institute of Technology, Harbin, China

zhaojingjing@hit.edu.cn,yangyan@hit.edu.cn, hitxb@hit.edu.cn

Abstract

A CNN method for sentiment classification task in Task 4A of SemEval 2017 is presented. To solve the problem of word2vec training word vector slowly, a method of training word vector by integrating word2vec and Convolutional Neural Network (CNN) is proposed. This training method not only improves the training speed of word2vec, but also makes the word vector more effective for the target task. Furthermore, the word2vec adopts a full connection between the input layer and the projection layer of the Continuous Bag-of-Words (CBOW) for acquiring the semantic information of the original sentence.

1 Introduction

The polarity of a Twitter message is classified into positive, negative and neutral in Twitter sentiment analysis. However, the difficulty of sentiment analysis greatly increases due to the ambiguity and the rhetorical of natural language (Liu, 2012). In recent years, the deep learning model has shown great potential in the task of sentiment classification (Socher et al., 2011; Poria et al., 2015; Socher et al., 2013). For short text data such as Twitter, Convolutional Neural Network (CNN) model (Kim, 2014; Dos Santos and Gatti, 2014; Chen et al., 2016) is the most widely and successfully used, and in the SemEval 2016-task4A competition, the system ranked first also uses CNN model (Deriu et al., 2016). So CNN model is used to complete the task in our system. The task 4A of SemEval 2017[1] is a polarity classification task which requires participated systems to classify a

---

[1] http://alt.qcri.org/semeval2017/task4/

given Twitter message into positive, negative or neutral (Rosenthal et al., 2017).

The system integrates the word2vec and CNN to train the labeled data, generating the word vector of each word in the data. This method can improve the training speed of word vector. In order to preserve the more semantic information of the original sentence effectively, the word2vec is fully connected between the input layer and the projection layer of the Continuous Bag-of-Words (CBOW).

2 System description

2.1 Word vector representation method

Word2vec can represent every word that appears in a large number of training texts as a lower dimension vector (usually 50-100 dimensions). (Mikolov et al., 2013b; Rong, 2014; Mikolov et al., 2013a) have a detail description of word2vec. Word2vec in our system uses Continuous Bag-of-Words (CBOW) model, and the structure is shown in Figure 1, in which w_i is a word, and the sequence $\langle w_{(i-c)}, ..., w_{(i-1)}, w_{(i+1)}, ..., w_{(i+c)} \rangle$ represents the context of the word w_i, and c is the window size. The word-vector length of the word w_i is d. The traditional word2vec adds $2c$ words' word vector on the input layer to the projection layer. (Mikolov et al., 2013b) has a detail description of this method, which has been exactly used in Google Word2vec released in 2013. However, in the sentiment analysis task, whether there is a negative word before the sentiment word will influence the identification of polarity (Liu, 2012). So in order to preserve more emotional semantic information, the input layer and the projection layer of CBOW are fully connected in this system.

The procedure of integrating word2vec and CNN to train the words vector follows four

689

Proceedings of the 11th International Workshop on Semantic Evaluations (SemEval-2017), pages 689–693,
Vancouver, Canada, August 3 - 4, 2017. ©2017 Association for Computational Linguistics

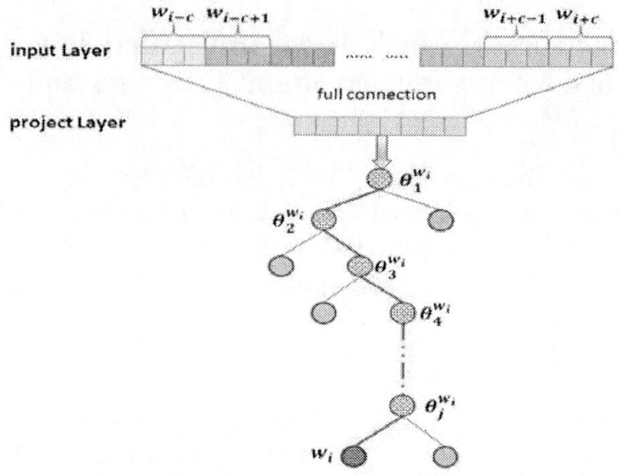

Figure 1: The structure of word2vec in the system.

steps: *(i)* initialization and pre-training: initialize word2vec and CNN parameters, and pre-train word2vec a certain number of iterations; *(ii)* CNN training: input the latest words vector from word2vec to CNN; *(iii)* word2vec training: input the latest words vector from CNN to word2vec; *(iv)* alternate the *(ii)* and *(iii)* steps until the training phase converges. CNN can help word2vec extract more effective text features. Experiments show that the model obtained by integrating CNN and word2vec performs better when the data is sufficient compared to adopting them separately.

2.2 Deep learning model

The system proposes CNN model to predict the sentiment polarity of a Twitter text. The CNN structure diagram is shown in Figure 2.

Word vector sequence: Each word is represented as a d-dimensional word vector, a sentence or a Twitter text containing n words can be expressed as n d-dimensional vectors, which are concatenated together into a matrix $X \in \mathbb{R}^{d \times n}$ form which represents a sentence or a Twitter text. Each row of matrix X is treated as a new vector, thus d n-dimensional vectors are obtained and concatenated as input to the CNN network.

Convolutional layer: The convolution layer uses full convolution operation. Let $F_i^l \in \mathbb{R}^{M_1}$ represents ith feature map at lth layer[2], and $m_{j,i}^l \in \mathbb{R}^{M_2}$ represents the convolutional kernel of the jth convolutional result C_j^{l+1} at $l + 1$th layer. So the

jth convolutional result C_j^{l+1} at $l + 1$th layer is the result of convolution operation between each feature map at lth layer and convolutional kernel $m_{j,i}^l$, i.e.,

$$C_j^{l+1} = \sum_j m_{j,i}^l * F_i^l \qquad (1)$$

k-**max pooling:** After the convolution operation, the max-pooling operation is performed which preserves the largest value in each convolution result. The system uses k-max pooling, which preserves the largest k values instead. For example:

$$(1, 6, 3, 8) \xrightarrow{2-max} (6, 8)$$

Where k is a parameter that needs to be set manually.

full-connection Layer: The full connection layer receives the output of the last layer of CNN and fully connects itself to the output layer, i.e. $W * x + b$ operation, where W and b can be trained during the network training phase.

output Layer: The output layer uses the Softmax operation and outputs the probability that the input sentence or Twitter text belongs to each class, and the class with the maximum probability is the predicted class judged by the system.

2.3 Combination prediction

Because of the insufficiency of training data and the great quantity bias in different classes' training data, the trained CNN can't work so well. So our system adds Support Vector Machine (SVM) (Suykens, 2001) model to predict jointly with

---

[2]Here, a layer refers to one convolutional and one pooling layer.

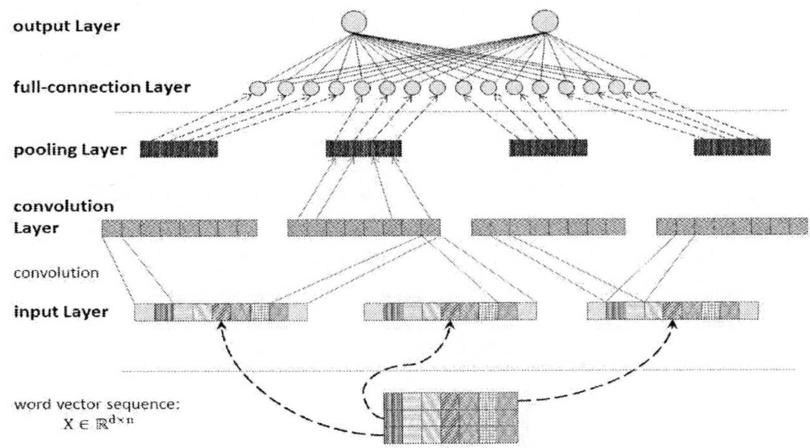

Figure 2: The structure of CNN in the system.

CNN. The steps of combination prediction are shown in Figure 3.

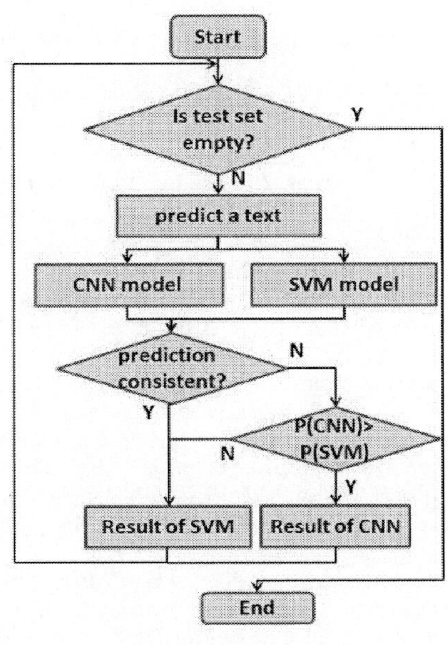

Figure 3: The steps of combination prediction.

3 Experimental datasets and model parameters

3.1 Experimental datasets

The datasets of the experiment is provided by SemEval 2017, and the specific datasets used are shown in Table 1.

Dataset	positive	negative	neutral	Total
train	18123	14354	21748	54225
dev	1000	500	1500	3000
test	2375	3972	5937	12284

Table 1: Datasets of the experiment.

3.2 Model parameters

The parameters set of word2vec and CNN in our system are shown in Table 2.

word2vec parameters	
Window size of context c	3
Number of hidden layer	1
Dimensionality of hidden layer	[50]
Convolutional Neural Network parameters	
Number of Convolutional layer	1
Number of max-pooling layer	1
Convolutional kernel size	7
Number of feature map at Convolutional	100
k-max pooling parameter k	2

Table 2: Parameters used in the word2vec and CNN.

4 Experimental results and analysis

4.1 Evaluation method

The measure metric of the Evaluation is average macro recall (Rosenthal et al., 2017). The formula is as follows:

$$\rho^{PUN} = \frac{\rho^P + \rho^U + \rho^N}{3} \qquad (2)$$

Here, ρ^P, ρ^U and ρ^N denote recall for the positive class, neutral class and negative class.

The other two measure metrics are the average macro F_1 and the average macro precision:

$$F_1^{PUN} = \frac{F_1^P + F_1^U + F_1^N}{3} \qquad (3)$$

$$P^{PUN} = \frac{P^P + P^U + P^N}{3} \qquad (4)$$

Here, F_1^P, F_1^U and F_1^N denote F_1 for the positive class, neutral class and negative class; P^P, P^U and P^N denote precision for the positive class, neutral class and negative class.

4.2 Analysis of experimental results

Table 3 lists the average macro recall for each model on the development dataset. From the table 3, the effect of word2vec+CNN model is better than SVM, and word2vec + CNN + SVM is the best of the three models, so the best results on the test set are submitted.

System	SVM	CNN	SVM+CNN
ρ^{PUN}	0.589	0.601	0.653

Table 3: The results of different models on the development dataset.

Table 4 shows the details of our system's result in comparison with the three top ranked systems' results. It can be seen from the table that our result's ρ^N is not good, but ρ^U is better than the top three systems. The decrease of experimental results is from the quantity bias in training data of different classes.

For deep learning models, a lot of training data are required. Due to the lack of Twitter texts, word2vec training is not sufficient and do not generate effective words vector representation. In the future, semi-supervisory mechanisms will be considered to expand the number of training data.

In the future, we can improve the system's performance from following points: *(i)* to expand the amount of training data; *(ii)* to improve the type of combination: the results can be combined with multiple CNN systems to predict; *(iii)* to add more emotional semantic features.

5 Conclusion

This paper presentes a method of training word vector by integrating word2vec with CNN and using the trained CNN to complete the Twitter sentiment analysis task. In the future work, we hope to continue to improve system's performance in multiple ways, such as trying to modify some parameters or improve the type of classifiers' combination, adding some sentiment features.

Acknowledgments

This work is supported by the National Natural Science Foundation of China (No. 61402134).

References

Peng Chen, Bing Xu, Muyun Yang, and Sheng Li. 2016. Clause sentiment identification based on convolutional neural network with context embedding. In *Natural Computation, Fuzzy Systems and Knowledge Discovery (ICNC-FSKD), 2016 12th International Conference on*. IEEE, pages 1532–1538.

Jan Deriu, Maurice Gonzenbach, Fatih Uzdilli, Aurelien Lucchi, Valeria De Luca, and Martin Jaggi. 2016. Swisscheese at semeval-2016 task 4: Sentiment classification using an ensemble of convolutional neural networks with distant supervision. *Proceedings of SemEval* pages 1124–1128.

Cícero Nogueira Dos Santos and Maira Gatti. 2014. Deep convolutional neural networks for sentiment analysis of short texts. In *COLING*. pages 69–78.

System	Positive			Negative			Neutral			Score
	P	ρ	F_1	P	ρ	F_1	P	ρ	F_1	ρ^{PUN}
DataStories(1)	0.6259	0.7023	0.6619	0.5929	**0.8291**	0.6914	0.7471	**0.5115**	0.6073	0.681
BB twtr(1)	0.6851	0.6522	0.6682	0.5848	**0.8776**	0.7019	0.7518	**0.5144**	0.6109	0.681
LIA (3)	0.6480	0.6518	0.6499	0.6082	**0.8170**	0.6973	0.7289	**0.5599**	0.6333	0.676
MI&T Lab	0.4780	0.5171	0.4968	0.5496	**0.5451**	0.5473	0.6066	**0.5902**	0.5983	**0.551**

Table 4: The details of our result and the three top ranked results.

Yoon Kim. 2014. Convolutional neural networks for sentence classification. *arXiv preprint arXiv:1408.5882* .

Bing Liu. 2012. Sentiment analysis and opinion mining. *Synthesis lectures on human language technologies* 5(1):1–167.

Tomas Mikolov, Kai Chen, Greg Corrado, and Jeffrey Dean. 2013a. Efficient estimation of word representations in vector space. *arXiv preprint arXiv:1301.3781* .

Tomas Mikolov, Ilya Sutskever, Kai Chen, Greg S Corrado, and Jeff Dean. 2013b. Distributed representations of words and phrases and their compositionality. In *Advances in neural information processing systems*. pages 3111–3119.

Soujanya Poria, Erik Cambria, and Alexander F Gelbukh. 2015. Deep convolutional neural network textual features and multiple kernel learning for utterance-level multimodal sentiment analysis. In *EMNLP*. pages 2539–2544.

Xin Rong. 2014. word2vec parameter learning explained. *arXiv preprint arXiv:1411.2738* .

Sara Rosenthal, Noura Farra, and Preslav Nakov. 2017. SemEval-2017 task 4: Sentiment analysis in Twitter. In *Proceedings of the 11th International Workshop on Semantic Evaluation*. Association for Computational Linguistics, Vancouver, Canada, SemEval '17.

Richard Socher, Jeffrey Pennington, Eric H Huang, Andrew Y Ng, and Christopher D Manning. 2011. Semi-supervised recursive autoencoders for predicting sentiment distributions. In *Proceedings of the conference on empirical methods in natural language processing*. Association for Computational Linguistics, pages 151–161.

Richard Socher, Alex Perelygin, Jean Y Wu, Jason Chuang, Christopher D Manning, Andrew Y Ng, Christopher Potts, et al. 2013. Recursive deep models for semantic compositionality over a sentiment treebank. In *Proceedings of the conference on empirical methods in natural language processing (EMNLP)*. Citeseer, volume 1631, page 1642.

Johan AK Suykens. 2001. Nonlinear modelling and support vector machines. In *Instrumentation and Measurement Technology Conference, 2001. IMTC 2001. Proceedings of the 18th IEEE*. IEEE, volume 1, pages 287–294.

SiTAKA at SemEval-2017 Task 4: Sentiment Analysis in Twitter Based on a Rich Set of Features

Mohammed Jabreel   **Antonio Moreno**

Intelligent Technologies for Advanced Knowledge Acquisition (ITAKA),
Departament d'Enginyeria Informàtica i Matemàtiques,
Universitat Rovira i Virgili,
Av. Països Catalans, 26, 43007 Tarragona, Spain
<first_name>.<last_name>@urv.cat

Abstract

This paper describes SiTAKA, our system that has been used in task 4A, English and Arabic languages, Sentiment Analysis in Twitter of SemEval2017. The system proposes the representation of tweets using a novel set of features, which include a bag of negated words and the information provided by some lexicons. The polarity of tweets is determined by a classifier based on a Support Vector Machine. Our system ranks 2nd among 8 systems in the Arabic language tweets and ranks 8th among 38 systems in the English-language tweets.

1   Introduction

Sentiment analysis in Twitter is the problem of identifying people's opinions expressed in tweets. It normally involves the classification of tweets into categories such as positive, negative and in some cases, neutral. The main challenges in designing a sentiment analysis system for Twitter are the following:

- Twitter limits the length of the message to 140 characters, which leads users to use novel abbreviations and often disregard standard sentence structures.

- The informal language and the numerous spelling errors.

Most of the existing systems are inspired by the work presented in (Pang et al., 2002). Machine Learning techniques have been used to build a classifier from a set of tweets with a manually annotated sentiment polarity. The success of the Machine Learning models is based on two main facts: a large amount of labeled data and the intelligent design of a set of features that can distinguish between the positive, negative and neutral samples.

With this approach, most studies have focused on designing a set of efficient features to obtain a good classification performance (Feldman, 2013; Liu, 2012; Pang and Lee, 2008). For instance, the authors in (Mohammad et al., 2013) used diverse sentiment lexicons and a variety of hand-crafted features.

This paper proposes the representation of tweets using a novel set of features, which include the information provided by seven lexicons and a bag of negated words (BonW). The concatenation of these features with a set of basic features improves the classification performance. The polarity of tweets is determined by a classifier based on a Support Vector Machine.

The system has been evaluated on the Arabic and English language test sets of the Twitter Sentiment Analysis Track in SemEval 2017, subtask A (Message Polarity Classification). Our system (SiTAKA) has been ranked 8th over 38 teams in the English language test set and 2nd out of 8 teams in the Arabic language test set.

The rest of the paper is structured as follows. Section 2 presents the tools and the resources that have been used. In Section 3 we describe the system. The experiments and results are presented and discussed in Section 4. Finally, in the last section the conclusions as well as further work are presented.

2   Resources

This section explains the tools and the resources that have been used in the SiTAKA system. Let us denote its Arabic language and English language versions by *Ar*-SiTAKA and *En*-SiTAKA, respectively.

Proceedings of the 11th International Workshop on Semantic Evaluations (SemEval-2017), pages 694–699,
Vancouver, Canada, August 3 - 4, 2017. ©2017 Association for Computational Linguistics

2.1 Sentiment Lexicons

2.1.1 *En*-SiTAKA Lexicons

We used for *En*-SiTAKA five lexicons in this work, namely: General Inquirer (Stone et al., 1968), Hu-Liu opinion lexicon (HL) (Hu and Liu, 2004), NRC hashtags lexicon (Mohammad et al., 2013), SenticNet (Cambria et al., 2014), and TS-Lex (Tang et al., 2014b). More details about each lexicon, such as how it was created, the polarity score for each term, and the statistical distribution of the lexicon, can be found in (Jabreel and Moreno, 2016).

2.1.2 *Ar*-SiTAKA Lexicons

In this version of the SiTAKA system, we used four lexicons created by (Saif M. Mohammad and Kiritchenko, 2016): Arabic Hashtag Lexicon, Dialectal Arabic Hashtag Lexicon, Arabic Bing Liu Lexicon and Arabic Sentiment140 Lexicon. The first two were created manually, whereas the rest were translated to Arabic from the English version using Google Translator.

2.2 Embeddings

We used two pre-trained embedding models in *En*-SiTAKA. The first one is word2vec which is provided by Google. It is trained on part of the Google News dataset (about 100 billion words) and it contains 300-dimensional vectors for 3M words and phrases (Mikolov et al., 2013b). The second one is SSWEu, which has been trained to capture the sentiment information of sentences as well as the syntactic contexts of words (Tang et al., 2014c). The SSWEu model contains 50-dimensional vectors for 100K words.

In *Ar*-SiTAKA we used the model Arabic-SKIP-G300 provided by (Zahran et al., 2015). Arabic-SKIP-G300 has been trained on a large corpus of Arabic text collected from different sources such as Arabic Wikipedia, Arabic Gigaword Corpus, Ksucorpus, King Saud University Corpus, Microsoft crawled Arabic Corpus, etc. It contains 300-dimensional vectors for 6M words and phrases.

3 System Description

This section explains the main steps of the SiTAKA system, the features used to describe a tweet and the classification method.

3.1 Preprocessing and Normalization

Some standard pre-processing methods are applied on the tweets:

- *Normalization*: Each tweet in English is converted to the lowercase. URLs and usernames are omitted. Non-Arabic letters are removed from each tweet in the Arabic-language sets. Words with repeated letters (i.e. elongated) are corrected.

- *Tokenization and POS tagging*: All English-language tweets are tokenized and tagged using Ark Tweet NLP (Gimpel et al., 2011), while all Arabic-language tweets are tokenized and tagged using Stanford Tagger (Green and Manning, 2010).

- *Negation*: A negated context can be defined as a segment of tweet that starts with a negation word (e.g. *no*, *don't* for English-language, لا و ليس for Arabic-language) and ends with a punctuation mark (Pang et al., 2002). Each tweet is negated by adding a suffix (".NEG" and "منفي-") to each word in the negated context.

It is necessary to mention that in *Ar*-SiTAKA we did not use all the Arabic negation words due to the ambiguity of some of them. For example, the first word ما, is a question mark in the following "ما رأيك في ما حدث؟"-What do you think about what happened?" and it means "which/that" in the following example "إن ما حدث اليوم سيء جدا"- The matter that happened today was very bad".

As shown in (Saif et al., 2014), stopwords tend to carry sentiment information; thus, note that they were not removed from the tweets.

3.2 Features Extraction

SiTAKA uses five types of features: *basic text*, *syntactic*, *lexicon*, *cluster* and *Word Embeddings*. These features are described in the following subsections:

3.2.1 Basic Features

These basic features are extracted from the text. They are the following:

Bag of Words (BoW): Bag of words or n-grams features introduce some contextual information.

The presence or absence of contiguous sequences of 1, 2, 3, and 4 tokens are used to represent the tweets.

Bag of Negated Words (BonW): Negated contexts are important keys in the sentiment analysis problem. Thus, we used the presence or absence of contiguous sequences of 1, 2, 3 and 4 tokens in the negated contexts as a set of features to represent the tweets.

3.2.2 Syntactic Features

Syntactic features are useful to discriminate between neutral and non-neutral texts.

Part of Speech (POS): Subjective and objective texts have different POS tags (Pak and Paroubek, 2010). According to (Zhou et al., 2014), non-neutral terms are more likely to exhibit the following POS tags in Twitter: nouns, adjectives, adverbs, abbreviations and interjections. The number of occurrences of each part of speech tag is used to represent each tweet.

Bi-tagged: Bi-tagged features are extracted by combining the tokens of the bi-grams with their POS tag e.g. *"feel_VBP good_JJ"* "جميل_JJ جداً_VBD". It has been shown in the literature that adjectives and adverbs are subjective in nature and they help to increase the degree of expressiveness (Agarwal et al., 2013; Pang et al., 2002).

3.2.3 Lexicon Features

Opinion lexicons play an important role in sentiment analysis systems, and the majority of the existing systems rely heavily on them (Rosenthal et al., 2014). For each of the chosen lexicons, a tweet is represented by calculating the following features: (1) *tweet polarity*, (2) *the average polarity of the positive terms*, (3) *the average polarity of the negative terms*, (4) *the score of the last positive term*, (5) *the score of the last negative term*, (6) *the maximum positive score* and (7) *the minimum negative score*.

The polarity of a tweet T given a lexicon L is calculated using the equation (1). First, the tweet is tokenized. Then, the number of positive (P) and negative (N) tokens found in the lexicon are counted. Finally, the polarity measure is calculated as follows:

$$polarity = \begin{cases} 1 - \frac{N}{P} & ; if\ P > N \\ 0 & ; if\ P = N \\ \frac{P}{N} - 1 & ; if\ P < N \end{cases} \quad (1)$$

3.2.4 Cluster Features

We used two set of clusters in *En*-SiTAKA to represent the English-language tweets by mapping each tweet to a set of clusters. The first one is the well known set of clusters provided by the Ark Tweet NLP tool which contains 1000 clusters produced with the Brown clustering algorithm from 56M English-language tweets. These 1000 clusters are used to represent each tweet by mapping each word in the tweet to its cluster. The second one is *Word2vec cluster ngrams*, which is provided by (Dong et al., 2015). They used the word2vec tool to learn 40-dimensional word embeddings of 255,657 words from a Twitter dataset and the K-means algorithm to cluster them into 4960 clusters. We were not able to find publicly available semantic clusters to be used in *Ar*-SiTAKA.

3.2.5 Embedding Features

Word embeddings are an approach for distributional semantics which represents words as vectors of real numbers. Such representation has useful clustering properties, since the words that are semantically and syntactically related are represented by similar vectors (Mikolov et al., 2013a). For example, the words "coffee" and "tea" will be very close in the created space.

We used *sum*, *standard-deviation*, *min* and *max* pooling functions (Collobert et al., 2011) to obtain the tweet representation in the embedding space. The result is the concatenation of vectors derived from different pooling functions. More formally, let us consider an embedding matrix $E \in \mathbb{R}^{d \times |V|}$ and a tweet $T = w_1, w_2, ..., w_n$, where d is the dimension size, $|V|$ is the length of the vocabulary (i.e. the number of words in the embedding model), w_i is the ith word in the tweet and n is the number of words. First, each word w_i is substituted by the corresponding vector v_i^j in the matrix E where j is the index of the word w_i in the vocabulary. This step ends with the matrix $W \in \mathbb{R}^{d \times n}$. The vector $V_{T,E}$ is computed using the following formula:

$$V_{T,E} = \bigcup_{pool \in \{max,min,sum,std\}} pool_{i=1}^n v_i \quad (2)$$

where $\bigcup$ denotes the concatenation operation. The pooling function is an element-wise function, and it converts texts with various lengths into a fixed-length vector allowing to capture the information throughout the entire text.

3.3 Classifier

Up to now, Support Vector Machines (SVM) (Cortes and Vapnik, 1995) have been used widely and reported as the best classifier in the sentiment analysis problem. Thus, we trained a SVM classifier on the training sets provided by the organizers. For the English-language we combined the training sets of SemEval 13-16 and testing sets of SemEval 13-15, and used them as a training set. Table 1 shows the numerical description of the datasets used in this work. We used the linear kernel with the value 0.5 for the cost parameter C. All the parameters and the set of features have been experimentally chosen based on the development sets.

System	Training set	Dev set
En-SiTAKA	27,700	20,632
Ar-SiTAKA	2684	671

Table 1: Numerical description of the set of tweets

4 Results

The evaluation metrics used by the task organizers were the macroaveraged recall (ρ), the F1 averaged across the positives and the negatives $F1^{PN}$ and the accuracy (Acc) (Rosenthal et al., 2017).

The system has been tested on 12,284 English-language tweets and 6100 Arabic-language tweets provided by the organizers. The golden answers of all the test tweets were omitted by the organizers. The official evaluation results of our system are reported along with the top 10 systems and the baseline results in Table 2 and 3. Our system ranks 8th among 38 systems in the English-language tweets and ranks 2nd among 8 systems in the Arabic language tweets. The baselines 1, 2 and 3 stand for the cases in which the system classifies all the tweets as positive, negative and neutral respectively.

5 Conclusion

We have presented a new set of rich sentimental features for the sentiment analysis of the messages posted on Twitter. A Support Vector Machine classifier has been trained using a set of basic features, information extracted from a set of useful and publicly available opinion lexicons, syntactic

#	System	ρ	$F1^{PN}$	Acc
1	DataStories	**0.681**₁	0.677₂	0.651₅
	BB_twtr	**0.681**₁	0.685₁	0.658₃
3	LIA	**0.676**₃	0.674₃	0.661₂
4	Senti17	**0.674**₄	0.665₄	0.652₄
5	NNEMBs	**0.669**₅	0.658₅	0.664₁
6	Tweester	**0.659**₆	0.648₆	0.648₆
7	INGEOTEC	**0.649**₇	0.645₇	0.633₁₁
8	*En*-**SiTAKA**	**0.645**₈	0.628₉	0.643₉
9	TSA-INF	**0.643**₉	0.620₁₁	0.616₁₇
10	UCSC-NLP	**0.642**₁₀	0.624₁₀	0.565₃₀
	baseline 1	0.333	0.162	0.193
	baseline 2	0.333	0.224	0.323
	baseline 3	0.333	0.00	0.483

Table 2: Results for SemEval-2017 Task 4, subtask A, English.

#	System	ρ	$F1^{PN}$	Acc
1	NileTMRG	**0.583**₁	0.610₁	0.581₁
2	*Ar*-**SiTAKA**	**0.550**₂	0.571₂	0.563₂
3	ELiRF-UPV	**0.478**₃	0.467₄	0.508₃
4	INGEOTEC	**0.477**₄	0.455₅	0.499₄
5	OMAM	**0.438**₅	0.422₆	0.430₈
	LSIS	**0.438**₅	0.469₃	0.445₆
7	1w-StAR	**0.431**₇	0.416₇	0.454₅
8	HLP@UPENN	**0.415**₈	0.320₈	0.443₇
	baseline 1	0.333	0.199	0.248
	baseline 2	0.333	0.267	0.364
	baseline 3	0.333	0.00	0.388

Table 3: Results for SemEval-2017 Task 4, subtask A, Arabic.

features, clusters and embeddings. Deep learning approaches have recently been used to build supervised, unsupervised or even semi-supervised methods to analyze the sentiment of texts and to build efficient opinion lexicons (Severyn and Moschitti, 2015; Tang et al., 2014a,c); thus, the authors are considering the possibility of also using this technique to build a sentiment analysis system.

Acknowledgment

This work was partially supported by URV Research Support Funds (2015PFR-URV-B2-60, 2016PFR-URV-B2-60 and Martí i Franqués PhD grant).

References

Basant Agarwal, Natasha Mittal, and Erik Cambria. 2013. Enhancing sentiment classification performance using bi-tagged phrases. In *Data Mining Workshops (ICDMW), 2013 IEEE 13th International Conference on*. IEEE, pages 892–895.

Erik Cambria, Daniel Olsher, and Dheeraj Rajagopal. 2014. SenticNet 3: a common and common-sense knowledge base for cognition-driven sentiment analysis. In *Twenty-eighth AAAI conference on artificial intelligence*.

Ronan Collobert, Jason Weston, Léon Bottou, Michael Karlen, Koray Kavukcuoglu, and Pavel Kuksa. 2011. Natural language processing (almost) from scratch. *Journal of Machine Learning Research* 12:2461–2505.

Corinna Cortes and Vladimir Vapnik. 1995. Support vector machine. *Machine learning* 20(3):273–297.

Li Dong, Furu Wei, Yichun Yin, Ming Zhou, and Ke Xu. 2015. Splusplus: A Feature-Rich Two-stage Classifier for Sentiment Analysis of Tweets. *SemEval-2015* page 515.

Ronen Feldman. 2013. Techniques and applications for sentiment analysis. *Communications of the ACM* 56(4):82–89.

Kevin Gimpel, Nathan Schneider, Brendan O'Connor, Dipanjan Das, Daniel Mills, Jacob Eisenstein, Michael Heilman, Dani Yogatama, Jeffrey Flanigan, and Noah A. Smith. 2011. Part-of-speech Tagging for Twitter: Annotation, Features, and Experiments. In *Proceedings of the 49th Annual Meeting of the Association for Computational Linguistics: Human Language Technologies: Short Papers - Volume 2*. Association for Computational Linguistics, Stroudsburg, PA, USA, HLT '11, pages 42–47.

Spence Green and Christopher D Manning. 2010. Better arabic parsing: Baselines, evaluations, and analysis. In *Proceedings of the 23rd International Conference on Computational Linguistics*. Association for Computational Linguistics, pages 394–402.

Minqing Hu and Bing Liu. 2004. Mining and summarizing customer reviews. In *Proceedings of the tenth ACM SIGKDD international conference on Knowledge discovery and data mining*. ACM, pages 168–177.

Mohammed Jabreel and Antonio Moreno. 2016. Sentirich: Sentiment analysis of tweets based on a rich set of features. In *Artificial Intelligence Research and Development - Proceedings of the 19th International Conference of the Catalan Association for Artificial Intelligence, Barcelona, Catalonia, Spain, October 19-21, 2016*. pages 137–146.

Bing Liu. 2012. Sentiment analysis and opinion mining. *Synthesis lectures on human language technologies* 5(1):1–167.

Tomas Mikolov, Kai Chen, Greg Corrado, and Jeffrey Dean. 2013a. Efficient estimation of word representations in vector space. *arXiv preprint arXiv:1301.3781*.

Tomas Mikolov, Ilya Sutskever, Kai Chen, Greg S Corrado, and Jeff Dean. 2013b. Distributed representations of words and phrases and their compositionality. In *Advances in neural information processing systems*. pages 3111–3119.

Saif Mohammad, Svetlana Kiritchenko, and Xiaodan Zhu. 2013. NRC-Canada: Building the State-of-the-Art in Sentiment Analysis of Tweets. In *Proceedings of the seventh international workshop on Semantic Evaluation Exercises (SemEval-2013)*. Atlanta, Georgia, USA.

Alexander Pak and Patrick Paroubek. 2010. Twitter as a Corpus for Sentiment Analysis and Opinion Mining. In *Proceedings of the Seventh conference on International Language Resources and Evaluation (LREC'10)*. European Language Resources Association (ELRA), Valletta, Malta.

Bo Pang and Lillian Lee. 2008. Opinion Mining and Sentiment Analysis. *Found. Trends Inf. Retr.* 2(1-2):1–135.

Bo Pang, Lillian Lee, and Shivakumar Vaithyanathan. 2002. Thumbs Up?: Sentiment Classification Using Machine Learning Techniques. In *Proceedings of the ACL-02 Conference on Empirical Methods in Natural Language Processing - Volume 10*. Association for Computational Linguistics, Stroudsburg, PA, USA, EMNLP '02, pages 79–86.

Sara Rosenthal, Noura Farra, and Preslav Nakov. 2017. SemEval-2017 task 4: Sentiment analysis in Twitter. In *Proceedings of the 11th International Workshop on Semantic Evaluation*. Association for Computational Linguistics, Vancouver, Canada, SemEval '17.

Sara Rosenthal, Alan Ritter, Preslav Nakov, and Veselin Stoyanov. 2014. Semeval-2014 task 9: Sentiment analysis in twitter. In *Proceedings of the 8th International Workshop on Semantic Evaluation (SemEval 2014)*. pages 73–80.

Hassan Saif, Miriam Fernández, Yulan He, and Harith Alani. 2014. On stopwords, filtering and data sparsity for sentiment analysis of Twitter. In *Proceedings of the 9th language resources and evaluation conference (LREC)*. Reykjavik, Iceland.

Mohammad Salameh Saif M. Mohammad and Svetlana Kiritchenko. 2016. Sentiment lexicons for arabic social media. In *Proceedings of 10th edition of the the Language Resources and Evaluation Conference (LREC)*. Portorož, Slovenia.

Aliaksei Severyn and Alessandro Moschitti. 2015. UNITN: Training deep convolutional neural network for Twitter sentiment classification. In *Proceedings of the 9th International Workshop on Semantic Evaluation (SemEval 2015), Association for Computational Linguistics, Denver, Colorado*. pages 464–469.

Philip Stone, Dexter C Dunphy, Marshall S Smith, and DM Ogilvie. 1968. The general inquirer: A computer approach to content analysis. *Journal of Regional Science* 8(1):113–116.

Duyu Tang, Furu Wei, Bing Qin, Ting Liu, and Ming Zhou. 2014a. Coooolll: A Deep Learning System for Twitter Sentiment Classification. In *Proceedings of the 8th International Workshop on Semantic Evaluation (SemEval 2014)*. Association for Computational Linguistics and Dublin City University, Dublin, Ireland, pages 208–212. http://www.aclweb.org/anthology/S14-2033.

Duyu Tang, Furu Wei, Bing Qin, Ming Zhou, and Ting Liu. 2014b. Building Large-Scale Twitter-Specific Sentiment Lexicon : A Representation Learning Approach. In *Proceedings of COLING 2014, the 25th International Conference on Computational Linguistics: Technical Papers*. Dublin City University and Association for Computational Linguistics, Dublin, Ireland, pages 172–182. http://www.aclweb.org/anthology/C14-1018.

Duyu Tang, Furu Wei, Nan Yang, Ming Zhou, Ting Liu, and Bing Qin. 2014c. Learning Sentiment-Specific Word Embedding for Twitter Sentiment Classification. In *Proceedings of the 52nd Annual Meeting of the Association for Computational Linguistics (Volume 1: Long Papers)*. Association for Computational Linguistics, Baltimore, Maryland, pages 1555–1565. http://www.aclweb.org/anthology/P14-1146.

Mohamed A Zahran, Ahmed Magooda, Ashraf Y Mahgoub, Hazem Raafat, Mohsen Rashwan, and Amir Atyia. 2015. Word representations in vector space and their applications for arabic. In *International Conference on Intelligent Text Processing and Computational Linguistics*. Springer, pages 430–443.

Zhixin Zhou, Xiuzhen Zhang, and Mark Sanderson. 2014. Sentiment analysis on twitter through topic-based lexicon expansion. In *Databases Theory and Applications*, Springer, pages 98–109.

Senti17 at SemEval-2017 Task 4: Ten Convolutional Neural Network Voters for Tweet Polarity Classification

Hussam Hamdan
Labex Observatoire de la vie littraire (OBVIL)
Laboratoire d'Informatique de Paris 6 (LIP6), Pierre and Marie Curie University, UMR 7606
4 place Jussieu, 75005, Paris, France
Hussam.Hamdan@lip6.fr

Abstract

This paper presents Senti17 system which uses ten convolutional neural networks (ConvNet) to assign a sentiment label to a tweet. The network consists of a convolutional layer followed by a fully-connected layer and a Soft- max on top. Ten instances of this network are initialized with the same word embeddings as inputs but with different initializations for the network weights. We combine the results of all instances by selecting the sentiment label given by the majority of the ten voters. This system is ranked fourth in SemEval-2017 Task4 over 38 systems with 67.4% average recall.

1 Introduction

Polarity classification is the basic task of sentiment analysis in which the polarity of a given text should be classified into three categories: positive, negative or neutral. In Twitter where the tweet is short and written in informal language, this task needs more attention. SemEval has proposed the task of Message Polarity Classification in Twitter since 2013, the objective is to classify a tweet into one of the three polarity labels (Rosenthal et al., 2017).

We can remark that in 2013, 2014 and 2015 most best systems were based on a rich feature extraction process with a traditional classifier such as SVM (Mohammad et al., 2013) or Logistic regression (Hamdan et al., 2015). In 2014, Kim (2014) proposed to use one convolutional neural network for sentence classification, he fixed the size of the input sentence and concatenated its word embeddings

for representing the sentence, this architecture has been exploited in many later works. Severyn and Moschitti (2015) adapted the convolutional network proposed by Kim (2014) for sentiment analysis in Twitter, their system was ranked second in SemEval-2015 while the first system (Hagen et al., 2015) combined four systems based on feature extraction and the third ranked system used logistic regression with different groups of features (Hamdan et al., 2015).

In 2016, we remark that the number of participations which use feature extraction systems were degraded, and the first four systems used Deep Learning, the majority used a convolutional network except the fourth one (Amir et al., 2016). Despite of that, using Deep Learning for sentiment analysis in Twitter has not yet shown a big improvement in comparison to feature extraction, the fifth and sixth systems (Hamdan, 2016) in 2016 which were built upon feature extraction process were only (3 and 3.5% respectively) less than the first system. But We think that Deep Learning is a promising direction in sentiment analysis. Therefore, we proposed to use convolutional networks for Twitter polarity classification.

Our proposed system consists of a convolutional layer followed by fully connected layer and a softmax on top. This is inspired by Kim (2014), we just added a fully connected layer. This architecture gives a good performance but it could be improved. Regarding the best system in 2016 (Deriu et al., 2016), it uses different word embeddings for initialisation then it combines the predictions of different nets using a meta-classifier, Word2vec and Glove have been used to vary the tweet representation.

Proceedings of the 11th International Workshop on Semantic Evaluations (SemEval-2017), pages 700–703,
Vancouver, Canada, August 3 - 4, 2017. ©2017 Association for Computational Linguistics

In our work, we propose to vary the neural network weights instead of tweet representation which can get the same effect of varying the word embeddings, therefore we vary the initial weights of the network to produce ten different nets, a voting system over the these ten voters will decide the sentiment label for a tweet.

The remaining of this paper is organized as follows: Section 2 describes the system architecture, Section 3 presents our experiments and results and Section 4 is devoted for the conclusion.

2 System Architecture

The architecture of our convolutional neural network for sentiment classification is shown on Fig. 1. Our network is composed of a single convolutional layer followed by a non-linearity, max pooling, Dropout, fully connected layer and a soft-max classification layer. Here we describe this architecture:

2.1 Tweet Representation

We first tokenize each tweet to get all terms using HappyTokenizer[1] which captures the words, emoticons and punctuations. We also replace each web link by the term *url* and each user name by *uuser*. Then, we used Structured Skip-Gram embeddings (SSG) (Ling et al., 2015) which was compiled by (Amir et al., 2016) using 52 million tweets.

Each term in the tweet is replaced by its SSG embedding which is a vector of d dimensions, all term vectors are concatenated to form the input matrix where the number of rows is d and the number of columns is set to be maxl: the max tweet length in the training dataset. This 2-dim matrix is the input layer for the neural network.

2.2 Convolutional Layers

We connect the input matrix with different convolutional layers, each one applies a convolution operation between the input matrix and a filter of size m x d. This is an element-wise operation which creates f vectors of $maxl\text{-}m\text{+}1$ dimension where f is the number of filters or feature maps.

This layer is supposed to capture the common patterns among the training tweets which have the same

___
[1] http://sentiment.christopherpotts.net/tokenizing.html

filter size but occur at any position of the tweet. To capture the common patterns which have different sizes we have to use more than one layer therefore we defined 8 different layers connected to the input matrix with different filter sizes but the same number of feature maps.

2.3 Activation Layer

Each convolutional layer is typically followed by a non-linear activation function, RELU (Rectified Linear Unit) layer will apply an element-wise operation to swap the negative numbers to 0. The output of a ReLU layer is the same size as the input, just with all the negative values removed. It speeds up the training and is supposed to produce more accurate results.

2.4 Max-Pooling Layer

This layer reduces the size of the output of activation layer, for each vector it selects the max value. Different variation of pooling layer can be used: average or k-max pooling.

2.5 Dropout Layer

Dropout is used after the max pooling to regularize the ConvNet and prevent overfitting. It assumes that we can still obtain a reasonable classification even when some of the neurones are dropped. Dropout consists in randomly setting a fraction p of input units to 0 at each update during training time.

2.6 Fully Conected Layer

We concatenate the results of all pooling layers after applying Dropout, these units are connected to a fully connected layer. This layer performs a matrix multiplication between its weights and the input units. A RELU non-linarity is applied on the results of this layer.

2.7 Softmax Layer

The output of the fully connected layer is passed to a Softmax layer. It computes the probability distribution over the labels in order to decide the most probable label for a tweet.

3 Experiments and Results

For training the network, we used about 30000 English tweets provided by SemEval organisers and

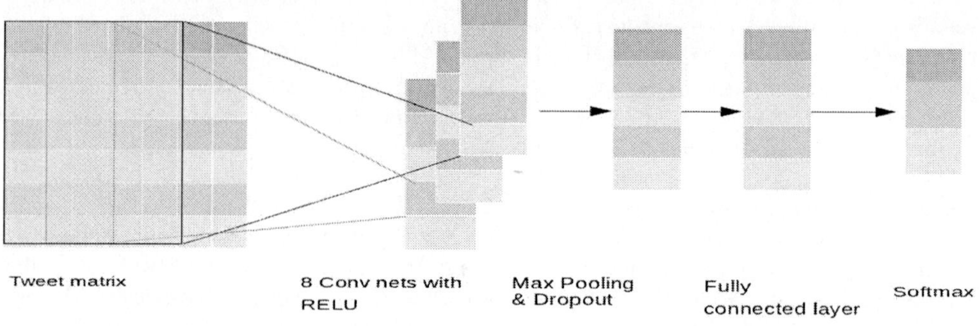

Figure 1: Network architecture.

the test set of 2016 which contains 12000 tweets as development set. The test set of 2017 is used to evaluate the system in SemEval-2017 competition. For implementing our system we used python and Keras[2].

We set the network parameters as follows: SSG embbeding size d is chosen to be 200, the tweet max legnth *maxl* is 99. For convolutional layers, we set the number of feature maps f to 50 and used 8 filter sizes (1,2,3,4,5,2,3,4). The p value of Dropout layer is set to 0.3. We used Nadam optimizer (Dozat, 2015) to update the weights of the network and back-propogation algorithm to compute the gradients. The batch size is set to be 50 and the training data is shuffled after each iteration.

We create ten instances of this network, we randomly initialize them using the uniform distribution, we repeat the random initialization for each instance 100 times, then we pick the networks which gives the highest average recall score as it is considered the official measure for system ranking. If the top network of each instance gives more than 95% of its results identical to another chosen network, we choose the next top networks to make sure that the ten networks are enough different.

Thus, we have ten classifiers, we count the number of classifiers which give the positive, negative and neutral sentiment label to each tweet and select the sentiment label which have the highest number of votes. For each new tweet from the test set, we convert it to 2-dim matrix, if the tweet is longer than

maxl, it will be truncated. We then feed it into the ten networks and pass the results to the voting system.

Official ranking: Our system is ranked fourth over 38 systems in terms of macro-average recall. Table 4 shows the results of our system on the test set of 2016 and 2017.

Test Dataset	Avg. Recall	Accuracy	F-score
Test 2017	0.674	0.652	0.665
Test 2016	0.692	0.650	0.643

Table 1: Table 1: Senti17 results on the test sets of 2016 and 2017.

4 Conclusion

We presented our deep learning approach to Twitter sentiment analysis. We used ten convolutional neural network voters to get the polarity of a tweet, each voter has been trained on the same training data using the same word embeddings but different initial weights. The results demonstrate that our system is competitive as it is ranked forth in SemEval-2017 task 4-A.

References

Silvio Amir, Ramn Fernndez Astudillo, Wang Ling, Mrio J. Silva, and Isabel Trancoso. 2016. INESC-ID at SemEval-2016 Task 4-A: Reducing the Problem of Out-of-Embedding Words. In *SemEval@NAACL-HLT*.

Jan Deriu, Maurice Gonzenbach, Fatih Uzdilli, Aurlien Lucchi, Valeria De Luca, and Martin Jaggi. 2016. SwissCheese at SemEval-2016 Task 4: Senti-

---

[2]https://keras.io

ment Classification Using an Ensemble of Convolutional Neural Networks with Distant Supervision. In *SemEval@NAACL-HLT*.

Timothy Dozat. 2015. Incorporating Nesterov Momentum into Adam.

Matthias Hagen, Martin Potthast, Michel Bchner, and Benno Stein. 2015. Webis: An Ensemble for Twitter Sentiment Detection.

Hussam Hamdan, Patrice Bellot, and Frederic Bechet. 2015. Lsislif: Feature Extraction and Label Weighting for Sentiment Analysis in Twitter. In *Proceedings of the 9th International Workshop on Semantic Evaluation (SemEval 2015)*, pages 568–573, Denver, Colorado, June. Association for Computational Linguistics.

Hussam Hamdan. 2016. SentiSys at SemEval-2016 Task 4: Feature-Based System for Sentiment Analysis in Twitter. In *SemEval@NAACL-HLT*.

Yoon Kim. 2014. Convolutional Neural Networks for Sentence Classification. *CoRR*, abs/1408.5882.

Wang Ling, Chris Dyer, Alan Black, and Isabel Trancoso. 2015. Two/Too Simple Adaptations of word2vec for Syntax Problems. In *Proceedings of the 2015 Conference of the North American Chapter of the Association for Computational Linguistics: Human Language Technologies*, Denver, Colorado. Association for Computational Linguistics.

Saif M. Mohammad, Svetlana Kiritchenko, and Xiaodan Zhu. 2013. NRCCanada: Building the State-of-the-Art in Sentiment Analysis of Tweets. In *In Proceedings of the International Workshop on Semantic Evaluation, SemEval 13*.

Sara Rosenthal, Noura Farra, and Preslav Nakov. 2017. SemEval-2017 Task 4: Sentiment Analysis in Twitter. In *Proceedings of the 11th International Workshop on Semantic Evaluation*, SemEval '17, Vancouver, Canada, August. Association for Computational Linguistics.

Aliaksei Severyn and Alessandro Moschitti. 2015. UNITN: Training Deep Convolutional Neural Network for Twitter Sentiment Classification. In *Proceedings of the 9th International Workshop on Semantic Evaluation (SemEval 2015)*, pages 464–469, Denver, Colorado, June. Association for Computational Linguistics.

DUTH at SemEval-2017 Task 4:
A Voting Classification Approach for Twitter Sentiment Analysis

Symeon Symeonidis **Dimitrios Effrosynidis** **John Kordonis** **Avi Arampatzis**

Database & Information Retrieval research unit,
Department of Electrical & Computer Engineering,
Democritus University of Thrace, Xanthi 67100, Greece
{ssymeoni,dimievfr,ioankordl,avi}@ee.duth.gr

Abstract

This report describes our participation to SemEval-2017 Task 4: Sentiment Analysis in Twitter, specifically in subtasks A, B, and C. The approach for text sentiment classification is based on a Majority Vote scheme and combined supervised machine learning methods with classical linguistic resources, including bag-of-words and sentiment lexicon features.

1 Introduction

For millions of users, microblogging services such as Twitter, a popular service where users can post no more than 140 characters status messages, have become an elemental part of daily life. By using tools and techniques from Natural Language Processing (NLP) and machine learning, Sentiment analysis is defined as the process to identify and analyze polarity from short texts, sentences, and documents (Pang et al., 2008).

In the last few years, people from different research disciplines are interested in Sentiment Analysis, and the SemEval workshop offers an opportunity to compete and work in this field. Our team has participated in SemEval-2017 task 4 on Sentiment Analysis in Twitter, more specifically on subtasks A (Message Polarity Classification), B, and C (Tweet Classification in either two-point or five-point scale respectively) (Rosenthal et al., 2017).

In this report, we present an ensemble text sentiment classification scheme, based on an extensive empirical analysis of several classifiers and other related works, e.g. (Balahur, 2013; Martínez-Cámara et al., 2014; Balikas and Amini, 2016; Onan et al., 2016). A voting scheme combines learning algorithms to identify and select an optimal set of base learning algorithms. These components were carefully combined and optimized to create a separate version of the system for each of the tackled subtasks.

The rest of this report is organized as follows. The description of proposed system we used and its feature extraction are presented in Section 2. Section 3 reports our experiments. Conclusions and directions for further work/research are summarized in Section 4.

2 System Description

The main objective of SemEval-2017 Task 4 is sentiment classification. The system we used is based on the bag-of-words representation, n-gram extraction, and usage of lexicons which have a pre-defined sentiment for every uni-gram and bi-gram. For the implementation of the system we used Python's Scikit-Learn (Pedregosa et al., 2011), as well as NLTK (Natural Language Toolkit) (Bird et al., 2009).

2.1 Pre-processing

The pre-processing steps that we followed were to remove and replace strings from the tweets that do not show any sentiment, as well as to remove duplicates and unicode strings:

- Removing duplicates: we found that some instances were duplicates, e.g. in Subtask A, so we removed them.

- Replacing hashtags, URLs and usernames: we first removed the "#" character in front of the words and replaced the twitter oriented strings @usernames and the URLs with tags such as "AT_USER" and "URL" respectively.

- Removing unicode strings: there were many Unicode strings especially in the testing data, e.g. strings like "\u002c" and "x96".

Proceedings of the 11th International Workshop on Semantic Evaluations (SemEval-2017), pages 704–708,
Vancouver, Canada, August 3 - 4, 2017. ©2017 Association for Computational Linguistics

	Positive	**Negative**	**Neutral**	**Total**
train	18377 (38%)	7442 (16%)	22012 (46%)	47831
dev	2412 (43%)	1056 (18%)	2185 (39%)	5653
test	2375 (19%)	3972 (32%)	5937 (49%)	12284

Table 1: Number of tweets in training (train), development (dev), and testing (test) data for subtask A.

- Removing numbers and punctuation: preliminary experiments showed better results when we removed all the numbers. Before removing punctuation, we detected useful punctuation signs such as "!" and "?" and replaced them with labels.

- Using lowercase and tokenization: the final tweets were lower-cased (after detecting words that had all of their character capitalized which were retained) and splitted into tokens.

- Removing stop words: stopwords are common function words with very high frequency among sentences and low content, so we removed them.

- Using stemming: stemming is the process of reducing a word to its base root form. Preliminary tests showed that stemming improves a lot the results.

Previous studies (Pak and Paroubek, 2010; Bakliwal et al., 2013) have made references on the influence of pre-processing and proposed a set of features to extract the maximum sentimental information.

2.2 Feature Engineering

We extracted features based on the lexical content of each tweet and we also used lexicons. Below we present all the features.

- Word n-grams: the word level uni-grams and bi-grams are adopted.

- Number of capitalized words

- Number of question marks, exclamation marks and the aggregation of them

- Number of elongated words: it indicates the number of elongated words in the raw text of the tweet.

To identify the sentiment polarity of tweets, we used three different sentiment lexicons during our experiments. Sentiment lexicons are lexical resources which are formed by a list of words without any additional information and are built by opinion words and some sentiment phrases (Martínez-Cámara et al., 2014).

In our system we used sentiment lexicons such as Bing Liu's lexicon (Hu and Liu, 2004), the NRC emotion lexicon (Mohammad and Turney, 2010), the MPQA lexicon (Wilson et al., 2005) and combinations of them. The above lexicons have a sentiment tag for each word and in our approach we count the occurrences of each sentiment class for each tweet's word. Finally, we compute the overall sentiment of the tweet, by adding its words sentiments.

3 Experiments

In this section, after the feature extraction, we analyse the classification process with the learning methods and classification algorithms that used in our system.

3.1 Datasets

The datasets were provided by the organizers and contained all datasets of the previous years with the addition of a new. For Subtask A the available datasets were all the training, development, and testing data from the years 2013 to 2016. For Subtask B the available datasets were from the years 2015 to 2016, and for Subtask C from the year 2016. We used a portion of the data for development and the rest for training. We present them in Tables 1–3.

	Positive	**Negative**	**Total**
train	12812 (79%)	3410 (21%)	16222
dev	2139 (78%)	604 (22%)	2743
test	2463 (40%)	3722 (60%)	6185

Table 2: Number of tweets in training (train), development (dev), testing (test) data for subtask B.

	2	1	0	-1	-2	Total
train	819 (3%)	10984 (41%)	11735 (44%)	2869 (11%)	225 (1%)	26632
dev	201 (5%)	1938 (48%)	1258 (31%)	529 (13%)	74 (3%)	4000
test	131 (1%)	2332 (19%)	6194 (50%)	3545 (29%)	177 (1%)	12379

Table 3: Number of tweets in training (train), development (dev), testing (test) data for subtask C.

As we can observe from the tables, the testing data that were provided by the organizers have different ratio among the classes, especially between the positives and negatives.

3.2 Evaluation Metrics

For Subtask A, we use the macro-average recall, which is the recall averaged across the three classes $R_{macro} = \frac{R_{pos} + R_{neu} + R_{neg}}{3}$. Subtask B maintains the same measure, but among the two classes $R_{macro} = \frac{R_{pos} + R_{neg}}{2}$. For Subtask C, the official metrics are the macro-averaged mean absolute error and the extension of macro-averaged recall for ordinal regression (Rosenthal et al., 2017) among 5 predefined classes.

3.3 Learning

Using all the features described above, we first trained several classifiers to the development data in order to tune the parameters of each classifier. The main target of tuning was the metric of this specific task, which is the macro-average recall. We tested a variety of classifiers that include the following:

- Ridge: an algorithm belonging to the Generalized Linear Models family that alleviates the multicollinearity amongst predictor variables.

- Logistic Regression: despite its name it is used for classification and fits a linear model. It is also known as Maximum Entropy, and uses a logistic function to model the probabilities that describe the output prediction.

- Stochastic Gradient Descent: a simple and efficient algorithm to fit linear models. It is suitable for very large number of features.

- Nearest Centroid: an algorithm that uses the center of a class, called centroid, to represent it and has no parameters.

- Bernoulli Naïve Bayes: an alternative of Naïve Bayes, where each term is equal to 1 if it exists in the sentence and 0 if not. Its difference from Boolean Naïve Bayes is that it takes into account terms that do not appear in the sentence.

- Linear SVC: an SVM algorithm, which tries to find a set of hyperplanes that separate space into dimensions representing classes. The hyperplanes are chosen in a way to maximize the distance from the nearest data point of each class.

- Passive-Aggressive: belongs to a family of algorithms for large-scale learning, which do not require a learning rate and includes a regularization parameter C (Pedregosa et al., 2011).

In order to vectorize the collection of raw documents, we used a Python's Scikit-Learn (Pedregosa et al., 2011) *tf-idf* transformation with a *max_df* parameter of 0.5. The value of this parameter was extracted by the tuning process and indicates that we ignore terms that have a frequency strictly higher than this threshold. The next step was to use these parameters to test our model with the help of 10-fold cross-validation on the training set.

3.3.1 Subtask A

Subtask A is a multi-class classification problem, where each tweet has to be classified in one among three classes. We found that the best combination for this task was the use of stemming and the three lexicons. Features like the number of exclamation marks, etc., under-performed. The three classifiers with the best results were the Bernoulli Naïve Bayes, the Stochastic Gradient Descent (SGD), and the Linear SVC.

The final step was to use the majority voting classification method that combines three different classifiers and outputs the class that the majority of them agreed. Using all possible combinations of every three classifiers, the best result was with the Bernoulli Naïve Bayes, SGD, and Nearest Centroid. Note that Nearest Centroid was one of the weakest classifiers in isolation, but presented an excellent contribution when combined with other two.

3.3.2 Subtask B

Subtask B is a topic-based binary classification problem, where each tweet belongs to a topic, and one has to classify whether the tweet conveys a positive or negative sentiment towards the topic. We used the same approach with Subtask A, with the addition of a weight for the topic which was added as a feature. The best combination was the use of stemming and the three lexicons, like in subtask A. The three best classifiers were the SGD, the Passive-Aggressive, and the Linear SVC.

The majority voting classifier outperformed all the single classifiers; here, the best result was with the SGD, Logistic Regression, and Ridge classifiers, showing once again that weak classifiers can contribute significantly when combined with others.

3.3.3 Subtask C

Subtask C is also a topic-based classification problem, where each tweet belongs to a topic, and one has to estimate the sentiment conveyed by the tweet towards the topic on a five-point scale. The same approach as with Subtask B was used, and the best result was achieved by the combination of the Logistic Regression, the Nearest Centroid, and the Bernoulli Naïve Bayes classifiers.

	ρ	F_1^{PN}	Acc
Task A	0.621	0.605	0.640
Task B	0.663	0.600	0.607
	(MAE^M)	(MAE^μ)	
Task C	0.895	0.544	

Table 4: DUTH's results for SemEval-2017 Task 4 on Sentiment Analysis in Twitter (Rosenthal et al., 2017).

4 Conclusions & Future work

By analyzing and classifying sentiments on Twitter, people can comprehend attitudes about particular topics, making Sentiment Analysis an attractive research area. In this report we presented an approach for Twitter sentiment analysis on two-point, three-point, and five-point scale, based on a voting classification method. This was our first contact with the task of sentiment analysis and compared with the top-ranked participating systems, there seems to be for us much room for improvement.

In future work, we consider to focus on adding more pre-processing methods such as spelling correction and POS tagging. We also consider adding more features such as emoticons, negation, character n-grams and more lexicons.

References

Akshat Bakliwal, Jennifer Foster, Jennifer van der Puil, Ron O'Brien, Lamia Tounsi, and Mark Hughes. 2013. Sentiment analysis of political tweets: Towards an accurate classifier. Association for Computational Linguistics.

Alexandra Balahur. 2013. Sentiment analysis in social media texts. In *4th workshop on computational approaches to subjectivity, sentiment and social media analysis*. pages 120–128.

Georgios Balikas and Massih-Reza Amini. 2016. Twise at semeval-2016 task 4: Twitter sentiment classification. In *Proceedings of the 10th International Workshop on Semantic Evaluation (SemEval-2016)*. Association for Computational Linguistics, San Diego, California, pages 85–91. http://www.aclweb.org/anthology/S16-1010.

Steven Bird, Ewan Klein, and Edward Loper. 2009. *Natural language processing with Python: analyzing text with the natural language toolkit.* " O'Reilly Media, Inc.".

Minqing Hu and Bing Liu. 2004. Mining and summarizing customer reviews. In *Proceedings of the Tenth ACM SIGKDD International Conference on Knowledge Discovery and Data Mining*. ACM, New York, NY, USA, KDD '04, pages 168–177. https://doi.org/10.1145/1014052.1014073.

Eugenio Martínez-Cámara, Salud María Jiménez-Zafra, Maite Martin, and L. Alfonso Urena Lopez. 2014. Sinai: Voting system for twitter sentiment analysis. In *Proceedings of the 8th International Workshop on Semantic Evaluation (SemEval 2014)*. Association for Computational Linguistics and Dublin City University, Dublin, Ireland, pages 572–577. http://www.aclweb.org/anthology/S14-2100.

Saif M. Mohammad and Peter D. Turney. 2010. Emotions evoked by common words and phrases: Using mechanical turk to create an emotion lexicon. In *Proceedings of the NAACL HLT 2010 Workshop on Computational Approaches to Analysis and Generation of Emotion in Text*. Association for Computational Linguistics, Stroudsburg, PA, USA, CAAGET '10, pages 26–34. http://dl.acm.org/citation.cfm?id=1860631.1860635.

Aytu Onan, Serdar Korukolu, and Hasan Bulut. 2016. A multiobjective weighted voting ensemble classifier based on differential evolution algorithm for text sentiment classification. *Expert Systems with Applications* 62:1 – 16.

Alexander Pak and Patrick Paroubek. 2010. Twitter as a corpus for sentiment analysis and opinion mining. In *LREc*. volume 10.

Bo Pang, Lillian Lee, et al. 2008. Opinion mining and sentiment analysis. *Foundations and Trends® in Information Retrieval* 2(1–2):1–135.

Fabian Pedregosa, Gaël Varoquaux, Alexandre Gramfort, Vincent Michel, Bertrand Thirion, Olivier Grisel, Mathieu Blondel, Peter Prettenhofer, Ron Weiss, Vincent Dubourg, Jake Vanderplas, Alexandre Passos, David Cournapeau, Matthieu Brucher, Matthieu Perrot, and Édouard Duchesnay. 2011. Scikit-learn: Machine learning in python. *J. Mach. Learn. Res.* 12:2825–2830. http://dl.acm.org/citation.cfm?id=1953048.2078195.

Sara Rosenthal, Noura Farra, and Preslav Nakov. 2017. Semeval-2017 task 4: Sentiment analysis in twitter. In *Proceedings of the 11th International Workshop on Semantic Evaluation (SemEval-2017)*. Association for Computational Linguistics, Vancouver, Canada, pages 501–516. http://www.aclweb.org/anthology/S17-2088.

Theresa Wilson, Janyce Wiebe, and Paul Hoffmann. 2005. Recognizing contextual polarity in phrase-level sentiment analysis. In *Proceedings of the Conference on Human Language Technology and Empirical Methods in Natural Language Processing*. Association for Computational Linguistics, Stroudsburg, PA, USA, HLT '05, pages 347–354. https://doi.org/10.3115/1220575.1220619.

SSN_MLRG1 at SemEval-2017 Task 4: Sentiment Analysis in Twitter Using Multi-Kernel Gaussian Process Classifier

Angel Deborah S, S Milton Rajendram, T T Mirnalinee
SSN College of Engineering
Kalavakkam 603 110, India
`angeldeboarahs@ssn.edu.in`

Abstract

The SSN_MLRG1 team for Semeval-2017 task 4 has applied Gaussian Process, with bag of words feature vectors and fixed rule multi-kernel learning, for sentiment analysis of tweets. Since tweets on the same topic, made at different times, may exhibit different emotions, their properties such as smoothness and periodicity also vary with time. Our experiments show that, compared to single kernel, multiple kernels are effective in learning the simultaneous presence of multiple properties.

1 Introduction

Twitter is a huge microblogging service with more than 500 million tweets per day from different locations of the world and in different languages (Nabil et al., 2016). The sentiment analysis in Twitter has been applied in various domains such as commerce (Jansen et al., 2009), disaster management (Verma et al., 2011) and health (Chew and Eysenbach, 2010). The task is challenging because of the informal writing style, the semantic diversity of content as well as the "unconventional" grammar. These challenges in building a classification model can be handled by using proper approaches to feature generation and machine learning.

The heart of every Gaussian process model is a covariance kernel. Multi Kernel Learning (MKL)—using multiple kernels instead of a single one—can be useful in two ways:

- Different kernels correspond to different notions of similarity, and instead of trying to find which works best, a learning method does the picking for us, or may use a combination of them. Using a specific kernel may be a source of bias which is avoided by allow- ing the learner to choose from among a set of kernels.
- Different kernels may use inputs coming from different representations, possibly from different sources or modalities.

(Gonen and Alpaydn, 2011) and (Wilson and Adams, 2013) explain how multiple kernels definitely give a powerful performance. (Gonen and Alpaydn, 2011) also describe in detail various methodologies to combine kernels. (Wilson and Adams, 2013) introduces simple closed form kernels that can be used with Gaussian Processes to discover patterns and enable extrapolation. The kernels support a broad class of stationary covariances, but Gaussian Process inference remains simple and analytic.

We studied the possibility of using multiple kernels to explain the relation between the input data and the labels. While there is a body of work on using Multi Kernel Learning (MKL) on numerical data and images, yet applying MKL on text is still an exploration.

2 Gaussian Process

Gaussian Process is a non-parametric Bayesian modelling in supervised setting. Gaussian process is a collection of random variables, any finite number of which have a joint Gaussian distribution (Rasmussen and Williams, 2006). Using a Gaussian process, we can define a distribution over functions $f(x)$,

$$f(\mathbf{x}) \sim GP(m(\mathbf{x}), k(\mathbf{x}, \mathbf{x}')) \qquad (1)$$

where $m(\mathbf{x})$ is the mean function, usually defined to be zero, and $k(\mathbf{x}, \mathbf{x}')$ is the covariance function (or kernel function) that defines the prior properties of the functions considered for inference. Gaussian Process has the following main advantages (Cohn and Specia, 2013; Cohn et al., 2014).

Proceedings of the 11th International Workshop on Semantic Evaluations (SemEval-2017), pages 709–712,
Vancouver, Canada, August 3 - 4, 2017. ©2017 Association for Computational Linguistics

- The kernel hyper-parameters can be learned via evidence maximization.
- GP provides full probabilistic prediction, and an estimate of uncertainty in the prediction.
- Unlike SVMs which need unbiased version of dataset for probabilistic prediction, yet does not take into account the uncertainty of $f(\mathbf{x})$, GP does not suffer from this problem.
- GP can be easily extended and incorporated into a hierarchical Bayesian model.
- GP works really well when combined with kernel models.
- GP works well for small datasets too.

2.1 Gaussian Process Classification

In Gaussian Process Classification (GPC), we place a GP prior over a latent function $f(\mathbf{x})$ and then "squash" this prior through the logistic function to obtain a prior on $\pi(\mathbf{x}) \triangleq p(y = +1|\mathbf{x}) = \sigma(f(\mathbf{x}))$. Note that π is a deterministic function of f, and since f is stochastic, so is π.

Inference is divided into two steps: first, computing the distribution of the latent variable corresponding to a test case

$$p(f_*|X, \mathbf{y}, \mathbf{x}_*) = \int p(f_*|X, \mathbf{x}_*, \mathbf{f})p(\mathbf{f}|X, \mathbf{y})d\mathbf{f} \tag{2}$$

where $p(\mathbf{f}|X, \mathbf{y}) = p(\mathbf{y}|\mathbf{f})p(\mathbf{f}|X)/p(\mathbf{y}|X)$ is the posterior over the latent variables, and subsequently using this distribution over the latent to produce a probabilistic prediction

$$\pi_*(x) \triangleq (y_* = +1|X, \mathbf{y}, \mathbf{x}_*) \tag{3}$$

$$= \int \sigma(f_*)p(f_*|X, \mathbf{y}, \mathbf{x}_*)df_* \tag{4}$$

In classification, the non-Gaussian likelihood in Equation 2 makes the integral analytically intractable. Similarly, Equation 4 can also be analytically intractable for certain sigmoid functions. Therefore, we need an analytical approximation of integrals. We can approximate the non-Gaussian joint posterior with a Gaussian one, using Expectation Propagation (EP) method (Minka, 2001). EP, however, uses the probit likelihood

$$p(y_i|f_i) = \Phi(f_i y_i), \tag{5}$$

which makes the posterior analytically intractable. To overcome this hurdle in the EP framework, the likelihood is approximated by a *local likelihood approximation* in the form of an un-normalized

Gaussian function in the latent variable f_i which defines the *site parameters* $\tilde{Z}_i$, $\tilde{\mu}_i$ and $\tilde{\sigma}_i^2$.

$$p(y_i|f_i) \simeq t_i(f_i|\tilde{Z}_i, \tilde{\mu}_i, \tilde{\sigma}_i^2) \triangleq \tilde{Z}_i \mathcal{N}(f_i|\tilde{\mu}_i, \tilde{\sigma}_i^2) \tag{6}$$

The posterior $p(\mathbf{f}|X, \mathbf{y})$ is approximated by $q(\mathbf{f}|X, \mathbf{y}) = \mathcal{N}(\mu, \Sigma)$, where $\mu = \Sigma\tilde{\Sigma}^{-1}\tilde{\mu}$, $\tilde{\Sigma}$ is diagonal with $\tilde{\Sigma}_{ii} = \tilde{\sigma}_i^2$, $\Sigma = (K^{-1} + \tilde{\Sigma}^{-1})^{-1}$, and K is the covariance matrix.

A practical implementation of Gaussian Process Classification (GPC) for binary class (Rasmussen and Williams, 2006) is outlined in the following algorithm:

Algorithm: Predictions for Expectation Propagation GPC.
Input:$\tilde{\nu}$, $\tilde{\tau}$ (Natural site param), X (Training inputs), $\mathbf{y}$ (Training targets), k (Covariance function), x_* (Test input).
Output: Predictive class probability.
1. $L := \text{cholesky}(I_n + \tilde{S}^{1/2}K\tilde{S}^{1/2})$
2. $z := \tilde{S}^{1/2}L^T\backslash(L\backslash\tilde{S}^{1/2}K\tilde{\nu})$
3. $\overline{f}_* := \mathbf{k}(\mathbf{x}_*)^T(\tilde{\nu} - z)$
4. $\mathbf{v} := L\backslash(\tilde{S}^{1/2}\mathbf{k}(\mathbf{x}_*))$
5. $V[f_*] := k(\mathbf{x}_*, \mathbf{x}_*) - \mathbf{v}^T\mathbf{v}$
6. $\overline{\pi}_* := \Phi(\overline{f}_*/\sqrt{1 + V[f_*]})$
7. **return**: $\overline{\pi}_*$ (predictive class probability)

The natural site parameters $\tilde{\nu}$ and $\tilde{\tau}$ for Expectation Propagation GPC are found using EP approximation algorithm. Multi-class classification can be performed using either one-versus-rest or one-versus-one for training and prediction. For Gaussian Process classification, "one-vs-one" might be computationally cheaper, so we have used it to for subtasks A and C.

2.2 Multiple Kernel Gaussian Process

The covariance kernel $\mathbf{k}$ of Gaussian Process directly specifies the covariance between every pair of input points in the dataset. The particular choice of covariance function determines the properties such as smoothness, length scales, and amplitude, drawn from the GP prior.

We have used Exponential kernel and Multi-Layer Perceptron kernel combined with Squared Exponential kernel, and found the combinations to give better results. The text data used in sentiment analysis is collected over a period of time. Comments on the same topic may exhibit different emotions, depending on the time it was made, and hence their properties, such as smoothness and periodicity, also vary with time. Since any one kernel learns only certain properties well, multiple kernels are effective in detecting the simultaneous presence of different emotions in the data.

The MKL algorithms use different learning methods for determining the kernel combination function. It is divided into five major categories: Fixed rules, Heuristic approaches, Optimization approaches, Bayesian approaches and Boosting approaches. The combination of kernels in different learning methods can be performed in one of the two basic ways, either using linear combination or using non-linear combination. Linear combination seems more promising (Gonen and Alpaydn, 2011), and have two basic categories: unweighted sum (i.e., using sum or mean of the kernels as the combined kernel) and weighted sum. Non-linear combination uses non-linear functions of kernels, namely multiplication, power, and exponentiation. We have studied the fixed rule linear combination in this work which can be represented as

$$\mathbf{k}(x, x') = \mathbf{k_1}(x, x') + \mathbf{k_2}(x, x') + \ldots + \mathbf{k_n}(x, x'). \tag{7}$$

For training, we have used one-step method together with the simultaneous approach. One-step methods, in a single pass, calculate both the parameters of the combination function, and those of the combined base learner; and the simultaneous approach ensures that both sets of parameters are learned together.

3 System Overview

The system comprises of the following modules: data extraction, preprocessing, feature vector generation, and multi-kernel Gaussian Process model building. The data is preprocessed with lemmatization and tokenization, using NLTK toolkit. Then train variable is assigned an integer value. A data dictionary is built using training sentences, and feature vectors for train sets are generated by encoding BoW representation. These feature vectors are given as input to build the MKGPC model.

The Multi-Kernel Gaussian Process Classification (MKGPC) model building is outlined in the following algorithm.

Algorithm: Build a Multi-Kernel Gaussian Process model.

Input: Input dataset with BoW feature representation.

Output: Learned model.

begin
1. Split the training dataset into XTrain which contains the features and YTrain that contains the emotion scores.
2. Build the initial classification model using appropriate kernel function.
3. Optimize the classification model with the hyper-parameters (length scale, variance, noise).
4. Return the learned model.

end

There are different kernels that can be used to build a GPC model. The *Squared Exponential (SE)* kernel, sometimes called the Gaussian or Radial Basis Function (RBF), has become the default kernel in GPs. To model the long-term smooth-rising trend, we use a Squared Exponential covariance term.

$$\mathbf{k}(x, x') = \sigma^2 \exp\left(-\frac{(x - x')^2}{2l^2}\right). \tag{8}$$

where σ^2 is the variance and l is the length-scale.

The usage of *Exponential kernel* is particularly common in machine learning and hence is also used in GPs. They perform tasks such as statistical classification, regression analysis, and cluster analysis on data in an implicit space.

$$\mathbf{k}(x, x') = \sigma^2 \exp\left(-\frac{(x - x')}{2l^2}\right) \tag{9}$$

The *Multi-Layer Perceptron* kernel has also found use in GP as it can learn the periodicity property present in the dataset; its $\mathbf{k}(x, x')$ is given by

$$\frac{2\sigma^2}{\pi} \sin^{-1} \frac{(\sigma_w^2 x^T x' + \sigma_b^2)}{\sqrt{\sigma_w^2 x^T x + \sigma_b^2 + 1}\sqrt{\sigma_w^2 x'^T x' \sigma_b^2 + 1}} \tag{10}$$

where σ^2 is the variance, σ_w^2 is the vector of the variances of the prior over input weights and σ_b^2 is the variance of the prior over bias parameters. The kernel can learn more effectively because of the additional parameters σ_w^2 and σ_b^2.

4 Results and Discussion

The output submitted for the task was obtained using MKGPC with Radial Basis Function kernel and Exponential Kernel. We also used Multi-Layer Perceptron Kernel. The results of the SGPC using SE kernel for subtask B and MKGPC for subtask B are shown in Table 1. The evaluation was done on SemEval-2017 labeled test dataset. Only 1000 tweets were used to train the model due to the time-complexity of GP and hardware limitations, and from among the remaining 9551 tweets test set was taken.

Table 1: A Performance Evaluation based on Recall, F-measure and Precision (all macro-averaged) for subtask B

Model	Recall	F-measure	Precision
SGPC	0.57	0.58	0.64
MKGPC(R+E)	0.56	0.56	0.63
MKGPC(R+M)	0.61	0.62	0.64
MKGPC(R+E+M)	0.62	0.63	0.64

The kernel combinations used in Table 1 are
SGPC: Single Kernel Gaussian Process Classifier with Radial Basis Function (RBF) kernel,
MKGPC(R+E): Multi Kernel Gaussian Process with sum of RBF and Exponential kernels,
MKGPC(R+E+M): Multi Kernel Gaussian Process Classifier with sum of RBF, Exponential, and Multi-Layer Perceptron kernels,
MKGPC(R+M): Multi Kernel Gaussian Process Classifier with sum of RBF and Multi-Layer Perceptron kernels.

We observe from Table 1 that though the macro-averaged precision of the MKGPC models is the same as SGPC, their macro-averaged recall and F-measure are better than SGPC (except for MKGPC(R+E)), because the Multi-Layer Perceptron kernel learns the periodicity better than RBF and Exponential kernels do. These different models, when evaluated on dataset for subtask A and subtask C, exhibited similar performance as in subtask B. The system underperform compared to the baseline system in task C, and to logistic regression on 1-gram in tasks A and B since only a small fraction of the dataset was used for training.

5 Official Evaluation

Our system scored a macro-averaged recall of 0.431 and was ranked 35 for subtask A, macro-averaged recall of 0.586 and was ranked 20 for subtask B, and macro-averaged mean absolute error of 1.325 and was ranked 15 for subtask C.

6 Conclusion

In this paper, we have presented a Gaussian Process classification model for sentiment analysis in Twitter. We used Bag of Words feature vectors and fixed rule multi kernel learning to build the GP model. We observed that combining Multi-Layer Perceptron kernel improves the performance of the system, perhaps due to its more effective learning of the periodicity property in the dataset. There is scope for enhancing the results by using different feature generation algorithms, different multi-kernel learning approaches, and increasing the data size.

References

C. Chew and G. Eysenbach. 2010. Pandemics in the age of twitter: content analysis of tweets during the 2009 h1n1 outbreak. *PloS ONE* 5(11):1–13.

Trevor Cohn, Daniel Beck, and Lucia Specia. 2014. Joint emotion analysis via multi-task gaussian processes. In *Proceedings of EMNLP 2014, the International Conference onEmpirical Methods in Natural Language Processing*. Journal of Machine Learning Research, pages 1798 – 1803.

Trevor Cohn and Lucia Specia. 2013. Modelling annotator bias with multi-task gaussian processes: An application to machine translation quality estimation. In *Proceedings of the 51st Annual Meeting of the ACL-2013*. ACL, pages 32–42.

Mehmet Gonen and Ethem Alpaydn. 2011. Multiple kernel learning algorithms. *Journal of Machine Learning Research* 24(11):2211 – 2268.

B. J. Jansen, M. Zhang, K. Sobel, and A. Chowdury. 2009. Twitter power: Tweets as electronic word of mouth. *Journal of the American Society for Information Science and Technology* 60(11):21692188.

T P Minka. 2001. *Family of Algorithms for Approximate Bayesian Inference*. PhD thesis, MIT.

Mahmoud Nabil, Mohamed Aly, and Amir F. Atiya. 2016. Cufe at semeval-2016 task 4: A gated recurrent model for sentiment classification. In *Proceedings of SemEval-2016*. ACL, pages 52 –57.

Carl Edward Rasmussen and Christopher K. I. Williams. 2006. *Gaussian processes for machine learning*, volume 1. MIT Press Cambridge.

S. Verma, S. Vieweg, W. J. Corvey, L. Palen, J. H. Martin, M. Palmer, A. Schram, and K. M. Anderson. 2011. Natural language processing to the rescue? extracting situational awareness tweets during mass emergency. In *Proceedings of 5th International Conference on Web and Social Media (ICWSM)*.

A. G. Wilson and R. P. Adams. 2013. Gaussian process kernels for pattern discovery and extrapolation. In *Proceedings of ICML 2013, the International Conference onMachine Learning*. Journal of Machine Learning Research, pages 1067 – 1075.

YNUDLG at SemEval-2017 Task 4: A GRU-SVM Model for Sentiment Classification and Quantification in Twitter

Min Wang[1], Biao Chu[1], Qingxun Liu[1], Xiaobing Zhou[1]

[1]School of Information Science and Engineering, Yunnan University, Yunnan, P.R. China
{1147192499, 372744991, 1243305076, zhouxb.yn}@qq.com

Abstract

Sentiment analysis is one of the central issues in Natural Language Processing and has become more and more important in many fields. Typical sentiment analysis classifies the sentiment of sentences into several discrete classes (e.g.,positive or negative). In this paper we describe our deep learning system(combining GRU and SVM) to solve both two-, three- and five- tweet polarity classifications. We first trained a gated recurrent neural network using pre-trained word embeddings, then we extracted features from GRU layer and input these features into support vector machine to fulfill both the classification and quantification subtasks. The proposed approach achieved 37th, 19th, and 14rd places in subtasks A, B, and C, respectively.

1 Introduction

Sentiment analysis (SA) is a field of knowledge which deals with the analysis of people's opinions, sentiments, evaluations, appraisals, attitudes and emotions towards particular entities (Liu, 2012). Typical approaches to sentiment analysis is to classify the sentiment of a sentence into several discrete classes such as positive and negative polarities, or six basic emotions: anger, happiness, fear, sadness, disgust and surprise (Ekman,1992). SA is widely considered to be one of the most popular and challenging, competitive and the hot research area in computational linguistics. There are many ways to tackle the sentiment classification problems, such as random forest, support vector machine (SVM), Bayes classifier. In addition, there are many cha-

llenges, such as analysis of noise texts (e.g. oral language) in natural language processing tasks, despite numerous notable advances in recently years (e.g., Breck et al,. 2007; Yessenalina and Cardie, 2011; Socher et al,. 2011). Based on this, our way is to extract features with Gated Recurrent Unit (GRU) and classify sentences by SVM using these features.

Task 4 subtask A is to classify a tweet's sentiment as positive, negative, or neutral. Subtask B (Tweet classification according to a two-point scale) requires classifying a tweet's sentiment towards the given topic. Similar to B, subtask C is a five-point scale (Nakov et al., 2016). Unlike typical classification approaches, ordinal classification can assign different ratings (e.g., very negative, negative, neutral, positive and very positive) according to the sentiment strength (Taboada et al., 2011; Li et al., 2011; Yu et al., 2013; Wang and Ester, 2014).

This paper presents a system that combine GRU and SVM to process subtasks A, B and C. Our system uses a GRU neural network with word embeddings (Mikolov et al,. 2013) that are slightly fine-tuned (Yoon Kim et al,. 2014) on each training set. The word embeddings were obtained by training GloVe (Jeffrey Pennington et al,. 2014) on 2 billion tweets that we crawled for this purpose. These word vectors are then used to build sentence vectors through a recurrent convolutional neural network.

The proposed gated recurrent neural network consists of the GRU layer and SVM classifier. The choice based on the following two reasons: (1) it is more computational efficient than Convolution Neural Network (CNN) models (Lai et al., 2015); (2) unlike CNN, it also can extract

713

Proceedings of the 11th International Workshop on Semantic Evaluations (SemEval-2017), pages 713–717,
Vancouver, Canada, August 3 - 4, 2017. ©2017 Association for Computational Linguistics

long semantic patterns without tuning the parameter when training the model. Our system architecture is composed of a word embedding layer, drop out layer, GRU layer, a hyperbolic relu layer, SVM classifier and softmax layer.

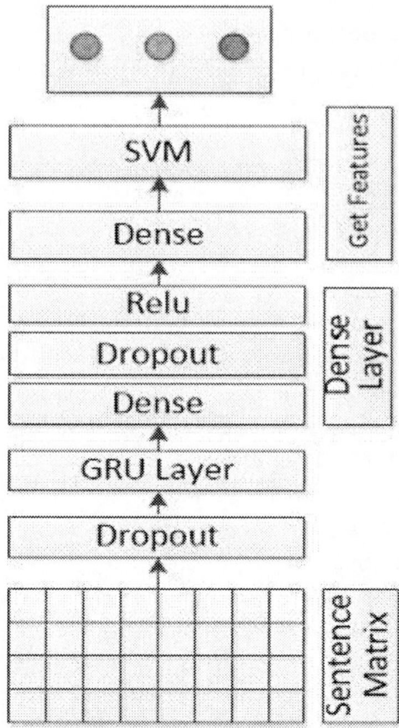

Figure 1: The architecture of the GRU + SVM system.

By capturing features from GRU layer, we obtain training and test data features, and integrate them with given labels as inputs, so SVM classifier can train the parameters.

2 Combining GRU and SVM for Sentences Classification

2.1 Embedding Layer

The first layer in the network , we let $x_i \in R_k$ be the k-dimensional word vector corresponding to the i-th word in the sentence. A sentence of length n (padded where necessary) is represented as:

$$x_{1:n} = x_1 \oplus x_2 \oplus \ldots \oplus x_n, \quad (1)$$

n is the maximum length of sentences and we set it to 50. When meeting short tweets we use fixed characters padding. Each word x_i is represented by embedding vectors $(w_1, w_2 \ldots w_l)$ where l is set to 200. For word embeddings, we use pre-trained word vectors from GloVe (Pennington et al., 2014). GloVe is an unsupervised learning technology for learning word representation. The purpose of training is to use statistical information to find similarities among words and based on co-occurrence matrix and statistical information. We use them to provide pre-trained word vectors trained on 27B tokens from Twitter and with a length of 200. Words not presented in the set of pre-trained words are initialized randomly.

2.2 GRU Layer

The main layer in our model, the input to it is the sequence of length L and each word in it having k dimension. The gated recurrent network proposed in (Bahdanauetal., 2014) is a recurrent neural network (a neural network with feedback connection, see(Atiya and Parlos, 2000)) where the activation hj of the neural unit j at time t is a linear interpolation between the previous activation h_t^j (Chung et al., 2014):

$$h_t^j = (1 - z_t^j)h_{t-1}^j + z_t^j h_t^j \quad (2)$$

Where z_t^j is the update gate that determines how much time the units update its content, h_t^j is the newly computed candidate state.

2.3 Dropout Layer

Dropout is a regularization technique for reducing overfitting in neural networks by preventing complex coadaptations on training data Dropout refers to randomly let the weight of some hidden layer of network does not work in model when training, those nodes does not work can temporarily thought is not part of the network but the weight of it is retained(just temporarily not update), because it may work again the next time throwing samples into it.

2.4 Relu Layer

This layer is to allow the network to make complex decision by learning non-linear classification boundaries. We used more efficient function Rectified Linear Units (ReLU).

2.5 Soft-Max Layer

The output of the GRU layer and dropout layer is passed to a fully connected softmax layer. This

714

layer calculates the classes probability distribution:

$$P(y=j\,|\,\mathbf{x},\mathbf{s},\mathbf{b})=\mathrm{softmax}_j(\mathbf{x}^T\mathbf{w}+\mathbf{b})$$

$$=\frac{\exp(x^T w_j + b_j)}{\sum_{k=1}^{K}\exp(x^T w_k + b_k)} \quad (3)$$

where w_k and b_k are the weight vector and bias of the k-th class, respectively. For subtask A and B, the difference is three neurons and two neurons used (i.e., K=3 or K=2).

2.6 SVM classifier

Support vector machines (SVMs) are a set of supervised learning methods used for classification, regression and outliers detection. Given a set of training examples, each training instance is marked as belonging to one or the other of the two categories, the SVM training algorithm to create a new instance will be assigned to one of two categories of models, making it a nonprobability binary linear classifier. Sklearn is a Python library of scientific computing and it provides several clustering algorithms. In our system, we from sklearn.svm import SVC module and redefine this function and parameters. As we all known, SVM is a binary classifier, but we also need process three and five classification problem. In the multiclass case, this is extended as per Wu et al. (2004). SVC and NuSVC implement the "one-against-one" approach (Knerr et al., 1990) for multi-class classification. If n_class is the number of classes, then n_class * (n_class - 1) / 2 classifiers are constructed and each one trains data from two classes. To provide a consistent interface with other classifiers, the decision_function_shape option allows to aggregate the results of the "one-against-one" classifiers to a decision function of shape (n_samples, n_classes).

3 Data

The training and development datasets used in our experiments were all datasets from SemEval 2013-2016 that labeled. Before training, we processed the data with the follow procedures:
1). The texts were lowercased by string.strip().lower(),
2).We only retain punctuation, exclamation mark, question mark and comma,

3). Tokenize each tweet using blank in sentences,
4). Emoticons like (^.^) have been deleted,
5).Using the patterns described in Table 1 to normalize each tweet.

Pattern	Examples	Normaliza
Usernames	@user1,@user2	UserName
Abbreviation	Don't	Do not
Abbreviation	2c or a90	Delete
Repeated letters	ahahhhh	ahahh
Numbers	123	NUM
URLs	www.google.co	URL
Topic (Subtask B only)	Microsoft	Entity

Table 1: Normalization Patterns

Datasets	Total	Pos	Neg	Neu
Twitter2013	13454	5124	2097	6233
SMS2013	2093	492	394	1207
Twitter2014	1853	982	202	669
LiveJournal2014	1142	427	304	411
Tw2014Sarcasm	86	33	40	13
Twitter2015	2390	1038	365	987
Twitter2016	29632	11259	4483	3985

Table 2: Overview of datasets and number of tweets we dowloaded. The data was divided into training, development and testing sets

4 Experiments and Results

All our experiments have been developed using Keras deep learning library with Theano backend, and with CUDA enabled. And all our experiments were performed on a computer with Intel Core(TM) i3 @3.4GHz 16GB of RAM and GeForce GTX 1060 GPU. The hyper-parameters of the network are chosen based on the performance on the dev-test data. We firstly carry out our system: put data into GRU model, as we known GRU can also train and test dataset at the same time we adjust some important parameters to make our GRU model to be the newest. Then we define a Theano function, and input para-meter is the GRU network portal, output is the GRU network dense layer before softmax layer. Using the Theano function, once we throw new data, we can get features that meeting our requirements. Last we throw these features into SVM so we can get classification results as we hope. After experiment we know our system performance well on two classification question, and poor on five classification. Some factors may cause this: small training data and in five-classification dataset many twitters belong to negative, neutral and positive; our deep model GRU maybe not actually called deep due to number of layers and our manually tuning.

4.1 Subtask A

Rank	System	$F1^{PN}$	ρ^{PN}	Acc
37	YNU-1510	0.201_{37}	0.340_{36}	0.387_{36}
baseline 1: all Positive		0.169	0.333	0.193
baseline 2: all Negative		0.244	0.333	0.323
baseline 3: all Neutral		0.000	0.333	0.483

Table 3: Result for Subtask A "Message Polarity classification", English. The systems are ordered by their F_1^{PN} score (higher is better).

4.2 Subtask B

Rank	System	ρ^{PN}	$F1^{PN}$	Acc
21	YNU-1510	0.516_{21}	0.499_{19}	0.499_{21}
baseline 1: all Positive		0.500	0.285	0.398
baseline 2: all Negative		0.500	0.376	0.602

Table 4: Results for Subtask B "Tweet classification according to a two-point scale", English. The systems are ordered by their ρ^{PN} score (higher is better).

4.3 Subtask C

Rank	System	MAE^{M}	MAE^{μ}
14	YNU-1510	1.262_{14}	0.764_{14}
baseline 1: Highly NEGATIVE		2.000	1.895
baseline 2: NEGATIVE		1.400	0.923
baseline 3: NEUTRAL		1.200	0.525
baseline 4: POSITIVE		1.400	1.127
baseline 5: Highly POSITIVE		2.000	2.105

Table 5: Results for Subtask C "Tweet classification according to a five-point scale", English. The systems are ordered by their MAEMscore (lower is better).

5 Conclusion

In this paper, we presented our GRU-SVM system used for SemEval 2017 Task4 (Subtasks A, B and C). The system used a gated recurrent layer as a core layer to extract features and then feed these features into SVM classifier.

Acknowledgments

This work was supported by the Natural Science Foundation of China No.61463050, and the NSF of Yunnan Province No. 2015FB113.

References

Bing Liu. 2012. Sentiment analysis and opinion mining Synthesis Lectures on Human Language Technologies. Morgan &Claypool publishers.

Paul Ekman. 1992. An argument for basic emotions. Cognition and Emotion, 6(3-4), 169-200.

Eric Breck, Yejin Choi, and Claire Cardie. 2007. Identifying expressions of opinion in context. In Manuela M. Veloso, editor, IJCAI 2007, Proceedings of the 20th International Joint Conference on Artificial Intelligence, Hyderabad, India, January 6-12,2007,pages 2683–2688.

Ainur Yessenalina and Claire Cardie. 2011. Compositional matrix-space models for sentiment a-nalysis. In Proceedings of the 2011 Conference on Empirical Methods in Natural Language Processing, EMNLP 2011, 27-31 July 2011, John McIntyre Conference Centre, Edinburgh, UK, A meeting of SIGDAT, a Special Interest Group of the ACL, pages 172–182.

Richard Socher, Jeffrey Pennington, Eric H. Huang, Andrew Y. Ng, and Christopher D. Manning. 2011. Semi-supervised recursive auto encoders for predicting sentiment distributions. In Proceedings of the 2011 Conference on Empirical Methods in Natural Language Processing, EMNLP 2011, 27-31 July 2011, John McIntyre Conference Centre, Edinburgh, UK, A meeting of SIGDAT, a Special Interest Group of the ACL, pages 151–161.ACL.

Preslav Nakov, Sara Rosenthal, Zornitsa Kozareva, Veselin Stoyanov, Alan Ritter, and Theresa Wilson. 2013. SemEval-2013 Task 2: Sentiment Analysis in Twitter. In Second Joint Conference on Lexical and Computational Semantics (*SEM), Volume 2: Proceedings of the Seventh International Workshopon Semantic Evaluation (SemEval 2013), pages 312–320, Atlanta, Georgia, USA, June. Association for Computational Linguistics.

Preslav Nakov, Alan Ritter, Sara Rosenthal, Fabrizio Sebastiani, and Veselin Stoyanov. 2016a. Evaluation measures for the SemEval-2016 task 4: "sentiment analysis in Twitter".

Preslav Nakov,Alan Ritter, Sara Rosenthal, VeselinStoyanov, and Fabrizio Sebastiani. 2016b. SemEval-2016 task 4: Sentiment analysis in Twitter. In Proceedings of the 10th International Workshop on Semantic Evaluation (SemEval 2016), San Diego, California, June. Association for Computational Linguistics.

Yoon Kim, Yacine Jernite, David Sontag, and Alexander M. Rush. 2015. Character-aware neural language models. CoRR, abs/1508.06615.

Richard Socher, Jeffrey Pennington, Eric H. Huang, Andrew Y. Ng, and Christopher D. Manning. 2011. Semisupervised recursive autoencoders for predicting sentiment distributions. In Proceedings of the 2011 Conference on Empirical Methods in Natural Language Processing, EMNLP 2011, 27-31 July 2011, John McIntyre Conference Centre, Edinburgh, UK, A meeting of SIGDAT, a Special Interest Group of the ACL, pages 151–161.ACL.

Dzmitry Bahdanau, Kyunghyun Cho, and Yoshua Bengio. 2014. Neural machine translation by jointly learning to align and translate. arXiv preprint arXiv: 1409.0473.

Amir F Atiya and Alexander G Parlos. 2000. New

results on recurrent network training: unifying the algorithms and accelerating convergence. NeuralNetworks, IEEE Transactions on, 11(3):697–709.

LSIS at SemEval-2017 Task 4: Using Adapted Sentiment Similarity Seed Words For English and Arabic Tweet Polarity Classification

Amal Htait*,**   **Sébastien Fournier***,**   **Patrice Bellot***,**

* Aix Marseille University

CNRS, ENSAM, Toulon University

LSIS UMR 7296,13397, Marseille, France.

** Aix-Marseille University

CNRS, CLEO OpenEdition

UMS 3287, 13451, Marseille, France.

{amal.htait, sebastien.fournier, patrice.bellot}@openedition.org

Abstract

We present, in this paper, our contribution in SemEval2017 task 4 : "Sentiment Analysis in Twitter", subtask A: "Message Polarity Classification", for English and Arabic languages. Our system is based on a list of sentiment seed words adapted for tweets. The sentiment relations between seed words and other terms are captured by cosine similarity between the word embedding representations (word2vec). These seed words are extracted from datasets of annotated tweets available online. Our tests, using these seed words, show significant improvement in results compared to the use of Turney and Littman's (2003) seed words, on polarity classification of tweet messages.

1 Introduction

Sentiment Analysis aims to obtain feelings expressed as positive, negative, neutral, or even expressed with different strength or intensity levels. One of the well known extracting sentiment approaches is the lexicon-based approach. A sentiment lexicon is a list of words and phrases, such as *excellent*, *awful* and *not bad*, each is being assigned with a positive or negative score reflecting its sentiment polarity. Therefore, sentiment lexicon provides rich sentiment information and forms the foundation of many sentiment analysis systems (Liu, 2012).

Our system is based on one of the most significant sentiment lexicon classification methods introduced by Turney and Littman (2003). The method is inspired by the semantic similarity measuring and applied to the sentiment analysis field as a sentiment similarity measuring. In a similar

method, Kanayama and Nasukawa (2006) worked on detecting a word's sentiment polarity by measuring the difference between its sentiment similarity with a positive seed word and a negative seed word, respectively. This method achieves better results with larger corpora, where there are more chances to find the word (to be classified) near the positive and negative seed words.

In SemEval2017 task 4, we're working with tweets which will lead to deal with slang words and informal phrases. Therefore, the classic seed words suggested by Turney and Littman (2003), listed below in Table 1, will not be very suitable. For example, the word *Superior* is rarely used in the modern "social media" English, and it is barely found in tweets compared to other seed words. In the tweets dataset of sentiment140 (Go et al., 2009), the word *Superior* is used 42 times, but the word *Nice* is used 23563 times. Thus, for the English tweets polarity classification task, we use the adapted for tweets seed words extracted in our previous work (Htait et al., 2017). And for the Arabic tweets polarity classification task, we apply the same method as in (Htait et al., 2017) to extract Arabic seed words adapted for tweets, to be used in our system.

positive	negative
good, nice, excellent, positive, fortunate, correct, superior.	bad, nasty, poor, negative, unfortunate, wrong, inferior.

Table 1: The classic seed words suggested by Turney and Littman (2003).

2 Related Work

The use of seed words was the base of many sentiment analysis experiments, some used the concept with supervised or semi-supervised methods.

Proceedings of the 11th International Workshop on Semantic Evaluations (SemEval-2017), pages 718–722,
Vancouver, Canada, August 3 - 4, 2017. ©2017 Association for Computational Linguistics

For example, Ju et al. (2012) worked on a semi-supervised method for sentiment classification that aims to train a classifier with a small number of labeled data (called seed data). Some other experiments used the concept with unsupervised methods which reduces the need of annotated training data. For example Turney (2002; 2003), which used statistical measures to calculate the similarities between words and a list of 14 seed words (Table 1), such as point wise mutual information (PMI). But we should note that Turney's seed words were manually selected based on restaurant reviews, which have different nature than tweets. Also we find that Maas et al. (2011) used the concept as "bag of words" but with cosine similarity measure on word embedding.

Our previous work (Htait et al., 2017) was on sentiment intensity prediction of tweets segments using SemEval2016 Task7[1] data. We extracted new seed words as more adapted for tweets seed words. We retrieved the most frequent words in Sentiment140 (Go et al., 2009) and then manually filtered the list to eliminate the neutral words. Our tests in (Htait et al., 2017) showed the efficiency of the new seed words over Turney's 14 seed words. Also, they showed that using cosine similarity measure of word embedding representations (word2vec) yields better results than using statistical measures like PMI to calculate the similarities between words. Therefore, and based on the above experiments, we decide to use for our system cosine similarity measure of word embedding representations, but also to use the adapted for tweets seed words from (Htait et al., 2017).

Even though the Arabic language processing faces more challenges than the English language, since words can have transitional meanings depending on position within a sentence and the type of sentence (verbal or nominal) (Farra et al., 2010), we can still find some interesting experiments in lexical-based sentiment analysis: El-Beltagy and Ali (2013) built a sentiment lexicon based on a manually constructed seed sentiment lexicon of 380 words. Using this lexicon, with assigned sentiment intensity score for each value, they were able to calculate the sentiment orientation for a set of tweets in Arabic language (Egyptian dialect). Another paper by Eskander and Rambow (2015) presented a large list of sentiment lexicon for Arabic language

called SLSA where each value is associated with a sentiment intensity score. The scores were assigned due to a link created between the English annotation of each Arabic entry to a synset from SentiWordNet (Cambria et al., 2010). For our system in Arabic language, we are following the same method as the system in English language. But since there is no previously created list of adapted for tweets seed words, we create the list following the same method in (Htait et al., 2017), and then use it with cosine similarity measure of word embedding representations.

3 Adapted seed words

3.1 English seed words

In (Htait et al., 2017), seed words were extracted from Sentiment140 dataset (Go et al., 2009). For the positive seeds, a list of the most frequent words in Sentiment140 positive tweets is retrieved and then manually filtered to eliminate the neutral words, and the same is applied for negative seeds. The list of English seed words adapted to tweets is as shown in Table 2.

Positive	Negative
love, like, good, win , lol, hope, best, thanks, funny, haha, god, amazing, fun,beautiful, nice, cute, cool, perfect, awesome, okay, special, hopefully, glad, congrats, excellent, dreams, sunshine, hehe, positive,fantastic, dance, correct, fabulous, superior, fortunate, relaxing, happy,great, kind, laugh, haven, wonderful, yay, enjoying, sweet,	ill, fucking, shit, fuck, hate, bad, break, sucks, cry, damn, sad, stupid, dead, pain, sick, wtf, lost, worst, fail, bored, scared, hurts, afraid, upset, broken, died, stuck, boring, horrible, negative, unfortunate, inferior, unfortunately,poor, need, suck, wrong, evil, missed, sore, alone, crap, hell, tired, nasty.

Table 2: The Tweets Adapted English seed words (Htait et al., 2017).

3.2 Arabic seed words

The Arabic language's experiences, in lexical-based sentiment analysis, were mostly oriented to sentiment lexicons than to seed words. Large lists of sentiment lexicons were built and used for sentiment analysis. For our system, we create a list of seed words following almost the same method as in (Htait et al., 2017). We search for the most common words in positive tweets and in negative tweets from two annotated corpora of Ara-

[1]http://alt.qcri.org/semeval2016/task7/

bic tweets (Arabic Sentiment Tweets Dataset[2] and Twitter data-set for Arabic Sentiment Analysis[3]). Then, to filter the list and to eliminate the neutral words, we use Mohammad et al.'s (2016) list. That list contain 240 positive and negative words of modern standard Arabic, therefore and due to Arabic dialects variety, using that list to filter will create a list of seed words in modern standard Arabic but adapted for tweets, and it can be used independently of dialects. The list of Arabic seed words adapted for tweets is as shown in Table 3.

Positive	Translation	Negative	Translation
خير	benevolent	بال	worn
الجمال	fairness	بشع	ugly
كبير	grand	وسخ	filthy
أعلى	superior	جائر	unjust
حسن	well	عيب	flaw
عظيم	great	خطير	dangerous
رائع	wonderful	حقير	despicable
نادر	exceptive	بايخ	vapid
جمال	beauty	حزين	sad
كريم	generous	قذر	dirty
أعظم	greatest	هائل	massive
نبيل	noble	مقرف	nasty
جميل	beautiful	باطل	invalid
صالح	valid	تافه	trifle
دقيق	accurate	ملعون	damned
مشرق	bright	مرفوض	unacceptable
طيب	delicious	مسكين	poor
حلو	sweet	فاسد	corrupt
جيد	good	مؤسف	regrettable
عبقري	genius	فظيع	horrible

Table 3: The Tweets Adapted Arabic seed words.

4 System of Sentiment classification

Our System is based on sentiment similarity cosine measure with Word Embedding representations (word2vec). For the English language, we use twitter word2vec model by Godin et al (Godin et al., 2015), since best results were achieved using that model in sentiment intensity prediction with the adapted seed words (Htait et al., 2017). This model is a word2vec model trained on 400 millions tweets in English language and it has word representations of dimensionality 400. For the Arabic language, there is no twitter word2vec

model available online (to the best of our knowledge). Therefore, we collect 42 millions tweets in Arabic language from archived twitter streams[4] to create our twitter word2vec model.

In Figure 1, we have the work flow of our system for tweets sentiment classification. First, each tweet is cleaned by removing links, user names, stop words, numeric tokens and characters except the common emoticons: ":-)", ":-(", ":)", ":(", ":'(". Also, words with repetitive characters are replaced by the corrected ones (e.g. coooool by cool). After that, the tweet is segmented into tokens or words. The similarity between each word with positive seed words and negative seed words is calculated using gensim tool[5] with the previously mentioned word2vec models for both languages English and Arabic.

Having the sentiment score of each word in a tweet, we aggregate by sum to combine these values. The final score specify the tweet's polarity. After many tests on old SemEval data (task "Message Polarity Classification" of 2013 and 2014), we found that the best scores achieved are by considering the following: if the score is higher than 1, the tweet is considered positive, else if the score is lower than -2, the tweet is considered negative, else it is considered neutral.

To test the efficiency of the adapted seed words on tweets polarity classification, we apply our system on SemEval data for the task : "Sentiment Analysis in Twitter" of years 2013[6] and 2014[7], using Turney's seed words (in Table1), and the adapted seed words. The Table 4, along with the results, shows clearly how the use of the adapted for tweets seed words increase the results compared to Turney's seed words.

2013	AvgF1	AvgR	Acc
Turney	0.262	0.381	0.480
Adapted	**0.564**	**0.571**	**0.508**
2014	AvgF1	AvgR	Acc
Turney	0.303	0.383	0.511
Adapted	**0.589**	**0.553**	**0.552**

Table 4: The comparison between Turney's seed words and the adapted seed words on semEval task's data of years 2013 and 2014.

The results of our participation at SemEval2017 Task4 (subtask A) for English and Arabic lan-

---

[2]http://www.mohamedaly.info/datasets/astd
[3]https://archive.ics.uci.edu
[4]https://archive.org/details/twitterstream
[5]https://pypi.python.org/pypi/gensim
[6]https://www.cs.york.ac.uk/semeval-2013/task2.html
[7]http://alt.qcri.org/semeval2014/task9/

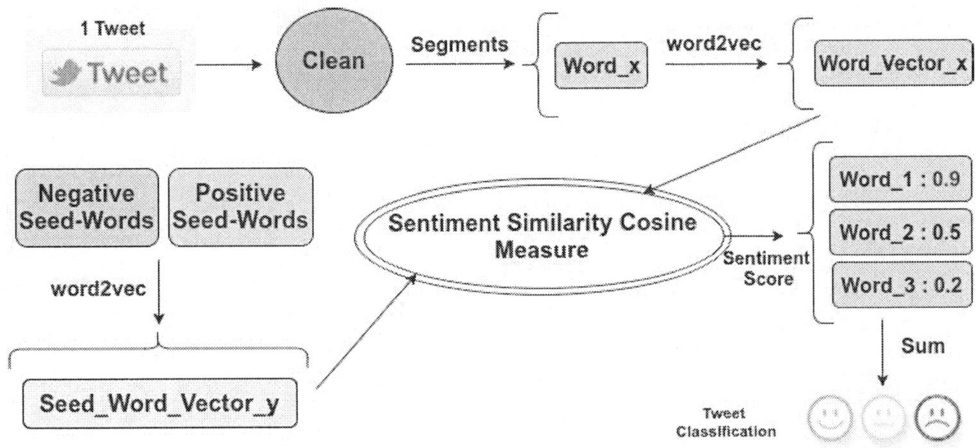

Figure 1: The work flow of tweets sentiment classification.

guages are in Table 5, with the best results accomplished in the subtask A.

English	Team	AvgF1	AvgR	Acc
	BB_twtr	0.685	0.681	0.658
	LSIS	0.561	0.571	0.521
Arabic	Team	AvgF1	AvgR	Acc
	NileTMRG	0.610	0.583	0.581
	LSIS	0.469	0.438	0.445

Table 5: The results at semEval2017 Task 4 subtask A - for English and Arabic Languages.

5 Conclusion

In this paper, we present our contribution in SemEval2017 task4: Sentiment Analysis in Twitter, subtask A: Message Polarity Classification, for English and Arabic languages. Our system is based on a list of sentiment seed words adapted for tweets, used in sentiment similarity cosine measure with word embedding representations (word2vec). Although the results are encouraging, further investigation is required concerning the detection of negations (e.g. not) and intensifiers(e.g. very) in the tweets, due to their big effect on reversing the polarity of a tweet.

Acknowledgments

This work was supported by the French program Investissements d'Avenir Equipex "A digital library for open humanities" of OpenEdition.org.

References

Erik Cambria, Robert Speer, Catherine Havasi, and Amir Hussain. 2010. Senticnet: A publicly available semantic resource for opinion mining. In *AAAI fall symposium: commonsense knowledge*. volume 10.

Samhaa R El-Beltagy and Ahmed Ali. 2013. Open issues in the sentiment analysis of arabic social media: A case study. In *Innovations in information technology (iit), 2013 9th international conference on*. IEEE, pages 215–220.

Ramy Eskander and Owen Rambow. 2015. Slsa: A sentiment lexicon for standard arabic. In *EMNLP*. pages 2545–2550.

Noura Farra, Elie Challita, Rawad Abou Assi, and Hazem Hajj. 2010. Sentence-level and document-level sentiment mining for arabic texts. In *Data Mining Workshops (ICDMW), 2010 IEEE International Conference on*. IEEE, pages 1114–1119.

Alec Go, Richa Bhayani, and Lei Huang. 2009. Twitter sentiment classification using distant supervision. *CS224N Project Report, Stanford* 1(12).

Fréderic Godin, Baptist Vandersmissen, Wesley De Neve, and Rik Van de Walle. 2015. Multimedia lab@ acl w-nut ner shared task: named entity recognition for twitter microposts using distributed word representations. *ACL-IJCNLP* 2015:146–153.

Amal Htait, Sébastien Fournier, and Patrice Bellot. 2017. Identification automatique de mots-germes pour l'analyse de sentiments et son intensité. In *RJCRI*. Marseille, France.

Shengfeng Ju, Shoushan Li, Yan Su, Guodong Zhou, Yu Hong, and Xiaojun Li. 2012. Dual word and document seed selection for semi-supervised sentiment classification. In *Proceedings of the 21st ACM international conference on Information and knowledge management*. ACM, pages 2295–2298.

Hiroshi Kanayama and Tetsuya Nasukawa. 2006. Fully automatic lexicon expansion for domain-oriented sentiment analysis. In *Proceedings of the 2006 conference on empirical methods in natural language processing*. Association for Computational Linguistics, pages 355–363.

Bing Liu. 2012. Sentiment analysis and opinion mining. *Synthesis lectures on human language technologies* 5(1):1–167.

Andrew L Maas, Raymond E Daly, Peter T Pham, Dan Huang, Andrew Y Ng, and Christopher Potts. 2011. Learning word vectors for sentiment analysis. In *Proceedings of the 49th Annual Meeting of the Association for Computational Linguistics: Human Language Technologies-Volume 1*. Association for Computational Linguistics, pages 142–150.

Saif Mohammad, Mohammad Salameh, and Svetlana Kiritchenko. 2016. Sentiment lexicons for arabic social media. In *LREC*. Portoro, Slovenia.

Peter D Turney. 2002. Thumbs up or thumbs down?: semantic orientation applied to unsupervised classification of reviews. In *Proceedings of the 40th annual meeting on association for computational linguistics*. Association for Computational Linguistics, pages 417–424.

Peter D Turney and Michael L Littman. 2003. Measuring praise and criticism: Inference of semantic orientation from association. *ACM Transactions on Information Systems (TOIS)* 21(4):315–346.

ELiRF-UPV at SemEval-2017 Task 4: Sentiment Analysis using Deep Learning

José-Ángel González, Ferran Pla, Lluís-F. Hurtado
Universitat Politècnica de València
Camí de Vera sn, 46022, València
{jogonba2|fpla|lhurtado}@dsic.upv.es

Abstract

This paper describes the participation of ELiRF-UPV team at task 4 of SemEval2017. Our approach is based on the use of convolutional and recurrent neural networks and the combination of general and specific word embeddings with polarity lexicons. We participated in all of the proposed subtasks both for English and Arabic languages using the same system with small variations.

1 Introduction

Twitter has become a source of a huge amount of information which introduces great possibilities of research in the field of Sentiment Analysis. Sentiment Analysis or Opinion Mining, is a research area within Natural Language Processing whose aim is to identify the underlying emotion of a certain document, sentence or aspect (Liu, 2012). Sentiment Analysis systems has been applied, among other, for classifying reviews (Turney, 2002; Pang et al., 2002), for generating aspect-based summaries (Hu and Liu, 2004), or political tendency identification (Pla and Hurtado, 2014).

SemEval-2017 task 4 organizers proposed five different subtasks. All five subtasks are related to sentiment analysis at global level in Twitter, but each one of them has significant differences. Additionally, in the 2017 edition, the five subtasks were also proposed in Arabic. Altogether, the participants could address ten different challenges.

Subtask A consists in predicting the message polarity as positive, negative, or neutral. In subtasks B and C, given a message and a topic systems should assign the message in a two-point scale or in a five-point scale respectively.

Subtasks D and E address the problem of tweet quantification, that is, given a set of tweets about a given topic, estimate the distribution of the tweets across two-point scale or in a five-point scale respectively.

The rest of this paper is organized as follows. Section 2 describes the general system architecture proposed in this work. Section 3 presents both the variations on the general system introduced to address the different subtasks and the results obtained in the subtasks. Finally, section 4 presents some conclusions and the future work.

2 System description

In this section, we describe the system architecture we used for all the Sentiment Analysis subtasks. This system is based on the use of convolutional and recurrent neural networks and the combination of general and specific word embeddings (Mikolov et al., 2013b,a) with polarity lexicons.

Slight modifications of the system have been applied to adapt it to each subtask. These modifications are motivated by the characteristics of each subtask and the available resources.

The system combines three Convolutional Recurrent Neural Network (CRNN) (Zhou et al., 2002) in order to learn high level abstractions (Lecun et al., 2015) from noisy representations (Jim et al., 1994). The input of these three networks are: out-domain embeddings, in-domain embeddings, and sequences of the polarities of the words. The output of the CRNNs is concatenated and used as input for a discriminating model implemented by a fully-connected Multilayer Perceptron (MLP). Figure 1 summarizes the proposed approach.

The CRNNs used have as a first layer a unidimensional convolutional layer that allows to extract spatial relations among the words of a sentence (Kim, 2014). In some subtasks, a down-

Proceedings of the 11th International Workshop on Semantic Evaluations (SemEval-2017), pages 723–727,
Vancouver, Canada, August 3 - 4, 2017. ©2017 Association for Computational Linguistics

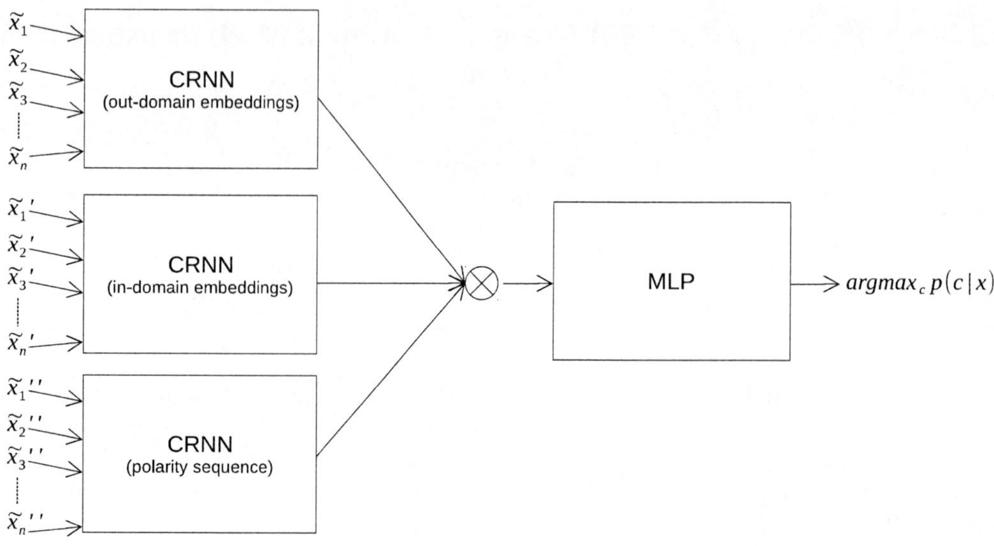

Figure 1: General system architecture.

sampling process by means of a *max pooling* layer was applied.

Then, the output of the convolutional layers (including *max pooling* in some subtasks) is used as input for a recurrent neural network (LSTM). Moreover, because the polarity of a subsequence of the sentence not only depends on the previous words but also depends on the next words, we used a Bidirectional Long-Short-Term Memory (BLSTM) network (Hochreiter and Schmidhuber, 1997; Schuster and Paliwal, 1997). In most subtasks, only one BLSTM layer has been used. The dimension for the output vector has been fixed between 32 and 256.

Figure 2 shows a graphical representation of the CRNN layers, where $\tilde{x}_i$ is a noisy version of the input, c_i are the kernels of the convolutional layer, p_i represent the operations of max pooling, and y_s is the output of the CRNNs.

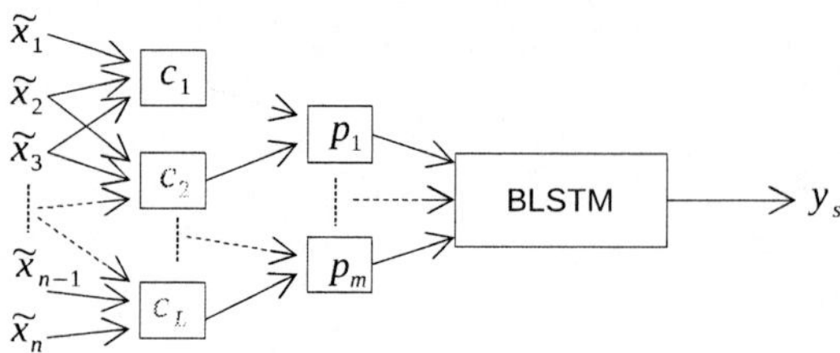

Figure 2: Implementation of the Convolutional Recurrent Neural Network.

The last network used in our system is a fully connected Multilayer Perceptron. Depending on the subtasks, we used between 1 and 3 hidden layers. The number of neurons also depended on the subtask. Softmax activation function was used in the output layer to estimate $p(c|x)$ (the number of neurons in that layer depends on the number of classes in the task).

A graphical representation of the MLP used can be seen in Figure 3, where y_i are the outputs of the CRNNs, which are used as input for the MLP. Note that, in this case, no noise is applied to the input because the chosen setup obtained better results during the tuning phase.

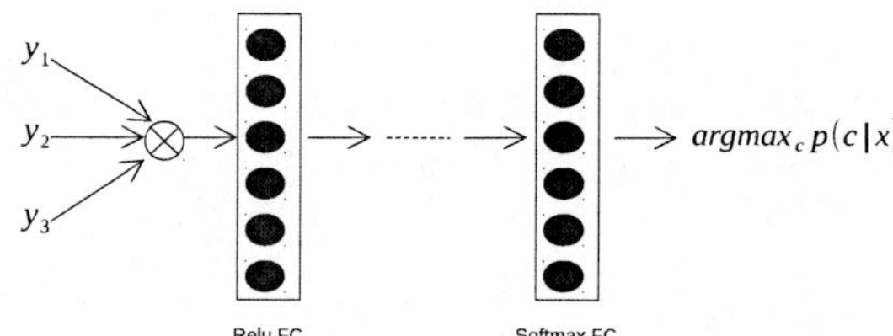

Figure 3: Implementation of the Multilayer Perceptron.

2.1 Resources

As we stated above, we used two different kind of embeddings (in-domain and out-domain) as input to the system for all the Arabic and English subtasks.

We used these two embeddings models in order to reduce the number of unseen words. In this way, we combined a specific representation that only considers the words seen in the training set (in-domain embeddings) with a more general one that has a great amount of words unseen in the training set but that can appear in the test set (out-domain embeddings).

For the English subtasks, we used as out-domain model the word2vec model learned by Fréderic Godin (Godin et al., 2015; Ritter et al., 2011) from 400 million tweets in English. For the Arabic subtasks, we learned a 400-dimensional word2vec model using the articles of the Wikipedia in Arabic (Wikipedia, 2017). With respect to the in-domain models, a word2vec model was trained for each subtask from the provided training corpus.

In addition to the two representations based on embeddings, we added polarity information to the input layer. To include this information, we considered a representation of tweets based on a sequence of C-dimensional one-hot vectors, where C is the number of sentiment classes. Each vector indicates the polarity of one word according to certain polarity lexicon. This way, a tweet is a sequence of C-dimensional vectors. Once again, the resources used depended on the language. We used the NRC lexicon (Mohammad et al., 2013) both for the Arabic and English subtasks and the *Afinn* lexicon (Hansen et al., 2011) only for the English subtasks.

3   Results

In this section, we present the modifications we made on the general schema for all the subtasks in which we participated. We also report and discuss the results we achieved in the different subtasks.

Due to the different sizes of the corpora used in every subtask, we made some changes from the generic model in order to reduce or increase the number of parameters to be estimated. These changes had been fixed for each subtask by means of a tuning process.

3.1   Subtask A: Message Polarity Classification

Subtask A consists in classifying the message as positive, negative, or neutral. Our model for this subtask consists of three CRNN merged with a three layer MLP, see general schema in Figure 1.

The results achieved by our system in Subtask A are shown in Table 1. The measure used to range the participants was macroaveraged recall (ρ). Two additional measures were also considered: F_1 averaged across the positives and the negatives (F_1^{PN}) and Accuracy (Acc). We have also included, for each measure, the position reached by our system compared with the other participants.

Subtask A	English		Arabic	
ρ	0.632	(14/38)	0.478	(3/8)
F_1^{PN}	0.619	(12/38)	0.467	(4/8)
Acc	0.599	(24/38)	0.508	(3/8)

Table 1: Results for Subtask A: Message Polarity Classification, English and Arabic.

Note the different ranking position achieved by our system considering ρ and Acc measures for English. ρ achieved the 14th position while Acc achieved the 24th position. We think this is due to the way we tackled with the imbalanced classes in the corpus. The decision was to balance the training set by eliminating some samples of those classes that appeared more times in the corpus.

In contrast, for the Arabic subtask, Accuracy results are not influenced by the way we managed the imbalanced problem, achieving similar position in all the measures considered.

3.2   Subtask B: Tweet classification according to a two-point scale

In subtask B, given a message and a topic, the participants must classify the message on two-point scale (positive and negative) towards that topic. Unfortunately, we did not include information of the topic in the model and, in consequence, our model consists of a variation of the generic model. In this case, max pooling layers were replaced with another convolutional layer, the number of neurons in MLP layers was reduced and we used Gaussian noise over MLP layers activations because better results are obtained over the validation set. For the Arabic language, we used the same topology, but we reduced the number of parameters due to the size of the training corpus.

The results achieved by our system in Subtask B are shown in Table 2. The measures considered were the same as in Subtask A.

The scores achieved in all measures are better than those obtained in task A. Perhaps, this sub-

Subtask B	English		Arabic	
ρ	0.766	(17/23)	0.721	(2/4)
F_1^{PN}	0.773	(16/23)	0.724	(2/4)
Acc	0.790	(13/23)	0.734	(2/4)

Table 2: Results for Subtask B: Tweet classification according to a two-point scale, English and Arabic.

task is easier because only two classes are considered. But, compared with the other participants, our system ranked lower in this subtask. We think this is because no information of the topic was included in the model. For this subtask, the behavior of the system for both languages is similar.

3.3 Subtask C: Tweet classification according to a five-point scale

In this subtask, given a message and a topic, participants must classify the message on a five-point scale towards that topic. As in Subtask B, we did not include topic information to the model. Our model was an extension of the generic model, with two convolutional layers and two max pooling layers in each CRNN. For the Arabic version, we used the generic model with less parameters because of the available data.

The results achieved by our system in Subtask C are shown in Table 3. The measure used to range the participants was macroaveraged Mean Absolute Error (MAE^M). An extension of macroaveraged recall for ordinal regression (MAE^μ) was also considered.

Subtask C	English		Arabic	
MAE^M	0.806	(7/15)	1.264	(2/2)
MAE^μ	0.586	(11/15)	0.787	(2/2)

Table 3: Results for Subtask C: Tweet classification according to a five-point scale, English and Arabic.

For the English language, our system achieved the 7th position (0.806), with big difference respect to the team that obtained the best results (0.481). Once again, not including information about the topic could be decisive in the performance of the system.

3.4 Subtask D: Tweet quantification according to a two-point scale

Subtask D consists of tweet quantification in a two-point scale. Given a set of tweets about a given topic, participants must estimate the distribution of the tweets across two-point scale (positive and negative). We used the output of Subtask B to estimate, by maximum likelihood, the distribution of the tweets.

The results achieved by our system in Subtask D are shown in Table 4. The measure used to range the participants was Kullback-Leibler Divergence (KLD). Two additional measures were also considered: absolute error (AE) and relative absolute error (RAE).

Subtask D	English		Arabic	
KLD	1.060	(14/15)	1.183	(3/3)
AE	0.593	(15/15)	0.537	(3/3)
RAE	7.991	(15/15)	11.434	(3/3)

Table 4: Results for Subtask D: Tweet quantification according to a two-point scale, English and Arabic.

We can partially explain these poor results due to the simplicity of the method used to estimate the probability distribution and because the output of Subtask B also included errors.

3.5 Subsection E: Tweet quantification according to a five-point scale

In a similar way that Subtask D, Subtask E was a tweet quantification task, but in a five-point scale. For this subtask, we used the output of Subtask C to estimate, by maximum likelihood, the distribution of the tweets.

The results achieved by our system in Subtask E are shown in Table 5. The measure used to range the participants was Earth Mover's Distance (EMD).

Subtask E	English		Arabic	
EMD	0.306	(4/12)	0.564	(2/2)

Table 5: Results for Subtask E: Tweet quantification according to a five-point scale, English and Arabic.

Our system achieved the 4th position (0.306) for English, with slight difference respect to the first system (0.245).

4 Conclusions

In this work, we have presented the system developed by ELiRF-UPV team for participating in the task 4 of SemEval2017. We used a general system with small modifications to participate in all the subtasks. The system was based on the use of convolutional and recurrent neural networks and the combination of general and specific word embeddings with polarity lexicons. The results achieved by our system were competitive in many subtasks.

As future work, we plan to study some problems not addressed in this work such as tackle with the imbalance problem, address tweet quantification problem properly, add topic information in the model for B and C subtasks, and consider additional resources for tweet representation.

Acknowledgements

This work has been funded by the MINECO and FEDER founds under TIN2014-54288-C4-3-R project: ASLP-MULAN: Audio, Speech and Language Processing for Multimedia Analytics.

References

Fréderic Godin, Baptist Vandersmissen, Wesley De Neve, and Rik Van de Walle. 2015. Multimedia lab@ acl w-nut ner shared task: named entity recognition for twitter microposts using distributed word representations. *ACL-IJCNLP* 2015:146–153.

Lars Kai Hansen, Adam Arvidsson, Finn Årup Nielsen, Elanor Colleoni, and Michael Etter. 2011. Good friends, bad news-affect and virality in twitter. In *Future information technology*, Springer, pages 34–43.

Sepp Hochreiter and Jürgen Schmidhuber. 1997. Long short-term memory. *Neural Comput.* 9(8):1735–1780. https://doi.org/10.1162/neco.1997.9.8.1735.

Minqing Hu and Bing Liu. 2004. Mining and summarizing customer reviews. In *Proceedings of the Tenth ACM SIGKDD International Conference on Knowledge Discovery and Data Mining*. ACM, New York, NY, USA, KDD '04, pages 168–177. https://doi.org/10.1145/1014052.1014073.

Kam Jim, Bill G. Horne, and C. Lee Giles. 1994. Effects of noise on convergence and generalization in recurrent networks. In *Proceedings of the 7th International Conference on Neural Information Processing Systems*. MIT Press, Cambridge, MA, USA, NIPS'94, pages 649–656. http://dl.acm.org/citation.cfm?id=2998687.2998768.

Yoon Kim. 2014. Convolutional neural networks for sentence classification. *CoRR* abs/1408.5882. http://arxiv.org/abs/1408.5882.

Yann Lecun, Yoshua Bengio, and Geoffrey Hinton. 2015. Deep learning. *Nature* 521(7553):436–444. https://doi.org/10.1038/nature14539.

Bing Liu. 2012. *Sentiment Analysis and Opinion Mining. A Comprehensive Introduction and Survey*. Morgan & Claypool Publishers.

Tomas Mikolov, Kai Chen, Greg Corrado, and Jeffrey Dean. 2013a. Efficient estimation of word representations in vector space. *CoRR* abs/1301.3781. http://arxiv.org/abs/1301.3781.

Tomas Mikolov, Ilya Sutskever, Kai Chen, Greg Corrado, and Jeffrey Dean. 2013b. Distributed representations of words and phrases and their compositionality. *CoRR* abs/1310.4546. http://arxiv.org/abs/1310.4546.

Saif M Mohammad, Svetlana Kiritchenko, and Xiaodan Zhu. 2013. Nrc-canada: Building the state-of-the-art in sentiment analysis of tweets. *arXiv preprint arXiv:1308.6242* .

Bo Pang, Lillian Lee, and Shivakumar Vaithyanathan. 2002. Thumbs up? sentiment classification using machine learning techniques. In *IN PROCEEDINGS OF EMNLP*. pages 79–86.

Ferran Pla and Lluís-F. Hurtado. 2014. Political tendency identification in twitter using sentiment analysis techniques. In *Proceedings of COLING 2014, the 25th International Conference on Computational Linguistics: Technical Papers*. Dublin City University and Association for Computational Linguistics, Dublin, Ireland, pages 183–192. http://www.aclweb.org/anthology/C14-1019.

Alan Ritter, Sam Clark, Mausam, and Oren Etzioni. 2011. Named entity recognition in tweets: An experimental study. In *Proceedings of the Conference on Empirical Methods in Natural Language Processing*. Association for Computational Linguistics, Stroudsburg, PA, USA, EMNLP '11, pages 1524–1534. http://dl.acm.org/citation.cfm?id=2145432.2145595.

M. Schuster and K.K. Paliwal. 1997. Bidirectional recurrent neural networks. *Trans. Sig. Proc.* 45(11):2673–2681. https://doi.org/10.1109/78.650093.

Peter D. Turney. 2002. Thumbs up or thumbs down? semantic orientation applied to unsupervised classification of reviews. In *ACL*. pages 417–424. https://doi.org/http://www.aclweb.org/anthology/P02-1053.pdf.

Wikipedia. 2017. Wikipedia arabic dumps. [Online; accessed 22-February-2017]. https://dumps.wikimedia.org/arwiki/.

Zhi-Hua Zhou, Jianxin Wu, and Wei Tang. 2002. Ensembling neural networks: Many could be better than all. *Artificial Intelligence* 137(1):239 – 263. https://doi.org/http://dx.doi.org/10.1016/S0004-3702(02)00190-X.

XJSA at SemEval-2017 Task 4 : A Deep System for Sentiment Classification in Twitter

Yazhou Hao
University of Xi'an Jiaotong
yazhouhao@gmail.com
Yufei Li
University of Xi'an Jiaotong
18391819285@163.com

Yangyang Lan
University of Xi'an Jiaotong
1564018606@qq.com
Chen Li
University of Xi'an Jiaotong
cli@xjtu.edu.cn

Abstract

This paper describes the XJSA System submission from XJTU. Our system was created for SemEval2017 Task 4 – subtask A which is very popular and fundamental. The system is based on convolutional neural network and word embedding. We used two pre-trained word vectors and adopt a dynamic strategy for k-max pooling.

1 Introduction

Several years ago, the typical approaches to sentiment analysis of tweets were based on classifiers trained using several hand-crafted features, in particular lexicons of words with an assigned polarity value. About since 2014 the deep neural network methods have got state-of-the-art results in many NLP tasks, especially in sentiment classification. The work of Harvard NLP group in 2014 and Kalchbrenner's work in 2014 have suggested that convolutional neural network and word embedding play important roles in this field. General word embedding has got excellent results. If we can embed sentiment information in vectors, we will get better results. There are some open word vectors on the web already such as Word2Vec (Mikolov et al., 2013), Glove (Pennington et al., 2014), SSWE (Tang et al., 2014). In our system we use Word2Vec and SSWE at the same time.

Deep learning models have achieved excellent results in computer vision and speech recognition in recent years. In the field of natural language processing, much work with deep learning methods has involved learning word vectors representations for their own task or problem (Bengio et al., 2003; Mikolov et al., 2013, Collobert C&W et al., 2011).The others exploit the open word vectors which was mentioned above.Word vectors is a transformation of the feature of letter,word,sentence and paragraph or even text. It's a lower dimensional, dense and continuous vectors. In this vector, the words have similar syntactic are close – in Euclidean or cosine distance in the vector space. So one can study and compare the syntactic functionality between different words via word vectors.

Convolutional neural network (CNN) utilize layers with convolutional filters that are applied to local features (LeCun et al., 1998). CNN originally invented for computer vision, recently CNN models have achieved remarkably results in many natural language processing problem, such as sentence modeling (Kalchbrenner et al., 2014), semantic parsing (Yih et al., 2014), sentiment classification (kim et al., 2014) and other traditional natural language processing tasks(Collobert C&W et al., 2011).

Our system was inspired by the work (kim et al., 2014) and another work (Tang et al., 2014). In the aspect of CNN, we use a simple 3 layers CNN to automatic extract features. In the aspect of pre-trained vectors, we use the Word2Vec and SSWE to filter our training set to get a proper input for CNN. The reason that we use the vectors trained by Mikolov et al. (2013) is the 100 billion words of Google News and the vectors are publicly for free. We use the SSWE vectors because the vectors was especially trained for sentiment classification by Tang et al (2014). SSWE contains sentiment information which is not in word vectors trained by Mikolov.

Proceedings of the 11th International Workshop on Semantic Evaluations (SemEval-2017), pages 728–731,
Vancouver, Canada, August 3 - 4, 2017. ©2017 Association for Computational Linguistics

2 Background

As is shown above,traditional methods typically model the syntactic context of words but ignore the sentiment information of text. As a result, words with opposite polarity are mapped into close vectors, such as good and bad, just as Word2Vec.So in our system,we use SSWE and Word2Vec at the same time for word embedding, SSWE first.

Tang et al.(2014) introduce SSWE model to learn word embedding for Twitter sentiment classification. In our task,We use the word vector trained by $SSWE_u$,which captures the sentiment information of sentences as well as the syntactic contexts of words. $SSWE_u$ is illustrated in Figure1.

Given an original(or corrupted)n-gram and the sentiment polarity of a sentence as the input, SSWE_u predicts a two-dimensional vector for each input n-gram. t is the original n-gram, t^r is the corrupted n-gram.The two scalars (f_0^u, f_1^u) stand for language model score and sentiment score of the input n-gram,where f_0^u stands the positive, f_1^u the negative.

The training goal of SSWE are that (1) the original n-gram should obtain a higher language model score $f_0^u(t)$ than the corrupted n-gram $f_0^u(t^r)$,and (2) the sentiment score of original n-gram $f_1^u(t)$ should be more consistent with the gold polarity annotation of sentence than corrupted n-gram $f_1^u(t^r)$ .The loss function of SSWE_u is shown behind,

$$loss_u(t,t^r) = \alpha \bullet loss_{cw}(t,t^r) +$$

$$(1-\alpha) \bullet loss_{us}(t,t^r) \qquad (1)$$

where $loss_{cw}(t,t^r)$ is the syntactic loss as given in Equation 1, $loss_{us}(t,t^r)$ is the sentiment loss as shown in Equation 2.The hyper-parameter α weights the two parts. $\delta_s(t)$ is an indicator function reflecting the sentiment polarity of a sentence.

$$loss_{us}(t,t^r) = \max(0,1 - \delta_s(t)f_1^u(t)$$

$$+ \delta_s(t)f_1^u(t^r)) \qquad (2)$$

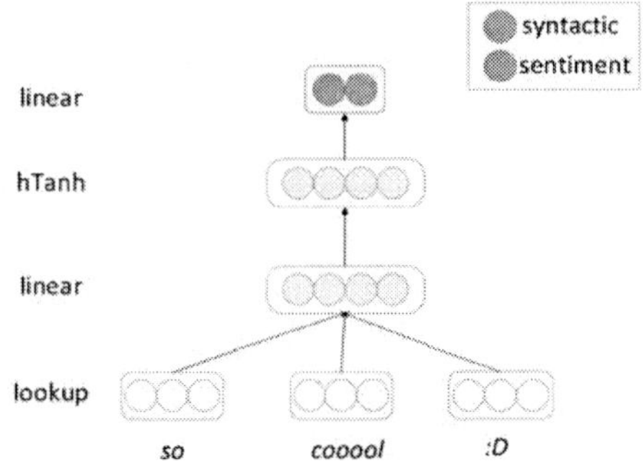

Figure 1:The SSWE_u model

3 Model

The architecture of our system shown in figure 2 is a simple 3 layers CNN just like the architecture of Kim et al (2013). $x_i \in \Re^k$ is the k-dimensional word vector corresponding to the i-th word in the sentence. A sentence of length n is described as

$$x_{1:n} = x_1 \oplus x_2 \oplus ... \oplus x_n, \qquad (3)$$

Where $\oplus$ is the concatenation operator. Then we let $x_{i:i+j}$ stand for the concatenation of words $x_i, x_{i+1},..., x_{i+j}$. A convolutional filter $w \in \Re^{hk}$ is applied to a window of h words to produce a new feature. For example, a feature c_i is generated from a window of words $x_{i:i+h-1}$ by

$$c_i = f(w \bullet x_{i:i+h=1} + b) \qquad (4)$$

where $b \in \Re$ is a bias term and f is a non-linear function. This filter is applied to each possible window of words in the sentence $\{x_{1:h}, x_{2:h+1},..., x_{n-h+1:n}\}$ to produce a feature map

$$c = [c_1, c_2,..., c_{n=h+1}], \qquad (5)$$

Here $c \in \Re^{n-h+1}$. Then a max-over-time pooling operation is applied just like Collobert C&W et al. (2011).over the feature map and take the maximum value $\hat{c} = \max\{ c\}$

4 Experimental Setup

We test our system on the following settings:

4.1 Hyper-parameters and Training

There are four models in Kim et al (2013):CNN-rand,CNN-static,CNN-non-static,CNN-multichannel.

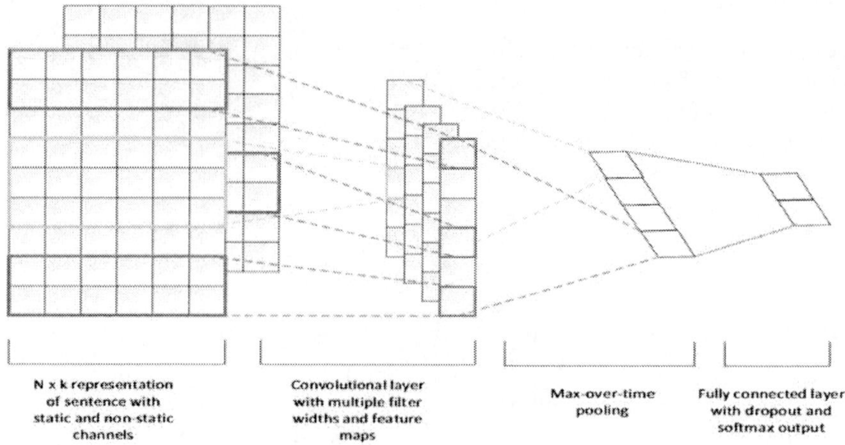

Figure 2: Architecture of XJSA

For all our experiments we use CNN-non-static: A model with pre-trained vectors from SSWE and wrd2vec.The pre-trained vectors are fine-tuned for each task.

We use rectified linear units, filter windows (h) of 3, 4, 5 with 100 feature maps each, dropout rate (p) of 0.5, l_2 constraint (s) of 3, and mini-batch size of 50. These values were chosen via a grid search on the dev sets.

4.2 Pre-trained Word Vectors

Initializing word vectors with those obtained from an unsupervised neural language model is a popular method to improve performance in the absence of a large supervised training set (Collobert C&W et al., 2011; Socher et al., 2011; Iyyer et al., 2014). First we use SSWE (Tang et al. 2014) which is a word vector contains sentiment information.We also use the publicly available word2vec vectors which were trained on 100 billion words from Google News. The vectors have dimensionality of 300 and were trained using the CBOW architecture.Because the dimensionality of vectors in SWEE is 50, so we extended it to 300 dimension by padding the 250 dimension randomly.

4.3 Environment of experiment

The experiments were run on a linux server with an nVIDIA GTX 1080 accelerated GPU.

5 Results

In order to compare the results of our system with other better system's results, here we show enough results generated by our system and the top one. The official submission achieved results presented in Table 1, compared to the top scoring system. We also list our detailed scores in Table 2

	P	R	F1
Positive	0.5791	0.6748	0.5423
Negative	0.5655	0.5592	0.5065
Neutral	0.5264	0.4340	0.4962
AvgP = 0.557, **AvgR** = 0.556, **AvgF1** = 0.519			
Overall score: 0.556			

Table 1: Official results of our submission compared to the top one.

system	AvegF1	AvegR	Acc
BB_twtr	0.685	0.681	0.658
XJSA	0.519	0.556	0.575

Table 2: Detailed scores of XJSA official submission.

6 Conclusion

Our work based on the method with deep learning neural network built on the top of word2vec and SSWE. We can find if we exploit the sentiment information in the pre-trained word vector we would get better result. Our work and some previous work mentioned in this paper show that unsupervised pre-training of word vectors plays an important role in deep learning for sentiment analysis.

References

Alfred. V. Aho and Jeffrey D. Ullman. 1972. *The Theory of Parsing, Translation and Compiling, volume 1*. Prentice-Hall, Englewood Cliffs, NJ.

American Psychological Association. 1983. *Publications Manual*. American Psychological Association, Washington, DC

Collobert, Ronan, and Jason Weston. "A Unified Architecture for Natural Language Processing: Deep Neural Networks with Multitask Learning." In Proceedings of the 25th International Conference on Machine Learning, 160–167. ACM, 2008. http://dl.acm.org/citation.cfm?id=1390177.

Collobert, J Weston, L.Bottou, M.Karlen, K.Kavukcugla, P.Kuksa. 2011"Natural Language Processing(Almost)from Scratch." Journal of Machine Learning Research 12:2493-2537

Kalchbrenner, Nal, Edward Grefenstette, and Phil Blunsom. "A Convolutional Neural Network for Modelling Sentences." arXiv Preprint arXiv:1404.2188, 2014. http://arxiv.org/abs/1404.2188.

Kim, Yoon. "Convolutional Neural Networks for Sentence Classification." arXiv Preprint arXiv:1408.5882, 2014. http://arxiv.org/abs/1408.5882.

Tang, Duyu, Furu Wei, Nan Yang, Ming Zhou, Ting Liu, and Bing Qin. "Learning Sentiment-Specific Word Embedding for Twitter Sentiment Classification." In ACL (1), 1555–1565, 2014. http://anthology.aclweb.org/P/P14/P14-1146.pdf.

Gao J, He X, Yih W, et al. Learning continuous phrase representations for translation modeling//In ACL. 2014.

Pennington J, Socher R, Manning C D. Glove: Global Vectors for Word Representation//EMNLP. 2014, 14: 1532-1543.

Socher R, Perelygin A, Wu J Y, et al. Recursive deep models for semantic compositionality over a sentiment treebank//Proceedings of the conference on empirical methods in natural language processing (EMNLP). 2013, 1631: 1642.

Iyyer M, Boyd-Graber J L, Claudino L M B, et al. A Neural Network for Factoid Question Answering over Paragraphs//EMNLP. 2014: 633-644.

Adullam at SemEval-2017 Task 4: Sentiment Analyzer based on Lexicon Integrated Convolutional Neural Networks with Attention

Joosung Yoon
Korea University
Seoul, South Korea
xelloss705@gmail.com

Kigon Lyu
Korea University
Seoul, South Korea
gon0121@korea.ac.kr

Hyeoncheol Kim
Korea University
Seoul, South Korea
hkim64@gmail.com

Abstract

We propose a sentiment analyzer for the prediction of document-level sentiments of English micro-blog messages from Twitter. The proposed method is based on lexicon integrated convolutional neural networks with attention (LCA). Its performance was evaluated using the datasets provided by SemEval competition (Task 4). The proposed sentiment analyzer obtained an average F1 of 55.2%, an average recall of 58.9% and an accuracy of 61.4%.

1 Introduction

Sentiment analysis is necessary to interpret the vast number of online opinions on social media platforms such as Twitter. This will allow governments and corporations to manage public relations and policies effectively. Existing sentiment analyzers are based on naïve bayes, SVM, RNN (Irsoy, 2014) and in particular convolutional neural networks (CNNs) (Kim, 2014).

In order to improve on existing CNN based sentiment analyzer, lexicon embedding and attention embedding were integrated into the proposed sentiment analyzer. Lexicon embedding allows extraction of sentimental score for each word and attention embedding enables the global view of the sentence.

The proposed LCA was both trained and evaluated using corpus from Twitter 2013 to 2016 provided by the SemEval-2017. Figure 1 shows the overview of the proposed sentiment analyzer. It consists of embedding, CNNs, concatenation, fully connected and softmax layer.

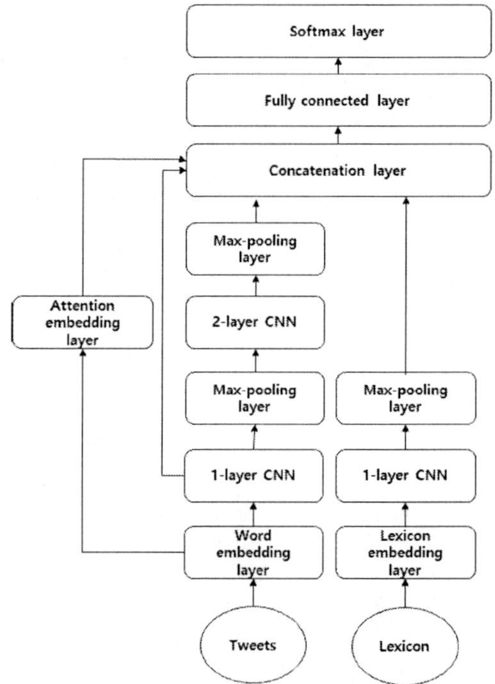

Figure 1: Architecture of proposed LCA.

2 Input Features & Architecture

The proposed LCA consists of three input features
(i)   Word embeddings
(ii)   Lexicon embeddings
(iii)   Attention embeddings.

Proceedings of the 11th International Workshop on Semantic Evaluations (SemEval-2017), pages 732–736,
Vancouver, Canada, August 3 - 4, 2017. ©2017 Association for Computational Linguistics

Word embeddings are trained by implementation of word2vec using skip-gram (Mikolov, 2014) and negative sampling. The word embeddings are trained using an unlabeled corpus of 1.6M tweets from Sentiment 140 dataset with different dimensions (50, 100, 200, 400). The dimensions of word embeddings are d and the number of words in a document is n

Lexicon embeddings are considered because they are useful features. Lexicon embeddings consist of set of words each paired with a score ranging from -1 to +1. Where a score of -1 represents a negative sentiment and +1, a positive sentiment. The lexicon document corresponding to each word is $s_l \in \mathbb{R}^{n \times e}$, where e is the dimension of lexicon embeddings and it is set by the number of lexicon corpus.

Attention embeddings are important for Deep Learning in terms of performance and explanation of models (Kelvin, 2015). CNN uses several filters which have length l. It considers l-gram features, but it only takes local views into account not considering the global view of sentence. Sentiment analysis must consider transitional cases such as negation. While attention embeddings can capture keywords to improve sentiment analysis, it also considers the global view of sentence. In order to do so, CNN for attention embedding used 1 as the length of filter. Then, it executes max pooling for each row of attention matrix. The output of max pooing is an attention vector which has probabilities assigned to each word vector that has d-dimension.

The architecture of LCA consists of
    (i)   a word and lexicon embedding layer,
    (ii)   CNNs,
    (iii)   a concatenation layer,
    (iv)   a fully connected layer
    (v)   and a softmax layer.

Word and lexicon embedding layer transform input data into vector representation. The input to our model is a document, treated as a sequence of words. Instead of hand-crafted features, we used word2vec (w2v) to represent words to vectors. We also converted lexicons to vectors, containing sentiment score. The Input document matrix is $s \in$

$\mathbb{R}^{n \times d}$ where n is the number of words in a document.

Convolutional neural networks are effective for extracting high level features. We modified the LCA architecture of Shin (2016). The proposed LCA consists of two layer CNNs with a nonlinearity, max pooling layers, a concatenation layer and a softmax classification layer with respect to the word embedding layer. The architecture of the proposed LCA was chosen empirically. The document matrix s is convolved by the filter $c \in \mathbb{R}^{l \times d}$, where l is the length of filters. In convolving lexicon embeddings by the filter, we used the separate convolution approach of Shin (2016).

Concatenation layer consists of 1-layer CNN, 2-layer CNN, lexicon and attention outputs. We deliberately designed our model so that the output of 1-layer CNN captures low level feature for getting additional information. The dimension of concatenation layer is $D_{concat} \in \mathbb{R}^{2m+d \times n_l}$, where m is the number of filters with the same length and n_l is the number of filters with different lengths.

Fully connected layer (FC) is used to create nonlinear combinations with rectified linear unit (ReLU) (Nair and Hinton, 2010). The input of fully connected layer is the output of concatenation layer. The dimension of weight is $W_{fc} \in \mathbb{R}^{D_{concat} \times n_c}$ and bias is $b_{fc} \in \mathbb{R}^{n_c}$, where n_c is the number of class.

Softmax layer is used to convert the output of FC layer into classification probabilities. In order to compute the probabilities, softmax function was used:

$$\text{softmax}(x_i) = \frac{e^{x_i}}{\sum_i e^{x_i}}$$

The output dimension is 3 because our model classified tweets into 3 classes (positive, neutral and negative).

Regularization is achieved by L_2 regularizer. In order to prevent overfitting from our CNN model, dropout is used at the output of CNN and fully connected layer. To do this, each node is randomly removed. We also apply L_2 regularization to the cost function by adding the term $\lambda \|\theta\|_2^2$, where λ

is the regularization strength and $\theta \in \Theta$ are the fully connected neural network parameters.

3. Data and Preprocessing

Tweets are used as the training and development dataset from Twitter 2013 to 2016 (The training and development dataset were provided by the SemEval-2017 competition.) In addition, sentiment 140 corpus are added for training word embedding.

Lexicons in the proposed LCA have six types of sentiment lexicons (that include sentimental score). Some lexicons only contain positive and negative sentiment polarities. Sentiment scores were normalized to the range from -1 to +1 because some lexicons have different scales. If some words are missing in a lexicon, we assigned neutral sentiment score of 0.

- SemEval-2015 English Twitter Sentiment Lexicon (2015).

- National Research Council Canada (NRC) Hashtag Affirmative and Negated Context Sentiment Lexicon (2014).

- NRC Sentiment140 Lexicon (2014).

- Yelp Restaurant Sentiment Lexicons (2014).

- NRC Hashtag Sentiment Lexicon (2013).

- Bing Liu Opinion Lexicon (2004).

Corpus	Total	Positive	Negative	Neutral
Train 2013	9,684	3,640	1,458	4,586
Dev 2013	1,654	575	340	739
Train 2015	489	170	6	253
Train 2016	6,000	3,094	863	2,043
Dev 2016	1,999	843	391	765
DevTest 2016	2,000	994	325	681
Test 2013	3,547	1,475	559	1,513
Test 2014	1,853	982	202	669
Test 2015	2,390	1,038	365	987
Test 2016	20,632	7,059	3,231	10,342
TwtSarc 2014	86	33	40	13
SMS 2013	2,094	492	394	1,208
LiveJournal 2014	1,142	427	304	411

Table 1: Overview of datasets

The following preprocessings were applied to every tweets and lexicon in the corpus:

- Lowercase: all the characters in tweets and lexicons are converted in lowercase.

- Tokenization: all tweets were tokenized using tokenizer.

- Cleaning: URLs and '#' token in hashtag were removed to reduce sparse representation.

4. Training and Hyperparameters

The parameters of our model were trained by *Adam* (Diederik et al., 2014) optimizer. To anneal the learning rate over time, the learning rate were calculated by exponential decay. The following configuration is our hyperparameters:

- Embedding dimension = (50, 100, 200, 400) for both word and attention embeddings.

- Filter size = (2,3,4,5,6) for capturing more n-gram features.

- Number of filters = (128) for convolving the document matrix s combined with lexicon and attention embeddings.

- Batch size = (64) for calculating losses to update weight parameters.

- Number of epochs = (80) for training our models.

- Starter learning rate = (0.0001) for updating weight parameters.

- Exponential decay steps and rate = (3000, 0.96) for annealing the learning rate.

- Dropout rate = (0.5) for avoiding overfitting from the last layer of CNN and FC layer

- L_2 Regularization lambda = (0.005) for avoiding overfitting from FC layer

5. Evaluation

The evaluation metric consisted of

(i)   macro-averaged F1 measure,
(ii)   recall
(iii)   and accuracy in the competition across the positive, negative and neutral classes.

	$d(50)$	$d(100)$	$d(200)$	$d(400)$
F1 score	0.6065	**0.6097**	0.594	0.5841

Table 2: F1 scores corresponding
to the dimension of word embedding

Model	Twt2013	Twt2014	Twt2015	Twt2016
All features	0.6116	**0.6202**	0.6109	0.6194
w/o lexicon	0.5460	0.5501	0.5414	0.5682
w/o w2v	0.5872	0.5825	0.5811	0.5810
w/o both	0.5256	0.5409	0.5187	0.5327

Table 3: Test score of F1

6. Results

The result of competition showed that our model was overfitting because our experimental results were higher than the actual result. In our experiment, lexicon and word embedding feature showed that it could improve our model. Table 2 presents the various dimensions of word embeddings that could change performance which is high when the dimension of word embedding is 100. Table 3 shows lexicons as the feature more important than word2vec because the overall performances of model with lexicon were higher than the overall performance with word2vec. Since the sentiment score of missing words (such as 0; neutral) has been replaced, the lexicon feature is not perfect. Nonetheless, lexicon is still an important and essential feature for sentiment analysis.

7. Conclusion

This paper proposes the integration of lexicon with attention on CNN as an approach to sentiment analysis. We considered various features to capture improved representations by concatenating the output of 1-layer and 2-layer CNN. Lexicon and word embedding showed that these features improved the model performance significantly.

Additional enhancements are viable by gathering more training dataset or lexicon dataset with distant supervision (Deriu et al, 2016), because it will extend the coverage of our model. Furthermore, in the aspect of models, the combined CNN-CRF model, recursive neural network and ensembles of multi-layer CNN can be applied.

Acknowledgments

This research was supported by Basic Science Research Program through the National Research Foundation of Korea (NRF) funded by the Ministry of Science, ICT & Future Planning (NRF-2017R1A2B4003558).

References

Yoon Kim. 2014. Convolutional Neural Networks for Sentence Classification. In *EMNLP 2014 - Empirical Methods in Natural Language Processing*, pages 1746–1751.

Bonggun Shin, Timothy Lee, and Jinho D. Choi. 2016. Lexicon Integrated CNN Models with Attention for Sentiment Analysis. *arXiv preprint arXiv:*1610.06272.

Mickael Rouvier, Benoit Favre. 2016. Polarity embedding fusion for robust sentiment analysis. *Proceedings of SemEval (2016)*: 202-208.

Jan, Deriu, et al. 2016. Sentiment classification using an ensemble of convolutional neural networks with distant supervision. *Proceedings of SemEval (2016)*: 1124-1128.

XingYi, Xu, Liang HuiZhi , and Baldwin Timothy. An Ensemble of Neural Networks and a Word2Vec Based Model for Sentiment Classification. *Proceedings of SemEval (2016)*: 183-189.

Kingma, Diederik, and Ba Jimmy. 2014. Adam: A method for stochastic optimization. *arXiv preprint arXiv:1412.6980 (2014)*.

Vinod Nair and Geoffrey E. Hinton. 2010. Rectified linear units improve restricted boltzmann machines. In *ICML 2010 - Proceedings of the 27th International Conference on Machine Learning*, pages 807–814.

Tomas, Mikolov, et al. 2013. Distributed representations of words and phrases and their compositionality. *Advances in neural information processing systems. 2013.*

Kelvin, Xu, et al. 2015. Show, Attend and Tell: Neural Image Caption Generation with Visual Attention. In *ICML. Vol. 14. 2015.*

rsoy, Ozan, and Cardie Claire. 2014. Opinion Mining with Deep Recurrent Neural Networks. In *EMNLP 2014 - Empirical Methods in Natural Language Processing*, pages 720-728.

Socher, Richard, et al. 2013. Recursive deep models for semantic compositionality over a sentiment treebank. In *Proceedings of the conference on empirical methods in natural language processing (EMNLP). Vol. 1631. 2013.*

EICA at SemEval-2017 Task 4: A Convolutional Neural Network for Topic-based Sentiment Classification

Maoquan Wang, Shiyun Chen, Yufei Xie, Jing Ma, Zhao Lu

Department of Computer Science and Technology,
East China Normal University, Shanghai, P.R.China

{maoquanwang,yufeixie,liangma,lzhao}@ica.stc.sh.cn, csyecnu@outlook.com

Abstract

This paper describes our approach for SemEval-2017 Task 4 - Sentiment Analysis in Twitter (SAT). Its five subtasks are divided into two categories: (1) sentiment classification, i.e., predicting topic-based tweet sentiment polarity, and (2) sentiment quantification, that is, estimating the sentiment distributions of a set of given tweets. We build a convolutional sentence classification system for the task of SAT. Official results show that the experimental results of our system are comparative.

1 Introduction

With the rapid growth of social media such as Twitter, sentiment classification towards the user generated texts has attracted increasing research interest. The objective of sentiment classification is identifying the sentiment of a text into binary polarity (Positive vs. Negative) or single-label multi-class (e.g., Very positive, Positive, Neutral, Negative, Very negative). Feature representation is one of key points for this kind of classification, which generally falls into two categories: (1) traditional feature engineering (Liu, 2012; Mohammad et al., 2013), such as sentiment lexicon, n-grams, dependency triple, etc. (2) deep learning methods (Zhao et al., 2015; Yang et al., 2016), which use exquisitely designed neural network to encode input texts and to get text feature representation. Recently, deep learning approaches emerge as powerful computational models for text sentiment classification, and have achieved new state-of-the-art result in some datasets.

SemEval-2017 provides a universal platform for researchers to explore the task of twitter sentiment analysis. In this paper, we explore Task 4 (Rosenthal et al., 2017), which includes five subtasks: subtask A, B and C are related to the task of sentiment classification, and subtask D and E are related to sentiment quantification (that is distributions of sentiments). Considering the length limitations of tweets, we view the subtasks of SAT as sentence-level sentiment analysis. We design a convolutional neural network for topic-based sentiment classification.

2 System Description

In this section, we describe the neural network architecture of our system. As shown in Figure 1, our system consists of six layers, an input layer, a convolutional layer, a max-pooling layer, a topic embedding layer, a concatenate layer, and an output layer.

Input layer. A tweet text can be denoted as a sentence sequence $\mathbf{x}$ with n words, $\mathbf{x} = [w_1, w_2, \cdots, w_i, \cdots, w_n]$. To obtain word vector of word w_i, we look-up word embedding matrix $\mathbf{E}$, where $e(w_i) \in \mathbf{R}^d$, $\mathbf{E} \in \mathbf{R}^{|V| \times d}$, $|V|$ is the vocabulary size. Then, we get an input matrix $\mathbf{X} = [e(w_1); \cdots; e(w_n)]$, where $\mathbf{X} \in \mathbf{R}^{n \times d}$.

Convolution layer. The convolution action has been used to capture n-gram information (Collobert et al., 2011), and n-gram has been shown useful for twitter sentiment analysis (Dos Santos and Gatti, 2014). In this layer, a set of m filters is applied to a sliding window of length h over each tweet matrix $\mathbf{X}$, and a feature $\mathbf{c_i} \in \mathbf{R}^{n-h+1}$ is generated from a window of words $e(w)_{i:i+h}$ by:

$$\mathbf{c_i} = f(F_k \cdot e(w)_{i:i+h} + b) \qquad (1)$$

where f is an activation function, and $b \in \mathbf{R}$ is a bias term. The vectors $\mathbf{c} = [\mathbf{c}_1 \oplus \cdots \oplus \mathbf{c}_m]$ are then aggregated over all m filters into a feature map matrix. We consider m is 3, and h is chosen in $\{3, 4, 5\}$.

Max-pooling layer. In order to get a fixed dimension vector, we exploit pooling techniques to

Proceedings of the 11th International Workshop on Semantic Evaluations (SemEval-2017), pages 737–740,
Vancouver, Canada, August 3 - 4, 2017. ©2017 Association for Computational Linguistics

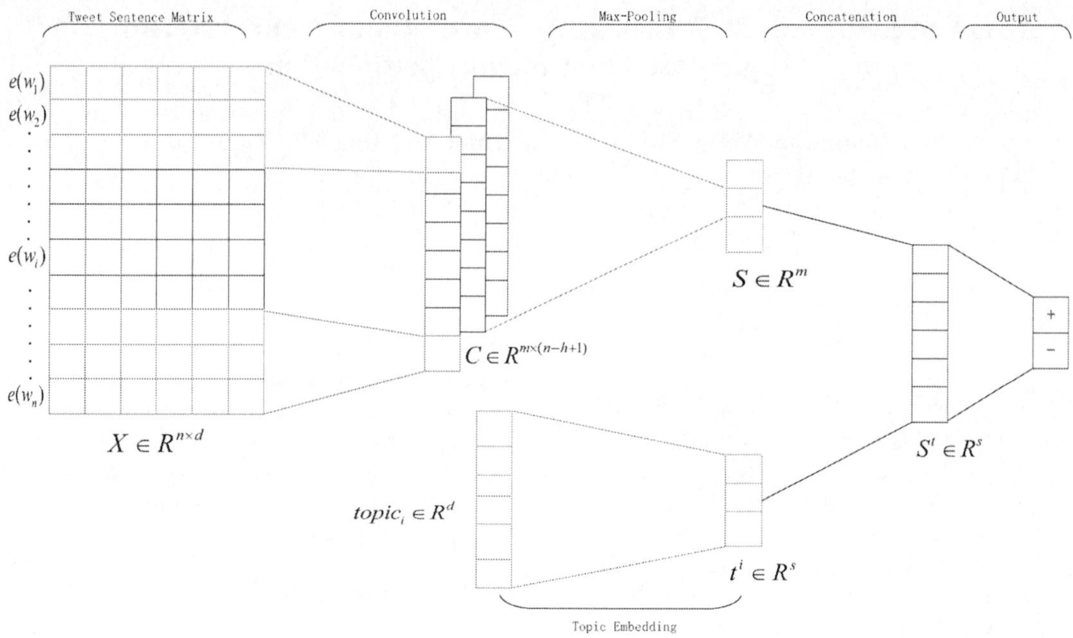

Figure 1: The framework of the simple CNN for topic-based sentiment classification.

get sentence representation $\mathbf{S} \in \mathbf{R}^m$, and we adopt max pooling function.

Topic embedding layer. To make the best use of topic information, we propose to learn an embedding vector $\mathbf{t}_i$ for each topic:

$$\mathbf{t}_i = tanh(W^{(1)} avg(e(\mathbf{w}_1), \cdots, e(\mathbf{w}_k))) \quad (2)$$

where $w_1, \cdots, w_k$ are topic words, $\mathbf{t_i} \in \mathbf{R}^s$, $avg(\cdot)$ is a element average function, and $W^{(1)} \in \mathbf{R}^{s \times d}$.

Concatenation layer. We use a concatenation layer to get tweet representation which can be formed as:

$$\mathbf{S^t} = tanh(W^{(2)} [\mathbf{S} \oplus \mathbf{t_i}]) \quad (3)$$

where $\oplus$ is the concatenation operator, $W^{(2)} \in \mathbf{R}^{s \times (s+m)}$.

Output layer. Finally, we use a softmax layer to get the class probability:

$$P_i = \frac{exp(W_{y_i}^T \mathbf{S}^{\mathbf{t}(i)} + b_{y_i})}{\sum_{j=1}^{C} exp(W_j^T \mathbf{S}^{\mathbf{t}(i)} + b_j)}. \quad (4)$$

Where $\mathbf{S}^{\mathbf{t}(\mathbf{i})}$ denotes the tweet representation with sentiment class y_i. W_j is jth column of parameter $W \in \mathbf{R}^{2s \times C}$ and C is number of categories.

Training process. The training goal is to minimize the cross-entropy loss over the training set T:

$$L(\theta) = -\sum_{x \in T} \sum_{i=1}^{C} P_i^g(x) \cdot logP_i(x) + \frac{\lambda}{2} \| \theta \|^2 \quad (5)$$

where C is the number of classes, x represents a tweet, θ is the model parameters, $P^g(x)$ is the goal probability, which has the same dimension as the number of classes, and only the corresponding goal dimension is 1, with all others being 0.

We use mini-batch gradient descent algorithm to train the network, with the batch size is 32 and a learning rage of 0.01. We also use Adadelta (Zeiler, 2012) to optimize the learning of θ, which is a effective method to train the neural networks. We initialize all the matrix and vector parameters with uniform samples in $\left(-\sqrt{6/(r+c)}, +\sqrt{6/(r+c)}\right)$ (Glorot and Bengio, 2010), where r is the rows numbers , and c is the column numbers.

Pre-training Word Embedding We adopted the word2vec tool[1] to obtain word embedding with

---

[1] https://code.google.com/archive/p/word2vec

the dimensionality of 100, trained on 238M tweet from Sentiment140[2].

3 Experiments

3.1 Datasets

Since only tweet IDs are provided by organizers, Some tweets are no longer available on Twitter due to tweets miss or system errors. Subtask B and D share one dataset, while subtask C and E share the other dataset. An overview statistics of the data available for download are given in Tables 1, 2, and 3, respectively.

	dataset	positive	neutral	negative	total
train	2013train	3,632	4,564	1,453	9,649
	2013test	1,473	1,513	559	3,545
	2015test	1,033	983	363	2,379
	2016train	3,078	2,036	861	5,975
	2016dev	842	765	390	1,997
	2016test	7,033	10,302	3,221	20,556
dev	2013dev	573	737	339	1,649
	2014test	982	669	202	1,853
	2015train	170	252	66	488
	2016devtest	994	681	323	1,998
test	2017test	2,375	5,937	3,972	12,284

Table 1: Statistics of datasets for subtask A, English. The data was divided into train, dev and test sets.

	dataset	positive	negative	total	topics
train	2015train	144	56	200	44
	2016train	3,579	754	4,333	60
	2016dev	985	339	1,324	20
	2016test	8,202	2,333	10,535	100
dev	2015test	863	260	1,123	137
	2016devtest	1,417	264	1,417	20
test	2017test	2,458	3,695	6,153	125

Table 2: Statistics of datasets for subtask B and D, English. The data was divided into train, dev and test sets.

	dataset	-2	-1	0	1	2	total	topics
train	2016train	87	665	1,651	3,139	433	5,975	60
	2016dev	43	296	675	930	53	1,997	20
	2016test	136	2,191	10,034	7,814	381	20,556	100
dev	2016devtest	31	232	582	1,005	148	1,998	20
test	2017test	177	3,505	6,149	2,323	130	12,284	125

Table 3: Statistics of datasets for subtask C and E, English. The data was divided into train, dev and test sets.

[2] http://help.sentiment140.com/
for-students/

3.2 Tweet Preparation.

We preprocessed all of our datasets as follows:

- The tweet text was lowercased.

- URLs and mentioned usernames were substituted by replacement tokens $<$ **LINK** $>$ and $<$ **MENTION** $>$ respectively. We also map numbers to a generic **NUMBER** token.

- All words that appear less than 5 times in the training were removed.

- Recovered the elongated words to their original forms, e.g., "goooooood " to "good".

- The NLTK[3] twitter tool was employed to tokenize tweets.

3.3 Result on Test Data

Subtask A. For this subtask, there is no topic information, so we removed the Concatenate and Topic Embedding parts in Figure 1. We report the result of our system in Table 4.

Metric	Our score	Best score	Rank
ρ	0.595	0.681	23/37
F_1^{PN}	0.599	0.677	24/37
Acc	0.555	0.651	24/37

Table 4: Our score and rank compared to the best team's result for Subtask A "Message Polarity Classification" , English.

As shown in Table 4, we obtained poor performance in Subtask A. In order to further analysis our system performance on three-point scale(positive, negative, neutral), we show the detail results in Table 5

Our system did not distinguish the positive and negative class, but it performed well in neutral class. The unbalanced train data distribution may influence our system: 49%(positive), 31%(neutral) , 20%(negative).

Subtask B and C. The results of our system for Subtasks B and C are reported in Table 6 and Table 7, individually. For these two subtasks, the organizers make available alternative metrics. We found that the choice of the scoring metric influences results considerably, for example, in Subtask C, our system ranked second by MAE^{μ} while ranked 8th in MAE^{M}.

[3] http://nltk.org/

Team		P	R	F1
	+	0.5086	0.6371	0.5656
EICA	-	0.6137	0.4907	0.5453
	=	0.6351	0.6561	0.6454
	+	0.6259	0.7023	0.6619
DataStories	-	0.5929	0.8291	0.6914
	=	0.7471	0.5115	0.6073
	+	0.6851	0.6522	0.6682
BB_twtr	-	0.5848	0.8776	0.7019
	=	0.7518	0.5144	0.6109

Table 5: More detail metric in task A. EICA is our team name, DataStories and BB_twtr are rank 1 teams which have same ρ score. +: positive. -: negative. =: neutral

Metric	Our score	Best score	Rank
ρ	0.790	0.882	14/23
F_1^{PN}	0.775	0.890	14/23
Acc	0.777	0.897	16/23

Table 6: Our score and rank compared to the best team's result for Subtask B "Tweet classification according to a two-point scale" , English.

4 Conclusion

In this paper, we used a simple convolution neural network to accomplish sentiment analysis towards sentence level (i.e., subtask A) and topic level (i.e., subtask B, C), without using any user information. In future work, we will focus on developing advanced neural network to model sentence with the aid of user information. we also would like to ensemble deep leaning based classifier with handcrafted features based classifier to improve the system performance, in the next SemEval competition.

Acknowledgements

This research was supported in part by Science and Technology Commission of Shanghai Municipality (No.16511102702).

References

Ronan Collobert, Jason Weston, Léon Bottou, Michael Karlen, Koray Kavukcuoglu, and Pavel Kuksa. 2011. Natural language processing (almost) from scratch. *Journal of Machine Learning Research* 12(Aug):2493–2537.

Cícero Nogueira Dos Santos and Maira Gatti. 2014.

Metric	Our score	Best score	Rank
MAE^M	0.823	0.481	8/15
MAE^μ	0.509	0.554	2/15

Table 7: Our score and rank compared to the best team's result for Subtask C "Tweet classification according to a five-point scale" , English

Deep convolutional neural networks for sentiment analysis of short texts. In *COLING*. pages 69–78.

Xavier Glorot and Yoshua Bengio. 2010. Understanding the difficulty of training deep feedforward neural networks. In *Aistats*. volume 9, pages 249–256.

Bing Liu. 2012. Sentiment analysis and opinion mining. *Synthesis lectures on human language technologies* 5(1):1–167.

Saif M Mohammad, Svetlana Kiritchenko, and Xiaodan Zhu. 2013. Nrc-canada: Building the state-of-the-art in sentiment analysis of tweets. *arXiv preprint arXiv:1308.6242* .

Sara Rosenthal, Noura Farra, and Preslav Nakov. 2017. SemEval-2017 task 4: Sentiment analysis in Twitter. In *Proceedings of the 11th International Workshop on Semantic Evaluation*. Association for Computational Linguistics, Vancouver, Canada, SemEval '17.

Zichao Yang, Diyi Yang, Chris Dyer, Xiaodong He, Alex Smola, and Eduard Hovy. 2016. Hierarchical attention networks for document classification. In *Proceedings of NAACL-HLT*. pages 1480–1489.

Matthew D Zeiler. 2012. Adadelta: an adaptive learning rate method. *arXiv preprint arXiv:1212.5701* .

Han Zhao, Zhengdong Lu, and Pascal Poupart. 2015. Self-adaptive hierarchical sentence model. *arXiv preprint arXiv:1504.05070* .

funSentiment at SemEval-2017 Task 4: Topic-Based Message Sentiment Classification by Exploiting Word Embeddings, Text Features and Target Contexts

Quanzhi Li, Armineh Nourbakhsh, Xiaomo Liu, Rui Fang, Sameena Shah

Research and Development
Thomson Reuters
3 Times Square, NYC, NY 10036
{quanzhi.li, armineh.nourbakhsh, xiaomo.liu, rui.fang, sameena.shah}@thomsonreuters.com

Abstract

This paper describes the approach we used for SemEval-2017 Task 4: Sentiment Analysis in Twitter. Topic-based (target-dependent) sentiment analysis has become attractive and been used in some applications recently, but it is still a challenging research task. In our approach, we take the left and right context of a target into consideration when generating polarity classification features. We use two types of word embeddings in our classifiers: the general word embeddings learned from 200 million tweets, and sentiment-specific word embeddings learned from 10 million tweets using distance supervision. We also incorporate a text feature model in our algorithm. This model produces features based on text negation, tf.idf weighting scheme, and a Rocchio text classification method. We participated in four subtasks (B, C, D & E for English), all of which are about topic-based message polarity classification. Our team is ranked #6 in subtask B, #3 by MAE^u and #9 by MAE^m in subtask C, #3 using RAE and #6 using KLD in subtask D, and #3 in subtask E.

1 Introduction

There have been many studies on message or sentence level sentiment classification (Go et al., 2009; Mohammand et al., 2013; Pang et al., 2002; Liu, 2012; Tang et al., 2014), but there are few studies on target-dependent, or topic-based, sentiment prediction (Jiang et al., 2011; Dong et al., 2014; Vo and Zhang, 2015). A target entity in a message does not necessarily have the same polarity type as the message, and different entities in the same message may have different polarities. For example, in the tweet "Linux is better than Windows", the two named entities, *Linux* and *Windows*, will have different sentiment polarities. In this paper, we describe our approach for the subtask B, C, D & E of

SemEval-17 Task 4: Sentiment Analysis in Twitter (Sara Rosenthal and Noura Farra and Preslav Nakov, 2017). All the four subtasks are on topic-based message sentiment classification. Task B and C are about topic-based message polarity classification. Given a message and a topic, in task B, we classify the message on a two-point scale: positive or negative sentiment towards the topic. And in task C, we classify the message on a five-point scale: sentiment conveyed by the tweet towards the topic on a five-point scale. Task D and E are about Tweet quantification. Given a set of tweets about a given topic, in task D, we want to estimate the distribution of the tweets across two-point scale - the positive and negative classes, and in task E, we estimate that on a five-point scale - the five classes of a five-point scale. Our approach uses word embeddings (WE) learned from general tweets, sentiment specific word embeddings (SSWE) learned from distance supervised tweets, and a weighted text feature model (WTM).

Learning features directly from tweet text has recently gained lot of attention. One approach is to generate sentence representations from word embeddings. Several word embedding generation algorithms have been proposed in previous studies (Collobert et al., 2011; Mikolov et al., 2013). Using the general word embeddings directly in sentiment classification is not effective, since they mainly model a word's semantic context, ignoring the sentiment clues in text. Therefore, words with opposite polarity, such as *worst* and *best*, are mapped onto vectors embeddings that are close to each other in some dimensions. Tang et al. (2014) propose a sentiment-specific word embedding (SSWE) method for sentiment analysis, by extending the word embedding algorithm.

Proceedings of the 11th International Workshop on Semantic Evaluations (SemEval-2017), pages 741–746,
Vancouver, Canada, August 3 - 4, 2017. ©2017 Association for Computational Linguistics

SSWE encodes sentiment information in the word embeddings.

In our approach, we incorporate WE, SSWE and a weighted text feature model (WTM) together. The WTM model generates two types of features. The first type is a negation feature based on the negation words in a tweet. The second set of features is created by computing the similarity between the tweet and each of the polarity types, using cosine similarity and the tf.idf word weighting scheme. Each polarity category is represented by a pseudo centroid tweet learned from training data. This is very similar to the Rocchio text classifier (Christopher et al., 2008), but here all the similarity values with all the polarity types are used as features, and fed to the classification algorithm. The rationale behind the second set of features is that the similarity values with the different polarity types will have some correlations, and using all of them as features will provide more information to the classifier. For example, a positive tweet usually will have a higher similarity value with neutral type than with the negative type. This will provide an additional signal to the classifier.

The context of an entity will affect its polarity value, and usually an entity has a left context and also a right one, unless it is at the beginning or end of a message. Both the context information and the interaction between these two contexts are included in the classification features of our approach. Our approach uses both SSWE and WE to represent these contexts, since WE and SSWE complement each other, and our experiment shows that using both increases the accuracy by more than 6%, compared to using only one of them.

In the following sections, we present the related studies, our methodology and the experiments and results for subtask B, C, D and E.

2 Related Work

Message Level Sentiment: Traditional sentiment classification approaches use sentiment lexicons (Mohammad et al., 2013; Thelwall et al., 2012; Turney, 2002) to generate various features. Pang et al. treat sentiment classification as a special case of text categorization, by applying learning algorithms (2002). Many studies follow Pang's approach by designing features and applying different learning algorithms on them (Feldman, 2013; Liu, 2012). Go et al. (2009) proposed a distance supervision approach to derive features from

tweets obtained by positive and negative emotions. Some studies (Hu et al., 2013; Liu, 2012; Pak and Paroubek 2010) follow this approach. Feature engineering plays an important role in tweet sentiment classification; Mohammad et al. (2013) implemented hundreds of hand-crafted features for tweet sentiment classification.

Deep learning has been used in the sentiment analysis tasks, mainly by applying word embeddings (Collobert et al., 2011; Mikolov et al., 2013). Learning the compositionality of phrase and sentence and then using them in sentiment classification is also explored by some studies (Hermann and Blunsom, 2013; Socher et al., 2011; Socher et al., 2013). Using the general word embeddings directly in sentiment classification may not be effective, since they mainly model a word's semantic context, ignoring the sentiment clues in text. Tang et al. (2014) propose a sentiment-specific word embedding method by extending the word embedding algorithm from (Collobert et al., 2011) and incorporating sentiment data in the learning of word embeddings.

Target-dependent Sentiment: Jiang et al. (2011) use both entity dependent and independent features generated based on a set of rules to assign polarity to entities. By using POS features and the CRF algorithm, Mitchell et al. (2013) identify polarities for people and organizations in tweets. Dong et al. (2014) apply adaptive recursive neural network on the entity level sentiment classification. These two approaches use syntax parsers to parse the tweet to generate related features. In our approach, we consider both the left and right contexts of a target when generating features.

3 Methodology

In this section, we describe the three main components used in our method, the WE, SSWE and WTM models, and how they are integrated together.

3.1 Word Embedding

Word embedding is a dense, low-dimensional and real-valued vector for a word. The embeddings of a word capture both the syntactic structure and semantics of the word. Traditional bag-of-words and bag-of-n-grams hardly capture the semantics of words. Word embeddings have been used in many NLP tasks. The C&W model (Collobert et al., 2011) and the word2vec model (Mikolov et al., 2013), which is used in this study to generate the WE embeddings, are the two popular word embedding models.

The embeddings are learned to optimize an objective function defined on the original text, such as likelihood for word occurrences. One implementation is the word2vec from Mikolov et al. (2013). This model has two training options, continuous bag of words and the Skip-gram model. The Skip-gram model is an efficient method for learning high-quality distributed vector representations that capture a large number of precise syntactic and semantic word relationships. This model is used in our method and here we briefly introduce it.

The training objective of the Skip-gram model is to find word representations that are useful for predicting the surrounding words in a sentence or a document. Given a sequence of training words W_1, W_2, W_3, . ., W_N , the Skip-gram model aims to maximize the average log probability

$$\frac{1}{N} \sum_{n=1}^{N} \sum_{-m \leq i \leq m, i \neq 0} \log p(W_{n+i} \mid W_n)$$

where m is the size of the training context. A larger m will result in more semantic information and can lead to a higher accuracy, at the expense of the training time. Generating word embeddings from text corpus is an unsupervised process. To get high quality embedding vectors, a large amount of training data is necessary. After training, each word, including all hashtags in the case of tweet text, is represented by a low-dimensional, dense and real-valued vector.

3.2   Sentiment-Specific Word Embedding

The C&W model (Collobert et al., 2011) learns word embeddings based on the syntactic contexts of words. It replaces the center word with a random word and derives a corrupted n-gram. The training objective is that the original n-gram is expected to obtain a higher language model score than the corrupted n-gram. The original and corrupted n-grams are treated as inputs of a feed-forward neural network, respectively.

SSWE extends the C&W model by incorporating the sentiment information into the neural network to learn the embeddings; it captures the sentiment information of sentences as well as the syntactic contexts of words (Tang et al., 2014). Given an original (or corrupted) n-gram and the sentiment polarity of a tweet as input, it predicts a two-dimensional vector (f_0, f_1), for each input

n-gram, where (f_0, f_1) are the language model score and sentiment score of the input n-gram, respectively. The training objectives are twofold: the original n-gram should get a higher language model score than the corrupted n-gram, and the polarity score of the original n-gram should be more aligned to the polarity label of the tweet than the corrupted one. The loss function is the linear combination of two losses - $loss_0$ (t, t') is the syntactic loss and $loss_1$ (t, t') is the sentiment loss:

$$loss\ (t, t') = \alpha * loss_0\ (t, t') + (1-\alpha) * loss_1\ (t, t')$$

The SSWE model used in this study was trained from massive distant-supervised tweets, collected using positive and negative emotions.

3.3 Weighted Text Feature Model (WTM)

WTM features: This model only uses the training data set to generate features; it does not use any external lexicon or other data sources, such as embeddings learned from millions of tweets. The feature generation process is simple, fast, and effective. This model generates two types of features for each training or test tweet:

- Negation feature - the number of negation words in the tweet. This is different from other studies that add a prefix to all the words that follow the negation word, e.g. NOT xxx becomes NOT_xxx. We use the following negation words: *no, not, cannot, rarely, seldom, neither, hardly, nor, n't, never*
- Features corresponding to the cosine similarity values between this tweet and the pseudo centroid tweet of each of the polarity types.

Pseudo centroid tweet: The pseudo centroid tweet for each sentiment type is built from training data, via the following steps:

- Tweet text is pre-processed as follow:
  - all URLs and mentions are removed
  - dates are converted to a symbol
  - all ratios are replaced by a special symbol
  - integers and decimals are normalized to two special symbols
  - all special characters, except hashtags, emoticons, question marks and exclamations, are removed
  - negation words that are already used in the negation features are removed
- A tf.idf value is calculated for each term in a polarity category. For tf.idf, each catego-

ry is treated as a document, and tf is normalized by its category size.

- A pseudo centroid tweet is generated for each sentiment type. We define a centroid as a vector containing the tf.idf value for each term in this category. Although we call it a "tweet", its length is much longer than a regular tweet.

Similarity value: For each training or test tweet, its similarity with a sentiment type is calculated as follows:

- The tweet text is pre-processed using the same steps mentioned above
- A tf.idf value is calculated for each remaining term
- A cosine similarity is calculated between this tweet and each sentiment type.

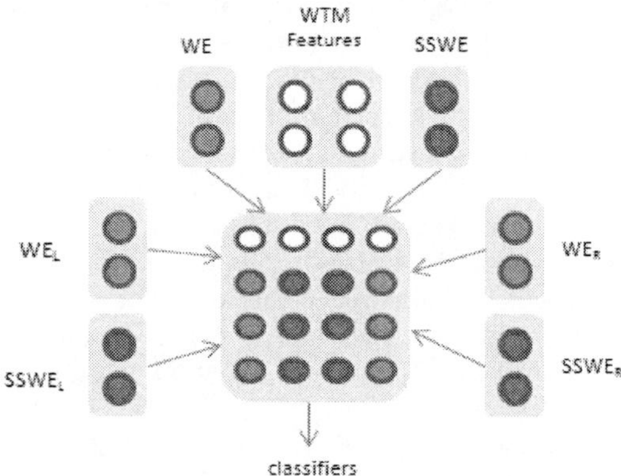

Figure 1. The features generated from different models.

3.4 Feature Generation

3.4.1 Features

Given a tweet and the target entity, eight types of features are generated based on WE, SSWE, and WTM models. They are integrated together to train the classifier. Figure 1 shows the eight types of features. Six types of features are generated from WE and SSWE embeddings for a target entity. Two types of features are generated from the WTM model. The red ones are SSWE embeddings, and the blue ones are WE embeddings. The subscript letter $_L$ and $_R$ refer to the left and right side of an entity, respectively. They are described below:

WE$_L$ and WE$_R$: These are the WE embeddings for the text on the left side and right side of the target entity, respectively. In the four subtasks, occasionally, the given topic (target) is a paraphrase of the actual target entity in the tweet text, and it is not easy to match these two. In this case, the whole tweet text is used for both the left and right contexts, and this case is handled in the same way when generating SSWE$_L$ and SSWE$_R$ described below.

SSWE$_L$ and SSWE$_R$: These are the SSWE embeddings for the text on the left side and right side of the target entity, respectively.

WE and SSWE: these are the embeddings generated from the whole message text, which means they are entity independent features. We use these two features to capture the whole message, which reflects the interaction between the left and right sides of the entity.

WTM features: It has two types of features: the negation feature and the features corresponding to the cosine similarity values between the tweet and the pseudo centroid tweet of each of the polarity types. We have described how to generate them in the previous section.

These eight types of features together capture different types of information we are interested: the entity's left and right contexts, the interaction of the two sides, the sentiment specific word embedding information, the general word embedding information, and the sentiment affected by negation terms.

3.4.2 Text Representation from Term Embeddings

There are different ways to obtain the representation of a text segment, such as a whole tweet or the left/right context of an entity, from word embeddings. In our approach, we use the concatenation convolution layer, which concatenates the layers of max, min and average of word embeddings, because this layer gives the best performance based in our pilot experiments.

Subtask	Metric, Score & Rank		
B	ρ	F_1^{PN}	Acc
	0.834_6	0.824_8	0.827_8
C	MAE^μ	MAE^m	
	0.530_3	$0.0.842_9$	
D	RAE	AE	KLD
	0.939_3	0.109_6	0.060_6
E	EMD		
	0.273_3		

Table 1. Evaluation result for subtask B, C, D & E. The subscript of each score is the rank of our approach by the corresponding metric for that task.

4 Experiments and Results

4.1 WE Model Construction

The tweets for building the WE model include tweets obtained through Twitter's public streaming API and the Decahose data (10% of Twitter's streaming data) obtained from Twitter. Only English tweets are included in this study. Totally there are about 200 million tweets. Each tweet text is preprocessed to get a clean version, following similar steps described in the WTM model subsection, except the stop removal step. Stop words are not removed, since they provide important information on how other words are used. Totally, about 2.9 billion words were used to train the WE model. Based on our pilot experiments, we set the embedding dimension size, word frequency threshold and window size as 300, 5 and 8, respectively. There are about 1.9 million unique words in this model.

4.2 SSWE Model Construction

The SSWE model for Twitter was trained from massive distant-supervised tweets (Tang et al., 2014), collected using positive and negative emoticons, such as *:), =), :(and :-(.* A total of 10 million tweets were collected, where 5 million contain positive emotions and the other 5 million contain negative ones. The embedding dimension size was set as 50 and the window size as 3.

4.3 Data Set and Results for Task 4

For subtask B and D, the sentiment classification and quantification based on a 2-point scale, the training data is from the related tasks of SemEval-2015 and SEmEval-2016. There are 20,538 tweets, but the actual tweet texts are not provided, due to privacy concerns. So we crawled these tweets from Twitter's REST API. However, we were unable to obtain all these tweets because some of them were already deleted or not available due to authorization status change. To build our classifier, we split this data set into three parts: 70% as training data, 20% as development data and 10% for testing our classifier. For these two subtasks, we applied several classification algorithms, such as SMO, LibLinear and logistic regression, to see which one performs the best. The result we reported is based on logistic regression, which performed the best.

For subtask C and E, the sentiment classification and quantification based on a 5-point scale, the training data is from the related tasks of SemEval-2016. There are 30,632 tweets, and

similarly to subtask B and D, we downloaded the tweets from Twitter's API and split them into three parts. The result we reported is based on SMO (Keerthi et al., 2001), which performed the best among several classifiers we tested. SMO is a sequential minimal optimization algorithm for training a support vector classifier.

Table 1 shows the results of our approach for the four subtasks. It lists the scores and ranks of our team for all the performance metrics used for each subtask. The subscript of each score is the rank of our team using that metric for that subtask.

The meanings of the measures used in Table 1 are explained below:

For task B: ρ is the macro-averaged recall, which is macro-averaged over the *positive* and the *negative* class. Accuracy and F1 measures are also used for subtask B. As subtask B is topic-based, each metric is computed individually for each topic, and then the results are averaged across the topics to yield the final score. This is the same for all the measures used in task C, D and E, which are all topic based tasks.

For task C: MAE^M is the macro-averaged mean absolute error, which is an ordinal classification measure. Note that MAE^M is a measure of error, not accuracy, and thus lower values are better. MAE^μ is an extension of macro-averaged recall for ordinal regression. More details about these two measures are described in (Baccianella et al., 2009; Nakov et al., 2016a).

For task D: KLD is the Kullback-Leibler Divergence measure, a measure of error, which means that lower values are better. AE is the absolute error and RAE is the relative absolute error.

For task E: Subtask E is an ordinal quantification task. As in binary quantification, the goal is to compute the distribution across classes, assuming a quantification setup. EMD is Earth Mover's Distance (Rubner et al., 2000), which is currently the only known measure for ordinal quantification. Like KLD and MAE, EMD is a measure of error, so lower values are better.

5 Conclusion

This paper describes the approach we used for subtask B, C, D and E of SemEval-2017 Task 4: Sentiment Analysis in Twitter. We use two types of word embeddings in our classifiers: general word embeddings learned from 200 million tweets, and sentiment-specific word embeddings learned from 10 million tweets using distance supervision. We also incorporate a weighted text feature model in our algorithm. Our team is ranked #6 in subtask B, #3 using MAE^u metric and #9 using MAE^m metric in subtask C, #3 using RAE and #6 using KLD in subtask D, and #3 in subtask E.

References

Stefano Baccianella, Andrea Esuli , Fabrizio Sebastiani, SentiWordNet 3.0: An Enhanced Lexical Resource for Sentiment Analysis and Opinion Mining, *LREC 2010*

Stefano Baccianella, Andrea Esuli, and Fabrizio Sebastiani. 2009. Evaluation measures for ordinal regression. *In Proceedings of the 9th IEEE International Conference on Intelligent Systems Design and Applications (ISDA 2009)*. Pisa, IT, pages 283–287.

Ronan Collobert, Jason Weston, Leon Bottou, Michael Karlen, Koray Kavukcuoglu, and Pavel Kuksa. Natural language processing (almost) from scratch. *Journal Machine Learning Research*, 12:2493–2537, 2011.

L. Dong, F. Wei, C. Tan, D. Tang, M. Zhou, K. Xu, adaptive recursive neural network for target-depedant twitter sentiment classification. In *Proceedings of ACL 2014*.

R.-E. Fan, K.-W. Chang, C.-J. Hsieh, X.-R. Wang, and C.-J. Lin. LIBLINEAR: A Library for Large Linear Classification, *Journal of Machine Learning Research*, 9(2008), 1871-1874.

Ronen Feldman. 2013. Techniques and applications for sentiment analysis. *Communications of the ACM*, 56(4):82–89.

Alec Go, Lei Huang, and Richa Bhayani. 2009. Twitter sentiment analysis. *Final Projects from CS224N for Spring 2008/2009* at The Stanford Natural Language Processing Group.

Karl M. Hermann and Phil Blunsom. 2013. The role of syntax in vector space models of compositional semantics. In *Proceedings ACL*, pages 894–904

Xia Hu, Jiliang Tang, Huiji Gao, and Huan Liu. 2013. Unsupervised sentiment analysis with emotional signals. In *Proceedings of the International World Wide Web Conference*, pages 607–618.

L. Jiang, M. Yu, M. Zhou, X. Liu, T. Zhao, target-depedant twitter sentiment classification, In *Proceedings of ACL* 2011

S.S. Keerthi, S.K. Shevade, C. Bhattacharyya, K.R.K. Murthy, 2001. Improvements to Platt's SMO Algorithm for SVM Classifier Design. *Neural Computation*. 13(3):637-649.

Bing Liu. 2012. Sentiment analysis and opinion mining. *Synthesis Lectures on Human Language Technologies*, 5(1):1–167

Tomas Mikolov, Ilya Sutskever, Kai Chen, Greg Corrado, and Jeffrey Dean. Distributed Representations of Words and Phrases and their Compositionality. In *Proceedings of NIPS*, 2013.

Christopher Manning, Prabhakar Raghavan and Hinrich Schütze, (2008), Vector space classification. *Introduction to Information Retrieval*. Cambridge University Press.

Margaret Mitchell, Jacqui Aguilar,Theresa Wilson, and Benjamin Van Durme. Open domain targeted sentiment. I *Proceedings of EMNLP*, 2013.

Saif M Mohammad, Svetlana Kiritchenko, and Xiaodan Zhu. 2013. Nrc-canada: Building the state-ofthe- art in sentiment analysis of tweets. In *Proceedings of SemEval* 2013.

P. Nakov, A. Ritter, S. Rosenthal, F. Sebastiani and V. Stoyanov. 2016. SemEval-2016 Tasks: Sentiment Analysis in Twitter. In *Proceedings of SemEval* 2016

Alexander Pak and Patrick Paroubek. 2010. Twitter as a corpus for sentiment analysis and opinion mining. In *Proceedings of Language Resources and Evaluation Conference*, volume 2010.

Bo Pang, Lillian Lee, and Shivakumar Vaithyanathan. 2002. Thumbs up? sentiment classification using machine learning techniques. In *Proceedings of EMNLP*, pages 79–86

J. Platt, Fast Training of Support Vector Machines using Sequential Minimal Optimization. In B. Schoelkopf and C. Burges and A. Smola, editors, *Advances in Kernel Methods - Support Vector Learning*, 1998

Sara Rosenthal and Noura Farra and Preslav Nakov, SemEval-2017 Task 4: Sentiment Analysis in Twitter. In *Proceedings of SemEval* 2017, Vancouver, Canada

Yossi Rubner, Carlo Tomasi, and Leonidas J. Guibas. 2000. The Earth Mover's Distance as a metric for image retrieval. *International Journal of Computer Vision,* 40(2):99–121.

Richard Socher, J. Pennington, E.H. Huang, A.Y. Ng, and C.D. Manning. 2011. Semi-supervised recursive autoencoders for predicting sentiment distributions. In *Proceedings of EMNLP* 2011, pages 151–161.

Richard Socher, Alex Perelygin, Jean Wu, Jason Chuang, Christopher D. Manning, Andrew Ng, and Christopher Potts. 2013. Recursive deep models for semantic compositionality over a sentiment treebank. In *Proceedings of EMNLP* 2013, pages 1631–1642.

Duyu Tang, Furu Wei, Nan Yang, Ming Zhou, Ting Liu, and Bing Qin. 2014. Learning sentimentspecific word embedding for twitter sentiment classification. In *Proceedings of ACL* 2014, pages 1555–1565.

Duyu Tang, Bing Qin, Xiaocheng Feng, Ting Liu, 2016. Effective LSTMs for Target-Dependent Sentiment Classification, In *Proceedings of COLING* 2016

Mike Thelwall, Kevan Buckley, and Georgios Paltoglou. 2012. Sentiment strength detection for the social web. *Journal of the American Society for Information Science and Technology*, 63(1):163–173.

Peter D Turney. 2002. Thumbs up or thumbs down?: semantic orientation applied to unsupervised classification of reviews. In *Proceedings of ACL*, pages 417–424

D. Vo and Y. Zhang, Target-dependant twitter sentiment classification with rich automatic features, *IJCAI 2015*.

Sida Wang and Christopher D Manning. 2012. Baselines and bigrams: Simple, good sentiment and topic classification. In *Proceedings of ACL* 2012, pages 90–94

DataStories at SemEval-2017 Task 4: Deep LSTM with Attention for Message-level and Topic-based Sentiment Analysis

Christos Baziotis, Nikos Pelekis, Christos Doulkeridis
University of Piraeus - Data Science Lab
Piraeus, Greece
mpsp14057@unipi.gr, npelekis@unipi.gr, cdoulk@unipi.gr

Abstract

In this paper we present two deep-learning systems that competed at SemEval-2017 Task 4 "Sentiment Analysis in Twitter". We participated in all subtasks for English tweets, involving message-level and topic-based sentiment polarity classification and quantification. We use Long Short-Term Memory (LSTM) networks augmented with two kinds of attention mechanisms, on top of word embeddings pre-trained on a big collection of Twitter messages. Also, we present a text processing tool suitable for social network messages, which performs tokenization, word normalization, segmentation and spell correction. Moreover, our approach uses no hand-crafted features or sentiment lexicons. We ranked 1st (tie) in Subtask A, and achieved very competitive results in the rest of the Subtasks. Both the word embeddings and our text processing tool[1] are available to the research community.

1 Introduction

Sentiment analysis is an area in Natural Language Processing (NLP), studying the identification and quantification of the sentiment expressed in text. Sentiment analysis in Twitter is a particularly challenging task, because of the informal and "creative" writing style, with improper use of grammar, figurative language, misspellings and slang.

In previous runs of the Task, sentiment analysis was usually tackled using hand-crafted features and/or sentiment lexicons (Mohammad et al., 2013; Kiritchenko et al., 2014; Palogiannidi et al., 2016), feeding them to classifiers such as Naive Bayes or Support Vector Machines (SVM). These approaches require a laborious feature-engineering process, which may also need domain-specific knowledge, usually resulting both in redundant and missing features. Whereas, artificial neural networks (Deriu et al., 2016; Rouvier and Favre, 2016) which perform feature learning, last year (Nakov et al., 2016) achieved very good results, outperforming the competition.

In this paper, we present two deep-learning systems that competed at SemEval-2017 Task 4 (Rosenthal et al., 2017). Our first model is designed for addressing the problem of message-level sentiment analysis. We employ a 2-layer Bidirectional LSTM, equipped with an attention mechanism (Rocktäschel et al., 2015). For the topic-based sentiment analysis tasks, we propose a Siamese Bidirectional LSTM with a context-aware attention mechanism (Yang et al., 2016). In contrast to top-performing systems of previous years, we do not rely on hand-crafted features, sentiment lexicons and we do not use model ensembles. We make the following contributions:

- A text processing tool for text tokenization, word normalization, word segmentation and spell correction, geared towards Twitter.

- A deep learning system for short-text sentiment analysis using an attention mechanism, in order to enforce the contribution of words that determine the sentiment of a message.

- A deep learning system for topic-based sentiment analysis, with a context-aware attention mechanism utilizing the topic information.

2 Overview

Figure 1 provides a high-level overview of our approach, which consists of two main steps and an optional task-dependent third step: (1) the *text processing*, where we use our own text processing tool for preparing the data for our neural network, (2) the *learning* step, where we train the neural

---

[1] github.com/cbaziotis/ekphrasis

Proceedings of the 11th International Workshop on Semantic Evaluations (SemEval-2017), pages 747–754,
Vancouver, Canada, August 3 - 4, 2017. ©2017 Association for Computational Linguistics

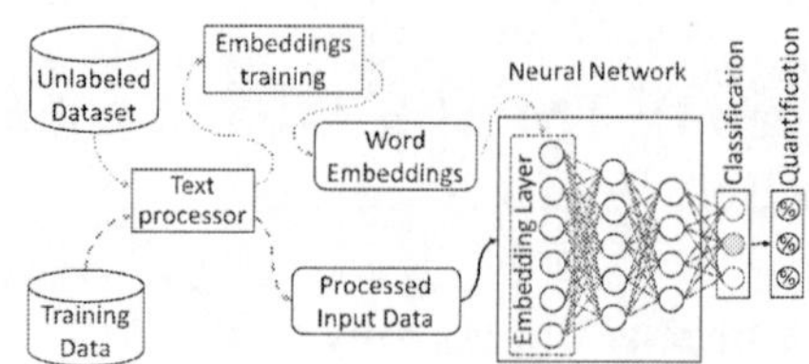

Figure 1: High-level overview of our approach

networks and (3) the *quantification* step for estimating the sentiment distribution for each topic.

Task definitions. In Subtask A, given a message we must classify whether the message expresses positive, negative, or neutral sentiment (3-point scale). In Subtasks B, C (topic-based sentiment polarity classification) we are given a message and a topic and must classify the message on 2-point scale (Subtask B) and a 5-point scale (Subtask C). In Subtasks D, E (quantification) we are given a set of messages about a set of topics and must estimate the distribution of the tweets across 2-point scale (Subtask D) and a 5-point scale (Subtask E).

Unlabeled Dataset. We collected a big dataset of 330M English Twitter messages, gathered from 12/2012 to 07/2016, which is used (1) for calculating words statistics needed by our text processor and (2) for training our word embeddings.

Pre-trained Word Embeddings. Word embeddings are dense vector representations of words (Collobert and Weston, 2008; Mikolov et al., 2013), capturing their semantic and syntactic information. We leverage our big collection of Twitter messages to generate word embeddings, with vocabulary size of 660K words, using GloVe (Pennington et al., 2014). The pre-trained word embeddings are used for initializing the first layer (embedding layer) of our neural networks.

2.1 Text Processor

We developed our own text processing tool, in order to utilize most of the information in text, performing sentiment-aware tokenization, spell correction, word normalization, word segmentation (for splitting hashtags) and word annotation.

Tokenizer. The difficulty in tokenization is to avoid splitting expressions or words that should be kept intact (as one token). Although there are some tokenizers geared towards Twitter (Potts, 2011; Gimpel et al., 2011) that recognize the Twitter markup and some basic sentiment expressions or simple emoticons, our tokenizer is able to identify most emoticons, emojis, expressions such as dates (e.g. 07/11/2011, April 23rd), times (e.g. 4:30pm, 11:00 am), currencies (e.g. \$10, 25mil, 50€), acronyms, censored words (e.g. s**t), words with emphasis (e.g. *very*) and more.

Text Postprocessing. After the tokenization we add an extra postprocessing step, performing modifications on the extracted tokens. This is where we perform spell correction, word normalization and segmentation and decide which tokens to omit, normalize or annotate (surround or replace with special tags). For the tasks of spell correction (Jurafsky and Martin, 2000) and word segmentation (Segaran and Hammerbacher, 2009) we used the Viterbi algorithm, utilizing word statistics (unigrams and bigrams) from our unlabeled dataset, to obtain word probabilities. Moreover, we lowercase all words, and normalize URLs, emails and user handles (@user).

After performing the aforementioned steps we decrease the vocabulary size, while keeping information that is usually lost during the tokenization phase. Table 1 shows an example of our text processing pipeline, on a Twitter message.

2.2 Neural Networks

Last year, most of the top scoring systems used Convolutional Neural Networks (CNN) (LeCun et al., 1998). Even though CNNs are designed for computer vision, the fact that they are fast and easy to train, makes them a popular choice for NLP problems. However CNNs have no notion of order, thus when applying them to NLP tasks the crucial information of the word order is lost.

2.2.1 Recurrent Neural Networks

A more natural choice is to use Recurrent Neural Networks (RNN). An RNN processes an input sequentially, in a way that resembles how humans do it. It performs the same operation, $h_t = f_W(x_t, h_{t-1})$, on every element of a sequence, where h_t is the hidden state a timestep t,

original	The *new* season of #TwinPeaks is coming on May 21, 2017. CANT WAIT \o/ !!! #tvseries #davidlynch :D
processed	the new <emphasis> season of <hashtag> twin peaks </hashtag> is coming on <date> . cant <allcaps> wait <allcaps> <happy> ! <repeated> <hashtag> tv series </hashtag> <hashtag> david lynch </hashtag> <laugh>

Table 1: Example of our text processor. The word annotations help the RNN to learn better features.

and W the weights of the network. The hidden state at each timestep depends on the previous hidden states. This is why the order of the elements (words) is important. This process also enables RNNs to handle inputs of variable length.

RNNs are difficult to train (Pascanu et al., 2013), because gradients may grow or decay exponentially over long sequences (Bengio et al., 1994; Hochreiter et al., 2001). A way to overcome these problems is by using one of the more sophisticated variants of the regular RNN, the Long Short-Term Memory (LSTM) network (Hochreiter and Schmidhuber, 1997) or the recently proposed Gated Recurrent Units (GRU) (Cho et al., 2014). Both variants introduce a gating mechanism, ensuring proper gradient propagation through the network. We use the LSTM, as it performed slightly better than GRU in our experiments.

Attention Mechanism. An RNN updates its hidden state h_i as it processes a sequence and at the end, the hidden state holds a summary of all the processed information. In order to amplify the contribution of important elements in the final representation we use an attention mechanism (Rocktäschel et al., 2015; Raffel and Ellis, 2015), that aggregates all the hidden states using their relative importance (see Figure 2).

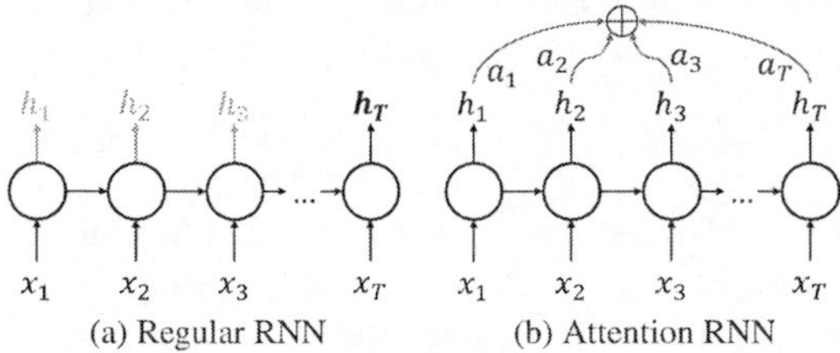

Figure 2: Comparison between the regular RNN and the RNN with attention.

2.3 Quantification

For the quantification tasks an obvious approach is the Classify & Count (Forman, 2008), where we simply compute the fraction of a topic's messages that a classifier predicts to belong to a class c. Another approach is the Probabilistic Classify & Count (PCC) (Gao and Sebastiani, 2016), in which first we train a classifier that produces a probability distribution over the classes and then we average the estimated probabilities for each class to obtain the final distribution. Let T be the set of topics in the training set and $p(c|tweet)$ the (posterior) probability that a tweet belongs to class c as

estimated by the classifier. Then we estimate the expected fraction of a topic's tweets that belong to class c as follows:

$$\hat{p}_T(c) = \frac{1}{|T|} \sum_{tweet \in T} p(c|tweet) \qquad (1)$$

3 Models Description

We propose two different models, a Message-level Sentiment Analysis (MSA) model for Subtask A (3.1) and a Topic-based Sentiment Analysis (TSA) (3.2) model for Subtasks B,C,D,E.

3.1 MSA Model (message-level)

Our message-level sentiment analysis model (MSA) consists of a 2-layer bidirectional LSTM (BiLSTM) with an attention mechanism, for identifying the most informative words.

Embedding Layer. The input to the network is a Twitter message, treated as a sequence of words. We use an Embedding layer to project the words $X = (x_1, x_2, ..., x_T)$ to a low-dimensional vector space R^E, where E the size of the Embedding layer and T the number of words in a tweet. We initialize the weights of the embedding layer with our pre-trained word embeddings.

BiLSTM Layers. An LSTM takes as input the words of a tweet and produces the word annotations $H = (h_1, h_2, ..., h_T)$, where h_i is the hidden state of the LSTM at time-step i, summarizing all the information of the sentence up to x_i. We use bidirectional LSTM (BiLSTM) in order to get word annotations that summarize the information from both directions. A bidirectional LSTM consists of a forward LSTM $\overrightarrow{f}$ that reads the sentence from x_1 to x_T and a backward LSTM $\overleftarrow{f}$ that reads the sentence from x_T to x_1. We obtain the final annotation for a given word x_i, by concatenating the annotations from both directions:

$$h_i = \overrightarrow{h_i} \parallel \overleftarrow{h_i}, \quad h_i \in R^{2L} \qquad (2)$$

where $\parallel$ denotes the concatenation operation and L the size of each LSTM. We stack two layers of BiLSTMs in order to learn more abstract features.

Attention Layer. Not all words contribute equally to the expression of the sentiment in a message. We use an attention mechanism to find the relative contribution (importance) of each word. The attention mechanism assigns a weight a_i to each word annotation. We compute the fixed representation r of the whole message as the weighted sum

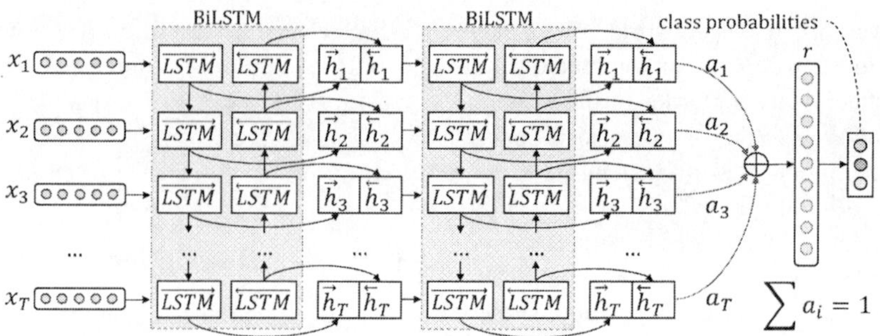

Figure 3: The MSA model: A 2-layer bidirectional LSTM with attention over that last layer.

of all the word annotations. Formally:

$$e_i = tanh(W_h h_i + b_h), \quad e_i \in [-1, 1] \quad (3)$$

$$a_i = \frac{exp(e_i)}{\sum_{t=1}^{T} exp(e_t)}, \quad \sum_{i=1}^{T} a_i = 1 \quad (4)$$

$$r = \sum_{i=1}^{T} a_i h_i, \quad r \in R^{2L} \quad (5)$$

where W_h and b_h are the attention layer's weights, optimized during training to assign bigger weights to the most important words of a sentence.

Output Layer. We use the representation r as feature vector for classification and we feed it to a final fully-connected softmax layer which outputs a probability distribution over all classes.

3.2 TSA Model (topic-based)

For the topic-based sentiment analysis tasks, we propose a Siamese[2] bidirectional LSTM network with a different attention mechanism than in MSA. Our model is comparable to the work of (Wang et al., 2016; Tang et al., 2015). However our model differs in the way it incorporates topic information and in the attention mechanism.

Embedding Layer. The network has two inputs, the sequence of words in the tweet $X^{tw} = (x_1^{tw}, x_2^{tw}, ..., x_{T_{tw}}^{tw})$, where T_{tw} the number of words in the tweet, and the sequence of words in the topic $X^{to} = (x_1^{to}, x_2^{to}, ..., x_{T_{to}}^{to})$, where T_{to} the number of words in the topic. We project all words to R^E, where E the size of the Embedding layer.

Siamese BiLSTM. We use a bidirectional LSTM with *shared weights* to map the words of the tweet and the topic to the *same* vector space, in order to be able to make meaningful comparison between the two. The BiLSTM produces the annotations for the words of the tweet

---

[2]Siamese are called the networks that have identical configuration and their weights are linked during training.

$H^{tw} = (h_1^{tw}, h_2^{tw}, ..., h_{T_{tw}}^{tw})$ and the topic $H^{to} = (h_1^{to}, h_2^{to}, ..., h_{T_{to}}^{to})$, where each word annotation consists of the concatenation of its forward and backward annotations:

$$h_i^j = \vec{h}_i^j \parallel \overleftarrow{h}_i^j, \quad h_i^j \in R^{2L}, \quad j \in \{tw, to\} \quad (6)$$

where $\parallel$ denotes the concatenation operation and L the size of each LSTM.

Mean-Pooling Layer. We use a *Mean-Pooling* layer over the word annotations of the topic H^{to} that aggregates them to produce a single annotation. The layer computes the *mean over time* to produce the topic annotation, $\overline{h^{to}} = \frac{1}{T_{to}} \sum_1^{T_{to}} h_i^{to}$.

Context-Aware Annotations. We *append* the topic annotation $\overline{h^{to}}$ to each word annotation to get the final *context-aware* annotation for each word:

$$h_i = h_i^{tw} \parallel \overline{h^{to}}, \quad h_i^j \in R^{4L} \quad (7)$$

Context-Attention Layer. We use a context-aware attention mechanism as in (Yang et al., 2016), in order to strengthen the contribution of words that express sentiment towards a given topic. This is done by adding a context vector u_h that can be interpreted as a fixed query, like "which words express sentiment towards the given topic", over the words of the message. Concretely:

$$e_i = tanh(W_h h_i + b_h), \quad e_i \in [-1, 1] \quad (8)$$

$$a_i = \frac{exp(e_i^\top u_h)}{\sum_{t=1}^{T_{tw}} exp(e_t^\top u_h)}, \quad \sum_{i=1}^{T_{tw}} a_i = 1 \quad (9)$$

$$r = \sum_{i=1}^{T_{tw}} a_i h_i, \quad r \in R^{4L} \quad (10)$$

where W_h, b_h and u_h are jointly learned weights.

Maxout Layer. We pass the representation r to a Maxout (Goodfellow et al., 2013) layer to make the final comparison between the tweet aspects

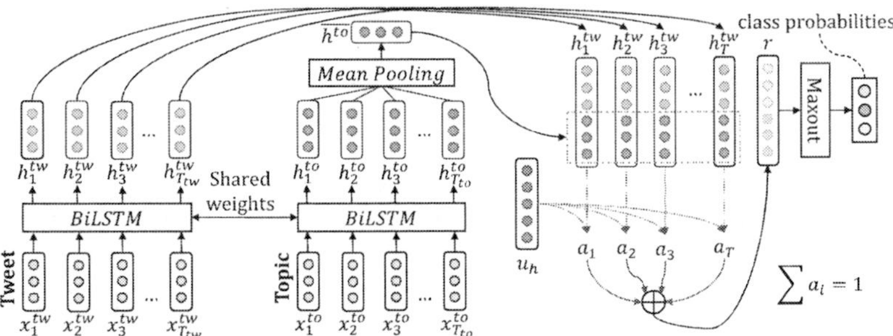

Figure 4: The TSA model: A Siamese Bidirectional LSTM with context-aware attention.

and the topic aspects. We selected Maxout as it amplifies the effects of dropout (Section 3.3).

Output Layer. We pass the output of the Maxout layer to a final fully-connected softmax layer which outputs a probability distribution over all classes.

3.3 Regularization

In both of our models we add Gaussian noise at the embedding layer, which can be interpreted as a random data augmentation technique, making our models more robust to overfitting. In addition to that, we use dropout (Srivastava et al., 2014) to randomly turn-off neurons in our network. Dropout prevents co-adaptation of neurons and can also be thought as a form of ensemble learning, because for each training example a subpart of the whole network is trained. Moreover, we apply dropout to the recurrent connections of the LSTM as in (Gal and Ghahramani, 2016). Furthermore we add L_2 regularization penalty (weight decay) to the loss function to discourage large weights. Also, we stop training after the validation loss has stopped decreasing (early-stopping).

Finally, we do not fine-tune the embedding layers. Words occurring in the training set, will be moved in the embedding space and the classifier will correlate certain regions (in embedding space) to certain sentiments. However, words in the test set and not in the training set, will remain at their initial position which may no longer reflect their "true" sentiment, leading to miss-classifications.

3.4 Class Weights

In the training data some classes have more training examples than others, introducing bias in our models. In order to deal with this problem we apply class weights to the loss function of our models, penalizing more the misclassification of underrepresented classes. Moreover, we introduce a smoothing factor in order to smooth out the weights in cases where the imbalances are very strong, which would otherwise lead to extremely large class weights. Let x be the vector with the class counts and α the smoothing factor, we obtain class weights with $w_i = \frac{max(x)}{x_i + \alpha \times max(x)}$. In Subtasks A, B, D we use no smoothing ($\alpha = 0$) and in Subtasks C and E we set $\alpha = 0.1$.

3.5 Training

We train all of our networks to minimize the cross-entropy loss, using back-propagation with stochastic gradient descent and mini-batches of size 128. We use Adam (Kingma and Ba, 2014) for tuning the learning rate and we clip the norm of the gradients (Pascanu et al., 2013) at 5, as an extra safety measure against exploding gradients.

Dataset. For training we use the available data from prior years (only tweets). Table 2 shows the statistics of the data we used. Also, we do not use any user information from the tweets (only text).

3.5.1 Hyper-parameters

In order to find good hyper-parameter values in a relative short time, compared to grid or random search, we adopt the Bayesian optimization (Bergstra et al., 2013) approach, performing a "smart" search in the high dimensional space of all the possible values.

MSA Model. The size of the embedding layer is 300, and the LSTM layers 150 (300 for BiLSTM). We add Gaussian noise with $\sigma = 0.2$ and dropout of 0.3 at the embedding layer, dropout of 0.5 at the LSTM layers and dropout of 0.25 at the recurrent connections of the LSTM. Finally, we add L_2 regularization of 0.0001 at the loss function.

TSA Model. The size of the embedding layer is 300, and the LSTM layers 64 (128 for BiLSTM). We insert Gaussian noise with $\sigma = 0.2$ at the embedding layer of both inputs and dropout of 0.3 at

Dataset	Task	Positive		Neutral	Negative		Total
		2	**1**	**0**	**-1**	**-2**	**Total**
Train	A	19652 (39.64%)		22195 (44.78%)	7723 (15.58%)		49570
	B,D	14897 (78.85%)		-	3997 (21.15%)		18894
	C,E	1016 (3.34%)	12852 (42.23%)	12888 (42.35%)	3380 (11.11%)	296 (0.97%)	30432
Test	A	2375 (19.33%)		5937 (48.33%)	3972 (32.33%)		12284
	B,D	2463 (39.82%)		-	3722 (60.18%)		6185
	C,E	131 (1.06%)	2332 (18.84%)	6194 (50.04%)	3545 (28.64%)	177 (1.43%)	12379

Table 2: Dataset statistics. Notice the difference in the ratio of positive-negative classes this year.

the embedding layer of the message, dropout of 0.2 at the LSTM layer and the recurrent connection of the LSTM layer and dropout of 0.3 at the attention layer and the Maxout layer. Finally, we add L_2 regularization of 0.001 at the loss function.

4 Experiments and Results

Semeval Results. Our official ranking (Rosenthal et al., 2017) is 1/38 (tie) in Subtask A, 2/24 in Subtask B, 2/16 in Subtask C, 2/16 in Subtask D and 11/12 in Subtask E. All of our models performed very good, with the exception of Subtask E. Since the quantification was performed on top of the classifier of Subtask C, which came in 2nd place, we conclude that our quantification approach was the reason for the bad results for Subtask E.

Attention Mechanism. In order to assess the impact of the attention mechanisms, we evaluated the performance of each model, with and without attention. We report (Table 3) the average scores of 10 runs for each system, on the official test set. The attention-based models performed better, but only by a small margin.

RNN	Subtask A (MSA)		Subtask B (TSA)	
	ρ	$F1^{pn}$	ρ	$F1^{pn}$
Regular	0.678	0.673	0.856	0.817
Attention	**0.682**	**0.675**	**0.863**	**0.82**

Table 3: Results of the impact of attention[3].

Quantification. To get a better insight into the quantification approaches, we compare the performance of CC and PCC. It is inconclusive as to which quantification approach is better. PCC outperformed CC in (Bella et al., 2010) but underperformed CC in (Esuli and Sebastiani, 2015). Following the results from (Gao and Sebastiani, 2016), which are reported on sentiment analysis in twitter, we decided to use PCC for both of our

quantification submissions. Table 4 shows the performance of our models. PCC performed better than CC for Subtask D but far worse than CC for Subtask E. We hypothesize that two possible reasons for the difference in performance between D and E, might be (1) the difference in the number of classes and (2) the big change in the ratio of *pos*-to-*neg* classes between the training and test sets.

Method	Subtask D			Subtask E
	KLD	AE	RAE	EMD
CC	0.060	**0.093**	**0.608**	**0.359**
PCC	**0.048**	0.095	0.848	0.595

Table 4: Results of the quantification approaches[4].

Experimental setup. For developing our models we used Keras (Chollet, 2015) with Theano (Theano Dev Team, 2016) as backend and Scikit-learn (Pedregosa et al., 2011). We trained our neural networks on a GTX750Ti (4GB). Lastly, we share the source code of our models [5].

5 Conclusion

In this paper, we present two deep-learning systems for short text sentiment analysis developed for SemEval-2017 Task 4 "Sentiment Analysis in Twitter". We use RNNs, utilizing well established methods in the literature. Additionally, we empower our networks with two different kinds of attention mechanisms in order to amplify the contribution of the most important words.

Our models achieved excellent results in the classification tasks, but mixed results in the quantification tasks. We would like to work more in this area and explore more quantification techniques in the future. Another interesting approach would be to design models operating on the character-level.

---

[3] ρ is the average recall and $F1^{pn}$ the macro-average F1 score of the positive and negative classes

[4] KLD is Kullback-Leibler Divergence, EMD is Earth Mover's Distance, AE is Absolute Error and RAE is Relative Absolute Error. For all metrics lower is better.

[5] https://github.com/cbaziotis/datastories-semeval2017-task4

References

Antonio Bella, Cesar Ferri, José Hernández-Orallo, and Maria Jose Ramirez-Quintana. 2010. Quantification via probability estimators. In *Proceedings of ICDM*. pages 737–742.

Yoshua Bengio, Patrice Simard, and Paolo Frasconi. 1994. Learning long-term dependencies with gradient descent is difficult. *IEEE Transactions on Neural Networks* 5(2):157–166.

James Bergstra, Daniel Yamins, and David D. Cox. 2013. Making a science of model search: Hyperparameter optimization in hundreds of dimensions for vision architectures. In *Proceedings of ICML*. pages 115–123.

Kyunghyun Cho, Bart Van Merriënboer, Caglar Gulcehre, Dzmitry Bahdanau, Fethi Bougares, Holger Schwenk, and Yoshua Bengio. 2014. Learning phrase representations using RNN encoder-decoder for statistical machine translation. *arXiv preprint arXiv:1406.1078* .

François Chollet. 2015. Keras. `https://github.com/fchollet/keras`.

Ronan Collobert and Jason Weston. 2008. A unified architecture for natural language processing: Deep neural networks with multitask learning. In *Proceedings of ICML*. pages 160–167.

Jan Deriu, Maurice Gonzenbach, Fatih Uzdilli, Aurélien Lucchi, Valeria De Luca, and Martin Jaggi. 2016. SwissCheese at SemEval-2016 Task 4: Sentiment classification using an ensemble of convolutional neural networks with distant supervision. In *Proceedings of SemEval*. pages 1124–1128.

Andrea Esuli and Fabrizio Sebastiani. 2015. Optimizing Text Quantifiers for Multivariate Loss Functions. *ACM Trans. Knowl. Discov. Data* 9(4):27:1–27:27.

George Forman. 2008. Quantifying counts and costs via classification. *Data Mining and Knowledge Discovery* 17(2):164–206.

Yarin Gal and Zoubin Ghahramani. 2016. A theoretically grounded application of dropout in recurrent neural networks. In *Proceedings of NIPS*. pages 1019–1027.

Wei Gao and Fabrizio Sebastiani. 2016. From classification to quantification in tweet sentiment analysis. *Social Network Analysis and Mining* 6(1).

Kevin Gimpel, Nathan Schneider, Brendan O'Connor, Dipanjan Das, Daniel Mills, Jacob Eisenstein, Michael Heilman, Dani Yogatama, Jeffrey Flanigan, and Noah A. Smith. 2011. Part-of-speech tagging for twitter: Annotation, features, and experiments. In *Proceedings of ACL*. pages 42–47.

Ian J. Goodfellow, David Warde-Farley, Mehdi Mirza, Aaron C. Courville, and Yoshua Bengio. 2013. Maxout networks. In *Proceedings of ICML*. pages 1319–1327.

Sepp Hochreiter, Yoshua Bengio, Paolo Frasconi, and Jürgen Schmidhuber. 2001. *Gradient Flow in Recurrent Nets: The Difficulty of Learning Long-Term Dependencies*. A field guide to dynamical recurrent neural networks. IEEE Press.

Sepp Hochreiter and Jürgen Schmidhuber. 1997. Long short-term memory. *Neural Computation* 9(8):1735–1780.

Daniel Jurafsky and James H. Martin. 2000. *Speech and Language Processing: An Introduction to Natural Language Processing, Computational Linguistics, and Speech Recognition*. Prentice Hall PTR, 1st edition.

Diederik Kingma and Jimmy Ba. 2014. Adam: A method for stochastic optimization. *arXiv preprint arXiv:1412.6980* .

Svetlana Kiritchenko, Xiaodan Zhu, and Saif M. Mohammad. 2014. Sentiment analysis of short informal texts. *Journal of Artificial Intelligence Research* 50:723–762.

Yann LeCun, Léon Bottou, Yoshua Bengio, and Patrick Haffner. 1998. Gradient-based learning applied to document recognition. *Proceedings of the IEEE* 86(11):2278–2324.

Tomas Mikolov, Ilya Sutskever, Kai Chen, Greg S. Corrado, and Jeff Dean. 2013. Distributed representations of words and phrases and their compositionality. In *Proceedings of NIPS*. pages 3111–3119.

Saif M. Mohammad, Svetlana Kiritchenko, and Xiaodan Zhu. 2013. NRC-Canada: Building the state-of-the-art in sentiment analysis of tweets. *arXiv preprint arXiv:1308.6242* .

Preslav Nakov, Alan Ritter, Sara Rosenthal, Fabrizio Sebastiani, and Veselin Stoyanov. 2016. Semeval-2016 Task 4: Sentiment analysis in Twitter. In *Proceedings of SemEval*. pages 1–18.

Elisavet Palogiannidi, Athanasia Kolovou, Fenia Christopoulou, Filippos Kokkinos, Elias Iosif, Nikolaos Malandrakis, Haris Papageorgiou, Shrikanth Narayanan, and Alexandros Potamianos. 2016. Tweester at SemEval-2016 Task 4: Sentiment analysis in Twitter using semantic-affective model adaptation. In *Proceedings of SemEval*. pages 155–163.

Razvan Pascanu, Tomas Mikolov, and Yoshua Bengio. 2013. On the difficulty of training recurrent neural networks. In *Proceedings of ICML*. pages 1310–1318.

Fabian Pedregosa, Gaël Varoquaux, Alexandre Gramfort, Vincent Michel, Bertrand Thirion, Olivier Grisel, Mathieu Blondel, Peter Prettenhofer, Ron Weiss, Vincent Dubourg, and others. 2011. Scikit-learn: Machine learning in Python. *Journal of Machine Learning Research* 12:2825–2830.

Jeffrey Pennington, Richard Socher, and Christopher D. Manning. 2014. Glove: Global Vectors for Word Representation. In *Proceedings of EMNLP*. pages 1532–1543.

Christopher Potts. 2011. Sentiment Symposium Tutorial: Tokenizing. `http://sentiment.christopherpotts.net/tokenizing.html`.

Colin Raffel and Daniel PW Ellis. 2015. Feedforward networks with attention can solve some long-term memory problems. *arXiv preprint arXiv:1512.08756* .

Tim Rocktäschel, Edward Grefenstette, Karl Moritz Hermann, Tomáš Kočiskáżş, and Phil Blunsom. 2015. Reasoning about entailment with neural attention. *arXiv preprint arXiv:1509.06664* .

Sara Rosenthal, Noura Farra, and Preslav Nakov. 2017. SemEval-2017 Task 4: Sentiment Analysis in Twitter. In *Proceedings of SemEval*. Vancouver, Canada.

Mickael Rouvier and Benoît Favre. 2016. SENSEI-LIF at SemEval-2016 Task 4: Polarity embedding fusion for robust sentiment analysis. In *Proceedings of SemEval*. pages 202–208.

Toby Segaran and Jeff Hammerbacher. 2009. *Beautiful Data: The Stories Behind Elegant Data Solutions*. "O'Reilly Media, Inc.".

Nitish Srivastava, Geoffrey E. Hinton, Alex Krizhevsky, Ilya Sutskever, and Ruslan Salakhutdinov. 2014. Dropout: A simple way to prevent neural networks from overfitting. *Journal of Machine Learning Research* 15(1):1929–1958.

Duyu Tang, Bing Qin, Xiaocheng Feng, and Ting Liu. 2015. Target-dependent sentiment classification with long short term memory. *CoRR, abs/1512.01100* .

Theano Dev Team. 2016. Theano: A Python framework for fast computation of mathematical expressions. *arXiv e-prints* abs/1605.02688.

Yequan Wang, Minlie Huang, Xiaoyan Zhu, and Li Zhao. 2016. Attention-based LSTM for aspect-level sentiment classification. In *Proceedings of EMNLP*. pages 606–615.

Zichao Yang, Diyi Yang, Chris Dyer, Xiaodong He, Alex Smola, and Eduard Hovy. 2016. Hierarchical attention networks for document classification. In *Proceedings of NAACL-HLT*. pages 1480–1489.

TwiSe at SemEval-2017 Task 4: Five-point Twitter Sentiment Classification and Quantification

Georgios Balikas

University of Grenoble Alps, CNRS, Grenoble INP - LIG

`georgios.balikas@imag.fr`

Abstract

The paper describes the participation of the team "TwiSE" in the SemEval-2017 challenge. Specifically, I participated at Task 4 entitled "Sentiment Analysis in Twitter" for which I implemented systems for five-point tweet classification (Subtask C) and five-point tweet quantification (Subtask E) for English tweets. In the feature extraction steps the systems rely on the vector space model, morpho-syntactic analysis of the tweets and several sentiment lexicons. The classification step of Subtask C uses a Logistic Regression trained with the one-versus-rest approach. Another instance of Logistic Regression combined with the classify-and-count approach is trained for the quantification task of Subtask E. In the official leaderboard the system is ranked *5/15* in Subtask C and *2/12* in Subtask E.

1 Introduction

Microblogging platforms like Twitter have lately become ubiquitous, democratizing the way people publish and access information. This vast amount of information that reflects the opinions, news or comments of people creates several opportunities for opinion mining. Among other platforms, Twitter is particularly popular for research due to its scale, representativeness and ease of access to the data it provides. Furthermore, to facilitate the study of opinion mining, high quality resources and data challenges are organized. The Task 4 of the SemEval-2017 challenges, entitled "Sentiment Analysis in Twitter" is among them.

The paper describes the participation of the team `Twitter Sentiment` (`TwiSe`) in two of the subtasks of Task 4 of SemEval-2017. Specifically,

I participated in Subtasks C and E. Both of them assume that sentiment is distributed across a five-point scale ranging from *VeryNegative* to *VeryPositive*. Subtask C is a sentiment classification task, where given a tweet the aim is to assign one of the five classes. Subtask E is a quantification task, whose aim is given a set of tweets referring to a subject to estimate the prevalence of each of the five classes. The tasks are described in more detail at (Rosenthal et al., 2017).

The rest of the paper is organized as follows: Section 2 describes the feature extraction steps performed in order to construct the representation of a tweet, which is the same for both subtasks C and E. Section 3 details the learning approaches used and Section 4 summarizes the achieved performance. Finally, Section 5 concludes with pointers for future work.

2 Feature Extraction

In this section I describe the details of the feature extraction process performed. My approach is heavily inspired by my previous participation in the "Twitter Sentiment Analysis" task of SemEval-2016, which is detailed at Balikas and Amini (2016). Importantly, the code for performing the feature extraction steps described below is publicly available at `https://github.com/balikasg/SemEval2016-Twitter_Sentiment_Evaluation`.

There are three sets of features extracted:

1. Word occurrence features,

2. Morpho-syntactic features like counts of punctuation and part-of-speech (POS) tags,

3. Semantic features based on sentiment lexicons and word embeddings.

Proceedings of the 11th International Workshop on Semantic Evaluations (SemEval-2017), pages 755–759,
Vancouver, Canada, August 3 - 4, 2017. ©2017 Association for Computational Linguistics

For the data pre-processing, cleaning and tokenization[1] as well as for most of the learning steps, I used Python's Scikit-Learn (Pedregosa et al., 2011) and NLTK (Bird et al., 2009).

2.1 Word occurrence and morpho-syntactic features

Following (Kiritchenko et al., 2014; Balikas and Amini, 2016) I extract features based on the words that occur in a tweet. The aim is to describe the lexical content of the tweets as well as to capture part of the words order. The latter is achieved using N-grams, with $N > 1$. To reduce the dimensionality of the representations when using N-grams, especially with noisy data such as tweets, I use the hashing trick. Hashing is a fast and space-efficient way for vectorizing text spans. It turns arbitrary features into vector indices of predefined size (Weinberger et al., 2009). For example, assume that after the vocabulary extraction step one has a vocabulary of dimensionality 50K. This would result in a very sparse vector space model and longer training for a classifier. Feature hashing can be seen as a dimensionality reduction process where a hash function given a textual input (vocabulary item) associates it to a number j within $0 \leq j \leq D$, where D is the dimension of the new representation.

The word-occurrence and morpho-syntactic features I extracted are:

- N-grams with $N \in [1, 4]$, projected to 20K-dimensional space using the hashing function,[2]

- character m-grams of dimension $m \in [4, 5]$, that is sequences of characters of length 4 or 5, projected to 25K-dimensional space using the same hashing function. The sizes of the output of the hashing function for N-grams and character m-grams (20K and 25K respectively) were decided using the validation set. Also, I applied the hashing trick only for these two types of features,

- # of exclamation marks, # of question marks, sum of exclamation and question marks, binary feature indicating if the last character of the tweet is a question or exclamation mark,

- # of capitalized words (*e.g.*, GREAT) and # of elongated words (*e.g. coool*), # of hashtags in a tweet,

- # of negative contexts. Negation is important as it can alter the meaning of a phrase. For instance, the meaning of the positive word "great" is altered if the word follows a negative word *e.g. "not great"*. We have used a list of negative words (like "not") to detect negation. We assumed that words after a negative word occur in a negative context, that finishes at the end of the tweet unless a punctuation symbol occurs before. Notice that negation also affects the N-gram features by transforming a word w in a negated context to w_NEG,

- # of positive emoticons, # of negative emoticons and a binary feature indicating if emoticons exist in a given tweet, and

- The distribution of part-of-speech (POS) tags (Gimpel et al., 2011) with respect to positive and negative contexts, that is how many verbs, adverbs etc., appear in a positive and in a negative context in a given tweet.

2.2 Semantic Features

With regard to the sentiment lexicons, I used:

- manual sentiment lexicons: the Bing liu's lexicon (Hu and Liu, 2004), the NRC emotion lexicon (Mohammad and Turney, 2010), and the MPQA lexicon (Wilson et al., 2005),

- # of words in positive and negative context belonging to the word clusters provided by the CMU Twitter NLP tool[3], # of words belonging to clusters obtained using skip-gram word embeddings,

- positional sentiment lexicons: the sentiment 140 lexicon (Go et al., 2009) and the Hashtag Sentiment Lexicon (Kiritchenko et al., 2014)

I make, here, more explicit the way I used the sentiment lexicons, using the Bing Liu's lexicon as an example. I treated the rest of the lexicons similarly, which is inspired by (Kiritchenko et al.,

---

[1] We adapted the tokenizer provided at `http://sentiment.christopherpotts.net/tokenizing.html`

[2] I used the signed 32-bit version of Murmurhash3 function, implemented as part of the `HashingVectorizer` class of scikit-learn.

[3] `http://www.cs.cmu.edu/~ark/TweetNLP/`

2014). For each tweet, using the Bing Liu's lexicon I generated a 104-dimensional vector. After tokenizing the tweet, I count how many words (i) in positive/negative contexts belong to the positive/negative lexicons (4 features) and I repeat the process for the hashtags (4 features). To this point one has 8 features. I repeat the generation process of those 8 features for the lowercase words and the uppercase words. Finally, for each of the 24 POS tags the (Gimpel et al., 2011) tagger generates, I count how many words in positive/negative contexts belong to the positive/negative lexicon. As a result, this generates $2 \times 8 + 24 \times 4 = 104$ features in total for each tweet based on the sentiment lexicons.

With respect to the features from text embeddings, I opt for cluster-based embeddings inspired by (Partalas et al., 2016). I used an in-house collection of ~ 40M tweets collected using the Twitter API between October and November 2016. Using the skip-gram model as implemented in the word2vec tool (Mikolov et al., 2013), I generated word embeddings for each word that appeared in the collected data more than 5 times. Therefore, each word is associated with a vector of dimension D, where I set $D = 100$, which I did not validate. Then, using the k-means algorithm I clustered the learned embeddings, initializing the clusters centroids with k-means++ (Arthur and Vassilvitskii, 2007). Having the result of the clustering step, I produced binary cluster membership features for the words of a tweet. For instance, assuming access to the results of k-means with $k = 50$, each tweet's representation is augmented with 50 features, denoting whether words of the tweet belong to each of the 50 clusters. The number of the clusters k in the k-meams algorithm is a hyper-parameter, which was set to $1,000$ after tuning it from $k \in \{100, 250, 500, 1000, 1500, 2000\}$.

3   The Learning Approach

The section describes the learning approach for Subtasks C and E. For each of them, I used a Logistic Regression optimized with the Broyden-Fletcher-Goldfarb-Shanno (BFGS) algorithm from the quasi-newton family of methods, and in particular its limited-memory (L-BFGS) approximation (Byrd et al., 1995).[4]

3.1   Fine-grained tweet classification

The output of the concatenation of the representation learning steps described at Section 2 is a 46,368-dimensional vector, out of which N-grams and character m-grams correspond to 45K elements. We normalize each instance using l_2 norm and this corresponds to the vector representation of the tweets. I train a Logistic Regression as implemented in Scikit-learn (Pedregosa et al., 2011) using L_2 regularization. The hyper-parameter C that controls the importance of the regularization term in the optimization problem is selected with grid-search from $C \in \{10^{-4}, 10^{-3}, \ldots, 10^4\}$. For grid-search I used a simple train-validation split, which is described in the next section. Once the C parameter is selected, I retrained the Logistic Regression in the union of the instances of the training and validation sets.

In addition, as shown in Figure 1 ("Class Distribution: Training data"), the classification problem is unbalanced as the distribution of the examples across the five sentiment categories is not uniform. To account for this, I assigned class weights to the examples when training the Logistic Regression. The goal is to penalize more misclassification errors in the less frequent classes. The weights are inversely proportional to the number of instances of each class.[5] This is also motivated by the fact that the official evaluation measure is the macro-averaged Mean Absolute Error (MAE_M) that is averaged across the different classes and accounts for the distance between the true and predicted class. More information about the evaluation metrics used can be found at (Rosenthal et al., 2017).

3.2   Fine-grained tweet quantification

While the aim of classification is to assign a category to each tweet, the aim of quantification is to estimate the prevalence of a category to a set of tweets. Several methods for quantification have been proposed: I cite for instance the work of G. Forman on classify and count and probabilistic classify and count (Forman, 2008) and the recently proposed ordinal quantification trees (Da San Martino et al., 2016). In this work, I focus on a classify and count approach, which simply requires classifying the tweets and then aggregating the classification results. The official evaluation measure is Earth Movers Distance (EMD) averaged over the

---

[4]From scikit-learn: 'LogisticRegression(solver='lbfgs').

[5]From scikit-learn: 'LogisticRegression(class_weight = 'balanced').

	Subtask C & E
Train2016	5,482
Development2016	1,810
DevTest2016	1,778
Test2016	20,632
Test2017	12,137

Table 1: Size of the data used for training and development purposes. We only relied on the SemEval 2016 datasets.

Subtask C		Subtask E	
Team	Score	Team	Score
BB_twtr	0.4811	BB_twtr	0.245
DataStories	0.5552	**TwiSe**	0.269
Amobee-C-137	0.5993	funSentiment	0.273
Tweester	0.6234	ELiRF-UPV	0.306
TwiSe	0.6400	NRU-HSE	0.317

Table 2: Top-5 systems ranks for Subtask C based on MAE_M and of Subtask E based on EMD.

subjects of the data, described in detail at (Rosenthal et al., 2017).

The classification and the quantification methods I use rely on efficient operations in terms of memory (hashing) and computational resources (linear models). The feature extraction and learning operations are naturally parallellizable. I believe that this is an important advantage, as the end-to-end system is robust and fast to train.

4 The Experimental Framework

The data Table 1 shows the data released by the task organizers. To tune the hyper-parameters of my models, I used a simple validation mechanism: I concatenated the "Train2016", "Development2016", and "DevTest2016" (9,070 tweets totally) to use them as training and I left the "Test2016" as validation data. I acknowledge that using the "Test2016" part of the data only for validation purposes may be limiting in terms of the achieved performance, since these data could have also used to train the system. I also highlight that by using more elaborate validation strategies like using the subjects of the tweets, one should be able to achieve better results for tuning.

Official Rankings Table 2 shows the performance the systems achieved. There are two main observations. For Subtask C, where TwiSe is ranked 5th, I note that the system is a slightly improved version of the system of (Balikas and Amini, 2016), ranked first in the Subtask in the 2016 edition. The only difference is the addition

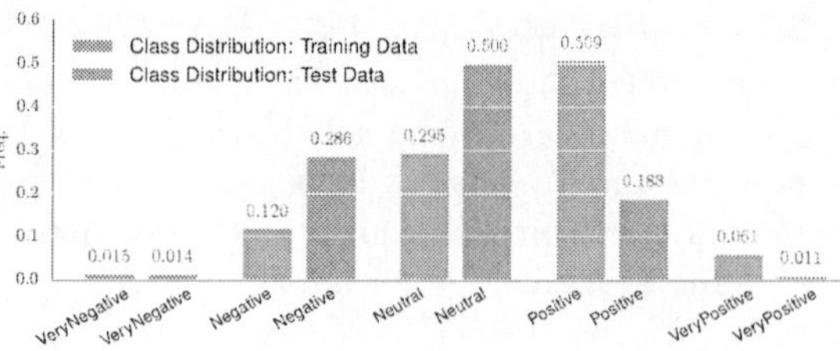

Figure 1: The distribution of the instances in the training and test sets among the five sentiment classes. The figure is rendered better with color.

of the extra features from clustering the word embeddings. This entails that significant progress was made to the task, which is either due to the extra data ("Test2016" we only used for validation) or more efficient algorithms. On the other hand, TwiSe is ranked 2nd in Subtask E. This, along with the simplicity of the approach used that is based on aggregating the counts of the classification step, entails that there is more work to be done in this direction.

Five-Scale Classification: Error Analysis Analyzing the classification errors, one finds out that the (macro-averaged) mean-absolute-error per sentiment category is distributed as follows: *VeryNegative*: 0.836, *Negative*: 0.566, *Neutral*: 0.584, *Positive*: 0.771, *VeryPositive*: 0.443. The system performed the best in the *VeryPositive* class (lowest error) and the worst in the *VeryNegative* class. Interestingly, the system did not do as well in the *Positive* class. To better understand why, Figure 1 plots the distribution of the instances across the five sentiment classes, for the training data we used and the test data. Notice how the Positive class is the dominant in the training data, while this changes in the test data. I believe that that the distribution drift, between the training and test data is indicative as of why the system performed poorly in the "Positive" class.

Five-Scale Quantification: Error Analysis I repeat, here, the error analysis process for the quantification task. The best performance was achieved in the subject "leonard cohen", whose EMD was 0.029 while the worst performance in the topics "maduro" (EMD=0.709) and "medicaid" (EMD=0.660). The distribution of sentiment for "leonard cohen" is very similar to the distribution of sentiment in the training set, Kullback-Leibner divergence of 0.140. On the other hand the Kullback-Leibner divergence for "maduro" and "medicaid", which are both skewed towards the negative sentiment, are 1.328 and 0.896 respectively. Although a more detailed error analysis is required in order to improve the performance of the system, I believe that the distribution drift between the training examples and the examples of a subject plays an important role. This may be further enhanced by the fact I used a classify and count approach which does not account for drifts.

5 Conclusion

The paper described the participation of `TwiSe` in the subtasks C and E of of the "Twitter Sentiment Evaluation" Task of SemEval-2017. Importantly, my system was ranked 2nd in Subtask E, "Five-point Sentiment Quantification" using a simple classify and count approach on top of a Logistic Regression. An interesting future work direction towards improving the system aims at better handling distribution drifts between the training and test data.

References

David Arthur and Sergei Vassilvitskii. 2007. k-means++: The advantages of careful seeding. In *Proceedings of the eighteenth annual ACM-SIAM symposium on Discrete algorithms*. Society for Industrial and Applied Mathematics, pages 1027–1035.

Georgios Balikas and Massih-Reza Amini. 2016. Twise at semeval-2016 task 4: Twitter sentiment classification. In *SemEval@NAACL-HLT 2016, San Diego, CA, USA, June 16-17, 2016*. pages 85–91.

Steven Bird, Ewan Klein, and Edward Loper. 2009. *Natural Language Processing with Python*. O'Reilly Media.

Richard H. Byrd, Peihuang Lu, Jorge Nocedal, and Ciyou Zhu. 1995. A limited memory algorithm for bound constrained optimization. *SIAM J. Scientific Computing* 16(5):1190–1208.

Giovanni Da San Martino, Wei Gao, and Fabrizio Sebastiani. 2016. Ordinal text quantification. In *Proceedings of the 39th International ACM SIGIR conference on Research and Development in Information Retrieval*. ACM, pages 937–940.

George Forman. 2008. Quantifying counts and costs via classification. *Data Mining and Knowledge Discovery* 17(2):164–206.

Kevin Gimpel, Nathan Schneider, Brendan O'Connor, Dipanjan Das, Daniel Mills, Jacob Eisenstein, Michael Heilman, Dani Yogatama, Jeffrey Flanigan, and Noah A Smith. 2011. Part-of-speech tagging for twitter: Annotation, features, and experiments. In *Proceedings of the 49th Annual Meeting of the Association for Computational Linguistics: Human Language Technologies: short papers-Volume 2*. Association for Computational Linguistics, pages 42–47.

Alec Go, Richa Bhayani, and Lei Huang. 2009. Twitter sentiment classification using distant supervision. *CS224N Project Report, Stanford* 1:12.

Minqing Hu and Bing Liu. 2004. Mining and summarizing customer reviews. In *Proceedings of the tenth ACM SIGKDD international conference on Knowledge discovery and data mining*. ACM, pages 168–177.

Svetlana Kiritchenko, Xiaodan Zhu, and Saif M Mohammad. 2014. Sentiment analysis of short informal texts. *Journal of Artificial Intelligence Research* pages 723–762.

Tomas Mikolov, Kai Chen, Greg Corrado, and Jeffrey Dean. 2013. Efficient estimation of word representations in vector space. *CoRR* abs/1301.3781.

Saif M Mohammad and Peter D Turney. 2010. Emotions evoked by common words and phrases: Using mechanical turk to create an emotion lexicon. In *Proceedings of the NAACL HLT 2010 workshop on computational approaches to analysis and generation of emotion in text*. Association for Computational Linguistics, pages 26–34.

Ioannis Partalas, Cédric Lopez, Nadia Derbas, and Ruslan Kalitvianski. 2016. Learning to search for recognizing named entities in twitter. *WNUT 2016* page 171.

F. Pedregosa, G. Varoquaux, A. Gramfort, V. Michel, B. Thirion, O. Grisel, M. Blondel, P. Prettenhofer, R. Weiss, V. Dubourg, J. Vanderplas, A. Passos, D. Cournapeau, M. Brucher, M. Perrot, and E. Duchesnay. 2011. Scikit-learn: Machine learning in Python. *Journal of Machine Learning Research* 12:2825–2830.

Sara Rosenthal, Noura Farra, and Preslav Nakov. 2017. SemEval-2017 task 4: Sentiment analysis in Twitter. In *Proceedings of the 11th International Workshop on Semantic Evaluation*. Association for Computational Linguistics, Vancouver, Canada, SemEval '17.

Kilian Weinberger, Anirban Dasgupta, John Langford, Alex Smola, and Josh Attenberg. 2009. Feature hashing for large scale multitask learning. In *Proceedings of the 26th Annual International Conference on Machine Learning*. ACM, pages 1113–1120.

Theresa Wilson, Janyce Wiebe, and Paul Hoffmann. 2005. Recognizing contextual polarity in phrase-level sentiment analysis. In *Proceedings of the conference on human language technology and empirical methods in natural language processing*. Association for Computational Linguistics, pages 347–354.

LIA at SemEval-2017 Task 4:
An Ensemble of Neural Networks for Sentiment Classification

Mickael Rouvier
LIA
University of Avignon
Avignon, France
mickael.rouvier@univ-avignon.fr

Abstract

This paper describes the system developed at
LIA for the SemEval-2017 evaluation campaign. The goal of Task 4.A was to identify sentiment polarity in tweets. The system is an ensemble of Deep Neural Network
(DNN) models: Convolutional Neural Network (CNN) and Recurrent Neural Network
Long Short-Term Memory (RNN-LSTM). We
initialize the input representation of DNN with
different sets of embeddings trained on large
datasets. The ensemble of DNNs are combined using a score-level fusion approach.
The system ranked 2nd at SemEval-2017 and
obtained an average recall of 67.6%.

1 Introduction

This paper describes the system developed at LIA
for the SemEval-2017 sentiment analysis evaluation
task 4 (Rosenthal et al., 2017).

We have participated in Subtask A: sentiment
analysis at the message level in English. It consists
in determining the message polarity of each tweet
in the test set. The sentiment polarity classification
task is set as a three-class problem: positive, negative and neutral.

The sentiment analysis task is often modeled as a
classification problem which relies on features extracted from the text in order to feed a classifier.
Recent work has shown that Deep Neural Networks
(DNN) using word representations as input are well
suited for sentence classification problems and have
been shown to produce state-of-the-art results for
sentiment polarity classification (Tang et al., 2014a;
Severyn and Moschitti, 2015). Two different types

of DNN models are used: Convolutional Neural
Network (CNN) and Recurrent Neural Network with
Long Short-Term Memory units (RNN-LSTM). Pre-
trained word embeddings are used to initialize the
word representations, which are then taken as input
of a text.

Our approach consists in learning classifiers for
four types of embeddings, based on the CNN and
RNN-LSTM architectures. Each set of word embeddings models the tweet according to a different point
of view. A final fusion step is applied.

Our contributions are as follows:

- We propose to apply a teacher-student ap-
  praoch for training the DNN models.
- We propose a new way to capture polarity in
  word embeddings.
- The source code of our system, the models
  trained for the evaluation, as well as the corpus
  collected for creating word embeddings, are all
  made available to the community in hope of
  helping future research [1].

The paper is structured as follows. Section 2
presents a quick overview of the system architecture, which is then detailed in sections 3 and 4, along
with the various word embeddings and other features used in our system. Results and discussion appear in Section 5.

2 Overview of the approach

The system was developed as a two-level architecture. Given a tweet, the first level extracts input representations based various word embeddings. These

---

[1] http://gitlia.univ-avignon.fr/rouvierm/semeval-2017-
sentiment-analysis

Proceedings of the 11th International Workshop on Semantic Evaluations (SemEval-2017), pages 760–765,
Vancouver, Canada, August 3 - 4, 2017. ©2017 Association for Computational Linguistics

embeddings are fed to a DNN model (CNN and RNN-LSTM). Four different sets of word embeddings are used: one lexical embedding and three different sentiment embeddings.

The second level inputs the concatenation of the scores obtained each input representation and Deep Neural Network (DNN and RNN-LSTM) from the first level. This representation is fed to a Multi-Layer Perceptron (MLP) which was trained to predict polarity.

3 Deep Neural Networks

3.1 Convolutional Neural Networks

CNNs represent one of the most used Deep Neural Network models in computer vision (LeCun and Bengio, 1995). Recent work has shown that CNNs are also well suited for sentence classification problems and can produce state-of-the-art results (Tang et al., 2014a; Severyn and Moschitti, 2015). The difference between CNNs applied to computer vision and their equivalent in NLP lies in the input dimensionality and format. In computer vision, inputs are usually single-channel (eg. grayscale) or multi-channel (eg. RGB) 2D or 3D matrices, usually of constant dimension.

In sentence classification, each input consists of a sequence of words of variable length. Each word w is represented with a n-dimensional vector (word embedding) e_w of constant size. All the word representations are then concatenated in their respective order and padded with zero-vectors.

The parameters of our model were chosen so as to maximize performance on the development set: the width of the convolution filters is set to 5 and the number of convolutional feature maps is 300. We use ReLU activation functions and a simple max-pooling. The fully-connected hidden layer is of size 512.

For this layer, a standard dropout of 0.4 is used (40 % of the neurons are disabled at each iteration). The back-propagation algorithm used for training is Adadelta. In our experiments we observed that the weight initialization of the convolution layer can lead to a high variation in terms of performance. Therefore, we trained 20 models and selected the one that obtained the best results on the development corpus.

3.2 Reccurent Neural Network with Long Short Term Memory

RNNs are popular models that have shown great promise in many Natural Language Processing (NLP) tasks. The main differentiating feature of RNNs is that the model take into account the ordering of words in the text as opposed to CNNs which take only a limited, small context window.

In a traditional neural network we assume that all inputs (and outputs) are independent of each other. RNNs can take into account the input but also what they perceived one step back in time. Hence recurrent networks have two sources of input, the present and the recent past, which combine to determine how to respond to new data, much as we do in life.

The parameters of our model were also chosen so as to maximize performance on the development set: the hidden layer is of size 128, a standard dropout of 0.2 is used. The back-propagation algorithm used for training is Adadelta.

3.3 Word embeddings

Word embeddings are an approach for distributional semantics which represents words as vectors of real numbers. Such a representation has useful clustering properties, since it groups together words that are semantically and syntactically similar (Mikolov et al., 2013). For example, the word "coffee" and "tea" will be very close in the created space. The goal is to use these features as input to a DNN classifier. However, with the sentiment analysis task in mind, typical word embeddings extracted from lexical context might not be the most accurate because antonyms tend to be placed at the same location in the created space.

This year, in SemEval-2017 we explored different approaches to integrate the sentiment polarity of the words. Four representations were explored:

Lexical embeddings: these embeddings are obtained with the classical skipgram model from (Mikolov et al., 2013). The representation is created by using the hidden layer of a linear neural network to predict a context window from a central word. For a given context $w_{i-2} \ldots w_{i+2}$, the input to the model is w_i, and the output could be w_{i-2}, w_{i-1}, w_{i+1}, w_{i+2}. This method typically extracts a representation which covers both syntax and semantics, to some extent.

Sentiment embeddings (multitask-learning): One

of the problems with the basic skipgram approach (lexical embeddings) is that the model ignores the sentiment polarity of the words. As a result, words with opposite polarity, such as "good" and "bad", are mapped into close vectors. In (Tang et al., 2014b), the authors propose to tackle this problem so that sentiment information is encoded in the continuous representation of words. They propose to create a neural network that predicts two tasks: the context of the word and the sentiment label of the whole sentence. Since it is expensive to manually label sentences with their polarity, the authors propose to use tweets that contain emoticons and rely on the polarity conveyed by the emoticons to label the sentences. Since they report that best performance is obtained by weighting both tasks equivalently, the model is the same as for lexical embeddings, except that the predicted context is formed of (word, sentiment) couples. For example, if s is the polarity of the sentence where the context $w_{i-2} \ldots w_{i+2}$ is extracted, the model gets w_i as input and has to predict $(w_{i-2}, s), (w_{i-1}, s), (w_{i+1}, s), (w_{i+2}, s)$.

Sentiment embeddings (distant-supervision): The distant-supervision is another solution to integrating sentiment polarity in words. A DNN (CNN or RNN-LSTM) is trained on massive distant-supervised tweets selected by positive and negative emoticons. The positive and negative emoticons are used as supervised labels. During training, the DNN will automatically refine the word embeddings in order to capture the sentiment polarity in words. The refined word embeddings can be used as a new representation.

Sentiment embeddings (negative-sampling): The negative-sampling approach is an efficient way of computing softmax. In order to deal with the difficulty of having too many output vectors that need to be updated, the main idea of negative sampling is to update not all the words but only a few words as negative samples (hence "negative sampling"). Instead of selecting random words, as is usual for this technique, we chose to select words with opposite polarities. For example, for the word "good" we select the words "bad", "terrific", etc. for negative sampling.

3.4 Extension of the DNN model

The DNN model relies on word embeddings as word representation. Unfortunately these models can only capture information at the word level. We propose to extract some sentence-level information and to inject this information into the model. In order to incorporate this source of information into the system, a set of sentence-level features are concatenated with the last hidden layer in the model.

The following features are extracted at the sentence level:

- **Lexicons**: frequency of lemmas that are matched in MPQA (Wiebe et al., 2005), Opinion Lexicon (Hu and Liu, 2004) and NRC Emotion lexicon (Mohammad and Turney, 2013).
- **Emoticons**: number of emoticons that are grouped in positive, negative and neutral categories.
- **All-caps**: number of words in all-caps.
- **Elongated units**: number of words in which characters are repeated more than twice (for example: loooooool).
- **Punctuation**: number of contiguous sequences of several periods, exclamation marks and question marks.

3.5 Mimic model

The teacher-student approach consists in training a state-of-the-art model (teacher model), and then training a new model (student model) to mimic the teacher model. The mimic model (student model) is not trained on the original labels, but it is trained to learn targets predicted by the teacher model. Remarkably, a mimic model trained on targets predicted by the teacher model can be more accurate than teacher model trained on the original labels. There are a variety of reasons why this can happen:

- If some labels have errors, the teacher model may eliminate some of these errors thus making it learning easier for the student.
- Learning from the original, hard 0/1 labels can be more difficult than learning from a teacher's conditional probabilities; but the mimic model sees non-zero targets for most outputs on most training cases, and the teacher can spread uncertainty over multiple outputs for difficult cases. The uncertainty from the teacher model is more informative to the student model than the original 0/1 labels.
- The mimic model can be seen as a form of regularization that helps prevent overfitting the model.

Corpus	Positive	Negative	Neutral	Total
SemEval$_{13-15}$	9.316	3.443	9.067	21.826
SemEval$_{16}$	7.059	3.231	10.342	20.632

Table 1: Statistics of the successfully downloaded part of the SemEval 2017 Twitter sentiment classification dataset.

4 Fusion system

The outputs from all Deep Neural Networks are concatenated to form a single feature vector. This vector is then fed into a Multi-Layer Perceptron (MLP) that is trained to predict the polarity. The MLP contains one hidden layer of 128 neurons and the activation function used is $tanh$.

5 Experiments

5.1 Corpus

We use the training corpus from Twitter'13 to 17 for training the various parts of the architecture. We split the corpus into two parts. The train, development and test corpora given in SemEval'13, 14, 15 form the first part, referred to as SemEval$_{13-15}$. The test corpus given in SemEval'16 forms part 2, referred to as SemEval$_{16}$. We perform 2-fold cross-validation, where one part is used as the training corpus and the other one is used as the development corpus. Note that we were unable to download all the training and development data because some tweets were deleted or not available due to modified authorization status. The sizes of the datasets are summarized in Table 1.

5.2 Word embedding training

To train the word embeddings, we have created a unannotated corpus of sentiment-bearing tweets in English. These tweets were recovered on the Twitter platform by searching for emotion keywords (from the sentiment lexicons) and unigrams, bigrams and trigrams extracted from the SemEval training corpus. This corpus consists of about 90 million tweets. A sub-corpus of about 20 million tweets containing at least one emoticon is used for training the sentiment embeddings. Both corpora are now publicly available [2].

In our experiments, lexical embeddings and part-of-speech embeddings are estimated using the word2vec toolkit (Mikolov et al., 2013). Sentiment

---

[2] http://gitlia.univ-avignon.fr/rouvierm/semeval-2017-sentiment-analysis

System	Rec^{Pos}	Rec^{Neu}	Rec^{Neg}	Avg-Rec
Fusion	64.6	57.7	80.4	67.6

Table 2: Overall performance of the LIA sentiment analysis systems. Rec^{Pos}, Rec^{Neu} and Rec^{Neg} are respectively the recall on positive, neutral and negative classe. Avg-Rec is the macro-averaged recall calculated over the three categories.

embeddings are estimated using word2vecf. This toolkit allows to replace linear bag-of-word contexts with arbitrary features. The embeddings are trained using the skipgram approach with a window of size 3 and 5 iterations. The dimension of the embeddings is set to 100. Part-of-speech tagging is performed with Tweet NLP (Owoputi et al., 2013; Gimpel et al., 2011).

5.3 Results

Overall performance: The evaluation metric used in the competition is the macro-averaged recall calculated over the three categories. Table 3 presents the overall performance of each of the systems used for the first level. We observe that the best first-level system is the CNN Mimic model using sentiment embedding (negative-sampling). The system obtained an average-recall of 66.91%. Concerning the word embedding, in generally sentiment embedding (negative-sampling) obtains for each DNN model the best results. Concerning the DNN models, the CNN approach provide better results than the RNN-LSTM models.

Impact of fusion: Table 2 presents the results obtained by the fusion system. It achieved the second rank on the Twitter 2017 data among 39 teams.

6 Conclusions

This paper describes the LIA participation in SemEval 2017. Our approach consists in running an ensemble of neural networks (CNN and RNN-LSTM) over different types of embeddings. A final fusion step is applied, based on concatenating the scores given by the neural networks and training a deep neural network for the fusion. The resulting system ranked 2nd at the SemEval-2017 evaluation campaign.

Acknowledgments

This project was financed by the project CHISTERA CALL - ANR: Access Multilingual Information opinionS (AMIS), (France - Europe).

References

Kevin Gimpel, Nathan Schneider, Brendan O'Connor, Dipanjan Das, Daniel Mills, Jacob Eisenstein, Michael Heilman, Dani Yogatama, Jeffrey Flanigan, and Noah A Smith. 2011. Part-of-speech tagging for twitter: Annotation, features, and experiments. In *Proceedings of the 49th Annual Meeting of the Association for Computational Linguistics: Human Language Technologies: short papers-Volume 2*, pages 42–47. Association for Computational Linguistics.

Minqing Hu and Bing Liu. 2004. Mining and summarizing customer reviews. In *SIGKDD*, pages 168–177.

Yann LeCun and Yoshua Bengio. 1995. Convolutional networks for images, speech, and time series. *The handbook of brain theory and neural networks*, 3361(10).

Tomas Mikolov, Kai Chen, Greg Corrado, and Jeffrey Dean. 2013. Efficient estimation of word representations in vector space. *arXiv preprint arXiv:1301.3781*.

Saif M Mohammad and Peter D Turney. 2013. Nrc emotion lexicon. Technical report, NRC Technical Report.

Olutobi Owoputi, Brendan O'Connor, Chris Dyer, Kevin Gimpel, Nathan Schneider, and Noah A Smith. 2013. Improved part-of-speech tagging for online conversational text with word clusters. Association for Computational Linguistics.

Sara Rosenthal, Noura Farra, and Preslav Nakov. 2017. SemEval-2017 task 4: Sentiment analysis in Twitter. In *Proceedings of the 11th International Workshop on Semantic Evaluation*, SemEval '17, Vancouver, Canada, August. Association for Computational Linguistics.

Aliaksei Severyn and Alessandro Moschitti. 2015. Unitn: Training deep convolutional neural network for twitter sentiment classification. In *Proceedings of the 9th International Workshop on Semantic Evaluation (SemEval 2015), Association for Computational Linguistics, Denver, Colorado*, pages 464–469.

Duyu Tang, Furu Wei, Bing Qin, Ting Liu, and Ming Zhou. 2014a. Coooolll: A deep learning system for twitter sentiment classification. In *Proceedings of the 8th International Workshop on Semantic Evaluation (SemEval 2014)*, pages 208–212.

Duyu Tang, Furu Wei, Nan Yang, Ming Zhou, Ting Liu, and Bing Qin. 2014b. Learning sentiment-specific word embedding for twitter sentiment classification. In *ACL (1)*, pages 1555–1565.

Janyce Wiebe, Theresa Wilson, and Claire Cardie. 2005. Annotating expressions of opinions and emotions in language. *Language resources and evaluation*, 39(2-3):165–210.

Appendix

System	Architecture	Word embeddings	Training corpus	Rec^{Pos}	Rec^{Neu}	Rec^{Neg}	Avg-Rec
1	CNN	lexical	SemEval_{13-15}	63.5	53.9	80.3	65.9
2	CNN	sentiment (multi-task learning)	SemEval_{13-15}	66.4	50.0	82.5	66.3
3	CNN	sentiment (distant-supervision)	SemEval_{13-15}	65.5	49.8	83.9	66.4
4	CNN	sentiment (negative-sampling)	SemEval_{13-15}	65.6	51.5	81.4	66.2
5	RNN-LSTM	lexical	SemEval_{13-15}	56.0	58.6	76.9	63.9
6	RNN-LSTM	sentiment (multi-task learning)	SemEval_{13-15}	62.4	52.4	78.0	64.3
7	RNN-LSTM	sentiment (distant-supervision)	SemEval_{13-15}	59.5	60.0	68.6	62.7
8	RNN-LSTM	sentiment (negative-sampling)	SemEval_{13-15}	61.5	60.9	72.2	64.9
9	CNN Mimic	lexical	SemEval_{13-15}	66.3	53.7	80.0	66.7
10	CNN Mimic	sentiment (multi-task learning)	SemEval_{13-15}	64.6	52.8	81.7	66.4
11	CNN Mimic	sentiment (distant-supervision)	SemEval_{13-15}	65.0	51.2	83.8	66.7
12	CNN Mimic	sentiment (negative-sampling)	SemEval_{13-15}	70.6	48.0	82.3	66.9
13	CNN	lexical	SemEval_{16}	57.0	58.6	80.9	65.5
14	CNN	sentiment (multi-task learning)	SemEval_{16}	53.2	53.5	84.2	63.6
15	CNN	sentiment (distant-supervision)	SemEval_{16}	56.3	58.3	82.1	65.5
16	CNN	sentiment (negative-sampling)	SemEval_{16}	60.3	45.8	88.7	64.9
17	RNN-LSTM	lexical	SemEval_{16}	55.8	58.4	78.2	61.4
18	RNN-LSTM	sentiment (multi-task learning)	SemEval_{16}	56.1	55.5	81.3	64.3
19	RNN-LSTM	sentiment (distant-supervision)	SemEval_{16}	52.6	48.0	83.7	61.5
20	RNN-LSTM	sentiment (negative-sampling)	SemEval_{16}	61.7	62.7	71.0	65.1
21	CNN Mimic	lexical	SemEval_{16}	57.5	53.3	84.1	65.0
22	CNN Mimic	sentiment (multi-task learning)	SemEval_{16}	59.8	53.9	82.9	65.5
23	CNN Mimic	sentiment (distant-supervision)	SemEval_{16}	58.9	53.8	83.3	65.3
24	CNN Mimic	sentiment (negative-sampling)	SemEval_{16}	62.1	52.6	83.8	66.2

Table 3: Overall performance of the DNN models using different word embeddings and training corpus. Rec^{Pos}, Rec^{Neu} and Rec^{Neg} are respectively the recall on positive, neutral and negative classe. Avg-Rec is the macro-averaged recall calculated over the three categories.

TopicThunder at SemEval-2017 Task 4: Sentiment Classification Using a Convolutional Neural Network with Distant Supervision

Simon Müller
Zurich University of Applied Sciences
Switzerland
muellsi3@students.zhaw.ch

Tobias Huonder
Zurich University of Applied Sciences
Switzerland
huondtob@students.zhaw.ch

Jan Deriu
Zurich University of Applied Sciences
Switzerland
deri@zhaw.ch

Mark Cieliebak
Zurich University of Applied Sciences
Switzerland
ciel@zhaw.ch

Abstract

In this paper, we propose a classifier for predicting topic-specific sentiments of English Twitter messages. Our method is based on a 2-layer CNN. With a distant supervised phase we leverage a large amount of weakly-labelled training data. Our system was evaluated on the data provided by the SemEval-2017 competition in the Topic-Based Message Polarity Classification subtask, where it ranked 4th place.

1 Introduction

The goal of sentiment analysis is to teach the machine the ability to understand emotions and opinions expressed in text. There are numerous challenges which make this task very difficult, for instance the complexity of natural language which makes use of intricate concepts like irony, sarcasm, and metaphors to name a few. Usually we are not interested in the overall sentiment of a tweet but rather in the sentiment the tweet expresses towards a topic of interest. Subtask B in SemEval-2017 (Rosenthal et al., 2017) consists of predicting the sentiment of a tweet towards a given topic as either positive or negative.

Convolutional neural networks (CNN) have shown to be very efficient at tackling the task of sentiment analysis, as they are able to learn features themselves instead of relying on manually crafted ones (Kalchbrenner et al., 2014; Kim, 2014). Our work is based on the system proposed by (De-

riu et al., 2016), which in turn is based on (Severyn and Moschitti, 2015). CNNs typically have a large number of parameters which need sufficient data to be trained efficiently. In this work, we leverage a large amount of data to train a multilayer CNN. The training is based on the following 3-phase procedure (see Figure 1): (i) creation of word embeddings based on an unsupervised corpus of 200M English tweets, (ii) a distant supervised phase using an additional 100M tweets, where the labels are inferred by weak sentiment indicators (e.g. smileys), and (iii) a supervised phase, where the pre-trained network is trained on the provided data.

We evaluated the approach on the datasets of SemEval-2017 for the subtask B, where it ranked 4th out of 23 submissions.

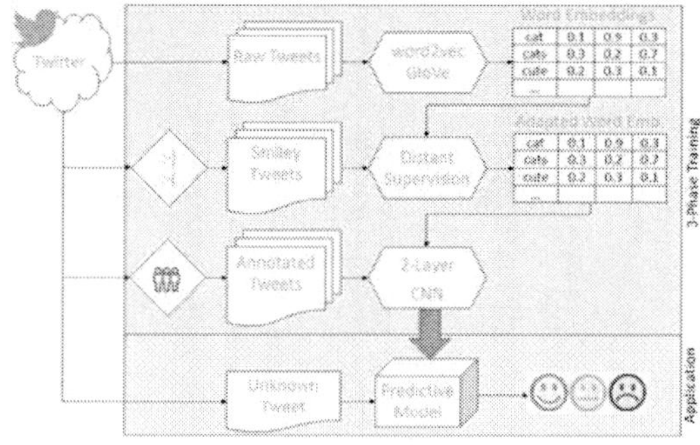

Figure 1: *Overview of the 3-Phase training procedure.*

Proceedings of the 11th International Workshop on Semantic Evaluations (SemEval-2017), pages 766–770,
Vancouver, Canada, August 3 - 4, 2017. ©2017 Association for Computational Linguistics

2 Model

Our system is based on the 2-layer CNN proposed by (Deriu et al., 2016), as depicted in Figure 2 and described in details below. We refer to a layer as one convolutional and one pooling layer, thus, a 2-layer network consists of two consecutive pairs of convolutional-pooling layers.

Word embeddings. The word embeddings are initialized using word2vec (Mikolov et al., 2013) and then trained on an unlabelled corpus of 200M tweets. We apply a skipgram model of window size 5 and filter words that occur less than 15 times. The dimensionality of the vector representation is set to $d = 52$. The resulting vocabulary is stored as a mapping $V : t \rightarrow i$ which maps a token to an index, where unknown tokens are mapped to a default index. The word embeddings are stored in a matrix $\mathbf{E} \in \mathbb{R}^{v \times d}$ where v is the size of the vocabulary and the i-th row represents the embedding for the token with index $V(t) = i$.

Preprocessing The preprocessing is done by: (i) lower-case the tweet, (ii) replace URLs and usernames with a special token, and (iii) tokenize the tweet using the *NLTK-TwitterTokenizer*[1].

Input Layer. Each tweet is converted to a set of indices by applying the aforementioned preprocessing. The tokens are mapped to their respective indices in the vocabulary V.

Sentence model. Each word is associated to a vector representation, which consists in a d-dimensional vector. A tweet is represented by the concatenation of the representations of its n constituent words. This yields a matrix $\mathbf{X} \in \mathbb{R}^{d \times n}$, which is used as input to the convolutional neural network.

Convolutional layer. In this layer, a set of m filters is applied to a sliding window of length h over each sentence. Let $\mathbf{X}_{[i:i+h]}$ denote the concatenation of word vectors $\mathbf{x}_i$ to $\mathbf{x}_{i+h}$. A feature c_i is generated for a given filter $\mathbf{F}$ by:

$$c_i := \sum_{k,j} (\mathbf{X}_{[i:i+h]})_{k,j} \cdot \mathbf{F}_{k,j} \qquad (1)$$

A concatenation of all vectors in a sentence produces a feature vector $\mathbf{c} \in \mathbb{R}^{n-h+1}$. The vectors $\mathbf{c}$ are then aggregated over all m filters into a feature map matrix $\mathbf{C} \in \mathbb{R}^{m \times (n-h+1)}$. The filters are

---

[1] http://www.nltk.org/api/nltk.tokenize.html

learned during the training phase of the neural network.

Max pooling. The output of the convolutional layer is passed through a non-linear activation function before entering a pooling layer. The latter aggregates vector elements by taking the maximum over a fixed set of non-overlapping intervals. The resulting pooled feature map matrix has the form: $\mathbf{C_{pooled}} \in \mathbb{R}^{m \times \frac{n-h+1}{s}}$, where s is the length of each interval. In the case of overlapping intervals with a stride value s_t, the pooled feature map matrix has the form $\mathbf{C_{pooled}} \in \mathbb{R}^{m \times \frac{n-h+1-s}{s_t}}$. Depending on whether the borders are included or not, the result of the fraction is rounded up or down respectively.

Hidden layer. A fully connected hidden layer computes the transformation $\alpha(\mathbf{W} * \mathbf{x} + \mathbf{b})$, where $\mathbf{W} \in \mathbb{R}^{m \times m}$ is the weight matrix, $\mathbf{b} \in \mathbb{R}^m$ the bias, and α the rectified linear ($relu$) activation function (Nair and Hinton, 2010). The output vector of this layer, $\mathbf{x} \in \mathbb{R}^m$, corresponds to the sentence embeddings for each tweet.

Softmax. Finally, the outputs of the final pooling layer $\mathbf{x} \in \mathbb{R}^m$ are fully connected to a softmax regression layer, which returns the class $\hat{y} \in [1, K]$ with largest probability. i.e.,

$$\hat{y} := \arg\max_j P(y = j | \mathbf{x}, \mathbf{w}, \mathbf{a})$$
$$= \arg\max_j \frac{e^{\mathbf{x}^\mathsf{T}\mathbf{w}_j + a_j}}{\sum_{k=1}^{K} e^{\mathbf{x}^\mathsf{T}\mathbf{w}_k + a_j}}, \qquad (2)$$

where $\mathbf{w}_j$ denotes the weights vector of class j and a_j the bias of class j.

Network parameters. Training the neural network consists in learning the set of parameters $\Theta = \{\mathbf{E}, \mathbf{F}_1, \mathbf{b}_1, \mathbf{F}_2, \mathbf{b}_2, \mathbf{W}, \mathbf{a}\}$, where $\mathbf{E}$ is the sentence matrix, with each row containing the d-dimensional embedding vector for a specific word; $\mathbf{F}_i, \mathbf{b}_i (i = \{1, 2\})$ the filter weights and biases of the first and second convolutional layers; $\mathbf{W}$ the concatenation of the weights $\mathbf{w}_j$ for every output class in the soft-max layer; and $\mathbf{a}$ the bias of the soft-max layer.

Training. We pre-train the word embeddings on an unsupervised corpus of 200M tweets. During the distant-supervised phase, we use emoticons to infer the polarity of a set of additional 100M tweets (Read, 2005; Go et al., 2009). The resulting dataset contains positive 79M tweets and 21M

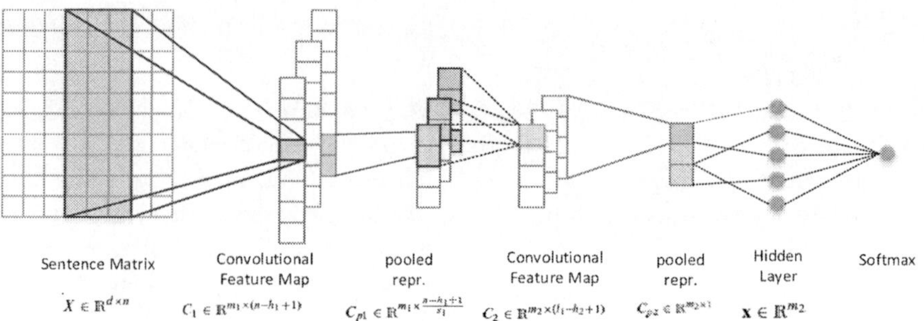

Figure 2: The architecture of the CNNs used in our approach.

negative tweets. The neural network is trained on these 100M tweets for one epoch. Then, the neural network is trained in a supervised phase on the labelled data provided by SemEval-2017. To avoid over-fitting we employed early-stopping, where we stop the training if the score on the validation set did not increase for 50 epochs. The word-embeddings $\mathbf{E} \in \mathbb{R}^{d \times n}$ are updated during both the distant and the supervised training phases, as back-propagation is applied through the entire network.

The network parameters are learned using *AdaDelta* (Zeiler, 2012), which adapts the learning rate for each dimension using only first order information. We used the hyper-parameters $\epsilon = 1e^{-6}$ and $\rho = 0.95$ as suggested by (Zeiler, 2012).

Computing Resources. The implementation of the system is written in *Python*. We used the *Keras* framework (Chollet, 2015) using the *Theano* (Theano Development Team, 2016) back-end. *Theano* allows to accelerate the computations using a GPU. We used an *NVIDIA TITAN X* GPU to conduct our experiments. To generate the word embeddings we used the *Gensim* framework (Řehůřek and Sojka, 2010) which implements the word2vec model in *Python*. It took about 2 days to generate the word embeddings. The distant phase takes approximately 5 hours and the supervised phase up to 10 minutes.

3 Experiments & Results

3.1 Data

We evaluate our system on the datasets provided by SemEval-2017 for subtask B (see Table 3.1). The training-set is composed by *Train 2016, Dev 2016*, and *DevTest 2016*, whereas we use *Test 2016* as validation set. The training and the validation

set have 100 topics each. Since our dataset of 200M tweets for the word embeddings consists primarily of tweets from 2013, some of the topics are not covered by the vocabulary. Thus, we download an additional 20M tweets where we use the topic-names as search key. This reduced the percentage of unknown words from 14% to 13%.

Dataset	Total	Posit.	Negat.	Topics
Train 2016	5355	2749	762	60
Dev 2016	1269	568	214	20
DevTest 2016	1779	883	276	20
Test: *Test 2016*	20632	7059	3231	100

Table 1: Overview of datasets and number of tweets (or sentences) provided in SemEval-2016. The data was divided into training, development and testing sets.

3.2 Setup

We use the following hyper parameters for the 2-layer CNN: In both layers we use 200 filters, a filter length of 6, and for the first layer we use a pooling length of 4 with striding 2.

In order to optimize our results, we varied the batch-sizes, we introduced class-weights to lessen the impact of the unbalanced training set, and we experimented with different schemes for shuffling the training set (see below). To determine the class-weight of class i we used the following formula: $\frac{n}{c * n_i}$, where n is the total number of samples in the training set, c is the number of classes, namely 2, and n_i is the number of samples that belong to class i.

3.3 Results

The following results are computed on *Test 2016*. We use the *macroaveraged recall* ρ as scoring mechanism for our experiments, which is more robust regarding class imbalances (Rosenthal et al.,

2017; Esuli and Sebastiani, 2015).

The results show that the usage of class weights increases the score by approximately 2 points from 0.8225 to 0.8403 points.

Figure 3 shows the score depending on the batch size used. The results show that higher batch sizes tend to give higher scores. This effect however subsides when batch sizes greater than 1200 are used.

Figure 4 shows the result when different schemes for shuffling the training set before training are applied. When we do not shuffle the training set, the *macroaveraged recall* score drops by 4-5 points. We compare two schemes for shuffling: (i) the *epoch based shuffling*, where the training set is shuffled entirely before each epoch, (ii) *batch based shuffling*, where the training set is split into batches and each batch is shuffled separately. The results in Figure 4 show that there is just a small difference of 1 point among the two strategies.

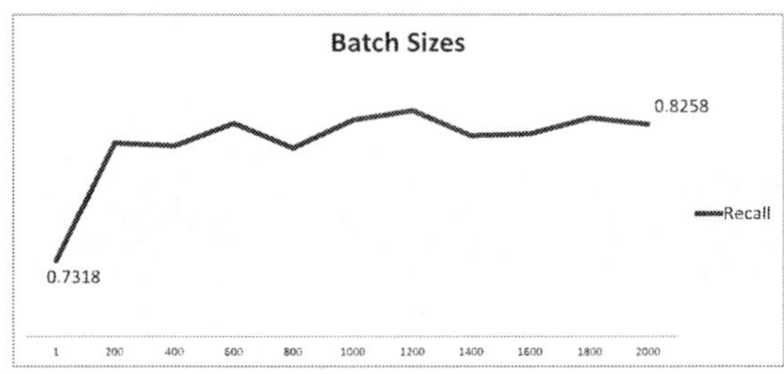

Figure 3: The architecture of the CNNs used in our approach.

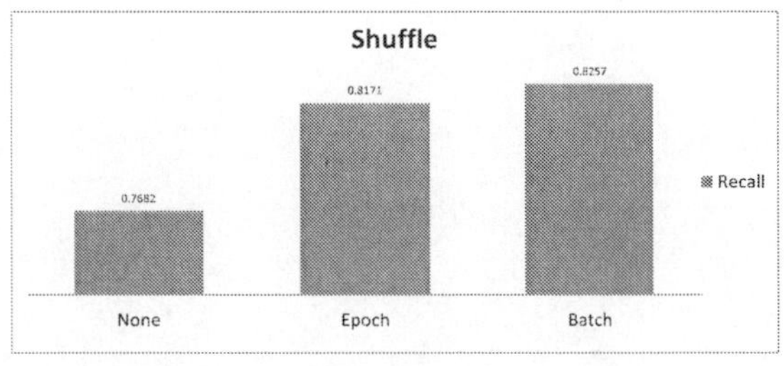

Figure 4: The architecture of the CNNs used in our approach.

Table 2 shows the results on the *Test 2017* set, which is the official test set of the competition. The system achieves a *macroaveraged recall* of 0.846, thus, ranking at 4th place. The *BB twtr* system, ranked 1st, outperforms our approach by 4 points, whereas the *DataStories* system and the *Tweester* system outperform our system by only 1 point.

System	ρ	F_1^{PN}	Acc
TopicThunder	0.846	0.847	0.854
BB twtr	0.882	0.890	0.897
DataStories	0.856	0.861	0.869
Tweester	0.854	0.854	0.863

Table 2: Official results on *Test 2017*. We compare our system to the systems that ranked 1st, 2nd, and 3rd.

4 Conclusion

We described a deep learning approach to solve the problem of topic-specific sentiment analysis on twitter. The approach is based on a 2-layer Convolutional Neural Network which is trained using a large amount of data. Furthermore, we experimented with different parameters to fine tune our system. The system was evaluated at SemEval-2017 for the task of Topic-Based Message Polarity Classification, ranking at 4th place.

References

Franois Chollet. 2015. keras. https://github.com/fchollet/keras.

Jan Deriu, Maurice Gonzenbach, Fatih Uzdilli, Aurelien Lucchi, Valeria De Luca, and Martin Jaggi. 2016. Swisscheese at semeval-2016 task 4: Sentiment classification using an ensemble of convolutional neural networks with distant supervision. *Proceedings of SemEval* pages 1124–1128.

Andrea Esuli and Fabrizio Sebastiani. 2015. Optimizing text quantifiers for multivariate loss functions. *ACM Transactions on Knowledge Discovery from Data (TKDD)* 9(4):27.

Alec Go, Richa Bhayani, and Lei Huang. 2009. Twitter sentiment classification using distant supervision. *CS224N Project Report, Stanford* 1:12.

Nal Kalchbrenner, Edward Grefenstette, and Phil Blunsom. 2014. A Convolutional Neural Network for Modelling Sentences. In *ACL - Proceedings of the 52nd Annual Meeting of the Association for Computational Linguistics*. Baltimore, Maryland, USA, pages 655–665.

Yoon Kim. 2014. Convolutional Neural Networks for Sentence Classification. In *EMNLP 2014 - Empirical Methods in Natural Language Processing*. pages 1746–1751.

Tomas Mikolov, Quoc V Le, and Ilya Sutskever. 2013. Exploiting Similarities among Languages for Machine Translation. *arXiv* .

Vinod Nair and Geoffrey E Hinton. 2010. Rectified linear units improve restricted boltzmann machines. In *Proceedings of the 27th International Conference on Machine Learning (ICML-10)*. pages 807–814.

Jonathon Read. 2005. Using emoticons to reduce dependency in machine learning techniques for sentiment classification. In *Proceedings of the ACL student research workshop*. Association for Computational Linguistics, pages 43–48.

Radim Řehůřek and Petr Sojka. 2010. Software Framework for Topic Modelling with Large Corpora. In *Proceedings of the LREC 2010 Workshop on New Challenges for NLP Frameworks*. ELRA, Valletta, Malta, pages 45–50. `http://is.muni.cz/publication/884893/en`.

Sara Rosenthal, Noura Farra, and Preslav Nakov. 2017. SemEval-2017 task 4: Sentiment analysis in Twitter. In *Proceedings of the 11th International Workshop on Semantic Evaluation*. Association for Computational Linguistics, Vancouver, Canada, SemEval '17.

Aliaksei Severyn and Alessandro Moschitti. 2015. Twitter sentiment analysis with deep convolutional neural networks. In *Proceedings of the 38th International ACM SIGIR Conference on Research and Development in Information Retrieval*. ACM, pages 959–962.

Theano Development Team. 2016. Theano: A Python framework for fast computation of mathematical expressions. *arXiv e-prints* abs/1605.02688. http://arxiv.org/abs/1605.02688.

Matthew D. Zeiler. 2012. ADADELTA: An Adaptive Learning Rate Method. *arXiv* page 6. http://arxiv.org/abs/1212.5701.

INGEOTEC at SemEval 2017 Task 4: A B4MSA Ensemble based on Genetic Programming for Twitter Sentiment Analysis

Sabino Miranda-Jiménez and **Mario Graff**[*] and **Eric S. Tellez**
CONACyT - INFOTEC, Aguascalientes, México
{sabino.miranda,mario.graff,eric.tellez}@infotec.mx

Daniela Moctezuma
CONACyT - CentroGEO, Aguascalientes, México
dmoctezuma@centrogeo.edu.mx

Abstract

This paper describes the system used in SemEval-2017 Task 4 (Subtask A): Message Polarity Classification for both English and Arabic languages. Our proposed system is an ensemble of two layers, the first one uses our generic framework for multilingual polarity classification (B4MSA) and the second layer combines all the decision function values predicted by B4MSA systems using a nonlinear function evolved using a Genetic Programming system, EvoDAG. With this approach, the best performances reached by our system were macro-recall 0.68 (English) and 0.477 (Arabic) which set us in sixth and fourth positions in the results table, respectively.

1 Introduction

Sentiment Analysis is the computational analysis of people's feelings or beliefs expressed in texts such as emotions, opinions, attitudes, appraisals, etc. (Liu and Zhang, 2012). At the same time, with the growth of social media (review websites, microblogging sites, etc.) on the Web, Twitter has received particular attention because it is a huge source of opinionated information ($6,000$ tweets each second) [1], and has potential uses for decision-making tasks from business applications to political campaigns.

In this context, SemEval is one of the forums that conducts evaluations of Sentiment Analysis Systems on Twitter at different levels such as polarity classification at global or topic-based message, tweet quantifications, among other tasks (Nakov et al., 2016; SemEval, 2017).

In this research, the sentiment analysis task is faced as a classification problem, thus supervised learning techniques are used to tackle this problem. Particularly, we used Support Vector Machines (SVM) and a Genetic Programming system called EvoDAG (Graff et al., 2016, 2017).

In this context, one crucial step is the procedure used to transform the data (i.e., tweets) into the inputs (vectors) of the supervised learning techniques used. Typically, Natural Language Processing (NLP) approaches for data representation use n-grams of words, linguistic information such as dependency relations, syntactic information, lexical units (e.g. lemmas, stems), affective lexicons, etc.; however, selecting the best configuration of those characteristics could be a huge problem. In fact, this selection can be seen as a combinatorial optimization problem where the objective is to improve the accuracy (or any performance measure) of the classifier being used. The proposed system uses our generic framework for multilingual polarity classification (B4MSA) (Tellez et al., 2016) to transform the data into the inputs of an SVM. Furthermore, B4MSA uses random search and hill climbing to find a suitable text transformation pipeline among the possible ones.

Looking at systems that obtained the best results in previous SemEval editions, it can be concluded that it is necessary to include more datasets, see for instance SwissCheese system (Deriu et al., 2016), besides the one given in the competition. Here, it was decided to follow this approach by including an extra dataset for English, and a number of datasets automatically labeled using a distant supervision approach in both languages, English and Arabic. Regarding this point, it was observed that it is important to have a good balance between quality and amount of samples. We take care of this issue by removing the repeated samples in our training set and at the same time using a lot of sam-

---

[*]Corresponding author: mario.graff@infotec.mx

[1]https://www.brandwatch.com/blog/44-twitter-stats-2016/

Proceedings of the 11th International Workshop on Semantic Evaluations (SemEval-2017), pages 771–776,
Vancouver, Canada, August 3 - 4, 2017. ©2017 Association for Computational Linguistics

ples.

In this paper, we describe our classification system used in SemEval-2017 contest for Task 4, subtask A: polarity classification at global message. This task consists in classifying given a tweet whether is positive, negative, or neutral sentiment according to its content. Our system was evaluated on the English and Arabic languages.

2 System Description

Our framework comprises two subsystems: B4MSA (Tellez et al., 2016), which is a supervised learning system based on SVM; and EvoDAG (Graff et al., 2016, 2017) that acts as integrator of agreements among the decision functions values predicted by a set of B4MSA systems. Figure 1 shows the architecture of our approach. The basic idea of this framework is to make maximum use of synergies between both approaches B4MSA and EvoDAG.

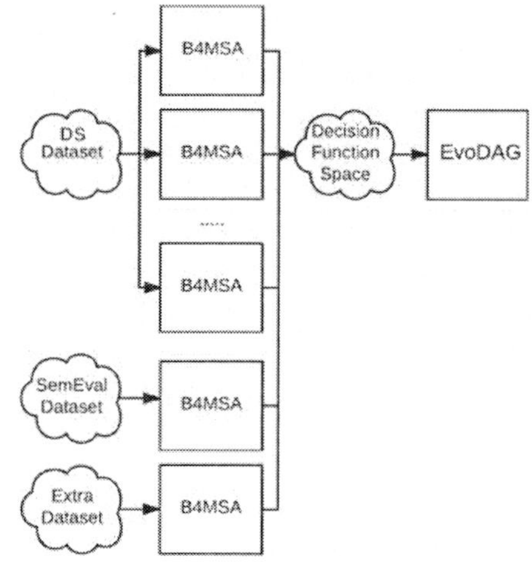

Figure 1: Prediction Scheme

Roughly speaking, our approach uses two layers. In the first layer, a set of B4MSA classifiers are trained with two kind of datasets; datasets labeled by human annotators: SemEval datasets from 2013-2016 and the English dataset of (Mozetič et al., 2016), called HL dataset, and also datasets generated by distant supervision approach, called DS dataset, (see section 3.2). In case of HL datasets, each B4MSA classifier produces three real output values, one for each sentiment (negative, neutral and positive).

In the case of DS, the entire collection is divided into a number of disjoint parts to obtain a number of individually trained B4MSA classifiers. Each B4MSA is only trained to predict if a tweet is positive or negative, based on the distant supervision procedure described in §3.2. Since there are only two classes, then each classifier produces a real output. To improve the classification performance, we fix the size of the parts to contain 30K tweets (positive and negative) for large datasets. Due to the large number of parts for very large DS collections, we take into account just a few classifiers, k, in the decision process. To select the k best classifiers, we define a vocabulary-affinity measure that scores what a classifier knows about the vocabulary (content) of a tweet to be classified. All B4MSA classifiers compute its vocabulary affinity; then, the top k classifiers are selected dynamically for each tweet according to its content using the vocabulary-affinity measure. The optimal k should be experimentally determined.

Finally, EvoDAG's inputs are the concatenation of all the decision functions predicted by B4MSA. The following subsections describe the internal parts of our approach. The precise configuration of our benchmarked system is described in §4.

2.1 B4MSA

B4MSA[2] (Tellez et al., 2016, 2017) is a framework to create multilingual sentiment analysis systems; in particular, it produces sentiment classifiers that are weakly linked to language dependent methods. For instance, B4MSA avoids the usage of computational expensive linguistic tasks such as lemmatization, stemming, part-of-speech tagging, etc., and take advantage of data representations, mostly based on simple text transformations and a number of text tokenizers.

The core idea of B4MSA is to determine automatically the best text transformation pipeline along with the best performing set of tokenizers, given a large set of possible configurations. In B4MSA, the whole process is stated as a combinatorial optimization problem, where the set of configurations define the possible solutions. In practice, the best text configuration for a particular problem has a high computational cost to evaluate each configuration, due to the large configuration space; however, a competitive solution can be found using hyper-heuristics.

We use a plain B4MSA setup, see Table 1 for details of text transformations used in our sys-

---

[2]https://github.com/INGEOTEC/b4msa

tem. This set of text transformations was selected among millions of possible configurations through the combinatorial optimization solution implemented in B4MSA.

2.2 EvoDAG

EvoDAG[3] (Graff et al., 2016, 2017) is a Genetic Programming system specifically tailored to tackle classification and regression problems on very high dimensional vector spaces and large datasets. In particular, EvoDAG uses the principles of Darwinian evolution to create models represented as a directed acyclic graph (DAG). An EvoDAG model has three distinct node's types; the inputs nodes, that as expected received the independent variables, the output node that corresponds to the label, and the inner nodes are the different numerical functions such as: sum, product, sin, cos, max, and min, among others. Due to lack of space, we refer the reader to (Graff et al., 2016) where EvoDAG is described, and, we followed, in this research, the steps mentioned there.

In order to provide an idea of the type of models being evolved, Figure 2 depicts a model evolved for the Arabic polarity classification at global message task. As can be seen, the model is represented using a DAG where direction of the edges indicates the dependency, e.g., cos depends on X_3, i.e., cosine function is applied to X_3. There are three types of nodes; the inputs nodes are colored in red, the inner nodes are blue (the intensity is related to the distance to the height, the darker the closer), and the green node is the output node. As mentioned previously, EvoDAG uses as inputs the decision functions of B4MSA, then first three inputs (i.e., X_0, X_1, and X_2) correspond to the decision function values of the negative, neutral, and positive polarity of B4MSA model trained with SemEval Arabic dataset, and the later two (i.e., X_3 and X_4) correspond to the decision function values of two B4MSA systems each one trained with our DS dataset. It is important to mention that EvoDAG does not have information regarding whether input X_i comes from a particular polarity decision function, consequently from EvoDAG point of view all inputs are equivalent.

3 Data Preparation

To determine the best configuration of parameters for text modeling, B4MSA integrates a hyper-

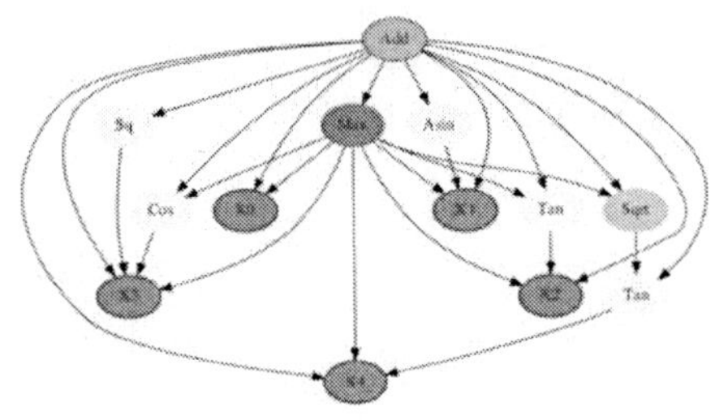

Figure 2: An evolved model for the arabic task.

parameter optimization phase that ensures the performance of the sentiment classifier based on the training data. The text modeling parameters determined for the English and Arabic languages related to text transformations, weighting scheme, and tokenizers are described in Table 1. A text transformation feature could be binary (yes/no) or ternary (group/delete/none) option. Tokenizers denote how texts must be split after applying the process of each text transformation to texts. Tokenizers generate text chunks in a range of lengths, all tokens generated are part of the text representation. B4MSA allows selecting tokenizers based on n-words, q-grams, and skip-grams, in any combination. We call n-words to the well-known word n-grams; in particular, we allow to use any combination of unigrams, bigrams, and trigrams. Also, the configuration space allows selecting any combination of character q-grams (or just q-grams) for $q = 3, 5, 7,$ and 9. Finally, we allow to use $(2, 1)$ and $(3, 1)$ skip-grams (two words separated by one word, and three words separated by a gap).

Our parameter set contains five binary features, four ternaries ones, and nine individual tokenizers; thus the configuration space contains $5^2 \times 4^3 \times (2^9 - 1) = 817,600$ different items. For instance, for the English dataset, a commodity workstation needs close to ten minutes to evaluate each configuration,[4] such that an exhaustive evaluation of the configuration space will take 15 years. We use a number of hyper-heuristics to find a competitive model in a few hours, the interested reader on the optimization process is referenced to (Tellez et al., 2016, 2017).

Table 1 shows the final configurations for each language, for example, *remove diacritics* is not applied to English, but it is applied to Arabic. Although *lowercase* transformation is weird for

---

[3]https://github.com/mgraffg/EvoDAG

[4]Only human labeled data, this time does not apply to the distant supervision dataset.

Text transformation	English	Arabic
remove diacritics	no	yes
remove duplicates	no	yes
remove punctuation	no	yes
emoticons	none	delete
lowercase	yes	yes
numbers	group	group
urls	group	delete
users	delete	none
Term weighting		
TF-IDF	yes	yes
Tokenizers		
n-words	$\{2,3\}$	$\{2\}$
q-grams	$\{3,5,9\}$	$\{3,5\}$
skip-grams	–	$\{(3,1)\}$

Table 1: Set of configurations for text modeling

Arabic since there is no such concept in Arabic text, it makes sense when text is not constrained to Arabic, e.g., tweets are full of text in other languages, it has URLs, user's names, or hashtags.

In case of English, the model selection procedure performed by B4MSA determined to use trigrams, bigrams, and character q-grams of sizes 3, 5, and 9. In case of Arabic, each tweet must be split into $(3,1)$-skip-grams, bigrams and trigrams of words, and 3-grams, 5-grams of characters. TF-IDF term weighting is applied to both languages.

The processes associated to text modeling, shown in Table 1, are applied to all datasets as text representation model.

3.1 Training Data

For this year, SemEval provides training data from 2013 to 2016 (Nakov et al., 2016) evaluations to train systems. In addition, we use an extra dataset annotated by humans around 73 thousand tweets and 2,000 available for English (Mozetič et al., 2016) and Arabic (NRC, 2017) languages, respectively. Table 2 shows the distribution of classes for English and Arabic datasets. We consider, essentially, three kind of datasets as training data: all datasets provided from SemEval are as a cross-domain dataset for evaluation on the contest, Extra-data as out-of-domain dataset of SemEval evaluations, and DS dataset (distant supervision) as general domain dataset, mainly, for learning affective vocabulary and related words. In case of DS dataset, we obtained 11 million tweets for English after processing a huge amount of tweets, and 16 thousand tweets for Arabic (see section 3.2). For Arabic, due to the lack of data, all human labeled tweets are considered as a dataset.

DataSet	Positive	Neutral	Negative	Total
Statistics of English training data				
train2013	3,662	4,600	1,466	9,728
dev2013	575	739	340	1,654
test2013	1,572	601	1,640	3,813
test2014	982	669	202	1,853
test2015	1,040	987	365	2,392
train2016	3,094	863	2,043	6,000
dev2016	844	765	391	2,000
devtest2016	994	681	325	2,000
test2016	7,059	10,342	3,231	20,632
Extra-data	21,166	33,620	18,454	73,240
DS-dataset	5.5M	-	5.5M	11M
Statistics of Arabic training data				
train2017	743	1,470	1,142	3,355
Extra-data	448	202	1,350	2,000
DS-dataset	8,108	-	8,108	16,216

Table 2: Statistics of English and Arabic training data. We used the labeled English extra-data from (Mozetič et al., 2016), and the Arabic extra data from (NRC, 2017).

3.2 External Data

In addition of the training datasets provided by SemEval'17, and annotated Extra-datasets, we generate an affective dataset using distant supervision approach. Distant supervision has been used for tasks such as information extraction (Mintz et al., 2009), or sentiment analysis (Go et al., 2009). In sentiment analysis, emoticons, some words, and hashtags are usually used as indicators of emotion in order to create labeled dataset without human assistance. These new labeled datasets are expected to improve the performance of systems based on training data. We introduce a set of heuristics for distant supervision based on affective lexicons to generate labeled datasets for positive and negative sentiment.

Our approach consists in filtering tweets considering the affective degree that each tweet contains based on its affective words. First, we have collected more than 220 million tweets for U.S. English according to their geolocation (from July to December 2016), and more than 130 thousand tweets for Arabic without restriction of geolocation (one week of January 2017). Later, tweets are filtered using a large affective lexicon built for this purpose. The tweets are selected based on its positive or negative words. Some heuristic rules are used, for example, if a tweet contains negative markers that could reverse the sentiment such as *no, not, although, however, but*, etc., question marks, or both positive and negative words, then the tweet is discarded; if a tweet has only positive or negative words (no contradiction), then it is selected and labeled with the corresponding sentiment according to the affective words. Also, English and Arabic stemmers from NLTK (Bird et al., 2009) are used in order to maximize the matches between affective words and tweets.

Our distant supervision approach uses an affective lexicon that was created based on the SentiSense lexicon (de Albornoz et al., 2012) to extract affective tags (sadness, anger, love, etc.) related to WordNet synsets (Miller, 1995). A synset defines a group of words with semantic similarities, thus, a synset label defined in SentiSense is applied to all words in the WordNet synset, these words are part of our lexicon. Negative emotions in SentiSense (sadness, fear, anger, hate, disgust) are mapped to negative tag, and positive emotions (love, joy, like) are mapped to positive tag. In addition, opinion words from Bing Liu's lexicon (Liu, 2017) are also added to our lexicon. In case of Arabic language, the affective lexicon was created translating the affective lexicon from English into Arabic by means of python translation package for Bing translator service (LittleCoder, 2017). The same heuristic rules for English are applied to Arabic to create the labeled dataset for positive and negative emotions.

Finally, we remove near duplicated tweets to reduce the final dataset (DS-dataset); the idea is to select only the essential dataset while the vocabulary around affective words is maximized. The process of near duplicate removal is performed as follows. We performed a linear scan of the retrieved dataset, we transform the tweet with a number of coarsening text transformations (all those supported by B4MSA, see Table 1). Whether the transformed text has not be seen; that is, if the text was already generated, the tweet is discarded. In the end, from an initial collection of 220 million tweets, we obtained around 11 million exemplars for English, and, from an initial set of more than 130K of Arabic tweets, around 16 thousand exemplars were obtained (see Table 2 for more details).

4   Results

We present the results of our system in subtask A for both the English and Arabic languages. Table 3 shows the performance on some configurations for EvoDAG. 2-HL indicates the use of two human labeled datasets, SemEval and the presented in (Možetič et al., 2016); 44-DS indicates the use of $k = 44$ for the 11 million DS-dataset. More detailed, the best 44 classifiers are chosen from 367; each classifier is trained over chunks of $30K$ tweets. The selection is made based on the vocabulary-affinity between an object and each classifier, see §2 for more details. In the end, this configuration produces 50 inputs for EvoDAG. Six inputs correspond to 2-HL since each dataset contributes with three inputs, i.e. the B4MSA's decision functions for positive, negative, and neutral classes. Also, the rest of the inputs correspond to 44 best B4MSA classifiers trained with our distant supervision process. Each value describes if a tweet is just positive or negative, as decided by the corresponding B4MSA classifier. We obtained 0.680 of macro-recall in our training stage, and achieve 0.649 in the SemEval's gold-standard.

In addition, we tested our system without using DS-dataset in order to show the improvement of our distant supervision approach (see 2-HL-train/4 configuration, Table 3). The training dataset was divided into 4 subsets to train our scheme with EvoDAG, this configuration, only with training dataset annotated by humans, is below nearly 3% of our best performance. Thus, we use the same DS approach for both English and Arabic languages.

In the case of Arabic, due to the lack of data, there are only five inputs for EvoDAG. As shown in Figure 2: three inputs come from a B4MSA trained with annotated datasets (1-HL), and two additional inputs come from trained classifiers with DS-dataset (16K tweets). The last dataset is partitioned into two subsets of around 8K tweets (2-DS), the only evaluation is shown in Table 4, we obtained 0.642 of macro-recall in our training stage and 0.477 in the SemEval's gold-standard.

configuration	macro-F1	macro-recall	accuracy
2-HL, 44-DS (11M)	0.649	**0.680**	0.667
2-HL, 44-DS (3.5M)	0.648	0.679	0.666
2-HL, train/4	0.632	0.652	0.655
Performance on gold standard of SemEval'17			
2-HL, 44-DS (11M)	0.645	**0.649**	0.633

Table 3: Results for substask A on English datasets. (HL) Human labeled, (DS) Distant supervision

configuration	macro-F1	macro-recall	accuracy
1-HL, 2-DS (16K)	0.642	**0.642**	0.662
Performance on gold standard of SemEval'17			
1-HL, 2-DS (16K)	0.455	**0.477**	0.499

Table 4: Results for substask A on Arabic datasets. (HL) Human labeled, (DS) Distant supervision

5 Conclusions

In this paper was presented the proposed approach combining a generic framework for multilingual polarity classification, B4MSA, with a genetic programming system, EvoDAG. For the training, we use several datasets: human annotated datasets, and our datasets generated with distant supervision approach. Our performance, macro-recall 0.649, brought us to the sixth position in the English language, and fourth position, macro-recall 0.477, for the Arabic language.

References

Steven Bird, Ewan Klein, and Edward Loper. 2009. *Natural Language Processing with Python*. O'Reilly Media.

Jorge Carrillo de Albornoz, Laura Plaza, and Pablo Gervás. 2012. Sentisense: An easily scalable concept-based affective lexicon for sentiment analysis. In *Proceedings of LREC 2012*. pages 3562–3567.

Jan Deriu, Maurice Gonzenbach, Fatih Uzdilli, Aurelien Lucchi, Valeria De Luca, and Martin Jaggi. 2016. Swisscheese at semeval-2016 task 4: Sentiment classification using an ensemble of convolutional neural networks with distant supervision. In *Proceedings of the 10th International Workshop on Semantic Evaluation (SemEval-2016)*. Association for Computational Linguistics, San Diego, California, pages 1124–1128. http://www.aclweb.org/anthology/S16-1173.

Alec Go, Richa Bhayani, and Lei Huang. 2009. Twitter sentiment classification using distant supervision. *CS224N Project Report, Stanford* 1(12).

M. Graff, E. S. Tellez, S. Miranda-Jiménez, and H. J. Escalante. 2016. Evodag: A semantic genetic programming python library. In *2016 IEEE International Autumn Meeting on Power, Electronics and Computing (ROPEC)*. pages 1–6. https://doi.org/10.1109/ROPEC.2016.7830633.

Mario Graff, Eric S. Tellez, Hugo Jair Escalante, and Sabino Miranda-Jiménez. 2017. Semantic Genetic Programming for Sentiment Analysis. In Oliver Schtze, Leonardo Trujillo, Pierrick Legrand, and Yazmin Maldonado, editors, *NEO 2015*, Springer International Publishing, number 663 in Studies in Computational Intelligence, pages 43–65. DOI: 10.1007/978-3-319-44003-3_2.

LittleCoder. 2017. Translation a python translation package based on website service. `https://pypi.python.org/pypi/translation`. Accessed 20-Jan-2017.

Bing Liu. 2017. English opinion lexicon. `https://www.cs.uic.edu/~liub/FBS/sentiment-analysis.html#lexicon`. Accessed 20-Jan-2017.

Bing Liu and Lei Zhang. 2012. *A Survey of Opinion Mining and Sentiment Analysis*, Springer US, Boston, MA, pages 415–463. https://doi.org/10.1007/978-1-4614-3223-4-13.

George A Miller. 1995. Wordnet: a lexical database for english. *Communications of the ACM* 38(11):39–41.

Mike Mintz, Steven Bills, Rion Snow, and Dan Jurafsky. 2009. Distant supervision for relation extraction without labeled data. In *Proceedings of the Joint Conference of the 47th Annual Meeting of the ACL and the 4th International Joint Conference on Natural Language Processing of the AFNLP: Volume 2-Volume 2*. Association for Computational Linguistics, pages 1003–1011.

Igor Mozetič, Miha Grčar, and Jasmina Smailović. 2016. Multilingual twitter sentiment classification: The role of human annotators. *PloS one* 11(5):e0155036.

Preslav Nakov, Alan Ritter, Sara Rosenthal, Veselin Stoyanov, and Fabrizio Sebastiani. 2016. SemEval-2016 task 4: Sentiment analysis in Twitter. In *Proceedings of the 10th International Workshop on Semantic Evaluation*. Association for Computational Linguistics, San Diego, California, SemEval '16.

NRC. 2017. Syrian tweets arabic sentiment analysis dataset. `http://saifmohammad.com/WebPages/ArabicSA.html`. Accessed 17-Feb-2017.

SemEval. 2017. Semeval-2017: Sentiment analysis task 4. `http://alt.qcri.org/semeval2017/task4/`. Accessed 17-Feb-2017.

Eric S. Tellez, Sabino Miranda-Jimnez, Mario Graff, Daniela Moctezuma, Oscar S. Siordia, and Elio A. Villaseor. 2017. A case study of spanish text transformations for twitter sentiment analysis. *Expert Systems with Applications* 81:457 – 471.

Eric Sadit Tellez, Sabino Miranda-Jiménez, Mario Graff, Daniela Moctezuma, Ranyart Rodrigo Suárez, and Oscar Sánchez Siordia. 2016. A simple approach to multilingual polarity classification in twitter. *CoRR* abs/1612.05270. http://arxiv.org/abs/1612.05270.

BUSEM at SemEval-2017 Task 4

Sentiment Analysis with Word Embedding and Long Short Term Memory RNN Approaches

Deger Ayata[1], Murat Saraclar [1], Arzucan Ozgur[2]
[1]Electrical & Electronical Engineering Department, Bogaziçi University
[2]Computer Engineering Department, Bogaziçi University
Istanbul , Turkey
{deger.ayata, murat.saraclar, arzucan.ozgur}@boun.edu.tr

Abstract

This paper describes our approach for SemEval-2017 Task 4: Sentiment Analysis in Twitter. We have participated in Subtask A: Message Polarity Classification subtask and developed two systems. The first system uses word embeddings for feature representation and Support Vector Machine, Random Forest and Naive Bayes algorithms for the classification of Twitter messages into negative, neutral and positive polarity. The second system is based on Long Short Term Memory Recurrent Neural Networks and uses word indexes as sequence of inputs for feature representation.

1 Introduction

Sentiment analysis is extracting subjective information from source materials, via natural language processing, computational linguistics, text mining and machine learning. Classification of users' reviews about a concept or political view may bring different opportunities including customer satisfaction rating, making right recommendations to right target, categorization of users etc. Sentiment Analysis is often referred to as subjectivity analysis, opinion mining and appraisal extraction with some connections to affective computing. Sometimes whole documents are studied as a sentiment unit (Turney and Littman, 2003), but it's generally agreed that sentiment resides in smaller linguistic units (Pang and Lee, 2008).

This paper describes our approach for SemEval-2017 Task 4: Sentiment Analysis in Twitter. We have participated in Subtask A: Message Polarity Classification subtask. We have developed two systems. The first system

uses word embeddings for feature representation and Support Vector Machine (SVM), Random Forest (RF) and Naive Bayes (NB) algorithms for classification Twitter messages into negative, neutral and positive polarity. The second system is based on Long Short Term Memory Recurrent Neural Networks (LSTM) and uses word indexes as sequence of inputs for feature representation.

The remainder of this article is structured as follows: Section 2 contains information about the system description and Section 3 explains methods, models, tools and software packages used in this work. Test cases and datasets are explained in Section 4. Results are given in Section 5 with discussions. Finally, section 6 summarizes the conclusions and future work.

2 System Description

We have developed two independent systems. The first system is word embedding centric and described in subsection 2.1. The second is LSTM based and described in subsection 2.2. Further details about both systems are given in Section 3.

2.1 Word Embedding based System Description

In word embedding centric system approach, each word in a tweet is represented with a vector. Tweets consist of words and vectorial values of words (word vectors) are used to represent tweets as vectorial values. Word Embedding system framework is shown Figure 1. Two methods are used to obtain word vectors in this work. The first method is based on generating word vectors via constructing a word2vec model from semeval corpus as depicted in Figure 1 steps 1 and 2. The second

Proceedings of the 11th International Workshop on Semantic Evaluations (SemEval-2017), pages 777–783,
Vancouver, Canada, August 3 - 4, 2017. ©2017 Association for Computational Linguistics

method is based on Google News pre-trained word vectors model (step 3).

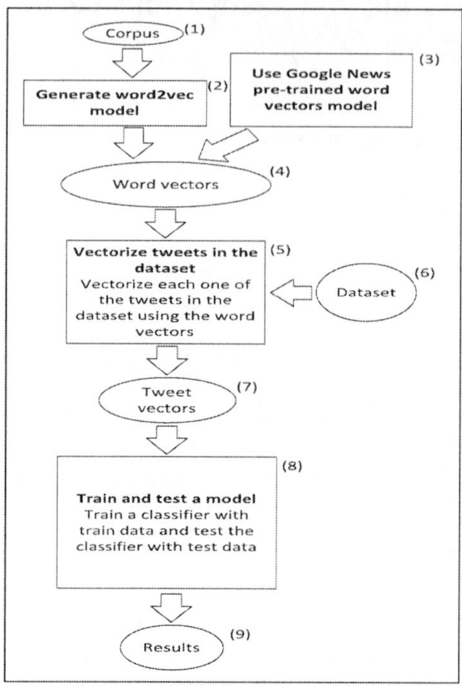

Figure 1: General framework of the system

In the first method, a word2vec model is construted by using the entire semeval tweet corpus and a vector space (word2vec model) has been created. This model contains vector values for all unique words in the corpus. Words which have similar contexts are positioned closer on this space. The parameters used in training word2vec model effect the performance of the whole framework. Therefore it is important to find optimal parameter values. This work is focused on the parameter named feature vector dimension size and its impact on the general performance. This parameter determines the dimensionality of the word vectors, which are generated via the word2vec model.

The second method is based on Google News pre-trained word vectors model. This method uses the Google News pre-trained word vectors model to obtain word vectors as shown in Figure 1 step 3. The Google news pre-trained model is a dictionary which contains word and vectorial value pairs, and it is generated via a word2vec model trained on the Google News text corpus.

Next stage includes using the obtained word vectors to vectorize tweets in the dataset which contains both training data and test data (steps 5 and 6). This stage includes also the preprocessing of the tweets, e.g. deleting http links and twitter user names included in the tweets, deleting the duplicate tweets which occur multiple times on the dataset etc. Later, preprocessed and formatted tweets are iterated to generate a tweet vector for each tweets by using the words they contained. Therefore, inputs of this stage are the dataset and the model which includes word vectors, while its output is a set containing tweet vectors, both for the train and the test data.

Outputted tweet vectors are in a numerical format which can be given as an input to multiple machine learning algorithms with the purpose of classifying them into categories or testing an existing model (step 8). At this stage, each tweet in the dataset is represented as a vector with multiple dimensions (step 7). It is possible to train a new classifier model or load a pre-trained and saved model. SVM, RF, and NB classifier models are trained in this work. Tweets are categorized into three classes which are negative, neutral and positive (step 9).

2.2 LSTM Based System Description

The pipeline of the second system consists of many steps : reading Tweets from Semeval datasets, preprocessing Tweets, representing each word with an index, then representing each Tweet with a set of word index sequence and training a LSTM classifier with sequence index array. The Flowchart of this system is shown in Figure 2.

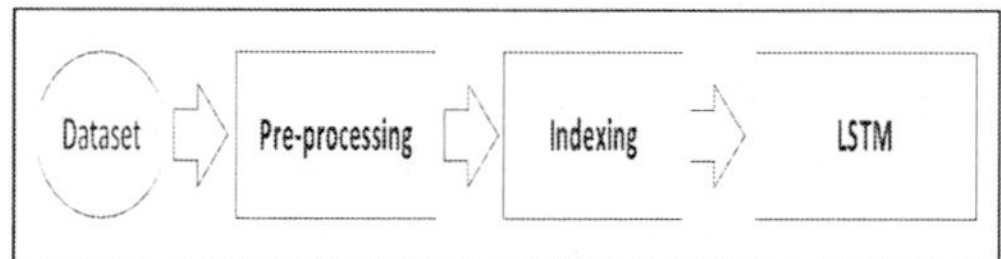

Figure 2: LSTM based system pipeline

3 Methods and Tools

3.1 Word Embedding

Word embedding stands for a set of natural language processing methods, where words or phrases from the vocabulary are mapped to vectorial values of real numbers (Bengio et al.,2003). Embeddings have been shown to boost the performance of natural language processing tasks such as sentiment analysis

(Socher et al., 2013). Vector representations of words can be used in vector operations like addition and subtraction. Vectors generated by word embedding can be used to represent sentences, tweets or whole documents as vectorial values. There are multiple methods to generate sentence vectors using the word vectors, a modified version of the sum representation method which is proposed by Blacoe is used in this work (Blacoe et al., 2012).

The sum representation model, in its original state, is generated via summing the vectorial embeddings of words which a sentence contains. The related equations are given below with E.1, E.2 and E.3:

Twt: $tweet$, $twtVec$: $tweet\ vector$,
w: $word$, $wdVec$: $word\ vector$,
n: $number\ of\ words\ in\ tweet$,
$Twt_i = \left(w_1{}^{(i)}, \dots, w_n{}^{(i)}\right)$: $words\ in\ tweet$

$$twtVec[j] = \sum_{k=1,\dots,n_i} wdVec_{w_k}[j] \qquad (E.1)$$

A modified version is used in this work. Derived version considers the number of words. The related equations are given below:

$$Twt_i = \left(w_1{}^{(i)}, \dots, w_n{}^{(i)}\right) \qquad (E.2)$$

$$twtVec[j] = \frac{\sum_{k=1,\dots,n_i} wdVec_{w_k}[j]}{n} \qquad (E.3)$$

3.2 Classification Models

3.2.1 Support Vector Machine

SVM finds a hyper plane seperating tweet vectors according to their classes while making the margin as large as possible. After training, it classifies test records according to which side of the hyperplane their positions are (Fradkin et al, 2000). We have used SVM with the following parameters = {Kernel = PolyKernel, batchSize=100}

3.2.2 Random Forest

Random forests, first proposed by Ho (Ho, 1995) and later improved by Breiman (Breiman, 2001), operate by generating multiple decision trees and generate the final decision by evaluating the results of these individual trees. The mathematical expression

is given in equation (E.4). We have used Random Forest with the following parameters ={bagSizePercent =100, batchSize=100}

$\{(x_i, y_i)\}_{i=1}^{n}$: $training\ set$,

$y*$: $predictions$,

x' : $new\ points\ to\ classify$,

$W(x_i, x')y_i$: $weight\ of\ the\ i'th\ function$,

W : $weight\ function$,

$$y^* = \frac{1}{m}\sum_{j=1}^{m}\sum_{i=1}^{n} W_j(x_i, x')y_i$$
$$= \sum_{i=1}^{n}\left(\frac{1}{m}\sum_{j=1}^{m} W_j(x_i, x')\right)y_i \qquad (E.4)$$

3.2.3 Naïve Bayes

Naïve-Bayes is a probabilistic classifier based on Bayes' theorem, based on independence of features (John et al, 1995). Mathematical expression is given in equation (E.5).

$c*$: $predicted\ class$ x : $sample$

h_{NB}: $naïve\ bayes\ func$
$c^* = h_{NB}(x)$

$$= argmax_{j=1\dots m}P(c_j)\prod P(X_i = x_i | c_j) \quad (E.5)$$

3.2.4 Long Short Term Memory Recurrent Neural Nets

LSTM networks have similiar architecture to Recurrent Neural Nets (RNNs), except that they use different functions and architecture to compute the hidden state. They were introduced by Hochreiter & Schmidhuber (1997) to avoid the long-term dependency problem and were refined and popularized by many people in next studies.

LSTMs have the form of a chain of repeating modules of a special kind of architecture. The memory in LSTMs are called *cells*. Internally, these cells decide what to keep in and what to erase from memory. They then combine the previous state output, the current memory and the input to produce current state output. It turns out that these types of units are very efficient at capturing long-term dependencies. Before feeding the LSTM Network, preprocessing and indexing steps have been applied as shown in Figure 2.

Preprocessing

We have pre-processed the dataset before we input it into the LSTM classifier. We used Deeplearning4J library[1] to remove punctuations from tweets, and convert all content into lowercase.

Indexing

Indexing is iterating over all tweets contained in the dataset to determine words used in them and enumerate them. The index values of words are combined sequentially so that each tweet is presented as a sequence of word index numbers.

The program iterates through the dataset, enumarates each word which has not been indexed before and generates a dictionary that contains word – index pairs. As a result, each tweet is represented as set of sequential indexes, each representation contains same number of values as the tweet word count.

Indexed tweets are in sequential structure and they can be given as input to neural networks directly. LSTM networks make it possible to take the data sequentially and take in consideration the order of words in the training and classifying stages. Therefore, we used LSTM upon indexed tweets. We have used categorical crossentropy as loss function and softmax function. Our model parameters are given in Table 1 and the model is shown in Figure 3.

3.3 Used Tools and Software Packages

3.3.1 Deeplearning4J

Deeplearning4j is a commercial-grade, open-source, distributed deep-learning library written for Java and Scala[1]. There are multiple parameters to adjust when training a deep-learning network. Deeplearning4j is used for generating a vectorized format of the Semeval dataset using the Google News trained word vectors model.

Table 1: Parameters for classifier stage

`max_features`	86000 : Maximum integer value of indexed dataset.
`maxlen`	25 : Indexed tweets padded into this value.
`batch_size`	32
`model`	Sequential(): sequential model
`Embedding`	max_features : Input dimension, size of the vocabulary. 128 : Dimension of the dense embedding. dropout=0.2
`LSTM`	128 : dimension of the internal projections and the final output dropout_W=0.2 : Fraction of the input units to drop for input gates. dropout_U=0.2 : Fraction of the input units to drop for recurrent connections.
`Dense`	3 : Output dimensions.
`Activation`	'softmax' : Normalized exponential function
`loss`	'sparse_categorical_crossentropy' :.
`optimizer`	'adam' : Adam optimizer.

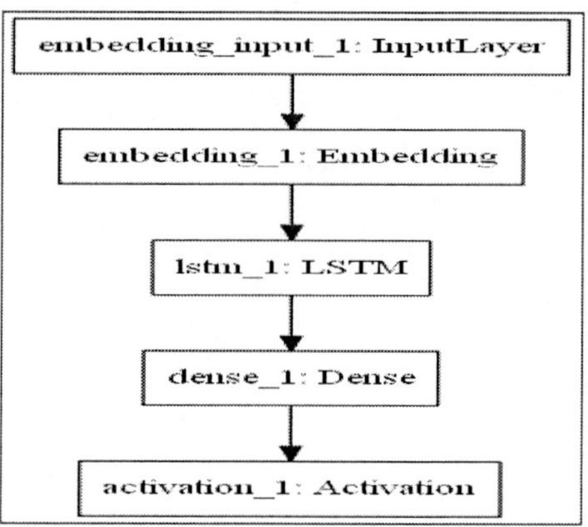

Figure 3: Plotted diagram of the LSTM classifier

3.3.2 Keras

Keras[2], developed by Chollet et al., is a high-level, open-source neural networks library written in Python (Chollet, 2015). It can use Theano or TensorFlow libraries as its backend. It is focused on fast experimentation with data. It includes implementations of commonly used neural network blocks such as layers, activation functions, etc., to enable its users to implement various neural networks in their work. We have used Keras library to develop LSTM network for tweet polarity classification.

[1] Deeplearning4j, http://deeplearning4j.org (Referenced Nov 2016)
[2] Keras, https://keras.io/ (Referenced February 2017)

3.3.3 Word2vec

Word2vec[3], is a group of models used to generate word embeddings (Mikalov et al., 2013). Word2vec models are based on two-layer neural networks which takes a large corpus of text as its input and produces a vector space of several hundred dimensions. Each unique word in the corpus is assigned a corresponding vector in this space. Embeddings are used to represent words as vectors which are closer to each other when words have similar meanings and far apart when they do not. Therefore, the system can generalize similar words.

Representing words as vectorial values makes it possible to treat words as vectors and use vectorial operations on them. A properly trained Word2vec model can calculate an operation like *[king] - [man] + [woman]* and give the approximate result of *[queen]*.

We have generated word2vec models in our tests from semeval datasets. We have run word2vec models with the parameters shown in Table 2.

Table 2: Parameters for word2vec generation stage

minWordFreq	MIN_WORD_FREQ = 5 : Minimal element frequency for elements found in the training corpus.
iterations	NETWORK_ITERATION = 25/50 :How many iterations should be done over batched sequences.
layerSize	FEATURE_VECTOR_DIMENSION_SIZE = 300/600/900 : Number of dimensions for outcome vectors.
seed	RANDOM_SEED = 42 : Sets seed for random numbers generator.
windowSize	WINDOW_SIZE = 25 : Sets window size for skip-Gram

3.3.4 Google News Trained Word2vec Model

Google news trained word vectors compose a word vector model which has been pre-trained on part of Google News corpus that includes 100 billion words. The model contains 300-dimensional vectors for 3 million words and phrases[4]. It is 3.39 GB in size which is observable from the equality, *3 million words * 300 features * 4bytes/feature = ~3.39GB.* Some stop words like "a", "and", "of" are excluded, but others like "the", "also", "should" are included. It also includes misspellings of words. For example, it includes both "mispelled" and "misspelled".

We have used Google News pre-trained word vectors to generate vector representations of tweets with FEATURE VECTOR DIMENSION SIZE equals to 300 configuration.

4 Dataset and Test Cases
4.1 Dataset

SemEval-2016 Task4 Subtask A's twitter train and test datasets have been used in this work[5]. The given datasets are dynamic which don't include the tweets that are deleted by their authors. Thus, the available data changes dynamically as users make their tweets available or deleted. We have used all previous years' tweets to construct the word embedding and classification models.

4.2 Test Cases

We have tested many configurations to find the best configuration to achieve the highest accuracy rate. We have conducted five main test cases. In the first, second and third test cases we have used word2vec model that has been constructed with previous years' semeval tweet datasets.

In Test 01, Test 02 and Test 03 we have trained word2vec model with SemEval Tweet dataset corpus. Also we have used different vector dimension sizes including 300, 600 and 900. In test case 04 we have used google news based(trained) word vectors. Also in each test case classification has been done with SVM, RF and NB. Test 05 id done with LSTM classifier on SemEval dataset. The test cases are listed in Table 3.

Table 3: Results obtained from tests

Test No.	Word Vectors	Dimension Size	SVM	RF	NB	LSTM
01	SemEval	600	√	√	√	
02	SemEval	300	√	√	√	
03	SemEval	900	√	√	√	
04	Google News trained	300	√	√	√	
05	N/A (index)	30				√

[3] Word2vec https://deeplearning4j.org/word2vec.html

[4] Google News trained word vectors model, https://code.google.com/archive/p/word2vec/

[5] SemEval Dataset, alt.qcri.org/semeval2017/task4/index.php?id=data-and-tools

5 Results and Discussion

5.1 Tests with Word Embedding and SVM, TF, NB

Purpose of the first three tests was observing the parameter feature vector dimension size's and classifier type impact on the general performance. We have used SemEval training and test datasets pertaining to 2013, 2014, 2015 and 2016 years to construct SemEval word2vec model. The tests have been done using this SemEval cumulative dataset. Results obtained from the classification tests are shown in Table 4.

Table 4: Accuracy / Results obtained from tests

Test No.	Word Vectors	Dim. Size	SVM %	RF %	NB %
01	Semeval	600	58.3	54.4	52.3
02	Semeval	300	57.3	45.7	51.8
03	Semeval	900	58.7	53.7	51.7
04	Google News trained word vectors	300	62.8	57.2	53.1

For SVM, the difference is minimal, but the value 900 worked best. For RF, the value 300 drastically reduced the overall performance while the value 600 worked best. NB accuracies are close to each other but it is observed that this method has the lowest overall accuracy values among three. With a word2vec model which is trained on the same dataset with the classifier, SVM method obtained the best results.

The fourth test has a different approach, which is not generating a word2vec model but obtaining the Google News pre-trained word vectors instead. This model has the standard value 300 for the feature vector dimension size and resulted in better accuracies for each one of the classification methods. It is observed that the model has positive impact on the overall system performance.

5.2 Tests with LSTM

Keras library is used to train and test LSTM Recurent Neural Net. Test 05 id done with LSTM classifier on SemEval cumulative dataset and 62.6% accuracy rate has been achieved.

5.3 Results over the SemEval 2017 Test Set

The test dataset is used to test the system's capability of predicting categories for unlabeled tweet data, and give them as an output. The original test dataset includes 12379 records, 95 of which are confirmed to be duplicates. These duplicate records are deleted from the dataset. Remaining 12284 records are evaluated in this test.

Preprocessing stage strips all punctuation from the dataset and converts all tweets into lower case. This means, twitter user names, e.g. @username, are stripped from their '@' symbol, but the user names themselves are preserved.

In SemEval 2017, the results are given with three scores: average F_1 (F_1 averaged across the positives and the negatives), average R (recall averaged across the three classes) and accuracy. The F_1 score measures test accuracy by considering precision and recall where a F_1 score reaches its worst value at 0 and best value at 1.

Using SemEval 2017 test data we have achieved the following scores : Average F_1 = 0.587, Average R = 0.605 and Accuracy = 0.603.

6 Conclusion and Future Work

The best result is obtained via support vector machine classifier, when Google News pre-trained word vectors are used, which is 62.8% accuracy in average when applied to previous years' training and test data.

On the Semeval 2017 Test Dataset by using same Word embedding + SVM pipeline (the first system), we have obtained 60.3% accuracy rate with the following scores scores : Average F_1 = 0.587, Average R = 0.605 and Accuracy = 0.603.

There may be many approches to create a better system. One possible way to further improve our system could be to transfer word embedding features to other classifiers (Recurrent Tensor Neural Networks, combining LSTM and Convolutional Neural Networks etc.). Another possible line of the future research is the combination of hand crafted features (bag of words, n-grams, lexicons) with word embedding features.

References

B. Pang, L. Lee, S. Vaithyanathan. 2002. *Thumbs up? Sentiment Classification using Machine Learning Techniques*, Proceedings of EMNLP 2002, pp. 79–86.

B. Pang and L. Lee. 2008. *Opinion mining and sentiment analysis*. Foundations and Trends in Information Retrieval.

Turney, P. & Littman, M. 2003. *Measuring praise and Criticism: Inference of semantic orientation from association.* ACM Transactions on Information Systems, 21(4), 315-346.

Y. Bengio, R. Ducharme, P. Vincent, C. Jauvin, *"A Neural Probabilistic Language Model,* Journal of Machine Learning Research 3 1137–1155, 2003

R. Socher, A. Perelygin, J. Wu, J. Chuang, C. Manning, A. Ng, C. Potts, *"Recursive Deep Models for Semantic Compositionality Over a Sentiment Treebank"*, Conference on Empirical Methods in Natural Language Processing, 2013

W. Blacoe, M. Lapata, *"A Comparison of Vector-based Representations for Semantic Composition"*, Proceedings of the 2012 Joint Conference on Empirical Methods in Natural Language Processing and Computational Natural Language Learning, 546–556, 2012

T. Mikolov, K. Chen, G. Corrado, J. Dean, *"Efficient Estimation of Word Representations in Vector Space"*, 2013

D. Fradkin, I. Muchnik, *"Support Vector Machines for Classification"*, DIMACS Series in Discrete Mathematics and Theoretical Computer Science, 2000

T. K. Ho, *"Random Decision Forests"*, ICDAR '95 Proceedings of the Third International Conference on Document Analysis and Recognition Vol.1, 1995

G. H. John, P. Langley, *"Estimating Continuous Distributions in Bayesian Classifiers"*, Proceedings of the Eleventh Conference on Uncertainty in Artificial Intelligence, 1995

S. Hochreiter and J. Schmidhuber, *"Long Short Term Memory"*, Neural Computation, vol. 9, no. 8, p. 1735–1780, 1997

F. Chollet, *"Keras: Deep Learning library for Tensor Flow and Theano"*, GitHub, https://github.com/fchollet/keras, 2015

L. Breiman, (2001). *"Random Forests"*. Machine Learning. 45 (1): 5-32. doi:10.1023/A:1010933404324.

TakeLab at SemEval-2017 Task 4: Recent Deaths and the Power of Nostalgia in Sentiment Analysis in Twitter

David Lozić, Doria Šarić, Ivan Tokić, Zoran Medić, Jan Šnajder
Text Analysis and Knowledge Engineering Lab
Faculty of Electrical Engineering and Computing, University of Zagreb
Unska 3, 10000 Zagreb, Croatia
`{name.surname}@fer.hr`

Abstract

This paper describes the system we submitted to SemEval-2017 Task 4 (Sentiment Analysis in Twitter), specifically subtasks A, B, and D. Our main focus was topic-based message polarity classification on a two-point scale (subtask B). The system we submitted uses a Support Vector Machine classifier with rich set of features, ranging from standard to more creative, task-specific features, including a series of rating-based features as well as features that account for sentimental reminiscence of past topics and deceased famous people. Our system ranked 14th out of 39 submissions in subtask A, 5th out of 24 submissions in subtask B, and 3rd out of 16 submissions in subtask D.

1 Introduction

Sentiment analysis (Pang et al., 2002), a task of determining polarity of text towards some topic, recently gained a lot of interest, mostly due to its applicability in various fields, such as public relations (Pang et al., 2008) and market analysis (He et al., 2013). Following the growing popularity of social networks and an increasing number of user comments that can be found there, sentiment analysis of texts on social networks, such as tweets from Twitter, has been the focus of much research.

However, determining the sentiment of a tweet is often not an easy task, since the length of the tweet is limited and language is mostly informal, including slang, abbreviations, and hashtags. Various systems have been proposed for tackling this problem, ranging from simple unsupervised models that use precompiled sentiment lexicons for evaluating polarity of tweets (O'Connor et al., 2010) to more complex supervised models that use textual feature representations in combination with machine learning algorithms such as Support Vector Machines (SVM) (Khan et al., 2015; Barbosa and Feng, 2010) or deep neural networks (Dos Santos and Gatti, 2014; Tang et al., 2014).

In this paper, we present our system for determining sentiment of tweets, which we submitted SemEval-2017 Task 4 (Rosenthal et al., 2017), more specifically to the English versions of subtasks A, B, and D. In subtask A, the goal was to predict the sentiment of a tweet as either positive, neutral, or negative. Subtask B consisted of predicting the sentiment of a given tweet on a 2-point scale (positive or negative) given a topic. In subtask D, the task was to determine the distribution of positive and negative tweets for each topic in a given set of tweets annotated with topics.

The system we submitted uses an SVM classifier with a linear kernel and a number of features. We experiment with basic features such as tf-idf and pretrained word embeddings, as well as more task-specific features including sentiment lexicons, ratings-based, "nostalgia features", and "recent deaths". Ratings-based features use external data from different online resources to leverage the information such as rating of a movie or an actor mentioned in a tweet. "Recent deaths" features make use of information about recent deaths of notable people, while "nostalgia feature" makes use of topic's "age" – the rationale being that people usually reminisce about past events in a sentimental and positive way. Our system ranked 3rd out of 16 teams in subtask D, 5th out of 24 teams in subtask B, and 14th out of 39 teams in subtask A.

2 Features

To build our model, we first preprocess tweets and extract various features. We use standard features such as bag-of-words (more precisely tf-idf), pre-

Proceedings of the 11th International Workshop on Semantic Evaluations (SemEval-2017), pages 784–789,
Vancouver, Canada, August 3 - 4, 2017. ©2017 Association for Computational Linguistics

trained word embeddings, and count-based stylistic features. Additionally, we design task-specific features based on publicly available ratings for certain topics. We next describe the preprocessing and the features in more detail.

2.1 Preprocessing of Tweets

As a first preprocessing step, we tokenize tweets using a basic Twitter-adapted tokenizer.[1] After tokenization, we lemmatize and stem tweets and remove stopwords from each tweet using the NLTK toolkit (Bird et al., 2009).

Additionally, since some of our features require recognizing named entities in a tweet, we use the named entity tagger, also from the NLTK toolkit, for recognizing entities in tweet. Unfortunately, using NLTK-provided named entity tagger yielded unsatisfactory results, i.e., many of named entities in tweets were not recognized correctly. We assume this is due to tweets generally having poor capitalization, which is something named entity taggers in general are rather sensitive to.

As a remedy, we replaced the tagger with a greedy search algorithm. This approach simply looks for an occurrence of any string in tweet in some of our named-entity databases (introduced in the following sections). This proved to be a working solution for named entities longer than one word, but led to problems with unigrams, which were falsely recognized as named entities due to the existence of a movie or a game with that exact name. For instance, the word *"her"* would falsely be recognized as the 2013 movie *"Her"*.

Finally, we settled for a combination of the two approaches. We introduced parameters for the length range of word sequences. For the named entity tagger, we set the length range to $[0, 1]$, while for the greedy search algorithm we used the range $[2, 7]$. This way, we try to reduce the number of falsely recognized named entities in the greedy search algorithm (by omitting single word entities from its scope), while ensuring that some single word entities still get recognized by the named entity chunker.

2.2 Standard Features

We use a number of standard features typically used in sentiment analysis and other text classification tasks.

Word embeddings. For word embeddings we use GloVe (Pennington et al., 2014). We use 200-dimensional word embeddings, pretrained on 2B tweets. Final vector representation of a tweet is calculated as an average of the sum of vectors of all the words in a tweet.

Tf–idf. The standard tf–idf vectorizer from Python's scikit–learn package.[2]

Counting features. For each tweet we count the number of occurrences of various stylistic features: exclamation marks, question marks, elongated words, capitalized words, emoticons, and hashtags.

User information. We collected the information about authors of the tweets using the script provided by the organizers. From this data we extracted the number of followers, friends, and tweets of each user.

Sentiment polarity lexicons. We use sentiment lexicons developed by Bravo-Marquez et al. (2016), which contain three weights per word, indicating word's positive, neutral, and negative sentiment. These lexicons are built from automatically annotated tweets and existing hand-made opinion lexicons. We use the most positive word sentiment and the most negative word sentiment in each tweet as features, together with the number of extremely positive and extremely negative words in a tweet. A word is considered extremely positive if its positive weight in lexicon is higher than 0.75, and extremely negative if its negative weight is higher than 0.8.

2.3 Nostalgia Feature

We presume that some topics, such as games, movies, and music from years ago, are usually mentioned in positive light due to nostalgia.[3] To leverage this, for many of our topic-based features we try to take the age of the certain topic into account.

We use the following metric for calculating nostalgia feature, where applicable:

$$nost(y) = \min(m, y_{curr} - y) \qquad (1)$$

where y is the year of the content's release, y_{curr} current year, and m empirically determined upper bound for age.

---

[1] http://sentiment.christopherpotts.net/codedata/happyfuntokenizing.py

[2] http://scikit-learn.org/

[3] Nostalgia is a sentimentality for the past, typically for a period or place with happy personal associations. (*Wikipedia*)

2.4 Ratings Features

We introduce a series of features that are calculated if a certain "rateable" topic is mentioned in a tweet. In order to build those features, we collected information from publicly available ratings for various domains: movies and TV shows, actors, games, musicians, historically influential people, and companies. It is worth noting that we are collecting these publicly available ratings independently of training the classifier, which makes our system applicable to tweets about new movies, TV shows, actors, etc.

Movies and TV shows. To gather movies' and TV shows' data, we used IMDb's publicly available plaintext database.[4] As the plaintext database is quite comprehensive, we filtered the data, leaving only movies and TV shows released in 2005 or later, with more than 50,000 user votes, and a minimum average rating of 4.0. This reduction left us with an acceptable amount of ~4,300 entries.

Movie-ratings features are implemented as a vector of 14 values: a binary value indicating if a movie was found in a tweet, movie's rating, number of user votes, movie's nostalgia value (as defined above), and 10 values representing user votes distribution per rating (from 0 to 9).

Actors. In the same manner as for the movies, we obtained the IMDb's plaintext database of actors using the same resource. We filtered out all actors that do not appear in the previously filtered movies database, to reduce the number of entries in an otherwise huge database. This left us with approximately 135,000 actor entries.

If an actor is mentioned in a tweet, his or her mention is represented with a single value in the feature vector – actor's rating. This rating is calculated by taking into account actor's appearances in various movies, as well as actor's position in movie's credits; the latter captures the intuition that each actor in a movie does not equally contribute to the movie's overall rating.

We calculated each actor's (a) rating for a single movie (m) as follows:

$$r(a, m) = r(m) \cdot \left(1 + c^{\frac{1 - pos(a,m)}{k}} - 1\right) \quad (2)$$

where c is the percentage of the movie's rating taken into account, k is the rate of how much the

position affects the rating, $r(m)$ is the movie's rating, and $pos(a, m)$ is the actor's position in the movie's credits. Actor's final rating is then defined as mean of their ratings in all the movies they participated in. During the evaluation, we set the hyperparameters c and k to 0.1 and 50, respectively.

Games. We obtained the data about video games by scraping *GameRankings*[5] website for all games with at least 10 reviews. This way we gathered about 8,500 game entries.

A mention of a game in a tweet is represented with three values in the feature vector: a binary value representing game's mention in a tweet, game's rating, and game's nostalgia metric, as defined in Section 2.3.

Musicians. For musicians' data, we scraped *Metacritic*'s *Music People* pages.[6] This gave us names, numbers of albums, and ratings for about 10,500 artists and bands.

Three values were added to the feature vector for musicians: a binary value representing musician's mention in a tweet, number of musician's albums, and musician's rating.

Important people. We use *MIT*'s *Pantheon*[7] list of historically influential people, with around 10,000 entries, to obtain a number of useful features. Based on this list, we compute 28 features, as follows:

- binary value indicating a person has been found in the obtained list;

- person's historic ranking on *Pantheon*;

- person's nostalgia value, derived from their birth year;

- person's Wikipedia page views;

- person's Wikipedia page views standard deviation;

- person's historic popularity;

- person's place of birth as a vector of 10 binary values representing the highest-ranked birth sites by *Pantheon*: U.S., U.K., France, Italy, Germany, Russia, Spain, Turkey, Poland, the Netherlands;

---

[4] ftp://ftp.fu-berlin.de/pub/misc/movies/database/

[5] http://www.gamerankings.com/
[6] http://www.metacritic.com/browse/albums/people
[7] http://pantheon.media.mit.edu/rankings/people/all/all/-4000/2010/H15

- person's occupation as a vector of 10 binary values representing the most historically influential occupations by *Pantheon*: Politician, Actor, Writer, Soccer Player, Religious Figure, Singer, Musician, Philosopher, Physicist, Composer.

Companies. Using *Good Company Ratings'* 2014 report,[8] we gathered the data about various companies, consisting of about 300 entries.

Company features contain four values: a binary value indicating company's mention in a tweet, its *Fortune* rank, seller ratings, and steward ratings.

2.5 Recent Deaths

Due to the impact celebrity deaths have on social media and the fact that people usually reminisce in a positive way about deceased people, we posit that the information whether a person mentioned in a tweet died recently would prove useful for sentiment analysis. To this end, we gathered from *Wikipedia*[9] a list of significant people who died in the last three years.

We represent deaths using a single value indicating the number of years that have passed from the person's death. While at first similar to nostalgia metric introduced above, the death metric accounts for recent events and, therefore, emphasizes values that are the opposite of the values obtained with nostalgia metric. The death metric is given by $1 - nost(y)$, where y is the year of death, with m set to 3 (last three years only).

2.6 Controversy

We encode controversial topics as 41 binary values, one for each of the currently controversial events listed in the *University of Michigan-Flint*'s *Frances Willson Thompson Library*.[10] To further improve the performance of correct identification of controversial topics, we additionally provide alternative phrases for some of the issues, for example *"Affordable Care Act"* is also triggered by its popular nickname *"Obamacare"*.

2.7 Curse Words

We use a list of 165 curse words often used in tweets, compiled by Kukovačec et al. (2017).

Presence of a curse word in a tweet is encoded with a single binary value, indicating whether a curse word was found in tweet or not.

2.8 Topics and Hashtags

We built the above-mentioned features for three cases: topic identified from tweet's text, topic explicitly given as tweet's topic in subtasks B and D, and for the topic that might appear in a hashtag as a part of tweet.

Since hashtags usually contain more than one word in a single string, we adapt the greedy splitting procedure proposed by Tutek et al. (2016), which uses a dictionary of known words to split a hashtag that is a concatenation of multiple words. Additionally, for each word obtained from hashtag splitting we generate sentiment lexicon features, acknowledging that sentiment is often expressed via a hashtag.

3 Evaluation

We started with a number of different classifiers and chose the one that gave the best result on a hold-out test set (2016 test set) (Nakov et al., 2016) for each subtask. After the official results were published, together with the gold labels for test sets, we additionally performed a simple feature analysis over predefined feature groups to analyze the impact each of these groups has on the final result.

3.1 Evaluation Metrics

We submitted our solution to three subtasks: A, B, and D. Subtask A uses macro-averaged recall (ρ) over all three classes (positive, neutral, and negative) as an official metric. For subtask B, macro-averaged recall over positive and negative classes (ρ^{PN}) is used, while subtask D uses Kullback-Leibler Divergence (KLD) as the official measure.

3.2 Classifier Selection

We experimented with a number of classification algorithms from the scikit-learn package (Pedregosa et al., 2011): Support Vector Machine with a linear kernel (SVM), Logistic Regression (LR), Multinomial Naive Bayes (MB), Random Forest (RF), and a Stohastic Gradient Descent classifier (SGD). For training, we used all the available data provided by the organizers, except for the 2016 test set, which we used for testing the classifiers. We performed 5-fold cross-validation

---

[8] http://www.goodcompanyindex.com/ratings/
[9] http://en.wikipedia.org/wiki/Lists_of_deaths_by_year
[10] http://libguides.umflint.edu/topics/current

Classifier	Subtask A (ρ)	Subtask B (ρ^{PN})
LR	0.620	0.742
NB	0.467	0.663
RF	0.487	0.549
SGD	0.488	0.614
SVM	**0.623**	**0.752**

Table 1: Results for subtasks A and B on 2016 test set using the official measures for both subtasks

Team	ρ^{PN}	Team	KLD
BB twtr	0.882	BB twtr	0.036
DataStories	0.856	DataStories	0.048
Tweester	0.854	**TakeLab**	**0.050**
TopicThunder	0.846	CrystalNest	0.056
TakeLab	**0.845**	Tweester	0.057
funSentiment	0.834	funSentiment	0.060
YNU-HPCC	0.834	NileTMRG	0.077

Table 2: Official results for subtasks B and D (top 7 teams only)

Excluded group	A (ρ)	B (ρ^{PN})	D (KLD)
None	0.615	0.849	0.054
Counting	0.616	**0.852**	**0.050**
Lexicon	**0.617**	0.850	0.052
Ratings	**0.617**	0.846	0.053
Tf-idf	0.610	0.840	0.061
User info	0.615	0.849	0.053
Word2vec	0.602	0.798	0.116

Table 3: Feature analysis results for all subtasks

on our training set for optimizing each classifier's parameters. We used all of the described features for evaluating classifiers for subtask B and a subset of features for subtask A (everything except rating features extracted from explicit topic, features extracted from hashtags, user information features, curse words presence, and controversial topics).[11]

We observed that macro-averaged recall in subtask B (the official measure) improved (from 0.705 to 0.752) when we completely excluded the ratings and user information features, although the accuracy notably dropped (from 0.899 to 0.855). For this reason, we decided to submit our solution to both subtasks B and D without those two feature groups, since it led to higher recall at the expense of lower overall accuracy.

Table 1 shows the results in terms of macro-averaged recall on the 2016 test set for subtasks A and B for all of the models we experimented with and the final set of features that we included in the final submissions. We chose SVM with a linear kernel for all of our submissions, as it gave the best result on both subtask A and B. For subtask D, we used the outputs of the classifier built for subtask B and calculated the distribution of tweets using a simple "classify and count" approach.

Our submissions ranked 14th on the leaderboard for subtask A, 5th for subtask B, and 3rd for subtask D. Table 2 shows scores of top 7 submissions for subtasks B and D.

3.3 Feature Analysis

After the testing phase finished, we carried out an analysis of the impact of the specific feature groups in classification, for each of the three subtasks we took part in. We performed an ablation study over all feature groups. The results of these analyses are shown in Table 3.

The analysis confirmed that excluding some feature groups indeed helps in obtaining higher recall in both subtask A and B. More specifically, excluding counting or lexicon features improved recall in subtask B, while excluding counting, lexicon, or ratings features from the set of features used for subtask A led to an increase in recall as well. Moreover, KLD score improves as well, when the group of counting features is excluded from complete set of features.

4 Conclusion

In this paper we described our solutions to SemEval 2017 Task 4 – subtasks A, B, and D. Our solution is based on a linear SVM classifier with some standard and a series of task-specific features, including rating-based features obtained from various websites as well as features that account for sentimental reminiscence of past topics and deceased famous people. Our system performed relatively well in all three subtasks. We ranked 14th out of 39 in subtask A, 5th out of 24th in subtask B, and 3rd out of 14 in subtask D.

For future work, it would be interesting to expand our model's feature set to non-covered domains (e.g., sports), and also to investigate how our model behaves on a more diverse set of topics. Expanding the system with a topic classifier as a pre-sentiment processing step might also be worth investigating, since the way sentiment is expressed varies across different domains.

---

[11]Unfortunately, we did not finish our system in time for the submission of subtask A, which resulted in differences between submissions for subtask A and the other two subtasks.

References

Luciano Barbosa and Junlan Feng. 2010. Robust sentiment detection on Twitter from biased and noisy data. In *Proceedings of the 23rd International Conference on Computational Linguistics: Posters*. Association for Computational Linguistics, pages 36–44.

Steven Bird, Ewan Klein, and Edward Loper. 2009. *Natural language processing with Python: analyzing text with the natural language toolkit*. O'Reilly Media, Inc.

Felipe Bravo-Marquez, Eibe Frank, and Bernhard Pfahringer. 2016. Building a Twitter opinion lexicon from automatically-annotated tweets. *Know.-Based Syst.* 108(C):65–78.

Cícero Nogueira Dos Santos and Maira Gatti. 2014. Deep convolutional neural networks for sentiment analysis of short texts. In *COLING*. pages 69–78.

Wu He, Shenghua Zha, and Ling Li. 2013. Social media competitive analysis and text mining: A case study in the pizza industry. *International Journal of Information Management* 33(3):464–472.

Aamera ZH Khan, Mohammad Atique, and VM Thakare. 2015. Combining lexicon-based and learning-based methods for Twitter sentiment analysis. *International Journal of Electronics, Communication and Soft Computing Science & Engineering (IJECSCSE)* page 89.

Marin Kukovačec, Juraj Malenica, Ivan Mršić, Antonio Šajatović, Domagoj Alagić, and Jan Šnajder. 2017. Takelab at semeval-2017 task 6: #rankinghumorin4pages. In *Proceedings of the 11th International Workshop on Semantic Evaluation (SemEval-2017)*. Association for Computational Linguistics, Vancouver, Canada, pages 395–399. http://www.aclweb.org/anthology/S17-2066.

Preslav Nakov, Alan Ritter, Sara Rosenthal, Fabrizio Sebastiani, and Veselin Stoyanov. 2016. SemEval-2016 Task 4: Sentiment analysis in Twitter. *Proceedings of SemEval* pages 1–18.

Brendan O'Connor, Ramnath Balasubramanyan, Bryan R Routledge, and Noah A Smith. 2010. From tweets to polls: Linking text sentiment to public opinion time series. *ICWSM* 11(122-129):1–2.

Bo Pang, Lillian Lee, and Shivakumar Vaithyanathan. 2002. Thumbs up?: Sentiment classification using machine learning techniques. In *Proceedings of the ACL-02 conference on Empirical methods in natural language processing-Volume 10*. Association for Computational Linguistics, pages 79–86.

Bo Pang, Lillian Lee, et al. 2008. Opinion mining and sentiment analysis. *Foundations and Trends® in Information Retrieval* 2(1–2):1–135.

Fabian Pedregosa, Gaël Varoquaux, Alexandre Gramfort, Vincent Michel, Bertrand Thirion, Olivier Grisel, Mathieu Blondel, Peter Prettenhofer, Ron Weiss, Vincent Dubourg, et al. 2011. Scikit-learn: Machine learning in Python. *Journal of Machine Learning Research* 12:2825–2830.

Jeffrey Pennington, Richard Socher, and Christopher D. Manning. 2014. Glove: Global vectors for word representation. In *Empirical Methods in Natural Language Processing (EMNLP)*. pages 1532–1543. http://www.aclweb.org/anthology/D14-1162.

Sara Rosenthal, Noura Farra, and Preslav Nakov. 2017. Semeval-2017 task 4: Sentiment analysis in twitter. In *Proceedings of the 11th International Workshop on Semantic Evaluation (SemEval-2017)*. Association for Computational Linguistics, Vancouver, Canada, pages 501–516. http://www.aclweb.org/anthology/S17-2088.

Duyu Tang, Furu Wei, Bing Qin, Ting Liu, and Ming Zhou. 2014. Coooolll: A deep learning system for Twitter sentiment classification. In *Proceedings of the 8th International Workshop on Semantic Evaluation (SemEval 2014)*. pages 208–212.

Martin Tutek, Ivan Sekulić, Paula Gombar, Ivan Paljak, Filip Čulinović, Filip Boltužić, Mladen Karan, Domagoj Alagić, and Jan Šnajder. 2016. TakeLab at SemEval-2016 Task 6: Stance classification in Tweets using a genetic algorithm based ensemble. *Proceedings of SemEval* pages 464–468.

NileTMRG at SemEval-2017 Task 4: Arabic Sentiment Analysis

Samhaa R. El-Beltagy[1], Mona El Kalamawy[2], Abu Bakr Soliman[1]
[1]Center for Informatics Sciences
Nile University, Juhayna Square, Sheikh Zayed City, Giza, Egypt
[2]Faculty of Computers and Information,
Cairo University, Ahmed Zewail St, Giza, Egypt
samhaa@computer.org, mona.elkalamawy@fci-cu.edu.eg, ab.soliman@nu.edu.eg

Abstract

This paper describes two systems that were used by the NileTMRG for addressing Arabic Sentiment Analysis as part of SemEval-2017, task 4. NileTMRG participated in three Arabic related subtasks which are: Subtask A (Message Polarity Classification), Subtask B (Topic-Based Message Polarity classification) and Subtask D (Tweet quantification). For subtask A, we made use of our previously developed sentiment analyzer which we augmented with a scored lexicon. For subtasks B and D, we used an ensemble of three different classifiers. The first classifier was a convolutional neural network for which we trained (word2vec) word embeddings. The second classifier consisted of a MultiLayer Perceptron while the third classifier was a Logistic regression model that takes the same input as the second classifier. Voting between the three classifiers was used to determine the final outcome. The output from task B, was quantified to produce the results for task D. In all three Arabic related tasks in which NileTMRG participated, the team ranked at number one.

1 Introduction

Because of the potential impact of understanding how people react to certain products, events, people, etc., sentiment analysis is an area that has attracted much attention over the past number of years. The consistent increase in Arabic social media content since 2011 (Neal 2013)(Anon 2012)(Farid 2013) resulted in increased interest in Arabic sentiment analysis. Lack of Arabic resources (datasets and lexicons), initially hindered research efforts in the area, but the area gradually gained attention, with research effort either focusing on building missing resources (El-Beltagy 2016; Refaee & Rieser 2014; El-Beltagy 2017), or on experimenting with different classifiers and features while creating needed resources as is briefly described in the related work section.

In this paper we present our approach to addressing the following three SemEval related sentiment analysis subtasks (Arabic):

A) Message Polarity Classification: given a tweet/some text the task is to determine whether the tweet reflects positive, negative, or neutral sentiment.

B) Topic-Based Message Polarity Classification: given some text and a topic, determine whether the sentiment embodied by the text is positive or negative towards the given topic.

D) Tweet quantification: given a set of tweets about a given topic, estimate their distribution across the positive and negative classes.

Two systems have been used to address these tasks. The first system is a slightly altered version of that presented in (El-Beltagy et al. 2016). The second is composed on an ensemble of three different classifiers: a convolutional neural network(Kim 2014), a Multi-Layer Perceptron, and a Logistic regression classifier.

Proceedings of the 11th International Workshop on Semantic Evaluations (SemEval-2017), pages 790–795,
Vancouver, Canada, August 3 - 4, 2017. ©2017 Association for Computational Linguistics

The rest of this paper is organized as follows: section 2 presents a brief overview of related work, section 3 describes the datasets used for training, section 4 overviews the developed systems, while section 5 presents the evaluation results, and section 6 concludes the paper.

2 Related Work

2.1 Task A

Research in Arabic Sentiment analysis has been gaining momentum over the past couple of years. The work of (El-Beltagy & Ali 2013) outlined challenges faced for carrying out Arabic sentiment analysis and presented a simple lexicon based approach for the task. (Abdulla et al. 2013) compared machine learning and lexicon based techniques for Arabic sentiment analysis on tweets written in the Jordanian dialect.

The best obtained results were reported to be those of SVM and Naive Bayes. The work presented in (Shoukry & Rafea 2012) targeted tweets written in the Egyptian dialect and was focused on examining the effect of different pre-processing steps on the task of sentiment analysis. The authors used a SVM classifier in all their experiments. (Salamah & Elkhlifi 2014) developed a system for extracting sentiment from the Kuwaiti-Dialect. They experimented with a manually annotated dataset comprised of 340,000 tweets, using SVM, J48, ADTREE, and Random Tree classifiers. The best result was obtained using SVM. (Duwairi et al. 2014) presented a sentiment analysis tool for Jordanian Arabic tweets. The authors experimented with Naïve Bayes (NB), SVM and KNN classifiers. The NB classifier performed best in their experiments. (Shoukry & Rafea 2015) presented an approach that combines sentiment scores obtained using a lexicon with a machine learning approach applied it on Egyptian tweets. The experiments conducted by the authors, show that adding the semantic orientation feature does in fact improve the result of the sentiment analysis task. (Khalil et al. 2015) experimented with various datasets, classifiers and features representations to determine which configurations work best for Arabic sentiment analysis. They concluded that Multi-nominal Naïve Bayes and Complement Naïve Bayes tend to work best, especially when term features are represented using their idf weights.

2.2 Tasks B and D

To the knowledge of the authors, no previous work on "Topic-Based Message Polarity Classification" has been attempted on Arabic. The same task has been introduced last year at SemEval-2016, so a number of systems have been developed to address this task in English. For this task, most participants preferred to use a deep learning approach. The Finki team for example (Stojanovski et al. 2016) developed a system composed of a merged convolutional neural network with a gated recurrent neural network. In their system, pre-trained Glove word embeddings were used to represent tweet tokens. The "thecerealkiller" team (Yadav 2016) on the other hand, used only a recurrent neural network. In their system, tweets were minimally pre-processed before being fed to the network. The "LyS" team (Vilares et al. 2016) used a convolutional neural network with support vector machines. They trained the SVM using hidden CNN activations with additional linguistic information. The "Tweester" team (Palogiannidi et al. 2016) used multiple independent classifiers: neural networks, semantic-affective models and topic modeling. Each classifier predicts the result and late fusion is done to generate the final result.

3 Used Data

3.1 Task A

The organizers provided a total of 3355 sentiment labeled tweets for training and an additional 671 labeled tweets for validation/development. Close examination of the provided labeled tweets revealed that some tweets in the training set were duplicated, sometimes even with conflicting labels. To use those for training, the data was cleaned as follows:

1) All tweets that had conflicting sentiment labels were removed.
2) A single copy of tweets which were duplicated, but had a consistent label, was kept.
3) Any tweet in the training dataset which was found in the development dataset, was deleted.

This brought down the number of training tweets to 2499. Initial experimentation using only this data for training resulted in rather low performance. Additional data in the form of the NBI dataset described in (El-Beltagy et al. 2016) was augmented to this training data after balancing it with some data from the Nile University (NU) dataset also described in (El-Beltagy et al. 2016). In addition, lexicon terms that had a score higher than a 0.8 threshold as determined by the work described in (El-Beltagy 2017) were added as entries to the training dataset with their polarity as a label. The final training dataset consisted of 13,292 tweets/entries.

3.2   Tasks B and D

The organizers provided 1322 tweets with topics and their sentiment labels for training and a further 332 tweets for validation/development. The only additional data that we have used, consisted of 4 million Arabic tweets which were used to train a word2vec model (Mikolov, Sutskever, et al. 2013; Mikolov, Corrado, et al. 2013) for use with a convolutional neural network (Kim 2014).

4   System Descriptions

4.1   The System used for Task A

As mentioned earlier, the system used for task A, is a modified version of the NU sentiment analyzer described in (El-Beltagy et al. 2016). The analyzer was built using a Complement Naïve Bayes classifier (Rennie et al. 2003) with a smoothing parameter of 1 and trained using the 13,292 Arabic tweets described in section 3.1. Complement Naïve Bayes was selected as a classifier based on the work presented in (Khalil et al. 2015). Input to the model consists of feature vector representations of input tweets. Each vector represents   unigrams and bigram terms with their idf weights and has an additional set of lexical features for the input tweet that can be summarized as follows:

- *startsWithLink*: a feature which is set to 1 if the input text starts with a link and to a 0 otherwise.
- *endsWithLink*: a feature which is set to 1 if the input text ends with a link and to 0 otherwise.
- *numOfPos*: a count of terms within the input text that have matched with positive entries in our sentiment lexicon.
- *numOfNeg*: a count of terms within the input text that have matched with negative entries in the sentiment lexicon.
- *length*: a feature that can take on one of three values {0,1,2} depending on the length of the input text. The numbers correspond to very short, short and normal.
- segments: a count for the number of distinct segments within the input text.

- *endsWithPostive*: a flag that indicates whether the last encountered sentiment word was a positive one or not.
- *endsWithNegative*: a flag that indicates whether the last encountered sentiment word was a negative one or not.
- *startsWithHashTag*: a flag that indicates whether the tweet starts with a hashtag.
- *numOfNegEmo*: the number of negative emoticons that have appeared in the tweet.
- *numOfPosEmo*: the number of positive emoticons that have appeared in the tweet.
- *endsWithQuestionMark*: a flag that indicates whether the tweets ends with a question mark or not.

In addition to these features that were originally described in (El-Beltagy et al. 2016), we have made use of our newly created weighted sentiment lexicon (El-Beltagy 2017) to add two additional features:

- *negScore*: a real number that represents that score of all negative terms in the input text.
- *posScore*: a real number that represents that score of all negative terms in the input text

It is worth noting that these two features replaced the *negPercentage* and *posPercentage* features described in (El-Beltagy et al. 2016). As stated in (El-Beltagy 2017), an amplification factor for these scores does enhance the classifier's performance. When experimenting using the supplied validation dataset, using these additional two features versus not using them, did make a difference. Additionally, the validation dataset was used to:

- Determine whether the removal of any of the listed features would impact system performance positively. In the end, all features were kept.
- Experiment with various training dataset combinations.
- Determine the amplification factor to use.

In task A, we only used the validation dataset for fine tuning. The model that performed best on the validation dataset, was the model used to generate sentiment labels for the test data. Additional pre-processing steps included character normalization, mention normalization, elongation removal, emoticon replacement, and light stemming. Further details on each of these steps can be found in (El-Beltagy et al. 2016).

4.2 The System used for Tasks B and D

The approach followed for addressing task B, was one in which three independent classifiers were built using the provided training data. Voting among the three classifiers, determined the final label for any given tweet. Task D is in fact highly dependent on task B, so we cannot say that we built a separate system for that task. Instead, the output of task B is simply counted and quantified to produce the output of task D. While validation data was used to fine tune this system, it was also augmented to the training data to build the final model which was used to generate labels for the test data. In the following subsections we described each of the used classifiers.

4.2.1 The convolutional Neural Network

The CNN model (Kim 2014) that we employed, is composed of 2 convolutional layers with filters of window sizes 3 and 4. A max pooling layer was added to extract the most important features, then a fully connected layer of size 25 nodes was connected to the pooling layer. A softmax layer generates the predicted class label. We have implemented this model using Keras (Chollet 2015).

Tweet Preprocessing

The following preprocessing steps were carried out on tweets that were used with this classifier:

- Hyperlinks and diacritics were removed

- Elongation was eliminated (ex. Yessss -> Yes)

- Text was normalized: $(آ ,إ ,أ) \rightarrow (ا)$, $(ي) \rightarrow (ى)$, $(ة) \rightarrow (ه)$

- Positive emoticons were replaced by the word "حب" (love), and negative emoticons by "غضب" (anger).

- The word "حب" (love) was added beside words that indicate positivity like: (شجاع, عظيم, ممتاز) (brave, excellent, great) and the word "غضب" (anger) next to words that indicate negativity like (حطم, يسئ, هابط) (broke/destroyed, harms, lowly)

- If the target topic was found in the tweet's text, it was replaced with a static keyword

Input to the CNN

Each word in a tweet is represented by its embeddings vector, the dimensionality of which is 100. The whole tweet is thus represented by the aggregate of vectors for each of its words which is essentially a matrix. As a CNN requires a fixed size input, we chose to set the matrix size to the max tweet length (which was 35 words in our case). For tweets smaller than the max, word embeddings were centered in the middle and padded with zeros around. Note that the number of rows is constant (embedding vector length). If a word wasn't found in the word2vec model, we set its embeddings vector to random numbers.

4.2.2 The Multi-Layer Perceptron & Logistic Regression Classifiers

We have grouped these two classifiers together as they essentially take in the same input features. Tweets are preprocessed for these classifiers in exactly the same way they are preprocessed for the CNN except that we don't replace the target topic with a static keyword.

Input to the Classifiers

The input to both the multi-layer perceptron and logistic regression classifiers is a set of feature vectors representing input tweets. A feature vector is composed to a bag of words representation of the tweet in addition to the following features:

1) **The overall sentiment** of the tweet (regardless of the target). The NU Sentiment analyzer (El-Beltagy et al. 2016) was used to set this feature. Since two teams were working in parallel on tasks A and B respectively, the team working on task B simply used the older version of the system with old training data. We believe that using the modified version that was described for task A, might yield better results.

2) **The number** of positive/negative words found in the tweet.

3) A flag indicating the presence of positive emoticons

4) A flag indicating the presence of negative emoticons

5) The position of the target in the tweet

6) A flag to indicate if there are positive **terms** around the target topic

7) A flag to indicate if there are negative **terms** around the target topic

8) A flag to indicate if there positive/negative **words** around the target?

9) The number of positive terms in the first half of the tweet

10) The number of negative terms in the first half of the tweet

11) The number of positive term in the second half of the tweet

12) The number of negative terms in the second half of the tweet

Features 1, 2, 6, and 7 were amplified to emphasize their importance.

5 Results

5.1 Task A

The supplied test data for task A consisted of 6100 unlabeled tweets. These tweets were classified using the system described in section 3.4. Based on the results supplied by the organizers of the task (Rosenthal et al. 2017), our system ranked at number 1 as shown in table 1.

#	System	P	F_1^{PN}	Acc
1	**NileTMRG**	0.583_1	0.610_1	0.581_1
2	SiTAKA	0.550_2	0.571_2	0.563_2
3	ELiRF-UPV	0.478_3	0.467_4	0.508_3
4	INGEOTEC	0.477_4	0.455_5	0.499_4
5	OMAM	0.438_5	0.422_6	0.430_8
6	LSIS	0.438_5	0.469_3	0.445_6
7	Iw-StAR	0.431_7	0.416_7	0.454_5
8	HLP@UPENN	0.415_8	0.320_8	0.443_7

Table 1: Results for Subtask A "Message Polarity Classification", Arabic. The systems are ordered by average recall ρ

5.2 Task B

The supplied test data for task B consisted of 2757 tweets with each having a given topic. Voting amongst the 3 classifiers described in section 4.2, determined the final label for the topic (positive or negative). The results for our system, which ranks us at number 1, are shown in table 2.

#	System	P	F_1^{PN}	Acc
1	**NileTMRG**	0.768_1	0.767_1	0.770_1
2	ELiRF-UPV	0.721_2	0.724_2	0.734_2
3	ASA	0.693_3	0.670_4	0.672_4
4	OMAM	0.687_4	0.678_3	0.679_3

Table 2: Results for Subtask B "Tweet classification according to a two-point scale", Arabic. The systems are ordered by average recall ρ

To better understand the performance of the voting system, the performance of the individual classifiers which participated in the voting process, is presented in table 3.

#	System	ρ	F_1^{PN}	Acc
1	MLP	0.728	0.720	0.720
2	**LR**	0.762	0.759	0.761
3	CNN	0.747	0.737	0.738

Table 3: Individual results of each of the used classifiers

5.3 Task D

Test data for task D was identical to that for task B. In order to obtain results for task B, a script was created that takes in the input from task B and converts it to the required output for task D. The results for our system, which ranks us at number 1, are shown in table 4.

#	System	KLD	AE	RAE
1	**NileTMRG**	0.127_1	0.170_1	2.462_1
2	OMAM	0.202_2	0.238_2	4.835_2
3	ELiRF-UPV	1.183_3	0.537_3	11.434_3

Table 4: Results for Subtask D "Tweet quantification according to a two-point scale", Arabic. The systems are ordered by their KLD score (lower is better)

6 Conclusion

In this paper, we have briefly described our submissions to SemEval task-4, subtasks A, B, and D (Arabic). For task A, we have augmented our previously developed sentiment analyzer with a scored lexicon and trained it using a little more that thirteen thousand tweets. For tasks B and D, we have used three independent classifiers and employed a voting strategy to determine the final label for a given topic. The evaluation results for all three tasks have ranked our systems at number one.

References

Abdulla, N.A. et al., 2013. Arabic sentiment analysis: Lexicon-based and corpus-based. In *Applied Electrical Engineering and Computing Technologies (AEECT), 2013 IEEE Jordan Conference on*. Amman: IEEE, pp. 1–6.

Anon, 2012. Facebook Statistics by Country. Available at: http://www.socialbakers.com/facebook-statistics/.

Chollet, F., 2015. Keras: Deep Learning library for Theano and TensorFlow. *GitHub Repository*.

Duwairi, R. et al., 2014. Sentiment Analysis in Arabic tweets. In *Information and Communication Systems (ICICS), 2014 5th International Conference*. Irbid: IEEE, pp. 1–6.

El-Beltagy, S.R. et al., 2016. Combining Lexical Features and a Supervised Learning Approach for Arabic Sentiment Analysis. In *CICLing 2016*. Konya, Turkey.

El-Beltagy, S.R., 2016. NileULex: A Phrase and Word Level Sentiment Lexicon for Egyptian and Modern Standard Arabic. In *proceedings of LREC 2016*. Portorož , Slovenia.

El-Beltagy, S.R., 2017. WeightedNileULex: A Scored Arabic Sentiment Lexicon for Improved Sentiment Analysis. In N. El-Gayar & C. Suen, eds. *Language Processing, Pattern Recognition and Intelligent Systems. Special Issue on Computational Linguistics, Speech& Image Processing for Arabic Language*. World Scientific Publishing Co.

El-Beltagy, S.R. & Ali, A., 2013. Open Issues in the Sentiment Analysis of Arabic Social Media : A Case Study. In *Proceedings of 9th the International Conference on Innovations and Information Technology (IIT2013)*. Al Ain, UAE.

Farid, D., 2013. Egypt has the largest number of Facebook users in the Arab world. *Daily News Egypt*. Available at: http://www.dailynewsegypt.com/2013/09/25/eg ypt-has-the-largest-number-of-facebook-users-in-the-arab-world-report/.

Khalil, T. et al., 2015. Which configuration works best? An experimental study on Supervised Arabic Twitter Sentiment Analysis. In *Proceedings of the First Conference on Arabic Computational Liguistics (ACLing 2015), co-located with CICLing 2015*. Cairo, Egypt, pp. 86–93.

Kim, Y., 2014. Convolutional Neural Networks for Sentence Classification. *Proceedings of the 2014 Conference on Empirical Methods in Natural Language Processing (EMNLP 2014)*, pp.1746–1751.

Mikolov, T., Sutskever, I., et al., 2013. Distributed Representations of Words and Phrases and their Compositionality. *Advances in neural information processing systems*, pp.3111–3119.

Mikolov, T., Corrado, G., et al., 2013. word2vec-v1. *Proceedings of the International Conference on Learning Representations (ICLR 2013)*, pp.1–12.

Neal, R.W., 2013. Twitter Usage Statistics: Which Country Has The Most Active Twitter Population? *International Business Times*. Available at: http://www.ibtimes.com/twitter-usage-statistics-which-country-has-most-active-twitter-population-1474852.

Palogiannidi, E. et al., 2016. Tweester at SemEval-2016 Task 4 : Sentiment Analysis in Twitter using Semantic-Affective Model Adaptation. , pp.160–168.

Refaee, E. & Rieser, V., 2014. Subjectivity and Sentiment Analysis of Arabic Twitter Feeds with Limited Resources. In *Proceedings of the Workshop on Free/Open-Source Arabic Corpora and Corpora Processing Tools*. Reykjavik, Iceland, pp. 16–21.

Rennie, J.D.M. et al., 2003. Tackling the Poor Assumptions of Naive Bayes Text Classifiers. *Proceedings of the Twentieth International Conference on Machine Learning (ICML)-2003)*, 20(1973), pp.616–623.

Rosenthal, S., Farra, N. & Nakov, P., 2017. {SemEval}-2017 Task 4: Sentiment Analysis in {T}witter. In *Proceedings of the 11th International Workshop on Semantic Evaluation*. SemEval '17. Vancouver, Canada: Association for Computational Linguistics.

Salamah, J. Ben & Elkhlifi, A., 2014. Microblogging Opinion Mining Approach for Kuwaiti Dialect. In *The International Conference on Computing Technology and Information Management (ICCTIM2014)*. pp. 388–396.

Shoukry, A. & Rafea, A., 2015. A Hybrid Approach for Sentiment Classification of Egyptian Dialect Tweets. In *First International Conference on Arabic Computational Linguistics (ACLing)*. Cairo, Egypt, pp. 78–85.

Shoukry, A. & Rafea, A., 2012. Preprocessing Egyptian Dialect Tweets for Sentiment Mining. In *Proceedings of the fourth workshop on Computational Approaches to Arabic Script-Based Languages*. San Diego, California, USA, pp. 47–56.

Stojanovski, D. et al., 2016. Finki at SemEval-2016 Task 4 : Deep Learning Architecture for Twitter Sentiment Analysis. *Proceedings of SemEval-2016*, (November), pp.154–159.

Vilares, D. et al., 2016. LyS at SemEval-2016 Task 4 : Exploiting Neural Activation Values for Twitter Sentiment Classification and Quantification *. , pp.79–84.

Yadav, V., 2016. thecerealkiller at SemEval-2016 Task 4 : Deep Learning based System for Classifying Sentiment of Tweets on Two Point Scale. , pp.100–102.

YNU-HPCC at SemEval 2017 Task 4: Using A Multi-Channel CNN-LSTM Model for Sentiment Classification

Haowei Zhang, Jin Wang, Jixian Zhang, Xuejie Zhang
School of Information Science and Engineering
Yunnan University
Kunming, P.R. China
Contact: xjzhang@ynu.edu.cn

Abstract

In this paper, we propose a multi-channel convolutional neural network-long short-term memory (CNN-LSTM) model that consists of two parts: multi-channel CNN and LSTM to analyze the sentiments of short English messages from Twitter. Unlike a conventional CNN, the proposed model applies a multi-channel strategy that uses several filters of different length to extract active local n-gram features in different scales. This information is then sequentially composed using LSTM. By combining both CNN and LSTM, we can consider both local information within tweets and long-distance dependency across tweets in the classification process. Officially released results show that our system outperforms the baseline algorithm.

1 Introduction

Social network services (SNSs) such as Twitter, Facebook, and Weibo are used daily to express thoughts, opinions, and emotions. In Twitter, 6000 short messages (tweets) are posted by users every second[1]. Therefore, Twitter is considered as one of the most concentrated opinion-expressing venues on the Internet. Subjective analysis of this type of user-generated content has become a vital task for politics, social networking, marketing, and advertising.

The potential application of sentiment analysis has been the motivation behind the SemEval 2017 Task 4, which is a competition involving a series of subtasks that focus on Twitter sentiment classifications. Subtask A involves message polarity classification, which requires a system to classify whether a message is of positive, negative, or neutral sentiment. Subtasks B and C involve topic-based message polarity classification, which require a system to classify a message on two- and five-point scales toward a certain topic.

Various approaches have been proposed to analyze sentiment of text, and deep neural network has achieved state-of-the-art results in recent years. Proven successful text classification methods include convolutional neural networks (CNN) (LeCun et al., 1990; Y. Kim, 2014; Kalchbrenner et al., 2014) and Long Short-Term Memory (LSTM) (Hochreiter et al, 1997; Tai et al., 2015). In general, CNN applies a convolutional layer to extract active local n-gram features, but lost the order of words. By contrast, LSTM can sequentially model texts. However, it focuses only on past information and draws conclusions from the tail part of texts. It fails to capture the local response from temporal data.

In this paper, we propose a multi-channel CNN-LSTM model for sentiment classification. It consists of two parts: multi-channel CNN, and LSTM. Unlike a conventional CNN model, we apply a multi-channel strategy that uses several filters of different length. The model is thus able to extract active n-gram features of different scales. LSTM is then applied to compose those features sequentially. By combining both CNN and LSTM, both local information within tweets and long-distance dependency across tweets can be considered in the classification process. To train the proposed neural model effectively using many parameters, we pretrained the model using a distant supervision approach (Go et al., 2009). In our experiment, we presented our participation of the proposed model for

---

[1] http://www.internetlivestats.com/twitter-statistics/

Proceedings of the 11th International Workshop on Semantic Evaluations (SemEval-2017), pages 796–801,
Vancouver, Canada, August 3 - 4, 2017. ©2017 Association for Computational Linguistics

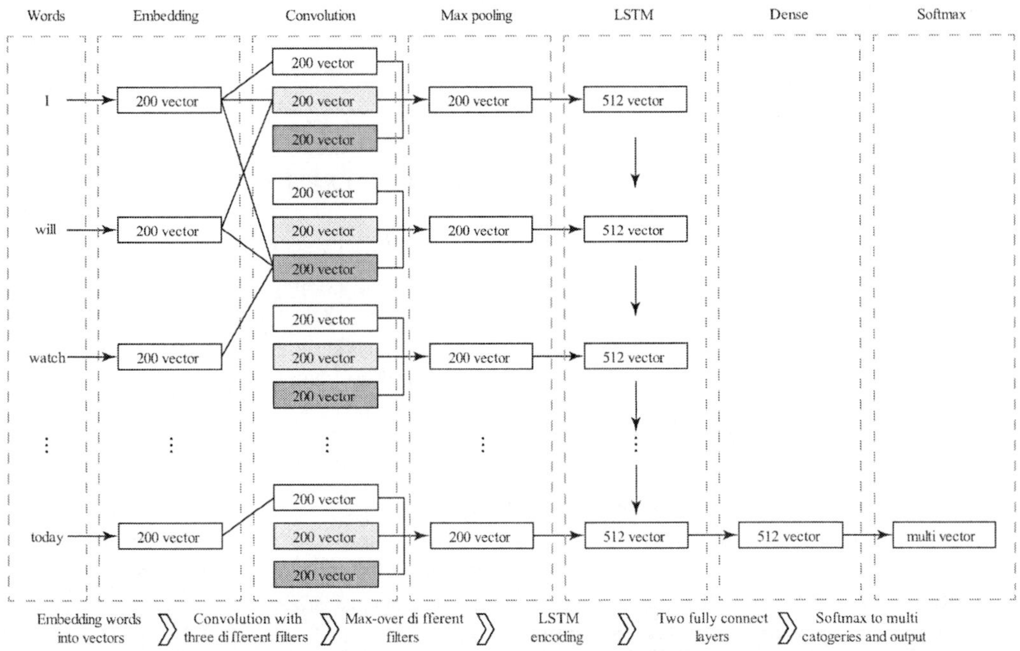

Figure 1: Architecture of the proposed CNN-LSTM model.

the SemEval 2017 Task 4 Subtasks A, B, and C (Rosenthal et al., 2017).

The remainder of this paper is organized as follows. In Section 2, we detail the architecture and multi-channel strategy of our model. Section 3 summarizes the comparative results of our proposed model against the baseline algorithm. Section 4 offers a conclusion.

2 Multi-Channel CNN-LSTM Model

Figure 1 shows the architecture of our model. The model consists of six types of layers: embedding, convolution, max-pooling, LSTM, dense, and softmax. First, a tweet is input as a series of vectors of constituent words and transformed into a feature matrix by an embedding layer. The feature matrix is then passed into three parallel CNNs having different filter lengths. The max pooling layer extracts the max-over different CNNs results that are intended to be the salient features, and input them to the LSTM layer. Then, normal dense and softmax layers use outputs from LSTM and output the final classification result.

2.1 Embedding Layer

The embedding layer is the first layer of the model. Each tweet is regarded as a sequence of word tokens t_1, t_2, …, t_N, where N is the length of the token vector. According to statistics of tweets collected from twitter in Section 3.1, about 95% tweets is shorter than 30 words. Thus, we empirically limit the maximum of N to 30. Any tweet longer than 30 tokens is truncated to 30, and any tweet shorter than 30 is padded to 30 using zero padding. Every word is mapped to a d-dimension word vector. The output of this layer is a matrix $T \in \Re^{N \times d}$.

2.2 CNN Layer

In each CNN layer, m filters are applied to a sliding window of width w over the matrix of previous embedding layer. Let $F \in \Re^{w \times d}$ denote a filter matrix and b a bias. Assuming that $T_{i:i+j}$ denotes the token vectors t_i, t_{i+1}, …, t_{i+j} (if $k > N$, $t_k = 0$), the result of each filter will be $f \in \Re^d$, where the i-th element of f is generated by:

$$f_i = T_{i:i+w-1} \otimes F + b \tag{1}$$

where $\otimes$ denotes convolution action. Before processing f to the next layer, a nonlinear activation function is applied. Here, we use ReLU function (Nair and Hinton, 2010) for faster calculation. Convolving filters with window width w can extract w-gram feature. By applying multiple convolving filters in this layer, we can extract active local n-gram features in different scales. To keep output sizes of different filters identical, we apply zero padding to token vectors before convolution.

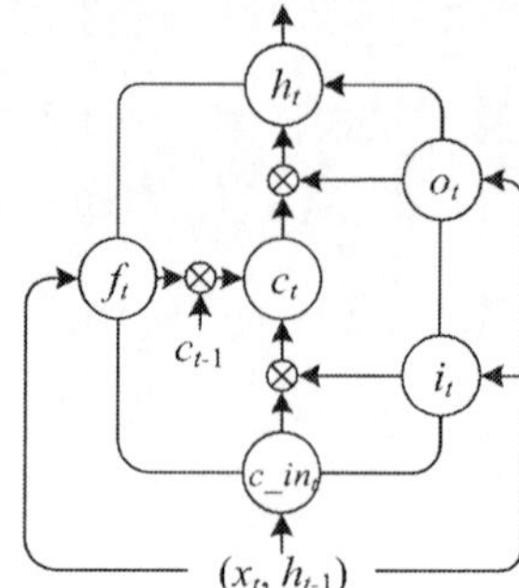

Figure 2: Architecture of LSTM cell.

2.3 Max-over Pooling Layer

In this layer, the maximum value from different filters is taken as the most salient feature. Because the CNN layer with window width w can extract w-gram features, the maximum values of the output from CNN layer are considered the most salient information in the target tweet. We choose max rather than mean pooling because the salient feature represents the most distinguishing trait of a tweet.

2.4 LSTM Layer

The architecture of a recurrent neural network (RNN) is suitable for processing sequential data. However, a simple RNN is usually difficult to train because of the gradient vanishing problem. To address this problem, LSTM introduces a gating structure that allows for explicit memory updates and deliveries. As shown in Figure 2, LSTM calculates hidden state h_t using the following equations:

- *Gates:*
$$i_t = \sigma(W_{xi}x_t + W_{hi}h_{t-1} + b_i)$$
$$f_t = \sigma(W_{xf}x_t + W_{hf}h_{t-1} + b_f) \qquad (2)$$
$$o_t = \sigma(W_{xo}x_t + W_{ho}h_{t-1} + b_i)$$

- *Input transformation:*
$$c\_in_t = \tanh(W_{xc}x_t + W_{hc}h_{t-1} + b_{c\_in}) \qquad (3)$$

- *State update:*
$$c_t = f_t \otimes c_{t-1} + i_t \otimes c\_in_t$$
$$h_t = o_t \otimes \tanh(c_t) \qquad (4)$$

where x_t is the input vector; c_t is the cell state vector; W, U, and b are layer parameters; f_t, i_t, and o_t are gate vectors; and σ is a sigmoid function. Note that $\otimes$ denotes the Hadamard product.

Content	Example	Result
Usernames start with @	@username1	<user>
URLs	http://t.co/short	<url>
Numbers	12,450	<number>
Hashtags	#topic	<hashtag>
Slash	/	or

Table 1: Example of pre-processing pattern.

2.5 Hidden Layer

This is a fully connected layer. It multiplies results from the previous layer with a weight matrix and adds a bias vector. The ReLU activation function is also applied. The result vectors are finally input to the output layer.

2.6 Output Layer

This layer outputs the final classification result. It is a fully connected layer using softmax as an activation function. The output of this layer is a vector calculated by:

$$P(y = j \mid x) = \frac{e^{x^T w_j}}{\sum_{k=1}^{K} e^{x^T w_j}} \qquad (5)$$

where x is the input vector, w is the weight vector, and K is the number of classes. Thus, the final classification result $\hat{y}$ will be:

$$\hat{y} = \arg\max_j P(y = j \mid x) \qquad (6)$$

3 Experiments and Evaluation

3.1 Data Preparation

We implemented a simple tokenizer to process tweets into array of tokens. Because we are only participating in English tasks, all characters other than English letters or punctuations are ignored. Every tweet is applied with the patterns shown in Table 1. We applied the first four patterns and lowered all letters to accommodate the known tokens in GloVe (Pennington et al., 2014) pretrained word vectors.

Before training on given tweets, we pretrained the model using data with distant supervision. Two external datasets were used. The first was crawled from Twitter. Thanks to the streaming API kindly provided by Twitter, we collected approximately 428 million tweets (all tweets were published between Nov. 2016 and Jan. 2017). Approximately one sixth of them had only one emoji or emoticon[2], which perfectly fit the condition for weak labeled.

---

[2] Emoji and emoticons list are based on https://en.wikipedia.org/wiki/List_of_emoticons

Subtask	Metrics	Final Result	Baseline	Rank	Participants
A	Average Recall	0.633	0.333	12	39
	Average F_1-Score	0.612	0.135	15	39
	Accuracy	0.647	0.333	7	39
B	Average Recall	0.834	0.5	6	23
	Average F_1-Score	0.816	0.317	10	23
	Accuracy	0.818	0.5	10	23
C	MAE^M	0.925	1.6	12	15
	MAE^μ	0.567	1.315	8	15

Table 2: The evaluation results on Subtask A, B, C of
SemEval 2017 Task 4: Sentiment analysis in Twitter.

The second dataset was from Sentiment140, which provided 1.6 million balanced-distribution tweets.

We used GloVe pretrained data[3] to initialize the weight of the embedding layer. GloVe is a popular unsupervised machine learning algorithm to acquire word embedding vectors. It is trained on global word co-occurrence counts and achieves state of the art performance on word analogy datasets. In this competition, we used the 200-dimension word vectors that were pretrained on two billion tweets.

3.2 Implementation

We used Keras with Theano (Bergstra et al., 2010) backend, which can fully utilize the GPU computing resource. CUDA (Nickolls et al., 2008) and cuDNN (Chetlur and Woolley, 2014) were used to accelerate the system. The optimizer we used was Adadelta (Zeiler, 2012).

The hyper-parameters were tuned in train and dev sets using the scikit-learn (Pedregosa et al., 2012) grid search function, which can iterate through all possible parameter combinations to identify the best performance. The best-tuned parameters include as follows. The CNN filter count is $m = 200$; the length of multi-convolving filters are 1, 2, and 3; and the dimension of the hidden layer in LSTM is 512. To prevent over-fitting, we also applied dropout (Tobergte and Curtis, 2013) after LSTM layer and fully connected layer at rate of 0.5. The training also runs with early stopping (Prechelt, 1998), terminating processing if validation loss has not improved within the last 5 epochs.

3.3 Evaluation Metrics

We evaluated our system on Subtasks A, B, and C. Subtask A was a message polarity classification of three points. Subtasks B and C involved ordinal sentiment classification of two and five points. Metrics of Subtasks A and B were average F_1-score,

average recall, and accuracy. The F_1-score was calculated as:

$$F_1^p = \frac{2\pi^p \rho^p}{\pi^p + \rho^p}, \tag{7}$$

where F_1^p is the F_1-score of one class (p denotes positive here as an example), π^p and ρ^p denote precision and recall, respectively.

Metrics of subtask C were MAE^M and MAE^μ, which were calculated as:

$$MAE^M(h, Te) = \frac{1}{|C|} \sum_{j=1}^{C} \frac{1}{Te_j} \sum_{x_i \in Te_j} |h(x_i) - y_i| \tag{8}$$

$$MAE^\mu = \frac{1}{|Te|} \sum_{x_i \in Te} |h(x_i) - y_i| \tag{9}$$

where y_i is the true label of item x_i, $h(x_i)$ is the predicted label, and Te_j is the set of test documents whose true class is c_j. A higher F_1-score, recall, accuracy, and a lower MAE^μ and MAE^M value indicate more accurate forecasting performance.

3.4 Results and Discussion

To prove the advantages of our system architecture, we ran a 5-fold cross validation on different sets of layers excepting embedding and hidden layers. A single LSTM achieved 0.617 accuracy on train and dev data. A single CNN achieved 0.606, a multi-channel CNN 0.563, and a single CNN with LSTM 0.603. Our multi-channel CNN with LSTM outperformed all other architecture with a 0.640 accuracy.

Table 2 presents the detailed results of our evaluation against the baseline algorithm. That our system achieved 0.647 accuracy on Subtask A is noteworthy, as the best score for this subtask was 0.651. The evaluation results revealed that our proposed system is considerably improved than the average baseline, which we attribute to our multi-channel CNN with LSTM architecture and distant supervision training. The proposed system can effectively

---

[3] http://nlp.stanford.edu/projects/glove/

extract features from tweets and classify sentiments of them.

4 Conclusion

In this paper, we described our system submissions to the SemEval 2017 Workshop Task 4, which involved sentiment analysis in Twitter. The proposed multi-channel CNN-LSTM model combines CNN and LSTM to extract both local information within tweets and long-distance dependency across tweets. A large number of tweets with distant supervision were leveraged to pretrain the model. Officially released results revealed that our system outperformed all baseline algorithms, and ranked 14th on Subtask A, 10th on Subtask B, and 8th on MAE^u of Subtask C. In the future, we will attempt to enhance the tokenizer and model architecture to achieve an improved classification system.

Acknowledgements

This work is supported by The Natural Science Foundation of Yunnan Province (Nos. 2013FB010).

References

James Bergstra, Olivier Breuleux, Frederic Frédéric Bastien, Pascal Lamblin, Razvan Pascanu, Guillaume Desjardins, Joseph Turian, David Warde-Farley, and Yoshua Bengio. 2010. Theano: a CPU and GPU math compiler in Python. *Proceedings of the Python for Scientific Computing Conference (SciPy)*(Scipy):1–7.

Sharan Chetlur and Cliff Woolley. 2014. cuDNN: Efficient Primitives for Deep Learning. *arXiv preprint arXiv:* ...:1–9.

Alec Go, Richa Bhayani, and Lei Huang. 2009. Twitter Sentiment Classification using Distant Supervision. *Processing*, 150(12):1–6. https://doi.org/10.1016/j.sedgeo.2006.07.004.

Sepp Hochreiter and Jürgen Schmidhuber. 1997. Long Short-Term Memory. *Neural Computation*, 9(8):1735–1780, November. https://doi.org/10.1162/neco.1997.9.8.1735.

Nal Kalchbrenner, Edward Grefenstette, and Phil Blunsom. 2014. A Convolutional Neural Network for Modelling Sentences. In *Proceedings of the 52nd Annual Meeting of the Association for Computational Linguistics (Volume 1: Long Papers)*, pages 655–665, Stroudsburg, PA, USA. Association for Computational Linguistics. https://doi.org/10.3115/v1/P14-1062.

Yoon Kim. 2014. Convolutional Neural Networks for Sentence Classification. *Proceedings of the 2014 Conference on Empirical Methods in Natural Language Processing (EMNLP 2014)*:1746–1751. https://doi.org/10.1109/LSP.2014.2325781.

L. D. Le Cun Jackel, B. Boser, J. S. Denker, D. Henderson, R. E. Howard, W. Hubbard, Bb Le Cun, Js Denker, and D. Henderson. 1990. Handwritten Digit Recognition with a Back-Propagation Network. *Advances in Neural Information Processing Systems*, 39(1pt2):396–404. https://doi.org/10.1111/dsu.12130.

Vinod Nair and Geoffrey E Hinton. 2010. Rectified Linear Units Improve Restricted Boltzmann Machines. *Proceedings of the 27th International Conference on Machine Learning*(3):807–814. https://doi.org/10.1.1.165.6419.

John Nickolls, Ian Buck, Michael Garland, and Kevin Skadron. 2008. Scalable parallel programming with CUDA. *ACM SIGGRAPH 2008 classes on - SIGGRAPH '08*(April):1. https://doi.org/10.1145/1401132.1401152.

Fabian Pedregosa, Gaël Varoquaux, Alexandre Gramfort, Vincent Michel, Bertrand Thirion, Olivier Grisel, Mathieu Blondel, Peter Prettenhofer, Ron Weiss, Vincent Dubourg, Jake Vanderplas, Alexandre Passos, David Cournapeau, Matthieu Brucher, Matthieu Perrot, and Édouard Duchesnay. 2012. Scikit-learn: Machine Learning in Python. *Journal of Machine Learning Research*, 12:2825–2830. https://doi.org/10.1007/s13398-014-0173-7.2.

Jeffrey Pennington, Richard Socher, and Christopher D Manning. 2014. GloVe: Global Vectors for Word Representation. *Proceedings of the 2014 Conference on Empirical Methods in Natural Language Processing*:1532–1543. https://doi.org/10.3115/v1/D14-1162.

Lutz Prechelt. 1998. Automatic early stopping using cross validation: quantifying the criteria. *Neural Networks*, 11(4):761–767, June. https://doi.org/10.1016/S0893-6080(98)00010-0.

Sara Rosenthal, Noura Farra, and Preslav Nakov. 2017. SemEval-2017 Task 4: Sentiment Analysis in Twitter. In *Proceedings of the 11th International Workshop on Semantic Evaluation*, Vancouver, Canada. Association for Computational Linguistics.

Kai Sheng Tai, Richard Socher, and Christopher D. Manning. 2015. Improved semantic representations from tree-structured long short-term memory networks. *Proceedings of ACL*:1556–1566. https://doi.org/10.1515/popets-2015-0023.

David R. Tobergte and Shirley Curtis. 2013. Improving Neural Networks with Dropout. *Journal of Chemical Information and Modeling*, 53(9):1689–1699. https://doi.org/10.1017/CBO9781107415324.004.

Matthew D. Zeiler. 2012. ADADELTA: An Adaptive
Learning Rate Method. *arXiv*:6.

TSA-INF at SemEval-2017 Task 4: An Ensemble of Deep Learning Architectures Including Lexicon Features for Twitter Sentiment Analysis

Amit Ajit Deshmane
Infosys Limited
Pune, Maharashtra 411057, India
amitad87@gmail.com

Jasper Friedrichs
Infosys Limited
Newark, CA 94560, USA
jasper_friedrichs@infosys.com

Abstract

This paper describes the submission of team TSA-INF to SemEval-2017 Task 4 Subtask A. The submitted system is an ensemble of three varying deep learning architectures for sentiment analysis. The core of the architecture is a convolutional neural network that performs well on text classification as is. The second subsystem is a gated recurrent neural network implementation. Additionally, the third system integrates opinion lexicons directly into a convolution neural network architecture. The resulting ensemble of the three architectures achieved a top ten ranking with a macro-averaged recall of 64.3%. Additional results comparing variations of the submitted system are not conclusive enough to determine a best architecture, but serve as a benchmark for further implementations.

1 Introduction

The SemEval competitions continually offer suitable dataset and resulting benchmarks for a variety of natural language processing tasks. The SemEval-2017 Task 4 Subtask A addresses the polarity classification task of informal texts (Rosenthal et al., 2017). Tweets serve as a very accessible sample of the abundant social media content. Submitted systems must classify tweets into the categories of negative, positive and neutral opinion. Submitted results are compared over macro-averaged recall.

In recent benchmarks across this task, deep learning implementations achieved top results (Nakov et al., 2016). We seek to combine three varying deep learning approaches in an ensemble. Conventional methods seem to become obsolete since convolutional neural networks (CNN) have first shown state-of-the-art results in sentiment analysis (Kim, 2014). SemEval has since seen successful results by similar models (Severyn and Moschitti, 2015) as well as ensembles of CNNs (Deriu et al., 2016). Long term short term recurrent neural networks (LSTM) (Hochreiter and Schmidhuber, 1997) have also been applied successfully in ensemble with a CNN (Xu et al., 2016). As an alternative to LSTMs gated recurrent neural networks (GRNN) have been shown to be competitive in other domains (Chung et al., 2014). These models are well suited to model sequential data and were successfully applied for sentiment analysis of larger documents (Yang et al., 2016). The core contribution of a recent non deep learning system to win this task (Kiritchenko et al., 2014) back to back in 2013 and 2014, was the integration of opinion lexicons into a support vector machine system. Opinion lexicons have since then also been integrated into CNN architectures (Rouvier and Favre, 2016; Shin et al., 2016). In this work we combine these diverse architectures.

We use a CNN, thoroughly optimized for text classification, as the foundation of our ensemble approach. We add a lexicon integrated CNN to take advantage of lexicon features. In order to diversify the approach we also include a GRNN architecture as a sequential model. The idea is to get better and more robust results with a broader architecture. Results show that adding the latter two systems does not improve overall results, though the results for the core CNN approach were already good. Furthermore, results for individual classes do improve, making this a viable option when prioritizing specific classes or evaluation metrics. With this work we seek to contribute to the growing body of literature that presents comparable and reproducible solutions for this task.

Proceedings of the 11th International Workshop on Semantic Evaluations (SemEval-2017), pages 802–806,
Vancouver, Canada, August 3 - 4, 2017. ©2017 Association for Computational Linguistics

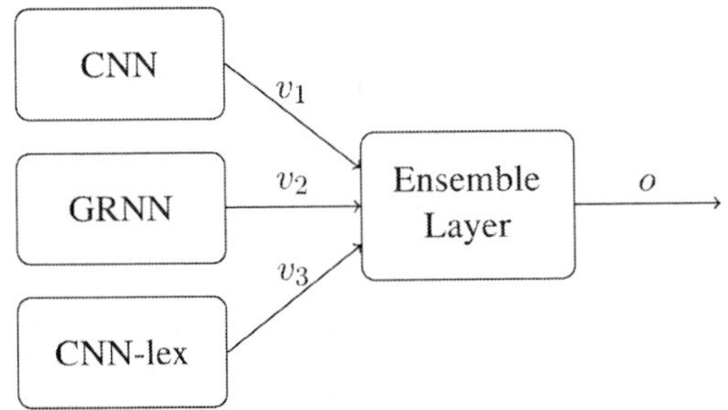

Figure 1: Ensemble component output vectors v_i are used as input to an ensemble, which determines a classification output vector o.

2 Approach

This section outlines the overall approach before detailing the subcomponents of the architecture. The purpose of the system is to classify an input tweet into an element of the opinion classes C, with $|C| = 3$. This is determined by the maximal value of an system output vector $o \in \mathbb{R}^{|C|}$. As outlined in Fig. 1 we propose an ensemble of three deep learning architectures to solve this task. A CNN and a GRNN over word embeddings as well as a CNN over lexicon embeddings. The ensemble components output vector representations $v_{1/2/3}$ can be considered an abstraction of the input tweet. These representations are the input to an ensemble system which determines the final output. We will describe preprocessing steps to create the ensemble layer input before outlining the ensemble architecture.

2.1 Preprocessing

First of all the tweet data is tokenized with NLP4J[1] as a preprocessing step for creating embeddings. In the following we refer to a tweet as a document, which is a sequence of tokens, constrained to $n = 120$. If the actual document is less in size, it is padded with zero vectors, otherwise it is truncated.

The tokens are then converted into either word embeddings of dimension d or lexicon embeddings of dimension l. We use pretrained word embeddings from Frederic Godin[2] (Godin et al., 2015), with $d = 400$. The embeddings were trained on 400 million tweets. The lexicon embeddings are polarity scores from three different lexicons, thus $l = 3$. We use Bing Liu's Opinion lexicon (Hu and Liu, 2004), the Hashtag Sentiment

Lexicon and the Sentiment 140 Lexicon (Mohammad et al., 2013) to form the complete lexicon embedding.

Tensorflow[3](Abadi et al., 2016) is used as the deep learning framework for implementing the system. The next subsections describe the components of this system, followed by an outline of how their outputs are combined into an ensemble.

2.2 Convolution Neural Network

This component is based on a standard CNN architecture used for text classification (Kim, 2014). We make small changes for fine tuning to the task. The input to this component are the word embeddings described in the preceding subsection. The embeddings of dimension d are formed into a document matrix $D \in \mathbb{R}^{n \times d}$ across the n input tokens. The document matrix D is passed through k filters of filter size s. The convolution weights belong to $\mathbb{R}^{s \times d}$. The convolutions result in k convolution output vectors of dimension $\mathbb{R}^{n-s+1}$. A max pool layer converts these vectors to a vector of size $\mathbb{R}^k$. We then add a normalization layer (Ioffe and Szegedy, 2015) so as to merge outputs from different filter sizes. With f filter sizes, we finally arrive at vector $v_1 \in \mathbb{R}^{k \times f}$. This vector is passed to a dense layer of 256 ReLu units. The dense layer is followed by an output softmax layer. We apply dropout (Hinton et al., 2012) at the beginning of the dense layer as well as the output layer. The implementation uses following the configuration:

- Weights are initialized using Xavier weight initialization (Glorot and Bengio, 2010).

- The Learning rate is set to 0.0001 with a batch size of 100.

- The architecture uses $f = 5$ filter sizes, [1,2,3,4,5], and $k = 256$ filters per filter size over $n = 120$ word embedding vectors of dimension $d = 400$.

- The input vector to the dense layer v_1 thus has a dimension of 1280.

- At the dense layer and output layer, we use dropout with a keep probability of 0.7.

- We run 200 training iterations and select the model that performed best on development data.

---

[1] https://github.com/emorynlp/nlp4j
[2] http://www.fredericgodin.com/software/
[3] https://www.tensorflow.org/

2.3 Gated Recurrent Neural Network

The GRNN is based on the gated recurrent unit (GRU) (Cho et al., 2014), which uses a gating mechanism while tracking the input sequence with a latent variable. GRUs seemed to perform better compared to other RNN cells like LSTM in our experiments, which go beyond the scope of this paper. The input to the GRNN are the word embeddings described in Section 2.1. The input is read sequentially by a GRU layer. The GRU cell is designed to learn how to represent a state, based on previous inputs and the current input. The GRU layer consists of g hidden units. After the last token of the sequence is processed, the output vector $v_2 \in \mathbb{R}^g$ of this layer is collected to be merged into other architectures. The implementation is configured by:

- $g = 256$ hidden units with tanh activation,

- resulting in the 256 dimensional output vector v_2.

2.4 Lexicon Integrated Convolution Neural Network

The lexicon integrated CNN (CNN-lex) is similar to the previously described CNN architecture. The fundamental difference is that convolutions are done over lexicon embeddings, described in Section 2.1. The input to this component is a document matrix $L \in \mathbb{R}^{n \times l}$ across the l dimensional lexicon embeddings of n input tokens. The architecture uses j filters per e convolution filter sizes. The convolution layer output is passed through a max pool and normalization layer. This results in an output vector $v_3 \in \mathbb{R}^{j \times e}$ that is collected to be merged into other architectures. The implementation uses following configuration:

- The architecture uses $e = 3$ filter sizes, [3,4,5], and $j = 64$ filters per filter size over $n = 120$ lexicon embeddings of dimension $l = 3$.

- The ensemble output vector v_3 thus has a dimension of 192.

2.5 Ensembles

The previously described architectures can be combined into ensemble systems. The CNN-lex and GRNN architectures are already defined as ensemble subsystems through their output vectors v_2 and v_3. While the CNN architecture was previous

introduced as a stand alone system it is naturally described as an ensemble component. The vector v_1 described in Section 2.2 is the output vector of the CNN as a subsystem. The three vectors are concatenated as inputs to the ensemble layer. The ensemble layer consists of a dense layer of 256 ReLu units followed by a softmax output layer, which results in the output vector o of dimension $|C|$. The CNN is combined into three ensembles by concatenating its input vector v_1 with v_2 (CNN, GRNN) and with v_3 (CNN, CNN-lex) as well as with both v_2 and v_3 (CNN, CNN-lex, GRNN). The latter is the submission architecture while the other two are evaluated for comparison. These ensembles are trained as a single system. Training is conducted as previously described for the CNN architecture.

3 Data

The training data for this approach was constrained to data published in the context of the SemEval workshops. Table 1 lists the data available to the authors. It is important to note that the data is heavily imbalanced. Before submission the system was tested with the 2016-test set as development test data. The results described in this paper focus on the 2017-test data, which was used to rank the submissions. All other data in Table 1 was combined into one data set, shuffled and split four to one into training and development data.

4 Results

The following results compare the core CNN architecture against ensembles with the CNN as a subsystem. The ranked submission marked by $*$ in Table 4 ranked ninth out of 37 participants.

Twitter Corpus	Pos	Neg	Neut	Total
2013-train	3640	1458	4586	9684
2013-dev	575	340	739	1654
2013-test	1475	559	1513	3547
2014-sarcasm	33	40	13	86
2014-test	982	202	669	1853
2015-test	1038	365	987	2390
2016-train	3094	863	2043	6000
2016-dev	843	391	765	1999
2016-devtest	994	325	681	2000
2016-test (A)	7059	3231	10342	20632
2017-test (B)	2375	3972	5937	12284

Table 1: SemEval data subsets as available to authors. Aside from development test (A) and test (B) split, all sets where combined for a train and dev split.

2017-test, detailed	Recall			Precision			F_1		
	pos	neg	neut	pos	neg	neut	pos	neg	neut
CNN	68.3	78.3	47.6	**54.8**	57.7	71.7	**60.8**	66.5	57.2
CNN, CNN-lex	**74.3**	**85.6**	33.1	50.3	54.7	**76.7**	60.0	**66.7**	46.3
CNN, GRNN	73.2	71.0	50.1	50.4	61.2	70.3	59.7	65.7	58.5
CNN, CNN-lex, GRNN ∗	74.1	64.0	**55.0**	50.9	**63.6**	67.6	60.3	63.8	**60.6**

Table 2: Per class results of recall precision and F1 on test data (2017-test, Table 1) for CNN and ensemble architectures, where ∗ marks the submission system

2016-test	ρ	F_1^{PN}	Acc.
CNN	**66.1**	**62.6**	62.8
CNN, CNN-lex	64.9	61.0	56.4
CNN, GRNN	64.2	61.9	61.3
CNN, CNN-lex, GRNN	64.0	62.4	**64.1**

Table 3: Macro-averaged recall ρ, negative positive macro-averaged F1 and accuracy on development test data (2016-test, Table 1) for CNN and ensemble architectures.

2017-test	ρ	F_1^{PN}	Acc.
CNN	64.7	**63.6**	61.5
CNN, CNN-lex	64.3	63.4	58.0
CNN, GRNN	**64.8**	62.7	61.3
CNN, CNN-lex, GRNN	64.3∗	62.0	**61.6**

Table 4: Macro-averaged recall ρ, negative positive macro-averaged F1 and accuracy on test data (2017-test, Table 1) for CNN and ensemble architectures, where ∗ marks the ranked submission.

For detailed rankings we refer to the task description (Nakov et al., 2016), we only put this result in context with the described architectures. Three ensembles are used for comparison, the basic CNN combined with either the GRNN or the lexicon integrated CNN as well as both. The two result data sets are the 2016-test set as pre-submission test data and the final 2017-test data set used to benchmark the submissions.

Overall the CNN performs en par or better than the ensembles on macro-averaged recall and macro-averaged positive negative F1. For both development test data in Table 3 and test data in Table 4 we observe that the CNN outperforms the ensembles across macro-averaged F1. Though there is a substantial difference between macro-averaged recall of the CNN versus the ensembles on the development test data, macro-averaged recall on the test data is consistent across all systems.

The strongest fluctuation in averaged results is the drop in accuracy for the CNN, CNN-lex ensemble across both data sets. Detailed results in Table 2 show that this is due to a steep drop in neutral class recall, a class the data is heavily biased towards (Table 1). We note that though macro-averaged recall stays consistent on the test data (Table 4), per class results do fluctuate substantially (Table 2). These class trends were generally consistent across both 2017-test and 2016-test data, thus the later results are omitted for brevity.

5 Conclusions

In the previous sections we described experiments of adding various deep learning architecture elements to a basic CNN. Results show that the derived ensembles of approaches did not improve performance over the more relevant metrics of macro-averaged recall and F1. To give further context it is important to mention that substantially more effort went into engineering and tuning of the CNN model than of the additional architectures. Just as the submission system, the CNN architecture itself would have ranked within the top ten of this sentiment analysis task. Room for improvement was thus limited. We do note that per class results do fluctuate quite a bit across ensembles, which means these architecture can be used to prioritize class specific recall and precision.

It remains open whether the more complex architectures perform more robustly across diverse datasets. We will seek more clarity on this issue by experimenting with different data sets. Another architecture choice to pursue is to include an attention mechanism so that the ensemble system can learn which subcomponents to prioritize.

Acknowledgments

We thank assistant professor Jinho D. Choi at Emory University for guidance.

References

Martín Abadi, Ashish Agarwal, Paul Barham, Eugene Brevdo, Zhifeng Chen, Craig Citro, Greg S Corrado, Andy Davis, Jeffrey Dean, Matthieu Devin, et al. 2016. Tensorflow: Large-scale machine learning on heterogeneous distributed systems. *arXiv preprint arXiv:1603.04467* .

Kyunghyun Cho, Bart Van Merriënboer, Dzmitry Bahdanau, and Yoshua Bengio. 2014. On the properties of neural machine translation: Encoder- decoder approaches. *arXiv preprint arXiv:1409.1259* .

Junyoung Chung, Caglar Gulcehre, KyungHyun Cho, and Yoshua Bengio. 2014. Empirical evaluation of gated recurrent neural networks on sequence modeling. *arXiv preprint arXiv:1412.3555* .

Jan Deriu, Maurice Gonzenbach, Fatih Uzdilli, Aurelien Lucchi, Valeria De Luca, and Martin Jaggi. 2016. Swisscheese at semeval-2016 task 4: Sentiment classification using an ensemble of convolutional neural networks with distant supervision. *Proceedings of SemEval* pages 1124–1128.

Xavier Glorot and Yoshua Bengio. 2010. Understanding the difficulty of training deep feedforward neural networks. In *Aistats*. volume 9, pages 249–256.

Fréderic Godin, Baptist Vandersmissen, Wesley De Neve, and Rik Van de Walle. 2015. Multimedia lab @ acl w-nut ner shared task: Named entity recognition for twitter microposts using distributed word representations. *ACL-IJCNLP* 2015:146–153.

Geoffrey E Hinton, Nitish Srivastava, Alex Krizhevsky, Ilya Sutskever, and Ruslan R Salakhutdinov. 2012. Improving neural networks by preventing coadaptation of feature detectors. *arXiv preprint arXiv:1207.0580* .

Sepp Hochreiter and Jürgen Schmidhuber. 1997. Long short-term memory. *Neural computation* 9(8):1735–1780.

Minqing Hu and Bing Liu. 2004. Mining and summarizing customer reviews. In *Proceedings of the tenth ACM SIGKDD international conference on Knowledge discovery and data mining*. ACM, pages 168–177.

Sergey Ioffe and Christian Szegedy. 2015. Batch normalization: Accelerating deep network training by reducing internal covariate shift. *arXiv preprint arXiv:1502.03167* .

Yoon Kim. 2014. Convolutional neural networks for sentence classification. *arXiv preprint arXiv:1408.5882* .

Svetlana Kiritchenko, Xiaodan Zhu, and Saif M Mohammad. 2014. Sentiment analysis of short informal texts. *Journal of Artificial Intelligence Research* 50:723–762.

Saif M. Mohammad, Svetlana Kiritchenko, and Xiaodan Zhu. 2013. Nrc-canada: Building the state-of-the-art in sentiment analysis of tweets. In *Proceedings of the seventh international workshop on Semantic Evaluation Exercises (SemEval-2013)*. Atlanta, Georgia, USA.

Preslav Nakov, Alan Ritter, Sara Rosenthal, Veselin Stoyanov, and Fabrizio Sebastiani. 2016. SemEval-2016 task 4: Sentiment analysis in Twitter. In *Proceedings of the 10th International Workshop on Semantic Evaluation (SemEval 2016)*. Association for Computational Linguistics, San Diego, California.

Sara Rosenthal, Noura Farra, and Preslav Nakov. 2017. SemEval-2017 task 4: Sentiment analysis in Twitter. In *Proceedings of the 11th International Workshop on Semantic Evaluation*. Association for Computational Linguistics, Vancouver, Canada, SemEval '17.

Mickael Rouvier and Benoit Favre. 2016. Sensei-lif at semeval-2016 task 4: Polarity embedding fusion for robust sentiment analysis. *Proceedings of SemEval* pages 202–208.

Aliaksei Severyn and Alessandro Moschitti. 2015. Unitn: Training deep convolutional neural network for twitter sentiment classification. In *Proceedings of the 9th International Workshop on Semantic Evaluation (SemEval 2015), Association for Computational Linguistics, Denver, Colorado*. pages 464–469.

Bonggun Shin, Timothy Lee, and Jinho D Choi. 2016. Lexicon integrated cnn models with attention for sentiment analysis. *arXiv preprint arXiv:1610.06272* .

XingYi Xu, HuiZhi Liang, and Timothy Baldwin. 2016. Unimelb at semeval-2016 tasks 4a and 4b: An ensemble of neural networks and a word2vec based model for sentiment classification. *Proceedings of SemEval* pages 183–189.

Zichao Yang, Diyi Yang, Chris Dyer, Xiaodong He, Alex Smola, and Eduard Hovy. 2016. Hierarchical attention networks for document classification. In *Proceedings of NAACL-HLT*. pages 1480–1489.

UCSC-NLP at SemEval-2017 Task 4: Sense n-grams for Sentiment Analysis in Twitter

José Abreu, Iván Castro,
Claudia Martínez, Sebastián Oliva

Catholic University of the Most Holy Conception

Alonso de Ribera 2850, Concepción, Chile

`{joseabreu,cmartinez}@ucsc.cl`

`{ilcastro,snoliva}@ing.ucsc.cl`

Yoan Gutiérrez

University of Alicante

Carretera de San Vicente s/n

Alicante, Spain

`ygutierrez@dlsi.ua.es`

Abstract

This paper describes the system submitted to SemEval-2017 Task 4-A Sentiment Analysis in Twitter developed by the UCSC-NLP team. We studied how relationships between sense n-grams and sentiment polarities can contribute to this task, i.e. co-occurrences of WordNet senses in the tweet, and the polarity. Furthermore, we evaluated the effect of discarding a large set of features based on char-grams reported in preceding works. Based on these elements, we developed a SVM system, which exploring SentiWordNet as a polarity lexicon. It achieves an $F_1 = 0.624$ of average. Among 39 submissions to this task, we ranked $10th$.

1 Introduction

To determine whether a text expresses a POSITIVE, NEGATIVE or NEUTRAL opinion has attracted an increasingly attention. In particular, sentiment classification of tweets has immediate applications in areas such as marketing, political, and social analysis (Nakov et al., 2016)

Different approaches have shown to be very promising for polarity classification of tweets such as Convolutional Neural Networks trained with large amounts of data (Deriu et al., 2016).

Several authors have studied Machine Learning approaches based on lexicon, surface and semantic features. The proposal of Mohammad et al. (2013) as well as an improved version of Zhu et al. (2014) show very competitive scores.

The latter approach was re-implemented by Hagen et al. (2015) as a part of an ensemble of twitter polarity classifier which is top-ranked in the SemEval 2015 Task 9: Sentiment Analysis in Twitter. Our system proposes to enrich the set of fea-

tures used by Mohammad et al. (2013). We describe here only the features more relevant for our experiments, further details in all features could be found in Mohammad et al. (2013); Hagen et al. (2015).

- Lexicon Based Features (LB)

NRC-Emotion, NRC-Sentiment140, NRC-Hashtag (Mohammad et al., 2013), BingLiu (Hu and Liu, 2004) and MPQA (Wilson et al., 2005) lexicons have been used to generate features. Given a tweet, the following features were computed:

- Number of words with positive score

- Number of words with negative score

- Sum of the positive scores

- Sum of the negative scores

- Maximum positive score

- Minimum negative score

- Score of the last positive word

- Score of the last negative word

For unigrams, bigrams and non-contiguous pairs were computed separated feature sets.

- N-gram Based Features (WG and CG)

Each 1 to 4-word n-gram present in the training corpus is associated with a feature which indicates if the tweet includes or not the n-gram. For characters, all different occurrences of 3 to 5 grams are considered.

Given its definition, the number of generated n-gram based features is variable and related with the training corpus. In experiments with SemEval

Proceedings of the 11th International Workshop on Semantic Evaluations (SemEval-2017), pages 807–811,
Vancouver, Canada, August 3 - 4, 2017. ©2017 Association for Computational Linguistics

2017 training data, we got near three million of features of this type that is much largest than the number of tweets.

- Cluster Based Features (CB)

For each one of the 1000 clusters identified by Owoputi et al. (2013) using Brown algorithm (Brown et al., 1992) a feature indicates whether the terms of the tweet belong to them.

Mohammad et al. (2013) studied the effect of removing individual set of features as well a whole group of them. Empirical results suggest that lexicon and n-gram based features are the most important since removing them causes the greatest drop on the classifier efficacy measured as the macro-average F-score in the test set.

In this work, we studied how to reduce the number of generated features by removing some of the n-gram based. Next sections describe further details of our approach.

2   System Description

We trained a Support Vector Machine (SVM) as in (Mohammad et al., 2013; Zhu et al., 2014; Hagen et al., 2015). SVM algorithm has proved to be very effective in the Sentiment Analysis task. Moreover, to better assess the effect of the removal or inclusion of new features we decided to use the same classifier as the aforementioned authors.

In the first stage of our system, the tweets were preprocessed like Hagen et al. (2015). To avoid missing some emoticon symbols we ensure UTF-8 encoding in all stages. In addition, instead of detect emoticons using a regular expression [1] we use the tag provided by the CMU pos-tagging tool. In our case, negation was not considered to generate the word n-gram features.

2.1   New Predictor Features

We aim to explore the relation between the polarity and the presence or not of certain sense combinations in the text. Due to synonymy, two semantically equivalent tweets could lead to very different word n-grams while the sense n-grams could be the same in both tweets.

After a word sense disambiguation (WSD) stage, we generated a new version of the tweet where each word is replaced by its sense. A set of new n-grams features are computed using the new text. This approach allows one sense n-gram

---

to represent two or more different word n-grams if the words have the same sense.

To enrich our model respect to those in (Mohammad et al., 2013; Hagen et al., 2015) we have considered SentiWordNet (Baccianella et al., 2010) as a polarity dictionary, idea explored in (Günther and Furrer, 2013). In this case, after WSD, we can use SentiWordNet to compute positive or negative scores for a given word generating features as with the other lexicons.

Considering that elongated (e.g. greaaaat) words could emphasize the sentiment expressed, similar features were computed but only allowing for the lengthened words in the tweet. In this case, we not considered bi-grams lexicons and normalized the elongated words before query the lexicons.

Finally, we studied the following set of new features.

- Additional Features

  - Sense n-grams (SG): one feature for each sense n-gram in the training corpus.

  - SentiWordNet polarity scores (SW): eight features similar to those defined to other lexicons in section 1.

  - Polarity scores of elongated words (EW): eight features similar to those defined to other lexicons in section 1 but only considering lengthened words if any. All lexicons but NRC-Sentiment140 and NRC-Hashtag for bi-grams were used.

  - Polarity of the last emoticon (LE), if any, accordingly to Hogenboom et al. (2015).

2.2   Model Ensemble

With the available training data, we trained several models using different combinations of feature types. Our final submission was an ensemble of the top 10 models trained. Classifiers was combined by weighted voting as explained by Kuncheva (2004). To classify a tweet, we query a model that output a single label and a weight for that label, proportional to the accuracy of the classifier for that class in previous tests. Querying the 10 models, the final classification of the tweet is the most voted class.

Given A_{ij}^{C} the accuracy of the model i over the class C in test data j the weight of that category for

C is computed as $w_i^C = \frac{\sum_{j=1}^{S} A_{ij}^C}{\sum_{m=1}^{M}\sum_{j=1}^{S} A_{mj}^C}$ where $j = 1$ refers to SemEval 2013 test data and so on to $S = 4$ and $M = 10$ is the number of models in the ensemble.

The next section describes the experiments we carried out to assess different feature sets, how weights were computed as well the results.

3 Experiments

Our predictor is based in an ensemble of Support Vector Machines with linear kernel, and $C = 0.005$ trained with all the features proposed by Mohammad et al. (2013); Hagen et al. (2015) plus the new ones detailed in section 2.1. LibLIN-EAR (Fan et al., 2008) implementation available in Weka (Frank et al., 2016) was used.

As Mohammad et al. (2013), we want to evaluate how removing n-gram and cluster based features affect the results of our models. Table 1 show eight base models resulting of removing combinations of features of the types WG, CG and CB; with X indicating the characteristic set included in the model.

Table 1: Base models

	1	2	3	4	5	6	7	8
WG	x	x	x	-	x	-	-	-
CG	x	x	-	x	-	x	-	-
CB	x	-	x	x	-	-	x	-

Table 2 show different arrangements of the new features which were combined with the based models for a total of 96 experiments.

Table 2: Combinations of new features.

Exp	1	2	3	4	5	6	7	8	9	10	11	12
SG	-	-	-	x	x	-	x	x	x	x	x	x
SW	-	-	-	-	x	-	-	x	-	x	-	x
EW	-	-	x	-	-	x	-	-	x	x	x	x
LE	-	x	-	-	-	x	x	x	-	-	x	x

We replicated twice the experiments that included SG, one time disambiguating with Lesk (Lesk, 1986) algorithm and other considering the most frequent sense for a word. In all experiments, we used implementations from the NLTK (Bird et al., 2009) to disambiguate. In total, 160 different models were evaluated. Note that some of these models just augmented the features in (Mohammad et al., 2013) with some of the new ones.

With the training data of previous SemEval, 2013 to 2016, we mock our participation in these competitions. We trained SVMs for each model and evaluated it with the corresponding test data using the F_1 score for the POSITIVE class. Table 3 show the best (B) and the worst (W) results for each test dataset.

These results allowed us to rank the models. A final ranking was computed averaging the different positions across different test data of the same model. However, a drawback of this approach is that, besides one model could be ranked better than other, the result difference between them could be very small. The 10 top ranked models are the result of the based model 3 (character n-grams discarded) combined with new features $[4, 2, 5, 9, 4*, 12, 9*, 8, 10, 1]$ where $*$ indicates that the WSD was using Lesk algorithm.

Given the results in all previous SemEval test data, the accuracy over each category was obtained for each model as well the weights for the top 10.

Finally, the system submitted was built as follow. We train versions of each of the top 10 models using the SemEval-2017 training data. After removing duplicates, we get $52,780$ tweets. The 10 trained classifiers were combined by weighted voting with weights computed as explained before. Table 4 show results for each category over the $12,284$ test tweets. As regard of the measures used to evaluate systems, our proposal gets an average recall of $\rho = 0.642$, $F_1^{PN} = 0.624$ and accuracy $Acc = 0.565$. The submitted system stood 10th among participants. Further details about the train and test datasets and results of other participants can be found in (Rosenthal et al., 2017)

4 Conclusions and Future Works

Our proposal is based in (Mohammad et al., 2013). We assessed a new set of features as well analyzed the effect of removing some of the features used in this system.

Data in Table 3 as well the top 10 model trained show that the inclusion of the new features cold improve results.

Experiments in (Mohammad et al., 2013) suggest that removing character n-grams attributes degrades the classifier outcome. We also got these results, but when the feature set is extended with the new ones, character n-grams exclusion seems to be convenient. A look of model results and rankings, show that all models in the top 10, furthermore, in the top 30 are models where character

Table 3: Best (B) and worst (W) results in previous SemEval test data. In parenthesis, the number of the base model. An * indicates that the WSD was using Lesk algorithm.

	2013		2014		2015		2016	
	B	W	B	W	B	W	B	W
1	70.82 (3)	65.34 (8)	70.85 (3)	67.58 (6)	66.02 (3)	61.13 (8)	59.30 (3)	56.80 (8)
2	70.92 (3)	65.24 (8)	70.77 (3)	63.67 (8)	63.37 (3)	58.85 (8)	59.00 (3)	55.30 (8)
3	70.52 (3)	65.58 (8)	70.6 (3)	64.3 (8)	65.66 (3)	61.89 (8)	59.40 (3)	56.70 (8)
4	71.33 (3)	66.75 (8)	71.64 (3)	67.54 (2)	66.24 (3)	61.67 (8)	59.5 (3)	57.10 (8)*
5	70.89 (3)	67.39 (8)	71.87 (7)	67.89 (4)	65.83 (3)	62.02 (8)	59.5 (3)	57.10 (8)
6	70.77 (3)	67.5 (8)	71.97 (7)	67.90 (6)	63.44 (1)	58.46 (8)	59.00 (3)	55.50 (8)
7	70.74 (3)	67.46 (8)	71.77 (7)	68.05 (4)	64.84 (3)	61.37 (8)	59.10 (3)	57.30 (6)
8	70.98 (3)	67.63 (8)	71.79 (7)	68.08 (2)	63.57 (3)*	60.4 (8)*	59.00 (3)*	57.30 (8)*
9	71.26 (3)	67.58 (8)*	71.86 (7)*	68.36 (6)*	65.96 (3)	61.76 (8)	59.50 (3)*	57.20 (8)*
10	70.96 (3)	67.62 (8)	72.01 (7)	68.09 (4)	65.88 (3)*	62.05 (8)*	59.60 (3)*	57.10 (8)
11	70.83 (3)	67.48 (8)	72.05 (7)	67.96 (4)	63.71 (3)*	60.80 (8)*	59.10 (3)	57.50 (6)
12	70.94 (3)	67.68 (8)	71.82 (7)*	68.25 (6)*	63.63 (3)*	60.31 (8)*	59.00 (3)*	57.40 (8)*

Table 4: Results in SemEval 2017 test, Precision (P), Recall (R) and F1.

	P	R	F1
POSITIVE	0.4505	0.8156	0.5804
NEGATIVE	0.5694	0.8072	0.6678
NEUTRAL	0.7617	0.3020	0.4325

n-grams were excluded but some of the new ones considered.

Another interesting fact is that systems seem to be more sensitive to word n-grams and cluster based attributes. The best ranked model without n-grams, stood 23 in our ranking. Character n-grams were also omitted in this model, which was extended with SG, SW and LE features. After the release of the gold labels, we evaluated the predictions of other models not submitted but also trained with the SemEval 2017 training data. The aforementioned model shows a $F_1^P N = 0.652$, better than the model we submitted. It is important to say that this model used only $822, 650$ features, substantially less than the $2, 993, 189$ used by the best of our single models over test data which only discards character n-grams plus SG, EW and LE features and achieves a $F_1^P N = 0.654$

These results open an interesting direction of future work, further study how to minimize the set of features used without a noticeable degradation of prediction results. Ideally, identifying a set of features of size independent of the corpus as the lexicon based ones.

Acknowledgments

This paper has been partially supported by the Catholic University of the Most Holy Conception through the research project DIN-01/2016 and by the Ministry of Education, Culture and Sport of Spain, the University of Alicante, the Generalitat Valenciana and the Spanish Government through projects TIN2015-65136-C2-2-R, TIN2015-65100-R, PROMETEOII/2014/001 and FUNDACIONBBVA2-16PREMIOI.

References

Stefano Baccianella, Andrea Esuli, and Fabrizio Sebastiani. 2010. Sentiwordnet 3.0: An enhanced lexical resource for sentiment analysis and opinion mining. In *LREC*. volume 10, pages 2200–2204.

Steven Bird, Ewan Klein, and Edward Loper. 2009. *Natural language processing with Python: analyzing text with the natural language toolkit*. " O'Reilly Media, Inc.".

Peter F Brown, Peter V Desouza, Robert L Mercer, Vincent J Della Pietra, and Jenifer C Lai. 1992. Class-based n-gram models of natural language. *Computational linguistics* 18(4):467–479.

Jan Deriu, Maurice Gonzenbach, Fatih Uzdilli, Aurelien Lucchi, Valeria De Luca, and Martin Jaggi. 2016. Swisscheese at semeval-2016 task 4: Sentiment classification using an ensemble of convolutional neural networks with distant supervision. In *Proceedings of the 10th International Workshop on Semantic Evaluation (SemEval-2016)*. Association for Computational Linguistics, San Diego, California, pages 1124–1128. http://www.aclweb.org/anthology/S16-1173.

Rong-En Fan, Kai-Wei Chang, Cho-Jui Hsieh, Xiang-Rui Wang, and Chih-Jen Lin. 2008. Liblinear - a library for large linear classification. The Weka classifier works with version 1.33 of LIBLINEAR. http://www.csie.ntu.edu.tw/c̃jlin/liblinear/.

Eibe Frank, Mark A. Hall, and Ian H. Witten. 2016. The weka workbench. online appendix for "data mining: Practical machine learning tools and techniques". Technical report.

Tobias Günther and Lenz Furrer. 2013. Gu-mlt-lt: Sentiment analysis of short messages using linguistic features and stochastic gradient descent. In *Second Joint Conference on Lexical and Computational Semantics (*SEM), Volume 2: Proceedings of the Seventh International Workshop on Semantic Evaluation (SemEval 2013)*. Association for Computational Linguistics, Atlanta, Georgia, USA, pages 328–332. http://www.aclweb.org/anthology/S13-2054.

Matthias Hagen, Martin Potthast, Michel Büchner, and Benno Stein. 2015. Webis: An ensemble for twitter sentiment detection. In *Proceedings of the 9th International Workshop on Semantic Evaluation (SemEval 2015)*. Association for Computational Linguistics, Denver, Colorado, pages 582–589. http://www.aclweb.org/anthology/S15-2097.

Alexander Hogenboom, Daniella Bal, Flavius Frasincar, Malissa Bal, Franciska De Jong, and Uzay Kaymak. 2015. Exploiting emoticons in polarity classification of text. *J. Web Eng.* 14(1&2):22–40.

Minqing Hu and Bing Liu. 2004. Mining and summarizing customer reviews. In *Proceedings of the tenth ACM SIGKDD international conference on Knowledge discovery and data mining*. ACM, pages 168–177.

Ludmila I Kuncheva. 2004. *Combining pattern classifiers: methods and algorithms*. John Wiley & Sons.

Michael Lesk. 1986. Automatic sense disambiguation using machine readable dictionaries: how to tell a pine cone from an ice cream cone. In *Proceedings of the 5th annual international conference on Systems documentation*. ACM, pages 24–26.

Saif Mohammad, Svetlana Kiritchenko, and Xiaodan Zhu. 2013. Nrc-canada: Building the state-of-the-art in sentiment analysis of tweets. In *Second Joint Conference on Lexical and Computational Semantics (*SEM), Volume 2: Proceedings of the Seventh International Workshop on Semantic Evaluation (SemEval 2013)*. Association for Computational Linguistics, Atlanta, Georgia, USA, pages 321–327. http://www.aclweb.org/anthology/S13-2053.

Preslav Nakov, Alan Ritter, Sara Rosenthal, Fabrizio Sebastiani, and Veselin Stoyanov. 2016. Semeval-2016 task 4: Sentiment analysis in twitter. In *Proceedings of the 10th International Workshop on Semantic Evaluation (SemEval-2016)*. Association for Computational Linguistics, San Diego, California, pages 1–18. http://www.aclweb.org/anthology/S16-1001.

Olutobi Owoputi, Brendan O'Connor, Chris Dyer, Kevin Gimpel, Nathan Schneider, and Noah A Smith. 2013. Improved part-of-speech tagging for online conversational text with word clusters. Association for Computational Linguistics.

Sara Rosenthal, Noura Farra, and Preslav Nakov. 2017. Semeval-2017 task 4: Sentiment analysis in twitter. In *Proceedings of the 11th International Workshop on Semantic Evaluation*. Vancouver, Canada, SemEval '17.

Theresa Wilson, Janyce Wiebe, and Paul Hoffmann. 2005. Recognizing contextual polarity in phrase-level sentiment analysis. In *Proceedings of the conference on human language technology and empirical methods in natural language processing*. Association for Computational Linguistics, pages 347–354.

Xiaodan Zhu, Svetlana Kiritchenko, and Saif Mohammad. 2014. Nrc-canada-2014: Recent improvements in the sentiment analysis of tweets. In *Proceedings of the 8th International Workshop on Semantic Evaluation (SemEval 2014)*. Association for Computational Linguistics and Dublin City University, Dublin, Ireland, pages 443–447. http://www.aclweb.org/anthology/S14-2077.

ECNU at SemEval-2017 Task 4: Evaluating Effective Features on Machine Learning Methods for Twitter Message Polarity Classification

Yunxiao Zhou[1]**, Man Lan**[1,2]***,Yuanbin Wu**[1,2]
[1]Department of Computer Science and Technology,
East China Normal University, Shanghai, P.R.China
[2]Shanghai Key Laboratory of Multidimensional Information Processing
51164500061@stu.ecnu.edu.cn, {mlan, ybwu}@cs.ecnu.edu.cn

Abstract

This paper reports our submission to subtask A of task 4 (Sentiment Analysis in Twitter, SAT) in SemEval 2017, i.e., Message Polarity Classification. We investigated several traditional Natural Language Processing (NLP) features, domain specific features and word embedding features together with supervised machine learning methods to address this task. Officially released results showed that our system ranked above average.

1   Introduction

In recent years, with the emergence of social media, more and more users have shared and obtained information through microblogging websites, such as Twitter. The study on this platform is increasingly drawing attention of many researchers and organizations. SemEval 2017 provides a universal platform for researchers to explore sentiment analysis in Twitter (Rosenthal et al., 2017) (Task 4, Sentiment Analysis in Twitter, SAT) which includes five subtasks, and we participated in subtask A: Message Polarity Classification. It aims at sentiment polarity classification of the whole tweet on a three-point scale(i.e., *Positive*, *Negative* and *Neutral*).

Given the character limitations on tweets, the sentiment orientation classification on tweets can be regarded as a sentence-level sentiment analysis task. Following previous work (Mohammad et al., 2013; Zhang et al., 2015; Wasi et al., 2014), we adopted a rich set of traditional NLP features, i.e., linguistic features (e.g., word n-gram, part-of-speech (POS) tags, etc), sentiment lexicon features (i.e., the scores calculated from eight sentiment lexicons), and domain content features (e.g., emoticons, capital words, elongated words, etc).

In consideration of rich information in the metadata of tweets, we also extracted metadata features from tweets. Moreover, several word embeddings (including general word embeddings and sentiment word vectors) were adopted. We performed a series of experiments to explore the effectiveness of each type of features and supervised machine learning algorithms.

2   System Description

We first performed data preprocessing, then extracted several types of features from tweets and metadata for sentiment analysis and constructed supervised classification models for this task.

2.1   Data Preprocessing

Firstly, we used about $5,000$ abbreviations and s-langs[1] to convert the informal writing into regular forms, e.g., "*3q*" replaced by "*thank you*", "*asap*" replaced by "*as soon as possible*", etc. And we recovered the elongated words to their original forms, e.g., "*soooooo*" to "*so*". Then the processed data was performed for tokenization, POS tagging, parsing, stemming and lemmatization using *Stanford CoreNLP* (Manning et al., 2014).

2.2   Feature Engineering

In this task, we evaluated four types of features, i.e, linguistic features, sentiment lexicon features, domain-specific features and word embedding features.

2.2.1   Linguistic Features

- *Word_RF n-grams:* We extracted *unigram*s, *bigram*s and *trigram*s features at two different levels, i.e., the original word level and the word stem level. Considering that different words make different contribution to sentimental expression, for each n-gram feature,

---

[1]https://github.com/haierlord/resource/blob/master/slangs

Proceedings of the 11th International Workshop on Semantic Evaluations (SemEval-2017), pages 812–816,
Vancouver, Canada, August 3 - 4, 2017. ©2017 Association for Computational Linguistics

we calculated *rf* (relevance frequency) value (Lan et al., 2009) to weight its importance.

- *POS:* Generally, the sentences carrying subjective emotions (i.e., positive and negative sentiment) are inclined to contain more adjectives and adverbs while the sentences without sentiment orientation (i.e., neutral) would contain more nouns. Therefore, we recorded the number of each POS tag in one sentence.

- *Negation:* Negation in a message always reverses its sentiment orientation. We manually collected 29 negations[2] from previous work in (Zhang et al., 2015) and designed two binary features. One is to indicate whether there is any negation in the tweet and the other is to record whether this tweet contains more than one negation.

2.2.2 Sentiment Lexicon Features (SentiLexi)

We employed the following eight sentiment lexicons to extract sentiment lexicon features: *Bing Liu lexicon*[3], *General Inquirer lexicon*[4], *IMDB*[5], *MPQA*[6], *NRC Emotion Sentiment Lexicon*[7], *AFINN*[8], *NRC Hashtag Sentiment Lexicon*[9], and *NRC Sentiment140 Lexicon*[10]. Since certain words may consist of mixed sentiments based on different contexts, it is not appropriate to assign only one sentiment score for this type of word. Therefore, the first five lexicons use two values for each word to represent its sentiment scores, i.e., one for positive sentiment and the other for negative sentiment. In order to unify the formats, we transformed the two scores into a one-dimensional value by subtracting negative emotion scores from positive emotion scores. Then in all sentiment lexicons, for each word the positive number indicates a positive emotion and the minus sign represents a negative emotion.

Given a tweet, we first converted all words into lowercase. Then on each sentiment lexicon, we calculated the following six scores for one message: (1) the ratio of positive words to all words, (2) the ratio of negative words to all words, (3) the maximum sentiment score, (4) the minimum sentiment score, (5) the sum of sentiment scores, (6) the sentiment score of the last word in tweet. If the word does not exist in one sentiment lexicon, its corresponding score is set to 0.

2.2.3 Domain-Specific Features

Domain-specific features are extracted from two sources. One is from the content of tweets and the other is from tweet metadata information.

Firstly, the domain specific features extracted from tweet content are shown as follows:

- *All-caps:* One binary feature is to check whether this tweet has words in uppercase.

- *Bag-of-Hashtags:* We constructed a vocabulary of hashtags appearing in the training data and then adopted the bag-of-hashtags method for each tweet.

- *Elongated:* It indicates whether the raw text of tweet contains words with one continuous character repeated more than two times, e.g., "gooooood".

- *Emoticon:* We manually collected 67 emoticons from Internet[11] and designed the following 4 binary features:
  - to record the presence or absence of positive and negative emoticons respectively in the tweet;
  - to record whether the last token is a positive or a negative emoticon.

- *Punctuation:* Punctuation marks (e.g, exclamation mark (!) and question mark (?)) usually indicate the expression of sentiment. Therefore, we designed the following 6 binary features to record:
  - whether the tweet contains an exclamation mark;
  - whether the tweet contains more than one exclamation mark;
  - whether the tweet has a question mark;
  - whether the tweet contains more than one question mark;

– whether the tweet contains both exclamation marks and question marks;

– whether the last token of this tweet is an exclamation or question mark.

Recently, several studies using tweet metadata are reported to have good performance on sentiment classification (Tang et al., 2015; Chen et al., 2016). Inspired by them, the second tweet domain-specific features we used are extracted from tweet metadata information. We first used Twitter API[12] to collect tweet metadata and then designed the following two types of features.

- *Tweet metadata*: Two binary features are to check whether this tweet has been *retweeted* and whether it has been *liked* by authenticating users. Furthermore, given one tweet, two numeric features are to record the count of *retweeted* and the count of *liked*. These two numeric features were standardized using [0-1] normalization.

- *User metadata*: In addition to the metadata of tweets, users who write tweets may also contain useful information. Thus the following 5 user metadata features are collected: *friends count, followers count, statuses count, verified* and *default profile image*. The first three numeric items are standardized using [0-1] normalization and the rest are binary values.

In total, we collected 9 metatdata features.

2.2.4 Word Embedding Features

Word embedding is a continuous-valued vector representation for each word, which usually carries syntactic and semantic information. In this work, we employed five different types of word embeddings. The *GoogleW2V* and *GloVe* are two pre-trained word vectors downloaded from Internet. The former is pre-trained on News domain and the latter is pre-trained on tweets. We also trained the *TweetW2V* on tweet domain using Google word2vec tool. Besides, taking into consideration the sentiment information of each word, previous work in (Tang et al., 2014) and (Lan et al., 2016) presented methods to learn sentiment word vectors rather than general word vectors. The last two word vectors i.e., *SWV* and *SSWE*, are expected to endow word embeddings with sentiment information and semantic information.

- *GoogleW2V:* The 300-dimensional word vectors are pre-trained on Google News with 100 billion words, available in Google[13].

- *GloVe:* The 100-dimensional word vectors are pre-trained on Twitter using GloVe, available in *GloVe*[14].

- *TweetW2V:* We adopted the *word2vec* tool[15] to obtain 100-dimensional word vectors (i.e., TweetW2V) on *NRC140 tweet corpus*(Go et al., 2009), where the corpus is made up of 1.6 million tweets (0.8 million positive and 0.8 million negative).

- *SWV:* Our previous work in (Lan et al., 2016) proposed a combined model to learn sentiment word vector (SWV) for sentiment analysis task. In this work, we learned the *SWV* on *NRC140 tweet corpus* and the dimension is set as 200.

- *SSWE:* The sentiment-specific word embedding (SSWE) model has been proposed by (Tang et al., 2014) used a multi-hidden-layers neural network to train *SSWE* on 10 million tweets with dimensionality of 50.

In order to obtain a sentence vector, we simply adopted the *min*, *max* and *mean* pooling operations on all words in a tweet message. Obviously, this combination strategy neglects the word sequence in tweet but it is simple and straightforward. As a result, the final sentence vector $V(s)$ was concatenated as $[V_{min}(s) \oplus V_{max}(s) \oplus V_{mean}(s)]$.

2.3 Learning Algorithms

We granted this task as a three-way classification task and explored four supervised machine learning algorithms: Logistic Regression (LR) implemented in *Liblinear*[16], Support Vector Machine (SVM), Stochastic Gradient Descent (SGD) and AdaBoost all implemented in *scikit-learn tools*[17].

2.4 Evaluation Metric

To evaluate the system performance, the official evaluation criterion is *macro-averaged recall*,

---

[12]https://dev.twitter.com/overview/api

[13]https://code.google.com/archive/p/word2vec
[14]http://nlp.stanford.edu/projects/glove
[15]https://code.google.com/archive/p/word2vec
[16]https://www.csie.ntu.edu.tw/ cjlin/liblinear/
[17]http://scikit-learn.org/stable/

which is calculated among three classes (i.e., positive, negative and neutral) as follows:

$$R_{macro} = \frac{R_{Pos} + R_{Neg} + R_{Neu}}{3}$$

3 Experiments

3.1 Datasets

For training set, the organizers provided only the list of tweet ID and a script for all participants to collect tweets and their corresponding metadata. However, since not all tweets and their metadata are available when downloading, participants may collect slightly different numbers of tweets for training data. Table 1 shows the statistics of the tweets we collected in our experiments. Similarly, due to missing tweets or metadata and system errors when downloading, the metadata of training, development and test set is not complete. Specifically, approximately 21% training, 18% development and 39% test sets lost their metadata information.

Dataset	Positive	Negative	Neutral	Total
train	7,310 (43%)	2,613 (15%)	7,077 (42%)	17,000
dev	7,059 (34%)	3,231 (16%)	10,342 (50%)	20,632
test	2,375 (19%)	3,972 (32%)	5,937 (48%)	12,284

Table 1: The statistics of data sets in training, development and test data. The numbers in brackets are the percentages of different classes in each data set.

3.2 Experiments on Training Data

Firstly, in order to explore the effectiveness of each feature type, we performed a series of experiments. Table 2 lists the comparison of different contributions made by different features on development set with *Logistic Regression* algorithm. We observe the following findings.

(1) All feature types make contributions to sentiment polarity classification. Their combination achieves the best performance (i.e., 63.14%).

(2) Linguistic features act as baseline and have shown their effectiveness for sentiment polarity prediction. Besides, SentiLexi makes more contributes than other domain-specific and word embeddings features. Since sentiment lexicons are constructed by expert knowledge, it is beneficial for tweet sentiment polarity prediction.

(3) The domain-specific metadata is not as effective as expected. One possible reason results

from the missing metadata downloaded by Twitter API.

Features	R_{macro}
Linguistic	0.584
.+SentiLexi	0.621 (+0.037)
.+Domain Metadata	0.623 (+0.002)
.+Domain Content	0.628 (+0.005)
.+Word Embedding	0.631 (+0.003)

Table 2: Performance of different features on development data. ".+" means to add current features to the previous feature set. The numbers in the brackets are the performance increments compared with the previous results.

Algorithms	R_{macro}
LR	0.631
SVM	0.612
SGD	0.623
AdaBoost	0.603

Table 3: Performance of different learning algorithms on development data.

Secondly, we also explored the performance of different learning algorithms. Table 3 lists the comparison of different supervised learning algorithms with all above features. Clearly, Logistic Regression algorithm outperformed other algorithms.

Therefore, the system configuration for submission is all features and LR algorithm.

3.3 Results on Test Data

Table 4 shows the results of our system and the top-ranked systems provided by organizers for this sentiment classification task. Compared with the top ranked systems, there is much room for improvement in our work. There are several possible reasons for this performance lag. First, although the linguistic features are effective, the dimensionality of *word_RF n-gram* features is quite huge (approximately $79K$ n-grams), which dominates the performance of classification rather than other low dimension features. Second, the usage of word embeddings is simple and straightforward, which neglects the word sequence and sentence structure. Third, the effects of metadata may be reduced due to lots of missing metadata.

Team ID	$R_{\mathbf{macro}}$	F_{macro}	Acc
ECNU	0.628 (15)	0.613 (13)	0.630 (12)
DataStories	0.681 (1)	0.677 (2)	0.651 (5)
BB_twtr	0.681 (1)	0.685 (1)	0.658 (3)
LIA	0.676 (3)	0.674 (3)	0.661 (2)

Table 4: Performance of our system and the top-ranked systems. The numbers in the brackets are the official rankings.

4 Conclusion

In this paper, we extracted several traditional NLP features, domain specific features and word embedding features from tweets and their metadata and adopted supervised machine learning algorithms to perform sentiment polarity classification. The system performance ranks above average. In future work, we consider to focus on developing neural networks method to model sentence with the aid of sentiment word vectors.

Acknowledgements

This research is supported by grants from Science and Technology Commission of Shanghai Municipality (14DZ2260800 and 15ZR1410700), Shanghai Collaborative Innovation Center of Trustworthy Software for Internet of Things (ZF1213) and NSFC (61402175).

References

Huimin Chen, Maosong Sun, Cunchao Tu, Yankai Lin, and Zhiyuan Liu. 2016. Neural sentiment classification with user and product attention. In *Proceedings of EMNLP*.

Alec Go, Richa Bhayani, and Lei Huang. 2009. Twitter sentiment classification using distant supervision. *CS224N Project Report, Stanford* pages 1–12.

Man Lan, Chew Lim Tan, Jian Su, and Yue Lu. 2009. Supervised and traditional term weighting methods for automatic text categorization. *IEEE transactions on pattern analysis and machine intelligence* 31(4):721–735.

Man Lan, Zhihua Zhang, Yue Lu, and Ju Wu. 2016. Three convolutional neural network-based models for learning sentiment word vectors towards sentiment analysis. In *Neural Networks (IJCNN), 2016 International Joint Conference on*. IEEE, pages 3172–3179.

Christopher D. Manning, Mihai Surdeanu, John Bauer, Jenny Finkel, Steven J. Bethard, and David McClosky. 2014. The Stanford CoreNLP natural language processing toolkit. In *Proceedings of 52nd Annual Meeting of the Association for Computational Linguistics: System Demonstrations*. pages 55–60.

Saif Mohammad, Svetlana Kiritchenko, and Xiaodan Zhu. 2013. NRC-Canada: Building the state-of-the-art in sentiment analysis of tweets. In *Second Joint Conference on Lexical and Computational Semantics (*SEM), Volume 2: Proceedings of the Seventh International Workshop on Semantic Evaluation (SemEval 2013)*. Atlanta, Georgia, USA, pages 321–327.

Sara Rosenthal, Noura Farra, and Preslav Nakov. 2017. SemEval-2017 task 4: Sentiment analysis in Twitter. In *Proceedings of the 11th International Workshop on Semantic Evaluation*. Association for Computational Linguistics, Vancouver, Canada, SemEval '17.

Duyu Tang, Bing Qin, and Ting Liu. 2015. Learning semantic representations of users and products for document level sentiment classification. In *ACL (1)*. pages 1014–1023.

Duyu Tang, Furu Wei, Nan Yang, Ming Zhou, Ting Liu, and Bing Qin. 2014. Learning sentiment-specific word embedding for twitter sentiment classification. In *The Annual Meeting of the Association for Computational Linguistics*. pages 1555–1565.

Sabih Bin Wasi, Rukhsar Neyaz, Houda Bouamor, and Behrang Mohit. 2014. Cmuq@ qatar: Using rich lexical features for sentiment analysis on twitter. *SemEval 2014* page 186.

Zhihua Zhang, Guoshun Wu, and Man Lan. 2015. Ecnu: Multi-level sentiment analysis on twitter using traditional linguistic features and word embedding features. *Proceedings of SemEval* pages 561–567.

Fortia-FBK at SemEval-2017 Task 5:
Bullish or Bearish?
Inferring Sentiment towards Brands from Financial News Headlines

Youness Mansar*, Lorenzo Gatti°, Sira Ferradans*, Marco Guerini°, and Jacopo Staiano*
*Fortia Financial Solutions, Paris, France
°Fondazione Bruno Kessler, Povo, Italy
{youness.mansar,sira.ferradans,jacopo.staiano}@fortia.fr
{l.gatti,guerini}@fbk.eu

Abstract

In this paper, we describe a methodology to infer *Bullish* or *Bearish* sentiment towards companies/brands. More specifically, our approach leverages affective lexica and word embeddings in combination with convolutional neural networks to infer the sentiment of financial news headlines towards a target company. Such architecture was used and evaluated in the context of the SemEval 2017 challenge (task 5, subtask 2), in which it obtained the best performance.

1 Introduction

Real time information is key for decision making in highly technical domains such as finance. The explosive growth of financial technology industry (*Fintech*) continued in 2016, partially due to the current interest in the market for Artificial Intelligence-based technologies[1].

Opinion-rich texts such as micro-blogging and news can have an important impact in the financial sector (*e.g.* raise or fall in stock value) or in the overall economy (*e.g.* the Greek public debt crisis). In such a context, having granular access to the opinions of an important part of the population is of key importance to any public and private actor in the field. In order to take advantage of this raw data, it is thus needed to develop machine learning methods allowing to convert unstructured text into information that can be managed and exploited.

In this paper, we address the sentiment analysis problem applied to financial headlines, where the goal is, for a given news headline and target company, to infer its polarity score *i.e.* how positive (or negative) the sentence is with respect to the target company. Previous research (Goonatilake and Herath, 2007) has highlighted the association between news items and market fluctiations; hence, in the financial domain, sentiment analysis can be used as a proxy for *bullish* (i.e. positive, upwards trend) or *bearish* (i.e. negative, downwards trend) attitude towards a specific financial actor, allowing to identify and monitor in real-time the sentiment associated with e.g. stocks or brands.

Our contribution leverages pre-trained word embeddings (GloVe, trained on wikipedia+gigaword corpus), the DepecheMood affective lexicon, and convolutional neural networks.

2 Related Works

While image and sound come with a natural high dimensional embedding, the issue of *which is the best representation* is still an open research problem in the context of natural language and text. It is beyond the scope of this paper to do a thorough overview of word representations, for this we refer the interest reader to the excellent review provided by (Mandelbaum and Shalev, 2016). Here, we will just introduce the main representations that are related to the proposed method.

Word embeddings. In the seminal paper (Bengio et al., 2003), the authors introduce a statistical language model computed in an unsupervised training context using shallow neural networks. The goal was to predict the following word, given the previous context in the sentence, showing a major advance with respect to n-grams. Collobert *et al.* (Collobert et al., 2011) empirically proved

---

[1] F. Desai, "The Age of Artificial Intelligence in Fintech" https://www.forbes.com/sites/falgunidesai/2016/06/30/the-age-of-artificial-intelligence-in-fintech

S. Delventhal, "Global Fintech Investment Hits Record High in 2016" http://www.investopedia.com/articles/markets/061316/global-fintech-investment-hits-record-high-2016.asp

Proceedings of the 11th International Workshop on Semantic Evaluations (SemEval-2017), pages 817–822,
Vancouver, Canada, August 3 - 4, 2017. ©2017 Association for Computational Linguistics

the usefulness of using unsupervised word representations for a variety of different NLP tasks and set the neural network architecture for many current approaches. Mikolov *et al.* (Mikolov et al., 2013) proposed a simplified model (`word2vec`) that allows to train on larger corpora, and showed how semantic relationships emerge from this training. Pennington *et al.* (Pennington et al., 2014), with the `GloVe` approach, maintain the semantic capacity of `word2vec` while introducing the statistical information from latent semantic analysis (LSA) showing that they can improve in semantic and syntactic tasks.

Sentiment and Affective Lexica. In recent years, several approaches have been proposed to build lexica containing prior sentiment polarities (sentiment lexica) or multi-dimensional affective scores (affective lexica). The goal of these methods is to associate such scores to raw tokens or tuples, e.g. `lemma#pos` where `lemma` is the lemma of a token, and `pos` its part of speech.

There is usually a trade-off between coverage (the amount of entries) and precision (the accuracy of the sentiment information). For instance, regarding sentiment lexica, *SentiWordNet* (Esuli and Sebastiani, 2006), (Baccianella et al., 2010), associates each entry with the numerical scores, ranging from 0 (negative) to 1 (positive); following this approach, it has been possible to automatically obtain a list of 155k words, compensating a low precision with a high coverage (Gatti et al., 2016). On the other side of the spectrum, we have methods such as (Bradley and Lang, 1999), (Taboada et al., 2011), (Warriner et al., 2013) with low coverage (from 1k to 14k words), but for which the precision is maximized. These scores were manually assigned by multiple annotators, and in some cases validated by crowd-sourcing (Taboada et al., 2011).

Finally, a binary sentiment score is provided in the *General Inquirer* lexicon (Stone et al., 1966), covering 4k sentiment-bearing words, and expanded to 6k words by (Wilson et al., 2005).

Turning to affective lexica, where multiple dimensions of affect are taken into account, we mention *WordNetAffect* (Strapparava and Valitutti, 2004), which provides manual affective annotations of WordNet synsets (ANGER, JOY, FEAR, etc.): it contains 900 annotated synsets and 1.6k words in the form `lemma#PoS#sense`, which correspond to roughly 1k `lemma#PoS` entries.

AffectNet (Cambria and Hussain, 2012), contains 10k words taken from ConceptNet and aligned with WordNetAffect, and extends the latter to concepts like 'have breakfast'. *Fuzzy Affect Lexicon* (Subasic and Huettner, 2001) contains roughly 4k `lemma#PoS` manually annotated by one linguist using 80 emotion labels. *EmoLex* (Mohammad and Turney, 2013) contains almost 10k lemmas annotated with an intensity label for each emotion using Mechanical Turk. Finally, *Affect database* is an extension of *SentiFul* (Neviarouskaya et al., 2007) and contains 2.5k words in the form `lemma#PoS`. The latter is the only lexicon providing words annotated also with emotion scores rather than only with labels.

In this work, we exploit the `DepecheMood` affective lexicon proposed by (Staiano and Guerini, 2014): this resource has been built in a completely unsupervised fashion, from affective scores assigned by readers to news articles; notably, due to its automated crowd-sourcing-based approach, `DepecheMood` allows for both high-coverage and high-precision. `DepecheMood` provides scores for more than 37k entries, on the following affective dimensions: *Afraid, Happy, Angry, Sad, Inspired, Don't Care, Inspired, Amused, Annoyed.* We refer the reader to (Staiano and Guerini, 2014; Guerini and Staiano, 2015) for more details.

The affective dimensions encoded in `DepecheMood` are directly connected to the emotions evoked by a news article in the readers, hence it seemed a natural choice for the SemEval 2017 task at hand.

Sentence Classification. A modification of (Collobert et al., 2011) was proposed by Kim (Kim, 2014) for sentence classification, showing how a simple model together with pre-trained word representations can be highly performing. Our method builds on this conv-net method. Further, we took advantage of the rule-based sentiment analyser VADER (Hutto and Gilbert, 2014) (for Valence Aware Dictionary for sEntiment Reasoning), which builds upon a sentiment lexicon and a predefined set of simple rules.

3 Data

The data consists of a set of financial news headlines, crawled from several online outlets such as Yahoo Finance, where each sentence contains one or more company names/brands.

Each tuple (headline, company) is annotated with a sentiment score ranging from -1 (very negative, bearish) to 1 (very positive, bullish). The training/test sets provided contain 1142 and 491 annotated sentences, respectively.

A sample instance is reported below:

> Headline: *"Morrisons book second consecutive quarter of sales growth"*
>
> Company name: *"Morrisons"*
>
> Sentiment score: *0.43*

4 Method

In Figure 1, we can see the overall architecture of our model.

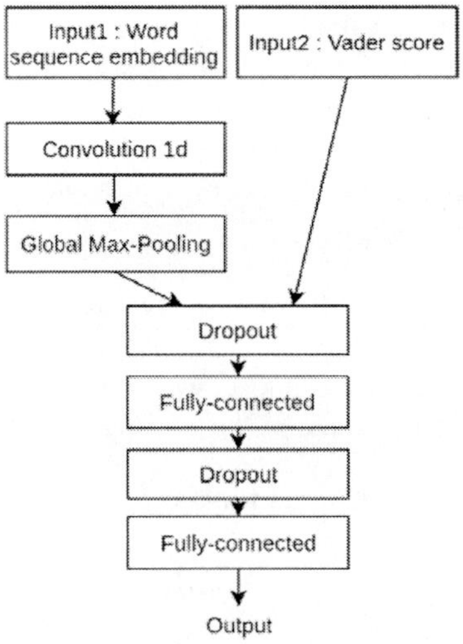

Figure 1: Network architecture

4.1 Sentence representation and preprocessing

Pre-processing. Minimal preprocessing was adopted in our approach: we replaced the target company's name with a fixed word <company> and numbers with <number>. The sentences were then tokenized using spaces as separator and keeping punctuation symbols as separate tokens.

Sentence representation. The words are represented as fixed length vectors u_i resulting from the concatenation of GloVe pre-trained embeddings and DepecheMood (Staiano and Guerini, 2014)

lexicon representation. Since we cannot directly concatenate token-based embeddings (provided in GloVe) with the lemma#PoS-based representation available in DepecheMood, we proceeded to re-build the latter in token-based form, applying the exact same methodology albeit with two differences: we started from a larger dataset (51.9K news articles instead of 25.3K) and used a frequency cut-off, *i.e.* keeping only those tokens that appear at least 5 times in the corpus[2].

These word-level representation are used as the first layer of our network. During training we allow the weights of the representation to be updated. We further add the VADER score for the sentence under analysis. The complete sentence representation is presented in Algorithm 1.

Algorithm 1: Sentence representation

Input : An input sentence s, and the GloVe word embeddings W

Output: The sentence embedding x

1   $v = \text{VADER}(s)$
2   **foreach** w_i *in* W **do**
3 | $u_i = [\text{GloVe}(w_i, W), \text{DepecheMood}(w_i)]$
4   **end**
5   $x = [v, \{u_i\}_{i=1,\dots,|W|}]$

4.2 Architectural Details

Convolutional Layer. A 1D convolutional layer with filters of multiple sizes $\{2, 3, 4\}$ is applied to the sequence of word embeddings. The filters are used to learn useful translation-invariant representations of the sequential input data. A global max-pooling is then applied across the sequence for each filter output.

Concat Layer. We apply the concatenation layer to the output of the global max-pooling and the output of VADER.

Activation functions. The activation function used between layers is ReLU (Nair and Hinton, 2010) except for the out layer where tanh is used to map the output into [-1, 1] range.

---

[2] Our tests showed that: (i) the larger dataset allowed improving both precision on the SemEval2007 Affective Text Task (Strapparava and Mihalcea, 2007) dataset, originally used for the evaluation of DepecheMood, and coverage (from the initial 183K unique tokens we went to 292K entries) of the lexicon; (ii) we found no significant difference in performance between lemma#PoS and token versions built starting from the same dataset.

Regularization. Dropout (Srivastava et al., 2014) was used to avoid over-fitting to the training data: it prevents the co-adaptation of the neurones and it also provides an inexpensive way to average an exponential number of networks. In addition, we averaged the output of multiple networks with the same architecture but trained independently with different random seeds in order to reduce noise.

Loss function. The loss function used is the cosine distance between the predicted scores and the gold standard for each batch. Even though stochastic optimization methods like Adam (Kingma and Ba, 2014) are usually applied to loss functions that are written as a sum of per-sample loss, which is not the case for the cosine, it converges to an acceptable solution. The loss can be written as :

$$\text{Loss} = \sum_{B \in \text{Batches}} 1 - \cos(\hat{\mathbf{V}}_B, \mathbf{V}_B), \quad (1)$$

where $\hat{\mathbf{V}}_B$ and $\mathbf{V}_B$ are the predicted and true sentiment scores for batch B, respectively.

The algorithm for training/testing our model is reported in Algorithm 2.

Algorithm 2: Training/Testing algorithm. To build our model, we set N=10.

Input	: A set of training instances S, with ground-truth scores y, and the set of test sentences S_o
Output	: A set of trained models M, and the predictions y_o for the test set S_o
Parameters:	The number N of models to train

```
1  preprocess(X) // see sec 3.1
2  foreach s_i in S do
3  |   X_i = sentence_representation(s_i)
   |       // see Alg. 1
4  end
5  foreach n ∈ N do
6  |   M_n = min Loss(X) // see Eq. 1
7  end
8  foreach n ∈ N do
9  |   y_n = evaluate(X_o, M_n)
10 end
11 y_o(u) = (1/N) Σ_n^N y_n(u)
```

---

5 Results

In this section, we report the results obtained by our model according to challenge official evaluation metric, which is based cosine-similarity and described in (Ghosh et al., 2015). Results are reported for three diverse configurations: (i) the full system; (ii) the system without using word embeddings (*i.e.* `Glove` and `DepecheMood`); and (iii) the system without using pre-processing. In Table 1 we show model's performances on the challenge training data, in a 5-fold cross-validation setting.

Algorithm	mean±std
Full	0.701 ±0.023
No embeddings	0.586 ±0.017
No pre-processing	0.648 ±0.022

Table 1: Cross-validation results

Further, the final performances obtained with our approach on the challenge test set are reported in Table 2. Consistently with the cross-validation performances shown earlier, we observe the beneficial impact of word-representations and basic pre-processing.

Algorithm	Test scores
Full	0.745
No embeddings	0.660
No pre-processing	0.678

Table 2: Final results

6 Conclusions

In this paper, we presented the network architecture used for the Fortia-FBK submission to the Semeval-2017 Task 5 (Cortis et al., 2017), Subtask 2 challenge, with the goal of predicting positive (bullish) or negative (bearish) attitude towards a target brand from financial news headlines. The proposed system ranked 1st in such challenge.

Our approach is based on 1d convolutions and uses fine-tuning of unsupervised word representations and a rule based sentiment model in its inputs. We showed that the use of pre-computed word representations allows to reduce over-fitting and to achieve significantly better generalization, while some basic pre-processing was needed to further improve the performance.

References

S. Baccianella, A. Esuli, and F. Sebastiani. 2010. Senti-WordNet 3.0: An enhanced lexical resource for sentiment analysis and opinion mining. In *Proceedings of LREC 2010*. Valletta, Malta, pages 2200–2204.

Yoshua Bengio, Réjean Ducharme, Pascal Vincent, and Christian Jauvin. 2003. A neural probabilistic language model. *Journal of machine learning research* 3(Feb):1137–1155.

M.M. Bradley and P.J. Lang. 1999. Affective norms for English words (ANEW): Instruction manual and affective ratings. *Technical Report C-1, University of Florida* .

Erik Cambria and Amir Hussain. 2012. *Sentic computing*. Springer.

Ronan Collobert, Jason Weston, Léon Bottou, Michael Karlen, Koray Kavukcuoglu, and Pavel Kuksa. 2011. Natural language processing (almost) from scratch. *Journal of Machine Learning Research* 12(Aug):2493–2537.

Keith Cortis, André Freitas, Tobias Dauert, Manuela Huerlimann, Manel Zarrouk, Siegfried Handschuh, and Brian Davis. 2017. Semeval-2017 task 5: Fine-grained sentiment analysis on financial microblogs and news. In *Proceedings of the 11th International Workshop on Semantic Evaluation (SemEval-2017)*. Association for Computational Linguistics, Vancouver, Canada, pages 517–533. http://www.aclweb.org/anthology/S17-2089.

A. Esuli and F. Sebastiani. 2006. SentiWordNet: A publicly available lexical resource for opinion mining. In *Proceedings of LREC 2006*. Genova, IT, pages 417–422.

Lorenzo Gatti, Marco Guerini, and Marco Turchi. 2016. SentiWords: Deriving a high precision and high coverage lexicon for sentiment analysis. *IEEE Transactions on Affective Computing* 7(4):409–421.

Aniruddha Ghosh, Guofu Li, Tony Veale, Paolo Rosso, Ekaterina Shutova, John Barnden, and Antonio Reyes. 2015. Semeval-2015 task 11: Sentiment analysis of figurative language in twitter. In *Proceedings of the 9th International Workshop on Semantic Evaluation (SemEval 2015)*. pages 470–478.

Rohitha Goonatilake and Susantha Herath. 2007. The volatility of the stock market and news. *International Research Journal of Finance and Economics* 3(11):53–65.

Marco Guerini and Jacopo Staiano. 2015. Deep feelings: A massive cross-lingual study on the relation between emotions and virality. In *Proceedings of WWW 2015*. pages 299–305.

C.J. Hutto and Eric Gilbert. 2014. Vader: A parsimonious rule-based model for sentiment analysis of social media text. In *Proceedings of ICWSM 2014*.

Yoon Kim. 2014. Convolutional neural networks for sentence classification. In *Proceedings of the 2014 Conference on Empirical Methods in Natural Language Processing, EMNLP 2014*. pages 1746–1751.

Diederik P. Kingma and Jimmy Ba. 2014. Adam: A method for stochastic optimization. *CoRR* abs/1412.6980. http://arxiv.org/abs/1412.6980.

Amit Mandelbaum and Adi Shalev. 2016. Word embeddings and their use in sentence classification tasks. *arXiv preprint arXiv:1610.08229* .

Tomas Mikolov, Kai Chen, Greg Corrado, and Jeffrey Dean. 2013. Efficient estimation of word representations in vector space. *arXiv preprint arXiv:1301.3781* .

Saif M Mohammad and Peter D Turney. 2013. Crowdsourcing a word–emotion association lexicon. *Computational Intelligence* 29(3):436–465.

Vinod Nair and Geoffrey E. Hinton. 2010. Rectified linear units improve restricted Boltzmann machines.

Alena Neviarouskaya, Helmut Prendinger, and Mitsuru Ishizuka. 2007. Textual affect sensing for sociable and expressive online communication. In *Affective Computing and Intelligent Interaction*, Springer Berlin Heidelberg, volume 4738, pages 218–229.

Jeffrey Pennington, Richard Socher, and Christopher D Manning. 2014. GloVe: Global vectors for word representation. In *Proceedings of EMNLP 2014*. volume 14, pages 1532–43.

Nitish Srivastava, Geoffrey E Hinton, Alex Krizhevsky, Ilya Sutskever, and Ruslan Salakhutdinov. 2014. Dropout: a simple way to prevent neural networks from overfitting. *Journal of Machine Learning Research* 15(1):1929–1958.

Jacopo Staiano and Marco Guerini. 2014. Depeche Mood: a lexicon for emotion analysis from crowd annotated news. In *Proceedings of ACL 2014*. The Association for Computer Linguistics, volume 2, pages 427–433.

P.J. Stone, D.C. Dunphy, and M.S. Smith. 1966. *The General Inquirer: A Computer Approach to Content Analysis*. MIT press.

C. Strapparava and A. Valitutti. 2004. WordNet-Affect: an affective extension of WordNet. In *Proceedings of LREC 2004*. Lisbon, pages 1083 – 1086.

Carlo Strapparava and Rada Mihalcea. 2007. Semeval-2007 task 14: Affective text. In *Proceedings of the 4th International Workshop on Semantic Evaluations*. Association for Computational Linguistics, pages 70–74.

Pero Subasic and Alison Huettner. 2001. Affect analysis of text using fuzzy semantic typing. *Fuzzy Systems, IEEE Transactions on* 9(4):483–496.

M. Taboada, J. Brooke, M. Tofiloski, K. Voll, and M. Stede. 2011. Lexicon-based methods for sentiment analysis. *Computational linguistics* 37(2):267–307.

Amy Beth Warriner, Victor Kuperman, and Marc Brysbaert. 2013. Norms of valence, arousal, and dominance for 13,915 English lemmas. *Behavior research methods* 45(4):1191–1207.

T. Wilson, J. Wiebe, and P. Hoffmann. 2005. Recognizing contextual polarity in phrase-level sentiment analysis. In *Proceedings of the conference on HLT/EMNLP 2005*. Vancouver, Canada.

SSN_MLRG1 at SemEval-2017 Task 5: Fine-Grained Sentiment Analysis Using Multiple Kernel Gaussian Process Regression Model

Angel Deborah S, S Milton Rajendram, T T Mirnalinee
SSN College of Engineering
Kalavakkam 603 110, India
angeldeboarahs@ssn.edu.in

Abstract

The system developed by the SSN_MLRG1 team for Semeval-2017 task 5 on fine-grained sentiment analysis uses Multiple Kernel Gaussian Process for identifying the optimistic and pessimistic sentiments associated with companies and stocks. Since the comments on the same companies and stocks may display different emotions depending on time, their properities like smoothness and periodicity may vary. Our experiments show that while single Kernel Gaussian Process can learn some properties well, Multiple Kernel Gaussian Process are effective in learning the presence of different properties.

1 Introduction

Sentiments have been widely studied as they play an important role in human intelligence, rational decision making, social interaction, perception, memory, learning and creativity (Pang and Lee, 2008; Strapparava and Mihalcea, 2008; Maas et al., 2011; Li et al., 2015). The ability to discern and understand human sentiments is critical for making interactive human-like computer agents, and requires the use of machine learning approaches (Alm et al., 2005).

2 Gaussian Process

Gaussian Process (GP) is a Bayesian non-parametric approach to machine learning. A Gaussian Process is a collection of random variables, any infinite number of which have a joint Gaussian distribution (Rasmussen and Williams, 2006). Using a Gaussian process, we can define a distribution over functions $f(x)$,

$$f(x) \sim GP(m(x), k(x, x')) \qquad (1)$$

where $m(x)$ is the mean function, usually defined to be zero, and $k(x, x')$ is the covariance function (or kernel function) that defines the prior properties of the functions considered for inference. Gaussian Process has the following main advantages (Cohn and Specia, 2013; Cohn et al., 2014).

- The kernel hyper-parameters can be learned via evidence maximization.
- GP provides full probabilistic prediction, and an estimate of uncertainty in the prediction.
- Compared to SVMs which need unbiased datasets for good performance, GPs do not usually suffer from this problem.
- GP can be easily extended and incorporated into a hierarchical Bayesian model.
- GP works really well when combined with kernel models.
- GP works well for small datasets too.

2.1 Gaussian Process Regression

The Gaussian Process regression framework assumes that, given an input x, output y is a noise corrupted version of a latent function evaluation. In a regression setting, we usually consider a Gaussian likelihood, which allows us to obtain a closed form solution for the test posterior (Ebden, 2008). Gaussian Process model, as they are applied in machine learning, is an attractive way of doing non-parametric Bayesian modeling for a supervised learning problem. GP-based modeling has the ability to learn hyper-parameters directly from data by maximizing the marginal likelihood. Like other kernel methods, the Gaussian Process can be optimized exactly, given the values of their hyper-parameters and this often allows a fine and precise trade-off between fitting the data and smoothing.

A practical implementation of Gaussian Process Regression (GPR) (Rasmussen and Williams, 2006) is outlined in the following algorithm:

Proceedings of the 11th International Workshop on Semantic Evaluations (SemEval-2017), pages 823–826,
Vancouver, Canada, August 3 - 4, 2017. ©2017 Association for Computational Linguistics

Algorithm: Predictions and log-marginal likelihood for GP regression.

Input: X (training inputs) , $\mathbf{y}$ (training targets), k (covariance function), σ_n^2 (noise level), x_* (test input).

Output: Predictive mean, variance and log-marginal likelihood.

1. $L := \text{cholesky}(K + \sigma_n^2 I)$
2. $\alpha := L^T \backslash (L \backslash y)$
3. $\overline{f}_* := \mathbf{k}_*{}^T \alpha$
4. $\mathbf{v} := L \backslash \mathbf{k}_*$
5. $V[f_*] := k(\mathbf{x}_*, \mathbf{x}_*) - \mathbf{v}^T \mathbf{v}$
6. $\log p(\mathbf{y}|X) := -\frac{1}{2}\mathbf{y}^T\alpha - \sum_i \log L_{ii} - \frac{n}{2}\log 2\pi$
7. return f_* (mean), $V[f_*]$ (variance), $\log p(\mathbf{y}|X)$ (log-marginal likelihood)

2.2 Multiple Kernel Gaussian Process

The heart of every Gaussian process model is a covariance kernel. The kernel $\mathbf{k}$ directly specifies the covariance between every pair of input points in the dataset. The particular choice of covariance function determines the properties such as smoothness, length scales, and amplitude, drawn from the GP prior. Therefore, it is an important part of GP modelling to select an appropriate covariance function for a particular problem. Multi Kernel Learning (MKL) — using multiple kernels instead of a single one — can be useful in two ways:

- Different kernels correspond to different notions of similarity, and instead of trying to find which works best, a learning method does the picking for us, or may use a combination of them. Using a specific kernel may be a source of bias which is avoided by allowing the learner to choose from among a set of kernels.

- Different kernels may use inputs coming from different representations, possibly from different sources or modalities.

(Gonen and Alpaydin, 2011; Wilson and Adams, 2013) explain how multiple kernels definitely give a powerful performance. (Gonen and Alpaydin, 2011) also describes in detail various methodologies to combine kernels. (Wilson and Adams, 2013) introduces simple closed form kernels that can be used with Gaussian Processes to discover patterns and enable extrapolation. The kernels support a broad class of stationary covariances, but Gaussian Process inference remains simple and analytic.

We studied the possibility of using multiple kernels to explain the relation between the input data and the labels. While there is a body of work on using Multi Kernel Learning (MKL) on numerical data and images, yet applying MKL on text is still an exploration. We have used Exponential kernel and Multi-Layer Perceptron kernel together with Squared Exponential kernel, and found the combinations to give better results. The text data used in sentiment analysis is collected over a period of time. Comments on the same topic may exhibit different emotions, depending on the time it was made, and hence their properties, such as smoothness and periodicity, also vary with time. Since any one kernel learns only certain properties well, multiple kernels will be effective in detecting the presence of different emotions in the data.

The MKL algorithms use different learning methods for determining the kernel combination function. It is divided into five major categories: Fixed rules, Heuristic approaches, Optimization approaches, Bayesian approaches and Boosting approaches. The combination of kernels in different learning methods can be performed in one of the two basic ways, either using linear combination or using non-linear combination. Linear combination seems more promising (Gonen and Alpaydin, 2011), and have two basic categories: unweighted sum (i.e., using sum or mean of the kernels as the combined kernel) and weighted sum. Non-linear combination use non-linear functions of kernels, namely multiplication, power, and exponentiation. We have studied the fixed rule linear combination in this work which can be represented as

$$\mathbf{k}(x, x') = \mathbf{k_1}(x, x') + \mathbf{k_2}(x, x') + \ldots + \mathbf{k_n}(x, x'). \tag{2}$$

For training, we have used one-step method together with the simultaneous approach. One-step methods, in a single pass, calculate both the parameters of the combination function, and those of the combined base learner; and the simultaneous approach ensures that both sets of parameters are learned together.

3 System Overview

The system comprises of the following modules: data extraction, preprocessing, feature vector generation, and multi-kernel Gaussian Process model building. The algorithm for preprocessing of the data and feature vector building is outlined below:

Algorithm: Preprocess the data and generate feature vectors.

Input: Input dataset.

Output: Dictionary with the key - value pair and BoW Feature vector.

begin

1. Perform lemmatization using `WordNet Lemmatizer` from the NLTK tool kit.
2. Perform tokenization using the `wordpunct` tokenize function of the NLTK toolkit.
3. Set the integer value for the `train` variable.
4. Build data dictionaries for training sentences.
5. Build a data dictionary with words mapped to their indices.
6. Generate feature vectors for the train sets that encode a BoW representation.
7. Build a dictionary with the key-value pairs. The key is the emotion and the value is a matrix where rows are BoW vectors.

end

The Multi-Kernel Gaussian Process (MKGP) model building is outlined in the following algorithm.

Algorithm: Build a Multi-Kernel Gaussian Process model.

Input: Input dataset with BoW feature representation.

Output: Learned model,

begin

1. Split the training dataset into XTrain which contains the features and YTrain that contains the emotion scores.
2. Build the initial regression model using appropriate kernel function.
3. Optimize the regression model with the hyper-parameters (length scale, variance, noise).
4. Return the learned model.

end

The Multi-Kernel Gaussian Process model is implemented using linear combination method which takes the unweighted sum of the kernels.

4 Comparison Using Different Kernels

The output submitted for the task was based on the linear combination of Squared Exponential kernel and Exponential kernel.

4.1 Kernels

The *Squared Exponential (SE)* kernel, sometimes called the Gaussian or Radial Basis Function (RBF), has become the default kernel in GPs. To model the long term smooth-rising trend we use a Squared Exponential covariance term.

$$\mathbf{k}(x, x') = \sigma^2 \exp\left(-\frac{(x - x')^2}{2l^2}\right). \quad (3)$$

where σ^2 is the variance and l is the length-scale.

The usage of *Exponential kernel* is particularly common in machine learning and hence is also used in GPs. They perform tasks such as statistical classification, regression analysis, and cluster analysis on data in an implicit space.

$$\mathbf{k}(x, x') = \sigma^2 \exp\left(-\frac{(x - x')}{2l^2}\right) \quad (4)$$

The *Multi-Layer Perceptron* kernel has also found use in GP as it can learn the periodicity property present in the dataset; its $\mathbf{k}(x, x')$ is given by

$$\frac{2\sigma^2}{\pi} \sin^{-1} \frac{(\sigma_w^2 x^T x' + \sigma_b^2)}{\sqrt{\sigma_w^2 x^T x + \sigma_b^2 + 1}\sqrt{\sigma_w^2 x'^T x' \sigma_b^2 + 1}} \quad (5)$$

where σ^2 is the variance, σ_w^2 is the vector of the variances of the prior over input weights and σ_b^2 is the variance of the prior over bias parameters. The kernel can learn more effectively because of the additional parameters σ_w^2 and σ_b^2.

4.2 Performance Evaluation

Other combinations of the kernel were also tried after submission. One such kernel used for experimentation purpose was Multi-Layer Perception Kernel. The results of the Single Kernel and Multi-Kernel GP on subtask 1 dataset are collated in Table 1. The results of the Single Kernel and

Table 1: A performance comparison based on Cosine Similarity (CS), Pearson Score (PS) and Mean Absolute Error (MAE) for subtask 1 dataset

Model	CS	PS	MAE
SGP	0.6942	0.6694	0.2003
MKGP(R+E)	0.7044	0.6809	0.1965
MKGP(R+E+M)	0.7099	0.6864	0.1931
MKGP(R+M)	**0.7106**	**0.6872**	**0.1930**

Multi-Kernel GP on subtask 2 dataset are shown in Table 2. The kernel combinations used in Table 1 and Table 2 are

Table 2: A performance comparison based on Cosine Similarity (CS), Pearson Score (PS) and Mean Absolute Error (MAE) for subtask 2 dataset

Model	CS	PS	MAE
SGP	0.5590	0.5615	0.2506
MKGP(R+E)	0.5530	0.5569	0.2558
MKGP(R+E+M)	0.5864	0.5870	0.2445
MKGP(R+M)	**0.5931**	**0.5928**	**0.2426**

SGP: Single Kernel Gaussian Process with Radial Basis Function (RBF) kernel,

MKGP(R+E): Multi Kernel Gaussian Process with sum of RBF and Exponential kernels,

MKGP(R+E+M): Multi Kernel Gaussian Process with sum of RBF, Exponential, and Multi-Layer Perceptron kernels,

MKGP(R+M): Multi Kernel Gaussian Process with sum of RBF and Multi-Layer Perceptron kernels.

The evaluation considered 70% of the dataset for training and 30% for testing. The greater the Cosine Similarity (CS) and the Pearson Score (PS), and the smaller the Mean Absolute Error (MAE), the better the performance of the system. The tables show that MKGP(R+M), Multi Kernel Gaussian Process with sum of Squared Exponential and Multi-Layer Perceptron kernels, performs better.

5   Official Evaluation

The systems developed were evaluated based on Cosine Similarity measure. Our system ranked fifth position with Cosine Similarity of 0.7347 for subtask 1 and fifteenth position with Cosine Similarity of 0.6657 for subtask 2.

6   Conclusion

In this paper, we have presented a Multi Kernel Gaussian Process(MKGP) regression model for fine-grained sentiment analysis of financial microblogs and news. We used Bag of Words input feature vectors as input and fixed rule multi kernel learning to build GP model and found it to perform better than single kernel learning. The results can be further enhanced by using different feature generation approaches and multi kernel learning approaches.

References

Cecilia Ovesdotter Alm, Dan Roth, and Richard Sproat. 2005. Emotions from text: Machine learning for text-based emotion prediction. In *Proceedings of Human Language Technology Conference and Conference on Empirical Methods in Natural Language Processing (HLT/EMNLP)-2005.* ACL, pages 579–586.

Trevor Cohn, Daniel Beck, and Lucia Specia. 2014. Joint emotion analysis via multi-task gaussian processes. In *Proceedings of EMNLP 2014, The International Conference on Empirical Methods in Natural Language Processing.* Journal of Machine Learning Research, pages 1798–1803.

Trevor Cohn and Lucia Specia. 2013. Modelling annotator bias with multi-task gaussian processes: An application to machine translation quality estimation. In *Proceedings of the 51st Annual Meeting of the ACL-2013.* ACL, pages 32–42.

M Ebden. 2008. Gaussian processes for regression: A quick introduction. *arXiv.org* .

Mehmet Gonen and Ethem Alpaydin. 2011. Multiple kernel learning algorithms. *Journal of Machine Learning Research* 24(11):2211–2268.

Shoushan Li, Lei Huang, Rong Wang, and Guodong Zhou. 2015. Sentence-level emotion classification with label and context dependence. In *Proceedings of the 53rd Annual Meeting of the ACL and the 7th International Joint Conference on Natural Language Processing.* ACL, pages 1045–1053.

Andrew L. Maas, Raymond E. Daly, Peter T. Pham, Dan Huang, Andrew Y. Ng, and Christopher Potts. 2011. Learning word vectors for sentiment analysis. In *PHLT '11 Proceedings of the 49th Annual Meeting of the ACL: Human Language Technologies.* ACL, pages 142–150.

Bo Pang and Lillian Lee. 2008. Opinion mining and sentiment analysis. *Foundations and Trends in Information Retrieval* 2(1):1–135.

Carl Edward Rasmussen and Christopher K. I. Williams. 2006. *Gaussian processes for machine learning*, volume 1. MIT Press Cambridge, Englewood Cliffs, NJ.

Carlo Strapparava and Rada Mihalcea. 2008. Learning to identify emotions in text. In *SAC '08 Proceedings of the 2008 ACM symposium on Applied computing.* pages 1556–1560.

A. G. Wilson and R. P. Adams. 2013. Gaussian process kernels for pattern discovery and extrapolation. In *Proceedings of ICML 2013, The International Conference on Machine Learning.* Journal of Machine Learning Research, pages 1067–1075.

IBA-Sys at SemEval-2017 Task 5: Fine-Grained Sentiment Analysis on Financial Microblogs and News

Zarmeen Nasim

Institute of Business Administration (IBA)
Karachi, Pakistan
znasim@khi.iba.edu.pk

Abstract

This paper presents the details of our system IBA-Sys that participated in SemEval Task: Fine-grained sentiment analysis on Financial Microblogs and News. Our system participated in both tracks. For microblogs track, a supervised learning approach was adopted and the regressor was trained using XgBoost regression algorithm on lexicon features. For news headlines track, an ensemble of regressors was used to predict sentiment score. One regressor was trained using TF-IDF features and another was trained using the n-gram features. The source code is available at Github [1]

1 Introduction

Sentiment Analysis has become a very active area of research during the last decade. The reason behind this rising popularity is twofold. First, sentiment analysis has a great number of applications varying from academia to commercial domains such as customer support, brand management, social media marketing e.t.c. Second, sentiment analysis involves a number of challenges such as handling unstructured and noisy text, anaphora resolution, context understanding and many others.

Sentiment Analysis now becomes an interesting area of research in the Financial domain also. Researchers have shown that the consumer opinions and sentiments have a profound impact on market dynamics [(Goonatilake and Herath, 2007),(Van de Kauter et al., 2015)]. This further leads to the research interest in predicting stock market from social media discussions and

news text (Bollen et al., 2011). Earlier attempts of sentiment analysis in Financial domain includes the work of McDonald and Loughran (Loughran and McDonald, 2011) in 2011. They developed the list of words with associated sentiment polarities for classifying sentiment in financial text. The SemEval 2017 Fine-grained sentiment analysis on financial microblogs and news task (Cortis et al., 2017) aims at identifying bullish(optimistic) and bearish(pessimistic) sentiment associated with companies and stocks. This task involved two tracks. Track 1 included microblog messages and track 2 included the dataset of news statements and headlines. In both tracks, the task was to predict the sentiment score for a stock (in track 1) and for a company (in track 2) in a given instance of text. The challenging part was that the sentiment values are on a continuous scale between -1(very negative) to +1(very positive) rather than discrete labels.

IBA-Sys participated in both subtasks. For subtask 1, our system was trained to predict the sentiment score on the given microblog with relevance to the given cashtag. For subtask 2, our system was trained to predict the sentiment score on the given piece of headline with relevance to the given company name. Our system IBA-Sys participated in both tracks. In track 1, we were among top 5 teams whereas, in track 2, our system secured 14th position.

The remainder of this paper is organized as follows. Section 2 describes the datasets in detail. Section 3 presents the preprocessing steps applied to clean the dataset. Section 4 and Section 5 discusses the features and methodology used to build our system. Section 6 discusses experimental results and official submission. Finally, Section 7 concludes this paper.

---

[1]https://github.com/zarmeen92/
IBA-Sys-SemEval-2017

827

Proceedings of the 11th International Workshop on Semantic Evaluations (SemEval-2017), pages 827–831,
Vancouver, Canada, August 3 - 4, 2017. ©2017 Association for Computational Linguistics

Table 1: Statistic of Dataset

Subtask	Training Set	Test Set
Microblogs	1694	799
News Headlines	1142	491

2 Datasets

This section presents the details of the datasets provided by SemEval organizers.

2.1 Subtask 1 - Microblogs

The dataset provided by SemEval for fine-grained sentiment analysis on Microblogs comprises of microblog messages related to the Financial domain. Each message is annotated with the following information. Table 1 presents statistics of dataset provided by SemEval organizers.

1. Source: Source identifies the name of the platform where the message was posted. This contains either "Twitter" or "Stocktwits".

2. Id: Id provides a unique identifier of the message.

3. Cashtag: Cashtag provides the stock ticker symbol to which the span and sentiment are related.

4. Sentiment: Sentiment is a floating point value between -1 and 1 (very negative to very positive).

5. Spans: Spans contains piece of message expressing sentiment.

The data set contains 1694 microblog messages for training and 799 microblog messages for evaluation purpose.

2.2 Subtask 2 - News Headlines

The dataset provided for this subtask consisted of news headlines. Each message is annotated with the following information. Table 1 presents statistics of dataset provided by SemEval organizers.

1. Id: Id provides a unique identifier of the message.

2. title: Title contains the textual content of headline.

3. Sentiment: Sentiment is a floating point value between -1 and 1 (very negative to very positive).

4. Company: Company contains the name of a company to which the sentiment is related to.

The data set contains 1142 headlines for training and 491 headlines for evaluation purpose.

3 Preprocessing

Preprocessing is an important step in any natural language processing task. This section describes the preprocessing steps applied on the datasets.

3.1 Subtask 1 - Microblogs

Microblogs often contain noisy text such as special characters, URLs, punctuations e.t.c. Preprocessing is an important step applied in machine learning before proceeding to train phase. For preprocessing the actual microblog message, following tasks were performed.

1. Removal of special characters, punctuations and numbers.

2. Removal of URLs, user names mentioned in a tweet message.

3. Removal of words with length less than three in order to reduce the dimensionality of feature space.

4. Conversion of tweet text into lower case.

5. Concatenation of *spans* to form a unified string. For the empty *spans* field, we considered the whole preprocessed message text for feature extraction.

3.2 Subtask 2 - News Headlines

The textual content of news headlines contains the name of organizations. In the train and test datasets, the organization for which the sentiment needs to be extracted was given. However, it was found that often more than one organization name was mentioned in the headline content. Therefore, we applied named entity recognition to extract names of organizations that were included in the given headline. To extract the names of organizations we used NLTK Named Entity Recognition (NER) Tagger (Bird et al., 2009). After applying NER tagging, following steps were performed.

1. Removal of special characters and punctuations and numbers.

2. Removal of words with length less than three in order to reduce the dimensionality of feature space.

3. News text often contains important words beginning with capital letter. After applying NER tagging, words with Named Entity tags other than {*Person, Organization*} were converted to lower case.

4 Features

This section describes features used in training our system for predicting sentiment score on the given microblog message or news headline.

4.1 Subtask 1 - Microblogs

Following features were used in system training for subtask 1.

4.1.1 Lexicon Features

We used sentiment lexicons constructed for the Financial domain to compute sentiment polarity score of the microblog message under consideration. Lexicons have been widely used for sentiment analysis. The use of domain-specific lexicon can greatly improve the performance of the system. We used following lexicons to compute lexicon based features.

1. **Loughran and McDonald Sentiment Word Lists**
   (Loughran and McDonald, 2011) identified that the sentiment lexicons constructed for other domains often misclassify words commonly used in financial blogs. They developed a list of positive and negative words used in the financial text. For modeling our system to predict sentiment score of microblog text, we used the word list constructed by (Loughran and McDonald, 2011). For each message, we compute a positive word count and negative word count. Positive word count refers to the number of positive words occurred in the message and negative word count refers to the number of negative words occurred in the message.

2. **Stock Market Lexicon**
   (Oliveira et al., 2016) created a lexicon using a large set of labeled messages from Stock-Twits. For each word with a Part of Speech (POS) tag in a lexicon, sentiment score in range $-\infty$ to $+\infty$ is determined in positive context and negated context. In order to compute sentiment score of a microblog message using Stock Market Lexicon, a message is tagged with POS tags using NLTK POS tagger (Bird et al., 2009). Then for each word in a message, a positive and negative sentiment score was determined using the lexicon. The total positivity of a message was determined by the sum of positive scores of each word in a message and the total negativity of a message was determined using the sum of negative scores of each word in a message.

4.1.2 Term Frequency - Inverse Document Frequency (TF-IDF)

TF-IDF feature determines the importance of a word to a document in a collection or corpus. TF-IDF assigns higher weights to to words occurring less frequently in a corpus. This helps in reducing the importance of commonly used words. A matrix of TF-IDF features was computed using sklearn library (Pedregosa et al., 2011).

4.2 Subtask 2 - News Headlines

Following features were used in system training for subtask 2.

4.2.1 Lexicon Features

For subtask 2, we used following lexicons to compute sentiment polarity scores.

1. **Loughran and McDonald Sentiment Word Lists**
   Lexicon scores using Loughran and McDonald Sentiment Word Lists were computed in a similar way as done for subtask 1.

2. **Harvard Inquirer Sentiment Lexicon**
   Harvard IV sentiment lexicon was used to determine the sentiment polarity of a given headline.

3. **NRC Hashtag Sentiment Lexicon** (Mohammad et al., 2013) constructed a list of words associated with a positive and negative sentiment score. Sentiment score is a real number, where values greater than zero indicates positive sentiment and values less than zero indicates negative sentiment. For each headline text, the polarity score was computed by summing the sentiment score of each word in the text.

4.2.2 Term Frequency - Inverse Document Frequency (TF-IDF)

TF-IDF feature determines the importance of a word to a document in a collection or corpus. A matrix of TF-IDF features was computed using sklearn library (Pedregosa et al., 2011).

4.2.3 N-gram Features

N-gram refers to the sequence of N words in the given text. In this paper, we used unigrams to learn a vocabulary from the given training set and then constructed a square matrix of size equal to the size of vocabulary. Each entry in a matrix represents the occurrence of a corresponding word in a given text.

5 Modeling

This section describes our approach for training system.

5.1 Subtask 1 - Microblogs

We trained our system on the provided training data using features described in Section 4. Since the task was determined the sentiment score as a real number ranging from -1 to +1, we trained our model using XGBoost Regression algorithm[2]. 3-fold cross-validation was also performed to tune XGBoost regression parameters.

5.2 Subtask 2 - News Headlines

For subtask 2, we used ensembling of two regressors trained on the different set of features. For model 1, we trained XgBoost Regressor on feature set including McDonald and Loughran Positive Word Count, McDonald and Loughran Negative Word Count, Sentiment score computed using NRC Hashtag sentiment lexicon, sentiment polarity score computed using Harvard IV sentiment lexicon and TF-IDF features.

Our second model was trained using XgBoost Regressor on features including same lexicon features as used in model 1 training and n-gram features. For predicting sentiment score on test data, we computed the average of the sentiment scores predicted by each of our models.

6 Results and Discussion

This section presents evaluation results of our system on subtask 1 and subtask 2. Evaluation of the

---

participating systems was based on cosine similarity metric. Cosine similarity was computed as follows,

$$cosine(G, P) = \frac{\sum_{i=1}^{n} G_i * P_i}{\sqrt{\sum_{i=1}^{n} G_i^2} * \sqrt{\sum_{i=1}^{n} P_i^2}}$$

where, G represents the vector of true sentiment polarity values and P represents the vector of predicted sentiment polarity values by the system.

Table 2 presents evaluation results of our official submission. Our system secured **4th** position in subtask 1 and **14th** position in subtask 2.

On subtask 2 which was related to News headlines dataset, our system did not perform well. The subtask2 was more challenging as compared to subtask 1. In subtask 1, participants are also given with the spans related to cashtag towards which the sentiment is expressed. Whereas, in subtask 2, spans were not given. It was quite challenging to identify the orientation of sentiment towards a company under consideration, in cases where more than one company is mentioned in the headline. We did not consider this issue while modeling our system and considered the whole text for extracting features.

Table 2: Official Results of System Evaluation

Subtask	Test Set	Cosine Similarity Score
Microblogs	799	0.655
News Headlines	491	0.547

7 Conclusion

This paper presented our approach to fine grained sentiment analysis on financial microblogs and news headlines SemEval Task 5. The task includes two subtasks including Sentiment analysis on Financial Microblogs and sentiment analysis on News Headlines. Our system was among top scorers for subtask 1. However, we did not performed well in subtask 2. In future, we can improve the system by further integrating dependency parsing to extract phrases from sentences. This will help in identifying different sentiments oriented towards specific companies with in the same text.

References

Steven Bird, Ewan Klein, and Edward Loper. 2009. *Natural language processing with Python: analyz-*

---

[2]https://github.com/dmlc/xgboost

ing text with the natural language toolkit. " O'Reilly Media, Inc.".

Johan Bollen, Huina Mao, and Xiaojun Zeng. 2011. Twitter mood predicts the stock market. *Journal of computational science* 2(1):1–8.

Keith Cortis, André Freitas, Tobias Dauert, Manuela Huerlimann, Manel Zarrouk, Siegfried Handschuh, and Brian Davis. 2017. Semeval-2017 task 5: Fine-grained sentiment analysis on financial microblogs and news. In *Proceedings of the 11th International Workshop on Semantic Evaluation (SemEval-2017)*. Association for Computational Linguistics, Vancouver, Canada, pages 517–533. http://www.aclweb.org/anthology/S17-2089.

Rohitha Goonatilake and Susantha Herath. 2007. The volatility of the stock market and news. *International Research Journal of Finance and Economics* 3(11):53–65.

Tim Loughran and Bill McDonald. 2011. When is a liability not a liability? textual analysis, dictionaries, and 10-ks. *The Journal of Finance* 66(1):35–65.

Saif M. Mohammad, Svetlana Kiritchenko, and Xiaodan Zhu. 2013. Nrc-canada: Building the state-of-the-art in sentiment analysis of tweets. In *Proceedings of the seventh international workshop on Semantic Evaluation Exercises (SemEval-2013)*. Atlanta, Georgia, USA.

Nuno Oliveira, Paulo Cortez, and Nelson Areal. 2016. Stock market sentiment lexicon acquisition using microblogging data and statistical measures. *Decision Support Systems* 85:62–73.

F. Pedregosa, G. Varoquaux, A. Gramfort, V. Michel, B. Thirion, O. Grisel, M. Blondel, P. Prettenhofer, R. Weiss, V. Dubourg, J. Vanderplas, A. Passos, D. Cournapeau, M. Brucher, M. Perrot, and E. Duchesnay. 2011. Scikit-learn: Machine learning in Python. *Journal of Machine Learning Research* 12:2825–2830.

Marjan Van de Kauter, Diane Breesch, and Véronique Hoste. 2015. Fine-grained analysis of explicit and implicit sentiment in financial news articles. *Expert Systems with applications* 42(11):4999–5010.

HHU at SemEval-2017 Task 5: Fine-Grained Sentiment Analysis on Financial Data using Machine Learning Methods

Tobias Cabanski, Julia Romberg, Stefan Conrad
Institute of Computer Science
Heinrich Heine University Düsseldorf
D-40225 Düsseldorf, Germany
`tobias.cabanski@hhu.de`
`{romberg,conrad}@cs.uni-duesseldorf.de`

Abstract

In this Paper a system for solving SemEval-2017 Task 5 is presented. This task is divided into two tracks where the sentiment of microblog messages and news headlines has to be predicted. Since two submissions were allowed, two different machine learning methods were developed to solve this task, a support vector machine approach and a recurrent neural network approach. To feed in data for these approaches, different feature extraction methods are used, mainly word representations and lexica. The best submissions for both tracks are provided by the recurrent neural network which achieves a score of 0.729 in track 1 and 0.702 in track 2.

1 Introduction

Analysing texts from the finance domain is a task that can help market traders to make important decisions because research has shown that sentiments and opinions can affect market dynamics (Goonatilake and Herath, 2007). In the meantime, the internet contains a huge corpus of finance news from news websites or social media platforms. Natural language processing methods can be used to analyse this data as, for instance, sentiment analysis. To improve the understanding of the special characteristics of the domain, SemEval-2017 provides Task 5.

2 Related Work

In the task of sentiment analysis, machine learning methods are widely used. One approach is shown in (Agarwal et al., 2011) where a sentiment analysis on twitter messages is performed by combining different features. It was found out that the use of multiple features processed by a support vector machine leads to good classification scores.

The work of (Yadav, 2016) shows that recurrent neural networks can provide a good performance for this task. A powerful system can be created even with doing only a little preprocessing on the text data.

3 Task Description

The SemEval-2017 Task 5 is divided into two tracks which each consider a different data basis (Cortis et al., 2017). The objective of both tracks is the prediction of a sentiment score with reference to a company or a stock in a given piece of text. The sentiment score is a number within the interval $[-1, 1]$ with -1 denoting a very bearish sentiment and $+1$ denoting a very bullish sentiment.

Track 1 is focused on microblog messages about stock market events. The data corpus consists of 1710 annotated messages taken from StockTwits[1] and Twitter[2], whereas a cashtag and the related spans are given in each case.

Track 2 refers to financially relevant news headlines. The annotated data given for the system's training comprises 1156 headlines. For every headline-score pair the corresponding company name is specified. Spans are not given.

4 System Description

Below, the system is outlined. In doing so, preprocessing steps, feature selection, and the used machine learning techniques are described.

4.1 Preprocessing

Preceding the feature extraction, the texts are processed by first expanding contractions and remov-

---

[1] https://stocktwits.com/
[2] https://twitter.com/

Proceedings of the 11th International Workshop on Semantic Evaluations (SemEval-2017), pages 832–836,
Vancouver, Canada, August 3 - 4, 2017. ©2017 Association for Computational Linguistics

ing URLs in the text.

Emotions generally take an important part in the microblog domain and it was shown that the consideration of punctuation and bracket characters can improve the score because they can express special meaning like facial expressions (Agarwal et al., 2011). After the revision of the data, it shows that these characters rarely occur in the data of track 1 and apparently never occur in the track 2 data. Therefore, these characters are removed.

Furthermore, character strings of multiple white spaces are normalized to length 1 and case insensitivity is introduced. Additional tokenization is done using SpaCy.[3]

4.2 Features

Two different types of features are examined for the construction of the system. In the first feature set the preprocessed data is transformed into a numerical word representation. The second feature set consists of multiple sentiment lexicon resources.

4.2.1 Text Representations

Textual input has to be transformed into a machine-readable representation. For this, the ensuing two approaches are selected.

Word2vec (Mikolov et al., 2013) generates a vector space based representation for a word in the text. Each unique word in the corpus is represented by a feature vector having similar words being positioned near each other in the space. A pre-trained Levy and Goldberg dependency-based model (Levy and Goldberg, 2014) from SpaCy is used as well as a self-trained model which is constructed using gensim[4]. In contrast to the pre-trained model, the self-trained model contains the whole input vocabulary, but bases on a smaller corpus.

4.2.2 Lexica

Since there is only a small amount of training data, it was decided to bring additional information into the system by using different lexica.

SentiWordNet (Baccianella et al., 2010) consists of WordNet's synset corpus (Fellbaum, 1998). Every synset term has a positive and a negative score between zero and one named PosScore and NegScore. It is also possible to calculate the objectivity of a word by subtracting one from the sum of PosScore and Negscore. Since a word can have more than one score according to different meanings, the final score for a word is the mean of all found scores in the SentiWordNet.

VADER lexicon (Hutto and Gilbert, 2014) is a gold-standard sentiment lexicon that is geared to social media platforms. Hence, words and symbols that are not included in conventional lexical resources are contained and scored with continuous values.

Opinion Lexicon (Hu and Liu, 2004) is a resource that is constantly being updated since 2004. The words in this lexicon are classified binary as positive or negative. Like in the VADER lexicon, this resource was also trained on social media data.

MaxDiff Twitter Sentiment Lexicon (Kiritchenko et al., 2014) is an additional lexicon that delivers a continuous score for words. This corpus is mainly trained on Twitter data.

Financial Sentiment Lexicon As word polarities might depend on a specific domain, a lexicon based on the training data from the respective track is created. The Financial Sentiment Lexicon is built from the training data: First, the score of a short message is assigned to all words of the message. Then a vocabulary of all distinct words is built and the scores of identical words are averaged. In the final pruning step words with occurrence less than 0.1% in the data are removed to prevent that very infrequent words have an impact on the score. Also words with occurrence greater than 10% in the data are removed so that very frequent words like stop words don't influence the score.

4.3 Regression Methods

On the one hand, support vector regression is applied. This regression method bases upon a support vector machine (SVM) which is a widely used machine learning method and which delivers good results for various tasks. The implementation of it is realized by the python package Scikit-Learn.[5]

The other regression method that is used is a recurrent neural network (RNN) using a Long Short-Term Memory Cell (Hochreiter and Schmidhuber, 1997). This is an improvement of a standard RNN in which the network is able to keep information

[3]https://spacy.io/
[4]https://radimrehurek.com/gensim/

[5]http://scikit-learn.org

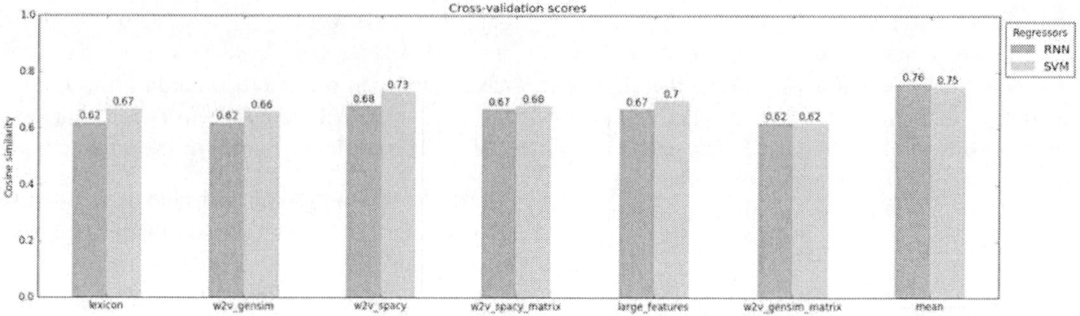

Figure 1: Results of the cross validation of Track 1

over a larger amount of time steps. Unlike the SVM, the RNN can process a message sequentially observing the sentence structure. The implementation is realized by the python package TensorFlow.[6] The model consists of two LSTM cells and a layer count of 10.

5 Results

For every track, the support vector regression and the RNN approach are tested on the testing data using the depicted features. The predicted values are rated by the cosine similarity between the gold standard and the predicted sentiment score. For evaluation of the system, cross-validation is used by creating five subsets out of the training data set.

5.1 Track 1

The results for track 1 are presented in Figure 1. The Figure shows the results of the regression of the features, which are determined by a recurrent neural network and a support vector machine. The presented combination of features has delivered the best result when the average score was formed.

The *lexicon* feature is the sentiment score of every single word in a message, aggregated to the mean for the whole message. *w2v_gensim* relates to the word2vec representation through gensim that has been described in chapter 4.2.1. All word vectors of a short message are averaged to a single feature vector. *w2v_spacy* refers to the second word2vec model named in chapter 4.2.1 which bases on SpaCy. Like described for w2v_gensim, the definite feature vector of a message consists of the average of every word's representation vector. The two matrix features *w2v_spacy_matrix* and *w2v_gensim_matrix* are created in the same way as the word vector features describes before,

but they don't average the single word vectors to one vector. Instead, every word vector is represented by a line of a matrix with a fixed count so that every matrix for a message has the same shape. This representation is optimized for the recurrent neural network because it can process one line at a single time step. To use the matrix features in a support vector machine, the matrix will be reshaped to a vector where all word vectors are concatenated to one single vector. The *large_features* are further matrix features, where a word representation is concatenated to the lexicon scores of a single word. For that, a 50-dimensional word vector is created by gensim and then a five-dimensional vector is built by looking up the score for the word in the lexica. This feature has a matrix representation with a fixed line count as in the matrix features described before.

All feature combinations were tested. Figure 1 shows the similarity scores obtained by the individual features and the mean score of all single feature predictions. As the figure shows, this aggregation leads to a cosine similarity which is higher than all single features. The combinations, that are not explicitly presented, did not lead to better results.

When comparing the scores of the SVM and the RNN, it is noticeable that the SVM scores for the single features are the same or better than those of the RNN. But after aggregating the results of the features for the final score, the RNN yields a slightly better result than the SVM. Another considerable thing is the comparison of the matrix feature scores. Due to the optimized representation for a RNN, it is expected that the score of the matrix features processed by the RNN is better than processing them by the SVM. Though, the evaluation shows a different result: The matrix features

<hr>

[6]https://tensorflow.org

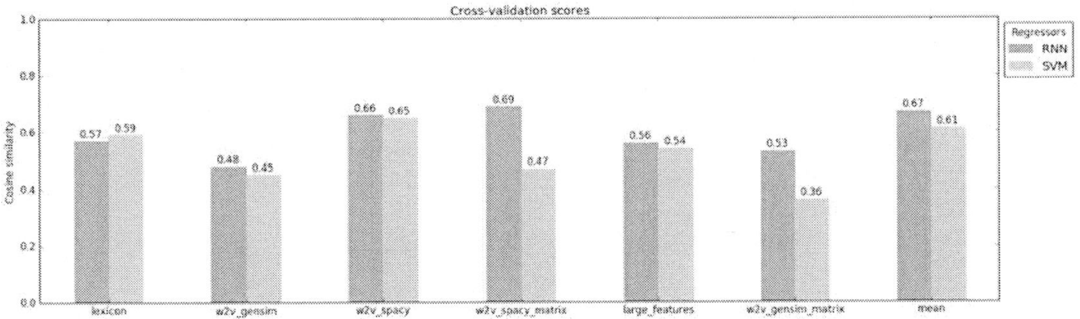

Figure 2: Results of the cross validation of Track 2

perform better when processed by a SVM. This could be caused by the length and structure of the data in track 1. Since the data only contains short snippets of the full message text, which is often only one word, the step-wise data processing of the RNN offers no advantage.

5.2 Track 2

The results of the cross-validation of track 2 are shown in Figure 2. The same features as in track 1 were used to make the results comparable. The mean over all single feature predictions has also been approved as best and been used for the final score.

In comparison to the first track, the cosine similarity is lower for most of the features. This might be due to the fact that, unlike track 1, the full text of a headline is delivered so that the average message length is higher and more words influence the score.

Another fact that is show in figure 2 is that the RNN outputs better results over most of the single features and also over the mean. This can be explained by the structure of the data. Since the full headline text has to be processed, a message consists of more words than in track 1. The three matrix features keep most of the information of the words in a message and the step-wise processing of the feature matrix by the RNN shows much better results than reshaping the matrix to a single vector and processing it by a SVM.

5.3 Official results

In this project, the prediction of the mean-feature-SVM approach and of the mean-feature-RNN approach were each chosen to be submitted.

The official evaluation for track 1 has resulted in a better score for the RNN approach with an overall rank of 6 and a score of 0.729. The SVM approach has a slightly worse result with a score of 0.720. In track 2, also the RNN approach reached a better score than the SVM with a rank of 7 and a cosine similarity of 0.702. The SVM achieved a similarity of 0.655. The official evaluation confirms the cross-validation results by the better performance of the RNN over the SVM.

6 Conclusion and Future Work

It has been shown that the extraction and aggregation of multiple features can lead to a score that performs better than every single feature score. The best single scores are represented by the word vectors where the cosine similarity is near the mean score for track 1 and in one case better than the mean score in track 2. It can also be emphasized that the RNN outputs better scores on longer messages than the SVM, especially when the stepwise procedure is used with the matrix-shaped features.

To further improve the results it is possible to weight the single features before averaging them. To learn the weights, a neural network can be used which takes all single feature scores as input and outputs one value as the sentiment prediction.

Another method to improve the scores is to notice the cashtag or company name. By adding features that take the dependency of the words into account, it is possible to find out which words have an influence on a specific entity. When using a RNN as regression method, it is also possible to pass the entity as an input, for example as a word vector.

References

Apoorv Agarwal, Boyi Xie, Ilia Vovsha, Owen Rambow, and Rebecca Passonneau. 2011. Sentiment Analysis of Twitter Data. In *Proceedings of the Workshop on Languages in Social Media*. Association for Computational Linguistics, pages 30–38.

Stefano Baccianella, Andrea Esuli, and Fabrizio Sebastiani. 2010. SentiWordNet 3.0: An Enhanced Lexical Resource for Sentiment Analysis and Opinion Mining. In *Proceedings of the Seventh International Conference on Language Resources and Evaluation (LREC'10)*. European Language Resources Association, pages 2200–2204.

Keith Cortis, André Freitas, Tobias Dauert, Manuela Huerlimann, Manel Zarrouk, Siegfried Handschuh, and Brian Davis. 2017. SemEval-2017 Task 5: Fine-Grained Sentiment Analysis on Financial Microblogs and News. In *Proceedings of the 11th International Workshop on Semantic Evaluation (SemEval-2017)*. Association for Computational Linguistics, pages 517–533.

Christiane Fellbaum. 1998. *WordNet: An Electronic Lexical Database*. Bradford Books.

Rohitha Goonatilake and Susantha Herath. 2007. The Volatility of the Stock Market and News. *International Research Journal of Finance and Economics* 3(11):53–65.

Sepp Hochreiter and Jürgen Schmidhuber. 1997. Long Short-term Memory. *Neural computation* 9(8):1735–1780.

Minqing Hu and Bing Liu. 2004. Mining and Summarizing Customer Reviews. In *Proceedings of the Tenth ACM SIGKDD International Conference on Knowledge Discovery and Data Mining*. ACM, pages 168–177.

Clayton Hutto and Eric Gilbert. 2014. VADER: A Parsimonious Rule-based Model for Sentiment Analysis of Social Media Text. In *Eighth International AAAI Conference on Web and Social Media*. Association for the Advancement of Artificial Intelligence, pages 216–225.

Svetlana Kiritchenko, Xiaodan Zhu, and Saif M Mohammad. 2014. Sentiment Analysis of Short Informal Texts. *Journal of Artificial Intelligence Research* 50:723–762.

Omer Levy and Yoav Goldberg. 2014. Dependency-Based Word Embeddings. In *Proceedings of the 52nd Annual Meeting of the Association for Computational Linguistics (Volume 2: Short Papers)*. Association for Computational Linguistics, pages 302–308.

Tomas Mikolov, Kai Chen, Greg Corrado, and Jeffrey Dean. 2013. Efficient Estimation of Word Representations in Vector Space. *arXiv preprint arXiv:1301.3781* .

Vikrant Yadav. 2016. thecerealkiller at SemEval-2016 Task 4: Deep Learning based System for Classifying Sentiment of Tweets on Two Point Scale. In *Proceedings of the 10th International Workshop on Semantic Evaluation (SemEval-2016)*. Association for Computational Linguistics, pages 100–102.

INF-UFRGS at SemEval-2017 Task 5: A Supervised Identification of Sentiment Score in Tweets and Headlines

Tiago Zini and **Marcelo Dias** and **Karin Becker**

Instituto de Informática (INF)

Universidade Federal do Rio Grande do Sul

Porto Alegre, RS, Brazil

{tiago.zini, marcelo.dias, karin.becker}@inf.ufrgs.br

Abstract

This paper describes a supervised solution for detecting the polarity scores of tweets or headline news in the financial domain, submitted to the SemEval 2017 Fine-Grained Sentiment Analysis on Financial Microblogs and News Task. The premise is that it is possible to understand market reaction over a company stock by measuring the positive/negative sentiment contained in the financial tweets and news headlines, where polarity is measured in a continuous scale ranging from -1.0 (very bearish) to 1.0 (very bullish). Our system receives as input the textual content of tweets or news headlines, together with their ids, stock cashtag or name of target company, and the polarity score gold standard for the training dataset. Our solution retrieves features from these text instances using n-gram, hashtags, sentiment score calculated by a external APIs and others features to train a regression model capable to detect continuous score of these sentiments with precision.

1 Introduction

Sentiment analysis involves the automatic identification of opinions, feelings, evaluations, attitudes expressed by people in the written language. A popular line of work in this field is opinion mining (Liu, 2012; Tsytsarau and Palpanas, 2012). Growing attention has been dedicated to sentiment analysis in the financial domain, given its links to market dynamics. The challenges are to detect how sentiment is expressed in documents in this domain, and how it can translate to a reaction over a company stock, ranging from bullish to bearish. This problem is addressed as part of SemEval-2017 (International Workshop on Semantic Evalu-

ation 2017), Task 5[1]. The task was defined as follows: "given a text instance (microblog message in Track 1, news statement or headline in Track 2), predict the sentiment score for each of the companies/stocks mentioned. Sentiment values need to be floating point values in the range of -1 (very negative/bearish) to 1 (very positive/bullish), with 0 designating neutral sentiment." The task was divided into two subtasks, according to the type of document (i.e. tweets and financial headlines) and sentiment target, and this paper describes our solution for both problems.

We addressed these sub-tasks by building a supervised model to do regression of sentiment value in the documents based solely on their textual content. The target of the sentiment in Task 5-1 is the company stocks for which two sets of annotated tweets were supplied: a training corpus with 1700 annotated tweets and a test corpus with 800 unannotated tweets for task evaluation purpose. Two sets of news headlines were made available as part of Task 5-2, where the target of opinion is a company. The training set was composed of 1142 annotated instances, and the test corpus has 491 unannotated instances for task evaluation. Details of Task 5 can be found at (Cortis et al., 2017).

The regression of sentiment in a text can be complex, because the sentiment can be related in different levels and complexities to the document or just with an aspect or even with a comparison between entities (Feldman, 2013). Our strategy was to address the regression as an opinion mining problem. In addition, sentiment score detection faces challenges common to sentiment analysis in general, such as use of vocabulary and slang specific of the stock market, orthography errors, sarcasm, etc.

Our method extracts a set of features from financial texts and associate this data with annotated

---

[1] http://alt.qcri.org/semeval2017/task5/

Proceedings of the 11th International Workshop on Semantic Evaluations (SemEval-2017), pages 837–841,
Vancouver, Canada, August 3 - 4, 2017. ©2017 Association for Computational Linguistics

sentiment score provided by each task to train a prediction model specific to sentiment found in tweets and an other for sentiment found in headlines. To explain the details of our solution the remaining of the paper describes the obtained results, the proposed solution and the experiments developed in the next sections respectively.

2 Results

Tasks 5-1 and 5-2 evaluated the proposed solutions according to the cosine similarity of bearish and bullish, considering the respective test dataset. The evaluation was based on cosine similarity as defined by Equation 3, where G_i is the gold standard of instance and P_i is value predicted by our system. The cosine similarity ranges from 0.0 to 1.0. We calculate the cosine similarity considering G like a single vector with all instances of the gold standard, and P with all instances of predictions.

$$cosine(G, P) = \frac{\sum_i^n G_i \cdot P_i}{\sqrt{\sum_i^n G_i} \cdot \sqrt{\sum_i^n P_i}} \quad (1)$$

$$weight\_cosine = \left| \frac{P}{G} \right| \quad (2)$$

$$final\_cs = weight\_cosine \cdot cosine(G, P) \quad (3)$$

In the Task 5-1, our solution was ranked 17th among 25 participants, with a cosine similarity of 0.6142038157. Similarly, in the Task 5-2, we ranked 21srt among 29 participants, with a cosine similarity of 0.6081537843.

3 The Process

This section explains the sequence of steps to preprocess the documents, extract features and train the regression model.

3.1 Text Pre-processing

Before extracting text features, we preprocessed the content of tweets and headlines messages. Full URLs, company cashtags and company names were replaced by the symbols "url", "$cashtag" and "company" respectively. Numbers, monetary values, percentages were replaced by the symbols "positive_number", "negative_number", "money", "positive_percentage", and "negative_percentage". We do the replacing of expression with numeric digits from the more complex to more simple ones, being the more simple case a numeric part of a sequence of characters being replaced by the "positive_number" word. Other substitutions were also

performed with dates and other types of numbers. Special character sequences, like emoticons, were replaced by symbols designating their positive or negative value. Emoji's special characters, when identified, were also replaced by the symbol "_emoji_". We also identified expressions that determine negation in a sentence, and replaced these expressions by the symbol "_NOT_", maintaining the adjacent related words unchanged.

Additional pre-processing was implemented over the spans field provided in each tweet input instance. The Span field corresponds to the part of the tweet message related to the target of annotated sentiment. The adjustment done is concatenating its text with the prefix "SPAN_" in order to differ the features derived from spans, from the ones extracted from the complete tweet text.

All these substitutions aim to preserve the original meaning and context of the expressions within the documents, given that these properties would be lost if the textual features were extracted before the pre-processing.

3.2 Features

We extracted the following groups of features from the preprocessed text instances:

Features Common For Both Tasks: The features present in the model of both tasks are:

a) n-grams: we experimented with different variations of n-grams ($n = [1..4]$), which were extracted from both tweet contents/headlines and tweet spans. To deal with sparsity and non-discriminant features, we removed all n-grams whose frequency was below and above given thresholds. Experimentally, we defined as minimum threshold at least 2 times, and as maximum threshold, at most in 95% or 100% of the instances. We chosen a Boolean representation for these features;

b) sentiment polarity and score: we used IBM Alchemy[2] API, providing the tweet text/headline as input. This choice was motivated by our earlier experience on the use of this tool (Dias and Becker, 2016).

Features For Tweets: These are features explored just for tweets:

a) has-hashtag: indicates the presence of hashtag in the document;

b) external stock features: based on the tweet

---

[2]http://www.alchemyapi.com/

date, we used the Python module Yahoo Finance[3] to get data about stock quotes of cashtag mentioned in the tweet at opening and close time of market. We also calculate the variation from the stock quote price from this date and a future date, using two lags: 7 days and 1 month. We used this data to build three features with the variation in percentage, and three aditional features with information about variation delta symbolized by "increase", "decrease" or "none". Despite the good results provided by the adoption of these features, they could not be not included in the final microblog model because, differently from training dataset, the test dataset had very few instances that included tweet creation date.

3.3 Training

We used the group of features selected for each subtask as detailed in Section 3.2 to train a regression model using a algorithm named Support Vector Regression (SVR), available in the Scikit-learn[4] tools for Python language. The SVR learning was configured only with parameters of linear kernel and $C = 1.0$.

3.4 Training Results

Using annotated sentiment score provided by the SSIX project (Davis et al., 2016), we run our regression models over the test data and compared the results to build a confusion matrix for each subtasks. Tables 1 and 2 describe these matrix in terms of precision and recall, where Bullish is represented by scores greater than 0, and Bearish by negative scores. It is interesting to observe that

---

[3]https://pypi.python.org/pypi/yahoo-finance
[4]http://scikit-learn.org

| | Predicted | | | |
	Bullish	Bearish	Neutral	Recall
Bullish	449	72	0	86.02
Bearish	96	161	0	62.64
Neutral	5	9	0	0
Precision	81.04	67.64	0	
F-score	83.46	65.05	0	

Table 1: Confusion Matrix - Microblog

| | Predicted | | | |
	Bullish	Bearish	Neutral	Recall
Bullish	208	68	0	75.36
Bearish	148	55	0	72.90
Neutral	6	6	0	0
Precision	77.32	66.66	0	
F-score	76.33	69.65	0	

Table 2: Confusion Matrix - News Headline

our solution did not predict any Neutral sentiment, probably because neutral score is exactly 0. It is also possible to observe that recall and precision for Bullish detection is much higher (about 15 percentage points), compared to Bearish. This result might be explained by the prevalence of positive scores in the training instances, as detailed on Table 3.

Subset	Polarity	Quantity
Microblog	Bullish	1092
Microblog	Bearish	581
Microblog	Neutral	27
Headline	Bullish	653
Headline	Bearish	451
Headline	Neutral	38

Table 3: Polarity Distribution in the Training Datasets

Our solution achieved a higher evaluation score in the first subtask, apparently because the tweets contained more textual information and were freely written using emoticons, Emojis, slangs, financial values and financial language. News headlines were shorter and written in a more formal and standard style. Thus, more discriminative features to train the regression model could be extracted from tweets.

Another difference was the use of cashtags, a compact form to identify one type of company stock, in the tweets. They simplified the detection of company, while the news headlines, in most cases, expressed the companies as composed names. Many news headlines were written entirely using upper case, complicating the distinction of proper names parts from words that have important meaning.

4 Experiments

We made experiments as the basis for our proposed solutions. The experiments for Tasks 5-1 and 5-2 are described in subsections 4.1 and 4.2, respectively. In the both experiments we use different baselines. For each subtask we add some features and test the improvements in cosine similarity measurements.

Based on the models built with improvement results reported in the experiment of each subtask (using 70% of instances for training the model and 30% of them to test the cosine similarity) we evaluate the test instances provided for each subtask.

4.1 Experiments for Subtask of Microblogs

The results of our experiments are reported in Table 4. To evaluate the performance of the proposed system, we adopted as baseline a simple model trained over n-grams (with $n = [1, 2, 3]$). As an improvement, we kept the same n-gram textual features that appeared least twice, and at most in 95% of tweets instances. Then we added the "has-hashtag' feature and the Alchemy score. These results are reported in Table 4 as *Final*, as it corresponds to the solution submitted to Task 5-1.

We further improved this model (labeled *Intermediate* in Table 4) using the previous features, and in addition, all external stock features mentioned in Section 3.2. The only exception was the feature *variation delta in tweet date*. Despite the better result, this model was not submitted to the task, because the features added were not trustworthy in the test data due to the reasons explained in Section 3.2.

4.2 Experiments for Subtask of Headlines

To evaluate the performance of the proposed system, we compare it to a baseline trained over n-grams with $n = [1, 2, 3, 4]$ and keeping only its features that are present at least two instances of headlines. Using the same algorithm we add the feature of sentiment polarity and score of Alchemy API. Results are reported in table 4.

Task	Baseline	Final	Intermediate
Microblog	0.487855	0.518896	0.524003
Headline	0.413345	0.468760	-

Table 4: Improvements gained after the changes in the initial baseline of models in the metric of cosine similarity

5 Conclusions and Future Work

The results obtained by the participants of SemEval Task 5-1 and Task-5-2 and specially our results reveals that polarity regression using cosine similarity as target metric is a hard problem, for which available solutions could evolve.

One of the difficulties we faced was assuming there were no significant differences in the structure of the tweets in the training and testing datasets. As the testing dataset contained very few instances with date information, we could not explore the external features that provided the best results in the training dataset. Another difficulty common to many participant of Task 5 was dealing with the ambiguity in the definition of similarity calculation of the cosine proposed in the description of the tasks. Maybe a standard regression measure like Mean Squared Error would have been a more direct evaluation choice.

The publication of the gold standard for the tasks of Task 5 will allows to us to improve the process, focusing mainly in strategies for increasing the performance with regard to the more complex sentences. Among the strategies are combine Alchemy score with score of others external APIs like Haven On Demand[5] and Vivekn[6] , and the investigation of pre-processed issues like Emojis sentiment. Another approach would be do experiments of deep learning approach.

Acknowledgments

Two of the authors would like to acknowledge Procempa - Brazil by the support provided to the development of this work. This research is partially sponsored in part by CNPq (Brazil) under Grant No. 459322/2014-1.

References

Keith Cortis, André Freitas, Tobias Dauert, Manuela Huerlimann, Manel Zarrouk, Siegfried Handschuh, and Brian Davis. 2017. Semeval-2017 task 5: Fine-grained sentiment analysis on financial microblogs and news. In *Proceedings of the 11th International Workshop on Semantic Evaluation (SemEval-2017)*. Association for Computational Linguistics, Vancouver, Canada, pages 517–533. http://www.aclweb.org/anthology/S17-2089.

Brian Davis, Keith Cortis, Laurentiu Vasiliu, Adamantios Koumpis, Ross McDermott, and Siegfried Handschuh. 2016. Social sentiment indices powered by x-scores. In *2nd International Conference on Big Data, Small Data, Linked Data and Open Data, ALLDATA 2016 Lisbon, Portugal.*

Marcelo Dias and Karin Becker. 2016. INF-UFRGS-OPINION-MINING at semeval-2016 task 6: Automatic generation of a training corpus for unsupervised identification of stance in tweets. In *Proceedings of the 10th International Workshop on Semantic Evaluation, San Diego, CA, USA, June 16-17, 2016.* pages 378–383.

Ronen Feldman. 2013. Techniques and applications for sentiment analysis. *Communications of the ACM* 56(4):82–89.

Bing Liu. 2012. Sentiment analysis and opinion mining. *Synthesis lectures on human language technologies* 5(1):1–167.

---

[5] https://www.havenondemand.com/
[6] http://sentiment.vivekn.com/docs/api/

Mikalai Tsytsarau and Themis Palpanas. 2012. Survey
on mining subjective data on the web. *Data Mining
and Knowledge Discovery* 24(3):478–514.

HCS at SemEval-2017 Task 5: Sentiment Detection in Business News Using Convolutional Neural Networks

Lidia Pivovarova   **Llorenç Escoter**   **Arto Klami**   **Roman Yangarber**

Department of Computer Science
University of Helsinki
Finland
`first.last@cs.helsinki.fi`

Abstract

Task 5 of SemEval-2017 involves fine-grained sentiment analysis on financial microblogs and news. Our solution for determining the sentiment score extends an earlier convolutional neural network for sentiment analysis in several ways. We explicitly encode a *focus* on a particular company, we apply a data augmentation scheme, and use a larger data collection to complement the small training data provided by the task organizers. The best results were achieved by training a model on an external dataset and then tuning it using the provided training dataset.

1 Introduction

This paper describes our approach to Task 5 of the SemEval-2017 Challenge—fine-grained sentiment analysis on financial microblogs and news. The task is to determine the *sentiment score* (positive or negative) of a mention of a given company in a business-related text document—a microblog message (Track 1) or a news headline (Track 2).

Our solution, "HCS," is a convolutional neural network to classify sentiment scores. The model's input takes two kinds of information: an article text, a list of *focus* points—positions in the text where a given company is mentioned. Foci allow the model to distinguish company mentions within the text, and to assign different scores to them.

The data provided by the task organisers, (Handschuh et al., 2016), is short, one-sentence messages, with a given focus company. To train the model on additional data, we use the Named Entity (NE) recognition module of PULS (Yangarber and Steinberger, 2009; Huttunen et al., 2013; Atkinson et al., 2011), a news monitoring system, to find company mentions in arbitrary text.

2 Data

The SemEval training set contains 1700 sentences for the microblog track and 1300 news headlines for the headline track, which is a very limited resource for training flexible models. To compensate for the small size of the provided training sets, we built an extended training set. The PULS news monitoring system[1] collects articles from a range of sources of business news (Pivovarova et al., 2013; Du et al., 2016). One of our data sources is a collection of news summaries written by business analysts, which contain metadata annotations.

The metadata does not include sentiment scores. However, the metadata does provide labels that indicate business *events* mentioned in the article, e.g., *Investment*, *Fraud* or *Merger*. The labels are not mutually exclusive, and some documents may have more than one label. There are approximately 300 labels, some of which imply— or weakly imply—positive or negative sentiment. However, most labels do not. We selected only those labels with the most clear sentiment implications: e.g. *Investment*, *New Product*, *Sponsorship*, etc., are considered "positive," while *Fraud*, *Layoff*, *Bankruptcy*, etc., are considered "negative." In total, we used 26 positive and 12 negative labels.

Using these labels, we collected a training set from the corpus of short articles. We selected only documents for which we can infer a clear sentiment score; if a document has event several labels with conflicting sentiment, it is not used for training. Further, we used only those documents, whose headline and first sentence mention exactly one company. The rationale for this is that two companies mentioned together may have different scores. Since our event labels do not provide such detailed information, we avoid these cases to keep the training data as clean as possible. A positive

---

[1]http://puls.cs.helsinki.fi

Proceedings of the 11th International Workshop on Semantic Evaluations (SemEval-2017), pages 842–846,
Vancouver, Canada, August 3 - 4, 2017. ©2017 Association for Computational Linguistics

label is considered to have a score of 1 and a negative label is -1.

The dataset produced in this fashion is highly skewed: 90% of the data are positive. We apply a *random undersampling* strategy (Stamatatos, 2008; Erenel and Altınçay, 2013) by randomly selecting a subset of positive documents so that positive and negative training data are more balanced. In our corpus, 100,000 documents have a negative label and mention exactly one company. Thus, the total dataset consists of 200,000 documents. Of these, 10% are used as a development set to determine when to stop training.

3 Approach

Our model is based on a convolutional neural network (Kim, 2014), which demonstrated state-of-the-art performance on sentiment analysis (Tai et al., 2015). The original model is relatively simple, and we adapt it for determining sentiment score for a given company. We add an indicator of *focus* to the input, i.e., the position of the company of interest, for which we wish to determine a sentiment score. We also augment the network by incorporating additional convolutional layers.

An overview of our model is shown in Figure 1. The inputs are fed into the network as zero-padded sentences of a fixed size, where each word is represented as a fixed-dimensional embedding, complemented with a scalar indicator of focus. The inputs are fed into a layer of convolutional filters with multiple widths, optionally followed by deeper convolutional layers. The results of the last convolutional layer are max-pooled, producing a vector with one scalar per filter, which is then fed into a fully-connected layer with dropout regularisation, and a soft-max output layer. The output is a 2-dimensional vector that is interpreted as probability distributions over two possible outcomes: positive and negative. Thus, if an instance has a sentiment score -1 it is mapped into [1, 0], a score of 1 is mapped into [0,1]. A cross-entropy loss function is computed between the network's output and the true value to update the network weights via back-propagation.

Next, we briefly describe the details of the components of the model.

Embeddings: Words are represented by 128-dimensional embeddings. The initial embeddings were trained using GloVe (Pennington et al., 2014) on a corpus of 5 million business news articles.

Each document was pre-processed using lemmatisation and named entity (NE) recognition. All NEs of a certain type are mapped to the same token, e.g., all company names have the same embedding.

Following the suggestion of Kim (2014), we tune the embeddings during training by updating them at each iteration. This allows the model to learn word properties that are significant for sentiment detection, such as the difference between antonyms, that are not necessarily captured well in the initial embeddings.

Focus: One crucial extension beyond the model in (Kim, 2014) is the *focus* vector, indicating the position(s) of a given company in the text. The focus vector is shown in darker grey in Figure 1, with the company position in a red frame. This provides an additional dimension to the word embedding, and helps to distinguish between training instances that differ only in focus and sentiment.

The reason for introducing focus is that sentiment is not a feature of the text as a whole, but of each company mention. Two mentions in the same text may have different sentiments and a model needs be able to distinguish them. In this sense, this task is similar to *aspect-based sentiment analysis* (Pontiki et al., 2016), where the task is not to classify a text or sentence, but an entity within the text. The notion of focus is similar to *attention* (Bahdanau et al., 2016; Yin et al., 2016), with the difference that attention is learned during training whereas focus is given as an additional input.

We experiment with three alternative representations for focus. The **baseline** model has no focus, and uses only lexical features without NEs. In the **binary** strategy, the focus vector contains ones in positions where the target company is appears, and zeros elsewhere. In the **smoothed** strategy, the focus value for each word indicates the *proximity* of the current word to the position of the nearest mention of the target company. Proximity is computed according to the formula:

$$Prox(p) = \frac{1}{1 + |p - m|}$$

where p is the position of the current word and m is the position of the nearest mention of the target company. Thus, proximity is 1 for a company mention, $1/2$ for its immediate neighbours, $1/3$ for the next neighbours, etc. It is never 0, which allows a convolution filter to use information about focus points, even if it exceeds the filter length.

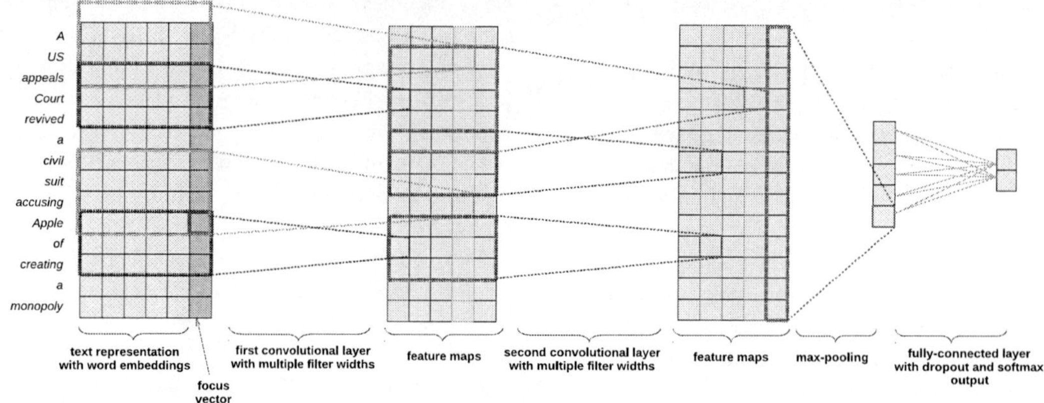

Figure 1: Model architecture with focus vector and two convolution layers

Data augmentation: Since the training set contains only "simple" instances—that mention exactly one company, as described in Section 2—we introduce a method for *data augmentation* which allows us to generate more realistic data. By feeding our model instances that mention *several* companies, we force the network to make use of the focus information, so it can learn to handle more complex test instances, producing a better model.

To augment the data we randomly select two simple instances—which gives them a 50% chance of having different sentiments—and concatenate them. We then randomly decide which of them should receive focus. As a result, we get an instance that mentions a focus company and a distractor company either on the left or on the right of the focus. We expect that using these examples the model would learn to ignore sentiment signals if they are far removed from the focus.

Model tuning: We have two different corpora—a large one collected by us and a small training set provided by the task organisers. We used a two-stage learning procedure, where the model is first trained using the large corpus and then it is refined using the shared task data. The core idea is that the first stage is used to learn a coarse solution for the problem on rich data, while the latter stage is used to fine-tune the model for the specific task at hand. In particular, in the second stage the model should calibrate an output to the exact values of the scores, since in the first stage all instances are labelled using only 1 or -1.

For the first training phase we used 10K sentences as a development set to determine when to

stop training. For the second phase we take another approach since we want to use as much data as possible for training. First, we split the data into two halves and tune the model, using the second half as a development set to define the number of steps before it overfits. Then we tune the model using the entire training set (and no development set) and allow it to train the same number of *epochs*, which means the model has seen each training instance the same number of times.

4   Results

Table 1 shows the results for a selection of models trained on our data and tested on the shared task's *training set*. For the experiments we use only English microblogs. The evaluation is done in terms of *cosine* similarity between a model's output and the correct answer, as well as *accuracy*.[2]

We explore several hyper-parameters of the model: the number of convolution layers and the number and size of convolution filters. We also report the effect of using (or not) the data augmentation scheme described above. We also manipulate the instances, where the same company is mentioned several times, by considering instances with (**many**) foci or splitting them into several instances with only **one** focus point.

As shown in the table, the data augmentation scheme does not help the performance for this par-

---

[2] To compute accuracy, we map the sentiment score into three classes: negative (-1:-0.2), neutral (-0.2:0.2), and positive (0.2:1). This is a rather arbitrary split into three classes, which provides a rough estimate of the model's accuracy. In actual training we optimise the *loss*, i.e. the cross-entropy between the model's output and the true value.

Au	Focus	FP	CL	Filter	Fi	Headlines		Blogs	
						acc	cos	acc	cos
no	no (baseline)	one	1	3,4,5	128	**70.67**	**53.92**	63.59	32.71
no	binary	one	1	3,4,5	128	69.88	52.53	**63.98**	30.40
no	binary	many	1	3,4,5	128	70.05	52.15	60.14	26.59
no	smooth	one	1	3,4,5	128	68.48	51.36	58.91	25.91
no	smooth	one	2	3,4,5	128	70.32	53.35	62.03	**33.19**
yes	smooth	one	1	3,4,5	128	69.53	51.14	61.83	31.41
yes	smooth	many	1	3,4,5	128	70.32	52.11	58.91	21.52
yes	binary	one	3	3,4,5	128	70.40	52.78	62.09	30.43
yes	binary	one	1	3,4,5	200	68.91	49.77	61.31	27.91
yes	binary	many	1	3,4,5	128	70.05	50.09	61.64	29.63
yes	binary	many	3	3,4,5	128	69.00	50.28	60.60	26.03
yes	smooth	one	1	3,7,11	128	70.05	50.29	58.19	24.90
yes	smooth	one	2	3,7,11	128	69.53	49.53	63.00	29.13
yes	smooth	many	2	3,7,11	128	69.26	49.68	61.64	25.12
yes	binary	one	6	3,8	40	64.27	42.68	57.35	24.22

Table 1: A selection of best-performing models. Legend: **Au**—augmentation, **FP**—number of focus points per instance, **CL**—number of convolution layers, **Fi**—number of filters (of each size).

	Example	True score	Model output
1	*Tesco names Deloitte as new auditor after accounting scandal.*	-0.452	0.289
2	*Tesco breaks its downward slide by cutting sales decline in half.*	0.172	-0.703

Table 2: Problematic examples.

	Headlines	Blogs
without tuning	51.30	36.03
with tuning	67.95	60.73

Table 3: Official results for SemEval 2017 Task 5: cosine similarity.

ticular task. Thus, we submitted a solution without augmentation. Using foci increases performance for microblogs but not for headlines, probably because most instances in the task have only one mention. However, we submitted a solution with (smooth) focus since we believe it will be crucial in more realistic settings.

It can also be seen from the table that, although the results for headlines and microblogs have comparable accuracy, microblog classification is substantially worse in terms of cosine similarity.

The model we chose for the SemEval submission (for both subtasks) is highlighted in blue in the table. For each subtask, we made two submissions: one without tuning—using only our data, and one with the tuning step—we continue refining the model, using headlines and microblog data respectively. The final results of the shared task are shown in Table 3. As can be seen in the table, tuning provides a substantial improvement—16% for headlines and 24% for microblogs. Table 2 shows some examples of the more problematic cases that we found during error analysis.

Example 1 would require processing of long-distance dependencies. In this sentence the key phrase *accounting scandal* is far from the focus company *Tesco*, so none of the convolutional filters is applied to the company name and the phrase at the same time. The focus mechanism reduces the weight of the phrase, since another company name appears between the focus and the phrase, which may indicate a drawback of our model on such short input strings. Some sentences are incorrectly classified due to a complicated syntactic structure.

Example 2 contains a string of strongly negative cues (*breaks, downward slide, cutting, sales decline*), which should cancel each other out, but correct processing of such sentences would require deeper semantic analysis. Note, that in this task we have rather short pieces of text; in a more realistic setting the model should classify an entire document, where the company of interest would be mentioned multiple times with different keywords in context.

Acknowledgements

We are thankful to Denny Britz, whose TensorFlow implementation[3] of (Kim, 2014) model was used as a starting point for our implementation.

---

[3] https://github.com/dennybritz/cnn-text-classification-tf

References

Martin Atkinson, Jakub Piskorski, Erik van der Goot, and Roman Yangarber. 2011. Multilingual real-time event extraction for border security intelligence gathering. In U. Kock Wiil, editor, *Counterterrorism and Open Source Intelligence*, Springer Lecture Notes in Social Networks, Vol. 2, pages 355–390.

Dzmitry Bahdanau, Jan Chorowski, Dmitriy Serdyuk, Philemon Brakel, and Yoshua Bengio. 2016. End-to-end attention-based large vocabulary speech recognition. In *Acoustics, Speech and Signal Processing (ICASSP), 2016 IEEE International Conference on*. IEEE, pages 4945–4949.

Mian Du, Lidia Pivovarova, and Roman Yangarber. 2016. PULS: natural language processing for business intelligence. In *Proceedings of the 2016 Workshop on Human Language Technology*. Go to Print Publisher, pages 1–8.

Zafer Erenel and Hakan Altınçay. 2013. Improving the precision-recall trade-off in undersampling-based binary text categorization using unanimity rule. *Neural Computing and Applications* 22(1):83–100.

Siegfried Handschuh, Adamantios Koumpis, Ross McDermott, Keith Cortis, Laurentiu Vasiliu, and Brian Davis. 2016. Social sentiment indices powered by x-scores. In *2nd International Conference on Big Data, Small Data, Linked Data and Open Data, ALLDATA 2016*. INSIGHT Centre for Data Analytics, NUI Galway, Ireland.

Silja Huttunen, Arto Vihavainen, Mian Du, and Roman Yangarber. 2013. Predicting relevance of event extraction for the end user. In Thierry Poibeau, Horacio Saggion, Jakub Piskorski, and Roman Yangarber, editors, *Multi-source, Multilingual Information Extraction and Summarization*, Springer Berlin, Theory and Applications of Natural Language Processing, pages 163–176.

Yoon Kim. 2014. Convolutional neural networks for sentence classification. In *EMNLP*.

Jeffrey Pennington, Richard Socher, and Christopher D. Manning. 2014. GloVe: Global vectors for word representation. In *Empirical Methods in Natural Language Processing (EMNLP)*. pages 1532–1543. http://www.aclweb.org/anthology/D14-1162.

Lidia Pivovarova, Silja Huttunen, and Roman Yangarber. 2013. Event representation across genre. In *Proceedins of the 1st Workshop on Events: Definition, Detection, Coreference, and Representation*. NAACL HLT.

Maria Pontiki, Dimitris Galanis, Haris Papageorgiou, Ion Androutsopoulos, Suresh Manandhar, Mohammad AL-Smadi, Mahmoud Al-Ayyoub, Yanyan Zhao, Bing Qin, Orphee De Clercq, Veronique Hoste, Marianna Apidianaki, Xavier Tannier, Natalia Loukachevitch, Evgeniy Kotelnikov, Núria Bel,

Salud María Jiménez-Zafra, and Gülşen Eryiğit. 2016. Semeval-2016 task 5: Aspect based sentiment analysis. In *Proceedings of the 10th International Workshop on Semantic Evaluation (SemEval-2016)*. Association for Computational Linguistics, San Diego, California, pages 19–30. http://www.aclweb.org/anthology/S16-1002.

Efstathios Stamatatos. 2008. Author identification: Using text sampling to handle the class imbalance problem. *Information Processing & Management* 44(2):790–799.

Kai Sheng Tai, Richard Socher, and Christopher D Manning. 2015. Improved semantic representations from tree-structured long short-term memory networks. In *ACL*.

Roman Yangarber and Ralf Steinberger. 2009. Automatic epidemiological surveillance from on-line news in MedISys and PULS. In *Proceedings of IMED-2009: International Meeting on Emerging Diseases and Surveillance*. Vienna, Austria.

Wenpeng Yin, Hinrich Schütze, Bing Xiang, and Bowen Zhou. 2016. ABCNN: Attention-based convolutional neural network for modeling sentence pairs. *Transactions of the Association for Computational Linguistics* 4:259–272.

NLG301 at SemEval-2017 Task 5:
Fine-Grained Sentiment Analysis on Financial Microblogs and News

Chung-Chi Chen, Hen-Hsen Huang and Hsin-Hsi Chen
Department of Computer Science and Information Engineering
National Taiwan University, Taipei, Taiwan
{cjchen, hhhuang}@nlg.csie.ntu.edu.tw; hhchen@ntu.edu.tw

Abstract

Short length, multi-targets, target relationship, monetary expressions, and outside reference are characteristics of financial tweets. This paper proposes methods to extract target spans from a tweet and its referencing web page. Total 15 publicly available sentiment dictionaries and one sentiment dictionary constructed from training set, containing sentiment scores in binary or real numbers, are used to compute the sentiment scores of text spans. Moreover, the correlation coefficients of the price return between any two stocks are learned with the price data from Bloomberg. They are used to capture the relationships between the interesting target and other stocks mentioned in a tweet. The best result of our method in both subtask are 56.68% and 55.43%, evaluated by evaluation method 2.

1. Introduction

Nowadays the discussion of finance on social media such as twitter reveals the feeling of a market in some degrees. Market sentiment analysis becomes an important financial technology in trading strategies (Kazemian, 2014). Financial tweet sentiment classification differs from traditional sentiment classification in several ways. Firstly, the sentiment degree is a real number rather than discrete numbers such as 1 (positive), 0 (neutral), and -1 (negative).

Secondly, a financial tweet usually concerns multiple targets. In the tweet, "Oil To Break Out: Adding Chevron https://t.co/IrZkAVxjiE $AXP $CLGRF $CSCO $ERX $IBM $MCD $SSRI $VLO $WMT $XOM $CVX", all companies denoted by the cashtag $ticker-symbol share only one description. The activity, oil to break out, is a good news for energy companies, but may be bad for shipping companies. Domain knowledge about the targets is necessary for suitable interpretation in this case.

Thirdly, numbers in the financial tweets are quite important. In the tweet, "MarketWatch: RT wmwitkowski: Guess who sold off about $800 million in $MDLZ after losing about $1 billion on $VRX???https://t.co/SHiJutyenv", large number means more negative. In contrast, in the tweet (named T1 hereafter), "$AAPL now up 2.2% w/div since my original call, while $SPY up only 0.6% even w/ this Fri's div. #EMH be damned. Still holding", the larger the number is, the more positive score the target will get. The activity related to numbers determines the polarity and its degree.

Fourthly, sentiment scores depend on the activity of the companies, and their relationships, e.g., the adversarial relation versus the cooperate relation. In the tweet, "Report: Apple signs up for Google's cloud, uses much less of Amazon's $AAPL $GOOG $GOOGL $AMZN $DROPB https://t.co/zN3KDGYvGT", $AAPL $GOOGL $AMZN and $DROPB are assigned sentiment scores 0.15, 0.443, -0.38 and -0.213, respectively, by human annotators because Amazon and Dropbox are two competitors of Google in the cloud market.

This paper explores various types of features selected from the text span related to the interesting targets for fine-grained financial tweet sentiment classification. Both human and machine labelled text spans are used and compared. This paper is organized as follows. Section 2 surveys the related work. Section 3 presents the identification of text spans and extraction of features from them.

Proceedings of the 11th International Workshop on Semantic Evaluations (SemEval-2017), pages 847–851,
Vancouver, Canada, August 3 - 4, 2017. ©2017 Association for Computational Linguistics

Section 4 shows and discusses the experimental results. Section 5 concludes the remarks.

2. Related Work

Go et al. (2009) employ Naïve Bayes, Maximum Entropy, and SVM to classify sentiment of Twitter messages to positive, neutral, and negative categories. Usernames, usage of links and repeated letters are taken as features. Jiang et al. (2011) consider target-dependent features and related tweets in the target-dependent Twitter sentiment classification, and achieve an accuracy of 68.2%. The sentiments of the tweets are still discrete, i.e., positive, negative, or neutral.

Takala et al. (2014) develop an evaluation dataset for topic-specific sentiment analysis in financial and economic domain, where financial news are sampled from Thomson Reuters newswire. Each news story is annotated by 7-point scale from very positive to very negative. The SemEval-2017 Task 5 deals with fine-grained sentiment analysis on financial microblogs and news. Financial tweets and news headlines are taken as evaluation data.

This paper is different from the above coarse-grained approaches. Multi-targets in a short text is one of the major issues to be tackled. We will find the sentiment of an interesting target in a tweet

3. Features

The twitter dataset in SemEval-2017 Task 5 is used in this study. It consists of 1,539 financial tweets. Total 55.6% of tweets contain more than one target. The sentiment scores of the targets in a tweet are labeled into the real numbers between -1 to 1 by 3 experts.

Figure 1 shows the structure of a financial tweet. The following sections will discuss how to extract features from each component. The 21 features used in the experiments are shown in Table 1.

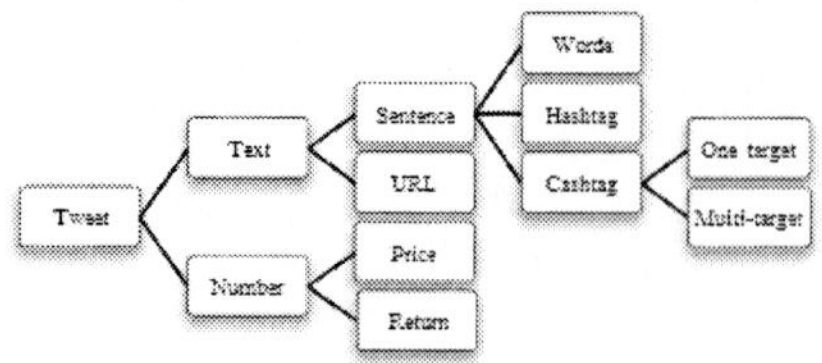

Figure 1. Structure of a financial tweet

Type	Source	Dictionary/Operations	#Features
text span	in tweet	15 dictionaries/average	15
text span	in tweet	trained dict/avg or max	2
text span	via URL	SenticNet 4/avg or max	2
number	in tweet	not applicable	1
relation	in tweet	not applicable	1

Table 1. Features

3.1 Text Span

In the SemEval-2017 dataset, experts labeled a "text span" for each target. In the tweet T1 specified in Section 1, the spans "$SPY up only 0.6%, Still holding" and "now up 2.2%, Still holding" are assigned to $SPY and $AAPL, respectively.

Besides human-annotated text span, we also explore two span determination algorithms shown as follows. Here, we collect a mapping table of tickers and company names from Bloomberg, and use it to find the canonical form of the company mentions in a tweet.

(1) Position-based approach (EP)

First, a tweet will be separated into sentences. Then, the sentence containing the cashtag or the company name of a target is deemed as the span for the target. The sentence without any company names or cashtags will be regarded as the span for all targets shown in the tweet. Here, a hashtag is regarded as a word.

(2) Dependency-based approach

(2.1) Stanford Parser (ED-S)

A tweet is parsed by Stanford dependency parser (Marneffe, 2006). To reduce the effects of out of vocabulary (OOV) words in parsing, cashtags and company names are replaced by common names like "Bob". A dependency tree for n-word tweet is composed of n triples in the form of $dep(word_i, word_j)$, where $word_i$ and $word_j$ has a dependency dep, $word_i$ is a parent of $word_j$, and $word_j$ is a child of $word_i$. We take the ancestors and the decedents of a target as its span.

(2.2) TweeboParser (ED-T)

TweeboParser is a dependency parser, designed for tweets (Kong et al., 2014). It tries to deal with the following challenges: token selection, multi-word expressions, multiple roots, and structure within noun phrases. The multiple roots property tends to provide shorter span than ED-S with the same extracted algorithm.

The average length of the tweets, manual spans, EP spans, ED-S and ED-T spans are 17.61, 6.26, 12.17, 10.27, and 7.78 words, respectively. Compared with 140-character word limit in twitter, a financial tweet is very short. In particular, manual spans are much shorter.

Besides text span in tweets, tweets may contain URLs as reference (shown in Figure 1). To collect as much information as possible, we parse the web page designated by the URL and retrieve the sentences containing the target. Those sentences are considered as additional text for sentiment classification.

Table 2 shows the example of span for the single target case: "$ATVI ooks pretty bullish for now. from a short-term perspective, it's got a good chance of maybe sliding back to 33.70 #stocks #investing"

Table 3 shows the example of span for: "Report: Apple signs up for Google's cloud, uses much less of Amazon's $AAPL $GOOG $GOOGL $AMZN $DROPB https://t.co/zN3KDGYvGT" The target of span is $AAPL.

As shown in the above two examples, ED-T method provides the shortest span and extracts the span more similar to Manual span. The extract results may sometimes include all words in tweet.

Manual	ooks pretty bullish for now
EP	'$ATVI ooks pretty bullish for now.', 'from a short-term perspective', " it's got a good chance of maybe sliding back to 33.70 #stocks #investing"
ED-S	Bob ooks pretty bullish for now from a short term perspective it s got a good chance of maybe sliding back to 33 70 stocks investing
ED-T	$atvi ooks pretty bullish for now

Table 2. Example of Single Target Span

Manual	Report: Apple signs up for Google's cloud
EP	Report: Apple signs up for Google's cloud, uses much less of Amazon's
ED-S	Report Bob signs up for Google s cloud uses much less
ED-T	apple signs up for google's cloud

Table 3. Example of Multi-Target Span

3.2 Ensemble of Sentiment Dictionaries

In the lexicon-based sentiment analysis, the sentiment score of a text span is determined by the sentiment scores of the sentiment words it contains. We use the max or the average of the sentiment scores of the related words as the features shown in Table 1. Total 15 sentiment dictionaries of two forms, real value and binary, are consulted. In addition to the publicly available dictionaries, we also construct a sentiment dictionary from the training set automatically.

(1)   Real value: SentiWordNet[1], SenticNet 4[2], NRC Hashtag Emotion Lexicon, NRC Hashtag Affirmative Context Sentiment Lexicon and NRC Hashtag Negated Context Sentiment Lexicon unigrams and bigrams, Yelp Restaurant Sentiment Lexicon unigrams and bigrams, Amazon Laptop Sentiment Lexicon unigrams and bigrams, Sentiment140 Affirmative Context Lexicon unigrams and bigrams, Emoticon Lexicon aka Sentiment140 Lexicon unigrams, bigrams[3]

(2)   Binary (1 for positive, -1 for negative): NRC Word-Emotion Association Lexicon, Macquarie Semantic Orientation Lexicon

SentiWordNet is quite different from the other sentiment dictionaries in the above. Words of different senses are assigned different sentiment scores. In the experiments, we use Babelfy (Moro et al., 2014) to disambiguate the word senses before consulting SentiWordNet.

We separated all words in training set, then counted the average sentiment score for each word to construct the other sentiment dictionary.

3.3 Numbers and Relationships

As described in Section 1, numbers such as monetary expressions are important cues for analyzing financial tweets. We use the position between a target and numbers to decide which number in a tweet is related to a target, and calculate the ratio of this number and sum of all numbers mentioned in the tweet as a feature.

In finance, the correlation coefficient of the price return between two stocks has been used to capture their relationship. We calculate the correlation coefficients by the stock prices during 2015/01/01 to 2016/10/31 downloaded from Bloomberg, and use them to compute the geometric mean of the absolute value of the correlation coefficients between the interesting target and other stocks in a tweet. The sign of this feature depends on the plurality voting.

4. Experimental Results

In coarse-grained classification, we classify the sentiment of a given target mentioned in a tweet into positive, negative, or neutral. The SVM model with the proposed 21 features are used. In fine-grained classification, we predict the sentiment score of the given target in real number. The SVR is adopt for this task. Both model followed the default parameters used in python Scikit-learn (Pedregosa et al., 2011) Accuracy and cosine similarity are used to measure the performance of the coarse-grained and the fine-grained tasks, respectively. The ground truth is represented as a vector of targets' sentiment scores in cosine measurement. Four-fold cross-validation is conducted.

Table 4 shows the experimental results. Using manual spans achieves the ideal performance because the critical text span for the target is known beforehand. Using EP spans is better than using the complete tweet, but worse than using manual spans. The performance of the ED-S Span approach does not meet our original expectation due to the noise results in dependency parsing in tweets, which are usually incomplete sentences. The ensemble of the first five methods show in

Table 4 show the best accuracy in the 4-fold validation for both coarse-grained and fine-grained case.

Methods	Coarse-grained	Fine-grained
Complete Tweet	64.91%	59.40%
Manual Span	86.94%	82.17%
EP Span	72.00%	62.83%
ED-S Span	64.52%	39.48%
ED-T Span	34.50%	34.05%
Ensemble	89.60%	82.60%

Table 4. Experimental Results

Although ED-T method provides the span whose average length is the closest to manual span, it gets the worse accuracy. It's worth to leave no stone unturned. We leave this part in the future works.

Due to the limited amount of submission, we submit two test results: manual span and the ensemble. The final result for the SemEval-2017 Task 5 by cosine similarity are 35.66% and 38.28%, and by evaluation method 2^4 are 55.34% and 56.68%, as the test of 4-fold validation that ensemble result got the best accuracy.

The same dictionaries and SVR model are used to subtask 2, using the news headline data. The best result is 55.43% using evaluation method 2.

5. Conclusion and Future Work

In this paper, we analyze the specific properties of the financial tweets, and propose methods to extract features from a tweet and its mentioned URL.

We illustrate some of the challenges of analyzing financial tweets. For the multi-targets problem, in order to extract the specific part of tweet for the target, we provide three methods, making the process automatically. The comparison of "spans" similarity will be provided in the future works. Moreover, we will also handle the number and the relationship between targets more precisely.

---

[4] Description of evaluation method 2 :
http://alt.qcri.org/semeval2017/task5/data/uploads/description_second_approach.pdf

References

Alec Go, Richa Bhayani and Lei Huang. 2009. Twitter sentiment classification using distant supervision. CS224N Project Report, Stanford 1, 12

Long Jiang, Mo Yu, Ming Zhou, Xiaohua Liu and Tiejun Zhao. 2011. Target-dependent twitter sentiment classification. Proceedings of the 49th Annual Meeting of the Association for Computational Linguistics, pages 151–160

Siavash Kazemian, Shunan Zhao, and Gerald Penn.2014. Evaluating sentiment analysis evaluation: A case study in securities trading. Proceedings of the 5th Workshop on Computational Approaches to Subjectivity, Sentiment and Social Media Analysis, pages 119–127

Pyry Takala, Pekka Malo, Ankur Sinha, and Oskar Ahlgren. 2014. Gold-standard for topic-specific sentiment analysis of economic texts. Proceedings of Ninth International Conference on Language Resources and Evaluation, pages 2152–2157

Marie-Catherine de Marneffe, Bill MacCartney and Christopher D. Manning. 2006. Generating Typed Dependency Parses from Phrase Structure Parses. In LREC 2006.

Lingpeng Kong, Nathan Schneider, Swabha Swayamdipta, Archna Bhatia, Chris Dyer, and Noah A. Smith. 2014. A Dependency Parser for Tweets. In EMNLP, 1001–1012

A. Moro, A. Raganato, R. Navigli. 2014. Entity Linking meets Word Sense Disambiguation: a Unified Approach. Transactions of the Association for Computational Linguistics (TACL), 2, pp. 231-244.

Pedregosa et al, 2011. Scikit-learn: Machine Learning in Python, JMLR 12, pp. 2825-2830

Baccianella, Stefano, Andrea Esuli, and Fabrizio Sebastiani. 2010. SentiWordNet 3.0: An enhanced lexical resource for sentiment analysis and opinion mining. In Proceedings of the Seventh Conference on International Language Resources and Evaluation (LREC'10), pages 2200–2204, Valletta.

E. Cambria et al., "SenticNet 4: A Semantic Resource for Sentiment Analysis based on Conceptual Primitives," Proc. 26th Int'l Conf. Computational Linguistics, 2016, pp. 2666–2677

Saif Mohammad and Peter Turney. 2013. Crowdsourcing a Word-Emotion Association Lexicon. Computational Intelligence, 29 (3), 436-465

Svetlana Kiritchenko, Xiaodan Zhu and Saif Mohammad. 2014. Sentiment Analysis of Short Informal Texts. Journal of Artificial Intelligence Research, volume 50, pages 723-762

Kiritchenko, S., Zhu, X., Cherry, C., 2014 Mohammad, S.M.: NRC-Canada-2014: Detecting aspects and sentiment in customer reviews. In: Proceedings of the International Workshop on Semantic Evaluation, SemEval '14, pp. 437–442

Svetlana Kiritchenko, Xiaodan Zhu and Saif Mohammad.2014. Sentiment Analysis of Short Informal Texts. Journal of Artificial Intelligence Research, volume 50, pages 723-762

Saif Mohammad and Peter Turney. 2010. Emotions Evoked by Common Words and Phrases: Using Mechanical Turk to Create an Emotion Lexicon, In Proceedings of the NAACL-HLT 2010 Workshop on Computational Approaches to Analysis and Generation of Emotion in Text, June 2010

Saif Mohammad, Bonnie Dorr, and Cody Dunne. 2009. Generating High-Coverage Semantic Orientation Lexicons From Overtly Marked Words and a Thesaurus, In Proceedings of the Conference on Empirical Methods in Natural Language Processing (EMNLP-2009)

Cortis, Keith and Freitas, Andr and Dauert, Tobias and Huerlimann, Manuela and Zarrouk, Manel and Handschuh, Siegfried and Davis, Brian. 2017. SemEval-2017 Task 5: Fine-Grained Sentiment Analysis on Financial Microblogs and News. Proceedings of the 11th International Workshop on Semantic Evaluation (SemEval-2017).

funSentiment at SemEval-2017 Task 5: Fine-Grained Sentiment Analysis on Financial Microblogs Using Word Vectors Built from StockTwits and Twitter

Quanzhi Li, Sameena Shah, Armineh Nourbakhsh, Rui Fang, Xiaomo Liu

Research and Development
Thomson Reuters
3 Times Square, NYC, NY 10036
{quanzhi.li, sameena.shah, armineh.nourbakhsh, rui.fang, xiaomo.liu}@thomsonreuters.com

Abstract

This paper describes the approach we used for SemEval-2017 Task 5: Fine-Grained Sentiment Analysis on Financial Microblogs. We use three types of word embeddings in our algorithm: word embeddings learned from 200 million tweets, sentiment-specific word embeddings learned from 10 million tweets using distance supervision, and word embeddings learned from 20 million StockTwits messages. In our approach, we also take the left and right context of the target company into consideration when generating polarity prediction features. All the features generated from different word embeddings and contexts are integrated together to train our algorithm.

1 Introduction

Domain specific Sentiment Analysis has received much attention recently. The financial domain is a high-impact use case for Sentiment Analysis because it has been shown that sentiments and opinions can affect market dynamics [9, 48]. Given the link between sentiment and market dynamics, the analysis of public sentiment becomes a powerful method to predict the market reaction. One main source of public sentiment is social media, such as Twitter and StockTiwts.

In this paper, we describe our approach for SemEval-2017 Task 5: Fine-Grained Sentiment Analysis on Financial Microblogs (Cortis et al., 2017). The task is: given a microblog message, predict the sentiment score for each of the companies/stocks mentioned. Sentiment values needed to be floating point values within the range of -1 (very negative/bearish) to 1 (very positive/ bullish), with 0 designating neutral sentiment. Our approach uses word embeddings (WE-Twitter) learned from general tweets, sentiment

specific word embeddings (SSWE) learned from distance supervised tweets, and word embeddings learned from StockTwits messages (WE-StockTwits).

Message or sentence level sentiment classification has been studied by many previous works (Go et al., 2009; Mohammand et al., 2013; Pang et al., 2002; Liu, 2012; Tang et al., 2014), but there are few studies on target-dependent, or entity level, sentiment prediction (Jiang et al., 2011; Dong et al., 2014; Vo and Zhang, 2015). A target entity in a message does not necessarily have the same polarity type as the message, and different entities in the same message may have different polarities. For example, in the tweet "iPhone is better than Blackberry", the two named entities, *iPhone* and *Blackberry*, will have different sentiment polarities. Recent studies have focused on learning features directly from tweet text. One approach is to generate sentence representations from word embeddings. Several word embedding generation algorithms have been proposed in previous studies (Collobert et al., 2011; Mikolov et al., 2013). Using the general word embeddings directly in sentiment analysis is not effective, since they mainly model a word's semantic context, ignoring the sentiment clues in text. Therefore, words with opposite polarity, such as *worst* and *best*, are mapped onto vectors embeddings that are close to each other in some dimensions. Tang et al. (2014) propose a sentiment-specific word embedding (SSWE) method for sentiment analysis, by extending the word embedding algorithm. SSWE encodes sentiment information in the word embeddings.

Many terms in financial market have different meanings, especially sentiment polarity, from that in other domains or sources, such as general news articles and Twitter. For example, terms

852

long, short, put and *call* have special meanings in stock market. Another example is the term *underestimate*, which is a negative term in general, but it can suggest an opportunity to buy when used in stock market messages. Therefore, in this study we also build word embedding specifically from StockTwits messages.

The context of an entity will affect its polarity value, and usually an entity has a left context and also a right one, unless it is at the beginning or end of a message. Both the context information and the interaction between these two contexts are included in the algorithm features of our approach. In this task, the financial microblogs are from StockTwits and Twitter, so in our approach, we incorporate features generated from WE-Twitter, SSWE and WE-StockTwits to represent these contexts, since they complement each other.

2 Previous Studies

Sentence or Message Level Sentiment: Traditional sentiment analysis approaches use sentiment lexicons (Mohammad et al., 2013; Thelwall et al., 2012; Turney, 2002) to generate various features. Pang et al. treat sentiment classification as a special case of text categorization, by applying learning algorithms (2002). Many studies follow Pang's approach by designing features and applying different learning algorithms on them (Feldman, 2013; Liu, 2012). Go et al. (2009) proposed a distance supervision approach to derive features from tweets obtained by positive and negative emotions. Some studies (Hu et al., 2013; Liu, 2012; Pak and Paroubek 2010) follow this approach. Feature engineering plays an important role in microblog sentiment analysis; Mohammad et al. (2013) implemented hundreds of hand-crafted features for tweet sentiment analysis.

Deep learning has been used in the sentiment analysis tasks, mainly by applying word embeddings (Collobert et al., 2011; Mikolov et al., 2013). Learning the compositionality of phrase and sentence and then using them in sentiment classification is also explored by some studies (Hermann and Blunsom, 2013; Socher et al., 2011; Socher et al., 2013). Using the general word embeddings directly in sentiment analysis may not be effective, since they mainly model a word's semantic context, ignoring the sentiment clues in text. Tang et al. (2014) propose a sentiment-specific word embedding method by extending

the word embedding algorithm from (Collobert et al., 2011) and incorporating sentiment data in the learning of word embeddings.

Entity or Target Level Sentiment: Jiang et al. (2011) use both entity dependent and independent features generated based on a set of rules to assign polarity to entities. By using POS features and the CRF algorithm, Mitchell et al. (2013) identify polarities for people and organizations in tweets. Dong et al. (2014) apply adaptive recursive neural network on the entity level sentiment classification. These two approaches use syntax parsers to parse the tweet to generate related features. In our approach, we consider both the left and right contexts of a target when generating features.

3 Methodology

In this section, we describe the three main components used in our method, the WE-Twitter, SSWE and WE-StockTwits models, and how the learning features are generated from them and integrated together.

3.1 WE-Twitter and WE-StockTwits Word Embedding

Word Embedding: A word embedding is a dense, low-dimensional and real-valued vector for a word. The embeddings of a word capture both the syntactic structure and semantics of the word. Traditional bag-of-words and bag-of-n-grams hardly capture the semantics of words. Word embeddings have been used in many NLP tasks. The C&W model (Collobert et al., 2011) and the word2vec model (Mikolov et al., 2013), which is used in this study to generate the WE-Twitter and WE-StockTwits embeddings, are the two popular models.

The embeddings are learned to optimize an objective function defined on the original text, such as likelihood for word occurrences. One implementation is the word2vec from Mikolov et al. (2013). This model has two training options, continuous bag of words and the Skip-gram model. The Skip-gram model is an efficient method for learning high-quality distributed vector representations that capture a large number of precise syntactic and semantic word relationships. This model is used in our method for building WE-Twitter and WE-StockTwits models. Generating word embeddings from text corpus is an unsupervised process. To get high quality embedding vectors, a large amount of training data is necessary. After training, each word, including all hashtags in the case of tweet, is represented by a low-dimensional, dense and real-valued vector.

WE-Twitter model construction: The tweets for building the WE-Twitter model include tweets obtained through Twitter's public streaming API and The Decahose data (10% of Twitter's streaming data) obtained from Twitter. Only English tweets are included in this study. In total there are about 200 million tweets. Each tweet text is preprocessed to get a clean version, following steps blow:

- all URLs and mentions are removed.
- dates are converted to a symbol.
- all ratios are replaced by a special symbol.
- integers and decimals are normalized to two special symbols.
- all special characters, except hashtags, cashtags, emoticons, question marks and exclamations, are removed.

Stop words are not removed, since they provide important information on how other words are used. In total, about 2.9 billion words were used to train the WE-Twitter model. Based on our pilot experiments, we set the embedding dimension size, word frequency threshold and window size as 300, 5 and 8, respectively. There are about 1.9 million unique words in this model.

WE-StockTwits model construction: StockTwits is a financial social network for sharing ideas among traders. Anyone on StockTwits can contribute content – short messages limited to 140 characters that cover ideas on specific investments. Most messages have a *cashtag*, which is a stock symbol, such as $aapl, to specify the entity (stock) this message is about. We received the permission from StockTwits to access their historical message archive from 2011 to 2016. We extract 20 million messages from this data set to build the WE-StockTwits model. Some preprocessing steps are performed to clean the messages:

- messages that contain only cashtags, URLs, or mentions are discarded, since they do not have meaningful terms.
- message text is converted to lower case.
- all URLs are removed.
- all mentions are converted to a special symbol, for privacy reason.
- all cashtags are replaced by a special symbol, to avoid cashtags to gain a polarity value related to a particular time period.

The embedding dimension size, word frequency threshold and window size are set as 300, 5 and 8, respectively.

3.2 Sentiment-Specific Word Embedding

SSWE: The C&W model (Collobert et al., 2011) learns word embeddings based on the syntactic contexts of words. It replaces the center word with a random word and derives a corrupted n-gram. The training objective is that the original n-gram is expected to obtain a higher language model score than the corrupted n-gram. The original and corrupted n-grams are treated as inputs of a feed-forward neural network, respectively.

SSWE extends the C&W model by incorporating the sentiment information into the neural network to learn the embeddings; it captures the sentiment information of sentences as well as the syntactic contexts of words (Tang et al., 2014). Given an original (or corrupted) n-gram and the sentiment polarity of a tweet as input, it predicts a two-dimensional vector (f_0, f_1), for each input n-gram, where (f_0, f_1) are the language model score and sentiment score of the input n-gram, respectively. The training objectives are twofold: the original n-gram should get a higher language model score than the corrupted n-gram, and the polarity score of the original n-gram should be more aligned to the polarity label of the tweet than the corrupted one. The loss function is the linear combination of two losses - $loss_0$ (t, t') is the syntactic loss and $loss_1$ (t, t') is the sentiment loss:

$$loss\ (t, t') = \alpha * loss_0\ (t, t') + (1-\alpha) * loss_1\ (t, t')$$

The SSWE model used in this study was trained from massive distant-supervised tweets, collected using positive and negative emotions.

SSWE model construction: The SSWE model for Twitter was trained from massive distant-supervised tweets, collected using positive and negative emoticons, such as *:), =), :(and :-(.* A total of 10 million tweets were collected, where 5 million contain positive emotions and the other 5 million contain negative ones. The embedding dimension size was set as 50 and the window size as 3.

3.3 Feature Generation

3.3.1 Features

Given a message and the target entity, nine types of features are generated based on WE-Twitter, SSWE, and WE-StockTwits models. They are integrated together to train the algorithm. Figure 1 shows the nine types of features. Three types of features are generated from SSWE embeddings for a target entity. The red ones are SSWE embeddings, and the blue ones are WE-Twitter and WE-StockTwits embeddings. The subscript letter $_L$ and $_R$ refer to the left and right side of an entity, respectively. These features are described below:

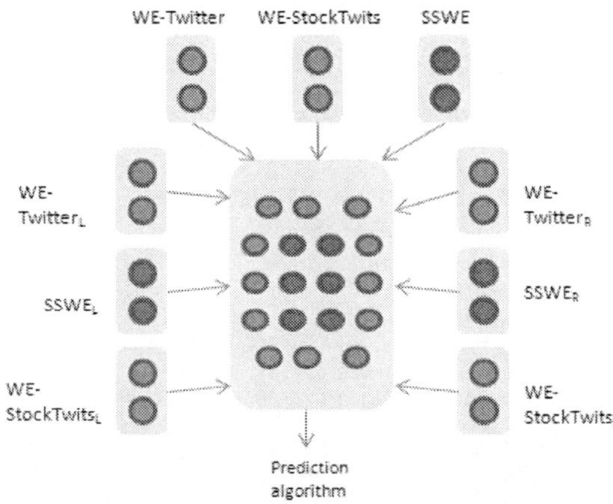

Figure 1. The features generated from different word embedding models and different contexts.

WE-Twitter$_L$ and WE-Twitter$_R$: These are the WE-Twitter embeddings for the text on the left side and right side of the target entity, respectively. In this task, occasionally, the given cashtag (company stock symbol) does not appear in the message text. In this case, the whole tweet text is used for both the left and right contexts, and this case is handled in the same way when generating WE-StockTwits$_L$, WE-StockTwits$_R$, SSWE$_L$ and SSWE$_R$ described below.

WE-StockTwits$_L$ and WE-StockTwits$_R$: These are the WE-StockTwits embeddings for the text on the left side and right side of the target entity, respectively.

SSWE$_L$ and SSWE$_R$: These are the SSWE embeddings for the text on the left side and right side of the target entity, respectively.

WE-Twitter, WE-StockTwits and SSWE: these are the embeddings generated from the whole message text, which means they are entity independent features. We use these three features to capture the whole message, which reflects the interaction between the left and right sides of the entity.

These nine types of embeddings together capture different types of information we are interested: the entity's left and right contexts, the interaction of the two sides, the sentiment specific word embedding information, and the general word embedding information learned from Twitter and StockTwits.

3.3.2 Text Representation from Term Embeddings

A message or text segment, such as the left/right context of an entity, has multiple words and each word has its own embedding vector. How to combine them together to represent this message so that all messages will have the same size of embedding vector needs to be explored. There are different ways to do this, e.g. for each embedding dimension, using the max value of all the words. In our approach, we use the concatenation convolution layer, which concatenates the layers of max, min and average of word embeddings, because this layer gives the best performance based on our pilot experiments. The concatenation layer is expressed as follow:

$$Z(t) = [Z_{max}(t), Z_{min}(t), Z_{ave}(t)]$$

where $Z(t)$ is the representation of text segment t.

4   Experiment and Result

For this task, the training data are provided by the task organizers. There are 1,704 tweets and StockTwits messages. We downloaded them from Twitter and StockTwits. To build our model, we split this data set into three parts: 80% as training data and 20% as development data. Since the predicted output in this task is a real value, so we use a liner regression algorithm in our approach. Based on the cosine similarity metric and the evaluation data set, which consists of 800 tweets and StockTwits messages (Cortis et al., 2017), the score of our approach is 0.7153, and our team is ranked at #6 among the 38 submissions.

5   Conclusion

This paper describes the approach we used for SemEval-2017 Task 5: Fine-Grained Sentiment Analysis on Financial Microblogs. We use three types of word embeddings in our algorithm: general word embeddings learned from 200 million tweets, sentiment-specific word embeddings learned from 10 million tweets using distance supervision, and word embeddings learned from 20 million StockTwits messages. We treat the task as a target-dependent sentiment analysis problem and consider the context of the target company.

References

Stefano Baccianella, Andrea Esuli , Fabrizio Sebastiani, SentiWordNet 3.0: An Enhanced Lexical Resource for Sentiment Analysis and Opinion Mining, *LREC 2010*

Stefano Baccianella, Andrea Esuli, and Fabrizio Sebastiani. 2009. Evaluation measures for ordinal regression. *In Proceedings of the 9th IEEE International Conference on Intelligent Systems Design and Applications (ISDA 2009)*. Pisa, IT, pages 283–287.

Ronan Collobert, Jason Weston, Leon Bottou, Michael Karlen, Koray Kavukcuoglu, and Pavel Kuksa. Natural language processing (almost) from scratch. *Journal Machine Learning Research*, 12:2493–2537, 2011.

Keith Cortis, Andre Freitas, Tobias Daudert, Manuela H¨urlimann, Manel Zarrouk, and Brian Davis, SemEval-2017 Task 5: Fine-Grained Sentiment Analysis on Financial Microblogs and News, SemEval-2017

L. Dong, F. Wei, C. Tan, D. Tang, M. Zhou, K. Xu, adaptive recurisive neural network for target-depedant twitter sentiment classification. In *Proceedings of ACL 2014.*

R.-E. Fan, K.-W. Chang, C.-J. Hsieh, X.-R. Wang, and C.-J. Lin. LIBLINEAR: A Library for Large Linear Classification, *Journal of Machine Learning Research,* 9(2008), 1871-1874.

Ronen Feldman. 2013. Techniques and applications for sentiment analysis. *Communications of the ACM*, 56(4):82–89.

Alec Go, Lei Huang, and Richa Bhayani. 2009. Twitter sentiment analysis. *Final Projects from CS224N for Spring 2008/2009* at The Stanford Natural Language Processing Group.

Karl M. Hermann and Phil Blunsom. 2013. The role of syntax in vector space models of compositional semantics. In *Proceedings ACL*, pages 894–904

Xia Hu, Jiliang Tang, Huiji Gao, and Huan Liu. 2013. Unsupervised sentiment analysis with emotional signals. In *Proceedings of the International World Wide Web Conference*, pages 607–618.

L. Jiang, M. Yu, M. Zhou, X. Liu, T. Zhao, target-depedant twitter sentiment classification, In *Proceedings of ACL 2011*

S.S. Keerthi, S.K. Shevade, C. Bhattacharyya, K.R.K. Murthy, 2001. Improvements to Platt's SMO Algorithm for SVM Classifier Design. *Neural Computation*. 13(3):637-649.

Bing Liu. 2012. Sentiment analysis and opinion mining. *Synthesis Lectures on Human Language Technologies*, 5(1):1–167

Tomas Mikolov, Ilya Sutskever, Kai Chen, Greg Corrado, and Jeffrey Dean. Distributed Representations of Words and Phrases and their Compositionality. In *Proceedings of NIPS*, 2013.

Christopher Manning, Prabhakar Raghavan and Hinrich Schütze, (2008), Vector space classification. *Introduction to Information Retrieval*. Cambridge University Press.

Margaret Mitchell, Jacqui Aguilar,Theresa Wilson, and Benjamin Van Durme. Open domain targeted sentiment. I *Proceedings of EMNLP*, 2013.

Saif M Mohammad, Svetlana Kiritchenko, and Xiaodan Zhu. 2013. Nrc-canada: Building the state-ofthe- art in sentiment analysis of tweets. In *Proceedings of SemEval* 2013.

P. Nakov, A. Ritter, S. Rosenthal, F. Sebastiani and V. Stoyanov. 2016. SemEval-2016 Tasks: Sentiment Analysis in Twitter. In *Proceedings of SemEval 2016*

Alexander Pak and Patrick Paroubek. 2010. Twitter as a corpus for sentiment analysis and opinion mining. In *Proceedings of Language Resources and Evaluation Conference*, volume 2010.

Bo Pang, Lillian Lee, and Shivakumar Vaithyanathan. 2002. Thumbs up? sentiment classification using machine learning techniques. In *Proceedings of EMNLP*, pages 79–86

J. Platt, Fast Training of Support Vector Machines using Sequential Minimal Optimization. In B. Schoelkopf and C. Burges and A. Smola, editors, *Advances in Kernel Methods - Support Vector Learning*, 1998

Yossi Rubner, Carlo Tomasi, and Leonidas J. Guibas. 2000. The Earth Mover's Distance as a metric for image retrieval. *International Journal of Computer Vision,* 40(2):99–121.

Richard Socher, J. Pennington, E.H. Huang, A.Y. Ng, and C.D. Manning. 2011. Semi-supervised recursive autoencoders for predicting sentiment distributions. In *Proceedings of EMNLP 2011*, pages 151–161.

Richard Socher, Alex Perelygin, Jean Wu, Jason Chuang, Christopher D. Manning, Andrew Ng, and Christopher Potts. 2013. Recursive deep models for semantic compositionality over a sentiment treebank. In *Proceedings of EMNLP 2013*, pages 1631–1642.

Duyu Tang, Furu Wei, Nan Yang, Ming Zhou, Ting Liu, and Bing Qin. 2014. Learning sentimentspecific word embedding for twitter sentiment classification. In *Proceedings of ACL 2014*, pages 1555–1565.

Duyu Tang, Bing Qin, Xiaocheng Feng, Ting Liu, 2016. Effective LSTMs for Target-Dependent Sentiment Classification, In *Proceedings of COLING 2016*

Mike Thelwall, Kevan Buckley, and Georgios Paltoglou. 2012. Sentiment strength detection for the social web. *Journal of the American Society for Information Science and Technology*, 63(1):163–173.

Peter D Turney. 2002. Thumbs up or thumbs down?: semantic orientation applied to unsupervised classification of reviews. In *Proceedings of ACL*, pages 417–424

D. Vo and Y. Zhang, Target-dependant twitter sentiment classification with rich automatic features, *IJCAI 2015.*

Sida Wang and Christopher D Manning. 2012. Baselines and bigrams: Simple, good sentiment and topic classification. In *Proceedings of ACL 2012*, pages 90–94

SentiHeros at SemEval-2017 Task 5: An application of Sentiment Analysis on Financial Tweets

Narges Tabari, Armin Seyeditabari, Wlodek Zadrozny

Narges Tabari: nseyedit@uncc.edu

Armin Seyeditabari: sseyedi1@uncc.edu

Wlodek Zadrozny: wzadrozn@uncc.edu

Abstract

Sentiment analysis is the process of identifying the opinion expressed in text. Recently it has been used to study behavioral finance, and in particular the effect of opinions and emotions on economic or financial decisions. SemEval-2017 task 5 focuses on the financial market as the domain for sentiment analysis of text; specifically, task 5, subtask 1 focuses on financial tweets about stock symbols. In this paper, we describe a machine learning classifier for binary classification of financial tweets. We used natural language processing techniques and the random forest algorithm to train our model, and tuned it for the training dataset of Task 5, subtask 1. Our system achieves the 7th rank on the leaderboard of the task.

1 Introduction

The recent explosion of textual data creates an unprecedented opportunity for investigating people's emotions and opinions, and for understanding human behavior. Although there are several methods to do this, sentiment analysis is an especially effective method of text categorization that assigns emotions to text (positive, negative, neutral, etc.). Sentiment analysis methods have been used widely on blogs, news, documents and microblogging platforms such as Twitter.

Although social media and blogging are popular and widely used platforms to discuss many different topics, they are challenging to analyze. This is to large extent due to the specific of vocabulary and syntax, which are dependent on topics, with the same words possibly expressing different sentiments in different contexts. For example, a word in a casual context might have positive or neutral sentiment (e.g., crush), while the same word generally has a negative sentiment in finance. Therefore, with the absence of general natural language understanding, context-dependent and domain-specific approaches allow us to increase the accuracy of sentiment analysis at a relatively low implementation cost.

Domain-specific sentiment analysis is being used to analyze or investigate various areas in finance, such as corporate finance and financial markets, investment and banking, asset and derivative pricing. Ultimately, the goal is to understand the impact of social media and news on financial markets and to predict the future prices of assets and stocks.

The proposed task in SemEval-2017 targets a sentiment analysis task, which we should identify a range of negative to positive affect on the stock of certain companies. The objective of the task was to predict the sentiment associated with companies and stock with floating point values in the interval from -1 to 1.

Previous research on textual analysis in a financial context has primarily relied on the use of bag of words methods, to measure tone (Tetlock, 2007) (Loughran & McDonald, 2011) which is one of the prominent efforts to improve sentiment analysis in financial domain, showed that using non-financial word lists for sentiment analysis will produce misclassifications and misleading results. To illustrate this, they used the Harvard-IV-4 list on financial reports, and found that 73.8% of the negative word counts were attributable to words that were not actually negative in a financial context.

Recently, there has been an increasing interest towards the use of machine learning techniques to get better sentiment result; e.g., naïve Bayesian classifier (Saif, He and Alani 2012) with various features got the accuracy of 83.90%. Other reported results include the use of support vector machines (SVMs) with the accuracy of 59.4% (O'Hare et al., 2009), and multiple-classifier

Proceedings of the 11th International Workshop on Semantic Evaluations (SemEval-2017), pages 857–860,
Vancouver, Canada, August 3 - 4, 2017. ©2017 Association for Computational Linguistics

voting systems with the 72% accuracy (Das & Chen, 2007).

In this paper, we describe our approach to building a supervised classifier predicting the sentiment scores of financial tweets provided by SemEval-2017. The classifier is fed preprocessed tweets as input and it predicts the binary labels of the tweets. Once tweets were preprocess and features were extracted, various classification models were applied using Weka tool (Hall et al., 2009). This environment contains a collection of machine learning-based algorithms for data mining tasks, such as, classification, regression, clustering, association rules, and visualization. We ultimately used Random Forest as our classifier as in our various tests it showed the best and accuracy in classifying the tweets. After predicting the binary labels, we then use the probability of the tweets being correctly classified to create a range of predictions from -1 to 1 as it was requested in the task.

2 Method

2.1 Preprocessing the data

SemEval task 5, subtask 1 provided a training dataset with 1800 tweets. Every tweet had a sentiment score between -1 to 1 and it showed its sentiment toward the stock symbol that was assigned to that tweet. Table 1 describes variables in the training dataset we used for analyzing the tweets:

Label	Description
ID	Each tweet was assigned a unique ID
Span	Part of tweet that was considered to carry the sentiment toward the company or stock.
Sentiment	Score provided to us with numbers between -1 to 1.
Cashtag	Stock symbol that was the target of each tweet, e.g. $GE.

Table 1. Attributes used to create the sentiment classification model.

To prepare the dataset for classification, we first converted the sentiment scores to -1, 0 and 1. Tweets with sentiments between -0.01 and 0.01 were labeled as zero, positive sentiments labeled as 1 and negative tweets were labeled as -1. We then disregarded the tweets with neutral sentiment, which left us 1560 tweets to train our mod-

el. Some tweets had multiple Spans, describing the sentiment toward the Cashtag. To keep things simple, we concatenated the spans of each tweet with each other. Then using the Python NLTK[1] library we deleted the punctuations, tokenized the spans, and deleted the stop words.

Since certain stop words in financial context can have impact on the sentiment of the tweets, we excluded them from the stop word list. Words like "up", and "down" were not removed from tweets. We also removed the negations from the stop word lists, as we later handle the negations on our own when creating the features.

2.2 Feature Selection Process

To add features to our training dataset, we used the McDonald's wordlist (Loughran & McDonald, 2011). This is a list of positive and negative words for financial 10-K reports containing the summary of the company's performance.

We calculated number of positive or negative words in each Span, using the McDonald's wordlist in the added features. There were some words, such as "short" which was not in any wordlist as a negative word, yet shorting a stock expresses a negative sentiment toward that stock. For this reason, we manually added positive or negative words to each list that to our best knowledge carry those sentiments. Table 2 shows some of the words were added to McDonald's wordlist:

Word	Sentiment
Profit	Positive
Long	Positive
Short	Negative
Decay	Negative

Table 2. Example of the words added to McDonald's wordlist. (See full list in Appendix A)

Adding these words to the wordlist improved our results. Then we realized in context of finance, co-occurrence of some words with each other in one tweet changes the sentiment of the tweet completely. For example, "short" and "sell" are both negative words in context of finance, but selling a short contains a positive sentiment in stock market context. Another example would be the co-occurrence of "go" and "down", or "pull" and "back" in our tweets. In a similar fashion we

---

[1] http://www.nltk.org/

also we handled the negations. Once we found these patterns, we normalized our data, i.e. we replaced the combinations of words in the tweet with a single positive or negative label, which we treated just as another positive or negative word. We then re-counted the number of positive or negative words in the tweet and updated our feature vectors. Table 3 shows examples of patterns we found in the tweet to have changed the sentiment of the word. The normalization had a benefit of increasing the counts of rarely occurring ex

Word 1	Word 2	Replaced with
Go	Up	OKAY
Go	Down	NOTOKAY
Sell	Short	OKAY
Pull	Back	NOTOKAY

Table 3. Example of the word couples and their replacements used to normalize the data (tweets). (See full list in Appendix B.)

2.3 Sentiment Prediction

Classifier	Accuracy	F-score	Precision	Recall
Random Forest	91.26%	86.5%	91.3%	82.2%
SVM	90.43%	85.4%	88.9%	82.2%
Logistic Regression	84.69%	79%	74.3%	84.3%
Naïve Bayes	83.73%	73.3%	83.3%	65.4%

Table 4. Results of different Weka classifiers using 10-fold cross validation and default settings.

After pre-processing our data and creating all our features (Tweet, Positive-Count, Negative-Count), we used WEKA to classify our tweets. Our feature vectors were the combination of document vectors generated by Weka's StringToWordVector filter, followed by the features extracted from the data as explained above. Among all the classification methods that we used, Random Forest did give us the best result with accuracy of 91.2%. Table 4 shows results from various classifiers using our training data. The random forest model in WEKA provided both a class prediction and class probability for each tweet in the training and test set.

Since the final float score needed to be between -1 and 1, for tweets classified as negative we made the sentiment score the negative of the class probability; for positive classifications, the sentiment score was simply the class probability.

2.4 Other Experiments

We have done several other experiments first to find a promising approach, and to gauge alternative methods of classification and data preprocessing.

In our initial experiment, after pre-processing the tweets, we first ran the tweets on WEKA to classify using only the feature vector, WEKA's StringToWordVector which is a term document matrix. Random forest and Logistic regression had the highest accuracy of 83.3% and 85.3% respectively. This experiment shows the impact of our additional features to be around 6%.

Before deciding on the final features of the model, we tried other types of features. Although many of them did not improve the model, we still thought they were worth mentioning, with description of them following:

Bigrams: In the first experiment, bigrams were used. (Kouloumpis, Wilson, & Moore, 2011) showed that using unigrams and bigrams are effective in improving sentiment analysis. (Dave et al., 2003) reported that bigrams and trigrams worked better than unigrams for polarity classification of product reviews. Unfortunately, bigrams reduced accuracy of Random Forest and Logistic regression to 76.7% and 73.9% respectively. We imagine that with a larger data set, bigrams might be valuable.

Feature selection using logistic regression: In another experiment, we used logistic regression to produce a list of words with the higher odds ratio. We then removed other words from tweets, in an attempt to amplify the stronger signals. However, applying filtered tweets, with various ranges of odds ratio did not help with improving the results. The best result was when words only with odds ratio of [-5, 5] stayed in our training set; this gave us the accuracy of 83.5%.

Using word embedding (GloVe vectors): GloVe vectors (Pennington, Socher, & Manning, 2014) are vector representations of the words. In two separate experiments, we used vectors based on the Common Crawl (840B tokens, 2.2M vocab, cased, 300 dimensions), and the pre-trained word vectors for Twitter (2B tweets, 27B tokens, 1.2M vocab, 200 dimensions). We represented every word in each tweet by a corresponding vector. We then calculated the tweet vector, using the mean of word vectors of the tweet. In this experiment, McDonald's (Loughran & McDonald, 2011) positive and negative wordlist again were used. That is, we created a positive and negative vector using words in those lists. Comparing the cosine similarity of tweet vectors with positive and negative vector, we classified the tweets. The accuracy of this method was 72% and 73.8% for tweet and common crawl respectively.

3   Conclusion

The purpose of this paper was to create a classification method for SemEval-2017 task 5, subtask 1. In our approach after pre-processing the data, negation handling, and feature selection approaches, we used Weka to classify our data using Random Forest algorithm. Our classifier was ranked 7th and achieved accuracy of 91.26%.

In the next step, we think it is important to capture more complex linguistic structure, irony, idioms, and poorly structured sentences in financial domain. To this regard, we would like to apply dependency parser trees for tweets to see if that would improve our results; it might also be necessary to capture some of the idiomatic constructions in this domain.

Also, SemEval-2017 training dataset was a relatively small dataset, which would prevent us from implementing any neural network models for prediction. Therefore, we think a step to create a better model is to increase the size of training dataset.

References

Das, S. R., & Chen, M. Y. (2007). Yahoo! for Amazon: Sentiment Extraction from Small Talk on the Web. *Management Science, 53*(9), 1375–1388. http://doi.org/10.1287/mnsc.1070.0704

Dave, K., Lawrence, S. & Pennock, D. M. (2003). Mining the peanut gallery: Opinion extraction and semantic classification of product reviews. *Proceedings of the 12th International Conference on World Wide Web*, 519–528. http://doi.org/10.1145/775152.775226

Kouloumpis, E., Wilson, T., & Moore, J. (2011). Twitter sentiment analysis: The good the bad and the omg! *Proceedings of the Fifth International AAAI Conference on Weblogs and Social Media (ICWSM 11)*, 538–541. Retrieved from http://www.aaai.org/ocs/index.php/ICWSM/ICWSM11/paper/download/2857/3251?iframe=true&width=90%25&height=90%25

Loughran, T. I. M., & McDonald, B. (2011). When is a Liability not a Liability? Textual Analysis , Dictionaries , and 10-Ks. Journal of Finance, 66(1).

O'Hare, N., Davy, M., Bermingham, A., Ferguson, P., Sheridan, P. P., Gurrin, C., … OHare, N. (2009). Topic-Dependent Sentiment Analysis of Financial Blogs. *International CIKM Workshop on Topic-Sentiment Analysis for Mass Opinion Measurement*, 9–16. http://doi.org/10.1145/1651461.1651464

Pennington, J., Socher, R., & Manning, C. D. (2014). GloVe: Global Vectors for Word Representation. *Proceedings of the 2014 Conference on Empirical Methods in Natural Language Processing*, 1532–1543. http://doi.org/10.3115/v1/D14-1162

Saif, H., He, Y., & Alani, H. (2012). Semantic sentiment analysis of twitter. *Lecture Notes in Computer Science (Including Subseries Lecture Notes in Artificial Intelligence and Lecture Notes in Bioinformatics), 7649 LNCS*(PART 1), 508–524. http://doi.org/10.1007/978-3-642-35176-1-32

Tetlock, P. C. (2007). Giving content to investor sentiment: The role of media in the stock market. *Journal of Finance, 62*(3), 1139–1168. http://doi.org/10.1111/j.1540-6261.2007.01232.x

Appendix A. Words Added to McDonald's Wordlist.

Negative words: cult, brutal, fucked, suck, decay, bubble, bounce, bounced, low, lower, selloff, disgust, meltdown, downtrend, bullshit, shit, breakup, dropping, cry, dumped, torture, short, shorts, shorting, fall, falling, sell, selling, sells, bearish, slipping, slip, sink, sinked, sinking, pain, shortput, nervous, damn, downtrends, censored, toppy, scam, censor, garbage, risk, steal, retreat, retreats, sad, dirt, flush, dump, plunge, crush, crushed, crying, unhappy, drop, broke, overbought.

Positive words: epic, highs, recover, profit, long, upside, love, interesting, loved, dip, dipping, secure, longs, longput, rise, able, buy, buying.

Appendix B. Full List of Word Couples to Detect the Semantic of a Tweet.

Positive word couples: (go, up), (short, trap), (exit, short), (sell, exhaust), (didnt, stop), (short, cover), (close, short), (short, break), (cant, risk), (not, sell), (dont, fall), (sold, call), (dont, short), (exit, bankruptcy), (not, bad), (short, nervous), (dont, underestimate), (not, slowdown), (aint, bad).

Negative word couples: (high, down), (lipstick, pig), (doesnt, well), (bounce, buy), (isnt, cheap), (fear, sell), (cant, down), (not, good), (wont, buy), (dont, trade), (buy, back), (didnt, like), (profit, exit), (go, down), (not, guaranteed), (not, profitable), (doesn't, upward), (not, dip), (pull, back), (not, optimistic).

DUTH at SemEval-2017 Task 5: Sentiment Predictability in Financial Microblogging and News Articles

Symeon Symeonidis   John Kordonis   Dimitrios Effrosynidis   Avi Arampatzis

Database & Information Retrieval research unit,
Department of Electrical & Computer Engineering,
Democritus University of Thrace, Xanthi 67100, Greece
{ssymeoni,ioankordl,dimievfr,avi}@ee.duth.gr

Abstract

We present the system developed by the team DUTH for the participation in Semeval-2017 task 5 - Fine-Grained Sentiment Analysis on Financial Microblogs and News, in subtasks A and B. Our approach to determine the sentiment of Microblog Messages and News Statements & Headlines is based on linguistic pre-processing, feature engineering, and supervised machine learning techniques. To train our model, we used Neural Network Regression, Linear Regression, Boosted Decision Tree Regression and Decision Forrest Regression classifiers to forecast sentiment scores. At the end, we present an error measure, so as to improve the performance about forecasting methods of the system.

1 Introduction

Social media sentiment is an important indicator of public opinion. Determining sentiment can be valuable in a number of applications including brand awareness, product launches, and detecting political trends. Many microblogging platforms such as Twitter and StockTwits have become very popular and are employed by many traders and investors. Recently, many studies (Piñeiro-Chousa et al., 2016; Van de Kauter et al., 2015; Kordonis et al., 2016) used sentiment from social media and financial news articles trying to analyze market movements.

This paper describes our submissions to SemEval 2017 task 5 (Cortis et al., 2017), which deals with sentiment analysis in microblog messages for SubTask A, and sentences for news headlines for SubTask B. In SubTask A, our model was ranked last because of a submission format error. We perform error measures in order to obtain a better understanding of the strengths of these particularly new tasks and to improve the performance about forecasting methods of our model (Armstrong and Collopy, 1992). For Subtask B, our team was ranked 24th from 29 teams.

The rest of this paper is structured as follows: Section 2 provides our system's description. Section 3 presents the experiments and some unofficial results used in analyzing the system's performance. Finally, conclusions and further directions for research are presented in Section 4.

2 System Description

In this section we present the details of our sentiment analysis system, feature extraction and some statistics about preprocessing.

2.1 Dataset

The Task 5 organizers (Cortis et al., 2017) provided a training and testing set for both subtasks. For subtask A, resources of Microblog messages were Stocktwits and Twitter, which have been annotated for fine-grained sentiment [1]. A collection of financially relevant news headlines which have been annotated for fine-grained sentiment, from sources such as Yahoo Finance, are given from Task Organizers for subtask B [2]. Some statistics about the datasets are presented in table 1.

2.2 Pre-processing and Feature Engineering

To make it suitable for reliable analysis, the data had to be pre-processed. Moreover, feature hashing was used as an approach according to (Da Silva et al., 2014), to reduce the number of features provided as input from pre-processing to

---

[1] https://bitbucket.org/ssix-project/semeval-2017-task-5-subtask-1/

[2] https://bitbucket.org/ssix-project/semeval-2017-task-5-subtask-2/

Proceedings of the 11th International Workshop on Semantic Evaluations (SemEval-2017), pages 861–865,
Vancouver, Canada, August 3 - 4, 2017. ©2017 Association for Computational Linguistics

	train	test
Task A	1534	799
Task B	1142	491

Table 1: Number of tweets in training (train) and testing (test) data for subtask A and B.

a learning algorithm. As first step of our approach we chose to normalize the tweet text by performing the following operations:

- Remove numbers

- Remove punctuation

- Replace all user mentions and URL addresses, which were normalized to "@user" and "URL"

- Convert to lower case

Furthermore, we chose to compute the counts and cumulative frequencies of the words in the tweets. The NLTK (Bird et al., 2009) package contains two tools to help:

- The regexp_tokenize function tokenizes the text. Tokenization is the process of dividing the text into its component tokens. In this case, the tokens are all words, since we are working with normalized text.

- The FreqDist function computes the frequency distribution of words in a text corpus. A Python Pandas data frame (McKinney, 2010) is then computed from the word frequency array.

The most frequent words are in the head of the new data frame. Of these 20 most frequent words none are likely to give much information on sentiment.

In addition, we implemented a method in order to create a bar plot of word frequency for the 60 most common words, as presented in Figure 1, to comprehend the vocabulary of microblogging messages and news headlines. Unfortunately, we saw that many of the most frequent words are stopwords, such as 'the', 'and', and 'you', which are not likely to be helpful in determining sentiment.

Another tool for examining the frequency of words in a corpus of documents is the cumulative distribution frequency (CDF) plot, as presented in Figure 2.

Figure 1: Frequencies of the most common words

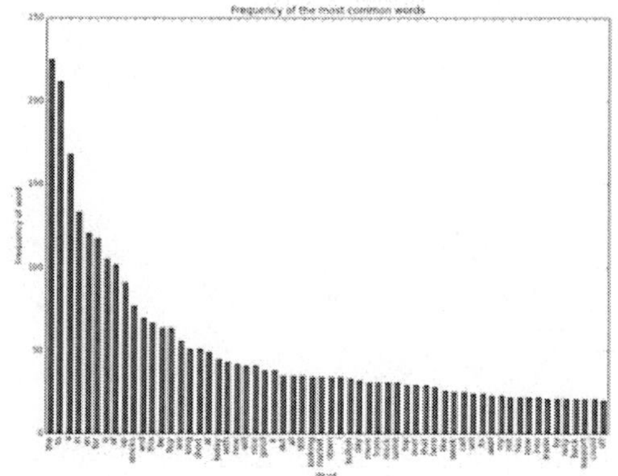

Figure 2: Cummulative fraction of total words vs. words

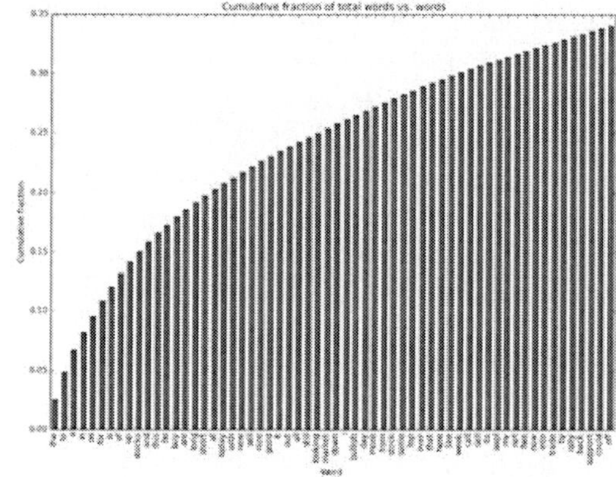

These frequent words, which are largely extraneous, are known as stopwords and should be removed from the text before further analysis, unlike with few studies which take stopwords as features (Mohammad et al., 2013). So, we implemented a method to remove the stopwords from each tweet using nested list comprehensions and execute the code from previous implementation in order to visualize the word frequency.

As before, Figure 3 shows a number of frequent words which are likely to convey sentiment. However, note that these 60 most frequent words only make up about 17% of the total words, where used in feature extraction.

Figure 3: Frequencies of the most common words after preprocessing

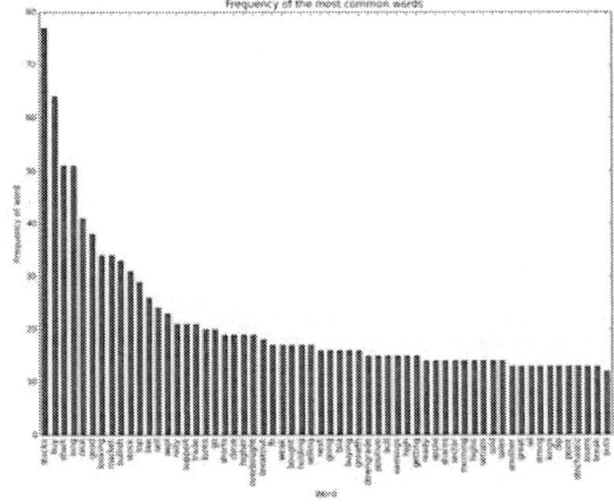

Figure 4: Wordcloud of frequent words after pre-processing

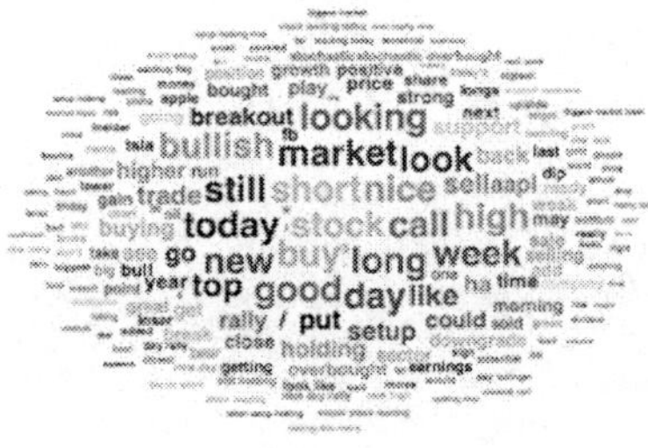

Figure 4 shows the most frequent words on dataset as a wordcloud and helps the researcher to understand if something went wrong in pre-processing.

Now, that we have cleaned the tweet text and removed stopwords, there is one last data preparation step required, stemming the words. Stemming is a process of reducing words to their stems or roots, reduce the vocabulary size and manage the case of data sparseness (Lin and He, 2009). For example, conjugated verbs such as 'goes', 'going', and 'gone' are stemmed to the word "go". Depending on suitable choice, the results can be more or less suitable for the application. In our case, we used the so popular Porter stemmer implemented by the PorterStemmer function in the nltk.stem.porter library.

In subsection 2.2, we described the preprocessing techniques and the features that were extracted for training our model. Section 3 presents the machine learning techniques and algorithms which were used for our experiments.

3 Experiments

In this section we present the main methodology implemented in our system for the SemEval 2017 Task 5. In order ti select the feature sets to use for each classifier, we have carried out a number of experiments.

3.1 Evaluation Metrics

The evaluation metric used by the task organizers was the cosine similarity, specifically, the metric of Ghosh et al. (2015). Sentiment scores had to be in scale between -1 and 1. The degree of agreement between predicted values and values from gold labels calculate the final result. In Section 4 the error metrics about our model are presented which are the following:

- Mean Absolute Error

- Root Mean Squared Error

- Relative Absolute Error

- Relative Squared Error

- Coefficient of Determination

The selection of error measures to calibrate our model are based on other related studies (Hippert et al., 2001; Armstrong and Collopy, 1992).

3.2 Machine Learning Methods

All system implementation was done using Python and the open-source machine learning toolkit scikit-learn (Pedregosa et al., 2011). In our system we implemented four classification techniques as follows:

- Linear Regression, which attemps to model the relationship between two variables by fitting a linear equation to the training data.

- Boosted Decision Tree Regression, which uses boosting to create an ensemble of regression trees. Boosting aims to learn any tree by fitting the continuing of the trees that preceded ands depends on prior trees. As a result, boosting in a decision tree ensemble contributes to small risk accruracy.

- Decision Forrest Regression, which is a model using an ensemble of decision trees.

- Neural Network Regression. Although neural networks are known for use in deep learning problems like recognition in images, and for regression problems they are adapted too. So, where a more traditional regression model is not fitting to a solution, neural network regression is suited to these problems.

The above four techniques were chosen empirically and based on related studies (Mittal and Goel, 2012; Ghiassi et al., 2013).

4 Results

Below, error measures of our model was done to improve our system's performance about forecasting methods of the system for subtask A. Figure 5 and 6 present the results for Mean Absolute Error, Root mean Squared Error, Relative Absolute Error, Relative Squared Error, and Coefficient of Determination. These metrics represent the performance of our system, without considering the metrics of Task. The results of error measures are promising for accuracy of our model and the prices of errors are not big to have disproportionate impacts for forecasting. According to Task Organizers results, our team got cosine score 0.5879725192 for Subtask B and 0.003076891426 for Subtask A (because of a submission format error).

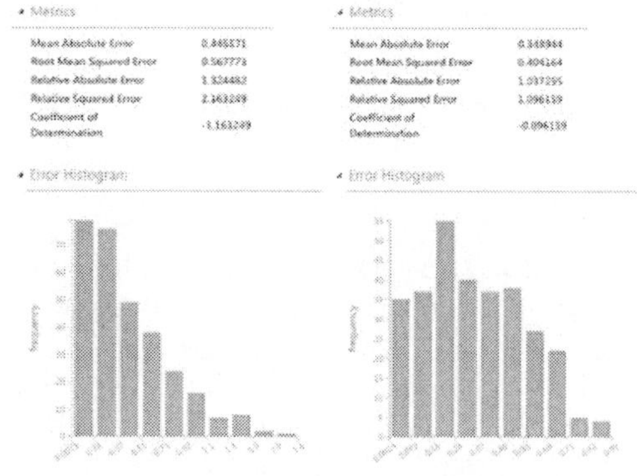

Figure 5: Linear Regression and Boosted Decision Tree Regression error metrics

5 Conclusions

We presented a supervised regression sentiment analysis system to detect the semantic interpretation of financial texts. Given the above error analysis results, we conclude that our methods for sentiment analysis on financial microblogs and news,

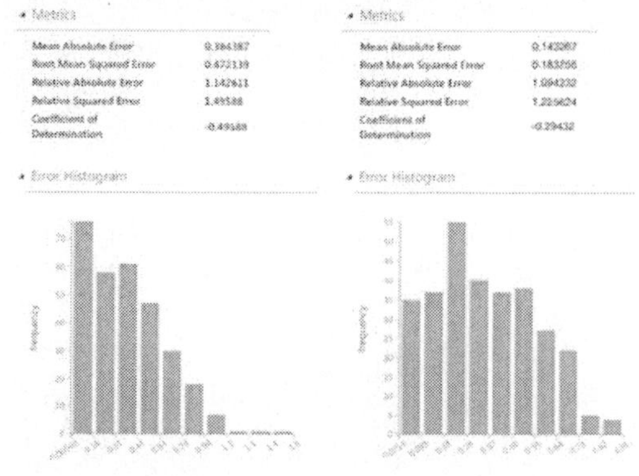

Figure 6: Decision Forrest Regression and Neural Network Regression error metrics

are promising. Future work will focus on feature selection and usage of some lexicons resources to achieve better results.

References

J. Scott Armstrong and Fred Collopy. 1992. Error measures for generalizing about forecasting methods: Empirical comparisons. *International Journal of Forecasting* 8(1):69–80. https://doi.org/10.1016/0169-2070(92)90008-W.

Steven Bird, Ewan Klein, and Edward Loper. 2009. *Natural Language Processing with Python.* O'Reilly Media, Inc., 1st edition.

Keith Cortis, André Freitas, Tobias Dauert, Manuela Huerlimann, Manel Zarrouk, Siegfried Handschuh, and Brian Davis. 2017. Semeval-2017 task 5: Fine-grained sentiment analysis on financial microblogs and news. In *Proceedings of the 11th International Workshop on Semantic Evaluation (SemEval-2017)*. Association for Computational Linguistics, Vancouver, Canada, pages 517–533. http://www.aclweb.org/anthology/S17-2089.

Nadia FF Da Silva, Eduardo R Hruschka, and Estevam R Hruschka. 2014. Tweet sentiment analysis with classifier ensembles. *Decision Support Systems* 66:170–179.

Manoochehr Ghiassi, James Skinner, and David Zimbra. 2013. Twitter brand sentiment analysis: A hybrid system using n-gram analysis and dynamic artificial neural network. *Expert Systems with applications* 40(16):6266–6282.

Aniruddha Ghosh, Guofu Li, Tony Veale, Paolo Rosso, Ekaterina Shutova, John Barnden, and Antonio Reyes. 2015. Semeval-2015 task 11: Sentiment analysis of figurative language in twitter. In *Proceedings of the 9th International Workshop on Semantic Evaluation (SemEval 2015)*. Association for Computational Linguistics, Denver, Colorado, pages

470–478. http://www.aclweb.org/anthology/S15-2080.

Henrique Steinherz Hippert, Carlos Eduardo Pedreira, and Reinaldo Castro Souza. 2001. Neural networks for short-term load forecasting: A review and evaluation. *IEEE Transactions on power systems* 16(1):44–55.

John Kordonis, Symeon Symeonidis, and Avi Arampatzis. 2016. Stock price forecasting via sentiment analysis on twitter. In *Proceedings of the 20th Pan-Hellenic Conference on Informatics*. ACM, New York, NY, USA, PCI '16, pages 36:1–36:6. https://doi.org/10.1145/3003733.3003787.

Chenghua Lin and Yulan He. 2009. Joint sentiment/topic model for sentiment analysis. In *Proceedings of the 18th ACM conference on Information and knowledge management*. ACM, pages 375–384.

Wes McKinney. 2010. Data structures for statistical computing in python. In Stéfan van der Walt and Jarrod Millman, editors, *Proceedings of the 9th Python in Science Conference*. pages 51 – 56.

Anshul Mittal and Arpit Goel. 2012. Stock Prediction Using Twitter Sentiment Analysis. *Tomx.Inf.Elte.Hu* (June).

Saif M Mohammad, Svetlana Kiritchenko, and Xiaodan Zhu. 2013. Nrc-canada: Building the state-of-the-art in sentiment analysis of tweets. *arXiv preprint arXiv:1308.6242* .

Fabian Pedregosa, Gaël Varoquaux, Alexandre Gramfort, Vincent Michel, Bertrand Thirion, Olivier Grisel, Mathieu Blondel, Peter Prettenhofer, Ron Weiss, Vincent Dubourg, Jake Vanderplas, Alexandre Passos, David Cournapeau, Matthieu Brucher, Matthieu Perrot, and Édouard Duchesnay. 2011. Scikit-learn: Machine Learning in Python. *J. Mach. Learn. Res.* 12:2825–2830. http://dl.acm.org/citation.cfm?id=1953048.2078195.

Juan Ramón Piñeiro-Chousa, M Ángeles López-Cabarcos, and Ada María Pérez-Pico. 2016. Examining the influence of stock market variables on microblogging sentiment. *Journal of Business Research* 69(6):2087–2092.

Marjan Van de Kauter, Diane Breesch, and Véronique Hoste. 2015. Fine-grained analysis of explicit and implicit sentiment in financial news articles. *Expert Syst. Appl.* 42(11):4999–5010. https://doi.org/10.1016/j.eswa.2015.02.007.

TakeLab at SemEval-2017 Task 5: Linear Aggregation of Word Embeddings for Fine-Grained Sentiment Analysis on Financial News

Leon Rotim, Martin Tutek, Jan Šnajder
Text Analysis and Knowledge Engineering Lab
Faculty of Electrical Engineering and Computing, University of Zagreb
Unska 3, 10000 Zagreb, Croatia
`{leon.rotim,martin.tutek,jan.snajder}@fer.hr`

Abstract

This paper describes our system for fine-grained sentiment scoring of news headlines submitted to SemEval 2017 task 5, subtask 2. Our system uses a feature-light method that consists of a Support Vector Regression (SVR) with various kernels and word embedding vectors as features. Our best-performing submission scored 3rd on the task out of 29 teams and 4th out of 45 submissions, with a cosine score of 0.733.

1 Introduction

Sentiment analysis (Pang and Lee, 2008) is a task of predicting whether the text expresses a positive, negative, or neutral opinion in general or with respect to an entity of interest. Developing systems capable of performing highly accurate sentiment analysis has attracted considerable attention over the last two decades. The topic has been one of the main research areas in recent shared tasks, with main focus on social media texts, which are of particular interest for social studies (O'Connor et al., 2010; Wang et al., 2012) and marketing analysis (He et al., 2013; Yu et al., 2013). At the same time, social media texts pose a big challenge for sentiment analysis due to their short, informal and often ungrammatical format.

This work focuses on the second subtask of SemEval-2017 Task 5, which aims to perform fine-grained sentiment analysis of the financial news. Given that sentiments can affect market dynamics (Goonatilake and Herath, 2007; Van de Kauter et al., 2015), sentiment analysis of financial news can be a powerful tool for predicting market reactions. Similar to social media posts, finance news are short texts, but, unlike social media posts, the text is edited and hence grammatically correct. On the other hand, news headlines are notorious for

the use of a specific language (Reah, 2002), which is often elliptical and compressed, and thus differs from the language used in the rest of the news story.

Many approaches to sentiment analysis resort to rich, domain-specific, hand-crafted features (Wilson et al., 2009; Abbasi et al., 2008). At the same time, there has been a growing interest in feature-light methods, including kernel-methods (Culotta and Sorensen, 2004; Lodhi et al., 2002a; Srivastava et al., 2013) and neural embeddings (Maas et al., 2011; Socher et al., 2013). These methods alleviate the need for manual creation of domain-specific features, while maintaining high accuracy. Most of the recently published work focuses on sentiment analysis problems that are framed as a classification task, while fine-grained analysis is framed as a regression problem. However, most of the high performing classification methods can be easily tuned to perform regression.

In this work we focus on feature-light methods as they do not require complex, time consuming feature engineering. More specifically, we focus on string kernels (Lodhi et al., 2002b) and methods using neural word embeddings (Mikolov et al., 2013a). Developing domain-specific, rich feature sets would probably make the method highly dependent to the specific problem and would be hardly applicable to similar problems in other domains. Feature-light methods have no such constrains: they typically offer satisfactory performance across different domains and may therefore be preferred to other domain-specific methods which use hand-crafted features.

2 Related Work

There has been considerable research focusing on sentiment analysis of short texts (Thelwall et al., 2010; Kiritchenko et al., 2014), especially within recent SemEval campaigns (Nakov et al., 2016;

866

Proceedings of the 11th International Workshop on Semantic Evaluations (SemEval-2017), pages 866–871,
Vancouver, Canada, August 3 - 4, 2017. ©2017 Association for Computational Linguistics

Rosenthal et al., 2015, 2014). A large body of recent work focuses on sentence-level sentiment prediction. Socher et al. (2012) and Socher et al. (2013) reported impressive results working with matrix-vector recursive neural network (MV-RNN) and recursive neural tensor networks models over sentence parse trees. Working with sentence parse trees Kim et al. (2015) and Srivastava et al. (2013) obtained competitive results using tree kernels as an alternative to recursive neural networks. These methods, while producing promising results, are highly dependent on parse trees. In practice, we often work with informal texts, where syntactic parsing often produces inaccurate results, which in turn heavily affects performances of the afore-mentioned methods. Furthermore, as noted by Le and Mikolov (2014), it is not straightforward how to extend these methods when working with text spans that range over multiple sentences.

There has been a growing amount of interest in methods that are not based on syntax. The most promising results have been achieved using neural word embeddings (Mikolov et al., 2013a), while string kernels (Zhang et al., 2008; Lodhi et al., 2002a; Leslie et al., 2002) offer a viable alterna-tive. Maas et al. (2011) and Tang et al. (2014) reported promising results by learning sentiment specific word embeddings. By extending word em-beddings to more complex paragraph embeddings Le and Mikolov (2014) reported state-of-the-art results on sentiment classification for both short and long English texts. Building on word embed-dings, Joulin et al. (2016) developed an end-to-end, domain independent, high-performance text classi-fication model.

3 Dataset

Our task was, given a news headline, to predict the sentiment score for a specific company mentioned in the headline. The dataset consisted of the name of the company, the text of the news headline and a value denoting the sentiment.

The sentiment was on a scale between -1 and 1 (inclusive), where -1 corresponds to very negative sentiment, 0 is considered neutral, while 1 stands for a very positive sentiment. The news headlines were on average 10 words in length and largely composed of abbreviations.

The training set was composed of 1142 news headlines, while the test set contained 491 head-lines, i.e., a 70:30 train-test split. The training set

id	5
company	Ryanair
title	EasyJet attracts more passengers in June but still lags Ryanair
sentiment	0.259

Table 1: Sample training data instance

and the test set mention 294 and 168 unique com-panies, respectively. The distribution of headlines for a specific company was not uniform, and only 58 companies in the train set were targets of more than 4 news headlines, while "Barclays" – the most frequently mentioned one – was the target 67 times. In total, 112 companies occur in both the train and test set.

An example of a training data instance is given in Table 1. This particular example also illustrates a possible difficulty regarding the headlines as they might refer to more than one company. Such exam-ples, however, are pretty rare in the dataset.

As for the class breakdown in the training set, we observe that the number of positively labeled instances is significantly larger than the number of negatively labeled instances (a ratio of 653 : 451 in favor of headlines with positive sentiment, in-cluding 38 headlines with a perfectly neutral score of 0.0). However, the distribution of the target variable has an almost zero mean value of 0.031 and a standard deviation of 0.39. All things con-sidered, we conclude that the dataset was fairly well-balanced and the dependent variable was not skewed towards either class.

4 Methods

While working on fine-grained sentiment analy-sis, we focus on feature-light, domain indepen-dent methods. In all considered methods, we use support vector regression (SVR) model for senti-ment prediction. The SVR allows us to experiment with both different features and kernels. Model training is performed using LIBSVM (Chang and Lin, 2011) for the non-linear kernel and LIBLIN-EAR (Fan et al., 2008) for the linear kernel.

BoW baseline. We use the standard bag-of-words (BoW) methods as a sensible baseline. BoW methods are implemented by creating a dictionary of words appearing in the train set. We imple-mented the BoW baseline using all uni-, bi-, and tri-grams that occur at least twice in the dataset, while filtering out words from the standard stopword list. We experiment with TF-IDF and Bernoulli weighting schemes for the word features. For generating the n-grams, we used NLTK toolkit (Bird et al., 2009), and filtered out n-grams consisting of stopwords.

String kernels. String kernels offer a dictionary-free alternative compared to other commonly-used methods. There are several known string kernels in use, the most popular being the spectrum kernel (SK) (Leslie et al., 2002) and the subsequence kernel (SSK) (Lodhi et al., 2002a). The SSK measures string similarity by first mapping each input string s to:

$$\varphi_u(s) = \sum_{i:u=s[i]} \lambda^{l(i)} \tag{1}$$

where u is a subsequence searched for in s, i is a vector of indices at which u appears in s, l is a function measuring the length of a matched subsequence and $\lambda \leq 1$ is a weighting parameter giving lower weights to longer subsequences. Using (1), the SSK kernel is defined as:

$$K_n(s,t) = \sum_{u \in \Sigma^n} \langle \varphi_u(s), \varphi_u(t) \rangle$$

where n is maximum subsequence length for which we calculate the kernel and Σ^n is a set of all finite strings of length n. Spectrum kernel can be defined as a special case of SSK where $\lambda = 1$ and i must yield continuous sequences. We experiment with both SK and SSK kernels, which we computed using the string similarity tool Harry.[1]

Word embeddings. Word embedding are task independent features, yet they offer competitive results on many text classification tasks. We experimented with pretrained word embeddings, namely GloVe (Pennington et al., 2014) and Skipgram (Mikolov et al., 2013b) trained on the Google News corpus.[2] We achieved the best results with the 300-dimensional Google News vectors.

The feature vector that is fed to the classifier is computed as the linear aggregate of the words making up the headline, simply as the average of the word embeddings of the individual words. Lowercasing the words that appear in the title gave us a considerable performance gain, which is expected

since most of the words appearing in news headlines are title-cased. We refer to this method as the *word embeddings method* (WEM).

We further experimented with additional filtering of the word tokens we use for building word embedding vectors. Our motivation was based on the observation that sentiment-bearing words typically exclude the named entities. We therefore used StanfordNLP (Manning et al., 2014) named entity recognition (NER) tools to filter out all named entities before building adding up the word embedding vectors. We refer to this method as the *filtered word embeddings method* (FWEM).

When using word embeddings as features, we experimented with the linear, RBF, and cosine kernel (CK). The latter is defined as:

$$CK(\boldsymbol{x}, \boldsymbol{y}) = \left[\frac{1}{2} \left(1 + \frac{\langle \boldsymbol{x}, \boldsymbol{y} \rangle}{\|\boldsymbol{x}\| \|\boldsymbol{y}\|} \right) \right]^\alpha$$

5   Results

Model evaluation was performed as defined on the task description page.[3] From the instances given in the test set, we create a vector containing ground truth annotations G and a vector containing our model predictions P. Model performance score is computed using cosine similarity between the two vectors, as follows:

$$cosine(G, P) = \frac{\sum_{i=1}^n G_i \cdot P_i}{\sqrt{\sum_{i=1}^n G_i^2} \sqrt{\sum_{i=1}^n P_i^2}} \tag{2}$$

To optimize the hyperparameters of the models (C for linear SVR, n and λ SSK, n for SK, α and C for cosine kernel, and C and γ for RBF kernel), we performed a grid search in a nested K-folded cross-validation on the train set, using 10 folds in the outer and 5 folds in the inner loop. To select the best parameters for a model, we choose the ones that consistently provided the best result across the 10 outer loops. Using the chosen hyperparameters, we finally train that model on the complete train set. The best results for all of the considered models are reported in Table 2.

While working with BoW models, the best results were obtained using the simple Bernoulli feature weighting scheme, indicating whether a term appeared in the headline with a weight of 1 and 0 otherwise.

---

[1] http://www.mlsec.org/harry/index.html
[2] https://code.google.com/archive/p/word2vec/

[3] http://alt.qcri.org/semeval2017/task5/index.php?id=evaluation

Method	Cosine score
$\text{BoW}_{Bernoulli}$	0.539
SSK	0.654
SK	0.671
WEM_{linear}	0.610
WEM_{RBF}	0.724
WEM_{Cosine}	0.730
FWEM_{linear}	0.612
FWEM_{RBF}	0.727
FWEM^{*}_{Cosine}	**0.733**

Table 2: Cosine similarity between ground truth annotations and model predictions (higher is better). Subscript displayed with (F)WEM methods indicate the kernel used to train the model. Model marked with (*) is the submitted model.

String kernels gave us a considerable performance gains in comparison to the BoW baseline. Interestingly, experiments showed that the SK kernel outperformed the SSK kernel.

Using word embeddings provided us with significant performance gains compared to the other two methods. Word embedding features combined with the linear kernel did not outperform string kernels. However, using non-linear kernel such as RBF and especially cosine kernel yielded substantial performance gains.

6 Conclusion

We described our system for fine-grained sentiment scoring of news headlines, which we submitted to the SemEval 2017 task 5, subtask 2. We implemented a number of feature-light methods for sentiment analysis with basic preprocessing. Our best performing method used skip-gram word embeddings trained on the Google News corpus, which were fed as features to a cosine kernel Support Vector Regression. We report our results on the gold set, where our system ranked 3rd place out of 29 teams, with a cosine score of 0.733.

It should be note that we did not use the information about which company the sentiment is measured for in any way. Arguably, not using this information leads to performance decreases when dealing with (1) headlines entirely unrelated to the company of interest and (2) headlines containing mentions of multiple companies. For future work, it would be interesting to consider encoding this information into the model or using additional pre-processing methods to detect specific parts of the headline related to the company of interest.

References

Ahmed Abbasi, Hsinchun Chen, and Arab Salem. 2008. Sentiment analysis in multiple languages: Feature selection for opinion classification in web forums. *ACM Transactions on Information Systems (TOIS)* 26(3):12.

Steven Bird, Ewan Klein, and Edward Loper. 2009. *Natural language processing with Python: analyzing text with the natural language toolkit*. " O'Reilly Media, Inc.".

Chih-Chung Chang and Chih-Jen Lin. 2011. LIBSVM: A library for support vector machines. *ACM Transactions on Intelligent Systems and Technology* 2:27:1–27:27.

Aron Culotta and Jeffrey Sorensen. 2004. Dependency tree kernels for relation extraction. In *Proceedings of the 42nd Annual Meeting on Association for Computational Linguistics*. Association for Computational Linguistics, page 423.

Rong-En Fan, Kai-Wei Chang, Cho-Jui Hsieh, Xiang-Rui Wang, and Chih-Jen Lin. 2008. LIBLINEAR: A library for large linear classification. *Journal of machine learning research* 9:1871–1874.

Rohitha Goonatilake and Susantha Herath. 2007. The volatility of the stock market and news. *International Research Journal of Finance and Economics* 3(11):53–65.

Wu He, Shenghua Zha, and Ling Li. 2013. Social media competitive analysis and text mining: A case study in the pizza industry. *International Journal of Information Management* 33(3):464–472.

Armand Joulin, Edouard Grave, Piotr Bojanowski, and Tomas Mikolov. 2016. Bag of tricks for efficient text classification. *arXiv preprint arXiv:1607.01759* .

Jonghoon Kim, Francois Rousseau, and Michalis Vazirgiannis. 2015. Convolutional sentence kernel from word embeddings for short text categorization. In *Proceedings of the 2015 Conference on Empirical Methods in Natural Language Processing (EMNLP)*. Association for Computational Linguistics, Lisbon, Portugal, pages 775–780.

Svetlana Kiritchenko, Xiaodan Zhu, and Saif M. Mohammad. 2014. Sentiment analysis of short informal texts. *Journal of Artificial Intelligence Research* 50:723–762.

Quoc V. Le and Tomas Mikolov. 2014. Distributed representations of sentences and documents. In *Proceedings of The 31st International Conference on Machine Learning (ICML)*. volume 14, pages 1188–1196.

Christina S Leslie, Eleazar Eskin, and William Stafford Noble. 2002. The spectrum kernel: A string kernel for svm protein classification. In *Proceedings of the Pacific Symposium on Biocomputing*. volume 7, pages 566–575.

Huma Lodhi, Craig Saunders, John Shawe-Taylor, Nello Cristianini, and Chris Watkins. 2002a. Text classification using string kernels. *Journal of Machine Learning Research* 2(Feb):419–444.

Huma Lodhi, Craig Saunders, John Shawe-Taylor, Nello Cristianini, and Chris Watkins. 2002b. Text classification using string kernels. *Journal of Machine Learning Research* 2(Feb):419–444.

Andrew L. Maas, Raymond E. Daly, Peter T. Pham, Dan Huang, Andrew Y Ng, and Christopher Potts. 2011. Learning word vectors for sentiment analysis. In *Proceedings of the 49th Annual Meeting of the Association for Computational Linguistics: Human Language Technologies-Volume 1*. Association for Computational Linguistics, Stroudsburg, PA, USA, pages 142–150.

Christopher D. Manning, Mihai Surdeanu, John Bauer, Jenny Finkel, Steven J. Bethard, and David McClosky. 2014. The Stanford CoreNLP natural language processing toolkit. In *Association for Computational Linguistics (ACL) System Demonstrations*. pages 55–60. http://www.aclweb.org/anthology/P/P14/P14-5010.

Tomas Mikolov, Kai Chen, Greg Corrado, and Jeffrey Dean. 2013a. Efficient estimation of word representations in vector space. *arXiv preprint arXiv:1301.3781*.

Tomas Mikolov, Ilya Sutskever, Kai Chen, Greg S Corrado, and Jeff Dean. 2013b. Distributed representations of words and phrases and their compositionality. In *Proceedings of the Neural Information Processing Systems Conference (NIPS 2013)*. Lake Tahoe, USA, pages 3111–3119.

Preslav Nakov, Alan Ritter, Sara Rosenthal, Fabrizio Sebastiani, and Veselin Stoyanov. 2016. Semeval-2016 Task 4: Sentiment analysis in Twitter. *Proceedings of SemEval* pages 1–18.

Brendan O'Connor, Ramnath Balasubramanyan, Bryan R Routledge, and Noah A. Smith. 2010. From tweets to polls: Linking text sentiment to public opinion time series. In *International Conference on Web and Social Media (ICWSM)*. Washington, DC, pages 122–129.

Bo Pang and Lillian Lee. 2008. Opinion mining and sentiment analysis. *Foundations and trends in information retrieval* 2(1-2):1–135.

Jeffrey Pennington, Richard Socher, and Christopher D. Manning. 2014. Glove: Global vectors for word representation. In *Empirical Methods in Natural Language Processing (EMNLP)*. pages 1532–1543. http://www.aclweb.org/anthology/D14-1162.

Danuta Reah. 2002. *The language of newspapers*. Psychology Press.

Sara Rosenthal, Preslav Nakov, Svetlana Kiritchenko, Saif M Mohammad, Alan Ritter, and Veselin Stoyanov. 2015. SemEval-2015 Task 10: Sentiment analysis in Twitter. In *Proceedings of the 9th international workshop on semantic evaluation (SemEval 2015)*. pages 451–463.

Sara Rosenthal, Alan Ritter, Preslav Nakov, and Veselin Stoyanov. 2014. SemEval-2014 Task 9: Sentiment analysis in Twitter. In *Proceedings of the 8th international workshop on semantic evaluation (SemEval 2014)*. Dublin, Ireland, pages 73–80.

Richard Socher, Brody Huval, Christopher D. Manning, and Andrew Y. Ng. 2012. Semantic compositionality through recursive matrix-vector spaces. In *Proceedings of the conference on empirical methods in natural language processing (EMNLP)*. Association for Computational Linguistics, pages 1201–1211.

Richard Socher, Alex Perelygin, Jean Y Wu, Jason Chuang, Christopher D Manning, Andrew Y Ng, and Christopher Potts. 2013. Recursive deep models for semantic compositionality over a sentiment treebank. In *Proceedings of the conference on empirical methods in natural language processing (EMNLP)*. volume 1631, page 1642.

Shashank Srivastava, Dirk Hovy, and Eduard H Hovy. 2013. A walk-based semantically enriched tree kernel over distributed word representations. In *Proceedings of the Conference on Empirical Methods in Natural Language Processing (EMNLP)*. Association for Computational Linguistics, Seattle, USA, pages 1411–1416.

Duyu Tang, Furu Wei, Nan Yang, Ming Zhou, Ting Liu, and Bing Qin. 2014. Learning sentiment-specific word embedding for twitter sentiment classification. In *The 52nd Annual Meeting of the Association for Computational Linguistics (ACL)*. Baltimore, MD, USA, pages 1555–1565.

Mike Thelwall, Kevan Buckley, Georgios Paltoglou, Di Cai, and Arvid Kappas. 2010. Sentiment strength detection in short informal text. *Journal of the American Society for Information Science and Technology* 61(12):2544–2558.

Marjan Van de Kauter, Diane Breesch, and Véronique Hoste. 2015. Fine-grained analysis of explicit and implicit sentiment in financial news articles. *Expert Systems with applications* 42(11):4999–5010.

Hao Wang, Dogan Can, Abe Kazemzadeh, François Bar, and Shrikanth Narayanan. 2012. A system for real-time twitter sentiment analysis of 2012 us presidential election cycle. In *Proceedings of the ACL 2012 System Demonstrations*. Association for Computational Linguistics, pages 115–120.

Theresa Wilson, Janyce Wiebe, and Paul Hoffmann. 2009. Recognizing contextual polarity: An exploration of features for phrase-level sentiment analysis. *Computational linguistics* 35(3):399–433.

Yang Yu, Wenjing Duan, and Qing Cao. 2013. The impact of social and conventional media on firm equity value: A sentiment analysis approach. *Decision Support Systems* 55(4):919–926.

Changli Zhang, Wanli Zuo, Tao Peng, and Fengling He. 2008. Sentiment classification for Chinese reviews using machine learning methods based on string kernel. In *Proceedings of the 3rd International Conference on Convergence Information (ICCIT)*. IEEE, Busan, Korea, volume 2, pages 909–914.

UW-FinSent at SemEval-2017 Task 5:
Sentiment Analysis on Financial News Headlines
using Training Dataset Augmentation

Vineet John
University of Waterloo
vineet.john@uwaterloo.ca

Olga Vechtomova
University of Waterloo
ovechtomova@uwaterloo.ca

Abstract

This paper discusses the approach taken by the UWaterloo team to arrive at a solution for the Fine-Grained Sentiment Analysis problem posed by Task 5 of SemEval 2017. The paper describes the document vectorization and sentiment score prediction techniques used, as well as the design and implementation decisions taken while building the system for this task. The system uses text vectorization models, such as N-gram, TF-IDF and paragraph embeddings, coupled with regression model variants to predict the sentiment scores. Amongst the methods examined, unigrams and bigrams coupled with simple linear regression obtained the best baseline accuracy. The paper also explores data augmentation methods to supplement the training dataset. This system was designed for Subtask 2 (News Statements and Headlines).

1 Introduction

The goal of this SemEval task is to identify fine-grained levels of sentiment polarity in financial news headlines and microblog posts. Specifically, the task aims at identifying bullish (optimistic) sentiment, expressing the belief that the stock price will increase, and bearish (pessimistic) sentiment, expressing the belief that the stock price will decline. The expressed sentiment is quantified as floating point values in the range of -1 (very negative/bearish) to 1 (very positive/bullish), with 0 denoting neutral sentiment. (Cortis et al., 2017). This paper describes our system developed for subtask 2 (News Statements and Headlines).

While developing the system for this subtask, we systematically evaluated a number of alternative solutions for each step in the pipeline. Specifically, we investigated different document vectorization approaches, such as N-gram models, TF-IDF and paragraph vectors. A number of regression models were evaluated, namely, Simple Linear Regression, Support Vector Regression and XGBoost Linear Regression.

One of the challenges with performing sentiment analysis in the financial domain is scarcity of training data. We explored different approaches to augment the training data provided by the task organizers with training data from other sources in the financial domain, as well as using out-of-domain sentiment resources.

2 Approach

The overall approach to predicting the sentiment of the test dataset headlines is detailed below.

- **Pre-Processing & Cleaning**

  This step is needed to simplify and sanitize the input set of headlines. In the context of this task, since the headlines were short snippets ranging from 5 to 15 words in length, the only pre-processing done was replacing the name of the organization being spoken of in the headlines, with a generic organization name, to reduce the feature space.

- **Text Vectorization**

  The objective is to vectorize the textual content of the headlines into a numeric representation that a statistical learning model can then be trained on. N-gram models, TF-IDF and Paragraph Vector implementations were explored for this purpose. N-gram models generally performed the best on the trial dataset, followed by TF-IDF, and Paragraph Vectors. Of the different N-gram configurations experimented with, word N-grams that

Proceedings of the 11th International Workshop on Semantic Evaluations (SemEval-2017), pages 872–876,
Vancouver, Canada, August 3 - 4, 2017. ©2017 Association for Computational Linguistics

used a combination of unigrams and bigrams achieved the best baseline scores. These techniques are further discussed in Section 3.

- **Statistical Model Learning**

  The objective is to use the vector representations of the headlines as features and learn a model to predict the sentiment scores. Simple Linear Regression, Support Vector Regression and XGBoost Linear Regression were the learning methods that were used. The linear regression methods consistently outperformed Support Vector Regression and XGBoost regression in experiments on the training dataset. These techniques are discussed in Section 4.

3 Document Vectorization

Document vectorization is needed to convert the text content of the SemEval headlines into a numeric vector representation that can be utilized as features, which can then be used to train a machine learning model on. The methods for vectorization used are listed in the subsections below.

3.1 N-gram Model

For the purpose of this task, a vectorizer implementation using Scikit-Learn (Pedregosa et al., 2011) was used to obtain vector representations of the SemEval headlines, since they have been proven to be an effective representation of textual content for sentiment classification in general (Wang and Manning, 2012).

3.2 TF-IDF Model

The TF-IDF implementation in Scikit-Learn (Pedregosa et al., 2011) was used to obtain vector representations of the SemEval headlines.

3.3 Paragraph Vector Model

A Paragraph Vector representation model is comprised of an unsupervised learning algorithm that learns fixed-size vector representations for variable-length pieces of texts such as sentences and documents (Le and Mikolov, 2014). The vector representations are learned to predict the surrounding words in contexts sampled from the paragraph. In the context of the SemEval headlines, the vector representations were learned for the complete headline.

Two distinct implementations were explored while attempting to vectorize the headlines using the Paragraph Vector approach.

- Doc2Vec: A Python library implementation in Gensim[1].

- FastText: A standalone implementation in C++ (Bojanowski et al., 2016) (Joulin et al., 2016).

Doc2Vec was the final choice that was opted for due to the ease of integration into the existing system. The paragraph embeddings for Doc2Vec are trained using the SemEval training headlines corpus.

4 Regression Models

Three different regression implementations were used to train models to predict the sentiment scores of the headlines:

- **Simple Linear Regression**

  This is the standard version of linear regression that simply learns the weights for the feature vector that minimize the cost function, which is represented as a Euclidean loss function.

- **Support Vector Regression**

  The idea of SVR is based on the computation of a linear regression function in a high dimensional feature space where the input data is mapped using a non-linear function (Basak et al., 2007).

  Instead of minimizing the observed training error, Support Vector Regression (SVR) attempts to minimize the generalization error bound so as to achieve generalized performance.

- **XGBoost Regression**

  This is an ensemble method for regression that coalesces several 'weak' learners into a single 'strong' learner by iteratively minimizing the least squares error or Euclidean loss incurred by the cost function (Chen and Guestrin, 2016).

  The hyper-parameters applicable are the regularization parameter (λ) and the gradient descent step-size / learning rate (α).

---

[1] https://radimrehurek.com/gensim/models/doc2vec.html

Vectorization Method	Learning Model	R^2 Score	Cosine Similarity
Unigrams & Bigrams	Simple Linear Regression	0.38	0.63
Unigrams & Bigrams	Support Vector Regression	0.38	0.63
Unigrams & Bigrams	XGBoost Regression	0.21	0.50
TF-IDF	Simple Linear Regression	-0.10	0.50
TF-IDF	Support Vector Regression	0.38	0.63
TF-IDF	XGBoost Regression	0.19	0.47
Doc2Vec	Simple Linear Regression	-4.69	0.04
Doc2Vec	Support Vector Regression	-0.05	0.08
Doc2Vec	XGBoost Regression	-0.06	0.06

Table 1: Experimental Results

The implementation library utilized for the Simple Linear Regression and Support Vector Regression techniques is Scikit-Learn (Pedregosa et al., 2011), whereas the XGB Python library was used for the XGBoost regression implementation.

5 Training Dataset Augmentation

A few different datasets were used to train the models on, in an attempt to identify the best representative training set. The dataset augmentation strategies used are enumerated below.

- **Article Content Expansion**

  To increase the number of features to train on, it was decided to retrieve the full text content of the articles corresponding to the article headlines. This was achieved by creating an application to search for the article headlines that were part of the training set using an online search engine, and to retrieve the full-text of the article by scraping the content from the source websites.

  This application is implemented in Java and is open-source[2]. The implementation can be extended to augment any set of headlines with the corresponding article content.

  The assumption made here is that the sentiment expressed in the article headline sufficiently proxies the sentiment in the actual article content.

- **Amazon Product Reviews**

  This corpus is a set of Amazon product reviews[3], each consisting of the review text and a star rating on the scale of 1-5. To normalize the dataset, the rating scores 1 & 2 are assumed to be associated with negative reviews, 3 with neutral and 4 & 5 with positive reviews. This score range was then mapped to a -1 to 1 scale to match the sentiment scores of the training data. In total, $100,000$ documents from this dataset were used to augment the existing training dataset.

- **Financial Phrasebank**

  This dataset is specific to the financial domain and is manually annotated (Malo et al., 2014). It is comprised of a set of financial snippets from stock market related news that have been annotated with the classes positive, negative and neutral.

  To normalize the labels, neutral was assigned a sentiment score of 0 and experiments were run for $positive \in (1, 0.5)$ and $negative \in (-1, -0.5)$.

None of the above strategies proved to be a good augmentation of the existing data, since their addition to the training datasets did not show any improvements in the overall cross-validated accuracy score.

6 System Implementation

The entire system was coded in Python with the use of the Scikit-Learn (Pedregosa et al., 2011), XGB and Gensim libraries. This includes a framework for automated testing of accuracy scores to arrive at the best hyper-parameters to be used for unigram & bigram word count combinations, as well as Doc2Vec hyper-parameters.

The system implementation includes all the plugins pertaining to the different document vector-

---

[2]https://github.com/v1n337/news-article-extractor
[3]http://jmcauley.ucsd.edu/data/amazon/

Vectorization Method	Learning Model	Cosine Similarity
Unigrams & Bigrams	Simple Linear Regression	0.644
Unigrams & Bigrams	XGBoost Regression	0.547

Table 2: SemEval Task 5 Submissions

ization techniques and statistical learning techniques discussed in sections 3 and 4 respectively.

The code is open source[4] and is available to replicate the results published in this paper along with the instructions to operate the system.

7 Experimental Results

For arriving at the baseline scores, an exhaustive set of tests were conducted using each of the document vectorization techniques in combination with the regression techniques described in the previous sections.

Using the automated test-suite included as part of the system, it was concluded that the Doc2Vec model performed best when the number of dimensions (features) of text is around 832 and the learning algorithm completes 40 passes before settling on a vector representation. It was also concluded, that a combinations of unigrams & bigrams had the best baseline accuracy scores for the training datasets.

The measure of accuracy used was the R^2 score, also called the co-efficient of determination. The R^2 score can be computed using the below formula:

$$R^2 = 1 - \frac{\sum_{i=1}^{N}(y_i - f_i)^2}{\sum_{i=1}^{N}(y_i - \bar{y})^2}$$

where y is the gold set score vector and f is the predicted score vector, and N is the number of test samples.

The experimental results for the Training and the Trial datasets are shown in Table 1. The best baselines scores seem to favor the simplest vectorization model, i.e. unigrams & bigrams.

8 System Evaluation

For the two submissions permitted by SemEval, the methods used for the submissions made are described in Table 2.

The evaluation was done using the task evaluation metric, the $cosine\_score$ (Cortis et al., 2017).

$$cosine\_score = cosine\_weight * cosine(G, P)$$

[4]https://github.com/v1n337/semeval2017-task5

where

$$cosine(G, P) = \frac{\sum_{i=1}^{N} G_i * P_i}{\sqrt{\sum_{i=1}^{N} G_i^2} * \sqrt{\sum_{i=1}^{N} P_i^2}}$$

and

$$cosine\_weight = \frac{|P|}{|G|}$$

and G, P are the gold set scores and the predicted scores respectively, for N test samples.

The simplest model implemented, using Unigrams & Bigrams, combined with Simple Linear Regression, was what yielded the best performance by the system, with a cosine similarity score of 0.644.

9 Conclusions and Future Work

This paper has described the UW-FinSent system developed by the UWaterloo team for Task 5, Subtask 2 during SemEval 2017.

The experimental results indicate that the usage of simpler techniques like N-gram text vectorization and linear regression to predict the continuous-valued scores achieve better results than bag-of-words or deep learning feature extraction techniques.

A recurring topic that needed to be addressed during the progress on this task was the fact there there were no reliable datasets that could accurately augment the training set. In the future, we plan to develop automatic methods for generating high quality, sentiment-annotated training datasets for the financial domain.

Acknowledgements

The authors are grateful to the organizers for their support for this task. The authors would also like to thank (Malo et al., 2014) for sharing the Financial Phrasebank Dataset for the purposes of our evaluation.

References

Debasish Basak, Srimanta Pal, and Dipak Chandra Patranabis. 2007. Support vector regression. *Neural Information Processing-Letters and Reviews* 11(10):203–224.

Piotr Bojanowski, Edouard Grave, Armand Joulin, and Tomas Mikolov. 2016. Enriching word vectors with subword information. *arXiv preprint arXiv:1607.04606* .

Tianqi Chen and Carlos Guestrin. 2016. Xgboost: A scalable tree boosting system. In *Proceedings of the 22Nd ACM SIGKDD International Conference on Knowledge Discovery and Data Mining*. ACM, pages 785–794.

Keith Cortis, André Freitas, Tobias Dauert, Manuela Huerlimann, Manel Zarrouk, Siegfried Handschuh, and Brian Davis. 2017. Semeval-2017 task 5: Fine-grained sentiment analysis on financial microblogs and news. In *Proceedings of the 11th International Workshop on Semantic Evaluation (SemEval-2017)*. Association for Computational Linguistics, Vancouver, Canada, pages 517–533. http://www.aclweb.org/anthology/S17-2089.

Armand Joulin, Edouard Grave, Piotr Bojanowski, and Tomas Mikolov. 2016. Bag of tricks for efficient text classification. *arXiv preprint arXiv:1607.01759* .

Quoc V Le and Tomas Mikolov. 2014. Distributed representations of sentences and documents. In *ICML*. volume 14, pages 1188–1196.

Pekka Malo, Ankur Sinha, Pekka Korhonen, Jyrki Wallenius, and Pyry Takala. 2014. Good debt or bad debt: Detecting semantic orientations in economic texts. *Journal of the Association for Information Science and Technology* 65(4):782–796.

Fabian Pedregosa, Gaël Varoquaux, Alexandre Gramfort, Vincent Michel, Bertrand Thirion, Olivier Grisel, Mathieu Blondel, Peter Prettenhofer, Ron Weiss, Vincent Dubourg, et al. 2011. Scikit-learn: Machine learning in python. *Journal of Machine Learning Research* 12(Oct):2825–2830.

Sida Wang and Christopher D Manning. 2012. Baselines and bigrams: Simple, good sentiment and topic classification. In *Proceedings of the 50th Annual Meeting of the Association for Computational Linguistics: Short Papers-Volume 2*. Association for Computational Linguistics, pages 90–94.

RiTUAL-UH at SemEval-2017 Task 5:
Sentiment Analysis on Financial Data Using Neural Networks

Sudipta Kar[*] and **Suraj Maharjan**[*] and **Thamar Solorio**
Department of Computer Science
University of Houston
Houston, TX 77204-3010
`{skar3, smaharjan2}@uh.edu, solorio@cs.uh.edu`

Abstract

In this paper, we present our systems for "SemEval-2017 Task-5 on Fine-Grained Sentiment Analysis on Financial Microblogs and News". In our system, we combined hand-engineered lexical, sentiment, and metadata features with the representations learned from Convolutional Neural Networks (CNN) and Bidirectional Gated Recurrent Unit (Bi-GRU) having Attention model applied on top. With this architecture we obtained weighted cosine similarity scores of 0.72 and 0.74 for subtask-1 and subtask-2, respectively. Using the official scoring system, our system ranked in the second place for subtask-2 and in the eighth place for the subtask-1. However, it ranked first in both subtasks when evaluated with an alternate scoring metric[1].

1 Introduction

Predicting sentiments of financial data has a wide range of applications. The most important application is being able to predict the ups and downs of the share market as the changes in sentiments and opinions can change the market dynamics (Goonatilake and Herath, 2007; Van de Kauter et al., 2015). Stock market related information is typically found in newspapers (Malo et al., 2013) and people discuss them in social media platforms like Twitter and StockTwits. Positive news has the capability to boost the market by increasing optimism among people (Van de Kauter et al., 2015; Schuster, 2003). SemEval-2017 Task 5 on 'Fine-Grained Sentiment Analysis on Financial Microblogs and News' aims at analyzing the polarity of public sentiments from financial data found in newspapers and social media. In this paper, we describe our systems, which exploit automatically learned representations using deep learning architecture based methods along with hand-engineered features in order to predict the sentiment polarity of financial data.

2 Dataset

Task	Training	Trial	Test
Subtask-1	1,694	10	799
Subtask-2	1,142	14	491

Table 1: Data distribution for subtask-1 and subtask-2.

Table 1 shows the distribution of training, trial, and test data for subtask-1 and subtask-2. For the subtask-1, the financial microblogs and tweets were collected from Twitter[2] and StockTwits[3] whereas for subtask-2, the financial news headlines were collected from different financial news sources such as Yahoo Finance[4]. Each instance was labeled with a floating point value ranging from -1 to +1, indicating the sentiment score. A score of -1 means very negative or bearish whereas, a score of +1 means very positive or bullish. A score of 0 means neutral sentiment. The dataset is noisy and contains URLs, cashtags, digits, usernames, and emoticons. The messages are short with an average number of 13 tokens for the microblog data and 10 tokens for the headlines data.

---

[*]Both authors contributed equally.

[1]`http://alt.qcri.org/semeval2017/task5/data/uploads/description_second_approach.pdf`

[2]`https://twitter.com`
[3]`https://stocktwits.com`
[4]`https://finance.yahoo.com`

Proceedings of the 11th International Workshop on Semantic Evaluations (SemEval-2017), pages 877–882,
Vancouver, Canada, August 3 - 4, 2017. ©2017 Association for Computational Linguistics

3 Methodology

We designed two systems for predicting sentiment polarity scores. The first system exploits the hand-engineered features and uses Support Vector Regression (SVR) to predict the sentiment scores. The next system combines the hand-engineered features with representation learned using CNN and Bi-GRU to predict the sentiment scores. These systems are explained below:

3.1 System 1

With the hand-engineered features explained in Section 3.1.1, we built a support vector regression (SVR) model with linear kernel using the implementation of Scikit-learn (Pedregosa et al., 2011). We only used linear kernel as most of the text classification problems are linearly separable (Joachims, 1998). We tuned the C parameter through grid search cross-validation over the values $\{10, 1, 0.1, \text{1e-02}, \text{1e-03}, \text{1e-04}, \text{1e-05}, \text{1e-06}\}$ during the training phase.

3.1.1 Hand-crafted Features

Before extracting the features, we first lowercased, applied stemming and removed stopwords from the messages. We also replaced named entities (NE), and digits with common identifiers to reduce noise.

Lexical: We extracted word n-grams (n=1,2,3) and character n-grams (n=3,4,5) from the messages as they are strong lexical representations (Cavnar and Trenkle, 1994; Mcnamee and Mayfield, 2004; Sureka and Jalote, 2010).

Sentiment: SenticNet (Cambria et al., 2016) have been used successfully in problems related to sentiment analysis (Bravo-Marquez et al., 2014; Poria et al., 2016; Maharjan et al., 2017) as it provides a collection of concept-level opinion lexicons with scores in five dimensions (*aptitude, attention, pleasantness, polarity, and sensitivity*). We used both of the stemmed and non-stemmed versions of the messages to extract concepts from the knowledge base. We modeled the concepts as bag-of-concepts (BoC) and used them as binary features. We averaged the concept scores of five dimensions for each text and used them as numeric features.

Word Embeddings: Word embeddings have been shown to capture semantic information. Hence, in order to capture the semantic representation of the messages, we used publicly available word vec-

tors[5] trained on Google News. It was trained by the method proposed by (Mikolov et al., 2013) and has 3M vocabulary entries. We averaged the word vectors of every word in the messages and represented them with a 300-dimensional vector. If any word is not available in the pre-trained vectors vocabulary, we skipped that word. The coverage of the Google word embedding is 73% and 82% for the microblog and headlines data, respectively.

Metadata: We used the message sources, cashtags and company names as metadata features.

3.2 System 2

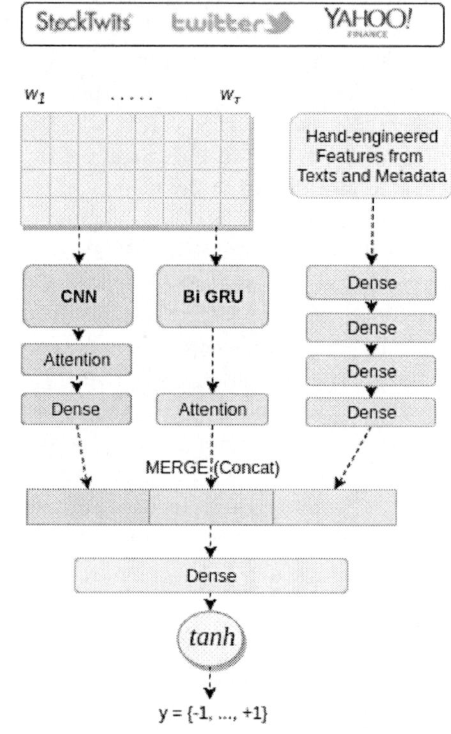

Figure 1: Architecture of System 2

Figure 1 shows the overall system architecture of our neural network model. The main motivation to use deep learning methods is the wide success these methods have achieved in various NLP tasks (Bahdanau et al., 2014; Attia et al., 2016; Samih et al., 2016; Collobert and Weston, 2008). It is a combination of two deep learning architecture based models and a multilayer perceptrons (MLP) model operating on hand-engineered fea-

---

[5] https://code.google.com/archive/p/word2vec/

878

tures discussed in Section 3.1.1.

$$S_i \rightarrow x_{1:T} = [x_1, x_2, ..., x_T] \qquad (1)$$

We tokenized each messages and represented them as sequences of word vectors as in Equation 1. The maximum length (T) of the sequences was set to 18 for headlines and 33 for microblogs. These lengths were determined from the training data. The embeddings for the words were initialized using pre-trained word embeddings. We used zero vectors to pad the shorter sequences and represent the missing words in the pre-trained vectors. We used Keras (Chollet, 2015) to build the model with Theano (Theano Development Team, 2016) as the back end.

3.2.1 Convolutional Neural Network (CNN)

We used two parallel deep learning architecture based models on the embeddings. As the first model, we used a Convolutional Neural Network (CNN) (LeCun et al., 1989). In this model, we stacked 4 sets of convolution modules with 512 filters each for filter sizes 1, 2, 3, and 4 to capture the n-grams ($n = 1$ to 4). The t-th convolution output using filter size c is defined by:

$$h_{c,t} = ReLU(W_c x_{t:t+c-1} + b_c) \qquad (2)$$

The filter is applied from window t to window $t + c - 1$ of size c. Each convolution unit calculates a convolution weight W_c and a bias b_c. Each filter of size c produces a high-level feature map h_c.

$$h_c = [h_{c,1}, h_{c,2}, ..., h_{c,T-c+1,}] \qquad (3)$$

On those filters, we apply pooling operation using an attention layer. Attention models have been used effectively in many problems related to computer vision (Mnih et al., 2014; Ba et al., 2014) and adopted successfully in natural language related problems (Bahdanau et al., 2014; Seo et al., 2016). An attention layer applied on top of a feature map h_i computes the weighted sum c_i.

$$c_i = \sum_j \alpha_{ij} h_{ij} \qquad (4)$$

The weight α_{ij} is defined by

$$\alpha_{ij} = \frac{exp(u_{ij}^\top u_w)}{\sum_j exp(u_{ij}^\top u_w)}, \qquad (5)$$

where

$$u_{ij} = tanh(W_w h_{ij} + b_w) \qquad (6)$$

Here, W_w, b_w and u_w are model parameters. A dense layer containing 128 neurons were applied on the attention layer to get the final representation for the high-level features produced by the CNN model.

3.2.2 Bidirectional GRU (Bi-GRU)

The second model was based on a bidirectional GRU (Bahdanau et al., 2014). It summarized the contextual information from both directions of a sequence and provided annotation for the words. The bidirectional GRU contains a forward GRU of 200 units and another backward GRU of 200 units. The forward GRU $\overrightarrow{f}$ reads a sequence s_i of size n from w_1 to w_n to calculate a sequence of *forward hidden states* $(\overrightarrow{h_1}, ..., \overrightarrow{h_n})$ and the backward GRU $\overleftarrow{f}$ reads the same sequence from w_n to w_1 to calculate a sequence of *backward hidden states* $(\overleftarrow{h_1}, ..., \overleftarrow{h_n})$. For each word w_j, we get an annotation h_j by concatenating the forward hidden state $\overrightarrow{h_j}$ and backward hidden state $\overleftarrow{h_j}$, i.e. $h_j = [\overrightarrow{h_j}; \overleftarrow{h_j}]$.

We applied an attention layer similar to CNN on the word annotations to find out the important features and got a vector of 200 dimensions.

3.2.3 Multilayer Perceptrons (MLP)

To use the hand-engineered features we employed a multilayer perceptron in parallel with the deep learning architecture based models. We fed the extracted features in the input layer and used four hidden dense layers having 200, 100, 50, and 10 neurons respectively. For the feature vector representation $\overrightarrow{x_i} = [x_{i,1}, x_{i,2}, ..., x_{i,T}]$ of message m_i, each neuron of a hidden layer j calculates a vector $\overrightarrow{h_j}$ defined by the following equation.

$$\overrightarrow{h_{ij}} = ReLU(W_{ij} x_i + b_j) \qquad (7)$$

Here, W_{ij} is the weight matrix and b_j is the bias vector of the layer j. This model produced a high-level feature representation in the output layer of size 10.

By concatenating the outputs of these three models we created a merged layer of size 338. It contained the three types of high-level features computed by three different types of models. CNN captured the local information, Bi-GRU captured the sequence information and MLP represented the hand-engineered features. We apply a dense layer of 128 neurons on top of this merged layer. It was similar to the layers used in the MLP model but we used *tanh* as the activation function instead of *ReLU* here. The outputs of this layer were passed to the activation layer containing only one neuron having *tanh* as the activation function. We used *tanh* in the final two layers as it produces val-

Model	ST-1 : Microblogs	ST-2 : Headlines
Baseline	0.29	0.68
System 1	**0.70**	0.67
MLP	0.66	0.64
CNN	0.58	0.65
Bi-GRU	0.68	0.68
System 2	0.69	**0.71**

Table 2: Results of 10-fold cross-validation on training and trail data with different models using the official scorer.

		ST-1 : Microblogs		ST-2 : Headlines	
Official	sub-2	0.72 (8)	sub-2	0.74 (2)	
scorer	sub-1	0.70 (11)	sub-1	0.74 (2)	
Alternate	sub-2	0.73 (1)	sub-2	0.71 (1)	
scorer	sub-1	0.70 (11)	sub-1	0.70 (3)	

Table 3: Weighted cosine scores with ranks achieved by the submissions using the official scorer and the alternate scorer.

	Text	True	Pred.
MB1	Worst performers today: $RIG -13% $EK -10% $MGM $IO -6% $CAR -5,5% / best stock: $WTS +15%	0.857	-0.365
MB2	$GDX $GDXJ $JNUG - strong move today for the Junior Gold Miners - keep an EYE out for a gap fill	0.750	0.750
MB3	Weird day $GPRO up $amba down	-0.649	0.588
HL1	MarketsWolseley shares wilt 8.8% after full year results	-0.787	0.192
HL2	Kingfisher share price: FY statutory pre-tax profit falls 20.5%	-0.426	-0.425
HL3	Shell eyes $700 million exit from Gabon - sources	0.562	-0.123

Table 4: Sample texts from both subtasks with annotated scores and predicted scores by the systems. (MB: Microblogs, HL: Headlines)

ues between -1 and +1 and it is also the range of sentiment scores.

4 Experiments and Results

As the trial dataset too small compared to the training data, we merged it with the training data and ran 10-fold cross-validation to evaluate different models. We tuned the hyper-parameters during the training phase through grid-search cross validation method for System 1. We also experimented with different architectures to build System 1 in this phase.

We evaluated our models using the official scoring system that measures the weighted cosine similarity, similar to the scorer used in Ghosh et al. (2015). As the predictions are continuous values between -1 and +1, cosine similarity measures the degree of alignment between the true values and the predictions. The final weighted score is computed by multiplying the cosine similarity with the ratio of predicted values against the number of test cases. As no official baseline scores were provided, we did a baseline experiment using a simple linear regression model with the hand-engineered features to compare our models.

Table 2 presents the weighted cosine scores achieved by the models we experimented with. System-1 achieved weighted cosine scores of 0.70 and 0.67 for subtask-1 and subtask-2, respectively. Among the neural network models, Bi-GRU performed better than the others. It achieved 0.68 for both of the subtasks. The combination of the three neural network based model (System-2) performed better than the individual models. The neural network models were trained for 10 epochs. We observed issue of overfitting when we increased the number of epochs beyond this.

From the results for subtask-1 we can see that all the other models performed better than CNN. It indicates that other features captured by Bi-GRU and hand-engineering process were more informative than the local information captured by

CNN. We can understand the strength of the hand-crafted features also by observing the performance of SVR. Although it did not perform as expected on the test data of subtask-1, it showed good performance on the validation set.

We submitted predictions by System-1 (sub-1) and System-2 (sub-2) for subtask-1 as they were the best models. Due to comparatively better performance of System-2 in subtask-2, we submitted predictions from two different models with this system but varied the number of epochs from 10 (sub-1) to 20 (sub-2). For subtask-1, sub-1 and sub-2 was ranked eleventh and eighth, respectively. For subtask-2, both of the submissions achieved almost similar scores and ranked second.

Submitted systems were evaluated simultaneously with an alternate scoring system that measures cosine similarity by grouping instances based on the related company. Our systems ranked the first for both subtasks when evaluated with this scorer.

Table 4 shows that our system worked well when there are more plain texts (*MB2, HL2*). But it struggles when the text contains more statistics (*e.g. $RIG -13% $EK -10%*) than plain texts or mix of words with strong positive and negative sentiments (*worst, strong, weird, wilt, falls, exit*). If we look at *MB1*, it is very difficult to determine the sentiment polarity from the message. The message starts with *'Worst performers today'*, which indicates a negative polarity. Rest of the message contains statistics for different companies. Among them four indicate a drop in prices and only one indicates a rise in the stock price. It is noticeable that, although the message started with negative impression, it ended with a positive impression by saying *'best stock: $WTS +15%'*. As this is the only possible reason for the highly positive true sentiment polarity score of 0.857 for this message, we get a hint that our systems might need to put more attention on how a message ends.

MB3 starts with the phrase *'Weird day'* followed by a positive and a negative news about stock prices of two companies and our model predicted 0.588 as the polarity score where gold score is -0.649. We tried to find out the possible reason behind our prediction by simply looking at the distribution of the words in this message. In the training data, the word *'weird'* appeared only once. 68% of the 241 messages that contain *'day'* are positive in the training data. Out of 270 messages that contain *'up'*, 201 messages (75%) are positives. We found 118 messages that contain *'down'* and 80 (68%) of them are negative. So, we can see that if a message contains *'up'* and *'down'*, chance of predicting it as positive is higher. Related cashtag $GPRO was found in three messages and $amba appeared only in one message.

Our model predicted a positive sentiment for *HL1* although it contains a clear indication of a negative polarity by the word *'wilt'*. To find out the reason we observed that, *'wilt'* did not appear in the headlines training data at all. Its polarity is -0.087 in the scale of -1 to +1 according to the SenticNet database we used. So we can say that, our model needs to handle this type of trigger word that can control the polarity itself.

5   Conclusions

In this paper, we presented our system for analyzing sentiments from microblogs and news headlines. We used deep learning architecture based models to automatically identify important local and sequential features from the texts and concate-

nated them with multilayer perceptron-based representation of hand-engineered features extracted from the data. Future works include analyzing the statistics of ups and downs in stock prices of companies from the messages to incorporate them as features of the model.

References

Mohammed Attia, Suraj Maharjan, Younes Samih, Laura Kallmeyer, and Thamar Solorio. 2016. Cogalex-v shared task: Ghhh - detecting semantic relations via word embeddings. In *Proceedings of the 5th Workshop on Cognitive Aspects of the Lexicon (CogALex - V)*. The COLING 2016 Organizing Committee, Osaka, Japan, pages 86–91. http://aclweb.org/anthology/W16-5311.

Jimmy Ba, Volodymyr Mnih, and Koray Kavukcuoglu. 2014. Multiple object recognition with visual attention. *CoRR* abs/1412.7755. http://arxiv.org/abs/1412.7755.

Dzmitry Bahdanau, Kyunghyun Cho, and Yoshua Bengio. 2014. Neural machine translation by jointly learning to align and translate. *CoRR* abs/1409.0473. http://arxiv.org/abs/1409.0473.

Felipe Bravo-Marquez, Marcelo Mendoza, and Barbara Poblete. 2014. Meta-level sentiment models for big social data analysis. *Knowledge-Based Systems* 69:86 – 99.

Erik Cambria, Soujanya Poria, Rajiv Bajpai, and Bjoern Schuller. 2016. Senticnet 4: A semantic resource for sentiment analysis based on conceptual primitives. In *Proceedings of COLING 2016, the 26th International Conference on Computational Linguistics: Technical Papers*. The COLING 2016 Organizing Committee, Osaka, Japan, pages 2666–2677. http://aclweb.org/anthology/C16-1251.

William B. Cavnar and John M. Trenkle. 1994. N-gram-based text categorization. In *In Proceedings of SDAIR-94, 3rd Annual Symposium on Document Analysis and Information Retrieval*. pages 161–175.

François Chollet. 2015. Keras. `https://github.com/fchollet/keras`.

Ronan Collobert and Jason Weston. 2008. A unified architecture for natural language processing: Deep neural networks with multitask learning. In *Proceedings of the 25th international conference on Machine learning*. ACM, pages 160–167.

Aniruddha Ghosh, Guofu Li, Tony Veale, Paolo Rosso, Ekaterina Shutova, John Barnden, and Antonio Reyes. 2015. Semeval-2015 task 11: Sentiment analysis of figurative language in twitter. In *Proceedings of the 9th International Workshop on Semantic Evaluation (SemEval 2015)*. Association for Computational Linguistics, Denver, Colorado, pages

470–478. http://www.aclweb.org/anthology/S15-2080.

Rohitha Goonatilake and Susantha Herath. 2007. The volatility of the stock market and news. *International Research Journal of Finance and Economics* 3(11):53–65.

Thorsten Joachims. 1998. Text categorization with suport vector machines: Learning with many relevant features. In *Proceedings of the 10th European Conference on Machine Learning*. Springer-Verlag, London, UK, UK, ECML '98, pages 137–142. http://dl.acm.org/citation.cfm?id=645326.649721.

Y. LeCun, B. Boser, J. S. Denker, D. Henderson, R. E. Howard, W. Hubbard, and L. D. Jackel. 1989. Backpropagation applied to handwritten zip code recognition. *Neural Comput.* 1(4):541–551. https://doi.org/10.1162/neco.1989.1.4.541.

Suraj Maharjan, John Arevalo, Manuel Montes, Fabio A. González, and Thamar Solorio. 2017. A multi-task approach to predict likability of books. In *Proceedings of the 15th Conference of the European Chapter of the Association for Computational Linguistics: Volume 1, Long Papers*. Association for Computational Linguistics, Valencia, Spain, pages 1217–1227. http://www.aclweb.org/anthology/E17-1114.

Pekka Malo, Ankur Sinha, Pyry Takala, Pekka J. Korhonen, and Jyrki Wallenius. 2013. Good debt or bad debt: Detecting semantic orientations in economic texts. *CoRR* abs/1307.5336. http://arxiv.org/abs/1307.5336.

Paul Mcnamee and James Mayfield. 2004. Character n-gram tokenization for european language text retrieval. *Inf. Retr.* 7(1-2):73–97.

Tomas Mikolov, Ilya Sutskever, Kai Chen, Greg Corrado, and Jeffrey Dean. 2013. Distributed representations of words and phrases and their compositionality. In *Proceedings of the 26th International Conference on Neural Information Processing Systems*. Curran Associates Inc., USA, NIPS'13, pages 3111–3119. http://dl.acm.org/citation.cfm?id=2999792.2999959.

Volodymyr Mnih, Nicolas Heess, Alex Graves, and Koray Kavukcuoglu. 2014. Recurrent models of visual attention. *CoRR* abs/1406.6247. http://arxiv.org/abs/1406.6247.

F. Pedregosa, G. Varoquaux, A. Gramfort, V. Michel, B. Thirion, O. Grisel, M. Blondel, P. Prettenhofer, R. Weiss, V. Dubourg, J. Vanderplas, A. Passos, D. Cournapeau, M. Brucher, M. Perrot, and E. Duchesnay. 2011. Scikit-learn: Machine learning in Python. *Journal of Machine Learning Research* 12:2825–2830.

Soujanya Poria, Erik Cambria, Newton Howard, Guang-Bin Huang, and Amir Hussain. 2016. Fusing audio, visual and textual clues for sentiment analysis from multimodal content. *Neurocomput.* 174(PA):50–59. https://doi.org/10.1016/j.neucom.2015.01.095.

Younes Samih, Suraj Maharjan, Mohammed Attia, Laura Kallmeyer, and Thamar Solorio. 2016. Multilingual code-switching identification via lstm recurrent neural networks. In *Proceedings of the Second Workshop on Computational Approaches to Code Switching*. Association for Computational Linguistics, Austin, Texas, pages 50–59. http://aclweb.org/anthology/W16-5806.

Thomas Schuster. 2003. Meta-communication and market dynamics. reflexive interactions of financial markets and the mass media. Finance, EconWPA.

Paul Hongsuck Seo, Zhe Lin, Scott Cohen, Xiaohui Shen, and Bohyung Han. 2016. Hierarchical attention networks. *CoRR* abs/1606.02393. http://arxiv.org/abs/1606.02393.

Ashish Sureka and Pankaj Jalote. 2010. Detecting duplicate bug report using character n-gram-based features. In *Proceedings of the 2010 Asia Pacific Software Engineering Conference*. IEEE Computer Society, Washington, DC, USA, APSEC '10, pages 366–374. https://doi.org/10.1109/APSEC.2010.49.

Theano Development Team. 2016. Theano: A Python framework for fast computation of mathematical expressions. *arXiv e-prints* abs/1605.02688. http://arxiv.org/abs/1605.02688.

Marjan Van de Kauter, Diane Breesch, and Véronique Hoste. 2015. Fine-grained analysis of explicit and implicit sentiment in financial news articles. *Expert Syst. Appl.* 42(11):4999–5010. https://doi.org/10.1016/j.eswa.2015.02.007.

COMMIT at SemEval-2017 Task 5: Ontology-based Method for Sentiment Analysis of Financial Headlines

Kim Schouten   **Flavius Frasincar**   **Franciska de Jong**

Erasmus University Rotterdam
P.O. Box 1738, NL-3000 DR
Rotterdam, The Netherlands
{schouten,frasincar}@ese.eur.nl
f.m.g.dejong@eshcc.eur.nl

Abstract

This paper describes our submission to Task 5 of SemEval 2017, *Fine-Grained Sentiment Analysis on Financial Microblogs and News*, where we limit ourselves to performing sentiment analysis on news headlines only (track 2). The approach presented in this paper uses a Support Vector Machine to do the required regression, and besides unigrams and a sentiment tool, we use various ontology-based features. To this end we created a domain ontology that models various concepts from the financial domain. This allows us to model the sentiment of actions depending on which entity they are affecting (e.g., *decreasing debt* is positive, but *decreasing profit* is negative). The presented approach yielded a cosine distance of 0.6810 on the official test data, resulting in the 12th position.

1   Introduction

Many companies in the financial sector are in the business of gathering and selling information, including news and sentiment analysis information, because of the profound influence this has on investor behavior (Van de Kauter et al., 2015). The relation between news and movements in the financial market is intricate, with news influencing the market (Schuster, 2003) as well as the market being a source of news itself. Price fluctuations of financial instruments can be linked to supply and demand and thus to the desirability of that financial product, which changes when new facts related to this product are published. Sentiment analysis in the context of financial news headlines aims to capture the change in desirability of a given product. Assigning a negative sentiment score to a certain news headline for a given product then represents a decrease in desirability and thus a decrease in price for that product, while assigning a positive sentiment has the opposite meaning.

In track 2 of Task 5 at SemEval 2017 (Cortis et al., 2017), each news headline contains one or more company names, and for a given company name, the sentiment, modeled as a real number between -1 and 1, needs to be determined. When multiple companies are mentioned, the same sentence can appear multiple times in the data, each time asking for the sentiment with respect to a different company. In financial headlines, there are two reasons why the expressed sentiment can differ for the various companies that are mentioned. The first is that expressed sentiment is often opposite for competitors, while the second is that news often reflects on the stock movements of the day mentioning both the biggest winners and biggest losers in the same headline.

Besides directly mentioning the stock movements of a company, news headlines often report on changes with respect to a certain aspect of a company (e.g., its profit or debt) or on actions that influence the company (e.g., opening stores or being sued). The expressed sentiment often depends on what particular aspect is in scope. A decrease in profit, for example, is considered negative, while a decrease in debt is generally considered positive.

The issue of aspect-dependent sentiment is addressed in our approach by classifying aspects and actions in such a way that an ontology reasoner, with the help of a set of class axioms, can infer which sentiment is expressed by a given pair of aspect and (increase or decrease) action. Besides aspect-dependent sentiment expressions, there are also sentiment expressions that always convey a positive (e.g., lift or good) or negative sentiment (e.g., drown or bad), and those are also stored in the ontology.

The ontology information is used a source of

Proceedings of the 11th International Workshop on Semantic Evaluations (SemEval-2017), pages 883–887,
Vancouver, Canada, August 3 - 4, 2017. ©2017 Association for Computational Linguistics

features for the Support Vector Regression model that is employed in our approach. Hence, we present an approach that is a hybrid between knowledge-based methods and machine learning methods (Cambria, 2016).

This paper is structured as follows. In Sect. 2, the method is presented, followed by an extensive evaluation in Sect. 3. Conclusions and suggestions for future work are given in Sect. 4.

2 Method

At the heart of the method is a Support Vector Regression (SVR) model, for which we use the Weka implementation (Frank et al., 2016; Shevade et al., 2000). To provide features that describe the news headline, all headlines are preprocessed using the Stanford CoreNLP library. This involves tokenization, Part-of-Speech tagging, lemmatization, dependency parsing, and sentiment annotation. Furthermore, after tokenization, the headlines are scanned for company names that are in the ontology, and all text is set to lowercase. The company field in the annotations is also linked to a URI in the ontology. The sentiment tool (Socher et al., 2013) that is part of the CoreNLP package assigns a sentiment score to various parts of the text (using the parse tree), but for this research we use only the sentiment assigned to the complete headline. This is a number in the range of -2 to 2, but in practice, sentence sentiment tends to be between -1 and 1. Besides the sentiment value, which is a feature for the SVR, we also use the presence or absence of unigrams as features (i.e., classical bag-of-words), denoting presence with 1 and absence with 0. This unigrams plus sentence sentiment forms our baseline method.

2.1 Ontology Design

To the baseline method, we add various ontology features. To that end, we first designed and manually populated an ontology that models expressions in the financial domain (Schouten et al., 2017). The ontology contains four main classes: `Sentiment`, modeling mentions of a certain sentiment value, `Entity`, modeling nouns that represent entities like companies or aspects of entities like profit and debt, `Property`, modeling adjectives like *lower*, *better*, etc., and `Action`, representing verbs in the text. Hence, the ontology is a model of mentions or expressions of the concepts in the financial domain rather than a model of the concepts themselves.

In accordance with the two main polar directions: up or increase, and down or decrease, all subclasses of `Entity` are split into two groups that correspond to these two directions. The first group consist of positively oriented entities for which an 'up' or 'increase' movement is positive (e.g., profit). The second group is comprised of negatively oriented entities for which a 'down' or 'decrease' movement is positive (e.g., debt).

Actions and properties are giving information about some entity and these are divided into four categories. The first two are aspect-dependent, representing an `Increase` and `Decrease` action, while the other two categories represent actions that are inherently `Positive` and `Negative`. Actions in the `Increase` or `Decrease` category can only be assigned a sentiment if they are linked with an entity from the ontology, while actions in the two sentiment classes always denote that sentiment value regardless of what entity they affect. A similar reasoning holds for properties. An overview of the main ontology classes is given in Figure 1.

2.2 Ontology Features

The presence or absence of subclasses of `Entity`, `Property`, and `Action`, which are the domain components of our ontology, are recorded as additional features for the SVR. To avoid fitting the model on certain companies that occur in predominantly positive (or negative) headlines in this particular set of news headlines, we filter out company name URLs from the set of features. Ontology concepts are linked to the text by means of lexicalizations that have been added to each non-abstract concept in the ontology. Once a concept has been found, all its superclasses are also added as features to the SVR model. Hence, if we find the action `Lift`, we also add the concepts `Action`, `Positive`, and `Sentiment`, since the concept `Lift` always denotes a positive sentiment in our domain ontology.

On top of these ontology lookup features, we define a set of class axioms that will allow the reasoner to infer the sentiment of a given combination of an `Entity` and either a `Property` or a `Action`, where the action or property on its own is not already a subclass of `Sentiment`. Using the two polar categories of entities (i.e., the positively oriented group and the negatively ori-

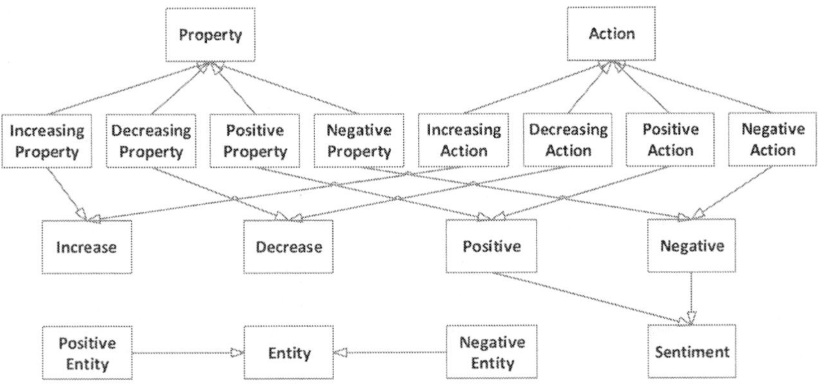

Figure 1: The main classes of the used ontology

ented group) in conjunction with the `Increase` and `Decrease` classes that contain actions and properties, we can infer the sentiment of the four different combinations that are possible. The class axioms that describe this behavior are:

1. $Increase \sqcap PosEntity \sqsubseteq Positive$
2. $Increase \sqcap NegEntity \sqsubseteq Negative$
3. $Decrease \sqcap PosEntity \sqsubseteq Negative$
4. $Decrease \sqcap NegEntity \sqsubseteq Positive$

Besides these general class axioms, we also defined a number of specific axioms that will allow the reasoner to infer the sentiment for certain particular expressions. For example, *closing a deal* is considered positive, while *closing stores* generally is not. While we could get the right behavior by classifying `Store` as a positively oriented entity, and `Deal` as a negatively oriented entity, this did not match with our intuition that a deal is something positive and more deals is not necessarily bad, which is a conclusion that would follow from classifying `Deal` as a negatively oriented entity. Hence we have specific axioms that deal with this scenario and the related `Open` action:

1. $Close \sqcap Deal \sqsubseteq Positive$
2. $Close \sqcap CompanyPart \sqsubseteq Negative$
3. $Open \sqcap CompanyPart \sqsubseteq Positive$

In the above axioms, a `CompanyPart` is the class that models all parts of a certain company, including things like headquarters, stores, webshops, departments, etc. An example of the reasoner in action is visualized in Figure 2.

2.3 Company-specific Sentiment

The above model, with all the described ontology features, would still result in a sentence-level sentiment algorithm that would not be able to give dif-

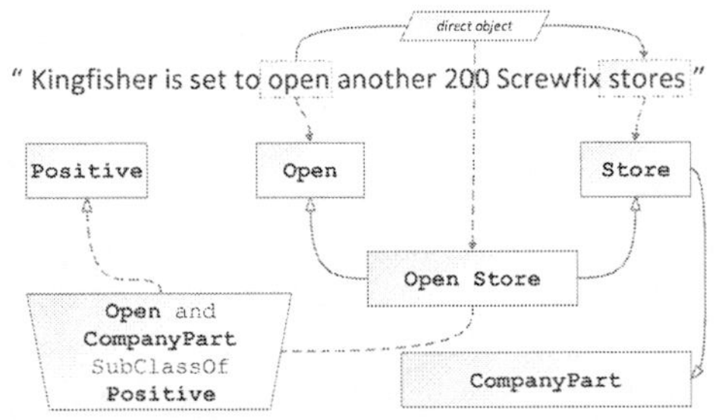

Figure 2: A schematic overview of the given reasoning example.

ferent sentiment scores for different companies in the same sentence. Since this problem does appear, we add a company-specific sentiment feature to the feature set. This feature denotes a positive (1), neutral (0), or negative (-1) sentiment score for the company that is mentioned in the company field of the annotation. Since we already annotated this field with a URL, we can locate the company within the headline. After that, we use the grammatical dependencies to find all words directly connected to the company. If these words are either a property or an action, we can use those to compute the company-specific sentiment as we can safely assume that directly connected words in the dependency graph pertain to that company.

Since a company is positively oriented entity, all actions and properties with superclass `Decrease` or `Negative` convey a negative sentiment towards the company, while `Increase` or `Positive` communicate a positive sentiment. A positive sentiment is quantified as +1, and a negative sentiment is represented by -1. Then, the company-specific sentiment feature is computed as the sum of all sentiment conveying words directly related in the dependency graph to the company mention in the headline.

3 Evaluation

In this section we evaluate our submission on the training data and report the results obtained on the official test data. The data consist of news headlines in the financial domain, and each headline is annotated with the name of the target company. For the training data the target sentiment score is also provided. Note that the same headline can appear multiple times in the data, each time with a different target company. On the official test data, a cosine distance of 0.6810 is achieved, resulting in the 12th position. The feature set experiments have been performed on the training data by running 5 times a 10-fold cross-validation setup, each time with different random folds, to ensure robust results.

To measure the effect of the various employed ontology features, the method is run with different subsets of all features. The results of this experiment are reported in Table 1. In this way, we can compare the benefit of adding entities, properties, and actions from the ontology, separately. From the reported results we can see that entities and properties are not particularly useful for sentiment analysis. For entities, this makes sense, as these convey no sentiment information. For properties, it is less intuitive, as adjectives, the word types that usually correspond to a subclass of `Property` from the ontology, are often strong indicators of sentiment (e.g., *good*, *bad*, etc.).

On the other hand, matching verbs in the text to subclasses of `Action` shows a large improvement to sentiment analysis. We hypothesize that the division into four categories (i.e., `Positive`, `Negative`, `Increase`, and `Decrease`) is a meaningful categorization in the domain of financial news. We observe that verbs are often the central word in conveying information to the reader, and hence, a lot of sentiment information is communicated using this type of concept.

Adding the class axioms to determine the sentiment of combinations with subclasses of `Increase` and `Decrease` is also useful, with a 2% increase compared to not using it. Adding the company specific sentiment, however, does not seem to help much.

Table 1: The change in performance when using different feature sets, reporting the average performance on the training data, using 5 runs with 10-fold cross-validation. Feature sets that are statistically indistinguishable from each other in terms of performance are grouped together

	avg. cosine distance	st.dev.
base (B)	0.6311	0.0482
B + entities (E)	0.6361	0.0455
B + properties (P)	0.6300	0.0478
B + actions (A)	0.6815	0.0498
B + E + P + A	0.6883	0.0502
B + E + P + A + class axioms	0.7041	0.0450
B + E + P + A + class axioms + company-specific sentiment	0.7050	0.0441

4 Conclusions

In this work we presented our submission to Task 5 of SemEval 2017: fine-grained sentiment analysis on financial news headlines (track 2). We showed that by categorizing entities (nouns), properties (adjectives), and actions (verbs), and linking them to concepts in an ontology, we can harness the power of the ontology reasoner to infer the sentiment of expressions that indicate a typical up/increase or down/decrease movement. This is achieved by defining class axioms within the ontology. In terms of contribution to performance, we can state that the categorization of actions into `Positive`, `Negative`, `Increase`, and `Decrease` gave the highest increase in performance, followed by adding class axioms for sentiment inference.

For future work, we want to invest more in the company-specific sentiment so we can assign different sentiment values to different companies in the news headline. Given the fact that headlines often contain companies with opposite sentiment, this is a highly desirable feature to have. By using a form of spreading activation, we could compute the sentiment for the whole dependency graph, not with respect to the root which would result in the sentence sentiment, but with respect to the node in the graph representing the company. Negators and other valence shifters can be used to properly spread the sentiment from one node to the next.

References

Erik Cambria. 2016. Affective Computing and Sentiment Analysis. *IEEE Intelligent Systems* 31(2):102–107.

Keith Cortis, André Freitas, Tobias Dauert, Manuela Huerlimann, Manel Zarrouk, Siegfried Handschuh, and Brian Davis. 2017. SemEval-2017 Task 5: Fine-Grained Sentiment Analysis on Financial Microblogs and News. In *Proceedings of the 11th International Workshop on Semantic Evaluation (SemEval-2017)*. Association for Computational Linguistics, pages 510–526.

Eibe Frank, Mark A. Hall, and Ian H. Witten. 2016. *The WEKA Workbench. Online Appendix for "Data Mining: Practical Machine Learning Tools and Techniques", Fourth Edition.* Morgan Kaufmann.

Kim Schouten, Flavius Frasincar, and Franciska de Jong. 2017. COMMIT at SemEval-2017 Task 5: Ontology-based Method for Sentiment Analysis of Financial Headlines - Ontology. http://www.kimschouten.com/publications/#semeval2017.

Thomas Schuster. 2003. Meta-Communication and Market Dynamics. Reflexive Interactions of Financial Markets and the Mass Media. Technical report, EconWPA. http://EconPapers.repec.org/RePEc:wpa:wuwpfi:0307014.

S.K. Shevade, S.S. Keerthi, C. Bhattacharyya, and K.R.K. Murthy. 2000. Improvements to the SMO Algorithm for SVM Regression. *IEEE Transactions on Neural Networks* 11(5):188 – 1993.

Richard Socher, Alex Perelygin, Jean Y Wu, Jason Chuang, Christopher D Manning, Andrew Y Ng, and Christopher Potts Potts. 2013. Recursive Deep Models for Semantic Compositionality Over a Sentiment Treebank. In *Proceedings of the 2013 Conference on Empirical Methods on Natural Language Processing (EMNLP 2013)*. Association for Computational Linguistics, pages 1631–1642.

Marjan Van de Kauter, Diane Breesch, and Véronique Hoste. 2015. Fine-grained Analysis of Explicit and Implicit Sentiment in Financial News Articles. *Expert Systems with Applications* 42(11):4999–5010.

ECNU at SemEval-2017 Task 5: An Ensemble of Regression Algorithms with Effective Features for Fine-Grained Sentiment Analysis in Financial Domain

Mengxiao Jiang[1], Man Lan[1,2]*, Yuanbin Wu[1,2]
[1]Department of Computer Science and Technology,
East China Normal University, Shanghai 200062, P.R.China
[2]Shanghai Key Laboratory of Multidimensional Information Processing
`51151201080@stu.ecnu.edu.cn, mlan,ybwu@cs.ecnu.edu.cn`

Abstract

This paper describes our systems submitted to the Fine-Grained Sentiment Analysis on Financial Microblogs and News task (i.e., Task 5) in SemEval-2017. This task includes two subtasks in microblogs and news headline domain respectively. To settle this problem, we extract four types of effective features, including linguistic features, sentiment lexicon features, domain-specific features and word embedding features. Then we employ these features to construct models by using ensemble regression algorithms. Our submissions rank 1st and rank 5th in subtask 1 and subtask 2 respectively.

1 Introduction

SemEval-2017 Task 5 is Fine-Grained Sentiment Analysis on Financial Microblogs and News(Cortis et al., 2017), focusing on identifying positive (bullish; believing that the stock price will increase) and negative (bearish; believing that the stock price will decline) sentiment associated with stocks and companies from microblogs and news domains. Unlike previous sentiment analysis, in this task, the fine-grained sentiment analysis not only contains sentiment orientation (i.e., positive or negative of the sentiment score) but also sentiment strength (i.e., the value of the sentiment score) attached to a particular company or stock explicitly or implicitly expressed in given texts.

Given a text instance (a microblog message from Twitter or StockTwits in subtask 1, a news statement or a headline in subtask 2), the goal of participants is to predict the sentiment score for each of the stocks and companies mentioned. The sentiment score is a floating value in the range of -1 (very negative) to 1 (very positive), with 0 designating neutral sentiment. Each microblog instance contains the following 5 items: "id", "source" (i.e., Twitter or StockTwits), "cashtag" (i.e., the company stock symbols to be predicted, e.g. "*$AAPL*"), "spans" and "sentiment score". And each news headline instance contains 4 items: "id", "company" (i.e., the company to be predicted), "title" and "sentiment score".

There are several differences between the spans in subtask 1 and the title in subtask 2: (1) The spans are sentence fragments related to the cashtag to be predicted, whereas the title is a complete sentence; (2) The spans almost regard one cashtag while the title usually contains one or more companies; (3) Due to (1) and (2), the spans contain less words but more effective information and less noises, which is contrary to the title.

In this work, the similar method is adopted for two subtasks. We extract a series of elaborately designed features. In addition to linguistic features, sentiment lexicon features and word embedding features, we also extract some domain-specific features for this task. Besides, we examine multiple different regression algorithms and ensemble methods are used to improve the performance of our models.

The rest of this paper is structured as follows. Section 2 describes our system in details, including data preprocessing, feature engineering, learning algorithms and evaluation measure. Section 3 reports datasets, experiments and results discussion. Finally, Section 4 concludes our work.

2 System Description

To solve these two subtasks, we extract lots of traditional NLP features combined with multiple machine learning algorithms to build supervised regression models. Due to the differences of data forms and data sources between the two subtasks, we adopt different features and algorithms

Proceedings of the 11th International Workshop on Semantic Evaluations (SemEval-2017), pages 888–893,
Vancouver, Canada, August 3 - 4, 2017. ©2017 Association for Computational Linguistics

for each subtask.

Specifically, for subtask 1, we rebuild the metadata of training and test set respectively with the official API of Twitter and StockTwits. The metadata contains the following information: tweets info or StockTwits info (e.g., "retweet_count"), users info (e.g., "favourites_count") and entities info (e.g., "sentiment"). As most of metadata of Twitter in test dataset is missing, we only extract the metadata features for StockTwits.

2.1 Data Preprocessing

Since the differences between the spans and the title described in section 1, for subtask 2, we replace the target company with *"TCOMPANY"* and replace other company with *"OCOMPNAY"* in the title.

For both subtasks, the subsequent preprocessing is the same. We firstly replace all URLs with "url" and transform the abbreviations, punctuation with a special format, slangs and elongated words to their normal format. Then, we use *Stanford CoreNLP tools*(Manning et al., 2014) for tokenization, POS tagging, named entity recognizing (NER) and parsing. Finally, the WordNet-based Lemmatizer implemented in NLTK[1] is adopted to lemmatize words to their base forms with the aid of their POS tags. And the word stemmer based on the Porter stemming algorithm and implemented in NLTK is adopted to remove morphological affixes from lemmatized words.

2.2 Feature Engineering

We extract the following four types of features to construct supervised regression models for two subtasks, i.e., linguistic features, sentiment lexicon features, domain-specific features and word embedding features.

2.2.1 Linguistic Features

N-grams: We remove the cashtag, punctuation, words that contain numbers and words with a length less than 2 from the sentence, and then extract 3 types of Bag-of-Words features as *N-grams* features, where N = {1,2,3} (i.e., *unigram, bigram*, and *trigram* features).

RF N-grams: Differ from the *N-grams* features where each token shares the same weight, we calculate the weight for each token similar to (Lan et al., 2009). We firstly count the number of oc-

currences of each token in the positive and negative samples in the training data. Then we calculate the weight (i.e., *rf*) for each token in *unigram, bigram* and *trigram* as follows:

$$rf = max\left(ln(2 + \frac{a}{max(1,c)}), \; ln(2 + \frac{c}{max(1,a)})\right)$$

where a is the number of sentences in the positive category that contain this token and c is the number of sentences in the negative category that contain this token.

Finally, using a method similar to the *N-grams* features, we extract 3 types of *RF N-grams* features, where N = {1,2,3}. The difference between these two features is that *RF N-grams* features use the corresponding *rf* weight whereas *N-grams* features use 1 to represent the occurrence of words.

Verb: Verbs usually contain more subjective tendencies. Thus, we also extract verbs (whose corresponding POS tags are VB, VBD, VBG, VBN, VBP and VBZ) from the sentence as *Verb* features with the Bag-of-Words form.

NER: Considering that the money, number and percent informations might be useful for predicting the sentiment score of stocks in financial domain, we extract 11 types of named entities (i.e., DATE, DURATION, LOCATION, MONEY, NUMBER, ORDINAL, ORGANIZATION, PERCENT, PERSON, SET, TIME) from the sentence and represent each type of named entity as a binary feature to check whether it appears in the current sentence.

Word Cluster: Since the high dimension of *N-grams* features, we also extract *word cluster* features to reduce the dimension of sentence representation (compared with *N-grams* features).

The *word cluster* features are extracted as follows: Firstly, we used the publicly available *Google word2vec*[2][3] that were trained on 100 billion words from Google News with the Skip-gram model (Mikolov et al., 2013) to get a 300-dimensional vector for each word in sentence. Then we use the *K*-means algorithm (k = 50) to cluster the words in the 300-dimensional vector space, and the value of k is chosen according to the preliminary experiment. After that, the word in sentence is replaced by its corresponding cluster assignment to get *word cluster* features.

---

[1] http://nltk.org

[2] https://code.google.com/archive/p/word2vec

[3] https://drive.google.com/file/d/0B7XkCwpI5KDYN1N UTTISS21pQmM/edit

2.2.2 Sentiment Lexicon Features

We also extract sentiment lexicon features (*SentiLexi*) to capture the sentiment information of the given sentence.

For each word in the sentence, we calculate five sentiment scores for each sentiment lexicon to construct *SentiLexi*: (1) the ratio of positive words, (2) the ratio of negative words, (3) the maximum sentiment score, (4) the minimum sentiment score, (5) the sum of sentiment scores. We transform the sentiment scores in all sentiment lexicons to the range of $[-1, 1]$, where "$-$" denotes negative sentiment. If the word does not exist in one sentiment lexicon, its corresponding score is set to zero. The following 8 sentiment lexicons are adopted in our systems: *Bing Liu opinion lexicon*[4], *General Inquirer lexicon*[5], *IMDB* (Zhu et al., 2013), *MPQA*[6], *AFINN*[7], *SentiWordNet*[8], *NRC Hashtag Sentiment Lexicon*[9], *NRC Sentiment140 Lexicon*[10].

2.2.3 Domain-specific Features

Observing data, we found that the data in financial domain usually contains numbers. These numbers can indicate the degree of bullish or bearish, which has an important impact on the sentiment score of stocks or companies in financial domain. Moreover, we found that "call" and "put" are terminologies usually used in microblog domain and related to sentiment score. Therefore, we design the following domain-specific features.

Number: We design 14 binary features to indicate whether there are the following types of numbers in the sentence: (1) *+num* (with a "+" in front of the number, e.g., "+5"); (2) *-num*; (3) *num%*; (4) *+num%*; (5) *-num%*; (6) *$num*; (7) *num_word* (the number mixed with characters, e.g., "5am"); (8) *ordinal number* (e.g., "2nd"); (9) *num-num*; (10) *num-num%*; (11) *num-num-num*; (12) *num/num*; (13) *num/num/num*; (14) *only number* (there are no symbols and characters before and after the number).

Keyword+Number: Based on the *Number* features, we defined 4-dimensional *Keyword+Number* features to indicate whether there

---

[4]http://www.cs.uic.edu/liub/FBS/sentiment-analysis.html
[5]http://www.wjh.harvard.edu/inquirer/homecat.htm
[6]http://mpqa.cs.pitt.edu/
[7]http://www2.imm.dtu.dk/pubdb/views/publication_details.php?id=6010
[8]http://sentiwordnet.isti.cnr.it/
[9]http://www.umiacs.umd.edu/saif/WebDocs/NRC-Hashtag-Sentiment-Lexicon-v0.1.zip
[10]http://help.sentiment140.com/for-students/

is "call" (or "calls", "called") or "put" (or "puts") before "*+num%*" or "*-num%*" in the sentence.

Metadata usually contains information on the user who posted this tweet or StockTwits. The user information is useful, because it reflects the degree of authority or confidence of the posed tweet and StockTwits. Moreover, it also includes some extra useful informations about this tweet or StockTwits. Therefore, we extract the following *Metadata* features.

Metadata: As most of metadata in Twitter is missing in test dataset, we used 8 items of the metadata in StockTwits to design following three types of features: (1) *Binary features* include the following items corresponding to the key in the metadata (json format): "source", "user/official", 'entities/sentiment", "liked_by_self" and "conversation/parent". (2) *Value features* contain the values of "conversation/replies" and "likes/total". And the *Value features* are standardized using [0-1] normalization. (3) *Other features*: "created_at" indicates whether the StockTwits is created in [0am, 9am), [9am, 3pm) or [3pm, 24pm). In total, we obtain 12 features from metadata.

Punctuation (Punc): People often use exclamation mark(!) and question mark(?) to express surprise or emphasis. Therefore, we extract the following 6 features: (1) whether there is "!" in sentence; (2) whether there is "?" in sentence; (3) the number of "!" in sentence; (4) the number of "?" in sentence; (5) the number of "$" in sentence; (6) the number of continuous "!" and "?" in sentence, e.g., "!!!", "????" or "!!??".

2.2.4 Word Embedding Features

The previous work (Zhang and Lan, 2016; Jiang et al., 2016) on sentiment analysis task has proved the effectiveness of word embedding features. In this part, we utilize the *Google word2vec* to get the representation of the sentence.

GoogleW2V: Unlike the *word cluster* features, the *Google word2vec* features (*GoogleW2V*) are extracted as follows: We firstly use the *Google word2vec* to get a 300-dimensional vector for each word in sentence. Then, the simple *min*, *max*, *average* pooling strategies are adopted to concatenate sentence vector representations with dimensionality of 900.

2.3 Learning Algorithms

For both tasks, we explore 7 algorithms as follows: AdaBoost Regressor (ABR), Bagging Regressor

(BR), Random Forest (RF), Gradient Boosting Regressor (GBR) and LASSO implemented in scikit-learn toolkit(Pedregosa et al., 2011), Support Vector Regression (SVR) implemented in liblinear toolkit(Fan et al., 2008) and XGBoost Regressor (XGB)[11] provided in (Friedman, 2001). All these algorithms are used with default parameters.

2.4 Evaluation Measure

To evaluate the performance of different systems, the official evaluation measure *weighted cosine similarity* (WCS) is adopted for two subtasks. Cosine similarity and cosine_weight will be calculated according the equation 1 and 2 respectively, where G is the vector of gold standard scores and P is the vector of scores predicted by the system. The final score is the product of the cosine and the weight (i.e., $WCS = cosine\_weight * cosine(G, P)$).

$$cosine(G, P) = \frac{\sum_{i=1}^{n} G_i \times P_i}{\sqrt{\sum_{i=1}^{n} G_i^2} \times \sqrt{\sum_{i=1}^{n} P_i^2}} \quad (1)$$

$$cosine\_weight = \frac{|P|}{|G|} \quad (2)$$

3 Experiment

3.1 Datasets

We conduct the experiments on the official datasets constructed by SSIX project (Davis et al., 2016), which consist of microblog messages (from Twitter or StockTwits) in subtask 1 and news headlines in subtask 2. Table 1 shows the statistics of the datasets used in our experiments.

Domain		Dataset	Instance	Metadata	Positive	Negative	Neutral
Microblog (subtask 1)	Twitter	train	765	603	246	510	9
		test	371	6	116	243	6
	StockTwits	train	934	926	330	586	18
		test	429	423	141	280	8
Headline (subtask 2)		train	1156	-	658	460	38
		test	491	-	276	203	12

Table 1: Statistics of training and test datasets of two subtasks. *Positive, Negative and Neural* stand for the number of corresponding instances whose sentiment score is positive, negative and zero.

3.2 Experiments on Training Data

3.2.1 Comparison of Different Algorithms

Table 2 shows the results of different algorithms using all features described before. Note that we

---

[11]https://github.com/dmlc/xgboost

did not use the *Metadata* feature in subtask 2 as there is no metadata in news headline domain. The 5-fold cross validation is performed for system development.

Method	Algorithm	Subtask 1	Subtask 2
Single	SVR	0.7450	0.7078
	XGB	0.7412	0.5875
	ABR	0.7382	0.6310
	BR	0.7441	0.5655
	RF	0.7373	0.5856
	GBR	0.7358	0.6763
	LASSO	0.3344	0.3297
Ensemble	SVR + GBR	0.7679	**0.7231**
	SVR + XGB + ABR + BR	**0.7827**	0.6875

Table 2: Results of algorithm selection experiments for two subtasks in terms of *WCS* on training datasets.

From Table 2, we find that for both subtasks, SVR outperforms other algorithms and LASSO performs the worst among all algorithms. Other algorithms perform differently on two subtasks. Therefore, we also perform experiments using an ensemble method. The last two rows in Table 2 list the results of using the top two and top four algorithms to build the ensemble regression models (named EN(2) and EN(4)), which average the output scores of all regression algorithm. From Table 2, we find that the ensemble classifier greatly increased the performance on both subtasks. Specifically, for subtask 1, the ensemble with top 4 algorithms improve 4% and for subtask 2, ensemble with top 2 improved 2% compared with the top score using a single regression algorithm. Therefore, we chose the EN(4) for subtask 1 and EN(2) for subtask 2 as the regression algorithm in following experiments.

3.2.2 Feature Selection

Table 3 shows the best feature sets for two subtasks. Based on previous ensemble algorithms, we adopt *hill climbing* algorithm to select best features. That is, keep adding one type of feature at a time until no further improvement can be achieved. From Table 3, we find that: (1) The *RF N-grams*, *Verb*, *Word Cluster*, *SentiLexi*, *Number*, *Punctuation* and *GoogleW2V* features are beneficial for both subtasks; (2) Specially, the *NER* features and *Keyword+Number* features are more effective in subtask 1 than subtask 2.

To further analysis the significance of different features, we conduct the ablation experiments for both systems. Table 4 lists the comparison of top

Features	Linguistic									SentiLexi	Domain-specific				Word embedding	WCS
	unigram	bigram	trigram	rf_1	rf_2	rf_3	Verb	NER	Word Cluster	SentiLexi	Number	Keyword+Number	Metadata	Punc	GoogleW2V	
Subtask 1	✓			✓		✓	✓	✓	✓	✓	✓	✓	✓	✓	✓	**0.7912**
Subtask 2				✓	✓	✓	✓		✓	✓	✓			✓	✓	**0.7264**

Table 3: Results of feature selection experiments for both subtasks on training datasets. rf_1, rf_2 and rf_3 stand for *rf_unigram*, *rf_bigram* and *rf_trigram* features respectively.

Subtask 1

Feature set	WCS	change (%)
Best features	0.7912	-
- rf_unigram	0.7643	-3.40
- SentiLexi	0.7664	-3.10
- metadata	0.7841	-0.90
- number	0.7869	-0.54

Subtask 2

Feature set	WCS	change (%)
Best features	0.7264	-
- GoogleW2V	0.6951	-4.31
- rf_unigram	0.6964	-4.13
- SentiLexi	0.7144	-1.65
- rf_bigram	0.7245	-0.27

Table 4: Ablation study: the comparison of top 4 most important features.

4 most important features.

From Table 3 and the ablation study results in Table 4, it is interesting to find that: (1) *rf_unigram* feature plays a key role in both subtasks and is more effective than *unigram* feature. The reason may be that *RF N-grams* features endow each word with a weight, which can capture how much the word contributes to the sentiment analysis of the sentence. Besides, the weight also contains some sentiment information. (2) *SentiLexi* features also make great contribution to both subtasks, which indicates that *SentiLexi* features are beneficial not only in traditional sentiment analysis tasks, but also in predicting the sentiment score of stocks in financial domain. (3) The *Number* features and *Keyword+Number* features are more effective in subtask 1 than subtask 2. The reason may be that there are plenty of numbers in the data of microblog domain but only a few numbers in news headline domain. (4) Although we only extract the *Metadata* features from the StockTwits, it perform better than most of other features, which indicates that the metadata is indeed significant. (5) The *GoogleW2V* feature is more effective in subtask 2 than subtask 1. The reason may be that

the spans in microblog domain contain less words and many word vectors of the spans can not be obtained from the pre-trained *Google word2vec*. (6) The *bigram* feature and *trigram* feature are not beneficial in both subtasks. The possible reason lies in the large dimensions of these two features leading to sparse representation in two domains.

Overall, the system configurations for two subtasks are: using the optimum feature sets shown in Table 3 and the algorithms described in section 3.2.1 (i.e., ensemble with top 4 regression algorithm for subtask 1 and ensemble with top 2 regression algorithm for subtask 2) to build supervised regression models.

3.3 Results and Discussion on Test Data

	Subtask 1	Subtask 2
Our system	0.7779	0.7107
Rank 1	0.7779	0.7452
Rank 2	0.7600	0.7437
Rank 3	0.7590	0.7327

Table 5: Performance of our systems and the top-ranked systems for two subtasks in terms of *WCS* on test datasets.

Using the system configurations described above, we train separate model for each subtask and evaluate them against the test set in SemEval-2017 Task 5.

Table 5 shows the results on test datasets. From Table 5, we find that: (1) Our system achieves lower performance on test data compared with the training data, the possible reason might be the different data distribution held between them. (2) Our results perform best among all submissions in subtask 1 and rank 5th in subtask 2, which proves the effectiveness of the method we proposed.

4 Conclusion and Future Work

In this paper, we extract four types of features, i.e., linguistic features, sentiment lexicon features, domain-specific features and word embedding features, and employ the ensemble regression models to predict the sentiment score for two subtasks. The results on test and training data show the effectiveness of our method for this task.

For the future work, we would explore domain-specific sentiment lexicons and use the deep learning method (e.g., attention neural networks) to improve the performance. Due to the limitation of annotated data, we would like to first pre-train a neural network model on similar tasks (e.g., aspect-level sentiment analysis task), and then fine tune the neural network model on the current fine-grained sentiment analysis task to boost the performance.

Acknowledgments

This research is supported by grants from Science and Technology Commission of Shanghai Municipality (14DZ2260800 and 15ZR1410700), Shanghai Collaborative Innovation Center of Trustworthy Software for Internet of Things (ZF1213) and NSFC (61402175).

References

Keith Cortis, André Freitas, Tobias Dauert, Manuela Huerlimann, Manel Zarrouk, Siegfried Handschuh, and Brian Davis. 2017. Semeval-2017 task 5: Fine-grained sentiment analysis on financial microblogs and news. In *Proceedings of the 11th International Workshop on Semantic Evaluation (SemEval-2017)*. Association for Computational Linguistics, Vancouver, Canada, pages 519–535. http://www.aclweb.org/anthology/S17-2089.

Brian Davis, Keith Cortis, Laurentiu Vasiliu, Adamantios Koumpis, Ross McDermott, and Siegfried Handschuh. 2016. Social sentiment indices powered by x-scores. *ALLDATA 2016* page 21.

Rong-En Fan, Kai-Wei Chang, Cho-Jui Hsieh, Xiang-Rui Wang, and Chih-Jen Lin. 2008. Liblinear: A library for large linear classification. *Journal of machine learning research* 9(Aug):1871–1874.

Jerome H Friedman. 2001. Greedy function approximation: a gradient boosting machine. *Annals of statistics* pages 1189–1232.

Mengxiao Jiang, Zhihua Zhang, and Man Lan. 2016. Ecnu at semeval-2016 task 5: Extracting effective features from relevant fragments in sentence for aspect-based sentiment analysis in reviews. *Proceedings of SemEval* pages 361–366.

Man Lan, Chew Lim Tan, Jian Su, and Yue Lu. 2009. Supervised and traditional term weighting methods for automatic text categorization. *IEEE transactions on pattern analysis and machine intelligence* 31(4):721–735.

Christopher D. Manning, Mihai Surdeanu, John Bauer, Jenny Finkel, Steven J. Bethard, and David McClosky. 2014. The Stanford CoreNLP natural language processing toolkit. In *Association for Computational Linguistics (ACL) System Demonstrations*. pages 55–60. http://www.aclweb.org/anthology/P/P14/P14-5010.

Tomas Mikolov, Ilya Sutskever, Kai Chen, Greg S Corrado, and Jeff Dean. 2013. Distributed representations of words and phrases and their compositionality. In *Advances in neural information processing systems*. pages 3111–3119.

Fabian Pedregosa, Gaël Varoquaux, Alexandre Gramfort, Vincent Michel, Bertrand Thirion, Olivier Grisel, Mathieu Blondel, Peter Prettenhofer, Ron Weiss, Vincent Dubourg, et al. 2011. Scikit-learn: Machine learning in python. *Journal of Machine Learning Research* 12(Oct):2825–2830.

Zhihua Zhang and Man Lan. 2016. Ecnu at semeval-2016 task 6: Relevant or not? supportive or not? a two-step learning system for automatic detecting stance in tweets. *Proceedings of SemEval* pages 451–457.

Tian Tian Zhu, Fang Xi Zhang, and Man Lan. 2013. Ecnucs: A surface information based system description of sentiment analysis in twitter in the semeval-2013 (task 2). *Atlanta, Georgia, USA* page 408.

IITPB at SemEval-2017 Task 5: Sentiment Prediction in Financial Text

Abhishek Kumar[a]**, Abhishek Sethi**[b]**, Md Shad Akhtar**[a]**, Asif Ekbal**[a]
Chris Biemann[c]**, Pushpak Bhattacharyya**[a,b]
[a]Indian Institute of Technology Patna, India
[b]Indian Institute of Technology Bombay, India
[c]Universität Hamburg, Germany
{abhishek.ee14,shad.pcs15,asif,pb}@iitp.ac.in
{abhisethi,pb}@cse.iitb.ac.in
biemann@informatik.uni-hamburg.de

Abstract

This paper reports team IITPB's participation in the SemEval 2017 Task 5 on 'Fine-grained sentiment analysis on financial microblogs and news'. We developed 2 systems for the two tracks. One system is based on an ensemble of Support Vector Classifier and Logistic Regression. This system relis on Distributional Thesaurus (DT), word embeddings and lexicon features to predict a continuous sentiment value between -1 and +1. The other system is based on Support Vector Regression using word embeddings, lexicon features, and PMI scores as features. Our systems are ranked 5th in track 1 and 8th in track 2.

1 Introduction

We are living in a world where stock market directly affects the economic system of a country. Therefore, a reliable and prompt delivery of information plays an important role in the financial market. Up until the last decade printed/television news were the major source of stock market-related information. However, with the introduction of micro-blogging websites (e.g. Twitter etc.) the trend has been shifted. The rise of Twitter and StockTwits has given the people and organizations an opportunity to vent out their feelings and views. This information can be used by an individual or an organization to make an informed prediction related to any company or stock (Si et al., 2013). This opens a new avenue for sentiment analysis in the financial domain of microblogs and news.

News headlines are a short piece of text describing the nature of an article. Due to space constraints, headlines normally follow a compact writing style, known as *headlinese*, which limits the usage of articles, the verb form of to be, conjunctions etc.

Similarly, social media platforms text is prone to noise. There is a very high possibility of the data lacking a proper structure, grammar and appropriate punctuations. These inconsistencies make it challenging to solve any NLP problems including sentiment analysis (Khanarian and Alwarez-Melis, 2012). Moreover, each tweet can have reference to multiple company names (or stock symbols) and the expressed sentiment can be different towards different companies. Hence, there is a need to perform fine-grained sentiment analysis wherein, generally, a context is used to decide the relevant portion of a tweet for a particular company. Another inherent challenge with the microblog and news data is the use of short languages, hashtag, emoticons and embedded URL. Special attention should be given to these as they can provide some important hidden information (Mohammad et al., 2013). Example - *#bullishMarket* and *#increasingProfit* can reflect *positive* sentiment. These are some of the major challenges associated with fine-grained sentiment analysis of microblogging and news data.

The SemEval-2017 task 5 (Fine-Grained Sentiment Analysis on Financial Microblogs and News) has two tracks (Cortis et al., 2017). For both the tracks, the overall aim was to assign a sentiment score to a cashtag/company over a continuous range of -1 (very negative/bearish) to 1 (very positive/bullish).

First track involves finding a sentiment score towards a given 'cashtag' (stock symbol preceded by a \$, e.g. \$AAPL for Apple Inc.) in microblog messages while the second track involves finding a sentiment score towards a given company name in the news headlines.Instances in track 1 datasets also contain 'span'. It is the section of a tweet from where sentiment score should be derived.

Proceedings of the 11th International Workshop on Semantic Evaluations (SemEval-2017), pages 894–898,
Vancouver, Canada, August 3 - 4, 2017. ©2017 Association for Computational Linguistics

Track 1	Microblogs
Message:	Putting on a little \$F short, prevailing wisdom notwithstanding.
Score:	-0.454
Span:	Putting on a little \$F short
Cashtag:	\$F

Track 2	News headlines
Message:	RBS and Barclays shares temporarily suspended amid heavy losses.
Score:	-0.941
Company:	Royal Bank of Scotland Group

Table 1: Instances of of microblog and news headline dataset.

We participated and submitted our system for both the tracks. A total of 27 and 29 teams participated in track 1 and track 2 respectively. Our system ranked 5th in the first track with a cosine similarity of 0.725. In the second track, our system scored cosine similarity of 0.695 and ranked 8th overall.

The rest of the paper is organized as follows: Section 2 briefly describes the proposed systems. Description of the feature set is given in Section 3. Section 4 is devoted to experimental result and error analysis. Lastly, we conclude in Section 5.

2 System Overview

In this section, we present a brief description of the proposed systems. We adopted a supervised approach for solving the problem of both the tasks. We employed Logistics Regression, Support Vector Machine (SVM) and Support Vector Regression (SVR) as the base classifier for the prediction. We tried various combinations of the feature set for training the model. Following this approach, we select a feature set that best suited for the problem at hand. To further improve the efficacy of the system we ensemble the outputs of various classifiers at the end. For ensemble, the final sentiment value was calculated by taking the harmonic mean of both the system's prediction and then, linearly scaling it in between -1 and +1.

2.1 Distributional Thesaurus

Missing words in word2vec or Glove vector representation makes it non-trivial to learn from the data. We employ Distributional Thesaurus (DT) (Biemann and Riedl, 2013) expansion strategy for those words whose representation was missing in word2vec or GloVe model. Distributional Thesaurus is an automatically computed word list which ranks words according to their semantic similarity. It finds words that tend to occur in similar contexts as the target word. We use a pre-trained DT model to expand a source word. If the representation of a word is not present in word2vec or GloVe model, then its corresponding most similar expanded word is used to replace it. If the replaced word does not have its corresponding representation also we select next similar word and so on. For a source word, we took top 5 similar words in the expanded list as targets. An example is listed in Table 2. For the source word 'drinks', its DT expanded word list contains 'beer', 'wine', 'coffee', 'liquids' and 'beverages'.

Word	DT expanded list
drinks	beer, wines, coffee, liquids, beverages
price	prices, pricing, cash, cost, pennies
laptop	pc, computer, notebook, tablet, imac

Table 2: Example of DT expansion

3 Feature set

We use following set of features for training the model.

3.1 Track 1 - Microblogs messages

- **Word Embedding:** Word embeddings are known to capture the syntactic and semantic similarity in a better and representative way. We used 200 dimensional twitter based pre-trained GloVe vectors[1] for word representation. Averaging of words representation was done for calculating sentence embeddings.

- **Tf-Idf Score:** We use Tf-Idf score as a feature value in the work. The score reflects how important a word is to a document in a corpus.

- **Sentiment Lexicon:** We compiled a list of positive and negative words using NRC Hashtag Sentiment Lexicon (Kiritchenko et al., 2014), MPQA Subjectivity Lexicon (Wilson et al., 2009) and Bing Liu Opinion Lexicon (Hu and Liu, 2004). Using these we created hand-engineered features. M_{pos} and

---

[1] http://nlp.stanford.edu/projects/glove/

M_{neg} are the number of positive and negative words in span and text.

- **Agreement Score:** It is the agreement value of the positive and negative words in the data instance. This was calculated both for span or text. If we have all positive or all negative words then A = 1. We have modified the proposal in (Rao and Srivastava, 2012) to make the feature more effective.

$$A = 1 - \sqrt{1 - \left| \frac{M_{pos} - M_{neg}}{M_{pos} + M_{neg}} \right|}$$

- **Polar word occurrence:** We count the number of occurrences of all positive and negative words in the text and assign values +1, -1 and 0 if the difference between M_{pos} & M_{neg} are positive, negative and zero respectively.

3.2 Track 2 - News headlines

- **Word Ngrams:** We extracted and used unigrams and bigrams as features for this task.

- **Sentiment Lexicon:** Sentiment lexicons have been known to be a decisive feature in sentiment analysis tasks. We use the following four sentiment lexicons to get lexicon based features:

  - Bing Liu's Sentiment Lexicon (Hu and Liu, 2004)
  - Harvard General Inquirer (Stone et al., 1966)
  - SentiWordNet (Baccianella et al., 2010)
  - Loughran and McDocnald's Finance Lexicon (Loughran and McDonald, 2011)

For each instance, we extract 3 features: positive score, negative score, and cumulative score. Each token is assigned a score of +1 or -1 if it belongs to positive or negative list respectively. We followed stated approach for all lexicons except SentiWordNet. In the case of SentiWordNet lexicon, we use the positive and negative score as given in the lexicon rather than +1 or -1.

- **Semantic Orientation (SO):** Semantic orientation (Hatzivassiloglou and McKeown,

1997) finds the association of a token with respect to its positivity and negativity. We calculate a score for each term in our training corpus to get the association value.

$$score(w) = PMI(w, pos) - PMI(w, neg)$$

where PMI is point-wise mutual information and calculated as follows:

$$PMI(w, pos) = \log_2 \frac{freq(w, pos) * N}{freq(w) * freq(pos)}$$

In the above equation *pos* is the collection of positive reviews and N is the total number of tokens in the corpus.

- **Word Embeddings:** We use the 300-dimensional pre-trained word2vec (Mikolov et al., 2013) vectors trained on part of Google News dataset (about 100 billion words). The sentence embedding is obtained by averaging the embedding vectors of all words in the sentence.

4 Experiments and Results

4.1 Dataset

The training datasets contains 1700 and 1142 instances of microblog messages and news headlines respectively. Test data comprises of 800 and 491 resp. of such instances for the two tracks. We use 20% of the training dataset as validation set.

4.2 Preprocessing

We used CMU ARK toolkit[2] for tokenization of microblog tweets. For preprocessing the text, each url, username and number was replaced by *<url>*, *<user>* and *<number>* respectively. Example - '*www.twitter.com*' by *<url>*, '*@johnSnow*' by *<user>* and '*9.7*' by *<number>*. Since the data was collected from the web all HTML entities were converted to their corresponding unicode characters e.g. '*&*' to '*and*'. Datasets analysis suggests that few hashtags convey explicit sentiment in the text. Therefore, we replace hashtags by '*#*' followed by the associated word with the hashtag. For example - '*#happy*' by '*# happy*'. Lastly, all the characters are converted to lower case and for the news headline we use NLTK[3] for the tokenization.

[2]http://www.cs.cmu.edu/~ark/
[3]http://www.nltk.org/

4.3 Experiments

We used python based machine learning package scikit-learn[4] for the implementation. As classification algorithm, we used Logistic Regression (LR), Support Vector Machine (SVM) and Support Vector Regression (SVR). As discussed earlier, each instance of the dataset need a score over a continuous range of -1 to +1. Since SVM predicts discrete class labels, as post-processing we use the probability of predicted class as the score. During validation phase we observed that models trained on SVM work better than that of SVR for the microblog datasets. In contrast, SVR works better than SVM in news headline datasets. The hyperparameters of the SVM were $C = 30$ and $\gamma = 0.01$, for SVR we used $C = 10$ and $\gamma = 0.01$ and for LR we set $C = 6$. Cosine similarity of various combinations of the feature set is listed in Table 3 and 4 for microblogs and news headlines validation set respectively. For fine tuning of hyper-parameters, we did an exhaustive grid search evaluated through ten-fold cross-validation on the training set.

Model	Cosine Similarity		
	LR	SVM	SVR
W.E	0.649	0.654	0.691
Tf-Idf	0.727	0.729	0.736
W.E + Lexicon	0.656	0.678	0.684
W.E + Tf-Idf	0.745	0.762	0.726
Tf-Idf + Lexicon	0.749	0.752	0.759
W.E + Tf-Idf + Lexicon	0.760	**0.775**	0.717

Table 3: Microblog messages: Cosine similarity on validation set.

Model	Cosine similarity		
	LR	SVM	SVR
Unigrams	0.507	0.58	0.566
Unigrams + Lexicon	0.598	0.609	0.640
(Uni+Bi)grams + Lexicon	0.603	0.609	0.648
(Uni+Bi)grams + Lexicon + SO	0.738	0.713	0.794
Unigrams + Lexicon + SO	0.736	0.713	0.789
W.E	0.619	0.584	0.673
W.E + Lexicon	0.613	0.580	0.639
W.E + Lexicon + PMI	0.746	0.708	**0.80**

Table 4: News headline: Cosine similarity on validation set.

As a result, we observed that the word embedding along with lexicon based features produce the

best cosine similarity for both the datasets. Further, we observed the output of different classifier are contrasting in nature, therefore we merge the outputs of different classifiers using averaging and harmonic mean. We found that harmonic mean of LR and SVM produces better cosine similarity score than other combinations for microblogs messages. However, for news headline performance did not improve on the ensemble, so we choose the best feature combination to train an SVR. Table 5 shows the results for harmonic mean of SVM and LR cosine similarities in microblogs datasets.

Model	Cosine similarity
W.E	0.687
Tf-Idf	0.733
W.E + Lexicon	0.697
W.E + Tf-Idf	0.768
Tf-Idf + Lexicon	0.755
W.E + Tf-Idf + Lexicon	**0.778**

Table 5: Microblog messages: Ensemble of SVM & LR on validation set.

After finalizing the proposed approach on validation set, we evaluated it on the test datasets. For microblogs messages we got the cosine similarity of 0.725. In news headline, our system produces cosine similarity of 0.695. Table 6 depicts evaluation results on test datasets.

Datasets	Cosine similarity
Track 1: Microblogs	0.725
Track 2: News headlines	0.695

Table 6: Cosine similarity on test dataset.

5 Conclusion

In this paper we proposed a supervised sentiment analyzer for financial texts as part of our participation in SemEval 2017 shared task. As base classification algorithm we used Logistic Regression (LR), Support Vector Machine (SVM) and Support Vector Regression (SVR) for predicting the sentiment score. In second stage we combine the predictions of two best performing models using harmonic mean. Evaluation shows encouraging results on the shared task dataset. In future we would like to explore other relevant features to improve the performance of the system.

---

[4] http://scikit-learn.org

References

Stefano Baccianella, Andrea Esuli, and Fabrizio Sebastiani. 2010. Sentiwordnet 3.0: An enhanced lexical resource for sentiment analysis and opinion mining. In *LREC*. volume 10, pages 2200–2204.

Chris Biemann and Martin Riedl. 2013. Text: now in 2D! A framework for lexical expansion with contextual similarity. *J. Language Modelling* 1(1):55–95. https://doi.org/10.15398/jlm.v1i1.60.

Keith Cortis, Andre Freitas, Tobias Daudert, Manuela Huerlimann, Manel Zarrouk, and Brian Davis. 2017. Semeval-2017 task 5: Fine-grained sentiment analysis on financial microblogs and news. *Proceedings of SemEval* .

Vasileios Hatzivassiloglou and Kathleen R. McKeown. 1997. Predicting the semantic orientation of adjectives. In *Proceedings of the 35th Annual Meeting of the Association for Computational Linguistics*. Association for Computational Linguistics, Madrid, Spain, pages 174–181. https://doi.org/10.3115/976909.979640.

Minqing Hu and Bing Liu. 2004. Mining and summarizing customer reviews. In *Proceedings of the tenth ACM SIGKDD international conference on Knowledge discovery and data mining*. ACM, pages 168–177.

Michael Khanarian and David Alwarez-Melis. 2012. Sentiment classification in twitter: A comparison between domain adaptation and distant supervision. Technical report, CSAIL, MIT. Statistical NLP Final Project. http://people.csail.mit.edu/davidam/docs/ SentClassifTwitter.pdf.

Svetlana Kiritchenko, Xiaodan Zhu, and Saif M. Mohammad. 2014. Sentiment analysis of short informal texts. *J. Artif. Intell. Res. (JAIR)* 50:723–762. https://doi.org/10.1613/jair.4272.

Tim Loughran and Bill McDonald. 2011. When is a liability not a liability? textual analysis, dictionaries, and 10-ks. *The Journal of Finance* 66(1):35–65.

Tomas Mikolov, Ilya Sutskever, Kai Chen, Greg S. Corrado, and Jeff Dean. 2013. Distributed representations of words and phrases and their compositionality. In *Advances in neural information processing systems*. Lake Tahoe, NV, USA, pages 3111–3119.

Saif Mohammad, Svetlana Kiritchenko, and Xiaodan Zhu. 2013. NRC-Canada: Building the state-of-the-art in sentiment analysis of tweets. In *Second Joint Conference on Lexical and Computational Semantics (*SEM), Volume 2: Proceedings of the Seventh International Workshop on Semantic Evaluation (SemEval 2013)*. Association for Computational Linguistics, Atlanta, Georgia, USA, pages 321–327. http://www.aclweb.org/anthology/S13-2053.

Tushar Rao and Saket Srivastava. 2012. Analyzing stock market movements using twitter sentiment analysis. In *Proceedings of the 2012 International Conference on Advances in Social Networks Analysis and Mining (ASONAM 2012)*. IEEE Computer Society, pages 119–123.

Jianfeng Si, Arjun Mukherjee, Bing Liu, Qing Li, Huayi Li, and Xiaotie Deng. 2013. Exploiting topic based twitter sentiment for stock prediction. In *Proceedings of the 51st Annual Meeting of the Association for Computational Linguistics (Volume 2: Short Papers)*. Association for Computational Linguistics, Sofia, Bulgaria, pages 24–29. http://www.aclweb.org/anthology/P13-2005.

Philip J. Stone, Dexter C. Dunphy, and Marshall S. Smith. 1966. The general inquirer: A computer approach to content analysis .

Theresa Wilson, Janyce Wiebe, and Paul Hoffmann. 2009. Recognizing contextual polarity: An exploration of features for phrase-level sentiment analysis. *Computational Linguistics* 35(3):399–433. https://doi.org/10.1162/coli.08-012-R1-06-90.

IITP at SemEval-2017 Task 5: An Ensemble of Deep Learning and Feature Based Models for Financial Sentiment Analysis

Deepanway Ghosal, Shobhit Bhatnagar, Md Shad Akhtar,
Asif Ekbal, Pushpak Bhattacharyya
Indian Institute of Technology Patna, India
{deepanway.me14,shobhit.ee14,shad.pcs15,asif,pb}@iitp.ac.in

Abstract

In this paper we propose an ensemble based model which combines state of the art deep learning sentiment analysis algorithms like Convolution Neural Network (CNN) and Long Short Term Memory (LSTM) along with feature based models to identify optimistic or pessimistic sentiments associated with companies and stocks in financial texts. We build our system to participate in a competition organized by Semantic Evaluation 2017 International Workshop. We combined predictions from various models using an artificial neural network to determine the opinion towards an entity in (a) Microblog Messages and (b) News Headlines data. Our models achieved a cosine similarity score of 0.751 and 0.697 for the above two tracks giving us the rank of 2nd and 7th best team respectively.

1 Introduction

Sentiment analysis of financial text is an important area of research. It has been shown that sentiments and opinions can affect market dynamics (Goonatilake and Herath, 2007). Social media has created a new world of venting customer voice. People tend to express their personal sentiment about the stock market through tweets. On the other hand, news presents the macroeconomic factors, company-specific or political information. Positive news tend to bring optimism and lift the market where as negative news effect the market in opposite direction (Van de Kauter et al., 2015). Sentiment analysis gives organizations the ability to observe the various social media sites in real time and then act accordingly. Twitter is considered to be an ocean of sentiment data.

A study indicates that sentiment analysis of public mood derived from Twitter feeds can be used to eventually forecast movements of individual stock prices (Smailović et al., 2014). All these evidences show us that financial sentiment analysis has a lot of untapped power and extensive research in the field can help us gain great insight about the financial market. The fundamental problem with classifying financial tweets is the presence of noise. The natural use of short, informal languages, emoticons, hashtag and sarcasm in tweets makes the sentiment analysis problem especially challenging.

News headlines usually use limited number of words to summarize the article. Moreover, aspects like language patterns, writing style, irony usage differs notably among different news categories and articles. Use of articles, verb form of 'to be', conjunction are very rare in practice.

In this paper we describe our proposed system as part of the 'SemEval-2017 Task 5 on Fine-Grained Sentiment Analysis for Financial Microblogs and News' (Cortis et al., 2017). We propose a multilayer perceptron (MLP) based ensemble method that leverages the combination of deep learning and feature based models for the prediction. Our system produces 4th and 8th best cosine similarity score for microblogs messages and news headline respectively. A total of 25 teams participated for the microblogs messages task while 29 teams submitted their systems for the news headline track.

The task defines sentiment score prediction in two separate tracks i.e. microblogs and news headlines. The objective of the task is to predict a sentiment score associated with a company/cashtag in the text. The sentiment score lies in a continuous range of -1(very bearish) to +1(very bullish). Cashtag refers to a stock symbol that uniquely identifies a company. For e.g. $AAPL represents

Proceedings of the 11th International Workshop on Semantic Evaluations (SemEval-2017), pages 899–903,
Vancouver, Canada, August 3 - 4, 2017. ©2017 Association for Computational Linguistics

stock symbol for the company Apple Inc. Every instance of microblogs messages also include a span which indicates a part of text from where prediction should be derived.

This rest of the paper is organized as follows: Section 2 illustrates our system architecture in detail. We present our experimental results in Section 3. Finally, Section 4 presents our conclusions.

2 System Description

In this section we discuss our proposed system for the task. We developed a multi-layer perceptron (MLP) based ensemble approach which learns on top of a convolution neural network (CNN), a long short term memory network (LSTM), a vector averaging MLP and a feature driven MLP model. We separately train and tune all the models and then feed the prediction scores of each model as input to an MLP for ensembling. Training and tuning of this system is performed separately. The resultant pipeline is used to predict the final sentiment score.

2.1 Word Embeddings

Word embeddings are generally helpful in many natural processing tasks due to it's excellence in capturing hidden semantic structures. For word embeddings we used two pre-trained embedding models: GloVe[1] and Word2Vec[2]. For microblogs messages we used GloVe (Pennington et al., 2014) and Word2Vec (Godin et al., 2015) twitter model trained on 2 billion and 400 million tweets respectively. For news headline we used GloVe common crawl model trained on 802 billion words and Word2Vec Google News model (Mikolov et al., 2013). We experimented with 200, 300 and 400 dimension vectors and observed that 200 & 300 dimension vectors are the near-optimal case for microblogs messages and news headlines respectively. We have used concatenation of word embeddings to form sentence embeddings.

2.2 Convolutional Neural Network (CNN)

Convolutional neural network consists of one or more convolution and pooling layers followed by one or more dense layers. Our system uses 2 convolution layers followed by a max pool layer, 2 dense layers and an output layer. Size of convolution filters dictates the hidden features to be extracted. We employ 50 such filters while sliding over 1, 2, 3 and 4 word(s) at a time.

2.3 Long Short Term Memory (LSTM)

LSTMs are special kind of recurrent neural network which can efficiently learn long-term dependencies. We use two layers of LSTM on top of each other followed by 2 dense layers and a output layer. We fix number of neurons on each LSTM layers as 100. For the dense layer we use 50 and 10 neurons in the hidden layers.

2.4 Multilayer Perceptron (MLP) - Vector Averaging Model

Concatenation of word vectors for generating sentence embeddings often face the curse of high-dimensionality. In an attempt to get a constant low-dimensional feature vector we employ vector averaging technique for producing sentence vector. We perform an element wise averaging of the word vectors in a tokenized tweet/headline. We then use the sentence embeddings to train a 3-layered neural network for the prediction.

2.5 Multilayer Perceptron (MLP) - Feature Driven Model

This model is based on various lexical and semantic features. We trained a multilayer perceptron on top of the following features.

- **Character ngrams:** tf-idf weighted counts of continuous sequences of 2, 3, and 4 characters;

- **Word ngrams:** tf-idf weighted counts of continuous sequences of 1, 2, 3, and 4 words;

- **POS-tag**: parts of speech tags of each token in the text;

- **Lexicons:**

  - Following set of features are used for each of the four lexicons: Opinion Lexicon (Liu et al., 2005), Loughran and McDonald Sentiment Word Lists (Loughran and McDonald, 2011), MPQA Lexicon [+1.0 for strong positive, +0.5 for weak positive, similarly for negative] (Wilson et al., 2005) and Harvard's General Inquirer (Stone et al., 1962):

    * **positive count:** number of positive tokens in a tweet/title.

---

* **negative count:** number of negative tokens in a tweet/title.
        * **net count:** positive count - negative count in tweet/title.
    - In addition we use four NRC Lexicons: Hashtag Context, Hashtag Sentiment, Sentiment140, Sentiment140 Context (Svetlana Kiritchenko and Mohammad, 2014; Mohammad et al., 2013) for the microblogs messages. Following set of features are extracted for each of them:
        * positive count, negative count and net count.
        * sum of positive scores, negative scores and all scores.
        * maximum of positive and negative scores.

* **Pointwise Mutual Information (PMI):** We calculate a sentiment score for each term in our training corpus to get the association of each term with positive as well as negative sentiment.

$$score(w) = PMI(w, pos) - PMI(w, neg)$$

PMI is calculated as follows:-

$$PMI(w, pos) = \log_2 \frac{freq(w, pos) * N}{freq(w) * freq(pos)}$$

In the above equation $freq(w, pos)$ is the frequency of word w in positive text, $freq(pos)$ is the number of words in positive headlines and N is the total number of tokens in the corpus.

* **Microblog Specific Features:** We use following features only for microblogs messages track:

    - the number of words with all characters in upper case.
    - the number of favorite and retweet counts of a message (tweet).
    - the number of hashtags in the message.

The multilayer perceptron network has three hidden layers and one output layer consisting of 500, 50, 10 and 1 neurons respectively.

2.6 Ensemble Model

Ensemble of various systems is an effective technique to improve the overall performance by assisting each other. Ensembling usually reduces the generalization error, which in turn reduces over-fitting. Here we discuss second stage of the our proposed system. We merge predicted sentiment scores of all four models (CNN, LSTM, Vector Averaging, Feature Driven) to create a new feature vector, and then fed it into a multilayer perceptron (MLP) network for training. Figure 1 shows, an overall schema of the proposed approach.

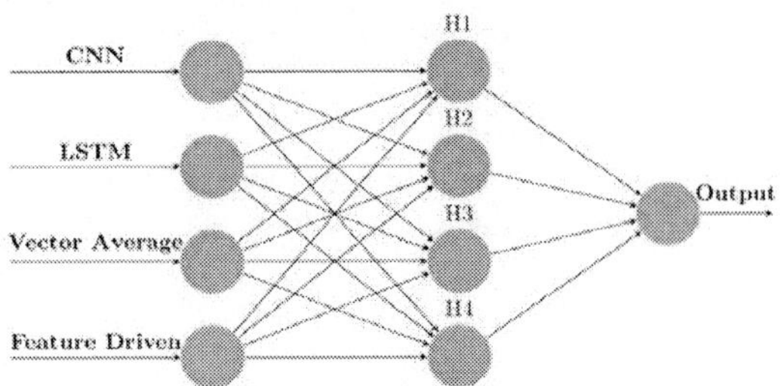

Figure 1: Ensembling Network Structure

3 Dataset, Experiments and Results

3.1 Datasets

The training datasets comprises of 1700 and 1142 instances of microblogs messages and news headlines respectively. We used the span in microblogs message track and the title in news headlines track as the textual feature for all our experiments described in this paper. For validation we did a 80:20, train:development split of the full datasets. The split was done such that the relative percentage of sources (twitter and stocktwits), mean and standard deviation of sentiment scores were same in the training and development data. We trained our model on the train data and selected models for ensembling, based on results on development data. Figure 2 and 3 shows the distribution of sentiment scores for the two datasets.

3.2 Experiments

We used python based neural network package Keras[3] for the implementation. We use ReLU activations for the intermediate layers and tanh activation for the final layer. Dropout (Srivastava et al., 2014) is a very effective regularization technique to prevent over-fitting of a network. It restrict convergence of weights to identical positions by randomly turning off the neurons during forward propagation. We use 15% dropout and '*Adam*' optimizer (Kingma and Ba, 2014) for regularization and optimization.

---

[3]www.keras.io

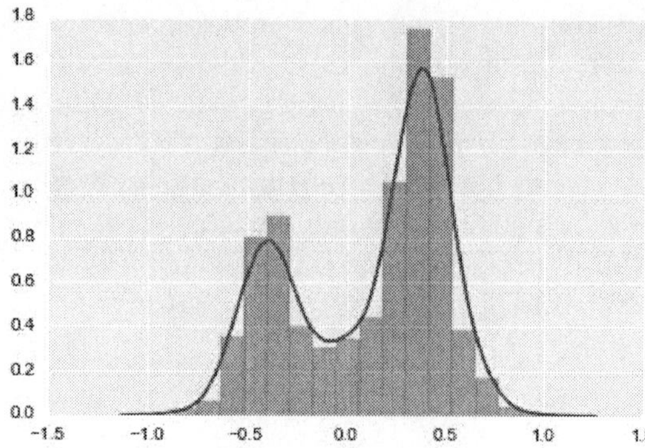

Figure 2: Histogram plot of sentiment scores in microblogs messages

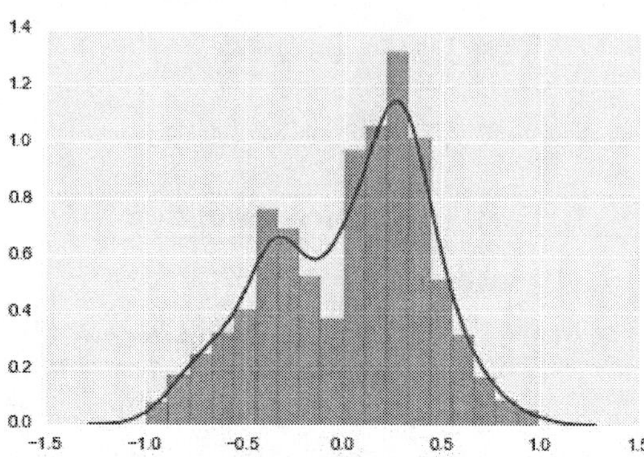

Figure 3: Histogram plot of sentiment scores in news headlines

SNo	Models	Cosine Similarity	
		Microblogs	**Headlines**
D1	W2V CNN	0.752	0.670
D2	W2V LSTM	0.725	0.652
D3	GloVe CNN	0.768	0.649
D4	GloVe LSTM	0.765	0.644
F1	Feature Based	0.792	0.784
V1	W2V Average	0.804	0.663
V2	GloVe Average	0.781	0.643
E1	D3 + D4 + F1 + V1	**0.834**	-
E2	D3 + F1 + V1	0.826	-
E3	D4 + F1 + V1	0.821	-
E4	D3 + D4 + V1	0.812	-
E5	D3 + D4 + F1	0.799	-
E6	D1 + D2 + F1 + V1	-	**0.802**
E7	D1 + F1 + V1	-	0.795
E8	D2 + F1 + V1	-	0.788
E9	D1 + D2 + V1	-	0.683
E10	D1 + D2 + F1	-	0.791

Table 1: Cosine similarity score on validation set.

Tracks	Cos Sim	Rank
Track-1: Microblogs Messages	0.751	2nd
Track-2: News Headlines	0.697	7th

Table 2: Cosine similarity score on test dataset.

We train and validate each model on 80% & 20% of the full data respectively. Table 1 shows our results of deep learning models (D), feature based model (F) and vector averaging models (V) on the validation set. It also depicts the results of our ensemble model (E) on the development set. It should be observed that use of ensemble improves the performance by a margin of 2-3%.

We submitted the E1 and E6 systems for the final evaluation and got a test cosine similarity score of 0.751 and 0.697 for microblogs messages and news headlines tracks respectively. Table 2 reports cosine similarity of our system.

4 Conclusion

In this paper we presented an MLP based ensemble technique for predicting the sentiment score. The proposed approach is a robust regression algorithm which predicts optimistic or pessimistic sentiments of associated stocks and companies in financial text. We implemented a variety of semantic and linguistic features for our analysis of the noisy text such as tweets and news headlines. We combined predictions of four models (i.e. CNN, LSTM, Vector Averaging MLP and Feature Driven MLP) for calculation of final prediction. Our submission stood 2nd and 7th in two tracks that involves microblogs messages and news headlines respectively in SemEval 2017 shared task on 'Fine-Grained Sentiment Analysis of Financial Microblogs and News'.

References

Keith Cortis, Andre Freitas, Tobias Daudert, Manuela Huerlimann, Manel Zarrouk, and Brian Davis. 2017. Semeval-2017 task 5: Fine-grained sentiment analysis on financial microblogs and news. *Proceedings of SemEval* .

Fréderic Godin, Baptist Vandersmissen, Wesley De Neve, and Rik Van de Walle. 2015. Multimedia lab@ acl w-nut ner shared task: named entity recognition for twitter microposts using distributed word representations. *ACL-IJCNLP* 2015:146–153.

Rohitha Goonatilake and Susantha Herath. 2007. The volatility of the stock market and news. *Interna-*

tional Research Journal of Finance and Economics 3(11):53–65.

Diederik P. Kingma and Jimmy Ba. 2014. Adam: A method for stochastic optimization. *CoRR* abs/1412.6980. http://dblp.uni-trier.de/db/journals/corr/corr1412.html.

Bing Liu, Minqing Hu, and Junsheng Cheng. 2005. Opinion observer: analyzing and comparing opinions on the web. In *Proceedings of the 14th international conference on World Wide Web*. ACM, pages 342–351.

Tim Loughran and Bill McDonald. 2011. When is a liability not a liability? textual analysis, dictionaries, and 10-ks. *The Journal of Finance* 66(1):35–65.

Tomas Mikolov, Ilya Sutskever, Kai Chen, Greg S Corrado, and Jeff Dean. 2013. Distributed representations of words and phrases and their compositionality. In *Advances in neural information processing systems*. pages 3111–3119.

Saif Mohammad, Svetlana Kiritchenko, and Xiaodan Zhu. 2013. Nrc-canada: Building the state-of-the-art in sentiment analysis of tweets. In *Proceedings of the seventh international workshop on Semantic Evaluation Exercises (SemEval-2013)*. Atlanta, Georgia, USA.

Jeffrey Pennington, Richard Socher, and Christopher D. Manning. 2014. Glove: Global vectors for word representation. In *Empirical Methods in Natural Language Processing (EMNLP)*. pages 1532–1543. http://www.aclweb.org/anthology/D14-1162.

Jasmina Smailović, Miha Grčar, Nada Lavrač, and Martin Žnidaršič. 2014. Stream-based active learning for sentiment analysis in the financial domain. *Information Sciences* 285:181–203.

Nitish Srivastava, Geoffrey Hinton, Alex Krizhevsky, Ilya Sutskever, and Ruslan Salakhutdinov. 2014. Dropout: A simple way to prevent neural networks from overfitting. *Journal of Machine Learning Research* 15:1929–1958. http://jmlr.org/papers/v15/srivastava14a.html.

Philip J Stone, Robert F Bales, J Zvi Namenwirth, and Daniel M Ogilvie. 1962. The general inquirer: A computer system for content analysis and retrieval based on the sentence as a unit of information. *Behavioral Science* 7(4):484–498.

Xiaodan Zhu Svetlana Kiritchenko and Saif M. Mohammad. 2014. Sentiment analysis of short informal texts 50:723–762.

Marjan Van de Kauter, Diane Breesch, and Véronique Hoste. 2015. Fine-grained analysis of explicit and implicit sentiment in financial news articles. *Expert Systems with applications* 42(11):4999–5010.

Theresa Wilson, Janyce Wiebe, and Paul Hoffmann. 2005. Recognizing contextual polarity in phrase-level sentiment analysis. In *Proceedings of the conference on human language technology and empirical methods in natural language processing*. Association for Computational Linguistics, pages 347–354.

FEUP at SemEval-2017 Task 5: Predicting Sentiment Polarity and Intensity with Financial Word Embeddings

Pedro Saleiro[1,2], **Eduarda Mendes Rodrigues**[1], **Carlos Soares**[1,3], **Eugénio Oliveira**[1,2]

Faculdade de Engenharia da Universidade do Porto[1],

LIACC[2], INESC-TEC[3]

Rua Dr. Roberto Frias, s/n, Porto, Portugal

{pssc,eduarda,csoares,eco}@fe.up.pt

Abstract

This paper presents the approach developed at the Faculty of Engineering of University of Porto, to participate in SemEval 2017, Task 5: Fine-grained Sentiment Analysis on Financial Microblogs and News. The task consisted in predicting a real continuous variable from -1.0 to +1.0 representing the polarity and intensity of sentiment concerning companies/stocks mentioned in short texts. We modeled the task as a regression analysis problem and combined traditional techniques such as pre-processing short texts, bag-of-words representations and lexical-based features with enhanced financial specific bag-of-embeddings. We used an external collection of tweets and news headlines mentioning companies/stocks from S&P 500 to create financial word embeddings which are able to capture domain-specific syntactic and semantic similarities. The resulting approach obtained a cosine similarity score of 0.69 in sub-task 5.1 - Microblogs and 0.68 in sub-task 5.2 - News Headlines.

1 Introduction

Sentiment Analysis on financial texts has received increased attention in recent years (Nardo et al., 2016). Nevertheless, there are some challenges yet to overcome (Smailović et al., 2014). Financial texts, such as microblogs or newswire, usually contain highly technical and specific vocabulary or jargon, making the develop of specific lexical and machine learning approaches necessary. Most of the research in Sentiment Analysis in the financial domain has focused in analyzing subjective text, labeled with explicitly expressed sentiment.

However, it is also common to express financial sentiment in an implicit way. Business news stories often refer to events that might indicate a positive or negative impact, such as in the news title "company X will cut 1000 jobs". Economic indicators, such as unemployment and future state modifiers such as drop or increase can also provide clues on the implicit sentiment (Musat and Trausan-Matu, 2010). Contrary to explicit expressions (subjective utterances), factual text types often contain objective statements that convey a desirable or undesirable fact (Liu, 2012).

Recent work proposes to consider all types of implicit sentiment expressions (Van de Kauter et al., 2015). The authors created a fine grained sentiment annotation procedure to identify polar expressions (implicit and explicit expressions of positive and negative sentiment). A target (company of interest) is identified in each polar expression to identify the sentiment expressions that are relevant. The annotation procedure also collected information about the polarity and the intensity of the sentiment expressed towards the target. However, there is still no automatic approach, either lexical-based or machine learning based, that tries to model this annotation scheme.

In this work, we propose to tackle the aforementioned problem by taking advantage of unsupervised learning of word embeddings in financial tweets and financial news headlines to construct a domain-specific syntactic and semantic representation of words. We combine bag-of-embeddings with traditional approaches, such as pre-processing techniques, bag-of-words and financial lexical-based features to train a regressor for sentiment polarity and intensity. We study how different regression algorithms perform using all features in two different sub-tasks at SemEval-2017 Task 5: microblogs and news headlines mentioning companies/stocks. Moreover, we compare

Proceedings of the 11th International Workshop on Semantic Evaluations (SemEval-2017), pages 904–908,
Vancouver, Canada, August 3 - 4, 2017. ©2017 Association for Computational Linguistics

Sub-task	Company	Text Span	Sentiment Score
5.1 - Microblogs	JPMorgan	"its time to sell banks"	-0.763
5.2 - Headlines	Glencore	"Glencore's annual results beat forecasts"	+0.900

Table 1: Training set examples for both sub-tasks.

how different combinations of features perform in both sub-tasks. The system source code and word embeddings developed for the competition are publicly available.[1]

The remainder of the paper is organized as follows. We start by describing SemEval-2017 Task 5 and how we created financial-specific word embeddings. In Section 4 we present the implementation details of the system created for the competition followed by the experimental setup. We then present the experimental results and analysis, ending with the conclusions of this work.

2　Task Description

The task 5 of SemEval 2017 (Cortis et al., 2017) consisted of fine-grained sentiment analysis of financial short texts and it was divided in two sub-tasks based on the type of text. Sub-task 5.1 – Microblogs – consisted of stocktwits and tweets focusing on stock market events and assessments from investors and traders. Companies/stocks were identified using stock symbols, the so called cashtags, e.g. "$AMZN" for the company Amazon.com, Inc. Sub-task 5.2 – News Headlines – consisted of sentences extracted from Yahoo Finance and other financial news sources on the internet. In this case, companies/stocks were identified using their canonical name and were previously annotated by the task organizers.

The goal of both sub-tasks was the following: predict the sentiment polarity and intensity for each of the companies/stocks mentioned in a short text instance (microblog message or news sentence). The sentiment score is a real continuous variable in the range of -1.0 (very negative/bearish) to +1.0 (very positive/bullish), with 0.0 designating neutral sentiment. Table 1 presents two examples from the training set. Task organizers provided 1700 microblog messages for training and 800 messages for testing in sub-task 5.1, while in sub-task 5.2, 1142 news sentences were provided for training and 491 for testing. Submissions were evaluated using the cosine similarity (Cortis et al., 2017).

3　Financial Word Embeddings

Mikolov et al. (2013a) created word2vec, a computational efficient method to learn distributed representation of words, where each word is represented by a distribution of weights (embeddings) across a fixed set of dimensions. Furthermore, Mikolov et al. (2013b) showed that this representation is able to encode syntactic and semantic similarities in the embedding space.

The training objective of the skip-gram model, defined by Mikolov et al. (2013b), is to learn the target word representation (embeddings) that maximize the prediction of its surrounding words in a context window. Given the w_t word in a vocabulary the objective is to maximize the average log probability:

$$\frac{1}{T} \sum_{t=1}^{T} \sum_{-c \leq j \leq c, j \neq 0} \log P(w_{t+j}|w_t) \qquad (1)$$

where c is the size of the context window, T is the total number of words in the vocabulary and w_{t+j} is a word in the context window of w_t. After training, a low dimensionality embedding matrix $\mathbf{E}$ encapsulates information about each word in the vocabulary and its use (surrounding contexts).

We used word2vec to learn word embeddings in the context of financial texts using unlabeled tweets and news headlines mentioning companies/stocks from S&P 500. Tweets were collected using the Twitter streaming API with cashtags of stocks titles serving as request parameters. Yahoo Finance API was used for requesting financial news feeds by querying the canonical name of companies/stocks. The datasets comprise a total of 1.7M tweets and 626K news titles.

We learned separate word embeddings for tweets and news headlines using the skip-gram model. We tried several configurations of word2vec hyperparameters. The setup resulting in the best performance in both sub-tasks was skip-gram with 50 dimensions, removing words occurring less than 5 times, using a context window of

---

[1]https://github.com/saleiro/
Financial-Sentiment-Analysis

5 words and 25 negative samples per positive example.

Even though the text collections for training embeddings were relatively small, the resulting embedding space exhibited the ability to capture semantic word similarities in the financial context. We performed simple algebraic operations to capture semantic relations between words, as described in Mikolov et al. (2013c). For instance, the skip-gram model trained on tweets shows that vector ("bearish") - vector("loss") + vector("gain") results in vector ("bullish") as most similar word representation.

4 Approach

In this section we describe the implementation details of the proposed approach.

4.1 Pre-Processing

A set of pre-processing operations are applied to every microblog message and news sentence in the training/test sets of sub-tasks 5.1 and 5.2, as well as in the external collections for training word embeddings:

- **Character encoding and stopwords**: every message and headline was encoded in UTF-8. Standard english stopword removal is also applied.

- **Company/stock and cash obfuscation**: both cashtags and canonical company names strings were replaced by the string _company_. Dollar or Euro signs followed by numbers were replaced by the string _cash_amount_.

- **Mapping numbers and signs**: numbers were mapped to strings using bins (0-10, 10-20, 20-50, 50-100, >100). Minus and plus signs were coverted to *minus* and *plus*, "B" and "M" to *billions* and *millions*, respectively. The % symbol was converted to *percent*. Question and exclamation marks were also converted to strings.

- **Tokenization, punctuation, lowercasing**: tokenization was performed using Twokenizer (Gimpel et al., 2011), the remaining punctuation was removed and all characters were converted to lowercase.

4.2 Features

We combined three different group of features: bag-of-words, lexical-based features and bag-of-embeddings.

- **Bag-of-words**: we apply standard bag-of-words as features. We tried unigrams, bigrams and tri-grams with unigrams proving to obtain higher cosine similarity in both sub-tasks.

- **Sentiment lexicon features**: we incorporate knowledge from manually curated sentiment lexicons for generic Sentiment Analysis as well as lexicons tailored for the financial domain. The Laughran-Mcdonald financial sentiment dictionary (Bodnaruk et al., 2015) has several types of word classes: positive, negative, constraining, litigious, uncertain and modal. For each word class we create a binary feature for the match with a word in a microblog/headline and a polarity score feature (positive - negative normalized by the text span length). As a general-purpose sentiment lexicon we use MPQA (Wilson et al., 2005) and created binary features for positive, negative and neutral words, as well as, the polarity score feature.

- **Bag-of-Embeddings**: we create bag-of-embeddings by taking the average of word vectors for each word in a text span. We used the corresponding embedding matrix trained on external Twitter and Yahoo Finance collections for sub-task 5.1 and sub-task 5.2, respectively.

5 Experimental Setup

In order to avoid overfitting we created a validation set from the original training datasets provided by the organizers. We used a 80%-20% split and sampled the validation set using the same distribution as the original training set. We sorted the examples in the training set by the target variable values and skipped every 5 examples. Results are evaluated using Cosine similarity (Cortis et al., 2017) and Mean Average Error (MAE). The former gives more importance to differences in the polarity of the predicted sentiment while the latter is concerned with how well the system predicts the intensity of the sentiment.

We opted to model both sub-tasks as single regression problems. Three different regressors were applied: Random Forests (RF), Support Vector Machines (SVM) and MultiLayer Perceptron (MLP). Parameter tuning was carried using 10 fold cross validation on the training sets.

6 Results and Analysis

In this section we present the experimental results obtained in both sub-tasks. We provide comparison of different learning algorithms using all features, as well as, a comparison of different subsets of features, to understand the information contained in each of them and also how they complement each other.

6.1 Task 5.1 - Microblogs

Table 2 presents the results obtained using all features in both validation set and test sets. Results in the test set are worse than in the validation set with the exception to MLP. The official score obtained in sub-task 5.1 was 0.6948 using Random Forests (RF), which is the regressor that achieves higher cosine similarity and lower MAE in both training and validation set.

Regressor	Set	Cosine	MAE
RF	Val	0.7960	0.1483
RF	**Test**	**0.6948**	**0.1886**
SVR	Val	0.7147	0.1944
SVR	**Test**	0.6227	0.2526
MLP	Val	0.6720	0.2370
MLP	**Test**	0.6789	0.2132

Table 2: Microblog results with all features on validation and test sets.

We compared the results obtained with different subsets of features using the best regressor, RF, as depicted in Table 3. Interestingly, bag-of-words (BoW) and bag-of-embeddings (BoE) complement each other, obtaining better cosine similarity than the system using all features. Financial word embeddings (BoE) capture relevant information regarding the target variables. As a single group of features it achieves a cosine similarity of 0.6118 and MAE of 0.2322. It is also able to boost the overall performance of BoW with gains of more than 0.06 in cosine similarity and reducing MAE more than 0.03.

The individual group of features with best performance is Bag-of-words while the worst is a system trained using Lex (only lexical-based features). While Lex alone exhibits poor perfor-

mance, having some value but marginal, when combined with another group of features, it improves the results of the latter, as in the case of BoE + Lex and BoW + Lex.

Features	Cosine	MAE
Lex	0.3156	0.3712
BoE	0.6118	0.2322
BoW	0.6386	0.2175
BoE + Lex	0.6454	0.2210
Bow + Lex	0.6618	0.2019
Bow + BoE	**0.7023**	**0.1902**
All	0.6948	0.1886

Table 3: Features performance breakdown on test set using RF.

6.2 Task 5.2 - News Headlines

Results obtained in news headlines are very different from the ones of the previous sub-task, proving that predicting sentiment polarity and intensity in news headlines is a complete different problem compared to microblogs. Table 4 shows that MLP obtains the best results in the test set using both metrics while SVR obtains the best performance in the validation set. The best regressor of sub-task 5.1, RF is outperformed by both SVR and MLP. The official result obtained at sub-task 5.2 was a cosine similarity of 0.68 using MLP.

Regressor	Set	Cosine	MAE
RF	Val	0.5316	0.2539
RF	**Test**	0.6562	0.2258
SVR	Val	0.6397	0.2422
SVR	**Test**	0.6621	0.2424
MLP	Val	0.6176	0.2398
MLP	**Test**	**0.6800**	**0.2271**

Table 4: News Headlines results with all features on validation and test sets.

Table 5 shows the results of the different groups of features in sub-task 5.2 for MLP regressor. The most evident observation is that word embeddings are not effective in this scenario. On the other hand, lexical based features have significantly better performance in news headlines than in microblogs. Despite this, the best results are obtained using all features.

6.3 Analysis

Financial word embeddings were able to encapsulate valuable information in sub-task 5.1 - Mi-

Features	Cosine	MAE
BoE	0.0383	0.3537
Lex	0.5538	0.2788
BoW	0.6420	0.2364
BoE + Lex	0.5495	0.2830
BoW + Lex	**0.6733**	**0.2269**
BoW + BoE	0.6417	0.2389
All	0.6800	0.2271

Table 5: Features performance breakdown on test set using MLP.

croblogs but not so much in the case of sub-task 5.2 - News Headlines. We hypothesize that as we had access to a much smaller dataset ($\sim$ 600K) for training financial word embeddings for news headlines, this resulted in reduced ability to capture semantic similarities in the financial domain. Other related works in Sentiment Analysis usually take advantage of a much larger dataset for training word embeddings (Deriu et al., 2016).

On the other hand, lexical features showed poor performance in microblog texts but seem to be very useful using news headlines. The fact that microblogs have poor grammatically constructed texts, slang and informal language reveals that financial lexicals created using well written and formal financial reports, result better in news headlines rather than in microblog texts.

7 Conclusions

Work reported in this paper is concerned with the problem of predicting sentiment polarity and intensity of financial short texts. Previous work showed that sentiment is often depicted in an implicit way in this domain. We created financial-specific continuous word representations in order to obtain domain specific syntactic and semantic relations between words. We combined traditional bag-of-words and lexical-based features with bag-of-embeddings to train a regressor of both sentiment polarity and intensity. Results show that different combination of features attained different performances on each sub-task. Future work will consist on collecting larger external datasets for training financial word embeddings of both microblogs and news headlines. We also have planned to perform the regression analysis using Deep Neural Networks.

References

Andriy Bodnaruk, Tim Loughran, and Bill McDonald. 2015. Using 10-k text to gauge financial constraints. *Journal of Financial and Quantitative Analysis* 50(04).

Keith Cortis, Andre Freitas, Tobias Daudert, Manuela Huerlimann, Manel Zarrouk, and Brian Davis. 2017. Semeval-2017 task 5: Fine-grained sentiment analysis on financial microblogs and news. *Proceedings of SemEval* .

J. Deriu, M. Gonzenbach, F. Uzdilli, A. Lucchi, V. De Luca, and M. Jaggi. 2016. Swisscheese at semeval-2016 task 4: Sentiment classification using an ensemble of convolutional neural networks with distant supervision. *Proceedings of SemEval* .

K. Gimpel, N. Schneider, B. O'Connor, D. Das, D. Mills, J. Eisenstein, M. Heilman, D. Yogatama, J. Flanigan, and Noah A Smith. 2011. Part-of-speech tagging for twitter: Annotation, features, and experiments. In *ACL HLT: short papers-Volume 2*.

Bing Liu. 2012. Sentiment analysis and opinion mining. *Synthesis lectures on human language technologies* 5(1).

Tomas Mikolov, Kai Chen, Greg Corrado, and Jeffrey Dean. 2013a. Efficient estimation of word representations in vector space. *arXiv preprint arXiv:1301.3781* .

Tomas Mikolov, Ilya Sutskever, Kai Chen, Greg S Corrado, and Jeff Dean. 2013b. Distributed representations of words and phrases and their compositionality. In *NIPS*.

Tomas Mikolov, Wen-tau Yih, and Geoffrey Zweig. 2013c. Linguistic regularities in continuous space word representations. In *Hlt-naacl*. volume 13.

Claudiu Musat and Stefan Trausan-Matu. 2010. The impact of valence shifters on mining implicit economic opinions. In *International Conference on Artificial Intelligence: Methodology, Systems, and Applications*. Springer.

Michela Nardo, Marco Petracco-Giudici, and Mins Naltsidis. 2016. Walking down wall street with a tablet: A survey of stock market predictions using the web. *Journal of Economic Surveys* 30(2).

Jasmina Smailović, Miha Grčar, Nada Lavrač, and Martin Žnidaršič. 2014. Stream-based active learning for sentiment analysis in the financial domain. *Information Sciences* 285.

Marjan Van de Kauter, Diane Breesch, and Véronique Hoste. 2015. Fine-grained analysis of explicit and implicit sentiment in financial news articles. *Expert Systems with applications* 42(11).

Theresa Wilson, Janyce Wiebe, and Paul Hoffmann. 2005. Recognizing contextual polarity in phrase-level sentiment analysis. In *EMNLP*.

UIT-DANGNT-CLNLP at SemEval-2017 Task 9: Building Scientific Concept Fixing Patterns for Improving CAMR

Khoa Dang Nguyen
Faculty of Computer Science
University of Information Technology
VNU-HCM
ndkhoa@nlke-group.net

Dang Tuan Nguyen
Faculty of Computer Science
University of Information Technology
VNU-HCM
dangnt@uit.edu.vn

Abstract

This paper describes the improvements that we have applied on CAMR baseline parser (Wang et al., 2016) at Task 8 of SemEval-2016. Our objective is to increase the performance of CAMR when parsing sentences from scientific articles, especially articles of biology domain more accurately. To achieve this goal, we built two wrapper layers for CAMR. The first layer, which covers the input data, will normalize, add necessary information to the input sentences to make the input dependency parser and the aligner better handle reference citations, scientific figures, formulas, etc. The second layer, which covers the output data, will modify and standardize output data based on a list of scientific concept fixing patterns. This will help CAMR better handle biological concepts which are not in the training dataset. Finally, after applying our approach, CAMR has scored 0.65 F-score[1] on the test set of Biomedical training data[2] and 0.61 F-score on the official blind test dataset.

1 Introduction

Since Abstract Meaning Representation (AMR) was published by Banarescu et al. (2013) for the first time in 2013, it has been considered by many researchers in Natural Language Processing domain. In this trend, the task of AMR has been held continuously for two years in SemEval-2016 and SemEval-2017. There have been many parsers

shown its outstanding performance for high F-score points like RIGA (Barzdins and Gosko, 2016), CAMR, CU-NLP (Foland and Martin, 2016), etc.

Inspired by the performance of CAMR in SemEval-2016 Task 8, we selected it as our baseline parser for SemEval-2017 Task 9 - Subtask 1: Parsing Biomedical Data. The parsing task of 2017 has a particular domain but there are many scientific terms, formulas, reference quotations, numbers, etc. That makes the task of 2017 very challenging.

According to Wang et al. (2015a,b), the accuracy of CAMR depends greatly on the accuracy of input dependency parser. When we conduct training and testing on Biomedical training data used for SemEval-2017, we have found that CAMR is not good in handling the reference citations, scientific figures, formulas, etc which are commonly used in scientific papers. This is partly due to the dependency parser not correctly handling this kind of information. And also, the aligner can not fulfill its mission. We have built the first wrapper to support solving the problem related to these information in input data.

At the same time, we found CAMR can memorize very well AMR structure of concepts which have appeared in the training data. However, when parsing testing sentences which have unknown concepts (concepts which are not in training corpus), the parser will not be able to parse and return a single node to indicate the unknown concept (the first error form described in Subsection 3.1). Another weakness of CAMR is the terminal condition. The parser will finish parsing the sentence when the number of elements in the queue has run out. In the output result, we found that many AMR structures of concepts are not in good form (the second error form described in Subsection 3.1). Therefore, we proposed to build a second wrap-

---

[1]Currently, the datasource for constructing the list of concept fixing patterns are the training, develop and test set of Biomedical training data

[2]This data is all freely available to download at http://amr.isi.edu/download.html

Proceedings of the 11th International Workshop on Semantic Evaluations (SemEval-2017), pages 909–913,
Vancouver, Canada, August 3 - 4, 2017. ©2017 Association for Computational Linguistics

per to fix the parsing error on output data, which will help CAMR deal with these issues better.

2 The first wrapper layer

Unlike the corpus used for Task 8 of SemEval-2016, the Biomedical training data corpus used for Task 9 of SemEval-2017 are sentences from scientific articles related to the topic cancer pathway discovery. Generally, the sentences from scientific papers contain a lot of reference citations, scientific figures, formulas, etc.

In the gold AMR structure, the reference citations are represented by node `describe-01`. This node appeared 2,756 times in the training set and the develop set of Biomedical training data. Similarly, in the test set, `describe-01` node appeared 263 times. The number of nodes `describe-01` accounted for a big amount in the corpus. Better handling of these reference citations will increase the accuracy of the parser significantly. However, with the following reference citation formats, input dependency parser is almost impossible to handle and consider the reference citations as meaningless symbols:

1. "[1]"

2. "(1), (2), (3)"

3. "(Wang. et al, 2016)"

Obviously, with the reference citation formats of 1, 2 above, dependency parser will handle these citations as usual numbers. With the reference citation format of 3, it is also not easy for dependency parser because "(Wang. et al, 2016)" does not have the structure of a normal sentence or a clause. Since dependency parser did not handle these quotation formats properly, the aligning and the training process would not achieve good results. For example with the reference citation format of 3, the word "et" can not be aligned to node `other` in the gold AMR. And in the training stage, CAMR won't be able to know that the word "et" is related to node `other`.

And there are also other difficulties such as: the reference citation formats in the corpus have more complex forms than the above examples like "(Wang. et al, 2016a; Wang. et al, 2016b)", there are XML annotations in the input sentences,...

To support solving this problem, we write a tool to remove all XML annotations in the input data,

Node	Wrapper OFF	Wrapper ON
describe-01	49	835
publication-91	2	497
person	871	993
other	406	501
and	4731	5180

Table 1: Number of successfully aligned node before and after the application of the first wrapper

then the tool updates these citation formats to the following patterns:

1. "[1]" → "(described in publication 1)"

2. "(1), (2), (3)" → "(described in publication 1 and 2 and 3)"

3. "(Wang. et al, 2016)" → "(described in publication of Wang and other members in 2016)"

For more complex forms of the reference citation formats, the tool also follows the above patterns. For example, "(Wang. et al, 2016a; Wang. et al, 2016b)" should be updated to "(described in publication of Wang and other members in 2016; described in publication of Wang and other members in 2016)".

These modifications not only help dependency parser can operate more accurately but also help the aligner (Flanigan et al., 2014) align more accurately, especially with node `describe-01` and its sub-nodes (`publication-91`, `person`, `other`, `and`) in the AMR structure.

In addition, we also have a few other modifications with the abbreviations of measuring unit and the abbreviations of scientific term on the first wrapper. The abbreviations of measuring unit can be find out easily by grepping out all `:unit` edges in the traning data. With the abbreviations of scientific term, we have to find them manually. These modifications include:

- Replace the abbreviations of measuring unit with its full form (for example "kDa" → "kilodalton", "pg/ml" → "picogram per milliliter", etc.)

- Replace the abbreviations of scientific term to its full form (for example "UM" → "uveal melanoma")

Selumetinib in combination with TMZ enhances DNA damage.

(a) CAMR parse

```
(x6 / enhance-01
 :ARG0 (x1 / selumetinib)
 :condition (x3 / combine-01
   :ARG2 (x5 / tmz))
 :ARG1 (x8 / damage-01
   :ARG1 (x7 / enzyme
     :name (n / name
     :op1 "DNA"))))
```

(b) CAMR parse + our addition

```
(x6 / enhance-01
 :ARG0 (x1 / small-molecule
   :name (n1 / name
     :op1 "selumetinib"))
 :condition (x3 / combine-01
   :ARG2 (x5 / small-molecule
   :name (n3 / name
     :op1 "TMZ"))
 :ARG1 (x8 / damage-01
   :ARG1 (x7 / nucleic-acid
   :name (n / name
     :op1 "DNA")
   :wiki "DNA")))
```

Figure 1: An example of CAMR parsing result and our addition

Table 1 represents the number of aligned nodes before and after the application of our first wrapper. Obviously the number of aligned nodes is increased substantially. Especially with nodes often appear in AMR structure describe the reference citations. The more successfully aligned nodes, the easier for CAMR in the traning stage.

3 The second wrapper layer

3.1 Parsing error detecting method

We classify parsing errors of CAMR into two main types. First, we propose methods to identify all the errors of the two types of the returned output of CAMR. Figure 1 represents the results of CAMR's original parsing result and the parsing result after being updated by our system.

The first error type usually happens with the unknown concept, which does not appear in the training set. When processing an unknown concept, CAMR will return an individual node such as (x1 / selumetinib) or (x5 / tmz). To be able to identify the errors of this type in the returned results, we will collect a list of all of node labels in gold AMR of training set. From this list, we will traverse through all nodes on AMR results, if any node label is not on this list, it's likely that node is a presentation for an unknown concept. For example, with the AMR in Figure 1b, then this list is: {enhance-01, small-molecule, name, "selumetinib", combine-01, "TMZ", damage-01 , nucleic-acid, "DNA"}. Node selumetinib and tmz (without quotes) are not in the list above, so these may be unknown concepts.

Second error form is related to the structure of the AMR node such as wrong concept type, missing important sub-node or having wrong sub-node, null node, null edge, etc. As in Figure 1a, the "DNA" node is identified as an enzyme. But in the training set, there is no enzyme node which has the :name edge connected to a "DNA" node. "DNA" is always a nucleic-acid in the training set. The method to identify this error type is the same as above, but instead just collect a list of node labels, we will collect a list of all concept nodes in the training set. A node is called concept node when it has a direct :name edge. We call this list is the list of the AMR structure concept. When traversing through all nodes in the result AMR, if there is a :name edge appeared in a node of the AMR structure, we will compare that node with these nodes in the list of the AMR structure concept. If the list doesn't contain that node, that mean this is a new node created by CAMR. And there is a probability that the node contains some errors. We just stop at identifying concept node in AMR structure which has the probability of containing errors. It still needs the help of a human expert to give out a final judgment that the concept node of AMR structure is correct or not.

3.2 Parsing error fixing method

From the two error lists above, we will build a new list with each element has the form "Label-Error AMR-Fixed AMR". We call this the list of concept fixing patterns. Two ingredients Label and Error AMR are taken directly from the two error lists above. Filling the Fixed AMR would require the support of human experts. Particularly for Biomedical training data, we refer the gold AMR in the test set of training data to fill out the Fixed AMR.

Table 2 represents the list of concept fixing patterns for the example in Figure 1.

After having the parsing result of CAMR as in Figure 1a. We will traverse all the

Label	selumetinib
Error AMR	`(x1 / selumetinib)`

Fixed AMR	`(x1 / small-molecule`
	`  :name (n1 / name`
	`    :op1 "selumetinib"))`

Label	tmz
Error AMR	`(x5 / tmz)`

Fixed AMR	`(x5 / small-molecule`
	`  :name (n3 / name`
	`    :op1 "TMZ"))`

Label	enzyme

Error AMR	`(x7 / enzyme`
	`  :name (n / name`
	`    :op1 "DNA"))`

Fixed AMR	`(x7 / nucleic-acid`
	`  :name (n / name`
	`    :op1 "DNA")`
	`  :wiki "DNA"))`

Table 2: The list of concept fixing patterns for the example in Figure 1

System	Precision	Recall	F-score
Baseline parser	0.67	0.50	0.57
OurSystem(W1)	0.70	0.53	0.60
OurSystem(W12)	0.73	0.58	0.65

Table 3: Comparison with the baseline parser

nodes in the result AMR. When traversing node `(x1 / selumetinib)`, we will find out these elements in the list of concept fixing patterns which have Label is `selumetinib`. We will compare the structure of traversing node with the structure in Error AMR part of these elements. If there are a structural matching, we will replace the traversing node structure with the structure in the Fixed AMR part of the corresponding element. Similarly, the structure `(x5 / tmz)` and `(x7 / enzyme :name (n / name :op1 "DNA"))` will also be updated to the Fixed AMR structure in the list of concept fixing patterns. The final output will the the same as the AMR structure in 1b.

4 Experiment

We used the Biomedical training data which have been split into training, develop and test set for experiments. About CAMR, we used the version which was described in (Wang et al., 2016) as a baseline parser with its default configurations. But, we have not used named entity tags and semantic role labels in the experiment stage. To evaluate the output result, we used the Smatch tool (Cai and Knight, 2013) at version 16.11.14.

Firstly, we implemented the first wrapper layer as the proposed method in Section 2. Then, we started training on two systems. The training data is the collection of all sentences in training set and develop set of Biomedical training data. On the

first system, CAMR was trained with the original training data, which had not been updated by our first wrapper layer. On the other system, the training data had been updated by our first wrapper layer. Both of two systems were trained in 10 iterations.

After that, two systems were tested with all sentences from the test set of Biomedical training data. In order to fix the parsing error of CAMR, we need to build the list of concept fixing patterns. We implemented a tool to detect the concept parsing errors. This tool will traverse all the nodes in the output result of CAMR when parsing test set of training data to collect a list of AMR node which has the probability of containing errors as the proposed method in Subsection 3.1. After finished detecting error, the tool will return the list of concept fixing patterns. Each element of the list will have form of "Label-Error AMR-Fixed AMR". We then refer the gold AMR in the training data to fill out the "Fixed AMR" part. We have to do this manually to guarantee that the detected error node actually contains error.

After having the list of concept fixing patterns, we will have another tool to update the parsing result based on the list. We only run this tool on the second system. The output result of the first system is keep original. Table 3 shows our experiment results. The first row is the evaluated score of the baseline parser. The second row is the score of our system when only used the first wrapper layer. The last row is the score of our system when have both two wrappers activated. There is a special note about wrapper 2: currently, we have to extract the data from the training, develop and test set of the Biology training data to fill out the "Fixed AMR" part.

With the official blind test set, our system used the first wrapper layer to normalize and update input sentences. Then, our system automatically used the above pre-built list of concept fixing patterns to fix the parsing error of CAMR before return the final output result. We achieved 0.61 F-score on the official blind test set.

5 Conclusion

The main contribution of this paper is the second wrapper layer which can be used very effective in finding concept parsing errors of AMR parsers. Although the improvements have been developed in CAMR, but both of these two wrappers can easily be applied to other AMR parsers.

However, currently, our approach requires manual processing to create the concept fixing patterns. In further work, we will focus on researching about automatically create the fixing patterns for a few particular domains. We intend to use open knowledge databases of these domains, the combination with supervised machine learning methods and pre-built corpus to create the concept fixing patterns automatically.

References

Laura Banarescu, Claire Bonial, Shu Cai, Madalina Georgescu, Kira Griffitt, Ulf Hermjakob, Kevin Knight, Philipp Koehn, Martha Palmer, and Nathan Schneider. 2013. Abstract meaning representation for sembanking. In *Proceedings of the 7th Linguistic Annotation Workshop and Interoperability with Discourse*. Association for Computational Linguistics, pages 178–186. http://www.aclweb.org/anthology/W13-2322.

Guntis Barzdins and Didzis Gosko. 2016. Riga at semeval-2016 task 8: Impact of smatch extensions and character-level neural translation on amr parsing accuracy. In *Proceedings of the 10th International Workshop on Semantic Evaluation (SemEval-2016)*. Association for Computational Linguistics, pages 1143–1147. https://doi.org/10.18653/v1/S16-1176.

Shu Cai and Kevin Knight. 2013. Smatch: an evaluation metric for semantic feature structures. In *Proceedings of the 51st Annual Meeting of the Association for Computational Linguistics (Volume 2: Short Papers)*. Association for Computational Linguistics, pages 748–752. http://aclweb.org/anthology/P13-2131.

Jeffrey Flanigan, Sam Thomson, Jaime Carbonell, Chris Dyer, and A. Noah Smith. 2014. A discriminative graph-based parser for the abstract meaning representation. In *Proceedings of the 52nd Annual Meeting of the Association for Computational Linguistics (Volume 1: Long Papers)*. Association for Computational Linguistics, pages 1426–1436. https://doi.org/10.3115/v1/P14-1134.

William Foland and H. James Martin. 2016. Cu-nlp at semeval-2016 task 8: Amr parsing using lstm-based recurrent neural networks. In *Proceedings of the 10th International Workshop on Semantic Evaluation (SemEval-2016)*. Association for Computational Linguistics, pages 1197–1201. https://doi.org/10.18653/v1/S16-1185.

Chuan Wang, Sameer Pradhan, Xiaoman Pan, Heng Ji, and Nianwen Xue. 2016. Camr at semeval-2016 task 8: An extended transition-based amr parser. In *Proceedings of the 10th International Workshop on Semantic Evaluation (SemEval-2016)*. Association for Computational Linguistics, San Diego, California, pages 1173–1178. http://www.aclweb.org/anthology/S16-1181.

Chuan Wang, Nianwen Xue, and Sameer Pradhan. 2015a. Boosting transition-based amr parsing with refined actions and auxiliary analyzers. In *Proceedings of the 53rd Annual Meeting of the Association for Computational Linguistics and the 7th International Joint Conference on Natural Language Processing (Volume 2: Short Papers)*. Association for Computational Linguistics, Beijing, China, pages 857–862. http://www.aclweb.org/anthology/P15-2141.

Chuan Wang, Nianwen Xue, and Sameer Pradhan. 2015b. A transition-based algorithm for amr parsing. In *Proceedings of the 2015 Conference of the North American Chapter of the Association for Computational Linguistics: Human Language Technologies*. Association for Computational Linguistics, Denver, Colorado, pages 366–375. http://www.aclweb.org/anthology/N15-1040.

Oxford at SemEval-2017 Task 9: Neural AMR Parsing with Pointer-Augmented Attention

Jan Buys[1] and Phil Blunsom[1,2]
[1]Department of Computer Science, University of Oxford   [2]DeepMind
{jan.buys,phil.blunsom}@cs.ox.ac.uk

Abstract

We present an end-to-end neural encoder-decoder AMR parser that extends an attention-based model by predicting the alignment between graph nodes and sentence tokens explicitly with a pointer mechanism. Candidate lemmas are predicted as a pre-processing step so that the lemmas of lexical concepts, as well as constant strings, are factored out of the graph linearization and recovered through the predicted alignments. The approach does not rely on syntactic parses or extensive external resources. Our parser obtained 59% Smatch on the SemEval test set.

1 Introduction

The task of parsing sentences to Abstract Meaning Representation (AMR) (Banarescu et al., 2013) has recently received increased attention. AMR represents sentence meaning with directed acyclic graphs (DAGs) with labelled nodes and edges. No assumptions are made about the relation between an AMR and the structure of the sentence it represents: the representation is not assumed to have any relation to the sentence syntax, no alignments are given and no distinction is made between concepts that correspond directly to lexemes in the input sentences and those that don't.

This underspecification creates significant challenges for training an end-to-end AMR parser, which are exacerbated by the relatively small sizes of available training sets. Consequently most AMR parsers are pipelines that make extensive use of additional resources. Neural encoder-decoders have previously been proposed for AMR parsing, but reported accuracies are well below the state-of-the-art (Barzdins and Gosko, 2016), even

with sophisticated pre-processing and categorization (Peng et al., 2017). The end-to-end neural approach contrasts with approaches based on a pipeline of multiple LSTMs (Foland Jr and Martin, 2016) or neural network classifiers inside a feature- and resource-rich parser (Damonte et al., 2017), which have performed competitively.

Our approach addresses these challenges in two ways: This first is to utilize (noisy) alignments, aligning each graph node to an input token. The alignments are predicted explicitly by the neural decoder with a pointer network (Vinyals et al., 2015), in addition to a standard attention mechanism. Our second contribution is to introduce more structure in the AMR linearization by distinguishing between lexical and non-lexical concepts, noting that lexical concepts (excluding sense labels) can be predicted with high accuracy from their lemmas. The decoder predicts only delexicalized concepts, recovering the lexicalization through the lemmas corresponding to the predicted alignments.

Experiments show that our extensions increase parsing accuracy by a large margin over a standard attention-based model.

2 Graph Linearization and Lemmatization

We start by discussing how to linearize AMR graphs to enable sequential prediction. AMR node labels are referred to as *concepts* and edge labels as *relations*. A special class of node modifiers, called *constants*, are used to denote the string values of named entities and numbers. An example AMR graph is visualized in Figure 1.

In AMR datasets, graphs are represented as spanning trees with designated root nodes. Edges whose direction in the spanning tree are reversed are marked by adding "-of" to the argument label.

Proceedings of the 11th International Workshop on Semantic Evaluations (SemEval 2017), pages 914–919,
Vancouver, Canada, August 3 - 4, 2017. ©2017 Association for Computational Linguistics

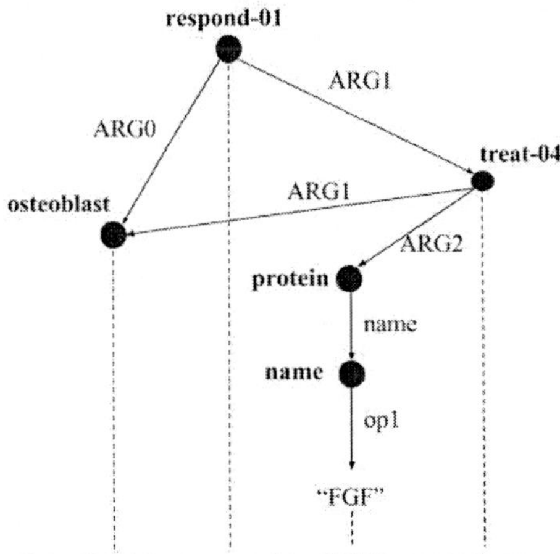

Figure 1: AMR graph aligned to the sentence it represents.

```
:focus( respond-01
  :ARG0( obsteoblast )
  :ARG1( treat-04
    :ARG1*( obsteoblast )
    :ARG2( protein
      :name( name
        :op1( "FGF" ) ) ) ) )
```

Figure 2: Standard linearized representation of the AMR in Figure 1.

Edges not included in the spanning tree (*reentrancies*) are indicated by adding dummy nodes pointing back to the original nodes.

The first linearization we propose (which we refer to as *standard*) is similar, except that nodes are identified through their concepts rather than explicit node identifiers. Constants are also treated as nodes. Reentrancy edges are marked with $\star$ and the concepts of their dependent nodes are simply repeated. During post-processing reentrancies are recovered heuristically by finding the closest nodes in the linear representation with the same concepts. An example of this representation is given in Figure 2.

In the second representation (*lexicalized*) every graph node is aligned to an input token. The alignments could be encoded as strings in the graph linerization, but in our model we will predict them separately. Every constant is replaced with a placeholder CONST token; the constant string is

```
:focus( <2> -01
  :ARG0( <1> -u )
  :ARG1( <5> -04
    :ARG1*( <1> -u )
    :ARG2( <4> protein
      :name( <4> name
        :op1( <4> CONST ) ) ) ) )
```

Figure 3: Delexicalized linearization, with alignments, of the AMR in Figure 1.

then recovered as a post-processing step through the predicted token alignment.

We classify concepts in an AMR graph as either lexical, i.e. corresponding directly to the meaning of an aligned token, or non-lexical. This distinction, together with alignments, is annotated explicitly in Minimal Recursion Semantics predicates in the English Resource Grammar (ERG) (Copestake et al., 2005). However for AMR we classify concepts heuristically, based on automatic alignments. We assume that each word in a sentence aligns to at most one lexical node in its AMR graph. Where multiple nodes are aligned to the same token, usually forming a subgraph, the lowest element is taken to be the lexical concept.

A subset of AMR concepts are predicates based on PropBank framesets (Palmer et al., 2005), represented as sense-labeled lemmas. The remaining lexical concepts are usually English words in lemma form, while non-lexical concepts are usually special keywords. Lemmas can be predicted with high accuracy from the words they align to.

Our third linearization (*delexicalized*) factorizes the lemmas of lexical concepts out of the linerization, so that they are represented by their alignments and sense labels, e.g. -01 for predicates and -u for other concepts. Candidate lemmas are predicted independently and lexicalized concepts are recovered as a post-processing step. This representation (see Figure 3) decreases the vocabulary of the decoder, which simplifies the learning problem and speeds up the parser.

2.1 Pre-processing

We tokenize the data with the Stanford CoreNLP toolkit (Manning et al., 2014). This tokenization corresponds more closely to AMR concepts and constants than other tokenizers we experimented with, especially due to its handling of hyphenation in the biomedical domain. We perform POS and

NE tagging with the same toolkit.

The training data is aligned with the rule-based JAMR aligner (Flanigan et al., 2014). However, our approach requires single-token alignments for all nodes, which JAMR is not guaranteed to give. We align each Wiki node to the token with the highest prefix overlap. Other nodes without alignments are aligned to the left-most alignment of their children (if they have any), otherwise to that of their parents. JAMR aligns multi-word named entities as single subgraph to token span alignments. We split these alignments to be 1-1 between tokens and constants. For other nodes with multi-token alignments we use the start of the given span.

For each token we predict candidate lexemes using a number of lexical resources. A summary of the resources used for each lexical type is given in Table 1. The first resource is dictionaries extracted from the aligned training data of each type, mapping each token or span of tokens to its most likely concept lemma or constant. A similar dictionary is extracted from Propbank framesets (included in LDC2016E25) for predicate lemmas. Next we use WordNet (Miller, 1995), as available through NLTK (Bird et al., 2009), to map words to verbalized forms (for predicates) or nominalized forms (for other concepts) via their synsets, where available. To predict constant strings corresponding to unseen named entities we use the forms predicted by the Stanford NE tagger (Finkel et al., 2005), which are broadly consistent with the conventions used for AMR annotation. The same procedure converts numbers to numerals. We use SU-Time (Chang and Manning, 2012) to extract normalized forms of dates and time expressions.

Input sentences and output graphs in the training data are pre-processed independently. This introduces some noise in the training data, but makes it more comparable to the setup used during testing. The (development set) oracle accuracy is 98.7% Smatch for the standard representation, 96.16% for the aligned lexicalized representation and 93.48% for the unlexicalized representation.

3 Pointer-augmented neural attention

Let $\mathbf{e}_{1:I}$ be a tokenized English sentence, $\mathbf{f}_{1:J}$ a sequential representation of its AMR graph and $\mathbf{a}_{1:J}$ an alignment sequence of integers in the range 1 to I. We propose an attention-based encoder-decoder model (Bahdanau et al., 2015) to encode

e and predict $\mathbf{f}$ and $\mathbf{a}$, the latter with a pointer network (Vinyals et al., 2015). We use a standard LSTM architecture (Jozefowicz et al., 2015).

For every token e we embed its word, POS tag and named entity (NE) tag as vectors; these embeddings are concatenated and passed through a linear layer such that the output $g(e)$ has the same dimension as the LSTM cell. This representation of e is then encoded with a bidirectional RNN. Each token e_i is represented by a hidden state h_i, which is the concatenation of its forward and backward LSTM state vectors.

Let s_j be the RNN decoder hidden state at output position j. We set s_0 to be the final RNN state of the backward encoder LSTM. The alignment a_j is predicted at each time-step with a pointer network (Vinyals et al., 2015), although it will only affect the output when f_j is a lexical concept or constant. The alignment logits are computed with an MLP (for $i = 1, \ldots, I$):

$$u_j^i = w^T \tanh(W^{(1)} h_i + W^{(2)} s_j).$$

The alignment distribution is then given by

$$p(a_j | \mathbf{a}_{1:j-1}, \mathbf{f}_{1:j-1}, \mathbf{e}) = \mathrm{softmax}(u_j).$$

Attention is computed similarly, but parameterized separately, and the attention distribution α_j is not observed. Instead $q_j = \sum_{i=1}^{i=I} \alpha_j^i h_i$ is a weighted average of the encoder states.

The output distribution is computed as follows: RNN state s_j, aligned encoder representation h_{a_j} and attention vector q_j are fed through a linear layer to obtain o_j, which is then projected to the output logits $v_j = Ro_j + b$, such that

$$p(f_j | \mathbf{f}_{1:j-1}, \mathbf{e}) = \mathrm{softmax}(v_j).$$

Let $v(f_j)$ be the decoder embedding of f_j. To compute the RNN state at the next time-step, let d_j be the output of a linear layer over $d(f_j)$, q_j and h_{a_j}. The next RNN state is then computed as

$$s_{j+1} = RNN(d_j, s_j).$$

We perform greedy decoding. We ensure that the output is well-formed by skipping over out-of-place symbols. Repeated occurrences of sibling subtrees are removed when equivalent up to the argument number of relations.

Candidate Type	JAMR alignments	PropBank	WordNet	NE Tagger	Lemmatizer
Predicates	✓	✓	✓	✗	✓
Other concepts	✓	✗	✓	✗	✓
Constants	✓	✗	✗	✓	✓
Wikification	✓	✗	✗	✓	✗

Table 1: Resources used to predict candidate lemmas for different types of AMR outputs. The left-most resource that has a prediction available is used.

Model	Smatch F1
Attention, no tags	54.60
Attention, with tags	57.27
Pointer, lexicalized	57.99
Pointer, delexicalized	59.18

Table 2: Development set results for the Bio AMR corpus.

4 Experiments

We train our models with the two AMR datasets provided for the shared task: LDC2016E25, a large corpus of newswire, weblog and discussion forum text with a training set of 35,498 sentences, and a smaller dataset in the biomedical domain (Bio AMR Corpus) with 5,542 training sentences. When training a parser for the biomedical domain with minibatch SGD, we sample Bio AMR sentences with a weight of 7 to each LDC sentence to balance the two sources in sampled minibatches.

Our models are implemented in Tensor-Flow (Abadi et al., 2015). We train models with Adam (Kingma and Ba, 2015) with learning rate 0.01 and minibatch size 64. Gradients norms are clipped to 5.0 (Pascanu et al., 2013). We use single-layer LSTMs with hidden state size 256, with dropout 0.3 on the input and output connections. The encoder takes word embeddings of size 512, initialized (in the first 100 dimensions) with embeddings trained with a structured skip-gram model (Ling et al., 2015), and POS and NE embeddings of size 32. Singleton tokens are replaced with an unknown word symbol with probability 0.5 during training.

We compare our pointer-based architecture against an attention-based encoder-decoder that does not make use of alignments or external lexical resources. We report results for two versions of this baseline: In the first, the input is purely word-based. The second embeds named entity and POS embeddings in the encoder, and utilizes pre-trained word embeddings. Development set

Metric	Neural AMR (average)
Smatch	59 (53.67)
Unlabeled	63 (57.83)
No WSD	59 (53.67)
Named Entities	66 (55.83)
Wikification	18 (33.00)
Negation	27 (23.17)
Concepts	74 (71.17)
Reentrancies	43 (34.17)
SRL	57 (50.33)

Table 3: SemEval test set results on various metrics, reported as rounded to the nearest percentage.

Model	Smatch F1
Bio AMR	59.27
LDC	61.89

Table 4: Test set results for the Bio AMR and LDC2016E25 corpora.

results are given in Table 2. We see that POS and NE embeddings give a substantial improvement. The performance of the baseline with richer embeddings is similar to that of the first pointer-based model. The main difference between these two models is that the latter uses pointers to predict constants, so the results show that the gain due to this improved generalization is relatively small. The delexicalized representation with separate lemma prediction improves accuracy by 1.2%.

Official results on the shared task test set are presented in Table 3. AMR graphs are evaluated with Smatch (Cai and Knight, 2013), and further analysis is done with the metrics proposed by Damonte et al. (2017). The performance of our model is consistently better than the shared task average on all metrics except for Wikification; the reason for this is that we are not using a Wikifier to predict Wiki entries. The performance on predicting reentrancies is particularly encouraging, as it shows that our pointer-based model is able to learn to point to concepts with multiple occurrences.

To enable future comparison we also report results on the Bio AMR test set, as well as for training and testing on the newswire and discussion forum data (LDC2016E25) only (Table 4).

5 Conclusion

We proposed a novel approach to neural AMR parsing. Results show that neural encoder-decoder models can obtain strong performance on AMR parsing by explicitly modelling structure implicit in AMR graphs.

Acknowledgments

The first author thanks the financial support of the Clarendon Fund and the Skye Foundation. We thank the anonymous reviewers for their feedback.

References

Martín Abadi, Ashish Agarwal, Paul Barham, Eugene Brevdo, Zhifeng Chen, Craig Citro, Greg S. Corrado, Andy Davis, Jeffrey Dean, Matthieu Devin, Sanjay Ghemawat, Ian Goodfellow, Andrew Harp, Geoffrey Irving, Michael Isard, Yangqing Jia, Rafal Jozefowicz, Lukasz Kaiser, Manjunath Kudlur, Josh Levenberg, Dan Mané, Rajat Monga, Sherry Moore, Derek Murray, Chris Olah, Mike Schuster, Jonathon Shlens, Benoit Steiner, Ilya Sutskever, Kunal Talwar, Paul Tucker, Vincent Vanhoucke, Vijay Vasudevan, Fernanda Viégas, Oriol Vinyals, Pete Warden, Martin Wattenberg, Martin Wicke, Yuan Yu, and Xiaoqiang Zheng. 2015. TensorFlow: Large-scale machine learning on heterogeneous systems. Software available from tensorflow.org. http://tensorflow.org/.

Dzmitry Bahdanau, Kyunghyun Cho, and Yoshua Bengio. 2015. Neural machine translation by jointly learning to align and translate. In *Proceedings of ICLR*. http://arxiv.org/abs/1409.0473.

Laura Banarescu, Claire Bonial, Shu Cai, Madalina Georgescu, Kira Griffitt, Ulf Hermjakob, Kevin Knight, Philipp Koehn, Martha Palmer, and Nathan Schneider. 2013. Abstract meaning representation for sembanking. In *Proceedings of the 7th Linguistic Annotation Workshop and Interoperability with Discourse*. pages 178–186. http://www.aclweb.org/anthology/W13-2322.

Guntis Barzdins and Didzis Gosko. 2016. Riga at semeval-2016 task 8: Impact of smatch extensions and character-level neural translation on AMR parsing accuracy. In *Proceedings of SemEval*.

Steven Bird, Ewan Klein, and Edward Loper. 2009. *Natural Language Processing with Python*. O'Reilly Media.

Shu Cai and Kevin Knight. 2013. Smatch: An evaluation metric for semantic feature structures. In *Proceedings of ACL (2)*.

Angel X Chang and Christopher D Manning. 2012. SUTime: A library for recognizing and normalizing time expressions. In *Proceedings of LREC*.

Ann Copestake, Dan Flickinger, Carl Pollard, and Ivan A Sag. 2005. Minimal recursion semantics: An introduction. *Research on Language and Computation* 3(2-3):281–332.

Marco Damonte, Shay B. Cohen, and Giorgio Satta. 2017. An incremental parser for abstract meaning representation. In *Proceedings of EACL*. pages 536–546. http://www.aclweb.org/anthology/E17-1051.

Jenny Rose Finkel, Trond Grenager, and Christopher Manning. 2005. Incorporating non-local information into information extraction systems by Gibbs sampling. In *Proceedings of ACL*. pages 363–370. http://dx.doi.org/10.3115/1219840.1219885.

Jeffrey Flanigan, Sam Thomson, Jaime G. Carbonell, Chris Dyer, and Noah A. Smith. 2014. A discriminative graph-based parser for the abstract meaning representation. In *Proceedings of ACL*. pages 1426–1436. http://aclweb.org/anthology/P/P14/P14-1134.pdf.

William R Foland Jr and James H Martin. 2016. CU-NLP at SemEval-2016 Task 8: AMR parsing using LSTM-based recurrent neural networks. In *Proceedings of SemEval*. pages 1197–1201.

Rafal Jozefowicz, Wojciech Zaremba, and Ilya Sutskever. 2015. An empirical exploration of recurrent network architectures. In *Proceedings of ICML*. pages 2342–2350.

Diederik P. Kingma and Jimmy Ba. 2015. Adam: A method for stochastic optimization. In *Proceedings of ICLR*. http://arxiv.org/abs/1412.6980.

Wang Ling, Chris Dyer, Alan W Black, and Isabel Trancoso. 2015. Two/too simple adaptations of word2vec for syntax problems. In *Proceedings of NAACL*. pages 1299–1304. http://www.aclweb.org/anthology/N15-1142.

Christopher D. Manning, Mihai Surdeanu, John Bauer, Jenny Finkel, Steven J. Bethard, and David McClosky. 2014. The Stanford CoreNLP natural language processing toolkit. In *ACL System Demonstrations*. pages 55–60. http://www.aclweb.org/anthology/P/P14/P14-5010.

George A. Miller. 1995. Wordnet: A lexical database for english. *Commun. ACM* 38(11):39–41. https://doi.org/10.1145/219717.219748.

Martha Palmer, Daniel Gildea, and Paul Kingsbury. 2005. The proposition bank: An annotated corpus of semantic roles. *Computational linguistics* 31(1):71–106.

Razvan Pascanu, Tomas Mikolov, and Yoshua Bengio.
2013. On the difficulty of training recurrent neural
networks. *Proceedings of ICML (3)* 28:1310–1318.

Xiaochang Peng, Chuan Wang, Daniel Gildea,
and Nianwen Xue. 2017. Addressing the
data sparsity issue in neural amr parsing.
In *Proceedings of EACL*. pages 366–375.
http://www.aclweb.org/anthology/E17-1035.

Oriol Vinyals, Meire Fortunato, and Navdeep
Jaitly. 2015. Pointer networks. In *Advances in Neural Information Processing Systems*, Curran Associates, Inc., pages 2692–
2700. http://papers.nips.cc/paper/5866-pointer-
networks.pdf.

FORGe at SemEval-2017 Task 9: Deep sentence generation based on a sequence of graph transducers

Simon Mille [1], Roberto Carlini [1], Alicia Burga [1], Leo Wanner [1,2]
[1] Universitat Pompeu Fabra, Roc Boronat 138, 08018 Barcelona, Spain
[2]Institució Catalana de Recerca i Estudis Avançats (ICREA),
Lluis Companys 23, 08010 Barcelona, Spain
`firstname.lastname@upf.edu`

Abstract

We present the contribution of Universitat Pompeu Fabra's NLP group to the SemEval Task 9.2 (AMR-to-English Generation). The proposed generation pipeline comprises: (i) a series of rule-based graph-transducers for the syntacticization of the input graphs and the resolution of morphological agreements, and (ii) an off-the-shelf statistical linearization component.

1 Setup of the system

The generator we presented for Task 9.2 of SemEval is a pipeline of graph transducers called *Fabra Open Rule-based Generator* (FORGe).[1] It is built upon work presented, e.g., in (Bohnet, 2006; Wanner et al., 2010). It can be also considered an extended rule-based version of (Ballesteros et al., 2015). The current generator has been mainly developed on the dependency Penn Treebank (Johansson and Nugues, 2007) automatically converted to predicate-argument structures, and adapted to the AMR inputs using SemEval's training and evaluation sets.

1.1 Overview of the pipeline

The core of the generator is rule-based: graph transduction grammars convert, in several steps, abstract AMRs into syntactic structures that contain all the morphological features needed to retrieve the final forms of all the words. The syntactic structures are then linearized with an off-the-shelf tool, and finally the final forms of the words are retrieved. Our generator follows the theoretical model of the Meaning-Text Theory (Mel'čuk, 1988); the names of the intermediate layers used in Table 1 come from the MTT terminology.

---

[1]A slightly updated version of the submitted system can be found at `https://www.upf.edu/web/taln/resources`

	Step	Layer_{mtt}	#rul.
0	Conversion of AMRs format into CoNLL'09 format	ConS	N/A
1	Mapping of AMRs onto predicate-argument graphs	SemS	190
2	Assignment of parts of speech	SemS_{pos}	96
3	Derivation of deep syntactic structure	DSyntS	267
4	Introduction of function words	SSyntS	294
5	Resolution of agreements	DMorphS	85
6	Linearization	SMorphS	N/A
7	Retrieval of surface forms	Text	1
8	Post-processing	Text_{final}	4

Table 1: Overview of the AMR-to-text pipeline.

1.2 Input format conversion

Since our generator cannot read the provided format, we converted the input AMRs to the CoNLL'09 format (Hajič et al., 2009). We assume that each sentence in the original file has two components: a three-line comment with some metadata (id, date, original sentence, etc.) and the AMR tree. In order to map the AMR tree to CoNLL, we assume that: (i) each node of the tree will be defined as either (a) slash-separated variable-value pair, (b) only the variable name, or (c) only the value, and (ii) each branch will be defined by a relation name preceded by a colon.

2 Generation from AMRs

There are 932 activated graph-transduction rules in the pipeline; Steps 0 and 1 are AMR-specific, while in the rest of the grammars, only one rule is AMR-specific rule (at Step 3).

2.1 Mapping of AMRs onto predicate-argument graphs

The mapping produces graphs that contain linguistic information only, which includes meaning bearing units and the following types of roles:

Proceedings of the 11th International Workshop on Semantic Evaluations (SemEval-2017), pages 920–923,
Vancouver, Canada, August 3 - 4, 2017. ©2017 Association for Computational Linguistics

Arguments and coordinations (*ARG0, ARG1, ...,
ARGn*), relations coming from AMR non-core
and prepositional roles (*NonCore*), and underspecified relations (*Elaboration*). Information that
does not need to be generated in the final sentence is excluded: ontological information such
as types of entities (e.g., "person", "date-entity")
and relations (e.g., "has-rel-role", "has-org-role",
"month"); meta-information such as the origin of
a label (e.g., "Wiki"); etc. For this purpose, we remove the corresponding nodes and relations and
connect the remaining nodes. Furthermore, the
AMR core roles are maintained, while all other
roles (non-core, prepositional, coordinations) are
mapped to one single role or to a subgraph that
contains one node and two edges, as, e.g., in the
following example:

$$N_1 \;\; N_2 \;\; \xrightarrow{purpose} \;\; N_1 \;\; N_{purpose} \;\; N_2$$

Since AMRs are provided in a tree format, there
are some reversed argumental relations (ARG0-of,
ARG1-of, etc.). For the sake of a consistent treatment of all argumental relations, these relations
are inverted back in our setting and the "-of" extension is removed.[2]

2.2 Assignment of parts of speech

Before building the syntactic structures, we assign
parts of speech to each node of the structure. This
tagging is very rudimentary and slow: rules check
in a lexicon if a node label matches an entry and
retrieve the part of speech from that entry. Since
more than one part of speech is often possible for
one string, rules consult the context in the graph,
if necessary, in order to take a decision.

2.3 Derivation of the deep syntactic structure

This transduction performs a top-down recursive
syntacticization of the semantic graph. It looks for
the syntactic root of the sentence, and from there
for its syntactic dependent(s), for the dependent(s)
of the dependent(s), and so on.

The rules are organized in a cluster of three
grammars. The purpose of the first two grammars
is to identify the root of a syntactic tree in case
the original input structure does not contain one.[3]

Obviously, verbs are the best candidates for being
the root; we pay special attention to the number
and complexity of dependents that a verb has (a
"heavier" verb is more likely to be a root), and to
the fact that a verb is not on the ARG2 side of a
node that comes from a non-core relation, since
this configuration makes syntacticization less natural in many cases. Consider the following AMR
graph:

$$I \;\; go \;\; have\text{-}condition \;\; you \;\; go$$

In this example, if the first "go" is chosen as the
root, the syntactic tree can unfold as "I go if you
go". But if the second "go", which is on the ARG2
side of the "have-condition" non-core node, is selected as the root, the generator is currently unable
to build a sentence, since it should be able to invert
the "if" and has no such information.[4]

For this task, the main challenge is to produce
a well-formed tree that covers as much of the input graph as possible, while avoiding the possible
dependency conflicts. One major issue to solve
is that one element can (legitimately) be the argument of several predicates, whereas (i) a syntactic structure is a tree-like structure in which every
node can have only one governor, (ii) some predicates *need* their argument(s) in syntax, and (iii)
some predicates cannot be realized with their ar-
gument(s). In other words, each argument has to
be assigned to the correct governor in syntax, and
duplicated when needed. The rules keep track of
whether a node has already been used and what it
has been used for.[5]

In the following example, "peek" is chosen as
the root, "dog" is its dependent, and the other predicates of which "dog" was an argument become its
syntactic dependents. Furthermore, "dog" is duplicated in order to create a relative clause (Left:
predicate-argument; Right: Deep-Syntax):

$$he \;\; peek \;\; dog \;\; black \;\; bark \qquad he \;\; peek \;\; dog \;\; black \;\; bark \;\; dog$$

---

[2] We are conscious that this transformation makes the task
more challenging. For instance, it sometimes creates cycles
in the graphs. Specific rules address this issue.

[3] Given that AMRs are provided in tree format, and the
root of this tree is the main node (the root) of the sentence,
this step can seem redundant. But since during Step 1 some
nodes are removed (see 2.1), it is possible that the original
root is missing, and the system needs to find a substitute.
More generally, we want our system to be able to generate
without any information about syntactic structure.

[4] Even for a human it is challenging to generate a natural
sentence; maybe something like "The fact that you go would
be the condition for me to go" would be acceptable.

[5] For more details on the deep-syntactic structures and
their relation with surface-syntactic structures, see (Ballesteros et al., 2016).

2.4 Introduction of function words

The next step towards the realization of the sentence is the introduction of all idiosyncratic words and of a fine-grained (surface-)syntactic structure that gives enough information for linearizing and resolving agreements between the different words. For this task, we use a valency (subcategorization) lexicon built automatically from PropBank (Kingsbury and Palmer, 2002) and NomBank (Meyers et al., 2004); see (Mille and Wanner, 2015). For instance, the entry corresponding to "peek" would contain the following information:

peek_VB_01{pos=VB gp={II={prep=at, rel=IOBJ}}}

It indicates that, according to PropBank, the second argument of "peek" needs the preposition "at". Hence, this preposition is introduced in the surface-syntactic structure, as shown in the following example:

he peek at dog the black bark that

AMRs are underspecified in terms of tense, aspect, number, and definiteness. For the task, a past progressive is equally correct as a simple present. Our generator is able to introduce all types of auxiliaries and/or modals, but we set the default verbal form to simple present. By default, nominal number is set to singular and definiteness to indefinite. However, the corresponding rule can take different decisions: in some cases, the presence of a definite determiner is usually more adequate–for instance, if the noun is modified by a relative clause (cf. the above example). During this transduction, anaphora are resolved, and personal pronouns are introduced in the tree (this includes possessive, relative and personal pronouns). Some syntactic post-processing rules fix ill-formed structures when possible.

2.5 Resolution of morpho-syntactic agreements

Every word must be assigned all necessary morphological information; some information comes from the deeper strata of the pipeline (as, e.g., verbal tense or finiteness), but some features come from some other elements of the tree. In English, for instance, verbs get their person and number from their subject. In order to resolve these agreements, the rules for this transduction check the governor/dependent pairs, together with the syntactic relation that links them together. During this step, parts of speech are set to match the training

data used for the linearizer, and question and exclamation marks are introduced.

2.6 Linearization

The surface-syntactic structures are linearized with an off-the-shelf tool used in the first SRST (Belz et al., 2011), a statistical tree linearizer that orders bottom-up each head and its children (Bohnet et al., 2011).

2.7 Retrieval of surface forms

With the morpho-syntactic information at hand for each word, we just need to find the corresponding surface form. We match the triple <lemma><POS><morpho-syntactic features> with an entry of a morphological dictionary and simply replace the triple by the surface form. In order to build such a dictionary, we analyzed a large amount of data[6] and retrieved all possible combinations of lemma, part of speech and morphological features; e.g., for verbs: peek<VB><GER>=peeking; peek<VB><FIN><PRES><3><SG>=peeks. If several surface forms are found for a combination of features, we keep the most frequent one. The final sentence corresponding to the running example would be *He peeks at the black dog that barks*.

2.8 Post-processing

A few post-processing rules make the output more readable: the first letter of a sentence is converted to upper case, punctuation signs are added, underscores are replaced by spaces, and spaces before contracted elements ("'s" and "n't") are removed.

3 Results and discussion

Metric	FORGe	Average
Win pct	43.64	36.668
win+tie pct	57.43	54.19
trueskill	**44.9**	**40.664**
BLEU	4.74	11.362

Table 2: Results of the task

It takes in average about 2 seconds to generate one sentence, 1.7 seconds of which is due to PoS assignment. Table 2 shows the results that our system obtained for the task, compared to the average results of the other systems; the first three metrics are derived from the ranking obtained during the human evaluation; BLEU is the result of an n-gram based automatic evaluation. According to

---

[6]For this, we used the Open ANC corpus http://www.anc.org/data/oanc/annotations/

922

the organizers of the task, *trueskill* (highlighted in bold) is considered the "main" metric for this task.

Our system obtained results slightly above average for the human-based evaluation, while the BLEU score is quite low, compared to that of the other systems. We believe that this is due to the fact that we prioritized the quality of the output over coverage: the submitted generator produces an output for 98.8% of the sentences, but the latter only contain 74.3% of the total of nodes contained in the predicate-argument graphs (see Section 2.1). Indeed, at two points of the pipeline, we choose not to generate or to remove content from the trees. First, during Step 3, when the generator is not sure what to do with one predicate-argument relation, it does not generate it. For instance, when the root of a sentence is on the ARG2 side of a node which originates from a non-core relation, the whole subgraph of this node is omitted (see Section 2.3). Second, during Step 4, if a subtree that is likely to be faulty is identified (as, e.g., a conjunction without a complement), it is removed.

Consider for example the following (partial) gold output: *Securing Reiss' release has been a diplomatic priority for France, with President Nicolas Sarkozy raising the case with other leaders.* Our fallback whole-coverage generator would output *diplomacy France prioritize secure like release Clotilde Reiss president Nicolas Sarkozy raise case with onbehalfof person intervene...*, while our actual output is *France prioritizes to secure the release of Clotilde Reiss.* Eventually, choosing the production of readable sentences over their completeness allowed us to get better human ratings. But this, combined to the fact that we always generate simple present tense and singular words, naturally has a negative impact with an n-gram-based metric (that includes a brevity penalty) such as BLEU.[7]

Finally let us point out that most rules in this system are language-independent. Experiments adapting it to Spanish, Polish and German show that with rich lexicons, the effort related to grammars for obtaining well-formed texts is minimal.[8]

Acknowledgments

The work described in this paper has been partially funded by the European Commission under the contract numbers FP7-ICT-610411, H2020-645012-RIA, H2020-700024-RIA, and H2020-DRS-01-2015.

---

[7]Note that our fallback generator obtained a BLEU that is only 18% inferior to the score of the submitted output.

[8]Currently, for indicative purposes, the approximate count of non language-independent rules is the following: 2% in Step 2, 14% in Step 3, 64% in Step 4, and 13% in Step 5.

References

Miguel Ballesteros, Bernd Bohnet, Simon Mille, and Leo Wanner. 2015. Data-driven sentence generation with non-isomorphic trees. In *Proceedings of NAACL:HLT*. ACL, Denver, CO, pages 387–397.

Miguel Ballesteros, Bernd Bohnet, Simon Mille, and Leo Wanner. 2016. Data-driven deep-syntactic dependency parsing. *Natural Language Engineering* 22(6):939–974.

Anja Belz, Mike White, Dominic Espinosa, Eric Kow, Deirdre Hogan, and Amanda Stent. 2011. The first Surface Realisation Shared Task: Overview and evaluation results. In *Proceedings of ENLG*. Nancy, France, pages 217–226.

Bernd Bohnet. 2006. *Textgenerierung durch Transduktion linguistischer Strukturen*. Ph.D. thesis, University Stuttgart.

Bernd Bohnet, Simon Mille, Benoît Favre, and Leo Wanner. 2011. StuMaBa: From deep representation to surface. In *Proceedings of ENLG*. Nancy, France, pages 232–235.

J. Hajič, M. Ciaramita, and R. Johansson et al. 2009. The CoNLL-2009 Shared Task: Syntactic and semantic dependencies in multiple languages. In *Proceedings of CoNLL*. Boulder, CO, USA, pages 1–18.

Richard Johansson and Pierre Nugues. 2007. Extended constituent-to-dependency conversion for English. In *Poceedings of NODALIDA*. Tartu, Estonia, pages 105–112.

Paul Kingsbury and Martha Palmer. 2002. From Tree-Bank to PropBank. In *Proceedings of LREC*. Las Palmas, Canary Islands, Spain, pages 1989–1993.

Igor Mel'čuk. 1988. *Dependency Syntax: Theory and Practice*. SUNY Press, Albany.

Adam Meyers, Ruth Reeves, Catherine Macleod, Rachel Szekely, Veronika Zielinska, Brian Young, and Ralph Grishman. 2004. The NomBank Project: An interim report. In *Proceedings of the Workshop on Frontiers in Corpus Annotation, (HLT/NAACL)*. Boston, MA, USA, pages 24–31.

Simon Mille and Leo Wanner. 2015. Towards large-coverage detailed lexical resources for data-to-text generation. In *Proceedings of the First International Workshop on D2T Generation*. Edinburgh, Scotland.

Leo Wanner, Bernd Bohnet, Nadjet Bouayad-Agha, François Lareau, and Daniel Nicklaß. 2010. MARQUIS: Generation of user-tailored multilingual air quality bulletins. *Applied Artificial Intelligence* 24(10):914–952.

RIGOTRIO at SemEval-2017 Task 9: Combining Machine Learning and Grammar Engineering for AMR Parsing and Generation

Normmunds Gruzitis[1], Didzis Gosko[2] and Guntis Barzdins[1]

[1]University of Latvia, IMCS / Rainis blvd. 29, Riga, Latvia
`normunds.gruzitis@lumii.lv, guntis.barzdins@lumii.lv`
[2]LETA / Marija street 2, Riga, Latvia
`didzis.gosko@leta.lv`

Abstract

By addressing both text-to-AMR parsing and AMR-to-text generation, SemEval-2017 Task 9 established AMR as a powerful semantic interlingua. We strengthen the interlingual aspect of AMR by applying the multilingual Grammatical Framework (GF) for AMR-to-text generation. Our current rule-based GF approach completely covered only 12.3% of the test AMRs, therefore we combined it with state-of-the-art JAMR Generator to see if the combination increases or decreases the overall performance. The combined system achieved the automatic BLEU score of 18.82 and the human Trueskill score of 107.2, to be compared to the plain JAMR Generator results. As for AMR parsing, we added NER extensions to our SemEval-2016 general-domain AMR parser to handle the biomedical genre, rich in organic compound names, achieving Smatch F1=54.0%.

1 Introduction

AMR (Banarescu et al., 2013) as a sentence-level semantic representation is evolving towards interlingua at SemEval-2017 Task 9 on Abstract Meaning Representation Parsing and Generation (May and Priyadarshi, 2017). The challenge was to improve over state-of-the-art systems for both text-to-AMR parsing (Barzdins and Gosko, 2016) and AMR-to-text generation (Flanigan et al., 2016).

AMR parsing subtask this year focused on specific genre of Biomedical scientific articles regarding cancer pathway discovery. Such texts are challenging to existing AMR parsers because they are rich in organic compound names with types "enzyme", "aminoacid", etc. not recognized by common NER tools that are often restricted to types "person", "organization", "location", etc.

The paper starts with NER extensions used for the Biomedical AMR parsing subtask, followed by a novel approach of using Grammatical Framework for AMR generation, and concludes with a brief analysis of our SemEval results.

2 Text-to-AMR parsing

Only two adaptations to the AMR parser from SemEval-2016 (Barzdins and Gosko, 2016) were implemented: it was retrained on the union of LDC2015E86, LDC2016E25, LDC2016E33 and Bio AMR Corpus, and a gazetteer was added to extend the NER coverage to organic compound names found in the Bio AMR Corpus (e.g. "B-Raf enzyme", "dabrafenib small-molecule", etc.). The gazetteer was generalized w.r.t. numbers used in the names.

Although we achieved an above average Smatch score (54.0% versus 53.6%) in the preliminary official scoring, the ablation metrics show that we scored below average for named entities (46.0% versus 55.8%) and wikification (0% versus 33.0%). Since we used gazetteers extracted from the training data for both named entities and wikification, this suggests that external data sources should have been used instead.

3 AMR-to-text generation

Our approach to text generation from AMR graphs stems from a recent feasibility study (Gruzitis and Barzdins, 2016) on the grammar-based generation of storyline highlights – a list of events extracted from a set of related documents. The events would be represented by pruned AMR graphs acquired by an abstractive text summarizer and verbalized afterwards.

Such storyline highlight extraction is a part of

Proceedings of the 11th International Workshop on Semantic Evaluations (SemEval-2017), pages 924–920,
Vancouver, Canada, August 3 - 4, 2017. ©2017 Association for Computational Linguistics

the H2020 research project SUMMA, *Scalable Understanding of Multilingual MediA*.[1] The storyline highlights are expected to be relatively simple and concise in terms of grammatical structure and, thus, in terms of the underlying meaning representation. In our use case, adequacy and semantic accuracy of the generated sentences, and the control of the generation process are more important than fluency. Therefore we are following a grammar-based approach for AMR-to-text generation. In the SemEval task, however, we are pushing the limits and scalability of such approach, as the task requires much more robust wide-coverage general-purpose generation.

The proposed approach builds on Grammatical Framework, GF (Ranta, 2011). GF is a grammar formalism and technology for implementing computational multilingual grammars. GF grammars are bi-directional; however, they are particularly well suited for language generation. Most importantly, GF provides a wide-coverage resource grammar library with a language-independent API – a shared abstract syntax. The idea is to transform the AMR graphs to the GF abstract syntax trees (AST), leaving the surface realization (linearization) of ASTs to the existing English resource grammar.[2] Since the GF resource grammar library supports many more languages, this approach automatically extends to multilingual AMR-to-text generation, provided that there is a wide-coverage translation lexicon which includes named entities.

Because the coverage of our hand-crafted AMR-to-AST transformation rules is currently far from complete, we use the JAMR generator (Flanigan et al., 2016) as a default option for AMRs not fully covered by the rules. In other words, we want to measure if sentences generated by the GF approach (from AMRs fully covered by the transformation rules) outperform the respective JAMR-generated sentences. If so, it would be worth developing this approach further.

3.1 Grammatical Framework

More precisely, GF is a categorial grammar formalism and a functional programming language, specialized for multilingual grammar development. It has a command interpreter and a batch compiler, as well as Haskell and C run-time systems for parsing and linearization. The C run-time system has Java and Python bindings, and it allows for probabilistic parsing as well. Compiled GF grammars can be embedded in applications written in other programming languages.[3]

The key feature of GF grammars is the division between the abstract syntax and the concrete syntax. The abstract syntax defines the language-independent semantic structure and terms, while the concrete syntax defines the surface realization of the abstract syntax for a particular language. The same abstract syntax can be equipped with many concrete syntaxes (and lexicons) – reversible mappings from ASTs to feature structures and strings – making the grammar multilingual (Ranta, 2004).

What makes the development of GF application grammars rapid and flexible is the general-purpose GF resource grammar library, RGL (Ranta, 2009). The library currently covers more than 30 languages that implement the same abstract syntax, a shared syntactic API. The API provides overloaded constructors like

$$\text{mkVP} : \text{V2} \rightarrow \text{NP} \rightarrow \text{VP}$$
$$\text{mkVP} : \text{VP} \rightarrow \text{Adv} \rightarrow \text{VP}$$

for building a verb phrase from a transitive verb and an object noun phrase, or for attaching an adverbial phrase to a verb phrase, etc. – all without the need of specifying low-level details like inflectional paradigms, syntactic agreement and word order. These details are handled by the language-specific resource grammars.

Note that the overloaded API constructors generalize over the actual functions of the abstract syntax. The respective RGL functions of the above given mkVP constructors are

$$\text{ComplV2} : \text{V2} \rightarrow \text{NP} \rightarrow \text{VP}$$
$$\text{AdvVP} : \text{VP} \rightarrow \text{Adv} \rightarrow \text{VP}$$

These constructors and functions are applied to build ASTs. For instance, the sentence

"The boys want an adventure."

is represented by the following AST w.r.t. RGL:

```
(PredVP
    (DetCN
        (DetQuant DefArt NumPl)
```

---
[1] http://summa-project.eu
[2] In terms of GF, linearization refers to resolving the word order, word forms (agreement), function words, etc.

---
[3] http://www.grammaticalframework.org

(UseN boy_N))
(ComplV2
    want_V2
    (DetCN
        (DetQuant IndefArt NumSg)
        (UseN adventure_N))))

The respective API constructor application tree is more general and simpler:

(mkCl
    (mkNP the_Quant pluralNum boy_N)
    (mkVP
        want_V2
        (mkNP a_Quant adventure_N)))

where want_V2, boy_N and adventure_N are nullary lexical functions, while the_Quant and a_Quant are predefined constructors for the function words, and pluralNum is a parameter for selecting the plural form of the noun. In GF, there is no formal distinction between syntactic and lexical functions.

We map AMRs to ASTs by a sequence of pattern-matching transformation rules, using RGL API constructors as a convenient intermediate layer. The language-specific linearization of the acquired ASTs is already defined by the English (or other language) resource grammar and lexicon.

3.2 AMR-to-AST transformation

The overall transformation process is as follows:

1. The input AMR is rewritten from the PENMAN notation to the the LISP-like bracketing tree syntax by a simple parsing expression grammar.
2. In case of a multi-sentence AMR, the graph is split into two or more graphs to be processed separately.
3. For each AMR graph represented as a LISP-like tree, a sequence of tree pattern-matching and transformation rules is applied, acquiring a fully or partially converted AST constructor application tree w.r.t. the API of RGL.
4. In case of a partially converted AST, the pending subtrees are just pruned.[4]
5. The resulting ASTs are passed to the GF interpreter for linearization.

Inspired by Butler (2016), we use the Stanford JavaNLP utilities Tregex and Tsurgeon (Levy and Andrew, 2006) for the pilot implementation of AMR-to-AST conversion.[5] The difference of our approach is that we convert AMR graphs to abstract instead of concrete syntax trees, and the choice of GF allows for further multilingual text generation, preserving grammatical and semantic accuracy.

In the time frame of the SemEval task, we defined around 200 transformation rules[6] covering many basic and advanced constructions used in AMR.[7] To illustrate the ruleset, let us consider the AMR graph given in Figure 1, and its expected AST in Figure 2, acquired by the ordered rules outlined in Figure 3. For each rule, P denotes a simplified Tregex pattern (a subtree to match), and R denotes the resulting subtree – after Tsurgeon operations like adjoin, move, relabel, delete have been applied (omitted in Figure 3). Note that we first slightly enrich the original AMR by adding frame-specific semantic roles to ARG2..ARGn. In our example, :ARG4 is rewritten to :ARG4-GOL, based on PropBank. Semantic roles are used to determine the preposition in a preposition phrase (see the ninth rule in Figure 3). Thus, we get GOL_Prep for the NP under :ARG4 of go-02, which, in the current prototype, is always linearized as the preposition "to". Although this preposition fits to our example, in general, other preposition can be used in the realization of GOL. More elaborated post-processing is needed to reconstruct the prepositions that are lost in the AMR representation of the input sentence. Statistics from the PropBank corpus (Palmer et al., 2005) would be helpful to decide whether there is a dominant frame-dependent preposition for the argument/role, or a dominant NP-dependent preposition, independently of the frame.

In addition to the regular AMR constructions, we have defined a number of rules for the treatment of the special frames: have-org-role-91 and have-rel-role-91. The special rules are applied before the regular ones. We have also introduced some post-editing rules over the resulting ASTs to

---

[4]For the SemEval submission, we took the respective JAMR-generated sentence instead, skipping the fifth step.

[6]More precisely, we have defined 198 Tregex patterns over AMR/AST trees. For each pattern, 2.5 Tsurgeon transformation operations are defined on average (493 in total).

[7]Roughly estimating, the development of the current ruleset took us less than two person months.

```
(w / want-01
  :ARG0 (b / boy)
  :ARG1 (g / go-02
    :ARG0 b
    :ARG4 (c / city
      :name (n / name
        :op1 "New"
        :op2 "York"
        :op3 "City")
      :wiki "New_York_City")))
```

Figure 1: An AMR representing the sentence "The boys want to go to New York City".

```
(mkText (mkUtt (mkS
 (mkCl
  (mkNP a_Quant (mkCN boy_N))
  (mkVP
   want_VV
   (mkVP
    (mkVP go_V)
    (mkAdv
     GOL_Prep
     (mkNP (mkPN "New York City")))))
))) fullStopPunct)
```

Figure 2: An AST acquired from the AMR given in Figure 1. When linearized, the AST yields "A boy wants to go to New York City" in English, or "En pojke vill gå till New York City" in Swedish.

make the final linearization more fluent. For instance, simple attributive relative clauses are converted to adjective modifiers; e.g. "luck that is good" gets converted to "good luck". Similarly, it would be often possible to convert general nouns modified by simple verbal relative clauses into more specific nouns omitting the use of relative clauses: "person that reports" – to "reporter", "organization that governs" – to "government", etc.

Regarding the RGL lexicon, it contains more than 60,000 lexical entries, providing a good coverage for general purpose applications. To handle out-of-vocabulary words and multi-word expressions which most frequently are named entities (e.g. "New York City"), we use low-level RGL constructors to specify fixed strings.

3.3 JAMR Generator

A pre-trained JAMR generation model (Flanigan et al., 2016) along with provided Gigaword corpus 4-grams were used.[8] The JAMR authors reported

[8]https://github.com/jflanigan/jamr/tree/Generator

1. mkVP : VV $\rightarrow$ VP $\rightarrow$ VP

   P   (*frame*$_A$ (:ARG1 (*var frame*$_B$)))
   R   (want-01$_A$ (mkVP go-02$_B$))

2. mkCl : VP $\rightarrow$ Cl

   P   (*var frame*$_A$)
   R   (mkCl (mkVP want-01$_A$))

3. mkCl : NP $\rightarrow$ VP $\rightarrow$ Cl

   P   (mkCl (mkVP (*frame*$_A$:ARG0)))
   R   (mkCl :ARG0 (mkVP want-01$_A$))

4. mkNP : Quant $\rightarrow$ CN $\rightarrow$ NP

   P   (:ARG0 (*var concept*$_A$))
   R   (mkNP a_Quant (mkCN (b boy$_A$)))

5. mkCN : N $\rightarrow$ CN

   P   (mkCN (*var concept*$_A$))
   R   (mkCN boy_N$_A$)

6. Recursively merge :op1 .. :op$_n$ under :op1

   P   (name (:op1 *literal*$_A$) (:op$_i$ *literal*$_B$))
   R   (name (:op1 "New$_A$ York$_A$ City$_B$"))

7. mkPN : Str $\rightarrow$ PN
   mkNP : PN $\rightarrow$ NP

   P   (*var* (name (:op1 *literal*$_A$)))
   R   (mkNP (mkPN "New York City"$_A$))

8. Excise a node chain: var - NE type - :name

   P   (*var* (*type* (:name mkNP)))
   R   (mkNP)

9. mkVP : VP $\rightarrow$ Adv $\rightarrow$ VP
   mkAdv : Prep $\rightarrow$ NP $\rightarrow$ Adv

   P   (mkVP (*frame*$_A$ (ARGn-*role*$_B$ mkNP)))
   R   (mkVP (mkVP go-02$_A$)
         (mkAdv GOL_Prep$_B$ mkNP))

10. Ignore (delete) :wiki nodes.

11. Relabel frames, depending on their syntactic valence in the resulting AST. Thus, want-01 becomes want_VV (a verb-phrase-complement verb), in contrast to want_V2 (see Section 3.1), and go-02 becomes just go_V (an intransitive verb).

Figure 3: A sample set of AMR-to-AST transformation rules for converting the AMR in Figure 1 into the AST in Figure 2. P – pattern, R – result. The terms in italic (P) refer to regular expressions.

their original results on Gigaword corpus 5-grams (Gigaword licence required) which is known to improve the BLEU score by approx. 1 point.

3.4 First results

By applying the transformation ruleset (see Section 3.2), we were able to fully convert and linearize 12.3% of the 1293 evaluation AMRs. Additionally, we acquired partially transformed trees and, consequently, partially generated sentences for another 36% of the evaluation AMRs, but we did not include those sentences in the final submission, since large subtrees often got pruned. Instead, we replaced them by sentences acquired by JAMR Generator (see Section 3.3).

With the combined JAMR and GF-based system, we achieved Trueskill 107.2 and BLEU 18.82 in the preliminary official scoring. The key open question is if the 12.3% GF-generated sentences scored better or worse in comparison to the JAMR output by human-evaluated Trueskill.

By BLEU-scoring the GF-generated sentences apart from the JAMR-generated sentences, the BLEU scores are 11.35 and 19.18 respectively. This suggests that BLEU favors the corpus-driven JAMR approach which tries to reproduce the original input sentence, while the grammar-driven GF approach sticks to AMR more literally, producing a paraphrase of the input sentence. Therefore we are primarily interested in Trueskill and less concerned about BLEU.

4 Conclusion

The SemEval subtask on AMR-to-text generation has given us confidence that it is worth to develop further the GF-based approach. We are particularly pleased to see that AMR equipped with GF is emerging as a powerful interlingua for semantic cross-lingual applications. Although it is difficult to reach a large coverage in a short term, a grammar-based approach complemented with statistics from AMR and PropBank-annotated corpora is competitive with other approaches in a longer term, at least for use cases where adequacy is more important than fluency.

Acknowledgments

This work was supported in part by the Latvian State research programmes SOPHIS and NexIT, the H2020 project SUMMA (grant No. 688139), and the European Regional Development Fund grant No. 1.1.1.1/16/A/219. We also thank Aarne Ranta, Alexandre Rademaker and Alastair Butler for encouraging and helpful discussions.

References

Laura Banarescu, Claire Bonial, Shu Cai, Madalina Georgescu, Kira Griffitt, Ulf Hermjakob, Kevin Knight, Philipp Koehn, Martha Palmer, and Nathan Schneider. 2013. Abstract Meaning Representation for Sembanking. In *Proceedings of the 7th Linguistic Annotation Workshop and Interoperability with Discourse*.

Guntis Barzdins and Didzis Gosko. 2016. RIGA at SemEval-2016 Task 8: Impact of Smatch extensions and character-level neural translation on AMR parsing accuracy. In *Proceedings of the 10th International Workshop on Semantic Evaluation*.

Alastair Butler. 2016. Deterministic natural language generation from meaning representations for machine translation. In *Proceedings of the 2nd Workshop on Semantics-Driven Machine Translation*.

Jeffrey Flanigan, Chris Dyer, Noah A. Smith, and Jaime Carbonell. 2016. Generation from Abstract Meaning Representation using Tree Transducers. In *Proceedings of the 2016 Conference of the North American Chapter of the Association for Computational Linguistics: Human Language Technologies*.

Normunds Gruzitis and Guntis Barzdins. 2016. The role of CNL and AMR in scalable abstractive summarization for multilingual media monitoring. In *Controlled Natural Language*, Springer, volume 9767 of *LNCS*.

Roger Levy and Galen Andrew. 2006. Tregex and Tsurgeon: Tools for querying and manipulating tree data structures. In *Proceedings of the 5th International Conference on Language Resources and Evaluation*.

Jonathan May and Jay Priyadarshi. 2017. Semeval-2017 task 9: Abstract meaning representation parsing and generation. In *Proceedings of the 11th International Workshop on Semantic Evaluation*.

Martha Palmer, Daniel Gildea, and Paul Kingsbury. 2005. The Proposition Bank: An Annotated Corpus of Semantic Roles. *Computational Linguistics* 31(1).

Aarne Ranta. 2004. Grammatical Framework: A Type-Theoretical Grammar Formalism. *Journal of Functional Programming* 14(2).

Aarne Ranta. 2009. The GF Resource Grammar Library. *Linguistic Issues in Language Technology* 2(2).

Aarne Ranta. 2011. *Grammatical Framework: Programming with Multilingual Grammars*. CSLI Publications, Stanford.

The Meaning Factory at SemEval-2017 Task 9: Producing AMRs with Neural Semantic Parsing

Rik van Noord
CLCG
University of Groningen
`r.i.k.van.noord@rug.nl`

Johan Bos
CLCG
University of Groningen
`johan.bos@rug.nl`

Abstract

We evaluate a semantic parser based on a character-based sequence-to-sequence model in the context of the SemEval-2017 shared task on semantic parsing for AMRs. With data augmentation, super characters, and POS-tagging we gain major improvements in performance compared to a baseline character-level model. Although we improve on previous character-based neural semantic parsing models, the overall accuracy is still lower than a state-of-the-art AMR parser. An ensemble combining our neural semantic parser with an existing, traditional parser, yields a small gain in performance.

1 Introduction

Traditional open-domain semantic parsers often use statistical syntactic parsers to derive syntactic structure on which to build a meaning representation. Recently there have been interesting attempts to view semantic parsing as a translation task, mapping a source language (here: English) to a target language (a logical form of some kind). Dong and Lapata (2016) used sequence-to-sequence and sequence-to-tree neural translation models to produce logical forms from sentences, while Barzdins and Gosko (2016) and Peng et al. (2017) used a similar method to produce AMRs. From a purely engineering point of view, these are interesting attempts as complex models of the semantic parsing process can be avoided. Yet little is known about the performance and fine-tuning of such parsers, and whether they can reach performance of traditional semantic parsers, or whether they could contribute to performance in an ensemble setting.

In the context of SemEval-2017 Task 9 we aim to shed more light on these questions. In particular we participated in Subtask 1, Parsing Biomedical Data, and work with parallel English-AMR training data comprising extracts of scientific articles about cancer pathway discovery.

More specifically, our objectives are (1) try to reproduce the results of Barzdins and Gosko (2016), who used character-level models for neural semantic parsing; (2) improve on their results by employing several novel techniques; and (3) combine the resulting neural semantic parser with an existing off-the-shelf AMR parser to reach state-of-the-art results.

2 Neural Semantic Parsing

2.1 Datasets

Our training set consists of the second LDC AMR release (LDC2016E25) containing 39,620 AMRs, as well as the training set of the bio AMR corpus that contains 5,452 AMRs. As development and test set we use the designated development and test partition of the bio AMR corpus, both containing 500 AMRs. HTML-tags are removed from the sentences.

2.2 Basic Translation Model

We use a seq2seq neural translation model to *translate* English sentences into AMRs. This is a bi-LSTM model with added attention mechanism, as described in Bahdanau et al. (2014). Similar to Barzdins and Gosko (2016), but contrasting with Peng et al. (2017), we train the model only on character-level input. Model specifics are shown in Table 1.

In a preprocessing step, we remove all variables from the AMR and duplicate co-referring nodes. An example of this is shown in Figure 1. The variables and co-referring nodes are restored after testing, using the restoring script from

Proceedings of the 11th International Workshop on Semantic Evaluations (SemEval-2017), pages 929–933,
Vancouver, Canada, August 3 - 4, 2017. ©2017 Association for Computational Linguistics

Parameter	Value
Layers	1
Nodes	400
Buckets	(510,510)
Epochs	25–35
Vocabulary	150–200
Learning rate	0.5
Decay factor	0.99
Gradient norm	5

Table 1: Model specifics for the seq2seq model.

Barzdins and Gosko (2016).[1] Wikipedia links are also removed from the training set, but get restored in a separate Wikification post-processing step.

```
(require-01
   :ARG0 (induce-01
      :ARG1 (cell)
      :ARG2 (migrate-01
         :ARG0 cell))
   :ARG1 (bind-01
      :ARG1 (protein
         :name (name :op1 "Crk"))
      :ARG2 (protein
         :name (name :op1 "CAS"))))
```

Figure 1: *"Crk binding to CAS is required for the induction of cell migration"* - seq2seq tree representation.

2.3   Improvements

In this section we describe the methods used to improve the neural semantic parser.

Augmentation   AMRs, as introduced by Banarescu et al. (2013), are rooted, directed, labeled graphs, in which the different nodes and triples are unordered by definition. However, in our tree representation of AMRs (see Figure 1), there is an order of branches. This means that we are able to permute this order into a more intuitive representation of the sentence, by matching the word order using the AMR-sentence alignments. An example of this method is shown in Figure 2.

This approach can also be used to augment the training data, since we are now able generate "new" AMR-sentence pairs that can be added to our training set. However, due to the exponential growth, there are often more than 1,000 different AMR permutations for long sentences. We ran multiple experiments to find the best way to use this oversupply of data. Ultimately, we found that

```
(require-01
   :ARG1 (bind-01
      :ARG1 (protein
         :name (name :op1 "Crk"))
      :ARG2 (protein
         :name (name :op1 "CAS"))))
   :ARG0 (induce-01
      :ARG1 (cell)
      :ARG2 (migrate-01
         :ARG0 cell))
```

Figure 2: *"Crk binding to CAS is required for the induction of cell migration"* - seq2seq representation that best matches the word order.

it is most beneficial to "double" the training data by adding the best matching AMR (based on word order) to the existing data set.

Super characters   We do not necessarily have to restrict ourselves to using only individual characters as input. For example, the AMR relations (e.g. `:ARG0`, `:domain`, `:mod`) can be seen as single entities instead of a collection of characters. This decreases the input length of the AMRs in feature space, but increases the total vocabulary. We refer to these entities as *super characters*. This way, we essentially create a model that is a combination of character and word level input.

POS-tagging   Character-level models might still be able to benefit from syntactic information, even when this is added directly to the input structure. Especially POS-tags can easily be added as features to the input data, while also providing valuable information. For example, proper nouns in a sentence often occur with the `:name` relation in the corresponding AMR, while adjectives correlate with the `:mod` relation. We append the corresponding POS-tag to each word in the sentence (using the C&C POS-tagger by Clark et al. (2003)), creating a new super character for each unique tag.

Post-processing   In a post-processing step, first the variables and co-referring nodes are restored. We try to fix invalidly produced AMRs by applying a few simple heuristics, such as inserting special characters (e.g. parentheses, quotes) or removing unfinished edges. If the AMR is still invalid, we output a smart default AMR.[2]

We also remove all double nodes, i.e., relation-concept pairs that occur more than once in a branch of the AMR. This form of duplicate output is a common problem with deep learning models,

---

[1] https://github.com/didzis/tensorflowAMR

[2] This was not necessary for the evaluation data.

since the model does not keep track of what it has already output. We refer to this method as *pruning*.

Wikification Our Wikification method is based on Bjerva et al. (2016), using Spotlight (Daiber et al., 2013). They initially removed wiki links from the input and then tried to restore them in the output by simply adding a wiki link to the AMR if it matches with the name in a :name relation. Even though this approach worked well for the LDC data, it did not work for the biomedical data.

This is mainly due to the fact that :name nodes are not consistently annotated with a wiki link in the gold biomedical data. 138 unique names that had a corresponding wiki link at least once in the gold data did not have this wiki link 100% of the time. For example *DNA* occurred 86 times as a :name in the gold data and was only annotated with a wiki link in 69 cases, while *ERK* occurred 228 times with only 3 annotated wiki links. For this reason we opt for a safe Wikification approach: we only add wiki links to names that were annotated with the same wiki link more than 50% of the time in the gold data. Following our previous example, this means that *DNA* does still get a wiki link, but *ERK* does not.

2.4 CAMR ensemble

As we know that our neural semantic parser is unlikely to outperform a state-of-the-art AMR parser, but is likely to complement it, our strategy is to use an ensemble-based approach. The ensemble comprises the off-the-shelf parser CAMR (Wang et al., 2015) and our neural semantic parser. The implementation of this ensemble is similar to Barzdins and Gosko (2016), choosing the AMR that obtains the highest pairwise Smatch (Cai and Knight, 2013) score when compared to the other AMRs generated for a sentence. This method is designed to ultimately choose the AMR with the most prevalent relations and concepts.

We train CAMR models based on the biomedical data only, the LDC data only and the combination of both data sets. Since CAMR is nondeterministic, we can also train multiple models on the same data set. Ultimately, the best ensemble on the test data consisted of three bio-only models, two bio + LDC models and one LDC-only model. This ensemble was used to parse the evaluation set.

3 Results and Discussion

3.1 Results on Test Set

Table 2 shows the results of all improvement methods tested in isolation on the test set of the biomedical data. Augmenting the data only helps very slightly, while the super characters are responsible for the largest increase in performance. This shows that we do not necessarily have to use only character or word level input in our models, but that a combination of the two might be optimal. The best result was obtained by combining the different methods. This model was then used to parse the evaluation data. Table 3 shows the results of retraining CAMR on different data sets, as well as an ensemble of those models. Adding our seq2seq model to the ensemble only yielded a very small gain in performance.

Feature	F-score	Increase
Baseline	0.422	
Pruning	0.425	0.7%
Wikification	0.423	0.2%
Augmentation	0.424	0.5%
Super characters	0.481	14.0%
POS-tagging	0.436	3.3%
All combined	0.504	19.4%

Table 2: Results of the different seq2seq models on the test set of the biomedical data.

	F-score
CAMR retrained on LDC	0.399
CAMR retrained on bio	0.585
CAMR retrained on LDC + bio	0.582
Ensemble CAMR	0.588
Ensemble CAMR + seq2seq	0.589

Table 3: Results of retraining CAMR and results of best ensemble models, tested on the biomedical test data.

3.2 Official Results

In Table 4 we see the detailed results of the best seq2seq model and best ensemble on the evaluation data, using the scripts from Damonte et al. (2017).[3] While CAMR has similar scores on the

---

[3] Unofficial score for seq2seq negation; due to a mistake, all :polarity nodes were removed in the official submission. This had no influence on the final F-score.

test data, the score of the seq2seq model decreases by 0.04. It is interesting to note that seq2seq scores equally well without word sense disambiguation, while there is no separate module that handles this.

Setting	seq2seq	Ensemble
Smatch	**0.460**	**0.576**
Unlabeled	0.504	0.623
No WSD	0.463	0.579
Named Entities	0.512	0.576
Wikification	0.458	0.396
Negation	0.141	0.244
Concepts	0.630	0.759
Reentrancies	0.290	0.352
SRL	0.427	0.543

Table 4: Official results on the evaluation set for both the ensemble and the seq-to-seq neural semantic parser.

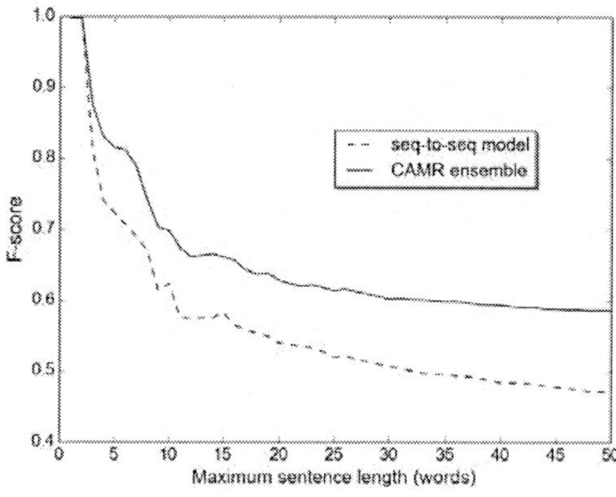

Figure 3: Comparison of CAMR and our seq-to-seq model for different sentence lengths.

3.3 Comparison with CAMR

Although CAMR outperformed our neural semantic parser by a large margin, the seq-to-seq model did produce a better AMR for 108 out of the 500 evaluation AMRs, based on Smatch score. If the CAMR + seq2seq ensemble was somehow able to always choose the best AMR, it obtains an F-score of 0.601, an increase of 2.2% instead of the current 0.2%. This suggests that the current method of combining neural semantic parsers with existing parsers is far from optimal, but that the neural methods do provide complementary information. A different way to incorporate this information would be to pick the most suitable parser based on the input sentence. A classifier that exploits the characteristics of the sentence could be trained to assign a parser to each individual (to be parsed) sentence.

Figure 3 shows the performance of the neural semantic parser and the CAMR ensemble per maximum sentence length. We see that seq-to-seq can keep up with CAMR for very short sentences, but is clearly outperformed on longer sentences. As the sentences get longer, the difference in performance gets bigger, but not much.

4 Conclusion and Future Work

We were able to reproduce the results of the character-level models for neural semantic parsing as proposed by Barzdins and Gosko (2016). Moreover, we showed improvement on their basic setting by using data-augmentation, part-of-speech as additional input, and using super characters. The latter setting showed that a combination of character and word level input might be optimal for neural semantic parsers. Despite these enhancements, the resulting AMR parser is still outperformed by more traditional, off-the-shelf AMR parsers. Adding our neural semantic parser to an ensemble including CAMR (Wang et al., 2015), a dependency-based parser, yielded no noteworthy improvements on the overall performance.

Do these results indicate that neural semantic parsers will never be competitive with more traditional statistical parsers? We don't think so. We have the feeling that we have just scratched the surface of possibilities that neural semantic parsing can offer us, and how they possibly can complement parsers using different strategies. In future work we will explore these.

Acknowledgements

We thank the two anonymous reviewers for their comments. We would also like to thank the Center for Information Technology of the University of Groningen for their support and for providing access to the Peregrine high performance computing cluster. We also used a Tesla K40 GPU, which was kindly donated by the NVIDIA Corporation. This work was funded by the NWO-VICI grant "Lost in Translation – Found in Meaning" (288-89-003).

References

Dzmitry Bahdanau, Kyunghyun Cho, and Yoshua Bengio. 2014. Neural machine translation by jointly learning to align and translate. *arXiv preprint arXiv:1409.0473* .

Laura Banarescu, Claire Bonial, Shu Cai, Madalina Georgescu, Kira Griffitt, Ulf Hermjakob, Kevin Knight, Philipp Koehn, Martha Palmer, and Nathan Schneider. 2013. Abstract meaning representation for sembanking. In *Proceedings of the 7th Linguistic Annotation Workshop and Interoperability with Discourse*. Association for Computational Linguistics, Sofia, Bulgaria, pages 178–186. http://www.aclweb.org/anthology/W13-2322.

Guntis Barzdins and Didzis Gosko. 2016. Riga at semeval-2016 task 8: Impact of smatch extensions and character-level neural translation on amr parsing accuracy. In *Proceedings of the 10th International Workshop on Semantic Evaluation (SemEval-2016)*. Association for Computational Linguistics, San Diego, California, pages 1143–1147. http://www.aclweb.org/anthology/S16-1176.

Johannes Bjerva, Johan Bos, and Hessel Haagsma. 2016. The meaning factory at semeval-2016 task 8: Producing amrs with boxer. In *Proceedings of the 10th International Workshop on Semantic Evaluation (SemEval-2016)*. Association for Computational Linguistics, San Diego, California, pages 1179–1184. http://www.aclweb.org/anthology/S16-1182.

Shu Cai and Kevin Knight. 2013. Smatch: an evaluation metric for semantic feature structures. In *Proceedings of the 51st Annual Meeting of the Association for Computational Linguistics (Volume 2: Short Papers)*. Association for Computational Linguistics, Sofia, Bulgaria, pages 748–752. http://www.aclweb.org/anthology/P13-2131.

Stephen Clark, James R Curran, and Miles Osborne. 2003. Bootstrapping pos taggers using unlabelled data. In *Proceedings of the seventh conference on Natural language learning at HLT-NAACL 2003-Volume 4*. Association for Computational Linguistics, pages 49–55. http://www.aclweb.org/anthology/W03-0407.

Joachim Daiber, Max Jakob, Chris Hokamp, and Pablo N. Mendes. 2013. Improving efficiency and accuracy in multilingual entity extraction. In *Proceedings of the 9th International Conference on Semantic Systems (I-Semantics)*.

Marco Damonte, Shay B. Cohen, and Giorgio Satta. 2017. An incremental parser for abstract meaning representation. In *Proceedings of the 15th Conference of the European Chapter of the Association for Computational Linguistics: Volume 1, Long Papers*. Association for Computational Linguistics, Valencia, Spain, pages 536–546. http://www.aclweb.org/anthology/E17-1051.

Li Dong and Mirella Lapata. 2016. Language to logical form with neural attention. In *Proceedings of the 54th Annual Meeting of the Association for Computational Linguistics (Volume 1: Long Papers)*. Association for Computational Linguistics, Berlin, Germany, pages 33–43. http://www.aclweb.org/anthology/P16-1004.

Xiaochang Peng, Chuan Wang, Daniel Gildea, and Nianwen Xue. 2017. Addressing the data sparsity issue in neural amr parsing. In *Proceedings of the 15th Conference of the European Chapter of the Association for Computational Linguistics: Volume 1, Long Papers*. Association for Computational Linguistics, Valencia, Spain, pages 366–375. http://www.aclweb.org/anthology/E17-1035.

Chuan Wang, Nianwen Xue, and Sameer Pradhan. 2015. A transition-based algorithm for amr parsing. In *Proceedings of the 2015 Conference of the North American Chapter of the Association for Computational Linguistics: Human Language Technologies*. Association for Computational Linguistics, Denver, Colorado, pages 366–375. http://www.aclweb.org/anthology/N15-1040.

PKU_ICL at SemEval-2017 Task 10: Keyphrase Extraction with Model Ensemble and External Knowledge

Liang Wang
Key Laboratory of
Computational Linguistics
Peking University, China
`intfloat@pku.edu.cn`

Sujian Li
Key Laboratory of
Computational Linguistics
Peking University, China
`lisujian@pku.edu.cn`

Abstract

This paper presents a system that participated in *SemEval 2017 Task 10* (subtask A and subtask B): *Extracting Keyphrases and Relations from Scientific Publications* (Augenstein et al., 2017). Our proposed approach utilizes external knowledge to enrich feature representation of candidate keyphrase, including Wikipedia, IEEE taxonomy and pre-trained word embeddings etc. Ensemble of unsupervised models, random forest and linear models are used for candidate keyphrase ranking and keyphrase type classification. Our system achieves the 3rd place in subtask A and 4th place in subtask B.

1 Introduction

Keyphrases summarize the most important aspects of a document. They can be helpful in many areas such as information retrieval, topic modeling and text classification. However, manually labeling keyphrase would be far too time-consuming, and unrealistic especially when dealing with web-scale collection of documents. Therefore, automatic keyphrase extraction has drawn growing interests among NLP research communities for years.

For state-of-the-art system on keyphrase extraction, Hasan and Ng(2014) presents a comprehensive survey. Their experiments demonstrate that unsupervised approaches including graph-based ranking and topic modeling techniques perform best on *News* and *Blogs* dataset. In *SemEval 2010 Task 5* (Kim et al., 2010) (Kim et al., 2013), which also aims to tackle the challenge of keyphrase extraction in scientific area, a majority of the participants adopt supervised approaches, and especially the top 2 systems are both supervised. Thus, in our work, we argue that super-

vised approaches can enable combination of rich features, with parameters learned efficiently and automatically, while their unsupervised counterparts often involve simply designed features and manually fine-tuned hyperparameters.

Based on the consideration above, for *SemEval 2017 Task 10*, our system is designed as a supervised one which also explore unsupervised techniques as auxiliaries. It involves three steps: *candidate generation*, *keyphrase ranking* and *keyphrase type classification*. For *candidate generation*, we use chunking-based approach to discover phrases that match a predefined part-of-speech pattern. Heuristic rules are manually designed by experience and applied to filter out those phrases which are unlikely to be keyphrases. For *keyphrase ranking* in subtask A, we use a straightforward regression-based pointwise ranking method. Here, two unsupervised algorithms *TextRank* (Mihalcea and Tarau, 2004) and *SGRank* (Danesh et al., 2015) are incorporated into random forest by providing their output as complementary features. In our experiments, we find that stacking linear model upon random forest can provide extra performance gain. For *keyphrase type classification* in subtask B, we model it as a three-way classification problem, with the same feature set and classifiers used in subtask A.

Feature engineering is a critical part for supervised model. The task of keyphrase extraction heavily relies on statistical features(such as TF-IDF) and semantic features. However, due to the limited size of labeled dataset, it is hard to get reliable estimation of phrases' IDF value or semantic representation. In this paper, we solve this problem by exploiting external knowledge resources such as *Wikipedia* and pre-trained word embeddings. Experiments show the effectiveness of our proposed feature set.

Proceedings of the 11th International Workshop on Semantic Evaluations (SemEval-2017), pages 934–937,
Vancouver, Canada, August 3 - 4, 2017. ©2017 Association for Computational Linguistics

2 Methodology

Our system works in a pipeline fashion. It involves *candidate generation, keyphrase ranking* for subtask A and *keyphrase type classification* for subtask B. As the third step use the same feature set and classifiers as second step, we omit its detailed description.

2.1 Keyphrase Candidate Generation

There are generally two approaches for candidate generation: n-grams and part-of-speech pattern matching. Even though n-grams strategy usually achieves higher recall, it also brings in more false positives, which could cause serious problem for classifiers. Our strategy is a combination of part-of-speech pattern matching and heuristic rules.

First, let's define the heuristic rules with the format of functions, which take a phrase p as an argument and output a boolean value. Assume $NP = (NN*|JJ*)*(NN*)$.

$$f_1(p) = \text{whether } p \text{ matches pattern } NP \quad (1)$$
$$f_2(p) = \text{whether } p \text{ consists of capital letters} \quad (2)$$
$$f_3(p) = \text{whether } p \text{ consists of} <5 \text{ words} \quad (3)$$
$$f_4(p) = \text{whether } p \text{ contains '[' or ']' or ','} \quad (4)$$
$$f_5(p) = \text{whether } p \text{ consists of only digits} \quad (5)$$

A phrase p becomes a keyphrase candidate if $(f_1(p) \vee f_2(p)) \wedge f_3(p) \wedge \neg f_4(p) \wedge \neg f_5(p)$ is *true*. Candidate generation is carried out at sentence level, we don't consider the possibility that a keyphrase may span across multiple sentences.

2.2 External Knowledge

To deal with the aforementioned problem, we exploit several external knowledge resources to get more reliable estimation of statistical and semantic features.

- **English Wikipedia.**[1] It consists of more than 5 million articles covering almost every area you can think of. We use this corpus D to calculate IDF of word t. Words with top $10k$ IDF score are kept.

$$IDF(t, D) = log \frac{|D|}{|\{d \in D : t \in d\}|} \quad (6)$$

- **IEEE taxonomy.** Official *IEEE taxonomy*[2] includes a list of manually summarized keyphrases related to technical areas. Articles in this shared task come from three domains: computer science, material science and physics. All three domains are covered by IEEE. We add a boolean feature which indicates whether the given candidate keyphrase appears in this list.

- **Pre-trained Glove embeddings.**[3] (Pennington et al., 2014) Word embeddings trained on billions of tokens provide a simple way to incorporate semantic knowledge. They prove to be helpful in many NLP tasks especially when labeled data is limited. In our system, we use IDF-weighted word embeddings for phrase representation. Given a phrase consisting of n words $w_1, w_2...w_n$, its representation is calculated as follows.

$$\frac{\sum_{i=1}^{n} IDF(w_i) \cdot E_{w_i}}{\sum_{i=1}^{n} IDF(w_i)} \quad (7)$$

E_{w_i} is the glove embedding of word w_i.

2.3 Feature Engineering

Based upon the experience of many previous work on keyphrase extraction and the unique characteristics of scientific publications, our system incorporates four types of features: linguistic features, context features, external knowledge based features and unsupervised model based features, as shown in Table 4.

feature type	feature definition
linguistic features	stemmed unigram
	avg/max/min of TF/IDF/TF·IDF
	whether p consists of capital letters
	part-of-speech for every word in p
	number of tokens/characters in p
context features	previous/next token of p
	POS of previous/next token of p
	distance between p and citation
	relative position of p in given text
external knowledge	whether p is in *IEEE taxonomy* list
	Wikipedia based avg/max/min IDF
	glove embedding of p
unsupervised feature	whether p is in top 20 keyphrases according to *TextRank* algorithm
	whether p is in top 20 keyphrases according to *SGRank* algorithm

Table 1: Features for a candidate keyphrase p.

2.4 Model Ensemble for Keyphrase Ranking

Model ensemble has been shown to be an effective way to boost generalization performance both

---

[1]https://dumps.wikimedia.org/enwiki/
[2]https://www.ieee.org/documents/taxonomy_v101.pdf
[3]http://nlp.stanford.edu/projects/glove/

in practice and theoretically (Zhou, 2012). Random forest itself is an ensemble model, with variant of decision trees combined via *Bagging*. In this shared task, we explore two layers of stacking.

At the first layer, we stack trees upon output from unsupervised algorithms. There are numerous algorithms for unsupervised keyphrase extraction based on clustering, graph-based ranking etc, different algorithms reflect different aspects of phrase. Stacking provides a convenient and powerful way to combine those information. In this paper, we use two algorithms: *TextRank* (Mihalcea and Tarau, 2004) and *SGRank* (Danesh et al., 2015).

At the second layer, we stack linear model upon random forest. Instead of treating decision tree as a classifier, it can be seen as learning to transform input features. Each leaf node corresponds to a feature transformation path from root node, and therefore can serve as a boolean feature. Linear model can be applied to learn the weights of those features. Logistic regression is usually used, however, we find linear SVM is more robust to overfitting in this shared task.

For keyphrase ranking in subtask A, probabilistic score is required, candidates with score no less than α are chosen as keyphrases. α is tuned on validation dataset to balance precision and recall. For keyphrase type classification in subtask B, it is a three-way classification problem.

In deep learning community, "stacking" usually means joint training of multiple layers. In this paper, "stacking" means that lower layers provide their output as features for upper layer, different layers are trained separately.

3 Experiments

For details about this shared task and dataset, please refer to *SemEval 2017 Task 10* description paper (Augenstein et al., 2017).

3.1 Experimental Setup

Preprocessing   We use *nltk* (Bird, 2006) to segment each paragraph into a list of sentences, tokenize every sentence and then get part-of-speech tag for every token. *Snowball Stemmer* is used for stemming. Stop words, punctuations and digits are removed for feature engineering, but not for keyphrase candidate generation. We use simple heuristics to parse the IEEE taxonomy pdf file and get 6978 phrases in total.

Configurations   Library *scikit-learn* is used for implementation of our supervised models. Random forest is set to have 200 trees and other parameters are set to default. Parameters of linear SVM are all set to default. We use 50-dimensional glove embeddings for calculating phrase representation. For subtask A, we choose threshold $\alpha = 0.15$ to balance recall and precision.

3.2 Results and Analysis

		precision	recall	f1-score
subtask A		0.522	0.498	**0.510**
subtask B	Material	0.464	0.456	0.460
	Process	0.441	0.364	0.399
	Task	0.286	0.041	0.072
	Average	0.450	0.374	**0.409**

Table 2: Official results on test set.

Our system's final results are shown in Table 2, f1-score for subtask A is 0.510 (3rd place), and micro-averaged f1-score for subtask B is 0.409 (4th place). The f1-score of the 1st place solution in a similar task *SemEval 2010 Task 5* is 27.5% (Kim et al., 2010). In comparison with the prior work, our system seems to be surprisingly well. We attribute such performance gap to unique characteristics of this shared task. Instead of keyphrase extraction from entire document, participants are only asked to extract keyphrase from single paragraph, and the density of keyphrases is higher.

Another interesting phenomenon is the poor numbers for *Task* keyphrases. Most of *Material* and *Process* keyphrases are noun phrases or have capital letters, they are relatively easy to discriminate by part-of-speech pattern. However, *Task* keyphrases cover a wide range of part-of-speech patterns, and some of them have verb or conjunction. It remains a challenge for our system to achieve satisfying performance for *Task* keyphrases.

	Material	Process	Task	Micro-average
recall	0.715	0.608	0.334	0.606

Table 3: Recall for keyphrases.

An important metric for our pipeline system is recall for keyphrases in candidate generation step. Table 3 shows that our heuristic rules cover 60.6% of keyphrases in training data, although it's possible to improve recall by introducing more part-of-

	subtask A			subtask B		
	precision	recall	f1-score	precision	recall	f1-score
unsupervised features	0.378	0.341	0.359	0.186	0.168	0.177
+ linguistic features	0.481	0.417	0.447	0.352	0.305	0.327
+ context features	0.499	0.497	0.498	0.371	0.369	0.370
+ external knowledge	**0.522**	**0.498**	**0.510**	**0.450**	**0.374**	**0.409**

Table 4: Performance with different combinations of features.

speech patterns, precision will go lower. There has to be a tradeoff between recall and precision.

	precision	recall	f1-score
tf-idf	0.163	0.216	0.186
rf	0.510	0.507	0.508
rf+svm	**0.524**	0.520	0.522
best	0.510	**0.610**	**0.560**

Table 5: Comparison of different models on test data. (a) *tf-idf* output phrases with top 15 tf-idf score; (b) *rf* stands for random forest; (c) *rf+svm* stacks a linear SVM upon random forest; (d) *best* is the 1st place solution for this shared task.

Table 5 shows the effectiveness of our approach. Even though *rf* and *rf+svm* share the same input features and random forest already has a built-in ensemble mechanism, *rf+svm* model still manages to improve all three metrics via stacking, with f1-score increasing by 1.4%, from 50.8% to 52.2%.

We also examine how different feature combinations would affect overall performance. Results are shown in Table 4. Unsupervised features are pretty impressive to discriminate keyphrase and non-keyphrase (subtask A), but they fail to reliably identify keyphrase type (subtask B). Incorporation of external knowledge is clearly a key to further boost system performance. All six metrics improve as more features are added. Once again it shows our model's ability to combine many features without worrying too much about overfitting. It is possible to add more relevant features.

4   Conclusion

This paper gives a brief description of our system at *SemEval 2017 Task 10* for keyphrase extraction of scientific papers. By incorporating multiple external knowledge resources, careful feature engineering and model ensemble, our system achieves competitive performance.

Acknowledgements

We would like to thank *SemEval 2017* organizers and anonymous reviewers for their helpful suggestions. This work was partially supported by National Natural Science Foundation of China (61572049 and 61333018). The correspondence author of this paper is Sujian Li.

References

Isabelle Augenstein, Mrinal Kanti Das, Sebastian Riedel, Lakshmi Nair Vikraman, and Andrew McCallum. 2017. SemEval 2017 Task 10: ScienceIE - Extracting Keyphrases and Relations from Scientific Publications. In *Proceedings of the International Workshop on Semantic Evaluation*. Association for Computational Linguistics, Vancouver, Canada.

Steven Bird. 2006. Nltk: the natural language toolkit. In *Proceedings of the COLING/ACL on Interactive presentation sessions*. Association for Computational Linguistics, pages 69–72.

Soheil Danesh, Tamara Sumner, and James H Martin. 2015. Sgrank: Combining statistical and graphical methods to improve the state of the art in unsupervised keyphrase extraction. *Lexical and Computational Semantics* page 117.

Kazi Saidul Hasan and Vincent Ng. 2014. Automatic keyphrase extraction: A survey of the state of the art. In *ACL (1)*. pages 1262–1273.

Su Nam Kim, Olena Medelyan, Min-Yen Kan, and Timothy Baldwin. 2010. Semeval-2010 task 5: Automatic keyphrase extraction from scientific articles. In *Proceedings of the 5th International Workshop on Semantic Evaluation*. Association for Computational Linguistics, pages 21–26.

Su Nam Kim, Olena Medelyan, Min-Yen Kan, and Timothy Baldwin. 2013. Automatic keyphrase extraction from scientific articles. *Language resources and evaluation* 47(3):723–742.

Rada Mihalcea and Paul Tarau. 2004. Textrank: Bringing order into texts. Association for Computational Linguistics.

Jeffrey Pennington, Richard Socher, and Christopher D Manning. 2014. Glove: Global vectors for word representation. In *EMNLP*. volume 14, pages 1532–1543.

Zhi-Hua Zhou. 2012. *Ensemble methods: foundations and algorithms*. CRC press.

NTNU-1@ScienceIE at SemEval-2017 Task 10:
Identifying and Labelling Keyphrases with Conditional Random Fields

Erwin Marsi, Utpal Skidar, Cristina Marco, Biswanath Barik, Rune Saetre
Department of Computer Science
Norwegian University of Science and Technology
`{emarsi,utpals,cristina.marco,biswanath.barik,saetre}@ntnu.no`

Abstract

We present NTNU's systems for Task A (prediction of keyphrases) and Task B (labelling as Material, Process or Task) at SemEval 2017 Task 10: Extracting Keyphrases and Relations from Scientific Publications (Augenstein et al., 2017). Our approach relies on supervised machine learning using Conditional Random Fields. Our system yields a micro F-score of 0.34 for Tasks A and B combined on the test data. For Task C (relation extraction), we relied on an independently developed system described in (Barik and Marsi, 2017). For the full Scenario 1 (including relations), our approach reaches a micro F-score of 0.33 (5th place). Here we describe our systems, report results and discuss errors.

1 Approach

We choose Conditional Random Fields (Lafferty et al., 2001) because they have produced state-of-art results on comparable sequence labelling tasks such as named entity recognition in biomedicine. Two systems were developed, using different feature sets and alternative CRF implementations.

Preprocessing Input text is linguistically analysed using the Spacy NLP pipeline (Honnibal and Johnson, 2015), including sentence splitting, tokenisation, lemmatisation and dependency parsing. Since CRFs cannot handle Brat's stand-off annotation format directly, keyphrase annotations are first converted to the Inside-Outside-Begin (IOB) tagging scheme by aligning their character offsets with the character offsets of tokens: if the start character offset of a token coincides with the start offset of an annotated keyphrase, the token receives a B (begin) tag; if the offset span of a token falls within the offset bounds of a keyphrase, the token gets an I (inside) tag, otherwise the token is assigned an O (outside) tag. Each sentence corresponds to a sequence of IOB tags, serving as the labelled sequence for the CRF. Separate IOB tags are derived for each of the three keyphrase classes (Material, Process, Task). Annotations and tokens do not always properly align; the resulting errors are discussed in Section 3.

System 1 relies on the CRFsuite implementation (Okazaki, 2007) as wrapped by the sklearn-crfsuite module for SciKit Learn. A dedicated classifier is trained for each of the three keyphrase classes. CRFs are used with default parameter setting. The following features were selected per class by cross-validation on the development data:

- Word features: word shape (e.g. 'Xxxx'), is-alpha, is-lower-case, is-ascii, is-capitalized, is-upper-case, is-punctuation, like-number, prefix-chars (2,3,4), suffix-chars (2,3,4), is-stopword, all in a window of size 3 for Material and Process;
- Lemma and POS, in a window of size 5 for Material and Process, in window of size 3 for Process;
- Wordnet (for Material only): synset names of all hypernyms (transitive closure), in a window of size 5

Supervised learning is generally hampered by skewed class distributions, where minority classes tend to be predicted poorly. In our case, the O tag is by far the most frequent tag. To reduce its weight, all sentences without a Material keyphrase are removed from training material of the CRF for predicting the Material class, and likewise for the other two classes.

Output is postprocessed with the intention of improving consistent labelling throughout a single

Proceedings of the 11th International Workshop on Semantic Evaluations (SemEval-2017), pages 938–941,
Vancouver, Canada, August 3 - 4, 2017. ©2017 Association for Computational Linguistics

text. For example, if a majority of the occurrences of the phrase '*carbon*' in a text is labelled as Material, then any unlabelled occurrences are by extension also labelled as Material.

System 2 consists of two steps: (1) detection of keyphrase boundaries; (2) labelling of keyphrases. Both steps are implemented using the C++ based CRF++ package[1]. The boundary detection model uses the the following features: local context: -2 to +2[2], POS, lemma, prefix-suffix-chars (1,2,3,4), is-word-length-with-upper-case < 5, word-frequency, shape, is-stopword, is-all-upper-case, is-beginning-upper-case, is-inner-upper-case, is-single-upper-case, is-words-in-training-data, is-all-digit and is-alpha-digit.

For labelling of keyphrases, separate classifiers are trained for each class, where the classifiers for Process and Task (but not Material) use the predicted keyphrase boundaries as a feature. The following features were used for Material:

- Word features: local-context (uni-gram and bi-gram, -2 to +3), is-all-digit (-1 to +2), is-single-upper-case (-2 to +2), is-all-upper-case (-2 to +1), is-inner-upper-case (-2 to +4), is-stopword (-1 to +3), shape (-2 to +1), prefix-chars (1), suffix-chars (1,2,3), is-word-length-with-upper-case < 5 (-2 to +3), is-word-in-training-data (-3 to +3)
- Babelfy Mention (-2 to +2): Checks if current word belongs to any Babelfy (Moro et al., 2014) named entities
- Lemma (-1 to +3) and POS (-1 to +2)
- Wordnet: Synonym and Hypernym (first 2 synset names and hypernyms of first and third synset names. If no hypernyms are found, we represent it as ND (not defined)).

The following features were used for Process:

- Word features: local-context (uni-gram and bi-gram: -4 to +2), is-digi-alpha (-1 to +4), is-all-digit (-3 to +3), is-inner-upper-case (-1 to +1), is-beginning-upper-case (-2 to +4), is-all-upper-case (-2 to +2), is-stopword (-2 to +1), shape (-2 to +3), word-frequency (-4 to +4), is-word-in-training-data (-3 to +1), prefix-chars (1,3), suffix-chars (1,3)

- keyphrase boundary according to boundary detection model (-2 to +4)
- POS (uni-gram and bi-gram: -4 to +1)
- Wordnet: Synonym and Hypernym (second synset names and hypernyms of first and third synset names)

The following features were used for Task:

- Word features: local-context (uni-gram and bi-gram, -4 to +1), is-digi-alpha (-3 to +3), is-all-digit (-3 to +4), shape (-1 to +4), is-word-in-training-data (-1 to +4), prefix-chars (1,4), suffix-chars (1,3,4)
- keyphrase boundary according to boundary detection model (-2 to +3)
- Babelfy Mention (-3 to +1)
- Lemma and POS (-4 to +3)
- Wordnet: Synonym and Hypernym (first synset names and hypernyms of fourth synset name)

System 3 System 3 is an optimal combination of the two preceding systems according to CV on the development data. Based on the precision value, System 2 was given higher priority when both systems identified the words as keyphrases. That is, we add any Task or Material keyphrases predicted by System 1 to those predicted by System 2, unless they happen to overlap with any System 2 predictions (Process remained unaltered).

IOB-to-Brat conversion The final step consists of merging the IOB tags predicted by the three separate models in order to produce labelled keyphrases in Brat format.

Experimental setup Cross-validation on the training data was used to select features and tune hyper-parameters. The best performing systems were tested on dev data to check for undesired overfitting. Finally the best systems were trained on the combination of train and dev data to make predictions on test data.

Relation extraction For Task C (relation extraction), we relied on an independently developed system described in (Barik and Marsi, 2017), which performs exhaustive pairwise classifications of keyphrase pairs of the same type within a sentence.

2 Results

Results for our three systems are shown in Table 1. Micro averages are weighted across the

---

[1] https://taku910.github.io/crfpp/
[2] Here '-' and '+' indicate the number of preceding and following words in the context window respectively.

three labels for keyphrases and the two relation types, but as the keyphrases are substantially more frequent, the weight of the relations is relatively small. System 1 performs worst and system 2 performs best, although the differences are small. System 1 mainly wins on precision. The combination of both in system 3 does not offer any advantages, except for higher recall. All system obtain best scores for Material and worst scores for Task. This can be partly explained by the support for each class: Material and Process instances are much more frequent than Task in the training data. Another part of the explanation may be that Process and Task are harder to distinguish from each other.

Results on test data are substantially lower than on the dev data, with 6 to 7 percent lower average F-scores. This suggests that the models were overfitted on the combination of train and dev data. This is somewhat surprising, because no such differences showed up between cross-validated scores on the training data and scores on the dev data.

Performance on relation extraction is rather poor when compared with the scores obtained with manually annotated keyphrases as input. This is to be expected, as errors in keyphrase extraction propagate to errors in relation extraction. For more analysis of the relation extraction system, see (Barik and Marsi, 2017).

3 Discussion

IOB tags The offsets of annotated phrases did not always properly align with the beginning or end of a token. This was partly due to tokenisation errors. In particular, Spacy tended to consider periods as part of an abbreviation instead of the end of a sentence. For example, it took the period after '*Co(II)OEP.*' as a part of an abbreviation rather than a sentence ending, which does not align with the annotated phrase '*Co(II)OEP*'. Likewise, words compounded with a dash or slash (e.g. '*solid-liquid*') were sometimes individually annotated as keyphrases, but not split by Spacy, or the other way around. There were also errors were annotators did not include all characters in the text span (e.g., '*ossil mass*' instead of '*fossil mass*', or unintentionally included extra characters (e.g. '*EBL and HSQ development, t*').

In order to estimate the impact of IOB conversion errors on the scores, we converted annotated keyphrases in Brat format to IOB format and then back to Brat format. We then used the eval.py script to compute the scores of the resulting 'predictions'. The number of misalignments and their impact on precision, recall and F-score are shown in Table 2. We conclude that the impact of conversion to IOB tags on F-score is relatively small: between 1 to 3 percent at maximum, assuming all predictions are correct.

Failed attempts We tried tuning the CRF hyperparameters using grid search (for run 1), optimising the micro-average F-score over the B and I tags. However, this criterion did not correspond well with the official scores reported by eval.py. In fact, CRFs with optimised hyper-parameters yielded official scores that were lower than for CRFs with default parameter setting. Optimising directly on the official scores is more expensive and complicated, because of the conversion of IOB tags to Brat annotation. However, doing so may improve performance.

Qualitative error analysis The analysis of errors has been conducted over a random sample of 10% of the documents from the test data under the best system (2). This analysis shows that almost half of the errors are words or phrases incorrectly tagged as keyphrases. The other half are due to either incorrect boundaries (19%), such as *ERP system* instead of *hybrid ERP system* in S0166361516300926; label (18%), e.g. *FIB instruments* as Material instead of Process in S0168583X14003929; or both incorrect boundaries and label (15%), e.g. *finding a group of optimized coefficients* in S0021999113002945 is automatically annotated as Process whereas *optimized coefficients* is Material in the test data.

Other types of errors are those in which the same phrase has been annotated with two different labels and only one of these is correct. For example, *SNR* (S096386951400070X) or *DP* (S0010938X15301268) are both Material and Process, but only the former exists in the gold standard data. This is especially frequent among acronyms.

It is worth mentioning that part of these errors are also due to errors already present on the annotated test data. For instance, *RH ceramics* in *value of the fracture toughness of RH ceramics* is clearly some kind of material, but it is unlabelled in the gold standard data.

Table 1: Results on dev and test data

System	Label	Dev			Test		
		Prec	Rec	F	Prec	Rec	F
System 1	Material	0.48	0.47	0.47	0.36	0.42	0.39
	Process	0.38	0.34	0.36	0.35	0.28	0.21
	Task	0.17	0.12	0.14	0.08	0.09	0.09
	Synonym-of	0.40	0.22	0.29	0.67	0.18	0.28
	Hyponym-of	0.29	0.08	0.13	0.05	0.03	0.04
	Micro Average	0.41	0.34	0.37	0.32	0.31	0.31
System 2	Material	0.54	0.40	0.46	0.41	0.40	**0.41**
	Process	0.44	0.33	0.38	0.39	0.29	**0.33**
	Task	0.18	0.16	0.17	0.10	0.12	**0.11**
	Synonym-of	0.41	0.27	0.32	0.65	0.21	0.32
	Hyponym-of	0.39	0.11	0.17	0.11	0.05	**0.07**
	Micro Average	0.45	0.32	0.37	**0.36**	0.31	**0.33**
System 3	Material	0.45	0.53	0.49	0.34	0.49	0.40
	Process	0.45	0.31	0.37	0.38	0.27	0.32
	Task	0.17	0.21	0.19	0.07	0.13	0.09
	Synonym-of	0.38	0.29	0.33	0.64	0.22	**0.33**
	Hyponym-of	0.26	0.11	0.16	0.05	0.05	0.05
	Micro Average	0.40	0.38	0.39	0.31	**0.34**	0.32

Table 2: IOB alignment errors and their impact

	#spans	#misalign	Prec	Rec	F-score
train	6721	138 (2.1%)	-0.01	-0.03	-0.02
dev	1154	16 (1.4%)	0.00	-0.02	-0.01
test	2051	47 (2.3%)	-0.01	-0.04	-0.03

Besides, this analysis shows that around more than three quarters of these errors are due to keyphrases incorrectly labelled as Material (43%) or Process (42%), whereas only 15% are Task. Interestingly, a similar proportion of keyphrases is observed in the training data: there is a considerably lower number of keyphrases labelled as Task (1132), than Process (2992) and Material (2608). For example, *nuclear fission reactors* in S0263822312000657 was labelled as Material but it is a Task in the gold standard data; *capture features in the solution* (S0021999113006955) was predicted as Task but it should be a Process; or *optimized coefficients* in S0021999113002945 was predicted as a Task but it is a Material.

Regarding coverage, 62 entities are not covered by System 2 at all. This amounts to 35% of the gold standard data. The distribution of errors is very similar to the one reported for precision, with 45% of the entities not covered being Material, 40% Process and 15% Task. For instance, in S0021999113006955 there are two instances of *true surface* that were ignored by the classifier. Interestingly, another mention of the same keyphrase in the same document was correctly annotated as Material. However, postprocessing of predictions to enforce consistent labelling in System 1 did not show any nett improvements.

References

Isabelle Augenstein, Mrinal Kanti Das, Sebastian Riedel, Lakshmi Nair Vikraman, and Andrew McCallum. 2017. SemEval 2017 Task 10: ScienceIE - Extracting Keyphrases and Relations from Scientific Publications. In *Proceedings of the International Workshop on Semantic Evaluation*. Association for Computational Linguistics, Vancouver, Canada.

Biswanath Barik and Erwin Marsi. 2017. NTNU-2 at SemEval-2017 Task 10: Identifying Synonym and Hyponym Relations among Keyphrases in Scientific Documents. In *Proceedings of the International Workshop on Semantic Evaluation*. Vancouver, Canada.

Matthew Honnibal and Mark Johnson. 2015. An improved non-monotonic transition system for dependency parsing. In *EMNLP*. Lisbon, Portugal, pages 1373–1378.

John Lafferty, Andrew McCallum, Fernando Pereira, et al. 2001. Conditional random fields: Probabilistic models for segmenting and labeling sequence data. In *Proceedings of the eighteenth international conference on machine learning, ICML*. volume 1, pages 282–289.

Andrea Moro, Alessandro Raganato, and Roberto Navigli. 2014. Entity linking meets word sense disambiguation: a unified approach. *TACL* 2:231–244.

Naoaki Okazaki. 2007. CRFsuite: a fast implementation of Conditional Random Fields (CRFs). http://www.chokkan.org/software/crfsuite/.

EELECTION at SemEval-2017 Task 10:
Ensemble of nEural Learners for kEyphrase ClassificaTION

Steffen Eger[†‡], Erik-Lân Do Dinh[†], Ilia Kuznetsov[†], Masoud Kiaeeha[†], Iryna Gurevych[†‡]
[†]Ubiquitous Knowledge Processing Lab (UKP-TUDA)
Department of Computer Science, Technische Universität Darmstadt
[‡]Ubiquitous Knowledge Processing Lab (UKP-DIPF)
German Institute for Educational Research and Educational Information
http://www.ukp.tu-darmstadt.de

Abstract

This paper describes our approach to the SemEval 2017 Task 10: "Extracting Keyphrases and Relations from Scientific Publications", specifically to Subtask (B): "Classification of identified keyphrases". We explored three different deep learning approaches: a character-level convolutional neural network (CNN), a stacked learner with an MLP meta-classifier, and an attention based Bi-LSTM. From these approaches, we created an ensemble of differently hyper-parameterized systems, achieving a micro-F_1-score of 0.63 on the test data. Our approach ranks 2nd (score of 1st placed system: 0.64) out of four according to this official score. However, we erroneously trained 2 out of 3 neural nets (the stacker and the CNN) on only roughly 15% of the full data, namely, the original development set. When trained on the full data (training+development), our ensemble has a micro-F_1-score of 0.69. Our code is available from https://github.com/UKPLab/semeval2017-scienceie.

1 Introduction

Although scientific experiments are often accompanied by vast amounts of structured data, full-text scientific publications still remain one of the main means for communicating academic knowledge. Given the dynamic nature of modern research and its ever-accelerating pace, it is crucial to automatically analyze new works in order to have a complete picture of advances in a given field.

Recently, some progress has been made in this direction for the fixed-domain use case[1]. However, creating a universal open-domain system still

remains a challenge due to significant domain differences between articles originating from different fields of research. The SemEval 2017 Task 10: ScienceIE (Augenstein et al., 2017) promotes the multi-domain use case, providing source articles from three domains: Computer Science, Material Sciences and Physics. The task consists of three subtasks, namely (A) identification of keyphrases, (B) classifying them into broad domain-independent classes and (C) inferring relations between the identified keyphrases.

For example, for the input sentence 'The thermodynamics of copper-zinc alloys (brass) was subject of numerous investigations' the following output would be expected:

(A) 1. The thermodynamics of copper-zinc alloys
    2. copper-zinc alloys
    3. brass

(B) 1. TASK
    2. MATERIAL
    3. MATERIAL

(C)   synonym(2,3)

Our submission focuses on (B) keyphrase classification given item boundaries. We avoid task-specific feature engineering, which would potentially render the system domain-dependent. Instead, we build an ensemble of several deep learning classifiers detailed in §3, whose inputs are word embeddings learned from general domains.

2 Task and Data

In the annotation scheme proposed by the task organizers, keyphrases denoting a scientific model, algorithm or process should be classified as *PROCESS* (P), which also comprises methods (e.g. 'backpropagation'), physical equipment (e.g. 'plasmatic nanosensors', 'electron microscope') and tools (e.g. 'MATLAB'). *TASK* (T) contains

---

[1] E.g. BioNLP: http://2016.bionlp-st.org/

Proceedings of the 11th International Workshop on Semantic Evaluations (SemEval-2017), pages 942–946,
Vancouver, Canada, August 3 - 4, 2017. ©2017 Association for Computational Linguistics

concrete research tasks (e.g. 'powder processing', 'dependency parsing') and research areas (e.g. 'machine learning'), while *MATERIAL* (M) includes physical materials (e.g. 'iron', 'nanotube'), and corpora or datasets (e.g. 'the CoNLL-2003 NER corpus').

The corpus for the shared task consisted of 500 journal articles retrieved from ScienceDirect[2], evenly distributed among Computer Science, Material Sciences and Physics domains. It was split into three segments of 350 (training), 50 (development), and 100 (test) documents. The corpus used in subtask (B) contains paragraphs of those articles, annotated with spans of keyphrases. Table 1 shows the distribution of the classes M, T, and P in the data. We note that class T is underrepresented and makes up less than 16% of all instances.

	Material	Process	Task
Train+Dev	40%	44%	16%
Test	44%	47%	9%

Table 1: Class distribution in the datasets.

Inter-annotator agreement for the dataset was published to be between 0.45 and 0.85 (Cohen's κ) (Augenstein et al., 2017). Reviewing similar annotation efforts (QasemiZadeh and Schumann, 2016) already shows that despite the seemingly simple annotation task, usually annotators do not reach high agreement neither on span of annotations nor the class assigned to each span[3].

3   Implemented Approaches

In this section, we describe the individual systems that form the basis of our experiments (see §4).

Our basic setup for all of our systems was as follows. For each keyphrase we extracted its **left context**, **right context** and the keyphrase itself (**center**). We represent each of the three contexts as the *concatenation* of their word tokens: to have fixed-size representations, we limit the left context to the ℓ previous tokens, the right context to the r following tokens and the center to the c initial tokens of the keyphrase. We consider ℓ, r and c as hyper-parameters of our modeling. If necessary, we pad up each respective context with 'empty' word tokens. We then map each token to a d-dimensional word embedding. The choices for

word embeddings are described below. To summarize, we frame our classification problem as a mapping f_θ (θ represents model parameters) from concatenated word embeddings to one of the three classes *MATERIAL*, *PROCESS*, and *TASK*:

$$f_\theta : \mathbb{R}^{\ell \cdot d} \times \mathbb{R}^{c \cdot d} \times \mathbb{R}^{r \cdot d} \rightarrow \{\mathrm{M}, \mathrm{P}, \mathrm{T}\}.$$

Next, we describe the embeddings that we used and subsequently the machine learning models f_θ.

Word Embeddings

We experimented with three kinds of word embeddings. We use the popular Glove embeddings (Pennington et al., 2014) (6B) of dimensions 50, 100, and 300, which largely capture semantic information. Further we employ the more syntactically oriented 300-dimensional embeddings of Levy and Goldberg (2014), as well as the 300-dimensional embeddings of Komninos and Manandhar (2016), which are trained to predict both dependency- and standard window-based context.

Deep Learning models

Our first model is a character-level convolutional neural network (**char-CNN**) illustrated in Figure 1. This model (A) considers each of the three contexts (left, center, right) independently, representing them by a 100-dimensional vector as follows. Each character is represented by a 1-hot vector, which is then mapped to a 32-dimensional

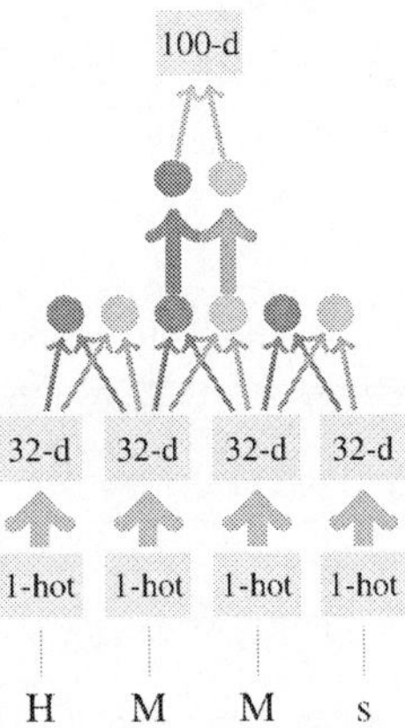

Figure 1: CNN. Each character is represented by a 1-hot vector, which is then mapped to a learned 32-d embedding vector. On these, m ($m = 2$ in the example) filters operate, which are combined to an m-dimensional vector via max-over-time-pooling. The output layer, with tanh activation, is 100-d and is fully connected with the m-dim layer that feeds into it. We represent the left context, right context, and center via the same illustrated CNN, and then concatenate the 100-d representations to a 300-d representation of the input.

---

[2] http://www.sciencedirect.com/
[3] F_1-scores ranging from 0.528 to 0.755 for span boundaries and from 0.471 to 0.635 for semantic categories.

embedding (not pre-trained, and updated during learning). Then m filters, each of size s, are applied on the embedding layer. Max-over-time pooling results in an m-dimensional layer which is fully connected with the 100-dimensional output layer, with tanh activation function. The 100-d representations of each context are then (B) concatenated, resulting in a 300-dimensional representation of the input. A final softmax layer predicts one of our three target classes. The hyper-parameters of this model—additional to ℓ, r, c mentioned above—are: number of filters m, filter size s, and a few others, such as the number of characters to consider in each context window.

Our second model, which operates on the token-level, is a "**stacked learner**". We take five *base classifiers* from scikit-learn (RandomForestClassifier with two different parameterizations; ExtraTreesClassifier with two different parameterizations; and XGBClassifier), and train them repeatedly on 90% of the training data, extracting their

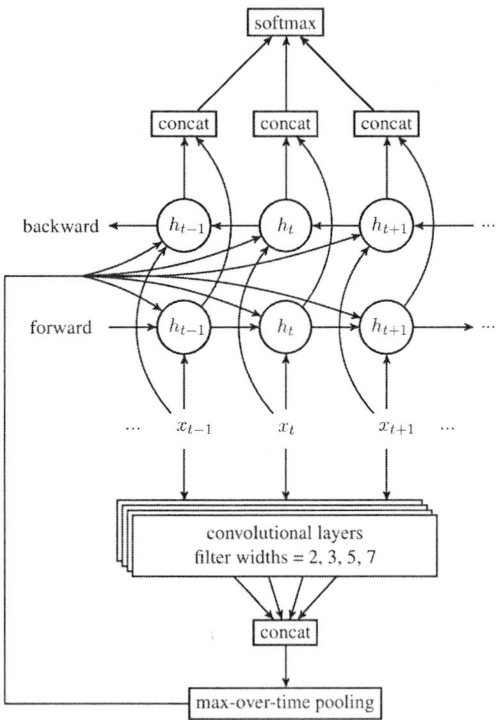

Figure 2: Bi-LSTM with attention. Pre-trained word embeddings x_t are fed to an ensemble of CNN layers with 4 different filter widths. For each timestep the outputs are concatenated and we employ max-over-time pooling. The resulting attention vector is supplied to the nodes in the forward and backward LSTM layers. The output of both LSTM layers is concatenated to a 128-dim vector, which is fed to the final softmax layer.

predictions on the remaining 10%. This process is iterated 10 times, in a cross-validation manner, so that we have a complete sample of predictions of the base classifiers on the training data. We then use a multi-layer perceptron (MLP) as a *meta-classifier* that is trained to combine the predictions of the base classifiers into a final output prediction. The MLP is trained for 100 epochs and the model with best performance on a 10% development set is chosen as the model to apply to unseen test data.

Our third model (Figure 2), also operating on the token level, is an attention based Bi-directional Long Short-Term Memory network (**AB-LSTM**)[4]. After loading pre-trained word embeddings, we apply 4 convolutional layers with filter sizes 2, 3, 5 and 7, followed by max-over-time-pooling. We concatenate the respective vectors to create an *attention vector*. The forward and backward LSTM layers (64-dimensional) are supplied with the pre-trained embeddings and the computed attention vector. Their output is concatenated and, after applying dropout of 0.5, is used by the final softmax layer to predict the label probabilities.

4 Submitted Systems

We set the c hyper-parameter to 4, and draw left and right context length hyper-parameters ℓ, r ($\ell = r$) from a discrete uniform distribution over the multi-set $\{1, 2, 2, 3, 3, 3, 4, 4, 4, 4, 5\}$.

Performance measure was micro-F_1 as computed by the task's evaluation script.[5] Table 2 shows average, maximum, and minimum performances of the systems we experimented with. We indicate the 'incorrect' systems (those trained on only the dev set) with a star. We tested 56 different CNNs—hyper-parameters randomly drawn from specific ranges; e.g., we draw the number of filters m from a normal distribution $\mathcal{N}(\mu = 250, \sigma = 50)$—90 different stackers, and 20 different AB-LSTMs. Our three submitted systems were simple majority votes of (1) the 90 stackers, (2) the 90 stackers and 56 CNNs, (3) the 90 stackers, 56 CNNs and 20 AB-LSTMs. Overall, majority voting is considerably better than the mean performances of each system.

---

[4] Code was adapted from https://github.com/codekansas/keras-language-modeling

[5] We report results without the "rel" flag, i.e., corresponding to the column "Overall" in Augenstein et al. (2017), Table 4. Setting "rel" leads to consistently higher results. E.g., with this flag, we have 72% micro-F_1 for our best ensemble (corresponding to column "B" in Augenstein et al. (2017), Table 4), rather than 69% as reported in our Table 2.

944

	Mean	Max	Min
CNN	58.32*/64.08	61*/65	54*/60
Stacker	61.57*/67.11	64*/68	59*/65
AB-LSTM	59.12	64	56
Majority	63*/69	63*/69	62*/68

Table 2: Micro-F_1 results in % for our systems.

For the stacker, the Komninos embeddings worked consistently best, with an average F_1-score of 63.83%. Levy embeddings were second (62.50), followed by Glove embeddings of size 50 (61%), size 300 (60.80) and size 100 (59.50). We assume this is due to the Komninos embeddings being 'richest' in nature, capturing both semantic and syntactic information. However, with more training data (corrected results), mean performances as a function of embedding type are closer: 67.77 (Komninos), 67.61 (Levy), 67.38 (Glove-300), 66.88 (Glove-50), 65.77 (Glove-100). The AB-LSTM could not capitalize as much on the syntactic information, and performed best with the Glove embeddings, size 100 (60.35%), and worst with the Levy embeddings (57.80).

The char-level CNN and the stacker performed individually considerably better than the AB-LSTM. However, including the AB-LSTM in the ensemble slightly increased the majority F_1-score on both the M and T class, as Table 3 shows.

Ensemble	M	P	T
(1) Stackers	76	71	46
(2) Stackers+CNNs	76	72	46
(3) Stackers+CNNs+AB-LSTMs	77	72	47

Table 3: F_1 results in % across different classes.

Error analysis: Table 4 details that *TASK* is often confused with *PROCESS*, and—though less often—vice versa, leading to drastically lower F_1-score than for the other two classes. This mismatch is because *PROCESS* and *TASK* can describe similar concepts, resulting in rather subtle differences. E.g., looking at various 'analysis' instances, we find that some are labeled as *PROCESS* and others as *TASK* in the gold data. This holds even for a few seemingly very similar keyphrases ('XRD analysis', 'FACS analysis'). The ensemble has trouble labeling this correctly, tagging 6 of 17 'analysis' instances wrongly. Beyond further suspicious labelings in the data (e.g.,

'nuclear fissions reactors' as Task), other cases could have been resolved by knowledge of syntax ('anionic *polymerization* of styrene' is a process, not a material) and/or POS tags, and by knowledge of common abbreviations such as 'PSD'.

We note that our submitted systems have the best F_1-score for the minority class *TASK* (45%*/47% vs. $\leq$28% for all other participants). Thus, our submission would have scored 1st using *macro-F_1* (60.66*/65.33 vs. $\leq$56.66), even in the erroneous setting of much less training data.

| | | Prediction | | |
		Material	Process	Task
Gold	Material	710	194	0
	Process	218	708	28
	Task	22	105	67

Table 4: Stackers+CNNs+AB-LSTMs confusion matrix.

5 Conclusion

We present an ensemble-based keyphrase classification system which has achieved close-to-the-best results in the ScienceIE Subtask (B) while using only a fraction of the available training data. With the full training data, our approach ranks 1st. To avoid using expert features has been one of our priorities, but we believe that incorporating additional task-neutral information beyond words and word order would benefit the system performance.

We also experimented with document embeddings, created from additionally crawled ScienceDirect[6] articles. Even though the stacker described in §3 acting as a document classifier obtained a reasonably high accuracy of ~87%, its predictions had little effect on the overall results.

Manual examination of system errors shows that using part-of-speech tags, syntactic relations and simple named entity recognition would very likely boost the performance of our systems.

Acknowledgments

This work has been supported by the Volkswagen Foundation, FAZIT, DIPF, KDSL, and the EU's Horizon 2020 research and innovation programme (H2020-EINFRA-2014-2) under grant agreement № 654021. It reflects only the authors' views and the EU is not liable for any use that may be made of the information contained therein.

---

[6] https://dev.elsevier.com/api_docs.html

References

Isabelle Augenstein, Mrinal Das, Sebastian Riedel, Lakshmi Vikraman, and Andrew McCallum. 2017. Semeval 2017 task 10: Scienceie - extracting keyphrases and relations from scientific publications. In *Proceedings of the 11th International Workshop on Semantic Evaluation (SemEval-2017)*. Association for Computational Linguistics, Vancouver, Canada, pages 544–553. http://www.aclweb.org/anthology/S17-2091.

Alexandros Komninos and Suresh Manandhar. 2016. Dependency Based Embeddings for Sentence Classification Tasks. In *Proceedings of NAACL-HLT '16*. ACL, San Diego, CA, USA, pages 1490–1500. http://www.aclweb.org/anthology/N16-1175.

Omer Levy and Yoav Goldberg. 2014. Dependency-Based Word Embeddings. In *Proceedings of ACL '14*. ACL, Baltimore, MD, USA, pages 302–308. http://aclweb.org/anthology/P/P14/P14-2050.pdf.

Jeffrey Pennington, Richard Socher, and Christopher D. Manning. 2014. Glove: Global Vectors for Word Representation. In *Proceedings of EMNLP '14*. ACL, Doha, Qatar, pages 1532–1543.

Behrang QasemiZadeh and Anne-Kathrin Schumann. 2016. The ACL RD-TEC 2.0: A Language Resource for Evaluating Term Extraction and Entity Recognition Methods. In *Proceedings of LREC '16*. ELRA, Portorož, Slovenia, pages 1862–1868.

LABDA at SemEval-2017 Task 10: Extracting Keyphrases from Scientific Publications by combining the BANNER tool and the UMLS Semantic Network

Isabel Segura-Bedmar, Cristóbal Colón-Ruiz, Paloma Martínez
Computer Science Department, Universidad Carlos III of Madrid
Avd. Universidad, 30, Leganés, 28911, Madrid, Spain
`isegura,ccolon,pmf@inf.uc3m.es`

Abstract

This paper describes the system presented by the LABDA group at SemEval 2017 Task 10 ScienceIE, specifically for the subtasks of identification and classification of keyphrases from scientific articles. For the task of identification, we use the BANNER tool, a named entity recognition system, which is based on conditional random fields (CRF) and has obtained successful results in the biomedical domain. To classify keyphrases, we study the UMLS semantic network and propose a possible linking between the keyphrase types and the UMLS semantic groups. Based on this semantic linking, we create a dictionary for each keyphrase type. Then, a feature indicating if a token is found in one of these dictionaries is incorporated to feature set used by the BANNER tool. The final results on the test dataset show that our system still needs to be improved, but the conditional random fields and, consequently, the BANNER system can be used as a first approximation to identify and classify keyphrases.

1 Introduction

In the era of big data, as it could not be otherwise, an enormous amount of scientific articles is available. Although during the last few years search engines have provided significant improvements in information access, researches still have to spend much time exploring the huge number of articles published in their research fields. This laborious task could be reduced if search engines were able to answer common questions such as: *which studies have dealt with a specific TASK?, which studies have explored a PROCESS? or which studies have employed such MATERIAL?*. The automatic detection and classification of keyphrases (which describe tasks, processes and materials) as well as the extraction of their relations between them from scientific articles can support to find the answers to the previous questions. This task is very important, but has hardly been explored at the present time (Augenstein and Sgaard, 2017).

The ScienceIE task at SemEval 2017 (Augenstein et al., 2017) aims the automatic extraction of keyphrases and their relations from scientific publications. The task consists of three subtasks: (1) the subtask A is focused on the identification of the keyphrases in a given article; (2) the subtask B is focused on the classification of keyphrases by one of the following types: MATERIAL, TASK, and PROCESS; and (3) the subtask C deals with the classification of the relationships between keyphrases by one of the following types: HYPONYM-OF, SYNONYM-OF, and NONE. For the evaluation of the task, the organizers have defined three different scenarios, which the participating teams can choose to submit their outputs. For example, in scenario 1, the test dataset consists of plain texts without any annotation and participants can submit their outputs for all subtasks; for the scenario 2, the texts in the test dataset also include the annotation of keyphrases with their offsets in texts, but without providing their types. In this case, the teams can only submit their outputs to the subtask B and C. Finally, in scenario 3, which is only valid for the subtask C, test documents contain the keyphrases annotated with their offsets and their types.

In this paper, we describe the participation of the group LABDA in the subtasks A and B. Our approach for identifying and classifying keyphrases from scientific articles combines the use of the BANNER tool (Leaman et al.,

947

2008) and the UMLS semantic network (McCray, 1989)[1]. The paper is organized as follows. Section 2 describes our approach. Experiments, results, and discussion are described in Section 3. Finally, the paper is concluded and future work is proposed in Section 4.

2 Combining the BANNER tool and UMLS to identify and classify keyphrases

This section describes the system proposed by the LABDA group for participation for subtask A and B. BANNER is a named entity recognition (NER) system, which is based on conditional random fields (CRF). CRF is a class of statistical modelling method for sequence labelling and makes use of a rich set of lexical and syntactic features. Based on successful results provided by this approach for NER in the biomedical domain (Krallinger et al., 2015; Wei et al., 2015; Segura-Bedmar et al., 2015), in this paper, we explore the recognition of keyphrases as a sequence labeling problem by using the BANNER tool. This tool is designed to maximize domain independence and allows to recognize named entities from different domains.

BANNER has a 3-stage pipeline, whose input is a sentence. The first process splits the sentence into tokens. Then, each token is represented by a set of features: lemma, prefixes and suffixes of up to 2, 3 and 4 characters, bigrams and trigrams, as well as a series of regular expressions to normalize numeric values. Moreover, the word-class feature also normalizes the possible forms of a token based on their letters by converting upper-case letters to 'A', lower-case ones to 'a' and numbers to '0'.

We also incorporate a new feature that indicates if the token is found in a given dictionary. In particular, for each type of keyphrase (TASK, MATERIAL, PROCESS), we define a dictionary based on the semantic groups of UMLS. To create these dictionaries, we studied in depth the UMLS semantic network and proposed the links between the keyphrase types and the UMLS semantic groups shown in Table 1. Then, we traverse the UMLS methatesaurus and their terms are stored in their corresponding dictionary based on the classification shown in Table 1. The UMLS semantic groups as well as their semantic types can

be found at https://semanticnetwork.nlm.nih.gov/. Thus, if a token is found in one of the three dictionaries, the feature is set to the name of the dictionary.

To label tokens, we try with different IOB tagging schemas (O=outside, B=beginning of an entity, I=inside of an entity, E=end of an entity, W=a single entity). Finally, a CRF model is trained using the features for each token from the training data. We consider the three types of keyphrases as the three possible types of entities to be recognized by BANNER. Thus, our approach performs both subtasks, identification and classification, as one only process. We train a single model for the three types.

3 Evaluation

As said before, we have only participated in the subtasks A (identification) and B (classification). That is, our experiments are performed on scenarios 1 and 2. Our approach for identification is evaluated on the scenario 1, where the test documents do not contain any annotation. Our approach for classification is evaluated on the scenario 2, where texts include the offsets of the keyphrases, but not their types. Actually, as said above, we use the same system to identify and classify keyphrases.

For evaluating the classification task on the scenario 2, we take the list of keyphrase mentions (without their types) provided as input of this scenario and compare it with the output of the BANNER tool, which was trained to classify the three types of keyphrases: MATERIAL, TASK and PROCESS. If the mention was classified as a keyphrase by BANNER, we return the type provided by BANNER. If the mention was classified with the tag O by BANNER (that is, outside token), our system was not be able to classify it. However, if it is actually a keyphrase (because it is in the input of the scenario 2), we decide to classify it with the most frequent type (PROCESS). The keyphrases classified by BANNER, but not found in the input of the scenario 2, are ignored.

Table 2 shows the results on the development set for each keyphrase type: MATERIAL, TASK and PROCESS. We tried with different variations of the IOB schema and with different combinations of the dictionaries defined from the UMLS semantic network.

The best results are achieved for the type MATERIAL with an F1 of 35.33%, followed by PRO-

---

[1] https://semanticnetwork.nlm.nih.gov/

Type	UMLS groups
MATERIAL	ANAT:Anatomy, CHEM:Chemicals and Drugs, GENE:Genes and Molecular sequences, LIVB:Living beings, OBJC:Objects, CONC:Concepts and Ideas
PROCESS	ACTI:Activities and Behaviors, DISO(T050:Experimental Model of Disease), OCCU:Occupations, PROC:Procedures, CONC:Concepts and Ideas (T185:Classification, T089:Regulation or Law, T170:Intellectual product, T171:Language, T080:Qualitative Concept, T081:Quantitative Concept, T079:Temporal Concept)
TASK	DISO:disorders(all concepts except those classified with the semantic type T050), PHEN:phenomena, PHYS:physology

Table 1: Linking between keyphrase types and UMLS semantic groups.

Type	IOB schema	dictionaries	Precision(%)	Recall(%)	F-Measure(%)
MATERIAL	IO	NO	59.45	23.48	33.67
	IO	Material	**59.74**	**25.08**	**35.33**
	IOB	Material	61.29	23.66	34.14
	IOBEW	Material	62.73	23.66	34.36
TASK	IO	NO	**18.51**	**7.29**	**10.47**
	IO	Task	16.12	7.29	10.05
	IOB	Task	17.02	5.83	8.69
	IOBEW	Task	19.51	5.83	8.98
PROCESS	IO	NO	39.93	25.82	**31.36**
	IO	Process	40.00	25.60	31.22
	IOB	Process	41.76	24.06	30.53
	IOBEW	Process	40.87	22.73	29.21

Table 2: Results on the development set for each type of keyphrase (scenario 1).

CESS with a 31.36% of F1. The system achieves the worst results for TASK (F1=10.47%). We study the list of keyphrases in the training dataset in order to know how many words form each keyphrase type. We observe that 41% of MATE-RIALS are formed by a single word, 32% of them are formed by two words, and the rest of MA-TERIALS (27%) are phrases with more than two words. Therefore, we can claim that a high percent of MATERIALS could be named entities. For the type of PROCESS, more than half are formed by one or two words (that is, they can be named entities), while the rest (48%) are phrases with more than two words. However, many of TASKS (74%) have three or more words. Thus, while CRF models have succeeded in the task of NER from the biomedical texts, the sequence labelling approach may not be the most appropriate for identifying keyphrases when they are formed by three or more words. Another possible cause of low results for TASK could be that the semantic linking between TASK and the UMLS semantic groups, which we defined for this work, is not suitable for the task.

Regarding the different settings, the IO schema seems to achieve the best results for the three keyphrase types. Only the use of the dictionary for MATERIALS achieves a significant improvement, while the rest of dictionaries do not seem to improve the performance. We proposed the three submitted runs based on the results on the development set.

The final results of the task show that our system achieved an F1 of 0.33 for the subtask A and 0.23 for the subtask B, when the system is evaluated on the scenario 1 (without annotations). As expected, our results are better for the subtask B when it is classified on the scenario 2 (the offsets of the keyphrases are provided for the participants), achieving an F1 of 0.51.

4 Conclusion

In this paper, we study if a sequence labelling approach is appropriate for the tasks of identification and classification of keyphrases from scientific publications. In particular, we use the BANNER tool, based on a CRF model and a rich set of lexical features. To classify the keyphrases, we study the UMLS semantic network and propose a linking between the keyphrases types and the UMLS semantic groups. Then, we extend the BANNER tool by incorporating a new feature that indicates if the token is found in one of the three dictionaries built from UMLS. Results are modest yet suggest promise for MATERIAL and PROCESS. As a future work, we plan to explore other dictionaries for the areas of computer science, physics and material science. Moreover, we plan to study an approach based on deep learning methods. Because keyphrases are usually longer phrases than named entities, we would like to create a phrase embedding model capable of measuring the similarity between keyphrases. This approach could be a solution to deal with nested keyphrases.

Acknowledgments

This work was supported by the Research Program of the Ministry of Economy and Competitiveness - Government of Spain, (eGovernAbility-Access project TIN2014-52665-C2-2-R).

References

Isabelle Augenstein, Mrinal Kanti Das, Sebastian Riedel, Lakshmi Nair Vikraman, and Andrew McCallum. 2017. SemEval 2017 Task 10: ScienceIE - Extracting Keyphrases and Relations from Scientific Publications. In *Proceedings of the International Workshop on Semantic Evaluation*. Association for Computational Linguistics, Vancouver, Canada.

Isabelle Augenstein and Anders Sgaard. 2017. Multi-Task Learning of Keyphrase Boundary Classification. In *Proceedings of the 55th Annual Meeting of the Association for Computational Linguistics*. Association for Computational Linguistics, Vancouver, Canada.

Martin Krallinger, Florian Leitner, Obdulia Rabal, Miguel Vazquez, Julen Oyarzabal, and Alfonso Valencia. 2015. Chemdner: The drugs and chemical names extraction challenge. *Journal of cheminformatics* 7(1):S1.

Robert Leaman, Graciela Gonzalez, et al. 2008. Banner: an executable survey of advances in biomedical named entity recognition. In *Pacific symposium on biocomputing*. volume 13, pages 652–663.

Alexa T McCray. 1989. The umls semantic network. In *Proceedings of the Annual Symposium on Computer Application in Medical Care.*. American Medical Informatics Association, pages 503–507.

Isabel Segura-Bedmar, Víctor Suárez-Paniagua, and Paloma Martínez. 2015. Combining conditional random fields and word embeddings for the chemdner-patents task. In *Proceedings of the fifth BioCreative challenge evaluation workshop, Sevilla, Spain*. pages 90–93.

Chih-Hsuan Wei, Yifan Peng, Robert Leaman, Allan Peter Davis, Carolyn J Mattingly, Jiao Li, Thomas C Wiegers, and Zhiyong Lu. 2015. Overview of the biocreative v chemical disease relation (cdr) task. In *Proceedings of the fifth BioCreative challenge evaluation workshop*. pages 154–166.

The NTNU System at SemEval-2017 Task 10:
Extracting Keyphrases and Relations from Scientific Publications
Using Multiple Conditional Random Fields

Lung-Hao Lee[1], Kuei-Ching Lee[2], Yuen-Hsien Tseng[1]
[1]Graduate Institute of Library and Information Studies, National Taiwan Normal University
[2]China Development Lab, IBM
[1]No. 162, Sec. 1, Heping East Road, Taipei 10610, Taiwan
[2]No. 13, Sanchong Road, Taipei 11501, Taiwan
`lhlee@ntnu.edu.tw, jklee@tw.ibm.com, samtseng@ntnu.edu.tw`

Abstract

This study describes the design of the NTNU system for the ScienceIE task at the SemEval 2017 workshop. We use self-defined feature templates and multiple conditional random fields with extracted features to identify keyphrases along with categorized labels and their relations from scientific publications. A total of 16 teams participated in evaluation scenario 1 (subtasks A, B, and C), with only 7 teams competing in all subtasks. Our best micro-averaging F1 across the three subtasks is 0.23, ranking in the middle among all 16 submissions.

1 Introduction

Keyphrases are usually regarded as phrases that capture the main topics mentioned in a given text. Automatically extracting keyphrases and determining their relations from scientific articles has various applications, such as recommending articles to readers, matching reviewers to submissions, facilitating the exploration of huge document collections, and so on. An adapted nominal group chunker and a supervised ranking method based on support vector machines have previously been used to extract keyphrase candidates (Eichler and Neumann, 2010). The conditional random field based keyphrase extraction method has been presented (Bhaskar et al., 2012). A naïve approach has been proposed to investigate characteristics of keyphrases with section information from well-structured scientific articles (Park et al., 2010). Features broadly used for the

supervised approaches in scientific articles have been assessed in the compilation of a comprehensive feature list (Kim and Kan, 2009). Maximal sequences and page ranking have been combined to discover latent keyphrases within scientific articles (Ortiz et al., 2010). Noun phrases containing multiple modifiers have been extracted from earth science publications and generalized by matching tree patterns to the syntax trees of the sources texts (Marsi and Öztürk, 2015). Keyphrase boundary classification has been regarded as a multi-task learning problem using deep recurrent neural network (Augenstein and Søgaard, 2017).

The ScienceIE task seeks solutions to automatically identify keyphrases within scientific publications, label them, and determine their relationships. Specifically, the ScienceIE task contains three subtasks: (A) *Identification of keyphrases*: to identify all the keyphrases within a given scientific publication; (B) *Classification of identified keyphrases*: to label each keyphrase as Process, Task, or Material; (C) *Extraction of relationships between two identified keyphrases*: to label keyphrases as Hyponym-of or Synonym-of.

The ScienceIE task presents three evaluation scenarios. In Scenario 1, only plain text is given for subtasks A, B, and C; in Scenario 2, plain text with manually annotated keyphrase boundaries are given for subtasks B and C; and in Scenario 3, plain text with manually annotated keyphrases and their types are given for subtask C. System output is matched against a gold standard to measure system performance. The micro-averaging precision, recall, and F1 across the subtask(s) are used in the task. Each participating team can submit at most

Proceedings of the 11th International Workshop on Semantic Evaluations (SemEval-2017), pages 951–955,
Vancouver, Canada, August 3 - 4, 2017. ©2017 Association for Computational Linguistics

three results and the best result for each evaluation scenario is taken as the performance of the participating team.

This article describes the NTNU (National Taiwan Normal University) system for the ScienceIE task at the SemEval 2017 workshop. Our solution uses multiple conditional random fields at the sentence level. Each sentence is parsed to obtain features, including words, lemmas, part-of-speech tags, and syntactic phrases. CRFs are then trained to learn sequential patterns using the datasets provided by task organizers. We participated in the evaluation scenario 1 with three subtasks. Our best micro-averaging F1 of 0.23 ranked in the middle of all 16 submissions.

The rest of this paper is organized as follows. Section 2 describes the details of the NTNU system for the ScienceIE task. Section 3 presents the evaluation results and performance comparisons. Section 4 discusses some findings. Conclusions are finally drawn in Section 5.

2 The NTNU System

Our proposed approach uses the Conditional Random Field (CRF) technique (Lafferty et al., 2001), a type of discriminative probabilistic graph model, by learning linguistically motivated features to extract the keyphrases from scientific articles and identify their relations. The linear chain CRF is empirically effective for predicting the sequence of labels given a sequence input. A word in a sentence is regarded as a state in our CRF. Given an observation and its adjacent states in terms of the distinguished features, the probability of reaching a state is determined based on the Stochastic Gradient Descent. In the testing phase, the proposed CRF reports the sequence of categories with the largest probability as the identified result.

The following four features are used for training the CRF model with the Stanford CoreNLP toolkit (Manning et al., 2014).

- *Word*: the original words in the sentence of a scientific article are directly used without any revision.

- *Lemma*: this is to reduce inflectional forms and derivationally related forms to determine the lemma of a word in terms of its intended meaning

- *Part-of-Speech*: noun, verb, adjective, adverb, pronoun, etc.

Word	Lemma	POS Tag	Syntactic Phrase
This	this	DT	S-NP
paper	paper	NN	S-NP
addresses	address	VBZ	x
the	the	DT	NP-NP
tasks	task	NNS	NP-NP
of	of	IN	x
named	name	VBN	NP-NP
entity	entity	NN	NP-NP
recognition	recognition	NN	NP-NP
(	-lrb-	-LRB-	x
NER	ner	NN	PRN-NP
)	-rrb-	-RRB-	x
.	.	.	x

Table 1: An example sentence with features.

Token	Task	Pro.	Mat.	Syn.	Hyp.
This	O	O	O	O	O
paper	O	O	O	O	O
addresses	O	O	O	O	O
the	O	O	O	O	O
tasks	O				
of	O	O	O	O	O
named	Task	O	O	Syn.	O
entity	Task	O	O	Syn.	O
recognition	Task	O	O	Syn.	O
(	O	O	O	O	O
NER	Task	O	O	Syn.	O
)	O	O	O	O	O
.	O	O	O	O	O

Table 2: An example sentence with encoding.

- *Syntactic Phrase*: a phrasal category which is a type of syntactic unit in the grammar structure. Noun phrases are usually regarded as keyphrases in scientific texts. Hence, we only adopt noun phrases and their upper phrasal category as features.

Table 1 shows an example sentence with its corresponding features. Each row denotes a token in the sequence. In addition to words, the remaining three features (i.e., lemmas, part-of-speech tags, and syntactically phrasal tags) are provided by the Stanford CoreNLP toolkit.

Table 2 shows the same example sentence with encoding for training multiple CRF models. We use the simplest IO encoding, which tags each token as either being in a particular type of keyphrase X or in no keyphrase (denoted as "O").

We regard the relations Synonym-of and Hyponym-of as individual types in this sequential labeling problem. The one-vs.-rest strategy, which involves training a single classifier per class, is adopted using class samples as positive instances and all the other samples as negatives. In total, we have five corresponding CRF models for each type (i.e., Task, Process, Material, Synonym-of, and Hyponym-of).

During the testing phase, all trained CRF models are parallel to label one of types. The tags predicting by both Synonym-of and Hyponym-of CRF models are reliable dependently on the other three models, because pairs of keyphrase should be identified first for relations. Hence, we check the pairs of keyphrases to keep those are identified by Task, Process and Material CRF models. Finally, we integrate all identified results as our system outputs without handling any conflicts.

3   Evaluation

3.1   Data

The datasets for the ScienceIE task were provided by task organizers (Augenstein et al., 2017). The collected corpus consisted of journal articles from ScienceDirect open access publications evenly distributed among Computer Science, Material Science and Physics. The training, development, and test datasets were comprised of sampled paragraphs, of which 350 were used for training data, 50 for development, and 100 for testing. These datasets were made available to participants without copyright restrictions.

No external resources were used to supplement the datasets. To pre/post-process the datasets, we transformed alphabet-based start/end counts into word-based positions.

3.2   Implementation

The CRF++ toolkit was used for system implementation. CRF++ is an open source implementation of conditional random fields for segmenting or labeling sequential data, and is available at https://taku910.github.io/crfpp/

Supplementary Material in the Appendix shows feature templates used in our implemented system. Each line denotes one template, in which the first characters "U" and "B" respectively represent unigram and bigram features. In each template, a special macro %[row, col] is used to specify a token in the input data, in which row specifies the relative position from the current focus token and col specifies the absolute position of the column.

The encoding scheme we used was one-hot. We had 5 columns, where the first four ones respectively denoted features, *i.e.*, Word, Lemma, Part-of-Speech and Syntactic Phrases, and the last was a given type, *e.g.*, Process or not, for training a specific CRF model to label a given type. In the testing phase, the same template file was used and the last column was an estimated type predicting by the trained CRF model.

3.3   Metrics

The traditional metrics precision, recall, and F1-score were computed to measure system performance for each subtask. The micro-averaging strategy was then used to obtain overall score across subtask(s).

3.4   Results

Table 3 shows our results for each defined type. "Task" for subtask B and "Hyponym-of" for subtask C clearly performed worse than other three types.

Table 4 shows our results for each subtask. Comparing subtask C with subtasks A and B shows the former is relative more difficult.

3.5   Comparisons

Of the total 16 submissions, 9 teams did not participate in subtask C. We participated in all subtasks, achieving a micro-average F1 of 0.23, thus ranked 9th of the 16 submissions.

Type	Precision	Recall	F1
Task	0.17	0.05	0.08
Process	0.44	0.17	0.25
Material	0.47	0.19	0.27
Synonym-of	0.73	0.07	0.13
Hyponym-of	1.00	0.01	0.02

Table 3: Our results for each type.

Type	Precision	Recall	F1
Subtask A only	0.53	0.21	0.30
Subtask A+B only	0.43	0.17	0.24
Subtask C only	0.75	0.04	0.08
Subtask A+B+C	0.44	0.16	0.23

Table 4: Our results for each subtask.

4 Discussion

For this task, we only use multiple CRF models with four defined features. In addition to the Stanford CoreNLP toolkit for extracting features, we do not use any other methods such as the NER tool. Our error analysis reflects that the NER may be useful to improve the performance of Task keyphrase identification. It is also difficult to extract the Hyponym-of relation due to the limitation of long distance using existing features templates.

During the development phrase, we attempted to identify the relations between extracted phrases using manually crafted rules. Our multiple CRF models with the help of rules improved the performance on the development set, but performed worse on the testing set. Hence, we do not adopt rules in the system module. Our observations suggest that human-crafted rules do not perform well due to the challenge of coverage.

5 Conclusions

This study describes the NTNU system in the ScienceIE task, including system design, implementation and evaluation. This is our first exploration of this research topic. Future work will explore other features to further improve performance.

Acknowledgments

This study was partially supported by the Ministry of Science and Technology, under the grant MOST 105-2221-E-003-020-MY2 and the "Aim for the Top University Project" and "Center of Learning Technology for Chinese" of National Taiwan Normal University, sponsored by the Ministry of Education, Taiwan.

References

Isabelle Augenstein, and Anders Søgaard. 2017. Multi-task learning of keyphrase boundary classification. In *Proceedings of ACL 2017, the 55th Annual Meeting of the Association for Computational Linguistics*. Association for Computational Linguistics.

Isabelle Augenstein, Mrinal Kanti Das, Sebastian Riedel, Lakshmi Nair Vikraman, and Andrew McCallum. 2017. SemEval 2017 task 10: ScienceIE – Extracting keyphrases and relations from scientific publications. In *Proceedings of SemEval 2017, the 11th International Workshop on Semantic Evaluation*. Association for Computational Linguistics.

Pinaki Bhaskar, Kishorjit Nongmeikapam, and Sivaji Bandyopadhyay. 2012. Keyphrase extraction in scientific articles: a supervised approach. In *Proceedings of COLING 2012, the 24th International Conference on Computational Linguistics: Demonstration Papers*. IIT Bombay and Association for Computational Linguistics, pages 17-24. http://aclweb.org/anthology/C12-3003

Kathrin Eichler, and Günter Neumann. 2010. DKFI KeyWE: ranking keyphrases extracted from scientific articles. In *Proceedings of SemEval 2010, the 5th International Workshop on Semantic Evaluation*. Association for Computational Linguistics, pages 150-153. http://aclweb.org/anthology/S10-1031

Su Nam Kim, and Min-Yen Kan. 2009. Re-examining automatic keyphrase extraction approaches in scientific articles. In *Proceedings of MWE 2009, the 5th Workshop on Multiword Expressions: Identification, Interpretation, Disambiguation and Applications*. Association for Computational Linguistics, pages 9-16. http://aclweb.org/anthology/W09-2902

John D. Lafferty, Andrew McCallum, and Fernando C. N. Pereira. 2001. Conditional Random Fields: probabilistic models for segmenting and labeling sequence data. In *Proceedings of ICML 2001, the 18th International Conference on Machine Learning*. Morgan Kaufmann Publishers, pages 282-289. http://dl.acm.org/citation.cfm?id=655813

Christopher Manning, Mihai Surdeanu, John Bauer, Jenny Finkel, Steven Bethard, and David McClosky. 2014. The Stanford CoreNLP natural language processing toolkit. In *Proceedings of ACL 2014, the 52nd Annual Meeting of the Association for Computational Linguistics: System Demonstrations*. Association for Computational Linguistics, pages 55-60. http://aclweb.org/anthology/P14-5010

Erwin Marsi, and Pinar Öztürk. 2015. Extraction and generalization of variables from scientific publications. In *Proceedings of EMNLP 2015, the 2015 conference on Empirical Methods in Natural Language Processing*. Association for Computational Linguistics, pages 505-511. http://aclweb.org/anthology/D15-1057

Roberto Ortiz, David Pinto, Mireya Tovar, and Héctor Jiménez-Salazar. 2010. BUAP: an unsupervised approach to automatic keyphrase extraction from scientific articles. In *Proceedings of SemEval 2010, the 5th International Workshop on Semantic Evaluation*. Association for Computational Linguistics, pages 174-177. http://aclweb.org/anthology/S10-1037

Jungyeul Park, Jong Gun Lee, and Béatrice Daille. 2010. UNPMC: native approach to extract keyphrases from scientific articles. In *Proceedings*

of SemEval 2010, the 5th International Workshop
on Semantic Evaluation. Association for Computational Linguistics, pages 178-181.
http://aclweb.org/anthology/S10-1038

A Supplementary Material

The feature templates used for training CRF models are shown as follows.

#Unigram
U01:%x[-2,0]
U02:%x[-1,0]
U03:%x[0,0]
U04:%x[1,0]
U05:%x[2,0]
U06:%x[-2,0]/%x[-1,0]
U07:%x[-1,0]/%x[0,0]
U08:%x[0,0]/%x[1,0]
U09:%x[1,0]/%x[2,0]
U11:%x[-2,1]
U12:%x[-1,1]
U13:%x[0,1]
U14:%x[1,1]
U15:%x[2,1]
U16:%x[-2,1]/%x[-1,1]
U17:%x[-1,1]/%x[0,1]
U18:%x[0,1]/%x[1,1]
U19:%x[1,1]/%x[2,1]
U21:%x[-2,2]
U22:%x[-1,2]
U23:%x[0,2]
U24:%x[1,2]
U25:%x[2,2]
U26:%x[-2,2]/%x[-1,2]
U27:%x[-1,2]/%x[0,2]
U28:%x[0,2]/%x[1,2]
U29:%x[1,2]/%x[2,2]
U31:%x[-2,3]
U32:%x[-1,3]
U33:%x[0,3]
U34:%x[1,3]
U35:%x[2,3]
U36:%x[-2,3]/%x[-1,3]
U37:%x[-1,3]/%x[0,3]
U38:%x[0,3]/%x[1,3]
U39:%x[1,3]/%x[2,3]
#Bigram
B

MayoNLP at SemEval 2017 Task 10: Word Embedding Distance Pattern for Keyphrase Classification in Scientific Publications

Sijia Liu[1,2], **Feichen Shen**[1], **Vipin Chaudhary**[2], and **Hongfang Liu**[1]

[1]Department of Health Science Research, Mayo Clinic, USA
{liu.sijia,shen.feichen,liu.hongfang}@mayo.edu
[2]Department of Computer Science and Engineering, SUNY at Buffalo, USA
vipin@buffalo.edu

Abstract

In this paper, we present MayoNLP's results from the participation in the ScienceIE share task at SemEval 2017. We focused on the keyphrase classification task (Subtask B). We explored semantic similarities and patterns of keyphrases in scientific publications using pre-trained word embedding models. Word Embedding Distance Pattern, which uses the head noun word embedding to generate distance patterns based on labeled keyphrases, is proposed as an incremental feature set to enhance the conventional Named Entity Recognition feature sets. Support vector machine is used as the supervised classifier for keyphrase classification. Our system achieved an overall F1 score of 0.67 for keyphrase classification and 0.64 for keyphrase classification and relation detection.

1 Introduction

In this paper, we present details of our participation in the SemEval 2017 Task 10, ScienceIE (Augenstein et al., 2017). Named Entity Recognition (NER) is one of the major challenges in Natural Language Processing (NLP) and text mining. The interesting entity types in NER tasks vary from communities and corpora. In general, NLP community mainly focused on the identification of proper nouns or noun phrases, e.g., locations, names and organizations in news corpora (Nadeau and Sekine, 2007). In contrast, biomedical community is more interested in finding biomedical or clinical terminologies (Leaman and Gonzalez, 2008; Tsuruoka and Tsujii, 2005) in biomedical texts and scientific literatures. There are several machine learning based methods used in biomedical NER, which include Support Vector Machine (SVM) (Lee et al., 2004), Hidden Markov Model (HMM) (Zhou and Su, 2004) and Conditional Random Field (CRF) (Tsai et al., 2006).

Semantic word embedding (Mikolov et al., 2013) is designed to capture different degrees of similarity between words using a vectorized representation, which preserves semantic and syntactic relationships. Word embeddings and word embedding based features have drawn increasing attention for classification tasks (Ma et al., 2015) and similarity prediction tasks (Afzal et al., 2016).

We leveraged pre-trained word embeddings to obtain head noun pattern features, and combined several other NER feature sets to improve the keyphrase classification performance. Although our team participated in Scenario 2 (keyphrase classification and relation detection), our efforts were focused on keyphrase classification task (Subtask B). For the relation detection problem (Subtask C), we implemented a straightforward rule-based system to detect synonyms and hyponyms given annotated keyphrases.

The rest of the paper is organized as follows. Section 2 briefly introduces the corpus used in this task. Section 3 discusses the methods proposed in our NER system. Section 4 addresses the experimental results in the development set, our submitted runs and official evaluation results. Finally, Section 5 concludes the paper with possible extensions for future work.

2 Materials

The corpus provided by the ScienceIE organizers consisted of 500 introductory paragraphs from ScienceDirect journal articles in Computer Science, Material Sciences and Physics. The corpus

956

Proceedings of the 11th International Workshop on Semantic Evaluations (SemEval-2017), pages 956–960,
Vancouver, Canada, August 3 - 4, 2017. ©2017 Association for Computational Linguistics

was divided into training, development and test sets, which contained 350, 50 and 100 documents, respectively. It is the first publicly available corpus with annotations focused on the research topics and goals of general domain scientific literature. The annotated keyphrases were relatively longer than other annotated corpora, which makes the boundary detection and classification task very challenging. More details of the corpus can be found in (Augenstein et al., 2017).

3 Methods

3.1 Preprocessing

To facilitate feature extraction for supervised classification, all plain text sentences and annotations were pre-processed by NLTK[1] for tokenizing, Part-of-Speech (POS) tagging and sentence detection.

3.2 Head Noun Extraction

Intuitively, the head noun of a keyphrase provides important information of its semantic category (Li, 2010). For example, in the phrase *"homonuclear chains of tangent Mie spherical CG segments"* from the ScienceIE 2017 corpus, the noun *"chains"* determines the phrase is from the category "Material". In another example, the category of the phrase *"applications of methodology of research"* is determined by the head noun *"application"*, which is an instance of "Task". Extracting the head noun can help eliminate ambiguous contexts while preserving the semantic information for the classification step. Therefore, we used the extracted head noun features, rather than the features from whole phrase, to determine the semantic category.

A shallow parsing approach is applied to extract the head nouns from given phrases. We removed the part at and after the preposition token "of", "with", "for" and "on", and kept only the features from the head noun for the feature extraction step. In the above examples, we extracted the head noun *"chains"* and *"applications"*.

3.3 Feature Set

Given a sentence and a head noun token w_i, we adopted several commonly used feature sets as the input of supervised classifiers for the baseline system.

____

[1] http://www.nltk.org/

Lexical features The lower case of tokens in ± 2 window.

Orthographic features The set of case, character and symbolic features of given token. Orthographic features are all binary features: if the token contains only upper case letters, if only the first letter is in upper case, if the token contains only alphabetic characters, if the token contains numbers, and if the token starts with alphabetic characters and ends with numbers.

Part-Of-Speech features The Part-Of-Speech (POS) tags for the tokens in ± 2 window.

Lemma features Lemmatized word of w_i and its verb form from WordNet. For example, for the token *"derivations"*, the lemmatized word is *"derivation"* and the verb form is *"derive"*.

3.4 Word Embedding Distance Pattern

The extraction of head nouns in keyphrases enables utilizing word embedding information as features in the keyphrase classification task.

To improve the performance using baseline NER features described above, we proposed Word Embedding Distance Pattern (WEDP). It is based on the assumption that the differences among the head nouns in each semantic category should follow similar patterns in semantic word vector space. We would like to validate and obtain the patterns in this keyphrase classification task.

We selected 10 most frequent head nouns from each category in the training corpus. After excluding the duplications, we obtained the following list of keywords $M=\{$*model, particle, data, system, film, problem, algorithm, function, effect, equation, reaction, method, surface, alloy, layer, structure*$\}$. We also added the category names (*task, material, process*) into M.

Given a token w, the word embedding distance to each of the k-th word-embedding above is calculated by

$$d_k(w) = dist(w2v(w), w2v(M_k)), \quad (1)$$

where $k = 1, \ldots, |K|$, the distance function $dist$ is the cosine distance, and $w2v$ is the dictionary lookup method, which returns the embedding of the input token from a pre-trained word to vector (word2vec) model. If the token w cannot be found in the word embedding dictionary, we set $d_k(w) = 1$ for all k.

In this study, we used the word embedding

" ()", ", where .", ", i.e.)",
" (i.e., in terms of)", ", or equivalently, .",
", which is the ,", ", the so-called ",
", which are called [,.]", ", which is called [,.]",
" (the)"

Table 1: Matching contexts for synonym detection, separated by comma (",")

model GloVe [2]. We tested the overall classification performance against different dimensions, ranging from 50 to 300, but found the differences are negligible. For better algorithm efficiency, we selected the 50-dimension model as the final solution.

3.5 Classification

In this study, we modeled the keyphrase classification task as a supervised multi-class classification problem. All features described in Section 3.3 were encoded into a sparse vector, and then combined with the WEDP as the input of supervised classifiers.

3.6 Relation Extraction

For the relation extraction subtask, we implemented a simple rule-based system. For each sentence, we considered all possible pairs of the entities as relation candidates. For each candidate, the context texts between two entities were extracted, including one character after the entity appeared later of the pair. The matching patterns we used are shown in Table 1. If any of those patterns matched with the context, we identified the pair as a detected relation. Relations sharing at least one entity were grouped together as one relation, according to the requirement of output format.

We used hearstPattern[3] which implements Hearst patterns (Hearst, 1992) for hyponym detection.

4 Results

We tested several supervised classification methods, The results on development set are shown in Table 2. The L2-loss linear kernel SVM was selected as the classifier and used the scikit-learn[4] implementation. The result also validated that

SVM can outperform other classification methods in high dimensional data (Chang and Lin, 2011). The hyperparameter C was tested in the range from 0.01 to 10. The F1 scores[5] range from 0.70 to 0.78 and yields the highest F1-score on the development set when C is set to 0.5.

Classifier	Material	Process	Task	Avg
ExtraTrees	0.77	0.69	0.45	0.68
SGD	0.76	0.67	0.35	0.65
5-NN	0.66	0.59	0.24	0.56
RBF-SVM	0.76	0.71	0.29	0.65
Linear SVM	0.88	0.75	0.45	**0.78**

Table 2: F1 scores for different classification methods on development set for Subtask B. (5-NN: 5 Nearest Neighbor; SGD: Stochastic Gradient Descent; RBF: Radial Basis Function)

Ablation experiments were conducted on the development set to find the importance of individual feature sets. The ablation results in F1 scores are shown in Table 3. From Table 3, we see that both the baseline feature sets and the WEDP contributed to the overall performance, since the combination of these two sets outperform the other feature settings.

Feature sets	F1 score
Lexical features, ± 1 window	0.68
+ ± 2 window	0.69
+ Orthographic features	0.71
+ POS features	0.72
+ Lemma feastures	0.72
baseline features only	0.72
WEDP features only	0.67
All	0.78

Table 3: Ablation F1 scores of keyphrase classification on the development set

The official evaluation uses the standard precision (P), recall (R) and F1 score as the metrics. We submitted two runs for official evaluation. Run 1 uses the feature set described in Section 3.3 with synonym detection result. Run 2 is derived by extending Run 1 by predicted hyponyms. Both runs achieved F1 score of 0.64 for Subtasks B and C. This was due to the insignificance from the positive cases of "Hyponym-of" relations on Run 2. The results of Run 2 are shown in

---

[2]http://nlp.stanford.edu/projects/glove/
[3]https://github.com/mmichelsonIF/hearst_patterns_python
[4]http://scikit-learn.org/

[5]Unless specified, the F1 scores mentioned in this section are micro-average F1 scores in keyphrase classification.

Category	P	R	F1 score	Support
Material	0.74	0.78	0.76	904
Process	0.69	0.64	0.66	954
Task	0.28	0.29	0.28	193
Synonym-of	0.42	0.27	0.33	112
Hyponym-of	0.16	0.03	0.05	95
Entity	0.67	0.67	0.67	2051
Relation	0.37	0.16	0.23	207
Overall	0.66	0.62	0.64	2258

Table 4: Official evaluation results of the best submitted run on the test set using annotated keyphrase boundaries (Scenario 2).

Table 4. From the results, "Task" is the most difficult category for our proposed method, but its relatively low proportion reduces its impact on the overall F1 score. Compared to the development set Table 2, the F1 scores of all three categories drop by at least 0.09, which indicates the selected classifier suffers from overfitting.

5 Conclusion

In this paper, we presented details of MayoNLP's participation in the ScienceIE share task at SemEval 2017. We used a supervised classifier for the keyphrase classification task using word embedding distance patterns, which improves the performance of conventional feature sets. Our system achieved an overall F1 score of 0.67 for keyphrase classification subtask and 0.64 for keyphrase classification and relation detection subtasks. It outperformed other participating systems in Scenario 2.

A future extension of this work is to test the patterns on different pre-trained word embeddings. We will also develop methods for more accurate key noun extraction such as dependency parsing, to improve the overall classification performance.

Acknowledgments

We would like to thank Yanshan Wang, Ravikumar Komandur Elayavilli, and Majid Rastegar-Mojarad for their valuable suggestions. This work is supported by NIH grants R01GM102282-01A1 and R01EB19403-01 and NSF IPA grant.

References

Naveed Afzal, Yanshan Wang, and Hongfang Liu. 2016. MayoNLP at SemEval-2016 Task 1: Semantic textual similarity based on lexical semantic net and deep learning semantic model. In *Proceedings of the 10th International Workshop on Semantic Evaluation (SemEval 2016)*. San Diego, CA, USA.

Isabelle Augenstein, Mrinal Kanti Das, Sebastian Riedel, Lakshmi Nair Vikraman, and Andrew McCallum. 2017. SemEval 2017 Task 10: ScienceIE - Extracting Keyphrases and Relations from Scientific Publications. In *Proceedings of the International Workshop on Semantic Evaluation*. Association for Computational Linguistics, Vancouver, Canada.

Chih-Chung Chang and Chih-Jen Lin. 2011. Libsvm: A library for support vector machines. *ACM Trans. Intell. Syst. Technol.* 2(3):27:1–27:27. https://doi.org/10.1145/1961189.1961199.

Marti A. Hearst. 1992. Automatic acquisition of hyponyms from large text corpora. In *Proceedings of the 14th Conference on Computational Linguistics - Volume 2*. Association for Computational Linguistics, Stroudsburg, PA, USA, COLING 1992, pages 539–545. https://doi.org/10.3115/992133.992154.

Robert Leaman and Graciela Gonzalez. 2008. Banner: An executable survey of advances in biomedical named entity recognition. In *Pacific Symposium on Biocomputing (PSB)*. pages 652–663.

Ki-Joong Lee, Young-Sook Hwang, Seonho Kim, and Hae-Chang Rim. 2004. Biomedical named entity recognition using two-phase model based on SVMs. *Journal of Biomedical Informatics* 37(6):436 – 447. Named Entity Recognition in Biomedicine. https://doi.org/10.1016/j.jbi.2004.08.012.

Xiao Li. 2010. Understanding the semantic structure of noun phrase queries. In *Proceedings of the 48th Annual Meeting of the Association for Computational Linguistics*. Association for Computational Linguistics, Stroudsburg, PA, USA, ACL '10, pages 1337–1345. http://dl.acm.org/citation.cfm?id=1858681.1858817.

Mingbo Ma, Liang Huang, Bing Xiang, and Bowen Zhou. 2015. Dependency-based convolutional neural networks for sentence embedding. In *Proceedings of the 53st Annual Meeting of the Association for Computational Linguistics (ACL)*. Association for Computational Linguistics, Beijing, China, pages 174–179. http://aclweb.org/anthology/P/P15/P15-2029.pdf.

Tomas Mikolov, Scott Wen-tau Yih, and Geoffrey Zweig. 2013. Linguistic regularities in continuous space word representations. In *Proceedings of the 2013 Conference of the North American Chapter of the Association for Computational Linguistics: Human Language Technologies (NAACL-HLT-2013)*. Association for Computational Linguistics.

David Nadeau and Satoshi Sekine. 2007. A survey of named entity recognition and classification. *Lingvistic Investigationes* 30(1):3–26. https://doi.org/10.1075/li.30.1.03nad.

Tzong-han Tsai, Wen-Chi Chou, Shih-Hung Wu, Ting-Yi Sung, Jieh Hsiang, and Wen-Lian Hsu. 2006. Integrating linguistic knowledge into a conditional random fieldframework to identify biomedical named entities. *Expert Syst. Appl.* 30(1):117–128. https://doi.org/10.1016/j.eswa.2005.09.072.

Yoshimasa Tsuruoka and Jun'ichi Tsujii. 2005. Bidirectional inference with the easiest-first strategy for tagging sequence data. In *Proceedings of the Conference on Human Language Technology and Empirical Methods in Natural Language Processing*. Association for Computational Linguistics, Stroudsburg, PA, USA, HLT '05, pages 467–474. https://doi.org/10.3115/1220575.1220634.

Guodong Zhou and Jiang Su. 2004. Exploring deep knowledge resources in biomedical name recognition. In *Proceedings of the International Joint Workshop on Natural Language Processing in Biomedicine and Its Applications*. Association for Computational Linguistics, Stroudsburg, PA, USA, JNLPBA '04, pages 96–99. http://dl.acm.org/citation.cfm?id=1567594.1567616.

Know-Center at SemEval-2017 Task 10: Sequence Classification with the CODE Annotator

Roman Kern
Know-Center GmbH
Inffeldgasse 13
Graz, 8010, Austria
rkern@know-center.at

Stefan Falk
Know-Center GmbH
Inffeldgasse 13
Graz, 8010, Austria
sfalk@know-center.at

Andi Rexha
Know-Center GmbH
Inffeldgasse 13
Graz, 8010, Austria
arexha@know-center.at

Abstract

This paper describes our participation in SemEval-2017 Task 10, named *ScienceIE (Machine Reading for Scientist)*. We competed in Subtask 1 and 2 which consist respectively in identifying all the key phrases in scientific publications and label them with one of the three categories: Task, Process, and Material. These scientific publications are selected from Computer Science, Material Sciences, and Physics domains. We followed a supervised approach for both subtasks by using a sequential classifier (CRF - Conditional Random Fields). For generating our solution we used a web-based application implemented in the EU-funded research project, named CODE. Our system achieved an F1 score of 0.39 for the Subtask 1 and 0.28 for the Subtask 2.

1 Introduction

Information Retrieval (IR) systems for scientific publications face different challenges compared to the standard approaches. This, mainly is due to the unavailability of the whole text from reviewed papers and the vague specification of the searching information. The identification and the extraction of the key phrases from such articles can partially overcome the limits described above by allowing search engines to access and use them as text features. Furthermore, the classification of the key phrases as a Task, a Process, or a Material, can help the researchers to correctly specify the type of information they are seeking.

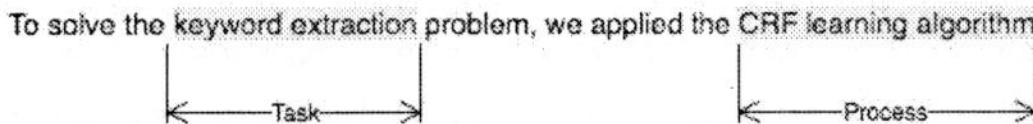

Figure 1: Example of a keyphrase with its associated label

The Subtasks 1 and 2 of Task 10 (Augenstein et al., 2017) in SemEval-2017 named *ScienceIE (Machine Reading for Scientist)*, tackle the aforementioned problems. This task consists in identifying (Subtask 1) and labeling (Subtask 2) all the key phrases in scientific publications from Computer Science, Material Science, and Physics.

For training and evaluating this task, it was provided a set of scientific papers together with the annotated key phrases and their associated labels. The annotations were represented with their start and end offsets in the text. The labels associated with each annotation can be from one of the three options: Task, Process, and Material. The example in Figure 1 illustrates the given dataset.

We followed a supervised approach for both subtasks. More specifically, we trained a sequential classifier CRF - Conditional Random Fields (Lafferty et al., 2001) and fed it with grammatical and text features. The model built from this classifier represents our solution for identifying and labeling the key phrases.

The rest of the paper is organized as follows. In the next section we describe our system's details. In section 3 we show the results of our systems and compare it with the other participants in the challenge. We end with section 4 summing up the con-

Proceedings of the 11th International Workshop on Semantic Evaluations (SemEval-2017), pages 961–964,
Vancouver, Canada, August 3 - 4, 2017. ©2017 Association for Computational Linguistics

clusions and foreseeing our future work.

2   System Description

In the ScienceIE (Machine Reading for Scientist) we
have followed a supervised approach. For classifying a certain number of elements as key phrases
and label them, we use a CRF (Conditional Random Field) classifier. Our system is part of an open-
source tool[1] that has been developed within a EU
funded research project, named CODE[2]. This system is a web-based application, which allows to
quickly annotate textual corpora imported directly
from Mendeley[3], an E-Mail server or a Zip-file containing Brat annotations.

Once the corpus has been imported, it is automatically pre-processed and indexed using a semantic
search engine. In order to make use of an automatic annotation of a corpus, a model needs to be
trained. This is conducted using solely the web interface of the tools, see Figure 2 for a screenshot
of the configuration panel where the model can be
trained. The submitted runs have been generated
using exclusively the CODE Annotator tool, only
a slight modification of the Brat annotation files as
supplied by the organisers were necessary.

2.1   Pre-Processing

Given the individual tokens and sentences we apply
a light pre-processing on the text. At first we apply
a part-of-speech tagger, namely OpenNLP[4], to derive the word form of each word within the sentence.
As our pre-processing pipeline is designed to work
with multiple languages, with each having its own
dedicated tagset, we defined our own uniform POS
tagset. This tagset consists of just 14 different word
forms, e.g. proper nouns and common nouns (including the tags that indicate plural) are all unified
into a single noun tag. We store the original POS
tags together with the unified tags within an internal
representation of the text.

---

[1] http://code-annotator.know-center.
tugraz.at/
[2] http://code-research.eu/
[3] http://mendeley.com/
[4] https://opennlp.apache.org/

2.2   Feature Generators

We used a series of feature generators that operate on
the pre-processed sentences to create features, which
are then fed to the classifiers.

Tokens   The token feature generator directly encodes the individual words as features, following a
bags of words approach. This generator offers the
configuration parameter to optionally normalise the
tokens, i.e. to bring them into a lower-case representation. For the submitted runs, we used the raw
tokens without further normalisation.

Token Character   The first and last characters of a
word are often indicative of its semantic and grammatical function. Therefore we crafted a feature
generated that generates character n-grams from the
prefix and suffix of the tokens. This generator provides options on the length of the generated n-gram
features. We finally ended up using 1, 2 and 3-
gram features, which are additionally normalised by
bringing them into a lower case representation.

Token Shape   In many different domains entities
are often abbreviations or specific words using combinations of special characters and numbers. To capture this, we designed a feature generator that maps
a word into a representation that should reflect the
words shape. All characters of a word are mapped
to a sequence of characters that represent: upper
case, lower case, special characters, and numbers.
For each word we create two representations: i) adjacent mappings are conflated into a single character, ii) adjacent mappings are merged into a single
character, but additionally the number of merged
characters is appended. For example, the entity
"NFAT/AP-1" will yield two features: "A/A-x"
and "A4/1A2-1x1".

Token POS Tag   This feature generator simply
adds the POS tagging to the set of features. We
used our unified tag set instead of the Penn Treebank
tagset, which is used by the POS tagger.

Context Window   This feature generator takes the
features from the surrounding words and adds them
to the feature set of the word in focus. We one can
specify the size of the sliding window - with the left
and right window size individually. Based on pre-

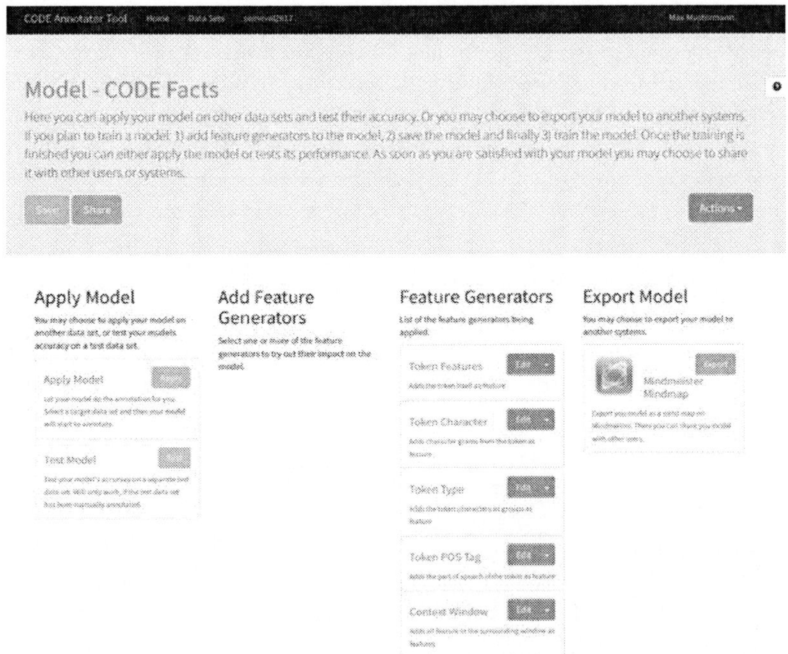

Figure 2: Screenshot of the CODE annotator tool, where users can tweak the model, trigger the learning process, evaluate the model on test corpora or apply a model on a corpus.

be more expressive, but may yield worse results in some scenarios.

The "BILOU" encoding scheme refers to classify each of the token as either: B) beginning of a (multi-token) key phrase, I) used for all tokens inside a (multi-token) key phrase, L) for the last token of a (multi-token) key phrase, O) used for tokens outside of a key phrase (i.e. all tokens not being part of a key phrase), and finally U) used for key phrases consisting of just a single token. See Figure 3 for an example how the labels are constructed.

To fit the current classifier with the Subtask 2, we encode each word contained in a key phrase as a concatenation of the key phrase's label with the corresponding "BILOU" encoding. Consider the key phrase "keyword extraction" in the example 3 and let's assume that its label is "Task". We would encode the word "keyword" as "Task-B" and the word "extraction" as "Task-L". The encoding returned from the CRF algorithm would determine then the label of the key phrase.

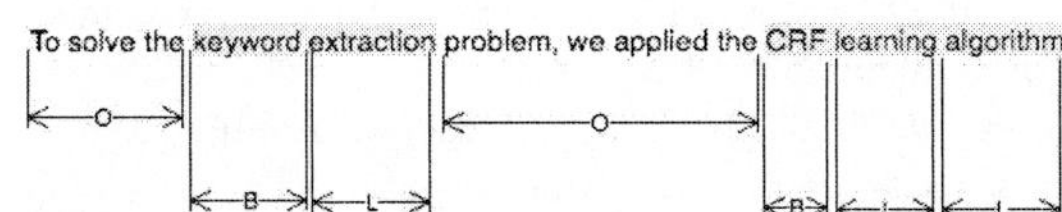

Figure 3: An example of the application of a sequence of words labelled with a BILOU encoding.

liminary test we opted to use a very short window of just 1 word to the left and right of each word.

2.3 Classification

To label words as part of key phrases, we followed a sequence classification approach. Here a single sentence is seen as a sequence of items, which are all assigned to a label.

Key Phrases As key phrases may consists of multiple words and multiple key phrases may directly succeed each other, one needs a labelling scheme that cater for this cases. The most common encoding schemes are "BIO" and "BILOU". Based on preliminary tests we opted for the latter, which should

Key Phrase Classification Algorithm We used the Conditional Random Field (CRF) algorithm as supplied by the Mallet[5] library. Mallet does allow to specify the order of the random field. Due to the small size of the training data set we were able to use a fully-connected model. Furthermore we were able to train the model until convergence, without the need to stop at a predefined threshold.

3 Results

Here we describe the results of the challenge and compare all the other participating teams. Table 1 shows the results for the two subtasks we have participated in.

System	F1 score for Subtask 1	F1 score for Subtask 2
TIAL_UW	0.56	0.44
s2_end2end	0.55	0.44
PKU_ICL	0.51	0.38
TTI_COIN	0.50	0.39
NTNTU-1	0.47	0.34
WING-NUS	0.46	0.33
SciX	0.42	0.21
IHS-RD-BELARUS	0.41	0.19
Know-Center	**0.39**	**0.28**
LIPN	0.38	0.21
SZTE-NLP	0.35	0.28
LABDA	0.33	0.23
NTNU	0.30	0.24
NITK_IT_PG	0.30	0.15
HCC-NLP	0.24	0.16
Surukam	0.24	0.1
GMBUAP	0.08	0.04

Table 1: Official results for the Subtask 1 and 2 of the Task 10 in Semeval-2017, named *ScienceIE (Machine Reading for Scientist)*

As illustrated, we have achieved a F1 score of 0.39 for the Subtask 1 and 0.28 for Subtask 2. The best performing team managed to achieve an F1 score of 0.56 and 0.44 respectively for each subtask. We ranked in the 9-th place for the Subtask 1 and 7-th for the Subtask 2.

4 Conclusions and Future Work

In this paper we presented our system for the SemEval-2017 Task 10, named *ScienceIE (Machine Reading for Scientist)*. We competed in Subtask 1 and 2, which consist, respectively, in identifying all the key phrases in scientific publications and label them. We achieved an F1 score of 0.39 for the Subtask 1 and 0.28 for the Subtask 2.

Our plan for the future work is to extend the set of used features and analyse their impact. Furthermore we intend to consider different classifications algorithm and tune their parameters.

Acknowledgments

The Know-Center GmbH Graz is funded within the Austrian COMET Program - Competence Centers for Excellent Technologies - under the auspices of the Austrian Federal Ministry of Transport, Innovation and Technology, the Austrian Federal Ministry of Economy, Family and Youth and by the State of Styria. COMET is managed by the Austrian Research Promotion Agency FFG.

References

[Augenstein et al.2017] Isabelle Augenstein, Mrinal Kanti Das, Sebastian Riedel, Lakshmi Nair Vikraman, and Andrew McCallum. 2017. SemEval 2017 Task 10: ScienceIE - Extracting Keyphrases and Relations from Scientific Publications. In *Proceedings of the International Workshop on Semantic Evaluation*, Vancouver, Canada, August. Association for Computational Linguistics.

[Lafferty et al.2001] John D. Lafferty, Andrew McCallum, and Fernando C. N. Pereira. 2001. Conditional random fields: Probabilistic models for segmenting and labeling sequence data. In *Proceedings of the Eighteenth International Conference on Machine Learning*, ICML '01, pages 282–289, San Francisco, CA, USA. Morgan Kaufmann Publishers Inc.

---

[5]`http://mallet.cs.umass.edu/` (Version 2.0.7)

NTNU-2 at SemEval-2017 Task 10: Identifying Synonym and Hyponym Relations among Keyphrases in Scientific Documents

Biswanath Barik, Erwin Marsi
Department of Computer Science
Norwegian University of Science and Technology
{biswanath.barik,emarsi}@ntnu.no

Abstract

This paper presents our relation extraction system for subtask C of SemEval-2017 Task 10: ScienceIE. Assuming that the keyphrases are already annotated in the input data, our work explores a wide range of linguistic features, applies various feature selection techniques, optimizes the hyper parameters and class weights and experiments with different problem formulations (single classification model vs individual classifiers for each keyphrase type, single-step classifier vs pipeline classifier for hyponym relations). Performance of five popular classification algorithms are evaluated for each problem formulation along with feature selection. The best setting achieved an F_1 score of 71.0% for synonym and 30.0% for hyponym relation on the test data.

1 Problem Description

Task C of ScienceIE at SemEval-2017 (Augenstein et al., 2017) concerns identifying sentence level 'SYNONYM-OF' (or 'same-as') and 'HYPONYM-OF' ('is-a') relations among three types of *keyphrases*: PROCESS (PR), TASK (TA) and MATERIAL (MA) in scientific documents. The 'SYNONYM-OF' relation is symmetric, whereas the 'HYPONYM-OF' relation is directed. Hyponym relation prediction is thus associated with two ordered subtasks: (1) predicting relations between pairs of keyphrases; (2) predicting the direction of the relation. It is assumed that there are no relations between keyphrase of different types. Automatic identification of synonym/hyponym relations is useful for many NLP applications, e.g. knowledge base completion and ontology construction.

2 Challenges

The relation prediction task of ScienceIE is challenging and quite different from other semantic relation prediction task like SemEval-2010 Task 8 (Hendrickx et al., 2009). In SemEval-2010 Task 8, there are two marked nominals in a sentence and the task is to predict if any of nine semantic relations hold between the nominal pair. Although there are more relations than ScienceIE (9 vs 2), ScienceIE poses different challenges. Instead of single-word nominals, the keyphrases of ScienceIE are arbitrarily large text spans referring to larger syntactico-semantic units. The top part of Table 1 shows the percentage of keyphrases longer than 10 tokens in the training (10.89%), development (8.76%) and test (6.71%) data. The problem with such large text spans is to identify features which best represent the keyphrase and contribute most to the relation prediction task.

Another challenge of ScienceIE is the occurrence of multiple keyphrases in one sentence, producing a large number of possible relations among keyphrase pairs, i.e., $n(n-1)/2$ for n keyphrases. As most of these are negative instances, the positive and negative classes are imbalanced.

A third challenge is the potentially long distance between keyphrase pairs. The middle part of Table 1 shows that there are 49.2%, 57.68% and 43.77% keyphrase pairs in training, development and test sets respectively which are separated by more than 19 tokens. In addtion, a number of other keyphrases can occur in between a pair of related keyphrases, as shown in Table 1.

Finally,the number of synonym and hyponym relations in the training and development datasets is limited. The bottom part of Table 2 shows the frequencies of relations in training and development datasets (ignoring inter-sentence keyphrase relations).

Proceedings of the 11th International Workshop on Semantic Evaluations (SemEval-2017), pages 965–968,
Vancouver, Canada, August 3 - 4, 2017. ©2017 Association for Computational Linguistics

Table 1: Keyphrase related statistics on data sets

keyphrase length (ℓ)	train	dev	test
$\ell = 1$ (single word)	8.49	13.13	12.87
$2 \leq \ell \leq 5$	58.11	58.08	63.44
$6 \leq \ell \leq 10$	22.51	20.03	16.98
$\ell \geq 11$	10.89	8.76	6.71
inter-keyphrase distance (λ)	**train**	**dev**	**test**
$\lambda = 0$ (adjacent)	0.05	0.02	0.06
$1 \leq \lambda \leq 10$	20.60	16.17	22.24
$11 \leq \lambda \leq 20$	29.52	26.13	32.94
$\lambda \geq 20$	49.82	57.68	43.77
# intervening keyphrases (n)	**train**	**dev**	**test**
$n = 0$ (adjacent)	51.40	43.14	55.53
$n = 1$	23.84	23.95	25.13
$n = 2$	11.64	12.84	11.30
$n = 3$	5.64	7.32	4.57
$n \geq 4$	7.48	12.72	3.46

Table 2: Relation related statistics on data sets

Relation Type	Dataset	PR	TA	MA	Total
SYNONYM	train	150	11	88	249
SYNONYM	dev	23	1	21	45
HYPONYM	train	188	48	178	414
HYPONYM	dev	41	8	71	120

3 Approach

Inspired by the best systems at SemEval-2010 Task 8 (Rink and Harabagiu, 2010), we developed our relation extraction system in a supervised learning framework with the dependency structure of the input sentence as the major resource. The main intuition is that Bunescu and Mooney (2005) showed that the shortest path between two entities in a dependency graph contains most of the information for identifying the relation between them. In causal relation extraction (Barik et al., 2017), we have experienced that such intuition is effective. We tried two alternative approaches.

Approach-1: Individual vs Single Classifier As relations only occur between keyphrases of the same type, our first experiment evaluates the performance of separate synonym and hyponym classifiers for each keyphrase type, resulting in six classification problems. The description of System-1 provides more details on the classifiers.

The main challenge of developing individual classifiers for each task is the limited number of instances in the dataset. For example, there are only 11 relation instances between TASK (TA) keyphrases in the training data and only a single one in the dev data. Hence individual classifiers might not generalize well enough. Therefore, an alternative approach is to train one synonym classifier and one hyponym classifier for all keyphrase pairs, ignoring their types. This gives a higher number of positive training instances – 249 for synonym and 414 for hyponym – as shown in Table 2. This is the approach taken with System-2.

In both of these problem formulations, synonym is a binary classification problem, whereas the hyponym relation is considered as ternary classification (i.e., *forward* relation, *backward* relation and *no* relation).

Approach-2: Hyponym Relation-Direction Prediction Since the hyponym relation is directed, another option is to predict its direction separately. Whereas in Approach-1 hyponym relations and their direction were predicted simultaneously as a three class problem, in Approach-2 we have developed two systems – for relation prediction and direction prediction – and connect them in a pipeline. System-3 thus refers to a pipelined classification of hyponym relations.

4 Experiments

Preprocessing Input text is linguistically analyzed with the Stanford CoreNLP library (Manning et al., 2014), which includes sentence boundary detection, tokenization, lemmatization, part-of-speech (POS) tagging and dependency parsing.

Feature Extraction Features are extracted for every possible keyphrase pair within a sentence. The feature extraction process dependents heavily on contextual information and dependency structures, specifically, the shortest dependency path between two keyphrase heads and the dependency subtree connecting two keyphrases as described in (Liu et al., 2015). The major feature categories are:

- *context features*: bag-of-word – unigram & bigram, lemma, POS, word-POS combination
- *before & after context features*: bag-of-word – unigram & bigram, lemma, POS, word-POS combination in certain window sizes
- *dependency features*: dependency head & dependents of each keyphrase of the considered pair, head of the in-between context, dependency path between two entity heads, ordering of keyphrases in dependency path, dis-

Table 3: Candidate Classification Algorithms

Sl.	Classification Algorithm	Parameters
1	Support Vector Machines (SVM)	C, w, loss
2	Multinomial Naive Bayes (MNB)	Alpha
3	Decision Tree (DT)	split, w, max_feat
4	Random Forest (RF)	n_est., w, criterion
5	k-Nearest Neighbours (kNN)	N, weight

Sl.	Feature Selection Method	Parameters
1	χ^2-based feature selection (X2)	k
2	Tree-based feature selection (TR)	ExtraTreesClf
3	Recursive Feature Elim. (REF)	SVM

tance between two keyphrase heads in a dependency path

- *other features*: open bracket in the context, capitalization in keyphrase, length of keyphrase, number of lemma common to both keyphrase, number of intervening keyphrases
- *intervening keyphrase features*: the intervening keyphrase features like head of the keyphrase, its relation with context head, etc.
- *WordNet features* : synonym/hyponym relation between heads of two keyphrases, lexical cues for synonym/hyponym relation, e.g., 'such as', 'is a', 'including' etc.

Classifiers Used Instead of choosing any particular classification algorithm, we have evaluated five different classifiers with hyper-parameters and class weights tuned for different systems, as listed in the top half of Table 3.

Feature Selection Methods As shown Table 1, the keyhrase length (ℓ) and the in-between context length (λ) can be arbitrarily large. As a result, the feature extraction process generates a large number of features, many of which are unlikely to provide any useful information. Therefore we investigated three different feature selection techniques, as shown in the bottom half of Table 3. Among these feature selection techniques, χ^2-based feature selection (X2) gave the best result.

Parameter Optimization through CV The training instances were extracted from 350 training files, indexed by training file name, followed by preprocessing and feature extraction as described above. The class weights, parameters for five classifiers and k (the top-k feature for χ^2-based feature selection) were optimized for the three different experimental setups (System 1-3) descibed below using five fold cross validation

with *grid search*, where training instances from the same training file are always in the same fold. Our implementation relied on classifiers, feature selection methods and CV grid search from Scikit-learn[1].

System-1 We ran CV experiments to optimize settings for the separate relation prediction tasks: synonym_process (SP), synonym_task (ST), synonym_material (SM), hyponym_process (HP), hyponym_task (HT) and hyponym_material (HM). For each task, we optimized the hyper-parameters of five classifiers as shown in Table 3. The performance of the best classifier was then evaluated on the development dataset. For the hyponym relation, we optimized on the micro-average score over the forward and backward relation.

System-2 System-2 consists of a combination of one synonym classifier and one hyponym classifier.

System-3 Hyponym relations and their directions were predicted by separate classifiers connected in a pipeline. Parameters were therefore optimized for relation and direction prediction separately. The synonym predictions of System-3 result from the combination of the synonym classifier of 1-4 and 2 where any keyphrase pair predicted by either classifier 1-4 or classifier 2 is considered as synonym.

5 Results

Table 4 shows the result of System 1-3 on development data, while Table 5 shows performance on test data. According to Table 4, the combined performance of individual classifiers (of System-1) for synonym (SM-SP-ST) and hyponym (HM-HP-HT) is 77% and 29%, which is slightly lower then the corresponding performance of system-2. This is consistent with performance on the test data.On the other-hand, the pipeline of System-3 shows a lower score than System-1 and System-2 for the hyponym relation.

5.1 Error Analysis

We have analyzed the mistakes produced by System 1-3 and found the following frequent error categories:

- *synonyms* - The synonyms with pattern KEYPHRASE1 (KEYPHRASE2 in abbrevi-

---

[1] http://scikit-learn.org/stable/

Table 4: Result of individual classifiers where hyponym relations are considered as three class problem with micro average of positive classes

Sys	Relation	Clf	Pr	Re	F_1
1-1	SM	SVM	0.93	0.62	0.74
1-2	SP	DT	0.78	0.78	0.78
1-3	ST	DT	1.00	1.00	1.00
1-4	SM-SP-ST	SVM-DT-DT	0.84	0.71	**0.77**
1-5	HM	RF	0.39	0.21	0.27
1-6	HP	SVM	0.51	0.27	0.35
1-7	HT	SVM	0.04	0.10	0.06
1-8	HM-HP-HT	RF-SVM-SVM	0.40	0.23	**0.29**
2	Syno	SVM	0.80	0.77	**0.78**
2	Hypo	DT	0.37	0.28	**0.32**
3	Syno 1-4+2	SVM	0.84	0.79	**0.81**
3	Rel	SVM	0.64	0.35	0.45
3	Dir	SVM	0.73	0.72	0.72
3	Rel $\rightarrow$ Dir	SVM-SVM	0.36	0.21	**0.26**

Table 5: Result of synonym and hyponym relation of System 1-3 on test data

System	Hyponym			Synonym		
	Pr	Re	F_1	Pr	Re	F_1
1	0.34	0.24	0.28	0.71	0.62	0.66
2	0.35	0.26	**0.30**	0.82	0.57	0.67
3	0.31	0.18	0.23	0.78	0.65	**0.71**

ation) like 'density of states (DOS)' are identified correctly. However, the opposite pattern like 'SRTM (Shuttle Radar Tropographical Mission)' are not well recognized.

- *hyponyms with conjunctions* - when a list of hyponyms is connected by conjunctions, often some hyponyms are missed.

- *hyponym to synonym* - In some cases hyponym patterns are quite similar to frequent synonym patterns and therefore misclassified. For example, in the sentence fragment, 'xR is the x-position of the receiving element (R)', the keyphrase 'R' is connected with 'receiving element' by a synonym relation, whereas the correct relation is hyponym.

- *synonym to hyponym* - In some cases a synonym relation is observed instead of a hyponym relation. For example, in 'constituent statistics (SB, SDSD, and LCS)', the keyphrases 'SDSD' and 'LCS' are correctly linked to the 'constituent statistics' by a hyponym relation, but 'SB' is incorrectly linked as a synonym.

6 Conclusion

We have described our system for predicting synonym and hyponym relations between keyphrases within a feature-based supervised learning framework. We have developed three systems for the synonym and hyponym prediction tasks. Experiments showed that with a relatively small dataset, training a single classifier for synonym and hyponym works slightly better than training separate classifiers for each keyphrase type. We also found that a pipeline of classifiers for relation and direction prediction of hyponym relations is not effective compared with predicting relation and direction simultaneously. As future work, we can investigate the performance of neural network-based relation classification approaches (specifically Convolution and Recurrent Neural Networks).

References

Isabelle Augenstein, Mrinal Kanti Das, Sebastian Riedel, Lakshmi Nair Vikraman, and Andrew McCallum. 2017. SemEval 2017 Task 10: ScienceIE - Extracting Keyphrases and Relations from Scientific Publications. In *Proceedings of the International Workshop on Semantic Evaluation*. Vancouver, Canada.

Biswanath Barik, Erwin Marsi, and Pinar Öztürk. 2017. Extracting Causal Relations among Complex Events in Natural Science Literature. In *Proceedings of the 22nd International Conference on Natural Language & Information Systems (NLDB)*. Liege, Belgium.

Razvan C Bunescu and Raymond J Mooney. 2005. A shortest path dependency kernel for relation extraction. In *Proceedings of the conference on human language technology and empirical methods in natural language processing*. pages 724–731.

Iris Hendrickx, Su Nam Kim, Zornitsa Kozareva, Preslav Nakov, Diarmuid Ó Séaghdha, Sebastian Padó, Marco Pennacchiotti, Lorenza Romano, and Stan Szpakowicz. 2009. Semeval-2010 task 8: Multi-way classification of semantic relations between pairs of nominals. In *Proceedings of the Workshop on Semantic Evaluations: Recent Achievements and Future Directions*. pages 94–99.

Yang Liu, Furu Wei, Sujian Li, Heng Ji, Ming Zhou, and Houfeng Wang. 2015. A dependency-based neural network for relation classification. *arXiv preprint arXiv:1507.04646* .

Christopher D Manning, Mihai Surdeanu, John Bauer, Jenny Rose Finkel, Steven Bethard, and David McClosky. 2014. The stanford corenlp natural language processing toolkit. In *ACL (System Demonstrations)*. pages 55–60.

Bryan Rink and Sanda Harabagiu. 2010. UTD: Classifying semantic relations by combining lexical and semantic resources. In *Proceedings of the 5th International Workshop on Semantic Evaluation*. pages 256–259.

LABDA at SemEval-2017 Task 10: Relation Classification between keyphrases via Convolutional Neural Network

Víctor Suárez-Paniagua, Isabel Segura-Bedmar and Paloma Martínez
Computer Science Department
Carlos III University of Madrid
Leganés 28911, Madrid, Spain
`vspaniag,isegura,pmf@inf.uc3m.es`

Abstract

In this paper, we describe our participation at the subtask of extraction of relationships between two identified keyphrases. This task can be very helpful in improving search engines for scientific articles. Our approach is based on the use of a convolutional neural network (CNN) trained on the training dataset. This deep learning model has already achieved successful results for the extraction relationships between named entities. Thus, our hypothesis is that this model can be also applied to extract relations between keyphrases. The official results of the task show that our architecture obtained an F1-score of 0.38% for Keyphrases Relation Classification. This performance is lower than the expected due to the generic preprocessing phase and the basic configuration of the CNN model, more complex architectures are proposed as future work to increase the classification rate.

1 Introduction

Nowadays, a deluge of scientific articles is published every year, which demonstrates that we are living in an emerging knowledge era. An important drawback of this situation is that the study of a given field or problem requires reviewing an huge number of scientific publications, becoming such a very arduous task. Most search engines apply linguistic normalization (such as lemmatization or stemming) and some of them also exploit the semantic analysis of texts in order to detect concepts to improve their recall. The goal of the ScienceIE Task at SemEval 2017 (Augenstein et al., 2017) is the extraction of keyphrases (such as MATE-RIALS, PROCESSES and TASKS) and relation-

ships between them from scientific articles. This competition provides a common evaluation framework to researches allowing a fair way to evaluate and compare their approaches. Our participation focuses on the subtask of extracting relationships between keyphrases. In particular, these relationships are HYPONYM-OF (for example, 'femur' is HYPONYM-OF 'bone'), SYNONYM-OF (for example, 'ophthalmologist' is SYNONYM-OF 'oculist'), and NONE. The detection of these relationships between keyphrases can improve the performance of current researches.

In this paper, we describe the participation of the group LaBDA for participating in the subtask C (extraction of relationships between keyphrases) evaluated on the scenario 3, where the test dataset includes texts as well as the annotations of their keyphrases (boundaries and types). Our approach is based on the CNN proposed in (Kim, 2014), which was the first work to exploit a CNN for the task of sentence classification. This model was able to infer the class of each sentence, and returned good results without the need for external information. To this end, the model computes an output vector, which describes the whole sentence, and applies convolving filters to the input through several windows of different sizes. Finally, this vector is used in a classification layer to assign a class label. Recently, CNN has succeeded providing the state-of-art results in some tasks of relation extraction such as the relationships between nominals (Zeng et al., 2014) or the extraction of drug-drug interactions (Zhao et al., 2016). Our aim is to explore if CNN is also a suitable method for extracting relationships between keyphrases.

2 Dataset

The valuable contribution of the ScienceIE challenge was to provide an annotated corpus for train-

Proceedings of the 11th International Workshop on Semantic Evaluations (SemEval-2017), pages 969–972,
Vancouver, Canada, August 3 - 4, 2017. ©2017 Association for Computational Linguistics

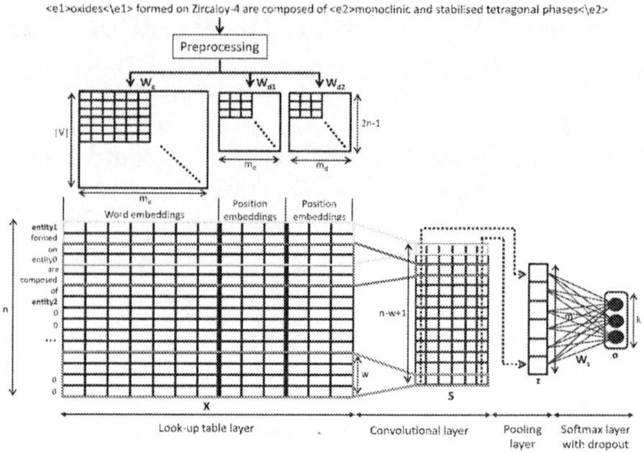

Figure 1: CNN model for the ScienceIE keyphrases Relation Classification task of SemEval 2017.

ing and evaluating supervised algorithms to extract Keyphrases from Scientific Publications. The whole corpus contains 500 journal articles about Computer Science, Material Sciences and Physics from ScienceDirect[1]. The corpus is split into training, development and testing sets with 350, 50 and 100 documents, respectively. A detailed description of the method used to collect and process documents can be found in (Augenstein et al., 2017).

2.1 Pre-processing phase

Each pair of keyphrases represents a possible relation instance. Each of these instances is classified by the CNN model in three classes HYPONYM-OF, SYNONYM-OF and NONE. The corpus is given in the paragraph level, that is why we use the NLTK[2] sentence splitter to separate the relations in the sentence level because we only have to annotate relations within a sentence.

Once we have each instance, following a similar approach as that described in (Kim, 2014), the sentences were tokenized and cleaned (converting all words to lower-case and separating special characters with white spaces by regular expressions). Then, the two keyphrases of each instance were replaced by the labels "entity1" and "entity2", and by "entity0" for the remaining keyphrases in the sentence. This method is known as entity blinding, and verifies the generalization of the model.

In the case of the HYPONYM-OF class the directionality must be considered. For instance, if an entity A is HYPONYM-OF B we annotated the relation of B with A as NONE. For the remain-

der classes, we annotated both directions with the same class label.

The keyphrases corpus contains a number of overlapped keyphrases. As this kind of mentions produces bad entity blinding, we decided to remove them. The classification of keyphrases involving overlapped entities is a challenging task which will be tackled in future work. One possible solution will consider different instances for each overlapped entities.

3 CNN model

In this section, we present a CNN model for the special case of sentences which describe keyphrases relationships. Figure 1 shows the whole process from its input, which is a sentence with marked entities, until the output, which is the classification of the instance into one of the keyphrases relation types.

3.1 Word table layer

After the pre-processing phase, we created an input matrix suitable for the CNN architecture. The input matrix should represent all training instances for the CNN model; therefore, they should have the same length. We determined the maximum length of the sentence in all the instances (denoted by n), and then extended those sentences with lengths shorter than n by padding with an auxiliary token "0".

Moreover, each word has to be represented by a vector. To do this, we considered to randomly initialize a vector for each different word which allows us to replace each word by its word embedding vector: $\mathbf{W}_e \in \mathbb{R}^{|V| \times m_e}$ where V is the

---

[1] http://www.sciencedirect.com/
[2] http://www.nltk.org

970

vocabulary size and m_e is the word embedding dimension. Finally, we obtained a vector $\mathbf{x} = [x_1; x_2; ...; x_n]$ for each instance where each word of the sentence is represented by its corresponding word vector from the word embedding matrix. We denote p_1 and p_2 as the positions in the sentence of the two entities to be classified.

The following step involves calculating the relative position of each word to the two interacting keyphrases as $i - p_1$ and $i - p_2$, where i is the word position in the sentence (padded word included), in the same way as (Zeng et al., 2014). In order to avoid negative values, we transformed the range $(-n + 1, n - 1)$ to the range $(1, 2n - 1)$. Then, we mapped these distances into a real value vector using two position embedding $\mathbf{W}_{d1} \in \mathbb{R}^{(2n-1) \times m_d}$ and $\mathbf{W}_{d2} \in \mathbb{R}^{(2n-1) \times m_d}$. Finally, we created an input matrix $\mathbf{X} \in \mathbb{R}^{n \times (m_e + 2m_d)}$ which is represented by the concatenation of the word embeddings and the two position embeddings for each word in the instance.

3.2 Convolutional layer

Once we obtained the input matrix, we applied a filter matrix $\mathbf{f} = [f_1; f_2; ...; f_w] \in \mathbb{R}^{w \times (m_e + 2m_d)}$ to a context window of size w in the convolutional layer to create higher level features. For each filter, we obtained a score sequence $\mathbf{s} = [s_1; s_2; ...; s_{n-w+1}] \in \mathbb{R}^{(n-w+1) \times 1}$ for the whole sentence as

$$s_i = g(\sum_{j=1}^{w} f_j x_{i+j-1}^T + b)$$

where b is a bias term and g is a non-linear function (such as tangent or sigmoid). Note that in Figure 1, we represent the total number of filters, denoted by m, with the same size w in a matrix $\mathbf{S} \in \mathbb{R}^{(n-w+1) \times m}$. However, the same process can be applied to filters with different sizes by creating additional matrices that would be concatenated in the following layer.

3.3 Pooling layer

Here, the goal is to extract the most relevant features of each filter using an aggregating function. We used the max function, which produces a single value in each filter as $z_f = max\{\mathbf{s}\} = max\{s_1; s_2; ...; s_{n-w+1}\}$. Thus, we created a vector $\mathbf{z} = [z_1, z_2, ..., z_m]$, whose dimension is the total number of filters m representing the relation instance. If there are filters with different sizes,

their output values should be concatenated in this layer.

3.4 Softmax layer

Prior to performing the classification, we performed a dropout to prevent overfitting. We obtained a reduced vector $\mathbf{z}_d$, randomly setting the elements of $\mathbf{z}$ to zero with a probability p following a Bernoulli distribution. After that, we fed this vector into a fully connected softmax layer with weights $\mathbf{W}_s \in \mathbb{R}^{m \times k}$ to compute the output prediction values for the classification as $\mathbf{o} = \mathbf{z}_d \mathbf{W}_s + d$ where d is a bias term; we have $k = 3$ classes in the dataset (HYPONYM-OF, SYNONYM-OF and NONE). At test time, the vector $\mathbf{z}$ of a new instance is directly classified by the softmax layer without a dropout.

3.5 Learning

For the training phase, we need to learn the CNN parameter set $\theta = (\mathbf{W}_e, \mathbf{W}_{d1}, \mathbf{W}_{d2}, \mathbf{W}_s, d, \mathbf{F}_m, b)$, where $\mathbf{F}_m$ are all of the m filters $\mathbf{f}$. For this purpose, we used the conditional probability of a relation r obtained by the softmax operation as

$$p(r|\mathbf{x}, \theta) = \frac{\exp(\mathbf{o}_r)}{\sum_{l=1}^{k} \exp(\mathbf{o}_l)}$$

to minimize the cross entropy function for all instances $(\mathbf{x}_i, y_i)$ in the training set T as follows

$$J(\theta) = \sum_{i=1}^{T} \log p(y_i|\mathbf{x}_i, \theta)$$

In addition, we minimize the objective function by using stochastic gradient descent over shuffled mini-batches and the Adam update rule (Kingma and Ba, 2014) to learn the parameters.

4 Results and Discussion

Firstly, we use a basic CNN predefined parameters to create a baseline system without a position embeddings. Secondly, the effects of the position embeddings were observed assigning a dimension $M_d = 10$. In addition, we define the parameters the same as in (Kim, 2014): word embeddings dimension $M_e = 300$, filters $m = 200$ with a window size $w = (3, 4, 5)$. For the training phase we use: a dropout rate $p = 50\%$, mini-batch size of size 50 and the Rectified Linear Unit (ReLU) as the non-linear function g. The parameter $n = 95$ which is determined by the maximum length sentence in the dataset. Only the number of epochs was fine-tuned in the validation set using the stopping criteria.

The results of the basic CNN configuration without position embeddings are showed in Table 1. We observe that the Recall performance in both classes are very low, the reason is that the parameters were not explored in detail and the model does not fit to this problem. In addition, the entities overlapped removal discard many examples that can improve the results.

	Precision	Recall	F1-score
HYPONYM-OF	0.27	0.07	0.12
SYNONYM-OF	0.65	0.32	0.43
Total	0.53	0.21	0.30

Table 1: Results over the dataset using a basic CNN.

The official results obtained by the CNN with position embeddings are showed in Table 2. We observe that the Precision increases considerably in the case of HYPONYM-OF and the Recall of SYNONYM-OF. This proves that sentences are best represented using position embeddings (+8% in F1-score against to CNN without position embeddings).

For both cases, the class SYNONYM-OF is classified better than the class HYPONYM-OF because the examples in the former class are very clear, e.g. in the sentence "trajectory surface hoping (TSH)" the keyphrase "trajectory surface hoping" is a SYNONYM-OF "TSH", and, also, we obtained the double of instances due to the class is the same in both directions. That is the main reason why the class HYPONYM-OF obtained low Recall in both models. For this reason, we will add some preprocessing to correct these classification errors with a rule-based system.

	Precision	Recall	F1-score
HYPONYM-OF	0.54	0.07	0.13
SYNONYM-OF	0.61	0.46	0.52
Total	0.60	0.28	0.38

Table 2: Results over the dataset using a CNN with position embedding size of 10.

5 Conclusions and Future work

We present the CNN model used by LaBDA Team for the ScienceIE keyphrases Relation Classification task of SemEval 2017. We find that the performance of the CNN model in this task is promising but the results are lower in comparison with other participant results. However, we only try a basic configuration with a generic preprocessing phase and without external features. The results suggest that the usage of the position embedding improves the performance in both classes.

As future work we will explore and fine-tune all the parameters of this architecture such as the size of the position embeddings, the number and the size of the filters. In addition, we will tackle the overlapped entities problem using each entity as different instances. Thus, more examples will be used for each class to increase the classification rate. Furthermore, we will train a CNN with different pre-trained word embedding models instead of using a random word embedding initialization and comparing results with and without position embeddings.

Funding

This work was supported by the Research Program of the Ministry of Economy and Competitiveness - Government of Spain, (eGovernAbility-Access project TIN2014-52665-C2-2-R).

References

Isabelle Augenstein, Mrinal Das, Sebastian Riedel, Lakshmi Vikraman, and Andrew McCallum. 2017. Semeval 2017 task 10: Scienceie - extracting keyphrases and relations from scientific publications. In *Proceedings of the 11th International Workshop on Semantic Evaluation (SemEval-2017)*. Association for Computational Linguistics, Vancouver, Canada, pages 546–555. http://www.aclweb.org/anthology/S17-2091.

Y. Kim. 2014. Convolutional neural networks for sentence classification. In *Proceedings of the 2014 Conference on Empirical Methods in Natural Language Processing (EMNLP)*. pages 1746–1751.

Diederik P. Kingma and Jimmy Ba. 2014. Adam: A method for stochastic optimization. *CoRR* abs/1412.6980.

Daojian Zeng, Kang Liu, Siwei Lai, Guangyou Zhou, and Jun Zhao. 2014. Relation classification via convolutional deep neural network. In *Proceedings of the 25th International Conference on Computational Linguistics (COLING 2014), Technical Papers*. Dublin City University and Association for Computational Linguistics, Dublin, Ireland, pages 2335–2344.

Zhehuan Zhao, Zhihao Yang, Ling Luo, Hongfei Lin, and Jian Wang. 2016. Drug drug interaction extraction from biomedical literature using syntax convolutional neural network. *Bioinformatics* .

WING-NUS at SemEval-2017 Task 10: Keyphrase Identification and Classification as Joint Sequence Labeling

Animesh Prasad **Min-Yen Kan**

School of Computing, National University of Singapore
Computing 1, 13 Computing Drive, Singapore 11741
`{animesh,kanmy}@comp.nus.edu.sg`

Abstract

We describe an end-to-end pipeline processing approach for SemEval 2017's Task 10 to extract keyphrases and their relations from scientific publications. We jointly identify and classify keyphrases by modeling the subtasks as sequential labeling. Our system utilizes standard, surface-level features along with the adjacent word features, and performs conditional decoding on whole text to extract keyphrases.

We focus only on the identification and typing of keyphrases (Subtasks A and B, together referred as extraction), but provide an end-to-end system inclusive of keyphrase relation identification (Subtask C) for completeness. Our top performing configuration achieves an F_1 of 0.27 for the end-to-end keyphrase extraction and relation identification scenario on the final test data, and compares on par to other top ranked systems for keyphrase extraction. Our system outperforms other techniques that do not employ global decoding and hence do not account for dependencies between keyphrases. We believe this is crucial for keyphrase classification in the given context of scientific document mining.

1 Introduction

Keyphrases are often used for representing the salient concepts of a document. In scientific documents, keyphrase extraction is an important prerequisite task that feeds downstream tasks such as summarization, clustering and indexing, among others. As such, automatic keyphrase extraction has garnered attention and become a focal point for many researchers (Kim et al., 2010). Usually,

the most common scenario of keyphrase extraction is to identify the keyphrases over the whole scientific document. Existing techniques in aforesaid setups use elaborate, hand-crafted features fed for selected candidate keyphrases to machine learning models such as support vector machines and multilayer perceptrons, to learn keyphrases (Kim et al., 2013). The scope of features vary from simple, surface-level features like character n-grams, token type, and part-of-speech tags – to features drawn from global statistics and lexical semantics, such as TF-IDF, keywordness, relation to document's logical structure (Nguyen and Kan, 2007).

However, the given task setup is inherently different as it requires to identify all the keyphrases of certain types (or classes – *Material*, *Process* and *Task*) over an excerpt of a scientific document. As inferred from our primary analysis of the training data, some of the crucial challenges of keyphrase extraction in this particular task setup are:

- Keyphrases occur more densely in the excerpts compared against the standard keyphrase extraction task where systems typically identify 5–25 keyphrases over an entire document;

- Keyphrases overlap significantly. For example "equally sized blocks" and "blocks" both need to be extracted as keyphrases of type *Materials*;

- Determining the keyphrase type depends on the context. For example "oxidation test" and "assessment of the corrosion condition" can potentially be either of *Task* or *Process*, depending on the context.

Considering these differences, we believe that sequence labeling based modeling is more suited than the standard, top K keyphrase extraction.

Proceedings of the 11th International Workshop on Semantic Evaluations (SemEval-2017), pages 973–977,
Vancouver, Canada, August 3 - 4, 2017. ©2017 Association for Computational Linguistics

Such a model also easily extends to a joint approach for both extraction and classification, which we investigated.

2 Method

To accomplish Subtasks A and B, we deploy the Conditional Random Field (CRF) (Lafferty et al., 2001), a model capable of capturing conditional dependencies from sequential information. A CRF is a decoder which labels unseen sequences using the parameters learned from annotated examples to maximize conditional probability $p(y|x)$. We describe the inventory of features we provisioned (parenthesized notation used in Table 1).

- Token (F0): The token itself.

- Lower (F1): The token, lowercased.

- N-gram Prefix and Suffix (F2–F9): The initial to first four characters (prefix) and ultimate to last four characters (suffix) of the token.

- Part-of-Speech (F10): The part of the speech tag, as obtained from tagging of the complete sequence using the *nltk.punkt* tagger.

- Capitalization (F11): The orthographic case of the original token; taking one of four values: ALLCAPS, MixedCaps, Startcap or lowercase.

- Alpha/numeric? (F12–F13): Where the token is solely an integer, word, mixed or contains special characters.

- ASCII? (F14): Whether the token consist of non-ASCII special characters (the larger UTF-8/ISO Latin set, commonly used as symbols in scientific writing).

- Quoted? (F15): Whether the token exists between quotes.

- Hyphenated? (F16): Whether the token contains a hyphen.

- Math operators? (F17): Whether the token contains equality or inequality operators.

- Occurs in Title? (F18): Whether the token is present in the title of the article and is not a stop word in *nltk.stopword* for English.

- Output for Previous Token (O): The prediction for the previous token, a contextual label feature.

To achieve Subtask C, we placed minimal effort, choosing to build the end-to-end pipeline for sake of completeness. For Subtask C, we employed the *sklearn.ensemble*'s random forest classifier, with syntactic similarity features. The features are computed over the keyphrase pairs annotated with a relation as an instance for that relation and randomly generated pairs between keywords as an instance of no-relation. These features are the substring overlap between the two keyphrases, probabilistic and binary scores for one keyphrase being short/expanded form of other. We note that this approach is suboptimal as it does not incorporate any semantic information required for understanding relatedness.

3 Experiments

We use the CRF++ implementation[1] of CRFs. CRF++ takes as input a feature template file, describing contextual positions (like previous token, next two tokens) to incorporate component features from (F0 – F18, O). The template also can direct CRF++ to compute more complex feature–bigrams. Our final model's expanded feature list includes many of the surrounding tokens features [2].

Dataset. We participate in SemEval-2017 Task 10 on science information extraction (Augenstein et al., 2017) using the dataset consisting of 350 training samples (*Train*), 50 development samples (*Dev*) and 100 testing samples (*Test*). Each data sample is an excerpt of a scientific document. Unlike previous work creating similar benchmark dataset (Handschuh and QasemiZadeh, 2014), the dataset excerpt is taken out of a random section of the document.

Tasks. The excerpt requires its keyphrases to be identified (Subtask A), typed among one of three types: *Materials*, *Process* and *Task* (Subtask B), then finally followed by *Synonym-of* and *Hyponym-of* identification among the extracted keyphrases (Subtask C). Our work focuses specifically only on Subtasks A and B; our effort on Subtask C is minimal.

---

[1] https://taku910.github.io/crfpp/
[2] Code available at https://github.com/animeshprasad/science_ie

	Features	Subtask A			Subtask B		
		Precision	Recall	F_1	Precision	Recall	F_1
1.	All	0.55	0.38	0.45	0.51	0.32	**0.40**
2.	All - (F0–F1)	0.49	0.34	0.40	0.44	0.26	0.34
3.	All - (F2–F9)	0.53	0.33	0.40	0.46	0.25	0.33
4.	All - F10	0.55	0.36	0.43	0.50	0.30	0.37
5.	All - (F11–F17)	0.55	0.37	0.44	0.51	0.31	0.38
6.	All - F18	0.56	0.39	**0.46**	0.51	0.32	0.39
7.	All - O	0.30	0.39	0.34	0.26	0.32	0.29

Table 1: Model performance over different feature ablation, as evaluated on *Dev*. Best performance is **bolded.**

Evaluation. The designed evaluations test complete end-to-end pipeline of keyphrase identification, classification and relationship identification (Scenario 1); classification and relationship identification, given extracted keyphrases (Scenario 2); and relationship identification, given the extracted and classified keyphrases (Scenario 3). As the most intuitive and challenging scope, we only examine Scenario 1 in depth here. In Scenario 1 all the tasks are performed over the (noisy) system output of previous tasks whenever applicable.

3.1 Feature Ablation

To assess the importance of the component features, we perform ablation testing over the *Dev* (Table 1). We see that the setup of using all features is largely validated, with only a slight 0.01 F_1 loss on Subtask A alone. The decay in performance due to ablation is stable: showing that sequential dependencies on the previous output (O), the token identity, prefixes and suffixes matter the most. These results are expected and validate earlier sequence labeling work for parsing bibliographic reference strings (Councill et al., 2008). As we are dealing with document excerpts taken from random sections, and possibly due to the sparsity of the feature, title occurrence (F18, Row 6) played the least role in performance and could have been omitted. However, it helps in Subtask B, making the overall Subtask B perform slightly better (F18, Row 1). For simplicity, we use all features (Row 1) for our subsequent CRF models.

3.2 Joint Modeling versus Individual Experts

A limitation of CRFs is that they discount overlapping, hierarchical sequence labels, assigning the

Setup	Precision	Recall	F_1
Joint	0.55	0.38	**0.45**
Unified	0.49	0.40	0.44

Table 2: Subtask A performance for *Joint* versus *Unified* models, as assessed on *Dev*. Best performance is **bolded.**

single most likely label sequence. As an example from *Train*, a *Material* occurring as substring of a *Task* could not be labeled correctly, as in "*[sequences of optimal walks of a growing length in weighted [digraph]$_{material}$]$_{task}$*". In contrast, separate CRF models for individual classes could label such structures; however, these separate models then have no contextual evidence of the existence of other labels in the sequence.

We test whether the aforementioned model (as in Table 1, referred to here as *Joint*) compares favorably to having individual expert models. We also test whether a single model only trained for identification (Subtask A) outperforms the *Joint* model which performs a relatively complex job. These additional models are:

- *Unified*: We collapse all three keyphrase types into a single type. This system acts as an expert for identifying keyphrases (Subtask A only).

- *Individual*: We use each of the three types of keyphrases to train an expert type-specific keyphrase extractors. This model can potentially predict overlapping (and sometimes conflicting) class instances.

We evaluate on the *Dev* with models trained on the *Train* (Tables 2 and 3). Interestingly, we can

Setup	Class	Precision	Recall	F_1
Joint	Material	0.61	0.36	**0.45**
	Process	0.45	0.34	**0.39**
	Task	0.29	0.12	**0.17**
	Micro Avg.	0.51	0.32	**0.40**
Individual	Material	0.50	0.28	0.36
	Process	0.29	0.23	0.26
	Task	0.22	0.07	0.11
	Micro Avg.	0.37	0.22	0.28

Table 3: Subtask B performance for *Joint* versus *Individual* models, as assessed on *Dev*. Best performance is **bolded.**

Class	Precision	Recall	F_1
Material	0.40	0.40	0.40 (-0.05)
Process	0.37	0.26	0.30 (-0.09)
Task	0.13	0.07	0.09 (-0.08)
Synonym-of	0.06	0.18	0.09
Hyponym-of	0.00	0.01	0.00
Micro Avg.	0.26	0.29	0.27

Table 4: Scores for evaluation on *Test*. Parenthetical numbers give differences from *Dev* performance.

see that the *Joint* model does better in both scenarios. In comparing the *Joint* versus the *Unified* model, we see that there is a useful signal in knowing the type of keyphrase. The *Unified* model benefits from having better annotation density, which could account for the higher recall. However, in the *Unified* model, the output feature (O) loses the information of the keyphrase type (if any) of the previous context. We conjecture that this loss of fidelity in the labels causes the drop in overall performance, particularly in precision. This is corroborated by our feature ablation experiments, where omitting the output feature causes the largest single drop in performance (Table 1, Row 7).

4 Official Run Results

We discuss the final reported system performance as officially recorded in the SemEval-2017 system runs for Task 10 blind *Test*. Table 4 reports the official results of our submitted run on the *Test*, trained over both *Train* and *Dev*.

We see a recognizable degradation of *Task* performance of over 50%, partially due to the skew in the distribution change between *Test* and *Dev* (Table 5). We note from the official run results, systems across the board experienced similar performance loss on *Task*.

Table 6 shows the breakdown of the Scenario 1 result for Subtasks A, B, and C. For Subtasks A

Dataset	Material	Process	Task
Dev	562(49%)	455(39%)	137(12%)
Test	904(44%)	954(46%)	193(9%)

Table 5: Type Count and Percentages.

Subtask	Precision	Recall	F_1
A	0.51	0.42	0.46
B	0.37	0.31	0.33
C	0.03	0.10	0.04

Table 6: Official scores on Subtask evaluations.

and B in terms of precision, our model performed close to the best performing system, with a difference of 0.04. Our recall was significantly lower, by around 0.1. We believe this is caused by the systematic modeling error that our model incurs as it cannot deal with overlapping (nested) annotated types. The results are further worsened by the strict score calculation that discards partially extracted keyphrases as incorrect. This implies that every time a nested instance appears, the model loses at least one keyphrase for recall. This evaluation, also, to a great level contributes to the observed lower performance on *Task* (Table 3) on an average as compared to other classes. As apparent from the dataset, *Task* have more tokens and occasionally encompass smaller *Material* token sequences making it more susceptible to not match completely and hence incur low precision.

5 Conclusion

We detail our approach in using the conditional random field to address the science information extraction task in SemEval-2017. We demonstrate that the CRF model, when applied jointly to the task of performing both identification and classification, outperforms sequential models for each task separately.

References

Isabelle Augenstein, Mrinal Kanti Das, Sebastian Riedel, Lakshmi Nair Vikraman, and Andrew McCallum. 2017. SemEval 2017 Task 10: ScienceIE - Extracting Keyphrases and Relations from Scientific Publications. In *Proceedings of the International Workshop on Semantic Evaluation*. Association for Computational Linguistics, Vancouver, Canada.

Isaac G. Councill, C. Lee Giles, and Min-Yen Kan. 2008. ParsCit: An open-source CRF reference string parsing package. In *Language Resources and Evaluation Conference*.

Siegfried Handschuh and Behrang QasemiZadeh. 2014. The ACL RD-TEC: a dataset for benchmarking terminology extraction and classification in computational linguistics. In *COLING 2014: 4th International Workshop on Computational Terminology*.

Su Nam Kim, Olena Medelyan, Min-Yen Kan, and Timothy Baldwin. 2010. Semeval-2010 task 5: Automatic keyphrase extraction from scientific articles. In *Proceedings of the 5th International Workshop on Semantic Evaluation*. Association for Computational Linguistics, pages 21–26.

Su Nam Kim, Olena Medelyan, Min-Yen Kan, and Timothy Baldwin. 2013. Automatic keyphrase extraction from scientific articles. *Language resources and evaluation* 47(3):723–742.

John Lafferty, Andrew McCallum, and Fernando Pereira. 2001. Conditional random fields: Probabilistic models for segmenting and labeling sequence data. In *Proceedings of the eighteenth international conference on machine learning, ICML*. volume 1, pages 282–289.

Thuy Dung Nguyen and Min-Yen Kan. 2007. Keyphrase extraction in scientific publications. In *Proceedings of the 10th international conference on Asian digital libraries: looking back 10 years and forging new frontiers*. Springer-Verlag, pages 317–326.

MIT at SemEval-2017 Task 10:
Relation Extraction with Convolutional Neural Networks

Ji Young Lee[*]
MIT
jjylee@mit.edu

Franck Dernoncourt[*]
MIT
francky@mit.edu

Peter Szolovits
MIT
psz@mit.edu

Abstract

Over 50 million scholarly articles have been published: they constitute a unique repository of knowledge. In particular, one may infer from them relations between scientific concepts. Artificial neural networks have recently been explored for relation extraction. In this work, we continue this line of work and present a system based on a convolutional neural network to extract relations. Our model ranked first in the SemEval-2017 task 10 (ScienceIE) for relation extraction in scientific articles (subtask C).

1 Introduction and related work

The number of articles published every year keeps increasing (Druss and Marcus, 2005; Larsen and Von Ins, 2010), with well over 50 million scholarly articles published so far (Jinha, 2010). While this repository of human knowledge contains invaluable information, it has become increasingly difficult to take advantage of all available information due to its sheer amount.

One challenge is that the knowledge present in scholarly articles is mostly unstructured. One approach to organize this knowledge is to classify each sentence (Kim et al., 2011; Amini et al., 2012; Hassanzadeh et al., 2014; Dernoncourt et al., 2016). Another approach is to extract entities and relations between them, which is the focus of the ScienceIE shared task at SemEval-2017 (Augenstein et al., 2017).

Relation extraction can be seen as a process comprising two steps that can be done jointly (Li and Ji, 2014) or separately: first, entities of interest need to be identified, and second, the relation among the entities has to be determined. In this work, we concentrate on the second step (often referred to as relation extraction or classification) and on binary relations, i.e. relations between two entities. Extracted relations can be used for a variety of tasks such as question-answering systems (Ravichandran and Hovy, 2002), ontology extension (Schutz and Buitelaar, 2005), and clinical trials (Frunza and Inkpen, 2011).

In this paper, we describe the system that we submitted for the ScienceIE shared task. Our system is based on convolutional neural networks and ranked first for relation extraction (subtask C).

Existing systems for relation extraction can be classified into five categories (Zettlemoyer, 2013): systems based on hand-built patterns (Yangarber and Grishman, 1998), bootstrapping methods (Brin, 1998), unsupervised methods (Gonzalez and Turmo, 2009), distant supervision (Snow et al., 2004), and supervised methods. We focus on supervised methods, as the ScienceIE shared task provides a labeled training set.

Supervised methods for relation extraction commonly employ support vector machines (Uzuner et al., 2010, 2011; Minard et al., 2011; GuoDong et al., 2005), naïve Bayes (Zayaraz and Kumara, 2015), maximum entropy (Sun and Grishman, 2012), or conditional random fields (Sutton and McCallum, 2006). These methods require the practitioner to handcraft features, such as surface, lexical, syntactic features (Grouin et al., 2010) or features derived from existing ontologies (Rink et al., 2011). The use of kernels based on dependency trees has also been explored (Bunescu and Mooney, 2005; Culotta and Sorensen, 2004; Zhou et al., 2007).

More recently, a few studies have investigated the use of artificial neural networks for relation extraction (Socher et al., 2012; Nguyen and Grishman, 2015; Hashimoto et al., 2013). Our approach follows this line of work.

---

[*] These authors contributed equally to this work.

Proceedings of the 11th International Workshop on Semantic Evaluations (SemEval-2017), pages 978–984,
Vancouver, Canada, August 3 - 4, 2017. ©2017 Association for Computational Linguistics

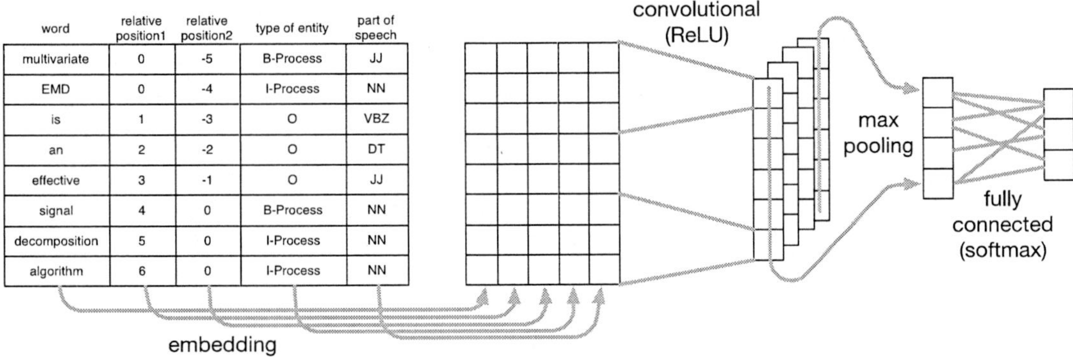

Figure 1: CNN architecture for relation extraction. The left table shows an example of input to the model.

Examples	Rule format	Relations detected
transmission electron microscopy (TEM)	A (B)	If B is an abbreviation of A, then A and B are synonyms.
high purity standard metals (Sn, Pb, Zn, Al, Ag, Ni)	A (B, C, ... , Z)	If any of B, C, ... , Z is a hyponym of A, then all of them are hyponyms of A.
(TEMs), scanning electron microscopes	(A) B	A and B have no relation.
DOTMA/DOPE	A/B	A and B have no relation.

Table 1: Rules used for postprocessing. We considered B to be an abbreviation of A if the first letters of each token in A form B. The examples are from the training and development sets

2 Model

Our model for relation extraction comprises three parts: preprocessing, convolutional neural network (CNN), and postprocessing.

2.1 Preprocessing

The preprocessing step takes as input each raw text (i.e., a paragraph of a scientific article in ScienceIE) as well as the location of all entities present in the text, and output several examples. Each example is represented as a list of tokens, each with four features: the relative positions of the two entity mentions, and their entity types and part-of-speech (POS) tags. Figure 1 shows an example from the ScienceIE corpus in the table on the left.

Sentence and token boundaries as well as POS tags are detected using the Stanford CoreNLP toolkit (Manning et al., 2014), and every pair of entity mentions of the same type within each sentence boundary are considered to be of a potential relation. We also remove any references (e.g. [1, 2]), which are irrelevant to the task, and ensure that the sentences are not too long by eliminating the tokens before the beginning of the first entity mention and after the end of the second entity mention.

2.2 CNN architecture

The CNN takes each preprocessed sentence as input, and predicts the relation between the two entities. The CNN architecture, illustrated in Figure 1, consists of four main layers, similar to the one used in text classification (Collobert et al., 2011; Kim, 2014; Lee and Dernoncourt, 2016; Gehrmann et al., 2017).

1. the **embedding layer** converts each feature (word, relative positions 1 and 2, type of entity, and POS tag) into an embedding vector via a lookup table and concatenates them.
2. the **convolutional layer** with ReLU activation transforms the embeddings into feature maps by sliding filters over the tokens.
3. the **max pooling layer** selects the highest feature value in each feature map by applying the max operator.
4. the **fully connected layer** with softmax activation outputs the probability of each relation.

2.3 Rule-based postprocessing

The postprocessing step uses the rules in Table 1 to correct the relations detected by the CNN, or to detect additional relations. These rules were developed from the examples in the training set, to be consistent with common sense.

annotation	A (arg1) is a Hyponym of (rel) B (arg2)					
order in text	... A ... B ...			... B ... A ...		
strategy	rel	arg1	arg2	rel	arg1	arg2
correct order	Hypo	A	B	Hypo	A	B
correct order w/ neg. smpl.	Hypo	A	B	Hypo	A	B
	None	B	A	None	B	A
fixed order	Hypo	A	B	Hyper	B	A
any order	Hypo	A	B	Hyper	A	B
	Hyper	B	A	Hypo	B	A

annotation	A (arg1) is a Synonym of (rel) B (arg2)					
order in text	... A ... B ...			... B ... A ...		
strategy	rel	arg1	arg2	rel	arg1	arg2
correct order	Syn	A	B	Syn	A	B
correct order w/ neg. smpl.	Syn	A	B	Syn	A	B
	Syn	B	A	Syn	B	A
fixed order	Syn	A	B	Syn	B	A
any order	Syn	A	B	Syn	A	B
	Syn	B	A	Syn	B	A

Table 2: Argument ordering strategies. "w/ neg. smpl.": with negative sampling (Xu et al., 2015), "rel": relation, "arg": argument. "Syn", "Hypo", "Hyper", and "None" refers to the "Synonym-of", "Hyponym-of", "Hypernym-of", and "None' relations. Note that the "Hypernym-of" relation is the reverse of the "Hyponym-of" relation, introduced in addition to the relations annotated for the dataset.

2.4 Implementation

During training, the objective is to maximize the log probability of the correct relation type. The model is trained using stochastic gradient descent with minibatch of size 16, updating all parameters, i.e., token embeddings, feature embeddings, CNN filter weights, and fully connected layer weights, at each gradient descent step. For regularization, dropout is applied before the fully connected layer, and early stop with a patience of 10 epochs is used based on the development set.

The token embeddings are initialized using publicly available[2] pre-trained token embeddings, namely GloVe (Pennington et al., 2014) trained on Wikipedia and Gigaword 5 (Parker et al., 2011). The feature embeddings and the other parameters of the neural network are initialized randomly.

To deal with class imbalance, we upsampled the synonym and hyponym classes by duplicating the examples in the positive classes so that the *upsampling ratio*, i.e., the ratio of the number of positive examples in each class to that of the negative examples, is at least 0.5. Without the upsampling, the trained model would have poor performances.

3 Experiments

3.1 Dataset

We evaluate our model on the ScienceIE dataset (Augenstein et al., 2017), which consists of 500 journal articles evenly distributed among the domains of computer science, material sciences and physics. Three types of entities are annotated: process, task, and material. The relation between each pair of entities of the same type within a sentence are annotated as either "Synonym-of",

"Hyponym-of", or "None". Table 3 shows the number of examples for each relation class.

Relation	Train	Dev	Test
Hyponym-of	420	123	95
Synonym-of	253	45	112
None	5355	1240	1503
Total	6028	1408	1710

Table 3: Number of examples for each relation class in ScienceIE. "Dev": Development.

3.2 Hyperparameters

Table 4 details the experiment ranges and choices of hyperparameters. The results were quite robust to the choice of hyperparameters within the specified ranges.

Hyperparameter	Choice	Experiment range
Token embedding dim.	100	$50-300$
Feature embedding dim.	10	$5-50$
CNN filter height	5	$3-15$
Number of CNN filters	200	$50-500$
Dropout probability	0.5	$0-1$
Upsampling ratio	3	$0.5-5$

Table 4: Experiment ranges and choices of hyperparameters.[3]

3.3 Argument ordering strategies

One of the main challenges in relation extraction is the ordering of arguments in relations, as many relations are *order-sensitive*. For example, consider the sentence "A dog is an animal." If we set "dog" to be the first argument and "animal" the second,

---

[2] http://nlp.stanford.edu/projects/glove/

[3] For these experiments, we used the official training set as the training/development set with a 75%/25% split, and the official development set as the test set.

Labels used	Training strategy	Evaluation strategy	Hyponym-of			Synonym-of			Micro-averaged		
			P	R	F1	P	R	F1	P	R	F1
All	correct order	any order	0.193	0.101	0.132	0.782	0.640	0.703	0.409	0.245	0.306
	corr. w/ n. s.	any order	0.431	0.127	0.196	0.826	0.756	0.788	**0.638**	0.295	0.404
	any order	any order	0.482	0.197	0.279	0.784	0.756	0.769	0.621	0.346	0.444
	any order	fixed order	**0.486**	0.195	0.278	0.773	0.753	0.763	0.621	0.345	0.443
	fixed order	any order	0.372	0.218	0.274	0.743	0.756	0.749	0.516	0.362	0.425
	fixed order	fixed order	0.425	0.213	0.283	0.803	0.753	0.777	0.578	0.358	0.441
Hyponym	correct order	any order	0.108	0.069	0.084	-	-	-	-	-	-
	corr. w/ n. s.	any order	0.215	0.115	0.148	-	-	-	-	-	-
	any order	any order	0.384	0.246	0.299	-	-	-	-	-	-
	any order	fixed order	0.410	0.235	0.298	-	-	-	-	-	-
	fixed order	any order	0.385	**0.249**	**0.301**	-	-	-	-	-	-
	fixed order	fixed order	0.409	0.237	0.297	-	-	-	-	-	-
Synonym	any order	any order	-	-	-	0.855	0.771	0.811	-	-	-
	any order	fixed order	-	-	-	0.852	**0.776**	**0.812**	-	-	-
Hyp+Syn	any + any	any + fixed	0.385	0.228	0.285	**0.857**	0.771	**0.812**	0.553	**0.373**	**0.445**

Table 5: Results for various ordering strategies on the development set of the ScienceIE dataset, averaged over 10 runs each.[3] "corr. w/ n. s.": correct order with negative sampling. Hyp+Syn is obtained by merging the output of the best hyponym classifier and that of the best synonym classifier.

then the corresponding relation is "Hyponym-of"; however, if we reverse the argument order, then the "Hyponym-of" relation does not hold any more.

Therefore, it is crucial to ensure that 1) the CNN is provided with the information about the argument order, and 2) it is able to utilize the given information efficiently. In our work, the former point is addressed by providing the CNN with the two relative position features compared to the first and the second argument of the relation respectively. In order to certify the latter point, we experimented with four strategies for argument ordering, outlined in Table 2.

4   Results and Discussion

Table 5 shows the results from experimenting with various argument ordering strategies. The correct order strategy performed the worst, but the negative sampling improved over it slightly, while the fixed order and any order strategies performed the best. The latter two strategies performed almost equally well in terms of micro-averaged F1-score. This implies that for relation extraction it may be advantageous to use both the original relation classes as well as their "reverse" relation classes for training, instead of using only the original relation classes with the "correct" argument ordering (with or without the negative sampling). Moreover, ordering the argument as the order of appearance in the text and training once per relation

(i.e., fixed order) is as efficient as training each relation as two examples in two possible argument ordering, one with the original relation class and the other with the reverse relation class (i.e., any order), despite the small size of the dataset.

The difference in performance between the correct order versus the fixed or any order strategies is more prominent for the "Hyponym-of" relation than for the "Synonym-of" relation. This is expected, since the argument ordering strategy is different only for the order-sensitive "Hyponym-of" relation. It is somewhat surprising though, that the correct order strategy performs worse than the other strategies even for order-insensitive "Synonym-of" relation. This may be due to the fact that the model does not see any training examples with the reversed argument ordering for the "Synonym-of" relation. In comparison, the negative sampling strategy, which learns from both the original and reversed argument ordering for the "Synonym-of" relation, the performance is comparable to the two best performing strategies.

We have also experimented with different evaluation strategies for the models trained with the any order and fixed order strategies. When the model is trained with the any order strategy, the choice of the evaluation strategy does not impact the performance. In contrast, when the model is trained with the fixed order strategy, it performs better if the same strategy is used for evaluation. This may be the reason why the model trained with the correct order strategy does not perform as well, since it has to be evaluated with a different strategy from training, namely the any order strategy, as we do not know the correct ordering of arguments for examples in the test set.

We have also tried training binary classifiers for the "Hyponym-of" and the "Synonym-of" relations separately and then merging the outputs of the best classifiers for each relations. While the binary classifiers individually performed better than the multi-way classifier for each corresponding relation class, the overall performance based on the micro-averaged F1-score did not improve over the multi-way classifier after merging the outputs of the hyponym and the synonym classifiers.

Based on the results from the argument ordering strategy experiments, we submitted the model trained using the fixed order strategy, which ranked number one in the challenge. The result is shown in Table 6.

Relation	Precision	Recall	F1-score
Synonym-of	0.820	0.813	0.816
Hyponym-of	0.455	0.421	0.437
Micro-averaged	0.658	0.633	0.645

Table 6: Result on the test set of the ScienceIE dataset, using the official train/dev/test split.

To quantify the importance of various features of our model, we trained the model by gradually adding more features one by one, from word embeddings, relative positions, and entity types to POS tags in order. The results on the importance of the features as well as postprocessing are shown in Figure 2. Adding the relative position features improved the performance the most, while adding the entity type improved it the least. Note that even without the postprocessing, the F1-score is 0.63, which still outperforms the second-best system with the F1-score of 0.54.

Figure 3 quantifies the impact of the two preprocessing steps, deleting brackets and cutting sentences, introduced to compensate for the small dataset size. Cutting the sentence before the first entity and after the second entity resulted in a dramatic impact on the performance, while deleting brackets (i.e., removing the reference marks) improve the performance modestly. This implies that the text between the two entities contains most of the information about the relation between them.

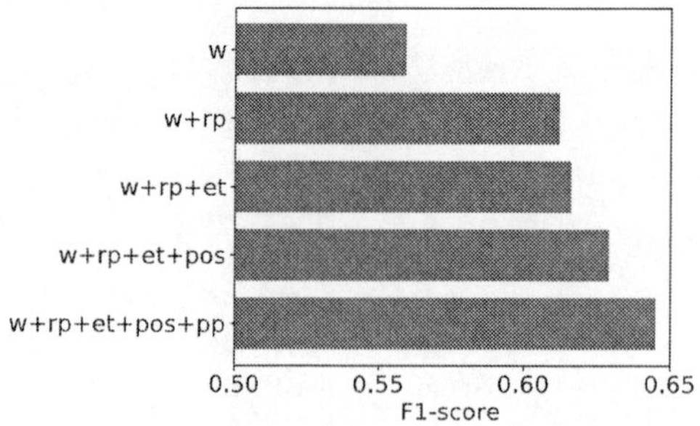

Figure 2: Importance of features of CNN and postprocessing rules. w: word embeddings, rp: relative positions to the first and the second arguments, et: entity types, pos: POS tags.

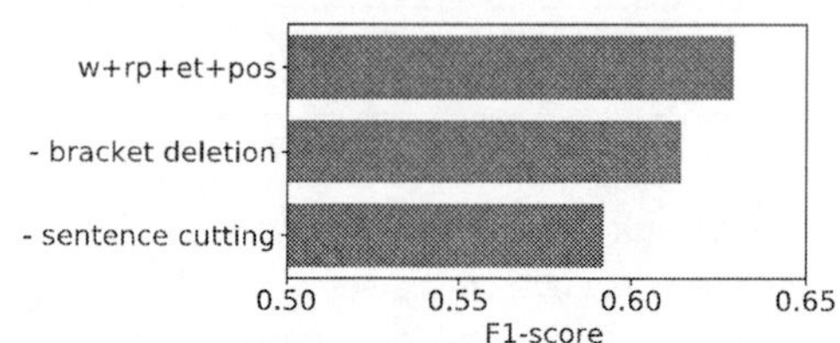

Figure 3: Impact of bracket deletion and sentence cutting. "w+rp+et+pos" represents the CNN model trained using all features with both bracket deletion and sentence cutting during preprocessing. "-bracket deletion" is the same model trained only without bracket deletion, and "-sentence cutting" only without sentence cutting.

5   Conclusion

In this article we have presented an ANN-based approach to relation extraction, which ranked first in the SemEval-2017 task 10 (ScienceIE) for relation extraction in scientific articles (subtask C). We have experimented with various strategies to incorporate argument ordering for ordering-sensitive relations, showing that an efficient strategy is to fix the arguments ordering as appears on the text by introducing reverse relations. We have also demonstrated that cutting the sentence before the first entity and after the second entity is effective for small datasets.

Acknowledgments

The authors would like to thank the ScienceIE organizers as well as the anonymous reviewers. The project was supported by Philips Research. The content is solely the responsibility of the authors and does not necessarily represent the official views of Philips Research.

References

Iman Amini, David Martinez, and Diego Molla. 2012. Overview of the ALTA 2012 Shared Task. In *Australasian Language Technology Association Workshop 2012*. volume 7, page 124.

Isabelle Augenstein, Mrinal Kanti Das, Sebastian Riedel, Lakshmi Nair Vikraman, and Andrew McCallum. 2017. SemEval 2017 Task 10: ScienceIE - Extracting Keyphrases and Relations from Scientific Publications. In *Proceedings of the International Workshop on Semantic Evaluation*. Association for Computational Linguistics, Vancouver, Canada.

Sergey Brin. 1998. Extracting patterns and relations from the world wide web. In *International Workshop on The World Wide Web and Databases*. Springer, pages 172–183.

Razvan C Bunescu and Raymond J Mooney. 2005. A shortest path dependency kernel for relation extraction. In *Proceedings of the conference on human language technology and empirical methods in natural language processing*. Association for Computational Linguistics, pages 724–731.

Ronan Collobert, Jason Weston, Léon Bottou, Michael Karlen, Koray Kavukcuoglu, and Pavel Kuksa. 2011. Natural language processing (almost) from scratch. *The Journal of Machine Learning Research* 12:2493–2537.

Aron Culotta and Jeffrey Sorensen. 2004. Dependency tree kernels for relation extraction. In *Proceedings of the 42nd annual meeting on association for computational linguistics*. Association for Computational Linguistics, page 423.

Franck Dernoncourt, Ji Young Lee, and Peter Szolovits. 2016. Neural networks for joint sentence classification in medical paper abstracts. *EACL 2017*.

Benjamin G Druss and Steven C Marcus. 2005. Growth and decentralization of the medical literature: implications for evidence-based medicine. *Journal of the Medical Library Association* 93(4):499.

Oana Frunza and Diana Inkpen. 2011. Extracting relations between diseases, treatments, and tests from clinical data. In *Canadian Conference on Artificial Intelligence*. Springer, pages 140–145.

Sebastian Gehrmann, Franck Dernoncourt, Yeran Li, Eric T. Carlson, Joy T. Wu, Jonathan Welt, David W. Grant, Patrick D. Tyler, and Leo A. Celi. 2017. Comparing rule-based and deep learning models for patient phenotyping. *arXiv:1703.08705*.

Edgar Gonzalez and Jordi Turmo. 2009. Unsupervised relation extraction by massive clustering. In *Data Mining, 2009. ICDM'09. Ninth IEEE International Conference on*. IEEE, pages 782–787.

Cyril Grouin, Asma Ben Abacha, Delphine Bernhard, Bruno Cartoni, Louise Deleger, Brigitte Grau, Anne-Laure Ligozat, Anne-Lyse Minard, Sophie Rosset, and Pierre Zweigenbaum. 2010. Caramba: concept, assertion, and relation annotation using machine-learning based approaches. In *i2b2 Medication Extraction Challenge Workshop*.

Zhou GuoDong, Su Jian, Zhang Jie, and Zhang Min. 2005. Exploring various knowledge in relation extraction. In *Proceedings of the 43rd annual meeting on association for computational linguistics*. Association for Computational Linguistics, pages 427–434.

Kazuma Hashimoto, Makoto Miwa, Yoshimasa Tsuruoka, and Takashi Chikayama. 2013. Simple customization of recursive neural networks for semantic relation classification. In *EMNLP*. pages 1372–1376.

Hamed Hassanzadeh, Tudor Groza, and Jane Hunter. 2014. Identifying scientific artefacts in biomedical literature: The evidence based medicine use case. *Journal of biomedical informatics* 49:159–170.

Arif E Jinha. 2010. Article 50 million: an estimate of the number of scholarly articles in existence. *Learned Publishing* 23(3):258–263.

Su Nam Kim, David Martinez, Lawrence Cavedon, and Lars Yencken. 2011. Automatic classification of sentences to support evidence based medicine. *BioMed Central (BMC) Bioinformatics* 12(2):1.

Yoon Kim. 2014. Convolutional neural networks for sentence classification. In *Proceedings of the 2014 Conference on Empirical Methods in Natural Language Processing (EMNLP)*. Association for Computational Linguistics (ACL), pages 1746–1751.

Peder Olesen Larsen and Markus Von Ins. 2010. The rate of growth in scientific publication and the decline in coverage provided by science citation index. *Scientometrics* 84(3):575–603.

Ji Young Lee and Franck Dernoncourt. 2016. Sequential short-text classification with recurrent and convolutional neural networks. In *Human Language Technologies 2016: The Conference of the North American Chapter of the Association for Computational Linguistics, NAACL HLT*.

Qi Li and Heng Ji. 2014. Incremental joint extraction of entity mentions and relations. In *ACL (1)*. pages 402–412.

Christopher D. Manning, Mihai Surdeanu, John Bauer, Jenny Finkel, Steven J. Bethard, and David McClosky. 2014. The Stanford CoreNLP natural language processing toolkit. In *Association for Computational Linguistics (ACL) System Demonstrations*. pages 55–60. http://www.aclweb.org/anthology/P/P14/P14-5010.

Anne-Lyse Minard, Anne-Laure Ligozat, and Brigitte Grau. 2011. Multi-class svm for relation extraction from clinical reports. In *Ranlp*. volume 59, pages 604–609.

Thien Huu Nguyen and Ralph Grishman. 2015. Relation extraction: Perspective from convolutional neural networks. In *Proceedings of NAACL-HLT*. pages 39–48.

Robert Parker, David Graff, Junbo Kong, Ke Chen, and Kazuaki Maeda. 2011. English Gigaword fifth edition. Technical report, Linguistic Data Consortium, Philadelphia.

Jeffrey Pennington, Richard Socher, and Christopher D Manning. 2014. GloVe: global vectors for word representation. *Proceedings of the Empiricial Methods in Natural Language Processing (EMNLP 2014)* 12:1532–1543.

Deepak Ravichandran and Eduard Hovy. 2002. Learning surface text patterns for a question answering system. In *Proceedings of the 40th annual meeting on association for computational linguistics*. Association for Computational Linguistics, pages 41–47.

Bryan Rink, Sanda Harabagiu, and Kirk Roberts. 2011. Automatic extraction of relations between medical concepts in clinical texts. *Journal of the American Medical Informatics Association* 18(5):594–600.

Alexander Schutz and Paul Buitelaar. 2005. Relext: A tool for relation extraction from text in ontology extension. In *International semantic web conference*. Springer, volume 2005, pages 593–606.

Rion Snow, Daniel Jurafsky, Andrew Y Ng, et al. 2004. Learning syntactic patterns for automatic hypernym discovery. In *NIPS*. volume 17, pages 1297–1304.

Richard Socher, Brody Huval, Christopher D Manning, and Andrew Y Ng. 2012. Semantic compositionality through recursive matrix-vector spaces. In *Proceedings of the 2012 Joint Conference on Empirical Methods in Natural Language Processing and Computational Natural Language Learning*. Association for Computational Linguistics, pages 1201–1211.

Ang Sun and Ralph Grishman. 2012. Active learning for relation type extension with local and global data views. In *Proceedings of the 21st ACM international conference on Information and knowledge management*. ACM, pages 1105–1112.

Charles Sutton and Andrew McCallum. 2006. An introduction to conditional random fields for relational learning. *Introduction to statistical relational learning* pages 93–128.

Ozlem Uzuner, Jonathan Mailoa, Russell Ryan, and Tawanda Sibanda. 2010. Semantic relations for problem-oriented medical records. *Artificial intelligence in medicine* 50(2):63–73.

Özlem Uzuner, Brett R South, Shuying Shen, and Scott L DuVall. 2011. 2010 i2b2/va challenge on concepts, assertions, and relations in clinical text. *Journal of the American Medical Informatics Association* 18(5):552–556.

Kun Xu, Yansong Feng, Songfang Huang, and Dongyan Zhao. 2015. Semantic relation classification via convolutional neural networks with simple negative sampling. In *Proceedings of the 2015 Conference on Empirical Methods in Natural Language Processing*. Association for Computational Linguistics, Lisbon, Portugal, pages 536–540. https://aclweb.org/anthology/D/D15/D15-1062.

Roman Yangarber and Ralph Grishman. 1998. Nyu: Description of the proteus/pet system as used for muc-7. In *In Proceedings of the Seventh Message Understanding Conference (MUC-7)*. Citeseer.

Godandapani Zayaraz and Suresh Kumara. 2015. Concept relation extraction using naïve bayes classifier for ontology-based question answering systems. *Journal of King Saud University-Computer and Information Sciences* 27(1):13–24.

Luke Zettlemoyer. 2013. Relation extraction. *CSE517: Natural Language Processing* .

Guodong Zhou, Min Zhang, Dong-Hong Ji, and Qiaoming Zhu. 2007. Tree kernel-based relation extraction with context-sensitive structured parse tree information. In *EMNLP-CoNLL*. Citeseer, volume 2007, pages 728–736.

TTI-COIN at SemEval-2017 Task 10: Investigating Embeddings for End-to-End Relation Extraction from Scientific Papers

Tomoki Tsujimura, **Makoto Miwa**, and **Yutaka Sasaki**
COmputational INtelligence Laboratory
Toyota Technological Institute
2-12-1 Hisakata, Tempaku-ku, Nagoya, Aichi, 468-8511, Japan
`{sd16420, makoto-miwa, yutaka.sasaki}@toyota-ti.ac.jp`

Abstract

This paper describes our TTI-COIN system that participated in SemEval-2017 Task 10. We investigated appropriate embeddings to adapt a neural end-to-end entity and relation extraction system LSTM-ER to this task. We participated in the full task setting of the entity segmentation, entity classification and relation classification (scenario 1) and the setting of relation classification only (scenario 3). The system was directly applied to the scenario 1 without modifying the codes thanks to its generality and flexibility. Our evaluation results show that the choice of appropriate pre-trained embeddings affected the performance significantly. With the best embeddings, our system was ranked third in the scenario 1 with the micro F1 score of 0.38. We also confirm that our system can produce the micro F1 score of 0.48 for the scenario 3 on the test data, and this score is close to the score of the 3rd ranked system in the task.

1 Introduction

Semantic relationships between entities are useful for building knowledge bases and semantic search engines. Their automatic extraction has been widely studied in the natural language processing (NLP) field (Li and Ji, 2014; Miwa and Sasaki, 2014; Miwa and Bansal, 2016). SemEval-2017 Task 10 (Augenstein et al., 2017) deals with relation extraction from scientific papers.

While entity detection and relation extraction have often been treated as separate tasks, several studies show that joint treatment of these tasks can improve extraction performance on both tasks (Li and Ji, 2014; Miwa and Sasaki, 2014). We em-

ployed the state-of-the-art neural network-based end-to-end entity and relation extraction system LSTM-ER[1] (Miwa and Bansal, 2016). The model of the system is built on pre-trained word embeddings, and it has a tree-structured bidirectional long short-term memory-based recurrent neural network (LSTM-RNN) layer stacked on a sequential bidirectional LSTM-RNN layer. It predicts entities and relations in an end-to-end manner with shared parameters, and the parameters in word embeddings and both LSTM-RNNs are updated simultaneously during training.

We first checked the applicability of the system in our evaluation. The system was originally developed for ACE (automatic content extraction) corpora, but it does not depend on specific tasks and has high configurability (Miwa and Ananiadou, 2015) since it prepares a separate configuration file, where task specific settings like hyperparameters can be specified. The system was successfully applied to the end-to-end relation extraction setting (scenario 1 in the task) without modifying the original codes in our experiments, although small modifications to the inputs were required. This shows the generality of the system.

Using this system, we also investigated how the pre-trained word embeddings affect the overall performance. Miwa and Bansal (2016) mostly focused on the model architectures and paid little attention to the differences in pre-trained embeddings. Our results show that selecting the appropriate initial embeddings is crucial since changing the pre-trained embeddings greatly affected the overall performance.

2 System description

In this section, we describe our base neural network system and pre-trained word embeddings

---

[1] `https://github.com/tticoin/LSTM-ER`

Proceedings of the 11th International Workshop on Semantic Evaluations (SemEval-2017), pages 985–989,
Vancouver, Canada, August 3 - 4, 2017. ©2017 Association for Computational Linguistics

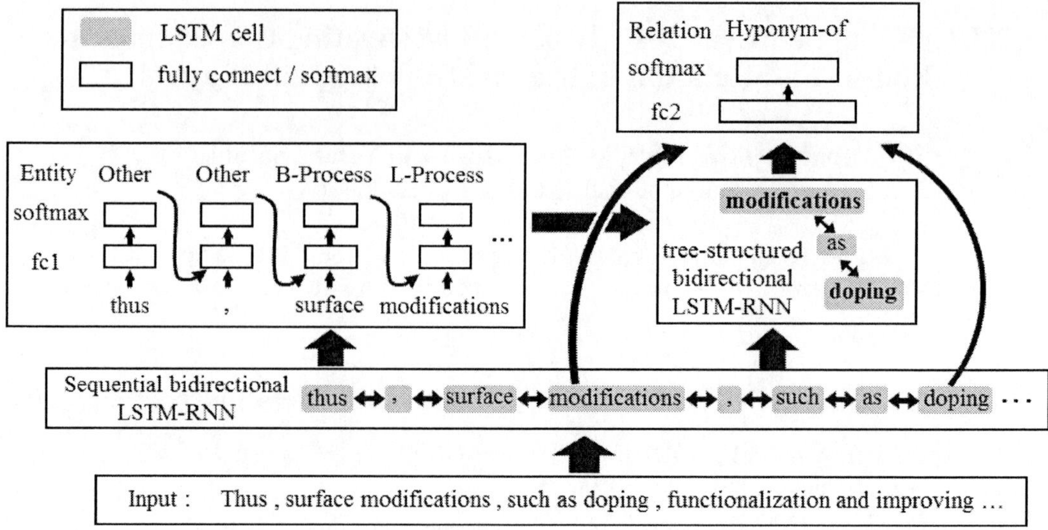

Figure 1: Model overview in extracting a *Hypernym-of* relation between *Process* entities "surface modifications" and "doping". Word and POS embeddings are input to the sequential bidirectional LSTM-RNN.

used for the initialization.

2.1 Base system

We employ the LSTM-ER system that implements a neural network-based model (Miwa and Bansal, 2016). The system has a high configurability, and it can be applied to new tasks with minimum manual efforts. Figure 1 illustrates the overview of the model. The model represents relations using tree-structured LSTM-RNNs and entities using a sequential LSTM-RNN, and stack these LSTM-RNNs to realize their end-to-end extraction.

This model first inputs the concatenation of word embeddings and part-of-speech (POS) embeddings to a sequential bidirectional LSTM-RNN. The output of the sequential bidirectional LSTM-RNN is obtained by concatenating the output of the forward sequential LSTM-RNN and the output of the backward sequential LSTM-RNN.

These outputs together with the embedding of the previous label are passed to the fully connected layer `fc1` with an activation tanh function, and then the model calculate the probabilities of the entity labels through a softmax layer. The model uses the BILOU (Begin, Inside, Last, Outside, Unit) scheme (Ratinov and Roth, 2009) for representing entities and assigns the labels to each word. Each entity label is decided in a greedy manner, starting from the beginning of a sentence to the end of the sentence. During this greedy decision, the model avoids illegal label assignments.

For example, if a t-th word is determined as *I-Material*, only either *I-Material* or *L-Material* can be selected for the next $(i + 1)$-th word and other illegal labels like *B-Task* are not chosen.

After detecting entities, for each target entity pair, the model picks up words that are contained in the shortest path between the last words of the pair. The model passes the outputs of the sequential bidirectional LSTM-RNN together with the entity-label and dependency embeddings relating to these words to a bidirectional tree-structured LSTM-RNN. In the bidirectional tree-structured LSTM-RNN, each cell of the bottom-up tree-structured LSTM-RNN receives multiple children states and calculates the parent state from them, while each cell of the top-down one takes a parent state and calculates the states of the children.

The output of the bi-directional tree-structured LSTM-RNN is obtained by concatenating the output of the root word from the bottom-up tree-structured LSTM-RNN and the outputs of last words of the entities from the top-down tree-structured LSTM-RNN. This output of the bi-directional tree-structured LSTM-RNN is passed to the fully connected layer `fc2` with the activation tanh function, together with the outputs of the last words in each target entity in the sequential bi-directional LSTM-RNN. The model then calculates the probability of each relation label through a softmax layer as in entity detection.

2.2 Investigating pre-trained word embedding

Word embeddings are frequently used for the inputs to neural network based models. It is well-known that the performance of neural models can be improved by initializing embeddings with pre-trained embeddings. Word2vec (Mikolov et al., 2013) is a widely-used toolkit to obtain such pre-trained embeddings from raw texts. Word2vec implements two models: continuous bag-of-words (CBOW) and skip-gram. CBOW learns embeddings by predicting the distribution of target word from the surrounding words, while skip-gram learns embeddings by predicting the distribution of each surrounding word from the input word. Ling et al. (2015) introduced the structured skip-gram model[2] based on word2vec in order to consider the ordering of co-occurrence words by incorporating an attention mechanism.

To investigate the effects of the pre-trained word embeddings, we employed two unlabeled data sets: Wikipedia articles[3] and PubMed abstracts[4]. After the preliminary experiments, we compared 100 dimensional word embeddings obtained by the skip-gram model on the Wikipedia articles and those by the structured skip-gram model on the PubMed abstracts. We used these embeddings for initialization, and we fine-tuned these embeddings during training.

3 Evaluation

3.1 Task

SemEval-2017 Task 10 (Augenstein et al., 2017) deals with a relation extraction problem that focuses on detecting entities of *Process*, *Task* and *Material* from research papers and extracting the *Synonym-of* and *Hypernym-of* relationships between the entities. In this task, 500 example paragraphs are extracted from the ScienceDirect open access publications, and they are manually annotated with the entities and their static relationships. 350 examples of them are used for training, 50 for development, and 100 for test. Each paragraph consists of multiple sentences. Each sentence may contain multiple entities and relationships, and an entity may overlap other entities. *Hypernym-of* relations are directed, while *Synonym-of* relations

Parameter	dimension
word embeddings	100
POS embeddings	10
bidirectional seq-LSTM	50×2
FC1	100
bidirectional tree-LSTM	100×2
FC2	100

Table 1: Dimensions of layers.

are undirected. The tasks consists of three sub-tasks: A, B and C. In subtask A, the participants need to detect segmentations of all entities without considering the entity types. In subtask B, the types of entities need to be labeled. Subtask C focuses on extracting relations between the entities. Three scenarios are provided With the subtasks: the system needs to solve subtasks A, B, and C in scenario 1, B and C in scenario 2, and C in scenario 3. We focus on scenarios 1 and 3.

3.2 Evaluation settings

Pre-trained word embeddings: We obtained pre-trained word embeddings by the skip-gram model and the structured skip-gram model with the same setting. We set the window size to 2, the number of negative samples to 10, the down-sampling rate to 1e-4. We also ignored the words that appear less than 26 times. Other parameters are kept as the default of the original word2vec toolkit[5].

POS tagging and dependency parsing: To deal with the data with the LSTM-ER system, we obtained POS tags and dependency trees for all training, development and test data sets by using the Stanford parser (Chen and Manning, 2014). Since the texts contained Unicode, we processed the data as Unicode texts.

Relation modification: We treated each relation as a directed relation. The *Synonym-of* relations are undirected, but we treated them as they always have left-to-right directions.

Out-of-vocabulary words: For the robustness, we treated out-of-vocabulary words as follows. We first counted the frequencies of words in the training dataset. We then picked up words that only appear once in the training dataset and replaced 1% of them with a symbol word "UNK" randomly. Embeddings for the words that do not appear in the vocabulary of pre-trained embed-

---

[2] https://github.com/wlin12/wang2vec
[3] https://dumps.wikimedia.org/enwiki/20150901/
[4] 2014 MEDLINE/PubMed baseline distribution

---

[5] https://code.google.com/archive/p/word2vec/

Model	Development			Test		
	A	A,B	C	A	A,B	C
End2end (Wikipedia)	0.55	0.46	0.37	0.49	0.36	0.20
End2end (PubMed)	0.58	0.50	0.39	0.50	0.39	0.21
Relation (Wikipedia)	-	-	0.50	-	-	0.43
Relation (PubMed)	-	-	0.52	-	-	0.48 (0.1)

Table 2: Micro F1 scores on the development and the test dataset for three task settings: subtask A, subtask A,B, and subtask C. The number in the parentheses for Rel (PubMed) shows our official score.

Model	Development			Test		
	A	A,B	C	A	A,B	C
structured skip-gram (PubMed)	0.58	0.50	0.39	0.50	0.39	0.21
skip-gram (PubMed)	0.57	0.48	0.36	0.51	0.39	0.22
skip-gram (Wikipedia)	0.55	0.46	0.37	0.49	0.36	0.20

Table 3: Results on the end-to-end model with several pre-trained word vectors.

dings and are not replaced with "UNK" are initialized with random values. The embedding of the "UNK" word is also initialized with random values. We also replaced all the out-of-vocabulary words in the development and test datasets with the "UNK" word.

Nested entities: Entities that were inside of other entity were ignored. The ignored entities were not used as training examples since the base model gives only one entity label to each word. Our system thus did not predict internal entities on the development and test datasets.

Hyper-parameter tuning: We tuned the dimensions of the embeddings and layers, the rates of the dropout, the coefficient of L2 generalization, and the learning late in a greedy manner. We used both the training and development data sets to train the final models for testing. These parameters were tuned by modifying the configuration file of the LSTM-ER system. Table 1 summarizes the dimensions of word/POS embeddings and layers we used for all models.

3.3 Results

Table 2 shows the F1 scores on the development and test datasets for each subtask. We show our (unofficial) evaluation results of our system for the relation classification task (scenario 3)[6]. In all the evaluations, the results with word embeddings obtained by the structured skip-gram model on the PubMed abstracts were better than those by the skip-gram model on the wikipedia abstracts.

Table 3 shows the results between the models using several pre-trained word embeddings.[7] When comparing the training models of pre-trained embeddings on the PubMed abstracts, our system with embeddings by the structured skip-gram model shows better performance than the system with those by the skip-gram model on the develop dataset does, but this is opposite for the test dataset. As for the difference on the training corpora for pre-training using the skip-gram model, the system with embeddings on PubMed shows consistently higher performance on the entities than the system with those on the Wikipedia articles, but there was no consistent performance change for the relations.

There were 11,026 kinds of lowercased words in the 500 examples in the data set in practice. The numbers of out-of-vocabulary words that were not initialized with the pre-trained embeddings were 2,984 for the Wikipedia dataset and 1,697 for the PubMed dataset. The PubMed abstracts are scientific articles in a different domain like the shared task data sets, and this may be one of the reasons why the pre-trained embeddings on PubMed covers more words than those on Wikipedia. In addition, the similarity in the writing between PubMed and ScienceDirect articles may lead the model to fit to the task on entities.

---

[6]We got this low result due to our mistakes in converting the results into the task format.

[7]We got results on the model with word embeddings by applying the skip-gram model to the PubMed abstracts after the competition.

4   Conclusion

We participated SemEval-2017 Task 10 with the
end-to-end entity and relation extraction system
proposed by Miwa and Bansal (2016). We successfully applied the system to the task without
modifying the codes. We improved all F1 scores
by replacing pre-trained word embeddings obtained from the structured skip-gram model on the
PubMed abstracts from those obtained from the
skip-gram model on the Wikipedia articles. We
achieved micro F1 score of 0.50 for the subtask
A, 0.39 for the subtask A and B and 0.21 for the
subtask C, and our system was ranked 3rd in the
end-to-end setting.

References

Isabelle Augenstein, Mrinal Kanti Das, Sebastian
Riedel, Lakshmi Nair Vikraman, and Andrew Mc-
Callum. 2017. SemEval 2017 Task 10: ScienceIE -
Extracting Keyphrases and Relations from Scientific
Publications. In *Proceedings of the International
Workshop on Semantic Evaluation*. Association for
Computational Linguistics, Vancouver, Canada.

Danqi Chen and Christopher Manning. 2014. A fast
and accurate dependency parser using neural networks. In *Proceedings of EMNLP*. ACL, Doha,
Qatar, pages 740–750.

Qi Li and Heng Ji. 2014. Incremental joint extraction
of entity mentions and relations. In *Proceedings of
ACL*. ACL, Baltimore, Maryland, pages 402–412.

Wang Ling, Chris Dyer, Alan W Black, and Isabel
Trancoso. 2015. Two/too simple adaptations of
word2vec for syntax problems. In *Proceedings of
ACL*. ACL, Denver, Colorado, pages 1299–1304.

Tomas Mikolov, Ilya Sutskever, Kai Chen, Greg S Corrado, and Jeff Dean. 2013. Distributed representations of words and phrases and their compositionality. In *NIPS*. pages 3111–3119.

Makoto Miwa and Sophia Ananiadou. 2015. Adaptable, high recall, event extraction system with minimal configuration. *BMC Bioinformatics* 16(Suppl
10.):S7.

Makoto Miwa and Mohit Bansal. 2016. End-to-end relation extraction using lstms on sequences and tree
structures. In *Proceedings of ACL*. ACL, Berlin,
Germany, pages 1105–1116.

Makoto Miwa and Yutaka Sasaki. 2014. Modeling
joint entity and relation extraction with table representation. In *Proceedings of EMNLP*. ACL, Doha,
Qatar, pages 1858–1869.

Lev Ratinov and Dan Roth. 2009. Design challenges
and misconceptions in named entity recognition. In
Proceedings of CoNLL. ACL, Boulder, Colorado,
pages 147–155.

SZTE-NLP at SemEval-2017 Task 10: A High Precision Sequence Model for Keyphrase Extraction Utilizing Sparse Coding for Feature Generation

Gábor Berend

Department of Informatics, University of Szeged
Árpád tér 2, H6720 Szeged, Hungary
`berendg@inf.u-szeged.hu`

Abstract

In this paper we introduce our system participating at the 2017 SemEval shared task on keyphrase extraction from scientific documents. We aimed at the creation of a keyphrase extraction approach which relies on as little external resources as possible. Without applying any hand-crafted external resources, and only utilizing a transformed version of word embeddings trained at Wikipedia, our proposed system manages to perform among the best participating systems in terms of precision.

1 Introduction

The sheer amount of scientific publications makes intelligent processing of papers increasingly important. Automated keyphrase extraction techniques can mitigate the severe difficulties arising when navigating in massive document collections. Hence, extracting keyphrases from scientific literature has generated substantial academic interest over the past years (Witten et al., 1999; Hulth, 2003; Kim et al., 2010; Berend, 2016a).

Continuous word representations such as `word2vec` (Mikolov et al., 2013) has gained increasing popularity recently. These representations assign some semantically meaningful low dimensional vector $\mathbf{w}_i$ to the vocabulary entries of large text corpora.

We demonstrated previously (Berend, 2016b) that useful features can be derived for various sequence labeling tasks by performing a sparse decomposition of the word embedding matrix. In this paper, we investigate the generalization properties of our proposed approach for the task of keyphrase extraction.

2 Sequence labeling framework

Our sequence labeling framework builds on top of our previous work which aimed at multiple different sequence labeling tasks, i.e. part-of-speech tagging and named entity recognition.

2.1 Feature representation

Each token in a sequence is described by a set of feature values and those of its direct neighbors in our model. We relied on multiple sources for deriving features, i.e.

- sparse coding of dense word embeddings,

- Brown clustering of words,

- word identity features and

- orthographic characteristics.

2.1.1 Sparse coding derived features

The main source of features was sparse coding performed on continuous word embeddings. We demonstrated in (Berend, 2016b) that sequence labeling tasks can largely benefit from the sparse decomposition of dense word embedding matrices. That is, given a word embedding matrix $W \in \mathbb{R}^{d \times |V|}$ – with its columns containing the d dimensional dense word embeddings – we seek for its decomposition into a product of $D \in \mathbb{R}^{d \times K}$ and $\alpha \in \mathbb{R}^{K \times |V|}$ – containing sparse linear combination coefficients for each of the word embeddings – such that $\|W - D\alpha\|_F^2 + \lambda\|\alpha\|_1$ gets minimized.

Features for some word w_i are then determined based on its corresponding vector $\boldsymbol{\alpha}_i$ by taking the signs and indices of its non-zero coefficients, i.e.

$$f(\mathbf{w}_i) = \{sign(\boldsymbol{\alpha}_i[j])j \mid \boldsymbol{\alpha}_i[j] \neq 0\},$$

where $\boldsymbol{\alpha}_i[j]$ denotes the jth coefficient in $\boldsymbol{\alpha}_i$.

Proceedings of the 11th International Workshop on Semantic Evaluations (SemEval-2017), pages 990–994,
Vancouver, Canada, August 3 - 4, 2017. ©2017 Association for Computational Linguistics

As we observed a consistent benefit of using polyglot (Al-Rfou et al., 2013) embeddings previously, we now also rely on those embeddings for keyphrase extraction.

2.1.2 Brown clustering

Brown clustering (Brown et al., 1992) defines a hierarchical clustering over words and cluster supersets can be easily turned into features. We used the commonly employed approach of deriving features from the length-p ($p \in \{4, 6, 10, 20\}$) prefixes of Brown cluster identifiers as it was done previously by Ratinov and Roth (2009); Turian et al. (2010) as well.

We used the implementation of Liang (2005) for determining 1024 Brown clusters[1] based on the same Wikipedia dump which was used upon the training of the freely available `polyglot` word embeddings[2] that we relied on for performing sparse decomposition.

2.1.3 Orthographic features

Orthographic clues can vastly help identifying keyphrases in scientific publications. For this reason the below listed indicator features get determined for some word w:

- $isNumber(w)$

- $isTitleCase(w)$

- $isNonAlnum(w)$

- $containsNonAlnum(w)$

- $prefix(w, i)$ for $1 \leq i \leq 4$

- $suffix(w, i)$ for $1 \leq i \leq 4$

2.2 Training the model

Features described in Section 2.1 were utilized in linear chain CRFs (Lafferty et al., 2001) relying on the CRFsuite (Okazaki, 2007) implementation. CRFSuite was applied with its default regularization parameters, i.e. 1.0 and 0.001 for ℓ_1 and ℓ_2 regularization, respectively.

The shared task also required the identification of keyphrase types beyond merely finding the keyphrases within the text. We handled the fact that keyphrase scopes of different keyphrase types could overlap by training a separate CRF model

	Sentence	Word form	Token
Train	35.10%	77.77%	94.59%
Dev	36.19%	86.77%	94.84%
Test	31.84%	83.48%	94.49%

(a) Overall word representation coverages.

	Material	Process	Task
Train	85.03%	91.65%	93.55%
Dev	82.60%	92.05%	96.21%
Test	80.35%	88.84%	93.14%

(b) Per-category token-level coverage breakdown.

Table 1: Coverages of the word embeddings.

for each keyphrase type and merging the predictions of the different models in a post-processing step. The models we trained employ the 5-class BIOES-augmented tagging scheme for the labels.

3 Experiments

In this section we report our evaluations on the SemEval-2017 Task 10 dataset which consists of 350 training, 50 development and 100 test text passages, respectively. Each text passage originates from either Computer Science, Material Sciences or Physics publications and the task was to identify and classify keyphrases into the types of *Material*, *Process* and *Task*.

The shared task included both a keyphrase type insensitive (Subtask A) and sensitive (Subtask B) evaluation. Further details about the dataset and the description of the keyphrase types can be accessed in (Augenstein et al., 2017).

The only preprocessing we performed on the shared task data was sentence splitting and tokenization of input sentences. These steps were executed relying on `spacy`[3]. In order the sparse word embedding and Brown clustering-based features to work effectively, it is important that the a substantial amount of tokens from the shared task data have word representation determined for, i.e. the coverage of the word representations is satisfactory.

Table 1 includes the coverage of the word representations for the training, development and test sets. Table 1a contains the proportion of sentences with all words having a word representation determined for, alongside with the same values for

---

[1]`https://github.com/percyliang/brown-cluster`

[2]`https://sites.google.com/site/rmyeid/projects/polyglot`

[3]`https://spacy.io`

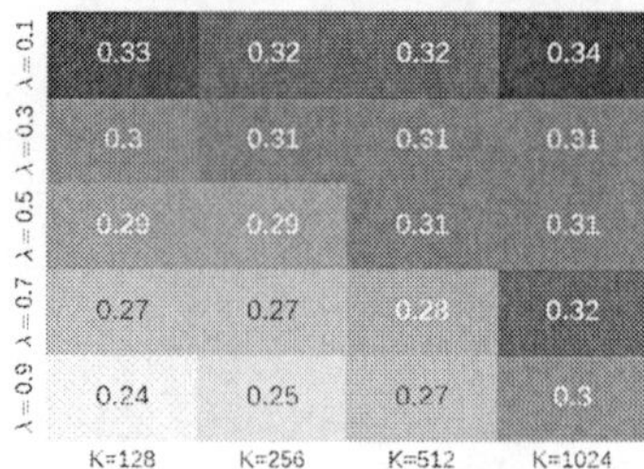

(a) Excluding word identity features

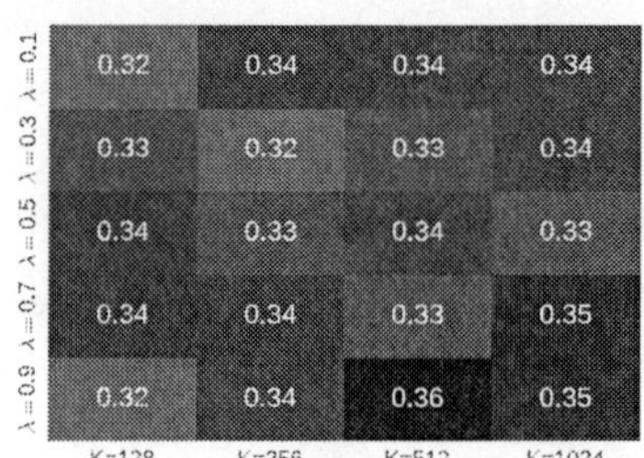

(b) Including word identity features

Figure 1: Micro-averaged F-scores for Subtask B as a function of varying λ and K parameters for sparse coding without Brown clustering-based and orthographic features being used.

	Precision	Recall	F-score
Subtask A	0.51	0.27	0.35
Subtask B avg.	0.40	0.21	0.28
Material	0.46	0.27	0.34
Process	0.39	0.19	0.26
Task	0.09	0.05	0.06

(a) Excluding word identity features.

	Precision	Recall	F-score
Subtask A	0.51	0.30	0.38
Subtask B avg.	0.39	0.23	0.29
Material	0.43	0.29	0.35
Process	0.38	0.20	0.27
Task	0.14	0.05	0.07

(b) Including word identity features.

Table 2: Results of the official submission on the test data with $K = 128, \lambda = 0.9$.

	Precision	Recall	F-score
Subtask A	0.49	0.25	0.33
Subtask B avg.	0.37	0.19	0.25
Material	0.42	0.26	0.32
Process	0.36	0.15	0.21
Task	0.13	0.05	0.07

Table 3: Results on the test set with all features used **except for** the sparse coding-derived ones.

word forms and tokens. Table 1b provides a more detailed breakdown of the coverages of word representations for the different keyphrase types also.

As subsequent results illustrate, higher word coverage for a certain type of keyphrase does not necessarily imply better performance on that type as e.g. *Task*-type keyphrases have the highest token coverage, nevertheless, scores are the lowest on that particular type (cf. Table 4).

3.1 Results on development data

Figure 1 illustrates the effect of varying the K and λ hyperparameters of sparse coding when not relying on orthographic or Brown clustering derived features. Figure 1b illustrates the effect of adding word identity features to the sparse coding derived ones, which suggests that the choice of $K = 1024$ seems to a reasonable choice for sparse coding since for that value of K, adding word identity features over the sparse coding derived ones yields marginal (or no) improvements. Inspecting Figure 1a also reveals that setting the regualrization parameter λ too high hurts performance.

Subsequently, we investigate how does adding orthographic and Brown clustering-derived features affect results for two extremely different hyperparameter combinations of sparse coding, i.e. $K = 128, \lambda = 0.9$ and $K = 1024, \lambda = 0.1$. These results are presented in Table 4a-4d. Table 4 reveals that when orthographic and/or Brown clustering-based features are used in conjunction with the sparse coding derived ones, results become more stable, i.e. they are much less affected by the choices of the K and λ. Simultaneously, the importance of word identity features diminishes once orthographic and/or Brown clustering-related ones get involved in the model. This effect is more pronounced when adding orthographic features.

Interestingly, when both orthographic and Brown clustering related features are employed, results become better for small values of K, however, this was not the case without the application of these additional feature classes.

	Sparse coding only			+Brown			+Orthograpy			+Brown+Orthography		
	P	R	F	P	R	F	P	R	F	P	R	F
Subtask A	0.69	0.18	0.28	0.64	0.25	0.36	0.63	0.32	0.42	0.61	0.34	0.44
Subtask B avg.	0.59	0.15	0.24	0.56	0.22	0.31	0.53	0.27	0.36	0.54	0.30	0.39
Material	0.63	0.22	0.33	0.64	0.28	0.39	0.62	0.34	0.44	0.63	0.36	0.46
Process	0.53	0.11	0.19	0.50	0.20	0.28	0.44	0.24	0.31	0.48	0.28	0.35
Task	0.20	0.01	0.01	0.25	0.05	0.08	0.45	0.10	0.17	0.32	0.13	0.19

(a) Results with $K = 128, \lambda = 0.9$, excluding word identity as features.

	Sparse coding only			+Brown			+Orthograpy			+Brown+Orthography		
	P	R	F	P	R	F	P	R	F	P	R	F
Subtask A	0.64	0.25	0.36	0.65	0.27	0.38	0.58	0.33	0.43	0.62	0.34	0.44
Subtask B avg.	0.57	0.22	0.32	0.59	0.25	0.35	0.50	0.29	0.37	0.55	0.30	0.39
Material	0.65	0.26	0.38	0.70	0.31	0.43	0.60	0.35	0.44	0.63	0.36	0.45
Process	0.51	0.21	0.30	0.50	0.22	0.31	0.44	0.25	0.32	0.49	0.29	0.36
Task	0.27	0.05	0.09	0.29	0.04	0.08	0.30	0.14	0.19	0.39	0.11	0.17

(b) Results with $K = 128, \lambda = 0.9$, including word identity as features.

	Sparse coding only			+Brown			+Orthograpy			+Brown+Orthography		
	P	R	F	P	R	F	P	R	F	P	R	F
Subtask A	0.56	0.29	0.38	0.57	0.30	0.40	0.57	0.33	0.42	0.55	0.33	0.41
Subtask B avg.	0.49	0.26	0.34	0.49	0.26	0.34	0.49	0.29	0.36	0.48	0.29	0.36
Material	0.59	0.31	0.40	0.61	0.31	0.41	0.60	0.35	0.44	0.59	0.35	0.44
Process	0.45	0.23	0.30	0.43	0.24	0.30	0.41	0.27	0.33	0.43	0.27	0.33
Task	0.25	0.15	0.19	0.21	0.11	0.14	0.25	0.10	0.14	0.20	0.12	0.15

(c) Results with $K = 1024, \lambda = 0.1$, excluding word identity as features.

	Sparse coding only			+Brown			+Orthograpy			+Brown+Orthography		
	P	R	F	P	R	F	P	R	F	P	R	F
Subtask A	0.56	0.30	0.39	0.59	0.29	0.39	0.58	0.33	0.42	0.58	0.34	0.42
Subtask B avg.	0.49	0.26	0.34	0.52	0.25	0.34	0.50	0.28	0.36	0.50	0.29	0.37
Material	0.65	0.26	0.38	0.70	0.31	0.43	0.60	0.35	0.44	0.63	0.36	0.45
Process	0.44	0.26	0.33	0.50	0.24	0.32	0.42	0.27	0.33	0.44	0.28	0.34
Task	0.21	0.06	0.09	0.18	0.08	0.11	0.24	0.07	0.11	0.20	0.09	0.12

(d) Results with $K = 1024, \lambda = 0.1$, including word identity as features.

Table 4: Ablation experiments on the development set. P=Precision, R=Recall, F=F-scores.

3.2 Results on test data

Based on our experiments on the development data, out official shared task submission employed $K = 128, \lambda = 0.9$ alongside with orthographic and Brown clustering-derived features. One of our official submissions relied on word form features, whereas the other dismissed such ones. The final results of our submissions are included in Table 2.

As our main goal was to verify the applicability of sparse coding derived features in keyphrase extraction as well, we checked the performance of the model which uses all features except for the sparse coding derived ones. The result of that model is presented in Table 3. By comparing these scores with those in Table 2, we can see that even when using a low value for K and a large regularization parameter λ we manage to get better F-scores when sparse coding related features are employed.

4 Conclusion

In this paper, we proposed an approach for extracting keyphrases from scientific publications. A key source of features in our approach were those derived from the sparse coding of continuous word embeddings.

In our approach we did not use any task-specific features (such as lists or gazetters), which implies that i) by relying on some extra task specific features, results could be easily improved on this task and ii) the proposed approach is likely to be successfully applicable to further sequence labeling tasks without severe modifications.

References

Rami Al-Rfou, Bryan Perozzi, and Steven Skiena. 2013. Polyglot: Distributed word representations for multilingual nlp. In *Proceedings of the Seventeenth Conference on Computational Natural Language Learning*. Association for Computational Linguistics, Sofia, Bulgaria, pages 183–192. http://www.aclweb.org/anthology/W13-3520.

Isabelle Augenstein, Mrinal Kanti Das, Sebastian Riedel, Lakshmi Nair Vikraman, and Andrew McCallum. 2017. SemEval 2017 Task 10: ScienceIE - Extracting Keyphrases and Relations from Scientific Publications. In *Proceedings of the International Workshop on Semantic Evaluation*. Association for Computational Linguistics, Vancouver, Canada.

Gábor Berend. 2016a. Exploiting extra-textual and linguistic information in keyphrase extraction. *Natural Language Engineering* 22(1):73–95. https://doi.org/10.1017/S1351324914000126.

Gábor Berend. 2016b. Sparse coding of neural word embeddings for multilingual sequence labeling. *CoRR* abs/1612.07130. http://arxiv.org/abs/1612.07130.

Peter F. Brown, Peter V. deSouza, Robert L. Mercer, Vincent J. Della Pietra, and Jenifer C. Lai. 1992. Class-based n-gram models of natural language. *Comput. Linguist.* 18(4):467–479. http://dl.acm.org/citation.cfm?id=176313.176316.

Anette Hulth. 2003. Improved automatic keyword extraction given more linguistic knowledge. In *Proceedings of the 2003 Conference on Empirical Methods in Natural Language Processing*. Association for Computational Linguistics, Stroudsburg, PA, USA, EMNLP '03, pages 216–223. https://doi.org/10.3115/1119355.1119383.

Su Nam Kim, Olena Medelyan, Min-Yen Kan, and Timothy Baldwin. 2010. SemEval-2010 task 5: Automatic keyphrase extraction from scientific articles. In *Proceedings of the 5th International Workshop on Semantic Evaluation*. ACL, Morristown, NJ, USA, SemEval '10, pages 21–26. http://portal.acm.org/citation.cfm?id=1859664.1859668.

John D. Lafferty, Andrew McCallum, and Fernando C. N. Pereira. 2001. Conditional random fields: Probabilistic models for segmenting and labeling sequence data. In *Proceedings of the Eighteenth International Conference on Machine Learning*. Morgan Kaufmann Publishers Inc., San Francisco, CA, USA, ICML '01, pages 282–289. http://dl.acm.org/citation.cfm?id=645530.655813.

P. Liang. 2005. *Semi-Supervised Learning for Natural Language*. Master's thesis, Massachusetts Institute of Technology.

Tomas Mikolov, Kai Chen, Greg Corrado, and Jeffrey Dean. 2013. Efficient estimation of word representations in vector space. *CoRR* abs/1301.3781. http://arxiv.org/abs/1301.3781.

Naoaki Okazaki. 2007. CRFsuite: a fast implementation of Conditional Random Fields (CRFs). http://www.chokkan.org/software/crfsuite/.

Lev Ratinov and Dan Roth. 2009. Design challenges and misconceptions in named entity recognition. In *Proceedings of the Thirteenth Conference on Computational Natural Language Learning*. Association for Computational Linguistics, Stroudsburg, PA, USA, CoNLL '09, pages 147–155. http://dl.acm.org/citation.cfm?id=1596374.1596399.

Joseph Turian, Lev Ratinov, and Yoshua Bengio. 2010. Word representations: A simple and general method for semi-supervised learning. In *Proceedings of the 48th Annual Meeting of the Association for Computational Linguistics*. Association for Computational Linguistics, Stroudsburg, PA, USA, ACL '10, pages 384–394. http://dl.acm.org/citation.cfm?id=1858681.1858721.

Ian H. Witten, Gordon W. Paynter, Eibe Frank, Carl Gutwin, and Craig G. Nevill-Manning. 1999. Kea: Practical automatic keyphrase extraction. In *ACM DL*. pages 254–255.

LIPN at SemEval-2017 Task 10: Filtering Candidate Keyphrases from Scientific Publications with Part-of-Speech Tag Sequences to Train a Sequence Labeling Model

Simon David Hernandez, Davide Buscaldi, Thierry Charnois
Laboratoire d'Informatique de Paris Nord, CNRS (UMR 7030)
Université Paris 13, Sorbonne Paris Cité, Villetaneuse, France
`{hernandez-perez,buscaldi,thierry.charnois}@lipn.univ-paris13.fr`

Abstract

This paper describes the system used by the team LIPN in SemEval 2017 Task 10: Extracting Keyphrases and Relations from Scientific Publications. The team participated in Scenario 1, that includes three subtasks, Identification of keyphrases (Subtask A), Classification of identified keyphrases (Subtask B) and Extraction of relationships between two identified keyphrases (Subtask C). The presented system was mainly focused on the use of part-of-speech tag sequences to filter candidate keyphrases for Subtask A. Subtasks A and B were addressed as a sequence labeling problem using Conditional Random Fields (CRFs) and even though Subtask C was out of the scope of this approach, one rule was included to identify synonyms.

1 Introduction

Identifying candidate keyphrases in texts is commonly a first step in systems for keyphrase extraction (Hasan and Ng, 2014; Haddoud et al., 2015), this can be done by filtering words or phrases from documents using heuristics to determine which can be candidate keyphrases.

The system uses *sequences of part-of-speech tags (PoS sequences)* as patterns to filter candidate keyphrases. These candidates are used to train two Conditional Random Field (CRF) models, one for keyphrase identification and other for keyphrase classification. CRF was trained with orthographic features, additionally to features from WordNet and titles from academic papers. The PoS sequences were extracted from the annotated keyphrases in the corpus provided for the task (Augenstein et al., 2017).

The PoS sequences used in this system are described in Section 2, there is an explanation of how they were used and how they were extracted from the training data. In Section 3 is detailed how CRF was trained with the candidate keyphrases and in Section 4 the features are described. In Section 5 there is an explanation of how CRF was applied to identify and classify keyphrases. Section 6 shows the post-processing steps and Section 7 introduces some experiments.

2 PoS sequences

In this paper, we use the term *PoS sequences* to refer to *sequences of part-of-speech tags*. PoS sequences are used in automatic keyphrase extraction as features (Kim and Kan, 2009; Hasan and Ng, 2014) or to filter candidate keyphrases (Kim and Kan, 2009; Haddoud et al., 2015; Hasan and Ng, 2014), for example, with small sets of patterns matching all noun phrases and prepositional phrases, avoiding patterns that increase error, like sequences containing adverbs (Kim and Kan, 2009).

In this system, PoS sequences are used only to filter candidate keyphrases. From the annotated keyphrases in the training data, were extracted 1445 different PoS sequences [1], Table 1 shows an example of PoS sequences, sorted by number of occurrences.

Each extracted PoS sequence was used as a pattern to filter candidate keyphrases in the training, development and test corpus, instead of generalize a smaller set of patterns as is proposed in other approaches.

---

[1]The full list of extracted POS sequences is available in
`https://github.com/snovd/corpus-data/`
`blob/master/SemEval2017Task10/`
`POSsequences.txt`

Proceedings of the 11th International Workshop on Semantic Evaluations (SemEval-2017), pages 995–999,
Vancouver, Canada, August 3 - 4, 2017. ©2017 Association for Computational Linguistics

Occurrences	POS sequence
1333	NN
559	NN NN
414	JJ NN
301	NN NNS
293	NNS
289	JJ NNS
⋮	⋮
61	VBG
54	NN NN NNS
52	JJ JJ NN
51	JJ
41	VBG NN
⋮	⋮

Table 1: Example of POS sequences extracted from the training data, ordered by number of occurrences.

2.1 Filtering candidate keyphrases

Each PoS sequence is compared with the part-of-speech[2] of a text, all the sequences of tokens matching the pattern are selected as candidate keyphrases.

> provides/VBZ an/DT approach/NN to/TO circumvent/VB the/DT sign/NN problem/NN in/IN numerical/JJ simulations/NNS

Figure 1: Extract from the development data[3].

For example, the extract of text in Figure 1 has the following annotations, *"sign problem"* is a keyphrase of type TASK and *"numerical simulations"* is part of a larger keyphrase of type PROCESS. From the same text, two sets of candidate keyphrases are shown in Table 2, the first set is obtained by matching all the PoS sequences and the second by matching the PoS sequences with at least 14 occurrences.

If we were using ngrams to propose candidate keyphrases, in same example, we get 45 different candidates, with ngrams from 1-grams to 5-grams, so there is a significant reduction of extracted phrases. Also, note that there is a reduction of candidate keyphrases between the two sets in Table 2 without excluding the annotated

---

[2]Getting the PoS with TreebankWordTokenizer and PerceptronTagger in NLTK

[3]File S0003491613001516.txt

Occurrences of PoS sequence	Extracted phrases
≥ 1	problem in numerical simulations
	the sign problem
	circumvent the sign problem
	sign
	sign problem in numerical simulations
	provides an approach
	numerical simulations
	the sign
	approach
	circumvent the sign
	approach to circumvent
	an approach
	problem in numerical
	problem
	an
	simulations
	problem in
	numerical
	the
	sign problem
≥ 14	problem in numerical simulations
	sign
	sign problem
	approach
	numerical simulations
	problem
	simulations
	numerical

Table 2: Two sets of candidate keyphrases. Generated with the PoS sequences filtered by the number of occurrences.

keyphrases, also the token *"provides"* is missing. We took advantage of this observation to improve the precision, see Section 7.

2.2 Keyphrases and Non-keyphrases

We extracted all the possible candidate keyphrases from the training corpus, using all the PoS sequences described before. An extracted candidate is labeled as KEYPHRASE if it is annotated as keyphrase in the training corpus, on the contrary it is labeled as NON-KEYPHRASE, like in a binary classification problem (Frank et al., 1999).

3 Training CRF

Using Conditional Random Fields (CRFs) to address Automatic Keyword Extraction as a sequence labeling problem has already been proposed (Bhaskar et al., 2012; Zhang, 2008; Augenstein et al., 2017).

We trained CRF [4] only with the candidate keyphrases, each one as a separated input, using BIO encoding[5] and the labels KEYPHRASE and NON-KEYPHRASE for Subtask A, like in the examples in Figures 2 and 3. Similarly, a second CRF model was trained for Subtask B, with labels TASK, PROCESS and MATERIAL.

the/O sign/B problem/I in/O

Figure 2: Example of KEYPHRASE/TASK 'sign problem' in BIO encoding.

'the/O sign/B problem/I in/I numerical/I simulations/I of/O'

Figure 3: Example of NON-KEYPHRASE 'sign problem in numerical simulations' in BIO encoding.

Note that in the sets in Table 2 there are repetitions of tokens in several candidate keyphrases. For example, *"sign problem"* is an annotated keyphrase, so it is labeled as KEYPHRASE/TASK, in contrast with *"circumvent the sign problem"* and *"sign problem in numerical simulations"* which are labeled as NON-KEYPHRASE, ignoring completely that these phrases contain a keyphrase. Also, text that doesn't match a PoS sequence is not used to train the model.

4 Features

For identification of keyphrases (Subtask A) and classification of identified keyphrases (Subtask B), we trained two different CRF models with the same candidate keyphrases, labeled differently depending on the subtask. Subtask B uses the same features that Subtask A, in addition to features from WordNet.

All the features were generated for each token in a given candidate, including the tokens that surround the start and end of the phrase, as shown in the examples of Figures 2 and 3. Text that is not present in the candidate keyphrases is ignored with the exception of these two context tokens as features.

4.1 Features - Subtask A

To train CRF for Subtask A, we used the features suggested in the documentation of python-crfsuite for the task of named entity recognition, we didn't make a deep exploration of them. Those features are the token in lowercase, its part-of-speech, the first two letters of the part-of-speech, the suffixes of one and two characters, and three binary features, which value depends on the letter case of the token, these are uppercase, lowercase or title case, also are included two tokens of context (previous, next) in lowercase. Finally, an indicator is added if the token is at the beginning or the end of the whole text.

4.1.1 Titles from academic papers

Information from titles has been useful in keyphrase extraction (Hasan and Ng, 2014; Grineva et al., 2009), so we generated a database with bigrams, trigrams and the part-of-speech of the trigrams, extracted from titles from academic papers[6]. Only titles in English were included[7].

We added four binary features for each token in a candidate keyphrase, the value depends on whether ngrams formed with its context exist or not in the database. For example, the token *'sign'* in Figure 1 forms the ngrams, *'the sign'*, *'sign problem'*, *'the sign problem'* and *'DT NN NN'*.

4.2 Features - Subtask B

We used binary features with information from WordNet 3.0, these are included only when the lemmatized token [8] has *noun synsets*. The first feature is True only if the synsets of the lemmatized token have holonyms, a second feature depends on whether it has derivationally related forms.

We also included a fixed set of synsets as binary features[9], which are the more probable synsets

---

[4]We used python-crfsuite with the default parameters for Named Entity Recognition, 'c1': 1.0, 'c2': 1e-3, 'max_iterations': 50, 'feature.possible_transitions': True, `https://github.com/scrapinghub/python-crfsuite`

[5]Indicating the (B)eginning of the phrase, (I)nside of the phrase or (O)ther.

[6]Microsoft Academic Graph, version 2016/02/05 `https://academicgraphwe.blob.core.windows.net/graph-2016-02-05/index.html`

[7]Were separated with guess_language `https://pypi.python.org/pypi/guess_language-spirit`

[8]Lemmatization with WordNetLemmatizer

[9]List of synsets used as binary features. `https://github.com/snovd/corpus-data/blob/master/SemEval2017Task10/SynsetsRelatedToTrainingData.txt`

from the annotations in the training corpus. To obtain the set, we merged the twenty[10] more probable synsets by label (PROCESS, MATERIAL and TASK). These features are True for a token if they are present in the hypernyms of the noun synsets.

5 Identifying and labeling keyphrases

First, CRF was trained as described in Section 3, then we extracted the candidate keyphrases from the development/test data with the PoS sequences having at least 14 occurrences in the training data with the method explained in Section 2. Then we excluded the candidates of one token if they exist in an exclusion list (described in Subsection 5.1).

Then CRF was applied to each candidate keyphrase with the features for Subtask A, if all the tokens in the candidate were labeled as KEYPHRASE, then the entire candidate was labeled as KEYPHRASE.

CRF was applied again to all the resulting keyphrases from the last steps, but this time with the model trained with the Subtask B features. Similarly, if the tokens in the keyphrase were labeled with the same type, then the keyphrase is labeled entirely with the corresponding type, PROCESS, MATERIAL or TASK. If the keyphrase was not labeled equally, it was marked as PROCESS by default.

5.1 Exclusion list

This list was generated from the training corpus to exclude very common tokens. It was generated by filtering the inverse document frequency (idf) of each token with a threshold. First, we calculated the idf for all the tokens in the papers from the training corpus. The threshold is the mean of the idfs minus four times the standard deviation. One token is added to the exclusion list only if its idf is lesser or equal than the threshold.

6 Post-processing

For the case of overlapping, as it is shown in Table 5, when a full keyphrase is contained inside other keyphrase, the largest keyphrase is chosen.

Finally, we included a simple rule to relate synonyms. By observation of the training data, we noticed that two keyphrases are marked as synonyms, if one is followed by another inside of parenthesis, been the second an acronym of the first.

---

[10]This number was chosen arbitrarily

7 Experiments

In Figures 4 (Precision), 5 (Recall) and 6 (F_1) are shown the results of different experiments for Subtask A. In these experiments we tested the effect of removing the least occurring PoS sequences in the training corpus to filter the candidate keyphrases in the development corpus. *"Candidate keyphrases + CRF + Titles"* represents the experiments of the system with all the features as described previously. *"Candidate keyphrases + CRF"* represents the experiments of the system without using the database of titles as features (Subsection 4.1.1). *"CRF"* and *"CRF + Titles"* are the results of applying CRF with the same features and without filtering candidate keyphrases. *"Candidate keyphrases"* is our baseline, these are the results of using candidate keyphrases directly as keyphrases.

As can be observed in Figure 6, the best F_1 score is reached when the candidate keyphrases from the development corpus were filtered with all the PoS sequences with an occurrence of at least 14 times in the training corpus, like in the example of Table 2 and as described in Section 5. In that case, the proposed system has a better result in F_1 score than *"CRF + Titles"*.

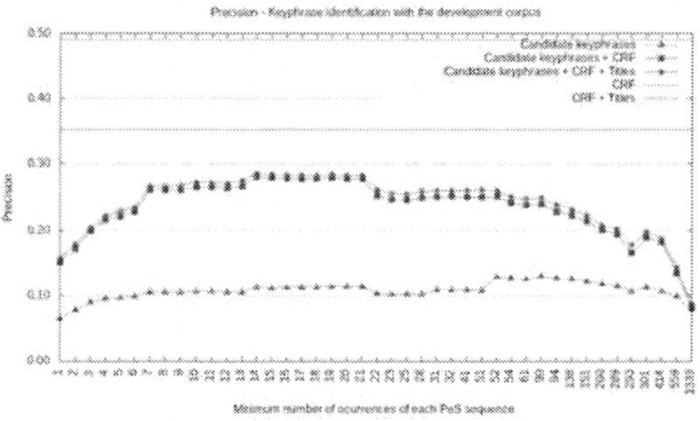

Figure 4: Precision: Experiments for Subtask A with the development corpus.

8 Results

Our final results are shown in Table 3, we ranked 11th in Scenario 1, 10th in Subtask A and 11th in Subtask B. We obtained our best performance in Subtask A, which is the main target of this work.

9 Conclusion

We tested the use of PoS sequences extracted from the training data to filter candidate keyphrases, in-

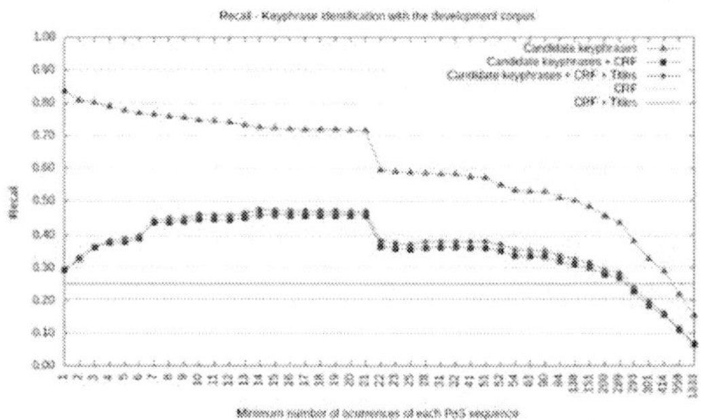

Figure 5: Recall: Experiments for Subtask A with the development corpus.

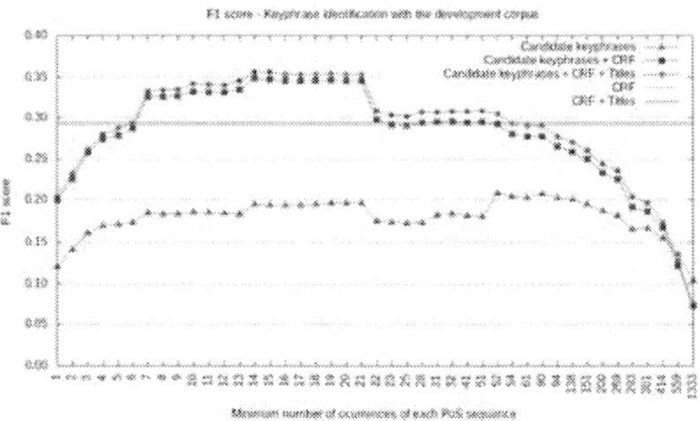

Figure 6: F_1 score: Experiments for Subtask A with the development corpus.

stead of filtering with a fixed set of patterns to match noun phrases or prepositional phrases as proposed in other approaches. Our experiments show that filtering candidate keyphrases to train CRF with this method helps to improve the results for Automatic Keyphrase Extraction by increasing the Recall, with the disadvantage of lost of Precision.

Subtask	P	R	F_1
Scenario 1	0.17	0.25	0.21
Subtask A	**0.31**	**0.49**	**0.38**
Subtask A+B	0.17	0.27	0.21
Subtask C	0.33	0.02	0.05

Table 3: Final results for team LIPN in SemEval 2017 Task 10

References

Isabelle Augenstein, Mrinal Das, Sebastian Riedel, Lakshmi Vikraman, and Andrew McCallum. 2017. Semeval 2017 task 10: Scienceie - extracting keyphrases and relations from scientific publications. In *Proceedings of the 11th International Workshop on Semantic Evaluation (SemEval-2017)*. Association for Computational Linguistics, Vancouver, Canada, pages 537–546. http://www.aclweb.org/anthology/S17-2091.

Pinaki Bhaskar, Kishorjit Nongmeikapam, and Sivaji Bandyopadhyay. 2012. Keyphrase extraction in scientific articles: A supervised approach. In *Proceedings of COLING 2012: Demonstration Papers*. The COLING 2012 Organizing Committee, Mumbai, India, pages 17–24. http://www.aclweb.org/anthology/C12-3003.

Eibe Frank, Gordon W. Paynter, Ian H. Witten, Carl Gutwin, and Craig G. Nevill-Manning. 1999. Domain-specific keyphrase extraction. In *Proceedings of the Sixteenth International Joint Conference on Artificial Intelligence*. Morgan Kaufmann Publishers Inc., San Francisco, CA, USA, IJCAI '99, pages 668–673. http://dl.acm.org/citation.cfm?id=646307.687591.

Maria Grineva, Maxim Grinev, and Dmitry Lizorkin. 2009. Extracting key terms from noisy and multi-theme documents. In *Proceedings of the 18th International Conference on World Wide Web*. ACM, New York, NY, USA, WWW '09, pages 661–670. https://doi.org/10.1145/1526709.1526798.

Mounia Haddoud, Aïcha Mokhtari, Thierry Lecroq, and Saïd Abdeddaïm. 2015. Accurate Keyphrase Extraction from Scientific Papers by Mining Linguistic Information. *Proceedings of the First Workshop on Mining Scientific Papers: Computational Linguistics and Bibliometrics co-located with 15th International Society of Scientometrics and Informetrics Conference (ISSI 2015) Istanbul, Turkey, June 29, 2015*. 1384:12–17. http://ceur-ws.org/Vol-1384/paper2.pdf.

Kazi Saidul Hasan and Vincent Ng. 2014. Automatic keyphrase extraction: A survey of the state of the art. In *Proceedings of the 52nd Annual Meeting of the Association for Computational Linguistics (Volume 1: Long Papers)*. Association for Computational Linguistics, Baltimore, Maryland, pages 1262–1273. http://www.aclweb.org/anthology/P/P14/P14-1119.

Su Nam Kim and Min-Yen Kan. 2009. Re-examining automatic keyphrase extraction approaches in scientific articles. In *Proceedings of the Workshop on Multiword Expressions: Identification, Interpretation, Disambiguation and Applications*. Association for Computational Linguistics, Singapore, pages 9–16. http://www.aclweb.org/anthology/W/W09/W09-2902.

Chengzhi Zhang. 2008. Automatic keyword extraction from documents using conditional random fields. *Journal of Computational Information Systems* 4(3):1169–1180.

EUDAMU at SemEval-2017 Task 11: Action Ranking and Type Matching for End-User Development

Marek Kubis and **Paweł Skórzewski** and **Tomasz Ziętkiewicz**
Faculty of Mathematics and Computer Science
Adam Mickiewicz University in Poznań
`{mkubis,pawel.skorzewski,tomasz.zietkiewicz}@amu.edu.pl`

Abstract

The paper describes a system for end-user development using natural language. Our approach uses a ranking model to identify the actions to be executed followed by reference and parameter matching models to select parameter values that should be set for the given commands. We discuss the results of evaluation and possible improvements for future work.

1 Introduction

The goal of the end-user development (EUD) is to provide users of software systems with the tools to create, extend or modify software (Lieberman et al., 2006). End-User Development using Natural Language is one of the tasks of SemEval-2017 International Workshop on Semantic Evaluation.

The idea of using tools for software development more accessible than programming languages has been discussed almost since the beginning of computers. The concept of programming with natural language commands and its consequences have been considered already in the 70s (Dijkstra, 1979). However, only in recent years these ideas could be put into practice with the rapid development of advanced natural language processing methods.

A comprehensive overview of recent trends and achievements in EUD has been presented by Paternò (2013). Although most common solution for EUD problem are various variations on graphical user interfaces, solutions using NLP are also present. One of the examples is the Koala (later: CoScripter) system (web browser extension), that uses "sloppy programming", i.e. pseudo-natural language instructions, to automate business processes on the web (Little et al., 2007). Other systems that use simple natural language commands to achieve programming-like goals, described in recent years, include SPOK, an EUD environment for smart homes (Coutaz et al., 2014), and NaturalMash, an EUD tool for creating web mashups (Aghaee and Pautasso, 2014).

This paper describes our system for the end-user development using natural language and reports its performance according to the SemEval 2017 Task 11 evaluation criteria (Sales et al., 2017).

2 Data preparation

We pre-process all the input data: both the action knowledge base and natural language commands. The pre-processing is done in several stages. It includes basic text processing as well as adding lexical features. We use these features to better match the commands to actions. The pre-processor operates on JSON files, in each step adding new fields to the JSON structure so the original data are not lost in the process and can be used in further steps. The input fields we annotate are: `desc`, `name`, `value`, `nl_command_statment`, `provider`, `sample`, `tags` and `api-name`.

The first pre-processing stage is sentence splitting. The sentence splitter is applied to `nl_command_statment` and `desc` fields only.

The second step is tokenization. The input data are amended not only with tokens, but also with token types. The following token types are recognized: text, number, phone number, monetary expression, punctuation, URL, e-mail address, hashtag, file name, other. Types of tokens are recognized using regular expressions. The set of token types has been specified manually in such way that they are useful in the context of both the original training dataset and other possible datasets. The token types are used in further processing stages: anaphora resolution, action detection and parameters matching.

Proceedings of the 11th International Workshop on Semantic Evaluations (SemEval-2017), pages 1000–1004,
Vancouver, Canada, August 3 - 4, 2017. ©2017 Association for Computational Linguistics

In the next step, we append features from SyntaxNet (Andor et al., 2016), Stanford CoreNLP (Manning et al., 2014) and NLTK (Bird et al., 2009) to the natural language commands. In particular, we introduce: part-of-speech tags from SyntaxNet to implement discourse annotation rules (cf. Section 3.1); word lemmata from NLTK for the purpose of preprocessing text for the action ranker (cf. Section 3.2); named entities and constituency parser annotations from CoreNLP (Finkel et al., 2005) for anaphora resolution.

The next pre-processing stage appends features extracted from the user knowledge base. Any reference to the user knowledge base entry that occurs in a command is annotated with the entry identifier and the name of the referred entry field.

The last pre-processing stage is to add anaphora information. Anaphora tags are appended to possible anaphoric terms like *it*, *him* etc. or nouns preceded with definite articles (e.g. *the file*). The antecedent expressions of the anaphora are identified on the basis of their part-of-speech tags, NER tags, token types or phrase categories. For this purpose we use token type annotations and selected features from CoreNLP: tokens, POS tags, NER tags and parse results.

3 System Overview

The main components of the system are presented in Figure 1. A natural language command that has been preprocessed according to the procedure described in Section 2 is passed to the discourse tagger which identifies phrases and relationships among them. Phrases are passed separately through action ranker which identifies candidate actions. Next, reference matcher identifies dependencies that link data values that are returned by the candidate actions with the parameters of their successor actions. Then, the parameter matcher aligns tokens that occur in the phrase to the parameters of the candidate actions that where not linked by the reference matcher. Finally, the phrases annotated with actions and parameter values are passed to the statement mapper which uses the discourse structure to output action instances that conform to the task specification.[1]

---

[1]For an example of a complete data flow that passes a natural language command through all the system modules, we refer the reader to (Kubis et al., 2017).

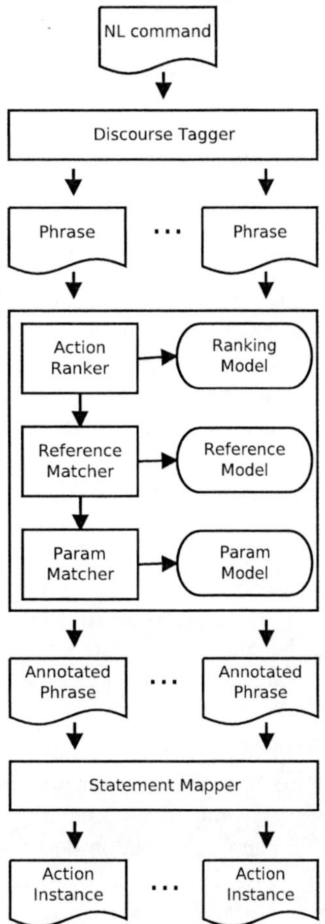

Figure 1: System Components

3.1 Discourse Tagger

The discourse tagger consists of a set of hard-coded rules that are responsible for splitting the command into separate phrases that can be passed to the action ranker independently. The rules are implemented as Python functions that check if a given token can be a split point and assign tags that identify the relationships that hold among phrases being separated. For example, the discourse tagger has a rule that checks if both sides of the *and* token contain tokens that are verbs (i.e. are annotated with the VERB part-of-speech tag) and if the condition is satisfied, the tagger splits the command into two phrases and annotates the second phrase with the AN tag. Beside the rules for separating sequences of actions, the tagger also contains rules that identify conditional statements and assign IF, DO and EL tags that indicate the condition, consequence and alternative parts. Since while loops occurred in the training set sparsely, we did not introduce tags to annotate them restricting our attention to sequences of actions and conditional statements only.

3.2 Action Ranker

For the purpose of ranking the actions we considered TF-IDF (Spärck Jones, 1972) and Doc2Vec (Le and Mikolov, 2014) document similarity models.[2] We represent the actions by documents that consist of the text collected from the selected fields of the action definitions specified in the `actionkb` file and natural language commands provided in the `mapping` file. The gathered text is lemmatized and stop words are eliminated. Furthermore, the natural language commands are delexicalized by replacing occurrences of named entities and quotations with placeholder tags. In order to determine candidate actions for the given command, we apply the same text preprocessing rules as above and select actions that correspond to the documents that are most similar to the preprocessed command.[3]

We performed 5-fold cross-validation on the training set to select features for our final model. We investigated the models that gather text from: action names (N), action descriptions (D), `provider` fields (P); names and descriptions of action parameters (Par); names and descriptions of action `data` fields (Dat); natural language commands from the `mapping` file (Com). The average Micro F1 scores and their standard deviations across validation folds are reported in Table 1. It may be noticed that results achieved by introduction of action descriptions and `provider` fields to the models surpass the results of the models that consists of the action names only. Conversely, the extension of the NDP (name, description and `provider`) model with the names and descriptions of action parameters (NDPPar) worsens the results. The same holds if we extend the NDP model with action data values (NDPDat). Finally, the feature that improves the results most consists of the aggressively normalized natural language commands from the `mapping` file (Com). This exemplifies that even a small sample of the annotated input data can improve the results significantly. Another interesting observation is that Dov2Vec

models perform considerably worse than TF-IDF models in the task regardless of the feature choice. Thus, for our final submission we selected the TF-IDF model that encompasses action names, their descriptions, `provider` fields from `actionkb` and natural language commands from `mapping` (NDP-Com).

3.3 Reference Matcher

The reference matcher is responsible for establishing links between the data returned by an action and the parameters of the succeeding actions. The mapping file distributed with the training data is used to populate the set of constraints for the acceptable links. For any two actions that are linked by an occurrence of the <return*> tag, the training procedure collects the identifiers of the linked actions and the names of the `data` and `params` fields being connected.

The matching procedure traverses consecutive phrases of the natural language command. If a phrase contains an anaphor, then the reference matcher checks whether the action instances of the antecedent and current phrases belong to the set of constraints learned during training. If the pair of actions belongs to the constraints set, the links between corresponding `data` and `params` fields are established.

3.4 Parameter Matcher

For the purpose of setting parameter values for actions we began with a sequence model based on the learning to search approach (Chang et al., 2015). Unfortunately, due to relatively small training set, the model became highly over-trained and did not prove to be useful for our final submission. Instead, we decided to use a parameter matcher that aligns data types between tokens that occur in the phrase and action parameters. The matcher consists of two components: parameter type and phrase type inducers.

The parameter type inducer restricts data types that can be accepted by action parameters. Data types are constrained on the basis of feature annotations gathered during the data preparation stage (cf. Section 2). The constraints are learned from the mappings file with the following algorithm:
For every phrase in the mapping file, for every action instance of the phrase, for every parameter of the action instance, let C be the set of constraints of the parameter, let S be the set of phrase tokens that match the parameter value:

---

[2] For training TF-IDF and Doc2Vec models we used Gensim (Řehůřek and Sojka, 2010).

[3] We limit our attention to up to 10 documents that are within 0.05 distance to the most similar candidate.

Model	Metric	N	ND	NDP	NDPPar	NDPDat	NDPCom
TF-IDF	micro-F1	0.0759	0.1079	0.1146	0.0960	0.1099	**0.2609**
	std. dev.	0.0274	0.0249	0.0302	0.0415	0.0288	0.0935
Doc2Vec	micro-F1	0.0049	0.0543	0.0737	0.0683	0.0866	0.2007
	std. dev.	0.0043	0.0186	0.0076	0.0215	0.0098	0.0531

Table 1: Average Micro F1-Score of TF-IDF and Doc2Vec action ranking models.

1. Add types of tokens in S to C.

2. Add named entity tags of tokens in S to C.

3. If S is encompassed by quotation signs, add the `quotation` *type to C.*

The phrase type inducer constraints data types of the phrase by applying the following procedure to every token T:
Let C be the set of constraints of T:

1. Add type of T to C.

2. Add named entity tags of T to C.

3. If T is encompassed by a quotation, add the `quotation` *type to C.*

4. If T is a reference to the entry E in the user knowledge base, add data types of all non-empty fields of E to C.

We assume that an action parameter has to be matched, if the intersection of the sets of constraints returned by both inducers is non-empty. Initialization of the parameter value is a 2-step procedure. If the token type belongs to the set of constraints returned by the parameter type inducer, then the raw text of the token is appended to the parameter value. Otherwise, if the token is a reference to the entry in the user knowledge base, the parameter value is populated with the value of an entry field that satisfies the constraints returned by the parameter type inducer.

3.5 Statement Mapper

As in the case of the discourse tagger, the statement mapper consists of a set of deterministic, hard-coded rules implemented in Python that are responsible for converting the phrases annotated with actions assigned by the action ranker, links established by the reference matcher and parameter values set by the parameter matcher to the output format described in the task definition. The relationships among phrases identified by the discourse tagger and encoded as `AN`, `IF`, `DO` and `EL`

tags are used by the statement mapper to create JSON objects that represent sequential and conditional execution of action instances in accordance with the task specification.

4 Results

The results of evaluation performed according to the official task criteria are gathered in Table 2. The detailed error analysis requires access to the annotated version of the test set which was not available at the time of writing. Nevertheless, some initial observations can be drawn. The TF-IDF model built from action names, their descriptions, provider names and exemplar phrases seems to be a reasonable baseline for determining the ranking of actions that results in solving of 13 out of 31 scenarios if the parameter values are not considered. On the other hand, the parameter matching strategy requires considerable improvement. We suspect that our per-token strategy leads to the parameter values that are only partially matched, hence do not contribute to the result. Another issue that has to be approached in the future is the problem of propagating data type constraints from parameters of actions that occur in the set of training commands to the parameters of actions for which the training instances are not available.

Criterion	Metric	Value
Individual actions solved ignoring parameter values	precision	0.5490
	recall	0.7066
Individual actions solved considering parameter values	precision	0.0533
	recall	0.0533
Scenarios solved ignoring parameter values	accuracy	41.93%
Scenarios solved considering parameter values	accuracy	0%

Table 2: Evaluation results.

References

Saeed Aghaee and Cesare Pautasso. 2014. End-user development of mashups with naturalmash. *Journal of Visual Languages & Computing* 25(4):414–432.

Daniel Andor, Chris Alberti, David Weiss, Aliaksei Severyn, Alessandro Presta, Kuzman Ganchev, Slav Petrov, and Michael Collins. 2016. Globally normalized transition-based neural networks. *arXiv preprint arXiv:1603.06042* .

Steven Bird, Ewan Klein, and Edward Loper. 2009. *Natural language processing with Python: analyzing text with the natural language toolkit.* " O'Reilly Media, Inc.".

Kai-Wei Chang, Akshay Krishnamurthy, Alekh Agarwal, Hal Daume, and John Langford. 2015. Learning to search better than your teacher. In David Blei and Francis Bach, editors, *Proceedings of the 32nd International Conference on Machine Learning (ICML-15)*. JMLR Workshop and Conference Proceedings, pages 2058–2066. http://jmlr.org/proceedings/papers/v37/changb15.pdf.

Joëlle Coutaz, Alexandre Demeure, Sybille Caffiau, and James L Crowley. 2014. Early lessons from the development of SPOK, an end-user development environment for smart homes. In *Proceedings of the 2014 ACM International Joint Conference on Pervasive and Ubiquitous Computing: Adjunct Publication*. ACM, pages 895–902.

Edsger W Dijkstra. 1979. On the foolishness of "natural language programming". In *Program Construction*, Springer, pages 51–53.

Jenny Rose Finkel, Trond Grenager, and Christopher Manning. 2005. Incorporating Non-local Information into Information Extraction Systems by Gibbs Sampling. In *Proceedings of the 43rd annual meeting on association for computational linguistics*. Association for Computational Linguistics, pages 363–370.

Marek Kubis, Paweł Skórzewski, and Tomasz Ziętkiewicz. 2017. EU-DAMU System Components Data Flow. https://bitbucket.org/mapato/eudamu/wiki/DataFlow.

Quoc V. Le and Tomas Mikolov. 2014. Distributed representations of sentences and documents. In *Proceedings of the 31th International Conference on Machine Learning, ICML 2014, Beijing, China, 21-26 June 2014*. pages 1188–1196. http://jmlr.org/proceedings/papers/v32/le14.html.

Henry Lieberman, Fabio Paternò, Markus Klann, and Volker Wulf. 2006. End-user development: An emerging paradigm. In *End user development*, Springer, pages 1–8.

Greg Little, Tessa A Lau, Allen Cypher, James Lin, Eben M Haber, and Eser Kandogan. 2007. Koala: capture, share, automate, personalize business processes on the web. In *Proceedings of the SIGCHI conference on Human factors in computing systems*. ACM, pages 943–946.

Christopher D. Manning, Mihai Surdeanu, John Bauer, Jenny Finkel, Steven J. Bethard, and David McClosky. 2014. The Stanford CoreNLP natural language processing toolkit. In *Association for Computational Linguistics (ACL) System Demonstrations*. pages 55–60. http://www.aclweb.org/anthology/P/P14/P14-5010.

Fabio Paternò. 2013. End user development: Survey of an emerging field for empowering people. *ISRN Software Engineering* 2013.

Radim Řehůřek and Petr Sojka. 2010. Software Framework for Topic Modelling with Large Corpora. In *Proceedings of the LREC 2010 Workshop on New Challenges for NLP Frameworks*. ELRA, Valletta, Malta, pages 45–50. http://is.muni.cz/publication/884893/en.

Juliano Sales, Siegfried Handschuh, and André Freitas. 2017. SemEval-2017 Task 11: End-User Development using Natural Language. In *Proceedings of the 11th International Workshop on Semantic Evaluation (SemEval-2017)*. Association for Computational Linguistics, Vancouver, Canada, pages 554–562. http://www.aclweb.org/anthology/S17-2092.

Karen Spärck Jones. 1972. A statistical interpretation of term specificity and its application in retrieval. *Journal of Documentation* 28(1):11–21.

Hitachi at SemEval-2017 Task 12: System for temporal information extraction from clinical notes

Sarath P R[1], Manikandan R[1], Yoshiki Niwa[2]
[1]Research and Development Center, Hitachi India Pvt Ltd, India
[2]Hitachi Ltd, Center for Exploratory Research, Japan
`{sarath,manikandan}@hitachi.co.in`
`yoshiki.niwa.tx@hitachi.com`

Abstract

This paper describes the system developed for the task of temporal information extraction from clinical narratives in the context of the 2017 Clinical TempEval challenge. Clinical TempEval 2017 addressed the problem of temporal reasoning in the clinical domain by providing annotated clinical notes, pathology and radiology reports in line with Clinical TempEval challenges 2015/16, across two different evaluation phases focusing on cross domain adaptation. Our team focused on subtasks involving extractions of temporal spans and relations for which the developed systems showed average F-score of 0.45 and 0.47 across the two phases of evaluations.

1 Introduction

Temporal information extraction has been a widely explored topic of research interest in the field of information extraction during recent years. It is essential for improving the performance of applications such as question answering, search, text classification and systems that establish timelines from clinical narratives. In this line over the years, research community challenges on clinical temporal information extraction have been organized; i.e., the 2012 Informatics for Integrating Biology and the Bedside (i2b2) challenge (Sun et al., 2013) the 2013/2014 CLEF/ShARe challenge (Mowery et al., 2014), and the 2015/16 Clinical TempEval challenge (Bethard et al., 2015, 2016). These challenges provide annotated corpora on temporal entities and relations, which facilitate comparisons of multiple systems and push the state of art in the development of clinical temporal information extraction methodologies.

The 2017 Clinical TempEval challenge is the most recent community challenge that addresses temporal information extraction from clinical notes. The challenge was in inline with 2015/16 challenge in terms of subtasks. However this year's challenge focussed on cross domain adaptation across two phases of evaluation. In phase one (unsupervised domain adaptation), the systems were evaluated on their results for all six sub-tasks on brain cancer notes given colon cancer notes (data of 2015/16 challenge) as inputs. In phase two (supervised domain adaptation), evaluation was carried out in line with phase one but a small number of annotations of brain cancer notes were also given as inputs.

In this paper, we describe an end-to-end system that addresses subtasks involving extractions of temporal spans and relations. We designed the system by adapting various insights and techniques from previous work on temporal information extraction in the clinical domain (Sarath et al., 2016; Abdulsalam et al., 2016; Johri et al., 2014) and ensemble modelling (Dzeroski and Zenko, 2004).

The rest of the paper is organised as follows: In section 2, we discuss datasets, methods and feature sets used for each of the subtasks. In section 3, we present the results for various subtasks and conclude our work in section 4 with some of our findings and possible implications on future work.

2 Dataset and Methods

The THYME corpus (Styler et al., 2014) used in this task consists of clinical, pathology and radiology notes for colon/brain cancer patients from Mayo clinic (Bethard et al., 2017).

We designed an end-to-end pipeline consisting of four modules which process the input text in three stages: In stage one, the first and second

1005

Proceedings of the 11th International Workshop on Semantic Evaluations (SemEval-2017), pages 1005–1009,
Vancouver, Canada, August 3 - 4, 2017. ©2017 Association for Computational Linguistics

modules extract time/event expressions and their spans. In stage two, the third module predicts document time relations between the event and document creation time expressions. Finally, all the outputs of stage one and two are used to extract container relations in stage three. For phase one (unsupervised domain adaptation) we used train, dev and test colon cancer datasets to train and evaluated on the brain cancer test dataset. While in phase two we retrained models with a mixture of colon cancer and additional brain cancer notes, each of which are explained in upcoming sections. For our temporal information extraction system we used following open source libraries. 1) Stanford-CoreNLP (Manning et al., 2014) 2) scikit-learn (Pedregosa et al., 2011) 3) NLTK (Loper and Bird, 2002) 4) XGBoost (Chen and Guestrin, 2016) 5) Apache CTAKES (Savova et al., 2010) 6) ClearTK (Bethard et al., 2014) 7) H2O[1]

2.1 Time span identification

In the first stage our system identifies the time expressions and their spans.

Our manual observation of the colon cancer and brain cancer notes revealed that different time expressions show specific set of characteristics (Sarath et al., 2016) unique to each of the TIMEX3 class. Such characteristics may limit the systems performance, if one tries to identify event mentions or time expressions of all types at once and then identify their types. Therefore, our system identifies the spans of times as well as their types simultaneously.

Based on above observations and previous works on entity recognition tasks in the clinical domain (Lin et al., 2016), five Conditional Random Field(CRF) classifiers (Lafferty et al., 2001) were employed to identify each class of TIMEX3 expression except "duration" class for which we built a simple rule based system using Stanford TokensRegex Framework (Chang and Manning, 2014). For training CRF we tagged each token with either O (outside of a time mention), B-type (beginning of a time mention of type), or I-type (inside of a time mention of type), where type can be any of the TIMEX3 types defined by the Clinical TempEval challenge.

Features: n-grams (uni-, bi-) of nearby words (window size of +/- 2), character n-grams (bi- and tri-) of each word, prefix and suffix of each word (up to three characters), and orthographic forms of each word (obtained by normalizing numbers, uppercase letters, and lowercase letters to #, A, and a, respectively, and by regular expression matching) and word shape features.

Unsupervised adaptation Run 1: CRF trained system only on colon cancer notes.

Supervised adaptation Run 1 & 2: Additionally we used additional 30 brain cancer notes.

2.2 Event span identification

Following the extraction of time expression, our system then identifies event expressions and their spans. Similar to time expression event expression also exhibited characterstic behaviour (Sarath et al., 2016; Abdulsalam et al., 2016).

A single CRF classifier was trained for extraction of event terms from clinical notes for which we used features that are described in section 2.1. Additionally we used following set of features.

Additional features: Word shape features of higher order, features showing disjunctions of words anywhere in the left or right, Conjoin of word shape and n-gram features. All the above features are described in Stanford-CoreNLP (2014)

Both supervised and unsupervised adaptations differ as described previously in section 2.1.

2.3 Document time relation identification

Given spans of event mentions, our system further identifies relations between events and the document creation time using an NER (Named entity recognition) classifier trained for BEFORE, OVERLAP, BEFORE-OVERLAP or AFTER types.

Unsupervised adaptation run 1: Uses ClearTK NER chunking classifier (CRF) and features specified in section 2.1 extracted from the window of ± 5 words.

Supervised adaptation run 1: Similar to unsupervised adaptation run 1 except usage of additional 30 brain cancer notes.

Supervised adaptation run 2: Similar to supervised adaptation run 1 except ClearTK NER was replaced by a two-layer perceptron NER using H2O toolkit and skip-gram based word2vec word embeddings.

---

[1](http://www.h2o.ai/)

2.4 TLINK:Contains identification

We divide the task of narrative container relation identification into four sub-problems based on two criteria: (1) whether the target narrative container relation is between two events or between an event and a time and (2) whether the two event/time mentions are within one sentence or within two adjacent sentences. For each sub-problem, we trained an different set of classifiers that identifies whether an ordered pair of two events/times (or a candidate pair) forms a TLINK of Contains type, using the scikit-learn package. Before training the classifiers, we apply the following steps in order to take into account the data distribution characteristics.

Firstly, since any two events/times can be a candidate pair to train a classifier, the number of candidate pairs becomes huge with small portion of positive instances among them. This may not be ideal for training a classifier. In order to reduce the number of prospective negative instances, we filtered out some of the candidate pairs that are highly unlikely to form a TLINK:Contains relation based on the THYME corpus annotation guidelines (Lee et al., 2016) and heuristic rules (Abdulsalam et al., 2016). Secondly we apply cost sensitive learning in order to balance the effect of the larger negative samples present in the final set used for training. For each class we assigned weight proportional to class frequency.

Unlike event and time expressions, where we used single classifier such as CRF or a single multi layer perceptron network, for container relations, based on our previous experiences in relation extraction we used stacking of multiple classifiers to further reduce the effect of negative class overfitting. As such we used ensemble of Gradient boosted trees, XGBoost, Extra Trees (Geurts et al., 2006), Random forest (Breiman, 2001) classifier for extraction of narrative containers with following features. During model development all the hyperparamters were tuned using grid search with colon cancer notes (training) and 50% of brain cancer notes (validation).

Common features: Event/time tokens and its POS features, Special punctuation characters between event/time mentions, other event/time mentions within the same sentence, number of other event/time mentions between the two event/time mentions, verb tenses, section headers, sentence length.

Special features: A flag to indicate the presence of a pair in colon cancer data and a flag to indicate if the pairs were identified by pretrained CTAKES model.

Unsupervised adaptation Run 1: Stacked ensemble of gradient boosted decision trees, random forest, extra trees classifier with special features.

Supervised adaptation Run 1 & 2: Stacked ensemble of bagged XGBoost classifier, random forest and extra trees classifier re-trained on additional 30 brain cancer notes with event/time tokens and special features removed.

3 Experiments and Results

In this section, we present our system performance of various runs across two different phases for each of the participated subtasks. Tables 1-2 show the results of temporal span extraction and tables 3-4 shows results of temporal relation extraction. Our systems showed average F-score of 0.45 for unsupervised runs and 0.47 for supervised runs across different sub-tasks.

Submission runs	P	R	F
Unsupervised run 1	0.63	0.33	0.43
Supervised run 1 & 2	0.53	0.48	0.51

Table 1: Results of time expression

Submission runs	P	R	F
Unsupervised run 1	0.67	0.69	0.68
Supervised run 1 &2	0.67	0.75	0.71

Table 2: Results of event expression

Submission runs	P	R	F
Unsupervised run 1	0.44	0.45	0.45
Supervised run 1	0.49	0.55	0.52
Supervised run 2	0.42	0.47	0.44

Table 3: Results of doctime relation expression

3.1 Discussion

In this paper we described the system developed for temporal information extraction from clinical notes, using which we achieved average result of 0.45 for unsupervised and 0.47 for supervised phases of evaluation. We adapted state of the art techniques for entity recognition and relation extraction. We also experimented and evaluated stacked ensemble models involving XGBoost, Extra trees, Random Forest, Gradient Boosted trees for narrative container relation extraction.

Submission runs	P	R	F
Unsupervised run 1	0.23	0.22	0.23
Supervised run 1 & 2	0.11	0.27	0.15

Table 4: Results of narrative container relations

For time and event expression extraction our result (table 1 and table 2) were consistent across two phases and was on average 6% behind the best performing system. Potential reasons for the difference in F-score are i) Difference of our results with respect to gold standard annotation due to inclusion/exclusion of prepositions in certain expressions. For example, while a DURATION type time is annotated for the phrase "for the last 40 years" in the gold set, our system predicted a DURATION for the phrase "the last 40 years" omitting the preposition "for" from the gold standard annotation; ii) Limitations of features selected; iii) False negatives in event expression concerned with mispredictions in pathology and radiology reports; iv) Structural difference between colon and brain cancer notes, which is in agreement with improvement of results in phase two with the introduction of 30 brain cancer notes; In our future work we plan to investigate rule based methods to reduce preposition errors and filtering false negative. Further we plan to address problem of lesser training data of target domain through data augmentation techniques using deep learning methods.

For the document time relation extraction subtask, the CRF-based classification approach again allowed for significant improvements, particularly in phase two. Table 3 shows the evaluation scores obtained on the test set for DocTimeRel relation using CRF model. The final scores achieved in phase two (0.52) are comparable to the scores achieved (0.44) in phase one. This allows us to make consistent conclusions about classifier performance with and without supervision. Further when compared we could see that the top performing system had 5% higher F-score for DR task. A possible explanation for this and our future areas of concentration for improvement would be usage of different features related to the section where the event occurs, temporal expressions surrounding the event, and tense and aspect features of the predicates in the event context.

Narrative container relation extraction was the most difficult among all the subtasks as it suffers from major problem of data imbalance. For this work we employed pair/class weight selection strategies previously described in section 2.4 based on extensive experiments on colon cancer test set. Even though we tuned our system to achieve the results of the top performing system of clinical TempEval 2016 our system achieved very low result as shown in table 4. Our results are average of 13% behind the best performing system across two phases in CR task. Following are the major reason for this behaviour i) During testing the number of event-event pairs generated were very high, which made us to remove event-event pairs and submit only time-event pairs; ii) Removal of special features; iii) During phase two, bagging XGBoost resulted in overfitting of the model; iv) Also candidate pairs spanning across multiple sentences were missed by our classifier. During our experiments we observed most of the false positives followed pattern where both the expressions in pairs fall under same concept type in UMLS. Further we found that some pairs failed to satisfy parent child relationship in UMLS concept tree. Thus we plan to investigate rule based methods using UMLS that can identify and remove these kind of false positives. In addition to reducing false positives, this would also counteract against model overfitting when combined with a machine learning method. Also we believe further exploration of future engineering is needed to capture the pairs that span across multiple sentences.

4 Conclusion

Temporal information extraction from clinical notes remains a challenging task. Our analysis of different machine learning approaches have been informative, and resulted in competitive results for the 2017 Clinical TempEval subtasks. From our experiments we observe that CRF's generalize fairly well for extraction of time and event expressions. At the same time we can see there is a large room for improvement (methods and standardizations) in area of narrative container relations extraction. In future we plan to further improve our system to show higher performance based on the above observations.

Acknowledgments

We thank Mayo clinic and Clinical TempEval organizers for providing access to THYME corpus and other helps provided for our participation in the competition.

References

Abdulrahman Al Abdulsalam, Sumithra Velupillai, and Stéphane Meystre. 2016. Utahbmi at semeval-2016 task 12: Extracting temporal information from clinical text. In *SemEval@NAACL-HLT*.

Steven Bethard, Leon Derczynski, Guergana K. Savova, James Pustejovsky, and Marc Verhagen. 2015. Semeval-2015 task 6: Clinical tempeval. In *SemEval@NAACL-HLT*.

Steven Bethard, Philip V. Ogren, and Lee Becker. 2014. Cleartk 2.0: Design patterns for machine learning in uima. In *LREC*.

Steven Bethard, Guergana K. Savova, Wei-Te Chen, Leon Derczynski, James Pustejovsky, and Marc Verhagen. 2016. Semeval-2016 task 12: Clinical tempeval. In *SemEval@NAACL-HLT*.

Steven Bethard, Guergana K. Savova, Wei-Te Chen, Leon Derczynski, James Pustejovsky, and Marc Verhagen. 2017. Semeval-2017 task 12: Clinical tempeval. In *SemEval@ACL*.

Leo Breiman. 2001. Random forests. *Machine Learning* 45:5–32.

Angel X. Chang and Christopher D. Manning. 2014. Tokensregex: Defining cascaded regular expressions over tokens.

Tianqi Chen and Carlos Guestrin. 2016. Xgboost: A scalable tree boosting system. In *KDD*.

Saso Dzeroski and Bernard Zenko. 2004. Is combining classifiers with stacking better than selecting the best one? *Machine Learning* 54:255–273.

Pierre Geurts, Damien Ernst, and Louis Wehenkel. 2006. Extremely randomized trees. *Machine Learning* 63:3–42.

Nishikant Johri, Yoshiki Niwa, and Veera Raghavendra Chikka. 2014. Optimizing apache ctakes for disease/disorder template filling: Team hitachi in the share/clef 2014 ehealth evaluation lab. In *CLEF*.

John D. Lafferty, Andrew McCallum, and Fernando Pereira. 2001. Conditional random fields: Probabilistic models for segmenting and labeling sequence data. In *ICML*.

Quoc V. Le and Tomas Mikolov. 2014. Distributed representations of sentences and documents. In *ICML*.

Hee-Jin Lee, Hua Xu, Jingqi Wang, Yaoyun Zhang, Sungrim Moon, Jun Xu, and Yonghui Wu. 2016. Uthealth at semeval-2016 task 12: an end-to-end system for temporal information extraction from clinical notes. In *SemEval@NAACL-HLT*.

Chen Lin, Dmitriy Dligach, Timothy A. Miller, Steven Bethard, and Guergana K. Savova. 2016. Multi-layered temporal modeling for the clinical domain. *JAMIA* 23:387–395.

Edward Loper and Steven Bird. 2002. Nltk: The natural language toolkit. *CoRR* cs.CL/0205028.

Christopher D. Manning, Mihai Surdeanu, John Bauer, Jenny Finkel, Steven J. Bethard, and David McClosky. 2014. The Stanford CoreNLP natural language processing toolkit. In *Association for Computational Linguistics (ACL) System Demonstrations*. pages 55–60. http://www.aclweb.org/anthology/P/P14/P14-5010.

Danielle L. Mowery, Sumithra Velupillai, Brett R. South, Lee M. Christensen, David Martínez, Liadh Kelly, Lorraine Goeuriot, Noémie Elhadad, Sameer Pradhan, Guergana K. Savova, and Wendy W. Chapman. 2014. Task 2: Share/clef ehealth evaluation lab 2014. In *CLEF*.

F. Pedregosa, G. Varoquaux, A. Gramfort, V. Michel, B. Thirion, O. Grisel, M. Blondel, P. Prettenhofer, R. Weiss, V. Dubourg, J. Vanderplas, A. Passos, D. Cournapeau, M. Brucher, M. Perrot, and E. Duchesnay. 2011. Scikit-learn: Machine learning in Python. *Journal of Machine Learning Research* 12:2825–2830.

Sarath, Manikandan R, and Yoshiki Niwa. 2016. Hitachi at semeval-2016 task 12: A hybrid approach for temporal information extraction from clinical notes. In *SemEval@NAACL-HLT*.

Guergana K. Savova, James J. Masanz, Philip V. Ogren, Jiaping Zheng, Sunghwan Sohn, Karin Kipper Schuler, and Christopher G. Chute. 2010. Mayo clinical text analysis and knowledge extraction system (ctakes): architecture, component evaluation and applications. *JAMIA* 17:507–513.

Scharolta Katharina Siencnik. 2015. Adapting word2vec to named entity recognition. In *NODAL-IDA*.

Stanford-CoreNLP. 2014. Stanford ner feature factory. https://tinyurl.com/zanvz7c.

William F. Styler, Steven Bethard, Sean Finan, Martha Palmer, Sameer Pradhan, Piet C. de Groen, Bradley James Erickson, Timothy A. Miller, Chen Lin, Guergana K. Savova, and James Pustejovsky. 2014. Temporal annotation in the clinical domain. *TACL* 2:143–154.

Weiyi Sun, Anna Rumshisky, and Ozlem Uzuner. 2013. Evaluating temporal relations in clinical text: 2012 i2b2 challenge. *JAMIA* 20.

NTU-1 at SemEval-2017 Task 12: Detection and classification of temporal events in clinical data with supervised domain adaptation

Po-Yu Huang[*], Hen-Hsen Huang[†], Yu-Wun Wang[†], Ching Huang[†], Hsin-Hsi Chen[†]

[*]School of Medicine
Taipei Medical University Taipei, Taiwan
[†]Department of Computer Science and Information Engineering
National Taiwan University Taipei, Taiwan
`b101100089@tmu.edu.tw, hhhuang@nlg.csie.ntu.edu.tw,`
`{b02902033, b02902042, hhchen}@ntu.edu.tw`

Abstract

This study proposes a system to automatically analyze clinical temporal events in a fine-grained level in SemEval-2017. Support vector machine (SVM) and conditional random field (CRF) were implemented in our system for different subtasks, including detecting clinical relevant events and time expression, determining their attributes, and identifying their relations with each other within the document. Domain adaptation was the main challenge this year. Unified Medical Language System was consulted to generalize events specific to each domain. The results showed our system's capability of domain adaptation.

1 Introduction

This study proposes a system to participate in the Clinical TempEval 2017 shared task, which focuses on the detection and classification of temporal events in clinical data. To better utilize the information in clinical data, temporal event extraction is fundamental in previous researches (Bethard et al., 2016). Unlike previous studies, the training and the test data are in different domains this year. The task is further separated into two phases: unsupervised domain adaption and supervised domain adaption. We took part in the supervised domain adaption where data of 591 records of colon cancer patients and 30 records of brain cancer patients from Mayo clinic were given. Based on the THYME corpus (Styler IV et al., 2014), we propose a framework that automatically analyzes clinical temporal events in a fine-grained level. Our framework identifies temporal events in unstructured text and further labels every event with its attributes.

The task consists of three major subtasks. The first one is to detect clinical relevant events and time expressions in a given medical record. From the unstructured text, both the spans of time expressions and the spans of event mentions are identified.

The second subtask is analyzing the attributes of time expressions and event mentions. A time expression will be classified into one of six types: DATE, TIME, DURATION, QUANTIFIER, PREPOSTEXP, and SET. An event mention contains four properties such as type of an event, polarity, degree and modality. Our model labels these four properties to every event mention.

The final subtask is to determine two kinds of relations within the text. DocTimeRel is the relation between the document creation time and an event mention. Four types of DocTimeRel including BEFORE, AFTER, OVERLAP, and BEFORE-OVERLAP are annotated in THYME. In addition to DocTimeRel, our model also recognizes the narrative container of an event mention called TLINK in this task. There are five types of TLINK, including BEFORE, CONTAIN, OVERLAP, BEGINS-ON, and ENDS-ON.

The outcomes of our system are not only the clinical temporal events, but also their detailed properties and their temporal relations with other events. The results of our framework can be further used to discover relationships between illnesses, symptoms, medications, and procedures.

2 Methods

Our system contains five modules: the first one identifies the span and the type of each event mention; the second one determines the other re-

Proceedings of the 11th International Workshop on Semantic Evaluations (SemEval-2017), pages 1010–1013,
Vancouver, Canada, August 3 - 4, 2017. ©2017 Association for Computational Linguistics

maining attributes of an event mention; the third one identifies the span and the type of each time expression; the fourth one determines the TLINK between each pair of event mention and time expression in the same sentence; the fifth one determines the TLINK between each pair of event mentions in the same sentence.

2.1 Preprocessing

We ran Stanford CoreNLP toolkit (Manning et al., 2014) on all the clinical data. This toolkit generated POS and NER for each word, and dependencies for each sentence in the clinical data. A dictionary was built based on Unified Medical Language System (UMLS) (Bodenreider, 2004) with five categories of different genre of medical related words, including DIAGNOSIS, EXAMINE, MEDICINE, POSITION and SURGERY. All of these were utilized in the following steps.

2.2 Event Mention Identification

In this module, we tried to identify the span denoting an event and its type. There are three types of event mentions, including ASPECTUAL, EVIDENTIAL, and N/A. ASPECTUAL event mentions often turn out to be verbs indicating something would happen later in the timeline, like "reoccur", "continue", etc. EVIDENTIAL events are usually verbs like "show", "reveal", and "confirm", which show how doctors come to identify and learn about other events. N/A events are mostly composed of medical related words like "nausea", "surgery", and "operate".

We built a four-way linear SVM classifier using scikit-learn (Pedregosa et al., 2011) to classify a word into ASPECTUAL, EVIDENTIAL, N/A, or non-event. In other words, span identification and type classification are done simultaneously. Features for our SVM classifier are listed as follows:

Lexical Feature: n-gram of nearby words, and character n-gram within the target word
POS Feature: POS n-gram of nearby words
Named Entity Type: type of named entities identified by NER
Orthographic Feature: orthographic n-gram of nearby words obtained by substituting all uppercase letters, lowercase letters, and digits with 'A', 'a', and '0'.
Structural Features: 1) position of the target word divided by the sentence length, and 2) the length of the path from the target word to the root in the dependency-parsing tree.
UMLS Category: the category of the target word based on UMLS.

Since training set and test set come from two different domains, i.e., colon cancers versus brain cancers, there may be some medical terms in test set but not appearing in training set. In this study, UMLS dictionary was consulted to cluster the medical terms into the five categories in order to deal with domain adaptation problem and reduce sparseness. For example, terms specific to colon cancer "right hemicolectomy" and "rectum" would be transformed into "SURGERY" and "POSITION", respectively, while building n-gram features.

2.3 Event Attribute Identification

Besides modality, polarity, and degree, we include DocTimeRel from the relation subtask here because it is also an attribute along with an event mention. We trained a multi-class linear SVM classifier for each of the four attributes. The features described in Section 2.2 were used. In additions, we introduced time related features for DocTimeRel, including tense of verbs within the same sentence, n-gram and POS n-gram of time related terms within the same sentence, and the relative position of the time related terms within the same sentence.

2.4 Time Expression Identification

Time expression identification is different from event mention identification because time expression is less affected by the change of domain. However, its spans are more diverse than those in event mention. For instance, a SET time expression is usually composed of multiple words like "three times a week". By contrast, a PRE-POSTEXP is mostly just one word only, like "preoperative". To deal with the issue of diverse spans, we used CRF[1] to develop this module because of its ability in sequence labeling. Similarly to Section 2.2, we also determined the span and the type simultaneously.

Besides those features (UMLS Category excluded) used in Section 2.2, we added some other features, including the existence of pre-post related characters ("pre", "post", "peri", and "intra"), the existence of a number, and whether there is a

---

[1] http://sklearn-crfsuite.readthedocs.io/en/latest/index.html

duration condition in the same sentence ("for", "since", "through", "until", and "in").

2.5 TLINKs between Event Mentions and Time Expressions

TLINK is determined between event mentions, and between event mentions and time expressions. TLINKs are mostly linked within the same sentence, thus we focused on identifying TLINKs within sentences.

Two multi-class SVM classifiers were built for five subtypes in TLINK: the first one was trained to identify TLINKs given a pair of time expression and event mention, which we called "TE classifier", and the second one was trained to identify TLINKS given a pair of event mentions, which we called "EE classifier".

Features we used are shown as follows:

Features for both classifiers: types, attributes, tokens and POS of the pair of mentions, punctuations between the pair of mentions, tense of the nearest verbs, and dependency path between the pair of mentions.

Features only for EE classifier: if exists a time expression which is linked to both event mention by the TE classifier, types of the two TLINKs were considered as features

3 Results

We used the clinical data provided in the supervised domain adaption, which contained 591 records of colon cancer patients and 30 records of brain cancer patients, to train our system. Table 1 shows the results of event mentions, time expression and relations, where F1 stands for F1 score, P stands for precision, and R stands for recall.

Brain cancer	F1	P	R
ES	0.73	0.62	0.87
ES: All attributes	0.41	0.35	0.50
ES: Modality	0.63	0.54	0.75
ES: Degree	0.72	0.62	0.86
ES: Polarity	0.70	0.60	0.84
ES: Type	0.70	0.60	0.85
DocTimeRel	0.49	0.42	0.59
TS	0.58	0.58	0.58
TS: Type	0.54	0.54	0.54
TLINK	0.26	0.20	0.37

Table 1: Results of event spans (ES), time spans (TS), TLINK, and their attributes tested on brain cancer patients.

To compare our system's performance while switching domain, we also provide Table 2 of the results for all three subtasks where training and testing data are all colon cancer patients.

Colon cancer	F1	P	R
ES	0.86	0.84	0.89
ES: All attributes	0.57	0.55	0.58
ES: Modality	0.78	0.76	0.81
ES: Degree	0.86	0.84	0.88
ES: Polarity	0.83	0.81	0.86
ES: Type	0.83	0.81	0.86
DocTimeRel	0.65	0.63	0.67
TS	0.75	0.83	0.68
TS: Type	0.73	0.80	0.66
TLINK	0.39	0.38	0.39

Table 2: Results of all subtasks tested on colon cancer patients.

4 Discussion

The F1 scores of event mentions in brain cancer patients are lower than in colon cancer patients. It is mostly contributed by the decrease in precision. Without the ground truths, we can only assume that our system still learned some domain-specific features to tell event apart from non-event under the replacement of words with classes according to UMLS. The scores of TLINK have the same problem as event mentions.

Interestingly, the performance of time expression, which we thought to be free from the challenge of domain adaptation, decreases drastically in all three scores. It is certain that some domain specific features played big roles in our system. However, without the ground truths, it is difficult to identify the problem.

CRF and SVM were both experimented for time expressions and shown in Table 3. With the same features, CRF performed better than SVM in F1 score and precision. The results show that CRF has a better performance in sequence labeling. Advanced deep learning model including convolution neural network (CNN) and recurrent neural network (RNN) will be explored in the future due to their advantages in sequence labeling.

Time	F1	P	R
SVM	0.69	0.67	0.70
CRF	0.73	0.80	0.66

Table 3: results of time expression identification with two different settings

Best vs. Us	F1	P	R
ES	0.76 (0.73)	0.69 (0.62)	0.85 (0.87)
ES: All attributes	0.52 (0.41)	0.47 (0.35)	0.58 (0.50)
ES: Modality	0.69 (0.63)	0.63 (0.54)	0.78 (0.75)
ES: Degree	0.75 (0.72)	0.68 (0.62)	0.84 (0.86)
ES: Polarity	0.75 (0.70)	0.68 (0.60)	0.83 (0.84)
ES: Type	0.75 (0.70)	0.68 (0.60)	0.83 (0.85)
DocTimeRel	0.59 (0.49)	0.53 (0.42)	0.66 (0.59)
TS	0.58 (0.58)	0.51 (0.58)	0.67 (0.58)
TS: Type	0.55 (0.54)	0.49 (0.54)	0.64 (0.54)
TLINK	0.32 (0.26)	0.25 (0.20)	0.43 (0.37)

Table 4: Comparison with the best results in F1 of the other runs in this shared task, where our results are listed inside the brackets.

Compared to the best results of other runs in this shared task, which is shown in Table 4, DocTimeRel is the most poorly predicted attribute by our system. DocTimeRel is the relationship between an event and its document creation time. However, the features we chose for this subtask were all confined to one sentence. Adding features capturing the time representations within neighboring sentences, within the section, or even within whole document should increase the performance.

TLINK is another attributes that our system performed notably worse than the first place. This is possibly due to the chain effect where TLINK was determined based on event mentions and time expressions that were already with worse performance. Once ruling out this possibility, we can then focus on how to improve our TLINK module.

5 Conclusion

In this paper, we proposed a system to participate in the Clinical TempEval 2017 shared task. Our system not only identified the clinical temporal events, but also their detailed properties and their temporal relations with other events. It can also take on the challenge of domain adaptation where only a few data from targeted domain was given while the other data were from different domain. Our system adopted SVM and CRF for different subtasks. The results were in the third place in supervised domain adaptation.

In future works, we will focus on the increasing the performance in DocTimeRel and explore deep learning algorithms.

References

Steven Bethard, Guergana Savova, Wei-Te Chen, Leon Derczynski, James Pustejovsky, and Marc Verhagen. (2016). Semeval-2016 task 12: Clinical tempeval. *Proceedings of SemEval*:1052-1062.

Oliver Bodenreider. (2004). The Unified Medical Language System (UMLS): integrating biomedical terminology. *Nucleic Acids Res, 32*(Database issue):D267-270. doi:10.1093/nar/gkh061

Christopher D Manning, Mihai Surdeanu, John Bauer, Jenny Rose Finkel, Steven Bethard, and David McClosky. (2014). *The stanford corenlp natural language processing toolkit.* In *Proceedings of the ACL (System Demonstrations)*, pages 55-60.

Fabian Pedregosa, Gaël Varoquaux, Alexandre Gramfort, Vincent Michel, Bertrand Thirion, Olivier Grisel, Mathieu Blondel, Peter Prettenhofer, Ron Weiss, and Vincent Dubourg. (2011). Scikit-learn: Machine learning in Python. *Journal of Machine Learning Research, 12*(Oct):2825-2830.

William F Styler IV, Steven Bethard, Sean Finan, Martha Palmer, Sameer Pradhan, Piet C de Groen, Brad Erickson, Timothy Miller, Chen Lin, and Guergana Savova. (2014). Temporal annotation in the clinical domain. *Transactions of the Association for Computational Linguistics, 2*:143-154.

XJNLP at SemEval-2017 Task 12: Clinical temporal information extraction with a Hybrid Model

Yu Long
University of Xi'an Jiaotong
yulongxbdx@163.com
Xuan Wang
University of Xi'an Jiaotong
m18829236255@163.com

Zhijing Li
University of Xi'an Jiaotong
tokyojackson@stu.xjtu.edu.cn
Chen Li
University of Xi'an Jiaotong
cli@xjtu.edu.cn

Abstract

Temporality is crucial in understanding the course of clinical events from a patient's electronic health records and temporal processing is becoming more and more important for improving access to content. SemEval 2017 Task 12 (Clinical TempEval) addressed this challenge using the THYME corpus, a corpus of clinical narratives annotated with a schema based on TimeML2 guidelines. We developed and evaluated approaches for: extraction of temporal expressions (TIMEX3) and EVENTs; EVENT attributes; document-time relations. Our approach is a hybrid model which is based on rule based methods, semi-supervised learning, and semantic features with addition of manually crafted rules.

1 Introduction

Extraction and interpretation of temporal information from clinical text is essential for clinical practitioners and researchers. Extracting temporal information from unstructured clinical narratives is an important step towards the accurate construction of a patient timeline over the course of clinical care. SemEval-2017 Task 12 (Clinical TempEval) is a direct successor to 2016 Clinical TempEval. Clinical TempEval is designed to address the challenge of understanding clinical timeline in medical narratives and it is based on the THYME corpus which includes temporal annotations.

Researchers have explored ways to extract temporal information from clinical text. Lee et al. (2016) developed an approach based on linear and structural (HMM) support vector machines using lexical, morphological, syntactic, discourse, and word representation features. P R, Sarath et al. (2016) used a hybrid approach(rule-based and

machine learning) for temporal information extraction from clinical notes. Velupillai et al. (2015) developed a pipeline based on ClearTK and SVM with lexical features to extract TIMEX3 and EVENT mentions. Most of the participants of these challenges used CRF and SVM for event and time expression extraction with features including the information gathered from different resources like UMLS (Unified Medical Language System), output of TARSQI toolkit, Brown Clustering, Wikipedia and Metamap (Aronson and Lang, 2010). Those machine-learning methods are complex and they cost much time to run. However, they can be not only flexible but also convenient when compared to the handcrafting label. Others also used some rule based methods, which are fast but not flexible enough. It seems that the combination of those two methods may gain the better result. Since in I2b2 2012 temporal challenge, all top performing teams used a combination of supervised classification and rule based methods for extracting temporal information and relations (Sun et al., 2013). Besides THYME corpus, there have been other efforts in clinical temporal annotation including works by Roberts et al. (2008), Savova et al. (2009), Galescu and Blaylock (2012) and so on. Recently, interest in temporal processing has moved forward in two directions: cross-document timeline extraction (Minard et al., 2015) and domain adaptation (Sun et al., 2013; Bethard et al., 2015). Based on the analysis above, our hybrid model utilize machine learning techniques and crafted rules which contains SVM (Support Vector Machine) classifier and RNN (Recurrent Neural Networks) classifier to extract Temporal Information from Clinical documents and make classifications.

Proceedings of the 11th International Workshop on Semantic Evaluations (SemEval-2017), pages 1014–1018,
Vancouver, Canada, August 3 - 4, 2017. ©2017 Association for Computational Linguistics

2 Data and Method

2.1 Data

We use THYME corpus for training and evaluating the methods, which consists of clinical and pathology notes of patients with colon cancer and brain cancer from Mayo Clinic. The THYME corpus is split into training, development, and test sets based on patient number, with 50% in training and 25% each in development and test sets. Table 2 shows the distributions of the different time and event classes in the THYME corpus. The training data about colon cancer contains 3,833 time expressions and 38,890 events, the development data contains 2,078 time expressions and 20,974 events. The training data about brain cancer contains 350 time expressions and 2,557 events.

	attribute	Coloncancer-Train	Braincancer-Train	Coloncancer-Dev
	Documents	293	30	147
E V E N T	ASPECTUAL	546	51	246
	EVIDENTIAL	2,206	85	1,314
	N/A	36,185	2,421	19,414
	MOST	96	2	45
	LITTLE	143	18	65
	N/A	38,698	2,537	20,864
	POSITIVE	34,832	2,386	18,795
	NEGATIVE	4,105	171	2,179
	ACTUAL	35,781	2,172	22,647
	HEDGED	889	81	443
	HYPOTHETICAL	1,656	88	829
	GENERIC	611	216	611
T I M E X	Date	2,588	204	1,422
	Duration	434	29	200
	PrePostExp	313	37	172
	Set	218	13	116
	Quantifier	162	9	109
	Time	118	58	59

Table 1: different time and event attributes in the THYME3 corpus

The data of colon cancer are more than others and the training data of brain cancer is too little but the test data is all about brain cancer, so the task will focus on domain adaptation. We can also see the unbalanced data distribution, for example, the data of N/A is 38,698, but the data of MOST is only 96, and maybe unbalanced data will have an impact on the results. We used the development set for optimizing learning parameters, then combined it with the training set to build the system used for reporting results in Section 4.

2.2 Task Description

Clinical TempEval 2017 was focused on designing approaches for information extraction in the clinical domain.There were 6 different tasks which are listed in Table 2.

Clinical TempEval is designed to address the challenge of understanding clinical timeline in medical narratives and it is based on the THYME corpus which includes temporal annotations.

Task	Description
TS	TIMEX3 spans
ES	EVENT spans
TA Class	Attributes of TIMEX3 <DATE, TIME, DURATION, QUANTIFIER, PREPOSTEXP, SET>
EA Modality Degree Polarity Type	Attributes of EVENTs <ACTUAL, HYPOTHETICAL, HEDGED,GENERIC> <MOST, LITTLE,N/A> <POS, NEG> <ASPECTUAL, EVIDENTIAL, N/A>
DR	Relation between EVENT and document time <BEFORE, OVERLAP, BE- FORE/OVERLAP, AFTER>
CR	Narrative container relations

Table 2: Tasks of clinical TempEval 2017

For extracting temporal information from clinical text, we utilize semi-supervised learning algorithms (SVM and RNN) with diverse sets of features for each task. We also utilize manually-crafted rules to improve the performance of the classifiers, when appropriate. We show the effectiveness of the designed features and the rules for different tasks.

3 Methodology

Our approach to the tasks is a hybrid model that is based on rule based methods and supervised learning using lexical, syntactic and semantic features extracted from the clinical text. We also designed custom rules for some tasks when appropriate. Details are outlined below:

3.1 TIMEX3 Span Detection and Time Expression Attribute Identification

Our tasks are about time expression span detection (TS) and time expression attribute identification (TA), which means that we should first extract the time expression and then identify which class it belongs to. As for time span, we use the rule based methods to detect the boundary of the time expression. We use Stanford NLP package to do the pre- processing and we normalize the digital expressions after it, we change every character to "0" as long as it is digit. (e. g. we normalize the "12:13" to "00:00".)

For the rule based methods, firstly we find all the prepositions, according to our experience and experimental statistics, we extract five tokens behind their own prepositions. Since we thought that many time expressions always show up behind a preposition, we then judge whether those five words are related to time expressions. We define a time dictionary to list the words which we think can be a part of the time expressions, like "month", "week, "day", "hour", "May", "Monday", "morning", "once" and so on. Next, we contrast the five tokens with time dictionary, and find whether it can represent a date or a precise time. Finally, we extract all the continuous tokens that we thought may relate to the time expressions (if there is a definite article before those tokens, extract it as well). There exist some expressions do not after a preposition and only contain one word and most of them have the same prefix like "pre", "post", "peri". So we use this prefix rule to find the remain expressions.

We also use the rule based methods to identify the classes of the time expression. And here are some examples of the rules for each class:

Class	Rules
Date	1999-11-08, yesterday, last Saturday, in 3 years, 3 months ago...
Duration	for 3 days, July to August, since last summer....
PrePostExp	post, preoperative, prior to the surgery....
Set	Twice per day, 3 times a day...
Quantifier	Twice, once...
Time	13:56, in the morning....

Table 3: examples of rules for each time expression class

3.2 Event Extraction Task

In this task, we need to extract medical events from the clinical text and identify attributes of the events which are showed in table 1.

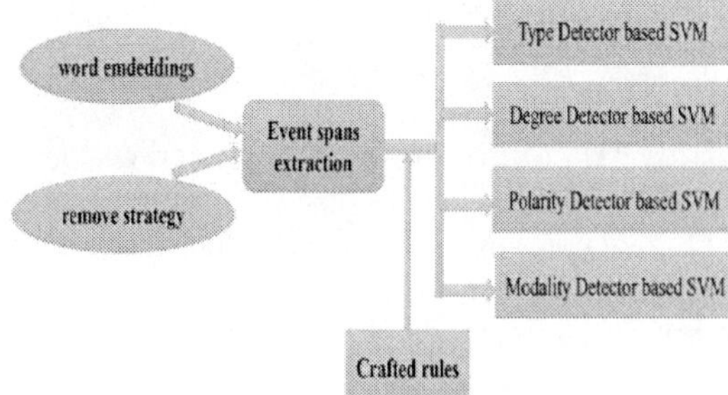

Figure 1 Event Extraction Architecture

Figure 1 illustrates the architecture of our EVENTs extraction system. First, we create word embeddings using the Wikipedia database. Then we extract event spans with a SVM classifier and a remove strategy. Finally we detect type, degree, modality, and polarity using four separate SVM classifiers and crafted rules.

3.2.1 Event Spans (ES) Extraction

To extract EVENT spans, first we train a separate Support Vector Machine to complete prediction. Then we make a colon corpus about colon cancer which comes from training data and Wikipedia. Finally, we remove the events which exist in the colon corpus from the prediction result.

The major feature we used for training the SVM classifier is word embeddings. We trained all word embeddings in this document with word2vec (Mikolov et al., 2013) using the Skipgram model on a text window size of 2 tokens, to obtain words vector representations of dimension 50. We also try to use the words vector representations of dimension 300, but the result is unexpected.

3.2.2 Identifying EVENTs Attributes (EA)

Table 1 shows the EVENTs attributes. Assigning these attributes to one of its values is an classification task. We train four separate Support Vector Machines for each attribute to classify their respective classes. We also use word embeddings as the major features for training separate SVM classifier for each attribute.

Furthermore, according to our observations of the corpus, different types of event mentions may show different rules. For instance, events with EVIDENTIAL type are usually represented with verbs such as "showed", "reported", "found", in contrast, the events with N/A type that are usually represented medical terms such as "nausea", "chemotherapy" or "colonoscopy". So we create such rules to help classifications.

3.3 Document-time Relation (DR)

Document-time relations (DR) are specific attributes of EVENTs indicating their temporal relation with the document creation time. There are 3 different types of DRs, namely, BEFORE, AFTER, and OVERLAP. For identifying the DR attribute types, we use RNN. RNN makes up for the inaccuracy of the convolution kernel and the pool size in the process of text processing, therefore, the generated RNN classifier has higher accuracy for text classification. We train classifier for each DR type using an set of features to what was used for EVENTs attributes detection. Verb tense and the modals in the sentence are also indicative of the sentence tense and can help in identifying the document-time relation. Figure 1 describes the additional features that we use for DR extraction. In addition to the base features, we consider features specific to the EVENTs annotation. We furthermore expanded the features by considering contextual features from the sentence and nearby time and date mentions. We try to optimized the RNN classifier--thread level speculation. Replace the calculated results of the other core to be weighted with speculative value, in that way, the parallel computing can be carried out smoothly. We used this method to classify the colon cancer data with golden annotations, the results are shown in the following table.

DR	P	R	F1
RNN	0.69	0.71	0.70
RNN+	0.90	0.91	0.90

Table 4: Document-time Relation of cancer data

From this table, we can see the value of precision, the value of recall and the value of F1 are relatively high, so the Optimized RNN classifier is effective. But we do not know whether it is suitable for the brain cancer data.

4 Experiments and Results

The 2017 Clinical TempEval task consisted of two evaluation phases. Phase1 is unsupervised domain adaptation and phase 2 is supervised domain adaptation. In phase 2, we participated in all tasks, except for CR.

We report the results on the test set for all subtasks, Results have been computed in terms of Precision (P), Recall (R) and F1. For comparison we will also report the maximum scores of the participating systems.

Subtask	P	R	F1
TIMEX3_SPAN	0.33	0.52	0.41
TIMEX3_Class	0.29	0.45	0.35

Table 5: results for TS and TA subtasks

However, the result is less than satisfactory. Table 5 shows the final result. We compared our results with the best results on the Semeval website. (https://competitions.codalab.org/) We think there are three reasons: First, our methods always extract two different expressions as one if they are very close to each other. Secondly, our dictionary is too small to cover enough words. Thirdly, we extract most of words in the raw text that have the prefix "pre", "post", "peri", but some of them are not time expressions. As for TA, we think that we only focus on the time expression itself but ignore much semantic information.

Subtask	P	R	F1
ES	0.55	0.69	0.61
Type	0.53	0.66	0.59
Degree	0.54	0.67	0.56
Polarity	0.49	0.61	0.54
Modality	0.46	0.57	0.51

Table 6: results for EVENTs subtasks

The results for EVENTs subtasks also show lower performance in comparison with the result of best system. Error analysis are as bellowed:

Firstly, we don't use a good and effective domain adaption method, and we do not have an effective way to solve the unbalanced data. Secondly, we don't integrate more domain specific features. Thirdly, in the process of Events Attributes identification, we ignore the importance of context analysis and Sentiment analysis. For example, "bleeding" can be the positive class of the Polarity attribute, and it also can be the negative class. This is up to the context analysis. In addition, we create word embeddings using the Wikipedia database. The temporal information from clinical is professional. So we need to use more database about clinic to improve the performance of the word embeddings. In the future, we plan to further improve our system to show higher performance based on the observations above.

Subtask	P	R	F1
DR	0.29	0.36	0.32

Table 7: results for DR subtasks

We use the results of EVENT extraction to forecast the document-time relation of brain cancer. So the results of EVENT_span and TIMEX3_span are very important, and we do not add the domain adaptation, so the result of DR of brain cancer are relatively low, the detailed results are shown in table7. We have identified some errors: first, wrong output of the pre-processing modules, especially the parsing process. Second, limitations of the features selected. Third, lack of domain specific knowledge.

5 Discussion and Conclusions

SemEval 2017 task 12 (Clinical TempEval) was focused on temporal information extraction from clinical narratives. Our methods employed rule based methods and machine learning classification scheme for all the tasks except for CR based on various sets of syntactic, lexical, and semantic features. We illustrated that incorporating manually crafted extraction rules improves results, but the rules should be improved.

For TIMEX3 subtasks, our approach was clearly not the best solution as our rules are simple and not perfect so that the system cannot obtain the high score. For EVENTs subtasks, our system is not ideal for unbalanced data classification, and we will enhance its effectiveness. For DR subtask, we showed that the optimized classifier can improve the accuracy but we do not know whether it is suitable for the brain cancer data. Besides, we do not consider the domain adaptation and our features were minimal. There are many options to improve the system, ranging from fine tuning the pre-processing phase in order to avoid offset misalignments, to the generation of better features for the ES and DR subtasks. In future work, we aim to implement all the improvements mentioned above.

References

Rodriguez P, Wiles J, Elman J L. A RNN that learns to count[J]. Connection Science, 1999.

Wang W J, Liao Y F, Chen S H. RNN-based prosodic modeling for mandarin speech and its application to speech-to-text conversion[J]. Speech Communication, 2002,36(3-4):247-265.

Cho K, Merrienboer B V, Gulcehre C, et al. Learning Phrase Representations using RNN Encoder-Decoder for Statistical Machine Translation[J]. Computer Science, 2014.

Jain A, Zamir A R, Savarese S, et al. Structural-RNN: Deep Learning on Spatio-Temporal Graphs[J]. Computer Science, 2015.

Namikawa J, Tani J. A model for learning to segment temporal sequences, utilizing a mixture of RNN experts together with adaptive variance[J]. Neural Networks, 2008, 21(10):1466-1475.

Shao H, Nonami K, Wojtara T, et al. Neuro-fuzzy position control of demining tele-operation system based on RNN modeling[J]. Robotics and Computer-Integrated Manufacturing, 2006, 22(1):25-32.

Routraya G, Kanungo P. Genetic Algorithm Based RNN Structure for Rayleigh Fading MIMO Channel Estimation[J]. Procedia Engineering, 2012, 30(30):77-84.

Chung J, Jang H, Jung K H, et al. Parallel approach for processing itinerary-based RNN queries in object tracking WSNs[J]. Telecommunication Systems, 2014, 55(1):55-69.

Patnaik P R. A RNN for a fed-batch fermentation with recombinant Escheria coli subject to inflow disturbances[J]. Process Biochemistry, 1997, 32(5):391-400.

Boronat M, Corma A, Gonzálezarellano C, et al. Synthesis of Electron-Rich CNN-Pincer Complexes, with N-Heterocyclic Carbene and (S)-Proline Moieties and Application to Asymmetric Hydrogenation[J]. Organometallics, 2014, 29(1):159-172.

Weiyi Sun, Anna Rumshisky, and OzlemUzuner. 2013. Evaluating temporal relations in clinical text: 2012 i2b2 challenge. Journal of the American Medical Informatics Association, 20(5).

Sumithra Velupillai, Danielle L Mowery, Samir Abdelrahman, Lee Christensen, and Wendy W Chapman. 2015. Blulab: Temporal information extraction for the 2015 clinical tempeval challenge. Association for Computational Linguistics.

Alan R Aronson and Franc, ois-Michel Lang. 2010. An overview of MetaMap: historical perspective and recent advances. Journal of the American Medical Informatics Association, 17(3):229–236.

Steven Bethard, Leon Derczynski, James Pustejovsky, and Marc Verhagen. 2015. Semeval-2015 task 6: Clinical tempeval. In Proceedings of the 9th International Workshop on Semantic Evaluation (SemEval 2015). Association for Computational Linguistics.

ULISBOA at SemEval-2017 Task 12: Extraction and classification of temporal expressions and events

Andre Lamurias[‡], Diana Sousa[1], Sofia Pereira[1], Luka A. Clarke[2] and Francisco M. Couto[1]

[1]LaSIGE, Faculdade de Ciências, Universidade de Lisboa, Portugal
[2]BioISI: Biosystems & Integrative Sciences Institute,
Faculdade de Ciências, Universidade de Lisboa, Portugal

Abstract

This paper presents our approach to participate in the SemEval 2017 Task 12: Clinical TempEval challenge, specifically in the event and time expressions span and attribute identification subtasks (ES, EA, TS, TA). Our approach consisted in training Conditional Random Fields (CRF) classifiers using the provided annotations, and in creating manually curated rules to classify the attributes of each event and time expression. We used a set of common features for the event and time CRF classifiers, and a set of features specific to each type of entity, based on domain knowledge. Training only on the source domain data, our best F-scores were 0.683 and 0.485 for event and time span identification subtasks. When adding target domain annotations to the training data, the best F-scores obtained were 0.729 and 0.554, for the same subtasks. We obtained the second highest F-score of the challenge on the event polarity subtask (0.708). The source code of our system, Clinical Timeline Annotation (CiTA), is available at `https://github.com/lasigeBioTM/CiTA`.

1 Introduction

This paper presents our system CiTA (Clinical Timeline Annotation) to participate in the SemEval 2017 Task 12: Clinical TempEval challenge. Our team participated in the subtasks corresponding to the identification of the following properties: time expression spans, event expression spans, time expression attributes, event expression attributes. Time expressions had only one attribute, type, which could be DATE, TIME, DURATION, QUANTIFIER, PREPOSTEXP or SET. Event attribute identification consisted of four attributes: type (N/A, ASPECTUAL or EVIDENTIAL), polarity (POS or NEG), degree (N/A, most or little) and modality (ACTUAL, HEDGED, HYPOTHETICAL or GENERIC).

For this challenge, we developed a system, named Clinical Timeline Annotation CiTA[1], which uses IBEnt (Lamurias et al., 2015) to identify the text spans of time and event entities based on machine learning and semantic techniques. CiTA also incorporates hand-crafted rules to assign the attributes to each entity. We trained one classifier for each entity type using Conditional Random Fields (CRF) and developed a set of rules for each attribute, based on the training data available at each phase. This paper describes the features and resources used for each subtask, presents our results and discusses the main issues found. CiTA is publicly available in a GitHub repository [2].

2 Methods

A corpus of clinical, pathology and radiology notes from the Mayo Clinic was available to the participants. This corpus contained notes for the source domain (colon cancer) and for the target domain (brain cancer). Each document was manually annotated with time and event expressions, as well as their attributes. The annotators and adjudicators followed a set of guidelines which were also available to the participants. During Phase 1 only annotated colon cancer reports were avail-

---

[‡]alamurias@lasige.di.fc.ul.pt

[1]`http://labs.fc.ul.pt/cita/`
[2]`https://github.com/lasigeBioTM/CiTA`

Proceedings of the 11th International Workshop on Semantic Evaluations (SemEval-2017), pages 1019–1023,
Vancouver, Canada, August 3 - 4, 2017. ©2017 Association for Computational Linguistics

able, and in Phase 2 thirty annotated brain cancer documents were also released.

The colon cancer dataset was partitioned in 3 sets: train, development and test. We trained the system with the train and development set, and optimized with the test set. In Phase 2, we enhanced the classifiers by adding the brain cancer annotated documents. We ignored sections of the colon cancer documents that were not annotated due to the guidelines.

2.1 Event / Time Entity Span Identification

For both ES and TS subtasks we trained CRF classifiers on the training data annotations. We trained a CRF classifier for events and another for time expressions, using CRFSuite (Okazaki, 2007). These classifiers identified only the spans of the entities so that we can evaluate and improve the results of this subtask before classifying the entity attributes. This is justified in the context of the competition since the attribute classification subtasks are dependent on the span identification subtasks, and a poor performance on the span identification subtasks would affect the other subtasks.

We used a set of common features for time and event expressions, based on previous experiments, that explored linguistic, orthographic, morphological and contextual properties of the tokens (Table 1). For most features, we considered a contextual window of size one, i.e., the value of the same feature for the previous and next token. Lemma and Part-of-Speech tags were obtained using Stanford CoreNLP (Manning et al., 2014).

Furthermore, we selected specific features for time and event expressions. For time expressions, we used the NER tags given by SUTime (Chang and Manning, 2012), part of Stanford CoreNLP. SUTime is able to detect general time and date expressions, which is the case of some of the time expressions in the gold standard. For the event classifier, we matched each word in the gold standard to a Unified Medical Language System (UMLS) concept and used it as a feature if the confidence level was higher than 0.8. The matching was performed using LDPMAP (Ren et al., 2014). Many words were matched to UMLS since it is large vocabulary. However, by applying a high threshold, we ensure that only high quality matches are considered.

During Phase 2, we analyzed some errors made

Feature	Context window	Entity
Prefix sizes 2-4	-1/1	All
Suffix sizes 2-4	-1/1	All
Contains number	0	All
Case	-1/1	All
Lemma	-1/1	All
POS tag	-1/1	All
Word class	-1/1	All
SUTIME tag	-1/1	Time
POS tag	-2/2	Event
UMLS	-1/1	Event

Table 1: Features used for TS and ES subtasks.

by the colon cancer classifiers on the brain cancer training set. To overcome these errors, we automatically created a list of common false positives and false negatives for time and event expressions. We applied the false positives list to the output of the CRF classifiers as a filter, and performed a dictionary search with the false negatives list to identify missed entities. We used these lists only on Run 2 of our Phase 2 submission.

2.2 Event / Time Entity Attribute Classification

Each event and time entity identified by CiTA was then classified according to the attributes defined by the task. To this end, we established a set of rules for each attribute using regular expressions. These rules were developed according to the annotation guidelines and training data. The rules developed for modality and polarity attributes were based on the context windows of each event. Furthermore, we chose the default values of each attribute based on the frequency of each value on the brain cancer annotations.

We found that several expressions used in the context window of the event affected its modality and polarity. For polarity, *avoid*, *absent* and *not* indicated a negative polarity. If the context of the event did not include any of the expressions of our list, we classified it as positive (95.9% of the cases). For modality, we selected *ACTUAL* as the default value (84.9% of the cases), since it is the most frequent value.

To choose the size of the context windows, various sizes were tested, both to the left and right of the event. We noticed that if we extended the window too much, some expressions that did not affect the event would be matched. However, shorter context windows would not include the relevant expressions. We fixed the window size of 5 for both polarity and modality. If the conjunctions *but* or *with* were found in the context window, we cut the window at that point. These conjunctions change the subject of the sentence from the respective event, and all words afterwards were ignored. Furthermore, we ignored any expressions that affected the polarity of an event if there was another event between the expression and that event. For example, if the expression *not* appears in the left context window of event A, but event B also appeared in the same window, between *not* and event A, then event A was classified as positive.

For the other attributes (event type and time type) we chose a different approach. Although we tried to formulate rules based on the context windows of each event and time entity we realized that it was more efficient to make a direct match between the attribute and the event or time entity. To classify type of events, as it was said on the set of the guidelines available to the participants, we realized that specific groups of verbs indicated a certain modality, for example, *evidence* (EVIDENTIAL) or *starting* (ASPECTUAL), making it easy to recognize which verbs belong to this class. We developed rules based on each modality class, except for the default value (N/A) (94.7% of the cases). The rules used to classify the type of time expressions were slightly different. We had to identify which of the six attributes was the default or the one that included the widest amplitude of expressions. We started by making rules for each attribute by identifying the patterns in the gold standard, quickly realizing that the default attribute was DATE (59.3% of the cases). So we focused our attention on the definition of the other five attributes (PREPOSEXP, SET, TIME, DURATION and QUANTIFIER) by matching the different type of time expressions and possible variations to each appropriated attribute.

3 Results

We submitted one run during Phase 1 and two runs during Phase 2. While during Phase 1 we only had access to source domain annotations, some target domain annotations were released for Phase 2. Hence, we were able to improve the performance of CiTA in relation to the target domain during Phase 2. Table 2 shows the official results for Phase 1 and Phase 2 Run 1 and 2. For each run, we present the precision, recall and F1-score obtained in each subtask.

Compared to the results of Phase 2, Phase 1 results were lower, particularly for Time span identification ($\Delta = 0.069$). The false positive filter applied on Phase 2 Run 2 improved the precision of the time span subtask, although at the expense of a lower recall. On the event span subtask it results in a lower precision, with almost no effect on recall. In both phases, the results for time expressions were lower than for events.

The results of the time and event attributes are shown in combination with the span identification. This means that an entity is considered positive if both the span and attribute are found in the gold standard. Hence, we can evaluate the effect of the rules on the test set by comparing the scores of each attribute to the span identification score. Furthermore, we evaluated the accuracy of the rules on the colon cancer and brain cancer train sets (Table 3). We assumed that the attribute value was correct if it matched the gold standard. Table 3 shows the results obtained using the rules developed for the second phase, which were tuned for the brain cancer data sets.

4 Discussion

The main challenge of this task was to adapt a system developed for a specific source domain to a different target domain. Systems trained on a specific domain, either using hand-crafted rules or machine learning, are biased for that domain. In real world scenarios, information extraction systems need to be able to perform well in multiple domains. Although at first it seemed like the only difference between the source and target domains was the type of cancer, we observed that the reports and annotations were also different in terms of form of the documents and terms used. These differences contributed to lower scores obtained on the target domain test set, when compared to the source domain test set used in the previous edition of this task (Bethard et al., 2016). Even using the brain cancer train set available during Phase 2, our best F1 score on the event span subtask was 0.16 lower than on the colon cancer test set.

Comparing to the other teams that submitted results to this task, our submission performed better on the event expressions subtasks. On Phase 1, we are the third best team on all event subtasks in terms of F1 score. On Phase 2, we are in second

	Phase 1			Phase 2 Run 1			Phase 2 Run 2			Phase 2 Top F1		
	P	R	F1	P	R	F1	P	R	F1	P	R	F1
Event span	0.618	0.765	0.683	**0.649**	**0.831**	**0.729**	0.637	0.830	0.721	0.69	0.85	0.76
Event modality	0.548	0.679	0.607	**0.571**	**0.731**	**0.641**	0.561	0.730	0.634	0.63	0.78	0.69
Event degree	0.610	0.756	0.675	**0.642**	**0.821**	**0.720**	0.630	0.820	0.713	0.68	0.84	0.75
Event polarity	0.600	0.744	0.664	**0.630**	**0.807**	**0.708**	0.619	0.806	0.700	0.68	0.83	0.75
Event type	0.598	0.741	0.662	**0.629**	**0.805**	**0.706**	0.617	0.804	0.698	0.68	0.83	0.75
Time span	0.441	0.538	0.485	0.517	**0.598**	**0.554**	**0.520**	0.588	0.552	0.57	0.62	0.59
Time type	0.393	0.479	0.432	0.483	**0.559**	**0.518**	**0.485**	0.548	0.515	0.54	0.59	0.56

Table 2: Results of our submission and for each task the results from the top F1 score submission of Phase 2. Notice that *Time type* represents *Time span + Class* column of the results table published by the organizers.

Gold standard	Colon	Brain
Event modality	**0.914**	0.891
Event degree	**0.995**	0.993
Event polarity	**0.969**	0.968
Event type	**0.972**	0.962
Time type	0.890	**0.971**

Table 3: Accuracy obtained using the rules developed for each attribute, on the colon cancer and brain cancer train sets.

place on the Event polarity subtask, maintaining the third place on all the other event subtasks, except modality. In time span and type we are in third place in terms of recall.

4.1 Error Analysis

Some of the more persistent errors while classifying the type of time entities were that some of the time expressions presented in the gold standard had double attribution. For example, *time* sometimes appeared classified as TIME and in others as DURATION, and *daily* was classified as DATE, SET and QUANTIFIER. Although initially we tried to introduce context windows of each time expression to help us solving this systematic error, we realized that there was no explicit difference in the context of most of these words, so introducing context windows only harmed our efforts to achieve better results.

Some event attributes were incorrectly classified due to the developed context window rules. For example, in *not limited to loss of appetite*, *appetite* was incorrectly classified with negative polarity since it had *not* in its left context window, and no event in-between. In some cases, the rule we implemented to ignore negation expressions between events resulted in incorrect positive polarities. In the expression *no second lesion seen in the brain*, *no* did not affect *seen* because another event, *lesion* appeared in its context window. However *seen* was supposed to be classified as negative.

One limitation of a rule-based approach is that it is necessary to take into account every expression that might affect an attribute. Since we had a limited amount of target domain training data, we missed some cases where more complex rules could have been applied. We had a rule that assigned the modality of an event as HYPOTHETICAL if the expression *may* appeared in the context window. This resulted in some errors, for example,with *and there may be increased cerebral blood volume*, the modality of *volume* should be HEDGED instead of HYPOTHETICAL.

5 Conclusions and Future Work

We obtained the second best F1 score on the event polarity subtask and third best on the event span and other event attributes subtasks. We made publicly available the source code of CiTA including the rules created to produce our results. The rules to classify event and time attributes were efficient, on the other hand the list of common false positive and negative created for Run 2 did not make a significant difference.

CiTA is dependent on training data, which suggests that domain-independent approaches should be explored. One approach is to apply semantic similarity measures to automatically identify similar expressions in terms of meaning, even if using different terms (Couto and Pinto, 2013). Another approach is to explore distant supervision (Lamurias et al., 2017) to train a predictive model using a knowledge base, for example by exploring Linked Data (Barros et al., 2016), instead of annotated text.

Acknowledgments

This work was supported by the Portuguese Fundação para a Ciência e Tecnologia (https://www.fct.mctes.pt/) through the PhD Grant ref. PD/BD/106083/2015 and UID/CEC/00408/2013 (LaSIGE). We thank Mayo Clinic for providing THYME corpus and Sebastião Almeida for his contributions to our participation.

References

Marcia Barros, Francisco M Couto, et al. 2016. Knowledge representation and management: a linked data perspective. *IMIA Yearbook* pages 178–183.

Steven Bethard, Wei-te Chen, James Pustejovsky, Leon Derczynski, and Marc Verhagen. 2016. SemEval-2016 Task 12 : Clinical TempEval pages 1052–1062.

Angel X Chang and Christopher D Manning. 2012. SUTime: A library for recognizing and normalizing time expressions. *Lrec* (iii):3735–3740.

Francisco M Couto and H Sofia Pinto. 2013. The next generation of similarity measures that fully explore the semantics in biomedical ontologies. *Journal of bioinformatics and computational biology* 11(05):1371001.

Andre Lamurias, Luka A Clarke, and Francisco M Couto. 2017. Extracting MicroRNA-gene relations from biomedical literature using distant supervision. *PLoS ONE* .

Andre Lamurias, João D Ferreira, and Francisco M. Couto. 2015. Improving chemical entity recognition through h-index based semantic similarity. *Journal of Cheminformatics* 7(Suppl 1):S13.

Christopher D Manning, John Bauer, Jenny Finkel, Steven J Bethard, Mihai Surdeanu, and David McClosky. 2014. The Stanford CoreNLP Natural Language Processing Toolkit. *Proceedings of 52nd Annual Meeting of the Association for Computational Linguistics: System Demonstrations* pages 55–60.

Naoaki Okazaki. 2007. Crfsuite: a fast implementation of conditional random fields (crfs).

Kaiyu Ren, Albert M Lai, Aveek Mukhopadhyay, Raghu Machiraju, Kun Huang, and Yang Xiang. 2014. Effectively processing medical term queries on the UMLS Metathesaurus by layered dynamic programming. *BMC Medical Genomics* 7(Suppl 1):S11.

GUIR at SemEval-2017 Task 12: A Framework for Cross-Domain Clinical Temporal Information Extraction

Sean MacAvaney, Arman Cohan, and Nazli Goharian
Information Retrieval Lab
Department of Computer Science
Georgetown University
{firstname}@ir.cs.georgetown.edu

Abstract

Clinical TempEval 2017 (SemEval 2017 Task 12) addresses the task of cross-domain temporal extraction from clinical text. We present a system for this task that uses supervised learning for the extraction of temporal expression and event spans with corresponding attributes and narrative container relations. Approaches include conditional random fields and decision tree ensembles, using lexical, syntactic, semantic, distributional, and rule-based features. Our system received best or second best scores in TIMEX3 span, EVENT span, and CONTAINS relation extraction.

1 Introduction

Clinical TempEval 2017 (Bethard et al., 2017) is designed to address the challenge of extracting clinical timelines from medical narratives. It is a successor to Clinical TempEval 2016 (Bethard et al., 2016), Clinical TempEval 2015 (Bethard et al., 2015), and the i2b2 temporal challenge (Sun et al., 2013).

Clinical TempEval evaluates systems using the THYME corpus (Styler IV et al., 2014), which is annotated with temporal expressions (TIMEX3), events (EVENT), and temporal relations (TLINK) per an extension of the TimeML specifications (Pustejovsky et al., 2003).

The focus of Clinical TempEval 2017 is domain adaptation. The source domain consists of clinical text about patients undergoing colon cancer treatments, while the target domain consists of clinical text about those with brain cancer. There are two phases in the task. In phase 1, the shared task provides no annotations for the target domain (unsupervised). In phase 2, the shared task provides

a small annotated training set from the target domain (supervised). Both phases evaluate system performance on thirteen tasks via precision, recall, and F1-score.

In Clinical TempEval 2016, the top-performing system employed structural support vector machines (SVM) for entity span extraction and linear support vector machines for attribute and relation extraction (Lee et al., 2016). For the previous iteration, Velupillai et al. (2015) developed a pipeline based on ClearTK and SVM with lexical and rule-based features to extract TIMEX3 and EVENT mentions. In the i2b2 2012 temporal challenge, all top performing teams used a combination of supervised classification and rule-based methods for extracting temporal information and relations (Sun et al., 2013). Other efforts in clinical temporal annotation include works by Roberts et al. (2008), Savova et al. (2009), and Galescu and Blaylock (2012).

Previous work has also investigated extracting temporal relations. Examples of these efforts in the general domain include: classification by SVM (Chambers et al., 2007), Integer Linear Programming (ILP) for temporal ordering (Chambers and Jurafsky, 2008), Markov Logic Networks (Yoshikawa et al., 2009), and SVM with Tree Kernels (Miller et al., 2013).

In this paper, we present a framework for temporal information extraction in clinical narratives. Specifically we utilize Conditional Random Fields (CRFs) and decision tree ensembles for extracting temporal entities and relations from clinical text. The features we use are covered in detail in Section 2. This work can be seen as an extension and refinement of the system used for Clinical TempEval 2016 by Cohan et al. (2016).

Proceedings of the 11th International Workshop on Semantic Evaluations (SemEval-2017), pages 1024–1029,
Vancouver, Canada, August 3 - 4, 2017. ©2017 Association for Computational Linguistics

2 Methodology

Our approach uses supervised learning algorithms with lexical, syntactic, semantic, distributional, and rule-based features for span, attribute, and relation extraction.

2.1 Span Extraction

Extraction of TIMEX3 and EVENT spans uses linear-chain CRFs.

We use BIO labels for the classification of spans of text from the tokenized source text: "B" indicates that the token begins a span, "I" indicates that the token is inside the span, and "O" indicates that the token is outside all spans. This approach allows for spans to represent one or more adjacent tokens. Non-contiguous spans, although not supported, have a low occurrence.

Basic lexical features computed for each token are as follows: lowercase form of the token; uppercase and lowercase flags; prefix and suffix; lemmatized form; shape; punctuation flag; and stop word flag. Syntactic features are coarse- and fine-grained part-of-speech tags. We used spaCy[1] for tokenization and basic features. In addition, we used the Unified Medical Language System (UMLS) ontology (Bodenreider, 2004) via MetaMap[2] to capture semantic concepts and use them as features. We limited the types to those indicative of clinical events (diagnostic procedure, disease or syndrome, and therapeutic procedure).

We also include regular expression-based features to capture more complicated and specialized token properties (summarized in Table 1). While the more generalized features we used (e.g. shape and suffix) capture some of the same information, this approach prioritizes likely generalizations and avoid over-fitting to specific cases. For instance, it allows the algorithm to generalize "Summer 2010" as "[Season] [Year]" instead of a more literal sequence.

We use distributional features for generalization. We construct Brown clusters (Brown et al., 1992) on the text with fifty clusters. The binary representation of each token's cluster is a feature. We also use word embeddings trained using Word2Vec (Mikolov et al., 2013) on the MIMIC-III dataset (Johnson et al., 2016) with a dimension of 100. The word embeddings also encode token usage context, and thus should generalize the

Feature	Examples
Date	12/3/2010, 1965-01-21
Month	January, Aug
Day	1st, 31
Day-of-week	Monday, Wed
Season	summer, spring
Year	2013, 1990s
Time	8:42, a.m.
Time Unit	minute, sec
Number	4, seventeen
Temporal preposition	in, after
Temporal adverb	daily, lately
Temporal prefix	pre, post

Table 1: Rule-based features and examples.

model.

For each token's feature set, we also include the features from the ± 1 adjacent tokens.

2.2 Attribute Extraction

We treat the extraction of the attributes of EVENT and TIMEX3 as a classification problem. Our system trains a CRF model for each attribute, with the labels of each model corresponding to the attribute values and the same features used in span extraction. An expanded window of ± 3 tokens is used for this task. Our system treats DOCTIMEREL (the EVENT's temporal relation to the document time) as attribute extraction.

2.3 Narrative Containers

Our approach trains gradient boosted trees (Friedman, 2001) on candidate relation pairs and uses this model to predict relations. Our system uses XGBoost (Chen and Guestrin, 2016) for this task.

Clinical TempEval 2017 only considers temporal links (TLINK) with a type of CONTAINS; other types of TLINKs are not evaluated due to lower inter-annotator agreements. Our system uses TLINK type labels when the relation exists, and a null label when the candidate relation does not represent an actual relation. We note that our approach extracts all relation types. Our system uses both entity features (describing each relation endpoint) and relation features (describing the relationship between the source and target).

Entity features include the entity type, entity attribute values, and the case-folded text value. Additionally, we use each token and related features (e.g. suffix) contained within the entity as features. We apply semantic Role Labeling (SRL) to the sentence containing the entity, which identifies semantic predicates in the sentence per PropBank guidelines (Palmer et al., 2005). If the entity text

---

[1] spacy.io

[2] https://metamap.nlm.nih.gov/; 2016 version

	TIMEX3 Spans			EVENT Spans		
	P	R	F1	P	R	F1
Phase 1 (Unsupervised)						
Our System	0.61	0.53	†**0.57**	0.64	‡**0.80**	‡**0.71**
Median	0.63	0.46	0.48	0.64	0.69	0.68
Phase 2 (Supervised)						
Our System	‡**0.57**	‡**0.62**	†**0.59**	‡**0.68**	0.82	‡**0.74**
Median	0.53	0.52	0.54	0.67	0.76	0.71
MEMORIZE	0.64	0.22	0.33	0.61	0.51	0.56

Table 2: Evaluation results for span extraction. †Top score. ‡Second highest score.

is found in a semantic predicate, we use the argument label as a feature for the model. We used the SENNA[3] implementation for SRL tagging.

Relation features capture information about the relationship between two entities. Basic relation features included are the character distance between the entities and the pair of entity types. Syntactic features applied capture the path along the constituent and dependency trees between the entities. Our system uses the spaCy toolkit for dependency parsing. We derive n-gram segments of the path, the full path, and the distance of the path, and use them as features.

We limit candidate relations to permutations of entities belonging to the same sentence. This approach precludes relations that cross sentence boundaries, but limits the extent of negative training samples.

2.4 Domain Adaptation

Our system splits the phase 2 text ("train10") into a dev set and a test set. A grid search is performed for span, property, and relation extraction over the applicable hyperparameters. Text from the source domain is used for training, and the dev set from the target domain is used for evaluation. The test set is used after the grid search to verify that the procedure did not overfit hyperparameters.

3 Experimental Setup

In phase 1, we train our system on all available annotations from the source domain. In phase 2, we train our system on all available data from the source domain and the "train10" dataset from the target domain.

Baselines The baselines are two rule-based systems (Bethard et al., 2015) that the shared task

provides along with the corpus. The MEMORIZE baseline, which is the baseline for all tasks except for narrative containers, memorizes the EVENT and TIMEX3 mentions and attributes based on the training data. Then it uses the memorized model to extract temporal information from new data. For narrative containers, the CLOSEST baseline predicts a TLINK relation with type CONTAINS between every TIMEX3 annotation and its closest EVENT.

Furthermore, we compare our results against the other submissions to Clinical TempEval 2017. We report the median value for each metric, as well as indicators when our system achieves either the top result (†), or second-highest result (‡). Only the systems that submitted values for a particular task are considered; systems reported as $p = 0.00$, $r = 1.00$, and $F1 = 0.00$ are ignored.

Evaluation metrics Clinical TempEval 2017 evaluates thirteen tasks. Each task reports the precision recall, and F1-score of the submitted results as compared to a human annotated and adjudicated ground truth. The following tasks are not reported in this paper for brevity: "All spans & all properties", "All spans only", "Time span & all properties", and "Event span & all properties".

4 Results and discussion

Our system outperformed other participating systems, receiving best or second best results extracting TIMEX3 spans, EVENT spans, and CONTAINS relations. Generally our domain adaptation procedure improved results, but it reduced the results of CONTAINS relations. Although we received top scores, we fell short of the single-domain performance achieved in Clinical TempEval 2016.

Table 2 shows the results for TIMEX3 and EVENT span extraction. Our system achieved the top F1 score for TIMEX3 spans and the second highest F1 score for EVENT spans in both phases. Furthermore, our system met or exceeded the median and MEMORIZE baseline in all but one metric (TIMEX3 precision), in which it had significant gains in recall. Table 3 shows the results for TIMEX3 and EVENT attribute extraction. We note that while our system performs well on some of these categories, on some other categories it underperforms the median results (e.g. such as EVENT Modality and EVENT Polarity). Our system performed well at CONTAINS relations, but only achieved median results at DOCTIMEREL

---

[3]http://ml.nec-labs.com/senna/

	TIMEX3 Class			EVENT Modality			EVENT Degree			EVENT Polarity			EVENT Type		
	P	R	F1	P	R	F1	P	R	F1	P	R	F1	P	R	F1
Phase 1 (Unsupervised)															
Our System	0.55	0.47	‡**0.51**	0.50	0.64	0.56	0.61	‡**0.77**	‡**0.68**	0.59	‡**0.74**	0.65	0.61	‡**0.76**	‡**0.68**
Median	0.56	0.45	0.46	0.55	0.63	0.59	0.62	0.71	0.68	0.60	0.70	0.66	0.61	0.70	0.66
Phase 2 (Supervised)															
Our System	‡**0.54**	‡**0.59**	†**0.56**	0.60	0.72	‡**0.66**	‡**0.67**	0.80	‡**0.73**	0.54	0.64	0.58	‡**0.66**	0.79	‡**0.72**
Median	0.49	0.48	0.48	0.57	0.68	0.63	0.66	0.77	0.71	0.62	0.70	0.66	0.65	0.76	0.70
MEMORIZE	0.49	0.17	0.25	0.29	0.24	0.26	0.47	0.40	0.43	0.56	0.47	0.51	0.50	0.42	0.46

Table 3: Evaluation results for attribute extraction. †Top score. ‡Second highest score.

	CONTAINS			DOCTIMEREL		
	P	R	F1	P	R	F1
Phase 1 (Unsupervised)						
Our System	†**0.52**	0.25	†**0.34**	0.36	0.45	0.40
Median	0.33	0.25	0.32	0.39	0.45	0.41
Phase 2 (Supervised)						
Our System	†**0.59**	0.16	0.25	0.45	0.55	0.50
Median	0.20	0.16	0.16	0.42	0.51	0.46
CLOSEST	0.33	0.08	0.12	-	-	-
MEMORIZE	-	-	-	0.22	0.18	0.20

Table 4: Evaluation results for relation extraction. †Top score.

relations (see Table 4). In phase 1, our system achieved the top results for CONTAINS precision and F1. Our domain adaptation procedure resulted in a drop in recall for CONTAINS relations. We suspect this is due to overfitting the model to the sample data. We suspect that including more contextual or semantic features would improve the performance of attribute extraction (including DOCTIMEREL).

4.1 Error Analysis

We conducted an unsupervised domain adaptation run against the "train10" dataset to get an idea of failure cases. (We could not use the full target domain test set because these data are not available.)

One issue with TIMEX3 extraction is previously unseen or atypical date formats, for instance "12Jun2013" (no hyphens). One way to resolve this issue could be to use a more generalized library for extracting time expressions (e.g. Heidel-Time), but even this library does not extract the example shown above. Furthermore, it would not generalize to new and otherwise unknown formats. The supervised training subset could be used in each domain to identify these kinds of conventions, but this is labor-intensive and prone to error.

Another issue is inconsistency in TIMEX3 annotation conventions (e.g. annotating a date and time separately sometimes and jointly in others). This complicates the model and leads to otherwise inexplicable annotation absences.

One example of an EVENT extraction failure is the false positive of "Cancer" in the phrase "Cancer Research Hospital". An approach to resolve this would be to use named entity recognition features, or by treating named entities as chunks that are annotated using a different technique. False positive EVENTs were common in certain sections of the notes (e.g. ongoing care; suggested interventions), indicating that document segmentation by section could be useful. This would only work in a supervised environment, unless domain sections have a great degree of overlap and can be mapped to one another.

TLINK error cases include the known limitation of intra-sentence relations. Other false negatives candidates seemed to be due to domain-specific language (e.g. "temozolomide"), suggesting that lexical features are overused, or the syntactic and semantic features we use are inadequate.

5 Conclusions

The results of Clinical TempEval 2017 show that there is still room to explore cross-domain temporal information extraction. We presented a system for both unsupervised and supervised temporal domain adaptation. It performed among best of participating teams, receiving best or second best scores in TIMEX3 span, EVENT span, and CONTAINS relation extraction. All teams fell short of meeting the top results for the source domain. Future work in this area could focus on techniques for using a small number of annotations to tune a system to other domains due to the modest improvements in phase 2.

References

Steven Bethard, Leon Derczynski, Guergana Savova, James Pustejovsky, and Marc Verhagen. 2015. Semeval-2015 task 6: Clinical tempeval. In *Proceedings of the 9th International Workshop on Semantic Evaluation (SemEval 2015)*. Association for Computational Linguistics Denver, Colorado, pages 806–814.

Steven Bethard, Guergana Savova, Wei-Te Chen, Leon Derczynski, James Pustejovsky, and Marc Verhagen. 2016. Semeval-2016 task 12: Clinical tempeval. *Proceedings of SemEval* pages 1052–1062.

Steven Bethard, Guergana Savova, Martha Palmer, and James Pustejovsky. 2017. Semeval-2017 task 12: Clinical tempeval. In *Proceedings of the 11th International Workshop on Semantic Evaluation (SemEval-2017)*. Association for Computational Linguistics, Vancouver, Canada, pages 563–570. http://www.aclweb.org/anthology/S17-2093.

Olivier Bodenreider. 2004. The unified medical language system (umls): integrating biomedical terminology. *Nucleic acids research* 32(suppl 1):D267–D270.

Peter F Brown, Peter V Desouza, Robert L Mercer, Vincent J Della Pietra, and Jenifer C Lai. 1992. Class-based n-gram models of natural language. *Computational linguistics* 18(4):467–479.

Nathanael Chambers and Dan Jurafsky. 2008. Jointly combining implicit constraints improves temporal ordering. In *Proceedings of the Conference on Empirical Methods in Natural Language Processing*. Association for Computational Linguistics, pages 698–706.

Nathanael Chambers, Shan Wang, and Dan Jurafsky. 2007. Classifying temporal relations between events. In *Proceedings of the 45th Annual Meeting of the ACL on Interactive Poster and Demonstration Sessions*. Association for Computational Linguistics, pages 173–176.

Tianqi Chen and Carlos Guestrin. 2016. Xgboost: A scalable tree boosting system. In *Proceedings of the 22Nd ACM SIGKDD International Conference on Knowledge Discovery and Data Mining*. ACM, pages 785–794.

Arman Cohan, Kevin Meurer, and Nazli Goharian. 2016. Guir at semeval-2016 task 12: Temporal information processing for clinical narratives. *Proceedings of SemEval* pages 1248–1255.

Jerome H Friedman. 2001. Greedy function approximation: a gradient boosting machine. *Annals of statistics* pages 1189–1232.

Lucian Galescu and Nate Blaylock. 2012. A corpus of clinical narratives annotated with temporal information. In *Proceedings of the 2nd ACM SIGHIT International Health Informatics Symposium*. ACM, pages 715–720.

Alistair EW Johnson, Tom J Pollard, Lu Shen, Liwei H Lehman, Mengling Feng, Mohammad Ghassemi, Benjamin Moody, Peter Szolovits, Leo Anthony Celi, and Roger G Mark. 2016. Mimic-iii, a freely accessible critical care database. *Scientific data* 3.

Hee-Jin Lee, Yaoyun Zhang, Jun Xu, Sungrim Moon, Jingqi Wang, Yonghui Wu, and Hua Xu. 2016. Uthealth at semeval-2016 task 12: an end-to-end system for temporal information extraction from clinical notes. *Proceedings of SemEval* pages 1292–1297.

Tomas Mikolov, Ilya Sutskever, Kai Chen, Greg S Corrado, and Jeff Dean. 2013. Distributed representations of words and phrases and their compositionality. In *Advances in neural information processing systems*. pages 3111–3119.

Timothy Miller, Steven Bethard, Dmitriy Dligach, Sameer Pradhan, Chen Lin, and Guergana Savova. 2013. Discovering temporal narrative containers in clinical text. In *Proceedings of the 2013 Workshop on Biomedical Natural Langua ge Processing*. pages 18–26.

Martha Palmer, Daniel Gildea, and Paul Kingsbury. 2005. The proposition bank: An annotated corpus of semantic roles. *Computational linguistics* 31(1):71–106.

James Pustejovsky, Patrick Hanks, Roser Sauri, Andrew See, Robert Gaizauskas, Andrea Setzer, Dragomir Radev, Beth Sundheim, David Day, Lisa Ferro, et al. 2003. The timebank corpus. In *Corpus linguistics*. volume 2003, page 40.

Angus Roberts, Robert Gaizauskas, Mark Hepple, George Demetriou, Yikun Guo, Andrea Setzer, and Ian Roberts. 2008. Semantic annotation of clinical text: The clef corpus. In *Proceedings of the LREC 2008 workshop on building and evaluating resources for biomedical text mining*. pages 19–26.

Guergana Savova, Steven Bethard, F William IV, IV Styler, James H Martin, Martha Palmer, James J Masanz, and Wayne H Ward. 2009. Towards temporal relation discovery from the clinical narrative. In *AMIA*. pages 568–572.

William F Styler IV, Steven Bethard, Sean Finan, Martha Palmer, Sameer Pradhan, Piet C de Groen, Brad Erickson, Timothy Miller, Chen Lin, Guergana Savova, et al. 2014. Temporal annotation in the clinical domain. *Transactions of the Association for Computational Linguistics* 2:143–154.

Weiyi Sun, Anna Rumshisky, and Ozlem Uzuner. 2013. Evaluating temporal relations in clinical text: 2012 i2b2 challenge. *Journal of the American Medical Informatics Association* 20(5):806–813.

Sumithra Velupillai, Danielle L Mowery, Samir Abdelrahman, Lee Christensen, and Wendy W Chapman. 2015. Blulab: Temporal information extraction for the 2015 clinical tempeval challenge. In *The 9th International Workshop on Semantic Evaluation (SemEval 2015), Denver, Colorado, June 4-5, 2015*. Association for Computational Linguistics, pages 815–819.

Katsumasa Yoshikawa, Sebastian Riedel, Masayuki Asahara, and Yuji Matsumoto. 2009. Jointly identifying temporal relations with markov logic. In *Proceedings of the Joint Conference of the 47th Annual Meeting of the ACL and the 4th International Joint Conference on Natural Language Processing of the AFNLP: Volume 1-Volume 1*. Association for Computational Linguistics, pages 405–413.

KULeuven-LIIR at SemEval-2017 Task 12:
Cross-Domain Temporal Information Extraction from Clinical Records

Artuur Leeuwenberg and **Marie-Francine Moens**
Department of Computer Science
KU Leuven, Belgium
{tuur.leeuwenberg, sien.moens}@cs.kuleuven.be

Abstract

In this paper, we describe the system of the KULeuven-LIIR submission for Clinical TempEval 2017. We participated in all six subtasks, using a combination of Support Vector Machines (SVM) for event and temporal expression detection, and a structured perceptron for extracting temporal relations. Moreover, we present and analyze the results from our submissions, and verify the effectiveness of several system components. Our system performed above average for all subtasks in both phases.

1 Introduction

In this paper, we describe the system used for the KULeuven-LIIR submissions at SemEval task 12, named Clinical TempEval 2017 (Bethard et al., 2017), which is concerned with temporal information extraction from clinical records. In Clinical TempEval extraction of temporal information is split into six subtasks. Our system participated in all tasks:

1. Detection of event spans (ES)

2. Identification of event attributes (EA)

3. Detection of temporal expressions (TS)

4. Attribute identification of temporal expressions (TA)

5. Extraction of document-creation-time relations for events (DR)

6. Extraction of narrative container relations (CR)

This year, a new aspect of Clinical TempEval is that systems will be evaluated across domains, which involves two phases: Firstly, *unsupervised domain adaptation* (Phase I), where the training data is in the colon cancer domain, and the test data in the brain cancer domain. And secondly, *supervised domain adaptation* (Phase II), where the vast majority of the training data are colon cancer reports, and a small number of brain cancer reports is made available for training as well. The test data is again in the brain cancer domain.

Our system consist of a combination of linear Support Vector Machines (SVM) for entity span and attribute recognition (tasks ES, EA, TS and TA), and a document-level structured perceptron (Leeuwenberg and Moens, 2017) for relation extraction tasks (tasks DR and CR). We used three system components for the domain adaptation: (1) assigning more weight to target-domain training data, (2) introduction of a UNK (unknown) token to model out-of-vocabulary words, and (3) exploitation of relational properties of temporality during prediction.

In Section 2, we provide a detailed description of our full system, and in Section 3 we discuss the results from our submissions.

2 Our System

Our system consist of three main components (1) preprocessing, (2) entity detection, and (3) relation extraction. In Figure 1, we show a schematic overview of our system.

2.1 Preprocessing

The corpus used in Clinical TempEval 2017 is the THYME corpus (Styler IV et al., 2014). For the unsupervised domain adaptation phase (Phase I), we use all colon cancer sections for training. For the supervised domain adaptation (Phase II) participants also received a small training section in

Proceedings of the 11th International Workshop on Semantic Evaluations (SemEval-2017), pages 1030–1034,
Vancouver, Canada, August 3 - 4, 2017. ©2017 Association for Computational Linguistics

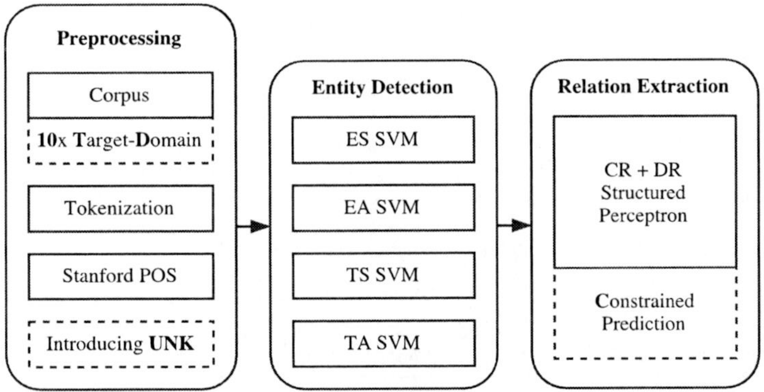

Figure 1: Schematic overview of our system. Components we expect to help domain adaptation are dashed.

the brain cancer domain. Some statistics about the dataset can be found in Table 1.

Table 1: Dataset statistics for the THYME sections used in our experiments.

Section	Documents
Training Colon Cancer	591
Training Brain Cancer	30
Test Brain Cancer	148

Our first simple method for adapting to a new domain, when given target-domain training data (Phase II), is to assign more weight to the target-domain data at training time (Jiang and Zhai, 2007). In our submissions we assigned a 10 times higher weight to the target-domain training data compared to the colon cancer training data.

In all experiments, we preprocess the text by using a very straightforward tokenization procedure considering punctuation[1] or newline tokens as individual tokens, and splitting on spaces. We also employ lowercasing, and conflate all digits to a single representation. An example would be:

October 20, 1991 ⇒ october 55 , 5555

For our part-of-speech features, we rely on the Stanford POS Tagger (Toutanova et al., 2003), with the English bidirectional tagger model. We also take the transitive closure of the CONTAINS relation on the training data, as this has shown to improve results in existing work (Mani et al., 2006).

Our second domain adaptation modification involves the introduction of an unknown word token (UNK) to the input vocabulary of the extraction models. This is a widely used technique in statistical language modeling to account for out-of-vocabulary (OOV) words. In a language modeling setting, we can expect that the proportion of OOV words in the test set can be modeled by using the proportion of one-time-occurring words from the training set, by Good Turing estimation (Gale and Sampson, 1995). In our system, we train the weights for the UNK token by replacing all tokens that occur only once in the training data by the UNK token. At prediction time we simply replace all words that are OOV by the UNK token. We expect this technique to be effective for domain adaptation as new words can be a serious problem when crossing domains.

2.2 Entity Detection

For all span and attribute tasks we employ linear SVM classifiers[2]. We only resort to token and POS features, and use the same features for span detection as for attribute detection. More elaborate feature descriptions are shown in Table 2. We consider all single tokens as EVENT candidates, and all token {1,2,3,4,5,6}-grams as TIMEX3 candidates (upper bound 6 is based on tuning on the colon cancer training data).

2.3 Relation Extraction

For relation extraction we rely on the linear document-level structured perceptron by

---

[1] ,./\"´=+-;:()!?<>%&$*|[]{}

[2] Trained using LIBLINEAR(Fan et al., 2008) with regularization constant C=1.0 (tuned on the colon cancer section of the training data from {0.1, 1.0, 10})

Table 2: Features of the local feature functions of each subtask: ϕ_{cr} for CR, ϕ_{dr} for DR, ϕ_{e*} for ES and EA, and ϕ_{t*} for TS and TA.

Features	ϕ_{dr}	ϕ_{cr}	ϕ_{e*}	ϕ_{t*}
Strings for tokens and POS of each entity	✓	✓	✓	✓
Strings for tokens and POS in a window of size $\{3, 5\}$, left and right of each entity	✓	✓	✓	✓
Booleans for entity attributes (event polarity, event modality, event degree, and type)	✓	✓		
Strings for tokens and POS of the closest verb	✓			
Strings for tokens and POS of the closest left and right entity	✓			
Strings for token $\{1, 2, 3\}$-grams and POS $\{1, 2, 3\}$-grams in-between the entities		✓		
Booleans on if the first argument occurs before the second (w.r.t. word order)		✓		

Table 3: Global DR (document-level) features.

Feature	Description
Φ_{sdr}	Bigram and trigram counts of subsequent DCTR-labels in the document

Leeuwenberg and Moens (2017)[3]. Their model employs a structured learning paradigm, assigning a score S to each label assignment. Prediction corresponds to finding the label assignment with the highest score. The score for a document-level label assignment is constructed by joining all local features (shown in Table 2) within a document for both tasks (DR and CR), together with a global DR feature shown in Table 3, resulting in a joint feature vector $\Phi(X, Y)$.

The joint features $\Phi(X, Y)$ are assigned a weight vector λ, resulting in the linear scoring function in Equation 1.

$$S(X, Y) = \lambda\Phi(X, Y) \tag{1}$$

The weight vector λ is trained using the structured perceptron algorithm (Collins, 2002), with averaging (Freund and Schapire, 1999).

At prediction time integer linear programming (ILP) is used to find the best label assignment Y^*, as shown in 2, using the Gurobi ILP Solver (Gurobi Optimization, 2015).

$$Y^* = \arg\max_Y S(X, Y) \tag{2}$$

We also experimented with the constraints on the output labeling formulated by Leeuwenberg and Moens (2017). The constraints enforce the model to output labeling to be temporally consistent, by enforcing relational properties onto the predictions. We only chose the properties relevant for the CR and DR subtasks, which are transitivity of containment, but also consistency between containment and the document-creation time relations of the events. The relational properties that we enforce as constraints during prediction are captured in the following rules (condition above, and conclusion below the horizontal line):

$$\frac{\text{contains}(x, y) \wedge \text{contains}(y, z)}{\text{contains}(x, z)} \tag{3}$$

$$\frac{\text{contains}(x, y) \wedge \text{before}(x, doctime)}{\text{before}(y, doctime)} \tag{4}$$

$$\frac{\text{contains}(x, y) \wedge \text{after}(x, doctime)}{\text{after}(y, doctime)} \tag{5}$$

Our hypothesis is that these constraints can help with assigning labels to unfamiliar input (e.g. from the target-domain), by ensuring that local assignments are consistent with surrounding labels.

3 Experiments and Results

We conducted a number of experiments with our system to test the effectiveness of the different system components[4]. We submitted in phase I, and in phase II. In Phase I, we used our system as shown in Figure 1, only with the UNK introduction, so without increased weight for target-domain training data (as there is none in Phase I), and without constraints. In Phase II, our system includes the full system, with all proposed components for domain adaptation.

When we look at the results of Phase I, in Figure 2, we can see that our system performs above average on all tasks, and for both attribute identification tasks, it performs best (for EA there is another system with best performance).

If we look at the results of Phase II, in Figure 2, our system again performs above average in all

---

[3]Using the code at https://github.com/tuur/SPTempRels

[4]Code at https://github.com/tuur/ClinicalTempEval2017

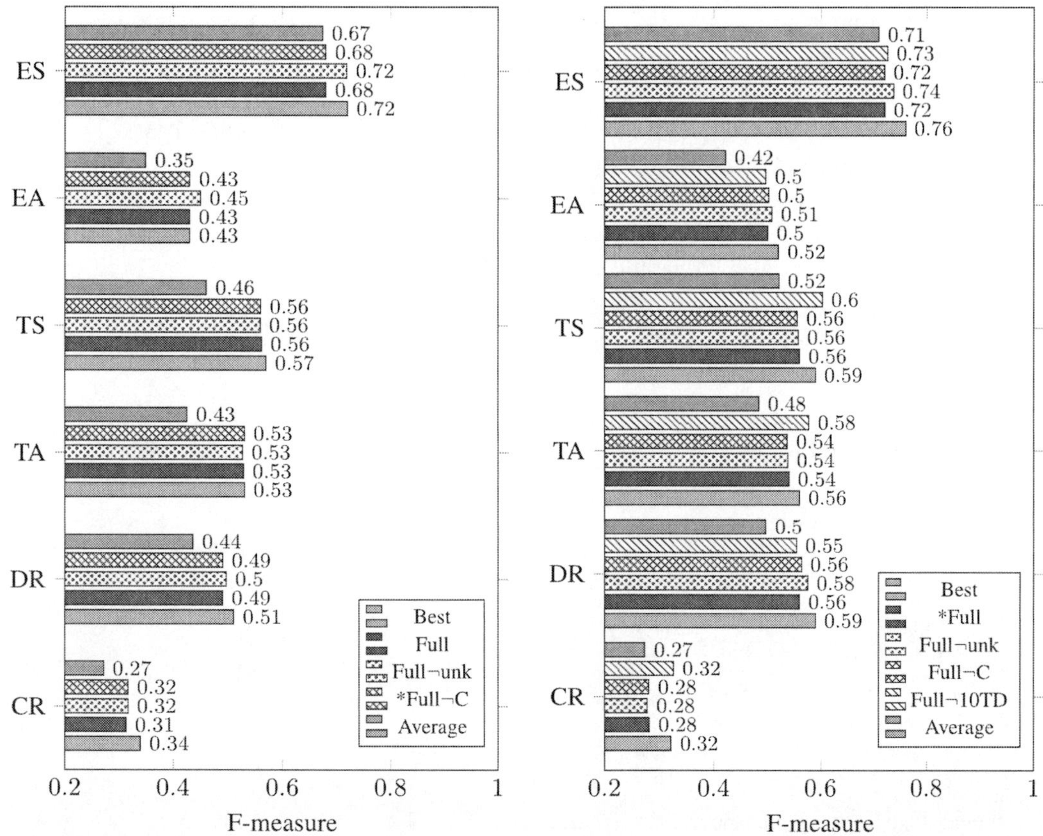

Figure 2: Results from Phase I (left) and Phase II (right): We compare our submission (indicated by *) to the best performing system, and to the average score of all participating systems in each task. Out of competition, an ablation of each modification is also evaluated (¬ indicates absence of a component).

cases. However, it seems our system does not lie as close to the best system as in Phase I, suggesting that we could have better exploited the target-domain training data.

When looking at the ablation of the system components in Figure 2, we can see that using the UNK modification (comparing Full with Full¬unk), decreases performance for the ES, EA and the DR subtask. Furthermore, employing temporal constraints (C) appears to have a slightly negative influence in Phase I for DR, and little influence in Phase II.

The effect of adding more weight to target-domain training data (10TD) is mixed, leaning towards a negative influence. For DR performance increased by 1 point (because of increase in precision). However, for CR, TS, TA and EA it seems to have a negative effect, for various reasons. For example, for CR mostly due to a big decrease in recall, but for TS due to a big decrease in precision

(hardly any difference in recall). This shows that the effectiveness of weighting the target-domain training data is highly task-dependent.

An interesting observation is that there is hardly improvement in CR performance in Phase II compared to Phase I (the best system score is even lower). This suggests that domain-adaptation for CR is more challenging than the other subtasks.

4 Conclusions

We described the KULeuven-LIIR system at Clinical TempEval 2017, for all six subtasks. Our system exploits SVM for entity detection and a document-level structured perceptron for relation extraction. Our system performed above average for all subtasks in both phases. For future research it would be interesting to analyze the errors that were made by the system, and explore methods to better exploit small amounts of target-domain training data, or unlabeled target-domain data.

Acknowledgments

The authors would like to thank the reviewers for their constructive comments, and the Mayo Clinic for permission to use the THYME corpus. This work was funded by the KU Leuven C22/15/16 project "MAchine Reading of patient recordS (MARS)", and by the IWT-SBO 150056 project "ACquiring CrUcial Medical information Using LAnguage TEchnology" (ACCUMULATE).

References

Steven Bethard, Guergana Savova, Martha Palmer, and James Pustejovsky. 2017. Semeval-2017 task 12: Clinical tempeval. In *Proceedings of SemEval-2017*. Association for Computational Linguistics, Vancouver, Canada, pages 563–570.

Michael Collins. 2002. Ranking algorithms for named-entity extraction: Boosting and the voted perceptron. In *Proceedings of ACL*. Association for Computational Linguistics, pages 489–496.

Rong-En Fan, Kai-Wei Chang, Cho-Jui Hsieh, Xiang-Rui Wang, and Chih-Jen Lin. 2008. Liblinear: A library for large linear classification. *Journal of machine learning research* 9(Aug):1871–1874.

Yoav Freund and Robert E Schapire. 1999. Large margin classification using the perceptron algorithm. *Machine Learning* 37(3):277–296.

William A Gale and Geoffrey Sampson. 1995. Good-turing frequency estimation without tears*. *Journal of Quantitative Linguistics* 2(3):217–237.

Inc. Gurobi Optimization. 2015. Gurobi optimizer reference manual. http://www.gurobi.com.

Jing Jiang and ChengXiang Zhai. 2007. Instance weighting for domain adaptation in NLP. In *Proceedings of ACL*. Association for Computational Linguistics, volume 7, pages 264–271.

Artuur Leeuwenberg and Marie-Francine Moens. 2017. Structured learning for temporal relation extraction from clinical records. In *Proceedings of EACL*. Association for Computational Linguistics, Valencia, Spain.

Inderjeet Mani, Marc Verhagen, Ben Wellner, Chong Min Lee, and James Pustejovsky. 2006. Machine learning of temporal relations. In *Proceedings of COLING–ACL*. Association for Computational Linguistics, pages 753–760.

William F Styler IV, Steven Bethard, Sean Finan, Martha Palmer, Sameer Pradhan, Piet C de Groen, Brad Erickson, Timothy Miller, Chen Lin, Guergana Savova, et al. 2014. Temporal annotation in the clinical domain. *Transactions of the Association for Computational Linguistics* 2:143–154.

Kristina Toutanova, Dan Klein, Christopher D. Manning, and Yoram Singer. 2003. Feature-rich part-of-speech tagging with a cyclic dependency network. In *Proceedings of NAACL-HLT*. Association for Computational Linguistics, pages 173–180.

Author Index

Association for Computational Linguistics
209 N. Eighth Street
Stroudsburg, Pennsylvania 18360